Collected Papers of the Pioneer of Constructivist Psychology

George A. Kelly

Not long after my father submitted his manuscript entitled *The psychology of personal constructs* to several publishers, I recall his remarking at our dinner table: "Oh, even if someone agrees to publish it, my book probably won't sell more than a few hundred copies. Some academics and a few grad students will buy it and that will be the end of it." My father was a visionary about so many things, but he could not have been more wrong about his Magnum Opus.

Here we are some seventy years later. Because of the ongoing interest in Personal Construct Psychology, David Winter and Nick Reed have seen fit to compile this collection of my father's writings in order that his ideas may be shared with a new generation of psychologists. I imagine that my father is looking down from on high, feeling genuinely surprised but also delighted by this latest turn of events.

Jacqueline Aldridge
September 2024

Collected Papers of the Pioneer of Constructivist Psychology

George A. Kelly

FIRST EDITION

Edited by

David A. Winter and Nick Reed

WILEY Blackwell

This edition first published 2026

Registered Offices
John Wiley & Sons, Inc., 111 River Street, Hoboken, NJ 07030, USA
John Wiley & Sons Ltd, New Era House, 8 Oldlands Way, Bognor Regis, West Sussex, PO22 9NQ, UK

For details of our global editorial offices, customer services, and more information about Wiley products visit us at www.wiley.com.

The manufacturer's authorized representative according to the EU General Product Safety Regulation is Wiley-VCH GmbH, Boschstr. 12, 69469 Weinheim, Germany, e-mail: Product_Safety@wiley.com.

Wiley also publishes its books in a variety of electronic formats and by print-on-demand. Some content that appears in standard print versions of this book may not be available in other formats.

Library of Congress Cataloging-in-Publication Data Applied for:

Hardback ISBN: **9781394153688**

Cover Design: Wiley
Cover Image: Courtesy of Jacqueline Aldridge

Set in 9.5/11.5pt Ehrhardt by Straive, Pondicherry, India

Printed and bound by CPI Group (UK) Ltd, Croydon, CR0 4YY

C9781394153688_080426

In these volumes, Winter and Reed have accomplished the improbable, if not the impossible, assembling the variegated life work of George Kelly, the founding figure of psychology's constructivist trend. In this impressive archaeology of knowledge, the editors have dug deeply into the archives of a pre-digital world to recover very nearly the whole of Kelly's life work, in all its audacity, perspicacity, originality, and sometimes even humor. Giving Kelly space to make his case poignantly and often playfully for a comprehensive psychology of personal constructs remains a welcome contribution to all contemporary psychologists and psychotherapists who share a vision of human beings as inveterate makers of meaning who co-create the significance of their lives, and in doing so, of their own identities as persons.

—Professor Robert A. Neimeyer, University of Memphis and Portland Institute for Loss and Transition, Author of *Constructivist Psychotherapy* and Editor of the *Journal of Constructivist Psychology*

Maybe few authors in the field of psychology and psychotherapy have seen so many books written by their followers, having published only one book, as George A. Kelly did. His *The psychology of personal constructs*, printed in 1955 in two volumes and derived from a view of knowledge as a personal construction, has paved the way for a radically new approach to psychology, personality, and psychotherapy. It is only some decades later that approaches sharing a similar view have become known and spread as varieties of psychological constructivism.

However, before and after 1955, Kelly created many other writings: journal articles, book chapters, conference papers and addresses, reports, book reviews, and a number of unpublished manuscripts. Seventeen were published in 1969 (two years after Kelly's premature death) in a collection edited by Brendan Maher, *Clinical psychology and personality: The selected papers of George Kelly*, and around a dozen appeared as single chapters in edited books. Those interested in deepening the roots of Kelly's ideas and their later developments had little chance of finding his other writings.

Winter and Reed have made an astounding archaeological work digging for known but hidden finds, discovering new ones, and gathering them—for a total of 127 writings—under suitable headings. Their *Collected papers of the pioneer of constructivist psychology: George A. Kelly* is an indispensable work not only for those interested in personal construct psychology and psychotherapy, but also for the wider community of practitioners who identify themselves with a constructivist perspective.

—Professor Gabriele Chiari, Director Emeritus of the School of Specialisation in Constructivist Narrative Psychotherapy, ICoNa, Padua, and of the Centro Studi SE, Florence

The work of George A. Kelly is widely known for his famous two volumes, *The psychology of personal constructs*, but the compilation that David Winter and Nick Reed offer to the scholarly and general readership today is a vast collection of other works that have been largely out of our awareness due to the difficulty of access to many of them. Even today, Kelly's writings represent a breath of fresh air in contemporary psychological theory and practice. Indeed, the luminosity, originality, lucidity, and depth of these writings make it difficult for Kelly's writings to perish, even after all these years. I believe that the personal construct approach, as created by Kelly and later developed by other researchers, provides an optimal theoretical and methodological framework for the study of meaning systems, the self, and identity.

—Professor Guillem Feixas, University of Barcelona

Winter and Reed's anthology of George Kelly's work makes an important contribution to constructivist psychology. It's a wonderful and valuable resource for students, academics and practitioners who are interested in Kelly's psychology of people. This book is a comprehensive and astonishing piece of work.

—Professor Peter Caputi, University of Wollongong

George A. Kelly was a towering figure in American Psychology and a founder of the discipline of Clinical Psychology. He published his Magnum Opus in the two volumes of *The psychology of personal constructs* in 1955, later reprinted by Routledge in 1991. This work was an enormous contribution, introducing the first serious and comprehensive alternative vision of how to conduct psychological therapy to the then dominant approaches of psychoanalysis and behaviour therapy. For Kelly, the client's perspective must be accepted and respected, not seen as problematic and flawed. The therapeutic relationship then becomes one of collaboration and partnership rather than the therapist playing the role of expert with the client in a one-down position. Therapists will of course have expertise of a general kind and will use the plethora of new approaches that Kelly developed for establishing how people struggling with difficulties make sense of their situations and how these are contributing to the problematic predicament for which they are seeking help. However, clients' views of the world, their *personal construct systems*, must remain the central consideration and the vehicle for change in the process of therapy.

But Kelly's work consists not just of a significant contribution to therapy and clinical psychology. Kelly brought in a dialectical understanding of the nature of meaning. Introducing this into the discipline of psychology was a brilliant move. This new understanding of how people construe the world has implications well beyond psychology, making it relevant to the human sciences in general, and indeed extending into philosophy. Kelly needs to be recognized as an important philosopher in his own right with a strong and coherent new logical and ethical basis with implications for how anyone should relate to their fellow humans at all levels from personal relationships, through to the importance of mutual respect and tolerance for differences of culture, gender and religious beliefs in society. This precept is based on his philosophy of *constructive alternativism*—that there are many valid ways of construing the world. There has never been more urgency in our current situation for this principle to be made fundamental in order to avoid escalation into conflict, violence and war.

For a long time now, researchers and practitioners have been relying on the 1955 volumes and the excellent collection of essays edited by Brendan Maher in 1969, as well as the extensive secondary literature published over the decades. These two volumes of Kelly's collected works, edited by David Winter and Nick Reed, will enable the laying of the groundwork for scholarly research into the whole corpus of Kelly's work and will expedite an assessment and understanding of his enormous contribution, which has not yet been fully appreciated by the mainstream community of academics and practitioners.

—Professor Harry Procter, University of Hertfordshire

Contents

Foreword

By Jonathan D. Raskin

In his review of George Kelly's 1955 magnum opus, *The psychology of personal constructs*, renowned cognitive psychologist Jerome Bruner presciently remarked that "these excellent, original, and infuriatingly prolix two volumes easily nominate themselves for the distinction of being the single greatest contribution of the past decade to the theory of personality functioning. Professor Kelly has written a major work" (Bruner, 1956, p. 355). Nearly 70 years later, Kelly's ideas still resonate. Considered one of the earliest constructivist thinkers in psychology, Kelly's conception of knowledge as an ever-evolving human invention, rather than a direct reflection of the world as it is, remains influential. Personal construct theory has generated an impressive body of research and writing in the fields of psychology, psychotherapy, and beyond.

However, because Kelly wrote significantly more than he published, readers have not been privy to much of his intellectual journey before and after authoring *The psychology of personal constructs*. Aside from his two-volume masterwork and the paperback version of its first three chapters, the only other published collection of Kelly's writings to date is the posthumous 1969 collection, *Clinical psychology and personality*, which contains a variety of previously unpublished manuscripts that Kelly was working on at the time of his death, along with reprints of several of Kelly's journal articles (Maher, 1969). Since then, no new collection of Kelly's writings has appeared—until now.

Thus, the present volume marks a momentous and long-overdue occasion. The writings collected here, many of which are being published for the first time, offer readers fascinating insights into both Kelly and his theory. They represent the most comprehensive compilation of George Kelly's works that is currently possible. Except for a few elusive pieces that appear lost to history, this book includes all of Kelly's known writings other than *The psychology of personal constructs*. It is a wide-ranging assortment. Some of these works enhance one's understanding of Kelly the theorist, while others transform one's impression of Kelly the man. However, all of them provide a fuller picture of Kelly's 50-year intellectual journey—ranging from a brief essay he wrote at age 16 to numerous papers left unpublished at the time of his death. Consequently, this compendium should prove to be an invaluable resource for anyone wishing to understand George Kelly or the psychology he envisioned.

Shortly before he died at the age of 61 in March 1967, George Kelly prepared his final bibliography of works citing personal construct theory. On the title page, he included the following epigraph: "The purpose of life is to be on with it" (Kelly, 1967). This statement quintessentially captures both the man and his theory. It also serves as excellent advice for readers embarking on a journey through Kelly's collected works: Be on with it!

References

Bruner, J. S. (1956). A cognitive theory of personality [Review of the book *The psychology of personal constructs: Vol. I. A theory of personality/Vol. II. Clinical diagnosis and psychotherapy*, by G. A. Kelly]. *Contemporary Psychology: A Journal of Reviews*, *1*(12), 355–357. https://doi.org/10.1037/005215

Kelly, G. A. (1967). 1967 personal construct theory bibliography supplement. Unpublished manuscript.

Maher, B. (1969). *Clinical psychology and personality: The selected papers of George Kelly*. John Wiley.

Preface

George Alexander Kelly (1905–1966) is best known as the creator of personal construct theory, a bold and prescient new psychology that he developed and articulated in 1955 in his two-volume magnum opus, *The psychology of personal constructs*. The first three chapters of this work were also published in 1963 as *A theory of personality: The psychology of personal constructs*. Although these were the only books that Kelly ever published, he produced a substantial number of scholarly and professional outputs, including journal articles, book chapters, unpublished books, lectures, and reports. At the time of his death, he was planning to compile a book consisting of some of this work, and selected papers were eventually published in a Wiley volume edited by Brendan Maher (1969). However, this is the first time that virtually all of these writings, the majority of which are either previously unpublished or out of print, have been gathered together. They document the extraordinary diversity of his scholarly explorations, as well as the style of his writing, which ranged from formal presentations of his theory to much more informal pieces, rich with humor and perceptiveness. While some writings, such as those on reading and speech disabilities, trigonometry, the design of aircraft instrument panels, and the use of television in education, may seem far removed from personal construct theory, we have decided to include them all in order to provide a comprehensive picture of the work of this polymath and the development of his ideas.

The writings collected herein illustrate how Kelly embodied his theory's metaphor of the person as a scientist, constantly formulating and experimenting with alternative constructions of the world. Although a work of this nature might conventionally commence with a brief biography of Kelly, we shall leave it to him to provide an account of his life through the autobiographical pieces that initiate this volume. Readers interested in learning more about Kelly the individual may refer to a forthcoming authoritative biography by Epting and Raskin (in progress), as well as to works by Fransella (1995), Butt (2008), and Chiari (2017). Those interested in recent developments in personal construct theory and its applications will find reviews in Walker and Winter (2007), Winter and Reed (2016), and Procter and Winter (2020).

We have divided the book into sections based on the broad themes of the contributions, which are, for the most part, ordered chronologically within each section. However, this classification, like previous attempts to pigeonhole Kelly's work, is artificial, as most of the writings span several of these themes. Although we were occasionally tempted to make adjustments to punctuation, we have resisted editorial alterations except when there were obvious errors in the original manuscripts. Some stylistic changes (e.g., in headings, references, and the use of American English) have been made in the interest of consistency throughout the book. We have not modified Kelly's language (e.g., the use of the male pronoun) to make it more compatible with contemporary standards. Therefore, while the reader may occasionally be surprised, or even offended, by some of Kelly's apparent departures from what might be regarded as currently acceptable forms of expression, we believe that his writing should be evaluated from the perspective of the time and social context in which he lived.

The completion of this project would not have been possible without the unwavering support of George Kelly's daughter, Jacqueline Aldridge. His late wife, Gladys, also initially provided copies of many of Kelly's papers to Fay Fransella, to whom we are indebted for assembling the Fransella Collection of works on personal construct theory, currently housed at the University of Hertfordshire, UK. This collection was further enriched by the addition of the Miller Mair Archive, made possible through the generosity of Ingrid Mair and Miller's children. We also owe particular debts to Gabriele Chiari, Franz Epting, and Jon Raskin, as well as to Mary-Ellen Ducey, who is responsible for the collection of Kelly's papers in the University Archives/Special Collections at the University of Nebraska—Lincoln libraries, USA. Countless others, too numerous to mention, have assisted us in the search for papers, and we are profoundly grateful to them, as well as to those who have granted permission for the republication of papers, as acknowledged in many of the individual chapters. Although we intended this volume to be a complete anthology of Kelly's work, there are a few documents that we have been unable to trace; these are listed in the Appendix.

George Kelly's work has exerted a profound influence on psychology, as evidenced by the acknowledgment of his contributions by subsequent leading figures across various fields. On a more personal level, it has also significantly impacted very many individuals, including ourselves. It has been an honor for us to edit this volume, which we hope will serve as a fitting tribute to Kelly—both the psychologist and the man.

David A. Winter and Nick Reed
August 2024

References

Butt, T. (2008). *George Kelly: The psychology of personal constructs*. Palgrave.

Chiari, G. (2017). *George A. Kelly and his personal construct theory*. George Kelly Society. https://itunes.apple.com/us/book/george-a-kelly/id1239028049?ls=1&mt=11

Epting, F. R., & Raskin, J. D. (in progress). *Audacious adventurer: The life and times of George Kelly and his psychology of personal constructs*. Cambridge University Press.

Fransella, F. (1995). *George Kelly*. Sage.

Kelly, G. A. (1955). *The psychology of personal constructs*. Norton.

Kelly, G. A. (1963). *A theory of personality: The psychology of personal constructs*. Norton.

Maher, B. (1969). *Clinical psychology and personality: The selected papers of George Kelly*. Wiley.

Procter, H., & Winter, D. A. (2020). *Personal and relational construct psychotherapy*. Palgrave.

Walker, B. M., & Winter, D. A. (2007). The elaboration of personal construct psychology. *Annual Review of Psychology*, *58*, 453–477.

Winter, D. A., & Reed, N. (Eds.). (2016). *Wiley handbook of personal construct psychology*. Wiley-Blackwell.

Section I

Autobiography

Kelly's *Autobiographical sketch* encompasses the period from his birth to his 20 years of employment at The Ohio State University. While the first version of the sketch is primarily a factual record, the second contains numerous anecdotes and much of his characteristic humor. The first version was completed in 1965, at the beginning of the year in which he relocated from Ohio to assume the Riklis Chair of Behavioral Science at Brandeis University. His health subsequently deteriorated, and he died in Boston on March 6, 1967, at the age of 61.

An epistle to the Western Hemisphere is an imaginary letter to a girlfriend, describing Kelly's experiences while studying in Edinburgh in 1929. Although the extent to which it is fictional remains unclear, it is included in this section on the assumption that it has some basis in events that transpired during his stay in Scotland and his construing of these.

The autobiography of a theory describes how the events of Kelly's life contributed to the development of personal construct theory and the therapeutic approaches derived from it.

In *Confusion and the clock*, which, like Chapter 15 in this volume, was intended to be a chapter in a book titled *The human feeling*, Kelly reflects on his feelings following a heart attack to contemplate matters such as anticipation, anxiety, and guilt.

Collected Papers of the Pioneer of Constructivist Psychology: George A. Kelly, First Edition. Edited by David A. Winter and Nick Reed.

1

Autobiographical Sketch[1]

I was born on a farm near Perth, Kansas on April 28, 1905, the only child of Theodore Vincent Kelly and Elfleda Merriam Kelly. My father had been educated for the Presbyterian ministry at Parsons College and at McCormick and Princeton Seminaries. My mother had been born on Barbados in the British West Indies where her father had taken his family after steam had driven his sailing ship out of the North Atlantic trade. Later Captain Merriam had become an Indian agent in South Dakota and it was at the border town of Brown's Valley, Minnesota that my parents had met. Not long after their marriage the career in the ministry was abandoned and the young couple moved to the farm where I was born.

In 1909 my father converted our lumber wagon into a covered wagon and moved the family to Eastern Colorado to take up a claim on some of the last free land offered settlers in the west. The venture failed because no water could be found under the land, and my parents moved back to the farm in Kansas.

My schooling was rather irregular and in Colorado was limited to the occasions when my parents could spend a few weeks in town. However, since they themselves were educated, they took seriously their responsibility for my studies at home.

My high school education was about as badly mixed up as my elementary schooling had been. After a few weeks commuting to a local high school it was decided to send me to Wichita. Thus it was that I lived away from home most of the time after I was thirteen, and I attended four different high schools.

In 1926, after three years at Friends University and one at Park College, I received a B.A. Degree at the latter institution in physics and mathematics. The original plan had been to continue in mechanical engineering, but my interest had begun to shift to social problems, partly because of experience in intercollegiate debates on such topics. The next fall, therefore, I enrolled in educational sociology at the University of Kansas, with minor studies in labor relations and sociology. My master's thesis was a study of Kansas City workers' distribution of leisure time activities.

The year at the University of Kansas was followed by a few months in Minneapolis where I taught part time in a labor college, conducted classes in speech for the American Bankers Association, and taught an Americanization class for prospective citizens. In the late winter of 1928 I went to the new public junior college in Sheldon, Iowa, where I met Gladys Thompson, a fellow teacher of English and dramatics in the high school, who later became my wife. After a year and a half there, a summer in sociology at the University of Minnesota, and a few months as an aeronautical engineer for the struggling Watkins Aircraft Company back in Wichita, I went to Edinburgh on an exchange fellowship. There I received the Bachelor of Education Degree in 1930, being permitted, after nine months of residence, to take examinations over both years of graduate work normally required beyond the Honors M.A. Degree. My thesis, under the direction of Sir Godfrey Thomson, dealt with the prediction of teaching success.

The next year, in the States, I enrolled in psychology for the first time in the fall of 1930, and the following June received a Ph.D. Degree from the State University of Iowa with a dissertation on common factors in speech and reading disabilities. Two days after commencement my wife and I were married in Sioux City.

At the end of a summer of teaching at the State University of Iowa we moved to Kansas, where I taught in the Ft. Hays Kansas State College until receiving a commission in the Navy as an aviation psychologist during World War II. During the period at Hays I found there was little occasion to pursue the physiological approaches to psychology in which I had recently become interested, but there was need for clinical psychology, especially in the schools of the state. Soon we received some legislative support for a program of traveling clinics that gave my students and me a chance to develop our psychological thinking in close contact with persons in distress.

[1] Editors' note: There are two versions of this sketch, both of which are included here in view of the additional anecdotal information that is contained in the second version. The first version is dated February 15, 1965. Published by permission of Jacqueline Aldridge.

Collected Papers of the Pioneer of Constructivist Psychology: George A. Kelly, First Edition. Edited by David A. Winter and Nick Reed.

With the beginning of the war in Europe I was placed in charge of the local civilian pilot training program and undertook to learn to fly myself. This interest in aviation continued after I was placed on duty as an officer in the Aviation Psychology Branch of the Navy's Bureau of Medicine and Surgery in Washington.

In 1945 I was appointed to an associate professorship at the University of Maryland and in 1946 I became Professor and Director of Clinical Psychology at the Ohio State University. After five years in this directorship the position was rotated to other members of the clinical staff, and only recently have I had to resume it again.

There have been supplementary appointments in my career—summer teaching at the University of Iowa in 1931, Ohio State University in 1933, University of Chicago in 1940, University of Nebraska in 1942, University of Southern California in 1957, Northwestern University in 1958, Brigham Young University in 1963, and the University of New Hampshire in 1964. In 1954 I spent several months directing an educational television research project at the Montclair State Teachers College in New Jersey, and in the spring of 1962 I was a visiting professor at the City College of New York.

I am a past president of the Clinical and Consulting Divisions of the American Psychological Association and of the American Board of Examiners in Professional Psychology.

My principal scholarly venture has been the development of a personality theory, the psychology of personal constructs, and the publication in 1955 of a two volume work describing the theory and its clinical implications. During the year 1960-61 my wife and I traveled around the world on a project financed by the Human Ecology Fund in an effort to apply the construct theory to certain international problems. During this trip I lectured at London, Oslo, Copenhagen, Louvain, Madrid, Prague, Warsaw, and Moscow. We have also made some academic forays into the Caribbean area and South America.

--- --- ---

I was born on a farm near Perth, Kansas on April 28, 1905, the only child of Theodore Vincent Kelly and Elfleda Merriam Kelly. My father had been trained for the Presbyterian ministry at Parsons College, and at Princeton and McCormick Seminaries, and, after serving for a brief period of years as a pastor in Minnesota had given up the ministry for farming. Twenty years later he was to return to the ministry. My mother was the daughter of a Nova Scotian captain of a sailing ship who had been driven off the North Atlantic trade routes by the advent of the steamship and had gone into the Caribbean trade, making his headquarters in Barbados where my mother had been born. After his ship burned he immigrated to the United States and became an Indian agent in South Dakota. It was there, or rather at the border town of Brown's Valley, Minnesota, that my parents met.

In 1909 my father bought the bows and canvas to convert our lumber wagon into a covered wagon and set out for eastern Colorado to take up a claim near Eads. But this effort was doomed to failure, for no water could be found on or near the claim, and he brought his family back to the Kansas farm in 1913. During part of the time we were in Colorado it had been impossible for me to go to school and my parents took over the responsibility for my education.

In the fall of 1918 I started my high school education in Caldwell, Kansas, but this arrangement did not work out and by the end of the first semester I had had only a few weeks of actual schooling. I was then sent to Wichita, where I had two and a half years in the junior high school and the senior high school. When I was sixteen I transferred to the Friends University Academy in Wichita and began taking a combination of college and academy courses. Thus it was that I did not actually graduate from high school, a fact that is sometimes hard to explain.

At the beginning of my senior year I transferred to Park College, Parkville, Missouri and completed my baccalaureate studies in the spring of 1926 with majors in physics and mathematics. My plan had always been to complete an engineering course after graduating from college, but an interest and some success in intercollege debate aroused my interest in social issues and made me question the ultimate value of a career in engineering. That fall, therefore, I enrolled in the University of Kansas, without any very clear notion of how to pursue my new-found interest, and enrolled for a major in educational sociology under the distinguished W. R. Smith, and undertook minor studies in sociology and labor economics. My master's thesis was on industrial workers' use of leisure time and was carried out with the support of certain labor unions in Kansas City.

In the fall of 1927, with my thesis still incomplete and no offers of a teaching job, in spite of many applications, I followed my roommate to Minneapolis, where he had a fellowship in psychology. There I managed to survive by teaching one night a week in each of three night schools, one a speech class for labor organizers, one a class for the American Bankers Association, and one an Americanization class for prospective citizens. I enrolled in the University of Minnesota in sociology and biometrics, but after several weeks it was discovered that I had been unable to pay my fees and I was told that I could no longer attend.

In the late winter of 1927-28 I was given a job teaching psychology and speech, including the coaching of dramatics, in the Sheldon Junior College at Sheldon, Iowa. The college, then in its second year, had had disciplinary problems and the previous teacher had been run out of town by the rowdy students. The superintendent of schools apparently decided that academic qualifications were of secondary importance and employed me. It was here that I met Gladys Thompson. We were assigned the same classroom and desk and, while the arrangement seemed a little cramped at first, we adjusted to it and decided to share our quarters on a permanent basis.

During the year I completed my masters thesis and returned to Minnesota for the summer as a legitimately enrolled graduate student in sociology. During the ensuing year I continued at Sheldon but applied for an exchange fellowship between the International Institute of Teachers College, Columbia University and the National Committee for the Training of Teachers in Scotland. It turned out there were only two applicants and Professor Monroe turned over the pictures of the two of us to his secretaries and asked them to make the selection. The other fellow had sent in a picture of himself dressed in a tuxedo and the girls evidently thought this was inappropriate, so they chose me.

During the summer of 1929 I got a job as a draftsman in the Watkins Aircraft Plant in Wichita but when it was discovered that I had some mathematics and physics background I was quickly moved into the position of assistant engineer with responsibilities for stress analysis and minor design. The engineering analysis was approved by the Department of Commerce and the plane flew quite successfully. But my exchange fellowship was waiting, so I resigned to go to Scotland.

In Scotland I elected to make my headquarters in Edinburgh and to enroll in the University while familiarizing myself with the Scottish schools. I had hoped that I might become a candidate for the Ph.D. but I could not meet the residence requirements in the one year I was to be there. It was suggested, however, that the two years of residency beyond the Honors Masters Degree, required for the Bachelor of Education Degree, might be waived if I could successfully complete the two year curriculum in one year. Thus it was that I completed the work for this degree the following spring and graduated in a class of eight candidates, having studied psychology under Prof. James Drever and education under Sir Godfrey Thomson, with a thesis under the latter.

Returning to the States in the fall of 1930 I found the depression had hit, the aircraft industry in which I had hoped to support myself until I could continue my education had collapsed and there was no work to be had. However, I was able to borrow money for another nine months of education and the question became, where could I get a doctoral degree without having to learn languages. My efforts to learn Latin in high school had resulted in a resounding failure and I had managed to avoid languages from that point on. A letter to Prof. Peter Sandiford at Toronto University brought back the information that I might be able to complete the requirements for a Doctor of Education Degree there, and, what was more to the point, I would not be required to learn a language.

On the way to Toronto I stopped at the University of Iowa, having heard that once they had substituted an advanced knowledge of statistics instead of a language proficiency. Besides, I had other interests in Iowa where Gladys Thompson was still teaching in Sheldon. Things went well until the dean of education found that I was much younger than I had at first appeared. It was then he decided I needed to plan on more than nine months and that I really needed some courses in clay modeling and other educational methods courses. But when I explained that this was financially out of the question he was kind enough to send me to Dean Carl Seashore of the Graduate School who was, as he told me, "A fool and might do anything."

It did not take Dean Seashore more than two or three minutes to make up his mind that I should transfer to the Department of Psychology, of which also he was the Chairman. But on the matter of languages he was adamant, telling me that he would give me just five days to learn French. Since the Toronto session did not start for another two or three weeks I had nothing to lose but my pride and there was not much of that left. Five days later I passed the French examination, with the help of one of the mobster students I had taught in Sheldon Junior College who was now a teaching assistant in the French Department at the University of Iowa. When I showed this to the "Iron Dean" a few minutes before the deadline, he replied laconically, "Fine, we'll give you your qualifying examination the day after tomorrow." I was too numbed from five almost sleepless days and nights of studying French to remonstrate, although the idea of taking a doctoral qualifying examination in a subject in which I had had only marginal interest up to that time struck me as a little strange.

The upshot was that nine months later I had a Ph.D. in psychology with a thesis in which I had developed the notion of a transient aphasia characteristic of all of us, but particularly apparent in persons who showed a combination of speech and reading disabilities. Two days after graduating Gladys and I were married and I returned to a summer of post-doctoral work at Iowa, a summer that was to provide me with an unexpected temporary instructorship when the professor of educational psychology became ill.

In the fall of 1931 we set out for Hays, Kansas to teach in the Fort Hays Kansas State College for what was to stretch out into twelve years mixed with wide open opportunities, rewarding associations with students, and bitter relations with the college administration and the community. It was here that I found there was little occasion to pursue work in physiological psychology and I turned to the kinds of psychological services that seemed to be most needed. It was here, too, that our two children, Jacqueline and Joe, were born and we survived the dust storms of the middle thirties. After seven years I was still teaching for less than the salary I had been promised for my first year, which, by the way, was never paid in full.

War clouds began to: appear on the horizon in the late thirties and I was put in charge of the flight training program allocated to the college by the Civil Aeronautics Administration. In the fall of 1943 I was commissioned in the U.S. Naval reserve and stationed in the Bureau of Medicine and Surgery. After a year at the University of Maryland in 1945-46 I was appointed to a professorship at The Ohio State University, a position which I still occupy.

2

An Epistle to the Western Hemisphere[1]

Saturday nite in Scotland

Mabel dear,—So far, I've been in Scotland four weeks and two Sundays. The sun they use here looks very much like our own except that they hang it in a different place and don't expose it so much.

I understand, Mabel, you want to know all about my experiences in this distant, far-off land. I'm going to write to you quite frankly now, and may the Peace Pact preserve me if this missile should fall into the hands of a native.

It is a problem to know which is the more startling: the fact that the people here are so much like those at home or the fact that they are so different. At one moment the discovery that all of them do not wear kilts, is most impressive; at another, their ability to put food into their mouths with an inverted fork held in the left hand sets them apart in one's own mind as a distinct species. If the Scots were either more or less like us, the task of making an illuminating description of them would be considerably simplified. For instance, it would be very easy to cite experiences which, taken alone, would give a very unfair impression of the people. I could tell of meeting a Scot, within a short time after my arrival, who vehemently asserted that he hated his country and all its people. Such a remark would probably create an impression which would be a complete reversal of the truth. How easy it must be for the American tourist who must make a short vacation carry him over so many cultures to carry home the wrong impression of the countries he has visited! You see, Mabel, how hard it would be for me to make a fair evaluation of my experiences. I shall, however, risk an attempt to describe some of the peculiar differences in manners and customs which are particularly striking.

To my mind, the first item on the list should be the heating scheme generally employed in Scottish homes. It had never occurred to me that anyone except those in the very outposts of civilisation relied upon an open fire for heating their home. Imagine my complete astonishment on being informed that open fires are used in the United Kingdom because they are more "cheery" than fires which keep you warm. For the first few days I wore my hat and overcoat in the house, and frequently discarded them when exercising outdoors. Then I changed my room on the understanding that my new landlady would put me in charge of the local coal supply.

From heating I turn to dogs, the next most striking item. Dogs! the canine population of Edinburgh is "most estawdinry," to use the British expression. Can you imagine looking out of your window and seeing full-grown men and women walking up and down the street carrying dogs on the ends of strings for the purpose of exercising these creatures? It's done here.

For the first few days Edinburgh traffic represented a continual hazard for my insurance company: no one drives on the right side of the street. I had not realized how the habit of looking first left, then right, had become reflexive.

No one can stay here long without absorbing some history. Shortly after my arrival I was taken aside by a confiding Scot who whispered in my ear that the edifice to my left was "very old;" I thought my eyesight was being made the butt of some sarcasm. Later I learned that the Scotsman's "very old" is equivalent to our "very old" with several exclamation points after it. Many of the buildings simply ooze with history, and the Scot carefully traces the development of every article he uses in his daily life. Innovations must have a metaphysical background before being admitted into Scottish society. Automobiles were able to invade Scotland only after it was pointed out that they were a development from Descartes.

Street cars here are two stories high and rock gently fore and aft when under way. A conductor who looks like the joint advertisement of a hardware establishment and a harness shop collects the moderate fares for the voyage. In spite of his peculiar garb, you always find him glad to help you in making your way about the intricate street systems of the city, and never yet have I seen one grow impatient when asked for detailed directions.

I must tell you, Mabel, of my first experience in a classroom. As I took a place in the large amphitheater and looked about me, I felt a touch of disappointment that there was nothing unusual about the students whom I saw. They filed in quite naturally, talking and laughing, and took

[1] Published in 1929 in *Moray House Magazine, XXIII*(1), 9-12. Republished by permission of Jacqueline Aldridge.

Collected Papers of the Pioneer of Constructivist Psychology: George A. Kelly, First Edition. Edited by David A. Winter and Nick Reed.

their places just as we do at home. I was on the point of kicking myself for having endured the perils of a trans-Atlantic voyage in vain, when in strode the teacher. I quickly reconsidered my diagnosis, for streaming from his shoulders was a long robe of some thin black material, worn unbuttoned all down the front. Ah! now here at last was the atmosphere of a real foreign classroom; anything might happen now. It did! The first sentence of the lecture had nearly come to a glorious climax when it was suddenly drowned by a thunderous stamping of feet. I gasped, ducked my head, shut my eyes, and held my breath until the counter-attack should come. There was no counter-attack. With a smile as broad as that of a Scot at a bargain counter the lecturer proceeded. I came up for air, but not for long. Sentence Number Two was greeted with more footwork. This time the feet were put through a sort of shuffling exercise. I was beginning to wonder what part the treadmill plays in Scottish education when a new sound broke upon my ears—a sort of clicking sound, as nearly as I can describe it—like the Russian Army entering upon a soup course. Understand, of course, that I have never seen the Russian Army, but I have seen soup and know some of its potentialities. Several people have attempted to explain the meaning of these symbols to me, but I find that I am able to understand them only in proportion to my acquaintance with the personality of the Scottish student himself.

Here, one's social career seems to be somewhat determined by his capacity for tea. They actually have a sort of meal between lunch and dinner which they call "tea." The tea far surpasses any I've ever tasted in America. At home, you know, many cafés do not even serve tea, and never had I seen milk used with it until I reached Scotland.

The most amusing thing I have noticed in Scotland is the way people will tell you how hard it is to make acquaintance with their countrymen. By their very acts of friendship and confidence they contradict their words. I only wish it had always been as easy for me to make friends as it has been here.

The people, I observe, are very fond of walking. They go at it as if they really enjoyed it. When you see some healthy, rosy-cheeked Scottish lassie with each arm swinging in a three-foot arc, bearing down on you, it is best to stand aside. In fact, it is altogether fitting that one should stand aside, for she probably has risen at an early hour, built the fire for the household, and prepared one of those ample Scottish breakfasts. Where is the American girl who could do that, or would if she could? Mabel, you know it too, don't you?

They have some very fine specimens of Old-World architecture here; there's the Edinburgh Castle overlooking one of the most interesting streets I have ever seen, and Holyrood Palace down by the gas works. Moray House itself, they tell me, used to be the scene of some of the old human barbecues back in the days of iron overcoats. It makes one tingle all over to stand by a brass plate engraved with the brief obituary of some noble whose career came to an untimely end at that spot. It we had had history chiseled into our doorsteps as these people have, it would have been a great incentive to increase our vocabulary of historical dates and events.

Mabel, when your boy friend comes home you won't know him. He will be saying "aye" instead of "sure," "auch" instead of "oh," and will accent his remarks with" jolly well," "chap," "estawdinry," and may even be able to sing out "cherio," although I'm not sure about the last. I've tried saying "cherio" on several occasions, but so far they have all turned out miserable failures; I can't get my tongue wrapped around it right. Well, this is Scotland as I'm seeing it and I must confess I rather like it.—As usual,

George A. Kelly.

P.S.—Let me know if you don't get this, for I shouldn't want it to go astray.

2nd. P.S.—That's all a mistake about them taking the census in Edinburgh by rolling a dollar down the street. Sorry!

3

The Autobiography of a Theory[1]

This is the autobiography of a certain theory in psychology known as the *psychology of personal constructs*. I feel myself uniquely qualified to write this account because I wrote the theory also, though I realize that writing a theory does not necessarily mean you know how you came by it. Undoubtedly what I wrote is hopelessly entangled in the ideas of my predecessors. However that may be, I can at least write about what I now recall.

Rather than starting with the basic premises of *personal construct theory*, the usual strategy for making a theory appear respectable, I would like to mention certain events and tentative conclusions reached and abandoned along the way to its formulation. This is not to say that the events shaped the theory—not that at all—but what I have to describe are the happenings out of which, in some accountable way, the theory has sought to make sense.

In the first course in psychology that I took I sat in the back row of a very large class, tilted my chair against the wall, made myself as comfortable as possible, and kept one ear cocked for anything interesting that might turn up. One day the professor, a very nice person who seemed to be trying hard to convince himself that psychology was something to be taken seriously, turned to the blackboard and wrote an "S," an arrow, and an "R." Thereupon I straightened up my chair and listened, thinking to myself that now, after two or three weeks of preliminaries, we might be getting to the meat of the matter.

Although I listened intently for several sessions after that the most I could make of it was that the "S" was what you had to have in order to account for the "R" and the "R" was put there so the "S" would have something to account for. I never did find out what that arrow stood for—not to this day—and I have pretty well given up trying to figure it out. I can see, of course, that once you step into this solipsism you can go round and round without feeling obligated to come out with anything useful.

Some of my friends have tried to explain to me that the world is filled with "S's" and "R's" and it is unrealistic of me to refuse to recognize them. But before they have talked themselves out they become pretty vague about which is which. Others, who are not so concretistic, argue that the formula represents only a relationship between events, not the events themselves. This makes a little more sense, and might continue to make sense if they didn't persist in talking about the matter, rubbing their forefingers across that arrow in the formula. That gets me all confused again, for they seem to be contradicting themselves and saying that it is the *arrow* that expresses the relationship between the events, not the "S" and the "R."

Out of all this I have gradually developed the notion that psychology is pretty much confined to the paradigms it employs and, while you can take off in a great many directions and travel a considerable distance in any of them—as indeed we have with stimulus-response psychology—there is no harm in consorting with a strange paradigm now and then. Indeed the notion has occurred to me that psychology may best be regarded as a collection of paradigms wooed by ex-physicists, ex-physiologists, and ex-preachers, as well as a lot of other intellectual renegades. Even more recently it has struck me that this is the nature of man; he is an inveterate collector of paradigms. But now I am getting ahead of myself again.

About three years later, after I had abandoned engineering as a career and had entered graduate school in an effort to learn something about sociology and labor relations, I decided it was high time I had a look at Freud. I can remember the occasion rather well. I was in the northeast corner of the reading room of the library at the University of Kansas. I don't remember which one of Freud's books I was trying to read, but I do remember the mounting feeling of incredulity that anyone could write such nonsense, much less publish it. It was not the pan-sexualism that makes Freud objectionable to some new readers, but the elastic meanings and arbitrary syntax that disturbed me. If I had any misgivings about having abandoned psychology so readily after my first encounters, I had very few regrets after reading Freud that day.

But this is not the end of the story. It might have been the end of the story if what psychologists say about learning and sociologists say about subcultures were true. What happened was that about four years later Dean Seashore, in person, conferred on me the Ph.D. in psychology,

[1] Dated 1963. Published in Maher, B. (Ed.). (1969). *Clinical psychology and personality: The selected papers of George Kelly* (pp. 46-65). Wiley. Republished by permission of Wiley.

Collected Papers of the Pioneer of Constructivist Psychology: George A. Kelly, First Edition. Edited by David A. Winter and Nick Reed.

prefacing his part of the ceremonies with a little speech about the Doctor of Philosophy Degree being the highest that any university could bestow. The events that filled this transitional period are not particularly relevant to this discussion, except, possibly, the fact that during the interval I had taught soap-box oratory in a labor college for labor organizers, government in an Americanization institute for prospective citizens, public speaking for the American Bankers Association, and dramatics in a junior college, that I had taken a Master's degree with a study of workers' use of leisure time, and an advanced professional degree in education at the University of Edinburgh, and that I had dabbled academically in education, sociology, economics, labor relations, biometrics, speech pathology, and cultural anthropology, and had majored in psychology for a grand total of nine months. This, I might say in case any of you are wondering, is not what I recommend for my own students.

Coping with Circumstances

Now, with a doctoral degree and the depression of 1931 on my hands, and with recently acquired aspirations in physiological psychology, I set out with my bride for what was soon to become the notorious dust bowl. During the following twelve years at a small college in western Kansas I had, shall we say, several more priceless opportunities to revise my outlook. I might add that during this time I had a minimum of intellectual interference from my colleagues in psychology, although I did, from time to time, find myself confronted with less formidable obstacles to intellectual progress, the nature of which I shall not inflict upon you.

It did not take many weeks in those depression times to reach the decision to pursue something more humanitarian than physiological psychology. Too many young people were wondering what, if anything, to do with their lives. The schools, only recently established at a secondary level in that part of the state, were only barely functioning as educational institutions, and there were many who thought public education should be abandoned altogether. It was a time for a teacher to talk of courage and adventure in the midst of despair. It was not a time for the "S," the arrow, and the "R!"

Again, let me state my conviction that it was not the circumstances that dictated the conclusions I reached. I could have used the same circumstances to confirm stimulus response psychology. It is to say, rather, that the premises with which I entered the situation no longer were useful to me. Or perhaps it would be more correct to say that it was the actions that derived from my premises that did not seem appropriate. Of course I would still have liked to pursue some exciting hunches I had about physiological psychology, and particularly something which had turned up and I had called "transient aphasia." As a matter of fact, it would have been even more fun to have stayed with my original love of engineering, for I have always found the drafting board an instrument of relaxation.

So why did I at this point turn from the things I spontaneously enjoyed to the heart-breaking tasks of the psychotherapist? Was it the circumstances? I think not. It was I! Was it a sense of inner duty to fellow man? If you mean by that that there was something called "duty" that intruded itself into my life and beckoned me to follow it, then the answer is definitely no. Nothing like that ever happened to me. As a matter of fact, when someone tries to tell me what my duty is I am not likely to take him very seriously, for it seems to me he is probably a busybody who, having failed to make something out of his own circumstances, wants someone else to fulfill his neglected aspirations.

In other words, I do not regard my career in psychology as a "calling." Everything around us "calls," if we choose to heed. Moreover, I have never been completely satisfied that becoming a psychologist was even a very good idea in the first place—a doubt that I am sure some of my colleagues share. The only thing that seems clear about my career in psychology is that it was I who got myself into it and I who have pursued it. But, again, I am ahead of myself, for this is part of the theory whose autobiography I am reciting.

A Psychology of Man Himself

It was somewhere around this point in my experience that it occurred to me that what seemed true of myself was probably no less true of others. If I initiated my actions, so did they. I suppose you might say that this position commits me to a psychology of man rather than of his circumstances. It is a psychology concerned with what we do and why we do it, rather than one that attempts to pinpoint the events that compel others to do what they do not choose to do. There is, I suspect, a lot of difference between these two psychologies. But so far, it must be said, there was nothing in my thinking that could be called a full-blown theory of personality—only a kind of convenient posture I assumed toward what confronted me.

But to believe that man is the author of his destiny is not to deny that he may be tragically limited by his circumstances. I saw too many unfortunate youngsters, some of them literally starving in that depression-ridden dust bowl, for me not to be aware of their tragic limitations. Clearly there were many things they might have liked to do that circumstances would not permit. But, nevertheless, this is not to say that they were victims of circumstances. However much there was denied them, there was still an infinity of possibilities open to them. The task was to generate the imagination needed to envision those possibilities. And this is a point of departure for a psychology of man, the canons of Nineteenth Century scientific determinism notwithstanding.

Man in Trouble

So I listened to people in trouble and I tried to help them figure out what they could do about it. None of the things I had studied or pursued in the years before seemed to have any very specific bearing on what confronted us, though at one time or another through this period I probably attempted to make some use of everything I knew.

Certainly there was not much point in pinning pathological diagnoses on the persons who came to me. That is one of the moves in *the referral game* that some clinical psychologists like to play. But it has to be played in metropolitan areas where there is a suitable proliferation of agencies and specialists on whom you can unload your less profitable clients. In western Kansas when a person came to me we were pretty much stuck with each other. Our job was to figure out what the two of us could do ourselves. Now that I look back on it this was an open invitation to approach psychology from an unconventional angle. And that is what I am afraid I did.

The strangest thing about this period is that I went back to Freud for a second look. My recollections of Rasmussen's *Principal Nervous Pathways* and of Thorndike's electrical condenser theory of learning applied at the synapses had not proved very helpful to people troubled about what was to become of them. But now that I had listened to the language of distress, Freud's writings made a new kind of sense. That fellow Freud, he was indeed a clinician! He too must have listened to these same cries echoing from deep down where there are no sentences, no words, and no syntax.

So it was that I became a "Freudian," if not by training, at least by persuasion. The Freudian language of explanation provided me with a way of understanding the difficulties of those who came to me for aid, of anticipating their thoughts, and of helping them regain the initiative in their lives. In short, I began to have what I thought was "insight." Through my Freudian interpretations, judiciously offered at those moments when clients seemed ready for them, a good many unfortunate persons seemed to be profoundly helped.

I suppose it is clear that none of this was under psychiatric supervision, nor under any kind of supervision, for that matter. My clients and I were on our own and, while I think I have come a long way since this period in my psychological career, we—my client and I—are still pretty much on our own whenever we buckle down to a difficult problem. It is important that this be understood in order to visualize what happened next.

Beware of the Obvious

There is something about the obvious things in this world that repeatedly rises to plague me. I know that many persons complain that they are tormented by the uncertainties of life, by its ambiguities, or by the fact that there seem to be no final answers. I think I know how they feel, and to some extent, I am troubled by such things too, though thus far I have no very serious complaints about my uncertainties. But those things I once thought I knew for sure, those are what get me into hot water, time after time. They are a lot more troublesome than those things I have known all along that I didn't understand. Moreover, a world jam-packed with lead pipe certainties, dictionary definitives, and doomsday finalities strikes me as a pretty gloomy place. How can there be any room in a world like that for such a nascent thing as life?

I suppose it would have to be conceded that life in the opposite kind of world—a world of chaos—might seem pretty hopeless after a while. But, as between the two—a world without hopes or a world without doubts—I think, for myself, I would prefer the world without hopes. Of course, I would prefer some of both, hopes and doubts. But, still, if I had to end my life on some final note I think I would like it to be a question, preferably a basic one, well posed and challenging, and beckoning me on to where only others after me may go, rather than a terminal conclusion—no matter how well-documented. There is something exciting about a question, even one you have no reasonable expectation of answering. But a final conclusion, why that is like the stroke of doom; after it—nothing, just nothing at all!

It was with some such thoughts as these in the back of my noggin that I began to be uncomfortable with my Freudian "insights." It was not that they were failing me so much as it was that I felt myself beginning to take them for granted. And ideas, like women, when too long taken for granted are likely to turn fickle.

So I began fabricating "insights." I deliberately offered "preposterous interpretations" to my clients. Some of them were about as un-Freudian as I could make them—first proposed somewhat cautiously, of course, and then, as I began to see what was happening, more boldly. My only criteria were that the explanation account for the crucial facts as the client saw them and that it carry implications for approaching the future in a different way. Now you can see what it meant to me not to be under supervision during this period.

What happened? Well, many of my preposterous explanations worked, some of them surprisingly well. To be sure, the wilder ones fell flat, but a reexamination of the interviews often suggested where the client's difficulty with them lay. Now I would not want to say that as a general rule, my fabricated "insights" worked as well as my Freudian ones. But I can say that some of them out-performed normal expectations.

Perhaps I should add that I have some doubts that this experiment could easily be repeated. Even my friends in western Kansas have picked up some Freudianisms in the past thirty years and if I tried this sort of thing again I might insult their sense of orthodoxy.

Certainly many of them would get the impression that I was not much of a psychologist. But in those days psychology was regarded locally as a pretty far-out kind of thing anyway, and if I said that a nervous stomach was rebelling against nourishment of all kinds—parental, educational, and nutritional—most of my clients were willing to try to make something of it.

Nowadays, of course, clients have a lot of preconceived sophistries about what has to happen in psychotherapy—notions about authority relationships, sexual potency, mother fixations, etc.—and besides they expect a detailed accounting for all the frustrations of childhood they can remember, as well as all the daily household episodes they can cram into their therapeutic hour. They want their autobiographies thoroughly psychologized—preferably Freudianized, if they can afford a little higher fee—and kept right up to date.

Psychotherapy: The Cooperative Venture

Before I go too far with this account I would like it made clear that I do not think a psychologist has the right to exploit his clients. There is a difference between exploitation and doing something unconventional in psychotherapy. Two considerations underlie this difference: first, the client has to be a participant in the experimental venture. He should himself be looking for new solutions emerging out of the experience and just as ready as the therapist to accept disconfirming evidence. What is proposed to him as an interpretation should always be in the form of a hypothesis, not in the form of a natural truth exempt from any human appraisal. In other words it should be clear that the psychologist is his fellow experimenter, not an unctuous priest. Second, both of them should keep themselves, moment by moment, as sensitive as possible to what emerges from the undertaking; no waiting for fifty cases to accumulate before concluding that your method has brought half of them to the brink of suicide.

There is something else, too. The therapist should do his best to prepare himself for the kind of responsibility he carries. This, as you can now readily see, means training himself as a scientist, not merely as a practitioner. It seems to me that the extensive training of therapists in theory and technique only, and failing to demonstrate scientific methodology as an actual interview-room procedure, is itself unethical. Only as the therapist approaches his client's problem as a scientist, and invites his client to do the same to the limit of his ability, can he avoid the tyranny of dogmatism and the professional exploitation of his clients.

It is much more feasible to get this kind of training now than it was thirty years ago, although a lot of the most prestigious preparation today seems to me to unfit the therapist for joining his client in a truly sensitive and humble exploration of the world. Too often the training substitutes doctrine for inquiry; it makes the therapist feel respectable rather than responsible—and there is a lot of difference between the two.

Something To Go On

As a result of this exploration of preposterous explanations, I developed the notion that what many clients needed was something they could use to give them a fresh approach to life, some explanation they could employ to cover a rather large number of future contingencies. While it might be helpful if the new constructions of events covered the original complaints, I was not at all sure this was essential. And when I say that what is needed is something to facilitate the composed anticipation of contingent events, I would like it to be clear that I refer to internal events such as those we commonly call "feelings," as well as to external events.

About this possibility of ignoring the original complaints; I reached this hypothesis more or less by accident. It came about in this way. After a time the requests for psychological help exceeded my spare hours. This was not particularly surprising. So it was that often, after listening to a person describe his difficulties, I had to explain to him that it would be months before I could see him.

It occurred to me that I had some responsibility to suggest some things he might do while waiting his turn. Sometimes this took the form of reminding him that there were others in distress too, and there were certain kinds of things that anyone might do to be helpful. This was not intended to "cure" him, but was merely something that needed to be done and he might as well make himself useful while waiting to see me. Besides, his contribution would be a measure of how much he wanted help for himself. I might add at this point that I charged no fees. In fact, after more than thirty years, I have still to collect my first fee for psychotherapeutic services.

To my surprise, a considerable number of these persons, when they were finally told their turn had come, reported either that they no longer felt the need for help, or that they had come to realize that other persons they knew needed it more than they, and that therefore they were willing to wait a few weeks longer. Most of them said that what they had done in the meantime had put their problem in a new perspective.

It was not so much that they had been "cured" by the experience, but that their troubles, though still with them, no longer seemed unmanageable. By this time I knew what most therapists have observed—that this kind of statement is often about what you get from so-called successfully treated clients, and that it actually suggests a better prognosis than the euphoric claims that some clients make in their fervent "flights into health."

Whether this means that my clients, whose treatment had been postponed and who made themselves useful in the meantime, were actually "therapized" by their altruistic efforts is a question I am not prepared to answer. It may not even be a very good question. What the experience does suggest is that the new structure that emerges from psychotherapy may not need to cover the old complaints at all. Indeed psychotherapy may not even need to deal with that elusive entity called "the self," regarded by so many of our colleagues as the focal point of their efforts.

The Role of Disproof

There was something else that began to dawn on me at this time, though I did not attempt to put it into words until years later. It is the notion that one does not have to disprove one proposition before entertaining one of its alternatives. A lot of footless controversy between scientists could be avoided if this possibility were explored. Each could go about his business without distraction long enough to see what he could turn up on his own, without becoming embroiled in controversy with his colleagues.

The same is probably true of all of us. One way of life need not be invalidated before the outcomes of another are examined. If a person in psychotherapy can free himself from the indicative moods of our language system long enough to entertain some novel hypotheses about other ways of living, he can save himself and his therapist a lot of trouble overcoming the "resistances" and "false premises" of his previous outlook. Therapy could then become concerned with alternatives instead of involving the participants in long, intricate, and reductionistic analyses designed to disabuse the client of his "neurotic" notions.

Words and Deeds

It is a short step from this psychological vantage point to which my psychotherapeutic efforts had thus far led me and the next idea in the sequence. But it took a long time to take that step—it took *me* a long time, that is.

Moreno's writings, when they began to come out in the 1930's, seemed intriguing to me as well as to others, particularly what he had to say about psychodrama. But whereas psychodrama for him led back into the classical personality theories implied in Greek drama, just as Freud's clinical experiences reminded him of classical themes, I was led no further back than to the development of the extemporaneous theater out of "method acting" in Europe after World War I. I suppose, too, in some way I may have been thinking about the James-Lange Theory of Emotion.

In any case I began to pursue the notion that one's current acts and undertakings might have as much to do with the development of his personality as did the imprint of the events with which he came in contact or the insights he was able to conjure up with the help of his therapist. To put it very simply, man was shaped by his commitments and what he did to fulfill them. Even a momentary commitment, experienced for no more than a fleeting instant during a psychotherapeutic interview or in a split second in some fast-breaking emergency on the highway might make a lifetime of difference.

There is much in man's social history that confirms this idea. It is said that the United States Presidency may make a statesman out of a politician, provided he commits himself to it. Professional controls may also make the man who dedicates himself to professional objectives. More than one of us has assumed the ways of scholarship by first undertaking the responsibilities of teaching.

But closely allied to these concepts of role commitment was something else that came to my attention in the late 1930's. Korzybski's newly published *Science and Sanity* raised questions about the ways in which language and thought are interrelated. His ideas about general semantics seemed to me to fit not only my own experiences in psychotherapy, but also what I thought I saw in psychodrama.

Not only did it seem that the words man uses give and hold the structure of his thought, but, more particularly, the names by which he calls himself give and hold the structure of his personality. Each of us invests his name with a particular kind of meaning. It has been so for thousands of years. The man who knew himself as "Saul" became the man who martyred himself as "Paul," perhaps in a way that would have been impossible if he had persisted in identifying himself as "Saul." Women, whose marriages confronted them with particular difficulties in complementing their husbands' lives, were greatly aided in the transition by the change in their names. I had seen this happen in cases where I had some intimate knowledge of what the woman had to overcome. Moreover, those professions which supposedly required the greatest sublimation of personal impulses often made the task easier for their members by attaching some title such as "Reverend" or "Doctor" to the man's name. This bit of disidentification with the rest of humanity does not, of course, work in all cases.

It is not, I am sure, that there is any special magic in names—only the magic that we invest in them. Behind the name is the identity that we put there. To the extent that we remain faithful to that identity we remain faithful to the name, and vice versa. If the identity is to be changed it does, of course, require more than a mere change in name. But the change in name, along with all the other terms of one's identity can have profound psychological implications.

Something More

But now where are we? We have seen persons change as a result of carrying out new commitments and we have seen them change as a consequence of their redefinitions of themselves. But enlightening as these glimpses of what a viable psychology of man might be, it still seems as if the objective eludes our grasp. How often the client in psychotherapy says, in effect, "I see what I want to do; I see now how to do it and where; and I see how someone like me could step out into an entirely new way of life; but I cannot picture myself— *me*—ever becoming anything other than what I am."

It hardly seems enough to say that such a person lacks "emotional insight," or even to say that there is something wrong with "the boundaries of his ego." Nor is it adequate to argue that his thoughts are straightened out, but not his behavior. There must be something more than emotion, thought, and behavior that goes to make the man. To find this "something" is the challenge of psychology, though I doubt that very many psychologists see it this way. And so this particular venture that started with the "S," the arrow, and the "R" on the classroom blackboard continued to blunder on its way, without, I am afraid, any very respectable identification with the mainstream of American psychology.

But howsoever thoughts may fail to progress, one's circumstances move ahead without waiting for him. So it was with me. With the unsolicited help of some legislators in western Kansas and the gratuitous opposition of the State's most prominent psychiatrist we were given a thousand dollars a year to conduct traveling psychological clinics. Mostly these clinics were sponsored by schools, though occasionally other agencies took the initiative, including, I am happy to say, some county medical societies which, while they characteristically found it difficult to cooperate on an equalitarian basis in any community enterprise, did have a certain intimate appreciation of the personal distress of the families on whom they made house calls.

Motives and Complaints

One of the salient features of this state-wide experience was the opportunity to examine the language of complaint used by teachers, parents, children, and others. Each person seeks to communicate his distress in the terms that make sense to him, but not necessarily in terms that make sense to others or to the person complained about. The result is a great deal of misunderstanding in psychological matters. Teachers do not understand how their pupils feel, pupils are unable to sympathize with their teachers' frustrations, and neither is able to put himself into the shoes of parents.

After a time it became abundantly clear that a complaint, as for example a teacher's complaint about a child, reflected primarily the disruption in her own life and did not necessarily state the issue or provide adequate grounds for approaching the person complained about. A teacher might complain that a child was "lazy," but when asked to observe him for several days to see how he went about being "lazy," come up with a description of some very active and purposeful behavior. "Laziness," then, although attributed to the child, had as its principal referrent, as far as the psychologist was concerned, the frustration the teacher experienced in trying to get the child to join her in something she thought they ought to be doing.

There was something more that came out of this experience—one of many more things, in fact. An analysis of the context of the language of complaint suggested that all of us are inclined to use motivational terms, such as "laziness," when others do not do what we think they should, and sometimes even when we do not do what we think we should. Yet it is neither accurate nor descriptive to say that someone does nothing at all. So with all motivational terms—they lose their descriptive value when one becomes intimate with what is going on in the world of another person.

Thus our state-wide travels brought us face-to-face with a strange paradox: the more we understood what was actually happening the less useful was our lexicon of psychodynamic terms. Already we had come a long way from Freud, even further than we then suspected. But nonetheless our next step was to be bolder than any we had yet taken.

An Experiment in Living

What if a person thinks he is neurotic—or even is neurotic—does he have to act that way, or continue to live that way? This may not be a well-posed question, but it was with some such proposition as this in our minds that my students and I undertook a radical approach to psychotherapy. Radical, but perhaps not altogether new!

Having observed that man often makes something of himself by undertaking a commitment—even a commitment undertaken without full conviction—and having observed that many of us refuse to budge from our neurotic positions without first stretching out a safety net of rationalizations—and hence never succeed in making anything of ourselves at all—it occurred to us that the key to therapy might be in getting the client to get on with a new way of life without waiting to acquire "insight." After all, is not that the way man has been treating himself for thousands of years? Rarely does one know where he is going when he launches out into a new way of life, and even less often does he know what is wrong with the pathway he abandons. It is only in a semantically rationalized and elaborately psychologized society that one insists on knowing all the *whys* before seeking to experience the *whats*.

So we set about asking each client to write a self-characterization and to Q-sort the Mailer Inventory cards containing self-descriptive statements. This was before the days of the Minnesota Multi-Phasic Inventory and before this kind of task was called Q-sorting. Then a group of three or four of us would take this information and write another sketch, as it might have been written by another person. Embodied in this sketch of ours would be a different outlook and some illustrations of how such an outlook led to characteristic social behavior. The therapist would then take this sketch back to the client, ask him to pretend that he was the other person, for perhaps two weeks, rehearse the part with him every day or two, and invite the client to pay particular attention to the results of the experiment.

There was, of course, a good deal more to it than play acting. We soon realized that there were tricks to writing the new role, ways of setting up real-life situations, and, particularly, a framework for presenting the undertaking to a skeptical and usually reluctant client who would ordinarily prefer to talk about himself. This is not the place to go into detail as to how this fixed-role therapy, as we have come to call it, was carried out. Let me say only that it produced some exciting results. A little later on in this account I shall come back to it and attempt to say what I think the experience contributed to the development of the theory whose autobiography I am pretending to write.

An Afternoon with the Obvious

It is commonly said that the clinician at his best is an artist and not a scientist, and that the scientist at his best is a man of cold intellect without passion or empathy. Sometimes it is conceded that the clinician might be regarded as an applied scientist, that is to say, a technician who takes what the true scientist has discovered and exploits it for the benefit of fellow man. But most psychologists believe that the scientist and the clinician are really two quite different kinds of persons.

Perhaps I have described enough of my experiences to make it clear that this distinction between the clinician and the scientist runs counter to what I have seen. Whatever progress I may have made in shaking loose from the old notions and in developing novel hypotheses out of intimate experience with man in distress was progress in science, and, as I soon hope to make clear, what I did as a clinician emerged out of my thinking more or less in the manner of a scientist. Indeed I suspect that the best scientist is one who approaches his subject intimately as a clinician may be expected to approach it, and the best clinician is one who invites his client to join him in a controlled investigation of life. Nowhere, it seems to me, is this intrinsic relationship more basic than in psychology, and no discipline stands to lose more by failing to recognize it.

One of my tasks in the 1930's was to direct graduate studies leading to the Master's degree. A typical afternoon might find me talking to a graduate student at one o'clock, doing all those familiar things that thesis directors have to do—encouraging the student to pinpoint the issues, to observe, to become intimate with the problem, to form hypotheses either inductively or deductively, to make some preliminary test runs, to relate his data to his predictions, to control his experiments so that he will know what led to what, to generalize cautiously, and to revise his thinking in the light of experience.

At two o'clock I might have an appointment with a client. During this interview I would not be taking the role of the scientist, but rather helping the distressed person work out some solutions to his life's problems. So what would I do? Why, I would try to get him to pinpoint the issues, to observe, to become intimate with the problem, to form hypotheses, to make test runs, to relate outcomes to anticipations, to control his ventures so that he will know what led to what, to generalize cautiously, and to revise his dogma in the light of experience.

At three o'clock I would see a student again. Likely as not he was either dragging his feet, hoping to design some world-shaking experiment before looking at his first subject to see first-hand what he was dealing with, or plunging into some massive ill-considered data-chasing expedition. So I would again try to get him to pinpoint the issues, to observe open-mindedly, to become intimate with the problem, to form hypotheses—all the things that I had had to do at one o'clock.

At four o'clock another client! Guess what! He would be dragging his feet, hoping to design a completely new personality before venturing his first change in behavior, or plunging into some ill-considered acting-out escapade, etc., etc. But this, of course, was not my hour for science; it was my hour for psychotherapy. And what I had done with that student back in the hour before, that was obviously not psychotherapy; it was science!

I must say that this sort of thing went on for a long time before it ever occurred to me that I was really doing the same sort of thing all afternoon long. It seems incredible now that it took me so long to realize this, but at the time it seemed so perfectly obvious that science and psychotherapy were different, even contrasting kinds of experience. Science was objective and cold; psychotherapy was subjective and warm. Science dealt with truth but psychotherapy dealt with humanity. But, as I have said before, all my life it has been the obvious things that have gotten me into trouble! I have even speculated that man's greatest challenge and noblest undertaking may be to transcend the obvious. And that is something I wish I knew how to do.

Right-Hand and Left-Hand Theories of Personality

There was something else that was slow in dawning on me. I must tell you about that before attempting to distill something out of blunt fixed-role therapy and my afternoons with the obvious.

Almost any textbook written before 1940, and, indeed, most of the textbooks in elementary psychology turned out in the decades since, made quite an issue out of psychology's being a science. Generally psychologists have emphasized the point that science is characterized more by its method than by its accumulated body of knowledge. This being so, they argue, psychology is really pretty scientific stuff, even though it does not have many solid facts to point to. In fact, psychologists, being self-conscious about their methodology, may have a wee bit better claim to being scientists than a lot of physicists who spend their time making engineering hay out of a few classic experiments.

In order to clarify what they meant the authors of these psychology texts would describe the essentials of scientific method, which is, as we all know, the inside story of how the scientist behaves. This fellow called the scientist pinpoints the issues, they said, he observes, he becomes intimate with the problem, he forms hypotheses inductively and deductively, he makes test runs, he relates his data to predictions, he controls his experiments so that he knows what leads to what, he generalizes cautiously, and he revises his thinking in the light of experimental outcomes. These are the operations that explain the behavior of a person who has achieved the status of a scientist. All of this is very interesting, particularly because it represents a particularly coherent theory of personality, albeit one that is reserved for scientists only.

But now, as the author of our textbook turns from his credentials to his contributions, he abandons this perceptive theory of personality and starts to tell us how ordinary human beings, which he usually prefers to call "organisms" rather than "scientists," function. In doing so he spins an altogether different kind of personality theory, or perhaps two or three such theories. Man, the organism, he says, responds to stimuli, learns what he is taught, is propelled by his motives, is helplessly suspended in his culture, and is swept along with the tides of social change.

Now that I look back on it I cannot understand how one could have failed to be struck immediately by the contrast in personality theories espoused by the same psychologist; on the one hand, the one he universally uses to explain himself and, on the other, the various concoctions he uses to explain ordinary mortals. Yet few of my colleagues find this paradox amusing. They say, "But of course the scientist is different!" But I must admit also that it was a long time before I myself became aware of this inconsistency, and perhaps if I had been more of a psychologist it would have been even longer.

Now it seems that it might prove interesting to do one of two things: either apply to psychologists themselves the psychologies they designed to explain the behavior of ordinary mortals, or to apply to man the psychology they designed to explain themselves. Since there are a lot more mortals in this world than there are psychologists, for the time being at least, we might run into more possibilities if we tried the latter. If we do so, then it may be said that our model of man is that of man-the-scientist and our questions will revolve about the issue of whether man can be understood in this manner, both in the floodlight of history and in the dark of his closet.

It has been only recently in my professional life that I have been willing to regard myself as either a philosopher or a theoretician in any measure whatsoever. A long time ago, however, I fell to fancying myself as a scientist of sorts. Now I am quite prepared to concede that I may not be very much of any of these, but at least nowadays if someone describes me as a personality theorist I do not protest as vigorously as I might have twenty years ago.

From time to time I wrote chapters and prepared condensed drafts of a handbook of clinical techniques for my students. But the serious writing always bogged down because it seemed as if I should say why something should be done as well as how to do it. Moreover I was confronted with the growing realization that I had got out of step with a good deal of the psychological thinking of my times and therefore my reasons for doing things in certain ways would not make much sense to my colleagues, even in cases where our techniques might happen to be identical.

How far out of the mainstream of psychology had I drifted and what was there about this outlook I had developed that was essentially unique? It seemed as if I were overdue for some extensive self-examination, and perhaps an overhaul. Could I state my position in a coherent fashion and, if I could, would it be something that would open any new vistas and stand up to the demands of rigorous testing?

I suppose the issue I faced was: could I put into words what I meant and, if I could, would I still mean it? As I describe these meanderings in the maze of human distress, as I now remember them, it may appear to my reader or listener that there are some converging lines of thought. Take the last two things I have mentioned—the afternoon of interviews alternating between psychotherapy and advice to researchers, and the two kinds of personality theory each textbook writer espoused. Both suggest that, in practice, the struggles of man the mortal and man the scientist were against the same obstacles and that those obstacles were to be surmounted in what has proved over the centuries to be the human way. And as we look back on our iconoclastic ventures with fixed-role therapy we can see these also as fitting into a personality theory that says, in effect, that the means by which man has, over the centuries, coped most successfully with his historical obstacles are in some general way the basic devices he can extend and improve in coping with his personal distress.

Fixed-role therapy is, according to this model, not a panacea but an experiment. In fact, we have learned that if it is presented as a panacea it fails its purpose and the client does not get on with the life process of finding out for himself. So do all panaceas tend to immobilize man at those moments when he ought to be exploring his alternatives creatively. The important thing about the fixed-role enactment is not that it gives the person an authentic way to live, but that it invites him to try a new way, calculated and venturesome, and to appraise its outcomes. Certainly the role as written may not turn out well at all. But that is true of the attempts of any life that is approached wholeheartedly. Not all the new things men try prove to be good, but, if nothing is ever tried, then even the old ways, which once might have been regarded as good, will become oppressively stagnant. The only valid way to live one's life is to get on with it.

Man lives best when he commits himself to getting on with his life. Since I see the concept of learning as nothing less than this, the term seems redundant when applied to a living creature. And so, too, with the objectives of therapy, for therapy is a way of helping man get on with it, to live wholeheartedly. However, if you prefer to call the whole thing "learning" then I have no objection to this use of the term—as long as its meaning is now narrowed down to something less than life's basic enterprise by the textbook writers.

The Outcome

This account is intended to describe the course of certain psychological experiences, as I now remember them, which led to the formulation of a particular position in psychology I have called *personal construct theory*. I should say also that as a result of trying to cope with these experiences I seem to have brought myself to a philosophical position for which I can think of no better term than *constructive alternativism*. When it appeared that clients in therapy could often make good use of my preposterous explanations and when it occurred to me that it was not necessary, or even desirable, to refute one proposition before investigating its alternatives—as one does not refute the old self in fixed-role therapy before inviting participation in the experiment—I was groping toward such a philosophical position.

To be sure, personal construct theory can be expounded in the conventionally logical manner. It has a basic postulate and a set of corollaries. And it has some constructs that arise from the pursuit of its implications. All this, if it were expounded, would make it seem more or less rational, I suppose. I know this is what a theorist is expected to do. But I am convinced that this is not the way theories happen. Certainly it is not the way personal construct theory came into being.

What I have done, therefore, is tell you how this theory happened. Or perhaps it would be more accurate to say that this is how, in retrospect, I think it happened. If I had kept a diary I might be surprised at what I would actually now find written there—perhaps something quite different from what I remember.

4

Confusion and the Clock[1]

Some Things I would Like to Know, but Not Yet

It has often occurred to me, as I am sure it has to you too, that it would be amusing to have a peek through the curtain of night at what tomorrow has in store. Suppose I could observe what I would be doing at this time tomorrow night. It might be interesting to watch the goings on from this present vantage point of the evening before, yet not to participate in them, nor to be concerned with whether I was doing what I was supposed to be doing, nor even to be in any danger of being recognized as an intruder. Such a thing would have to be done surreptitiously, however, for I am sure if I were to be caught at my eavesdropping, my tomorrow's I (How do you say that?) would become self-conscious about the arrangement and start acting in an unnatural manner. He might not even do things the way he was destined to do them, and the whole affair might fall apart in a shambles of irreality.

But if I could manage to keep out of sight, so that all the performers in tomorrow evening's episode would act the way the sum-total of their previous experiences supposedly required them to act, that is, would act naturally, the affair might come off pretty well. Now that I think of it, the other people, other than myself-tomorrow and myself-today, ought to be easy enough to fool, even if they did get a glimpse of me eavesdropping. They would probably no more than mistake me for myself-tomorrow, and think it quite natural that I should be there—unless, of course, I was wearing a different colored shirt, or hadn't shined my shoes, as I haven't tonight. So that part of the arrangement has a reasonable chance of being worked out, in spite of what some of my more skeptical readers—not you; I didn't mean you!—are likely to think.

Where I would get into trouble, if I weren't extremely careful, is with myself. Perhaps if I arrived in some kind of disguise, it would keep me from finding myself out. Now, let's see: I could go as my Cousin Leander. I don't know him very well, and if I looked a little familiar to myself, there would be a perfectly logical explanation.

Leander, however, if I remember correctly, is a little nearsighted, and, unless his nearsightedness has been offset by presbyopia during the last ten years, he might miss a good deal of what was going on. Besides, I doubt if Cousin Leander would be very much interested in what I am going to do tomorrow night. That wouldn't be a real obstacle, of course, since I would only be pretending to myself that I was Cousin Leander.

Still, the performance would have to be pretty good—pretty realistic, I mean—to fool me, because I am sure that I would know right off that the real Cousin Leander was not genuinely interested enough to be acting so alert to all the things that would need watching. So, if I let myself get too closely involved with the events of the evening, I am sure that my tomorrow's self would suspect that something unusual was up and start asking pointed questions. And, whenever that happens, I mean when I start to ask myself pointed questions, I get confused and my stories don't hang together.

Before the evening was over I am sure I would be found out and I would have to come back to today, if it weren't too late, which is where I am now. Then, I would simply have to wait it out until tomorrow came around and I found out what I want to know by the time-honored method of living through it. While this wait-and-see approach to the problem seems unnecessarily conservative—even reactionary—I doubt I shall be able to do much in the way of improving it, at least until I have given the matter a great deal more thought.

Still, I don't like to give up on this project too quickly; people who give up too quickly are apt to earn the reputation of being *unwise*; like my grandfather who once bought a thousand acres of rice land in Texas. He sold it a year or two later, just before oil was discovered on it; which was unwise. He did not know that he was selling a part of the fabulously rich Beaumont Field.

Then, on the other hand, there is my neighbor, I mean there was my neighbor—that is to say, he is now a neighbor to where I used to live—who has been convinced for years and years that there is oil underneath his farm. He thinks there is oil under mine, too, but only the edge of the oil deposit is under mine. The center of it, where the gushers are going to be, is under his.

[1] Written in 1960 and first published as Kelly, G.A. (1978). Confusion and the clock. In F. Fransella (Ed.). (1978). *Personal Construct Psychology 1977* (pp. 209-232). Academic Press (ISBN: 9780122654602). Italian translation, La confusione e l'orologio, published in *Costruttivismi*, 2015, *2*, 20-37. Republished here with permission by Elsevier, who hold the copyright.

Collected Papers of the Pioneer of Constructivist Psychology: George A. Kelly, First Edition. Edited by David A. Winter and Nick Reed.

Now some people think he is being a little fanciful about the matter, but if he holds on year after year, and some day they do find oil on his place, he will, unlike my grandfather, be acclaimed as a very wise man, if he is still alive; and if he isn't still alive, they will probably acclaim him as an even wiser man. On the other hand, if they don't find oil, all he has to do is to sit and wait until something else turns up—maybe a new market for sandburrs—and after that he will be considered almost as wise as if it had turned out to be oil.

So, let me try again. While I probably will not succeed this time either, I can at least establish the reputation of being a person of vision. Then, if something does turn up later and people can tell what is going to happen to them twenty-four hours in advance, I can put in my claim to wisdom.

****

Since writing the paragraphs above, I have been thinking very hard and I believe I have reached a conclusion. The real sticker in this business of predicting the future is the danger of my remembering in the midst of tomorrow night's activities that I have already been there, and who that fellow over there who claims to be Cousin Leander really is. Now I think, at last, we have got to the nub of the matter, like isolating the schizococcus, and it should only be a matter of time until we achieve a major break-through, and the whole thing will seem as simple as A-B-C.

We shall need funds, of course, to achieve this break-through. Perhaps someone will organize a *Tomorrow Research Fund* and put on campaigns with the neighbors around the block collecting coins from each other. Or a *March of Times* might do the trick. Now that we know what the problem is—our discovery that the human mind takes account of what it has foreseen—our research will have a wholly different emphasis.

The task will be to help people forget what they foresaw just before it happens. This would enable them to step across the threshold of any new situation with a freshly opened mind, completely emptied of its expectations. In a word, we would replace memory with foresight. Thus, we would always know in advance what was going to happen, but we would not be hampered at the instant of occurrence by looking for it or remembering what it was.

My! My! We could predict events faithfully, right down to the last sneeze, even down to the sneeze that doesn't quite come off, but we would be just as pleasantly surprised as ever at the final ka-choo! Sneezes would appear to have slipped up on us unawares, just as they do now. And, while we would know that the next sneeze that fails to come off was not really supposed to come off anyway, we could enjoy the suspense and the tingling sensation that precedes sneezes that don't come off. The sneeze that doesn't happen is an event, too, you know, or didn't you realize that?

****

This brings me to an obstacle. I know that wise men always surmount obstacles, so I suppose I should try to be wise enough to climb over this one too, just as I have been scrambling over a good many others during the past few minutes—*your* minutes, *my* hours—that some of you might have considered insurmountable. The obstacle is this: If something like a sneeze doesn't happen, and you already knew in advance that it wasn't going to happen, why is its failure to explode into reality *an event*? Are all the things that don't happen events just like the things that do? Can something be an event without ever happening, or something happen without being an event?

Looked at this way, our little peeks into the future are going to be very complicated, because we will have to see displayed before us all the things that are not going to happen as well as the one thing that will. Sorting out the one from all the others will be like finding a needle in a haystack. It may not even be worth the trouble it would take. My grandfather, for example, would have had to paw through an awfully big clutter of things that were not going to happen to his land before coming across the one thing that was not not-going-to-happen: discovery of oil. Even he, though he was a prodigiously energetic man, might not have felt it was worth the bother.

There is one possibility that I have not considered. Now that I think of it, it seems so obvious that I wonder why it did not occur to me before. Perhaps man already knows how to anticipate the future and the reason he thinks he doesn't is that he always forgets what he has predicted just before it happens. Or, just before it doesn't happen, whichever is the case—I mean if he predicts that it will not happen and, sure enough, it doesn't, then, instead of saying, "This is just what I expected," he forgets, and finds himself just as surprised as he would be if he hadn't ever known. This is just what we were talking about, isn't it—forgetting our predictions so as not to spoil the taste of things when they actually happen?

Now take me. The night before last I was wondering what would happen the next night—remember? So I wrote about it, and if you have been reading this chapter straight through, you must have come across what I had to say. Well, now, that next night has come and gone—the night I wanted to foresee. There was nothing very unusual about it, nothing that I noticed, anyway. Nothing seemed incongruous with what had happened the night before, and I don't remember thinking of anything that was expected to come off and didn't. Cousin Leander didn't show up and even the TV show turned out the way it was supposed to, as far as I could tell.

Now, while I may have forgotten what it was I predicted, let us suppose that when I wrote about forecasting, I could actually tell just what was going to happen, and that when last night rolled around, I promptly forgot what I had predicted. Would that not explain why I felt that I was experiencing things for the first time?

A curious thing! I had the feeling that everything was going along reasonably enough, even though I couldn't think what was supposed to happen, I wonder if that was because, while I had forgotten what was supposed to happen, I had not forgotten the fact that I had been expecting it. This kept me from being flabbergasted at everything my wife said, although I had no idea of what it was to be. Thus, the whole evening went by pretty much as if I were being reminded of something. Altogether, it was a very pleasant experience—not a bit shocking—just a series of interesting reminders. There is even the fact that I didn't get very much written yesterday. That is always a source of minor annoyance. But even that did not surprise me very much. You know, I don't think I expected to, anyway!

In a way, I wish that I could remember what I must have known I was going to do this afternoon. In particular, I wish I could remember—but of course, I can't—what it was I was destined to write this afternoon. Especially I would like to remember how it was going to be said. It seems like such a long ways from the kind of discourse in which I am now involved to the point where I will be saying anything you can agree with, or that will make the whole passage come together, coherent and reasonable. If I could only remember now, then I would have nothing to do except type it off in a hurry and use the extra time before supper to putter around in the basement shop. Somehow, I have the feeling that puttering around in the shop is not in the cards for me this afternoon.

It has doubtless occurred to you that we could check up on this hunch about forgetting one's infallible predictions if we simply wrote down our predictions at the time we made them, and then came back to see if things had turned out the way the writing said they would. This assumes that we would remember having written something down. But, in any case, my wife would probably find the manuscript and ask if I was ready to have it burned with the trash; and if I had already started to forget I would probably tell her to go ahead.

I must confess this bothers me, and casts some doubt on my entire line of reasoning. A while ago, I thought it was going to turn out all right, but now I am not so sure. It must be that everpresent forgetting process again; it has just now erased my prophesy of what I was going to say.

****

Thirteen months and an ocean now separate me from the time and place at which that last of the sentences above was written. As it happens, the manuscript was not burned with the trash. Yet, as I re-read it, I find that at no point did I do what I was talking about doing and make specific predictions of what would occur during the ensuing days. Perhaps the part of the manuscript containing the predictions was destroyed, though I doubt it. It would be especially interesting to read what I might have said was not going to happen. But nothing like that was put down and I cannot be sure how much of what did go on was anticipated. This I know: Nothing that came about was wholly expected and nothing was wholly unexpected. This raises a question of whether one is ever capable of being completely surprised, either by the things that happen or those that don't. But, that is something we can take up later.

What took place, among other things, was this. I was writing during the week-end, and on Saturday had rather a good day of it, probably because I was letting my mind wander unhampered into all kinds of logical traps without concerning myself with how I was going to reason my way out of them. Then came Sunday; as usual, a lazy day. That was the day I was to disguise myself as Cousin Leander. Perhaps I was waiting for something special to happen, and rather proving to myself that nothing special actually would.

On Monday the going was tortuous, as it usually is even when I pretend that I am typing out a message to the most fascinated and wide-eyed listener my imagination can dream up. I remarked to you in that day's manuscript that there wasn't anything particularly special about the evening before. As the writing shows, I even wished on Monday that the conjured fates would take over and tell me what to say, so I could get on with it.

Tuesday and Wednesday my muse deserted me altogether. This was no great surprise. She often leaves me like this, without warning, and, while I don't like it and I occasionally complain to her about her fickleness, I have decided that she must find herself cramped by my efforts to put her soft breath into precise psychological terms, and she must slip away to recover her composure, or perhaps to avoid quarreling with me openly. If so, it is better that way, for I would not want matters between her and me to come to such a state that we would break up permanently.

If you have a few moments to spare, perhaps you wouldn't mind my trying to describe our relationship a little more fully. If you are in a hurry, just skip ahead, since the following passage has very little to do with what I set out to tell you.

BEMUSED
Whose muse are youse?

Last night, the cushioned hours
Piled deep and soft,
You whispered close.
Your voice was in my ear.
"You're mine," I thought.

"All mine!"

So I set down
The throbbing syllables.
And then, at dawn,
I read those lines
I'd written in your spell
And—. What-th'hell!

No sign!

No trace of all
Those sentient moments we
Alone had shared.
You'd slipped away
And stealthily closed the door
And where we lay—

See!

The pillows there.
Each one puffed smooth and bare.
And where, where
Are you? Just where
Are you? And look! In my hands
These incoherent words!

So!

Today, I played
The game a different way.
Within my den,
The hours stacked high
With books upon the floor,
I read from men

Of yore.

I sought only words
That meant just what they said,
And nothing more.
Then twilight came.
The print began to fade,
And there, instead—!

You jade!

You wench! You whore!
Our secrets of the night before
You'd been whispering into others' ears
a thousand years

Or more!

Tonight, recluse,
I sit. No man nor muse
Dares pass that door!
In dark silence sit.
Until, across the room,
I hear a sigh.

She's here!

Already here,
She sits as lone as I;
Ten thousand years
Without a love.
Of all the consorts she
Has had, none wooed

Her true!

Each one pressed close
The eager lips to snatch
Some precious words
As dowry pay
From her supply, to shout
Themselves, all day.

Hard gold!

And so had I;
Just so had failed to clasp
My lonely wraith

In love!

From now I woos m'muse!

Well, that's that.

Thursday, with some reluctance, I went to see my doctor about a pain I had in a certain place where I had always supposed my stomach to be. It's not that I have ever taken much interest in anatomy—internal anatomy, that is. It's rather, that in a general sort of way I like to know where my vital possessions are. I remember distinctly that my seventh grade physiology book at Pleasant Valley School had a picture in it that showed precisely where the things I swallowed got formally admitted to the stomach. Moreover, I know from experience that on those rare occasions when admission is denied, or rescinded, this is the spot where the rumpus starts.

Perhaps I had better explain my reluctance. It's not that I don't like to talk to my friend, the doctor. I do like to talk to him. He happens to be a scholar, and is therefore both humble and fascinated by a variety of things. Medicine, of course, is one of them, though I doubt if he recognizes the vital relationship between it and country club membership. Indeed, I would be surprised if it should turn out that he ever belonged to a country club. No, the reason for my reluctance was that I always feel rather embarrassed in going to him about a furtive pain, or a persistent wart, or an ambulent itchy spot that has developed in the inaccessible reaches of my back. I know he finds medicine just as puzzling as I find psychology, and it seems a little unfair to keep presenting him with problems like these that may trip him up.

But still, he is a man who has faced up to the vagaries of medical practice, and therefore, has sense enough to make me share some of the responsibility for the decisions that are made. Moreover, he seems to recognize my inalienable and constitutional right to manage my own insides, and would never think of giving me "doctor's orders." Nor has he ever audibly invoked "The Medical Profession" in my presence. Instead, when I turn up with something pretty vague or obscure we are both likely to be embarrassed, so we sit there and look at each other and try to think of something to say that will relieve the other's discomfort.

As a physician he has his more enterprising moments, just as I have, and on these occasions he show great ingenuity in thinking of places that can be looked into. This is the way he was on this particular Thursday. In no time at all he had wangled an appointment for a series of tests in a laboratory the next day.

None of this seemed particularly surprising, nor, on the other hand, was it anything I could have precisely predicted. It was all, more or less, within the pattern of life according to which I lived day by day. I felt no more than the usual relief that something systematic could be done, the usual annoyance at further intrusions on an already unproductive week, and the usual undertone of curiosity about how much more of this life I would be privileged to see.

That evening the Thursday Nighters gathered. These are the patient souls who accept the standing invitation my wife and I extend to all those who are willing to listen and comment on whatever manuscript I have produced during the preceding week. Needless to say, I often greet them with apprehension, an apprehension I try to hide beneath my role as host.

This evening I read the latest installment of this manuscript—right up to the end. They were puzzled, as they had been with the previous installments of this particular undertaking, and not particularly pleased with what I was doing. What literary reputation I have among them is that of an expository writer with a commitment to a certain amount of scientific discipline, and, while they knew I was off on a different track this time, they did not see that I was going anywhere. But they were momentarily interested in the propositions conjured up by my whimsy and, somewhat to my relief, turned the discussion to such questions as whether *anticipation* was a posture one assumed toward the future and if it should be distinguished from *prediction*, the latter being something which may be better understood as a probability statement about events. And, too, they raised the question of "phenomenal time" and wondered if anticipation were bounded by that. According to my notes, we did not, on this occasion, get into a discussion of anxiety, the central topic of this chapter.

Early the following morning I had an acute coronary attack—my first. Some years ago I watched my mother die from a coronary. It took two weeks of agony. It has seemed to me, particularly since that experience, that mankind ought to find a better way to go about this business. I'm all for putting it off as long as it is decently possible, of course, but when the time comes it should be possible for a person to pass on with a little more dignity. I have in mind that one ought to be able to think noble thoughts on such an occasion, or, if he finds it hard to think noble thoughts on his own, he ought to have a chance to recall the lines of Thanotopsis, which are pretty noble, I think, or something like that.

While I have noticed that death often does give other people in the vicinity a certain amount of inspiration—particularly those whose lives are not too intimately tied up in the deceased—it is apt to be a very distracting and messy business for the person who is doing the dying and for those who lose part of their own lives along with him. The fact that death, in many cases, is preceded by months or years of physical and mental deterioration adds to the indignity.

In this case, of course, I didn't die. Moreover, I managed, I think, to retain a certain amount of dignity, though not as much as one might wish, and I kept it until I got to the hospital. There, in spite of my best efforts, professionals who are highly trained in such techniques took most of what I had left away from me.

The pain, at first, was terribly distracting and, when I realized what was going on inside me, which was within an hour or so after the commotion started, I supposed that the odds were pretty much against me—a mistaken conception, as I was to discover later. So, here I was, with a Fire Department inhalator over my face, and, so I thought, on the brink of one of life's greatest ventures. I was facing for myself the one thing in the world that has most stirred mankind's imagination, yet has offered him the least literal verification of his outflung hypotheses. I remember thinking of this, in the split seconds between cramps, retches, and gasps.

I remember thinking, and being somewhat relieved to discover, that there was nothing particularly frightening about it. I even thought about one of the allegorical tales of Sir Garth, I believe it was, from the Idylls of the King in which the same theme was expressed, and I thought to myself how true it was. It might have been interesting to mention this point to some of the people close to me, later on when I could talk. But it was a thought not particularly appropriate to the kind of torture they were going through and it seemed in rather bad taste to bring it up at the time. No, there was nothing frightening, as far as I was concerned about the imminent prospect of dying. Nor was the climactic experience I was having utterly strange or confused.

I remember thinking, while we were waiting for the ambulance, that since this had developed into a nip-and-tuck affair, I was going to put up the fight of my life. I felt, strangely enough, that I was ready to put up such a fight. I had been in a similar spot before, holding on by my teeth against losing consciousness, and I had won. Besides, if this was to be my last fight, I wanted it to be a good one. And I remember thinking, too, that in the months I might be able to hang on, even if I survived this first attack, there would probably be some everyday things to be done in order to make the transition as easy as possible for my family. But this was about as far as my planning went. I was much too involved with immediate matters to try to go into these speculations in any detail.

Again, let me come back to the theme of this chapter, which is really the only excuse for talking about these rather personal matters. Was all this that happened something that was, in some measure, anticipated? Had I seen them behind my Cousin Leander's mask? Yes, I think so. I had indeed eavesdropped on myself in this moment many times before, but had never been clear as to what I saw going on or as to when it was happening. Perhaps this was because of Cousin Leander's nearsightedness, or perhaps his tendency not to be greatly interested in my personal affairs.

And, another question: Was the experience itself characterized by further anticipations? I think it was that, too! I have already mentioned my fleeting glimpses of what the future might be. But there was more of anticipation in the experience than that. Even among the tortured moments, each gasping pain was a preview of the next, telling me what to expect moment by moment, and the contortions into which I twisted myself were as much postures against the next onslaught as they were reactions to the last. Nor did I, before undertaking each spasm, have to reason to myself that the next stab was coming; my preparatory efforts were as spontaneous as life itself. As life itself!

In general, then, was it not, on the one hand, a passage of human experience whose strange unprecedented notes derived significance that early morning from the underlying theme of my life, which they so sharply embellished, and, on the other, one whose meaning stemmed less from the repetitive familiarity of its details than from what it seemed to foretell.

But now I am arguing, I suspect, and this book is not intended to prove anything; only to be an adventure in human feelings, one in which I have asked you to join me, so that, when we are finished, we can each ask the other where we have been and what we have found out.

So far, in talking about this experience, I have reported only those feelings that had to do with my direct personal relationship to the events. There were also other things that crossed my mind. Like those I have already mentioned, one half these were experienced both in their reassuring and in their disquieting dimensions. In fact, I am not sure I can always tell the difference between what is reassuring and what is not, or between what is pleasant and what is not. Such qualities often seem not to be so much properties of the things that happen as they are ways of coping with them.

There are some things, I grant, that I would find terribly difficult to regard as pleasant. The pain I had was an example. I didn't like that, not one bit! The knack of enjoying it was an art I had not mastered at all, possibly because I've never really tried. But I am not so sure that there aren't some people who would be delighted by such misery. I'll go even further; I know that there are people who are thrilled by such experiences. I have seen them at it. And, now that I think of it, I can remember there have been times when I have myself enjoyed sharp pains, as in playing football, for example. But that was "sport" and, so far, I have not taken up coronaries as a form of sport.

As for regarding some of my experiences as intrinsically disquieting, that, too, is hard to pin down. I have referred to the pain as "distracting." It turned my attention away from what I was doing; got me away from this manuscript for a whole year, as you see. But this flat label may be a misnomer. During the months when I was trying to get caught up with other things, so I could get back to writing, I thought many times about the discussion in which I was engaged when my work was interrupted. In a sense, then, the effect has been quite the opposite of distraction; instead of being turned from what I was doing, I have found myself preoccupied with it. Moreover, this is not a reaction against—a turning away from—the illness, in some sort of counter-play, but actually a viewing of it in a new perspective. As one can see, I am now turning out page after page of manuscript, splashing the events of last year across the outlines of this chapter. So, as I say, even my cautious adjective, "distracting," may be too arbitrary a term for what happened.

And as for what is inherently disquieting or reassuring, or whether the feelings I have described so far were essentially calm or turbulent; that, too, I cannot set down definitively. I can talk about those feelings from the standpoint of the calmness I perceived. And, I can talk also about turbulence—as I have, in some degree! But what were the feelings, really? I don't think I can answer that question. And, I think I would be very skeptical of anyone who tried to answer for me.

There are some scholars who make a big to-do about getting down to the genuineness of human experience—the existentialists, for example, whoever they may be (I have never been quite able to identify them). Or, the followers of Carl Rogers who concentrate upon the full acceptance of feelings as they naturally are (These folks are easier to identify)! I can't say I disapprove of such efforts to reach a terminal point in human inquiry; it is only when someone claims to have arrived that I get that restless feeling again.

So now, as I start to talk about the other things I found in the experience—the ones I did not mention in the paragraphs above—I want to enter an advance protest. I still do not know whether the events were of themselves good or bad, painful or pleasant, reassuring or disquieting. All I can do is report what I made of them; that is to say, what I thought, or what I remember thinking. To do this I have to align my perspective along various preconceived axes, else it would be practically impossible to have any sense of ever having been there at all. The dimensions I use are the dimensions I have myself devised, both for description of such events in general and for the fullest possible appreciation of the particular experience itself. Who knows how adequate these terms of reference are! This is what I do about such matters, and the best I can do about this special matter, and probably something of the sort is the best anyone can do in coming to grips with such affairs.

I remember looking up at my wife and thinking of the chilling shock she must be experiencing at that moment. Yet there was no outward sign, only an alertness and a quick efficiency, as she turned here and there to do the things that had to be done. It crossed my mind that I was very proud of her, that she was probably stronger than I was accustomed to give her credit for being, and that there are great resources in the human personality which one can easily overlook in day-by-day casual living. But there, inside, there was none-the-less the icy grip of reality; I knew that for sure, in spite of all the resources she might be mobilizing against it. And there I was, sprawled and twisting on the bed, making a shameful spectacle of myself, and, moment by moment, making matters all the worse for her. All these were scarcely more than fleeting thoughts, of course.

There was also a dimension of reprehensibility that ran through these feelings. That is to say, I could not escape thinking that I was responsible for the mess we all were in. If I had listened to the experts and heeded their dire warnings, I might have been able to live the life of a healthy organism. In that case, I would have been waking up just about then, bouncing into a cold shower, eating a hearty but leisurely breakfast of prunes and yogurt, and getting ready for a snappy day at the office, during which I would delegate responsibility right and left, make clear-cut simple-minded decisions, clear my desk promptly, and—with never a backward glance at the inanities I had perpetrated—arrive on time for three o'clock golf, followed by an inspirational dinner meeting on the subject of "Why isn't everybody smart and successful." I cannot say that I thought in exactly these terms, but this was the gist of it.

While I felt uncomfortably responsible for the confused state of affairs into which it appeared I had plunged us all, I remember I still felt rebellious against doing the things that people say would have avoided it. So, not only did I feel ashamed, responsible, and stupid; I also felt unrepentant. And, then a whole new round of thought threatened to start; I was beginning to feel ashamed of being unrepentant. As long as I was on this track, I was caught between being a virtuous vegetable and an independent corpse. Stretched out along this axis of appraisal—this yardstick—I found myself confused, disorganized, put upon, and, as if I were trying to go two ways at once.

Now let's have no misunderstanding about this. I know perfectly well, and I knew then, that the way to avoid this kind of feeling is to conform to some readymade doctrine. And if you get caught and find that you have already slipped up, you start kicking yourself in the shins and make some special display of your eagerness to conform. In some cultures this is called "repentance," in others, "self- criticism." Of course, nobody claims that self-abnegation will keep unpleasant things from happening to you—well, *almost* nobody these days—but there is ample evidence to indicate that it keeps you from being upset over the messes you stumble into.

There are still other people who take the view that the sort of confusion I experienced at this point constitutes bed-rock realistic thinking. Things actually are in a mess—all-over—everywhere! They say we are all inclined to ignore the trouble we are in and we go blithely about making it worse by engaging in such diversions as watching TV, whistling, dressing up to go places, and being polite to each other. Finally, when we are all alone and it is too late to do anything about it, there is nothing left to do but look at the nightmare that has been shadowing the backs of our minds all the time.

To subscribe to this kind of notion takes a bit of preliminary thinking. You have to start out by assuming that the stark naked truth of man's existence is to be seen just by turning around and looking at it. We just open our eyes, stare in the right direction, and the whole thing stands there perfectly clear. You don't understand things by experimenting with interpretations of them—you understand them directly, by confronting them. Just around the corner of your facade you can face up to what's what!

Well, this is one way to go at it. When we start out with such a notion in mind, it happens that each time we turn a corner and see something rather grim we are likely to think, "This is it. We have arrived. This is the end." Still, there always seem to be more corners to turn and a starker nakeder truth that someone claims to have glimpsed in the dusk just ahead. It's awfully hard to settle on something grim enough to suit everybody.

So, while I was quite miserable, in some ways, about the goings-on that Friday morning, I was not then, nor am I now, convinced that I was face to face with the ultimate meaning of my life—or even very close to it, for that matter. Almost anybody—certainly any of my readers—could think up something a great deal more stark than what I have described. As a matter of fact, if I may address myself to you personally, haven't you already done so while reading this? As for me, if there was a nightmare catching up with me, I was well aware that it was the one I had personally manufactured and not the ultimate logos.

It seems to me that it must make a considerable difference whether one assumes that the ultimate facts of life are close at hand or that there are vast remote truths toward which we progress but slowly. The former view often seems quite practical—quite workable. You figure something out, and you believe it's there, and you believe in it, and you cling to it, and its everyday workability seems to support your feeling of having hit upon something solid. Like money, for example: there are so many things you can do with money, and, day after day, quite consistently, money gets results. So most of us put a lot of faith in it. Moreover, if we were smart enough, we could probably do a good deal more with money than we do.

But now consider the latter view, the view that there are vast remote truths toward which we progress but slowly. That is the kind of outlook that can encourage mysticism. You are always expecting tomorrow to be different, and you get fooled because it turns out to be the same, thousands of times in succession. Pretty soon you begin to look like an utter nincompoop. So you go through life half believing that anything is possible, no matter how unlikely it may be.

If every day were under a firm contract to duplicate every other day the bed rock realism of the former view should be the more comfortable of the two. The vast majority of one's days are indeed pretty much alike—at least we can get by construing them so—just as Sunday night about which I speculated in the first part of this chapter could be interpreted as pretty much like any other Sunday night. I wrote a remark—which I intend to retain in the manuscript—about this on Monday, the day my muse was packing up to leave. Having experienced a good many thousands of such everyday appearing days I suppose one could hardly blame himself for concluding that he had a pretty realistic slant on life.

But then you come to a day, just one day out of all the thousands, that does not fit the realistic way you cross off your calendar. Perhaps it is the day you die. Then, *then* if you try to cope with that day as just another Sunday night, or Friday morning, you may very well get the impression that you have been missing the truth of things and it is too late to do anything about it.

So, I lay there, that one day that was different from the thousands I had known before, that Friday morning, and I felt twinges of anguish. The anguish was a mixture of things: the ambiguity of my being—future, past, and present—the disarray in the orderliness of mind and body I had come to rely upon, and the unspeakable loneliness of guilt which threatened to cut me off from those closest to me. In fact, I suspect if I had been a very practical or exacting idealist I would have felt that truth had played me false, and, from that point on, the whole thing would have gotten badly out of hand. ("Practical Idealist!" No incompatibility of terms here, if we take the view that an idealist is anyone who carries a clear image of perfection around in his head!)

But, even in those moments, I could not honestly believe that truth had played me false simply because I can't take truth very literally. Of course, I believe in truth, believe in it very deeply, but not literally like some people who hold up a book and say, "This is it, the only infallible rule of faith and practice," or who intone some sonorous phrase, loaded with seventeen incompatible implications, and then say, "Ah!" or "Amen!" or "Court's adjourned!" Why don't they say instead, "This is the story of men's quest of God. As you see, they haven't got very far. But it's a better guide to our further quests than the pronouncements of any one man, no matter how devout he may be." Or, at least they could say, "Ah, there must be more there than I can understand; I'll go home and think it over." Or, when they rap the gavel, instead of saying, "Court's adjourned!" why don't they say, "Sorry! That's the best we can do today!"

Now that I think of it, I have never staked my existence wholly on the practical "facts of life," though I have repeatedly told myself that I should. But how can one spend his whole life, the one and only life that is given him, taking notes on things as they are, without once using his pencil to make a little sketch in the margin depicting things as they might be. Must we always pretend that truth is only what is? Even on the day, the one that is different from the thousands before, must we still pretend that?

All I need to say about keeping my anguish from enveloping me with practical disruptions is that I am not very practical anyway, and what idealism I carried over from my youth still tends to be vaguely wistful and inexact. I have never known beforehand precisely what I wanted or what I wanted to be, unless it was to be so many things that I could not decide what to eliminate. But this lack of singular purpose does not mean I have altogether failed to strive for what generally seemed worthwhile, or that I did not, in the erratic course of this striving, often find myself sitting with my arms around the very thing I wanted most. Moreover, a gratifying proportion of this striving I have managed, with a few annoying distortions here and there, to piece together into a vocation—a stroke of good fortune, in this vocation-oriented society of ours, for which I frequently have feelings of profound gratitude and amazement.

I hope, for Heaven's sake, it is clear that I am talking about my own experiences here, and not presuming to utter some basic truth about how your life can be made to conform to your most cherished expectations, or how your expectations can be stretched to conform to your life. You will have to figure out for yourself how to do that; although what I have written may suggest either ways to go about it or inadvertancies you will want to avoid. Besides, there are plenty of occasions when I find myself in circumstances I have not bargained for, and, while in retrospect I am often able to speculate on where I have made my mistakes, there are many outcomes that still have me bamfoozled. So, don't take my medicine unless you want my headaches, too.

I must tell you, too, that, as far as I can see, things do not turn out in others' lives the way they have in mine. To be sure, most people do not approach life the way I do, but, even if they did, there is nothing to guarantee that their experiences would add up the same way. There are some people, for example, who have had a very bad time of it—altogether too many people! And, of these, there are those who are overwhelmed and there are those who write successful books about their misfortunes and then contrive to repeat the inspirational cycle. Each person has his own entanglements and it is often convenient for him to preserve them. I know this. Among those who have spent long periods in psychotherapy with me, the cherished intricacies are vastly different, and one has to rise to very high levels of abstraction, indeed, if he is to formulate any simple over-arching principles that can be regarded, even tentatively, as inevitably governing all men's lives.

But, it is still Friday morning. I remember the faces of our daughter and son. There was deep concern there, but not, as far as I could see, any sign of panic. My job was cut out for me; it was to survive, if I could. But what were they to do? They could not help but be aware, even in that first hour, of the difficulties that my death would plunge them into. How well I managed to forestall those difficulties? Not very well!

There were a thousand and one thoughts, intangible, important, that I had long imagined myself sharing with them, but always these had seemed to require a more propitious moment. So, not only was I lying there in a most unfatherly exhibition of helplessness that must give them none of the sense of security that children have a right to expect of a father in times of emergency, not only was I at the point of leaving them without having properly planned for their future, but I was about to be cut off from the last hope of ever saying to them what was always in my heart. I felt all this, not in sentences, as it is written down here, but altogether in one choking lump.

Then, there was this thought; it was a separate thought, I believe: Here I was creating additional strain for our pregnant daughter who, with her husband serving overseas, was already under too much stress. And I thought of our first grandchild, expected in a few weeks, whom I might never see, and to whom I might never tell the wonderful stories that all grandchildren should hear.

There were other moments, when I looked at our son and realized how like him it would be to try to sacrifice his own opportunities to make life easier for his widowed mother. He would undertake the sacrifices I had failed to make.

It occurred to me, too, how families always feel guilty when one of them dies, and everyone is inwardly depressed because he remembers how badly he treated the deceased. I know how terrible the pain of this kind of guilt can be, and how much one appreciates some sort of timely reassurance. So, I wanted to reassure the three members of my family standing there—to tell them how perfectly wonderful they had been. But how could I say that, without dramatizing a "death-bed" scene! So I thought the better of it and kept my mouth shut. Besides, the doctor and the Emergency Squad people were standing around, and it was strictly none of their business.

The cruelest clutch of all came during those moments when I thought of the widow's loneliness I might be bringing down on my wife. There seemed to be nothing I could do about this except to try desperately to stay alive. How does this business of human relationships work out? With one person you share too little, and when you go you leave in his memory only the shreds of the legacy he might have had; with another, you share too much, and when you go you leave in his memory altogether too great an emptiness.

There were other thoughts during this day that was like no other, many that do not lend themselves to words, and many too intimate to mention here. What I have said ought to be enough to indicate how, on such a day, things can become a bit messy, and may even fall apart completely if there is nothing to stop them. In my case, there was one thing that helped immensely—I didn't die. So that is something that comes later! But no matter; it seems clear now that death was not itself the bugaboo I faced. The pain: That was to be taken more seriously, and I must say it occupied a lot of my attention. But pain is not the worst; it can be helped, and, in my case, it soon was.

What is not so easy to help is the failure of those "truths" that have served to make so many thousands of days turn out as expected. We believe them because how else is one to know what is really so, or how else to bridge the chasm between past and future over which we always find ourselves suspended, how else to find continuity and thus to live. These "truths"—they can be little tick-tock-tick-tock truths that keep repeating themselves in the corner—and always so impersonal about what is going on that you don't mind having them around—or they can be big round shining truths—brittle as all perfect things must be—that roll along majestically until they crash against the day that was not meant for them, and leave you with nothing but their fragments, a litter of words—leave you shattered too.

I suppose one solution is to forge bigger, rounder, fuller truths—really perfect truths this time, or, if not perfect, so hard they will not be shattered by the crash of single events. Then, when that one day comes along, we can simply regard it as exception to the rule, a statistical improbability, or, if it is something nice, as a miracle. The trouble with this is that once you come face to face with this pesky statistical improbability you have to be an awfully fast talker to keep yourself convinced that it is not genuine. But then, some of us are awfully fast talkers, and quite ready to believe something does not exist if we keep telling ourselves it is not there.

But how about grasping the perfect incontrovertible truth, the frozen ultimate, the knowledge of the way things really *really* are; would not that end the confusion of having something happen unexpectedly, end it once and for all? With such knowledge in our possession nothing could possibly occur unexpectedly and our lives would be lived out perfectly in peaceful contemplation of what was coming next.

This, it seems to me, is like a man teetering on what he thinks is the edge of the universe and daring anyone to push him off. He feels perfectly safe because he thinks he knows what is what and there is obviously no such thing as ever going beyond the limits of reality. Still, occasionally he makes a pretense of looking over the edge, just for laughs, and he says, "See, there really isn't anything there—just a lot of nonsense." Then, out of the corner of his eye he does catch a glimpse of something moving out there in the nothing; at first, perhaps, no more than the shadows of his own imagination. All night long he wonders what is the perfect truth about them, how much further out their limits lie. So he secretly tests these shadows, tries to see if he can make them move. Soon he is working with his hands.

In time, there arise out there in the nowhere whole new cities, built outside the walls against which he once leaned so confidently. Now his world is different. Now his once "perfect" truths tell him what he can see is not so, and, faithful as he may try to be, he can offer no more than lip service to them. Now, each time he looks up from his work and peers beyond his latest achievement, he wonders who he is to have imagined such things, and what he is doing, and he shudders to think how much of his life was spent behind the old barriers, or what unseen walls may imprison him now. And then he wonders more; to what destinies has he been false—and why has the evening grown so late?

This tail-spin of thinking starts as all tail-spins do, from the stall that occurs when one tries to stand still in mid-flight. From the moment we assume that truth is a stationary achievement, rather than a stage in a lively quest, it is only a matter of time until things start spinning round and round. Truth is neither reality nor phantasy. It needs to be understood, instead, as a continually emerging relationship between reality and ingenuity, and thus never something that can be skewered by a phrase, a moment, or a place. But can man ever trust[2] himself aloft to such aerodynamics? Will he ever be able to get his mind off the ground and fly?

****

I looked at my family that morning and it occured to me that if I had wished for the most wonderful thing in the world to happen it would turn out to be just such a family. And I realized that while life had given me only a small proportion of all the miscellany I had, at one time or another, grasped for, it had generally ended up supplying me with the very best that could be managed under the circumstances, better than anything I could claim to have deserved.

There is a certain injustice in this kind of outcome. Perhaps it would be more just for us all to get exactly what we demand; it might serve us right. This is a familiar theme that runs through our folklore. The moral usually drawn is that we should not reach for anything at all, that we should sit around waiting patiently for our just reward. I must confess that I do not find the idea of living in a community of such deserving people very attractive. We would all be trying to out-deserve each other, and such a public exhibition of deservingness could become obnoxiously unctious. What a way to live!

But anyway, this is not the way things are. Instead, the world is filled with injustices, heart-rending injustices for the weak, disgusting injustices for the strong. Added to these are a lot of outcomes that are hard to appraise one way or the other, for our notions about what constitutes justice, and whose job it is to see that it happens, are still pretty foggy. I suppose we are inclined to think that justice is something to be dispensed by Providence or by incorruptible public officials, rather than something that has to be figured out by all of us. Thus, we tend to regard it like truth, something all packaged, rather than something continually in the process of definition.

I suppose I could have treated this undeserved reward so closely gathered around me as an insult to my sense of true justice, and only further evidence that the world was badly managed. Or, I could have held on to my proper misery by claiming that the reward was illusory, that only a little family-bound parochial mind would describe these three dimwitted anthropoids as "wonderful." Thus my Olympean sense of pure and perfect justice could be kept intact, along with any long-standing complaints I might have against God and man for their loose administration of such important matters.

[2] Editors' note: [sic]

None of this occurred to me that morning. What did occur to me was that it was a shame to waste these precious moments in self-recrimination when there before me was the best that a man could want, and that simply their being the kind of persons they were was the best of all the things I could have wished for them. Whatever else I might have provided, none would have been as valuable as what they already possessed. Whether all this was a reward intended for me, or whether it was deserved by me, was quite beside the point. If there was anything tragic about my state that morning, it was my momentary failure to see what was there before my very eyes. This is what I thought.

But what about my own reprehensibility? Did the fact that I felt rewarded prove I was any less guilty? Of course not! It was just as clear as ever that the role I had enacted in life was not all it should have been. How smug would I have had to be to claim otherwise! Certainly the more one scrutinizes his relations with his fellow-man, the more he should be able to find wrong with them. And the more he tinkers with those relationships to make them better, the more practical faults will turn up. So, it seems to me that a sense of wrong-doing is what inevitably results from examining yourself and from making efforts to do better.

Perhaps if one only sits around and rationalizes, he may be able to set his house in apparent order, and keep it that way. But that assumes that he neither examines the facts critically nor experiments with improvements. Once one starts experimenting, the bugs, as they say in manufacturing circles, are bound to show up. The more you try to do right, the more you find wrong with yourself.

One way to assuage those horrible guilt feelings is to regard a mistake as something to be punished rather than an occasion for revision of outlook. This tends to keep you from experimenting and hence from discovering new faults. Such a view helps one stabilize himself, and, of course, keeps him from making any genuine progress.

Closely allied with this view is the belief that a mistake is any deviation from the blueprint that has been laid down for us. All one has to do, then, to slough off the guilt is to get himself punished and thereafter keep his finger more firmly on the blueprint. This is the view a lot of people take towards sin, and it seems pretty superficial to me. To be frank about it, punishment and conformity usually work even harder for the perpetuation of evil than for the achievement of goodness.

There are philosophers who agree that punishment and conformity are not a cure for sin. That is good. So they try to figure out what has gone wrong. That is good too. The more they think about it the more of a clutter they discover in man's affairs. Naturally! But there they stop the enterprise and start caterwauling. They generate a lot of anguish in themselves, they are overwhelmed by their guilt feelings, and they are often furiously angry at anyone who refuses to share their misery.

Suppose one takes the rather practical view that a mistake—or sin, if the point is to be made more dramatically—is something to be examined and corrected. This is what I think repentance means; but, then, most people don't agree with me. Once you do this, you start turning up new complexities, old values become shaky, new values begin to shape themselves, and you find that you have been making a host of blunders that you had never recognized before. Moreover, the simple perfections on which you used to pin your faith begin to look brutally primitive.

So far, there is really nothing dangerous about this line of inference. But if you lose sight of your objective at this point, and start telling yourself that punishment is the cure for all these freshly revealed mistakes, and that you are not fit to belong to society, then you are immediately in trouble—deep trouble. So there is a real hazard in examining your mistakes, unless you keep firmly in mind that the sole object is to provide grounds for trying out better ways of doing your part. The sense of guilt, then, can be harmful or helpful, depending upon what we think should be done about it.

So when I looked up at the faces so dear to me and mustered sense enough to recognize what had really happened in spite of my shortcomings, I felt a great surge of reassurance. The moment is still very clear to me. As for my feelings of inadequacy, of wrong-doing, or of sin, it became clear that they were important to me only if I lived to do something about them.

It occurred to me, also, that most people were wise enough not to expect me to be perfect, that I had myself long since outgrown such an exalted image of my destiny, and even if I did make a flat-out attempt at here-and-now perfection, I would probably stiffen up into just as foolish a posture as have the other people I have seen make that attempt. Besides, I still could not put my finger on where all my mistakes had been—mostly I knew only where I had deviated from convention—or whether all of them had actually been mistakes; nor did I know what could readily be done even if they had been mistakes. Naturally, I had some clues, here and there, but, in the main, these were questions it would take years to work out, and, if I did well with them, they would be followed by further, more perspicacious questions.

So that was that! It was at this point in the proceedings that I found myself free to go single-mindedly about the immediate task of surviving and trying to restore to my family whatever composure my antics had destroyed.

Taken altogether, what happened that week at the beginning of which I asked you to join me in imagining what it would be like to look in on our tomorrows? I don't know what happened to you, but one thing for sure, a lot of me was thrown into disarray—my insides, my orientation toward my surroundings, the enactment of my role as a responsible person, and, to some extent, my dynamic and delicately balanced status as a human being. My insides could not get into step with my heart, my mind could not pace itself to the successive moments that tumbled down on me, my pattern of life failed to lead up smoothly to the new turns of events, and, to make a long story short, the whole system of anticipations—who expects what to happen when—got badly mixed up. The zigs stopped matching the zags.

Depending on the level at which we focus attention on this confusion, we can call it "pain," "anxiety," "guilt," or—if you prefer an up-to-date soul-shaking term for chaos—call it "anguish." But the anxiety was not as devastating as I suspect it might have been if I had not, in some general way, already envisioned such a state of affairs. I had indeed eavesdropped on this moment, and 1 was not altogether without some notion of how things might be managed.

The part of the experience that more particularly might be called "guilt"—the sense of loss of role, the failure to live up to my own expectations in relation to those closest to me—was the most difficult part to get hold of. It was to abate only when I looked more carefully at what was there in front of me and when I was to realize that guilt feelings are for the person who has some time to do something about them.

Q. And what do I now think of the whole incident?
A. I can't say that I liked it.
Q. So?
A. I wonder what will happen next week.
Q. Haven't I learned not to wonder about such things?
A. Oh, No! Quite the contrary!
Q. But won't speculation about them tend to make them happen?
A. Perhaps, but I insist on having some continuity in my life.
Q. What am I going to write about next?
A. Joy and depression.
Q. Is that to be based on experience too?
A. I don't know – yet!

Section II

Theory and Philosophy

In *Essay on the doctrine of mental energy*, which, like *Social inheritance* (Chapter 86), was written when the 25-year-old Kelly was based at the University of Edinburgh, he considers the various uses of this doctrine by psychologists to illustrate that the criterion of a good hypothesis is its utility, rather than its truth.

A brief introduction to personal construct theory was written to articulate Kelly's theory in a new book on personal construct research that he never completed. Since it outlines the theory's philosophical assumptions, fundamental postulate, corollaries, and some of its professional constructs, it is included, out of chronological sequence, towards the beginning of this section for the benefit of readers who are less familiar with Kelly's ideas. Of particular interest to those who are well acquainted with his theory may be the fact that it contains an admission that, in his magnum opus, the Commonality Corollary was wrongly worded.

In *The psychology of personal constructs*, Kelly, four years prior to the publication of his two volumes of the same name and "not . . . without considerable anxiety," presents the emerging Fundamental Postulate and a few of the corollaries of his theory for the first time to an audience other than his research team. *Theoretical behavior* presents the notion of a theory as "a way of behaving," and introduces the view of the person as a scientist, highlighting the consequent similarities between the supervision of graduate students and the process of psychotherapy—themes to which he returned in several later papers. *Alternatives* elucidates the notion of bipolar constructs, introduces the methodology of the role construct repertory test, and posits a view of psychotherapy as a means of enabling individuals to structure their lives in terms of testable alternatives. *A theoretical approach to psychological movement*, based on the PhD dissertation of one of Kelly's students, presents a perspective on movement that is pertinent to fostering change in both therapeutic and educational contexts by facilitating the perception of contrasts between an individual's present and past states.

Other papers delineate aspects of the theory to audiences following the publication of the two volumes. *Personal construct theory as a line of inference* focuses again on the view of the person as a scientist and on aspects of the Dichotomy Corollary, asserting the bipolarity of constructs. In *Behavior is an experiment*, Kelly, in a lighthearted and informal style, elaborates on his view of the person as being as much a scientist as the professional psychologist, and as someone who tests hypotheses through his or her behavior. *Ontological acceleration* and *Behavior is a question* (which reiterates much of the material from *The autobiography of a theory*) also elaborate on the view of behavior as an independent variable rather than, as it is often regarded in psychology, a dependent variable.

Feelings for and feelings of (The ontology of feelings) was intended to be one of the chapters in *The human feeling*, a book that Kelly began working on due to his concern that personal construct theory was being categorized as a cognitive theory. Other papers in the present volume focus on Kelly's approach to "emotions" as constructs of transition. In *How to be comfortable with threat*, he introduces readers to the personal construct views of threat, anxiety, and fear and of how to deal with these. *Hostility* and *The threat of aggression* provide explanations of Kelly's views on two of his "constructs of transition" and the differences between them, including, in the latter paper, how these differences may offer a resolution of the "humanistic psychologist's dilemma" of "how to protect human audacity from human audacity without stifling human audacity." In addition to the distinction between *cognition* and *emotion*, various traditional dichotomies are challenged in several papers; for example, those between values and knowledge and between free will and determinism in *Values, knowledge and social control*. *Man's construction of his alternatives*, although first presented at a conference on "The assessment of human motives," eschews the notion of motivation and instead portrays the individual as "a form of movement" making choices based on their capacity to enhance the anticipation of events.

Collected Papers of the Pioneer of Constructivist Psychology: George A. Kelly, First Edition. Edited by David A. Winter and Nick Reed.

Prediction and control presents a view of control as involving the extension of prediction to one's own behavior. In *The language of hypothesis*, Kelly argues for the use of language in an invitational mood and explores the implications of this in areas ranging from psychotherapy to international affairs. *The psychology of the unknown* contrasts accumulative fragmentalism with constructive alternativism and considers how a person can "transcend the obvious" and get along with the unknown by completing full experience cycles.

In *Aldous, the personable computer*, Kelly takes a lighthearted swipe at some attempts at computer simulation of personality, pointing out that all people, from the personal construct theory perspective, are themselves simulators and indicating how a person's psychological space can be represented by a repertory grid matrix. In *Epilogue: Don Juan*, he uses the central character of Mozart's opera *Don Giovanni* to illustrate how an individual may be construed in alternative ways and that the person's own self-construction may be discounted. *Onta,* an undated poem, consists of ontological reflections.

5

Essay on the Doctrine of Mental Energy[1]

Some Greek must get the credit, in this case, say, Aristotle for he, on observing "change and decay" or thc pre-Galileo equivalent of the concept that "the world moves," used the term "energeia" to express the manifestation of change. The latent ability for change he called, "dunamis." So much for the classic Greek.

Post-Renaissance physicists constructed or borrowed two useful concepts from the thinking of Aristotle. They conceived energy as an essence or hypothetical persistent constant to which change was superficial. Energy was of two forms, kinetic and potential. Kinetic energy was energy the manifestation of which was in a state of flux and potential energy was energy the manifestation of which was non-variant. Neither of these concepts coincides with either of Aristotle's. Fatal admission! Yet kinetic energy playfully frisks about his quiet and introvert brother, potential energy, in every modern physicist's nursery.

The test of a hypothesis is not so much its truth as its utility in helping us discover laws of prediction. Unless the initial hypothesis contains some element embodied in the terminal law it may later be discarded without invalidating one's ability to forecast sequences of physical change. There is no need to prove a hypothesis "true" as long as its utility is demonstrative. Take the energy hypothesis: it is simply a device or convenient vehicle for carrying along the physicist's thought. There was a time when the two-fluid theory of heat, the two-fluid theory of electricity, and the corpuscular theory of light furnished probably the most useful working conceptions for the sciences of heat, electricity, and light. If the lens makers of Holland had waited for the wave theory of light before developing Galileo's telescope the age of plumbago scientists might be still upon us.

But the children of the physicist have a "poor relation," stunted and handicapped from birth yet gifted with that peculiar persistence which is characteristic of so many runts: it is the doctrine of mental energy. This doctrine in its more physiological or neural forms is adhered to by such scientists as McDougall, James, Ladd, and Woodworth. Spearman (1)[2] would have us include with these Maudsley, Ribot, Lasswitz, Spiller, Claparède, Ioteyko, Lehmann, Woodrow, Pyle, Goddard, and Thurstone. The more psychical versions of the doctrine are held by Spearman himself, Bergson, Wildon Carr, Höffding, della Valle, Wirth, the school of Brentano, and such noted psychiatrists as Breuer, Freud, Jung, Janet, Déjérine, Gauckler, Deschamps, Regis, Hesnard, and Lévy. On the other hand the behavioristic school and a great number of other physiological psychologists are contemptuous in their rejection of it: in fact, the majority of psychologists are inclined to look upon mental energy as a survival of Medieval thinking.

Before considering the conflicting viewpoints and arguments it will do no harm to review the various forms in which the mental energy hypothesis has cropped up. With the more physiological or neural interpretations it is difficult to distinguish between the concept of mental or neural energy and the generally accepted concept of nerve impulse, if indeed there be any difference intended.

Dr. Fraser Harris (2) gives us the following account citing the familiar anecdote of Johannes Muller's prophecy and Helmholtz's experiment:

> "For a long time nerve-energy, as nerve-impulses were called, was thought of as identical with electric energy, at the time when the fundamental phenomena of electricity had just been discovered by Galvani and Volta in Italy, it was natural to conclude that nerve-energy was either the same as electricity or acted with a similar speed. For indeed neural operations seemed to be carried out with the speed of lightning. The "twinkling of an eye" had always meant something inconceivably short, the speed of thought was a synonym for what was brief indeed. So eminent and cautious a physiologist as Johannes Muller wrote as lately as 1835—'We shall probably never attain the power of measuring the velocity of nervous action, for we have not the opportunity of comparing its propagation through immense spaces as we have in the case of light'. Within fifteen years after this prophecy was made, a fellow-countryman of Muller, the great mathematical physicist and physiologist, Hermann von Helmholtz, then Professor of Physiology at Königsberg, measured the rapidity of the propagation of the nerve-impulse in one of the motor nerves of the frog, and found it something, relatively speaking, of quite a low order of velocity, namely, ninety feet (thirty meters) a second."

[1] Unpublished manuscript, University of Edinburgh, May, 1930. Published by permission of Jacqueline Aldridge.

[2] Editors' note: citation style and the bibliography have been kept as in the original manuscript.

Collected Papers of the Pioneer of Constructivist Psychology: George A. Kelly, First Edition. Edited by David A. Winter and Nick Reed.

The usual velocity of a nerve impulse in the motor nerves of man is about 150 feet a second. Conductivity, the power of propagating nerve impulses, may be considerably increased with increased temperature and the velocity of conduction may be doubled in the case of frogs' nerves by the change from 17 degrees C to 35 degrees C. It is to be noted that this velocity of propagation varies throughout the animal kingdom very nearly as the intensity of vitality in the different species varies.

Together with the nerve-impulse and perhaps accounting for the idea that nerve-impulses were once thought electric, is invariably an electric accompaniment. The action current, as this electric accompaniment is called, is taken as the most sensitive detector of the passage of an impulse. As an impulse passes along a nerve fiber the surface of the active region develops a negative potential with respect to the neighboring inactive regions. If one region on the nerve fiber is connected by electrodes, through a galvanometer, to another current will be found to flow at a maximum when the nerve-impulse passes one of the electrodes.

Again, the "all or none" relation between a stimulus and the transmission of a corresponding nerve-impulse holds true, that is to say there are no gradations in the size of nerve-impulses: either an impulse is completely released, or "set off" in a nerve fiber by the stimulus or it is not released at all. On the other hand a strong stimulus will irritate more fibers and release impulses in each one more frequently than will a weak stimulus.

Now these brief details of the behavior of a nerve-impulse are cited here because they resemble so closely the phenomena for the explanation of which the physicist uses his energy hypothesis. There is a resemblance between the laws governing the thermal radiation from a perfect radiator and this "all or none" law governing the transmission of a nerve-impulse released by a stimulus. In order to account for the stability of the atom the electrons must be conceived as moving in elliptical[3] orbits. This demands that for each electron in its orbit a certain definite amount of energy be postulated according to the size of the orbit and the positions of other electrons in the same atom. The only time an atom could be conceived of as losing energy would be when an electron was thrust from one orbit to another. Thus in order to explain the laws governing the thermal radiation from a perfect radiator the physicist, Planck, had been led to formulate the hypothesis that an accelerated electron did not radiate energy continuously, as demanded by the classical electromagnetic theory of light but only intermittently, each emission consisting of a definite burst or quantum of energy. More recently (1905) Einstein had made the further assumption that the radiation itself traveled in minute bundles each possessing a quantum according to its frequency. This quantum theory is in reality not a theory: no theoretical basis has yet been found for it. It is a fundamental law governing the exchange of energy between radiation and matter, and in all cases in which it has been tested has been found to express the phenomena with great exactitude. There is still another resemblance between these phenomena of the physicist and those of the physiologist: the electromagnetic waves comprising light are known to travel, not continuously, each wave followed by another just like it, but in bursts interspersed by stretches in which there are apparently no waves at all.

The ejection or injection of energy in definite quanta by the atom and the bursts of ether waves are phenomena suggesting, the "all or none" transmission and the "waves" of nerve-impulse. The physicist tests his laws upon the hypothesis that the universe is a closed system of energy and he sets for himself the task of measuring and accounting for each loss or gain of energy in the objects of his experiment. The neurologist and psychologist have so far found it nearly impossible to set themselves to such a rigid task and so have either disregarded any hypothesis of energy, or, having hypothesized it, let the illusive creature slip through their fingers unmeasured and un-accounted for.

But hitherto we have been speaking of the well-known and generally admitted phenomenon of nerve-impulse and assuming a kind of identity, equivalency, or close relationship between it and some sort of energy hypothesis. Our only justification for such assumption is the fact that the current literature on the subject falls into the same way. It is difficult, for instance, whether McDougall (3) intends his "neurin" or nerve-energy as a hypothetical cause or as a concrete manifestation, for he describes it as a sort of fluid which "constitutes a reservoir of energy upon which the various forms (of the nervous system) draw in turn as they become active." In 1908 McDougall wrote, "another conception of the whole operation of nervous energy which goes back as far as Descartes: the conception namely, that the energy liberated by chemical change, by katabolic process in one part of the nervous system may be conducted through the nervous channels and may operate in other parts of the nervous system. . ..Now it seems impossible to get the physiologists of the laboratory....who are chiefly concerned with the organs rather than the organism, to consider this conception seriously, and on its merits. If they occasionally refer to it, it is only to put it aside contemptuously as a naive survival from the Dark Ages. Yet those who are in the habit of dealing with the problems of the organism as a whole, the physician and the psychologist, constantly make use of this conception, for they find it impossible to make progress in the understanding of their problems without it." Here in speaking of the energy released by katabolic processes and placed at the disposal of the various parts of the nervous system through the "nervous channels" i.e., by nerve-impulses, probably: McDougall is not postulating anything more or less than the physicist's energy. Katabolic process is a physical process and its known product is simply other forms of the physicist's energy. This fact, he himself appears to recognize for in another place he says, "Every part of each neuron is irritable, i.e. is capable of responding to a stimulus with a katabolic change which initiates a "nervous impulse." This katabolic change results in the conversion of chemical potential energy into free nervous energy, just as the decomposition of such a substance as nitro-glycerine results

[3] Editors' note: 'elipsical' in the original.

in the liberation of energy from the chemical potential form. But the process of liberation of energy in the neuron differs from processes of a similar kind that occur outside living tissues in one very important respect, namely, the quantity of energy liberated in the neuron varies with the intensity of the stimulus, a feeble stimulus produces a small quantity of chemical change and the liberation of a small quantity of energy, and a strong stimulus produces a correspondingly large quantity of change and liberates a large quantity of energy. The energy so set free seems to behave like other forms of free energy, e.g., heat and electrical energy, in that it tends to flow from any place of high potential to places of lower potential along conducting substances." Again he says of this form of energy, "This energy, which in the present state of our ignorance can be most profitably regarded as a fluid, tends always to flow, like heat, electricity, or water, from places of higher to places of lower potential, following the paths of least resistance, and for convenience of description it may be called 'neurin.'" Now this "neurin" hypothesis set forth by McDougall cannot be regarded as a separate energy hypothesis running parallel to that of the physicist for we see that he himself speaks of it as a form of energy released by katabolic or chemical process and quite within the closed systems so carefully observed by the physicists. McDougall's theory then becomes, not a new postulate, but an advocate of physiochemical methods of investigation and interpretation of neural events.

Until this point we have considered the most physiological version of the doctrine of mental energy. The more philosophical and psychical versions though not capable of such lucid and accurate description nevertheless constitute excellent trapezia upon which to perform mental gymnastics. I shall boldly turn our faces to the task.

In the exclusive inner circles of Philosophy I am told that such terms as "pressure," "strain," "stress," "energy," "resistance," "impact," "action," "force," "impulse," "effective agency" are all considered "terms of causation." For my part I see no reason why such terms as "stimulus," "contact," "presence," "tonic," etc. should not be included, and, in fact, why all terms of sequence or coexistence should not fall within the lawful compass of "causation." Be that as it may, Stout (4) tells us that, "In common language such words as *pressure*, *strain*, *stress*, *energy*, *impact*, imply something more than can be included in the mere description of the space relations and the changes of the space relations of the parts of matter. This something more is certainly rather indistinctly conceived. There is, however, no room for doubting that it consists in an assumed inner state of material bodies,—a state imperceptible to the external observer and uninterpretable in terms of the data yielded by external observation....Without going into details, which for the present purposes would be superfluous, it is enough to remark that the animistic bias of ordinary thought which leads us to represent moving and resisting bodies as if, in some vague way, they had an inner experience of their own activity, is traceable backwards to that primitive stage in the history of culture in which earth, sky, stars, stones, plants, animals, and men were all regarded as on the same plane of conscious life." Stout is trying to show that his own use of the term, "mental activity," is objectively scientific rather than subjectively metamorphic. He argues that it is useless for the purposes of explanation to postulate an underlying "state imperceptible to the external observer and uninterpretable in terms of the data yielded by external observation." Such a prime cause, or underlying irreducible constant propension, is to him a useless coinage of a primitive mind. He goes so far as to say, "Causation for the 'plain man' involves more than mere priority and subsequence: it carries with it a vague, and, for science, a futile representation of what Professor Pearson calls 'enforcement'. The traces of this bias are often found even in scientific exposition. Thus it is plainly in evidence whenever 'force' is referred to as cause of motion or a reason why a body moves. This is the case, for example, in Newton's second law of motion: 'change of motion is proportional to force applied, and takes place in the direction of the straight line in which the force acts.'" Stout wishes to use these terms of causation as indicators of dispassionate mechanistic conditions of priority and co-existence without reading into them any irreducible subjective substrate of effort or "enforcement." But his criticism of Newton's second law of motion as erroneously containing this implication in no way invalidates the law or, as far as I can see, any application of the law. The use which the physicist makes of the terms "force," "energy," etc. may for him imply this animistic substrate while he works, but in its application it is just as pure and dispassionately causal as any interpretation which Stout wishes to place upon his "mental activity." Thus we see, Stout's concept of "mental activity" is a hypothesis no more mechanistic than the ordinary concepts of physics, and, like them, coined to form an underlying constant substrate, objective and adapted to treatment by scientific methods. It is on no different plane and fulfills no different level of purposes than do such terms as "pressure," "neurin," and "energy".

Ladd (5) in his "Elements of Physiological Psychology," 1896, in discussing the psycho-physical problem and conceiving of the brain as the "seat" of the mind says: "There would be no advantage to the mind in being 'seated' in the brain—that is, in being under any special relations to a given extent of nervous matter—unless it were somehow influenced or acted upon by this nervous matter, and could in turn influence and act upon it....To act and to be acted upon is equivalent to standing in the relation of cause and effect." Energy, according to Ladd, is one of the terms which may be used in expressing this "cause and effect" relationship. He continues: "All forms of energy must be classified as respects quality, by the kind of their motion, and, as respects degree, by the amount of their motion....But between the mind whether regarded as merely the formal subject of consciousness or as a real unit-being whose faculty or power it is to be conscious, and the physical basis of mind in the brain, no correlation, no passing back and forth of energy, can occur....No atom is transferred from brain to mind....The stricter we make our application of the law of the correlation and conservation of energy within the physical realm, the more impossible does it become to apply it to all the relations of body and mind." In this manner Ladd argues against the application of the doctrine of mental energy to both psychic and physiological phenomena although admitting that these stand in some sort of cause and effect relationship. But suppose we lean to a more monistic doctrine of the relation between mind and body. If we consider the mind as the manifestation of bodily activities, the sum and organization of organic workings, we can find a place for the doctrine of mental energy, not as a medium of exchange between the two, but as a factor in the composition of each. Ladd's argument against use of the hypothesis of mental energy to explain the relationship between body and mind on the grounds that no atoms are transferred between the two is a metaphysical difficulty not easily to be surmounted. From things mental Ladd has, by definition, excluded things atomic, and hence things resolvable into energy units. Should he discover any atomic transfer between body and some part of the thing which he now calls mind, his method of discrimination between the two would require him to correspondingly increase the boundaries of his "body" concept to include the new organ, and to shift his "mind" concept to exclude it. Ladd's "mind" then becomes a will o' the wisp separated from analysis in terms of energy by the metaphysical limitations which he has placed upon it. Such metaphysical dogmatization can scarcely lend itself either to objective methods or to refutation of the mental energy hypothesis.

The argument of Ladd, however, leads us to an important consideration which we shall treat briefly. An essential part of the physicist's concept of energy is his law of conservation of energy. He considers the universe a closed system into which no new energy can be injected or old energy be ejected, only the forms of energy may change into equivalent forms. In its first forms the doctrine of mental energy involved considering the individual soul a closed system, or at least open only to or through a supreme being. Beneke and others following him did conceive of an open system but a purely psychical one, that is, he conceived of the psychical system being closed to the physical system. Such concepts of closed or partially closed systems were used to defend a belief in immortality. More recent doctrines have attacked the problem from the standpoint of including the psychical system and physical system as one, and have attempted to explain psychic phenomena as new forms of the universally present physical energy.

There is, for example, a school which treats mental energy in an almost purely metaphysical way. I suppose the school might be said to lay a purely psychical interpretation upon the doctrine of mental energy. I quote H. Wildon Carr in his translator's preface to Henri Bergson's "Mind Energy" (6): "In affirming Mind-Energy the intention is not to include the activity of the mind in the system of radiant energy which constitutes the science of physics. On the contrary, what is intended is that the science of mind, quite as much as the science of matter, can only be constituted by means of a concept which allows of the formulation of a law of conservation. Mind is not a phenomenon which flares up at nothing and relapses into nothing, it can only be understood when it is conceived as a continuity of existence....Activity seeking expression is the concept of Mind-Energy."

Here is a system which conceives mental energy as running parallel to but never trespassing upon the closed system of physical energy. Bergson cites consciousness, memory, and attention as concepts of activity within a closed system which therefore require an energy postulate. He uses "Mind-Energy" as opposed to "mind stuff." He places consciousness coextensive with life, hence, with activity, and he speaks of reality as fundamentally spiritual activity. He speaks of his Mind-Energy as a "dynamic concept of psychical reality." To quote directly a part of his argument for a closed system of mental energy, from the phenomena of memory: "All consciousness, then, is memory,—conservation and accumulation of the past in the present.... But all consciousness is *also* anticipation of the future....Attention is expectation, and there is no consciousness without a certain attention to life." The energy of Bergson rests upon purely metaphysical bases and does not apparently lend itself of objective examination and measurement. Its value to experimental or applied psychology is therefore to be doubted.

Today, in Britain, at least, Spearman's "general factor of intelligence" is probably the most prominent of the more psychical versions of the doctrine of mental energy. Unlike most of the others who resort to the psychical versions of the hypothesis he attempts to rest his arguments upon experimentation and statistical applications.

If we measure a number of different kinds of mental performance by a number of different tests, say, A, B, C, D, etc. it will be found that the scores a, b, c, d, etc. on the respective tests will be correlated. If the coefficients of intercorrelation, r_{ab}, r_{ac}, r_{ad}, r_{bc}, r_{bd}, r_{cd}, etc. are placed in a table of cells, each r being placed at the intersection of the column and the row at the end of which appear the corresponding tests it will be found the order of the tests both vertically and horizontally can be constructed so as to give a hierarchical order to the values of the coefficients of correlation, that is, say, values of the coefficients will be greater in the upper and left cells and will decrease as one goes down and to the right. As a measure of this hierarchical order one may consider the values of the tetrad equations—the determinant members of any four coefficients standing in a square relationship on the table. In every table of correlations between mental abilities the values of these "tetrad differences" tend to cluster about zero, closely if the hierarchical order is marked and more scattered if the hierarchical order is less marked.

Now a correlation may be conceived as being caused by an overlapping of the two variables concerned. The coefficient of correlation r_{ab} may be conceived as being due to the fact that tests A and B have measured some of the same specific abilities. When there are a limited number of specific abilities to be encompassed by tests A, B, C, D, etc. the probability is great that every test will measure a number of the same specific abilities. Those tests which measure more specific abilities will, according to this conception of correlation, correlate more highly with one another simply because there is a tendency for them to measure more of the same specific abilities. Thus if we arrange the tests on our table in order of the number of specific factors involved we will get the hierarchical order known to exist. Again if we take into account the fact that a correlation coefficient might be greater or less than its most "probable" value as determined by the number of specific abilities most likely to be measured twice by two tests, we have an explanation of the fact that the tetrad differences cluster about rather than equal zero. This phenomenon, however, Spearman accounts for as due to errors in the measurements of the general abilities.

Spearmen puts the following interpretation upon these findings. He maintains that the correlations are due to the tests measuring in common of varying amounts of one "general factor." Factors not generally measured in common are called by him specific factors, although these specific factors may be at times entered between two or more tests. This "eclectic" or two-factor doctrine advanced by Spearman accounts for all the facts except the scatter of the tetrad differences quite as satisfactorily as does Thomson's "chance combination" doctrine which I have briefly stated.

Now the issues between these two keen rivals do not appear to be clearly perceived by them. Spearman says of Thomson's doctrine: "And as regards the opposite view which holds that the hierarchy must needs occur by mere 'chance', this—even if it were accepted—could by no possibility enter into conflict with the doctrine given above. The foregoing equations would not be altered by a hair's breadth, nor even would any of the accompanying comments require so much as a change of emphasis. The utmost that could ensue would be to indicate that the g (Spearman's general factor) may somehow be the product of numerous elements distributed in a 'chance' manner. This, no doubt, is a view as to the nature of g which deserves due consideration." In another place he says concerning this "other view as to the nature of g,": "The term chance has two almost opposite meanings. In the one, it implies the wildest irregularities, such as the shiftings of a weathercock in a storm. In the other meaning, it becomes regular and accordingly follows laws." He goes on to discuss the laws of chance for card-cutting, coin tosses, and throws of dice. He then argues that "in the course of ordinary life—as distinguished from the artificialities of card-cutting, dice-throwing, etc.—any such uniform probabilities together with additional influences that neutralize each other in the long run would appear to be surprisingly rare." He then goes on to argue that the exigencies of life and mental events are not comparable to the regularity of "chance" drawings of cards, throwing of dice, etc. He concludes his argument as follows: "The very core of this doctrine of "chance," throughout all its possible varieties in detail, is that every individual should have a uniformly fair throw of the dice for each of very numerous ability-elements. Now, if this really happened, then every individual would in any pool of many different operations tend to equality with every other individual. Anything more opposed to the known facts could hardly be imagined." Now it seems to me that the issue of the whole controversy lies right here. Spearman has admitted that the doctrine of "chance" satisfies his equations and has even gone so far as to say at a point earlier in his argument that "the utmost that could ensue would be to indicate that the g may somehow be the product of numerous elements distributed in a 'chance' manner. This, no doubt is a view as to the nature of g which deserves due consideration." At this point Spearman has fallen back to an argument from analogy saying that it is more *like* life to have orderly groupings of abilities—to have the dice loaded. He also says that chance distributions of abilities among individuals would tend to give them all equal general endowments, and asserts that such is not the case. Here are the principal points upon which Spearman's theory rests. With respect to his argument from analogy he should not expect us to admit that "chance" is an unorderly and unruly anarchy, for the best definition of chance is that it is the total effect of the operation of unknown laws. Chance is orderly and the events of life do tend to distribute themselves in a symmetrical fashion suggesting the Gaussian curve. With respect to the argument that the doctrine of chance distribution would eventually mean that individuals would all receive equal general endowments: But here he is arguing against his own theory as much as against Thomson's, for they both rest upon the same *mathematical* assumptions regarding distribution of abilities. Or, to attack the argument directly it can be pointed out that the general endowments of individuals *do* tend to be more closely clustered about an average than are their specific abilities. This is equivalent to the well-known fact that the standard deviation of a group of means is less than the standard deviation of the original raw scores. Now it seems to me that g might at once be considered as a general factor and as a number of "chance" factors held in common by different general abilities, if it were not for the fact of the scatter of the tetrad differences. This mathematical fact is explained by Spearman on the grounds of errors of measurement, while according to the doctrine of "chance" operations it is to be expected as evidence of the overlap between some but not all of the tests. Spearman also has advanced the concept that some of the "specific abilities" may overlap between two or more tests but strangely enough he does not employ it to account for the scatter of the tetrad differences. In view of this last mentioned concept of Spearman's we may offer this interpretation of Spearman's theory. The factor, g, is the quantitative value of the minimum overlap between tests, the factor s for each test is total of that which the test measures less g, and the s factors which overlap according to Spearman are, according to the "chance" doctrine, the overlapping factors reduced by the value g.

Spearman makes a further contention which brings this discussion into the scope of this essay. He proposes that g be considered a measure of mental energy and the different s factors be considered measures of organic facilitations or engines for transforming mental energy into thought. He suggests the hypothesis to explain the phenomena of limited span of attention, of decreased muscular efficiency during mental distraction, mental fatigue, and some other phenomena which he designates as those of "retentivity, conative control, and primordial potencies." The phenomenon of limited span of attention he enlarges upon under the heading of "universal mental competition." This competition he contrasts with the co-operation of the organic bodily functions. Competition, he asserts, is a fundamental law covering phenomena of conative and affective life as well as of cognitive life. The wavering of the will between two or more courses of projected action, the crowding out of affections, and the limited span of attention are the phenomena which he cites. Finally he says, "the facts of general psychology—quite apart from those of individual differences—strongly support the suggestion of mental energy and engines. Moreover, such an energy would seem to be just what is wanted to explain g, whilst the engines might go far towards explaining the s's."

The purpose of this paper has been to show the many tendencies to hypothesize mental energy or some such causal concept as an explanation or fundamental persistent constant to which psychologists may relate their thinking. Although nearly every psychologist has advanced the doctrine as an explanation of a different phenomenon it seems to have been a natural assumption derived from the same undercurrent of thought. Apparently no work has been hindered by the assumption of the hypothesis, and, in fact, the only difficulty apparently encountered was a metaphysical one. Taking usefulness as our criterion of a good hypothesis I think it safe to say that no one should prejudice himself against the findings or formulations of laws of predictions by scientists simply because they adopt the mental energy hypothesis for the purposes of their own thinking.

Bibliography

1 Spearman, C., *The Abilities of Man*. 1927
2 Harris, D. Fraser, *Nerves*. 1913
3 McDougall, Wm., *Physiological Psychology*. 1905 *Body and Mind*. 1911
4 Stout G. F., *Analytic Psychology*. 1896
5 Ladd, G. T., *Elements of Physiological Psychology*. 1896
6 Bergson, Henri. Trans. by H. Wildon Carr, *Mind-Energy*. 1920
7 Aveling, F. A., *Directing Mental Energy*. 1927
8 James, Wm., *The Energies of Man*. 1906

6

A Brief Introduction to Personal Construct Theory[1]

Who can say what nature is? Is it what now exists about us, including all the tiny hidden things that wait so patiently to be discovered? Or is it the vista of all that is destined to occur, whether tomorrow or in some distant eon of time? Or is nature, infinitely more varied than this, the myriad trains of events that might ensue if we were to be so bold, ingenious, and irreverent as to take a hand in its management?

Personal construct theory neither offers nor demands a firm answer to any of these questions, and in this respect it is unique. Rather than depending upon bedrock assumptions about the inherent nature of the universe, or upon fragments of truth believed to have been accumulated, it is a notion about how man may launch out from a position of admitted ignorance, and how he may aspire from one day to the next to transcend his own dogmatisms. It is, then, a theory of man's personal inquiry—a psychology of human quest. It does not say what has or will be found, but proposes rather how we might go about looking for it.

Philosophical Position

Like other theories, the psychology of personal constructs is the implementation of a philosophical assumption. In this case the assumption is that whatever nature may be, or howsoever the quest for truth will turn out in the end, the events we face today are subject to as great a variety of construction as our wits will enable us to contrive. This is not to say that one construction is as good as any other, nor is it to deny that at some infinite point in time human vision will behold reality out to the utmost reaches of existence. But it does remind us that all our present perceptions are open to question and reconsideration, and it does broadly suggest that even the most obvious occurrences of everyday life might appear utterly transformed if we were inventive enough to construe them differently.

This philosophical position we have called *constructive alternativism*, and its implications keep cropping up in the psychology of personal constructs. It can be contrasted with the prevalent epistemological assumption of *accumulative fragmentalism*, which is that truth is collected piece by piece. While constructive alternativism does not argue against the collection of information, neither does it measure truth by the size of the collection. Indeed it leads one to regard a large accumulation of facts as an open invitation to some far-reaching reconstruction which will reduce them to a mass of trivialities.

A person who spends a great deal of his time hoarding facts is not likely to be happy at the prospect of seeing them converted into rubbish. He is more likely to want them bound and preserved, a memorial to his personal achievement. A scientist, for example, who thinks this way, and especially a psychologist who does so, depends upon his facts to furnish the ultimate proof of his propositions. With these shining nuggets of truth in his grasp it seems unnecessary for him to take responsibility for the conclusions he claims they thrust upon him. To suggest to him at this point that further human reconstruction can completely alter the appearance of the precious fragments he has accumulated, as well as the direction of their arguments, is to threaten his scientific conclusions, his philosophical position, and even his moral security. No wonder, then, that, in the eyes of such a conservatively minded person, our assumption that all facts are subject—are wholly subject—to alternative constructions looms up as culpably subjective and dangerously subversive to the scientific establishment.

[1] This essay was written in 1966 to introduce a projected book on research in personal construct theory. It was first published in Bannister, D. (Ed.). (1970). *Perspectives in personal construct theory* (pp. 1-29). Academic Press and (with the title of 'A summary statement of a cognitively-oriented comprehensive theory of behavior') in Mancuso, J. C. (Ed.) (1970). *Readings for a cognitive theory of personality* (pp. 27-58). Holt, Rinehart & Winston. It was republished in Fransella, F. (Ed.) (2003). *International handbook of personal construct psychology* (pp. 3-20). It is published here by permission of Jacqueline Aldridge.

Collected Papers of the Pioneer of Constructivist Psychology: George A. Kelly, First Edition. Edited by David A. Winter and Nick Reed.

Facts and Conclusions

But wherein does responsibility lie? Can we ever make facts, even facts that turn out as predicted, responsible for conclusions? I think not. Whatever the world may be, man can come to grips with it only by placing his own interpretations upon what he sees. While his ingenuity in devising suitable constructions may be limited, and many misfortunes therefore come to pass, still it is he, not facts, who holds the key to the ultimate future. This, it seems to me, makes him responsible, and suggests that it is quite inappropriate for him ever to claim that his conclusions have been dictated by any nature other than his own.

This, of course, is how I construe it; and in this undertaking I, too, have chosen to bear responsibility for where my constructive alternativism is leading me. So, also, my reader, if he accepts this invitation to join me, will, like any other Adam or Eve who chooses to understand for himself, be held responsible for his choice—though no more so than I should think him responsible for any other choice he might make, including the choice of *not* accepting this invitation.

None of this is a denial that men customarily share each other's insights and prejudices. Our ingenuity in devising alternative constructions is limited by our feeble wits and our timid reliance upon what is familiar. So we usually do things the way we have done them before or the way others appear to do them. Moreover, novel ideas, when openly expressed, can be disruptive to ourselves and disturbing to others. We therefore often avoid them, disguise them, keep them bottled up in our minds where they cannot develop in the social context, or disavow them in what we believe to be loyalty to the common interest. And often, against our better judgment, we accept the dictates of authority instead, thinking thus to escape any personal responsibility for what happens.

But though our devices for interpreting circumstances are still meager, and the human adventure continues to be fraught with dire uncertainties, it does not follow that facts ever dictate our conclusions, except by the rules we impose upon our acts. Events do not tell us what to do, nor do they carry their meanings engraved on their backs for us to discover. For better or worse we ourselves create the only meanings they will ever convey during our lifetime. The facts of life may even be brutal, but they are nonetheless innocent of any evil intent, and we can scarcely accuse them of taking sides in our epistemological disputes. Our ever present task is to devise ways of anticipating their occurrences, and thus to prepare ourselves for assuming a more and more responsible role in the management of the universe.

The Meaning of Events

Constructive alternativism stresses the importance of events. But it looks to man to propose what the character of their import shall be. The meaning of an event—that is to say, the meaning we ascribe to it—is anchored in its antecedents and its consequents. Thus meaning displays itself to us mainly in the dimension of time. This is much more than saying that meanings are rehearsals of outcomes, a proposition implicit in behavioristic theory, or that the ends justify the means—the ethical statement of the same proposition.

Besides including anticipated outcomes, meaning includes also the means by which events are anticipated. This is to suggest that different meanings are involved when identical events are correctly anticipated by different sets of inferences. It suggests also the implication of quite different meanings when the basic assumptions are different, even when the chains of inference are otherwise more or less similar.

In all of this we look to events to confirm our predictions and to encourage our venturesome constructions. Yet the same events may confirm different constructions, and different, or even incompatible, events may appear to validate the same construction. So, for each of us, meaning assumes the shape of the arguments which lead him to his predictions, and the only outside check on his personal constructions are the events which confirm or disconfirm his expectations. This is a long way from saying that meaning is revealed by what happens, or that meaning is something to be discovered in the natural course of events, or that events shape men and ideas. Thus in constructive alternativism events are crucial, but only man can devise a meaning for them to challenge.

When we place a construction of our own upon a situation, and then pursue its implications to the point of expecting something to happen, we issue a little invitation to nature to intervene in our personal experience. If what we expect does happen, or appears to happen, our expectation is confirmed and we are likely to think that we must have had a pretty good slant on the trend of affairs, else we would have lost our bet. But if we think the matter over carefully we may begin to have doubts. Perhaps a totally different interpretation would have led to an equally successful prediction; and it may, besides, have been more straightforward, or more consistent with our conscience. Or perhaps our vivid expectations overlaid our perception of what actually happened.

So, on second thought, even when events are reconciled with a construction, we cannot be sure that they have proved it true. There are always other constructions, and there is the lurking likelihood that some of them will turn out to be better. The best we can ever do is project our anticipations with frank uncertainty and observe the outcomes in terms in which we have a bit more confidence. But neither anticipation nor outcome is ever a matter of absolute certainty from the dark in which we mortals crouch. And, hence, even the most valuable construction we have yet contrived—even our particular notion of God Himself—is one for which we shall have to continue to take personal responsibility—at least until someone turns up with a better one. And I suspect he will! This is what we mean by *constructive alternativism*. Our view might even be called a philosophical position of *epistemological responsibility*.

The Conduct of Inquiry

One of the most exciting aspects of constructive alternativism is its bearing upon the conduct of human inquiry. According to the canons of logic a statement, if meaningful, is either true or not true. Indeed, the logical positivists have reversed the logic and argued that the criterion for meaningfulness is whether or not a statement can be proved true or not true. This means, I take it, that we should not ask a question until we have answered it. But constructive alternativism suggests that the canon itself is not fruitful, or at least that it tends to stultify fruitful endeavor. Besides, I note that most of the members of the famous Vienna Circle abandoned their extreme position—bursting with unanswerable questions, no doubt.

Since ultimate truth is such a long way off, it seems as inappropriate to try to capture it by, say, five o'clock on Tuesday as it is to claim we already have it in our grasp. Thus any proposition we contrive must be regarded as a crude formulation of a question which, at best, can serve only as an invitation to further inquiry, and one that can be answered only through personal experience and in terms of the *ad interim* criterion of anticipated events. Indeed, the answer we get is not likely to be exactly an answer to our question at all, but an answer to some other question we have not yet thought to ask.

To this way of thinking the verbs in all significant statements a man makes are implicitly cast in an "invitational mood," rather than in the indicative mood, or in one of the other moods recognized by English grammar. "What," he says, "would happen if....?" We suspect, furthermore, that this is psychologically characteristic of man whenever he is not in a defensive posture, and that it characterizes his unspoken impulses as well as his articulate sentences. "Please," he means to say, "join me in pursuing the implications of this pose I have assumed."

In this light, then, it is not necessary to disprove one proposition before entertaining alternatives to it. In certain situations, as in psychotherapy for example, it may even be disastrous to start with disproof, at least until we know what alternatives will drop into place once the disproof is taken seriously. Constructive alternativism is therefore an invitation to immediate adventure. By not insisting on disproof as a precondition for initiative it saves a lot of wear and tear on nerves and it should release a great deal of scholarly manpower for more productive and less disputatious occupations.

So, under constructive alternativism, even the appearance of some objective certainty may be taken as a flagrant challenge to throw—without waiting for the courage that disillusionment provides—a new light on the very circumstances that make it seem so obvious. Yet constructive alternativism tells us also that the reconstructive enterprise may be forestalled even earlier in the sequence. If one cautiously insists that truth must be compiled and cross-validated in fragments before he ever ventures further in the human quest, he may never reach the point where he can sense the challenge of upending smug certainties. He will be so eager to nail down his bits of truth once and for all that he will never back off and treat himself to a fresh look.

Generally, propositions cannot be effectively refuted unless we accept their terms of reference. But unless the terms are better stated than they usually are, it may be more appropriate to discard an old proposition than to go through the contortions necessary to disprove it. This seems to be mostly what we do with old propositions anyway! In any case, constructive alternativism suggests that we need not become bogged down in tedious refutations and that audacious proposals, including some that are badly put, may well serve as springboards for novel inquiry—even while we still retain a preference for their traditional alternatives.

Generating Psychological Theory

But now, since we are already on the threshold of psychological theorizing, we might as well get on with it, even though there is much more that could be said about the philosophical position of constructive alternativism. So let us talk about personal construct theory itself. We can come back to philosophy later if necessary.

The question of just how a theory is generated is about as complicated as the whole of human psychology. Since theories—so far, at least—are devised by men, it seems unreasonable to claim that they are shaped by any process other than a psychological one. Yet for a long time we have been saying that one moves from old propositions to new ones by the logical procedures of induction or deduction, as if this could happen independently of the personal disposition of man. Indeed, I have come to doubt that the notions of induction and deduction tell us very much about what goes on. In the one case I suppose it means we listen to ourselves making a clutter of assertions only to end up trying to say them all in one mouthful. In the other we let loose with a high-sounding remark and then, like a four-year-old child trying to "read" his own "writing," struggle to figure out what we meant by it.

In formulating the theory I have called *the psychology of personal constructs* I cannot say that I actually launched out deductively from the assumption of constructive alternativism as I have phrased it here, though now I can see how, with the help of a certain amount of idiosyncratic bias along the way, one could start with constructive alternativism and end up with personal construct theory. And I believe I can see how the clutter of events I experienced was important. Now that I think of it, I can remember a lot of relevant things that happened over the years. But not for one moment would I claim that these events converged to shape my theory. They seemed only to keep challenging it—and not always to be very constructive about it either. It may even be that I can remember these incidents now only because, on hindsight, they seem to confirm what my present formulation would forecast. And I am sure that I found myself perplexed and aggravated by many circumstances I have long since forgotten, and that what I came to think as a psychologist was what, over the years, I had jury-rigged as a man to cope with what was going on.

So let us not be hasty. Perhaps constructive alternativism was my basic assumption all along. I may only have delayed putting it into words. I recall that I have often felt that personal construct theory was as much an account of what had long been running through my noggin as it was the outcome of my labored thinking after I told myself to go ahead and dare to write a theory.

All of this is to suggest that the psychological postures, mine included, that we accent with words, or dignify in philosophical terms, may be quite personal and may considerably antedate our verbal statements about them. There is even reason to dread bringing such nascent constructions to light lest they betray us as foolish or even crazy. And I must say, at some risk to myself I suppose, that to propose a statement of such sweeping proportions as constructive alternativism is to flirt with grandiosity—a symptom more often associated with psychosis than with genius. But just as good cannot be accomplished without risking evil, so enlightenment cannot be sought wholeheartedly without approaching the brink of what may turn out to be insanity. There is no such thing as adventure with safety guaranteed in advance, not even when sitting alone with a typewriter. Not that I have ever lost any sleep over that matter!

Scientific Behavior as a Paradigm of Human Behavior

Legend has it that many theories originated with simple observations, often occurring under the most commonplace of circumstances. Archimedes is supposed to have been dallying in his bath when he made the observation that led to the notion of specific gravity. And there is the story about Newton napping under the apple tree. Then there is Bernoulli. I have long had my suspicions about what Bernoulli was doing.

Not to be outdone in fictionalizing itself, personal construct theory also can lay claim to an initial anecdote. In this case it is an observation of an amusing human, and even better than that, a psychologists' foible—which happily lowers it, I think, to the level of a caricature. So let us say that personal construct theory is a bit of humor that examined its own implications. And what, may I ask, could be more candidly psychological than that?

Psychologists are likely to be very much in earnest about making their discipline into a science. (Unfortunately, not many are as concerned as they might be about making science into something). And they are never more deadly serious about staking a claim to scientific respectability than they are when they are writing elementary textbooks. It struck me rather suddenly one day that all the elementary texts I had read contained at least two theories of personality—one covert, lucid, and facile, and the others labeled, abstruse, and labored.

"Psychology is a science," each author would say as soon as he had finished his initial exhortation to his young readers to stop relying upon common sense, "and a scientist is one who observes, construes relationships, articulates theories, generates hypotheses, ventures predictions, experiments under controlled conditions, and takes candid account of outcomes." This is to say that if the student is to understand a psychologist's commitment to life, here is the way to make sense out of it. Not bad! It gives us a pretty clear picture of what it is like to be a psychologist. Altogether it is a most penetrating and perceptive theory of personality, albeit one reserved for the scientifically elite.

Later on in the book, after the writer has explained that the eye really sees things upside down, that dogs' mouths water when they hear the dinner bell, and that the child's confrontation with the school system at age sixteen turns out about the same way it did when he was six (proving that it is *the child's* intelligence that does not change) he takes up the matter of personality theories, making it clear that he is really talking about organisms and being careful not to anthropomorphize his explanations—even his explanations of man. And how do organisms, such as human organisms (still being careful to avoid the use of such a compromising term as *persons*), behave? Why, they are *conditioned* (meaning that learning is something they must have had done to them—probably when they weren't looking), they are propelled by drives (anyone can see that otherwise they would just sit and do nothing at all), deluded by their motives (why else would they disagree with us?), and stalked by the ghosts of their childhood fantasies (note how they read the comic strips in the newspaper).

But what would happen if one were to envision all human endeavor in those same terms the psychologists have found so illuminating in explaining themselves to their students? And, indeed, might it not be that in doing so one would see the course of individual life, as well as human progress over the centuries, in clearer perspective? Scientists are men, and, while it does not follow that men are scientists, it is quite appropriate to ask if it is not their human character that makes scientists what they are. This leads us to the question of how that human character can better be construed so as to account for scientists, and whether our construction can still explain as well the accomplishments that fall far short of what we, at this transient moment in history, think good science is.

This is not a question of whether or not men do, in fact, live by the canons of science? That, except to an accumulative fragmentalist, is not even an appropriate question. We are not in search of such a neat conclusion, but of a strategic advantage in a long term quest for understanding. No theory can offer us more than that. The issue, then, is what this constructive alternative of seeing man as an incipient scientist will contribute at the present state in the search for a psychological understanding of him. Who knows—a by-product of this venture may be new light on scientific endeavor itself. In fact, I think I can see such a by-product emerging as personal construct theory suggests ways in which psychological processes we have hitherto spurned may enliven the scientific enterprise.

Basic Postulate

A person's processes are psychologically channelized by the ways in which he anticipates events. This is what we have proposed as a fundamental postulate for the psychology of personal constructs. The assumptions of constructive alternativism are embedded in this statement, although it may not be apparent until later in our exposition of the theme just how it is that they are.

We start with a *person*. Organisms, lower animals, and societies can wait. We are talking about someone we know, or would like to know—such as you, or myself. More particularly, we are talking about that person as an event—the processes that express his personality. And, since we enter the system we are about to elaborate at the point of a process—or life—rather than at the point of a body or a material substance, we should not have to invoke any special notions, such as dynamics, drives, motivation, or force to explain why our object does not remain inert. As far as the theory is concerned, it never was inert. As we pursue the theoretical line emerging from this postulate I think it becomes clear also why we do not need such notions to account for the direction of movement—any more than we need them to explain the movement itself.

This is to be a psychological theory. Mostly this is a way of announcing in the basic postulate that we make no commitment to the terms of other disciplines, such as physiology or chemistry. Our philosophical position permits us to see those other disciplines as based on man-made constructions, rather than as disclosures of raw realities, and hence there is no need for the psychologist to accept them as final, or to limit his proposals to statements consistent with them.

In addition, I think the theory sounds more or less like the other theories that are known as psychological. This gives me an inclusive, as well as an exclusive reason for calling it a psychological theory, although this is more or less a matter of taste rather than of definition. Certainly I have no intention of trying to define psychology; there are just too many things called psychological that I do not care to take responsibility for.

Some have suggested that personal construct theory not be called a psychological theory at all, but a metatheory. That is all right with me. It suggests that it is a theory about theories, and that is pretty much what I have in mind. But I hope that it is clear that it is not limited to being a metatheory of formal theories, or even of articulate ones.

There is also the question of whether or not it is a cognitive theory. Some have said that it was; others have classed it as existential. Quite an accomplishment; not many theories have been accused of being both cognitive and existential! But this, too, is all right with me. As a matter of fact, I am delighted. There are categorical systems in which I think the greater amount of ambiguity I stir up, the better. Cognition, for example, strikes me as a particularly misleading category, and, since it is one designed to distinguish itself from affect and conation, those terms, too, might well be discarded as inappropriately restrictive.

Personal construct theory has also been categorized by responsible scholars as an emotional theory, a learning theory, a psychoanalytic theory (Freudian, Adlerian, and Jungian—all three), a typically American theory, a Marxist theory, a humanistic theory, a logical positivistic theory, a Zen Buddhistic theory, a Thomistic theory, a behavioristic theory, an Apollonian theory, a pragmatistic theory, a reflective theory, and no theory at all. It has also been classified as nonsense, which indeed, by its own admission, it will likely some day turn out to be. In each case there were some convincing arguments offered for the categorization, but I have forgotten what most of them were. I fear that no one of these categorizations will be of much help to the reader in understanding personal construct theory, but perhaps having a whole lap full of them all at once will suggest what might be done with them.

The fourth term in the postulate—*channelized*—was chosen as one less likely than others to imply dynamics. This is because there is no wish to suggest that we are dealing with anything not already in motion. What is to be explained is the direction of the processes, not the transformation of states into processes. We see states only as an *ad interim* device to get time to stand still long enough for us to see what is going on. In other words, we have assumed that a process can be profitably regarded as more basic than an inert substance. We have had to do this notwithstanding the commitments of the centuries to quite another kind of language system. There are some disadvantages that come with this notion of what is basic, but we are willing to accept them for the time being in order to explore the Heraclitean implications more fully than psychologists have ever done before.

In specifying *ways of anticipating events* as the directive referent for human processes we cut ourselves free of the stimulus-response version of nineteenth century scientific determinism. I am aware that this is a drastic step indeed, and I suspect that others who claim to have taken similar steps have not always seriously taken stock of the difficulties to be encountered. For one thing, the very syntax of the language we must employ to voice our protest is built on a world view that regards objects as agents and outcomes as the products of those agents.

In our present undertaking the psychological initiative always remains a property of the person—never the property of anything else. What is more, neither past nor future events are themselves ever regarded as basic determinants of the course of human action—not even the events of childhood. But one's way of anticipating them, whether in the short range or in the long view—this is the basic theme in the human process of living. Moreover, it is that events are anticipated, not merely that man gravitates toward more and more comfortable organic states. Confirmation and disconfirmation of one's predictions are accorded greater psychological significance than rewards, punishments, or the drive reduction that reinforcements produce.

There are, of course, some predictions we would like to see disconfirmed, as well as some we hope will indeed materialize. We should not make the mistake of translating personal construct theory back into stimulus-response theory and saying to ourselves that confirmation is the same as a positive reinforcement, and that disconfirmation nullifies the meaning of an experience. Disconfirmation, even in those cases where it is disconcerting, provides grounds for reconstruction—or of repentance, in the proper sense of that term—and it may be used to improve the accuracy and significance of further anticipations. Thus we envision the nature of life in its outreach for the future, and not in its perpetuation of its prior conditions or in its incessant reverberation of past events.

Personal construct theory is elaborated by a string of eleven corollaries which may be loosely inferred from its basic postulate. Beyond these are certain notions of more limited applicability which fall in line with personal construct thinking—notions about such matters as anxiety, guilt, hostility, decision making, creativity, the strategy of psychological research, and other typical concerns of professional psychologists. These latter notions need not be considered part of the formal structure of the theory, although our theoretical efforts may not come to life in the mind of the reader until he has seen their applicability to the daily problems he faces.

Construction Corollary

A person anticipates events by construing their replications. Since events never repeat themselves, else they would lose their identity, one can look forward to them only by devising some construction which permits him to perceive two of them in a similar manner. His construction must also permit him to be selective about which two are to be perceived similarly. Thus the same construction that serves to infer their similarity must serve also to differentiate them from others. Under a system that provides only for the identification of similarities the world dissolves into homogeneity; under one that provides only for differentiation it is shattered into hopelessly unrelated fragments.

Perhaps it is true that events, as most of us would like to believe, really do repeat aspects of previous occurrences. But unless one thinks he is precocious enough to have hit upon what those aspects will ultimately turn out to be, or holy enough to have had them revealed to him, he must modestly concede that the appearance of replication is a reflection of his own fallible construction of what is going on. Thus the recurrent themes that make life seem so full of meaning are the original symphonic compositions of a man bent on finding the present in his past, and the future in his present.

Individuality Corollary

Persons differ from each other in their constructions of events. Having assumed that construction is a personal affair, it seems unlikely that any two persons would ever happen to concoct identical systems. I would go further now than when I originally proposed this corollary and suggest that even particular constructions are never identical events. And I would extend it the other way too, and say that I doubt that two persons ever put their construction systems together in terms of the same logical relationships. For myself, I find this a most encouraging line of speculation, for it seems to open the door to more advanced systems of thinking and inference yet to be devised by man. Certainly it suggests that scientific research can rely more heavily on individual imagination than it usually dares.

Organization Corollary

Each person characteristically evolves, for his convenience in anticipating events, a construction system embracing ordinal relationships between constructs. If a person is to live actively within his construction system it must provide him with some clear avenues of inference and movement. There must be ways for him to resolve the more crucial contradictions and conflicts that inevitably arise. This is not to say that all inconsistencies must be resolved at once. Some private paradoxes can be allowed to stand indefinitely, and, in the face of them, one can remain indecisive or can vacillate between alternative expectations of what the future holds in store for him.

So it seems that each person arranges his constructions so that he can move from one to another in some orderly fashion, either by assigning priorities to those which are to take precedence when doubts or contradictions arise, or by arranging implicative relationships, as in Boolean algebra, so that he may infer that one construction follows from another. Thus one's commitments may take priority over his opportunities, his political affiliations may turn him from compassion to power, and his moral imperatives may render him insensitive to the brute that tugs at his sleeve. These are the typical prices men pay to escape inner chaos.

Dichotomy Corollary

A person's construction system is composed of a. finite number of dichotomous constructs. Experience has shown me that this is the point where many of my readers first encounter difficulty in agreeing with me. What I am saying is that a construct is a 'black and white' affair, never a matter of shadings or of 'grays'. On the face of it, this sounds bad, for it seems to imply categorical or absolutistic thinking rather than any acceptance of relativism or conditionalism. Yet I would insist that there is nothing categorical about a construct.

When we look closely the initial point of difficulty in following personal construct theory usually turns out to lie in certain unrecognized assumptions made earlier while reading the exposition, or even carried over from previous habits of thought. Let us see if we can get the matter straightened out before any irreparable damage is done.

Neither our constructs nor our construing systems come to us from nature, except, of course, from our own nature. It must be noted that this philosophical position of constructive alternativism has much more powerful epistemological implications than one might at first suppose. We cannot say that constructs are essences distilled by the mind out of available reality. They are imposed *upon* events, not abstracted *from* them. There is only one place they come from; that is from the person who is to use them. He devises them. Moreover, they do not stand for anything or represent anything, as a symbol, for example, is supposed to do.

So what are they? They are reference axes, upon which one may project events in an effort to make some sense out of what is going on. In this sense they are like Cartesian coordinates, the x, y and z axes of analytic geometry. Events correspond to the points plotted within Cartesian space. We can locate the points and express relations between points by specifying x, y and z distances. The Cartesian axes *do not represent* the points projected upon them, but serve as guidelines for locating those points. That, also, is what constructs do for events, including ones that have not yet occurred. They help us locate them, understand them, and anticipate them.

But we must not take the Cartesian analogy too literally. Descartes' axes were lines or scales, each containing in order an infinite number of imaginary points. Certainly his x or y-axis embodied well enough the notion of shadings or a succession of grays. Yet a construct is not quite such an axis.

A construct is the basic contrast between two groups. When it is imposed it serves both to distinguish between its elements and to group them. Thus the construct refers to the nature of the distinction one attempts to make between events, not to the array in which his events appear to stand when he gets through applying the distinction between each of them and all the others.

Suppose one is dealing with the construct of good versus bad. Such a construct is not a representation of all things that are good, and an implicit exclusion of all that are bad. Nor is it a representation of all that are bad. It is not even a representation of all things that can be called either good or bad. The construct, of itself, is the kind of contrast one perceives and not in any way a representation of objects. As far as the construct is concerned there is no good-better-best scale, or any bad-worse-worst array.

But, while constructs do not represent or symbolize events, they do enable us to cope with events, which is a statement of quite a different order. They also enable us to put events into arrays or scales, if we wish. Suppose, for example, we apply our construct to elements, say persons, or to their acts. Consider three persons. One may make a good-bad distinction between them which will say that two of them are good in relation to the third, and the third is bad in relation to the two good ones. Then he may, in turn, apply his construct between the two good ones and say one of them is good with respect to the other formerly 'good' one and the one already labeled 'bad'.

This, of course, makes one of the persons, or acts, good in terms of one cleavage that has been made and bad in relation to the other. But this relativism applies only to the objects; the construct of good versus bad is itself absolute. It may not be accurate, and it may not be stable from time to time, but, as a construct, it has to be absolute. Still, by its successive application to events one may create a scale with a great number of points differentiating along its length. Now a person who likes grays can have them—as many as he likes.

But let us make no mistake: A scale, in comparison to a construct, is a pretty concrete affair. Yet one can scarcely have himself a scale unless he has a construct working for him. Only if he has some basis for discrimination and association can he get on with the job of marking off a scale.

Now note something else. We have really had to fall back on our philosophical position of constructive alternativism in order to come up with this kind of an abstraction. If we had not first disabused ourselves of the idea that events are the source of our construct, we would have had a hard time coming around to the point where we could envision the underlying basis of discrimination and association we call the construct.

The Geometry of Psychological Space

While we are at it, let us keep on going with this kind of abstract thinking and envision an equally abstract construction system made up of many constructs. If we can hold on we shall be well on our way to understanding personal construct theory's underlying mathematics or metaphysics. But we dare not fall back on our Cartesian analogy, once we have reached this point in the argument, lest we find ourselves envisioning systems of lines intersecting at common points. That may be all right for dimensioning physical space—though I am not so sure—but certainly it will not do for structuring psychological space.

To catch a glimpse of psychological space we may imagine a system of planes, each with two sides or aspects, slicing through a galaxy of events. One does not measure distances on these planes, he notes only, at any one instant of application, which side of each plane faces which events when the set is suspended in the galaxy. The set, or construct system, can, of course, be moved around in the galaxy in the manner I have described when a single construct is used to devise a scale. If the set is moved into all possible positions it generates a paracartesian hyperspace with its relatively concrete scalar axes. But that is a rather large undertaking, and one likely to fall through because man is inventive enough to keep thinking of new constructs he would like to add to the system. Another way of saying this is to suggest that even the simplest personal construct system can hardly get around to putting all events in order, and, unless the man is pretty unimaginative, he will have to keep starting over each time he thinks of a new way to discriminate or associate.

One thing more has to be said. In order to make the point, I have had to talk about constructs in such an explicit manner that I have probably given the impression that a construct is as highly articulate and cognitive as my discussion has had to be. If I had been able to say what I have said in metaphor or hyperbole I might have left the impression that a construct had something to do with feeling or with formless urges too fluid to be pinned down by labels. But personal construct theory is no more a cognitive theory than it is an affective or a conative one. There are grounds for distinction that operate in one's life that seem to elude verbal expression. We see them in infants, as well as in our own spontaneous aversions and infatuations. These discriminative bases are no less constructs than those the reader may have been imagining during the reading of the preceding paragraphs. Certainly it is important not to consider a construct as another term for a concept, else a major sector of the arena in which constructs function will be obscured from view.

Choice Corollary

A person chooses for himself that alternative in a dichotomized construct through which he anticipates the greater possibility for the elaboration of his system. It seems to me to follow that if a person makes so much use of his constructs, and is so dependent upon them, he will make choices which promise to develop their usefulness. Developing the usefulness of a construction system involves, as far as I can see, two things: defining it and extending it. One defines his system, by extension at least, by making it clear how its construct components are applied to objects or are linked with each other. He amplifies his system by using it to reach out for new fields of application. In the one case he consolidates his position and in the other he extends it.

Note that the choice is between alternatives expressed in the construct, not, as one might expect, between objects divided by means of the construct. There is a subtle point here. Personal construct theory is a psychological theory and therefore has to do with the behavior of man, not with the intrinsic nature of objects. A construct governs what the man does, not what the object does. In a strict sense, therefore, man makes decisions which initially affect himself, and which affect other objects only subsequently—and then only if he manages to take some effective action. Making a choice, then, has to do with involving oneself, and cannot be defined in terms of the external object chosen. Besides, one does not always get the object he chooses to gain. But his anticipation does have to do with his own processes, as I tried to say in formulating the basic postulate.

So when a man makes a choice what he does is align himself in terms of his constructs. He does not necessarily succeed, poor fellow, in doing anything to the objects he seeks to approach or avoid. Trying to define human behavior in terms of the externalities sought or affected, rather than the seeking process, gets the psychologist pretty far off the track. It makes more of a physicist of him than a psychologist, and a rather poor one, at that. So what we must say is that a person, in deciding whether to believe or do something, uses his construct system to proportion his field, and then moves himself strategically and tactically within its presumed domain.

Men change things by changing themselves first, and they accomplish their objectives, if at all, only by paying the price of altering themselves—as some have found to their sorrow and others to their salvation. The choices that men make are choices of their own acts, and the alternatives are distinguished by their own constructs. The results of the choices, however, may range all the way from nothing to catastrophe, on the one hand, or to consummation, on the other.

Range Corollary

A construct is convenient for the anticipation of a finite range of events only. A personal construct system can hardly be said to have universal utility. Not everything that happens in the world can be projected upon all the dichotomies that make up a person's outlook. Indeed I doubt that anyone has ever devised a construct that could cover the entire range of events of which he was aware. There are patches of clouds in every man's sky. This is to say that the geometry of the mind is never a complete system. The lines of reference here and there become lost in irrelevancies and make it practically impossible to write formulas that are universally applicable.

The classical notion of a *concept* is that it embraces all elements having a common property, and excludes all others. But this kind of notion will not do for *constructs*. A construct is a distinction which has the effect of distributing objects tentatively into two associations. If one says that a man is tall he does more than exclude all objects that are not tall. He denies that the man is short. He asserts that there are other objects that are both not tall and are short. And he excludes only those objects which are outside his range of concern.

Logicians, accustomed to thinking about concepts and not yet altogether clear about what I mean by constructs, might take issue with me at this point. They might say that all one has disclaimed is the possibility that the man is not tall. But we must remind ourselves that here we are talking about the psychology of man's actions and intents, and we can be sure that if the person who makes the remark has nothing more on his mind than what formal logic suggests, he will keep his mouth shut. Psychologically, the only point in commenting on the man's being tall is to deny some alternative that needed denying. What is excluded, therefore, includes some pretty important considerations, as well as some irrelevancies.

If we are to understand a person's statement we had better take into account just what it was he felt he must negate, as well as what he used as the subject or the predicate of his sentence. This, again, is a way of saying that the construct is a basis of making a distinction and, by the same act, creating an association, as one does when saying that a man is tall and implying thereby that he is like some other objects in that respect. Especially, one must keep in mind that a construct is not a class of objects, or an abstraction of a class, but a dichotomous reference axis.

A construct has its *focus of convenience*—a set of objects with which it works especially well. Over a somewhat larger range it may work only reasonably well; that is its *range of convenience*. But beyond that it fades into uselessness and we can say the outer array of objects simply lies beyond that range of convenience.

It would be nice, mathematically, if every event in a man's world could be projected onto every construct he had. Then we might hope to check out the whole system and all its internal relationships. It would be even nicer if every event could be projected upon every construct of every man. Then we could check one man's outlook precisely against another's—hoping that neither would change his mind before the wallpaper came out of the computer. But I don't think this is very likely to happen, at least not during the natural life of personal construct theory.

Experience Corollary

A person's construction system varies as he successively construes the replications of events. Here again our analytic geometry model does not quite fit the mathematics of psychological space. Rather than remaining altogether fixed, as the axes of analytic geometry do when points are plotted within them, the tendency is for personal constructs to shift when events are projected upon them. The distinctions they implement are likely to be altered in three ways: (1) The construct may be applied at a different point in the galaxy, (2) it may become a somewhat different kind of distinction, and (3) its relations to other constructs may be altered.

In the first of these shifts it is a matter of a change in the location of the construct's application, and hence not exactly an intrinsic change in the construct itself. In the second case, however, it is the abstraction itself which is altered, although the change may not be radical enough for the psychologist to say a new construct has been substituted. Finally, in the third case, the angular relations with other constructs are necessarily affected by the transition, unless, by some chance, the construct system were rotated as a whole. But that is not a very likely contingency.

The first kind of shift might be observed when a person moves to an urban community. Some of the actions he once regarded as aloof and unneighborly he may come to accept as relatively friendly in the new social context. But he may also rotate the axis of his construct as he gains familiarity with city life, and, as a result, come to see "aloofness" as a neighborly respect for his privacy, something he had never had very clearly in mind before. This would be an example of the second kind of shift. The third kind of shift comes when he alters his notion of respect as a result of the experience, perhaps coming to sense it not so much a matter of subservience or adulation but more a matter of empathy and consideration. As a matter of fact, we might regard the whole transition as leading him in the direction of greater maturity.

Keeping in mind that events do not actually repeat themselves and that the replication we talk about is a replication of ascribed aspects only, it begins to be clear that the succession we call experience is based on the constructions we place on what goes on. If those constructions are never altered, all that happens during a man's years is a sequence of parallel events having no psychological impact on his life. But if he invests himself—the most intimate event of all—in the enterprise, the outcome, to the extent that it differs from his expectation or enlarges upon it, dislodges the man's construction of himself. In recognizing the inconsistency between his anticipation and the outcome, he concedes a discrepancy between what he was and what he is. A succession of such investments and dislodgments constitutes the human experience.

A subtle point comes to light at this juncture. Confirmation may lead to reconstruing quite as much as disconfirmation—perhaps even more. A confirmation gives one an anchorage in some area of his life, leaving him free to set afoot adventuresome explorations nearby, as, for example, in the case of a child whose security at home emboldens him to be the first to explore what lies in the neighbor's yard.

The unit of experience is, therefore, a cycle embracing five phases: anticipation, investment, encounter, confirmation or disconformation, and constructive revision. This is followed, of course, by new anticipations, as the first phase of a subsequent experiential cycle gets underway. Certainly in personal construct theory's line of reasoning experience is not composed of encounters alone.

Stated simply, the amount of a man's experience is not measured by the number of events with which he collides, but by the investments he has made in his anticipations and the revisions of his constructions that have followed upon his facing up to consequences. A man whose only wager in life is upon reaching heaven by immunizing himself against the miseries of his neighbors, or upon following a bloody party-line straight to utopia, is prepared to gain little experience until he arrives—either there, or somewhere else clearly recognized as not the place he was looking for. Then, if he is not too distracted by finding that his architectural specifications have been blatantly disregarded, or that the wrong kind of people have started moving in, I suppose he may begin to think of some other investments he might better have been making in the meantime. Of course, a little hell along the way, if taken more to heart than most heaven-bound people seem to take it, may have given him a better idea of what to expect, before it was too late to get a bit of worthwhile experience and make something out of himself.

Modulation Corollary

The variation in a person's construction system is limited by the permeability of the constructs within whose ranges of convenience the variants lie. While the Experience Corollary suggests that a man can revise his constructions on the basis of events and his invested anticipations of them there are limitations that must be taken into account. He must have a construct system which is sufficiently open to novel events to let him know when he has encountered them, else the experience cycle will fail to function in its terminal phases. He must have a system which also will admit the revised construct that emerges at the end of the cycle. If the revised construct is left to stand as an isolated axis of reference it will be difficult for him to chart any coordinated course of action that takes account of it; he therefore can do little with respect to it except vacillate.

Perhaps it is clear from these remarks that what is meant by permeability is not a construct's plasticity, or its amenability to change within itself, but its capacity to be used as a referent for novel events and to accept new subordinate constructions within its range of convenience. A notion of God, for example, which includes an unabridged dictionary of all things holy is likely to be impermeable. Anything new that turns up—such as an unbiblical event or idea—is likely to be excluded from the construct's realm of concern. Unless the novelty can fit elsewhere into some more permeable part of the construct system, it is likely to be ignored.

Fragmentation Corollary

A person may successively employ a variety of construction subsystems which are inferentially incompatible with each other. We must be careful not to interpret the Modulation Corollary to mean that a construct system has to be logically intact. Perhaps in any proximate transition in the human process there is an inferential relationship between antecedent and consequent at some constructive level in the person's system. But persons move from *a* to *b* and on to *c* without always taking into account the fact that their overview of *c* cannot be inferred from their overview of *a*. A man may move from an act of love to an act of jealousy, and from there to an act of hate, even though hate is not something that would be inferred from love, even in his peculiar system. This is the kind of psychological fact to which the Fragmentation Corollary calls particular attention.

Perhaps I should add that I do not see this kind of "irrationality" as necessarily a bad thing. For man logic and inference can be as much an obstacle to his ontological ventures as a guide to them. Often it is the uninferred fragment of a man's construction system that makes him great, whereas if he were an integrated whole—taking into account all that the whole would have to embrace—the poor fellow would be no better than his "natural self."

Commonality Corollary

To the extent that one person employs a *construction of experience which is similar to that employed by another, his processes are psychologically similar to those of the other person.*[2] On the face of it, this corollary appears to assert pretty much what personal construct theory seems to stand for: The notion that behavior is governed by constructs. But there is more to it than what such a simplified statement might be taken to imply.

If we do as most behavioristically influenced psychologists do, and use behavior as a synonym for all human process, we then might, I suppose, substitute the term "behaviors" for "processes" in stating this corollary. But what thoughtful behaviorists have in mind when they make behavior the focus of their concern is the logical positivist position that anything that cannot be identified as behavior is untestable and therefore a scientific distraction. If we were to take this stand—as I would prefer not—we would be concerned only with that phase of the experiential cycle I have called "personal investment." Personal construct theory would lead us, I think, to be concerned with the whole experiential cycle and the process which it represents, rather than with the behavioral phase only.

There is something more. I have used the expression, "construction of experience," rather than "construction of events." I wanted it to be clear that the construction would have to cover the experience itself, as well as the external events with which experience was ostensibly concerned. At the end of an experiential cycle one not only has a revised construction of the events he originally sought to anticipate, but he has also a construction of the process by which he reached his new conclusions about them. In launching his next venture, whatever its concern might be, he will have reason to take account of the effectiveness of the experiential procedures he employed in his last.

To be sure, in writing this corollary it would have been literally correct to say simply, "construction of events," a phrase that appears so frequently in this exposition. This would have included "experience," since an experience, once it has been enacted, is

[2] To my mild dismay I have only now realized that the word "psychological" was misplaced in my original phrasing of this corollary. Instead of modifying "processes," as I originally had it, the term should modify "similar," as constructive alternativism would suggest. Sorry about that!

itself an event. But experience is such an important event in charting what comes next, it seemed important to single it out for special mention. Besides, since experience, as I have defined it, already embraces the events with which the experiencing person has involved himself, the term is sufficiently inclusive, as well as exclusive, to pinpoint what needs to be said. What I especially want to make clear is that the extent of the psychological similarity between the processes of two persons depends upon the similarity of their constructions of their personal experiences, as well as upon the similarity in their conclusions about external events.

But let us also be especially clear about something this corollary does not say, and what that means for the psychology of man in motion. It does not say that the two persons must have experienced "the same" events and it does not say their two experiential cycles have to be "the same." And, to go further, it does not even say they must have experienced "similar" events or that the two experiential cycles must actually have been similar in some way. What has to be similar, in order for their processes to be similar in the same degree, is their construction of experience. And that includes similarity of the construction of events that emerges in the terminal phase of the experiential cycle.

The reason for this being so important is that the outcome of an experience is not merely a tendency to repeat or to avoid it thereafter, as reinforcement theory presumes, but that the conclusions reached through experience are likely to be in the form of new questions which set the stage for new ventures. One does not fully understand human behavior, or human processes, except as he understands also the flashes of ingenuity that intersperse human monotonies. While novel undertakings can be construed in ways which show replications, as the Construction Corollary suggests, it is not behavior or process itself which is concretely re-enacted. But in construing replications, rather than in claiming he has seen concrete repetitions, one may project a view of man engaged in ventures, rather than always repeating concretely what has been reinforced.

This corollary makes it possible to say that two persons who have confronted quite different events, and who might have gone through experiential cycles which actually seem to us to be quite different, might nevertheless end up with similar constructions of their experiences, and, because of that, thereafter pursue psychologically similar processes of further inquiry. Thus personal construct theory further releases psychology from assumptions about the identity of events and man's dependence upon them. It leaves us free to envision man coping with "familiar" events in new ways and co-operating with other men to produce novelties which make their world a different place to live in. Neither behaviorism nor phenomenology, as I see them, provides a psychological basis for this kind of forward movement in man.

Sociality Corollary

To the extent that one person construes the construction processes of another, he may play a role in a social process involving the other person. The implications of this corollary are probably the most far reaching of any I have yet attempted to propound. It establishes grounds for understanding *role* as a psychological term, and for envisioning thereupon a truly psychological basis for society. As far as I can see, the term has only extrapsychological meaning elsewhere. This view offers, moreover, an approach to certain puzzling aspects of psychopathy, and it permits one to understand guilt in far more intimate terms than are possible within more conventional "personality" theories, or within current theological doctrines. It leads us also to a position from which we can distinguish personality theories from others.

Perceptive psychologists are keenly aware that there must be some important relationship between what they call "role," "guilt," and "psychopathic personality" on the one hand, and the viability of society on the other. Yet there is little in the stimulus-response kind of theorizing that throws psychological light on what the relationship may be. There is scarcely more to be found in the so-called dynamic theories, although the literature associated with them richly documents a vaguely disquieting awareness of what may be transpiring in the community of man.

Let me start by trying to differentiate two levels at which I may try to understand another person—say, my reader. It is not hard for me to imagine him—*you*, I mean—at this moment a figure bending over a book. It—the figure—is skimming the paragraphs with the right fore-finger in a position to turn to the pages that follow. The eye movements zig zag down the page and quickly the next leaf is flipped, or perhaps a whole section—a chapter or more—is lifted with the left thumb and drawn horizontally aside.

What I am envisioning is a moving object, and whether or not I am correctly describing the movements that are taking place can be reasonably well confirmed—or disconfirmed—by an observer who has been watching you for the past few moments, or if he saw a motion picture film of what has been taking place. This is to say I have couched my picture of you in the terms of "objective" psychology. I have offered a hypothesized description of a "behaving organism."

Ordinarily, if I wanted to play the game by the rules of objectivity, I would not stoop to ask you outright whether or not my description of your actions was correct; the noises you might make in reply could be taken in so many different ways I can be sure of being "a scientist" only if I stick to what can be confirmed. Being a "scientist" may be so important to me that I dare not risk sullying myself with your delusions. I shall therefore play my part and retain my membership in Sigma Xi by referring to your reply as a "vocal response" of a "behaving organism." *Hello there, Behaving Organism*!

But now let me say it quite another way. There you are, my reader, wondering, I fear, what on earth I am trying so hard to say, and smiling to yourself as the thought crosses your mind that it all might be put in a familiar phrase or two—as indeed it may. You are hunched uncomfortably over the book, impatiently scanning the paragraphs for a cogent expression or a poignant sentence that may make the experience worth the time you are stealing from more urgent duties. The right forefinger is restlessly poised to lift the page and go on to discover if perhaps anything more sensible follows.

Let me confess that I feel at this moment like urging you not to try so hard. While it has taken me hours to write some of these paragraphs—the four preceding ones, for example—and I would like to think the outcome has been worth some of your time too, they were not meant to be hammered into your consciousness. They are intended, instead, to set off trains of thought. And, in following them, I earnestly hope we shall find ourselves walking along the same paths.

There now, isn't that the way it really is? It isn't? Then, tell me, what *are* you doing? And while we are at it, tell me also how my efforts strike you—I mean, what do you think I am trying to do, not merely whether I am making sense or not. Only please do not tell me that all I am really doing is pounding a typewriter in an effort to keep my wife awake; I have other psychoanalytically oriented friends who are only too happy to offer me that kind of "interpretation."

Although these two descriptions of my view of the reader both represent a wide departure from accepted literary style, I hope they will make clear the contrast between construing the construction processes of another person and construing his behavior merely. In the first instance, I construed only your behavior. There is nothing wrong with that, as far as it goes. In the second case I went further and placed a construction upon the way in which I imagined you might be thinking. The chances are that I was more or less mistaken in both instances, particularly in the second. But the point I want to make lies in the difference in my mode of construing you. In both formulations I was indeed concerned with your behavior, but only in the second did I strive for some notion of the construction which might be giving your behavior its form, or your future behavior its form. If immediate accuracy is what I must preserve at all costs, then I had better stick to the first level of construction. But if I am to anticipate you, I must take some chances and try to sense what you are up to.

One does not have to be a psychologist to treat another person as an automaton, though training in "experimental psychology" may help. Conversely, treating him that way does not make one into a scientist—though some of my colleagues may wish to dispute this. It is easy enough to treat persons we have never met as behaving organisms only, and many of us think that is the sophisticated way to go about secondary human relations. We may even treat our neighbors that way, especially if there are more of them than we care to know. I have even observed parents who go so far as to treat their children so, and they sometimes come to me for psychological advice on how to do it. I sometimes suspect it is because they have more children than they care to know. To be very frank about it, my construction of you, while writing some of these passages, has often lapsed into no more than that. And, if you are like me in this respect, there must have been moments when you regarded me as a disembodied typewriter, or as an Irish name on the title page of a book, or as a kind of animated sentence ejector.

Points about Roles to be Emphasized

I know from past experience in attempting to explain this notion of role that two things need especially to be made clear, particularly if I am trying to explain it to a thoroughly trained fellow psychologist. First, my construing of your construction processes need not be accurate in order for me to play a role in a social process that involves you. I have seen a person play a role, and do it most effectively—even in a manner quite acceptable to his colleagues—when he grossly misperceived their outlooks, and they knew it. But because he did what he did on the basis of what he thought they understood, not merely on the basis of their overt acts, he was able to play a collaborative role in a social process whose experiential cycle led them all somewhere. Experiential cycles which are based on automaton-like constructions do not, I think, generate social processes, though they may lead to revisions of the manipulative devices by which men try to control each other's actions.

The second point that experience has led me to stress is that my construction of your outlook does not make me a compliant companion, nor does it keep us from working at cross purposes. I may even use my construction of your view as a basis for trying to undo your efforts. But there is something interesting about this; there is still a good chance of a social process emerging out of our conflict, and we will both end up a good way from where we started—in my case, because the experiential cycle will reflect back upon my construction of your outlook, not of your behavior only, and, in your case, because you would find that something beyond your overt behavior was being taken into account, and you might revise your investments accordingly.

There is a third point that sometimes needs mentioning. What I have proposed is a psychological definition of role, and therefore it does not lean upon sociological assumptions about the nature of society or economic assumptions about the coordination of human labor. Being psychological, it attempts to derive its terms from the experience of the individual, though, once the derivations have been made, there are no necessary restrictions on pursuing implications on out into the world of the sociologist, or even into that of the mathematician.

What comes out, then, is a definition that permits us to say that roles are not necessarily reciprocal; you may indeed enact a role based on your construction of my outlook, but my failure to construe you as anything more than a "behaving organism" may prevent me from enacting a role in relation to you. The social process that results from such an exchange stems from you but not from me. It involves you because your behavior tests out a version of my outlook, and the experiential cycle in which you invest yourself leads you to a reinterpretation of our social relationship. It does not involve me because the only hypotheses to which I have made an experiential commitment are hypotheses about your overt behavior.

Role and Experience

If I fail to invest in a role, and relate myself to you only mechanically, then the only thing that disconfirmation can teach me is that the organism I presume you to be is not wired up to produce the behaviors I thought it would—just as my typewriter does not always behave in the way I expect it to. When my typewriter behaves unpredictably I look to see if there isn't a screw loose, or if something hasn't gotten into the works. Sometimes I find I have struck the wrong key; I'll strike a different one next time.

And if I insist on construing you as I do my typewriter, I shall probably take my predictive failures as an indication only that I should look to see if there isn't "a screw loose somewhere" in you. Or perhaps I shall wonder if I haven't "struck the wrong key," or if something hasn't "gotten into your works," like a "motive" or a "need," for example. I may even conclude that you are a brand of "typewriter" that has been badly put together. Certainly if this is the way I go about concluding my experiential cycle, I can scarcely claim that I have engaged myself in a social process. Mine might be the kind of experience that gets the commonwealth's work done, but it would not be the sort that builds viable societies.

When one construes another person's outlook, and proceeds to build an experiential cycle of his own upon that construction, he involves himself, willy nilly, in an interesting way. He can test his construction only by activating in himself the version of the other person's outlook it offers. This subtly places a demand upon him, one he cannot lightly reject if his own experience is to be completed. He must put himself tentatively in the other person's shoes. Only by enacting that role can he sense the impact of what happens as a result of taking the point of view he thinks his friend must have.

This means making a behavioral investment of his own, following the hypothesized lines, and experiencing the consequences. The enactment by which he pursues this experiential venture comes close to what is popularly regarded as role-taking. While not all enactments constitute roles in the personal construct sense, and not all role enactments culminate in completed experiential cycles, these brief comments may serve to suggest why the term *role* has been given such a salient part in the development of this theory.

Guilt

It is in the context of the Sociality Corollary that one can begin to develop a truly psychological definition of *guilt*. This is not to say that such a definition has to be at odds with ecclesiastical or legal definitions, though it may indeed suggest quite different courses of human action where misdemeanor is involved. We shall be speaking, of course, about the experience of guilt and what it is like, psychologically.

Most psychological theories, both "mechanistic" ones and "dynamic" ones, regard the experience of guilt as a derivative of punishment. One feels guilty because he thinks he has made himself eligible for punishment. But suppose one does not see punishment as the appropriate treatment of wrong-doing, only as revenge by injured persons serving simply to make clear that they have been hurt. Or suppose one does not see wrong-doing as something for which he has been systematically punished. Can he still feel guilty? I think he can. I think Jesus thought so too, though very few ecclesiastics appear to agree with either of us on this point. Even the term "repentance," which I think might better be taken to mean rethinking or reconstruing, as its etymology suggests, has come to stand for undertaking something irrelevantly unpleasant or punitive in compensation for disobedience, rather than doing something which will throw light on past mistakes.

As far as I can see, both from what I have observed and what I have figured out for myself, a person who chronically resorts to this kind of penitence to bring his guilt feelings back into comfortable equilibrium, or to write off his wrong-doing, ends up as a well-balanced sanctimonious psychopath. His only possible virtue is obedience and the society he perpetuates has no purpose except to uphold its own laws. I suspect, furthermore, that this is the net effect of any stimulus-response-reinforcement kind of theory, whether in psychology, religion or politics. And I have been moved to say, on occasion, that a psychopath is a stimulus-response psychologist who takes it seriously—a remark I find does not endear me to all my colleagues.

From the standpoint of personal construct theory, guilt is the sense of having lost one's core role structure. A core structure is any one that is maintained as a basic referent of life itself. Without it a person has no guidelines for staying alive. To the extent that one's core structure embodies his role also, as we have defined role, he is vulnerable to the experience of guilt. He has only to perceive himself dislodged from such a role to suffer the inner torment most of us know so well.

To feel guilty is to sense that one has lost his grasp on the outlook of his fellow man, or has unwittingly played his part in a manner irrelevant to that outlook by following invalid guidelines. If the role is based on one's construction of God's outlook, or The Party's, he has only to fail to play it or to find that in playing it he has grossly misinterpreted its principal dimensions, to experience a religious sense of guilt. With this goes a feeling of alienation from God, or man, or from both. It is not a pleasant experience, and if the perception of excommunication is extensive or the core role deeply disrupted, it may be impossible for life to continue. Indeed, among primitive people, life may be extinguished within a few days, and, among more civilized ones, it may be abandoned by suicide.

A person who has never developed a role, or who has never allowed his life to depend on it, need not experience guilt. Guilt follows only from the loss of such a central part in the affairs of man. Persons who have always lacked a sense of role, such as psychopaths are said to be, may become confused or even anxious, as they contemplate the disconfirming outcomes of their experiences, but what they display is usually clinically distinguishable from guilt. But, then, neither do such persons play any substantial part in the developments by which societies emerge. Guilt is thus a concomitant risk in any creative social process by which man may seek to transcend blind obedience. The author of the Book of Genesis seems to have perceived this a good deal more clearly than his readers have.

Hostility

At this point let us turn back to the Experience Corollary and examine its contribution to our understanding of another puzzling matter—hostility. The experience cycle described in that section included a terminal phase embodying an assessment of the construction in terms of which the initial anticipation had been cast and the behavioral commitment had been made. If outcomes emerging successively from ventures based on the same construction continue to leave a trail of disconfirmations behind, it becomes increasingly clear, even to the most dim-witted adventurer, that something is wrong with his reference axes.

Of course, all he has to do when this happens is to start revising his constructs. But, if he procrastinates too long or if his core constructs are involved, this may prove to be a major undertaking. Constructs which are in the process of revision are likely to be pretty shaky, and if he has a great deal of importance resting on one of them, with no others nearby to take up the load, he may find himself on the verge of confusion, or even guilt.

Ordinarily one can loosen his constructs by falling back on more permeable constructions, as suggested by the Modulation Corollary. But if his superordinate constructs are impermeable he will find himself unable to range any new constructions under them. He will then be confronted with a far more extensive revision of his system than he would if he had more open-ended constructions to fall back upon. The upshot of all this may be that he will find himself precariously poised between the minor chaos that his recent disconfirmations have disclosed, and the major chaos that might engulf him if he attempted to make the needed repairs in his reference axes. In this predicament he may look for some way to avoid both.

One way to avoid the immediate chaos is to tinker with the validational evidence which has recently been giving trouble. There are several ways of doing this. One is to stop short of completing one's experiments. Graduate students are quick to catch on to this one. Another is to loosen up one's construction of outcomes, though this is likely to invite charges of being unrealistic. Still another is to claim rewards as valid substitutes for confirmations, the way doting parents and reinforcement theorists do. One does this by exploiting his dependency on people who are over eager to be helpful.

But there is still another way. That is to force the circumstances to confirm one's prediction of them. A parent who finds that his child does not love him as much as he expected may extort tokens of affection from the helpless youngster. A nation whose political philosophy has broken down in practice may precipitate a war to draft support for its outlook. A meek and trembly spinster, confronted at last by the fact that it is her impregnable posture that renders her unmarriageable, may "prove" the validity of her stand by enticing one of the male brutes to victimize her. A child, unwilling to concede his parents' better judgment because of its far-reaching implications for himself, may seize upon the first opportunity to engage in spiteful obedience by following their advice legalistically in a situation to which it obviously does not apply.

Each of these illustrates an instance of hostility. What personal construct theory has to offer in this matter differs radically from what conventional psychological theory implies. As with other topics with which it deals, personal construct theory attempts to define psychological constructs in terms of the personal experience of the individual to which they are to be applied. Thus, in defining hostility, we do not say that it is essentially an impulse to destroy—even though that may be its consequence—for that sounds more like a complaint of the victim than a prime effort of the hostile person. Instead, hostility is defined as the continued effort to extort validational evidence in favor of a type of social prediction which has already proved itself a failure.

Further Implications of Personal Construct Theory

Since this presentation is intended to be a brief introduction to personal construct theory, rather than a condensation of it, much has had to be omitted. The important decision cycles and creativity cycles which the theory envisions remain unmentioned until this moment, as does a radically different view of dependency. There are strictly psychological definitions of threat, impulsivity, anxiety, transference, preemption, constellatoriness, and propositionality. There is a linguistic system called the language of hypothesis, an ontology exemplified in orchestrated approaches to psychotherapy, and a methodology of psychological research. The notions of motivation, needs and psychodynamics vanish under the light of the Basic Postulate which accepts man as alive to begin with, and the principle of the elaborative choice which takes care of the directionality of man's moves without invoking special motivational agents to account for each of them.

The concept of learning evaporates. The boundary between cognition and affect is obliterated, rendering both terms meaningless. Fixed role therapy illustrates one of a variety of psychotherapeutic approaches which, at first glance, appear to violate most accepted canons of mental treatment by recognizing man as his own scientist. A new view of schizophrenia emerges, as well as fresh interpretations of "the unconscious," depression, and aggression.

But this is enough to mention now. All it has been possible to accomplish in these pages is to state the basic propositions from which hypotheses may be drawn, to illustrate a few of the lines of inference that may be pursued, and to encourage the more impatient readers to seek out the theory's most exciting implications for themselves.

7

The Psychology of Personal Constructs[1]

This evening I would like to share with you some thoughts regarding the philosophical and scientific bases of our common interest in the problem of mental health. A discussion of this sort is not prepared without considerable anxiety. This is the first time I have attempted to discuss, outside of our own closely knit research teams, the basic postulate upon which the psychology of personal constructs is founded. In preparing such a discussion as this, one wonders how it will sound to strange ears, whether the group to whom he wishes to communicate what he believes to be novel ideas has not itself developed its own characteristic approach to the very same problems, whether they will be able to follow one's own provincial scientific dialect, whether words will mean the same to them as to himself and, finally, whether he will be unintentionally desecrating the icons of his listeners' scientific faith.

As one would infer from the words, "personal constructs," this approach to personality theory is focused upon the individual and personal nature of people's ways of construing their worlds.

Some thirteen years ago, Dr Gordon Allport posed a basic problem in personality theory. He pointed out that there were two approaches to the understanding of personality. One, the nomothetic approach; the other, the idiographic approach. The nomothetic approach is used when one attempts to make many separate observations on different people and from this sample of observations, however limited or extensive, attempts to make inferences regarding people or classes of people. In its pure form a nomothetic approach is one in which the number of people observed[2]. The contrasting approach, and that espoused by Dr Allport, he calls the idiographic approach. When one uses this approach the universe is not a population of all the people in the world, out of which we have drawn a sample, but rather the universe is one person and the population from which our sample of observations is drawn is a population of all possible observations of a certain type made upon one person. In its purest form this approach involves multiple observations on one person only.

Now, as I am sure you have already discovered if you have presented these two points of view to students, interns, or residents, the first response of the listener is usually to take sides. If the listener is "case oriented" and tends to be sympathetic with his patients, the chances are that he will first seize upon the idiographic approach as best expressing a scientific point-of-view. If, by contrast, and I hope that this contrast will not be considered odious, your listener is management oriented and problem oriented, he is more likely to seize first upon the nomothetic approach as best representing a scientific point-of-view.

Let us examine very briefly what happens when each of the approaches is criticized from the point-of-view of the other. If you believe in the nomothetic approach you will probably criticize the idiographic approach in some such manner as the following: The idiographic approach leads one nowhere except in his own private world. The idiographic observer cannot be a true observer for the system in which he seeks to operate has no frame of reference. He cannot say that a patient is aggressive because he has established no norms which would indicate that the patient is more or less aggressive than other patients or other people. His conclusions, reached upon the basis of his pseudo-observation of a universe of behaviors in one person, have no relevance to any other person. Knowledge gained in relation to one patient provides no basis for predicting or understanding future patients. Indeed the nomothetic protagonist will say that in a practical sense it is impossible for one to be scientifically idiographic, for even the perception of behavior of another person can be accomplished only in relating to reference points established through previous experience with other patients and other people.

But let us see how the idiographic protagonist defends himself. I have never seen it better expressed than by a certain courageous student of mine who was defending his dissertation in an oral examination with an advanced degree at stake. His research had involved some experimentation with different therapeutic approaches to a small number of patients. Sure enough, one of the examiners asked him, with a strong hint of sarcasm in his voice, how in the world he thought he could prove anything with less than a hundred cases. The student was ready for that question! He said, "Professor Blank, have you ever seen a two headed calf and how many of them did you have to see before you believed it?" What the student had sensed is what all followers of the idiographic approach must sense: that nature

[1] Presented at the US Veterans Administration Hospital, Houston, Texas, 20 March, 1951. Published by permission of Jacqueline Aldridge.

[2] Editors' note: although this sentence is incomplete, it is a correct reproduction of the original.

Collected Papers of the Pioneer of Constructivist Psychology: George A. Kelly, First Edition. Edited by David A. Winter and Nick Reed.

herself does not have to prove her validity. Here we can all agree. One patient suffering from anxiety is just as true a phenomenon and may be known with as much scientific exactitude as a thousand patients who reject Card IV on the Rorschach Test.

Both the nomothetic and idiographic approaches have been fruitful in helping us develop more precise psychological tools. The nomothetic approach has contributed to the field of personnel selection in which it has been possible, through actuarial statistics, to save industry and the military forces billions of dollars and man hours in training men for highly skilled jobs. The instruments developed through the idiographic approach, while not as highly developed as personnel tests, seem to be proving useful in clinical situations. It would be unfortunate if we would have to settle upon one approach to the exclusion of the other. Rather it appears more meaningful to say, at this point in our development of a philosophy of science, that the nomothetic-idiographic dichotomy is not a true one; at least not a true one in the way it is usually expressed.

Let us rather look at the problem in a fashion which the following illustration should make clear. Let us suppose you are experimenting with two different types of mental status interviews. As a standard procedure, at the end of each type of interview, the experimental design requires that you offer to shake hands with the patient. Let us suppose that you have selected two carefully matched groups of fifty patients each, one group of fifty to be given interview Type A and the other group of fifty to be given interview Type B. When your experiment is finished you find that forty out of the fifty patients who received interview Type A grasped your offered hand firmly and, similarly, forty-two of the patients who received interview Type B, also grasped your offered hand firmly. If you made no more than this single observation on each patient you would have to conclude that the slight difference between groups A and B could just as well be explained by chance as by the difference in the type of interview to which they had been subjected.

But now let us suppose you have taken more into account than merely the patient's single act of grasping your offered hand. Let us suppose that you take into account what he does with your hand after he grasps it. Suppose you take into account also what he says, the pitch of his voice, and various other behavioral factors. But let us suppose also that you consider only one patient, first interviewed by method A and second by method B. Let us suppose that after this single patient has been interviewed by method A he shakes your hand warmly and expresses gratitude for your helpfulness in a well-modulated voice and let us suppose that after interview B he again grasps your hand, attempts to put a hammer look on you and swears at you. Now you know something important about this particular patient but you still know little about the probable relative efficacy of interviews A and B on other patients.

Next let us suppose we combine the methods. Let us suppose we observe more than mere hand grasping, as we have done in the latter instance, and let us suppose that we study more than one patient. Suppose that the forty people out of fifty who were interviewed by method A and who accepted your offered hand, shook your hand warmly and thanked you for what you had done and suppose that the forty-two people, out of the fifty in group B who also grasped your hand firmly, all said something unpleasant and attempted physical violence against you. Now we have some meaningful data regarding the efficacy of the interviews. To be sure one must be careful to construe the outcome in the light of sampling considerations, extraneous factors, etc. but the point to be made is that the datum which is lifted from each individual case is more meaningful in the total experimental design if it is itself the outcome, or the generalization, of a series of idiographic observations within the case. In our last illustration the datum lifted from each case was not the firmness of the hand grasp but rather the pattern of aggression or acceptance in the behavior of the patient, this, in turn, having been derived idiographically from a series of observations of which the firmness of handclasp was only one. Briefly stated then, the issue of the nomothetic versus idiographic approach to personality is really the issue of the level of abstraction or generality at which a datum should be lifted from the individual case and thrown into a nomothetic or social framework. An adequate theory of personality should provide within its framework room for this kind of thinking.

At this point we must ask ourselves again, as all of us do so frequently, what is the basis and characteristic nature of science? We are all familiar with the definition of the goal of science as prediction and control. Presumably if, as a result of our scientific endeavors, we can make more precise predictions we can, through those predictions, set the stage for control of the natural world around us, including the world of other people. Let us have a look at how we learn to make precise predictions. The basis of our approaches is always some kind of theoretical frame of reference. Indeed that is what the scientific theory is for—to provide us with a basis for making precise predictions. These predictions that we make are formulated in terms of hypotheses and then subjected to test. Now the outcome of the test may be essentially that which was predicted. If the test or experiment was properly designed one may then conclude, with a certain but always limited amount of confidence that the hypothesis is substantiated.

The substantiation of hypotheses is really not quite as simple as I have tried to make it sound. The catch is, of course, in the design of the experiment. If the experiment is so designed that other obvious hypotheses would have expressed the same prediction the experimenter made, the question arises as to which hypothesis was verified by the experiment. As a matter of fact, in scientific research one never quite finds the ultimate proof of a given hypothesis. About the time he thinks he has such proof within his grasp another scientist comes along with another hypothesis which provides just as plausible an explanation of the experimental results. The usual practice is to design the experiment so that the results, whatever they turn out to be, can best be expressed as the outcome of either of two hypotheses, the *experimental hypothesis* and the *null hypothesis*. The experimental hypothesis is the one derived from one's theoretical position or some other systematic source. The null hypothesis represents one's prediction under random or chance conditions. If the data furnished by the experiment turn out to be a rather unlikely outcome of chance conditions, which is what one usually hopes for, the null hypothesis is discredited, to the main, and one can then turn to the experimental hypothesis as the first and most likely alternative. For example, if the data are such as would be expected less than one time out of a hundred under the regime of chance the experimenter is happy and reports that he has at least found evidence in favor of his experimental hypothesis at the coveted one per cent level of confidence. The relevant point, for the purposes of this discussion, is that even the precise hypotheses which one derives from a good scientific theory are never substantiated with absolute finality no matter how many experiments are performed. As we have seen we are always dependent upon a kind of second-hand proof that the unlikelihood of the null hypothesis provides. We should also point out that the null hypothesis never wholly relinquishes its claim on the data.

Now there are roughly three ways of coming up with a testable hypothesis in scientific investigation: 1) One may deduce it from explicit theory, 2) one may induce it from observation e.g., from clinical experiences, 3) one may eschew logical procedures and go after the hypothesis with a statistical dragnet. Each of these methods circumvents some of the disadvantages of the other two. The hypothetico-deductive method proceeds from a theory which, for the time being, is and must be considered inflexible. Sooner or later, however, the impact of unexpected experimental results must filter back and shake the logical structure of the theory either at the hypothetical level or at the level of the core of the theory itself. In scientific practice the question becomes one of deciding upon the stage in an experiment or in an experimental program at which one must begin to bow to the facts and alter his hypotheses or his theory. That stage, wherever it is, marks the point at which one ceases to be wholly deductive and starts again to be inductive i.e., starts to learn from the facts of nature.

The hypothetico-inductive method yields to facts from the outset. Even the hypotheses are formed as minor generalizations of the observed facts and the explicit theoretical superstructure is allowed to take shape more or less as an afterthought. Again in practice it seems impossible to adhere faithfully to the method all the time. Facts can be seen only through the eyes of observers and thus are subject to whatever selections and distortions the observers' viewpoints impose upon them. Realistically then, the hypotheses formulated are personally construed facts. They may really be thought of as being deduced in a sense from the observers' implicit personal theory as much as being induced from phenomenal facts.

The third method, that of the statistical dragnet, also appears to accept the priority of facts. It differs somewhat from the hypothetico-inductive or clinical method of deriving hypotheses in two principal ways: the logical structure both of hypotheses and theory is minimized; and the facts that are brought into focus are made available by a variety of prior observations made with a variety of biases. Now statistical hypotheses usually are stated in a much less general form and, even though supported by cross-validation procedure, cannot be extended to other situations without making certain precarious assumptions regarding the representativeness of the known samples. The hypotheses are usually no more than single items on a test, for example, which are predicted to be discriminative between two sub-samples separated solely on the basis of some kind of "criterion."

A dragnet picks up whatever is lying around loose. The statistical method of formulating hypotheses does just that. Variables which do not account for a sizeable proportion of the measured variance of the population are not picked up by the method even though they may be extremely significant in bringing about personal readjustments or social changes. In a sense it is correct to say that the hypotheses which are dredged up by the statistical dragnet reflect only the massed bias in the status quo. It is primarily for this reason that hypotheses picked up by this method are usually considered more valuable for descriptive, or administrative purposes than for understanding the mental processes of a patient which may be mobilized to bring about therapeutic change.

From the standpoint of clinical application most of us find more useful the scientific approaches represented by the hypothetico-deductive and the hypothetico-inductive methods of deriving hypotheses. Our discussion this evening, having to do with theory, turns our attention primarily to the former of these, since it is through the adequate development of psychological theory that we are able to employ most usefully the hypothetico-deductive method of setting up scientific hypotheses for experimentation.

Let us consider the function of a theory. A theory may be looked upon as a handy way of binding together a mixture of facts so that one may comprehend them all at once. When the theory enables us to make reasonably precise predictions, one may call it scientific. If its predictions are so elastic that a wide variety of conceivable events can be construed as being corroborative, the theory fails to meet the elementary requirements of science. Let us hasten to add, however, that a theory need not be scientific to be useful. All of us order the daily events of our lives by ... constructions that are usually somewhat less than scientific.... of everyday events, while not Scientifically.... nevertheless....our lives with.... life does not seem wholly capricious we are prepared to take each day's new experience in our stride[3].

But this is not all. If men's theories did no more than provide ornamented armchairs for a passive acquiescence to events, mankind would be no more than a throng of stony-faced spectators witnessing the pageant of creation. Men do play roles in the shaping of events. How they can do this and still themselves be construed as lawful beings is a basic issue in any psychological theory.

The answer lies, first of all, in our recognition of the essentially active nature of our universe. The world is not an abandoned monument, built by God and left to crumble with the ages; it is an event of tremendous proportions, happening today, the conclusion of which is not yet apparent to us. The theories that men employ to construe this massive event are themselves incidents in successive approximations to a larger scheme of things which we are able slowly to unfold. Thus, a theory is a tentative expression of determinism ascribed to subordinate events and at the same time it is superordinate and free of any control these events might place upon it. A theory is bound only by the construction system of which it is a part and at that, the binding is only temporary, lasting only as long as the superordinate system is employed.

But theories are the thinkings of men. To the extent that these thinkings subsume the events of men's lives, there is a possibility of men exercising control over their destinies. Mankind is, therefore, just as free as his valid predictions, but no more so.

Scientific theory must enable one to make such precise predictions that he can subject them to incontrovertible verification. This means that a scientific theory should, through deductive reasoning, yield hypotheses which are brittle enough to be shattered whenever the facts they lead

[3] Editors' note: ellipses indicate missing sections of text in the original.

one to anticipate fail to materialize. The theory itself, of course, need not be quite so fragile as the offspring hypotheses. Rarely does the scientific theory wholly stand or fall with the outcome of a single experiment.

An acceptable scientific theory should meet certain additional requirements. While it need not portray the kind of self-evident truth that a cold fact manifests, it should, in the hands of thoughtful people, yield a succession of hypotheses which actually do turn out to be true. Thus, a good scientific theory must first meet the requirement of furnishing testable hypotheses and second become known both for the accuracy of its hypotheses and its fertility in producing them.

In our introductory remarks we tried to point out the necessity for a modern, scientific psychological theory to take account of some sort of combination of the idiographic and nomothetic approaches to the understanding of human behavior. We are attempting to make clear our conviction that a psychological theory of personality would have to provide both a frame of reference for understanding the succession of behaviors in an individual and a frame of reference for understanding common behaviors in many individuals.

Our list of requirements and specifications for an adequate psychological theory of personality are mounting. Let us add another specification. There is one construct or concept that has particularly caused difficulty when applied to the realm of psychology. That is the construct of energy. As we all know this construct was originally introduced in man's thinking to explain physical change or movement and since its introduction it has indeed been a vital feature in a variety of scientific theories. The construct of energy is really an outgrowth of certain fundamental assumptions that physicists have found it convenient and profitable to make. By assuming that matter is basically comprised of static units, it became immediately necessary for them to account for the obvious fact that what they observed was not always static but frequently quite patently active. What made the units wriggle about? "Why, let's call it energy!" they said.

Now when men attempted to apply scientific theorizing in the realm of psychology, they came up with the notion of *mental* energy to account for the obvious mental processes that were going on. By buying the notion of energy second-hand from the physicists, the psychologists implicitly bought the same basic assumption of static units which had first made energy a necessary construct for the physicists.

Was this purchase necessary? Did it not prove to be an inconvenience in the construction of an adequate scientific psychological theory? These questions and a host of related ones can only be answered by the tentative construction of a theory of psychology which does not employ the energy construct analogue. Having constructed such a theory, we may then set about to put it to use. If it serves us well, we may, tentatively inscribe it as "true;" at least true until a more useful and more comprehensive theory can be formulated.

All carefully constructed scientific theories are based upon explicitly stated postulates. Once the fundamental postulate of a theory is laid down, the variables, dimensions, and constructs with which one must be concerned tend to become pretty well fixed. Now let us try to lay down a postulate which will meet the specifications we have outlined.

Postulate 1. A person's psychological processes evolve toward what he construes to be an optimal anticipation of events.

Before we go on to examine the explicit meanings and the ensuing implications of this rather simple declarative sentence, let us have a brief look at what we mean by a fundamental postulate in a scientific theory. A postulate is, of course, an assumption. But it is an assumption so basic in nature that it antecedes everything which is said in the logical system which it supports. Now, a person may question the truth of a statement which is proposed as a fundamental postulate: indeed we are always free, as scientists, to question the truth of anything. But we should bear in mind, that the moment that we do question the truth of a statement proposed as a postulate, that statement is no longer a postulate in our subsequent discourse. A statement therefore is a postulate only if we accord it that status. If we bring the statement into dispute, as well we may in some instances, we must recognize that we are then arguing from other postulates either explicitly stated or implicitly believed. Thus in scientific reasoning nothing antecedes the postulate, as long as it is a postulate and the truth of the statement is never questioned as long as that statement is in use as a postulate.

What we have really said then is, "Let us suppose, for the sake of the discussion which is to follow, that a person's psychological processes evolve toward what he construes to be an optimal anticipation of events and let us see where the assumption of this postulate leads us." Now let it be clearly understood that we are not proposing this postulate as an *ultimate* statement of truth. In modern scientific circles, it is always customary to accept postulates as tentative or *ad interim* statements of truth.

Let us look at the words we have carefully chosen for this fundamental postulate. In the first place, you heard me use the term "person." This term is used to indicate that the individual person is the primary phenomenon with which the theory is concerned. The theory has to do with individuals as persons having internal private structure and the existence of separate persons is thus implied from the outset. It is believed that a theory has optimal psychological implications if it concerns itself primarily with a person.

Secondly, we have used the term "psychological"—a person's psychological processes. This is a theory in a limited realm which does not necessarily include physiology on the one hand or sociology on the other. Thus, contradictions of theoretical formulations having primarily to do with phenomena in other realms, are to be ignored during this theory's presumably temporary life of usefulness.

Processes. Instead of postulating an inert substance, a step which would inevitably lead to the necessity for establishing as a corollary the existence of some sort of mental energy, the substance of psychology is assumed at the outset to be a process. We shall want to say more about this later.

A person's psychological processes evolve. The word "evolve" is used because it is assumed that the patterns of psychological process undergo progressive change in themselves as they function.

We have used the word "toward." Thus the directionality of psychological processes is built into the fundamental postulate.

A person's psychological processes evolve toward what he construes. Now the phrase "what he construes," indicates that the person himself sets his objectives and he does it by attributing meaning, by framing events with significance.

A person's psychological processes evolve toward what he construes to be an optimal anticipation of events. Here then is what the person is after, an optimal anticipation of events. The direction of mental processes is established to be determined by predictive or anticipatory values. As a matter of fact, this is really an extension of the commonly accepted notion regarding the goal of science, which we discussed a few moments ago. By using the term, "optimal anticipation" it is recognized that some sort of reconciliation of potentially contradictory anticipations must be assumed as taking place in the individual. Not all of the pieces will fit together perfectly. A person's construct system is not necessarily represented by a scheme of tightly knit verbal logic but rather by a system where the emphasis is placed upon optimal logical structure, even at the sub-verbal level. Thus the person will accept a pragmatic determination of truth as long as it does not threaten his poise in anticipating events.

And now we come to the final term—"events." While not essential for the development of this limited theory, it is wholly consistent with our basic assumption regarding the nature of psychological substance to consider events rather than objects to be the stuff out of which a person's environment is made. A notion of events goes well with a notion of prediction. It makes more sense to speak of predicting or anticipating events than to speak of predicting or anticipating objects.

Now we may derive immediately from this fundamental postulate four corollaries which may be very simply stated. The first corollary is that a person's construction system, that is, the system by which he construes, varies as he successively construes experience. We might well call this the learning or experience corollary. Our second corollary, which would appear to follow naturally from our postulate, is that persons must differ in their constructions or their construing of experience. The third corollary follows from the fundamental postulate and from the two preceding corollaries. To the extent that one person employs the same constructions of experience as another he may duplicate the other person's psychological processes. In other words, he may act and think and feel like him. And finally the fourth corollary is that, to the extent that one person's construction system subsumes that of another, he may play a role in a social process involving that other person.

Now we intend, for the purpose of this evening's discussion, to skim over some of the interesting implications of our theoretical venture. One of those implications, which we shall not take the time to discuss, is that we now have a theory which is not dynamic, as that term is usually used. The theory does not involve the concept of energy or the concept of force, those constructs being invented solely out of the necessity for explaining why objects originally postulated as inert were observed really to move. We have avoided the construct of force or energy and with it all anthropomorphic concepts such as ego, id, inner man, etc. by recognizing from the outset in our postulate that the person is a process not an inert object which has to be prodded into action. Movement and process, like the kitchen cabinet, is "built-in" to the basic assumptive structure of the theory.

We shall skip over the implications of the theory for the psychology of learning and for the psychology of individual differences. Moreover, we shall skip over the implications of the theory as expressed in the third corollary, the corollary about people duplicating each other's psychological processes if they employ the same constructions of experience and the implications of that corollary for the study of culture and psychological adjustment in culture groups, and turn our attention to the fourth corollary, which reads "To the extent that one person's construction system subsumes that of another, he may play a role in a social process involving that other person." By this we mean that for people to be able to understand each other it takes more than a similarity or commonality in their thinking. In order for people to get along harmoniously with each other, each must have some understanding of the other. This is different from saying that each must understand things in the same way as the other and this delicate point has profound implications for psychotherapy. To the extent that people understand each other or, stated in the language of our theory, to the extent that their construction systems subsume each other, their activities in relation to each other may be called, "roles," a role being a course of activity which is played out in the light of one's understanding of the behavior of one or more other people.

Let us make sure that we have not slighted the point that there is a difference between two people holding the same construction system and two people understanding each other so that they can play roles in relation to each other. Consider the differences in the characteristic approaches to life of men and women. None of us would claim, I believe, that men and women construe life in the same way and yet nature has provided us with no finer example of role relationships and constructive social interacting than in the sexes. If we look at the testimony of nature, we shall have to admit that it takes a man to understand a woman and a woman to understand a man and there is no greater tragedy than the failure to arrive at these understandings which permit this kind of role inter-relationship.

The ultimate test of a theory, as we attempted to say earlier, is its fertility in supplying testable and verifiable hypotheses. If our attempt at theory-building is to meet this ultimate test, it will have to be fertile in suggesting new approaches to scientific problems, new experiments to be performed, new clinical procedures to be tried. This, of course, is not the time or the place to try to catalog all the hypotheses that one might infer from this theoretical structure. But you would be unhappy, I am sure, and I would feel ineffectual if I failed to provide you with at least one or two illustrations of what kinds of psychological inference might be drawn from this theoretical formulation.

Let us take our example in the field of practical psychotherapy in which I presume all of us are interested. We are all more or less familiar with the psychoanalytic concept of transference. The analysts, at least more of them, believe that transference is basic to deep therapy. As a phenomenon transference means simply that the patient puts on the spectacles with which he has looked at his parents and other important early figures in his life and looks at the therapist through them. In other words, he transfers to the therapist meanings and feelings that should normally be reserved solely for these receding figures of the past and starts to treat the therapist as if he were the effigy of the patient's father or his mother.

Now notice how this concept of transference takes shape as we look at it from the standpoint of the psychology of personal constructs. Now we are less concerned about what historically the patient's father did to him or the patient's mother did to him and we are less concerned about the dammed-up energies that threaten to burst forth and flood his ego and we turn our attention directly to the problem of the construct system by which he has come to see the important figures that have populated his childhood world. We are less concerned with what they really were than we are with how he now sees them. What spectacles is he wearing when he is angry with you? What spectacles is he wearing when he effects coy mannerisms? Indeed we shall be primarily concerned with his stock of spectacles or the repertory of personal constructs by means of which he must perceive the people in his world. If the patient becomes abusive, we shall not understand it as manifest aggression toward us but rather we shall ask ourselves what personal construct is he employing to deal with us now. What is the nature of that construct? Why does he feel it is the most practical alternative at this moment?

The analysts say that transference itself must be analyzed. If we take the point of view of the psychology of personal constructs, we can see this admonition not as another one of the many rules to be followed by analysis but as the obvious and basic approach to the remediation of unfortunate personal constructs.

But a theory can be useful, not only because it enables us to see things in different ways: a theory can actually make a difference in what we do, to what we set about to accomplish in the actual moment-by-moment techniques by which we seek to achieve therapeutic goals. So with this theoretical formulation. And here is an illustration of how it so operates. If we see matters this way in a psychotherapeutic relation, we shall deliberately give the patient opportunities to try on his different sets of spectacles, to exhibit, and thus to submit to his observation and to ours, his repertory of personal constructs. Here is how it works. A patient, at a certain stage in therapy, appears to be ready to express strong feelings of resentment toward his father. If he expresses these feelings of resentment vehemently, he will cast himself in the role of an ungrateful son and suffer sharp and almost unbearable pangs of guilt. If he expresses them toward the therapist he may have some similar feelings, though, as we all know, if the therapeutic relationship has been well handled, the guilt feelings are somewhat more manageable and less disturbing to the patient.

But now let us suppose that the therapist sets up a few minutes of a brief role-playing exchange. The therapist may say, "Let us do a little pretending. Let us suppose that I am a father of a boy something like you used to be and let us suppose that you are a boy something like the kind of a boy you actually were. Now, as the father I would say this, and this and this."

In this kind of indirect relationship, it is frequently possible for the patient to express, behind the protective screen of the artificial role, his basic personal constructs, as they relate to his conception of the role of his father and the role of himself in relation to his father, which are causing him difficulty. It is not usually necessary for such role-playing episodes to last more than a few minutes. Sometimes it is not even necessary that words be spoken though usually the role-playing is more efficient in eliciting the personal role constructs if words are used on both sides. In order to clarify the situation it is frequently advisable to follow up the role-playing with another role-playing episode in which the roles are reversed—again, a very brief one. As one patient recently said, "For the first time in my life, I was able to see things as they really were."And it was possible to mark the initial use of this simple role-playing technique as the point at which therapeutic movement became marked and rapid in this patient.

As the use of role-playing progresses, it is possible to bring the roles closer and closer to real and present life until finally it is possible for the patient to say, "I see now the problem is really the way I *have acted* towards my father and the way I *thought* he was acting towards me; but now as I play out his role I can see that he was not really acting that way. He makes a lot more sense to me now."

The ways in which this simple type of role-playing can be used are innumerable. One technique is to set up a situation in which the therapist plays the part of the parent and the patient is asked to play the part of a therapist to whom the parent has come for consultation regarding his difficulties in understanding and getting along with his child. Indeed wherever it appears to be difficult for the patient to express feeling or an idea, there is the possibility that the use of a simple role-playing situation may permit the therapist to explore with the patient his personal role construct system immediately and explicitly without too great threat to the patient.

We have attempted to cover a great deal of ground in a very short time. I have no idea whether or not I have successfully communicated my thinking. We have attempted to point out some of the specifications for an adequate psychological theory and we have given in part the assumptive structure of such a theory. Finally we have attempted to show how such a theory may have real practical implications as to the way in which we undertake to accomplish the treatment of the patient.

Some three weeks ago, I asked my research team at Ohio State how much of this theoretical position they thought I dare attempt to expound in this manner. There was some difference of opinion but in general it was their judgement that I ought to have a try at explaining some aspect of the theory that we have been working upon. After a sort of summary statement one of the team said, "Well, we hope at best that your listeners will agree with you enthusiastically. As a second best alternative, we hope that they will disagree with you violently. The worst that could happen would be that they would accord you a polite acceptance and forget the next day whether they agreed with you or disagreed with you."

8

Theoretical Behavior[1]

A theory is a way of looking at things. A person's way of looking at things may be a function of what it is he has sought to examine. If a person has spent most of his life looking under beds for lost shoes, he may develop a peculiarly inverted way of looking at the world in general. What I have to say has been greatly influenced by what I have been looking at during the last twenty years. I have been asked to talk about theory. You are entitled to know what I was looking at when I developed my peculiar theoretical position.

A good share of my professional life has been spent sitting across the desk from psycho-neurotic patients and graduate students. Sometimes the graduate students were the psychoneurotic patients. It was inevitable that sooner or later it would occur to me that dealing with one was very much like dealing with the other.

Patients are frequently anxious, so are graduate students. Patients are frequently anxious about things that won't ever hurt them, so are graduate students. Patients often fail to recognize the real threats in their lives, so do graduate students. Patients frequently do not want to experiment with the reality of life, similarly, graduate students postpone their research. Patients frequently fail to recognize when they have done something exceptionally well, so do graduate students. Ah-ha, patients and graduate students are indeed much alike!

Not only is it possible to see that patients and graduate students have many of the same presenting symptoms, but more and more it is possible for one to see that conducting psychotherapy is very much like directing research. For example, a graduate student comes to you with a rather vague notion that research must be a good thing, since everybody talks about it, and that now he is growing up to be a big graduate student it is about time that he undertook the adult responsibility of doing a thesis. He has a great feeling of apprehension regarding the actual job. He feels guilty that he hasn't started sooner and he seems to have the implicit notion that you are going to cut off his ears and throw them in the wastebasket if he does either of two things: (a) if he admits that he doesn't perceive research as the epitome of all virtues; and (b) if he dares question any of your biases. It is within this context of feeling that he timidly asks for an appointment to talk over research. The patient also may approach you in a manner which is not unlike this. He, too, has a vague feeling that you are going to scold him for not being more mature. He has the feeling that you are going to order him to go out and do things which he doesn't want to do. He may feel, furthermore, like the graduate student, that he does not dare express his real doubts about certain issues with respect to which he feels he has no right to be skeptic.

With the graduate student, usually one of our first tasks is to get him to express his ideas in terms of hypotheses. Ordinarily he doesn't mind this so much at first. Later on he is likely to feel that you have played a dirty trick on him. He may be quite angry at you for putting him on the spot by getting him to make a statement which he firmly believes to be true but which his research proves to be false. It was not his intention when he came to you to crawl out on a limb, much less, to crawl out on a limb which he himself is expected to saw off.

The patient is likely to feel very much the same way. If you ask him to express himself explicitly and vigorously he may become angry at you because he feels that you have let him commit himself to statements which can perhaps be proved true or false. It may not have been his idea when he came to you that he would allow himself to express anything which later could be subjected to validating experience.

Some graduate students come to us with the idea that they want to prove something. Personally. I have no particular objection to a graduate student who starts out in that way. The job of the research adviser at this point is to help the graduate student to make some statement of what it is he wants to prove. By the time one has finished this job he probably will have the initial outline of the student's theoretical system. It usually does not take long to find out that what the student wished to prove involves much more than a validation of some new projective technique or the vindication of some particular group of misunderstood souls. Usually it turns out that the student has privately put much more at stake in his projected research than was necessary. The task is to get him to limit his hypotheses and help him to see that no matter which way the data turns out he can construct his experimental design in such a way

[1] Presented at Purdue University, Lafayette, Indiana, USA, May 20, 1952. Published by permission of Jacqueline Aldridge.

Collected Papers of the Pioneer of Constructivist Psychology: George A. Kelly, First Edition. Edited by David A. Winter and Nick Reed.

as to make progress in his thinking. Thus we seek to substitute the attitude of "finding" for the attitude of "proving" in the research activities of the graduate student.

In dealing with the patient we go through a very similar procedure. The patient makes certain dogmatic statements. He enlists the therapist's support in proving to his parents or to his spouse or to the world in general that he is right. He may even propose taking certain violent actions in order to show the world how right he is. Again the task of the adviser, in this case a psychotherapist, is to encourage the patient to elaborate and find out what it is he is seeking to prove. As in the case of the graduate student, it may very well develop that the patient is seeking to prove too much all at once. Again the therapist can help the patient formulate his persuasions in terms of hypotheses which can stand or fall without necessarily bringing the whole structure of the patient's personality system down on his head. Again the idea of substituting "finding" for "proving" is a basic step in dealing with the client's problem.

Let us turn back to the graduate student for a moment. How many times we have heard the wail, "But, Professor, what will my committee do to me if I get negative results?" A student will delay his research month after month and sometimes even for years because he does not want to get negative results. He looks for the "dream problem," the one in which all his hypotheses are certain to be verified at the one tenth of one percent level. Sooner or later he finds himself disillusioned with the realization that when positive results are certain there is no point in collecting evidence and that anything which needs to be investigated is likely to show unexpected outcomes.

So it is with the patient. We may say that he is escaping. We may say that he is not testing reality. Perhaps he spends his early adolescence daydreaming about the kind of person he will be when he grows up but never takes any steps toward growing. Perhaps he stays in school year after year hoping to become something but never takes any steps to find out whether or not he can become what he hopes to be. He too postpones his dissertation. He too wonders what they will do to him if he gets negative results.

Just as the graduate student is reluctant to act upon the basis of his convictions, so the patient is often reluctant to act upon the basis of his convictions. Just as the graduate student hopes, if he does act upon the basis of his convictions, to be sure that the outcome will prove him right; so the patient, when he seeks to act upon the basis of his convictions, is eager not to come up against unexpected outcomes.

All of us have had experience with a graduate student who shows perseveration of the undergraduate attitude toward authority. He wants the right answer. He does not want to experiment with the wrong answer in mind. For him, critical thinking is hostile thinking. He fears to engage in it lest he be subjected to retaliation.

How often in dealing with a patient have we run against the same thing? He wants the right answers. He wants the therapist to tell him what to do. He does not want to be critical of his parents because for him criticism means hostility. Sometimes the only way in which he can allow himself to think critically about the pattern of behavior exemplified for him in his home is to go through a stage of hostile reactions toward his parents.

But perhaps I have labored this point too long. Human beings are human beings whether they talk about scientific hunches or personal feelings. Suppose we put all of this together and came up with a fundamental question. Is the scientist, as exemplified by a graduate student, a separate species of animal? Is the thinking of the scientist necessarily so different in form from the thinking of everyone else? When the scientist gets mixed up in a problem, is it so different from the situation that obtains when a patient gets mixed up in dealing with a problem? We say, for example, that the scientist tends to deduce his hypotheses from some core of theoretical or partial theoretical formulation. Is he alone in this tendency? May we not consider that this is the way that all people lay wagers on life? Up to a certain degree all people proceed to structure their experience, to make progress to mature by means of formulating hypotheses which are subject to subsequent and immediate validating evidence.

The scientist proceeds from theory. He also induces the theory. If you wish to understand the scientist's position or to attempt to correct his point of view you need to know what his theory is. Is this any less true of a person who does not happen to be called a scientist? Is it not also necessary that we know what his theory is?

We say that the goal of the scientist is prediction. If a scientist can do a good job of prediction he is happy. Isn't this what makes other people happy too? Is the scientist really paid off in another kind of coin? Or do not scientists and non-scientists fundamentally aspire to the same goals?

What happens if we develop a theory of personality with science itself as the model? For the past three years some of us have been pursuing this line of thought to see where it would lead us. The further we go the more intriguing the whole idea becomes. What actually happens when you start looking at other persons as if they too had a point of view, as if they too were fellow scientists engaged in pursuing a line of research and investigation, experimenting with hypotheses, some of them well formed, some poorly formed, some crucial experiments long overdue, and some outcomes subject to alternative interpretations. We can concern ourselves with the individual theories that all men have and not merely with the individual affairs that certain men, called scientists, have. Here we have a personality theory which is itself a theory of personal theories. Under this scheme of thinking, a personality theory has to do with the personal systems of individuals in a manner which is analogous to the way in which a philosophy of science has to do with the various theoretical systems of scientists. Indeed, our conceptualization of a theory of personality is much like the general current conceptualization of a philosophy of science. A theory of personality is a subsuming system within which the various sub-systems of individuals can be seen to make sense, can be seen to have elements in common, and can be seen to be modifiable.

Perhaps this is the point at which we should give our approach a name. We have been calling this approach the Psychology of Personal Constructs. It is a theory about theories. It is a psychology which has something to say about psychologies. It is a psychological philosophy of science, with science so liberally defined that any person's construction system can tentatively be accepted as scientific.

A theory is something which does not exist wholly independently of people. Actually a theory is a way of construing the behavior of people. This is just as true of a theory in physics as it is true of a theory in psychology. A theory in physics provides us with a way of understanding why the physicist does what he does. A theory in the field of social science provides us with a way of understanding why the social scientist makes the kind of inquiries he does—why he totes up his columns of observations in the way he does. Thus we say, any theory is a way of construing the behavior of people.

Another way of saying the same thing is to say that a theory is a way of behaving. If I adhere to the quantum theory in physics it means simply that my behavior is structured with respect to that theory. Again, a theory is a way of behaving and this whole paper has to do with theoretical behavior, as its title implies. Theoretical behavior is a kind of behavior. People behave theoretically. I am trying to behave theoretically this evening. The kind of noises I am making are theoretical noises and what I have been saying is that it might be exciting to look at all behavior as basically theoretical behavior, that is, behavior that emerges from a way of looking at things. We said at the outset a theory is a way of looking at things. We are saying now also a theory is a way of behaving. These two statements actually are not much different from each other.

Theories do make a difference. It is granted that many different people do the same things under the aegis of supposedly different theoretical positions. If we look at patients we find that two different patients may engage in what appears to be the same behavior under the aegis of two different types of insights. Furthermore, two patients apparently voicing the same insights do frequently appear to behave differently. Does this necessarily mean that their insights are not relevant to their ways of behaving or does it mean merely that while their verbalizations are identical, private meanings of their words are such that they actually are expressing two different kinds of insight systems. For the time being at least I am inclined to accept the latter interpretation.

We do know that when patients start behaving differently this difference is usually accompanied by a different kind of talk, by a different kind of verbalized insight. We know that patients when they start behaving differently, start explaining things on a different kind of ground. Thus the change in their verbal explanations is likely a cue to the fact that their basic outlook and their behavioral pattern has been undergoing some change. Now we have to be careful not to reverse our logic and assume that because a person's verbalizations can be made to change that his behavior will necessarily follow suit. It is relatively easy to get a patient to use new words to express old ideas. We do it in the classroom all the time. In the classroom we are inclined to call this effect a pseudo-sophistication. The kind of verbal concomitant that I am talking about now is the one which is a reflection of basic constructive change in the individual rather than a determinant of constructive change. A change in outlook therefore, does not necessarily follow upon a change of words, but a change of words is quite likely to follow from a real change in outlook. When we talk about outlook we are talking about basic personal theory or one's personal construction system. If we wish to infer one's personal construction system from the words he uses we must make sure that he is not merely trying to talk back to us in our own language but that the words he uses are natural and spontaneous reflections of his personal outlook.

A theory is a way of behaving and theories do make a difference. Only last week a student of mine in a class had an interesting (Ah-ha!) experience. He was a person who had shown some indication of being basically disturbed. He had expressed feelings of insecurity and of lack of confidence in himself. During the course of a discussion I had occasion to challenge the stimulus-response theoretical position held by so many of our colleagues. Apparently it suddenly occurred to him that throughout his life he had been looking upon himself as if he had been victimized by his stimuli. He had been looking at himself as though he were a bundle of human responses being tossed about in a sea of external circumstantial stimuli. The idea that he himself could be a stimulus to himself had not occurred to him. He had seen himself as the product of his past as the inevitable outcome of things which had already happened to him and which could not now be undone. The very thought that he could reconstrue life and that the reconstruction possibilities were infinite seemed suddenly to open to him a whole new outlook. While this was a classroom experience, it is paralleled by a number of similar experiences I have had in psychotherapy and it does suggest dramatically that people can paint themselves into a corner by their theoretical behavior.

Now I do not wish to become involved deeply with the criticism of stimulus-response psychology. Undoubtedly, this student's interpretation of stimulus-response psychology as it applied to himself is not the only kind of interpretation which could be made. My point for the moment is simply that one's theoretical position, and I should say personal theoretical position, is a potent determiner of what he is able to see as available pathways to adjustment.

Let us take another kind of illustration. Consider for example the person who has a basically psychoanalytic point of view. Let us suppose that psychoanalysis is more than just a series of words grafted on to his former prejudices and that the theoretical position expressed by Freud and his followers has in a large measure been incorporated into the thinking of the person. Does it make a difference in the way he behaves? I think it does. I am not too certain about this but I believe I can now detect a large proportion of those persons who have had deep psychoanalysis on the basis of their behavior and conversation in a simple social situation. Many of my colleagues feel similarly. What is it that we observe? For one thing the psychoanalyzed person, when he talks to you, frequently seems less willing to deal with your ideas than with your motives. With respect to your motives he seems to take the view that either your ideas are enlightened or unenlightened and that there is not very much that he can do about them except reject or accept them. With respect to your motives, he seems to have a greater tendency than most people to deal with what you say from the standpoint of your personal needs. As a result the psychoanalyzed person seems frequently to treat you as if you were an irrational being.

Another characteristic which some of us feel characterizes the deeply analyzed person is the reduction in spontaneity. Some of my colleagues say that psychoanalysis has made dull sophists out of a lot of once interesting personalities. Some refer to it as a kind of "burned out affect." Others refer to it as a reduction in spontaneity with the person behaving as if he were controlling those deep feelings of hostility which, through analysis, he has discovered underlying his own motivation.

Now this is not necessarily bad. A lot of interesting personalities could afford to be a little less interesting in order to make life a little more pleasant to themselves and other people. Moreover, a lot of people are better off to do a little sitting on their own hostilities. They may as a result accomplish more and, indeed, permit other people to accomplish more. Our sole point at this juncture is that a thorough-going psychoanalytic point of view is itself a kind of theoretical behavior which generalizes to the office and to the dinner table. I am suggesting that if you wish to understand personalities of certain psychoanalyzed people, you need to understand their psychoanalytic theoretical behavior. Psychoanalytic theoretical behavior thus, in some instances, becomes the content with which an overall personality theory must deal if it is to understand the behavior of certain people. Psychoanalysts are a kind of people. Stimulus-response devotees are a kind of people. In the latter case one certainly does not have to have a psychology major in order to be governed by the stimulus-response outlook on life.

It should be possible to point out how other general theoretical positions can affect one's outlook and day by day behavior. For example, the notion of energy as a causal and explanatory agent is widely accepted in our culture by people at various levels of sophistication. Most of our current theories of personality are based more or less on an energy postulate. We do know of course that the assumption of energy is not absolutely necessary in the formulation of a theory, either a theory of personality or a theory of physical action. The physicists have found it convenient to accept the energy postulate, though I understand that some theoretical physicists have been toying with the idea of a non-energetic system. Psychology has been ambivalent about the notion of energy. Some psychologists say that we can accept the notion of energy to explain physiological phenomena but that we should avoid the use of the energy postulate when talking about mental phenomena. This, of course, raises the question as to what is a physical phenomenon versus what is a mental phenomenon. After all, our universe is made up of unlabeled phenomena. We put the tags on them. Sometimes we put different tags on the same phenomenon, that is, we take a given phenomenon and construe it psychologically on the one hand and physiologically on the other. The system within which we construe the phenomenon is a matter of convenience. Therefore, when we say that we may use energy when dealing with physiological or physical phenomena but that we may not use it when dealing with psychological phenomena, we have no real basis for concluding that a given phenomenon is itself either physiological or psychological. Our statement then reduces itself simply to the idea that energy is a construct that physiologists and physicists use when dealing with the world of events but it is a notion which does not fit in well with the rest of the psychologist's language.

There are some psychologists who say that the construct of energy should be used throughout all of our scientific systems. There are other psychologists who maintain that the notion should not be used in any system. Whether or not we use the construct of energy in an attempt to construe our world in an orderly fashion, is largely a matter of convenience. Does it enable us to make predictions of the kind that are worth making? It seems that it might be worthwhile to try constructing a psychological system which does not have to invoke the energy construct and see what it will do for us.

Now if we are to avoid use of the energy construct we shall have to be careful to avoid the use of any equivalent construct and we must remember that there are in psychology a great many of equivalent constructs. Our early notions of stimulus carried with them an implication of energy. A stimulus somehow caused a response. Stimulus injected something into the organism which made it react. We have tried very hard to get rid of this interpretation of the stimulus and as far as I can see we have been only partially successful. Instead of speaking of stimulus energy now we speak of stimulus value, but we go on treating the stimulus value as if it were an energetic thing. Instead of speaking of demons or humors we use such terms as motives, but these in turn we treat as if they were energies. In a further attempt to get away from energy thinking we sometimes talk of incentives. Or if we wish to place more emphasis upon the organism itself, we say needs. But all of these notions are treated by psychologists as if they were energies in themselves. The fact that they were learned (whatever that means) somehow is supposed to make them a little more acceptable.

Once one has grown up with the notion of energy, it is very difficult to get away from it. I find myself no exception. I also find my patients more or less dependent upon energy thinking. Furthermore, I find I must take into account their point of view in dealing with them therapeutically. Ordinarily rather than to attempt to change their attitudes toward energy or towards psychoanalysis, or towards stimulus-response thinking, or whatever type of deep conviction they have, it seems much more profitable to try to help them work out their adjustment within the system which they have. Thus in approaching a patient, I use a system about systems. My attempt is to use a theory which is sufficiently catholic to subsume their various systems, even though their systems are ones which I myself would not choose to espouse. All of this follows from taking the position that a theory is a way of behaving and that patients' behavior may be considered in a sense theoretical behavior. It follows from the recognition of the similarity between directing the research of graduate students and directing the personal explorations of patients. This is what we find ourselves doing if we consider that a patient can be looked at in much the same way that we look at a fellow scientist who adheres to a point of view somewhat different from our own but who is nevertheless a sincere though baffled seeker after truth.

Let us pursue the implications of this kind of thinking further. The scientist is interested in prediction. In general we think we can explain scientific behavior by saying that it is behavior bent on prediction. We design our experiments around the notion of prediction. Sampling theory, which is, by the way, not the only logical means by which we can make inferences, is basically an approach to prediction. What characterizes scientific behavior? Prediction. What makes a scientist tick? Why prediction, of course. What makes the scientist's life worth living? Why nothing less than the opportunity to improve his prediction system. What motivates the scientist? Nothing less than the anticipation of bigger and better anticipations.

Now we are ready to make our leap into the formulation of a fundamental postulate which is to underly personality theory covering all persons, not merely so-called scientists. Instead of saying that anticipation is the one motive that underlies the behavior of all scientists, we shall try broadening our postulate and say that anticipation is the one motive that underlies the behavior of all persons. This is a venturesome postulate. The only way we can find out where it will eventually lead us is to give it a whirl and see what happens.

Now if a person's behavior is construed as a way of seeking a kind of dynamic homeostasis in which he is seeking to behave in the most predictable fashion among the most predictable environmental elements we soon find ourselves arriving at a kind of rat race theory of motivation. We can't let that happen. A venture which ends up the first night in a rat race is not a very exciting venture. We can take comfort from the fact that scientists do not end up in rat races, at least none of them has just yet.

Let us state our fundamental postulate quite carefully. Here is the form which we have worked out by successive approximations. We have been able to keep it in this form for about a year and a half now and it may be something that we can live with. *A person's psychological processes evolve toward what he construes to be an optimal anticipation of events.* Here we place the emphasis upon *evolve*. That is the principal verb in our sentence. The phraseology implies, we hope, that one's anticipatory system unfolds by successive approximations. Our statement also places the emphasis upon the way the person construes his anticipations of events. We do not say that a person's psychological processes evolve toward an optimal anticipation of events. We have said only that they evolve toward what he *construes* to be an optimal anticipation of events. At this point we have placed the emphasis on the person's own construing. We lay the ground work for a psychology of personal constructs or a theory of theoretical behavior. We are, however, still treating the person as if he were a scientist seeking to predict, as all good scientists do.

What happens to mental energy and to motivation under this system if one follows this postulate? In the first place the noun in our sentence which is used as the subject is the word, "processes." A person's psychological processes evolve. In other words we start out with a process rather than an inanimate thing or a static state of affairs. The show is on the road at the time we first join it. We, therefore, do not need any special agent to explain why a static object is prodded into action. Our object is not static in the first place, it is originally moving. We are dealing with processes. As far as getting action is concerned we do not need the notion of motives, incentives, libido, or *elan vital*. Parenthetically I might remark at this point, since I have used the expression *elan vital*, that while Henri Bergson was the great exponent of duration or process he nevertheless insisted upon retaining a notion of energy, a conservation which it seems to me was made unnecessary when he reformulated Descartes' "I am a thing which thinks" to "I am a thing which endures." Be that as it may, our basic postulate starts us out with a world which is alive and kicking and not one which must be pushed around by external energies.

Moreover we have in our basic postulate the notion of directionality. We got it from the oft-repeated statement regarding the goal of science. These processes which we take as givens also have their directionality given. Thus our fundamental postulate gives us both process and direction of process. Since the direction of process is given us we do not need such terms as needs or goals. "A person's psychological processes evolve toward what he construes to be an optimal anticipation of events." This is our basic postulate, this is what we will start with. One always has to start somewhere. The postulate, of course, can be questioned and it can be rejected. If it is questioned it must be questioned on some grounds. Those grounds then must be accepted as themselves postulates which are even more basic than the one stated. All one can do in a discussion of this sort is to propose a postulate. It is like saying, now let us suppose, for the sake of argument, for the sake of experimentation, or for the sheer fun of it, that the following is true. "A person's psychological processes evolve toward what he construes to be an optimal anticipation of events." You don't have to buy it. This postulate simply states the ground for a discussion and a development.

Since we are dealing with processes, the person, in order to see similarity to the events of life, has to chop up the continuity in terms of cycles. In this sense then, things are essentially repetitive cycles. A day is a convenient cycle for us to construe: at least at intermediate latitudes. Near the north pole it is not quite so easy to construe a day, particularly if you are traveling without a compass and have no familiar land marks against which to gauge the passage of the sun. One of the reasons that we divide things up into cycles is that it permits us to make predictions. When the sun comes up in the morning we have an I.P. for predicting where the sun will be at 10 o'clock and when it will go down beyond the horizon. If we had no such construct as the construct of day it would be difficult for us to make these kinds of predictions. Constructs we formulate in order to see the cycles of life are really ways in which we can make predictions. A cycle is a scheme toward making temporal predictions.

Now all of us find that our experience will make much more sense if we put it into cycles or phrases of this sort. We might say that the phrasing of experience is a way a man gives his experience meaning, life, and vitality. We could use the analogy of music, some people play simply a succession of notes and it sounds like the dickens. Others, by their skill in phrasing, are able to make the same sequence of notes interesting, meaningful, and moving. The patterns by which we phrase experience are held in place by constructs. When we perform a learning experiment, the experimenter is likely to think of the experience being phrased in terms of trials, each of which has a beginning and an ending according to the experimenter's particular preconceived plan. The subject, however, may phrase things quite differently, as indeed our experience with partial reinforcement might lead us to believe. He sees other kinds of cycles, two-trial cycles, three-trial cycles, whole-experiment cycles. As he phrases his experience in terms of large and small cycles he is able to construe it; in other words to set it up so that it becomes predictable within larger and smaller frames of reference. The way a subject does this personally gives us some clue as to how long he will perseverate in a pattern of behavior, when he will find it necessary to revise it in the light of expectations which fail to materialize, and possibly how he will anticipate the future. A personal construct then is a personal way of phrasing experience. A psychologist, if he wishes to understand the subjective experience of the patient or the student, will need to develop some idea of how the individual is making his personal construction. Thus we say we have a psychology of personal constructs.

Lest our use of the term personal constructs may mislead some into believing that we have here a phenomenological theory of personality let me hasten to point out that this is not a classical phenomenological theory. While we are dealing with individualities we are dealing with them within a public frame of reference. We are suggesting that the psychologist have a theory of theoretical behavior and that he have grounds for subsuming the great variety of theoretical positions and view points which different individuals hold. This then is not what we are accustomed to call the phenomenological or even the neo-phenomenological position.

We have emphasized the process nature of this psychological universe. We have invoked the model of scientific prediction to explain human motivation. We have pointed out that man is able to catch meanings within the ceaseless flow of time by attuning his ear to repetitive themes and by the phrasing of experience. He captures the cycles by means of constructs. In the lecture which is a companion to this we have attempted to discuss the constructs in greater detail. He avoids monotony by seeing little cycles as fitting into greater cycles, by seeing the little roles that he plays in day-by-day situations fitting into a life role, and finally, by seeing his own life role fitting into an even larger pattern or scheme of things. These constructs are essentially prediction-consummation cycles. Now let us have a look at how man learns from experience.

We have started from the postulate that a person's psychological processes evolve toward what he construes to be an optimal anticipation of events. Our system would be incomplete if we provided no check point at which one's anticipation would be validated against events, at least against the events as he construes them. The validation of predictions is an essential feature of this theoretical position. When we predict that the sun will go down at the end of a day, an important question is, does it go down or does it do something that we cannot construe as going down. When you predict that the patient will have a dream involving the transference relationship with his therapist between now and the next session, the validation end of our prediction cycle comes upon us in our next session. Does the patient have such dreams or does he not? What we perceive as validation is also, at another level, a matter of construction. Let us suppose the patient says that he has a dream about a man seven feet tall who is trying to lash him with a black snake whip. The therapist, not being seven feet tall may say, "Oh, shucks, I missed my prediction." Another therapist would say, "Oh, lo, that dream is a perfect example of a patient's fear of masculine punishment from the therapist." Alternatively the patient may say, "I just can't remember having dreamt a thing. I am sure I didn't dream a thing. Why should I dream? Why should I dream every time? I just slept every night as sound as a rock. I just didn't dream about anybody." Now our first therapist might say, "I fear I missed my prediction." The second therapist might call attention to the patient's defensiveness and to his implication that his dream, if he had had one, would have been about a certain person. He might say, therefore, "Yes, my patient obviously dreamt about the therapist but he is so threatened that he cannot even remember his dream."

How many of us have had the experience in dealing with a patient by encouraging him to make certain experimental ventures and then finding that the results were not accepted as satisfactory by the patient. Yet those results night ordinarily lead us to believe that he had had a heart-warming and reinforcing experience. Yet the patient seems frustrated over the results of his experience almost as if he were annoyed at having gotten along so well. This is a common experience in dealing with hypochondriac patients. For example, you may have a patient who does a great deal of complaining about being sick and says what a wonderful thing it would be to be well. He is sure that he has a cancer. You send him to a physician or, more likely still, to a string of physicians. He gets the final report that there is not a sign of cancer. Is he happy? No. He is angry at you. The experience has been frustrating. He now finds himself forced to build painfully and elaborately another semi-plausible complaint. What has happened is that the patient has lost a bet. His construction of life has not been validated and he is anxious. Something inside of him went out when the results of his predictions became known. From the standpoint of the psychology of personal constructs it then becomes more important to know what his prediction cycles are, what hypotheses he is experimenting with, and how comprehensively those hypotheses have been formulated, if we wish to know what will be the outcome of confronting him with validating experience.

We have sketched only in barest outline form a theoretical position. We have tried to build it upon the model of science. We have given only a few illustrations, but perhaps we have been able to say enough to arouse your curiosity and perhaps, in some cases, to encourage your participation actively or vicariously in this venture. There is much yet to be learned. We recognize that a theoretical position is a matter of convenience and not orthodox doctrine. You are, of course, all welcome to discard these ideas as unpromising, to utilize them, to revise them, or even to construe them in some novel way.

9

Alternatives[1]

One of the characteristics of scientific method is its reliance upon precise logical form. This is true whether scientific method is applied in the laboratory or in the psychotherapeutic conference room. Many of the more precise logical forms which we use have been collected under the rubric of "mathematics". When we describe our observations in terms to which mathematics is applicable we say that we have "quantified" our data. It is frequently said that the quantification of one's observations is an essential first step in treating them scientifically.

Now, as any good clinician knows, there have been many sins committed in the name of quantification. We have seen many of our fellow psychologists, in their zeal for finding the final and mathematical answers to all of life's problems, make an appalling number of human sacrifices to the god of objectivity. A fervent but fundamentalistic belief in the doctrine of science has led all too frequently to the interpretation of objectivity as nothing more than literalism. Literalism has come all too frequently to be substituted for objectivity. Thus intelligence was "objectively" defined as the arithmetic quotient one got by dividing mental age by chronological age or a "trial" in a learning experiment was a phrase[2] of experience as literally interpreted by the experimenter rather than an anticipation-consummation cycle as construed by the subject. We might say that in the hands of many psychologists, bent upon objectivity at any price, quantification has been reduced to a sort of civil service status. Scores are added up, allowances made for longevity, and veterans' preference, efficiency ratings taken into account, and, lo, one comes out with an "objective" measurement of the person's qualifications. This is quantification at its worst.

There is no need to argue at length against a Civil Service kind of misapplication of the scientific method. But is the alternative an impressionistic approach? Is it possible for a clinician to be both sensitive and objective? This is an important question and the way psychologists generally answer it will, have a great deal to do with the development of psychology during the next fifty years.

It is a common misconception that quantified values are necessarily values which can be placed along a scale or continuum. Thus for many students the idea of quantification is synonymous with the idea of gradations. They come to believe that to deal with the world quantitatively is to give up dealing with it in terms of black and white contrasts. Quantification seems to mean the employment of scalar values rather than dichotomous ones. Perhaps the fact that we have grown up with a decimal number system rather than a binary number system makes it easy for us to come to this conclusion.

But it is possible to reduce all scales to values which represent the products of dichotomies. A decimal number system can be reduced to a binary number system. For example, the numbers 0, 1, 2, 3, 4, 5, 6, 7, 8, 9, 10, 11, 12 can be reduced to the numbers within a binary system of 0, 1, 10, 11, 100, 101, 110, 111, 1000, 1001 etc. Here we have a scale which is based upon dichotomous alternatives combined by multiplication just as we combine our decimal system by multiplication when we go from digits to tens, and from tens to hundreds. The recent developments with electronic computers have dramatically called our attention to the fact that all quantities can be expressed in terms of the multiplication of dichotomous alternatives. Perhaps our world of values can also be reduced to terms of black and white. Indeed we have arising in psychology today the so called information theories which are based upon cybernetic analogs and which lend themselves to the treatment of complex ideas as well as to neuronic discharges.

Some of you may be disturbed at our saying that perhaps the world may best be construed in terms of blacks and whites. It may seem like saying that the world is made up of two kinds of people—good and bad people, and all of us who are clinicians realize what problems arise among patients who feel that they must discriminate between people primarily on these grounds. Those of us who are parents have also faced the problem when taking our children to see the movies. If the movie is a western and the child has learned to distinguish between the "good" men and the "bad" men, without being long held in suspense, everything goes along fairly smoothly. But how many of us remember the occasions when we have taken our children to see a more complicated play and have listened to a querulous voice all the way home saying. "But, Daddy, was he a good man or a bad man?"

[1] Unpublished address, Purdue University, 1952. Published by permission of Jacqueline Aldridge.

[2] Editors' note: [sic]

Collected Papers of the Pioneer of Constructivist Psychology: George A. Kelly, First Edition. Edited by David A. Winter and Nick Reed.

Lest we be too patronizing of the child's difficulty in structuring his social world, let us remember our experiences in counseling a university student who is having difficulty recovering from a love affair which has gone on the rocks. Have we not heard such complaints as this, "But, Doctor, how could she be a good woman and do the things she has done to me?" The university student when first coming face to face with the complexities of women is obviously no less handicapped than the child when he can deal with the women in his life only in terms of good and bad.

Now when we say that the world can be reduced for purposes of science to dichotomies we are not saying that the world must be approached with the naïveté of a child. The child's difficulty is that he is unable to multiply his dichotomies. That is to say he is dealing with the world in terms of a one-place, binary number system comprised solely of 0 and 1. He cannot yet count his world in terms of 10's and 11's, 100's and 101's, etc. He is trying to make the dichotomy of good and bad cover all of the important characteristics of the people with whom he comes in contact. He has yet to learn that some things that people do are good and some things that the same people do are bad, and when you take into account all of the kinds of things that people do, you come up with a complicated quantification of their behavior.

Now there are two ways of dealing with the evaluation of complicated behavior. We can say, on the one hand, that a given person is somewhat good and somewhat bad; in other words, make a so-so evaluation. This is like saying that a given parson is about average or that he is mediocre. This is also a way of avoiding the issue of goodness and badness or a way of saying that the dichotomy is inapplicable to a given situation. It is a way of casting the world in terms of grays rather than blacks and whites. The other approach is to say that while, as a whole, we cannot evaluate the person as either black or white, there must be elements in the situation which can be evaluated as black or white—good or bad. The first is actually a way of avoiding the making of a precise evaluation or prediction. It is a way of ignoring the alternatives. The second way is a way of accepting certain specified alternatives—a way of making precise predictions or evaluations, a way of quantifying the data within a binary system. Now which of these approaches is more meaningful, which is more scientific?

When we perform a scientific experiment it is considered appropriate that we establish an experimental hypothesis and that our experiment be designed so that our hypothesis be considered as supported only if an alternative hypothesis can be shown to be an unlikely explanation for our data. Ordinarily the alternative hypothesis is a "null" hypothesis. Actually, we have to do more than this. We have to design our experiment in such a way that our experimental hypothesis represents the most plausible explanation *if* the null hypothesis is discredited. Now frequently it does occur that we can reject the null hypothesis at the one percent level of confidence, and this happy event is usually considered grounds for celebrations. Yet it may very well be that even when the null hypothesis is rejected at the one percent level of confidence we cannot safely conclude that the experimental hypothesis is the only alternative. Actually, we have to set up our experiment with a sort of vague hope that our critics will be inclined to agree that the experimental hypothesis is the most reasonable alternative to the null hypothesis. Thus in scientific research we always attempt to set up our experiment in terms of a competition between two hypotheses. One, an experimental hypothesis which represents cosmos, and the other, a null hypothesis which represents chaos. Only as we are able to design experiments around this kind of dichotomy do we feel that we are making scientific progress.

Now up to this point we have approached our proposition from two angles. One, we have said that in order to quantify our scientific observations and make them amenable to the precise logical forms of mathematics, we must reduce them to discrete alternatives. Furthermore, we have suggested that it is possible to set up the alternatives in terms of pairs or dichotomies and that we may use a binary number system in dealing with them mathematically. Second, we have invited attention to the fact that scientific progress has been more satisfactory when experiments are designed around alternative hypotheses, one alternative being the experimental hypothesis and the other being the null hypothesis.

Next let us approach our proposition from still another angle. It is commonly said that the goal of science is prediction and control. Indeed it might be possible to make this expression even more succinct if we said simply that the goal of science is prediction, since control may be conceived as only a special form of prediction. Be that as it may it is prediction that we emphasize in modern scientific method. Of course, in making predictions of events, it is not necessary that the prediction be made before the event itself occurs. It is only necessary that we make a prediction before we have other knowledge of the event which we are seeking to predict. Thus it is possible to have a science of archeology with the archeologist predicting what he will turn up next, even though the events with which he is dealing happened thousands of years ago. It is possible also for the astronomer to make predictions of astronomical phenomena which happened millions of years ago but which, because millions of light years of space separate him from them, are only just now becoming observable.

In order for a prediction to make any sense, it needs to be cast in the form of definite alternatives. It doesn't make much sense to predict that tomorrow will be a wonderful day unless tomorrow, when it arrives, would be manifestly wonderful or not wonderful. It is like making a wager on a football game. It is not very meaningful to say "I bet $5 that the Purdue team will play a great game tomorrow." Rather one has to declare his bet in terms of definite alternatives. He would have to say, for example. "I bet the Purdue team will win tomorrow by a margin of 14 or more points." The alternatives are clearly stated. Either the Purdue team will win by 14 or more points or it will not win by 14 or more points. It may not win for a variety of reasons. The game may not be played, they may win but by a smaller margin, they may lose, they may tie, they may make at least 14 points more than their opponents but have to forfeit the game on account of eligibility, etc., etc. But the wager is definite—either the Purdue team will win by 14 or more points or it will not win by 14 or more points. The prediction has been stated in terms of a dichotomy of alternatives. One does not have to be a scientist in order to see that in making wagers at least one has to express his predictions in terms of definite alternatives.

Not only is it customary to express predictions in terms of alternatives, preferably of the dichotomous form, but we do not learn much from making predictions unless we so express them. Actually we make progress by laying wagers on life—a point which I have tried to develop in the manuscript which is a companion to this. If our wagers are so formed that we do not win or lose on them within a reasonable time, there is very little profit gained from having made them. Continuing growth or adjustment of the personality requires that one subject his outlook to the validating effects of experience. If one never expresses his outlook in terms of precise predictions or in terms of alternatives, he simply loses out on the receipt of validating information. Experience is wasted on him. He is like the administrator who had only one year of experience, repeated twenty times. Thus, if we make predictions either as scientists or gamblers, or indeed, as any kind of human being attempting to anticipate life, we are able to validate those predictions only if we express them in terms of precise alternatives. Thus, just as the scientist in order to make progress must lay his predictions on the line in terms of hypotheses, so any individual in order to make progress must lay his predictions on the line in terms of alternatives if he is to make his daily comings and goings add up to meaningful experience.

Let us approach our thesis from still another angle: one which is perhaps more familiar to sophisticated graduate students in psychology. Consider learning. When a psychologist sets up a learning experiment he has to indicate clearly what he considers a trial and what he considers not a trial. He also tries to determine precisely what is a reinforcement and what is not a reinforcement. He hopes, though I doubt if he is often successful, that what he perceives as a trial will inevitably be what the subject perceives as a reinforcement. I am sorely tempted to digress at this point and talk about the clumsiness of current learning theories in this respect. However, the thesis which I am seeking to develop in this lecture is to be one which is as much supported by current learning theory as by the other theoretical approaches to personality. The shortcomings of learning theory are therefore not especially relevant to our present discussion. We need only say that experience with learning would lead us to believe that only as we perceive the problems of life in terms of alternatives are we able to improve our scores, eliminate our mistakes, profit from our trials, or work out the solutions to new problems.

What we have been saying may perhaps be readily seen as a way in which a scientist would approach life. But does this mean that it is a new way for the clinician to approach his patient, assuming for the moment that a clinician is not necessarily a scientist. Does a clinician, particularly an accepting clinician, tend to cast his cases in terms of alternatives? Is not this the antithesis of the all-important attitude of acceptance? Does he not rather try to "see his case as a whole"? And does he not try to avoid categorization of his patient?

Again I would emphasize that unless a clinician, like the scientist or anyone else can learn to anticipate his patients' behavior he will gain very little from his day by day experience. A good clinician lays wagers on what his patient will do from moment to moment and from day to day. He lays these wagers in forms which permit him to get definite evidence later as to how his predictions are turning out. One of the best ways I know of training clinicians in clinical sensitivity, is to require them to stick their necks out and predict what their patients will do between conferences, what kind of dreams they will have, what kind of complaints they will have on the next conference, what kind of experiments they will report having tried out in the interim, and how they will respond to various kinds of comments made by the therapist.

A particular way of getting a clinician to predict his patient or lay wagers upon him is to ask him to role play the parts of his patients. By this means one may see if he has a perceptual structure which enables him to predict spontaneously what they will do in various kinds of situations. The supervisor can set the stage by himself taking various parts and asking the student clinician to portray his patient. The clinician who does not stick his neck out and make predictions as to what the patient will do is never surprised at anything the patient does, never has any reason for changing his viewpoint, never learns anything from one patient which will help him to do a better job with the next one. Like the administrator with one year of experience repeated twenty times he has only had experience with one patient, an experience which was repeated twenty or more times.

Sometimes it is difficult for clinicians to see themselves as utilizing the scientific method because they realize that they must deal with so many pairs of alternatives at the same time. This makes them feel that they must despair of using anything which is analogous to the scientific procedure they use when doing their doctoral research. Let us have a look at the typical doctoral dissertation design. For one thing it is usually designed around one or two principal experimental hypotheses. To be sure we usually throw in one or two long shot hypotheses, one or two so-so hypotheses and one or two hypotheses which are essentially methodological. If our principal hypotheses are not supported we may get something very exciting or surprising in one of the long shot hypotheses or we can retreat to a second line of defense and say that at least our so-so hypotheses have been supported by the data. If all of this fails we can fall back on our methodological hypotheses and say, "Look, we haven't proved anything but see the wonderful methodological approach we have developed for investigating this kind of phenomena."

Now a clinician cannot operate in exactly this way. When he goes through the diagnostic or therapy planning stage of dealing with a patient, he has as many hypotheses as he has test findings. Indeed, in a clinical setting, any test finding should be treated as a hypothesis rather than as a conclusion. Furthermore, in every interview, exploratory or therapeutic, the alert clinician is confronted with a parade of hypotheses or alternatives, any two or three of which, if thoroughly run down, might be the basis of a doctoral dissertation. The reason that it is difficult for some clinicians to see themselves operating as scientists is that they must deal with so many pairs of alternatives at a time. Yet this fact does not mean that the clinician must use some other form of logic. It only means (1) that he must act upon less conclusive evidence in accepting or rejecting hypotheses and (2) that he is not required to extend his range of generalization to all people in all cultures but rather only to the patient at hand. This latter point makes it somewhat easier for him to operate with a minimum amount of crucial data.

In doctoral research we usually treat our hypotheses as if they were independent of each other. In terms of our binary number system model it is concerned only with digits and not with two and three place numbers. We might say in the language of the cyberneticists that in the doctoral dissertation one is concerned only with bits (a contraction of binary digit) but the clinician must take into account the permutations of his alternatives. In other words he must deal with two, three, four, or six place binary numbers. For example, if the patient identifies himself in terms of behaviors of the opposite sex, this fact also places a different value upon his domestic behavior and in turn that must be considered in combination with his relationship to authority figures in his job. Actually the clinician makes many observations in terms of alternatives and comes to conclusions regarding his patient by a process of multiplying alternatives or taking them in combination with each other.

The clinician's task is also complicated by the fact that the alternatives with which he deals are of unequal frequency of incidence among his patients and among people in general. For example, a relatively smaller number of people consider themselves to be stutterers than consider themselves not to be stutterers. Thus the individuality and the generalized characteristics of a patient are somewhat more precisely determined when he is observed to consider himself a stutterer than when he is observed to consider himself not a stutterer.

A clinician's dealing with alternatives is also further complicated by the fact that the kinds of alternatives which he uses tend to be inter-related rather than independent. For example, to use a very simple illustration, age, sex and the incidence of stuttering are somewhat inter-related variables. The ratio of male stutterers to female stutterers at adult ages is far greater than it is in early childhood. To identify a person as a thirty year old female stutterer is likely to be more meaningful than to identify the person as a five year old female stutterer or a thirty year old male stutterer. Now it may very well be that as we come to understand better the alternatives with which we deal in a clinical situation we will be able to reduce them to independent dichotomies. In terms of factor analysis we may actually be able to rotate axes in order to get orthogonal structure. But for the most part in clinical practice we are not dealing with orthogonal structure and the alternatives with which we deal are constellar or inter-related.

Another thing to be taken into account in considering how the clinician deals with alternatives is to remember that he reformulates his patterns of alternatives as he goes. In other words, he sets up his hypotheses by successive approximations. He abandons those which appear to be unfruitful as soon as their unfruitfulness begins to become apparent. When he writes his doctoral thesis, however, he is expected to state his hypotheses at the beginning of the fixed research stage of his investigation and stay with them to the bloody end. There is a possibility of compromising between these two approaches if the researcher is skilled in using the statistical methods of sequential analysis. At least the use of such computations makes the end a little less delayed and a little less bloody. But the clinician must always reformulate his alternatives by successive approximation. He should always be sure that his successive reformulations are in terms of alternatives, or in terms of hypotheses. It is easy to interpret successive approximation as meaning that one is always in the position of just having abandoned one set of hypotheses but not yet having stated his next set of hypotheses.

There is another way in which the good clinician is truly a scientist in respect to this matter of using alternatives. Consider the matter of diagnosis. It used to be that we made diagnoses primarily in order to have something to enter on the face sheet of a clinical record. Then it became apparent that the diagnostic categories in which we placed patients had a great influence on what we attempted to do for them. For example, if we diagnosed a patient as a schizophrenic, it usually meant that we put him away. If we diagnosed them as neurotic we would attempt psychotherapy. If we diagnosed them as manic we put them in a straightjacket and waited for nature to take its course. Gradually it dawned upon us that clinical diagnoses are meaningful only as they determine alternative methods of treatment. Thus, more and more, we now attempt to make so-called dynamic diagnoses, that is, diagnoses which not only will give us some idea of what treatment to attempt but also some idea of what ways to proceed in the treatment. With steps in the treatment perceived as the important alternatives with which the clinician must deal, diagnoses tend to take on different forms and a lot more meaning.

When a clinician deals with patients in terms of treatment alternatives he sometimes finds that the null hypothesis does not best express the alternative to his clinical hypothesis. Let us suppose that I am suspected of having a brain tumor, the treatment alternatives may on the surface be simply whether to operate or whether not to operate. Let us suppose that the mortality rate for this particular kind of operation is five percent. Well, I may be willing to accept the five percent level of confidence in dealing with certain impersonal psychological research but ordinarily I would set a much higher fiducial limit where the null hypothesis is replaced by the death hypothesis. Accepting a five percent level of confidence in such a matter is too much like playing Russian roulette.

But now let us suppose that we have another kind of alternative in the situation. Let us suppose that the chances are fifty-fifty that I die if I do not have the operation. Now the practical alternatives stack up altogether differently. The wise clinician realizes that he is not dealing merely with the five percent level of confidence but with a fifty percent level of confidence. The question is whether the patient will be given nineteen chances out of twenty for survival or only ten chances. The clinician is now confronted with reality in terms of alternatives and he deals with his patient in a far more realistic manner because of this. A good clinician, then, not only sees alternatives but he makes some effort to determine the stakes involved.

We have been talking about the clinician structuring life in terms of alternatives. Is it possible to see a patient also structuring life in terms of alternatives? We have already mentioned the child who has difficulty in dealing with a movie or a play in which the bad men are not clearly distinguished from the good men. Apparently such a child is using alternatives in dealing with people. We have also talked about the university student who, disappointed in a love affair, seeks unfortunately to construe all women in terms of a simple alternative scheme. We may say that both of these represent illogical behavior. But do they? The logic of course is not adequate but it is there nonetheless. The difficulty is that the person is trying to count everything in terms of one place numbers when actually the array of experience requires one, two, three, four and five place numbers.

Behind this question is a more fundamental question of whether it is possible to treat illogical behavior as if it were logical. There was a time when it was thought that the behavior of the natural elements was capricious and illogical. It was thought therefore to be impossible to apply logical schemes in predicting it. Nowadays it is pretty generally conceived that mother nature is completely amenable to logic and that she is predictable. Yet there are people who are still holding out for the idea that human nature, in contrast to mother nature, is itself so illogical that we cannot apply logic in construing it. They seem to believe that we should therefore ignore a subject's or a patient's verbal behavior as being utterly meaningless and attempt to explain him solely in terms of those behaviors which are analogous to animal behaviors. Those of us who believe that human nature is no less logical than mother nature believe that it is profitable to investigate how the patient himself structures his life in terms of alternatives. What are the choices that he sees that he must make? What are the categories that he uses in dealing with his fellow men? Does he stick his neck out and make predictions which can be validated in the immediate future or does he protect himself by making predictions which can only be invalidated or validated long after it is too late for him to revise his prediction system? What is his personal scheme for making predictions—for choosing alternatives?

Now up to this point we have been attempting to develop the thesis that life may be structured in terms of alternatives. We have argued that the clinician as well as the scientist will find this approach advantageous. We have gone even further: we have suggested that not only should the person who is trying to do something for others make his approach in terms of alternatives but that he may, in turn, see his subject or his patient as one who himself uses alternatives. Thus, constructions in terms of alternatives may be not only the method of psychology but also the content of psychology.

Now let us see what it is like to deal with a patient as one who himself construes his world in terms of alternatives. Let us say that the pattern or form of a construing act may be called a construct. A construct is a unit of abstraction-for-the-sake-of-generalization which is stated in terms of a dichotomy or two alternatives. We may say that a construct is just another name for a concept. Indeed the two terms are comparable. I have preferred to use the term construct because it tends to carry with it certain experimental implications. However, I might have used the term concept.

A construct is a way in which certain things are like each other and yet different from certain other things. In its minimum context a construct would be a way in which two things are alike and yet at the same time different from a third. It should be kept in mind that the *way* in which the two things are like each other is the same as the *way* in which they are different from the third. Thus, the minimum context for a construct is three things. These three things are abstracted in such a way that two of them are like each other and both of them are unlike the third. It is important that the way in which the two things are alike should be the same as the way the two are unlike the third thing. To say that two things are alike and not to imply that their likeness makes them in the same way different from something else is meaningless. It amounts to no more than saying that all things in the world are alike in a way which distinguishes them from nothing.

When we emphasize both the alikeness and the distinction which a construct involves it is another way of saying that the old associationistic laws of similarity and contrast were really the same law for there is no similarity save as it implies a contrast and there is no contrast save as it implies a similarity.

Sometimes we try to avoid being explicit about what is similar and what is dissimilar. We may say, for example, "Mary and Alice have gentle dispositions but neither of them is as attractive as Jane." Here, actually we have invoked two constructs. If we were to express them explicitly we would have to say something like this, "Mary and Alice are gentle, Jane is not." Or we might say, "Jane is more attractive than Mary or Alice."

When we say that "Mary and Alice have gentle dispositions but neither of them is as attractive as Jane,"we may be implying two different constructs, gentleness and attractiveness. The selection of an adjective to describe two persons or even to describe one person usually means that the speaker has formed a category which, for him, has the simultaneous inclusive and exclusive properties of a construct. To say that Mary is gentle is to imply that at least one other person is gentle also and that at least one other person is not gentle, or it may imply only that at least two other persons are not gentle.

In any case the minimum context for a construct is three things. We cannot express a construct either explicitly or implicitly without involving at least two things which have a likeness and one which is, by the same token, different. To say that Mary and Alice are gentle and not imply that somewhere in the world there is someone who is not gentle is illogical. More than that, it is unpsychological.

Now a person may be heard to say, "Mary and Alice are gentle and I cannot conceive of anyone not being gentle." Such a speaker may be attempting to avoid placing himself in a position of one who sees ungentleness. Like the second monkey, he sees no evil. His statement may thus provide an important lead for the psychologist who is seeking to understand him. On the other hand the speaker may be restricting the reference of the construct to an idiographic frame. He may if we ask him indicate that he really means "Mary and Alice are gentle not now as contrasted with some other time but gentleness is not a construct which distinguishes people from each other but rather distinguishes day to day variations in persons." This construction of gentleness also throws considerable light on the speaker's own pattern of mood changes. It is certainly profitable to listen carefully to a speaker's use of constructs.

Sometimes a person will attempt to limit the context to two things which are *unlike* in some way. He may say, "Mary is gentle, Jane is not. I know of no one else who is like either of them." It may be a little bit more difficult to see but this also represents a breakdown of conceptualization. Mary and Jane have already been distinguished when they entered the discussion identified by their names. To say that they are further distinguished by their gentleness or lack of it is to add nothing to the distinction unless that further distinction by indicating a kinship of at least one of them with a third person classifies them. While this kind of conceptual breakdown is not as common as that described a moment ago, it does indicate that the speaker is having trouble communicating the kinship he covertly construes between Mary and Jane and the other people in his social world. The missing like element in expression of his construct is quite possibly denied because he himself is it. To say that his conceptualization of Mary and Jane is concretistic is not enough. He is really in trouble about Mary and Jane.

It is not our purpose at this point to illustrate all of the ways which an analysis of people's constructs can contribute to an understanding of their personalities. It is enough to indicate that constructs can have submerged ends. That is, people may be unwilling to express clearly one of the alternatives with which the construct deals.

Now let us turn to another implication of the construct and its alternatives. If we consider that the construct is the form in which life is given structure or the form in which life is construed we can readily see that constructs are the channels in which one's mental processes run. They are the paths by which we reach conclusions. They make it possible to anticipate the on-rushing flood of events. They represent the patterns along which we may organize our behavior. The limitations of one's construction system then also become the limitations of the ways in which he may adjust himself to life, for constructs may be considered as controls.

Moreover, it is possible for a person by the nature of his construction system to find himself painted into a corner. The alternatives with which he confronts himself may turn out to be dilemmas. Indeed, all of us who have had experience with psychotherapy can readily see that many patients are disturbed because of the way in which they construe their world rather than because of what the world has done to them. We know that in therapy if we always accept the patient's version of his problem we may soon find ourselves confronted with the same unpleasant alternatives which he faces. We know also that it is frequently possible to get a patient to cast his problem in new light and find that the alternatives which he had originally set for himself are not inevitable alternatives after all and that the problem can be cast in other terms or by means of other constructs.

Now something very interesting happens when a person first seeks to readjust his life within the framework of his personal system of constructs. The dimensions, of course, are really the dichotomous dimensions or alternatives that our constructs provide us. These dimensions tend to remain the same. The person's freedom of movement, therefore, at first appears to him to be only along the axes which he has already established for himself. Let us suppose that he has oriented his own role with respect to the personal construct of gentleness. Let us suppose that he has classified himself as like the gentle people in his construct context. He is one of the gentle ones. Now suppose the act starts to misfire. He misses his cues, garbles his lines; it becomes apparent that he must do something about his role. The most obvious thing to do is to start reclassifying his role within the context of some of his personal role constructs. Suppose he decides to move his role along the gentleness-ungentleness axis. A few weeks later his friends remark, "What's happened to Casper? My, my, how he has changed!"

The chances are that Casper has not really changed his adjustment *system* but has tried to reidentify himself within whatever limited construction system he already had to work with. It may be that his construction system left him no alternative save to move in the direction of ungentleness. An examination of so-called marked personality changes, such as those appearing in the manic-depressive cycle, confirms the fact that most of the radical movements that we see appearing in people's behavior do[2] represent basic changes in their blueprints of life, but rather an attempt to shift within the rigid frameworks which provide their only cues to the understanding of human relationships. If a clinician is aware of a patient's dimensional system or system of alternatives he can make some prediction of the direction in which the patient will probably have to move if he is to move at all.

A psychotherapist who seeks to force his patient to move too rapidly runs into exactly this kind of problem. He forces his patient to move along the only axes the patient has pre-established for himself and the results may be catastrophic. Even if the psychotherapist moves slowly but is not aware of what the personal construct system is he may find his patient moving in totally unexpected, but logically meaningful directions.

The point we wish to make here, then, is that the construct, being a pair of alternatives, is also an available path of movement, and as we construe our world in terms of constructs we also lay down the network of streets and avenues along which it is possible to make personality readjustments.

[3] Editors' note: Although this is 'do' in the original, it should probably be 'do not'.

For the past two or three years we have been experimenting with approaches to personality which would place emphasis upon the understanding of the construct system of patients. One of these approaches is tentatively called the Role Construct Repertory Test. More recently we have been inclined to shorten this jaw-breaking name simply to the Rep Test. The approach is to provide the patient with a list of role titles. The role titles are such identifications as, "your father," "your mother," "a teacher you can remember having liked at about the time you were in the sixth grade," "a girl friend you went with just before you started going with your present girl friend," etc. The subject is asked to identify these people by name and then he is asked to sort them as one might sort the blocks in a Vygotsky Test.

There are various approaches to this sorting. One of the ways is to present the names, three at a time, and ask him to say in what important way he feels that two of them are alike and yet different from the third. He is then asked to write this way down, or perhaps the examiner writes down the term. Next the patient is asked what he considers to be the contrasting construct or the contrasting end of the construct. By this way it is possible to get some idea of the alternatives in terms of which he classifies important figures of his intimate world. It is possible also by analyzing the Rep Test results to get some idea of the way in which his constructs fall into constellations, for we may find that he uses words somewhat loosely. For example, he may say on one sort that the similarity end of the construct is gentleness. He may identify the contrasting end as cruelty. On another sort he may say that a pair of figures are aggressive and that the contrasting end of the construct is also gentleness. This would seem to indicate that the two construct dimensions or pairs of alternatives are actually similar. We say, therefore, that the two fall into a constellation.

This is, of course, an exceedingly brief sketch of the Rep Test and actually we have done a good deal more with it than compute constellations. In fact we have been having a good deal of fun with it lately and several pieces of research have been designed around it or around the conceptualizations which are evolving out of its use.

It is possible to analyze Rep Test protocols and in order to get some idea of how adequate a patient's constructs are. For example, we find that some patients tend to perceive people in terms of alternatives which are so fixed that it would be impossible to re-perceive people in any other way. For example, a patient in a mental hospital, after we had worked through his constellations, appeared to have only two constructs that he used for dealing with the people in his role title list. There were those people who were relatives of his *versus* those who were not relatives of his and there were those who were hospitalized people and those who were on the outside. Now this patient had essentially painted himself into a corner in such a way that he could not possibly see people as changing nor until he developed a more adequate repertory of constructs could he be expected to work out any new adjustments to people.

The number of constructs one uses to deal with people may be an element in his capacity for adjustment and perhaps it is one of the features to be taken into account when deciding whether psychotherapy will be effective. We are not sure yet how important mere number of constructs is. If we consider all of our constructs as dichotomous, and I believe that fundamentally they are dichotomous, though we may mix them in such a way that they may appear to be scalar at some times, we can get a rough measure of the adequacy of one's construct repertory from the well-known information theory formula of Log2n, where *n* is the number of people to be distinguished from each other and the *base 2* refers to the fact that this is done in terms of dichotomies. The value of Log2n is the number of constructs which it is necessary for one to have in order to distinguish *n* number of people from each other. For example, if one is to distinguish 16 people from each other it would be necessary to have at least four constructs. Actually in practice the formula is not quite as simple as this since people do tend to deal in constructs which are not absolutely independent of each other and since also the pair of alternatives which each construct represents is not equally weighted.

I have spoken of the Rep Test approach to understanding patients. We may also use the notion of construct alternatives as a basis for doing psychotherapy. We may say that therapy is a way of getting people to structure their life in terms of reasonable alternatives. We may also say that therapy is a way of getting them to structure life in terms of such alternatives as will enable them to lay precise wagers on life. Just as one of the tasks in directing graduate students is to get them to express their hypotheses in testable form so it is reasonable to see psychotherapy as a way of getting patients to express their hypotheses (or constructs) in ways that are testable. One of the jobs of the psychotherapist is to help the patient formulate reasonable constructs and then to go out and use those constructs to make predictions which can be validated within a reasonable time. I said "go out and use constructs." Actually it may be possible for the patient to validate the construct within the psychotherapy room. Indeed, the psychotherapy room may be likened to a laboratory in which the patient may try, in test tube sizes, the experiments by means of which his hypotheses or constructs can be tested.

Another function of psychotherapy is to help the patient to develop a more complex and adequate system of constructs, so that he can deal with more complicated material and not be in the unfortunate position of the patient I described who had only two relatively useless constructs with which he was trying to go through life.

Another function of psychotherapy is to help the patient to reconstrue his alternatives or, in other words, to revise his construct system on the basis of the results he gets from his experimentations, both in the psychotherapy room and outside. This is analogous to saying that in psychotherapy we do what we try to do in research—to get the patient to structure his experience in such a way that he can make some sense out of it, so that he can get some results, and then, in turn, to re-construe his alternatives and reformulate his hypotheses in such a way that they will enable him to make some systematic progress.

I have tried to develop the idea that life may be construed in terms of alternatives. I have tried to go on further and say that perhaps life always is psychologically construed in terms of alternatives. Then I have tried to develop the idea that it is possible to study patients in terms of the alternative systems they have established for themselves and that it is possible to go on and apply this kind of thinking in the psychotherapy room as well as in the laboratory. I trust that this attempt to develop a point of view will support the view, as I am sure many of you have sought to support the view, that scientific psychology and clinical psychology are essentially one and the same thing. Just as the scientist attempts to deal with his world in terms of testable hypotheses which he revises on the basis of experiments, so clinical psychology attempts to help patients state their hypotheses in testable form, to try them out, and to revise them on the basis of results. Psychotherapy as well as science can profit from the efficacious use of well chosen alternatives.

10

A Theoretical Approach to Psychological Movement[1]

Scientists almost universally agree that their manifold efforts are directed toward prediction and control of their subjects, animate or inanimate, human or not. In this paper, we are concerned with the human being, specifically the maladjusted individual, and the changes he evidences over a given time interval. We feel that movement is of prime interest to the student of human behavior and that a fuller comprehension of this phenomenon will enhance the effectiveness of therapeutic (broadly defined) techniques.

It is assumed that the therapeutic situation is one that is designed to hasten the process of change. We infer also that all changes in behavior follow upon the construing of these changes (Kelly, 1951). Behavioral changes do not just happen; they are man-made. Therapy provides a framework wherein accelerated change may occur.

Saying that our ideas, our aspirations, precede the actual working out of these ideas and aspirations is another way of stating that behavioral change follows the construction of change. For example, today we plan an investigation which necessarily must precede our doing the investigation. Our ideas tend to run ahead of our "actual" performance, or our "actual" behavior. A further example, simple but cogent, is furnished in the area of literary composition. We tend to compose our thoughts faster than we can put them on paper. In the sense that we are aware of what we intend to write, we anticipate extensive movement. But if we were halted at any given point and our (actual) movement measured to that point, it would appear that little change had occurred. The writer, however, affected by his over-all construction of the situation, perceives his own movement in terms of this greater plan and thereby distorts his perceptions to that extent. More will be said of this contrasting process below.

In therapy, we offer the patient a situation in which the construction of change may be facilitated. The therapeutic situation provides him with a framework in which he may structure changes taking place. Although he may accomplish this to some extent in "unguided real life," his therapist aids him in a more rapid realization of what is transpiring. Under the therapist's guidance, he becomes more effective in perceiving the changes, extensive and limited, that he has undergone. In addition, the patient is helped to become more aware of future changes. He broadens his perspective to include more distant goals; his construction of events runs ahead of the more readily observable behavioral changes.

The reader may have noted the synonymous utilization of the terms, "movement" and "change." It is necessary that our present use of these terms be understood. In general, we regard movement or change as a constantly varying behavioral process. The individual manifests behavioral variations throughout his existence. Measurement is accomplished through arbitrary segmentation along the time dimension. Movement is here discussed in two contexts, measured and perceived. *Measured movement* refers to the variation ascribed to an individual's behavior by "outside" observers. It is the change noted in behavior deriving from observation of the individual on two separate occasions. *Perceived movement* denotes the variation ascribed by the individual to himself at two instants in time. This is a more complex process than appears at first glance. It is not simply a matter of twice reporting on himself. At one instant, his perceiving of present status will also be somewhat affected by his anticipation of future movement, and, to an even lesser degree, by constructions of prior events. At the second instant, his perception of past status is slightly affected by anticipation of future movement, and, to a much greater degree, influenced by a reorganization of the past derived through the construction of the present. In any event, the individual's perception of the temporal changes in himself can be expected to be more distorted than that of a "neutral" observer. Examination of the effect of future anticipations upon behavior remains largely for later study. More fully treated below is the perception of past status.

[1] First published as Howard, A.R. & Kelly, G.A. (1954). A theoretical approach to psychological movement. *Journal of Abnormal Psychology, 49 (3)*, 399-404. Now in the public domain and republished by permission of Jacqueline Aldridge. Drawn from a dissertation submitted by Howard, with the direction and assistance of Kelly, to the Department of Psychology, The Ohio State University, in partial fulfillment of the requirements for the Ph.D. degree. Grateful acknowledgement for their generous aid was made also to Drs. H. Gordon Hullfish, Francis P. Robinson, Julian B. Rotter, and Robert J. Wherry

Collected Papers of the Pioneer of Constructivist Psychology: George A. Kelly, First Edition. Edited by David A. Winter and Nick Reed.

It is hypothesized that perceived movement is greater than measured movement. It is our contention that this derives from a "contrast" phenomenon not unlike that which may be ascribed to the work of such investigators as Bartlett (1932), Zeigarnik (1927), and Ovsiankina (1928). As a result of Bartlett's pioneer efforts, for example, we have since accepted the notion that perception is functionally selective. He demonstrated effectively that past experiences influence present perceptions and that recall of these perceptions changes with time through reorganization of the past. In the repeated reproduction of stories, for example, certain elements are successively distorted so that they become increasingly removed from the originals. This process of distortion we have chosen to term a contrast from the measured (or original) perception. The studies of Zeigarnik and Ovsiankina may be similarly viewed. They demonstrated the tendency of individuals to recall interrupted tasks more often than tasks which had been completed. The aim was completion, and when the aim was not met, the contrast was sufficiently great to engender greater remembrance of the failures.

It is, then, our view that upon recalling past events the individual tends to focus upon the most contrasting of these events—the sharper details out of a time telescoped; that is, an individual's segmentation of time differs from an "actual" time interval. The past becomes a comparatively more undifferentiated mass in which earlier and later events merge or telescope. From this mass the individual recalls only the "figures" or "sharper details." Concomitant with "actual" movement, the individual perceives himself to be "playing a new role(s)." As a result of these new constructions, any degree of change tends to be "overexaggerated" so that the contrast between past and present events is "overenhanced." Perceiving movement in himself, the individual will, upon contrasting what to him is the relatively static past with the ever-moving present, tend to construe a continually widening gap between his present and past behavior.

An illustration of the manner in which contrast-enhancement is deemed to operate may be helpful (Fig. 1). Let us suppose that a given individual is requested to render three self-evaluations (SE): *(a)* at instant A concerning current status at A (SE-A); *(b)* at instant L (for later) concerning current status at this subsequent point in time (SE-L); *(c)* also at instant L but concerning status at instant A (SE-LA). Let us further suppose that, when rendering SE-LA, this individual perceives himself to feel much better at instant L than he felt at an earlier point in time, A. The construction system at A, now perceived relative to the (forward) construction system at L, is viewed in "sharper contrast," i.e., the individual says, in effect: "I see this constellation at L which depicts my assets and liabilities. Now (L) I have more assets than liabilities and I know I wasn't feeling as well before this (A). In fact, according to the way I feel now, I must have been pretty low at that time." Thus, as a result of contrasting past and present, a "distorted" evaluation appears at LA. A formerly perceived threat is now recalled as a strength, and vice versa; a formerly perceived strength is now recalled as a strength of even greater intensity, etc. This apparent perceptual distortion leads one to hypothesize that perceived movement is greater than measured movement, i.e., the difference perceived by the individual as represented by his evaluations at L and LA exceeds the difference noted by external observers at L and A. Thus L serves as a kind of buffer through which perceptions of the past are filtered and distorted. The "figures" of the pattern constituting A are heightened by this contrasting process and the "ground" becomes even further removed. But the figures are not carried over to LA unchanged. In the course of time, and as the result of filtering through L, they undergo alteration. The "outside" observer, noting behavior merely on two separate occasions does not respond to these "filtering" conditions.

A further basis for understanding the process of movement presents itself. An individual becomes aware of the variance in his construction system as events are successively construed by him. At L he construes only limited variation in that he tends to confine his perceptions to a relatively shorter period of time than he does at LA. At "point" L in the evaluation of his psychological processes, he is aware of changes which have transpired, but to a greater degree on a level of "less cognitive awareness" (Kelly, 1951). At LA he

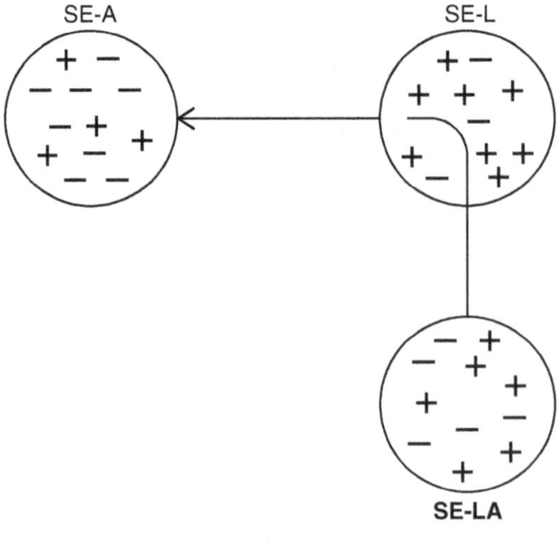

Fig. 1 Operation of Contrast-Enhancement on Perceived Strength(+) and Perceived Threat(-)

is requested to bring this awareness to a higher (more cognitively aware) level whereupon three processes occur: *(a)* removal from restrictions of less cognitive awareness at L; *(b)* "conscious" perception of a greater number of successive constructions occurring over a longer time span tending to remove the person further from the limited perspective at L; *(c)* evaluation of the concept of change itself. Movement may be regarded as a manifestation of the rate of organization of experience along a time line. Differences in the degree of movement between individuals may be viewed as the result of differences arising in such rates. If two persons exposed to the same (therapeutic) situation reveal significantly discrepant degrees of movement, one is obviously assimilating at a slower rate than the other. If we hold as a therapeutic objective the maximum absorption in the briefest time, we must devise means for gauging a particular individual's organization rate. As the point of diminishing returns is approached, the process of termination may be profitably initiated. If, then, we examine historical factors in order to group various "kinds" of subjects, we should be able to predict the extent of their movement in a given situation and within a specified period of time.

In this regard it is felt that case histories may indeed afford a fruitful source of hypotheses. Our predictions would cluster about the "hunch" that certain construction systems held earlier, or certain cultural characteristics to which an individual has been exposed, tend to hinder movement; others tend to facilitate movement. For example, the person who construes life apart from his mother as unbearable would be expected to anticipate backward movement in an institutional framework. On the other hand, the individual who has been actively striving for years to sever the umbilical cord may welcome a hospital environment relatively free of patronizing authority figures and construe forward movement within such a situation. We would hypothesize "regression" also on the part of adherents to an atmosphere of cultural propriety when they are exposed to the customary inelegancies of institutional existence.

We have tended to view the fundamental aim of therapy, broadly conceived, as the stimulation of more rapid change in the patient than would result from his own unguided efforts. The individual who perceives himself as remaining relatively stationary—"I don't seem to be getting anywhere"—lacks the experience of felt movement. Left to his own devices, it would appear that his future chances for rapid movement are rather slight. If therapy is to prove successful, the patient must feel that he is changing, or at least perceive himself to be capable of changing.

Extending our discussion to the classroom, we note that the teacher teaches and the learner learns. Some pupils assimilate knowledge at a faster rate than others. If a student is to realize the maximum from his attendance, he must somehow develop the notion that he is in the process of changing; for if he perceives no change, he may inquire, "What good is an education?" As he perceives that he is learning, as he perceives that school experiences are making him different from what he was earlier, his assimilation rate may be expected to accelerate (at least for a time). Perhaps test results and grades (the measured change) will fail to reveal movement as extensive as that perceived by the student; nevertheless, if he perceives a greater change in terms of some personal norm, it should, for the serious student at least, provide sufficient incentive for further change. As long as he contrasts a prior status with his "better educated" status of the moment, he will continue to view his school experiences as desirable events.

Perhaps then, our use of objective tests (in school and elsewhere), group norms, and grades has too long overemphasized status and disregarded the essential aim, movement. More stress must be placed upon the individual's perceptions of the learning process. If he views a situation to be beneficial to him, his continuance in that situation should be facilitated. If he feels that he is learning something in the classroom, he will seek further education. Why risk stifling incentive, particularly in the formative years, with our noneradicable "final grades" which so frequently result in the inference of "final" attainment rather than in the inference of having achieved merely a given termination? Perhaps a more useful approach would be to "ask him" what he believes he has learned, and then clarify the "facts" relating to those issues on which he appears to be misinformed. In this manner, we first pay heed to the person's perceptions, and we do not hamper initiative to the degree that may occur when an arbitrary standard (a desired measured status) is imposed from above.

Viewing the phenomenon of change in terms of "contrast" permits us to link the not-too-dissimiiar areas of (formal) education and therapy. In the former, we attempt to convey diverse information, often relying, in our textbooks and lectures, upon examples which tend to clarify the issues under discussion. As a result, frequently we resort to overenhancement of differences and similarities; we draw sharp contrasts, emphasizing discrepancies; and we offer oversimplified analogies, highlighting likenesses, in order to "make the point stick." Similarly, in therapy, we draw upon a relatively minor change that the patient has perceived in himself at an earlier date and utilize this to stimulate further change. We recall to him the movement he reported earlier, contrasting it with a movement he now reports, in our endeavor to encourage his anticipation of further change. As in the educational situation, we resort to overenhancement. We are relatively uninterested in the actual, or true, change that occurs. We value more highly the *perception* of change taking place than a more objective appraisal of what is "actually" occurring.

In the school this means that we foster the perception that one is learning, that one is different from what he was at a period when he knew less. Our sharp, clear-cut examples readily register with the student, with the result that he perceives movement in his rapid grasp of a concept, a solution, or a technique. In the therapeutic situation, this means that we guide the patient in the perception of contrast between earlier behaviors and contemporary ones. We strive to get him to see that he is changing or has changed. In both situations, so long as the individual perceives that he has benefited, he is less likely to terminate inopportunely. It matters little if, by all objective criteria, he has evidenced less movement than he has perceived. Indicating that he is capable of perceiving movement, he has indicated that he is capable of continuing such behavior in the future. In both situations, we help the individual adopt a point of view by means of which he considers himself to be a continuing learner; we guide him toward establishing a framework of thinking within which he may structure future changes as a learner, or as an "improved" patient. One useful principle leading toward the attainment of this goal is that of "contrast," whereby the teacher or the therapist may help the person feel that his change may well be considered more extensive than it might be in terms of some arbitrary measured standard.

We have, at several points, referred briefly to anticipations of future movement. Similarly, the sole mention of the direction movement may take has been confined to illustrative material. Simultaneous elaboration of both areas is possible.

The fundamental postulate in Kelly's "psychology of personal constructs" reads: "A person's psychological processes evolve toward what he construes to be an optimal anticipation of events" (Kelly, 1951, p. 29). It is the "evolutionary" aspect of the postulate upon which primary stress must be placed at this point. Perhaps the person who revamps his construction system to the extent that he perceives more change in himself than does another observer (even if this is not now improvement in the customary sense) is actually in the process of anticipating greater prediction and control of his behavior in the future. As an individual initiates movement, a wider range of subsequent movement becomes potentially available to him. The more movement occurring, the more numerous the chances of eventual satisfactory "anticipation of events."

We have said that therapy is designed to hasten movement. If one "kind" of therapy is more accelerating than another, we would expect persons in the former situation to have available to them even more opportunities for anticipating events. For example, if we select two groups of hospital patients on the basis of whether this is the first confinement or a subsequent one, we would hypothesize a greater degree of movement on the part of the new admission. This would apply equally to both perceived and measured movement and derives from the theoretical deduction that first admissions are in a more accelerated therapy situation than are readmissions for two reasons. First, the new patient has not been in the same milieu before. He thus perceives more freedom to move, in whatever direction; he may either be frightened by the novelty and therefore move backward, or take advantage of the new environment and the removal from one in which he was poorly adjusted and thus change "for the better." Second, institution personnel tend to minister to the first admission patient to a greater degree than to the readmission patient. The psychiatrist conducts a more detailed initial interview with him. In rapid succession, he undergoes a series of routine examinations—physical, psychological, social service. Again he may move in either direction—backward or forward. All this attention may serve to make him feel that people are helping to cure him, or it may result in his feeling that he must indeed be very ill to have so many persons consulting him.

We have, then, what is essentially an accelerated therapy situation for the first admission. The readmission, on the other hand, has undergone the hospitalization process a number of times. For him, there is less novelty, less contrast from one confinement to the next. The routine is the same, the personnel are the same, the wards are the same. Returned to the same situation, he remains less likely to perceive changes in himself and less likely to be observed by others to have changed.

Thus we note that before an individual can change, he must construe change as being potentially available to him. Therapy may aid by structuring the need for change. Once such construction has occurred, certain behaviors will be observable to others. The person who perceives that he is moving forward will be noted to be moving forward; the person who perceives that he is moving backward will be noted to move in a backward direction. Analogous observation will be made of the person who perceives that he is at a standstill, that he is "getting nowhere." There are occasions however, wherein an individual is observed to be changing to a greater degree than he perceives. It is felt that this trend will become reversed, in view of our earlier statement concerning behavior following one's construction system. This person will soon be observed to be behaving more in accord with his own perceptions. If he perceives backward movement, or no movement at all, his behavior will likewise reflect this. Should his perception of movement alter so that now he sees more movement in himself than others do, we have then the situation originally posited.

Thus the personal construct system is reflected through successive modifications of behavior. By periodically observing behavior we may infer the nature of the perceptual system. Rather than content ourselves with a cessation of operations at that point, we would undoubtedly desire to gauge the extent to which a person's behavior is a consequence of his construction system. One method would be to request periodic self-evaluations of an individual. During the intervals between the rendering of these, observational records of the individual's behavior in various activities should be maintained. The primary objective would be to predict from any given self-evaluation, i.e., the construction system at a given point in time, the behavior that the individual is likely to exhibit during a specified future period. The observer's records would serve as a check on the predictions made and, of greater import, may be expected to yield principles of prediction applicable to other situations.

An approach to psychological movement, or change, has been presented. Stress has been placed on the role of therapy in accelerating movement. Earlier investigations have afforded the basis for currently offering a "contrast" phenomenon to explain certain aspects of movement and to link the fields of (formal) education and therapy. Implications of these and other fields are noted.

References

Bartlett, F. C. (1932). *Remembering*. Cambridge University Press.

Kelly, G. A. (1951). *The psychological construction of life*. Unpublished manuscript, Psychology Clinic Library, Ohio State University.

Ovsiankina, M. (1928) Die Wiederaufnalime von unter-brochener Handlungen. *Psychol. Forsch.*, *11*,302–389. (In *Psychol, Abstr.*, 1929, *3*, 2599.)

Zeigarnik, B. (1927). Das Behalten erledigter und unerledigter Handlungen. *Psychol. Forsch.*, *9*, 1–85. (In *Psychol. Abstr.*, 1927, *1*, 2365.)

11

Hostility[1]

It is a common experience among those who, in the headlong pursuit of their occupation, pause occasionally to sketch some guidelines for their patterns of thought to discover that the principles they have so carefully defined were once artfully portrayed in Greek legend. I have had this particular experience in connection with this afternoon's topic. It is a disconcerting experience for not only does it lead one to question his personal capacity for original thinking but it also casts doubt upon the wisdom of all those explicit verbal definitions upon which modern science so largely depends. Of the two, it is perhaps less upsetting to give up one's claim to originality. But definition—if one cannot define, how can he ever hope to progress? Yet it seems to be the irony of explicit thinking that such great emphasis is placed on the outer boundaries that it never touches the heart of the idea.

Not so the Greeks. They, while they might be accused of being perfectionists, were certainly never literalists, and even now it seems as if they were freer then to say what they meant than we are. So, before I start rounding up the precise scientific meaning of this *hostility* construct by modern-day methods of circumlocution, let me just tell you very briefly how the Greeks got to the heart of the matter and said it all much more simply than I would ever dare to.

There was a young man by the name of Theseus who had been reared under the domination of his mother. One day, out in the garage or some place, he ran onto an old sword and a pair of shoes that had belonged to his father. Right then and there he decided to make a break for it and go look up his father, who, it appears, had gone away to a national convention a number of years before and somehow had managed to stay away on urgent business ever since. Just how his father managed this is part of the story that has never been quite clear to me. I did hear, once, that some scandal was involved, but since it seemed to be none of my business I never looked into the matter. I am sure that it is not an important part of the story.

Now this young victim of "momism," as it existed in the classic Greek era, became quite a hero by the time he caught up with his old man—a combination of fact which, it seems to me, some alert publicity-minded psychiatrist ought to be able to capitalize on. For one thing, along the road, Theseus ran into a character by the name of Procrustes.

This fellow had bought a small place way out in the country where the road wound through a deserted canyon. Some people say his real name was Damastes, while others insist it was Polypamon. The mixup was probably because people going by were always in such a hurry that they didn't take time to read the Greek letters on his mailbox. In any case, people thereabouts all called him by his nickname, "Stretch," which is what the word "procrustes" means in English.

Stretch Damastes was hostile. That, of course, is the whole point of telling this story. I don't think he ever meant to be hostile. His feelings would probably have been hurt if anyone had even suggested the idea. As a matter of fact, it is quite possible that no one ever did mention it to him. In those times not many people went in for psychoanalysis and you could easily go for weeks without so much as once having someone interpret your unconscious motivation to you.

I am sure that Stretch was not really out to hurt people. The fact that his guests always seemed to have such a bad time of it was just one of those unfortunate things that so often seem to happen in spite of everything you do to make people comfortable.

Because he happened to be hostile, Stretch was one of those unlucky souls in this world whose fate it is to be grossly misunderstood. Why? In the first place he was genuinely interested in people. I mean genuinely! He had bought this little chicken ranch, or whatever it was, with the express purpose of setting up a kind of wayside motel where travelers who found themselves in this lonely spot at nightfall could be assured of some old-fashioned hospitality. Moreover, he had in mind that he would give them their supper and their lodging free. Breakfast, too, if they happened to want it! He was as thoughtful as that.

Stretch, like most hostile people, had a pretty clear idea of how guests should be treated. He really fancied himself as a host and along about sundown he used to stand out by the front gate, lean against the mailbox, and wait to see if he could persuade some

[1] Presidential Address, 1957, Clinical Division, American Psychological Association. Published in Maher, B. (Ed.). (1969), *Clinical psychology and personality: The selected papers of George Kelly* (pp. 267–280).Wiley. Republished by permission of Wiley.

Collected Papers of the Pioneer of Constructivist Psychology: George A. Kelly, First Edition. Edited by David A. Winter and Nick Reed.

traveler to stop in for supper. At the table he always proved to be an excellent conversationalist and, before his guest realized how late it had gotten to be, it would be time to go to bed.

There was a bed, as those of you who know the story probably remember. Some say there were two beds, but most everyone now agrees that there was only this one. Stretch was especially concerned that his guest would find the bed just right. He would fluff up the pillows, press down on the mattress to show how soft it was, and keep murmuring something about how much he hoped that the bed would be neither too long nor too short. In fact, he would fuss around long after the guest was yawning and ready to turn in. Showing all this solicitude was what really got him into trouble.

In fact, the poor man would get himself so worked up over his social role as a host that later, back in his own room and long after his guest was comfortably asleep, he would be tossing and turning, worrying himself sick over the possibility that there might be some flaw in his hospitality. Was his guest comfortable or not? Had he used the dainty guest towels in the bathroom? And the guest bed—that was what worried him most. Did it fit? Maybe he was a little too tall for it; maybe a little too short—which was it? Throughout the restless night the thoughts nagged and mounted until they were unbearable.

You can guess what happened, if you do not already know. In the wee hours of the morning Stretch would tiptoe to the door of the guest room, open it ever so softly, and peek in, just to make sure. You can also guess what he saw and what utter consternation seized him at finding his guest either too short or too long—never a perfect fit. And now, knowing how it was that Stretch was trying so hard to be a perfect host, it is quite easy to see that next he simply had to do what he did.

There are some folks—not very practical folks, I'm afraid—who think that what he should have done was cut off the bed to fit the guest; or stretch it, as the case might be. But if such people would only stop to think for a moment, they would readily perceive that this would not be socially adaptive behavior. It would be bound to make the bed the wrong size for the next guest, not to mention the damage to an expensive piece of furniture. Of course, Stretch could have gone back to bed, pulled the covers over his head and said, "To heck with it!" as some folks who do not have a sincere interest in people, no doubt, would do.

The rest of the story is not very important, now that we all appreciate Stretch's predicament and have feelings of genuine acceptance for him as a person. You know, of course, that Theseus, who was not a particularly sensitive person, did Procrustes in—not because of any deep sense of hostile regard, I'm afraid, but only because Procrustes happened to get in his way. Theseus was young and ambitious and had his heart set on being a hero. To his immature mind, life was simply an aggressive adventure and he still lacked that subtle capacity for exactitude in the interpretation of human nature that genuinely hostile people have.

Let me turn now from this classical mode of expression to the form of semantic discourse with which we are more familiar. It will take longer to say the same thing, and much of the meaning will be lost in literalism, but it will sound more scientific and much more like what a psychologist is expected to say on an occasion like this.

Over a period of a good many years—many of them not very productive of publications, I fear—I have attempted to come to grips with the psychology of man as if I had only recently come across the species. It was like pretending to be someone from Mars who had just dropped in to meet these earth-creatures for the first time and was trying to understand them. More and more, it seemed to me that what I wanted, in my role as a stranger on earth, was man's own account of things as he saw them, as he experienced them, and not merely what outsiders said about him.

Early in my clinical experience I found myself repeating over and over to my students, "If you don't know what is troubling a child, ask him, maybe he'll tell you." And often he did; although it never proved easy for a clinician to quiet down and hear what the child was saying. To do so he had to brush away his literalistic biases about what words naturally meant and pay more attention to what the child meant. He had to set aside also many of his diagnostic presentiments about what kinds of packages children come wrapped up in. And as for listening to adults; that is even harder. So often the adult has long since lost track himself of what it was he started out to say, many years ago. By the time he meets the clinician he can repeat only words and words, wearily making the kinds of vocal sounds that quickly reverberate themselves away into lexical emptiness.

If we were to develop a psychology of man from his own point of view—a psychology of man himself—it could obviously be neither a prejudiced kind of psychology, nor an objective one. I repeat—*neither prejudiced, nor objective*! Under no condition could it be the kind of psychology that merely points objectively to a man and says, "That thing out there; let me prod it. I want to see which way it will hop." Instead, it would have to be an experiential kind of psychology that would enable one to look all about him and say, "So this is how it is to be a man. So this is the way the world looks through his eyes. So this is the sense of his behavior. So this is his framework of cause and effect. So this, at last, is the mind of man."

At first we—my students and I—started calling this new psychological point of view, "role theory." The term seemed a likely name for what we were thinking. Not only was our route to the understanding of clients via an appreciation of the part they were attempting to enact, but psychotherapy, we soon discovered, could often be developed in terms of a way of life—a role—rather than in terms of so-called insights which reduced behavior to motivation, and motivation, in turn, to atavism.

Soon, however, the term "role" began to appear widely in psychological literature in quite a different sense. So we temporarily abandoned use of the term and began talking about a psychology of personal constructs. By this we did not mean merely a kind of perceptual theory, nor did we mean merely the realm of objects that fall within a given man's purview. Rather, we had in mind a psychology that dealt with the manner in which man comes to grips with his world of reality. The task was not so much to choose a theory of psychology for ourselves but, first of all, to establish a frame of reference in terms of which we might appreciate any man's personal theory of psychology. For, it seemed to us, it would have to be at the level of the personal construction of events, without which construction no man has any psychological footing, that the task of the psychologist must begin. Indeed, only at this level of the man's personal construction, can it ever be said that an event becomes a stimulus for him, or that an action becomes an expression of motives within him, or that his behavior is learned. To overlook this crucial point at which events start to be interpreted as psychological variables is to become enmeshed in what Bertrand Russell and others have called the subject-predicate error of the Indo-European mode of thought.

So we turned to a psychology of personal constructs. The venture, so far, has been exciting. There have been hidden surprises waiting for us along the way. Some of them have been occasions for dismay. I have already mentioned one surprise when I said that we would have to abandon prejudice and *objectivity* both! The very thought of abandoning objectivity sounds just as wicked to the narrowly indoctrinated psychologist of today as the idea of abandoning other forms of revealed truth sounded to the fundamentalists of another generation. Yet the doctrine of objectivity, as currently practiced in our world of psychology, looks to events as if they somehow abstracted themselves and spoke out in their own direct revelations of profound truth.

As we pursue further our line of thinking the concept of *stimulus* drops out also. There is simply no way to keep it in. *Reinforcement* becomes a question-begging term, at least in the sense in which it is commonly used. The whole conceptual area of *motivation*, as we know it in psychology today, vanished. Even *learning* is washed up; when the theory gets through with it it sounds like a synonym for the verb *to become*. In brief, this is not a theory for anyone who likes to display his Ph.D. diploma on the wall of his office, for several times a day he will find it glowering down on him in silent disapproval.

Now, having stirred up this hornets' nest of scientific convictions, let us deal with a limited part of the confusion we have attempted to create. (This is known as establishing an initial atmosphere of unacceptance, in the hope that in what follows the listener will grasp more eagerly for a little of something he can make sense out of.) We have chosen the topic of hostility. Hostility is one of the clinician's most crucial concerns. Let us see what happens when we apply this kind of thinking to it. What will it help him to notice? What will it lead him to look for? What new openings to psychotherapeutic movement will it provide for his client?

In the psychological realm of discourse, as contrasted with some of our better developed realms of discourse such as physics, most of our concepts are projections of two principal axes of reference—pleasure versus pain and good versus evil. Since it is assumed that each of us automatically heads for pleasure and away from pain while trying to get other people to head for good and away from evil, our psychological dimensions all begin to look like one-way streets, every one of them leading in the same general direction. One is reminded of the fellow who offered to solve any city's traffic problem, simply by marking a system of one-way streets, all leading out of town. The hitch in such a traffic system is that it does not provide the citizens with any true mobility. So it is with much of our psychological thinking; our conceptual network is so aligned that it does not permit us much mobility in dealing with our personal problems.

The concept of hostility, as commonly understood, is just such a notion. If you have got it, it may be fun but it's bad. If the fellow next door has got it, you may get hurt. The only thing to do with hostility is get rid of it or get away from it. Nice people try to keep it bottled up and psychoanalyzed people try to dump it out somewhere where it won't do any harm.

The usual understanding of hostility is that it is an impulse to hurt someone, to cause pain. This definition, it must be noticed, puts the limiting condition in the experience of the other person, not in the experience of the hostile person himself. Yet if we are to have a psychology of man's own experiences we must anchor our basic concepts in that personal experience, not in the experiences he causes others to have or which he appears to seek to cause others to have. Thus, if we wish to use a concept of hostility at all, we have to ask, what is the experiential nature of hostility from the standpoint of the person who has it. Only by answering this question in some sensible way will we arrive at a concept which makes pure psychological sense, rather than sociological or moral sense merely.

What is it like to be hostile? How does it feel? How does hostility creep into the human enterprise? In order to get the answers to these questions we have to talk to people like Procrustes, rather than Theseus. It is in this respect that psychoanalysis has made two priceless contributions to the symptomatic understanding of hostility, although I fear the analyses have done little to develop hostility as a psychological concept.

One of these contributions has to do with the recognition of what is symptomatically called, "passive hostility." This is seen as a way of inflicting injury by letting people stew in their own juice. It involves keeping someone's juice as hot as possible in eager anticipation of his falling in and, when he does fall in, piously pointing out to him how hot it is.

The other psychoanalytic contribution to our understanding of hostility symptoms is the description of incorporative hostility that robs others of their individuality and brings them helplessly into the orbit of the hostile person's world. This is what is sometimes called, in the poetic idiom of psychoanalysis, *oral hostility*. One of its manifestations has been coined into the currently popular phrase, "smother love."

But while the clinical experience of psychoanalysts, as well as that of psychotherapists of other persuasions, has led us all to a greater sensitivity to the variety of symptoms through which hostility is expressed, it has not so far resulted in better conceptualization, nor has it contributed much to the improvement of psychological theory dealing with the essential nature of hostility. Hostility is still seen as the urge to hurt someone, sometimes as the urge to hurt one's self. Even guilt is seen as the urge to hurt turned against the self as substitute—preparing one's own juice to be stewed in. Oral hostility, still viewed as the urge to hurt, is described as the impulse to destroy as one destroys food by eating it.

But I think the Greeks, at least the early Greeks who mostly understood the impulses of man in terms of his adventures, probably sensed something about hostility that is easily missed by those who feel they must deal with man in terms of his pathological symptoms. In this early story of Procrustes they appear to have embodied part of what they knew about the nature of the hostile man. There is something humanly plausible about Procrustes. He did what people do. He could not bear the thought of being wrong in his estimate of the stature of his guests. Rather than change his estimate he corrected his guests. And so this part of the Thesean story has lived and the poetic imagery of the Procrustean bed has survived to this day.

It is at the point of Procrustes' failure to anticipate correctly the stature of his guests that the legend places the fulcrum of his hostility. But this point of frustration is still only the fulcrum. It takes a massive weight of personal meaning to tip the scales. In my paraphrasing I have underscored one original feature of the tale by describing Procrustes as an ardent host who was genuinely interested in people. It was only because so much of his world was centered in his claim to knowing the true dimensions of man that the invalidating evidence assumed such overwhelming proportions. When he peeked through the bedroom door that world of his threatened to collapse.

How to save it! If his bed—his only bed—did not fit his guest, his guest must be made to fit the bed. Regardless of the cost, the validity of his bed and the integrity of his world—which were one and the same thing—must be sustained. That piece of psychological furniture was for him, not just a bed, but a vital institution—more important by far than the physical well-being of just one guest. It was a key to his way of life. Under the circumstances he did the only thing as far as he could see, that made sense. And, as I said before, it is really too bad that Theseus did not sense the situation and do something constructive about it. Ambitious people are so often dull-witted about such matters.

From the standpoint of a psychology of personal constructs, each person, like Procrustes, devises as best he can a structure for making sense out of a world of humanity in which he finds himself. Some of this personal structure is cast in terms of words and he can name the parts for us. But most of it is expressed only in terms of talk—which is something quite different from semantic communication—and some of it stands way back in the shadows of human expression as a background pattern that is never traced with the fine lines of verbal detail.

Without such patterned structure it would appear that no man can come to grips with his seething world of people, nor can he establish himself as a psychological entity. If one wishes, he can look upon this personal structure of man as a network of hypotheses about human nature. But if he does think of it in terms of hypotheses he should be prepared to envision hypotheses that are not verbally formulated as well as the kind of explicitly stated hypotheses that are familiar to research settings. In any case, like all psychological structure and all hypotheses, this personal construct system tempts man to make predictions. And predictions, in turn, have a way of either occurring or not occurring, and usually being rather obvious about it. It is in terms of his predictions, then, that the mind of man comes at last into firm contact with reality. I would go even further and say that *it is only in terms of his predictions* that man ever touches the real world about him.

Having gone this far with our theorizing it seems that we have involved ourselves in kind of a psychological theory in which the notion of validation will have to play a major part. This is quite all right with us. It fits our clinical experience. It fits the report[2] experiences of others. It offers promise of a psychology that will turn its attention to man's plastic future rather than to his fateful past.

Man predicts what will happen. If it happens, his prediction is validated, the grounds he used in making it are strengthened, and he can venture further next time. If it does not happen, his prediction is invalidated, the structure he used in making the prediction is brought into question, and the road ahead becomes less clear.

If now we wish to understand the implications of an event in a person's life, we shall, in terms of his kind of psychology, look not only at the event but also at the kind of wager that was laid on it. Events come and go without necessarily having anything to do with a person's psychological processes. Of themselves, they are neither validating nor invalidating, nor is it meaningful to describe some of them as reinforcements. Validity is a matter of the relationship between the event as it happened and what the person expected to happen. More correctly stated, it is the relationship between the event as he construed it to happen and what he anticipated.

It is in this relationship between anticipation and realization that the real fate of man lies. It is a fate in which he himself is always a key participant, not simply the victim. To miss this point and to allow ourselves to become preoccupied with independent forces, sociodynamics, psychodynamics, leprechaun theory, demonology, or stimulus-response mechanics, is to lose sight of the essential feature of the whole human enterprise.

Now let us strip the Procrustean legend of its rich narrative structure and trace the central theme of hostility in the more barren terminology of personal construct theory. A person has a construct system. It gives him identity. Right or wrong, it serves to put him in touch with reality. It provides him with grounds for formulating his anticipations; including his anticipations about people. Then, one day, perhaps after a long wait, his expectations are not confirmed. He is staggered by the implications of his disconfirmation for he has wagered more of his construct system on the outcome of his venture than he can afford to lose. If he accepts the outcome and all its presumed implications he will be left in a state of deep and pervading confusion.

But wait! There is still something he can do to save the situation. If he acts quickly he may be able to force the outcome to conform to his original expectations and give him a last-minute confirmation of his major premises about human nature. This is the hostile

[2] Editors' note: [sic]

choice. The key to understanding hostility from the standpoint of the person himself is in this instant of decision. Or is it an instant of impulse—it makes no difference; this is where it is!

In the language of research, we may say that the hostile person distorts his data to fit his hypotheses. In the language of the classroom, he puts people in their place. In the language of economics, he extorts tokens of subservience to his system of values. In the language of the child, he threatens to scream loud enough to prove to the neighbors that his parents have made a horrible mistake. In the language of the divorce court, since his spouse did not conform to his idealized image of what a wife should be, the husband sees to it that she is exhibited to the world as the other kind of woman, "the kind of person he has always known most women were." Ditto, hostile wives and "the kind of person they always knew men were!" In the language of nations—we all know how clearly everything the enemy does expresses "his cruel and vicious nature."

Instead of saying that such goings-on are the outcroppings of hostility—hostility being an extrapersonal force that is supposed to invest the organism—we are saying that they are the hostility. The essence of hostility is not in its motivational property—anyone who is alive is on the move—but in its characteristic way of following up one's mistakes. It is the substitution of extortion for problem solving. It is the attempt to collect a bet on a horse that has already lost. The hostile person turns from events as they are to payoffs that belie reality. "See," he says, "I got paid, didn't I? That means I was right all along."

Psychologists make frequent use of the frustration-aggression hypothesis—the notion that the greater one's disappointment the more violently he will react to it. What we have been saying may appear to be a restatement of that hypothesis. But there are important differences. Hostility is not aggression, although the two terms are frequently used synonymously. The simplest way to look at aggression is to view it as adventuresomeness. It means actively formulating one's expectations specifically about many things, about big things and, sometimes, about remote matters. It means taking steps to bring one's hunches to test. And it often means betting large stakes on the outcome.

While an aggressive person sticks his neck out, he is not necessarily hostile. He does not necessarily extort confirmation of personal hypotheses that have already proved themselves to be invalid. An aggressive conversationalist may press a point to the place where his companions have to come out and say exactly what they think. That, of course, is what the aggressive but nonhostile person wants to know. His companions may be furious at finding themselves smoked out but, unless their aggressive friend has a streak of hostility in him, he will not try to compromise them into agreeing with him. He only wants to know.

If we take the traditional view that hostility is the impulse to hurt, it is easy to see how aggression can be interpreted as hostility. The moment someone is hurt he cries "foul" or "ouch," and the aggressive person is immediately labeled as hostile, not so much because of any psychological property of his own make-up but because of the make-up of the person who is hurt. Of course, if we are rigorous about it, we can hold to the definition that hostility is present only when the actor *wants* to hurt someone. But this definition is hard to maintain in a world of social thought that describes persons in terms of how they are reacted to, rather than in terms of what they are up to. A psychology that is based on the outlook of man himself does not find it very helpful to define hostility in terms of its anticipated effect on others. It asks, instead, for an understanding of the hostile person in terms of what is at stake in his own life. If we want to understand Procrustes we talk to Procrustes, not Theseus. We talk to him about his bed. We talk to him about his role as a host. We find out what he expects guests to be like.

Now it is quite possible for an aggressive person to become hostile and, conversely, it is quite possible for a hostile person to pursue his extortionism by aggressive means. The aggressive conversationalist we mentioned may, for example, get himself so far out on a limb that when he discovers what his friends actually do think he may not be able to take it. He may then go to pieces in anxious confusion. Or he may pull in his horns. But he may—he just may—take the hostile course of action and try to put his friends in some kind of spot where they appear to confirm his point in spite of the realities of the social situation. On the other hand, take the person who is hostile to begin with. In his frantic efforts to make the data fit the hypothesis he may resort to vigorous measures. We can then say he is also aggressive. Not all hostile people do it this way; some express their hostility very effectively by the most passive of means. But they can. And when they do, it is correct to speak of aggressive hostility.

The frustration-aggression hypothesis, as any psychologist will tell you, is not a simple formula to apply. In order to use the formula one has to introduce a number of qualifications, both as to what is to be labeled frustration and what is to be construed as aggression. Nor can we, from the standpoint of the psychology of personal constructs, relabel the formula as a frustration-hostility hypothesis. The hostility is not proportional to the frustration—to say that would be to reduce the formula to the stimulus-response paradigm. The hostility is in the type of solution the person attempts—that is the personal construct theoretical view.

What about the person who is sadistic? Can we say that he is simply trying to make his experiment with social relations yield affirmative evidence? What if he feels like jumping up and down with glee and excitement every time he sees a person writhing in pain? Or what about the military flyers who slap each other on the back and show great delight at having scored a hit on a military target? Are they thinking of the agony they have left there on the ground? In either of these instances, our understanding of hostility would not place the psychological value primarily on the pain others experienced—even though we may reserve the right to judge such acts in terms of moral or social values—but on what is confirmed in the act. The sadist may (indeed, from our clinical experience we believe that he does) see in the other person's injury a long overdue confirmation of his own outlook, a confirmation that has been denied him in the natural state of affairs. The military aviator probably tries not to think of what is going on down on the ground in the target area in the wake of his bomb. In his case the suffering is less likely to be a relevant psychological variable. In both cases, what is happening to the other person is incidental, what is happening to the person himself is what is crucial.

It may be helpful to see hostility in the flesh. Before we illustrate in terms of case material, however, let us review the essential features of hostility from the standpoint of the psychology of personal constructs. A person construes human nature in his own way. He makes social predictions on the basis of this construction. To set the stage they must be crucial predictions; that is to say, he must have wagered more on them than he can afford to lose—more of his construct system, that is. He turns up invalidating evidence. It is clear that he was wrong about people. He can no longer ignore the fact. Moreover, he was overwhelmingly wrong—basically wrong. In the face of the harsh facts he can, of course, revise his outlook. But the revision would shake him so deeply that he is reluctant to undertake it. Alternatively, he could let matters ride—say to himself, "So I just don't understand people very well." But this too is an alternative he is reluctant to choose. Finally, he can close his eyes to reality and attempt to make people fit the construct bed his system provides. This is the hostile choice.

Consider a young woman, aged thirty. She grew up in a home where she was secure in her parents' love, where her father was a stable and constant figure and the neighborhood, with its beaches and sand dunes, was a safe and ever-interesting place to roam in search of childhood adventure. The only important male figure in her life, aside from her father, was a boy who was fenced out of that world with social taboos. At the turn of adolescence her girlfriends start to desert her and the forms of play they have enjoyed together and direct their attention to the female pursuit of catching boys with their newly found charms. What she had discovered, up to this time, to be true about both males and females now seems to be invalid. At first she is only puzzled. Later she is more than puzzled—she is confused and anxious. Her mother, too, seems perturbed that she seems so immature. What the child does not realize, of course, is that the mother knows that her own years are rapidly running out and she is unduly apprehensive lest her daughter still be a child when the time comes to go it alone. Soon the mother's death comes. The father is prostrated with grief and he is perceived by the child as letting her down. Her first efforts are to get herself another man. She will have a man, the kind of strong man her outlook insists men must be. Even cruelty is acceptable, if it is accompanied by strength. Yet, whatever male substitute she finds, the apparent failure of her father to live up to her expectations of him is still, to her, an inescapable fact. For a time she extorts from him the tokens of paternal support—clothes, luxuries, indulgences. This is hostility. But hostility is difficult to contain within reasonable bounds. She now has a disillusioned version of what men are—all men. To make a long story short, she fits all men, including her husband, into this Procrustean Bed. They are often surprised at how neatly she tricks them into confirming her hypotheses about the contemptible weak-kneed creatures. And so, to some extent, is she. Her gay and tantalizing manner is misleading. Like Procrustes, she is interested in people, she cannot live without their company. Like Procrustes, she is an excellent conversationalist. And, like Procrustes, she has a bed. Soon each man in her life wakes up to find that he has been chopped down to just the right size to fit it. This is hostility in the flesh.

Most psychotherapists understand, regardless of their theoretical persuasion, that the key to the alleviation of hostility lies in the proper use of aggression. The psychoanalysts and others look upon aggression as the dynamic feature of the hostile pattern and insist that it must be allowed to vent itself before it can be brought under self-control. The Rogerians provide an atmosphere of acceptance for their clients, in which we could say, in terms of the frustration-aggression hypothesis, that the frustration is minimized in order to keep the aggressive pressure down to a point where the person can gently come to terms with himself. (There is, of course, much more to both of these points of view.) Certainly both of these outlooks, I would insist, can be taken as grounds by clinicians for doing something effective about the hostility.

From the standpoint of the psychology of personal constructs, however, the emphasis is placed not on the conceptualization forces driving the individual in spite of himself but on what he himself does. Hostility is not a dynamism in the personality, it is part of the personality pattern. Unfortunate people are not acted upon by hostility, they themselves make the choices which are describable as hostile. The psychotherapist turns to aggressive experimentation under proper psychotherapeutic controls, not to drain it out, but in order to help the client find other ways of dealing with the invalidity that confronts him. He reinstates imaginative adventure, but with fresh ways of dealing with the outcomes. He helps the client to make use of negative evidence instead of displacing it with extorted and unrealistic positive evidence.

Probably all of us have daily bouts in some measure with hostility. Most of us are traditionally inclined to see this hostility as a force welling up within us. When seen in others, it is easy to interpret only as a desire to hurt, especially if we must bear the brunt. Yet whether we experience it in ourselves, or have to deal with it in our associates, the key to its understanding is an appreciation of the person himself. Behind the mask of his hostility, we find these key features: deep concern with social relations, his far-reaching convictions regarding human nature, the wager that he could not afford to lose, and his frantic effort to collect winnings long after the race was run and hopelessly lost.

12

Man's Construction of His Alternatives[1]

This paper, throughout, deals with half-truths only. Nothing that it contains is, or is intended to be, wholly true. The theoretical statements propounded are no more than partially accurate constructions of events which, in turn, are no more than partially perceived. Moreover, what we propose, even in its truer aspects, will eventually be overthrown and displaced by something with more truth in it. Indeed, our theory is frankly designed to contribute effectively to its own eventual overthrow and displacement.

We think this is a good way for psychologists to theorize. When a scientist propounds a theory he has two choices: he can claim that what he says has been dictated to him by the real nature of things, or he can take sole responsibility for what he says and claim only that he has offered one man's hopeful construction of the realities of nature. In the first instance he makes a claim to objectivity in behalf of his theory, the scientist's equivalent of a claim to infallibility. In the second instance he offers only the hope that he may have hit upon some partial truth that may serve as a clue to inventing something better and he invites others to follow this clue to see what they can make of it. In this latter instance he does not hold up his theoretical proposal to be judged so much in terms of whether it is the truth at last or not—for he assumes from the outset that ultimate truth is not so readily at hand—but to be judged in terms of whether his proposition seems to lead toward and give way to fresh propositions; propositions which, in turn, may be more true than anything else has been thus far.

One of the troubles with what are, otherwise, good theories in the various fields of science is the claim to infallibility that is so often built into their structure. Even those theories which are built upon objective observation or upon first-hand experience make this claim by their failure to admit that what is observed is not revealed but only construed. In fact, the more objectively supported the theory at the time of its inception, the more likely it is to cause trouble after it has served its purpose. A conclusion supported by the facts is likely to be a good one at the time it is drawn. But, because facts themselves are open to reconstruction, such a theory soon becomes a dogmatism that may serve only to blind us to new perceptions of the facts.

Take, for example, the body of theoretical assumptions that Freud propounded out of his experience with psychoanalysis. There was so much truth in what he said—so much new truth. But like most theories of our times, psychoanalysis, as a theory, was conceived as an absolute truth, and, moreover, it was designed in such a manner that it tended to defy both logical examination and experimental validation. As the years go by, Freudianism, which deserves to be remembered as a brave outpost on the early frontier of psychological thought, is condemned to end its days as a crumbling stockade of proprietary dogmatism. Thus, as with other far-seeing claims to absolute truth, history will have a difficult time deciding if Freudianism did more to accelerate psychological progress during the first half of the Twentieth Century than it did to impede progress during the last half.

This business of absolutism in modern science and the havoc it creates is a matter that has been given a good deal of thought in recent decades. It has been attacked on several fronts. First of all, modern science has itself attacked dogmatism through its widespread use of the method of experimentation. But experimentation, if assumed to be a way of receiving direct revelations from nature, can often be found living quite happily side by side with dogmatisms of the lowest order.

There is nothing especially revelational about events that happen in a laboratory—other events that happen elsewhere are just as real and are just as worth taking account of. Even the fact that an event took place in a manner predicted by the experimenter gives it no particular claim to being a special revelation from nature. If an experimenter's predictions come true, it means only that he has hit upon one of many possible systems for making predictions that come true. He may be no more than a wee bit closer to a genuine understanding of things as they really are. Indeed, the fact that he has hit upon one such way of predicting outcomes may even blind him to alternatives which might have proved far more productive in the long run.

Absolutism is coming under other forms of attack. It has been pointed out, for example, that the subject-predicate form of our Indo-European languages has led us to confound objects with what is said about them. Thus every time we open our mouths to say

[1] First published in Lindzey, G. (Ed.). (1958). *The assessment of human motives* (pp. 33–64). Holt, Rinehart, Winston. Republished in Maher, B. (Ed.). (1969). *Clinical psychology and personality: The selected papers of George Kelly* (pp. 66–93). Wiley. Published here by permission of Wiley.

Collected Papers of the Pioneer of Constructivist Psychology: George A. Kelly, First Edition. Edited by David A. Winter and Nick Reed.

something, we break forth with a dogmatism. Each sentence, instead of sounding like a proposal of an idea to be examined in the light of personal experience, echoes through the room like the disembodied rumblings of an oracle. Even as we try to describe a theory of personal constructions of events, one that stands in contrast to theories that claim to spring from events directly, we are caught up in the assumptions and structure of the very language upon which we depend for communication. In view of this fact, we can think of no better way of disclaiming the assumptions of our language than by introducing this paper with the paradoxical statement that we are proposing half-truths only.

A second feature of this paper is its outright repudiation of the notion of motivation. Since the topic of the conference stories, in which we have been so graciously invited to participate, is "The Assessment of Human Motives," such a repudiation may appear to be in bad taste. It seems a little like being honored with an invitation to preach a sermon in church, and then taking advantage of the solemn occasion in order to present the case for atheism. Yet the forthcoming volume on the assessment of human motives may not lose flavor from this kind of seasoning. Perhaps one chapter of heresy may even strengthen the reader's convictions about human motives, just as an occasional rousing speech on atheism might do more than a monotony of sermons to bring a church congregation face-to-face with its own convictions—or lack of them.

Certainly the repudiation of "motives" as a construct is a major undertaking, not to be ventured into without giving some thought to its consequences. For a period roughly corresponding to the Christian era, metaphysics, including psychology, has conceptualized its spiritual realm in terms of a trichotomy just as Christianity has envisioned itself in terms of a trinity. The classic trichotomy is variously called by such terms as cognition, conation, and affection; or intellect, will, and emotion; or even, in somewhat more modem terms, thought, action and feeling. Psychologists keep coming back to this trichotomous division, perhaps because they have never been able to venture beyond it. For us to say now that we propose to abandon motives will seem to many listeners to be a kind of unforgivable sin, something like the unforgivable sin of rejecting the Holy Ghost.

In the classic psychological trichotomy, cognition, on the one hand, has been viewed as a realm governed by verbalized rationality, while affection, on the other, has been viewed as a very chaotic, though often pleasant place, where inarticulate irrationality is in command. Conation, the middle category which deals with behavior or determination to act, has been caught between the other two, sometimes believed to be swayed by the rationality of the cognitive mind, but at other times, suspected of having a secret allegiance to the whimsical irrationality of feeling and emotion.

Because the topic of motivation falls into this disputed area where modem man has had such a difficult time reconciling rationality with irrationality, we propose to start our serious discussion at this particular point. We would like to deal with those matters which are called rational—and, therefore, by quirk of our language structure assumed actually to be rational—together with those matters which are called irrational—for the same reason—both in the very same psychological terms. In doing so we shall, if our previous experiences repeat themselves, be perceived by some as capitulating to the classic rationalism of Thomas Aquinas, and by others as giving hostages to the supposed intuitive irrationality of Freud, Rogers, or Sullivan. Not that we really mind being bracketed with any of these great names; but rather the burden of our comments, it seems to us, rests on other grounds.

This is the risk we take. Why? Why will some see this as conforming to classical rationality and others see it as lapsing into irrationality? We have already mentioned the tendency to confound objects with what is said about them. Some philosophers, Bertrand Russell being possibly the first and foremost, have seen this tendency to confound words and facts as being embedded in the subject-predicate structure of our language. But it involves also the highly questionable *law of the excluded middle*, a law accepted as a basic principle of logic for the past twenty-four hundred years, though now under sporadic attack.

What this law proposes is that for any proposition there is only one alternative. I call an object a spade. There is only one alternative to calling it a spade—to call it not a spade! I can't say, "to heck with it," or "who cares," or "who brought that up," or that the object cannot be sensibly called either a spade or not a spade; I have to stick with one or the other. Once the object is accused of being a spade it has to plead innocent or guilty, or I have to plead its innocence or guilt in its behalf.

Now if we combine this dictum with the subject-predicate mode of thought we put ourselves in a stringent position with respect to our world. We call an object a spade. Not only do we, therefore, imply that it is a spade because we cannot say that it is not a spade, but we put the onus of choosing between the two alternatives on the object itself. We disclaim responsibility for our propositions and try to make the objects we talk about hang themselves on the horns of the dilemmas we invent for dealing with them. If a woman is accused of being a witch, she has to be either a witch or not a witch—it is up to her. The speaker disclaims all responsibility for the dilemma he has imposed upon her.

For centuries Western Man has roamed his world impaling every object he has met on the horns of the dilemmas he chose to fashion out of his language. In fact, an individual, if he was very bright and had a vocabulary well stocked with psychological terms, could do a pretty substantial job of impaling himself. Recently so many people have learned to do it in so many ingenious ways that it appears that half the world will have to be trained in psychotherapy in order to keep the other half off its own hooks. Yet, even at that, it may be what most of the psychotherapists are doing is lifting people off one set of hooks and hanging them on other more comfortable, more socially acceptable, hooks.

Let us see if we can make this point a little clearer. For example, on occasion I may say of myself—in fact, on occasion I *do* say of myself—"I am an introvert." "I," the subject, "am an introvert," the predicate. The language form of the statement clearly places the onus of being an introvert on the subject—me. What I actually am, the words say, is an introvert.

The listener, being the more or less credulous person to whom I make the statement, says to himself, "So George Kelly is an introvert—I always suspected he was." Or he may say, "Him an introvert? He's no introvert," a response which implies scarcely less credulity on the part of my listener. Yet the proper interpretation of my statement is that *I construe* myself to be an introvert, or, if I am merely being coy or devious, I am inveigling *my listener into construing me* in terms of introversion. The point that gets lost in the shuffle of words is the psychological fact that I have identified myself in terms of a personal construct—"introversion." If my listener is uncritical enough to be taken in by this quirk of language, he may waste a lot of time either in believing that he must construe me as an introvert or in disputing the point.

In clinical interviewing, and particularly in psychotherapeutic interviewing, when the clinician is unable to deal with such a statement as a personal construction rather than as fact or fallacy, the hour is likely to come to a close with both parties annoyed with each other and both dreading their next appointment. But more than this, if I say of myself that I am an introvert, I am likely to be caught in my own subject-predicate trap. Even the inner self—my self—becomes burdened with the onus of actually being an introvert or of finding some way to be rid of the introversion that has climbed on my back. What has happened is that I named myself with a name and, having done so, too quickly forgot who invented the name and what he had on his mind at the time. From now on I try frantically to cope with what I have called myself. Moreover, my family and friends are often quite willing to join in the struggle.

Now back specifically to the law of the excluded middle. Here, too, we find a failure to take into account a psychological fact, the fact that human thought is essentially constructive in nature and that even the thinking of logicians and mathematicians is no exception. I say that I am an introvert, whatever that is. If I now go ahead and apply the law of the excluded middle, I come up with the dilemma that I must continue to claim either to be an introvert or not an introvert—one or the other. But is this necessarily so: may not introversion turn out to be a construct which is altogether irrelevant? If it is not relevant is it any more meaningful to say that I am not an introvert than to say that I am? Yet classical logic fails to make any distinction between its negatives and its irrelevancies; while modern psychology ought to make it increasingly clear to each of us that no proposition has more than a limited range of relevance, beyond which it makes no sense either to affirm or deny. So we now ought to visualize propositions which are not universal in their range of application but useful only within a restricted range of convenience. For each proposition, then, we see three alternatives, not two: it can be affirmed, it can be denied, or it can be declared irrelevant in the context to which it is applied. Thus, we argue, not for the inclusion of the long excluded middle—something between the yes and the no—but for a third possibility that is beyond the meaningful range of yes and no.

Apply this more psychological way of thinking to the proposition, "I am an introvert." Instead of lying awake trying to decide whether I am or am not an introvert, or taking frantic steps, as so many do, to prove that I am not, I simply go off to sleep with the thought that, until the construct of introversion is demonstrated to be of some practical usefulness in my case, there is no point of trying to decide whether I am or not or what to do about it if I am. Thus we treat the subject-predicate problem and the excluded middle problem in pretty much the same way—we insist on demonstrating relevance before we lose any sleep over a proposition,

Let us try to summarize our criticisms of the two features of Western thought which have gone unchallenged for more than two thousand years. First of all, there is the dogmatism of subject-predicate language structure that is often presented under the guise of objectivity. According to this dogmatism, when I say that Professor Lindzey's left shoe is an "introvert," everyone looks at his shoe as if this were something his shoe was responsible for. Or if I say that Professor Cattell's head is "discursive," everyone looks over at him, as if the proposition had popped out of his head instead of out of mine. Don't look at his head! Don't look at that shoe! Look at me; I'm the one who is responsible for the statement. After you figure out what I mean you can look over there to see if you make any sense out of shoes and heads by construing them the way I do. It will not be easy to do this, for it means abandoning one of the most ancient ways of thinking and talking to ourselves.

As far as the law of the excluded middle in this particular context is concerned, it does not matter whether a person has ever heard of this law or not, or whether he has ever sat down to puzzle out a similar notion on his own. The law is an everyday feature of nearly every educated man's more intellectualized thought processes. The law says, assuming that the term "introvert" ever has meaning, that that shoe, at which we looked a moment ago, has to be construed either as an introvert or as not an introvert; it has simply got to be seen as one or the other. There is no middle ground.

Some people argue against the law of the excluded middle by claiming that the shoe could be a little introvertish, but not completely introvert, or that it could be a little nonintrovertish, though not wholly nonintrovert. This is the notion of shades of gray that can be perceived between black and white. But this notion of reifying the excluded middle by talking about grays is not what we are proposing. In fact, we see this gray thinking as a form of concretism that merely equivocates and fails to get off the ground into the atmosphere of abstraction.

What we are saying, instead, is that "introversion" may well enough be a term that has meaning in some contexts, but that it does not go well with shoes. Since it does not apply to shoes, it makes no more sense to say that Professor Lindzey's left shoe is not an introvert than to say that it is. Thus we see three possibilities, not two as the law would insist: the shoe is an introvert; the shoe is not an introvert; and the shoes do not fall within the context of the construct of introversion versus nonintroversion. The third possibility is not a middle proposition in any intermediate sense, but rather a kind of outside, beyond the pale, kind of proposition.

So much for a summary of this section of our discourse. In spite of our criticisms let us not say that the inadequacies we have pointed out prevented our language and thought from leading us along a path of progress. Remember that we believe that half-truths serve to pave the way toward better truths. Time spent with a half-truth is not necessarily wasted; it may have been exceedingly profitable. In order to appreciate a half-truth one has to examine two things: what it replaced, and what it led up to. Let us see what the kind of thing we have been criticizing actually replaced. Let us compare it with more primitive modes of language and thought.

Western thinking, which has pretty much overrun the world recently, takes the very practical view that a word is beholden to the object it is used to describe. The object determines it. This is a moderate improvement over the so-called magical way of thinking which has it that the object is beholden to the word. The improvement has been the basis of scientific thinking, particularly the experimentalism that has psychologists and others bubbling with so much excitement these days.

Let us see how the improvement works. Say the word and the object will jump out at you—that is magical thinking; very bad! Prod the object and the word will jump out at you—that is objective thinking; very good! Worth publishing! Say "Genie, come genie" and hope that a genie will pop out of the bottle—that is magical; no good! Kick the bottle until either a genie pops out or does not pop out—now that is *science!*

But there is something one can do besides shouting, "Genie, come genie," or kicking the bottle through a series of statistically controlled experiments. He can ask himself, and the other people who have worked themselves up over the genie business, just what they are trying to get at. This is what the skilled psychotherapist does in dealing with the thoughts of man. It is based on the notion that "genie" is a construct that someone erected in order to find his way through a maze of events. The approach is not a substitute for experimentation but a useful prelude to it. It is a proper substitute, however, for random measurement of verbalizations.

This is the way we see the matter: magical thinking has it that the object is beholden to the word—when the word is spoken the object must produce itself. So-called objective thinking, under which it has been possible to make great scientific progress, says that the word is beholden to the object—kick the bottle to validate the word. If, however, we build our sciences on a recognition of the psychological nature of thought we take a third position—the word is beholden to the person who utters it, or, more properly speaking, to the *construction* system, that complex of personal constructs of which it is a part.

This concern with personal meaning should prove no less valuable to the scientist than it has to the psychotherapist. It stems from the notion that when a person uses a word he is expressing, in part, his own construction of events. One comes to understand the communication, therefore, not by assuming the magical existence of the word's counterpart in reality and then invoking that counterpart by incantation; nor does he understand it by scrounging through a pile of accumulated facts to see if one of them will own up to the word, but rather he understands the communication by examining the personal construction system within which the word arose and came to have intimate meaning for the individual who attempted to communicate.

How does this apply to motives? We have already said that we do not even use the term as a part of our own construction system, yet it enters our system, perforce, as a matter to be construed. If one catches his friends in the act of using such a term as "motives," how does he act? Does he put his fingers in his ears? Does he start kicking the bottle of reality to see if it produces the phenomenon? If it fails shall he accuse his friends of irrationality? We think not.

Again, if we so much as start to inquire into motivation as a construct, do we not thereby reify it? Or if we deal with a realm which so many believe is essentially irrational in nature, are we not capitulating ourselves to irrationality? And if we attempt to think rationally about the behavior of an individual who is acting irrationally, are we not closing our eyes to an irrationality that actually exists? Are we not hiding behind a safe intellectualism? All of these are questions that rise out of the long-accepted assumptions of a subject-predicate mode of thought that tries to make reality responsible for the words that are used to construe it. Because of the currency of this kind of interpretation we run the risk we mentioned a few moments ago—the risk of being bracketed with either the classic rationalists or the modern intuitionists.

Actually we are neither. Our position is that of a psychology of personal constructs, a psychologist's system for construing persons who themselves construe in all kinds of other ways. Thus I, Person A, use[2] Construct A′, a component construct within my own construction system, to understand Construct B′, a component construct within Person B's construction system. His B′ is not a truth revealed to him by nature. Nor is my A′ revealed to me by his human nature. Construct A′ is my responsibility, just as B′ is his. In each case the validity of the construct rests, among other things, upon its prophetic effectiveness, not upon any claim to external origin, either divine or natural.

Now let us hope we are in a safe position to deal with the assessment of human motives without appearing either to reify them or to talk nonsense. Our discussion might as well start where our thinking started.

Some twenty years or more ago a group of us were attempting to provide a traveling psychological clinic service to the schools in the state of Kansas. One of the principal sources of referrals was, of course, teachers. A teacher complained about a pupil. This word-bound complaint was taken as prima facie grounds for kicking the bottle—I mean examining the pupil. If we kicked the pupil around long enough and hard enough we could usually find some grounds to justify any teacher's complaint. This procedure was called in those days, just as it is still called, "diagnosis." It was in this manner that we conformed to the widely accepted requirements of the scientific method—we matched hypothesis with evidence and thus arrived at objective truth. In due course of time we

[2] Editors' note: This word has been inserted as a verb was missing in the original.

became quite proficient in making something out of teachers' complaints and we got so we could adduce some mighty subtle evidence. In short, we began to fancy ourselves as pretty sensitive clinicians.

Now as every scientist and every clinician knows and is fond of repeating, treatment depends upon diagnosis. First you find out what is wrong—really wrong. Then you treat it. In treatment you have several alternatives; you can cut it out of the person, or you can remove the child from the object, or you can alter the mechanism he employs to deal with the object, or you can compensate for the child's behavior by taking up a hobby in the basement, or teach the child to compensate for it, or if nothing better turns up, you can sympathize with everybody who has to put up with the youngster. But first, always first, you must kick the bottle to make it either confirm or reject your diagnostic hunches. So in Kansas we diagnosed pupils and, having impaled ourselves and our clients within our diagnoses, we cast about more or less frantically for ways of escape.

After persevering in this classical stupidity—the treatment-depends-on-objective-diagnosis stupidity—for more years than we like to count, we began to suspect that we were being trapped in some pretty fallacious reasoning. We would have liked to blame the teachers for getting us off on the wrong track. But we had verified their complaints, hadn't we? We had even made "differential diagnoses," a way of choosing up sides in the name-calling games commonly played in clinical staff meetings.

Two things became apparent. The first was that the teacher's complaint was not necessarily something to be verified or disproved by the facts in the case, but was, rather a construction of events in a way that, within the limits and assumptions of her personal construction system, made the most sense to her at the moment. The second was the realization that, in assuming diagnosis to be the independent variable and treatment the dependent variable, we had placed the cart before the horse. It would have been better if we had made our diagnoses in the light of changes that do occur in children or that can be made to occur, rather than trying to shape those changes to independent but irrelevant psychometric measurements or biographical descriptions.

What we would like to make clear is that both these difficulties have the same root—the traditional rationale of science that leads us to look for the locus of meaning of words in their objects of reference rather than in their subjects of origin. We hear a word and look to what is talked about rather than listen to the person who utters it. A teacher often complained that a child was "lazy." We turned to the child to determine whether she was right or not. If we found clear evidence that would support a hypothesis of laziness, then laziness was what it was—nothing else—and diagnosis was complete. Diagnosis having been accomplished, treatment was supposed to ensue. What does one do to cure laziness? While, of course, it was not quite as simple as this, the paradigm is essentially the one we followed.

Later we began to put "laziness" in quotes. We found that a careful appraisal of the teacher's construction system gave us a much better understanding of the meaning of the complaint. This, together with some further inquiry into the child's outlook, often enabled us to arrive at a vantage point from which one could deal with the problem in various ways. It occurred to us that we might, for example, help the teacher reconstrue the child in terms other than "laziness"—terms which gave her more latitude for exercising her own particular creative talents in dealing with him. Again, we might help the child deal with the teacher so as to alleviate her discomfort. And, of course, there was sometimes the possibility that a broader reorientation of the child toward himself and school matters in general would prove helpful.

We have chosen the complaint of "laziness" as our example for a more special reason. "Laziness" happens to be a popular motivational concept that has widespread currency among adults who try to get others to make something out of themselves. Moreover, our disillusionment with motivational conceptualization in general started with this particular term and arose out of the specific context of school psychological services.

Our present position regarding human motives was approached by stages. First we realized that even when a hypothesis of laziness was confirmed, there was little that could be said or done in consequence of such a finding. While this originally appeared to be less true of other motivational constructs, such as appetite or affection, in each instance the key to treatment, or even to differential prediction of outcomes, appeared to reside within the framework of other types of constructs.

Another observation along the way was that the teachers who used the construct of "laziness" were usually those who had widespread difficulties in their classrooms. Soon we reached the point in our practice where we routinely used the complaint of "laziness" as a point of departure for reorienting the teacher. It usually happened that there was more to be done with her than with the child. So it was, also, with other complaints cast in motivational terms. In general, then, we found that the most practical approach to so-called motivational problems was to try to reorient the people who thought in such terms. Complaints about motivation told us much more about the complainants than it did about their pupils.

This is a generalization that seems to get more and more support from our clinical experience. When we find a person who is more interested in manipulating people for his own purposes, we usually find him making complaints about their motives. When we find a person who is concerned about motives, he usually turns out to be one who is threatened by his fellowmen and wants to put them in their place. There is no doubt but that the construct of motives is one which is widely used but it usually turns out to be a part of the language of complaint about the behavior of other people. When it appears in the language of the client himself, as it does occasionally, it always—literally always—appears in the context of a kind of rationalization apparently designed to appease the therapist, not in the spontaneous utterances of the client who is in good rapport with his therapist.

One technique we came to use was to ask the teacher what the child would do if she did not try to motivate him. Often the teacher would insist that the child would do nothing—absolutely nothing—just sit! Then we would suggest that she try a nonmotivational approach and let him "just sit." We would ask her to observe how he went about "just sitting." Invariably the teacher would be able to report some extremely interesting goings-on. An analysis of what the "lazy" child did while he was being lazy often furnished her with her first glimpse into the child's world and provided her with her first solid grounds for communication with him. Some teachers found that their laziest pupils were those who could produce the most novel ideas; others that the term "laziness" had been applied to activities that they had simply been unable to understand or appreciate.

It was some time later that we sat down and tried to formulate the general principles that undergirded our clinical experiences with teachers and their pupils. The more we thought about it, the more it seemed that our problems had always resolved themselves into questions of what the child would do if left to his own devices rather than questions about the amount of his motivation. These questions of what the child would do seemed to hinge primarily on what alternatives his personal construction of the situation allowed him to sense. While his construed alternatives were not necessarily couched in language symbols, nor could the child always clearly represent his alternatives, even to himself, they nonetheless set the outside limits on his day-to-day behavior. In brief, whenever we got embroiled in questions of motivation we bogged down, the teachers bogged down, and the children continued to aggravate everybody within earshot. When we forgot about motives and set about understanding the practical alternatives which children felt they were confronted by, the aggravations began to resolve themselves.

What we have said about our experiences with children also turned up in our psychotherapeutic experiences with adults. After months or, in some cases, years of psychotherapy with the same client, it did often prove to be possible to predict his behavior in terms of motives. This, of course, was gratifying, but predictive efficiency is not the only criterion of a good construction, for one's understanding of a client should also point the way to resolving his difficulties. It was precisely at this point that motivational constructs failed to be of practical service, just as they had failed to be of service in helping children and teachers get along with each other. Always the psychotherapeutic solution turned out to be a reconstruing process, not a mere labeling of the client's motives. To be sure, there were clients who never reduced their reconstructions to precise verbal terms, yet still were able to extricate themselves from vexing circumstances. And there were clients who get along best under conditions of support and reassurance with a minimum of verbal structuring on the part of the therapist. But even in these cases, the solutions were not worked out in terms of anything that could properly be called motives, and the evidence always pointed to some kind of reconstruing process that enabled the client to make his choice between new sets of alternatives not previously open to him in a psychological sense.

Now, perhaps, it is time to launch into the third phase of our discussion. We started by making some remarks of a philosophical nature and from there we dropped back to recall some of the practical experience that first led us to question the construct of motivation. Let us turn now to the formulation of psychological theory and to the part that motivation plays in it.

A half century ago William McDougall published his little volume, *Physiological Psychology*. In the opening pages he called his contemporary psychologists' attention to the fact that the concept of *energy* had been invented by physicists in order to account for movement of objects, and that some psychologists had blandly assumed that they too would have to find a place for it in their systems. While McDougall was to go on in his lifetime to formulate a theoretical system based on instinctual drives and thus, it seems to us, failed to heed his own warning, what he said about the construct of energy still provides us with a springboard for expounding a quite different theoretical position.

The physical world presented itself to preclassical man as a world of solid objects. He saw matter as an essentially inert substance, rather than as a complex of related motion. His axes of reference were spatial dimensions—length, breadth, depth—rather than temporal dimensions. The flow of time was something he could do very little about and he was inclined to take a passive attitude toward it. Even mass, a dimension which lent itself to more dynamic interpretations, was likely to be construed in terms of size equivalents.

Classical man, as he emerged upon the scene, gradually became aware of motion as something that had eluded his predecessors. But, for him, motion was still superimposed upon nature's rocks and hills. Inert matter was still the phenomenon, motion was only the epiphenomenon. Action, vitality, and energy were the breath of life that had to be breathed into the inertness of nature's realities. In Classical Greece this thought was magnificently expressed in new forms of architecture and sculpture that made the marble quarried from the Greek islands reach for the open sky, or ripple like a soft garment in the warm Aegean breeze. But motion, though an intrinsic feature of the Greek idiom, was always something superimposed, something added. It belonged to the world of the ideal and not to the hard world of reality.

Today our modern psychology approaches its study of man from the same vantage point. He is viewed as something static in his natural state, hence, something upon which motion, life, and action have to be superimposed. In substance he is still perceived as like the marble out of which the Greeks carved their statues of flowing motion and ethereal grace. He comes alive, according to most of the psychology of our day, only through the application of special enlivening forces. We call these forces by such names as "motives," "incentives," "needs," and "drives." Thus, just as the physicists had to erect the construct of energy to fill the gap left by their premature assumption of a basically static universe, so psychology has had to burden itself with a construct made necessary by its inadequate assumption about the basic nature of man.

We now arrive at the same point in our theoretical reasoning at which we arrived some years earlier in appraising our clinical experience. In each case we find that efforts to assess human motives run into practical difficulty because they assume inherently static properties in human nature. It seems appropriate, therefore, at this juncture to reexamine our implied assumptions about human nature. If we then decide to base our thinking upon new assumptions, we can next turn to the array of new constructs that may be erected for the proper elaboration of the fresh theoretical position.

There are several ways in which we can approach our problem. We could, for example, suggest to ourselves, as we once suggested to certain unperceptive classroom teachers, that we examine what a person does when he is not being motivated. Does he turn into some kind of inert substance? If not—and he won't—should we not follow up our observation with a basic assumption that any person is motivated, motivated for no other reason than that he is alive? Life itself could be defined as a form of process or movement. Thus, in designating man as our object of psychological inquiry, we would be taking it for granted that movement was an essential property of his being, not something that had to be accounted for separately. We would be talking about a form of movement—man—not something that had to be motivated.

Pursuant to this line of reasoning, motivation ceases to be a special topic of psychology. Nor, on the other hand, can it be said that motivation constitutes the whole of psychological substance; although from the standpoint of another theoretical system, it might be proper to characterize our position so. *Within our system*, however, the term, "motivation," can only appear as a redundancy.

How else can we characterize this stand with respect to motivation? Perhaps this will help: motivational theories can be divided into two types, push theories and pull theories. Under push theories we find such terms as drive, motive, or even stimulus. Pull theories use such constructs as purpose, value, or need. In terms of a well-known metaphor, these are the pitch fork theories on the one hand and the carrot theories on the other. But our theory is neither of these. Since we prefer to look to the nature of the animal himself, ours is probably best called a jackass theory.

Thus far our reasoning has led us to a point of view from which the construct of "human motives" appears redundant—redundant, that is, as far as accounting for human action is concerned. But traditional motivational theory is not quite so easily dismissed. There is another issue that now comes to the fore. It is the question of what directions human actions can be expected to take.

We must recognize that the construct of "motive" has been traditionally used for two purposes: to account for the fact that the person is active rather than inert, and also for the fact that he chooses to move in some directions rather than in others. It is not surprising that, in the past, a single construct has been used to cover both issues; for if we take the view that the human organism is set in motion only by the impact of special forces, it is reasonable to assume also that those forces must give it direction as well as impetus. But now, if we accept the view that the organism is already in motion simply by virtue of its being alive, then we have to ask ourselves if we do not still require the services of "motives" to explain the directionality of the movement. Our answer to this question is, no. Let us see why.

Here, as before, we turn first to our experiences as a clinician to find the earliest inklings of a new theoretical position. Specifically, we turn to experiences in psychotherapy.

When a psychologist undertakes psychotherapy with a client he can approach his task from any one of a number of viewpoints. He can, as many do, devote most of his attention to a kind of running criticism of the mistakes the client makes, his fallacies, his irrationalities, his misperceptions, his resistances, his primitive mechanisms. Or, as others do, he can keep measuring his client; so much progress today, so much loss yesterday, gains in this respect, relapses in that. If he prefers, he can keep his attention upon his own role, or the relationship between himself and his client, with the thought that it is not actually given to him ever to know how the client's mind works, nor is it his responsibility to make sure that it works correctly, but only that he should provide the kind of warm and responsive human setting in which the client can best solve his own problems.

Any one of these approaches may prove helpful to the client. But there is still another approach that, from our personal experience, can prove most helpful both to the client and to the psychotherapist. Instead of assuming, on the one hand, that the therapist is obliged to bring the client's thinking into line, or, on the other, that the client will mysteriously bring his own thinking into line once he has been given the proper setting, we can take the stand that client and therapist are conjoining in an exploratory venture. The therapist assumes neither the position of judge nor that of the sympathetic bystander. He is sincere about this; he is willing to learn along with his client. He is the client's fellow researcher who seeks first to understand, then to examine, and finally to assist the client in subjecting alternatives to experimental test and revision.

The psychologist who goes at psychotherapy this way says to himself, "I am about to have the rare opportunity of examining the inner workings of that most intricate creation of all of nature, a human personality. While many scholars have written about the complexity of this human personality, I am now about to see for myself how one particular personality functions. Moreover, I am about to have an experienced colleague join me in this venture, the very person whose personality is to be examined. He will help me as best he can, but there will be times when he cannot help, when he will be as puzzled and confused as I am."

When psychotherapy is carried out in this vein the therapist, instead of asking himself continually whether his client is right or not, or whether he himself is behaving properly, peers intently into the intimate psychological processes the unusual relationship permits him to see. He inquires rather than condemns; he explores rather than rejects or approves. How does this creature, man, actually think? How does he make choices that seem to be outside the conventionalized modes of thought? What is the nature of his logic—quite apart from how logicians define logic? How does he solve his problems? What ideas does he express for which he has no words?

Out of this kind of experience with psychotherapy we found ourselves becoming increasingly impatient with certain standard psychotherapeutic concepts. "Insight" was one of the first to have a hollow sound. It soon became apparent that, in any single case, there was any number of different possible insights that could be used to structure the same facts, all of them more or less true. As one acquires a variety of psychotherapeutic experience he begins to be amazed by how sick or deviant some clients can be and still surmount their difficulties, and how well or insightful others can be and yet fall apart at every turn. Certainly the therapist who approaches his task primarily as a scientist is soon compelled to concede that unconventional insights often work as well or better than the standardized insights prescribed by some current psychological theory.

Another popular psychotherapeutic concept that made less and less sense was "resistance." To most therapists resistance is a kind of perverse stubbornness in the client. Most therapists are annoyed by it. Some accuse the client of resisting whenever their therapeutic efforts begin to bog down. But our own experiences with resistance were a good deal like our experiences with laziness—they bespoke more of the therapist's perplexity than of the client's rebellion. If we had been dependent entirely on psychotherapeutic experiences with our own clients we might have missed this point; it would have been too easy for us, like the others, to blame our difficulties on the motives of the client. But we were fortunate enough to also have opportunities for supervising therapists and here, because we were not ourselves quite so intimately involved, it was possible to see resistance in terms of the therapist's naivete.

When the so-called resistance was finally broken through—to use a psychotherapist's idiom—it seemed proper, instead of congratulating ourselves on our victory over a stubborn client, to ask ourselves and our client just what had happened. There were, of course, the usual kinds of reply, "I just couldn't say that to you then," or "I knew I was being evasive, but I just didn't know what to do about it," etc.

But was this stubbornness? Some clients went further and expressed it this way, "To have said then what I have said today would not have meant the same thing." This may seem like a peculiar remark, but from the standpoint of personal construct theory it makes perfectly good sense. A client can express himself only within the framework of his construct system. Words alone do not convey meaning. What this client appears to be saying is this! When he has the constructs for expressing himself the words that he uses ally themselves with those constructs and they make sense when he utters them. To force him to utter words which do not parallel his constructs, or to mention events which are precariously construed, is to plunge him into a chaos of personal nonsense, however it may clarify matters for the therapist. In short, our experience with psychotherapy led us to believe that it was not orneriness that made the client hold out so-called important therapeutic material, but a genuine inability to express himself in terms that would not appear, from his point of view, to be utterly misconstrued.

Perhaps these brief recollections of therapeutic experience will suffice to show how we began to be as skeptical of motives as direction-finding devices as we were skeptical of them as action-producing forces. Over and over again, it appeared that our clients were making their choices, not in terms of the alternatives we saw open to them, but in terms of the alternatives they saw open to them. It was their network of constructions that made up the daily mazes that they ran, not the pure realities that appeared to us to surround them. To try to explain a temper tantrum or an acute schizophrenic episode in terms of motives only was to miss the whole point of the client's system of personal dilemmas. The child's temper tantrum is, for him, one of the few remaining choices left to him. So for the psychotic; with his pathways structured the way they are in his mind, he has simply chosen from a particular limited set of alternatives. How else can he behave? His other alternatives are even less acceptable.

We have still not quite answered the question of explaining directionality. We have described only the extent to which our therapeutic experiences led us to question the value of motives. But, after all, we have not yet found, from our experience, that clients do what they do because there is nothing else they can do. We have observed only that they do what they do because their choice systems are definitely limited. But, even by this line of reasoning, they do have choices, often bad ones, to be sure, but still choices. So our question of directionality of behavior is narrowed down by the realization that a person's behavior must take place within the limited dimensions of his personal construct system. Yet as long as his system does have dimensions it must provide him with some sets of alternatives. And so long as he has some alternatives of his own making we must seek to explain why he chooses some of them in preference to others.

Before we leave off talking about clinical experience and take up the next and most difficult phase of our discussion, it will do no harm to digress for a few moments and talk about the so-called neurotic paradox. O.H. Mowrer has described this as "the paradox of behavior which is at one and the same time self-perpetuating and self-defeating." We can state the paradox in the form of a question. "Why does a person sometimes persist in unrewarding behavior?" Reinforcement theory finds this an embarrassing question, while contiguity theory, to which some psychologists have turned in their embarrassment, finds the converse question equally embarrassing. "Why does a person sometimes *not* persist in unrewarding behavior?"

From the standpoint of the psychology of personal constructs, however, there is no neurotic paradox. Or, to be more correct, the paradox is the jam certain learning theorists get themselves into rather than the jam their clients get themselves into. Not that clients stay out of jams, but they have their own ingenious ways of getting into them and they need no assistance from us psychologists. To say it another way, the behavior of a so-called neurotic client does not seem paradoxical to him until he tries to rationalize it in terms his therapist can understand. It is when he tries to use his therapist's construction system that the paradox appears. Within the client's own limited construction system he may be faced with a dilemma but not with a paradox.

Perhaps this little digression into the neurotic paradox will help prepare the ground for the next phase of our discussion. Certainly it will help if it makes clear that the criteria by which a person chooses between the alternatives, in terms of which he has structured his world, are themselves cast in terms of constructions. Men not only construe their alternatives, but they construe also criteria for choosing between them. For us psychologists who try to understand what is going on in the minds of our clients it is not as simple as saying that the client will persist in rewarding behavior, or even that he will vacillate between immediate and remote rewards. We have to know what this person construes to be a reward, or, better still, we can bypass such motivational terms as "reward," which ought to be redefined for each new client and on each new occasion, and abstract from human behavior some psychological principle that will transcend the tedious varieties of personalized motives.

If we succeed in this achievement we may be able to escape that common pitfall of so-called objective thinking, the tendency to reify our constructs and treat them as if they were not constructs at all, but actually all the things that they were originally only intended to construe. Such a formulation may even make it safer for us to write operational definitions for purposes of research, without becoming lost in the subject-predicate fallacy. In clinical language it may enable us to avoid concretistic thinking—the so-called brain-injured type of thinking—which is what we call operationalism when we happen to find it in a client who is frantically holding on to his mental faculties.

Now we have been procrastinating long enough. Let us get on to the most difficult part of our discussion. We have talked about experiences with clients who, because they hoped we might be of help to them, honored us with invitations to the rare intimacies of their personal lives and ventured to show us the shadowy processes by which their lives were ordered. We turned aside briefly in our discussion to talk about the neurotic paradox, hoping that what we could point to there would help the listener anticipate what needed to come next. Now we turn again to a more theoretical form of discourse.

If man, as the psychologist is to see him, exists primarily in the dimensions of time, and only secondarily in the dimensions of space, then the terms which we erect for understanding him ought to take primary account of this view. If we want to know why man does what he does, then the terms of our whys should extend themselves in time rather than in space; they should be events rather than things; they should be mileposts rather than destinations. Clearly, man lives in the present. He stands firmly astride the chasm that separates the past from the future. He is the only connecting link between these two universes. He, and only he, can bring them into harmony with each other. To be sure, there are other forms of existence that have belonged to the past and, presumably, will also belong to the future. A rock that has rested firm for ages may well exist in the future also, but it does not link the past with the future. In its mute way it links only past with past. It does not anticipate; it does not reach out both ways to snatch handfuls from each of the two worlds in order to bring them together and subject them to the same stern laws. Only man does that.

If this is the picture of man, as the psychologist envisions him—man, a form of movement; man, always quick enough, as long as he is alive, to stay astride the darting present—then we cannot expect to explain him either entirely in terms of the past or entirely in terms of the future. We can only explain him, psychologically, as a link between the two. Let us, therefore, formulate our basic postulate for psychological theory in the light of this conjunctive vision of man. We can say it this way: *a person's processes are psychologically channelized by the ways in which he anticipates events.*

Taking this proposition as point of departure we can quickly begin to sketch a theoretical structure for psychology that will, undoubtedly, turn out to be novel in many unexpected ways. We can say next that man develops his ways of anticipating events by construing—by scratching out his channels of thought. Thus he builds his own maze. His runways are the constructs he forms, each a two-way street, each essentially a pair of alternatives between which he can choose.

Another person, attempting to enter this labyrinth, soon gets lost. Even a therapist has to be led patiently back and forth through the system, sometimes for months on end, before he can find his way without the client's help, or tell to what overt behavior each passageway will lead. Many of the runways are conveniently posted with word signs, but most of them are dark, cryptically labeled, or without any word signs at all. Some are rarely traveled. Some the client is reluctant to disclose to his guest. Often therapists lose patience and prematurely start trying to blast shortcuts in which both they and their clients soon become trapped. But worst of all, there are those therapists who refuse to believe that they are in the strangely structured world of man, insisting only that the meanderings in which they are led are merely the play of whimsical motives upon their blind and helpless client.

Our figure of speech should not be taken too literally. The labyrinth is conceived as a network of constructs, each of which is essentially an abstraction and, as such, can be picked up and laid down over many, many different events in order to bring them into focus and clothe them with personal meaning. Moreover, the constructs are subject to continual revision, although the complex interdependent relationship between constructs in the system often makes it precarious for the person to revise one construct without taking into account the disruptive effect upon major segments of the system.

In our efforts to communicate the notion of a personal construct system we repeatedly ran into difficulty because listeners identify personal constructs with the classic view of a concept. Concepts have long been known as units of logic and are treated as if they existed independently of any particular person's psychological processes. But when we use the notion of "construct" we have nothing of this sort in mind; we are talking about a psychological process in a living person. Such construct has, for us, no existence independent of the person whose thinking it characterizes. The question of whether it is logical or not has no bearing on its existence, for it is wholly a psychological rather than a logical affair. Furthermore, since it is a psychological affair, it has no necessary allegiance to the verbal forms in which classical concepts have been traditionally cast. The personal construct we talk about bears no essential relation to grammatical structure, syntax, words, language, or even communication; nor does it imply consciousness. It is simply a psychologically construed unit for understanding human processes.

We must confess that we often run into another kind of difficulty. In an effort to understand what we are talking about a listener often asks if the personal construct is an intellectual affair. We find that, willy-nilly, we invite this kind of question because of our use of such terms as thought and thinking. Moreover, we are speaking in the terms of a language system whose words stand for traditional divisions of mental life, such as "intellectual."

Let us answer this way. A construct owes no special allegiance to the intellect, as against the will or the emotions. In fact, we do not find it either necessary or desirable to make that classic trichotomous division of mental life. After all, there is so much that is "emotional" in those behaviors commonly called "intellectual" and there is so much "intellectualized" contamination in typical "emotional" upheavals that the distinction merely becomes a burdensome nuisance. For some time now we have been quite happy to chuck all these notions of intellect, will, and emotion, and, so far, we cannot say we have experienced any serious loss.

Now we are at the point in our discourse where we hope our listeners are ready to assume, either from conviction or for the sake of argument, that man, from a psychological viewpoint, makes of himself a bridge between past and future in a manner that is unique among creatures, that, again from a psychological viewpoint, his processes are channelized by the personal constructs he erects in order to perform this function, and finally, that he organizes his constructs into a personal system that is no more conscious than it is unconscious and no more intellectual than it is emotional. This personal construct system provides him both with freedom of decision and limitation of action—freedom, because it permits him to deal with the meanings of events rather than being helplessly pushed about by them, and limitation, because he can never make choices outside the world of alternatives he has erected for himself.

We have left to the last the question of what determines man's behavioral choices between his self-construed alternatives. Each choice that he makes has implications for his future. Each turn of the road he chooses to travel brings him to a fresh vantage point from which he can judge the validity of his past choices and elaborate his present pattern of alternatives for choices yet to be made. Always the future beckons him and always he reaches out in tremulous anticipation to touch it. He lives in anticipation; we mean this literally; *he lives in anticipation!* His behavior is governed, not simply by *what* he anticipates—whether good or bad, pleasant or unpleasant, self-vindicating or self-confounding—but by *where* he believes his choices will place him in respect to the remaining turns in the road. If he chooses this fork in the road will it lead to a better vantage point from which to see the road beyond or will it be the one that abruptly brings him face-to-face with a blank wall?

What we are saying about the criteria of man's choices is not a second theoretical assumption, added to our basic postulate to take the place of the traditional beliefs in separate motives, but is a natural outgrowth of that postulate—a corollary to it. Let us state it so. *A person chooses for himself that alternative in a dichotomized construct through which he anticipates the greater possibility for extension and definition of his system.*

Such a corollary appears to us to be implicit in our postulate that a person's processes are psychologically channelized by the ways in which he anticipates events. For the sake of simplification we have skipped over the formal statement of some of the intervening corollaries of personal construct theory: the corollary that deals with construing, the corollary that deals with construct system, and the corollary that deals with the dichotomous nature of constructs. But we have probably covered these intervening ideas well enough in the course of our exposition.

What we are saying is this crucial *Choice Corollary* gives us the final ground for dismissing motivation as a necessary psychological construct. It is that if a person's processes are channelized by the ways in which he anticipates events, he will make his choices in such a way as to define or extend his system of channels, for this must necessarily be his comprehensive way of anticipating events.

At the risk of being tedious, let us recapitulate again. We shall be brief. Perhaps we can condense it into three sentences. First we saw no need for a closet full of motives to explain the fact that man was active rather than inert; there was no sense in assuming that he was inert in the first place. And now we see no need to invoke a concept of motives to explain the directions that his actions take; the fact that he lives in anticipation automatically takes care of that. Result: no catalog of motives to clutter up our system and, we hope, a much more coherent psychological theory about living man.

At this point our discourse substantially concludes itself. What we have left to offer are essentially footnotes that are intended to be either defensive or provocative, perhaps both! Questions naturally arise the moment one begins to pursue the implications of this kind of theorizing. One can scarcely take more than a few steps before he begins to stumble over a lot of ancient landmarks that remain to serve no purpose except to get in the way. Perhaps it is only fair that we spotlight some of these relics in the hope of sparing our listeners some barked intellectual shins.

Is this a dynamic theory? This is the kind of question our clinical colleagues are likely to ask. We are tempted to give a flat no to that question. No, this is not what is ordinarily called a dynamic theory: it intentionally parts company with psychoanalysis, for example—respectfully but nonetheless intentionally. However, if what is meant by a "dynamic theory" is a theory that envisions man as active rather than inert, then this is an all-out dynamic theory. It is so dynamic that it does not need any special system of dynamics to keep it running! What must be made clear, else our whole discourse falls flat on its face, is that we do not envision the behavior of man in terms of the external forces bearing upon him; that is a view we are quite ready to leave to the dialectic materialists and to some of their unwitting allies who keep chattering about scientific determinism and other subject-predicate forms of nonsense.

Is this rationalism revisited? We anticipated this question at the beginning of our discussion. We are tempted to answer now by claiming that it is one of the few genuine departures from rationalism, perhaps the first in the field of psychology. But here is a tricky question, because it is not often clear whether one is referring to extra-psychological rationalism or to an essential-psychological rationalism that is often imperfect when judged by classical standards and often branded as "irrationality," or whether the question refers simply to any verbalized structure applied to the behavior of man in an effort to understand him.

Certainly ours is not an extra-psychological rationalism. Instead it frankly attempts to deal with the essential rationalism that is actually demonstrated in the thinking of man. In doing so it deals with what is sometimes called the world of the irrational and nonrational.

But in another sense our interpretation, in its own right and quite apart from its subject matter, is a psychologist's rationale designed to help him understand how man comes to believe and act the way he does. Such a rationale approaches its task the way it does, not because it believes that logic has to be as it is because there is no other way for it to be, not because it believes that man behaves the way he does because there is no other way for him to react to external determining forces, nor even because the rationale's own construction of man provides him with no alternatives, but rather, because we have the hunch that the way to understand all things, even the ramblings of a regressed schizophrenic client, is to construe them so as to make them predictable. To some this spells rationalism, pure and simple, probably because they are firmly convinced that the nether world of man's motives is so hopelessly irrational that anyone who tries to understand that world sensibly must surely be avoiding contact with man as he really is.

Finally, there is the most important question of all: how does the system work? That is a topic to be postponed to another time and occasion. Of course, we think it does work. We use it in psychotherapy and in psychodiagnostic planning for psychotherapy. We also find a place for it in dealing with many of the affairs of everyday life. But there is no place here for the recitation of such details. We hope only that, so far as we have gone, we have been reasonably clear, and a mite provocative, for only by being both clear and provocative can we give our listeners something they can set their teeth into.

Addendum

The invitation to prepare this paper was accompanied by a list of nine issues upon which, it was presumed, would hinge the major differences to be found among any group of motivational theorists. On the face of it such a list seems altogether fair. But one can scarcely pose even one such question, much less nine of them, without exacting hostages to his own theoretical loyalties. And if a correspondent answers in the terminology of the questions posed, he, in turn, immediately bases his discourse on the assumptions of an alien theory. Once he has done that he will, sooner or later, have to talk as if the differences he seeks to emphasize are merely semantical.

Yet the nine questions need to be met, if not head on, at least candidly enough to be disposed of.

1 Is it essential in assessing motives to provide some appraisal of the ego processes, directive mechanisms, or cognitive controls that intervene between the motive and its expression?
"Ego" is a psychoanalytic term; we still don't know what it means. "Cognitive" is a classical term that implies a natural cleavage between psychological processes, a cleavage that confuses everything and clarifies nothing; let's forget it. The notion of a "motive" on the one hand and "its expression" on the other commits one to the view that what is expressed is not the person but the motivational gremlins that have possessed him. Finally, if the term "directive mechanisms" is taken in a generic sense, then we can say that we see these as in the form of constructs formulated by the person himself and in terms of which he casts his alternatives. What needs to be assessed are these personal constructs if one wishes to understand what a person is up to.

2 How important are conscious as opposed to unconscious motives in understanding human behavior? Are there conditions under which one type of motivation is likely to be of particular importance?
We do not use the conscious-unconscious dichotomy, but we do recognize that some of the personal constructs a person seeks to subsume within his system prove to be fleeting or elusive. Sometimes this is because they are loose rather than tight, as in the first phase of the creative cycle. Sometimes it is because they are not bound by the symbolisms of words or other acts. But of this we are sure, if they are important in a person's life it is a mistake to say they are unconscious or that he is unaware of them. Every day he experiences them, often all too poignantly, except he cannot put his finger on them nor tell for sure whether they are at the spot the therapist has probed for them.

When does a person fall back upon such loosened thinking? Or when does he depend upon constructs that are not easily subsumed? Ordinarily when one is confronted with confusion (anxiety) the first tendency is to tighten up, but beyond some breaking point there is a tendency to discard tight constructions and fall back upon constructs that are loose or which have no convenient symbolizations. It is in the human crises that it becomes most important to understand the nature of a person's secondary lines of defense.

3 What is the relative importance of direct as opposed to indirect techniques for assessing human motives? Under what circumstances is the contribution of each type of technique likely to be greatest?
Let us change the word "motives" to "constructs." They are not equivalent, of course, but "motives" play no part in our system while "constructs" do. If we ask a person to express his constructs in words, and we take his words literally, then we may say, perhaps, that we are assessing his constructs "directly." If we assume that his words and acts have less patent meanings and that we must construe him in terms of a background understanding of his construct system, shall we say that we have used a more "indirect" technique? But is anything more direct than this? Perhaps the method that takes literal meanings for granted is actually the more indirect, for it lets the dictionary intervene between the client and the psychologist. If time permits we vote for seeking to understand the person in the light of his personal construct system.

4 In assessing human motives how important is it to specify the situational context within which the motives operate?
Each of a client's constructs has a limited range of convenience in helping him deal with his circumstances. Beyond that range the construct is irrelevant as far as he is concerned. This is the point that was so long obscured by the Law of the Excluded Middle. Knowledge, therefore, of the range of convenience of any personal construct formulated by a client is essential to an understanding of the behavior he structures by that construct.

5 How necessary is knowledge of the past in the assessment of the contemporary motivation?
It is not absolutely necessary but it is often convenient. Events of the past may disclose the kind of constructions that the client has used; presumably he may use them again. Events of the past, taken in conjunction with the anticipations they confirmed at the time, may indicate what has been proved to his satisfaction. Again, events of the past may indicate what a client has had to make sense out of, and thus enable us to surmise what constructions he may have had to erect in order to cope with his circumstances. Finally, since some clients insist on playing the part of martyrs to their biographical destinies, therapy cannot be concluded successfully until their therapists have conducted them on a grand tour of childhood recollections.

6 At this time is the area of motivation more in need of developing precise and highly objective measures of known motives or identifying significant new motivational variables?
Neither.

7 Is there a unique and important contribution to the understanding of human motive that can be made to present through the medium of comparative or lower animal studies that cannot be duplicated by means of investigations utilizing human subjects?
No.

8 In attempting to understand human motivation is it advisable at present to focus upon one or a small number of motivational variables or should an effort be made to appraise a wide array of variables?
Human impetus should be assumed as a principle rather than treated as a variable or group of variables.

9 What is the relative importance of detailed studies of individual cases as compared to carefully controlled experimental research and large-scale investigation?
All three have their place in the course of developing psychological understanding. The detailed case studies provide excellent grounds for generating constructs. Experimental research, in turn, permits us to test out constructs in artificial isolation. Large-scale investigations help us put constructs into a demographic framework.

13

Prediction and Control[1]

It is frequently said that science sets as its objective the prediction and control of events. Both terms, of course, imply doing something about matters that have not happened yet. If the objective of science were stated in terms of following out some course of action which had already been set, or in pursuing some divine will, or in fulfilling man's potentialities, the whole character of the scientific effort would assume quite a different shape. But in plotting the course of science in terms of anticipated events, rather than in terms of forces that must blow themselves out we have, whether intended to or not, actually said something about the psychology of man; not merely the cult of man who attempts to set themselves apart in a special breed to be known as scientists, but all mankind. Personal construct theory starts with this kind of notion about what makes man do what he does.

But is it the eagerness to predict or the eagerness to control that sets man on his way? So far we have always mentioned both when we describe the nature of the scientific effort. From a theoretician's point of view it would be desirable to state the objective in monolithic terms—one goal, one explanatory principle, one key to both the force and direction of human movement. Do we already have such a principle at hand? May we ask if prediction and control add up to the same thing or if there is something that underlies them both, something that can be stated in a simple declarative sentence.

In setting up the basic postulate of the psychology of personal constructs I chose prediction as the central principle and dismissed control as a special case of using the prediction principle. In a later section of the discourse I deal with if–then relationships as a special kind of construct in which a word or time line was specified. At another point I dealt with control in the context of a discussion of determinism and free will. There I described control as the opposite side of the coin we call free will. To be free is to be free to control and to be controlled is to be subject to some freely made decision. Thus freedom and control were not seen either as absolutes or as antitheses, but rather as independent and dependent variables.

Now I would like to say something more explicit about control in its relation to prediction. To set up a prediction is to imagine an event, or the proportions of an event, in such a way that when the series of real events starts unwinding we can point to one of them and say, "There, that is the one I predicted." Or we may say, "There is precisely the spot I predicted my event would turn up; but what I see there is not what I expected." The prediction is not a full-blown picture of an event, conjured up before its time, but an abstracted formulation—a plot of coordinates in a personal construct grid.

Prediction has an advantage over realization. When the time comes for this real event to occur, it crowds out all alternative events. The time line is so thin that there is room for only one event to sit down at a time—all the competitors must either wait their turn or give up the hope of ever materializing. But when one is dealing only with predictions he can juggle his anticipated realities without their getting seriously in each other's way. If he doesn't like the looks of one thing he predicts he can look around to see what conditions would enable him to predict something he would rather have happen. When he finds that one of the key changes in predicating conditions is a change in his own actions, he is in luck. He does what needs to be done and thus sets up conditions under which he can predict something he would like to have happen. If his prediction system is valid—and this is something he has to keep cheeking in any case—he has achieved control.

Thus control of events at least hinges upon prediction. The prediction, however, has to include the prediction of what one is able to do himself; otherwise prediction is bound to fall short of control. We might put it this way; a prediction system that includes an understanding of the predictor's own behavior has the elements of a system of control. If it does not include any understanding of one's self, it amounts to no more than a system for worrying over things one is helpless to do anything about.

[1] Dated 1958. Published by permission of Jacqueline Aldridge.

Collected Papers of the Pioneer of Constructivist Psychology: George A. Kelly, First Edition. Edited by David A. Winter and Nick Reed.

There is a sense, of course, in which prediction, since it comes right down to being a human act, is a kind of control—a control the person sets over his own mental processes. When a person makes a prediction he is at least committing himself to something. As a matter of fact a person cannot do anything, not even predict something, without taking himself in hand. And when he does that he controls. Indeed, what direction would his life take unless it were oriented toward what he expected to happen?

Prediction is still the key, not only to understanding man's scientific effort but also to understanding all man's effort, of which scientific effort is only a refinement. Control, which is also no less human than it is scientific, emerges when prediction is extended to one's own behavior and, like all prediction, gets better and better as he revises and validates his prediction system.

14

How to be Comfortable with Threat[1]

This is a theoretical discussion of threat and is not meant to be "useful." The topic is of interest because many of the assignments in this organization involve difficulties with threat. Thus, its basic nature is important to us.

Before discussing threat, as such, it is necessary to take up some other matters. One of these is the Subject-Predicate Error (of the Indo-European mode of thought). We have become so adapted to this 2500 year old premise that we no longer see it as an error; therefore, we are stuck with it. We don't even have the language to describe it as an error. Bertrand Russell has used this error to solve many of the classical paradoxes of mathematics.

Definition of the Subject-Predicate Error: In our language, verbs[2] are used to describe the subject of a sentence. The person making the statement has no responsibility for what is said. Thus, in the sentence, "The dog is large," *large* is a quality which adheres to the dog. What we really should be saying is, "I deal with a dog with a concept of largeness." Similarly, the statement "Ed's spectacles are introvert" can have no meaning if one considers the spectacles rather than the speaker. The meaning, and the usefulness, of this statement adheres to the speaker. Thus, the Subject-Predicate Error is in assuming that properties and concepts are carried in the events (the subject of the sentence) rather than being the responsibility of the person who imposes the meaning. This line of reasoning is contrary to the usual concept of objectivity.

There are five lines of reasoning which end at the same criticism of the Subject- Predicate Error: a) the nature of truth, b) the nature of reality, c) the experimental approach, d) psychological approaches, and e) clinical evidence. Each of these will be described in turn.

a In science, we tend to think that new ideas are a replacement of errors by truth. With each changing version of truth, we tend to treat what is past as erroneous; does this mean that we have been wrong all the time? Indeed, as this process goes on, more and more rapidly, we are forced to say that all knowledge is error. We need some system to allow saying that truth is replaceable. If we do not assume that truth adheres to reality, to nature, then we can say that truth is one way of construing (interpreting) nature. This gives us a basis for reconstruction and gives us freedom to make successive interpretations and predictions (Constructive Altemativism).

b What is real? Berkeley believed that reality existed only in the mind of God, that we could only approximate it through sensory experience. In this way of thinking, we assume that there is reality somewhere, that it truly exists. However, we can never reach it but only approach it by successive approximations. Well, if we can't reach it, why bother to use it at all? Like the concept of infinity, it has a certain usefulness. Reality is an outer point important for understanding our progression of thinking, necessary for understanding our successive revisions.

c Experimental sciences are based on inverse logic, a kind of arguing from ignorance. We say, "Since we don't know any better, it must be so." That is, we set up an experiment with rival hypotheses, the experimental H_1 and the null H_0. We collect data, and ask these data to choose between the two hypotheses. The experimentalist tilts against the null hypothesis, against the hypothesis of chaos. The rejection of H_0 is seen as proof for the experimental hypothesis. But this begs the question; the fact that H_1 *could*, doesn't mean that H_1 *did* produce the given results. There are two kinds of errors here. First, H_1 is not the only, or the best, hypothesis; it is the only one that the experimenter thought of. Secondly, just because H_0 does explain the results, at a $p = .50$, for example, this is no reason that H_0 is the only explanation. It is "stupid" to assume that the universe in a disorganized state is simpler than the universe in an organized state; the simplest explanation (i.e., H_0) is not always the best. This kind of back-door proof forces us to the point of view that there must be alternative explanations.

d Psychologists describe themselves as scientists interested in the problems of prediction and control. But this interest is not ascribed to other men's behavior; their behavior is explained by biography, accidents of error, whims, motives, affects, etc.—by some other system than prediction and control. What might happen if we say: i) all psychologists are men, ii) all men are incipient psychologists,

[1] Notes taken by three people (initials LKB, NK, and JFW) attending a seminar given by Kelly as Consultant to Accident and Emergency Department staff, Washington, January 15, 1958. Published by permission of Jacqueline Aldridge.
[2] Editors' note: [sic]

Collected Papers of the Pioneer of Constructivist Psychology: George A. Kelly, First Edition. Edited by David A. Winter and Nick Reed.

iii) all human behavior is based on prediction and control. Then we would ask people "What is your system of psychology?" and would look for his frame of reference. Psychology would thus become a psychology about psychologists. This is the basis for the Psychology of Personal Constructs.

e Clinical evidence indicates that, during psychotherapy, not only the sense of values seems to change but also the frame of reference. That is, there may be a change in the principal dimensions by which the world is perceived. Every assertion (made by a patient) implies also a negation. Thus, a patient who asserts "I believe people are loving" is negating something. It might be that he means that if people are not loving, he himself might be hateful, and who knows what might happen then. In other words, the axis (dimension, construct) loving-not loving is an important one to this individual.

This leads us to certain philosophical propositions or considerations:

a Whatever exists (is real) can be approached by construing (interpreting).
b Whatever exists can be reconstructed at any time, no matter how useful may be the present construing. Thus one can hope for a world of freedom with knowledge.
c The fact that everything can be reconstrued does not mean that it makes no difference how things are construed; these constructions vary in usefulness.
d The possibility of more useful and less useful constructions always exists, but the more useful constructions tend to increase while the less useful ones tend to decrease.

Let us look now at a psychological theory based on the considerations outlined above. The basic postulate of such a theory sees each person as an incipient scientist; a person's psychological processes are channelized by the way in which he construes events. These constructions are organized or systematized into a network of constructs (called by Kelly, the construct system). This is not phenomenology which treats each individual as a separate, distinct, unrelated universe since many individuals may have the same construct system. (These constructs, incidentally, are not necessarily verbalized by the individual holding them but must be inferred from behavior).

Since each person organizes his behavior in terms of his constructs, his investment in his construct system is great. If you destroy this network, leaving the individual no channels within which to operate, he becomes scared, upset. This sense of lost or invalidated channels is termed *anxiety*. Whenever one tries to make a profound change in his way of thinking or doing things, he is, in a sense, "caught with his constructs down." That is, he becomes anxious.

Some of our channels are so important that our very being depends on them. A person feels threatened when he is faced with an imminent change in his core system. The anticipation of such a change is threat. This is not hedonism which defines threat as imminent punishment. In battle, fear (danger of injury) is balanced against threat (dislodgment as a person) and threat wins out since to give in would mean that the individual will be destroyed as a person. Thus, threat is an internal condition of the individual, not a condition of events.

In this organization, it is important that Case Officers with certain assignments have something (trench-coat) which will allows them to maintain their core construct system (sense of identity) regardless of the tasks performed. It is important to remember that threat is not a derivative of fear but is something used to describe an individual. (The distinction between anxiety, fear, and threat will be taken up again in a later section).

Landfield, (a former student of Kelly) carrying the study of threat a little further, has come up with two hypotheses concerning the kinds of people who are threatening. Everyone sees himself as changing or developing. To look back, as, for example, to adolescence, may be threatening because of the imminence of slipping back to a still plausible mode of behavior. Assuming that one construes himself as having changed, and not fixed, he is threatened by those a) who exemplify the old, still plausible, not-yet-completely discarded behavior and by those b) who expect him to behave in the old way. Thus, the recently reformed alcoholic is threatened by his old associates who represent to him a still plausible behavior.

How does this apply to our situation? A person may be threatened by the Communist Party either because he has tendencies in that direction or because he has recently escaped from it. He becomes anxious, upset, irritable, rigid, because to him this alternative is plausible.

Discussion

Does the number of constructs which one has serve as a protection against threat? Threat depends upon one's particular construct system and the imminence of the plausible change. A multiplicity of constructs gives some protection in that other alternatives may be present, but more important is the nature of one's construct network.

Differentiation between Anxiety, Fear, and Threat

Anxiety is "being caught with one's constructs down," to be in a condition of chaos where there are no highways, no guideposts.

Threat faces one with two worlds, one of which involves a complete reorganization of the core construct system. One is faced, in threat, with another tempting plausible way of life. For example, the oral examination (at doctorate level) always brings a certain amount of anxiety because one doesn't know the dimensions, the rules. He will feel threat if he sees some incompatible modes of behavior cropping out in himself (e.g., losing temper, blowing up, etc.) Threat in the oral examination situation is often seen in women. Here, women almost don't want to pass the examination. While anxiety involves chaos and threat involves a total change, *fear* involves the loss of part of reality (limb, life). No change in the construct system is anticipated; there is no chaos present, but one's anchoring points may be lost.

Threat is more than "conflict" in the traditional sense. It must be perceived, but may not be verbalized, appearing only at the "gut level" of psychology. Since Kelly rejects both the pitchfork and the carrot theory of psychology, he also rejects the notion of "conflict."

Tolerance to threat? A person's "tolerance to threat" is a misnomer, since threat is internal, not a condition of the events themselves. What is important and meaningful is "What things threatening to most people are not threatening to this person?" One can deal with threat:

(1) by giving a person some sort of identity which won't be invalidated by any experience,
(2) by providing him with enough structure about how other people act and feel so that he won't be disillusioned when he meets them, or
(3) by talking through the threat of the other self he might become so that it is no longer an alternative but can be subsumed under some present larger construct. Threat, thus, is eliminated by providing stability or by minimizing the imminent change.

One minimizes anxiety by providing structure, by giving either specific predictions or a general framework within which to operate in times of chaos. This builds up tolerance for ambiguity.

Fear, of a specific, can be dealt with by making something else appear more monstrous. Thus, a soldier comes to feel that cowardly behavior is less tolerable than the physical danger to which he is exposed. In addition, providing knowledge of what goes beyond this particular bit of reality also helps; that is, by giving the knowledge that even if one should lose his hand (his life), the battle (job, mission) still goes on.

15

Feelings For and Feelings Of[1]: (The Ontology of Feelings)

Light Touch on a Thick Skin

There was a fellow one time, a colleague of mine, who had a hide like a rhinoceros[2]. Oh, was his skin thick! Nothing you could say could possibly embarrass him or, more important, none of the blunderheaded things he himself used to say ever embarrassed him. Not that he was stupid; I don't suppose he could have been stupid—not completely stupid. How could he have been—somebody had conferred a Ph.D on him a number of years before, undoubtedly "with all honors, rights, and privileges appertaining thereto"—and in *psychology*, no less! Of course, knowing now what I did not know then, that you can easily trick pompous people into giving you a Ph.D by meticulously following their advice, I suppose I could entertain the hypothesis that he was stupid. Or perhaps that is one of the privileges that "appertains" to the Ph.D.

Still, it could not really have been that he was stupid. *Bona Fide* ignoramuses exhibit their feelings, perhaps even more than most people. In fact, it is often because their feelings stick out that they are called stupid. This is perfectly all right, of course, for children, and for young women in bathing suits; no one minds if their feelings stick out and keep them from appearing to be very intellectual[3]. This is an interesting angle, and now that it has come up I wonder if it is not something we ought to plan to talk about. But later, in another chapter!

As I remember it, this fellow's callousness was tied up with his intellect in some way. Like the well-drilled R.O.T.C. cadet his mind was trained to march in square corners. He simply could not follow the winding paths of free-flowing thought, nor, as a teacher, could

[1] Dated 1951, this is a draft of Chapter 1 of a book that Kelly was writing on *The Human Feeling* (1959). It is published by permission of Jacqueline Aldridge.

[2] You have been duly warned in the Preface, if you read it as you were supposed to, against paying attention to any of these footnotes. They are bound to confuse you, just as they do me. Most certainly they will take a lot of the fun out of reading what otherwise I had hoped might be a rather congenial and amusing visit between us.

Now take this particular footnote, for example; what I have in mind to say here is that this whole chapter is to do with the ontology of affect, and how feelings can be construed within a rational system of thought. This, I am convinced, is not at all the same as saying that all human experience is essentially rational—not, for that matter, that any of it is, on its own account, irrational either.

Confusing, isn't it? Now you see why you were urged to leave these footnotes alone. If you must know, they are written solely for those constitutionally anxious flibbertigibbets who cannot sit down and enjoy a book without everlastingly puzzling over what the book is supposed to be about. Now you aren't *that* kind of a person—are you?

[3] Nowadays they're supposed to have "talent," but that is something else, again. It isn't what they've got when they disport themselves, the young ladies, I mean—but the feeling we get when we look at them; that is what "talent" is. Psychologists used to call this "stimulus error." More generally it should be called "the subject-predicate error."**

** Don't look at these footnotes; they only dampen your interest in what you are about to read!

So, since brides
do not have hides
like rhinoceroses' sides
they are likely
to be touchy.

Contrariwise,
I would guess
that nothing less
than a thermal dermal duplicate
would ever thrill
a rhino's mate.

Collected Papers of the Pioneer of Constructivist Psychology: George A. Kelly, First Edition. Edited by David A. Winter and Nick Reed.

he manage to catch the wistful inflections of a student in search of an idea without a name. It seemed to me that he missed a good deal that he might have enjoyed, as well as some of the things that make the rest of us cringe.

Then, too, he never seemed to know when he had hurt someone. Or perhaps I should say that he did not show the usual signs of remorse—apologetic mannerisms, shamefacedness, agitation, withdrawal. He was the kind of fellow who would go down the reception line, shake hands with the bride, and ask her what happened to her ex-fiancé and if she expected to have a baby before the end of the current school year.

Some brides, to be sure, are not greatly upset by such remarks; it keeps the formal affair from becoming stuffy. But still many a bride is likely to be hurt; the ex-fiancé may have run off with a sorority sister and the question about the baby may be one to which she herself is waiting to learn the answer.

This naturally brings us to the matter of my colleague's wife. At this point, I suddenly realize that the figure of speech is almost too well proportioned, and I think it is better that I leave off and come back to the topic I started to talk about.

I used to be greatly upset by my lubberly colleague. It was not so much, I think, because of the way he treated me face-to-face, although that was often annoying enough, as the way he generally managed situations, including his relations with others. The blunders could have been overlooked. What I could not overlook was his lack of concern for having made them.

Occasionally I would try to do something about it; remarks that might prick whatever feelings were under that thick skin: "As a responsible person, what do you think will happen now," or "What was the matter with your other foot," and perhaps adding "Couldn't you put it in too?"

Such remarks never fazed him. They served only to re-double my own discomfort. Not only was I proving myself ineffectual, but I was engaging in the same doltish behavior I found so objectionable in him. It was far more disturbing to find the threat within myself than to have to observe it in him[4].

Objective or Subjective

But why should I have had these feelings in the first place? Was it that I was such a sensitive and empathic soul that I could not bear to see his victims suffer? Did I naturally have feelings for them? Was I merely seeking to enjoy the luxury of righteous indignation?

Or was it this, that when I blundered in my own human relations, the realization of the blunder brought a discomfort such as he was able to escape? Why did I have to suffer and not he? If I must feel like an outcast, should he not be excommunicated too? Was it this?

Or was it this? Not only was I a blunderer too, but so was I calloused. Was I threatened because he escaped the pain of remorse, or because I was guilty of wanting to escape it—to be like him? Did I then envy him, or was I fighting off the temptation to imitate and my aroused feelings were no more than a superficial check on my own impulses? Perhaps I was about to lose a battle with myself, or to retreat from some hard-won position I had only precariously gained?

Now[5] that I come to think of it, what did my colleague have to do with my feelings anyway, except to provide an appropriate occasion for them? Was it he who made me have them? Did he cause my discomfort, or was it I who was mainly responsible for that? Granted, it was a considerable relief to get away from him, but whose doing was that? His?

I am not suggesting that one, and only one, of these explanations is the true one. Truth in these matters is not so easily pinned down. What I have suggested are some various levels of interpretation. There could be others, probably hundreds of others.

But what were my real feelings? That is a question that can be answered only if one looks at feelings as they are experienced and not merely in terms of why they are experienced.

Still, I am never quite sure that I can do that.

I think, as I remember it, I had a feeling of threat. That sentence has a ring of reality about it. But threatened, what by? Frankly, I cannot be sure. Or what for? I cannot be sure of that either. Was it for my colleague? For the people he hurt? For myself? But still it was, in itself, a feeling of threat. So I think I know what it was a feeling of but I suspect I do not know what it was a feeling for.

[4] The psychological concept of threat is being developed here. It is one of the basic constructs for understanding human behavior though, by no means would I say it was the most important.

[5] Editors' note: "Not" in the original.

16

Values, Knowledge and Social Control[1]

The subject of this symposium has three parts: values, knowledge, and social control. Professor Bauer has directed his remarks mainly at the third of these, social control. He suggests that too much control will not be the fault of too much knowledge, but rather the lack of it. In other words, he does not think rigidly controlled societies make sense, and knowledgeable leaders will know enough not to waste their time with them.

In principle I agree. But we still have a problem on our hands. We still try to keep some kinds of knowledge away from the Soviet Union for fear they will turn it against us before we have had a chance to turn it against ourselves. We still see psychological knowledge used to get vulnerable people to buy what they cannot afford, and then shudder when they take violent steps to guarantee themselves an income which will allow them to keep up the payments. We still find statesmanship subordinated to the short-term facts of public relations, campaign tactics, and the timing of press releases. None of these may be very smart, but will more knowledge, merely more of the stuff, automatically bring things back into balance? Is preparation for the Ph.D. prelims a cure for insanity?

Certainly knowledge is not adequately described in quantitative terms alone—it is not a matter of how much or how little. Some kinds of knowledge, if applied to mankind in the absence of other kinds, become self-defeating. With the world in the state it is, this point probably needs no particular supporting argument from me. The problem is how to keep knowledge in perspective, not necessarily by suppressing its more precocious developments, but by paying attention to over-riding considerations, or, as we call them, values. As I see it, values represent knowledge in perspective, hence are themselves a superior form of knowledge.

Thus, of the two remaining sub-topics that Professor Bauer has left me to talk about, knowledge and values, I feel better prepared to talk about values. This may be a subjective decision. For a long time now, living under the scrutiny of graduate students, I have been kept acutely aware of my limitations in the world of knowledge, but, believe me, I have values. Just what they are has always been somewhat of a secret puzzle to me, but there is no doubt about my having them. In fact, just about every time I start out to do something interesting, there they are!

Seriously, I too would like to say something about social control, but I feel that I can't until I have lined up my values in order to get some perspective. Perhaps I am in the position of the poor soul the existentialists feel so sorry for—assuming the existentialist can feel sorry *for* anyone; maybe he just feels sorry. Perhaps I am one who is so preoccupied with the examination of his values that he never gives them a chance to take over. Or, perhaps, as my Indonesian friend, Professor Pribadi, says: At man's highest ontological level, the level of creative integration with the universe, values are of no account; it is only when man immobilizes himself and stares back at his footprints that he becomes strictured by values.

But still I want to talk about values. And I think I know why it is. It is because I am talking to scientists, and scientists, while they mostly do not mind admitting to having values during weekends and off hours, are usually horrified at the idea of bringing values into the laboratory. In this connection I have wondered if the typical convention of the American Psychological Association is an off-hours or a during-hours activity.

While scientists may be reluctant to become embroiled in any discussion of values, even the laying down of emphatic rules about what science is to be and what it is not to be represents the imposition of a value system. The only way out that I can see is for psychologists to quit trying so hard to be scientists and to get on with their business. If what they do works out, Sigma Xi will, under one pretext or another, start calling it Science. And if what they do looks good, the moralists will claim it too. As far as I can tell, neither of these prospects is any more grim than the other.

In talking about the prevalent convictions among scientists—well, among psychologists at least—that it is bad for a research man to be concerned with values during working hours, I am reminded of two old aphorisms. One goes like this, "A preposition is a bad

[1] Part of a symposium of the American Psychological Association, Cincinnatti, 1959. Read by E.L. Kelly in view of the author's illness. Published by permission of Nick Reed.

Collected Papers of the Pioneer of Constructivist Psychology: George A. Kelly, First Edition. Edited by David A. Winter and Nick Reed.

thing to end a sentence with." The other reads, "It is wrong to ever split an infinitive." There is a more subtle one especially for psychologists: "One should never make black and white judgments about people; I have no use for those who do."

While it may be paradoxical for scientists, and especially psychologists, to be skittish about bringing values into the realm of scientific discourse, there are explanations, explanations that ought to be taken into account whenever we talk about the relation between knowledge and values. One explanation is a very simple historical one. Nearly every major scientific advance has had to push its way through a barrier of opposing traditions. This has led the more impatient scholars to come out against all traditions, merely because they are traditions and stand in the way of change. Moreover, since human values are among the things that tradition tends to legalize, literalize, fossilize and generally reduce to irrational forms, scientists are apt to consider it, along with all such things, a nuisance.

One may point out, of course, that this century's scientific achievement, no less than its other traditions, is likely to stand in the way of the next century's scientific break-through. It is the fate of many a great idea that it releases man's thoughts during the first phase of its life-span, and shackles them during the last. The psychoanalytic contributions of Freud and his successors, for example, show signs of following such a life cycle. Thus science itself tends to become traditionalized and value laden, and an obstacle in the way of its own progress.

But there may be a reply to this too. Some scientists may point out that it is not science that stands in the way of its own later progress, but the values which accumulate around it. And they may go further to point out that the persons who are guilty of this value accretion are not really scientists, but only those who apply science, who exploit it, who do so not because they understand how it works but because they have learned only that it is a good thing—they have learned to value it. One would then argue that it is not psychoanalysis that stands in the way of further psychological progress during the last half of the twentieth century, but the practicing psychoanalysts who promote it, who have invested a lot of time and money in it, and who believe it is a good thing. Indeed, throughout medicine—and especially psychiatry, where there is such a wide chasm between research and practice—it is thought that the only way to break through the traditional value system is to oppose it with counter values; opposing with scientific knowledge alone will scarcely suffice.

There is another reason for the difficulty we have in putting knowledge and values into the same system of discourse. For a long time Western man has envisioned an essential cleavage between what seemed to him to be rational, reasonable, and sensible, on the one hand, and what seemed to belong to that irrational world, that unpredictable world of feeling, on the other. What he has taken to be an awareness of the former he has called cognition, and what has seemed to be his experience of the latter he has called by such names as affection, feeling, or emotion. Since Western man also pretends to be objective, that is, to ascribe his insights wholly to the objects he is looking at, rather than to his way of looking at them, he long ago got into the habit of thinking that the things he could understand were rational by nature, and those he could not understand were essentially irrational.

In this connection does it not seem a bit curious that some of us who make so much of the so-called first postulate of science—that all nature is organized—are so ready to go on to say that human nature is not organized? And is it not surprising that some psychologists who are dedicated to the notion of universal natural law will still go to great lengths to describe schizophrenia as personality in a disorganized state? But this is the objective way of going at it.

It should be pointed out that Freud achieved a major break-through against the stalemate of objective thinking by pointing out the irrational component in all so-called rational thinking. He showed that cognition was always contaminated with the irrational affective demands of the Id, on the one hand, or the irrational value-laden demands of the Super-Ego, on the other. But still he failed to note the inappropriateness of the distinction; for him it was simply a mixture of two essentially distinct things, cognition and its reality principle, on the one hand, and, on the other, libidinal impulse and its pleasure principle.

And so we still have the cleavage, even after the monumental work of Freud. Still the first thing that is asked when a new personality theory is proposed is whether it is a cognitive theory, or a motivational theory. Does it say that a man acts the way he thinks, or does it say a man acts the way he feels? Freud said that a man's actions are a mixture of both. But he did not by any means resolve the age-old issue of rationality versus irrationality, reality versus pleasure, understanding versus motivation, reason versus impulse, understanding versus motivation[2], knowledge versus values.

So it comes about that value-laden behavior is likely to be lumped with the things we find hard to understand, especially when we see it in other people, and, being well-indoctrinated objective observers of human behavior—objective and no more—we conclude that the irrationality must be an intrinsic feature of the values themselves. This is enough, according to some people, to exclude them from any scholarly discourse. *De gustibus non est disputandum!*

There is another angle, a more philosophical one, and with it another difficulty for the scholar who wants to cope with values. Western science, and more recently Soviet science, has been ontologically based on the assumptions of materialistic realism. In the Soviet Union this stand has been conscious and intentional; in America it has crept up on us. By the way, they call our version simply a "vulgar materialism." Remember, I am talking about science only, not necessarily about the general public outlook.

The materialistic realist thinks that truth is something to be discovered, ready-made, and naturally structured by the hard facts of life. This revelational notion of truth is not so different from the classical notion of revealed truth, except that it suggests that one is supposed to work hard and dig for it, and that it is more likely to be found buried in a laboratory than on top of Mount Sinai. But

[2] Editors' note: [sic]

still it is thought to be there, all assembled and waiting, and, even though you may have to dig it up a piece at a time, the job is to discover it—no more.

Values, on the other hand, are obviously invented, not discovered. Man makes them up to suit himself. This seems, clearly enough to the materialistic realist, to exclude them altogether from the discourse of science, or even in some eyes from all the discourse of scholars. And any attempt to include values can accomplish nothing except to corrupt science—and that would be *bad!* It's a little confusing, but I suppose *this particular "bad" is not considered to be a value term.*

What I have been saying up to this point is that we are all concerned with values, even as scholars and scientists we are concerned with them. We are concerned with them whether they are the entrenched values which we see held by society in the path of the progress we hope to make, whether they are the values about which we are inarticulate, and hence, to some persons' ways of thinking, essentially irrational, or whether they are judged to be insubstantial because they are invented rather than discovered. In none of these cases are we any less concerned with values, nor do we hold to our own values any less tenaciously. The problem is not whether the scientist must rule values outside his scientific realm of concern, as psychologists and others often say, but rather what can a scientist do when he finds his values at odds with those of others.

If we are willing to concede broadly, without becoming embroiled in a dispute over pragmatism, that the ultimate test of truth is in its infinite outcomes and that the heuristic test of truth is in its immediate outcomes, then the scientist's testing of truth differs from the moralist's testing of truth primarily in the time lapse between prediction and ultimate verification. The scientist, of course, may not want to express his ultimates in terms of heaven and hell, or even in terms of cosmos and chaos, but that is a semantic problem.

To this way of thinking values differ from most other forms of belief mainly in a dimension of time lapse—the lapse between anticipation and realization. Science is a system of anticipations; so are values. Science looks for verifications to appear as soon as possible. In the case of values, one waits. The scientist is prepared to change his anticipations in the light of tomorrow's outcomes. But values are likely to get changed only when people forget what it was they were wagering on. While no outcome ever quite provides a final verification of the anticipations laid for it, we are placed in the position of having to accept, in the case of values, conclusions which are much further in advance of their ultimate evidence. In the case of other forms of knowledge, especially the scientific forms, the validating evidence we employ seems to be much closer to its final form. This is a way of saying that we have ahead of us a lot more yet to be learned about values than about other things.

We can take it for granted that, in a practical sense, nothing we will ever come across can satisfy the criterion of finality. Even this is a tentative conclusion. But since we are resigned to living day by day in a world of tentative conclusions, we can accept it for the moment. Furthermore, even though we live in a world of tentative conclusions, it is possible to represent, symbolically, and in a measure to be guided by, ultimate conclusions, conclusions we shall never be able to lay our finger on. We have done this for some time now, algebraically, with our use of the "numbers" *infinity* and *zero*. And we do it geometrically with the use of asymptotic lines. Furthermore, such representations are probably no less useful in the scientific and social world than they are in the mathematical world. I am convinced that scientists can talk about the things they do not know yet, indeed, talk about the things they will never know, just as profitably as the mathematician can talk about things too big or too small to enumerate.

What, then, in simple terms, is the evidence of truth? No more than this; what we believe today is validated against what we believe tomorrow, and what we believe tomorrow is tested against what we believe the day after that, or some day after that. Must we, then, assume by and large, that man is making progress and the approach to truth is measured by that progress? Yes! This is, in fact, the way it is done, and at the moment, I cannot imagine any other way of going about it.

My point is that values and knowledge do belong in the same system of discourse and that they do hinge upon the same general criteria of truth. It is not because of any mental lapse that the scholar is discovered making as much of his values as he does of his knowledge. It would be silly for him not to. The distinction we often try to draw between values and knowledge is another one of those unfortunate dualisms that has become so concretized that it prevents one's gaining perspective. The mind-matter dualism, in its concretized or objective form, is another.

What, then, should behavioral scientists, particularly psychologists, be about that they are not about already? When one talks to physical scientists about their responsibilities he usually points to a nuclear bomb mushrooming in the sky, or at the screeching cars at a highway intersection, or even at the lowly television set blinking and squalling in the corner, and then he goes on to say, ominously, that scientists simply cannot expect to go on forever doing things without assuming some responsibility for the consequences.

Now, what to say to behavioral scientists! Perhaps I can point with alarm at such things as brainwashing, popcorn subception, or the flood of uncritical interpersonal acceptance that is available to anyone who is willing to misbehave to get it, and then invite your horrified attention to the consequences of turning such powerful devices loose in the world. Think of it! Do psychologists any longer dare say they have no responsibility for what happens when such creations get into the hands of the wrong people? Or are psychologists, because they are dedicated scientists, less responsible than other people for the consequences of their acts? Are they, as tough-minded scientists, for example, less responsible than the equally tough-minded employers who dump their employees onto the relief rolls during slack seasons, or the realistic landowners who allow their indigent sharecroppers to lapse into serfdom?

At this point, as you probably suspect, I am not being wholly serious about the danger of putting psychological knowledge in the hands of a dictator. I am, I would say, about half serious. But this is something about which one can become wholly serious when he examines, not the dictators, but the people who believe in them. Professor Bauer has referred to what his colleague, Professor Inkeles, calls the "mothball dictatorship." This, I take it, is a society in which what each person now wants is supplied or withheld from him in just the right proportion to keep him from ever getting interested in anything else. No doubt such a community of cultivated addicts might constitute a Utopia completely free of controversy.

Is it, then, appropriate to ask, what happens to freedom in a dictatorship, or, more broadly, what constitutes freedom within any kind of societal control? Obviously the question is a special case of the still broader age-old issue of determinism versus free will. Historically, in this arena, scientists and Presbyterians plumped first. Moreover, both scientists and Presbyterians have gotten into a lot of trouble over the matter. Nobody really believes them when they say that everything is determined, or *predestined,* if you prefer the more old-fashioned term.

The trouble is that determinism[3] and free will have been construed as incompatible with each other, rather than as antithetical. As incompatibles they cannot coexist, but as antitheses each gives meaning to the other. Good and evil, hope and despair, north and south, are such antitheses—without one the other would make no sense. So it is with determinism and free will. What is it to exercise free will, except to determine something? Would one ever be free if he could not make any commitments? One could not set out for his office with the hope of ever getting there, or start to eat his breakfast, or reach down to tie his shoes, because there would be no likelihood of his ever finishing before he changed his mind. On the other hand, an exclusively deterministic version of the universe would be equally chaotic. To speak of a chain of inevitable events without implying some freely chosen point of origin makes no sense. If everything happens in one way and in one way only, then it makes no sense to say that it happened the way it did because of something, or in consequence of something, or to say that it was determined by something but for which it would have turned out differently.

Actually, determinism and free will are the polar ends of one construct dimension, one which must always be handled abstractly rather than concretely, just as north and south must be handled abstractly rather than concretely. When we read a sequence of events back through their antecedents we are looking at them deterministically. When we compare two or more courses of action we are thinking freely. When we choose a point of departure we are exercising freedom and when we set off in pursuit of its consequences we are accepting determinism. Without the freely chosen point of departure there would be no way of determining anything, and without the deterministic pursuit of outcomes any free choice one might make would be robbed instantly of all its consequences.

Take the impulsive client often seen in psychotherapy; his choices range freely over a wide field, but they never mean anything to him because he never lets himself be bound by them. All the time he is so busy reaching into the grab bag that he never gets to open one of the packages. In contrast to this, the most independent person in the world is, in a sense, a victim of his own decisions, and the man who is caught up on circumstances is free either to adjust to them in a thousand different ways or to figure out some means of altering them.

I do not wish to minimize the value of a free society. On the contrary, I think it ought to be taken seriously and its decisions allowed to amount to something. Failure to make something of a society's free choices is to reduce the community to a state of impulsive neuroticism and grab bag economy. Nor would I minimize the value of a controlled society, either; indeed, it ought to be the same society as the free one. But here control should stem from a freely chosen position, or from a variety of freely chosen positions, else it becomes monolithic and oppressive.

I agree with Professor Bauer that for a man to try to be a dictator is stupid, and I would go on to say that the acceptance of his dictatorship is even more stupid, even if he claims to limit his dictation to politics and values—the things that scholars don't want to be bothered with. Suppose a man could be found who was inculcated with the exact modal long range values of his society, as well as endowed with its completely abstracted short range knowledge; it would still be stupid to make a dictator out of him and thus discard the other ninety-nine percent of available human ingenuity.

So, what, then, is dictatorship? A lot of social control? Certainly not, for that is equally the mark of a free society that goes ahead and makes something out of its freedom. Is it a minimum of freedom? Not necessarily that either, for the society's members may have no alternatives to suggest even when given more freedom to express themselves. Dictatorship is, I think, the acceptance on the part of the few of a host of responsibilities, already abandoned by the many.

What I am saying is that it makes no more sense for scholars to ignore their stake in social control than it does to abandon their values in the campus parking lot, and it makes no more sense for them to shun values than it does to insist on filtering all new knowledge through the skull of a dictator who thinks he already knows everything.

[3] Editorial change from 'determination' in the original.

17

Personal Construct Theory as a Line of Inference[1]

One could wish, at a time like this, that the English language were constructed differently. Take the moods of our verbs, for example. If I use a verb in the indicative mood, I imply an identity between what I say and what I am talking about. Right now I don't want to do this. And I don't want to use my verbs in the imperative mood either. Nor does the subjunctive mood quite fit the spirit in which I would like to address you.

The Invitational Mood

For what I want to say there ought to be such a thing as an *invitational mood* into which verbs could be cast. Thus each remark I made would not have to be taken as an effort to state the *indicative* what *is*, or the *imperative* what *ought* to be, or the *subjunctive* what *might* be, but would, instead, be an *invitation* to the listener to join me in *imagining for the moment,* that such and such is so. It would be an invitation for you to come along on an excursion of thought, without worrying too much about whether each statement along the way is true, or good, or whether it is even possible: but solely for the purpose of discovering where the adventure leads us. At the end of our journey we can both ask whether we want to be where we then find ourselves.

So will you join me, for this hour, in pretending that English verbs do have an invitational mood, and that all my predicates are cast in this grammatical form. In other words let's not worry too much about whether my initial remarks have a sound realistic, moral, or practical base. Instead, let us see where this winding passage of inference leads.

Epistemology

My topic this afternoon is *personal construct theory*. As a matter of fact, without having mentioned it, I have already launched into my subject, for what I have been saying is not merely a device for bringing an idea to your favorable attention, it is an example of the kind of epistemology on which personal construct theory is based. Simply stated, this is an epistemology that gauges the limits of knowledge by the points to which our lines of reasoning ultimately lead us.

"Ultimately" means a long ways off of course. But no matter. Even if such points of final reckoning do happen to lie in the infinitely remote future, they nevertheless have something important to do with the lines of inference we pursue here and now, just as the term *infinity* at the end of certain mathematical equations, a something which no one can concretely put his finger on or count up to, is essential to the immediate meaning of these equations. Our *ultimate* test of truth, then, is not how many things we can account for all at once, not the closeness of correspondence between our thoughts and our senses, not even the number of full professors who agree with us, but it is, rather, the way our guesses turn out in the end. Our *immediate* test of truth is then, by the same token, how things turn out tomorrow.

So you see, it was natural enough for me to start out by *inviting* you to take the afternoon off, leave behind any psychological certainties that might spoil the fun, and come along with me for the ride. Now it happens that not only do I think there is a way of arriving at some interesting places we might not otherwise come across, but I suspect this is how mankind generally progresses—perhaps even a little in spite of himself.

[1] Lecture presented at Harvard University, May 6, 1960. Published by permission of Jacqueline Aldridge.

Collected Papers of the Pioneer of Constructivist Psychology: George A. Kelly, First Edition. Edited by David A. Winter and Nick Reed.

A Line of Inference

At this point it should not be hard for you to see how I regard personal construct theory. It is a continuing adventure and, like any adventure needs to be judged, not so much by its point of departure as by its points of arrival. Will you join me then in seeing personal construct theory not so much as a set of fixed spatial dimensions in terms of which moving things, such as human behavior, can be made to stand still long enough to be looked at. It is that, of course. But even more may we regard it this afternoon as an ongoing train of inferences that could give us some fascinating glimpses of what is going on in the mind of man.

Let me hasten to add that the historical beginnings of this train of inferences are quite lost to me. I know others must have started out along these lines, probably centuries ago, and some must have pursued the quest further than I have, but just where they left off or where I picked up from them I am at a complete loss to say. This is something I don't intend to worry about, at least not this afternoon. Moreover, I have no particular proprietary feelings about personal construct theorizing. It is a road anyone can travel as he pleases, and there probably are as many short-cuts as there are people who have set foot on the path.

Every line of thought involves the alternating play of induction and deduction. This is true of my own theorizing ventures. For example, my daily calendar of appointments used to involve a mixture of people who came in to talk about their research and people who came in to talk about their intimate problems. In fact, my calendar still involves such a mixture and it is the sort of mixture I recommend highly for persons who want to have a close-up view of human experiences. The first kind of appointment is supposed to be concerned with scientific inquiry and the second with psychotherapy.

Two Kinds of Referents

I must confess that I was a little slow in catching on, but it did finally dawn on me that both types of interviews were basically concerned with the same issues. The social amenities and the terms of reference were somewhat different—usually. But the obstacles were much the same. For example, at two o'clock we might be confronted with some elastic hypotheses about data that had recently been collected. And at three o'clock we might have to cope with some elastic interpretations of what had happened at the home the night before. At four o'clock I might find myself confronted with a person who was reluctant to stake his prejudices on the outcome of a systematic inquiry. And at five I might find myself facing a poor trembling soul who likewise was reluctant to put his feelings in the form of questions.

The thing that struck me was that for one person I was trying to reduce human behavior to the terms of science—prediction, control, systematic observation, hypothesis testing, experimentation, and perhaps even a little creative thinking now and then. In the other case I was trying to reduce human experience to the terms that psychologists reserve for describing behavior other than their own—motives, needs, anxiety, the residue of childhood misfortunes, unconscious desires, and perverse resistance to realistic insight.

I can't say that one set of referents was working out any better than the other, for by the time I realized that I was dealing with the same basic problems all afternoon I realized that my methods had already begun to fuse with each other. By and large, though, it seemed that my interviewee and I were a little freer to try out something constructive when we were attempting to think together like scientists than when we were trying to negotiate an agreement between patient and therapist. Not that there weren't advantages to the clinical way of thinking; often when we were engaged in what we regarded as psychotherapy we were more imaginative and better able to generate hypotheses. But, too often these sensitive hypotheses were rejected out of hand as obvious "defenses" or, accepted uncritically as "insights." To be sure, in psychotherapy it seemed that we were coming to grips with something way down deep, with those surges of human experience that rarely reach the light of language. But our way of dealing with those surges was mostly by speculative talk, punctuated with soulful silences, heavy sighs, a few tears, wistful glances, moments of ecstasy, and the like. We did not very often reduce our clinical hypotheses to operational terms in order to try them out experientially. So I doubt if we were making as much use of our capacities for human experience as we pretended we were. What we did ended up mostly in talk. And our reasoning tended to be post hoc and safely speculative, rather than the ad hoc risk-taking kind of intellectual venturesomeness that characterizes modern experimentally oriented science.

What I am talking about here is the kind of inductive reasoning that has gone into personal construct theorizing. There were many other inductive passages, of course, such as those which ensued from our explorations of enactment, or from the whimsically fabricated interpretations we tried out in psychotherapy, or from our experiences with the complaints of teachers about their pupils—but perhaps this one line of inference is sufficient to illustrate our point. So let us follow this particular line a little further in order to illustrate how the inductive phases of our theorizing begin to link up with the deductive phases.

The Referents of Science

If science and therapy both find themselves confronted with the same day-to-day problems, cannot we therefore cast those problems into the same terms? And, furthermore, may this not be a good thing to do? Suppose we view the client as we do the scientist and see him, as he struggles to accomplish whatever it is he is trying to accomplish, using the same basic manipulative devices. If the scientist makes use of prediction as a way of life, does he do this only because he is trained as a scientist, or because he is, first of all, a man, using the instruments that men universally employ to accomplish their ends?

Such speculation points to another figure among the various images of man which have been erected through the ages. Instead of man the glutton, or man the tragedian, or man the victim of women, or man the mentally backward god, or man the precocious animal, we have here—man the scientist, the anticipator of what is about to happen. This view puts human behavior squarely on a time dimension, rather than regarding it first in spatial terms and then superimposing some kind of dynamics to account for behavior as a process.

A Postulate with Corollaries

We can state this view of man as a postulate, and then proceed deductively to see how well our inferences turn out. Put it this way, "A person's processes are psychologically channelized by the ways in which he anticipates events." This is a start, and there are several ways we can go from here. One corollary statement that occurs to me right off is that a person anticipates events by construing replications among them. Since time presumably never repeats itself it is up to man, even when he is an infant, to construe experience so that some events seem like what has happened before. Persons do this differently; if this were not so it would be hard to tell one person from another. And each person builds up his own *system* of constructions. Now you see right off we have stated three corollaries, a "Construction Corollary," an "Individuality Corollary," and an "Organization Corollary." You say you might have inferred others. Of course! I agree. You probably would. Indeed, I have already conceded the point. I said—"each person builds up his own system of constructions."

The Dichotomy Corollary

But let's go on. Now we come to one that may be more controversial. "A person's construction system is composed of a finite number of dichotomous constructs." It is a popular notion that we should avoid making black and white judgments about anything. But I am prepared to hold, both on deductive and inductive grounds, that these are the only kinds of judgments that any of us are psychologically prepared to make. Let us see how this works.

Suppose we start with the familiar logical form, *A is either B or not B,* and consider it from two angles. In order to make this a little more wide awake on a late Friday afternoon let us substitute some more vivid terms of reference. Let us put it this way, for the sake of our discussion: *your psychology professor is either interested in you or he is not interested in you.* Now let us consider *this* statement from our two angles.

Some psychologists say that one must first determine whether this is a nonsensical statement. If the idea that one person is *interested* in another is inconceivable, then there is no way of proceeding with the argument. But suppose this is a statement that is conceivable to you but not to me. You have been able to set up a construct of one person being interested in another or not, and have been able to employ it in a variety of situations and to a variety of people, but I haven't the faintest glimmer as to how such an abstraction works. From the standpoint of personal construct theory, then, the question is not whether the *proposition makes sense* of itself or not, but whether it expresses the kind of sense that *you or I make* out of our interpersonal relations. This is a way of saying that, from the standpoint of the theory, constructs are personal.

Now it may occur that even you find the proposition inconceivable in certain realms of events. For example, you may be able to think of a parent being interested in a child, or a student being interested in another student, or even of a student being interested in a professor, but the notion of a professor being interested in a student may seem about as sensible as the idea that Plymouth rock might have been interested in a pilgrim. Here is an instance of where you have the construct all right, but its range of convenience does not extend to such things as professors. Here again the question is not so much whether the construct makes sense or not but where it makes sense as well as to whom. The notion, then, of the range of convenience of the personal construct is an important one in the scheme of things that personal construct theorizing brews.

Now suppose we take the second angle from which this statement about your professor can be viewed, the *either…or* in the sentence. Your psychology professor is *either* interested in you or he is not interested in you. It's got to be one or the other. Now it is possible that you can imagine his being interested in you on some occasions and not on others. In fact he may show interest in you in preference to certain students but not in preference to others. Depending upon the number of occasions, the variety of settings, and the context in which he displays interest rather than no interest you may make some judgment of the *amount* of interest he shows.

Now I have no quarrel with the notion of *amount* or of *shadings of gray* used in this sense. But the notion of *amount* is another construct, also dichotomous with poles of *much* or *little,* which is here combined with the construct of interest. You may say of your professor, then, that he shows a considerable amount of interest in you by combining constructs of *interest versus no interest,* and *much versus little*. But as for your primary working construct of interest, as distinguished from the final plot of your professor, there is only one distinction implied, the distinction between interest and not interest. And there is only one similarity implied too, though one that lumps interested people together and, by the same token, lumps uninterested people together.

Two Poles but Only One Similarity

In making this last statement we have gotten a little ahead of ourselves. The structure of our language and our Western standards of logic will permit us to agree readily enough that there is a similarity between people implied when it is said that they are interested in us. But is there a similarity between the people of whom it is said that they are not interested in us? The line of theorizing we are following this afternoon leads us to say that there is such a similarity. Moreover, it leads us to regard it as essentially the same abstraction that links the interested persons with each other.

Suppose we go back to Plymouth Rock, as I understand it is quite appropriate to do when in these parts. Suppose I said that after considering the matter quite carefully I had concluded that Plymouth Rock was never actually interested in a pilgrim. Such a remark would imply that Plymouth Rock was within the range of convenience of my construct of interest all right enough, and that it therefore made some particular sense to me to conclude that Plymouth Rock was *not interested*. Here I *am* construing the behavior of the rock and I am affirming something about that behavior. Perhaps I am drawing my inference from the fact that it is willing just to lie there and be looked at, without in the slightest ever inching over to the iron fence through which people peer at it, or without ever responding to any of the rude remarks made in its presence. I may even speculate that this monumental lack of interest stems from the Rock's inner conviction that it will outlast both its critics and idolizers, so why should it bother with either. But I have accepted the rock within the range of convenience of the construct and I have likened it to other objects, including possibly some psychology professors, which have bravely withstood the temptation to become interested in people.

During this passage in our line of inference I am supposed to be theorizing deductively. But theory building is not simply one big wave of induction followed by one big trough of deduction. There are a lot of ripples too in the pattern of thought, and I still have something important to say about the dichotomy corollary. I think we can say it best by following an *inductive* line of inference.

The Implicit Pole of a Construct

Take the child who repeats, during clinical interviews, such expressions as "He gets mad," or "They had fits," or "Somebody was looking for a fight," or "She blows up," etc. Are these terms which merely distinguish some sense of turbulence from everything else in the world, from a rooster's tail, from a slip of the tongue, from the time of day, from a big bass drum? Or is he saying that there is another pole to his dimension, perhaps a pole of tranquility that he longs for or has once caught a glimpse of. Or is he saying that there is a gay and carefree way for people to get along with each other, if they would only hit on it. Then again may he not be saying that the persons he knows *do* angry things but that, as persons, this is not wholly the way he seems to them? Or is this it: "I am not an angry person, it is only that I am *surrounded* by anger?" Perhaps he means that only after an explosion has taken place can one be sure that he is no longer on the verge of catastrophe. Is he reminding his gently mannered interviewer that this is not the way people in his world interact with each other? Actually, our clinical experience teaches us that we know comparatively little about what he means until the construct he is using is fully explicated in its dichotomous form, until the implicit contrast becomes clear.

Or take the student who keeps saying, "I believe people should be *accepted* as they are. I believe students should be encouraged to choose their own intellectual pursuits. On examinations they should be allowed to say what they really think. We need more faith in our fellow man." As clinicians we ask ourselves, what is the student saying?

What is the complete construct?

Every construct seems to involve two assertions. In this case the assertion that people should be "accepted" is only one of them. The student is also asserting something else. In fact, the something else is likely to be what he is primarily addressing himself to. If he looks you straight in the eye while making these remarks you may suspect that he is drawing some kind of contrast which puts you on one side of the fence and himself on the other. He may be implying that some people *control* others, or perhaps that he feels *himself controlled* by outside forces, or that there is a helplessness, a sense of utter dependency, for which he sees social permissiveness as the only remedy.

But experience in psychotherapy will lead us to suspect that there may be even more here. Not only is there an attitude being expressed which needs to be understood both in terms of its thesis *and* its anti-thesis, but the student is cutting out for himself a conceptual slot along which he can move himself. Such a mental slot gives direction to his own behavior. If his social posture proves impossible to maintain, this construct dimension that he has just expressed makes it clear what he can do about it. He can move from one end to the other. He can stop putting up with people as they *are* and start making them into what they ought to be. He can demand that his professors provide more positive leadership, that they stand for something! He can insist that examinations measure what students really know. And he can become alert to the hidden motivations of his fellow man—these in contrast to what he said about *accepting* people as they are, *encouraging students* to choose, letting them speak their minds on examinations, and having *faith* in fellow man.

This is perhaps enough to say about the dichotomy corollary in general and about the kind of inductive inferences in particular that go into it. We can return to deduction for awhile. I might talk about the body oriented patient who for months had puzzled his therapist with his complaints that he was sick, sick, sick. The therapist, after elaborating with him the idea of sickness, as well as trying a number of other things, decided to examine the construct from the point of view of the dichotomy corollary and asked him what it would mean not to be sick. The patient, surprised at being asked such an obvious question, looked up and said immediately, "Why, to be *free*." After that the two of them began to make some progress.

A Cognitive Theory or an Affective Theory

You will recognize that I have formulated human behavior in terms of dichotomous units—units called "constructs" because they are erected to cope with circumstances and, furthermore, called "personal constructs" because they are erected by the persons who use them. You have perhaps noted that these are abstracted units of behavior which may or may not carry word labels in the mind of the user. Perhaps it is clear, too, that this is not a cognitive theory any more than it is an affective theory. The only reason I can think of for anyone's calling it a cognitive theory is that he was accustomed to think of anything that can be understood dispassionately by a psychologist as inherently lacking in passion. This background of belief in a necessary and immediate homology of construct and object sometimes causes confusion in understanding personal construct theory. To understand it properly one needs to approach the theory from the epistemological position of constructive alternativism, a position which most scientists half believe in, but find hard to apply because neither our culture nor our language permit us to talk that way.

Abstraction

There is something more that needs to be said about the "Dichotomy Corollary" that may help one to understand how he can regard a construct as essentially a black versus white affair, yet use that construct to plot objects concretely along a scale. The construct is an abstraction. I have already said that, haven't I! This is to say it is portable, like a measuring stick that can be picked up and laid down to compare a great variety of lengths, or like a compass that always points either north or south—never a little north or a little south—but which can be moved about to tell which is north of which or what is south of what. And, like the compass, the construct tells us specifically that what is north is not south, not merely the one-ended fact that what is north is different from up or down, east or west, rooster tails, slips of the tongue, times of the day, big bass drums. The psychologic, if we may pull a word apart in order to cram some meaning into it, is of the form, *A is either B or C*, rather than of the classical form, *A is either B or not B*. Your professor is either interested in you *or he is a stinker*. This may not be logical, but it is psychological! It seems to us that live human beings do not compare a something with a nothing, not even a professor. I doubt if they even can. They think by comparing something with something—an interested professor or a stinker.

I said that this corollary had something to do with the mathematics of personal construct theory. Without trying to elaborate the point this late in our discussion, perhaps you will simply agree with me that the construct, viewed as we view it—as an abstraction, and as dichotomous, and as having two affirmative poles—is a kind of binary mathematical unit. We will not go into the further implications of this, except to say that it permits one to predict such things as a Gaussian distribution of responses on an attitude scale whose constructs do not match the constructs of the respondent, and a U-shaped curve in certain instances where they do: and to say that it permits the use of binary factorial analyses of personal construct systems that have been explicated in certain ways.

Well, we have been hung up for the major portion of this paper on the dichotomy corollary. Perhaps that was to be expected, for dichotomous constructs *are* forms of self-prepared dilemmas, and people *do* hang themselves up on the horns of them, and tender minded clinical psychologists often try to haul people off these painful perches; sometimes by generously offering the use of their own dilemmas.

Other Corollaries

There are other corollaries along the path of inference we have chosen. Having set up his dichotomy we suspect a person chooses for himself the alternative which appears either to stabilize the core of his system or to extend its perimeter. Call that one a "Choice Corollary." And constructs have limited ranges of convenience, at least the ones we have seen seem to have. Call that the "Range Corollary." We have already mentioned it. And construct systems change with the rolling succession of predictions and outcomes that characterize life's experience. Call that the "Experience Corollary." But there are limits to one's flexibility in revising his system, limits that are pretty much set by how well one can use his existing constructs to embrace new things. That one we can call the "Modulation Corollary." Of course, a construction system is not altogether internally consistent. That is the "Fragmentation Corollary." And if we look at human goings-on in this personal construct way we are led to say that to the extent that one person employs a construction of experience which is similar to that of another, his psychological processes are similar. That we can call a "Commonality Corollary." Finally, we can say that to the extent that one person construes in some way or other the construction processes of another, he may play a role in a social process involving the other person. That is the "Sociality Corollary." From it stem a lot of things that have to do with the way people deal with each other, as well as right useful theories of guilt, hostility, and psychotherapeutic relationships. But we won't worry about these this afternoon.

And Now, the View

What I wanted to talk about was personal construct theory, not so much as a fixed *point* of view, but as a *line* of successive inferences, a line which each of you, I am sure, would have traced out along a somewhat different route. But you have been kind enough to let me drive during this outing. As you see, I've placed as much emphasis upon human *experience* as I have upon human *behavior,* both for man in general as well as for you who accepted the invitational mood of my verbs and came along on this ride. You have been patient with my driving, which you must have found pretty bumpy in spots. But at last we've parked the car at what I consider a vantage point. Now you can look around, see what there is to be seen, and ask yourself if you like the view.

18

The Psychology of the Unknown[1]

The psychologist who attempts to understand human behavior often finds it convenient to envision man's actions in terms of what the man knows—or thinks he knows. When this device works it is said that the behavior is *rational*. Strictly speaking, however, it is not the behavior that is rational; it is the explanation that is rational. This is an important point, and I think that it, or something like it, will keep cropping up as a recurrent theme in what I have undertaken to say.

When, on the other hand, the device fails and the psychologist tries in vain to see a logical relationship between what his friend knows and does, he is inclined to give up and say simply that the behavior is *irrational*. But here again the psychologist's failure to apply the rationality paradigm successfully can just as well be regarded as a failure of the paradigm to meet the situation as it can be attributed to some essential property of the behavior.

In order not to be left high and dry when his rationality paradigm fails him, the psychologist is likely to seek other modes of explanation when he is confronted with what he has called "irrational behavior" in a friend. Most often he attributes such behavior to some special force or motive which operates semi-autonomously within his friend's personality and distorts the normal process of making inferences. The poor man, it seems to the psychologist, is not altogether free to cope with situations as he sees them; he must, instead, continually compromise with the intruding psychodynamics of his own personality.

As a by-product of this kind of psychologizing we have in our society a growing belief that, while a person may be held responsible for his "rational behavior." it is unfair to make him account for his "irrational behavior." In the subcultures where this belief has taken root it becomes quite clear how any of us who finds personal responsibility bothersome may conduct himself so as to be rid of it. All he has to do is to act as if he were the unwitting victim of his psychodynamics. No one can hold him responsible for that!

Cognitive *versus* Dynamic Theories of Personality

When a personality theory is constructed in a rational form it becomes known, quite naturally, as "a rational theory." And, because we find it so easy to confound the rationality of the constructs we erect with the presumed intrinsic rationality of what they seek to explain, we are likely to take it for granted that such a theory is useful only in understanding those behavior we have long regarded as essentially "rational." Moreover, because "rational behavior" is supposed to be based on what the behaving person knows, such a theory is likely to be classified further as "a cognitive theory." and its applications are presumed to be limited to the knowing process in man, that is to say, to *epistemology*.

But a theory may have a rational structure without the theorist having to claim that his own rationale is identical with that of the person he seeks to understand. Certainly the purpose of a psychological theory is not simply to reproduce symbolically the human processes through which man's behavior emerges, but, more appropriately, to enable the psychologist to gain some overview of them, and thus to achieve a level of understanding that will enable him to transcend them. Psychology is not the simulation of human behavior, hither, thither, and yon, but the comprehensive overview of man—man whose full range of behaviors' has yet to unfold itself. It is therefore quite appropriate to erect a theoretical structure on rational grounds and apply it to any man, no matter how incompetent he is, or to any act of man, no matter how impulsive it is.

Much the same can be said about theories that have been designed to explain "irrational behavior." Since we have been inclined to think of theories as simulations of reality, rather than approaches to it, we are likely to suppose that such experiences as love, hostility,

[1] Dated 1963 and published in Bannister, D. (Ed). (1977). *New perspectives in personal construct psychology* (pp. 1–19). Academic Press. Republished by permission of Jacqueline Aldridge.

Collected Papers of the Pioneer of Constructivist Psychology: George A. Kelly, First Edition. Edited by David A. Winter and Nick Reed.

and anxiety cannot be regarded as the calculated outcomes of one's intentions, but as the involuntary products of such corresponding agencies as "motives," "drives," and "psychodynamics." For example, a person in love is not likely to claim that he reached this state of mind by adding up facts. He is more likely to say that love was something that came over him, perhaps "overwhelmed" him. If, then, the theorist is to explain this man's experience it may seem as if he, too, must explain it in terms of "something that came over him." Again, this is a case of the subject matter being confounded with the constructs one has devised in order to understand it. This confounding of objects and constructs is what characterizes, it seems to me, the so-called dynamic theories in psychology.

Representing Events *versus* Construing Them

The man in love may see nothing rational in his experience, and he may go so far as to regard himself as the unwitting victim of psychodynamics or love potions. But that does not mean that we must limit ourselves to the same terms he uses. Our job is to understand his experience in general, not merely to simulate it in particular. To do this with any perspicacity we must devise our own constructions. Our constructs must enable us to subsume his constructs, not merely simulate them. If he thinks in terms of psychodynamics, that is something we ought to understand and appreciate. But it is not necessary for us to resort to psychodynamic explanations ourselves in order to understand his construct of "psychodynamics."

Furthermore, it seems clear that if we are to talk psychologically about any subject matter at all we cannot allow ourselves to rely upon *simulative* terms alone. We must use *constructive* terms, and these are terms for which we must hold ourselves—not their objects—firmly responsible. Thus, in the natural sense, even the words, "love," "hostility," and "anxiety" refer to notions we have ourselves erected, not to events so obvious as to be invulnerable to human interpretation.

So it remains important for us to keep in mind that, even though our only access to events is through the psychological devices we create for looking at them, it is always proper to raise pointed questions about which is which, and about the appropriateness of our personal constructs to their intended objects. "Love," for example, may hold an ever so important position in one's construct system—as I, for one, believe it should. But it may be fitting, nonetheless, for you to ask if what I regard as "love" might not better be construed as "dependency," or even as "hostility." Similarly, one may, in some cases, ask if what a reluctant mother dreads as "self-denial" she might not better experience as "love."

But is love *actually* rational? The answer to this question must, I believe, remain unknown in our generation. Yet our psychology must enable us to cope with such unknowns. If we are careful to distinguish between love as an experience, on the one hand, and our rational construction of it, on the other, the question need not arise. Whatever it will turn out to be in the end, we should not be inhibited in examining it through the spectacles of rationality. As long as we remember what spectacles we are wearing, love, itself, need not be distorted by such inspection.

But a second question: Can love be completely understood if it is regarded in rational terms only? Probably not; we have not yet developed a completely rational understanding of much of anything, even things that seem much less complex than love. Does this not mean, therefore, that we ought to resort to irrational psychodynamic terms? Not necessarily that either; they may cause us to miss even more of what there is to be seen.

And now a third question: Is not the understanding of love implicit in the experience of love? If you can fall in love, does that not mean that you understand it? The experience does indeed provide a kind of understanding, but being in love with someone does not always carry with it a certain understanding of the love that another feels. And that is the root of many a tragedy.

It is sometimes said that man is the only animal who can represent his environment. The implication is that this ability to simulate reality is the principal psychological feature of man, and, hence, something we all ought to cultivate. To be sure, the reproduction of reality is one of the *post hoc* tests of understanding—prediction, for example, is another. But the mere reproduction of reality adds precious little to one's understanding of it. Man can and does do better than that! This, of course, is something every artist knows.

As for the artist, so for all of us; to construe the surrounding world is to visualize it in more than one dimension. And this is no less true for the psychological theorist. He, like the artist—and man—must transcend the obvious. A simulative theory is not enough; in fact it is no theory at all, only a technician's blueprint for the reproduction of something, say, for example, the reproduction of some well known bit of behavior through the presentation of a "stimulus." To serve as a theory one's psychological formulation must not only give him mechanistic prediction and control over the familiar acts of man, but provide access to human potentialities not yet realized. This means that a theory must be *constructive*, not merely *representative*.

To transcend the obvious—this is the basic psychological problem of man. Inevitably it is a problem we must all seek to solve, whether we fancy ourselves as psychologists or not. What has already happened in our experience may seem obvious enough, now that we have been through it. But literally it is something that will never happen again. It can't, for time refuses to run around in circles. If then, as we live our lives, we do no more than erect a row of historical markers on the spots where we have had our experiences, we shall soon find ourselves surrounded by a cemetery of monuments, and overburdened with biographical mementos.

But to represent an event by means of a construct is to go beyond what is known. It is to see that event in a way that could possibly happen again. Thus, being human and capable of construing, we can do more than point realistically to what has happened in the past; we can actually set the stage for what may happen in the future—something, perhaps in some respects, very different. Thus we transcend the obvious!

By construing we reach beyond anything that man has heretofore known—often reach in vain, to be sure, but sometimes with remarkable prescience. This paper has to do with how man, from his position of relative ignorance, can hope to reach out for knowledge that no one has yet attained. This, as I see it, is a primary problem for the psychologist, though I doubt that most psychologists see it that way.

Constructive Alternativism

It is precisely because we may venture to look ahead only by construing never-to-be-repeated events, rather than merely recording or duplicating them, that we must continually and adventurously hold all matters open to the possibility of fresh reconstruction. No one knows yet what all the alternative constructions are, except that, if the history of human thought offers us any clue, there must still be an awful lot of them.

Even the constructions we daily take for granted are probably open to an incalculable number of radical improvements. But, our imaginations being limited as they are, it may be a long time before we get around to looking at familiar things in new ways. What we tend to do is to accept familiar constructs as downright objective observations of what is really there, and to view with great suspicion anything whose subjective origin is recent enough to recognize. The fact that familiar constructs have equally subjective—though possibly more remote—origins usually escapes us. We continue to refer to them as objective observations, as the "givens" in the theorems of daily existence. Yet it is doubtful that any of the "givens" we accept so "realistically" has yet been cast in its final form.

It may, on first thought, be disturbing to visualize ourselves trying to make progress in a world where there are no firm points of departure immediately accessible to us, no "givens." nothing that we start out by saying we know for sure. There are, of course, those who stoutly maintain that this is not indeed the case, that we do have such unimpeachable sources of evidence, that they know what those sources are, and that we too had better believe in them. One such person—the idealist, in the philosophical sense—may say that his anchor point is a god who maintains a certain point of view, or he may hold to a principle or dogma from which he attempts to deduce everything else he needs to know. On the other hand, the materialist, always skeptical of abstractions, anchors his ideas in his senses, or, in the case of the dialectical materialist, in a line of inference which seeks to synthesize physical and social facts. Each, however—idealist and materialist—thinks he must initially have an anchor point, a known reality from which he may safely launch out, and without which it would be futile to proceed.

Yet the "known realities" keep slipping out from under us. Our senses play all kinds of tricks and prove themselves to be the most unreliable informants. And our theologies, far-seeing as they appear to be, do, in time, lead to such indecent practices that sensitive men refuse any longer to take them literally. Thus we find ourselves repeatedly cut off from what once we thought we knew for sure, and we must reluctantly abandon the very faiths from which we originally launched our most fruitful enterprises.

The upshot of all this is that we can no longer rest assured that human progress may proceed step by step in an orderly fashion from the known to the unknown. Neither our senses nor our doctrines provide us with the immediate knowledge required for such a philosophy of science. What we think we know is anchored only in our own assumptions, not in the bed rock of truth itself, and that world we seek to understand remains always on the horizons of our thoughts. To grasp this principle fully is to concede that everything we believe to exist appears to us the way it does because of our present constructions of it. Thus even the most obvious things in this world are wide open to reconstruction in the future. This is what we mean by the expression *constructive alternativism*, the term with which we identify our philosophical position.

But let us assume also that there is indeed a real world out there, one that is largely independent of our assumptions. Moreover, it is a world that moves along and we are, willy nilly, caught up in its stream of time. To understand this objective world is to be able to do more than trace its permanent features; we must anticipate the flow of its events. Now it is precisely at this point that our line of reasoning veers away from classical phenomenology. While we do hold that perceptions are anchored in constructs, we hold also that some constructions serve us better than others in our efforts to anticipate comprehensively what is actually going on. The big question is, of course, which ones, and how do we know.

In Which Direction Lies the Truth?

Since our experiences lie mostly behind us, we are likely to think of the past as defining as well as encompassing all the things we know for sure. And, since, at any given moment, we cannot tell what the future holds in store, we are likely to regard everything that lies up front as somewhat chaotic. If, then, we are asked to say something that is "true" we are likely to mention something we have experienced—something from our past—rather than something we are looking for.

Moreover, when we sit down to try to figure out what will happen in the future, it usually seems as if the thing to do is to start with what we already know. This progression from the known to the unknown is characteristic of logical thought, and it probably accounts for the fact that logical thinking has so often proved itself to be an obstacle to intellectual progress. It is a device for perpetuating the assumptions of the past.

Perhaps at the root of this kind of thinking is the conviction that ultimate truth—at least some solid bits of it—is something embedded in our personal experience. While this is not the view I want to endorse, neither would I care to spend much time quarreling with it. It does occur to me, however, that one of the reasons for thinking this way is our common preference for certainty over meaning; we would rather know some things for sure, even though they don't shed much light on what is going on. Knowing a little something for sure, something gleaned out of one's experience, is often a way of knowing one's self for sure, and thus of holding on to an identity, even an unhappy identity. And this, in turn, is a way of saying that our identities often stand on trivial grounds. If I can't be a man I can, at least, be an expert.

There is another reason for the wide-spread conviction that we must look backwards if we want to see truth. If we regard the attainment of knowledge as a matter of the accumulation of information, then we will see truth as something put together bit by bit, with each individual fact verified and then nailed down to stay. If you want to point to truth, then, you have only to look back at what has been nailed down. A scientist is supposed to start his inquiries with what is already known and published. Only from such a point of departure is it believed that he can best explore the realm of uncertainty.

Having accepted this viewpoint, some scientists in the last century speculated as to what proportion of all possible knowledge had already been accumulated. It was a large proportion, if I remember correctly, somewhat over half. And they guessed that within a century or so everything would be pretty well settled. Now, however—a century later—the day when we will know everything of importance seems a good deal further off. Moreover, a lot of those matters we thought we had settled are having to be reconsidered.

Experience, Knowledge and Truth

I suppose that science can be regarded as moving ahead step by step—whatever that means. But with each step that brings into focus some new facet of the universe something, which before we thought was all settled, begins to look questionable. It is not that each new fact displaces an old one, but that gradually, almost imperceptibly as our ventures progress, a darkening shadow of doubt begins to spread over the coastline behind us.

A student, for example, who starts his career by making certain conventional assumptions about scientific determinism thereafter comes across many things in his lifetime, and may end up with serious doubts about scientific determinism itself. This is not to say that his assumptions trapped him in blind alleys. Indeed, only by pursuing their implications as avidly as he did was he able to arrive where he did. Still, from the very vantage point to which they eventually led him, those assumptions appeared much more questionable than they originally did, and he would now hesitate to use them again.

Now the question is, did the truth lie ahead of him or behind him? Did he, using his partial knowledge as a base, launch an invasion of the remaining world of things he did not know? Or did he, starting from a position of admissible ignorance and using only his faulty vision of an ultimate truth, proceed toward what he—ignorant man that he was—dared hope to understand?

Perhaps we had better make a distinction between knowing something and believing it to be the truth. Since knowing something can also be regarded as a subjective experience—that is to say an *awareness*, and need not imply that what is thus known is significant of anything except the experience itself, it would seem reasonable to say that the student had indeed proceeded from the "known" into the realm of what had once been for him the "unknown." What he knew was how he felt, and what he did not know was how he would later feel. Yet his point of departure seemed less valid when he looked back on it. And if he had been forewarned of the extent to which the outlooks of scholars are likely to change during a lifetime, he would not have felt, when he started out, that he really knew very much at all.

Now we can say that truth becomes known only *through experience*. This is not the same as the more trivial proposition, mentioned a moment ago, that bits of truth are embedded in one's experience. One can make a stronger case for the *through experience* proposition, and I shall have something to say presently about the importance of it. But, before I do, let me remark that it is tempting to infer from this proposition that there is no point in venturing beyond one's own experience in searching for truth.

I suppose it does seem a little silly for man to attempt to transcend himself? That is a prerogative which, since the Greeks, we have left to the gods, is it not—or to the priests who, after all, have proved themselves much more articulate than gods ever were, or, nowadays, to the medics who have turned out to be more enterprising in telling us just what to do with ourselves than either gods or priests? If, then, it is personal experience alone that counts, I suppose it would seem logical for us mortals to focus the attention of all psychology upon the self, the self which is both the agent and the beneficiary of all experiential outcomes.

There is indeed a point here, and if man were no more than a bystander to that procession we call the universe, or if the universe were itself no more than a spatially distributed display of interesting objects, then we might reasonably regard experience and truth as facsimiles of each other. But what man thinks he sees leads him to conjure with what he has not seen, and what he has experienced makes him wonder what he has missed. So imagination, once stirred, often leads to initiative, and initiative to action, and action produces something unexpected for men to contemplate and experience, and, finally, the newest experience throws the recollections of prior experiences into fresh perspective, thus reducing them to the level of mere chronicler's facts, facts whose historical meaning takes its shape from present rather than past interpretations.

What, for example, is experienced on the battlefield as fear and desperation is recast as heroism and noble purpose; what once was experienced as tenderness in courtship is sometimes re-experienced in the life of a married man as possessiveness; adventure becomes boredom, and boredom in a classroom is translated by some magic of retrospect and academic acclaim into scholarly enterprise. Certainly shifting perspectives can do strange things to experience.

Where, then, lies the truth? In experience? And if in experience, then in what experience—the experience of the past, or in the experience of the future? And can it be said that experience is the key to what is known? If so, then what is it that is known? Is it only experience itself that is known—one's past experience, perhaps, or the experience of the fleeting instant—as psychologists of the actual genetic school would say—or of the phenomenal present—as the true phenomenologist might say? If so, then what about the desperate soldier on the battlefield, alternately performing acts of tender mercy and deeds of enormous cruelty—for one or the other of which he may later be decorated by Act of Congress, or perhaps even elected to public office—does he know only his immediate experience, and will he never know anything else? Is killing and rescuing and being killed all "just for kicks"? Is experience both end and means, both truth and evidence, premise and conclusion? In short, is the universe of man a vast redundancy?

Or would it not be better to say that one can never know his immediate experience until he has looked back on it again and again—long after it has ceased to be immediate—and even then will he know it only partially until he looks back on it still again? And is it not better to say that a man of experience is one who has done more than collide with a series of events, that he is, instead, a person who, by anticipating and taking account of those events, has been moved to reconstrue them in many dimensions to gain fresh perspectives on everything around him? Yes, I rather think such a definition of human experience has more to offer than the notion of immediate *self-involvement*—important as I believe *being-in-the-world* is in the full realization of existence.

Even *commitment*, which is *self-involvement* plus *affirmative anticipation*, does not altogether unlock the potentialities of human experience, for it often leaves man a hostage to his past involvements, rather than the beneficiary of them, and it indentures him to the immature expectations of his youth. Only by adding *reconstruing* to the sequence of psychological processes can the full cycle of human experience be completed and man freed from his Sisyphean labors. The cycle of human experience remains incomplete unless it terminates in fresh hopes never before envisioned. This, as I see it, is no less true for the puzzled scientist than for the distraught person who seeks psychotherapeutic escape from the psychological redundancies that he has allowed to encompass him, or, for that matter, for the experienced sinner who finds in repentance, not reincapsulation within a dogmatic system, but the full restoration of his initiative.

The Role of Experience in a World Where Nothing Is Yet Known for Sure

It is true that most psychologists concede that the full possession of the ultimate truth is an accomplishment which still lies far ahead of us. But the structure of the scientific establishment they usually work to build is founded on the notion of an ultimate truth that is pieced together bit by bit, and fragment by fragment. This is to say that if one knows A and B to be true, he can safely proceed to the discovery of C, and be that much further along toward having the whole jig-saw puzzle of the universe properly assembled. But if he is mistaken about A or B he can scarcely hope to arrive at C. This is the *fragmental* notion of truth, and science, according to this notion, progresses by a series of technical "break-throughs." So the business of the scientist is to get things nailed down, one at a time, and, using each established fact or law as a point of departure, to make further inferences and test them by experimentation. If the data confirm the hypotheses, then one will have something more to nail down, and the total job of simulating the universe will be that much nearer completion. I suppose when the task is complete they hope to declare a scientists' "sabbath" and rest from their labors.

But what I am now led to say differs fundamentally from this notion of *fragmental* truth, though I think it has been implicit in scientific enterprise for some time. Moreover, I see in it profound implications for the science of the future, and especially for psychology. Let us say that the whole of truth lies ahead of us, rather than that some parts of it ahead and some behind. What we possess, or what we have achieved so far, are *approximations* of the truth, not *fragments* of it. Hopefully we are getting closer, in some sort of asymptotic progression, and, at some infinite point in time, science and reality may indeed converge.

What we do then is not so much to go about sifting out nuggets of truth to add to our treasure chest, as it is to invent new constructions to place upon the events of the universe in which we have engaged ourselves. The constructions are admittedly inadequate—the history of scientific thought should, if nothing else, lead us to regard them so. But, even though they are inadequate expressions of what we will eventually conclude, they do provide practical grounds for more intimate involvement, for more alert anticipation, for more courageous commitment, and, eventually, for the very reconstructions which will supplant them. None of us knows how many alternative constructions are tenable, but I think the variety must always—this side of eternity—be considerable.

So we have called this outlook on the scientific undertaking *constructive alternativism*. It is itself an alternative to the notion of *accumulative fragmentalism*, upon which it now appears we have, in fact, been building our scientific edifice. And I should hasten to add that *constructive alternativism* is a philosophical outlook that has as much significance for the distressed individual who seeks psychotherapy—or even for the artist—as it does for the scientist. But, for the moment, let us speak only to the issues of science, or to that particular program of human effort we are momentarily inclined to call "science."

Our venture as scientists, then, is not to press down with one hand on what is presumed to be known for sure and reach out with the other into the unknown for more bits of the puzzle, but rather to proceed from propositions which are admittedly faulty, in the hope that we can complete fully the experiential cycles which will enable us to formulate new propositions that are perhaps less faulty. It is not that we, as scientists, know just so much, and are out to add to the store, but rather that our experiences, pressed full cycle, will lead us to question more freely, to be less taken in by the "obvious," to see fresh possibilities of relationships, to put facts together into more productive combinations, and to entertain sweeping alternative constructions of events where once we could only "feel" and "perceive" and "learn" what was already "known"—in the manner that "psychologists" write so much about.

Transcending the Obvious

Now what is there about this human experience, pursued in full cycle, that enables man to rise above what he thinks he knows and so often to do better than he knows how? How does he transcend the obvious? If a man, say a psychologist, remains aloof from the human enterprise he sees only what is visible from the outside. But if he engages himself he will be caught up in the realities of human existence in ways that would never have occurred to him. He will breast the onrush of events. He will see, he will feel, he will be frightened, he will be exhilarated, and he will find himself feared, hated, and loved. Every resource at his disposal, not merely his cognitive and .professional talents, will be challenged. So involved will he be that, in order to survive, he will have to cope with his circumstances inarticulately as well as verbally, primitively as well as intelligently, and he will have to pull himself together physically, socially, biologically, and spiritually.

Now add to this *involvement* the further ingredient of *commitment*. Not only does he fling himself into the path of events but he also undertakes to anticipate them and to deflect their course. He becomes a significant event himself, and hence a factor in what happens. So not only must he cope with what has engulfed him, but he must bear some responsibility for the turn of events. So cast, he becomes, in some measure, the architect of his own hazards and catastrophes, and thus what was once so obvious to him as an external observer is emptied of its previous meaning.

It is true that a person so caught up in the tide of circumstances, or so committed to the control of them, can scarcely be accredited as an unbiased observer. But, from the standpoint of constructive alternativism, the issue is not bias versus unbias, but the question of what the bias is and how long it takes to see things in a new light. There are indeed times in one's life when the stream of events flows so rapidly that he becomes preoccupied with his own survival and he fails to see the world in any but a momentary perspective. But give him time to look back on an experience, not as a bystander to it, but as one who has survived it. Or let him involve himself in more massive affairs. These are the ways of gaining perspective, and not disengagement from the human enterprise in an effort to achieve the fiction of being an "unbiased" observer.

It is not an uncommon occurrence that men who have faced death or tragedy come to see their worlds in quite different ways. Is it that misfortune is merely a rude reminder of some earlier conviction? I think not. It is the experience, with its self-involvement and, in some cases, its commitment, that mobilizes their reconstruing resources. Before the crisis such a man may have lived in a day-to-day world of obvious meanings. It was "obvious" that he must drive his car at high speed—else he would miss his appointment. It was "obvious" that he had to burn the candle at both ends—else he would not get his job done, or what he thought was his job. It was "obvious" that starvation was the result of perversity. But, through an experience in which he himself was involved and committed, he quickly found a way to transcend such "obvious" things.

A man who is not engaged with life has to explain his behavior in terms of "motivations"—how else can he? But a man who is fully engaged and committed never thinks of such things. He has purposes and expectations, but not motives. A man who experiments as a way of coping with his life may devise something new, but the fellow who is merely an experimentalist can scarcely hope to see anything that he does not already presume is there. In the one case an experiment is a recourse to experience, in the other it is a formalistic exercise intended to take the place of such a grubby occupation.

Using the Full Cycle of Experience

I hope it is clear at this point that I see personal experience as a key to human progress, both individual and scientific. This is the reason I have identified myself with clinical psychology, even though I have no particular interest in applied psychology. In fact, it is precisely because I do not wish to be an applied psychologist that I have taken up the more intimate approach to man. Except as I involve myself deeply with a person whose life is at the turning point, unless I seek to anticipate the outcomes of his decisions at this point, unless I myself make some commitment to joining him in a common undertaking, and unless in this situation I am ready to *reconstrue* psychology rather than *apply* it merely, then I think that, as a psychologist, I shall accomplish little more than to accumulate a bibliography to attach to my next application for a job.

But, while *constructive alternativism* turns me to *experience* as a way of transcending the obvious, it is, as I have said before, the full cycle of experience—that is to say, my involvement in the life of man, unequivocal prediction, the recognition of confirmation and disconfirmation, and ingenious reapproximation—rather than one phase of the cycle only that must concern me. So, along with the emphasis I place on experience, I hope it is equally clear that I am not proposing phenomenology as the key to scientific advancement—nor existentialism—nor cognitive theory. I realize that *personal construct theory*, with which my name has been identified, has been placed by various writers in each of these categories; but I think it belongs in none of them. I even once found it categorized as a "learning theory," a discovery which has given me considerable amusement, since, in proposing the theory, I went to some lengths to urge psychologists to consider the advantages of abandoning the concept of "learning" altogether.

May I take a moment to point out what *constructive alternativism*, and its implementation through personal experience, means to the graduate student in psychology. A student interested in the topic of creativity, for example, would first try to see it in the flesh. What he thought he "knew" about it would be assumed to be an approximation to truth only, and completely open to reconstruction, rather than as so much known for sure with a little more about to come.

He might, of course, round up some creative people and measure them. This is what some psychologists who are interested in creativity are doing, and they are no longer graduate students. But there is not very much self-involvement in that. There would be a little more involvement if the student observed these "organisms" in the act of being creative, and still more if he found some way to participate. Then he could have a go at being creative himself, unless his dissertation adviser were too upset by that sort of thing.

But, more than this, the full use of experience implies that the student would seek to understand the difference between the creative moments and the uncreative moments in one's life, and the possible complementary relationship between them. This is not the same as trying to find dimensions in which the creative person differs from the less creative person; it has, rather, to do with the fluctuations in the creative process itself and their particular dimensions, and it provides better grounds for participating in the experience.

But, thus far, the student has undertaken only the personal involvement phase of the experiential cycle. It is the sort of thing any phenomenologist might suggest. Now we can move from involvement to commitment, as Camus did when breaking with post-war French existentialism. And we do this by adding anticipation, that is to say, the setting of goals, trying to make something happen with a vision of what it might be, and the prediction of outcomes. Can the graduate student do something to make himself more creative at a given time, or make his associates more creative, or help them find their creative moments, and can he say explicitly what he has done, or can they? If they undertake the task together will their commitment to the task and to each other throw any light on the matter?

Next, there is the matter of assessing the outcomes of their undertakings, and, again, it is just as important, I think, for the so-called subjects in this phase of the inquiry to assess the outcomes as it is for the person who initiated the experiment. This is to say that it is proper to exploit all the available experience of all the persons who have it.

Finally, there is the reconstruing phase of the cycle. Can conventional psychological theory adequately cover both the experience and its apparent outcomes? Does the student dare tamper with theory enough to adapt it to the facts?

After all this—*after*—there is the formal experiment. That may invite some experience too, but not necessarily very much. Experiments are usually designed to test out some element of a theory, or to add another brick to the scientific establishment, but rarely are they designed to put the experimenter into an advantageous position for seeing things in a new light or for reapproximating truth.

But, nevertheless, experiments must be done if degrees are to be awarded, and, in general, I am in favor of them—both experiments and degrees. A formal experiment is a test to see if one has a reasonably good rule for predicting what will happen, or for making it happen. At this point it may be safe for the student to see his experimental design committee, though that often turns out to be a deadly thing to do.

What happens next is well known and psychologists reverently allude to it as "research"—sometimes as "re-search," which is, perhaps, a better term for what they do. To be a "scientist" one must reduce his experience to a set of rules and techniques, so that anyone can accomplish the same result without having to know what he is doing. From here on the job is legalistic and technical, and our profession abounds in the kind of people who are good at this sort of thing; some graduate departments will hardly employ anyone else.

But this is all right. The student who has made sure that he is clinically familiar with "creativity," or whatever else he has chosen to explore, who has produced the phenomenon under face-to-face operating conditions, who has experienced its personal components, and who is patient enough to listen respectfully to the research technicians without losing track of what he is doing, has little to worry about. In fact, at this point—if, indeed he has actually reached it—he probably doesn't even need a clinical psychologist as a dissertation adviser.

Faith and the Unknown

While I have proposed this before, it may not hurt to express, in this context, the idea that one has to start with his own construction of a situation—not because he believes it to be true, or out of any conviction that he knows anything for sure, or even after assuring himself that it is the best of all available alternatives. On the contrary, he must, if he has any sense of historical perspective, realize that his psychology must, in the light of coming centuries, still be considered a psychology of the unknown—this, rather than a psychology that has been partly substantiated—and that knowledge, certainly, and truth all lie a considerable distance ahead of him.

This does not, by any means, make psychology a footless undertaking. What man starts with is not a certainty of the way things are, but a *faith*, a faith that, by systematic effort, he can get a little closer to the way they are. One need not assume he has possession of any shining bits of "revealed truth," picked up either on Mt. Sinai or in a psychological laboratory. But it is important to appreciate the fact that there have been some mighty ingenious approximations to truth, and some of them can be shown to be a lot better than others. Still, ingenious as these approximations are, one may live in the *faith* that better ones can be contrived. It is this *faith* that distinguishes the psychology of the unknown from simple psychological agnosticism. And it is *experience*, sought in full cycle, that is the implementation of the *faith*.

So one's construction of a situation, for which he must always take full personal responsibility—whether he can put it into words or not—provides the initial grounds for seeking experience with events. This is to say that one's personal constructs—not physical accidents—are the springboard to self-involvement. I become aware of a situation by construing it in my own terms, and on these terms I seek to come to grips with it. Some psychologists call this "opening the self to experience." But there is more to experience than mere collision with events—a lot more. I dare anticipate what will happen and I wager my life that what happens will be different because I have intruded myself. This, as I see it, is *commitment*—what I have called "self-involvement plus anticipation."

But, as I have suggested, flinging oneself into the path of onrushing events does not make the experienced man. People do that sort of thing all the time, and over and over in the same way. Nor is experience ever complete at the instant the last impact with an event has taken place, unless, of course, the man fails to survive. No sooner has the impact occurred than the experience-prone man starts reconstruing its significance. With a little ingenuity he should, by sundown, have come up with several versions of what happened.

With his reconstructions he should be prepared to face another day, to involve himself with it in a somewhat different way, to anticipate the day's being different because of his designs upon it, and to nurse still another bloody nose when evening comes. Now that, I submit, is experience! His point of departure is characterized by what the fellow did not know. But a lifetime of such diurnal cycles should bring him a lot closer to knowing something about the way the world is run. It is not the bumps that teach him, nor his bull-headed commitment, nor what he thinks about when he is putting cold compresses on his nose, but the full cycle of experience. What he thought when he started it all will probably seem a lot different a few years later, yet it must be remembered that it was the initial basis for launching himself into the experience. And let us keep in mind that he must all along have had some faith that at least he could begin to get the hang of it.

Where Does the Responsibility for Explanation Lie?

Now I have come to the last paragraphs of this paper, and I must confess that I have not yet even mentioned the most important thing I wanted to say. But no matter; if what I have said so far is clear enough, there should be no difficulty in making my point.

You will recall that I started out by saying that psychology does not have to be irrational or to resort to motivational explanations, even in accounting for the kinds of behavior that do not appear to make sense. The difficulties we have are intrinsic to the theories we employ and to the persons who use them, and need not be attributed to the behavior itself. And as for psychological constructs, it is the man who applies them who must take responsibility for them. The objects of his constructions should not be blamed for his failures to predict accurately.

In going on to speak of the psychology of the unknown, I suggested that there are many alternative constructions one can place upon events—such as the acts of a friend—and the chances are that none of those that occur to us in our lifetimes will turn out to be precisely right. What we do is embark upon the psychological enterprise with a faith that, given a new vantage point through experience, we can formulate better versions of what is going on in the mind of man. It is not that we may ever start with the certainty that we know just so much and are about to uncover a little more.

So how do we make the plunge? By undertaking experience! And experience comes about in a sequence of cycles, not just in one cycle, or in part of one cycle. It comprises, first of all, self-involvement—our jumping into something with both feet. In psychology I think that means undertaking intimate relationships with man—as, for example, in clinical psychology, and, more particularly, in psychotherapy. To this is added anticipation, and thus experience includes commitment. But even that is not enough, for then reconstruction is required, else no progress is accomplished.

Experience need not be an irrational undertaking, as so many psychologists claim, though it may be very hard to account for what happens in experience on available rational grounds. That difficulty is another matter. The point here is that experience, because it mobilizes all of man's resources—intellectual, inarticulate, implicit, physical, social, and even his will to change matters— enables him to transcend the obvious. And that is something that is very hard to do when you stick to the psychology of the known, or when you keep thinking about science in terms of *accumulative fragmentalism*.

Constructive alternativism, however, provides, in contrast to *accumulative fragmentalism*, an approach in which experience has a systematic role. And, in addition to putting such matters as the role of experience into a clearer psychological perspective, it suggests some startlingly fresh answers to some very old questions. Take, for example, that old favorite, *free will versus determinism*. Not only is this a basic issue in science, but it is of peculiar importance to the psychologist whose primary concern is the alleged agent of free will himself, as well as its often pitied victim.

Determinism and Freedom

I have suggested elsewhere that freedom and determinism are two sides of the same coin. That is to say that each implies the existence of the other, and, indeed, would make no sense without the presence of the other. The argument is very simple—at least it seems so to me. Free will would not make much sense unless, by exercising it, I could make something happen. That means exercising a deterministic influence on subsequent events.

If, as a free man with all the supposed rights of citizenship, I decide to tie my shoe, I make a little bargain with myself and hold myself to it until the shoe is properly tied. That means that I make a decision and subsequently bind myself by its deterministic influence. But if my decision imposes no obligation on my subsequent actions, if I am as fancy free as ever to change my mind before I so much as stoop to reach my shoe laces, the freedom with which I make the original decision is futile. Freedom is freedom only if it is the freedom to determine something. And I reap the rewards of freedom only by obligating myself. Of course, if I am running down stairs in a five-o'clock subway crowd, I may find the exercise of my constitutional freedoms somewhat hazardous.

Determinism, conversely, implies an option exercised at some prior point. I do not see how a given event can be regarded as the outcome of a deterministic linkage if there was never any possibility of its being anything other than what it is. To say that it was determined is to say that it is as it is because, but for certain circumstances, it might have turned out differently. Somewhere along the line the die was cast. Up until the moment it was cast there was still the possibility of the event later turning out in some other way. So determinism implies a prior moment of decision, and, while "free will" may seem like too anthropomorphic a term, we do imply that there was an instant when matters were still free to head one way or another.

What we do, in fact, is to apply the constructs of freedom and determinism alternatively. In the sequence; A is followed by B, which, in turn, is followed by C; the term C can be regarded as "determined" by B—the point of choice. But, if we wish, we can go back to A and call it the moment of choice—the instant of "freedom." And why not?

Or if you prefer to turn the illustration around, you can start with A and define it as a point of choice to start with. This is a way of saying that B and C were determined by it. But then, if you don't like to admit that it was Grandfather A's choice that started it all, you can start, instead, with Father B—only one generation up the line—and blame what happened to C on him. Or, if you are a psychiatrist with a lot of counter transference on C, you may rather say that it was Mrs. B—the mother—who was at fault.

Now what I have been doing is applying the principle of *constructive alternativism* to a problem that is both old and urgent. Some day we may know who to blame for a child's troubles, or we may give up the construct of "blame" altogether. But as of now, all we have are some approximations to the understanding of psychological problems—not the perplexing nuggets of truth the accumulative fragmentalist thinks he has collected. Let us not say that "blame" is intrinsic to the man to whom it is applied. It is our construct, and we who use it are the ones who must take primary responsibility for its appropriateness. We are the ones who must take the blame for "blame."

Free will, with its implicit moral responsibility, and *determinism*, with its hope that everything can be accounted for in some grand plan, are alternative constructions that we currently employ in our quest for better approximations to the complete understanding of man. And they are not altogether antithetical as principles, unless one makes the mistake of regarding them as intrinsic to the events which we attempt to construe by means of them. Of course it is difficult to regard an event as *intrinsically* both a consequent and as a determinant in the same progression. But the contradiction vanishes when we realize that whether an event is regarded as a determinant or a consequent is a matter of construction, and it should not, this side of eternity, be identified as being of itself one or the other. Moreover, the constructions of determinism and free will are matters for which we must ever hold ourselves and our theories responsible, not the events themselves. But this I have said before.

There is a Psychology for Getting Along with the Unknown

But where does all this about encouraging rational theories of "irrational' behavior about the antics of organisms not really being explained by psychodynamics, about experience transcending "the obvious" and taking the place of inferences from known facts, about the possible abandonment of those fragments of truth that students memorize for their qualifying examinations, and the dialectic about freedom and determinism each being propped up by logic of the other—now where does all this lead us? Do I not believe the universe is organized? My answer to that is that I would not claim to know that it is. Whether it is organized or not is still one of those things that are unknown. I don't even know whether it is a good question or not.

But while I don't know the answer to the question, I need not be immobilized. There is a psychology for getting along with the unknown. It is a psychology that says in effect, "Why not go ahead and construe it to be organized—or disorganized, if you prefer—and do something about it. In the world of unknowns seek experience, and seek it full cycle. That is to say, if you go ahead and involve yourself, rather than remaining alienated from the human struggle, if you strike out and implement your anticipations, if you dare to commit yourself, if you prepare to assess the outcomes as systematically as you can, and if you master the courage to abandon your favorite psychologisms and intellectualisms and reconstrue life altogether; well, you may not find that you guessed right, but you will stand a chance of transcending more freely those 'obvious' facts that now appear to determine your affairs, and you just may get a little closer to the truth that lies somewhere over the horizon."

19

Discussion: Aldous, The Personable Computer[1]

Since most of the participants in this conference have been prefacing their remarks by saying that they really have no business being here, I would like to insert my claim to a similar distinction. I think I can make a more convincing case than the others who have tried.

Not only am I innocent of any intimacies with computers, but I am the fellow who has sworn off using most of the psychological constructs that have been tossed around during the last three days. For example, some time ago I discarded "motives" and have been living quite happily without recourse to "motivation" ever since. "Affect" makes no sense to me anymore; nor do "drives," "reinforcements," "stimuli," "responses," "emotion," or "cognition." As a matter of fact, I decided to abandon "learning" some years ago, a bold step that opened up a whole exciting new world to me. Having had a taste of this exhilarating way of life, it seems quite unthinkable now that I should ever return to the days when I allowed my time to be taken up with learning things rather than making something out of them, with being pushed around by what people kept telling me were my motives, or with being forever prodded into some senseless activity by events that happened to be labeled "stimuli."

But while I, myself, have abandoned most of the vocabulary of those who keep the American Psychological Association journals going, I do regress, from time to time, in the interest of classical humanism. So just to make it clear I have not lost respect for the older generation who imagined there really were such things as "affect," etc., I have tried to put some of the thoughts expressed in this conference into poetical form:

There once was an ardent young suitor
Who programmed a female computer,
But he failed to connect
The affective effect,
So there wasn't a thing he could do to 'er.

I suppose I really shouldn't have recited that—the sentiment being quite antithetical to my own personal convictions. But I find, sometimes, it is helpful to give my opponents an argument or two with which to defend their positions. It makes for better feeling when we get through.

Following World War I the intellectuals of Central Europe were searching desperately for values to replace the romanticism they believed they had lost. During the Twenties a play by Karel Capek appeared, entitled "R.U.R.—Rossun's Universal Robots." The word "robot" was new in those days and I remember there was considerable discussion of how it should be pronounced—"rah'but," "row-boat," "ro-bow." In any case, what happened was that, in the play, the robots, whose outlook on life was pretty much what we would call that of the "hard scientists" nowadays, got out of hand and began to take over from the natives. Just about the time the last inefficiently sentimental human being was being mowed down by machine gun fire, a couple of the late model robots began to exhibit some quite unrobot-like behavior. A girl robot and a boy robot fell in love with each other. Thus, right at the moment of triumph for the ingeniously constructed simulators, the whole project collapsed. The robots got to acting so much like human beings that they actually became human. All of which goes to show you can't really win at this game of simulating the human personality; for the moment you succeed, you are right back where you started. If I may paraphrase Camus, simulation is a Sisyphean enterprise.

As a matter of fact, at the Ohio State University we have taken this hazard into account and have developed a simulator that goes just about as far as you can expect to go in this direction without getting set back to where you started. The model is called the OSU-401.

[1] Discussion at a conference on *Computer simulation of personality: Frontier of psychological theory* held at Educational Testing Service and Princeton University, Princeton, NJ, June 13–15, 1962. First published in Tomkins, S. S. & Messick, S. (Eds.). (1963). *Computer simulation of personality* (pp. 221–229). Wiley. Republished by permission of Wiley.

Collected Papers of the Pioneer of Constructivist Psychology: George A. Kelly, First Edition. Edited by David A. Winter and Nick Reed.

We have quite a number of units of this device available for research in the Department of Psychology, although from time to time the more objective members of the staff express doubts about how well it simulates the human personality and, indeed, occasionally raise some very grave questions about its statistical reliability. (Perhaps I should say that 401 is the number of our elementary psychology course and the units are made available to us free of charge through an arrangement that requires students enrolled in the course to serve as subjects in experiments.) But as I say, this is getting perilously close to the ultimate in personality simulation, so I wouldn't blame some of you if you voiced objections over the extent to which we have allowed our enthusiasm for computer verisimilitude to override our obligations to science.

Actually it was some years ago, when I was in the Navy during the war, that I discovered that you could carry this simulation business too far. It had been suggested that the Navy should purchase some Link Trainers and rig them so that primary flight instruction could be given in them. This was known as "The Visual Link Project." The Link Trainer is a mock-up of an airplane cockpit which can be rotated on three axes by the occupant's using stick and rudder. It has little stub wings sticking out from the side that are supposed to suggest the wings of an airplane. I might add that this bit of simulated realism always struck me as extremely amusing because of what it revealed about the mentality of Naval officers.

Be that as it may, one of the problems that seemed to stand in the way of the use of the Link Trainer as a primary flight instructional device was the fact that it could not simulate the noise, the laboring of the engine in a climb, the vibration, and the acceleration effects one experiences in a turn. As they thought it over, the engineers decided they could simulate everything except the acceleration effects. But those effects are especially important in the early stages of learning to fly.

After giving the matter some thought myself, I came up with a definitive solution to all aspects of the problem. I suggested that the Link Trainer be enlarged so that a real engine could be installed, that the stub wings be extended, and that certain other modifications could be adopted to provide greater realism. I was able to point out an interesting feature of my proposal—the fact that the cost of all this would be only about one thirtieth that of a regular Link Trainer, which was a pretty expensive gadget. But this is where I made my first mistake; no one was interested in reducing the cost of anything. Enthusiasm for my project immediately declined.

But this was only my first blunder; the whole project completely collapsed when they discovered that my invention would actually fly. "Why," they said, "that would be nothing but an airplane!" They were right, of course; I had made the fatal mistake that all computer enthusiasts run the risk of making—the mistake of carrying simulation too far. If I had only doubled the cost, instead of cutting it, and had stopped just short of something that would actually fly, I am sure I could have won a Green Commendation Ribbon.

At this point perhaps I should make my own theoretical position clear, so as to forestall any frivolity that may grow out of my outspoken enthusiasm for computer simulation of personality. I think truth can be approached by simulation, and by simulation only. This is the thesis behind the phrase, "the psychology of personal constructs" (Kelly, 1955). Man gets at the truth of things, not by some special revelation on Mount Sinai or in a laboratory, but by erecting constructs to simulate it as best he can. The point at which the simulation and the reality will converge is, I assume, a very long way off.

So we devise machines to simulate—not man directly—but theories about man. The machines are actually two steps removed from personality. The circuitry of the machines is designed to simulate the logical connections within the theories they are supposed to approximate. The theories, in turn, are constructed to simulate the human processes they are supposed to explain.

But the simulation does not stop there. The persons themselves are simulators. They attempt to simulate each other—too much, some say. They simulate their parents, their gods, a presumed rational way of life, and the expectations of others. In fact, a lot of people even make a big to-do about simulating themselves. This is known as "trying to be yourself" and is often regarded as quite an accomplishment. Sometimes people simulate machines. This is sometimes called "being objective." Doctor Blum (1963) has even programmed his people to behave like computers. Some psychologists undoubtedly will take this to mean that he has succeeded in getting people to behave psychologically. All this, it seems to me, brings us to a situation of infinite regression—like that of the cat looking in the mirror at a cat looking in a mirror at..., etc. Persons act like models that are supposed to act like persons that act like models that are supposed..., etc.

Some persons raise the objection to computer simulation, as they have for many years objected to factor analysis, that "you get out of the system only what you put into it." For my own part, I cannot see this as anything to fuss over. It would be a sorry state of affairs if it turned out that you didn't get out of it what you put into it. If that were true, you could never use the computer to test the outcome of anything, for you could never tell whether you were getting out of it the consequences of something you put into it or the consequences of something you didn't put into it.

I suppose what the critics who raise this objection mean is that you don't really discover anything by firing up your computers, that the outcome is biased by what you have invented, not governed by what nature really is. But since, as I have already indicated, the inventive approach to truth is the only one that works anyway, I see no fault in this kind of bias.

To be candid about it, there is considerable virtue in the fact that computers do not simulate persons perfectly. If they did, they would produce some pretty complex results. We would probably have to go looking for some human simulators to give us a down-to-earth version of what was going on—a version we could grasp. To be sure, we would have the blueprint that had been used in manufacturing the gadget, but that would not mean we could tell what was happening inside the mechanism, nor would it mean we could read backwards from a similar bit of human behavior and say it came about in the same way.

As long as the task of science is to reduce matters to terms our pedestrian minds can grasp, the instruments of science will have to select, distort, and simplify the vast complexities of nature. In other words, I hope Aldous does not behave like a human being. He would turn out to be quite a problem if he did.

There are two major ways in which I see a computer simulation program contributing to an experimental science of psychology. First, as I have already intimated, it can simulate the logic of a theoretical system and, with a series of inputs, explicate the theory and its implications in ways the original theoretician would take a lifetime to figure out on his own. Moreover, the output should, at various stages here and there, be sufficiently parallel to human observables to enable the theoretician to check himself against the behavior of a human subject.

The second contribution can be to the processing of data provided by a given subject, as suggested by Doctor Colby's research (Colby, 1963). This, too, can be compared with the subsequent behavior of the subject at various check points along the line.

In this connection I would like to make a plug for the psychology of personal constructs (Kelly, 1955). Not only is it a system built on the notion that scientists and human beings, alike, approach truth by erecting simulation devices—called constructs—but it is a theory deliberately formulated in a language system which is based on binary elements and which does not accept the so-called subject-predicate error of the Indo-European language system.

Without burdening you with the radical assumptions of the theory, may I simply mention the fact that a personal construct is defined by extension through being applied to a series of events. The events are not regarded as stimuli but as objects of construction. If we imagine a matrix with events ranged along the top, then a construct, defined by extension, would be a horizontal row of plusses and minuses within the matrix—or, better, incidents and voids. The construct would be symbolically defined as such a row pattern. Another construct would be defined as a somewhat different row pattern. There is a theorem here to the effect that if two constructs match, cell by cell, throughout the length of their rows, clear out to infinity, they are identical.

Such a matrix is a representation of a person's psychological space. The dimensions are his, not necessarily those of his psychologist or of his culture. They are not likely to be orthogonal to each other. There are many interesting matrix relationships that can be directly explored by means of machine processes, using personal construct data produced by an individual person or by a group of persons. Such exploration may throw light upon the dimensions which define the space in which individuals are free to move and live their lives.

While Aldous, as he is now constituted, would not, of course, be prepared to explicate the theory of personal constructs, I am sure Doctor Loehlin[2] could, if he wished, sire a fellow called Suodla who could explicate the theory. Suodla is simply Aldous spelled backwards.

Of course, Suodla would, and should at best, be an imperfect simulator. I am sure that for some this would spell disappointment.

There once was a passionate dame
Who wanted some things made plain,
So she punched up the cards,
Filled tape by the yards,
But—somehow—*it just wasn't the same!*

References

Blum, G.S. (1963). Programming people to simulate machines. In S.S. Tomkins & S. Messick (Eds.), *Computer simulation of personality* (pp. 127–157). Wiley.

Colby, K.M. (1963). Computer simulation of a neurotic process. In S.S. Tomkins & S. Messick (Eds.), *Computer simulation of personality* (pp. 165–180). Wiley.

Kelly, G.A. (1955). *The psychology of personal constructs*. Norton.

[2] Editors' note: This refers to Loehlin, J.C. (1963). A computer program that simulates personality. In S.S. Tomkins & S. Messick (Eds.), *Computer simulation of personality* (pp. 189–211). Wiley.

20

The Language of Hypothesis: Man's Psychological Instrument[1]

For about three centuries now Anglo-Saxon man has labored under the somewhat misleading assumption that knowledge is transmitted through the senses. This was John Locke's great notion in 1690. In expressing it, he provided the essential spadework for both modern experimental psychology and the courageous empiricism of Sigmund Freud. But great ideas, like great men, sometimes have a way of eventually blocking the very progress they once so courageously initiated.

Thus it is, even after continued experience in psychotherapy, most of us still hold doggedly to the belief that one man's understanding of the universe can be somehow encoded within a signal system and then transmitted intact to another man via the senses. The signal system is often called "language." Indeed, Pavlov's psychological term for "language" was simply "the second signal system." And it is interesting to note in this connection that today much of Soviet education, psychotherapy, and prisoner rehabilitation—as well as the dreaded "brainwashing" routine—is supposedly directed at the installation of an accurately tuned signal system for the undistorted reception of messages.

But, senses notwithstanding, we are coming at last to realize that language occupies a puzzling and paradoxical position between man and his circumstances. On the one hand, it is a device he uses to represent his circumstances, and, on the other, it may interpose itself as a compromise between tender phantasies and harsh realities. It enables man to understand what is going on around him, but it is equally useful in helping him put out of mind what he fears to understand. It provides both the sensitivity for following subtle events and the rigidity for standing against the tides of human affairs. It is a vehicle for communicating with other men, but it often serves us effectively when we want to distort the communications others seek to have with us.

Nowhere are these contradictory usages of language more apparent than in the realm of psychology. A parent, for example, may use language to gain some insight into the mind of his child. But he may also use diagnostic labels and verbal rationalizations to avoid being enmeshed in the magic of childlike perceptions. The experimental psychologist often betrays his ambivalence about having an intimate understanding of other persons by erecting a complex system of categories between himself and his subjects. Even a psychotherapist may employ verbal interpretations of his client's remarks to keep from being taken in by them.

This evening I would like to talk about language in a very special sense. I would like to talk about it as a human device for anticipating the events that are about to happen to us. This is to say I shall not be talking about it so much as a means of representing reality, or of shielding us from it, nor so much as a means of communication between persons, but more as an instrument for probing the future and, at the same time, maintaining our composure in the face of onrushing events.

If I say "The floor is hard," I employ a language system in which the subject-predicate relationship inheres in the subject itself. It is the floor which is hard, and that is its nature, regardless of who says so. The statement stands, not because the speaker said it, but because the floor happened to be what it is. The sentence's validity stems from the floor and not from the speaker.

Contrast with this the phenomenological use of language in which it is presumed that such a statement portrays a state of mind of the speaker and does not necessarily represent anything more than that. While our common language forms are not constructed so as to designate this kind of interpretation specifically, phenomenology has begun to enter the thinking of psychologists at least, and this kind of meaning is much less difficult to understand and live with than it was twenty or thirty years ago. Moreover, this use of language has proved to have some utility in the psychotherapeutic exchange, though many psychologists are skeptical of its ultimate value and find themselves quite uncomfortable when they try to use it.

But suppose we consider the possibility of using language in a third way—neither objectively nor phenomenologically. Suppose our verbs could be cast in the *invitational mood*. This is to say that instead of being used in the popular *indicative mood* of objective speech,

[1] Address at the American Society of Adlerian Psychology and the Alfred Adler Institute graduation exercises, New York, May 16th, 1964, and also published in the *Journal of Individual Psychology*, 1964, *20*, pp. 137–152. Republished in Maher, B. (Ed.). (1969). *Clinical psychology and personality: The selected papers of George Kelly* (pp. 147–162). Wiley, and in *Costruttivismi, 1*, 5–15. Published here by permission of University of Texas Press and Wiley.

Collected Papers of the Pioneer of Constructivist Psychology: George A. Kelly, First Edition. Edited by David A. Winter and Nick Reed.

or in one of the other moods recognized by our language—*conditional*, *subjunctive*, or *imperative*—a verb could be cast in a form which would suggest to the listener that a certain novel interpretation of an object might be entertained. For example, I might say, "Suppose we regard the floor as if it were hard."

If I make such a statement I immediately find myself in an interesting position. The statement leaves both the speaker and the listener, not with a conclusion on their hands, but in a posture of expectancy—suppose we do regard the floor as if it were hard, what then? A verb employed in the invitational mood, assuming our language had such a mood, would have the effect of orienting one to the future, not merely to the present or to the past. It would set the stage for prediction of what is to ensue. It suggests that the floor is open to a variety of interpretations or constructions. It invites the listener to cope with his circumstances—in this case, the floor—in new ways. But more than this, it suggests that the view of the floor as something hard is one that is not imposed upon us from without, nor is it isolated from external evidence, as a phenomenological proposition would be, but is one that can be pursued, tested, abandoned, or reconsidered at a later time. "Suppose we regard the floor as if it were hard; what follows and what do we do about it?"

Toward the end of the last century a German philosopher, Hans Vaihinger began to develop a system of philosophy he called the "philosophy of 'as if.' "[2] In it he offered a system of thought in which God and reality might best be represented as paradigms. This was not to say that either God or reality was any less certain than anything else in the realm of man's awareness, but only that all matters confronting man might best be regarded in hypothetical ways. In some measure, I suppose, I am suggesting that Vaihinger's position has particular value for psychology.[3] At least, let us pursue the topic—which is probably just the way Vaihinger would have proposed that we go at it.

Make-Believe as an Essential Feature of Science

Science is often understood by students as a way of avoiding subjective judgments and getting down to the hard facts of reality. But I am suggesting that the avoidance of subjectivity is not the way to get down to hard realities. Subjective thinking is, rather, an essential step in the process the scientist must follow in grasping the nature of the universe. Let me see if I can make this point clear.

When we know something, or think we do, we make up sentences about it, using verbs cast in the indicative mood. We talk about it in a way that appears to be objective. But science tends to make its progress by entertaining propositions which appear initially to be preposterous. Quite often this is done secretly, the scientist being careful not to let people know what he is imagining until after he has accumulated some evidence to support his position. After he has a foothold in evidence he can, of course, claim that he was simply a careful observer and that, being a careful observer, he "discovered" something. But unless he had been willing, at some point in the sequence, to open his mind to possibilities contrary to what was regarded as perfectly obvious, he would have been unable to come up with anything new.

The novelist starts his exploration of the world in much the same way. But there are two differences between him and the scientist; he is more willing to confide his make-believe—even publish it—and he is willing to postpone the accumulation of factual evidence to support the generality of characters and themes he has narrated.

But neither of these differences between the novelist and the scientist is very fundamental. Both men employ nonetheless typically human tactics. The fact that the scientist is ashamed to admit his phantasy probably accomplishes little more than to make it appear that he fits a popular notion of the way scientists think. And the fact that a novelist does not continue his project to the point of collecting data in support of his portrayals and generalizations suggests only that he hopes that the experiences of man will, in the end, prove him right without anyone's resorting to formal proof.

But the brilliant scientist and the brilliant writer are pretty likely to end up saying the same thing—given, of course, a lot of time to converge upon each other. The poor scientist and the poor writer, moreover, fail in much the same way—neither of them is able to transcend the obvious. Both fail in their make-believe.

[2] Vaihinger, H. (1924). *The philosophy of 'as if': A system of the theoretical, practical and religious fictions of mankind.* Translated by C. K. Ogden. Routledge & Kegan Paul.

[3] The writer is indebted to Dr. H. L. Ansbacher for calling attention to the important fact that Alfred Adler, who had studied Vaihinger and had grasped the psychological significance of "as if" philosophy, regarded such notions as "unconscious" and "inferiority complex" as inventions, rather than discoveries.

In 1937 Adler wrote, "I, myself, as the inventor of the 'inferiority complex' have never thought of it as of a spirit, knowing that it has never been in the consciousness or unconsciousness of the patient but only in my own consciousness, and have used it rather for illumination so that the patient could see his attitude in the right coherence" (Psychiatric aspects regarding individual and social disorganization. *Amer. J. Sociol.*, 1937, 42, 773-780).

Thus Adler's philosophy of science differed sharply from that of Freud, who, in the now-fading Nineteenth Century tradition, regarded the scientific enterprise as an effort to discover bits of truth or to uncover things in the mind heretofore concealed.

Make-Believe as a Way of Coping with Threat

There are few experiences in the biography of a man more distressing than that of feeling himself utterly confused. How disturbing the person finds this confusion in his life depends somewhat on the area in which he experiences it. For example, it does not disturb me greatly when a student says things I cannot understand—I am rather used to that. But when my wife starts saying things I cannot understand I get the feeling that my world is beginning to wobble on its axis. And when I myself start saying things I cannot understand I am likely to become downright upset. Actually, however, all of these add up to about the same thing; the more deeply the confusion enters into my life the more alarmed I become.

Yet almost everything new starts in some moment of confusion. In fact, I cannot imagine just now how it could be otherwise. But this is not to say that confusion always serves to produce something new. It can just as well have the opposite effect, especially if the person finds the confusion so intolerable that he reverts to some older interpretation of what is going on. Here then is the element of risk for the person who ventures confusion in order to create something; he may end up regressing in order to control his panic.

But there is another stage in the creative process that stands midway between the confusion that we try to dispel by seeking either something new or regressing to something old, and the structured view of our surroundings that makes it appear that we know what's what. It is that transitional moment when the confusion has partly cleared and we catch a glimpse of what is emerging, but with it are confronted with the stark realization that we are to be profoundly affected if we continue on course. This is the moment of threat. It is the threshold between confusion and certainty, between anxiety and boredom. It is precisely at this moment when we are most tempted to turn back.

Let us concentrate on this moment of threat—or these moments of threat—in the life of man. Let me suggest that if we can find some way of helping man pass this kind of crisis we will have helped him in one of the most important ways imaginable. It is here that we can employ that part of the language of hypothesis that I have called "the invitational mood." Instead of insisting that old truths are about to give way to new, that we are shifting from one indicative to another, we can take the view that it is not the truth that is changing, but rather that we are tentatively exploring the possibilities of a new approach to the truth. "Suppose we regard the floor as if it were hard." We approach the truth through the door of make-believe.

Probably nothing has contributed so much to the adventuresome development of scientific thinking as the understanding of hypothetical reasoning. A hypothesis is not to be asserted as a fact, for if it is it immediately ceases to serve its purpose. It does not even need to be regarded as an inference, although some scientists, still easily embarrassed at being caught in their unrealistic moments, prefer to limit themselves to what they call the hypothetico-deductive method. At least that makes them appear rational, if not realistic.

The point that needs emphasis, it seems to me, is that the hypothesis serves to make an unrealistic conclusion tenable, or tenable for a sufficient period of time for the person to pursue its implications *as if* it were true. The fact that it is regarded as a hypothesis, and as a hypothesis only, has great psychological importance in man, for it enables him to break through his moment of threat. It is, after all, only make-believe.

Hypotheses for the Psychologist, Client, and Graduate Student

Let me turn our discussion from abstractions to certain problems in psychology. It is supposed to be good for psychologists to act like scientists and many of us, I fear, spend more time acting like scientists than we do trying to understand persons. Suppose, instead of trying to apply scientific methods, as we know them, to psychological problems, we embark on an altogether different undertaking. Suppose we attempt to understand the psychology of scientific endeavor.

I have hinted at what such an inquiry might cover—the dread of confusion, the obstacle the scientist confronts at the moment of threat, the psychological role of the hypothesis, and the possible use of verbs in an invitational mood. I have also suggested that people who fancy themselves as scientists are very much afraid of being caught doing anything that is not recognized as scientific, and especially so, if what they are doing has anything to do with their professional field. I suppose it would be very upsetting to a good many of our colleagues if it were seriously suggested to them that they might stop trying to be scientific and get on with the job of understanding man. Yet I am confident that such an abandonment of what we now know as "science" would, in the end, be a good thing both for psychology and for science. In fact I suspect that as the results began to be known the Sigma Xi cult might be only too happy to claim psychology as a "basic science."

For a good many years I have been impressed with the similarities between psychotherapeutic and research activities. The difficulties the client seems to confront in his psychotherapeutic experience seem much like those the graduate student finds most frustrating. Let me illustrate.

Both have difficulty formulating testable hypotheses, and, even when they do, they hesitate to lay them on the line experimentally. Sometimes it appears that they dread to test them lest they be disconfirmed, though often I suspect it is because they fear the evidence *will* confirm the hypotheses and they will be threatened with a new set of verbs, all cast, of course, in the indicative mood. A person, whether in his scientist role or in his patient role, can be threatened by finding himself on the brink of a changed outlook, even though it may be regarded as a rewarding one.

Moreover, both in the client and in the graduate student, the remedy seems to lie in pointing out that what is being tested is, after all, only a hypothesis. The ultimate truth, it is important to recognize, lies far beyond the immediate experiment. It is when the student realizes this that he begins to feel more comfortable investing his efforts in something less than a magnum opus and can get some satisfaction out of making progress rather than coming up with a major achievement. The same is true of the client. What he is, or what he is to be, does not stand or fall by what he does today or tomorrow; he needs only to make some kind of progress, not transform his life into some final state of perfection all at once.

Probably there is nothing more exciting in the whole field of clinical psychology than the notion that persons in distress can couch their problems in the language of hypothesis, and that one can think with verbs in the invitational mood, even though our language has no structural form for designating such verbs. A client who regards himself as a victim of his unfortunate youth may, of course, mobilize all sorts of evidence in support of his conclusion. He may talk of himself objectively, marshalling evidence in interview after interview to support the indicative mood of the verbs he uses in describing himself.

As long as this goes on he himself is likely to be *immobilized.* We can call it intellectualization on his part, if we like, but, whatever it is, the outlook he expresses seems to him to be realistic. Sometimes we try to break up the rigid pattern of his self-perception by inviting him to be incoherent, as in the loosening efforts psychoanalysts often employ. Out of the confusion that ensues there may come some new construction of himself and his circumstances—particularly of his future. But confusion is anxiety and he *may* simply regress. Indeed certain patients are quite likely to regress to more primitive constructions when loosened psychoanalytically.

Sometimes the psychotherapist meets his greatest resistance just when his client is on the threshold of some important new insight. This, of course, is the moment of threat that I have been mentioning. And, of course, there are many other obstacles to be overcome in psychotherapy that have their parallels in other forms of human endeavor, as in art and in science.

Clinical Psychology as Pure Science

I suppose this is as good a time as any for me to say that I have very little interest in applied psychology, and that is why I think clinical psychology is so important! An applied scientist puts his verbs in the indicative mood, while the pure scientist uses the invitational mood. The psychologist is at his best when he speaks the language of hypothesis rather than imposes psychological certainties on his clients. There are, unfortunately, a large number of psychologists—the majority of them perhaps—who think they dare not use the language of hypothesis when talking directly to persons; it is, they think, a language to be employed only when dealing with more remote matters. Most of them regard themselves as experimental psychologists, or perhaps more accurately as the experimental psychologists. But for me the most exciting experimental situation is the therapy room, and the most stimulating colleague in the research enterprise is my client.

This is not to say I find psychotherapy always a comforting and rewarding experience. It is sometimes, but mostly it is anything but that. I said only that it was exciting and stimulating. My clients and I go through some difficult times together. Both of us find ourselves trapped by the subject-predicate error of so-called objective speech. Both of us experience confusion, or *anxiety* if you prefer a clinical term, in which we become a little frightened at our own incoherence. Sometimes out of this confusion comes something new; sometimes we only regress.

I can, of course, insist that only my client, and not I myself, shall be permitted to risk confusion; and sometimes I do just that. Neither of us can put up with too much chaos at any one moment. But if I insist on risking no confusion in myself whatsoever I don't learn anything. I am only an applied psychologist. Without risking confusion, without venturing preposterous thoughts occasionally, I do not come to understand my client, I only diagnose him and I substitute my "interpretations" for the genuine experience of knowing him.

Of course I can make life easier if I entrench myself in some orthodoxy and, through repeated and patient interpretations, drill my client in my way of looking at things. When he agrees with me I tell him he has "insight" and when he doesn't I tell him he is "resisting"—both of these being terms that grow out of objective speech and the prestigeful use of the indicative mood in talking about psychological matters.

But clinical psychology does not have to be an applied discipline. It can, in the very best sense, be truly scientific. And when I say this I do not mean that the clinical psychologist uses his clients as unwitting guinea pigs in an experiment for which they have no responsibility. I mean that clinical psychology *can* be scientific in the therapy room, that the client *can* be—and indeed properly *is*—a colleague, and that the client and his therapist may come to talk to each other in the language of hypothesis.

The Threat of Profound Change

But there is more than anxiety to be encouraged and used productively in the psychotherapeutic situation. There is threat, the experience that occurs at the moment when we stand on the brink of a profound change in ourselves and can see just enough of what lies ahead to know that so much of what we are now will be left behind forever, once we take that next step. It is here that the language of hypothesis can be of particular help, both to the psychotherapist who senses the warning that his own experience with the client will not leave him unchanged, and to the client who can see that he is about to invalidate much of what he has deeply believed over many years of his life. It is at this point that it becomes particularly useful to say, "Suppose—just suppose—we regard the floor as if it were hard." Except we shall probably be saying something like, "Suppose we regard your boss as if he were frightened," or "Suppose we regard your feelings as if they were a shield against the hazards of loving someone."

As I said before, the language of hypothesis invites one to get on with the task of understanding life, to test, to calculate new experiences, and to profit from mistakes, rather than to be overwhelmed with guilt on realizing that he has made them. There is something in stating a new outlook in the form of a hypothesis that leaves the person himself intact and whole. It implies that being has an integrity of its own and that we approach it, whether it is a truth about the external world or about ourselves, by successive approximations, each of which is subject to further examination. Truth, then, is regarded as something to be adventured and tested, not something that is revealed to us whole by God or nature—not even by one's psychotherapist.

This moment of threat, in which so many human enterprises are abandoned, is not found exclusively in psychotherapy. The scientist experiences it in his own life, and so does the novelist and the artist. It is, no doubt, what the existentialists have in mind when they talk about "the leap," although I would not want to pretend that I have a very clear idea of all the things existentialists talk about.

On the night of November 10th, or shortly thereafter—the records are not altogether clear—in the year of 1619, Rene Descartes had three dreams. In the first dream he was a cripple seeking shelter in a church; in the second he heard thunder and saw fire; and in the third he was reading the words, "What way of life shall I follow," a quotation from a poem that was currently popular. What is perhaps more important than his dream thoughts is the notion which he claimed preceded them. That notion was that the methods of analytic geometry might be broadly applied to other disciplines—hardly enough to scare one into church, we might suppose, but then Descartes was a very well-educated man whose intellectual ventures penetrated far deeper than the superficial mimicry that ordinarily passes for cognition, and, besides, the year was 1619. So upset was Descartes at the notion of applying analytic geometrical solutions to a wide variety of man's problems that he discontinued his inquiries and went on a long trip, lasting several months, in order to escape the threat that confronted him.

Descartes was a man greatly concerned with the reality of existence—"*Cogito ergo sum.*" He sought, moreover, to proceed in his intellectual endeavors by the exclusive use of objective language. The times did not provide him with a language of hypothesis, though he was clearly aware of alternative explanations for what he observed and he did experiment actively. For him, however, experimentation was a way of discovering which of several explanations was the true one. Thus he had not quite reached the point where he could use the language of hypothesis to its full advantage. If he had been able to use it, he might have saved himself a lot of discomfort and perhaps have accomplished some things that even his great mind fell short of achieving. Even a Descartes can experience his moment of threat and be disconcerted by it.

Being Oneself is Not Enough

A good deal is said these days about being oneself. It is supposed to be healthy to be oneself. While it is a little hard for me to understand how one could be anything else, I suppose what is meant is that one should not strive to become anything other than what he is. This strikes me as a very dull way of living; in fact, I would be inclined to argue that all of us would be better off if we set out to be something other than what we are. Well, I'm not so sure we would all be *better* off—perhaps it would be more accurate to say life would be a lot more *interesting*.

There is another meaning that might be attached to this admonition to be oneself; that one should not try to disguise himself. I suspect this comes nearer to what *psychologists* mean when they urge people to be themselves. It is presumed that the person who faces the world barefaced is more spontaneous, that he expresses himself more fully, and that he has a better chance of developing all his resources if he assumes no disguises.

But this doctrine of psychological nakedness in human affairs, so much talked about today and which allows the self neither make-up nor costume, leaves very little to the imagination. Nor does it invite one to be venturesome. I suspect, for example, that in the Garden of Eden it might have occurred to Adam to take a chance much sooner than he did if Eve had been paying a little more attention to her wardrobe. As it was I hear she had to bribe him with an apple. Later on they say she contrived a saucy little something out of fig leaves.

What I am saying is that it is not so much what man is that counts as it is what he ventures to make of himself. To make the leap he must do more than disclose himself; he must risk a certain amount of confusion. Then, as soon as he does catch a glimpse of a different kind of life, he needs to find some way of overcoming the paralyzing moment of threat, for this is the instant when he wonders what he really is—whether he is what he just was or is what he is about to be. Adam must have experienced such a moment. With him perhaps, as with modern Anglo-Saxon man, the indicative mood of his verbs might have put him in a quandary, forced him upon the horns of his own dilemma, rendered him ambivalent, perhaps even impotent.

It may be helpful at this point to ask ourselves a question about children at Halloween. Is the little youngster who comes to your door on the night of October 30th, all dressed up in his costume and behind a mask, piping "trick or treat, trick or treat"—is that youngster *disguising* himself or is he *revealing* himself? Is he failing to be spontaneous? Is he *not* being himself? Which is the *real* child—the child behind the mask or the barefaced child who must stand up in front of adults and say "please" and "thank you"? I suspect costumes and masks worn at Halloween time, as well as uniforms worn by officers on duty, doctoral degrees, and the other devices we employ to avoid being seen as we are, are all ways we have of extricating ourselves from predicaments into which we have been cast by the language of objectivity. They represent devices for coping with the world in the language of hypothesis.

But masks have a way of sticking to our faces when worn too long. Verbs cease to express the invitational mood after the invitation has been accepted and experience has left its mark. To suggest to a person that he be what he has already become is not much of an invitation. Thus it is that the man who has worn a uniform long enough to explore all its possibilities begins to think that he really is an officer. Once this happens he may have to go through a lot of chaos before he can make anything more of himself. A student who is awarded a Ph.D. degree can find a lot of adventure in being called "doctor" and the academic mask may enable him to experiment with his life in ways that would have seemed much too preposterous before his dissertation was accepted. But trouble sets in when he begins to think that he really is a doctor, or a professor, or a scholar. When that happens he will have to spend most of his time making noises like doctors, professors, or scholars, with the resultant failure from that time on to undertake anything interesting. He becomes trapped by verbs that have lapsed into the indicative mood when he wasn't looking.

After Confirmation, What?

It may seem that I am advocating the use of a language in which nothing is ever confirmed. In a sense this is true—I am! The moment we find it practicable to regard the floor as if it were hard we don't walk away from it leaving it hard, but we always tack a little note on it that says, "But maybe it's something else too"—or instead, "I'll be back later to see."

One of the most amusing yet baffling experiences in psychotherapy is the way today's "insight" can become tomorrow's "resistance." Psychotherapists often stand on their heads to retain what they once hailed as a remarkable insight in their patient's step-by-step analysis. A few weeks later they may find themselves saying, "But that isn't exactly what I thought you meant." The therapist ends up trying to dress up his client's insight to fit the current circumstances and the new stage to which they—he and his client—have progressed in their mutual enterprise. And before he knows it his own dilemma has tricked him into lecturing his colleague in ways no respectable therapist is supposed to do. If he had regarded the client's new construction as a hypothesis rather than an insight in the first place, he could have saved himself a lot of anxiety once it became clear to both of them that the therapy must move on to other levels of construction. Moreover, it is precisely at this point in the psychotherapeutic progression that the language of hypothesis must be reemployed.

There is more to this than tactics in psychotherapy. It is very commonly believed by people who should know better that one is obligated to disconfirm one explanation before he dares entertain seriously the possibilities of any other. Scholars waste a great deal of time trying to disprove what others have claimed in order to make room for their own alternative explanations. If the floor is hard—really is—I am not going to get to first base with any notion of its being soft. Therefore, it seems that I must first prove that those who say it is hard are dead wrong. This is all a terrible waste of time, in my opinion.

Suppose, instead, we employ the language of hypothesis. We say, in effect, "To be sure the floor may be regarded as hard, and we know something of what ensues when we cope with it in the light of such an assumption. Not bad! But now let us see what happens when we regard it as soft." Out of this further exploration may come, not so much confirmation that it really is hard or that it really is soft—as Descartes would have reasoned—but a sequence of fresh experiences that invite the formulation of new hypotheses. For example, one may come up with a notion of relativism, that is to say, the floor is harder than some things and softer than others. Or he may come up with a notion of properties, the hardness aspect of the floor and its softness aspect. Or he may come to regard hardness not as anything that inheres in the floor, but as a dimension of appraisal useful in understanding floors. From this position he may launch out and contrive the notions of resilience and plasticity to account for what happened when he treated the floor as if it were soft.

The Invitational Mood in International Affairs

Here then we have a language which can be employed in many situations, not the least of which are in the realm of international affairs. Suppose we regard the Soviet Union as "a democracy." Sounds heretical, doesn't it! But why not see what comes out of such a hypothesis? Now we are going to have a problem on our hands if we ask our John Bircher friends to explore this issue. To most of them, I suspect, such a proposal sounds like an invitation to jump off the edge of the world. As long as it sounds this way to them I doubt that they will be much tempted, and I doubt that it would do much good to point out such facts as that before a vote is taken at any echelon of Soviet government, from individual citizens on up, every effort is made to have it discussed in a face-to-face situation, and that such town meeting discussions involve about eighty percent of the voters. Nor would it do much good to point out to a fellow who thinks he has been invited to walk the plank that the unanimity the Soviet system demands is a rather mild version of our jury system in which unanimity is demanded of all twelve jurymen—a requirement that brings the minority members of a jury under almost intolerable pressure to go along with the vocal faction, just as it does in a Soviet election.

If our Bircher friends did allow themselves to consider facts such as these they might be brought to the brink of concluding that some features, at least, of the Soviet system are more democratic than the corresponding features in our own system. This, I am sure, would bring them to that moment of threat to which their limited notions of democracy have left them so vulnerable. Will the language of hypothesis enable our friends to surmount this intellectual barrier and examine matters further? Well, I don't know. Perhaps I have chosen too difficult an illustration; it may be asking too much of a sworn chauvinist to suggest that he employ the language of hypothesis in order to reach a better understanding of international issues.

One thing, of course, we shall not ask the Bircher to concede; we shall not ask him to deny that the Soviet system is based on dictatorship. And here is my point. It is not necessary for that hypothesis to be discontinued before another is entertained. Nor do we ask him, or ourselves, to agree that the Soviet system *is essentially* democratic. That would not be using the language of hypothesis. All we ask is that we apply the criteria of democracy to what goes on in that society and examine the outcomes of such an honest inquiry on our own part.

It does not follow that we must eventually choose between the hypothesis of dictatorship and the hypothesis of democracy. As in the case of our propositions about the floor, the explorations that ensue from the two hypothetical propositions may lead us to formulate some much better ones—ones that may throw as much light upon directions our own society may take as upon our proper posture toward the Soviet Union. Unlike Descartes, we shall look forward to a better statement of issues rather than to some knock-down-drag-out decision on issues that may be badly posed. It seems much more likely in Soviet-American relations that, if the conflict can be settled at all by means other than war, it will turn out that history will regard neither side as the perfect embodiment of democracy, and more thoughtful generations will find better ways to pose the issues than we, in our dread of political confusion, have yet found. Still, the chauvinists on one side or the other may finally have their way, and men, here or elsewhere, who oppose them will have to die in defense of their right to pursue their own propositions and to seek enlightenment for all.

Conclusion

There is a good deal more to the language of hypothesis than what I have tried to cover thus far in this discussion. I might have pointed out that it is a dimensional language rather than a language of attributes. By that I mean that when I say, "Suppose we regard the floor as if it were hard," I am inviting my listener to envision a dimension or parameter that is not a part of the floor, but exists supposedly independently of the floor. Having constructed such a dimension, or personal construct, the listener is invited to plot the position of the floor with respect to such a hypothetical dimension. This to say that the language has its particular way of using nouns and adjectives as well as its verbs. In the case of the floor, about which I talk in this language, the basic noun has to do with a dimension or guideline erected by myself, one which I hope will enable me to plot the position of "floor" in my own psychological space. My adjectives are not so much relativistic adjectives as they are statements of where a given event is to be plotted with respect to the dimension symbolized by my noun.

But enough of this; the object of this discourse is only to suggest how a certain kind of language form can enable us to extricate ourselves from the kind of realism to which our so-called objective language system has bound us. Nowhere is this semantic enslavement clearer than in the psychotherapy room. It is there one can see most clearly how man can be trapped by his indicative verbs and how, in turn, he has been led to believe that he must choose between mutually exclusive versions of reality. Not only does he find that he must risk the chaos of anxiety in order to come up with something new, but also he discovers that once he has managed a new version of the important issues in his life he must face a moment of terrible estrangement from all that he has been if he is to make the existential leap. It is here—at the moment I have called the moment of threat—that the language of hypothesis enables his therapist to say, "But only suppose the floor is to be regarded as if it were hard," or, "But only suppose your posture is designed to protect you from ever again having feelings like those you once had for your mother."

I hope that, as well as inviting you to consider the use of another language for coping with man's problems both in the therapy room and in international affairs, I have led you to explore the implications of a particular proposition, the somewhat unorthodox one of, "Suppose we regard clinical psychology as if it were the purest of sciences."

21

The Threat of Aggression[1]

This conference has been convened to consider the topic of humanism in psychology. But I am not sure I have a very clear idea of what humanism is. Ostensibly it has something to do with man, though I have often doubted that it had to do with anyone I know. Nevertheless, I suppose that when psychologists get together and say that we ought to revive humanism it is because they are alarmed by the tendency of their disciplines to ignore man, except as an inexhaustible source of data, and to become preoccupied, instead, with their own bibliographies, expendable animals, and the rituals of laboratory science. A humanistic turn of events would, then, be one, I presume, in which the focal importance of living man would be reaffirmed, and psychology would no longer be pursued for its own sake.

Those who attempt to revive humanism are likely to point to the culture of classic Greece as an example of what they would like to restore. That culture, as I understand it, was characterized by man's audacity in the face of adversities imposed by the gods or by nature. Its heroes asserted themselves as men, as men they dared challenge what their history and their gods told them was inevitable, and as men they often suffered frustration and defeat. Yet while history, more often than not, continued to reaffirm its verdicts, the men we as humanists want to remember are those who refused to acquiesce to the facts of life.

Humanism and Classicism

But neohumanism, it seems to me, is often no more than a form of classicism; that is to say, a preoccupation with adventure as an historical fact, rather than a present enterprise, a preoccupation with a state of affairs to be revered and restored, phrase by phrase and stone by stone. And the modern classicist is related to the humanist's heroes of the Fourth Century B.C. or the Fifteenth Century A.D. in about the same way the Twentieth Century Daughters of the American Revolution are related to the Eighteenth Century signers of the Declaration of Independence.

There were, undoubtedly, classicists among the Greeks too, and it may be a little unfair to try to assess their role from this distance. Whatever it was they stood for, they were probably pretty skeptical of what was going on and I am sure they were always trying to revive something. I do not know what they managed to accomplish, but there is little reason to believe it was their influence that made Greek culture either humanistic or classic. Nor does our admiration for the humanism of other times and places make humanists of us now, any more than does tracing our ancestry to a hero who fought for civil rights in the American Revolution mean that we have any stomach for the civil rights battles of our own generation. Indeed, I must note that the most heroic figures in today's struggle for human values regard their ancestors more in pity than in pride.

Humanism is then, as I see it, not something we revive. Revivals are the work of classicists. Humanism, instead, has to do with the present, the novel, the defiant, the alive, and with what the classicists often argue cannot be done. Where the classicist documents historical certainties, the true humanist fumbles with present uncertainties. The classicist seeks to be historically right; the humanist continually risks being historically wrong in order to set something right. The humanist is aggressive, and hopes thus to achieve better things, but the classicist, threatened by the humanistic enterprise, equates aggression with hostility, and hostility, in turn, with destruction.

[1] Prepared for a conference on humanistic psychology, Old Saybrook, Connecticut, November 27–29, 1964, and first published as Kelly, G.A. (1965). The threat of aggression. *Journal of Humanistic Psychology*, *V*, 195–201. Republished in Maher, B. (Ed.). (1969). *Clinical psychology and personality: The selected papers of George Kelly* (pp. 281–288). Wiley. Published here by permission of Sage and Wiley.

Collected Papers of the Pioneer of Constructivist Psychology: George A. Kelly, First Edition. Edited by David A. Winter and Nick Reed.

The Humanist Paradox

Now there is another theme in humanism. It is a secondary theme that derives from the first, and I think it makes sense only when expressed in the context of human audacity. This is the theme that whatever is truly characteristic of man is good and should therefore be preserved and protected against any distorting influence. Man, in the light of his audacious achievements, should be encouraged to go on being the kind of person he has so aptly proved himself to be; he should express himself; he should go right ahead and be audacious. But he should not be permitted to tamper with human nature; that is carrying audacity too far!

It is this secondary theme—a theme sometimes identified as permissiveness, sometimes as nonaggression, sometimes as respect for the dignity of man—that often colors the meaning of humanism. Thus, humanism appears to have created for itself a paradox. The audacity of man in general has proved to be so valuable a human asset that the audacity of any particular man must be restrained from impinging upon it. Man must express himself—that is very, very important—but never, never must he express himself in such a way that anything human will be affected.

One way out of this paradox is to believe that the nature of man is such that if he does express himself—his true self—he will harmonize with all other men who truly express themselves. This is to say that the intrinsic nature of man is intrinsically compatible with its collective self, and that disharmonies arise only out of extrinsic distortions, or, possibly, out of temporary immaturities.

Another way out is to say that man cannot be manipulated except as his nature conspires. Whatever he does, it is he who does it. And the fact that he does it under certain imposed conditions in no way denies his dignity, but, instead, stands as a credit to his personal achievement ("under optimal psychological conditions," as we sometimes say). A child learns to play the piano well by being forced to practice four hours a day. That is not suppression; that is a human accomplishment. When he grows up he will probably be proud of it—and perhaps think of himself as a first class humanist. A depressed person is disciplined to a hospital routine of scrubbing floors and scouring toilets. As a result he finds himself too busy to worry. So, again, man prevails! See how the organism's ingenious adaptability has contrived to substitute reality for imagination? How fortunate! Not everyone is able to do that!

But it is difficult for me to see how either of these constructions can provide an escape from the humanist's paradox. The interpretation of man as a naturally harmonious being, who likes other people in proportion to his admiration of himself, seems to ignore the fact of human tyranny. Whether he can rise above this unpleasant fact is another question. But it appears to me to be as presumptuous to regard man as naturally good as it is to label him as inherently evil. Moreover, we are still much too busy sorting out good from evil to be altogether clear about which is which, or whether man is wholly one or the other.

The other construction of man—the construction of him as an ingenious conformist, a slave who is smart enough to know his place—is not very encouraging to the fellow who doesn't want to be a slave, or practice his music lessons, or live in Levittown, but on the banks of Walden Pond. He persists in thinking that under other circumstances he might accomplish a lot more. He may be right. And then, again, he may be wrong, for some men do accomplish more under a reinforcement schedule than when left to their own devices. And what is the humanist going to say about that?

The Meaning of Threat

The human enterprise is, at best, a touch-and-go proposition. Any assumptions we make about what is good, or what is evil, or what will open the door to the future, are best regarded as only temporary, and any conclusions we draw from our experiences are best seen as approximations of what we may eventually understand. The human quest is not about to be concluded, nor is truth already partly packaged for distribution and consumption. Instead, it seems likely that whatever may now appear to be the most obvious fact will look quite different when regarded from the vantage point of tomorrow's fresh theoretical positions. Yet it is a misfortune that man should be so set on being right at the very outset that he dares not risk stupidities in an effort to devise something better than what he has.

This brings us back to the audacity of man, which, as you already know, I have come to regard as the primary humanistic theme. I like that theme. But let us not overlook the fact that this audacity is the very thing that men fear when they see it about to be expressed—and as often admire when it has run its course. In a world where vast experiments are being undertaken, where new psychological devices are being employed, and strange societies are being constituted, we dread the far-reaching implications of what is about to happen to us.

This is threat. To feel that one is on the threshold of deep changes in himself and his way of life is, I think, its essential feature. Threat is, from this point of view, an impending personal experience, not a set of ominous circumstances. Moreover, it is in the context of threat—or dread—that the two terms, aggression and hostility, become subjectively synonymous. This is to say that to encounter either in the actions of another person is to raise the specter of transformation in oneself. And may I point out also the curious fact that the two terms have become synonyms both in the language that diplomats use and in the language that psychologists use—as well, it seems, as in the language that humanists speak.

So how do we encourage human audacity without inviting one man's initiative to suppress another's? This is the humanist's dilemma. It is also the dilemma of democracy—how do you give political sovereignty to a people, or a state, bent on suppressing its minorities?

So, also, it is the problem of the economist—how can you have a free enterprise system that produces the Bell Telephone Company, and still claim that you have anything that even remotely resembles free enterprise? And it is the problem of the liberal scholar—what happens when you are liberal with the board of trustees of a state university?

Aggression

Before trying to find a humanistic answer to these questions, let me turn to a psychological matter. We call aggressive men hostile because what they do seems destructive, especially when it is pointed in our direction. We don't want them to meddle with our lives. Thus we judge them not so much by the character of their acts as by our own characteristic response to their initiative.

But what happens to us is not to be confounded with what is happening within them. What they undertake is not measured by what we experience. If one is to have an adequate psychology of man, it must be a psychology of the actor, not the victim. This is to say that behavior needs to be explained within the fact, not before or after the fact. Our own reaction to what another person attempts is scarcely enough to account for what he is trying to accomplish. Nor do our hurt feelings constitute a psychological analysis of his behavior.

Now may I go on to say that this equating of aggression with our projection of destructive intent is the outcome of Nineteenth Century notions about scientific determinism. To think scientifically about the psychology of man has seemed to mean that we must regard him as an intervening variable—called an "organism"—in a stimulus-response couplet. Our ventures collapse when challenged by an aggressive colleague. How shall we explain it? Simple! The collapse is the observed response; he is the obvious stimulus; and we are the organismic victim caught in the S-R squeeze. His aggression caused our downfall; and what more do you need to explain what the rascal was up to?

A stimulus-response psychology is, of course, one in which human responses are explained in terms of their external antecedents—their stimuli. And stimuli, in such a system, are reciprocally explained in terms of what they produce—their responses. That is the solipsism, or "equation," as we prefer to call it in mathematics. If I am threatened, then the person whom I see as the stimulus explains my experience. If I can cope with his aggression only by contemplating a profound change in myself, then the scoundrel must be hostile. Psychotherapists will recognize this as something that turns up rather frequently among their patients. But it is much more widespread than that; it is a conclusion commonly reached by all those who live out their lives according to the formula of stimulus-response.

But stimulus-response psychology is not the only possible kind of psychology. We can, if we wish, employ a psychology which casts its explanations in terms of what the person himself is doing, not what others do to him or what they think he has done to them. Aggression, in such a psychological system, is more akin to initiative. It is an expression of the audacity of man, even as he ventures into the realm of psychology. The aggressive man—like the humanist—may be one who risks being wrong in order to set something right—or in order to find out what rightly explains his fellow man.

Hostility

Now hostility, in this way of thinking, may, or may not, involve aggression, and aggression may, or may not, involve hostility. The two constructs are propositionally independent of each other. If we are to employ a notion of hostility within this kind of psychological system we must understand the hostile person's enterprise in terms of his own outlook, not merely in terms of the threat that others experience when they seek to come to terms with him.

Since any system of psychology must provide some explanation of the means by which a person checks up on himself, it becomes important to understand how the implications of such a checkup are incorporated. In stimulus-response theory the checkup is cast in terms of reinforcement, that is to say, by ascribing some kind of stimulus quality to the response itself, or to its consequences, which will feed back into the system. But in personal construct theory the checkup is provided by confirmation of expectations. This is to say that if the expectations that follow from one's construction of events continually fail to materialize, a revision of the construction system is called for. This means that defeat must be recognized, failure identified, and even tragedy experienced if man is to survive, and all the more so if man is to achieve anything of epic proportions.

But a major revision of one's construct system can threaten him with immediate change, or chaos, or anxiety. Thus it often seems better to extort confirmation of one's anticipations—and therefore of the system that produced them—rather than to risk the utter confusion of those moments of transition. It is this extortion of confirmation that characterizes hostility.

A nation, before admitting that its long leap forward in the defense of human life has proved invalid, may destroy millions of lives when they disclose evidence of the failure of the system. A country may go to war to displace responsibility for its mistakes. A man may commit murder to discredit what has proved him wrong. And, since hostility may as easily employ passivity as aggression, we may resort either to spiteful "obedience" or "respect for law" to simulate the missing validity in a crumbling societal system. Or, in a family whose structure is no longer viable, we may offer indulgence to replace affection and to smother a child's unexpected independence.

Nevertheless, whether undertaken by aggressive or passive means, hostility is, in a personal construct theoretical system, an extortional undertaking designed by the person to protect a heavy investment in his own construction of life. And if, perchance, his hostility proves destructive of others, then that, unfortunately, is the way it must be. The economy must be preserved; the fact that the elderly starve in India or on the other side of town is incidental. Heresy must be controlled; too bad that intellectual curiosity on the campus must be denied. Bombs must be dropped; to be sure children will die, but who can say it was we who put them in the target area? From our point of view, it is a precious way of life that we defend—Cadillacs and all. But what the hostile man does not know is that it is he who is the eventual victim of his own extortion. With the adoption of hostility he surrenders his capacity to judge the outcome of his way of life, and without that capacity he must inevitably go astray.

The acknowledgment of defeat or tragedy is not a destructive step for man to take. It characterizes, instead, the negative outcome of any crucial test of our way of life, and it is, therefore, an essential feature of human progress toward more positive outcomes. Hostility does not, for this very reason, contribute to human achievement. Primarily because it denies failure it leads, instead, to the abatement of human enterprise, and substitutes for nobler undertakings a mask of complacency.

A Step for the Humanist

In this way of thinking, which I have proposed for the humanistically inclined psychologist, there are three key notions that must be lifted from the context of stimulus-response psychology and recast in the light of a psychology of the man himself. They are *threat, aggression,* and *hostility*. Threat, for the man himself, is the experience of being on the brink of a major shift in his core construct system. Aggression, for the man himself, is one's own initiative, not what that initiative may lead another to do or feel. And so with hostility, too; hostility is the extortion of confirming evidence to present to oneself when there seems too much at stake to undertake the personal changes that natural evidence requires.

The humanistic psychologist's dilemma—how to protect human audacity from human audacity without stifling human audacity—finds another kind of solution when we manage to step outside the stimulus-response solipsism. It is the hostile, and not necessarily the aggressive enterprise, that must be guarded against. The aggressive effort to understand man, or to experiment with ways of accomplishing psychological feats never before achieved, is not intrinsically destructive. It may, of course, be hazardous. It does become destructive, however, when one tries to make it appear that disconfirming events did not actually arise, or that what failed to occur actually happened. And this, in turn, is generated by the notion that we ought always to be right before we commit ourselves, a notion that later makes it very hard to concede our mistakes, or to revise our construction of the world when our heavily invested anticipations fail to materialize.

Humanism reflects audacity in man. But this audacity, when it substitutes extortion for disconfirmation, disengages itself from the world and abandons the future of mankind. Humanism, while it openly experiences defeat, does not succumb to it, for to do that would be to give up man's aggressive undertakings altogether, and, with them, all the aspirations that arise from being tragically human. Thus, the experience of tragedy, and not the sense of certainty, is the basis of all hope, and is indeed the most essential step in the bold pursuit of better things. And that, I submit, is a notion that lies close to the heart of the human enterprise.

22

Epilogue: Don Juan[1]

It happens that twice in the past year I have gone to see the same opera. This is not by any means a normal thing for me to do. But for several months after seeing this particular opera for the first time I had had the nagging feeling that I must have missed something that should have been quite obvious. So a few weeks ago, when I saw that Mozart's Don Giovanni was to be produced, I persuaded my wife that we should buy tickets.

I particularly wanted my wife to be with me this time. She notices many things that escape my attention and I rather hoped that, after seeing the production, she could explain to me in simple language just what was supposed to be going on.

So we sat through it, craning our necks to see around the high stalls that partition off the crannies of the Paris Opera House, and now and then catching rewarding glimpses of some magnificent staging. The building was apparently designed by a music lover who thought it might be just as well if the audience listened rather than looked, or else by an architect who had worked his way up from designing horse barns. I suspect the latter. I spent the evening with the sense that there must be a manger and feedbox somewhere in the shadows behind me. As a matter of fact there was nothing of the sort, only a little couch in a dark comer behind the half dozen or so chairs, presumably intended for those who might be overpowered by the emotional impact of great operatic moments.

When it was over my wife called my attention to the fact that the music was great—which it was, I must agree; that people appreciated the drama—which they did seem to; and that a lot of folks, including some close relatives of ours who are musicians, would have their feelings hurt if I described the way the opera had appeared to me the first time I saw it. This last, of course, remains to be seen. But she is probably right. She usually is about such things.

But I can see now that none of this makes sense unless I go back a few months and describe my impressions the first time I saw Don Giovanni. On that occasion the architecture had a very definite bearing on what happened; that, and the thing they give you to read before the performance, the paper that is supposed to tell you what to expect.

I was by myself on that occasion. After arriving fairly early for the performance and settling down in my seat behind a post, I discovered it was much too dark to read anything. When I looked around the slowly filling gallery I saw that most of the seats were behind posts and there was scarcely enough light for reading anywhere. This, too, was an opera house built either by a music lover or by an architect with an obsession. If he was a music lover he must have expected such thunderous applauses that only a forest of supporting columns would keep the balconies from tumbling down. But, then, perhaps he was only a farsighted architect who figured it would be a long, long time before the "Met" would replace the building and he had better draw up something that would stand. In any case, between the designer and his posts and the manager's conservation of electricity, I was effectively prevented from reading what the usherette had thrust into my hand when she showed or rather, led, me to my seat.

I suppose I could have gone back to the lobby to read my program. It was light enough there. But I had been standing outside in the winter rain for some time waiting to snag a ticket, my feet were tired and wet, I was cold, and the plush seat felt too good to leave. Besides, I was not sure I could find my way back.

So, not being informed in advance of precisely what I should see, I was on my own. What I actually did see was probably the faintly coherent patterns of my own particular kind of outlook, reflected off the rapidly shifting events of the play.

You should know, I suppose, that my outlook, while it embodies many things, incorporates something of what my fellow psychologists believe (although I find most of their beliefs highly questionable), a little of what psychiatrists are trying to propagate—which sounds to me pretty wild when it is pitched at any level of abstraction above that of straightforward clinical observation—and much of what I have picked up on my own during a good many years spent more or less trying to help people disentangle themselves and trying to figure out how they got that way. All of this I find very confusing. So when I describe what I saw, it is *my* Don Giovanni, not Mozart's. Or, better, it is the reflections of my personal world shimmering off the polished facets of Mozart's magnificent creation.

[1] Written in 1960 and first published in Maher, B. (Ed.). (1969). *Clinical psychology and personality: The selected papers of George Kelly* (pp. 333–351). Wiley. Republished by permission of Wiley.

Collected Papers of the Pioneer of Constructivist Psychology: George A. Kelly, First Edition. Edited by David A. Winter and Nick Reed.

I am sure that I am not the first to see Don Giovanni with a nude mind. In every audience there must be many individuals who have not been told what they are supposed to see. What unique stories they might disclose if only they dared. For one it might be the everlasting antiphony of strength and weakness, of timidity and daring; for another, the story of one honest man, true to his passions, aware of his impulses, open in his thoughts, and caught up in a world of hypocrites; for another, an orgy of delicious indulgence, vicariously enjoyed and unmarred by any feelings of guilt, since in the end the full price of punishment is to be paid, and unmixed with fear, since it is Don Giovanni who is to do the paying. But people are usually ashamed of seeing what they are not supposed to see, so these are the stories that are never told.

I, too, might not be reporting what I saw if it were not for the vivid impression I got out of the experience. Nothing occurred to interfere with this impression until I read the printed story. That was after the performance was over, the impression was too deep to be easily erased, and I had returned to the hotel room where the light, while not particularly good, was still good enough to read by. By that time I was ready to be stubborn about the whole thing.

As I had watched and listened everything seemed to hang together and make pretty good sense. It was dramatic too. I had heard enough about operas to know they are all supposed to be dramatic. Knowing this much in advance, the dramatic features were perfectly obvious to me. But it turned out that there were other things I did not know in advance, so, naturally, those were the things that I missed altogether.

What I saw was that Squire John, to give him—more appropriately I think—an old-fashioned American name instead of Don Giovanni or the more familiar Don Juan, was obviously in trouble from the word "Go." Throughout the evening I had felt rather sorry for him. There he was, in scene after scene, keeping up such a brave front, while being slowly driven to exasperation by one frustration after another. Imagine, then, my surprise when after the performance I read that he was supposed to have been having himself a fine time, right up to the last when he was clump-clumped off to hell by the solid marble ghost of the man he had murdered. It was incredible. In spite of the official document there in my hands I could not believe that that was the way it had happened.

My own interpretation of his final scene, as I had listened to the story come to its soul-stirring climax, was that here at last someone was taking a personal interest in John. It seemed quite appropriate, dramatically, that it should be the spirit of the very man he had done in. Since it was so obvious that John had never gotten along well with his parents, the long-delayed fatherly advice and guidance were particularly touching, especially coming from a municipal statue out of the park.

Up to that moment there was precious little warmth and sympathy to be had from the live people whom John had picked up as companions. And how like life that was! Through moistened eyes I witnessed this final triumph of tenderness over a lifetime full of cruel misunderstandings. Moreover, the Paris production, although it treated this final scene quite differently, seemed to make even clearer the new-found feeling between John and his father-figure.

But now I find I am ahead of myself again. To tell this story properly one should start from the beginning.

The curtain rises. It is night. There on the stage is our maladroit hero for the evening, introducing himself to the audience by pretending to rape some woman, whom he obviously cannot see too clearly, and doing it there right in her own front yard. The venture would appear to have started out as an effort at seduction. But things had not gone well, and John, who must not have been able to measure up to expectations, was being chased out of the house. The whole audience, if not John, could see that he was embroiled with a very much aroused female who was half again his age and fully twice his size. Despite the fact that she was bundled up to the ears in a huge padded nightgown we could see that she was bent on making the situation look like a classic case of rape, if she could only keep him from getting away.

John had his hands full. Not being very perceptive, he was doing his best to go along with the act the way she wanted it, and at the same time protect himself from the frustrated and enraged prima donna. He clutched at her as best he could, but every time she shrugged her shoulders his feet would fly off the ground. The truth was that both of them were getting pretty well fed up with each other and there were moments when I was sure she was about to send him sprawling, like the time he got his head in the way when it came her turn to sing.

And, my, how she could sing! If only John had had the sense to sit on his hands during the evening and listen to her sing instead of making a pass at her. She would have liked that, I am sure, and it would have kept her mind off matters that were peculiarly troublesome to her.

Well, this is the way it went. One could not help but feel sorry for the fellow, right from the very start. His taste in women was as bad as his understanding of them. It must have been painful to discover that he had failed to meet the girl's standards of what a masculine lover should be, and he had allowed the whole thing to break down into a clumsy juvenile effort at bold conquest. Here was our hero, now fully introduced to the audience as a man who, like so many unfortunate people in the world, was totally unprepared to play his part in an adult relationship.

But let us go on with the scene and see how gross human tragedy is compounded out of persistent faults and petty virtues. It now happens that the girl's father, who has been watching from the wings, is unable to restrain himself any longer. So he comes barging in to try to straighten things out before they get any worse. But he is too late. By this time John, frustrated in his efforts to be manly, is furious at himself, the girl, and about everything in sight, and he is in no mood to listen to advice. He turns his rage on the father, as if somehow here was the fiend behind this maddening woman. In a moment the old man, who I am sure only wanted to be helpful, is dead, the victim of John's nimble sword and wildly diffused hostility.

That pretty much concludes the opening passage of the opera. Here in a brief and deftly contrived scene, presented on a partially darkened stage with a few beautifully composed operatic lines, the tragic plight of this young man and of so much of mankind was unerringly sketched. Now, human nature being what it is, there remained only the task of unfolding the inevitable consequences.

Anna, now an orphan and free to embellish her own mistakes, has a fiancé—also a dope—by the name of Ottavio. It isn't quite clear what explanation she gives him for being out in the front yard in her nightgown with another man, especially when she can't even say who the fellow was or what he looked like. But anyway, instead of letting the matter drop at a point where it might eventually have been forgotten, she sets out to get Ottavio mixed up in the affair. Somebody must be punished. That is the way to untangle human affairs. Ottavio is quickly taken in, he agrees to take a conventional stand in the matter, and he swears he will run the fellow through if Anna can ever point him out. Anna, who knows perfectly well who it was, decides to hold off a little longer to see what she can stir up. Maybe she can make it into something really big.

Not long after this happened, dear old John, who seems incapable of learning from experience, swaggers into another trap. This time he is spotted at a distance by a cute little flirt named Zerlina. Here is a sharp-eyed earthy creature who has no difficulty reading her male. No doubt she has heard of John, suspects he might be amusing, and, attracted by the idea of having a fling on the eve of her nuptials, decides to unzip his ego. The moment she sees him up close she pinpoints his weakness and knows she will be perfectly safe as long as help is within screaming distance. She is.

Where Anna had made trouble for John because she failed utterly to understand him, Zerlina's unerring insight was her implement for mischief-making. Meanwhile, Zerlina's fiancé, who, in turn, has seen through her for some time but doesn't have the courage to do anything about it, takes advantage of the opportunity to go off and "have a round with the boys." Let her tease someone else for a change. Besides, good-hearted John has offered to drop in later and pay for the drinks.

A pair of the most clever and amusing scenes in the whole opera come next. The first shows John being trussed up for his tryst with Zerlina. It is a two-man job. No casual slacks and smoking jacket for our John! With the help of his valet, who laces him up the back, he encases himself in layer after layer of upholstery material. Needless to say, the valet, who can readily imagine what is going to happen at the critical moment, finds this vastly amusing. In fact, he has been keeping a diary of such misadventures and is not above reciting from it whenever he meets someone who is inclined to take John seriously.

Now the next scene shows John escorting Zerlina off to look at the etchings she was so eager to see. After a few moments—scarcely enough time to formulate a critical appraisal of more than one or two of them—there is a scream, a pause, and they are back, John's inaccessible back-lacings still tied in hard knots, and Zerlina wide-eyed with surprise. The same old John! Quite obviously, if he had been intending to make a pass at the girl, he had failed, as before, to think the situation through.

John then tries to explain to everybody that it was his valet, Leporello, who had slipped up on Zerlina while he himself was up in the attic trying to remember where he had put those blasted etchings. Though this is the truth, no one believes it. I thought that Zerlina might have vouched for his story at this point, but she didn't. Perhaps she was too much upset over the fact that her carefully planned strategy had left her rear unprotected.

Anyway, John gets out of there just in time to save his skin from a jealous mob who would have unlaced him fast enough if they had ever got their hands on him. Now he is in more trouble than ever, and he has two strikes against him.

Not all of John's girlfriends were unsympathetic. There was Elvira, who had visions of making a man of him. But he would not listen. He wanted to do the job himself and in his own way. She was annoyed by that, as one is always annoyed when a friend refuses to be made over.

But still Elvira keeps hoping that John will end up making such a fool of himself he will be ready to listen to reason. Leporello, who likes nothing better than to see situations deteriorate, pulls out his notebook and does his best to convince Elvira that John is a hopeless fool already. But it is only when she falls in with the self-righteously indignant Anna and her stooge Ottavio that she is finally willing to abandon her project and take up the official line.

I suppose we should not be too critical of this institutionalized animosity. No man is above the law, as they always say. After all, John was now a murderer and, in his present disturbed state of mind, really quite dangerous. If this had not happened before the days of Organized Medicine someone could have complained, and in less time than it would have taken to tie his gussets he would have been quietly clamped into a "protective environment."

But now that we think of it, John was not the only dangerous person to have running around loose at night. Ottavio, too, was dangerous. He was pledged to kill the first man Anna pointed out to him. So, in turn, Anna, also, was dangerous. Then there was Leporello, the cynic who delighted in seeing people disillusioned; he was dangerous in an accessory-before-the-fact sort of way. And Zerlina, who was forever playing with matches, was likely to start fires that could not be put out.

In fact, we can see how each one, in his own way, was dangerous—Ottavio with the pledged loyalty of a soldier, Anna who could not distinguish between justice and punishment, Leporello who could not see beyond facts, Zerlina with her love of danger itself, and Elvira, who was ready to abandon what she could not mold; all of these—but it was our dim-witted John who got cracked at the end of the whip.

And now the stage goes dark again. John walks the empty streets in the chill of night, clanking his sword and trying to think brave thoughts. Dogging his footsteps is the gloating realist, Leporello. Before them, out of the shadows, looms the statue of Anna's father, the man John had murdered in blind rage. In his loneliness John reaches out to this wise old man and expresses aloud his wish that tonight of all nights they might be having supper together and talking about matters that so much filled his heart. Slowly, the massive head nods assent. Needless to say, at this point Leporello is flabbergasted; in his world things like this can't really happen!

But this is no hallucination. Supper is served, there is a knock at the door, and there stands the marble ghost. In open defiance of the facts of life he has dismounted from his horse in the park and come all the way on foot.

Yet, for all the wisdom of his years, the old man is still human. Like many a well-meaning father he opens the conversation by asking John to "repent." Repent? Of what should he repent? Can John repent his own stupidity—how can one repent what he cannot comprehend? Should he repent his misery—how does one renounce his own punishment? Repent his efforts to find love in the arms of a woman—where better to seek it? To us, who have developed repentance to a fine art, these may seem like stupid questions, but we must remember that John was not overly bright and these were the only ways he knew to pose the issues.

But soon wisdom and fatherly concern prevail. The two men clasp hands. For a moment John's knees weaken, but he is sustained by the firm hand that holds his. In the background someone has built a heart-warming fire against the dreadful cold of this long night, and, with a comforting arm around his shoulder, John strides confidently off to meet his destiny.

Left behind are the petty characters of the drama, their scapegoat no longer to bear the brunt of their half-ventures, talking among themselves about how quiet things are with John gone, and thinking that perhaps they ought to find some way of getting along with each other. None of them seems very happy about the prospects and one suspects that sooner or later they will find themselves another Don Juan.

There are some, no doubt those who read their programs in advance instead of letting the opera speak for itself, who insist that John was being ushered off to hell. To hell, indeed! And just what do they think they were looking at all evening! No, they are wrong. Surely Mozart's sense of dramatic integrity would never have led him to add mere fire and brimstone to the tortures already displayed.

Then there are some who say the music itself sounds the notes of doom and thus tells a story quite different from mine. But who has heard the notes of doom and lived to write them down? The music speaks of power, yes, and of massive forces rising in crescendo to bring the story to its conclusion. It speaks of destiny, too. But what destiny is worthy of the mighty chords with which Mozart has rendered these final scenes—a trash fire at the city dump (Jerusalem's gahanna), or is it compassion's recovery of man's soul from torments he can neither understand nor endure?

* * *

Now that I have told my story, it is only fair to say what the classical yarn is. I suppose that in the end I shall be forced to concede that it was the classical story that Mozart had in mind. But—still—let me stand firm on my personal experience a little longer. Think of this: may there not be two levels of wisdom—the protective screen of words behind which we think thoughts that have no words of their own, and the torrent of words with which those feelings sometimes burst through? May not the classical story of Don Juan, then, have been the screen behind which Mozart dared conjure with the forbidden feelings of a troubled man, and the opera itself—the one I thought I saw—have been the torrent bursting through to express what he could not say?

The classical Don Juan is written down as a man of courage, fearing neither man, fate, nor conscience. Surrounded by lesser beings who crave adventure but fear to seize it on their own, he stirs the envy of men and the hearts of women. Openly he does, or seduces them into doing, what they secretly wish they might do on their own. But by this he stirs their animosity too, for what woman wants to wake up in the morning and find both her lover and her virtue gone, or what man will stand idly by and see his own just rewards embraced by another. So Don Juan leaps from bed to bed and fight to fight, no less successful in one than in the other. What are we to do with him? Surely the eventual triumph of such wickedness must be forestalled at all costs. So nothing less than hell itself must be invoked at the end of the story to ensure the justice that man himself cannot contrive.

But is this the happy end of evil? Look! There Don Juan strides through the very gates of hell. He has refused to cringe. Behind, we, the timidly innocent, are left gaping. So what has been proved? A question: Is virtue only another name for fear? Having struck this unresolved chord, the classic story ends. Now poets and philosophers—and perhaps all of us—continually find ourselves drawn back to this libertine and the question he poses.

For my own part, as you already know, I think the composer, or the production staff, or the artists, had spontaneously found an answer and portrayed it well. But could they bring themselves to say they had found it, or even let themselves think they had found it? Probably not! Such naivete would have brought ridicule down upon their heads, and people who study their programs in advance, as I am sure they must, are not ones to invite ridicule.

* * *

There is another version of Don Juan, a psychiatric version. Perhaps we might say there are two such versions, the one narrowly medical and the other Freudian. The latter makes more interesting reading. And, besides, it was by using the broader logic of medicine that Freud attempted to construct his particular humanistic model of man. That makes it somewhat medical and a reasonable representation of how psychiatry thinks about John.

Freud's Don Juan dangles helplessly from the end of his biography, and the sooner he comes to realize it the sooner he can squirm himself into a comfortable position. The amorphous forces that awaken infant life are quickly shaped by experience. It is only after it is too late to reshape them that John, or anyone else, can step in and take a hand. By then he is outnumbered by the grotesque gremlins who have moved in on him. Now, as with any member of a minority group, his task is to gain insight into his master's foibles and get busy practicing the subtle art of compromise. The Don Juan we see barging around is little more than an imperceptive and impulse-ridden baby for whom the necessary compromises have been too long delayed.

To understand Don Juan, then, we must first understand the amoral impulses of an infant. As he seeks his place in the family he first competes for, and then loses, the enveloping affection of the one woman in his life—his mother. Yet he often finds himself allied with her against the man who has defeated him—his father. So what does that make of him?

Who is he? What is he? Whatever his infantile answer to those questions might be, he cannot accept it. So he spends the rest of his life frantically trying to prove what he cannot believe. He seduces women, some of them young and beautiful—the kind of prize for which strong men compete—or maternal women, who will play mother to his appealing wistfulness. But none is the embodiment of the prize he once sought and lost. He allies himself with restless women against their kind of men, but that is not a man's game. He destroys men in combat, but does not thereby himself become a man. Still, in its way, each of these conquests results in a momentary victory. But it is momentary only, so soon he must try again. How is such a child to know that the conclusive achievements of adulthood are quite another order of experience?

Our psychiatric Don Juan, then, is a desperate man, precariously balanced between infancy and maturity, between masculinity and feminity, between cuddling softness and brutal assault. He acts out the parts he cannot think through. For all his gay boyish appeal he is as dangerous to himself as he is to others. He is as quick to plunge into the fires of hell as he is to thrust others into them. His conscience, having no firm anchorage in early loyalties, fails to serve him in the moments of his infantile crises. Not a very pretty picture, this psychiatric Don Juan, nor very heroic, either.

The psychiatric version of Don Juan does not attempt to cope with the issues posed by the classical story. The question of good and evil, and how one may be made to triumph over the other, is ignored. Fear and innocence remain as much confounded as ever. There is nothing toward which man fumbles his way except to be comfortably at peace with himself. Nothing out yonder! The horizon is the end of the world.

John is a patient, a very sick one, who needs professional care. And if he is sick we are all sick and we had better turn ourselves in for treatment. If we are not too resistant to our psychoanalysts we may eventually be able to hobble around on our own, but every day we must remember who our masters are and make the necessary concessions to keep peace with them.

Where the classic story sets forth the question of man's destiny, the psychiatric diagnosis fetches up John's case history. The Don Juan of literature challenges our ontology: He tempts us, frightens us, enrages us, sets us wondering what we have become. The sickly John simply turns us over in bed to have a look at our psychodynamics.

* * *

Now that we have three versions of Don Juan, and one more to come, there will be those—there always are—who will want to be told which is the correct one. This presupposes that there really is, or was, such a person in the first place. At least, it seems to presuppose that! But, instead of accepting the presupposition, we had better put it in the form of a prior question: Was there ever really such a person?

We might hedge a little and say, "Well, I suppose there must have been, at some time or other, somewhere, a fellow they called, 'Don Juan'." As a matter of fact there may have been as many as fifty-six fellows who were called that, including forty-three who were christened with that name, eight who earned it on their own, and four who were falsely accused. Suppose there were; it seems reasonable enough. So we reply, "Yes; there really was a Don Juan." That, of course, is not what was asked, but, perhaps, the obliqueness of our reply will be overlooked.

But this does not help us much. We have to ask our question another way. Let's be specific: Was there ever such a person as Mozart thought he saw, or as Freud thought he saw, or as I thought I saw? That sounds a little better. But is it not the same question we started out with, stated in another way, and just as hard to answer? Take my "Don Juan," whom, as you would probably guess, I am rather fond of; if there was, indeed, such a person, then such was the person there was. That makes my version of him self-evidently the correct one. What does this do to Freud's version? Nothing at all; we have only to look for another fellow who fits it. So our whole line of discourse falls apart because we have not agreed on an object of reference. Perhaps we never can agree—really!

And if there never was anyone resembling any of the Don Juans described by Mozart, Freud, or me, then the question of which version is the correct version makes no sense at all. You can't go around asking what is the "correct version" of something that doesn't exist. And if it does exist, before I can answer your question, you will have to tell me about it or present it to me in some way before I can be expected to say what the "correct version" really is. When you get through I will have to think over very carefully what you have said or shown me and come up with an answer.

And what will I say? Limited, as I am, to your representation, I have no grounds for saying that you do not know what you are talking about. Unless I can claim some other access to what you describe, what is there for me to say, indeed, except, "Yes, that is absolutely the correct version," or, simply, "So that is that!" Who am I to say you are wrong or what you have shown me is wrong? So, as these things go, you are right, Mozart is right, Freud is right, I am right, and just about anybody can be right. Good Heavens! There must be something wrong with our question!

Perhaps the trouble is we can't make up our minds what we are talking about. Let's see if being "objective" will get us off the hook. You just point to the fellow we are to talk about—don't say anything, mind you—just point to him, and then we can get down to the question of whose version of him is the correct one.

Good! Now suppose he has his Sunday suit on, or the suit Don Giovanni wore to the party for Zerlina. You wait till he is all fixed up, then you point to him and grunt or make some nonverbal signal to indicate he/she/it is what you have in mind. Keep the words out of it; that will let the creature speak for itself!

But wait a minute; haven't you been a little prejudiced in his favor and have you not chosen to point him out under particularly favorable conditions?

You could ask him to take his suit off, I suppose. But that is hardly fair either, since normally he must wear some kind of clothes, if only the tops of his pajamas. If we have him stand there without anything on we can hardly say he looks himself. Moreover, if all this takes place in the dime store or in the First National Bank, won't we get a biased impression of some sort?

Now I see I've used up a whole page of manuscript and I'm still no closer to telling you what the correct version of Don Juan is. I haven't even mentioned yet the distortion that this renegade himself will put into the picture. Suppose when we ask him to take his clothes off, he calls the police and has us thrown into jail. Not only is this likely to damage our ability to judge him fairly, but it points up the fact that he will resort to all kinds of underhanded tricks to keep us from seeing him as he really is.

It is just because of things like this that the whole science of psychology is in such a bad fix. People insist on acting up, distorting themselves, misleading us, and otherwise refusing to let us make objective scientific observations that are free from all biases. If people would only be natural, and if we could only point them out to each other without having them show up in some particular biased way, we might develop a very fine system of psychology to explain what makes them tick. It might even be that psychology could become a precise science like physics, where everyone, except a few of the most brilliantly confused scientists—whom we rarely see anyway—knows what he is talking about, and where you can always ask such questions as, "What is the correct version of Don Juan?"

Let's try again. Our task has turned out to be to nail down an objective reference point against which we can determine who has the correct version of Don Juan. Let us concede, reluctantly, that whomsoever we point out as the authentic Don Juan will be a fellow who is bound to be acting so as to give a distorted picture of himself. That is to say, we shall admit that it is natural of a man to act unnaturally. Almost anybody you can think of is likely to be presenting his own biased version of himself in some way, either to his public, his wife, his children, his associates, the people he imagines are looking at him—but aren't—, even to himself. If "being yourself" is anything different from trying to be something other than yourself, then it is hopeless to try to put a finger on what it is.

We shall have to make another concession. Whomsoever we point to and say, "There, that is Don Juan, climbing in the window," will, by the very way we point him out, be cast into a particular version of him. Even if we felt that this was too suggestive of a particular kind of mission, it would do no good to hold off. We would only end up a few moments later exclaiming, "Oh look; there he is now, jumping out the window."

We could say, simply and in a level monotone, "There, that is Don Juan," pointing to the fellow sitting on the curb with his head in his hands, and being careful not to say one word more. But most people would see through this sort of camouflage and, just as sure as the world, some young lady is going to burst out, "You mean thing! Why did you have to go and point him out just now, right when he has that awful headache? You should have shown him to everybody last night, when he had his guitar. Yummy! You should have seen him then!"

So you see how difficult it is going to be with all the different versions that creep in: Don Juan's public relations version, our version in the way we point him out, and the version of the people we point him out to. But, as I say, we can't let this stop us. We shall just have to let Don Juan put on whatever kind of act he wants, we shall have to point him out regardless of what he happens to be doing at the moment, and people will just have to picture him through their own rose-colored impulses. There just is no such thing as being neutral in such matters.

This clears the way for us to point to something and to say, "There, that's it. Whose version of that is correct?" We may not be quite as hopeful of getting an ultimately satisfactory answer as we were before, but at least we now have some grounds for trying.

Since, at last, that difficult matter is decided, I would like to suggest that we point to the Don Giovanni I saw that first night at the opera. That rather pins down what we are talking about. The fact that the singer may have been a family man who shudders every time a frustrated female calls him "Darling," is quite beside the point. Moreover, none of us really has the faintest idea how, in real life, he reacts to women on the loose. No, we shall confine ourselves to what we saw of him on the stage.

To be sure this selection of a person, against whom to test our versions for their correctness, gives a slight edge in the controversy to Mozart and me and rather puts Freud at a disadvantage. Still, the fellow who played the part that night may have been psychoanalyzed. Like as not he had; a lot of artists are these days. If he had—and it had "taken"—he would be bound by the sacred code of *Insight* to portray a Freudianized version of the opera's hero[2]. That would put Freud back in the running along with Mozart and me.

[2] "*Insight*" is what you are left with after you have been stripped of your imagination.

Now that we know what we are talking about, how shall we decide whose version is correct? In making this decision we must not overlook the fact that a lot goes on that is never put into words. Everybody knows that, and some people are always making a big point of it. So let's not limit our considerations to what the actor sang, or what Mozart wrote down, or what I said. There must have been many times when the singer's version of Don Giovanni led him quite spontaneously to make subtle discriminations and, on the basis of them, turn this way or that, inflect one way rather than another, or catch his breath here instead of there.

So with Mozart, too; he might despair of writing out a logical explanation containing the whole truth of why, at a particular place, he put one note in the score in place of another, even though he wrote under quite rigidly formal rules. He might only suggest that it was put there because it fitted some distinctive repetitive theme that was reflected from deep inside the character of the Don Giovanni he envisioned. Indeed, that must have been the very nature of Mozart's hero, a rich pattern of such likenesses and differences—subtle, interwoven, and action laden. But, more than that, Mozart must have sensed that his listeners for generations to come would discover their own lives shot through with these same unnamed constructs. So he wrote the notes and story of the legendary figure and wagered that they would stir men and women of another generation in strangely familiar ways.

So Mozart's version is the right one, after all, is it not? And why? Simply this: His fine distinctions delineate a theme which runs basically unchanged, from boudoir to hell, and straight through whatever lies between. Only a theme of immense power and compelling validity can ring true when struck against such widely varying circumstances.

This happened: Not only did Mozart erect a man out of the distinctions and similarities he personally envisioned, he tested that structure, and found its brutal integrity defied all the vicissitudes of human whims and circumstances. Gradually now the genius is possessed by what it has produced. The composer's hand is guided across the pages of the manuscript and he can scarcely bring the opera to its conclusion in any way except that dictated by Don Giovanni. The image he constructed became the man about whom he wrote. Thus it happens that imagination put to test, becomes the key to realization. The world of reality has no other key. Nor does truth have any other access.

As we look further afield we find even broader grounds for believing that Mozart's image of Don Juan was a correct one. Here was an image that projected itself into the future, moment by moment, scene by scene, enabling Mozart to anticipate what he was about to write, or what it was that his Don Giovanni would do next. That much we have already guessed. But as we continue to look we see that others found it was, or could be, their image too. And in the structure of its basic lines they, also, found the story unfolding itself naturally and predictably. Once they grasped Mozart's basic constructs, they could no longer be utterly amazed by what was about to happen on the stage.

There is still more to attest the correctness of Mozart's Don Giovanni. At the end of the performance, as the audience rose to put on coats and go out to shout for taxicabs, they were to find the same story, first here, then there, among friends or in the depths of their own unspoken desires. Echoed again and again in the winter air were still to be heard the distinctive notes that had given continuity to what had happened on the stage, still valid, still foretelling what lies ahead along the dark paths we walk.

* * *

Now that we have done so handsomely by Mozart's Don Giovanni what are we to do with Freud's animated figure of Don Juan, whom we left a few pages back frantically chasing his tail. If Mozart is right then Freud must be wrong—so goes the logic of our times. Or take my lowly bungleheaded John, of whom I am no less fond than before: I must be terribly wrong about him.

If we follow the time-honored notion that what has proved to be correct displaces all versions that disagree with it, then the magnificent Giovanni takes over, and, sure enough, once more it has to be poor old John who is in the wrong. He is not even an honest-to-goodness version of himself!

We could say, I suppose that one was more or less right and the other more or less wrong. But isn't that only a polite way of avoiding the issue? The kind of logic which assumes that there can be only one correct version is only a little worse than the logic which says one only partially replaces the other. Both are the kind of grounds upon which dogmatism, absolute or partial, rests. And dogmatism, while often a great comfort to faltering minds and restless swords, is the implicit enemy of creative thought.

But certainly it is proper to pit alternatives against each other—Mozart's Giovanni against Freud's Juan and my John—and see what follows. What, then, is to happen to the ones who come out second or third best in the competition? Is my John valid only to the extent he is found to be in agreement with Giovanni? Is that the way to judge the truth, by testing its conformity to what is already believed to be correct? Not at all! The test for John must be the same as the test for Giovanni; how well does the construction of the figure anticipate what happens or what can be made to happen—in the story, among the audience, in the world off stage, and in the hours and years that follow.

Giovanni has survived these tests well. John has been tested only in the world of my own experience. Undoubtedly there are such things as partial truths; I have not said there weren't. Some are more sweeping than others; they cover a wider range of human experience or they have spanned a greater period of time. And, in this case, there are truths that have been subjected to more thorough tests than others; over a broader range of events or over a greater span of time. But it is not the partialness or the weighty documentation of truth I am talking about; it is the tentativeness with which we may ever say that we have stated the correct version of something.

Nor am I saying that what exists in the light of our understanding today may cease to exist in the light of what we shall know tomorrow. I am saying only that it is the understanding that is likely to change. What is to be emphasized is the temporariness with which any man's version of the Don Juan story can be said to be the correct one. That, you will recognize, is quite a different thing from saying that correctness is partial, or that it is relative, or that it changes with the times, or that it is what people agree upon or that it is only what one chooses to believe.

John, then, stands in his own right as an alternative construction of the story. Through the impulses of how many of my readers he can live and breathe as a human being, I do not know. His bungling may seem odd and inconceivable. Nor do I know how long he can survive through changing times. But of this I am reasonably sure, his validity does not depend on how closely he conforms to Don Giovanni, nor does it require any proof that Don Giovanni is false. It is only in a world run by tradition-bound dogmatists that the bungling John must bow to the masterful Giovanni, and only in a world run by envious ones that Giovanni would be forced to relinquish his claim to greatness in favor of the proletarian John.

* * *

There is a fourth version of Don Juan that enjoys a unique access to reality. It is his—Jack's—own intimate story. While Mozart constructed a figure and let the structure guide his hand until the opera was done Jack conjured up an image and let it guide his life until it was done. So he, too, built in his own image. Moreover, this kind of building was for him, as it must be for everyone, his way of living. Before he knew it he was what he made of himself, though, no doubt, the project never seemed quite complete.

What Jack was was a puzzled man sketching and resketching plans to be executed. What Jack was was a man following and discarding blueprints he had given himself—some clear, some illegible, but nevertheless the only ones he had to go by. What Jack was was the outcome of what he had done. He was architect, builder, and occupant of the structure—all three. And these three aspects of his daily existence were linked so that the occupant turned out to be a builder by trade and an architect by disposition. This, just this, was what was going on as we tried to follow the antics of this strange man.

Perhaps it is this triple redundancy that makes us so reluctant to hear what Jack has to say about himself. Some say it is because we cannot depend on him to tell the truth about himself. Others argue that he cannot be expected to find words for feelings that are too deep to fathom. Still others claim that he simply does not know what he is up to. So each observer, sensing the redundancy of man—architect, builder, and occupant—finds a different reason for disregarding the version of Don Juan to be found in Jack himself.

I am not sure what we can do about the redundancy business. We have already talked about it when we examined the simpler redundancy that occurs when any observer looks at Don Juan through his own spectacles. But I don't think that our own redundancies, as observers, are any more tolerable than Jack's would be. Besides, before we get through, we are going to be more or less stuck with both sets of redundancies anyway, for what we can observe, albeit with whatever objectivity we can muster, it is still going to be the act that Jack puts on. And, in turn, whatever Jack's expurgated version of himself may be, we will still have to twist and turn it into alignment with our own terms before we can bring it into any kind of focus.

As for Jack's intellectual honesty, we ought to admit that if he were able to tell the whole truth about himself—or even if he wanted to—he would have to be quite a different kind of person from the fellow we are after. We would have to call him "Frank," "Earnest," or "Camile," or something like that. It just wouldn't be our Jack. And besides, what would a person who was perfectly honest about himself do about the conflicting truths of different levels of his personality, or the changing states of mind that make him different from moment to moment? Wouldn't he have to gloss over these in order to be "honest"? Or, if he didn't gloss them over, wouldn't he have first to bring himself to some uniform dead level of existence, and bring to a halt all those life processes that make what was true and poignant at one moment trite and obsolete when applied to the next? I think we had better take Jack in all the ways that he is, and as fast as he comes.

As for the inadequacy of words to denote what is going on, that is true. But not all expression is through the denotations of words. There are connotations too—a lot more of them. Besides, man has other ways of expressing himself than by making noises in the air or squiggles on a piece of paper. And, come to think of it, what is wrong with the words he is able to use? Does the fact that ours are better—if, indeed, they are—make his not worth listening to? I suspect this whole objection has something to do with the kind of logic we were talking about a page or two ago, the kind that assumes there is never room for more than one interpretation of what exists. And, to top it all off, we are going to be using our words to talk about his words, sooner or later anyway, so why not hear him out?

One more objection to be dealt with, the objection that he does not know what he is up to. Well, who of us does?

So let's listen to Jack's version.

Now, where on earth did he go? Has anybody seen him around in the past half hour?

Jack! JACK!!!

Jack, if you are reading this, won't you please speak up; we would like to hear your version of what it is like to be a Don Juan. Not that anybody is going to take you too seriously; we still prefer our own versions of what you are. Still, what you have to say might prove to be amusing. Naive, of course, but amusing!

23

Ontological Acceleration[1]

Modern psychology is concerned with the scientific study of human behavior. Unfortunately this is usually taken to mean that the psychologist wants only to find out how he can predict human actions, or, at most, how to control them. But human behavior can be regarded as an expression of anticipation, as well as something to be anticipated. Moreover, it can be regarded as man's means of controlling himself and his surroundings, as well as something to be controlled. This makes it not only an object of human inquiry, scientific or otherwise, but a vital instrument of human investigation. Behavior, therefore, commands the interest of the psychologist, not merely as a set of events he would like to forecast and manage, but as something he can scarcely hope to understand until its own forecasting and managing capabilities are envisioned.

As I see it, what I have just proposed is not an abandonment of the principle of sequential explanation, of which ordinary notions of prediction and control are limited examples, but rather a proper extension of that principle. To be sure, to predict what will happen can be an exciting psychological experience, particularly if it is something the like of which has never occurred before. But human anticipation— the stuff that life is made of—unfolds its full meaning only when one is keenly appreciative of what might actually happen instead, and when he comes to forecast the events of his future in the rich context of all else that may be possible.

Applied to human behavior, then, the principle of sequential explanation challenges us not only to predict correctly what a man will do under given conditions—or to master him momentarily by creating circumstances with which the poor fellow has not yet devised any alternative means of coping—but also to join him in testing the limits of his unsuspected talents, including especially those that would enable him to surmount the circumstances by which we have hitherto sought to control him.

A full-fledged psychological inquiry into the behavior of a baby, for example, is not confined to calculating what he will pop into his mouth next, nor to training him to do what we want by frustrating all his ingenious efforts to escape the strictures we have imposed, but invites us to look at him and wonder what vast and unforeseen alternatives might lie ahead. More than that, no psychologist, I think, is all that he might be until he has undertaken to join the child's most audacious venture beyond the frontiers of social conventions and to share its most unexpected outcomes.

The psychological question is not merely what will this child be, given the worldy conditions we have allowed ourselves to take for granted, nor what we can make of him, assuming our own unfulfilled aspirations are to be hung around his neck, but what might he become. Of course we should not be so unreasonable as to expect him to actualize all his potentials; he can live only one life at a time. But even when it is clear that he has not become all that is possible, the significance of what he has actually achieved comes into focus only when it is outlined against a background of what might have been.

To ask a question is to invite the unexpected. If any man seriously asks the question of what his possibilities are—as indeed men are now doing at an accelerating pace—something shocking is likely to come of it, as indeed it has. The very process of posing questions about himself with deeds rather than words transforms the questioner, even before he is aware of any rewarding answers. As long as most men were so overawed by nature that they treated events as stimuli to which their behavior must be attuned, man appeared as an object so vestigial that psychologists could explain him as a tail wagged by the dog of antecedent events. But no modern man, no race, no people—its fears and its scholars notwithstanding—accepts this post-Darwinian premise indefinitely. Instead, behavior that probes his possibilities transforms a man beyond the scholar's recognition—as it is known to transform a child. The bolder the questions the more remarkable the transformation. And what is psychology to say about that!

[1] Dated 1966. Published in Maher, B. (Ed.). (1969). *Clinical psychology and personality: The selected papers of George Kelly* (pp. 7–45). Wiley. Republished by permission of Wiley.

Collected Papers of the Pioneer of Constructivist Psychology: George A. Kelly, First Edition. Edited by David A. Winter and Nick Reed.

Psychological Explanation Implies Contrast

What I have said in these initial paragraphs is no more than a sketchy introduction to a theme I would now like to develop in some psychological detail. Rather than pursuing the exposition in the usual structural manner, piling point upon point, I shall try to expound components of the theme recurrently through varying passages, bringing the reader back again and again to the same idea at a new level. In attempting this I shall be seeking to conform to an aspect of one of the things I shall be talking about—sequential explanation.

Let us start with what at first will appear to be some strange brand of logic rather than psychology. Yet I hope it will become clear that it stems as much from the psychological observation of inarticulate human experience as from the conventions of logic or of linguistic systems. Particularly I hope no one will think I am talking about "cognition," as contrasted with "affect." As a matter of fact, I can associate nothing with either of those terms that would justify treating it as a category rather than a dimension of appraisal—and one of doubtful utility, at that.

The classical notion of a concept as a property attributable to two or more objects which are otherwise distinguished from each other ignores an important psychological fact. That fact is that, while a concept may be defined academically in this way, it serves no human purpose unless the user is immediately concerned with at least one other object in which he intends to negate the property. If he were not immediately concerned with such a negation his current reference to a common property would be indiscriminate and psychologically footless. Thus a concept as defined in the dictionary is of little concern to a psychologist. But a concept on the occasion of its use is quite another matter.

It is not enough to say that when a man employs a concept he has simply embraced a set of objects and ignored all others, the way a dictionary does. To be sure, not all the excluded objects could possibly have had relevance to him at the moment the concept was invoked. Some, therefore, could properly be ignored. But other excluded objects surely did have relevance, else he would have had nothing to say. If the realm of a concept embraces all objects relevant to the occasion, then it must embrace some that were implicitly chosen for exclusion as well as those ostensibly included in the abstraction. Sometimes what is implicitly denied is more focal to the person's intent than what was affirmed, as when the disgruntled first mate entered in the ship's log that "the captain was sober tonight."

All this is to remind us of what is generally well enough understood in everyday discourse between persons. Construction, when it arises as a human act and thereby becomes a subject of psychological inquiry, serves, whether it is verbal or preverbal, symbolized or portrayed, to differentiate objects as well as to associate them. Indeed, it must do both at once, for association implies that objects are thereby differentiated from others of immediate relevance, and differentiation implies that objects are thereby selectively identified with others in contrasting classes. Otherwise, human conceptualization is psychologically pointless—that is to say, who would bother to bring the matter up!

But instead of using the term *concept*, and thus offer ever more reluctant hostages to a language which already threatens our thoughts with excommunication, let us at least employ a more modern term—construct. It will be easier for us to envision *construct* as something devised by man for his own lively purposes. And that is precisely what we want to conjure up. As for *concept*, that is too likely to be presumed a latent category of nature—something for man's diligence to discover rather than for his ingenuity to contrive. Moreover, a *construct* is more easily perceived as a structural member of a system erected by man, and, therefore, as having dimensionality or two-endedness.

Dimensionality Provides Grounds for Relevance

Dimensionality is important. It has universal utility in the life of man, even though I propose we regard it as dichotomous rather than continuous. This is to say that a construct is at heart a black and white affair, rather than a scale of grays. Indeed, it is precisely because constructs do comprise pairs of sharply drawn contradistinctions that they enable man to make his choices and get on with the human enterprise.

But it must be noted that I have not said that objects fall naturally into black and white categories. It is the constructs that are dichotomous, not the objects. If we had assumed that constructs were properties of objects or something distilled out of them, as is often intended when concepts are mentioned, we would be in hot water the instant we called them categorically black or white.

It must always be clear that the construct is a reference axis devised by a man for establishing a personal orientation toward the various events he encounters. It is not itself a category of events or even the focus of a class—as we usually imagine a concept to be. Man can, in turn, use this portable device for ordering symbols along scales, for placing events into categories, or for defining classes in the various familiar ways that suit his needs. Being a reference axis, rather than representation of something, the construct is much more clearly a psychological guideline against which objects may be referred, than it is either a limited collection of things or a common essence distilled out of them.

The use of the construct rather than the concept as a unit opens for the scientist a door to quite a different line of thinking. It enables him to regard science, along with other modes of endeavor, as a system of ventures open to psychological study, quite apart from their material referents and outcomes. More than this, it turns our attention to the matter of relevance, a matter that has aroused the special concerns both of the Vienna Circle and of the critics of the atom bomb.

Where a construct is used in the dimensional sense we have proposed, the important distinction drawn between elements is not simply between what is included within the realm of the construct and what is excluded, but is in the way selected elements are projected onto the contrasting poles of the construct. To be sure, there are elements that fall outside the realm of personal concern—or, better, beyond the construct's range of convenience. Those elements, I have already conceded, are irrelevant to it. But relevance, in the manner of thinking I have proposed, is not limited either to one pole of construction or to events that have already occurred. What is most important in the life of man is what may yet occur, and the part he will choose to play in its realization.

Whatever one says about any event gathers its meaning from what contrasting things could otherwise have been said about it, as much as from the other events of which the same might have been said or those occurrences of which a contrasting statement might have been made. Since every perception we have, as well as every statement we make, is no less a denial than it is an assertion, it becomes important to note what is perceptually negated as well as what is verbally affirmed. For example, what one does in life can be subjected to moral judgment only in the context of what he might have done—and didn't. It is in such a manner that construct theory embraces both relevance and responsibility. There is little elsewhere in science that goes as far as that.

Appraising Human Behavior in a Context of Relevance

Construct theory, or better, *personal construct theory*—a term which implies that a construct is as much a personal undertaking as it is a disembodied scheme for putting nature in its place—suggests that human behavior is to be understood in a context of relevance. That is to say that the mere prediction of what a person will do, even if it is subsequently confirmed, does not demonstrate a full understanding of his behavior, any more than it defines his responsibility for his acts. A fuller explanation requires us to be aware of what he might have done. The construct dimension that lends structure to the behavioral event does so by providing contrasting poles, and unless we take the trouble to explicate both of them the directional trend of the behavior we have observed cannot be plotted.

Note that we have not claimed that a person's act is set off by all that it is not. To say that would invoke a host of irrelevancies. But it is brought into a relevant perspective by our structured awareness of what it might have been. That awareness is sharpened by the bipolar constructs we have erected for surveying such acts.

To be sure, this makes it very difficult to ever claim that we finally understand a human act, for the behavioral possibilities it must have displaced could not be displayed. But we can sometimes infer them from other experiences. Constructs help us do that.

Likewise, it is a tricky matter to pass moral judgment on something that has not been undertaken or before its consequences have played themselves out. But the fact that we cannot foresee outcomes does not prevent them from occurring, nor does it permit us to disavow our own contribution to the state of affairs that later materializes. Sin is not a self-evident property of any act and therefore to be avoided by the inhibitions of self-conscious innocence. Sin is a risk that every well-intentioned man must take and innocence is subject to harsh judgment for what it does not venture to try. Constructs help us anticipate what the risk and judgment might be.

But perhaps we are in too much of a hurry to come to conclusions about human behavior anyway, and thereafter to stop wondering what undisclosed potentialities it has. Indeed, I suspect that historically the questions men have asked have turned out to be more important than the conclusions they reached. Questions breed actions that lead to further questions, and these, in turn, to the boldness of further inquiring acts. Conclusions, however, perpetuate themselves and often serve to limit, if not stultify, both action and thought. Thus the living history of man is the story of the questions he has enacted, rather than the conclusions he has anchored in science or dogma.

Besides, it is for "the last judgment," whenever that may come about, to write all human epitaphs. Perhaps this is the reason that awesome event is identified with the end of the world. Such a definitive pronouncement of truth would scarcely dare leave questions remaining to be asked, and certainly none that man might reopen by his latter deeds. The questioning endeavor we know as the human enterprise would simply have to come to an abrupt halt. In reaching terminal conclusions, moral or psychological, man commits the ultimate suicide of his race.

So I am not greatly disturbed by the fact that I have proposed a criterion for understanding human behavior that makes stable conclusions about it virtually impossible. As a matter of fact, I hope the criterion of relevant contrast will serve to keep us from deciding once and for all that our confirmed predictions of any man's acts encapsulate all that may ever be expected of him. A science that respects relevance simply cannot rest upon conclusions, save as tentative grounds for further questions. And I think there is no place where this is more true or more pertinent than in the science of human behavior. So I hope my criterion will keep all conclusions quivering on their empirical foundations and will confront us with such disturbing questions about the potentialities of man that all sorts of imaginative inquiries will be provoked.

What has just been said about the tentative outcomes of successful prediction can be said also—and perhaps with even greater emphasis—about control. The claim that a man can, on demand, be compelled to live the life of a slave, or a soldier, or a doctor, or a criminal, or an intellectual—even if true—does not mean that his behavior is thus comprehensively defined. Nor does it mean that a life so successfully shackled to circumstances must have been psychologically understood—not even when its every act has been precisely regulated, right down to the batting of an eyelash. There is always the relevant and morally responsible issue of what would have enabled the slave to explore the reaches of freedom, what the soldier might have disciplined himself to do besides march and shoot, or what the intellectual might have understood if he had allowed his thoughts to be shaped by compassion.

Behavior is Man's Way of Posing a Question

What I have managed to say up to this point still falls far short of what I have hoped to convey. It is not enough to argue that an enlightened psychology projects the behavior of man against a background of his unrealized potentialities. It must do more than that. And it does. It incorporates behavior as the instrument of its own exploration. In this respect a good psychologist is like a man, for behavior, I have observed, happens also to be man's favorite way of posing a question.

It is perhaps best, in developing this point of view, to start out by noting just how the psychologist uses his own behavior to pose questions. Generally he tries to follow the canons of science, and particularly those of experimental science. This means that he does not content himself with armchair speculation, nor does he regard his logical inferences as anything but tentative. He makes predictions which are expressions of hypotheses. What he hypothesizes then becomes a basis for his ventures in action. These ventures he calls experiments. In performing them he takes a certain personal risk and, if he survives, he reassesses his position in the light of the outcomes. Being a scientist he never wholly trusts either his arguments or his forecasts; he is much too aware of the fallibility of uncommitted thought. So he must try things out for himself. Thus experimental science, at its best, turns out to be a humble blending of piercing ingenuity and wide-eyed ingenuousness.

It is easy enough to see that a psychologist who believes in active experimentation uses his own behavior as his instrument of inquiry. However, those psychologists who are not so obviously scientific in their approach to man also invest themselves in action. They go out of their way to talk about what they believe is so. They make claims. They publish. And what makes it clear that they really are asking questions all the while is the way they prick up their ears when what they have done appears to provoke a reaction.

Thus psychologists who are less self-consciously scientific can be seen to initiate their actions in order to present themselves with outcomes they think they can assess. They launch inquiries by means of their behavior, even when they seem to be demanding against odds that all results confirm their anticipations. In fact I have noted that the more dogmatic they are the more they betray their distress and covertly express the hope that vigorous declarations and actions will dispel the lurking doubts that trouble their minds—replacing uncertainties with convictions they need not continually defend. For them, I think, no less than for their more disciplined cousins, behavior is the expression of a question. More often than we suppose it may be a question of frantic proportions.

To be sure, the issues unctuous men raise may center more around the public credibility of their claims than the essential truth expressed.

They want to know, I suppose, what they can sell. As with salesmen, truth may appear to be a consensus of customers. But then we should not be too impatient with such colleagues, for science itself leans more heavily on credibility than on revelation. At least the behavior of would-be prophets offers a challenge to more circumspect men.

But if there is a fallacy in the outlook of most psychologists, it is not that they sometimes put their questions in the form of overeager assertions—for an assertion, once one is bold or imaginative enough to make it, tends to set in motion the processes that will ultimately test its validity—but that they deny to other men the penchant for behaviorally implemented inquiry they find so crucial to their own endeavors.

What is so special about a psychologist? He experiments? Who doesn't? He enacts his questions? Don't we all? His inquiries produce more questions than answers: Who has ever found it to be otherwise? Not Adam! Not Eve! Not Pandora! Not John Alden! Not Robert Oppenheimer!

Now that we think of it, does the psychologist do anything that other men do not do, except, possibly, that he does it less spontaneously? And if he did do what other men do not, would he be much of a psychologist? Is he a scientist—a creature apart—whose own behavior is explained by his undertakings, while the behavior of other men is to be explained only in terms of stimuli, motives, physiology, and the momentum of their biographies? Or is he not as often the pompous and unwitting subject in the experiments less pretentious intellects perform—perhaps his perceptive wife, his wide-eyed children, his whispering students, and even those whom he has employed to enact the parts he prescribes for "subjects." As I see it, being a psychologist is doing what man does, though perhaps more systematically than most men, and concentrating all the while on behavior for its own sake rather than on physics, government, art, commerce, recreation, or any of the particular enterprises in which human efforts are channeled.

If a psychologist's own life is taken up in behaviorally expressed modes of inquiry, is it not appropriate to examine the lives other men lead to see how they may similarly be up to their ears in asking questions? And if behavior is the way other men ask questions too, what does that mean to the perceptive student of human behavior? Is the scientific formula of "predict and control" still to be applied to human behavior in the same way it is applied to electricity or the weather? I think not, though, as I have already said, I see no need for psychologists to abandon the broad principle of sequential explanation.

The Psychologist's Shifting Task

What I think this view of man as the paradigm of the scientist—and vice versa—does mean is that the ultimate explanation of human behavior lies in examining man's undertakings, the questions he asks, the lines of inquiry he initiates, and the strategies he employs, rather than in analyzing the logical pattern and impact of the events with which he collides. Until one has grasped the nature of a man's undertakings, he can scarcely hope to make sense out of the muscular movements he observes or the words he hears spoken. In dealing with human behavior we inevitably find ourselves confronted with the human ingenuity it expresses. And that is the point of confrontation at which most psychology breaks down.

While human ingenuity is something that is continually challenged by circumstances, it is never dictated by them. History confirms that. Besides, it would hardly make sense for one to claim ingenuity in producing what had been dictated by his circumstances.

As I tried to say in my introductory paragraphs, behavior cannot be fully understood except in the context of all that is humanly possible, and mere circumstances are stone silent as to what that may be. Still, the constructs against which human behavior is to be reflected to give it meaning must, as I have noted, take some account of what is relevantly excluded.

Furthermore, our best constructs notwithstanding, we cannot know for sure what is possible until we try. This goes for all of us. The behavior of Twentieth Century Man will be much better understood when the Twenty-First Century has rolled around and we see what has come of man's present undertakings. While we may continue in that century to make progress in understanding the psychology of man, the end will still not be in sight. New ventures will be under way, and the appraisal of the behaviors channelized by them will await their still later outcomes. Thus human behavior will prove to be a changing phenomenon, caught up in the constantly expanding human enterprise, and its explanation will be a continually reopened question. Since man persists in being creative it will probably be no easier to predict his most significant acts in the coming generations than it will be to forecast the research imaginative psychologists will contrive and what will come of it.

In the perspective of this viewpoint the task of the psychologist is not simply to tabulate the categorial ways in which men presently behave, and the circumstances in which each occurs, but to engage himself with fellow men in exploring the uncharted realms into which the human quest may be expanded. And in this mutual enterprise one may well wonder what outcomes will ensue and to what unexpected vantage points their joint experience will lead. So now, in order to survive, psychology must invent as well as discover. That will make it a discipline disconcertingly alien to the one in which most of us were once trained.

What a Teacher Has Yet to Learn

So where does this put us? Perhaps I had better start by putting the question to myself. I am a teacher. I have been a teacher for about thirty-five years, not counting some time spent doing other things. During the graying years I have picked up a few tricks of the trade—how to enable students to buckle down and learn what I think they should know, some persuasive arguments for their learning by teaching each other instead of asking me to explain everything to them myself, a little about how to build morale in a class or in an educational program, some ways of disengaging myself from footless dialogs with students who would rather be clever than explore the breathless wonderment of a world reserved for self-acknowledged idiots, devices for managing a large class without too much investment of time and effort, phrases that teach a few and entertain the rest, and, in my rarer moments of genius, how to get students to forget what I once told them. Early in my career I developed some talent for predicting which students would go far; at least I bet on some pretty unlikely candidates and—often to the consternation of my colleagues and my own egotistical delight—have won.

I recall that ten of the ninety or so seniors of the Class of 1938 at the Fort Hays Kansas State College continued elsewhere to earn the Ph.D. in psychology, and, regardless of what the facts may be, I am reluctant to let anyone convince me that I did not have something to do with that. If I remember correctly, when I went to western Kansas to teach in the fall of 1931, only four graduates in the history of the college had ever completed doctoral degrees in any field. So much for one teacher's experience with prediction and control.

But what eludes me still is an understanding of human behavior, and particularly that of my students. I have only the faintest idea of what they might have achieved if they had made the most of their opportunities, or what failures otherwise awaited them in that depression-ridden, drought-stricken dustbowl of the 1930's. Only in the context of what was possible can I make a proper assessment of their behavior, or of mine.

Now and then, over the years, I have caught passing glimpses of students exploring life by acting out their questions. On occasion I have accepted an invitation to join one of them in his efforts. But mostly I have remained on the sidelines, a psychologist living in the world he has known, and content to predict and control behavior without participating in its venture.

Now I wonder how much more of a psychologist I would have been if I had seen behavior, not as something merely to be forecast and managed, but as an investment in questions, as man's projection of himself into the enterprise of inquiry. If I had I might by now have formed some clearer notion of human nature from observing how it is variously engaged and what can come of it.

So, what do I find myself saying? I must be confessing that I can understand even my own behavior only in a context of what it might have been, and I can measure it only in alignment with the construct dimensions in which its diminishing future potentialities may be seen to lie.

Psychotherapy is Practiced by Whom?

Besides being a teacher, I am a psychotherapist. I have engaged in psychotherapy almost as long as I have taught. During a good deal of that time I have supervised psychotherapists, as well as offered more formal instruction in psychotherapeutic procedures. So what kind of a psychologist does this make me? Does it mean that I have some experience in the control of human behavior? And, if so, does it also mean that I understand it?

I regret to say that it took me a long time and the persistent efforts of a number of able and determined patients to make it clear to me that psychotherapy is not simply a form of treatment by which they could be managed. At last they were somehow able to demonstrate that what I did to them did not make them well or compel them to conduct themselves with propriety. It was their behavior that eventually made them well, just as their original distress had been an ill-fated undertaking of their own contrivance. They were not patients who submitted to my treatment—at least the ones who got well weren't—but clients who made some use of me. This proved to be no less true of hospitalized psychotics than of those who came to my office.

What I did, I think, was pose issues for them, sometimes by what I attempted on my own initiative, sometimes by my rejoinders to their initiatives, and sometimes only by my presence at an opportune moment when they were ready to reach for some human resource. They sought to cope with me—sometimes, I suppose, because they could see no alternative—and often they resented their dependent commitment to me. The transference neurosis, long before noted by Freud, proved to be one from which the patient must extricate himself. So always the inquiring venture turned out to be my clients' own. What I offered may have been something worth their effort—either to seek or escape—and a facility they could use to explicate their questions in terms they could enact and comprehend.

Gradually my clients taught me that a symptom was an issue one expresses through the act of being his present self, not a malignancy that fastens itself upon a man. What they experienced as symptoms were urgent questions, behaviorally expressed, which had somehow lost the threads that lead either to answers or to better questions. The symptom was even a fragment of a proper human experiment—one designed in childhood, perhaps, and repeated again and again in later years. Yet the experiment could never be carried through to its conclusion because the generating hypotheses had lost their contexts or because the current outcomes had slipped out of focus. It was for the psychotherapist to help his client pick up the elusive theme and follow it to its psychological conclusion—that is to say, to some point where its consequences would be reflected back upon its anticipations and its implications expressed in the enactment of more fruitful questions.

But if I managed to help my clients overcome symptoms, as I am sure I sometimes did, does this provide an adequate measure of my psychological understanding of man? Only partly so, I think, for the "normal" behavior that replaced the "abnormal" symptoms may have been only the acceptable neurosis of the times. Ask, rather, what was possible.

Now if I only knew the answer to that question—or even had some better approximation to an answer—I might be able to appraise my understanding of those who seek psychotherapeutic help. The significance of any successful clinical prediction we make, or any therapeutic cure we effect, is not disclosed by the degree of success in reaching a goal, but looms up only in the context of what might have happened. So we, together with those who do not claim to be the psychologists we are, continue to test those missing potentialities through the curiosity of our own deeds.

Behavior is What Behavior Asks

What I said earlier about understanding behavior as a questioning act engaged in exploring its own contextual possibilities raised the urgent question of where psychology must now find itself. The actuarial relations between antecedents and consequents, in terms of which stimulus response psychology has heretofore been attempting to explain behavior, is being changed by the very thing it seeks to explain. Is psychology then scrambling head over heels in the ever more swiftly moving transitions that human behavior itself produces? I think it is.

Actuarial explanations take no account of projected future developments. They concern themselves instead with the regularity with which human actions are associated with antecedent events. What they measure, then, is not man's imagination, but his lack of it. Yet the pace of man's imaginative ventures is accelerating. He is asking ingenious questions—a great many of them—and the behavior in terms of which he asks them is as free of antecedent events as imagination is free of tradition.

A quick look at what man has been doing with himself in the last three decades should be enough to make one suspect what is going on. Behavior is man's way of changing his circumstances, not proof that he has submitted to them. What on earth, then, can present-day psychology be thinking about when it says that it intends only to predict and control behavior scientifically? Does it intend to halt the human enterprise in its tracks?

Since I am a psychologist—or have been representing myself as one long enough to establish considerable seniority over most of my colleagues—it seemed that I had better ask myself if I too have been practicing a psychology of the unimaginative man. Do I understand behavior's achievements, or only its repetitive failures? That is a fair question.

In the preceding paragraphs I reminded myself that, in some degree, I have been able to predict and control the behavior I observed. But now it strikes me that is not enough. With man's efforts actualizing unheard-of possibilities on every hand, my predictive and managerial accomplishments of the past begin to look rather puny. It is small consolation to note that the successes of so many of my "behavioristic" colleagues seem even more petty.

So let us be bold enough to pursue our venture further. In suggesting new criteria for a genuine understanding of human behavior, and in seeing psychology as a science that must try to make predictions about behavior in an exploding universe of human accomplishments, I may have a bear by the tail. If I want to continue posing as a psychologist, I may get carried along a good deal further than I ever intended to go. Yet, for the moment at least, I am willing to be drawn into the wake of my own behavior. As a youngster riding a horse through flood waters I learned that the safest thing to do is to swim downstream.

Anticipation

None of what I have been saying should be taken to suggest that prediction and control are footless undertakings when they are assigned their proper place in sequential explanation. As I said at the outset, the principle of sequential explanation, of which prediction and control are only cases in point, also challenges us to join man in testing the limits of his unsuspected talents. What must be kept in mind throughout is that behavior is our questioning act.

Behavior puts itself into perspective by exploring its own possibilities, as well as by allowing itself to be the object of our psychological inquiries. For psychologists to continue to assign it a passive role puts them, and all who take them seriously, out of touch with the accelerating pace of human adventure. Behavior is not the *answer* to the psychologist's question; it *is* the question. And, just as all questions are anticipatory, behavior is anticipatory too. Let us see what this may mean.

To ask a question is to invite a reply. If the question is relevant to anything of human account then presumably the reply will change one's perception of himself and his world. Sometimes one anticipates a reply which will confirm a position he has already taken, that is to say, one from which he has been accustomed to launch his inquiries. But the confirmation, if it occurs, will nonetheless alter his experience—if only because it puts his position in a more presumptuous light. He must know that.

Sometimes one anticipates a reply which will disconfirm his present outlook. In that case he may assert his position with particular vigor on the occasions when it is most likely to be challenged. A person who seems to go out of his way to fail does that. Again, sometimes, one appears to ask for no particular reply, only for something he can grasp. In this case the relevance of the question may give us a clue to a construct dimension we might envision within his system. That, in turn, should give us some hint as to the kind of reply he is prepared to accept.

The tricky part of all this, both for him and for us, is that replies seldom end up being acceptable conclusions. At best they are grounds for further inquiries. The best answer to a question is two better ones. Any of us may, of course, think he has had a conclusion revealed to him, and therefore discontinue making adventuresome inquiries. But if he stops asking questions altogether someone will probably have to take him out and bury him. At least we can be reasonably sure his wife will start looking for another man who is not so sure the answers he knew twenty years ago still hold.

Questions are restless bedfellows. When they are behaviorally activated they disturb all sleep nestled in foregone conclusions and elicit dreams of unprecedented replies. Ask the most foolish question you can imagine and, sure enough, someone will offer an answer. Even a stunned silence in the midst of an animated conversation is an outcome not to be ignored. And before the questioner's ears have told him what is happening in the room he will begin to sense his own internal response to the venture. One so often remembers his foolish questions longer than he does his sensible ones, and he wonders over and over why on earth he asked them. Behavior is like that; it puts itself into perspective by exploring its own outlandish possibilities.

If man's behavior poses important questions, something of one sort or another is bound to come of it, even the stunned silence that follows a bomb. It will not do to say that what comes of it will always be conclusive. History, the long-term behavioral record of man, gives us precious few conclusions. The few it does appear to offer keep turning themselves unexpectedly into the most urgent questions of the day. The longer they are held as conclusions, it seems, the bigger questions they turn out to be.

And whoever heard of a child who took a pat answer and let it go at that? Or, if he did acquiesce to a pat answer, how much more overwhelming a question it proved to be in his adult moments of extremity! All of this explosive emergence in the enterprises of man sets a particularly exasperating task for the psychologist who is out to account for behavior in terms of its antecedent events—as if the ventures of man were a phenomenon already fixed in space and time, and curiosity a lawless state that befalls the unwary mind.

Human Behavior is Itself an Evolutionary Process

Psychology, emerging in the late Nineteenth and Twentieth Centuries, sought to identify itself with a science it had no part in creating. It seemed enough that the science of the day was wonderful and good. In the world that scientists envisioned nature was a relatively stable entity. Evolution had run its course. At last the outcome of the long slow process could be studied to see what nature's assembled menagerie had turned out to be.

But it is increasingly clear that human behavior has not settled into orbit. It is, indeed, the one part of nature that now is most in transition—perhaps transforming itself at a pace no other aspect of nature has ever matched. Man, inquisitive chap, is irrepressibly engaging in new enterprises, just as psychologists themselves seek to do, and the formulas we derive for binding events to his subsequent actions keep losing touch with the novel human engagements of our day. Man is not content to cope with his circumstances forever in the same way. At an ever-increasing tempo he casts his anticipation in fresh varieties of searching questions and, to pose them, the behavior that psychologists want so much to explain is redeployed in an ever-varying encounter with circumstances.

For example, the psychological interpretations that brilliantly illuminated the plight of Viennese women in Freud's time have become less and less appropriate to the troubles in which women now involve themselves. The mind-body dualism of the mid-Victorian era provided a woman with a ready-made protective barrier she could place between herself and humiliation—both public and private. She had only to invoke the mechanism of conversion, safely portraying in what she supposed to be medical terms the sweetly petulant and vulgar questions she had caught herself experiencing in mental terms. Nowadays, with the bulkheads of mind-body dualism gradually giving way, and the terms of feminine humiliation and vulgarity almost reversed, women are puzzled about stranger matters, and when they behave they articulate the wordless queries of our times.

Abandonment of Substantial Explanation

There are those who argue that since we know reality only in the dubious terms of our own construction of it, there is no point in assuming that it exists at all, except as a figment of our imagination. Our own contrived constructions—sometimes called "experience"—are all we shall ever have, they say, and we had better make up our minds to be content with them. This is not to deny there is heavy thinking to be done, for our subjective perceptions often turn out to be at odds with each other. But if something upsetting occurs, such as a death in the family, the problem is not in what has happened, but in how to reconcile our grief-stricken thoughts of today with our compound evasions of years past.

This phenomenological view keeps all the turmoil within the man and offers him neither the challenge of external threats nor the comfort of resources beyond himself. In its light no circumstances lying beyond the outermost layer of his skin can be seen to constrain his impulses or to offer any hint of the enticing mysteries of anticipations. There is nothing, absolutely nothing save the image he himself conjures up, to dictate his acts, to disclose their consequences, or to suggest that anything other than chaos awaits him. There is no venture, and hence no ominous risk and no hairbreadth escape. All the story will ever tell is what he will set down for himself to read.

Life provides this man with no scientific footholds on reality, suggests to him no narrative plots, offers no rhythmic metaphor to confirm the moving resonance of a human theme. If he chooses to write tragedy, then tragedy it will be; if comedy, then that is what will come of it; and if burlesque, he, the sole reader, must learn to laugh at its misanthropic caricatures of the only person he knows—himself.

Most of all, phenomenological man cannot share his subjective plight, for even his most beloved companion is a manikin fabricated out of his own moods. A blind poet, imprisoned alone in a cell whose walls he cannot touch, the only sound man hears is a ringing in his ears. With no voices to haunt him, no future to dread, no consequences to stir remorse, he experiences the absolute freedom that only utter emptiness can guarantee the human soul.

This rather dismal phenomenological picture I have sketched should be enough to warn the reader that I have something else in mind to suggest. If he has not sensed it, let me remind him of what I have said about understanding man, not so much in the context of his present circumstances, but in the context of all his behavioral possibilities, both manifest and potential. As long as man can enact his questions the world of which he is a moving part can scarcely stand still—and neither can he. One is not finally engulfed by circumstances he can still manipulate.

Besides, I am neither phenomenologist enough to advocate the kind of encapsulated redundancy I have described, nor realist enough to believe it is forced upon me. The fact that my only approach to reality is through offering some responsible construction of it does not discourage me from postulating that it is there. The open question for man is not whether reality exists or not, but what he can make of it. If he does make something of it he can stop worrying about whether it exists or not. If he doesn't make something of it he might better worry about whether he exists or not.

Moreover, I see no reason why I cannot approach some objective which men such as I may hope to achieve only at some infinitely remote point in time. Like Sisyphus, one may commit himself to a continuing endeavor as well as to more limited projects. Perhaps if I were a Euclidean psychologist, sharply dividing events into those which do happen before my eyes and those which can never happen, I would be overwhelmed by a growing awareness of man's failure to reach any ultimate conclusions about nature. I might then be tempted to throw in the sponge and concede that the lines of human construction and outer reality can never, never touch.

But I prefer the more cosmic view which supposes these two progressions may ultimately join hands, though that auspicious moment may prove to be an infinity of years away. Now that seems to me to be a proposition of quite a different order. It is, I suspect, only a once naive realist, now too suddenly disillusioned to cope with his own transition, who ends up with no remaining alternative save the extreme existentialism I have described. He steps into a trap. It is one into which men, who have grown up expecting science or religion to offer conclusions rather than ways of asking further questions, are prone to fall. To be sure, I am such a man, but, my biography notwithstanding, I do not choose to stumble into this particular manhole.

Explanation by Manipulation

Phenomenology's abandonment of all hope of finding substantial explanations of the behavior of man need not be man's own final answer. He can assume a reality without having to believe that his life is run by it. He can assume that he, with other men, is a part of that reality, and may act accordingly. And he can assume that when he ventures to act nature is refreshed. The response to the question his behavior poses confronts him with new and mystifying natural occurrences about which he may dare ask even more meddlesome questions.

Even the questioning act of man is a disturbance of nature, as well as a provocation to it. The more interrogations he presses upon his world, and the more vigorously he plies his resources, the more altered his world of resources becomes. His act of questioning even changes himself, to the consternation of psychologists who want to understand him as the stabilized product of antecedent events—evolutionary, biographical, and official. Thus a man comes to understand for himself what is happening—within and without—not as an academic dilettante whose ethereal propositions impinge on nothing, but as the impact of his own actions demonstrates what is possible.

This brings us to the point where we can selectively agree and disagree with phenomenology. We can agree that we cannot find the explanation of human behavior neatly wrapped up in antecedent events. Events do not prophesy. Besides, we know as little intrinsically, and perhaps even less, about those events as we might know simply from asking a man to account for himself. The properties one may attribute to occurrences in nature seem limitless and our perceptions of what they are shift again and again as time affords us with different perspectives. It is not hard to agree that it is the personal experience of the observer that makes one event appear different from another and one account of it turn out to be at odds with another.

But we can disagree with phenomenology by declining to accept its implicit assumption that perception is passive. Let us say, rather, that we know an event through our own act of approach to it. We ask questions about it, not academically merely, but experimentally. We intervene and there are outcomes. We invent and new accomplishments materialize. We traverse space and strange objects heave into view. Academic impossibilities yield to demonstrated achievements. The scholar has only to look outside his study window to see less educated men doing what he once said could not occur. The psychologist has only to participate in the human enterprise to find that man does what "intelligence" tests have said he can't.

Personal Construct Theory

None of what we have been talking about need be taken to prove that human behavior is unpredictable. To be sure, it cannot be predicted solely from circumstances; we have already noted that man is too recalcitrant to allow that to happen. Furthermore, as time goes on, he seems less and less disposed to accept the dictatorship of circumstances.

Even God, the most powerful circumstance of them all, is nowadays said to be dead. Such a statement is obviously not atheistic, or even agnostic. In a general way it concedes the creation of circumstances and does not deny their historical importance, yet in a peculiar theological way it is a sweeping declaration of independence on the part of men who are ready to accept responsibility for their acts and are ceasing to acknowledge the guiding power of any circumstances, even the greatest of them—God. As theologians sometimes do—to the amazement of scientists who rather think of themselves as being more precise with words—these men state the new humanistic proposition most succinctly. They say simply, "God is dead." When this sort of thing begins to happen it becomes very difficult indeed for psychologists to predict human behavior from any circumstances at all, regardless of what prior "learning processes" have been observed.

But does all this mean that the psychologist must from now on disregard God or any other set of circumstances altogether and pin everything on some unanalyzable and inaccessible experience of the individual man? I think not. There ought to be some way for psychology to outgrow circumstantial explanation without having to choose between dissection and metaphor.

Events can be construed. There is a particular way to do this. One may chart his psychological space in many dimensions—certainly many more than the three we ascribe to physical space, or four, if we enlarge our notion of space and include time, or five, if we enlarge it still more and include Michelsonian observation. The dimensions we ascribe are expressed in terms of reference axes, and the events we experience can be located in our personal hyperspace by projecting them onto these axes. The more independent axes upon which we project an event the greater the psychological depth in which we see it, and the more meaningful it becomes to us.

In personal construct theory these dimensions of one's psychological space, in terms of which meaning emerges for him, are the constructs about which we spoke earlier. They are not, as I tried to make clear, intrinsic properties of the events—either real or imagined. One asks of an event only that it can be plotted with reference to an axis, not that it somehow produce the axis out of itself or that it confess to him the full depth of its meaning—as if all well-bred events spoke Shakespearian English.

It is to be noted that no disruptive analysis is performed on the event by construing it. This becomes an important point when man or a bit of human behavior is construed. In this respect personal construct theory is a form of mathematics, not a natural science. On the other hand, it is a scientific theory to the extent that it postulates that each man devises his own construction system, a statement that offers numerous experimental derivatives.

To suggest that each man contrives his own system and plots events within it is not to say that each of us is bottled up forever in his own private world. Different men can construe the same events, though each starts out by doing it in his own way. Two people, say a mother and a newborn child, may not have a full intellectual meeting of minds the first time they try to enter into a discourse with each other in the maternity ward. But by sharing their encounter with events—including the events produced by their own behavior—some mothers and daughters do develop a fair understanding, each of what the other is talking about. Each may rely upon her own system, but the constructs of one system can be devised to plot the approximate positions of those of the other.

Children and men, therefore, cease to be altogether alone when they try to see events through the spectacles others use, even while reserving the privilege of using their own. And when they couch this interrogatory effort in behavioral terms they make roles for themselves—in the special sense in which "role" is regarded in personal construct theory. A society thrives on the roles its members play. It can emerge and remain viable as long as men see each other as construing beings rather than merely reactive objects, as long as questions are asked through deeds, and as long as the reconstruing of outcomes continues apace.

Events, then, are of supreme psychological significance, even though we do not see man's behavior dictated by them. The circumstances that encompass a man are his always resources, and his shackles only on those occasions when his behavior does not alter them. Events play their crucial part, not only because two men may encounter the same event, but also because each may ask a question of the other by putting it into the form of an event for the other to construe. Similarly, man can even ask an important question of himself—or of inanimate nature—through his behavior. This is sometimes called psychotherapy, sometimes commitment. To be sure, he sometimes confronts himself with more than he is prepared to manage. But then, no one has yet gone so far as to say that experimentation is a safe undertaking. All I have said so far is that in a universe on the move it is the only undertaking that counts.

Can Psychology Ever be Part of the Ongoing Human Enterprise?

What I have said so far represents a far-reaching effort to show how enormous the problems confronting modern psychology are. I picked up the thread of what I wanted to say by pointing out how hard it is to say one understands the behavior of a man until he has some idea of what other behavioral possibilities were open to him. Let us look closely. If a man is observed doing one of two things only, can we say we understand his behavior if we develop a formula for predicting which of the two he will do tomorrow? If it should be that there are these two possibilities and these two only, then I suppose it would be good enough to be able to predict accurately which of the two it would turn out to be. It might even be good enough if there were a third possibility—if we could be sure he would not think of it. But it certainly would not be good enough if he did think of the third possibility—not even if he refrained from attempting it. He just might change his mind and try it one of these days. And even if he doesn't, one can scarcely say he understands the man's behavior until he knows why that dangling third possibility is allowed to remain dangling.

But men can do more than two things—more than three. That makes the problem a little more complex. But what begins to make it seem so vastly difficult for today's psychology is the fact that men can do things that once were considered utterly impossible—at least to psychologists. That ought to be enough to make us suspect they can do in the future what now seems incredible. Furthermore, we see men doing things that men of a century ago did not even think to try. Does this not suggest that men will be accomplishing feats a hundred years hence so strange that psychologists do not now have even enough foresight to declare them impossible?

Now, if we take all these vaguely suspected possibilities into account, what happens to our sense of understanding human behavior? Can we say we understand what it is until we have some idea of what it might be instead? I think not.

Psychology has pretty much gone about its business under the "Darwinian" assumption—though I am not sure Darwin himself would have made it—that mankind has finally stopped evolving and all psychologists have to do now is see how the individual man grows up. But it is becoming increasingly hard to ignore the fact that the cultural and behavioral patterns of man are changing explosively. In the midst of such rapid transitions I don't think modern "experimental" psychology—as we know it anyway—can accomplish anything except identify itself more and more with cultural and behavioral obsolescence. I fear that it may end up being no more than a nuisance to the human enterprise. Men would rather find out what they can do by actually attempting it, than to be told what they can't do by a psychologist who assumes the future of all men but himself must be a repetition of the past.

The point is that the men the psychologist seeks to understand are resorting to experimentation as much as he is. When a man does that he does not behave as he did last year, or in the fall of 1929, nor does he treat his circumstances in the familiar ways that have been repeatedly "reinforced." He tries something different, just as a reasonably inventive psychologist does. He even ventures to do it without a Ph.D. or a state license to innovate. Psychologists, having observed only his past behavior, may undertake to tell him what he can or cannot do. But he, recalcitrant chap that he is, will go ahead and try something anyway. When he succeeds he will turn to the psychologist and tell him what he can do—or what both of them can do!

Probability and Innovation

Now it is time to point this discussion more directly to the problems involved in trying to explain behavior in terms of sequences of events. I have made several glancing references to a principle of sequential explanation, enough to suggest that I am not for an abandonment of that idea. I have indeed argued as effectively as I know how that in today's plunging stream of human innovations the acts which implement those innovations cannot be adequately understood as a mere product of antecedent stimuli. Yet I have continued to insist also that life is essentially anticipatory, if for no other reason, by virtue of the fact that his most significant behavior is man's expectant way of posing an honest and courageous question. Such anticipation must imply that, in spite of what I have said about stimulus response psychology, there is indeed some kind of antecedent-consequent relationship between my present and my future. What that relationship may be is of prime concern to any psychologist who cares to participate in the quickening human enterprise. Let us deal with it so.

Admittedly, most of what I do today is easily enough construed as similar to what I did yesterday. Friends who have known me during the past few years have little difficulty recognizing my walk, my posture, my facial expression, my voice, and even some of the ideas I express. Probabilistically, then, it would be a poor bet for anyone to wager that my personality tomorrow would be unrecognizably different from what I have exhibited in the past.

But statistical probability is not the same as psychological significance. The most important things in a man's life are mostly those which have never happened to him before—his birth, his marriage, his first child, the departure of grown children from his home, the loss of a loved one, his retirement, his feeble years alone, his death. To be sure, we can sometimes predict—in a very superficial way—these very personal experiences from what we have seen others go through. But none of us, when he approaches them in his own life, finds much in his past that tells him what it will be like when his turn comes.

Yet forecasts are made, and most of us come up with some versions, variously intellectualized, of what we think is going to happen to us. When some of these important events do occur for the first time in our own lives the similarities and contrasts between anticipation and realization stand out with shocking clarity. Few would say in such a poignant moment that what was occurring was so unusual there was no point in taking it seriously.

There are first-time occurrences in the history of mankind too. Again, as in the lifetime of the individual, it is these, rather than the repetitions of history, to which thoughtful appraisal must, in retrospect, attach greater significance. Yet human history records no event so novel it was utterly unexpected. The posture of anticipation, which is the identifying psychological feature of life itself, silently forms questions, and earnest questions erupt in actions. Unprecedented consequences ensue. But when the novel contingencies occur, who, knowing how it was they came about, can say they fell wholly outside the realm of human anticipation? Moreover, it is the historical events precipitated in this manner, rather than those having greater actuarial probability, which tell us most about man in his hastening transitions.

A psychology that pins its anticipations on the repetitions of events it calls "stimuli," or on the concatenations of events it calls "reinforcements," can scarcely hope to survive as man's audacities multiply. More and more it will find its accurate predictions confined to the trivialities of man's least imaginative moments and to the automatisms of persons given in to despair. It seems to me that most of what we know as "modern psychology" is a monotonous tale told of men left behind by the quickening tempo of human undertakings. It is such men, and such men only I suspect, who enact nothing save what has been reinforced, who are carried on by the momentum of their biographies rather than compose their diaries afresh each day, and who become transfixed by their identities. And yet I doubt that there are ever men who are altogether like this. Perhaps it only seems that way from listening to psychologists.

Prediction Within a System of Constructs

Earlier in this discussion I pointed out how man begins to cope with events by devising reference axes called *constructs*. A system of such referrents permits him to put the events he encounters in some kind of perspective. What he devises is not dictated by the events, nor is it a property extracted from them. Nevertheless its utility in enabling him to make accurate predictions is constantly subject to check. Although what a man anticipates is not necessarily a reenactment of what has gone on before, its referrents, in terms of which he pinpoints his forecast, may have been subject to prior tests of their utility.

Whether the phenomenon that occurs can ever be said to be the one that was anticipated is a question not easily answered. One's anticipation of a future incident is scarcely more than a plotted position within a system of personal constructs. If subsequent observations made within the same system seem to coincide with the forecasted plot, one may say, within the referrents of his system, that his anticipation has been confirmed. Later, of course, he may devise other reference axes against which the occurrence may take on new meaning. Then he may wonder if what happened is what he would have anticipated if he had been using the new reference axes at the time he made his original forecast. But this is a question he can scarcely hope to answer. The best he can do is make another forecast, this time in terms of his augmented dimensional system.

Does a succession of accurate predictions serve to demonstrate that one has hit upon the truth at last? Perhaps it might if all the possible reference axes were taken into account in plotting the prediction. But such omniscience is next to impossible. From the point of view I have been expounding this cannot even be considered a good question. One may well keep in mind that it is improbable that any fragment of truth can be nailed down in such a finite manner.

But, more than this, what needs to be noted in the second place is that a construct is not a facsimile of any set of events; only one of an ad hoc system of guidelines for apprehending events. It is hardly appropriate, then, to argue about whether or not a construct is true to reality. A more appropriate question is whether or not it provides a perspective in which anticipations can be checked against realizations. But even if it does serve this purpose, there always remains the likelihood that further constructions will be devised to do the job better.

There is a third, and even more important, consideration. Does a construct, or system of constructs, open up the vastness of a man's psychological space and permit him to dream in new dimensions? And does it provide such definition within its realm that he can implement what he imagines? In short, is it fertile?

Accurate prediction, then, can scarcely be taken as evidence that one has pinned down a fragment of ultimate truth, though this is generally how it is regarded in psychological research. The accuracy confirms only the interim utility of today's limited set of constructs. Tomorrow's genius will erect new dimensions, open up unsuspected degrees of freedom, and invite new experimental controls.

And yet, however useful prediction may be in testing the transient utility of one's construction system, the superior test of what he has devised is its capacity to implement imaginative action. It is by his actions that man learns what his capabilities are, and what he achieves is the most tangible psychological measure of his behavior. It is a mistake to always assume that behavior must be the psychologist's dependent variable. For man, it is the independent variable.

The Stultifying Effect of Actuarial Prediction

Back in the 1920's the Soviet Union shifted its educational policy in a way that puzzled many Western educators. It removed chapters on individual differences from its psychology textbooks and it took a stand against all psychological testing. It is interesting to note that a similar movement is afoot in this country today, though I am inclined to believe it is not the communists who are behind it. It does appear, however, to be led by persons with an uncanny ability to identify communism's faults and virtues, for what is good they consistently oppose and what is evil, they imitate.

Moscow planned to industrialize. The choice had proved urgent. Having alienated itself from the economic and humanistic obligations honored by industrialized nations, and being therefore no longer in a relationship of mutual trust with the rest of the world, it could scarcely hope to attain economic viability unless it could produce by itself the goods upon which modern civilization in part depends. But Soviet scholars, including psychologists, could find little in the behavioral record and measured aptitudes of the people to support the hope they could ever operate machines and man factories, much less supply the vast needs of an industrialized society for advanced engineering and technical skills. What was the USSR to do? The choice was to listen to the experts or throw away the book. They threw away the book.

What happened is becoming history. Through two generations human behavior has been used as an instrument to explore its own potentials. While it seems clear that communism still has much to learn about the potential of the individual—perhaps as much as corporate Western Society seems bent on forgetting—no one can now say, as actuarialists would once have said, that the USSR cannot reach the moon.

Similar predictions were voiced when Egypt took over the Suez Canal. Egyptians could not develop the skills required of the Canal's pilots. Yet with Soviet help and encouragement, now grounded on experience doing what behavior experts once said was impossible, the Egyptians took on the job. Soon they were operating the Canal more efficiently than their predecessors. These were instances in which human actions came to be understood better in the context of their own potentialities. Actuarial prediction, however it may have previously been confirmed in both cases, proved to be grossly misleading. When human behavior was taken as an independent rather than a dependent variable, its functional relationship with other variables was radically changed. This is something for psychology to note if it intends to survive the Twentieth Century.

Behavior as the Psychologist's Independent Variable

It has been customary for psychologists to attempt to explain behavior as dependent variable. They point out its antecedents, as if in saying what brought it about, they could demonstrate their understanding of it. Yet there is much more to psychological explanation than that. As I have been insisting, behavior can scarcely be understood until one has caught a glimpse of what it might be as well as of what it is. What one does comes into perspective as a contrast to what he might have done. This is to say that human behavior takes on additional meaning when one sees it as a contrast, a denial, an abandonment of alternatives, or as a choice which has left other possibilities unexplored.

To see behavior in this kind of perspective one needs reference axes within which he can plot what he actually does in a structured context of what he might possibly do. Without such a framework there are no grounds for assessing relevance and one's understanding of human behavior is limited to the lowest order of mechanistic description. The reference axes are the constructs devised by man, and each person erects a system of his own, though it is not necessarily a verbalized one. Within the realm of relevance his personal construct system defines for him, each man initiates what he says and does. Thus his words and his acts are not mere events consequent upon previous occurrences, but are expressions of what is relevantly affirmed and denied within his system.

A man curses. What he says is scarcely understood by looking up the purple phrases in a dictionary. One must understand the relevance of his verbal expression—what his curses emphatically deny, and what it would mean to him if he could not disavow what is so important to him to negate. Any word, whether an oath or a benediction, has a meaning in the context of its usage and within the construct system of the speaker that no dictionary can make clear. This is because dictionaries cannot provide the framework of relevance that makes language come alive.

Or a man makes love. One does not understand such an act from a description of its motor and physiological properties. There are the circumstances to be taken into account. But even a description of these—the moon and the girl—does not tell us all the act means. There is the structure of relevance, a highly personal matter that is often so difficult for others to understand, and, perhaps on a later occasion, even difficult for the man himself to understand. What did his affection assert? What did it deny? What are the boldly outlined dimensions that channelized his enactment so spontaneously it seemed to run its course without intent? It is within these parameters that his love-making begins to make sense, rather than following simply as the next link in a primordially forged chain of natural events.

But the context of relevance, as dimensioned by a man's personal construct system, is still not all that is needed to understand his behavior. Accomplishments must be noted too, for it is through his behavior and through his behavioral investment only, that man makes his entrance into the world of reality. When he acts he poses a question, and what ensues gives the question its import, the act its potency, and his life its meaning.

Behavior is man's independent variable in the experiment of creating his own existence. But to the extent that he loses sight of this fact and, thinking that he is being "psychological," regards his actions as a dependent variable, he denies himself a role in the human enterprise. And that, I think, amounts to abdicating his existence, except as an after-the-fact occurrence. A psychology that presumes to make a man an echo of once meaningful events must ultimately destroy him altogether, and, doing so, engrave its own final epitaph as well.

Behavior must be the independent variable for the psychologist too, just as it is for all children and for most men who have managed to stay clear of modern psychology. Rather than drawing from their actuarial studies the inference that human initiative is only what it has heretofore been, psychology's greater task is to join mankind in the exploration of what human behavior might be, and what would happen if it were. This is not merely a speculative or an artistic undertaking; it can be just as rigorously scientific as the psychology that treats behavior as its dependent variable—indeed, more so.

Guidelines

For psychology to launch into such a venturesome participation in the human enterprise it must concern itself with the guidelines that give behavior its directionality. The temptation is to say, in the tradition of Nineteenth Century determinism, that the guidelines are no more than reverberations of what has gone on before, and the best man can do is resonate to them. But if the psychologist does say that, humanity's present entry to the on-going human experiment we call existence is negated. And if he should go so far as to believe it of himself, his own experiment will collapse too. Psychology would then have no basis in ontology.

A psychology that participates in the human enterprise must perceive that the guidelines channelizing a person's processes are drawn by the person himself—that they are therefore personal constructs, and may be redrawn and revalidated by the user to structure anew his thought and his behavior. They are not the residue of biographical incidents, nor are they projected facsimiles of reality. They are, instead, the axes of reference man contrives to put his psychological space in order and to plot his varying courses of action.

With such personal constructs a man can make his entrance into the world of reality by acting with initiative and ingenuity. Failing to erect them he can only repeat concretely what has been "reinforced," in the circular manner that psychological journals—themselves deliberately acting, I fear, as products of their own concrete satisfactions—describe. It is difficult to see how a psychology so addicted to its reinforcements can ever participate imaginatively in the mounting behavioral ventures of the coming generation.

Prediction

What has been said so far about understanding human behavior might be cataloged under three headings. First, one must recognize behavioral alternatives—what man might do as well as what he does. In this generation men are exploring their behavioral alternatives at a pace never before equaled in the history of man. A psychology preoccupied with human behavior as a system of events primordially linked to prior occurrences can look forward to no substantial part for itself in this expanding human enterprise.

Second, neither science nor psychology can continue to ignore the relevance of what man does. Human behavior makes the world a different kind of place—though not always a very good one to live in. Man tampers with the scheme of things. But what do we know about what is happening to that scheme while it is being meddled with, except as we have some awareness of the dimensions of the psychological space within which the intrusive ventures are initiated? Yet the only dimensions we know are those erected by man himself—by *each* man himself. We call them constructs. Without them novel human acts can only appear as disruptive, disjunctive, chaotic, and somehow precipitated by hidden antecedents. But with them one can begin to see behavior probing for new avenues for man to extricate himself from prior circumstances and seeking them in a context of relevance to the current transition in human affairs.

Third, the meaning of human behavior cannot be assessed until its accomplishments are noted. It is through his behavioral initiative that man makes his entry into the real world of human events. He seizes life by starting something, and he becomes aware of his existence by noting what happens as a consequence. This is to say that life is anticipatory, not in a mere passive sense, but in an active, participative one.

Most scientists would agree with me, I am sure, if I said that the advancement of knowledge depends on the confirmation of predictions. Indeed, I do want to say just that. But I want to say more too. Before I do say more, however, let me make a few comments about the confirmation of predictions.

If we can agree that there is a reality beyond what pure phenomenology is willing to concede we can concern ourselves with the procedures by which man makes contact with it. We might say, of course, that if we keep our eyes and our ears open, sooner or later nature will reveal herself to us. But I think she is more coy than that. Instead of taking the initiative in disclosing herself to a passive man, or responding directly to a cross-examination logically phrased in plain English, I think that she, being every bit as feminine as they say she is, more likely lowers her lashes and murmurs, "Try me and see."

If this seems a much too anthropomorphic explanation for mechanistic stomachs, let me simply turn it around and suggest that feminine women know how to behave naturally. Is that better? But it's really all the same. It is just that when metaphors are turned around they don't sound so prejudicial. In any case, this view of the matter passes the initiative along to man—where it probably belongs if he is ever going to amount to anything—and generally makes him responsible for nature's reputation, called "science," as well as for his own existence.

If man is to comprehend natural events at any level—even at preverbal levels—he must anticipate them. This means predicting in some manner when and how they will occur. If what turns up resembles what he expected he can say his prediction was confirmed, at least in part. If it does not, he had better do something about it or reconcile himself to being left out of the goings-on.

The apparent failure of a prediction calls for reassessment. That may mean reidentifying the events from which inferences were drawn, reconsidering the inferences themselves, or questioning the constructs one has employed in structuring his psychological space. On the other hand, the apparent success of a prediction also leaves much in doubt. The confirming occurrence may not have depended on what the adventurer thought it did; it may look like what he expected only as long as he does not examine it too closely, or both his prediction and the outcome may have been so loosely defined that they could not possibly have turned out to be at odds with each other.

There is also the matter of just what it is a successful prediction confirms. Does it confirm only the specific prediction itself? Does it confirm the general hypothesis from which the prediction was derived? Or does it confirm something else—as when a person who thinks his neighbors are prejudiced against him finds his prediction well enough confirmed when he keeps complaining about it?

As a matter of fact, no confirmed prediction can be taken as evidence that one has struck bedrock truth. If one thinks science is a simple digging operation by which solid bits of truth are uncovered, he is likely to be in for some disappointments, especially if he relies upon the confirmation of his predictions as firm evidence that he has struck something conclusive.

At best, the confirmation of a prediction is no more than tentative evidence that one may be on the track of something. The psychology of living in a world that is largely unknown—and in rapid transition, besides—leads us to hope for little more than ad interim support for our beliefs. The confirmation of our local predictions, equivocal as that may be, is about the most we can expect. No, there is one thing more, vastly important—our ability, while alive, to pose further questions by our invested behavior, and thus to enter the stream of nature's fluid enterprise as an entity in our own right.

One thing more about confirmation of predictions: the basis upon which a prediction is formulated is more generalized and more tenuous than the observation which confirms or disconfirms it. A man predicts he can reach the moon. He can ordinarily be less sure about the accuracy of his advance calculations than he can about his observation of whether he reached it or not. There are a number of grounds for this—consensus of observers, previous validation of criteria, exhaustiveness of the construct axes of reference, multidimensional fix of the observed event, etc.—none of them absolute, of course. But, at least for the moment, it appears he can tie his unsure predictions to outcomes that seem sufficiently obvious. While this usually turns out to be shortlived scholarship, as it was in the case of Columbus who hurried home to tell Isabella that he had been right all along about reaching India—and had "Indians" to prove it—it probably serves to account well enough for so many scientific practitioners believing their task is only a matter of accumulating information about such linkages with "the obvious," bit by bit, and holding off replications of their experiments long enough to publish their results. However, this is not the place to discuss that particular fallacy at greater length than we already have.

Control

If one can control events, as well as predict them, can he then allow himself to believe he understands them? Or, to make the question applicable to psychology, if one can control another's behavior does it means he understands that person's actions? Or, to bring the question within the realm of personal experience, does it mean that I understand my own behavior if I succeed in making it conform to a chosen pattern?

When the question is thus pinpointed it is easier to see how the answer has to be "no." At the very least the answer has to be "no" in the light of what has been said about understanding behavior in the context of its alternatives. A man who commits suicide probably knows very little about his own behavior, simply because its alternatives are so chaotically perceived by him. Yet there can be no doubt about his controlling it definitively.

Still it must be taken for granted that there have been some cases—Socrates and Jesus, for example—when the act leading to death was understood in the light of a careful examination of its alternatives. Even if we apply our third criterion for understanding human behavior—awareness of its consequents—one would still have to concede that some suicidal attempts may be fairly well understood by those who make them, though certainly most of such acts are pretty shortsighted. In any case, the point is that even this most definitive control of one's subsequent behavior cannot be taken as evidence it is understood. And as for what it means to be able to control the behavior of others, I am most reluctant to agree that all tyrants are proven psychologists.

It appears that I have set up an impossible standard for judging human behavior psychologically. That is true; I have. But it is a good one, nonetheless. I am less concerned, anyway, about definitive criteria than I am about usable ones which enable us to get on with the human enterprise. The task of the psychologist is to enable human behavior to make something out itself, not nail it dead to rights! This is a moving universe, especially those aspects of it with which the psychologist ought to be concerned, and the psychologist who thinks he cannot understand it until it settles down to a routine is the one who has really set an impossible standard for himself.

Yet to control behavior, as to predict it successfully, is to put it into a sequence; in the case of control, to make it follow upon intent, and, in the case of prediction, to envision outcomes before they happen. Both imply reaching a threshold of understanding, though the success of either has often been taken by psychologists as grounds for stopping short of understanding, and has thereafter led to grief. Both are anticipatory, and therefore express, in some degree, the spirit of human life. Both are useful to the human quest, particularly if they are taken to mean only that one may be on the track of something. Both represent, in part, the methodology of sequential explanation, by which psychologists can participate intelligently in the expanding human enterprise without asking it to stand still or spin around in orbital facsimiles of itself.

Sequential Explanation of Behavior

The principle of sequential explanation comprehends a number of things. There is the notion that human behavior falls into a progressively moving sequence, an orbit of infinite proportions, and is not restricted to the little stimulus response circuit some psychologists examine so minutely in their laboratories. The exciting thing about the psychology of man is that he, for one, tries what he has never tried before and thus transforms himself before the psychologist's eyes, not that so much of his life at the same time continues to be routinely repetitive. And what makes it all the more exciting is that the pace of sequential transformation is accelerating, causing the task of the "Darwinian" psychologist, who assumes the evolution of human behavior has leveled off, to get so far out of hand he is threatened with extinction.

Not only must the principle of sequential explanation take into account the possibilities of behavioral orbits having infinite elements, but it must concern itself with successions pursuant upon entries undertaken at various points in the sequence of human events. In spite of some disparaging remarks I have made about stimulus response psychology, I am in no position to deny that a psychologist may intervene at the point of a "stimulus" and profitably observe what ensues as a behavioral "response." But he can also, and more often with profit I think, intervene in the cycle at the point marked, "response," and observe what stimulating events follow in the sequence. This is what I meant when I urged psychology to treat behavior as the independent variable in the ongoing experiment we call human existence.

The sequence of events that follows from a behavioral innovation contributes quite as much—even more—to our understanding of the action as do the action's antecedents. What it is important for man to know about the psychology of his behavior is what its alternatives are and what each might lead to, not how monotonously repetitive it is. The principle of sequential explanation must never be regarded as limited to an account of the succession of things that have already happened. To be sure, a prediction confirmed in the past is a case of sequential explanation, and it most certainly means something, but if it is taken as ground for a terminal conclusion, supposedly rendering inevitable what man may do tomorrow, the principle itself is violated.

Where human behavior is concerned, one must always take into account the sequential implications of unprecedented behavioral undertakings. As those implications begin to be suspected it is pretty likely that someone will venture the unprecedented undertakings, regardless of what stimulus response psychology predicts he will do. He may not get a research grant from the National Science Foundation for his venture, but that will not necessarily stop him.

The notion of relevance fits in here too. Increasingly men have projects up their sleeves. Without a hint as to what those projects might be some of their behavior may look very strange, and psychologists who can explain behavior only by looking to the stimulus events that have impinged upon these persons are likely to have a hard time of it. They may have to break with psychological tradition and ask the persons outright what they are up to.

But even asking a man what his objectives are may not throw much light on his behavior. Objectives have to be plotted in psychological space, and if one does not know the coordinate axes being used he may not be able to locate the objective. In that case his respondent's plotted courses of action will remain as obscure as his objective. One can scarcely trace a sequence wandering around through uncharted space, much less rely upon it to make something clear.

The reference axes—personal constructs—used by man must be inferred if one is to understand how a sequence goes and what bearing human objectives have upon the direction of human behavior. Thus the principle of sequential explanation, the wide-angled view of what follows what or what might follow what in this volatile world, demands that antecedents and consequents be plotted within the same construction system, or at least within construction systems that are cognate to each other. All of this is a rather philosophical way of saying that behavior is not understood until its relevance is straightened out.

So psychology needs to make use of sequential explanation when it deals with a subject so much in transition as human behavior. This means more than reliance upon confirmed predictions of human acts and the successful control of men. The events falling in sequence upon behavioral innovations must be considered. Behavioral alternatives must be envisioned if explanations of manifest behavior are to be entertained. Relevance must come to light, and not be dismissed as a "value" beyond the concern of scientific psychology. It can come to light if the dimensional structure of psychological space is explored, and the course of events, behavioral and otherwise, is plotted within personal construct systems that hopefully are cognate to each other.

Living with Sequential Explanation

What constitutes an adequate explanation in science or elsewhere is a matter of some perplexity to man, just as it is to a child who is asked to explain his behavior to his teacher or his parent. For some it seems to require a sort of proof that an event could not have occurred otherwise than the way it did. This usually backs up the explanation to antecedent events which are expected to take the rap for what has happened, and this, in turn, involves us in an assumption of a primordial linkage of natural occurrences in some sort of inevitable succession. For others explanation means the removal of all contradictions between what happened and all other things known to exist. For still others it means that an event is explained by its essential membership in a complex which, as a whole, can be taken for granted, or that the event can be designated precisely by terms derived from axioms. Then there are those who consider it enough to point out that the event was premeditated.

Before you get very far in this kind of discussion the question gets itself mixed up with the issue of freedom versus determinism, an issue I prefer to discuss elsewhere. But to a psychologist, explanation, in my opinion, turns out to be pretty much a matter of convenience. We want to get on with what we are doing and the kind of explanation that helps us in the undertaking, or suggests more attractive undertakings, is the one we are likely to accept.

Finding the ultimate explanation of something is about the same kind of quest as trying to capture certainty in a formula or truth in a dogma. For the time being, we are going to have to accept explanations that fall short of such conclusive pronouncements. Besides, I am not sure most of us would care to be dragged, kicking and screaming, through life by its certainties, or to have our burning curiosities extinguished by being doused with a bucketful of truth.

But we seem to be safe enough for the time being. No one seems to have pinned down the primordial explanatory event from which all others must ensue, nor has anyone come up with a terminal explanation which blockades all alternative routes. Since we cannot see either the beginning or the end very clearly, we shall just have to work our way out from the middle—which is where we find ourselves. As I see it, the way to do that is to have a look at what follows what, and in what order. We can, for example, look at what has already followed what. But that is not enough, unless we are content to walk through life facing backwards. We had better have a look also at what is going to follow what, since the world, especially the world of human behavior seems to be turning up a lot of novelties. It is even more challenging to look at what else could be undertaken and consider what might follow in sequence from that.

Explanation in a humanistic or psychological sense seems to me to be a matter of seeing where something fits into a sequence. We can explain events by looking at their antecedents, as the stimulus response psychologists do, or we can explain them by lining them up with their consequents, or we can look at alternative successions to see what would have ensued—or would ensue—if they had been initiated. Such an explanation might not be of much comfort to a philosopher who generally dislikes having to live with his ignorance—or with ours. But as psychologists, we have to get along with our human handicaps, and the limited knowledge we can glean about what follows what is enough to enable us to get along gratefully with whatever it is we are trying to do.

In any case, whether it is satisfying or not, this is what the principle of sequential explanation means, and this is why the psychology of human behavior can live with it. Mostly the point I want to make about it is that ordinary notions of prediction and control, while they are limited examples of sequential explanation, are insufficient for a psychology that must not only remain out of touch with primordial beginnings and ultimate endings but must also find itself swept along in a mounting tide of behavioral innovations and their consequences as well.

Behavior is Both the Problem and Man's Way of Solving It

Most of all, psychology, if it is to provide us with an understanding of human behavior, must help us see that man's behavior is his admission ticket to human existence. It is through behavior that questions are posed, and without it there is little that is new or worth anticipating in the realm of human events. What man does, whether in the outer world of international affairs or in the inner world of his mind, is what makes things turn out differently for him.

It will not be easy for a psychology modeled on Nineteenth Century science—and a science that believed that evolution had leveled off, at that—to participate in the accelerated behavioral innovations that promise to change the shape of the human affairs that confront it. Did I say, "not be easy?" I should have said, "be incredible!" Yet I think it should be possible for psychologists, who are less self-conscious about being scientists, to participate in the quickening human enterprise, once they appreciate the creative role of behavior in the affairs of man.

24

Behavior is a Question[1]

This story has its beginning more than forty years ago. The setting was a large classroom and I was sitting on the back row with my chair tilted back against the wall. I was taking my first—and what I hoped would be my last—course in psychology.

At the time I was an undergraduate majoring in mathematics and physics, and entertaining aspirations to study engineering after completion of a liberal arts degree. But, being short of funds, I was very much afraid I would have to teach for a year or two, in order to earn enough to extend my studies beyond the baccalaureate degree. The necessity of having to earn money in this way was something that I regarded as a misfortune. If anyone had told me then that I would still be teaching after all these years, I would have been deeply depressed. And if they had told me furthermore that I would be teaching psychology, I probably would have entertained serious doubts that life was worth-while.

In order to teach, one had to have a certificate and, in order to get a certificate in those days, just as now, one had to do a lot of silly things. One of them was to take an elementary course in psychology. That was why I was in the classroom dozing through my first course in psychology.

One day the professor, a very kindly and dignified gentleman who seemed to be trying hard to convince himself that psychology was something to be taken seriously, turned to the blackboard and wrote an "S," an "arrow," and an "R." I can remember the incident very clearly and I remember how I straightened up my chair and began to listen, thinking to myself that now, after two or three weeks of preliminary nonsense, we might be getting to the meat of the matter.

Although I listened intently for several sessions after that, the most I could make of it was that the S was what you had to have in order to account for the R. There were Rs all around us and it was unthinkable that people should do things just because they wanted to or felt like it. So it was obvious that we had to go and look for Ss in the environment that would account for what people did.

When we turned to the R, it was explained that that symbol occurred in the formula so that the Ss would have something to account for. I never did find out what that arrow stood for—not to this day—and I have pretty well given up trying to figure it out. I can see, of course, that once you step into this little solipsism, you can go round and round for publication after publication without being obligated to come out with anything particularly useful. This, for academic people, is obviously an advantage, for what an academician wants is to be useful. Moreover, the formula enables you to avoid asking people directly what they are doing. That, too, is a great advantage for a scientist, for it is all too well-known that people give disgracefully subjective answers to such a question. And any person with a disciplined mind, knows very well that you cannot base a science on hearsay evidence.

Some of my friends have tried to explain to me that the world is filled with Ss and Rs and it is unrealistic of me to refuse to recognize their existence. But, before they have talked themselves out, they become pretty vague about which is which. Others, who are not so concretistic, argue that the formula represents only a relationship between events, not the events themselves. This makes a little more sense and might continue to make sense if they didn't persist in talking about the matter, always rubbing their forefingers across that arrow in the formula. That gets me all confused again, for they seem to be contradicting themselves in saying that it is the *arrow* that expresses the relationship between the events, not the S and the R.

Out of all this, I have gradually developed the notion that psychology is pretty much confined to the paradigms it employs and, while you can take off in a great many directions and travel a considerable distance in any one of them—as indeed we have with stimulus-response psychology—there is no harm in consorting with a strange paradigm now and then. Indeed, the notion has occurred to me that psychology may best be regarded as a collection of paradigms wooed by ex-physicists, ex-physiologists and ex-clergymen, as well as a lot of other intellectual renegades. Even more recently, it has struck me that this is the nature of man: he is an inveterate collector and user of paradigms. But now I am getting ahead of myself.

[1] Prepared for presentation at the Xth Inter–American Congress of Psychology, Lima, Peru, April 3–7, 1966. Not delivered because of illness. Published by permission of Jacqueline Aldridge.

Collected Papers of the Pioneer of Constructivist Psychology: George A. Kelly, First Edition. Edited by David A. Winter and Nick Reed.

The second scene in this story occurred about three years later, after I had abandoned engineering as a career and had entered graduate school in an effort to learn something about sociology and labor relations. I decided it was high time I had a look at Freud. I can remember the occasion rather well. I was in the northeast corner of the reading room of the Library at the University of Kansas. I had decided to take the afternoon off in order to learn all about Freud, about whom I had heard some pornographic rumors.

I don't remember which of Freud's books I was trying to read, but I do recall the mounting feeling of incredibility that anyone could write such nonsense, much less find a publisher for it. It was not the pan-sexualism that made Freud objectionable to me. As a matter of fact, I found the Freudian writings rather disappointing as pornography. What did disturb me was his words with elastic meanings placed in an arbitrary scientific syntax. In any case, after a few hours, I gathered up the books from the table and dumped them all down the return chute with the comfortable feeling that now I knew all about Freud that I would ever need to know.

But this is not the end of the story. It might have been the end of the story if what psychologists say about learning and sociologists say about sub-cultures were true. But in my case neither what I had learned up to this point nor the culture with which I was identified would have suggested that four years later I would have been receiving a Ph.D. in psychology. I don't think for one moment that the intervening events shaped my life. Nor do I suspect that I have turned out to be a psychologist because of my constitution. If I became a psychologist it was because I chose to do something psychological about the events I faced and, to a considerable extent, chose the events about which I wished to do something.

I have to tell you what happened next. It was the summer of 1931. With a doctoral degree in psychology on my hands and the early stages of the depression of the 1930s already apparent, and with some recently acquired aspirations in physiological psychology, I set out with my bride for what was soon to become the notorious dust bowl of west-central United States. During the following twelve years, at a small college in Western Kansas, I had, shall we say, several more priceless opportunities to revise my outlook. I might add that, during this time, I had a minimum of intellectual interference from my colleagues in psychology.

It did not take many weeks in those depression times to reach the decision to pursue something more humanitarian than physiological psychology. Too many young people were wondering what, if anything, to do with their lives. The schools, only recently established at the secondary level in that part of the state, were only barely functioning as educational institutions, and there were many who thought public education should be abandoned altogether until economic recovery had taken place. It was time for a teacher to talk of courage and adventure in the midst of despair. It was not a time for the S, the arrow, and the R.

Again let me state my conviction that it was not the circumstances that dictated the conclusions I reached. I could have used the same circumstances to confirm stimulus-response psychology or cultural determinism. It was, rather, that the paradigms with which I entered the situation no longer seemed appropriate. The fact that I felt this way probably proves that I was not really a psychologist. At least, it suggests that I was more interested in what was going on in the world of human affairs than I was in psychology.

As a matter of fact, I am not sure that I have ever been very much interested in psychology. Engineering still holds more fascination for me. So why did I, at this point, turn from the things I spontaneously had enjoyed to the heartbreaking tasks of the psychotherapist? Was it circumstances? I think not. It was I. Was it an inner sense of duty to fellow man? If you mean that there was something called "duty" that intruded itself into my life and beckoned me to follow it, then the answer is no. As a matter of fact, when someone tries to tell me what my duty is, I am not likely to take him very seriously for, it seems to me, he is probably a busybody who, having failed to make something out of his own circumstances, wants someone else to fulfill his neglected aspirations.

What happened was that I found myself confronted with circumstances I had not wholly anticipated. So, instead of worrying about why I behaved as I did, I sought to use my behavior to cope with the circumstances and to inquire into methods of altering them. My behavior was not something to be explained by an S, but was my instrument of inquiry. You might say that I had taken the arrow in that formula that had been written on the blackboard in my elementary course in psychology and had turned it around.

Perhaps I had better pause at this point and ask you to look ahead to see where I mean to lead you. In the mid-1950s, I published a theory of personality which I called *The Psychology of Personal Constructs*. The events I am describing lead up to this theory.

As you can probably guess, the psychology of personal constructs makes no use of the notions of stimulus or response. There is no stimulus generalization, no affect, no cognition, no feeling, no emotion, and no reinforcement. The concept of insight is abandoned, together with the ideas of psychotherapeutic resistance, the unconscious, and psychosomatics. There is no ego, no id, no superego. There is no conditioning, no motivation, and no learning. And, just to suggest how far my wickedness has gone, let me say that it implies black and white judgments rather than shadings of gray.

To be sure, some well-known terms are used in the theory, but most of them are completely redefined; terms like hostility, aggression, guilt, anxiety, transference, identification, role, acceptance, dependency, validity, determinism, freedom, variable, construct, and even truth. Now that I have warned you let us go back to the 1930s.

It was somewhere around this point in my experience that it occurred to me that what seemed true of myself was probably no less true of others. If I initiated my action to cope with circumstances and to inquire into ways of altering them so did they. I suppose that this position commits me to a psychology of man rather than the psychology of man's circumstances. It is a psychology concerned with what behavior may accomplish rather than what causes it. In the one case, behavior is a way of formulating a question. In the other case, we have a psychology in which behavior is the answer to a question. There is, I suspect, a lot of difference between these two psychologies.

But to believe that man is the author of his destiny is not to be blind to the fact that he may be tragically limited by his circumstances. I saw too many unfortunate youngsters, some of them literally starving in that depression-ridden dust bowl, for me not to be aware of their tragic limitations. Clearly, there were many things they might have liked to do that circumstances would not permit. But this is not to say that they were the victims of those circumstances. However much was denied them, there was still an infinity of possibilities open to them. The task was to generate the imagination needed to envision these possibilities. Man can always reconstrue what he may not deny, and this is a point of departure tor a psychology of man, the canons of 19th century determinism notwithstanding.

So I listened to two people in trouble and I tried to help them figure out what they could do about it. None of the things I had studied or pursued in the years before seemed to have any very specific bearing on what confronted us, though, at one time or another through this period, I probably had attempted to make some use of everything I knew.

The strangest thing about this period is that I went back to Freud for a second look. My recollections of Rasmussen's *Principal Nervous Pathways*, and of Thorndike's electrical condensor theory of learning applied at the synapses had not proved very helpful to people troubled about what was to become of them. But, now that I had listened to the language of distress, Freud's writings made a new kind of sense. That fellow Freud, he was indeed a clinician! He, too, must have listened to these same cries echoing from deep down where there are no sentences, no words, and no syntax.

So it was that I became a "Freudian," if not by training, at least by persuasion. The Freudian language of explanation provided me with a way of understanding the difficulties of those who came to me for aid, of anticipating their thoughts, and of helping them regain the initiative in their lives. In short, I began to have what I thought was insight. Through my Freudian interpretations, judiciously offered at those moments when a client seemed ready for them, a good many unfortunate persons seemed to be helped profoundly.

I suppose it is clear that none of this was under psychiatric supervision nor under any kind of supervision for that matter. My clients and I were on our own and, while I think I have come a long way since this period in my psychological career, we—my client and I—are still pretty much on our own whenever we buckle down to a difficult problem. It is important that this be understood in order to visualize what would happen next.

There is something about the obvious things in this world that repeatedly rises to plague me. I know that many persons complain that they are tormented by the uncertainties of life, by its ambiguities, or by the fact that there seemed to be no final answers. I think I know how they feel and, to some extent, I am troubled by such thinkings too, though thus far I have no very serious complaints about my uncertainties. But, those things I once thought I knew for sure, those are what get me into trouble time after time. They are a lot more troublesome than those things I have known all along that I didn't understand.

I have told you enough about my experience for you to see how this was true in my own life. As an undergraduate, I was wrong about psychology. The one subject I found the most useless in my undergraduate years, and the teaching career which I found so repulsive, turned out to be the very things to which I have devoted the major part of my life's efforts. I was wrong about Freud too. Freud is not something to be accepted or rejected out of a textbook, but something to be used as an instrument of man's venture. Nor is it that we need to be so greatly concerned about whether or not Freudian theory is valid. It is the validity of the human venture itself about which we are most deeply concerned.

So, in the 1930s, people in distress came to see me. I listened to them. I had insights. Then they listened to me and they had insights. Lives were changed. Altogether things worked out rather well. It seemed obvious that after my years of floundering I had finally stumbled upon the true faith.

Obvious? It was then that I recalled that it had been when things seemed most obvious to me that I had turned out to be most wrong. It was with some such thought as this in the back of my mind that I began to be uncomfortable with my Freudian "insights." It was not that they were failing me so much as it was that I felt myself beginning to take them for granted, and ideas, like women, when too long taken for granted are likely to turn fickle.

So I began fabricating "insights." I deliberately offered preposterous interpretations to my clients. Some of them were about as un-Freudian as I could make them. I proceeded somewhat cautiously at first, and then, as I began to see what was happening, more boldly. My only criteria were that the explanation account for the crucial facts as the clients saw them, and that it carries implications for approaching the future in a different way. My fabrications had become not so much conclusions about life as they were grounds for the behavioral expression of questions about it.

What happened? Well, some of my preposterous explanations worked, some of them surprisingly well. To be sure, the wilder ones fell flat. But a re-examination of the interviews often suggested where the client's difficulty with them lay. Now I would not say that, as a general rule, my fabricated insights worked as well as my Freudian ones. But I can say that some of them out-performed normal expectations.

And now where was I? Must I now conclude that life has no conclusions? Should I say that fiction and truth are equally valid as far as human behavior is concerned? What kind of behavior is the answer to the question? How should a man live his life? If psychology is a science and the objective of science is to predict and control, should not I, as a psychologist, be primarily concerned with the prediction and control of behavior? Or is there something else about behavior that I did not at this point in my career understand?

As a result of my exploration of preposterous explanations, I developed the notion that what many clients needed was something they could use to give them a fresh approach to life, some explanation they could employ to cover a rather large number of future contingencies. While it might be helpful if a new construction of events covered the original complaints, I was not at all sure this was essential. And, when I suggest that what may be needed is something to facilitate the composed anticipation of contingent events, I would like it to be clear that I refer to internal events such as those we commonly call "feelings," as well as to external occurrences.

About this possibility of ignoring the original complaints: I reached this hypothesis more or less by accident. It came about in this way. After a time the requests for psychological help exceeded my spare hours. This was not particularly surprising. So often, after listening to a person describe his difficulties, I had to explain to him that it would be months before I could see him on a regular basis.

It occurred to me that I had some responsibility to suggest things that he might do while waiting his turn. Sometimes this took the form of reminding him that there were others in distress too, and there were certain kinds of things that anyone might do to be helpful. This was not intended to "cure" him, but it was merely something that needed to be done and he might as well make himself useful while waiting to see me. Besides, his contribution would be a measure of how much he wanted help for himself. I might add at this point that I charged no fees. In fact, after more than thirty years practicing psychotherapy, I have still to collect my first fee for psychotherapeutic services. Some of my colleagues consider this immoral on my part.

To my surprise, a considerable number of these potential clients, when they were finally told their turn had come, reported either that they no longer felt the need for help or that they had come to realize that other persons they knew needed it more than they, and that therefore they were willing to wait a few weeks longer. Most of them said that what they had done in the meantime had put their problem in a new perspective.

It was not so much that they had been cured by the experience but that their troubles, though still with them, no longer seemed unmanageable. There were things they could do. By this time I knew what most therapists have observed—that this kind of statement is often about what you get from so-called successfully treated clients, and that it actually suggests a better prognosis than the euphoric claims that some clients make in their frantic "flights into health."

Whether this means that my clients, whose treatment had been postponed and who made themselves useful in the meantime, were actually therapized by their altruistic efforts is a question I am not prepared to answer. I suspect it may not even be a very good question. What the experience does suggest is that the new structure that emerges from psychotherapy may not need to cover the old complaints at all. Indeed psychotherapy itself may not need to deal with that elusive entity called the self, regarded by so many of our colleagues as the focal point of their efforts. If anything at all worth-while had happened to my neglected clients it was that they had used their own behavior, turned not into themselves but toward others, as their instrument of inquiry about themselves. This suggests that the way to inquire about one's self is to see what he can do about others.

As you see I was still floundering and every time I hit upon what appeared to be a certainty I came to distrust it, to test it, and find that it was not the only possible answer. My conclusions kept turning into questions. In particular, my conclusions about behavior kept coming back to the notion that behavior itself could not ever be regarded as a conclusion but only as a way of posing a question.

It is a short step from this doubtful psychological vantage point, to which my psychotherapeutic efforts had thus far led me, and the next idea in the sequence, but it took a long time to take that step. At least it took *me* a long time.

The writings of two men began to intrigue me—Moreno and Korzybski. One suggested that enactment, even though not wholly spontaneous, might yield answers otherwise not forthcoming. The other suggested that the self might be regarded as a semantic term capable of redefinition.

In any case I began to pursue the notion that one's current acts and undertakings might have as much to do with the development of his personality as did the imprint of the events with which he came in contact, or the insights he was able to conjure up with the help of his therapist. To put it very simply, man shaped himself by his commitments and what he did to fulfill them.

There is much in man's social history that confirms this idea. It is said that the United States presidency may make a man out of a politician, provided he commits himself to it. Professional controls may also make a man out of one who dedicates himself to professional objectives. More than one of us has assumed the ways of scholarship by undertaking first the responsibilities of teaching.

Not only did it seem that the words man uses give and hold the structure of his thoughts but, more particularly, the names by which he calls himself give and hold the structure of his personality. Each of us invests his name with a particular kind of meaning, and it has been so for thousands of years. The man who knew himself as "Saul" became the man who martyred himself as "Paul," perhaps in a way that would have been impossible if he had persisted in identifying himself as "Saul." Women whose marriages confronted them with particular difficulties in complementing their husbands' lives were greatly aided in the transition by the change in their names. I had seen this actually happen in cases where I had some intimate knowledge of what the individual woman had to overcome. Moreover, those professions which supposedly required the greatest sublimation of personal impulses often made the task easier for their members by attaching some title such as Reverend, Doctor, or Colonel to the man's name. This bit of disidentification with the rest of humanity does not of course work in all cases.

It is not, I am sure, that there is any special magic in names—only the magic that we invest in them. Behind the name is the identity that *we* put there. To the extent that we remain faithful to that identity, we remain faithful to the name and vice versa. If the identity is to be changed it does, of course, require more than a mere change in name. But the change in name, along with all the other terms of one's identity, can have profound psychological implications.

But now where are we? We have seen persons change as the result of carrying out new commitments. We have seen them change as a consequence of their redefinitions of themselves. But, enlightening as these glimpses of what a viable psychology of man might be, it still seems as if the objective eludes our grasp. How often the client in psychotherapy says, in effect, "I see what I want to do, I see now how to do it and where, and I see how someone like me could step out into an entirely new way of life, but I cannot picture myself—*me*—ever becoming anything other than what I am."

Perhaps it is characteristic of man that he uses his own behavior to ask questions. If this is true then might it not be better for psychologists to make use of this deeply human method of inquiry, rather than to suppress it by trying merely to predict and control behavior? Should not psychologists concern themselves with behavior as man's instrument for solving problems rather than as a problem in itself?

So what about a person who is psychologically disturbed? Shall we try to "correct" his behavior? Is not correcting the behavior of a neurotic person a good deal like telling him what questions to ask, the way ecclesiastics set up a catechism and force children to ask questions that would never otherwise occur to them—except that the questions in the catechism are not really questions at all?

So what if a person does think he is neurotic—or even *is* neurotic—does he have to act that way or continue to live that way? This may not itself be a well-posed question but it was with some such proposition as this in our minds that my students and I undertook a radical approach to psychotherapy. Radical, but perhaps not altogether new!

Having observed that man often makes something of himself by undertaking a commitment—even a commitment without full conviction—and having observed that many of us refuse to budge from our neurotic positions without first stretching out a safety net of rationalizations—and hence never succeed in making anything of ourselves at all—it occurred to us that the key to therapy might be in getting the client to get on with a new way of life without waiting to acquire "insight." After all, is that not the way man has been treating himself for thousands of years? Rarely does one know *where* he is going when he launches out into a new way of life, and even less often does he know what is wrong with the pathway he abandons. It is only in a semantically rationalized and elaborately psychologized society that one insists on knowing all the *whys* before seeking to experience the *whats*.

So we set about asking some of our clients to write self characterizations. Then a group of three or four of us would examine this information and write another sketch as it might have been written by another person. Embodied in this second sketch of ours would be a different outlook and some illustrations of how such an outlook led to characteristic social behavior. The therapist would then take this sketch back to the client to pay particular attention to the results of the experiment. We found it important to make clear to the client that the new sketch did not represent a solution for his difficulties but only a new way of inquiring into problems of interpersonal relations.

There was, of course, a good deal more to it than play-acting. We soon realized that there were tricks to writing the new role, ways of setting up real-life situations, and particularly a framework for presenting the undertaking to a skeptical and reluctant client who would ordinarily prefer to talk about himself.

This is not the place to go into details as to how this fixed-role therapy, as we have come to call it, was carried out. Let me say only that it produced some exciting results. It produced those results when the client realized that he could use his own behavior as an instrument of inquiry, and it tended to fail as a device when the client saw it as a prescription for living his life. It worked when behavior was seen as a question, and it tended to fail when the behavior it suggested was seen as a proposed answer.

It is commonly said that the clinician at his best is an artist and not a scientist, and that the scientist at his best is a man of cold intellect without passion or empathy. Sometimes it is conceded that the clinician might be regarded as an "applied" scientist, that is to say, a technician who takes what the true scientist has discovered and exploits it for the benefit of fellow man. And most psychologists believe that the scientist and the clinician are really two quite different kinds of persons.

Perhaps I have described enough of my experiences to make it clear that this distinction between the clinician and the scientist runs counter to what I have observed. Whatever progress I may have made in shaking loose from the old notions and in developing novel hypotheses out of intimate experience with man in distress was indeed progress in science as well. And, as I hope to make it clear, what I did as a clinician emerged out of my thinking more or less in the manner of a scientist. Indeed I suspect that the best scientist is one who approaches his subject intimately as a clinician may be expected to approach it, and the best clinician is one who invites his client to join him as a scientist of sorts in a controlled investigation of life. Nowhere, it seems to me, is this intrinsic relationship more basic than in psychology, and no discipline stands to lose more by failing to recognize it.

One of my tasks in the 1930s was to direct graduate studies leading to the Master's degree. A typical afternoon might find me talking to a graduate student at one o'clock, doing all those familiar things that thesis directors have to do—encouraging the student to pinpoint the issues, to observe, to become intimate with the problem, to form hypotheses either inductively or deductively, to make some preliminary test runs, to relate his data to his predictions, to control his experiments so that he will know what led to what, to generalize cautiously, and to revise his hypotheses in the light of experience.

At two o'clock I might have an appointment with a client. During that interview I would not intentionally be taking the role of the scientist, but, rather, helping the distressed person work out some solutions to his life's problems. So what would I do? Why I would try to get him to pinpoint the issues, to observe, to become intimate with the problem, to form hypotheses, to make test runs, to relate outcomes to anticipations, to control his adventures so that he will know what led to what, to generalize cautiously, and to revise his dogma in the light of experience.

At three o'clock I would see a student again. Likely as not he was either dragging his feet hoping to design some world-shaking experiment before looking at his first subject to see first-hand what he was dealing with, or plunging into some massive and ill-considered data-chasing expedition. So I would again try to get him to pinpoint the issues, to observe open-mindedly, to become intimate with the problem, to form hypotheses—all the things I had had to do at one o'clock.

At four o'clock another client! Guess what! He would be dragging his feet, hoping to design a completely new personality before venturing his first change in behavior, or plunging into some ill-considered acting-out escapade, etc. etc. But this of course was not my hour for science; it was my hour for psychotherapy. And what I had done with that student back in the hour before; that "obviously" was not psychotherapy; it was science!

I must say that this sort of thing went on for a long time before it ever occurred to me that I was really doing the same sort of thing all afternoon long. It seems incredible now that it took me so long to realize this, but at the time it seemed so perfectly obvious that science and psychotherapy were different, even contrasting kinds of experience. Science was objective and cold. Psychotherapy was subjective and warm. Science dealt with truth but psychotherapy dealt with humanity. But, as I have said before, all my life it has been the obvious things that have gotten me into trouble. I've even speculated that man's greatest challenge and noblest undertaking may be to transcend the obvious. And that is something I wish I knew how to do.

There was something else that was slow in dawning on me. I must tell you about that before attempting to distill something out of blunt fixed-role therapy on my afternoons with the obvious.

Almost any textbook written before 1940, and indeed most of the textbooks in elementary psychology turned out in the decades since, makes quite an issue out of psychology as being a science. Generally, psychologists have emphasized the point that science is characterized more by its method than by its accumulated body of knowledge. This being so, they argue, psychology is really pretty scientific stuff, even though it does not have many solid facts to point to. In fact, psychologists, being rather self-conscious about their methodology, may have a wee bit better claim to being scientists than a lot of physicists who spend their time making engineering hay out of a few classic experiments.

In order to make clear what they meant, the authors of these psychology textbooks would describe the essentials of scientific method, which are, as we all know, the inside story of how the scientist behaves. This fellow called the scientist pinpoints the issues, they said. He observes, he becomes intimate with the problem, he forms hypotheses inductively and deductively, he makes test runs, he relates his data to predictions, he controls his experiments so that he knows what leads to what, he generalizes cautiously, and he revises his thinking in the light of experimental outcomes. These are the operations that explain the behavior of a person who has achieved the status of a scientist. All of this is very interesting, particularly because it represents an especially coherent theory of personality, albeit one that is reserved for scientists only.

But now, as the author of our textbooks turns from his credentials to his contributions, he abandons this perceptive theory of personality and starts to tell us how ordinary human beings, which he usually prefers to call organisms rather than scientists, function. In doing so he spins an altogether different kind of personality theory, or perhaps two or three such theories. Man, the organism, he says, responds to stimuli, learns what he is taught, is propelled by his motives, is helplessly suspended in his culture, is sucked into the vacuums created by his needs, and is swept along with the tides of social change.

Now that I look back on it I cannot understand how one could have failed to be struck immediately by the contrast in personality theories espoused by the same writer; on the one hand, the one he universally uses to explain himself and, on the other, the various concoctions he uses to explain ordinary mortals. Yet few of my colleagues find this paradox amusing. They say, "But of course the scientist is different." But I must admit also that it was a long time before I, myself, became aware of this inconsistency and perhaps, if I had been more of a psychologist, it would have been even longer.

Now it seems that it might prove interesting to do one of two things; either apply to psychologists themselves the psychologies they have designed to explain the behavior of ordinary mortals, or to apply to man the psychology they have designed to explain themselves. Since there are a lot more mortals in this world than there are psychologists, for the time being at least, we might run into more possibilities if we tried the latter. If we do so, then it may be said that our model of man is that of "man-the-scientist" and our questions will revolve about the issue of whether man can be understood in this manner, both within the floodlight of history and in the dark of his closet.

Now that I look at my experiences, in my afternoons alternating between graduate students and clients and in my years of unperceptive reading of psychology textbooks, I am impressed with the fact that the scientist is a person who has learned how to use his behavior to ask questions, and the client is a person who has made the mistake of asking a psychotherapist to provide him with behavioral answers. Yet the outcome of psychotherapy is rarely very imaginative or hopeful until the client has come to realize that he too, like the scientist, can use his behavior as an instrument of inquiry.

And now something else occurs to me. Man has had his great historical moments. One such moment was in Greece—the moment we now call classical, though I suspect there was nothing classical about it when it happened. That was a moment when it seemed to man that he could use his own capacity for behavior as a means of adventure. It was not so much a moment in which he tried to decide to what patterns of behavior he must conform, but rather one in which he realized that he could use his behavior to challenge the prerogatives of the Gods.

There were other moments, as for example the moments of the renaissance, when a small city such as Florence produced a breathtaking array of geniuses. The men whose names we remember out of that exciting period are not so much men who sought legalistic rules of behavior to which they could conform, but rather used their own venturesome spirits and their own capacity for action to inquire into the world around them. Through their actions, their surroundings were enlivened and filled with hitherto unimagined potentialities.

And has it not been so throughout the history of man? His greatest moments have been the moments in which his behavior has expressed his questions, and his most dismal centuries have been those in which behavior—prescribed, circumscribed, and predetermined—has been his answer.

Two men look at a child. One sees the child's immaturity and his fumbling attempts to do what adults can do better. So he sets about to train the child to behave more as an adult would behave. He seeks, on behalf of the child, a behavioral answer.

The man who sees the child in this way will become concerned with conditioning, with learning, with behavior modification, with the question of how the child should behave, with the question of controlling behavior, and, of course, with the matter of how the child's behavior can be predicted from circumstances. This man is a psychologist, whether he is an experimental psychologist or a psychoanalyst.

But there is another way of looking at the child. This is to see a child's behavior as an incipient question. One who looks at the child in this manner will be concerned about the nature of the question and how the child may pose the question in such a way as to resolve it into better questions, and to invite more exciting outcomes.

A child "misbehaves." From a psychological point of view, what is the problem? Is it to get him to stop misbehaving? Is it to get him to behave in a nice way? Or is it to understand what question the child is asking—as if the child were a graduate student performing an experiment? And, if it is the latter, what do you do about children's behavior—give them catechisms with prescribed questions and authentic answers? Certainly that is not the way we treat graduate students. Nor is it, I suspect, the best way of dealing with children. I imagine instead, that if behavior is regarded as a question, the psychologist will become concerned with helping the child pose the question in better forms, so as to get answers which themselves imply new and better questions.

So now I come back to my first course in psychology, and the S, the arrow, and the R. That formula suggests that behavior is the answer. But in a career characterized by being wrong more often than right, I suspect that the arrow needs to be turned around. So that the behavioral response initiates the question, and the novel events we have called "stimuli" become his answers.

25

Behavior is an Experiment[1]

This afternoon I am in the embarrassing position of being reminded of a funny story, and, at the same time, realizing that I was not invited to come here to tell jokes. To make matters worse, I have already let slip the fact that I think the story is funny. If you are like most audiences I am sure you would have preferred to let the story speak for itself.

Humor, on most occasions, is intended to illustrate some minor point the speaker hopes to make. You can therefore take it or leave it. Now and then a thoughtful speaker will invite laughter out of consideration for the digestive processes that must accompany every address scheduled so soon after lunch as this one was. He may have a weak stomach himself. More often it occurs, however, and in spite of anything the speaker may intend, the story succeeds only in diverting attention from what, if anything, he means to say. Thus it can serve admirably the intentions of the audience—making the whole performance palatable for those who came mainly because they thought they ought to, as well as bearable for those conventioneers who came because their feet hurt and they wanted to sit down.

But the humor I have in mind has a certain lethal quality to it. If you should get the point of the joke there would be no way you could escape the point of the speech. Moreover, I am caught in this predicament myself; there is no way for me to make the speech and avoid the joke. The best I can do under the circumstances is to string out the story long enough to make it sound like the speech. Perhaps it won't seem so devastatingly funny that way.

Psychology Tries to Join the Science Club

There is something pathetically incongruous about a textbook in psychology—every one I can remember reading, at least. It took me nearly fifteen years to notice what it was. When I did I think I became a more empathic psychologist. I have been chuckling and wondering to myself ever since. Even the sometimes dreary rituals of our profession have become more endurable. Perhaps it is appropriate, therefore, to pass along my private formula for happy psychologizing to my colleagues, some of whom must lead incredibly dull lives, if one may judge from what they publish.

Probably what took me so long to catch on was that whenever I read a book I read it as a loyal member of the Straight Faced Society of Publishing Psychologists, rather than as a man freely observant of the human scene. I believed that psychology textbooks expounded what psychology was, rather than exhibited what psychologists were. It was a long time before it ever occurred to me that I was witnessing the curious things a person, once he had started thinking of himself as a psychologist, could be led to say.

Now there is a rather touching story behind the spectacular rise of modern psychology. Charles Darwin figures in it somewhere, though I doubt that he ever intended it to turn out the way it did. It seems that, once upon a time, psychologists became enamored of science. It was quite a passionate affair, but very one-sided. Psychologists were deeply hurt by the harsh turn of events. But instead of abandoning their suit, as any objectively minded psychologist would advise others to do, they loudly protested their continuing infatuation, taking advantage of everyone who could be made to stand still and listen. This usually turned out to be students, who, though they would rather talk to psychologists about matters of greater concern to themselves and their friends, were mostly willing to lend a sympathetic ear. Young people are notoriously tolerant in affairs of the heart.

I used to think this public display of blighted affection bordered on the ridiculous. Why didn't psychologists get on with the job of understanding man? If they did their job well the Scientific Establishment would soon enough lay claim to all they had achieved—perhaps too soon for them ever to find out what was wrong with it. Such things have happened before in the demure flirtations of scholars.

[1] Invited address, Division of School Psychologists, American Psychological Association, 1966. It was published in Bannister, D. (Ed.). (1970). *Perspectives in personal construct theory* (pp. 255–269). Academic Press. Republished by permission of Jacqueline Aldridge.

Collected Papers of the Pioneer of Constructivist Psychology: George A. Kelly, First Edition. Edited by David A. Winter and Nick Reed.

There are too many characters abroad who know a going thing when they see it, and they will seize upon the slightest shred of knowledge as justification for arrogant practices, rather than reading it as a passing notation in the draft of a scholarly composition. Not all such fellows, may I say, smoke pipes, wear white coats, or drive Cadillacs.

So I was amused. The over-serious involvement with science had culminated in rejection. Yet the psychology I found so amusing is the harlequin among the sciences. In that classic theme man is reminded that the clown he observes is himself. The audience may become contemptuous of the harlequin's pomposity, be annoyed by the effrontery into which it degenerates, and linger to laugh all the louder at his subsequent frustration. But this is never the end of the encounter, for the laughter is followed by the sense that the fool has portrayed with a depth he cannot understand, and that, in turn, by the sharp realization that the harlequin is one's own pathetic self. So it is with psychology, a discipline so entangled in its own consistencies that it moves from pomposity to pathos, and, in doing so, portrays man better than it knows.

Some Curious Things Scientists Believe

By hanging onto the notion that they were scientists, psychologists have confronted themselves with the task of spelling out just what it is the scientist does that makes it possible for them to say they are like him. The ensuing descriptions of the processes of science may prove to be the only thing of great human significance psychologists have so far attempted. Yet this may be just what we are looking for. Perhaps to the extent and depth we can understand science we can begin to understand human behavior, for science is one of man's most revealing activities.

Surely we cannot hope to grasp the potentialities of man without paying some attention to the most adventuresome things he does. Specifically, this suggests to me that unless mankind is seen in the terms we psychologists—who are no more than men ourselves—use to understand our own initiative, what we shall do will remain forever alien to the human enterprise.

But not many psychologists, I am afraid, are prepared to agree with me just yet. Most of us may be like the lonely lover who tosses about in his sleep dreaming of a lady-love far away who will have nothing to do with him. At dawn he rolls over and finds she is—finds she is just *leaving*. But now I am ahead of myself. Psychologists haven't rolled over yet.

If this concern with the process of science is as important as I think it is, it will be worth our while to have a look into how psychologists deal with it.

Textbook authors usually make their pitch for science in the introductory chapter. They start the discourse with a gratuitous concession to logic, which, like most scientific concessions to logic, turns out to be premature. Science, they say, knows from the outset that nature is organized, except, possibly, human nature; *that* sometimes is easier seen as disorganized, as in schizophrenia. (But this is an exception not likely to be mentioned in the first chapter, where everything is made to appear as rational as possible.)

Knowing all this, though I am not quite clear as to how they know it or why it should be necessary to make a point of it, psychologists go on to argue that the job of science is to test the truth of everything man believes. The idea seems to be that in a deterministic world everything has to be nailed down. The possibility that there may be more appropriate grounds for exercising scientific curiosity is not likely to be mentioned.

Nevertheless, as in the case of "organized nature," there is one convenient exception to this consuming eagerness to test everything. That is in the case of determinism itself. There is no testing that, unless you take as a test of it the fact that scientists disregard it outright when making up their minds about what they themselves want to do. But then I suppose if initiative should ever cease to be a special prerogative reserved for scientists, and should be rashly conceded to human nature in general, the whole present structure of psychology would collapse. As long as there is no test of determinism it should be possible to stave off such a proletarian disaster.

Exceptions, exceptions! But perhaps it is just as well. Otherwise, the ultimate truth of the universe might snap shut on us and there would be no place to go—except, possibly, to heaven, where I understand one might be indulged with some latitude in amusing himself, in a more or less predetermined sort of way, and as long as he was careful not to turn up anything unscheduled or unexpected. That is probably the reason the place is reserved exclusively for dead people. Live ones might not fit into such an orderly scheme of things, no matter how scientifically enlightened the management might be.

The Psychology of Man-the-Scientist

But when the psychologist stops making dogmatic claims in the name of science, and starts describing how scientists behave, the reading perks up. The scientist, he says, plays guessing games. These little affairs start with hypotheses and one plays by wagering as little as possible of his own time, and as much as possible of the Government's money, on what will happen when they are put into operation. Some hypotheses are supposed to be worth more than others. There are those who think that when they bet on them they should use only the special blue chips provided by the National Science Foundation.

The hypotheses, the writer continues, are sometimes deduced from theory, which is supposed to be the most elegant way to come by them, or they are induced from years of observation—all right for Darwin, but too tedious if you want to get ahead in these more competitive times—or, in some cases, one goes after them with a dragnet, commonly known as "collecting items". There is some difference of opinion as to whether the object of the game is to confirm hypotheses or disconfirm them. Most graduate students I have talked to seem to be of the opinion that it is better to confirm them. For my own part I am inclined to think it depends mostly on what people may run out into the street and start doing when they read about it in the paper, or what kind of research the scientist will try next.

The nice thing about hypotheses is that you don't have to believe them. This, I think, is a key to the genius of the scientific method. It permits you to be inconsistent with what you know long enough to see what will happen. Children do that. What is so wonderful about the language of hypothesis is its refreshing ability to free the scientist from the entangling consistencies of adulthood. For a few precious moments he can think again like a child, and, like a child, learn from his experience rather than adhere stubbornly to his professional identity. But now I'm getting ahead of myself again.

The chapter goes on to tell about how experiments are designed, controls are instituted, comparable observations are made, and anticipations are pitted against the outcomes. Hypotheses stand or fall—though I have noted privately over the years that mostly they sort of lean, at about the .08 level of confidence. When the experiment is over the scientist picks up the pieces and reflects on the whole undertaking, wondering if his sample was unrepresentative, his hypotheses improperly drawn, his controls ineffectual, or if there might be something at fault with the theoretical foundation on which the enterprise was based. You want to know about the scientist? This is the inconclusive story of his life. It is also the continuing story of man.

Psychology's Hidden Personality Theory

Now, as I have suggested before, the trouble with most of this is that we take it, as I once did, as no more than a faithful description of something quite external to man—called science—rather than as a perceptive account of a man who thinks he is a scientist. But is it not a most illuminating way to see the striving of all mankind in the perspective of human accomplishments and disillusionments?

In this over-view man can be seen moving through the centuries, as well as through the seasons of his own life. He does not endlessly repeat himself, waiting for some unusual concatenation of stimuli to point his nose in a new direction. He is not driven by the forces he inherits, nor is he helplessly buffeted by his circumstances. Instead, he repeats what seems promising, he mobilizes the forces at his command, and he recognizes his circumstances as his best resources. Like a growing child, he finds the meaning of his behavior, not in the inculcated habits that restrain its impulses, but in what his imagination can do with it.

What a personality theory! It is such a marvelously enlightening way of looking at man that I suppose one should not be surprised that psychologists should try to reserve it exclusively for explaining themselves. And that is precisely what they do.

When the writers get around to explaining the behavior of ordinary men—usually in the last chapters of the book—you should see what they say. What man does is a response to stimuli to which he was plugged in when he wasn't looking. He is lashed into slavish endeavors by his motives, sucked into vacuums created by his needs, betrayed by his upbringing, addicted to his reinforcements, and, when he gives up looking for any sense in all this, he yields to self-destruction. And no wonder!

When one stumbles into this kind of reading he can be sure he has reached the section on "personality theories." The creatures described are not philosophers. They are not physicists. They are not even psychologists. Yet the persons you and I know—children and adults—are all of these. The would-be scientist who wrote the book is having his nightmares, unaware of what has been lying softly beside him from the moment he finished the first chapter.

The Function of a Theory

If one is to use the paradigm of the scientist as the basis of a personality theory, it is important to be clear about what a theory is. To begin with, we shall have to rule out two common notions. It is not a collection of information, regardless of how carefully cataloged it may be. Nor is it an account of a sequence of events, no matter how well authenticated.

In essence a theory is simply a way of highlighting events so they may be viewed in some kind of perspective. And yet, regardless of how well events are illuminated, it is quite unreasonable to hope they ever can be so completely revealed there will be nothing left to look for. The best one can ever expect of a theory is that it will enable him to see what he has never seen before, and that it will be succeeded in time by another theory which will disclose some of what still remains hidden.

Starting, then, with the psychology textbook writer's account of the behavior of the scientist and regarding it in a more general way as a theory of the behavior of all men, we can proceed to the next step. If we do, it will be interesting to note that we shall not retreat into the mentalism which some of our humanistic colleagues see as the only alternative to behaviorism. Behavior will remain one of the most important concerns of psychology. But its role in the life of man will be seen as vastly different from that envisioned by either psychoanalysis or classic behaviorism.

Behavior Is Always a Means; It Rarely Remains an End

Instead of being a problem of threatening proportions, requiring the utmost explanation and control to keep man out of trouble, behavior presents itself as man's principal instrument of inquiry. Without it his questions are academic and he gets nowhere. When it is prescribed for him he runs around in dogmatic circles. But when he uses it boldly to ask questions, a flood of unexpected answers rises to tax his utmost capacity to understand.

It is true that in most of psychology's inquiries some patently desirable behavior is sought as an answer to the question posed. But the quest always proves to be elusive. In the restless and wonderful world of humanistic endeavor, behavior, however it may once have been intended as the embodiment of a conclusive answer, inevitably transforms itself into a further question—a question so compellingly posed by its enactment that, willy nilly, the actor finds that he has launched another experiment. Behavior is indeed a question posed in such a way as to commit man to the role and obligations of an experimenter.

In pursuing the theoretical venture I have proposed we shall not so much be asking *what makes* people behave the way they do, nor *how to get* them all to behave in the way that threatens no one, but we shall ask, instead, how can *behavior be employed* to seek the answers that stir human curiosity. And when we see behavior that distresses us we will spend less time wondering what conditioned it and ask, instead, what is the experiment that is being performed, what hypotheses are being tested, how the outcomes are to be assessed, and whether it opens or closes the door to any man's further adventure.

From the vantage point offered by this kind of theorizing behavior is not to be regarded as the terminal goal of the psychologist's effort. His objective is not to get man to display himself in all the enlightened ways of which he is capable, or even to exhibit the healthiest living habits prescribed by licensed psychiatry. How man is to act will rather be determined by the nature of his vital inquiries. What may represent actions of great self fulfillment today will properly be considered senseless repetitions when it comes time to ask tomorrow's questions. No scientist performs the same experiment over and over just because it gives him a warm feeling inside. If he does perform the same experiment over and over, as I have noted some of them do, I shall suspect he is still looking for the answer to a question he knows no better way of asking.

A School for Experimental Behavior

Let us now try looking at some behavior in this theoretical perspective and see what comes to light. For the past two years Mrs. Penelope Upton, a trained teacher and herself the mother of five, has been operating the Banbury Cross Nursery School along lines suggested by personal construct theory—a theory which embodies the point of view I have been outlining. The effort is frankly experimental, which will come as no surprise after what I have just said. It would have to be, if it were human, though one would not need to be as frank in admitting it as Mrs. Upton is. Being honest with herself about what she is doing she makes a running analysis of what goes on, and this, in turn, has produced a continuing series of methodological transitions. In other words, she uses her own behavior to ask questions, just as the theory would suggest, and she examines her children's behavior to see what questions they may be asking and how their questions may be better posed.

The primary object of a good school is not to control behavior, or even to "give" the child experience—two goals frequently cited by educators. In a society convinced that freedom is more than a happy personal convenience, that it also enables men to make the most of their capacity to help each other, a school cannot allow itself to become an instrument for keeping the underprivileged in line by squelching their impulses. Moreover, the school cannot permit itself to take the position that experience, instead of being a prerogative of all human life, is to be doled out in calculated amounts by the educational establishment. Yet none of this is to say that limits on behavior are to be abandoned or that experience cannot proceed in an orderly fashion.

In Mrs. Upton's words, "The *primary* object of the school is to give each child the opportunity to discover through his own ventures who he is—and what he might become." In such a setting one becomes aware that the limits are as often imposed by the child as by the teacher. It is her observation that "the most stringent boundaries seem to be self-imposed." But regardless of who imposes them, they serve as guard rails permitting freer experimentation within presumed limits of safety. Occasionally one finds the limits have been set altogether too far out and a child shrinks back from exploration. Sometimes they are set too close in and he explores coherently only within infantile orbits. When he must function outside the limits his behaviorally posed questions are observed to be frantic and his experiments inconclusive.

As for *experience* in such a school, it is recognized, first of all, that it must be the outcome of the child's own experimental efforts carried through to some point of conclusion; it is not the direct consequence of his being bombarded at an early age with pedagogical demands, as seems to be envisioned by Project Head Start. The teacher's role is to help, as best she can, to design and implement each child's own undertakings, as well as to assist in interpreting the outcomes and in devising more cogent behavioral inquiries. But usually she has to begin, as any apprentice begins, by implementing what others have designed; in this case, what her children have initiated.

To be a fully accredited participant in the experimental enterprise she must gain some sense of what is being seen through the child's eyes. That is to say, she must do what personal construct theory technically terms, "enact a role". Otherwise the experiment performed will be hers and not the child's, and the hypotheses apparently confirmed or disconfirmed will bear solely on her own venture, while those versions enacted by the child, and confirmed or disconfirmed by his experience, will be secret ones to which she remains oblivious. Children do not learn from events just because they happen, but from contrived adventures in coping with them.

What Happened at Banbury Cross

Instead of teaching the children "how to play games," Mrs. Upton seeks to play a contributory part in the games children play. The following excerpts are taken from her notes. They describe three incidents in the life of Larry, a boy who has difficulty modulating his behavior outside the safety of the boundaries he has imposed on himself. She starts by making observations of how two other children have transcended boundaries. She writes,

"Debby, in the mother role, tells me *not* to go up Centre Street. When I ask her what her own mother might do if she—Debby—were *a little girl* and ran up the street, she replied, 'She would turn *the girl* into soup.' Ann's father also reported to me that Ann, after having been spanked by him for taking Polly's toys, started waving her hands over the baby and said, 'I'm Polly's fairy godmother. I'm turning she into a cow'."

To be sure, the boundaries explored by these two children were not altogether self-imposed. The one Debby transcended was defined by taking her mother's role while Ann used her ingenuity to examine the far side of one her father had tried to impose by spanking her. Nevertheless, from these child-inventions Mrs. Upton develops a notion of how Larry may experiment more conclusively outside his present enclosure. Her notes go on to say,

"These two exchanges suggested to me that some children transcend a boundary, or contemplate the results of such a transcendence, by employing fantasy to explore what lies beyond. It occurred to me, therefore, that this device might provide me with an approach to Larry, whose locus of control seems to be largely internal and whose boundaries stand in the way of reciprocal relations with other children. So I arbitrarily cast him into a fantasy role through which I hoped he might be able to make some kind of effective contact with his peers.

"The first day I attempted this approach, I tried to contact him the same way I thought he might initially choose to contact another person—either child or adult. This is to say, I entered what I thought might be *his* game, rather than suggesting that he enter *mine*. I did this by 'driving a truck up behind his and crashing into it.'

"'Hi, Joe,' I said.

"Larry looked startled, then laughed and said, 'Didn't you see the red light?'

"It was interesting to note that thereupon, in the role of 'Joe,' he did have some success interacting with his peers. Debby spontaneously joined the game and entered into the spirit by helping 'Joe' load lumber onto his truck. When the lumber had been hauled to its destination, Ben joined in and helped Larry unload the lumber and construct a house. The participation of both children was accepted collaboratively by the fictional 'Joe' without the friction characteristic of Larry when he is forced to contact children outside the perimeter of his own entrenchments.

"Later, at clean-up time, 'Joe,' at my request, put the lumber back on the truck and put it away. This is not what Larry would ordinarily have done."

Mrs. Upton's notes then tell us more about Larry. "Larry," she says, "has a particularly difficult time entering into activities in the circle." By "the circle," she means a group activity in which children sit in a ring facing each other and take part in some kind of community activity, such as singing or story-telling. She comments, "He is wild, imaginative, and appears to be totally absorbed in a private game." She goes on to say,

"In a father role the following day, Larry again had difficulty making contact with his peers. He insisted upon throwing every single tiny piece of equipment into the toy sink. Sally, who was playing a mother role, was furious and kept putting things away. Finally, after Larry had thrown everything into the sink for the third time, Sally left the game.

"Larry then climbed up on a tall divider, transgressing a teacher-imposed boundary. There, at my suggestion, he 'repaired the roof' and then climbed down. I had hoped to give him a reason for being up there and a way of getting down without losing face. He seemed quite willing to go along with my suggestion, but the game he and Sally had been playing had ended abruptly and apparently inconclusively."

Two months later Mrs. Upton comments,

"Larry and I had a conversation about hunting during which I mentioned that pygmies used darts dipped in poison for hunting and for defense. This intrigued Larry. Half an hour later he approached me with a stick and jabbed it into my leg.

"'There, Don, she's dead.'

"I slumped over, playing my part in the game.

"Larry became very excited and shouted, 'Let's bury her, Don!' As he tried to pick me up I collapsed on the floor and Larry started shoveling imaginary sand on top of me. Sally came into the room and, finding me 'dead' threw her arms around my neck and started to cry. I reassured her, and then noticed Larry curled up on the floor behind me.

"'I wonder what you are doing?'

"'I'm just lying here feeling sorry for you, Mrs. Upton'."

Mrs. Upton concludes,

> "In this experiment, Larry, having had the opportunity to act the whole scene out, was able to experience feelings bound naturally to the consequences of his actions, as well as those immediately identified with the actions themselves. Had he not *carried it through* we may have seen the same experimental fragment—jabbing with a dart—repeated over and over."

Analysis of a Four-year-old's Experiment

In these briefly recounted anecdotes we see first the teacher's sensitivity to the nature of human inquiry. She notes the limits Larry maintains, outside of which he finds himself confused by unspecified variables and his behavior unmodulated. So also the accredited scientist sets limits, which he calls "experimental controls", in order to avoid becoming lost in a multivariant universe. She sees, furthermore, that Larry, as many another scientist, is both hemmed in by the boundaries he has defined and is rendered ineffectual outside them. This is science in the flesh—the personal methodology of man. If this truly natural science is to be understood in depth it must be examined psychologically, not merely formalistically.

So the teacher goes on to help design an experiment—a human one. In this case the methodology she employed for transcending Larry's constrictive controls was ingeniously derived from the observation of two children, Debby and Ann, who, being incipient scientists too, had something to offer a puzzled teacher. She calls the methodology simply "fantasy," and she hopes it will help Larry get on with his experimental project. Via the imaginary "Joe" she reaches behind what the logic of science formally calls "hypothesis" and picks up the basic human process by which all hypotheses are derived.

Larry then, in posing his question behaviorally and in the terms of this basic form of hypothesis, finds out what other scientists who employ the language of hypothesis also learn. He finds that as "Joe" he can produce outcomes not attainable by the "Larry" in terms of whom he ordinarily approaches his world.

In the next episode we find Larry posing a question in a familiar way, again behaviorally, and having to face up to what appears to be an inconclusive outcome, or at least one that must be contemplated from the height of the room divider. We do not know what hypothesis is being tested—probably not another "Joe," but possibly an aspect of what he assumes to be "Larry," The experiment takes an abrupt turn when Sally, presumably his principal subject, walks out on him. The teacher then attempts to salvage something from the project by having him "repair the roof" up there. Then, like the reluctant gods, who, as their human experiments go awry, must eventually descend from their lofty contemplations atop Mount Olympus, he comes down.

In the last episode, two months later, Larry is engaged in a much more penetrating inquiry, and we are given a glimpse of the resolving effect of a completed experiment. Designed by himself, and carried, with the teacher's co-operation, through its full natural cycle, the experiment reaches the point of being a significant experience when Larry, finally prostrate on the floor beside his "victim," says, "I'm just lying here feeling sorry for you, Mrs. Upton." How much more psychologically significant this was than to have offered a guilty apology for what he had done. I cannot refrain from mentioning a parenthetical comment I found in Mrs. Upton's notes for this day. She says, "There is so much that goes on in the course of the morning that never is noted it distresses me."

Pete Smith: Panacea or Experiment?

Let me turn quickly now to two more illustrations of the way in which human behavior can be regarded as experimental—"fixed role therapy" and "behavior therapy". The first suggests how a person may use his behavior to pose hypotheses about a different kind of self, and, by being alert to the outcomes, attain a better vantage point from which to launch the sequence of further experimental ventures we call "life." The second suggests how much more lucidly a procedure, in which *a subject* is usually envisioned as being "treated," may be understood if the person is regarded instead as *an experimenter,* and his behavior changes as an orderly progression of hypotheses.

About twenty-five years ago A. J. Robinson (1941) and Ethel Harkness Edwards (1943) collaborated with me in developing a form of psychotherapy that has come to be called "fixed role therapy." It makes no use of psychodynamic or motivational concepts, or of "insight" into one's customary behavior, or of past influences in a person's life, or of learning by reward or contiguity, or of calculated verbal reinforcements, or of affective support, or of environmental control. In fact it discards about everything either the hard scientists or the soft scientists claim is essential—everything, that is, except that outcropping of intrinsically human methodology we call "science." The particular method consists in the design and execution of an experiment. And it is carried by the client through a full experimental cycle to a point of conclusion, one where it may become a significant personal experience in his life.

The client—call him John Jones—is shown a tailor-made self-characterization sketch "written" by a fictional person called, say, Pete Smith. If, on reading the sketch with the therapist, Pete seems like a genuine person and one whom he would like to know, John is asked to imagine that he himself is going to the mountains for a two-week holiday, and in his place there materializes Pete, whose part the client is to enact as faithfully as he can, twenty-four hours a day. He is to think of himself as Pete, talk like Pete, treat others as Pete would, execute Pete's daily habit pattern, entertain himself as Pete might, and, if he can, even dream as Pete would dream.

In frequent sessions during the enactment the therapist rehearses the part with the client, paying particular attention to situations involving the client's peers, his supervisors, his spouse or girl friends, his parents, and his religious outlook. At the end of the period the therapist insists that John Jones come back and take over. After John has returned, and done what he can to pick up the pieces, the client is free to make what he wants out of his experience, and to go ahead and start making something out of his life.

Of course there is much more to it than this. Before the enactment is proposed John has written his own self-characterization, and there are serious pitfalls that experience has shown can be avoided when this step is taken. The Pete Smith characterization, that binds together the clustered hypotheses of the experiment, must not omit certain features, notably a clear axis of contrast between Pete and John, and *role constructs*—as that notion is precisely defined in personal construct theory. It is important that the enactment not break down into a conglomeration of impulsive bits of self-expression whose outcomes can have no apparent bearing on any clearly perceived component of the undertaking. Without the theme of Pete Smith the experiment becomes incoherent.

Finally, it needs to be clear that the part of Pete Smith is not a doctor's prescription for the improvement of John's mental health. Pete may turn out to have more faults than John. Nor can any evaluation of John be inferred from the proposal itself. Besides, the therapist, his fee structure notwithstanding, is only an inquiring scientist himself, and not a prophet. He is in no position to know precisely what is best for his erstwhile research colleague, and he had better be frank about it. Both of them must wait for the data to come in.

The central purpose of the enactment—which both therapist and client must keep in constant focus—is to see what ensues when the hypothesis of Pete Smith is put to thc world—and to one's self—in the terms of a behavioral commitment. No matter that Pete Smith is not the client's presumed self; a hypothesis is always a venturesome departure from the dogmatic world of certainty. And that indeed is its genius, a genius practiced spontaneously by children and self-consciously by scientists.

Since what is proposed is never intended to be a panacea for the vacationing John Jones, who was too grown up to imagine being anything but himself, outcomes can scarcely be judged as patent successes or failures. But how much more exciting it is anyway to be confronted with some of the amazing things that may happen in a world that is differently approached. When it is all over, the returning John Jones, who just once in his life was a Pete Smith, can decide, from among the countless variations his own ingenuity might contrive, what kind of a person he wants to be, and get on with the undertaking.

Perhaps I should add parenthetically that fixed role therapy is not a method I choose to employ in all cases—perhaps only one in fifteen. There are too many other novel and exciting approaches to the world of psychotherapy. As a therapist, I, too, can be a Pete Smith instead of a John Jones. Besides, fixed role therapy is hard work. There ought to be still more facile ways to help man participate in the human enterprise.

In Behavior Therapy, Who is the Experimenter?

Now what about "behavior therapy," which is supposed to be at odds with humanistic psychology, and precisely so because it is "rigorously scientific?" To my mind the only thing wrong with the accounts of behavior therapy I have read is that they fail to mention who the principal investigator was. They call him a "subject," while the fellow with the doctoral degree, who turns out to be only the technician in the project, is given credit for doing the experiment. Sounds familiar, doesn't it? Nevertheless, the psychologists who write about this sort of thing may be about to turn over and find what is in bed with them. But they haven't done so yet.

Take, for example, the reverse snake charming experiment, which has become the popular prototype for behavior therapy. The task is for a person who shudders at the sight of snakes to come to appreciate how very charming a snake can be. The first step is to entertain the hypothesis; although, like any proper hypothesis, it may not appear to be very realistic—at least not for the person engaged in the undertaking. The next step is to make a behavioral investment, that is to say, to pose the question behaviorally. That may not be what a philosopher would do, but it is what a scientist, who always doubts uncommitted rationality, must do. So the part to be played is the part of a scientist.

But a man making up to snakes may find himself floundering about in a multivariant predicament. Like Larry, when he had to approach other children outside the safety of his guard rails, one may find, in the presence of too many snakes, that his behavior has lost its composed directionality. If the old boundaries of safety are to be transcended in his approach to snakes, and there is to be a conclusion to the experiment, new boundaries must be established *ad hoc*. In research language this means that each successive experiment must be "controlled" if the researcher is not to become lost in a sea of "variables." Moreover, the specific hypotheses in each sequential inquiry must be clearly defined, else the principal researcher will not be able to determine what is confirmed by what.

And there is one final ingredient in the science of being charmed by snakes. The scientist—I'm still talking about the fellow who is trying out a new slant on snakes—must be left free at the conclusion of each step to decide just what experiment is to come next. Here, as elsewhere, the outcomes of scientific endeavors are often best judged by what the scientist, after searching his own reactions to his completed undertakings, decides to do next. It is preposterous to assume that the mere overt outcomes of one experiment make the scientist's next venture a cut-and-dried affair.

Now let us notice how the Wolpe type of behavior therapy artfully contrives a procedure to enable the patient to become his own experimenter. Preliminary interviewing focuses attention on the general hypothesis that he can learn to live with snakes. It is, of course, only a hypothesis and therefore a ventured departure from the reality of the patient's world. The criteria against which accurate predictions will be assessed are defined in terms of the state of relaxation the patient may experience. He then practices relaxation so he will recognize it when he sees it.

Next the patient's fear is calibrated and a useful scale of aversion is constructed out of a graduated series of pictures of snakes, or actual distances measured from the snake itself. Experimental controls are established as *ad hoc* boundaries which can be successively moved out as the patient becomes bolder. Fantasy, or make-believe, is employed as the patient imagines his approach to the snake before he actually attempts it. This, as in the case of Larry, constitutes the formulation of intermediate hypotheses in terms of which his experimental behavior is to be attempted, step by step.

The patient is not pushed beyond the limits established for the current phase of his inquiry. Before each successive venture he must decide where the guard rails are to be placed, and he is free to return to their protective enclosure whenever he is threatened with incoherence. He does not surrender his initiative to another investigator. He observes carefully what happens—how frightened he is, or, rather, how relaxed he is, relaxation being operationally a better defined criterion for him than fright—and he notes how differently the snake appears as he approaches it. Finally, it is the patient, now a scientist planning his own actions, who decides what the next step in the experimental series will be. In this kind of therapy, behavior is so clearly an experiment.

Behavior is the Method of Man-the-Scientist

In conclusion let me suggest only that when psychology, that harlequin who turns out to be ourselves, rolls over it may realize that, while intellectualization is the method of man the incipient philosopher, behavior is the method of man the scientist. The philosopher asks questions by disengaging from facts; the scientist inquires by confronting himself with events of his own creation. This is true, whether the scientist is a psychologist, a Larry, a John Jones, or Adam's impressionable girl friend who thinks "snakes really have *a lot* to offer."

References

Edwards, E.D. (1943). *Observation of use and efficiency of changing a patient's concept of his role: A psychotherapeutic device.* Unpublished MA thesis, Fort Hays Kansas State College.
Kelly, G.A. (1955). *The psychology of personal constructs.* Vols 1 and 2, Norton.
Kelly, G.A. (1964). The language of hypothesis. *Journal of Individual Psychology*, *20*, 137–152.
Kelly, G.A. (1965). The strategy of psychological research. *Bulletin of the British Psychological Society*, *18*, 1–15.
Kelly, G.A. (1966). Sin and psychotherapy. In O.H. Mowrer (Ed.), *Religion and mental health* (pp. 365–381). Rand McNally.
Kelly, G.A. (1967). A psychology of the optimal man. In A.W. Mahrer (Ed.), *Goals of psychotherapy* (pp. 238–258), Appleton-Century-Crofts.
Krasner, L. and Ullmann, L.P. (1965). *Research in behavior modification: New developments and implications.* Holt, Rinehart & Winston.
Lazarus, A.A. (1964). Crucial procedural factors in desensitization therapy. *Behaviour Research and Therapy*, *2*, 65–70.
Robinson, A.J. (1941). *A further validation of role therapy.* Unpublished MA thesis, Fort Hays Kansas State College.
Wolpe, J. (1958). *Psychotherapy by reciprocal inhibition.* Stanford University Press.

26

ONTA[1]

1.

(Parmenides) Is so!

The men who grasp and clutch at objects say,
"Now look; this is reality.
It's firm. It's bold and clear.
So straight would be tomorrow's flimsy way
If you would only deign to see
Just that that's here, that's here."

To this what shall I say?

One cannot but agree.

I too am surely here.

2.

(Alexander) But why for man?

The men who talk and talk in order to be wise
Yap loud and long at shadows in our night
And snarl at strangers constantly.
Alone, they strive their dreams to guard with peering eyes
Till dawn, or death—or both—shall prove them right
And what is not at last shall be.

But who utters truth until he tries?

To save their dreams all men must fight.

My world shall take its shape from me!

[1] Dated between 1929 and 1945. Included in Fransella, F. (1995). *George Kelly* (pp. 46–48). London: Sage Publications. Published by permission of Jacqueline Aldridge.

Collected Papers of the Pioneer of Constructivist Psychology: George A. Kelly, First Edition. Edited by David A. Winter and Nick Reed.

3.

(Paul) Man lives. Man dies. What then?

The men who climb the distant heights to gain some crystal tower,
From thence to visualize the space beyond their time.
Chart past and future as one coursing stream,
Find themselves, borne in its flow, transcending troubled hours.
So thus, in lives with greater destinies aligned,
Self's immortality is seen.

And I? Why dare not I attune to greater power?

Indeed, all's lost, astray from its majestic line.

I'll dangle neither truth nor gods upon a string!

4.

(Xenos) Once this I knew and had forgot

The men who lived to live, whose names are lost among discarded years,
No pedant questions posed. Their words stood not for things apart
But only served to draw them close to what was theirs.
Self was for them a woman's voice, a tiny hand, a storm, a tear,
A sorrow etched in love. They left no legacy of art,
Yet overhead we hear their children climbing up the stairs.

To whom but them has what is real approached so near?

This is no alien world; its keys are in my heart.

I touch, I try, I scan, I feel, and stumble up my stairs.

Section III

Research, Measurement, and Experimental Psychology

Some common factors in reading and speech disabilities presents findings from Kelly's PhD thesis. Findings relevant to the understanding of reading disability are also presented in *Some observations on the relation of cerebral dominance to the perception of symbols* and *Some observations on the relation of the principle of psychological polarity and symmetry and the doctrine of cerebral dominance to the perception of symbols*. Kelly also draws upon the difficulties in establishing a relationship between intelligence and reading ability, as well as, interestingly, in making decisions in the area of warfare, in *The assumption of an originally homogeneous universe and some of its statistical implications* in support of his thesis that the universe is an "indefinite, incoherent homogeneity" and that "all variables are emergent."

A projective method of personality investigation is the abstract for a presentation of a diagnostic personality inventory based on individuals' identification with characters in stories. This work was co-authored with one of Kelly's students, as was *Clinical validity and conceptual consistency*, another paper that illustrates Kelly's interest in projective techniques during this period. The latter paper presents research in which predictions of Rorschach test scores were made from non-Rorschach behaviors, employing a novel approach in which both the test scores and the predictors were conceptualized in terms of Rorschach personality dimensions, rather than in terms alien to this framework. It can, therefore, be regarded as an illustration of Kelly's "credulous approach"—in this instance, applied to the construct system of the Rorschach user.

The reader may be tempted to skip *The theory and technique of assessment*, a review of the literature on psychological assessment; however, it is noteworthy in that Kelly successfully synthesizes, with considerable humor, what one might consider the dry content of over 300 publications. The paper includes a statement of his "first principle" that "If you don't know what is going on in a person's mind, ask him; he may tell you," as well as such gems as the following: "When the subject is asked to guess what the examiner is thinking, we call it an objective test; when the examiner tries to guess what the subject is thinking, we call it a projective device. Most intelligence tests belong to the former group, which probably accounts for the fact that intelligence testing has made very little contribution to our understanding of the psychological processes of anyone except psychologists."

Other chapters present Kelly's own approaches to psychological assessment. *Instructions: Role Construct Repertory Test (Rep Test) and Situational Resources Test (Res Test)* is a brief practical guide to the administration of these two techniques. In *A mathematical approach to psychology*, Kelly introduces his audience in Moscow to the notion of a matrix consisting of construct and element axes, illustrating the findings that may be obtained from such a matrix. *The abstraction of human processes* is essentially a presentation of the repertory grid technique to an audience of personality researchers. In *Nonparametric factor analysis of personality theories*, Kelly illustrates the advantages of a nonparametric approach by applying it to Q-sorts regarding a suicidal client completed by himself and five other leading clinicians in Farberow and Shneidman's project on suicide, to which he contributed (see Chapter 68 in this volume).

In *The strategy of psychological research*, Kelly argues against an approach to research based on logical positivism and instead advocates for a logic of questions rather than one of answers. The strategy promoted is one based upon constructive alternativism rather than accumulative fragmentalism, and it encompasses a creativity cycle that alternates between loosening and tightening. *Humanistic methodology in psychological research* cautions against the "danger that humanistic psychology, in looking back over its shoulder, may, as behaviorism did, lose track of where it is going." It argues against the abandonment of technology by psychologists because "humanistic psychology needs a technology through which to express its humane intentions."

Collected Papers of the Pioneer of Constructivist Psychology: George A. Kelly, First Edition. Edited by David A. Winter and Nick Reed.

27

Some Common Factors in Reading and Speech Disabilities[1]

Historical

The deep-seated and diffuse nature of the stutterer's defect has been emphasized by Travis (1931). He has discovered numerous motor disturbances which accompany the activities of the stutterer but which are apparently unrelated to his speech. The explanation offered is that in the stutterer there is a tendency toward decentralized neural control resulting primarily from a lack of inherent bias for cerebral dominance or from lesions which reduce the ascendency of the higher motor centers. The result of this decentralized control is dysintegration of the nervous system, manifest in the case of stuttering in speech. The present study is an investigation of this and other factors which may be common to reading and speech disabilities.

Travis (1927) and Fossler (1930) have shown that the breathing of the stutterer during overt speech is dysintegrated from the standpoint of effectively producing normal speech. Murray (1931), following these workers, has shown that similar dysintegrations occur in the breathing of stutterers during silent reading and reasoning. He has also pointed out the tendency toward a silent reading disability among stutterers.

Orton (1925) reported that about 2 per cent of the school population have reading defects of the "word-blindness" type. He attributed this type of manifest defect to a difficulty in the building of associations between the visual and auditory spheres at the third functional level, the lowest level on which cerebral dominance plays any significant part. The natural inconsistency between visual and auditory stimuli is normally eradicated at this level, but, due to a lack of inherent bias toward cerebral dominance or to lesions, is in this type of reading defect the cause of "congenital word blindness" (*strephosymbolia*). On this associational level the memorial images of the two visual cortices are mirrored counterparts of each other; thus a lack of dominance of one cortex over the other confuses the visual memory images and prevents normal imagery.

It is generally maintained that Wernicke's (auditory speech) center is directly involved in the production of overt speech. Cases have been recorded of bilateral lesion of this area producing loss of hearing and loss of speech, the motor centers being unaffected. This is called Wernicke's sensory aphasia. Mott (1910) reports a clear-cut case of this sort. This direct connection with overt speech is not evident to the same extent in the case of the visual cortices of the occipital lobe. While lesions of the visual centers have been frequently observed they are not known to be entirely responsible for the loss of overt speech.

Bartley and Perkins (1931) in comparing action currents obtained from the different areas of the dog's brain under varying circumstances found that the activity tended to be focalized in not less than two of the following areas, auditory, visual, motor. At one time the activity might be focalized in the auditory and visual areas with comparative quiescence in the motor area; at another time the activity might be focalized in the auditory and motor areas with comparative quiescence in the visual area; at another time the activity might be focalized in the visual and motor areas with comparative quiescence in the auditory area. Never was activity focalized in one area only.

Bluemel (1913) at one time expressed the thesis that "the stammerer's difficulty is transient auditory amnesia." At that time he emphasized the contention that the stammerer was an "auditomoteur" type and his stammering was due to a loss of the memorial image of the sound which should follow that on which he stammers. More recently, however, he has expanded his conception of this transitory phenomenon. His recent thesis is that the stammerer is confronted with a discontinuity in the whole of his consciousness.

Ranschburg (1925) attributed reading defects among children to lack of development of the carotid arteries with corresponding reduction of the oxygen supply. Starr (1922) reported low vital capacity and insufficient ventilation in stutterers. He has also found a high carbon dioxide content and a low calcium concentration associated with stutterers. For certain types of stutterers (psychopathic) he has found low hydrogen ion concentrations; for others (normals) he reports extremely high hydrogen ion concentrations.

Studies of imaginal habits, mostly based upon introspection technique, have had perennial revivals since Galton (1883) made his classic study of "types." A review of the literature concerning these studies would be a dissertation in itself. One study of particular significance in the present connection is that reported by Golla and Antonovitch (1929). A box plethysmograph, said by the authors to be unusually sensitive,

[1] First published in 1932 in *Psychological Monographs, 43,* 175–201. Now in the public domain and republished by permission of Jacqueline Aldridge.

Collected Papers of the Pioneer of Constructivist Psychology: George A. Kelly, First Edition. Edited by David A. Winter and Nick Reed.

was used in connection with a smoked drum kymograph for the recording of the subjects' breathing over a long period of time. Of 67 cases whose rest breathing was recorded over a considerable period of time, 34 were classed as "regular" breathers, 33 of which were "visual" types, and one was an "auditory" type. Of the 32 "irregular" breathers 28 were "auditory" types and 4 were "visual" types (1 case rejected). When given a problem to solve which required the use of visual imagery 25 of the 30 "irregular" breathers breathed regularly and the remaining five abandoned attempts to solve the problem. The breathing of the "regular" breathers remained unchanged during the solution of the problem. Such a striking conclusion as this appears to be, if verified, would have far-reaching significance in psychology and education. In the present investigation a check was made upon this finding and, as will be shown later, showed it not to be without partial substantiation.

Most of the experimental work with breathing curves, exclusive of studies of speech production, has attempted to link respiratory rhythm with changes of attention or with emotional states. Skaggs (1930) reported shallow and more rapid breathing during silent reasoning and somewhat deeper, though rapid, breathing during emotional states. One of the first studies in the field was made in Wundt's laboratory by Zoneff and Meumann (1903) and revealed changes in respiratory rhythm with fluctuations of attention.

Probably one of the most significant investigations from the standpoint of the present study is that recently reported by Bills (1931). In studying the decrements of work curves for homogeneous serial tasks he has observed certain periodicities in production efficiency which occur in rhythmic succession at the rate of about three a minute. The periods of efficiency were separated by periods of blocking when the tasks were performed slowly and imperfectly. Furthermore, the moments of maximum efficiency tended to be separated by just half a phase-length from the movements of minimum efficiency, thus indicating a truly cyclical phenomenon.

At about the same time Knight (1931) observed periodicities in the occurrence of errors made by sixth grade children in solving multiplication problems involving several places in the multiplier. Errors occurred most frequently at the end of the problem and least frequently at the beginning. The rhythm of efficiency and inefficiency tended to adjust itself to changes in the tasks, that is, efficiency was partly restored at the beginning of each new problem. A finding of this nature is of primary importance in the field of educational method.

In 1927 Farnsworth, Seashore, and Tinker published the results of a study which showed as high a correlation as +.53 between certain serial reaction times and Army Alpha intelligence scores. The correlation was considerably lower between serial reaction times and scores made on those intelligence tests which placed less emphasis upon the speed factor. The correlation of simple reaction times with intelligence scores was insignificant. Gaskill (1928) reported a relationship between simple reaction times and the phase of breathing, the shortest reaction times occurring when the stimulus was given during the period between the phases of breathing, that is, when breathing movements were momentarily suspended.

Method

The first hypothesis taken into consideration by the present investigation was that those individuals who are defective in silent reading would exhibit dysintegrations in breathing during silent reading similar to those of the stutterers during silent reading. Accordingly six groups of *O*s were chosen from the men of the 1930–31 freshman class of the University of Iowa. They were chosen on the basis of the entrance tests given to all freshmen who enter the University and on the basis of scores on the Iowa Silent Reading Comprehension Tests which were administered to nearly all freshmen as a part of a survey made by the Department of Speech. The groups were selected in the following manner: in one group were eight *O*s whose percentile ranks in the Iowa Silent Reading Comprehension Test were not only low, but considerably lower than their percentile ranks in the General Qualifying Examination, a test highly correlated with intelligence tests. In another group were eight *O*s matched with these on the basis of percentile ranks in the General Qualifying Examination but whose percentile ranks in the reading test were approximately the same as their ranks in the General Qualifying Examination. In another group were eight *O*s matched with the *O*s in the other two groups on the basis of percentile ranks in the General Qualifying Examination but whose percentile ranks on the reading test were relatively high. Similarly, there were four (it being impossible to match one score) *O*s whose percentile ranks in the reading test were high but whose percentile ranks in the General Qualifying Examination were higher, five matched on the basis of the percentile ranks in the General Qualifying Examination but with reading ranks approximately equivalent, and five matched on the basis of the percentile ranks in the General Qualifying Examination but with reading ranks relatively high.

The *O*s were called into the laboratory singly. Each *O* was seated in a chair facing a table on which were placed the materials which he used during the experiment. His breathing was recorded by means of two Boulitte pneumographs, one placed over the thorax at the level of the armpits and the other over the diaphragm about one inch inferior to the xiphoid process. The record was made with black Skrip ink on white paper with a Renshaw polygraph. The pulse from the left carotid artery was recorded similarly by means of a very sensitive tambour. A Boulitte laryngeograph was used to record laryngeal movements simultaneously with the pulse and breathing movements. The polygraph was placed behind *O*. *E* sat at the right and slightly back of him.

The experimental series consisted of the following items, many of which are identical with those used by Murray (1931) in his study of the breathing of stutterers during silent reading.

1 A period of adjustment for *O* during which he conversed freely with *E* and became accustomed to the hum of the polygraph.
2 A five-minute period of rest-breathing during which *O* sat without moving or speaking while listening to the ticking of a Jacquet chronometer. He was instructed not to think about anything too intently and to bring his attention to the ticking if he found any other subject absorbing his interest.

3 Two minutes' silent reading of fairly difficult prose.
4 Answering in writing multiple-choice questions, visually presented, over the material he had just read.
5 Two minutes' silent reading of poetry.
6 Questions.
7 Two minutes' silent reading of light prose.
8 Questions.
9 One minute rest.
10 Solving and writing the answers to problems in mental arithmetic auditorially presented by the experimenter.
11 Visualizing the face of a clock. In this part of the experiment *O* was given a series of problems such as this: "Suppose it were twenty-three minutes past seven: what time would it be if the positions of the two hands of the clock were interchanged? Write your answer."
12 Silent reasoning. *O* was presented with a proposition such as this: "A falsehood is justifiable if to one's knowledge it will save the reputation of a friend." He was then told to make a decision as to the truth or falsity of the statement and to formulate three reasons for his answer. After *O* had indicated that his answer and reasons were ready he was asked to dictate them into an Ediphone. Five of these propositions were presented.
13 Memorizing from a visual stimulus. *O* was given a typewritten selection of an abstract nature and told that he would be given five minutes to memorize it.
14 Solving Golla's "visual imagery" problem. The exact procedure was as follows: *E* said, "Now imagine a number of blocks like the ones you used to play with when you were a child. Imagine you have built of them a cube, three blocks on a side; that is, a perfect cube, three blocks high, three blocks long and three blocks wide. Now imagine that you have painted it red all over and taken it apart. How many of the little blocks will have three sides red,—how many will have two sides red,—how many will have one side red? Lift your hand when you have the right answer The cube was three blocks on a side."
15 Memorizing from auditory stimulus. *E* repeated four times a short selection similar to the one memorized from visual stimulus.
16 Visual aphasia test. In this test the presentations were made by means of a band of white paper stretched between the drums of a small kymograph. For the length of the band a black line appeared. Alternately above and below this line appeared pairs of digits about 8 mm. high. A cardboard shield containing a window 22 mm. wide was placed around one of the kymograph drums so that when the kymograph was set in motion the pairs of digits were exposed successively. Following each pair of digits above the line appeared a pair of digits below the line, one of which had appeared in the previous pair and one of which was unlike either of the digits in the preceding pair. *O* was asked to pick out and write down the unrepeated digit in each pair of digits appearing below the line. Forty-five presentations were made at about 2 sec. intervals. A short practice period preceded the test.
17 Auditory aphasia test. In this test the presentations were made by means of an Ediphone record. Each presentation consisted of a three-place number spoken as follows: "Three hundred and twenty-nine!" *O* was asked to write the number with the positions of the first two digits interchanged, that is, in the above illustration he would write, "2 3 9". Forty presentations were made at 3 sec. intervals.

During the whole experiment, which usually consumed from an hour and a half to two hours, the polygraph was kept running and a continuous record of breathing, pulse, and laryngeal movements was made.

As criteria of breathing irregularity Murray (1931) used the coefficients of variation of the following four variables: (a) duration of expiration, (b) duration of inspiration, (c) amplitude of expiration, (d) amplitude of inspiration. This involved making four measurements of each breathing curve and if carried out in the present study would have entailed measuring with a millimeter scale some 600,000 curves. Accordingly another method was devised, although for the breathing curves during silent reading individual measurements were made and coefficients of variation computed. Durations of expiration and of inspiration during the five minutes of rest breathing were measured, the means and standard deviations computed, and the normal range of values found, assuming a normal distribution to extend three standard deviations on either side of the mean. Thus a value of each of the two variables, duration of inspiration and duration of expiration, was found, values below which would fall outside the normal probable distribution. Likewise another value was found, values above which would fall outside the normal probable distribution. Thus with rest breathing as a standard, irregularity of breathing during the different tasks of the series could quickly be observed. Three measures of breathing irregularity were used, (a) the number of inspirations whose durations fell outside the normal distribution of inspiration durations for rest breathing, divided by the time in seconds; (b) the number of expirations whose durations fell outside the normal distribution of expiration durations for rest breathing, divided by the time in seconds; (c) defining any expiration or inspiration whose duration was greater than the normal duration in rest breathing as a "block," the total duration of all blocks in seconds divided by the total time in seconds. Measure "c" might be designated as the ratio of blocking time to total time.

Data and Discussion: Breathing Irregularities of Reading Disability Cases

By none of the three criteria of breathing irregularity was any consistent relation between breathing dysintegration and reading disability found, either with or without intelligence taken into consideration. Coefficients of variation based on individual measurements of each curve also showed no consistent difference between the groups of cases. The findings with respect to the hypothesis that reading defectives would show breathing irregularities during silent reading as do stutterers were essentially negative. They were consistent, however, with the findings reported elsewhere in this study.

General Relation of Reading and Speech Defects

The next question to be answered was whether or not there was any relation between speech and reading defects. Murray (1931) reports that "stutterers appear to be approximately one grade below normal in rate of reading. The disparity is emphasized further at least one-half grade when their reading achievement is considered in relation to their true intelligence." The question remaining to be answered was whether or not the converse is true; are reading defectives defective speakers? It is to be remembered in this connection that stuttering is only a very specialized kind of speech disability while in the present connection no distinction between kinds of reading disability has been made.

Analysis of the Speech of Reading Disability Cases

In the present investigation an analysis was made of the speech of the 31 *O*s who made records under item 12 in the procedure described above. Five different criteria of speaking ability were used: (a) the number of words spoken a second under the conditions of the experiment; (b) counting each hesitation of one second or less at a place where the thought content did not require a pause as a block of one second, the ratio of hesitation or blocking time to total time of speaking; (c) the ratio of repeated vowel sounds, excluding completed words, to the total number of words spoken; (d) the ratio of repeated words to the total number of words spoken; (e) the ratio of slurred words to the total number of words spoken. Slurred words were defined as those indistinctly spoken, either because of too short a phonation time or omission of one or more syllables.

The results of this analysis are shown in Table I. It is evident from this table that there is quite a definite relation between silent reading ability and speaking ability with intelligence held constant. Especially in the rate of speaking is the relationship brought out. These averages were computed on the basis of about 200 spoken words for each individual.

Analysis of Silent Reading Scores on General Speech Disability Cases

As a further check on the coincidence of reading and speech defects an analysis was made of the data obtained by the Department of Speech at the University of Iowa in its general survey of speech abilities among the members of the 1930–1931 freshman class. During the first semester of the year each freshman was given a general effectiveness rating on his speech by a committee chosen from the staff of the Department. For the 101, approximately the lowest decile, who were indicated as being defective speakers the mean percentile rank on the Iowa Silent Reading Test was 44.8, or very nearly at the median. Since general intelligence was operative both in determining the speech rating and the reading test rank it can scarcely be maintained on the basis of this finding alone that any other factor was responsible for the slightly low reading average.

By subtracting the percentile rank of each freshman on the reading test from his percentile rank on the General Qualifying Examination a measure of the discrepancy between the two could be obtained. For these freshmen rated as speech defectives (the same

Table I Analysis of speech records in relation to silent reading and intelligence

	No. of cases	*Words per sec.*	*Block time: total time*	*Repeated vowels: total words*	*Repeated words: total words*	*Slurred words: total words*
Reading ability and intelligence both relatively *low;* groups matched in intelligence						
Reading ability relatively lower..............	7	1.66	.46	.23	.06	.05
Reading ability relatively same...............	7	1.94	.34	.06	.03	.05
Reading ability relatively higher..............	7	2.24	.36	.04	.01	.04
Reading ability and intelligence both relatively *high;* groups matched in intelligence						
Reading ability relatively lower..............	3	1.97	.44	.13	.06	.12
Reading ability relatively same..............	4	2.20	.18	.03	.02	.04
Reading ability relatively higher..............	3	2.63	.30	.10	.04	.04

group described in the previous paragraph) the mean of these percentile differences was only +1.1, indicating quite definitely that here there was no relation between speech and reading disability other than perhaps a low general intelligence. At this point it became apparent that if there were a relationship between reading disability and speech disability it must be of a particular rather than of a general nature.

Analysis of the Relation of Different Aspects of the Speech Survey to Silent Reading Disability

In rating each freshman's general effectiveness in speech the committee in charge of the survey scored on a scale of 1 to 10 each individual's ability in each of the following aspects of speech: articulation, voice, organization of materials, and symbolic formulation and expression. The intercorrelations between these scores and the raw scores on the silent reading tests are shown in Table II. From this table it can be seen that except for "halo" effects between scores on certain of the aspects of the speech rating the general interrelationship is insignificant. Coefficients were computed on the basis of random samples of 250 cases.

Analysis of the Relation of Different Aspects of the Silent Reading Test to Speech Disability

Since organization of materials was taken into consideration in rating each freshman's general effectiveness in speech it was thought that inability to organize might comprise a common element in speech and reading defects. For the 113 freshmen rated as deficient in speech organization the mean percentile rank in sentence organization as measured by the Iowa Silent Reading Comprehension Test was 46.36, or nearly at the median. Similarly, for the same group the mean percentile rank in paragraph organization as measured by the Iowa Silent Reading Comprehension Test was 46.77, again nearly at median. Apparently there is little relation between speech organization and sentence or paragraph organization during silent reading.

Relation Between Speech Comprehension and Silent Reading Comprehension

If general intelligence or general ability to comprehend language represented the only common element in speech and reading ability one would expect to find scores in silent reading comprehension and speech comprehension very highly correlated. Such, however, was not found to be the case. In connection with the same survey of speech abilities in the freshman class as was mentioned above, the Travis-Barnes Speech Comprehension Test was given. In giving this test the tester reads aloud a selection, after which the testee selects from four printed selections the one which he believes to be identical with the one read. Fifty selections are read in the entire test and the testee's score is the number which he is able correctly to identify on the printed page.

A coefficient of correlation of $+.575 \pm .030$ was obtained between this test and the Iowa Silent Reading Comprehension Test. This coefficient is far below that which would be expected if intelligence or general ability to comprehend language were the only factor involved. Scores on an auditory acuity test made in the general speech survey revealed no consistency with the scores on the Travis-Barnes Speech Comprehension Test. Thus it becomes evident that some factor other than general intelligence or even general language comprehension is operative in one or the other or both of these tests.

Relation of Speech Rhythm Defects to Silent Reading Disability

One aspect of the speech survey did appear to be definitely related to silent reading disability. For the 67 cases which were diagnosed as being defective in the rhythm of speech the mean percentile ranking on the General Qualifying Examination was 45.25 and the mean percentile ranking on the Iowa Silent Reading Test was 40.87, a discrepancy of 4.39. In this connection it should be borne in mind that silent reading comprehension is a very considerable element in any written examination and that therefore the above numerical difference is probably too small.

This finding checks with the analysis made of the records of the 31 cases whose speech was recorded on the Ediphone. All the measures used in that analysis were essentially measures of speech rhythm (see Table I). Thus on the basis of two studies defective

Table II Intercorrelations between aspects of the speech ratings and scores of the Iowa Silent Reading Test

	Reading	*Articulation*	*Voice*	*Speech organization*	*Symbolic formulation and expression*
Reading		.080	.035	.090	.110
Articulation			.338	.219	.300
Voice				.260	.230
Speech organization					.549
Symbolic formulation and expression					

speech rhythm was found to be related to reading disability. This pointed toward a common element in speech and reading defects which is essentially transient in nature.

Relation of Silent Reading Disability to Cerebral Dominance as Manifest in Ambidextrality and Sinistrality

For a further explanation of this essentially transient element the present investigation followed the lead of Orton (1925) who emphasized the importance of "word blindness" or *strephosymbolia* in reading disability. It is true that Orton limited this defect to about 2 per cent of the school population, but it is conceivable that the defect is present to some extent in everyone. With *strephosymbolia* and stuttering (essentially a defect in speech rhythm), both being attributable to lack of cerebral dominance, it became a matter of prime importance to study the reading disabilities of those whose cerebral dominance was somewhat doubtful, that is, left handed and ambidextrous individuals.

Of 28 individuals who reported left handedness or ambidexterity in the speech survey 22 or 79 per cent had a lower percentile ranking in silent reading comprehension than in the General Qualifying Examination. The mean percentile ranking for this group on the Iowa Silent Reading Comprehension Test was 41.0 and the mean percentile ranking on the General Qualifying Examination was 47.6, a discrepancy of 6.6 percentiles. Again it should be pointed out that any silent reading disability would tend to influence unfavorably scores on the General Qualifying Examination.

In the speech survey 22 individuals reported having been changed from the left to the right hand at some time in their lives. Silent reading ranks were available for only 16 of these individuals; however, for this small group the mean reading percentile was 43.7 and the mean qualifying percentile was 47.9. It is interesting to note in passing that four of these individuals were stutterers.

Relation of Transient Sensory Aphasia to Silent Reading Disabilities

It is evident from the foregoing paragraphs that although there is a common element, essentially transient in nature, in reading and speech rhythm defect, there is still some discrepancy and the presence of one type of defect in an individual does not insure the presence of the other type of defect. An analysis of the two tests for transient aphasia will throw some light on this discrepancy. Table III shows the results. From this table it can be seen that the percentage of errors made on the visual aphasia test, described under item 16 in the experimental series, is a fair measure of the silent reading ability with the intelligence held constant. The auditory aphasia test, described under item 17 in the experimental series, does not appear to be as closely related to silent reading ability.

Relation of Transient Sensory Aphasia to Defective Speech Rhythm

After examining the results shown in Table III the question arose whether or not the auditory test might be more closely related to speech rhythm defects. In order to test this hypothesis a much longer auditory aphasia test and a much longer visual aphasia test were constructed. The nature of the tests and the methods of presentation were retained but the number of presentations was increased to 133 in the auditory test and to 197 in the visual test. Time intervals between presentations remained unchanged in each case.

For the experiment 12 stutterers and an equivalent number of normal speakers were matched on the basis of age and advancement in school. All the individuals were either undergraduate or graduate students in the university. Table IV shows the results of this experiment. The differences are striking; here both visual aphasia and auditory aphasia tests appear to be closely related to stuttering. It can be seen, however, that those individuals who made a high percentage of errors on one test did not necessarily make a high percentage of errors on the other.

Table III Percentages of errors in the transient aphasia tests according to groups selected on the basis of the discrepancy between silent reading percentile ranks and percentile ranks in intelligence as measured on the Iowa General Qualifying Examination

Groups:					
Intelligence low			*Intelligence high*		
Reading lower	*Reading same*	*Reading higher*	*Reading lower*	*Reading same*	*Reading higher*
Transient Visual Aphasia Test					
20.0% (7 cases)	11.9% (7 cases)	5.9% (7 cases)	1.0% (3 cases)	3.7% (5 cases)	2.7% (3 cases)
Transient Auditory Aphasia Test					
42.2% (7 cases)	26.2% (7 cases)	28.2% (7 cases)	15.0% (3 cases)	17.5% (5 cases)	21.8% (3 cases)

Table IV Stutterers and normals compared on basis of percentage of errors made on aphasia tests

Normals			*Stutterers*		
O	*Auditory aphasia test in %*	*Visual aphasia test in %*	*O*	*Auditory aphasia test in %*	*Visual aphasia test in %*
Cr	.75	0	Ba	28.80	7.61
Ha	7.51	7.61	Be	61.60	34 50
Ke	.75	3.55	Fr	68.40	11.16
Ly	0	0	Cr	54 90	19 30
Ma	36.80	9.14	Ne	67.60	3.04
Na	5.26	1.52	He	19.53	10.64
Pa	17.30	3.05	Ja	7.50	13.20
Pr	28.60	8.01	Jo	6.76	10.15
Ti	21.80	0	Ma	100.00	100.00
Wa	6.01	1.52	Sc	24.80	8.10
Wh	3.76	0	Sw	43.60	17.76
Wi	6.76	1.01	Va	42.10	12.70
Means:	11.28	2.95		43.80	20.68

Preliminary Generalizations

At this point it is possible to generalize from the foregoing results to some extent. In the first place the connection of reading disability to defective speech rhythm independent of general intelligence indicates a common element of a transient nature. In the second place the connection of reading disability to lack of cerebral dominance indicates the presence in reading disability cases of the same sort of neurological condition as that involved in stuttering. In the third place the more particular connection of transient aphasia in the visual test to reading disability and the more particular connection of transient aphasia in the auditory test to stuttering indicates a certain amount of differentiation between the sensory fields involved in this neurological condition. It would appear, then, that "neural blocking" due to lack of cerebral dominance results in a transient sensory aphasia which may or may not be apparent in both visual and auditory fields, although there is a general tendency for both fields to be involved. To the extent that both fields are involved, speech and reading defects have, independently of low intelligence, a common element.

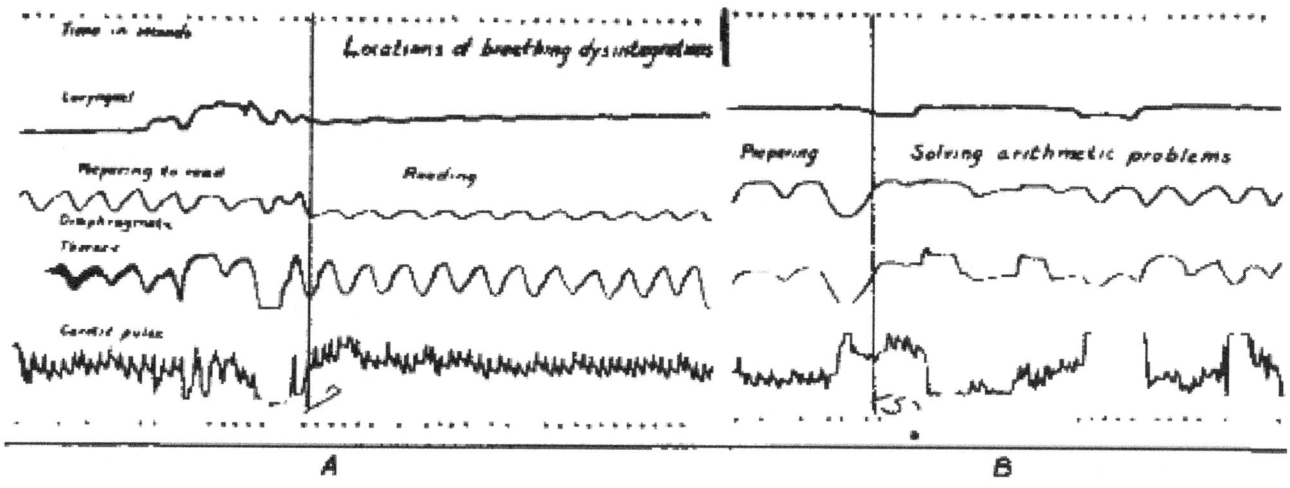

Plate I In the experimental series irregular breathing usually occurred at the beginning of a task. Two examples of the location of irregular breathing are shown. In case A the irregularity occurred just before the task was begun; in case B it occurred something after the task was begun. The solid line reaching vertically across the entire record indicates the point at which the signal to start was given. Curves of both thoracic and diaphragmatic breathing are indicated. The top line is the record of laryngeal movements.

Introspective Evidence

Two interesting incidents in the giving of the tests for visual and auditory aphasia lend weight to this conclusion. One *O* was having considerable difficulty with the test for auditory aphasia and as the test went on his difficulty increased, as was common with *O*s taking this test. At the 97th presentation he had missed 29 of the numbers. Suddenly he announced that he would miss no more, and from that point on appeared to make the responses with a minimum of difficulty. The remaining responses were all correctly made. When asked to explain his "trick" he said that while before he had tried to recall the sounds of the numbers, in the latter part of the test he visualized the numbers as they were presented to him and simply "copied" from the visual image. This indicates that the transient aphasia of this subject involved his auditory imagery more particularly than his visual imagery.

Another *O*, a stutterer, reported that he could "feel" the transient auditory aphasic states "coming on." He reported having at these times the same kinaesthetic sensations in his chest as he was accustomed to have at the onset of stuttering.

Relation of Auditory Imagery to Control of Breathing during Non-Speaking Intervals

The close relationship between transient auditory aphasia and disorders of speech rhythm opens the question of the extent to which auditory imagery is related to control of the speech organs, particularly those involved in breathing, during non-speaking intervals. Golla and Antonovitch's (1929) claim that rest breathing variability is very closely associated with auditory-motor types is not entirely substantiated by the present investigation. Table V shows a comparison between the six *O*s of the first experiment who reported habitual use of auditory imagery and the six *O*s who most definitely reported visual imagery. Of the latter group, however, *Sa* reported ability to recall very definite kinaesthetic images of such activities as playing golf, walking down the street, etc. It will be noticed that his breathing more nearly resembled that of the auditory group than that of the visual group into which the definiteness of his reported visual imagery required that he be placed.

The coefficients of variability for the durations of diaphragmatic expiration during rest breathing were only slightly larger in the case of the auditory group and there is considerable over-lapping. Golla and Antonovitch report only a 7.5 per cent discrepancy between irregular breathing and auditory imagery.

Table V Auditory and visual types of individuals compared on the basis of ratios of expiration duration to inspiration duration and variability of breathing during rest, silent reading, memorizing from a visual stimulus, and solving Golla's "visual" problem

	Auditory types				
	Ratio of expiration duration to inspiration duration		*Coefficient of variation of expiration durations during rest breathing*	*Blocking time: total time*	
	Rest	*Silent reading*		*Memorizing from visual stimulus*	*Solving Golla's visual problem*
Al	2.12	2.19	19.9	.6580	.1766
Br	2.27	1.86	13.1	.2622	.1486
Da	1.85	1.78	15.2	.1882	.4960
Ge	1.71	2.08	24.5	.4200	.0667
Nu	2.00	2.13	25.5	.6930	.0318
Su	2.26	2.36	25.1	.0373	.0895
Means:	2.03	2.07	20.5	.3764	.1682
	Visual types				
	Ratio of expiration duration to inspiration duration		*Coefficient of variation of expiration durations during rest breathing*	*Blocking time: total time*	
	Rest	*reading*		*Memorizing from visual stimulus*	*Solving Golla's visual problem*
Ba	1.85	1.40	13.3	.0866	0
Ca	1.25	1.49	18.6	.1800	.2850
De	1.46	1.49	22.0	.0138	0
Fl	1.58	1.32	13.6	.0165	.0495
Kn	1.32	1.48	14.4	0	.0375
Means	1.57	1.51	15.4	.0707	.0620
			Visual-kinæsthetic type		
Sa	1.98	1.88	10.4	.1272	0

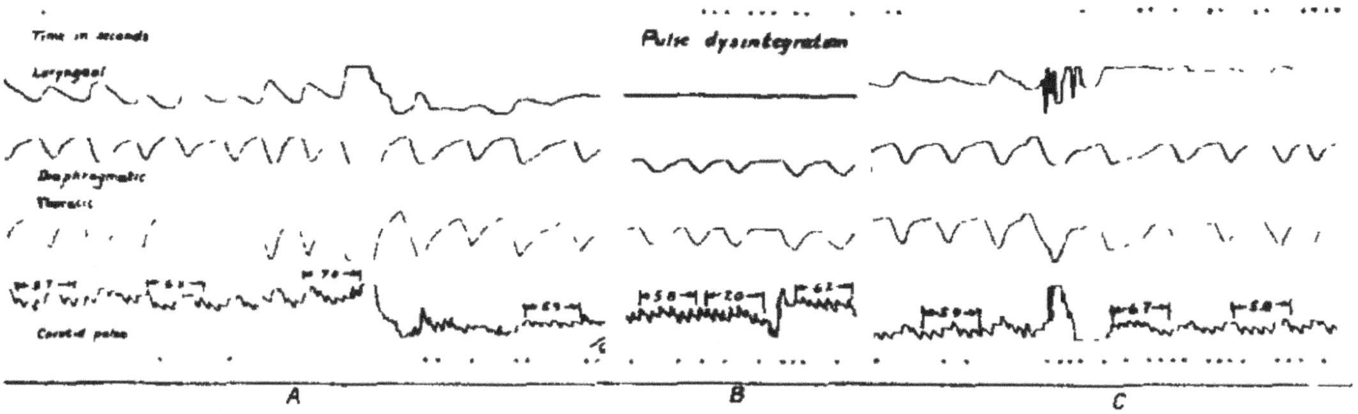

Plate II Irregularity in breathing was accompanied in almost every instance with a simultaneous increase in the heart-pulse rate. Three example are shown. Measurements of the number of beats in some of the 5 sec. intervals are indicated. In case A there were 5.7 beats in the first 5 sec. interval indicated, while in the third 5 sec. interval, which was coincident with an irregularity in the breathing, there were 7.0 beats. The same sort of increase in pulse rate occurring over a very short interval of time is shown in case B. Case C is another example of the same sort of thing. As in Plate I the top line is the record of laryngeal movements, the second of diaphragmatic breathing, the third of thoracic breathing, and the bottom line a record of the heart-pulse taken from the right carotid artery.

Much more significant in rest breathing was the difference between the two groups in the ratios of diaphragmatic expiration durations to diaphragmatic inspiration durations. The relatively long expirations and short inspirations of the auditory types suggest breathing during overt speech. Continual employment of verbalization during silent reading and studying probably implanted a speech-like pattern of breathing in the individual. The fact that the *O*s were supposedly directing their attention to the ticking of a chronometer when these records were being made indicates that this type of breathing persisted whether or not the individual was verbalizing at the time.

The ratio of expiration duration to inspiration duration during the silent reading periods is also shown in Table V. About the same difference between the two groups as in rest-breathing is indicated.

The most striking difference between the two groups appears in their breathing during a period of memorizing from a visual stimulus (described under item 13 in the experimental series). The measure here used was the ratio of blocking time to total time, or the ratio of the time during which the individual was making unusually long expirations or inspirations to the total time. Here the auditory types, due to their employment of verbalization in memorizing the passage, made relatively long expirations.

It was Golla and Antonovitch's (1929) claim that auditory types showed regular breathing patterns while solving a problem in which they were forced to employ visual imagery. The same problem (see item 14 in the experimental series) which these investigators used was employed in the present investigation, but with different results (see Plate III). In no case did the breathing become more regular and in most cases the problem was solved before a fair sample of breathing curves could be obtained. In Table V the ratios of blocking times to total times for visual and auditory types are shown. The auditory group is shown to be much more irregular in breathing than the visual group. That this irregularity was largely due to a tendency to verbalize on this "visual" problem could easily be observed by *E*.

In passing it is not inappropriate to remark that while Titchener (1929) and other authorities generally agree that about 75 per cent of the population-at-large are visual types the authors of the preceding study found 29 auditory types in a group of 67 cases. The present study revealed only six clear-cut auditory types out of 38 cases.

Synchronization of Breathing with Mental Processes

The foregoing data indicate a relatively close relationship between auditory imagery and the habitual pattern of respiration. In addition we may assume that there is also a relation between the breathing rhythm and visual imagery, although that relation is not nearly as marked as in the case of auditory imagery. During both visual and auditory tests the breathing of all *O*s tended to be synchronized with the presentations on the tests (see Plate IV). Four general types of synchronization were employed by the *O*s. In most cases *O* would employ one of these types consistently throughout the test. The most common form of synchronization was to regulate the breathing so that each presentation occurred during an expiration. Usually the breathing was regulated so that presentations came on successive expirations. A variation of this form of synchronization occurred in the cases of some of the auditory type of *O*s; it was to regulate each expiration so as to include two presentations (see D, Plate IV). This enabled *O* to breathe more slowly and more nearly at his normal rate. Another method of synchronization employed by some *O*s was to allow the presentation to occur at the change of breathing phase when the respiration movements were momentarily suspended. In some cases this tended to occur during the change from expiration to inspiration and in others it tended to occur during the change from inspiration to expiration. A variation of this method was to allow the presentation to occur at every third change of phase. The *O*s who

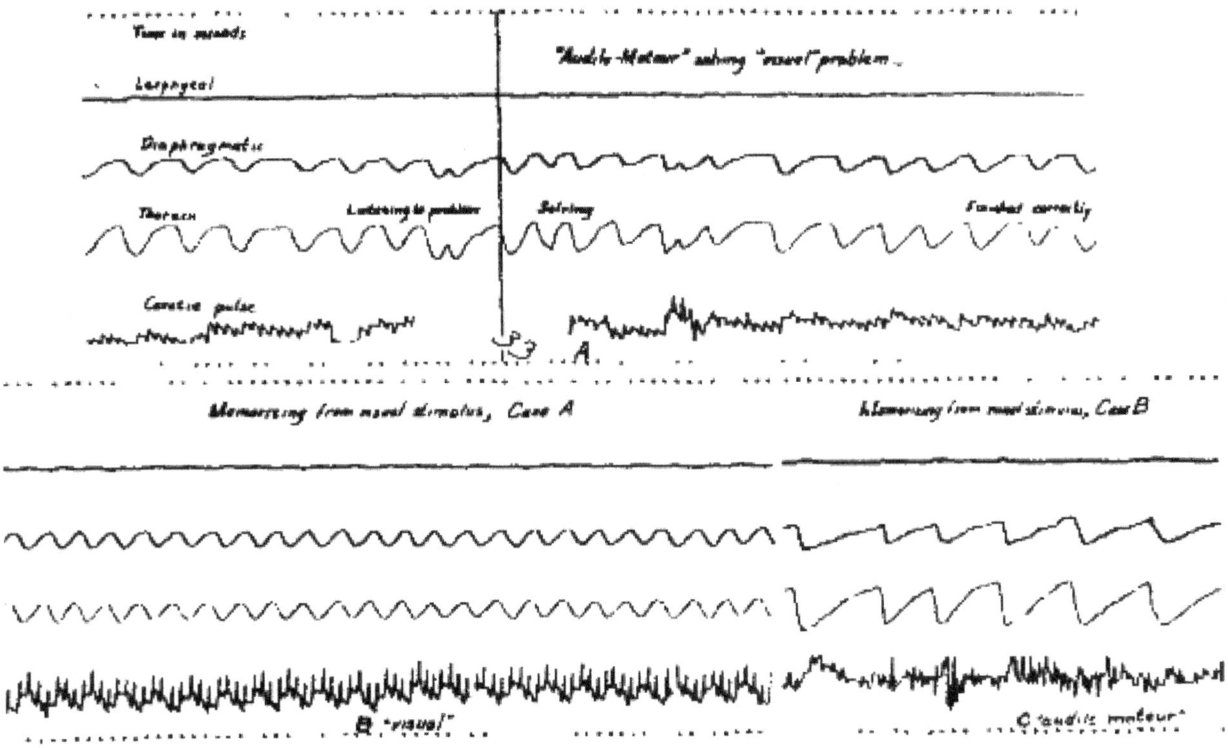

Plate III *Golla* and *Antonovitch* report that auditory types of individuals are irregular breathers during rest periods but that when given a "visual" problem to solve their breathing become regular. A shows the breathing of a typical auditory type of individual before and during the solution of the same "visual" problem upon which these investigators based their conclusion. Three point in refutation of their finding are illustrated. In the first place, breathing was not more regular during the period in which the problem was solved; secondly, the problem was solved correctly before a fair sample of breathing curves could be obtained; and thirdly, the last seven curves suggest verbalization or use of auditory-kinæsthetic imagery. The findings of this study with regard to the difference between visual and auditory types are illustrated in B and C. The most marked differences occurred during the period of memorizing a typewritten selection. Case A is the record of a visual type of *O* while memorizing the selection and Case B is the record of an auditory type of *O* while memorizing the same selection. The latter *O* was simply verbalizing or making use of auditory-kinæsthetic imagery. A similar, though much less marked, difference in the breathing curves of the two types of *O*s was observed during rest breathing. In each record the top line indicates the laryngeal movement, the second diaphragmatic breathing, the third thoracic breathing, and the bottom line the pulse of the carotid artery. Movements of those muscles of the neck involved in breathing and in verbalization naturally affected the record of the carotid pulse.

used this method would regulate their breathing so that one presentation would occur during the change from expiration to inspiration and the following presentation would occur during a change from inspiration to expiration. either one or three phase-lengths later. The synchronization of the breathing with the presentations of the tests of aphasia was particularly marked with the auditory types of *O*s and with all *O*s while taking the auditory aphasia test (see Plate IV).

Location of Breathing Dysintegrations

Suspension or blocking of the respiration, when it occurred during the experimental series, usually did so at the beginning of a task, either just before the task was undertaken or just after it was undertaken (see Plate I). With some *O*s, however, prolonged expirations or inspirations occurred periodically throughout the performance of a task.

Relation of Pulse Rate to Breathing Dysintegrations

Since the pulse from the right carotid artery was recorded on the same record as the breathing, it was possible to observe changes in pulse rate in relation to breathing irregularities. With all *O*s the pulse rate tended to be markedly increased at the same instant that a prolonged expiration or inspiration was begun (see Plate II). Since the increase in pulse rate occurred in some cases even before the breathing phase had reached a state of prolongation, it would appear that the phenomenon can not be entirely attributed to carbon dioxide stimulation in the lungs. A more likely explanation is that an underlying neural disturbance interferes with the rhythm of both heart-pulse and respiration.

As a measure of the variability of the pulse rate in individual cases the number of pulsations during every third 5 sec. period throughout the six minutes of silent reading in the experimental series was recorded. The mean difference between successive measurements was used as a measure of the heart-pulse. The coefficient of correlation between variability of heart-pulse as measured in this manner and the variability of breathing as measured by the coefficient of variation of thoracic inspiration duration was $+.63 \pm .07$.

Hydrogen Ion Concentration in the Mixed Saliva of Stutterers

The hydrogen ion concentration in the mixed saliva of nine of the stutterers after they had taken the visual and auditory aphasia tests was determined. A sample of the saliva was collected from each stutterer and kept under 2 c.c. of oil in a 15 c.c. vial. Determinations were made by the electrometric method. Following are the pH values for the nine stutterers:

O	*pH*
Ma	7.05
Va	5.75
Ho	5.25
Ba	6.90
Sc	5.00
Fr	5.60
Gr	6.00
Sw	6.30
Ja	6.10

All but two of the pH values are considerably below the normal range of pH values for normal individuals under ordinary conditions of mental work. Accepting the interpretation of Starr (1922) this would mean the presence of a considerable amount of carbon-dioxide in the blood, due to inefficient breathing. That the inefficient breathing in turn is due to dysintegration in the functioning of the nervous system is reasonable to suppose, since the accompanying aphasic condition is related to a peculiar neural situation.

Summary of Results

1 Individuals representing cases of silent reading disability were found to be as regular in their breathing during silent reading and associated mental processes as were normal readers.
2 Individuals representing cases of silent reading ability inconsistent with their general intelligence were found to be as regular in their breathing during silent reading and associated mental processes as were individuals whose reading ability was consistent with their intelligence.
3 Individuals whose silent reading ability was low in relation to their general intelligence were most deficient in the rhythm of their speech; individuals whose silent reading ability was high in relation to their general intelligence were least deficient in the rhythm of their speech; and individuals whose silent reading ability was consistent with their intelligence were midway between the other two groups in the rhythm of their speech.
4 Individuals who were diagnosed as deficient in the rhythm of their speech were found to be not only low in silent reading ability but low in proportion to their intelligence.
5 Silent reading comprehension and speech comprehension were not found to be highly correlated.
6 Individuals who were diagnosed as speech defectives, as a group, did not show any significant silent reading disability.
7 Individuals who were diagnosed as deficient in ability to organize a speech were deficient in neither sentence organization nor paragraph organization in silent reading.
8 None of the following aspects of speech were significantly correlated with silent reading ability: articulation, voice, organization of materials in a speech, symbolic formulation and expression.
9 Left handed and ambidextrous individuals were found to be not only low in silent reading ability but low in proportion to their intelligence.
10 Transient visual aphasia was found to be associated with silent reading disability independently of intelligence.
11 Transient auditory aphasia was found to be associated with stuttering.
12 The rest-breathing of auditory-motor types of individuals was found to be nearly as regular as the rest-breathing of visual types of individuals.

13 The duration of expiration among auditory types at all times, but especially when memorizing from a visual stimulus, was relatively long as compared with the duration of inspiration.
14 Breathing of both visual and auditory types of individuals was found to be synchronized with successive presentations of visual or of auditory stimuli in the aphasia tests.
15 Suspension or blocking of breathing, when it occurred, was most apt to occur at the beginning of a task.
16 Heart-pulse rate was found to increase momentarily during prolonged expirations or inspirations.
17 Variability in heart-pulse rate was highly correlated with variability in breathing rhythm.
18 Hydrogen ion concentration in stutterers after taking the aphasia tests was generally high.

Major Conclusions

1 The connection of reading disability to defective speech rhythm and of defective speech rhythm to reading disability independent of general intelligence indicates a common element of an essentially transient nature in speech and reading defects.
2 The connection of speech rhythm defects, such as stuttering, to lack of cerebral dominance—according to Travis (1931)—and the connection of reading disabilities independent of intelligence to lack of cerebral dominance indicates the same sort of neurological condition underlying each type of defect.
3 The more particular connection of transient visual aphasia to reading disability and of transient auditory aphasia to stuttering indicates a certain amount of differentiation between the sensory fields affected by the underlying neural situation.
4 Neural blocking, due to a lack of cerebral dominance, results in a transient sensory aphasia which may or may not involve both visual and auditory sensations.
5 To the extent that transient aphasia involves both visual and auditory sensations, speech and reading defects have, independently of low intelligence, a common element.

Minor Conclusions

1 A pattern of breathing resembling that necessary for the production of overt speech implants itself upon those individuals who customarily employ auditory-kinaesthetic imagery in the mechanism of their thought.
2 The rhythm of breathing tends to be synchronous with the rhythm of thought or fluctuations of attention over short-time intervals.
3 The rhythm of breathing is closely associated with the rhythm of the vaso-motor system and interruptions in the former alter the rate of the latter.
4 Most stutterers have a high hydrogen ion concentration.

Bibliography

Bartley, S., and Perkins, T. (1931). Cerebral action currents in the dog. Paper presented before the Midwest section of the American Psychological Association.
Bills, A. G. (1931). Blocking: a new principle of mental fatigue, *Psychological Bulletin*, *28*, 208; *American Journal of Psychology*, *43*, 230–245.
Bluemel, C. S. (1913). *Stammering and cognate defects of speech*. Stechert, 2 vols.
Bryngelson, B. (1926). *A study of the articulatory difficulties of thirteen stutterers*. Unpublished thesis, University of Iowa.
Farnsworth, P. R., Seashore, R. H., & Tinker, M. A. (1927). Speed in simple and serial action as related to performance in certain "intelligence" tests. *The Pedagogical Seminary and Journal of Genetic Psychology*, *34*, 537–551.
Fossler, H. R. (1930) Disturbances in breathing during stuttering. *Psychological Monographs*, *40*(1), 1–32.
Galton, F. (1883), *Inquiries into human faculty and its development*. Macmillan.
Gaskill, H. V. (1928) The relation of reaction time to the phase of breathing. *Journal of Experimental Psychology*, *11*, 364–369.
Golla, F. L., & Antonovitch, S. (1929). Respiratory rhythm in its relation to mechanism of thought. *Brain*, *52*(4), 491–500.
Knight, F. B. (1931). Certain periodicities in the work curves of sixth grade pupils in arithmetic. Paper read before the Iowa Academy of Sciences.
Mott, F. (1910). *The brain and the voice in speech and song*. Harper.
Murray, E. (1931). Dysintegration of breathing and eye-movements of stutterers during silent reading and associated mental processes. *Psychological Monographs*, *42*, No. 5, 218–275.
Orton, S. T. (1925). "Word-blindness" in school children. *Archives of Neurology and Psychiatry*, *14*, 581–615.

Ranschburg, P. (1925). Die Lese- und Schrusstörungen des Kindesalters. Ihre Psychologie, Physiologie, heilpadagogische und medizinische Therapie. Halle a. S., C. Marhold. (*Psychological Abstracts*, 1929, *3*, No. 482, 64.)

Skaggs, E. B. (1930). Studies in attention and emotion. *Journal of Comparative Psychol*ogy, *10*, 374–419.

Starr, H. E. (1922). The hydrogen ion concentration of the mixed saliva considered as an index of fatigue and of emotional excitation, and applied to a study of the metabolic etiology of stammering. *American Journal of Psychology*, *33*, 394–418.

Titchener, E. B. (1929). *Experimental psychology: instructor's manual, qualitative*. Macmillan.

Travis, L. E. (1927). Studies in stuttering, I. Dysintegration of the breathing movements during stuttering. *Archives of Neurology and Psychiatry*, *18*, 673–690.

Travis, L. E. (1931). *Speech pathology*. Appleton.

Zoneff, P., & Meumann, E. (1903). Ueber Begleiterscheinungen psychischer Vorgange in athem und Puls, Erster Artikel. *Philosophische Studien*, *18*, 1–113.

28

Some Observations on the Relation of Cerebral Dominance to the Perception of Symbols[1]

Orton, a pioneer worker in the field of word-blindness (strephosymbolia), has maintained that the tendency of many children to reverse and invert written symbols is related to a lack of cerebral dominance. Travis has also shown a relationship between general neural disintegration which is manifest in stuttering and the lack of cerebral dominance. The present writer has suggested elsewhere that a symptom of this neural disintegration is a functional disorder of the nature of transient aphasia. The present investigation seeks to discover the difference in the orientations of the mnemonic images governed by the two cerebral hemispheres.

[1] Abstract of paper presented at the Proceedings of the Eighth Annual Meeting of the Midwestern Psychological Association, May 18, 19, 20, 1933. Published in 1933 in *Psychological Bulletin, 30,* 583–584. Now in the public domain and republished by permission of Jacqueline Aldridge.

Collected Papers of the Pioneer of Constructivist Psychology: George A. Kelly, First Edition. Edited by David A. Winter and Nick Reed.

Published 2026 by John Wiley & Sons Ltd.

29

Some Observations on the Relation of the Principle of Physiological Polarity and Symmetry and the Doctrine of Cerebral Dominance to the Perception of Symbols[1]

Orton (1925), a pioneer worker in the field of word-blindness *(strephosymbolia)*, has maintained that the tendency of many children to reverse and invert written symbols is related to a lack of a sufficient margin of dominance of one of the cerebral hemispheres over the other. According to his view the mnemonic images governed by the two hemispheres are not in the same orientation but on the "third functional level" are mirrored counterparts of each other. The human organism, being symmetrical about the median plane but polaric about the transverse and horizontal planes, is predisposed to make similar responses to reverse patterns of stimulation if they are presented on opposite but counterpart sides of the median plane. Lack of dominance of one hemisphere over the other makes difficult the differentiation of one pattern from the other.

Any reference to the spatial orientation of mnemonic images is likely to provoke the criticism that images are not spatial phenomena but are physiological processes. The answer is that the physiological processes are really serial processes in spatially distributed organs and hence have the property of spatial direction.

In Fig. 1 let us first suppose that the left hemisphere is dominant when a stimulus '*d*' is presented. Let us suppose that the resulting percept is indicated by the arrow marked, '1.' Of course it would be improper to assume either that the contour or that the spatial orientation of the percept is like that of the stimulus; one can only say that whatever contour or spatial orientation the percept possesses *stands for* or *symbolizes* the *stimulus in its relation to the organism.* In recognition of this fact the percept has been represented in the diagram by an irregular arrow. Although the left cerebral hemisphere is the seat of the highest authority in this gradient the dynamic unity of the entire nervous system must not be overlooked. Obviously there must be some related process in the right cerebral hemisphere. Travis (1931) has been successful in showing this experimentally. If the process in the left hemisphere is principally in a peripheral or abductive direction as indicated by the arrow '1' the physiologically symmetrical process in the right hemisphere is also in a peripheral or abductive direction as indicated by the faint arrow marked, '2.'

[1] First published in 1935 in *Journal of Experimental Psychology*, *18*, 202–213. Republished by permission of Jacqueline Aldridge.

Collected Papers of the Pioneer of Constructivist Psychology: George A. Kelly, First Edition. Edited by David A. Winter and Nick Reed.

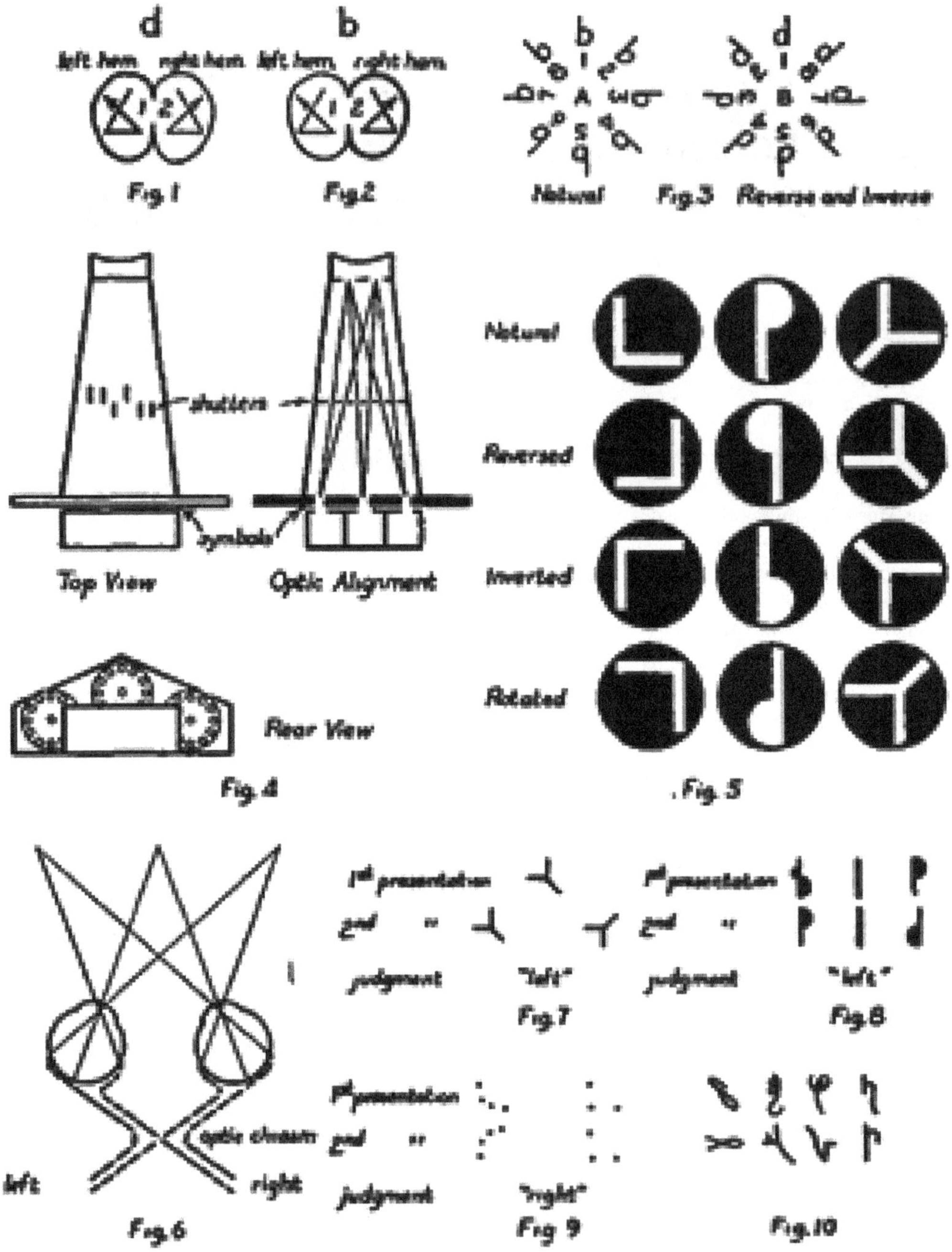

Now let us suppose that because of fatigue or lack either of inherent or cultivated bias the left hemisphere becomes recessive and the right hemisphere becomes dominant. A new gradient is set up in which the highest authority is located in the right hemisphere. Let us suppose that the stimulus '*b*,' a spatially reversed stimulus, is presented. *In relation to the new gradient* this stimulus calls for another peripheral or abductive process and the resulting percept may be indicated by the heavy arrow '2' in Fig. 2. Physiologically the arrows in both figures correspond to each other, all representing abduction, hence the stimuli '*d*' and '*b*' are judged congruous.

We have attempted briefly to explain the relation of the doctrine of cerebral dominance to the perception of the spatial orientation of symbols on the basis of similar processes in the two hemispheres. We have argued that since a percept consists of serial processes in spatially distributed organs it may have a spatial trend or direction. Our explanation would be even less awkward if we turned behaviorist and assumed that percepts were to be identified by the corresponding movements of peripheral structures, gestures of the limbs, articulatory movements of the vocal mechanisms, etc.

Before proceeding further with a discussion of theory it would be well to summarize the facts to be explained. There is an infinite number of positions or orientations in which a symbol may be presented. The orientations may be divided into two groups, a natural series and an inverse series. In each series the symbol may be moved from one position to another by rotation. Fig. 3 illustrates the difference between these two series. On the basis of symmetry about the median plane 1A would be confused with 1B, 2A with 2B, 3A with 3B, etc. On the basis of symmetry about the horizontal plane 1A would be confused with 5B, 2A with 6B, 3A with 7B, etc. On the basis of symmetry about both median and horizontal planes 1A would be confused with 5A, 2A with 6A, 3A with 7A, etc. Since the doctrine of cerebral dominance accounts only for symmetry about the median plane it implies that only symbols in corresponding positions in different series should be confused. Is this the case? According to some reports it is not. Cases of word-blindness have been observed in which both reversed and inverted handwriting have appeared. One observer, Bluemel (1933), discards the doctrine of cerebral dominance principally upon this evidence. We have found in our own clinical experience that some children with reading disabilities possess an unusual facility in reading inverted and rotated symbols as well as reversed symbols. Obviously this cannot be explained upon the basis of symmetrical processes or gestures about the median plane alone. Confusion of inverted symbols would indicate symmetrical processes about some horizontal plane. Confusion of rotated symbols would indicate symmetry about both median and horizontal planes at the same time. One would then suppose that confusion of rotated symbols would be the least frequent; and indeed that seems to be the clinical experience. One thing now appears to be clear; if we are to explain confused perception of the spatial orientation of symbols on the basis of symmetrical physiological processes or gestures we must consider both median and horizontal planes as axes of symmetry.

There are further facts to be explained. Whereas the preceding discussion has been concerned with spatial orientations there are clinical observations of temporal confusions to be considered. Temporal confusion, if explained upon the basis of symmetrical processes, implies symmetry about a point in time. That is to say, if I am to smooth my hair, pull my ear, and open my mouth the symmetrical series of gestures is to close my mouth, push my ear, and ruffle my hair. Travis (1931) has shown temporal confusion in the breathing movements and neural action currents of stutterers. He has shown that the stutterer frequently tries to speak during inspiration and that some muscles are acting as if the individual were inspiring at the same time that other muscles are acting as if the individual were expiring. A clinical case has come to our attention which illustrates the point. A fourteen-year-old girl frequently writes the last letter of a word first, then the next to the last letter, and so on. Many words are pronounced as if they were spelled backwards. This is symmetry about a point in time, not about a plane in space, and yet in this same case we have symptoms which indicate a spatial symmetry of response about the median plane. Frequently she will change her chalk or pencil from one hand to the other after starting to write the letters of a word in reverse order and rewrite the word correctly. For instance, in writing the word 'little' she wrote with the left hand 'e l t,' then hesitated, changed the chalk to her right hand, and wrote 'little.' Here it appears as if temporal confusion is related to spatial confusion about the median plane; but what theory, mechanistic or otherwise, accounts for such a fact?

We have been able to show elsewhere (Kelly, 1932) that reading disability is related to disorders in the rhythm of speech and have suggested that on the functional side the common factor between the two types of disorders is a transient aphasia. This transient aphasia also is related to the lack of cerebral dominance. Any transient disorder immediately suggests problems of refractory phase lengths and mental fatigue. If symmetry about both median and horizontal planes, symmetry about a point in time, and refractory phase are all related to stuttering, word-blindness, and transient aphasia about all that can be advanced by way of explanation is some doctrine of general neural disintegration—which may mean almost anything.

Before attempting further explanation of the confusion of differently oriented symbols it seems advisable to consider three questions. (1) Is cerebral dominance related at all to the perception of differently oriented symbols? (2) Are gestural responses of the adductor-abductor type always used in the perception of symbols? (3) What kind of change in the orientation of symbols is most likely to cause confusion?

We have undertaken a series of experiments in order to throw light upon these questions. For two of these experiments a special piece of apparatus has been constructed (Fig. 4). This apparatus is a tachistoscope by means of which short time exposures can be made in various parts of the field of peripheral vision separately for each eye. It consists of a light-proof box into which the observer looks. Symbols are presented by lighting lamps placed behind appropriately formed translucent screens. A system of shutters enables the experimenter to control the exposures to either eye independently and without the knowledge of the observer. A timing device consisting of a pendulum with movable counter-balances and sliding mercury cup drop switches enables the experimenter to make presentations in any order and for any period of time.

In the first experiment there were three symbols used (Fig. 5). Each was presented in one of the four possible orientations, natural, reversed, inverted, and rotated 180^0. In each observation the observer was allowed to fixate with both eyes a symbol in the median plane for a period of 1700 σ. At the end of this period the light behind the symbol was turned off and the lights behind two side symbols situated so as to stimulate non-foveal retinal areas were turned on for a period of 100 σ. This brief presentation of the side symbols should have made it difficult for the observer to move his eyes into a position of fixation on either side symbol since the reaction time for light is probably considerably greater than 100 σ. In each observation the shutters were so arranged that both eyes could be fixated on the median symbol but only one eye could be stimulated by each of the side symbols. Figure 6 illustrates the retinal areas, principal neural paths, and hemispheres involved.

In each observation the side symbols were similar in form to the median symbol. The observer was asked to report whether the left, the right, both, or neither of the side symbols was in the same orientation as the median symbol (Fig. 7). The presentation series was so constructed that each symbol in all of the possible combinations of orientations was presented through each of the four neural tracts.

Records were kept of the conditions under which errors were made. 18 observers, men and women, graduate and undergraduate students in psychology made 72 observations each.

An attempt was made to control the factor of manual preference since this is supposed to be a clue to cerebral dominance. 13 observers reported that they were right handed and 5 reported that they were left handed. When the phi-phenomenon technique (Jasper, 1932) was used as an objective check 7 observers indicated right central dominance, 7 indicated left central dominance, 3 indicated right peripheral dominance, and 1 indicated left peripheral dominance. There was no correlation between the reports of handedness and the phi-phenomenon criterion; furthermore both left and right handed groups showed similar reports in the experiment. No further attempt was made to control the factor of cerebral dominance among the observers. The factor of cerebral symmetry, however, continued to be an object of investigation.

There were 314 errors of judgment distributed as follows: 70 when the principal neural path lay from the right eye to the left hemisphere, 66 when it lay from the left eye to the left hemisphere, 73 when it lay from the right eye to the right hemisphere, and 105 when it lay from the left eye to the right hemisphere. The greatest number of errors was made when the principal neural path lay through those organs which are considered as usually non-dominant. Statistically, however, the mean number of errors made under this condition differed from the mean number made under the first condition only by about 2½ times the probable error of the difference between the means. This difference may be interpreted to be somewhat statistically significant but by no means conclusive.

About all that can be concluded from this experiment is that among observers in whom we have reason to believe there is a normally well established neural integration there is a tendency to make errors in detecting differences in the orientation of symbols when the non-dominant eye and hemisphere are involved in the principal neural tract. Our first question cannot be answered satisfactorily but there remains some evidence for believing that there is a relation between cerebral dominance and the perception of symbol orientation.

The second question, are gestural responses of the adductor-abductor type always used in the perception of symbols, is difficult to answer because gestural responses are not easily controlled. Our experiments yielded four kinds of evidence on this point. In the first place the observers reported that they "kept the symbols straight" by moving their hands or pointing their fingers to the right or left while fixating the median symbol. By maintaining this posture they were able to make a direct comparison with the side symbols in the second phase of the observation. Some observers verbalized, using such expressions as "*q*," "*p*," "*y* leaning to the left," "down right," etc. We suppose that this is another case where the conscientious behaviorist is tempted to accept introspective evidence.

In the second place we may consider the answer to our third question together with the answer to the second and call attention to the conditions of orientation under which errors were made. There were 51 errors in which symbols in reverse orientation were judged as in the same, 37 in which symbols in inverted orientation were judged as in the same, and 27 in which symbols in rotated orientation were judged as in the same. The number of presentations was the same in each instance. From this it appears that reversals are most confusing and rotations least confusing. Support for this same conclusion is obtained from the following: When symbols in the same orientation were presented with symbols in reverse orientation there were 84 errors, when presented with symbols in inverted orientation there were 62 errors, and when presented with symbols in rotated orientation there were 53 errors.

If we consider rotated symbols as symbols which have been both reversed and inverted we may say that while gestures of the adductor-abductor type might have been used to identify reversals and gestures of the elevation-depression type might have been used to identify inversions either kind of gesture could have been used to identify the rotations. The infrequent misjudgment of rotations might be due to the double check which the observer might apply to them. The frequent misjudgment of reversals fits very neatly into the argument in favor of the doctrine of cerebral dominance. The misjudgments of inversions might be explained upon two grounds; first, the observer would have to depend only upon one kind of gesture, the elevation-depression type, or second, the tendency to make the initial gesture with one hand or on one side might confuse the observer when a symbol in the second phase of the presentation appeared on the opposite side of the body. In the latter case there would have to be a transfer of gesture across the median plane. This in itself would be confusing. All of this, then, is consistent with the view that gestures are perceptual concomitants.

A third kind of evidence, however, casts doubt upon the gestural hypothesis. This evidence was gotten by varying the experimental series so as to discourage the use of gestures. This was done by requiring the observer to keep in mind two symbols at a time instead of one. The same apparatus was used. In the first part of each presentation a fixation light was presented in the median plane. After 1700 σ the light was removed and two side symbols presented for 100 σ. After an interval varying from 5 to 8 seconds the fixation light was presented again and followed by two side symbols. (Fig. 8). If both of the second pair of symbols were the same as the first pair the observer reported, "both;" if neither, "neither;" etc. Series were arranged so as to balance the different combinations of eyes, orientations, symbols, and sides of presentation. 18 observers, undergraduate students in psychology, were used as observers. All reported dextrality, or right handedness. Records of the conditions under which errors were made may be summarized as follows: There was an average of 4.28 errors in judging symbols in the same orientation, an average of 4.34 errors in judging symbols in reversed orientation, an average of 5.66 errors in judging symbols in inverted orientation, and an average of 4.21 errors in judging symbols in rotated orientation. (The first and last figures were corrected for an attenuation logically arising out of the nature of the presentation material.) The results of this experiment may be summarized by saying that when the use of gestural cues was discouraged by complicating the presentations only the inversion remained particularly difficult to identify. The hypothesis of symmetrical gestures or processes about a median plane will not explain this fact.

A variation of the above experiment was performed with presentations made in the tactile rather than in the visual mode. Raised figures were formed by driving small brads into wood cubes and leaving the heads projecting slightly above the surface.

The observer, blindfolded, held his hands on a frame while presentations were made by pressing the cubes against the lower surface of the first digits. Pairs of unlike symbols were presented for a period of about 3 seconds. After the presentation of a second pair the observer was asked to report which of the symbols in the second pair were like symbols presented in the first pair. The experimental and the control series were mixed. In the control series the same symbol was presented on the same side in the second presentation (Fig. 9). In the experimental series the same symbol was presented on the opposite side. Twenty observers made twelve observations each. The results were entirely negative. There was no significant difference in the number of errors made in each series or in the kind of change or orientation which provoked errors. If this arrangement by controlling the movement of the hands might be said to control the use of gestural cues it may be argued that the elimination of such cues makes the misjudgment of inversions and rotations as common as the misjudgment of reversals.

A fourth kind of evidence bearing upon the question of gestural responses in perception was obtained by devising more complex symbols which would be difficult to interpret in terms of gestures. 24 such symbols were devised (Fig. 10). The observers, in groups of approximately 10 were seated 3 to 3½ meters in front of a screen. Before each presentation was made the observers were asked to fixate a small red disk in the center of the screen. They were asked to keep this fixation during the presentation. The presentation was made by the experimenter who stood behind the screen and held two cards, one at either side of the screen, for a period of about 1 second. The cards bore symbols 6 cm. high. A learning series of 12 pairs of symbols and a recognition series of 12 pairs of symbols were presented. In the recognition series 6 symbols were presented on the same side and in the same orientation, 6 on the opposite side but in the same orientation, 6 on the same side but in reverse orientation, and 6 on the opposite side but in the reverse orientation. The symbols in the learning and recognition series were rearranged several times during the experiment so as to eliminate the effect of varying complexities. There were 135 observers, all undergraduate students with training in experimental psychology. The observers reported that it was impossible consciously to use gestural responses. The results were negative. In the recognition series there was no more tendency to misjudge the reversed symbols appearing on the opposite side than to misjudge the same symbols appearing on the opposite side. There was a slight but statistically insignificant tendency for symbols appearing on the opposite side to be misjudged more frequently than symbols appearing on the same side. Here again we have evidence that gestural responses of the adductor-abductor type are not always used in the perception of symbols and that when they are not so used reversals are as easy to detect as are the other changes in orientation.

The evidence cited has already thrown light upon the third question; what kind of a change in the orientation of symbols is most likely to cause confusion? We answer the question by saying that when gestural responses are discouraged inversions are most confusing but when the presentations are made through the tactile mode one kind of a change in orientation is as difficult to detect as another.

From the experiments we venture to make the following tentative conclusions: (1) Physiological symmetry is a significant factor in the perception of symbols only when gestural cues are used. (2) Inversion is peculiarly difficult to detect in the visual mode. (3) There is no known check on cerebral dominance which is sufficiently dependable to enable one to investigate the influence of that factor on the perception of the orientation of symbols.

Bibliography

Bluemel, C. S. (1933). The dominant gradient in stammering, *Quarterly Journal of Speech*, *19*, 233–242.

Childs, C. M. (1924). *Physiological foundations of behavior*. H. Holt & Co.

Jasper, H. H. (1932). A laboratory study of diagnostic indices of bilateral neuromuscular organization in stutterers and normal speakers, *Psychological Monographs*, *43*, 72–174.

Kelly, G. A. (1932). Some common factors in reading and speech disabilities, *Psychological Monographs*, *43*, 175–201.

Orton, S. T. (1925). 'Word-blindness' in school children, *Archives of Neurology & Psychiatry*, *14*, 81–615.

Travis, L. E. (1931). *Speech pathology*. Appleton.

30

The Assumption of an Originally Homogeneous Universe and some of its Statistical Implications[1]

Spencer's definition of evolution as "a change from an indefinite, incoherent homogeneity to a definite, coherent heterogeneity" describes a natural course of development which might well be taken as a basis in scientific reasoning.

Development in Scientists' Formulation of Their Fundamental Problem

From time to time scientists have formulated their problems differently. It should be possible to trace this development by a study of their tools. Consider mathematics. Mathematics is the most restricted and representative form of logic used in science. A consideration of it should yield to us by implication some knowledge of the problems which were envisaged by the men who used it.

From a historical point of view the simple comparison of size is the most primitive mathematical process. Later we find simple distinction between singularity and plurality followed by enumeration or counting. Addition and subtraction developed as substitutes for counting forwards and backwards. Multiplication and division were used instead of addition and subtraction when equally sized groups were considered. In all of these processes the student assumed that originally he had been given units which were clearly distinct from each other. As proof of this distinction he required no evidence other than that of his own senses. One sheep added to what was obviously another sheep made two sheep. It was unnecessary to make sure that the second sheep was not simply another aspect of the first sheep.

When scientists began to experiment they demanded of mathematics formulas which would enable them to predict and control the outcome of their experiments. The entities which they used were envisaged as many different forces influencing their findings. Aristotle had believed that all influence proceeded from one great comprehensive agency and that man's puny efforts to tamper with that agency were futile and unnatural. But the experimentalists sought and attempted to hold in their hands the various little influences with which they peopled their surroundings. They asked mathematics to express functional relationships and to designate independent and dependent variables. They generally assumed their data to be multifarious, definite, and unrelated until proved to be otherwise. Expressed in a general form, the problem which these so-called Aristotelian scientists set for themselves is:

Given: $a, b, c, d, \ldots$

Prove: $a = f(b) + f(c) + f(d) + \ldots$

Here we have given us the separate and originally unrelated factors, *a, b, c, d, etc.* It is assumed that these factors were originally recognized by someone in their isolated condition. Indeed, in the physical world, such naive observation generally does yield workable units. No scientific analysis is necessary to distinguish one sheep from another, fire from water, or earth from air. Recently, when scientists tried to state their social problems in this form they found themselves unable to distinguish the given quantities; or, having distinguished them, were unable to discover any complete statement of the functional relationships between them.

For example, in seeking control of the causes of war, political scientists have passed neutrality legislation specifying that "neutral" "nations" shall not "ship" "munitions" to "belligerents" in the event of "war." No sooner is the legislation completed than the administration finds it impractical to apply to the bloody conflicts in Ethiopia, Spain, or China because the given quantities ("neutral," "nations," "ship," "munitions," "belligerents," "war") are not clearly distinguishable in the situation. But even suppose they are distinguishable, that is to say in terms of the Aristotelian problem, even suppose the separate and originally unrelated factors,

[1] First published as Kelly, G.A. (1938). The assumption of an originally homogeneous universe and some of its statistical implications. *The Journal of Psychology, 5,* 201–208. Now in the public domain and republished by permission of Jacqueline Aldridge.

Collected Papers of the Pioneer of Constructivist Psychology: George A. Kelly, First Edition. Edited by David A. Winter and Nick Reed.

a, b, c, d, etc., are given, political scientists generally fail to discover any complete statement of a point to point functional relationship between them such as:

$$a\text{-}war = f\left(b - shipment\ \ of\ \ munitions\right) + f\left(c - belligerent\ \ nations\right) + f\left(d - \ \right) + \ldots$$

Similarly in the field of psychology the supposedly given factors of *adjustment, frustration, intelligence, fear,* and *energy output* can neither be isolated nor satisfactorily expressed in such a formula.

The Notions of Probability and Correlation

The notion of probability has recently been brought into use. The quantity *a* is not expressed as a function of *b* in the old mathematical sense, but is expressed as a function of *b* within a certain probability. This compromise results in the following statement of the scientific problem:

Given: $a, b, c, d, \ldots$

Prove: $a = f(b) \pm PE + f(c) \pm PE + f(d) \pm PE + \ldots.$

where *a* is the dependent variable, *b, c, d, etc.*, are the independent variables and *PE* is the probable error in each functional relationship. This is to say that *a* depends upon *b* but that some unknown amount may have to be added or subtracted. The variable *a* is an approximate function of *b*. In this equation the notion of mathematical dependence is retained, but the dependent variable is allowed certain degrees of freedom. The allowance is a concession to various outlaw factors or "chance." Here again we find the presumption of heterogeneity. The Gaussian or normal probability curve is expressed in terms of the expanded binomial $(p + q)^n$. It is significant that thus far nature has not clearly revealed any entities which fit the categories of *p* and *q*.

A variant and improvement of the probability concept is the notion of correlation. Stated in terms of correlation the scientific problem is:

Given: $a, b, c, d, \ldots$

Prove: $r_{ab} = k, r_{ac} = k, r_{ad} = k, \ldots$

where r_{ab} is the coefficient of correlation between *a* and *b*. Here there is no designation of dependent and independent variables. Instead of setting for themselves the task of proving that the given *a* is a certain function of the given *b* scientists attempted to show *how much* relationship exists between *a* and *b*; thus the concept of correlation was substituted for the concept of function. The problem of distinguishing the factors *a, b, c, d, etc.*, remains unrecognized and unsolved. There is also a second difficulty, a practical one, which arises in connection with the use of the coefficient of correlation. While theoretically the coefficient of correlation makes no commitment regarding the functional or causal relationship between the variables, in practice, such a meaning is almost universally read into it. Indeed any scientific report of correlations which did not carry causal implications would be too passively mechanistic to interest even the most cautious of scientists.

There are a number of other disappointing features of the coefficient of correlation. While a more complete enumeration of them is reserved for another paper, one in particular should be mentioned here because of its bearing upon the present problem. It is also of interest to the writer because it was once the subject of considerable embarrassment to him. Professor Cyril Burt sitting as External Examiner in Degree Examinations proposed the question of whether or not certain unsatisfactory correlation coefficients obtained on a training college population could be due to the selectivity of the teaching profession. The writer gave a negative answer, which was, of course, incorrect.

Consider a simple illustration. Suppose we compute the coefficient of correlation between intelligence test scores and reading test scores on the group of pupils who comprise the four upper grades of a certain elementary school, and then compute separate coefficients for each of the grades. Since the group of pupils in any one of the grades may be expected to represent a smaller range of intellectual ability than does the group as a whole we may expect its coefficient to be significantly smaller than that computed on the group as a whole. It seems patently ridiculous to say that there is less relation between intelligence and reading in the various grades than in the school which they comprise. Nor is this discrepancy due to the relative sizes of the groups; it would be true theoretically if their populations were infinitely large. Statisticians would call the correlations obtained on the separate grades "attenuated because of our failure to obtain an unselected sample," but there is the question of whether or not it is possible ever to secure an unselected sample. Long ago statisticians learned not to use the variable of chronological age in a correlation problem, yet the same considerations which led to the rejection of chronological age are essentially operative in all other variables which can be measured with a reasonable degree of accuracy.

The supposed attenuation of the coefficient of correlation such as that due to the limited range of intelligence in each of the separate grades of the elementary school is the subject of a correction formula by T. L. Kelley. It is:

$$\frac{\sigma}{\Sigma} = \frac{\sqrt{1 - R}}{\sqrt{1 - r}}$$

where σ is the standard deviation of a variable in the limited sample, Σ is the standard deviation the sample would have if it were unselected, *R* is the corrected coefficient of correlation, and *r* is the uncorrected coefficient of correlation. If, in our illustration, the coefficient of correlation between intelligence and reading in one of the grade groups were .40, the standard deviation of intelligence 1, and the standard deviation of intelligence in the entire school 2, Kelley's formula would yield a corrected coefficient of correlation of .85.

Stated in non-mathematical language the situation is this: In a class where the pupils all have nearly the same amount of intelligence it is relatively difficult to predict individual reading scores from a knowledge of the small differences in intelligence, but, in a school where the intelligence ranges from that of tiny youngsters to that of adolescents, it is relatively easy to segregate pupils into groups of varying levels of reading ability after giving an intelligence test. But this certainly does not mean that intelligence plays any greater role in learning to read when a child is listed as a member of one group than when he is listed as a member of another.

Now let us consider intelligence, not simply as a discrete factor given to us by naive observation in its clearly isolated form with a certain limited standard deviation (such as that observable in a fourth grade class), but as a comprehensive variable ranging from the lowest levels exhibited by fourth grade pupils to the highest levels exhibited by eighth grade pupils. Look further. See it range from the levels of low grade idiots to the levels of "Army Alpha Geniuses." Consider it again and see it extend from the levels of animal mind to the constructive contributions of an Aristotle. Even then we overlook the lower levels of adjustment found in plant life. Consider reading in the same way. Consider it as the ability to interpret symbols visually presented. Trace it downward past the phonetic alphabet, the pictorial writings, the expression on a mother's face, the trainer's threatening gesture. Trace it upward past diagrams, through current events, social trends, to signs of the times, and beyond. With intelligence and reading thus recognized an obtained correlation coefficient of .40 between them is a measure only of one thing; the narrowness of the restrictions which our definitions have imposed upon our observations. Give someone complete control of the temperature at the North Pole and he can demonstrate a perfect correlation between that variable and the length of rabbits' ears in Wyoming—or any other thing in our natural universe.

The Assumption of an Originally Homogeneous Universe

Obviously such extension of our everyday definitions as was suggested above would lead us to a point at which it would be impossible for us to distinguish intelligence from reading or from anything else. Our variables would become completely lost in an "incoherent, indefinite homogeneity." As James might say, man would be brought to face the world as he originally found it, as "a blooming buzzing confusion." Science must proceed in the opposite direction. Its problem is:

Given: X

Prove: $f_1(X) = a_1 + b_1 + c_1 + \ldots,$

$$f_2(X) = a_2 + b_2 + c_2 + \ldots,$$

$$f_3(X) = a_3 + b_3 + c_3 + \ldots,$$

where $f_1(X), f_2(X), f_3(X), \ldots$ are various functions of the natural universe X or *phenomena*, and $a_1, b_1, c_1, \ldots a_2, b_2, c_2, \ldots a_3, b_3, c_3, \ldots$ are measurable units or *convenient abstractions* chosen so that $a \neq b \neq c \ldots$ or $r_{ab} = 0, r_{ac} = 0, r_{bc} = 0, \ldots$ This is to say that science is given the unknown homogeneity X. Certain functions of this X (operational concepts, as some scientists would call them) emerge from the given universe to be apprehended by scientists and comprehended in the simple convenient terms *a, b, c,* etc., which we can all keep in mind. In political science the phenomenon of war, which we may call the war function of our natural universe, $f_{war}(X)$, is to be expressed in terms of familiar units. The desired alteration in this function is to be brought about with a minimum of disturbance to the other functions of our natural universe such as our economic life, $f_{econ}(X)$, our liberty, $f_{lib}(X)$, and our championing of justice, $f_{jus}(X)$. But how extensive is this war which we seek to control; is it only war as formally declared by some nations in the past, or do we mean to control all conflict? If the former, it ought to be susceptible to control with a minimum of disturbance to our economic life, liberty, and championing of justice; indeed that sort of war seems already to have been effectively discouraged. If the latter more extended definition is used, we oblige ourselves to alter our whole mode of living in order to bring it under control. Not even the most ardent pacifist can claim to be opposed to all forms of conflict, since such a position would deny him the right to express his opposition. Certainly democracy cannot oppose conflict as long as it is based upon the principle that the majority's might makes right. Spread over some limited extent of this great range of human conflict we expect to find just the war which we seek to bring under reasonable control. Thus as the political scientist advances in his work $f_{war}(X)$ may emerge as a reasonably definite palpable entity.

In the same way the psychologist must recognize such natural functions of the phenomenological world as intelligence, reading ability, and personal adjustment emerging as distinct and reasonably defined entities. Even primitive man counting his flock must recognize individual sheep emerging from the whole and equate each of them to simple non-overlapping units of number for his own convenience. It is fundamental to recognize that *all phenomena are emergent and that the task of science is to express them in terms of simple, convenient, distinct, uncorrelated abstractions.*

Statistical Implications

The statement that "all phenomena are emergent" is based upon the assumption of an originally homogeneous universe. Expressing our thesis in the more formal language of mathematics we might write:

POSTULATE: *The universe is originally an "indefinite, incoherent homogeneity."*

AXIOM: *All variables are emergent.*

CORRELATE I: *All sample populations must be considered as selected on the basis of the definition of the emergent variable measured in them. (There is no such thing as an unselected sample.)*

CORRELATE II: *The coefficient of correlation between any two variables is a measure of the homogeneity remaining in that function of the universe which they jointly represent.* (A coefficient of correlation between two variables which is equal to zero indicates in general that one or both of the variables has been so limited by definition or selection of the sample population that it is no longer merged with the other.)

In the light of this reasoning probably any mention of the value of a correlation should be accompanied by a specific statement of the absolute dispersion allowed each variable by its definition as well as the basis upon which the population was selected. Any statistical technique such as multiple regression or factor analysis which is based upon the degree of relationship expressed by the coefficient of correlation should be accompanied by such a statement. Certainly, in factor analysis, if one is to "discover" specific factors as "operative" he should make it clear to his readers that such discoveries are true only within the limitations which his definitions have imposed upon the dispersions, and that a "discovered" factor's "operative-ness" may be altered entirely by a more liberal definition of some of the measured variables. Thus energy output, as measured among the members of a certain fourth grade class, may not appear to affect the factor constellation in terms of which the class's performance on a battery of tests is described; but, in the cases of certain children, a clinical psychologist may be forced to recognize excessively low or excessively high energy outputs as the crucial factors in their test performances. A factor analysis would therefore be of little value to a clinical psychologist unless it specified that sufficiently extensive definitions of such variables were allowed.

These statistical implications are only suggestive. There are many others which might be investigated and reported. Psychologists interested in topology may find such mathematical investigations fruitful and the findings systematically consistent with their point of view.

References

Hogben, L. (1933). Limits of applicability of correlation technique in human genetics. *Journal of Genetics*, *27*, 379–406.
Kelley, T. L. (1924). *Statistical Method*. Macmillan.
Sanders, B. (1934). The inadequacy of correlation method in genetic research. *Journal of American Statistical Association*, *29*, 59–65.
Thurstone, L. L. (1937). Current misuse of the factorial methods. *Psychometrika*, *2*, 73–76.
Thurstone, L. L. (1935). *The Vectors of Mind*. University of Chicago Press.

31

A Projective Method of Personality Investigation[1]

A diagnostic personality inventory constructed from the presupposition that people identify themselves with strong characters in stories they read. A series of story plots are presented in which the subject selects the solution of the conflict. Solution selected indicates nature of maladjustment. Validated by independent diagnosis using other clinical techniques.

[1] This abstract from the Proceedings of the Seventeenth Annual Meeting of the Midwestern Psychological Association was first published as Bishop, F. & Kelly, G. A. (1942). A projective method of personality investigation. *Psychological Bulletin, 39(8)*, 599. It is now in the public domain and is republished by permission of Jacqueline Aldridge.

Collected Papers of the Pioneer of Constructivist Psychology: George A. Kelly, First Edition. Edited by David A. Winter and Nick Reed.
 Published 2026 by John Wiley & Sons Ltd.

32

Clinical Validity and Conceptual Consistency[1]

Psychologists still have some vexing questions to answer about the validity of their clinical instruments. Some of the most disturbing have to do with the Rorschach Test. Yet most clinical psychologists continue to make use of this instrument, some with brazen indifference to the mounting statistical and experimental evidence against it, others with mixed feelings and guilty consciences. Those of us who have used the Rorschach over the years to help clarify clinical situations are not convinced that its invalidity has been established by relevant experimental procedures, nor does candor permit us to make any substantial claims for its contribution to our work. It seems, therefore, that, as scientists, we are obligated to do some pretty heavy thinking about the continued use of this particular test, as well as our continued use of certain other tests in the face of contrary evidence. This article represents an attempt to do some of this kind of thinking, and to follow it up with a special kind of experimental venture.

Problem

First of all, let us step back and view the psychologist's clinical instruments in the context of the settings in which they are used. Each device attempts to locate its subjects as precisely as possible in relation to certain reference axes along which it has been scaled. The reference axes are not God-given but are simply products of the psychologist's conceptual art. They are erected for his convenience and he, as a scientist, applies certain criteria for determining how well they serve his purposes.

While some clinicians are perfectly content with instruments that merely give them a comfortable feeling in the presence of their clients or a staff-conference vocabulary that wins nods of approval from like-minded clinicians, the thoughtful psychologist seeks something more. What it is he seeks depends largely on what he is trying to do with his clients. If he is mainly interested in stable classification, he will construct reference axes with respect to which each client will show a minimum of change from day to day or from year to year; in no event does he want any client to get up off the continuum and wander over to its other end. But if the psychologist is mainly interested in psychotherapy, he will definitely want his client to move. In that case he will seek to erect a combination of reference axes that will suggest the important pathways that are open. The former type of psychologist will go for the IQ test and the fatalistic psychology which surrounds it. The latter psychologist will seek to throw light upon key attitudes of his client which, if altered, might bring about a chain-reaction of healthy improvement.

Most of our methodology for determining the validity of tests has been developed to serve the needs of the first type of psychologist—the one who wants every client to stay put, regardless of what happens to him. Yet clinical instruments are mainly used by psychologists who have the latter kind of need—the need to open important new pathways of movement for each of their clients. Testing validity, as well as reliability, in the latter kind of setting is a somewhat different matter. Validity has to be seen, not so much as an attribute of a particular test, but more as an attribute of a dimensional scheme in terms of which the psychologist may envision his client's opportunities.

Clinical validity runs headlong into another problem. Our thinking about clients always tends to be eclectic and complex. We erect all kinds of dimensional schemes around them and we often shift our reference axes as we move from fact to fact. What this means is that we are likely to arrange our criterion data along one axis and then try to check validity by correlating them with prediction data that have been conceptualized along another axis. Personality, being the complex kind of affair that it is, can be schematized in so many different ways that any two dimensions are at random quite unlikely to have similar alignments. The result is a distressing array of low validity coefficients. Tests, such as the Rorschach with which some of us attempt to throw light upon the therapeutic potentialities of a client are likely to be particularly hard hit.

[1] Unpublished manuscript by G.M. Collet & G.A. Kelly, 1954. It is based on Grace Collet's doctoral dissertation at The Ohio State University, *Prediction and communication problems illustrated by the Rorschach*, and is probably a revised version of a paper with this title (available from the editors on request) that had been submitted for publication. Published by permission of Jacqueline Aldridge.

Collected Papers of the Pioneer of Constructivist Psychology: George A. Kelly, First Edition. Edited by David A. Winter and Nick Reed.

Methodology

Now what would happen if we took particular pains to arrange our criterion data in terms of the same conceptual scheme as our predictor data? This would bring the axes of information into alignment with each other. If we spoke of the property of "*X-ness*" in the criterion we would also make sure that we were referring to the very same property of "*X-ness*" when we talked about the predictor. Both criterion and predictor would be structured within the same system.

For example, suppose we took the Rorschach Test—since it is one of the most conspicuous offenders against our scientific conscience—and paid especial attention to its unique system of personality dimensions. We would keep in mind, of course, that the ten ink blots do not themselves provide a set of dimensions, but rather that there has been a unique set of dimensions evolved by the persons who use them. We would recognize that Rorschach thinking has developed, in a considerable measure, its own system of concepts. We would look at this miniature system that has grown up in the thinking of Rorschachers and start dealing with it as an abstractive system, rather than as a concretive set of responses and scores.

Consider the *R-score,* for example—the total number of percepts reported by the examinee as he looks at the ten cards in succession. We can see *R*, not merely in a concrete manner as a score, but, in a more abstractive sense, as a dimension of psychologizing about people. Is *R-ness*—or *perceptual responsiveness* to give it a more descriptive name—a dimension along which a wide variety of client behaviors can be consistently generalized? Let us take this as an intermediate hypothesis and see where we get with it.

To begin with, we shall have to become accustomed to thinking about clients in terms of this dimension. We must come to see *perceptual responsiveness*, or whatever we call it, not merely as a score made by a given client on a given day, nor even as a continuum of scores made by different clients, but as a far-reaching dimension of any person's living. Nor will we let slip, as it is so easy to do, and consider our construct to be simply interchangeable with more familiar constructs such as "intellectual striving," "verbal productivity," or "oral compulsivity." The new term must freshly abstract and firmly hold its own nexus of meaning.

We can fall into another kind of semantic trap, too. We shall be tempted to derive the meaning of the new dimension from the name we have chosen to give it—*perceptual responsiveness*. But this may not turn out to be a good representation of Rorschach *R-ness*. Instead, we need initially to derive the meaning solely from various clients' behavior during Rorschach testing, the kind of behavior that affects the size of their R-scores. It is this score-influencing meaning, not semiotic meaning, that is then to provide structure for interpreting the broader aspects of the client's life. Thus we will need, not only to know a good deal about clients in general, but also a good deal about the features of their behavior that enter into their Rorschach performances.

We have mentioned the *R-score*. We can approach other important constructs in the same abstractive way. *Form-plus*, for example, can be given the new conceptual look. So can color, approach, and other Rorschach "scores."

What we are describing is a way of seeking conceptual consistency as a first step toward determining the validity of any psychological instrument, especially one which is to be used in a clinical setting. If both predictor and criterion are carefully cast in the same dimensions of discourse we should have far better grounds for determining how much we can learn about a person from giving him a certain test. This article is, therefore, not primarily about the validity of the Rorschach Test[2], but rather an article about what happens when one carefully examines his epistemological position before launching out into a study of validity. The choice of the Rorschach Test, rather than some other clinical instrument, and the operations by which our particular predictor and criterion variables were defined, are quite incidental.

Method

Now for the experiment itself. On the one side we have Rorschach scores; on the other we have various kinds of non-Rorschach information. The validity problem is to see how well we can predict the one after being informed of the other. The question of which is to be considered the predictor and which the criterion is not statistically important; in either case the correlational operation is the same. But the question of which is which does have a bearing on the way we develop our data[3]. Since we have decided to structure both sets of data in terms of Rorschach constructs, let us say that the Rorschach scores are on the criterion side and the non-Rorschach information is the predictor. This is a switch from the usual manner of approach, but it should help keep our thinking straight in the matter of conceptual consistency.

The study was conducted in three stages; a "free research" stage involving 13 hospitalized adults, followed by the conventional two stages of "fixed research" required by cross-validational experimental design. Thirty similar cases were involved in each of the latter two stages. During the first stage primary emphasis was placed on the reconceptualization of the predictor data. At the beginning of the second stage we

[2] Strictly speaking, it is improper to refer to a test or to its scores as having a property of validity. Nor is it sufficient merely to specify that a test is valid for a certain specific purpose. Instead, validity is a property of the predictions one makes, and not of the test data he chooses to construe—or misconstrue—in making his wagers.

[3] One could argue—although this is not the place for it—that the criterion should always be the variable based on the smaller range of available data and that it should always dictate the conceptual system or subsystem in which the experimental discourse is to be carried on. The predictor should be the variable based on the more multifarious data and should yield, for purposes of precision, its structure to the system employed for dealing with the criterion.

turned our attention to pinning down the operational referents. Before entering the last stage we selected variables by the Wherry-Doolittle Test Selection Method (Stead et al., 1940) and laid our final wagers in terms of multiple regression equations.

During the final stage especially tight controls were maintained against contamination of either predictor or criterion data. The clinician who administered and scored the Rorschach had no prior access to the predictions made by the clinician who construed the non-Rorschach data, nor were Rorschach scores made available to the predicting clinician until after the predictions had been recorded.

In the first stage we began by considering thirty-six different Rorschach dimensions—*number of responses* (R), *approach* (App), *good form per cent* (F+%), *shading shock* (SS), etc. and attempted to construe then conceptually as generalized dimensions in the lives of thirteen patients in a private sanitarium. We took into account the available case history information, the nosological classification made by the psychiatric staff (without knowledge of Rorschach information, of course), Wechsler-Bellevue Intelligence Scale data, Hanfmann-Kasanin Concept Formation Test data, Bolles-Rosen-Landis Sorting Test (BRL) data and Thematic Apperception Test (TAT) data. We tried to look at this non-Rorschach information through the templets of Rorschach constructs. Of course, we could not make direct translations from the data categories, for our task was to reconceptualize the data, and not merely to attempt literal or mathematical transformation from one conceptual scheme to another.

For example, when we looked at the case history information we tried to conceptualize the *R-ness* properties, then we tried to see the *F+%-ness*, then the *SS-ness*, etc. Certainly this, rather than the mathematical computations, was the crucial part of the experimental operation; yet how does one describe it? Especially, now does one describe it in those common language terms which are themselves the figments of another conceptual system, terms laden with all the prejudice of familiarity? Indeed, it was now our task to escape from such familiar concretized notions, not to use them as pre-supposed facts.

We began with the problem of conceptualizing Rorschach *R-ness*. Initially we guessed that this might be a property that could be abstracted from five sets of objects obtained from non-Rorschach sources.

The five were:

a "IQ score" from the Wechsler-Bellevue Intelligence Scale
b "Drive" from the Vygotsky Test
c "Perceptual impact" from the Thematic Apperception Test
d "Defense mechanisms" from psychiatric "diagnosis"
e "Achievement" from vocational and educational history

But the nascent reconceptualization of information that has already been conventionally classified and verbalized proved to be a frustrating task. We were only partially successful in our conceptual pioneering effort. After all, the *R-ness* we were struggling to conceive was neither "IQ," nor "drive," nor "perceptual impact," nor "defense mechanism," nor socio-economic "achievement." It was instead, we hoped, a new quality of psychological appraisal, one that had begun to take shape in the thinking of Rorschachers, but not one that had yet been generalized to non-Rorschach behaviors.

At the end of the first stage of our venture we gave up, as far as the present study was concerned, our efforts to generalize 18 of the original 36 Rorschach concepts. Continuing to entertain some hopes of extending the remaining concepts to non-Rorschach data, we then undertook to define them so as to achieve some reasonable degree of objectivity. For example in the case of *R-ness,* our next job was to pin it down to features of the five kinds of non-Rorschach data listed above.

In the matter of reading *R-ness* into IQ data it was immediately apparent that much of the quality of the subject's performance had been lost by the time the data were made available to us. Thus we had to guess how the *R-ness* property had operated in order to produce the score he got. We were, in part, though not altogether, thrown back on a literal transformation of IQ scores. While we regretted this retreat back in the direction of conventional conceptualization, we deemed it necessary in order to achieve objectivity. If we had it to do over again we would not be inclined to make this much of a concession.

In assessing the *R-ness* of intelligence test data we guessed that an IQ score of less than ninety was compatible with less than 15 responses on the Rorschach, that an IQ of 90 to 99 would reveal the same *R-ness* quality that 15 to 24 responses on the Rorschach would imply, and so on through five steps of an *R-ness* scale.

In the case of Vygotsky "drive" we also set up five steps, each operationally defined by a paragraph. The paragraph which best described the subject's Vygotsky behavior became the indicator of the amount of *R-ness*, or, simply, the number of responses predicted for his Rorschach performance. For example, the following describes the performance that was predicted would go with less than 15 Rorschach responses:

> Quits, lack of confidence; pathological or congenital inability to understand the task,

while the following, at the top of the scale, led to the prediction of 45 or more responses:

> Great persistence with intolerance of help even though he can't solve the problems; enjoys the task and would stick at it for hours, no fluidity and remains abstract; may also get it in a relatively short time but has revealed drive and need to achieve.

When we came to the TAT we had, of course, full protocols. Thus in judging "perceptual impact" we had much richer information to conceptualize. This may account for our later success in validating our abstraction of this particular operant. Thirteen descriptive paragraphs were set up, the subject was matched to the paragraph which seemed to fit him best, and the prediction of his Rorschach R was taken from the scalar value assigned to the paragraph.

The "defense mechanisms" which we guessed might bear upon our concept of *R-ness* were inferred simply from the psychiatric "diagnoses." For example, we guessed that the damaged patients; those who were coarctated or inhibited; and the suspicious, abulic, etc., i.e., those lacking outgoing drive or ability, would make less than 15 Rorschach responses. We simply lumped these as the diagnosed "depressives," the "organic," the "simple schizophrenics," and the "deteriorated paranoid schizophrenics." At the top of our five point scale we put the "acute or pre-schizophrenics," the "obsessive-compulsives," and the "hypomanics," and we guessed that they might make more than 45 responses.

"Achievement," as it was revealed in the case history, was already highly structured in terms of the concepts and values of our times and culture. About all that we could do was set up a transformation scale for years of "education" or "occupational level." We were not greatly surprised when we found later that we had not successfully abstracted the *R-ness* quality among these conventionalized data.

So much for *R-ness*. We approached the seventeen other Rorschach "concepts" in a similar manner, using various kinds of non-Rorschach information that are commonly available in the clinic. As the reader can imagine, this was somewhat more than a Sunday afternoon job. To give a detailed description of all the paragraphs and trial scales would demand more printer's ink than the exposition of our present thesis needs. Besides, it would tend to direct attention away from the philosophical notion of conceptual consistency and give some readers the impression that we were promulgating a concrete scale of psychological behaviors or that we were trying to prove that the Rorschach has inherent validity. To be sure, the proof of our pudding lies in the accuracy of the predictions we were able to make, but we would not argue for a moment that anyone should re-use the scales we built. Indeed, we would not use them again ourselves, even the ones that enabled us to make valid predictions. And as for the Rorschach, we think it will be a long time before anyone can claim it is a fool-proof instrument. All we propose to argue here is that there is evidence in favor of approaching this kind of problem through paying some attention to the conceptual consistency with which predictor and criterion data are handled. But now we are getting ahead of ourselves in reporting our venture.

At the end of the second stage of the study we had in hand a series of multiple regression equations based on operationally defined Rorschach-type concepts applied to non-Rorschach data as independent variables on one side and, on the other side, predicted Rorschach scores expressed as dependent variables. The independent variables in each equation had been chosen by the Wherry-Doolittle method. The 18 concepts with which we entered the second stage had dwindled to 12, six having made a poor showing on the 30 cases just studied. These 12 were now to be subjected to the rigorous test of cross-validation in the third and final stage of the study.

Results

An effort was made to match the nosological composition of the two groups of 30 subjects studied in the last two stages of the investigation. When chi-square was used to check the probability that the two groups came from the same nosologically defined population a p of .99 was obtained. As far as nosology is concerned the groups may, therefore, be considered random samples of the same population.

Table 1 shows the experimental results. The chi-square test of significance on a four-fold table was used to measure the validity of all 12 types of predictions and, where applicable, the Pearsonian correlation coefficient was also computed. Rorschach scores in the left hand column are designated by the conventional Rorschach symbols. In the case of four Rorschach scores the final sample of 30 cases did not distribute themselves in the same way as the preceding sample. While this meant that the scores had to be dichotomized at different points in order to form four-fold tables for chi-square computations, it did not involve any alteration of the hypothesized relationships. Nor did it affect the Pearsonian scattergrams. The four were: FC, CF, C, and F: M: C.

Predictions reached the .05 level of significance on six of the 12 Rorschach dimensions when measured by chi-square and on seven of the dimensions when measured by the Pearsonian correlation coefficient. Altogether, satisfactory predictions were made on eight of the 12 dimensions, if we accept X^2 and r as alternative measures of relationship. These eight were: R, App, F+%, M, FC, CF, Coarc, and F: M: C. Those dimensions in which predictions failed were: C, S, FCh, and Fc.

Discussion

The task of reconceptualizing psychological facts is extremely difficult. The facts themselves, by the time they reach our data sheets, are already the hostages of the established conceptual systems of common language and thought. They are by-products of those systems.

Table 1 Reliability of Prediction of Rorschach Scores

Score	X^2	*p*	*r*	*p*
R	11.7	<.001	.79	<.001
App	6.6	<.02	.48	<.01
F+%	9.4	<.001	.71	<.01
M	4.0	<.05	.52	<.01
FC	.7	<.50	.49	<.01
CF	.1	<.70	.54	<.01
C	1.0	<.40	–	–
Coarc	4.9	<0.5	.75	<.01
F:M:C	7.5	<.01	.29	<.20
S	.1	<.80	–	–
FCh	.2	<.70	–	–
Fc	.1	<.80	–	–

Moreover, we ran into other kinds of difficulty. The study was a doctoral dissertation and, according to the usual custom, had to be designed to meet psychologists' conventional standards. It was not enough that the novel approach should lead to valid predictions, but also it was required that the variables should be couched in "objective," i.e., familiar, terms. We had to conform to the conventional view that validity is somehow a property that inheres in a test rather than in the predictions made by the users of the test. Thus we found ourselves continually yielding here and yielding there to established customs of psychological thought. The outcome was that we did not reconceptualize our non-Rorschach data anywhere nearly as thoroughly as we had intended. We could only partially escape from the dimensions of our academic *Flatland*.

Yet, in spite of our difficulties in holding fast to a program of reconceptualizing non-Rorschach information, the yield of statistically significant predictions is remarkably promising, as Rorschach studies go. Bearing in mind that it is the conceptual consistency approach to the validation of clinical instruments that is at stake, we now have evidence that will clearly justify further efforts along this line. The particular prediction formulas we used are, as we have said before, not important—indeed we are for throwing them out, even if they did lead to some fairly respectable *p*-values. But the conceptual approach we are now ready to buy.

There is, of course, no way of knowing whether the four dimensions of prediction that failed still offer any promising possibilities. It is true that we ran into distribution troubles with them on the cross-validation sample. This is an all-too-familiar problem in research with clinical instruments.

To be sure, we used a small number of cases in our final sample. There are arguments on both sides, but we have generally taken the position that, the clinical setting being what it is, research with clinical instruments might better limit itself to small samples. A trend which can be reliably indicated only in a sample of several hundred cases may be important in a massive personnel selection program, but may be unimportant in dealing with patients who must be managed, one way or another, in the clinical setting.

Then there is the notion of validity itself. Psychologists are traditionally in favor of validity. They also have conventional ways of measuring it. And when an unconventional study such as ours turns up, there is an implicit invitation to stand up and say just how it uniquely conceptualizes validity.

We have already said that we are thinking of validity as a property of the predictions that people make, and not necessarily of the instruments from which they make inferences. This is important for our purposes. But we can say something more penetrating than this. Let us look at it this way. If we envision ourselves living in a world of given particulars—i.e., ready-made facts—then the task of the statistically-minded psychologist is to scrounge around for mislaid correlations between these taken-for-granted facts. When found, we can call them "validity coefficients." But if we see our world as one originally presented to us as an undifferentiated homogeneity—a vast rolling prairie of public domain unmarred by surveyors' stakes—then we may well ask what effect our conceptual bench marks and transit lines will have upon the relationships we shall later "discover" (Kelly, 1938, 1955). From this moment the quest for validity takes us off in quite a different direction.

At any given turning point in our lives there is, all around us, the panorama of the present; and there is also the future, shrouded always in fog. From what we can see now we try to guess what we shall discover when the fog begins to clear. Validity is the measure of how well we do this.

In the setting we have envisioned, the quest for validity becomes basically a search for concepts that will structure both present and future along the same dimensional lines. Only by such a conceptual alignment can we hope to measure the present and, from our measurements, forecast a well-structured future.

What the psychologist sees when he gives a patient the Rorschach Test is a little bit of the present. What he seeks to predict are the concluding chapters of the patient's biography, as it might be written under certain assumed conditions. The first problem of validity is not so much what the ten little magic blots have to say about the patient's future, but in what way, if any, the patient's behavior on seeing the blots for the first time and his behavior on seeing tomorrow's sunrise for the first time can be invested with the same conceptual properties. Once the very same property is seen in both, we stand some chance of saying something valid about an aspect of tomorrow's behavior. Perhaps these remarks about the problem of validity will help to make clear what we were in search of when we set out to make this study.

Summary

The validity of a test used for clinical purposes involves issues that are often overlooked. Not only must reference axes be erected along which it is possible to see patients move during the course of their treatment, but also we need to be consistent about the axes when we compare predictor and criterion data.

When we apply the second of these considerations to the Rorschach Test, for example, we find that the concepts used to structure a patient's Rorschach performance are not necessarily compatible with those commonly used to structure non-Rorschach information about him. We therefore asked the question what would happen if we generalized Rorschach concepts to patients' non-Rorschach behavior and then did a conventional cross-validation study of predictions. In effect, this meant treating Rorschach scores as criterion data and non-Rorschach information, construed in terms of Rorschach-type constructs, as predictor data. When such a study is made it must be kept clearly in mind that validity is essentially a property of the predictions we make and not necessarily a property of the test we use in making the predictions.

Considerable difficulty was experienced in reconceptualizing non-Rorschach information along the lines of Rorschach-type concepts. In spite of this, it was possible to make statistically significant predictions in a cross-validational sample along eight out of 12 dimensional lines. The makeshift formulas used for reconceptualizing the non-Rorschach information are not considered important or worth repeating. The methodology, however, does seem to be one which promises to throw new light upon the utility of clinical tests such as the Rorschach. The study points up the practical necessity of approaching questions of validity through reconceptualization rather than looking for gratuitous relationships among miscellaneous data.

References

Kelly, G. A. (1938). The assumption of an originally homogeneous universe and some of its statistical implications. *J. Psychol.*, *5*, 201–208.
Kelly, G.A. (1955). *The psychology of personal constructs*. Norton. 2 Vols.
Stead, W. H., Shartle, C. L., Otis, J. L., et al. (1940). *Occupational counseling*, Appendix 5. American Book.

Bibliography

American Psychiatric Association (1952). *Diagnostic and statistical manual of mental disorders*. American Psychiatric Association.
Beck, S. J. (1950). *Rorschach's test*. Vol. 1. *Basic processes* (2nd Ed.). Grune and Stratton.
Collet, G. (1953). *Prediction and communication problems illustrated with the Rorschach*. Unpublished doctor's dissertation, Ohio State Univer.
Cronbach, L. J. (1949). Statistical methods applied to Rorschach scores. *Psychol. Bull.*, *46*, 393–429.
Klopfer, B., & Kelley, D. M. (1942). *The Rorschach technique*. World Book.
Rapaport, D., Gill, M. M., & Schafer, R. (1946). *Diagnostic psychological testing*. Year Book, 2 vols.

33

Instructions Role Construct Repertory Test (Rep Test) and Situational Resources Test (Res Test)*[1]

Role Construct Repertory Test (Rep Test)

This test comprises of three parts: (1) Grid, (2) Overlay Sheet, and (3) this set of Instructions. The test is designed to help the examiner to understand you and some of the people who have played a part in your life.

1 Start with the Overlay Sheet. Beginning with your own name in the first blank write the first name of each of the persons described. If you cannot remember a person's first name, write his last name or something about him which will bring him clearly to your mind when you go back over the sheet.

2 Next lay the Overlay Sheet sidewise across the top of the Grid so that the numbered blanks correspond to the numbered columns in the Grid. Note that on the Grid the letters "M" and "F" appear at the head of each column. If you are a man, encircle the "M" at the head of the first column. If you are a woman, encircle the "F" to indicate that you are a female. In the same way indicate whether each of the persons in the remaining columns is male (M) or female (F).

3 Now move the Overlay Sheet down over the Grid until it is just above the first row of squares. Note that the three squares at the extreme right have circles in them. This means that you are first to consider the three people whose names appear on your Overlay Sheet in the last three columns—Columns 20, 21, and 22. Think about these three people. Are two of them *alike in some important way that distinguishes them from the third person*? Keep thinking about them until you remember the important way in which two of them are alike and which sets them off from the third person.

When you have decided which two it is, and the important way in which they are alike, put an "X" in the two circles corresponding to the two who are alike. Do not put any mark in the third circle.

Now write in the blank under "*Construct*" the word or short phrase that tells how these two are alike.

Next write in the blank under "*Contrast*" what you consider to be opposite of this characteristic.

4 Now consider each of the other nineteen persons whose names appear at the heads of Columns 1 to 19. In addition to the two persons whom you have marked with an "X," which ones also have this important characteristic? Put a check mark (✓)—not an "X"—under the name of each other person who has this important characteristic.

5 Now slide the Overlay Sheet down to the second row. Think about persons Number 17, 18, and 19—the three who have circles under their names. In what important way are two of these distinguished from the third? Put "X's" in the circles to show which two are alike.

Write the *Construct* and the *Contrast* in the blanks on the right just as you did before. Then consider the other nineteen persons. Check "✓" the ones who also have the characteristic you have noted.

6 Complete the test in the way you have done the first two rows. Write your name and date on the Grid and give it to the examiner. If he requests the Overlay Sheet, give him that also.

* For detailed instructions see, Kelly, G.A. (1955). *The psychology of personal constructs*. Vol. 1. *A theory of personality*. Norton.

1 Dated 26 June, 1956. Published by permission of Jacqueline Aldridge.

Collected Papers of the Pioneer of Constructivist Psychology: George A. Kelly, First Edition. Edited by David A. Winter and Nick Reed.

Situational Resources Test (Res Test)

This test comprises three parts: (1) Grid, (2) Overlay Sheet, and (3) This set of Instructions.

A Start with the Overlay Sheet. Beginning with your own name in the first blank write the first name of each of the persons described. If you cannot remember a person's first name, write his last name or something about him which will bring him clearly to your mind when you go back over the sheet.

B Next lay the Overlay Sheet sidewise across the top of the Grid so that the numbered blanks correspond to the numbered columns in the Grid. Note that on the Grid the letters "M" and "F" appear at the head of each column. If you are a man encircle the "M" at the head of the first column. If you are a woman encircle the "F" to indicate that you are a female. In the same way indicate whether each of the persons in the remaining columns is male (M) or female (F).

C The next step is to finish filling out the Grid. Everyone faces some personal problems at one time or another in his life. Here are some very general types of problems that everyone confronts in one way or another.

1 Think of the time in your life when you were most perplexed about what kind of a job or vocation you ought to go into. Write the *year* when it happened in the first blank under "*Construct*" on the Grid. Now write the *place* where it happened, just to the right under "*Contrast*." This is to help you identify the incident later in this test.

Now suppose each of the other twenty-one people whose names you have written at the tops of the columns of the Grid had been around at that time. Which ones, if any, do you feel you could have turned to for help? Put an "X" below each of their names in the first row of squares opposite the date and place. Place an "X" under your own name also, if you feel you could have worked out the problem by yourself.

2 Next think of the time in your life when you had the greatest difficulty understanding how to get along with people of the opposite sex. Write the year and place in the second row. Then put an "X" in the second row under each person you feel you might have turned to for help if he had been there. Also, if you think you could have worked out the problem by yourself, put an "X" under your own name.

Now you can go on to the rest of the items in the same way. Do not repeat situations. If a situation has already been listed simply make a second choice.

3 The time when things seemed to be going against you—when your luck was particularly bad.
4 The time when you were most hard up financially.
5 The time when you were in poorest health or had a long period of sickness.
6 The time when someone took advantage of you because you did not know what you were doing.
7 The time when you made one of the most serious mistakes in your life.
8 The time when you failed to accomplish something you tried very hard to do.
9 The time when you were most lonely.
10 The time when you felt most discouraged about the future.
11 The time when you wondered if you would not be better off dead or when you came nearest to feeling that way.
12 The time when you felt most misunderstood by others or when it seemed as if people were ganging up on you.
13 The time when you lost your temper or got very angry.
14 The time when you hurt someone's feelings in a way they did not deserve.
15 The time when you felt most ashamed of yourself.
16 The time when you were most frightened or fearful about what might become of you.
17 The time in recent years when you acted childishly or like a "sissy."
18 The time when you felt jealous of someone's affection.
19 The time in your life when you felt most mixed up or confused about things in general.
20 The time when you had serious trouble with your parents or came nearest having trouble with them.
21 The time when you had trouble with your brother, sister, or a close relative—or the time when you came nearest to having trouble with one of them.
22 The time when you had trouble with your wife (husband) or closest friend of the opposite sex—or the time when you came nearest to having trouble with that person.

*Now go back over the twenty-two situations you have listed and put a check mark "✓" opposite the **five** which have caused you the most worry during your life.*

Overlay Sheet

(For Use with the Rep Test or the Res Test)*

Figure List

1. Write your own name in the first blank here.
2. Write your mother's first name here. If you grew up with a stepmother, write her name instead.
3. Write your father's first name here. If you grew up with a stepfather, write his name instead.
4. Write the name of your brother who is nearest your own age. If you had no brother, write the name of a boy near your own ge who was most like a brother to you during your early teens.
5. Write the name of your sister who is nearest your own age. If you had no sister, write the name of a girl near your own age who was most like a sister to you during your early teens.

FROM THIS POINT ON DO NOT REPEAT ANY NAMES. IF A PERSON HAS ALREADY BEEN LISTED, SIMPLY MAKE A SECOND CHOICE.

6. Your wife (or husband) or, if you are not married, your closest present friend of the opposite sex.
7. Your closest friend of the opposite sex, immediately preceding the person listed above.
8. Your closest present friend of the same sex as yourself.
9. A person of the same sex as yourself whom you once thought was a good friend but in whom you were badly disappointed later.
10. The minister, priest, or rabbi whom you know personally and with whom you would be most willing to talk over your personal feelings about religion.
11. Your physician.
12. The present neighbor whom you know best.
13. A person with whom you have been associated who, for some unexplained reason, appeared to dislike you.
14. A person whom you would most like to help or for whom you feel sorry.
15. A person with whom you feel most uncomfortable.
16. A person whom you have recently met whom you would like to know better.
17. The teacher who influenced you most when you were in your teens.
18. The teacher whose point of view you have found most objectionable.
19. An employer, supervisor, or officer under whom you served during a period of great stress.
20. The most successful person whom you know personally.
21. The happiest person whom you know personally.
22. The person known to you personally who appears to meet the highest ethical standards.

← CONSTRUCT

← CONTRAST

* For detailed instructions see, Kelly, G.A. (1955). *The psychology of personal constructs.* Vol. 1. *A theory of personality*. Norton.

NB

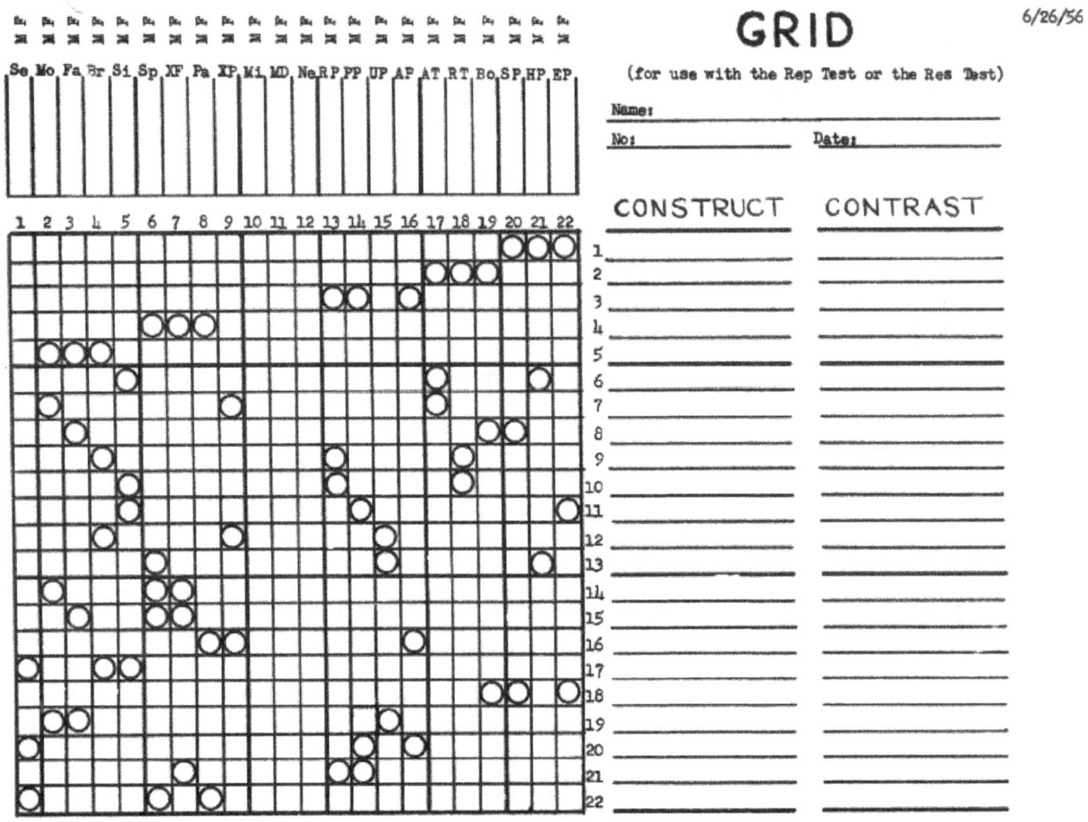
GRID
6/26/56
(for use with the Rep Test or the Res Test)
Name:
No:
Date:
CONSTRUCT
CONTRAST
Se Mo Fa Br Si Sp XF Pa XP Mi MD Ne RP PP UP AP AT RT Bo SP HP EP

34

The Theory and Technique of Assessment[1,2,3,4]

Discover or Invent?

It may take a while for it to happen, but surely someday scientists will be able to rid themselves of the notion that, while things can be invented ideas can only be discovered. It would be far better to believe that all ideas are sheer fabrications and that it is only the palpable things that sit around waiting to be discovered. Such a view would help to advance creative thinking to its proper phase in the cycle of scientific reasoning. It would also cast empiricism in its proper role—the discovery of what things ensue from the courageous application of invented ideas.

In the meantime, we shall continue to go poking about among our experiences pretending to uncover ideas, all the while believing that such notions as "anxiety," "hostility," or "hypochondriasis" are either the revelations of nature, or of dynamically oriented psychiatrists. As for using our inventive talents since we are, as we say, scientists, supposedly the only use for them is in the devising of such practical things as tests, gadgets, or mathematical scales which appear to conform to nature's expressed ideas.

To our way of thinking, this is about where the psychology of assessment now stands. We are still inventing a few new testing devices for it is legitimate to invent things. We are doing a little better in the prediction of specific criteria, which is largely a matter of refinement of technique. And we have backed away from our computational activities far enough to begin to worry about such matters as "construct validity." But if, at last, we have paused to inquire about the dimensions of man, it is still only to ask where they may be found, not to turn to the bold task of erecting them.

There are, nonetheless, a few straws in the wind. Surprisingly enough (or is it surprising?) some have blown up from the direction of mental deficiency which is, at the moment, psychology's most conceptually barren field. Cantor & Cromwell make a timely case against reductionism, the belief that descriptions should be reduced to conceptual terms that are most "real" (1). Yet, more familiar voices still recite the old convictions. Hunt, who is certainly no fool, punctuates his scholarly Salmon Lectures throughout with pledges of ultimate loyalty to physiological ideas (2).

Some look upon factor analysis as a happy compromise between discovery and invention. But it is essentially a collecting procedure, though it may, through its functional arrangements and graphic displays, make it easier for the psychologist to reconceptualize his dimensions of assessment. By including both predictor and criterion measures in the same factorial matrix, Bair, Lockman & Martoccia found themselves aided in defining the factors derived from predictor measures alone (3). There is also a new nonparametric factorization procedure resembling a code-breaking device, which permits the psychologist to begin with whatever makes personal sense to him and to assess his data in that familiar frame of reference (4, 5). But those who group data by factorization, whether by function or variance, are still attempting to discover what can only be invented (6, 7), while the whole or partial correlational procedures used by others are essentially belated attempts to put the flesh of meaning upon some very, very dry bones (8).

The challenge to invent ideas often seems to come directly from those who are assessed; some persons defy being explained, at least in the traditional terms (9, 10). One study even reports that ambiguous statements are more valid than either positive or negative statements, when forced choices are used to predict scholastic achievement (11). The revolt of subjects against the black and white values of psychologists must be well under way.

What would we do if we had to start from scratch in an assessment program on Mars? That would indeed be an invitation to invent new axes of reference. Or, to take a simpler problem instead, the assessment of vocational choice among the Apache Indians. The

[1] Republished by permission of Annual Reviews, Inc. from Kelly, G.A. (1958). The theory and technique of assessment. *Annual Review of Psychology, 9,* 323–352. Permission conveyed through Copyright Clearance Center, Inc.

[2] The survey of the literature pertaining to this review was concluded in May, 1957.

[3] The following abbreviations will be used in this chapter: MMPI (Minnesota Multiphasic Personality Inventory) and TAT (Thematic Apperception Test).

[4] Editors' note: The in-text citations and the reference list in this chapter have been kept in the same referencing style as the original.

Collected Papers of the Pioneer of Constructivist Psychology: George A. Kelly, First Edition. Edited by David A. Winter and Nick Reed.

Rosses found this simpler problem quite baffling enough (12). They resorted to giving Rorschachs! But they promised to come back the following summer with better ideas.

Thinking

There are other harbingers of a fertile spring to come. Following by only a year Johnson's systematization of the "ill-defined field" of thinking (13), Bruner, Goodnow & Austin have come up with a series of studies firmly rooted in the modern philosophy of science (14). Conceptualization is envisioned by them as only one of the stages in a cycle which includes explicit identification of objects in terms of abstractions, decision making, and consequences—the payoff matrix of a decision. Thus, "the pale cast of thought" with which this field has so long been "sicklied o'er" may soon regain "the name of action." It is only a short step from here to the study of the psychologists' own thinking and what they could do if they put their minds to it.

Thinking has, of course, long been a topic in psychology, but much of the impetus for the new trend can be traced to Goldstein and the efforts of others like him to share the private thoughts of schizophrenic patients. Already McGaughran & Moran have challenged Goldstein's conceptual level hypothesis with a carefully defined notion of conceptual area, based on two dimensions: private-public and open-closed (15). They propose the use of an "Autistic Index" in assessment and they report data supporting the utility of their point of view.

Levy & Dugan have now reported the original study in the factorial analysis of personal constructs (16). It was this study, which employed conventional factorization procedures, that inspired the development of non-parametric methods for coming to grips with personal constructs. Other factorization studies in the field of thinking are still based on inter- rather than intraindividual variances (17, 18).

Can people change their axes of reference? This is a question that has important bearing on the thinking of psychologists as well as that of their clients. Levy finds that they can if they do not see too much interrelatedness between their axes; otherwise it is difficult (19). This may be an important way of assessing individuals. As for psychologists themselves, this finding may mean that the more correlations they publish the more rapid their thinking will become.

The assessment of the personal constructs in terms of which people do their thinking is not limited to the laboratory or to the clinic. One free-protocol study even comes out of General Motors (20).

If it had not been for schizophrenia and its puzzling trains of thought, psychologists might never have gotten around to the assessment of thinking. Or is it the other way around? At least, schizophrenics show impairment in their thinking, we believe. Binder says it is an over-all intellectual impairment, rather than the differential impairment found in normal aging (21), and Chambers says it is an impairment in judgment without loss of accuracy in learning (22). Davis & Harrington note that the presence of other persons interrupts problem solving in schizophrenics (23). This may tie in with the privacy dimension emphasized by McGaughran & Moran (15).

Molish, still concerned with the classificatory problem of conventional diagnosis, but with a new look, seeks the schizophrenic components he may use (24). Guertin does the same by factoring the activities of schizophrenic patients (25), and Otgel classifies in terms of data that fall out of the case folders when they are dusted off (26).

Stotsky has begun the important task of developing vocational tests for the placement of schizophrenic patients, an especially important task, since it now appears that the isolated mental hospital, as we now know it, is rapidly disappearing in favor of a local in-and-out, out-and-in pattern of life for schizophrenics (27).

Gorham reports an unusually thorough study on the use of the proverbs test—a thinking approach, we are impelled to say—in screening military personnel for schizoid tendencies (28). Goldstein & Carr, apparently aroused by the current suspicions about mothers, take a look at the mothers of schizophrenic patients (29). There are no differences in the kinds of responses, but the mothers of catatonics omit four and a half times as many items as the mothers of paranoids. We wish they would pursue the matter further.

There were, of course, other studies concerned with the assessment of schizophrenic manners in terms of physiological dimensions such as subshock insulin (30)—significant only at the "Oh Shucks!" level of significance—;[5] prefrontal lobotomy (31)—same level—; and brain dysfunction (32)—highly significant at the personal conviction level.

Assessment in Terms of Conventional Constructs

Since, as we have seen, it is hard to change an axis of reference when it has a wide range of interdependency (19), it is not surprising that psychologists are still trying to measure in terms of such sweeping constructs as anxiety and aggression. Nevertheless, Wirt & Broen, taking a close look, conclude that what is measured on the Children's Manifest Anxiety Scale is not the same as what is called anxiety in the clinic (33). Zimet & Brackbill find this to be true of other measures also (34), and Siegman gallantly concludes that the Taylor Manifest Anxiety scores must have more construct validity than criterion validity (35). Sullivan & Calvin's findings in a vocabulary study generally support Siegman's conclusion (36).

[5] An expurgated version of a fiducial limit originally used by R. E. Jones in an oral communication.

Sinick reverses the current trend in findings on the relationship between encouragement, anxiety, and test performance (37), but Zweibelson finds that anxious children do better on a second test (38). Heath shows that anxiety goes with response disorganization; but then, so also does lack of abstract conceptual ability (39). Rorschach color takes another beating as a measure of anxiety, this time in an arabic-greco-latin square design, no less (40). Intellectual performance correlates (person-to-person variance) with Taylor anxiety, but not with changes in Taylor anxiety [within-person variance (41)]. And sure enough, just as Taylor has said, intelligent people can, if they try, cover their anxiety in taking her test (42).

Dibner has developed a measure of anxiety based on cues given in interviews (43). Ambiguity makes the interview more productive of such cues. If this holds up against outside criteria, it should be of great help in improving the sensitivity both of psychodiagnostic and of psychotherapeutic interviewing.

One more last look at digit span, an old friend in the anxiety circuit: Blackburn & Benton achieve greater reliability by giving more digit span items (44). The reader should repeat ten digits backward before he comments on this one! Goodstein & Farber hypothesized that the relation between Taylor anxiety scores and digit symbol performance was nonmonotonic but it was not (45). Interestingly enough, someone has now come up with a "short form" of the Manifest Anxiety Scale (46). Miss Taylor, shake hands with Mr. Wechsler, who knows all about how it feels to have his test reduced to "short forms!" Incidentally, neither of you need worry about clammy hands; Lotsof & Downing (47) and Calvin et al. (48) all assure you that your hands will not betray your anxiety.

Does aggressive fantasy aroused by pictures lead to overt acts of aggression? The fate of comic books, movies, and television may hang on the outcome of this one. Fantasy of outright fighting is at least associated with playground fights, says Kagan, but other aggressive themes are not (49). Lindzey & Tejessy also have trouble assessing covert aggression from pictures (50). But within the realm of intraindividual variance, Goldstein & Rawn show the effect of induced aggression on drawings, primarily in terms of graphomotor factors rather than symbolic representations—again something more overt than covert (51).

Two scales come in for appraisal. A study using the Palo Alto Aggressive Content Scale shows normals turning hostility outward, schizophrenics inward (52), and the Iowa Hostility Inventory gets some clinical validation, especially among women subjects (53).

Impulsivity and inhibition continue to recur as a reference axis in assessment. Two factorial studies produce displays that may well be seen in terms of this dimension (54, 55). In another, cognitive inhibition time is significantly related to Rorschach M, but not to the Erlebnistype ratio (56). Two other studies corroborate the significance of M, one showing high M to be associated with ability to inhibit laughter (57) and the other showing it to be related to the control of impulsivity, in a digit symbol test (58). Perhaps it is time that psychologists take another hard look at impulsivity and inhibition.

Empathy is another conventional construct which plays an important part in the communications of psychologists. Jarrard examines it from the standpoint of an industrial psychologist, considers its applications, and concludes that a high degree of empathic ability goes with high morale (59). Lundy, approaching it from the standpoint of assimilative projection, finds that when judges concentrate on their own behavior they are inclined to see others as more and more like themselves, but if they concentrate on others' behavior, they begin to sense how others see themselves (60). May we infer from this that psychotherapists who become overly concerned with their technique or their interpretations of client remarks, end up convinced that their clients have improved because they appear to be more like their masters? Borke & Fiske, however, find no relation between the four experimental interview conditions they tried and the way therapists empathize with clients (61).

When clients say they have improved, their therapists, as likely as not, will disagree, but when they say they have not improved, their therapists concur (62). Finally, Murstein (64), using the Dymond Individual Empathy Test, criticizes the findings of Norman & Leiding on the relationship between individual and mass empathy measures (63).

Since the publication of the Adorno report psychologists have been concerned with the construct of rigidity and have been reexamining the Einstellung phenomenon. Levitt, in a review of eight years of research, concludes that the water-jar test, as a psychological test, is a very poor one (65). It produces U-shaped distributions. From the writer's vantage point, however, this is a criterion of a good test, although we have no particular interest in filling and refilling water jars. Maher failed to find the water-jar performance related to the personal use of dynamic perceptions of other people, but he did find a relationship with achievement anxiety (66). He sees support in this for the view that situational or field variables play a significant role in the production of rigid behavior. There is a study which fails to find a relationship between tree drawings and Rorschach signs of rigidity (67) and another which discusses the general application of rigidity principles to the measurement of personality disturbance (68).

The tendency toward antisocial behavior is one of society's most urgent problems. Purcell reports that, "The superego variable as measured by anticipated internal punishments was found to be of far greater significance in inhibiting antisocial behavior than fear of retaliatory punishment ..." (69). In fact, antisocial subjects utilized themes of external punishment as an outright justification for their fantasy aggressions. In another study he uses the Qualitative Maze Test to assess antisocial behavior tendencies and concludes that impulsivity is a basic variable in assessment (70).

Dependency also comes in for assessment. Bernardin & Jessor report a construct validation study in this connection, using the Edwards Personal Preference Schedule (71). The seeking of approval and help figured in the validated construct, but conformity did not.

Sexual identification and deviation are proving difficult to assess. Most of the measures turn out to be indications of general maladjustment. Cutter reports that sex responses to Rorschach Cards 6 and 7 are associated with the estimated severity of disturbance but not with the degree of overt sexual deviation (72, 73). From their relationship with other personality measures he concludes that sex responses to these cards are simply indications of acute anxiety. Davids, Joelson & McArthur find Rorschach "signs" in overt homosexuals (74). They offer a new Rorschach "sign" and five new TAT "signs." Sexual characteristics in human figure drawings show no relationship to sexual adjustment (75). They are more self-portraits than indications of role identification (76). The theory of cultural sex symbolisms in formal designs gets strong support (77). The MMPI sexual deviation scale also proves to be more a measure of gross maladjustment (78).

Clinical psychologists expend a great deal of effort in assessing "organic deficit." When they find it, and they often do, the train of their thought processes usually stops. But the reductionistic influence in psychological thinking is still so strong that once he has arrived at organicity the psychologist feels that he has achieved some goal.

Rosvold et al. (79) have developed a continuous performance test based on the hypothesis that the hypersynchrony of brain-damaged patients indicates reduced attention. This is one finding that may have some functional implications.

The free-hand drawing people are taking a second look at their organicity signs. Silverstein & Robinson report that three-fourths of their subjects appeared to represent their disability in their drawings, but experienced judges still could not use the 55 scoring signs to match up the drawings of disabled and control subjects (80). Bolin, Schneps & Thorne tested the hypothesis that the height of the lightning scar represented in the drawing of a tree was related to the age at which personal trauma was experienced—no relation (81)! However, Reznikoff & Tomblen find signs in drawings which significantly discriminate patients with chronic brain syndromes (82). Two studies find relationships between brain injury and rotation; one study using drawings (83) and one using block designs (84). On a memory-for-designs test Wahler finds that the brain-damaged patients had fewer correct reproductions but they did not differ in the types of errors they made (85).

The spiral after-effect discriminates brain damage significantly, says Gallese (86), but not quite as well as originally reported, say Page et al. (87). Walker has now revised the Hooper Visual Organization Test so that it is workable (88).

Intellectual deficit is viewed from both physiological and psychological points of view by Reitan (89). He finds psychological variables more highly intercorrelated; at least Wechsler-Bellevue subtest scores are more highly intercorrelated than are Halstead's ten subtest scores. Mason reports the estimates of pre-illness intelligence of 510 patients and finds no differential relationship to their maladjustment, except in certain types of schizophrenic patients (90). Still body-bound, Jost & Epstein report that taking the Rorschach produces physiological stress (91).

A little gem comes to us from across the water which will bring a nostalgic tear to many who lived through the golden age of psychogalvanic response. O'Connor & Venables report a significant negative (-.40) correlation between skin conductance and Binet IQ (92). Finger dexterity correlates .48 with IQ and -.21 with skin conductance.

Factors that Affect Test Results in Extraneous Ways

When subjects are told that a Rorschach test is intended "to discover emotional disturbances," Henry & Rotter find that they give fewer responses, especially fewer aggressive responses, and more good form (93). Phares & Rotter report that when subjects are sitting in an English class they show more preference for academic rewards (94). When they are in their Gym class they claim more interest in athletic reinforcements, and when in their Woodworking class they say they want manual skill items. Bernstein finds that the presence of the examiner makes a significant difference in TAT stories (95). Matarazzo, Saslow & Guze find that subjects are more susceptible to changes in the behavior of the individual interviewer than to the differences between interviewers (96).

There are two important notes on the interactions of judges or examiners with their clients. Levy points up the value of a factorial design to control this interaction, especially when case file data are investigated (97), while Gage, Leavitt & Stone report a careful study on the use of an intermediary key to point up the variances which may cloud the relationships between judges and those whom they judge (98).

Social desirability makes a difference in the way subjects respond to test items, especially to those in the MMPI K-Scale (99, 100). It also affects the responses of high school subjects to about the same extent as it does college subjects on the Edwards Personal Preference Schedule (101). In studies comparing the self with the ideal self it is an especially important factor to be controlled, if the ideal is to be used as a reference point (102).

The ability of subjects to "fake" responses in certain types of inventories causes psychologists some concern. In general, however, results are not invalidated by the intentional distortion of responses (103 to 106) although Fisher & Morton report that fantasy measures on the TAT predict best those measures of hospital behavior which are least subject to camouflage (107).

Wiener reports that those subjects who are prone to be distrustful (MMPI) are significantly more impaired in intellectual behavior (108). This seems to put intellectual behavior in the social realm, or at least in the realm of intercommunication, where it probably belongs.

This brings us to the problem of assessment in the context of other cultures. Jahoda concludes from experiences in the Gold Coast that tests of abstract ability are no more culture-free than ordinary tests of intelligence (109). Sperling reports his experiences with the administration of psychological tests in Europe (110), and Wickert tells of his difficulties in testing security police candidates in Vietnam (111). Two MMPI studies, an Australian (112) and a German (113), together with a Spanish Language Form of the Oral Directions Test of Intelligence (114), are reported; interesting but not startling! Woods & Toal reverse other findings by reporting that Negroes perform better than whites on tests which require perceptual speed and accuracy (115). Beier & Hanfmann describe their use of California authoritarian projective questions in interviews with former Soviet citizens (116). The answers reflect general concern with problems of stark survival.

The Meaning and Use of Personal Judgments

If you don't know what is going on in a person's mind, ask him; he may tell you. This practical bit of advice to clinical psychologists is the basis of a number of assessment techniques used by psychologists, including sociometry, *Q*-sorts, personality inventories, and rating scales.

Bjerstedt offers a critical survey of sociometric theory, and the computational procedures associated with it (117, 118, 119). Gronlund reports that teachers underestimate the halo effect from situation to situation when trying to guess how their pupils will make their sociometric selections (120). Nevertheless, there seems to be a general ability factor among teachers for this kind of guesswork (121). Maher suspected that nominators might tend to choose persons of their own age, but has to report that they don't (122).

What makes one a good judge of others? Taft says that social attitudes are the most important factors (123). Good judges are achievement-oriented while poor judges are more concerned with personal qualities in relation to social situations. Members of rural and minority groups, together with those who do not have working experience, do poorly. Fisher hypothesized that "deep" interpretations would seem less plausible to psychologists and psychiatrists, but found quite the reverse to be true (124). We love our esoterica. Bendig thought the personality of judges might affect their agreement with experts in assessing clinical case histories (125). He says he was wrong. And Sorenson & Gross warn against setting too complex a task for raters; it spoils their ratings and gets them all confused (126).

In another study, Bendig reports that intellectual, interest, and educational variables are not related to the reliability with which judges rate case histories, but intelligence and education produce greater rater bias (127). He says also that reliability of such judgments is not a general trait (128).

In a well-controlled study, Johnson & Vidulich report their experimental manipulation of halo effect in ratings (129). They were able to eliminate the interaction variance between rater and rater, but at the expense of certain side-effects. Psychiatric diagnosis, a form of rating in currently bad repute, gets a gold star from Schmidt & Fonda (130). Psychiatrists who are concerned about such matters will be happy to read what Schmidt & Fonda have to say. Shontz reports that judges agree on what makes a healthy person, but not on what makes an ideal hospital patient (131). Two other studies report special rating procedures (132, 133), and Mann's review of experimental studies of role-playing concludes with the assertion that valid and reliable role-playing tests can eventually be developed (134).

Q-sorting has stirred up some lively by-play among psychologists with highly developed statistical consciences. Conger, Sawrey & Krause point out that inter-rater differences spuriously affected the findings in Beck's "Six Schizophrenias" (135). Stephenson replies that the factor arrays were intended to be related to theoretical considerations, rather than to certain concrete factors or classes (136). Conger, Sawrey & Krause retort that Stephenson confounds raters with patients (137).

Kogan et al. find *Q*-sorts affected by the close relationship (r of .89) between a social desirability factor and an emotional health-sickness factor (138). Livson & Nichols recommend *Q*-sorts forced into a rectangular distribution (139), while Jones recommends free *Q*-sorts (140). This reviewer likes to see free sorts fall into a U-distribution, for reasons that cannot be elaborated here.

Lorr, Holsopple & Turk report their carefully developed behavior scale for measuring the severity of illness (141), and Gordon, Bindley & May report the development of a similar scale for measuring change in psychiatric illness (142). Patients' leisure activities are related to their diagnosis but not to their response to treatment (143). The Discomfort-Relief Quotient does poorly when applied to individual differences rather than to changes within a series of interviews with a single patient (144). Study habits and attitudes, a somewhat different kind of rating, significantly (r's of .48-.51) predict subsequent academic rank upon graduation from high school (145).

Tests that Assume the Examiner is Right

When the subject is asked to guess what the examiner is thinking, we call it an objective test; when the examiner tries to guess what the subject is thinking we call it a projective device. Most intelligence tests belong to the former group, which probably accounts for the fact that intelligence testing has made very little contribution to our understanding of the psychological processes of anyone except psychologists.

The Personnel and Guidance Journal carries a series of articles on the best-known factored intelligence tests. The articles are written by the test authors and evaluated by Super (146 to 154). This series should prove worth keeping, even if the journal does take up a lot of precious shelf space.

About 76 percent of the variance of Jastak's Altitude Quotient (based on a subject's highest scores in a battery) is associated with IQ (155). The Davis-Eells Games test turns out to be correlated with reading achievement in the middle and upper socioeconomic groups, but not so much in the lowest group (156).

It may be wishful thinking, but perhaps more new approaches to the assessment of intellectual ability are appearing on the scene. Copple has developed a sentence-completion test of intelligence that correlates quite satisfactorily with academic achievement and Binet intelligence, even within a restricted age sample (157). It may provide much more access to the child's intellectual processes than the guess-what-I'm-thinking kind of tests that psychologists ordinarily give to youngsters. In quite a different direction, Pinard et al. report the development of their differential tests of intelligence at Montreal (158). They attempted to incorporate some of the types of items that have proved useful in concept-formation testing in recent years, although it appears that their statistical criteria are driving them back to the older type of test item. Let us hope they will not have to retreat all the way.

There is stubborn concern about subtest analysis—one for it (159), one against (160), and one abstention (161). Gerberich has a kit of objective achievement test items, together with detailed instructions, for do-it-yourself hobbyists (162). Maurendeau & Pinard have a method for locating items on an age scale (163), and the stop-watch people have come up with a number of more or less conventional reports of inter-correlations between different intelligence tests, forms of the same tests, and between tests and achievement criteria (164 to 171). It is also useful to know that *Personnel Psychology* runs two series of information exchanges edited by D. L. Grant, one on normative data of different tests, and another on validity information.

In the area of infant testing, Wittenborn's monographs on adoptive children provide some validity information (172) and an appraisal of environmental considerations (173). Simon & Bass find higher re-examination contingencies when adjustments are made for the depressing effect of non-optimal conditions which affected the child's performance in the original test (174). The Cattell Scale provides a poor predictive index at six months of age and the effect of premature birth upon scores disappears after about eighteen months (175). Kogan gets good results with a picture information test with cerebral palsied children who cannot take the Stanford-Binet.

Finally, there is the usual flurry of interest in "short forms" of intelligence tests. This is an annual affair (177 to 182).

Tests that Assume the Subject is Right

While Henry's book, *The Analysis of Fantasy*, deals with the TAT, it follows the recent trend that places greater emphasis upon understanding the psychological processes that are assessed, rather that upon the technique of assessment itself (183). Three studies throw light on the use of the TAT (184, 185, 186), and one (187) shows the sensitivity of another picture response test (188) to a realistic situation.

Two reviews assess the current status of the Rorschach test, one a review by Woltman of nine books on the subject (189), and the other a symposium (190 to 194) in which the article by Zubin, Eron & Sultan sounds the keynote (190). It is pointed out that Rorschach conceived an experiment in which inkblot space was substituted for real space. As a result, global clinical evaluations are often regarded as successful, experimental approaches rarely yield positive results, and content scales tend to show more validity than do perceptual scores. The authors say we need to develop more hypotheses about perception itself. This reviewer could not agree more heartily. Let's invent.

Bieri & Blacker find generality of cognitive complexity between one's perception of people and both his Rorschach determinants and his Rorschach content (195). Consalvi & Canter also find important cognitive factors (196), as do Sinnett & Roberts (197). Three studies place the emphasis upon the stimulus factors in the inkblots (198, 199, 200) in a way that invites attention to the importance of stimulus ambiguity in various areas of assessment.

Page finds M related to daydreaming (201), Mann finds significant relationships between M and C measures on the one hand and an association task on the other (202), but Canter finds the role of C has been overemphasized (203). Cards 4 and 7 do not remind subjects of their parents, current theory notwithstanding (204). A kaleidoscope quickly produces more useful percepts in certain unproductive subjects than do the Rorschach cards (205). So do the Projective Sequences materials (206).

Supplemental norms for the affective ratio involving cards 8, 9 and 10 are reported (207), but Maradie prefers to explain productivity on these cards in terms of the goal-spurt hypothesis (208). Rorschach validity is investigated in three studies with moderate results (209, 210, 211). Leventhal finds Wand Z scores somewhat affected by perceptual training (212). The individual administration of the Rorschach yields more anatomy percentage and more responses on Cards 8, 9 and 10 (213). Beck's sampling is criticized (214) and the Howard inkblots yield more M- and more pure C than do the regular cards (215).

Of special interest is a symposium, on the use of the Rorschach as a research tool in personality development studies, in which the participants offer rather guarded statements about the future of inkblots (216 to 220). Two studies report unusual validity possibilities (221, 222), another deals with the achromatic set of cards (223) and three are concerned with dimensions that generalize across tests (224, 225, 226).

The projective use of subjects' drawings continues. There is a quality scale available (227). The use of 16 crayons, rather than the usual eight, accentuates the chromatic phase of the House-Tree-Person (H-T-P) technique (228). The Family Drawing Test shows significant differences in sex, race, and economic status (229). Children and institutionalized aged differ in their drawings of the human figure (230). Scorer reliability on the H-T-P is adequate for group prediction, but of doubtful value in clinical use (231). The Goodenough Scale is satisfactory for measuring the intellectual ability of mentally deficient adults, but not that of normals or of the maladjusted mentally deficient (232).

Tolor has normative findings on types of associations to the Bender-Gestalt figures (233), and he finds diagnostic validity when the figures are used as a recall test for organicity (234). Reznikoff & Olin (235) report similar findings. Aaronson reports a slight relationship between Bender-Gestalt recall and Porteus Maze performance (236).

Rohde has now published her book, *The Sentence Completion Method* (237), and this popular technique is being explored as to its test-retest consistency—it is consistent in certain respects (238); its use in the measurement of attitudes toward superiors and subordinates—clouded by the interpersonal remoteness of the interactionaries (239); its variations—simply using the word "because" as a stem 20 times (240); and its portrayal of defensiveness—it fails (241).

The reliability of the Blacky Test, using only the multiple choice type of scoring, is reported to be low among TB patients, except for castration anxiety measurement (242). If it were possible to combine the other three types of scoring, results might be different (243, 244).

Inventories

Often it seems that people develop their philosophies in the imagery of their tools. This seems to be true of psychologists, whether they use 10 cards marked with fluid blots, 20 cards representing people, or 550 cards containing disjunctive sentences. Consider the sentence people. Never has a group of psychologists accepted so uncritically the intuitive diagnostic statements of psychiatrists and, at the same time, complained so loudly against clinical intuition. This apparent incoherence may be explained, possibly, by the fact that these people see two quite disjunctive types of sentences involved; criterion statements on the one hand, and predictor statements, on the other.

Empiricism, which is greatly admired up Minnesota way as well as in this reviewer's household, always takes its criteria for granted. It must, for that is the only way it can come to be so tough-minded about its predictors. Thus, his simple-minded credulity in one situation permits the psychologist to be sophisticatedly skeptical in another. But he needs to watch out lest the sweeping conclusions he draws from his skepticism undermine his criterion before he knows it, as appears to have occurred in MMPI research.

Hathaway (245) and Meehl (246), having well passed the point of no return on this flight of discourse, and supported by the kind of literalistic study that Wirt reports (247), ably present the Minnesota point of view, perhaps better than it has ever been presented before. Dahlstrom reviews 1955 research in clinical psychology through the Minnesota spectacles (248) and, with Welsh (249), offers 66 basic readings and 700 references on the MMPI. Kimber has an alphabetized list of the MMPI items, in case someone drops his deck (250). Four articles deal with response bias, one in comparison with another test (251), and three expressed in terms of Berg's Deviation Hypothesis (252, 253, 254). The MMPI is also checked out against: feelings induced by music—scattered correlations (255); escaping from prison—it works (256); firemen versus fire captains—it doesn't (257); hysteria and K-corrected hypochondriasis—it predicts psychiatrists (258); and the Edwards Personal Preference Schedule—maybe (259).

Gough's California Psychological Inventory, with its 18 scales and its announced emphasis upon what makes psychological sense, is now ready for mass use in the schools (260). There is a biographical inventory with 10 scales (261, 262), an activity inventory based on Kuder categories (263), and a short-cut inventory comprising conventional items (264).

There are some special criticisms of individual tests. Barry concludes that the McKinney Reporting Test needs further refinement (265); Tamkin questions the construct validity of Barron's Ego-Strength Scale (266); the usefulness of the Mooney Problem Checklist is upheld (267); and there are some additional normative data on the Edwards Personal Preference Schedule (268).

Special Assessments

Interviewing and observation are still the basic assessment procedures, and tests are best regarded as special refinements of them. Hunt, Herrmann & Noble report that brief psychiatric interviews prove valid in two of the three types of military situations they studied (269). Merton, Fiske & Kendall have a manual for interviewing that is directed toward determining the reactions of persons to situations (270); Wittenborn reports interviewing techniques in his study of adoptive children (271); Back looked for rigidity in factual interviewing (272); and Yonge is starting a campaign to determine general interview effectiveness (273). You can tell a captain's blood pressure by what he thinks he hears in the murmurings of indistinct speech (274). Hass has a disguised personality test based on proverbs (275), and Phillipson has a TAT-type object relations technique (276).

"If you could not be human what kind of animal would you like to be and what kind would you not like to be?" Pigem's interviewing of children is based on this type of question (277). "What could not possibly be happening in this picture?" This kind of question peps up the repressed psychic content of TAT protocol (278). Peixotto tells us the popular responses to the Despert Fables (279).

Dorken reviews the Mosaic Test literature of the last five years (280) and Levin reports sweepingly negative results with it (281).

Psychologists may do a better job when they think less of pure diagnosis and attempt more assessments of prognosis, as in recovery from tuberculosis (282, 283); in the effectiveness of psychotherapy (284); in the relationship to the therapist (285); in postsurgical invalidism (286); in rehabilitation of the blind (287, 288); in alcoholics' response to drug therapy (289); in the development of administrative work patterns (290, 291); or even in the progress of graduate students in psychology (292).

Always there is the self. But Levy's neat results lead him to believe that we have overgeneralized it (293). The generality actually lies in the discrepancy we see between what is actual and what is ideal. Perhaps this principle explains the essays written by the 18 self theorists and published in Moustakas' anthology (294). Psychologists say that men emphasize their self-concepts while women emphasize their body-images (295); that acceptance of self need not balance acceptance of others (296); that one's identification with his parent is in terms of traits rather than of sex (297); and that persons in management positions are more realistic in estimating their own proficiency while those in semiskilled and unskilled positions rate themselves in reverse (298).

In a free society, where one can gravitate toward an occupation that suits him, the job may, in part, be a valid measure of the man. In such a society, if we ever achieve it, the study of occupations will become intimately associated with the assessment of personality from all angles. Roe's book, while written for today's conditions, makes particular sense in the light of this speculation (299). So, also does the report of an extensive interdisciplinary project on the conceptual framework of occupational choice (300). Darley & Hagenah's book on vocational interests should be examined in this light (301), as should the book by Jacques (302), and the analysis by Ghiselli (303).

There are new theories afoot which may profoundly affect assessment in the future. If G.S. Hall captured our imagination with the phrase, "Ontogeny recapitulates phylogeny," so Kragh may turn the tide of thought with the notion that each perceptive act is a momentary recapitulation of ontogenesis (304, 305). There is Leary with his emphasis upon the time-binding of impulse (306). Brower & Abt's second volume on progress in clinical psychology has been published (307). Stern, Stein & Bloom have published their book on methods of personality assessment (308), and Marzolf has produced a timely volume on assessment in the schools (309).

Kavruck sketches the history of test development in the U. S. Civil Service Commission (310), and Guertin, Frank & Rabin summarize the research since 1950 on the Wechsler-Bellevue Intelligence Scale (311). The Veterans Administration has a directory of its medical research (312). Two basic articles on assessment, one by Horst (313) and one by Cronbach (314) should keep psychologists from becoming complacent about either their statistics or their French. Finally, everyone should know that the animal folks have taken up assessment (315). At last the psychology of assessment is pure!

Literature Cited

1 Cantor, O. N., and Cromwell, R. L., "The Principle of Reductionism and Mental Deficiency," Am. J. Mental Deficiency, 61, 461–66 (1957)
2 Hunt, W. A., *The Clinical Psychologist* (Charles C Thomas, Springfield, III., 206 pp., 1956)
3 Bair, J. T., Lockman, R. F., and Martoccia, C. T., "Validity and Factor Analyses of Naval Air Training Predictor and Criterion Measures," J. Appl. Psychol., 40, 213–19 (1956)
4 du Mas, F. M., *Manifest Structure Analysis* (Montana State Univ. Press, Missoula, Mont., 193 pp., 1955)
5 du Mas, F. M., Frost, C. H., and Rashleigh, C. H., "A Manifest Structure Analysis of Information Files," J. Clin. Psychol., 12, 139–43 (1956)
6 Cattell, R. B., and Baggaley, A. R., "The Objective Measurement of Attitude Motivation: Development and Evaluation of Principles and Devices," J. Personality, 24, 401–23 (1956)
7 Cattell, R. B., "Second-Order Personality Factors in the Questionnaire Realm," J. Consulting Psychol., 20, 411–18 (1956)
8 Ghiselli, E. E., "Correlates of Initiative," Personnel Psychol., 9, 311–20 (1956)
9 Ghiselli, E. E., "Differentiation of Individuals in Terms of Their Predictability," J. Appl. Psychol., 40, 374–77 (1956)
10 Levy, L. H., Brody, J. R., and Windman, G. O., "The Relationship between the Inferential Potential of Rorschach and TAT Protocols," J. Consulting Psychol., 20, 27–28 (1956)
11 Isard, E. S., "The Relationship between Item Ambiguity and Discriminating Power in a Forced-Choice Scale," J. Appl. Psychol., 40, 266–68 (1956)
12 Ross, W. T., and Ross. G. van B., "Backgrounds of Vocational Choice: An Apache Study," Personnel and Guidance J., 35, 270–75 (1957)
13 Johnson, D. M., *The Psychology of Thought and Judgment* (Harper & Brothers, New York, N. Y., 515 pp., 1955)
14 Bruner, J. S., Goodnow, J., and Austin, G. A., *A Study of Thinking* (J. Wiley & Sons, Inc., New York, N. Y., 330 pp., 1956)
15 McGaughran, L. S., and Moran, L. J., "'Conceptual Level' vs. 'Conceptual Area' Analysis of Object-Sorting Behavior of Schizophrenic and Nonpsychiatric Groups," J. Abnormal Social Psychol., 52, 43 50 (1956)
16 Levy, L.H., and Dugan, R. D., "A Factorial Study of Personal Constructs," J. Consulting Psychol., 20, 53–57 (1956)
17 Karson, S., and Pool, K. B., "The Abstract Thinking Abilities of Mental Patients," J. Clin. Psychol., 13, 126–32 (1957)
18 Mitchell, J. V., Jr., "A Comparison of the Factorial Structures of Cognitive Functions for a High and Low Status Group," J. Educ. Psychol., 47, 397–14 (1956)
19 Levy, L. H., "Personal Constructs and Predictive Behavior," J. Abnormal Social Psychol., 53, 54–58 (1956)
20 Thompson, A. S., and Davis, J. A., "What Workers Mean by Security," Personnel Psychol., 9, 229–41 (1956)
21 Binder, A., "Schizophrenic Intellectual Impairment: Uniform or Differential?" J. Abnormal Social Psychol., 52, 11–18 (1956)
22 Chambers, J. L, "Perceptual Judgment and Associative Learning Ability of Schizophrenics and Nonpsychotics," J. Consulting Psychol., 20, 211–14 (1956)
23 Davis, R. H., and Harrington, R. W., "The Effect of Stimulus Class on the Problem-Solving Behavior of Schizophrenics and Normals," J. Abnormal Social Psychol., 54, 126–28 (1956)
24 Molish, H. B., *Schizophrenic Reaction Types* (Bureau of Medicine and Surgery, Navy Dept., Washington, D. C., 100 pp., 1956)
25 Guertin, W. H., "A Factor Analysis of Schizophrenics Rated on the Activity Rating Scale," J. Clin. Psychol., 12, 163–66 (1956)

26 Otgel, S. A., "Differential Classification of Hebephrenic and Paranoid Schizophrenics from Case Material," J. Clin. Psychol., 13, 159–61 (1957)
27 Stotsky, B. A., "Vocational Tests as Measures of Performance of Schizophrenics in Two Rehabilitation Activities," J. Clin. Psychol., 12, 236 42 (1956)
28 Gorham, D. R., "Use of the Proverbs Test for Differentiating Schizophrenics from Normals," J. Consulting Psychol., 20, 435-40 (1956)
29 Goldstein, A. P., and Carr, A. C., "The Attitudes of the Mothers of Male Catatonic and Paranoid Schizophrenics toward Child Behavior," J. Consulting Psychol., 20, 190 (1956)
30 Peters, H. N., "Circular Pencil Maze Performance in Chronic Schizophrenics," J. Clin. Psychol., 12, 170–73 (1956)
31 Winne, J. F., and Scherer, I. W., "A Second Study of Psychological Changes During the First Year Following Prefrontal Lobotomy," J. Consulting Psychol., 20, 281 85 (1956)
32 Brackbill, G. A., "Studies of Brain Dysfunction in Schizophrenia," Psychol. Bull., 53, 210–26 (1956)
33 Wirt, R. D., and Broen, W. E., Jr., "The Relation of the Children's Manifest Anxiety Scale to the Concept of Anxiety as Used in the Clinic," J. Consulting Psychol., 20, 482 (1956)
34 Zimet, C. N., and Brackbill, G. A., "The Role of Anxiety in Psychodiagnosis," J. Clinical Psychol., 12, 173 77 (1956)
35 Siegman, A., "Cognitive, Affective, and Psychopathological Correlates of the Taylor Manifest Anxiety Scale," J. Consulting Psychol., 20, 137–41 (1956)
36 Sullivan, M. W., and Calvin, A. D., "Spoken and Written Vocabulary; Their Relation to a Standard Vocabulary Test, Intelligence and Anxiety," J. Consulting Psychol., 21, 160 (1957)
37 Sinick, D., "Encouragement, Anxiety, and Test Performance," J. Applied Psychol., 40, 315 18 (1956)
38 Zweibelson, I., "Test Anxiety and Intelligence Test Performance," J. Consulting Psychol., 20, 479–81 (1956)
39 Heath, D. H., "Individual Anxiety Thresholds and Their Effect on Intellectual Performance," J. Abnormal Social Psychol., 52, 403–8 (1956)
40 Rockett, F. C., "Speed of Form Recognition as a Function of Stimulus Factors and Text Anxiety," J. Abnormal Social Psychol., 52, 197–202 (1956)
41 Sarason, I. G., "The Relationship of Anxiety and 'Lack of Defensiveness' to Intellectual Performance," J. Consulting Psychol., 20, 220–22 (1956)
42 Voas, R. B., "Intelligence and the Distortion of Responses on the Taylor Anxiety Scale," Psychol. Repts., 2, 87–89 (1956)
43 Dibner, A. S., "Cue-Counting: A Measure of Anxiety in Interviews," J. Consulting Psychol., 20, 475–78 (1956)
44 Blackburn, H. L., and Benton, A. L., "Revised Administration and Scoring of the Digit Span Test," J. Consulting Psychol., 21, 139 43 (1957)
45 Goodstein, L. D., and Farber, I. E., "On the Relation Between A-Scale Scores and Digit Symbol Performance," J. Consulting Psychol., 21, 152–54 (1957)
46 Bendig, A. W., "The Development of a Short Form of the Manifest Anxiety Scale," J. Consulting Psychol., 20, 384 (1956)
47 Lotsof, E. J., and Downing, W. L., "Two Measures of Anxiety," J. Consulting Psychol., 20, 170 (1956)
48 Calvin, A. D., McGuigan, F. J., Tyrrell, S., and Soyars, M., "Manifest Anxiety and the Palmar Perspiration Index," J. Consulting Psychol., 20, 356 (1956)
49 Kagan, J., "The Measurement of Overt Aggression from Fantasy." J. Abnormal Social Psychol., 52, 390–93 (1956)
50 Lindzey, G., and Tejessy, C., "Thematic Apperception Test: Indices of Aggression in Relation to Measures of Overt and Covert Behavior," Am. J. Orthopsychiat., 26, 567–76 (1956)
51 Goldstein, A. P., and Rawn, M. L., "The Validity of Interpretive Signs of Aggression in the Drawing of the Human Figure," J. Clin. Psychol., 13, 169–71 (1957)
52 Wirt, R. D., "Ideational Expression of Hostile Impulses," J. Consulting Psychol., 20, 185–89 (1956)
53 Buss, A. H., Durkee, A., and Baer, M. B., "The Measurement of Hostility in Clinical Situations," J. Abnormal Social Psychol., 62, 84–86 (1956)
54 Singer, J. I., Wilensky, H., and McCraven, V. G., "Delaying Capacity, Fantasy, and Planning Ability: A Factorial Study of Some Basic Ego Functions," J. Consulting Psychol., 20, 375–83 (1956)
55 Twain, D. C., "Factor Analysis of a Particular Aspect of Behavioral Control: Impulsivity," J. Clin. Psychol., 13, 133–36 (1957)
56 Levine, M., and Meltzoff, J., "Cognitive Inhibition and Rorschach Human Responses," J. Consulting Psychol., 20, 119–22 (1956)
57 Meltzoff, J., and Litwin, D., "Affective Control and Rorschach Human Movement Responses," J. Consulting Psychol., 20, 463–65 (1956)
58 Levine, M., Glass, H., and Meltzoff, J., "The Inhibition Process, Rorschach Human Movement Responses, and Intelligence," J. Consulting Psychol., 21, 41–45 (1957)
59 Jarrard, L. E., "Empathy: The Concept and Industrial Applications," Personnel Psychol., 9, 157–67 (1956)
60 Lundy, R. M., "Assimilative Projection and Accuracy of Prediction in Interpersonal Perceptions," J. Abnormal Social Psychol., 52, 33–38 (1956)
61 Borke, H., and Fiske, D. W., "Factors Influencing the Prediction of Behavior from a Diagnostic Interview," J. Consulting Psychol., 21, 78–80 (1957)
62 Robertson, M. H., "A Comparison of Client and Therapist Ratings on Two Psychotherapeutic Variables," J. Consulting Psychol., 21, 110 (1957)
63 Norman, R., and Leiding, W. C., "The Relationship between Measures of Individual and Mass Empathy," J. Consulting Psychol., 20, 79–82 (1956)
64 Murstein, B. I., "Some Comments on the Measurement of Projection and Empathy," J. Consulting Psychol., 21, 81–82 (1957)
65 Levitt, E. E., "The Water-Jar Einstellung Test as a Measure of Rigidity," Psychol. Bull., 53, 347–70 (1956)
66 Maher, B. A., "Personality, Problem Solving, and the Einstellung Effect," J. Abnormal Social Psychol., 54, 70–74 (1957)
67 Tolor, A., "The Stability of Tree Drawings as Related to Several Rorschach Signs of Rigidity," J. Clinical Psychol., 13, 162–64 (1957)
68 Fisher, S., and Fisher, R. L., "Application of Rigidity Principles to the Measurement of Personality Disturbance," J. Personality, 24, 86–93 (1956)
69 Purcell, K., "The TAT and Antisocial Behavior," J. Consulting Psychol., 20, 449 (1956)
70 Purcell, K., "A Note on Porteus Maze and Wechsler-Bellevue Scores as Related to Antisocial Behavior," J. Consulting Psychol., 20, 361 64 (1956)
71 Bernardin, A. C., and Jessor, R., "A Construct Validation of the Edwards Personal Preference Schedule with Respect to Dependency," J. Consulting Psychol., 21, 63 67 (1957)
72 Cutter, F., "Rorschach Sex Responses and Overt Deviations," J. Clin. Psychol., 13, 83–86 (1957)
73 Cutter, F., "Sexual Differentiation in Figure Drawings and Overt Deviation," J. Clin. Psychol., 12, 369–72 (1956)
74 Davids, A., Joelson, M., and McArthur, C., "Rorschach and TAT Indices of Homosexuality in Overt Homosexuals, Neurotics, and Normal Males," J. Abnormal Social Psychol., 53, 161–72 (1956)

75 Sipprelle, C. N., and Swenson, C. H., "Relationship of Sexual Adjustment to Certain Sexual Characteristics of Human Figure Drawings," J. Consulting Psychol., 20, 197 98 (1956)
76 Murphy, M. M., "Sexual Differentiation of Male and Female Job Applicants on the Draw-A-Person Test," J. Clin. Psychol., 13, 87 88 (1957)
77 Winter, W. D., and Prescott, J. W., "A Cross Validation of Stater's Test of Cultural Symbolism," J. Consulting Psychol., 21, 22 (1957)
78 Peek, R. M., and Storms, L. H., "Validity of the Marsh-Hilliard-Liechti MMPI Sexual Deviation Scale in a State Hospital Population," J. Consulting Psychol., 20, 133–36 (1956)
79 Rosvold, H. E., Mirsky, A. F., Sarason, I., Bransome, E. D., Jr., and Beck, L. H., "A Continuous Performance Test of Brain Damage," J. Consulting Psychol., 20, 343–50 (1956)
80 Silverstein, A. B., and Robinson, H. A., "The Representation of Orthopedic Disability in Children's Figure Drawings," J. Consulting Psychol., 20, 333 41 (1956)
81 Bolin, B. J., Schneps, A., and Thorne, V. E., "Further Examination of the Tree-Scar-Trauma Hypothesis," J. Clin. Psychol., 12, 395 97 (1956)
82 Reznikoff, M., and Tomblen, D., "The Use of Human Figure Drawings in the Diagnosis of Organic Pathology," J. Consulting Psychol., 20, 467–70 (1956)
83 Yates, A. J., "The Rotation of Drawings by Brain-Damaged Patients," J. Abnormal Social Psychol., 53, 178–81 (1956)
84 Williams, H. L., Lubin, A., Gieseking, C., and Rubinstein, I., "The Relation of Brain Injury and Visual Perception to Block Design Rotation," J. Consulting Psychol., 20, 275–80 (1956)
85 Wahler, H. J., "A Comparison of Reproduction Errors Made by Brain-Damaged and Control Patients on a Memory-for-Designs Test," J. Abnormal Social Psychol., 52, 251–55 (1956)
86 Gallese, A. J., Jr., "Spiral Aftereffect as a Test of Organic Brain Damage," J. Clin. Psychol., 12, 254–58 (1956)
87 Page, H. A., Rakita, G., Kaplan, H. K., and Smith, N. B. "Another Application of the Spiral Aftereffect in the Determination of Brain Damage," J. Consulting Psychol., 21, 89–91 (1957)
88 Walker, R. G., "The Revised Hooper Visual Organization Test as a Measure of Brain Damage," J. Clin. Psychol., 387–88 (1956)
89 Reitan, R. M., "Investigation of Relationships between 'Psychometric' and 'Biological' Intelligence," J. Nervous Mental Disease, 123, 536–41 (1956)
90 Mason, C. F., "Pre-Illness Intelligence of Mental Hospital Patients," J. Consulting Psychol., 20, 297–300 (1956)
91 Jost, H., and Epstein, I. J., "The Rorschach as a Physiological Stress," J. Clin. Psychol., 12, 257–63 (1956)
92 O'Connor, N., and Venables, P. H., "A Note on the Basal Level of Skin Conductance and Binet I. Q.," Brit. J. Psychol., 47, 148–49 (1956)
93 Henry, E. M., and Rotter, J. B., "Situational Influences on Rorschach Responses," J. Consulting Psychol., 20, 457–62 (1956)
94 Phares, E. J., and Rotter, J. B., "An Effect of the Situation on Psychological Testing," J. Consulting Psychol., 20, 291–93 (1956)
95 Bernstein, L., "The Examiner as an Inhibiting Factor in Clinical Testing," J. Consulting Psychol., 20, 287–90 (1956)
96 Matarazzo, J. D., Saslow, G., and Guze, S. B., "Stability of Interaction Patterns During Interviews: A Replication," J. Consulting Psychol., 20, 267–74 (1956)
97 Levy, L. H., "A Note on Research Methodology Used in Testing for Examiner Influence in Clinical Test Performance," J. Consulting Psychol., 20, 286 (1956)
98 Gage, N. L., Leavitt, G. S., and Stone, G. C., "The Intermediary Key in the Analysis of Interpersonal Perception," Psychol. Bull., 53, 258–65 (1956)
99 Fordyce, W. F., "Social Desirability in the MMPI," J. Consulting Psychol., 20, 171–75 (1956)
100 Hanley, C., "Social Desirability and Responses to Items from Three MMPI Scales: D, Sc, and K," J. Appl. Psychol., 40, 324–28 (1956)
101 Klett, C. J., "The Stability of the Social Desirability Scale Values in the Edwards Personal Preference Schedule," J. Consulting Psychol., 21, 183–85 (1957)
102 Kenny, D. T., "The Influence of Social Desirability on Discrepancy Measures between Real Self and Ideal Self," J. Consulting Psychol., 20, 315–18 (1956)
103 Grayson, H. M., and Olinger, L. B., "Simulation of 'Normalcy' by Psychiatric Patients on the MMPI," J. Consulting Psychol., 21, 73–77 (1957)
104 Sorenson, A. G., "A Note on the 'Fakability' of the Minnesota Teacher Attitude Inventory," J. Appl. Psychol., 40, 192–94 (1956)
105 Rusmore, J. T., "Fakability of the Gordon Personal Profile," J. Appl. Psychol., 40, 175–77 (1956)
106 Gordon, L. V., and Stapleton, E. S., "Fakability of a Forced-Choice Personality Test under Realistic High School Employment Conditions," J. Appl. Psychol., 40, 258–62 (1956)
107 Fisher, S., and Morton, R. B., "Levels of Prediction from the TAT," J. Consulting Psychol., 21, 115–20 (1957)
108 Wiener, G., "The Effect of Distrust on Some Aspects of Intelligence Test Behavior," J. Consulting Psychol., 21, 127–30 (1957)
109 Jahoda, G., "Assessment of Abstract Behavior in a Non-Western Culture "J. Abnormal Social Psychol., 53, 237–43 (1956)
110 Sperling, P. L, "Administering Psychological Tests in Europe," Am. Psychol., 12,33–34 (1956)
111 Wickert, F. R., "An Adventure in Psychological Testing Abroad," Am. Psychol., 12,86–88 (1956)
112 Taft, R., "A Cross-Cultural Comparison of the MMPI," J. Consulting Psychol., 21, 161–64 (1957)
113 Sundberg, N. D., "The Use of the MMPI for Cross-Cultural Personality Study: A Preliminary Report on the German Translation,". J. Abnormal Social Psychol., 52, 281 83 (1956)
114 Sarnia, V. D., "A Note on the Spanish Language form of the Oral Directions Test of Intelligence," J. Applied Psychol., 40, 350 52 (1956)
115 Woods, W. A., and Toal, R., "Subtest Disparity of Negro and White Groups Matched for IQs on the Revised Beta Test," J. Consulting Psychol., 21, 136 38 (1957)
116 Beier, H., and Hanfmann, E., "Emotional Attitudes of Former Soviet Citizens, as Studied by the Technique of Projective Questions," J. Abnormal Social Psychol., 53, 143–53 (1956)
117 Bjerstedt, A., *Interpretations of Sociometric Choice Status* (Hakan Ohlssons Boktryckeri, Lund, Sweden, 408 pp., 1956)
118 Bjerstedt, A., "The Methodology of Preferential Sociometry," Sociometry Monog., (37), 155 pp. (1956)

119 Bjerstedt, A., "The Interpretation of Sociometric Status Scores in the Classroom," Acta Psychol., 12, 1–14 (1956)
120 Gronlund, N. E., "Generality of Teachers' Sociometric Perceptions: Relative Judgment Accuracy on Several Sociometric Criteria," J. Educ. Psychol., 47, 25–31 (1956)
121 Gronlund, N. E., "The General Ability to Judge Sociometric Status: Elementary Student Teachers' Sociometric Perceptions of Classmates and Pupils," J. Educ. Psychol., 47, 147–57 (1956)
122 Maher, H., "Age of Nominator and Scores Assigned Nominees of Various Ages," J. Appl. Psychol., 40, 55–56 (1956)
123 Taft, R., "Some Characteristics of Good Judges of Others," Brit. J. Psychol., 47. 19 29 (1956)
124 Fisher, S., "Plausibility and Depth of Interpretation," J. Consulting Psychol., 20, 249–56 (1956)
125 Bendig, A. W., "The Personality of Judges and Their Agreement with Experts in Judging Clinical Case Histories," J. Consulting Psychol., 20, 422 (1956)
126 Sorenson, A. G., and Gross, C. F., "Inter-Rater Reliability from the Viewpoint of the Rater," Personnel and Guidance J., 35, 365–68 (1957)
127 Bendig, A. W., "Reliability of Case History Ratings and Intellectual Ability of Graduate Raters," J. Consulting Psychol., 20, 142–44 (1956)
128 Bendig, A. W., "Ranking Methodology: The Generality of Ranking Reliability with Different Sets of Clinical Case Histories," J. Clin. Psychol., 12, 151–55 (1956)
129 Johnson, D. M., and Vidulich, R. N., "Experimental Manipulation of the Halo Effect," J. Appl. Psychol., 40, 130–34 (1956)
130 Schmidt, H. O., and Fonda, C. P., "The Reliability of Psychiatric Diagnosis: A New Look," J. Abnormal Social Psychol., 52, 262–67 (1956)
131 Shontz, F. C., "Evaluative Conceptualizations as the Basis for Clinical Judgments," J. Consulting Psychol., 20, 223–26 (1956)
132 Taylor, E. K., and Hastman, R., "Relation of Format and Administration to the Characteristics of Graphic Rating Scales," Personnel Psychol., 9, 181–206 (1956)
133 Webb, W. B., "A Procedure for Obtaining Self-Ratings and Group Ratings," J. Consulting Psychol., 20, 233–36 (1956)
134 Mann, J. H., "Experimental Evaluations of Role Playing," Psychol. Bull., 53, 227–34 (1956)
135 Conger, J. J., Sawrey, W. L., and Krause, L. F., "A Reanalysis of Beck's Six Schizophrenias," J. Consulting Psychol., 20, 83–87 (1956)
136 Stephenson, W., "A Reply to the Reanalysis of Becks' Six Schizophrenias," J. Consulting Psychol., 20, 88–89 (1956)
137 Conger, J. J., Sawrey, W. L., and Krause, L. F., "Reply to Dr. Stephenson," J. Consulting Psychol., 20,90–92 (1956)
138 Kogan, W. S., Quinn, R., Ax, A. F., and Ripley, H. S., "Some Methodological Problems in the Quantification of Clinical Assessment by Q Array," J. Consulting Psychol., 21, 57–62 (1957)
139 I.ivson, N. H., and Nichols, T. F., "Discrimination and Reliability in Q-Sort Personality Descriptions," J. Abnormal Social Psychol., 52, 159–65 (1956)
140 Jones, A., "Distributions of Traits in Current Q-Sort Methodology," J. Abnormal Social Psychol., 53, 90–95 (1956)
141 Lorr, M., Holsopple, J. Q., and Turk, E., "A Measure of Severity of Illness," J. Clin. Psychol., 12, 384–86 (1956)
142 Gordon, M. H., Lindley, S. B., and May, R. B., "A Criterion Measure of Within-Hospital Change in Psychiatric Illness," J. Clin. Psychol., 13, 145–47 (1957)
143 Robertson, J. P. S., "Leisure Activities in Relation to Neuropsychiatric Diagnosis and Treatment," J. Clin. Psychol., 13, 56–58 (1957)
144 Auld, F., Jr., and Mahl, G. F., "A Comparison of the DRQ with Ratings of Emotion," J. Abnormal Social Psychol., 53, 368–88 (1956)
145 Brown, W. F., and Holtzman, W. H., "Use of the Survey of Study Habits and Attitudes for Counseling Students," Personnel and Guidance J., 35, 214–18 (1956)
146 Super, D. E., "Use of Multifactor Test Batteries in Guidance," Personnel and Guidance J., 35, 9–15 (1956)
147 Bennett, G. K., Seashore, H. G., and Wesman, A. G., "The Differential Aptitude Tests: An Overview," Personnel and Guidance J., 35, 81–93 (1956) (With Comment by D. E. Super)
148 Dvorak, B. J., "The General Aptitude Test Battery," Personnel and Guidance J., 35, 145–54 (1956) (With Comment by D. E. Super)
149 Guilford, J. P., "The Guilford-Zimmerman Aptitude Survey," Personnel and Guidance J., 35, 219–24 (1956) (With Comments by D. E. Super)
150 Crowder, N. A., "The Holzinger-Crowder Uni-Factor Tests," Personnel and Guidance J., 35, 281–88 (1957) (With Comments by D. E. Super)
151 King, J. E., "Factored Aptitude Series of Business and Industrial Tests," Personnel and Guidance J., 35, 351–60 (1957) (With Comments by D. E. Super)
152 Segel, D., "The Multiple Aptitude Tests," Personnel and Guidance J., 35, 424–34 (1957) (With Comments by D. E. Super)
153 Flanagan, J. C., "The Flanagan Aptitude Classification Tests," Personnel and Guidance J., 35, 495–507 (1957) (With Comments by D. E. Super)
154 Thurstone, T. G., "The Tests of Primary Mental Abilities," Personnel and Guidance J., 35, 569–78 (1957) (With Comments by D. E. Super)
155 Brown, M. H., and Bryan, G. E., "The Altitude Quotient as a Measurement of Intellectual Potential," J. Clin. Psychol., 13, 135–40 (1957)
156 Love, M. I., and Beach, S., "Performance of Children on the Davis-Eells Games and Other Measures of Ability," J. Consulting Psychol., 21, 29–32 (1957)
157 Copple, G. E., "Effective Intelligence as Measured by an Unstructured Sentence-Completion Technique," J. Consulting Psychol., 20, 357 60 (1957)
158 Pinard, A., Barbeau, G. L., Laurendeau, M., and Parant, C., *Tests Differentials d'Intelligence* (Institut de Psychologic, Universite de Montreal, Montreal, Canada, 332 pp., 1954)
159 Voile, F. O., "A Proposal for 'Testing the Limits' with Mental Defectives for Purposes of Subtest Analysis of the WISC Verbal Scale," J. Clin. Psychol., 13, 64–67 (1957)
160 Jones, H. G., "The Evaluation of the Significance of Differences between Scaled Scores on the WAIS: The Perpetuation of a Fallacy," J. Consulting Psychol., 20, 319 -20 (1956)
161 Dana, R. H., "A Comparison of Four Verbal Subtests on the Wechsler-Bellevue, Form I, and the WAIS," J. Clin. Psychol., 13, 70 71 (1957)
162 Gerberich, J. K., *Specimen Objective Test Items: A Guide to Achievement Test Construction* (Longmans, Green & Co., New York, N. Y., 436 pp., 1956)
163 Maurendeau, M., and Pinard, A., "Une Methode Rationnelle de Localization des Echelles d'Age," Can. J. Psychol., 11, 33–17 (1957)

164 Goolishian, H. A., and Ramsay, R., "The Wechsler-Bellevue Form I and the WAIS: A Comparison," J. Clin. Psychol., 12, 1 17 51 (1956)

165 Harlow, J. E., Jr., Price, A. C., Tatham, L. J., and Davidson, J. F., "Preliminary Study of Comparison between Wechsler Intelligence Scale for Children and Form L of Revised Stanford Binet Scale at Three Age Levels," J. Clin. Psychol., 13, 72–73 (1957)

166 Gehman, I. H., and Matyas, R. P, "Stability of the WISC and Binet Tests," J. Consulting Psychol., 20, ISO 52 (1956)

167 Nimity, A., and Toal, R, "Reliability (Internal Consistency) of the Weschler Memory Scale and Correlation with the Wechsler-Bellevue Intelligence Scale," J. Consulting Psychol., 21, 131 35 (1957)

168 Barratt, E. S., "The Relationship of the Progressive Matrices (1938) and the Columbia Mental Maturity Scale to the WISC," J. Consulting Psychol., 20, 294–96 (1956)

169 Hall, J. C., "Correlation of a Modified Form of Raven's Progressive Matrices (1938) with the Wechsler Adult Intelligence Scale," J. Consulting Psychol., 21, 23–26 (1597)

170 Weaver, H. B., and Boneau, C. A., "Equivalence of forms of the Wonderlic Personnel Test: A Study of Reliability and Interchangeability," J. Appl. Psychol., 40, 127 -29 (1956)

171 Altus, G. T., "Some Correlates of the Davis-Eells Tests," J. Consulting Psychol., 20, 227–32 (1956)

172 Wittenborn, J. R., and Others, "A Study of Adoptive Children: II. The Predictive Validity of the Yale Developmental Examination of Infant Behavior," Psychol. Monog., 70, 59–92 (1956)

173 Wittenborn, J. R., and Others, "A Study of Adoptive Children: III. Relationships between Some Aspects of Development and Some Aspects of Environment for Adoptive Children," Psychol. Monog., 70, 93–115 (1956)

174 Simon, A. J., and Bass, L. G., "Toward a Validation of Infant Testing," Am. J. Orthopsychiat., 26, 340–50 (1956)

175 Cavanaugh, M. C., Cohen, L., Dunphy, D., Ringwall, E. A., and Goldberg, I. D., "Prediction from the Cattell Infant Intelligence Scale," J. Consulting Psychol., 21, 33–37 (1957)

176 Kogan, K. I., "A Method of Assessing Capacity in Preschool Cerebral Palsied Children," J. Clin. Psychol., 13, 54–56 (1957)

177 Himelstein, P., "Evaluation of an Abbreviated WAIS in a Psychiatric Population," J. Clin. Psychol., 13, 68–69 (1957)

178 Caldwell, M. B., and Davis, J. C., "A Short Form of the Wechsler-Bellevue Intelligence Scale Form II for a Psychotic Population," J. Clin. Psychol., 12, 402–3 (1956)

179 Murphy, D. B., and Langton, R. D., "A Short Form of the Wechsler-Bellevue and the Army Classification Battery as Measures of Intelligence," J. Consulting Psychol., 20, 405 (1956)

180 Olin, T. D., and Reznikoff, T, M., "The Use of Doppelt's Short Form of the Wechsler Adult Intelligence Scale with Psychiatric Patients," J. Consulting Psychol., 21, 27–28 (1957)

181 Maxwell, E., "Validities of Abbreviated WAIS Scales," J. Consulting Psychol., 21, 121–26 (1957)

182 Levinson, B. M., "The Knox Cube Backward (KCB) as a Performance Test of General Intelligence," J. Clin. Psychol., 12, 185–87 (1956)

183 Henry, W. E., *The Analysis of Fantasy* (J. Wiley & Sons, Inc., New York, N.Y., 305 pp,, 1956)

184 Cline, V. B., Egbert, R., Forgy, E., and Meeland, T., "Reaction of Men Under Stress to a Picture Projective Test," J. Clin. Psychol., 13, 141–44 (1957)

185 Winch, R. F., and More, D. M., "Does TAT Add Information to Interviews? Statistical Analysis of the Increment," J. Clin. Psychol., 12, 316–21 (1956)

186 Lindzey, G., and Heinemann, S. H., "Thematic Apperception Test: Individual and Group Administration," J. Personality, 24, 34–55 (1956)

187 Veroff, J., "Development and Validation of a Projective Measure of Power Motivation," J. Abnormal Social Psychol., 54, 1–8 (1957)

188 McClelland, D. C., Atkinson, J. W., Clark, R., and Lowell, E. L., *The Achievement Motive* (Appleton-Century-Crofts, Inc., New York, N.Y., 384 pp., 1953)

189 Woltmann, A. G., "Recent Rorschach Literature," Am. J. Orthopsychiat., 26, 193–203 (1956)

190 Zubin, J., Eron, L. D., and Sultan, F., "A Psychometric Evaluation of the Rorschach Experiment," Am. J. Orthopsychiat., 26, 773–82 (1956)

191 Benton, A. L., "The Rorschach Test and the Diagnosis of Cerebral Pathology in Children," Am. J. Orthopsychiat., 26, 783–91 (1956)

192 Beck, S. J., Molish, H. B., and Sinclair, J., "Concerning Researchers' Thinking in Schizophrenia Research," Am. J. Orthopsychiat., 26, 792–800 (1956)

193 Knopf, I. J., "The Rorschach Test and Psychotherapy," Am. J. Orthopsychiat., 26, 801–6 (1956)

194 Molish, H. B., "The Rorschach Test in Military Psychology and Psychiatry," Am. J. Orthopsychiat., 26, 807–17 (1956)

195 Bieri, J., and Blacker, E., "The Generality of Cognitive Complexity in the Perception of People and Inkblots," J. Abnormal Social Psychol., 53, 112–17 (1956)

196 Consalvi, C., and Canter, A., "Rorschach Scores as a Function of Four Factors," J. Consulting Psychol., 21, 47–51 (1957)

197 Sinnett, W. R., and Roberts, R., "Rorschach Approach Type and the Organization of Cognitive Material," J. Consulting Psychol., 20, 109 13 (1956)

198 Lawton, M. P., "Stimulus Structure as a Determinant of the Perceptual Response," J. Consulting Psychol., 20, 351 55 (1956)

199 Eckhardt, W., "Stimulus-Determinants of 'Shading' Responses," J. Clin. Psychol., 13, 172–73 (1957)

200 Kraus, A. R., "Shifts in the Levels of Operating Defenses Induced by Blurring of Inkblot Slides," J. Clin. Psychol., 12, 337–41 (1956)

201 Page, H. A., "Studies in Fantasy—Daydreaming Frequency and Rorschach Scoring Categories," J. Consulting Psychol., 21, 1 1 1–14 (1957)

202 Mann, L. "The Relation of Rorschach Indices of Extratension and Introversion to a Measure of Responsiveness to the Immediate Environment," J. Consulting Psychol., 20, 114–18 (1956)

203 Canter, A., "Rorschach Response Characteristics as a Function of Color and Degree of Emotional Constriction," J. Consulting Psychol., 21, 46 (1957)

204 Charen, S., "Pitfalls in Interpretation of Parental Symbolism in Rorschach Cards IV and VII," J. Consulting Psychol., 21, 52–56 (1957)

205 Starer, E., "The Use of the Kaleidoscope as an Adjunct to the Rorschach," J. Consulting Psychol., 20, 466 (1956)

206 Lundin, W. H., and Breiger, B., "A Comparison of Productivity and Fantasy on the Rorschach and Projective Movement Sequences," J. Consulting Psychol., 20, 342 (1956)
207 Taulbee, E. S., Sisson, B. D, and Gaston, C. O., "Affective Ratio and 8-9-10 Per Cent on the Rorschach Test for Normals and Psychiatric Groups," J. Consulting Psychol., 20, 105–8 (1956)
208 Maradie, L. J., "The Goal-Spurt Hypothesis and the Rorschach Test," J. Consulting Psychol., 30, 205 10 (1956)
209 Chambers, G. S., and Hamlin, R. M., "The Validity of Judgments Based on 'Blind' Rorschach Records," J. Consulting Psychol., 21, 105 9 (1957)
210 Knopf, I. J., "Rorschach Summary Scores in Differential Diagnosis," J. Consulting Psychol., 20, 99–104 (1956)
211 Wirt, R. D, "Pattern Analysis of the Rorschach," J. Clin. Psychol., 12, 282–84 (1956)
212 Leventhal, H., "The Effects of Perceptual Training on the Rorschach Wand Z Scores," J. Consulting Psychol., 20, 93–98 (1956)
213 Rohrer, J. H., and Edmonson, B. W., "An Experimental Study of the Effects of Individual and Group Presentation of the Rorschach Plates," J. Clin. Psychol., 12, 249–54 (1956)
214 Auld, F., Jr., "Is Beck's Sample of Rorschach Testees Representative?" J. Gen. Psychol., 56, 135–36 (1957)
215 Scott, E. M., and Douglas, F., "A Comparison of Rorschach and Howard Tests on a Schizophrenic Population," J. Clin. Psychol., 13, 79 81 (1957)
216 Crandall, V. J., "Observations on the Use of Projective Techniques in Child Development Research," J. Projective Techniques, 20, 251–55 (1956)
217 Ricciuti, H. N., "Use of the Rorschach Test in Longitudinal Studies of Personality Development," J. Projective Techniques, 20, 256–60 (1956)
218 Sigel, I. E., and Hoffman, M. L., "The Predictive Potential of Projective Tests for Nonclinical Populations," J. Projective Techniques, 20, 261–64 (1956)
219 Reichard, S., "Discussion: Projective Techniques as Research Tools in Studies of Normal Personality Development," J. Projective Techniques, 20, 265–68 (1956)
220 Kass, W., "Projective Techniques as Research Tools in Studies of Normal Personality Development," J. Projective Techniques, 20, 269–72 (1956)
221 Symonds, P. M., and Dudek, S., "Use of the Rorschach in the Diagnosis of Teacher Effectiveness," J. Projective Techniques, 20, 227–34 (1956)
222 Kaplan, B, Rickers-Ovsiankina, M. A., and Joseph, A., "An Attempt to Sort Rorschach Records from Four Cultures," J. Projective Techniques, 20, 172–80 (1956)
223 Crumpton, E., "The Influence of Color on the Rorschach Test," J. Projective Techniques, 20, 150–58 (1956)
224 Spiegelman, M., "Rorschach Form-Level, Intellectual Functioning and Potential," J. Projective Techniques, 20, 335–13 (1956)
225 McFarland, R. I.,Two Dimensions of Test Structure in Rorschach-Like Projective Tests," J. Projective Techniques, 20, 398–404 (1956)
226 Carr, A. C., "The Relation of Certain Rorschach Variables to Expression of Affect in the TAT and SCT," J. Projective Techniques, 20, 137–42 (1956)
227 Wagner, M. E., and Schubert, H. J. P., *Draw-a-Person Quality Scale* (Dr. M. E. Wagner, Buffalo, N.Y., 195 pp.)
228 Jolles, I., "Some Advances in Interpretation of the Chromatic Phase of the H-T-P," J. Clin. Psychol, 13, 81–83 (1957)
229 Reznikoff, M., and Reznikoff, H. R., "The Family Drawing Test: A Comparative Study of Children's Drawings," J. Clin. Psychol., 12, 167–69 (1956)
230 Lakin, M., "Certain Formal Characteristics of Human Figure Drawings by Institutionalized Aged and by Normal Children," J. Consulting Psychol., 20, 471–74 (1956)
231 Bieliauskas, V. J., "Scorer's Reliability in the Quantitative Scoring of the H-T-P Technique," J. Clin. Psychol., 12, 366–69 (1956)
232 Murphy, M. M., "A Goodenough Scale Evaluation of Human Figure Drawings of Three Non-Psychotic Groups of Adults," J. Clin. Psychol., 12, 397–99 (1956)
233 Tolor, A, "Structural Properties of Bender Gestalt Test Associations," J. Clin. Psychol., 13, 176–78 (1957)
234 Tolor, A., "A Comparison of the Bender-Gestalt Test and the Digit-Span Test as Measures of Recall," J. Consulting Psychol., 20, 305–9 (1956)
235 Reznikoff, M., and Olin, T. D., "Recall of the Bender-Gestalt Designs by Organic and Schizophrenic Patients: A Comparative Study," J. Clin. Psychol., 13, 183–86 (1957)
236 Aaronson, B. S., "The Porteus Mazes and Bender Gestalt Recall," J. Clinical Psychol., 13, 186–87 (1957)
237 Rohde, A. R., *The Sentence Completion Method* (The Ronald Press Co., New York, N.Y., 301 pp., 1957)
238 Osterweil, J., and Fiske, D. W., "Intra-Individual Variability in Sentence Completion Responses," J. Abnormal Social Psychol., 52, 195–99 (1956)
239 Burwen, L. S., Campbell, D. T., and Kidd, J., "The Use of a Sentence Completion Test in Measuring Attitudes Toward Superiors and Subordinates," J. Appl. Psychol., 40, 248–50 (1956)
240 Michaux, W. W., "The Sentence Composition Test," J. Clin. Psychol., 13, 174–75 (1957)
241 Wiener, M., Carpenter, B, and Carpenter, J. T., "Determination of Defense Mechanisms for Conflict Areas from Verbal Material," J. Consulting Psychol., 20, 215 19 (1956)
242 Charen, S., "Reliability of the Blacky Test," J. Consulting Psychol., 20, 16 (1956)
243 Blum, G. S., "Reliability of the Blacky Test: A Reply to Charen," J. Consulting Psychol., 20, 406 (1956)
244 Charen, S., "A Reply to Blum," J. Consulting Psychol., 20, 407 (1956)
245 Hathaway, S. R., "Clinical Intuition and Inferential Accuracy," J. Personality, 24, 223–50 (1956)
246 Meehl, P. E., "Wanted—A Good Cookbook," Am. Psychol., 11, 263–72 (1956)
247 Wirt, R. D., "Actuarial Prediction," J. Consulting Psychol., 20, 123 2–1 (1956)
248 Dahlstrom, W. G., "Research in Clinical Psychology: 1955," J. Clin. Psychol., 12, 222 28 (1956)
249 Welsh, G. S., and Dahlstrom, W. G., *Basic Headings on the MMPI in Psychology* (Univ. of Minnesota Press, Minneapolis, Minn., 656 pp., 1956)
250 Kimber, J. A. M., "An Alphabetical List of MM PI Items," J. Clin. Psychol., 13, 197–202 (1957)
251 Fricke, B. G., "Response Set as a Suppressor Variable in the OAIS and MMPI." J. Consulting Psychol., 20, 161–69 (1956)
252 Berg, I. A., "Response Bias and Personality: The Deviation Hypothesis," J. Psychol., 40, 61–72 (1955)
253 Barnes, E. H., "Response Bias and the MMPI," J. Consulting Psychol., 20, 371–74 (1956)

254 Barnes, E. H., "Factors, Response Bias, and the MMPI," J. Consulting Psychol., 20, 419-21 (1956)
255 Sopchak, A. L., "Relation between MMPI Scores and Musical Projective Test Scores," J. Clin. Psychol., 13, 165–68 (1957)
256 Beall, H. S., and Panton, J. H., "Use of the Minnesota Multiphasic Personality Inventory as an Index to 'Escapism,' "J. Clin. Psychol., 12, 392–94 (1956)
257 Olmsted, D. W., and Monachesi, E. D., "A Validity Check on MMPI Scales of Responsibility and Dominance," J. Abnormal Social Psychol., 53, 140–55 (1956)
258 Fricke, B. G., "Conversion Hysterics and the MMPI," J. Clin. Psychol., 12, 322–26 (1956)
259 Merrill, R. M., and Heathers, L. B., "The Relation of the MMPI to the Edwards Personal Preference Schedule on a College Counseling Center Sample," J. Consulting Psychol., 20, 310–14 (1956)
260 Gough, H. G., *California Psychological Inventory* (Consulting Psychologists Press, Palo Alto, Calif., 39 pp., 1956)
261 Siegel, L., "A Biographical Inventory for Students: I. Construction and Standardization of the Instrument," J. Appl. Psychol., 40, 5 TO (1956)
262 Siegel, L., "A Biographical Inventory for Students: II. Validation of the Instrument," J. Appl. Psychol., 40, 122–26 (1956)
265 Ewens, W. P., "The Development and Standardization of a Preliminary Form of an Activity Experience Inventory: A Measure of Manifest Interest," J. Appl. Psychol., 40, 169–74 (1956)
264 Heron, A., "A Two-Part Personality Measure for Use as a Research Criterion," Brit. J. Psychol, 47, 243–51 (1956)
265 Barry, J. R., "A Further Study of the McKinney Reporting Test Scores," J. Abnormal Social Psychol., 53, 258–60 (1956)
266 Tamkin, A. S., "An Evaluation of the Construct Validity of Barron's Ego-Strength Scale," J. Clin. Psychol., 13, 156–58 (1957)
267 Singer, S. L., and Stefflre, B., "The Concurrent Validity of the Mooney Problem Check List," Personnel and Guidance J., 35, 298–301 (1957)
268 Klett, C. J., "Performance of High School Students on the Edwards Personal Preference Schedule," J. Consulting Psychol., 21, 68–72 (1957)
269 Hunt, W. A., Herrmann, R. S., and Noble, H., "The Specificity of the Psychiatric Interview," J. Clin. Psychol., 13, 49–53 (1957)
270 Merton, R. K., Fiske, M., and Kendall, P. L., *The Focused Interview* (Free Press, Glencoe, 111., 186 pp., 1956)
271 Wittenborn, J. R., and Others, "A Study of Adoptive Children: I. Interviews as a Source of Scores for Children and Their Homes," Psychol. Monog., 70, 1–58 (1956)
272 Back, K. W., "The Einstellung Test and Performance in Factual Interviewing," J. Abnormal Social Psychol, 52, 28–32 (1956)
273 Yonge, K. A., "The Value of the Interview: An Orientation and a Pilot Study," J. Appl. Psychol, 40, 25–31 (1956)
274 Starkweather, J. A., "Content-Free Speech as a Source of Information about the Speaker," J. Abnormal Social Psychol., 52, 394–102 (1956)
275 Bass, B. M., "Development of a Structured Disguised Personality Test," J. Appl. Psychol., 40, 393–97 (1956)
276 Phillipson, H., *The Object Relations Technique* (Free Press, Glencoe, Ill, 224 pp., 1956)
277 van Krevelen, D. A., "The Use of Pigem's Test with Children," J. Projective Techniques, 20, 233–12 (1956)
278 Jones, R. M., "The Negation TAT; a Projective Method for Eliciting Repressed Thought Content," J. Projective Techniques, 20, 297–303 (1956)
279 Peixotto, H. E., "Popular Responses for the Despert Fables," J. Clin. Psychol, 13, 73 79 (1957)
280 Dorkcn, H., Jr., "The Mosaic Test: A Second Review," J. Projective Techniques, 20, 166–71 (1956)
281 Levin, M. L., "Validation of the Lowenfeld Mosaic Test," J. Consulting Psychol., 20, 239–48 (1956)
282 Moran, L. J., Fairweather, G. W., and Morton, R. B., "Some Determinants of Successful and Unsuccessful Adaptation to Hospital Treatment of Tuberculosis," J. Consulting Psychol., 20, 125–31 (1956)
283 Moran, L. J., Fairweather, G. W., Fisher, S., and Morton, R. B., "Psychological Concomitants to Rate of Recovery from Tuberculosis," J. Consulting Psychol, 20, 199–203 (1956)
284 Leary, T., and Harvey, J. S., "A Methodology for Measuring Personality Changes in Psychotherapy," J. Clin. Psychol, 12, 123–32 (1956)
285 Bibo, I. M., "The Projective Expression of Patient-Therapist Attraction," J. Clin. Psychol, 13, 33 36 (1957)
286 Bard, M., and Waxenberg, S. E., "Relationship of Cornell Medical Index Responses to Postsurgical Invalidism," J. Clin. Psychol., 13, 151–53 (1957)
287 Sargent, H. D., "Insight Test Prognosis in Successful and Unsuccessful Rehabilitation of the Blind," J. Projective Techniques, 20, 429–41 (1956)
288 Dean, S. L, "Adjustment Testing and Personality Factors of the Blind," J. Consulting Psychol., 21, 171–77 (1957)
289 Ellsworth, R. B., and Clark, L. D., "Prediction of the Response of Chronic Schizophrenics to Drug Therapy: A Preliminary Report of the Relationship between Palmar Sweat and the Behavior Effects of Tranquilizing Drugs," J. Clin. Psychol., 13, 59–61 (1957)
290 Stogdill, R. M., Shartle, C. L., Scott, E. S., Coons, A. E., and Jaynes, W. E., *A Predictive Study of Administrative Work Patterns* (Ohio State University, Columbus, Ohio, 68 pp., 1956)
291 Shartle, C. L., *Executive Performance and Leadership* (Prentice-Hall Inc., Englewood Cliffs, N.J., 302 pp., 1956)
292 Hyman, S. R., "The Miller Analogies Test and University of Pittsburgh Ph.D. in Psychology," Am. Psychol, 12, 35 36 (1957)
293 Levy, L. H., "The Meaning and Generality of Perceived Actual-Ideal Discrepancies," J. Consulting Psychol, 20, 396–98 (1956)
294 Moustakas, C. E., Ed., *The Self-Explorations in Personal Growth* (Harper & Bros., New York, N. Y., 284 pp., 1956)
295 Journard, S. M., and Remy, R. M., "Individual Variance Score: An Index of the Degree of Differentiation of the Self and the Body Image,". J. Clin. Psychol, 13, 62 63 (1956)
296 Fey, W. F., "Correlates of Certain Subjective Altitudes toward Self and Others," J. Clin. Psychol., 13, 44–49 (1957)
297 Porter, L. G., and Stacey, L. A "Study of the Relationships between Self-Ratings and Parent-Ratings for a Group of College Students," J. Clin. Psychol., 12, 241 48 (1956)
298 Ghiselli, E. E., "Occupational Level Measured through Self Perception," Personnel Psychol, 9, 169–80 (1956)
299 Roe, A., *The Psychology of Occupations* (J. Wiley & Sons, Inc., New York, N. Y., 340 pp., 1956)
300 Blau, P. M., Gustad, J. W., Jessor, R., Parnes, H. S., and Wilcock, R. C., "Occupational Choice: A Conceptual Framework," Ind. Labor Relations Rev., 9, 531–43 (1956)
301 Darley, J.G., and Hagenah, T., *Vocational Interest Measurement* (Univ. Minnesota Press, Minneapolis, Minn., 279 pp., 1955)

302 Jacques, E., *Measurement of Responsibility: A Study of Work, Payment, and Individual Capacity* (Harvard Univ. Press., Cambridge, Mass., 143 pp., 1956)
303 Ghiselli, E. E., "The Placement of Workers: Concepts and Problems," Personnel Psychol, 9, 1–16 (1956)
304 Kragh, U., *The Actual-Genetic Model of Perception-Personality* (Berlingska Boktryckeriet, Lund, Sweden, 394 pp., 1955)
305 Bjerstedt, A., "Levels of Strictness with Respect to Micro-Macro Correspondences. A Note on the 'Actual-Genetic' Model," Theoria, 22, 199–203 (1956)
306 Leary, T., *Interpersonal Diagnosis of Personality* (The Ronald Press Co., New York, N.Y., 518 pp., 1957)
307 Brower, D., and Abt, L. E., Eds., *Progress in Clinical Psychology, II* (Grime & Stratton, Inc., New York, N.Y., 364 pp., 1956)
308 Stern, G. G., Stein, M. I., and Bloom, B. S., *Methods in Personality Assessment* (Free Press, Glencoe, 111., 271 pp., 1956)
309 Marzolf, S. S., *Psychological Diagnosis and Counseling in the Schools* (Henry Holt, New York, N. Y., 401 pp., 1956)
310 Kavruck, S., "Thirty-Three Years of Test Research: A Short History of Test Development in the U. S. Civil Service Commission," Am. Psychol., 11, 329-333 (1956)
311 Guertin, W. H., Frank, G. H., and Rabin, A. I., "Research with the Wechsler-Bellevue Intelligence Scale: 1950-1955," Psychol. Bull., 53, 235–57 (1956)
312 U. S. Veterans Administration, Medical Research in the Veterans Administration, Print No. 50 (House Committee, 85th Cong., 1st Session, U. S. Government Print. Office, Washington, D. C., 945 pp., 1957)
313 Horst, P., "The Uniqueness of Configural Test Item Scores," J. Clin. Psychol., 13, 107–14 (1957)
314 Cronbach, L. J., "Les Exigences de la Validation des Techniques Projectives," Rev. Psychol. Appliqué, 5, 245–53 (1955)
315 Hirsch, J., and Tryon, R. C., "Mass Screening and Reliable Individual Measurement in the Experimental Behavior Genetics of Lower Organisms," Psychol. Bull., 53, 402–10 (1956)

35

The Abstraction of Human Processes[1]

One of the basic problems confronting both philosophy and science is that of representing *change* in terms simple enough to be understood, yet valid enough to make the change predictable.

This problem may be regarded initially as one of abstraction. In some areas man has made considerable progress in solving it. For example, where it is possible to represent the principal parameters, including time, in terms of spatial concepts, many elaborate temporal changes can be abstracted by the methods of analytic geometry.

But when we turn to biology, and from there to history and contemporary politics, the problem of abstraction becomes increasingly difficult. It may seem most difficult of all to the psychologist who is concerned with the assessment of personality, for the assessment of personality begins with the effort to abstract the changing patterns of personal thought and action into terms which are readily understandable and which permit the calculation of human events in advance of their occurrence.

"Personality" is an Abstraction and Generalization

Personality itself is, then, our abstraction of the activity of a person and our subsequent generalization of this abstraction to all matters of his relationship to other persons, known and unknown, as well as to anything else that may seem particularly valuable. Thus there are three points to be kept in mind in dealing with personality: (1) It is a venture in abstract thinking undertaken by psychologists who examine the processes of the individual person, and not an object simply to be discovered by them; (2) it cannot ignore the person's relationship to other persons; and (3) it is bound to be value-laden.

But abstraction and generalization of human activity are not the exclusive prerogatives of professional psychologists. What they do any person may do. Indeed every person does! Each individual the psychologists study abstracts and generalizes on his own, for he is even more vitally interested than they can ever be in the task of understanding himself and his relationship to other persons and values. Thus the psychology of personality is not simply a matter of disinterested psychologists assessing a disinterested organism, but of psychologists, who happen to be professionally and casually interested in their chosen subject matter, assessing a non-professional psychologist who, on his part, is intimately and urgently involved with the job of making sense out of the life upon which his existence depends. Moreover, this non-professional psychologist—who is any person we assess—does much of his abstracting and generalizing in precipitate ways he cannot easily depict for us in words or gestures.

For the person who assesses his own behavior, no less than for the scientists who examine it from the outside, the abstractions he makes enable him to see where he is going. At the personal level this is science too. But there is a special redundancy in the scientific determinism one applies to himself, for the same abstractions that enable one to forecast what he is about to do may serve also to determine how to act in order to fulfill or forestall his predictions.

Now we have four points to be kept in mind. Not only, as we have said before, is assessment of personality based on the abstraction of a person's known activity so it can be generalized to his unknown activity, not only is it particularly concerned with a person's relationship to other persons, not only is it bound up with values, but also assessment must take into account the person's own abstractions and generalizations about himself, even when they are imperfectly symbolized. These four considerations call for a psychology of personal constructs and for the development of techniques for appraising personal constructs.

[1] Presented at a Symposium on Personality Research and Applied Personality Assessments at XIV International Congress of Applied Psychology, Christiansborg Castle, Copenhagen, August 13-19, 1961. Originally published as Kelly. G.A. (1961). The abstraction of human processes. Proceedings of the XIV International Congress of Applied Psychology, Copenhagen, Denmark, 220–229. Republished by permission of the International Association of Applied Psychology.

Collected Papers of the Pioneer of Constructivist Psychology: George A. Kelly, First Edition. Edited by David A. Winter and Nick Reed.

The Nature of Abstraction

In order to develop a psychology of personal constructs for assessing personality it is necessary to concern ourselves with the psychological nature of the abstraction process itself. Whatever we may already understand abstraction to be from the standpoint of classical logic, it is necessary in addition to ask what it is from the standpoint of psychology.

Do persons indeed do their abstracting in classical form? Apparently not. Probably the most important deviation of psychological logic from classical logic is in its use of contrasts. For example, two women with whom one is acquainted may be abstracted as similar not only because they are feminine but just as much because their femininity contrasts with the masculinity of men. Thus speaking of femininity makes psychological sense only if one also implies the masculinity with which it stands in meaningful contrast.

This principle holds true for all the other abstractions with which human beings psychologically structure their world. To sum it up, then, we may say that each of us finds meaning in his life not only by identifying things for what they are, but also by noting what they are not. Moreover, in noting what they are not we clarify the alternatives that are open to us, thus establishing the psychological basis of what is most important of all—human freedom.

There are other features which seem to distinguish psychological logic from classical logic, and the study of all of them would probably be a lifetime undertaking, But perhaps I have said enough to trace the general line of inquiry I have been following and to suggest the basis for the methods of personality assessment I am about to describe.

Methods of Assessing Personal Constructs

Perhaps the best place to start the discussion of methodology is with the description of a particular technique. Then later I can attempt to describe the broader methodology of which this technique is a particular example.

Suppose I were to give one of you a card and ask you to write on it the name of your mother. Then I would give you another and ask you to write the name of your father. On a third you might write the name of your wife, and on a fourth the name of the girl you almost married—but didn't! We could continue until you had as many as twenty or thirty cards, each showing the name of a person important in your life.

Then suppose I should select three of these cards, perhaps the ones of your father, your mother, and your boss or supervisor. Suppose I should ask you to think of some important way in which any two of them seem to be alike and in contrast to the third. What will you say? Perhaps you will say that your mother and your boss have always seemed to know the answers to the questions you asked but that your father hesitated or told you to seek out your own answers.

Now if this is a distinction you can apply to your father, your mother, and your boss, can you extend it also to the other persons you have named? You probably can. The important fact is that as you apply it to person after person you are not only characterizing those persons but you are also providing an operational definition of what you have in mind. Applied to enough persons this operational definition provides a more extensive definition of a particular channel of your thought than do words you may use to symbolize it.

Now suppose I select another three cards, perhaps the ones with the names of your mother, your wife, and the girl you did not marry. What about them? Is there an important way in which two of them—any two—differ from the third? Perhaps you will respond immediately by saying that your wife and your mother are loving but that the girl you did not marry turned out to be harsh.

And how will you extend this personal construct to the other persons who are important in your life? Now let me suppose—for the sake of this discussion—something which I doubt would be true of anyone in this audience. Let me suppose that each person you characterize as "loving" is a person you have previously characterized as ready to answer your questions, and each person you characterize as "harsh" is one you previously characterized as sending you off to look for your own answers. Suppose this were true in case after case, on out to infinity. What could we say then? Would we then be ready to say that the two constructs were identical in everything but name?

Not quite! In our illustration the two constructs have been applied only to persons as whole entities. There is still the question of whether the constructs are applied identically to the separate acts of persons. To go even further, this suggests that, in general, the equivalence of constructs is determined by their similar application to all types of events, not merely to human events alone.

Moreover, we need also to make sure that both constructs occupy exactly the same range of convenience. That is to say, can the first construct in my illustration—the response-rejection construct—be applied to all the events to which the second construct—the loving-harsh construct—can be applied; and, of course vice versa? If there are some events that can be classified by the person as responsive or rejecting but which he cannot treat in terms of lovingness or harshness, then the ranges of convenience of the two constructs are different and the constructs themselves are therefore not quite the same.

All of this is a mathematical or logical problem and it leads to the formulation of one of the theorems underlying personal construct theory. Since, however, this paper is more concerned with the methodology of personal construct theory than with its mathematics, I shall limit myself to pointing out merely that such propositions exist.

Let us return to our deck of cards. We can represent the data produced so far in a flat matrix with events—in this case the names appearing on the cards—ranged along the top from left to right, and with the constructs ranged along the side from top to bottom. The entries in the matrix are single digit binary numbers, indicating simply whether the event is regarded one way or the other in terms of the construct. For example, if you regarded your mother as loving, this particular datum would be represented in the matrix by the numeral "1" in the first cell of the second row—below "mother" and opposite "loving-harsh." If you regarded your father as harsh the numeral "0" would be entered in the next cell, etc.

Now we may go on to expand the matrix until it is large enough to give us a stable idea of how the person construes his world. Starting with different triads of cards we can successively produce row after row of matrix entries.

This is not an interminable undertaking. Experience shows that only persons with the most complex or schizoid outlooks require more than twenty of thirty rows to express their repertory of constructs. Repertories used in everyday affairs are generally quite limited, and, especially so it appears, among those who prefer to act rather than reflect.

As you can see, the matrix can be factor-analyzed to see to what extent the person is employing a variety of constructs, or only a few constructs masquerading under different names. We can examine the columns in the matrix to see which figures in his life are viewed as similar to others, or whether, indeed, there is any great variety perceived among them. For example, does the subject see himself as like his father, or does he see his psychotherapist as like his father—as psychoanalytic theory suggests he should at certain stages of his treatment?

Incidentally, with regard to this particular psychoanalytic hypothesis, the research does not confirm psychoanalytic thinking. Patients entering into long-term psychotherapy seem rather to view their therapists as more and more like their family physicians.

Again, there are some men who can see complex differences among men, but only one-dimensional differences among women. There are some who have attempted to reduce all their interpersonal relations to the simple structure of one dimension—some military men, for example, and there are some who have done this in an effort to control the multi-dimensional confusion of their anxiety.

Research seems to indicate that there are advantages in having a complex repertory of personal constructs, but there are disadvantages, too, particularly in decision-making. It appears that schizoid persons have a complex repertory, but that constructs lack sufficient ranges of convenience to enable the person to relate one of them to another. Thus the system fails to function as a whole and we find erratic sequences in the matrix.

Up to this point we have emphasized the mathematical analysis of the matrix and have ignored the words the person uses to name his constructs. But the words may be examined also. A recent study by Landfield indicates that a verbal analysis distinguishes between university students who are socially well adjusted from those who are not (p values to below .01), that it sometimes gives a slight prior indication of which maladjusted ones will improve under psychotherapy ($p < .0$), and that it reflects the degree of improvement of the maladjusted ones under psychotherapy ($r_{bis} = .64$, $p < .001$).

But let us turn away from the particular kind of matrix we have described—which, after all, is only one example of the application of the methodology—and look at other kinds of personal construct matrices. Suppose, instead of asking you to write the name of a person on each of the cards I gave you, I would ask you to list an important experience you had had. Suppose, for example, I asked you to think of your wedding and make a note of it on the first card. On the second card you might note the occasion when you had a serious quarrel with your parents, on the third the time when you believed you were near death, on the fourth the ceremony at which you were awarded your university degree, then the meeting when a paper you presented was most severely criticized, and so on. Then suppose you were to construe these events, three at a time as you did the persons in your life, and then extended the constructs to all the other events you had mentioned. This would generate another kind of matrix whose columns and rows, as well as its verbal content, could be analyzed.

Or you might list only the catastrophes in your life and then ask yourself which of the persons you had named could, if they had been available at the time, have been helpful to you in meeting each emergency. Such a matrix provides information about one's allocation of his interpersonal dependencies—whether he has faced difficulties in which he feels no one could be of help, whether he turns to one or two persons only for all kinds of help, or whether he is indiscriminate in his selection of persons upon whom to depend.

Some researchers have used the methodology to come to an understanding of how a young person confronted with making a vocational choice views the different occupations and professions open to him. Others have used it to analyze personal factors in job dissatisfaction. Some have studied changes in the construing process during a year of university training, and others, have studied similar changes during psychotherapy.

Theoretical Implications of Personal Construct Methodology

Let us return now to some of the theoretical implications of this kind of methodology. As you see, our inquiry takes us into the field of personal constructs, their operations in relation to events as well as to words, and their interrelations with each other. While the constructs are personal and each individual has his own repertory of them, they are not so inaccessibly private that we human beings must despair of ever understanding each other. On the contrary, the methodology of matrices enables us to comprehend the complexities of differing personalities without having to reduce them to single-dimensional behavioral formulas, to physiological terms, to historical determinisms, to autonomous motives, or to any of the other reductionistic schemes that psychologists commonly employ. The psychology of personal constructs is then essentially a methodological psychology rather than the usual content psychology, though, of course, it yields content as a secondary product.

Personal Constructs and Change

At the beginning of this paper I referred to the basic difficulty encountered by science and philosophy in understanding change and to the particular acuteness of that difficulty in the field of psychology. It may not be clear at this point how what I have said bears on the matter of change.

The system of personal constructs, with their paired alternatives, may be regarded as a limited universe of dimensions in terms of which the individual structures his psychological space. Where his space has dimensions he is free to move and is hampered only by his dread of consequences, But where he has no dimensions there is no space as far as he is concerned. He cannot go there. He cannot step out and around in what is for him an inconceivable fourth dimension.

Thus, just as one first needs to construe ordinary space before he can manage the movement of physical bodies, so man is psychologically limited in what he may do with himself by the dimensions of the psychological space in his personal world. A personal construct represents, then, a psychological channel which the person's construing has opened up to him—a dimension of his personal freedom. Perhaps it is not necessary for me to add that human freedom—which is always personal if it is truly freedom—is the primary stake in the awful games that are being played between nations today.

As I have said before, we should not limit our notion of personal constructs merely to what the person can label with words or can represent logically. Whatever channels of movement are expressed in a person's life, no matter how subtly, these are his personal constructs. They define the psychological space in which he is free to breathe and move and their inter-relationships define the matrix which psychologists may examine in their efforts to understand the ever-shifting pattern of movement which we call the human personality.

36

A Mathematical Approach to Psychology[1]

Many different approaches to psychology are possible, but most of them have not been invented yet. The purpose of this paper is to describe an approach that is now in the process of being invented. Like all the others which have preceded it, as well as those to come later, it is a construction and not a discovery. I must make this clear at the outset; I did not find this theory lurking among the data of an experiment nor was it disclosed to me on a mountain top or in a laboratory. I have, in my own clumsy way, been making it up.

Invention and Discovery in Science

A scientist's inventions assist him in two ways: they tell him what to expect and they help him see it when it happens. Those that tell him what to expect are theoretical inventions and those that enable him to observe outcomes are instrumental inventions. The two types are never wholly independent of each other, and they usually stem from the same assumptions. This is unavoidable. Moreover, without his inventions, both theoretical and instrumental, man would be both disoriented and blind. He would not know where to look or how to see.

While invention is the key to progress in science, as well as in other forms of human inquiry, discovery is important also. But when we speak of discovery we must be explicit about what we mean, else we shall find ourselves enmeshed in the same difficulties as those who think that the natural events of the world go around introducing themselves by name and whispering theoretical revelations into the ears of deserving scientists.

First of all, theoretical inventions are used to make predictions. Then, still using inventions, but of a more instrumental type, we examine the outcomes to see if there is any correspondence between what we have predicted and what our instrumentalized perceptions tell us has occurred. If we find such a correspondence, we call it a discovery. We do not discover our theory; we do not discover our prediction; we do not even discover the ensuing event. What is discovered is a correspondence—a practical correspondence—between what our theoretical invention leads us to anticipate and what, subsequently, our instrumental invention leads us to observe.

When a scientist repeatedly fails to find any correspondence between what appears to happen and what his theoretical invention has led him to expect, he is likely to conclude, sooner or later, that his theory is worthless. Thus, if the invention I am about to describe to you fails to produce expectations that materialize, I, too, am likely to conclude, sooner or later, that my invention is worthless. Others may reach this conclusion sooner than I, for, having gone to the trouble of inventing the theory and writing papers about it, I shall want to explore its possibilities extensively before abandoning it. Some of you may be happy to abandon the theory at the very outset, while others may wish to pursue it, along with me, for some distance, if only out of sheer curiosity to see where it leads.

This paper, then, begins with a personal invitation to you to join me aboard my theoretical vessel and set out on a voyage of discovery, and, sharing with me such instruments as I have on board, to observe the islands we pass. If, at any time, you despair of discovering any correspondence between what we seek and what looms up on the horizon, you are free to turn back. I, too, may turn back at some point, if I become discouraged with the outcomes of our venture, while some of you, who are not so easily discouraged, may press the voyage further.

Constructive Alternativism

These statements I have been making so far are more epistemological than psychological. But let me continue further with them, for they have a bearing on the psychological statements I shall want to make later.

[1] Prepared at the invitation of the Moscow Psychological Society and presented in Moscow, April 10, 1961. Published in Maher, B. (Ed.). (1969). *Clinical psychology and personality: The selected papers of George Kelly* (pp. 94–113). Wiley. Republished by permission of Wiley.

For a long time scientists have assumed that before they could advance a new theory they must first prove something wrong with the old ones. I do not consider this a necessary assumption. It is true that our disappointments with one kind of explanation do often serve to set us off in search of a better one. There is nothing wrong with that. But does one always have to wait until he is frustrated and embittered before he dares start looking for new horizons? I think not.

The adventure in which I have invited you to join me for a little while does not, therefore, require you to deny anything you now believe or to destroy anything you now find useful. That is why I have said that you are free to return whenever you find the voyage discouragingly unproductive. You need not scuttle your present ships in order to embark on this one. Nor need you wait until you are discouraged before you quit my vessel for another.

The question of whether a theory is true or false, good or bad, useful or futile is not identical with the question of whether or not to explore its implications. These two types of questions arise properly at different times, and therefore are not to be answered concurrently. This is a point of view which is a convenience in dealing with what I have to offer; but it is more than that—it is an essential feature of the theory itself, as I hope to show during the course of this paper.

The underlying philosophical position which I have sketched briefly in the preceding paragraphs may be called "constructive alternativism." This is to say that reality is subject to many alternative constructions, some of which may prove to be more fruitful than others. The discovery of an ultimate correspondence between the constructions we are able to devise and the flow of actual events is an infinitely long way off. In the meantime, we shall have to be content to make a little progress at a time, to invent new alternative constructions—even before we have become dissatisfied with the old ones, and hope that, in general, we are moving in the right direction.

Converging Lines of Inference

I. Generalization of the Psychology of Scientific Behavior

Now, having said something philosophical, we are prepared to go on to say something more psychological. Since, as I am sure Professor Luria will agree, it is helpful to have a verbal response for something if we are to control all our other reactions to it, let me say that the theory I am about to describe may be called "the psychology of personal constructs."

The theory may be said to represent the convergence of several lines of inference. Naturally, I shall not attempt to describe all of them, but it is appropriate to mention one or two.

One thing that has struck me is that nearly every psychologist of our time inadvertently uses two quite different systems for explaining human behavior. While I see nothing particularly wrong in this, as you already know from my discussion of constructive alternativism, it does raise the fascinating question of whether one or the other of the two systems might not suffice to explain the whole spectrum of human behavior.

Let me try to explain what I mean. Most psychologists consider themselves scientists. This is true in my country as well as in yours. They see *science* as progressing according to certain principles and by means of certain methodologies. But when these same psychologists turn their attention to *man*, they speak in another language. In the first chapter of their books they say that *science* progresses by inducing or deducing theoretical statements, by formulation of hypotheses, by specifying predictions, by experimentation, by observing outcomes and comparing them with expectations, and by constant revision of one's line of reasoning. But in the ensuing chapters they forget all about this and they attempt to describe *man's* behavior in quite different terms, the particular terms depending somewhat upon their theoretical orientation at the moment.

But science is itself a form of human behavior, and a pretty important one, at that. Why, then, should we feel compelled to use one set of parameters when we describe *man-the-scientist* and another set when we describe *man-the-laboratory-subject*? I pose this question, not as one to be answered immediately by logical inference, or to be dismissed with the supposition that scientific behavior must require a unique psychology because it constitutes so small a part of human behavior, but as a question to be explored. I pose it, not as a philosophical question, but as a psychological one—and hence one to be answered or reformulated by scientific inquiry.

Answering a question of this sort, as I am sure you will agree, involves a good deal more than one simple laboratory experiment. One way of exploring this question is to take our notions of scientific progress, philosophical notions of what science is and how it proceeds, remove them from the context of a speculative philosophy and logic, and elaborate them as a system of psychological theory of man's behavior. Thus we would prepare our question for scientific investigation. We could then deduct hypotheses, raise issues, develop methodologies, devise instruments, generate data, perform experiments, induce further hypotheses, and revise our theoretical formulations. The psychology of personal constructs is an attempt to prepare our question in just such a way.

Converging Lines of Inference

II. The Double Entity Choice

Let me mention another of the converging lines of inference, merely one of many, which points to the psychology of personal constructs. From the time of Aristotle we have understood propositional speech as a way of denoting entities. We may say, "A is B."

This statement is a way of asserting a conclusion, the antithesis of which would have been to say, "A is not B." This is a familiar logical form and its intrinsic validity is generally taken for granted.

But we can look at this matter as psychologists and pose a scientific question about it. When one says that "A is B," is he, in fact, merely abandoning the alternative proposition that "A is not B"? Or is he, in fact, denying some other alternative? This is a question about human behavior, not a question of classical logic. Since it is a question about human behavior, it should be open to psychological examination.

Experience with clients undergoing psychotherapy, as well as with persons in the process of changing their lives under other conditions, leads one to suspect that a person never makes his choice merely between an entity and a nonentity. When he says that "A is B" it seems that he is also asserting that "A is not C." The choice he makes is not, therefore, between "B" and "not-B," but between "B" and "C"—between two entities. Let us call this "the double entity choice," to distinguish it from "the single entity choice" envisioned by classical logic.

If you prefer, we can state this observation in behavioral terms. We may then say that a person never chooses between behaving in a certain way and not behaving at all. Rather, he chooses between one behavior and another. He does not choose between activity and inactivity; instead, he chooses between alternative kinds of activity. At least, for the moment, this is the way it seems.

It must be clear that what I am offering here is an incident observation only. But it is an observation that can be pursued psychologically to see whether, as a generalization, it can be supported in a scientific manner. In order to examine it psychologically it is best that we first elaborate it in some theoretical form, preferably in one that is simple, coherent, communicable, productive of reasonably explicit hypotheses, and amenable to the operational definition of experimental terms.

And so, this time by a different route, we come again to the psychology of personal constructs, a theory which, among other things, attempts to do just this. It takes our incidental observation of the double entity choice in human behavior and incorporates it in a theoretical structure. The constructed theory, because of all its predictive implications, then becomes a basis upon which a series of scientific inquiries can be undertaken. Eventually, this series of inquiries should reveal to us whether or not we have invented anything useful.

Theoretical Composition of the Psychology of Personal Constructs

Thus far in this paper we have mentioned only three main ideas. The first is *constructive alternativism*, a philosophical position which simultaneously sustains a vast variety of competing theoretical formulations, and the research that stems from them, even though some of those formulations appear as alternatives to what is currently acceptable. The other two ideas are the two incidental observations that give rise to converging lines of inference. The first of these suggests the possibility of *generalizing the psychology of scientific behavior* to all human behavior, and the second suggests the possibility of incorporating the *double entity choice* into a psychological theory. There are, of course, many other initial ideas and observations that might have been mentioned as leading to this theory, but these three are sufficient for this paper. Actually most of our further discussion will center around the third idea, the idea of the double entity choice, since this is the one that leads us most directly to an unusual kind of mathematical approach to psychology.

Suppose a child distinguishes between two objects, say, a ball and a cube. On the following day let us say he distinguishes between another ball and another cube. Why are his two performances similar? One thing we can say is that because the pairs of objects were physically similar on the successive days the child's responses were similar. This explanation is based on the assumption that the child is under the control of the objects and therefore similar pairs of objects must always elicit similar responses. This is one type of explanation, and it is satisfactory, as far as it goes.

But suppose we make use of the principle of constructive alternativism and seek other kinds of explanation. Suppose we turn our attention to the child, rather than to the objects, and ask how it is that he was able to do with them what he did. Suppose we say it is not enough that the objects be similar; what more is required is that the child have some capability that enables him to respond as if they were similar. The psychological point I want to emphasize is that he construed the objects similarly, in spite of the fact that the occasions were different and the particular concrete objects were different.

One way of throwing light on the child's behavior is to examine the history of his performances. Such an examination has the advantage of enabling us to apply theories of conditioning or other historical types of explanation directly to particular acts. But, without burdening myself with the task of finding fault with such explanations—or others with the task of defending them—let me simply continue to take advantage of constructive alternativism and ask how the child, conditioned or not, copes with balls and cubes when they are presented to him.

One thing is obvious; the psychological feature we are seeking is itself neither a ball, a cube, a day, or a set of circumstances—we are not looking for stimuli. The feature must be, instead, the child's own way of dealing with balls and cubes, his own way of channelizing his response to them, regardless of changing circumstances, and, therefore, one that he need not abandon at the end of the day when he goes to bed. Moreover, it is based on his personal construction of balls and cubes, a construction which he did not discover but which, as a kind of scientist, he invented. Since he is a "scientist" who is alive and active we may presume he is experimenting with his invention and is in the process of discovering its predictive utility.

It is at this point in the elaboration of the theory that I must pause to make a special stipulation. Nothing that I have said implies that the child's way of managing balls and cubes is necessarily based upon language or upon so-called conscious thinking. Nor do I mean to suggest that there are classical ideas or concepts floating around in his head. I have done no more than to invite your attention first to what the child actually does, and now I am asking you to go one step further with me and pay particular attention to his ways of doing it. Thus, from now on, I shall be referring to the *forms* his life processes take, rather than to concrete processes themselves. The question of whether or not the processes are naturally physiological, mental, cognitive, spiritual, verbal, or unconscious is not relevant to what I have to say. We shall be talking about the ways these processes operate, not about their essences.

Assessing the Personal Construct

Now that we have left behind the particulars of human behavior and are dealing with the abstractions of human behavior which we hope will provide the grounds for systematic scientific inquiry, we can start to delineate the forms into which we may cast those abstractions. We shall take our cue, as I have already indicated, from the observation that persons appear to make a double entity choice, rather than a single entity choice. Thus a child, in identifying a ball, appears to distinguish it from some other type of object—perhaps a cube—rather than merely picking it out, all at once, from all the things in the world which are not balls. If it appears to us that he picks it out all at once we may suppose that this is only because he has applied a sequential series of distinctions, and the types of objects he has eliminated along the way are not easily recognizable in his final identification of the ball.

If we give the child a ball, a cube, and a disc, and then ask him to put together the two that are alike, he can respond in at least three ways. (1) He can put the disc and the ball together, in which case we suspect that he has erected some construction that distinguishes a curvilinearity he ascribes to those two objects from an angularity. (2) He can put the cube and the disc together, in which case we suspect that the underlying distinction is between flatness and convexity. (3) Or he can put the cube and the ball together, in which case we might guess that he is distinguishing between thickness and thinness.

But how can we be sure? Suppose he actually puts the cube and the disc together, thus distinguishing them from the ball. Can we be sure that this means he has construed in the form, "convex versus flat?" Unless we are confident we can rely upon an exchange of language symbols with him, we must resort to the further explication of his construct by other means.

Suppose we next give him a lozenge and a feather. Suppose, instead of placing the convex lozenge beside the ball and the flat feather beside the cube and the disc, he does the reverse. Now he has the feather and the ball together, and on the other side he has the lozenge, the cube, and the disc.

Now that his construct has been explicated through five objects we may have a somewhat better understanding of the pattern his behavior follows. But we may still find it hard to predict accurately how he will arrange additional objects. We may hypothesize, at this point, that we can predict his further arrangements by using ourselves a construct of stable objects, such as the cube, the disc, and the lozenge, versus mobile objects which are easily dislodged, such as the ball and the feather. But this is only our hypothesis. Still, if by using it we do accurately predict his sorting of the next twenty objects given him, we may begin to feel some confidence that we have devised a useful notion of how his construct enables him to function in this simple laboratory situation.

The Personal Construct as an Abstraction of Human Behavior

When a person identifies an object we may say he has applied a construct to it. This is to say he has abstracted his behavior into a form we call the personal construct, and that he can now move consistently from situation to situation by the generalized application of this form. Indeed, when a person behaves discriminatingly it is quite likely that he has made use of several personal constructs. His employment of several constructs enables him to fix both objects and behaviors multidimensionally, as one fixes points geometrically in hyperspace.

The application of a construct to an object has certain implications. Let me put two of these implications systematically, so they may become an explicit part of the theory we are developing. The first implication is that there is at least one other imaginable object which stands in contrast to the one immediately construed. The second implication is that there is at least a third object which is similar to one of the other two.

You will recognize the first of these two systematic statements as a theoretical formulation based on the incidental observation I mentioned earlier—that persons make double entity choices. The second statement is required if we are to deal with the abstraction of behavior, rather than isolated incidents of behavior. We may go on to say, then, that the minimum context in which a construct can be said to exist is three objects, or, to be more precise, three incidents. No less than three is required. As a matter of fact, of course, personal constructs are usually employed in much larger contexts.

It must also be understood that the personal construct abstracts similarity and difference simultaneously. One cannot be abstracted without implying the other. For a person to treat two incidents as different is to imply that one of them appears to be like another he knows. Conversely, for a person to treat two incidents as similar is to imply that he contrasts both of them with at least one other incident he knows. We intend this to be considered as an essential feature of the personal construct by means of which we hope to understand the psychology of human behavior.

The Personal Construct as a Mathematical Function

We come now to a more difficult point. I must confess that I find this point hard to explain to my students and colleagues. The discussion usually starts with the innocent question, "Do you envision the personal construct as a dichotomy or as a continuum?" My answer is, "I envision it as a dichotomy." But when I give this answer trouble starts. It appears to my listeners that I have said that human behavior must conform only to stereotypes and that everything in the world is judged as either black or white—never in shades of gray. This, of course, is not true.

I think I am beginning to understand what the root of the difficulty is. Most of us think about psychological matters concretely rather than abstractly. When we think of the form of human behavior we think of reflexes, of material learned, of decisions made, much as the child who, when he thinks of the mathematical value "four," thinks of "four apples," "four pieces of candy," "four pencils," or "four wheels."

Perhaps if we step outside the field of psychology for a moment we can make sure we have recovered our ability to think abstractly. Let us step into the field of geography. Consider the geographical construct of "north versus south." This is a dichotomous construct, and it is abstract. As far as the construct itself is concerned, there are no "partial norths" or "partial souths" crammed in between "north" and "south." And there certainly are no objects which are, of themselves, "north" or "south."

However, it is a simple matter to use this dichotomous construct to create an array of objects ranged from north to south. All we have to do is take advantage of the fact that the construct is abstract, and therefore readily available for use in a wide variety of circumstances. We may then apply it sequentially to the different objects we want to place in the array. But the array of objects we have thus set in order is not the construct; it is only one kind of concrete explication of the construct.

We can go further. We can use our abstract construct to build a scale, as for example, a scale of degrees along a meridian. This is simply a matter of creating an array of symbols which have been differentiated by our construct. Such a device has the advantage of being somewhat portable—and it is undoubtedly convenient. But never should it be confounded with the abstract construct of "north versus south," which is the basis for the device, and without which such a scale could never have been imagined.

Let us turn back, now, to psychology and visualize this same kind of dichotomous abstraction taking place. Let us visualize it taking place, not only with respect to geography, but with respect to all matters with which men, consciously or unconsciously, must cope. The particular behavioral content may vary from subject to subject and from person to person, but we propose the term, "personal construct" for the general form in which construing takes place.

As for the question of whether men deal with their world in terms of categories or continua, that is a heuristic matter. The fact is they do both, as we all well know. But the baseline, from which we may proceed to erect either categories or continua, and upon which we are free to project any behavior in our effort to understand it, may be regarded as essentially a dichotomous differentiating and integrating unit—the personal construct. It is in this sense, and in this sense only, that it properly becomes a mathematical function.

The Geometry of Psychological Space

Now that we have our basic unit, the personal construct, partially defined, we can turn our attention to the question of how the world appears when structured in such terms. Perhaps it is already clear that our psychological geometry is a geometry of dichotomies rather than the geometry of areas envisioned by the classical logic of concepts, or the geometry of lines envisioned by classical mathematical geometries. Each of our dichotomies has both a differentiating and an integrating function. That is to say it is the generalized form of the differentiating and integrating act by which man intervenes in his world. By such an act he interposes a difference between incidents—incidents that would otherwise be imperceptible to him because they are infinitely homogeneous. But also, by such an intervening act, he ascribes integrity to incidents that are otherwise imperceptible because they are infinitesimally fragmented.

For the present we do not need to ask how man performs this intervening act—whether with his brain, his stomach, or his glands. Nor do we need to concern ourselves just yet with the essence of the act—whether it is cognitive, conative, or affective. Finally we need not agree on what kind of substance fills the psychological space we have structured—whether the space is stuffed with physiological things, social things, or mental things. All these matters are, at most, no more than subsequent issues, and indeed, as I personally suspect, may prove to be no issues at all, after we have put our mathematics to work.

In this kind of geometrically structured world there are no distances. Each axis of reference represents not a line or a continuum, as in analytic geometry, but one, and only one, distinction. However, there are angles. These are represented by contingencies or overlapping frequencies of incidents. Moreover, these angles of relationship between personal constructs change with the context of incidents to which the constructs are applied. Thus our psychological space is a space without distance, and, as in the case of non-Euclidian geometries, the relationships between directions change with the context.

If we turn from the geometry of the psychology of personal constructs to its arithmetic, we find that the computation is essentially digital rather than analogical, nonparametric rather than parametric. Quantification takes on a different meaning in psychology. But these further implications of our line of theoretical reasoning, exciting as they are, should not be discussed further until after we have talked about more practical matters.

Data in Terms of Personal Constructs

Let us now look at some of the instrumental inventions produced by the psychology of personal constructs, some of the questions the theory poses for psychologists, some of the methodology for answering these questions, and some of the answers that are beginning to appear.

Probably all of you are familiar with the methods used by Vygotsky to investigate concept formation. One of his methods was to have his subject make a systematic arrangement of small wooden blocks of different sizes, shapes, and colors. The purpose was to see what categories or concepts the subject spontaneously employed, how coherent he was, and whether he could effectively alter his system of categories to meet varying requirements imposed by the experimenter.

Now suppose we consider only the first of these objectives—the observation of what categories the subject spontaneously employs. We shall disregard, for the present, the question of how competent he is or how diligently he complies with the experimenter's whims. Suppose, also, that we are more concerned with the question of how he deals with people than with the question of how he deals with blocks or other inanimate objects. Finally—and this is most important of all—let us look behind the separate categories themselves and focus our attention on the differentiation and integration processes that underlie these categories. In doing all this we shall have digressed widely from what Vygotsky had in mind, though we shall be nonetheless indebted to him for establishing a useful methodological point of departure.

Now, where does this put us? Instead of sorting blocks we shall ask our subject to sort persons he knows. Instead of pointing to the categories into which he places them we shall examine the various ways in which he sees them as different and similar to each other. In other words, instead of cataloging classical concepts, we shall be eliciting psychological data in terms of our basic mathematical unit, the personal construct.

Suppose I give one of you a card and ask you to write on it the name of your mother. Then suppose I give you another and ask for the name of your father. On a third you may write the name of your wife, on a fourth the name of the girl you might have married but did not, on a fifth the name of the professor who influenced you most, and so on until you have a pack of cards containing the names of the most important persons in your life.

Next, suppose I take this pack of cards and select three of them for your particular attention. Perhaps they are the ones on which are written the names of your father, your former professor, and your present supervisor. I give them to you and ask you to think of some important way in which you regard two of them as similar to each other but in contrast to the third. You look at the cards and then put at one side the two containing the names of your professor and your supervisor, saying, "These two persons have always seemed to know the answers to the questions I asked, but this one here—my father—usually urged me to seek the answers elsewhere."

Now I may give you the card with the name of your brother and ask you where you will place it—with your professor and your supervisor, on the one side, or with your father, on the other. Perhaps you will place him with the father, saying that he, too, was inclined to advise people to find their own answers. Then may come the card with your wife's name on it. How do you apply this differentiation and integration to her? Perhaps, with respect to this particular personal construct of yours, she seems to be more like your professor and your supervisor; that is to say, she thinks she knows the answers to all questions. And so we may go through all the cards in your pack.

The data you have produced may be placed in a simple array with the names of persons arranged in a horizontal row and below them a corresponding row of symbols—pluses and minuses—indicating in each instance whether you regarded each person as more like your professor and supervisor, or more like your father. The personal construct, insofar as it has been explicated by the data you have produced, is now represented in two ways: (1) verbally, by the words you have used to symbolize it, and (2) incidentally, by the row of pluses and minuses. The context in which you have explicated the construct is represented by the particular group of human figures whose names appear on the cards.

What we have done so far may be repeated, starting with another combination of cards. If I give you the names of your wife, your mother, and the girl you nearly married, what outstanding similarity and difference will you see? Perhaps you will say that your wife and mother are sympathetic, but the girl you once thought you loved turned out to be cruel. And what will you say about each of the other persons in this respect? Again, as before, your arrangement of the cards may be recorded as a row of pluses and minuses.

The Functional Identity Theorem

We can now examine the two rows of symbols you have produced to see how similar they are. Consider, first, the rather unlikely possibility that the rows are exactly alike, that each person you identified as willing to answer your questions you also judged as sympathetic, and that each person who urged you to find your own answers was also judged as cruel. Consider, further, the limiting case in which these two constructs might be explicated through an infinity of persons and events, but, throughout, would display exactly the same pattern of pluses and minuses. What may we conclude?

If we assume that the rows of pluses and minuses constitute the complete operational definitions of the two constructs involved, we may now conclude that the two constructs are functionally identical, even though you have used different words to describe them. There is an important theorem here to the effect that two constructs which produce an infinite series of identical operations are themselves identical. Of course, in this particular instance, one may raise the objection that since you have used different words in describing the two constructs the operations are not quite infinitely identical. But this is an issue that would force us to turn aside and deal with the whole question of symbols and their peculiar psychological status as events. This is not the occasion for such a digression.

The Construction Matrix

We may now pick up our pack of cards again. Starting from various combinations of three cards each, you may produce row after row of comparable data. When we stop we will have displayed before us a rectangular matrix containing a finite number of rows and a finite number of columns of nonparametric entries. At this point we may, if we wish, discard the words you have used to symbolize your constructs and consider only the configuration of incidents in the matrix. We may also discard the names of persons, too, but let us not do that just yet.

It is possible to do many things with this matrix. For example, we may factor-analyze it to see if there are clusters of similar rows or if it may be reduced to two or three row patterns without losing an undue amount of its discriminating power. We can also look at the columns and ask similar questions. What types of people inhabit your world? Are there many types or only a few? And whom do you identify with whom? Is your wife construed as more like your mother than like any other person you know? Are your father and your supervisor similar in all the respects you have displayed? Do you identify yourself with your father?

Now a host of fresh questions begins to arise, and new issues, both theoretical and practical, emerge. There are questions about the matrix itself. How many of the persons in your life and what sampling of persons is necessary for stable replication of a set of constructs? The indications, so far, suggest that not much is added if more than thirty or forty persons are represented in the matrix. How many constructs should be elicited in order to make the matrix representative of the person's ultimate matrix? This number appears to be smaller; twenty-five or thirty will suffice. The necessary and sufficient matrix is therefore likely to be one that is longer in its horizontal dimension than in its vertical dimension, but we have reason to suspect that these proportions, as well as the required size of the matrix, change as one becomes more mature.

What about changes that take place in the matrix? Do persons undergoing intensive psychotherapy, and who therefore are presumed to be changing radically, see their therapists as more and more like their fathers, as psychoanalytic theory suggests? No; they see them more and more like doctors or like persons who exercise arbitrary authority. Do persons undergoing therapy develop more generalized constructs? To answer this question we must change the subject's sorting task slightly, permitting him to discard those names of persons to whom he cannot apply a given construct. Then we get the interesting answer that in the early stages of psychotherapy the person becomes more restricted in his ways of construing the people he knows. But there is a paradox here. Another study showed that the less restricted he is at the beginning of hospital treatment, the more likely he is to make therapeutic progress—but still that this progress is itself accompanied by constriction!

But is this what happens in education? No; students during their first year away from home in college seem to change in the opposite way. Their personal constructs become more generalized, particularly constructs which emerge from their new social contacts and experiences.

Genetic Changes in the Matrix

There are questions that may be asked about human development, or the changes that commonly occur as one grows from childhood through adolescence and into adulthood. Not much has been done to answer these questions yet, but there are indications that children in general, as well as certain adults who have failed to adapt themselves to the responsibilities of mature life, tend to rely more upon figures and less upon constructs of the type we have been using for illustration. This is to say the persons they already know are used as direct measures of the persons they meet. For example, when they meet a person for the first time the principal judgment they make is whether that person is totally like or totally unlike their mother. Thus the figure of the mother serves as a kind of concretized personal construct. But as one becomes more mature it appears that his more abstract personal constructs, such as the construct, "sympathetic versus cruel," become the more important reference axes in his psychological space.

There are further changes that seem to come with maturity. In early adolescence one expects to find mere use of constructs having an immediate personal reference, such as the "sympathetic versus cruel" construct I have been using as an illustration. But, while such constructs are likely to continue in use through early adulthood, there are others of a more outgoing type that are likely to emerge and assume prior importance. The construct, "willing to answer questions versus tending to refer questioners elsewhere," is an example of this somewhat more mature construction.

But these changes may happen gradually. In my earlier illustration of the relationship between two constructs I suggested that this latter construct might prove to be operationally similar to the other construct—that sympathetic people were ones who answered one's questions, and cruel people were ones who send you away to find your answers elsewhere. To suggest that you might construe such a relationship was, of course, rather unfair, as I am sure you sensed at the time I mentioned it. It is, instead, the sort of relationship one would most likely find in middle adolescence. Nevertheless, the fact that a person is able to distinguish two such constructs at all suggests that one of them is beginning to separate itself from the other—that these two axes of reference are beginning to rotate away from each other in the person's psychological space. Later on we may even find the relationship somewhat reversed, with a kind of cruelty perceived in those who suppress our curiosity with too facile answers and a kind of basic sympathy recognized in those who respect the questioner's need to become self-reliant. But it should also be said that by the time this happens both constructs will have been operationally changed, and, indeed, the whole matrix may have been altered considerably.

The Generalization of Experience

But now let us turn to another class of questions. If we think of man as we think of a scientist—though we need not always think of him as a "good" scientist—what shall we say happens to his matrix, his theoretical system, when he gets negative results from his experiments. There are several possibilities. He may simply change his particular prediction of what his friends will do, without making other changes in the operations of his personal constructs. Or he may change the grounds for his prediction from one construct to another already present in his repertory. He may also change the operational patterns of the constructs he uses in making his prediction. He may invent new constructs. He may refuse to accept the verdicts given by his data and ignore them, distort his perception of them, or manipulate them in such a way that they will appear to confirm his hypothesis. (Incidentally, this latter manipulative reaction provides the basis for a fresh theoretical understanding of hostility—but that is a matter outside the scope of this paper.) Finally, he may change other constructs in his system which, while not used directly in the prediction that has failed, are nonetheless functionally related to those constructs he did use. All these, and others too, are types of changes that can and do occur, but under different conditions.

The limits of this occasion do not allow discussion of all these types of change, but it may be of interest to look more closely into one of them, perhaps the last one I mentioned—changes in constructs not directly used in making the predictions that have failed. For example, if you fail repeatedly when you make predictions of human behavior based on your construct of "sympathetic versus cruel," what happens to that other construct you use—the one that contrasted those who were ready to answer questions with those who send their questioners elsewhere?

While we are at it, we might as well mention the cognate question; what happens, for example, to your construction of your mother when your wife, whom you have construed to be much like her, turns out to be unpredictable? The first question has to do with rows in the matrix, and the second with columns. But you will also recognize in the first question the classic issue of response generalization and in the second the classic issue of stimulus generalization, although the matrix provides a different set of parameters for dealing with these problems.

According to the usual notion of a generalization gradient, we would be led to suppose that responses that are physiologically much like the one which is changed will be changed also, and that stimuli which are physically much like the one which was misjudged are likely to be reappraised also. Moreover, the more the gradient falls away from the critical response or stimulus, the more unlike it the other responses or stimuli are.

But our matrix enables us to deal with this problem in other terms. Instead of looking to see how physiologically similar to the critical response other responses are, we can look at the matrix and ask how psychologically similar they are. And the same is true in the case of stimuli; instead of taking account only of their physical similarity, we can examine their functional similarity. Thus we do not ask how much physiological similarity there is between one's responding to persons who appear sympathetic and responding to those who answer questions; we ask. instead, if the conditions for eliciting the responses are the same. And on the stimulus side, we do not ask if your mother and your wife are actually alike; we ask, instead, if your responses to them are usually the same.

Now, with the problem of generalization set up in the psychomathematical terms of the matrix instead of the physiological and physical terms we have customarily used, what do we find? The results, so far, are not conclusive but they strongly suggest that the popular notion of the generalization gradient does not hold when reduced to these terms. If your construct of "sympathetic versus cruel" fails you and you change it, and if your construct of "answering versus sending you after your own answers" is functionally similar—though not too similar—you may, instead of making a moderate change in your use of the latter construct, become quite rigid. Similarly, if your wife and your mother are construed in much the same fashion, your disillusionment with your wife is likely to be accompanied by an idealization of your mother. Your wife, so important to you, must be reconstrued in many ways, but you are unwilling to reappraise your mother, also important to you, in any way whatsoever.

Suppose we look at the reverse situation. What happens when one's predictions are consistently confirmed? Still dealing in the same parameters and with the same tentativeness about conclusions, we find our gradients inverted. It seems, then, that at those points where one is certain of his outcomes he holds fast to his constructions but becomes freer to explore variations in adjacent areas. If you are sure of your wife you can take chances with your mother, or if you are confident of your mother you can be flexibly responsive to changes in your wife—though this is predicated on your original construction of them as similar to each other. Conversely, if you are sure about the meaning of sympathy and cruelty, you can take a second and more mature look at what it means to give glib answers to questions—though this, too, is predicated on an initially close functional relationship between these two constructs.

Tentative as they are, these still are conclusions which gain support from incidental sources. Clinical experience suggests that the child who has a reliable understanding of what is happening at home is the first to venture into the next street where he suspects strange things are going on. And we have seen that children who have found their homes chaotic may develop irrational and inflexible attitudes toward those who function as parents. Or in psychotherapy: there it often proves helpful for the therapist to establish himself as a reliable fatherlike figure before that timid fellow-scientist of his—the patient—dares reexamine and experiment with his parental relations.

There are other parameters, derivable from the matrix, which bear on this problem of generalization, but perhaps I have said enough to indicate that the matrix is a fertile ground for exploration and that the mathematical operations it supports can be put to good use.

The Construction Matrix as a General Mathematical Form

Now I would like to correct a false impression I may have allowed to occur. I have talked about the matrix as if it were a particular psychological instrument, with persons ranged along one axis and constructs ranged along the other. But this is only a particular case. We could have substituted occupations or job assignments instead of persons and, as one investigator has done, examine the resulting matrix to see how workers construe their tasks and why they do some of the things they do. Or, if we are dealing with children, we could use the matrix to explicate the relationship between toys and games. Or, if we are dealing with rats, we could set up conditioning series to different triads of signals, and then examine the matrix to see what relationships emerge, and the effects of extinction on the patterns of relationship.

Finally, as I think of the uses to which the matrix might be put, I find myself a little depressed. Suppose someone would surreptitiously put "stimuli" instead of persons along one margin of the matrix, and "responses" instead of constructs along the other. If that should ever happen I am sure I would feel that I had been brought back, full circle to where I started. But perhaps no one will be so unkind as to do this; perhaps the most that will happen is that someone will put Leningrad "signals" along one axis and Tbilisi "sets" along the other. In any case, let us say broadly that the matrix is a general mathematical operation for relating events and behavior, and that the concurrence of these two psychological values can be expressed in terms of the psycho-mathematical function I have described—the personal construct.

37

Nonparametric Factor Analysis of Personality Theories[1]

N. I. Farberow and E. S. Shneidman (1961) have recently published a book in which eight different personality theorists deal with the clinical problem of suicide. In order to focalize the points of theoretical similarity and difference the authors presented to each theorist-clinician the summary of a protocol prepared by N. D. Tabachnick, psychiatrist. The protocol was a summarized report of a series of anamnestic interviews with Mr. A. S., a 23-year-old man who had made a serious attempt at suicide. The contributors were asked to expound their systematic positions with respect to suicide in general and then to make a blind analysis of the protocol summary. In addition, the participants were given a set of 76 cards on each of which appeared a different statement that might or might not be judged as applicable to the patient. They were then asked to Q-sort the statements into a format normally distributed into nine categories. Six participants replied to this request. A few illustrative items are reproduced in Table 1.

One of the theorists, H. L. Ansbacher, has raised the question of what a factor analysis may reveal about the relationships between the clinical judgments. Do Q-sorts applied to a particular case throw light on the differences between the clinical implications of various theories? This information of itself would be of considerable psychological interest, since recent studies have raised doubt as to whether the theoretical orientations of experienced clinicians actually make any difference in the way they go about handling their cases.

But there is also another intriguing possibility. If we put our minds to it, we may be able to contrive some new and discriminating device for bringing to light the essential likenesses and differences among any given set of theories. That also seems worth trying.

Now let us see what we can do with these two possibilities. Suppose we start with Farberow and Shneidman's intercorrelations between the Q-sort data they obtained. These are shown in Table 2. Upon a suggestion by Ansbacher, Harold Gulliksen in discussion with Sam Messick and Henrietta Gallagher computed a parametric factor analysis of the data. His factor loadings and communalities are shown in Table 3.

Information Provided by Factor Analysis

It is to be noted that Gulliksen's factorial composition of three factors is anchored in terms of theoreticians. If we are sure we know what the theoreticians stand for, we can make an educated guess as to what the factors represent. But suppose whatever the theoreticians stand for is precisely what we want to find out. In this case our guess will not be so educated, though we can make some secondary inferences from the net of interrelationships represented by the factors.

An alternative approach would have been to anchor the factorial construction in terms of items. But in this case we tend to lose track of the theories. Whether, in the final analysis, such an alternative approach would yield any meaning not produced by the standard approach is a matter of some difference of opinion among factor analysts, though it seems to me that in a problem of this sort the two methods do permit one to make inferences which supplement each other.

[1] Originally published as Kelly, G.A. (1963). Nonparametric factor analysis of personality theories. *Journal of Individual Psychology*, *19*, 115–147. Republished in Maher, B. (Ed.). (1969). *Clinical psychology and personality: The selected papers of George Kelly* (pp. 301–332). Wiley. Published here by permission of University of Texas Press and Wiley.

Collected Papers of the Pioneer of Constructivist Psychology: George A. Kelly, First Edition. Edited by David A. Winter and Nick Reed.

Table 1 Illustrative Items from the Q-Sort Deck and Their Ratings by Six Theoreticians.[a]

	Theoreticians' Ratings					
No.	*Fut.*	*Klo.*	*Ans.*	*Gre.*	*Kel.*	*Dia.*
1. He likes and seeks the companionship of others	4	2	3	3	2	3
2. He usually withdraws in social situations	2	6	5	4	6	4
3. He is obviously uncomfortable in his contacts with authority.	4	3	6	5	5	1
4. He gives in immediately when attacked	6	4	5	4	6	7
5. He seems to adapt to this environment quite well.	6	5	6	5	7	8
6. Nearly all his interpersonal relationships are superficial.	2	7	4	3	1	4
7. He meets aggression from others with counter-aggression.	9	5	5	8	3	5
8. He has very few friends.	4	4	2	3	3	3
9. He blames himself when criticized.	1	3	4	3	5	5
10. He has difficulty in relating to people.	4	5	5	4	3	1
16. He is rather cold and impersonal in his interactions with women.	5	8	7	5	5	2
17. He goes out of his way to please people.	6	1	6	2	5	3
20. He tends to retreat from the stress and strain of everyday living.	7	5	1	3	1	3
31. He retreats when other people become aggressive toward him.	3	4	3	4	6	5
39. He faces unpleasant situations in a direct manner.	5	7	9	7	9	7
46. His relations with mother figures are fairly happy.	9	4	3	7	2	5
72. He adapts fairly easily to authority demands.	7	3	2	4	4	9
74. He is rather neutral toward others.	4	6	4	5	5	6

[a] From *The cry for help*, by N. L. Farberow & E. S. Shneidman (eds.), pp. 307–310. Copyright 1961. McGraw-Hill Book Company, Inc. Used by permission.
[b] Samuel Futterman, Bruno Klopfer, Heinz L. Ansbacher, Maurice R. Green, George A. Kelly, Solomon Diamond.

Table 2 Interrelations Between Theoreticians on Q-Sorts for Mr. A. S.[a]

	Futterman	*Klopfer*	*Ansbacher*	*Green*	*Kelly*	*Diamond*
Futterman		.21	.21	.38	.06	.23
Klopfer			.48	.33	.16	.13
Ansbacher				.53	.56	.28
Green					.38	.33
Kelly						.50
Diamond						

[a] From *The cry for help*, by N. L. Farberow & E. S. Shneidman (Eds.), P. 312. Copyright 1961. McGraw-Hill Book Company, Inc. Used by permission.

Table 3 Conventional Factor Analysis of Theoretical Differences.[a]

		Factor Loadings			
Clinician	*Theory*	*1*	*2*	*3*	h^2 *3f*
Futterman	Freudian	.38	−.37	.38	.43
Klopfer	Jungian	.48	−.33	−.23	.39
Ansbacher	Adlerian	.79	−.06	−.32	.74
Green	Sullivanian	.68	−.19	.11	.51
Kelly	Personal construct	.69	.47	−.04	.71
Diamond	Nondirective	.54	.27	.32	.46

[a] From personal communication by Harold Gulliksen to H. L. Ansbacher.

Questions One Is Bound to Ask

In either case certain basic questions arise to plague the person who wants to know something about the practical implications of theories. If the factors are expressed in terms of theoreticians only, how can that tell us anything about the substance of the agreements and disagreements? On the other hand, if the factors are expressed in terms of items only, how will we know what the analysis has to do with theories?

While we are at it, let us ask some other questions, too. Can one ascribe meaningful names to the three factors produced by Gulliksen, and are there ways, other than name calling, to ascribe meaning to them? Are there alternative methods of mathematical treatment which might provide us with a better understanding of Mr. A. S., or of the clinical differences between the six theoreticians? To what extent can we generalize about the operational differences between clinicians or about the differences between theories when only one target case is involved? Are Farberow and Shneidman's items of such a nature as to explicate the full range of theoretical differences?

Then there are those cases in which the clinician has difficulty applying a categorical statement to the patient in the face of a history of contrasting or gradually shifting behaviors. For example, in the case of Mr. A. S. there is a report of numerous childhood fights, yet he describes his avoidance, as an adult, of interpersonal conflicts he felt he could not win. In the light of such a report how does one come out with a flat statement that he either was or was not inclined to give in immediately when attacked (Item 4)? Obviously this kind of difficulty is inherent in the application of any kind of trait theory, as well as in outright typology.

There are also some basic issues, such as those that always puzzle one when he attempts to understand persons from the way in which they cope with prefabricated propositions. For example, some clinicians use the terms "hostility" and "aggression" practically synonymously, while others see a vast difference in what is implied by the two terms. This is more than a matter of mere semantics; it has to do with dispositional patterns in the ways human behavior is perceived—quite apart from differences in the technical usage of terms. Is there any way to surmount this discrepancy, or must one retreat into pure phenomenology?

A glance at some of the differences in theoreticians' judgments serves to indicate how complex a matter it is to use the Q-sort items to spell out the substance of theoretical distinctions. For example, Ansbacher and Kelly assign the highest rating to the statement, "He tends to retreat from the stress and strain of everyday living" (Item 20), yet Futterman rates this statement at 7, indicating that he believes it is significantly untrue of the patient. But on Item 31 Futterman and Ansbacher agree that "He retreats when people become aggressive toward him," while Kelly is inclined to disagree. Here is an instance in which theoreticians not only disagree with each other, but two of them may appear to be disagreeing with themselves.

We could, of course, say that there is an "error factor" operating here. But there is also the likelihood that the three men have different notions about the nature of retreat, of stress and strain, and of aggressiveness. Can we then say that the pattern of differences in judgment reflect theory-based differences in the way the patient is seen, or do they reflect theory-based differences in the way the terms are seen?

There is another intriguing point. The factorial pattern produced by Gulliksen's analysis would likely have been substantially different if Herbert Hendin, who commented on the protocol from a modified Freudian point of view, and Louis E. De Rosis, who takes the Horney point of view, also had done the Q-sorts. Now what shall we say has happened to meaning? Isn't it a little silly to argue that what is basic to Futterman and Klopfer changes when data from Hendin and De Rosis snuggle up alongside it? To draw such a conclusion would be to let gnosiological relativism run wild. It must be obvious, therefore, that factor analysis does not produce what is commonly understood to be substantive meaning. At least, it fails to do in this kind of matrix.

What Dependable Meanings Emerge?

What kind of meaning referents, then, does this factor analysis erect? First of all, it tells us something holistically about the particular pool of judgments coming from the six theoreticians. But it tells us nothing absolute about the men—only how their judgments are related to the pool. Following the logic of Thurstone (1935), it is simply an economical way of representing the complex array of data provided by the six sets of Q-sorts.

It is always a little disappointing to be frustrated in our search for the absolute. Yet as long as we live in a world where we are dependent on partial or transient systems of knowledge, we must understand things in terms of their similarities and contrasts with other things, and with constellations of other things.

Still, it is worth something to know that the factorial description of the pool of information does throw some light on the interindividual differences of opinion. Consider Gulliksen's third factor, for example. Evidently it would be economical to say that there is a constellation of issues at stake in the Q-sorted data which pits Futterman and Diamond against Ansbacher and Klopfer and leaves Green and Kelly in the middle. Since this is a parametric factor analysis it does not say that this set of issues is one in which Futterman and Diamond say something is true and important in the case of Mr. A. S. while Ansbacher and Klopfer merely say it is unimportant or only half true and half untrue. As far as the factorial information is concerned, it might be that it is a case of Futterman and Diamond taking the ho-hum stand, with Ansbacher and Klopfer making a federal case out of it. Yet, it is interesting to know there is some scalar alignment to be envisioned among the clinicians, and it may help one guess what one theory involves from his prior knowledge of what some of the others involve. But it remains for him to guess just what that may be.

Some additional meaning is provided by the communality values (h^2) in Table 3. With the factorial composition developed along these particular lines, it occurs that varying amounts of individual communality are "explained." Again, this gives us no particular insight into the unique meanings of the six theoretical systems, but rather indicates only the comparative extent to which the three-factor system has drawn upon each of the six sets of Q-sort information.

The Minimax Problem Posed by Human Limitations

There is a more general way in which the function of factor analysis can be stated. Factor analysis provides one kind of answer to a minimax problem—how to encompass the maximum amount of information within the minimum number of parameters. The problem can also be stated as one of minimizing the differences between small units, such as test items, while maximizing the differences between large units, such as factorial constellations. How small and multiplex the items must be before it becomes desirable to minimize their differences, and how large and sweeping the factors can become before they become top-heavy with overgeneralizations, is basically dependent on something else—the limitations and capacities of the human mind, or of particular human minds.

If one could think in terms of 76 dimensions at once, there would be no point in factor analyzing the Q-sort data in Farberow and Shneidman's book. On the other hand, if one's thinking about personality matters is limited to one dimension, the three factors produced by the analysis will still leave him confused by the complexity of the information at hand. Points such as these were ably made by T. L. Kelley in his volume on factor analysis, published in 1935, incidentally within a few weeks of L. L. Thurstone's classic work, dealing with the same subject. T. L. Kelley had mentioned the point, though less lucidly, in 1928 (Kelley, 1928).

Conforming to Precast Structure

Beyond the minimax problem of producing a manageable compromise between the simplification and proliferation of information, there is the problem of bringing the information into alignment with the construct systems of those who are expected to understand it. Suppose a theoretician could think in 76 directions at once—or even three directions, for that matter—it does not follow that he can think clearly in line with the particular 76 constructs involved in the deck of Q-sort items, or the three constellated constructs represented by Gulliksen's factor pattern.

Nevertheless, the factor analysis may enable him to bring the information into alignment with the dimensions of his own personal system in two ways. First, an examination of the items comprised by one of the factors in an "inverted" factor analysis and the pattern of a factor's loadings on the six clinicians in a "conventional" factor analysis may give him some faint clues as to which constructs selected out of his own repertory may be appropriately invoked. Second, a successive reading of the items and a continued examination of the pattern of factor loadings may enable him to do some fresh abstracting on his own. If so, he can be expected to add suitable constructs to his own personal repertory, constructs that he may, with a little practice, be able to generalize beyond the fragments of data at hand.

It is in these respects that factor analysis has conceptual utility as an instrument for bringing information within man's reach, even though it does not uncover natural meanings or of itself create ideas.

Theoretical Restriction of the Data

Before proceeding to the description of our nonparametric approach to this problem, it is appropriate to take account of other kinds of limitation in the data. If one examines the items of the Q-sort deck, he will note a certain similarity running through most of them. Nearly all the items have to do with interpersonal relations. Such items tend to have the advantage of being more directly related to observable behavior than are more abstract or "psychodynamic" items. But they do limit the diversity of the clinicians' responses. Furthermore, it may occur that a particular type of item may be in closer alignment with the terms of reference of some personality theories than with the terminology of others. The Adlerian and Sullivanian systems, for example, tend to place considerable emphasis upon interpersonal relations, while the Freudian system reduces its observations to a considerably different set of terms. This may mean that Ansbacher and Green, who represented the Adlerian and Sullivanian systems, might have been able to make more complete statements of their positions in terms of the Q-sorts than was Futterman, who represented the Freudian system.

Adding Other Types of Items

It would be possible, of course, to add other types of items to the Q-sort deck, and thus provide for a more complete explication of some of the theoretical viewpoints. One would have to do his best to keep the new items within a common clinical language. For example, suppose he introduces an item having to do with the patient's use of the "conversion mechanism." While the item might make sense to a Freudian and provide him with a terminological framework in which he could express his appraisal of the case more fully, it might, at the same time, introduce a meaningless complication to the nondirectivist, in whose system such a term is likely to be peripheral, if not ambiguous.

There are down-to-earth practical items, however, that represent issues likely to be faced by any clinician, regardless of his conceptual network. An examination of what the different clinicians have said about Mr. A. S.'s treatment suggests a number of such common issues. For example, one item might be, "He will respond best if some form of psychotherapy is started immediately rather than being delayed," or another might be, "He is subject to wide and unpredictable mood swings."

Theoretical Restrictions of the Protocol

There is another respect—unavoidable—in which instrumentation of this study bears unequally on the different theoretical positions. The protocol itself, upon which the different theoreticians had to base their assessments, cannot be considered as theoretically sterile. While Tabachnick, who elicited the protocol, is to be congratulated for his consistent efforts to avoid theoretical bias, it is clear that one's outlook determines what kind of relationship he will establish with the patient, what questions he will ask, what observations he will be alert enough to make, which ones he will consider important enough to report, and how he will paraphrase what the patient has said. For example, this writer, in reading the protocol summary preliminary to making his appraisal, was struck with the congruency between what was reported and what an Adlerian theoretician would probably consider to be important. This was what led to his comments on the style-of-life paradigm (Farberow & Shneidman, 1961, p. 259). This is not to say that the interviewing clinician was careless or that he was an Adlerian; it is to say, rather, that he had to be *something* and evidently he sensed this particular perspective as closest to the unvarnished facts. What neither he nor any other clinician can escape is the tendency for facts to come into focus only in the light of prior personal assumptions—assumptions that are theoretically either explicit or implicit in the practical way one looks at things.

The Patient's Theoretical Orientation

But we must recognize that there were other theoretical impulses at work here. As we have already suggested, there is a theoretical commitment underlying the Q-sort items, and there is the commitment of the clinician who elicited the protocol—one without which he would have been unable to make any clinical contact with the patient. Beyond these there is the commitment of the patient. His outlook had something to do with the kind of relationship he was prepared to establish with the interviewer, the questions he must have asked or avoided asking, those he chose to answer and how he chose to interpret them, what he remembered, what he considered important enough to report, and how he put his observations into the formal language of words. No matter how clever the rest of us may be, it was this fellow's deeply engrained theory that structured the field, not merely as to what was produced in the protocol, but as to the very course of the events in his own turbulent life.

Limitations in Format

This brings us to the last of the possible built-in biases which might have made some theoreticians more comfortable with the protocol than were others. Tabachnick, in his effort to make his report as theoretically sterile as possible, on occasion quite properly fell back upon direct quotations from Mr. A. S. This produced the kind of protocol to which personal construct theory, with its emphasis on the personal constructions of the patient, and nondirectivism, with its empathic emphasis upon acceptance of expressed feelings, both tend to give considerable credence. Freudians, however, are not so likely to take such initial statements at face value. During the early stages of therapy they depend, instead, on what they consider to be more subtle cues to underlying mechanisms, many of which are not communicated by a literal transcription of what the patient has said. The Jungian also is inclined to discount such literal transcriptions.

These relationships between direct quotations in the anamnesis and the different theoretical positions of the clinicians do not suggest that the personal construct theorist and the nondirectivist could do a better job of interpreting the quotations. It suggests only that they may have been more comfortable with such information and hence possibly better able to use it to stabilize their conclusions, such as they were. On the other hand, Tabachnick's choice of statements worth quoting appears to be more in line with the sort of thing that would make a psychoanalyst prick up his ears, and somewhat less in line with what would alert the personal construct theorist and nondirectivist.

There are, therefore, many interesting technical and adventitious relations between the patient and the theoreticians, the items of the Q-sort, and the protocol, as well as theoretical divergencies among them. It would be difficult, indeed, to determine from the data whether one of the systematic points of view is more comprehensive in its general logical form or more precise in its particular application to this case than are the others. What the data may reveal, however—and this is of importance—is something about the issues at stake between the different theories. But to bring these issues into focus we shall need to employ a different mathematical approach.

Nonparametric Approach

Consider an item in the Q-sort series such as No. 72, "He adapts fairly easily to authority demands," on which there is considerable difference of opinion among the six clinicians. (See Table 1.) Ansbacher and Klopfer agree that this statement significantly describes Mr. A. S., the former rating it 2, that is, one of the eight most applicable statements, and the latter rating it a 3, one of the 18 most applicable statements. But Diamond rates this item a 9, one of the three most inapplicable statements, and Futterman tends to agree with him, rating it a 7, one of the 18 most inapplicable statements. Green and Kelly give it an intermediate rating of 4, only one of the 30 applicable statements.

Interpretation of Data in the Intermediate Range

Perhaps Green and Kelly saw Mr. A. S. as being near normal in this matter, or so mixed in his responses to authority demands that no clear-cut statement could be made. Or perhaps the statement seemed so ambiguous to them that they could do no better than assign it an intermediate position, hoping thus to avoid committing themselves. There is the further possibility that one or both of them considered the statement true enough, but not of sufficient clinical importance to place it among the items they were required to select as best describing the psychological structure of the case. Finally, they may simply have considered the item irrelevant. So what shall we say their intermediate ratings mean?

This problem of interpreting intermediate range data is always perplexing. Looking at the problem psychologically, this writer is inclined toward the use of dichotomous constructions, with all items omitted, rather than assigning an intermediate scalar value, when they cannot be clearly identified with one construct pole or the other. If, for some reason, Q-sorts in more than two categories do have to be made, then at least it might be better to specify that they conform to a U-shaped distribution rather than to a Gaussian curve. This matter has been discussed by the writer elsewhere (Kelly, 1955, p. 144) and Cromwell and Caldwell (1962) have produced experimental evidence indicating the relationship between a U-shaped distribution and personally relevant meaning. But all of this has to do with a set of issues which cannot be treated at length here.

Equivalent Patterns

To come back to our present data, we have, with respect to the ratings on Item 72, a pattern of differences between the theoreticians, with Ansbacher and Klopfer pitted against Diamond and Futterman, while Green and Kelly straddle the fence.

Now if we examine the ratings on Item 16, "He is rather cold and impersonal in his interactions with women," we will note a somewhat similar pattern. Ansbacher, who rates it a 7, and Klopfer, who rates it an 8, are still pitted against Diamond, who gives it a 2, though Futterman, the Freudian, has deserted his erstwhile nondirectivist colleague and joined Green and Kelly on the fence, all 5's. Still, except for the reversal of ratings, the two items reflect about the same pattern of disagreement between the theoreticians. Can we say, therefore, there is a common factor underlying the two patterns?

This is a tricky question. If we say the items share a common denominator, we must be careful to imply only that they provide grounds for a similar pattern of practical disagreement between theoreticians, and not that the substance of the two items is necessarily similar. But this pattern of disagreement—and agreement—narrows down our search for the substance of theoretical differences. We may, therefore, profitably delineate the pattern further by searching for other items where it is manifested.

Parametric versus Nonparametric Factors

But suppose, instead of inquiring specifically about the pattern we have observed in Items 16 and 72, we ask a more general question.

Suppose we ask ourselves if there is a pattern—any pattern—of agreement and disagreement between the theoreticians that is commonly reflected in a considerable number of items. That is to say, let us look for big things first, whatever they may be.

We can ask this question in two ways; we can ask if there is such a pattern that occurs regardless of the absolute ratings given by the theoreticians, or we can consider certain absolute ratings and ask which items conform closely to them. The first procedure involves a parametric factor analysis. Thus, if one item yielded a pattern of ratings of 1, 2, 3, 4, 5, and 6, respectively, for the six theoreticians, it would be parametrically the same as another item which yielded a pattern of 4, 5, 6, 7, 8, and 9, respectively, for the same theoreticians. The ordinal sequences being the same, the factorial composition would be considered parametrically identical.

The second approach involves a nonparametric analysis, and the two item patterns would be considered identical only if they disclosed exactly the same cardinal ratings by the respective theoreticians.

Most factor analytic methods are based on the parametric approach, but when it is desirable to find relationships which will permit the prediction of the absolute ratings of one particular item from the ratings assigned to another, a nonparametric approach is preferable. The writer has elsewhere proposed a nonparametric approach to the factor analysis of dichotomous personal constructions of events (Kelly, 1955). While there are certain inherent difficulties in such an analysis, some of which have been pointed out, the more common criticisms of the method have been based on the mistaken assumption that a factor must always be conceived parametrically.

Successive Approximations: First Trial

Let us see how a nonparametric method of analysis may be applied to the nine-step ratings in the present problem. Suppose we approach each factor by successive approximations. To start with, we shall be looking for a rating pattern that will match as closely as possible the largest possible number of items, but not one that is so general that it foils our efforts to discriminate theoretical differences. This is to say we must keep our minimax criterion in mind.

Perhaps the most obvious first step would be to determine the mean of each theoretician's ratings. The pattern of means would obviously be the best fit for the total of the items. But each clinician was instructed precisely as to how many ratings of each value he could make and, if he followed his instructions, he would come out with a mean rating of five. A pattern of fives for all six clinicians would then be the best fit for the 76 items and the items which fitted the pattern best would be those given intermediate or neutral values—hardly a very exciting basis for understanding theoretical differences.

In order to locate those items which elicited more extreme judgments, and thus possibly make meaning stand out in greater relief, we can go through all the items with a pattern of fives—a process called "scanning"—to cast out the ones that match such a drab pattern. Item 74, "He is rather neutral towards others," for example, has a pattern of 4, 6, 4, 5, 5, and 6. Obviously no one crawled very far out on either limb of this statement. Our scanning pattern of all-fives comes within four points of matching it. This is pretty close, so we may tentatively eliminate the item from the pool as not being likely to shed much light on theoretical issues.

Suppose we arbitrarily eliminate from the pool all items whose match with the scanning pattern of all-fives is less than ten points. This leaves us with the items marked with an asterisk (*) in the column head "$\Sigma(X — 5)$" in Table 4. We may now total the ratings for each clinician among these remaining items only. In adding these totals we shall, in effect, reverse some of the items, just as if they had been stated in the opposite way. Take Item 39, "He faces unpleasant situations in a direct manner," with a pattern of 5, 7, 9, 7, 9, and 7, for example. If we consider this item reversed, e.g., "He does *not* face unpleasant situations in a direct manner," the ratings would presumably be 5, 3, 1, 3, 1, and 3. We shall therefore balance the table by aligning all items so that extreme ratings will tend to be represented by low numbers only, rather than by low and high numbers both. This reversal of items, corresponding to "reflection" in conventional factor analysis, is accomplished simply enough if one turns end-for-end all items in which the average rating of the six clinicians is greater than five. The columnar totals are shown in the first row of Table 5 and the average (mean) of each clinician's ratings is shown in the next row beneath.

We may now set up our first trial scanning pattern for Factor One (f_{1t1}). It is derived from the 31 items selected by our casting out the "flat" ones. (See left-hand column, Table 5.) We would, of course, tend to get, though not always, the best total matching score for all the selected items if we scanned with the means in Table 5. But we shall not do this for two reasons. First, such a scanning pattern would require us to tote up fractional amounts, and it seems preferable to keep our task simple by sticking to

Table 4 *Nonparametric Analysis of Q-Sort Items, Items 21–75 Omitted.*[a]

	Theoreticians' Ratings							*First Factor Trials*				*Matching Scores Second Factor Trials*		*Third Factor Trials*		
Item No.	*Fut.*	*Klo.*	*Ans.*	*Gre.*	*Kel.*	*Dia.*	$\Sigma(X-5)$	*1*	*2*	*3*	*4*	*1*	*2*	*1*	*2*	*3*
1.	4	2	3	3	2	3	13*	5*	4*	5*	4*		11			12
2.	2	6	5	4	6	4	7	±17	±12	±11	10	8	5*			−6*
3.	4	3	6	5	5	1	8	14	11	12	11	13	8*			−9
4.	6	4	5	4	6	7	6	−14	±11	±10	−9		6			7
5.	6	5	6	5	7	8	7	−11	−8	−7	−6*		±11			10
6.	2	7	4	3	1	4	13*	13	10	9	8		±13			−12
7.	9	5	5	8	3	5	9	−17	±14	±13	− 12	−6*	−7*			12
8.	4	4	2	3	3	3	11	5*	4*	3*	2**		11			12
9.	1	3	4	3	5	5	9	13	8	9	8		5			12
10.	4	5	5	4	3	1	7	12	9	8	7		10			−11
11.	4	5	5	8	7	4	7	−11	−8	−7	−8		9			−10
12.	5	4	6	2	5	3	7	9*	8	7	8		9			−10
13.	4	4	7	7	9	6	11*	−9*	−6*	−5*	−6*		11			−12
14.	3	8	5	5	5	5	5	−15	−10	−11	± 12	−10*	−7*			−6
15.	4	7	7	7	6	6	9	−8*	−2*	−3*	−4*		−9			
16.	5	8	7	5	5	2	8	−14	−9	−10	−11	−13	−10	−9	−7*	−5
17.	6	1	6	2	5	3	11*	11	10	11	12	10*	11	8	12	±14
18.	2	3	5	5	4	6	7	15	10	11	10	8*	5*			8
19.	7	5	6	5	8	8	9	−11	−10	−9	−8		−11			10
20.	7	5	1	3	1	3	14*	6*	9	8	9		−14			13
76.	3	5	4	5	2	2	9	11	10	9	8		11			−10

[a]From Farberow and Shneidman (pp. 307–310).

Table 5 Successive Approximations of First Factor.

		Theoreticians' Ratings						
Successive Trials		*Fut.*	*Klo.*	*Ans.*	*Gre.*	*Kel.*	*Dia.*	*Criteria*
f_{1t1} $(N = 31)$	Totals	137	115	87	97	101	113	$\sum(X - 5) > 9$
	Means	4.4	3.7	2.8	3.1	3.3	3.6	
	Pattern	5	3	1	2	2	3	
f_{1t2} $(N = 27)$	Totals	128	91	69	78	82	98	
	Means	4.7	3.4	2.6	2.9	3.0	3.6	$f_{1t1} < 10$
	Pattern	5	3	3	3	3	3	
f_{1t3} $(N = 21)$	Totals	102	74	54	71	68	80	
	Means	4.9	3.5	2.6	3.4	3.2	3.8	$f_{1t2} < 7$
	Pattern	5	4	3	3	3	4	
f_{1t4} $(N = 22)$	Totals	97	77	59	72	73	83	
	Means	4.4	3.5	2.7	3.3	3.3	3.8	$f_{1t3} < 7$
	Pattern	4	4	3	3	3	4	
f_{1t5} $(N = 23)$	Totals	98	93	68	77	79	88	
	Means	4.3	4.0	3.0	3.3	3.4	3.7	$f_{1t4} < 7$
	Pattern	4	4	3	3	3	4	
F_1	Gulliksen's F_1 loadings	.38	.48	.79	.68	.69	.54	

whole numbers. Second, the pattern is still rather "flat" and we are looking for sharper differences between the clinicians, even if we have to sacrifice some generality in our first factor.

In order to increase the possibility of getting sharper differences among the clinicians into our first factor pattern, we shall expand the range of ratings in the pattern. We do this by assigning arbitrarily a rating of 1 to the lowest average (2.8)—appearing in Ansbacher's column—and a rating of 5 to the highest average (4.4)—appearing in Futterman's column. The other expanded values are determined by interpolation, and are rounded to the nearest whole number. The first trial scanning pattern in our search for a first factor (f_{It1}) produced by this method is shown in the third row of the first panel in Table 5. We shall use this pattern as a first approximation to the first factor, although it is obvious that in subsequent trials we shall have to let the regression effect pull some of the extreme scores (e.g., Ansbacher's artificial 1) down to more moderate values.

The matching value for each item is shown in Table 4, in the first column under "First factor trials," e.g., Item 1 matching this pattern with a value of 5. In this column where the match is better—lower matching score—for the item when it is reflected, the score is shown as a negative number, e.g., Item 4. In some cases the match is the same for the item when it is reflected as when it is not. In such a case, e.g., Item 2, the score is preceded by ±.

We shall apply this first trial scanning pattern to all items, including those we temporarily eliminated from the pool. The lower the matching score shown in the column, the closer the item matches the trial scanning pattern. From these lower matching scores we may determine which items show promise of fitting together to shape up our first factor. Suppose we say, somewhat arbitrarily to be sure, that any item shows promise when its ratings average one and a half points or less from the ratings in the scanning pattern. These would be the items with a value of less than ten in the column. They are marked with an asterisk (*) in Table 4. There are 27 of them, and that fact is noted at the left of the second panel in Table 5. Our new criterion for selecting the items from which to derive the second scanning pattern—a matching score of less than 10 when scanned with the preceding pattern—is noted in the right-hand column of Table 5 ($f_{It1} < 10$). Our "criterion" column in this table also indicates that we have dropped our initial requirement, applied only in the derivation of the first trial pattern, that items not match the all-fives pattern too closely.

Scanning with the Second Trial Pattern

Now suppose we add each theoretician's ratings of the starred items only, taking care to use reflected values for items whose matching scores for f_{It1} were negative. The totals and means are shown in the second panel of Table 5. These new values, when rounded, constitute the second trial scanning pattern, f_{It2} The item-by-item matching values obtained with this trial pattern are shown in the second column under "First factor trials," in Table 4.

Now suppose we tighten up our criterion of what we shall consider a promising item. Suppose we limit ourselves to those items with matching scores of six or less in the f_{It2} column. The theoretician totals and averages are shown in the next panel of Table 5, as before. From the rounded averages the third trial pattern emerges, f_{It3}. It is slightly different from the preceding trial pattern, so we shall run it through in a similar fashion, with matching scores shown in the next column in Table 4.

Using the same criterion for a "promising item," $f_{It3} < 7$, we may proceed to develop additional scanning patterns until the successive approximations come to a standstill. This actually occurs when it turns out that the f_{It5} rounded scanning pattern turns out to be the same as the preceding f_{It4} scanning pattern. No column 5, therefore, is shown in Table 4.

We now have our "first factor." It is shown in the fractional scanning pattern ("Means") in the next to the bottom panel of Table 5, or in the rounded values ("Pattern") in the row beneath. It is also shown in terms of the closely matching items whose matching scores are shown in the fourth column of first factor trials in Table 4. The items which match the scanning pattern best (3 or less) are marked ** and those matching fairly well (6 or less) are marked *. A list of the first factor items, together with their matching scores, appears in Table 6.

Table 6 *Some Items in the Q-Sorts and Their Factorial Assignments.*[a]

Item No.	*Principal Items in Order of Conformity to Factorial Scanning Pattern*	*Matching Score*	*Other Factor*
	Composition of first nonparametric factor		
	Fut. 4, Klo. 4, Ans. 3, Gre. 3, Kel. 3, Dia. 4 (last pattern, Table 5)		
8.	He has very few friends.	2	
45.	His friendships seem rather stable and have relatively few conflicts.	−2	
53.	Friendly gestures from others arouse his suspicion and hostility.	−3	
1.	He likes and seeks the companionship of others.	4	
15.	He is constantly fighting his environment.	−4	
25.	He becomes quite aggressive in most social situations.	−4	
32.	He competes very strongly with father figures.	−4	
41.	He gets along well with most people.	−4	
51.	He runs away from hostility in others.	4	
22.	He escapes in fantasy when threatened.	5	
24.	He is uneasy and uncomfortable around other men.	5	
29.	He reacts in a hostile and aggressive fashion in his interpersonal contacts.	−5	(F_2 − 6)
55.	He rarely responds to positive gestures from others.	−5	
62.	He responds in a realistic fashion to hostility in others.	−5	
65.	Even the mere presence of other people produces immediate withdrawal in him.	−5	
5.	He seems to adapt to his environment quite well.	−6	
13.	He has quite a few relatively warm interpersonal relationships.	−6	
21.	He meets the demands of his environment in a rather reasonable fashion.	−6	
23.	He tries to manipulate those around him to serve his own ends.	6	
26.	He generally feels accepted by others.	−6	
	Composition of second nonparametric factor		
	Fut. 3, Klo. 3, Ans. 5, Gre. 4, Kel. 6, Dia. 5 (last pattern, Table 7)		
31	He retreats when people become aggressive toward him.	6	($F_2$3)
43.	He is quite passive in most of his interpersonal contacts.	6	
73.	He becomes negativistic when people show a friendly interest in him.	−6	(F_3 − 6)
	Composition of second nonparametric factor		
	Fut. 3, Klo. 3, Ans. 5, Gre. 4, Kel. 6, Dia. 5 (last pattern, Table 7)		
31.	He retreats when people become aggressive toward him.	3	($F_1$6)
57.	When others show an interest in him, he immediately becomes aggressive and demanding.	−3	
35.	He becomes actively hostile when he is criticized.	−4	
47.	He yields meekly to the demands of others.	4	
2.	He usually withdraws in social situations.	5	
9.	He blames himself when criticized.	5	
18.	He accepts rather passively any impositions made upon him	5	
30.	He is unable to recognize affection when it is offered to him.	5	
49.	Rejection from others only makes him more aggressive.	−5	
50.	He is tactful and considerate with other people.	5	
4.	He gives in immediately when attacked.	6	
29.	He reacts in a hostile and aggressive fashion in his interpersonal contacts.	−6	(F_1 - 5)
59.	He is responsive to the needs and wishes of others.	6	
	Composition of third nonparametric factor		
	Fut. 7, Klo. 3, Ans. 3, Gre. 5, Kel. 4, Dia. 7 (last pattern, Table 8)		
72.	He adapts fairly easily to authority demands.	4	
16.	He is rather cold and impersonal in his interactions with women.	−5	
14.	He does not invest affect in his interpersonal relationships.	−6	
38.	He is quite responsive when people show an interest in his welfare.	6	
64.	He actively seeks social contacts.	6	
73.	He becomes negativistic when people show a friendly interest in him.	−6	(F_1 - 6)

[a] From Farberow and Shneidman (pp. 307–310).

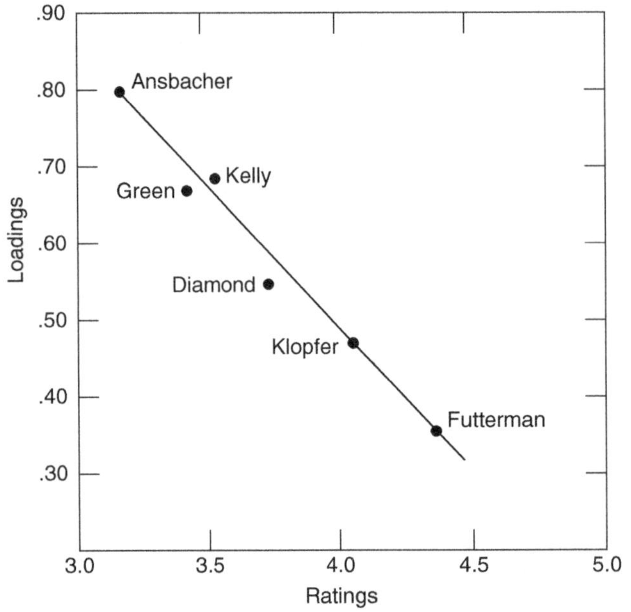

Figure 1 Mean ratings of items in first nonparametric factor versus loadings of first parametric factor.

What is the nature of this factor? Obviously it is one in which Ansbacher (average rating of 3.0) is at one end of the continuum and Futterman (average rating of 4.3) is at the other (Table 5). Green and Kelly tend to agree with Ansbacher, Diamond agrees slightly, and Klopfer tends to concur in Futterman's judgment that the type of item is not particularly applicable to the case, one way or the other.

How shall we "name" it? If we return to Table 6 we find the best matching scores are found opposite Items 8, "He has very few friends"; 45, "His friendships seem rather stable and have relatively few conflicts"—reflected; and 53, "Friendly gestures from others arouse his suspicion and hostility"—reflected. Some of the other items that match the scanning pattern closely are 1, "He likes and seeks the companionship of others"; 15, "He is constantly fighting his environment"—reflected; 25, "He becomes quite aggressive in most social situations"—reflected; 32, "He competes very strongly with father figures"—reflected; 41, "He gets along well with most people"— reflected; and 51, "He runs away from hostility in others."

It should be kept in mind that this first nonparametric factor is not to be taken as a statement of the main or outstanding feature of Mr. A. S.'s case. That is something revealed simply by extreme ratings. It is, rather, a cluster of issues in which there is consistent agreement and disagreement among the clinicians. It is, therefore more descriptive of the clinicians as a heterogeneous group, than of the group's consensus of opinion or the "real" dynamics of the case.

It is possible to compare the first factor obtained by this nonparametric method with the first factor in Gulliksen's conventional analysis. Figure 1 shows a plot of the loading of Gulliksen's first factor against the mean rating totals taken from the next to the last panel of our Table 5. The alignment is remarkably regular, probably more so than one could ordinarily expect, since the two factors, the one parametric and the other nonparametric, are only remotely comparable.

Second Factor

Now we can examine the items not generalized by the first factor and see if there is another scanning pattern which will economically represent a considerable group of them. Suppose we say that any item which does not match our first factor scanning pattern with a score of less than 10 has not yet been adequately represented. This is to say that the scanning pattern is acceptable for an item if it averages no more than one and a half points of matching the item ratings. This is an arbitrary decision, but then, so are all decisions regarding acceptable fiducial limits. This criterion is stated in the right-hand column of Table 7, with the notation $\sum(X - Xi) > 9$.

According to our criterion there are 17 items that fall outside the constellation of the first factor. In developing our scanning patterns for the second factor we shall confine our attention to these items. Our first trial scanning pattern for these 17 items is developed as it was for the first factor—by averaging each clinician's ratings, taking account of reflections, and then by expanding the scanning pattern. In this case, however, the expansion is from one (Futterman and Klopfer) to six (Kelly), since Kelly's average rating for these items is greater than five. The average and expanded values are shown in the first panel of Table 7. The matching scores are shown, as before, in the first column under "Second factor trials" in Table 4.

Table 7 Successive Approximations of Second Factor.

Successive Trials		*Theoreticians' Ratings*						*Criteria*
		Fut.	*Klo.*	*Ans.*	*Gre.*	*Kel.*	*Dia.*	
f_{2t1}	Totals	59	57	81	72	88	82	(a) $\sum(X - X_1) > 9$
($N = 17$)	Means	3.5	3.3	4.8	4.2	5.2	4.8	
	Pattern	1	1	5	3	6	5	
f_{2t2}	Totals	28	35	58	41	64	55	(a) $\sum(X - X_1) > 9$
($N = 11$)	Means	2.5	3.2	5.3	3.7	5.8	5.0	(b) $f_{2t1} < 11$
	Pattern	3	3	5	4	6	5	
f_{2t3}	Totals	38	43	67	50	72	65	(a) $\sum(X - X_1) > 9$
($N = 13$)	Means	2.9	3.3	5.2	3.9	5.5	5.0	(b) $f_{2t2} < 10$
	Pattern	3	3	5	4	6	5	
F_2	Gulliksen's F_2 loadings	–.37	–.33	–.06	–.19	.48	.27	

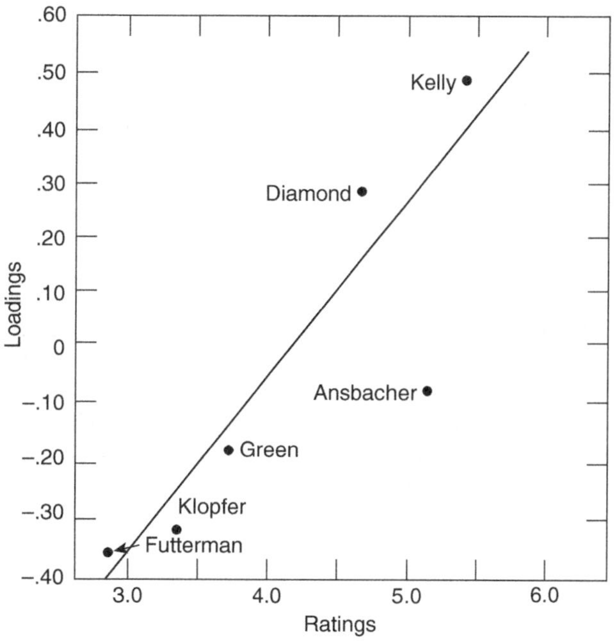

Figure 2 Mean ratings of items in second nonparametric factor versus loadings of second parametric factor.

We now proceed to the second trial scanning pattern for the second factor, f_{2t2}. There are two criteria now to be met in selecting the items, a minimum matching score with the scanning pattern of the first factor—to keep the two factors at arm's length from each other—and a maximum matching score with the scanning pattern of f_{2t1}. If we hold to the same criterion in the first instance, a matching score of greater than nine with the first factor scanning pattern, and then impose the additional requirement of a low matching score on the trial scanning pattern we have just used, there will be scarcely any of our 17 items left. In order, therefore, to keep our pool of items from shrinking unreasonably we shall apply a more liberal second criterion and accept any item that matched the first trial scanning pattern, f_{2t1}, with a score of ten or less. There are 11 items which now meet both criteria. Each is marked with an asterisk in column 1 under "Second factor trials" in Table 4. The averages are shown in Table 7.

In developing our third trial scanning pattern for the second factor we can, at last, afford to tighten up our second criterion very slightly, just as we did in developing the first factor. For f_{2t3} items we shall require that the f_{2t2} scanning pattern have matched the item ratings with an average score of nine or less. Thirteen items meet the tightened criteria; their average ratings, still taking reflections into account, are shown in the next panel of Table 7 and are marked with asterisks. The rounded values of these averages show no change from those of the preceding trial scanning pattern, so we may consider that we had already reached a satisfactory statement of the second factor in the second trial. No third trial column is shown in Table 4.

Figure 2 is a plot of our second factor average ratings against Gulliksen's second factor loadings. Again, there appears to be a closer relationship than one might normally expect.

There are 13 items which match our second factor scanning pattern with a score of six or less, and 40 which match it with a score of nine or less. (See Table 6.) Some of the items, of course, match both factors rather closely, e.g., Item 31, "He retreats when people become aggressive toward him." The two scanning patterns match each other with a score of nine, indicating that they are by no means orthogonal to each other.

Third Factor

There is some question about the value of proceeding to the development of a third factor. If we apply the same criterion as we did before in selecting our remaining "unexplained" items (matching scores of greater than nine with both preceding factors) we shall have only four surviving holdouts—Nos. 16, 17, 46, and 72. This hardly seems enough to make a fuss over. Nevertheless, we shall persist in our enterprise to see what comes out.

The procedure is the same as before, except that we have two criteria to meet in selecting our initial pool of items—matching scores of more than nine on *both* factors one and two. In developing the scanning pattern f_{3t2} we shall impose a third criterion—a matching score of less than 12 with the preceding pattern f_{3t1}. We can tighten up this requirement in developing f_{3t3} and require that items match f_{3t2} with a score of nine or less. This calls for the sacrifice of one of our precious four items, No. 17, but we are carrying out our ground rules literally. When we start to construct f_{3t4} we find that we shall be dealing with the same three items. There is no point in continuing further, so we shall let f_{3t3} stand as our final F_3 scanning pattern. The successive trial scanning patterns for this factor are all shown in Table 8.

Figure 3 is a plot of our third nonparametric factor against Gulliksen's third parametric factor. The correlation is genuinely surprising in this case, since our factor was based on only four leftover items, hardly a very stable basis for approximating the mathematically more elegant conventional factor analysis.

Relations Between the Factors

The method of counting the matches between patterns gives us a measure of the relationship between them, but since they are not construed as scales, i.e., are nonparametrically construed, it is not immediately apparent what degree of mismatching would correspond to orthogonality, or complete independence between factors. To compute such a measure would require our making some assumptions about the probability of two patterns matching each other by chance. As far as this study goes, this does not seem particularly worthwhile. It is of interest, however, to report how closely the three factor patterns match each other. The pattern of the first factor, F_1, matches that of F_2 with a score of nine, and F_3 with a score of 10. The pattern F_2 matches that of F_3 with a score of 11. The factors are thus spaced about as far apart as one would expect, considering the criteria we applied.

Inferences

At the beginning of this paper we posed a number of questions. Some proved to be unanswerable and therefore remain with us as warnings against the temptation to nail down our conclusions too tightly. Others could be answered on logical grounds. Still others were deferred until after we had developed a method of analysis. Now that the mathematics has been completed, we are ready to return to the dangling issues.

Table 8 Successive Approximations of Third Factor.

Successive Trials		*Theoreticians' Ratings*						*Criteria*
		Fut.	*Klo.*	*Ans.*	*Gre.*	*Kel.*	*Dia.*	
f_{3t1} $(N = 4)$	Totals	23	14	20	20	18	17	(a) $\sum(X - X_1) > 9$
	Means	5.7	3.5	5.0	5.0	4.5	4.2	(b) $\sum(X - X_2) > 9$
	Pattern	7	2	5	5	4	4	
f_{3t2} $(N = 4)$	Totals	27	10	14	18	16	25	(a) $\sum(X - X_1) > 9$
	Means	6.7	2.5	3.5	4.5	4.0	6.2	(b) $\sum(X - X_2) > 9$
	Pattern	7	3	4	5	4	6	(c) $\sum \quad f_{3t1} < 12$
f_{3t3} $(N = 3)$	Totals	21	9	8	16	11	22	(a) $\sum(X - X_1) > 9$
	Means	7.0	3.0	2.7	5.3	3.7	7.3	(b) $\sum(X - X_2) > 9$
	Pattern	7	3	3	5	4	7	(c) $f_{3t2} < 10$
F_3	Gulliksen's F_3 loadings	.38	–.23	–.32	.11	–.04	.32	

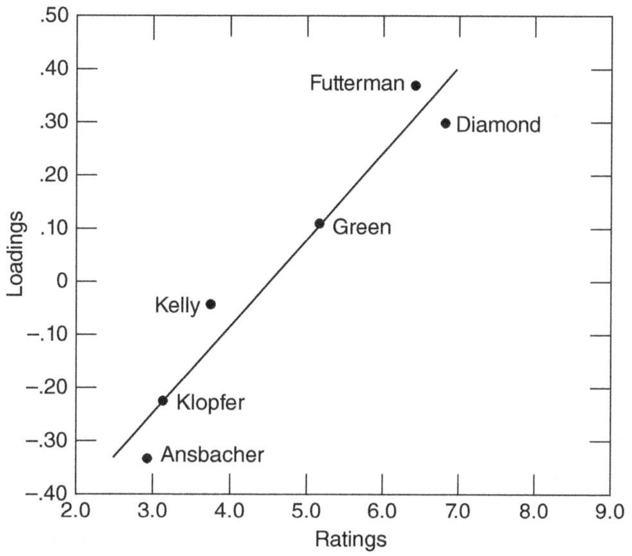

Figure 3 Mean ratings of items in third nonparametric factor versus loadings of third parametric factor.

Items and Theoreticians

In a problem of this sort the conventional method of factor analysis would base its factors either on items or theoreticians. Yet it would not do both at the same time. That is to say, it would not refer to theoreticians and items in the same factorial terms. The method we propose does do both at the same time. It discloses plausible patterns of agreements and disagreements between theoreticians, and it points out the specific items in which each pattern is consistently manifest. Thus the method pinpoints theoretical alignments in terms of who says what.

Since the factors emerging from this computation are expressed nonparametrically, they invite attention to those items which certain theoreticians believe to be both true and important in the clinical case under observation. If the factors were regarded parametrically they might have greater abstractive transitivity, but they would not point up the issues in this manner.

The Grasp of Meaning

Factor analysis can be regarded as a way of displaying information in an economical way. As we have suggested before, this is the answer to a minimax problem—how to reduce a maximum of information to a minimum of terms. It is the baffling complexity of psychological processes that makes psychologists seek to encompass a maximum of information, and it is the limited ability of the human mind to orient itself in hyperspace that makes them try to keep the number of factors at a minimum.

But there is another problem, too. Man has difficulty construing along unfamiliar lines, even when they are drawn with mathematical simplicity. His notions are held fast in a network of personal constructs and any ideas or feelings that have not yet found their place in that network are likely to remain exasperatingly elusive. Science, therefore, not only has the task of coming to simple terms with events, but it also has the psychological task of achieving some accommodation between what man believes and what, indeed, confronts him.

Following this line of reasoning, it is possible, and often desirable, to compute nonparametric factors in such a way that they tend to be aligned with those items which seem to make the most sense (Kelly, 1955). But thus far we have not done so in this case. We shall, therefore, first try to make sense out of our factors by verbal inference only.

Name Calling

Table 6 displays items arranged according to their alignment with the nonparametric factors we have computed. Items are arranged in each factorial group in order of the closeness with which they match the factor's scanning pattern. From these arrays of items one can formulate some kind of modal statements to represent the factors.

In some instances an item matches the scanning pattern of more than one factor. This is shown in the right-hand column. Item 73, for example, matches the scanning patterns of F_1 and F_3 equally well. We shall have to exercise some caution, therefore, in making inferences from such items.

Each factor's scanning pattern is shown also. The rounded scanning pattern of the first factor, F_1, is seen to be one in which Ansbacher, Green, and Kelly are pitted against Futterman, Klopfer, and Diamond. Moreover, it is a pattern in which one group judges an item to be somewhat true and significant, while the other sees it to be possibly true, but not significantly so. With this pattern spread before us and without knowledge of what the theoreticians have said about their theories we can make some educated guesses about what the factor refers to.

Where a matching score is shown to be negative in either of the last two columns of Table 6, it indicates that the meaning of the item must be reflected in order to be aligned with the factorial scanning pattern. In the first factor, F_1 for example, Item 15, "He is constantly fighting environment," must be considered in a reverse sense, while Item 8, "He has very few friends," can be taken as it stands.

First Factor: Emphasis on Interpersonal Relationships

As we examine the items listed under the first factor in Table 6 we find the closest matching scores in Nos. 8, 45, and 53—all concerned with friendships. But as we go further down the list to the less closely related items, we unveil a picture of a person who seeks friendships but who fails because he cannot muster the aggression, in the sense of initiative, necessary to hold his own.

It is this kind of item that Ansbacher, the Adlerian, thinks is both true and important in Mr. A. S. while Futterman, the Freudian, is inclined to pass it up. Green, the Sullivanian, and Kelly, the personal construct theorist, also make more of this "social" type of item, while Klopfer, the Jungian, and Diamond, the nondirectivist, regard it more as Futterman does (Figure 1 and Table 5). This alignment of theoreticians suggests that the issue at stake may be the comparative emphasis on interpersonal relationships, on the one hand, and interpersonal dynamics on the other.

Second Factor: Distinguishing between Aggression and Hostility

The second factor is one which pits Futterman and Klopfer, average ratings of 2.9 and 3.3, respectively, against Kelly, whose average rating of 5.5 puts him slightly on the opposite side of the fence. Diamond is strictly neutral, if we may interpret a rating of 5.0 to mean neutrality. Ansbacher leans ever so slightly toward Kelly's somewhat negative position (Figure 2 and Table 7).

As we run down the list of items in order of their matching scores, we see the kind of aggressiveness—or lack of it—that the Freudian and Jungian think is important in this case. To this writer, who makes a point of distinguishing between hostility and aggression and regards the latter as a dimension ranging from initiative to inertia, these items seem more to imply hostility, and Mr. A. S. appears to him to have some of it.

The editors, Farberow and Shneidman, point out—quite correctly—that the terms are commonly used synonymously and therefore—questionably perhaps—draw their generalized conclusions in the case without distinguishing between them (pp. 299–300). But the factor analysis suggests that here is a possible major issue between the theoretical approaches.

Third Factor: Emphasis on Authority Relationships

The third factor is one in which the Freudian and the Rogerian team up against the Adlerian and the Jungian (Figure 3 and Table 8). This is enough to raise anyone's curiosity. The most distinctive item in this constellation appears to be No. 72, "He adapts fairly easily to authority demands." Diamond and Futterman make a point of saying that he does not; Ansbacher and Klopfer insist that he does. Is this alertness to difficulties with authority the predisposition that makes bedfellows of the Freudians and the nondirectivists, and distinguishes them from the Adlerians and Jungians?

After examining the factorial structure, Ansbacher gives the following interpretation which seems to sum it up quite well.

> Factor three would be the bias to assume hostility toward all authority figures. According to the various items pertinent here, assumption of a negative attitude to mother, women, authority figures, men—a general hostility, is involved. This would be in accordance with Freudian theory of suicide as an act of aggression primarily. That this bias should also be present in the Rogerian, could be made plausible by remembering that Rogers, maybe more than others, believes permissiveness to be curative. The Jungian and the Adlerian, possibly the most optimistic, do not show this bias of assuming a generalized negativism and hostility (personal communication).

Our three-factor analysis leaves one orphan item, No. 17, "He goes out of his way to please people." Klopfer selects this as one of his three most descriptive statements.

Testing Hypotheses

What has been accomplished so far is a mathematical display of information that may provide grounds for making inferences about the theoretical issues at stake among the six clinicians who judged the Mr. A. S. protocol. But we need not stop here. On the basis of our inferences we can set up hypotheses and, using the same computational scheme, test them out. Mathematics and clinical judgment may be used in an interlocking fashion, notwithstanding the prejudices of mathematicians and clinicians against each other.

The Aggression-Hostility Hypothesis

In discussing the second factor the writer said he suspected the theoreticians differed from each other in the way they clinically construed aggression and hostility. Suppose we test this hunch.

When the writer uses the term, "aggression," he thinks of an axis of reference running from initiative to inertia on which a person may be described as well up toward the initiative end. He regards "hostility," on the other hand, as a dimension of appraisal at one end of which are represented efforts to immobilize persons or to extort their conformity to one's outmoded predictions of them. The opposite pole would be, not inactivity, but a liberalism of curiosity directed toward providing the greatest freedom of movement for others at the expense of one's preconceptions of them. Whether or not others are hurt is irrelevant, but any effort to incapacitate them would be regarded as hostile. Similarly, the aggressive person, who keeps upsetting apple carts, may be regarded as hurtful by those who do not like to be disturbed or have their circumstances altered. But that does not mean that the actor is hostile. This distinction between aggression and hostility is anchored in personal construct theory—but that is a long story and there is no need to go into that here.

In originally making the Q-sorts, the writer had to do the best he could with items obviously written by someone who did not use the terms in the same way he did and who probably also did not consider it important to distinguish between behavior along such reference lines.

Now suppose we impose this hypothesis about the distinction between hostility and aggression upon the data, such as they are. First the writer selected eight items that seemed to him to suggest the aggression axis, ranging from initiative to inertia. These items were used as an initial pool from which to derive an "aggression factor." Using the same method of nonparametric factor analysis, a scanning pattern was developed against the rather tight criterion of a matching score of no more than four. Only three of the items survived, but five additional items were picked up from elsewhere in the deck. The structure of this "aggression factor" is shown in Table 9.

Next the writer chose twelve other items that might suggest the hostility axis, ranging from extortion to curiosity. Six of these items survived and two additional items were picked up, as also shown in Table 9. It is to be noted that here, as in the "aggression factor" items, both the terms "aggression" and "hostility" are to be found.

There is another point of interest. All eight of the "aggression factor" items turn out to be critical items in Factor I and none is from Factor II. Of the eight "hostility factor" items seven turn out to have been critical items in Factor II and none was a critical item in either of the other factors. Not only does our hunch about the issue of aggression and hostility appear to be confirmed, but it also appears that aggression—as I understand it—is a principal component in our big general Factor I.

Table 9 Composition of Hypothesized Factors.

Item No.	*Principal Items in Order of Conformity to Factorial Scanning Pattern*	*Matching Score*
	Aggression factor	
	Fut. 5, Klo. 4, Ans. 2, Gre. 3, Kel. 4, Dia. 5	
65.	Even the mere presence of other people produces immediate withdrawal in him.	1
73.	He becomes negativistic when people show a friendly interest in him.	−2
53.	Friendly gestures from others arouse his suspicion and hostility.	−3
8.	He has very few friends.	4
15.	He is constantly fighting his environment.	−4
25.	He becomes quite aggressive in most social situations.	−4
32.	He competes very strongly with father figures.	−4
43.	He is quite passive in most of his interpersonal contacts.	4
	Hostility factor	
	Fut. 2, Klo. 4, Ans. 4, Gre. 4, Kel. 6, Dia. 5	
47.	He yields meekly to the demands of others.	1
31.	He retreats when people become aggressive toward him.	2
49.	Rejection from others only makes him more aggressive.	−2
35.	He becomes actively hostile when he is criticized.	−3
2.	He usually withdraws in social situations.	4
9.	He blames himself when criticized.	4
40.	His immediate response when threatened is to fight back.	−4
57.	When others show an interest in him, he immediately becomes aggressive and demanding.	−4

Differences Between Theoreticians

Now let us see what this means in terms of theoreticians. The two scanning patterns are shown in Table 9. If we compare the scanning patterns we can see that the antithesis of "hostility"—as I construe it—is something that Futterman reads into the case as important, but the antithesis of my kind of "aggression" is not. Ansbacher does not see my "hostility" as particularly important, but the opposite of my "aggression" he does. As for myself, I apparently saw Mr. A. S. as slightly hostile but also somewhat inert. The other theoreticians do not distinguish significantly between these two factors.

Conclusions

Our nonparametric method of factor analysis permits us to examine comparative clinical judgments in terms of items and clinicians, both at the same time. While the data at hand have certain limitations that limit the amount of analysis one might attempt in an ideal situation, it is possible to see within these clinical judgments certain systematic differences. This suggests that theoreticians do make clinical decisions related to their theoretical systems.

The Emerging Theoretical Issues

On the first time around, a broad general factor of difference between theoreticians seems to be the relative *emphasis placed upon interpersonal relationships*. The Adlerian placed greatest emphasis on this factor, with the Sullivanian, the personal construct theorist, the nondirectivist, the Jungian, and the Freudian, following in that order.

The second factor, a somewhat narrower one, I guess has something to do with *distinguishing between what I would call "aggression" and "hostility*." It puts the Freudian and the personal construct theorist at opposite ends, with the Jungian and the Sullivanian leaning toward the Freudian, and the nondirectivist and the Adlerian indifferent.

The third factor, a very narrow one, finds some of the theoreticians taking diametrically opposed views. It has to do with *emphasis on affect and authority relationships*. The Freudian and the nondirectivist regard it as important that Mr. A. S. cannot manage such matters. The Adlerian and the Jungian take the opposite view, while the others take an intermediate stand.

In testing the hypothesis that there is an issue at stake related to the distinction between hostility and aggression two clear-cut factors emerge. One of them, aggression, appears to account for a significant component of Factor I (interpersonal relations), but not the other. The Freudian sees the lack of hostility as important, but not the lack of aggression. The Adlerian does not see hostility or the lack of it as important, but the lack of aggression. The personal construct theorist sees Mr. A. S. as slightly hostile, but also exhibiting some lack of aggression. The others make no important distinction. I would take this as confirming my hypothesis about some theoretical confusion in the area of hostility and aggression.

Summary

Factor analysis, so often regarded as a means of forcing data to yield up neatly packaged meanings, leaves much to be desired. The use of Q-sort items also has many pitfalls. But for the purpose of clarifying the differences between theoretical positions, a nonparametric method of factor-analyzing Q-sorts, which embraces both items and theoreticians in the same factorial composition, may prove to be of assistance. In an illustrative case involving a suicidal attempt, where six theoreticians Q-sorted items after study of a blind protocol, certain interesting alignments between a Freudian, a Jungian, an Adlerian, a Sullivanian, a personal construct theorist, and a nondirectivist were suggested.

References

Cromwell, R. L., & Caldwell, D. F. (1962). A comparison of ratings based on personal constructs of self and others. *Journal of Clinical Psychology, 18*, 43–46.
Farberow, N. L., & Shneidman, E. S. (Eds.) (1961). *The cry for help*. McGraw- Hill.
Kelley, T. L. (1928). *Crossroads in the mind of man*. Stanford University Press.
Kelley, T. L. (1935). *Essential traits of mental life*. Harvard University.
Kelly, G. A. (1955). *The psychology of personal constructs. Vol. 1*. Norton.
Thurstone, L. L. (1935). *The vectors of mind*. University of Chicago Press.

38

The Strategy of Psychological Research[1]

Man does not always think logically. Some take this as a serious misfortune. But I doubt that it is. If there is a misfortune I think it more likely resides in the fact that, so far, the canons of logic have failed to capture all the ingenuities of man, and, perhaps, also in the fact that so many men have abandoned their ingenuities in order to think "logically" and irresponsibly. For each of us the exercise of ingenuity leads him directly to a confrontation with his personal responsibility for what happens. But, of course, he can avoid that distressing confrontation if, through his conformity to rules, he can make it appear that he has displaced the responsibility to the natural order of the universe.

It is, of course, possible to restate many of the achievements of man in terms of the logic we have so far formalized. But this does not tell us much about how the achievements came about. Nor does it help at all in finding how to disengage ourselves from the logic by which those achievements are presently sustained so we can go on to greater ones. For example, most of our formalized logic has to do with the establishment of certainties. But human progress depends also upon the selective creation of uncertainties; that is to say, the pinpointing of preposterous doubts and the formulation of new questions and issues.

Answers Without Questions

We have a logic of answers; now what about a logic of questions? To be sure, the logical positivists urged that we focus our attention upon questions that invite empirical answers. And that helped. At least it helped the research technicians who always like to have something to show for their efforts. But in ruling out all the questions for which no empirical answers could be foreseen the logical positivists aborted the embryonic questions out of which viable issues develop. Fortunately, as they grew older, most of these men sensed the sterility of the system they had been on the point of creating. For all their concern about the validity of questions they appeared to have had little awareness of the psychological processes by which doubts are systematically created and new issues take shape.

Yet doubts and issues are important and answers make no sense without them. Whatever one knows, or thinks he knows, he once approached with vague apprehension and he now experiences within a network of subjectively paired alternatives. If, then, we are to comprehend what he knows, or what he wants to know, or what he thinks, or feels, or dreads, or does, we must understand the system of contradictions within which his possibilities hold their shape and his choices—deliberate or impulsive—are made. These contrasts are, moreover, his own contrivances—his own constructions placed upon reality—and the network, with its restrictive channels of thought, feeling and action, is what we may call his "personal construct system."

But while an answer makes no sense when there is no issue, it is too often assumed that once an answer has been found that is the end of the matter and there is no further point in raising issues. This is to say simply that a pat answer is the enemy of a fresh question. As long as we regard an answer as an objective conclusion we are inclined to make external nature take full responsibility for it. The possibility that it is acceptable as a conclusion, only because it resolves the question we have chosen to ask, does not readily occur to us.

In a naturalistic science, in contrast to a constructive science, the only ground for raising new questions is clear evidence that the old answers are incorrect. If, then, progress is to be made in such an epistemological climate, all alternative constructions must be discredited before a single new one can be seriously entertained. While this makes for lively debate it tends to block any new thinking before it has much of a chance to find out what it can accomplish.

[1] Presented at Brunel College, London, on November 18, 1964 in a seminar series on personal construct theory conducted by Neil Warren, and later published in the *Bulletin of the British Psychological Society*, 1965, 18, 1–15. Subsequently published in Maher, B. (Ed.). (1969). *Clinical psychology and personality: The selected papers of George Kelly* (pp. 114–132). Wiley. Republished by permission of the British Psychological Society and Wiley.

Collected Papers of the Pioneer of Constructivist Psychology: George A. Kelly, First Edition. Edited by David A. Winter and Nick Reed.

But this kind of epistemological totalitarianism need not occur if human thought is envisioned in psychological rather than prescriptive terms merely. Nature can be regarded as open to an infinite variety of alternative constructions—some of them better than others, to be sure—and with most of the best ones yet to be concocted. In such a system the function of an answer is not to make further questioning unnecessary but to hold things together until a round of better questions has been thought up.

Posing Questions

This brings us to an important feature of effective strategy in psychological research. It should be constructive. I mean this in both senses of the term—in the sense that it approaches matters by placing a construction upon them and also in the sense that it produces something new rather than preoccupies itself with discrediting prior constructions. Now I want to be careful how I say this, for one of the criteria of a good experiment is that it opens the door to precise disconfirmation. But to attempt to disconfirm an old answer explicitly is implicitly to confirm the old question, while important research, I think, generally starts with fresh questions.

For example, it seems to me to be a waste of time to undertake some massive disproof of Hullian learning theory for that theory, like most elaborated theories can, with a little letting out and taking in here and there, be made to account for most all of what the stimulus-response psychologists like to call "learning." Indeed I have begun to suspect, like psychoanalysis, it can be stretched to account for almost anything human, as well as a lot of things that aren't. But what might be more exciting would be to disengage ourselves from the very notion of "learning"—not because it is wrong but because any human notion is prejudicial—then to recast the issues of intellectual endeavor and see what possibilities emerge for mankind. Good research, in this manner, starts by concerning itself with the kind of questions to be asked, not with answers to questions thoughtlessly posed or taken for granted.

So any statement we make can well be regarded as the answer to a question we ask—a biased question—and emerges as an indicated choice between alternatives previously posed. Furthermore any act, or experience, can be regarded as having such dimensional properties. We go rather than stay. We feel happy not just because we are in a state of mind, but we feel happy rather than sad or bored. We experience daytime in the dimension of night and day. Any act, or feeling, or statement bears equally upon its subjective antithesis without which it has no psychological significance to the person involved. The strategy of research concerns itself with knowing what the antithesis, for the person, is—what the question was, what the dimension of his appraisal may be or, to put it in terms I prefer, what kind of personal construct provides the relevant axis of reference.

The Analysis of Uniqueness

A perennial problem among Darwinians is the question of uniqueness among organisms. It strikes me as a rather tautological issue, one that would never have arisen if biologists had not so bound themselves to a limited matrix of appraisal. Among psychologists, however, where the axes of reference have not been so parsimoniously devised, the issue scarcely arises at all. Anyone who has tried very hard to understand the human personality has not spent much of his time wondering if people were really different from each other. For him the problem has been, rather, how to transcend the uniqueness of man in order to see him in terms of a comprehensive system simple enough to be understood.

In recent years, in order to cope with the problem of too much uniqueness, psychological research has placed increasing emphasis on multivariant methods. This means designing matrices of input and measurement in which a number of variables are plotted simultaneously. Such a matrix of inquiry provides a model of a psychological hyperspace within which one may understand man in depth rather than continue plotting him one dimension at a time, as, for example, we try to do when we look for the correlates of intelligence. And some psychologists have gone beyond this and have advocated a multivariant multimethod approach to research. This is to suggest that not only should we see man in more than one dimension at a time but also that we should vary the devices by which we manipulate and measure along each of those dimensions.

One way to envision the multivariant approach in research is to see it in terms of an interweave of events and constructs—or, if you prefer, an interweave of observations and issues. Each fixes the other in psychological space. Imagine an array of events, or objects, which are to be understood in a complex manner. We can arrange those events according to some issue—or construct—placing those to which one pole of the issue is more appropriately applied on the one side and those to which the other pole is more applicable on the other. Having done that, we can scramble the events and rearrange them in terms of another construct. As this rearranging proceeds, each event becomes locked into psychological space in greater depth. That is to say, an event seen only in terms of its placement on one dimension is scarcely more than a mere datum. And about all you can do with a datum is just let it sit on its own continuum. But as the event finds its place in terms of many dimensions of consideration it develops psychological character and uniqueness.

Now suppose we want to understand women. This is not an unprecedented undertaking. A good many persons have already tried their hand at this kind of research. So we start out by getting ourselves some women, perhaps all we can lay our hands on. This, too, is not an unprecedented research strategy and one that has been employed by those who find women particularly puzzling or have never figured out just what to do with them.

Now that we have our women, what is to be our question? Which ones are feminine and which masculine? Yes, if we wish, we can sort them out that way. But when we get through we will probably not yet know much about them. So we sort them in other ways, according to other constructs: busy-busy-busy women and oh-so-languid women, provocative women and bland women, passionate women and impacted women, women who look better dressed in expensive clothes and women who look better not dressed in expensive clothes. Now if we are able to keep all these constructs in mind—and not everyone can or wants to—each woman in our sample will begin to look different from all the others. She will appear unique.

But we need to extend our matrix both by adding constructs and by adding events. We should include men too. In understanding women it is as important to understand how they resemble and distinguish themselves from men as it is to assume simply that women are not men. And we need to extend our matrix in other ways. We need to understand how one woman changes her moods, how she responds differently to different men and, ultimately, how she builds her own matrix of appraisal. Only as we undertake this last assessment do we place ourselves in a position to play a role in relation to her.

The Minimax Problem in Psychology and in Science

One of the popular prescriptions for science is Occam's Razor or the so-called law of parsimony. It is the rather unimaginative notion that the simpler of two explanations is always the better as long as it covers the facts at hand. I suppose if every conclusion we reach is to be regarded as a terminal point of human inquiry this might not be such a bad rule to follow. But simple explanations are not necessarily the most fertile ones and, since I have a feeling that has been encouraged by the recent American elections[2]—a feeling that the world is going to go on for a while—I think it is more important to come up with explanations that lead somewhere rather than those whose only merit is that they can be punched into IBM cards.

But the law of parsimony can be regarded as a crude attempt to state a psychological principle and that principle is important to the strategy of psychological research. One of man's most pressing psychological problems is to understand his circumstances in variety as well as in depth—most of all to understand himself and his fellow man in variety and in depth. Of course variety and depth are related, but we need not go into that now.

One way to be aware of greater variety is to conjure up more constructs. But the number of constructs needed does not increase in direct ratio to the number of events to be distinguished. So what we have is a minimax problem; how to discriminate meaningfully the greatest variety of events with the least number of constructs. Since constructs are not only hard to come by but are difficult to keep in mind after you get them, it becomes psychologically strategic to devise a system which will do the most with the least.

Now this is not the law of parsimony, but I think it is clear how the law of parsimony must have been formulated by some poor striving student who found himself as much overwhelmed by the multiplicity of his ideas as by the multiplicity of his circumstances. He must have faced his personal minimax problem: how to probe the maximum complexity of events with the minimum complexity of construction. And this, as I see it, is strictly a psychological compromise.

Moreover, the minimax solution must vary within certain human limits from person to person. So its practical variability needs to be respected by the researcher. He must have some idea of what his own limits of construction complexity are, or what the limits are of the colleagues with whom he must test out his hunches. This, and not some legalistic principle for getting at the essence of nature, is the issue. Of course there is more to it than this, but perhaps I have said enough to suggest the relevance of the minimax principle to the strategy of research and to the model of the rectangular repertory grid with its interweave of events and constructs in unequal proportions.

Collectivization and Individualization

I know that psychological research is frequently regarded as a way of extricating the scientist from the clutter of personal individuality in order to cope with mankind collectively. This leads to a science of categories and pigeonholes rather than to a science of dimensions and units. In one case the generalizations are concrete; in the other, abstract. In one case objects are arranged; in the other, differentiated. But this psychology of categorization, with which we are all too familiar, is quite different from the psychology of differentiation.

I hope I have said enough thus far to tempt you to conjure up in your minds a notion of research headed in the opposite direction—a research that has the effect of making each individual stand out in clearer perspective as a unique person yet accomplishing this new perspective without resorting to the kind of holism that repeats the cliche, "the individual as a whole," and which rejects all precise distinctions. It is, instead, a psychology that is neither fragmental nor holistic. It is constructive; that is to say it uses abstractions

[2] The lecture was delivered shortly after the election of Lyndon B. Johnson over his opponent, Barry Goldwater (note by B. Maher).

and generalizations not to collectivize man, nor to protect him from analysis, but to differentiate him. And by that I mean not merely to differentiate him from other men but to differentiate among his acts and to differentiate between what he once was, what he now is, and what he may choose to become.

So there are, indeed, general things that can well be said about the psychology of man, but they are not the sort of things that most psychologists have been saying. They have to do, instead, with such matters as the methodology of man and the methodology of man's attempts—our attempts—to understand man. They have to do also with the units of psychological science—such as the abstracted "construct" I have proposed—and with the structure of the matrices within which the individual man can see himself and others in greater depth and within which he can be seen in greater depth and perspective. In short, I am proposing the same psychology for the researcher as for the man he studies. Each can profit from employing the psychology of the other; but perhaps of the two the researcher can profit more. Let me now see if I can make this point clear.

Individual Differences and "The Variables"

When I glance through a research prospectus before settling down to read it in detail there are a number of special things I look for. For example, I usually turn to the appendix if the writer has been kind enough to include it in the preliminary draft. Even before I know what his problem is I want to see if he knows what it is. One way to tell is to look at his instrumentation, the part of the study that is usually relegated to the appendix. I want to see if it appears to reflect any particular sensitization to the experience of his subjects. If he is merely applying an instrument he did not devise or derive from an intimate study of persons, I wonder if he has any first-hand familiarity with the problem he proposes to investigate and if he is not interposing the instrument between himself and the persons he would rather not know too well. Is he merely playing games with data? If so, it is what I call "slot machine psychology" or "Las Vegas humanism." I shall have more to say about this later.

Then I look to see if the writer has posed his questions well enough to work out his statistical analysis before he has set out to collect his final round of data. While I am not utterly opposed to some post hoc statistical analysis, after misfortune has struck and the student's children are growing pale and hungry, I believe that one should have tried to set up his statistics and his tables before starting the final round of data collection. Only the numerical entries and arithmetic computations should come after. And later I shall have more to say about this too.

But what I want to mention now is that very suspicious little clue to bad research—the "control group." Of course I realize that control groups in psychological research, like apologies for giving low marks in a classroom, are occasionally unavoidable. But when they appear in an experimental design I immediately wonder if the writer wants to understand persons or distribute them.

Now to understand my aversion to control groups let me talk about psychological variables. I don't much like the term "variables" either, for it appears to refer to the things that vary. It shouldn't. It should designate the selected reference axes with respect to which objects can be understood to vary. But then the reference axes should stand still. So it is the objects that vary with respect to the invariant reference axes. But no respectable scientist would say that the objects are the variables he talks about, even though he might concede that they are the only things that vary. It's all very confusing.

Well, anyway, when I mention "variables" you will all know that I am referring to reference axes with respect to which objects can be perceived as variable, and that, although I have not come right out and said so, I really mean *constructs* having dimensional properties—*personal* constructs that is. Sometimes I hear a colleague say something about "taking into account all the relevant variables." That always strikes me as a little expansive—something like taking an inventory of all the lines in hyperspace or going on an expedition to "find" the North Pole.

"Scientists" Out Looking for Those Pesky Mislaid "Variables"

I have no objection to the notion that persons might vary; of course not. What seems to me to be considerably less than scientific is the notion that they have variables in their insides and that we should go looking for them. Individuals do vary, both within themselves and among themselves. The problem of the psychologist is to come up with some notions that will enable him to impose structure upon that variation. It is his responsibility to devise some dimensions, if he is capable of such abstractions, in terms of which the variation will make sense.

There are several ways of doing this. The most common way is to collect some subjects, already distributed into obvious categories—like women and men, or sane people and people we lock up for their own good. Then we try to figure out what is the difference. We have had moderate success in the one case, but in the other the distinction is still pretty hazy. In the case of the people we lock up we usually examine them—not the people who lock them up—or subject them to experimental conditions to determine what there is about them that makes them so obviously different. It might be more appropriate to find out what there is about us that makes us judge them as different.

But even that does not quite get to the point. To be sure, the fact that some are locked up suggests that the deterministic choice point resides in the person who made the decision and that probably he himself has not been locked up—at least not yet. But the explanation of the categorization he employed does lie in the constructs accepted by himself and all those who make such decisions. If we want to understand why some people are locked up and some not we should examine the construction system in terms of which the decisions are made. Then we can go further and see if that construction system is truly predictive of what it claims to be. And we can go still further to see if the system is *necessarily* predictive of what the outcome of their lives *might* be.

But the variables—you now know what I mean by "variables"— that explain the differences between persons are not to be confounded with the ones that explain what happens to people or what can happen to them. So when we look for variables by which persons can be distinguished from each other we should not expect to find "the variables" of psychology by which personal lives have variety and accomplish change.

The Paradox of Variables Revealed

Now about those control groups. They suggest to me that what the person is mainly interested in controlling is interindividual differences. Of course this is all right if he is an administrator and this is really the level of his psychological ingenuity. But usually he is smarter than this—most psychologists are nowadays—and it has occurred to him that psychology might be concerned with variables that could mean something in one's personal life. In that case he has something I think is worth pursuing. But his bland use of control groups suggests that he thinks he can control such intraindividual variables by specifying interindividual variables that have the same names.

Now sometimes they do turn out to be comparable variables or axes of reference. I must concede that. But the glib incorporation of control groups in an experimental design implies that the researcher has assumed that a variable is a variable, and once you have found it there it is, and you will have to control it from now on out.

Well, I don't mean to say I won't go ahead and read the prospectus. There are times when it is pretty hard to control the variation that needs to be specified and you have to settle for a substitute. Still, most of the research I have seen could have been wrapped up into a much tighter design with all the controls defined in intraindividual terms. And this seems to me to be a much better research strategy. Besides, haven't you noticed how much more lenient the formula for the t-test is in such cases and how much more powerfully—to use the statisticians' improbable term—an analysis of variance square takes care of things when you subject each person to all experimental conditions?

Baiting the Psychological Trap

Now I have the feeling that I have left something dangling here. Let's see! Women—we were talking about women. This is a problem that seems to preoccupy so many psychologists: are there *really* sex differences and, if so, what on earth might they be? Well, I wouldn't want to ignore the ladies and, even in my serious role as a "psychologist," I have no intention of doing so. Moreover I have been convinced in my own mind for some time now that there are indeed interesting differences between women and men. The constructs—excuse me, "variables"—that isolate women from men are exciting, no doubt, though the ones that psychologists keep coming up with are not the ones I use in identifying women or relating to them. My colleagues come up with variables like "being able to get better marks in literature courses than in mathematics" or "having more mechanical skill in handling soft objects made of cloth than hard objects such as plumbers' tools." So in these ways women do differ from men.

But what happens to your own life when you attempt to vary it along such an axis? What happens indeed! What happens when you use it to structure intraindividual change? Well, you can become more feminine or you can become more masculine. A lot of people fuss and fuss over that decision. You can take up plumbing or you can take up dressmaking; you can do the things that women do or the things that men do. And that, I am sorry to say, is about the only channel of freedom that many persons have. It is not surprising, therefore, that so many of those who structure their lives, or attempt to alter their predicament, in terms of this dimension complain to their therapists that they "never seem to get anywhere." Certainly the sense of futility in a person whose role as a man or a woman is cast only in terms of sex differences is well known clinically. His problem is not that he doesn't know the difference between women and men. His problem is, rather, that his own life must go on. And since he has no other clear reference axes he can do no better than to vacillate psychologically between gross masculinity and femininity. Not even the idea of taking up plumbing and marrying a dressmaker is likely to occur to him.

But this was not intended to be a discussion of sex roles. It was meant, rather, to do with the strategy of psychological research and I have tried to illustrate, in this particular case, the paradox posed by a psychology of individual differences that presumes to offer structure for the processes by which human lives are lived. Now it is time to go on to something else.

The Problem of Disengagement

Let me try to distinguish between two views of the scientific enterprise. There is the view that science makes its progress step by step. This is usually taken to mean that we discover nature a fragment at a time, that as each fragment is verified it is fitted into place—much like a piece in a jigsaw puzzle. Some day we'll get it all put together.

The other view is a constructive one. We understand our world by placing constructions on it. And that is the way we alter it too. There is no finite end to the alternative constructions we may employ; only our imagination sets the limits. Still, some constructions serve better than others, and the task of science is to come up with better and better ones. Moreover we have some handy criteria for selecting better ones; at least we think we have, and they, too, are subject to reconstruction.

Now the first view we can call *accumulative fragmentalism*—a term pretentious enough to encourage most readers to leave the definition up to the author—and the second *constructive alternativism*—also a fairly good sized mouthful. They make a difference. In the first case science seeks to verify a hypothesis—determine whether it is really true. In the second case science seeks to confirm predictions—that is to say, observes how well its hypothesis has worked.

All right, so far so good, but the difference still seems to be a matter of semantics. The effective difference comes in what happens next. The man who has verified his hypothesis has, he supposes, a little chunk of 24-carat truth to add to his inventory. The man who has confirmed his prediction has, in the form of the hypothesis he has devised, only another pearl-handled extrapolator for approximating the future. For him there may remain many other ways and, likely as not, some of them will turn out to be better than what he has. The first man thinks he has captured an essence; the second knows only that he has devised a method.

Now what happens? This, by the way, is a question that is always appropriate, whether we are talking about science or the client who has resolved his transference neurosis and bids a healthy farewell to his psychotherapist. To the accumulative fragmentalist the next step is to find another nugget of truth or another paying client. To the constructive alternativist the next step is to see if he can improve his hypothesis, perhaps by formulating his questions in new ways or by pursuing the implications of some fresh assumption that occurred to him when he was writing up the conclusions to his last experiment. But for the accumulative fragmentalist the only grounds for entertaining further questions about the matter is evidence that he was wrong. Since this kind of nuisance may pop up at any time he is careful to replicate his experiments and make sure the answer to his question is absolutely, positively, and irrevocably right!

Once a man has "verified" his hypotheses he guards his findings jealously. If alternatives to such "proven conclusions" are proposed he immediately suspects someone is trying to snatch his nuggets away from him and his howls of protest will echo from one end of Academia to the other. They will have to prove he is dead wrong before he will release his clutch on what he has acquired in the name of Science. Ltd.—an outfit in which he believes he has become a major stockholder. But to the constructive alternativist it is a matter of no more than momentary interest whether his colleague's findings are disconfirmed or not. To propose a new question does not require the denial of an old answer. Indeed every neat answer makes him wonder what would have happened if the question had been posed differently.

Here, then, is the difference between the two points of view. It has to do with what ensues from the outcome of a successful experiment. It has to do with gracious and respectful disengagement from old and valuable ways of looking at things. In the one case disengagement can come only after brutal disconfirmation; in the other, disengagement is expected from the outset and may be undertaken deliberately and precariously as a step toward a better science. In the case where disconfirmation must precede the posing of new questions, disengagement can take place only in the state of chaos produced by disconfirmation. In the other case one does not wait for chaos to overtake him; he uses those previous conclusions to provide whatever security he may need to order his life while he is out looking for alternatives to them.

While I have been talking about scientists everything I have been saying applies equally to persons who do not claim to be scientists. A psychotherapy patient who accumulates things in pieces such as "good habits," "clever solutions," "sound knowledge," and tokens of "meritorious achievements" is likely to let his life get into pretty bad shape before he starts letting go of what he has acquired. And when he does start to let go everything seems to crumble at once. He had assumed that once his conclusions were verified there would be no point in exploring further what had already been demonstrated to be true. To make matters worse, every proposition his therapist offers or encourages becomes a threat, for it implies a sweeping invalidation of his way of life and a further spread of the chaos that has already engulfed him. The therapist will find himself called upon to exercise great skill in helping such a person collect his wits enough to venture anything new.

So one's epistemology does make a difference, whether in science or in one's personal life. And what I may not have emphasized enough is the depth of the construction that can become involved in this problem of disengagement. I am not talking about formal verbal propositions only; I have in mind all levels of discrimination, including those levels which are frequently cataloged as "somatic."

Steps in Creative Thinking

But disengagement is only one small aspect of the process of creative endeavor. Nor should psychological research be regarded merely as the counter-punctate composition of observations and newly formalized propositions; that is to say, a play between experience at two levels only—levels such as "cognition" and "perception." Research involves all the levels of experience that man is capable of having. This is especially true of psychological research. It is an orchestration of all the talents of man, just as psychotherapy is such an orchestration, not the implementation of some talents and the denial of others. And there is a way to put them all together—many, many ways I'm sure.

Let us turn now to what may be called the *creativity cycle*. This is a cycle that starts with a phase of loosened construction and terminates with a phase of tightened construction. These phases are not to be regarded as alternative states but as transitional stages in a continuity in which the vague, unexpected and dreamlike constructions that emerge during the loose phase are not altogether abandoned in favor of tight and neatly defined constructions in the later phase but are, instead, gently lifted from the miasma of incoherence and sensitively shaped to definition without being subjected to prematurely harsh tests of consistency—either tests of consistency with themselves or consistency with other constructions more tightly held. As these constructions take shape they are more tightly formulated and are prepared for an eventual rigorous test and for the confirmation or disconfirmation of all the human anticipations they invoke.

The trick, of course, is to deliver these nascent constructions alive without losing track of what they are or becoming frightened by their monstrous implications. It also requires considerable overall integrity to reach far into the preverbal constructions of our lives without becoming so involved that we want to stay there, or to reserve such self-gratifying indulgences apart for those special occasions when we want to escape responsibilities and "regress in service of our egos." It also requires integrity at the other end of the cycle and so to test reality for whatever it is, or, having tested it, not to hold too fast to its certainties for whatever security they seem to provide against personal chaos.

Without going into further detail let me suggest that the utmost employment of this kind of cyclical continuity is involved in the strategy of psychological research. But I should say also that for any one person there are limits in the extent to which he can go in either direction and still retrieve himself. I once tried to state this consideration as a "modulation corollary" to personal construct theory's basic postulate like this: "The variation in a person's construction system is limited by the permeability of the constructs within whose ranges of convenience the variants lie." Not everyone has set out to erect constructs for himself that are permeable enough to encompass and modulate the extremes of loose and tight thinking. And not many teachers have ever thought to suggest that he should.

The Role of Personal Involvement

Research does not start with the ranging of objective evidence against formal propositions. There is much that goes on before. Indeed this is only the terminal incident in the tightening phase of the creativity cycle. Behind it lies the disengagement from previous conclusions, the loosening, the emerging of new constructions and the posing of fresh questions—all of which I have mentioned.

But what I have not dealt with adequately up to this point are the devices for enlisting the ingenuities of man. Those ingenuities can be tapped only if he takes certain courageous steps to involve himself wholly in what he has undertaken. Otherwise he will think logically about his problem and let it go at that. He may use only those constructions he can put into words and can identify coherently within his favorite rational system.

But every man has other constructs held far back in reserve upon which he will likely rely if he gets into a jam. Some of them are verbally available to him; some are not. If he is to tap such resources he needs to get himself into a predicament, or at least put himself in a position where it will not suffice to act like an academician. There are ways of doing this.

One of the first measures for involving all the ingenuities of man is to go to where the problem is acute, to have him place himself, as best he can, in the midst of the circumstances upon which psychological structure is to be imposed. Not only does this involve the senses, the social "pressures" and the feeling of personal responsibility, but it provides one with an abundance of minor cues which he may weave into the fabric of his new construction. For example, I never conceptualized some of the psychological dimensions of poverty until I smelled the country market in Port-au-Prince, Haiti. Not even the wretchedness of certain parts of India placed the plight of poverty-stricken man in as deep perspective as that sensuous experience did.

Then there is involvement. This, if I understand them correctly, is what the existentialists mean when they talk about being "in the world." It is what we hope will happen when a researcher places himself in the circumstances he wishes to construe psychologically. But it may not happen, even in those circumstances, for one must see *himself as one of those circumstances*, and there are some who are so alien to the world that it is impossible for them to experience themselves as part of it. Still the fact that he himself is there, he himself is there going about being the kind of person he is and doing the things he does; that, too, is one of the circumstances he must cope with. And he may realize, further, that his presence there serves to make matters worse all around. To be involved is to realize that whatever happens, happens to oneself too, that whatever is done, he, too, has had a part in doing it. That is involvement.

Once involved the researcher is confronted with the chilling fact that the constructions, verbal and preverbal, by which his own life is ordered, have had a part in structuring events for which it would never otherwise have occurred to him he had any responsibility. I think it is only when one involves himself in psychotherapy with a disturbed person, for example, that he comes to realize that his own impulses and aversions, or ones like them in others, have had a part in making the person what he is, and that inevitably they will have a part in making him what he is to become. And this kind of realization will also put his research prospectus in quite a new light and will make it clear that man, the researcher, can no more be a stranger to mankind than man, the psychotherapist.

Commitment

But involvement is not enough to generate effective strategy in psychological research. There is commitment. The human venture is not an exercise in passive receptivity, nor is understanding developed out of sensory experience alone. As for the child who must manipulate the world in his mouth or with his ever-moving hands, so for the psychologist, too, who comes to know man only by doing something with men. So he commits himself to a human course of action. Without doing so he can never know what relevance his own construction of life has to the lives that others live.

Commitment, I fully realize, means aggression—personal aggression—and if the outcome brings a sense of having violated his role, the psychologist will experience guilt. Thus commitment can never be undertaken without risking one's virtue and sometimes losing it, nor without the possibility of emerging as a villain and sometimes actually doing just that. So in undertaking commitment the strategy of psychological research requires one to take deep personal risks. No wonder so many of us would like to become scientists and be content to win prizes without having to take an awful responsibility for people.

Appraisal

But even commitment is not enough; and here we part company with the existentialists. There must be appraisal and reconstruction. A commitment is not a blind undertaking—at least it should not be. Whatever one does under commitment he must continue throughout to face the possibility that he was wrong and as his experience brings him to new vantage points he must stand ready to reconstrue his whole undertaking. Thus he will stand as his own accuser, and the most penetrating judgments of his failures will be handed down by himself. That hurts, but it is necessary if the human enterprise is to progress. Only with this step is the experiential process complete, and it is complete only to the extent that it sets the stage for the next round. Nor is psychological research, merely because it purports to be scientific, exempt from this step in the human process through which mankind seeks his objectives.

Practical Steps

Translated into the more familiar terms of the psychological laboratory, what I have been saying suggests that the researcher is more likely to mobilize his ingenuities in devising important hypotheses if he goes to where the psychological problems are. In my own case I interpret this to mean going to where persons are disturbed enough to try to make something new out of their lives as, for example, where children are, for they are continually trying to make something new out of themselves—counting each year as they grow up and making plans for what they will do when they escape the restraints of size, age, vocabulary, and parental control. Or it may mean going to where adults have taken a critical look at themselves as, for example, to the clinic or the psychotherapy room. Wherever man is struggling mightily to make something of himself there is a fertile place for the researcher to be.

But, in a practical sense, research strategy means commitment too. That is to say the psychologist who wants to find out something about mankind had better join in the human enterprise else he will never know what it is all about. In my own case this has meant nearly thirty-five years of part-time service as a psychotherapist—not because feeling useful was the primary reward I sought but because I knew of no better way to bring all my resources to bear on the problems of scientific psychology with which I had undertaken to cope.

And, of course, there is, for the research strategist, reappraisal. When I look back on those years there are many regrets and many pangs of guilt. But that was the risk I took. Moreover, I am always perplexed at how long it took me to reach certain "obvious conclusions," as, for example, the *naivete* of stimulus-response psychology, or the utter irresponsibility of such a notion as "motivation."

But how does one who has had the full round of generalized experience get his research project under way? I think, first of all, he takes his particular problem through the same cycle of experience. He should go to where his newly posed problem is most acute. He should plunge into some reasonable involvement. And he should appraise what then happens to man—to others and, particularly, to himself.

I urge students, for example, who want to investigate "schizoid" thought to have a round of experience with it themselves. They should talk to their teammates, trying out their hunches about what it is to be a "schizoid" thinker. And they should ask their teammates to do the same thing and report what they observe and what they experience. Then they should see how others react to "schizoid" thought. And, lest the possibility should escape them, they should check their portrayals with experts, that is with "genuine schizophrenics" and the professors who study them.

They should also take advantage of the creativity cycle—lifting from their own loosened thinking tender hypotheses to be developed and, when clearly enough defined, to be rigorously tested in precast experimental designs in which all the statistical logic has been specified before the collection of the final round of data begins.

And, finally, they should not overlook what their subjects have to contribute, for psychological research, as I see it, is a cooperative enterprise in which the subject joins the psychologist in making an inquiry. I am very skeptical of any piece of human research in which the subjects' questions and contributions have not been elicited or have been ignored in the final analysis of results.

Summary

The strategy of psychological research has its philosophical roots and its everyday techniques. It employs man's intellectualisms, but it makes full use also of what many still regard as his irrational stupidities. It concerns itself with constructions that successively approximate the truth, not with the mere accumulation of fragments of truth. It disengages from old scholastic conclusions and reengages with man. It experiences. It tests. It reappraises. But, most of all, it seeks to mobilize all the resources of man—experimenter and subject—and not those of formalized logic alone.

39

Humanistic Methodology in Psychological Research[1]

Humanism is usually regarded as the guiding motif in the intellectual transitions that took place in Western Europe during "The Humanistic Century" of 1450 to 1550, A.D. During those years the cultures of classic Greece and Rome were examined in a new light. Whereas the medieval scholastics had rationalized the classics, the humanists put themselves in the place of the men who wrote them. When they did they caught glimpses of the freedom, innovation, and variety that had made the great classical achievements possible.

To the extent that humanism grasped an outlook rather than recapitulated an era it could combine with other forces to write an exhilarating chapter in the story of man. In its course the new study of the classics mobilized aspirations and utilized instruments it did not always intend. Ironically it was the very breath and wit of his humanism that made the classicist Erasmus the unwilling ally of the activist Luther. But the alliance shaped the conscience of man. And without gunpowder, which challenged the impregnability of baronical castles sitting astride the world's highways, and the printing press, which invited every man to become a scholar or a priest in his own right, humanism might have amounted to little more than return to classicism.

The Humanistic Intent

Classicism reveres the past; humanism is inspired by it. The classicist engrosses himself in the thought of other times; the humanist uses history as a fulcrum to pry himself loose from the prejudices of his own. Yet humanism's emancipation of the mind accomplishes little except as it molds man's conscience to new subtleties and marshals his technology to create fresh and challenging circumstances. A conscience so preoccupied with the evils of other times that it is insensitive to the wretchedness of its own, or a technology that serves only as an instrument of subjugation, renders bootless whatever freedom of thought the disadvantaged are allowed to retain. Soon enough empty-handed men abandon their intellectual freedoms to the prophecies of ideologies and the claims of the most vocal leaders.

One does not need to derive humanism from classicism. Indeed, to the extent that humanism produces novelty it distinguishes itself from classicism[2]. As I see it, classicism[3] was historical incidental humanism—no more. It seems to me, therefore, that the humanist's research in particular should not restrict itself either to classical topics or to classical methodologies. If a researcher does recapture the outlook of some prescient moment of the past—perhaps one when men were less subservient to deterministic doctrine than they are now—he may do so simply to start his inquiries afresh, rather than to retreat to the precedents of earlier beliefs.

Yet it must be said that much that passes for humanism today is more backward-wishing than forward-seeking, more antitechnological than instrumental. If looking backward will serve to disengage us from the strictures of today's intellectualisms, well and good. But if it renders us insensitive to living man, his immobilizing circumstances and his untried potentialities it will turn us down the path of scholasticism rather than of renaissance.

[1] Dated 1966. First published in Maher, B. (Ed.). (1969). *Clinical psychology and personality: The selected papers of George Kelly* (pp. 133–146). Wiley. Republished in 1969 in *Journal of Humanistic Psychology, 9*, 53–65. Published here by permission of Wiley.
[2] Editors' note: 'classism' in the original.
[3] Editors' note: 'classism' in the original.

Collected Papers of the Pioneer of Constructivist Psychology: George A. Kelly, First Edition. Edited by David A. Winter and Nick Reed.

Humanistic Psychology and Instrumentalism

It would, in my opinion, be a serious mistake for psychologists who hope to raise man from the position of an unwitting subject in an experiment to a posture of greater dignity, to abandon technology. The spirit of man is not enlarged by withholding his tools. Just, as I have recalled, it took the technology of gunpowder and the printing press to turn humanism into something more than classicism, so now it requires an appropriate technology for humanistic psychology to realize its objectives. A man without instruments may look dignified enough to those who do not stand in his shoes, but he most certainly will be incapable of making the most of his potentialities.

Besides, like B. F. Skinner, there are moments when I have doubts about what is meant by "the dignity of man." I can remember my father saying when I was a youngster that as far as he could see dignity often turned out to be stupidity in disguise, and moreover, the disguise was often an honorary degree such as Doctor of Divinity—which he, an erstwhile clergyman, humorously paraphrased as "Doctor of Dignity." I can't say that I altogether agree with him, but of this I am sure: a genuine respect for the dignity of man includes placing the instruments of effective action in his service and it cannot be expressed adequately by making claims for his noble nature or by erecting a statue of him sitting on a stone horse in the park.

Now American psychology has contributed enormously to the literature of behavior modification and instrumental conditioning. Psychologists who see themselves as humanistically inclined are likely to disparage this contribution and, often as not, are alarmed by it. They see it as a giant technological effort to make mankind jump through hoops. They fear the instruments will govern the intentions of those who wield them, as indeed for some men they do.

If this were all there was to it I would be alarmed too. But I must remember that the psychologist who makes it possible for me to accomplish a difficult leap has done me no disservice unless I am endangered by my own impulses. He has shown me how to realize one of my hidden potentialities. That is humanism. What I am still convinced I cannot do I am scarcely free to attempt, but what I have been shown can be done adds a new dimension to my freedom and makes it all the more real. Of course, I must admit that if I am continually prodded by the applied psychologists to make jumps I would prefer to avoid I am likely to become irritable.

If Skinner, the currently popular whipping boy for humanistic psychologists, can make it possible for men to actualize their intentions I would not want to accuse him of being antihumanistic. Or even if he went no further than to show what an imaginative psychologist can do to his subjects I would scarcely bring myself to say he has offered no humanistic inspiration to me, his fellow psychologist. In that event he would at least have demonstrated to me what is possible, rather than left me to the doubtful mercies of the inevitable. That is precisely one of the things I think a good humanist should do. Yet, by comparison, some of my literary colleagues leave me with the impression that "the nature of man" puts more out of my reach than within my grasp. I expect better of them.

This is crucial: humanistic psychology needs a technology through which to express its humane intentions. Humanity needs to be implemented, not merely characterized and eulogized. It is only when the subject, rather than the experimenter, becomes the model of the psychologist's man, or psychology's technology is mistaken for its theory, or theory encapsulates the reality it seeks to envision that humanistic ends are necessarily frustrated. It is not that man is what Skinner makes of him, but rather that what Skinner can do man can do—and more. Skinner's subjects are not the model of man; Skinner is.

The Role of the Subject in Humanistic Research

Since the model of man in humanistic research is the experimenter rather than the subject, it follows that the humanistic psychologist will make the most of what those whom he has enlisted to help him have to say (Kelly, 1965a). Too often it turns out that the experiment the psychologist thinks he is performing is not the one in which his subject is engaged. If the two experimenters are to collaborate each needs some idea of what the other is doing. What is frequently regarded merely as the subject's "behavior" may be for him no less of a venture, and have no less extensive implications, than the "experimenter's" efforts. This can be particularly true when students from elementary classes in psychology are required to serve as subjects in dissertation research in order to get satisfactory marks. For many students this provides an intriguing opportunity for some venturesome experimentation with psychologists. In any case, what is confirmed or disconfirmed by a student's experience, even when imperfectly articulated or reluctantly confided, is likely to be vastly more relevant to the outcomes—or the interpretations that should be placed upon the outcomes—than the hypotheses the "experimenter" has secretly perpetrated.

At the very least humanistic research means that each person who participates should at some point be apprised of what the "experimenter" thinks he is doing, and what he considers evidence of what. It is of equal importance to ask what the "subject" thinks is being done, and what he considers evidence of what. Since this can change during the course of the experiment it is appropriate to ask "subjects" what their perception of the experimental design was at each important juncture in the procedure[4].

[4] I recall the insistence of one of my teachers, Christian Ruckmick—a Titchenerian—that the subjects in my dissertation research be called "Observers." It has taken me a long time to realize how perceptive he was.

This is not merely a concession to scientific ethics; it can make a great deal of difference in what conclusions are drawn. It is therefore an essential step for any researcher who is intellectually curious enough to want to know what is going on in his own laboratory. To look only at "behaviors" is to lose sight of man, and to dismiss as "too unreliable" what men have to say about what they believed was at stake is to remain willfully ignorant of the experimentation that was actually performed.

But this candor in the exchange between experimenter and subject is only a minimum requisite of humanistically oriented research. An all-out pursuit of humanistic objectives draws much more into its orbit. Even the design of the experiment, including both the intended intervention and the control of other suspected interventions, can take shape from collaboration among those who participate. Moreover, the subject's convictions and doubts about what must govern his efforts to cope with the experimental circumstances are themselves implicit hypotheses in the existential undertaking, regardless of what the experimenter hypothesizes. They ought therefore to be built systematically into the assumptive structure the research is designed to test. The null hypothesis may not be the most ubiquitous alternative in competition with an experimenter's hunch; it often turns out that his subjects' hypotheses are.

It seems to me to be important in advance of setting up the final fixed design of an experiment—after which it is usually too late to do anything very imaginative—or examine anything very perceptively—for the experimenter to collaborate with a number of subjects, setting up hypotheses in the light of their experience with the kind of procedure he has started to develop. For example, Jennings (1963), in generating empirical evidence in support of a "creativity cycle" as propounded by personal construct theory, spent several years trying to set up operations that met the criteria of the theory. At first he treated subjects as subjects. But when, at last, he took them into his confidence and collaborated intimately with them to devise a procedure that produced and separated their experiences of "tightening" and "loosening" as postulated by the theory (Kelly, 1955), he was able to set up a very simple fixed design that could test the notion of a productive creativity cycle in subsequent subjects. When he took this humanistic step a long and discouraging experimental voyage got off the rocks. It stands particularly to his credit that the urgency of completing a dissertation did not frighten him into making a conventional study of "the differences between creative and noncreative individuals," which I am sure he could have completed and published within a few months using the "good guys versus the bad guys" criterion that has proved so popular with psychological journal editors.

The Role of the Experimenter in Humanistic Research

Much of what has been said about the role of the subject in humanistic research had as much to do with the role of the experimenter as with the role of the subject. That was because I regard subjects as experimenters—or, more generally, man as an experimenting creature, of which a scientist is an example. What can be added now is the humanistic perception that every scientist is, in an important sense, a subject in his own research. What he comes to think or what happens to him as a result of the experiment he performs is an important empirical outcome, perhaps even more important than the changes that are observed in his subjects. Just how far-reaching the implications of this notion are, and what their immediate bearing on research methodology is, require a little explaining.

Perhaps more was said at the outset of this discussion than was necessary to make it clear that the humanism I have in mind when I talk about research methodology is not classicism. But the point seemed worth emphasizing because I suspect some of my colleagues who defend humanism will want to disagree with me. If they do I hope that between us and the reader it will be clear what the points of disagreement are. The humanism I have in mind is as free of traditionalism as the adventuresome Greeks appear to have been. For it seems they were not classicists in their own time, at least not classicists as some tradition-bound men who now espouse classicism are.

Yet I must still agree that it is important for the psychological researcher to see the efforts of man in the perspective of the centuries. To me the striking thing that is revealed in this perspective is the way yesterday's alarming impulse becomes today's enlivening insight, tomorrow's repressive doctrine, and after that subsides into a petty superstition. But I am not cynical enough to believe therefore that these epochal transitions are futile, or that the quest for truth is illusory. I remind myself that a voyage upon which no man has ever embarked produces no landfalls, but one which men have pursued to its mysterious destination may then be abandoned to launch a wiser venture. Ships are built to be sailed. Ideas are meant to be enacted rather than preserved. I doubt that they can be both. The fact that their immediate function is to govern transition renders them no less valuable to the ultimate enterprise. The truths we seek may be everlasting, but the ones that must pattern our search are as transient as they are vital to the success of the human venture. This is no less than a humanistic notion, if I read history correctly. It is also a sort of empiric notion, though not in the usual epistemological sense.

All of this may sound more philosophical than methodological, but it has a lot to do with the way the experimenter structures his role. If he is one who imagines himself accumulating nuggets of ultimate truth he will place his primary research emphasis on the unassailability of his fragmentary findings. If he supports something at the .05 level of confidence he is encouraged; if he pushes it to the .01 level he is gratified; if it turns out at the .001 level he is ecstatic; and if it reaches the .0001 level he wonders how one writes an application for the Nobel Prize. The research objective of such a man is to nail something down, once and for all. His eternity is in his data. If he is a psychologist he will regard mankind as an accomplished fact, not as a current enterprise.

But if the experimenter sees himself exploring only one of many alternative constructions of man, with the best ones yet to be devised, he will be on a continual lookout for fresh perspectives emerging out of his research experience. What values he places upon his hypotheses will lie in the fertility of the experience in which they engage him, rather than in the certainty and parsimony of the explanations they offer. He will design his experiments to make his experience an optimal one. Thus he can not lose sight of the fact that he is himself the principal subject of his own experimental intervention. His psychology will not then be so much a study of what inescapable state impales man at this immature moment in history as it will be an exploration of what man may next become. He will approach his task with the horizon-scanning vision of a constructive alternativist rather than with the squint of an accumulative fragmentalist.

This is not to say that the humanistic psychologist need be unconcerned with precision in his research, though the scope of his outlook may often make him appear that way. If precise measurement will reveal faint cues to what is going on it should not be befogged by the global phraseologies of existentialism and phenomenology. The object of precision is to provide greater sensitivity to psychological processes not easily perceived, not to build impregnability into one's findings by adding decimal places.

Research as Experience

There are several ways in which the humanistic psychologist can maximize his confrontation with the phenomena he studies. The intimate collaboration with his subjects, mentioned in a preceding section, is one of them. Subjecting himself to the same experimental procedures he proposes for his subjects is another. To the full extent that he is capable he should experience what his subjects experience. Sights and sounds emanating from outside himself are not the only available clues to what is taking place. From internally manifested experience one may be alerted to crucial external events that otherwise would escape his notice. This is no less true when experimenting with children than when experimenting with adults; indeed, I suspect it is even more true. Close observation of everything that happens, rather than confining one's attention to those events for which the experimental design has preconceived categories, is not only humanistically appropriate; it is good basic scientific method.

I think it is safe to say that when any experimental conclusion, regardless of the statistical level at which it appears to be supported, violates one's sense of experiential reality it should be regarded with more than usual skepticism. This is not the same as saying that subjective judgment is better than objective judgment, but rather, in the best humanistic tradition, they will confirm each other. What man knows best is established by what he fully experiences, not exclusively by what he is compelled to concede.

The reader may have noted that in talking about experience I have been careful not to use either of the terms, "emotional" or "affective." I have been equally careful not to invoke the notion of "cognition." The classic distinction that separates these two constructs has, in the manner of most classic distinctions that once were useful, become a barrier to sensitive psychological inquiry. When one so divides the experience of man it becomes difficult to make the most of the holistic aspirations that may infuse the science of psychology with new life, and may replace the classicism now implicit even in the most "behavioristic" research. This too, as I see it, is a part of "the challenge of humanistic psychology."

Preliminary Stages of Research

Perhaps the role of the experimenter in humanistic psychology is most dramatically affected in the stages of research that precede the statement of a formal experimental design. Most of psychology's discourses on research, and certainly almost all of its published research reports, start with an assumed hypothesis, and tell us in obsessive detail what happens from there on. But the most exciting stages of research occur before this and are seldom mentioned—often not even recognized.

Humanistic psychology's research starts with man and initially leads the researcher to the most intimate understanding of the human experience he is capable of gaining. This may take a long time. It frightens some researchers and they protest that it endangers their "scientific objectivity." Unfortunately some of them never have any sense of confrontation with the phenomena they pretend to investigate. Yet they will argue that their research is definitive.

There is much to be said for a research strategy that insists on the psychologist having a first-hand clinical understanding of what he proposes to investigate before he sits down to write formal hypotheses about it. Certainly much time and expense could be saved if investigators would take the trouble to make the objects of their inquiries palpable before they start talking about intervening variables and mediational processes. Once the psychologist has seen "hostility," for example, with his own eyes, heard its sounds from both victim and obsessed, felt its pangs, restrained its impulses, lifted its myriad masks, struggled with its lingering consequences, and sensed its infinite variations he is in a far better position to undertake the disciplined task of formalizing the test of its properties.

Once during World War II, I was asked to consult with the officer in charge of an experimental research project dealing with a suspected psychological factor in some unexplained crashes experienced by naval aviators while flying in formation at night. A distinguished psychologist had published a paper in which he had dropped the remark that the autokinetic phenomenon might be involved in some way. The remark caught the eye of an ambitious reader and the entire project had been set up to test the hypothesis. The writer of the article, by then a naval officer himself and stationed a few minutes away, had not been consulted.

When I arrived it was immediately apparent that the flight surgeon in charge of the research, a personable chap with three stripes and obviously with a distinguished career ahead of him in the Navy, had probably never identified autokinetic movement in his own experience. He was blandly using a light source about fifty diameters too big. Within a few minutes, with the aid of a pin, a piece of cardboard and a small flashlight, it was possible to demonstrate what it was he was supposed to be investigating. "Well, whaddya know!" he exclaimed in amazement. Yet he had already spent upwards of $75,000 on a special research installation, tied up a number of highly trained enlisted aviation technicians badly needed elsewhere, and collected reams of yard-wide multiple polygraph tracings. He wanted me to detail "a psychologist or two to come over and analyze the data" since he admittedly did not "know anything about statistics." Needless to say, I used all the bureaucratic tricks at my command to get out from under that one. The last I heard of him he had an important role in the national space program.

It is easy enough for psychologists to poke fun at this fellow, since he was not a psychologist as we are, and particularly because he was a physician and a military man. Such stories about the military establishment are always making the rounds, as well as stories of medical efforts to assert proprietary control of all psychological research. Yet I have seen clinically inexperienced "experimental" psychologists set out to measure and manipulate "personality variables" which they would not think of observing in the flesh, and attempt to do so with scarcely a glance at the subjects who arrived at fifteen-minute intervals to sit behind a laboratory screen and push buttons in response to red and green lights. This kind of disengagement with man and the phenomena supposedly under investigation stands, as did the flight surgeon's project, in sharp contrast to the humanistic approach to psychological research.

Experimental Psychology and Humanistic Psychology

It is incredible that humanistic psychology should allow itself to stand opposed to the study of behavior, as suggested by some of our colleagues. Quite to the contrary, exploration by means of man's behavior is what once set humanism apart from scholasticism. But what now separates humanism from the behaviorism that arose in the early decades of this century—and lingered beyond its time—is that behavior is more to be used than explained. Indeed what best explains behavior is what it does, just as what best explains man is what he does. So the humanist asks what behavior can do.

The behaviorist worries about what made human acts inevitable in the scheme of material things. But I cannot imagine a lively humanist so preoccupied with a guilt-laden inquisition into why behavior had to happen in the otherwise rational life of man. But he may well inquire into the unfortunate undertakings that have brought man so close to the brink of disaster, both in his personal life and in his societal life. He might do so, not so much seeking what to blame them on—for the responsibility must ultimately be borne by man rather than by his circumstances—as seeking the constructions men have erected to channel their efforts so.

So the humanist studies behavior intently, but with an exciting difference. A psychological study of intelligence, for example, turns itself to the realization of various forms of unrecognized intelligent behavior rather than to the limits imposed by one's IQ. A psychological study of delinquency, for example, becomes a study of man's behavioral struggle to cope with his circumstances rather than a search for what can be done to make him obey the law. A psychological study of the psychotherapeutic process, for example, becomes an imaginative inquiry into how an immobilized person can utilize his own capacity for experimental behavior to answer important questions that seem now only to confront him with inexorable conclusions (Kelly, 1966). Behavior is the humanist's way of groping in the dark that engulfs us all not his bête noire. Wherein one can act he need not forever fear.

It should be added at this point that the use of the language of hypothesis is also of particular instrumental value to the humanistic psychologist, for it invites active inquiry rather than logic-tight answers, and it enables the researcher to entertain propositions "obviously untrue" long enough to find out whether they are as untrue as he and everyone else had supposed. But since the use of hypothesis is not an issue between humanistic psychologists and others, as the respective views of behavior are, there is no need to deal at length with the topic here (Kelly, 1964). The only issue here is what kind of hypotheses are worth investigating, and we have already had something to say about that.

Because of the present uncertainty of its stand on experimental research I fear there is a real danger of the recent humanistic psychology movement fizzling out. In their outright opposition to so much that is considered synonymous with "scientific research" and "experimental psychology," humanists may convince themselves and others that they oppose research in general and experimentation in particular. Nothing could be more incongruous than for humanistic psychology to become frozen in this posture. What could be more vital to psychology than to recognize that experimentation is even more characteristically human than it is scientific?

More than any of the other themes which guide psychologists, humanism invites their audacity and encourages their willingness to attempt what others believe to be preposterous. It would rather be absurd than subservient. In this respect it is allied to existentialism. The humanistic researcher looks for what man can do that he has never done before, rather than for conclusive explanations for what man has been doing all the time—and which, unfortunately, he may continue to do indefinitely should he allow himself to believe that he is what circumstances have made of him, or that he is destined to "be himself" and himself only.

Man's actions are best understood in an expanding context of all that is seen to be possible for him, rather than within the boundaries of his presumed nature, his reflexes, his brain, his complexes, his chronological age, his intelligence, or his culture. This, of course, means that, as unsuspected potentialities materialize, we shall probably have to keep changing the coordinates in terms of which we plot his life processes. But it does suggest, at the same time, that psychology can become a vital part of the on-going human enterprise. It is scarcely that now.

The Extent of Humanistic Research Methodology

What has been emphasized in this discussion is the broad methodology of humanistic research and a view of mankind that suggests to the scientist what he might be looking for. Little has been said about techniques, except to remind the reader that it expresses the genius of humanism for the psychologist to devise them and to place them within grasp of all men. Humanism, as I see it, must dispute the aristocratic claims of a self-appointed intellectual class, not identify with them. To the humanist every man is a scientist by disposition as well as by right, every subject is an incipient experimenter, and every person is by daily necessity a fellow psychologist.

While we have dwelt largely in the area of personality research, humanism has implications in less obvious arenas. Just as Freud listened patiently and emphasized[5] before he interpreted, so Darwin before him had observed and experienced in every way he was humanly capable. And before that Linnaeus had conceptualized what he had taken infinite pains to examine. Yet none was a passive observer. Each projected himself into his undertaking and thus marked it with his own character. Freud employed his originally eclectic technique, Darwin set sail in the *Beagle*, and Linnaeus collected his plants afield.

Nor is the research of the humanistic scientist an experience of himself alone. Galileo undertook to project his notion of a heliocentric universe into the everyday experience of man. It was for that he was condemned, not for proposing it as an academician's hypothesis, as Copernicus before him had done. Humanistic science is science in the grasp of men, not men in the grasp of science. It orchestrates all the talents of man. In pursuing its course it makes the most of man's range of experiential capacities, even those that are inarticulate. And as it progresses its outcomes are incorporated into the intentions of all men.

Behavior plays a crucial role, and behavior is best explained by what man finds he can do with it. More and more his ventures tell him what that may be. Thus, to the ever-alert humanist, the frame of reference within which the explanation of behavior takes shape is continually changing, and, in doing so, throws man's acts into new psychological and sociological perspectives.

To provide an enabling structure for the progressively shifting referents of behavior is to realize the psychological freedom of man. Such a structure is more substantial to human freedom than tearing down the ghettos in which men without hope congregate or insulating timid souls from the manipulative efforts of applied psychologists. I hope it is clear that this humanistic version of freedom is far removed from that which, too often, men have been able to envision for themselves only in civil chaos, in undisciplined liberty, in hallucinatory indulgence, or in a polite disengagement of man from man (Kelly, 1966).

The antecedents of behavior do not determine what it must be, but, like humanism's antecedent classicism, offer us a breathcatching glimpse of what man's capacity for behavior exploration might accomplish beyond those trackless seas that are too much accepted as the outer boundaries of our psychological world. Yet there is danger that humanistic psychology, in looking back over its shoulder, may, as behaviorism did, lose track of where it is going.

References

Jennings, C. L. (1963). *Personal construct theory and the creativity cycle*. Unpublished doctoral dissertation, Ohio State University.

Kelly, G. A (1955). *The psychology of personal constructs*, 2 vols. Norton.

Kelly, G. A. (1964). The language of hypothesis. *Journal of Individual Psychology*, *20*, 137–152.

Kelly, G. A. (1965a). The strategy of psychological research. *Bulletin of the British Psychological Society*, *18*, 1–15.

Kelly, G. A. (1965b). The threat of aggression. *Journal of Humanistic Psychology*, *5*, 195–201.

Kelly, G. A. (1967). A psychology of the optimal man. In A.R. Mahrer (Ed.), *Goals of psychotherapy* (pp. 238–258). Appleton-Century-Crofts.

[5] Editors' note: [sic]

Section IV

Interpersonal and International Relations

In *The sincere motive*, the idealistic 19-year-old Kelly makes a plea for peace to be borne from "our own hearts." A year later, in *Forgotten issues*, he articulates what he considers to be the ingredients of "ultimate civilization": democracy, self-determination, universal law, mutual confidence, organization, and the greatest loyalty to the largest group.

Kelly was a practicing Christian, and *Some preliminary thoughts on what one should seek first* consists of two addresses that he delivered on "Layman's Sunday" at his Presbyterian church. Among the points he makes is the observation that his country's significant spiritual revivals during that period were primarily occurring outside the church. Additionally, he emphasizes the importance of seeking and questioning, rather than merely accepting ready-made answers.

In whom confide: On whom depend for what? articulates Kelly's specific perspective on dependency, while also emphasizing the significance of mutual sociality in interdependent relationships.

In typical fashion, Kelly begins his invited paper for the 10th Annual Nebraska Symposium on Motivation, *Europe's matrix of decision,* with the assertion that he has "no use for the concept of motivation." The paper draws on data collected during his and his wife's world tour in an attempt to explore the "decision matrices," or constructs, used by individuals in different countries. In doing so, he illustrates how the endeavor to understand another person whose views appear markedly different from one's own can be threatening, and how resorting to motivational explanations can serve as an escape from such threats. *Nicholas Square*, which seems to consist of notes for, or fragments of, a book chapter, continues this theme in a more poetic manner and appears to derive from his experiences in the Soviet Union during the world tour.

Man, crises, and commitments: A stated purpose and a plan for an Institute for Advanced Psychological Studies, which is undated, outlines a number of crises that individuals have created within themselves and in their relationships with others, including in the context of international relations. Unfortunately, it was unfinished, and thus the reader is never able to discern Kelly's vision for the Institute that is tantalizingly referenced in the title of the paper.

Collected Papers of the Pioneer of Constructivist Psychology: George A. Kelly, First Edition. Edited by David A. Winter and Nick Reed.

40

The Sincere Motive[1]

Four years ago the streets of our city teemed with an expectant throng. The Forum was packed. The sidewalks were congested and Boy Scouts worked beneath a morning sun holding back an ever surging crowd. Here a youth eagerly pushed forward to catch a glimpse of the coming hero, while there a man staunchly held his position wondering even at his own interest in the expected procession. Meanwhile on the outskirts of the town, a special train came to a grinding stop and with the grating of those brakes, I see the finger of Mortality touch the soaring hopes of mankind and send them fluttering to the earth; while back in the crowd the people waited for the hero who would never come. Woodrow Wilson had run the course.

That morning sun of hope has turned to the languid glare of noon-day. The eager Youth has turned to his visions and the staunch Man has gone back to his dreams. The Hero is dead. And the throng is still the Throng. But what of the cause, the motivating ideal of the desire that burned within that Dreamer's soul? Was it for naught? Was it a fantastic dream of Eutopia's shores, or was it interred within the Dreamer's tomb?

I come not to laud a statesman nor to condemn the Throng, the Youth, or the Man. I come to waken their drugged souls. The shadow of war lingers upon our threshold. Old women stumbling into the city at dusk, bearing rotten firewood upon their scantily clad shoulders, are paying the price of a war, while the god of war shakes the very rocks of Olympus with his guffaws. This in Europe—and in America? In America our statesmen cry for peace and at the same time spend our taxes to create the demons of destruction. Our chemists toil long hours in the laboratory, concocting new fiends of death, while maudlin demagogues devise new phrases to fan the flame of our pristine passion into martial rhapsodies. One regiment of soldiers contains more efficient organization than all the peace societies in the United States. Our super-dreadnaughts lie waiting. Our poison gas factories are equipped. We are sowing the dragon's teeth of Cadmus and the crop is as inevitable; for two thousand years ago the man of Tarsus said that "Whatsoever we sow that also shall we reap."

And when that harvest does come, it will indeed be a crop for the grim reaper. When social civilization fails to keep pace with scientific, there the tottering castles of human hope crumble and bury themselves in the dust of aeons. How frail is the thread which holds civilization's vibrating ball. One atom out of tune and the mass is hurled into the deep eternity below, which even the flitting pinions of Memory know not. And my friends, war is that discord. When war stalks, men's very hearts are out of tune.

The Prince of Peace may knock in vain, but when false Mars flings his edicts in bugle blasts legion slaves hasten to his bidding. You may scoff at the entreaties of the lowly Nazarene, but if you falter at the summons of the demon of hate, you are a slacker, a traitor, a coward. The mad demagogues lead the maddened Throng and the Youth and the Man follow because their passion is fired and their souls drugged. All are slaves fighting for democracy which they know not, dying for liberty which is not. They are told that it is a righteous war and that the very height of the ideal will keep them from sin. But go to Germany's nameless orphans and ask if war has no sin. Then tread the still glowing embers at Smyrna and ask those scorched bones if war has no sin. Speak into the oracles of uncovered graves and ask if hate respects ideals. And when you startle at the answer, remember that two thousand years ago the apostle of Christ taught that "the wages of sin is death." Death, death from burning gas, death from hideous disease, death from merciless shrapnel, death everywhere. Our mothers, our sisters, the victims while the war-god grins at the lucky hit and grinds his heel deeper into our own ruined lives. That will be a next war.

Then when the thunder has died and the cannon have rusted for the want of plunder, when the best of society have gone to feed this martial Minotaur, the dregs set about to pay the price. The price is the hope of a civilization which might have been, the dream of brotherly love which should have been, and the vision of thoughts which would have been. Nothing is left but the stagnation of polluted ideals and the poverty of spent youth. Upon the lavish walls of that jeweled palace at Versailles they place the inscription, "To the Glory of War" and those old women dragging rotten firewood into the city at dusk pay for that inscription. Old women dragging rotten firewood when there is coal in Louisane.[2] Old women stumbling into the city at dusk where there should be youth dancing from the city at morning. Old slaves with faces tinged by the

[1] This oration was awarded first place in the peace Oratorical Contest held at Friends' University, Wichita, Kansas, March 28, 1924. It was published in 1924 in The Messenger of Peace, XLIX (5), 76–80, and is republished by permission of Jacqueline Aldridge.
[2] Editors' note: [sic]

Collected Papers of the Pioneer of Constructivist Psychology: George A. Kelly, First Edition. Edited by David A. Winter and Nick Reed.

pallid glint from the rows of crosses on yonder hillside;—rows of crosses where there should be perfume of growing crops. "The pitcher broken at the fountain, and the sound of the grinding become low." The price of a war,—dusk, darkness, death. Mars is collecting his tribute. Disturb him if you dare. That will be the aftermath of a next war.

And why have war? The militants say that we have war to develop manhood. To develop manhood from the dregs that infest the aftermath of a war? To develop a manhood from the unbalanced, shell-shocked millions that stagger home when taps have sounded? To develop a manhood from these cowards who let those old women drag home their scanty firewood when there is coal in Lousiane?[3] War has no manhood, save that of the half-endowed children who through war, learn to hate war.

Why have war? The psychologist says that war is inevitable, that man is destined to struggle, and that to refuse to fight is cowardly. To refuse to struggle is cowardly, but there is more honorable struggle than that which hurls both our neighbor and ourselves toward the dark oblivion from which even modern genius of civilization cannot rescue. A true manhood finds realms to conquer other than his neighbor's territory. The nation that must live by thrusting others down from the ladder of civilization is the impostor in international society.

The scientists says that war stimulates invention. Yes, stimulates invention in the art of destruction. It were far better to curb invention than to become a race of parasites sucking one another's national vitality. A true race of scientists needs no field of hate to raise a fruitful crop of inventors.

Why have war? Listen to the blinded Throng repeating in motley babel the catch-phrases of their war-drunken leaders. "We must have war to protect our national honor." Protect our national honor by a process that knows no honor? We cannot have peace as long as we place this so-called national honor above international responsibility.

Man and Youth of America, if you be minions of this god of war, then relax yourselves into the stupor of bartered souls, but if you be champions of peace, then extract yourselves from this blinded Throng and learn a lesson from that dreamer, Woodrow Wilson, who saw the pinnacles of his fondest dreams crumble before the old world diplomacy at Versailles and who, gathering the shattered fragments to his breast, died for them. We need not embrace those same specific ideals, but until we catch that spirit of idealism, there is little hope for the dawn of peace.

"Vain idealism," you say? And yet, is not that the very factor which is lacking in our conquest for peace? Our present desire for peace comes from a realization that peace is an economic necessity, a matter of political expediency or religious responsibility. We desire peace because we realize that we must destroy war before war destroys us. We desire peace because of its benefits, not because we hate the sin of war. We say that nations must disarm, that minorities must be protected, and that democracy must be established, yet the paramount change from the chaos of war to the dawn of peace must take place not in these materialistic peace programs alone, but in our own attitude toward war. This evolution from the old regime to the new, must take place in us, the Man and Youth of America. These materialistic problems are but the hard icy crust that inevitably forms when the idealistic motive for peace is quenched by a so-called practical civilization. We must plow deeper in the field of international relations and stir that subsoil, the motivating ideals of our own desires, for until there are ideals which are consistent with our desires, this problematic crust will continue to form. And again I say that this greatest step lies in you. It is a sincere desire for peace, for the very love of peace itself. Out of such a motive will come a solidly grounded public opinion which will not tolerate war. The dawn of peace will come not on the distant horizon of national policy nor international organization, but first within our own hearts.

O, Man and Youth, this must be your motivating ideal either to hold high or cast away into the dark abyss below. These are the flaming problems, these are the burning facts from which you must forge the plastic ideals of tomorrow. Here is your pattern, the visions of myriads of peace martyrs. Here is your hammer, the weight of a free public opinion. Here is your anvil, the Rock of Eternal Truth, on which we must pit our undying faith in the possibility of peace. And here, O Workman, is your reward. A world of freemen no longer under the martial yoke. A world of happiness, to posterity, who need never know war. And in the words of the Prophet Isaiah, ""Then shall thy light break forth as the morning, and thine health spring up speedily, and thy righteousness shall go before thee; and the glory of the Lord shall be thy reward." Here is thy FLAMING TORCH. Canst thou drop it?

[3] Editors' note: [sic]

41

Forgotten Issues[1,2]

Democracy, self-determination, universal law, mutual confidence, organization, greatest loyalty to the largest group! These are patriot's dreams,—Yes,—idle dreams. Yet they mark the dividing line between civilization and barbarism.

In that stage of the development of our political institutions in which nations were being formed, the autocratic and hierarchical ruling caste reigned infallible, shrouded in dogmas, sanctified by superstitious religions. Ultra-conservatism was made doubly secure by a belief that the existing institutions were the fruits of divine edicts and none dared criticize or suggest. Rulers were of papal power. Fatalism was the religious order. A man's social role was determined a century before he stepped upon the stage of human political drama. History tells us that in that age only the despot was free.

Evolving society has learned that with such a thinking man as is necessary for ultimate civilization, such autocracy, though efficient, is irksome, for the thinking man has a soul and the greater his thoughts the greater his soul. Society has learned that the man with a soul is an individual and that a government of individuals must be a government in which the individual can express himself. Hence it must be a democracy.

Russia was autocratic. Her despots were free. She was efficient. She remained efficient as long as she retained her autocratic government, but when Russians began to think, their efficient government fell, for autocracy. . .thinking men, men with souls, individuals, is dangerous. It is impossible. Democracy, then, is the first ingredient of ultimate civilization, yet democracy is not all. . .democracy to the individual man so is self-determination to the individual group. Minority groups would be cherished in a perfect democracy if there were no self-determination of peoples. The first unit of human government is the individual himself, hence a democracy for the expression of that individual. The second unit of human government is the group, the sect, the denomination, the clan, the colleagues who hold similar tenets, the men who think alike, act alike, believe alike. In the ultimate civilized government these too, must express themselves. Democracy,—self-determination—the first and second ingredients of ultimate civilization. Yet even these are not all.

Universal law, equality of law, for thinking men are jealous! They are proud. Yet if you would have civilization you must have thinking men, the kind of men who tolerate no inequality of government. Laws are instituted among men in order to establish equilibrium of opportunities but if the laws themselves are not equitable, they fail in their own purpose and become despotic to. . .high, low; black, white; first and last must be ruled by a common law, a universal law. They may institute. . . laws, within themselves and by themselves, but between themselves there must be one universal law.

Now, my friends, equity of law does not presuppose equality of men. There are probably no two equal men in existence. But unequal men demand equal law for civilization must have thinkers even though they be unequal and thinkers are proud and jealous and will tolerate no inequality in government. Universal law,—the third requisite of ultimate civilization! But laws are useless unless sustained by organization and organization is impossible where there is no mutual confidence.

Hardly had the gaseous fumes cleared away from the battle fields of the Great World Conflict before. . .where treaties were scorned. . .of a golden west set sail a new A. . ..sail from a land of prosperity. . .and old traditions, where democracy. . .which both high and low share. . .prove to ourselves that we trust our brother shall we become fully trustworthy. Then shall mutual confidence be established and the way paved for organized mankind.

Organization, mutual effort, efficiency in striving to attain a goal. Whatever the chief end of men, whether it be service, happiness, or glorification of the Deity, whatever the purpose of human life, that goal can be attained more quickly, more thoroughly, and more completely by organized effort. Organization, properly founded, will enable mankind to put forth his best effort whether in science or commerce, whether in religion or pedagogy. Organization is the machinery of men and things and the more perfect it is the more perfectly these may act. Surely organization is a requisite of ultimate civilization. But organization is not all.

[1] Talk given at Friends University, Wichita, Kansas, 1925. Published by permission of Jacqueline Aldridge.

[2] Editors' note: The original manuscript is partially destroyed. Missing text is indicated by ellipses.

Collected Papers of the Pioneer of Constructivist Psychology: George A. Kelly, First Edition. Edited by David A. Winter and Nick Reed.
 Published 2026 by John Wiley & Sons Ltd.

There must be loyalty, interloyalty, loyalty between individuals, loyalty of individuals to groups, and the larger the group the greater should be the loyalty devoted to it. To care more for the welfare of a smaller group than for the welfare of a larger group is selfishness and selfishness can have no place in civilized government. Loyalty must not be exclusive, but inclusive. Loyalty must not be narrow and clannish but universal. It must not be blind but comprehensive. The world must learn that life, interests, welfare, are just as important whether they are those of a Jew or a Christian, whether they are those of a Negro or a White, whether they are those of a countryman or a foreigner, yes, or even whether they are those of a stranger or a kinsman. The question of the inequalities of individuals must not enter into the problem of protecting the welfare of those individuals. Greatest loyalty to the largest group is the greatest requisite to ultimate civilization.

To the primitive barbarian the highest. . .of devotion was self and he acted accordingly. But as gradually the light of civilization began to pervade his life. . .of his devotion became first, the family, then the tribe and finally the nation. And the new Argosy's sails were white with the purity of its purpose, and the purity of purpose lit the whole of the horizon. On its deck stood a statesman. And he, too, was untainted by the old schools, impractical to the old diplomats, a dreamer, Woodrow Wilson. And his clarion cry was "self-determination! universal law! organization!"

The high priests of the old order were astonished, were alarmed. The populace was intoxicated with the new-born hope. In Italy the peasants burned candles before the portrait of Wilson. In Poland, university men grasped hands and exclaimed, "Wilson" as their greeting. His words were emblazoned on every pagoda in Turin. His "fourteen points" were the topics of the day in London. They hoped that he would establish the new order—the new order—the something better—the something greater—the unknown something that had always been just beyond. Hope, joy, promise reigned in the world during the first days of that peace conference at Versailles.

But within that conference Wilson fought in vain for open diplomacy. In vain he fought against the old diplomatic order, for their eyes were clouded with traditions and their ears were stopped with legends, and their reason was dulled with distrust.

Some day! Some day the world will learn that only the dreamer is practical, that only the ideal is practicable. Yet through it all we must be aware that things must come in their proper sequence and that we cannot expect the results of ideal civilization until one by one the foundations of that civilization. . .laid and perfected. We must realize that. . .be codified.

. . .vanished because mutual confidence. . .Civilization had reached the. . .that there must be democracy. . . .universal law but mutual confidence. . ..not dare trust their brother. . .to our brother that we trust. . .trustworthy and only when we can finally the nation. In the ultimate civilization this sphere of devotion must be widened until it will include all of mankind. In the United States the citizen devotes greater loyalty to his state than to his county and he devotes greater loyalty to his nation than to his state. In just the same way and for the same reasons must individuals allow the nation to become subordinated to the larger units of organization.

This principle of the greatest loyalty to the largest group is but an extension of the principle of democracy applied to our devotion. We believe in the majority rule in government, then why not majority rule in the claiming of our devotion? Loyalty is the cord that binds men together into effective organization. If organization is a requisite to ultimate civilization, then the greatest loyalty to the largest group is a requisite to ultimate civilization for organization without loyalty devoted to it becomes impotent machinery.

These six ingredients of ultimate civilization amid the blinded scurry of maddened demagogues, amid the flickering shadows of intrigue and secrecy, amid the hate and jealousies of age-old feuds, are fast fading—becoming forgotten issues in the parliaments of man. To you, to you who sit before me tonight, not to some far-away mystic power, but to you alone come these nigh forgotten issues.

Democracy, self-determination, universal law, mutual confidence, organization, greatest loyalty to the largest group. These are patriot's dreams. Yes—idle dreams? Yet they mark the dividing line between civilization and barbarism.

42

Some Preliminary Thoughts on What One Should Seek First[1]

This is Layman's Sunday. What you are about to hear are the remarks of three laymen, of whom I am fortunate enough to be the first. All of us have been well briefed on what we are supposed to say. As long as none of us steps out of line the ones who follow should have very little difficulty picking up the prescribed line of thought and making the points that the people at Presbyterian Headquarters in Philadelphia think Presbyterian laymen ought to make when they are asked to speak spontaneously. But the man who follows a speaker who gets out of line is likely to have a bad time of it.

In preparing these remarks—an exercise euphemistically described as "putting the ideas into your own words"—a passage from one of George Bernard Shaw's plays kept popping into my mind. Suspecting that it might be not be the kind of thing people would like to hear mentioned in church, I kept lifting it up gently and setting it down outside the fringe of my consciousness, much as one does with an overly affectionate kitten that keeps jumping up onto his lap when he is trying to do something painstaking. But the pesky little thing would not go away and, while I am sure it is nothing that the people in Philadelphia believe a layman should be thinking about on Layman's Sunday—particularly the kind of good Organization Man that a Presbyterian Layman is supposed to be—the thing is going to have to come out.

At this particular turn of Shaw's play, *The Applecart*, which has to do with the future workings of the British Monarchy, the King is being charged by his ministers with having altogether too much power in the affairs of state. They argue that he will have to stop delivering his speeches in person. The King remonstrates that he can't see what harm it does, since they are the ones who write every word he is allowed to utter in public. But, they reply, Your Majesty has a perfectly nasty habit of winking while reading some of our most delicately phrased passages.

(Perhaps I should add, for those who are interested in the plot of the play, as well as what I am trying to illustrate, that the King, a rather popular chap, finally threatened to run for election to Parliament. Shortly after that the politicians decide that the whole thing ought to be dropped.)

Our outline this morning suggests that laymen are often "tired, anxious, and frustrated;" that they often "worry;" that the decisions they have to make may seem to be "slowly killing" them. I suspect this is true. In fact, I have reason to know it is true. Certainly this is not one of the passages at which I would be tempted to wink.

But what is this struggle all about that so many of us should find it so burdensome? Do we get frustrated because our goals are so high that it requires super-human effort to attain them? I don't really think so. It is, instead I think, that so often our goals seem less and less real, less and less important, the longer we strive for them. It is the struggle for a goal that no longer seems worth struggling for that becomes unbearable. Or it is one that loses its shape and definition the closer it is approached. In the first instance we strive furiously year after year for something that keeps looking more and more like something we don't want. In the second instance we dedicate our lives to a cause that fades into meaninglessness; we even have trouble picturing in our minds just what it was we set out to achieve. In either instance, we get tired, anxious, worried and the daily decisions we feel driven to make seem to be killing us.

The Church says that it has something worth striving for. Does this mean that all we have to do is go to church and listen to the exhortations and our days of seeking will be over? But people do get ulcers doing church work and the quiet evening at home with one's family, or the uncluttered hours of meditation, both of them so well depicted by the *Presbyterian Life* magazine and other church publications, is obviously not for the layman who gets himself involved in what is customarily called, "Christian fellowship," "stewardship of time," etc. Indeed, the layman who looks for direction in his life—the goal that does not prove to be worthless on the eve of its attainment or lose its form and substance the closer it is approached—may well ask of his church, as well as his business, just what is going on here? Is the church really any different from other rat races?

[1] Delivered at the first and second services of the Presbyterian Church, Worthing, October 19, 1958. Published by permission of Jacqueline Aldridge.

Collected Papers of the Pioneer of Constructivist Psychology: George A. Kelly, First Edition. Edited by David A. Winter and Nick Reed.

We are told that there is a religious revival in America today. As evidence the fact is cited that more people are attending church than ever before. To those of us who have grown up with the idea that the church was the bastion of everything good, this is an encouraging statistic. But is it not fair to ask, "What for? Why are so many of us going to church these days?" Does this identification with churchly goings-on represent any deepening of man's sense of his own direction, the sense that enables one to go out after something without suffering all the currently popular neurotic ailments? Or does all this church attendance come about simply because people are more and more afraid of being left out of something?

Serious students of the religious upswing in America have characterized it as the most shallow of all the series of revivals that have come and gone in the three hundred years of American cultural history. They have only to point to the self-centered power and success motif that makes Herman Vincent Peale one of our most quoted ecclesiastics, or to the popularly phrased nostalgia with which Billy Graham takes us by the hand and softly leads us back to the uncomplicated religion of our childhood. One dresses religion in the ethic of Nineteenth Century Business; the other gives it the dimensions of a fourth grade Sunday School lesson. Both are devout men, both are helpful, both are to be admired. I would not think of disparaging them as dedicated persons. It is their listeners who make them leaders of contemporary religious thought.

On the other hand, the students of the religious revival have only to point to the sobering fact that the great spiritual revivals that do exist in this country today, such as those dealing with inter-racial relations, with economic exploitation of the unfortunate, and the dignity of man regardless of his state of mind, are mainly outside the church and have of themselves a deep virility that cannot he matched by anything to be seen in the church.

Do we always need someone to tell us just what it is we seek, or where it can be found, safe and waiting for us? I think not, for the man who is looking for something obviously does not know where it is. If he did he would no longer be seeking. So with the Christian layman. If his life is a genuine quest for what is worth achieving, he will ask questions of his church, he will examine the claims of those who insist that they have just what he is looking for, and he will always wonder if he as a part of the church organization and its ongoing program knows where he is going, just because he is identified with a religious body.

Many laymen will be called on to speak on Laymen's Sunday. You may be one of them. In most cases laymen will be expected to speak on the theme. These comments on the theme are made for whatever help they may be as you think about what you are going to say.

"SEEK FIRST." This is not an invitation to sight-seeing. This is nothing at all like "See America First." This direction, "Seek First," has to do with all the living we do all the time. It has to do with the next move you make. It has to do with your last thought on earth.

Are you tired, anxious, frustrated? Do you worry all the time? Are the decisions you have to make slowly killing you? Are you a bundle of tensions? Maybe you need to be tranquilized. On the other hand, maybe you just need to be energized. One thing is certain. Your wailing and self-pity will get you nowhere because nobody is listening. By the way, what have you done recently to improve the world? Maybe the time has come for us to realize that the human condition does not materially change from day to day or even from age to age. Our manipulation of the environment changes but we are really no better or worse off than those who gathered to hear Jesus twenty centuries ago. We may live longer and be better fed, housed, and clothed, but millions living on this earth today do not live longer and are not as well fed, housed, and clothed. We know infinitely more about the structure of life and the universe than did those anxious people who sat at the feet of Jesus. Yet they were just as close and just as far from His kingdom as you and I. The Kingdom was theirs to seek. It is also ours to seek. One gathers that it is the seeking that's important, ". . .seek first his kingdom and his righteousness. . ."

One of our difficulties is that we keep going off in all directions. We are not quite sure where we are headed or why. A lot of us have no more lofty goals than respectability (keeping up with Smiths) and security (job, old age, health and all the rest). Sooner or later we discover that keeping up with one set of Smiths only leads to a desperate effort to keep up with another set and still another. And it eventually dawns on us that life at best is really a risky piece of business and that the security we seek simply cannot be had. No wonder we get frantic. Pursuing the course we do, the more respectability and material security we get the more we have to lose so the more risky life becomes and the more insecure we feel. It's enough to drive us mad. And Jesus simply asks why we go on like this when we need only "seek first his kingdom and his righteousness."

What in life do you want anyway? What in death do you want? What is your great objective? Where are you headed? Jesus made it pretty clear that we are free to choose either life or death, His kingdom or the kingdoms of this world, His righteousness or our own evil, heaven or hell. Put it any way you like, it is an either or choice and the choice, that which a man seeks first, will determine all the rest of his life.

Now, as all of us know, seeking first His kingdom and His righteousness is not as easy as it sounds and when face to face with the choice, as we are all the time, we react in different ways. This is not surprising in view of the fact that we have little or no idea about His kingdom and would be hard put to it to define His righteousness. It is expected that we shall always see but dimly through a dark glass. Our Father knows that we are but human. He did not give us the capacity to see and know all things. He did give us the ability to "seek first his kingdom and his righteousness" and He did promise us that if we did so all would be well with us. Did you ever stop to think about how wonderful it is that God did not deliver the blueprints of His kingdom to us. Had we the blueprints how utterly insufferable we would be. The point is that His kingdom is not for us to build. It is for us to seek. The purpose of the National Council of Presbyterian Men is "to promote the Kingdom of God world-wide. . ." This really means that we are promoting kingdom seeking among all men. Can you imagine what life would be like if all men everywhere sought "first his kingdom and his righteousness." Hard to visualize, isn't it? That's because each generation has a full quota of people who think they have already found His kingdom or a "practical" substitute. History is filled with their mighty works. These men are capable of either massive benevolence or mass murder. All are well intentioned—all are ultimately rejected. You find it difficult to picture a society of kingdom seekers. That's because only the humble "seek first his kingdom and his righteousness." Humility among men is always in short supply. In our arrogance we persist in placing our confidence in our own imperfectly conceived and imperfectly executed designs for life. All too often we move from "Trust in God" to "Trust in God and keep your powder dry" to "Keep your powder dry" because we make powder and we have confidence in what we make. But the meek shall ultimately inherit because they "seek first his kingdom and his righteousness." People always get what they want—Jesus His Father's favor—Judas his silver. You really do get that for which you "seek First." It is really true that "all these things shall be yours as well."

Are you tired, anxious, frustrated? Are you filled with despair? Do Sputniks, Vanguards, hydrogen bombs and all the possible consequences of radioactive fall-out give you the shakes? Take it easy, fellow. You are in no greater danger than Abel was in the Company of Cain. By the way, you are in no less danger either. You think it's just awful that we live in this kind of world. Take heart. Our Lord lived in it and survived it gloriously. His design for living is instructive. He fixed His eyes on His Father and moved in perfect confidence. He neither sought trouble nor avoided it. He was concerned with neither security nor danger. He was not interested in being well adjusted in the community. He was concerned with His Father's approval. His life never depended on what other people did or did not do. He was not satisfied to be the product of his environment. The directing force in His life was His Father. He spoke from rich experience when He urged men to "seek first his kingdom and his righteousness. . ."

"SEEK FIRST." Interested? It requires effort, you know. It's true we can only see dimly through a dark glass but that's no excuse for not looking at all. It's true that we are not going to get our hands on the blueprints of the kingdom but that doesn't justify us in sitting around just waiting for something to happen. It's true that we are not going to reshape this world to our liking in this generation but this is no command to us to do nothing but twiddle our thumbs. The first thing we can do is to decide whether or not God matters in our lives. He will either matter a great deal or He will not matter at all. He will either be our first concern or He will be of no concern. We are living among many people who simply give God no thought at all. They do not know Him and think they cannot know Him. It is the Christian's professed belief that God can be and is known because He has revealed and continues to reveal Himself to us. Through the Scriptures, through Jesus Christ, through prayer, through the Holy Spirit we can know what God is like and the course He would have us take, the disposition He would have us make of our lives. It does take effort, an effort most people are not going to make unless they are related to others making the same effort. This is one of the things the Church is all about. In the Church we are most likely to find kingdom seeking people. In the nurture of the Church we are most likely to discover what God is like and to find His design for our lives. In the company of others who also "Seek First" we are most likely to approach His kingdom and His righteousness. And we are most likely to keep seeking.

"SEEK FIRST." Warning! We cannot know all the consequences of our pursuit of His kingdom and His righteousness. As this world judges things, the pursuit could be quite expensive. The promises of God are not paid off in long lives, good health, material security, or solid comfort. But our faith is that the promises are kept and in terms that are largely irrelevant in the value systems of this world. And who knows? Enough people seeking "first his kingdom and his righteousness" just might serve to transform this earth into something pleasing in His sight. Curiously enough, any number of men who sought His kingdom have found themselves a part of it. Or so they seem to be. Seeing them, one is inclined to believe it.

43

In Whom Confide: On Whom Depend for What?[1]

Let me express my appreciation of the opportunity to address this Society and to share with you, on this occasion, the memory of a distinguished and dedicated member of our profession.

"In whom confide? On whom depend for what?" Probably no experienced clinician can listen to these questions without being reminded of something he has heard many times before. Often it has been expressed in furtive undertones, as in the case of a frightened person who dares not ask the question out loud lest he receive the dreaded answer. Sometimes the question is explicit, but purely rhetorical, as in the case of one who is in the act of raising a barrier between himself and an intruding world.

It is of no matter, for the purposes of this discussion, that we customarily say of the one person that he is "neurotic" and of the other that he is "paranoid." I shall not try to classify symptoms nor to trace the pattern of learning that makes people say such things. You are invited, instead, to join me in an attempt to understand what each person *means* by such questions and the nature of the *experience* which, by asking them, he has offered to share.

Our point of departure is the place where we find man caught in the midst of a socially complex world for which he is psychologically unprepared—a world in which so few are able to face life at the one cocktail level of confidence. There are two popular explanations of how man has gotten in over his head. One is the "Frankenstein" thesis. It holds that material developments have outrun social progress. The other is the "babes in the wood" theory. It is that the complexities of society are beyond the psychological capacities of an animal who has only recently evolved from a lower form.

We should look at these two themes for a moment before proceeding along the alternative line I wish to develop with you. First, is it the imbalance between social and material progress that has gotten us into trouble? I think not. Indeed, our particular materialistic advance is itself as much a social development as it is the accumulation of wealth and hardware. It is the particular social form of this highly developed materialistic society whose viability is being urgently brought into question. Without the social structure and psychological outlook that takes them as its premises rather than its implements, neither wealth nor hardware would need be much of a threat to us. Granted, of course, societies have been built on other assumptions that turned out to be equally questionable.

As for the second popular theme, the one that man is still too much of a monkey to cope with civilization, I think this also is artifactual. The naïveté is not so much a vestigial trait, carried over from man's simian ancestry, as it is a tenet of the psychology he has devised for his everyday use. This version of psychology, which is the version in which you and I were trained, holds that our neighbors are precocious beasts to be enticed by food and sex or roused out of their naturally inert state to be propelled one way or another by motives and dynamics. The approach to such behaving organisms—I hesitate to say "persons" lest I be accused of being unscientific—is in terms of a psychology derived from the Nineteenth Century physiological model. The social upshot of this scientism is a particular kind of manipulative approach to interpersonal relations which has come to characterize and dehumanize our culture.

Now our theme, which stands in contrast to these two popular clichés, does not argue that the world is simpler than we think. If it were so simple, I might have to concede that man could as well remain simple too, and that it is possible for him to survive with no more psychological understanding than he had in primitive times.

But it is clear the world is not simple anymore. And it is equally clear that man is not coping with it as he ought. Moreover, the difficulty is something for us to pitch in and solve, not something we should lie down and be treated for. In other words, I regard the problem as one that can profitably be cast in *psychological* terms, though not in the sort of psychologisms I challenged at the beginning of this discussion[2].

[1] The Fourth Annual Samuel H. Flowerman Memorial Lecture presented to the New York Society of Clinical Psychologists on December 7, 1962. First published by kind permission of the Society in Maher, B. (Ed.). (1969). *Clinical psychology and personality: The selected papers of George Kelly* (pp. 189–206). Wiley. Republished by permission of Wiley.

[2] The main body of this paper was preceded by a brief, informal summary of Professor Kelly's abandonment of motivational concepts, such as "affect," "needs," "psychodynamics," etc.

Collected Papers of the Pioneer of Constructivist Psychology: George A. Kelly, First Edition. Edited by David A. Winter and Nick Reed.

The Dependent Society

It is true that Twentieth Century society is so complicated it is hard to understand, and that this causes difficulties. But what is more important is that it is a society in which each person finds himself dependent upon many fragmentary sources of supply. To put it another way, we may say that civilized man has an intricate social system of dependencies. He must continually analyze and fractionate his personal wants so as to allocate them appropriately within this complex. The person upon whom he depends for one kind of support is not the one who is likely to help him in other ways. Moreover, a person must be sensitively aware of what he has to offer others in return if he is to make his own personal matrix of reciprocal supplies and demands actually function. Otherwise his associates will soon come to regard him as an overly "dependent" nuisance, and he will eventually become a very lonely man.

Yet so complex is the typical dependency matrix that rarely do two partners match themselves so well that each supplies all the wants of the other. What more often happens is that the reciprocal dependency breaks down, leaving one person clinging and wistful where the other is restless and impatient. Where one seeks, the other tries to escape, and where one tries to disengage, the other finds himself clutching desperately at every passing coat sleeve to satisfy his unfulfilled dependency.

It is in this sense that we can say that civilized man is a very dependent man. What others can give him and what he can give others are so narrowly specialized that he is hard put to it to make the two match up in any comprehensive set of interpersonal relationships.

There is also a complementary sense in which civilized man is a particularly dependent creature. Not only are his sources of supply complex, and his services to others specialized, but his own shopping list is bulky and often illegible. The simple pleasures and obvious necessities of an older generation are no longer enough. Thus not only does he have to differentiate and allocate his dependencies within a complicated system involving mutual relationships, but he vaguely craves a lot of things his hard-pressed grandparents were too busy to think of.

The point I have tried to make so far is that civilized man, as we know him, is a particularly dependent man, that it is difficult for him to allocate his dependencies on a reciprocal basis, and that he is often lonely—not with the loneliness of a person who has no companions at all, but with the loneliness of one who cannot reach the companions he has.

Adults Are More Dependent than Children

Let me press a little further this translation of civilization into terms of dependency. It is customary to characterize a child as "dependent" and an adult as "independent." But this is misleading. To be sure, a child cannot take care of himself, but then, when you come right down to it, neither can an adult. An adult appears to be self-reliant merely because he is often better able to distribute his dependencies in proper relation to his potential resources.

But how many adults can survive on what is sufficient for a child? Indeed, in some cases, children are more adept in placing their dependencies than are their parents. A child's ability to love and the utter simplicity of his demands often places him in a more secure position. There is a sense, also, in which he is freer to express himself, to think independently, and to rely upon his own imaginative devices for exploring his world. He may not have the power his parents have, but he often has more independence.

Of course, this state of affairs in the child's world is changing. Children are more and more being caught up in the complex dependency matrix of global wants and fragmentary supplies that characterizes modern adult life. The worlds of work and play are separated by a gulf that grows wider and wider. Many children never see their fathers at work, much less join them in it. Young people are excluded from society's productive functions and reciprocal dependencies, both by law and union regulations.

What, then, are the kids supposed to do? Why, they are supposed to enjoy themselves, just like any clean-cut, normal, healthy, young American psychopath! Enjoy themselves—play it smart! Play it cool— enjoy themselves! If, in the midst of all this emphasis on the self for the sake of the psyche, they turn out to be delinquent, then what they need is—you guessed it—*recreational facilities*! That will bring them "the joy of self-fulfillment!"

Playgrounds are supervised by specialists. Even joy has to come in pieces. Schools, in turn, assume an increasing authority over the child's life, and then divide it up into departmentalized instruction—a further fragmentation of the child's sources of supply. In certain sectors of our culture—often called the privileged ones—even the functional relationships and reciprocal dependencies of home life are replaced by a boarding school regimen.

Yet in spite of this growing complication in the matrices of children's dependencies, and the well-publicized "overdependencies" of youth, I still believe it is clear that they remain somewhat more independent than their parents. While it is true that they are somewhat restrained by an adult society—a somewhat incoherent adult society, nowadays—and they are often disciplined legalistically rather than humanistically, still it is the young child, not the overadaptive adult, who dares try what others tacitly regard as preposterous, who is able to fulfill his wants by spontaneous play rather than by conforming to the arbitrary demands of an employer, and who would rather be guided by the best he knows than acquiesce to the shenanigans of local racketeers.

And it is the adult, not the child, who yields his independence, bit by bit, in exchange for power, until at last, when he gets the power he no longer has either the vision or the initiative to direct it. He even forgets why he wanted it in the first place. Worst of all, when the adult is confronted by leisure and its long-awaited gift of independence, he is ill at ease because it provides no obvious demands with which he can comply.

Now I am not saying that adult dependencies have to be auctioned off and distributed in this particular way; I am saying only that this is the way things have been working out. What I have described is not the elemental nature of man; it is a particular psychological invention he has cooked up for himself—no more—and, for the time being, the poor fellow is trying to survive on it. Nor am I saying that a lot of dependency is a bad thing. I am trying to show that we have a society that handles it badly, so badly, in fact, that power without imagination has become the accepted criterion of the "mature" citizen. In many sectors of our society the man who is regarded as mature is the one who is placed in influential positions because he knows just enough not to experiment with untried formulas. He may be regarded as even more mature if he prefers facts to ideas, is concretistic in his thinking, and suppresses anything that appears to be a figment of eggheaded imagination. Even among psychologists the term "mature" has come to have an honorific meaning, though it is not very clear what it means to them, other than being something characteristic of older persons.

I can go further. We do not even need to take for granted, as most people do, that maturity, in the sense of adulthood, is a good thing. Perhaps it is childhood that is the good thing. In other words, I am simply trying to analyze a cultural state of affairs from a psychological viewpoint, keeping in mind that social leadership and personal initiative are not synonymous, and that we have a society in which independence characterizes neither its adults nor its most civilized members.

What I have been saying about the en bloc exchange of independence for power, so often observed in the modern adult, can be criticized by your pointing out to me that without the implements of power, such as money, credit, professional status, control of the channels of mass communication, or mastery of the devices by which pressure can be brought to bear on people who want to get ahead and are therefore vulnerable to such things—without such implements an imaginative person is not likely to have much impact on society. That is true. Imagination without any power at all may fail to produce a thing, except, possibly, on paper, or in the minds of a few impressionable bystanders. But the contrasting alternative—power without imagination—is worse. That is simple tyranny!

Dependency as a Problem in Psychotherapy

As experienced psychotherapists, I scarcely need remind you that there is no point in the course of treatment where the psychologist gets into more trouble than when he tries to get his client to act independently and responsibly. If you are accustomed to think about this problem in psychoanalytic terms, you probably recognize it as that stage of psychotherapy where the analysis of transference begins. Those who think in other terms will define the stage differently, though generally there will be little disagreement as to the nature of the behavioral phenomena we all observe.

Often what we see is a client who wants to live his new life in the therapy room and solely with his therapist, while continuing on the outside in the same old ways. Sometimes the impatient therapist will attempt to build a fire under his clinging client to make him jump, as when fees are assessed for "therapeutic reasons." In the analytic therapies the client is confronted, in one way or another, with his childlike dependency—a dependency that was readily accepted by the therapist during the early stages of the transference relationship, but now starkly reveals itself to the therapist as evidence of his client's helplessness. It is at this point in the confrontation that the client—now driven to a state of exasperation—most often expresses aggressive hostility toward his therapist. This is also the point where the *acting-out* behavior, which most therapists unnecessarily dread, is most likely to assume abortive proportions, and where panic is most likely to appear.

To put it simply, the client is often threatened by a stark exposure of his dependency, a dependency that is not only unworthy of the adult he pretends to be, but one which threatens to render him permanently impotent. Even the classical cases of so-called homosexual panic are, I believe, essentially derived from sensing this kind of hopeless dependency. To be sure, where there is homosexuality there is likely to be some guilt involved, too. But nothing is quite so likely to panic a client as the prospect of utter dependence, regardless of whether or not there is any homosexuality involved. It can happen even when the dependency is identified with someone other than the therapist. But it is particularly likely to happen when it is the therapist on whom he feels dependent, and when it is the therapist himself who calls attention to it. Moreover, it is amplified when the client realizes that his relationship with that nourishing person is temporary, that there is no reciprocal dependency that might bind the therapist to him permanently, and that he has exposed himself not to a companion, but to a practitioner who has nothing but a professional commitment to the relationship. It is then that he becomes frantic.

A client of mine once put it this way. "There is no one I can talk to; not really. Of course, there are lots of people who want to talk, but all they give you is crap! Nobody really cares, not a single person in this whole world. Not one single person!"

"What about me?" I asked.

"Oh, yes, *you* care," she answered immediately. "But you don't count. You are *supposed* to care. It's your job."

What a tragedy it must be to realize that your best friend is a psychologist!

But why? Why should the realization of one's dependency on a therapist be so much more disturbing than the host of other dependencies that encompass one's life? Or why should this particular matter of dependency be singled out from among all the other things in the client's life that have obviously been going wrong? To answer these questions I would like to turn to theory again for a few moments.

No Cognition, No Affect, No Hostages to Classicism

I have said enough already to suggest that the problem of dependency boils down to the issue of how human wants and resources are differentiated, not *how much* dependency we have. The client who becomes alarmed over the *amount* of dependency he has transferred to his therapist is overwhelmed by the fact that he cannot move to make any decisions without running back to his couch, and by the fact, also, that his relationship with his therapist is artificial and temporary. But if this massive dependency were properly distributed and many sources of supply identified he would not feel so trapped. Of course he does not see this. The reason he cannot see it is simply because he cannot, at this point, differentiate between aspects of his own dependency. He experiences the objective of his striving as a massive yearning, not as something that can be divided up, achieved by stages, or supplied from a variety of sources.

This brings us into an area of psychology that is still held hostage to classical notions of logic. How does one identify something—either an object accessible to the senses, or the objective of his own strivings? I think we know by now that our senses do not automatically tell us what an object is, nor do they, by themselves, even tell us that it is there. Certainly senses do not discriminate one object from another; that remains a much more complicated task involving the surveying of boundaries between events and the abstraction of some similarity of one event to others.

Classical logic is based on the assumption that events present themselves to us already separated from each other and distinguishable as entities. All we have to do is take these obviously distinct events and put them together in various ways. This process is called *conceptualization*, and the ways the events end up being put together are called *concepts*.

It is commonly supposed, even by some psychologists, that these concepts—or ways of putting things together—do not really emerge until they have been symbolized in some way, usually by words. Thus, conceptualization has become known characteristically as a verbal process and theories of psychology that concern themselves with the ways things are lumped together are likely to be called cognitive theories.

But the events of this world do not march up to us single file, differentiate themselves by announcing their names, and wait to be assigned to classes, or organized into working teams charged with the responsibility of making something happen. William James said that for the child it was more like a blooming, buzzing confusion. And Herbert Spencer, viewing the matter more macroscopically, once spoke of evolution as a change from an indefinite incoherent homogeneity to a definite coherent heterogeneity. The task of man, emerging psychologically in this Twentieth Century, as never before, is to pull his innermost experience apart and then to put it together again, a task requiring both analysis and synthesis!

Now I don't think that either cognition or conceptualization provides an adequate basis for understanding how persons may best order their lives. The inadequacy of this kind of thinking is particularly apparent when we try to help a client differentiate and allocate his dependencies.

Construing: A New Look at the Psychological Reconstruction of Events

When a person makes a distinction between two objects, he does not assign one of them to a restricted class and relegate the other to a wastepaper basket containing everything else in the universe. Instead, he deals significantly and somewhat locally with both objects. Another way of saying this is to point out that one does not classify one object at a time; he distinguishes *between* that object and certain others that are relevant to the distinction, not between that object and *all* other objects. Objects not relevant to the distinction *are not psychologically* part of the context.

One thing more! When one makes a distinction, it makes no sense for him to say to himself that the two objects *differ* from each other unless, by doing so, he identifies one or the other of the objects as having some property that *links* it to additional objects that enter into the construction. Otherwise, he is saying only that "A is A and B is B," whatever that means.

So in making distinctions, whether between external objects or internal experiences, two functions are served simultaneously. Objects within one's field of attention *are separated and linked to other objects*. Now let me emphasize that this is accomplished by the same psychological act, not by two separate or successive acts. The very same process that sets one's experiences apart also puts them together in different ways. It is impossible to do one without accomplishing the other. This is a key to understanding basic psychological processes in man.

Now what I am describing is not *conceptualization*, as psychologists and logicians commonly understand that notion. It may not even be very good *logic*. But it is descriptive of the way man starts to make sense out of his blooming buzzing confusion. Instead of trying to classify this particular process loosely as one of "conception" or "cognition," let us abandon these formalistic notions altogether and designate it as the psychological process of *construing*, or of forming *personal constructs*. And I must insist that the elemental *construct* I am postulating bears little resemblance to a *concept* and that construing is a far cry from *cognition*.

It would be quite understandable, linguistic traditions being what they are, if you were to visualize construing as a verbalized or conscious act. But that need not be so. Constructs can be *preverbally symbolized* and, as far as *consciousness*—whatever that may be—is concerned, a person may have a hard time representing constructs to himself, except as raw experience. There is not necessarily anything either cognitive or affective about this kind of construing. In fact, as I have already said, I do not think that these terms are very useful to the psychologist.

To come back from theory to clinical observation again, I believe there is no better place to observe this psychological process of *construing*—particularly *preverbal construing*—than in the client who, in the midst of psychotherapy, is struggling to make new sense out of some experience that lies just beyond the reach of his semantic language. But it can be observed in some degree at even less accessible levels, levels that lie even beyond the reach of his primitive semiotic speech. This can be done if one is careful to note the transitions and repetitions of his unsignified acts. The details of just how the clinician does this lie somewhat beyond the scope of this discourse. If you are skeptical about there being such a possibility, as at this point you have every right to be, I shall have to ask you to accept the claim on faith, for the time being. The point is not absolutely essential to the further development of my argument, though it would make subsequent matters clearer if we could first agree on it. Perhaps the particular issue can be handled more satisfactorily in some other context.

The Personal Construct as a Dimension of Freedom in Human Interaction

Now we are ready to come back to dependency and the personal emancipation implied in its proper differentiation and distribution. Perhaps now it will make more sense to say that dependency is something to be handled by *construing*, not by *conceptualization*. Let us see how this works.

When I first mentioned the discriminating assignment of dependencies. I am sure that it seemed as though I were talking about some formalized sorting process involving the decision to do *this* with *that* and *something else* with the *other*. And I am sure, as clinicians, you knew that the surging experience of dependency could rarely, if ever, be handled quite so simply. The person who senses his own dependency often experiences it as a nameless craving only, a massive loneliness, or a desperate urgency to find something or be with someone. But no matter how oceanic the experience appears to be, it is, nevertheless, something that is construed—often with preverbal constructs. For every experience, to the extent that it stands out at all, stands out in terms of its similarities and distinctions. Thus the wistful person always senses that what he craves is something like . . . but not . . . He may even try to tell you what he wants in terms of words, though often he confesses later that his effort was scarcely more than an overwrought verbal gesture.

A construct is like a reference axis, a basic dimension of appraisal, often unverbalized, frequently unsymbolized, and occasionally unsignified in any manner except by the elemental processes it governs. Behaviorally, it can be regarded as an open channel of movement, and a *system of constructs* provides each man with his own personal network of action pathways, serving both to limit his movements and to open up to him passages of freedom which otherwise would be psychologically nonexistent.

The process of psychotherapy can be viewed as one of dealing with such basic psychological units of human life. Psychotherapy in its simplest form—though some would prefer not to dignify this kind of thing with the label "psychotherapy"—can be nothing more than getting a client to rattle back and forth in one of his construct slots. It has its place. Beyond it, however, there are many therapeutic possibilities, on up to the rather ambitious undertaking of replacing *core constructs*.

"Slot-Rattling" Between Dependence and Independence

Without trying to spell out all the personal subtleties in how dependency is construed, let me say simply that the construct of *dependence versus independence* is, in one form or another, a major reference axis in the lives of most people. I think we shall have no trouble agreeing on that. Because it is a major axis in most personal construct systems, it is one of those likely to be invoked when one finds himself in an untenable position and must find his way out. I trust it is clear by now that I am not saying that it has to be invoked semantically, or even semiotically. I am saying simply that it is likely to be used as an avenue of movement when things get hot. The person who has his fill of what he diagnoses as "independence" will, if he uses the dependence-independence construct, be likely to consider "dependence" as an alternative. And the person who senses that he is about to be overwhelmed by "dependence" will, if he has no time to figure out a more subtle way, be likely to dash to the other end of the first slot he sees open to him and start acting in ways that he considers to be "independent."

The worst of it is that many therapists see the problem the same way as their clients. They see dependency as a consequence of transference—which to some extent it is—and believe, therefore, that if the client's transference goes, so will his dependency. Moreover, they are keenly aware of the fact that his dependency *on them* is unproductive and cannot go on forever, and because they, too, are trapped by the syntactical proposition that independence is the alternative to dependency, urge the client to get busy and start acting "independently." Or perhaps, the therapist, now that his own psychodiagnostic curiosity has been satiated wants to talk to someone more interesting. Or, possibly, the therapist is getting tired having such a big baby to take care of.

In any case, this is one of the stages in the psychotherapeutic relationship when the client is likely to do a good deal of impulsive slot-rattling. And the reason for it may be his own construction of the alternatives to dependency—and sometimes the therapist's construction, too.

But the issue, as I tried to make clear in the earlier part of this discussion, can be drawn in a different way. Both civilization and adulthood are characterized by a great deal of dependency. The problem is to construe dependencies differentially, and also to identify and distinguish a wide range of resources which functionally match those dependencies. While it is admittedly difficult to match up complex dependencies and resources, even after they have been identified, this is still one of the essential tasks of psychotherapy.

The Economics of Dependency

It might simplify matters if we could set up a system of monetary exchange under which each of us could translate his dependencies into terms of money. Then with our pockets full of loose change we could put a coin into the slot whenever we saw something we wanted. We wouldn't have to worry about our own psychological skills in eliciting the responses we wanted.

Some people, I am sure, think this is about what civilization amounts to, or what maturity means. Why barter for anything; just buy it! To get what you want you first exchange your services for money. You may have to sacrifice some of your independence, but you will acquire power, and power is what it takes to get anything in this world. Any kind of perceptive giving—giving affection, offering sensitive support to someone in trouble at a timely moment, or personifying the fulfillment of another's hopes—if these acts do not fit into the economic scheme, they are old-fashioned and waste of time.

If people don't like you, subsidize them! If the waiter doesn't think you are important enough, tip him! If you want to have a lot of friends, don't waste time getting acquainted with individuals, throw a cocktail party! If you want some tender affection, buy a mink coat. No! No! *Not for yourself*! And if you don't know for sure what you want, but, whatever it is, you want it awful bad, look in the yellow pages—for a psychologist! He already has a pretty good idea of what it is you want, and he has the professional "know-how" to get it for you "wholesale."

Perhaps I should be generous enough to include psychiatrists in this image of the commercialized erogenator, since I seem to be implying the usurpation of the long-established prerogatives of an older profession—the oldest. But this lecture is about clinical psychology—which has quite enough perplexities of its own—not about psychiatry, so I shall not presume to inflict my remarks on our brethren of the medical persuasion. Anyhow, quite apart from the prior claims of the ancient ego-healing arts, medical or otherwise, the idea of an economy based on the universal convertibility of psychological wants and supplies into a pocketable medium of exchange is not altogether new.

Well, as you probably suspect, I don't think this is a very good way to run a railroad. And as responsible psychotherapists, you don't either! It is just as important to differentiate the dependencies of those upon whom you, in turn, depend, as it is to purchase what you yourself have found essential. The differential understanding of others' dependencies also is a *construing task*—in the sense I have developed the notion of *construing* in the earlier parts of this discussion.

But there are some differences between the two tasks. One's own preverbal construing plays a much less obvious part in differentiating the dependencies of another person, although it still is involved in some degree, as any sensitive therapist knows. On the other hand, the task of construing others is made more difficult by the particular kind of psychological training most of us have had. So let me talk about that very important matter for awhile.

Deterministic Thinking as an Obstacle to Understanding

The science of the last century has gone in for determinism in a big way, as everybody knows. What may not be quite so apparent to us is the extent to which this kind of thinking has affected our culture and biased the way we try to get along with each other. Now I don't want to become embroiled in a criticism of scientific determinism to the extent that we will all forget about our topic, and especially it would be unwise to stir up the scientific dogmatists so near the end of the lecture. So let us avoid the issue of whether or not determinism actually exists or whether it is a good thing and concentrate simply on what has happened to us in the course of our thinking about each other in terms of present-day scientific determinism.

Simply stated, scientific determinism is the belief that one event is bound to lead to another. Put your finger on that event and you are well on your way to the prediction and control of what ensues. Applied to human affairs this means that you look to see what antecedents are necessary and sufficient to make such matters predictable. Applied to psychology this means that you look for the stimulus that accounts for man's response. Punch him here and he jumps there. Tickle her here and she—well! And all that sort of thing!

I scarcely need to point out that this is a strictly manipulative approach to human relations. There is no particular point in trying to understand a child if every time you give him candy he does what he is supposed to do. And if, whenever you buy something for your wife, she caresses you and fixes an extra nice supper, what else could you conceivably want to know about her? If each time you make a loan to a Latin American country, it votes with you in the United Nations, who can possibly say that you don't understand Latin Americans? It's all very scientific and it's psychological, too. And this is the way it generally works out.

But *how well* does it work out? How often it is we hear a man, who appears to be successful in handling his employees, complain that he is not really wanted at home. All his family expects of him is "financial support." His children expect candy and agree among themselves that all they need to do to satisfy the old geezer is avoid crossing him. His wife expects gifts from him rather than understanding, and she has found that all she needs to do to make him perform is prepare his favorite meal and rub the back of his neck with the tips of her fingers—while she occupies her own mind with a romantic story in the *Ladies Home Journal*. While all this scientifically valid psychology is being practiced in the home, probably both of them have been seeing psychotherapists for some time now, and the children have likely been placed in some good school, chosen because of its staff of well-trained counselors.

But now suppose—just suppose—the prevailing psychology of our times was not a stimulus-response psychology or even a psychology of biographical determinants. Suppose it was instead a psychology that concerned itself with how men construe the world around them, and particularly with how they construe each other. Suppose this was not only the psychology employed by psychologists, but the psychology employed by all of us. That is to say, it would represent the psychological outlook of our culture and times. What difference would it make?

First of all, it would be a good idea to identify two levels of construing. The first would be concerned with events and with men treated as events. By that I mean we would construe men's behaviors rather than their outlooks. Another person would be simply another moving object on our horizon. This is one level of construing.

But then suppose there were a second level of construing. This would be concerned with construing the constructs of other men. Instead of making our own sense out of what others did we would try to understand what sense they made out of what they did. Instead of putting together the events in their lives in the most scientifically parsimonious way, we would ask how they put things together, regardless of whether their schemes were parsimonious or not.

Construing as a Basis for Interdependency

It is this second level of construing that opens the door to the reciprocal handling of dependency. We have already seen that dependency in our society is not so much a matter of the failure of independence as it is the failure to discriminate wants and resources and to allocate the one in proper relation to the other. We have seen, moreover, that where human interdependence is involved, the breakdown often comes when each person employs a psychology that tries to get what he wants from the other without being concerned with the other's outlook. If there is any reciprocity it is likely to be a simple transaction in which each person tries to give the other explicitly what he *says* he wants without trying *to understand, what it is like to have such a want.*

But now let us apply this second level of construing to interpersonal relationships. This would not put the interdependent relationship between two persons on the basis of a simple transactional exchange of services. It would not be enough for each to give the other what he asked or appeared to need. Far more important than the transaction, or the exchange, would be the framework of understanding within which it took place. Even if one person did not get what he wanted from the other, the fact that his outlook was understood by the other, that the other could see what it was like to have such wants, and that the other can agree that, from the same point of view, he, too would experience a similar yearning—all this is likely to provide greater security in the dependency relationship than getting literally what was asked for.

It is because the psychotherapist often seems to be the one person in the world who has this kind of understanding that so many members of our society think they would rather associate with psychologists than people. And when one confides, whether to a psychologist or to a stranger, it is often with the momentary hope that here at last is a person who is more interested in outlooks than in payoffs. It is in the moment of disillusionment, when it becomes clear that, like everyone else, the stranger and the psychologist both regard human relationships as simple matters of put and take, the confiding person comes to regret the stupid mistake he has made, and he continues on his wistful way. After further encounters of this sort he may continue to confide, not because he has any real hope, but because he knows no other way to pursue his quest for a human relationship.

Fortunately, not all clients experience disillusionment with their therapists, for often psychologists are better than their psychological upbringing would lead you to expect. Moreover, as the therapeutic encounter comes to be recognized as a fertile soil in which basic psychological ideas can germinate, rather than as a field of applied science with a little status attached, the more we may hope that the psychological theories of the future will have significance for all human beings, their longings, and the way they trust and depend upon each other. A profession that does not deal intimately with man's dependencies, as one does deal intimately with them in psychotherapy, cannot ever hope to understand the undertow of psychological distress that flows beneath a troubled society.

Is it only that Society has Become Specialized?

Is what I have said merely that society has become intricately specialized and this is bad? If so, then you have heard this lecture before—many times! But there is a good deal more to my thesis than this familiar sociological cliché.

It is true that our *society* has become a vast complex of specialized *services*. But let us look at it from the standpoint of the *individual*—just as I have been urging throughout my remarks. Looking at the supply of services only, it is clear enough that each individual plays his part by serving in only one or a few of the many specialties that must be articulated in an organized social economy.

But when we turn from the *services* a person renders to the *wants* he has, we find a contrasting state of affairs. Instead of each individual coming to specialize in what he wants, he is likely to do the reverse and extend his dependency over an ever wider range of demands. Thus we have *a psychological condition* which is much more problematical than the well-known *sociological condition*. What the individual wants from others is broad, complex, and undifferentiated, but what he has to offer them in return is narrow, concrete, and specific. The outcome is a society in which a lot of miscellany is available, but few people are able to find in all the clutter what they most earnestly crave.

Part of the solution lies in a reconsideration of the problem of dependency as experienced by the individual man. If, instead of trying to be "independent," he can differentiate his wants by construing them, so that what now looms up as a vague longing can be partly replaced by specific objectives, he will have a better chance of allocating his dependencies appropriately among the complex resources of a specialized society. This is a worthwhile psychological undertaking. It is one in which the clinical psychologist can help on a case-to-case basis.

But such an undertaking, I am sure, will not be enough. The man of the future, just as men of the past, is likely to find himself beset by mysterious yearnings, no matter how many of his previous wishes have been shaped into specific demands. He will continue always, in some degree, to depend in massive undifferentiated ways upon particular persons who share his most intimate life. This is to say he will still seek someone in whom to confide and the desires he cannot comprehend. But how can he hope to find anyone who will listen to him for long if he cannot listen in return? For this kind of mutual understanding both he and his confidant must be prepared to employ a psychology of personal constructs through which each may direct his attention broadly and sensitively to how the other construes his world, and not limit himself merely to the motives and stimuli that account for miscellaneous acts.

Conclusion of an Unpsychologistic Discourse

Now we come to the conclusion of what was intended to be an *unpsychologistic* discourse. In whom confide? On whom depend for what? I have tried to answer these questions in terms of a current society which unrealistically regards simple independence as the solution to all personal dependency problems, and which fails to recognize the need for an everyman's psychology that will accept a great amount of dependency and look for ways of allocating it. Such a new psychology is one based on the *process of construing*—which has practically nothing to do with conceptualization or cognition. Moreover, in a society where this kind of psychology directs attention primarily to the understanding of outlooks rather than the manipulation of behaviors, and to human striving rather than transactional exchanges of services, it should be possible to find suitable persons in whom to confide and on whom to depend.

Now, may I point out that, with the exception of the notion of *construing*—which I warned you would be my only technicality in tonight's discussion—I have spent the evening talking about psychology without resorting to psychological conventions. I have not invoked either stimuli or psychodynamics to explain human experience. And if, during the course of this discussion, you found yourself occasionally mumbling such words to yourself, I can only say that I did my best to stop you. My, it certainly is hard to give up bad habits! But—I understand! I even had the same outlook myself—once!

44

Europe's Matrix of Decision[1,2]

There is something you all should know at the outset of this paper: I have no use for the concept of motivation. Professor Jones was well aware of this last summer when he invited me to come here. We were having coffee together in Copenhagen—at least I remember it as coffee, although Dr. Jones says it was tea. I believe our wives were with us at the time. He doesn't remember that either. At any rate, he remembers that he invited me to come here. At the time, we both found the idea of my having to talk in public about motivation highly amusing. He probably still thinks it is funny, but, after the toil of preparing this paper, I am not so sure I still do. Nevertheless, here I am.

Since that conversation I have pondered on a number of things, including the whimsical possibility of writing such a convincing paper that you would be moved to change the topic of this annual Nebraska conclave to "Snakes in Ireland." How much more to the point it would be if the topic were something like this: "What Is Everybody up to These Days?" or "What in the World Is Mankind about To Do to Itself?" or perhaps this one: "Isn't There Any Other Way of Coping with a Problem Besides Lying Down and Being Treated for It?" A good short title could, I think, be lifted from Hans Fallada's 1932 novel, *Little Man, What Now?* "The Nebraska Symposium on *What Now*"—not bad!

Let us be honest with ourselves—isn't this the persistent question we hope to answer by all our talk about motivation: How can we forecast human behavior when it is left on its own? Not that this is a particularly well-posed question either, for I am sure you could argue, on the one hand, that human behavior is never on its own, or, on the other, that it is always on its own. Nevertheless, what we are trying to get at are the internal predicates of behavior, as contrasted with those external predicates we can more clearly and comfortably envision, such as stimuli or the inescapable logic we assume to be inherent in the way things are.

What it Means to Understand Men in Terms of Their Constructs

This paper is essentially a continuation of one I presented in the spring of 1957 as part of the *Syracuse University Symposium on the Assessment of Human Motives*. In that paper—which was published, along with the other contributions, under the editorship of Gardner Lindzey, and is now available in a paperback edition (Kelly, 1958)—I stated my theoretical position under the title, "Man's Construction of His Alternatives."

In my present paper I want to talk about the application of the theory to a specific international problem; the European man's construction of his alternatives. In this way I hope, not only to show how the theory works, but also to throw some light on an important substantive problem. You see, I have brazenly gone ahead with my distortion of the topic of this symposium and am speaking as if it were already "The Nebraska Symposium on *What Now*."

Theoretical Springboard

Before I launch into today's topic, however, I had better sketch some of the more important features of my theoretical position. Motivation is an invented construct. It cropped up a long time ago as a by-product of certain pre-Socratic assumptions about the fundamental nature of things. Once upon a time, there was a division of opinion between the Eleatic School of Parmenides, which assumed that fundamentally objects were solid and inert, and Heraclitus, who wanted to start with the assumption that change was the one inescapable fact of

[1] Paper presented at the 10th. Annual Nebraska Symposium on Motivation, Spring, 1962. First published as Kelly, G.A. (1962). Europe's matrix of decision. In M.R. Jones (Ed.), *Nebraska Symposium on Motivation 1962* (pp. 83–123). University of Nebraska Press. Republished in Kalekin-Fishman, D., & Walker, B.M. (Eds.). (1996). *The construction of group realities: Culture, society, and personal construct theory* (pp. 27–63). Krieger. Published here by permission of University of Nebraska Press, who hold the copyright.

[2] The experiences upon which this paper is based were made possible by a grant to the writer and his wife from the Human Ecology Fund.

Collected Papers of the Pioneer of Constructivist Psychology: George A. Kelly, First Edition. Edited by David A. Winter and Nick Reed.

existence. Neither side won the argument outright, but, as far as history is concerned, Heraclitus came out the worse. Atomism, which was a sort of compromise worked out later by Democritus and others, eventually caught hold and, off and on, has pretty much held its own ever since.

The crux of the matter is that if you start with the assumption that whatever the world is made of must be inherently inert, you then have to go ahead and guess that it changes only as force is applied to it. Here you are, saddled with two distinct constructs; objects, and the force that makes them move. As long as you are a materialist—and nearly everybody is, in spite of what he says—there is not much else you can do except think in terms of primary objects, such as the atoms of Democritus, being pushed around by secondary forces.

Apply this basic thinking to physiology, and you have the notion of a body being actuated by energy; apply it to psychology, and you come up with the notion of a person either being propelled by "motives" in spite of himself, or stuck tight in his fundament. As I say, there is just not much else you can do about it, unless you are willing to go back to about 420 B.C. and start thinking all over.

Well, I suggested in the Syracuse Symposium that we should go back and start over. Suppose we began by assuming that the fundamental thing about life is that it goes on. It isn't that something *makes* it go on; the going on *is the thing itself.* It isn't that motives *make* man come alert and do things; his alertness is an aspect of his very being. Talking about activating motives is simply redundant talky-talk, for once you've got a human being on your hands, you already have alertness and movement, and sometimes a lot more of it than you know what to make of.

There is another habit of thinking that Western Man more or less fell into fortuitously. As long as he was assuming that human beings are propelled by motives, it seemed reasonable to imagine also that the motives give direction to the movement; if they push, they must push in some direction. Now if we could only find out what is pushing, we could predict where everybody is going, as well as how soon he would get there.

So for two thousand years we have been looking for the thing that is doing the pushing, and often trying to define it by the directions it pushes. We haven't found it yet; naturally we haven't found it, but during the centuries we have built up a tremendous lexicon of push and pull terms. Even our language has fallen heir to the design of our quest, and we have committed ourselves to a grammar of motives (Burke, 1945) that controls our speech and channels our thinking about human behavior. Now we can scarcely say anything about what a person has done, or is about to do, without using a language form that implies that he has been pushed into it. We are even inclined to think that way about our own behavior, and when we do, it usually means we are in trouble.

But there is another way of accounting for the direction man's behavior takes, besides assuming that it must be imparted by the same forces that make him behave in the first place. We can start by saying that man copes with his environment by construing it into similarities and contrasts. It is not necessary to assume that this is a verbal or conscious undertaking. The associations and distinctions can be made at a very low level of awareness, as psychological research on reflexes has amply demonstrated.

The Personal Construct

The unit form of this construing can be designated as the *construct*, an abstraction of the linkage and differentiation which, inside each man's own tight little world, constitutes a generalized pair of alternatives. The construct, being an abstraction, can be picked up, carried around, and fitted to a great variety of circumstances. If it has a verbal handle on it, so much the better; it is easier to transport. A system of constructs constitutes a ready-made format for future thinking, and for lower order processes as well. To have constructed such a system means that a person has somewhat prepared himself to cope with all sorts of strange things that have not happened yet. But without it he is not free to think, to act, or even to get the gist of what is going on.

When a person can apply a construct to his own behavior, consciously or unconsciously, it opens for him a channel of choice along which he is more or less free to move. But without such a channel his freedom has no dimension, no extent; he cannot even strive toward objectives, nor can he hope for things to come, nor long for something out of reach, for he has no idea of what he is missing, nor even any sense of missing at all. He can no more move about in lines he has not construed than he can use the fourth dimension to side-step a locked door. This is why, throughout the history of the world, men seeking what they supposed to be freedom have struggled heroically to change their masters, but have made only feeble efforts to loosen their chains.

Get some notion of what a person's system of channels is like and you have a rough sketch of the network within which he is prepared to exercise his human right to freedom. Observe the shrinkage of a man's system, and you find yourself a witness to a gradual human enslavement, enslavement without barbed wire or coercion. It is this enslavement by atrophy of ideas that we sometimes call institutionalized behavior. We are usually thinking about mental hospitals, prisons, and orphans' asylums when we use the term, but the same kind of enslavement can occur in societies and in nations. Understanding a man's construct system is, then, the first, and most important, step in understanding what is commonly known by that vaguest of psychological terms, "motivation." And it is also the first step in comprehending the actual extent of a man's freedom. I was talking about this first step when I presented my Syracuse paper on "Man's Construction of His Alternatives."

Having construed his alternatives, a man still has to make choices between them if he is to commit himself to any undertaking. As a matter of fact, there are two kinds of choices he must make; the selection from his repertory of the most relevant construct to apply to his circumstances, and his choice between the pair of alternatives which that construct presents. There are some psychological principles that govern these choices, but there is no need to expound them here.

This concludes the review of what I said at Syracuse University. It was a theoretical statement, and it was my effort to extricate our thinking from the underlying assumptions upon which the notion of motivation is based, as well as from the deeply ingrained notion of motivation itself.

A Method of Studying Attitudes

This kind of theorizing leads us next, as all good theorizing should, to a methodology, and from methodology to substance, all the while being subject to successive revisions in the light of its outcomes. There are many ramifications of the methodology I am about to describe; ramifications in psychotherapy, in teaching, in negotiation, and in psychometrics. But let me confine myself to one area only; the theory's methodological implications in the appraisal of attitudes having international implications.

It is customary, in studying attitudes, to focus upon certain parameters. We may examine the object or the class of objects embraced by the attitude. We may take account of the attitude's generality across a wide variety of objects. We may judge its consonance with the rest of the attitudinal system and its stability from moment to moment. We may estimate its tendency to express itself in overt action. We may attempt to measure its intensity by estimating the amount of effort that is likely to be mobilized in its behalf. We may note its rigidity in the face of negating experience; and we may appraise its rational status, or look to see how deeply it is rooted in unconscious processes.

All these approaches are similar in one respect; they assume that an attitude is a one-sided affair—a man likes blondes or he does not. The attitude presumably has to do with blondes, and blondes only, which, I am sure some of you will agree, is a pretty one-sided way of looking at things. What in the world does it mean, merely to say that a man likes blondes? Does it mean he likes them rather than hates them, that he likes them better than brunettes, or does it mean he likes them better than doing his own cooking? We suppose there is some dimension along which differentiation is being made, but unless we look for the direction in which the opposite pole lies, we cannot tell what the bewildered fellow has on his mind.

A man says he despises capitalism. Does this mean he is a communist? Or does it mean he favors an economic democracy analogous to the political democracy that was achieved in Western Europe after centuries of struggle and bloodshed? Or can we stretch his statement to mean, on the contrary, that he opposes all forms of government by consent of the governed?

We don't really know what the statement means to the man who made it until we know the issue at stake. One of us might say that, in order to make such a remark, he would have to be a totalitarian of some sort—either a communist or a fascist—because it seems so downright certain that those are the only logical alternatives to capitalism. At least, the fellow must be against human dignity, because we are convinced the capitalism he despises is the natural expression of any society where personal liberties are respected. We may be right, of course—perfectly right; but let us keep in mind that these are the similarities and contrasts of our personal construct system, not necessarily of his. It is by such channels that our flow of thought is facilitated and constrained. But his intellectual efforts may be just as inescapably guided by the ruts worn deep in his way of life, even though they may seem utterly irrational to us.

Personal construct theory approaches attitudes by examining issues. It finds these issues, not so much in man's circumstances, as in his way of making sense out of what surrounds him. Purposeful behavior is a matter of setting up alternatives among his surroundings and, when the time comes, choosing between them. This is not an altogether novel approach; Mark Twain, in a behavioristic description of an elephant written long before John B. Watson's time, once made use of it (Clemens, 1896)[3].

Seeking Access to an Alien Dimension of Life

How can we use this approach of personal construct theory, in place of the motivational approach, to understand our friend who says he despises capitalism? Before we make the attempt, it is only fair to warn you that it is always hazardous to look at things through another person's glasses, whether he is a Russian, an Eichmann, a Negro, a psychotic patient, or one's own child—perhaps most of all, one's own child. Looking through glasses that are not your own can permanently affect your eyesight. It is much safer to attribute the behavior of other people to their *Motivation*—much safer. Now, you've been warned!

Let us suppose this man we are talking about is a Georgian, a citizen of that ancient little country, now one of the Soviet Republics, that lies just south of the main ridge of the Caucasus Mountains. When he talks about capitalism he undoubtedly has a vivid picture in mind of the privately controlled economic power of pre-revolutionary Georgian landowners—called princes—who held that it was a waste of time and money to teach farmers to read and write.

There is a painting in the world-famed Hermitage Museum in Leningrad that gives poignant meaning to this Georgian's thoughts about capitalism. It depicts a boy in ragged clothes listening furtively at the crack of a school room door. This picture has deep and far-reaching

[3] "He will leave Bibles to eat bricks, he will leave bricks to eat bottles, he will leave bottles to eat clothing, he will leave clothing to eat cats, he will leave cats to eat oysters, he will leave oysters to eat ham, he will leave ham to eat sugar, he will leave sugar to eat pie, he will leave pie to eat potatoes, he will leave potatoes to eat bran, he will leave bran to eat hay, he will leave hay to eat oats, he will leave oats to eat rice, for he was mainly raised on it. There is nothing whatever that he will not eat but European butter, and he would eat that if he could taste it."

significance to the people of Eastern Europe. It would probably mean something quite different to an American who imagines the only normal response of a boy to school is to play hooky.

The picture is not only symbolic; it is accurately representative. I talked to a man who, as a child, had done just that in his native country of Georgia. But he was soon caught in his delinquency, and the door was slammed in his face. Some time after, his father, touched by the boy's disappointment, managed to save back a sack of grain from the family's meager food supplies, and, taking his boy by the hand, carried the grain to the house of the prince. He told the prince the sack of grain was all he had and he asked if, in return for it, his son could be taught to read and write. The prince called the boy to his desk, showed him how to write his name, and then said, "There, young man; that is all the reading and writing you will ever need to know."

The prince kept the grain, possibly as an object lesson in sound economics. Indeed, one must admit that not many people would consider education a proper form of *capital* investment, particularly for one's last sack of grain. This is not to overlook the fact that there are always some people, even in our own country, who will yell for unrealistic expenditures on education—right up to the last Cadillac.

There was, until a few years ago, a somewhat less defensible practice which land-owners in that part of the world were able to enforce by means of their private control of the capital resources of the agricultural community. Brides were required to sleep with the land-owner before they could be claimed by their husbands. This was not quite as bad as it sounds. There was a way out for the groom, if he happened to be an enterprising young man. He was always perfectly free to give up his farm and look for another landlord—one whom he would be more willing to have sleep with his bride, or one who could be bought off for a price within his means. If he were a really imaginative young fellow he could look for a bride with whom nobody would want to sleep; then he could keep his home, his farm, and have a chaste wife besides.

I don't want to leave the wrong impression about Georgia either; this sort of practice was discontinued after the communist revolution and the advent of a man greatly admired in those parts, a fellow by the name of Joseph Stalin. Moreover, none of this has much to do with American capitalism, for it is obviously not the sort of practice that many American landlords could enforce and survive long enough to brag about it. I am only describing the system of capitalistic free enterprise my Georgian friend has in mind when he says he "despises capitalism." Moreover, I suspect this glimpse of the world through his glasses helps us understand what makes him tick better than would any concept of motivation. But as I warned you before, such surreptitious peeks are likely to affect our own eyesight; so it might be just as well if you forgot what I have just told you.

My other friend, the one who wanted to learn to read and write, also made out pretty well in the end, which goes to show what initiative and gumption will do. He took advantage of the confusion of World War I to escape to America. He is now an author and sculptor, and his writings are full of warmth, humor, and love of this country, with none of the bitterness one might expect (Papashvily & Papashvily, 1945, 1946a, 1946b). He is also a great hero back in Georgia, where we shared some experiences together during a recent visit. His American-born wife, in speaking the next morning of one reception they were given the day before, said it was the first time she had been kissed by a whole town.

A Prelude to Action

The other young men of Georgia also took matters in their own hands. My wife and I visited one of their schools a few months ago, along with the friends I have been talking about. We saw the emphasis upon the fundamentals of education—mathematics, languages, science, etc., just as you have heard it reported. One of the men teachers, overwhelmed at meeting the famous Georgian-American author, whose books he had read, embraced him and said, "You are the only person who ever made me cry."

The next day we visited one of the Pioneer Palaces and saw something of the program that provides for the hours, the days, and the months when young people are not in school. Here, in a program as extensive, as competently staffed, and more lavishly equipped than that of the schools, we saw what would be called "frills" in American education. Some observers have come back from the Soviet Union dismissing the Pioneer program as "something like the Boy Scouts." The comparison is preposterous, and the inference, so frequently made, that Soviet education is confined to good old fundamentals, is completely out of line with the facts.

I am still trying to illustrate the application of personal construct theory, in contrast to motivational theory, to the understanding of human behavior. I am trying to sketch a personal dimension of thought which, simply because it is personal and bears on immediate circumstances, represents so clearly the channel of choice for millions of people in Eastern Europe. The channel has to do with education and, strange as it may seem, I think you will agree it also has to do with the dignity of man, or perhaps you will at least agree that it has to do with the dignity of brides. I am inviting you to examine this principal construct dimension, not from our own point of view or as if it were the channel of choice which must govern our own actions, but from the point of view of those whose behavior we hope to understand.

Look at it. On the one end is the private control of capital and on the other, communism—the first step toward which is regarded as state capitalism, the present stage of the Soviet society. I am sure the line between these poles will remain the visible channel of choice until the people of that country are able to conceptualize their circumstances along other dimensions.

Can we "motivate" these people to go in other directions? I think not. Put pressure on them, put them under extreme conditions of need, jam their families into one-room apartments, deny them Cadillacs, Zims or Volgas, even take away their spare sacks of grain to support the schools, and you will not shoo them like a flock of chickens into our form of society. They will only sigh and say, "Times are hard, food is scarce, and something may be rotten in the administration. Still misfortune has not completely overtaken us; our children are being educated and our wives are respected. Perhaps we will have to go back to the days of 'capitalism'—but it hasn't happened yet. And anyone who wants to drive us back had better remember Stalingrad!" (Or would they say "Volgograd" now?)

Nothing that I have said should be taken to mean that the Soviet empire is ideologically monolithic. To be sure, one finds a remarkable internalization of the ideological controls, to use Don Marquis' phrase for it. People actually do think in the grooves marked out for them, certainly to a much larger extent than do the people of Czechoslovakia, where there are memories of a different kind of society. There are, again, some other dimensions of Georgian thought which permit a vision of the future not approved by Moscow. Nevertheless, whatever those other dimensions are, the one channel I have described is crystal clear to Georgians and is a key to their behavior.

The Construct as a Daily Way of Life

In delineating this Georgian construct I have dwelt mostly on community behavior, that is to say, the forms of behavior that are either articulated outright by group consensus or simply perpetuated by tacit compliance. But what does the construct mean at the level of everyday "spontaneous" behavior—if I may use a familiar, but relatively meaningless, motivational term. Or, to put it this way, which is better, does this construct have anything to say about what people do when they haven't bothered to go through any complicated process of making up their minds to it? If it does not have anything to do with such everyday individual matters, then our reading of this dimension of Soviet life is probably academic and does not meet the validity criteria that personal construct theory requires. Let us see.

Before entering the Soviet Union my wife and I were more or less aware, as 1 suppose most Americans are, of the Union's vigorous efforts to put education on a broad popular base, one that is even broader than our own, and not only to permit, but to insure the advanced education of every capable student, regardless of his age, his financial resources, or his formal educational credentials. We knew that some observers have questioned the breadth of this popular base—apart from the fact that the Soviets do not as yet have the total resources comparable to those America has mobilized for the support of education—and we pressed to find out what the restrictions might be. Our observations were mixed and inconclusive on this point, but that the base is very broad, there can be little doubt[4]. I need not go into the detailed ramifications of this complex matter, and besides, they involve dimensions of Soviet life that I cannot, at the present time, unfold to my own satisfaction.

One other fact, which is not so generally known, is that each year the Soviet Union publishes about four times as many new books as the United States—the next most productive country in the publication of this form of literature. With this tremendous publication list they not only seek to satisfy the voracious demand of Soviet citizens for serious reading material, but they make much needed educational materials available for underdeveloped countries. That these educational materials have a communist slant and put the Soviet Union in an unrealistically favorable light, goes without saying. But, more important than this, they constitute tangible evidence abroad of the

[4] The American Embassy in Moscow interprets the recent policy changes requiring applicants for university admission to have had two years of work experience—except in fields such as science and engineering technology where personnel shortages exist, or in cases of unusual scholarship—to mean that ideological tests are to be used more ruthlessly in screening students. The student strike at the University of Leningrad in support of the Hungarian uprising, caused Moscow no little concern. Still, outside of the disappearance of the leaders of the strike, presumably to spend the rest of their lives raising corn in areas of Asia where rainfall is at a minimum, and trying to remedy the chaotic condition of Soviet agriculture, no conspicuous measures were taken to enforce ideological conformity among students. There may have been, however, more gradual and subtle measures taken that I do not know about.

Regarding restriction of the popular base of higher education, other reports suggest a quiet but systematic elimination of Jewish students from the universities. We ourselves saw nothing that would confirm these reports, and such information as we were able to infer suggested that the main restriction might be on somewhat different grounds. For example, the promise of occupational productivity within the socialistic system, particularly in skills believed to be underdeveloped, did seem to be extensively used in selecting students. This selection restriction roughly corresponds to our own preferential support for athletes who show promise of making sports page headlines, and for engineering students who have committed their services to large industrial organizations. It was amusing to see how some students circumvent these preferential restrictions, just as they do in this country.

There is nothing that quite seems to parallel our recent large-scale movement toward restricting higher education to students of more than average means, through the sharp increases of student fees in state-supported universities—measures which are intentionally undertaken—and through our growing imbalance of financial resources between the lower third and the upper two-thirds of our population—a development our society has not yet faced up to. The closest Soviet parallel appears to be the class preference given to the children of "workers." This preference was originally said to be justified as a correction constant for the cultural decrement in their measures of intellectual competence. But the term "worker" has come to have a rather limited and meretricious meaning in Soviet society. It is used to refer particularly to factory workers and to those officials who represent themselves as identified with them. Thus what was once an equalizing factor in student selection appears to have become a distorting factor. Whether this distortion is as great as our own growing distortion, which tends to restrict higher education opportunities to the economically more privileged families, is hard to tell. In any case, I suspect the source of their distortion may be harder to dislodge than ours, for theirs has a built-in feature, via communist dogma, that up to now we have not had in our concept of democracy.

What will happen, however, if we decide that our society does not have *democracy* as its central concept, as some leaders are now suggesting, but has instead, *capitalism*, or something of that sort, as its central theme, is another matter. However defensible private capitalism may be, or how broadly we define it, there is nothing in the concept that is likely to serve as grounds for making education equally available to all. We shall have to see how the American society's image of itself develops during the next ten years. And it will be equally important to watch for new developments in Soviet society, too. Such is the central psychological significance of the cold war.

Soviet Union's commitment to universal education, free of cost to all persons. This commitment stands very close to the center of the Soviet system, more so, I am now convinced, than does any such commitment in our society.

We visited a bookstore in Leningrad a few days after entering the Soviet Union. It was a beehive of activity. Indeed, it was the only instance of merchandising we saw where the demand appeared to be in excess of the supply. We saw no such throngs in the gastronomes—grocery shops—in the department stores, or even at the theater box offices. In the bookstore we observed the types of books being bought. They were serious books, not murder mysteries or comic books such as one sees displayed at most American bookstands. There were books on mathematics, electronics, history, political science, economics, and geography. The bookstores have a practice of accepting used books as partial payment for new ones, with liberal trade-in allowances. Thus it appears likely that a considerable proportion of the new books published each year are read by more than one reader[5].

It was not an uncommon sight on a Moscow bus, at the end of a working day, to see begrimed laborers reading technical books which, if the illustrations I could see over the men's shoulders were any indication, were quite advanced. When we were in the Moscow airport waiting for the jet plane to take us to Tbilisi, news arrived that astronaut Gagarin was in orbit. During the flight to Tbilisi we received frequent bulletins, concluding with the bulletin that he had safely landed. There was applause and excited conversation, both in the Moscow airport and on the plane. But I noticed that between the flurries of activity two of the men in front of us returned to the books they were reading. One of the books had illustrations of complicated wiring diagrams and pages of mathematical equations. I couldn't see the other one.

Now here we have some observational evidence of the viability of the construct we have been tracing in such detail. The pursuit of learning is not merely a legalized opportunity or a perfunctory ritual, it is a daily fact—a way of life demonstrated by individuals left to the impulse of the moment. It represents a dimension of human freedom which is used, not merely talked about.

Nations and the Shape of Things to Come

In terms of these everyday goings-on one cannot help but draw comparisons between the meaning of education in the Soviet Union and its meaning to those of us who take it for granted, or who take as little of it as is necessary for a college degree. There is no question but that education is a tenet of our political philosophy and an important fact of our economy. It has been so ever since a century ago when Horace Mann uttered his dictum that "Education is the chief defense of the nation," and was accused of being a communist for his advocation of free public schools. But in addition to this formalized position in America, what part does education play in the way we live? What does it mean, for example, to have our universities rated in terms of their football teams instead of their scholarship?[6] What does it mean in terms of such little things as what one reads on the way home from work, the choice of a television program, or the conversation between two young people in the corner drug store?

To be a valid element in a decision matrix a construct must also have visible implications for the future. So let us ask that question, too. Does all this fascination for book learning betray a weakness in Soviet moral fiber and a fatal inability to envision the solid, neon-lighted values of our God-fearing economy; or is it a portent of unfamiliar things to come? And what on earth do you suppose will be the outcome of another thirty years of their society going their way, and our society going ours? These are not detached, academic speculations. They are brutally realistic questions that should not require too much imagination to answer. And, to come back to our central theme, I don't believe these are questions that can be satisfactorily answered in motivational terms.

At this point I feel impelled to reiterate a point which may already be clear enough. I have been talking about one construct dimension of the decision matrix of the Soviet way of life. It is an important one, but not the only one. While it provides a clear enough picture of a road along which Soviet society may now march or retreat, there are other constructs which are important because they channel behavior in other directions, and some that are important because of their absence. A more accurate statement of how the Soviet citizen of the future will live, or what the comparative positions of Soviet and American cultures will be thirty years from now, would certainly require the delineation of more than one of the components of the decision matrices within which the two societies function.

The Dread of Understanding Man Too Well

Now let me do something else, while certain thoughts are fresh in our minds. You will recall that earlier in this paper I invited your attention to the fact that the understanding of human behavior could be threatening. Because of this I suspected that we often employ motivational terms in order to manage human behavior without having to understand it. I suggested, furthermore, that when one comes to understand another person, there are likely to be irreversible changes in his own personality.

[5] This was in Leningrad, of course, which is still Russia's "window to the West." Probably no other city in the Union is as interested in the horizons that lie beyond the drabness that encompasses its daily life.

[6] This is not to imply that sports fail to play an important part in Soviet life. One of our group discussions at the Psychological Institute of the Georgian Academy of Sciences had to be cut short because of the intersectional football game scheduled that afternoon. Crowds had begun to gather at the stadium in the late morning, just as they do in an American university town. The Republic of Georgia was playing the Republic of Lithuania, one of the Baltic countries overrun by the Soviet Union and lying some 1300 miles to the northwest. But sports are sports and not a dog-wagging tail of higher education. Nor does one sense the tension when sports are discussed that he senses when the subject of universal education is brought up by a "capitalist" from America.

It is this imminence of change within ourselves that gives the experience of threat its peculiar feeling quality. There is the sense that our faith is about to be undermined, as, indeed it may well be undermined. For any bold venture into human understanding leaves the wreckage of sacred ideas in its wake. Once we are caught up in this enterprise, the immediate prospect of what we are about to witness may even make us angry, or, if we must avoid the raw experience of anger at any cost, it may lead us to dismiss what we see as merely some evidence of obscure "motivation."

And here is the crucial point of what I am trying to do at this juncture of my discussion of decision matrices: If I have portrayed vividly enough the Soviet construct of private capitalism *versus* individual opportunity, some of you will personally have experienced the kind of threat I have been talking about—experienced it right here and now. Perhaps some of you found yourselves apprehensive in the face of the threat of a new understanding, or was it a shadow of despair that crossed your mind? Possibly some of you were angry at what you interpreted to be my lack of faith in the present posture of America, and some equally angry because the 19th Century promise of this great democracy has been so widely betrayed by 20th Century abuse of the freedoms it guaranteed. These were risks I took when I ventured to lift a corner of the Iron Curtain ever so slightly to give you a first hand glimpse of what lies behind. Finally, some of you may have been simply annoyed that so elusive a matter as human values should be dragged into a scientific symposium. If any of you has actually experienced these reactions, then you surely must know by now that it was not just wild speculation when I said that the prospect of understanding human behavior in other than motivational terms can be deeply threatening.

Now I must hasten on, for there remains a great deal more to be told before this paper fulfills its promise to deal with Europe's decision matrices. All that I have said so far has been my effort to disabuse you of any inclination to think in terms of motives, to paint for you a compellingly vivid picture of one alien personal construct, and to alert you to the way your own feelings are likely to become embroiled the moment you decide to join me in this quest. If you can escape from motivational habits of thought, and if you can retain both the picture and the stabilizing introspective mood I have tried to create, then what I have yet to say should make good psychological sense.

Matrix Dimensions

On the morning of June 9th, 1960 my wife and I boarded United Airlines Flight 610 at the spanking new air terminal in Columbus, Ohio. We were about to start a journey that would take us around the world and bring us face to face with people in 37 countries. My pocket was sagging with a two-inch-thick packet of tickets that were good for one year, and we were determined not to miss a single day of the adventure they promised us. The last entry on the last ticket read, "Chicago to Columbus, 5:10 P.M., June 8th, 1961"—we had allowed ourselves only seven hours to spare!

Every article in our suitcases had been selected, tested, weighed, and evaluated with the greatest of care, for not only had we to be prepared for arctic cold and tropical heat, but each of us must also stay within the economy class baggage limit of 44 lbs. And, besides, we had to find room within that limit for a typewriter, a tape recorder, and special color films for the camera that dangled around my neck. During the year we were to pack and unpack those bags on the average of every 3.2 days, and take them across an international boundary on the average of every five days. I must admit that our overcoat pockets bulged suspiciously, for there were some additional articles that seemed essential for our undertaking, such as the International Directory of Psychologists, that would have tipped the airport scales over our allowance. Over the great distances we were to fly any excess charges would have wrought havoc on a delicately balanced budget.

This once-in-a-lifetime argosy had been more than a year in the planning. There had been moments when it had all seemed like a child's phantasy; it could not really happen. And there had also been some chilling moments when it seemed that indeed it could not happen, for shortly after the original plans were laid I had an acute coronary attack that immobilized me for several months. But, for once, the p-values, against which all psychologists must gamble their scientific careers, could be ignored. The administrators of The Human Ecology Fund, without whose assistance the project would have been quite impossible, were patient, and time, that persistent meddler in human affairs, decided to play on our side. And so, on that bright June morning, when we mounted the ramp and turned to wave to the members of our family who had come to see us off, we realized at last that this was no dream.

Lemcke's Questions

There had been some intensive psychological preparation for this undertaking. We had prepared ourselves, my wife and I, to ask some provocative questions and, what seemed even more important, to listen in certain ways. Dr. Frances Lemcke, also with the assistance of The Human Ecology Fund, had developed some group discussion procedures which we had pre-tested. We hoped that the use of these procedures would enable us to reach a first approximation of some of the important international decision matrices, as well as to hit upon a more sure-fire way of making such assessments.

Actually, Dr. Lemcke's procedure was only one of six approaches that we came to use, and, while it was relatively informal as psychological procedures go, it was the most elaborate, the most difficult to apply, and altogether the most fruitful. Let me describe it first.

We envisioned small groups, comprising three to fifteen persons, who might be willing to let us influence the course of their conversation for an hour or two. Since we wanted to see how they construed issues, rather than asking them to choose between alternatives we might propose, it was important that the questions with which we initiated the discussion should be more suggestive of a topical area than that they would be precise or objective. Moreover, we wanted as much as possible to put our friends in the position of asking each other questions and of seeking themselves the clarification of each other's responses. The more they interrogated each other the better would be the final statement of the issues as they saw them. After all, it was their system of personal constructs we were seeking to understand, not how they might inadvertently trap themselves within the web of our own dimensional scheme.

There were six lead questions in Lemcke's group discussion plan—the result of nine months exploration within the American context. In Europe I often took the liberty of altering them somewhat. My entry questions usually ran somewhat as follows:

1 In your country how do people such as yourselves come to choose to become psychologists (philosophers) (psychiatrists) (social scientists)?
2 In each person's life it appears that there are points at which major lifetime decisions must be made. In this country what are the typical personal decisions that people such as yourselves must make, aside from the choice of a profession?
3 Many people in the world today are concerned about the possibility of a major catastrophe—an atom bomb perhaps, a collision of the earth with some celestial body, a devastating earthquake, or something of that sort. Suppose there should be such a catastrophe in this country, destroying perhaps half the population, half the transportation, half the buildings, etc. What would the typical psychologist do?
4 A few months ago I was sitting in a room with three of my colleagues. I allowed myself to have a phantasy about these three persons and myself. I thought, "Suppose these three individuals were stranded on an ice floe and I were a helicopter pilot sent to rescue them. The helicopter will hold no more than three persons, including the pilot, all four of us are capable of flying it, the ice floe is breaking up, and there is no possibility of making a second trip. What would I do? Suppose the typical psychologist in your country were confronted with a similar problem. How would he go about solving it? If you wish, I can describe each of my colleagues, since I know them well. However, you will have to tell me exactly what you need to know about them.
5 Here is a question involving even more phantasy. Suppose each of us were to be taken to another planet and told that we would be allowed to return to earth only if we chose to be some kind of animal. We know, of course, that certain animals are regarded quite differently in various cultures and that the attributes ascribed to animals often represent important national values. What kind of animal do you suppose the typical psychologist in your country would choose to be?[7]
6 One more question: Suppose about twenty years from now another American psychologist were to come here and ask the same questions of a similar group of your countrymen. How do you suppose the answers might be different after twenty years?

No one could claim that simple categorical answers to these six questions would throw much light on constructs or on construct systems. For this kind of insight it is necessary to probe much deeper in order to develop statements of the alternatives among which the group envisioned its choices being made. For example, to the question about how psychologists in their country came to choose their profession, the first round of replies usually represented some effort to explain the choice in motivational terms. Now I have no particular objection to other people's explanation of their behavior in motivational terms, if those are actually the terms in which they think. But I have serious doubts that many of us actually make our decisions in such terms. I have, instead, the distinct impression that motivational terms injected into this kind of discussion serve only to make one's behavior appear rational, or, if not rational, at least psychological, and therefore, for whatever it is worth, coherent.

Constructs Underlying Occupational Choice

But there were several things one could do to clarify the underlying constructs behind the choice of psychology as a vocation. For example, most of the replies to this question had to do with the person's own choice, rather than the choice of the "typical psychologist." It was appropriate to ask, therefore, against what alternatives was the choice made. What vocational opportunities did the person abandon when he chose to be a psychologist? And on what issues was the decision finally made? What occupations did he see as standing in particularly sharp contrast to the group of occupations he had considered favorably—contrasting occupations especially to be avoided? Could he generalize the similarities and contrasts he had mentioned; that is to say, could he express the theses and their corresponding antitheses? To what extent did the group see this set of constructs operative in the vocational choice of other psychologists they knew?

As I suspect you have already begun to surmise, the wealth of information accruing from this method of inquiry was far greater than one could hope to report in a single paper. Not only did construct dimensions begin to appear, but other things as well—frustrations, compromises, stubborn hopes for the future, disillusionments, despair, conflicts between social groups and between economic groups, impatience with entrenched professors or university policies—all of the overtones of a complex decision matrix. Still, the important outcome of our inquiry was the dimensions themselves—the system of alternatives these persons conceptualized, and therefore the only pathways psychologically available to them. These, by the way, are the ultimate dimensions of human freedom. No others can be of any human use!

[7] This is essentially one of the questions used by the Spanish psychiatrist, Pigem (1949) in his examination of children.

Constructs and Personal Freedom

Perhaps at this point I should take a moment to illustrate how personal construct dimensions open up pathways of freedom in what otherwise may seem to be a deadlocked situation. During our visit to the Institute of Psychology in Moscow one of the psychological assistants employed in the Institute was assigned to us as a translator. She was an attractive little girl, very serious, conscientious in her choice of technical words, but quite expressive in her inflection and gesture, and with a manner of relating herself to people that was both open and ingenuous. How had she come to choose psychology as a vocation?

First of all, she did not wish to be a psychologist; her longstanding ambition was to become an actress—a serious actress. But the University of Moscow budgets the support it gives to students according to the faculties in which they study and according to an appraisal of needs of the Soviet society. In her case she had been unable to secure support for her study of dramatic arts, but, being a bright student, could qualify for support in other fields that were more heavily subsidized. As she examined her objectives more closely she was able to conceptualize a relationship between psychology and dramatics. She proceeded to qualify herself in psychology, completed the psychology curriculum, and found employment in the Psychological Institute.

She had also studied English, both as preparation for a career as an actress and as a skill considered highly valuable in the Soviet Union, especially wherever psychological research is carried on. Moreover, the Institute was downtown on the old university campus, close to the city's theater activities. Having established herself as a full-time research psychologist, with useful language skills and the responsibility for interpreting the ideas and feelings of English-speaking people, she was free to study drama in the evening, also a task of interpreting the ideas and feelings of characters who might not otherwise be properly understood.

At first glance her record might be regarded as no more than the result of a compromise within a rigid system that denied her the freedom she would have liked to have. But it was much more than that; she did not sell so much of her time to the Institute merely in order to earn the money to do what she wanted in the hours that remained. She reconceptualized her objectives, rather than compromised them, and by putting them in a different perspective established a decision matrix for herself that permitted her to move ahead with a minimum of artificial compromise and a maximum of intellectual integrity. She was not merely "putting in hours" and "earning money" in the Institute; she was training herself in the art of interpreting human behavior. Thus she was fulfilling her life rather than subjecting it to economic circumstances. She was no less of a psychologist than the other research workers in the Institute, and scarcely less of a student of the theater, I dare say, than the others who shared her evening classes. She had thought through a dimension of life and, in doing so, had found a measure of freedom in a society where personal freedom is not easy to come by.

And may I say just one more thing while I am about it—just to forestall any tendency some of you may have at this moment to lapse back into motivational thinking. I don't think the intensity of this young lady's motivation, assuming there is any such thing for a person to have, had anything to do with what she was doing. If there had been nothing but a burning desire to be an actress the temptation would have been, not to conceptualize, but to compromise. She would have sold herself to the best-paying job she could find, saved every kopek, hated herself all day long, daydreamed of the stage, and come alive only in those stolen moments she could spend at the theater.

Other Approaches

So far, I have described only one of the approaches my wife and I employed—the Lemcke Series—and, for the most part, I have been speaking of the first question only in that series, the question about vocational choice. Since this first question served mainly to initiate the discussion at a practical level, and generally did not involve as much abstraction as the five subsequent questions, you can readily see that I am having to leave out some of the most important parts of the methodology.

More often than not it was impossible to assemble a group for the kind of discussion the Lemcke approach envisioned. Even when a group was assembled, it was not always feasible to press them into this kind of conversation. In some instances, as in Denmark, for example, it was obvious that the group, assembled around the table in a home and under the most convivial circumstances, was less than enthusiastic about anything that smacked of a psychological inquiry. In some instances I found that we were members of a group that wanted to ask questions about psychology in America or about my own theoretical stand in psychology. Often I found myself limited to what could be learned in a conversation with one or two persons during a half hour's visit across a professor's desk.

As it turned out, we found ourselves using essentially six types of approaches, or combinations of them, depending on the circumstances or the mood of our hosts. The first, and most elaborate, was the group discussion based on Lemcke's questions, which I have already sketched. The second group method, used most effectively in places such as Prague, Warsaw, and Moscow, was a lecture given at the invitation of the local university or academy of science people, and dealing with personal construct theory. These lectures were usually followed by lively discussions lasting until late in the evening. There were also some occasions when I was asked to describe American graduate training in psychology. These naturally led us to problems of decision-making for psychologists and others in similar occupations. Some information could be gleaned from discussions of local research projects, since the laboratory walk is a standard part of any psychologist's visit to another university.

Where friendships developed beyond the formality of the initial visit, the conversation often turned to wartime and immediate post-war experiences. Most Europeans have vivid memories of this catastrophe, for the last war affected civilians in unprecedented ways that are hard for Americans to envision. For most Europeans their recollections of wartime experiences are tightly bound to their construction of life and any discussion of these traumatic events is likely to lead to some kind of effort to structure and evaluate the course of human affairs.

Finally, there was a question I found particularly useful when I was limited to a brief visit with men in their offices, in their laboratories, or at the lunch table. It ran like this: "I am impressed with the rapid changes that are going on in Europe these days. Undoubtedly these are going to have far-reaching consequences in your country as well as in others during the next decade or so. What role do you see psychologists, or the science of psychology, playing in the developments that lie ahead?"

The answers to this question varied greatly from country to country and in ways that seemed reasonably representative of the prevailing decision matrix. In Norway, for example, the young psychologists saw psychology as a major dynamic factor in the new society they believed to be emerging, while in Austria the answer was a flat, "none"—an answer reminiscent of the prewar German intellectuals' disclaimer of any responsible part in the ominous course of events leading up to the Nazi tyranny.

Ways To Listen

As I have already said, as much depended on the ways my wife and I listened as on the ways we posed questions. As a matter of fact, asking and listening must go together, for the act of asking a question attunes one's ear to the sort of answer he expects, and one usually asks his questions in the light of what he thinks he has heard.

Basically, personal construct theory ought to alert one to the implied similarities and contrasts in a respondent's use of terms or in his descriptions of events. If two incidents are described in the same context, one examines both content and syntax to detect, if he can, what the speaker sees as similar between them, and in what way he sees them in contrast with each other. These similarities and contrasts are the traces of the construct dimensions being used. The incidents mentioned are the operations designating the poles of these constructs and hence serve to define them by what is known in logic as the method of extension.

Often the contrasts are clearly implied by the use of introductory phrases in sentences, as, for example, when a sentence is introduced by the phrase, "In *this* country...." or "Our students are...." It is clear that what follows in the sentence is believed by the speaker to stand in contrast to something he thinks is true in some other country, or of another group of students. Often the speaker is distinguishing between what is true of his country or of his students and what he believes to be true of America or of American students, although the context of the conversation may suggest that he has some other contrast in mind.

Indeed, almost anything that a person chooses to say in a conversation may be regarded in either of two ways; a further elaboration of something that has just been said or of something the presence of his listener implies to him, or, on the other hand, it may be regarded as a statement having salience; that is to say, something that stands out in clear contrast to what has just been said by others, or distinguishes itself from what the listener is believed to represent. To catch the full meaning of what is being said, therefore, one must not limit his listening merely to an absorption of the content or to following a sequence of images, no matter how vivid they may be. He must alert himself to the construct dimensions which serve to conjoin and separate the elements of the conversation. Without such structuring dimensions a conversation would be no more than a kaleidoscopic succession of images.

In an ordinary conversation a speaker will go over and over the same construct dimensions, varying the content, from time to time appearing to change the subject, and approaching the same dimension of thought or feeling, first at one pole and then at the other. One soon senses, if he tries, that the speaker is trying to impress an abstract meaning on his listener by continually shifting its concrete underpinnings. It is up to the listener not to limit himself to stringing these bits of information on his own most convenient axes of reference, but to attempt to abstract from what is being said the true axes of the speaker's system.

There is an axiom often useful in psychotherapeutic interviewing: *The patient may readily change the subject, but only rarely does he change the theme*. In fact, it is by tracing the theme from subject to subject that the therapist gradually distills what is pervasive from what is merely illustrative. This is precisely what one must do in listening to any conversation if he is to detect its underlying essentials. Yet the illustrative material is often so shocking or so dull that the listener becomes preoccupied with it and fails to comprehend what is of central importance.

At a more technical level I might mention listening for the "buts," the "on the other hands," and the "therefores." These are obvious signs of contrasts and linkages. One can look for synonymous usages of terms. He can be alert to compounded modifiers of nouns, chains of modifiers, sweeping generalizations, and name-calling, all of which are common features of propaganda and are therefore likely to carry loose personal meanings which are quite remote from the dictionary meanings of the words used. He can make note of distance-making modifiers; "that versus this," "they versus we," "that class of people," etc. He can be aware of terms that seem to serve more as signals than as conveyors of semantic meanings—"the Germans," "the Nazis," "the Fascists," etc. Here again there may be evidence of a generalization which the person is not prepared to break down into its component parts.

It is often important to watch for artificial breaks in the chain of conversation, for interruptions by other members of the group, for sudden silences, for breaks in a line of discussion to ask the listener a question. There may be sudden blockages in the fluidity of the discussion, or inferential leaps that leave obvious logical gaps in the chain of reasoning, or there may be frantic efforts to disengage from a topic altogether. These are clues to the possibility that the contrasting pole of the construct is threatening and to the fact that the speakers are reluctant to disclose it.

One looks for areas in which discussion is spontaneous and where spontaneity breaks down. He observes constructs where one pole is discussed freely but the contrasting pole is avoided. There are likely to be some matters brought up when one is alone with the speaker which are never mentioned when a third person is present. This is particularly true behind the Iron Curtain. We were somewhat surprised to discover that constructs underlying such surreptitious conversations are likely to be fairly clearly expressed. In some cases there may be over-documentation of certain conclusions. This suggests that the speaker has some apprehension regarding the antitheses of those conclusions.

Who and Where

In planning this preliminary study of Europe's decision matrices, we had to make some decisions about sampling. We were less concerned with reaching a final statement regarding the decision matrix of a given country than we were about testing the feasibility of the methods derived from personal construct theory. Any final formulation of a particular decision matrix would have to be based on extensive experience within a single country, with proper regard for subcultures, for sizes of samples, and the rate at which patterns were changing. Furthermore, to concentrate on one country alone in our survey, would have led us to become overly involved with the similarities and contrasts between that country and our own. It seemed that only by maximizing the differences between the national cultures we visited that we could hope to get a proper perspective on our method and to determine whether or not it might be expected to reflect major cultural differences.

But we wanted to do something else, too, partly from the standpoint of convenience and partly from the standpoint of methodology. Obviously our most ready access to persons abroad was through our identification with a university and with the discipline of psychology. The fact that my own psychological interests at the present time are largely theoretical also provided a rather broad meeting-ground for conversations with psychologists abroad. Psychologists throughout the world know a good deal about each other, and university people, regardless of discipline and nationality, are likely to sense a common bond among themselves. We, therefore, had what was more or less a readymade access to universities in general and to psychologists in particular.

But even without this common interest in psychology, it would have been desirable to concentrate the study upon a particular kind of subculture. We were not seeking to distinguish the decision matrices of classes, but of national groups. It is to be assumed that the differences between socio-economic classes reflect distinctive differences in decision matrices. Indeed, one of the primary ways in which socio-economic classes are identified by sociologists is in terms of privileges, which are certainly closely related to the freedom of action within a kind of decision matrix. While I believe there is a lot of stereotyped nonsense in the unidimensional way social scientists talk about classes—"upper lower class," "lower middle class," and all that sort of thing, there are, nonetheless, sub-cultural differences worth taking into account. In making our plans it therefore seemed desirable to keep to the same type of sub-culture as we moved from country to country in our effort to become sensitive to national differences.

Now I suspect it may be true that the differences between psychologists from country to country are less remarkable than the differences between other types of sub-culture—merchants, for example, or perhaps miners. From this point of view our methodology is open to valid criticism. But I am not sure we can tell *a priori* what these subcultures are in which we may find greater national differences reflected.

There was a third reason for choosing to talk mostly to psychologists. We were trying out a set of psychological techniques and our target was a psychological problem. It was therefore possible to discuss frankly with our respondents just what we were doing and to enlist their comments on the spot. Psychologists tend to be pretty articulate people and we were often grateful for the opportunity to discuss with them just what we were trying to accomplish.

I should point out that our discussions were not limited to psychologists. There were often philosophers in our groups, as well as sociologists, psychiatrists, and individuals from other disciplines, who had a personal ancillary interest in the behavioral sciences. I should mention also the fact that we had very little contact with Americans during our year abroad. We did not mingle with embassy people, with military or technical assistance people, or with tourists, except on rare occasions, and then only briefly. In other words, we concentrated on psychologists and people like them and saw very little of "The American Community" in cities we visited. In some ways, I suppose, this was a disadvantage, but we thought, everything considered, it was best to maximize our contacts with foreign friends.

Altogether, then, our sampling specifications were simple enough: Concentrate on Europe, maximize national differences, and minimize sub-cultural differences by sticking to university communities and talking to psychologists and their friends. We did, of course, have a good many contacts outside university communities and with persons in non-professional occupations. But our very tentative observations in these cases are not part of the study I am reporting.

A Scandinavian Construct

While the differences in national outlook among the five Scandinavian countries (Denmark, Finland, Iceland, Norway, and Sweden) are often surprisingly great, there is one construct dimension which stands out in their appraisal of international affairs. Scandinavians, partly because of their relatively high standards of living and their high level of literary activity, often visit the United States and take a keen interest in comparing their way of life with ours. The Finns, because of the unique system of fellowships for study in the United States operating over the past forty years, are particularly alert to similarities and differences between their society and ours. Their friendship for America runs deep. This seems to be especially true among university people. While the Finns were defeated in two wars occurring in rapid succession, in one of which they found themselves aligned against us, and while they have been and are still being systematically plundered by the Soviet Union, our erstwhile ally, they have made an amazing recovery. Some measure of that recovery can be attributed to the leadership of persons who had training in the United States.

The Danes and the Norwegians have had particularly close contact with us since the war, and Americans who travel abroad are likely to agree that there is no place in Europe where an American feels more comfortable and accepted than in the homes and on the streets of Copenhagen. The story is somewhat different in Sweden, where local scholars feel they have been cut off from America because of their country's refusal to join NATO.

It is painfully different in Iceland where the presence of Americans is regarded as akin to a military occupation. Our activities are deeply resented there, even though they are conceded to be a necessary safeguard against Soviet aggression.

All this contact with America leads Scandinavians to attempt some sort of generalization of the differences they see between their way of life and ours. It is a generalization that appears to arise spontaneously among individuals, rather than following from some official ethnocentric line.

Probably the most shocking thing a Scandinavian sees when he visits the United States is the unbelievable squalor of our cities, towns, and country-side. However he may be impressed with our highways, our universities, and our productive capacity—and he is indeed impressed by these things—he carries away with him a sickening image of the abject hopelessness of the less privileged fourth of our population—of Negroes living in despair, of dilapidated farms, of mental hospitals that look like mismanaged zoos, of fear and violence stalking our city streets, of prisons and courts that have little relation to impartial justice or to the restoration of self-respect, an image of the sick and the helpless being stripped of their dignity the moment they are driven to seek aid. Alongside this he sees profligate spending, arrogant expense accounts of men in private industry, the poor being taunted because of their poverty, and wealth flaunted in the face of the needy. He hears Americans in comfortable surroundings extolling something they call private enterprise in the midst of an economy that has obviously been taken over by corporate enterprise, and he hears of the virtues of self-reliance from people whose fortunes were handed down to them. He wonders why, in a country where self-reliance is regarded so highly, there are so many who seem to have given up in despair and, where equality is so often talked about, there are so many who have no part to play. He concludes that in America it is a disgrace to be colored, to be poor, to be a child without parents, to be sick after you have spent your last dollar on doctor bills, or to be old and helpless.

Almost without exception he is deeply shocked by what he sees, and particularly so because he likes the Americans he meets, and is unfailingly impressed by their courtesy, hospitality, and personal generosity to him. Yet there are few Scandinavians now who do not think of America as the grand contemporary example of extremes of wealth and poverty—not the extremes of a five per cent wealthy against a ninety-five per cent impoverished, but the extremes of a three-fourths self-righteously successful against a one-fourth contemptibly derelict. Against what he sees and hears here the Dane or the Swede cannot help but draw contrasts from his own country and the responsibilities its citizens feel incumbent upon them; for none of the things I have mentioned among his observations could easily be said of a country like Denmark or Sweden, not even if one takes into account a certain amount of poverty to be found there.

I suspect this is a point where I would be well advised to ask you to recall just what it was we were attempting to do. Our task—remember—was, and is, to examine the decision matrices of Europe and to clarify as best we can the construct dimensions in terms of which the people of Europe do what they do and stand prepared to do whatever it is they will do in times of national emergency. The particular construct I have been delineating is not typically an American construct; few Americans see their society, or other societies, in terms of this dimension. And, furthermore, as if it were not abundantly obvious during the last few minutes, may I remind you that looking through other people's glasses is hard on the eyes. Is anyone for changing the topic back to something more academic—such as "motivation?"

Idealism and Materialism

During our visits to university cities it was a simple matter to stop by bookstores in the student districts and observe what books were being displayed and bought. We were surprised in many instances to find what a large proportion were American books. In Helsinki, for example, a rough check indicated that about half the textbooks displayed were American, with the remainder distributed among Finnish, Swedish, British, and German titles. The topics ranged from science to history and literature. I expressed this surprise to a group of Finnish university people one day and was rewarded by an enlightening reply from these astute observers of world affairs who survive under the shadow of the Soviet Union only by intensive research in political science and keeping their wits about them from week to week.

While Finnish authors are reputed to publish more books in proportion to the population than do those of any other country in the world, except perhaps Iceland, they were, up until the beginning of the last war, greatly dependent upon German textbooks. Like many other people, they looked to Germany as a fountainhead of both science and literature. America, by contrast, was the country where automobiles, airplanes, movie stars, illiterate millionaires, and addle-headed tourists came from. To a somewhat similar extent this axis of German scholarship versus American simple-minded materialism structured the thinking in other countries of Europe as well.

But there has been a curious shuffle since the war. The same construct dimension still holds, but America and Germany have exchanged positions. Now it is the Germans who are the materialistic, money-conscious, crude-mannered, vulgarians of the world, and it is the

Americans who are exporting scholarship. German economic growth has been spectacular while American economic growth seems on the point of grinding to a halt. Reactionary voices call America back, not to the dynamics of the nineteenth century but to the status of the nineteenth century, not to the forward look of our pioneers, but the backward look of those who keep talking about them. Since the war we have displayed a strange inability to get things done or to implement any programs comparable to Europe's Common Market. More and more the Germans are making the world's automobiles, the Dutch its medicines, the Italians its business machines.

But when we look at the other pole of this dimension we see something that we can scarcely believe ourselves. America is exporting scholarship as no nation of modern times has ever exported it. American scientific research on a broad front is outdistancing the contributions of other countries. In almost any field you can mention American textbooks are far ahead of those available elsewhere. American artists are exhibiting and performing with exciting new style and competence. America is rapidly coming to mean scholarship and intellectual leadership. This is indeed a switch of images.

Now I have been elaborating considerably on what was actually told me that evening in Finland. This elaboration, however, is based on observations in other parts of Europe and it substantially represents, I believe, an important dimension in the thinking of social scientists in a number of countries—though certainly not in all. Moreover, I doubt if all segments of the societies in which I observed this dimension make the same use of the contrast I have described, or, if they did, if they would all see American scholarship in such a favorable light. Our study is sharply limited to preliminary observations in the kind of sub-cultures we chose to visit.

Nevertheless, I believe we have something important here. So let me go on and describe the remarkable way in which this dimension of thought has guided the affairs of nations during the last decade and a half.

German idealism has always been an important pole of Germanic thinking. While idealism might at first glance appear to be antagonistic to empirical science, it has not always worked out that way in Germany. Indeed it often supported experimentation. The logical positivists of the Vienna Circle, taking their cue from Bertrand Russell of Britain and the American pragmatists, attempted to clean house in German science and sweep out the vestiges of idealism. But German idealism was not to be junked so easily; it was instead about to assume its most grotesque form and plunge the world into a Nazi nightmare.

Germany came out of the war with its idealism discredited, both at home and abroad. How deep this sense of invalidation was is hard to say. But at least it was acute enough on the surface. In the face of such invalidation, then, what was there for the German mind to do? Certainly if one finds his position untenable he must change it, if he is to survive. But how? How do you shift your position, except to move in the most obvious direction from where you stand and along the broadest avenue your mind has been able to pave for itself? For the German, this avenue ran straight from "German" idealism to "American" materialism. What could be more obvious—and with the American occupation forces, from Army sergeants to State Department officials, to show just how it could be done!

But I must point out that such massive shifts are not made along lines that are laid down by strangers from across the Atlantic, or by the immutable logic of the universe, but along lines that are construed by the human mind itself. The idealism the German felt himself forced to abandon was not the Nazism Americans perceived, but the Nazism he himself had experienced. Nor was that idealism some island perched out in natural space, existing independently of what man perceives, it was what the German experienced it to be in his own generation. And the materialism he envisioned as the alternative now open to him was not the America we experience, but the America he perceived us to be. Hence the shift became what it was. Western Germany, and to a considerable extent Eastern Germany too, has moved toward what they and most of the rest of Europe believed was "successful Americanism!" It has made this move with some misgivings on both sides of the Atlantic, for it was not altogether in the direction of their sober convictions or of what we deeply believe.

That this move may prove to be superficial must go without saying. Indeed, Americans might fervently hope that it is superficial, and that, instead of slipping back again into the old slot toward fascism the moment the American glamor has worn off, the German mind will conceptualize some new dimensions of national life. But we should not expect too much. We must remember that while war and defeat may challenge men to find new pathways along which civilization may move, the suddenness and shock of a great catastrophe too often cause men to turn and run back along old familiar alleys.

One Man's Matrix of Decision

Thus far I have attempted to sketch only two dimensions of European cultural change—one that I have called the Scandinavian dimension of *Humanitarianism versus Opportunism*, and the other that might be called the German dimension of *Ideas versus Wealth*. Rather than going on to catalog other dimensions and trace more complex matrices—which, as you see, takes time—let me show how this simple two-dimensional matrix defines some anxious choices in the life of an individual man and how it channels the destinies of nations in moments when great decisions are made.

A few months before the Berlin wall was put up, my wife and I had the opportunity to make the acquaintance of some young university instructors in Humboldt University, the old and respected "University of Berlin." It happens that this university lies just inside the Soviet sector of the city. Since the war an impressive new university, called the Free University of Berlin, has been erected in the American sector with the generous help of American funds. But one does not construct universities simply by building buildings and recruiting a distinguished staff. In some strange way, quite apart from these important features, each university seems to have its own integrity and character. Humboldt University, though it is now plastered with communist slogans and humming with programs for communizing Latin America, still retains some of its distinction as a center of scholarship. In some of its departments professors are under continual or intermittent harassment, yet are able to carry on in some degree in the old scholarly tradition. In spite of all their handicaps their work stands out in contrast to that in corresponding departments of the Free University where all the gleaming new buildings and equipment are. Psychology is one of those departments.

During one of a number of conversations a young man spoke of the pleasure he and his wife experienced on those occasions when they could leave the darkened rubble-covered streets of East Berlin and take the S-Bahn train over to West Berlin. He expressed himself something like this: "Do you know, even if I were to be offered a position with higher rank and pay in another city of the People's Democratic Republic, my wife and I have agreed that we would turn it down. It would be worth the sacrifice just to be able to retain the opportunity to go to West Berlin when our spirits are low, to walk the wide clean streets, to mingle with the happy crowds, to be caught up in the bright lights, and to look at the endless displays of beautiful things behind big plate glass windows. For us who live in East Berlin it is an exciting privilege just to go over there and breathe the air."

An American, hearing this kind of remark, is likely to feel a lump in his throat and sense a bond of kinship between himself and his new-found friend. I was no exception. After all, there is something about West Berlin that stands for America and its hopes for a war-chastened people, and one cannot help but be thrilled to hear this young man, reared under Nazi tyranny, scarred by combat, starved in a military prison camp, and living in the bleakness of communist oppression, speak of breathing the air of ... Here he is, a man who, in spite of all that tried to warp his life, has caught a glimpse of that dimension in which all human life seems to pulsate, that dimension so dear to the American heart.

Oppression versus Freedom!

We asked this young man, almost in our next breath, if he was planning to flee the Eastern Sector, something that at that time would have been easy enough to do. The immediate reply was, "No! Why?" The answer, with its overtones, ran something like this: "Well, the rents are very high over there—four or five times as much as we pay. To be sure there are employment opportunities now, but some day something you cannot help will happen. You may lose your position and if you lose your position in Western Germany your financial resources dwindle away very rapidly, very rapidly indeed. Before you know it, you and your wife and your children may be thrown out into the street. That sort of thing happens over there. Medical care is terribly expensive over there. The doctors like to live expensively, and if you can't pay for medical care you don't get it. No, we are going to stay right here. While the pay is poor, and the streets are dark, and you are under continual criticism if someone does not think you are following quite the correct line, still I know this: My family will always have a roof over their heads, I will always have an income, and there will always be free medical care for our children and ourselves, absolutely free—*good* medical care. I remember very well what it was like to be without these things, when children were deserted in the streets, and some starved while others ate. Then I look at my own children, and I know what my decision must be. No, I'm staying here. My family comes first!"

"Oh ho!" you may say. "It's easy enough to see what's wrong with this fellow. He just doesn't have the motivation. All people like him want is security, security! He expects everything to be soft and easy. He thinks the world owes him a living. He's a coward; he's afraid to face up to life. It takes a real man to enjoy freedom and he obviously doesn't measure up."

These comments are, of course, in the language of motivational psychology. They are not the sort of thing one says if he is looking for a glimpse of the world through the other fellow's glasses. They are an outsider's explanation, or, more correctly, a way of dismissing any claim this man may have to validity for the matrix of his decision. The psychology of motivation is like that!

But I have committed you to understanding this man in terms of the psychology of personal constructs. Let us, therefore, look more closely to see if we can detect the principal dimensions of his thought. He has expressed two main ideas, the first, the feeling he and his wife have when they walk the crowded streets of West Berlin, and the second his sense of over-riding responsibility to his family. The second is easy enough to understand in terms of what we called our "Scandinavian dimension of *Humanitarianism versus Opportunism.*" He sees matters in terms of this issue and he chooses for himself the pole of humanitarianism, presumably, of course, with certain personal modifications of the construct.

But what about the first statement? Was it the air of "freedom" that he and his wife were breathing on those walks along the brightly-lit Kurfurstendam—"freedom" as Americans understand it? I suspect it was not, really, just as I am sure it is not for all too many Americans. What they were breathing was the air of excitement, of glamor, of lavish wealth, of the endless display of goods—shiny things, soft things, luscious things—the air of the abundance of material possessions. No doubt they remembered something too, something that happened when they were youngsters—trumpets and flags, the quickened heart-beat that keeps time with marching feet, the spectacle of the launching of a thousand-year Reich, the power of brushing away all the villainous adversaries that fouled the path to greatness, the realization that they themselves, that they were not only Aryan but German. It has been twenty years now, but who can ever forget the bursting thrill of idealism rising in the adolescent breast.

But all that is gone now. Nazi idealism has proved itself to be cruel and wrong, and it has led to bitter reprisals from those who did not share that dream, just as all great ideals of faith, of hope, and deep conviction prove to be cruel and wrong when they are held too dearly. Ideals are as dangerous as they are powerful, and they lead to death and bitterness. One scarcely dares think of those adolescent moments now, or try to remember how he felt, much less mention such things aloud. So "idealism" is dead now. It perished with the millions of Jews it slaughtered and is buried with them in the same mass graves.

As this young man and his wife mingle with the shopping crowds in the KaDeWe, or stroll among the sidewalk diners at Krantzler's, I am sure they must hear the echo of distant drums, and sense a rising excitement. I am sure not even that dark ruined tower of the Gedächtniskirche, left standing high in the center of West Berlin's most brightly lighted district as a stark reminder of evil days, can slow the pulse or draw one's attention altogether away from the lush splendor of the Berlin-Hilton Hotel. This time it will be different. It is not the Nazi thrill one should have now, but the thrill of prosperity—like they are always talking about in America.

I have, to be sure, taken some liberty here in interpreting the personal experiences of our friends. And while I may be mistaken in some factual details, our inquiries into the dimensions of European thought lend strong support for the conclusion that one of the principal axes involved in the German's changing world is that of *Ideas versus Wealth*.

A Premature Conclusion

And now I am near the end of this paper. There were so many things I started out to say, and so few that got said. I suppose I should have fulfilled the promise of my title—The Decision Matrices of Europe—by cataloguing more of the dimensions of European thought and by suggesting what the cultural shifts may be if sudden emergencies should arise. I would like to have told you about the French, the wildest free-for-all discussion of Lemcke's questions one could ever imagine, their tolerance of intellectual innovation, their shocking proposals of standards by which to evaluate life. Or the Spanish; I would like to tell you about them, how they gracefully stalked me as a matador stalks a bull, making thrusts, stepping neatly aside, dangling false questions, until at last they were satisfied and let me hear what they were bursting all the time to say. I would like to try to make you feel that personal construct and how it bears upon the ever-approaching choice between Franco-ism and communism, a choice that might have been between Franco-ism and democracy—twenty-five years ago! Most of all, I would like to have told you about the exciting things that are happening to Marxist theory in Poland, and the wisp of hope they hold out for a more tolerant world. But the time is nearly gone, and I want to close with a little incident.

Just a few weeks after our return from the Orient last summer, my wife and I made a second trip to Europe. We met one of our East Berlin friends again. Just a few days before, the Berlin wall had gone up. No more happy walks along the Kurfurstendam, no more neon lights, no more window shopping! At the moment we talked to him there was still a legitimate way to flee to West Germany, and to take his family with him. He was facing his personal matrix of decision, just as today, or perhaps tomorrow, all Europe, and many other countries of the world as well, face the matrices of decision they have erected for themselves. It was obvious that he was under considerable tension. His voice quivered at times; he sought us out as old friends; he kept looking at us as if there were a question he wanted to ask, but he knew it was one we could not answer for him. For us, of course, with our own type of decision matrix, the choice might have been considerably less difficult. But each man decides within his own matrix. Our talks, on several occasions during those days last August, were warm and friendly, and we spoke briefly of the crisis in his life. But we did not press him to disclose what his decision might be. After all, human decency sets limits to psychological inquiry, and we did not have the heart to probe the anguish of his already troubled mind.

How is it that James Russell Lowell's (1897) poem runs—"Once to every man and nation comes the moment to decide..."?

References

Bieri, J. (1961). Complexity-simplicity as a personality variable in cognitive and preferential behavior. In D. Fiske & S. Maddi (Eds.), *Functions of varied experience* (pp. 355–379). Dorsey.

Burke, K. (1945). *A grammar of motives*. Prentice-Hall.

Clemens, S. L. (Mark Twain) (1896). The stolen white elephant. In *Tom Sawyer abroad; Tom Sawyer, Detective, and other stories*. Harper.

Ditzen, R. (Hans Fallada) (1933). *Little man what now* (trans. by Eric Sutton). Simon & Schuster.

Kelly, G. A. (1958). Man's construction of his alternatives. In G. Lindzey (Ed.), *Assessment of human motives* (pp. 33–64). Rinehart.

Kelly, G. A. (1955). *The psychology of personal constructs* (Vols. 1 and 2). Norton.

Kelly, G. A. (1961). Suicide: The personal construct point of view. In N. L. Farberow & E. S. Schneidman (Eds.), *The cry for help* (pp. 255–280). McGraw-Hill.

Lowell, J. R. (1897). *The complete poetical works of James Russell Lowell*. Houghton Mifflin.

Papashvily, G., & Papashvily, H. (1945). *Anything can happen*. Harper.

Papashvily, G., & Papashvily, H. (1946a). *Thanks to Noah*. Harper.

Papashvily, G., & Papashvily, H. (1946b). *Yes and no stories*. Harper.

Pigem, J. M. (1949). *La prueba de la expression desiderativa*. Libreria de Ciencias Medic.

45

Nicholas Square[1]

There is, they say, a common failing found in all of us:
We overlook the forest when we stop to gaze at trees.
And, I suppose, this is a serious fault, but, nonetheless,
I have the failing too. So, if you ask, what did I see
When I passed through that vast gray forest that lies in ominous wait
Behind the Iron Curtain, I can only speak of trees—
Some persons, that is, who brushed against my sleeve along the way,
Of how they looked, of what they did, and what they said to me.

Repeating what these people said may sound like treason, if one feels
It's time to silence every voice that challenges us to prove
Our speech is unfettered, our thoughts unwarped, that our liberties are real
Or if one thinks warfare[2] alone will answer or remove
The far-flung challenge the Soviets make that our prosperous way of life
Does not envision freedom for all men, but is reserved
For those who dedicate their souls to financial enterprise,
Whose fortunes are their virtue, and whose booty is deserved.

So I saw only trees. But why not speak of trees—except
Perhaps, there were too many to be seen and understood
In the homespun terms one understands his friends. Indeed, our sets
Of mind too often lack the depth to cope with neighborhood
Affairs. How could one ever hope to feel akin to those
He dreads, whose distant faces constitute a vandal horde.
Never-the-less, I'll sharpen the focus of what I have to say. Suppose
I mention only the encounters of one day—no more.

There is a certain city—Leningrad
Among the golden spires and cupolas
That decorate its sky there is a square
A broad gray square entirely paved
Except for a fenced-in plot along one side.
The place is named for Nicholas the First.

[1] Undated, unfinished, and unpublished manuscript, headed Chapter 4 but with no indication of where it was intended to appear. There are several alternative versions of the text that is reproduced here. Published by permission of Jacqueline Aldridge.
[2] Editors' note: "the bomb" was an alternative wording in one of Kelly's versions of this.

Collected Papers of the Pioneer of Constructivist Psychology: George A. Kelly, First Edition. Edited by David A. Winter and Nick Reed.

46

Man, Crises and Commitments: A Stated Purpose and a Plan for an *Institute for Advanced Psychological Studies*[1]

This is an invitation to join in a concerted attack upon the most persistent problems of man, and particularly against the avalanche of crises that twentieth century man has created within himself, and between himself and others.

Is the Advancement of Psychological Knowledge Necessarily a Good Thing?

Such a venture is not without risk. Whether it is by his invention of nuclear devices or his creation of equally explosive societies, man's accomplishments in the recent decades of this century have brought him nearer to destruction than he has ever been before. If now he were to turn the full force of his ingenuity upon his own psychological processes, would he not thereby create the likelihood of unforeseen cataclysms within himself as monstrous as those which now threaten him from the outside? This is a perfectly fair question, and one that should be faced squarely before anyone accepts this invitation to a further twentieth century adventure.

Decisions on issues of this sort are rarely made between the simple alternatives of doing something or doing nothing. It is impossible to do nothing, and those who try are likely to find themselves unwittingly committed to enterprises that are not of their own choosing. So unless one believes it is better to be victimized by history than to take the awful responsibility for it, he had better lay out in advance the alternatives open to him.

How does one lay out the alternatives and elaborate their possibilities? One may look backwards across the span of his own lifetime and say, "There, in scarcely more than a single generation, we have taken a great country that was founded on ideals of personal freedom, individual determination, and high purpose and have succeeded in converting its cities into communities of hatred, and we have turned its parks into jungles where neither child, grown woman, nor armed man dares walk at night." He may look across to Europe, point and say, "There, only a little while ago, a nation noted for its advanced culture turned itself overnight into an agency of brutality for which the history of savagery holds no precedent. And the great unanswered question is, 'Did this happen because they were Germans, or because they too were men like us?'" He may gaze further towards the far reaches of the East and exclaim, "Out there is the greatest mass enslavement the world has ever known, but it was not achieved by invading armies; it was achieved by the slaves themselves." He may look up to the sky and think to himself, "At last man has the stars almost within his grasp, and already he has laid the plans for making them pathways of destruction." And if one turns away from all this menace and looks hopefully into the minds of his friends, he discovers there only an increasing emptiness that leaves them with no way of coping with a problem other than to lie down and be treated for it.

Granted, these are easy generalizations. They point to nothing very specific other than that there is a genuine cause for alarm in the fact that man has created powerful machines and massively coordinated organizations without taking pains to develop the wisdom he needs to use them well. Yet demagogues, political and otherwise, use such statements every day to frighten us into adopting all sorts of ready-made nostrums. And we do go ahead and adopt them, simply, if for no other reason, because there are, as yet, no other clearly visible measures to be taken.

One such nostrum of desperation is to identify *bona fide* enemies and then hold a gun on them. But unless we destroy the enemies while we have the chance, this measure serves no purpose other than to buy us a little more time. To be sure, if we use this time to find and apply positive solutions our militant posture may serve us well. But this then raises the question of how vigorously we are pursuing the development of such solutions.

But what do we do when our enemy is identified as the neighbor next door? If he supports some suspicious cause, either actively or passively, shall we keep him under police surveillance? And if we do that, how long will it be before he has us under police surveillance?

Or what do we do when we come to suspect that the destructive forces are within ourselves? Purge ourselves? Quench every spark of impulse lest it start a fire? History is filled with the destructive escapades of men who thought they had purged themselves of all selfish motives.

[1] Undated and unfinished. Published by permission of Jacqueline Aldridge.

Collected Papers of the Pioneer of Constructivist Psychology: George A. Kelly, First Edition. Edited by David A. Winter and Nick Reed.

Some say that modern man has misplaced some important element of his character and he better go back and look for it. Of these, some say he lost it when he ceased to be a pioneer, others say it was when he stopped going to Sunday School, and still others believe he lost it a very long time ago, perhaps in the middle ages.

Finally, there are those who argue that the first thing to do is to put a ban on progress until man has had a chance to catch up with himself psychologically. This is another time-buying scheme, just as a strong military posture is a time-buying scheme. But this one, if successful, would itself be an extremely advanced psychological measure. And if we had this much psychological leverage on the imagination of man it would not be unreasonable to expect a comparable psychological leverage on the problems he faces. In that case there would be no need for suppression and progress could again proceed spontaneously.

Where does this leave us? Each of the alternative measures discussed so far is either a stop-gap device only, or it contains a highly negative or reactionary component. Assuming that none of these is good enough, we return to the venture proposed at the outset. Having returned, it remains for us to develop the theme of this venture and the devices by which it may be implemented.

A Theme

The stated theme of this venture is "man, his crises, and his commitments." While the proposed approach is secular rather than sectarian, it does not envision a type of secularism that studiously avoids the religious side of man in order to appear liberal, nor a science that excludes all value judgments because it believes them insubstantial. There is altogether too much likelihood that these matters, which this generation has so carefully avoided in order to break with certain intransigencies of the past, must now be reconsidered as realms of refreshing discourse, open to any scholar who seeks to understand the depths and potentialities of the human mind.

The danger of a venture of this sort is that it will define its problems too narrowly at the outset. This is likely to result in academic boundaries which restrict scholarship to what is sophisticated instead of directing inquiries toward what is vital. Man is vital. The crises he faces are vital. The commitments with which he dedicates his life—these inevitably prove to be vital too. But take only the narrowly defined aspects of man—man the tax payer, man the motorist, man the customer—and note how much of that vitality disappears. Once scholarship is delimited to pre-supposed aspects of problems it runs the risk of overlooking the changing shape of the problems themselves. For it is in the nature of human affairs that problems keep looming up in unexpected ways. That is why it is so important to keep an eye on them.

Man's Crises

Having stated the theme of the project in terms broad enough to be vital, it is possible to turn to particular issues to illustrate and embellish—but not to de-vitalize—that theme. Let us mention six broad areas of crisis and leave goodness knows how many others unmentioned.

Crisis in the Home

It is easy enough to point to the difficulties arising in the homes and family life of our times; perhaps too easy, for there are undoubtedly many ways in which the modern family and its home life are superior to their counterparts of a generation ago. Nevertheless, the estrangement of husband and wife, and of parents and children, can, once it gets started, quickly get out of hand. There is so little in our way of life that tends to heal such breaches, once they occur. Husbands and wives find it hard enough to remember what it is they are supposed to share. And adolescents, caught up in the fulfillment of their parents' ambitions, too easily find themselves alienated from the tolerant affection they once experienced as pre-school children. In some, the loneliness that results seems to call for alcohol, for rebellion in others, for driving business and professional success in men who hope thereby to find a place of meaning in their households, for divorce and the empty freedom it offers, for suicide, or for a psychotherapist who is paid by the hour to listen and understand.

Crisis in the Community

Delinquency, especially juvenile delinquency, seems to be on the increase. It is well enough to attempt to cope with it by means of settlement houses, organized neighborhood activities, supervised recreation, improved police methods, and better housing. But, beyond these practical socio-economic measures which do seem to have some bearing on the problem, the psychological nature of the personal disintegration that has been taking place needs to be understood. This is to say, while we know some of the correlates of the problem, we still have much to learn about the intrinsic changes in the lives of men that constitute the ...[2] problem.

After all, the young people of other times and other countries have lived in poverty too, and often under seemingly worse conditions, but not all of them have reacted in the same way we now see our young people reacting. So what is the difference? What is the

[2] Editors' note: Illegible words

nature of the demoralization which we have been trying to combat by providing more and more of the twentieth century's material comforts? Are we not providing more and more visible things and at the same time managing somehow to deprive our youth more and more of what they need to survive as human beings? Is it not time for a fresh look at what is actually going on?[3]

Crisis in the Means of Survival

Unemployment due to technological changes in industry, such as automation, is daily topic in our newspapers. But there is no place where large scale displacement is occurring more rapidly than on our farms. This is sometimes called a "farm problem," but it is actually less of a farm problem than it is a city problem. Displaced farmers move to the city and add to the city's problems. More and more farm machinery, like factory machinery, requires highly skilled technicians who know a good deal more than the minimum about engineering principles and about such things as cost accounting, soil chemistry, labor efficiency, and marketing as well. Those who cannot meet these requirements go elsewhere and often cause trouble.

But the new dimensions of the problem do not stop here. In fact, farming is cited here simply to illustrate the fact that the problem is not limited to industry. Take such an unlikely field as education. To be sure, more teachers are needed, not fewer teachers. But the teachers that are needed most are the superior ones. The market for teachers of low competence shows signs of drying up. And so we can go from occupation to occupation and foresee the time when the services of only the most able persons will be needed to keep our present type of economy going. What happens to the rest of us? Or better, what is already happening to the rest of us? Do we not have a rapidly mounting surplus of mediocrity that is proving far more burdensome than the much-publicized "farm surplus?"

But what is the nature of this human mediocrity? Is it inbred, or does it have a psychological component accessible to manipulation? How much of it is due to lack of educational facilities and subsidies? How much of it is due to lack of vision or lack of purpose in those who lapse into mediocrity? These are questions that require a more comprehensive look into the current psychological state of man.

The Crisis of Fear

When the USSR was nothing more than a den of wickedness we needed to know only that it was dangerous to look at the world through Marxist eyes. Now that the USSR bristles with rockets pointed in our direction, our carefully cultivated and over-simplified versions of the Soviet outlook are recognized throughout the world as the hallmark of America's vulnerability.

To be sure, we know how to make them afraid and how to back them into a corner, from which they may come out fighting. But do we know how to resolve the conflict? To be sure, some of our more articulate American psychologists are full of "expert" suggestions on how to play the little game called, "Conditioning Kruschev," but the target of their efforts seems to be so bent on winning his own game that he overlooks all the bells and whistles that are supposed to alter his reflexes.

To be sure, we know how to compete with the communist bloc by giving economic and technical aid to underdeveloped countries. But do we know how to give anything else? Certainly the communists have found ways of giving something else, something that is often more potent than all we have to offer;

The Crisis of Ignorance

Once the world was run by men who knew how to rule others. Then it was run by people who had learned how to rule themselves. Now, all around the perimeter of the Iron Curtain, government is being put in the hands of peoples who have learned neither how to rule others nor how to rule themselves. This is progress. Everyone agrees the initial steps should have been taken long ago. But it is headlong and frightening progress. Some say that it is the kind of progress that ought to be slowed down until widespread ignorance has been dissipated. But, as we have said before, if we were able to create the psychological conditions which would stop the march of progress, we could probably also create, at the same time, the psychological conditions that would make such progress less hazardous.

What does man need to govern himself in justice and in peace? Education alone will not do it—in case anyone still believes that educated men are always wise and cautious in the ways of government. Democratic constitutions will not do it—constitutions are suspended without the slightest hesitation when self-government collapses. Wealth will not do it—it is often the presence of the wealthy that provokes violence. What, then, is the state of mind that needs to be sought and cultivated? There—is a good question!

The Crisis of Disinvolvement[4]

[3] Editors' note: The placement of this paragraph in the manuscript is unclear.

[4] Editors' note: The original manuscript ends here.

Section V

Clinical Psychology and Psychotherapy

The handbook of clinical practice, which Kelly prepared for his students at Fort Hays Kansas State College, was credited by him as a precursor to *The psychology of personal constructs*. Of particular interest are the 34 rules it contains for students working in the psychological clinic that Kelly established at the college. *Stories from the clinic* and *Clinic ranks high in speech department* report on the activities of the clinic and subsequent traveling clinics for children that Kelly set up. Various abstracts from conference proceedings during Kelly's time in Kansas (*A comprehensive plan for case summaries*; *Some practical considerations in the formulation of clinical recommendations*; *The psychological clinic's use of practical rather than ideal recommendations*; and *A further validation of role therapy*) also concern aspects of clinical practice based on the work of the clinic, including the "role therapy" that he was developing and an analysis, further elaborated in *The practical effectiveness of certain general types of recommendations made by a psychological clinic*, of recommendations made regarding children attending the clinic. *Morale for tomorrow's generation* is an advertisement for the clinic, including a list of typical questions that the psychologist might be asked.

Differential diagnosis in the psychological clinic is the abstract of a conference paper that criticized clinical psychologists for modeling their diagnostic procedures on those of medical practitioners and presented a diagnostic approach designed to indicate therapy. In *A method of diagnosing personality in the psychological clinic*, Kelly again critiques the "current inadequate approach to diagnosis" and, long before this was widely promoted as an alternative to psychiatric diagnosis, emphasizes the importance of helping clients formulate their own understandings of their difficulties. Approximately 30 years later, in *The role of classification in personality theory*, addressing a conference on classification in psychiatry and psychopathology, he returns to critique a categorical system, rather than one based on the propositional use of "reference axes."

The person as a laboratory subject, as a statistical case, and as a clinical client is the abstract of a conference paper in which Kelly illustrated the problems that psychologists might be expected to address in the new (for the 1930s) role of working with clinical clients. *Problems of mental health* presents three case examples of conflicting expectancy systems related to individuals' social roles that, in Kelly's view, had "implications for [the] spiritual and moral foundations of American culture."

A series of documents provides insights into the clinical psychology program that Kelly directed at The Ohio State University. *The problem of clinical psychology* considers the question of whether the program should continue to turn away 90% of graduate students who seek clinical psychology training. *Seminar on psychotherapy*, consisting of notes for 10 sessions delivered in 1949, is of particular interest, as it contains an early presentation of the "limited theory of personality" that he was developing and sets out initial statements of what were to become its fundamental postulate, corollaries, and diagnostic constructs. Also noteworthy is Kelly's classification of different psychiatric diagnoses in terms of psychopathological adjustments to threat. *Psychotherapy: Syllabus—Psychology 865L*, from 10 years later, naturally includes much more material based on Kelly's theory and provides indications of his view of the process of psychotherapy. *Psychology 862 Psychopathology: Course outline* clearly indicates that students were encouraged to take a critical perspective to the traditional approaches on which they received input. Thus, among the course's objectives were "To span the so-called facts of psychopathology" and "to familiarize the student with the changing grounds upon which contemporary psychopathology rests and to prepare him for radical revisions in psychopathology in the near future." These revisions included "Abandonment of concepts of illness and disease together with their attendant social expectations." The course's examination questions display Kelly's ingenuity and humor; for example: "Suppose all the authors whose writings you have been asked to read for this course were to have mental break-down. Choose three from the following list whose psychiatric diagnoses you think you might be able to anticipate from having read their writings. In each case, indicate what you think the precise psychiatric diagnosis might be and what your reasons are for thinking so." *A student's outline of graduate training in clinical psychology at The Ohio State University* provides

Collected Papers of the Pioneer of Constructivist Psychology: George A. Kelly, First Edition. Edited by David A. Winter and Nick Reed.

students with an idea of what to expect during their training and in their future careers, and makes clear that "Students who want to live in an ordered world of answers rather than in a strange world of questions are likely to be unhappy in the field."

Two later reports, *Needs and uses of space in clinical psychology* and *Space needs for clinical psychology 1965–1975*, are of interest in providing not only a comprehensive list of the space requirements for the Clinical Psychology area of the Department of Psychology at The Ohio State University, but also further insights into the organization of this area of the department, including its functions of teaching, research, and provision of clinical services, as well as the principles upon which its style of graduate education was based. One of these principles, echoed in many chapters of this book, was a perspective on clinical psychology not as an applied science, which Kelly viewed as imposing an external framework upon the client, but rather as a collaborative application of the scientific method by both the psychologist and the client. The other principle involved a system of professors working with small groups of students. *Progress report: Ohio State University's graduate program in clinical psychology*, completed during Kelly's last year at the university, describes the program as having once been the best in the country, while also outlining Kelly's assessment of the obstacles that the program faced at the time of the report. *A doctoral program in clinical psychology*, prepared as a proposal for the City College of New York, can be considered as articulating his vision of an ideal program.

In *Psychological approaches to the management of patients*, presented four years prior to the publication of Kelly's magnum opus, descriptions are provided of certain aspects of the theory he was developing, as well as of techniques derived from it. Thus, although what would later be termed "constructs" are referred to in this work as "concepts," notions such as *permeability* and *looseness* are utilized, along with descriptions of what eventually became known as the *role construct repertory test* and *fixed-role therapy*. The presentation was clearly aimed at a diverse range of disciplines, not solely psychologists, and offers insights into topics such as the institutionalization and rehabilitation of psychiatric inpatients.

Contribution to symposium on contributions of learning theory to psychopathology takes a dim view of such contributions, contending that learning theories and methodologies are not well-suited to the domain of psychopathology. *Where do little hypotheses come from?* posits that clinical observations should be treated as hypotheses, and differentiates between big and little hypotheses, the former concerned with traditional diagnostic categories and the latter produced in a theoretico-deductive, clinico-inductive, or statistical dragnet way. It asserts that theory inevitably underpins the clinical psychologist's work.

In *Psychotherapy and the nature of man,* Kelly utilizes the story of Adam and Eve to contend that the nature of "man" is more likely to be elucidated through psychotherapy with individuals experiencing extraordinary moments in their lives than through normative approaches to psychology. *Suicide: the personal construct point of view* represents Kelly's contribution to an exercise in which eight personality theorists were invited to present their perspectives on suicide and to analyze the protocol of a man who had made a serious suicide attempt (see also Chapter 34 in this volume). Kelly's endeavor to comprehend suicide from the viewpoint of the individual attempting a suicidal act includes a differentiation between suicide as a *dedicated act* and mere suicide, conducted under conditions of either *realism* or *indeterminacy*.

The function of interpretation in psychotherapy, among the most significant of Kelly's previously unpublished works, is a series of three lectures delivered as part of an institute for post-doctoral training in psychotherapy. In the first paper, in which he presents the view of the person as an "incorrigible interpreter," he moves from the philosophical basis of his theory to the exploration of patterns of construing through repertory grid technique, and anticipates future applications of the grid, for example, in investigating the construing of traumatic events and reconstruction during psychotherapy. In the second paper, the focus is on reconstruction. Some of the professional constructs of the theory are introduced, and among the points made is that, although validation of constructions of a particular person consolidates the individual's construing of this person, it may lead to the reconstruing of other, similar individuals, and vice versa. In the third paper, the focus is on how the therapist may facilitate reinterpretation, working collaboratively with the client as a psychotherapeutic team, and it is emphasized that interpretations are "testable hypotheses" rather than "authoritative dicta."

Kelly's response to the question, *Is treatment a good idea?* is "no" due to the passive role it assigns to the recipient of treatment. *Innovations in psychotherapy* anticipates a future in which the term "mental illness" is no longer utilized, and examines the models from which new approaches to psychotherapy may be developed as alternatives to conventional treatment methods.

Personal construct theory and the psychotherapeutic interview delineates the ways in which a personal construct psychotherapist and their client can go about their task, and then provides a rare transcript of excerpts from Kelly's sessions with a client, accompanied by his commentary on both the client's and the therapist's remarks. In *Sin and psychotherapy,* Kelly examines the ways in which people escape from issues of good and evil and strategies for coping with such issues. He articulates the personal construct perspective on guilt, asserting that the psychotherapist's "task is to assist the individual man in what is singularly the most important undertaking in his life, the fullest possible understanding of the nature of good and evil."

The psychotherapeutic relationship examines the distinctions between personal construct theory and alternative approaches. It subsequently presents a perspective on psychotherapy as not relying on any particular set of techniques or type of relationship but rather as orchestrating techniques and relationships as a means of enabling the client to utilize their behavior to pose important questions. In *A psychology of the optimal man*, Kelly delineates the goals of psychotherapy from a personal construct perspective. Although personal construct psychotherapy may incorporate a variety of techniques, some of which are borrowed from other theoretical frameworks, the technique about which Kelly provides a detailed description in *Fixed role therapy* was specifically devised from his theory, albeit utilized by him with only about 1 in 15 of his clients.

Experimental dependency appears to be the introduction to an unfinished paper on the therapeutic process, with particular reference to interpersonal dependency. The manuscript includes a poem; however, this may not have been a part of the paper.

Clinical psychology is a section authored by Kelly within an entry of the *Encyclopedia Britannica* that Kelly co-authored with colleagues.

47

Differential Diagnosis in the Psychological Clinic[1]

Clinical psychologists have erred in attempting to pattern all of their diagnostic procedures after those of the medical profession. Psychological practice differs markedly from medical practice in its greater emphasis upon the rational therapies. It needs therefore a type of diagnosis which is designed to indicate the therapy rather than the syndrome. Present-day standardized tests and personality inventories are mostly impractical for use in the clinic because they have been designed without regard for this need.

A form of individual diagnostic examination is offered which is designed to indicate therapy. Each item in the twenty-six groups has been selected because at some time in the past three years it has been a point of major importance in treating a case; thus no items have been included merely because of their academic or systematic interest.

[1] Abstract from the Proceedings of the 43rd. Annual Meeting of the American Psychological Association, Ann Arbor, Michigan, September 4, 5, 6, 7, 1935. Published in 1935 in *Psychological Bulletin*, *32*(9), 684–685. Now in the public domain, and republished by permission of Jacqueline Aldridge.

Collected Papers of the Pioneer of Constructivist Psychology: George A. Kelly, First Edition. Edited by David A. Winter and Nick Reed.

48

The Handbook of Clinic Practice[1]

I Scope of Practice

1. **Cases admitted:** All cases applying to a psychological clinic for services[2] are normally eligible for such services[3]. It has been the custom in some quarters to discourage the registration of cases in which some pathology other than psychopathology is suspected. This is not justifiable.

RULE 1: EVERY APPLICANT FOR PSYCHOLOGICAL SERVICE POSSESSES A PSYCHOLOGICAL CONSTITUTION. THIS CONSTITUTION MAY LEGITIMATELY BE INVESTIGATED BY THE CLINIC WITHOUT INCURRING RESPONSIBILITY FOR NONPSYCHOLOGICAL DIAGNOSIS.

The psychological anamnesis should be so arranged and interpreted that other pathologies may be suspected and the case referred to the proper agencies for their diagnosis and treatment. This, however, should not be construed as a professional responsibility of the clinic.

2. **Cases not admitted:** The psychological clinic should never undertake responsibility for any case which is not committed to the clinic for diagnosis and treatment. Parents, teachers, physicians, and others who confer with the psychologist about cases but who do not present the cases must be made to understand that the responsibility is entirely theirs. Recommendations in such instances must be limited to the general rules of mental hygiene which may be applied safely in any case by any layman.

RULE 2: THE PSYCHOLOGICAL CLINIC SHOULD NEVER ASSUME RESPONSIBILITY BEYOND THAT WHICH IS DELEGATED TO IT.

No case should be administered therapy unless it has been specifically requested by himself or by those who present the case. Application for psychological diagnosis should not be construed as application for therapy[4].

No case should be administered therapy unless upon entering the clinic he has been made to understand as clearly as he is capable of understanding the purpose for which the clinical examination is being made and the general functions of a psychological clinic. The practice of admitting cases under false pretenses is never justified even under the most extenuating circumstances.

RULE 3: NO PRACTICE UNDER FALSE PRETENSES.

3. **Relation to medicine:** There is only one tenable position in distinguishing the field of psychology from the field of medicine: psychology deals with the psychological and medicine with the physiological. Any disregard for this boundary by either discipline must be considered a usurpation of responsibility. This distinction is otherwise known as the distinction between the functional and the organic.

4. **Relation to psychiatry:** Psychiatry is commonly known as a branch of medicine which deals with mental disorders. Many psychiatrists are trainees both in psychopathology and in the related organic pathologies. Strictly speaking, psychiatry is not necessarily a branch of medical practice. Psychiatry overlaps clinical psychology to the extent that it deals with functional or psychological problems. The attitude of clinical psychologists toward the practice of psychotherapy by psychiatrists should be based upon a

[1] This is the fourth edition of the handbook written by Kelly, and dated 1936, for his students in the Psychological Clinic at Fort Hays Kansas State College. It was published as Kelly, G. A., Jackson, T.T., Zelhart, P.F., & Markley, R.P. (1985), The handbook of clinic practice. *Fort Hays Studies Series, 49*. A fifth edition, entitled *Handbook of Psychological Clinic Procedure*, was published in 1941. However, since a fully legible version of this is not available, we are republishing the 1936 version, with the permission of Forsyth Library Special Collections, Fort Hays State University, but, by permission of University Archives/Special Collections—University of Lincoln-Nebraska, including in footnotes and an Appendix all legible changes that were made to this in the 1941 version. Kelly subsequently began work on a further edition of the handbook, but did not complete this.

[2] In the 1941 edition, 'services' is replaced by 'service'.

[3] In the 1941 edition, 'services' is replaced by 'service'.

[4] In the 1941 edition, this paragraph appears before the statement of Rule 2.

Collected Papers of the Pioneer of Constructivist Psychology: George A. Kelly, First Edition. Edited by David A. Winter and Nick Reed.

consideration of the preparation of the individual practitioners. This preparation should include basic studies as described in a later section of this handbook. The attitude of clinical psychologists toward the practice of organic therapies by psychiatrists should be that of one discipline toward another.

5. **Relation to law:** There have been a few instances when the position of the clinical psychologist as a recipient of confidential information has created delicate legal situations. The clinical psychologist must maintain an attitude of helpfulness in all legal matters. Information, however, which is received in confidence by a psychologist acting in a professional capacity must be kept in confidence. Written records must be kept and guarded accordingly.

6. **Relation to religion:** The clinical psychologist must recognize as belonging to religion all matters of right and wrong. When a therapeutic recommendation of a psychologist conflicts with the patient's conscience the psychologist should point out the consequences involved and, if possible, make alternative recommendations (e.g., when a psychologist recommends social dancing to a patient who holds scruples against this form of recreation, the attitude of the patient must be respected.)

7. **Relation to education:** Clinical psychology in its broadest sense is an educative function. If there is a distinction it is that clinical psychology places primary emphasis upon the individual aim of education. Education is thought by some to be more properly a socializing process.[5]

RULE 4: CLINICAL PSYCHOLOGY IS DISTINGUISHED FROM THOSE DISCIPLINES WHICH DEAL WITH ORGANIC OR PHYSIOLOGICAL PROBLEMS ON THE ONE HAND AND THOSE WHICH DEAL WITH SOCIAL AND RELIGIOUS PROBLEMS ON THE OTHER.

8. **Future of clinical psychology:** Somewhat more than half of the hospital beds in this country are being occupied by patients with diagnosed mental illness. When this fact is considered together with the fact that psychotherapy usually requires more time on the part of the clinician than does physiotherapy and with the fact that there is still considerable reticence on the part of patients in seeking psychotherapy it can be seen that an adequately organized profession for dealing with these disorders must be provided on a large scale. Such a profession must be organized as an integral unit and not as a subsidiary of another profession.

II Qualifications of Clinicians

1. **Intelligence:** Psychological treatment differs in certain fundamental respects from medical treatment. One of these respects is in its greater dependence upon the indirect therapies and the accompanying necessity of discovering specific etiologies. Each case possesses a unique syndrome and constellation of causative factors which usually must be thoroughly understood by the clinician. In the solution of such novel problems there is no substitute for native mental ability.

RULE 5: EACH CASE MUST BE TREATED AS A UNIQUE ENTITY.

2. **Mental health:** A clinician must be prepared to shoulder vicariously a great many difficult personal problems. If he is in a poor state of mental health himself or has only lately recovered from such a state he may be overtaxed. Every clinician before completing his training must undergo a psychological diagnosis and, if so advised, must accept psychotherapy.

RULE 6: EVERY CLINICIAN IS HIMSELF A CASE.

3. **Training:** The curriculum for clinicians should include the following subjects in addition to specialized clinical psychology.

experimental psychology
differential psychology
educational psychology
systematic psychology
comparative psychology
abnormal psychology
anatomy
social pathology
educational methods
genetic psychology
statistics and measurements
social psychology
history of psychology
physiological psychology
physiology
sociology
criminology

[5] In the 1941 edition, there are two further sections at this point:
8. **Relation to social work:** Clinical psychologists should recognize the skill of well-trained social workers in manipulating social forces in a community and in creating a generally wholesome society. Their understanding of methods for securing effective social cooperation should not be mistaken for or substituted for psychological insight.
9. **Professional priority:** The question frequently arises as to what profession should have prior authority in a case, and which profession should act in an advisory capacity only. This is simply a matter of convenience which must be determined in individual cases; unless, of course, one wishes to legislate an answer to the old question of what science is "basic." Frequently it is preferable for the psychologist to retain the initiative in a case.

All clinicians should plan to complete doctorate study and must have made definite provisions for masters study at the beginning of their preparation.

4. **Attitude toward work:** The responsibility of a clinician toward his case transcends all other responsibilities. Illness, study, vacations and all personal matters must be considered secondary. A psychological problem is generally more important than a problem of bodily health and the clinician can scarcely feel his responsibility too deeply. Individuals who are unwilling to assume this attitude should not attempt to become clinical psychologists.

III The Anamnesis

1. **Registration** (Form 1.1): Every case must be registered and all addresses recorded accurately so that the case may be followed by correspondence (see Form 1.1). The questions are to be answered by the person who registers the case and who wishes to have recommendations regarding its treatment. Below the starred line the clinician records the place or town at which the case is seen, the date on which the case was first seen, the auspices under which the clinical service was rendered, his own name, and the number of the case in the local clinic. Under Psychometrics the recommended tests are listed. The blanks for memoranda may be used by any clinician in calling special attention of any other clinician to some point.

All available supplementary information such as reports of other clinics, medical reports, health reports and social workers' histories are part of the clinic's permanent file. After a clinician has made recommendations regarding a case he should enter a preliminary diagnosis in the blanks provided.

During an oral registration it is a common experience to have the registrant or patient ask questions concerning the probable diagnosis or concerning the efficacy of corrective measures which have been used. A parent will ask, "Do you think my child is feebleminded?" Instead of reassuring the parent the clinician should say, "Of course that is possible. Our examination will cover that point and if we should discover that he is feebleminded we shall tell you so quite frankly." If parents or patients are reassured at the time of registration it places the psychologist in an embarrassing position if an unfavorable diagnosis must be reported. Such reassurance also encourages the withholding of valuable but morbid information which otherwise might be volunteered.

RULE 7: REASSURANCE SHOULD NOT BE INDISCRIMINATELY OFFERED: IT CLOSES THE CASE AND COMPROMISES THE DIAGNOSIS.

2[6]. **Appointments** (Form 1.21): When the anamnesis requires several appointments scattered over a period of time informants should be given a written schedule of appointments. Clinicians should always be careful to make appointments clear and definite. Extension clinics require a careful listing of appointments. Form 1.21 is to be filled from the registration in advance of an extension clinic. One copy is to be sent to the sponsor so that he may arrange to have all clients appear for their appointments, the other becomes a permanent record of the extension clinic's enrollment. On the form, Cl refers to case 1, P3 refers to parent 3, T6 refers to teacher 6, and F8 refers to friend 8. Names should be entered in the blanks.

3. **Schedule** (Forms 1.51, 1.52): This form enables a clinician to see at a glance the schedule of his day's work. The schedule is arranged so that no two clinicians need be using the same apparatus at the same time; it permits the psychologist to check all conferences, and it provides for group tests to be administrated by the supervisor without conflict with the clinicians. If a guidance conference is to be substituted for an individual psychometric and a physiological examination, the clinician will find at least fifty minutes of consecutive time available. If a parent has two children in a clinic he is registered as Pl and P2, or P4 and P5, etc. The schedule is arranged so that the parent may have double the usual conference time with the same clinician.

4. **Education** (Form 2): Form 2 is designed to be filled out by the clinician in conference with the case's classroom teacher. With some instruction the teacher may fill in Items 1-8, and 13 himself. As with the other forms, the clinician should attempt to secure answers for as many items as possible if[7] the proper conferee is not available.

All information which the clinician considers significant to the diagnosis should be plainly encircled. Thus the psychologist, in making his first perusal of the form, may look for encircled material only.

In item 1 "age" refers to age of case at the time he entered the grade, "repeat" is to be encircled if that grade was repeated once. In Item 2 the x's under "dislike-like" comprise a profile. If the subject listed spelling and the child dislikes it slightly the clinician should encircle the x just to the left of the large middle X in the profile. The large X is to be encircled if there is a normal amount of traits. "Remedies" refer to remedies attempted. In Item 4 a number of vocational subjects are listed and may be encircled when taught. Other vocational subjects taught may be listed in the blanks. In Item 7 the initials and names are requested so that the clinic may seek the cooperation of these individuals if such cooperation appears to be necessary in the treatment of the case. In Item 10 "conference" should be encircled

[6] In the 1941 edition, this section is preceded by:
Survey: All psychological work should be done with a clear view of the social setting in which the psychological problems arose and in which they must be solved. Ideal resources for carrying out psychological recommendations are rarely available but the psychologist can do much to mobilize available resources if he is aware of them. The survey form is sent to extension clinic sponsors. (Editors' note: The survey form is included in the Appendix to this chapter.)

[7] In the 1941 edition, 'even' precedes 'if.'

FORT HAYS KANSAS STATE COLLEGE PSYCHOLOGICAL CLINIC

Form 1.1 Registration

________________________________ ________________________________
Name of case Mailing address

________________________________ ________________________________
Name of parent or guardian Mailing address

________________________________ ________________________________
Name of superintendent or principal Mailing address

________________________________ ________________________________
Name of most interested classroom teacher Mailing address

________________ ________________ ________________
Name of person filling out this form Relation to case Mailing address

1. Upon what problems do you wish the Clinic to advise you? ________________________________
____
____
2. When were these problems first noticed? ________________________________
3. Under what conditions did these problems appear? ________________________________
____
____
4. What corrective measures have been taken? ________________________________
____
____
5. What changes have come with treatment or the passing of time? ________________________________
____
____
6. Under what conditions are the problems most noticeable? ________________________________
____
____
7. Under what conditions are the problems least noticeable? ________________________________
____
________________________________[8]

xxxxxxxxxxxxxxxxxxxxxxxxxxxxxxxxxxxxxxxxxxxxxxxxxxxxxxxxxxxxxxxxxxxxxxxxxxxxxxxxxxxxxxxxxxxxxxxxxxxxxxxxxxxxxxxxxx

__________ __________ __________ __________ __________
Place Date Auspices[9] Clinician No.[10]

Psychometrics[11]: 1 __________ 2 __________ 3 __________
4 __________ 5 __________ 6 __________ 7 __________

(Picture) Memoranda[12]: ________________________________
____
____

Diagnosis: 1__________ 2 __________ 3 __________
(Final) 1 __________ 2 __________ 3 __________

Follow-up: Person	Sent form no.	Date	Recd. reply date	Conf. date	Clin.

[8] In the 1941 edition, this is followed by:
8. Write a short paragraph describing and characterizing the case. This form should be accompanied by an abstract of school records, case history, and other available materials which will enable the Clinic to plan its work more effectively. (Use the reverse side of this page if necessary.)
[9] In the 1941 edition, this is followed by:
Authority __________ Address __________
[10] In the 1941 edition, this is Case No.
[11] In the 1941 edition, this is Recommended psychometrics, and is followed by five rather than seven spaces for answers.
[12] None of the following material is included in the form in the 1941 edition.

FORT HAYS KANSAS STATE COLLEGE PSYCHOLOGICAL CLINIC

Form 1.21 Appointments

Town __________________Auspices_______________________ Date__________________________

Appointment hours are hectographed immediately below the names of those whom the clinic wished to see. When one of the case's conferences may be eliminated the earlier arrival hour is stricken out. All individuals should be informed in advance of the date of the clinic and the exact hours of their appointments.

C1 ________: Arrive 7:50 or 8:30 Finish 11:10	P1 ________: Arrival 8:00 Finish 12:10	T1 ________: Arrive 7:50 Finish 9:20 Tchrs' conf 5-6	F1
C2 ________ Arrive 9:40 or 10:30 Finish 2:30	P2 ________ Arrive 10:05 Finish 3:20	T2 ________ Arrive 10:50 Finish 12:25 Tchrs' conf 5-6	F2
C3 ________: Arrive 10:30 Finish 4:40	P3 ________: Arrive 3:10 Finish 5:05	T3 ________: Arrive 1:50 Finish 3:40 Tchrs' conf 5-6	F3
C4 ________ Arrive 7:50-8:30 Finish 11:30	P4 ________ Arrive 7:50 Finish 12:25	T4 ________ Arrive 8:20 Finish 9:50 Tchrs' conf 5-6	F4
C4 ________ Arrive 9:50 or 10:50 Finish 2:40	P5 ________ Arrive 10:20 Finish 2:55	T5 ________ Arrive 10:05 Finish 10:55 Tchrs' conf 5-6	F5
C6 ________ Arrive 10:40 to 1:20 Finish 4:40	P6 ________ Arrive 3:00 Finish 5:05	T6 ________ Arrive 1:50 Finish 2:30 Tchrs' conf 5-6	F6
C7 ________ Arrive 7:50 or 8:50 Finish 11:30	P7 ________ Arrive 7:50 Finish 11: 50	T7 ________ Arrive 8:20 Finish 9:00 Tchrs' conf 5-6	F7
C8 ________ Arrive 9:40 Finish 2:40	P8 ________ Arrive 8:33 Finish 2:55	T8 ________ Arrive 9:05 Finish 10:00 Tchrs' conf 5-6	F8
C9 ________ Arrive 1:20 Finish 4:40	P9 ________ Arrive 1:20 Finish 5:00	T9 ________ Arrive 11:00 Finish 12:25 Tchrs' conf 5-6	F9
C10 ________ Arrive 10:30 Finish 4:20	P10 ________ Arrive 2:45 Finish 4:45	T10 ________ Arrive 11:30 Finish 12:25 Tchrs' conf 5-6	F10

FORT HAYS KANSAS STATE COLLEGE PSYCHOLOGICAL CLINIC

Form 1.51 Schedule

Time		Psychologist	Clinician I	Clinician II	Clinician III	Supervisor										
8:	00.	General.	T1	P4	P7	.	1.	2.	3.	4.	5.	6.	7.	8.	9.	10
	05.	confer-	.		.	.	.	o.	o.	.	o.	o.	.	o.	o.	o.
	10.	ence.		.	.	.	.	o.	o.	.	o.	o.	.	o.	o.	o.
	15.	.	P1.	.	.	.	.	o.	o.	.	o.	o.	.	o.	o.	o.
	20.	.	.	.	.	.	.	o.	o.	.	o.	o.	.	o.	o.	o.
	25.	.	.	.	.	.	.	o.	o.	.	o.	o.	.	o.	o.	o.
	30.	.	.	T4	P7	.	.	o.	o.	.	o.	o.	.	o.	o.	o.
	35.	.	.	.	.	.	.	o.	o.	.	o.	o.	.	o.	o.	o.
	40.	P7.	.	.	.	.	.	o.	o.	.	o.	o.	.	o.	o.	o.
	45.		C1 Test	C4 Personality	P8	.	.	o.	o.	.	o.	o.	.	o.	o.	o.
	50.	T7	.	.		.	x.	o.	o.	x.	o.	o.	.	o.	o.	o.
						.	x.	o.	o.	x.	o.	o.	.	o.	o.	o.
	55.	....	....	....	....	.	x.	o.	o.	x.	o.	o.	.	o.	o.	o.
9.	00	C7	.	.		.	x.	o.	o.	x.	o.	o.	x.	o.	o.	o.
	05.	.	.	.	.	.	x.	o.	o.	x.	o.	o.	x.	o.	o.	o.
	10.	T1	.	.	.	.	x.	o.	o.	x.	o.	o.	.	o.	o.	o.
	15.			C4 Test		.	x.	o.	o.	x.	o.	o.	.	o.	o.	o.
	20.	P1.														
	25.	.	C1 Physiological.			.	x.	o.	o.	x.	o.	o.	.	o.	o.	o.
	30	P4.			C7 Personality	.	x.	o.	o.	x.	o.	o.	x.	o.	o.	o.
	35.		.			.	x.	.	o.	x.	o.	o.	x.	o.	o.	o.
	40.	T4.				.	x.	.	o.	x.	o.	o.	x.	o.	o.	o.
	45.		C1 Personality			.	x.	.	o.	x.	o.	o.	x.	o.	o.	o.
	50.	T8				.	x.	.	o.	x.	o.	o.	x.	.	o.	o.
	55.		....	C4 Physiological		.	x.	.	o.	x.	o.	o.	x.	.	o.	o.
10:	00	P8			C7 Test	.	x.	.	o.	x.	.	o.	x.	.	o.	o.
	05.					.	x.	.	o.	x.	.	o.	x.	.	o.	o.
	10.	C8				.	x.	.	o.	x.	.	o.	x.	x.	o.	o.
	15.		P2	T5		.	.	.	o.	x.	.	o.	x.	x.	o.	o.
	20.	C1				.	x.	.	o.	.	.	o.	x.	.	o.	o.
	25.					.	x.	.	o.	.	.	o.	x.	.	o.	o.
	30.	C4		P5		.	.	.	o.	x.	.	o.	x.	.	o.	.
	35.					.	.	.	o.	x.	.	o.	x.	.	o.	.
	40.	T5			C7 Physiological	.	.	.	.	.	.	.	x.	.	o.	.
	45.		C2 Test.			.	.	x.	.	.	.	x.	.	o.	.	.
	50.	T2				.	.	x.	.	.	.	x.	.	o.	.	.
	55.	....	....	....	....	.	.	x.	.	.	.	.	x.	.	o.	.
11:	00.	P2.	.	C5 Physiological	C8 Personality	.	.	x.	.	.	.	.	x.	x.	o.	.
	05.		.	.	.	.	.	x.	.	.	x.	.	.	x.	o.	.
	10.	T9	.	.	.	.	.	x.	.	.	x.	.	.	x.	o.	.
	15.					.	.	x.	.	.	x.	.	.	x.	o.	.
	20.			C5 Test.		.	.	x.	.	.	x.	.	.	x.	o.	.
	25.		C2 Physiological			.	.	x.	.	.	x.	.	.	x.	o.	.
	30.	Staff 1, 4, 7			Staff 7	.	T10									
	35															
	40.					.										
	45.		Staff 1		P7 Report	C10			Test							
	50.	.	.	.	.	.										
	55.	....	....	....	C8 Physiological	....										
12.	00	P1 Report.	Staff 4	.	.	. . .										
	05.	.	.	.	.	.										
	10.	T2	.	.	.	.										
	15.	T10	.	P4 Report.	T9	.										
	20.															

FORT HAYS KANSAS STATE COLLEGE PSYCHOLOGICAL CLINIC

Form 1.52 Afternoon

Time	Psychologist	Clinician I	Clinician II	Clinician III	Supervisor	1.	2.	3.	4.	5.	6.	7.	8.	9.	10.
1: 30.	P9	C2 Personality	C5 Personality	C8 Test											
35.						o.	x.	.	o.	x.	.	o.	x.	.	.
40.	C9.					o.	x.	.	o.	x.	.	o.	x.	x.	.
45.						o.	x.	.	o.	x.	.	o.	x.	x.	.
50.	P5					o.	x.	.	o.	x.	.	o.	x.	x.	.
55.						o.	x.	.	o.	x.	.	o.	x.	x.	.
2: 00	C5	T3	T6			o.	.	.	o.	x.	.	o.	x.	.	.
05.															
10.	C2			P9		o.	x.	.	o.	.	.	o.	.	.	.
15.		C3 Test	C6 Physiological			o.	x.	x.	o.	.	x.	o.	.	.	.
20.	T6					o.	.	x.	o.	.	x.	o.	.	.	.
25.						o.	.	x.	o.	.	x.	o.	.	.	.
30.	Staff 2, 5. 8					o.	.	x.	o.	.	x.	o.	.	.	.
35.			Staff 5			o.	.	x.	o.	.	x.	o.	.	.	.
40.				Staff 8	C10 Physiological										
45.															
50.			P5 Report												
55.		Staff 2.			P8 Report.										
3: 00.			C6 Test		.P10										
0.5.					C9 Personality										
10.	P6	Report													
15.															
20.	P3.	C3 Physiological													
25.															
30.	T3				C10 Personality										
35.				C9 Physiological											
40.	C6	P3.		P6.											
45.															
50.	C3														
55.				C9 Test											
4: 00.	P10				Draft recommendations.										
05.															
10.	C10.	C3 Personality.		C6 Personality											
15.															
20.	Staff 3, 6., 9, 10				Staff 10										
25.															
30.															
35.															
				Staff 9	P10 Report										
40.		Staff 3		Staff 6											
45.					Pack										
50.					P9 Report.										
55.		P3 Report.		P6 Report.											
5: 00															

5: 05.
10.
15.
20.
25.
30.
35.
40. TEACHERS' CONFERENCE
45.
50.
55.
6: 00
05.

FORT HAYS KANSAS STATE COLLEGE PSYCHOLOGICAL CLINIC

Form 2 Education

Case	Informant	Relation	Clinician	Date
______	______	______	______	______

1. History

Grade	Age	Year	Repeat	School	Teacher	Superintendent	Ave Mark
Preschool		______	______	______	______	______	F D C B A
I	______	______	______	______	______	______	F D C B A
II	______	______	______	______	______	______	F D C B A
III	______	______	______	______	______	______	F D C B A
IV	______	______	______	______	______	______	F D C B A
V	______	______	______	______	______	______	F D C B A
VI	______	______	______	______	______	______	F D C B A
VII	______	______	______	______	______	______	F D C B A
VIII	______	______	______	______	______	______	F D C B A
IX	______	______	______	______	______	______	F D C B A
X	______	______	______	______	______	______	F D C B A
XI	______	______	______	______	______	______	F D C B A
XII	______	______	______	______	______	______	F D C B A

2. Recently studied subjects

		Dislike –marks	Difficulties Remedies
1. ______	x x x x x x x x x x	F D C B A	______
2. ______	x x x x x x x x x x	F D C B A	______
3. ______	x x x x x x x x x x	F D C B A	______
4. ______	x x x x x x x x x x	F D C B A	______
5. ______	x x x x x x x x x x	F D C B A	______
6. ______	x x x x x x x x x x	F D C B A	______
7. ______	x x x x x x x x x x	F D C B A	______

3. Vocation: case's aim ______ School's aim ______
4. Vocational subjects taught: 1 ______ 2 ______
   domestic-science domestic-art mechanics agriculture economics craft typing stenography book-keeping carpentry animal-husbandry crops market
5. Avocational interests of case: ______
   studies music projects dramatics societies companions parties dances movies gangs athletics mechanics pets collections domestic-interests
6. Avocational training of case by school: music dancing art sewing dramatics social-usage athletics current-events excursions organizations reading debate oratory declamation
7. Present sponsors of avocational training: (give initials and names)
   1. ______ 2. ______ 3. ______
8. Further schooling: no. years expected ______ obstacles ______
9. Absences: _____ Mo. ill work truant unknown remedies ______
10. Parental cooperation: x x X x x conference insight pressure instab critic
11. Behavior problems in last month:

Behavior problems in last month	Measures taken	Reaction of case
1. ______	______	______
2. ______	______	______
3. ______	______	______
4. ______	______	______
5. ______	______	______

12. Member of what organization: 1 ______ pres off 2 ______ pres off
    3 ______ pres off 4 ______ pres off 5 ______ pres off
13. Attitudes

Dependent-Independent	x x X x x	Rebellious-Cooperative	x x X x x
Lazy-Industrious	x x X x x	Tired-Energetic	x x X x x
Quiet-Noisy	x x X x x	Relaxed-Restless	x x X x x
Disinterested-Interested	x x X x x	Distracted-Calm	x x X x x
Quiet-Talkative	x x X x x	Cries easily-Mature	x x X x x
Interests narrow-Broad	x x X x x	Follower –Leader	x x X x x
Quarrelsome-Friendly	x x X x x	Unpopular-Popular	x x X x x

14. Rapport: x x x X x x x

if the teacher has had a conference with the case's parents regarding his progress, "insight" is for parent's insight into case, "pressure" for parental pressure on case of success, "instab" for emotional instability of parents, and "critic" for critical attitude on part of parents.

In Item 12 "pres" is for a presidency and "off" is for any other official position. Item 13 is a personality profile, and Item 14 refers to the rapport between clinician and conferee during the taking of the educational history.

If the case is not in school as much of the educational history as possible should be obtained from whatever sources are available.

5. **Sociology** (Form 3): Forms 3, 4 and 5 are designed to be filled out by the clinician in conference with the parent. No part can be filled satisfactorily by the parent himself. The clinician should say at the outset, "There are a great many questions which we always ask before giving any advice concerning a child. Let's work rapidly and get all the information before us that we can."

It is the practice in some quarters to make the case history interview as casual and conversational as possible, making no notes during the conversation. An opposite point of view is much more desirable; cases who present themselves in a clinic have already become serious about their problems and in general appreciate a thorough and business-like procedure. The blank should be filled at the time each answer is given. No time should be wasted.

RULE 8: DELICATE QUESTIONS SHOULD BE ASKED IN SUCH A WAY AS TO ENCOURAGE AFFIRMATIVE ANSWERS.

RULE 9: THE CLINICIAN MUST NEVER SHOW SURPRISE, DISAPPROVAL, OR REASSURANCE EITHER BY WORD, EXPRESSION OR GESTURE, NO MATTER HOW MORBID OR UNUSUAL THE INFORMATION GIVEN HIM.

It will be noticed that in the present (1936-37) edition, forms 3, 4, 5, 6, and 8 carry an analysis table in the margin. In Form 3 this table permits the clinician to scan for encircled items which bear upon vocational orientation, recreational orientation, personal orientation, school orientation, community orientation, friends, household, security, absorption of personality, independence, possessions, and control, respectively. If an item, such as Item 2, principally throws light upon the case's community orientation an x is to be found opposite that item and under "Com Or." If it also throws light upon friends and personal orientation o's will be found under "Friends" and "Pers Or." When the clinician records information which appears to be clinically significant he should encircle it and all of the o's and x's which appear in the same row in the analysis table.

Items 1-4 and 6 do not require names. Individuals may be identified by their relationships to the case, their sex and approximate ages. In Item 6 intimacy should be indicated as specifically as possible. Terms such as "playmate," "dates," "kissing," "sexual intercourse" should be used. In Item 18 the abbreviations are to be interpreted as follows, "mus" music, "dan" dancing, "voc" vocational training. In Item 21 "shr" is for shared and "own" is for very own or unshared belongings. Item 24 refers to the usual method of spending evenings; Item 25 refers to literature in the home suitable for the child. Item 27 calls for indicating those who help the case in his school work, and whether such help was requested by the school. Abbreviations in Item 30 are as follows: "sep" separated sexes for undressing, "mod" extremely modest attitude, "fea" fearful of undressing, "sex" sexual gestures, and "help" required for undressing. In Item 31 abbreviations are as follows "rstls" restless, "indf" indifferent, "deprs" depresses[13], "exalt" exalted, "brood" brooding, and "susp" suspicious.

6. **Development** (Form 4): The developmental history blank is designed so that it can be filled during a conference with the parent. When the case is an adult the information is difficult to obtain and the clinician may have to consult several sources in addition to the case. All sources should be indicated at the head of the form.

The same general rules which apply to the taking of the sociological history also apply to the taking of the developmental history.

There will be greater difficulty in keeping the conversation under control. Sometimes a parent will stop the clinician in the midst of the citation of problems and say, "My child has had none of those things." In this, the clinician must explain that few children have had many of the problems but that it is very important to know what problems have been met.

In Forms 4 and 8, terms which represent pathologies are capitalized.

In Item 1 abbreviations are for mother's age at the time of birth, period of pregnancy in months, malnutrition, use of alcohol, narcotics, and hard work during pregnancy. The question regarding malnutrition is best asked as follows, "Did you get all the kinds of foods you needed during your pregnancy?" The question regarding narcotics may be asked, "Did you require narcotics during pregnancy?" The abbreviations may be encircled.

[13] Editors' note: [sic]

In Item 2 the complete expressions are delivery period in hours, delivery without physician, delivery at home, breech case, instruments used, birth injury, breathing difficulty and cyanosis.

Item 3 gives a check on early growth with weights at various ages as the parent remembers them.

In Item 4 the terms refer to unusual conditions of the nose and throat, mouth, breathing, ear, eyes, and infections.

In Item 5 "sev" is for unusually severe.

In Item 6 "temp" is for maximum temperature and "No-md" is for no physician in attendance. In Item 7 the blanks are for the age of the appearance of the first tooth in months, weaning from breast, weaning from bottle, difficulty in weaning, achievement of bowel control, bladder control, age of sitting up, walking, talking, dressing self, lacing shoes, use of spoon, cup, age of reaching puberty in years. Item 8 gives the number of medical calls a year, dental calls, and administration of medicine in a month. In Item 9 the total hours of sleep in 24 hours is recorded, together with the norm.

Sometimes children are allowed to sleep with their parents occasionally after the regular practice has been discontinued. In such a case the clinician should be sure to obtain the information because of its bearing upon absorption of the personality. Particularly should regular or occasional sleeping with the parent of the opposite sex be recorded. Item 10 calls for bowel movements a day, urinations a day, washing of hands and face a day, and baths a week. In Item 12 encircle or write in the nature of the sex questions asked by case. Abbreviations are for asking where babies come from, questions regarding puberty of self and others, questions on sex differences, and questions of marriage. The clinician may indicate the nature of the answer by encircling the appropriate abbreviation on the next line: complete answer, reference to a book (get the name of the book), answer more complete than needed, inhibited attitude on part of parent, "doctor brings babies," "stork brings babies," "answer postponed," "God sends babies."

Items 13-28 refer to special problems exhibited by the case during his life: the ages at which they appeared and the corrective measure attempted. Abbreviations are as follows: 14-nightmares, 17-temper tantrums, 20-thumb sucking, tongue sucking, 22-table manners, 23-peculiar food preferences and aversions, 27-strephosymbolia, 28-peculiar mannerisms.

7. **Family** (Form 5): The family history is frequently difficult to fill because parents sometimes are unable to see its bearing upon the case. Another explanation may well be made before the form is attempted, the clinician saying that it is necessary to know the child's family as if he were a member of it in order to make helpful recommendations.

In this form names are not required, individuals being identified by order of birth and relation to case. The list of abbreviations at the top of the form permit the rapid recording of the family record in a small space. The items at the top of the columns indicate the order in which information should be recorded. Material important to the diagnosis should always be encircled. Item 6 refers to separations of parents for several months. Item 8 refers to the case. Item 11 abbreviations are for: retiring from active community participation, anxiety, projections, escape, irritability, excesses such as drunkenness, dependent attitude, and attitude of disillusionment. Item 12 abbreviations are for: religious denomination, attendances a month, active church participation, saying grace at table, religious because of felt need for comfort, because of family custom, and because of felt need for community status. Item 13 abbreviations are for: supervision of case's companions, use of car prohibited, card playing prohibited, Sunday playing prohibited, smoking prohibited, dancing prohibited, attendance at parties prohibited, and drinking prohibited. Item 15 abbreviations are for: definite division of labor in the family, community of interest among members of the family, overt expression of affection between members of family, and strong tendency of members of family to protect each other. Items 8-17 may sometimes be filled without asking direct questions depending upon inference from the earlier part of the interview.

Forms 3, 4, and 5 should be mastered completely enough so that they can be all filled in a period of thirty minutes. The beginner will find this no easy task as he will realize after he has spent some ninety minutes in his first trial. A question should be asked as soon as the answer to the previous question has been given: the clinician recording an answer, while the next question is being answered. This requires a good attention span, habitual phrasing of memorized questions, and an ability to appear interested in what the person is saying even though writing information on the form. It also requires thorough familiarity with the system of abbreviations appearing in the forms and customarily used for recording information.

FORT HAYS KANSAS STATE COLLEGE PSYCHOLOGICAL CLINIC

Form 3 Sociology

Case				Informant				Relation				Clinician Date Number
Voc Or	Recr Or	Pers Or	Sch Or	Com Or	Friends	House	Security	Absorb	Indep	Possess	Control	For attitudes give ages, sexes, & relations of person male-m punished by-pun love – lov female –f fight –fgt protect – prt nagged by – nag quarrel – qrl inseparable - insp
.	.	o	.	,.	.	x	o	,o	o	.	o	1. Household: 1 . . . . 2. . . . .
.	.	o	.	,.	.	x	o	,o	o	.	o	3 . . . . 4 . . . . 5 . . . .
.	.	o	.	,.		x	o	,o	o	.	o	6. . . . . 7. . . . . .8. . . . .
.	.	o	.	,.		x	o	,o	o	.	o	9. . . . . .10. . . . . .11 . . . .
.	.	o	.	,x	o	.	.	,.	.	.	o	2. Adult Neighbors: . . . . 1. . . . . 2. . . . .
.	.	o	.	,x	o	.	.	,.	.	.	o	3. . . . . .4. . . . . 5. . . . .
.	.	o	.	,x	o	.	.	,.	.	.	o	6. . . . . .7. . . . . 8. . . . .
.	.	.	x	,.	.	.	.	,o	o	.	o	3. Teachers: I . . . . II. . . . .
.	.	.	x	,.	.	.	.	,o	o	.	o	III . . . . IV . . . . V. . . . .
.	.	.	x	,.	.	.	.	,o	o	.	o	VI . . . . VII . . . . VIII. . . . .
.	.	.	x	,.	.	.	.	,o	o	.	o	HS 1 . . . . 2 . . . . 3. . . . .
.	.	.	x	,.	.	.	.	,o	o	.	o	4 . . . . 5 . . . . 6 . . . .
.	o	.	.	,.	x	o	.	,o	o	.	.	4. Companions: 1-2yrs. . . . . 2-5. . . . .
.	o	.	.	,.	x	.	.	,o	o	.	.	5-9 . . . . 9-14. . . . . .14-19. . . . .
.	o	.	.	,.	x	.	.	,o	o	.	.	Present: 1 . . . . .2. . . . .
.	o	.	.	,.	x	.	.	,o	o	.	.	3 . . . . .4 . . . . .5. . . . .
.	o	.	.	,.	x	.	.	,o	o	.	.	Younger Older Boys Girls Noisy Quiet Wander Rough
.	o	.	.	,.	x	.	.	,o	o	.	.	5. Groups: (Indicate official positions) 1. . . . .
.	o	.	.	,.	x	o	.	,o	o	.	.	2. . . . . .3. . . . .
.	.	o	.	,.	x	.	o	,o	o	.	.	6. Loves: Age, Age of other, terminates by, intimacy
.	.	o	.	,.	x	.	o	,o	o	.	.	1. . . . .
.	.	o	.	,.	x	.	o	,o	o	.	.	2. . . . .
.	.	o	.	,.	x	.	o	,o	o	.	.	3. . . . .
.	.	o	.	,.	o	o	o	,x	o	.	o	7. Manner of expressing affection: help hug lap kiss
.	.	o	.	,.	o	o	o	,o	x	.	o	8. Dominates. . . . .
.	.	o	.	,.	o	o	o	,o	o	.	x	9. Dominated by . . . .
.	.	o	.	,o	o	o	o	,o	o	.	x	10. Escapades. measures. . . . .
.	.	o	.	,.	.	o	o	,o	o	.	x	11. Punished by. . . . . for. . . . . .reaction. . . . .
.	.	o	.	,o	o	o	o	,o	o	.	x	12. Criticized by. . . . . for. . . . . .reaction. . . . .
.	.	o	.	,.	.	.	o	,o	o	.	x	13. Taboos. . . . . .reaction. . . . .
.	x	.	.	,o	.	.	o	,.	.	.	.	14. Trips. . . . . .1. . . . . .2. . . . . 3. . . . .
x	.	.	.	,.	.	o	o	,x	o	.	o	15. Parents' Ambitions for Case: . . . .
x	.	.	.	,.	.	.	o	,o	o	.	.	16. Case's ambitions: . . . . fulfilled. . . . .
x	o	o	.	,.	.	.	o	,.	o	.	.	17. Talents: . . . .
x	o	o	.	,.	.	.	o	,o	o	.	o	18. Special training: mus art dan sew voc. . . . .
o	.	.	.	,.	.	.	o	,o	x	o	o	19. Spending money: $______ _______mo, earn how. . . . .
x	.	.	.	,.	.	.	o	,o	o	o	o	20. Job: . . . . found own fire. . . . .
.	o	o	.	,.	.	o	o	,o	x	x	o	21. Belongings: shr. . . . . .own. . . . .
.	o	o	.	,.	.	.	o	,o	o	x	.	22. Pets. .collections. . . . .
o	x	o	.	,.	.	.	o	,o	o	o	.	23. Hobbies. . . . .
o	x	o	.	,.	.	.	o	,o	o	.	o	24. Evening . . . .
o	x	o	o	,.	.	.	o	,o	o	,	o	25. Literature. . . . . .read. . . . .
.	x	.	.	,.	.	.	.	,.	.	.	.	26. Movies: _________per mo Sports: . . . .
o	.	o	x	,x	o	o	o	,o	o	.	o	27. Help in school work: moth fath sis bro request. . . . .
o	o	o	x	,.	.	o	o	,o	o	.	o	28. Absences to work: . . . . .Kind of work. . . . .
.	.	.	.	,.	.	o	o	,o	x	.	o	29. Bedfellow: .Room-mate. . . . .
.	.	.	.	,.	.	o	o	,o	x	.	o	30. Undressing: sep mod fea open sex help. . . . .
.	.	x	.	,.	.	.	o	,o	o	.	.	31. Moods: rstls indf deprs exalt brood susp moody. . . . .
.	.	.	.	,.	.	.	.	,.	.	.	.	32. Rapport: x x X x x

FORT HAYS KANSAS STATE COLLEGE PSYCHOLOGICAL CLINIC

Form 4 Development

Case ______	Informant ______	Relation ______
Clinician ______	Date ______	Number ______

Injury	Constitution	Care	Training	Maturation	Stability	Tension	Status	Social or.	Assertion	Motor	Indep-Absoro	
O	X	O	.	,O	O	.	.	,.	.	.	.	1. Birth: :Date______m-age____pd______mc MAL ALC MARWK
X	O	O	.	,	O	.	.	,.	.	.	.	2. Deliver:_______ hrs. ALON HOME BRCH INST INJ BIRTH CY
.	O	O	.	,X	O	.	.	,.	.	.	.	3. Weight: birth
O	X	O	.	,.	.	.	.	,.	.	O	.	4. Condition: NOSE THROAT MOUTH-BREATH EAR EYES INF.
X	O	O	.	,.	O	.	.	,.	.	O	.	5. Injuries :AGE KIND SEV, AGE KIND SEV.
O	X	O	.	,O	O	.	.	,.	.	O	O	6. Diseases: AGE DURATION SEVERITY TEMP NO-MD.
O	X	O	.	,O	O	.	.	,.	.	O	O	a. ______ ______ ______ ______ ______ ______ ______
O	X	O	.	,O	O	.	.	,.	.	O	O	b. ______ ______ ______ ______ ______ ______ ______
O	X	O	.	,O	O	.	.	,.	.	O	O	c. ______ ______ ______ ______ ______ ______ ______
O	X	O	.	,O	O	.	.	,.	.	O	O	d. ______ ______ ______ ______ ______ ______ ______
O	X	O	.	,O	O	.	.	,.	.	O	O	e. ______ ______ ______ ______ ______ ______ ______
O	X	O	.	,O	O	.	.	,.	.	O	O	CONVULSIONS EPILEPSY RICKETS SCARLET TYPHOID
O	O	O	O	,X	.	.	.	,.	.	O	O	7. Maturation: tooth____mo; breast____ mo, bottle ______DIFF
O	O	O	O	,X	.	.	.	,.	.	O	O	Bwl____mo, Bldr____mo, Sit____ mo, Wlk ____ mo, Tlk____ mo.
O	O	O	O	,X	.	.	.	,.	.	O	O	Drs___mo, Lace____ mo, Spn ____ mo, Cup ____ mo, Pub____ mo.
O	O	X	.	,.	O	.	.	,.	.	O	O	8. Medication: m-d___/yr, dent____/yr, Medicine____/mo.
.	O	X	O	,O	O	O	.	,.	.	O	O	9. Sleep: retire______rise_____reg nap____hrs. tot___nrm___
.	.	.	O	,.	.	.	.	,.	.	.	X	Age stop nap____ since sleeping with parent_________
.	O	O	X	,O	.	.	.	,.	.	.	O	10. Toilet: bwl______/dy urn_____/wsh____/dy bth______/wk
.	O	X	O	,.	O	.	.	,.	.	O	.	11. Diet: reg fam mlk frt f-veg meat grs hot cdy var
.	.	O	X	,.	.	O	.	,.	.		O	12. Sex Instruction: Quest: baby puberty sex marriage
.	.	O	X	,.	.	O	.	,.	.		O	Ans: ans BOOK EXCESS INNB DR STORK POSTPONE GOD
.	.	.	.	,.	.	.	.	,.	.	.	.	PROBLEM AGE MEASURES TAKEN
.	.	.	.	,.	O	X	O	,.	.	.	O	13. NERVOUS RESTLESS WORRY PHOBIA___ ______
.	O	O	O	,.	O	O	O	,.	.	X	.	14. SLEEPLESS STEEP-WALK NIGHT MA__ ______
.	.	.	O	,.	O	O	O	,O	X	.	O	15. TIMID SHY SECLUSIVE EXHIBITION___ ______
.	.	.	O	,.	O	O	O	,O	X	.	O	16. STUBBORN RUDE NAG DISOBEDIENT___ ______
.	.	.	O	,.	O	O	O	,O	X	.	O	17. T-T CRY QUARREL FIGHT JEALOUS____ ______
.	.	.	O	,.	O	O	X	,O	O	.	O	18. RUN-AWAY TRUANT QUIT-SCHOOL_____ ______
.	.	.	O	,.	O	.	O	,O	X	.	O	19. SELFISH STEAL BOAST LIE SWEAR____ ______
.	O	O	O	,X	.	.	.	,.	O	O	O	20. SMOKE DRINK THUMB-SUCK TONGUE _____ ______
.	O	O	.	,O	O	O	O	,O	O	X	O	22. FIRES DESTRUCTION TABLE-MNRS_____ ______
.	.	.	O	,O	.	.	O	,O	X	O	O	23. CONSTIPATION ENURESIS FOODS____ ______
.	O	O	X	,O	O	.	O	,.	O	O	O	24. VOMIT FAINT HEADACHE EXHAUST _____ ______
.	O	O	O	,O	O	O	O	,O	O	O	X	25. MASTURBATION SEX IRREGULARITY _____ ______
.	.	.	X	,O	O	O	O	,.	O	O	O	26. STUTTER ARTICULATION LEFT-HAND____ ______
.	.	.	O	,O	.	O	.	,O	.	X	.	27. APHASIA MIRROR-WRITE STREPHO-___ ______
.	.	.	O	,O	.	.	.	,O	.	X	.	28. TIC POSTURE CHOREA GAIT MANNER___ ______
.	.	.	O	,O	.	.	.	,O	,	X	.	

RAPPORT x x x X x x x

FORT HAYS KANSAS STATE COLLEGE PSYCHOLOGICAL CLINIC

Form 5 Family

Case	Informant	Relation	Clinician	Date
Male . . . . . . m	Married . . . . . . mar	Deafness . . . . . . df	Epilepsy . . . . . . epl	
Female . . . . . . f	Divorced . . . . . . dvr	Speech defect . . . . . . sp	Genius . . . . . . g	
Died . . . . . . d	Separated . . . . . . sep	Sinistrality . . . . . . si	Feebleminded . . . . . . fm	
Foreign born . . . . . . B	Miscarriage . . . . . . mag	Nervousness . . . . . . n	Insanity . . . . . . ins	
White . . . . . . W	Illegitimate . . . . . . ilg	Headaches . . . . . . h	Narcotism . . . . . . nrc	
Negro . . . . . . N	Poverty . . . . . . pvt	Convulsions cv	Alcoholism . . . . . . alc	
Mixed blood . . . . . . M	Suicide . . . . . . sui	Paralysis . . . . . . prl	Criminality . . . . . . crm	
Consanguinity C	Blindness . . . . . . bl	Tuberculosis . . . . . . tb	Delinquency . . . . . . dlq	

Encircle parents' Parentheses in Item 3 and child's in Item 4.

Sex Death Age Cause Disease Marital Children Econom Social School — Sex Death Age Cause Disease Marital Children Econom Social School

PATERNAL . . . . MATERNAL . . . .

PATERNAL	MATERNAL
1. Grand.	1. Grand . . . .
2. Grand.	2. Grand. . . . .
3. Parent, uncles and aunts	3. Parent, uncles and aunts
(1)	(1) . . . .
(2)	(2) . . . .
(3)	(3) . . . .
(4)	(4) . . . .
(5)	(5) . . . .
(6)	(6) . . . .
(7)	(7) . . . .
(8)	(8) . . . .
(9)	(9) . . . .
(10)	(10) . . . .
4. Case and siblings. Indicate step-siblings.	
(1)	(6) . . . .
(2)	(7) . . . .
(3)	(8) . . . .
(4)	(9) . . . .
(5)	(10) . . . .

5. Occupations of parents since birth of case.

Occupation	Location	Time	Occupation	Location	Time
(1)______	______	______	(1) ______	______	______
(2)______	______	______	(2) ______	______	______
(3)______	______	______	(3) ______	______	______
(4)______	______	______	(4) ______	______	______

6. Separation : ___mo. in____because__________,._________mo. in______ because_____________mo. in_____ because_____________, _____________ mo. in ______because____________________
7. Remarriage: ____________________________ Dates ____________________.
8. Tension: Intra-________________________Overt known to case____________________.
   Extra-School Church Neighbor Organization Arrest Lawsuit Overt Known
9. Economic Status: Ample Secure Uncertain Debt Temporarily-low WPA Relief
10. Inadequate for: Food Shelter Clothing Education Entertainment Medicine.
11. Reaction of Parents: Retir Ans Proj Esc Irrit Excess Depend Disillus
12. Religious Denom ___________Att _____________mo. Active Grace Cust Comf Status
13. Taboos: Supr-comp Car Cards Sunday Smoke Dance Party Drink
14. Control: Patriarchal Matriarchal Democratic Anarchical
15. Integration: Divis-labor Com-interest _________________ Affection Protection.
16. Language:_________ Recreation_______________ Literature____________________________.
17. Rapport x x x X x x x

FORT HAYS KANSAS STATE COLLEGE PSYCHOLOGICAL CLINIC

Form 6 Physiology

Case ____________________ Age ________ Sex ________ Clinician ____________ Date ________ Number ________

Name ____________________

Dictation ____________________

Vision	Audition	Other sens	Nutrition	Elimination	Infection	Endocrin	Calcium	Anatomy	Ventilation	Cardi-motor	Motor		
.	1	2	.	.	.	.	.	.	.	.	.	1. Akoasm	2. Anesthesia
.	.	.	1	2	.	.	1	.	.	.	.	3. Paraly________Conv.	4. Chronic enuresis
.	.	.	.	½	.	.	.	.	.	.	.	5. Chronic diarrhea	6. Chronic constipation
.	.	.	.	½	.	.	.	.	.	.	.	7. Bowel move hr.______ t.___	8. Nausea anorexia allergy
.	.	.	.	.	.	.	.	1	.	.	2	9. Menses age ____ per ______	10. Vertigo
½	.	.	½	½	½	.	.	.	.	.	½	11. Headaches front vert. bitemp. occip. tender.	
½	.	.	½	½	½	.	.	.	.	.	½	12. Headaches time ________ occasion ________ hypochon.	
.	.	.	.	½	½	.	.	.	½	½	½	13. Other pains time ________ occasion _______ hypochon.	
.	.	.	.	.	.	.	.	.	.	.	½	14. Voice mono. nasal thick harsh trem. stut. art.	
.	.	.	.	.	.	.	.	.	.	.	½	15. Breathing trem. abt-init. lon-exp int-insp,	
.	.	.	.	.	½	.	.	½	.	.	.	16. Feet dirty infected odorous malformed________________	
.	.	.	2	.	.	2	.	2	.	.	½	17. Pat. reflex L____ R _____	18. Weight __________lbs.
.	.	.	½	.	.	½	.	½	.	.	½	19. Height ________inches	20. Norm______lbs. % _______
.	.	.	½	.	½	.	½	½	.	.	.	21. Teeth stained dirty Hutchinson's irregular soft	
.	.	.	½	.	½	.	½	½	.	.	.	T. U. 6 5 4 3 2 1 1 2 3 4 5 6 d-decay	
.	.	.	½	.	½	.	½	½	.	.	.	T. L, 6 5 4 3 2 1 1 2 3 4 5 6 o-out	
.	.	.	½	.	½	.	½	½	.	.	.	P. U, W 7 6 5 4 3 2 1 1 2 3 4 5 6 7 W L – loose	
.	.	.	½	.	½	.	½	½	.	.	.	P. L. W 7 6 5 4 3 2 1 1 2 3 4 5 6 7 W	
.	.	.	½	.	2	.	.	.	.	.	.	22. Gums enlarged inf.	23. Mouth inf. mal.________
.	.	.	.	.	1	.	.	2	.	.	.	24. Tonsils lrg. inf.	25. Palate cft. C-uv. Hare
.	.	.	.	½	.	.	.	½	.	.	.	26. Tongue coat macro micro fis trem tie f-tie hem	
.	.	.	.	.	.	.	.	½	.	.	.	27. Locution undershot over-mal. malf-jaw.	
.	.	.	.	.	½	.	.	½	.	.	.	28. Skull exct. Mucus micro-macro-hydro- mongol.	
.	.	.	.	.	½	½	.	.	.	.	.	29. Scalp dirty inf.	30. Ears dirty inf malfor.
.	.	.	.	.	.	½	.	.	.	.	.	31. Hair coarse dry soft bald thin thick color ____________	
.	.	.	.	.	½	½	.	.	.	.	.	32. Skin dry moist dirty inf. color________ birthm ________	
.	.	.	.	.	1	2	.	.	.	.	.	33. Cerv. Lymph nodes	34. Thyroid enlarged
.	.	.	.	.	1	2	.	.	.	.	.	35. Thorax abnormality	36. Abdomen pdnt flat arc
.	.	.	.	.	½	.	½	.	.	.	.	37. Rib rosettes	38. Scaphoid tendency
.	.	.	.	.	.	.	½	½	.	.	.	39. Body spins torso-leg_______	
												pyknic asthenic athl.	
.	.	.	.	.	.	.	1	½	.	.	.	40. Bowlegs knock-knees	41. Posture _________________
.	.	.	½	.	.	1	.	1	.	.	.	42. Fat sub-cut_____________	43. Mal-nut. sympt.
.	.	.	.	.	.	2	.	½	.	.	.	44. Hernia atro. asym.	45. Enlarged bones perspire.
.	.	.	.	.	.	.	.	½	.	.	.	46. Atonicity grip L 1____2___3___	
												R 1____2___3___kg.	
.	.	.	.	.	.	.	.	.	.	.	½	47. Handedness L R	48. Pupil ref. ______coor.______
.	.	.	2	2	2	2	.	.	.	2	1	49. Methodist Episcopal	50. Temperature____________F
.	.	.	.	.	.	.	.	.	.	½	.	51. Blood pres. S D	52. Pulse rate 1____2____
.	.	.	.	.	.	.	.	.	2	.	½	53. Breath rate 1____2	54. Pulse irregularity________
.	.	.	.	.	.	.	.	.	.	.	½	55. Toe stand ____________ sec.	56. Fatigue complaint.
½	.	.	.	.	2	2	.	2	.	.	1	57. Strabismus ver. c p	58. Eye color____inf. prot.
.	.	.	.	.	.	.	.	.	1	.	2	59. Cough adn. asth. sin.	60. Space perception______
.	.	.	.	.	.	2	.	.	.	.	½	61. Tremor fing. intent.	62. Nails dry soft bitten
.	.	½	.	.	.	.	.	.	.	.	.	63. Olfaction Gustation ___ pain (area)___________	
1	.	2	.	.	.	.	.	.	.	.	.	64. Color RG BY tot agn	65. Asteregnosis kinesthesis
.	.	.	.	.	.	.	.	2	.	.	½	66. Romberg long. Trans.	67. Line walk L C R ataxia
2	1	.	.	.	.	.	.	.	.	.	.	68. Audition L_____R_____	69. Vision L_______R_______
½	.	.	.	.	.	.	.	.	.	.	.	70. Astigmatism L 0 30 60 90 120 150	
												R 0 30 60 90 120 150	

Rapport x x X x x

8. **Physiology** (Form 6): The object of the physiological examination is to throw additional light upon the psychological diagnosis, not to attempt a medical diagnosis. From the physiological examination the clinician may conclude that an additional medical examination is necessary although he can never permit his recommendation to indicate that such an examination is not necessary or that the findings of such an examination would be positive. None of the information obtained on the physiological form may be put into the psychological recommendations to the case or others: for instance, if the eye examination shows that a child possesses less than 10/20 vision in each eye the psychologist can only recommend an eye examination, never say that the child needs glasses.

The items of the examination are arranged in the order in which they are to be administered. The physiological equipment should be arranged as follows: The physiologist's case should be placed on a table at the light end of a room at least twenty feet long. One side or the back should face the distant end of the room. The physiologist should have a chair facing the front of the physiologist's case. The chair for the subject should face the physiologist's chair and the scales should be placed in front of it. The steel rule should be used to measure off twenty feet from the case with marks on the floor every four feet: then the rule is to be tacked to the wall back of the physiologist. All other material should be left in the case except when in actual use.

When the subject enters the room he is asked to write his name and a dictated passage, then to remove his shoes. While he is removing them he is asked questions on Items 1-12. Items 14-16 may be filled from observation. Item 17 is checked next and while the results are being recorded the subject is asked to weigh himself. The clinician checks the weight and while recording it asks the subject to stand with his back against the steel rule. Height is checked by holding the right angle of the age-height-weight norm card against the rule above the subject's head. If the subject removes his shoes quickly some of the Items 1-13 may be postponed until after Item 19 and filled while the subject is replacing his shoes. The physiologist should be able to check Items 21-27 after one careful observation of the mouth. If he does so he will save considerable time in the examination. Items 28-45 should be filled at one time.

On Items 52 and 53 the first part is to be filled and then the subject told to step on and off a chair to a count of four. The counting should be spaced at about one second intervals and the subject required to mount the chair eight times. The pulse and breathing rate are counted immediately and simultaneously for fifteen seconds and the results multiplied by four to augment the value to rate a minute. Item 56 is checked immediately after Item 55. Item 60 is checked by holding a pencil about twenty inches in front of the subject and asking him to extend his arm horizontally at one side then rapidly touch the point of the pencil with the index finger. Space perception is a test with both arms separately and with both eyes open. Item 61 is tested by having the subject hold a sheet of paper on the tips of his fingers. Olfaction is tested by asking the subject to recognize the odor of peppermint oil. If necessary the subject may be given the vial of water and the vial of peppermint oil and asked to tell which one smells better. Pain is tested with an algesiometer fully loaded for adults and half loaded for children six years of age. Tests are made on the back of both hands with the eyes diverted, also on the back of the neck, on the back of the shoulder and on the calf of the leg. The subject is asked if the point is sharp or dull. Color blindness is checked with the Ishihara test, astereognosis by having the subject close his eyes and distinguish a ball and cube held in either hand, and kinesthesis by distinguishing between a nine gram weight and a fifteen gram weight of the same size. For children below nine years of age the regular Stanford-Binet Block test should be used. The line walk is carried out by directing the subject to walk to the twenty foot mark at the opposite end of the room with his eyes closed and his hands over his eyes. When he arrives at the mark his vision is tested for each eye separately, the light on the letters of symbols. The physiologist must be careful to hold the astigmatic chart at a level with the subject's eyes and perpendicular to his line of sight. Audition is tested with each ear separately, the subject facing the side and holding his hand over the far ear. He is asked to count a series of clicks of the acoumeter or to say "tick" each time he hears the acoumeter.

The analysis table in the margin of the form contains three symbols, 1, 2, and 1/2. 1 indicates that the left hand item in that row is involved, 2 indicates that the right hand item is involved and 1/2 indicates that both are involved.

Abbreviations are as follows by items: 3, paralysis with a note as to location, recent convulsions, or seizures; 7, time of usual bowel movements, frequency a day; 9, age of puberty; length of menstrual cycle; 11, frontal, vertical, bitemporal, occipital, excessive tenderness; 12-13, hypochondriacal attitude toward headaches and pains; 14, monotone, focal tremor, abrupt initiation of sound, long expirations, interrupted inspirations; 17, patellar reflex; 20, percent under or over weight (use plus and minus); 21, temporary and permanent teeth; and upper and lower; 22-24, infected, malformed, excessively large; 25, cleft palate, cleft uvula, hair lip; 26, tongue coated, large, small, fissured, tremor, tie, functional tongue tie, hemiatrophy; 27, overshot, malocution, malformed jaw; 28, skull exotosis, mucus patches, microcephaly, macrocephaly, hydrocephaly, mongoloid; 29, ears malformed; 32, birthmarks (usually significant only if conspicuous); 33, enlarged cervical lymph nodes; 36, abdomen pendant, *arc de cercle*; 39, torso leg ratio (approximate), athletic; 42, sub-cutaneous fat locations; 43, symptoms of malnutrition; 44, atrophies, asymmetries; 45, excessive perspirations; 46, left and right hand three trials on hand dynamometer; 48, pupillary reflex, coordinated (reflex in nonstimulated eye); 49, speech; 51, systolic, diastolic; 57, vertical, central, peripheral; 58, protruding eyes; 59, adenoids, asthma, sinus congestion; 61, finger tremor, intention tremor; 64, red-green blindness, blue-yellow, total, agnosia (does not know color); 66, longitudinal, transverse; 67, left, center, right; 70, numbers refer to degrees of angle at which lines seem darkest.

The clinician should master the physiological form sufficiently well to enable him to administer it in an average time of twenty minutes. He should be able to set up the equipment in three minutes.

9. **Psychometry** (Forms 7.1, 7.2, 7.3[14]): Advanced clinicians qualifying in psychometry must complete the following preparation:

Test	Number of Practice Administrations	Degree of Proficiency
Stanford-Binet	20	without manual or blank
Herring-Binet	10	with manual and blank
Pintner-Paterson	15	with blank only
	3 throughout entire scale	with blank only
Pintner Non-Language Mental	3	with manual
Detroit First Grade Intelligence	2	with manual
Detroit Primary Intelligence	2	with manual
Henmon-Nelson Mental Ability 3-8	1	with manual
Henmon-Nelson Mental Ability 7-12	1	with manual
Modern School Achievement	1	with manual
Pintner Achievement	1	with manual
Iowa High School Content	1	with manual
Monroe Reading Aptitude	3	with manual
Gray Oral Reading	2 of each set	with manual
Nelson-Denny Silent Reading for Senior High Schools and Colleges	1	with manual
Nelson Silent Reading 5-8	1	with manual
Kelly Speech and Reading Scale	10	with blank only
Clapp-Young Arithmetic	1	with manual
Nelson English	1	with manual
Stenquist Mechanical Aptitude I	1	with manual
Stenquist Mechanical Aptitude II	1	with manual
Pressey X-O	3	with manual

Binet tests and the speech and reading examination must be given in strict privacy. The Pintner-Paterson may be given in a room with other people who are not observing the case. The group tests may be given in a room with other people provided there is no disturbance.

A case should not be tested more than three hours in one day. The basic test for any case is the intelligence test. Cases in which there are suspected social inhibitions should be given a group test. Those who have educational difficulties in subjects involving reading difficulty should have a performance test.

Unless starred tests are specified, the longer form of the Stanford-Binet Scale should be given. Tests in the selected group of the Durrell Scale for non-readers are underlined. If a reading disability is suspected the M.A. on the Durrell Scale should be computed and compared with the other. Parts of tests completed should be encircled, the numbers of completed tests should be encircled and the year numerals of complete year levels should be encircled. C.A. and M.A. should be given in months. Test materials must be kept in the box when not actually in use so that the subject will not be distracted. The lid of the box must be kept up in such a way as to obscure the materials not in use. The form should be kept out of sight as much as possible. Children under eight should be asked if they need to go to the toilet before starting the examination.

Unless otherwise specified Group E (entire test) of the Herring-Binet Scale should be given. The Herring revision is preferred for use in extension clinics when time is short. When records are to be compared with those of other clinics the Stanford revision is preferred.

[14] The 1941 edition does not include the Stanford-Binet record sheet, but does contain record sheets for the Terman-Merrill, Gesell, and Cornell-Coxe tests.

FORT HAYS KANSAS STATE COLLEGE PSYCHOLOGICAL CLINIC

Form 7.1 Stanford-Binet

Case	Examiner	Date	Testing Time	Number
Sex Age /	Date of birth / CA / MA /	School /	Parent's name /	Parent's address

#III * Body/nose-eyes-mouth-hair
*2 Objects/ key-1c-knife-watch-pencil
*3 Pictures / Dutch-canoe-postoffice
4 Give sex
5 Give last name
*6 Repeat/I have-The dog-In summer
A Repeat digits/642-352-837
#IV. *1 Compare lines/1 2 3 (4 5 6)
2 Forms/ 1 2 3 4 5 6 7 8 9 10
*3 Counting four pennies
*4 Copying square (use back)
*5 Comprehension/sleepy-cold-hungry
6 Digits/4739-2854-7261
A Repeat/ The boy's-train- we are
#V. *1 Weights (3 & 15) / a- b - c
*2 Colors/red-yellow-blue-green
*3 Aesthetic comparison/a - b - c
4 Definitions/chair-horse-fork doll-pencil-table
5 Patience/a - b - c
*6 Three commissions/key-door-box
A Give age
#VI. *1 Right & left/hand-ear-eye
*2 Missing parts/a - b - c - d
*3 Thirteen pennies
*4 Comprehension/rain-fire-train
5 Coins /5c - 1c - 25 c- 10 c
6 Repeat/time-vacation-walk
A Forenoon and afternoon
#VII. *1 Fingers/one-other-both
2 Pictures /Dutch-canoe-postoffice
3 Digits/31759-42835-98176
4 Bow knot/t____ double-single
*5 Differences/fly-stone-wood
*6 Copy diamond/a - b - c (use back)
A1 Days of week/t ____checks a-b-c
A2 Digits bkws/283-427-958
#VIII. *1 Ball and field/inf-sup
*2 Count bkws/t_____ e______
*3 Comprehension/
broken-late-hits
*4 Likenesses/wood-apple-iron-ship
5 Define/ballon
tiger-football-
soldier
6 Vocabulary/1st____
2nd______
A1 Coins 71-25-10 $1-50
A2 Dictation

*IX. *1 Date/day of wk. mo. day of mo.
*2 Weights/a - b - c
3 Make change / (4 10) – (12 15) – (4 25)
*4 Digits bkws/6528-4937-9629
*5 Make sentence/bov-work-deserts
6 Rhymes/day _____mill_____ spring________
A1 Months/t ____checks a - b - c
A2 Stamps/t_____
#X *1 Vocabulary/1st____ 2nd_____
*2 Absurdity/hill-cars-body-48 rider
3 Designs/A_____ B_____ (use back)
4 Reading and report/t ____e _____mems
*5 Comprehend/opinion-begin-actions
*6 Words/½____ 1_____ 1½_____ 2½____ 3____ t
A1 Digits/374359-521746
A2 Repeat/apple-halfpast-summer
A3 Healy-Fernald puzzle a/t
#XII. *1 Vocabulary/1st_2nd____.
2 Definitions/pity-revenge-charity envy-justice
3 Ball and field/inf.-sup.
*4 Dissected sentences/a - b - c
*5 Fables/a____ b____ c_____ d_____ e____ t____
*6 Digits bkws/ 31979-69482-52961
*7 Pictures/Dutch-canoe-post.-colon.
*8 Like-snake-book-wool-knife-rose
#XIV. *1 Vocabulary/1st _____2nd_______
2 Induction/ans.-rule (give XVIII lst)
*3 Pres. & king/accession-tenure-pow.
*4 Questions/man-death-bicycle
*5 Arithmetic reasoning/50-20-35c
6 Clock/6:22-8:08-2:46
A Digits/2183439-9728475
#XVI. *1 Vocabulary/1st____ 2nd_____
*2 Fables/a____ b_____ c_____ d_____ e_____ t____
3 Differences/laziness-evolution- poverty-character
*4 Boxes/ (2 1) - (2 2) - (3 3) - (4 4)
*5 Digits bkws/471952-583294-752638 6 code/t___ e___
A1 Repeat/Walter-yesterday
A2 Physical relations/cannon-rish-rifle
#XVIII. *1 Vocabulary/1st__2nd____
2 Paper cutting test
*3 Digits/72534896-49853762-83795482
*4 Thought/a-b (record verbatum)
*5 Digits bkws/4162593-3826475-/ 33795482$
6 Ingenuity/ 3 & 5 get 7-5 & 7 get 8

FORT HAYS KANSAS STATE COLLEGE PSYCHOLOGICAL CLINIC

Form 7.2 Herring-Binet

Case	Clinician	Date	Testing time	Number

Sex	Date birth	CA	MA	School	Parent's name	Parent's address

GROUP A

1. Pictures/ 1____2____3____4____ 12 ( )
2. Number series/ a b c d e f g h 3 ( )
3. Thought/ 13 ( )
4. Digit bkws/ 1 2 3 4 5 6 7 8 9 10 9 ( )

MA _______ GROUP A TOTAL _______
Tests 1-4

GROUP B

5. -9 Body/ knee-finger-ear-foot 4 ( )
6. -9 Syllables/want-winter-bed 3 ( )
7. -15 Size/ 1 2 3 3 ( )
8. -19 Aesthetic comp./ 1 2 3 4 4 ( )
9. -25 Colors/ black-gray-white 3 ( )
10. -41 Situations/ lost-lessons buy-eat-failed-good 6 ( )
11. Read & report / score – 2 9 ( )
12. 6 – Define / obedience – hope-pride-culture-hostility severity- prejudice 7 ( )
13. 23- Read & report/score – 2 6 ( )

MA _______ GROUP B TOTAL _______
Tests 1 -15

GROUP C

14. -29 Situations/empty-ocean dropping-muddy-autos 5 ()
15. -31 Absurdities/$5-friends-$100-thief-Smith-25c 1&2 – lights 8 ()
16. -31 Make sentences/ hen-play-money-ball 4 ()
17. -37 Rhymes/ball-map-bad-rim 4 ()
18. -37 Similarities/wheel-sling ink-star-cloud-stone 6 ()
19. 6- Proverbs/canoe-fire-mild-Rome-woods 5 ()
20. 10- Read & report/score -2 7 ()
21. 10-Mixed sentences/ 1 2 3 (one minute) 3 ()
22. 22-Problem reading/ 1 2 3 6 ()

MA _______ GROUP C TOTAL _______
Tests 1-22

GROUP D

23. -25. Syllables/ school- snowballs-add-ice 4 ( )
24. 31 Directions/ 1 2 3 3 ( )
25. -31 Directions/ 1 2 3 4 4 ( )
26. -31 Similarities /baseball-rain wood-bed 4 ( )
27. Generalization / 5 ( )
28. 1C- Comprehension/ 3 ( )
29. 19- Sentence completion /5. 5 (two minutes) 5 ( )
30. 1C- Problem reading/ (two minutes) 5 ( )

MA _______ GROUP D TOTAL _______
Tests 1-30

GROUP E

31. -9 Name objects/nail-button-safety pin-hair pin-string 5 ( )
32. -15 Firm comparison/score-2 5 ( )
33. -29 Commissions/ 4 ( )
34. News route/

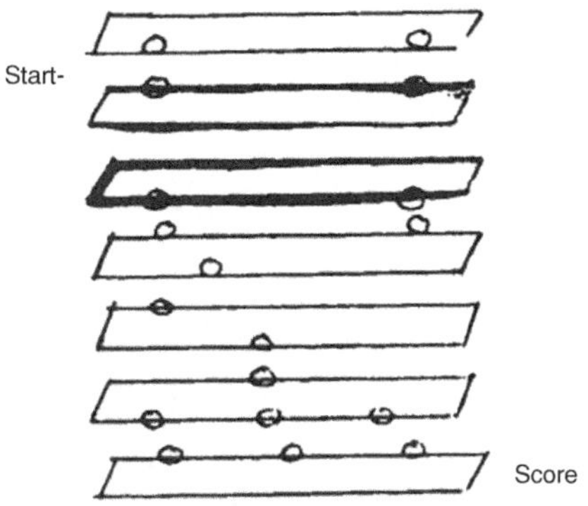

35. Digits forward/ 10 ( )
36. 10-Syllables/ 1 2 3 3 ( )
37. 10-Roast/ ½-1½-3-3½ 5 ( )
38. 10-Code/letters-2 (five minutes) 6 ( )

MA _______ GROUP E TOTAL _______
Tests 1-38

YEAR-MONTH EQUIVALENTS FOR CONVENIENCE IN COMPUTING CHRONOLOGICAL AGE
1-12, 2-24, 3-36, 4-48, 5-60, 6-72, 7-34, 8-96, 9-108, 10-120, 11-132, 12-144, 13-156, 14-168, 15-180, 16 and over-192

FORT HAYS KANSAS STATE COLLEGE PSYCHOLOGICAL CLINIC

Form 7.3 Pintner-Paterson

Case ________ Clinician ________ Date ________

Testing time ________ Date of birth ________ Age ________ C A ________ M A ________ Grade ________ Requested by ________

			4 5 6 7 8 9 10 11 12 13 14 15 A
1.	Mare	T	160--91--76--58--48--44--39----------32
		E	11---4---------------------------2
2.	Seguin (3)	T	43--29--25--21--19------------15---------------12
3.	Five Figure	T	300-224-145-131-106--90--84--62
		E	31--18--11---78----------------------4
4.	Two Figure	T	300-283-115--93------------63--5--42
		E	45--39--20--17-------------14------------------11
5.	Casuist	T	300-279-164------------127--98----------------------83
		E	30--14-------------11---7----------------------5
6.	Triangle	T	300-289-122---------------83----------------85--------59
		E	36--30--17------------------13---------------10---------6
7.	Diagonal	T	300-173------------140--83----------------48--38
		E	40--21------------16--10----------------5
8.	Healy A	T	300-----257----144-----95--77--65
		M	100-----50---38---31---26--20
9.	Manikin	S	2--------------3------------4---------5
10.	Profile	T	300-236-------------------311-189
11.	Ship	S	1---7---9---15--17--17--18-----------------19
12.	Picture	S	5--43--99--178-271-327-366-396-410
13.	Substitution	(T)	
		(E)	600--------384-248-194-163-142-122-118-109
14.	Adaptation	S	1---2---3------4---------------5
15.	Cube	S	1---2---3---4------5------------6-------------7----8
			4---5----6-----7---8---9---10---11----12---13--14--15--A

Picture Completion. (Part scores)
1 2 3 4 5 6 7 8 9 10

In each item the first number is the number of the test, the second is the score in Group A which qualifies the subject for taking the test. For instance, -9 in Test 5 indicates that if the subject made a score of 9 or less in Group A he is to take Test 5. The notation 9- would indicate that if he made a score of 9 or more in Group A he is to take the test. When the score in Group A exceeds this qualifying range full credit is given without administering the test. The number just before the blank indicates the maximum score on that test.

In form 7.3 the upper row of figures opposite each test refers to time in seconds and the lower row either to moves or errors. The score made is indicated by a check mark interpolated approximately between the two adjacent standardized scores. Scores better than the best standardized are indicated by drawing a line out to the right-hand margin. Ordinarily, it is not necessary to compute the mental age; the concentration of check marks indicates that value as closely as the discriminative power of the test justifies.

The Pintner-Paterson materials should be packed in their cases in the reverse order to that in which they are used. The subject should not see the top of any form board until he is ready to take the test. The method is to turn the form board upside down on a piece of cardboard to remove the blocks, then turn it on its edge with the back toward the subject, arrange the pieces using the board as a shield, give the instructions, drop the board toward the subject, and start the stop-watch.

RULE 10: THE PSYCHOMETRIST SHOULD NOT REPORT THE RESULTS OF AN INTELLIGENCE TEST TO THE CASE OR HIS PARENTS UNLESS DIRECTED TO DO SO BY THE CLINIC AUTHORITY[15].

10. **Speech and Reading** (Form 7.5[16]): The diagnosis of the symbolic functions requires a special examination covering both physiological and psychological aspects of reading, writing, and speech. The materials used in administering Tests 1-12, 18, and 20-37 of the examinations are contained in a special manual. They consist of the following: a Van Riper Angle Board for Item 20, a peep hole card for item 18, a list of sentences containing speech sounds in initial, medial and terminal positions together with the corresponding phonetic symbols for use in Items 26-37, a list of word groups for use in Items 21-35, a set of reading passages with flaps and questions for Items 1-22, a mirror for observing eye movements in Items 1-12 which can be folded into an A-stand for Item 15, four sets of words for use in Item 15, and a word finder for use in pointing out single words to the subject.

The abbreviations under the section on eye movements indicate the following: passage method of reading, total fixations made, reversals, questions answered correctly, six-year norm, eight-year norm, twelve-year norm, adult norm, and superior adult norm.

In tests 1-4 the reading is oral and in tests 5-8 it is silent. The time is the total reading time for the passage, and in each case the norm encircled is the one next below the performance. In Items 9-12 the abbreviations stand for abnormally long fixations, number of binocular aphasic divergences, extent of verbalization, and eye tremors. It is recommended that the Gray Oral Reading Test be used for Test 13 and the Nelson or Nelson-Denny Silent Reading Examination for Test 14. Scores should be converted to age norms.

Test 16 requires the copying of the sentences with each hand, forwards and backwards. The sentence contains all the letters of the alphabet. Test 17 is for simultaneous writing reversals. The clinician holds his hand over the subject's eyes, the subject stands close to the blackboard with arms well extended to sides (beyond tips of shoulders), the instructions are given to write with both hands at once, and the letters are pronounced in the order listed, the subject is encouraged to write spontaneously and rapidly and is not allowed to see the results of his efforts until the test is finished. The letters reversed or partially reversed by each hand are encircled. Reversals made by the unpreferred hand in naive subjects should not be considered serious evidence of lack of cerebral dominance.

Ocular dominance is tested by using a card with a hole in the center. The subject holds the card first in the left, then right, and then in both hands; each time dropping the card to the side after an observation. In bringing the card to the front of the face the subject is asked to bring it from the bottom for the first trials, then from the right, then from the left, and then from the top. The clinician stands about fifteen feet away and asks for reports on whether the pencil he holds in his hand is pointed up or down. The clinician should move about between observations and encourage a different set for each observation. Ten trials are taken and the number of each trial encircled opposite L or R depending upon the eye used.

Item 19 calls for the following: Hand preferred in writing, hand in taking pencil offered in the median plane (three trials), hand used in using scissors, and foot used in kicking baseboard (three trials). In offering the pencil the subject is instructed to sit squarely with table and with hands clasped tightly in front of him. The pencil is then laid about six inches in front of the subject's hands with the point toward the subject. The subject is instructed to pick up the pencil as quickly as possible after a signal is given. The kick test is administered with the subject standing close to and facing the wall. He is instructed to kick the wall three times as quickly as possible after the signal.

Test 20 is made with a modification of the Van Riper Angle Board. Simultaneous writing while blindfolded is required. The procedure is similar to that of Test 17. The two letters and the word are written with the angle board in each of the indicated positions. Reversed letters are encircled according to the hand used in reversing them.

The abbreviations in Item 21 stand for the following phrases: Transient aphasia, articulatory aphasia, agraphia, and alexia. In filling the blank opposite Item 27 the phonetic script for the proper sound is placed above the line and the substituted sound immediately

[15] In the 1941 edition, this rule is stated before the last two paragraphs.

[16] This form is not included in the 1941 edition.

below the line. The sounds are given on the speech and reading test cards. The test is administered orally by the examiner who must be careful to pronounce the sentences correctly himself. Each sentence contains words in which the sound appears in initial, median, and terminal positions. Several trials may be given on any one sound. The object is to discover which sounds cannot be formed and which sounds are habitually altered. The first abbreviation in Item 31 stands for malformed dental arch. In Item 38 hypert-turb stands for hypertrophied turbinates.

Tests 15-20 are for a lack of cerebral dominance. In Test 15 the number of erect words read should be larger than the number in any of the other lists. The rotated words will normally be read with somewhat greater difficulty. The reversed and inverted words are usually read with about equal difficulty unless the subject has had experience with type-setting. If the reversed words are read nearly as easily as the erect words, or much more easily than the inverted words, there is evidence of a lack of cerebral dominance.

In Item 16 the letters formed with the non-preferred hand should be of poorer quality and should contain more reversals when the writing is done left to right. When the writing is done right to left, the greater number of reversals should be made with the preferred hand although the quality of the letters should continue to be poorer when they are made with the non-preferred hand. The following indicate a cerebral dominance opposite to the manual preference: A better quality of writing with the non-preferred hand, reversals with the preferred hand in writing left to right, and a greater number of reversals with the non-preferred hand in writing right to left.

In test 17 the best integration is shown when there is no tendency to reverse with either hand; naïve subjects will commonly reverse with the non-preferred hand, subjects without dominance will reverse with both hands, and subjects whose manual preference is inconsistent with cerebral dominance will reverse principally with the preferred hand. Tests 18-20 are for native cerebral dominance.

Tests 1-12 require considerable skill and practice for successful administration. Some students find the technique too difficult to master but most students can get fairly accurate results after ten complete administrations.

The entire speech and reading examination should be given whenever a speech or reading defect is suspected. These defects are so interrelated that it is unwise to attempt to separate them in the examination[17].

11. **Personality** (Form 8)[18]: The form of the personality examination should be memorized but its administration must be flexible. While the primary purpose of the examination is diagnostic it so happens that it may aid therapy because of its tendency to objectify the patient's thinking and encourage a controlled catharsis. In some cases, however, it is best to administer only a part of the examination at a time consistently with the rules of therapy listed later in this handbook.

The personality examination was originally compiled from a record of replies of successfully treated cases to the question of what contributed most to their improvement. The cases were individuals who had been treated by the rational psychotherapeutic methods: those depend upon the patient effecting his own cure through investigating and understanding his own problem. The objective of a personality examination was considered to be the immediate and efficient elicitation of clinically significant material. Through keeping a record of the material considered clinically significant by the patients successfully treated by rational methods, it was possible to construct a personality examination which approached this objective. Originally then, each item in Form 8 represented a turning point in the actual treatment of some case. Since compiling the original form other items have been added which the psychologist has found by experience to have enabled him to predict the outcome of a case or to lead up more effectively to significant material. The items of the examination are semi-objectively compiled and their arrangement clinically determined.

In this form reactions which are generally considered pathological are capitalized. Whenever a capitalized abbreviation is encircled the O's and the X in the same row of the analytic margin should also be encircled. Items comprising the short form of the examination are starred. Item 1 should never be omitted from the first conference. Inclusion of it is a matter of professional ethics and an application of Rule 3.

Abbreviations are as follows: Analysis table; vocational orientation, recreational orientation, personal orientation, social orientation, motivation, ego strength and accessibility, energy output, integrity of personality, nature of censorship, nature of routing, kind and source of pressure, status, traumata, anxiety, phantasy life, delusionary structure, emotional adequacy, appetitive organization, mechanism of symptom formation.

Item 1: Escape, denial of problem's existence, projection of responsibility, Pollyanna, systematization of causes, anxiety, query and seeking of help from clinician, reasonable insight into problem.Item 2: Subversive attempt, protest of inability, systematic attempt.

Item 4: studies, music, projects, dramatics, society, companions, participant attitude, movies, gangs, athletics, mechanics, garden, pet, collection, toy, doll, game, family, narrow interests.

Item 5: swing, trapeze, sand pile, shack, wagon, tool, doll, pet, too few play facilities, parent, adult, older recreational companions, younger, sibling companions, friends, indoor recreation, outdoor, phantasy, social, bored, unplanned recreation.

Item 6: vocational ambition, source, major study, hobbies, preferred age of marriage, preferred number of children, preferred maximum level of education.

[17] In the 1941 edition, this is followed by:

Gesell: This is a comprehensive form for summarizing results on the Gesell Inventory.

Cornell-Coxe: Preme data on the administration of the test are recorded down the right margin. A graphic profile of individual test performance is drawn at the left.

[18] In the 1941 edition, this is followed by: See Kelly, G.A. A method of diagnosing personality in the psychological clinic. *Psychological Record, 2*, 1938, 95-111. A printed form for this examination is available in which key words are spelled in full and not abbreviated.

FORT HAYS KANSAS STATE COLLEGE PSYCHOLOGICAL CLINIC

Form 7.5 Speech and Reading

______________ ______________ ______________
Case Clinician Date

READING (EYE MOVEMENTS)

P.	Me.	Fix.	Nev.	.	6	8	12	Ad1	S. Ad1	13	(ORAL READING) (TEST)
1.	Or.	_____	_____	a	5	3	2	--	-		Age Norm: Rate ____
2.	Or.	_____	_____	a	7	5	4	3	-		Errors____________
3.	Or.	_____	_____	a	16	11	8	6	4		
4.	Or.			ab	54	29	24	19	12	14.	(SILENT READING Test)
5.	Si.	_____	_____	ab	80	53	40	30	15		Age Norm: Vocabulary__________
	(Time	_____	sec.	43	28	19	13	10)			Paragraph__________
6.	Si.	_____	_____	abc	-	82	33	46	21		
	(Time		sec.		-	49	27	18	14)	15.	(MIRROR READING)
7.	Si.	_____	_____	abc	-	-	82	57	31		Erect: __________words
	(Time	_____	sec.		-	-	44	26	20)		Rotated _________ words
8.	Si.	_____	_____	abc	-	-	-	71	36		Reversed _________words
	(Time		sec.		-	-	-	30	21		Inverted ___________ words
9.	Long	Fix.	_____								
10.	Aph.	Div.	_____								
11.	Verb	_____									
12.	Eye	Trem.									

WRITING 16. "Pack my box with five dozen liquor jugs."

L ____

R ____

"sguj rouqil nezod evif htiw xob ym kcaP"

____

____

17.	Simult.	Writing	Rever.	18.	Ocular	Dominance	19.	Write	Take	Kick
	L: o e m	b a c	4 7 3 6		1 2 3 4 5	6 7 8 9 10	L	LLL	L	LLL
	R: o e m	b a c	4 7 3 6		1 2 3 4 5	6 7 8 9 10	R	RRR	R	RRR

20. 0° 15° 30° 45° 60° 70° 90°
Van- L c n the 1 a cat o y dog e m hat f t log k m pig s w key

SPEECH (RHYTHM

21. Clon spm Ton Spm Thor Abdom Dys Breath Trem
22. Abrupt Init Prolong Insp Interrup Exp Vocal Trem
23. Tonal Rigid Intertonal Sound
24. Trans Aph Art Aph Aud Aph Agraphia Alexia
25. Verbal Syntatical Nominal Semantic

SPEECH (ARTICULATION AND TONATION

26. General Pathology____________________
27. Sound ____
    Substitution:
28. Tongue : Tumor macro- micro- tic hemiatrophy
29. Uvula: long thick bifurcated double
30. Palate : cleft high hare – lip
31. Teeth: malform - arch malocution obtruded intruded defective open
32. Jaws: overshot undershot
33. Cavities : adenoid tonsil nasal-polypi hepert-turb septum stenosis lary laryngitis sinus paralysis perichontritis
34. Audition : L______/ ____R______/ __________
35. Ataxia:
36. Rapport___________.

Item 7: motive unknown, exhibitionism, popularity, security, wealth, mastery, self assertion, romance, escape, domination of persons.

Item 8: intelligence quotient, education, opposition from people, poverty, physique, age responsibilities, wife, children, parents.

Item 9: financial, health, education, social opportunities, personal recognition, death, love, children.

Item 10: suicidal tendency, depression, anxiety, elation, euphoria, excitability, exhaustion, length of cycle.

Item 11: financial, health education, social opportunities, personal recognition, death, love, pregnancy, castration, mate, parent, child, sex, responsibilities, religion, philosophy, homosexuality, seizure, anger, obsession, dreams, accidents, employment, only temporarily anxious.

Item 12: nyctophobia, homophobia, monstrophobia, accidents, thanatophobia, acrophobia, pathophobia, hydrophobia, astraphobia, agoraphobia, claustrophobia, monophobia, neophobia, distance.

Item 13: mate, sibling, parent, in-law, community, law, school, church, employer.

Item 14: marked tendency to defend members of the family, tendency to project upon members of the family, anxious attitude in home, overt domestic tension, feeling of insecurity in home, feeling that family is over-critical, feeling of being unaccepted in family, uncertainty regarding status in family.

Item 15: situations which arouse the case's anger, people, enemies, people with whom the case fights, does the case usually win, lose, is the fight usually stopped by an outsider, how is the disagreement usually solved, anxiety regarding anger, fear of temper, self-contempt because of lack of self-control, projection of blame for conflicts, anger phantasies, feelings of deep guilt because of anger.

Item 16: objects, situations, kind of people, friends.

Item 17: experience of conversion, mysticism, ritualism, taboos, fear, agnosticism, cynicism, rationalism, pantheism, social, gospel, attitude, denomination, customary grade at table, regular prayers, Sunday school attendances a month, church, principal sources of religious influence.

Item 18: general, specific, compulsive, felt need for expiation, guilty ideas, ambivalence, fear, self-contempt, rationalization.

Item 19: religion, service, social, moral thrift, success, education, responsibility.

Item 20: superstition, thoughts, destructive tendencies, sexual-compulsions, compulsions to count, eat, lock doors and belongings, expect accidents.

Item 21: controlled principally by father, mother, sister, brother, boss, hero worship, sense of duty, expected reward.

Item 22: slow, apathetic, resistant, stiff, automatic obedience, catatonic, stereotype, left handed, right handed, hyperkinetic, hypokinetic, restless, tic, choretic movement, tense, peculiarity of facial expression.

Item 23: verbigeration, flight of ideas, divertability of attention, neologisms, auditory aphasia, short attention span, artificial speech, speech disorder.

Item 24: fear, death, pursuit, animals, falling, drowning, naked, guilt, sex, homosexual, oedipal, flying, fighting, eating, smoking, smothering, amnesia for dreams.

Item 25: insomnia, toss at night, somnambulism, unrested in morning, snores excessively, regular sleeping habits, fresh air, bed fellow.

Item 27: continued daydream story, repeated, systematized, bizarre, condensed, euphoria, many characters, self represented, represented as conquering hero, suffering hero.

Item 28: visual mode, parasthesia, Gedankenlautwerden in left ear, in right ear, men talking, women talking, voices recognized, considered real by case, experience under control, case's explanation of cause content of communication, prophetic value attached, thought to be voice of conscience, necromancy, *deja vu*.

Item 29: cephalic orbital, aural, dental, respiratory, cardiac, gastric, elimination, cancer, rheumatic, lumbar, *arc de cercle*, displaced organs, paralysis, taxis, kinesthesia, toxia, castration.

Item 30: persecution, watched, talked about, jealous, wronged, influences used against case, plans for revenge, grandeur, strength, power, wealth, noble birth, adventure, nihilism, adoption, systematized delusions, bizarre.

Item 31: grand mal, petit mal, absence, depersonalization.

Item 32: mate or lover, time love affair has lasted, ambivalent attitude toward mate or opposite sex, erotic attitude, inhibited attitude, anxious attitude, fearful, guilty, disgust, negative attitude toward opposite sex, satisfied with heterosexual status, number of kissing experiences, number of people kissed (exclusion of family), experience of petting (stimulating bodily contact other than kissing and holding hands), mutual masturbation, sexual intercourse, times, people, accept pay or reward for intercourse, witnessed intercourse, seduced.

Item 33: bisexuality, overt homosexual experience, invert, attitude of acceptance, anxiety, masturbation frequency.

Item 34: reaction to examination, depressed, anxiety, crying, systematization, hope, tremor, transference, asked for another appointment.

Item 35: Appearance of case: virile, weak, large, small, not dressed in taste, lack of social intelligence, lack of integration and security, moody, fearful, poor form, poor expression, not neat, dirty, poor manners, peculiar mannerisms, poor taxia, poor clothes.

Elaborations of items are as follows:

Item 1: This item must never be omitted from the first conference. Inclusion of it as a matter of professional ethics and an application of RULE 3. As in a number of the items, more than one of the abbreviations may properly be encircled. A child who has been registered because of a tendency to steal is asked, "You seem to have been in some trouble with your school principal lately; what was the matter?" If the child does not mention stealing, the clinician asks, "What about stealing?" The purpose of the questions is not to force a confession or to compel the child to talk about an unpleasant subject but first to give him a chance to give his own version of the problem and thus come to an understanding of the reason for his being in the clinic and then, if it appears that he still does not know why he is registered, to ask a direct question which will indicate what the clinician has in mind. This method of approach may appear too direct to the inexperienced worker, but it saves misunderstanding and actually serves to protect the case. Frequently the case is glad to have the worst "over with" before he has time to build up a story. If a case does not admit guilt the clinician does not force the issue or indicate disapproval. The clinician is not a legalist or a moralist at this stage; his task, primarily, is to come to an understanding of the case's personality rather than the case's guilt. Then there is always the chance that the case has been falsely accused. Cases which are registered for other reasons are approached in a similar manner.

Item 2: This item is for children only. It is a test of volition and honesty. The pencil trick (which can be demonstrated better than explained) is demonstrated and the case is given one minute to repeat the trick while the examiner looks away. The time the case continues trying to repeat the trick is recorded and also the method. The toestand is also administered for a maximum of one minute. A practice trial of ten seconds should be used.

Item 3: The following questions are numbered according to intellectual levels: (1) 'I don't know you very well yet. Won't you tell me something about yourself? What kind of a little boy are you? Are you a good little boy or a bad little boy?" (2) "Tell me about yourself. What sort of personality do you have? Do you have a good personality or are you rather disagreeable? What sort of an impression do you make upon people?"

Item 4: (1) "What sort of things do you like to do?" (2) "What are your principal interests in life? What sort of an impression do you make upon people?"

Item 5: (1) "Do you like to play? What do you like to play? What do you like to play with? Whom do you play with? Where and in what places do you play? Tell me some of the things you have to play with." (2) "What sort of recreation do you get? With whom do you usually take your recreation?"

Item 6: (1) "What do you want to be when you grow up? Did you decide that all by yourself? Do you want to get married and have children of your own? How far do you want to go in school?" (2) "What do you want to do when you get out of school? Who influenced you in deciding that? What subjects are you specializing in? Do you want to get married? How many children do you think you would like to have? How far do you intend to go in school?" (3) "What is your vocational ambition? Who has influenced that choice? What is your major? Your Minor? What are your hobbies? etc."

Item 7: (1) "What is there about ________ that you like so much? Why do you like to do that?" (2) "What is your motive in choosing that? Does that sort of thing mean a great deal to you? What are some of the other things that you want to get out of life? What would you say that life means to you in general?"

Item 8: (1) "Is there anything that might keep you from doing that? Do you think you will be able to do that?" (2) "What obstacle stands in your way? What are some of the things which you will have to overcome before you can achieve your ambition?"

Item 9: (1) "Has anything happened lately to make you feel bad? What are some of the things which make you feel unhappy?" (2) "Have you had any serious disappointment lately, such as disappointments in love, deaths in the family, or financial catastrophe?"

Item 10: (1) "Are you a happy boy or are you a sad boy? How happy do you feel? How sad do you feel? Do you ever feel you do not want to live any longer? Do you ever feel so happy that you just do not know what to do with yourself?" (2) "Do you get the blues frequently, or are you usually quite happy? How excited do you get when you are happiest? How do you feel at those times? How do you feel when you get the blues? Do you feel sick and exhausted? Do you feel as if you want to kill yourself? How often do you feel that way? Do those feelings come regularly?" (3) "Do you frequently feel melancholy? How excited do you get when you are feeling good? Have you ever considered suicide? Tell me about it. Do your feelings of elation and depression come in regular cycles or at regular times?"

Item 11: (1) "When you feel sad what do you feel sad about?" (2) "When you feel unhappy what do you think about?" (3) "What do you worry about mostly? Do you worry in spite of your better judgment? Do you feel yourself compelled to worry even though you do not feel that there is any cause for worry? Is this just a temporary worry or do you have it frequently?"

Item 12: (1) "What are you afraid of? Are you afraid of the dark or are you afraid of some people, etc.?" (2) "Do you have any fears? Are you afraid of the dark, etc.?"

Item 13: (1) "How do you get along with your brothers and sisters? Are they nice to you? How do you get along with your papa and mama? Do you like them? Do they like you? Which do you like better, etc.?" (2) "How do you get along with your girl friend? How do you get along in your family, especially with your brothers and sisters? Do you avoid each other or are you quite close to each other in your companionship, etc.?" (3) "How do you get along with your wife? Do you sometimes have tension which arises between you? What is the nature of these tensions or difficulties, etc.?"

Item 14: (1) "How do you get along at home? Do you think you have a nice home? Do you stick together? How is the household run?"

Item 15: (1) "Do you ever get mad? Tell me about some time that you got mad? What happened? Whom did you get mad at? Are there any people who don't like you? Did you ever get in a fight? Who won? Who stopped the fight? After that what did you do about it? How do you feel about the fight? After that what did you do about it? How do you feel about it now?" (2) "What sort of situations make you angry? What kind of people make you angry? Tell me about two or three of your enemies, etc."

Item 16: (1) "What one of your toys do you like best? Tell me about some place you like to be. What kind of people do you like best? Who is your best friend? Do you have any other people who are as nice to you as that?" (2) "What things or objects are you most attached to? What belonging means most to you? What places or situations are most attractive to you? What kind of people do you prefer as companions, etc.?"

Item 17: "Do you go to church? What church do you go to? Do you like church? Do you pray? What is there about church that you like? What is there about church that you do not like?" (2) "What is your attitude toward religion? Have you ever been converted? Do you feel that you have a religious calling? What part of religion appeals to you most, etc.?"

Item 18: (1) "Do you ever feel that you have been a bad boy? What is bad about you? What do you think you should do about it?" (2) Do you ever have a feeling of guilt? What do you feel guilty about mostly? Is it things that you think or things that you do that are bad? What have you been doing about it? What do you think you ought to do about it?"

Item 19: (1) "What do you think is the best thing in the world? What do you think is nicest of all?" (2) "What kind of ideals do you have? Tell me some of the ideals which you think are most important."

Item 20: (1) "Do you ever do things when you feel that you just can't help it? Do you ever think things that you don't want to think?" (2) "Do you sometimes find yourself doing things for no reason at all, yet you can't help doing them? Do thoughts ever come to your mind and refuse to leave? Do you have some ideas which seem to be forced upon you? Tell me about them."

Item 21: (1) "What keeps you from doing naughty things? Does somebody watch you so that you will be good, or are you good just because you want to be? What is there to keep you from being bad?" (2) "How is your life kept under control? Is it controlled by people who watch you? What is there to keep you from becoming immoral or bad? What kind of self control do you exercise?"

Items 22 and 23 can be indicated at this point in the examination without asking further specific questions.

Item 24: "Do you dream? Did you ever have a dream? Tell me your last dream."

Item 25: "Is it easy for you to go to sleep at night? Do you go to sleep at the same time every night? Do you sleep with the window open, etc?"

Item 26: In this blank record parts of a recent dream.

Item 27: (1) "What do you think about when you are all by yourself and there is nothing to do? Do you ever tell yourself a story or just play like things were happening? Tell me one of those stories." (2) "Do you ever daydream or imagine things happening to you just for the fun of it? Tell me one of your daydreams, etc."

Item 28: (1) "Do you ever think that you see things and then find out that they are really not there at all? Do you ever feel things crawling over you when there really is nothing at all? Do you ever hear people talking to you when there really isn't anyone there at all, etc.?" (2) "Do you ever have visions that seem almost as real as actual events? Do you sometimes have the sensation of having things crawling over you? Do you hear words or sounds when there is no one around to account for them, etc.?"

Item 29: (1) "Does your head sometimes hurt? Do your eyes sometimes hurt, etc.?" (2) "Do you have frequent headaches? Do your eyes bother you, etc.?"

Item 31: (1) "Do you ever have fits? Do you ever feel as if you were floating away or as if you did not really live?" (2) "Do you ever have seizures when you are not yourself? Tell me about it."

Item 32: (1) "Do you have a girl friend? How long have you had this girl friend? Do you sometimes like and sometimes hate her? Do you love her and want to touch her? Are you afraid to talk to her? Did you ever do anything together that was naughty? What? Were you afraid? How do you feel about it? Are you happy with this girl friend? Did you ever kiss a girl? How many times have you kissed a girl? Do you hold on to each other real tight sometimes? Do you ever touch each other under your clothes? How close did you get to each other? How many times did you do that? How many girls have you done that with? Did you ever pay a girl for that? Did you ever see anybody else do that? Did any girl ever try to get you to do that?" (2) Similar questions may be asked, but with the use of somewhat more adult language.

Item 33: (1) "Is it just as easy for you to like another boy as it is for you to like a girl? Have you ever been in love with a boy? Did you ever touch each other under the clothes? Or did you just feel like it? What are you going to do about it? Did you ever play with yourself where you shouldn't?" (2) Same questions will be asked in somewhat more adult phraseology.

Items 34, 35, and 36 can be answered without specific questions.

At the end of the examination the clinician must realize that he has probably probed quite deeply into the intimate life of the case and while the case may benefit somewhat from having this more objective point of view established, he is likely to feel somewhat disorganized and fearful. Not infrequently, the case will feel that a criticism is implied from the nature of the questions in the last part of the examination. It may be necessary to encourage the case to suspend judgment until the next conference and not allow himself to be worried about anything that has been said. If the case is depressed and no further conferences are in prospect, it is absolutely essential that the clinician reassure the case and leave him with a constructive point of view[19].

[19] In the 1941 edition, this is followed by:
Pressey X-O: The Pressey X-O test is used as an exploratory inventory which may reveal information not readily accessible in an interview. The form provides for a graphic profile record.
The 1941 edition also includes the record form for this test.

FORT HAYS KANSAS STATE COLLEGE PSYCHOLOGICAL CLINIC

Form 8 Personality

Case ____________ Clinician ____________ Date ____________ No. ____________

Voc Or, Rec Or, Pers Or., Soc. Or., Motiv., Ego, Energy, Integrit, Censor, Routine, Pressur, Status, Traumat, Anxiety, Phantas, Relusic, Emot, Appetite, Sympt.	
. . . . : o . o . : . o . o : o o . X	1. *Problem: ESC DEN ACPT PROJ POL SYST ANX quer insgt
. . . . X . o o . : . . . . :	2. Volition: Pencil sec. Toe sec. SUBV PROT syst
. . . o : X . o . : . . . . o	3. *Communication: xxxXxxx Self-defense: xxxXxxx
o o o o X . . . . o . . . . o	4. Interest: stud mus proj dram soc compn part movie gang athl mech gar pet coll toy doll game fam NARROW
o X . o o . . . . : . . . . :	5. Recreation: swng trap sand shk wgn tool doll pet
. X . . : . . . . : . . . . :	par ADLT OLD YNG sib frnd indr odr PHAN soc BPD UNPLN
. X . o : o . o . : . . . . o	6. *Ambition: Voc 1 _ 2 __SRC__ maj ____________ min ____________
X . . . o o . o . : o . . . :	Hob 1__2 ________Mar ____________Cha ____________Educ ____________
O X . O O . . . . : . . . . :	7. *Motive: ? EXH POP SEC WEA SER MAS ASR AVN ROM RSC DOM
O O O O X O . . . : O O . O :	8. *Obstacle: IQ EDUC OPP PVT PHYS AGE RESP WIF CHD PAR
O . . . O O . . O O O . X O :	9. Disappointment: FIN HEA EDUC SOC REOG DEA LOV CHILD
. . O . : O . . . : O . X O : . O . .	10. *Melancholia: xxXxSUI DEPR ANX ELA EUPH EXCI EXH CYC
. . . . : O O . : . . . . X : . O . .	11. *Anxiety: FIN HEA EDU SOC ROG DEA LOV PRG OST MAT PAR
. . . . : O . . . : O . O X : . O . .	CHI SEX REL PHL HOM SEZ ANG OBS DRM ACD EMP TEM
. . . . : O . . . : O . O X : . O . .	12. *Phobia: DARK PERSONS ANIMALS ACCIDENTS DEATH HIGH
. . . . : O . . O : . . O X O O O . .	DISEASE WATER STORMS OPEN CLOSED ALONE NEV DISTANT
. . . . : O . . O : . . O X O O O . .	13. *Tension : MATE SIB PAR IN-LAW COM-LAE SCH CHURCH EMPL
. . . X : . . . . O O O O . : O . . .	14. *Family: DEFEND PROJ ANX TEN INSEC CRIT UNACCEPT UNCER
. . . X : . . . O O O O O O :	15. *Anger: 1st ________PEO ________ENI__________ FGT____________
. . . X : . O . O : O O . . : . O . .	WIN LOSE STOP SOL ____ ANX PEAR OMPT PROJ PHANT GLT
. . . X : . O . O : O O . . : . O . .	16. Attachment: obj _____ sit ____ peo ____________ fr ____________
. . . X : . . . . : . . . . : . . O .	17. *Religion: CON CAL MYS RIT TAB FEA CYN RAT PAN SOC
. . O O O O . . X O O . . . O	denom ________________ gre pry ss ____ mo. cn mo. src ____________
. . O O O O . . X O O . . . O	18. *Guilt: GEN SPC CPL XPT IDE AMB FEA CPT RAT ____________
. . O . : . . . X O O . . O O O O . O	19. Ideal: rel___ser___soc___mor___thr _____suc___ddu___rep__________
. . O . O . . . O : . . . . X . O . .	20. * Compulsion: SUPRS THOT DEST SEX COUNT EAT LOCK ACCID
. . . . : O . . X : . . . . O . . O O	21. Control: FATH MOTH SIS BRO BOSS HERO DUT REW ____________
. . . O : O . O . O O X O	22. Motor: SLOW APATH RESIST STIFF AUTO-OB CATA STEREO
. . . . : O X . : . . . . . :	1 r HYPER HYPO RESTL TIC CHOR TENSE FACE-EXPR
. . . . : O X . : . . . . . :	23. Speech: VRBS FLIGIT DVRT NEOL A-APH SHT ATT ARTF DER
. . . . : O X . : . . . . . O O O . .	24. *Dream: FEA DEA PUR ANI FAL DRO NAK CLT SEX ROM CED
. . . . : . . . . : . . . . X . . O .	FLY FGT EAT SMO SMOTHER AMN____________
. . . . : . . . . : . . . . X . . O .	25. Sleep: INSOMN TOSS SOMNAM UNREST SNOR reg air fel____________
. . . O : X . . O : . . . . :	26. *Memory:________________________________
. . . . : O . . . : . . X O O	27. *Daydream: CNT RPT SYS BTZ CND EUP CHR SLF DNO BUF
. . O . O O . . . : . O . X O O O O O	28. Hallucination: VIS PARESTH GLAUT L R MEN WmN RCG
. . . . : O . . O : . . O O X O . . .	REAL CNTRL CAUSE ________CONIENT ______ PROPH CNSC NEC D-V
. . . . : O . . O : . . O O X O . . .	29. *Hypochondria: CEPH ORB AUR DENT RESP CARD CAST GL-H
. . . . : O . . . : . . O O X O O O O	ELIM CANC RHEU LUMB ARC DISP PRYL TAX KNSTH TCX CAST
. . . . : O . . . : . . O O X O O O O	30. Delusion PRSC WAT TLK JLS WRNG INFL PLN GRND STGTH
. . . . : O . . . : . . . O X O . . .	POW WEA BIR ADV NIHIL ADPT SYST BIZ____________
. . . . : O . . . : . . . O X O . . .	31. *Seizure: G-IAAL ABSENCE DEPERS____________
. . . . : O . : O : . . O o X O . . O	32. Heterosexuality: mat t AMB ERO INH ANX FRF GLT DSG
. . O . : O . . O : . . O O : . O X .	NEG sat KIS T__P __ PAY WIT SEDU
. . O . : O . . O : . . O O : . O X .	33. *Homosexuality: BISEX OVERT INVERT ACCPT ANX MSTRB____________
. . O . : O . . O : . . O O : . O X .	34. Reaction: DPR ANX CRY syst hope TREM TRANSF APPT
. . . . : O . . . : . . . . : . . . X	35. Appearance: virl WEAK LRG SML TAST S-INT IN-SEC MDY
. . . . : O O . : . . . X . :	FEA FRM EXPR NEAT DIRT MANR MANRSM TAX CLTHS
. . . . : X . . . : . . . . :	36. RAPPORT x x x X x x x

FORT HAYS KANSAS STATE COLLEGE PSYCHOLOGICAL CLINIC

Form 8.2. Special Information[20]

Case ____________ Clinician ____________ Date ________ No. ________

1. ____________ ____________ ____________
Informant Relation Remarks

Informant's Traits:

		1. Emotional Stability	x x x X x x x
2. Emotional Adequacy	x x x X x x x	3. Self Insight	x x x X x x x
4. Family Insight	x x x X x x x	5. School Insight	x x x X x x x
6. Case Insight	x x x X x x x	7. Interest in Case	x x x X x x x
8. Professional Training	x x x X x x x	9. Professional Attitude	x x x X x x x
10. Completeness of Inform	x x x X x x x	11. Cooperate in Treat	x x x X x x x

____________ ____________ ____________
Informant Relation Remarks

1. Emotional Stability	x x x X x x x	2. Emotional Adequacy	x x x X x x x
3. Self Insight	x x x X x x x	4. Family Insight	x x x X x x x
5. School Insight	x x x X x x x	6. Case Insight	x x x X x x x
7. Interest in Case	x x x X x x x	8. Professional Training	x x x X x x x
9. Professional Attitude	x x x X x x x	10. Completeness of Inform	x x x X x x x
11. Cooperate in Treat	x x x X x x x		

[20] As indicated in footnote 15, the version of this form in the 1941 edition includes a page for additional information.

12. **Special Information** (Form 8.2): Form 8.2 is simply a blank form on which special information about the case may be recorded. This information is usually of such a nature as not to be called for in the regular anamnesis. The personality profiles permit the clinician to score the individual with whom he holds his conference quickly and inconspicuously[21].

IV The Diagnosis

1. **Advisability of differential diagnosis:** In clinical psychology the need for exact classification of mental disorders is not as great as one might suspect. A distinction needs to be made between those which are to be treated by direct methods and those which are to be treated by rational methods. The former do require a more or less clear-cut diagnosis before therapy is undertaken, the latter do not. Nearly all psychological practice requires an emphasis upon etiology which is far greater than many clinicians have suspected. A complete case history is not merely an aid to treatment but usually an integral part of that treatment. In these respects clinical psychology differs markedly from clinical medicine.

The following rules or principles are peculiar to indirect psychotherapy.

RULE 11: ONLY THE PATIENT CAN EFFECT A CURE.
RULE 12: THE PATIENT'S DIAGNOSIS IS SYNONYMOUS WITH THE CURE.
RULE 13: IMPROVEMENT IS IN PROPORTION TO THE INSIGHT WHICH THE PATIENT ACQUIRES INTO THE TRUE NATURE OF HIS DIFFICULTY.

In view of these principles it can be seen that the purpose of the preliminary diagnosis is merely to indicate the general type of therapy to be used. If direct therapy is indicated, then the clinician should proceed to a more or less clear-cut diagnosis; but if indirect therapy is indicated only the general procedures can be determined.

There is still another reason why the preliminary diagnosis need not be exact. In the field of the neuroses one never encounters two neuroses which are exactly alike nor does he ever encounter an unmixed neurosis. For instance, paranoid symptoms are almost universally present in the neuroses and yet their presence may be of secondary importance. Again, one may undertake the treatment of what at first appears to be an anxiety hysteria with some compulsive complications; after a short treatment the acute hysteriform symptoms may be dispersed, leaving only the mild but persistent compulsive symptoms to be dealt with. It is not particularly important whether the preliminary diagnosis is anxiety hysteria or compulsion neuroses. The only important decision is the one as to whether or not the case possesses the ego strength and accessibility necessary for psychoanalytic therapy.

2. **Recommendations** (Form 9.1): The most satisfactory plan is to go directly from the facts derived from the anamnesis to the therapeutic recommendations.

RULE 14: ALL RECOMMENDATIONS SHOULD BE WRITTEN IN DUPLICATE, ADDRESSED TO SOME INDIVIDUAL AND SIGNED BY THE AUTHORIZED DIAGNOSTIC CLINICIAN.

[21] In the 1941 edition, this is followed by:
On the back of the form is an outline for the check interview with the patient. The key is as follows:
(a) Patient's attitude to school and other crucial problems and his plans for the future.
(b) The patient's attitude toward and characterization of himself.
(c) Inventory of emotion-arousing situations.
(d) Relation to family and society.
(e) The patient's memories.
(f) Physiological check of mouth, eyes, skin, hands. . ..anatomy.
(g) A check of motor manifestations, including gait, posture; and speech.
(h) Observation of aphasic symptoms—oral, auditory, visual, writing, and strephosymbolia.
(i) The patient's formulation of the problem.
(j) A psychological formulation of the problem.
(k) Tentative listing of therapies (1-90). This is a list of therapies commonly recommended. It is not exhaustive.

It is important that wherever a diagnosis is reported that it be reported in writing. An illustration of need for this procedure is the following: Suppose that a psychological clinic is using the pupils of a public school for practice testing in the training of its clinicians; suppose that the principal of the school asks for reports on the results of the testing. Until those results have been checked carefully by experienced clinicians no report, either oral or written, should be made. The making of an oral report in such an instance would not save the reputation of the Clinic. Next let us suppose the Clinic checks the results of the testing and is ready to make a report on each case which is limited to the intelligence quotient. If the report is not made in writing the school may claim to have received certain recommendations which the Clinic does not wish to underwrite. The making of all recommendations in writing protects the Clinic against charges of unjustified recommendations as well as against distortion of recommendations.

Sometimes a clinician wishes to discuss certain aspects of a case which fall outside the province of a psychologist. Ordinarily such discussions are to be avoided since they open the clinician to charges of encroachment upon another profession. When a clinician wishes to discuss a case "off the record" he must be very sure to make clear to his listeners that he is not speaking professionally, and also, he should be very sure that he has given his listener a written psychological recommendation so that if ever there is question concerning the recommendations of the clinic a record of those recommendations will be available and can be clearly seen to be of a strictly psychological nature.

A psychologist must be very sure to make recommendations in as practical a form as possible, but at the same time make them complete enough so that he cannot be charged with overlooking any important elements in the diagnosis. Let us suppose that the following situations have arisen: A child needs opportunity room training, the parents of the child are unable to afford such advantages; the psychologist should have made a report which outlines a treatment of the child that is possible of attainment, but he should be sure to add to the report a recommendation that the child have opportunity room training if possible. In that way the psychologist protects himself against the charge of having overlooked the need for opportunity room training in the case.

Another important principle to be followed in making recommendations is that the psychologist stay within his field. None of the items in the physiological form may be reported in the diagnosis since those items are within the field of medicine. A case may have obviously defective vision, but the psychologist cannot suggest that the child has defective vision, or that he needs glasses. In such a case the psychologist should recommend that the case have a "thorough eye examination" and that he should not be expected to succeed in school until the recommendations of an oculist have been followed. This distinction between professional areas may appear at first to be somewhat artificial and perfunctory but is nevertheless extremely important.

Sometimes the question arises as to what extent the psychologist may discuss his findings with a physician. The following principle applies in this situation: a psychologist may discuss psychological aspects of a case with any one whom he considers professionally responsible to the case but only to such an extent as he is sure that the listener will not misinterpret his statements; for instance, a psychologist may report the intelligence quotient of a case to a physician who is also working on the case only if he is sure that the physician understands the limitations, significance and general methods involved in the intelligence quotient.

When therapy is a matter of improvement of hygienic conditions in the home or school, the recommendation should be written in detail, summarized under points, and discussed with the case or with the responsible parties. If psychotherapy in the clinic is recommended, a simple written statement is all that is required[22].

3. **Classification of psychological disorders:** There are several clinical classifications now in use. The following is recommended for use at the present time. The categories refer to final diagnosis.

[22] The 1941 edition then states 'Following is an outline for making recommendations in a child guidance clinic.' This is followed by 'Out-patient Clinic: Steps in the Formulation of Psychological Recommendations' and 'Institutional Clinic,' both of which can be found in the Appendix to this chapter.

FORT HAYS KANSAS STATE COLLEGE PSYCHOLOGICAL CLINIC

Form 9.1 Recommendations

To____________________________ Concerning ____________________________

Date__________________193_____________

The diagnosis of the Clinic is limited to the psychological aspects of the case. It does not assume any **responsibility** for medical aspects . It is suggested that every case be taken to a medical physician for a thorough health examination in addition to the psychological examination.

Unless the following recommendations are carried out, little value can be attached to the services of the clinic. In general psychological problems are very persistent and their treatment must be no less persistent if improvement is to be expected.

RECOMMENDATIONS

In the home: 1. ____________________________

2. ____________________________

3. ____________________________

4. ____________________________

5. ____________________________

In the school: 1. ____________________________

2. ____________________________

3. ____________________________

4. ____________________________

5. ____________________________

Other examinations recommended: 1. ________________

2. ________________ 3. ________________

4. ________________ 5. ________________

____

Psychologist

- General Mental Deficiency
  - Special Deficiencies
    - Speech, Reading, and Thought
      - Rhythmic
        - Stuttering
        - Articulatory Aphasia
        - Auditory Aphasia
        - Agraphia
        - Alesia
        - Strophosymbolia
        - Verbal Aphasia
        - Syntactical Aphasia
        - Nominal Aphasia
        - Semantic Aphasia
        - Transient Aphasia
        - Dyslogia
      - Articulatory and Phonic
        - Mutism
        - Lisp
        - Idiolalia
        - Barbaralalia
        - Dysphenia
      - Subject Disabilities
        - Arithmetic
        - Spelling
        - Arrested Development
      - Sensory Disabilities
        - Auditory
        - Visual
        - Others
    - Disciplinary Deficiency
    - Social Deficiency
    - Occupational Deficiency
    - Educational Deficiency

- Neurosis
  - Hysteriform Neurosis
    - Hysteria
    - Anxiety Hysteria
    - Hypochondria
    - Anxiety
    - Neurasthenia
    - Pathoneurosis
    - Organ Neurosis
    - Inhibited State
    - Traumatic Neurosis
  - Psychasthenia
    - Obsessive
    - Motor Compulsive Neurosis
    - Bisexuality
    - Homosexuality
    - Nymphomania
    - Satyriasis
    - Sadism
    - Masochism
    - Addiction
  - Psychosis
    - Paranoid State
    - Schizothymia
    - Schizophrenia
      - Paranoid
      - Catatonic
      - Simple
      - Hebephrenic
  - Cyclothymia
  - Manic-Depressive Psychosis
    - Melancholia
    - Maniacal
    - Bi-Phasic

4. **Reporting diagnosis to the case:** Those cases which require a specific diagnosis before treatment should ordinarily be informed of that diagnosis. Those cases for whom the leap is made directly from facts to recommendations should know the recommendations and by the time the specific diagnosis is made during the course of their treatment they should be in position to receive that diagnosis. In general, then, it may be said:

RULE 15: THE PATIENT SHOULD BE INFORMED OF THE DIAGNOSIS AS SOON AS IT IS COMPLETED.

This rule applies to the reporting of intelligence test scores to the patient but not to the parents.

5. **Special diagnosis of study habits** (Form 9.2): Clinicians are frequently called upon to diagnose problems of students who are doing unsatisfactory work in college. The following form of interview will usually enable the clinician to make a rapid survey of the situation. Certain items may be followed up somewhat more at length than indicated in the form. This interview should never be used unless the student requests the diagnosis. Students who are sent to the clinician by instructors should be asked if they want all their problems discussed or would prefer to have the conference limited to an investigation of study habits only. The clinician in following this plan is simply observing RULE 2 which states that "The psychological clinic should never assume responsibility beyond that which is specifically delegated to it." The clinician should be very sure that the conferee specifically wants the entire interview before going into any personal matters.

(Ask all numbered questions. Ask indented questions only if previous answers indicate that they should be asked.)

1. What is your name?
2. What seems to be your difficulty?
3. How many hours are you carrying?
4. What are your subjects?
5. How are you getting along in (English)? (Also other subjects)?
6. What grades did you make last semester? (or in high school)?
   a. What was the matter in English? (also in other subjects)?
7. Are you working outside of school?
   a. For whom do you work?
   b. How many hours do you work per week?
   c. Are the hours regular? (Be specific).
8. Do you "batch"?
   a. How many of you are batching together?
   b. Do you get along all right with each other?
9. How are your finances?
   a. Are you in debt?
   b. Are you running up bills that your folks do not know about?
10. Do you see your way clearly throughout the rest of the semester?
11. Do you get plenty of social life?
12. What extra-curricular activities do you participate in?
13. Do you have all the dates that you want?
    a. Do you get along without dates because you want to or because you can't get the ones you want?
    b. Are things going along smoothly between you and your girl friend?
14. Are you under severe criticism from your parents or anyone else?
15. Have you had any serious disappointments lately: such as disappointments in love, deaths in the family, financial catastrophes, etc.?
    a. Have you made a satisfactory adjustment to it or does it bother you considerably in spite of your better judgment?
16. How old are you?
    a. What have you been doing since graduating from high school?
17. Why did you come to college?
18. Do you have any special goal in mind toward which you are working? a. Did you select that vocation yourself or did your parents select it for you?
19. Why are you taking (Psychology)? (Also other courses)?
20. How many hours a week do you spend studying (English)? (Also other subjects).
21. Do you study each subject at the same time each day?
22. Do you study each subject the same length of time each day?
23. Do you have trouble with your mind wandering while you are trying to study?
24. Do you find that you study the wrong things?
25. Do you formulate and answer questions over the material as you study?
26. Do you think of your lessons at odd moments when you are not actually studying and try to get new slants on the material?
27. Do you waste time?
    a. How much?
    b. Do you want me to help you arrange a time budget?
28. How badly do you want to solve your problem?

In addition to the results of the interview the clinician should consult the college personnel records for entrance test results and other information.

Of course it should be clearly borne in mind that any irregularity in the personal habits of a student may disrupt his entire emotional structure and render him unfit for study regardless of the number of hours spent with each book. Probably not more than half of the difficulties encountered by students in their preparations are attributable to improper study habits per se. Various anxieties are likely to be the cause of improper study habits and as such should be dealt with directly.[23]

[23] In the 1941 edition, this is followed by: Narrative summary: To provide for a quick review of case record by the follow up clinician or other clinicians at a later date, a carefully written narrative summary of each case is written on Form 9.3. This summary should be couched in exact psychological terms as it is for use in the clinic only. [The Narrative Summary form is included as an Appendix to this chapter, as is an Analytical Summary form, which was also contained in the 1941 edition of the handbook.]

FORT HAYS KANSAS STATE COLLEGE PSYCHOLOGICAL CLINIC

Form 9.2 Study Habits

Case ______________________ Clinician ______________________________ Date ______________

Questionnaire

1. Problem ____
2. Present subjects Grades Hrs. study wk. Daily time Difficulties
   a. ____
   b. ____
   c. ____
   d. ____
   e. ____
   f. ____
3. Last semester subjects Grades Difficulties
   a. ____
   b. ____
   c. ____
   d. ____
   e. ____
   f. ____

4. Work ______________	12. Expend. $ __________ mo.	20. Criticisms ______________
5. Schedule ______________	13. Debts ______________	21. Activities ______________
6. Hrs. per wk. ______________	14. Secret bills ______________	22. Traumata ______________
7. Batch ______________	15. Probable outcome	23. Adjustments ______________
8. Number ______________	16. Social outlet ______________	24. Age ______________
9. Congeniality ______________	17. Dates ______________ wk.	25. Recent occupations ______________
10. Finances ______________	18. Reason ______________	26. Vocational aim ______________
11. Income $ __________ mo.	19. Quarrels ______________	27. Reason in school ______________

28. Aims of courses ______________________________
29. Study: Distraction wrong selection of topics with questions
30. Maturation Waste time Disinterest Ambiguous aim
31. Rapport ______________

____

RECOMMENDATIONS:

1. Advance preparation
2. Recitation
3. Maturation
4. Anticipation
5. Formulation
6. Notes
7. Lists: Tech. terms Vocab. Persons Rules Theories Principles Quest.
8. Attitude
9. Self discipline
10. Silent reading
11. Study periods definite
12. Schedule
13. Library study
14. Recreation
15. Free time
16. Social life
17. Psychotherapy
18. Reduced schedule
19. See Dean
20. See instructors
21. Eye examination
22. General health examination
23. ______________________________

____

____

____

____

____

6. **Rules for study:** On the basis of the foregoing interview, any or all of the following study rules may be advised. It is best, whenever possible, to limit the rules given to the student to those which particularly fit his situation. **Advance preparation:** Prepare well in advance so that—**Recitation:** you may take full advantages of and participate in class discussion. Get the front seat habit; that may not be the most modest way to learn, but it is the easiest. **Maturation:** Study should be spaced so that there will be opportunity to turn the material casually over in the mind during walks to and from classes, odd moments, etc., before the class recitation. Students who study just before class session do not have time to let the material "ferment." Students who study for a certain time and then attempt to "forget about it all" do just that: they forget. Two kinds of preparation are required; intensive study and casual maturation. **Anticipation:** In preparation it is necessary to anticipate what is coming next. If one has no curiosity or attitude toward the successive paragraphs, he will miss any important points in them. **Formulation:** Lessons should be formulated into the same form as instructors use in examinations. If the instructor uses a short answer system in his test the student should formulate his subject matter into the same form of questions and answers. If the instructor emphasizes oral recitation in response to discussion questions, the student should formulate such discussion questions and practice answering them orally as if in class.

7. **Notes:** If difficulty is encountered during class work, the student must resort to an adequate system of notes covering both reading and class discussions. **Lists:** Supplementary lists are usually advisable. They may be lists of technical **terms or vocabulary, prominent personalities, and rules, theories or principles**. Class notes should be supplemented by lists of questions asked in class either by students or instructors.

A happy and aggressive **attitude** toward school work frequently changes ineffective study to effective study. If the work is taken as drudgery, the student is not likely to succeed and probably should not succeed.

8. **Silent reading**: Of all the skills of greatest general value to college students that of silent reading has been shown to be of surpassing value. Silent reading efficiency can usually be improved at least sixty percent with a few sessions of clinical guidance. **Study periods** should be of predetermined length in a naive student's case. The student should be in his seat at the beginning time and remain just as determinedly until the closing as if he were in class. During this period he should study as intensely as possible. At the close of the period he should stop whether he has finished his task or not, later on he may adjust this system so as to make it a little more flexible.

9. **Study schedule**: The following general rules apply to the making of a time budget. **Reasonable:** Most study budgets fail during the second week because they have been arranged too rigidly and do not allow a generous amount of time for idleness. **Free time:** There should be at least one hour each day when a student may feel himself absolutely free of responsibility. He should not study or do anything of a pressing nature during this time. **Similar daily progress:** Vacant periods should always be used for study, especially if they come at a time corresponding to class times on other days. Recreation and physical exercise should not be scheduled at a time which is customarily spent in study. Evenings should be left as free as possible, especially free of routine preparation. Sunday should be left free. **Library:** Students should be advised to study at the library until their habits have been well established. In general, students waste time getting meals and making toilets. These duties should be scheduled rigidly.

10. **Subject Disabilities:** Certain subject disabilities present characteristic clinical pictures. The following outlines of attack are designed to enable the clinician to make a quick diagnosis. The factors possibly contributing to the disorder are listed in the order in which they should be investigated.

1. Reading disability.
   - A. Insufficient motivation:
     - a. Home: Do the parents demonstrate the need of reading proficiency? Do they read? Does reading occupy an important position in the domestic life?
     - b. Recreation: Has reading been presented as a form of recreation? Is literature available which is adapted to age of the case?
   - B. Insufficient vocabulary:
     Has the case had opportunity to familiarize himself with a reasonably large vocabulary? Are foreign languages spoken in the home?
   - C. Oral inaccuracy in speech:
     Oral speech is the original language function and precedes reading. If it is defective the defect may give rise to the use of approximations in all language function. This is particularly true in young children or in cases where intelligence is below normal.
   - D. Rhythmic disturbance of speech:
     In addition to the handicap in the original language function the disordered rhythm may indicate transient aphasia.
   - E. Inconsistent disability:
     Does the defect vary greatly in prominence from day to day?
     Emotional disturbances characterize nearly all cyclical behavior.
   - F. Slow:
     Slow reading may merely be habitual.
   - G. Defective vision:

This affects reading proficiency but is not usually the cause of a special disability in that subject.

H. Defective eye movements:

I. Small fixation units:
These may be due to bad habits or an inability to integrate images appearing on the non-foveal unilaterally enervated areas of the retina.

2. Language disability:
   A. Poor usage in the environment:
   Check usage of friends, teachers, and parents.
   B. Insufficient instruction:
   Administer remedial grammar.
   C. Insufficient motivation:
   Encourage success and disapprove failure, give opportunities for creative writing. Encourage free expression, both written and oral.
3. Spelling disability:
   Clinical experience seems to indicate that this disability is one of the least important in the diagnosis of general mental deficiency.
   A. Distraction:
   Look for emotional disturbances such as those found in anxiety.
   B. Lack of phonetic cues:
   Correct by phonetic training.
   C. Inaccurate pronunciation:
   Administer speech corrective exercises.
   D. Peculiar associations:
   Approach by analytic methods.
   E. Aphasia:
   Administer the general corrective measures for the aphasia disorders or try mnemonics as a stop-gap.

4. Arithmetic disability:
   A. Mental deficiency:
   Because of its more exact standards the study of arithmetic is more likely to reveal general mental deficiency than other studies. For this reason many cases which are reported as specific arithmetic deficiencies are really cases of low intelligence. Give a general intelligence test first.
   B. Distraction:
   As in spelling.
   C. Dissociation with extra-curricular situations: Remedy by use of concrete concepts and construction of models to scale.
   D. Inadequate practice:
   Use diagnostic tests and correlated remedial exercises.
5. Geography and history disabilities:
   A. Motivation:
   In the clinic the most common cause of these disabilities is insufficient motivation of the part of the teacher.
   B. Home criticism:
   Look for aversion to these subjects in the parents.
   C. Poorly trained teacher:
   D. Lack of concrete projects:
   E. Chance unfortunate associations with the subjects:
   Treat by analysis.
6. Writing disability:
   A. Lack of general motor coordination.
   Administer general corrective measures.
   B. Interference with native manual preference:
   Determine degree and side of preference and treat by shift or tie-up accordingly.
   C. Hyperkinesis:
   Remove tensions and if difficulty persists analyze for hysteriform disorders.
7. Speech disability:
   Distinguish between the articulatory and phonic and the rhythmic disturbance. Treat former by direct therapy as for other idiomotor disorders. Treat latter by indirect therapy and by such methods as are used in correcting aphasias.

V Therapy

1. **Records and reports:** All records of the case should be kept together and, when not carried on the person of the clinician, should be kept securely locked. Under no condition should they be shown outside the clinic or left where unauthorized persons might examine them.

RULE 16: EVERY CONFERENCE CARRIED OUT UNDER THE AUSPICES OF THE CLINIC MUST BE REPORTED IN DETAIL.
RULE 17: CLINIC RECORDS MUST NOT BE SEEN BY UNAUTHORIZED PERSONS.

2. **Clinician's daily report** (Form 10.1): The conference reports are numbered serially, the number in the series being inserted at A in occupational therapy, discipline, motor training, speech correction, reassurance, suggestive therapy, motivation, active therapy, catharsis, psychoanalysis, child psychoanalysis. F refers to questions asked by clinician. Elements of the dream are written in the numbered sections at G and their associations in the corresponding sections under H. K refers to assignment made to case, L his reaction to it, and M to the degree of rapport between clinician and case.

3. **First follow-up letter** (Forms 10.2 and 10.3): The letter should be adjusted to the recommendations made in the case, should appear personal, and should follow the rules of correspondence given later in this handbook. Routine follow-ups should be made at two, six and twelve weeks. Replies to follow-up letters should be answered by the clinic immediately with additional suggestions, reiteration of original suggestions, and encouragement.[24]

4. **Progress** (Form 10.5): This form may be used for initial and terminal measurement of results where such results must be put into some quantitative form. A rough average adjustment score may be obtained by averaging the scores in Items 1-36. Items 37, 39, 42, 44, 46, and 48 are weighted by ten, Items 38 and 41 by five, Item 40 by thirty, Item 43 by three, Item 45 by seven, and Item 47 by fifteen.[25]

5. **General Conference rules**: While methods must always be adapted to the needs of the case, there are certain general conference techniques which apply to all cases.

The conference should be planned in ten-minute blocks. The plans need not be strictly adhered to.

RULE 18: THERE MUST BE A PLAN HELD IN RESERVE FOR EVERY CONFERENCE.
RULE 19: CALL FOR AND DELIVER CASES UNDER FOURTEEN UNTIL CERTAIN THAT THEY WILL COME AND GO PROMPTLY ALONE.

When a young case is taken from school or from home, the clinician should escort him both to and from the conference. This protects the clinic from responsibility for loitering or accidents.

RULE 20: APPOINTMENTS MUST BE SPECIFIC AS TO THE TIME AND PLACE.
RULE 21: ALLOW TEN MINUTES FOR CASE TO APPEAR FOR APPOINTMENT. IF THE APPOINTMENT IS NOT KEPT, DISCOVER THE CAUSE AND MAKE ANOTHER APPOINTMENT AS SOON AS POSSIBLE.
RULE 22: MAKE INSTRUCTION DEFINITE AND DISTINGUISH CLEARLY BETWEEN SUGGESTIONS AND INSTRUCTIONS.

The clinic does not recognize any excuse for a clinician failing to keep a case under control. Disciplinary problems arise only when there is some question as to the clinician's authority or ability to enforce instructions. The clinician is expected to take whatever measures are necessary to maintain control and take them quickly. There should never be a delay of more than a few seconds. This rule is not difficult to follow if all instructions are made sparingly and thoughtfully.

RULE 23: THE CLINICIAN MUST CONTROL HIS CASE. ONE FAILING TO DO SO WILL RESULT IN HIS IMMEDIATE DISCHARGE FROM THE CLINIC.

The clinician should avoid any manifestation of emotion. One ill-timed gasp of surprise or disapproval may do more damage to a case than a series of conferences can correct. Some cases assume a jolly attitude toward the conferences, but the clinician should never permit this to mislead him into laughing either with or at the case. Good humor is desirable, but mirth, cynicism or satire destroy the clinical situation. Adverse criticism, of course, should never be offered unless for a definite purpose.

[24] In the 1941 edition, this is followed by:
Teacher's report: In certain instances where special teaching methods have been recommended, it is desirable for the teacher to make daily general reports to the clinic.
(Editors' note: The teacher's report form, which is contained in the 1941 edition, is included in the Appendix to this chapter).

[25] In the 1941 edition, this is followed by:
Report of cathartic conferences: When teachers are doing important cathartic work with children it is frequently valuable for them to report the results of their interviews on a standard form. See Mason's handbook for teachers using cathartic methods.

FORT HAYS KANSAS STATE COLLEGE PSYCHOLOGICAL CLINIC

Form 10.1 Clinician's Daily_Report

A ______________________ ______________________ 193 ________ ________ to ________

No Case Clinician Date Time

B THERAPIES USED: Rem Dvs Oth Dsc Mtr Sp Rsr Sug Mtv Ath Cath Psa Cpsa

C PROGRAM FOLLOWED:

Nature of Exercise	Time	Reason for Exercise	Reaction of Case
1 ____________	____	____________	____________
____________	____	____________	____________
2 ____________	____	____________	____________
____________	____	____________	____________
3 ____________	____	____________	____________
____________	____	____________	____________
4 ____________	____	____________	____________
____________	____	____________	____________

D QUESTIONS ASKED BY CASE: ______________________

E INFORMATION VOLUNTEERED: ______________________

G DREAMS REPORTED: 1 ______ 2 ______ 3 ______
4 ______ 5 ______ 6 ______ 7 ______
8 ______ 9 ______ 10 ______ 11 ______
12 ______ 13 ______ 14 ______ 15 ______

H DREAM ASSOCIATION: 1 ______ 2 ______ 3 ______
4 ______ 5 ______ 6 ______ 7 ______
8 ______ 9 ______ 10 ______ 11 ______
12 ______ 13 ______ 14 ______ 15 ______

I WORD ASSOCIATION: ______________________

J FREE ASSOCIATION: ______________________

K ASSIGNMENT: ____________ L REACTION: ____________ M RAPPORT ____________

N NEXT SESSION: ______________________

O DISCUSSION OF SESSION: ______________________

P QUESTIONS AS TO THERAPY: ______________________

Q REVIEWERS REMARKS: ______________________

R REVIEWER: ______________________

FORT HAYS KANSAS STATE COLLEGE PSYCHOLOGICAL CLINIC

Form 10.2

(Reply to Dr. Geo. A. Kelly, Fort Hays Kansas State College, Hays)

To ______________________________ ______________________________

Address

Concerning ______________________________ ______________________________

Date sent Date returned

Which of the following suggestions were you able to carry out?

1.

2.

3.

4.

5.

What sort of progress is being made in school now?

Under what conditions do you notice most improvement?

Under what conditions is the improvement least noticeable?

To what extent are you receiving cooperation?

Are there further problems which have arisen since the clinic or further services which we can render you?

October 14, 1936

Mr. John D. Doe
Superintendent of Schools

Jonesburgh, Kansas

My Dear Mr. Doe:

Since the Jonesburgh clinic, September twenty-sixth, we have been interested in following the progress of Mary Curtis. Were you able to carry out the suggestions which we made? Has Mary been able to adjust herself to the fifteen-minute periods of routine?

The extension clinic conferences were necessarily so short that we could scarcely do more than get acquainted with your pupil's problems. Now we would like to keep in touch with you and be of any assistance we can in making helpful adjustments in the school and home.

We would appreciate receiving a nice long letter from you within the next few days. Remember that our only excuse for existing is that we may be of some help to you. Please make use of us in every possible way.

The enclosed form may be used in your reply.

Yours very truly,

Harry Mason
Graduate Assistant

HM/fk
10 . 3

FORT HAYS KANSAS STATE COLLEGE PSYCHOLOGICAL CLINIC

Form 10.5 Progress

(Address replies to Dr. Geo. A. Kelly, Hays, Kansas)

To_________________ Concerning _______________ sent __________ Met _________ cl ____

We are anxious to follow the progress of this person in a definite way in order to determine the extent to which our work has been effective. Because of your interest and contacts we are asking you to report on the convenient form below. Where two opposite traits are listed and this person in your estimation rates about average or half way between the traits you should encircle the middle figure, otherwise encircle the figure somewhat to the right or left depending upon the amount of the right or left trait.

	Trait		Score					Change since_______________ Worse - Better				
1.	Docile	-Aggressive	-2	-1	0	1	2	-2	-1	0	1	2
2.	Lazy	-Industrious	-2	-1	0	1	2	-2	-1	0	1	2
3.	Complaining	-Cheerful	-2	-1	0	1	2	-2	-1	0	1	2
4.	Tired	-Energetic	-2	-1	0	1	2	-2	-1	0	1	2
5.	Disinterested	-Interested	-2	-1	0	1	2	-2	-1	0	1	2
6.	Distracted	-Calm	-2	-1	0	1	2	-2	-1	0	1	2
7.	Inaccessible	-Communicative	-2	-1	0	1	2	-2	-1	0	1	2
8.	Tardy	-Prompt	-2	-1	0	1	2	-2	-1	0	1	2
9.	Secretive	-Open	-2	-1	0	1	2	-2	-1	0	1	2
10.	Posture poor	-Good	-2	-1	0	1	2	-2	-1	0	1	2
11.	Dependent	-Independent	-2	-1	0	1	2	-2	-1	0	1	2
12.	Rebellious	-Cooperative	-2	-1	0	1	2	-2	-1	0	1	2
13.	Sleepy	-Wide awake	-2	-1	0	1	2	-2	-1	0	1	2
14.	Day dreams	-Alert	-2	-1	0	1	2	-2	-1	0	1	2
15.	Restless	-Composed	-2	-1	0	1	2	-2	-1	0	1	2
16.	Nagging	-Reasonable	-2	-1	0	1	2	-2	-1	0	1	2
17.	Cries easily	-Mature	-2	-1	0	1	2	-2	-1	0	1	2
18.	Shows off	-Modest	-2	-1	0	1	2	-2	-1	0	1	2
19.	Fearful	-Courageous	-2	-1	0	1	2	-2	-1	0	1	2
20.	Wastes time	-Efficient	-2	-1	0	1	2	-2	-1	0	1	2
21.	Interest narrow	-Broad	-2	-1	0	1	2	-2	-1	0	1	2
22.	Quarrelsome	-Friendly	-2	-1	0	1	2	-2	-1	0	1	2
23.	Shows temper	-Good humor	-2	-1	0	1	2	-2	-1	0	1	2
24.	Delinquent	-Good	-2	-1	0	1	2	-2	-1	0	1	2
25.	Inactive	-Active	-2	-1	0	1	2	-2	-1	0	1	2
26.	Follower	-Leader	-2	-1	0	1	2	-2	-1	0	1	2
27.	Unpopular	-Popular	-2	-1	0	1	2	-2	-1	0	1	2
28.	Cries easily	-Mature	-2	-1	0	1	2	-2	-1	0	1	2
29.	Truant	-Dependable	-2	-1	0	1	2	-2	-1	0	1	2
30.	Deceitful	-Truthful	-2	-1	0	1	2	-2	-1	0	1	2
31.	Worried	-Happy	-2	-1	0	1	2	-2	-1	0	1	2
32.	Dirty	-Clean	-2	-1	0	1	2	-2	-1	0	1	2
33.	Slovenly	-Neat	-2	-1	0	1	2	-2	-1	0	1	2
34.	Dowdy	-Tasteful	-2	-1	0	1	2	-2	-1	0	1	2
35.	Helpless	-Self–reliant	-2	-1	0	1	2	-2	-1	0	1	2

36. Absences during last month_________ x -1
37. Number of fights __________ x -10
38. Minor disciplines ________ x -5
39. Major punishments_________ x -10
40. Delinquencies___________ x -30
41. Complaints from parents teacher or adults ______ x -5
42. Average Grades F (20) D (-10) c (0) B (10) A (20) D (-10)
43. Member clubs ________x -3
44. Residencies ________________x 10
45. Other Offices ________________ x -7
46. Has job (10) _____________ mos. x 5
47. Fired ______________ x -15
48. Quit _______________ x-10

RULE 24: A CLINICIAN SHOULD NEVER GIVE ANY INDICATION OF EMOTION, SURPRISE, DISAPPROVAL OR MIRTH DURING A CONFERENCE UNLESS SUCH AN INDICATION IS DEFINITELY A PART OF THE PLANNED THERAPEUTIC PROCEDURE.

The clinician-case relationship is not a personal friendship in any sense, it is not a give-and-take situation. In general, the case should not be met socially until after the treatment has been completed, better still, not at all.

RULE 25: THE CLINICIAN MUST NOT UNDER ANY CONDITION CONFIDE IN THE PATIENT.

The clinical conference requires the utmost alertness on the part of the clinician. At every moment mechanisms are revealed by the case which even the best of clinicians is likely to overlook. It is a great mistake for a clinician ever to assume that "nothing is happening." The conference is always a strenuous experience for a clinician.

RULE 26: IMPORTANT FACTS ARE BEING REVEALED EVERY MOMENT OF A CONFERENCE.

The transference situation is important in every conference, but it should remain flexible and should not be based upon a personal attachment for the clinician as a real person. In order to keep the transference from developing to a primary affection, the clinician should avoid all physical contact with the case. Shaking hands and helping with coats should be avoided as much as is consistent with good manners. Children should never be 'hugged' or touched unnecessarily. This applies to children of the same sex as that of the clinician as well as to those of opposite sex.

RULE 27: AVOID PHYSICAL CONTACT WITH THE PATIENT.

A certain degree of depression tends to stimulate catharsis and the revelation of information which the case is usually reluctant to disclose. It is the task of the clinician to prevent the patient from becoming too depressed in any conference. A moderate amount of crying in anxiety cases is permissible and frequently to be encouraged, but protracted crying should be avoided. Reassurance, redirection of the conversation, summary of facts of an objective nature, and termination of the conference may all be used to stem catharsis.

RULE 28: DO NOT PERMIT THE PATIENT TO BECOME TOO DEPRESSED IN ANY ONE CONFERENCE.

Frequently a patient will invite the clinician to concur in an opinion concerning right and wrong, religion, behavior of friends, etc. Since such an opinion may be an ego defense on the part of the patient, the clinician's concurrence will tend to repress the counter opinion in the patient and thus prevent a needed catharsis.

RULE 29: DO NOT CONCUR IN THE PATIENT'S OPINION ON PERSONAL OR CONTROVERSIAL MATTERS.

A clinician is sometimes tempted to correct defects in the attitude of the conferee's associates or in the social status of the patient. If these defects can be conveniently and legitimately changed and if they are truly abnormal, the clinician is justified in attempting the corrections. Ordinarily, this is not best.

RULE 30: TREAT THE CASE.

This rule is frequently applicable when a parent asks to have his child treated; the parent, being the one who has presented himself, should be dealt with first.

A conference with an adult case may be preceded by casual conversation. When the clinician seats himself, it should be taken as a signal to begin the clinical conference.

RULE 31: THE CONFERENCE BEGINS WITH THE SEATING OF THE CLINICIAN.

Immature clinicians are sometimes tempted to suggest escapes and rationalizations in helping the patient over difficulties.

RULE 32: A FAILURE MAY BE REORIENTED BUT NEVER ESCAPED.

It is usually considered a good sign when the patient develops an independence of the clinician. It indicates that the transference is broken and with it the need for transference. This normal termination of transference must not be confused with the ambivalent changes which a patient develops from time to time. The latter reveal quite clearly a personal feeling tone for the clinician and are colored distinctly with a critical, wounded or martyr attitude on the part of the patient. The ambivalent changes are usually brought about after a symptom has been counter-suggested, a difficult explanation made or the recollection of a particularly distasteful experience which the patient has decided not to reveal to the clinician. The second conference after the breaking of transference is the normal time for terminating the series of conferences unless a new series or cycle with a new transference situation is undertaken in order to dislodge more or different symptoms. When a case which is still in a stage of transference is discontinued by the clinician a transference neurosis resembling a traumatic neurosis is likely to develop.

RULE 33: TERMINATE THE THERAPEUTIC SERIES ON THE SECOND CONFERENCE AFTER TRANSFERENCE IS RESOLVED, UNLESS A COMPLETE NEW SERIES IS TO BE UNDERTAKEN.

RULE 34: USE REASSURANCE LIBERALLY IN THE LAST CONFERENCE OF A THERAPEUTIC SERIES.

6. Classification of therapeutic methods: The following classifications of general therapeutic methods are recognized in the psychological clinic.

Direct
- Remedial Training in Special Subjects
- Motor Training
- Speech Correction

Diversional
- Discipline
- General Diversion
- Occupational Therapy

Suggestive
- Reassurance
- Motivation
- Counter-suggestion
- Hypnosis

Cathartic
- Active Therapy
- Pure Catharsis
- Psychoanalysis
- Child Psychoanalysis

The direct methods are self-explanatory. The diversional methods are designed to redirect the patient's energies into constructive channels; to drain libido from the symptom. Discipline does not necessarily mean adverse criticism of the case, as used in the Clinic it means systematization of the patient's daily program. It is an extremely valuable method and will frequently yield results when all other methods appear to fail. General diversion consists in directing the attention of the patient to non-catharted ideas during a conference. It is used when a patient has already had enough catharsis during a conference or when conditions are such that complete therapy is not practical and the clinician is unwilling to open the case. In general, any occupational therapy is safe for any case provided it does not carry with it too much responsibility. The choice of an occupation or hobby should be based upon the desirability of an increased responsibility for the patient.

Reassurance (See RULE 7) is not the safe method which many clinicians think it to be. In general it should be used only at the close of a therapeutic series or when catharsis must be temporarily checked.

Hypnosis should ordinarily be avoided in the clinic. It is an outmoded procedure. Motivation is the adoption of the enthusiastic dynamic attitude on the part of the clinician and is used to break mild depressions or give general stimulation. It is a rather safe method if the patient identifies himself with the clinician, otherwise the patient may feel depressed when comparing himself with the clinician.

Counter-suggestion destroys *rapport* between clinician and case. It should be used with the greatest of caution. Although it may easily remove the symptoms against which it is directed, unless the patient has been well prepared, another symptom will be substituted for those removed. Sometimes it is necessary to "give back the symptom" if counter-suggestion is prematurely applied. Properly used counter-suggestion will speed up a therapy which otherwise would be unduly protracted.

Active therapy is treatment by giving definite instructions to a case which are to be followed out before the next conference. It possesses some of the disadvantages of counter-suggestion, but is generally safer. If the instructions are not carried out, the patient becomes secretive and ashamed and the clinician loses rapport.

Pure catharsis is the free expression of catharted ideas. It is invaluable as a therapeutic method, but must not be permitted to go too far, i.e., precipitates a protracted depression. Inexperienced clinicians should use the cathartic method cautiously until they are able to estimate the probable effects on different cases. Catharsis never fails to develop immediately a state of transference in the case. The transference may be negative in some cases. Clinicians must bear this in mind. The case must be treated thereafter as one in which there is a state of transference. In nearly every instance, a certain amount of relief may be expected following the first cathartic conference. This relief is frequently only temporary and becomes permanent only after the patient develops insight into his condition.

The psychoanalytic method, as developed by Freud and his followers, is very complex, but if properly used is quite safe for any case. Certain modifications such as those used in the seating of the patient, etc., adapt it for use in the psychological clinic. Because of its complexity, no attempt is made to discuss it here. The method of child analysis is that developed by Anna Freud and Klein. It is complex and no attempt is made to discuss it here.

7. **Principles of therapy for rhythmic disorders of speech, reading and thought**: Two principles are involved; the first is that of setting up a new neutral gradient for the disordered function, the second is that of integrating the disordered function into a larger and more stable neutral gradient. If, for instance, stuttering is to be treated the therapy becomes a matter first of setting up a

new speech gradient by changing the pattern of speech as much as possible, and second, of integrating speech into a larger gradient which includes writing, gesture, more extensive symbolism in thought, etc.

There are two main considerations to be followed in getting up the larger gradient: the relative stability of the new elements and the extent of symbolic formulation possible in the new elements. Thus if dysrhythmic speech is to be integrated with movements of the hands the clinician should first make sure that the subject has good control of his hands. Furthermore, since there is reversed symmetry both in the structure and the function of the two hands the speech should be integrated with the gestures of one hand only. The hand chosen should be the one preferred by the subject unless there is reasonable evidence for believing that the gradient of the other is inherently more stable. In the second place the clinician should require the movements of the hands to be highly symbolic if he wishes symbolic speech to be absorbed by the larger gradient. Simple swinging of the hands, snapping of the fingers, etc., are too simple to dominate speech or make any appreciable change in its gradient.

Precipitating causes of rhythmic disturbances may be somewhat alleviated by helping the case to make emotional adjustments. Either direct or indirect therapy may be used. A good form of direct therapy is that devised by Van Riper. It consists of assigning difficult social situations to which the case is to adjust himself. The situations are to be met in the order of their difficulty.

8. **General conference aids**: Ordinarily it is best to have the patient sit across the table from the clinician. The table furnishes support for the elbows and aids the interview. Four to six feet of space should separate patient and clinician. During continuous free association, the patient should have his face turned toward a blank wall. During catharsis it is usually best for the patient to look at the clinician since some measure of confidence is gained from observing the clinician's facial expression. Some patients, however, develop better catharsis while looking away. Seating should be arranged so that neither conferee will have to face the source of light. As far as possible the clinician should avoid mannerisms or distracting movements. Ordinarily the conference report should not be written during a cathartic conference. A report may be made, however, during a strictly diagnostic interview.

Some cases have difficulty responding to the cathartic method. Considerable patience is required in instructing them during the first two or three conferences. The following instructions may be used: "I want you to start out today by telling me everything that comes to your mind. I want you to say just exactly what you think. It won't make a bit of difference to me, you can't shock me no matter what you say. If you feel like crying, I want you to cry. You can laugh, sing, swear, tell me what you think of me—anything. If you don't know where to start, start by telling me the things which you have most dreaded telling me. Perhaps there are some things which you had thought you would rather hold back. Suppose you start with those. You can fill in the explanation later."

If a patient appears to be on the point of giving some information but is embarrassed, the clinician may say, "You are a little embarrassed aren't you? It is quite all right, I probably could guess very nearly what it is you have to say but it will be better if you say it yourself first. You see we deal with problems like yours every day and while this may all seem very serious and unusual to you, I will not be shocked or surprised at all. Go ahead."

In continuous free association the patient is likely to make logical associations instead of free ones. The clinician may interrupt and say, "No, now you are explaining! Just say what comes to your mind. If I hear something that I think should be followed up I'll interrupt you." Sometimes a patient complains that he can think of nothing to say. The clinician may permit the conference to lapse into a silence of a full three or four minutes and then say, "What are you thinking of now?"

There are various ways of conducting word associations. The words may be given orally and may represent words from a dream or previous conversation. At other times words may be presented from a standard list, each word on a card. The usual plan is to pronounce the word and lay down the card before the patient at the same time. The case may be instructed to make a single spontaneous association or to make a series of associations. Sometimes the words are administered rapidly and every effort made to hurry the case. In this instance cards upon which the patient blocks or for which he makes unusual responses are thrown out into a separate pile and are presented again with the request that the patient explain his unusual response. This method should never be used with a case who obviously has something in mind that he knows bears upon the diagnosis. The method is a direct attack upon the patient's integrity and should be used only when true resistance is being met.

A great many patients consciously withhold information. If they are made to understand that there will be no condemnation if they revise previous remarks, there should be little difficulty. The most willing and sincere patients will sometimes withhold information until the next conference.

Amnesia for dreams is nearly always a problem which will tax the clinician's ingenuity if he places any reliance upon this source of information. Some cases will develop an amnesia for dreams as soon as the therapeutic series is started. Others will develop an amnesia as soon as explanations have been offered. Still others report that they never dream. Of course, as every clinician knows, all cases start remembering dreams after the first few conferences. Sometimes a case may be told that he will dream during the following night and that he is to review the dream in his mind as soon as he awakes. The suggestion usually works, but sometimes the case reports that he can remember no details of the dream. Another plan is to have the case write the dreams as soon as he awakes in the morning, and still another is to have him determine to write the dream as soon as he dreams it, perhaps writing in the dark. Of course there is no such thing as a standardized translation of a dream; it all depends upon what the particular patient associates with the elements of the dream. Retelling of the dream and observation of the new details is always good practice.

In a general way, it may be said that the object of an analysis of an hysteriform disorder is to trace development back to the Oedipus situation, while in the case of an obsessional disorder, development must be traced back to pregenital stages. In each instance the intervening material must be well clarified for the case. The hysteriform case will usually show marked improvement after the recall of the Oedipus. The obsessional case does not respond so markedly to the reaching of the pregenital material. In many cases it is unnecessary to make a complete analysis.

In dealing with psychotic reactions one must usually employ some active therapy. In the schizoid types the analysis can profitably go back to the bisexual and masturbatory problems. Disciplinary therapy is not particularly advisable for schizoid types but is a very good therapy for cycloid types.

9. **Schemata of the psychopathology of the neuroses**: The following schemata are given as aids to therapy rather than as aids to diagnosis.

Neurosis	Symptom Formation	Conflict	Level
Hysteria	Conversion	Ego-Id	Regress to Oedipus
Anxiety	Displacement or Escape	Id-Real then Ego Real	Oedipus
Actual Neurosis Hypochondria	Regression to Narcissism	Ego-Real	Pregenital
Anxiety	Regression to Narcissism	Id-Real	Pregenital
Neurasthenia	Regression to Narcissism	Ego-Real	Pregenital (arrested)
Pathoneurosis	Regression to Narcissism	Organ-Real	Mature
Organ neurosis	Conversion to Narcissism	Ego-Id	Genital or Pregenital
Inhibited States	Ego Inhibition	Super Ego-Ego's sex	Genital or Pregenital
Traumatic Neurosis	Direct Defense	Id-Real	Mature
Psychasthenia	Displacement Ego Transference	Super Ego-Ego	Pregenital Anal Sadist

Solution	Principles	Common Symptoms
Compromise in symptom formation	Somatic compliance Identification Secondary gain Displacement upwards Genitalization of organs	Seizure Paralysis *Arc de cercle* No palatal reflex Absence Hyperfunction Disturbed vision *Globus hystericus* Heminesthesia
Ego flight Id wins in symptom	Phobic Façade	Anxiety Phobias
Masochism		Hypochondria
Id flight		Anxiety
Id impoverished		Depression Asthenia
Organ wins Hypercathexis	Follows organic treatment	Post-operative anxiety
Compromise on Id fixed on single organ	Single organ	Cardiac Respiratory Muscular, etc.
Super Ego propitiated Ego impoverished		Inhibitions
Real Wins		Shock
Super Ego wins Ego split	Expiation Atonement Internalization Isolation Undoing Depersonalization Relations rather than memories are repressed Secondary gain	Obsessions Compulsions Biphasic symptoms Bisexuality Ambivalence Affective emptiness Sexualizations of thinking Systematization Magic Rumination Hair-splitting Doubt Symptom related to masturbation

10. **Rules of mental hygiene**: Sometimes clinicians are asked to recommend rules of mental hygiene. Such rules are really nothing more than popular statements of common human needs, their formulation is a matter of convenience more than of principle. The statements should be brief enough to be readily remembered and simple enough to be readily applied. Following are some suggested rules of mental hygiene, clinicians may modify them or add others as circumstances require. Two statements are given for each rule, one for adults and one for children.

1. Cling to the indestructibles. Get your heart upon things which cannot easily be taken away from you.
2. Develop widely varying interests. Learn to be interested in many different kinds of things. Misfortune and a changing society frequently require radical readjustment of one's interests.
3. Treat all love affairs with respect. When people fall in love with each other, treat them with respect.
4. Avoid projections. When things go wrong be very careful not to blame other people or things too much. Blaming people is a bad habit and will make a person very unhappy.
5. Meet difficult problems with some emotion more effective than fear. Learn to be careful without being afraid.
6. Make conscience your friend. When you think you want to do something that is wrong and your conscience will not let you just remember that that is the way your conscience has of keeping you from being unhappy.

11. **Instructions to a patient about to undergo psychoanalysis**: In general, the following rules should be given to a patient in the first conference in a psychoanalytic series:

1. During each psychoanalytic conference, unless instructed otherwise, you are to express your thoughts just as freely as you can. Do not try to be logical or explain why different things have come to your mind, just express them as they come. Sometimes you may wonder if your thoughts are important enough to express. The answer is that if they are important enough to come to your mind at all, they are important enough to express. There must be absolutely no withholding of ideas: you must be your real self and talk just as you think.
2. Your relations with your clinician are utterly impersonal. He is not to be looked upon either as a friend or a critic. What you say makes no personal difference to him whatever. He is interested in you not as a person but as a very important case which he is extremely anxious to cure. Nothing that you can say will make him either like you or dislike you.
3. Outside the conference room, your relations with your clinician are only to be those of very casual acquaintances. You should not attempt to speak to him except in matters relating to appointments or details of your analysis. Under no condition should you attempt to meet him or his family socially.
4. As much as possible, avoid any attempt to estimate your clinician's opinion of you. You are not on display and personal attitudes are unimportant.
5. Avoid self-evaluation. Frequently a patient wonders if he is good or bad, the point is that it makes no difference as far as the analysis is concerned. The only purpose of the analysis is to put the patient in complete command of himself.
6. Do not discuss your analysis with anyone but your clinician until after it is finished. If you wish you may admit that you are under analysis, but your discussion should go no further.
7. At times you may develop very positive attitudes toward situations, people, or things. As much as possible, keep these attitudes from becoming fixed too soon; suspend judgment.
8. Do not make any major decisions regarding your life plan, marital relations or career while under analysis. They are likely not to be permanent.
9. Sometimes ideas will come to mind between conferences which seem very hard to retain or which seem repulsive. These are likely to be important to the analysis and you should make every effort to express them in the next conference.
10. Report in conference all dreams and emotional experiences.
11. You need not feel that the clinician is withholding explanation from you unnecessarily. The real solution of your problems will come to you first and with it will come the feeling of adequacy necessary to solve the problem. At times you may feel that you know the real source of your difficulty.
12. Ultimately you will cure yourself. Your clinician will have acted only in the role of an adviser, the real cure will be administered by yourself, no one else can administer it for you.

In addition to a general background in Psychology and an intensive training in abnormal psychology, clinicians should be familiar with the following books:

Adler, *The Practice and Theory of Individual Psychology*
Baker and Traphagan, *The Diagnosis of Behavior Problem Children*
Brown and Potter, *The Psychiatric Study of Problem Children*
Burt, *The Young Delinquent*

Cheney, *Outlines for Psychiatric Examination*
Fenichel, *Outline for Clinical Psychoanalysis*
Freud, *New Introductory Lectures on Psychoanalysis*
Garrett, *A Manual of Psychological and Physiological Tests*
Healy, Bronner, and Bowers, *Structure and Meaning of Psychoanalysis*
Henderson and Gillespie, *Textbook of Psychiatry*
Herrick, *Introduction to Neurology*
Malamud, *Psychopathology*
Morgan, *Psychology of the Unadjusted School Child*
Rasmussen, *The Principal Nervous Pathways*
Terman, *The Measurement of Intelligence*
Travis, *Speech Pathology*
White, *Outlines of Psychiatry*[26]

VI Vocational Guidance

In the conduct of a work project for non-school young people arranged through the cooperation of the National Youth Administration (N.Y.A.), the clinic has developed some procedures for vocational guidance. These procedures have been developed principally by Miss Opal Emmons, Mr. John Hadley, Mr. Harry Mason, Miss Margaret Pankaskie, and Miss Iris Stevenson.

Every vocational guidance case must have a sponsor who is in a position of authority or influence with respect to the case and who is not connected with the Clinic. Since the Clinic cannot solicit clients and since each case must have some introduction to the work of the Clinic, this measure is necessary.

RULE 1. EACH VOCATIONAL GUIDANCE CASE MUST HAVE A SPONSOR WHO ASSUMES THE RESPONSIBILITY FOR MAKING THE REGISTRATION.

The most satisfactory arrangement has been to have young people who are working on a N.Y.A. county work project assigned to the Clinic for supervision of their N.Y.A. work. This brings them into immediate contact with the Clinic and enables the Clinic to observe their working habits and carry out systematic prevocational training.

The proper conduct of a vocational guidance project consists of several stages as follows:

1. **Occupational survey:** A survey of occupations available in the community, employers, representative skilled workmen, who might supervise apprentices or advise the Clinic on training requirements, permanency of occupations, new occupations likely to develop, industrial changes taking place in the community, and prevailing wage scales and working conditions.
2. **Job analyses:** Job analyses of vocations which appear to present possibilities for the Clinic's clients.
3. **Sponsor selection:** Selection of sponsors for each client and original contact between client and Clinic.
4. **Social history:** Compilation of a social history on each case through contact with social agencies, former employers, and the Works Project Administration (W.P.A.) office.
5. **Diagnosis:** Diagnosis of occupational aptitudes and opportunities (Form 3.1, Vocational Sociology; Form 7.6. Vocational Skills; and Form 8.1, Vocational Personality). These diagnostic examinations are mostly modifications of the other examinations used in the Clinic. When clients are assigned to the Clinic for their N.Y.A. time, these examinations are supplemented by observation of their working habits, promptness, skills, social adjustment, etc.
6. **Training:** Prevocational training in basic skills and habits necessary for the occupation indicated by the diagnosis. This training is carried out under an individualized prevocational training syllabus prepared especially for each case.
7. **Placement:** Placement in apprenticeships or vocations.
8. **Supervision:** Supervision of apprenticeships and early employment. Where the client is placed in an apprenticeship the Clinic is responsible for very close supervision of the working conditions and the requirement of frequent reports on the progress of the client. The Clinic should work out the apprenticeships in cooperation with organized labor in those occupations where organized labor maintains standards of skills and proficiency. The great danger is that apprenticeships set up by the Clinic may reduce standards of wage and working conditions. This can be prevented by proper care.
9. **Vocational Sociology** (Form 3.1)[27]. Following are suggested questions to aid the examiner in administering this form.

[26] In the 1941 edition, this list also includes: Rogers, *The Clinical Treatment of the Problem Child.*

[27] This section, and the associated form, are not included in the 1941 edition.

1. Do you like to spend most of your time at home or do you like frequent changes? Are you more content with friends or relations or do you prefer to be with strangers? Do you travel much?
2. What school did you attend last? What grade were you in when you quit school? Which subject did you like best; which did you dislike? Who was your favorite teacher? Why? Which teacher did you dislike? Why? Did you like school?
3. Name some of the books which you have read. What magazines do you read? Do you read papers? Name them. How often do you attend the movies? Do you play cards, dance, go to parties? Do you belong to any gangs? Are you interested in athletics? Do you participate? What is your favorite amusement? How much money do you spend on amusements? How do you earn it?
4. Have you ever belonged to an organization? Did you hold an office? Fill in the blanks with the name of the organization. If the case has held an office in one of the organizations encircle the number following officer which corresponds to the number of the organization in which the office was held and write the name of the office in the blank.
5. Are your friends younger or older than you, girls or boys, etc.? Who is your best friend? What does he do? What do you like about him?
6. What church do you attend? Are you a member? How often do you attend? What is it in religion that appeals to you? The abbreviations stand for denomination, member, the number of times case attends church per month, escape, romance, security.
7. What do your parents want you to be? How do you get along with your family? Encircle any of the special attitudes shown by the case.
8. Who is living in your home at the present time? List members in the blanks.
9. Are you self-supporting? Do you have anyone else to support? Do you have some special duties at home or elsewhere?
10. Do you have someone that you usually go to for advice? Do you usually make up your own mind or do you wait for suggestions from others? Do you give advice to or boss anyone?
11. Are you happy? What do you worry about? Encircle the words indicating the nature of the case's worries. Abbreviations stand for health, finance, family, friend, education, social, death, love, recognition.
12. Are you sick very much? Do you have any physical handicaps? List physical disabilities.
13. Do you have any property of your own? Do you have some belongings which you share with someone else?
14. Who criticizes you? What are you criticized for? Who punishes you? How? For what?
15. Have you ever been in love? Who was your lover? How old was he? How old were you? How did you get along? What caused your friendship to end?

FORT HAYS KANSAS STATE COLLEGE PSYCHOLOGICAL CLINIC

Form 3.1 Vocational Sociology

Case Age Sex Clinician Date

Voc. Cr. Rec. Cr. School Security Family Friends Responsib Properly				
. . . .	1.	Domesticity		like home, travel, stranger change
. . . .	2.	School like-dislike	x x x x x x x	Fav. subj. ______ least liked ______ school Grade ___________ Favorite teacher least liked
. . . .	3.	Amusements Narrow-broad	x x x x x x x x	read books____ mag. _________ Paper ____ movies __________ cards _________ dance ______ Party ______ gangs __________ Athletics ________ favorite amusement money spent earned
. . . .	4.	Follower-leader	x x x x x x x x	organizations 1 ________________ 2 ___________________ 3 _______________ officer 1 2 3
. . . .	5.	Unpop-pop	x x x x x x x x	Friends, younger, older, boys, girls, noisy, quiet, wander, rough, married, single, leader, follower, names.
. . . .	6.	Religion		den __________ member ___________ att toward fam, affect, proud critical, ashamed.
. . . .	7.	Family tie slight-strong	x x x x x x x x	par. amb. for case _____________ att toward fam, effect, proud critical, ashamed.
. . . .	8.	Household		members 1___________ 2 ____________ 3 ____________ 4 _______________________ 5 _______________________
. . . .	9.	Respon-irres.		Dependents ______________________________________ home duties ______________________________________ other duties
. . . .	10.	Aggressive-docile		dominated _______________________________________ dominated by
. . . .	11.	Worry-cheerful		Health, fin, fam, friend, edu soc, dea, lov, recog.
. . . .	12.	Health good-poor	x x x x x x x	physical disabilities _______________________________
. . . .	13.	Belongings		share ____________________own ____________________
. . . .	14.	Tensions		Criticized by ____________________________________ for ____ punished by _____________________________________ for
. . . .	15.	Love affair		lover _____________age ____________________________ age of case _____________________________ cause of termination

The examiner should check the personality profile opposite each item after he has received the case's answer or reaction to the questions. In Item 2 if the case liked school, encircle an x to the left, if he disliked school encircle an x to the right. Follow this procedure for the remaining items. Abbreviations in Item 5 stand for unpopular or popular, in Item 9 for responsible or irresponsible.

Encircle the "." in the analysis margin opposite each item in which something of significance is found.

10. **Vocational Personality** (Form 8.1)[28]: In examining vocational guidance cases one of the first problems of the Clinic is to find out what kind of things the case is interested in, what he would like to do, and what he has had experience in doing. Besides determining his vocational interests it is also necessary to know something about his personal stability. Form 8.1 has been devised for this purpose. Below are some suggested questions and explanatory notes which should aid the examiner in administering this form.

1. List in the blanks the things which the case states that he is interested in. "What are you interested in? What things do you like to do?"
2. "What do you want to be? What would you like to do?" Abbreviations stand for social, finance, service, exhibitionism, mastery, and prestige. Encircle significant items.
3. "What kind of work have you done? Have you ever worked in a store, office, cafe, etc.?" Encircle the items which the case has had experience. List any others which you mentioned.
4. "Do you have a job at the present time? What do you do? Who is your employer? Where do you work? What were your duties? How much do you make?" Ask these questions about previous jobs, getting the date employed, and a cause of termination. Blanks are provided at the bottom of the sheet for this information.

Abbreviations in item 4 stand for: now employed, last employed, termination of the job.

5. "Do you dance, sing, play a musical instrument, sew, or take part in dramatics? Do you have any other talents?"
6. "Do you prefer to work indoors or out?"

Abbreviations stand for: neophobia, social, escape, dependent, independent. Encircle the abbreviations which seem to have a significant connection with the responses of the case as to the kind of surroundings he prefers.

7. "Do you like to learn a job and then stick to it or do you like to change jobs often? Do you like to travel?"
8. "Do you like to be bossed or would you rather boss? Do you like to feel responsible for a certain job?"
9. "Are you entirely self-supporting? If not, who helps support you? Do you support anyone?"
10. "How do you spend your free time? How much does your recreation cost?"

Abbreviations stand for escape, social, projection, sadism, masochism, homosexuality. Examiner should encircle the words which describe the form of satisfaction derived from the indicated recreation.

11. "Can you typewrite? Can you do carpentry work?" List special mechanical abilities.
12. "Can you cook? Do you sew? Do you go downtown to buy the groceries for the family? Do you do any other shopping for the family or yourself? Have you had any experience taking care of children?"
13. List other abilities.
14. "Who is your ideal person? What is his vocation? (It is often times necessary to state this question differently as to explain just what is meant by ideal.)
15. "Have you had any chances for a job? Did you accept? Why?" Write the case's reaction or answer in the blank.
16. "What was the first job you held? Did you like it? Did you quit or were you fired? Why?"
17. "Who was your favorite employer? Why? Which employer did you dislike the most? Why?"

[28] This section, and the associated form, are not included in the 1941 edition.

FORT HAYS KANSAS STATE COLLEGE PSYCHOLOGICAL CLINIC

Form 8.1 Vocational Personality

Case ______ Age ______ Sex ______ Clinician ______ Date ______

Amb	Aggr	Dev. ta	Stab	forsi	mat			
.	X	X	.	X	X	1.	Interested in	List 1. ______ 2. ______ 3. ______ 4. ______
.	X	X	.	X	X	2.	Amb. Vag-dex x x x X x x x	soc, fin, ser, exh, mas, pres
X	X	X	.	.	.	3.	Experienced x x x X x x x	farm, office, store, café, others
.	.	.	.	.	.	4.	Act-inact x x x X x x x	now, emp, last emp, termin of job
.	X	X	X	X	.	5.	Talented x x x X x x x	mus, dan, art, sew, drama, sing, others
.	.	.	X	.	.	6.	Surroundings prefer	hec, soc, osc, dep, indep, indoors-out
.	X	.	X	.	.	7.	Stability x x x X x x x	change, travel, routine
.	X	.	.	.	X	8.	Aggressive x x x X x x x	boss, take orders, respon,
X	X	.	.	.	.	9.	Non-self suppot x x x X x x x	other sources of income support others
.	.	.	X	.	X	10.	Recreation	type______ cost ______ esc, soc, proj, sadist masc, home,
X	X	X	.	.	.	11.	Mec. Ability	typing, carpentry
X	X	X	.	.	.	12.	Domestic Ability	cook, sew, market, child care
X	X	X	.	.	.	13.	Other Abilities	
X	.	.	.	.	X	14.	Ideal	person vocation of
.	.	.	X	.	.	15.	Opportunities had	accept ______ Why? ______ reaction
.	.	.	.	X	X	16.	First job like-dislike x x x X x x x	termination ______
.	.	.	.	.	.	17.	Employer	best liked ______ least liked

Job:	Employer:	Place:	Date:	Duties:	Salary:	Terminated:
______ :	______ :	______ :	______ :	______ :	______ :	______
______ :	______ :	______ :	______ :	______ :	______ :	______
______ :	______ :	______ :	______ :	______ :	______ :	______
______ :	______ :	______ :	______ :	______ :	______ :	______
______ :	______ :	______ :	______ :	______ :	______ :	______

The examiner should check the profile from the answers given to the questions asked in the items opposite each one.

In Item 2 of the profile encircle an x to the left if the case's ambition is vague, encircle one to the right if the case has a definite ambition. In Item 3, encircle an x to the left if the case has had little experience, encircle an x to the right if the case is experienced in some vocation. Use the same procedure in checking the remaining items. The abbreviations in Item 4 stand for active or inactive, and in Item 9 for non-self-supporting or self-supporting.

The x's in the analysis margin should be encircled opposite each item whenever anything of significance is discovered in the item. The abbreviations stand for ambition, aggressiveness, developed talents, stability, foresight, and maturity.

11. **Vocational Skills** (Form 7.6): The items are arranged in an order that is calculated to make administration as easy as possible, but this order need not be adhered to.

The first item is a test of oral propositional speech. Administering this test calls for considerable skill upon the part of the clinician, not as to manipulation of apparatus or memorizing instructions, but as to using the approach which will indicate spontaneous speech. The first approach might be, "Tell me what you think of the election," or "Tell me how you would spend a day if you could do anything you wanted to do," would be fair. "Tell me what you have been doing this Fall," might be all right if it would not embarrass the subject. In some cases, this item should be passed up and filled out by the person who has administered the vocational personality form. Two rules must be complied with. If the first suggestion intended to initiate propositional speech fails, another should not be given until after several items have been passed. Second, the subject should not be put upon his guard so that he might know that his speech is being checked. Abbreviations of pathologies to be watched for are: speech dysrhythm, poor grammar, faulty syntax, alogical speech, faulty pronunciation, incomplete sentences.

The second item is the Gray Oral Reading Check List. This should be list number four. It should be administered and scored in accordance with the author's instructions, and in addition, the abbreviations at the left should be noted and encircled if the pathology indicated is present. The abbreviations stand for: tonic block, clonic block, mispronunciation, halting style, articulatory speech defect, and peculiar accent.

The third item is the Pintner Achievement Test. It is given and the total score recorded at the right by writing in the score made in the position which it would assume in the series given, and encircling it. The part scores should be recorded at the left after abbreviations of their totals.

Number four is the Stenquist Mechanical Aptitude Test, Form II. It is given according to the author's direction, and the score recorded at the right as in the above test. Any pathology noticed while administering the test should be noted in the left hand margin. The abbreviations stand for frustration, sluggishness, and aphasia. If aphasia is noted, write down the approximate time of the aphasic periods.

Item number five, Eye Movements, is checked from the Speech and Reading Examination, passage number six. Pathologies to be noted are long fixations, aphasic divergencies and reversals. The small "abc" refers to the answers to the questions which are to be asked. If they are answered correctly the letters are encircled.

Item number six is a proof reading test for which copy has been hectographed and folded. The copy, folded, should be laid upon a sheet of carbon paper which has the carbon side up, and the following directions given. "This is a proof reading test. The material which is written here has mistakes in it, and you are to indicate which ones must be corrected before the material can be printed for publication. Take your pencil and encircle each mistake. Use a fairly heavy touch, and do the work as quickly as you can but remember that you must correct all the mistakes." If the subject asks "What kind of mistakes?" simply say, "Correct all the mistakes you can find." Time and score are both recorded. Items marked wrong that are right are deducted from the score, and three additional points are given if the right hand margin is marked for irregularity.

Item seven is a card sorting test. The cards should be thoroughly shuffled before they are brought out. Instructions follow: "The cards have been mixed up. You will notice that each one has a number on it. I want you to sort the cards into piles so that every card in a pile has the same middle digit or number. Sort them as quickly as possible but be sure to sort them correctly." If the subject does not understand the instructions, explain and demonstrate by putting the first four cards in piles, explaining why a certain card goes in a certain pile, but make a note on the record blank that extra instructions have been necessary. Time and errors are recorded. Abbreviations stand for clumsiness, alogical attack, incoordination of muscles, and long reaction time.

Item eight refers to a test of rapid calculation. The copy for this test is on hectographed sheets. The first part is oral, and the examiner should hold the paper during this part. Instructions to be read are at the top of the sheet. The examiner should say the digits at a rate of a little more than one per second, and wait ten seconds for a reply. Under A, if problem 1 is not completed or done properly, problem 2 should be given. In any case, give only enough problems under any one letter to allow the subject to get one right answer. Write down the answer given beside each problem. When the oral part is finished, give the subject the paper and tell him to do the operations indicated as quickly as possible, being sure to get the right answers. Keep time. Scratch paper may be provided for figuring. Key answers will be provided with which to check. Pathologies abbreviated for encircling in the left margin are alogical attack, mechanical errors, trouble in multiplication, addition, subtraction, and carrying.

Item nine refers to the test for following instructions. These tests are hectographed, and instructions to be read by the examiner in the oral test follow. The instructions for the written test are included in the hectographed copy. Pathologies which may be noticed, and for which abbreviations have been included are: short attention span, inability to comprehend, auditory aphasia, alexia, transient aphasia.

FORT HAYS KANSAS STATE COLLEGE PSYCHOLOGICAL CLINIC

Form 7.6 Vocational Skills

Case____________________ Clinician ____________________ Date __________

			IV V VI VII VIII Ad1. S. 10 11 12 13 14 15 17	Ad1.
1.	ORAL PROP. SPEECH		x x x x x x x x x x x x	Dys. Cr. Syn. Alog. Pron. Inop.
2.	GRAY ORAL	(time)	69 64 60	Ton. clon. pron. halt. art. acc
		(errors)	6 5 4	
3.	PINT. ACHIEV.		20 30 35 40 50	Inf. Aplg. Read. Arth. Voc.
4.	STENZ. MECH II		24 28 31 34 36	Frust. Slugg. Aphasic
5.	EYE MOVEMENTS (6)	(Fix)	55 46 31	Lg. Fix. Rev. Aph. Div. abc
		(Time)	40 27 10	
6.	PROOF READ.	(time)	4:0 3 ½ 3:0 2½ 2:0	1½ sp. Punc. Alog.
		(score)	8 10 15 18 23	
7.	CARD SORT.	(time)	3 ½ 3:0 2½ 2:0 1½	Clums. Alog. Incoo. Lg. R
		(errors)	6 4 3 2 1 0	
8.	RAPID CALC.	(oral)	3 4 5 6 7	Alg. Meck. Mult, Add.
	Written	(time)	3:0 4:0 6:0 50 4½	Sub. Carr.
		(errors)	5 3 2 1 0	
9.	Follow INST.	(oral)	3 4 5 7 8 9 10	Sh. Sp. Comp. Aud. Aph. Alex.
		(writ.)	3 4	
10.	LETTER WRIT.	(cond)	4 5 6 7 8	Spl. Syn SS. Penm. Neat.
		(form)	x x x x x x x x	Alg. Gram.
11.	Bounc. Ball		5 10 15 20	Bas. Rhy. Assym. Incoo.
12.	SPACE PERCEP.		3 5 6 7 8 9 10	
13.	ASTEREGG.	(tactile)	1 2 2 4 5	Alog.
14.	ASTEREDD	(visual)	122 118 109	
15.	MEASUREMENT	(Calip)	3 4 5 6 7	Rough Alog.
		(rule)	3 4 5 6 7	
16.	SAW TO LINE		4 8 16	Inep. Incoo. Stst. Assym.
17.	PERS . APPEAR	(GEN)	x x x x X x x x x	
	CLEANLINESS	(bod.)	x x x x X x x x x	Hds. Fac. Ear. Hair. Bo. Nails
		(clothes)	x x x x X x x x x	
		(mouth Hyg.)	x x x x X x x x x	Teeth Tong. Hal. Path.
	NEATNESS	(cloth)	x x x x X x x x x	Rag. Mend. Larg. Small.
		(hair)	x x x x X x x x x	Toup. Cut. Uncomb. Muss.
	TASTE	(gen)	x x x x X x x x x	Loud. Reouls. Shap.
	Approp to occas.		x x x x X x x x x	Ovrd. Undor.
	Approp to figure		x x x x X x x x x	Tight. Loose. Emph.
	SHOES		x x x x X x x x x	Shine. Runov. Fit.
18.	COLOR BLINDNESS		x x x x X x x x x	RG YB Tot. Agna.
19.	BODY TYPE		x x x x X x x x x	Malnut. Asut.Pynik Athl.
20.	FING. TREMOR		x x x x X x x x x	Int. Trem. Dysr.
21.	ANASTHESIA		x x x x X x x x x	Conv. Mypoc.
22.	PULSE		f d c b a	Sit. Ac. 30 60 90 120 180
23.	RESP.			Sit. Ac.
24.	HAND DYNAMOM.		x x x x X x x x x	Max. Stab. Time
25.	ROMBERG		x x x x X x x x x	Long. Trans.
26.	LINE WALK		x x x x X x x x x	Atax. Het. hip. SSL Pg. Sh.
27.	VISION		x x x x X x x x x	L------/ 20-----/ 20--------
28.	ASTIG.		x x x x X x x x x	Scale Below
29.	AUDITION		x x x x X x x x x	L___/ 20R__/20_______

L 0 30 60 90 120 150

R 0 30 60 90 120 150

REMARKS:

Oral Instruction Test: "Now in order to hold a job you must do everything y

our boss tells you to do. You must listen closely to all he says and be sure to do things exactly as he tells you. I am going to tell you some things to do and I want you to do them exactly as I say, as quickly as you can, and without asking questions."

"Look at the papers which I have given to you. There are a number of different forms such as squares, circles, triangles, etc. Each line is numbered. When you have finished line number 1, I will ask you to do something with line No. 2."

"When I say 'pencils up,' you are to lift your pencil regardless of what you are doing. Do not put your pencil down on the paper until I say 'begin'."

1. "Pencils up. Look at the rectangles at 1. When I say begin, but not before, make a circle in the first rectangle and also a letter A in the third. Begin." (5 seconds)
2. "Pencils up. Look at the rectangle and square and oval at 2 . When I say begin, make a figure 1 in the space that is in the oval but not in the square and rectangle, and make an x in the space that is in the square but not in the oval and rectangle. Begin." (10 seconds)
3. "Pencils up. Look at 3. When I say begin, put in the first circle the right answer to the question. How many days are there in a week? In the second and third do nothing, but in the fifth put in any number which is wrong as an answer to the question which I asked you. Begin." (10 seconds)
4. "Pencils up. Look at the shoes and chairs, etc. in No. 4. When I say begin, make a mark from the chair to the book going under the barrel and over the pitcher. Begin." (10 seconds)
5. "Pencils up. Look at 6. When I say begin, cross out the letter just before E and also draw a line under the second letter after H. Begin." (10 seconds)
6. "Pencils up. Look at 6 . If 10 is more than 8 , then when I say go, cross out the number 6 unless 6 is more than 9 in which case draw a line under the number 4 . Begin." (10 seconds)
7. "Pencils up. Look at 7. When I say begin, draw a line through every odd number that is not in a circle and also through every even number that is in a square by itself. Begin." (10 seconds)
8. "Pencils up. Look at 8. Notice the three blanks and the three words. When I say begin, place in the first blank the last letter of the first word, in the second, the first letter of the last word, and in the last, the last letter of the middle word. Begin." (10 seconds)
9. "Pencils up. Look at 9. If automobiles are older than horses put a cross in the first square. If not, draw a circle around the word no. Begin." (10 seconds)
10. "Pencils up. Look at 10. Notice that the drawing is divided into five parts. When I say begin, put an A or B in the two largest parts and any number from 5 to 7 in the smallest part. Begin." (10 seconds)

Item 10 refers to a test of letter writing ability, and should be administered as follows: the examiner should say, "We want to find out how good a letter you can write. Let us suppose that you are applying for a job (indicate the type of job from the subject's preference or statement of interest in vocational personality examination) — to (indicate the name and address of an appropriate firm). Write as good and as neat a letter as you can. Be sure to include everything which your employer should know about you, but make the letter concise and to the point.

Item 11 refers to a bouncing ball contact. A board with two holes in it is provided as a compass, and with this, a pencil, and a piece of chalk, a circle is drawn on the floor. The diameter of this circle is two feet. The subject takes the ball and bounces it in the circle, dribbling with alternate hands, continuing until an error is committed. An error consists in bouncing the ball outside the circle, catching the ball, or dribbling twice in succession with the same hand. Five trials are given, and the number of bounces in the most successful trial is recorded as the score. If the first trial results in a score of twenty or more, no further trials need be given. Abbreviations refer to poor basis rhythm, bodily asymmetry, either of build or of movement, and incoordination of muscles.

Item 12 refers to a test of space perception, performed with a special machine. The subject sits in a chair at a distance of ten feet from the front of the machine, with the center of the machine directly in front of him and the front of the machine parallel to a plane through his hips and shoulders. The examiner moves the right hand target to a fixed position and tells the subject to pull the one connected to the string (which the subject holds in his hand) as that is at the same distance from the screen at the front of the machine as the one which has been set. The examiner stands to one side until the subject has indicated that he has the target set, when the examiner notes the difference in the reading of the two scales. He then moves the right-hand target an inch or so from the first position, and a second trial is made. A third trial is made with the fixed target an inch or more in the opposite direction from the first position. The test is scored by computing the average of the three trials and giving credit as follows: Score of 10 indicates that the average error is less than ¼". For each ¼" average error, one point is deducted. For example, a score of nine is given where the average error is just one quarter-inch, or less than one half-inch. A score of eight is given for values between one-half and three quarters, etc. Abbreviations stand for plus deviations predominating (target or string closer to screen), minus deviations, and alogical attack.

Item 13 refers to a test of ability to recognize forms held in the hand. A block is presented to the subject in each hand, starting with the ball and the block nearest like a ball. He is asked to hand back the one most like a ball. If the correct one is handed back, a score of five is given. If the wrong one is handed back, and the ball retained, the others are presented in descending order as to roundness. A score of five is recorded if a perfect record is made, and one deducted for each additional presentation required before the difference is noted. The abbreviation is for alogical attack.

Item 14 refers to the usual Pintner-Paterson Substitution Test. This test is given and scored in the usual manner, and the score recorded in the right margin.

Item 15 refers to a measurement test. Six small steel blocks are provided, also a pair of five inch spring calipers. The blocks should be presented in helter-skelter order and the following instructions given. "Here are some blocks which vary slightly in size across this polished face" (Indicate with fingers used like spring calipers). "Take these calipers and line the blocks in order of size so that the largest will be here (indicate) and the smallest here (indicate)." A score of seven is given for perfect arrangement. One is deducted for every pair reversed. If a block is two places out of place, two points are deducted. Abbreviations stand for: roughness, alogical attack.

Item 16 refers to a test of ability to saw a line. A two-by-four is marked off so that it should be square on the end if sawed to a line marked around it. The subject should be given the piece of two-by-four and told to place it over a low bench or chair (these must sit with their legs square on the floor) and told to saw the line or just saw next to it; he should be told that he may do either, just so that he does one or the other consistently. The test is scored by placing a try-square across the sawed end and measuring down from the square to the wood at the point where the wood is farthest from the edge of the square. If the board is sawed within a sixteenth of an inch of square, the 16 on the record blank is encircled; if within an eighth, the 8 is encircled; and if within a quarter, the 4 is encircled. The pathologies which are abbreviated at the left are: general ineptitude, bodily incoordination, lack of systematization in attempt, and bodily asymmetry.

Item 17 is a check upon various items of personal appearance, to indicate what changes should be made and where improvement is necessary. The various items are subjectively judged and pathologies are abbreviated in the left-hand margin. This margin can also be used for notes concerning the various items. The first item is general appearance. The second item is bodily cleanliness, and the abbreviations noted are for hands, face, ears, hair, and body odor. A blank for cleanliness of clothing is also provided. Next is mouth hygiene, which is noted by an examination of the mouth, looking for pathologies, whether or not they are related to personal appearance. Teeth, gums, tongue, tonsils, dental arch should all be checked. The abbreviations are for teeth, tongue, halitosis, other pathologies. The next topic is neatness of clothing, and abbreviations stand for ragged, mended, large, and small. The next line is for hair, the abbreviations being as follows: "Toupee", which refers to appearance, rather than to actually having a wig, needs haircut, hair uncombed, hair messy. The next topic is taste in clothing and appearance generally; the abbreviations standing for loud, repulsive, and shabby. The next item is appropriateness to the occasion, and abbreviations are for overdressing and underdressing, relating to dressing beyond the requirements of the occasions, or without enough regard for the requirements of the occasion. The next line refers to appropriateness of clothing to the figure. The abbreviations are for tightness, looseness, and wrong emphasis. The next item is shoes, and abbreviations are for need of shine, runover appearance, and poor fit.

In Item 19, the body type is encircled, and the x's at the margin are used to indicate whether or not the figure might be a handicap in vocational or emotional adjustment. Good adjustment-value is indicated at the right, poor at the left. The abbreviations are for malnutrition symptoms, asthenic type, rhythmic type, athletic type.

The items from 18 on are physiological checks, the first one being for color blindness, using the Ishihara Color-blindness Test. The abbreviations are: total color-blindness, and chromatic agnosia.

Item 21. Finger tremor is indicated subjectively, the numbers being put down for a projected test which is not yet developed. Tremor can be tested with the elbow rested on the table, hand extended at an angle of about twenty degrees above the table top, and a sheet of paper laid on the fingers. Tremor is indicated on the number scale as if it were an x scale, much tremor at the left, and little at the right. The abbreviation in the margin is for intention tremor, which should be tested for by asking the subject to pick up some object from a table.

Item 21. Anesthesia may be determined by use of an algesiometer and asking a question concerning places upon the body where pain cannot be felt. The abbreviations are for suspected conversion symptom and for hypochondriacal attitude.

Item 22 refers to a check of pulse. The pulse is taken for a full minute with the subject in a sitting position. Then the subject is required to do twenty steps standing run, being sure that a good high step is taken. Pulse is recorded for the first 15 seconds after the run has ceased. Then the examiner waits 15 seconds, and takes the pulse for 15 more seconds, recording after the number 30. Then waits 15 more seconds, takes pulse for 15 seconds, and records after 60 . Similarly, the examiner waits 15 seconds and takes pulse for 15 seconds, and records after 90 seconds, etc. For rating of A, the record after 30, when multiplied by 4, should be no larger than the normal rate. For rating of B, rating after 60 is multiplied by 4 and compared with the normal rate. If pulse is not down to normal by this time, rating is D or F, and if pulse does not accelerate after standing run, rating is F. In the last mentioned case, the subject should consult a physician.

Item number 23, Respiration, is counted before the standing run, and for fifteen or thirty seconds immediately after. The number of full breaths per minute before the run is recorded after the abbreviation sit, which means sitting, and the number of full breaths per minute just after the standing run is recorded after the abbreviations Ac. which means accelerated.

Item 24. In the absence of a hand dynamometer, a small pair of bathroom scales, calibrated in pounds is used. This scale is grasped with both hands and gripped as hard a possible, the subject being told that he is to hold it there as long as he can. Maximum is recorded, then the point at which it is stabilized, the number of seconds before rapid decrease sets in. Abbreviations are for maximum, stabilized reading, and time of holding period.

Item 25. Romberg sign is tested in the usual manner.

Item 26. In using the line walk, the subject is first asked to walk toward a point with his eyes closed and covered by his hands. Then he is observed in natural walking. The abbreviations stand for ataxia, heel and toe walking, excessive hip movement, short and long steps, short steps, pigeon-toe walking. If deviation is more than 2 feet in 20, the examiner should note the direction of it.

Item 27, 28, 29. Vision and astigmatism are checked in the usual way with eye charts, and audition is checked with an akemeter, the examiner recording the fraction of twenty feet at which the click of the akemeter can be heard.

Appendix: Forms included in 1941 but not 1936 edition

FORT HAYS KANSAS STATE COLLEGE PSYCHOLOGICAL CLINIC

Form 1.11 Survey

Name of person filling out form ______________________________

Community ______________________ Date ______________

Since the Psychological Clinic is dependent upon the resources available in your community for carrying out the recommendations which it makes it considers it extremely important to know just what these resources are. Our recommendations are frequently planned with reference to ideal conditions. Even though your community may not have as many facilities for helping young people as might be desired, we are still interested in finding ways of guiding each case who is referred to the clinic. The following information will be of great assistance to us in rendering a truly helpful service in your community.

Vocational Guidance—

1. Has any service club, such as the Rotary, in your community formulated a plan by which each member could take some young person in need of vocational guidance for two or three hours a week and teach him his trade? _______ Who is in charge of this plan? ___________
2. Estimate the total number of man-hours of individualized work of this sort available from members of such service clubs or other local organizations. ___________
3. Are there other men in your community who would be willing to take young people into their businesses for training of an apprenticeship type? _____________ If so, please give the names and trades of these individuals.

   ____

Health Recommendations—

1. If we should recommend a general health examination to a case who could not afford to pay its cost, what public agency might undertake the expense?

   ____
   ____
   ____

2. If we should recommend a dental examination to a case who could not afford to pay its cost, what public agency might undertake the expense?

   ____
   ____
   ____

3. If we should recommend a visual examination to a case who could not afford to pay its cost, what public agency might undertake the expense?

   ____
   ____
   ____

4. If we should recommend an endocrinological examination to a case who could not afford to pay its cost, what public agency might undertake the expense?

   ____
   ____
   ____

5. If we should recommend a neurological examination to a case who could not afford to pay its cost, what public agency might undertake the expense?

____

____

____

Are you willing to take the responsibility for seeing that such recommendations are carried out? ____________________
Will your county medical association or some other local agencies (Red Cross, schools, churches, social welfare department or clubs) cooperate in assuming this responsibility? ____________________

Recreational Facilities –
If we should recommend participation in some club or recreational activity, what facilities could be used in the different schools and organizations of your community? Include in your list academic clubs (English and Spanish clubs, etc.), craft clubs, social clubs, athletic clubs or organized activities and the activity clubs (music, art, drama, etc.).

1. High School

1. ________	2. ________
3. ________	4. ________
5. ________	6. ________
7. ________	8. ________
9. ________	10. ________

2. Junior High School

1. ________	2. ________
3. ________	4. ________
5. ________	6. ________
7. ________	8. ________
9. ________	10. ________

3. Elementary School

1. ________	2. ________
3. ________	4. ________
5. ________	6. ________
7. ________	8. ________
9. ________	10. ________

4. Parochial School

1. ________	2. ________
3. ________	4. ________
5. ________	6. ________
7. ________	8. ________
9. ________	10. ________

5. List other organizations, such as scouts, church and Sunday School clubs, campfire girls, Y.M.C.A., Y.W.C.A., and local service clubs which might cooperate in furnishing recreational activities for the young people in your community. What individuals would be in charge of such movements?

1. ________	2. ________
3. ________	4. ________
5. ________	6. ________

6. List the places or forms of recreation available outside the home for *a boy between the ages of ten and fourteen:*

Time	Mon.	Tue.	Wed.	Thu.	Fri.
From 4 to 6 p.m.	1 2 3 4 5				
From 7 to 9 p.m.	1 2 3 4 5				

What can boys this age do on Saturday and Sunday afternoons from 2 to 5 p.m.?
Girls—ages ten to fourteen:

Time	Mon.	Tue.	Wed.	Thu.	Fri.
From 4 to 6 p.m.	1 2 3 4 5				
From 7 to 9 p.m.	1 2 3 4 5				

What can girls this age do on Saturday and Sunday afternoons from 2 to 5 p.m.?
Boys—ages fourteen to eighteen:

Time	Mon.	Tue.	Wed.	Thu.	Fri.
From 4 to 6 p.m.	1 2 3 4 5				
From 7 to 9 p.m.	1 2 3 4 5				

What can boys of this age do on Saturday and Sunday afternoons from 2 to 5 p.m.?
Girls—ages fourteen to eighteen:

Time	Mon.	Tue.	Wed.	Thu.	Fri.
From 4 to 6 p.m.	1 2 3 4 5				
From 7 to 9 p.m.	1 2 3 4 5				

What can girls of this age do on Saturday and Sunday afternoons from 2 to 5 p.m.?

Opportunity Rooms and Individual Instruction—

1. Is there an opportunity room or special room for retarded children in your community? ____
2. If not, are you looking forward to establishing an opportunity or special room? Would you be interested in having us work out a plan for establishing such a room at a minimum of expense? ____
3. If we should recommend individualized training for some case can we depend upon the teachers to give such training? ____________________ Please list the number of teacher hours per week available for individual training of special students.

High School Teachers-- ______________ hrs.

Junior High School Teachers-- ______________ hrs.

Elementary School Teachers-- ______________ hrs.

Are you willing to keep us in touch with the progress of the cases whom we see for a period of at least two years? ____________

OUT-PATIENT CLINIC

STEPS IN THE FORMULATION OF PSYCHOLOGICAL RECOMMENDATIONS

1. Determine
   a. sociopathology
   b. psychopathology
   c. particular mechanisms—personal
   d. special defects
2. Recommend
   a. Descriptive (key statement only)
   b. Crucial
      (1) agencies to be employed
   c. Incidental
      (1) agencies to be employed
   d. Predictive
      (1) possibilities and probabilities
      (2) suggested goals and plans
         (a) agencies
   e. Curricular adjustment
   f. Methodology
   g. Situation procedure
   h. Categorical answers to registration (number)
   i. Supplementary

INSTITUTIONAL CLINIC

1. Academic Prospectus
   a. I.Q. Max. M.A.
   b. prospective grade list
   c. optimum grade list
   d. major course
   e. remedial needs
2. Emotional Needs
   a. filial
   b. connubial
   c. social security
   d. personal-social
3. Expressive Needs
   a. esthetic
   b. cathartic
   c. physical
   d. gregarious
   e. integrity
4. Vocational Prospectus
   a. occupational level
   b. suggested occupation
   c. training facilities (present)
   d. needed training facilities
5. Establishment of Rapport
6. Diagnosis of Psychopathology
7. Lay Characterization

FORT HAYS KANSAS STATE COLLEGE PSYCHOLOGICAL CLINIC

Form 9.3 Narrative Summary

1. Case narrative

____

____

____

____

____

2. Test results: Test Results Clinical check

   a. ____

   b. ____

   c. ____

   d. ____

   e. ____

3. Most significant positive findings upon which recommendations are based:

____

____

____

4. Preliminary diagnosis:

____

____

5. Final diagnosis:

____

____

6. Prognosis:

____

____

FORT HAYS KANSAS STATE COLLEGE PSYCHOLOGICAL CLINIC

Form 9.3 Analytical Summary

IDENTIFICATION

Name_______________________________ Number _______________

Clinicians ____

Psychologist ___________________________ Summarized by _______________

Typed by_______________________________

_______________________ is a child _______ years of age living with

_______________________ at _______________________ (She) (He)

attends the_______________________ of_______________________ where _______________

is now in the_______________________ (She) (He) was referred to the Fort Hays Psychological Clinic at _______________

Kansas by_______________________ on_______________________, 1941

PROBLEM

At registration_______________________ stated the problem of

____

____

____

____

____

____

____

____

The routine psychological examination was given by_______________________

During the interviews_______________ additional problems were stated by those interested in _______________ welfare.

The classroom teacher stated the problems of

____

____

____

The (father) (mother) mentioned the problems of

____

____

____

The social worker called attention to problems of

____

____

____

APPEARANCE

When ______________________ (name) appeared at the Clinic ______________________________

(descriptive statements of appearance)

____

____

____

(statements describing action)

____

____

____

On being asked (some question)

____

____

____

________________ replied

"____

____

____

During the routine examination many clinically significant variants were considered.

DEVELOPMENT

The factor of

1. maturation
   A. was investigated
      (a) It was considered particularly significant because________________
      (b) Our test results show________________________________
      (c) but no important facts were discovered.
   B. was not investigated
      (w) because this factor was regarded as unimportant in the case.
      (x) because no adequate sources of information were available.
      (y) because of insufficient time for complete investigation.
      (z) but probably should have been.
   C. This factor was considered to be
      3. a strong favorable factor.
      2. a helpful factor
      1. a favorable factor
      0. a satisfactory factor
      -1. an unfavorable factor
      -2. a detrimental factor
      -3. an exceptionally unfavorable factor

2. training
   (A) a___ b___ c___ (B) w___ x___ y___ z___
   (C) 3___ 2___ 1___ 0___ -1___ -2___ -3___

3. care

   (A) a___ b___ c___ (B) w___ x___ y___ z___

   (C) 3___ 2___ 1___ 0___ -1___ -2___ -3___

4. constitution

   (A) a___ b___ c___ (B) w___ x___ y___ z___

   (C) 3___ 2___ 1___ 0___ -1___ -2___ -3___

5. injury

   (A) a___ b___ c___ (B) w___ x___ y___ z___

   (C) 3___ 2___ 1___ 0___ -1___ -2___ -3___

6. motor control

   (A) a___ b___ c___ (B) w___ x___ y___ z___

   (C) 3___ 2___ 1___ 0___ -1___ -2___ -3___

7. nutrition

   (A) a___ b___ c___ (B) w___ x___ y___ z___

   (C) 3___ 2___ 1___ 0___ -1___ -2___ -3___

8. elimination

   (A) a___ b___ c___ (B) w___ x___ y___ z___

   (C) 3___ 2___ 1___ 0___ -1___ -2___ -3___

9. infection

   (A) a___ b___ c___ (B) w___ x___ y___ z___

   (C) 3___ 2___ 1___ 0___ -1___ -2___ -3___

10. cardiac-motor disorders

    (A) a___ b___ c___ (B) w___ x___ y___ z___

    (C) 3___ 2___ 1___ 0___ -1___ -2___ -3___

11. ventilation

    (A) a___ b___ c___ (B) w___ x___ y___ z___

    (C) 3___ 2___ 1___ 0___ -1___ -2___ -3___

12. anatomy

    (A) a___ b___ c___ (B) w___ x___ y___ z___

    (C) 3___ 2___ 1___ 0___ -1___ -2___ -3___

13. calcium deficiency

    (A) a___ b___ c___ (B) w___ x___ y___ z___

    (C) 3___ 2___ 1___ 0___ -1___ -2___ -3___

14. endocrine disorders

    (A) a___ b___ c___ (B) w___ x___ y___ z___

    (C) 3___ 2___ 1___ 0___ -1___ -2___ -3___

15. audition

    (A) a___ b___ c___ (B) w___ x___ y___ z___

    (C) 3___ 2___ 1___ 0___ -1___ -2___ -3___

16. vision

    (A) a___ b___ c___ (B) w___ x___ y___ z___

    (C) 3___ 2___ 1___ 0___ -1___ -2___ -3___

17. other sensory disturbance

    (A) a___ b___ c___ (B) w___ x___ y___ z___

    (C) 3___ 2___ 1___ 0___ -1___ -2___ -3___

PSYCHOMETRICS

18. mental ability

(A) a___ b___ c___ (B) w___ x___ y___ z___

(C) 3___ 2___ 1___ 0___ -1___ -2___ -3___

19. skills

(A) a___ b___ c___ (B) w___ x___ y___ z___

(C) 3___ 2___ 1___ 0___ -1___ -2___ -3___

20. exploitable traits

(A) a___ b___ c___ (B) w___ x___ y___ z___

(C) 3___ 2___ 1___ 0___ -1___ -2___ -3___

SOCIAL

21. responsibilities

(A) a___ b___ c___ (B) w___ x___ y___ z___

(C) 3___ 2___ 1___ 0___ -1___ -2___ -3___

22. opportunities

(A) a___ b___ c___ (B) w___ x___ y___ z___

(C) 3___ 2___ 1___ 0___ -1___ -2___ -3___

23. vocational orientation

(A) a___ b___ c___ (B) w___ x___ y___ z___

(C) 3___ 2___ 1___ 0___ -1___ -2___ -3___

24. school orientation

(A) a___ b___ c___ (B) w___ x___ y___ z___

(C) 3___ 2___ 1___ 0___ -1___ -2___ -3___

25. community orientation

(A) a___ b___ c___ (B) w___ x___ y___ z___

(C) 3___ 2___ 1___ 0___ -1___ -2___ -3___

26. recreational orientation

(A) a___ b___ c___ (B) w___ x___ y___ z___

(C) 3___ 2___ 1___ 0___ -1___ -2___ -3___

27. personal orientation

(A) a___ b___ c___ (B) w___ x___ y___ z___

(C) 3___ 2___ 1___ 0___ -1___ -2___ -3___

28. friends

(A) a___ b___ c___ (B) w___ x___ y___ z___

(C) 3___ 2___ 1___ 0___ -1___ -2___ -3___

29. household organization

(A) a___ b___ c___ (B) w___ x___ y___ z___

(C) 3___ 2___ 1___ 0___ -1___ -2___ -3___

30. social security

(A) a___ b___ c___ (B) w___ x___ y___ z___

(C) 3___ 2___ 1___ 0___ -1___ -2___ -3___

31. social status

(A) a___ b___ c___ (B) w___ x___ y___ z___

(C) 3___ 2___ 1___ 0___ -1___ -2___ -3___

32. possessions
    (A) a___ b___ c___ (B) w___ x___ y___ z___
    (C) 3___ 2___ 1___ 0___ -1___ -2___ -3___
33. self-assurance
    (A) a___ b___ c___ (B) w___ x___ y___ z___
    (C) 3___ 2___ 1___ 0___ -1___ -2___ -3___
34. independence
    (A) a___ b___ c___ (B) w___ x___ y___ z___
    (C) 3___ 2___ 1___ 0___ -1___ -2___ -3___
35. absorption
    (A) a___ b___ c___ (B) w___ x___ y___ z___
    (C) 3___ 2___ 1___ 0___ -1___ -2___ -3___
36. tension
    (A) a___ b___ c___ (B) w___ x___ y___ z___
    (C) 3___ 2___ 1___ 0___ -1___ -2___ -3___

PERSONAL

37. stability
    (A) a___ b___ c___ (B) w___ x___ y___ z___
    (C) 3___ 2___ 1___ 0___ -1___ -2___ -3___
38. perceived status
    (A) a___ b___ c___ (B) w___ x___ y___ z___
    (C) 3___ 2___ 1___ 0___ -1___ -2___ -3___
39. pressure resistance
    (A) a___ b___ c___ (B) w___ x___ y___ z___
    (C) 3___ 2___ 1___ 0___ -1___ -2___ -3___
40. motivation
    (A) a___ b___ c___ (B) w___ x___ y___ z___
    (C) 3___ 2___ 1___ 0___ -1___ -2___ -3___
41. control
    (A) a___ b___ c___ (B) w___ x___ y___ z___
    (C) 3___ 2___ 1___ 0___ -1___ -2___ -3___
42. ego strength
    (A) a___ b___ c___ (B) w___ x___ y___ z___
    (C) 3___ 2___ 1___ 0___ -1___ -2___ -3___
43. censorship
    (A) a___ b___ c___ (B) w___ x___ y___ z___
    (C) 3___ 2___ 1___ 0___ -1___ -2___ -3___
44. appetitive organization
    (A) a___ b___ c___ (B) w___ x___ y___ z___
    (C) 3___ 2___ 1___ 0___ -1___ -2___ -3___
45. integration
    (A) a___ b___ c___ (B) w___ x___ y___ z___
    (C) 3___ 2___ 1___ 0___ -1___ -2___ -3___

46. emotional adequacy
    (A) a___ b___ c___ (B) w___ x___ y___ z___
    (C) 3___ 2___ 1___ 0___ -1___ -2___ -3___
47. energy output
    (A) a___ b___ c___ (B) w___ x___ y___ z___
    (C) 3___ 2___ 1___ 0___ -1___ -2___ -3___
48. routine
    (A) a___ b___ c___ (B) w___ x___ y___ z___
    (C) 3___ 2___ 1___ 0___ -1___ -2___ -3___
49. traumata
    (A) a___ b___ c___ (B) w___ x___ y___ z___
    (C) 3___ 2___ 1___ 0___ -1___ -2___ -3___
50. anxiety
    (A) a___ b___ c___ (B) w___ x___ y___ z___
    (C) 3___ 2___ 1___ 0___ -1___ -2___ -3___
51. phantasy
    (A) a___ b___ c___ (B) w___ x___ y___ z___
    (C) 3___ 2___ 1___ 0___ -1___ -2___ -3___
52. symptom formation
    (A) a___ b___ c___ (B) w___ x___ y___ z___
    (C) 3___ 2___ 1___ 0___ -1___ -2___ -3___
53. delusory structure
    (A) a___ b___ c___ (B) w___ x___ y___ z___
    (C) 3___ 2___ 1___ 0___ -1___ -2___ -3___

EXOGENOUS

54. familial psychopathology
    (A) a___ b___ c___ (B) w___ x___ y___ z___
    (C) 3___ 2___ 1___ 0___ -1___ -2___ -3___
55. familial sociopathology
    (A) a___ b___ c___ (B) w___ x___ y___ z___
    (C) 3___ 2___ 1___ 0___ -1___ -2___ -3___
56. familial indigency
    (A) a___ b___ c___ (B) w___ x___ y___ z___
    (C) 3___ 2___ 1___ 0___ -1___ -2___ -3___
57. familial parasitism
    (A) a___ b___ c___ (B) w___ x___ y___ z___
    (C) 3___ 2___ 1___ 0___ -1___ -2___ -3___
58. familial stigmata
    (A) a___ b___ c___ (B) w___ x___ y___ z___
    (C) 3___ 2___ 1___ 0___ -1___ -2___ -3___
59. ethnology
    (A) a___ b___ c___ (B) w___ x___ y___ z___
    (C) 3___ 2___ 1___ 0___ -1___ -2___ -3___

60. religion
    (A) a___ b___ c___ (B) w___ x___ y___ z___
    (C) 3___ 2___ 1___ 0___ -1___ -2___ -3___
61. community
    (A) a___ b___ c___ (B) w___ x___ y___ z___
    (C) 3___ 2___ 1___ 0___ -1___ -2___ -3___
62. school
    (A) a___ b___ c___ (B) w___ x___ y___ z___
    (C) 3___ 2___ 1___ 0___ -1___ -2___ -3___

RECOMMENDATION

The preliminary diagnosis was

After completion of the examination the final diagnosis was

Recommendations:

PROGNOSIS

If the recommendations are followed ______________________________ may be expected to

Our follow-up work has shown ______________________ (Name) progress on ______________ (Date) as reported by ____________________ to be

______________________ (Name of person reporting) reported on ____________ (Date)
______________________'s (Name) progress to be

The case was closed.

FORT HAYS KANSAS STATE COLLEGE PSYCHOLOGICAL CLINIC

Form 10.4 Teacher's Report

A. ____

Serial No. Pupil Teacher Date Time

B. General Plan of Instruction Outcome

C. Narrative report

D. Examples of Student's writing, drawing, etc.

E. Physical condition

1. Inflamed throat ______
2. Inflamed eyes ______
3. Mouth sores ______
4. Sores in other parts of body ______
5. Infection of any kind ______

49

Stories from the Psychological Clinic[1]

Leo Pearson stood four feet two inches in his "holy" socks. On the scale, while his bare toes wiggled up and down, he weighed seventy-one pounds. For a twelve-year-old boy, Leo possessed a peculiar physique, almost as peculiar as the expression on his face which had caused his teacher's worry. A few days before, Leo's fourth grade teacher had come to the psychologist with the request that Leo be given psychological service. Something was wrong with the boy, she said. There was a peculiar shifty look in his eye and, while he had never been found guilty of stealing or other misdemeanors on the playground, she felt that he might be one of those people whom the psychologists talk about, the ones who are destined to become delinquents and criminals.

With this boy as its first case the psychological clinic at the Fort Hays Kansas State College came into being five years ago this fall. It is customary to describe the work of an organization or the program of a movement without a primary emphasis on individual cases. Case histories are usually used for illustrative material and not for basic information. But in the case of a psychological clinic the program is of secondary importance. Always the case must come first, even though it means endangering the reputation of the clinic. That dictum is one of the first which the student clinical psychologist must learn. Paragraph four of the handbook now used by the Fort Hays clinicians reads as follows:

"4. **Attitude toward work:** The responsibility of a clinician toward his case transcends all other responsibilities. Illness, study, vacations and all personal matters must be considered secondary. A psychological problem is generally extremely important and the clinician can scarcely feel his responsibility too deeply. Individuals who are unwilling to assume this attitude should not attempt to become clinical psychologists."

So we have started our history with the description of a case because cases are so important. We must follow Leo further. While our boy is awkwardly tying his shoes, Miss Avenelle Spangler continues her examination. A careful look into his eyes reveals a slight rhythmic tremor which forces the eyeballs rapidly from side to side. From her study of the second chapter in her abnormal psychology text she has learned that this peculiar condition is a physical disorder called nystagmus. As quick as that some of the mystery is cleared from the case. Leo is no longer a candidate for the reformatory or penitentiary because of his "shifty eyes."

The examination continues. Miss Spangler administers several tests, including the well-known and thorough Stanford Revision of the Binet-Simon test. Two hours later the initial examination is finished. Perhaps on the basis of its findings, the date of December 18, 1931 may become a turning point in the life of this peculiar-appearing boy. The case is followed with a series of treatments consisting of training in motor control, training in methods of study which are adapted to his physical disability and fundamental exercises designed to adjust him to the work of his room. Leo Pearson has ceased to be an active case in the Hays clinic, but his clinician, Avenelle Spangler, is now occupying an important position in the newly established Detroit Parole Clinic.

Other clinicians have followed her. Doctor Yuba Hunsley, now chief psychologist-psychiatrist in the Sioux City schools, started her training soon after this incident. At the request of students, courses in clinical psychology were listed in the catalog of the college and have been regularly taught since. Standards of work have been raised. Requirements of applicants for admission to the clinical courses have been raised each year. Only a small percentage, somewhat less than half of those who apply for clinical training, are admitted, even though in some cases the scholastic-record of those rejected has been unusually high. The morale of clinicians is considered of primary importance.

[1] First published as Kelly, G.A. (1937). Stories from the psychology clinic. *The Aerend: Kansas Quarterly, 8*. 1 (Winter), 57–61. Reproduced by permission of Forsyth Library Special Collections, Fort Hays State University.

Collected Papers of the Pioneer of Constructivist Psychology: George A. Kelly, First Edition. Edited by David A. Winter and Nick Reed.

In not every case has the clinic been successful. There was Harold Carson, another fictitious name of course but not a fictitious case, who was referred to the clinic soon after Leo. It is hard to tell if the clinic's work with Harold was more of a benefit or a hindrance. Probably it was of some help, although since his appearance in the clinic he has been sent to a state penal institution. Probably if the clinic had the case again today it could do a somewhat better job.

There have been other cases, some of them spectacular in the improvements which were achieved, others of them meeting with only indifferent success and still others in which improvement was reached because of other agencies or Mother Nature. One never knows. The forces which play upon human life are so complex and the human personality so intricate that the thread of cause and result is soon lost and the psychological clinician is left to guess at the part he has played. That there is a psychological problem in every one of us and that it is ultimately possible to attack that problem through psychological study he is definitely persuaded. He also believes that effective tools for dealing with personal problems can only be forged in the clinic, that shop in which the theories of the psychological laboratory must meet the actual problems of every-day life.

Much of the success which the Fort Hays Kansas State College clinic claims for itself is due to the faith which teachers, physicians, students, parents and others have placed in its work. Because Superintendent Glenn believed in the work of the clinic and was willing to ask for its first extension appointment at Webster, the newly established system of extension clinics was started. As we look back upon it now, what a peculiar day that was that we spent at Webster that October 21, 1933. There was a lecture to parents in the morning and, because there had been a rumor that the peculiar pupils of the school would be stood on the platform as living illustrations of the points of the lecture, there was a large representation of parents and a conspicuous scarcity of pupils. After the lecture, however, a number of parents went home to get their children and before the day had ended seventeen young people had asked for psychological diagnosis and advice. This number was so much larger than that which the clinic was prepared to handle that the clinicians had their evening meal somewhat after ten o'clock at night. Since that time the clinic has learned to limit its registrations to twelve cases in a day and even at that the five members of the staff find that they must know their procedure letter-perfect in order not to waste valuable time. And speaking of heavy registrations, there was that December day in Ness City, 1933, when cases kept coming in all day long until thirty-one had asked to see the psychologist.

The early extension clinics had to face the problem of a well-coordinated schedule almost as much as they had to face the psychological problems of the cases brought to them. Procedure has changed. Now at least three of the four clinicians taken with the psychologist on an extension clinic must be prepared to carry out all phases of the clinic's work, family history, social history, educational history, physical tests, psychometrics and the interview designed to reveal the personality and ambitions of the case, the one which requires so much skill. The clinician must also know how to make recommendations of a practical nature. It is one thing to find out what is wrong with a case and quite another to make clear-cut recommendations which are within the reach of a case, helpful to those who work with him, and which have a reasonable possibility of being followed. It takes a great deal of skill in this new field of clinical psychology, where there is so much misunderstanding and so much charlatanism, to explain the nature of a clinical diagnosis, remove some of the unfounded fears which frequently creep up, and leave the case or his parent informed and determined to do something effective. A case which leaves the clinic discouraged, embarrassed and resentful has been a failure, no matter how accurately the diagnosis has been made. The purpose of the clinic is to assist a case in making personal adjustments, not to throw the case out of adjustment.

Kansas as a state is rapidly increasing its demands for psychological service. During the fiscal year ending June 30, 1936, under the special appropriation secured by friends of the clinic in the state legislature, twenty-six days of clinical service were rendered in communities outside of Hays. In Cherryvale and Leavenworth on the east to little western schools such as the consolidated school at Friend the work of the clinic was requested. Six days in all were spent in the Girls' Industrial School at Beloit. Recognition of the clinic led to the establishment of internships in cooperation with the University of Iowa, under which candidates for the doctor's degree in clinical psychology in that university will spend one semester in Hays. During the current year the Kansas Emergency Relief Committee, through the various poor commissioners, have made numerous requests for clinical service. Through cooperation with the state and district NYA offices a project has been set up to enable the clinic to render its services to young people of Hays who are not in school in an attempt to find and prepare them for vocational occupations which are reasonably stable and secure.

But no clinic at Hays, even though its staff spends much of its time in the field, can hope adequately to meet the problems requiring psychological guidance in the state. Already requests have come from the city schools of Wichita and from service groups in McPherson County and Dickinson County for the authorization of branch clinics with a resident staff. These branch clinics will be organized in cooperation with the state clinic at Hays and much of the service will be supervised directly from Hays. A few other clinics in various parts of the state are attempting to organize facilities and to secure recognition as branches of the Hays clinic.

So the work goes on, always a fascinating field, always with a challenge of personal and human service clearly before it, always offering a first-hand contact with life to those students who train themselves to answer its calling.

50

The Psychological Clinic's Use of Practical Rather than Ideal Recommendations[1]

The data consist of the follow-up records of eight hundred cases on which the Fort Hays Kansas State College Psychological Clinic has made recommendations to teachers and parents. Certain types of clinical recommendations, such as emotional catharsis, relaxation, removal of motivation, basing control upon a different assumed level of maturity, absorption of personality, use of impersonal methods, remedial teaching, increasing or decreasing social responsibility, supplementary examination, etc., are considered from the standpoint of (1) the client's ability to understand the principles involved in the recommendations, (2) his attitude of receptiveness to the recommendations, (3) his persistence in carrying out the recommendations, and (4) his reported success with the case. Certain recommendations protect the professional status of the clinic even though there is little chance of their being followed.

[1] Abstract from the Proceedings of the 45th. Annual Meeting of the American Psychological Association, Minneapolis, Minnesota, September 1-4, 1937. Published in 1937 in *Psychological Bulletin, 34 (9)*, 746. Now in the public domain, and republished by permission of Jacqueline Aldridge.

Collected Papers of the Pioneer of Constructivist Psychology: George A. Kelly, First Edition. Edited by David A. Winter and Nick Reed.

51

The Practical Effectiveness of Certain General Types of Recommendations Made by a Psychological Clinic[1,2]

Satisfactory results in the work of the psychological clinic depend largely upon the number of factors which the psychologist can control and which relate to the life of his case. The practice of disregarding certain factors simply because they may not technically be termed psychological is open to serious question. There may be a certain degree of professional protection for the psychologist in his being conscientiously blind to certain items which appear to be outside of his field, but such blindness offers no protection for his case.

During the past six years of development the Fort Hays Kansas State College Psychological Clinic has attempted to place the psychological welfare of its cases above any consideration that might arise out of the academic meaning of the term "psychology." This point of view has led it to make many adjustments in its methods of procedure, adjustments which were dictated by the peculiar circumstances in which the Clinic worked, but nevertheless, adjustments which ought eventually to be submitted to rigorous scientific study. If certain types of ideal recommendations have been discarded it has been because they appeared to be sociologically impracticable. Other ideal recommendations have been discarded because of lack of knowledge or facilities among the clients sufficient to carry the recommendations through to a successful conclusion. With respect to still other types of recommendations the Clinic is attempting to conduct controlled studies in the validity of the psychotherapeutic devices upon which they are based. But that is outside of the scope of this paper. Here we are interested in a discussion of the practical effectiveness of certain clinical recommendations as revealed by follow-up reports from the field. Nine general types of clinical recommendations have been considered. The records of approximately 800 cases for whom the Clinic has written recommendations in the last two years comprise the data of the study. Cases appearing in the Clinic before this period have not been considered because many of the methods and types of recommendations used by the Clinic more than two years ago have been completely discarded. The criteria of effectiveness have been, of course, largely subjectively determined but have been based upon reports of the clients themselves. We shall consider the types of recommendations separately.

Catharsis

Frequently the Clinic has been led to believe that a certain case would benefit from having a special opportunity to discuss his personal problems spontaneously and in detail with a sympathetic listener. In the group of 800 cases studied this form of simple catharsis was recommended about 90 times. Of course, catharsis was not the fundamental recommendation in every case. Usually the one recommended to take the catharsis was the parent or the teacher. In most cases, at the beginning the client was willing to undertake the responsibility and seemed to feel quite confident in his ability to follow the recommendation. It seemed an easy thing to sit down and patiently and lovingly listen to a child pour out his heart. In practice such catharsis proved difficult to obtain. Many clients reported that the children refused to express themselves or that there was difficulty in "breaking the ice." Other clients reported that their cases improved, but that they had not found it necessary to hold definite conferences. In these cases it was believed that the improvement was due simply to more sympathetic attitudes of the parents or teachers toward their cases. As the work developed and more follow-up reports were received, it became increasingly obvious that there was very little actual cathartic work being carried on, even where the recommendations of the

[1] First published in 1938 in *Journal of General Psychology, 19*, 211-217. Now in public domain, and republished by permission of Jacqueline Aldridge.
[2] Acknowledgment is due all members of the staff of the Fort Hays Kansas State College Psychological Clinic for assisting in the development of the Clinic's practical program.

Collected Papers of the Pioneer of Constructivist Psychology: George A. Kelly, First Edition. Edited by David A. Winter and Nick Reed.

Clinic seemed to have been helpful. In order to give teachers greater assistance in undertaking catharsis, a handbook[3] (one of several which have been prepared by the Clinic as teachers' aids) was prepared. It contained suggestive questions, illustrations, a minimum of theoretical discussion and a number of practical suggestions for conducting cathartic interviews. The Clinic also spent more time discussing in detail with the clients the procedures which had been recommended. In a few cases very complete follow-up reports were obtained, and after a few months it appeared that the following use of the handbook was frequently made. The teacher would ask all the questions she could find in the book in a firm, clear voice and would record the answers exactly and uncritically, a procedure which painfully reminds one of a psychologist applying a personality inventory in his study of personality. Within a few days there would be a letter from the teacher saying that she had asked all the questions in the book and were there any more that she should ask. In general, the results of the cathartic recommendation have been very discouraging except in a few cases, approximately 20, in which teachers have appeared to be able to conduct the cathartic conference somewhat satisfactorily. In those instances the effect of the conference upon the case has been, without exception, favorable.

Relaxation

In the 800 cases under consideration some form of relaxation has been recommended about 110 times. Various forms have been recommended. The simplest form has been the interpolation of one or more rest periods during the school day. In other cases idle play has been recommended, in others, relaxed attention, that is to say, attention characterized by a relaxed bodily attitude and at the same time an easy and spontaneous interest in the focal stimuli. In a few cases the Clinic has tried recommending systematic and progressive relaxation (no attempt is made to argue that such relaxation would be as complete as the progressive relaxation of Jacobson). With the exception of the systematic and progressive relaxation the results have been gratifying. In every case where there was reasonable persistence on the part of the client satisfactory or partially satisfactory results have been obtained. The recommendation has been simple and easily understood. In general the results have been more apparent two or three months after the program has been initiated, although some teachers report improvement in the children's attitudes and scholastic work after two days.

Reduction of Motivation

Regardless of what experiments on the value of motivation may reveal concerning specific improvements under the influence of that factor, the Clinic has become thoroughly persuaded that in many cases the total situation is improved by reducing the intensity of interests as well as the severity of social demands. Removal of pressure for success, including the removal of both rewards and punishments, has been recommended about 260 times. Increase of pressure has been recommended about 50 times. In about 40 percent of the cases in which the removal of pressure has been recommended, satisfactory results have been obtained if we may believe the reports of teachers and parents. In fact, the most spectacular results of the Clinic may be directly attributed to this type of recommendation. In another 40 percent of the cases in which this recommendation has been made partially satisfactory results have been obtained. In 20 percent of the cases complete failure has resulted, but it is interesting to notice that in these 20 percent almost all of the teachers have been unwilling to believe or unable to understand the purpose of the recommendation. The principle of unlimited educational motivation seems to be deeply embedded in the conscience of most teachers.

Basing Control Upon a Differently Assumed Level of Maturity

In about 80 cases it has been recommended that the child be treated as if he were older or younger than the age at which his control had previously been adjusted. Sometimes this meant simply that the Clinic has recommended that parents treat their twelve-year-old son like a twelve-year-old rather than like an eight-year-old. In other cases the Clinic has recommended that they treat the child as if he were younger than his chronological age. This type of recommendation is frequently convenient because it comprises a rather complete picture of the procedure which is to be used in treating the case. By nature the recommendation is one which has been most frequently used in cases where parents have been neurotic, usually placing a great deal of transference upon their children. Reasonable success has been reported in about 25 percent of the cases and partial success in about 60 percent of the cases. Because of the nature of the situation in which this recommendation has usually been made, these results would appear more favorable than the percentages indicate.

[3] Prepared by Harry Mason, Graduate Assistant, Fort Hays Kansas State College Psychological Clinic, 1936.

Avoiding Absorption of Personality

Like the previous recommendation, this recommendation has usually been given in cases where parents had developed such intimate and personal controls of their children that both parent and child had lacked sufficient independence to develop normal outside attachments. Usually it has been recommended that the parent develop outside interests and that the teacher alienate the child's affections in an attempt to break the unhealthful relationship between child and parent. Naturally this recommendation had to be used with caution and the fact that it has been successful in most of the 35 cases in which it has been recommended may reflect the caution of the Clinic in using it rather than the effectiveness of the recommendation if it had been used in all cases where it has seemed to be indicated.

Use of Impersonal Methods

This recommendation had been given frequently during the first four years of the Clinic's existence. It has been given especially to teachers. When follow-up reports indicated that many teachers had been using the recommendation to relieve themselves of responsibility for their cases, the Clinic began using the recommendation much more cautiously. During the past two years it has been offered only about 50 times. With these cases it has been almost universally successful although much of that success is due to the extreme caution with which the recommendation has been made.

Remedial Teaching

Naturally a large number of the problems presented to a psychological clinic by the schools require some form of remedial teaching. Remedial teaching has been recommended by the Clinic in 130 of the 800 cases and in nearly all cases has been partially successful. The important point which should be made, however, is that the success of remedial teaching has depended almost entirely upon the school which the child attended. Poorly trained teachers usually know almost nothing of remedial methods, while well trained teachers usually have some access to information regarding remedial methods if not actual familiarity with the methods themselves. Where remedial methods have not been successful when recommended by the Clinic the failure can, in almost every case, be attributed either to a lack of basic training on the part of the teacher or to a crowded program which robs the teacher of time for giving the necessary individual attention. Here is one field of clinical recommendations which is comparatively simple and which, because of its didactic method, is usually better understood by teachers than are the more subtle recommendations regarding personality.

Change in Amount of Social Responsibility

In about 60 cases an increase or a decrease in social responsibility has been recommended. In general this recommendation has been partially successful, completely failing only in about 10 of the cases. Most teachers have been pretty well drilled in the advantages of giving pupils responsibility, while on the other hand, being timid souls themselves, can be quite sympathetic with the situation when they are advised to reduce the responsibility of a child.

Supplementary Examinations

In about two-thirds of the cases medical examinations have been recommended. In many of these cases general health examinations had been given by physicians, but it has seemed advisable to seek more thorough medical attention. In most of the cases in which medical examinations were not recommended such examinations had already been made. This explanation is cited not because in practice the Clinic has found many medical examinations valuable, but because the professional status of the Clinic is protected when it recommends specific medical examinations. As everyone who has worked with cases knows, the public health situation, even where medical examinations are given, is appalling. Physicians are discouraged with the way in which they are required to examine relief clients and, in many cases, even with the work of the Red Cross. In general, medical examinations have been carried out when the Clinic placed definite responsibility for them upon a resident social worker. In general, the examinations have not been carried out when the responsibility for them has been placed upon teachers or parents. In general, when examinations have been carried out cases have neither been reassured nor assisted. In the way of medical treatment, tonsillectomies are the easiest to obtain and neurological examinations the hardest.

Summary

From the Clinic's experience it is led to believe that much needs to be done in training teachers in the basic principles of personality adjustment. When such training is undertaken seriously, there will not need to be so much discrepancy between practical and ideal recommendations in the work of the psychological clinic.

52

A Method of Diagnosing Personality in the Psychological Clinic[1]

The Present Inadequate Approach to Diagnosis

Clinical psychologists have been inclined to pattern their diagnostic procedures after those of the medical profession. The typical medical procedure is to ask the patient what hurts, observe his manifest symptoms, and sometimes test for pathologies. Upon the basis of information thus obtained the physician names the disorder (called diagnosing the case) and prescribes a treatment to be administered by the patient himself, members of his family, or a nurse. Everything depends upon the proper naming of the disorder. Once that is done the treatment consists in a direct mechanical or chemical attack upon the disease entity or in making certain concessions to the disability.

When clinical psychologists attempt to follow this pattern they get along all right as long as they confine themselves to speech disorders, motor disorders, simple educational deficiencies, feeble-mindedness, etc. but when they get into their own strictly psychological field of personality disorders they make little practical progress. Either they find themselves unable to name the disorder in such a way as to make a clear distinction between it and others of its kind or, having named it, they find that the name does not answer the question of what to do about it. One might suspect that their inability to find a satisfactory solution for this problem is the reason that many psychological clinics deliberately concede the strictly psychological problems of personality (of all things!) to the medical profession and become preoccupied with neurology (of all things!), standardization of "quizzes" (group norms being the object!), and factor analysis of personality inventories (where one hour is spent by an assistant administering the questionnaire to a large group of carefully unselected cases and six months are spent by a psychologist making "psychological" analyses of the scores!).

The Unique Role of Diagnosis in Psychotherapy

Personality disorders are usually best treated by some form of *rational* therapy. Rational therapy consists in showing the patient how to "think through" his difficulty. Medical practice furnishes no precedent for the clinical psychologist here. Consider the following illustration: A patient seeks medical aid for a broken leg sustained in a motor car accident. The physician examines neither the motor car nor the accident; he examines the leg and treats the fracture. That is *direct* therapy. Six months later the patient hobbles into the psychological clinic with hot water bottles strapped around his leg and complains bitterly of the policies of the highway commission. The psychologist does not examine the leg; he examines first the accident and then its personal consequences. Together he and the patient discover just how it has given him convenient grounds for staving off a threatened rift between the patient and his wife. That is *rational* therapy. In rational therapy the task is an educative one in which the subject taught is the individual etiology or "how the patient got that way," the teacher is the psychologist, and the pupil is the patient himself. Successful education depends upon the difficulty of the subject taught, the skill of the teacher, the intelligence of the pupil, and the pupil's willingness to learn.

Since in a clinic the ultimate object of a diagnosis is to help the patient to get well there is no point in making a diagnosis which does not contribute to a better therapy. A practical procedure in the psychological clinic is to make a type of diagnosis which will enable the psychologist first to set aside the group of disorders which can best be treated by some form of direct therapy and with them follow a conventional diagnostic procedure; with the remaining group, however, the diagnosis should indicate the patient's ability to benefit from rational therapy. Beyond that point further diagnosis becomes an integral part of the treatment.

[1] Originally published as Kelly, G.A. (1938). A method of diagnosing personality in the psychological clinic. *The Psychological Record, 2* (3), 95–111. Reprinted from Copyright Clearance Center on behalf of Springer Nature.

Collected Papers of the Pioneer of Constructivist Psychology: George A. Kelly, First Edition. Edited by David A. Winter and Nick Reed.

In our illustration of the man with the broken leg the psychologist first diagnoses the difficulty as one of personality from the hypochondriacal attitude of the patient, second, he attempts to estimate the patient's intelligence either from conversation or test, his grasp upon reality, his emotional adequacy, and his willingness to accept psychological treatment, and third, he starts the therapy which consists in studying through with the patient the etiology of his case. This combination of diagnosis and therapy is facilitated by the observation of certain significant mechanisms. The complaint against the highway commission suggests compensation and secondary gain. Other mechanisms come to light one by one until the pupil finally grasps the significance of his illness. It is important to notice first, that the differential diagnosis of the disease entity did not need to be made before therapy was begun; second, that it probably could not have been made satisfactorily at that time; and third, that it did not need to be made at all. Extensive inventories of symptoms are of far less importance in such cases than the careful delineation of one or two mechanisms employed by the individual patient. The variety of superficial introspections which the patient is able to make during the course of the interview throws less light upon the diagnosis than the end-product to which the course of the interview leads him.

Construction of the Diagnostic Instrument

In order to devise a diagnostic instrument for personality disorders which would meet the unique requirements of combined diagnosis and rational psychotherapy we have kept records of successful clinic treatments. These records answer the following three questions:

1 What discoveries do the patients who have been treated by rational psychotherapy say helped them?
2 At what stages of their treatment were they able to make those discoveries?
3 How did the clinician elicit the important information?

The answers to the first question were relatively easy to obtain since from the very nature of the rational method patients are led to make some formulation of their important discoveries. A large majority of patients talk of their discoveries freely at the end of the psychotherapeutic series of conferences, frequently explaining in detail some mechanisms which had not been clearly observed by the psychologist. A few patients prefer not to reveal all of their discoveries and may make some statement such as this: "I think I see now what my trouble has been and I would like to try to handle it myself. If I can't I'll come back and have you help me some more." While this sort of termination of a psychotherapeutic series is ordinarily discouraged, in practice, it is sometimes unavoidable and more often than not turns out to be satisfactory enough.

The answers to the second question were difficult to summarize. Important discoveries may be made at various stages in the treatment. It is common knowledge that what a patient may be able to accept and use as formulation of his problem at the end of a series may be utterly unacceptable to him in the earlier conferences. Nevertheless it is surprisingly easy for a psychologist to fumble in handling his case by making an unnecessary delay in raising crucial issues.

The answers to the third question were difficult to objectify for they involve the whole technique of dealing with cases. About the best that could be done at the moment was to list illustrative questions phrased for different vocabulary levels.

Form of the Diagnostic Instrument

The accompanying form sheet is, of course, intended to be used as a supplement to the usual psychological studies of a case. In our own practice the work of the clinic with the case is divided into eleven chapters as follows:

1 Registration and Statement of Observed Problems
2 Educational History, Status, Plans, and Facilities
3 Sociological History and Role
4 Developmental History
5 Family History
6 Physiological Examination
7 Psychometric Examinations
8 Personality Examination
9 Recommendations (These are always made in the light of the patient's social circumstances and frequently a special study is made of the community and of the people with whom the patient lives. Special supplementary examinations to be conducted by cooperating professions are included in this chapter.)
10 Therapy
11 Subsequent History

The present instrument is for use in connection with Chapter Eight above and to a less extent with Chapters Nine and Ten.

1 In all starred (*) items in the form one of the reactions listed has, at some time in the last six years, represented a turning point in the rational therapy of a case. The form is therefore directly derived from clinical experience. In this way the efficacy of its items has been established prior to their inclusion in the form.

Psychological Clinic *Form 8 Personality*

Case *Clinician*

Number *Date* *Time in conference*

Vocational Orientation	*Recreational Orientation*	*Personal Orientation*	*Social Orientation*	*Motivation*	*Ego Strength*	*Energy Output*	*Integration*	*Censorship*	*Routine*	*Pressure Resistance*	*Perceived Status*	*Traumata*	*Anxiety*	*Phantasy*	*Delusory Structure*	*Emotional Adequacy*	*Appetitive Organization*	*Symptom Formation*	
.	.	0	.	.	0	.	0	.	.	.	0	.	0	.	0	0	.	x	*1. *Problem*: ESCAPE DENIAL ACCEPTANCE PROJECTION POLLYANNA SYSTEMATIZATION ANXIETY query insight
.	.	.	.	x	0	0	0	0	.	.	.	.	.	.	.	.	.	.	2. *Volition*: Pencil trick .... seconds Toe stand .... seconds SUBVERSIVE-ATTEMPT PROTEST-OF-INABILITY systematic attempt
.	.	.	0	.	x	.	0	.	.	.	0	.	.	0	.	.	.	0	*3. *Communication*: x x x X x x x subjective objective SELF DEFENSE x x x X x x x
0	0	0	0	x	.	0	.	.	0	.	.	.	.	.	.	.	.	.	4. *Interest*: studies music projects dramatics society companions participant-attitude movies gangs athletics mechanics garden pet collection toy doll game family NARROW-INTERESTS
0	x	0	0	0	0	0	0	0	0	.	.	.	.	0	.	.	.	.	5. *Recreation:* swing trapeze sand-pile shack wagon tools doll pet TOO-LITTLE-EQUIPMENT-FOR-PLAY plays-with-parents-principally ADULTS OLDER-CHILDREN YOUNGER-CHILDREN siblings friends indoors outdoors PHANTASY-PLAY socialized-play BORED UNPLANNED-PLAY UNCONSTRUCTIVE-PLAY
x	0	0	0	0	0	.	0	0	.	0	.	.	.	.	.	.	0	.	6. *Ambition*: Vocational preference 1 . . .. 2.............. PERSON INFLUENCING CHOICE . . .. Major study .... Minor study . . .. Hobbies 1. . . .. 2. .... Preferred age of marriage . . .. Preferred number of children . . .. Preferred education . . ..
0	0	0	0	x	0	.	.	0	.	0	0	0	0	0	0	.	.	.	*7. *Motive*: NOT-RECOGNIZED EXHIBITIONISM POPULARITY SECURITY WEALTH SERVICE MASTERY SELF-ASSERTION ADVENTURE ROMANCE ESCAPE DOMINATION-OF-PEOPLE
0	.	0	.	0	0	.	.	0	0	0	.	x	0	.	.	0	.	.	*8. *Obstacle*: INSUFFICIENT-INTELLIGENCE EDUCATION PEOPLE POVERTY PHYSIQUE AGE RESPONSIBILITIES WIFE CHILDREN PARENTS
.	.	0	.	.	0	.	.	.	.	0	.	x	0	.	.	0	.	.	*9. *Disappointment*: FINANCIAL HEALTH EDUCATION SOCIAL OPPORTUNITIES PERSONAL-RECOGNITION DEATH LOVE CHILDREN
.	.	.	.	.	0	0	.	.	.	.	.	0	x	.	.	0	.	.	*10. *Melancholia*: x x x X x x x SUICIDE DEPRESSION ANXIETY ELATION EUPHORIA EXCITABLE EXHAUSTION CYCLICAL . . . . INTERVAL
.	.	.	0	.	0	.	0	.	.	0	0	0	x	.	.	0	.	.	*11. *Anxiety*: FINANCE HEALTH EDUCATION SOCIAL-STATUS RECOGNITION DEATH LOVE PREGNANCY CASTRATION MATE PARENT CHILD SEX RESPONSIBILITIES RELIGION PHILOSOPHY HOMOSEXUALITY SEIZURES ANGER OBSESSIONS DREAMS ACCIDENTS EMPLOYMENT ONLY-TEMPORARY-ANXIETY
.	.	.	.	.	0	.	.	0	.	.	.	0	x	0	0	0	.	.	*12. *Phobia*: DARK PERSONS ANIMALS ACCIDENTS DEATH HIGH-PLACES DISEASE WATER STORMS OPEN-PLACES CLOSED-PLACES SOLITUDE NEW-THINGS DISTANT-THINGS

.	.	.	x	.	.	.	.	0	0	0	0	0	.	.	0	.	.	.	*13. *Tension*: MATE SIBLINGS PARENTS IN-LAWS COMMUNITY LAW SCHOOL CHURCH EMPLOYER
.	.	.	x	.	.	.	.	0	0	0	0	0	0	.	.	.	.	.	*14. *Family*: DEFENDS - THEM PROJECTS - ON - THEM ANXIOUS-IN-HOME OVERT-TENSION INSECURITY FAMILY-OVER-CRITICAL UNACCEPTED UNCERTAIN-FAMILY-STATUS
.	.	.	x	.	.	0	0	0	.	0	0	0	.	.	.	0	.	.	*15. *Anger*: SITUATIONS. . . . . TYPES OF PEOPLE . . . . SPECIAL ENEMIES . . . . FIGHT WIN LOSE WHO-STOPPED-IT PRESENT-SOLUTION .... ANXIOUS-REGARDING-ANGER FEAR-IT SELF-CONTEMPTUOUS PROJECT-BLAME ANGER-PHANTASIES FEELING-OF-GUILT
.	.	.	x	.	.	.	.	.	.	.	.	0	.	.	.	.	0	.	16. *Attachments*: objects . . . . situations . . . . types of people . . . . special friends . . . .
.	.	0	0	0	0	.	0	x	0	0	.	.	.	0	.	.	.	.	*17. *Religion*: CONVERTED CALLING MYSTICISM RITUALISM TABOOS FEAR AGNOSTICISM CYNICISM RATIONALISM PANTHEISM SOCIAL-GOSPEL denomination . . . . pray Sunday School ... . per month Worship .... per month Other exercises . . . . Source of religious beliefs . . . .
.	.	0	.	.	0	.	.	x	0	0	.	.	0	0	0	0	.	0	*18. *Guilt*: GENERAL SPECIFIC COMPULSIVE EXPIATION GUILTY IDEAS AMBIVALENT FEARFUL SELFCONTEMPT RATIONALIZED . . . .
.	.	0	.	0	.	.	.	0	.	.	.	.	.	x	.	0	.	.	19. *Ideal*: religion .... service . . . . social .... moral . . . . thrift .... success . . . . education .... responsibility . . . .
.	.	.	.	.	0	.	0	x	.	.	.	.	.	0	0	.	0	0	*20. *Compulsion*: SUPERSTITION THOUGHTS DESTRUCTIVE-TENDENCIES SEX COUNTING EATING LOCKING EXPECT-ACCIDENTS
.	.	.	0	.	0	.	0	0	x	0	0	.	.	.	.	.	.	.	*21. *Control*: FATHER MOTHER SISTER BROTHER BOSS HERO SENSE-OF-DUTY REWARDS . . . .
.	.	.	.	.	.	0	x	.	.	.	.	.	.	.	.	.	.	.	22. *Motor*: SLOW APATHETIC RESISTANT STIFF AUTOMATIC-OBEDIENCE CATATONIC STEREOTYPY left-handed right-handed HYPERKINETIC HYPOKINETIC RESTLESS TIC CHORETIC TENSE FACIAL-EXPRESSION . . . .
.	.	.	.	.	.	0	x	.	.	.	.	.	.	0	0	0	.	.	23. *Speech*: VERBIGERATION FLIGHT-OF-IDEAS DIVERTIBILITY-OF-ATTENTION NEOLOGISMS AUDITORY-APHASIA SHORT-ATTENTION-SPAN ARTIFICIALITY DEFECT
.	.	.	.	.	.	.	.	.	.	.	.	.	.	x	.	.	0	.	*24. *Dream*: FEAR DEATH PURSUIT ANIMALS FALLING DROWNING NAKED GUILT SEX HOMOSEXUAL OEDIPAL FLYING F IGHTING EATING SMOKING SMOTHERING AMNESIA-FOR-DREAMS ....
.	.	.	.	.	.	x	.	.	0	.	.	.	.	.	.	.	0	.	25. *Sleep*: INSOMNIA TOSSING SOMNAMBULISM UNRESTFUL SNORING regular fresh-air bed-fellow . . . .

(*Continued*)

Psychological Clinic *Form 8 Personality*

Case *Clinician*

Number *Date* *Time in conference*

Vocational Orientation	*Recreational Orientation*	*Personal Orientation*	*Social Orientation*	*Motivation*	*Ego Strength*	*Energy Output*	*Integration*	*Censorship*	*Routine*	*Pressure Resistance*	*Perceived Status*	*Traumata*	*Anxiety*	*Phantasy*	*Delusory Structure*	*Emotional Adequacy*	*Appetitive Organization*	*Symptom Formation*	
.	.	.	.	.	0	.	.	.	.	.	.	x	0	0	.	.	.	.	*26. *Memory*: most vivid memories . . . .
.	.	0	.	0	0	.	.	.	.	.	.	.	0	x	0	.	0	0	*27. *Daydream*: CONTINUED-STORY REPEATED-STORY SYSTEMATIZED BIZARRE CONDENSED EUPHORIC MANY-CHARACTERS SELF-REPRESENTED CONQUERING-HERO SUFFERING-HERO
.	.	.	.	.	0	.	.	0	.	.	.	0	0	x	0	0	.	0	28. *Hallucinations*: VISUAL PARESTHESIA AUDITORY MEN WOMEN RECOGNIZED-VOICES CONSIDERED-REAL CONTROLLED BELIEVED-CAUSE . . . . CONTENT . . . . PROPHETIC VOICE-OF-CONSCIENCE NECROMANCY DEJA-VU
.	.	.	.	.	0	.	.	.	.	.	.	0	0	x	0	0	0	0	*29. *Hypochondria*: CEPHALIC ORBITAL AURAL DENTAL RESPIRATORY CARDIAC GASTRIC GLOBUSHYSTERICUS ELIMINATORY CANCER RHEUMATIC LUMBAR ARC-DE-CERCLE DISPLACED-ORGANS PARALYTIC TAXIC KINESTHETIC TOXIC CASTRATIVE
.	.	.	.	.	0	.	0	.	.	.	.	.	.	0	x	0	.	.	*30. *Delusion*: PERSECUTED WATCHED TALKED-ABOUT JEALOUS WRONGED SINISTER-INFLUENCE PLANS - FOR - REVENGE GRANDEUR STRENGTH POWER WEALTH NOBLE-BIRTH ADVENTURE NIHILISM ADOPTION SYSTEMATIZED BIZARRE
.	.	.	.	.	0	.	.	0	.	.	.	0	0	x	0	.	.	0	*31. *Seizure*: GRAND-MAL PETIT-MAL ABSENCE DEPERSONALIZATION
.	.	0	.	.	0	.	.	0	.	.	.	0	0	.	.	0	x	.	*32. *Heterosexuality*: selected-mate .... for months AMBIVALENT EROTIC INHIBITED ANXIOUS FEARFUL GUILTY DISGUSTED NEGATIVE satisfied KISS .... times kind of places . . . . PET MUTUAL-MASTURBATION INTERCOURSE times kind of places . . . . METHOD-OF-CONTRACEPTION PAID WITNESSED SEDUCED
.	.	0	.	.	0	.	.	0	0	.	.	0	0	0	.	0	x	0	*33. *Homosexuality*: BI-SEXUAL OVERT-EXPERIENCE INVERT PASSIVELY-ACCEPTED ANXIOUS MASTURBATION
.	.	.	.	0	x	.	.	.	.	.	0	.	0	.	0	0	.	0	34. *Reaction*: reaction to interview DEPRESSED ANXIOUS CRIED systematic-attitude hopeful TREMOROUS TRANSFERENCE asked-for-another-appointment
																			35. *Rapport*: x x x X x x x

2 The starred items are based upon approximately seven hundred psychotherapeutic conferences with one hundred and thirty patients in which the rational method was used.
3 Part or all of the form has been used in approximately fifteen hundred diagnostic interviews with one thousand patients.
4 Unstarred items are included in the form either because they throw light upon the general diagnosis and the prescription of further procedure or because experience indicates that they tend to establish *rapport* and naturally lead to the more crucial issues.
5 Arrangement of the items in the form is a matter of subjective judgment. Several types of arrangement have been tried. The present one seems to permit the interview to proceed smoothly from one item to another and to approach the more difficult material only after *rapport* has been partially established.
6 An exception to the above plan of arrangement occurs in Item One. In our practice we have held to the principle that there should be no practice under false pretense; that as far as he is capable the patient should always understand what problem the psychologist has in mind and should have an opportunity to give his version before the interview begins. Inclusion of this item at the beginning of the diagnostic interview is considered a matter of professional ethics.
7 Item One indicates the initial point at which the rational therapy must start. Since volition or perseverance is essential to rational therapy an attempt is made to measure that trait in Item Two. Children are given two tasks and the time and method of continuing their efforts is recorded. Adults are simply asked, "How badly do you want to solve your problem? Are you willing to approach it from the psychological angle?" In Item Three an attempt is made to discover the accessibility of the patient. Next the clinician must know something of how the patient is oriented with respect to various goals, what motives can be appealed to. In the first seven items the psychoanalyst will recognize an attempt to reveal what he is accustomed to call *ego* strength and accessibility. Items Eight to Twelve deal with frustrations, traumata, and the typically traumatic reactions. Items Thirteen to Sixteen deal with the patient's attachments and orientation toward people. Items Seventeen to Twenty-one deal with *super-ego* structure, Twenty-two to Twenty-three with overt reactions, and Twenty-four to Twenty-eight with phantasy mechanisms or reality substitutions. Items Twenty-nine to Thirty deal with delusional structure. Items Thirty-one to Thirty-three deal with vasomotor reactions and may throw some light upon *id* demands.
8 In order to keep a record of the interview which may be reviewed quickly words indicating the patient's reaction to various items are encircled by the examiner as he uses the form.
9 Words which usually indicate pathological conditions are capitalized.
10 An *analytic margin* for use in structuralizing the results of the interview appears at the left of the form. At the top of the margin there are listed nineteen concepts which seem to be useful in evaluating a case. When some word in an item is likely to bear upon one of these concepts an *x* or an *o* appears at the intersection of the appropriate row and column. The *x* appears under the concept which is principally involved and the *o's* under other concepts which are frequently involved. In using the form the psychologist may encircle the *x* and *o's* in any row in which he has also encircled a capitalized term.
11 It should be unnecessary to mention the fact that the form was developed and is intended to be used as a device for gaining *entrée* to the personality and that little can be expected of it if the clinician fails to follow immediately the leads which it reveals during the course of the interview. It sometimes occurs that the principal difficulty can be diagnosed very soon after the start of the interview by following some of the early leads. Categorical answers to any set of questions, no matter how well phrased and how comprehensive, are not likely to throw much light upon the personality. Psychologists who are looking for diagnostic instruments which they may place in the hands of their assistants for data gathering purposes will find little consolation in this form although there are certain to be some who will attempt to evaluate it from that angle only.
12 Since the phrasing of questions is an important consideration in the technique of any interview, the following illustrative phrasings are suggested. Alternative phrasing for different vocabulary levels is illustrated.

Item 1: This item must never be omitted from the first conference. As in a number of the items more than one of the abbreviations may properly be encircled. A child who has been registered because of a tendency to steal is asked, "You seem to have been in some trouble with your school principal lately; what was the matter?" If the child does not mention stealing the clinician asks, "What about stealing?" The purpose of the questions is not to force a confession or to compel the child to talk about an unpleasant subject, but first to give him a chance to give his own version of the problem and thus come to an understanding of the reason for his being in the clinic and then, if it appears that he still does not know why he is registered, to ask a direct question which will indicate what the clinician has in mind. This method of approach may appear too direct to the inexperienced worker, but it saves misunderstanding and actually serves to protect the patient. Frequently the patient is glad to have the worst "over with" before he has time to build up a story. Clients who are registered for other reasons are approached in a similar manner.

Item 3: (a) "I don't know you very well yet. Won't you tell me something about yourself? What kind of a little boy are you? Are you a good little boy or a bad little boy?" (b) "Tell me about yourself. What sort of a personality do you have? Do you have a good personality or are you rather disagreeable? What sort of an impression do you make upon people?"

Item 4: (a) "What sort of things do you like to do?" (b) "What are your principal interests in life?"

Item 5: (a) "Do you like to play? What do you like to play? What do you like to play with? Whom do you play with? Where and in what places do you play? Tell me some of the things you have to play with." (b) "What sort of recreation do you get? With whom do you usually take your recreation?"

Item 6: (a) "What do you want to be when you grow up? Did you decide that all by yourself? Do you want to get married and have children of your own? How far do you want to go in school?" (b) "What do you want to do when you get out of school? Who influenced you in deciding that? What subjects are you specializing in? Do you want to get married? How many children do you think you would like to have? How far do you intend to go in school?" (c) "What is your vocational ambition? Who has influenced that choice? What is your major? Your minor? What are your hobbies?"

Item 7: (a) "What is there about . . . . that you like so much? Why do you like to do that?" (b) "What is your motive in choosing that? Does that sort of thing mean a great deal to you? What are some of the other things that you want to get out of life? What would you say that life meant to you in general?"

Item 8: (a) "Is there anything that might keep you from doing that? Do you think you will be able to do that?" (b) "What obstacle stands in your way? What are some of the things which you will have to overcome before you can achieve your ambition?"

Item 9: (a) "Has anything happened lately to make you feel bad? What are some of the things which make you feel unhappy?" (b) "Have you had any serious disappointment lately, such as disappointments in love, deaths in the family, or financial catastrophe?"

Item 10: (a) "Are you a happy boy or are you a sad boy? How happy do you feel? How sad do you feel? Do you ever feel you do not want to live any longer? Do you ever feel so happy that you just do not know what to do with yourself?" (b) "Do you get the blues frequently, or are you usually quite happy? How excited do you get when you are happiest? How do you feel at those times? How do you feel when you get the blues? Do you feel sick and exhausted? Do you feel as if you want to kill yourself? How often do you feel that way? Do those feelings come regularly?" (c) "Do you frequently feel melancholy? How excited do you get when you are feeling good? Have you ever considered suicide? Tell me about it. Do your feelings of elation and depression come in regular cycles or at regular times?"

Item 11: (a) "When you feel sad what do you feel sad about?" (b) "When you feel unhappy what do you think about?" (c) "What do you worry about mostly? Do you worry in spite of your better judgment? Do you feel yourself compelled to worry even though you do not believe that there is any cause for worry? Is this just a temporary worry or do you have it frequently?"

Item 12: (a) "What are you afraid of? Are you afraid of the dark? Are you afraid of some people, etc.?" (b) "Do you have any fears? Are you afraid of the dark, etc.?"

Item 13: (a) "How do you get along with your brothers and sisters? Are they nice to you? How do you get along with your papa and mama? Do you like them? Do they like you? Which do you like better, etc.?" (b) "How do you get along with your girl friend? How do you get along in your family, especially with your brothers and sisters? Do you avoid each other or are you quite close to each other in your companionship, etc.?" (c) "How do you get along with your wife? Do you sometimes have a tension which arises between you? What is the nature of these tensions or difficulties, etc.?"

Item 14: (a) "How do you get along at home? Do you think you have a nice home?" (b) "Do you stick together? How is the household run?"

Item 15: (a) "Do you ever get mad? Tell me about some time that you got mad. What happened? Whom did you get mad at? Are there any people who don't like you? Did you ever get in a fight? Who won? Who stopped the fight? After that what did you do about it? How do you feel about it now?" (b) "What sort of situations make you angry? What kind of people make you angry? Tell me about two or three of your enemies."

Item 16: (a) "What one of your toys do you like best? Tell me about some place you like to be. What kind of people do you like best? Who is your best friend? Do you have any other people who are as nice to you as that?" (b) "What things or objects are you most attached to? What belonging means most to you? What places or situations are most attractive to you? What kind of people do you prefer as companions, etc.?"

Item 17: (a) "Do you go to church? What church do you go to? Do you like church? Do you pray? What is there about church that you like? What is there about church that you do not like?" (b) "What is your attitude toward religion? Have you ever been converted? Do you feel that you have a religious calling? What part of religion appeals to you most, etc.?"

Item 18: (a) "Do you ever feel that you have been a bad boy? What is bad about you? What do you think you should do about it?" (b) "Do you ever have a feeling of guilt? What do you feel guilty about mostly? Is it things that you think or things that you do that are bad? What have you been doing about it? What do you think you ought to do about it?"

Item 19: (a) "What do you think is the best thing in the world? What do you think is nicest of all?" (b) "What kind of ideals do you have? Tell me some of the ideals which you think are most important."

Item 20: (a) "Do you ever do things when you feel that you just can't help it? Do you ever think things that you don't want to think?" (b) "Do you sometimes find yourself doing things for no reason at all yet you can't help doing them? Do thoughts ever come to your mind and refuse to leave? Do you have some idea which seems to be forced upon you? Tell me about it."

Item 21: (a) "What keeps you from doing naughty things? Does somebody watch you so that you will be good, or are you good just because you want to be? What is there to keep you from being bad" (b) "How is your life kept under control? Is it controlled by people who watch you? What is there to keep you from becoming immoral or bad? What kind of self control do you exercise?"

Items 22 and 23 can be indicated at this point in the examination without asking further specific questions.

Item 24: "Do you dream? Did you ever have a dream? Tell me your last dream."

Item 25: "Is it easy for you to go to sleep at night? Do you go to sleep at the same time every night? Do you sleep with the window open, etc.?"

Item 27: (a) "What do you think about when you are all by yourself and there is nothing to do? Do you ever tell yourself a story or just play like things were happening? Tell me one of those stories." (b) "Do you ever daydream or imagine things happening to you just for the fun of it? Tell me one of your daydreams, etc."

Item 28: (a) "Do you ever think that you see things and then find out that they are really not there at all? Do you ever feel things crawling over you when there really is nothing at all? Do you ever hear people talking to you when there really isn't any one there at all, etc.?" (b) "Do you ever have visions that seem almost as real as actual events? Do you sometimes have the sensation of having things crawling over you? Do you hear words or sounds when there is no one around to account for them, etc.?"

Item 29: (a) "Does your head sometimes hurt? Do your eyes sometimes hurt, etc.?" (b) "Do you have frequent headaches? Do your eyes bother you, etc.?" At this point the psychologist must keep in mind that he is exploring hypochondriacal attitudes regardless of whether or not there are organic disorders.

Item 31: (a) "Did you ever have a fit? Did you ever feel as if you were floating away or as if you did not really live?" (b) "Do you ever have times when you are not yourself? Tell me about them."

Item 32: (a) "Do you have a girl friend? How long have you had this girl friend? Do you sometimes like and sometimes hate her? Do you love her and want to touch her? Are you afraid to talk to her? Did you ever do anything together that was naughty? What? Were you afraid? How do you feel about it? Are you happy with this girl friend? Did you ever kiss a girl? How many times have you kissed a girl? Do you hold on to each other real tight sometimes? Do you ever touch each other under your clothes? How close did you get to each other? How many times did you do that? How many girls have you done that with? Did you ever pay a girl for that? Did you ever see anybody else do that? Did any girl ever try to get you to do that?"

Item 33: (a) "Is it just as easy for you to like another boy as it is for you to like a girl? Have you ever been in love with a boy? Did you ever touch each other under the clothes? Or did you just feel like it? What are you going to do about it? Did you ever play with yourself where you shouldn't?"

Summary

Since the strictly psychological field of personality disorders usually requires rational psychotherapeutic measures diagnosis in this field assumes a unique role. The formulation of his problem which a patient is able to make at the end of his diagnostic interview is more important than a tabulation of his reactions during the course of his interview. In order to facilitate the rapid progress of the interview toward the revelation of important material and to lead more rapidly to a satisfactory formulation of the patient's problems a diagnostic interview form is presented. Its items consist principally of points which have been the recognized turning points in the successful rational psychotherapy of actual cases. Arrangement of the items has been determined by simple experimentation. Illustrative phrasing of initial questions is suggested.

Bibliography

Baker, H. J. and Traphagan, V. (1935). *The diagnosis and treatment of behavior problem children.* Macmillan.

Brown, S. and Potter, H. W. (1930). *The psychiatric study of problem children.* State Hospitals Press.

Cheney, C. O. (1934). *Outlines for psychiatric examinations.* State Hospitals Press.

Kelly, G. A. (1936). *Handbook of clinical practice, 3rd Ed.* Fort Hays Psychological Clinic.

Kelly, G.A. (1938). The practical effectiveness of certain general types of recommendations made by a psychological clinic. *Journal of General Psychology, 19*, 211–217.

53

Clinic Ranks High in Speech Department: Outline of the Activities of Psychological Clinic Here[1]

The work of the psychological clinic was started in a modest way in the fall of 1931 when a group of students from one of the classes in psychology undertook, as its special project, a clinical study of a child from Picken School. The following semester and summer courses in clinical psychology were introduced and special remedial work was undertaken for a limited number of children. During the first four years of its operation, the psychological clinic service was operated upon a total of thirty-five dollars. In 1933 a traveling clinic service was established upon request of communities who wished to have diagnosis of children done locally.

In 1935, at the initiative of one of the state legislators, a small special appropriation was made to extend the work of the traveling clinics. Under a special state act this clinic was made the official child guidance clinic of Kansas and its services have extended as far as Atchison, Leavenworth, Cherryvale, Ulysses, and Goodland. This service touches about three hundred fifty children each year. Cases seen in traveling clinics are followed for a period of two years by an extensive system of correspondence.

Clinic in Highest Bracket

The clinic has been interested in speech correction and in June, 1937, Consumers' Digest, published by Consumers' Research, gave approved rating to twenty-five clinics in the United States for correction of stuttering. Five clinics received the highest rating, including Fort Hays, University of Iowa, Northwestern University, University of California, and the University of Minnesota. Well-known speech clinics such as those of the University of Michigan, Ohio State, Purdue, and Colombia were placed in the lower rating bracket.

A large portion of the work of the clinic consists in developing carefully selected students who plan to receive doctorate degrees in this field. Two former students of the clinic have received Ph.D.s in clinical psychology. One is a prominent psychiatric social worker, and there are nine who are completing doctoral work in various universities. All of these have been awarded substantial fellowships which permit them to be self-supporting while completing their training.

Opportunity School Maintained

The clinic maintains a full-time Opportunity School for handicapped children. It also maintains, for two hours a day, a nursery school for children between the ages of three and five. Through a special arrangement with the State and District offices of the National Youth Administration the clinic conducts a special vocational guidance project for non-school youth in this area. The project employs twenty selected college young people in addition to five students who are assigned to the clinic on regular college N.Y.A. and two fellowship students.

With this staff the clinic offers vocational guidance to non-school youth, including psychological diagnosis, investigation of sociological background, a survey of community economic trends and employment conditions, actual supervision of the labor of some of these youth in private employment, and occupational adjustment after the employment has been undertaken. This project is in its third year.

[1] First published as Kelly, G.A. (1939). Clinic ranks high in Speech Department: Outline of the activities of psychological clinic here. *Fort Hays State Alumni News: A Supplement of the K.S.C. Leader, XXXII*, 30, Thursday May 30. Republished by permission of Forsyth Library Special Collections, Fort Hays State University.

Collected Papers of the Pioneer of Constructivist Psychology: George A. Kelly, First Edition. Edited by David A. Winter and Nick Reed.

Conduct Special Projects

During each year the clinic spends a number of days in the State Girls' Industrial School at Beloit, making psychological diagnosis and assisting in making plans for rehabilitation of the students there. From time to time the clinic conducts special projects. A considerable number of out-patients are brought to the clinic at Hays for special diagnosis. There have been out-patient clinics held especially for teachers who wish to have the clinic deal with problems of their own personality adjustment. In addition there is a limited number of adults who receive psychotherapy through a series of conferences. Each year the clinic operates reading clinics for college students who wish to improve upon their reading and study habits.

In the course of its development the clinic has produced a considerable amount of research, some of it having been published in the national professional journals of psychology. In the course of its seven and one half years of work the clinic has dealt with nearly fifteen hundred cases. The clinic is also interested in the establishment of local mental hygiene societies and is continually promoting through lectures and other means the formation of local community interests in the development of psychological facilities. Due to the extent of the clinic's undertaking, a large part of its responsibilities are carried by the college students themselves who have been selected for training toward professional service in this field.

54

The Person as a Laboratory Subject, as a Statistical Case, and as a Clinical Client[1]

The definition of the science of psychology eventually will be written by those who are not psychologists. It is difficult for anyone except a confirmed psychologist to see the laboratory subjects of the academic psychologists as the same human beings who inhabit the land. It is somewhat easier for an administrator, an economist, or a social worker to recognize the statistician's case as a workable entity. Great numbers of intelligent and interested laymen who have been newly awakened to so-called human values are thinking in terms of clinical clients and what the psychologist does for them. This forcing of the psychologist's hand may draw him into scientific inaccuracies or may cast for him a new and more vital role. Illustrations of the problems which psychologists will be expected to solve are offered.

[1] Abstract published as Kelly, G. A. (1938). The person as a laboratory subject, as a statistical case, and as a clinical client. In P. Weatherwax (Ed.), *Proceedings of the Indiana Academy of Science*, *48*, 186. Republished by permission of the Indiana Academy of Science.

Collected Papers of the Pioneer of Constructivist Psychology: George A. Kelly, First Edition. Edited by David A. Winter and Nick Reed.

55

Some Practical Considerations in the Formulation of Clinical Recommendations[1]

Both for psychologists and for the recipients of the psychologist's recommendations, devices are needed which will give character and pattern to individual case studies. Clinical recommendations are more likely to be followed if they include characterization and prediction in addition to comprehensive, crucial, incidental, and supplementary recommendations.

[1] Abstract from the Proceedings of the Fifteenth Annual Meeting of the Midwestern Psychological Association. Published in 1940 in *Psychological Bulletin, 37(8)*, 576. Now in the public domain, and republished by permission of Jacqueline Aldridge.

Collected Papers of the Pioneer of Constructivist Psychology: George A. Kelly, First Edition. Edited by David A. Winter and Nick Reed.

56

A Comprehensive Plan for Case Summaries[1]

Sixty-three clinically significant variants were isolated in a review of case records in the file of the Fort Hays Kansas State College Psychological Clinic. Now all new case records are made to touch specifically on each of these variants. This plan provides for restructuralization of otherwise fragmented case records.

[1] Abstract published as Hemphill, J. K., & Kelly, G. A. (1941). A comprehensive plan for case summaries. In R. H. Seashore (Ed.), Proceedings of the Sixteenth Annual Meeting of the Midwestern Psychological Association. *Psychological Bulletin*, *38*(8), 704–721. https://doi.org/10.1037/h0050662. In the public domain. Republished by permission of Jacqueline Aldridge.

Collected Papers of the Pioneer of Constructivist Psychology: George A. Kelly, First Edition. Edited by David A. Winter and Nick Reed.

57

A Further Validation of Role Therapy[1]

The present study has shown simplified ways for the clinician to derive the role to be used in "role therapy" and to validate it before it is tried out on the patient. The five role-dramatizing sessions have been reduced to a standard form.

[1] This abstract from the Proceedings of the Seventeenth Annual Meeting of the Midwestern Psychological Association was first published as Robinson, A.J., & Kelly, G. A. (1942). A further validation of role therapy. *Psychological Bulletin, 39(8)*, 596. It is now in the public domain and is republished by permission of Jacqueline Aldridge.

Collected Papers of the Pioneer of Constructivist Psychology: George A. Kelly, First Edition. Edited by David A. Winter and Nick Reed.

58

Morale for Tomorrow's Generation[1]

ANNOUNCING
Psychological Clinic Services
made available at nominal cost by the State of Kansas to—
Schools
Social Agencies
Civic Organizations
Professional Groups
Individuals

Two types of services are available.

Appointment Service:

By writing the Director of the Psychological Clinic, Fort Hays Kansas State College, any resident of the State may make an appointment for a psychological examination at Hays.

Appointments are usually made for ten o'clock in the morning and recommendations are usually completed in the afternoon of the same day.

A child presented for examination should be accompanied by his parents and his teacher.

There is no charge for this service.

Traveling Child Guidance Clinics:

Responsible community organizations may sponsor one or two-day clinics locally. The sponsor makes the necessary prearrangements and the Fort Hays Kansas State College Psychological Clinic provides a staff of one psychologist and four assistants.

Recommendations to parents are given privately. Recommendations to teachers, physicians, social workers and other local professional workers are developed in an evening joint staff conference.

The only charge for this service is one dollar a case or ten dollars for each day of service.

For further information write:

Psychological Clinic
Fort Hays Kansas State College
Hays, Kansas

Ask the Psychologist…

How can I help my daughter to get along in School?
Why can't Jimmy be one of the gang?
Must that girl always annoy her teachers?
How can I become a nurse?

[1] Published by permission of University Archives/Special Collections—University of Lincoln-Nebraska and Jacqueline Aldridge.

Collected Papers of the Pioneer of Constructivist Psychology: George A. Kelly, First Edition. Edited by David A. Winter and Nick Reed.

How can a child with so much ability be kept interested?
They've never been able to understand me!
Can she ever be like other children?
But he can't read!

Should he try to keep up medicine in spite of his handicap?
I can't get the silly idea out of my mind!
Why won't my boy ever confide in me?
Will he grow out of it?

Is it asking too much of my family to treat me like one of them?
To think of all that ability going to waste!
I've tried everything!
Is that simply baby-talk?

What can we do to keep Mary from being always so unhappy?
I keep thinking about it and it frightens me!
What can I do about my son's companions?
What makes her so nervous?

She starts crying when anyone even looks at her!
Won't that cause a nervous breakdown?
Does he have real musical talent?
I'm at my wit's end!

I'm doing something wrong with Carl. What is it?
Should I punish him for that?
What makes her so nervous?
He's afraid of everything!

How can we learn to get along with each other?
Can't her talents be developed?
Should I quit school?
I'm so ashamed!

Arithmetic has always been hard for me!
Should we rock him to sleep?
What kind of a home should she have?
Why don't my pupils trust me?

Why can't I be like other people?
I can't keep my mind on my work!
But he really isn't a bad boy!
Why won't they leave me alone?

59

Seminar on Psychotherapy[1]

Session I, October 3, 1949

The principal procedural approaches to psychotherapy.

A Psychoanalytic procedures.
  1 Freudian origins
    a Hypnosis via Mesmer, animal magnetism, Bergson, the Freudian School and Charcot.
    b Catharsis via exorcism, Aristotle, and Breuer.
    c Associationism via Locke and British School.
  2 Present-day psychoanalytic technique
    c Diffusion
    d Association
  Ref. Bjerre, History of Psychoanalysis.
  Fenichel, The Psychoanalytic Theory of the Neuroses.
  Fenichel, Problems of Psychoanalytic Technique.
B Client-centered procedures.
  1 Origins in Plato, Freud, Rank, Taft, and Rogers.
  2 The transference issue.
  3 Reflection technique.
  4 Theoretical frames
    a Self, Raimy
    b Phenomenology and Gestalt
    c Neophenomenology, Snygg and Combs
    d Self-consistency, Lecky.
  Ref. Hendrick, Facts and Theories of Psychoanalysis.
  Taft, The Dynamics of Therapy.
  Rogers, Counseling and Psychotherapy.
  Snygg and Combs, Individual Behavior.
  Lecky, Self-consistency.
  Boring, History of Experimental Psychology.
C Meyerian procedures.
  1 Biological and biographical origins
    a The case history
    b Anamnesis
    c Common sense and culture pattern
      The socio-psycho-biologic unity in a given setting at a given time
    d Symbolism and Tension
    e Suggestion and Restructuration

[1] Published by permission of Jacqueline Aldridge.

Collected Papers of the Pioneer of Constructivist Psychology: George A. Kelly, First Edition. Edited by David A. Winter and Nick Reed.

2 Role approaches
  a Cameron
  b Moreno

Ref. Lief, The Commonsense Psychiatry of Adolf Meyer.
Kraines, The Therapy of the Neuroses and Psychoses.
Cameron, The Psychology of Behavior Disorders.

Session II, October 10, 1949

Essentials of a Personality Theory

A theory is an economical system of explicitly stated assumptions, the logical relations between which provide one with a precise representation of many separately observed facts and a means for correctly anticipating certain classes of events.

Issues:

1 Determinism and free will.
2 Assumptions providing a logical place for therapy.
3 Common implicit assumptions (e.g., independence of observations).
4 The tentative nature of assumptions and desirability for economy in their use.
5 The relation between assumption, postulate, construct, and concept.
6 The relation between observation, perception, image, symbol, experience, fact and event.
7 The place of the hypothesis.
8 The binding effect of a system.
9 Prediction and validation.
10 Causation and the time factor.
11 Theory fertility.
12 The ultimate test of a theory: technical control.

Readings: LIFE: *Oppenheimer*, 10 Oct. 1949.
Lecky, Self-consistency
Fenichel, The psychoanalytic theory of neurosis
Johnson, H.H., Psychoanalytic therapy versus psychoanalytic rationale *Amer. Psychologist*, 1948, *3*, 337 (abstract)
Sears, Robert, Survey of Objective Studies of Psychoanalytic Concepts *Soc. Sci. Res. Coun. Bull. 156*, 1943, No. 51, pp XIV.
Cameron, Psychology of behavior disorders.

Session III, October 17, 1949

A Limited Theory of Personality

Fundamental Postulate

Mental process is in the apparent direction of prediction and control.

Definitions

1 Mental. An adjective denoting the kind of phenomena with which this limited theory is concerned.
2 Process. A non-repetitive activity in which elements are predictable from prior elements.
3 Apparent. An adjective denoting that which is perceived by someone; in this case, by the one who is mentally proceeding. (One might say, "in the construed direction.")
4 Prediction. An established expectancy.
5 Control. A re-combination of expectancies providing a new and more comprehensive expectancy.

Axiom I

Persons vary in their constructions of experience, hence what is apparent in one way to one person is not necessarily apparent in the same way to another person. Operational agreement between persons, as exemplified by concerted behavior through language communication, does not signify that they have identical perceptions.

Axiom II

To the extent that one person can employ the constructions of experience that are used by another, he may predict that person's immediate mental processes.

Axiom III

To the extent that one person can elicit a variety of constructions and, in turn, a variety of expectations in another, he may establish new and more comprehensive expectancies in that other person.

Session IV, October 24, 1949

Postulate B: A person may utilize a variety of construction systems which are logically incompatible with each other, i.e., which infer different predictions.

These systems may be used in such rapid alternation that only the smallest sequences of mental process are actually construed by the person within a single one of his systems.

Definition of active personal adjustment: When, following a series of alternating uses of incompatible systems, a person reorganizes his perceptual field on a more comprehensive level so as to eliminate the incompatibility, the change is designated as an "active personal adjustment."

Definition of passive personal adjustment: When one minimizes the apparent incompatibility of his construction systems by limiting his perceptual field, the relatively repetitive mental process that takes place is designated as a "passive personal adjustment."

Definition of active social adjustment: When one achieves control of his associates in a manner compatible with their level of active personal adjustment, he has made an "active social adjustment."

Definition of passive social adjustment: When one's behavior becomes predictable by his associates and does not interfere with their adjustment, he has made a "passive social adjustment."

Additional topics:

1 Occasions when prediction denies control. Fatalism. Stereotypy. Words.
2 The fear-anxiety-guilt-suicide sequence.

Session V, October 31, 1949

Restatements of postulates and corollaries of a limited theory of personality.

Postulate A, Fundamental Postulate: Mental process is in the construed direction of prediction and control.

Definitions:

1 Mental. An adjective denoting the kind of phenomena with which this limited theory is concerned.
2 Process. An activity in which the elements are not identical but which are predictable from prior elements.
3 Construed. An adjective denoting a person's particular perceptual referents.
4 Prediction. An established expectancy.
5 Control. The recombining of expectancies in such a manner to preserve certain established ones.

Postulate A is designed to establish a take-off point for the limited theory which will establish immediately a *direction* for mental processes and the reference point (the person's own construction) from which the mental process makes the most sense. The notions of valence, preference, liking and disliking, urges, etc. are subordinated to this postulate since mental process is here postulated as always taking place in the direction of prediction and control as seen by the person. The notion of mental energy is not employed in the theory since an activity or process is postulated as always going on. The so-called "self-concept" is not employed in the usual sense. The theory is concerned not merely with the conceptualization or construing *of the self by the self*, but the construing *of the direction in which one may achieve prediction and control of many kinds of events*!

Corollary I. *Individuality: Persons vary in their constructions of experience.* What is apparent in one way to one person is not necessarily apparent in the same way to another person. Operational agreement between persons, as exemplified by concerted behavior through language communication, does not signify that they have identical perceptions.

Corollary II. *Sociality: To the extent that one person employs the constructions of experience that are used by another, he may predict that person's mental processes.*

Postulate B. *Fragmentations: A person may utilize a variety of construction systems which are logically incompatible with each other.* In extreme instances these systems may be used in such rapid alternation that only the smallest sequences of mental process are actually construed by the person within a single one of his systems.

Definition:

6 Logically incompatible systems. Systems which infer different predictions, i.e., the events predicted by the different systems cannot be construed by the person as being equivalent.

The idea of validity of predictions is subsumed under Postulates A and B. A person infers or predicts an event. He then perceives that something happens. His perceiving involves construing the event in some way that makes sense. If he construes it within the same system in which he anticipated it, his anticipation system is validated to some extent. If he construes it within a system that is logically incompatible with the one in which he anticipated it, his anticipation system is invalidated to some extent.

Corollary III. *Adjustment*: A person's tolerance of incompatibility is limited.

At some point, varying with the organization levels of different individuals, fragmentation reaches a maximum and is certain to be followed by reconstruction of the perceptual field. This reconstruction is identified as adjustment. Incidentally, a particular adjustment may be construed by other persons as good or bad, but from the standpoint of the person who is adjusting it is inescapable.

Definitions:

7 Threat. Events which a person can construe only in a manner which is incompatible with a comprehensive system upon which he has come to rely are, for that person at that moment, a threat. If he can ignore or reconstrue the events in a compatible manner, or if he can reorganize his comprehensive system so as to contain them, they cease to stand in a threatening relation to him.

Types of adjustments (Personal)

8 Dilation. When, following a series of alternating uses of incompatible systems, a person broadens his perceptual field by reorganizing it on a more comprehensive level, the adjustment is called dilation. The dilation may eliminate the incompatibility as it was experienced but it may set the stage for new incompatibilities as new events enter the perceptual field, i.e., the reorganized system may prove to be invalid.

9 Constriction. When one minimizes the apparent incompatibility of his construction systems by limiting his perceptual field, the relatively repetitive mental process that takes place is designated as constriction.

Types of adjustments (Social)

10 Progressive Leadership. When one achieves control of his associates in a manner compatible with their dilating adjustments, he shows progressive leadership.

11 Suppressive Leadership. When one achieves control of his associates in a manner compatible only with their constricting adjustments, he shows suppressive leadership.

12 Passive social adjustment. When one's behavior becomes predictable by his associates and does not make adjustments necessary on their parts, he has made a passive social adjustment.

Session VI

A The construction systems employed by a person may be considered to differ in three principal respects:

1 Core structures are those which govern a person's maintenance processes, i.e., those by which he maintains his identity and his health.

2 Peripheral structures are those which can be altered without serious modification of core structuration.

3 Comprehensive structures are those which subsume a wide variety of events. In healthy persons core structures are included in this category.
4 Incidental structures are those which subsume a small variety of events. Under certain conditions of illness a part of one's core structure may become incidental. When this takes place one's identity or health is maintained in a highly specific and narrow manner. This precarious existence minimizes the use of comprehensive structures. For the most part, in healthy persons, incidental structure is peripheral and relates to everyday experience in which one's identity is not too deeply involved.
5 Firm structures are those which provide unvarying predictions.
6 Pliable structures are those which vary but which, for practical purposes, may be said to retain their identity.

In general the healthy person's mental processes follow core structures which are comprehensive and firm. Among his peripheral structures, however, some are comprehensive and some are incidental, some firm and some pliable.

Fear and Anxiety

Threat involves an imminent change in one's core structure. When the threat is perceived as the substance of an incidental structure we may call it "fear"; when the events comprising the identified threat are embraced in a comprehensive structure we may call it "anxiety." Guilt is something else!

Role and Guilt

Within one's core structure there are those frames which enable one to predict and control the interactions of himself with other persons and with societal groups of persons. Altogether these comprise his conceptualization of his "role." Taken separately they demark the facets of his role and explain a person's varicolored reflections under changing social illumination. One's deepest understanding of himself being maintained as a social being is his concept of his "role." Threat against this structure may be called "guilt."

The conventional notion of guilt as man's awareness of the evil within him is not antithetical to this formulation; nor is the psychoanalytic notion of guilt as a kind of superego spanking. The proposed formulation is designed to free the research-minded psychologist from the absolutism of the concept of "evil," on the one hand, and from the automatism of the concept of "superego," on the other.

Session VII, November 14, 1949

Suspension of Ideas

Forgetting, dissociation and repression are conceived in much the same ways. In order for an experience to be perceived clearly, it must be supported within a structure. When a structure is resolved in favor of another one, some of the elements tend to drop out, especially those which do not fit so well in the new structure. Again our present theory does not place the emphasis upon remembering what is pleasant or forgetting what is unpleasant but rather upon remembering what is structured and forgetting what is unstructured.

A kind of forgetting takes place when a structure is rejected as incompatible. An experience may be clearly contained in such an incompatible structure but the structure itself may constitute such a threat that it, together with the experiences it contains, may be held in abeyance. This kind of forgetting is called "repression" in some theories. Here let us tentatively call such forgetting suspension of ideas. In contrast with some notions of repression suspension means that the idea or element of experience is forgotten simply because the person can, at the moment, entertain no structure within which the idea would have meaning. Once he can entertain such a structure, the idea may become active within it.

Ideas are not suspended because of their intrinsic nature but rather because their implications are intolerable.

Hysteria

Certain facets of one's role have to do with his dependencies upon persons in his immediate environment, particularly his parents. These facets are developed early in life and are readily identified as child-like patterns. Some forms of expressing affection are within these dependency patterns. In their early forms the dependency patterns are selfish and involve much more receiving of support than giving of it to others.

When a person who has rigidly adhered to an early form of dependency pattern finds himself threatened by newly apparent patterns involving his own organic behavior, he may employ the suspension of some of the new ideas and reconstrue his organic behavior in a manner consistent with his dependency structure. Thus the realization of emerging sexual patterns of behavior in the adolescent may threaten rigidly established dependencies. Some of the emerging ideas are suspended within the rejected sex structure. Somatic patterning is modified to contain others and, at the same time, to comply with the dependency facet of the person's role. This is hysteria.

Characteristically the hysteria patient behaves like an over-demanding, love-needing, dependent child. He tends to relate himself in a dependent way to almost anyone, showing suggestibility to another person's ideas, rejecting the other's dependency upon him, and generally exhibiting inability to give in proportion to what he receives. Somatically he may develop dependency-creating symptoms which contain only a part of the elements in the threatening organic (possibly sex) pattern.

In broad outline therapy may be directed toward remedying the rigidity in the dependency pattern. The dependency pattern may be allowed to function in the therapy situation. After it has been established in detail, and not before, an attempt is made to incorporate new experiences into the system. As in other types of mental disturbances, therapy may attempt to handle the patient's conceptual rigidity by *loosening* techniques such as physical relaxation, phantasy verbalization, discussion of dreams, use of ambiguous stimuli, etc. The loosening techniques should be directed primarily toward the dependency structure in the patient's self-conceived role. As loosening takes place the therapist may use *dilating* techniques, especially with respect to physiological material.

Session VIII, November 28, 1949

Paranoia

Like hysteria, paranoia is a way of maintaining oneself in a role. Unlike hysteria, paranoia is not limited to the dependency facets of one's role. From the standpoint of this theory of personality the two disorders have much in common, a fact that may have usefulness in developing adequate treatment procedures for paranoia.

Paranoia develops when one's concept of his role is threatened by the everyday interpersonal events of his life. The person's anticipations of what he and others will do in a social relationship do not work out. Contradictory evidence piles up while the person doggedly refuses to modify his conceptualization of his role in such a manner as to contain the new perceptions. For a time he may suspend some of the contradictory ideas. But perceptions of social events are not all as easily ignored as sex impulses or perceptions which threaten only the dependency facets of one's role. When finally the incompatibility between role and manifest social events becomes intolerable the person is faced with the loss of the major portion of his role structure. The *threat,* specifically *guilt* in this connection, may be handled by the paranoid construction.

By placing a paranoid construction upon the threatening events the person reconstrues them as making sense within an inimical scheme being carried out by others. By this device he at once saves his old conceptualization of his role, brings the hitherto incompatible events into a compatible construction system, and saves himself from the awful feeling of guilt.

Once having employed this paranoid adjustment technique the person is likely to find that he has only this one way of adding on to his system. His interpersonal relationships continue to yield new data which must be construed. The plots against him must be intricate indeed to contain all that needs explaining. New perceptions must quickly be brought within the control of some external system which is compatible with his concept of his role. The person finds it necessary to be intellectually alert, especially as regards human relations, if he is to continue using the paranoid manner of adjustment to maintain his role. His perceptual field tends to dilate.

The person may find that the paranoid construction of interpersonal experience may invite certain additions and elaborations of his concept of his role. He does not destroy his old constructions in making these changes, rather he adds to them, making himself historically or politically important in a manner worthy of the plot in which he is the central figure.

This theoretical interpretation of paranoia suggests a form of psychotherapy. It suggests that the therapist reactivate some of the patient's early dependency patterns so as to enable him to maintain his role at an early childlike level without the threat that arises out of mis-prediction of interpersonal social reactions. The patient should be surrounded with social expectancies that call for his behaving like a person with hysterical tendencies. The treatment probably should be intramural with the patient made as dependent as possible upon two or three staff members to whom he would have to turn for every little need and from whom he would receive indulgent care. Shock, illness, and other dependency producing events may help, provided there are persons upon whom the patient may develop his feeling of dependence. When a dependency role is established the therapist may proceed cautiously with loosening techniques as with hysteria but with a minimum of dilation of the perceptual field. Any tendency toward recurrence of the paranoid construction should be met immediately with dependency producing treatment and constriction of the perceptual field.

Session IX, December 5, 1949

Manic and Depressive Solutions

The manic and depressive approaches to structure do not necessarily exclude the use of the specific solutions of hysteria and paranoia. The patient's difficulty is in establishing a core structure of his role as distinct from peripheral structures. Both the manic and the depressive patient tend to try to incorporate too much in their core structures. Each new event then becomes something involving their whole personalities, not merely something to be incorporated in a peripheral or partly detached structure.

The patient with this type of unstable over-extended conception of his core-role tends to over-identify himself with the events in his perceptual field. In his so-called manic state he makes everybody's business his own, he adapts his own role to nearly everything falling within his perceptual field and he tends to judge the behavior of others as if it were his own. In the so-called depressive state he is aware of his failure to incorporate his whole world into his role and the threat to his role is experienced, as always, in the form of guilt. He has no stable core which remains intact in the face of the unstructured events with which he sees himself surrounded. Somehow the events have swept him and his role up and carry him along. He yields to passivity or perhaps attempts to stem the tide by a final stroke of self-destruction.

If we use this theoretical construction of the manic depressive disturbance the following hypotheses as to therapy might be formulated.

Hypothesis 1: Therapy will tend to be effective when it is directed toward developing for the patient a limited but adequate conception of his role. The new conception should be sufficiently comprehensive to contain the expectancies of maturity and sex-identification with which his society will surround him. A temporary dependency or hospital citizen role would not suffice, except possibly to narrow his perceptual field or to restore his physical energy for the "great encirclement."

Hypothesis 2: Therapy will tend to be effective when it is directed toward isolating certain perceived events and containing them wholly within the patient's peripheral structures. Hospital routine, discipline, fixed regularities in which the patient has no responsibility or freedom of choice may come to be seen within these peripheral conceptual structures.

Session X, December 12, 1949

Aggression

In the presence of threat, as we have said before, one can ignore or reconstrue the threatening events in a compatible manner or, if he can reorganize his comprehensive system so as to contain them, he may incorporate them in a non-threatening relationship. Each of these courses of mental process may involve behavior which one's fellows may interpret as aggressive because it constitutes threat to their own comprehensive structures.

If the threat is handled by an attempt to ignore the events of which it is comprised, the person is construed by others as "resistive."

If the threat is handled by an attempt to reconstrue the events in a manner compatible with one's own comprehensive structure others may see themselves as unwillingly subordinated.

If the threat is handled by an attempt to reorganize one's comprehensive system so as contain the threatening events in a new non-threatening relationship, there is the possibility that others may find themselves involved to an unwanted degree.

The behavior which is most commonly described by one's fellows as aggressive is that which takes place in the second instance. If the reconstruction threatens the comprehensive system of the other person, it is likely to be called by him "aggression." It is important to recognize that this "aggression" is, for the subject himself, likely to be a hoped-for alternative for guilt. If the threat to the basic role looms large, the guilt becomes awful, and reconstructions of other people and their roles may become high-handed and threatening to them.

Obsessive-Compulsive Adjustments

The obsessive-compulsive adjustment is one that takes place in many types of situations and is, in itself, not necessarily pathological. Like most of the other reactions described above it is a way of handling new experience. As new experiences begin to pile up without being structured within existing systems, they approach threatening proportions. If one attempts to handle them solely by giving them their own independent structures, he may soon clutter his attic with psychological knick-knacks which bear no functional relation to his life.

The possible new implications of recent experiences may, in some cases, demand more serious attention. They may mount to the proportions of threats. The role may be threatened. Guilt as well as anxiety may be experienced.

If the person can make no fundamental adjustments and finds himself frantically structuring new experiences into unrelated miscellaneous systems, he is exhibiting obsessive-compulsive reactions. Little rituals for containing guilt, what-not shelves for various social graces, neatly indexed ideas at low levels of abstraction, a tendency to hold experience off at arm's length from one's self by giving it its own independent interpretation; these are the mechanisms of obsession and compulsion. Fragments of words, a phrase of song, an act here, another one there, the obsessive-compulsive person has his hands full.

Schizophrenic Thinking

Kraepelin was not too far off when he characterized this process as a kind of dementia. Basically schizophrenia may be conceived as the breakdown of conceptualization. Because the experiential content of the schizophrenic's perceptual field includes much that may once have been fairly well structured and his verbal symbols correspond to high level socially communicable ideas, he appears quite different from the feeble-minded person whose conceptualization also is loose. Most characteristically schizoid thinking is thinking which is conceptually loose but containing residuals of earlier and higher order concepts. Schizophrenia as a concept itself, therefore, should not be considered as of the same order as the concept of manic-depressive psychosis or hysteria. Schizoid thinking, i.e., marked loosening of conceptualization, may occur with any of the disorders previously discussed or by itself.

Viewed in this fashion we may consider that schizoid thinking takes place, on occasion, in almost anyone; that it is characteristic of transitional stages in one's mental development, that it is even characteristic of the transitional stages in solving an ordinary problem, and that it must appear to some degree in any readjustment. The loosening of association, the uncritical reporting of thoughts, and the general structure of psychoanalytic therapy calls for the patient to indulge in schizoid thinking as far as he is capable, though the alert therapist will try to keep the situation in hand.

Schizoid thinking has sufficient pliancy to make so-called creative thinking possible in some instances. Since the development of new concepts requires some loosening of the old, creative thinkers must go through a schizoid stage in formulating their ideas. If one's thinking remains schizoid all of the time he will never be able to develop a new concept with sufficient clarity to communicate it and devise it to the cultural inheritance. If, out of schizoid looseness, one may formulate vague new structure which may then be tightened up, he may achieve creativeness.

Paranoid Schizophrenia

When paranoia is shot through with schizoid thinking, the delusional conceptualization is necessarily loosened. The guilt features of paranoia are likely to be observable, but the patient's handling of them is likely to be loose. The conditions immediately preceding the onset of the disorder may suggest the threat to role although a long-standing tendency to looseness in thinking is likely to be evident.

Simple Schizophrenia

When the role is constricted so that threat and guilt do not touch it, the person may achieve a kind of long-term adjustment on a very simple level. Conceptualization may be loose but the experiential elements structured within the person's role are so limited that he is able to handle them within a very simple, concretistic, but conceptually adequate structure.

Catatonic Schizophrenia

A person whose loose conceptualization is unacceptable to him may try to "suspend operations" as if to try to catch up. Like the stock market on Roosevelt's bank holiday, when things start falling apart too badly the person attempts to hold off the flood of new experience until he can structure what he has at hand. His "freezing" of the flow of mental process is exhibited physiologically.

Somatic Complaints Associated with Schizoid Thinking

In many conceptual disorders the person may salvage some of the structure of his role by falling back upon its dependency substructures. If he can hold this last line of defense there is a possibility that some of the lost ground can later be regained. In other cases even this last claim to integrity is quickly over-run and the patient is swallowed up in conceptual chaos.

Resume of Psychopathological Adjustments

Let us suppose a person is confronted with threat.

1 If he suspends the ideas that he cannot handle and retreats into a dependency role he is adjusting by *hysteria*.
2 If he lumps the ideas that he cannot handle into a neatly structured plot against his role he is adjusting by *paranoia*.
3 If he tries to incorporate all new experience immediately into the present structure of his role he is adjusting as a *manic*. When he stops for a major overhaul of his role with its attendant feeling of guilt he is adjusting as a *depressive*.
4 If he runs around putting the ideas he cannot handle into neat but separate piles so that they will not get into his way in playing his role, he is adjusting as an *obsessive-compulsive*.
5 If he loosens his concepts so as vaguely to contain new experiences he is engaging in *schizoid thinking*.
6 If he vacillates between whole role patterns as events change, he is adjusting as a *psychopath*.
7 If in the face of ideas he cannot handle he withdraws into a simple role and beats out a little daily path he is adjusting by *simple schizophrenia*.
8 If he tries to freeze the flow of all mental process he is adjusting by *catatonia*.
9 If he is merely anxious in the face of threat and has not adopted any adjustment yet, he may be described as in an *anxiety state*.

60

Problems of Mental Health[1]

Each of us lives and moves in a world of expectancies. In part, this world is made up of what others expect of us and, in part, it is made up of what we expect of ourselves. The way in which we conform or seek compromises within this expectancy system, constitutes our life role. To the extent that one can work out his role in a manner that is reasonably consistent with new and old expectancies, he enjoys mental health. To the extent that the individual is assisted in this task by having consistent demands made upon him by society, he may be said to be supported by the spiritual and moral foundations of that society.

It goes without saying that the basic consistency of expectation which constitutes the spiritual and moral foundations of our society, must take into account long-range as well as short-range objectives. The demands of society must also be consistent both in respect to traditional needs and with respect to new and evolving needs. In other words, what is required is not only a static consistency in what society expects of its members, but also a dynamic consistency of what society comes to expect of its members in each succeeding decade.

The achievement of a clearly defined life role, satisfying both the changing expectancies of society and the emerging conceptualizations of oneself, is not always easy. One may be faced with contradictory expectations. For example, in our society the expectancies are such that you cannot have a wife and enjoy the affection and mutual support that go with a marital relationship, unless you can also bear the financial responsibility of maintaining a household and supporting children. Thus society's expectations regarding marital economy, and the individual's expectations regarding tender relationships, appear to be irreconcilable.

There are other irreconcilables which appear to be less a function of the times and more a function of natural law. For example, it is extremely difficult for a man to establish an adequate husband and wife relationship with two women at the same time.

Then there are those contradictions in our expectancy systems which can be resolved if we look more deeply into society's demands, or if we explore more thoughtfully the possibilities of our own life role. It is with these contradictions that I should like to deal this morning, citing three cases of people who faced this kind of contradiction.

The first case is that of a teacher of English in a high school in a small town. A group of us had been invited to hold a psychological clinic under the auspices of the school, in an attempt to help the staff formulate the psychological problems of pupils in such a way that they might handle them more effectively and happily. After the final conference, this teacher approached me and asked if she might discuss with me, personally, some of her own mental hygiene problems. In that conference she spoke quite frankly. She said, "Some of the problems that our youngsters are having are my fault, and I have a feeling that you know it as well as I do. You should have blamed me more than you did. I know that I am not a good teacher, but I hate teaching. I used to think that I might 'get by' teaching English because I had enjoyed that subject when I was in high school, but now I hate it. I hate the students, and they cordially hate me. They certainly have no interest in what I have to say and, frankly, I do not see any reason why they should. I hate the students, and I hate myself for hating them."

Then she went on to tell me more about her background. She said that she was the sole source of support for her parents who were aging and ill. She had found it necessary to give up much of what she had wanted in life in order to earn support for them. Teaching was the only kind of a job that she felt she could get. She ended up by saying, "The way I have it figured, I can last out perhaps through another year, but at the end of that time, I am certain that I will have a nervous breakdown."

The difficulties this teacher faced in working out her life role in such a manner as to conform adequately to all of the expectancies with which she saw herself surrounded, seemed to me to be typical of the difficulties which many young adults must face. This young woman faced problems of mental ill health for which the moral and spiritual foundations of American culture did not present a ready solution. The speakers who follow me will have something to say regarding this type of problem. While it is not essential for

[1] Address to *College of Education conference in celebration of the 75th Anniversary of the Ohio State University, 1950.* Published in *Role of education in American life: A College of Education conference in celebration of the 75th anniversary of the Ohio State University*, University Hall Chapel (pp. 84–91). Columbus, OH: College of Education, Ohio State University. Republished by permission of Jacqueline Aldridge.

Collected Papers of the Pioneer of Constructivist Psychology: George A. Kelly, First Edition. Edited by David A. Winter and Nick Reed.

our discussion this morning to say what the outcome of this particular case was, it would not be inappropriate to say that a year later this teacher was described as one of the most effective and enthusiastic teachers in the school. The change appeared to come about largely through the intelligent and well-planned efforts of one of her colleagues which helped her reconceptualize her social role.

Let us consider a second case involving the moral and spiritual foundations of American culture, and indicating a particular mental health problem. This is the case of a woman of forty-five. Her children were grown, had married, and had gone out into the community. Her husband's work required him to travel a good deal and to be away from home one or two nights a week. She had been a good mother in the sense that she had devoted her life to her children and their comfort, and now she attempted to fill her hours by doing the housework. She did not have many friends, and it had never been easy for her to make friends. She was friendly but not socially aggressive. She had had a reasonably good education which had prepared her for that phase of life which had just drawn to a close, but which for some reason or other had not prepared her for the phase of life into which she was now entering.

This woman came to an educational institution for the solution of her problems, and it was largely through the facilities of the fine arts department of that institution that she was able eventually to work out a happy solution. I have not told you what the problems were. During the long hours in the empty house, she began to find herself having fantasies. At first they were harmless little fantasies of conversations with friends and little domestic adventures. Soon she began to have fantasies that were more elaborate, and which seemed to her to violate her own expectancies for herself. As her social role began to deteriorate, she also began to have feelings of guilt regarding her fantasies. Yet her fantasies continued. There were fantasies of having a young man come to her house to make love to her. There were fantasies of being a wicked woman and of being pointed out as being a wicked woman in the community.

Realizing something was wrong, she asked for help and said, "What is the matter with me?" At this point one might make a diagnosis of her case and say to her, "Here is the explanation. You have some hormones, and at your age certain things begin to happen. What you need to do is to get out of the house more, to have more friends, to take part more in social activities, etc." Giving a person that kind of advice is about on the same level as telling an anxiety-ridden person that he should "stop worrying."

Since, in this case, it was a teacher of the fine arts, using what was probably the basic approach of the fine arts, who helped the woman to eventual recovery, we will all be particularly interested to hear what, in general, is the contribution of the arts to the strengthening of the moral and spiritual foundations of American culture.

The third case is that of a young man in a university. There are so many cases like this one that I am not going to describe a particular person, but rather a composite person. He is having a great deal of difficulty with his subjects. On the entrance tests, administered by the university, he has made a very low score. The machinery of the university eventually catches up with him and refers him for "guidance." In the guidance laboratory he is given more tests and finally undergoes an interview that runs about like this. "Young man. College is not easy. It requires the kind of skill that we call academic. Not all people are gifted in this particular way, and unless one finds that he has a great deal of talent for book learning, he should plan his career so as to take advantage of other types of talents which are just as respectable and which, ultimately, are just as capable of satisfying a person's vocational aspirations. Now, take your case. What have you considered doing besides going into college?"

"Nothing," says the student.

"Well, now, take mechanics for example. You would probably be very good as a mechanic."

"I don't want to be a mechanic," says the student to the counselor. I want to go to college. This is where I want to be. These are the kind of people I want to associate with. Here are the kind of ideas I want to hear about."

"But," says the counselor, "look at your grades."

"Oh, my grades—they are not so hot, are they? I think I'd like to be a teacher," he says, "because teachers deal with the sort of things that you people in college are dealing with, don't they?"

"Well, yes," says the counselor, "but now this matter of academic aptitude—you remember I said that there were all kinds of aptitudes. Some of us have the aptitude to work with our hands, and that is a wonderful thing. You can create beautiful things with your hands—plumbing and automobiles, for example. Now take this book stuff that you have been trying to do at the university, you don't really want to do book stuff, do you?"

"But I do want to do book things. I mean, while I can't read the books very well, and I can't get much out of them, books are the things I want to talk about. These are the ideas that I am interested in."

"Well," says the counselor, "all right, I guess you'll just have to try it for another quarter."

Another quarter goes by, the grades come back—"B" in mathematics, "F" in everything else.

Another interview. "Well, Mr. Jones, we talked about this thing last quarter. Now, it's hard on people to fail all the time. You don't want to go through life failing all the time, and, obviously, you must not be interested in that English course and that history course, etc. I'm not blaming you for failing."

"What about my 'B' in math?"

"That does look pretty good, but of course the test shows that it's mechanical things you must be interested in, because obviously you're not interested in academic things."

"But," he says, "I'm not dumb, or I couldn't have made a 'B' in mathematics."

"Well, of course, grades in one course, a large class, papers get mixed."

"Look, I'm going to go to school next quarter."

"All right, all right, go ahead next quarter."

Soon the student has coasted through two years of college with "D" grades, and an occasional "B" in certain subjects. He is still insisting that he is interested in the things that are talked about in the courses in which he gets low grades. Finally, it is decided that the trouble is that the student needs special training in silent reading, so he is put through a course in remedial reading. He does a little better work in his subjects, but all in all, there is very little improvement. In the meantime, the student has decided that he wishes to take graduate work. The counselor is horrified.

"Now look, you simply can't do that. That simply isn't being done. Graduate schools are crowded—only the best get in. You haven't a chance of being admitted."

But the student insists and then one fine day he comes in and says, "Look, Doc, I guess I haven't been very fair with you. I've studied all right, and I've tried, and I've told you the truth when I've told you that these are the things that I was interested in, but I've been hearing about things in these courses that make me think perhaps my problem is much broader than I thought it was. Maybe part of it is personal. Let me tell you about it,

"I've been engaged to a girl for several years. My parents are orthodox Jewish, and the girl is a Gentile. My mother, whom I would not offend for the world—I simply couldn't bear to offend her—wants me to make something of myself. Well, I want to make something of myself and marry the girl too. Things are a mess. I guess I've been feeling that if I could show my mother that I could make something of myself, perhaps she'd eventually let me marry the girl. I guess I think about all of this an awful lot. Sometimes it gets me mixed up when I am studying, although when I get interested in mathematics, sometimes I can forget about it. I just can't find the answer. I guess there isn't any answer, is there?"

This young man is caught up in a conflicting set of expectancy systems in which he can see nothing but irreconcilables. His spiritual resources were being taxed to the limit, and he has been unable so far to develop any clear-cut concept of his life role.

These three cases appear to me to be ones which involve mental health problems and, at the same time, to have implications for spiritual and moral foundations of American culture. I do not know whether the speakers who will follow will want to deal with these cases specifically, or to point out general approaches in solving the problems of all people who are caught up in personal and social conflict.

61

The Problem of Clinical Psychology[1]

The Basic Question

Shall we continue to turn away ninety per cent of the qualified graduate students who seek training in clinical psychology?

Over four hundred qualified people who sought graduate training in psychology were turned away this fall.

Over two hundred of them were seeking graduate training in clinical psychology.

Table 1 Applicants for Admission to Graduate Training in Psychology at Ohio State University in the Fall of 1950 (Tally as of Sept. 15, 1950)

1	Entrance Board tally of requests for consideration:	726
2	Entrance Board tally of those persisting in their applications after a letter was sent which was designed to discourage applicants and reduce their number:	443
3	"Persistent applicants" judged to be qualified and invited to submit detailed applications:	310
4	Inferred number of original "requestors" who were qualified: (Item 3 divided by Item 2 multiplied by Item 1.)	508
5	Personnel Committee tally of detailed application forms submitted after invitations were sent to selected persistent applications:	191
6	Total invited detailed applications in all major areas of the Department: (Five people applied in two areas each.)	196
7	Total accepted for graduate training in psychology:	77
8	Inferred qualified requestors and acceptances by major areas of the Department: (Entries in Column 2 are obtained by dividing the entries in Column 3 by Item 6 and multiplying by Item 4.)	

1. Area of Psychology	2. Qualified Requestors	3. Accepted	4. Per Cent
Academic Personnel	52	14	27
Clinical	223	20	9
Educational	65	16	25
General	106	15	14
Industrial	44	7	16
Statistics	18	5	28
Overall	508	77	15

What are the Alternatives?

Plan One. Maintenance of the graduate training program in clinical psychology at the present capacity only.

16 admissions per year
51 in all phases of training
9 Ph.D. completions per year

[1] Dated 1950. Published by permission of Jacqueline Aldridge.

Collected Papers of the Pioneer of Constructivist Psychology: George A. Kelly, First Edition. Edited by David A. Winter and Nick Reed.

Plan Two. Limited expansion.

28 admissions per year
91 in all phases of training
15 Ph.D. completions per year

Plan Three. Retrenchment to adjust to diminishing staff resources.

11 admissions per year
30 in all phases of training
6 Ph.D. completions per year

What does Plan One, Maintenance, Involve?

This plan involves the employment of two assistant professors in new positions, one to be placed on duty January 1, 1951, to meet the emergency occasioned by the loss of Dr. Courtney's services, and the other to be placed on duty October 1, 1951, to meet the minimum needs of graduate students majoring in other areas of the Department.

In the fall of 1948, Clinical Psychology lost one full time teaching position under a blanket University rule that prohibited the replacement of teaching staff at the instructor level. This rule was promulgated in the belief that the shifting balance enrollment to the junior and senior years would decrease the need for teaching staff at the instructor level. Ironically, the instructor we lost was not serving at the underclass level, nor even at the upper-class level, he was almost exclusively involved in graduate instruction!

During the past two years, Dr. Courtney has come to share a large portion of the burden of graduate training, although his salary was paid from funds earmarked for field services in the Bureau of Special and Adult Education. His resignation, effective Nov. 1, 1950, leaves an already overloaded training program in an untenable position.

For the past four years, we have attempted to meet the most urgent demands for clinical training with stop-gap measures which are not ultimately defensible. Graduate student fees have been used to employ assistant instructors, themselves graduate students.

They were assigned to teach graduate courses exclusively, mostly in the basic sequence! During the past year, eight of the twenty-two basic 800-level laboratories and practicums were taught, not by fully qualified professors as they should be but by other graduate students! Both of the two 600-level laboratory sections offered were taught by graduate students. Even third year graduate students are being taught by other graduate students who receive such overall supervision as senior staff members are able to provide.

What does Plan Two, Limited Expansion, Involve?

One assistant professor employed immediately and five others placed on duty October 1, 1951.

This plan would place the training program in a defensible position and permit gradual expansion over a four-year period to increase our training capacity by 80%. It would bring the selection ratio for clinical psychology majors up to 13%, a figure which would still be the most rigorous in the Department.

What does Plan Three, Retrenchment, Involve?

A realistic retrenchment to reduce the program to a size commensurate with the training resources the University provides.

An immediate attempt would be made to reduce the number of graduate majors on a voluntary basis by 40% in order to leave the staff in a position to train the remainder of the students adequately and to take care of a considerable proportion of students already majoring in other areas. If this fails it will be necessary to exclude from the basic clinical course sequence approximately 50% of the applicants who are majoring in other areas of the Department and 100% of graduate students from outside the Department.

In any case admissions must be dropped to 5 per year for two years and then allowed to mount gradually to a maximum of 11 per year.

How Many Students would be Admitted and Trained Under Each of the Three Plans?

Table 2 Selection and Training Under Alternative Plans

Plan One: Maintenance Only (Eventual Output 9 Ph.D.'s Per Year)

		1950–1	*1951–2*	*1952–3*	*1953–4*	*1954–5*	*1955–6*
1	Selection Ratio	9%*	6%	7%	7%	7%	7%
2	1st Yr. Grad. Majors	15	14	15	16	16	16
3	2nd Yr. Grad. Majors	17	12	11	12	13	13
4	3rd Yr. Grad. Majors	7	14	10	9	10	11
5	4th Yr. Grad. Majors	13	6	13	9	9	9
6	5th Yr. Grad. Majors (carried over)	9	8	3	3	2	2
7	Total	61	54	52	49	50	51
8	Ph.D. Completions	13	11	12	9	8	8
9	Discontinuations	8	6	7	6	7	7
10	Senior Training Staff	5	6	6	6	6	6
11	Senior Service Staff	1	1	1	1	1	1

* Nineteen new graduate students actually enrolled, including four 2nd Yr. students.

Plan Two: Limited Expansion (Eventual Output 15 Ph.D's. per year)

		1950–1	*1951–2*	*1952–3*	*1953–4*	*1954–5*	*1955–6*
1	Selection Ratio	9%	13%	13%	13%	13%	13%
2	1st Yr. Grad. Majors	15	28	28	28	28	28
3	2nd Yr. Grad. Majors	17	12	23	23	23	23
4	3rd Yr. Grad. Majors	7	14	10	19	19	19
5	4th Yr. Grad. Majors	13	6	13	9	17	17
6	5th Yr. Grad. Majors (carried over)	9	8	3	3	2	4
7	Total	61	68	77	82	89	91
8	Ph.D. Completions	13	11	12	9	13	15
9	Discontinuations	8	8	11	12	13	13
10	Senior Training Staff	5	10	10	10	10	10
11	Senior Service Staff	1	1	1	1	1	1

Plan Three: Retrenchment (Eventual Output 6 Ph.D's. per year)

		1950–1	*1951–2*	*1952–3*	*1953–4*	*1954–5*	*1955–6*
1	Selection Ratio	9%	2%	2%	4%	5%	5%
2	1st Yr. Grad. Majors	15	5	5	8	11	11
3	2nd Yr. Grad. Majors	17	12	4	4	6	9
4	3rd Yr. Grad. Majors	7	14	10	3	3	5
5	4th Yr. Grad. Majors	13	6	13	9	3	3
6	5th Yr. Grad. Majors (carried over)	9	8	3	3	2	1
6a	Involuntary Carry-overs	–	3	4	6	5	0
7	Total	61	48	39	33	30	29
8	Ph.D. Completions	10*	10	10	10	9	3
9	Discontinuations	8	4	4	4	3	5
10	Senior Training Staff	4	4	4	4	4	4
11	Senior Service Staff	1	1	1	1	1	1

Comparison with Selection Ratio in College of Medicine

While the data are not precisely comparable some rough comparisons can be drawn between the psychology selection ratios and the current ratio in the College of Medicine. The 1950 beginning class of 150 medical students was selected from approximately 600 applicants who subjected themselves to the complete screening process. This may be compared to the 77 new graduate students in psychology who were selected from 191 who were permitted to go through the complete screening process and who did so. It should be pointed out, however, that these 191 were pre-selected on the basis of a preliminary screen and had been discouraged from pursuing their applications beyond the inquiry stage.

Selection Ratios Compared with College of Medicine

				Ratio	
	Initial Qualified Applicants	*Final Qualified Applicants*	*Selected*	*Initial*	*Final*
College of Medicine (1950)	–	600 (app.)	150	–	25%
Psychology (1950)	508	191	77	15%	40%
Clinical Psychology (1950)	223	86	20	9%	23%

How Would the Clinical Training Staff be Employed Under Each of the Three Plans?

Table 3 Employment of Training Staff

Under Alternative Plans (9 Months Basis)

Plan One: *Maintenance at present level only*. (Add 2 Ass't. Profs. "E-F")

Prof.	A	B	C	D	(E)	(F)	Ass't. Instr.	Totals
Undergraduate Course Sections	1	-	-	-	-	3	-	4
Special Interest Course Sections	3	1	-	1	4	-	-	9
Basic Courses (Lecture)	1	2	2	2	-	1	-	8
Basic Courses (Lab)	2	1	5	3	4	6	5	26
Seminars	1	1	1	1	-	-	-	4
Field Courses	-	3	-	-	-	-	-	3
Research Advisees	8	9	9	9	8	8	-	51
Introductory Research Colloquy	-	2	-	-	-	-	-	2

Plan Two: *Limited Expansion* (Add 6 Ass't. Profs. "E- J")

Prof.	A	B	C	D	(E)	(F)	(G)	(H)	(I)	(J)	Asst. Instr.	Tots.	Additions
Undergraduate Course Sec.	1	-	-	-	-	3	-	-	-	-	-	4	0
Special Interest Course Sec.	1	-	-	-	3	-	2	2	1	1	-	10	1
Basic Course (Lecture)	1	2	2	2	1	2	1	2	1	1	-	15	7
Basic Courses (Lab.)	2	1	2	1	3	3	6	5	6	6	5	40	14
Seminars	1	1	2	2	1	-	-	-	-	-	-	7	3
Field Courses	-	3	-	-	-	-	-	-	-	-	-	3	0
Research Advisees	10	10	10	10	9	9	9	8	8	8	-	91	40
Introd. Research Coll.	-	2	-	2	-	-	-	-	-	-	-	4	2

Plan Three: *Retrenchment* (No new staff)

Prof.	A	B	C	D	Asst. Instr.	Total	Reductions
Undergraduate Course Sections	1	-	-	-	-	1	-3
Special Interest Course Sections	3	1	-	1	-	5	-4
Basic Courses (Lecture)	1	2	3	2	-	8	0
Basic Courses (Lab.)	2	1	6	3	5	17	-9
Seminars	1	1	1	1	-	4	0
Field Courses	-	3	-	-	-	3	0
Research Advisees	7	8	8	8	-	30	-20
Introd. Research Coll.	-	2	-	-	-	2	0

What Staff Resources Have Been Used During the Past Year for Training?

During the academic year, 1949–50, three professors and one associate professor were used full time in the training program.

One of them carried administrative duties.
One associate professor was used part-time.
One associate professor, who has for a number of years been committed to mental hygiene services, was not free to contribute substantially to the training program.
In addition, two assistant instructors (students) were used full-time and one part-time.
One lecturer was employed one quarter to teach a practicum section.

Table 4 Summary of Formal Teaching of Training Staff in 1949–50

	Level	*Total Credits*	*Number Sectn's*	*Total Enroll*	*Aver. Enroll.*	*Ideal Aver. Enroll.*
Undergraduate	Undergrad.	3	1	85	85	30
Special Interest (incl. lab)	Mostly Grad.	37	13	690	53	30
Basic Courses (Lecture)	All Grad.	23	7	151	25	18
Basic Courses (Lab)	All Grad.	41	22	159	7	6
Seminars	All Grad.	8	4	44	11	10
Field Courses	All Grad.	16 av.	4	50	12	12
Research	All Grad.	Varies	indiv.	134	–	–
Research Teams	All Grad.	–	15	149	10	6
Intro. Res. Colloquy	All Grad.	–	2	24	12	12

Where Does the Burden of Training Principally Fall?

In two places: (a) advanced practicum training in handling complex psychological problems of an intimate nature and (b) research.

Instruction and close supervision in advanced practicums simply cannot be watered down. The implications of slip-shod work may be fully as catastrophic for clients as they are for fourth year graduate students.

Research in the field of personality imposes peculiar difficulties for the student in making theoretical inferences and in the formulation of experimental designs. The beginning graduate student must have continued instruction and contact with research issues in clinical psychology if he is to be prepared for a scientific career in the field.

All graduate students in clinical psychology are kept active in research as members of research teams. The research team is the focal point of the training program both for students and for professors.

All present research teams are considered to be excessively large.

Table 5 Summary of Research Advisees (Teams) (Fall 1950)

		Number in Team	*Ideal*
Professor	A*	9	6
	B	11	6
	C	13	6
	D	13	6
	E	13	6
	F**	5	6
Unassigned		1	–
	Total	65	36

* Resigning as of November 1, 1950. Replacement requires *new* position.

** Emergency load now borne by service professor. Should be transferred to a training professor as soon as possible.

Table 6 Psychological Clinic Teams

Fall Quarter 1950

Team	*Name*	*Status*	*Stipend*	*Year*
Courtney	1. Castaneda, A.	reg.	USPH - 2	2
	2. Chance, J.	reg.	USPH - 3	3
	3. Fitzgerald, B.	reg.	VA - 2	2
	4. Hamilton, J.	reg.	Teach. Asst.	3
	5. Lyle, W.	reg.	VA - 2	2
	6. Rafferty, J.	reg.	Teach. Asst.	4
	7. Soklefald, B.	reg.	Asst. (910)	2
	8. Rohrer, J.	prov.	-	4
	9. Tyler, B.	prov.	Grad. Asst.	2
Durea	1. Albrecht, R.	reg.	VA - 4	4
	2. Cravens, R.	reg.	Grad. Asst.	2
	3. Gottwald, S.	reg.	On leave	4
	4. Goodrich, E.	prov.	VA - 2	2
	5. Brown, B.	prov.	Teach. Asst	2
	6. Levy, L.	prov.	VA - 1	1
	7. Rosenberg, M.	prov.	Grad. Asst.	1
	8. Worell, Mrs.	prov.	Grad. Asst.	1
	9. Baker, C.	prov.	VA - 1	1
	10. Vickers, E.	prov.	-	1
	11. Neems, R.	prov.	VA - 1	1
Kelly (with M. Mathews)	1. Bixler, R.	reg.	U. Louisville	4
	2. Boesel, F.	reg.	Toledo Schools	4
	3. Burton, J.	reg.	Asst. (PH)	2
	4. Hilgeman, L.	reg.	Merrill-Palmer	4
	5. Hunt, D.	reg.	USPH - 2	2
	6. Landfield, A.	reg.	Intern	4
	7. McGaughran, L.	reg.	Univ. Tenn.	4
	8. Poch, S.	reg.	Teach. Asst.	4
	9. Trapp, P.	reg.	Intern	4
	10. Howard, A.	prov.	VA - 4	4
	11. Jones, R.	prov.	USPH - 1	1
	12. Dorn, D.	prov.	VA - 1	1
	13. Bieri, J.	prov.	VA - 1	1
McCandless (with J. Lacey)	1. Baker, G.	reg.	Milwaukee G. W. Ind.	4
	2. Bardwell, A.	reg.	Intern	3
	3. Blyth, D.	reg.	Col. VA Clinic	4
	4. Dean, S.	reg.	VA - 3	3
	5. Kalhorn, J.	reg.	Fels Inst.	4
	6. Mahrer, A.	reg.	VA - 2	2
	7. Masling, J.	reg.	Teach. Asst.	4
	8. Rosenblum, S.	reg.	VA - 2	2
	9. Tyler, F.	reg.	Teach. Asst.	3
	10. Lasko, A.	prov.	VA - 3	3
	11. Strange, P.	prov.	VA - 2	2
	12. Rhodes, W.	prov.	Georgia P. H.	2
	13. Fager, R.	prov.	Asst. (PH)	2
Rotter	1. Abou-Ghorra, I.	reg.	Egypt. Gov.	3
	2. Dunlap, R.	reg.	USPH - 2	2
	3. Good, R.	reg.	Asst. Instr. (PH)	4
	4. Jessor, L.	reg.	Asst. Instr.	4
	5. Jessor, R.	reg.	SSRC Fellow	4
	6. Leef, C.	reg.	Boston U.	4
	7. Lotsof, E.	reg.	Teach. Asst.	4
	8. Rockwell, A.	reg.	Child. M.H. Cent.	4
	9. Bowen, W.	prov.	VA - 4	4

Table 6 (Continued)

Fall Quarter 1950				
Team	*Name*	*Status*	*Stipend*	*Year*
	10. Collet, G.	prov.	Harding San.	3
	11. Grandison, F.	prov.	Asst. (PH)	1
	12. Rosenthal, K.	prov.	VA - 2	2
	13. Maher, B.	prov.	-	1
Stogdill	1. Hirshenhart, A.	prov.	-	1
	2. Worell, L.	prov.	VA - 1	1
	3. Lundy, R.	prov.	VA - 1	1
	4. Cromwell, R.	prov.	VA - 1	1
	5. Joyce, J.	prov.	VA - 1	1
Unassigned	1. Heilman, A.	-	Ill. C.P. Hosp.	4
In VA Program with Speech Major	1. Carlton, R.	-	VA - 3	3

Assistants	1. Cravens, R.	Grad. Asst.	Assisting Durea
	2.	Grad. Asst.	Assisting Stogdill
	3. Burton, J.	Asst. (PH)	Assisting Kelly
	4. Grandison, F.	Asst. (PH)	Assisting Rotter
	5. Fager, R.	Asst. (910)	Assisting McCandless
	6. Soklefald, B.	Asst. (910)	Assisting Courtney

Is the Training Staff Able to Meet Demands other than those for the Training of Clinical Psychology Majors?

No. The demand for clinical training which has become so accentuated during the post-war years is reflected in the psychology graduate group as a whole. A survey made last year indicated that rate of flow through the basic clinical graduate course sequence would have to be stepped up from 24 to 59 per year if all students who wanted admission to these courses were served. In addition there appeared to be a backlog of 67 graduate students.

Will any of the Three Alternative Plans Allow for an Increase in Clinical Services?

With the exception of Dr. Stogdill's services which have become established over a period of more than 20 years, the clinic group has long since abandoned any services to the University or to the community which are not absolutely essential to training. This decision was made reluctantly and solely because it was believed that, under present conditions, long-term social needs would be best met if training were given priority.

Even the plan for expansion does not envision any increase in services, except that which would be incidental to an enlarged training program.

Is the Space Now Used by the Clinical Training Program Adequate for an Expanded Training Program?

No. It is approximately a third of that required for an adequate program of the present size.

What Would it Take to Provide Graduate Training for all Qualified Applicants as Most of the Other Departments of the University are Able to Do?

It would take a major outlay of funds which the University Administration would probably not have the audacity to advocate.

How Many of the Students in Clinical Psychology Plan to Complete the Ph.D. Degree?

Almost without exception. This is a function of the rigorous selection ratio.

What is the Attrition Rate?

Of 89 graduate students who were enrolled in 1946–7, 64 have discontinued training without receiving the Ph.D. degree or have been diverted to other major curricula because of lack of training facilities.

Of 20 entering in 1947–8, 9 have been advised to discontinue.
Of 14 entering in 1948–9, 6 have been advised to discontinue.
Of 16 entering in 1949–50, 3 have been advised to discontinue.
Of 19 entering in 1950–1, 0 have been advised to discontinue.

How Long does it Take to Get a Ph.D in Clinical Psychology?

The average for post-war Ph.D.'s at this university is shaping up between 4½ and 4¾ years, including summers.

The minimum is four academic years including nine months of supervised and approved internship during which the student remains active in research under his advisor and continues some academic work.

Is it Possible to Place all Graduates?

Yes. We could easily place twice as many graduates in today's market.

The United States Department of Labor on August 3, 1950, listed "Clinical Psychologist" as one of the 23 "professional and related occupations" classified as "critical."

The United States Public Health Service in 1946 estimated that the supply of trained clinical psychologists was 8% of the number the country could then absorb.

To What Kind of Positions do Ph.D. Graduates Go?

Table 7 Positions Accepted by the Ten Most Recent Ph.D.'s

Person	*Position*	*Annual Salary*
A.	Hospital	$4560
B.	Clinic plus teaching	$7250
C.	University plus consulting	$5100
D.	Hospital	$6400
E.	Hospital	$6400
F.	University	$5500
G.	Hospital plus teaching	$7600
H.	Research Institute	$5000
I.	Private Clinic	$7500
J.	University	$5000
	Average Salary	**$6026**

What About Applicants Who Apply at More than one University?

A study made at the University of Michigan two years ago and covering all applicants for the Veterans Administration-subsidized program throughout the country indicated that the average applicant applied at 4.8 universities.

Why are there Too Many Students Now in the Program?

The Department has been under continual pressure from private and public sources to admit more students. It has been possible to use funds from extra-University sources to support certain phases of the training program although in a long-term program these do not take the place of basic salary commitments by the University. As in the case of Dr. Courtney, some expansion of training facilities was possible by "bootlegging" the time of people who were paid for service functions. Finally, this fall, five more students were accepted than the quota originally agreed upon. It was expected that the group would shrink by enrollment time. It did not shrink.

Why has this Situation been Allowed to Develop?

In the spring of 1947, six months after the Clinic Director came to the campus, a detailed report of the situation, as it was then shaping up, was prepared. Illustrative charts, suitable for display purposes, and tables were prepared. Proposals were formulated. These were forwarded through channels to the University Administration and followed up by a request for an interview with the President by the Acting Dean of the College, the Chairman of the Department and the Director of the Clinic. The would-be interviewers got as far as the office of the Assistant to the President, no further! No acknowledgement of receipt of the report was ever received from the President's Office. There is no reason to believe that he ever saw it.

How Many Approved Ph.D. Level Training Institutions are There in the United States and how does Ohio State University Rank?

Forty university programs in clinical psychology are approved by the Committee on Training in Clinical Psychology of the American Psychological Association.

Ohio State is one of nine having the highest rating.

Ohio State University has one of the oldest and, over the years, one of the largest programs.

Table 8 Approved Training Programs in Clinical Psychology

Boston University
University of California at Berkeley
University of California at Los Angeles
Catholic University
University of Chicago
Clark University
University of Colorado
Duke University
Fordham University
Harvard University
University of Illinois
Indiana University
State University of Iowa
University of Kansas
University of Kentucky
University of Michigan
Michigan State College
University of Minnesota
University of Nebraska
New York University
University of North Carolina
Northwestern University
Ohio State University
Pennsylvania State College
University of Pennsylvania
University of Pittsburgh
Purdue University

(*Continued*)

Table 8 (Continued)

University of Rochester
University of Southern California
Stanford University
Syracuse University
Teachers College, Columbia
University of Tennessee
University of Texas
Tulane University
Washington University (St. Louis)
University of Washington (Seattle)
Western Reserve University
University of Wisconsin
Yale University

THE PROGRAM HAS BEEN CARRIED ALONG FOR FOUR YEARS ON A TEMPORIZING BASIS.

STAFF MEMBERS HAVE CARRIED EMERGENCY LOADS WHICH THEY CANNOT CONTINUE INDEFINITELY.
THE DEMAND FOR TRAINING AND THE DEMAND FOR TRAINED PEOPLE HAVE RISEN STEADILY AND ARE STILL RISING.
NOW THE UNIVERSITY IS FACED WITH MAKING AN EXPLICIT LONG-TERM DECISION ON WHAT IT WILL DO ABOUT GRADUATE WORK IN CLINICAL PSYCHOLOGY.

ON THE HUMAN SIDE

1 The Department's Personnel Committee has the responsibility of recommending selected admissions of qualified applicants according to the quotas established in different areas of the Department. They have tried to select the best qualified students on a completely impersonal basis.
2 Attached is a folder of a typical applicant who had to be rejected. Her recommendations are good and she has an undergraduate point-hour ratio of 3.37 in her major and 3.15 overall.
3 In a number of instances our public relations have suffered as a result of the necessity for limiting graduate admissions. For example, last year a professor of psychology in an Ohio College fell in the rejection column. He protested vigorously by long distance telephone, accused the Committee of bigotry. A few days later the Governor's Office called to get the facts regarding his rejection. In a previous year another Ohio College professor of psychology protested bitterly and in public regarding his rejection.
4 A number of students seek admission to the Department under the less restrictive quotas of other areas. Then as minors in clinical psychology they enroll in all of the basic clinical sequence courses in which they can find room. They hope to make scholastic records which will enable them to transfer to a clinical major. This fall one student was admitted to the clinical major who had spent two years as a major in another trying to establish herself as an acceptable candidate for a clinical major. Last fall another student gave up after two years waiting and doing satisfactory, but not spectacular, work in another area of the Department.
5 Selections are made about the first of April each year. Already a number of application forms, mostly clinical, for the fall of 1951 have been filed with the Entrance Board.
6 One case perhaps exemplifies the human side of the problem better than any figures. The Ohio State University offers a scholarship to valedictorians of other Ohio Colleges. This summer one such valedictorian arrived to enroll in clinical psychology. Informed that all quotas were long since filled, this disappointed candidate elected to wait a year in the hope of being admitted under next year's quota.

62

Psychological Approaches to the Management of Patients[1]

This afternoon I would like to talk to you about some psychological approaches to the management of patients. Since this is a lecture rather than a workshop or a practicum, it seems more appropriate for us to deal with the topic of *approaches,* implying as it does more generalized statements, than with the topic of *techniques*. Most of what I shall have to say this afternoon has to do with concepts and concept formation. We also shall be using the term "construct" which means about the same thing but which, to our way of thinking, carries a little more precise meaning in certain contexts. We shall be talking about the concepts and the construction systems of patients, not merely about the construction systems which clinicians and theorists employ in their own thinking *about* patients.

Dr. F.H. Sanford, now the Executive Secretary of the American Psychological Association, once classified personality theories, in a private communication, into "parlor" theories, "kitchen" theories, and "bathroom" theories. In this day and age when mental health workers vie with each other to see who can give the most earthy interpretation of human behavior, I feel that I probably should apologize in advance for the approach I intend to use this afternoon. I shall not use the bathroom approach, nor the kitchen approach; this I must shamefully admit is a parlor approach to the understanding of the patient.

This introduction to our discussion should suffice to make clear that we shall be concerned this afternoon with the way the patient sees things.

Let us look just at the problem of institutionalization itself. Let us see if we can see the problem of the institutionalization of the patient as seen through the eyes of the patient. Unless the patient has had some early experience with institutions as a non-patient, perhaps by having seen members of his family institutionalized, he is likely to look upon institutionalization as a last resort for "crazy" people or for people who have "lost" their minds. If he comes to the institution with this concept, he is likely on admission to have mixed feelings. On the one hand he may feel utterly discouraged at having been brought to this extremity where he no longer has control over his personal destiny and where he will be given a label which he will bear for the rest of his life. On the other hand, he may have mixed in with this feeling of discouragement the feeling of relief that he is no longer really responsible for what he does. These feelings, as we are all keenly aware, are not necessarily highly verbalized or explicitly expressed. The confused patient who arrives at the admission ward may even forget, in the course of weeks, the circumstances surrounding his arrival. But this does not mean that the implicit meaning of the experience is obliterated by his confusion at the moment or by the passage of time. Many patients who cannot remember explicitly the circumstances surrounding their arrival appear to carry with them permanently the generalized meanings which they attributed to that experience at the time.

If the patient is to be rehabilitated either as a hospital citizen or as a citizen of the outside world, he needs to be able to make some sense out of the admission experience. He needs to have an answer to the questions, "Why was I brought here?," "How can I reconcile my having been brought to a place like this with any feeling of status and personal worth?," "How can I reconcile it in the future with my role as a citizen of the world outside?" This is the problem of the admission trauma, and I mention it here because it is my impression that hospitals do a great deal better job of handling this problem now than they were able to do in generations past. The concept of *illness*, with its implication of temporary duration, is now frequently used in explaining to patients why they are where they are. In general, I believe patients now are given more help in understanding why they have to be institutionalized; and, instead of being given the idea that they have had to be "put away," are given the idea that they are in the hospital "to get well."

From the patient's point of view, institutionalization means a second kind of experience; the experience of finding other patients who are mentally ill. I will not say that the patient experiences this as the discovery of finding other people who are *like* himself. My impression is that few patients have that experience in the early stages of institutionalization. Indeed, we might even investigate, with a reasonable chance of getting definitive results, the hypothesis that as soon as the patient begins to see that his wardmates are "like himself," that perception is accompanied by some sort of therapeutic movement or readjustment. We do know that after patients have been in the hospital a time, they are more likely to say, "That fellow over there is more like I *was* when I came in." That

[1] Presented at the U.S. Veterans Administration Hospital, Houston, Texas, March 20, 1951. Published by permission of Jacqueline Aldridge.

Collected Papers of the Pioneer of Constructivist Psychology: George A. Kelly, First Edition. Edited by David A. Winter and Nick Reed.

too may be a sign of some kind of therapeutic movement. But the patient does begin to get some kind of understanding of other people through seeing other patients who are ill. This experience of seeing others who are ill and in need of help has both its threatening and supporting effects. It may threaten the patient, as it sometimes does the new clinician, by arousing within him dormant feelings of guilt and inadequacy. It may support him by providing him with a basis for the discovery that he is not the sole target of the world's hatreds; and, as Pollyanna would say, "things could be worse." The patient soon has to learn to be tolerant of other disturbed patients on his ward and this very understanding and need to adjust to others who are ill or irresponsible is itself likely to have some rehabilitating effect upon the patient.

But as the patient continues his institutional stay, he gets to see, if the situation is allowed to demonstrate it for him, certain reflections of his own personality in the behavior of other patients. Like the reflection technique in client-centered counseling, this may have important psychotherapeutic implications.

There appears to be among hospitals a tremendous difference in the ways patients on the ward are allowed and encouraged to understand other patients, and through their observation of other patients to see helpful reflections of facets of their own personalities. The implementation and careful control of this kind of ward milieu psychotherapy is a challenging task for attendants and nurses as well as for physicians. I have the impression that its psychological importance is not likely to be underestimated. The understanding of others, through seeing one's reflection in the behavior of others, can be seen, of course, most dramatically in group psychotherapy of the cathartic-discussion type.

There is a third important implication of institutionalization as seen through the eyes of the patient, and that is the simplification of the patient's world of experience and the controls which are necessary in order to maintain oneself in that world. Institutionalization does mean, of course, routine—a regular time for getting up, a regular time for eating, a regular diet, standardized social relations with attendants and nurses at least, and the reduction of many of the social processes of life to a minimum of complication and a maximum of regimentation and routine. A need for self control is lessened and the patient soon finds himself in a rut. To the patient whose problem has grown out of his inability to adjust himself to overwhelming dependency needs, this simplification of experience and its further dependency implications will be extremely threatening. He will see institutionalization as having the effect of forcing him deeper into the whirlpool of his confusion. He may fight back, he may take violent measures to lash out at what he sees as a regressive influence. To the patient who is anxious about other matters or who has allowed himself to regress to a stage of infantile dependency without further struggle toward adjustment, institutionalization may be a welcome change from the confusion and the problems he has experienced on the outside.

A fourth implication of institutionalization has to do with the relationship the patient is able to see between intra-institutional adjustment and extra-institutional adjustment. This is a problem which all of us, who have been concerned with institutional management, have discussed at great length, but for which, for the most part, we have been unable to work out any very satisfactory solution. We are well aware of the fact that intra-institutional adjustment does not necessarily augur well for subsequent extra-institutional adjustment. The patient may feel that same problem. He may vaguely sense that kinds of adjustments that he has to make within the institution are essentially maladjustments to extra-institutional life. Those of you who have dealt with the problem of penal institutional adjustments will recognize this problem as being extremely acute in that particular area. But it is a problem also in hospitalization and it is an implicit problem in the mind of the patient too. All too frequently, as we are all aware, the patient may attempt to make a trade; he may say, in effect, I will play like I am making an intra-institutional adjustment, but I will protect myself by making sure that it is only a pose. I will not let myself really want to make the intra-institutional adjustment and I will be very careful not to let my inner thinking be influenced by this pose I am going to assume. Then when they are satisfied and let me out I will not be incapacitated for making the kind of extra-institutional adjustment I feel is necessary. You will, of course, recognize that this kind of trade or pseudo-intrainstitutional adjustment is quite characteristic of certain types of paranoid patients.

So much for institutionalization and its implications in the mind of the patient. Let us consider next the problem of trauma and what its psychological implications are for the patient. There are, of course, dozens of theories as to the nature of the trauma. Theories of what is involved in electric shock are examples of our confusion in thinking about this problem. I believe someone recently made a tabulation and found eighty-odd different theoretical explanations. Instead of becoming too much involved in theory for the moment, let us make some generalizations of clinical observations which most of us share. We shall, of course, be talking not merely about electric shock but also about the effect of various forms of traumatic experience. For one thing, traumatic experience seems to arouse in the patient latent attitudes or latent ways of construing experience. They may arouse construction systems or ways of construing experience which appear to have been embedded in the patient's early childhood. We do know from psychological experimentation that, in the presence of threat, people tend to regress to the use of more primitive or more childlike patterns of adjustment. Now this is not necessarily bad; indeed, it may, for the patient whose illness is really quite recent, be a good thing, in that it will throw him back upon his basic beliefs and attitudes. The effect of trauma, of course, is in a sense, the arousal of a necessity for one's mobilizing his resources. But we should bear in mind that the resources which are mobilized may not always be mature and effective.

The second effect of traumatic experience, and frequently an undesirable one, is the tendency for the traumatic experience to act as further subjective documentation or proof of the patient's own maladaptive conceptual framework. Not only is the traumatized patient thrown back upon older and more infantile constructions of life, but he is likely, through this further experience, to find documentation for those constructions. It is correct to say of traumatic experience then that it usually "freezes people in their tracks." Now the patient for whom hospitalization has been traumatic will at the time of admission tend to be frozen in his tracks, and he may even find the admission in some ways a further documentation of the worst attitudes he has had toward himself and his world. The clinician, whether he be attendant, nurse, or physician, may find it very helpful to recognize this freezing effect when he sees it in the new patient.

A third effect of trauma we have already mentioned in connection with the patient's understanding of institutionalization and that is the tendency of traumatic experience to arouse in the patient his deeper feelings of dependency. And, if he happens to be a patient who has been fighting off dependency needs, to arouse in him also violent evasive action against the threat of seeing himself as a dependent person.

Let us now say something about insight. This is a term which has been used in so many different ways that I am sure it has baffled all of us even though in a vague way we feel that for many patients insight is like the pouring of sunlight through the windows of the patient's soul. For the most part in psychotherapy, the term, "insight," has been used to describe a kind of self-understanding, though the term has been used in psychological writing in general to refer to a sudden closure in a perceptual patterning of experience. It has been used also to refer to perception of objects and people outside of the self, but in psychotherapy the term traditionally has been used in the narrower sense of self-insight, or a reasonable and rational explanation of some particular problem involving one's self. In this more limited sense, there have been at least three approaches to the development of patient insight. There is the historical approach upon which the psychoanalysts place so much emphasis. By historical, of course, I mean historical from the point of view of the individual patient and the insight achieved through the historical approach is an insight or an understanding or an interpretation in the mind of the patient of how he got the way he is, what in his childhood resulted in his being ill, what developments and changes and successions of events meant to him, and how all of this has a bearing upon what he can now do to change the course of events and start writing a new history for himself from this point on. This is the historical approach to insight and while it is one made good use of, it is one which cannot be employed economically in a hospital setting. The interpretation of historical events in the life of the patient, if undertaken in a very brief sequence of psychotherapeutic conferences or if undertaken on the ward, is quite likely to be more confusing than helpful to the patient.

The second approach to the development of patient insight we may call the dynamic approach. Psychoanalysts use this approach also and some of them, including Fenichel, are careful to distinguish between dynamic insights and historical insights. When one approaches patient insight from the standpoint of dynamics he tries to help the patient understand what forces, what needs, what demands, what energies are operating to produce his problem of the moment. In attempting to develop this kind of insight, in a patient, the clinican is likely to use either in a formal discussion in the office or in an informal discussion on the ward such terms as needs, wants, wishes, and desires. The clinician may also speak of what the patient should or should not *have*. When the patient goes to occupational therapy and the occupational therapist says, "this is good for you," or "this will get it out of your system" or "now you can work out your feelings here," she is essentially using the dynamic approach to patient insight. Our language is full of dynamic terms and in the field of psychotherapy the term, "dynamic," has come to have a meritritious flavor. Dynamic psychology is "always a good thing." Now while I have my own personal doubts about this, let us recognize that there is a dynamic approach to patient insight and that it is very commonly used and that it is implied in most of the casual communications between clinicians and patients as well as in formal psychotherapeutic interviews. The patient who gets his insight by the dynamic route is led to believe that there are forces or needs which determine the course of his behavior and that his job is to find socially acceptable ways of releasing those forces or satisfying those needs. The patient who operates on this basis, of course, may do no more than attempt to palliate the forces and needs which he has come to believe are making demands upon him. Now this approach to insight may be somewhat more economically employed in a hospital situation, indeed it is the one which is most commonly employed; but it is a rather abstract approach as far as the patient is concerned. It is hard for a patient to say, "ah ha! This anger that I have now is really the expression of an internal need. Now what I must do is work something out. Oh ho! I have just the thing—I will do a finger painting with lots of red paint and bold lines." It is extremely difficult for a patient, and for us too, to feel, in the midst of an excited moment, that all that is operating is some internal force to which he must give outlet.

There is a third approach to patient insight which is not necessarily exclusive of the other two and which we may call the commonality approach. This approach is a didactic one in which the patient is presumed to have insight when he comes to agree with the clinician's construction of affairs. This, of course, may quickly degenerate into a kind of indoctrination or military training approach to mental hygiene. As clinicians we are all inclined to disparage this way of treating patients, but if we are realistic we must keep in mind that sometimes it works, that indoctrination is indeed one of the ways of getting people to get along with each other in a closely packed living space. This approach may sometimes be called the cultural approach; when used in this sense, insight is attempted by getting the patient to see things like members of his cultural group or social class see them; and, if he cannot do that, to change his membership to another cultural group or social class.

As we have seen, insight in the patient is essentially a matter of the development of an adequate concept of himself and his world. If insight then is to play such an important part in the rehabilitation of the patient and if it is essentially a matter of forming a new conceptual system, it is important for us to consider both the psychological nature of concepts and the way in which concepts are generated or changed.

Now, a concept is frequently referred to as a kind of abstraction and generalization. It is essentially a way of looking at old things in such a manner that we are prepared to meet new things which have not yet entered the field of our experience. Thus, a concept is different from a percept—a percept being simply an understanding of something as it is, and of that thing only. But the concept is an understanding of several things and an understanding of them in such a way that room is left in our thinking for the addition of other things in the same class as those other things may arise in our experience. A concept, then, is in a sense an open-ended system of percepts. A conceptual system is a scheme of things which permits us to embrace the future with familiarity and gratification.

Reduced to its lowest terms, concept formation is a matter of seeing how two things are alike yet different from a third. If we show the patient the names of three people with whom he has had intimate dealings in the past, each name written on a different card, perhaps on one card the name of his mother, on another card the name of his wife, and on another card the name of his commanding officer during combat, and if we ask him to tell us in what important way any two of these people are alike yet different from the third, we shall be asking him to express a concept regarding persons he knows. Now actually this technique, which I have used here merely as an illustration, is turning out to be, in some of our researches at the Ohio State University conducted by Mr. Alvin Landfield and Mr. David Hunt, an exceedingly interesting approach to the understanding of the patient's world. Now if we go on and ask the patient to sort other cards with the names of other people from his personal-social milieu and to express the concepts by which he sorts them, we soon find that he starts to repeat himself and that the repertory of concepts by which he understands the people who have populated his intimate world, is in fact limited and by the time the patient has reached his thirtieth sort approximately ninety per cent of the concepts elicited by the technique are duplications of concepts he has already used in previous sorts. Thus it is possible both from the standpoint of theoretical psychology and from the standpoint of a practical technique to discover the perceptual armamentarium or repertory that the patient has at his disposal for meeting new people in his social world. As the patient becomes acquainted with one of us, he plots our personalities with respect to the axes of these concepts; and we may indeed be surprised and amused or disturbed at the way he must pin-point our individualities in order to deal with us. In a sense we may say the patient is like Procrustes, he invites us to lie down in a guest bed and then, either by lopping off our feet and heads to make us short enough for the bed or by stretching us, he finds a way to make us fit the bed rather than for the bed to fit us.

Now it is possible by careful listening to many patients, as they express themselves in a relatively free and unstructured interview, to get some crude idea of the conceptual system which the patients employ in dealing with people. The more skillful the clinician and the more sensitive he is to nuances of personal expression and private language the easier it is for him to get some useful notion of what the patient's conceptual world is like from listening to the ramblings of his free speech. Most of us, however, are not sensitive enough to be able to pick up these understandings from such unstructured material. Fortunately, it is not necessary always for us to develop this degree of sensitivity in order to achieve an adequate understanding. As I have already suggested, it is possible to do the job by using a more precise test.

Not only is it possible to understand the patient better by understanding the conceptual frames that he placed around people but it is also possible to understand him better if we study those frames or concepts as to their level of generalization and their level of utility. In a recent careful research, done by one of our students, Dr. L.S. McGaughran, it was found possible to demonstrate in a practical, useful way, that concepts, as used by people, both patients and normal people, might well be classified along a scale of permeability; the permeable concepts being essentially those which are open-ended enough to permit the patient to take new experience in his stride and to add new people to the class which the concept represents. The impermeable concepts are those which have been closed-out or finished; the file of people and ideas, which the concept represents, is complete and no more people or ideas can be added to it. This latter kind of concept is, of course, not very useful to a person in meeting new problems and assimilating new experience. The former kind of a concept may or may not help one meet new situations adequately, depending upon how useful and practical it is for helping one develop a socially acceptable role. Now, in a sense, it is a good thing that we have let some of our concepts become impermeable, particularly those concepts of people which have such maladaptive implications for the behavior of the patient that if he were to try them on new people in his world he would likely run into difficulty in getting along with those new people. If the patient has the concept of malicious and scheming people which he has applied to a number of persons or behaviors of persons in his past, it may, if impossible actually to change the concepts, be somewhat helpful if he can at least limit the concepts to those particular people and the particular past behaviors of those people. In that sense it is possible for a patient to close-out this kind of thinking and relegate it to an inactive status along with the past experiences which it once structured.

Concepts do have a way of deteriorating in this manner. In fact, what was once a nice open-ended concept, may, with frequent literalistic use, degenerate into a stereotype or a fixed perception of certain people or things. Thus it is important for us to be alert as to the level of the conceptualization which the patient uses and not assume that, because the word he uses represents for most people a good permeable concept, the patient is using the word to denote a permeable concept. The concept may have long since deteriorated into an impermeable one, or to a stereotype, or simply to a fixed and non-useful idea. If the patient's concept has actually degenerated to this extremity it may not be essential to try to develop a change in it. It may already be so ossified that it has ceased to be functional in his dealings with his world. The violent descriptive language, which a patient may employ to describe certain people, may represent no more than a deteriorated concept which does not really stand in the way of his inner readjustment to society.

We are now ready to consider the ways in which the various clinicians who participate in the rehabilitation of the patient may help bring about desirable and useful conceptual changes in the patient. We have already said that traumatic experiences tend to freeze the patient in his tracks. Now by that, of course, we do not mean necessarily that the patient is inactive or mute when he is traumatized. Indeed he may be exceedingly active and verbose in the face of a trauma. What we mean to say is that the effect of traumatic experience is to freeze his *thinking* in its tracks. Frightened people do not develop new ideas. This is just as important a statement regarding the life of a patient as it is an important statement in understanding the effect of war upon cultural developments or the rapid rise of a new kind of civilization on the North American continent. First of all, therefore, if we wish to help the patient bring about an important conceptual change in his thinking, we will have to make sure that he is not continually faced with traumatic experiences. This is really another way of saying that the patient must experience a certain amount of security in his interpersonal relationships if he is to undertake the task, which is a ticklish one for him, of changing the frames of reference or the basic construction system which he employs in handling his social world.

A second way of setting the stage for conceptual change has its analog in nature. During periods of rest, relaxation, and sleep, all of us tend to become more autistic and more subjective in our thinking. Rather than considering this to be a kind of deterioration in our intellectual processes, let us say that these are periods when we are freer to explore vaguely new ideas and concepts, that sleep itself provides us with an opportunity for shaking loose the rigidities which the traumata of the day has driven us to assume. In psychoanalytic therapy, those autistic approaches to the formation of new concepts are deliberately used. The patient is encouraged to talk about his dreams, he is encouraged to use free association, and he is encouraged to express very "loose" concepts. We know that, out of this kind of autistic thinking, the patient may come to express new concepts which, if followed up and properly documented, may actually provide more precise and useful ways of dealing with the real world. This also is what the occupational therapist, who employs finger painting or artistic work, is doing. The vague and almost imperceptible beginnings of new concepts of the world can frequently be traced to the patient's work with clay or with paints. It is extremely important that the clinician, who has this exciting opportunity to see the very earliest beginnings of therapeutic change in the patient, be keenly sensitive to new notes and overtones in the patient's expressions and be careful to take full advantage of her resources for encouraging these novel developments.

The third way in which concepts can be changed is a rather obvious one. It is the same way in which scientists set about systematically to change their concepts. It is the way of experimentation. Indeed it may be said, that only as the patient explores new kinds of behavior is it possible for him to accomplish any basic psychotherapeutic goals. Even experimentation with the "wrong" behaviors is a basic way in which the patient may come to find valid new approaches to life. All too frequently, because our wards are crowded and our duties arduous, we are inclined to discourage the patient's experimentation with new behaviors and respond adequately to him only if he behaves in ways which we have come to expect and to understand. Of course it should be pointed out that experimentation is dangerous. It is always dangerous, whether it is carried out by a patient looking for new ways of handling his world or carried out by a chemist who is not quite sure how big a bang his latest concoction will make when it explodes. The patient's experimentation needs to be, of course, controlled, but it does need to be carried out, if he is ever to develop any really new understandings of his world.

Let me talk for a few moments about a very specific kind of experimentation which we have come to believe has great possibilities for the future improvement and acceleration of rehabilitative developments in the patient. Let us consider role-playing. When you ask a patient, either in a group situation or in a person-to-person relationship to play a role, either a fixed one, which is carefully outlined for him, in advance, or a relatively free one, which he is permitted to develop in his own way, the patient is given a basis for experimenting with new forms of behavior behind the protective screen of the artificial role. John Jones playing the role of a fictitious character named Pete Smith, may make Pete Smith experiment with a lot of new behaviors. Yet it is John Jones who tried out the experimentation and learns from it. It is John Jones who formulates the hypotheses, in a sense, just as a scientist may formulate and test out hypotheses.

In addition to trying out new behaviors for himself, John Jones may have an opportunity to try out new ways of seeing other people, as he ascribes to the person playing opposite him various new and strictly experimental characteristics. Thus, if John Jones is playing a role opposite someone who represents an authority figure he may first try various forms of behavior for himself in dealing with the authority figure and then later he may, through the reversal or exchange of roles, try out new ways of understanding the authority figure. He may indeed, through his experimentations, find new ways of interpreting the authority figure and his therapeutic movements may in the end be more related to his new interpretations of other people than to his new ways of behaving himself. Frequently therapy turns out to be not so much a matter of getting people to behave differently as it is a matter of getting them to see other people's behavior differently.

Another advantage of role-playing approaches to the changing of concepts is the way in which such a procedure basically protects the identity of the patient. The patient is not told that he must, in the role of his own identity, go out and be different or experiment with different kinds of behavior. John Jones is not asked to be anything other than John Jones. Not really, that is! All that he is asked to do is to "play like" Pete Smith. Now this is really a way of protecting the identity of John Jones during the period of explorations. The new exploratory behavior, with all its potentiality for creating guilt and anxiety in the patient, is wrapped up neatly and labeled, "Pete Smith," not John Jones. Thus John Jones is protected during the crucial period of his experimentation when, if it were not for his artificial role identification, he might be so frightened that he would be unable to experiment at all.

Let us consider another approach to the changing of patients' concepts. Let us consider communication as a kind of interpersonal relation which has an important bearing upon therapy. As a matter of fact, of course, most therapy is carried out in an intercommunication situation. Most therapy is carried out more or less through the use of words. Words are important to all of us, and particularly so if those words represent attempts to establish relationships with other people. As the patient communicates with other people, with clinicians of various professions, and, even in some cases, with other patients, he finds that his feelings must be put into words and that, in turn, the words tend to bind the feelings. Words then are wrapping cords with which we bind up our experiences into neat packages which can be handled and managed. Words initiated by the patient, in an attempt to communicate, may become also for him a way in which he can handle the buzzing confusion of his world.

We may look also upon communication and expression as a way in which the patient may clarify his own understanding or perception of himself. Sometimes we learn things about ourselves when we hear ourselves talk. A patient's speech or attempt to express himself is, even though quite bizarre, not necessarily a mere indication of his disturbance. It is thus likely to be important for a patient to keep on expressing himself even though he is not successful in making himself understood and even though he appears to have only a minimal interest in getting people to understand what he means.

There is another way in which communication is important. As patients communicate with each other and with clinicians it is almost unavoidable that they will, in some measure come to identify themselves with the people who appear to understand them. Thus the patient, who attempts to communicate with you or who merely sees you as attempting to understand him, begins to form in a vague way a feeling of identification with you. This identification with another person is, one might say, the beginnings of a concept regarding one's self, for it is a way of seeing that he and you are alike but different from a third person. And as the patient forms a concept of himself, not merely a percept, and, if that concept is permeable rather than impermeable, he begins to have a way of seeing himself change, of seeing a new self, and that, of course, is what every patient must be able to see if he is to make full use of his opportunities for rehabilitation. Thus it appears to be important for the clinician, in a measured way, to encourage a certain amount of identification of the patient with himself. It is important that the clinician attempt to do this in order to give the patient a truly permeable self concept and provide him with a conceptual basis for seeing himself in a new role.

Our discussion this afternoon has necessarily been general rather than specific. If it has accomplished no other purpose, I hope at least that it has made us all more keenly aware of the psychological processes which are manifested in the patients' daily behavior, and that it has served to emphasize that much of what the clinician does day-by-day has a profound effect upon the patient's rehabilitation. Psychotherapy is not merely something that takes place with a patient lying on a couch in a psychoanalyst's office. Therapeutic movement takes place in a wide variety of ways and under a wide variety of stimulation. Psychological approaches to the rehabilitation of the patient need not be considered mysterious nor need they be considered the professional property of any one occupational clique. Since the days of the enlightenment that closed the middle ages, knowledge has been considered to be in the public domain, and no one of us needs to feel that he must accept any legacy of ignorance because of his occupational label. Psychological approaches to the rehabilitation of the patient can and should be employed by all of us, regardless of whether or not we identify ourselves with the organized profession of psychology. Psychologists, like any enlightened group, ask only that the ideas which are associated with their discipline be thoughtfully studied and skillfully employed.

63

Contribution to Symposium on Contributions of Learning Theory to Psychopathology[1]

In taking a dim view of the contributions of learning theory to psychopathology I hope I shall be playing the role of a skeptic rather than that of a cynic.

The areas with which psychologists concern themselves—learning, physiological psychology, perception, interpersonal relations, etc.—are not altogether areas of *content*; they would be more accurately termed *alternative theories* or *variants of psychological methodology*. That is because they are conceptualized on such a level of abstraction that they may be possibly considered to have implications over a broad range of overlapping content. Thus, for example, the psychologist when he studies learning is not likely to be limiting himself to a certain group of phenomena, but rather to be applying a certain kind of theory or a certain kind of methodology to a wide variety of psychological problems. The learning psychologist no longer modestly couches his theoretical inferences, as Hull once did, in terms of the *area of rote learning*, but rather expresses his generalizations in sweeping terms without regard for the possible limitations of the span of its relevance. This is not necessarily bad, provided, of course, that the learning psychologists have something which will help you get along with your wife as well as rid the house of white rats, condition the baby, and save steps in the kitchen. The first point, then, I wish to make is that *learning* has come to represent in the minds of most psychologists not an area of problems but rather a kind of theoretical and methodological approach that some people think is applicable to all of the phenomenal areas of psychology.

Psychopathology, on the other hand, is ordinarily considered to be a *phenomenal* area. When one studies psychopathology he studies certain *things* by whatever methodological tools he is handy with. The problem, then, simply is this. Do the theories and methodologies which have been designed primarily to deal with the area of learning and which are, therefore, called learning theories and methodologies, suit themselves to the area of psychopathology, an area which they, admittedly, were primarily designed for? Bluntly stated, my view is that they do not. This is a negative position, and like all negative positions, is a difficult one to defend on logical grounds. Defending it is something like trying to prove the null hypothesis—a logical task which is basically indeterminate. Maybe tomorrow someone will come along and show just how our problems in the area of psychopathology can be structured in terms of learning theory and, having so structured, then will throw light upon how they should be handled.

The issue before us can perhaps be stated succinctly by saying that we want, of course, eventually to develop precise laws for important human phenomena or proceed first by attempting to develop approximate laws for important phenomena. We are assuming that laws must be invented and developed by the scientist and that he does not derive them by assuming that nature has hidden them from us and that he must therefore go out and start lifting up old boards and miscellaneous pieces of laboratory apparatus in order to discover where they have been secreted. We take the view that the derivation of primary laws, or the parameters whose relationships they express, is a process of abstraction or concept formation which must first be attempted in the phenomenal area in which they are initially to be of service.

Before we get into this matter too deeply, let us take stock of where we stand with respect to the philosophical as well as the procedural issues involved. It is pretty hard ever to prove that a given theory is true or untrue. What we have to do is set up some yardsticks by which we judge the adequacy of the theory. One common yardstick is the efficiency of the theory in explaining a given set of events. Can the theory be used to explain them without the theorist having to stand on his head and to juggle a lot of words. A second criterion is whether or not they enable the theorist to make ad hoc predictions. In other words, does it enable the scientist to lay wagers which will pay off. A third criterion of the value of theory is its fertility. In other words, does it provoke the scientist to express new hunches, does it generate new hypotheses, and does it suggest new technical inventions. All three of these criteria or yardsticks—(1) simple structure, (2) predictive efficiency, (3) fertility—are the values which I propose to use in this discussion.

It is obvious then, that we can arrive at no ultimate answer to the question of whether or not learning theories can make an adequate contribution to psychopathology. In a practical day by day sense there is as yet no such thing as a wholly true theory in the field of

[1] Presented at Midwestern Psychological Association Meeting, Hotel Drake, Chicago, Illinois, May 1, 1953. Published by permission of Jacqueline Aldridge.

Collected Papers of the Pioneer of Constructivist Psychology: George A. Kelly, First Edition. Edited by David A. Winter and Nick Reed.

psychopathology. For that matter, there probably is no such thing as a true or ultimate theory yet available to us in anything. What we have is a series of alternative approaches to psychopathology each of which has certain systematic advantages and each of which has certain systematic disadvantages. You pay your money and you take your choice.

We have tried to state what our yardsticks were for measuring the value of learning theory. Now, if I am to come to grips with the issue proposed in the symposium topic, I shall have to indicate what I consider to be the essentials of learning theory as contrasted with other psychological theories. As every graduate student is painfully aware, there is a variety of theories extant, all of which may be called learning theories. In fact, if you wish to take a broad enough view of learning, you can say that all psychological theories must of necessity have something to do with learning as a phenomenal area and, therefore, all are in some measure learning theories. We shall have to be more discriminating than this, however, and come to some agreement as to what kinds of theorizing we shall call *learning* and what kinds we shall call *not learning*. Let's go about it in this way. It seems to me that most people who have made contributions to what is commonly called learning theory have started with a notion of "scientific determinism." Simply stated, this means that one is concerned with the following kind of question. "If I want my dog to bark, which button do I push?" Let us lump in with the learning theorists, another group of people who ask this kind of question; "There goes my dog barking again. Who pushed what button?" This, of course, is the developmental approach, and is only loosely lumped with learning theory. The third approach can be stated simply in the form of the question, "What in the world is my dog barking at this time?"

The first approach implies the following question: Which of two S's will be the more likely to cause a given R. The second approach implies the following: Which of the two S's was the more likely indeed to have caused a given R. The third approach involves quite a different kind of logic. It runs like this: From a series of R's, how may we best abstract an S factor. In the last type of theory, the S is not given but rather is a kind of property of the given R. This approach, as I see it, is not characteristic of what are commonly called the learning theories. Now if you are willing to accept my definition of learning theory perhaps I can go ahead to make more explicit my reasons for taking a dim view of it in the field of psychopathology.

First of all, I think learning theories are too concretistic to serve our purposes well in the field of psychopathology. Most of us agree that psychology is and rightfully should be an experimental science. But we are deluding ourselves if we assume that experimentalism has no characteristic pitfalls. When one performs an experiment he has to reduce his thinking to operational terms. This means that he reduces his variables to concrete objects and simple fragments of behavior. Thus if a person is investigating some variable such as hunger, the temptation is not to abstract from a series of hunger situations the stimulus properties of hunger, but rather to concretize the stimulus of hunger in terms of such whole objects as pellets of food. By this line of reasoning the experimenter comes to see the stimulus as the concrete pellet of food rather than as a property which a pellet of food holds in common with other objects.

This tendency of the experimental method to lead the experimenter into concretistic modes of reasoning need not cause us to abandon the experimental method altogether but it should lead us to set up certain safeguards against concretistic thinking.

Now I realize that people who espouse learning theory have not been blind to the dangers of concretism arising out of operational experimentation. It has often been pointed out that a stimulus should always be identified as a quality or as a property rather than a given set of objects. This is another way of saying that it is the abstraction of a property rather than the collection of objects that defines the antecedent condition we call "stimulus." Now where does the abstraction come from? Is it furnished by the objects which are abstracted? Is it furnished by nature? Is it furnished by the experimenter? Or is it furnished by the responding organism. If we follow what I have called learning theory we must believe at best that the abstraction is furnished by nature or by the experimenter. Thus the learning theorist enters his experiment with his stimuli defined and concretized. If any abstracting is done it is he who does it and not his subjects. Thus, I would add a second criticism to learning theory to my first criticism that it tends to be concretistic. My second criticism is that when it does abstract stimulus properties, it does it either under the assumption that the abstractions exist in nature or under the assumption that they can be performed only by the experimenter. They tend to ignore the possibility that the subject, himself, abstracts stimulus properties and that these abstractions should only in proper turn be abstracted by the experimenter.

Now, as all of us know, this approach has been productive in dealing with animals. Animals tend to be rather concretistic in their approach to stimuli. They tend to respond to objects or collections of objects rather than to properties of objects, though it should be recognized that they are not wholly without abstracting capacity. Moreover, the approach works fairly well with children. They, too, tend to be somewhat concretistic and if we impose the assumption of concretism upon their behavior, we do not make too many mistakes in venturing to predict what they will do. The method also is not wholly inappropriate to the study of brain injured adults since they, too, tend to be concretistic in their identification of stimuli. But when we approach the problem of dealing with adults who are quite capable of abstraction but who employ unconventional concepts it is the experimenter who is likely to be acting as if something were wrong with his brain rather than the subject. Let us take an example. Not long ago, I was conducting a psychotherapeutic interview with a patient whom I had been treating for some time and whom I thought I knew pretty well. His progress under treatment had seemed to be satisfactory. And yet, in this interview, I discovered to my dismay that I had been from time to time making the mistake of congratulating him mildly on the new found poise he had shown in dealing with certain social situations. I discovered, also, that some of his friends had made the same mistake and that he had even gone so far as to avoid some of those who had congratulated him too enthusiastically. Now, of course, all of this had a good many ramifications but the simple point I wish to make is that what would normally be considered a "reinforcement" was in this particular case a threat. He and I both knew a good deal of why it was a threat but if I had continued to approach his case from the standpoint of learning theory, I suspect I might still be threatening him by showing approval of some of his new mature behavior.

My third reason for believing that learning theory, as I have defined it, is not making satisfactory contributions to psychopathology is that by its nature it does not enable us to make meaningful inferences regarding the behavior of intelligent adults. I would, therefore, prefer a theoretical approach to psychopathology which would recognize first of all the abstracting process which goes on in the mind of the subject and would lift each datum from an individual subject not in a concrete, behavioristic form but rather at a level of abstraction commensurate with the perception of the subject.

I have made three criticisms of learning theory's approach to psychopathology. (1) in attempting to meet the practical demands of experimental operationalism it tends to become concretistic in its reasoning about stimuli; (2) when it does take an abstract view it tends to assume either that the abstractions are given by nature or that they can be performed only by the experimenter; and (3) because intelligent psychopathologically disturbed adults do a great deal of surreptitious abstracting on their own, learning theories are particularly unsuited to that particular field. These are relatively specific criticisms. They would, of course, have to be withdrawn if someone would come along tomorrow and demonstrate the utility of learning theory in dealing with psychopathological conditions.

Finally let us see how our view of learning theory stacks up against the three yardsticks for the evaluation of a theory which I proposed in the forepart of this discussion—(1) simple structure, (2) predictive efficiency and (3) fertility.

With respect to *simple structure* learning theory does not do too badly in the area of psychopathology. The units of stimulus and response that the learning theorists envision are easily identifiable and the notion of associative conditioning is sufficiently broad to account for all sorts of accidental combinations. With respect to *predictive efficiency* learning theory comes out rather poorly in the area of adult psychopathology because of its failure to anticipate the abstractions or the personal constructions by means of which different persons distinguish between the properties of events that they choose to react to. The third yardstick, fertility, seems to me to be the one where learning theory tends to fall down most of all, not only with respect to the invention of novel procedures in dealing with psychopathological problems but also in the development of measures of psychological distortions. With respect to measures we are still almost wholly dependent upon perceptual theoretical approaches such as those involving projective methodology.

64

Where Do Little Hypotheses Come from?[1]

Undoubtedly all of us would agree that a good clinician is an observant person. He picks up cues readily. He relates them to each other in more or less systematic fashion. If he is a therapeutically oriented clinician—and fortunately clinical psychologists are becoming more and more therapeutically oriented these days—he will use his systematized observations to look ahead and see what further developments may reasonably be expected to take place in his patient's life. With such foresight he may even be able to do his patient some good. Now if this is what it takes to be a good clinician, what does theory have to do with it?

Years ago I used to think that the proper clinical approach was to make as many observations as possible on a given patient and then to try to sort out the miscellaneous facts into some kind of pattern that would make sense. Each case was dealt with as a kind of concept formation problem, that is, the clinical concepts were created on the spot and were tailor-made to fit the case. At least that is what I thought I was doing.

In its way it was good practice. It demanded a kind of alertness which kept me from going to sleep during a therapy session or merely looking for diagnostic signs during an intake interview. But it was exhausting. I began to be aware of more and more things that I ought to look for. My inventories and interview outlines got longer and longer. I ended up with a twenty-four page psychological examination outline—exclusive of tests—which was a mass of closely packed abbreviations for the clinician to use in seeking entrée points to the patient's problem.

Eventually it became apparent that even what I was capable of observing was itself a function of the particular vantage point I had chosen to stand on. Yet from that same vantage point other perfectly simple facts were utterly obscured from view. This is the point, undoubtedly, at which John Locke would have gone home to write the first pages of *An Essay Concerning Human Understanding*.

In the light of modern thinking regarding the logic of science, as well as in the light of this personal experience, two things become increasingly apparent:

(1) Even a simple observation is itself a form of hypothesis which emerges out of a more or less organized theoretical point of view and (2) it is extremely difficult to be aware of the unique nature of one's own point of view. Let us pursue these two points a little further to see what may be their implications for the training of clinical psychologists.

Consider first the notion that an observation is itself a form of hypothesis. The clinician must be a versatile observer. That is to say he must be prepared to produce a rich variety of hypotheses in dealing with a case. Now there are differences of opinion among field staff psychologists as to how psychological interns should be trained. There are those who ask the intern to maximize the variety of their findings when reporting the results of diagnostic testing or the progress of a series of psychotherapeutic interviews. They ask the intern to verbalize all of his vague hunches and then to document them as best he can. Then there are other field supervisors who say that this is training which leads psychology back down the road to impressionism and makes it unlikely that the intern will ever adopt a scientific point of view. These supervisors would say rather that the intern should voice only that which he can call findings of the type to which other observers would be expected to agree readily.

We could, of course, treat this as an issue between impressionism and objectivity in current clinical practice. But as I see it there is a far more important issue involved. It is a matter of what constitutes the nature of a clinical observation. More and more some of us are insisting that clinical students not report their experiences with patients as "psychological findings," as if these so-called findings were reality-binding facts, not subject to re-construing. In psychology it is all too easy to confound objectivity with literalism. Rather we are asking our students and interns to report their experiences in terms of hypotheses. Then, of course, each student is asked to document his hypotheses as best he can. But more than that is required. He is asked to indicate what kinds of further exploration and what kinds of further documentation would be necessary to provide higher levels of proof and disproof for the tenuously held hypotheses. In this manner the student is encouraged to point

[1] Paper presented at the Midwestern Psychological Association symposium, The role of theory in training clinical psychologists, 1953. Published in *Constructs (The Newsletter of the Centre for Personal Construct Psychology)*, 1985, *3*(4), 3–5. Republished by permission of Nick Reed and Jacqueline Aldridge. In the original a large number of words were underlined, but the underlining has been removed as it seemed that it probably served as an aid to Kelly in presenting the paper.

Collected Papers of the Pioneer of Constructivist Psychology: George A. Kelly, First Edition. Edited by David A. Winter and Nick Reed.

his clinical formulations toward the future rather than merely to provide a neat rationalization for what has already been observed. Probably the most useful of all the types of clinical hypotheses are those which can be validated or invalidated by some clinician's subsequent therapeutic efforts. These are the kinds of hypotheses which can be said to make a practical difference in the patient's life.

If we take the view that clinical observations should be treated as hypotheses subject to subsequent further validation or invalidation, we can find grounds for taking a firm stand on this issue of whether or not a clinician should venture to express all of his clinical hunches. The answer is yes. As a scientist he must, however, say as explicitly as he can what his present evidence is and suggest what further practical steps may be taken to validate or invalidate his hypotheses. In fact the more and the better organized the clinical hypotheses a person can generate under these conditions the better a clinician he is likely to be. This is just another way of saying that a good clinician is a versatile observer.

The clinician should be prepared to produce a rich variety of hypotheses in dealing with a case. He needs to get little hypotheses about what is going on in the patient's life from day to day and from moment to moment during a psychotherapeutic interview as well as big hypotheses having to do with such matters as the gross diagnostic categories in which the whole case may be placed. The big hypotheses are not so hard to come by. But where do little hypotheses come from? Are they delivered to us by the patient alive and kicking? The clinician himself has to produce them one by one and he must apply them to the patient experimentally.

As I see it there are about three readily distinguishable ways of producing little hypotheses. Let us call these three ways, (1) the theoretico-deductive way, (2) the clinico-inductive way, and (3) the statistical dragnet way. The theoretico-deductive way is to formulate an elaborate explicit theory and from it deduce hypotheses about the way all patients tend to behave. Then we may delineate special deductive sequences about the ways particular patients behave. This means working basically from an elaborated theory about which we have forced ourselves to become articulate. There is a shortage of such theories in psychology today, especially of those which delineate deductive sequences about the ways different individual patients can be expected to behave.

The clinico-inductive way of generating little hypotheses is the one I used to rely upon wholly. One starts with the patient. The clinician accumulates many facts. Of course these facts, as one perceives them, are themselves hypotheses. But they are even littler hypotheses than the clinical hypotheses by means of which we expect to bridge our day-to-day relationships with the patient. We sort and re-sort our observations as one would sort and re-sort the objects in a concept formation test. Gradually we generate hypotheses which have implications for the patient's future and which can be tested during our subsequent contacts with the patient.

The statistical dragnet way is like the way of the personnel test technician. He scrounges items from wherever he can find them lying around loose. When he gets a tub full he locks the patients out of his office and starts making tally marks. The hodgepodge of biases and theory out of which the items were originally produced do not concern him. He is a theoretical opportunist, ignoring but always ready to make profit out of the theoretical reasoning of others. Now if one has to develop a selection test to meet a national emergency this method is undoubtedly a good one to follow. It may, however, provide little assistance to a discipline which is interested in a long-range scientific advancement or to the clinician who must do a little special theory construction every time he must work through a case.

All of these sources of little hypotheses are utilizable in some measure by the clinical psychologist. He may tend to lean more heavily upon the clinico-inductive method, but even that method, because it depends upon observations which are themselves a kind of littler hypothesis, is based upon implicit, if not explicit, theoretical biases. What we are saying is that theory, implicit or explicit, unified or hodgepodge, must inevitably determine what it is that a clinical psychologist is able to see in his patient. Perception itself is systematically biased. Even the clinician's observations are little hypotheses which became visible to him only because he took his stand at a particular theoretical vantage point.

The question remaining is whether or not it is worthwhile to bother to make clinical psychologists aware of their theoretical biases or to suggest that they try some variations in their theoretical positions. I called attention to the fact that it is extremely difficult for one to be aware of the unique nature of his own point of view. Perception involves, among other things, the awareness of contrasts. One can be aware of the uniqueness of his own point of view only if he has been aware of the important characteristics of some other point of view against which his own stands out in contrast.

The graduate student who comes to you and says that he wants to deal with patients as they really are and that he therefore has no time to waste with all of this theoretical stuff is one who may be unable to realize the nature of his perceptual biases in his dealings with his patient. He has not seen enough of the contrasts between his position and those of others to be aware of what is going on when he makes an observation of his patient. Even if it is true that he is a good clinician, perhaps because his theoretical vantage point, though not explicitly stated, is one which does give him a fairly broad perspective in dealing with a patient, he is likely not to become a much better clinician after he has memorized all of the current clinical techniques. As psychological theory advances he is unlikely to be able to advance with it. He stands to become a victim of a sort of high level technological unemployment which we see taking its toll from among many of our colleagues who were trained a decade or more ago.

Basically then I see theory as playing an inevitable role in the work of the clinical psychologist. The question is shall we insist that it be an explicit theory. I think most graduate students in clinical psychology should be considered grown up enough to be told where the little hypotheses they use from day to day actually come from, and that they should not be left with the notion that clinical observations are always found under cabbages.

65

A Student's Outline of Graduate Training in Clinical Psychology in the Ohio State University: A Guide to Help the Prospective Graduate Student Formulate His Career Objectives and Plan His Training[1]

A Brief Look at the Profession of Psychology

Psychology embraces an amazing variety of activities. While some psychologists are making careful analyses of the phantasy life of preschool children, others are developing personnel record systems in industry, still others are designing aircraft instrument panel and radar network displays to conform to the perceptual limitations of the human observer and still others are studying the impact of new ideas on people who have long since settled down to a fixed way of life.

Can such a variety of interests be successfully subsumed in a single profession? Some psychologists say "no. we cannot." Most psychologists say, "yes, we can." But if we are to find a common core for all psychological thinking we must approach our field with a comprehensiveness of viewpoint which no other profession has yet been able to achieve. Of course no one psychologist can ever hope to master more than a small proportion of the specific techniques which various psychologists use. Yet if he is to be a member of a unified profession he must learn to *understand* them. This is a large order. It is no job for a constricted mind.

In the morning the student may find himself learning to listen intelligently to the word salad produced by a disturbed patient in a psychopathic ward of a hospital, in the afternoon he may present a paper in a seminar dealing with the Aristotelean view of concept formation and in the evening he may go home to study for an examination in mathematical probability theory. A student whose heart is set on the life of a technician will not be happy with such a schedule. Nor is it a simple matter for a four-year graduate training program to present the field of psychology with a proper distribution of emphasis upon detail and perspective. This little brochure describes how the problem is approached at the Ohio State University.

The Department

Ohio State has long had the largest and one of the most influential departments of psychology in the world. In clinical psychology it was one of the first to establish a graduate training program and now maintains the highest rating given by the Education Training Board of the American Psychological Association. A considerable proportion of the clinical psychologists of the country received their training here under a succession of distinguished past clinic directors: Henry Goddard, Carl Rogers, F.N. Maxfield, and C. M. Louttit. The roster of the Senior staff now lists the following names:

Name	*Field of Psychology*
Collins Burnett, Ph.D	Academic Personnel
H. E. Burtt, Ph.D. Chairman	Industrial
Mervin A. Durea, Ph.D.	Clinical
Horace B. English, Ph.D.	Educational
Paul M. Fitts, Ph.D.	Aviation
Frank M. Fletcher, Ph.D.	Industrial

[1] Prepared by George A. Kelly and the Clinical Staff, The Ohio State University, Columbus, Ohio; revised April 1st., 1953. Published by permission of Jacqueline Aldridge.

Collected Papers of the Pioneer of Constructivist Psychology: George A. Kelly, First Edition. Edited by David A. Winter and Nick Reed.

Name	*Field of Psychology*
Henry H. Goddard, Ph.D. (Emer.)	Clinical
Louis D. Hartson, Ph.D.	Educational
John K. Homphill, Ph.D.	Industrial
John E. Horrocks, Ph.D.	Educational
George A. Kelly, Ph.D.	Clinical
John R. Kinzer, Ph.D.	Academic Personnel
Erwin Lotsof, Ph.D.	Clinical
Donald R. Meyer, Ph.D.	Experimental
Paul H. Mussen, Ph.D.	Clinical
Harold B. Pepinsky, Ph.D.	Academic Personnel
Sidney L. Pressey, Ph.D.	Educational
Philburn Ratoosh, Ph.D.	Experimental
Samuel Renshaw, Ph.D.	Experimental
Francis P. Robinson, Ph.D	Academic Personnel
Julian B. Rotter, Ph.D.	Director, Psychological Clinic

Staff	
Alvin Scodel, Ph.D.	Clinical
Emily Leatherman Stogdill, Ph.D.	Clinical
Herbert A. Toops, Ph.D.	Statistics
Robert J. Wherry, Ph.D.	Statistics
Delos D. Wickens, Ph.D.	General
Robert D. Williams, Ph.D. (Emer.)	General
Carroll L. Shartle, Ph.D.	Clinical
Lauren G. Wispe, Ph.D.	Social

Field Staff in Clinical Psycology
Maurice Newberger, Ph.D.
Harold Paine, Ph.D.
Mervin Patterson, Ph.D.
Ruth Patterson, Ph.D.
Persis Simmons, Ph.D.
Dorothea Smith, Ph.D.
Alberta Turner, Ph. D.
Ranald Wolfe, Ph.D.
Henry Samuels, Ph.D.

Careers in Psychology

When the American Psychological Association was organized in 1892, less than half of its 35 members could lay claim to being psychologists. Today there are over 11,000 psychologists who are members of whom about fifteen per cent are in the Clinical Division. The occupations in which psychologists engage have become so diverse that some psychologists are expressing doubt that they can much longer be identified by a common core of knowledge.

The following represent some of the diverse occupations that make up psychology:

Biomechanics
  Design of equipment to suit human limitations
Clinical Psychology
  Institutions, clinics, agencies, preventive mental hygiene
Community Relations
  Analysis and alleviation of inter-cultural conflicts
Industrial Personnel
  Selecting, training, employee relations

Market Research and Opinion Polling
  Consumer analysis, public attitudes
Occupational Analysis
  Job classification, efficiency, operation specifications
Psychoeducational Clinic Services
  Learning and educational adjustment problems
Teaching
  Various academic and service fields
Test Construction
  Design of special measuring instruments
Educational Personnel
  School Counselors, deans' offices, student affairs
Military Psychology
  Personnel, human engineering, morale, psychological warfare, training, leadership, teamwork.

Kinds of Employment Suitable for Clinical Psychologists Typical Salaries 1953

Position	*Training*	*Starting*	*After 10 Years*
School (9 mos.)	M.A.	$3000-4000	$3000-4500
	Ph.D.	4000-5000	4000-5500
Colleges & Universities (9 mos.)	Ph.D.	4000-5000	5000-8000
State Hospitals	Ph.D.	3500-4500	3500-6000
U.S. Hospitals (VA & USPH)	Ph.D.	6000	7200-8400
Neuropsychiatric Clinics	Ph.D.	4500-5500	5000-8000
Child Guidance Clinics	Ph.D.	4500-5500	5000-8000
Social Agencies	Ph.D.	4500-5500	5000-7000
Penal Institutions	Ph.D.	4500-5500	5000-6000
Military Services	Ph.D.	5000-6000	5500-7500
Industry	Ph.D.	4500-6000	6000-12000
Private Practice	Ph.D.	2000-4000	4000-12000
Research	Ph.D.	3000-6000	3000-8000

In some respects the figures cited are misleading. For example, the salaries listed for Ph.D.'s in state hospitals and schools are higher than the amount commonly offered. They are more representative of what a very small number of psychologists are currently accepting. In other words, the majority of such positions are still going begging because of failure to offer salaries commensurate with professional training.

We have not listed salaries for psychologists who have only the M.A. degree except in the case of school psychologists. More and more psychology is moving toward an all Ph.D. profession, especially in the area of clinical psychology. For example, the Veterans Administration is abandoning all of its sub-doctoral positions in clinical psychology. The U.S. Public Health Service discontinued the employment of non Ph.D. clinical psychologists immediately after World War II.

This employment prospectus would not be complete without some reference to the pre-war situation. During depression times the standard starting rank and salary for newly graduated Ph.D. in many first-class universities was "instructor" at $1800. Some paid as little as $1200. Moreover, many of the employing institutions had no provision for advancement, either in rank or in salary. One state university reduced its department chairman to an annual salary of $1960 and made it stick.

It is impossible to predict what salary scales would prevail in the event of another economic depression and with a greatly increased number of psychologists:

Basic Qualifications

Interests

No one has yet been able to establish an empirical basis for predicting a person's eventual job satisfaction in clinical psychology from the pattern of interests he displayed before he was trained. Clinical psychologists report all sorts of pre-professional aspirations: engineering, theology, philosophy, education, literature, medicine, social work, law and other unexpected occupations. Perhaps the best way to evaluate one's interests in relation to the field is to look into the records of people who have found clinical training and practice uninteresting or distasteful.

Research

Commonest among the reasons for regretting the choice of clinical psychology seems to be an unexpected distaste for research. Research requires a combination of imagination and objectivity, two traits not often combined in the same person.

Disillusionment regarding research is not far around the corner when a graduate student makes one of the following statements:

1 "My adviser won't give me any idea of what he wants me to do."
2 "I want to do a problem that doesn't involve statistics."
3 "I don't want to spend a lot of time on a problem and then have it turn up negative results."
4 "This test does everything and I want to do research on it."
5 "I'm going to collect a lot of data and then find some way to work it up."
6 "I'm going to start with a questionnaire and then . . . . . ."
7 "I have just thought of a new projective technique."
8 "Every thesis topic I get somebody finds something wrong with."
9 "I'm tired of all this negativistic approach to everything."
10 "Can't I just do the Smith experiment over again and see if I get the same results?"
11 "First I'm going to get all my course work out of the way."
12 "I'm going to do my thesis during the summer quarter."

Carrying Cases

It may be late in the clinical graduate student's training course when he first discovers how it feels to have a case hung on him. Of course the needs of his patient get the right-of-way over his own. Then he begins to see stretching ahead of him a career comprised of thousands of days spent facing a lot of very unreasonable people who are always getting in the way of his advancement. If he is one who dreads carrying a burden of personal responsibility he may at this point start indulging himself with fantasies of neat and plausible "lectures" on the subject of "clinical" psychology. The next year he gets a teaching job!

I Want to Understand People

It must be wonderful to feel that one understands people, but the well trained clinical psychologist never reaps that reward! For him the questions always outnumber the answers and even the answers are dated and subject to reformulation. Never can he hope to lay claim to such a luscious title as, "*recognized psychological authority*." American Psychologists scrupulously avoid reliance upon the authority of any psychologist, no matter how distinguished. In psychology there is no "authority," only "evidence."

Students who want to live in an ordered world of answers rather than in a strange world of questions are likely to be unhappy in the field. To have preferred the ordered world is no indictment of their character, only a guidepost directing them from clinical psychology.

Status

The student who deeply fears that his contributions will not be heeded and who looks forward to being reverently called "doctor" usually ends up taking a M.D. degree, or wishing that he had! In contrast there is a sense in which the clinical psychologist, by choosing to be first of all a scientist, condemns himself to the role of a layman in his own field. There is no clergy to invest him either with safe doctrine or special privileges. Indeed, in most states clinical psychologists have no legal status and in some, the laws are written in such a way as to make his proper activities precarious.

On the whole psychologists have not, at least, until recently been a status minded group. There is a reason for this. Psychology has taken the matter of being a *science* quite seriously. Perhaps more than any other group, psychologists have tried to analyze just what it means for a discipline to become a science.

The outcome of this thinking is the widespread conviction among psychologists that no one can maintain his scientist's integrity if he even so much as keeps one eye cocked for popular approval of his work. Each separate work must stand solely on its own merits. There must never be the slightest reliance upon the worker's status, his reputation, or even his previous record as a successful research worker. Above all truth must always be allowed to stand in her own right and never be presumed to rest upon any kind of official pronouncement.

This self-conscious adherence to objectivity has led psychologists to assume some unusual positions. For a long time the American Psychological Association refused to endorse or support any kind of professionalization in the field. Only recently has it partly reconsidered its stand against "regimentation." Now the Association is frantically and ambivalently engaged in belated attempts to meet the public responsibilities of a leading profession while still maintaining the intellectual freedoms necessary for the advancement of psychology as a science. Psychology's insecure status as a profession is therefore undoubtedly a good reason for certain students' reconsidering their vocational choice.

Ability

A high. I.Q. is a useful gift but provides no definite insurance against failure in this field: Most of the people who fail in clinical psychology have enough ability to make acceptable marks in their courses but do not possess the other qualifications necessary for success.

The median centile of O.S.U. clinical graduate students on the Ohio State Psychological Examination is the 99th. Some, however, have done promising work although they rank below the 90th. Roughly, it appears that a person who is unable to score above an I.Q. of 130 on an intelligence test may be somewhat handicapped by his lack of intellectual facility but that differential values above 130 have relatively little prognostic significance.

For admission to the Graduate School the University requires a point-hour ratio of 2.5 (midway between C and B) in all credited undergraduate work and 2.7 in the major. This requirement is so liberal as to be misleading as far as graduate training in clinical psychology is concerned. On the other hand, even this regulation may keep out a few really promising students. Some students have low point-hour ratios simply because they have not been able to apply themselves effectively.

Perhaps a more helpful gauge of ability is the student's own candid answer to the question: "Could I, without an unreasonable amount of drudgery, have maintained a point-hour ratio of 3.5 or better?" The student who fails to answer the question honestly sets his career on precarious grounds and endangers his own feeling of personal security over the coming years.

Assessment of Basic Qualifications

Students who are about to commit themselves to training in clinical psychology will usually find it helpful to get an outside appraisal of their interests and abilities in relation to the field. Certainly the judgment of one's undergraduate psychology teacher should be sought. If a university guidance bureau such as the Occupational Opportunities Service at Ohio State University is available, a day spent there will give the student some grounds upon which to lay his plans.

Vigor

The strain of completing doctoral training in clinical psychology can scarcely be over-estimated. Not only must the candidate assimilate the factual background and complex theory, and meet the traditionally high scientific research standards of psychology, but he must acquire an armamentarium of clinical techniques sufficiently complete to enable him to team up on equal professional grounds with physicians and social workers whose training has been wholly directed toward professional practice. That is a double order. Poor health, advancing years, distracting family obligations, a too long dormant interest in book learning, or motivation solely by the fear of losing one's job, all are warning signs that the road to the doctoral degree will extract a heavy toll.

One's Purpose

The clinical psychologist "works with people" and normally enjoys it very much, yet many students who expect to enjoy clinical psychology because they too like to work with people are disappointed. Usually their mistake is in believing that the psychologist is a "super-influencer" and can "change people." The student should examine his motives carefully and see if he should not choose some other occupation which utilizes persuasive skills primarily.

So-called "warmth" of personality is highly desirable in a clinical psychologist. From the patient's point of view a psychologist is "warm" when he is instantly responsive to the feelings of the patient and seems to join him in those feelings either by reflecting them spontaneously or by adopting a complementary role. If one's interest in "working with people" naturally expresses itself in "warmth," at least one of the desirable personal qualities of clinical psychologist is present.

The altruistic and selfish components in one's strivings are probably not antithetical. In a theoretical sense one's purposes can be plotted with reference to either axis. In a practical sense a student should be able to orient his daily work satisfactorily with reference to the altruistic parameter without frequently having to chart his course in relation to personal needs. This is especially important in maintaining morale in the clinical psychology profession.

The Training Program Viewed as a Whole

Basic Aims

There is a rapidly growing mass of experimental and theoretical literature in the field of psychology and the student of clinical psychology must establish reading habits at the outset of his training which will enable him to catch up and keep up with it, Reading should include all fields of psychology, not clinical psychology alone. One of the aims of the Ohio State program is to train people to be students of all of psychology all of their lives.

A second aim is to provide the student with a broad enough background of information and training to enable him to serve usefully in a great variety of positions, including some positions that are not designated as clinical. Students who come to the Clinic asking to be trained solely as "hospital" psychologists or "court" or "school" psychologists are usually advised to take the Master's degree only and to enroll in another area of the Department or in another university. This training can be followed if desired, by a series of "refresher" courses. The Ph.D. degree in clinical psychology at Ohio State is reserved for those who wish to maintain a broad occupational motility.

The training program is also designed to be liberal in the best sense of the term. The coming decades promise many changes in the conceptual frames employed by scientists. The student who is trained as an avowed disciple of *Gestalt Theory, Nondirectivism, or Psychoanalysis* is too much in danger of being stuck with his pigeon hole system long after it has lost its usefulness. Not only is the program intended to place more than one conceptual system at the disposal of the student but it is hoped that he can be made free to re-constitute his conceptual system from time to time during his career. Thus it is planned that teaching will free students' concepts as well as fix them.

The Core

In contrast with many other training programs, the clinical program at Ohio State is organized around research as a core. If the psychologist has one accomplishment not widely shared, it is his research orientation and methodology in a field where the scientific approach is peculiarly difficult. It is believed that the clinical psychologist, if severed from this core, would soon degenerate into an "indoctrinated practitioner."

The student is urgently advised to write two dissertations. The first, if not submitted for a Master's degree, may be designated as a "minor problem." This arrangement either with or without the Master's degree, should involve no lengthening of the graduate program.

Duration of Training

The Ph.D. in clinical psychology normally requires at least twelve quarters, including three quarters under qualified psychological supervision in an approved internship. Students rarely are able to complete all requirements in the minimum time.

The first year is the technician's year. The Clinical Staff is eager that advanced theoretical discussions be preceded by some basic experience in handling the interpersonal relations and behavioral observations that comprise the groundwork for psychological theorizing. First year students are urged to complete their language requirements as soon as possible.

The second year is weighted more heavily with traditional psychology and personality theory. The student is expected to make some plans for his doctoral research and pass his preliminary and qualifying examinations.

The third year is an intern year. Research continues. Participation in seminars continues also. At the end of the intern year the student should be able to demonstrate reasonable skill in the basic clinical techniques as well as an understanding of the clinical material elicited by them.

The fourth year is devoted to research, to training in long term treatment and to occasional seminars. An examination over the doctoral dissertation completes the program.

Financial Aid

Few students complete doctoral training without taking advantage of opportunities for financial assistance. The principal forms of assistance at Ohio State are:

a Graduate Assistantships paying $900 for nine months service at fifteen hours a week. Encumbents may carry four-fifths of a normal schedule and are exempted from payment of fees during the three quarters of their employment and the next succeeding quarter.

b Teaching Assistantships paying $1350 for nine months service. Encumbents may carry two-thirds of a normal load and are exempted from payments of fees.

c U.S. Public Health Scholarships paying $1200, $1600, $2000, and $2400 respectively for the four years of graduate training. Scholars are exempted from payment of fees and are expected to devote their time exclusively to training. The number of these scholarships is quite limited.

d Veterans Administration Training Appointments paying from $750 to $3300 a year. This is a cooperative program involving the Veterans Administration and the Ohio State University. Payments are made at hourly rates for services rendered by trainees in V.A. installations. Employment is arranged and supervised so as to meet the requirements for internship, on the one hand, and the minimum of two years experience required by the U.S. Civil Service Commission for federal employment when the trainee graduates.

First year trainees may start to earn their stipends during the summer quarter following three quarters of campus study. They earn approximately $750 for 480 hours of service. Second year trainees earn approximately $1900 for 960 hours of service. Third year trainees earn approximately $3300 for 1440 hours of service. Fourth year trainees earn approximately $2300 for 960 hours of service. The Department's instructional program is supplemented in order to facilitate the plan. In addition to regular fees trainees pay a field laboratory fee of $70 to $210 a year depending on the amount of field supervision required.

Migration

The liberal tradition of the Ph.D. degree involves a graduate student's migrating from university to university in order to familiarize himself with varying points of view. The "ibid" degree has, in time past, been described as the poorest degree a university can give. The present day shortage of training facilities in the various universities of the country makes this traditional migration difficult and some cases, though still desirable, even impractical.

There are, of course, other ways in which the advantages of migration may be attained. To some extent the internship provides some protection against too much inbreeding of ideas. A careful choice of positions immediately following the completion of training may also provide some protection. In any case the graduate student should give some thought to the breadth of views with which he comes in contact and should take appropriate steps to avoid academic provincialism.

Breadth of Course Work

The work of the Department is classified into six areas:

1 General Psychology (including theoretical, experimental, comparative, and social)
2 Educational Psychology (including Mental and Educational tests)
3 Clinical and Abnormal Psychology
4 Statistics
5 Industrial Psychology
6 Personnel (student)

In addition to the clinical and general areas, where the clinical student concentrates his course work, the Department expects each doctoral candidate to have taken at least six credit hours in each of the other four areas. Credit taken on the undergraduate level as well as work taken on the graduate level satisfies this requirement. Credits transferred from other universities may be evaluated with relation to these areas. This requirement is to make sure that the student actually makes contact with instruction in a variety of psychological areas. In addition the student should plan to take nine hours of credit outside the Department.

The Department sets a second, and more formal requirement to insure breadth of training. The preliminary examination requires the student to write a series of examinations in topical areas. These areas are detailed in the Department's "Manual for Graduate Students."

A third provision for helping the student acquire an extra string for his bow is the requirement of a minor area. This may be an area within the Department or in another Department. The qualifying examination covers both major and minor areas.

A fourth provision is in the nature of recommendation. The Department urges students to take at least nine hours in other Departments.

Breadth of training, however, cannot be completely attained by following regulations. It can come about only when the student himself takes the initiative in widening his range of intellectual awareness.

Taking Advantage of Staff Resources

The names of the psychologists with whom a student has studied become a permanent and important part of his record. In psychological circles they carry much more weight than the course titles recorded on the student's transcript. When a psychologist represents himself as having a Ph.D. from Ohio State his colleagues expect him to be able to explain faithfully the viewpoints of the professors who were on the staff when his degree was taken. This means that the student, in signing up for a course or seminar, undertakes more than the mastery of a bulk of subject matter. As a student who is later to identify this professor as one of his teachers he undertakes a scholar's obligation both to understand and to appreciate his teacher's contribution.

Relations to Staff

Sometimes students complain that they dare not express ideas of their own in the presence of staff members. Staff members are not, of course, wholly immune to intellectual attack and may defend themselves in various characteristic ways. Listening to a professor's vigorous intellectual defense of his own viewpoint is an exhilarating experience. No student should be frightened by it.

In general, the tactics which make a student feel that he is being gagged are the very same ones which make the professor feel that his own ideas are not being given a scholarly consideration. Obstacles to good intellectual discussion usually arise when the student makes one of the following tactical errors.

- a Blocks the professor's orderly development of a topic by insisting upon immediate open discussion whenever traces of doubt begin to cross his mind.
- b Repeatedly challenges the professor's viewpoint without being in a position to indicate that he has first tried to understand it and to organize his own thinking regarding it.
- c Refuses to accept the professor's invitation to participate in discussion even when he is unable to reconcile his own view with that apparently expressed by the professor. Discussion may have been requested by the professor in order to give himself a chance to correct misinterpretation of his presentations.
- d Expresses the attitude that since he is a "clinical psychologist" the non-clinical professor's ideas are not particularly relevant to his training.

Relations to Fellow Students

It is virtually impossible for a graduate student to develop himself satisfactorily without keeping in close intellectual contact with his colleagues. He should make sure that he is a congenial member of at least one small, informal group who enjoy intellectually stimulating discussions of psychological topics. Fellow members of one's own research team comprise a natural nucleus for such associations. Whenever possible, the professor who is a member of the research team will want to participate in such discussions, for he too would like to profit from this intellectual association.

Basically, the research team idea, employed at the Ohio State University in clinical psychology, is to be both an intellectual synthesizing activity and an organization for group action on research projects. It is in the research team that the student should find himself most intimately involved in all of the activities which characterize an enthusiastic clinical psychologist. If the student fails to make himself an effective participating member of his team he should not be surprised to discover that he has lost his richest opportunities for professional and scientific development.

The beginning graduate student will find that his own research will progress much more smoothly if he first has had some experience assisting the fellow members of his team carry out their own research projects. In no other part of his student's training program does so much labor appear to be "lost" as in research. Almost any significant study could be repeated by the original task. The best way for one to minimize "wasted" effort is to invest some time working with one's colleagues, shrewdly noting their mistakes and discovering how their research could have been more efficiently conducted. A student usually finds his investment of time amply repaid in a greater facility for designing his own research and in planning the labors involved in its execution.

While a student's closest collaboration in research activities is likely to be with fellow members of his research team he will frequently find that students in other areas of the Department will make unexpected and stimulating contributions to his thinking. He should therefore not allow his enthusiasm for clinical psychology to degenerate into provincialism. Since there are 200 graduate students in psychology at the Ohio State University, he will need to take the initiative in bringing himself into intellectual contact with students in other areas of the Department.

One other factor should be mentioned. Among one's fellow students are the "distinguished psychologists" of the coming generation. The psychologist in his student days has such in opportunity as he will never again enjoy to develop fast friendships with professional colleagues.

Planning a Career in Clinical Psychology

A career in clinical psychology is, of course, much more than a succession of jobs and places of employment. It is foremost an actively pursued course of personal growth; or, as some of us would phrase it, a development of a life-role. The stages by which the life-role emerges are implied in the following series of characterizations: "bright boy," "serious student," "a member of the psychological profession," "a responsible representative of the psychological profession." A graduate student should attempt to bring his concept of his own life-role to the top rung of this ladder. Those who rise no higher than the first or second rungs may in their later years be unwelcome adherents to the profession.

It probably would be a mistake for any young person now training himself for the profession of clinical psychologist to assume that in his generation the concept of a profession would continue to be the same as that which has dominated medicine and other professions in the past generation. Science and society are on the march. Just as the concept of the witch doctor with supernatural authority had to give way to the concept of a professional man exercising authority by virtue of formalized training, so this latter concept must eventually yield to the concept of a professional man being, first of all, a scientist.

Needless to say, this transition will be resisted by many, both by those in the ranks of the professions, who will insist that it is enough to learn the skills of the practitioner; and by those who have identified themselves as "scientists," who, ignoring their own research findings in this context, will protest that research competence is a very special gift that only a few dare claim. Notwithstanding these objections, the training program in clinical psychology at Ohio State is founded upon the notion that clinical psychology, at least, shall be a new kind of profession—a genuinely scientific profession. It is based upon the idea that neither the attitudes nor the competencies implicit in such a profession are as elusive as we once believed.

To be sure, our concepts both of research and of clinical practice will have to be restructured within this new concept of the profession. But it is time that should be done away[2]! Both research and practice in psychology have been conceived too narrowly. Indeed research has been conceived so narrowly that most of the great ideas which have eventually proved stimulating to research in psychology during the past forty years have arisen and acquired their early growth under aegis of extramural groups, e.g., Gestalt psychology and psychoanalysis.

Practice also has been conceived narrowly. There have been strong movements afoot to train practitioners without giving them an understanding of the scientific logic upon which their techniques must rest. Such practitioners necessarily emerge from training imbued with fixed doctrine rather than with the attitudes and skills which will permit them to evaluate their experiences and move forward with their times.

On the scientific side, the basic difficulty has been our traditional failure to recognize that the most important and difficult stage of research is that which precedes and leads to the formation of testable hypotheses. Research does not really start with the testable hypothesis, though many students have been taught to believe so. In clinical psychology the best testable hypotheses arise out of the experiences of the sensitive, theoretically oriented clinician.

It seems now to be time to discontinue teaching our students that good natural hypotheses are found under cabbages. The fact that some have already learned the truth for themselves suggests that the facts of life will become known somewhere—in a Freudian alley, if not elsewhere.

At the other end of the research scale is the old-fashioned clinician, alert and responsive to the murmurings of nature but unmindful of the scientific implications of what he sees and hears. He has been told, and he believes it, that he is not a scientist and what little of science he has seen he will have none of it! Like the savage in a rich and fertile land, he lives close to nature unmindful of the cultural wealth which surrounds him.

If the clinician can be taught to formulate his experience into the most tentative hypotheses and the scientist, on the other hand, can be given an appreciation of how new systems and hypotheses come into being, we shall create a synthesis of these two contrasts; a new concept of an integrated profession will arise and both science and practice should develop the more rapidly.

The student planning a career in clinical psychology is urged to use this conceptual framework. If he accepts it, he will, of course, continue to be a research man as well as a practitioner. The formulation of research hypotheses out of his daily clinical experience will come just as "naturally" as the act of picking up his paycheck at the end of the month. For those clinical psychologists whose activities are focalized upon the other end of the research continuum, the formation of testable hypotheses out of actual clinical experience will come just as naturally as catching the rabbit before making a rabbit pie.

This is the comprehensive view of the profession of clinical psychology upon which the student is asked to base his plans for a career.

Marginal Notes on a Career in Clinical Psychology

As soon as the student enters training in clinical psychology, he should identify himself as a Student Affiliate of the American Psychological Association. This level of membership will put him on the mailing list for the *Psychological Abstracts* and the *American Psychologist*. The former is a journal which will abstract all published articles in psychology during his professional lifetime. Psychologists normally accumulate a complete file. The *American Psychologist* is the Association's news journal. It also carries articles of professional and scientific interest.

In addition to identifying himself with the American Psychological Association, the student should plan to attend regularly meetings either of the American Psychological Association or of his regional association. The regional psychological association to which Ohio State psychologists belong is the Midwestern Psychological Association. Membership is required for those whose papers are placed on its programs. Attendance at meetings is one of the best ways to "keep up" professionally.

If possible the student should seek for himself the experience of reading a paper at a psychological meeting. He may find the reception of his ideas in such meetings more exciting than that to which he has been accustomed. The experience is not likely to be one which he will soon forget nor one from which he will fail to profit.

[2] Editors' note: (sic).

State Association Membership and License

Many of the states now have state psychological associations which are affiliated with the American Psychological Association. As soon as the newly-graduated psychologist arrives on the grounds to undertake his first job, he should seek out the appropriate state psychological association and join it. Membership in a state psychological association is an important step in identifying oneself with the psychological profession. If the state in which he assumes his first position is one of the increasing number which provide licensing and certification, he should inquire immediately as to the standards expected and take appropriate steps to secure the proper designation as soon as possible. The Ohio Psychological Association, for example, maintains a Board of Examiners and any psychologist practising in Ohio should seek to be certified by it.

Diplomate Status

At approximately the same time that he qualifies for fellowship in the American Psychological Association a candidate who has designed his career properly should be ready to apply to the American Board of Examiners in Professional Psychology for a diploma in the specialty of clinical psychology. To be eligible for the diploma the candidate must show at least five years of good experience in his specialty during which he has attained among his colleagues and in his community stature as a representative of psychology. At the present time not all of this experience must be post-doctoral but by the time present students are eligible it is expected that all of it must be post-doctoral. The record of his performance during his years of experience should lend positive support to his claim to being a well-qualified specialist in his field.

If the applicant's credentials meet the standards of the American Board of Examiners in Professional Psychology, his professional and scientific training will be examined, he will be admitted to a two-stage examination, the first a written examination and the second an oral examination. The examinations cover the broad aspects of his training, his special field, his particular area of post-doctoral study, and his technical competence.

Service to the Nation

The national welfare increasingly depends upon the mobilization of scientific talent. When his training is approximately complete the clinical psychologist will wish to consider the nature of his responsibilities as a scientifically trained citizen and take appropriate steps to make his services, whether in a military or in a non-combatant category, available in the event of national emergency. A commission as a reserve officer with an appropriate identification as a psychologist will do much to avoid the confusion which came about in the last war when some psychologists were improperly assigned to duties. A member of the Psychological Clinic staff will be glad to help the student work out this phase of his career.

The socially oriented psychologist will further recognize a long-term obligation to contribute his talents to the improvement of human relations so that national emergencies may be less likely to occur. His contributions should be most effective on the side of improving understandings and the psychological processes by which men are prepared to accept or reject new concepts. This psychologists should be able to do well.

As political philosopher or as an agitator, he is probably no more wise or effective than any other well-meaning person.

Interprofessional Relations

One of the skills which the clinical psychologist must learn particularly is that of harmonious and effective relationship with other professions, such as social work, education, psychiatry, and pediatrics. Such inter-professional relations require much more than a pleasant disposition and general good will. They require genuine insight into the points of view characteristic of these professional groups. Even if the clinical psychologist yields all the so-called professional prerogatives, he still will be unable to cooperate properly in interprofessional relationships unless he has a genuine appreciation of values held in high esteem by his colleagues. For this reason the clinical psychologist is urged to take at least one course in social work and at least one course in education before going on internship. In most instances the internship relationship will give him an opportunity for developing appreciations and skills which will enable him to cooperate successfully with other professions. The importance of this phase of career preparation can scarcely be over-emphasized.

First Position

The student on completing his doctoral training should give a great deal of thought to the choice of his first position. First of all he should consider the opportunities for a combination of service and intellectual stimulation of the job. The graduate who goes to an isolated position in a teacher's college or in a state hospital must be especially careful to make sure that he does not become professionally insulated and lose the chance for normal job advancement, either because his achievements remain unknown or because the march of profession and science passes him by.

Even if the graduate is fortunate enough to go to a "big league" position, he should keep alive his contacts with his former professors and make sure that they know how his career is progressing. The better positions in psychology are always filled on the basis of a recommendation initiated, not by the candidate, but by someone who has prestige in the field who knows him well and who has his name on the tip of his tongue at the opportune moment.

Private Practice

There appears to be a growing opportunity for clinical psychologists in private practice. A private practice is, however, still a rather hazardous undertaking. In general, it would appear that a psychologist would be well advised to attain diplomate status with the rich experience background which that implies before attempting it.

It is doubtful that anyone can establish a private practice satisfactorily simply by going into a strange community and hanging out his shingle. He will stand a much better chance of succeeding if he has been invited by the local psychological organization and has their public endorsement to insure that they will support his activities. In addition, the clinical psychologist going into private practice should do so at the invitation of key medical and welfare agency people in the community. The more people who feel some degree of responsibility for the initiation of his practice, the more likely he is to succeed in it.

It seems that it might be advisable for the clinical psychologist in private practice to establish close relations with one or two pediatricians or internists together with one or two psychiatrists or neurologists. The psychologist should plan to place his office in the same building with these professional colleagues so that he may have frequent communication with them regarding cases and may frequently seek their opinions on professional matters. Any psychologist working alone will profit from the counsel of wise people, whether they are of his professional stripe or not. Unless a psychologist can make arrangements to "staff" a sizable proportion of his cases, he runs the serious risk of developing screwy ways of doing things which may verge on malpractice.

The psychologist who enters into private practice may find that he can enter gradually by maintaining a half-time salaried position in some community clinic or school system while developing his private practice.

Reading

Early in his training, the clinical psychologist should establish the habit of reading regularly certain journals in his professional field. For the clinical psychologist, *The American Psychologist, The Journal of Consulting Psychology, The Journal of Clinical Psychology, The Journal of Personality*, and *The Journal of Abnormal and Social Psychology* are usually considered "must" reading. In another section of this handbook there appears a list of journals available in the Ohio State College of Education Library,

Service

The clinical psychologist is trained as a professional worker is well as a scientist and he carries an implicit obligation throughout his lifetime to put his skills to use whenever and wherever they are most urgently needed. Training in clinical psychology involves a large public outlay of funds for university instruction. At the present time training is feasible only for a small proportion of those who seek it. The student who is fortunate enough to procure training may well consider himself obligated to render the service which others might have rendered if they had been given his opportunity.

Scientific Integrity

It is difficult to define integrity but among psychologists scientific integrity has come to mean a certain humility regarding one's own opinion and a certain eagerness to conduct scientific investigations in a spirit of open-minded questioning rather than in an attempt to design a convincing demonstration. It implies also that one sees himself as a searcher for truth rather than as an attorney arguing in her defense. Of course, intentional misrepresentation of data or careless inferences from data are the most flagrant violations of the psychologist's code of scientific integrity. Now that psychology, and particularly clinical psychology, is recognizing its professional obligations as well as its scientific obligations, it must also assert its stand for professional integrity.

Ethics

At the present time there are codes of ethics being developed by the American Psychological Association and by some of the specialty fields within psychology. These codes are now published in tentative form. The student is urged to study these formulations and to give some thought to his moral and social responsibilities as a scientist and a professional man as well as to develop as early as possible in his career a clear sensibility as to his own position.

Research and Publication

While in training the student has an excellent opportunity to develop his research skills, and he should plan to initiate the pattern of research and publication which he expects to follow in pursuing his career as a clinical psychologist. Publications need not be frequent but, as far as possible, they should be of such a quality or of such a level of definiteness that they will be useful to other psychologists. The object of publications is, of course, not to make one's self famous, but to place in the hands of colleagues the results of experiences and thinking which may be of help to them in forwarding the science and profession of psychology. Seen in this light, a brief technique may be more useful and more worthy of publication than a more erudite composition which is not sufficiently complete to make sense for other psychologists.

Preparation for Graduate Work

The undergraduate who expects to enter graduate training in clinical psychology should prepare himself as broadly as possible in the psychological field. His major, as far as possible, should include some training in experimental methodology, human development, physiological psychology, social psychology, abnormal psychology, and especially statistical methods. It is not necessary for the undergraduate major to include a great deal of material with a clinical flavor. It is suggested, however, that he make sufficient contact with the content of clinical psychology to make sure that that is the field in which he wishes to work.

He should also start rending psychological journals. The student who arrives at graduate school without ever having digested a single scientific article is bound to be conspicuous.

The undergraduate should also plan his training so that he has some background in other social and natural sciences. The graduate curriculum has all too little place for the study of other disciplines.

Since by inflexible tradition, a candidate for the Ph.D. degree must pass language examinations, the undergraduate is urged to prepare himself for these examinations before entering graduate school.

At the Ohio State University a reading knowledge of two languages (in each of which there is a significant amount of psychological literature) or "comprehensive" knowledge of one language is required. If a student leaves this preparation until some time after he has started his graduate work, he is likely to find his graduate training period lengthened by whatever time it takes him to prepare himself for his language examinations. It would be ideal if the beginning graduate student would get his language requirements out of the way during his first quarter of graduate work.

A number of factors must be taken into account in the selection of languages, one of which is the fact that the selection can never, never be revised once it has been made a matter of record in the Graduate School. The student should consult his adviser before declaring his selection officially.

For further information regarding language requirements, see "Manual for Graduate Students" prepared by the Department of Psychology.

Admission to Graduate Training in Clinical Psychology

At the present time nation wide facilities for graduate training in clinical psychology are inadequate, both from the standpoint of the number of people seeking training and from the standpoint of the number of demands for trained psychologists. At the Ohio State University, selections are made on the basis of recommendations originating in the Department's Personnel Committee and are based upon vacancies reported by the Staff of the clinical area. Students who wish to be admitted to training in September should have all application materials in the hands of the Personnel Committee by the first of the preceding March. Approximately forty graduate students in clinical psychology are carried in the various stages of the four-year graduate curriculum.

Outline of Requirements and Stages of Training

The Research Team

On starting his graduate training in clinical psychology, the student is assigned to a research team under the leadership of a senior staff member. The activities of the research team are considered to be the core of the training program, and the student may expect to be an active participant in a research team throughout his training period. In the research team he finds fellow students actively engaged in developing research problems and he is expected to join with them in this activity. The research team meets regularly and the new or "provisional" members of the team may be asked to assist the "regular" members of the team in pursuing research which is already under way.

At the end of the first quarter, if the student's own research ideas have not germinated, he is rotated to another research team as a provisional member.

Pilgrimage

When the beginning graduate student has developed his own research enthusiasms to the point where he feels that he can discuss them with staff members, he goes on what has been locally termed "the pilgrimage." The pilgrimage consists in making a series of one hour appointments with each member of the senior staff in Clinical Psychology, plus any other people whom he may wish to include. In each appointment he first discusses his own research enthusiasms and second explores the research enthusiasms of the staff member and his team. As a preparation for his pilgrimage the student may visit other research team meetings.

At the end of the pilgrimage the student approaches the leader of the team of his choice and requests acceptance as a regular member. If he is accepted he reports the acceptance to the Director and the assignment is made effective immediately. He remains a member of the team until his research project, either Master's or Doctoral, is completed. On the completion of Master's research, he is reassigned to a team as a provisional member and later undertakes a second pilgrimage to determine the team on which he will work out his Ph.D. dissertation.

As much as possible the student is expected to utilize the resources of his research team, to rely heavily upon their advice, and particularly, of course, to learn from the team leader, who is also considered his "major adviser."

The All-Clinic Colloquy

From time to time all graduate students in clinical psychology are called together for a meeting of general interest. These meetings have to do with research, theoretical or professional problems.

Students' Diagnostic Examination

When the student has completed approximately forty-five quarter hours in psychology (including undergraduate hours) he is asked to take a diagnostic examination designed to indicate what further instruction he needs in order to round out his basic training in psychology. (See "Manual for Graduate Students.")

Language Requirement

As indicated before, the graduate student is expected to pass an examination covering a reading knowledge of two appropriate languages or pass a more comprehensive examination in a single language. *The student is urged to prepare himself for these examinations before entering graduate work.* The summer preceding admission to graduate school usually provides an opportunity for this purpose. He should not declare his choice of language officially until he has discussed his needs with his adviser. (See "Manual for Graduate Students.")

Departmental Course Areas

The department's offerings are organized into six areas. The graduate student in clinical psychology will, of course, be expected to concentrate his training in the areas of clinical psychology and general psychology. In addition, he should take at least six hours (either graduate or undergraduate hours) in each of the four other areas of the department: statistical psychology, industrial psychology, academic personnel psychology, and educational psychology. (See "Manual for Graduate Students" for complete lists of courses in each of these areas.)

Total Credits

A Ph.D. in clinical psychology requires a total of 135 hours of credit, exclusive of field work or internship credit. Of this number, approximately forty-five are credited to the doctoral dissertation and five to the Master's thesis. The remaining credits represent the minimum to be acquired through taking courses. Usually a graduate student takes many more hours than the minimum before he feels himself prepared for his preliminary and qualifying examinations. He, therefore, need not be greatly concerned as to whether or not every fragment of his work is being officially "credited" by the Registrar.

Master's Thesis

While not technically required as a preliminary to the doctoral degree, the completion of Master's degree work, including a thesis is expected of graduate students in clinical psychology. Usually a student can approach his doctoral dissertation with much more assurance if he has had experience with a complete cycle of research, from the formulation of a problem through the statement of experimental hypotheses, design, execution, analysis of data, and report. In certain cases a completed research project may be accepted in lieu of a Master's degree.

Doctoral Dissertation

Doctoral research should get under way during the second year of his graduate training. Experience with research enables the student to bring together many aspects of his training and will enable him to gain perspective over the field of psychology as a whole. The research activity which lies at the core of graduate training in psychology makes the difference between book-learning and mere technical skill on the one hand and scientific and professional insight on the other.

Advisory Committees

The Master's examination is conducted by a committee of three staff members, at least one of whom is from outside the student's major area. For the doctoral dissertation, a committee of three members, at least one of whom is outside the student's major area, comprises the advisory committee. The chairman is, of course, the team leader or thesis adviser. The doctoral dissertation committee is responsible for guiding a student in planning research, as well as for evaluating completed research. (See "Manual for Graduate Students.")

Preliminary Examinations

Approximately at the close of his second complete year of graduate training, the student is expected to pass his "prelims." The Preliminary Examination is usually considered by graduate students to be one of the biggest hurdles they have to clear. It is given twice a year, fall and spring, by a rotating committee of the department. It comprises six examinations of three hours each. The student should lean heavily upon his adviser's advice in preparation for the Preliminary Examination and should seek the adviser's appraisal of his competence on an informal basis before presenting himself for the examination. A student would be unwise to present himself for the Preliminary Examination if his adviser, who is in the best position to judge his level of training, considers him unprepared. (See "Manual for Graduate Students" for lists of topics and suggested basic bibliography).

Qualifying Examination

In the quarter immediately succeeding the Preliminary Examination, the clinical student is advised to take his Qualifying Examination. This examination is the one which is officially recognized by the Graduate School. The Qualifying Examination consists of a five-hour written examination in the major field and a two and one-half hour written examination in the minor field. In the case of a clinical psychology student, the major field is clinical psychology and the minor field is selected from one of the five remaining areas of the department. If the written examinations are satisfactory, they are followed immediately by an oral examination upon the successful completion of which the student is admitted to "candidacy" for the Ph.D. degree. The Qualifying Examination is administered by a committee of five, normally comprised of the student's adviser, the two other members of his dissertation advisory committee, and two other professors, one of whom is designated as the representative of the Graduate School.

Two or three months before presenting himself for the Qualifying Examination, the clinical student is advised to set up "kangaroo" orals for himself, by having fellow graduate students, particularly those who have already completed their Qualifying Examinations, play the roles of the five examiners in the Qualifying Examination. The student may experience a reasonable facsimile of what he is to go through later. The "kangaroo" orals enable the student to follow lines of questioning to improve his tactics in conducting his own side of the discussion, and to secure the appraisals of his fellow students as to areas in which he needs further preparation. The situation also is useful to those graduate students who play the roles of staff members, since after graduation, they may find themselves members of graduate faculties with the responsibility of conducting oral examinations. The student's team leader may well act as a moderator of the "kangaroo" orals, and make suitable comments on the performances of the "candidate" and the "Examining Committee".

For Further Information Regarding the Qualifying Examination, "Manual for Graduate Students."

Internship

The graduate student in clinical psychology is expected to complete three quarters of approved internship as an integral part of his course of study. Normally, the internship comprises the third year of graduate training. Only those internships which are approved may be offered in fulfillment of this requirement.

Final Examination

Upon completion of all the other requirements for the degree, the student, on advice of his adviser, presents himself for a final oral examination. While not necessarily restricted to a discussion of the dissertation, the student's completed doctoral research is usually the principal topic.

Course Offerings in Clinical Psychology

The clinical area courses are divided into two groups: (a) the graduate sequence for majors and minors and (b) a group of service courses for other students.

The Graduate Sequence

861. Clinical Methodology, 5 hrs. (incl. laboratory) Autumn.
862. Psychopathology, 5 hrs. (incl. laboratory) Winter.
863. Psychodynamics, 5 hrs. (incl. laboratory) Spring.
864. Psychodiagnostics, 5 hrs. (incl. laboratory) Autumn.
718. Group Psychotherapy, 2 hrs. Spring.
865 (825) Advanced Psychological Clinic.
2-13 hrs. (incl. 4 hrs. lectures and 9 hrs. practicum, both A and B types). Lectures Autumn through Winter, practicums Autumn, Winter, or Spring.

Courses 861, 2, 3, 4, 5 comprise a thirty-five credit sequence which must be taken in order except that 865 may be carried concurrently with 864. Admission is by permission of the instructor and no one is admitted to the next course in the sequence unless the staff is reasonably sure that he is prepared to carry the responsibilities involved. This implies more than merely a mark of "B" in the preceding course.

Course 861, Clinical Methodology is placed first in the sequence because of the staff's firm belief that an understanding of the clinical method, as one of the psychological approaches to personality, is basic. The aim is to enable the student to see the so-called "disease entities" and "facts" which he learns later, as constructs of clinical experience and valid only to the extent that the methods through which they were inferred are valid. The laboratory in this course first concerns itself with basic methods of observation and interview, then approaches the more precise methods of psychological examination as extensions of these methodologies.

The second course, Psychopathology, is a heavy reading course into which is crowded most of the traditional "content" of clinical psychology. The laboratory is a continuation of clinical method, arranged to support the student's understanding of pathological types. For example, at approximately the same time schizophrenia is discussed the student does a practice examination of a hospitalized schizophrenic patient, Similarly a delinquent child, a deafened child, a visually handicapped child; a reading deficiency case, a senile patient and types of mental defectives are examined in relation to the course's lecture syllabus.

The third course, Psychodynamics, is designed to give the student an overview of a person's development, both past and future. It should enable the student to utilize various theoretical frameworks in planning therapeutic or rehabilitative programs for individuals or groups, Again, the laboratory, now a live-run practicum, is correlated, with the student working as a junior member of a clinical staff actually engaged in therapeutic or rehabilitative services.

The fourth course, Psychodiagnostics, involves intensive study of the most advanced psychodiagnostic procedures and their evaluation in terms of the psychodynamic systems studied in the preceding course.

The fifth course, Advanced Psychological Clinic, involves a study of advanced psychotherapeutic principles and techniques, together with supervised practicum training of two types: type A, psychological advisory service, primarily for children in collaboration with schools, institutions and other community agencies; and type B, psychological treatment services primarily for children, their parents, or university students who are referred for problems requiring psychological. treatment of a clinical type.

In addition, the student takes a course in Group Psychotherapy in which lecture and practicum instruction are combined. As much as possible, he takes practicum work with different practical approaches. At Ohio State each member of the Clinic Staff takes at least one turn at service duty during the year to "keep his hand in." In addition to the core courses the student familiarizes himself with the advanced points-of-view of the various members of the senior staff through participation in current advanced seminars. With the exception of seminars all the courses in clinical psychology combine practicum instruction with the more conventional methods of instruction.

The Service Group

These courses are designed primarily for students who are not graduate majors in clinical psychology.

1 *For Personal Assistance*
408. Mental Hygiene, 3 hrs. All quarters.

2 *For Theory and Classified Information*
541. Abnormal Psychology, 3 hrs. Winter.

609. Exceptional Child, 3 hrs. Autumn, Winter, Spring.
678. Personality, 3 hrs. Spring.

3 *For Special Problems Areas*

611. Intellectual Deviate, 3 hrs. Winter.
622. Delinquent Child, 3 hrs. Spring.

4 *For Methods*

671. Treatment of Behavior Problem Child, 3 hrs. Winter, Summer.
690. Mental Hygiene for Professional Workers, 3 hrs. Autumn, Summer.
695. Introduction to Clinical Method, 5 hrs. (incl. laboratory). Spring, Summer.

Course Syllabi in the Graduate Sequence

Psychology 861. Clinical Methodology. 5 hrs. Mussen and Assistants. Autumn.

I a Clinical observation of free behavior, the complaint, observation structure, time sampling, scheduling, psychodrama, and sociometry.
b Laboratory practice in time sampling and one-way screen technique.
II a Collateral interviewing, sources of information, personal involvement, preparatory interviewing, and method. of broadening the psychological field.
b Laboratory practice in collateral interviewing.
III a Free interviewing, self-conceptualization, the subjective phenomenon, and case integrity.
b Laboratory practice in free interviewing, recording of interviews, analysis of form, content, technique, and interpersonal behavior manifest in the interview.
IV a Fixed interviewing, anamnesis, testing forms, and introduction to intelligence testing.
b Laboratory practice in Wechsler-Bellevue testing, recording, and monitoring.
V a Specific test techniques, Wechsler-Bellevue, Stanford-Binet, Arthur, Goodenough, and representative group tests.
b Continuation of laboratory practice in individual psychometrics.
VI a Clinical psychology as a profession, historical background, practical aspects of interprofessional relations, present status of the profession, professional standards, ethics, and professional advancement.
b Continuation of laboratory practice in individual psychometrics.
VII a Accumulation and analysis of documentary information, school records, medical records, employment records, social work records, institutional records, court records, family records, and autobiography.
b Laboratory practice in relating documentary information to test selection and interpretation,
VIII a Case structurization, means of formulating a meaningful conceptualization of a case problem, progressive approximation of treatment, a play-by-play study of a case.
b Laboratory practice in cross-checking psychometrics.
IX a Clinical records and reporting, referrals, pre-screening of cases, development of a community psychological service, organization and conduct of different types of staff conference, records and files, follow-up procedures, anticipation of research uses, reporting to clients, parents, teachers, agencies.
b Laboratory practice in reporting simple psychometric findings.
X a Completion of a psychological case study, projecting treatment, distinction between static and dynamic factors.
b Laboratory practice in simulating types of subject behavior and in detecting invalidating factors in a test situation.

Psychology 862. Psychopathology. 5 hrs. Kelly and Assistants. Winter.

I Orientation to Psychopathology.
a Descriptive nosologies, medical orientation, special problems in adaptation, institutions, emerging concepts.
II Infant psychopathology
a Techniques in the examination of infants, infant problems.
b Examination of infants in St. Ann's Orphanage.
III Psychopathology of early childhood.
a Enuresis, cerebral palsy, malnutrition, convulsions, encephalitis, behavior problems.
IV Educational deficiencies.
a Reading and various subject matter disabilities, psychomotor disabilities.
b Psychological examinations in the Boy's Trade School.

V Mental mechanisms and processes.
  a Review of technical terminology.
VI Principal clinical constructs used in diagnosis.
  a Anxiety, affect, emotional inadequacy and inappropriateness, psychomotor activity, ideational content, reality contact, conceptualization.
  b Psychological examinations in the Columbus State Hospital.
VII Observation and informal testing.
  a Reactive signs, structural signs, social signs, social frames of reference, informal testing.
VIII Nosological systems.
  a History of classification systems, recent developments, legal and social considerations.
IX Conversion and anxiety reactions
  a Symptom choice, common symptoms, diagnostic principles, phobic reaction, anxiety reaction.
X Psychosomatic reactions.
  a Epistemological problem, differential diagnosis.
XI Affective disorders
  a Differentiation, melancholia, manic-depressive reactions, neurotic depression.
XII Schizophrenic disorders.
  a Ideation, symptoms, types.
XIII Sexual deviation and paranoid disorders
  a sex role, correlates, diagnostic procedures, types.
XIV Personality disorders
  a Principles, types, new classifications, situational factors.
  b Psychological testing in the State School for the Deaf.
XV Addictions and infections
  a Alcoholic disorders, drug addictions, syphilis, encephalitis, chorea.
  b Psychological testing in the State School for the Blind.
XVI Convulsive disorders
  a Types, pathology.
  b Psychological testing in the Columbus State School.
XVII Degenerative disorders
  a Cerebral accident, lobotomy, shock therapy, cretinism.
XVIII Aphasias
  a History, pathology, treatment.
XIX Mental Deficiency
  a Views, organic types, anatomy.
XX Education of the retarded child
  a Conceptualization, institutional adjustments, misinterpretations, parental adjustments.

Psychology 863. Psychodynamics. 5 hrs. Lectures, Rotter; Practicum, Paine, Turner, Lotsof. Spring.

This course deals with the common methods of psychological treatment and the theoretical structures on which they are based. The laboratory practice is loosely related to classroom lectures and is designed to give the student practice in examination of actual clinical cases and participating in conferences in which treatment plans are formulated. An outline of lecture topics is given below.

Part I. General

a The place of theory in clinical psychology
b The nature of constructs and description in personality
c Dimensions on which theories may be compared.

Part II. Individual Treatment Techniques

a Psychoanalysis
  1 Classical
  2 Modern - Alexander and French
b Adler's Individual Psychology
c Jung's contribution
d Analytic derivatives, play therapies

1 Levy's release therapy
2 Free play therapy
3 Puppets and expressive therapies
4 Psychodrama

e Rank and Rankian Derivatives
1 Jessie Taft
2 Allen's relationship therapy
3 Rogers' Client-Centered therapy.

f Role Therapy

g Learning Approaches
1 Sullivan
2 Dollard, Miller, and Mowrer
3 Implications of Social-learning theory

Part III. Integrative Concepts

a Catharsis
b Insight
c Support and reassurance
d Retraining

Part IV. Environmental approaches to children's problems.

a Institutions
b Foster home placement
c Camps and clubs
d Treatment of parents
e Use of the schools

Psychology 864, Psychodiagnostics. 5 hrs. (incl. lab.) Rotter and Scodel. Autumn.

This course deals with the nature, validity and underlying assumptions of the major "diagnostic" clinical tests. Emphasis is placed on the more difficult "projective" tests. The laboratory is integrated with the lectures and aims at giving the student initial practice in the administration and interpretation of the techniques discussed in lectures.

Part I. General Diagnostic Theory

a The function of diagnostic tests
b Criteria for useful clinical instruments
c Methods and problems of validation
d Projective, objective, and behavioral approaches

Part II. Projective Methods

a Rorschach
b Thematic Apperception Test
c Bender-Gestalt
d Incomplete Sentences
e Picture-Frustration
f Survey of other formal techniques
g Survey of informal techniques

Part III. Objective Tests

a Wechsler-Bellevue Analysis
b Babcock Test and Binet Analysis
c Concept formation and sorting tests
d Memory tests
e Special tests of aphasia

Part IV. Behavioral Approaches

a Role Playing
b Level of Aspiration
c Assessment techniques

Psychology 865. Advanced Psychological Clinic. 2-13 hrs. Kelly, Mussen, Rotter, Scodel. Lectures Autumn through Winter. Practicum Autumn, Winter, Spring.

Two lectures a week on advanced psychotherapeutic principles continuing through the Autumn and Winter Quarters with two hours credit each Winter or a total of four hours credit for the lecture portion of the course.

Two types of practicum are offered in connection with the community services of the Psychological Clinic: Type A, psychological advisory services, primarily for children in collaboration with schools, institutions and other community agencies; and Type B, psychological treatment services, primarily for children or for university students who are referred for problems requiring psychological treatment of a clinical type. Each unit of practicum requires a minimum of six hours of supervised duty per week throughout a quarter in addition to special preparations for the particular types of cases seen. Practicums are taken concurrently with or subsequently to the lectures. Three hours of credit are allowed for each practicum with a maximum total of nine hours of practicum credit. The student may not receive credit for more than two practicums of one type.

Lecture Section, Kelly

1st week: Considerations in the establishment of agency quality.
2nd week: Principles of receiving and thinking and making interprofessional referrals, the nature of basic records, which must be kept by a community agency.
3rd-4th week: Principles governing interdisciplinary professional relations. Introduction to the principles and operations of the so-called mental hygiene team. Functions and operations of the interdisciplinary staff conference. Functions and operations of the specialized staff conference.
5th-6th week: Preparation of first approximation of case information. Analysis of complaint and elaboration of case history to establish the psychological variables. Signs indicating need for specialized collaboration of other disciplines. Exploratory interview procedures. The technique of the fixed anamnesis. The technique of associative anamnesis.
7th week: On-the-spot analysis of psychological status. The mental status examination. The home visit. The ward round.
8th week: Principles and procedures involved in the interpretation of psychological findings to parents and teachers.
9th week: The use of fixed role technique in psychological readjustment. The use of a free role technique in psychological readjustment.
10th-11th week: The techniques and principles in handling transference and resistance phenomena.
12th week: The technique and principles governing the use of supportive and reassurance techniques.
13th week: Concept formation procedures in psychotherapy. The handing of rigidity.
14th-15th week: Analysis of dreams, fantasy, and reminiscence material and its interpretation to the client.
16th week: Warning signs indicating inability to handle material during psychotherapy or in the acceptance of psychological information. Control of anxiety and guilt.
18th week: Utilization of cultural determinants in psychotherapy. The place of vocational and situational planning.
19th week: Procedures for setting limits on behavior in child psychotherapy.
20th week: Institutionalization and custody as basic methods of treatment for children and methods of treatment for children and adults. The use of fixed limits in out-patient treatment of adults.
21st week: Utilization of occupational therapy procedures. Utilization of social facilitation procedures.
22nd-23rd week: Principles and procedures involved in planning a comprehensive psychological rehabilitation program for individual patients, and the setting of psychotherapeutic goals for the therapist.

Psychology 826, Personal Adjustment. 3 hrs. per quarter, Stogdill. Autumn, Winter, Spring.

One of the laboratories of Psychology 865 may be supplanted by a quarter of Psychology 826, Personal Adjustment. This practicum is identified with the Mental Hygiene Service carried on by the Psychological Clinic in conjunction with the "Remedial Aids Service" of the Department of Psychology.

Psychology 718, Group Psychotherapy. 2 hrs. Mussen, Scodel. Spring.

Two quarter hours, given in spring quarter, lecture and participation, the latter predominating as far as time spent is concerned. A study of the underlying principles of group psychotherapy, emphasis on the psychodynamics of the individual as they operate in a group situation. The student learns the basic principles of and participates in the various group therapy techniques—the free discussion, psychodrama, activity therapy, etc., yet with his point-of-view constantly being directed toward the revelation and working-out of the problems of the individual. Differences in methods for children, adults, the mentally ill, the mentally retarded are discussed, as are comparative merits of active and passive therapy, importance of acceptance and permissiveness, and the role played by catharsis. Some lectures are given by Social Administration and Neuropsychiatry Staffs.

lst week: Introduction to group therapy, definition, scope.
2nd week: Survey of group therapeutic methods and related methods such as socio-drama. Possible application of group therapy methods to such social institutions as the school, athletic and social clubs, and to the understanding of group dynamics. Principles of selection for group therapy. (Two lectures by Social Administration Staff.)
3rd - 4th week: Detailed description of child and adolescent methods (Slavson, Shoob, Redl, and others.)
5th week: Detailed description of adult methods used in psychiatric hospitals for mentally disordered cases (Department of Neuropsychiatry).
6th week: Detailed description of adult counseling methods for the less seriously disturbed (Moreno, Rogers, and others).
7th week: The active and passive therapist. Discussion of their roles and theoretical positions.
8th week: The role of acceptance and permissiveness. The role of insight and education.
9th week: The role of catharsis.
10th week: Factors and influences inherent in the group situation; significance of community factors (Social Administration). Significance of intra-group psychology.
11th week: Summary of principles of group therapy.

(Note: At least one third of the time is spent in practicum--role playing demonstrations of techniques, etc.)

Psychology 806, Seminar in Clinical Psychology. 2 hrs. per quarter. Mussen, Rotter, Scodel, Kelly.

The student is expected to carry from three to five quarters of Psychology 806, preferably with different staff members. These seminars are designed to enable the individual staff member to present his most advanced point of view and to enable the student to understand and appreciate the contributions of individual staff members,

Psychology Journals Available in the College of Education Library

Basic Journals for Clinical Psychologists

The American Psychologist
The Journal of Consulting Psychology
The Journal of Clinical and Abnormal Psychology
The Journal of Clinical Psychology
The Journal of Personality

Other Journals in Psychology

Acta Psychologica
American Journal of Mental Deficiency
American Journal of Orthopsychiatry
American Society for Psychical Research
American Psychologist
Archiv fur die Gesamte Psychologie
Archives de Psychologie
British Journal of Educational Psychology
British Journal of Psychology, Medical Section
Bulletin of Menninger Clinic
Canadian Psychological Association
Child Development
Child Development Monograph
Educational and Psychological Measurements
Genetic Psychology Monographs
Indian Journal of Psychology
International Journal of Psychoanalysis
International Zeitschrift fur Individual Psychologie

Japanese Journal of Psychology
Journal de Psychologie Normale et Pathologie
Journal of Child Psychiatry
Journal of Clinical Psychology
Journal of Comparative Psychology
Journal of Consulting Psychology
Journal of Educational Psychology
Journal of Experimental Psychology
Journal of General Psychology
Journal of Parapsychology
Journal of Psychology
Journal of Social Issues
Journal of Social Psychology
Nervous Child
Psychiatric Quarterly
Psychoanalytic Review
Psychological Bulletin
Psychological Monographs
Psychological Record
Psychologische Forschung
Psychometrika
Review of Educational Research
Revista de Neuro-psiquiatrie
Revista de Criminologia and Psiquiatrie
Revista de Disciplinas and Psiquiatrie
Rivista de Pedagogia and Psiquiatrie
Rorschach Research Exchange
Society for Psychological Study of Social Issues
Sociometry
Studies in Psychology and Psychiatry
Zeitschift fur Angewandte Psychologie
Zeitschrift fur Arbeitspsychologie
Zeitschrift fur die Gesamte Neurologie and Psychologie
Zeitschrift fur Jugendkunde
Zeitschrift fur Pedagogische Psychologle

Suggested Curriculum for Clinical Psychology Majors in the Department of Psychology

The following courses or equivalents will be considered to be included in the undergraduate training of clinical psychology major. If these courses have not been taken then, they will have to be taken at the graduate level.

601 – 3 hrs.
605 – 3 hrs.
613 – 3 hrs.
637 – 3 hrs.
645 – 3 hrs.

Graduate Program
Courses in Clinical Psychology:

718 – 2 hrs.
861 – 5 hrs.
862 – 5 hrs.
863 – 5 hrs.

864 – 5 hrs.
865 – 10 hrs.
806 – 8 hrs.
910 – (V. A. students only) 16 hrs. (6 hrs. only credited toward residence)
950 – 30 hrs.
826 – 3 hrs. (optional)

Courses in General Psychology:

624 – 3 hrs.
626 – 5 hrs.
646 – 3 hrs.
647 – 3 hrs.
811 – 3 hrs.
805 – 1 hrs.
825 – 5 hrs.
606 – 3 hrs.
802 – 2 hrs. (optional)
668 – 3 hrs. (optional)

Statistics:

608 – 4 hrs.
814 – 4 hrs.
815 – 2 hrs. (optional)
816 – 4 hrs. (optional)

Industrial Psychology:

689 – 3 hrs.
807 – 2 hrs. (optional)

Social Psychology:

648 – 3 hrs.
812 – 3 hrs.
679 – 3 hrs. (optional)
813 – 3 hrs. (optional)

Academic Personnel:

684 – 3 hrs.
781 – 3 hrs.
785 – 3 hrs. (optional)
822 – 3 hrs. (optional)

Educational Psychology:

631 – 3 hrs.
840 – 3 hrs.
683 – 3 hrs. (optional)
803 – 2 hrs. (optional)
850 – 2 hrs. (optional)

Sociology and Anthropology:

Soc. 624 – 3 hrs.
Soc. 622 – 3 hrs.
Soc. 900 – 2 hrs. (optional)

Speech Pathology:

Sp. 694 – 3 hrs. (optional)

Excluding the special 910 course for the V.A. students, this totals 128 hours of courses strongly recommended and 42 hours of courses listed as optional.

Check List for Graduate Students in Clinical Psychology

On the following pages is a check list for graduate students in psychology similar to that which is used by the staff of the Psychological Clinic in keeping a record of individual students' progress. At the beginning of his graduate training the student should enter target dates for each of the major milestones of his course. These target dates should also be on file with the Director of the Psychological Clinic and may be made out in consultation with him. Revisions in target dates should be reported to the Director of the Psychological Clinic and, as each milestone is passed, the appropriate asterisk in one of the columns at the right should be encircled. The locations of the asterisks in the columns at the right indicate the normal quarter and year in which the milestone should be passed: for example, the Preliminary Examination should normally be passed in the spring quarter of the second graduate year.

The next sections indicate the clinical courses which are normally part of the graduate student's preparation. The number of credit. hours is entered at the right in columns which suggest the quarters in which the courses are available, and in which they would normally be taken. In the next section is a similar list for courses in the general area of psychology.

On the next page are some of the area requirements. The student should keep the Director of the Psychological Clinic informed as to current enrollments and as to courses completed, so that the Clinic Staff may be fully informed as to his progress and needs. Current enrollments are usually indicated by a check mark opposite the credit hour figure, and completions are usually indicated by circling the credit hour figure.

Check List

Name______________________________ From________________

Month, Year	1st	2nd					3rd			4th		
Target Dates	A	W	S	A	W	S	A	W	S	A	W	S
First Language________	*	.	.	.	.	.	.	.		.	.	.
Second Language ________	.	*	.	.	.	.	.	.	.	.	.	.
Diagnostic Exam. ________	.	*	.	.	.	.	.	.	.	.	.	.
First Pilgrimage _______	.	.	*		.	.	.	.	.	.	.	.
M. A. Degree________	.	.	.	*	.	.	.	.	.	.	.	.
Preliminary Exam. _____	.	.	.	.	.	*	.	.	.	.	.	.
Second Pilgrimage_____	.	.	.	.	.	*	.	.	.	.	.	.
Qualifying Exams._____	.	.	.	.	.	.	*	.	.	.	.	.
Internship__________	.	.	.	.	.	.	*	*	*	.	.	.
Ph.D. Degree____	.	.	.	.	.	.	.	.	.	.	.	*

Clinical Courses	Credit Hours											
861 Clinical Method	5	.	.	.	.	.	.	.	.	.	.	.
862 Psychopathology	.	5	.	.	.	.	.	.	.	.	.	.
863 Psychodynamics	1	.	5	.	.	.	.	.	.	.	.	.
864 Psychodiagnostics	.	.	.	5	.	.	.	.	.	.	.	.
718 Group Psychotherapy	.	.	2	.	.	.	.	.	.	.	.	.
865 Advanced Clinic	.	.	.	2	2	.	.	.	.	.	.	.
Lab A	.	.	.	.	3	–	–	.	.	.	.	.
Lab B (or 826)	.	.	.	.	–	3	3	.	.	.	.	.
806 Seminar (3-5 q.)	.	.	.	2	2	2	.	.	.	–	–	–

Generalized Courses

608 Stat. Methods	4	.	.	.	.	.	.	.	.	–	–	–
613 Mental Tests	3	.	.	.	.	.	.	.	.	.	.	.
626 Human Learning	.	.	.	5	.	.	.	.	.	.	.	.
812 (813) Adv. Social	.	.	.	3	.	.	.	.	.	.	.	.
624 Perception	.	.	.	.	3	.	.	.	.	.	.	.
814 Adv. Statistics	.	.	.	.	4	.	.	.	.	.	.	.
646 (645) (647) Views	.	.	.	.	3	.	.	.	.	.	.	.
811 Adv. Theoretical	.	.	.	.	.	3	.	.	.	.	.	.
825 Exper. Method.	.	.	.	.	.	5	.	.	.	.	.	.

Take credit in six hours, at least, in each of the following psychological areas, either as a graduate or as an undergraduate.

	1st Yr.			2nd Yr.		
Statistics Courses	A	W	S	A	W	S
815 Seminar in Statistics	.	.	.	2	–	.
816 Special Statistics	.	.	.	.	.	4
Industrial Courses						
689 Occupational Information	3	–	–	.	.	.
807 Seminar in Industrial	.	.	.	.	–	2
Academic Personnel Courses						
684 Counseling Practices	3	–	.	.	.	.
781 Remedial Counselling Lab.	.	.	3	–	–	.
785 Guidance Lab.	.	.	3	.	.	–
822 Seminar in Student Personnel	.	.	.	.	.	2
Educational Courses						
631 Individual Difference	3	.	.	.	.	.
683 Reading	.	3	.	.	.	.
803 Seminar in Educational	.	.	.	.	2	.
840 Human Development	.	3	.	.	.	.
850 Old Age	.	.	.	.	.	2

Out-of-Department Courses (9 graduate hrs.)

______________ ________ ________

______________ ________ ________

______________ ________ ________

______________ ________ ________

______________ ________ ________

66

Personal Construct Theory and the Psychotherapeutic Interview[1]

Biography of a Theory

A good many years ago when I first set for myself the task of writing a manual of clinical procedures it was with the idea that psychologists needed to get their feet on the ground, and I was out to help them do it. Other scientists had gotten their feet on the ground; why couldn't we? Elsewhere all about us there were those hardy breeds who had penetrated the frontiers of reality with boldness and forthrightness. Practical men they were who, with each bedrock discovery, discredited all those generations of anemic philosophers who never dared venture beyond the comforts of their own redundancies. And yet here was the gloomiest vista of all, the mind of man, only one step away—a deep cavern so close behind our very own eyes and still enshadowed in Delphian mystery. And here we were, psychologists, standing on one foot wanting very much to be scientists—and more than a little defensive about it, too—chattering away and so frightened of what we might see that we never dared take a close look.

Fancying myself thus as a practical man and seeing science as something which was, above all things, practical, it seemed that whatever I could do to bring psychologists into contact with human beings, novel as that might be, would help extricate psychology from the mishmash of its abstruse definitions. So I proposed to write as much as I knew about how to come to terms with living persons. I took as my prototypes the ones who confided in me, particularly those who were in trouble, because, as I saw it, when a person is in trouble he acts more like what he is and less like something dangling from the strings of social convention. Out of such an undertaking, if enough psychologists were willing to join in, I could envision a gradual awakening of the ancient half-conscious mind of man and the ultimate fruition of its vast potentialities. It should be obvious that all this fantasy took place when I was very young.

That manual was never written, at least not that kind of manual. The business of being practical turned out to be not as simple as I thought. After more delay than should have been necessary, even for one short of wits, the notion finally struck me that, no matter how close I came to the man or woman who sought my help, I always saw him through my own peculiar spectacles, and never did he perceive what I was frantically signaling to him, except through his. From this moment I ceased, as I am now convinced every psychotherapist does whether he wants to admit it or not, being a realist. More important, I could now stop representing psychology to clients as packaged reality, warranted genuine and untouched by human minds.

Perhaps "realism" is not a good term for what I am talking about. It is obvious, of course, that I am not talking about Platonic realism. Nobody talks about that any more. The realism from which my clients and I are always trying to wriggle loose might possibly be called "materialistic realism." At least it is the hardheaded unimaginative variety nowadays so popular among scientists, businessmen, and neurotics.

Realism and Dogmatism

What happened was this. Like most therapists with a background of liberal scholarship rather than strictly professional training, I soon became aware that dogmatic interpretations of clients' problems often did more harm than good. It was not only the client who suffered; therapists were affected in much the same way he was. Dogmatism produces a kind of mental rigidity that replaces thoughts with words, stifles the zest for free inquiry, and tries to seal the personality up tight at the conclusion of the last psychotherapeutic interview.

Understand, I am not yet ready to say that dogmatism has no place whatsoever in psychotherapy, especially when weighed against certain grimmer alternatives. It may even prove valuable to all of us as a firm point from which to rebel. But these are other matters.

[1] First published in Maher, B. (Ed.). (1969). *Clinical psychology and personality: The selected papers of George Kelly* (pp. 224-264). Wiley. Reprinted in 1977 in *Cognitive Therapy and Research*, *1*, 355-362. Republished by permission of Wiley.

Collected Papers of the Pioneer of Constructivist Psychology: George A. Kelly, First Edition. Edited by David A. Winter and Nick Reed.

What actually jarred me loose was the observation that clients who felt themselves confronted with down-to-earth realities during the course of psychotherapy became much like those who were confronted with downright dogmatic interpretations of either the religious or psychological variety. On the heels of this observation came the notion that dogmatism—the belief that one has the word of truth right from the horse's mouth—and modern realism—the belief that one has the word of truth right from nature's mouth—add up to the same thing. To go even further, I now suspect that neither of these assumptions about the revealed nature of truth is any more useful to scientists than it is to clients. But especially I am sure that both assumptions get square in the way of that supreme ontological venture we call psychotherapy and that they serve only to perpetuate its present unhappy captivity to fee-based medical materialism.

While my original views of ontology—and I am insisting that it is the same ontological process that runs its course whether the man is in the role of a client, a psychotherapist, a physicist, or an artist—have changed in some respects with the years, one of my original convictions remains with me. It still seems important for the psychologist to deal directly with persons on the most forthright terms possible. This is why I think of clinical psychology, not as an applied field of psychology, but as a focal and essential area and method of scientific inquiry. On the other hand, traditional psychology, it seems to me, is still much too self-consciously scientific and still much too peripheral to its subject matter. Instead of being so careful to do nothing that a scientist would not do, it would be more appropriate for the psychologist to get on with his job of understanding human nature. To the extent that he is successful, "Science" will eventually be only too glad to catch up and claim his methods as its own.

As for dogmatism, I certainly am not the first to say that it often works badly in therapy. Nor am I the first to recognize that the client has a point of view worth taking into account. But if one is to avoid dogmatism entirely he needs to alert himself against realism also, for realism, as I have already implied, is a special form of dogmatism and one which is quite as likely to stifle the client's creative efforts. A client who is confronted with what are conceded to be stark realities can be as badly immobilized as one confronted with a thickheaded therapist. Even the presumed realism of his own raw feelings can convince a client that he has reached a dead end.

Alternativism

As my client's therapist I can temporarily avoid pushing him over the brink of reality by being passive or by accepting as nonjudgmentally as possible anything and everything he says or does. There is no doubt but that in this atmosphere of intimate ambiguity many clients will figure out sensible things to do in spite of a therapist's shortsightedness. This is good and, for a therapist who thinks he has to act like a realist, it is about as far as one can go without betraying the dogmatism implicit in his realism. But I am not a realist—not anymore—and I do not believe either the client or the therapist has to lie down and let facts crawl over him. Right here is where the theoretical viewpoint I call *the psychology of personal constructs* stakes out its basic philosophical claim.

There is nothing so obvious that its appearance is not altered when it is seen in a different light. This is the faith that sustains the troubled person when he undertakes psychotherapy seriously. It is the same as the faith expressed in the *Book of Job*—not so much in the overwritten poetic lines as in the development of the theme. To state this faith as a philosophical premise: *Whatever exists can be reconstrued*. This is to say that none of today's constructions—which are, of course, our only means of portraying reality—is perfect and, as the history of human thought repeatedly suggests, none is final.

Moreover, this is the premise upon which most psychotherapy has to be built, if not in the mind of the therapist, at least in the mind of the client. To be sure, one may go to a therapist with his facts clutched in his hand and asking only what he ought to do with them. But this is merely seeking technical advice, not therapy. Indeed, what else would one seek unless he suspected that the obstacles now shaping up in front of him are not yet cast in the ultimate form of reality? As a matter of fact, I have yet to see a realistic client who sought the help of a therapist in changing his outlook. To the realist, outlook and reality are made of the same inert stuff. On the other hand, a client who has found his therapeutic experience helpful often says, "In many ways things are the same as they were before, but how differently I see them!"

This abandonment of realism may alarm some readers. It may seem like opening the door to wishful thinking, and to most psychologists wishful thinking is a way of coming unhinged. Perhaps this is why so many of them will never admit to having any imagination, at least until after they suppose they have realistically demonstrated that what they secretly imagined was there all the time, waiting to be discovered. But for me to say that *whatever exists can be reconstrued* is by no manner or means to say that it makes no difference *how* it is construed. Quite the contrary. It often makes a world of difference. Some reconstructions may open fresh channels for a rich and productive life. Others may offer one no alternative save suicide.

A Theoretical Postulate

Here, then, is where one takes the next step, a step that leads him from a philosophical premise—called *constructive alternativism*—to a psychological postulate. Put it this way: *A person's processes are psychologically channelized by the ways in which he anticipates events*. Next, combining this statement with the gist of some of its ensuing corollaries, we can say simply: *A person lives his life by reaching out for what comes next and the only channels he has for reaching are the personal constructions he is able to place upon what may actually be happening.* If in this effort he fails, by whatever criterion, the prudence of his constructions is laid open to question and his grasp upon the future is shaken.

Let us make no mistake; here we come to the exact point where we all have trouble. If our misleading construction is based on dogmatic belief, that is to say it is held to be true because someone like God or the Supreme Soviet said so, we are not likely to have the audacity to try to revise it. Similarly, if it is believed to have had its origin in nature rather than in our own noggin—the position of "realism" I have been talking about—we are left with no choice except to adjust and make the best of matters as they stand. Or if realizing that it was altogether our own mistaken notions that led us afield, if it seems now that there is nothing left to do except to scrap our convictions, one and all, then utter chaos will start closing in on all sides. Any of these is bad. Fortunately, there are always other alternatives when predictions go awry. For the person who does not see any of them—psychotherapy!

View of Psychotherapy

We have ruled out the notion of psychotherapy as the confrontation of the client with stark reality, whether it is put to him in the form of dogma, natural science, or the surges of his own feelings. Instead, we see him approaching reality in the same ways that all of us have to approach it if we are to get anywhere. The methods range all the way from those of the artist to those of the scientist. Like them both and all the people in between, the client needs to assume that something can be created that is not already known or is not already there.

In this undertaking the fortunate client has a partner, the psychotherapist. But the psychotherapist does not know the final answer either—so they face the problem together. Under the circumstances there is nothing for them to do except for both to inquire and both to risk occasional mistakes. So that it can be a genuinely cooperative effort, each must try to understand what the other is proposing and each must do what he can to help the other understand what he himself is ready to try next. They formulate their hypotheses jointly. They even experiment jointly and upon each other. Together they take stock of outcomes and revise their common hunches. Neither is the boss, nor are they merely well-bred neighbors who keep their distance from unpleasant affairs. It is, as far as they are able to make it so, a partnership.

The psychotherapy room is a protected laboratory where hypotheses can be formulated, test-tube sized experiments can be performed, field trials planned, and outcomes evaluated. Among other things, the interview can be regarded as itself an experiment in behavior. The client says things to see what will happen. So does the therapist. Then they ask themselves and each other if the outcomes confirmed their expectations.

Often a beginning therapist finds it helpful to close his cerebral dictionary and listen primarily to the subcortical sounds and themes that run through his client's talk. Stop wondering what the words literally mean. Try to recall, instead, what it is they sound like. Disregard content for the moment; attend to theme. Remember that a client can abruptly change content—thus throwing a literal-minded therapist completely off the scent—but he rarely changes the theme so easily. Or think of these vocal sounds, not as words, but as preverbal outcries, impulsive sound gestures, stylized oral grimaces, or hopelessly mumbled questions.

But at other times the therapist will bend every effort to help the client find a word, the precise word, for a newly emerged idea. Such an exact labeling of elusive thoughts is, at the proper time, crucial to making further inquiries and to the experimental testing of hypotheses. Particularly is this true when the team—client and therapist—is elaborating personal constructs. But before we can discuss this matter further we need to say something about the nature of personal constructs from the point of view of the theory.

Personal Constructs

We have said that a person lives his life by reaching out for what comes next and the only channels through which he can reach are the personal constructions he is able to place upon what appears to be going on. One deals with the events of life, not as entirely strange and unique occurrences but as recurrences. There is a property, a human quality of our own manufacture, that makes today seem like yesterday and leads us to expect that tomorrow may be another such day. To see this is to construe similarity among one's days. Without this view the future would seem chaotic indeed.

But to say that one's days are all alike, and nothing more, is to lose them amidst the hours and the years. What makes days seem alike is also precisely what sets them apart. We construe, then, by ascribing some property that serves both to link an event with certain other events and to set it in contrast to those with which it might most likely become confused. This construed dimension, embodying both likeness and difference, this reference axis, is what we call a construct. And constructs are personal affairs; regardless of the words he uses, each person does his own construing.

In this world—past, present, and future—ordered by each of us in his own way, constructs and events are interwoven so that events give definition to constructs and constructs give meaning to events. Take the client. The events, for example, that he recalls from childhood during the course of a psychotherapeutic interview serve to define the constructs that often he can otherwise express only through "intellectualization" or by "acting out." But constructs, on the other hand, give current meaning both to his memories and to his future plans and, particularly when they are precisely verbalized, they lay the ground for profitable experimentation.

The constructs one applies to himself and his interpersonal relationships have particular importance. Psychotherapy finds itself mainly concerned with them. While always fewer in number than one might wish, they nevertheless set the pattern of human resources available to the client and, when they are applied to his own changes of mood or behavior, they become wide-open pathways for shifting his position and altering the course of his life. Knowledge of them helps the therapist predict and control the client's possible reactions to threat, including the implicit threat that, to some extent, is always implied by psychotherapy itself.

The Varying Techniques of Psychotherapy

The team of client and therapist can go about their task in a variety of ways. Essentially these are the same ways that, on one kind of occasion or another, man has always employed for dealing with perplexities. (1) The two of them can decide that the client should reverse his position with respect to one of the more obvious reference axes. Call this slot rattling, if you please. It has its place. (2) Or they can select another construct from the client's ready repertory and apply it to matters at hand. This, also, is a rather straightforward approach. Usually the client has already tried it. (3) They can make more explicit those preverbal constructs by which all of us order our lives in considerable degree. Some think of this as dredging the unconscious. The figure is one that a few have found useful; but I would prefer not to use it. (4) They can elaborate the construct system to test it for internal consistency. (5) They can test constructs for their predictive validity. (6) They can increase the range of convenience of certain constructs, that is, apply them more generally. They can also decrease the range of convenience and thus reduce a construct to a kind of obsolescence. (7) They can alter the meaning of certain constructs; rotate the reference axes. (8) They can erect new reference axes. This is the most ambitious undertaking of all.

Alteration or replacement of constructs—the last two methods mentioned—is essentially a creative kind of effort. Both involve first a loosening of the client's constructions, either by the use of fantasy, dreams, free association, or the introduction of varied and illusive content into the therapeutic interview. But creativity is not a single mode of thought; it follows a cycle. The second phase of the cycle involves tightening and validation of the newly placed or newly formed constructs.

I have summarized what goes on in therapy under eight headings. More might have been used. It is necessary only that I offer some sketch of how psychotherapy can be envisioned in terms of personal construct theory, that I try to make clear that what I am talking about is not restricted to the process tradition calls "cognition" (a term for which I find little practical use lately), that psychotherapy runs the gamut of man's devices for coming to grips with reality, and that the client and his therapist embark together as shipmates on the very same adventure.

Illustrative Interview

On the following pages is a verbatim transcript of an interview between one of my clients and myself. The client was kind enough to give his permission to have this interview published and discussed. All names of persons and places have been altered and even a few of the descriptions have been deleted or changed to protect the client's identity as well as that of others who are peripherally involved.

No one interview can illustrate all the facets of a theoretical point of view. The reader is, of course, already aware of that. Unless one takes the position that psychotherapy is wholly a matter of technique and couchside manner, the most that he can hope to see in one interview is how a particular client-therapist team has dealt with their problem at a particular stage of their venture. It is like dropping in on a research conference; what goes on depends on the make-up of the research team and the phase of their investigation at which one has caught them at work. Indeed, from the standpoint of personal construct theory, psychotherapy is a form of joint research effort.

This client was, at the time, a twenty-eight year old unmarried veteran who was attending a university. A man of superior intellectual ability, he was well-read and he exhibited spontaneous scholarly interests. Yet he was unable to make a go of it in either employment or classes. Before going into service, he had been able to finish a year or more of university study; but that was all. His most recent efforts had ended up in a succession of dismal failures. He completed none of the courses in which he had successively enrolled at the beginning of several recent sessions. This general failure pattern was the manifest complaint and the primary grounds upon which he applied for help.

He soon made it clear that he envisioned his current enrollment as a last ditch try. In fact, he told his father that he "could have his insurance money" if this effort did not pay off. While this suicidal comment represented certain situational features, it was not something to be ignored, especially in view of the client's exhaustion of the alternatives available to him under his current construct system. The following interview is of particular interest because of its bearing on this feature of the case.

A diagnostic appraisal of the case was made in order to set up the initial plan for the therapeutic program. While there is no necessity for describing that appraisal in detail, one feature of it is of particular interest. On the REP Test, a concept formation type of procedure in which persons associated with the client are sorted rather than blocks or objects, he showed an inability to deal with people except in concretistic ways. That is to say, his constructs showed limited ranges of convenience; they could be applied readily to certain figures only, whether as grounds for seeing persons as alike or for distinguishing between them. This is not to say that he lacked a general capacity for thinking abstractly, but rather that his construct repertory for dealing with role relations between persons lacked adequate span.

In the early interviews the client showed an interesting combination of interpersonal distance and undefended vulnerability. On the one hand, his use of language was overprecise and literal and his manner of speech was somewhat stylized. In the vernacular of psychotherapists he was obviously "an intellectualizer." But, on the other hand, he made it clear that he expected therapy to deal with the most difficult and painful matters. He dreaded it. But it would have to be done. He expected to be hurt—not right away, please, but we shall have to get down to business soon. In fact, he lost little time in bringing up matters he had not discussed with anyone before and about which he felt deeply disturbed and guilty. He expressed his outlook toward therapy by saying that, first of all, he expected it to be objective and that he thought client and therapist should not feel themselves close to each other lest the therapist would hold off hurting the client and the client would try too hard to stay in the favor of the therapist.

The Client's View of Psychotherapy

The following passages, taken from an interview that occurred after the language pattern had responded to efforts to free it from its literalisms, dramatically illustrate his perception of the role of the therapist. Out of context these passages may seem unduly fanciful. In context, however, and in the light of the kind of exploration he and the therapist were undertaking at this stage, they portray vividly what he thought he was letting himself in for. The passages are taken from the eleventh interview.

C: You build a wall so that as you think back and hit that wall, you don't go beyond it and you don't redo the uncomfortable experience, or painful experience. And you keep building these and eventually all you've got is scar tissue and no ... no abilities, so, ahh, as we are discussing here, I'm trying, I'm trying to the, now, I may be wrong, I don't know, in doing this. I don't know, ahh, if that's the direction of your question. But ahh, I'm trying to keep it so that if we should come to one of those and you ask me questions which tend to probe into or beyond it, I will not have any desire on my part to tint the situation, dodge the situation. I'll what, be as objective and, what, to describe the villain of the piece, diabolically clever with the scalpel as he grins and has some nice macabre music in the background and so on, and digs away with what, to get the proper stage lighting and everything in there.

T: And who is the villain, I?

C: No, no I'm just describing a, a situation. I was saying, ahh, instead of coming to the situation, coming to the place where there is a block as a friendly surgeon who's scared to really injure the patient ... to come as a, ahh, what, ahh, the, ahh, soap-opera villain with his long mustache and, ahh, the slight off-color lights in the background and some slightly jarring music and a fiendish grin and chuckle and a sharp scalpel, just go in and devil take the hindmost.

T: Ummhuh, yeah. This is preferable to have the, having the physician who is afraid to operate because it might hurt the patient.

C: Well, I don't know that it's preferable but I would say that ahh, it certainly should. That's from the point of view I'm taking right now. It should get through, or at least, ahh, get through some of the scar tissue. I'm saying that if, ahh, there was a relationship, a friendship in here or something like that, ahh, each time we approached one of those situations, I would be like the friendly surgeon. Ahhhh, ahhhh, ahhhh . . . instead of going ahead and going right on in.

T: Ummhuh. So you'd like to create a situation here where you or I or both of us together could be just as diabolical as necessary in order to get through the scar tissue. That may be a little rougher phraseology than would fit the case, but, it . . .

C: Sounded pretty rough, yes. (laughs)

T: Sounded pretty rough.

C: But the idea in comparison, yes, rather than each time coming to a scar tissue, sort of backing off and, and, what, playing around, going around and so on, just going on in.

T: This version of therapy then makes it look pretty rough, doesn't it?

C: I wouldn't say it's particularly rough. I'd say it's necessary, or at least based upon the description I have had of the situ, of how the mind would built this up . . . and I've read some factors which say that the mind's total capability from the experiences we have early in life that are unpleasant are slowly cut off more and more and more portions of the mind to where we're only using 2 or 3 percent when we're fully grown.

T: Yes. So it's going to take something pretty courageous . . .

C: (pause) Well, I would say it wouldn't take a chicken-hearted surgeon to do it.

T: You don't want to be chicken-hearted and you don't want me to be chicken-hearted in here, huh?

C: Ahhh, (pause) no. I would say, let's not be chicken-hearted, that is be afraid to get into it.

* * *

C: Yeah. I don't want to go into this thing and then, what, be at a complete loss as to what we've covered, to have to have you play back the record or something so that I can understand ahhh, what's happened. I want to be able, as we go along, now it may take longer, it may be the wrong approach, I don't know. I can just say what I feel. I feel if the approach is made this way, ahhh, the result will fit together like building blocks.

T: So you're saying essentially, as much as you feel you *can* say and still be (pause) appropriate, "For God's sake, don't throw me into chaos, all at once."

C: (laughs) Yeah, yeah, yeah, that's it! I hadn't thought of it from that point of view, but ahh, it fits, it fits what I've said very clearly.

* * *

C: It's like I'm, I am one of the convicts in the Spanish prison when Columbus comes along and says, let's go sail across the seas. He knows where he's going, but I don't. I don't think he really did, but at least he had a better idea than I would as the highly prejudiced—what we would consider ignorant nowadays—individual blindly stepping off into nowhere.

T: And in a sense, the prisoner might say, "Sure I want to be out of prison. But this is very sudden!"

C: Well, I think the attitude of many of the prisoners that were released probably was it's good to be out of prison. I don't think there's any argument there. However, the idea of Columbus, at that time there were two conflicting points of view, one the world was flat like a table top, the other that it was round. Well, Columbus took off sailing west on the assumption the world was round and he would run into the Indies. The prisoner I imagine, unless there were some educated ones amongst them which could happen at that time; even so, they were sailing out and eventually they'd just disappear into a void of nothing or a void of which, not a void, it wouldn't be, but a space in which there were sea demons and terrible dragons and all kinds of ahhh, concoctions and ahhh. . .

T: And here they were in a tight little imprisoned world with solid walls around them. At least they knew where they were.

C: Yeah.

T: And they knew the dimensions of their cells.

C: And it probably was very unpleasant.

T: Yeah, it was very unpleasant.

C: And unpleasant as shipboard duty would be with Columbus at least it was something. It was better than where they were.

T: Yeah.

C: But as they sailed west they approached this mythical drop off . . .

T: Yes.

C: They got more and more scared and probably were thinking, gosh, that cell looks awful darn nice.

T: Almost they wished for the walls again.

C: Yeah, I'll bet they did.

T: And you can sympathize with that.

C: I can see that.

T: The ahh, the metaphor fits you a little, huh?

C: Yeah, I would say it would, in this instance.

T: And here you have been within walls—and you have described it sometimes as "walls" I'm not sure just exactly *when*, but you've used the metaphor . . .

C: Yeah.

T: This simile before. Within the walls; you weren't very happy within these walls that limited your freedom.

C: Yeah.

T: Some of the walls were the walls of your home, maybe, but limited your freedom. What other kinds of walls?

C: There were walls there.

T: There were walls there, but at least you feel the dimensions of them in part.

C: Yeah. And I kept running into them in the most unexpected places too.

The preceding excerpt from an earlier interview should provide a fairly clear picture of how this client was approaching his psychotherapeutic task. In one sense his approach made him vulnerable and denied to him the comforting support that many clients get by transferring their childlike dependencies to the therapy room. In another sense, however, his verbalized determination to keep track of where he was going provided him a structured control over the situation, a control that he could use for coping with the turbulence he was expecting at any moment.

Objectives of This Particular Interview

The following interview is the twentieth in the psychotherapeutic series. The client's earlier manner of speech had been considerably modified by this time. It was more spontaneous (in our theoretical terms it showed more *impulsivity*), he was more willing to employ imprecise terms in order to catch fleeting thoughts before they escaped him (grasping for *preverbal constructs*), and he was beginning to portray fluctuating ideas without overconcern for their apparent contradictions (*loosening*). Moreover, he had dealt frankly with a few incidents which had been a long-time source of embarrassment to him (documentation of *guilt* and *threat*).

While up to a point these developments were therapeutically valuable, it was the therapist's judgment that this was a trend not to be continued indefinitely. Certainly therapy is not the simple task of laying bare vast areas of confusion and trusting in the client's utter dependence upon his therapist to keep matters in hand. There are always practical limits. Especially in the case of this particular client it is hard to see how a responsible therapist would want to lead him any great distance away from firm structure or let him sink much further into passive dependency.

We have here, therefore, not only a point of decision in dealing with this particular client, but a fulcrum across which to balance the weight of what different psychological systems have to offer. What is therapy? Is it an uncovering ritual that strips the client of all psychological clothing and reveals him as a naked brute? Is it stark realism warmed to body temperature by the therapist's attitude of acceptance? Are the forces that victimize us so irrational that they cannot be dealt with intellectually? Is psychology a science that throws light only on what is bestial, what is fatalistic, or what is senseless? Or can psychological science offer an ontological way for these two, client and therapist, to do together what neither of them can accomplish separately?

The following interview was chosen because it illustrates the kind of decision the personal construct theorist feels called upon to make. What was done in this interview may not have been wise. It may not be what personal construct theory would suggest to other therapists. But the issue envisioned is one that looms up in the light of this particular theory.

The moment-to-moment decisions facing the therapist during this interview hinge on two main considerations. First, this client is one who has built for himself a brittle verbalized structure to deal with peripheral matters but who has allowed more central matters to degenerate into a chaotic condition. The constructs with which these more central matters are bound remain loose and poorly symbolized. He has, therefore, no satisfactory way to bring them into his sensible world, and hence no way to experiment with them or to revise them. Before we plunge too deeply into this chaos we need to tighten up what he has been saying about his world of feeling, label it with symbols that he can use, and prepare to put his constructs to some cautious experimental tests.

But there is a second consideration that makes this a risky business. If he spells out this vaguely expressed dimension in definitive terms, it will lie there, wide open before him. Will he use such a broad pathway to destroy himself in some moment of impulse? The reader will readily see in the middle passages of the interview how the construct tightening process followed by the client and the therapist clarified the two ends of the continuum—rational hope *versus* irrational despair. The therapist decided that the time had come to put this pair of alternatives into clearer terms and the client seemed to agree with him. Were we wise? We can say only that it seemed so.

The tempo of the interview was speeded up somewhat above that of the preceding interviews. The therapist responded frequently in the passive supportive affirmative—indicated in the following protocol by the conventional typescript spelling, "yeah" to distinguish it from the active assertive affirmative, "yes." Digressions into situational or concrete illustrative material were not discouraged during the interview because, as the reader may be able to see, they represented the client's attempts to reduce vague feelings, for which there were no adequate symbols, to terms which were, at least, tangible. This was a part of the process of tightening construction, and tightening was what we were trying to accomplish.

The emphasis upon precise word-finding will particularly attract the attention of some readers with therapeutic experience. In the present session this emphasis is as intentional as the lack of such emphasis was in some of the preceding interviews. The object of this interview was not to exude feelings, but to bring the construct dimensions, through which feelings threatened to run riot, into clearer focus and to bind them with adequate symbols for future reference.

Protocol and Comments

T1: Come in. (long pause) How are your resolutions for the New Year?
C1: Didn't make any.
T2: Have you before, in other years?
C2: Ohh, I think maybe once or twice I have.

What may appear to be "small talk" at the beginning of this interview was undertaken deliberately. This client was one who had resolved many times to set his house in order but who had been unable to keep impulses from throwing his tightly drawn plans into disarray. It was important to know whether we would be dealing with another such attempt to manage with tight constructions.

T3: (pause) Ummhuh. (pause) Now, where do we stand? Are we at a place where we ought to start digging in deeper?
C3: Well, I think at the moment, perhaps, we've gone as far as we can on the surface.
T4: Yes, I have that feeling too.
C4: You mentioned last time that we'd probably ought to be digging in deeper.
T5: Yeah.
C5: And I don't suppose I could say I've been *thinking* it over, that is—what—setting aside time to think it over or anything like that. But whenever I happened to—the thought crosses my mind—I've been—what—mulling it over a little bit.

T6: Ummhuh.
C6: Ahh, it makes sense.
T7: I don't believe our time has been wasted, doing it the way we have. As a matter of fact, there's some depth to the things that have—that have transpired here. Yet I think that we have to—(pause) We have to communicate on another level too. (pause) I may not be easy. I don't know. Maybe easier than—ahh, than either of us would expect, when we try it.

The client introduces content in the following passage and immediately uses it to document a construction of his own behavior. He points out his own reaction to the breakthrough of impulsive behavior and then goes on quickly to anchor his construction in other events. Of course, at this stage he has neither the words nor the syntax to express his constructs effectively. He must therefore weave back and forth between efforts to say words that will delineate the constructions and the citation of selected events upon which the constructs are focused.

C7: Ahh, one thing came up this week. I don't know. I suppose it has some importance. I don't know. Ahhh. (pause) Yesterday, ahh, I was killing some time, ahh, down on the pool table in the basement.
T8: Umhuh.
C8: And Mom came down and began to iron and began to chat a little and, ahh, there developed in me (pause) a desire to get up and go—run—get out—a, ahh, (pause) a feeling that, at the time, I described as "hate"—"hatred" towards my mother.
T9: Ummhuh.
C9: Now, this does not, what, this presents a problem immediately in that, ahh, in my picture this is not the feeling I should have.
T10: No, of course not.
C10: But, just the same, it was there.
T11: Yeah.
C11: And, ahh, I thought I'd bring that up. (pause) Another thing I, ahh, that came to mind and I suppose I have indicated already in my discussion—discussions *with* you, but, ahh, for some reason it didn't come through *clear* to me until just recently. And that is, ahh, when I have these explosions or blowups, they are triggered by an outside force—some *event* happening other than involving myself, and they *may* involve myself.
T12: Yeah.
C12: But, sometimes they don't. So I'm just using an outside force and, ahh, at least the most recent one which I happened, I think, since our last discussion, ahhh, immediately or, frequently after the immediate—the first—explosion, the first feeling of anger—
T13: Yeah.
C13: —against some *external* being—person—, ahh, there was a, (pause) you know, like a rubber ball bouncing off a wall, the feeling came back at *myself*, a feeling of disgust, a feeling of anger at myself for having (laughs) the original *feeling*.
T14: Yeah.
C14: —for losing control, and it seemed to me, that of the two, this was the most severe.
T15: Ummhuh.
C15: And, ahh.
T16: (pause) The ball comes back harder even than you thought?
C16: Definitely! or, at least, this is the *impression* I get the most experience.
T17: Yeah.
C17: The one that's most clear in my mind. Now the others I, I don't remember seeing them in these two distinct categories.
T18: Ummhuh.
C18: But it, what, *seems*, it feels, like this is the way they've gone.
T19: Yeah, (pause) Did you feel this way after, after your recognition of your, of this impulse of this feeling toward your mother yesterday?
C19: Yes, and, ahhh, I got out of the house and drove off. Now that was at 4:10 and I got back to the house at about five, ten minutes to five, about forty minutes.
T20: Yeah.
C20: And I'd say at least a *half* an hour of that time was spent in *anger* of varying degrees—
T21: Yeah.
C21: Against myself, (pause) primarily, for, what, having this feeling and trying to piece it out. Ahh, there was no, ahh, any, no progressive thought pattern or no constant progression of thought. It was just, ahh, (pause) I suppose, like a little kid with a hammer and stone, trying to break it up. He pounds at it any ol' way it happens to be turned up.
T22: Yeah.
C22: So that's just the way I was going at it.
T23: No logical sequences.

C23: No logical sequence, no pattern or anything, just, ahhh,—oh, I'd drive for awhile and then I'd think of something and then I'd pound at that, and then I'd, ahh, get nowhere, I suppose, is the only way to say. I *got* nowhere trying to figure the thing out, except that some of this is, was developed at that time. Ahhh, developed I won't say, ahhh, the *ideas emerged* at that time, but they became more crystallized, more, they fitted in more during that time. But I'd say half an hour of the time was spent blowing off steam. I don't know, I drove down Avon and up and around, and came out north of Barton Road across from the Calumet coming down Sixty-one and Digby Road, and it wasn't until about the time, well, are you familiar with that territory out there at all?

T24: More or less—yes.

The client has just confronted himself with the lack of logical sequence in what has happened. He turns to a recitation of times and places. It would be easy to call this resistance. But from the point of view of personal construct theory, resistance is a poorly drawn psychologist's construct and might better be abandoned. The client is groping his way through the experience here in the therapy room, just as he groped his way through it on the day he is describing. Like anyone who gropes he reaches out for tangible objects. And he asks others to verify their presence.

C24: There's a road that goes up parallel to Calumet. It's got quite a few houses, new development out there, relatively new, four or five years old.

T25: West side of the Calumet, isn't it?

C25: It's on the west side of Calumet, parallel to it and relatively close to it.

T26: Yes, I know that road.

C26: Well, I went up that road and crossed over, ahh, north of Barton Road, I don't know what road I was on, but it goes out to Eton on one—. If I'd turned left going west, going to Eton, and I turned right, came over to Sixty-one, and down Sixty-one, Ahhh, it comes out. You know that antique shop on Digby Road?

T27: I know there is something—.

C27: There is one. There's a filling station that's next to it. Or something. There's two right there, and there's an antique shop on one side. Got some, oh, wagon wheels laying up against a fence there.

T28: That is a beautiful drive up on the west side there.

C28: Yeah, well, just as, I'd say about halfway up that drive this feeling of anger and so on completely left, well, completely—essentially—completely left me. There was some still little stirring of it but I began to notice (pause) my surroundings. That is, it wasn't a case of knowing that they were there and not being able to, ahh, think about them or anything, because of the break-ins of this anger or whatever.

T29: Yeah.

C29: And then I drove around, watched the skaters on the Calumet and drove home. (long pause) Now, that's one thing. There's something else that has come up in my mind and I don't know how you intended it . . . (pause) Ahh, last time I was in here, you began to ask me the why behind my idea of going into the ministry.

T30: Yeah.

C30: And there was a little question there, on one part, ahh, the decision, of this as a possibility has been coming more and more crystalized.

T31: Ummhuh.

C31: And there's a little possibility—little question there of whether or not you were questioning whether or not that's where I fitted. I didn't know whether you were or not.

T32: Pretty hard to, ahh, *not* to wonder, isn't it?

C32: Well, it is. Well, what, there are *two halves* of me.

T33: Yes.

The client now turns to an attempt to spell out a principal construct dimension. The therapist now has to decide how tightly this dimension ought to be drawn. If the client sees his alternatives in these terms only and if the implications gather up his whole life's pattern, will he not be endangered the next time he is caught up in impulsivity? This is a point of therapeutic risk. The decision is to go ahead and make the construct as explicit as possible.

There are, of course, many different kinds of comments that could be made about each passage—the kind of externalized control the client uses, his returns to anger and guilt, the fact that the full picture of hostility is not yet sketched in the interview series, the relation with the mother which is almost entirely construed preverbally at this time, the emphasis upon the notion of being "triggered" together with its gunlike or sexual implications and its association with his mother, and many other matters.

C33: And when the black half is in command it makes absolutely no sense to even have this idea as—well, actually, there are two, *two* ways of looking at even *this* half. You can say, "no, this isn't it," and, on the other hand, you can say, "yes," because in the search for this perhaps I can help someone else. When I'm in my bright mood, like I feel like I am right now, it makes sense. (pause) Another thing, ahh, sometimes I have these dark moods: I get mad and then I get mad at myself in return, and I start mentally browbeating or whatever.

T34: Yeah.

C34: If there is something on the outside. But then, I can turn this off, like a radio. Now, ahh, and what, present an outside cheery appearance. Say, I'm down—usually, this is when I'm alone, I mean it's not when I'm in a group—but if I'm alone, something else will—becomes—more than, if one, unless it's my mother. I can still retain my anger when she's present—my father to some extent, but not so much—my brother, usually I turn it off.

T35: Ummhuh.

C35: But it's somewhat like a radio. *You, I turn it off*, and assume a different attitude! And this, I don't know, whether it just is turned off and suppressed or just dies out of its own accord.

T36: There has to be something external or an occasion?

C36: External, ahh, *to turn it off*!

T37: Yes.

C37: But, ahh, I can let it die out in, I suppose, anywheres from twenty minutes to half an hour or so, based on a rough estimate of time from previous occasions and on the time it took this last, ahh—

T38: Yeah.

C38: —situation to cool off.

T39: (pause) What is the contrast between these two parts, the two main parts of yourself as you're describing them now?

C39: Well, I doubt, I doubt if, ahh, they're this extreme, but they're sort of like black and white. One side is—

T40: That's quite a contrast, isn't it?

C40: Well, yeah, ahh, well, as I say, I don't think they're quite as extreme, but they *seem to be*, ahh, *pretty close*. On one hand I feel good, cheery, ahh, present myself, ahh, fairly well to the outside—

T41: Yes.

C41: Ahh, get along fine with friends. (long pause) On the other hand, when I'm by myself and ahh, what, kick myself when I'm down ahh, (pause) this black feeling kinda snowballs.

T42: Yes.

C42: And down, and down, and *down* and DOWN! And it's, ahh, a steep curve going into and a gradual curve coming out.

T43: Yeah. Unless some event intervenes, where you just postpone it.

C43: Yeah, ahh, where, I don't know what you'd say. I do not desire the out—the other, the other people to see myself in this condition.

T44: Well, I can see where, in one case, you see *yourself* as seeing the world as bright. In the other case, it's—

C44: It's not so much the outside world, as it's, ahhh—

T45: "Me," huh?

C45: Me! My own feelings!

T46: Yeah.

C46: Because, ahh, I take this assumption simply from the fact that I can *switch*.

T47: Yeah.

C47: So that when I'm what . . .

T48: (pause) There's no question as to whether, as to where the mood arises, *actually* arises. It arises within you then?

C48: Though it's usually *triggered* by something, some event.

T49: It's triggered. Something outside?

C49: Something outside!

T50: Yeah. And you turn it off some—

C50: Now I got *very, very* upset, ahh, last Wednesday, New Year's. Ahh, I was best man in a wedding Saturday.

T51: Yeah.

C51: And we had the wedding gifts that had to be delivered. And, ahhh, Mom was making the suggestion that Dad take them over and then when she suggested Dad take them over she said, "Do you want to take my present at the same time?" Then she said, "Maybe you'd better not." "Yes." "No." It went—four distinct different movements—yes, no, yes, no. Ahh, and I *exploded*! More violently than I had in a long time! And it took me, ahh, two to three hours to cool off enough so that I came back up. I went down to my room and stretched out and read some comic books and ahh— there was another book, I don't know what it was—but cooled off.

T52: This was between your father and your mother.

C52: No, between my mother and myself.

T53: Oh, between your mother and yourself.

C53: Though, I can be triggered, for instance, when my mother and my brother were discussing something.

T54: Ummhuh.

C54: I mentioned that either last time or sometime recently in the past, I was triggered. And I can be *triggered* when my father and my mother are discussing. It's not as likely.

T55: Anything that involves haggling *could* trigger you.

C55: Yeah.
T56: Particularly, if you get involved *directly*.
C56: Well, not necessarily. It's not necessary for myself to become involved directly.
T57: Just even to sit on the sidelines gets you triggered sometimes?
C57: Yeah. And yet, other times, it doesn't bother me at all.
T58: Yeah. You can remain detached at other times.
C58: I can remain detached at other times. I imagine it's, ahh, just how I'm feeling at that particular moment, whether I'm susceptible or not.
T59: Yeah. Now there are two men by the name of Zeons, you then would say.
C59: Yeah.
T60: Looking at these two men from the outside, not just superficially, but I mean judging them as objectively as you can, or judging them whatever way you can, what is the difference between these two men? . . . On what dimension does it lie?
C60: (very long pause) I'm not too sure exactly what you want. I, I'm a little puzzled here.
T61: Well, let's look at these two men. Can you tell me what the difference is between them? (pause) The two men aren't here now. I'm pulling you out from them—.
C61: Yeah, I'm trying to, trying to, ahh, what, find something to, ahh, to, to, first I'm trying to find out what they are like and then trying to see where they differ, ahh, because, ahh, I haven't, what, looked at them from the outside, I've only described to you how *I* feel.
T62: How *you* felt.
C62: When, ahh, when I'm in these moods.
T63: Yeah.
C63: Ahhh, how I don't know that this is an adequate description. These are estimates, stabs in the dark. The one seems too cheery, outward looking, that is, I'm using "outward" as opposed to, what, I was going to describe the other one as "inward looking."
T64: Yeah.
C64: Then of course, the other one is moody, dark, that's what I use the two black and white terms, ahh, light and dark. Ahh, (very long pause) the one—Now, ahh, I'm also ascribing, what, absolutes to these, to these charac, characters which may or may not fit. But, trends in this direction may fit.
T65: Yeah.
C65: Ahhh, the light one would be ahh, cheery, outward looking, enjoys life—.
T66: Rational?
C66: (pause) That does not necessarily fit, I don't believe.
T67: That's another dimension.
C67: Ahhh, the *other* one, I definitely add "irrational" to the dark one.
T68: Yeah.
C68: And, and if you—if you want to put opposite in there, I suppose you'd add "rational" to the light one, but it doesn't necessarily fit, it seems to me. Ahhh, "puzzled," "disturbed," "confused," "irrational," in that this, nothing seems to make sense.
T69: Which one of them wants to go to the seminary?
C69: The light, the cheery one. Well, I think they both do.
T70: They both do.
C70: But for different reasons.
T71: O.K.
C71: The cheery one because of the, ahh, because of the ahh, of what this is a step towards, in that it is a service to people, helping people.
T72: Yeah.
C72: The other one in helping self, trying to find some pattern. This can all be sifted out and made to fit into some sort of relative pattern, some sort of, some sort of an outline or at least *something* so it isn't a confused jumble of emotion and irrationalities.
T73: Looking for some way to extricate one's self from this jumble.
C73: Yeah. (pause) And, when I'm in a dark mood, it seems to me this idea, ahh, of the light mood, of going through seminary and so on, may be a rationalization, a reason which I build up for myself so that this one makes sense, but that is, so that it doesn't seem like I'm doing this strictly for a purpose of self. Which also seems to fit.
T74: When in a dark mood you're skeptical of the bright mood, huh?
C74: Yeah! In other words, what reasons I can give when I'm feeling cheery, feeling good, ahh, when I'm in a dark mood. I wonder if I don't *make* these reasons.
T75: Of course.
C75: So that these don't *appear* as if I'm doing purely as a matter of self.
T76: So when you're in a dark mood you think *that* really is the real self; the other one is a superficial overlay, sometimes?

C76: Yeah. And, ahh, when I think about it, when I'm in a cheery mood, I can progress toward the darker mood because I'm thinking *towards myself*, which I do when I am in the dark mood. And, oh, I don't know, I just start edging over towards that way.

T77: So even when you're in a cheery mood, cheerful mood, and you wonder which of the two selves is real—

C77: Oh yeah.

T78: And you begin to wonder if it isn't the dark one.

C78: (pause) The dark one, in some ways, seems more real. It presents somewhat of a challenge to try and find out why I am the way I am. I think that's, ahh, I don't know. I don't know why the term "why" keeps coming up. But so many times, in fact, I think almost always—I could go so far as to say "always"—the term "why" comes into the question. Why am I the way I am? Why do I have these dark moods? Why? (sigh) Well, I suppose, by any approach to it, using the term "why" comes up.

T79: So "why" is always in this outcry.

C79: Yeah, What is behind it?

T80: (long pause) What do you think?

C80: (laughs) That's why I'm here. I don't know. (long pause) I suppose, somewhat it's background, the experiences I've had in life, both at home, school, work, play, what have you. And I imagine it's the fact that I have not allowed myself or forced myself, depending upon which viewpoint I take, to make very many friends. I am not particularly comfortable in a social atmosphere. (pause) But when I'm in my cheery mood I get along with people fine. When I'm in a dark mood I have to force myself.

T81: Ummhuh.

C81: Though I can force myself into a fairly acceptable cheery mood.

T82: That's this turning off that you mentioned awhile ago.

C82: Yeah. But it's, ahh, I tell you when I'm doing that, ahh, I'm tense. I definitely feel like I'm forcing myself.

T83: Ummhuh.

C83: Ahhh, I, I, I don't know how to say this. It's not—there are times when that's the case, and times when that's not the case. For instance, one time I was mad at myself, I was downstairs, my brother called that I had a phone call.

T84: Ummhuh.

C84: No problem. Just turn it off. Now, I think I was fairly well out of darkness. I was pretty well up towards, ahh, average between the two, or whatever you want to call it.

T85: Ummhuh.

C85: There are other times though, when I would be in a situation, where I'd be continually tense. I think this is becoming . . . less the pattern than it was in the past.

T86: Good.

C86: But it's still there! Particularly, it's there when I'm not prepared for class—or any other circumstances where I am *uncertain of the results*. I can build up a blacker picture than may be the case.

T87: So whenever you're confronted with something of any kind of importance, where you don't know what's going to happen—.

C87: Yeah. (pause) My imagination can get going, and, ahh, I don't know, the impossible makes it seem pretty rugged. Whereas—usually I'll say al—always—it's never *that* bad—as I paint it.

T88: But you do a good job of painting.

C88: Yeah.

T89: What *does* your imagination do at these moments of uncertainty? What are some of the worst of things that can happen?

C89: I don't know if I can describe any of them. When you ask for a description of something, ahh, there is—

T90: Just a whole lot of—

C90: Nothing comes to mind.

T91: Is that the worst that can happen to you? Sheer, utter confusion? (pause) Not knowing?

C91: (sigh) I don't know as I can say that. I was merely describing my feeling right now.

T92: Yeah. O.K., you might say it a little differently on other occasions.

C92: Ahhhh. (pause) Whenever I'm faced with a problem which I don't know, I'm uncertain about the (pause) event. (pause) Well, I'd say, ahh, I'm scared, which I assume to be normal. I assume that, ahh, when approaching an uncertainty or an unknown, most people are a little bit scared. But, I'd say I build upon this. I present the barriers as greater than they actually turn out to be. The problem is greater. I don't know whether I would say it's more serious, or more important than it was. Sometimes this happens.

T93: Ummhuh.

C93: But I'd say usually. It's just that the difficulty of *doing it* becomes greater in my mind. Although actually, when I arrive at the doing of it, it is not any more difficult than it would have been anyway. (pause) White-washed it instead of painting it black!

T94: Yeah. But the feeling—

C94: (pause) Fear that I'd fail, I think, is the simplest way of putting it.

T95: (pause) What would happen if you failed?

C95: I'd be in a black mood—kick myself.

T96: And then what?
C96: (pause) Well, after applying the club rather thoroughly, I imagine I'd (pause) get over with it—go on.
T97: But that isn't the way you feel at the moment. You're not thinking about getting over it. You're thinking of the worst that can happen, aren't you?
C97: Yeah.
T98: What is this worst that can happen?
C98: (pause) Be in a shameful position.
T99: Yeah.
C99: (silence).

We are now in a position where the black-white construct has a certain amount of tightness to it and it has been wrapped up in verbal terms to some extent. We now move back in the direction of documentation, choosing this time to get further away from local events. As we do this we may expect the construct to be tested out against other memories and, as a result of examination in other contexts, to be altered somewhat. The alteration is not something we can expect to happen in this interview, but perhaps in later ones.

T100: Lose face like when? What are some of the times when you've lost face in the worst possible ways? (very long pause) That's a hard question to ask, isn't it? But I think I should.
C100: (pause) Looking at it, from again the two viewpoints, there is one I can think of recently. Now, outside of home, I mean, whenever I get mad at myself I lose face with myself. But, other than lose face with myself, and, ahh, this again is strictly from the dark side viewpoint. (pause)
T101: Yeah.
C101: I blew up once in Freeport City, in the office. But, it was of a very short duration and it worked out exceptionally well, once I faced the problem—looked it—. It was a case I had to make a decision. I was the only person in the office that could make the decision. So, I think what actually I did, I rebelled against making the decision, at first. (pause) As near as I can remember, the secretary there placed faith in the decision and, and I said, "I can't do it!" She said, "You've got to. You're the only person here that can." In a minute or two I cooled and went ahead and made a decision and it worked out fine.
T102: That was loss of face, that is that you couldn't—
C102: That's from the black side of it.
T103: Yeah.
Cl03: I mean, from the other side of it I could see, ahh, that it's just a natural thing. But I mean, from the black side, I don't know if I'd say loss of face.
T104: What was the loss of face? That you were required to make the decision, or that *when* you were asked—?
C104: No, when I was asked, I blew up.
T105: Ummhuh.
C105: I rebelled against making the decision.
T106: And that was a face-losing thing to do.
C106: To blow up. Looking at it, I can see that it, I mean, looking at it rationally, I can see that it's, ahhh, natural to do it and so forth. But I, what, emotionally, was disgusted about—
T107: There's something shameful about losing your temper?
C107: (long pause) I don't know whether I'd use those words, but, yes, that meaning.
T108: Personally.
C108: I mean that *direction* of meaning.
T109: Yeah. Say it better for me, can you?
C109: Well, I was going to say, "disgusting," but I suppose, in, some ways, that's the same thing as "shameful"—"disturbing." Although I think that "disgusting," "disturbing," in that it is "disgusting," er, more than just "disturbing."
T110: Yeah, yeah. "Disgusting." To say that it's disgusting—(pause) in some way, some ways, is to condemn it more. Isn't it?
C110: You mean than shameful?
T111: Yeah. (pause) Is it repulsive? (pause) Is a person who loses his temper the way you lose it, as you see it in a black mood . . ?
C111: Yesss. (pause) I don't know that I'd say it. It, ahh, isn't something that clicks. But the idea fits, as I think about it. It does not seem to—it's just a little stronger—
T112: Oh.
Cl12: Than "disgusting"—"repulsive." I'd say it fits, but it's stronger.
T113: Ummhuh. O.K.
C113: I'd say "shameful" is less strong.
T114: So the situation in Freeport City was an example of where you thought you'd lose face.
Cl 14: From the black side of it.

T115: From the black side, yes. Looking at it from—
Cl 15: The white, light side—
T116: What does it look like?
Cl 16: Well, rationally, I can picture it as a natural happening.
T117: Yeah.
C117: Or, if not natural, at least reasonable. I don't know if "reasonable" is a word to use there either. (pause) Actually, to find something in which I lost face with some group outside of myself, ahh, it's hard to do. It's very easy to picture myself losing face *to* myself, which seems to happen more often, which seems to have (pause) more *continual* bearing upon myself.

In continuing to explore the range of convenience of the construct we turn to the more remote past. It is important to understand how this is viewed in personal construct terms. The past is not seen as a simple determinant of present behavior. What he is about to describe is not "what made him that way." Instead, what he is about to bring up is a memory that serves to document, or make tangible, the preverbal construct with which he is currently approaching his world. In fact he says as much; he is not sure it ever actually happened. But the "memory" still serves its purpose admirably.

T118: O.K. When you were a child, how did you lose face?
C118: (very long pause) Well, two events come to mind. And again, from the white side, they are perfectly natural events to have happened. And I cannot tell you, I know in one instance how I felt, that is, I know how I felt as *described by my parents*.
T119: Yeah.
C119: I know how I felt in the other instance because I can picture myself in the instance. The first instance would be about 1933. It would put me about two or three years old. I can picture, without even closing my eyes, the place. Now I've got—only got—I know there's a photo of the front of the house. Now that much has aided, I mean my picture of the place is aided by that. But in back of it, the only thing I have is a picture of it as aided by descriptions of it from my mother. But I can, I could see it before she started to enhance the description, and very clearly. Over a, what, a ravine or a creek. I mean it wasn't a ravine, it was, well, of course, I don't know. I can only picture it through, as I remember, as that occasion it was very deep, and I imagine it was, and I imagine it wasn't any deeper than this—
T120: Yeah.
C120: From the floor, but, at that age it looked deep. Ahhh, a hexagonal or octagonal porch timber, that is timber, unpeeled logs, so big, forming the railing, the floor, plank floor. And on this porch, out from behind the house, over this ravine, they stretched a net hammock.
T121: Ummhuh.
C121: I was in that hammock and got tangled up in it and I got (laugh) mad. Now, I don't, again this does not seem to be a natural event, and to my cheery side, my light side, it also seems to be a natural event.
T122: Yeah. It could seem—
C122: To my dark side, as I think about it, I get irritated by it. I won't say I get mad. Though. I'd say, using these two as points, irritated and mad, I'm about here, not *quite* as strong as "mad," but a good bit stronger than "irritated."
T123: Well, you must have felt helpless at that time, *at the moment*.
C123: Definitely. Well, there wasn't anything I could do! I was wrapped up like a, what, a fish does when it gets in a fish net. I suppose that's essentially, what, this was, I don't remember. It *seems* to be a—net about this big in my mind. I don't know what size the net was. It could very well have been a fish net, made into a hammock.
T124: And what was the other event there? I would like to come back to this if you don't mind. Before you forget—
C124: Ahhhhhh, now, the year I cannot place, (pause) nor the location. It was either '37 or, I believe, '38: '36-'37 or '37-'38. Two years when my Dad came down here to Goodfield we rented homes, one in Hinton, one in Ilma. That is, there was one each year, whichever way it was, I don't know. Anyway, in the back there was a fish pond. I imagine this was in Ilma because it doesn't fit Hinton, 'cause Dad pointed out the street where the house was and it doesn't fit. Oh, I don't imagine the pond at the deepest wasn't any deeper than that.
T125: Yeah.
C125: And it was well, dumbbell shaped. Shaped like this.
T126: Ummhuh.
C126: Oh the center part was oh, yeah, wide, and the ends, that much wider on both sides, but it went out and then around. And the goldfish you saw in there. Anyway, I was along the side and a friend pushed me in and, ahh, I came out mad—what, madder than a wet hen, as the saying goes. Now this emotional reaction, I do not, did not remember until my folks told me how I felt coming out. Now, on the light side this seems perfectly natural and rational, and yet on the other side,—what bothers me I think is that *I had the feeling*! I had the feeling of *madness* over this, which does not fit from the, looking at it from the *rational* point of view. I mean, I can say I look at it rationally, that is, from the light side, and it appears perfectly natural to have been mad over it.
T127: Ummhuh.

C127: You, as I don't know, whether I was standing alongside, or bending over looking at the goldfish or what. I—Even, now, well, I don't know if you are tempted sometimes, when you see someone like that, to push them in just for the horseplay or heck of it.

T128: Ummhuh.

C128: And yet, from the other point of view, it seems, I don't know what to say—irrational to get mad, I don't know, it isn't, but that was the feeling I had about it, I *have* about it, not what I *had* about it, I don't know *how* I felt. I can't picture myself in that situation, except as *I feel now*.

T129: It still is attached (pause) to the memory, the feeling—?

C129: Yes, Now, I don't know whether the feeling was one that developed *at the time* or whether it is one I have developed *in looking back on it*, through the description I have of it.

T130: Good point.

C130: When I thought of those two instances, I, in both instances, I don't know whether the feeling is one I have developed *from* the instance or whether it's one I developed *in reflecting* upon the instances.

T131: But the instance seems to illustrate the feelings.

C131: Yeah.

T132: This is probably the more important thing, anyway.

C132: Now, whether it is something I have assigned to this particular instance which has no bearing whatsoever to the instance, I don't know.

T133: At least, as you think of it now, they are good examples of an old feeling.

C133: To find something out of the air and grab hold of it, I'd say this is it. Ahhh, I, it's pretty foggy.

T134: Yeah.

C134: But these are two situations which I can reflect upon. Now, any, to picture anything, I can remember the pond, looking at it, as in the second instance. I can remember the porch, the first instance. Now whether I can, I can remember myself looking at it from another, from an outside viewpoint, of being tangled up in the net. In other words I can see it from an outside viewpoint. So how I felt, or what I saw *in the net*, I don't remember. That is, it is not clear. It is from an outside viewpoint. The same thing, ahh, from the pool instance. Now we have a picture of the pool, have a picture of me standing there, water pouring off and so on. And I can picture myself in that instance, looking at it from the outside, not from the inside.

T135: You say you do have a real picture of yourself, or is it just a mental picture of yourself?

C135: I think that we have a picture of me. I think we actually have a picture of me that was taken at the time. I don't know, but I think so.

T136: Would that have added to your humiliation—having your picture taken?

C136: From this side, no. It's perfectly natural to want to take a picture, I don't know! I don't know.

T137: But if this had been an instance in which you had been upset, had a great feeling of helplessness or something and had that—had that moment been crystallized in film—might have meant something?

C137: As a constant reminder of it. That is, here is something anytime you see it immediately you have these emotions, the emotions that you had at the time are brought to the surface again.

T138: As you look back on it, from the dark side?

C138: Now actually, seeing this picture the first time, I can't remember any emotions about it. But my folks. When I was told by my parents what happened here then I, what, I developed a story about it.

T139: You had a feeling about it.

C139: I had a feeling, well, I don't know if I had a feeling, I developed a story about it. I, what, what, whether what I have told you is one hundred percent true, I don't know. It was a emot . . . , an emotional—motion picture of what was happening at the time, *as I see it now*. What happened then, I couldn't tell you. For that reason, I think it was, ahh, thinking about it now, this is not something I have thought about in the past, but it makes sense, at least from this point of view, which is how I predict—happen to feel about it now. Ahhh, that this is a story which I built up from descriptions given.

T140: The fact that it is a story that seems to fit a mood is probably more important than whether the details actually happened in all the ways that you remember them this afternoon. (pause) So the story might be *emotionally* true without necessarily being altogether *historically* true.

The existentialist should have a heyday with the following passage.

C140: Yeah, I'll go along with that. (long pause) One thing puzzles me right here. In describing these situations, I have described them as an outsider looking at the situation. I have not felt, and cannot *see* myself as the individual in the situation. And, in reflecting upon other situations, not these, joyous, sad, or anything, now it's the same way. Now is this common, or is it?

T141: Partly a function of your being on your guard when you're in here.

C141: I mean this is, this is normal *all* the time. It's not—just when I, I mean, this is the way I think!

T142: But in the dark woods you have feelings.

C142: Yes. But they are all *strictly limited*, what, well, I suppose, if you were going to draw a picture of it, it'd be like this, looking down on it. That's a nose (laughs) believe it or not. . .

T143: Yeah.
C143: Ears, eyes. Looking down on the top, it seems to be limited right here. That's my emotional, in other words, it's all—
T144: Right on top of your head?
C144: Well, not entirely. I'm looking at a—
T145: It's in the plane view.
C145: Looking at a side view, I draw a square the same way.
T146: Yeah.
C146: Inside my head, or inside the being I am.
T147: Ummhuh.
C147: I don't have, ahh, ahh, ahh, a picture even of myself.
T148: Ummhuh.
C148: It's all inside.
T149: Ummhuh.
C149: And whereas, the other view, I cannot see myself in, I only see myself, what, looking at myself from the outside, as another person, or at least that seems to be the way it seems right now.
T150: Ummhuh. (pause) So there's a kind of, it's sort of undifferentiated, isn't it? (pause) It's ahhh—

Note how the client spontaneously comes back to the construct. Already he is ready to relocate one of its poles. There is progress in this interview, and it has been achieved by weaving between construction and documentation.

C150: Umh. Another thought just came to me. Ahhhh, (pause) (sigh) the description of the black is correct. The description of the white is only partially correct, because when I'm looking at myself and discussing my feelings, I look at myself as an outsider looking at myself. But, if I'm with another group, I was thinking of, I just spent the past two hours over in the Union in the coffee shop, drinking coffee.
T151: Ummhuh.
C151: Now, during this time, it was not a case of myself looking at myself as an outsider.
T152: Ummhuh. (pause) Instead?
C152: I don't know—it seems from the inside out. It's like right now—as I'm talking to you I'm looking from the inside out. As I'm talking to myself, I'm looking from the outside in.
C153: Ummhuh.
T153: Not outside *in* but outside at.
T154: O.K.
C154: I'm looking at myself, what, from the *surface* in.
T155: Ummhuh.
C155: From the outside to the surface, I'm looking at myself from the cheery side.
T156: Ummhuh.
C156: From the black side, from the surface *in*.
T157: Ummhuh.
C157: (sigh) If that makes sense. Kinda to try to—
T158: So that it may have made sense—
C158: To summarize my feelings, my ideas.
T159: So then, in a situation such as that of the last two hours, you're not particularly introspective.
T159: No, no. Although what we were doing ended up with just the four veterans talking things over.
T160: Ummhuh.
C160: And we were, what, reminiscing.
T161: Ummhum.
C161: And it was entirely, well, I was drawing upon experiences which I had (pause) enjoyable ones, and I suppose they were doing the same thing—told tall tales, rather around the table.
T162: Ummhuh. (pause) Well, there are two phases to the mood, I take it then. One is whatever it seems to be at the moment it's set off and the other, whatever it is, when you realize you've *got it*, as in the incident yesterday. There was the anger you felt towards your mother.
C162: Yeah.
T163: When she sought to engage you in conversation.
C163: Ummhuh
T164: And then the even blacker part of it came when you realized you were angry at your own mother.
C164: Yeah.
T165: (pause) And this snowballs. If I am a person that gets angry at his own mother, (pause) what kind of a person am I?

C165: Yeah.
T166: And how hopeless my life is.
C166: Yeah. There seems to be nothing upon which—well, just a black morass of, well, I suppose a situation which would fit the tar-pit description given of the dinosaur age.
T167: Ummhuh. Oh.
C167: Bottomless pit of nothing, errr, not nothing but something there, I mean—(sigh)
T168: Almost like the dinosaur struggling out of the tar pit, huh, trying to struggle?
C168: Yeah. Quicksand, going down. A feeling of, well, I don't know. One term I've used recently, I notice, is "corruption."
T169: Oh?
C169: Ahhh, ahhh, I think in the, the, ahhh, medical sense, that is, a stinking mess—*plus*! And this in itself some—
T170: Ummhuh.
C170: As an apt word appears, it, ahhh, builds upon itself.
T171: Ummhuh.
C171: You might say, a perfect example of making a mountain out of a molehill or something. (sigh) That's looking at it from this side. Looking at it from this side (laughs) it's a mountain.
T172: In both instances you recall, or formulate, or use to illustrate from childhood the hammock incident, the fish pond incident. What did they have in common? Feeling-wise, yes, they had this—they are examples of this black feeling.
C172: A feeling, what, well, the word came to me, "to strike out"— "retaliate."
T173: Ummhuh.
C173: And yet, in absolute helplessness! In the first incident, I was tangled in a hammock. Not a darn thing I could do, I'd *had* it (laughs)!
T174: Ummhuh.
C174: Until Mom came with her—whether or—Mom, I think it was my mother, extricated me.
T175: Suppose she laughed at you?
C175: Well, I suppose so, it's a—
T176: Probably would—
C176: Something which you, ahhh, I mean, if I saw someone, *I'd* probably laugh too if I was helping them out. It's a logical thing.
T177: So even if she didn't, the very fact that you could see that it was laughable—
C177: Yeah.
T178: Was just enough?
C178: Its justification enough for the feeling.
T179: Yeah. Because you felt that you were *in* a laughable position.
C179: I would say it's perfectly logical. In *both* instances—it was a laughable condition.
T180: Ummhuh.
C180: I seem to picture myself coming out of the fish, outside of the fish pond, and I wouldn't say I'm anything, ahhh, (sigh) *not laughable at*.
T181: So the outside self would say this, "This, whether anybody laughs at it or not, it is laughable."
C181: Oh, yes, looking at it from this point of view, it's a perfectly enjoyable, laughable condition.
T182: Yeah.
C182: That is, from looking at it from the outside. Looking at it from the inside it's a (sigh) made me just *mad*, thinking about being laughed at for the situation. Two viewpoints, the same situation, both perfectly natural.
T183: Yeah.
C183: And when I'm in a good mood, I look at it one way, and when I'm in a black mood, I look at it another way. If I'm in a black mood, I usually do not recognize the good mood, until I begin to shade out.
T184: Ummhuh. Yeah.
C184: When I'm in the good mood I can recognize the black mood exists.
T185: Ummhuh.
C185: Or was, or did exist, or what. The viewpoint is existent, and yet it does not seem to bother me.
T186: Ummhuh.
C186: I mean, it bothers, yes, but it does not seem to be of major importance, only of minor importance.
T187: Well, then when you are in the black mood you must almost hate yourself as you are.
C187: *Definitely! Definitely!*
T188: Particularly as you are in the good mood. You don't like that—
C188: Ahhh . . .
T189: Bright person, huh?
C189: Ummh, I don't know. I never thought of it that way. When I'm in a *black mood*, I just plain hate myself.
T190: At least you're suspicious of the good mood—suspicious of its motivations.

C190: Well, I didn't, I don't even think of the good mood.
T191: I see.
C191: It's, it's *completely* cut off.
T192: Ummhuh.
C192: Until I begin to shake out if it, ahhh . . .
T193: Yeah.
C193: That is, I'm using the term "shake out"—I suppose it's as good as any.
T194: Yeah, I think I follow that.
C194: Climb out of the pit, or whatever.
T195: Climb out of the pit like you climbed out of the fish pond.
C195: Well, I was thinking, ahhh, combining, ahhh, color quality and this sinking feeling of a well. I mean, this is not how I feel like I'm climbing out of a well.
T196: Yeah.
C196: But, as say, a description of the situation, absolute blackness in the well, climbing out as you get clearer, closer to the light it becomes a lighter shade—
T197: Ummhuh.
C197: Therefore, combining the two feelings.
T198: Yeah.
C198: (pause) Now, I don't know. This just brought up something in my mind (sighs). I get this black feeling as, I can't say this is how it feels 'cause I don't think anybody *knows*. It feels like I'm in quicksand. The harder I struggle, down I go.
T199: Ummhuh.
C199: Or a tar—a tar pool.
T200: Ummhuh.
C200: Pool of tar—it's the same thing. Down you go! Black and blacker!
T201: Ummhuh.
C201: And now I don't know. This thought pattern just came to me. The harder I struggle, the harder I try to find the reason, the blacker it gets and yet, when I relax, that is, when I give up, it planes off. The emotion planes off.
T202: Ummhuh.
C202: The intenser the emotion, the darker it is, the relaxing of the emotion, the well, the term came "boredom" of the emotion, I don't know—
T203: Ummhuh.
C203: Ahhh, if that word even fits, but the word came to mind.
T204: Ummhuh.
C204: Ahhh, it fades out.
T205: So it's almost as if while you're trying to fight it, you only lose.
C205: I don't know as that fits. It does. It doesn't. I'd say as long as I fight it *intensely* . . .
T206: Ummhuh.
C206: And what do I say, get *mad* at it . . .
T207: Yeah.
C207: I lose. But as I relax, ahhh, I cannot say this is how it happens—this seems to fit in the description. As I relax . . . the feeling disappears.
T208: Ummhuh.
C208: It doesn't disappear; it fades.
T209: Fades.
C209: But there continues a recollection of the feeling—I suppose, even a hatred of the feeling, a distinct dislike that the feeling even existed.
T210: Umh. (pause) So that's the next phase.
C210: I say it's a constant fade.
T211: Oh.
C211: I mean, it isn't fade, it is, what (sign) . . . well, back to my diagrams. (pause) If I were to draw it, this, just arbitrary, normal.
T212: Ummhuh.
C212: The black would be down here, and it planes off, and this would be normal, maybe even below normal, I don't know.
T213: Ummhuh.
C213: And this is my cheery self. Now this line, I don't know what—
T214: Ummhuh.
C214: Steepness it would be, or—

T215: Ummhuh.
C215: But, there seems to be, when the anger becomes, vertical or very steep.
T216: Ummhuh.
C216: And then it planes off slowly, even more slowly than I've shown it here.
T217: So when you go into it, it's a real plunge.
C217: It seems to, ahh, thinking back on it, it seems to be.
T218: Yeah.
C218: And then it shades off and then this feeling of recollection, I don't know if it'd be at the norm I've drawn here or below it or above it or where, but then as I, what, feel better, more cheery, more joyful, ahh, it gets above it and this, ahh, this part here is forgotten. Unless something brings my mind back to it.
T219: Ummhuh.
C219: And then I can go back down towards that—dark feeling.
T220: So it's hard even to think about it without being drawn back into it.
C220: Well, I wouldn't want to make an answer that couldn't be changed, but I'd say, "yes."
T221: Ummhuh, O.K.
C221: (pause) I wouldn't want to make *any* answer that couldn't be changed.
T222: Yes, of course.
C222: Each time you ask a question, there's, ahh, I wouldn't say *each* time but most, most, often, there is a complete blank, a lack of an immediate answer popping up and I have to sort of, what, battle around to try to find something that describes it and the terminology used, I make no guarantee of its accuracy.
T223: O.K., now Friday at four?
C223: Friday at four, Monday at four, Friday at four, and that is all we have scheduled at present.
T224: That carries us up for quite awhile.
C224: Goodbye.
T225: Goodbye.

In a later interview the client described his fishpond experience not so much as one of anger as one of chaotic confusion. He had had little experience in playing with other children and to have a playmate behave in such an unpredictable way was simply incomprehensible. He had experienced a massive invalidation of the limited construct system on which he depended for dealing with interpersonal relations. In terms of personal construct theory he experienced *anxiety*—loss of structure.

Later interviews returned, of course, to the mother topic. But in this case as well as from the standpoint of personal construct theory, the objective was not catharsis or venting of feelings. Instead the objective of such further exploration was to dispel the long-standing anxiety by finding adequate structure for dealing with her, as well as with companions who behaved in unexpected ways.

Eventually the task was to carry forward the reformulation of constructs into a series of planned experimental experiences outside the therapy room. These were the "field trials," planned in the laboratory and later analyzed there to provide bases for reformulations and further trials. Thus the model of scientific enterprise is utilized in psychotherapy. And why not? Should not a client be allowed to become his own psychologist?

67

Psychology 862: Psychopathology Course Outline[1]

Bibliography

Psychology 862 (Rev.1–1-58)

Text

1 Henderson, D. & Gillespie, R. D. *A textbook of psychiatry* (8th Ed.), London: Oxford Univer. Press, 1956. (Ed. Library, Health Center Library, Soc. Adm. Lib.).

Principal References

* *Committee on Nomenclature and Statistics of the American Psychiatric Assoc. Diagnostic and Statistical Manual-Mental Disorders.* Washington: Amer. Psychiat. Assoc., 1952. (Psy. Clinic Lib. - Soc. Adm. Lib.).
*2 Cattell, P. *The measurement of intelligence in infants and young children.* New York: Psychological Corp., 1940. (Educ. Library).
3 Coleman, J. C. *Abnormal psychology and modern life.* (2nd Ed.), New York: Scott Foresman, 1956. (Educ. Library).
*4 Cruickshank, W. M. *Psychology of exceptional children and youth.* New York: Prentice Hall, 1955.
5 English, H. B. *Dictionary of psychological and psychoanalytic terms.* New York: Longmans Green, (in press). (Ed. Library, Health Center Lib., Bur. of Educ. Research).
6 English, O. S. & Finch, S. M. *Introduction to psychiatry.* New York: Norton, 1954. (Soc. Adm. Lib., Health Center).
*7 Gates, A. *The improvement of reading.* New York: Macmillan, 1947. (Ed. Lib., Main).
*8 Gesell, A. & Amatruda, C. S. *Developmental diagnosis.* New York: Hober, 1941. (Ed Library, Health Center, Main Library).
*9 Hinsie, L. E. Shatzky, J. *Psychiatric dictionary.* New York: Oxford, 1953. (Health Center, Soc. Adm. Lib. & also Part II.).
*10 Hunt, W. A. *The Clinical Psychologist.* Springfield, Ill.: Thomas, 1956.
*11 Kelly, G. A. *The psychology of personal constructs.* 2 vols., New York: Norton, 1955. (Educ. Lib., Main Lib.).
*12 Rotter, J. B. *Social learning and clinical psychology.* New York: Prentice Hall, 1954. (Educ. Lib.).
*13 Goldstein, K, *Language and language disturbances.* New York: Grune & Stratton, 1948.
*14 Sarason, S. B. *Psychological problems in mental deficiency.* (2nd Ed.) New York: Harper, 1953. (Ed. Lib., Soc.. Adm. Lib.).
*15 Symonds, P. M. *Dynamics of human adjustment.* New York: Appleton-Century, 1946. (Educ. Lib.).
16 *Dynamic psychology.* New York: Appleton-Century, 1949. (Ed. Lib.).
*17 Tredgold, A. F. *A textbook of mental deficiency.* (7th Ed.) London: Baillieri, Tendall and Cox, 1947. (Educ. Lib., Health Center Lib., 101 Hamilton Hall).
*18 U. S. Children's Bureau. *Infant care.* Washington: U. S. Govt. Print. Off., 1945. (Soc. Adm. Lib.).
*19 *Your child from one to six.* Washington; U. S Govt. Print. Off., 1945. (Soc. Adm. Lib.).
*20 Warren, H.C. *Dictionary of psychology.* Boston: Houghton Mifflin, 1934. (Ed. Lib., Main Lib).
*21 Wells, F. L. & Ruesch, V. *Mental examiner's handbook.* New York: Psychological Corp., 1942. (Ed. Lib.).
22 White, R. W. *The abnormal personality.* (2nd Ed.), New York: Ronald, 1956. (Ed Lib. - Health Center).

*Psychological Clinic Library.

[1] Unpublished MS, Ohio State University, revised 1 January, 1958. Published by permission of University Archives/Special Collections—University of Lincoln-Nebraska and Jacqueline Aldridge.

Collected Papers of the Pioneer of Constructivist Psychology: George A. Kelly, First Edition. Edited by David A. Winter and Nick Reed.

Psychology 862: Psychopathology

Topic 1

A Psychological Orientation to Psychopathology

References: English and Finch, pp. 292–331
Henderson and Gillespie, pp. 84–88 (Psychosomatic Med.)
Kelly, pp. 3–23, 50–55, 612–615, 807–809, 920–926
Rotter, pp. 25–44, 88–97, 222–234

1 The orientation of the clinical psychology sequence at OSU
  a The inter-relationship of theory and practice
  b The teaching of common and deviant points of view
    1 The emphasis of common points of view in the eight-sixty sequence and personal points of view in the seminars
  c The eight-sixty sequence is a professional sequence in which the primary focus is not upon the student but upon the student's eventual client
    2 Professional responsibility is required in the laboratory rather than scholarship merely
  d The presentation of facts within the framework of method
2 The objectives of this course (Psychopathology)
  a To span the so-called facts of psychopathology
  b To familiarize the student with prevalent nosological systems
  c To acquire some practical knowledge of informal clinical techniques
  d To become aware of the practical but tenuous relationship between clinical observations and conventionalized syndromes
  e To learn to translate clinical observations into hypotheses rather than into presumed "findings"
  f To familiarize the student with the unique features of the psychiatric point of view
  g To prepare the student to participate effectively as a psychologist in an interdisciplinary setting
3 The epistemological viewpoint assumed in this course
  a Dualistic issues in psychopathology
  b The functional-organic dichotomy
  c Psychosomatic medicine
  d Constructive alternativism
  e Constructive alternativism as a basis for interdisciplinary collaboration
4 The nature of causation and its implications for treatment
  a Treatment vs. prevention
  b Prevention may involve reconstruction of "causes"

Topic 2

Trends in the Conceptualization of Psychopathology

References: English and Finch, pp. 3–12
Henderson and Gillespie, pp. 1–16 (History)
Tredgold, pp. 1–57 (Concept of MD and Incidence)
Hunt, Chap. II

The object of this teaching unit is to familiarize the student with the changing grounds upon which contemporary psychopathology rests and to prepare him for radical revisions in psychopathology in the near future.

1 The continuing emergence of new concepts in psychopathology
  a The psychiatric sequence from Lombroso to Kraepelin to Bleuler
  b The psychodynamic sequence from Charcot to Freud to Sullivan
  c The lost sequence that began with Meyer and was then diffused without any clear systematic trace

- d The pragmatic sequence from James to Dewey to Minnesota
- e The mechanistic sequence from Thorndike to Watson to Kohler to Mowrer

2 Descriptive vs. dynamic psychiatry
- a Descriptive psychiatry's failure to satisfy psychotherapists
- b Dynamic psychiatry's loss of contact with objectivity and experimental rigor

3 Psychiatry's effort to extricate itself from dualism
- a Psychiatry's attempt to retain medical identification
- b Psychoanalysis and the loss of psychiatry's scientific substructure
- c Attempts to solve dualism by professional arrogation
- d Attempts to solve dualism by interaction and hyphenism
- e The "functional-organic" dichotomy

4 Dualism as a problem in psychopathology

5 Dualism as a problem in interprofessional relations

6 Critiques of diagnosis
- a Psychoanalytic critique
- b Rogerian critique
- c Physiological critique
- d Culture critique

7 Emerging trends in diagnosis.
- a Cybernetics
- b Transitive diagnosis
- c Abandonment of concepts of illness and disease together with their attendant social expectations

Topic 3

Mental Mechanisms and Processes

References: Symonds (either volume)
English and Finch, pp. 53–68, 207–209, 214–217.
English, as needed.
Warren, as needed.
Hinsie and Shatzky, as needed.

The student is advised to familiarize himself with the exact meanings of the following terms as they are used professionally. There will be no formal lecture presentation of this topic.

1. Abreaction
2. Aggression
3. Ambivalence
4. Anxiety
5. Autoeroticism
6. Catharsis
7. Character Defense
8. Compensation
9. Compulsion
10. Conversion
11. Defense Mechanism
12. Displacement
13. Empathy
14. Erogeneity
15. Escape
16. Exorcism
17. Expiation
18. Fixation
19. Flight
20. Frustration
21. Guilt
22. Hostility
23. Identification
24. Inhibition
25. Introjection
26. Masochism
27. Narcissism
28. Obsession
29. Projection
30. Rationalization
31. Reaction Formation
32. Regression
33. Repression
34. Resistance
35. Sublimation
36. Sympathy
37. Transference

Topic 4

Nosological Systems

References: English and Finch, pp. 13–100.
Henderson and Gillespie, Chap. II, III, and IV.
Tredgold, Chap. I, II, III, and IV.
Sarason, Chap. I and II.
Statistical Manual, pp. 1–72.

The student is expected to start familiarizing himself with the everyday clinical use of the categories described in the Statistical Manual, pp. 12–43. By the end of the course he should be able to identify accurately the nosological classification to which the Manual assigns any listed group of symptoms.

1 History of classification systems
  a American Psychiatric Association 1917
  b New York Academy of Medicine 1927–1933
  c Veterans Administration Nomenclature 1946
  d Revised International Statistical Classification 1948
  e American Psychiatric Association 1952
2 Royal Medical Psychological Association classification
3 Features of the 1952 classification
  a Shift from disease entities to reactions
  b Emphasis upon statistical records and eventual diagnosis
  c Greater flexibility
  d Influence of psychoanalysis and psychotherapeutics
  e Stress, predisposition and impairment are three factors to be evaluated in every diagnosis
    1 Legal and social implications
4 Critique of disease entity
  a Reification of constructs
  b Conception of disease as an essentially alien process
  c Alternative approaches
    1 Abstracted properties of behavior
    2 Dimensions or axes of reference
    3 Mechanics (e.g., cybernetics)
    4 Pathways of movement

Topic 5

The Primary Clinical Cues

References: Henderson and Gillespie, Chapters IV, V, and VI.

This topic includes those cues that are commonly used by experienced clinicians in diagnosis, regardless of varying dynamic interpretations. The object is to prepare the student to use these cues when he is confronted with clients. Enactment is extensively used as a teaching device. The student, in turn, is expected to learn to portray the cues himself.

1 Anxiety
2 Affect
  a Flattening and blunting
  b Apathy and indifference
  c "La belle indifference"
  d Elation and euphoria
  e Depression
    1 Similarity to manic elation
    2 Difficulty in decision making

3 Pessimism
4 Guilt and unworthiness
5 Motor retardation
6 Variations (menopausal, etc.)
3 Emotional inadequacy and inappropriateness
4 Psychomotor activity
a Retardation and difficulty in thinking
b Automatisms
c Stereotype
d Cyclic and episodic manifestations
e Distractibility
f Perseveration
5 Ideational content
a Ideas of reference
b Systematization
c Delusion
d Hallucination
e Preoccupation
f Depersonalization
6 Reality contact
a Ego strength and accessibility
b Preoccupation
c Fantasy and autistic thinking
d Clouding
e Memory
f Orientation
g Judgment and practicality
h Depersonalization
i Stupor and perplexity
j Pane of glass
1 Obliqueness
2 Ellipsis
k Vigilance
7 Conceptualization
a Looseness and fragmentation
b Flight of ideas
c Circumstantiality
d Fabulation and confabulation
8 Miscellaneous
a Somatization
b Somatic compliance
c Secondary gain
d Suggestibility
e Deterioration
f Regression
1 Critical symptoms

Topic 6

Observation and Informal Testing

References: Wells and Ruesch (Scan all).
Kelly, pp. 774–829

This teaching unit is intended to give the student an introduction to the tremendous variety of relevant observations that may be made by a skilled clinician during a brief contact with a patient. It is expected that the student will immediately start developing a wide-angled view of his client, a view that should continue to develop during all the years of his professional experience.

1 Clinical observations not requiring obvious examination
  a Reactive signs
    1 Oral gestures, massage, posture
    2 Smoking pattern, reposturization, grimacing, hand sweating, vaso-motor changes
    3 Speech: pitch, rhythm, intensity, modulation, deference, querulousness, cluttering
    4 Tremors, loss of emotional adequacy, explosiveness eye-movement patterns, breathing patterns, functional asymmetry.
    5 Audition
    6 Vision—glasses
    7 Writing
    8 Handedness
    9 Odors
  b Structural signs
    1 Structural asymmetry
    2 Stigmata
    3 Distribution of fat and hair
    4 Eyes
    5 Head
    6 Nails and hands
    7 Feet
2 The impersonal clinical examination
  a Physical signs
    1 Head
    2 Eyes
    3 Mouth: shape, tongue, teeth, gums, throat
    4 Motor
    5 Sensory acuity
    6 Reflexes
    7 Glands
  b Social signs
    1 Occupational status and irregularity
    2 Community and socio-economic district
    3 Migration and community identification
    4 Nearness of relatives and their problems
    5 Size of family and ratio of wage earners to total number in household
    6 Dress
    7 Luxury-necessity patterns
    8 Vocabulary level in relation to occupation and community as a measure of social striving
    9 Companionship and socio-economic frame of reference
    10 Recreational pattern
    11 Language as a key to cultural identification and stress
    12 Catastrophic indicators
    13 Breaks in household continuity
    14 Trips and horizons
    15 Shared space and belongings
    16 Nature of organizational control under which a person carries out his vocation
    17 Projected ambitions
    18 Occupational skills, interests, and orientations
3 Informal testing with a demonstration of illustrative tests from Wells and Ruesch Handbook

Topic 7

Infant Psychopathologies

References: Cattell, Read pp. 93–268, Scan pp. 11–92
Infant Care, Scan pp. 1–222

The student should become familiar with the unique technical problems that arise in the clinical appraisal of infants, as well as become aware of the nature of psychopathological behavior at the infant level.

1 Special considerations in the examination of infants
   a Differs from other testing in that emphasis is placed upon maximum performance rather than conformity to the examiner's controls
      1 Emphasis upon differentiation of non-verbal stimuli
      2 Examiner should avoid mass response
      3 Distinction between apathy, distractibility, and fatigue
      4 Evaluation of fleeting responses, regardless of when they occur
      5 Recognize stimulus values rather than physical intensity of distracting stimuli
   b Appraise time and situation concomitants
   c Control of stimulation
      1 Use of familiar person
      2 Use of familiar and unfamiliar surroundings as means of cross-checking results
      3 Control of stimulation in relation to sleep, eating, and fatigue cycles
   d Emphasis upon behavior record as well as upon responses during examination
      1 Parents' accounts and their proper appraisal
      2 Use of the Vineland Scale
   e Emphasis upon biographical record in relation to environment
   f Using the test situation as a way of evaluating parent's response to the infant
      1 Infant needs response as well as stimulation
      2 Note physical aspects of stimulus and response in the infant's home situation
   g Kinds of response to be noted
      1 Vocal
      2 Bodily movement
      3 Prehensive and manipulative responses
      4 Eyes
      5 Adjustive responses
      6 Persistive responses
      7 Apathy
2 Common symptoms of infant psychopathology
   a Thanatoid syndrome
   b Feeding problems
      1 Self-regulation and scheduling
      2 Relation to other cycles
      3 Distraction
      4 Interruption of feeding
      5 Illness
   c Sleep problems
      1 Stimulation cycles
      2 Preparatory routine
      3 Warmth and security
   d Thumb sucking
      1 Manipulative and exploratory tendencies
      2 Relation to feeding
   e Crying and quiescence
      1 Experimental approaches
      2 Evaluation of symptom
   f Anxiety and fear
   g Toilet training.

Topic 8

Psychopathologies of Early Childhood

References: English and Finch, pp. 101–138, 575–592.
Sarason, Chap. 7.
Gesell, (Scan pp. 109–349).
Your Child, (Scan pp. 1–43).

1 Enuresis
  a Organic approaches
  b Negativism
  c Construed as a control phenomenon
    1 Sibling rivalry
    2 Parental disciplinary measures
  d Maturation
2 Malnutrition
  a Apathy and distraction
  b Failure of control and of modulation
  c Relation to over-stimulation
  d Erroneous interpretation of "excess energy"
  e Relation to reading and other long attention span activities
  f Perseveration
3 Convulsions
  a Physio-chemical factors
  b Epileptic types
  c Electroencephalographic approaches
4 Night terrors
5 Temper tantrums
6 Childhood schizophrenia
  a Bizarre behavior
  b Lack of diagnostic principles
7 Delinquency
  a Determine what it is that the child is delinquent in relation to
  b Appraise the danger of the child's not being delinquent
  c Depressive features in delinquency
  d Schizoid symbolism in delinquency

Topic 9

Sensory Handicaps

Reference: Cruickshank, pp. 120–183, 214–283.

1 Visual defect
  a The Hayes Binet
  b Motor difficulties
  c Sight saving techniques
  d Relation to other forms of organicity
  e Neurotic use of partial vision
  f Postural signs
  g Disguises for partial vision
  h Educational difficulties

2 Hearing defect
  a Relation to speech difficulties
  b Selective pitch
  c Postural signs
  d Informal methods of testing
  e Difficulties in the use of hearing aids
    1 Amplification of ambient noise
    2 Use of defect to provide a way of withdrawing
  f Projective filling
  g Suspicion
  h Hypersensitivity to noise in the hard-of-hearing
  i The case for lip reading vs. manual speech
  j Occupational deafness

Topic 10

Motor Handicaps

1 Crippledness
  a Early crippledness
  b Implications of later crippledness
2 Amputees
  a Occupational difficulties
  b Symbolic values attributed to lost member of amputee
  c Hostility and compensatory devices
3 Cerebral Palsy
  a Organicity
  b Athetosis and spasticity
  c Treatment experiments
  d Stages of psychological development
    1 Prehension hurdle
    2 Communication hurdle
  e Appraising the parents' role
  f Problems of psychological assessment
4 Encephalitis
  a Difficulty of tracing original fever
  b Personality characteristics
  c Manifest symptoms

Topic 11

Organicity

Reference: English and Finch, pp. 424–527

1 Cerebral deficit and damage in children
  a Psychometric pattern
  b Educational pattern
  c Perceptual orientation
  d Use of symbols
  e Teaching aids

2 Cerebral deficit and damage in adults
   a Reversal of psychometric pattern seen in children
   b Concretism
   c Perseveration
   d Substitution of rigid methodology for free exploration
   e Deterioration of concepts
   f Use of literalism
   g Use of pseudo-practicality
3 Senescence
   a Memory pattern
   b Value pattern
   c Adaptive psychotherapy
   d Maintenance of functional role

Topic 12

Psychosomatics

Reference: English and Finch, pp. 292–231.

1 General features of the statistical classification
   a Relation to somatization
   b Relation to psychophysiologic autonomic and visceral disorders
   c Characteristic bodily locations and their presumed implications
2 Differentiation from conversion
   a Involvement of organs and viscera innervated by autonomic nervous system
   b Failure to alleviate anxiety
   c Physiological rather than symbolic origin of symptoms
   d Frequent production of structural changes which may threaten life
3 Differentiation from anxiety reactions
   a Persistent involvement of a single organ system
4 Role of emotional factors
5 Differentiation from addictions
6 Differentiation from schizophrenic reactions
   a Not regressive or deteriorative

Topic 13

Educational Disabilities

References: Gates (Scan book)
The purpose of this teaching unit is to provide an illustrative introduction to the diagnostic difficulties involved in dealing with problems arising in the school setting and to make clear to the student educational difficulties cannot properly be construed as localized in the school setting nor as being peculiar to the classroom.

1 Reading disabilities
   a Cultural evaluation of the reading functions
   b Diagnosis
      1 Performance vs. verbal abilities
      2 Anxiety
      3 Educational methodology in the production of reading disabilities, as well as in their alleviation
      4 Psycho-social pattern in the home
      5 Specific psycho-motor functions

6 Reading readiness
  a Vocabulary
  b Interest level
  c Strephosymbolia
  d Speech
  e Ocular-motor factors
  f Eye-hand coordination
7 Demonstration of parts of Monroe Reading Aptitude Test

2 Arithmetic disability
  a Cultural evaluation of arithmetic functions
  b Sex-role considerations
  c Mathematics treated as concrete or as abstract
  d Instrumental use of mathematics
3 Psychomotor disabilities
  a Symbolic values
  b Relation to motor patterns in general

Topic 14

Aphasias

Reference: Goldstein, Chapter 4.
This is a large and complicated topical area. The student is expected to acquire no more than a simple introductory knowledge of it.

1 Historical information
  a Henry Head
  b Kurt Goldstein
  c The concept of disorders of symbolic organization and expression
  d The assumption of organicity and brain localization
  e Strephosymbolia and the Iowa School
    1 Samuel Orton
    2 L.E. Travis
2 Classification systems
  a Semantic, syntactical, nominal
  b Organic, functional, transient
  c Symptomatic
    1 Aphonia, alexia, agraphia, apraxia, Wernike's, etc.
    2 Dysphonia, dyslexia, etc.
  d Lesion areas
3 Treatment
  a Educative
    1 Stimulation
    2 Integrative exercises
  b Spontaneous recovery
4 Informal tests

Topic 15

Feeblemindedness

References: Henderson and Gillespie, Chapter 16.
Mental Defect Sarason, Chapter 6.
Tredgold, Chapters, 1, 13, and 14.
Tredgold, Chapters 1, 13, and 14.

1 Changing views
  a Goddard's earlier view
  b Symptomatic view
    1 Organic process types
    2 Social deprivation
    3 Constitutional types
2 Hydrocephaly
3 Macrocephaly
4 Microcephaly
5 Amaurotic family idiocy
6 Rh incompatibility
7 Consanguinity
8 Malnutrition
9 Mongolism
  a Etiology
  b Conventional "signs."
    (1) Slanted eyes
    (2) Flat occiput
    (3) Oval face
    (4) Unopposed thumb
    (5) Flexible joints
    (6) Fissured tongue
    (7) High narrow hard palate
    (8) History of mucous catarrhs
    (9) Mimicry
    (10) Sociability
    (11) Epicanthic fold
    (12) Flat profile
    (13) Short digits
    (14) Single lined hand
    (15) Large tongue
    (16) Low soft palate
    (17) Large torso-leg ratio
    (18) Low family incidence
    (19) Mental deficiency
10 Cretinism
  a Differentiation from mongolism
  b Speech disorders and voice quality

Topic 16

Management of the Retarded Child

References: Sarason, Chapters 10, 11, and 12
Tredgold, (Scan Chapter 17).

1 Conceptualization in the retarded child
  a Concretism
  b Perceptual dependency
  c Routine and self control
  d Distinction between conceptual level and perceptual complexity
2 The special room approach
  a Equipment
  b Syllabus
  c Methodology
  d Objectives
3 Administrative procedures
  a Failing grades
  b Pre-reading assessment
  c Confounding with reading disability
4 Feebleminded equivalents
  a Institutional behavior patterns
5 Planning for institutionalization

6 Interpretation of feeblemindedness to parents
   a Planning parental roles
   b Structure of the child's future
   c Effect on siblings
   d Interpretation of school's role

Topic 17

Conversion and Hypochondriasis

References: English and Finch, Chapter 7 (Conversion).
Henderson and Gillespie, Chapter 7 (Psychoneurotic Reactions).

1 Distinction between conversion and hypochondriasis
2 The mechanism of conversion
3 Principles covering symptom choice
   a Secondary gain
   b Somatic compliance
   c Displacement upwards
   d Genitalization of organs
   e Introjection and suggestibility
   f Cultural determinants
   g Popular notions of anatomy
4 Common symptoms
   a Type of crying
   b Effect of counter-suggestion
   c Narcosynthesis effects
   d Globus hystericus
   e Anesthesias
   f Arc le cercle
5 Diagnostic principles
   a Impracticality
   b Dependency
   c La belle indifference
   d Beautiful suffering
   e Acting out
   f Dissociative features
6 Deterioration in hypochondriasis
7 Psychotic outcomes

Topic 18

The Principal Anxiety Syndromes

References: English and Finch, Chapters 6, 8 and 9
Kelly, pp. 894–901, 1113–1117.

1 Anxiety reaction
   a Somatization
   b Free floating anxiety
   c Visceral reactions
      1 Supposed implication of head symptoms
      2 Supposed implication of abdominal symptoms
      3 Supposed difference between "inside" and "outside" symptoms
   d Relation to anxiety state
   e Differentiation from schizoid agitation

2 Weeping
  a Diffuse-inarticulate type
  b Infantile weeping
  c Regressive weeping
  d Loose weeping
  e Situational weeping
  f Histrionic weeping
  g Hostile weeping
  h Constrictive weeping
  i Agitated weeping
  j Facade weeping
3 Phobic reaction
  a Symbolic fears
  b Displacement mechanism
  c Relation to "anxiety hysteria"

Topic 19

The Affective Disorders

References: Henderson and Gillespie, Chapters 8 and 9.
Kelly, 901–908.

1 Differentiation of psychosis and neurosis
  a Reality orientation
  b Diffusion of response
  c Degree of distortion
  d Conceptual loosening
  e Coexistence of neurotic and psychotic patterns
  f Control of anxiety through psychosis
  g The pre-psychotic neurosis
2 The psychiatric view of affect vs. ideation
  a Emotional tone
  b Prolonged history of disorder argues for ideational disturbance
  c Episodic features of affective disorders
  d Realistic features of affective disorders
3 Involutional melancholia
  a Organic features
  b Constriction and change of life-role
  c Sex linkage
  d Absence of history of depression
  e Guilt, agitation and somatic concerns
4 Manic depressive reactions
  a Relation to extraversion
  b Mood swings
  c Contrast symptoms
  d Cycles
  e Retardation and acceleration
  f Stages of suicidal risk
  g Flight of ideas
  h Orality
  i Excited depression
  j Exhaustion
  k Hypomania

- l Perplexity and stupor
- m Precipitating factors

5 Neurotic depression
- a Relation to reality
- b Maintenance of a personal relationship
- c Threats to the patient
- d Therapeutic control of patient
- e Danger of generalized interpretations

Topic 20

The Schizophrenic Disorders

References: Henderson and Gillespie, Chapter 10
Kelly, 853–866

1 Identifying schizophrenia with ideation

2 Diagnostic criteria
- a Reality distortion within a private system
- b Conceptual loosening
- c Confabulation
- d Supposed retreat from reality
- e The clinician's "pane of glass" experience
- f Emotional inappropriateness
- g Affective flattening
- h Shallow affect
- i Regression
- j Deterioration

3 Types of Schizophrenia
- a Simple
  - 1 Apathy
  - 2 Retreat
  - 3 Long history
  - 4 Change in diagnostic criteria and recent years
  - 5 The flophouse type
- b Hebephrenia
  - 1 Regression
  - 2 Fetal position
  - 3 Laughter
  - 4 Humor
  - 5 Excitement
- c Paranoid type
  - 1 Persecution without complete systematization
  - 2 Less ability to control expression of persecutory delusions
  - 3 Ideas of reference
  - 4 Ideas of grandeur
  - 5 Hostility
  - 6 Systematize hypochondria
  - 7 Vigilance
  - 8 Intellectualization
- d Catatonic type
  - 1 Motor expressions
  - 2 Resistiveness
  - 3 Hazards in dealing with

    4 Episodic nature
    5 Inhibition
    6 Stupor, mutism, explosiveness, negativism, *cerea flexibilitas*
    7 Excitement
  e Acute types
    1 Episodic nature
    2 Dissociation
    3 So-called multiple personality
    4 Amnesia
    5 Quick remission
    6 Affective coloration
    7 Cases of first attack
    8 Response to institutionalization
  f Chronic or "old-schiz" types
  g So-called schizo-affective types

Topic 21

Sexual Deviation

1 The concept of sex role
  a Threat to the sex role and the displacement of cathexis
  b Inferiority feelings
  c Misperceptions of sexual function
  d Active and passive types of homosexuality
2 Correlations of sexual deviation
  a Organic involvements
  b Physique
  c Social expectations
  d Endocrinology
  e Group life
  f Vocations
  g Institutional deprivation—men, women
  h Culture linkages
3 Diagnostic procedures
  a Behavior cycles
  b Symbolisms
  c Impression on opposite sex
  d Selection of therapist
4 Latent sexual inversion
  a Excessive sexual demands
  b Homosexual panic
  c Oral and anal eroticism

Topic 22

Paranoid Syndromes

References: Henderson and Gillespie, Chapter 11

1 Relation of paranoia to guilt and failure in sex role
  a Manifest symptoms
  b Latent symptoms

2 Dynamic interpretations
  a Projection
  b Guilt
  c Systematization
  d Conceptualization
  e Intellectualization
  f Persecution feelings
  g Delusions of grandeur
3 Types of paranoid disorder
  a "Pure" paranoia
    1 Intricacy of system
    2 Slow development
    3 Intactness of rest of thought system
    4 Absence of hallucinations
    5 Rare incidence
  b Paranoid state
    1 Intermediate between paranoia and paranoid schizophrenia
    2 May be acute
  c Paranoid schizophrenia
    1 Fragmentation features predominate
    2 System less intact
    3 Deterioration more marked
    4 Common use of ideas of reference
    5 Includes systematized paranoid hypochondriacal states
    6 Hallucinations
  d Paranoid personality
    1 Neither psychotic nor neurotic
    2 Absence of anxiety
    3 May be evidence of physical immaturity or constitutional inadequacy
    4 Life-long pattern
    5 Supposedly unresponsive to therapy
    6 Some schizoid characteristics
    7 Automatic use of projective mechanism

Topic 23

Personality Disorders

Reference: English and Finch, Chapter 12
Henderson and Gillespie, Chapter 12 (Psychopathic States)

1 Principles
  a Developmental defect
  b Not usually regressive
  c Supposed not to be susceptible to treatment
  d Failure to develop "super-ego"
  e Organic signs
  f Revealed by pattern of behavior rather than by mental and emotional signs or by response to test and interview
  g Not psychotic because of absence of delusions and of distortions of reality. Not neurotic because not anxious
2 Inadequate personality
  a Inadaptability, ineptness, poor judgment
  b Lack of stamina
  c Social incompatibility

3 Schizoid personality
  a Withdrawal, aloofness and shyness
  b Inability to express aggression
  c Autistic thinking
  d Eccentricity
4 Cyclothymic personality
  a Extroversion
  b Internally conditioned moods
5 Paranoid personality
6 Emotionally unstable personality
  a Instability under stress
7 Passive-aggressive personality
  a Passive-dependent type
  b Passive-aggressive type
  c Aggressive type
8 Compulsive personality
  a Obsessive concern with standards
  b Capacity for work
  c Inability to relax
  d The decompensating compulsive personality
  e Psychotic breakthrough
9 Sociopathic personality disturbances
  a Failure to conform to society and culture
  b Place in psychological category if possible
10 Antisocial reaction
  a Includes cases formerly classified as "constitutional psychopathic state" and "psychopathic personality."
  b Lack of loyalties as revealed in record
  c Ability to use popular rationale
11 Dissocial reaction
  a Disregard for conventions as a result of abnormal moral environment
  b May have intra-group loyalties
12 Sexual deviation
  a Includes homosexuality, transvestism, pedophilia, fetishism, and sexual sadism
13 Addictions (See topic dealing with this)
14 Transient situational personality disorders

Topic 24

Addictions

References: Henderson and Gillespie, Chapter 14.

1 Alcoholic disorders
  a Personality characteristics
  b Psychotherapeutic difficulties
    1 Alcoholics Anonymous
    2 Drug treatment
    3 Psychotherapy
  c Dipsomania
    1 Cyclic nature
  d Alcoholic hallucinosis
    1 Not necessarily alcoholic
  e Polyneuritis
    1 Avitaminosis
  f Pathological intoxication
    1 Relation to brain injury

g Delirium tremens
 1 Hallucinations
 2 Withdrawal of alcohol from addict
 3 Course
h Korsakow's psychosis
 1 Confabulation
 2 Retrospective falsification
 3 Greater evidence in older females
 4 Spatial orientation less affected
 5 Suggestibility
 6 Course
i Chronic alcoholism
 1 Deterioration
2 Drug addiction
 a Character changes
 b Institutional treatment
 c Use of placebo and gradual withdrawal
 d Characteristic symptoms
  1 Opium and morphine
  2 Cocaine
  3 Marijuana
  4 Bromides

Topic 25

Infections

1 Paresis or general paralysis
 a Personality alterations
 b Deterioration
 c Tests
  1 Clinical
  2 Chemical
  3 Formal
 d Delusions
2 Cerebro-spinal syphilis
3 Tabes dorsalis (locomotor ataxia)
 a Motor symptoms
4 Encephalitis lethargica
5 Parkinsonian syndrome (paralysis agitans.)
 a Palsy
 b Gait
6 Chorea
 a Choreiform Movements
 b Sydenham's (ordinary)
 c Huntington's (hereditary)

Topic 26

Convulsive and Traumatic Disorders

References: Henderson and Gillespie, Chapter 15
Sarason, Chapter 8.

1 Epilepsy as a related group of syndromes rather than as a disease entity
2 Symptomatic types of epilepsy
    a Idiopathic or essential epilepsy
        1 The epileptic personality
        2 Prodramata and aura
        3 Cry and loss of consciousness
        4 Tonic spasm starting on one side
        5 Cyanosis
        6 Clonic stage
        7 Coma
        8 Grand mal
            a High voltage fast waves in EEG
        9 Petit mal
            a Bilaterally diffused EEG
            b Sharp spikes, three per second
            c Nausea
        10 Psychomotor seizure
            a High voltage, three per second
        11 Clouding, daze, anxiety, excitement, hallucinations, fears, violent outbreaks
    b Epileptic equivalents
        1 Asymptomatic diagnosis on basis of EEG
        2 Delta waves one to five per second
    c Jacksonian epilepsy
        1 Localized spasms
    d Narcolepsy
    e Epileptic fugue
    f Symptomatic epilepsy
    g Hysteriform epilepsy
3 Hyperventilation effects
4 Metabolic disturbances
5 Neoplasms
6 External trauma

Topic 27

Degenerative Disorders

References: Tredgold, Chapters 13 and 14.
Sarason, Chapters 3, 4, and 5.

1 Arteriosclerosis
    a Stroke
        1 Facial muscles
        2 Reflexes
        3 Memory
        4 One-sidedness
    b Mental losses
        1 Names and other specific memories
        2 Irritability
        3 Conceptual rigidity
        4 Concretism
        5 Retention of formal intellectual skills
        6 Test performance

2 Prefrontal lobotomy (leucotomy)
  a Types
    1 Standard
    2 Transorbital
    3 Topectomy
    4 Undercutting
  b Indications for
  c Personality changes
    1 Behavioral
    2 Test
    3 Prognosis
3 Shock therapies
  a Insulin
  b Metrazol
  c Electro-shock (ECT)
    1 Ancient usage
    2 Electronarcosis
    3 Standard Shock series
    4 Soft shock
    5 Regressive shock therapy
    6 Use of the electro-stimulator
    7 Hazards
    8 Indicators
    9 Sequelae
    10 Test effects
    11 Use in transorbital lobotomy

Psychology 862, Winter, 1953
First Mid-Term
examination
January 30, 1953

Do not write your name on this test. Use the number assigned you.
YOUR NUMBER.______________________

1 From the epistemological viewpoint assumed in this course how would you respond to the proposition that "since paresis is an organic disease only a psychiatrist should be permitted to handle a paretic patient"? State the basic position and indicate how the answer follows from it.
2 What would you consider the normal age in months for accomplishment of each of the following? List one figure only. A range of tolerance will be used in scoring.
  a Drinks from a cup held by another person
  b Takes first three steps unsupported
  c Sits up unsupported
  d Uses thumb opposition
  e Imitates drawing of a straight line
  f Gives up 2 A.M. feeding
  g Eyes follow a bright object
  h Acquires bowel control
  i Acquires bladder control
  j Speaks three word sentences
  k Laces and ties shoes
  l Turns a crank
  m Acquires first tooth

3 A teacher asks you to make a clinical evaluation of a seven-year-old child to determine whether or not she should put him into a beginning reading class or not. What skills and achievements would you examine or take into account? What relevance to her question does each of them have?

4 Compare and contrast each of the following pairs of terms:
   a conversion and displacement
   b catharsis and abreaction
   c aggression and hostility
   d introjection and empathy
   e anxiety and guilt

5 What clinical signs would you use to distinguish between *flattened affect* and *depression*.
   b When a psychiatrist asks to have a patient's *ego strength* and *accessibility* evaluated, what type of treatment does he probably have under consideration?
   c What does Henderson include under *somatic* demands?

6 What is the essential characteristic of each of the following?
   a *deja vu*
   b *la belle indifference*
   c *Folie a deux*
   d *Pseudologia phantastica*
   e *Nihilistic delusion*

KEY TO PSYCHOLOGY 862 FIRST MIDTERM EXAMINATION

Given January 30, 1953

Question	*Key*
1	Three points for each of the following: Statement of the position of constructive alternativism, statement of the causation fallacy, and statement of the application of either view to the question. Add one point for well integrated answer. Total 10 points.
2	One point for each answer that falls within the following brackets: a 4–10 b 12–15 c 7–9 d 6–11 e 20–32 f 1–2 g 1–3 h 15–20 i 20–30 j 20–30 k 70–90 l 25–35 m 5–8 Total 13 points
3	One point for mentioning each of the following and one point for mentioning proper relevance of each: a Sensory motor b Vocabulary c Experience and interests d Intelligence and conceptualization e Speech f Home training g Social relationships Total 14 points

Question	Key	
4	One point for proper comparison and one point for proper contrast of each of the following:	
	Comparison	*Contrast*
	a. Conflict	Affect
	b. Subordinate relationship	Reliving of experience
	c. Instinctual and forceful	Destructive
	d. Incorporation	Intellectual identification
	e. Apprehension of danger	Origin of danger in self
	Total 10 points	
5a	One point for each of the following equivalent:	
	a. Superficial approach vs. emotional withdrawal	
	b. Monotony vs. retardation	
	c. Undercontrolled pursuit of a topic vs. overcontrolled handling of material	
	Total 3 points	
5b	Psychoanalysis	3 points
	or Rational therapy	2 points
	or Psychotherapy	1 point
	Maximum 3 points	
5c	One point for each of the following: push and energy as evidenced by speech, interest in activities, sex activities.	
	Total 3 points	
6	a. Already seen	1 pt.
	Delusional	1.pt.
	b. Pseudo-avoidance	1.pt.
	Exhibitionistic	1.pt.
	c. Similarity	1.pt.
	Communicated	1.pt.
	d. Lying	1.pt.
	Pathological	1.pt.
	e. Denial of existence	2. pt.
	Total 10 points	
Class Distribution		
		*- Clinic Majors
		x-Others

66
↓
50–*
49–*
48
47–*x
46–x
45–*
44–x
43–*
42
41–x
40
39–*
38–x
37
36
35–x
34–x
33–xx*
32
31–xx
30–xxx
29
28–xxx
↓
9–x

Psychology 862
Second Mid-term
Examination
February 11, 1953

Write your name on the attached card, note the number assigned you, and return the card to the proctor. Do not put your name on your paper. Use only the number for identification.

Number______________________

1 What two diagnostic principles are generally accepted for distinguishing a neurosis from a psychosis?
2 In addition to expressing a diagnosis in terms of a nosological category modern psychiatric procedure recognizes that legal and social considerations make it advisable to make evaluative statements on each of three supplementary factors. What are the three factors?
3 How does one give the "serial sevens" test?
4 In what way did Freud modify Charcot's psychotherapeutic techniques?
5 Who is considered the originator of the eclectic point of view which underlies "total push" therapy?
6 What feature of conversion hysteria did Janet emphasize?
7 Compare and contrast the following pairs of terms:
   a Somatization and somatic compliance
   b Phobic reaction and anxiety reaction
   c Reaction formation and rationalization
   d Regression and transference
   e Character defense and resistance
8 When the cause of a particular type of mental deficiency is entirely exogenous what term does Tredgold use to designate the type?
9 What is the hypothesis of blastophoria?
10 In the British classification system what term is approximately parallel to our term of "moron"?
11 Under what rubrics do "hysteria", "psychasthenia" and "neurasthenia" fall in the more recent nosological systems?
12 What is the obvious clinical feature of each of the following?
   a Anorexia nervosa
   b Dermatographia
   c Ganser syndrome
   d Fugue
13 Criticize the concept of psychosomatics from a philosophical or systematic point of view.
14 Is the conversion hysteria patient who exhibits a "glove anesthesia" a philosophical monist? Discuss.

KEY TO PSYCHOLOGY 862 SECOND MIDTERM EXAMINATION GIVEN FEB. 11, 1953.

1 Two points each for:
   a contact with reality
   b extent of disorganization

Total 4 points

2 One point each for following:
   a Predisposition
   b Stress
   c impairment

Total 3 points

3 Total 3 points
4 One point each for:
   a added relaxation
   b added free association
   c subtracted hypnosis

Total 3 points

5 Adolph Meyer — Total 1 point
6 Suggestibility, la belle indifference, dissociation or failure of synthesis in a particular area.

Total 3 points

7 Two points each for the following, one for comparison and one for contrast:
   a Expression of a conflict vs. in an organ or organ symbolism vs. basis for choice of a symptom.
   b Displaced fear vs. free floating quality.
   c Both symptom defenses but reaction formation is denial through opposites and rationalization is logical subterfuge.
   d Both throwbacks but regression is behavioral and involves reversal of development while transference is perceptual and not necessarily a reversal.
   e Both defenses against anxiety but character defense is against internal forces and resistance is against external forces.

Total 10 points

8 Two points for secondary amentia.

Total 2 points

9 Two points for injury to genes.

Total 2 points

10 Feebleminded - one point.
11 Hysteria—conversion reaction - 2 points
or anxiety or dissociative - 1 point
Psychasthenia—compulsive or obsessional - 2 points
Neurasthenia—psychophysiologic reaction or asthenic reaction - 2 points

Total 16 points

12 One point for each of following:
a loss of appetite
b redness of skin when rubbed
c lying or tangential answers
d amnesia or flight

Total 4 points

13 Up to five points for clear expression of pseudo-monism attempted through interactionism.

Total 5 points

14 Up to five points

Total 5 points

Class Distribution
52
↓
47 - *
46
45 - x
44
43
42
41 - **
39 - x
38 - xxx*
37 - x
36 - x*
35
34 - x*
33 - *
32 -xx
31 - x
30 - xx
29
28
27 - x
26 - x
↓
17 - x

Psychology 862
Make-up Exam
Feb. 19, 1953

1 Kraepelin conceived of all the mental functions as being divided into three dimensions. Tell the origin of this tripartite division and describe each dimension.
2 According to Henderson and Gillespie, what are three disadvantages of a psychological classification of mental disorders?
3 According to Henderson and Gillespie, why is the term *reaction types* preferred to *mental diseases*?

4 Why does Tredgold adopt the "material" conception of mind?
5 List and briefly define the three criteria of feeblemindedness that Tredgold advocates.
6 Write two definitions of the psychosomatic disorders, one from the philosophical position of constructive alternativism and one from the standpoint of interactionism.
7 Identify the following:
Exogenous
Prefrontal leucotomy
Consanguinity
Primary amentia
Moral defectives

Psychology 862
Third Mid-term Examination
February 27, 1953

Write your name on the attached card, note the number assigned you and return the card to the proctor. Do not put your name on your paper. Use only the number for identification.

Number______________________

1 (8 pts.) On what four grounds are psychosomatic reactions ordinarily distinguished from conversion reactions?
2 (2 pts.) When a disorder is classified as an "affective" disorder, from what kind of disorders is it thus presumed to be distinguished?
3 (4 pts.) Write a brief description of a thirty-five year old woman who might reasonably be expected to become an involutional melancholia patient at the age of fifty.
4 (2 pts.) At which stage of psychosexual development, according to the psychoanalysts, are the basic mechanisms of manic depressive psychosis anchored?
5 (4 pts.) There is some difference of opinion as to whether a depressive psychotic is really anxious or not. Discuss.
6 (18 pts.)Following are some "classical" symptoms. If a symptom is generally considered to be characteristic of conversion reaction write "c" after the term, if characteristic of manic depressive psychosis write "m", if schizophrenia write "s".
a Displacement upwards
b Conceptual loosening
c Smearing
d Flight of ideas
e Affective flattening
f Secondary gain
g Lump in the throat
h Confabulation
i Infectious hilarity
j Verbigeration
k Functional blindness
l Deterioration
m Waxy flexibility
n Systematized delusion
o Mood swings
p Catatonia
q Cycloid features
r Acting out
7 (6 pts.) Which of the types of schizophrenia is most likely to show spontaneous recovery? Which is most likely to show regression? Which wander lust?
8 (12 pts.) Associate each of the terms on the left with one of those on the right. State the basis of your association.

Compulsion	Masochism
Reaction formation	Autoeroticism
Guilt	Resistance
Abreaction	Exorcism
Displacement	Ambivalence
Transference	Conversion
	Expiation
	Introjection

9 (6 pts.) "Write a short paragraph on the value of the Ph.D. in psychology."
   a Respond to this question as you might if you were a paranoid schizophrenic.
   b Respond as you might if you were a manic depressive in a depressed state.
   c Respond as you might if you were a manic depressive in a manic state.

KEY TO PSYCHOLOGY 862 THIRD MIDTERM EXAMINATION GIVEN FEB. 27, 1953

1 Two points each for following:
   a Involve autonomic organs
   b Failure to alleviate anxiety
   c Non-symbolic
   d Involve structural changes

Total 8 points

2 One point each for following:
   a Ideational
   b Schizoid

Total 2 points

3 Constriction 2 points
   Marital attitudes 1 point
   Object values 1 point (or equivalents)

Total 4 points

4 Two points for oral or
   one point for pregenital

Total 2 points

5 Two points each for:
   a Psychotic defense against anxiety
   b Quality of discussion

Total 4 points

6 One point for each of the following

a – c	g – c	m – s
b – s	h – s	n – s
c – s	i – m	o – m
d – m	j – s	p – s
e – c	k – c	q – m
f – c	l – s	r – c

Total 18 points

7 Two points for each of following:
   a Catatonic or acute
   b Hebephrenia
   c Simple

Total 6 points

8 One point for each key association plus one point for each rationale.
   a compulsion—masochism
   b reaction formation—ambivalence
   c guilt—expiation or masochism
   d abreaction—exorcism
   e displacement—conversion
   f transference—resistance

Total 12 points

9 One point for each feature:
   a persecutive
      systematized
   b brevity
      guilt or failure
   c dilation
      flight of ideas, etc.

Total 6 points

Feb. 27th
Class Distribution

62 maximum
61
60*
59
58
57x
56*
55*
54*
53
52x
51
50x**
49xxx
48x
47x
46
45xx
44xx
43x
42xxx
41
40
39
38x
37
36
34

Psychology 862
Final Examination
March 17, 1953

Write your name on the attached card, note the number assigned you and return the card to the proctor. Do not put your name on the paper. Use only the number identification.

Your number______________

1 In the psychological examination of infants it is customary for the examiner to make certain departures from standard procedure which he would not make if he were administering a test to older children. What are these departures? 3 pts.
2 In what way does the use of curare contribute to the treatment of spasticity? 3 pts.
3 An elementary school child has a lesion in the area of Broca. List two of the school subjects which you would expect him to find most difficult and two that would not necessarily be affected. 4 pts.
4 A physician observes both an Argyll Robertson pupil and a tabetic gait in a patient. What disease is he therefore likely to suspect? 2 pts.
5 When an electroencephalogram (EEG) reveals a slow rhythm with sharp spikes what type of epilepsy is to be suspected? 2 pts.
6 What are the principal sensory characteristics of amaurotic family idiocy? What is the usual prognosis of a case of this disorder? 4 pts.
7 What type of amentia is associated with an extremely low metabolic rate? 2 pts.
8 Describe the gait of a patient with Parkinsonian syndrome. 3 pts.
9 Describe the so-called "typical" *grand mal* attack. 8 pts.
10 You are on a camping trip with an elderly friend. He becomes ill and is unable to walk without support. You suspect a light "stroke" or minor cerebral hemorrhage. What simple informal tests could you employ and what responses to them would tend to verify your suspicion? 4 pts.
11 In taking an anamnesis or case history from a patient with Korsakow's syndrome the clinician should be particularly alerted to what features in the patient's behavior? 4 pts.

12 List eight anatomical characteristics of the mongoloid patient. 8 pts.
13 In the manic-depressive cycle at what point is the suicidal risk greatest? 4 pts.
14 Following are five trios of terms. Look at the first trio and decide how two of the terms can be construed as being alike and yet different from the third. Indicate which two you construe as being alike. Make a statement justifying your division of the terms. Do the same for the next trio, etc. 10 pts.
  a. Repression, inhibition, sublimation
  b. Introjection, identification, empathy
  c. Narcissism, masochism, regression
  d. Anxiety, fear, guilt
  e. Aggression, hostility, escape.
15 When clients come to our psychological clinic at Ohio State University, they are asked to fill out referral statements indicating the problems on which they wish help.
  a Suppose that you are a case of "conversion hysteria". In three or four sentences make the kind of a statement that you might write on the referral form. 5 pts.
  b Suppose that you are a case of "compulsion neurosis". In three or four sentences make the kind of a statement that you might write on the referral form. 5 pts.
16 Following is a new projective test. The subject is asked to say what he thinks the following sentence might mean.
  Curl furbnit shillu strat ionetique secks, therefore wha "cup" pe look at quwe? Fuffst!
  a Suppose you are a patient with confabulatory tendencies. How might you respond to this item? 5 pts.
  b Suppose you are a patient on the verge of a homosexual panic. How might you respond to this item? 5 pts.
  c Suppose you are an obsessive-compulsive neurotic patient. How might you respond to this item? 5 pts.

Psychology 862
Final Examination Key
March 17, 1953

Question	*Answer to be noted*		*Part Points*	*Total Points*
1.	Repetition of items		1 or	3
	Substitution of later passes for earlier failures		2 or	
	Principle of determination of *possibility* of response rather than social *conformity* to the examiner's control		3	
2.	Relaxes musculature		1 or	3
	Relaxes antagonistic muscles		2 or	
	Relaxes antagonistic muscles during motor learning		3	
3.	Any language subjects (two)		1 each +	4
	Any manual or non-symbolic subjects (two)		1 each	
4.	Syphilis or lues		1 or	2
	G.P., paresis, or syphilis of nervous system		2	
5.	Petit Mal		2	2
6.	Audition		1+	4
	Vision		1+	
	Loss of senses or no cure		1 or	
	Early death		2	
7.	Cretinism or myxedema		2	2
8.	Stiffness		1 or	3
	Lack of compensatory movements		3	
9.	Aura	Tonic spasm	1	8
	Cry	Cyanosis		
	Loss of consciousness	Clonic Spasm		
	Fall	Coma or automatism		
10.	Asymmetric motor response		1+	4
	Facial musculature affected		1+	
	Whistle test		1+	
	Speech affected		1	
11.	Memory gaps		2+	4
	Confabulation		2	

Question	*Answer to be noted*		*Part Points*	*Total Points*
12.	Slant eyes	Unopposed thumb	1 each	8
	Epicanthic fold	Single lined hand		
	Nasal palpae	Flexible joints		
	Flat occiput	Large tongue		
	Flat profile	Fissured tongue		
	Oval face	Low soft palate		
	Short digits	High narrow hard palate Large torso-leg ratio		
13.	In first phase of recovery from depression		4	4
14.	Any meaningful linkage		1+	10
	Any meaningful differentiation along same dimensional line		1	
15. a.	Martyr		1+	5
	No insight		1+	
	Somatization of complaint		1+	
	Histrionics		1+	
	Dependency		1	
b.	Legalism		1+	5
	Meticulousness		1+	
	Tries to rationalize or explain symptoms systematically		1+	
	Use of technical terms		1+	
	Intellectualism without spontaneity		1	
16. a.	Invokes additional stimulus material Tells story or theme		1 or	5
	Invents plausible story or theme (fanciful)		2 or	
	Invents extravagant and impossible theme 5		4 or	
			5	
	b. Displays anxiety		1 or	5
	Perceives impersonal hostility in stimulus Perceives hostility directed at self Expresses hostility toward test or examiner		2 or	
			3 or	
	Perceives sex (only if hostility also)		4 +	
			1	
c.	Stimulus bound or literalistic		1+	5
	Rumination		1+	
	"Discovering" words		1+	
	Dealing with punctuation		1+	
	Inability to make definitive statement		1+	10

CLASS DISTRIBUTION ON FINAL EXAMINATION

86 Maximum

↓

70 *
69
68 x
67
66 *
65 x*
64
63 xx*
62
61 *
60 xx
59 xxxx*
58 x
57
56 x

55
54 x
53 x
52
51 x
50 x
49
↓
40 x

Psychology 862, Winter, 1955
First Mid-Term Examination
January 28, 1955

Do not write your name on this test. Use the number assigned you.
Your Number____________________

1 In what general way do the objectives of this course differ from those of all the other courses in clinical psychology at this university?
2 Suppose you are a monist and are asked to give a definition of a psychosomatic disorder. How would you respond?
3 We are considering the development of a "Professional Maturity Scale" designed along the lines of the Vineland Scale for use among psychologists. Keeping in mind the structure of the Vineland Scale, set up a tentative draft of an eight-item scale that might be tried out.
4 Assuming that there is a relationship between compulsivity and toilet training, offer two competitive theoretical explanations for such an assumed relationship.
5 What are the two principal psychological hurdles that the cerebral palsied child must overcome if he is to avoid intellectual retardation?
6 What separate factors does the Monroe Reading Aptitude Test attempt to measure?
7 Compare and contrast each of the following pairs of terms.
   a Catharsis and exorcism
   b Repression and inhibition
   c Conversion and displacement
   d Introjection and identification
   e Conversion and reaction formation
8 What kind of examination procedure do Henderson and Gillespie recommend for evaluating a patient's "apperception"?
9 List six of the descriptive terms which Henderson and Gillespie use in evaluating "stream of talk".
10 The belief in reincarnation is probably anchored in one of the types of memory disturbance. Which one?
11 What are the clinical signs of *depersonalization*?
12 Under what conditions is a symptom a symbolization?

Psychology 862
Second Mid-Term Examination
February 16, 1955

Do not write your name on this test.
Use the number assigned you.
Your Number ____________________

Good morning students! How are you feeling this morning? How are you getting along in Psychology 862?

This test calls for role-playing on paper. Below are some symptom-concepts which are widely used in the impressionistic clinical appraisal of patients. Take each concept in turn and write a short paragraph of response to the class "greeting" above in such a way that a clinician reading the paragraph would clearly get the impression that you had the symptom. Make sure that your clinician gets the impression called for.

1 La belle indifference
2 Reference
3 Depersonalization
4 Lack of ego strength
5 Vigilance
6 Clouding
7 Flattening

Psychology 862
Psychopathology
Final Examination March 17, 1955

Do not write your name on this test. Use the number you have drawn.
Your Number____________

1 Find the term on the right that is the BEST associate for the term on the left. Copy its identifying letter in the blank provided. Letters may be used more than once and some letters may be left over.

________(1) Pane of glass	A. Symbolized conflict
________(2) Retardation	B. Lack of ego strength
________(3) Somatic compliance	C. Quotidian procrastination
________(4) Depression	D. Failure to gain spontaneous interaction with the patient.
________(5) Reference	O. Inability to deal with personal problems abstractly
________(6) Anxiety	L. A symptom value not related to basic anxiety
________(7) Acting Out	T. Uncertainty about what is taking place
________(8) Preoccupation	E. Labored thinking
________(9) Somatization	Z. Erecting an artificial story to hold together loosely perceived events
________(10) Secondary gain	N. Consistently avoiding the immediate situation in order to pursue one's own themes
________(11) Euphoria	H. A posture peculiar to conversion hysteria
________(12) Confabulation	G. Lump in the throat
________(13) Stomach ulcers	P. Choosing the most plausible symptom
________(14) Clouding	R. Feeling that one is being directed or influenced
________(15) Flattening	S. Awareness of confusion in one's self
________(16) Concretism	I. Uniformity in emotional tone
________(17) Autistic thinking	F. Amentia
	J. Nocturnal enuresis
	K. Depersonalization
	M. Necromancy

2 Here is another group of items of the same type.

________(1) Fragmented personality	A. Super ego
________(2) Systematized delusions	Z. Involutional melancholia
________(3) Introjected values	Y. Alcoholism
________(4) Euphoria	S. Conversion reaction
________(5) Non-conformism	E. Schizophrenia
________(6) The intra-psychic agency of one's mother	M. Broca's area
________(7) Dementia praecox	D. Paranoid reaction
________(8) St. Vitus' dance	B. Mongolism
________(9) Manic episode	U. Compulsion neurosis
________(10) Emotional inappropriateness	T. Paresis
________(11) Hysteria	K. Demoniacal possession
________(12) Regression	F. Hypnosis
________(13) Delusions of grandeur	C. Cretinism
________(14) Fastidiousness	O. Epilepsy
________(15) Aura	H. Catharsis
________(16) Korsakoff's psychosis	R. Affective disorder
________(17) Electroencephalographic spikes	G. Sociopathic personality
________(18) Precarious sex role	L. Narcosynthesis
________(19) Medical electricity	V. Chorea
________(20) Can't get a tune out of your mind	
________(21) Flat occiput	

Following are twenty diagnostic labels. Pin one on each of the syndromes described in the succeeding paragraphs. Use the letters to indicate your selections.

P. Traumatic brain damage
G. Addiction without brain damage
R. Mongolism

L. Manic depressive reaction, depressed type
A. Schizophrenic reaction, simple type
K. Schizophrenic reaction, catatonic type
D. Schizophrenic reaction, hebephrenic type
E. Schizophrenic reaction, paranoid type
M. Involutional psychotic reaction
S. Paranoid state
I. Psychophysiologic autonomic or visceral disorder
W. Anxiety reaction
F. Dissociative reaction
O. Conversion reaction
U. Depressive reaction
C. Obsessive compulsive reaction
N. Cyclothymic personality
H. Inadequate personality
T. Familial amaurosis
B. Passive-aggressive personality

3 A child does not learn to talk until age five. By age seven he has stopped talking. He has nightmares, seems to be afraid of everything, and reacts to everyone as if they are about to hurt him. Just before his chronic poor health culminates in death at age ten he has become almost totally deaf and partially blind.

4 A fifty-six year old farm woman, the devoted mother of seven married children, has been known as an excellent housekeeper all her life. Within the past two years she has become slovenly and withdrawn. She claims her husband doesn't love her anymore, that she must have committed an unpardonable sin for which God is punishing her in this way. The husband, who has been doing most of the housework lately, admits that he has become irritated with her during the past year. He cannot recall her ever being like this before.

5 A thirty year old unmarried man has been attending the university for the past seven years and is about to squeak through to a B.S. degree in agriculture. This was his choice of a major after having tried business administration, art, English, and psychology. Prior to his attending the university his work experience consisted of two years washing cans in his father's creamery and three months in the army. He is a regular and accepted member of a local church youth group. He insists that people are generally mean and narrow and will take advantage of anyone who tries to be kind to them. He is punctual about some things but quite haphazard about others. About the only complaint that members of the youth group make is that he does not take baths as often as he should.

6 A seventeen year old girl is generally considered spoiled, although her manner is appealing on first acquaintance. She makes much ado about every little triumph and disappointment in her life, including each of the passing episodes with a parade of boyfriends. She attaches herself closely to each new boyfriend but the relationship always breaks up dramatically after two or three months. She is a good student and is majoring in French. She hopes to become a writer of French plays for television in Quebec. Recently she has developed very painful arthritic pains in the back for which the physician is giving her massive vitamin shots in the hope that she can accept an invitation to the St. Patrick's Day Dance, if it should be offered.

7 A young man, aged twenty-four, has developed severe panic reactions to the prospect of taking the final examinations this spring quarter. He says two of his professors claim to have discovered something disgraceful about his recent relationships to one of the male graduate assistants to whom he has been quite attached until two weeks ago. He now refuses to leave his room lest he "do something he would be sorry for." He has been amusing himself during the past few days making calculations about the end of British rule in the Suez area based on the Great Pyramid's geometric data.

8 A woman of forty has become extremely upset because she lost all her check stubs for the period 1948 to 1952. It turns out that she has remarkably complete records of everything she has ever done and a day-by-day calendar schedule of all her planned activities for the coming year, including the evening she will go to the movie. She has become so upset over her loss of the check stubs that she has asked her psychology professor if she may take her final examination in a room separate from the rest of the class.

9 A seventeen year old university sophomore has asked his roommate to help him keep track of his examination schedule this week. The roommate describes him as being unusually absent-minded and vaguely upset over something during the past several months. For example, he dashed over to University Hall Sunday evening, saying that he has almost forgotten that that was the time eight o'clock Monday classes were scheduled to take examinations.

10 A twenty-two year old woman patient in the Columbus Hospital is an enthusiastic devotee of all-day suckers and dolls. She sits on the floor, soils herself and plays with rubber dolls for hours at a time, laughing and crying to herself, but never taking part in any kind of social interaction on the ward.

Psychology 862, Winter 1956
First Mid-Term. Examination
January 23, 1956

Do not write your name on this test. Use the number assigned to you,
Your Number______________

1 Why is a psychiatric textbook used in this course rather than a psychological textbook?
2 What did Freud learn from Charcot?
3 Suppose you met a psychiatrist and wanted to find out whether he was a so-called "dynamically oriented" psychiatrist or not. What key question would you ask him and what kind of an answer would you expect him to give if he were not this type of psychiatrist?
4 Suppose the principles of infant intelligence testing were applied to the testing of intelligence among members of this class. Set up a test item and write the instructions for its administration and scoring in such a way as to indicate clearly that you understand how such a change in approach would affect the testing of adult intelligence.
5 If early toilet training does not cause compulsivity in the mature personality how could you explain why it appears that so many compulsive persons show records of unusually early toilet training?
6 What kind of treatment needs to accompany the use of curare in dealing with spastic children?
7 From the epistemological position of this course how would you define a psycho-somatic disorder?
8 What would you consider the normal age in months for accomplishment of each of the following? List one figure only. A range of tolerance will be used in scoring.
  a Drinks from a cup held by another person
  b Takes first three steps unsupported
  c Sits up unsupported
  d Uses thumb opposition
  e Imitates drawing of a straight line
  f Gives up 2 a.m. feeding
  g Eyes follow a bright object
  h Acquires bowel control
  i Acquires bladder control
  j Speaks three-word sentences
  k Laces and ties shoes
  l Turns a crank
  m Acquires first tooth
9 According to "dynamic psychiatry" at what stage of psycho-sexual development does the child first develop rebelliousness?
10 Reproduce the classification scheme which English and Finch use for children's emotional disorders.

Psychology 862
First Mid-Term Examination
January 28, 1957

Do not write your name on this test. Use the number assigned you.
Your Number______________

1 Using the epistemological position assumed in this course, state as clearly as you can in each of the following cases the essential difference between the two terms listed. (6 points)
  a Psychology and Physiology
  b The responsibility of the clinical psychologist and the responsibility of the psychiatrist
  c The factor that causes a disorder and the factor that should be treated in order to alleviate the disorder
2 In what sense could you say that each of the following statements might be considered true? (6 points)
  a The person who uses the conversion mechanism is obviously a dualist
  b To the extent that a schizophrenic patient can be made anxious he can be made to recover from his psychosis
  c A character defense, even though mild, cannot be treated by psychotherapy
3 Suppose each of three first-year graduate students has been asked to present to this research team a tentative project for his Master's Thesis. One student has a tendency toward ideas of reference, the second has a tendency toward depression, and the third has a tendency toward feelings of depersonalization. Yet each puts forth a plan which is tentatively acceptable to the adviser and to the research team as a whole. Put yourself, in turn, in the place of each student and draft a research proposal, no more than half a dozen sentences in length. Explain why each student might write his proposal the way you have drafted it for him. (12 points)

KEY
MIDTERM EXAMINATION, JANUARY 28, 1957
PSYCHOLOGY 862

1.	a Psychology and physiology	2 conceptual systems	1 pt.
		plus not events themselves	2 pts.
	b Clin. Psychologist & psychiatrist	to view from different viewpoints	1 pt.
		plus to make the best predictions and outcomes his system will sustain	2 pts.
	c factor causing & factor to be treated	different	1 pt.
		cause of alleviation	2 pts.
2.	a conversion and dualism	use of physiological disguise	1 pt.
		quality answer	2 pts.
	b anxiety to help schizophrenic	accessibility	1 pt.
		psychotic defense	1 pt.
	c psychotherapy for character defense	ego insight will not produce change	1 pt.
		no desire to align with society	1 pt.
3.	a reference	suspicion only	1 pt.
		reference	2 pts.
		subtlety	3 pts.
		plausibility	4 pts.
	b depression	obvious depression only	1 pt.
		unworthiness	2 pts.
		implied depression in content	3 pts.
		plausible	4 pts.
	c depersonalization	obvious separation from	
		project	1 pt.
		perplexity	2 pts.
		implied in content	3 pts.
		plausible design	4 pts.

24
↓
18–111
17 - 11
16 - 1111
15 - 1
14 - 111
13 - 111
12 - 111
11 - 1
10 -
9 - 1

Psychology 862, Psychopathology
Mid-Term Examination
February 29, 1957

Do not write your name on this test.
Use the number assigned you.
Your number______________

1 Which of the following do English and Finch *not* include under "psychophysiologic disorders?"
  a Migraine
  b Hypertension
  c Korsakoff's psychosis
  d Psychomotor equivalent
  e Paroxysmal tachycardia
  f Asthma
  g Dyspepsia
  h Vaginismus
  i Pruritus

j Gastric ulcer
k Urinary urgency

2 What types of enuresis in children do English and Finch identify?
3 How does Tredgold distinguish between primary and secondary amentia?
4 According to Tredgold, why are mental defectives particularly liable to psychosis?
5 According to Cruickshank what are the three principal adjustment patterns of persons with impaired hearing?
6 List four of the seven hypotheses offered by Sarason to explain the nonbiological transmission of feeblemindedness in families.
7 What are the principal causal factors in delirium tremens?
8 Given one minute to make your examination, and being without equipment, how might you distinguish between each of the following?
   a A cretin and a mongoloid
   b A case of amaurotic family idiocy and amentia due to encephalitis lethargica
   c Athetosis and Parkinsonism
9 What is each of the following used to measure?
   a Kent EGY
   b Serial Sevens
   c Vineland Scale
   d Sorting Test (any type)
   e Pellet Test
   f Mirror Writing Test
   g Rum Cay

Psychology 862, Psychopathology
Mid-Term Examination
February 29, 1957

Do not write your name on this test. Use the number assigned you.
Your number____________

1 Which of the following do English and Finch *not* include under "psychophysiologic disorders ?"
   a Migraine
   b Hypertension
   c *Korsakoff's psychosis* – [Score 3 plus Rights minus Wrongs]
   d *Psychomotor equivalent*
5 pts. e Paroxysmal tachycardia
   f Asthma
   g Dyspepsia
   h Vaginismus
   i Pruritus
   j Gastric ulcer
   k Urinary urgency

4 pts 2 What types of enuresis in children do English and Finch identify?
   Revenge — Lack of training
   Regression — Fancied injury

2 pts 3 How does Tredgold distinguish between primary and secondary amentia?
   germ vs. accident

2 pts 4 According to Tredgold, why are mental defectives particularly liable topsychosis? Bad stock

6 pts. 5 According to Cruickshank what are the three principal adjustment patterns of persons with impaired hearing?
   constriction, protest of normality, and commonality

4 pts. 6 List four of the seven hypotheses offered by Sarason to explain the non-biological transmission of feeblemindedness in families.
   1. poor planning
   2. indifference
   3. inappropriate response
   4. bad scheduling
   5. neglect in large family
   6. lack of encouragement
   7. lack of *cultural* interests

4 pts 7 What are the principal causal factors in delirium tremens?
   alcohol, withdrawal, avitaminosis

8 Given one minute to make your examination, and being without equipment, how might you distinguish between each of the following?

2 pts. a. A cretin and a mongoloid - skin - mongoloid signs
b. A case of amaurotic family idiocy and amentia due to encephalitis lethargica - blindness, mask, gait
c. Athetosis and Parkinsonism - vermiform movements, block on intention

7 pts. 9 What is each of the following used to measure?

a. Kent EGY	intelligence
b. Serial Sevens	attention
c. Vineland Scale	social development
d. Sorting Test (any type)	concept formation
e. Pellet Test	motor skills
f. Mirror Writing Test	strephosymbolia
g. Rum Cay	thematic structure

4 pts. 10 Give a definition of the function of a state university:

a. As it might be phrased by a distinguished university administrator in the prime of life.	abstract
b. As it might be phrased by him two years after recovering—as far as vocabulary is concerned—from a major cerebral accident	concretistic

8 pts. 11 Here are four items from an analogies test designed especially to measure aptitude for clinical psychology. Complete each analogy by inserting a word from the list below.
a. Sympathy is to empathy as identification is to *introjection*
b. Repression is to inhibition as obsession is to *compulsion*
c. Masochism is to hostility as expiation is to *guilt*
d. Catharsis is to reaction formation as *aggression* is to *projection.*

(guilt ½) (conversion ½)

Exorcism	Introjection
Projection	Anxiety
Guilt	Erogeneity
Transference	Compulsion
Conversion	Narcissism
Fixation	Ambivalence

---

52 pts. – max.
Class Distribution
52
↓
45
44
43
42 – 1
41
40 – 11
39 – 1
38 – 11
37
36
35 – 111
34 – 1
33 – 1
32 – 1
31
30 – 11
29
28 – 111
27 – 1
26

25 – 1
24
23
22 – 1
21
20
19 – 1

Psychology 862, Psychology
Final Examination
March 12, 1957

Do not write your name on this examination. Use the number assigned you.
YOUR NUMBER________________

1 Draw a picture of a worm's-eye view of a cow. Suppose a patient is shown this picture and asked to say what it looks like.
  a What might a patient who was suffering from psychoneurotic obsessive compulsive reaction say?
  b What might a patient who was suffering from mildly regressive schizophrenia say? Write the response so as to make clear the distinction between the personality of this patient and that of the one in "a" above. 5 pts
  c What might a patient who was suffering from involutional melancholia say? Make clear the distinction from "a" and "b" personalities. 5 pts.
  d What might a patient who was suffering from paranoid personality say? Distinguish, etc. 5 pts.
2 On what grounds would you make a differential diagnosis between each of the following?
  a Psychoneurotic depressive reaction (reactive depression) and psychotic depressive reaction. 5 pts.
  b Severe anxiety reaction and mild phobic reaction. 5 pts.
  c Passive aggressive personality and inadequate personality. 5 pts.
3 Match the following categories with the symptoms which are most clearly associated with them. Indicate your answers by writing the appropriate letters in the blanks. You may use the same letter more than once

________ 1. Alzheimer's Disease
________ 2. Myxedema
________ 3. Pellagra
________ 4. Huntington's Chorea
________ 5. General Paresis
________ 6. Frigidity
________ 7. Cocaine Addiction
________ 8. Homosexuality
________ 9. Idiopathic Epilepsy
________ 10. Catatonic Schizophrenia
________ 11. Psychotic Depressive Reaction
________ 12. Sociopathic Personality, Antisocial Type
________ 13. Cyclothymic Personality
________ 14. Hebephrenia

A. Difficulty in pronouncing "Medical Electricity"
B. Peculiar Laughter
C. Flat Occiput
D. Paralysis Agitans
E. Waxy Flexibility
F. La Belle Indifference 14 pts.
H. Free Floating Hostility
I. Chronic Lassitude
J. Chromatic Agnosia
L. Dancing Gait
M. Constitutional Psychopathic State
N. Vaginismus
O. Paresthesia
P. Distorted Feelings of Guilt
R. Aura
S. Transvestitism
T. Scanty Hair in Eyebrows
U. Irregular Mood Swings
X. Pseudologia Phantastica
Y. Premature Senility
Z. Anamnesis

FINAL EXAMINATION (CONT.)

MARCH 12, 1957

1 Suppose you were asked to revise the Diagnostic and Statistical Manual of the American Psychiatric Association. List eight diagnosis categories you believe should be abandoned or replaced. In each instance explain how, and on what grounds, you would reclassify the cases that are now commonly assigned to the category. 16 pts.

Max. = 65 pts.

Class Distribution

65	43
↓	
57–11	42 – 1
56 – 1	41 – 11
55	40 – 1
54	39
53 – 1	38
52 – 1	37 – 1
51 – 1	36 – 1111
50 – 1	
49	
48	
47 – 1	
46 – 1	
45 – 1	
44 – 1	

MAKE -UP FINAL

PSYCHOLOGY 862

March 14, 1957

1 Select eight pairs of diagnostic categories recognized by the Diagnostic and Statistical Manual of the American Psychiatric Association. Indicate how you believe these pairs could be combined into four single diagnostic categories without doing violence to one's understanding of the patients assigned to them.
2 Suppose you were to ask the following question to a patient during the intake interview at a mental hospital: "What kind of treatment here do you think would be most helpful to you?" Write the response you might get____
   a —if the patient were an alcoholic
   b —if the patient were an involutional melancholic
   c —if the patient were an obsessive compulsive psychoneurotic
   d — if the patient were a sociopath, antisocial type.
3 What relation do you see between physio-chemical factors and situational reactions of a psychoneurotic type?
4 If you were to take charge of a newly-built institution for feebleminded, what diagnostic categories would you use and how would your management of individual patients be related to these categories?

Psychology 862, Psychopathology
First Mid-Term Examination
January 27, 1958

Do not write your name on your paper. Use your identification number and place it on each page.

1 (20 pts.) The American Psychiatric Association's Diagnostic and Statistical Manual defines "Schizophrenic Reactions" in terms of their characteristic "disturbances" and their principal psychological "tendencies."
   a What are these disturbances and tendencies?
   b The Manual lists nine types or sub-categories of "Schizophrenic Reactions." Name them.
2 (12 pts.) Can you identify the following important figures in the history of psychiatry?
   1 This man officially authorized the establishment of one of the first mental hospitals at London. It was later known as "Bedlam".
   2 Shortly after the French Revolution this man removed the chains from inmates of La Bicetre Hospital in Paris to prove that the mentally ill should be treated with kindness.
   3 This man developed in 1906 the first blood test for syphilis.
   4 Who were the founders of the Nancy school of thought which placed a strong psychological emphasis upon the understanding of hysteria in the latter part of the Nineteenth Century?
   5 In 1895, Freud went to Paris to study under this distinguished psychopathologist.
   6 Author of "A Mind That Found Itself" and founder of the modern organized mental hygiene movement in the United States.
   7 This woman is credited with the establishment of thirty-two modern mental hospitals and rounded out her amazing career by organizing the nursing forces of the Northern armies during the Civil War.

8 Author of "The Discovery of Witchcraft" published in 1584, an exposé of witchcraft superstitions. King James I of England ordered his book seized and burned.
9 An influential philosopher who argued that since reason was independent of man and immortal in nature it could not be attacked by illness.
10 A real old-timer who recommended marriage as the best remedy for hysteria.
11 This man is one of those who aided the survival of Greek medical thought and its relatively humane attitudes during the time when Christian lands were treating mentally disturbed persons with increasing cruelty.
12 Established the Zurich School of thought as an off-shoot of Freud's school and emphasized the "collective unconscious."

3 (20 pts.) On what principal dimensions would you compare and contrast the basic positions of Tredgold, Sarason and Cruickshank? Indicate where you would place each of these persons with respect to each of the dimensions you propose.

4 (20 pts.) What is the most important difference you noticed in the way English and Finch go about making a psychiatric examination and the way Henderson and Gillespie recommend? Illustrate.

5 (20 pts.) What descriptive terms do Henderson and Gillespie use in describing the "stream of talk" at a symptomatic level?

6 (15 pts.)

a Following is a quotation from one of the references in your reading list. While you are not expected to remember all that you read verbatim, your understanding of the various points of view will narrow down the possibilities to one or two. List three references in one of which you think this might be found .

"The inborn forces are commonly called instincts. They are primary data, being given in the innate equipment of the organism. . . The prevailing instinctive forces, however, are the same in man and animals. There are probably only two, *self-preservation* and *sex*. . . At birth in man the instincts have but few patterns of expression, but these multiply (under environmental influences) as the age of the individual increases, so that there are two varieties of pattern of instinctive expression—inherited and acquired."

b Now three guesses on this one.

"The tendency to categorize people into dichotomies or into one of a *limited* number of classes or types or to see in every behavior the expression of some basic personality characteristic or essence, is probably a special case of the error of overgeneralization. It is the source of so much wasted effort in present clinical practice and of great enough significance that it requires special treatment. . . . .

What are the characteristics of a 'neurotic'. . . . ?. . . . we would not consider this a useful question to ask.

c Who do you suppose said this? It ought to be easy, but you still have three chances.

"We have found the following classification useful for nervous disorders in children in general. Only the first four are additional to the syndromes, . . . in adults.

1 Disorders of personality: Timidity, obstinacy, irritability, sensitiveness, shyness, . . .
2 Behavior disorders: Truancy, wandering, temper tantrums, lying, stealing, begging, . . .
3 Habit disorders: Nail biting, thumb-sucking, incontinence (nocturnal and diurnal), constipation, . . .
4 Disorders of the so-called 'glycopenic' variety: Migraine, crises of collapse, insomnia, night terrors, . . ."

7 Suppose a ten months-old child was brought into the room where you are now taking this examination. You are asked to examine him immediately and make the best estimate you can of his level of intellectual development. You may use only such materials as you normally carry in your purse or pockets. Exactly what would you do and what observations would you make? For each of the things you would do indicate what response you would accept as evidence of a normal but not necessarily superior mental level.

Psychology 862 Psychopathology
Second Mid-Term Examination
February 21, 1958

DO NOT WRITE YOUR NAME ON YOUR EXAMINATION PAPER. USE THE IDENTIFICATION NUMBER YOU HAVE DRAWN.

The student may keep this copy of the examination.

1 This is a straight vocabulary item. Identify each of the descriptive statements by inserting the proper letter from the right hand column in the blank provided. Insert one letter only in each blank.

1 A disturbance due to a recent paralysis of the muscles used in speaking.	W. Deteriorative Proxemia
2 A disturbance resulting from a lesion in the area of Broca.	S. Amnesic-Apraxic
3 Excessive fear of water.	B. Dysrhythmic paralexia
4 An inability to produce letters which is not accompanied by any lack of ability to recognize them.	P. Dysarthria
5 So-called "word-blindness."	G. Rote Extinctis nervosa
6 Inability to reproduce letters because of a lack of a clear idea of how they are formed. The person is otherwise literate.	O. Alexia
	E. Peripheral Motor Aphasia

7 The loss of the ability to deal with numbers as quantitative values, leaving only the ability to deal with them as in counting serially or in following the mechanical steps of multiplication, etc.
8 Loss of memory.

N. Ideatoric Apraxia
A. Failure of abstraction or of simultaneous function
H. Parataxis
Z. Muscue Voluntantes
V. Intra-psychic Constriction
L. Amnesia
R. Paraphenolic Concretism
T. Agnostic mnemosis
M. Hydrophobia
Y. Aphonia
J. Mutism

2 It is known that one frequently finds children having difficulty in distinguishing between the symbols, b, d, p, q. There are two schools of thought in this matter. What are they? To which one does Gates belong?
3 How would you expect the weeping of a conversion hysteria patient to differ from the weeping of a depressed person?
4 Consider the following four diagnostic categories: (1) Anxiety Reaction, (2) Conversion Reaction, (3) Dissociative Reaction, and (4) Phobic Reaction.
   a In which would you expect the anxiety to be most "free-floating?"
   b In which would you most expect to find "beautiful indifference?"
   c In which would you most expect to find "fugue?"
   d In which would you be most likely to find constriction?
   e Which is most difficult to distinguish from schizoid reactions?
   f Which type of patient is least willing to deal with the psychological etiology of his case?
   g Which type of patient is most likely to have gastro-intestinal disorders growing out of the later stages of the process, rather than being present at the outset?
   h On which one did Freud cut his therapeutic teeth?
   i Which one is presumed to be almost wholly concerned with the Oedipal stage of psychosexual development?
   j Which is most likely to show retrograde amnesia?
   k Which is most likely to show anterograde amnesia?
5 Suppose you were given three minutes to inspect two ten year-old children and to determine which of them was a Mongoloid and which was a cretin. What criteria would you use to determine which diagnosis?
6 What do psychiatrists generally agree are the criteria for distinguishing generally between a psychosis and a psychoneurosis?
7 What are the principal symptoms of Korsakow's Psychosis?
8 A physician advised the parents of a twelve year old child to have him committed to an institution for the feebleminded. They come to you for an opinion. What information would you require in order to advise them and how would you weight that information with respect to the issue of institutionalization?
9 Make a concluding statement about this examination that would suggest that you were suffering from neurasthenia. Since the term does not appear in the most recent nosological systems, how would you, for the sake of the clinic records, classify a person who showed this kind of symptom?

Psychology 862, Psychopathology
Key to Second Mid-term Examination
February 21, 1958

1 (1) P (2) E (3) M (4) S (5) O (6) N (7) A (8) L
   One point each. Max. 8 points
2 Strephosymbolia, cerebral dominance theory, or equivalent vs. Lack of maturation, learning, form discrimination, or equivalent 5 points Gates belongs to latter 5 points. Max. 10 points
3 Histrionic, Attention to suffering, Wail, Hostile vs. Convulsive, Progressive, Constrictive, Self-deprecation. Max. 10 points
4 (a) 1 (b) 2 (c) 3 (d) 4 (e) 3 (f) 2 (g) 1 (h) 2 (i) 2 (j) 3 (k) 3. One point each. Max. 11 points
5 One point for flat occiput vs. normal occiput. Up to four additional points for other clearly discriminative differences.

Five points for quality—principally clarity Max. 10 points

6 Contact with reality
Extent of disorganization
Awareness of problem in self ("insight")
Interpersonal accessibility
Expression of unconscious wishes vs. disguise
Lack of true anxiety in psychotic
Max. 10 points

7 Memory gaps (4 pts.) filled by confabulation (3 pts.) with moral deterioration (2 pts.) and additional qualities (1 pt.) Max. 10 points

8 Nature and extent of disability, including IQ
Health of child
Household composition and age of parents
Training resources in home
Community resources
Effect of retention on others concerned
Attitudes of others concerned
Institutions available within family's reach
Max. 10 points

9 Fatigue or lassitude role-played (5 pts.)
Psychophysiologic nervous system reaction (5 pts.)
or anxiety (1 pt.)
or conversion (1 pt.)
Max. 10 points
Total 99 points

Psychology 862, Psychopathology
Final Examination
March 14, 1958

Do not write your name on this examination. Use the number assigned you.

1 Match the following categories with the symptoms which are most clearly associated with them. Indicate your answers by writing the appropriate letters in the blanks. You may use the same letter more than once. (14 pts.)

________1. Alzheimer's Disease
________2. Myxedema
________3. Pellagra
________4. Huntington's Chorea
________5. General Paresis
________6. Frigidity
________7. Cocaine Addiction
________8. Homosexuality
________9. Idiopathic Epilepsy
_______10. Catatonic Schizophrenia
_______11. Psychotic Depressive Reaction
_______12. Sociopathic Personality, Antisocial Type
_______13. Cyclothymic Personality
_______14. Hebephrenia

A. Chronic Lassitude
B. Flat Occiput
C. Difficulty in pronouncing "Medical Electricity"
D. Anamnesis
E. Peculiar Laughter
F. Free Floating Hostility
G. Chromatic Agnosia

H. Scanty Hair in Eyebrows
I. Constitutional Psychopathic State
J. Pseudologia Phantastic
K. La Belle Indifference
L. Waxy Flexibility
M. Paresthesia
N. Paralysis Agitans
O. Vaginismus
P. Transvestitism
Q. Larithmics
R. Cyanosis
S. Distorted Feelings of Guilt
T. Dancing Gait
U. Aura
V. Irregular Mood Swings
W. Premature Senility

2 Kraepelin is often accused of falling into the Aristotelian trap. But now that this has been pointed out, could you avoid such a trap yourself? (20 Pts.)
   a Demonstrate your skill by proposing a personality diagnosis of one of the authors whose book is on the reference list of this course. Temptation notwithstanding, please exclude from your consideration any authors whom you may know personally.
   b Explain how you believe you avoided the trap in your response to (a) above.
3 Suppose you were asked to summarize the last three class discussions in this course. (20 points)
   a Write what you think you might say if you were suffering from Korsakoff's Psychosis.
   b Write what you think you might say if you were suffering from hebephrenia.
   c Write what you think you might say if you were suffering from paranoid schizophrenia.
   d Write what you think you might say if you were hypomanic.
4 What is each of the following used to measure? (8 points)
   a Kent EGY
   b Serial Sevens
   c Vineland Scale
   d Sorting Test (any type)
   e Pellet Test
   f Writing Test
   g Rum Cay
   h Methodist Episcopal
5 Suppose you were given three minutes to inspect two ten-year old children and to determine which of them was a Mongoloid and which was a cretin. What criteria would you use to determine which diagnosis? (10 points)
6 How would you distinguish between the following? (10 points)
   a Between Sydenham's Chorea and Huntington's Chorea?
   b Between idiopathic epilepsy and Jacksonian Epilepsy?
   c Between locomotor ataxia and the Parkinsonian syndrome?
   d Between transorbital lobotomy and topectomy.
   e Between involutional melancholia and neurotic depression?

Psychology 862: Psychopathology
First Mid-Term Examination
January 26, 1959
Do not write your name on your paper. Use your identification number and place it on each page.

1 a. The appearance of such influences as the Nancy School, Freudianism, and others like them has posed certain practical epistemological problems which psychiatry had not squarely faced before, and which such recognized psychiatric authorities as Henderson, Gillespie, English, and Finch have not been able to resolve entirely. Other psychiatric writers, such as Tredgold, seem not even to have tried. What are these problems?
   b Rotter has proposed a way for the clinician to resolve such issues in his own thinking, and Kelly has offered a somewhat similar solution. What is the essential feature which their proposals have in common?

2 Consider, in turn, each of the following triads of terms. In each case, select two which, in some important respect, are similar and which stand in contrast to the third. Indicate (1) which two you see as similar, (2) how they are similar, and (3) how they contrast with the third.
  a Abreaction, Catharsis, Aggression
  b Empathy, Sympathy, Introjection
  c Transference, Projection, Identification
  d Guilt, Anxiety, Masochism
  e Reaction Formation, Displacement, Conversion
3 a. If you had a patient whom you suspected was aphasic, what two informal tests might you use to throw further light on the question?
  b —and what two if you suspected that he was disoriented?
  c —if you suspected he was distracted?
  d —if you suspected a recent cerebral accident or "stroke?"
  e —if you suspected general paresis?
4 In the measurement of intelligence is it possible to circumvent sensory deprivations, such as blindness and deafness?
5 What are the principal contrasts between Tredgold and Sarason in their approaches to the problem of feeblemindedness?

Psychology 862: Psychopathology
Second Mid-Term Examination
March 2, 1959

Do not write your name on this test.
Use the number assigned you.
Your number____________________

Find the term on the right that is the best possible associate for each term on the left., Copy its identifying letter in the blank provided. letters may be used more than once and some letters may be left over. (17 points)

________ (1) Concretism
________ (2) Clouding
________ (3) Confabulation
________ (4) Secondary gain
________ (5) Preoccupation
________ (6) Anxiety
________ (7) Depression
________ (8) Retardation
________ (9) Pane of glass
________ (10) Somatic compliance
________ (11) Reference
________ (12) Acting out
________ (13) Somatization
________ (14) Euphoria
________ (15) Stomach Ulcers
________ (16) Flattening
________ (17) Autistic Thinking

A. Symbolized conflict
B. Lack of ego strength
C. Quotidian procrastination
D. Failure to gain spontaneous interaction with the patient
E. Labored thinking
F. Amentia
G. Lump in the throat
H. A posture peculiar to conversion hysteria
I. Uniformity in emotional tone
J. Nocturnal enuresis
K. Depersonalization
L. A symptom value not related to basic anxiety
M. Necromancy
N. Consistently avoiding the immediate situation in order to pursue one's own themes
O. Inability to deal with personal problems abstractly
P. Choosing the most plausible symptom
R. Feeling that one is being directed or influenced
S. Awareness of confusion in one's self
T. Uncertainty about what is taking place
Z. Erecting an artificial story to hold together loosely perceived events

2 Psychotherapy with institutionalized mentally deficient persons is a highly controversial subject. What are the issues? (10 points)

3 According to the Diagnostic and Statistical Manual of the American Psychiatric Association the following disorders fall into three classes. Name the classes and indicate the one into which each disorder falls. (14 points)

a Phobic reaction
b Compulsive personality
c Antisocial reaction
d Conversion reaction
e Addiction
f Manic depressive reaction, depressed type
g Paranoid state
h Passive-aggressive personality
i Depressive reaction
j Schizophrenic reaction, schizo-affective type
k Schizoid personality

4 Suppose all the authors whose writings you have been asked to read for this course were to have mental break-down. Choose three from the following list whose psychiatric diagnoses you think you might be able to anticipate from having read their writings. In each case indicate what you think the precise psychiatric diagnosis might be and what your reasons are for thinking so. (15 points)

a Henderson or Gillespie
b Tredgold
c English or Finch
d Sarason
e Goldstein
f Gates
g Symonds
h Hunt
i Gesell
j Cattell

Make-Up Examination
Psychology 862
March 6, 1959

1 Following are five trios of terms. Look at the first trio and decide how two of the terms can be construed as being alike and yet different from the third. Indicate which two you construe as being alike. Make a statement justifying your division of the terms. Do the same for the next trio, etc. (10 pts.)

a Repression, inhibition, sublimation
b Introjection, identification, empathy
c Narcissism, masochism, regression
d Anxiety, fear, guilt
e Aggression, hostility, escape

2 What are the types of schizoid psychosis listed in the Handbook of the American Psychiatric Association? (10 pts.)

3 You are confronted with an extremely agitated patient in the admission ward of a mental hospital. You need to make an initial estimate of whether the patient is "neurotic" or "psychotic." List three questions you might ask, and for each question give two answers, one indicating that he is neurotic and the other indicating he is psychotic. The answers must be consistent with the fact that he is extremely agitated. (9 pts.)

4 Suppose each of the following authors of reference works assigned in this course were to be confronted with a college student who has come to the Dean's office because of bad marks in his course. What line of inquiry do you suppose each author would use and why? (15 pts.)

1 Henderson or Gillespie
2 Tredgold
3 Goldstein
4 English or Finch
5 Gates

Psychology 862: Psychopathology
Final Examination
March 16, 1959

Do not write your name on your paper. Use the number assigned you.

1 From the standpoint of current American psychiatric practice what are the differentiating symptoms of each of the following disorders?
  a "Korsakoff 's psychosis"
  b "Familial amaurosis"
  c "Involutional psychotic reaction"
  d "Mongolism"
  e "Psychotic depressive reaction"
  f "Manic depressive reaction, depressed type"
  g "Paranoid state"
  h "Schizophrenic reaction, paranoid type"
  i "Schizophrenic reaction, hebephrenic type"
  j "Neurodermatosis"
  k "Conversion reaction"
  l "Dissociative reaction"
  m "Cyclothymic personality"
  n "Jacksonian epilepsy"
  o "Parkinsonian syndrome"

2 What are the distinguishing features of the following clinical tests and what do the tests presume to measure?
  a Kent EGY
  b Serial Sevens
  c Sentence Building
  d Sway Test
  e Vygotsky Test
  f Picture Arrangement

3 You are asked to make a careful psychological examination of three babies, aged three months, six months, and nine months, respectively. List as many specific accomplishments and performances as you can which would normally distinguish between children of these ages. Indicate clearly what the standard would be for each age.

4 You are asked to go to the "back ward" of Chillicothe VA Hospital and select approximately twenty percent of the patients for transfer to a newly organized "intensive treatment" ward. How will you, as an enlightened psychologist who disparages "categorization" and all that sort of thing, select the patients? Describe the procedure well enough to enable another clinician, working with you, to make the same selections you would make. In other words, be explicit.

Psychology 862
First Mid-term Examination
January 25, 1960
(Topics 1–10)

Write your name on the card you have drawn, place it in the envelope, and return to proctor at beginning of the hour. Do not write your name on this test. Use only the number you have drawn.
Your number ____________________________

1 In a recent class session it was asked if Dr. Rotter had not actually succumbed to dualism in spite of himself when he referred to the interaction of the organism and its environment. Now, what about "constructive alternativism," my position? Is it not really dualistic—or worse, pluralistic? Defend your answer.

2 What informal tests can be used to detect various forms of aphasia?

3 What is the essential characteristic of each of the following?
  a deja vu
  b la belle indifference
  c folie a deux
  d pseudologia phantastica
  e nihilistic delusion

4 In what ways can you account for the common clinical observation that feelings of guilt and hostility are likely to be intermingled?
5 What are the clinical signs of malnutrition in a child'?

Psychology 862, Psychopathology
Second Mid-Term Examination
February 24, 1960

Do not write your name on your paper. Use the number you have drawn.
Number ____________________

1 Limiting yourself to the usual methodology of clinical psychology, what observations would you take as supporting a hypothesis of cerebral deficit and damage in a fifty-year old adult? (10 points)
2 Match diagnostic category with symptom by entering one appropriate letter in each blank. A letter may be used more than once. (15 points)

1. ________ Hydrocephaly
2. ________ Amaurotic Familial Idiocy
3. ________ Mongolism
4. ________ Latent Sexual Inversion
5. ________ Cocaine Addiction
6. ________ Conversion Hysteria
7. ________ Pellagra
8. ________ Cretinism
9. ________ Cerebral Palsy
10. ________ Hypochondriasis
11. ________ Alzheimer's Disease
12. ________ Huntington's Chorea
13. ________ Hebephrentia
14. ________ Involutional Melancholia
15. ________ Korsakow's Psychosis

A. Personality regression
B. Sensation of bright flashes of light
C. Continuous movements of the head, trunk, and limbs
D. Tactile hallucinations
E. Progressively increasing memory gaps
F. Rejection of society's mores
G. Dry skin
H. Generalized delusions of illness
I. Symbolic lump in the throat
J. Soft fingernails
K. Sense of having committed an unpardonable sin
L. Excessive sexual activity
M. Swelling at the fontanelle
N. Sore mouth
O. Progressive neural deterioration producing blindness and early death
P. Presbyopic literalis
Q. Failure to recognize words within sharply limited content areas
R. Rhythmic oscillation of the eyeballs
S. Chromatic agnosia
T. Faulty reciprocal inhibition of antagonistic muscles
U. High narrow palatal arch
V. Excessive fear of snakes
W. Nocturnal swelling of the ear lobes
X. Akoasm
Y. Tongue tremors
Z. Inability to concentrate while taking written examinations

3 Compare and contrast the following pairs of terms. (Two points each—one for a suitable comparison and one for a suitable contrast)
   a Somatization and somatic compliance
   b Phobic reaction and anxiety reaction
   c Reaction formation and rationalization
   d Regression and transference
   e Character defense and resistance
4 Suppose I were to tell you that you would have been able to do a better job on this test if you had not been so preoccupied with your own sexual impulses. Respond to this comment: (15 points)
   a —as you would if you were a typical female case of conversion hysteria.
   b —as you would if you were a typical male case of obsessive-compulsive.
   c —as you would if you were a typical middle-aged case of anxiety neurosis.

Psychology 862, Psychopathology
Final Examination
March 17, 1960

Do not write your name on your paper. Use the number you have drawn.
Number ____________________

1 In the current edition of the Diagnostic and Statistical Manual of the American Psychiatric Association there appears for the first time the term "reaction" in a number of the categorical titles. Why? (10 points)
2 Freudian descriptions of psychopathologies are often classified as "dynamic" in contrast with the Kraepelinian views which, by way of contrast, are often called "Aristotelian." But it can be argued that "dynamic" thinking, particularly the Freudian variety, is actually more primitive than Kraepelinian thinking. While you may not agree with this interpretation of "dynamic" thinking, can you, nevertheless, develop the argument in support of this view of its primitiveness? (10 points)
3 Suppose, whether you like the concept or not, you are required to work in an interdisciplinary mental hygiene team where you were expected to pin the "schizophrenic" label on a considerable proportion of your patients. Assuming that you conformed to this expectation, what diagnostic principles would you follow in determining whether or not a patient was "schizophrenic?" (10 points)
4 Under what conditions is it supposedly proper to use the diagnostic label, "sociopathic personality disturbance?" (5 points)
5 What two developmental hurdles is it most important that the cerebral palsied child overcome? (5 points)
6 Describe the sequence of symptoms in the classical grand mal episode. (10 points)
7 List eight anatomical characteristics of the mongoloid patient. (10 points)
8 Draw a picture of your own face as you think it might be seen by a homunculus who has been peering out from behind this sheet of paper while you have been taking this examination. Using the picture as your sole evidence, make the best analysis you can of the homunculus's personality. Specify the features of the picture which support your hypotheses. (10 points)

Testing and Field Trip Schedule for Laboratory Sections, Psychology 862

*Date**	*Institution*	*Tests*
1. Jan. 20–25	Juvenile Diagnostic Center 2280 W. Broad	1 WISC or Stanford Binet
2. Jan. 16	Juvenile Diagnostic Center	Field Trip
3. Jan. 23	Field Trip—School for Deaf	
4. Jan. 30	Field Trip—School for Blind	
5. Jan. 27-Feb. 4	School for the Deaf 500 Morse Road	2 Grace Arthurs
6. Feb. 3–7	School for the Blind 5220 North High Street	1 Hayes Binet
7. Feb. 6	Talk by Dr. Simmons of Columbus State School (410 Arps)	
8. Feb. 8	Field Trip to Columbus Cerebral Palsy Center - Treatment Center - 533 E. Towne	
9. Feb. 16–14	Columbus State School 1601 W. Broad Street	2 WISC or WAIS
10. Feb. 17–21	St. Ann's Hospital for Women 1555 Bryden Road	2 Psyche Cattels
11. Feb. 24-Mar. 7	Columbus State Hospital 1960 W. Broad	2 WAIS and one observation

* Exact dates for the Winter, '59 Quarter will be presented later.

Juvenile Diagnostic Center

LOCATION: 2280 W. Broad St. The Diagnostic Center is located at the west end of the Columbus State School grounds. Go to the building with the white pillars

GENERAL: This institution is concerned primarily with making diagnostic studies and referral recommendations of children referred to them by the courts. The usual stay at the Center is from 10 to 16 weeks with a few cases remaining as long as a year. Most of the children will be tested during this first week at the Center. This can be an especially difficult time for him and this should be kept in mind. One test will be required of each student and the WISC will be used. Two blanks and stop watches must be provided by the student. Two sets of WISC materials will be sent to the Center where they will remain during the period of testing. Two or three people may test each day, Monday through Friday. The hours of testing are 9:00 A.M. to 12 Noon and 1:15 to 3:1.5 P.M. Arrive *promptly*.

PROCEDURE:

1 Go to the receptionist just inside the entrance and identify yourself. Ask for Mrs. Harmon, who is Dr. Patterson's secretary (Chief Psychologist at the institution). She will tell you how to get to the room assigned to you for testing. The age range we shall see will be approximately years 12 to 14.
2 Tell the child you are testing him *for* his Center psychologist. Hold discussion to a minimum. *Do not probe*. Do *not* discuss the Center or the child's possible time of leaving. *Do not* ask the child why he is there. In establishing rapport you may ask how long they have been there, how they like it, etc. It is recognized that some children may want to talk about themselves but try to keep this to a minimum without being abrupt with the child. They will probably have been seen once by their psychologist prior to the testing.
3 You may get a very resistive child. If this is the case it is quite all right to go along with a child—none of these children *have* to be tested. If they are resistive do not force the issue at all. Report it to Dr. Patterson and he will make other arrangements.
4 When the testing is completed make a copy of the record blank and take the copy with you, leaving the original at the Center. If desired, you may request to see the child's clinical record—ask Mrs. Harmon.
5 Test write-ups *must* be turned in within one week of the administration. The reports should include the usual test results and analysis plus any observations and hypotheses which you may pick up in the test proper or in the general situation. It is often helpful if direct quotes can be given of the child's pertinent verbalizations. Administer the draw-a-person; if child cooperates.

Columbus State School for the Deaf

LOCATION: 500 East Morse Road (called Rathbone Road as it continues west from High Street). Take bus to Jeffrey Place. Walk east on Morse about ½ mile to school entrance. Keep bearing right. Mr. Nelson's office is in the intermediate building. His office will be the place to report for a subject.

GENERAL: Two tests will be required of each student, both Grace-Arthurs. Arthur kits will be left at the office but take your own blanks and stop watches. Two people may test during each morning and afternoon. *Report promptly* and be ready to test at precisely the following times:

9:00–10:15 A.M.,	12:45–2:30 P.M.
10:15–11:30 A.M.	2:15–4:00 P.M.

They would rather children were not interrupted during a period but you may run over into another period when testing if it is necessary. Should you be unable to complete both tests at one time, make another appointment with the principal's office according to your own time demands. Needless to say, such an arrangement should rarely happen, and indeed, it reflects badly on the Psychological Clinic.

REPORT: Too much dependence will not be placed on the report but don't go too far out on a limb regardless. Use pretty much the usual report but be sure what you say is communicable. Give some evaluation of level of functioning and state of conditions—if rapport was poor or if any portion of the test is invalid be sure to say so! Keep the write-up fairly brief and concise.

If you run into a difficult child do not push but report it to Mr. Nelson and he will make other arrangements. The children's folders are available to you if you wish to look them over.

We can expect subjects to be 9 years of age or older.

Ohio State School for the Blind

LOCATION: 5220 North High Street, just north of Jeffrey Place. There is a large sign on North High, marking the entrance to the school.

GENERAL: Each student will be required to give one Hayes-Binet test at this institution. Mrs. Alexander is the psychologist in charge of testing. However, all you need do is check with the receptionist (directly beyond the main entrance) and she will direct you to a room and child. We will be testing children 7 years of age or older, but only a few of high school age. Mrs. Alexander has requested a test protocol, in addition to a write-up. Consequently, each lab member will submit two copies of the test protocol with the final write-up.

TESTING HOURS: We have arranged for 3 testing periods. They must be met *on time* or a child will not be released from class. *Always arrive somewhat early*:

8:30–10:30 A.M.
10:30–12:00 Noon
1:00–2:30 P.M.

Materials for testing (manuals and blanks) will be at the school.

Columbus State School (Reception Center)

LOCATION: Go out Sullivant Ave. and enter the grounds from there. Keiser Hospital will be the first building you see on the right. Go to the entrance on the East and enter through the sun porch. Ask for Dr. Simmons.

GENERAL: This institution is the State School for the feebleminded child. The IQ's however run from 1 to the 90s. Most of the clinical types are represented in the population and if you express interest Dr. Simmons will be glad to explain the set-up and show you around. You may take your lunch and eat it there. Coffee, etc., is available in the canteen. Three people at one time can be accommodated. Hours are 9:00 to 11:00 and 12:30 to 4:30; *be prompt.* Two tests are required of each student and you may be asked to give a Binet, WISC, Arthur or Wechsler (you will have some idea beforehand). The test materials will be left there; you provide *blanks and stopwatches.*

PROCEDURE:

1 Report to the Psychology Office, where you will get the subject and be shown where to test. Introduce yourself to Dr. Simmons.
2 When testing is completed, notify the secretary in the office and she will call the unit. Wait with the child until someone comes for him.
3 No probing into the subject's problems—just accept what the child offers. If a child asks for anything, suggest he ask his attendant.
4 If you have an older subject and you wish to smoke it is only courteous to offer him a cigarette just as you would anywhere. You must furnish cigarettes, of course.
5 Reports: Must be turned in within *2 days* following the administration of the test. Prepare the usual test write-up with special attention to practical indications for placing the person. Comments on the subject's cooperativeness, your impressions and observations are highly desirable. Conversation which seems important or indicative should be quoted whenever possible. Suggestions of possible brain damage are also relevant but of course should be very guardedly made.
6 A report of your observations will also be required, typed on an informal (low-level) page to accompany the write-up.

St. Ann's Hospital for Women

LOCATION: 1555 Bryden Road (Note: Bryden Road is an extension of Towne going East)

GENERAL: This institution is supported by the Catholic Welfare Bureau and is intended to serve both wed and unwed mothers and their children. Most of the illegitimate children are eventually placed in adoptive or foster homes. The reports submitted may be used for adoption purposes, but they will not be the only test used. You will be asked to give two Cattell exams here and the children may be anywhere from three months to two years of age. Cattell kits will be available there so you will need to take only test blanks. Two people may test at a time. The testing schedule has been arranged so that the children will not be interrupted during rest periods. Testing periods: 9:30 - 11:00 A.M. and 1:15 - 3:00 P.M. Monday thru Saturday.

PROCEDURE: Simply identify yourself at the desk in the main lobby and ask for Sister Cecelia. You will be directed to her office and all of the arrangements for a room, gown, child, etc., will be made. Mrs. Osman, a Nursery Aide, may be of assistance to you in handling the child, etc. If you are at all uneasy about carrying the child please ask her to help.

Columbus State Hospital

LOCATION: 1960 West Broad Street

GENERAL: Each student will be required to do two full-scale WAIS's and at least one hour's observation which will be written up. Dr. Carter is in charge of the student testing and should be consulted on all problems. Dr. Carter is the Chief Psychologist. Two students can be accommodated each morning and two each afternoon. In order to test in the morning you must arrive no later than 9:00; in the afternoon, 1:00. Reports must be in no later *than four days* following the administration of the test. W-B materials will be left at the hospital but you must furnish your own test blanks and stopwatches.

PROCEDURE:

1 Go to the administration building and tell the girl at the information desk that you wish to see Dr. Carter. He will be expecting you and will give you the general orientation, telling you where to go from there. Passes to the wards will be provided by him.

2 Go to the ward office and identify yourself to either the nurse or the charge attendant, giving your name and the name of the patient you are to test. The nurse or attendant will get the patient for you. *Do not* go on the ward looking for the patient. Ask the attendant to show you the testing space allotted and tell the attendant or the nurse where you will be with the patient and for approximately how long.

3 Smoking is not permitted anywhere except in the offices or in the testing room. If it appears safe the patient may be allowed to smoke. Light his cigarette for him, but *under no circumstances* give him any matches for later. Cigarettes are provided for the patient and you are under no obligation to offer any: however, it is permissible and sometimes helpful in establishing initial rapport.

4 Do not probe—accept only what the patient offers beyond generalities. Case histories are available if you wish to look them over.

5 There is the possibility that a patient may become disturbed. If this occurs call the attendant immediately rather than trying to handle it yourself.

6 When you are through return the patient to the attendant.

7 Report:

   a Pretty much the usual type of write-up, beginning with general comments on behavior, etc.

   b Overall results: IQ, etc.

   c Breakdown of test, details, subtest picture, scatter, etc.

   d Content analysis, utilize content wherever possible. Report bizarre or unusual comments as well as anything else that appears relevant in quotes whenever possible.

   e Some estimate of deterioration with a rough estimate of possible pre-psychotic intelligence.

   f A diagnosis is not necessary. However if the student wishes to advance a tentative diagnosis based on his observations and test findings he may do so. Be *very* cautious however. Alternate diagnoses may be advanced if you desire.

   g The student should not try to elicit orientation information, or to establish the presence or absence of hallucinations or delusions.

   h Reports must be in within four days following testing.

68

Syllabus[1]: Psychology 865L: Psychotherapy Revised Version

Bibliography

Psychology 865L: Psychotherapy

Revised 1-1-59

1 Allen, F. H. *Psychotherapy with children.* New York: Norton, 1942.
2 American Psychological Association. *Ethical standards of psychologists.* Washington: American Psychological Association, 1954.
3 — *Psychology and its relations with other professions.* Washington: American Psychological Association, 1954.
4 Axline, Virginia M. *Play therapy.* Boston: Houghton Mifflin, 1947.
5 Daniel, R. S., & Louttit, C. M. *Professional problems in psychology.* New York: Prentice-Hall, 1953.
6 Deutsch, F. *Applied psychoanalysis.* New York: Grune & Stratton, 1949.
7 Dreikurs, R. *Fundamentals of Adlerian psychology.* New York: Greenberg, 1950.
8 Fenichel, O. *The psychoanalytic theory of the neuroses.* New York: Norton, 1945.
9 Fromm-Reichmann, Freida. *Principles of intensive psychotherapy.* Chicago: University of Chicago Press, 1950.
10 Gill, M., Newman, R., Redlich, F. C., & Sommers, Margaret. *The initial interview in psychiatric practice.* New York: International Universities Press, 1954.
11 Glover, E. *The technique of psychoanalysis.* New York: International Universities Press, 1955.
12 Harrower, Molly (Ed.). *Medical and psychological teamwork in the care of the chronically ill.* Springfield, Ill.: Charles C. Thomas, 1955.
13 Kelly, G. A. *The function of interpretation in psychotherapy.* Three unpublished mss., 1958.
14 — *The organization of an agency.* Unpublished ms., 1950.
15 — *Outline for case study.* Unpublished ms., 1938.
16 — *Personal construct theory and the psychotherapeutic interview.* Unpublished ms., 1958 (In forthcoming volume on the psychotherapeutic interview, J. Seeman, Ed.).
17 — *Practices in interdisciplinary collaboration.* Unpublished ms., 1948.
18 — *Interdisciplinary collaboration. Newsletter: Division of Consulting Psychology, American Psychological Association.* (Presidential Address, 1955) November, 1955.
19 — *The psychology of personal constructs.* 2 vols. New York: Norton, 1955.
20 — *Theory and therapy in suicide: The personal construct point of view.* Unpublished ms., 1958. (In forthcoming volume on theory and therapy in suicide, E. Schneidmann & N. Farberow, Eds.).
21 Lindzey, G. (Ed.). *Assessment of human motives.* New York: Rinehart, 1958.
22 Miner, R. (Ed.). *Annals of the New York Academy of Sciences*: Vol. 63. New York: New York Academy of Sciences, 1955.
23 Raimy, V. C. (Ed.). *Training in clinical psychology (Boulder Conference Report).* New York: Prentice-Hall, 1950.
24 Rogers, C. R. A process conception of psychotherapy. *American Psychologist*, 1958, *13*, 142–149.
25 — *Client-centered therapy.* Boston: Houghton Mifflin, 1951.
26 Rotter, J. B. *Social learning and clinical psychology.* New York: Prentice-Hall, 1954.
27 Rubenstein, E. A., & Lorr, M. *Survey of clinical practice in psychology.* New York: International Universities Press, 1954
28 Slavson, S. R. *An introduction to group therapy.* New York: International Universities Press, 1952.

[1] Unpublished MS, Ohio State University, revised 1.1.59. Published by permission of Jacqueline Aldridge.

Collected Papers of the Pioneer of Constructivist Psychology: George A. Kelly, First Edition. Edited by David A. Winter and Nick Reed.

29 Strother, C. R. (Ed.). *Psychology and mental health.* Washington: American Psychological Association, 1957.
30 Sullivan, H. S. *The psychiatric interview.* New York: Norton, 1954.
31 Watson, R. I. *Psychology as a profession.* Garden City, N.Y.: Doubleday, 1954.
32 Wolberg, L. R. *The technique of psychotherapy.* New York: Grune & Stratton, 1954.

Dates of course ____________________

Class Roster	*Examination Schedule*
1. ______________________________	first-quarter mid-term ____________
2. ______________________________	first-quarter final ______________
3. ______________________________	second-quarter mid-term __________
4. ______________________________	second-quarter final _____________
5. ______________________________	
6. ______________________________	
7. ______________________________	
8. ______________________________	Special Readings
9. ______________________________	
10. ______________________________	
11. ______________________________	
12. ______________________________	
13. ______________________________	
14. ______________________________	
15. ______________________________	
16. ______________________________	
17. ______________________________	
18. ______________________________	
19. ______________________________	
20. ______________________________	

Topic 1: Psychology as a Profession

Ref. 1 APA (2). Scan all. Read pp. 1–19 of Summary.
2 Daniel & Louttit (5). pp. 1–32.
3 Harrower (12). pp. 125–170.
4 Watson (31). pp. 1–65

A **Organization of American Psychological Association**
1 Legislative and administrative structure
2 Board of Directors
3 Policy and Planning Board
4 Board of Professional Affairs
5 Education and Training Board
6 Board of Scientific Affairs
7 American Board of Psychological Services
8 American Board of Examiners in Professional Psychology
9 Divisions
10 State Organizations
11 Regional Organizations

B **Combining science and profession**
1 Historical resistance to professionalization of psychology
2 Boulder Conference
3 Thayer Conference
4 Palo Alto Conference
5 Miami Conference

Topic 2: The Clinical Setting

Ref. 1 APA (3). All pp.
2 Harrower (12). pp. 65–91
3 Kelly (14). All pp.
4 Kelly (17). All pp.
5 Kelly (18). All pp.
6 Rubinstein & Lorr (27). Scan all. Read pp. 19–31, 46–56, 69–108.
7 Strother (29). pp. 4–40.

A **Legal status of psychologists in relation to therapy**
- 1 Privileged communication
- 2 Medical practice acts
- 3 Court rulings

B **Current policies of American Psychological Association**
- 1 Restriction of practice
- 2 Legal defense
- 3 Assistance to states

C **Legislative position of American psychology**
- 1 Certification and licensing
- 2 Model laws
- 3 Certification boards
- 4 Definition and restriction of practice
- 5 Exemptions
  - a Students
  - b Employee status
  - c Other professions
  - d Reciprocity
  - e Temporary resident
  - f National certification
- 6 Examinations
- 7 Grandfather clauses
- 8 Suspension and revocation
- 9 Penalties
- 10 Disclaimers
- 11 Codes of ethics

D **Interprofessional relations of national organizations**
- 1 Psychology and psychiatry
- 2 Psychology and medicine
- 3 Psychology and pediatrics
- 4 Psychology and sociology
- 5 Psychology and education
- 6 Psychology and social work

E **Psychologists in tables of organization**
- 1 Military organizations
- 2 Veterans Administration
- 3 State agencies
- 4 Hospitals
- 5 Schools
- 6 Small clinics

F **Recent trends and developments**

G **Considerations in judging agency quality**
- 1 Administrative structure
  - a Formation of a flexible and representative policy hoard
  - b Incorporation
  - c Separation of policy-making and executive functions
  - d Focalization of executive functions

2 Finance
 a Use of contingent funds
 b Financial resiliency
 c Fee structure
 d Financial participation
3 Professional structure
 a Formation of a professional advisory board
 b Use of the case conference in maintaining professional standing
 c The team approach
 d The departmental approach
4 Accreditation and recognition
 a Accreditation agencies (AMA, APA, State, City)
 b Licensing
 c Accreditation of staff
5 Staffing
 a Terms and contracts
 b Salaries
 c Evaluation of credentials
 d Recruitment
 e Verbal commitments to candidates
6 Scheduled activities
 a Types of case and staff conferences
 b Client appointments
 c Community non-professional contacts
 d Adjunctive assistance
 e Study activities
 f Inter-disciplinary vs. intra-disciplinary collaboration
 g Refresher training
7 Public relations
 a Representation of services in the press, etc.
 b Announcements of services
 c Reception
 d Telephone and letters

Topic 3: Referrals and Records

A **Types of referrals**
 1 Interagency referral
 2 Interprofessional referral
 3 Voluntary self-referral
 4 Intra-agency non-voluntary referral
B **Determination of validity of referrals**
 1 Proper relationship of referral agent to client
 2 Circumvention of parents or client
 3 Disguised referrals
 4 Right to return report
 5 Referral channels
 6 Unacceptability of referrals which by-pass psychological discretion, e.g., “for test results only.”
 7 Referrals and case conferences attempted without the client’s knowledge.
 8 Attorney’s referrals
 9 Administrative referrals
 10 Prejudiced referrals
 11 Validity of self-referral

C **Content of referrals**
  1 Full information referrals
  2 Limited information referrals
  3 Conferences with professional representatives of an agency
  4 Reporting of tentative opinion
  5 Written referral authorization
  6 Cross indexing of case files

D **Acceptance of self-referrals**
  1 The emergency case
  2 Judgment of suicidal and homicidal risks
  3 Judgment of medical emergency
  4 Use of the re-referral and protective follow-up
  5 Obligations attendant upon merely listening to a complaint
  6 Written referral
  7 Delay in services
  8 Pre-examination by other professional services
  9 Authorization for transmission of case information
  10 Implicit understandings regarding outcomes

E **Reports to referring agencies**
  1 Level of generalization and interpretation
  2 Illustrative techniques
  3 Language of report
  4 Use of evidence
  5 Predictive implications

F **Face sheets**
  1 Identifying information
  2 Authorization signature and identification
  3 Complaint
  4 Record of measures taken and present status of other professional services
  5 Log of all contacts
  6 Cognizant staff members

G **Content**
  1 Notes
  2 Tests
  3 Hypotheses
  4 Records of staff discussions
  5 Opinions
  6 Reports
  7 Correspondence and memos of telephone contacts

H **Files**
  1 Numbering
  2 Indexing
  3 Research files
  4 Cross indexing with other agencies
  5 Removal of files
  6 Protection of confidential information
  7 Copying and masking of identity

I **Statistical reports**
  1 Meaningful categories
  2 Implication of case load
  3 Cost accounting

J **General problems in communication**
  1 Psychiatric conceptual systems
  2 General medical conceptual systems
  3 The nurses' approach
  4 Teachers' ways of viewing problems

5 Parents' viewpoints
6 Social workers' viewpoints
7 Court and lawyers' vocabulary
8 Communication with clergy
9 The language of psychologists
10 Local terms and concepts

Topic 4: Basic Approaches to Therapy

Ref. 1 Kelly (19). Vol. I, Ch. 9 and 10; Vol. II, Ch. 11 and 12.

A **Acceptance**
- 1 Definition
- 2 Use
- 3 Credulous approach
- 4 The client's construction of therapy
- 5 The client's construction of the therapist

B **Dependency**
- 1 Relation to core constructs
- 2 Nourishment
- 3 Independence in a civilized culture
- 4 Allocation of dependency
- 5 Differentiation of sources of supply

C **Transference**
- 1 Psychoanalytic view is based on a conception of catharsis
  - a Psychoanalytic catharsis combines vestiges of exorcism, classical catharsis, physiological purgative and mental energy.
  - b Psychoanalytic catharsis as a way of relieving the unconscious of cathected ideas.
  - c A modern psychological view of catharsis might express it as a making of implicit constructs explicit.
- 2 Rankian views of transference
  - a Taft
  - b Allen
  - c Rogers
- 3 Negative transference
- 4 Counter transference
- 5 Transference neurosis
- 6 Primary and secondary transference
- 7 Transference as role construction

D **The concept of resistance**
- 1 Negative transference
- 2 Protection against counter-transference
- 3 Anxiety
- 4 Censorship
- 5 Super-ego control
- 6 Interdiction of pleasure principle
- 7 Deflection of attention
- 8 Constructs incompatible with one's role construct which nevertheless govern one's behavior at lower levels

E **The phenomena of transference**
- 1 Early clinical signs
- 2 Clinical signs of deep transference
- 3 Signs of primary transference
- 4 Resolving primary transference
- 5 Resolving secondary transference
- 6 Causes of negative transference
- 7 Control of guilt in negative transference
- 8 The transference cycle

9 Initiating a new type of cycle
10 Termination of psychotherapy
11 Handling counter-transference
  a Rogerian view
12 Use of the dependency construct system, e.g., in paranoid reactions

F **The phenomena of resistance**
1 Clinical signs
2 Protection and resistance
3 Structuring the interview series
4 Structuring the individual interview
5 Containing the role in the interview situation
6 Use of relaxation
7 Use of tension
8 Premature interpretation
9 Resistance as distraction
10 Resistance as an interference phenomenon
11 Role playing to handle resistance
12 Use of context to overcome resistance
13 Use of transference in handling resistance
14 Precursory signs of the dropping of resistance
15 Use of resistance to attain therapeutic goals

G **Reassurance as a reconstructive technique**
(Reassurance is a superordinate construction placed upon the clinical situation which is communicated to the patient so that his behavior and ideas temporarily appear to him to be consistent, acceptable, and organized.)
1 Therapist assumes initiative and superimposes a construction system under which the clients' personal constructs may remain intact and operative.
2 Reduction of anxiety by reassurance
3 Effect of reassurance when not substantiated by subsequent events
4 Reassurance as confirmation of symptom and maladjustive mechanisms
5 Reassurance and primary transference
6 Reassurance and secondary transference

H **Reassurance techniques**
1 Prediction of outcomes
2 Postdiction of outcomes
3 Establishment of a frame of anticipation surrounding all new clinical information. Acceptance of client's identity. Structuring the interview situation.
4 Posture, voice, and control of agitation in the therapist
5 Reassurance by value labels
6 Creation of resistance by reassurance
7 Reassurance by value labels
8 Temporary reinstatements of a symptom or defense
9 Minimum use of reassurance

I **Support** is a broad response pattern on the part of the therapist in relation to which the client successfully experiments with a variety of constructs and behaviors.
1 Therapist's acceptance of client's dependency role
2 Client's acceptance of his own dependency role
3 Support may lead to guilt feelings as the client initially construes his dependency role
4 Support requires an expanding repertory on the part of the therapist.

J **Support techniques**
1 Keeping appointments
2 Recalling clinical material at appropriate times
3 Construing material correctly within the client's construction system
4 Immediate adjustment to changes in the client's construction system without emphasizing the disparities involved
5 Minimum verbalization of new rationale or superordinate rationale
6 Pliancy
7 Services

K **Acceptable uses of reassurance and support**
1 Reassurance
a Only when willing to accept the slowing up of movement which goes with it. Use when therapeutic movement is too rapid and threatens to leave the patient without a basic structure upon which he can depend
b Use as a temporary preventive of fragmentation
c Use to encourage loosening conceptualization
d Controlling anxiety between sessions or during a period of suspended sessions
e Use as a very temporary expedient during the course of an interview to keep a chain of associations from being broken
f Use during temporary traumatic situations
2 Support
a Use in anxiety cases, particularly those with marked psychosomatic symptoms
b Use as a preliminary to helping a patient understand his dependency needs through having him play a dependent role
c Use to stabilize a situation such as in a home where the patient's frantic effort to solve his problems may precipitate new social difficulties which he cannot handle
d Use as a preliminary basis for helping patient revise his role construct repertory
e Use should be limited to cases or to phases of treatment where the client cannot handle all modes of reality or, more specifically, cannot take unexpected events in his stride. For such a client support minimizes the negative results growing out of his experimentation.

Topic 5: Diagnosis in a Clinical Setting

Ref. 1 Gill et al. (10). pp. 1–109
2 Kelly (19). Vol. I, Ch. 4; Vol. II, Ch. 15.
A **Diagnosis as a planning procedure**
B **Clinical issues**
1 The analysis of deviant behavior
a Psychological description of the manifest deviant behavior patterns (symptoms)
b Psychological evaluation of the gains and losses accruing to the patient through his symptoms
2 Analysis of subjective factors, particularly as they relate to the "depth" of the therapy to be undertaken
a The patient's conceptualization of his life-role and its problematic aspects
b The patient's accessibility and level of communication
c The patient's areas of integrity and disorganization
d The patient's areas and levels of mobility and rigidity
3 Analysis of psychodynamic structure which may be considered basic and within which reorientation is to be sought
a The patient's methodological approach to problems
b The expectancy system within which the patient must make his life-role function
4 Development of basic content to support the reintegrative process
a Assessment of the socio-economic potentialities in the case
b Preparation of the contextual background for establishing and maintaining therapeutic relationships
5 Determinants of immediate procedural steps
a Consideration of the organic implications of the psychological data
b Evaluation of the urgency of the case
6 Planning management and treatment
a Selection of the central therapeutic approach
b Designation of the principally responsible clinician
c Selection of adjunctive resources to be utilized
d Designation of the responsible clinician's advisory staff
e Determination of the *ad interim* status of the patient
f Setting of dates or conditions under which progress reports will be reviewed by the advisory staff
C **The six issues can be stated colloquially as six questions:**
1 In what ways does this patient act peculiarly and where does it get him?
2 How do things stack up in the patient's mind and what are the chances of getting to him with new concepts and making them stick?
3 What is there about this patient's world that you are just going to have to accept?
4 What is there in the whole case that can be put to good use?

5 Where does he go next?
6 How is he going to get well?

D **Reporting in an interdisciplinary setting**
1 The role of each discipline
a Social work—relation to individual history and society
b Teaching—relation to learning and child society
c Pediatrics—relation to development and health
d Psychiatry—clinical inferences
e Psychology—scientific inferences
2 Psychiatric issues
a Nosological diagnosis
1 Organic involvement
b Treatment of choice
1 Shock
2 Lobotomy
3 Institutional control
4 Psychotherapy
a Inpatient or outpatient
b Type and duration
c The economics of psychiatry
3 The interdisciplinary psychological report
a Diagnostic impression
b Order of abstraction of data reported
c Use of a common conceptual system
d Conceptual integrity and rigidity
e Control and decompensation
f Figures
g Nature of social relationships
h "Psychodynamics"
i Ego strength and accessibility
j Exemplification

E **Reporting in an intradisciplinary setting**
1 Observations and test data
2 Normative evaluations
3 Use of psychological theory
4 Clinical hypotheses and documentation
5 Systematic testing of hypotheses
6 Free formulation of hypotheses in first approximation of findings
7 Intra-mural records
8 Detailed report
9 Interdisciplinary report
10 Client's report

Topic 6: Use of Historical and Behavioral Information

Ref. 1 Kelly (15). Read all.
2 Kelly (19). Vol. II, Ch. 13 and 14.
3 Lindzey (21). pp. 33–64.
4 Sullivan (30). pp. 138–182.

A **Admission of case**
1 General background information
2 Other resources to be utilized or to be taken into account

B **Educational background**
1 School
2 Community
3 Family

C **Social background**
  1 Household
  2 Companions
  3 Work setting
  4 Travel
  5 Economic resources
  6 Activity interests and skills

D **Developmental history**
  1 Illness and injury
  2 Social and psychological settings
  3 Sequence of social roles
  4 Behavior problems by stages
  5 Nutrition and rest

E **Family**
  1 Direct line
  2 Collateral line
  3 Expectations
  4 History of structure
  5 Cultural identifications

F **Physiology**
  1 Observations
  2 Medical examination
  3 Medical measures
  4 Psychological appraisal of physiological and anatomical features

G **Employment record**
  1 Job shifts
  2 Shifts in academic interests

H **The client's construction of his background**
  1 Values
  2 Cultural contrasts as seen by client
  3 Descriptions offered by client

I **Observation of behavior**
  1 Behavior in groups
  2 Free behavior
  3 Mannerisms

Topic 7: The Psychotherapeutic Process

Ref. 1 Kelly (19). Vol. II, ch. 16 and 17.
  2 Rogers (24). Read all.
  3 Slavson (28). pp. 1–236.
  4 Sullivan (30). pp. 113–137.

A **Learning concepts**
  1 S-R approach
  2 Practice
  3 Closure
  4 Reflection of culture
  5 Anticipation and validation

B **The therapeutic experience**
  1 Intellectualization
  2 Acting out
  3 Loosening and tightening
  4 Creativity cycle
  5 Decision-making cycle

C **Threat**
1 Concept
2 Relation to fear
3 Areas of threat
4 Control
5 Superordinate constructs

D **Aggression in therapy**
1 Hypothesis formulation
2 Testing
3 Response to invalidating evidence
4 Segmental aggression

E **Hostility in therapy**
1 Relation to invalidation
2 Resolving by initiative

F **Role and guilt**
1 Adaptation of role
2 Protection of role relationships
3 Control of guilt feelings

G **Anxiety**
1 Signs
2 Segments
3 Control
4 Nature of confidence

H **Stages in therapy**
1 Symptom display
2 Seeking of causation
3 Dilation of issues
4 Dependency
5 Transference cycles
6 Experimentation
7 Resolving of transference

I **Group psychotherapy stages**
1 Building of support
2 Construction of primary role relationships
3 Mutual enterprises
4 Exploration of personal problems
5 Development of secondary role relationships
6 Secondary enterprises

Topic 8: Client-Therapist Relationships

Ref. 1 Kelly (16). Read all.
2 Rogers (25). pp. 197–231.
3 Rotter (26). pp. 335–398.
4 Wolberg (32). pp. 488–493.

A **The therapist as a colleague**
1 Communication levels
2 Formulation of hypotheses
3 Use of propositional constructs
4 Joint anticipations
5 The therapist as an *ad interim* validator

B **The therapy room as a laboratory**
1 Planning experiments
2 Controlling unexpected outcomes
3 Making inferences from outcomes

C **Planning field tests**
1 Abortive efforts
2 Undoing
3 Timing of trials
4 Reformulation at later stages of therapy

D **Transference**
1 Interpretation
2 Hostility
3 Danger of overgeneralized interpretations

E **Dependency in therapy**
1 Signs
2 Resolution

Topic 9: Exploratory Procedures

1 Glover (11). pp. 3–137.
2 Kelly (17). Vol. II, ch. 18 and 19.

A **What constitutes deviant behavior**
1 Deviation from norms implicit in the clinician's own experience
2 Incompatibility with the ways of the patient's accepted primary group
3 Incompatibility of the patient's behavior with his own norms
4 Inconsistency or unpredictability under commonly recognized systems of interpretation
5 Frequent abandonment of attempted adjustment patterns
6 Deviation versus transparency
7 The complaint itself as deviant behavior

B **Sources of information**
1 The nominal complaint
2 The patient's description of his own behavior
3 Initial status examination
4 Personnel records
5 Ward and reception behavior
6 The patient's family
7 Other associates

C **What constitutes manifest behavior**
1 Levels of interpretation

D **Elicitation and description of the complaint**
1 Complaint as the layman's formulation of the psychological problem
2 Subjective meanings in the language of complaint
3 Social patterns in complaints

E **Temporal patterns in the deviant behavior**
1 Cues to a history of emotional crises
2 Periodicity
3 Life-line plotting
4 Diurnal cycles
5 Phase descriptions
6 Prognosis

F **Situational concomitants**
1 Cultural context
2 Personal-social context
3 Stress concomitants

G **The occupational pattern**
1 Occupational history
2 History of occupational aims
3 Occupational adjustments and failures
4 Subjective values attached to the occupational record by the patient

H **The domestic pattern**
  1 Domestic and personal attachment history
  2 History of domestic and personal-affective aims
  3 Adjustments and failures
  4 Values attached to the record by the patient
I **Non-deviant collateral patterns**
  1 Relation to the deviant patterns
J **Analysis of losses and gains accruing to the patient through his symptoms**
  1 Compensation demands and formal disability claims
  2 Emotional equivalencies (cathexes)
  3 Control of associates and family (aggressions)
  4 Postponements and escapes from issues
  5 Attention, affection, and sympathy
  6 Incorporation of analysis with interviews
  7 Caution against hedonistic interpretations
K **Historical signs indicating need for specialized collaboration of other disciplines**
  1 Physiological complaints—temporal pattern, pathological inferences
  2 Psychological complaints not consistent with social history
  3 "Protective" habits in occupational and recreational history
  4 Familial disorders
  5 Medical contacts and vocabulary
  6 Diurnal patterns
  7 Special retardations or ineptitudes in school subjects
L **Clinical observations not requiring obvious examination**
  1 Reactive signs
    a Oral gestures, massage, posture during interview, etc.
    b Smoking pattern, reposturization, grimacing, hand sweating, vaso-motor changes
    c Speech—pitch, rhythm, intensity, modulation, deference querulousness, cluttering
    d Tremors, loss of emotional adequacy, explosiveness, eye movement patterns, breathing patterns, functional asymmetry
    e Audition
    f Vision—glasses
    g Writing
    h Handedness
    i Odors
  2 Structural signs
    a Structural asymmetry
    b Stigmata
    c Distribution of fat and hair
    d Eyes
    e Head
    f Nails and hands
    g Feet
M **The impersonal clinical examination**
  1 Physical signs
    a Head
    b Eyes
    c Mouth, shape, tongue, teeth, gums, throat
    d Motor
    e Sensory acuity
    f Reflexes
    g Glands
  2 Social signs
    a Occupational status and irregularity
    b Community and socio-economic district
    c Migration and community identification
    d Nearness of relatives and their problems

- e Size of family and ratio of wage earners to size of household
- f Dress
- g Luxury-necessity patterns
- h Vocabulary level in relation to occupation and community as a measure of social striving
- i Companionships and socio-economic frame of reference
- j Recreational pattern
- k Language as a key to cultural identification and stress
- l Catastrophic indicators
- m Breaks in household continuity
- n Trips and horizons
- o Shared space and belongings
- p Nature of organizational control under which a person carries out his vocation
- q Projected ambitions
- r Occupational skills, interests, and orientations

N **Fixed interview techniques**

- 1 Confrontation
  - a Complaint
  - b Life-role structure
  - c Willingness to accept therapy
  - d Interpretation client expects to give data
- 2 Control of anxiety
  - a Use of an outline
  - b Note taking
  - c Movement in interview
  - d Speed and shift
  - e Implications of reassurance
  - f Impersonal approaches
  - g Concretism and hypostasis
  - h Control by structuration
- 3 Implications for effective treatment
  - a Plan of action
  - b Routine
  - c A type of "active" therapy
  - d Participation
  - e Dilating and controlling the perceptual field

O **Free interview techniques**

- 1 Associative anamnesis
- 2 Self-description
  - a Spontaneous self-description
  - b Structured self-description
  - c Dis-identified self-description (role-protection)
  - d Way technique
- 3 Non-directive development of material
  - a Reflection
  - b Acceptance
- 4 Control of interviewer's participation
  - a Language of acceptance
  - b Measured reassurance
  - c Posture, gesture and facial expression
  - d Speed of reaction
- 5 Control of patient's participation
  - a Control of "loaded" material
  - b Probing

1 Immediate
2 Circular or delayed
c Relaxation
d Teaching therapeutic behavior
e Catharsis and abreaction and their implications for further therapy
f Length of interview
6 Types of anxiety which are superficially observable
a Pure anxiety—decompensation
b Neurasthenic anxiety
c Anxiety-hysteria
d Conversion anxiety
e Depressive anxiety
f Hypochondriacal anxiety
g Schizoid anxiety
h Agitation

P **On-the-spot analysis of psychological status**
1 The mental status examination
a Psychiatric use
1 Immediate decisions regarding patient management
2 Gross indication of progress
3 Check on over-treatment
b Outline
1 Complaint
2 Contact
3 Orientation
4 Memory
5 Affect
6 Activity
7 Intellect
2 The home visit
a An alternative to the clinic examination situation. Infant testing in the home.
b The setting of the patient's problem
1 The social structure in which the problem appears
2 The expectancies of the patient
3 The situation to which adjustment is to be made
4 The therapeutic goals
c An interview springboard
d The 5 p.m. to 10 p.m. time sample
3 The ward round
a As a setting for consultation
b As a training measure
c As a measure for facilitating interdisciplinary collaboration
d As a measure to facilitate emergency or "on call" treatment

Q **The Winter V. A. Hospital Schematic Outline for Psychological Examination** (By Helen Sargent, Martin Mayman and Karl Menninger)
1 General observations
a Circumstances
b Visualization
c Quotation
2 Perception (reality contact)
a Normal features: alertness, accuracy
b Deficiencies: sensory, attention, loss of contact, disorientation
c Excess and inappropriateness: sensory, attention false perceptions
3 Intellection (cognitive functions)
a Level and range

1 Normal features: intelligence, memory, abstraction, knowledge
2 Deficiencies: stupidity, hypomnesia, concretism
3 Excesses: hyper-intelligence, hypermnesia, syncrotism
4 Inappropriateness: disorders of judgment
b Thought processes
1 Normal features: tempo, rhythm, organization
2 Deficiencies: retardation, blocking, incoherence, irrelevance
3 Excesses and inappropriateness: obsessions, fixed ideas, delusions
4 Emotion (affective processes)
a Level and range
1 Normal features: intensity, modulation, mood quality
2 Excesses: elation, rage, depression, fear, guilt feelings
3 Deficiencies: blandness, apathy
4 Inappropriateness: disharmony, incongruity
b Physiological concomitants: autonomic, neuromuscular manifestations
5 Action (expressive behavior)
a Level and range
1 Normal features: vigor, persistence, constructiveness, etc.
2 Excesses: hyperkinesis, impulsiveness, destructiveness, assaultiveness
3 Deficiencies: inertia, stupor, paralysis, inhibition, rigidity
4 Inappropriateness: compulsions, tics, rituals, mannerisms, peculiar habits, stereotype, catalepsy, posturing
b Behavior traits: ambitious, honest, generous, etc.
6 Integrative and adjustive processes (personality)
a Interpersonal relationships
1 Normal features: selectivity, intensity, constancy, flexibility, modality
2 Excesses: diversity, superficiality, over-intensity
3 Deficiencies: sparsity, lack of depth
4 Inappropriateness: peculiar object choices and modalities, sexual perversion, etc.
b Self-concept
1 Normal variations: ego-identity, role playing, level of aspiration, ego ideals, goals
2 Excesses: grandiosity, arrogance, etc.
3 Deficiencies: feelings of inadequacy, nihilism
4 Inappropriateness: detachment, estrangement, depersonalization
c Sublimations
1 Normal variations: work and play interests, activities, satisfactions
2 Excesses and inappropriateness: peculiar substitute gratifications
3 Deficiencies: absence of sublimation, uncontrolled direct gratification
d Tension relieving devices
1 Normal tension relieving devices: humor, tears, phantasy, activity, etc.
2 Consciousness of ego tension (anxiety feeling): frequency, intensity, persistency, special provocation
3 Pathological tension relieving devices
a First order (emergency or alarm reaction): exaggeration of normal defenses
b Second order (partial withdrawal and attempted compensation): dissociation, displacement, sacrifice perversion
c Third order (ego rupture or exhaustive stage): discontinuous, continuous
d Fourth order (complete failure of ego control): suicidal attempts
7 Summary
a Assets: level of sublimation, normal ego functions, adequacy of tension relief
b Liabilities: extent of secondary tension relieving devices, ego disorganization
c Tentative differential impression of psychological status
d Prognostic impression

Topic 10: Client Control

Ref. 1 Kelly (20). Read all
2 Wolberg (32). pp. 340–358, 583–640

A **Structuring psychotherapy**
1 Defining limits
2 Defining relation to therapist
3 Breaking off uncontrollable relationships
4 Defining limits of other professional services

B **Hospitalization**
1 Involuntary commitment
2 Voluntary commitment

C **Protected environment**
1 Half-way house
2 Sheltered workshop
3 Hostelry
4 In-and-out program
5 Jail
6 Isolation
7 Orphanage
8 Retreat

D **Social controls**
1 Family
2 Neighborhood
3 Religious
4 Military
5 Alcoholics anonymous
6 Occupational

Topic 11: Psychotherapeutic Interpretation

Ref. 1 Fenichel (8). pp. 547–589
2 Fromm-Reichmann (9) pp. 69–194
3 Kelly (13). Read all.
4 Wolberg (32). pp. 411–487

A **The nature of personal construction**
1 Dimensions as well as values
2 Verbal misperceptions
3 Pre-verbal constructions

B **Interpretation and movement**
1 Slot movement
2 Impulsivity
3 The decision cycle (C-P-C)
4 Preemptive thinking

C **Interpretation at core levels**
1 "Emotional insight"
2 Experience as interpretation
3 Enactment as interpretation

D **Choosing other available axes of reference**
1 The role construct repertory
2 Closing out constructions

E **Reconstruing axes of reference**
  1 New axes
  2 Exploration at relatively unstructured levels
  3 Anxiety and interpretation
F **Overgeneralization in interpretation**
  1 Hostility
  2 Depression
  3 Loosening
  4 Paranoid reactions

Topic 12: Use of Autistic Material

Ref. 1 Kelly (19). Vol. II, ch. 19

A In therapy, in contrast with other forms of teaching, one deals with vague concepts and implicit communications. The material is frequently autistic and one has difficulty finding neat precise ideas which can be accepted objectively.
  1 The therapist has to teach the patient how to express less explicit ideas. He may teach the patient to loosen his conceptualization.
    a Free association
    b Slow tempo of conference
    c Use of physical relaxation
    d Encourage fragmentation, or even demonstrate it
      1 Break up discourses
      2 Ask for "tag ends" of ideas
      3 Avoid the "important"
      4 Develop a "wig-wag" system
    e Use of dreams
      1 Suggestion of dreams
      2 Principal actor
      3 Mood
      4 Break points
      5 Association "away from"
      6 Circular approaches
      7 Blocks in reporting
      8 Retelling
      9 Recall of associated dreams
      10 Experience qualities
      11 Use one's knowledge of common anxieties
      12 Delay use of symbolism. Get associations first.
      13 The "something-like" technique
      14 The plot is not likely to be a tight expression of the conceptual frame but is more likely to give the moods or affective settings of antecedents and consequents that the patient's conceptual frame generates.
    f Various other manifestations of implicit thinking may be employed as a basis of eliciting autistic material of interpretation.
  2 In contrast to teaching the patient how to express less explicit ideas and concepts, the therapist has also to teach the patient how to formulate and use more explicit ideas and concepts.
    a Talking vs. acting-out
    b Explaining feelings to therapist
    c Instructing therapist in role playing and reversed role playing
    d Analysis of historical basis
    e Use of the basic concept formation formula, "how are two of these alike yet different from the third?"
    f The "how do you know that" technique
    g The "who are you (WAY)" technique
  3 Alternation between levels of thinking is the basic feature of all interpretation.
    a Fenichel's Scylla and Charybdis

1 Too much intellectualizing
2 Too much eagerness in interpretation
3 Too much floating in the patient's unconscious, "learning his language," etc.
b Closing up before a break in series of sessions and opening up after the break
c The psychoanalytic technique of isolating first and then interpreting
d Dividing the person's psychological processes into judging and experiencing sectors. In other words, all interpretation involves not only the formulation and extended documentation of new concepts but also the ranking of concepts and conceptualization processes into subordinate and superordinate levels. This must start with the first interpretive session.
e Too rapid alternation of levels of judging and experiencing tends to destroy the patient's ability to do both, although as therapy progresses he is likely to be able to alternate more rapidly.
1 Usually the judging or higher level stages of the interview are at the end, though sometimes at the very beginning.
2 In early stages of therapy there may be a considerable succession of interviews at the experience level.
4 Forms of interpretation
a Is this like "a." How is this like "a.?"
b Placing two ideas in a contiguous relationship.
c "Is this what you meant by . . . ?"
d "Let's see if we can state the general formula."
e "Try this on for size."
f "If you had wanted_______, then it would have meant that you would _____, and _____ and _____."
5 Fixing or extending interpretations
a Documentation or "working through"
b Weaving
c Isolating
d Modifying concepts reached at an earlier level of therapy
e Deterioration and substituting concepts
f The tendency of a too rigid interpretation to break the transference cycle prematurely
6 Signs of adequate conceptualization
a Surprise or "Ah Ha"
b Spontaneous documentation
c Range of generalization
d Open-endedness
e Change in mood without too marked a change in daily behavior
f Use of patient summaries either written or oral
g Change in autistic material
7 Signs of inadequate new conceptualization
a Inadequate verbalization
b Bizarre documentation
c Over-simplification
d Sharp behavior changes and "flight into health"
e Literalistic and rigid applications
f Check anxiety behavior in therapist as a possible cause of superficial insights in patient.
g Check excessive anxiety in patient in sessions preceding the interpretive sessions.
h Check over-eager acceptances of patient's formulations.

Topic 13: Concept Formation in Psychotherapy

Ref. 1 Kelly (19). Vol. II, ch. 20

A **All psychotherapy may be construed as accelerated concept formation.**
1 As such, psychotherapy may be construed as being directed primarily against conceptual rigidity (antistasis).
2 The patient may be asked to re-sort his friends, his responsibilities or his past experiences in order to arrange them under new conceptual headings.
3 Some methods of psychotherapy, e.g., psychoanalysis, seek a widespread loosening of the patient's concepts as a preliminary to conceptual re-organization.
a Use of dream material to tap potentialities of new conceptual relationships.
b Danger of too much loosening
c Use of transference and dependency to keep patient stable while his concepts are in a precariously loosened state

4 Some methods of psychotherapy are based on a direct attempt to substitute new concepts for old on a one-to-one replacement basis.
   a "Directive" methods of certain types
   b Fixed role methods
5 Some methods of psychotherapy attempt reconceptualization by bringing into clear focus the inadequacies of the patient's current system.
   a Non-directive methods
   b "Diagnostic" methods (Morton's TAT)
6 Some methods attempt reconceptualization by extricating the patient from a system of social control in which his behavior is manifestly expected to conform to a pre-determined set of expectancies.
   a Change of situation
   b Leaving home
   c The psychotherapy interview situation
   d Free role playing
   e By this approach it is hoped that the patients' natural growth process of tendency to form new concepts in the face of unfolding events will provide enough new conceptualization to achieve therapeutic results.
7 Most actual methods of psychotherapy combine two or more of the above reconceptualization approaches.

B **It should be recognized that the prime factor in the reconstruction of experience is new experience.**
1 Therapy is *new* experience even though it may re-hash old experience.
2 First of all, therefore, therapy must be built around the selection of novel experience which challenges the patient's conceptual system but does not threaten its core structure.
   a To maximize reconceptualization, the therapist should place some emphasis upon the novelty of the therapeutic situation.
   b The patient may refuse to accept therapy as a new experience and rigidly insist upon construing the therapy as a social situation to be governed by the same ground rules as other social situations with which he is familiar.
3 Therapy must inevitably lead to exploratory behavior.
   a There is a tendency of people to seek verification of their construction systems in new experience. This tends to make one's concepts self-perpetuating to the extent that they predetermine the kind of experience one has.
   b As therapy progresses the patient needs to seek new experience for two reasons.
      1 To challenge his old concepts
      2 To verify his new concepts
   c In free or incidental role playing, for example, new social experiences are explored in test-tube quantities.
   d This amounts to a partial refusal to experience new events as being new.
   e In extreme withdrawal cases it may amount to a partial refusal to have experience, per se.

C **The clinician must learn how to use the patient's concept system to some degree.**
1 This is necessary in order both to establish communication and to set the stage for reconstructing the system.
2 When the clinician appears to be able to use the system the patient feels less threatened by the incompatibilities that the clinician seems able to bridge.

D **Reconceptualization of experience**
1 The patient may be asked to recall early childhood experiences and by putting them together in an adult frame of reference may be able to reconstrue them.
2 The effect of this reconstruction is actually to alter the memory content. As the reconstruction takes place the clinician finds the patient remembering different kinds of experience.
3 Viewed in this way it seems not so important to find out what happened to a person but rather to find out the system which governs his selection of things to recall.
   a Every therapist is likely to be impressed by the tendency of the patient to paint a much different picture of his childhood after successful therapy. The naive therapist is likely to be "taken in" by the black picture (sometimes white picture) that the patient paints of his past in the early stages of therapy.
4 Viewed in this way also dream material becomes significant, not so much as the disguised murmurings of unconscious forces, but as ideation selected in the light of the patient's current construction system.
5 Once the patient starts tentatively to develop a new system, the therapist may, if he chooses to use a somewhat directive rational approach, help the patient to expand the system by reconstruing more and more of the patient's experience in terms of the new system.
6 The therapist may, in some cases, successfully impose a wholly new system upon the patient and teach the patient how to use it. Some analysts do this.
7 The system imposed upon the patient need not be scientific nor even "believed" by the therapist. There is, of course, danger that the therapist may not be able to keep such a system sufficiently intact for the patient to develop an effective use for it.

8 A new system may be presented in story form.
 a Biography may help a person place a new construction upon one's life-role.
 b Folk-lore may be understood as the cultural imposition of a society's construct system upon its members.
 c Tailor-made stories may be used with great effectiveness upon the concept system of a child.
 d The Thematic Apperception Test is an attempt to understand the patient's construction of experience in the time dimension.

E **Reconstruction of persons**
1 Not only events, but people, are reconstrued as the result of therapy.
2 Interpretive therapy is primarily directed at this type of reconstruction.
3 Role playing, particularly as the patient plays the role of another real person, helps the patient reconstrue the figure played.
4 In role playing the patient has his conceptualization of the figure challenged and he finds it necessary to add facets to the character he plays.
5 The therapist may add facets to the character of some real person as he plays it out.
6 Again exploratory behavior must grow out of the therapeutic experience both to challenge the patient's old role construct repertory and to validate new characters and figures that come to inhabit his social world.
7 The reconstruction of other persons may actually be built into fixed role procedures although primarily these procedures are directed toward reconceptualization of the patient's self.
8 As the patient attempts to rationalize other persons, merely through description and illustration, he begins to reconceptualize them.
 a The training of a clinical psychologist has its psychotherapeutic implications for the student himself.
9 The test of a patient's role concept repertory may indicate the points at which reconceptualization of persons may be undertaken.

F **Reconceptualization of self**
1 The conceptual frame in which the self is viewed is essentially the same as that in which other people are viewed.
 a The values assigned to one's self on the dimensions may be markedly different from those assigned to others but the dimensions themselves which one strikes through the interpersonal field are the same.
2 Self description may be an important diagnostic procedure.
 a Clinicians have trouble keeping in mind the way in which self descriptions can most profitably be analyzed.
  1 They tend to look for the person's placement of himself on the dimensions of description rather than to look at the patient's choice of dimensions.
  2 It is the patient's choice of dimensions that reveals the basic system in which he deals.
  3 It is the dimensions of description rather than one's self-identified position on these dimensions that therapy must deal with.
  4 When the clinician requires the patient to use an outline in writing his self description he is imposing his own dimensional or conceptual system upon the patient.
3 Fixed role procedure is a new concept of the patient's own role, tentatively imposed upon him and providing a new set of expectancies regarding his own behavior and secondarily eliciting new behaviors on the part of others which then become anticipatable in terms of the new conceptual frame.
4 It is possible, in certain relatively superficial therapies, to help the patient to reidentify himself in terms of his own system.
 a This may take the form of reassurance.
 b It may take the form of reporting test results to him, etc.
 c Social roles, e.g., uniforms, office, new names, new appearances, may provide this form of reconceptualization.
5 The method of new identification is a classical procedure for reorganizing one's conceptual system.
 a e.g., the classical theme of the king who is temporarily misidentified as a jester.
6 The therapist may use semantic methods of re-identifying the patient, using newly defined words, etc.
 a Fractionation of concepts, e.g., the time and place subscripts of the general semanticists, may block the over-generalization of concepts or word-bound concepts.
 b The therapist may use semantic devices which help the patient to disidentify himself with his past role as he construes it.
  1 The past tense as an indicator of therapeutic movement and the "time binding".
  2 Emphasis of time and space distance to extricate the patient from rigid constructions of his role.
  3 Fractionation of concepts may be used to bring them under control.
7 Use of concept deterioration
 a Repetition appears to make concepts deteriorate and become more concrete and stereotyped.
  1 This principle may be used if the therapist wishes to reduce a troublesome concept to finite proportions and restrict its generalizing control over the patient's behavior.

Topic 14: The Use of Free Protocol

Ref. 1 Deutsch (6). pp. 1–167
2 Kelly (19). Vol. I, ch. 7

A **Analysis of self-characterization**
1 Topic sentences
2 Topic paragraphs
3 Sequence and transition
4 Organization
5 Reflection against context
6 Collation of terms
7 Restatements
8 Contextual areas
9 Thematic analysis
10 Dimensional analysis

B **Biography**
1 Symbolic formulations
2 Movement and theme
3 Related events described
4 Related characters described

C **Letters**
1 Inferred reader
2 Inferred reply
3 Format
4 Occasion
5 Documentation

D **Conversation**
1 Non-verbal analysis
2 Words as means of acting out
3 Movement

Topic 15: Enactment Procedures

Ref. 1 Kelly (19). Vol. I. ch. 8; Vol. II, ch. 22.

A **Theoretical constructions of role techniques**
1 Psychoanalytic theory
a Catharsis
b "Emotional" insight
c Transference
2 Learning theory
a Beta hypothesis
b Conditioning
c Establishment of freedom of movement through provision for a proximal goal and an experimental pathway
3 Construction theory
a Inventory of role concepts
b Control of threat to core structures
c Reconstruction
d Time binding and word binding

B **Free role techniques**
1 Psychodrama
a Auxiliary ego
b Participant spectator (classic Greek notion)
2 Sociodrama
c Skill learning
d Occupational role definition

3 Assessment
  a Behavior sampling
  b Criterion building
4 Teaching
  a Organized demonstration
  b Achievement testing
5 Group psychotherapy
  a Mobilization of group support
  b Freedom for experimentation
  c Non-verbal communication
6 Individual psychotherapy
  a Selection of roles and timing them
  b Extricating patient from involvements
  c Non-verbal role playing
  d Controlling perspective and distance
  e Role reversing
  f Controlling reflective features

C **Fixed role techniques**
1 Diagnostic basis
2 Self-characterization
  a Typical instructions for writing role characterization
  I want you to write a character sketch of______ ______.
  (short pause)
  just as if (s)he were the principal character in a play.
  (pause)
  Write it as it might be written by a friend who knows you very intimately and very sympathetically—
  (short pause)
  perhaps better than anyone ever really *could* know you.
  (short pause)
  Be sure to write it in the third person; for example, start out by saying, "__________ __________ is . . . ."
  (pause)
  Note: If the subject asks how long it should be, say "This is to be a kind of thumb-nail sketch of ______ ________. Write it so the reader will understand what kind of person(s) he really is."
  b Loosely structured instructions
  c Stage of insight or relation to other therapeutic programs
3 Supplementary diagnostic aids
4 Analysis of self-characterization
  a Topic sentences
  b Return to themes
  c Content organization
  d Strengths and threats expressed
  e Comprehensive implications
5 Writing new role
  a Acceptance of individuality
  b Organization
  c Avoiding partial changes
6 Securing acceptance of new role
7 Structuring period of role playing
8 Situations
  a School or work
  b Companionship
  c Religion or philosophy
  d Mate
  e Parents
9 Rehearsals
10 Safeguards
11 Types of successes and failures

Topic 16: Child Therapy

Ref. 1 Allen (1) pp. 45–121.
2 Axline (4). pp. 75–138.
3 Rotter (26). pp. 399–434.

A **Play therapy**
1 Nature of setting
2 Limits
3 Relationship
4 Materials

B **Relation of therapist to parents**
1 Inconsistencies in control
2 Rivalry
3 Parent observation

C **Activity**
1 Over-stimulation
2 Thematic interpretation
3 Expression of construct repertory
4 Feed-back

D **Children in groups**
1 Establishing role relationships
2 Cooperative play
3 Dramatic play
4 Competitive play
5 Creative play

Topic 17: The School Setting

A **Appraisal of a school setting**
1 Physical setting
2 Community setting
3 Observed activities
4 Classroom
5 Administration
6 Teachers

B **The psychologist's role in the school**
1 Learning
2 Individual deviations
3 Personnel
4 Teaching
5 Social control
6 Personal services to teachers
7 Analysis of administrative measures

C **Definition of remediation:** Readjustment in relation to goals mutually and explicitly understood between client and clinician accomplished through the use of explicit communication and obvious activities on the part of the client.
1 Remediation involves a minimal use of autistic or historical material.
2 The client is permitted to see himself as the operator and the problems upon which he operates as external rather than personal.
3 Remediation may have profound effect upon the mental health of the client.
a Relief of anxiety
b Gaining social acceptance
c Acquiring the tools for self-adjustment

D **General considerations governing the decision to use the remediation approach**

1 Need for objective assessment of level of disability in relation to the client's social frame and in relation to his level of aspiration. This may give the answer as to whether or not the problem can be approached by remediation procedures.

2 Need for assessment of possible secondary gains.

3 Need to assess damage and rigidities growing out of previous efforts toward remediation. These are always present in school children who are referred to a clinic for remediation.

4 Need to get client's formulation of the problem and especially to understand his use of the concepts of motivation and laziness in relation to the problem.

5 Need to get client's conceptualization of the remediation goal and its full implications with respect to other aspects of his life. Relation to role.

6 Need to study the pattern of disabilities

- a Verbal vs. performance I.Q.
- b Speech and reading linkages
- c Familial patterns
- d Collateral health disabilities
- e Subject matter patterns

7 Parents frequently consider speech and reading as the essence of education and may insist upon a remedial approach without regard for the more fundamental problems or for the psychological damage that may result from continued remedial efforts.

8 Disability needs to be understood in terms of the client's identification with his culture group. The example of the family with respect to, say, arithmetic uses may have more to do with the child's performance in learning arithmetic than the parent's interest in his report card.

E **Misleading features in remedial programs**

1 The regression effect
2 The referral effect
3 The growth effect
4 The anxiety effect

F **Remediation of speech disabilities**

1 Speech disabilities and social role

- a Situational approaches
- b Functional approaches
- c Expressive approaches

2 Dysrhythmic disabilities

- a Aphasic disorders
  - 1 Classic
  - 2 Transient
- b Stuttering
- c Negative practice
- d Drainage and facilitation
- e Milieu approach
- f Disorganizational approaches
- g Social support
- h Successive obstacles

3 Articulatory disorders

- a Auditory involvements. Substitution of pitch cues.
- b Method of successive approximations
- c Method of stimulations
- d Method of practice
- e Situational approaches

G **Remediation of reading disabilities**

1 Noting relation to speech
2 Visual involvements (near and far)
3 Eye movements
4 Increasing perceptual span
5 Verbalization

6 Relation between speed and comprehension
7 Syntactical approaches
8 Pacing approaches
9 Strategic approaches
10 Balancing interest and vocabulary levels
11 Phrase vs. letter methods
12 Form perception difficulties (putting legs on them)
13 Strephosymbolia
14 Drainage and facilitation. Oral reading
15 Reading readiness building
16 Dependency relations and reading

H **Remediation of arithmetic disabilities**
1 Relation to sex role.
2 Level of conceptualization.
3 Use of concrete tasks. Functional approaches.
4 Relation to other types of disabilities.
5 Diagnosis of specific conceptual faults.

Topic 18. Extramural Resources

Ref. 1 Dreikurs (7). pp. 1–136.

A **The home as a psychotherapeutic agency**
1 Using parental relations
2 Using child relations
3 Using sibling relations

B **The church as a psychotherapeutic agency**
1 Clergymen
2 Church workers
3 Church organizations

C **Organized community agencies**
1 Red Cross
2 YWCA, etc.
3 Recreation centers
4 Social work agencies
5 Industrial agencies

D **Special services**
1 Occupational therapy
2 Educational opportunities
3 Library
4 Recreational resources
5 Physical rehabilitation

Topic 19: Collateral Interviewing

A **Giving recommendations is like attempting short term therapy**
1 The child as a personal problem to parents
2 The child as a personal problem to teachers
3 The development of recommendations in an interview
a Stage at which it is possible to develop recommendations
b Trying on for size as a test of interviewee's personal concept level
c Use of the language of complaint
d Use of basic English
e Use of general rules
4 Recommendations should be developed orally first and then memorialized in writing
a Failures with oral recommendations only

1 Retroactive falsification
2 Retroactive reemphasis
3 Selective recollection
4 General feeling tone of interview is about all that is remembered

b Failures with written recommendations only
1 Failure to communicate
2 Failure to meet objections
3 Failure to establish confidence that the psychologist understands the respondent's situation
4 Failure to establish exemplary ways of acting

c Use of an open professional staff conference

d Need to develop recommendations immediately

B **Necessity for establishing a framework within which the psychologist can deal with the problems of parents and teachers**
1 Public announcements
2 On-the-spot statements of function
3 Use of a course in teachers' training as a frame for future contacts of a psychological nature
4 Previous contacts in the community
a Lectures
b Clinic staffs
c Clinic services
d Field seminars

C **Outline for recommendations**
1 "This is how the psychologist sees the case."
2 "The principal recommendation is . . .."
3 "The next most important recommendations are . . .."
4 "In addition the following should be done . . .. . ."
5 "If these recommendations are carried out one may reasonably expect . . .."
6 "Additional examinations should be carried out as follows . . .."
7 "Check back with us."

D **Helping teachers establish a working situation in which the carrying out of recommendations is feasible**
1 Pressures on teacher's time
2 Use of a key teacher
3 Use of staff conferences and action committees
4 Allocation of responsibility
5 Putting the spotlight on a teacher's work with an individual child
6 Providing the teacher with an outlet and reference point for problems arising in the treatment of the case
7 Use of non-professional personnel
8 Use of non-teaching community resources
9 Pointing out mile-posts and failure signs in the course of treatment and their significances for changing approaches
10 Unbinding teachers' time

E **Special types of finding**
1 I.Q.
a High.
b Low
2 Anxiety
3 Rejection
4 Pressure and motivation
5 Maturity level
6 Freeing interest potentialities
7 "Laziness"
8 "Attention getting"
9 Establishing priority of social and emotional factors in learning
10 Structuring the future
a In school
b At home
c In institution
d In career
11 Formulation of goals and target dates

Topic 20: Training and Supervision of Therapists

Ref. 1 Miner (22). pp. 319–432.
2 Raimy (23). pp. 93–117.

A **Responsibilities of the therapist**
1 Stage of training
2 Relation to training in diagnosis

B **Personal therapy**
1 Functions
2 When desirable
3 Should supervisor be the student's therapist?
4 Relation to understanding threat, resistance, and dependency

C **Theoretical orientation**

D **Supervisory techniques**

E **Cross-monitoring**

F **Career planning**

G **Research and therapy**

H **Science and therapy**

Psychology 865L, Psychotherapy
Special Final Examination
March 9, 1960

1 According to Rogers what are the successive stages in "process psychotherapy?"
2 According to psychoanalytic theory can transference ever be a rational process? Explain your answer briefly.
3 If one abandons the notion of motivation as a psychological construct, what are the two types of phenomena for which he must find an alternative explanation?
4 Consider the clinically related phenomena of guilt and hostility. Explain this relationship (a) from the standpoint of psychoanalytic theory and (b) from the standpoint of personal construct theory.
5 How would you contrast Rotter's view of dependency with Rogers' view?
6 How would you compare Slavson's view of the psychotherapeutic relationship with that of Sullivan?
7 According to Fenichel what is the single most important subject that must be interpreted in the course of psychotherapy?
8 In terms of what constructs does personal construct theory principally seek to explain suicidal attempts?
9 Why is it not necessary in psychotherapy for the client to report his dreams accurately?

Psychology 865L,
Psychotherapy
Final Examination March 14, 1960

Do not write your name on your paper. Use the number assigned you. ____________________

1 What are the principal roles in which the psychotherapeutic client initially casts his therapist?
2 What is the difference between primary and secondary transference in psychotherapy and by what different methods does the therapist dissolve each type?
3 In what way does the construct of motivation in psychology stem from our basic assumptions about the nature of the universe?
4 Did Socrates and Jesus essentially commit suicide? If you believe they did, can you have any faith in their teachings? If you believe they did not, must you not agree that they were both legalistic conformists to the juridicial system of their days?
5 What are the five basic questions that must be answered in clinical diagnosis?
6 Rogers, Rotter, and I all have misgivings about the psychoanalysts' use of dependency as a therapeutic agent. But we attempt to resolve the issue in three quite different ways. What are these ways?
7 The psychoanalysts in dealing with the interpretation of dreams say that one's wishes are often symbolized by their opposites. Thus a woman whose therapist is short and fat may dream that she is being seduced by a tall slender man. A personal construct therapist may also take account of the same dream but he explains the relationship differently. How does he account for such a dream?

8 Contrast Slavson's view of the group psychotherapeutic process with what you would expect Rogers' view would be.
9 Explain from a personal construct point of view how hostility serves as a means of controlling anxiety.

Psychology 865L,
Psychotherapy Final
Examination (second section)
March 19, 1959

Do not write your name on your paper. Use the number assigned you.__________

1 When a client becomes too anxious during a psychotherapeutic session, what principal methods may be employed to reduce the anxiety? Illustrate how each method may be employed. Describe the rationale of each and indicate what hazards are inherent in its injudicious use.
2 Some psychotherapists argue that a client never makes important progress until he has expressed an irrational hostility toward his therapist. In what sense do you believe this to be true?
3 Describe the principal conditions under which a psychotherapist should reinstate a defense mechanism.
4 Under what conditions is it especially appropriate to use loosening of construction during psychotherapy, and when particularly should it be avoided?
5 A twenty-eight year old clinical psychologist who has recently received his Ph.D. degree is employed as a counselor in a life insurance firm. A young matron who works as the private secretary to the Executive Vice-President is referred to him because she is "unhappy in her job and does not relate well to other members of the office force." After eight interviews she breaks down and tearfully confesses to the psychologist that she has a crush on him, that she cannot get him out of her mind, that she drives by his apartment every evening to see if the lights are on, and that she writes impassioned love notes to him each night in her diary—which, by the way, she keeps "in the back of the knife and fork drawer in the kitchen where her husband won't find it."

Is this a transference phenomenon? How do you describe it psychologically? Can the relationship be put to good therapeutic use? Assuming that the girl's husband is bigger than the psychologist, how can the psychologist maneuver himself into a less vulnerable position without abandoning his professional responsibility? What should he tell the Executive Vice-President, when he comments that the girl "seems more distractible since going to see you" and wants to know "if anything has happened to make her that way?"

First Quarter Examination
Psychology 865 (lecture)
December 12, 1953

1 Suppose you are in private practice as a clinical psychologist. A local psychiatrist, whom you know only casually, asks you to "do a Rorschach" on one of his patients and send him the protocol, together with a psychological interpretation.
   a What are the professional issues that are implicitly raised by this kind of request? How should they be resolved?
   b What are the psychometric issues raised by the request? How should they be resolved?
2 Is there any place for the formulation of statements about a client on the basis of his test performance when such statements are not definitively supported?
3 What is the difference between the concepts of validation and reinforcement as they are applied to a clinical situation?
4 Distinguish between the following and give illustrations of each of the following in a therapeutic situation.
   a Acceptance
   b Support
   c Reassurance
5 In what ways is threat an almost inescapable feature of a successful psychotherapeutic experience?
6 What is the argument against modern realism as a philosophical ground upon which to structure psychotherapy?
7 What are the most likely symptomatic possibilities in cases involving extreme constriction?
8 Immediately before expressing a new and useful insight in one of his psychotherapeutic sessions a client is likely to report the recall of events that seem to have been long forgotten. What relationship can be assumed to exist between the recollections and the insight?
9 How can the therapist reduce primary dependency transference?

69

The Function of Interpretation in Psychotherapy[1]

Interpretation as a Way of Life

There is a sense in which, whether we like it or not, all of us are caught up in our circumstances. I am quite convinced of this. I have been convinced of it for some time. For example, I have long since discovered that if the sun shines on me it makes me warm—at least it usually does. I have discovered that if I am out in the rain I am likely to get wet. When people talk to me I am apt to hear sounds. Moreover, I have found that these outcomes are also what other people have come to expect when these things happen to them. In fact, when such things occur no one ever seems to think of them as something he himself especially had to arrange for; he just takes them for granted as the natural consequences of sun, rain, or talk.

But while people are generally right about what follows upon sun, rain, or talk, and such outcomes are undoubtedly what anyone normally ought to expect, none of these consequents is exactly inevitable and that is something I would like to discuss. Consider the alternatives. There is always the remote possibility that sunshine on Ground Hog Day may give me the shivers as I contemplate its traditional forecast of six more weeks of winter. There is also the possibility that the rain may not get me wet if I have remembered to bring along my raincoat or if I have rubbed my skin with silicones. And, as for people talking to me, already I have, like many professional people who like to pursue their own lines of thought, taught myself to disregard the sound of voices when they seem to have nothing to say.

Yet, just to keep the record straight, I have not in any of these hypothetical instances succeeded in abrogating the sun, and the rain, and the talk. Nor have I managed to escape the reality of their existence. They are still with me. What I may have done is reverse the usual warming effect of the sun, or protect myself from the wetness of the rain, or deal with the welter of talk so as not to be distracted by it. Thus, while I am undeniably caught up in these circumstances and in hosts of others like them, I fear, and I must, willy nilly, cope with them all, I have reserved to myself the right to interpret such intrusions in my own way, and so to provide alternative outcomes for myself. In this way, without denying either the reality of the world about me or my essential involvement with it, I may still refuse to be victimized by it. What ultimately happens as a result of sun, rain, and talk is still my affair. Being human, I have already found some ways to make it so. Being human, I am determined to find more.

Here we have man's own special key to life—his ability to interpret what he may not deny. It is especially this ability to interpret—more specifically, his ability to *reinterpret*—that psychotherapy usually seeks to invoke in a man. Without this key psychotherapy would be reduced, perforce, to the manipulation of a person's surroundings, as if only to shoo him along in the general direction he is supposed to go.

There are, of course, some psychologists who maintain that this manipulation of circumstances is all that psychotherapy can ever be. As therapists, provided they actually take themselves seriously, they have to busy themselves maneuvering and manipulating in order to achieve the most salutary combination of circumstances for their clients to be driven by. Sometimes clients, too, prefer this kind of treatment. But such clients, when their stars again conspire against them, must either run away from their circumstances or scurry back to their therapists.

But assuming that man's interpretative ability rather than his circumstances is primarily what therapy depends upon, there are some questions to be asked. Basically we ought to ask if there is any systematic way in which we can analyze man's modes of interpretation. Can we get a genuine overview of man's way of construing the circumstances in which he is caught up? Given such an overview, how may the therapist best take advantage of man's ability to interpret? Does the therapist start with his own interpretative ability or

[1] A post-doctoral institute in verbal communication in psychotherapy. A series of three lectures given to the Los Angeles Society of Clinical Psychologists in Private Practice (a Division of the South California Psychological Association) and the Department of Psychology, University of California, Los Angeles, January 17–18, 1959. Published by permission of Nick Reed.

Collected Papers of the Pioneer of Constructivist Psychology: George A. Kelly, First Edition. Edited by David A. Winter and Nick Reed.

with his client's? Is it the therapist's responsibility to seize the initiative whenever he can and offer his client new nouns for his circumstances and adjectives for the new ways he is supposed to feel about them? Or is this a footless effort, interpretation by its very nature remaining solely the prerogative of the client: Or perhaps interpretation is something that emerges spontaneously from an interpersonal relationship, quite independently of any descriptive words used by the client or his therapist, and no matter how well such words are chosen. These are basic questions with which this series of three papers will seek to cope.

A Systematic Position

Before I go on to deal with these questions, let me formalize what I have already said so informally. As one can easily recognize, my introductory remarks amount to a philosophical position. After having stated this position more succinctly, I can then go on to say something systematic about psychology in general and about psychotherapy in particular.

Put it this way: Whatever exists is open to construction. Many alternative constructions are possible, some better than others, some worse. The ultimate meaning of even the simplest things is never settled, although we can tentatively use those judgments about which we have the least doubt as reference points for plotting more uncertain matters. Let us call this philosophical position *constructive alternativism.* It means that there are always other ways of looking at things, some of which must certainly be better than what we have.

Now let us take a hard look at science as a human enterprise. If we take the view that science is essentially a refinement of the human enterprise, rather than merely a special case of it, we can use science itself as a basic psychological model. This is to say we can look to science, not merely as we have been accustomed to look at it—as a methodology and a body of knowledge to be employed when one investigates the human mind—but as itself a paradigm of how that human mind works. We shall say that to study science is ultimately to study human psychology; to know science, together with its antecedents, is to know something about the basic workings of the mind of man.

Let me pursue the point. Consider prediction. Science has a well-known concern with prediction. But suppose, instead of saying merely that the objective of *science* is to predict—or to anticipate tomorrow's outlook—let us say more generally that it is *man* whose objective it is to predict—to anticipate how things will look from another vantage point in time. Instead of saying merely that *the scientist* formulates a succession of questionable theories and tests them out against observations about which he feels more certain, let us say, in a more general way, that it is *man* who invents theories and checks them against what he regards as obvious. To go on, instead of talking about *scientific constructs* only, let us talk about *personal constructs.* Instead of seeking to understand man as a super-rat, suppose we seek to understand him as the incipient scientist that, over the ranges of time, he has proved himself to be. Thus, in our search for the model of man, we shall figuratively turn away from Darwin's ape and take a careful look at the Darwin himself.

All this makes for another kind of psychology, quite different from anything we are accustomed to identify as psychology. It is different partly because it is pitched at a new level of abstraction. In a sense, it is a psychology of philosophy—or of personal philosophies—rather than a psychology of physiology or a philosophy of psychology. It is a psychology that undertakes to explain how logic comes about, rather than one that looks to traditional logic to explain what psychology is up to.

A Postulate

Taking man's science as the model of his psychology and, in turn, focusing attention upon science's aim to predict successfully things to come, I can think of no better way of putting it than to say that what a person does is psychologically channelized by the ways in which he anticipates events. We can take this as our initial postulate, although, of course, it is somewhat imprecise as logical postulates are supposed to go.

When I use the word "psychologically" in this postulate, I am hedging my statement. Frankly, I am not trying to lay the groundwork for a complete system of biosocial science. My effort is limited, for the present, to what can readily be subsumed under psychology.

The statement may sound teleological. While there is nothing particularly wrong with being teleological if one can get away with it, what I have said is that it is his ways of anticipating events that sets the course of man's behavior, not that he is drawn on by events that have not happened yet. If man is drawn on, it is by what he expects, not by what is actually going to happen. What is going to happen doesn't even exist yet. This notion sets the locus of psychological determination in current conditions, not in future conditions. It is one's current interpretation of the past and his current inferences as to the future that mark the route he undertakes.

Is this position historical or ahistorical? While I have no absolute objection to either of these systematic positions, neither does my postulate permit me to align myself exclusively with either of them. Historicalism is usually taken to mean that the course of events, once it is set in motion, elbows its way past the present and thrusts itself into the future. Present conditions can even be skipped over entirely, as if the reality of any existence were no more than a momentary obstacle in the way of history's headlong pursuit of its natural consequences. Such is the fuller implication of the historicalistic postulate. This is not for me.

Ahistoricalism, likewise, is sometimes taken to imply commitment which this postulate does not compel us to undertake. Even if one went so far as to assume that all of the determinants of the future are bound to be present at any given moment, he would still find it profitable to examine what had been happening up to now. The phenomenal present is a pretty small sample to work from, much too small, I'm afraid. Most of us lack the capacity to generate penetrating conceptualizations from such a limited range of data. So ahistoricalism, while emphasizing certain phenomenal points that stem from our postulate also, still tends to blot out parts of the record that we would have to consider important. Indeed, our model of man-the-scientist perhaps attributes a greater significance to the sweep of human history than does any other current psychological scheme.

Is this a phenomenological theory: Granted that, like ahistoricalism, phenomenology comes in various shapes and sizes, our postulate does not make the usual phenomenological commitments. We did not say, for example, that one is surrounded only by his perceptions. In fact, we started this discussion by asserting that there is a sense in which all of us are caught up in our circumstances. Nor do we say that each personal world is an island universe. The words "personal" and "private" are certainly not synonyms. I think the tree that falls in the primeval forest makes a bang just like any other tree. Moreover, we might sometime, although at the moment I cannot say how, take an interest in the noise that centuries ago nobody heard and eventually make something scientifically important out of it.

Perhaps our postulate makes it seem that I am winding up to deliver a self theory of personality. Here the answer is definitely "no." Quite the opposite. Self theories, without exception as far as I am able to learn, envision psychological processes as converging upon the point of their own origin—the self. While one may argue rather convincingly that a person whose own identity has become perfectly clear to him will be more likely to live and let live, or even that such a person will be freer to putter around with such altruistic projects as do not threaten to involve his self, the direction of the essential movement envisioned by self theories remains centripetal and regressive. Our postulate, in clear contrast, envisions incipient human movement as outgoing and concerned with the future.

One more question; is this a perceptual theory? If by "perceptual" one means a theory that assumes all matters of psychological importance in a man's life can be clearly communicated by him, the answer is "no." Certainly man's ways of anticipating events are not all verbal. Many of them are based on discriminations and generalizations that he cannot describe by any ordinary means. Yet they are there. He lives them out day by day and thus he expresses fully and completely what he cannot begin to describe. To be sure, another person may successfully put into words a psychological description of a pattern of life that the person himself cannot say much about. Yet one's pattern of life is still very much his own no matter how inarticulate he is; it is based on discriminations and anticipations all his own; it is he who makes all choices. If this conviction is the essence of perceptual theorizing, then we have embarked upon a perceptual theory. If not—and I am inclined to believe that it is not—then I doubt if what I am proposing should be classified as another perceptual theory.

Construing

Having said that a person's processes are psychologically channelized by the ways in which he anticipates events, we turn naturally to the question of what these ways are like. We could say that one of his ways is to look to the past in the expectation that what has already happened will happen again. Or we could say that one always anticipates what is optimal for his survival. Perhaps he chooses to expect those events which he can portray most vividly in his mind's eye. Certainly there are many different approaches to understanding man's ways of anticipating events.

But our line of theoretical reasoning, instead of leading us to choose between such alternatives, turns our attention to the process of construing. Man deals with events by placing constructions upon them. More exactly, he deals with events by construing their replications. This is to say that, although events never actually repeat themselves, he is able to construe them as if they did. In fact, if man were completely realistic about what was going on he would also be completely confused. (This is a point that has got the existentialists all in a dither.)

Instead of looking at an event in the raw, or even instead of looking at it as a whole, it is possible to look at it in a more limited way, to ascribe to it some kind of property, a kind of property so designed that it can be ascribed to other events as well. This takes ingenuity, especially human ingenuity. Having contrived to see an event in terms of imagined properties it becomes possible for one to look around him to see what other events can have one or more of these properties ascribed to them. He can even predict that an event having such and such a combination of properties attributable to it will occur in the future. He can then keep his eye open to discover whether any event that can be so construed actually turns up.

What we are describing here is an interplay between invention and discovery, and it is most important to get it straight which is which and what you can do with one that you cannot do with the other. If scientists, and especially psychologists, were to get this fixed in their minds they could rid themselves of a lot of impediments to their thinking—including a lot of this stimulus-response nonsense that clutters up the psychological journals.

We deal with events, not by waiting to be kicked around by them, but by inventing constructions to be placed upon them. We validate our constructions, not by memorizing them, but by discovering whether or not the events they lead us to expect actually turn up. Ideas are not discovered, they are invented. It is events that one discovers.

Suppose we try to do it the other way around. We would be putting our ear to the wall and patiently waiting for nature to whisper some great revelation of truth. That would be discovery. Then we would go out and check our discovery by inventing observations we could cite as evidence of the truth or falsity of what had been whispered to us. Sounds ridiculous, doesn't it?

While human psychology does not basically work this way, let us suppose that someone thought it did. After so long a time with his ear flattened to the wall he would probably hear something. Assuming that he has been waiting long enough to become impatient, or that his sense of what is about to happen to him has become so chaotic that matters are urgent, he is likely to think he is hearing a direct revelation. It will, of course, sound like something he has already invented or suspected, but he sternly overlooks this possibility and insists he discovered this truth with his own ears coming to him right through the wall. "Tough minded chap," we say. "Now there's a fellow who is concerned only with facts. Too bad he's a little paranoid."

We can, of course, go all the way in the other direction and argue, along with the philosophical idealist, that even the most palpable discoveries are, after all, merely man's best interpretation of material reality. I agree. And I am sure most of you do too, although you may be a little shy about admitting it as long as you are applying for membership in Sigma Xi. But we do not need to go on to say that it is pointless to talk about any firm reality other than man's perceptions, or about anything that lies beyond the immediate reach of man's perceptions. As in the case of the vigorous discourse of the behaviorists a generation ago, such an argument becomes absolutistic and, like all monopolar thinking, gives us no dimension for putting psychology in perspective.

If we must insist on having either a realistic interpretation of personal construct theory or a phenomenalistic interpretation, we might say that realistically an invention is an open-ended discovery that extends out of sight over our perceptual horizons and that, phenomenalistically, a discovery is an invention that is so close at hand we are willing to accept it, for the time being, as obvious to everyone.

Modern science makes a great deal of the event which occurs in fulfillment of a prediction that someone has ventured to lay on the line. The importance attached to such an event lies not so much in the fact that it happened as in the fact that it happened when it was supposed to. By turning up on schedule it tends to validate the inference that led to its being expected and leads the scientist to hope that by construing matters as he has, he has secured for himself the key to many other things that will happen or can be made to happen.

But why say "scientist"? Is this a fact any less true of the genus than of the species? Why not say "man"? That is what we had agreed to do, hadn't we? Is it not vastly more exciting for any of us to discover that we possess the conceptual goose that lays the golden eggs than it is to have one of the egg-facts dropped unexpectedly into our laps? It is not only the scientist who is looking for the goose.

To construe, then, is to see events, not merely for what they are, but for the evidence they provide. It is an attempt to understand them, not in their totality or uniqueness but in their commonality and individuality. To construe is to invent, pure and simple. As far as discovery is concerned, all that one ever discovers is whether or not the predictions, to which his inventions have led him, actually pan out.

If then we wish to understand the consequences of a given event in a person's life, whether he is a scientist concentrating in his laboratory or a child having the time of his life at a picnic, we need to know how it fits into the anticipations laid for it and what system of personal construction of the world, in turn, hangs on these anticipations. Rarely does the single wager represent all there is at stake. One's whole anticipatory system may be involved. To stare at an event—a mere event—without framing it in these personally significant terms, is to stare at it vacantly. And to try to base a psychology wholly on the natural consequences of events, *qua* events, as stimulus-response theory attempts to do, is to come up with an utterly vacuous psychology.

A Psychology Frankly Based on Black and White Distinctions

Much of what has been said up to this point sounds like some form of relativism. It may come as a surprise, therefore, to hear that the personal construct approach we are proposing is anchored in dichotomous, or black and white, evaluations. I am well aware that dichotomous evaluations are usually associated with intolerant and punitive social behavior. They are also considered by many to be synonymous with absolutistic thinking. But in proposing the dichotomous construct as a basic unit in terms of which to understand the psychology of man we are neither advocating intolerance nor absolutism, but rather a unit that meets the psychologist's logical and experimental needs both, much as a binary system of numbers lends itself to the computational convenience of the engineer and the notion of positive vs. negative charge serves the physicist in his dealing with electromagnetic phenomena. Indeed we are proposing such a unit as a way of dealing with all man's thinking, not merely as an observed feature of certain thought systems now prevalent in the world of physics and engineering.

In order to understand the use of the personal construct as a psychological unit we need to recognize that every behavioral act, whether involving a gross muscular movement or a flitting fantasy that can scarcely catch the observer's eye, whether involving verbal forms or a momentary palpitation of the heart, expresses both an affirmation and a denial. Here is a statement that takes us away from the beaten path of psychological discourse. Let us illustrate it as lucidly as we can. Suppose we choose our illustration from the realm of verbal behavior, not because what we say is limited to verbal, intellectual, or conscious behavior, but because it is easier to illustrate verbal behavior in terms of the words that one must use in a paper such as this. If I say, "This is a table," I am not only affirming a construction of the object before me but I seem to be implying two other things: (1) that there must be something else around that is not a table, and (2) that by being a table this object is excluded from some other class of objects. Both of these denials are implicit in the affirmation; if they were not, such a remark would have no psychological function; and, in case a reminder is necessary at this point, we are still talking about psychology—human psychology.

Putting it more colloquially; there would be no psychological sense in saying this was a table, or if, in saying that it was a table, one failed to distinguish it from anything else. I suppose one might argue on some sort of logical grounds that the statement could make sense in the absence of these implicit denials, but from a psychological point of view it seems far better to recognize the psychologically implicit denials as a way of understanding the person who makes the statement and his manner of expressing himself.

Let me bring in another feature of this unit of psychology we call the personal construct—the fact that it is abstract. I am well aware of the common notion that abstract behavior, or abstracting behavior, can only take place on a language level and must be intellectual rather than emotional and that it, furthermore, must be fully conscious—whatever that means. Yet, if psychoanalysis has taught us anything it has made it clear not only that the roots of verbal behavior lie much deeper than the dictionary meanings of the words one uses, but also that human interpretations of the world are actually abstracted and symbolized at levels far below anything we had ever before suspected. It is this latter fact that needs to be borne in mind if one is to grasp the psychological utility of the personal construct; otherwise the term will limit our thinking to a kind of classical intellectual psychology.

To construe an event is not to hoist it aboard one's mind in all its concrete totality but to deal with it only in those respects in which we can also view other events. Therefore, when we construe an object as a table, we are not picking up the whole object, lock, stock, and barrel, but only that property we can imagine as its table-ness. And this property, in turn, can be lifted only if, in the context of our thinking, there are other objects that can be similarly or contrastingly construed.

It may be merely an academic point, but this line of reasoning leads us to the conclusion that the minimum context in which a construct can be erected is three objects. The effect of the construct is to reduce them to two contrasting categories for purposes of dealing with them psychologically. If this is to be construed as a table, there must be at least two other objects to anchor the construct, at least one of which must appear to stand in clear contrast in respect to its table-ness. The third object must either be like the object we started with, in respect to table-ness, or like the contrasting object. Otherwise we deal with the objects as unique wholes, that is, concretistically. In any case, for the construct to make sense it must be an abstraction, it must establish a clear-cut contrast and it must identify a clear-cut similarity.

To see how this psychological unit, the personal construct, applies to one kind of practical problem, let us turn to a psychotherapeutic situation. Take the *client remark,* the concrete unit which the Rogerians have used so extensively in their research. There is a type of remark that very commonly appears in psychotherapy protocols—the phrase, "I know this is foolish". For the therapist to sit back and interpret this remark to mean only that the antecedent of the pronoun "this" is categorically "foolish," or only that it is regarded by the client as "foolish," is to miss the full import.

Let us look more carefully. By saying it is "foolish" the client is implying a linkage with other "its," perhaps saying it is like other things he has done or like things he has seen others do. But more than this, he is saying that what he is thinking of stands in clear contrast to other behaviors which he regards as distinguished by their "non-foolishness." And here it is important to realize that he is not contrasting a present object of immediate attention with remote and irrelevant matters, but with immediate behaviors highly relevant to the "foolishness-non-foolishness" axis of his thinking. The therapist must keep such an axis of reference—another name for the personal construct—in mind and not limit his attention to the concrete object the client described as "foolish."

Something else the therapist must keep in mind: When the client says he "knows this is foolish" he may be calling attention to the fact that there is a difference between knowing what one's behavior is, on the one hand, and controlling it, on the other. It may imply that there are many such things that he knows, but knowing them is not enough. Indeed, often such a statement is a way of saying, "Let's get this therapy onto another level. We are wasting too much time with the pat and the obvious."

We could go on and examine this client remark further, using the personal construct as our psychological unit, but at this juncture these two brief illustrations probably suffice to serve our major purpose. They may, however, fail to carry our further point that the personal construct, while abstract in nature, is not merely a verbal unit of language or communication, nor is it applicable only in the so-called realm of consciousness. Yet, rather than argue this latter point further, I would rather come back to the matter of dichotomy, or black and white thinking.

The construct is a notion of similarity and contrast, simultaneously perceived. It therefore establishes a dimension, albeit a two-point dimension. We can call it a dimension of psychological response, if we wish, or an axis of reference, or a unit of discrimination. But whatever terms we may prefer, it carries with it the idea of similarity and contrast so wrapped up together that neither makes sense without the other.

This two-point notion gets us into trouble if we fail to see the personal construct unit of psychology as abstract. If we say that objects, in their concrete totality or in their multi-dimensional construction, are altogether either black or white, we run into the kind of rigid thinking that the social psychologists find so distressing. It is the construct, not the total object, that is cast in dichotomous terms, just as the north versus south dimension is a clear-cut dichotomy that we use to determine various degrees of northerliness and southerliness of objects. North and south are not spots on the globe, nor must we say all terrestrial objects are located precisely at one of these points or the other. To say that would be to bog down in utterly concretistic thinking. But there is no equivocation about what north and south are in respect to each other, as long as we see this dichotomy as a compass that can be picked up and laid down next to many different objects to tell which is north of which and which is south of the other. To say that northishness is always mixed with a little bit of southishness is to destroy the sense of the construct. We can say this of objects, as we look at them in a complex or multidimensional fashion, but not of the basic personal construct units themselves.

Patterns of Interpretation

While it is impossible to take in a new philosophy, a new theory, and a new methodology all in one gulp, it would be disappointing not to carry our discussion far enough to give at least the flavor of what all of this might taste like when it is mixed into general psychological inquiry. Later we can extend the implications more specifically to clinical settings.

We have been talking about interpretation as a comprehensive psychological process and about a system of psychology based on such a notion. We have proposed the personal construct as a basic unit for thinking about psychological questions, a unit which is abstract, not necessarily verbal or intellectual in any traditional sense, and one which, because it channelizes one's anticipations of future events, can be checked against outcomes to see whether its channels lead in the right directions. We have been talking about the single construct and emphasizing its dichotomous nature. Now let us turn to a personal system made up of a whole lot of constructs. Such a system is a complex or, if you don't mind the term, a conceptual grid within which events can be seen in depth or in their psychological dimensions.

Consider an initial series of events: *a, b, c,* ......*k*. To cope with these events one construes them with a Construct *å*. He can now discriminate between them, at least to the extent of lumping them into two categories. He can also scale out the events by picking up, so to speak, his Construct *å* and laying it down in different places so as to arrange the events successively with respect to each other into some kind of order or sequence. This, as we have already indicated, involves the abstract use of a black-white construct.

But he may also deal with this series of events in a more complex fashion if he employs a second construct, Construct *β*. Now, even without taking advantage of the abstractness or portability of his constructs, one may put his events into as many as four categories. With a third construct, Construct *ç*, he can accomplish eight categories, the number of such concrete groupings being equal to 2^n, where *n* is the number of constructs applied.

By this same process events are ascribed individuality—I won't say "uniqueness," since that implies concrete discontinuity between events—but an individuality which makes each event distinguishable from all other events, distinguishable, not because of its unrelatedness to them but because it is indeed related to them in a complex pattern of likenesses and relevant differences. For purposes of psychological response, then, each event becomes *psychologically* a sequence of plusses and minuses as it is scanned in succession by a series of constructs.

This patterning of events in terms of constructs also serves to provide operational referents for the constructs. Events make sense because of the rows of constructs with which they are interlaced and constructs show form because of the columns of events which they put into order. Each takes on meaning in terms of the other.

A child gets a piece of candy. This is an event. Getting the candy begins to have meaning when he sees it as having properties in common with other events—kind words, other gifts, laughter, appeasement of appetite, etc. And it makes sense also because it stands in contrast with other events—scoldings, being deprived of toys, weeping, hunger, etc. The candy begins to have more meaning if he construes it also in terms of another theme—overeating, stomach ache, castor oil, etc. But so do the other events come into perspective when seen in terms of this health dimension. Thus the event of receiving candy gets to be seen in more and more psychological depth as additional constructs are applied to it, and the constructs, in turn, are explicated in terms of such palpable events as scoldings, hunger, etc.

We can represent this relationship as a rectangular grid—a Repertory Grid—with the events *a, b, c, k* arranged along the top with each event respectively heading a column of cells, and with the constructs *å, β, ə, ..., Ķ* arranged along the vertical margin, each at the left end of a row of cells. Since the constructs are bi-polar we can make an entry in each cell to indicate whether the construct in that row is applied one way or the other to the event represented by that column. (See Fig. 1)

Once the grid is filled out we have events and constructs defined in relation to each other. The system is, to be sure, solipsistic, but in the logically acceptable sense, as is any proper mathematical system. We can, if we wish to be purely mathematical about it, abandon the words originally used to label the events and to describe the poles of the different constructs, and deal only with the cell entries which we may call *emergent incidents* and *contrast incidents*, or simply plusses and minuses. Symbolically, then, a construct is a row pattern and an event is a column pattern of such entries.

Applying this model to our child with the candy, the event of *receiving candy* is psychologically construed in depth by the child by the column of cell entries which represent the way his repertory of constructs is applied to it. His construct of *security versus insecurity* is anchored by the row of cell entries that indicate how the construct is applied to various events in his life, of which receiving candy is only one.

It should be clear that this is a psychological model, that we use it because we understand that anything has to be construed in some manner if it is to be understood at all. The grid is the psychologist's personal way of construing—and it is designed to lay out for analysis his subject's personal ways of construing. That is the way it goes.

Now, a question: Should we go looking for grids in subjects to see if they really have them? I think not, any more than we would go looking for the North Pole to see if there really was one. Should we go looking for the ways grids operate in different subjects: Yes; that is a different question, and such a quest would be quite appropriate, just as it is appropriate to try to see what things are like in the place we call the North Pole. If our navigation gets crossed up because of the ambiguity of the construct we are using—either the construct of the Repertory Grid or of the North Pole—or if the use of either construct takes us into a blind alley, then we can say the thing was not a very good idea and we had better figure out another approach.

Actually, what we are proposing is analogous to the similarly solipsistic psychological model we call the stimulus-response model. The term *stimulus* can be made sensible only by inventing something to be called a *response* to go with it, and the term *response*, in turn, has to be set up

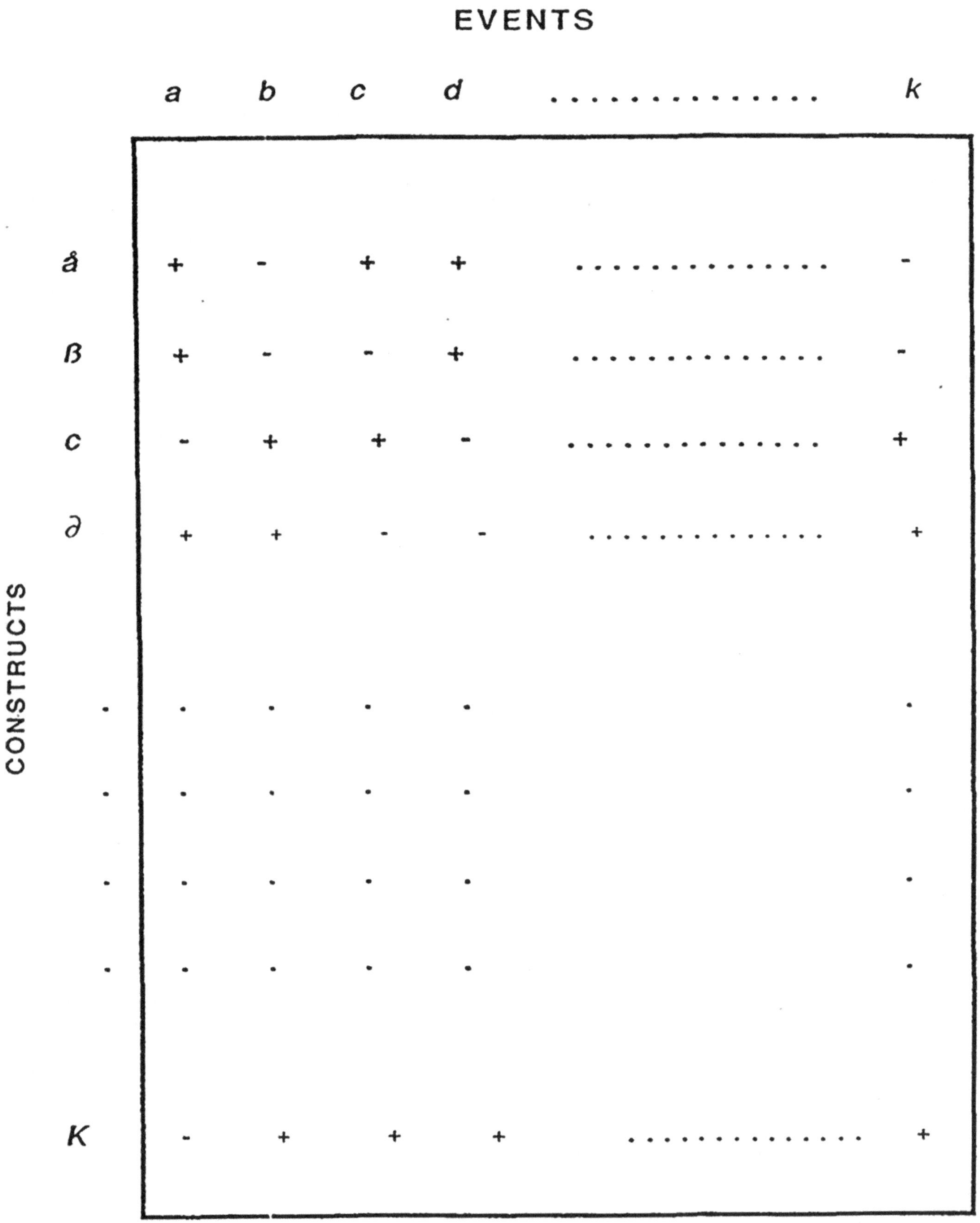

Fig. 1 Simple Repertory Grid.

in order to say what it is that a *stimulus* accounts for. One does not go out to see if there is such a thing as a stimulus or not, nor does he ever get his doctoral dissertation approved for discovering that there really is such a thing as a response—well, hardly ever! This particular psychologist's model has, in my opinion, proved itself sterile, not so much because it is logically inept; rather, because it is functionally restrictive. And, since it is only a model, any of us is perfectly free to try another model without being accused of closing his eyes to reality.

So the appropriate question to ask at this point is not whether there are actually grids that cross-hatch the human psyche, but whether this grid model helps us do anything we could not do better by some other obvious means. How successfully can we interpret the human psyche by laying it out on a grid?

We need to put in some disclaimers and qualifications at this point. For one thing, not all constructs can be conceived as applying to all the events which impinge on a person. Some constructs have a rather narrow range of convenience; others have a wide range. A complete grid of a person's construction system, if one were ever able to draw up such a thing, would therefore have a lot of blank cells in it. Practically, it is very difficult to deal with a grid mathematically unless all of the cells can be meaningfully entered.

Another point. It can be argued, and quite reasonably that the events which are interwoven with constructs are themselves constructs. This is true in two senses. They come into psychological being by the constructs that hold them in place and they are themselves simple generalities imposed upon natural phenomena. But, even though the latter is true, they can be treated as one order of experience, called the constructs, to create a fabric of psychological substance.

The way we have been describing the Repertory Grid may make it appear to be limited to events and constructs which are point-to-able and readily verbalized. But, as we pointed out earlier, we see no reason to limit personal construct theory to this kind of field. Why not other kinds of data too? Why not vaguely perceived impulses and unverbalizable experiences? Just because language custom and age-old thinking have refused to see impulses in any way except as explosively disorganized behaviors or as gremlin-directed forces is no reason for not setting them up in personal construct units and laying them out on a grid where we can look at them.

Predicting Behaviors in Terms of the Repertory Grid

We have described a grid in terms of the incident intersections between events *a, b, c, k* and the constructs *å, β, ə, …,Ķ*. We can then ask ourselves two kinds of questions:

1 How will a given construct *å* from this series be extended through a new series of columns representing events *m, n, o, …,z*;
2 How will a given event *a* be construed by a sequence of new constructs *μ, ¶, Ω,…, W*? Once these two questions are answered one can also infer and test all the cell entries of the fourth quadrant of the extended grid, the quadrant represented by the intersects of *m, n, o, …,z* and *μ, ¶, …, W*. (See Fig. 2.)

In order to answer the first question one has to be given a foothold in the new quadrant in one of two ways. He must know how at least one construct is extended through the new series of events by his subject, or he must, through his own identification with his subject's construct rows, make inferences as to how one or more of the rows (*1*) extend themselves into the new quadrant. From there on, in either case, he can infer what the cell entries would be for any given unknown row, such as the row for Construct *å*.

In order to answer the second question—how will old events be construed in terms of new constructs—the procedure is symmetrical, except that in this case it is more precarious for the psychologist to impose his own partial versions of what the new constructs will be.

Let us express this in less mathematical terms. Once one knows what events his subject construes in what ways, and has adequately extended these inter-relationships so that all the events in the initial series are viewed in terms of all the constructs in the initial series and vice versa, he can ask how new events will be construed by the subject in these same terms and he can ask how the same events will be construed in new terms. In the one case he has to extend the subject's way of thinking partially into the new series of events before he can start to make inferences. In the other case he has to extend the present events partially into the new system of reference before he can begin to make complete inferences about how his subject will apply new terms to old matters.

We can now move into the fourth quadrant we talked about a while ago; how will the subject deal with new events, once he has acquired a new set of constructs? The answers to this question can be inferred both from the way he extends old constructs to new events and from the way old events are structured by new constructs. From this methodology we actually make two sets of inferences about how our subject will deal with new events in new terms. Furthermore, our inferred cell entries can be tested empirically, giving us, in the case of each cell, three sources of information.

It is possible to adapt the Repertory Grid to many different kinds of data. One of the most common applications of the model is to ask the subject to select certain important persons in his life and treat them as events through which he attempts to thread important personal constructs. Another application is to take certain traumatic or near-traumatic events in his personal history and weave constructs through them. Still another application is to take such traumatic events and relate them to the persons in his life who could have been of assistance to him at the time. This, in effect, makes the persons the symbols of a form of dependency constructs,

EVENTS

CONSTRUCTS	a	b	c	d	...	k	l	m	n	o	p	...	z
á	+	-	+	+	...	-	+	$i_{\acute{a}m}$	$i_{\acute{a}n}$	$i_{\acute{a}o}$	$i_{\acute{a}p}$	...	$i_{\acute{a}z}$
ß	+	-	-	+	...	-	-	.	.	.	.	...	.
c	-	+	+	-	...	+	+	.	.	.	.	...	.
∂	+	+	-	-	...	+	-	.	.	.	.	...	.
.	.	.	.	.	...	.	.	.	.	.	.	...	.
.	.	.	.	.	...	.	.	.	.	.	.	...	.
.	.	.	.	.	...	.	.	.	.	.	.	...	.
K	-	+	+	+	...	+	+	.	.	.	.	...	.
§	+	+	-	-	...	+	-	-	+	-	+	...	+
μ	$i_{\mu a}$	.	.	.	...	.	+	.	.	.	.	...	.
¶	$i_{¶a}$	.	.	.	...	.	+	.	.	.	.	...	.
Ω	$i_{\Omega a}$	.	.	.	...	.	-	.	.	.	.	...	.
Π	$i_{\pi a}$	.	.	.	...	.	-	.	.	.	.	...	.
.	.	.	.	.	...	.	.	.	.	.	.	...	.
.	.	.	.	.	...	.	.	.	.	.	.	...	.
.	.	.	.	.	...	.	.	.	.	.	.	...	.
W	i_{wa}	.	.	.	...	.	+	.	.	.	.	...	.

Fig. 2 Four-Quadrant Repertory Grid.

often ones which the subject could not symbolize with any other kind of noun. Then, of course, in dealing with mentally deficient subjects, one may use pictures of the persons who serve as events and he may use concrete action questions such as sociometric questions or even paper doll play to delineate the construct rows. Non-verbal material in general can be used as events, situations can be used as occasions for constructs—a different situation for each successive row and two-choice behavior responses can be used as cell entries.

Perhaps I should add that the Repertory Grid can be factor-analyzed so one can see what simplifications of the various construct rows and of the various event columns are implicit in the subject's construct system. The effect of invalidating experiences can be studied also, not only as they alter the operational definitions of the terms one uses and the events he perceives, but also as these alterations are generalized to rows and columns not specifically involved in the invalidating experiences. One popular type of inquiry is the analysis of the subject's identification with other persons, such as members of his family, or with specified types of persons, such as women or homosexual men. One may also examine the similarities in certain selected dimensions which he perceives between his therapist and various figures in his life, such as his father or his mother, and he may examine the changes in these perceptions that come during the course of therapy. By using situations to elicit constructs (behavior choices), as well as events such as lights and bells, one may develop a Repertory Grid representing the construct system of an animal—a fact that ought to make those psychologists happy who harbor a deep distrust of human beings and the words they use. In fact, there is room for everybody, even those who part their hair the S-R way: "Stimuli" can be substituted for events, situations for constructs, and dichotomous behavior choices for incident cell entries.

Conclusion

What we have tried to do in this first paper is present the matter of interpretation, not as a particular kind of technique in human relations, nor as a special psychological function, but more broadly as a way of psychologizing. Man has been represented as an incorrigible interpreter, one who must interpret at all levels of awareness in order to live, even in order to be credited with being alive. The implications of this viewpoint have been traced through their epistemology, their logic, their theoretical form, and the generalized model of all psychological inquiry which arises from them. The next paper will deal with interpretation as the individual man's way of gaining personal stature as he lives out his life a day at a time.

Reinterpretation and Personal Growth

In the first paper of this series I sketched an epistemological position that assumed the reality of events, independently of how they are perceived. In taking this stand I broke off with the position known as phenomenology; at least I broke off with phenomenology to the extent that it is a form of pure philosophical idealism. I went on, however, to say some things that are very much like what the neo-phenomenologists say.

I said that events present themselves to us in a fluid state, offering no patent definitions of themselves, either as to their beginnings and endings or as to any essential similarities and distinctions by means of which they can be related to each other. It is up to man to chop them up into suitable lengths so that he can deal with them piecemeal—so he can compare and contrast them—and, by such imposed interpretations, manage to anticipate what is about to happen. I urged that this is not a special rite to be performed only by scientists and psychotherapists, but that it should be regarded as a psychological characteristic that imbues the whole human enterprise. This is what mankind does. This is what the individual man does. This is what a patient does. Interpretation is the basic fact of human psychology.

I went on to point out that the life process can be psychologically construed as an anticipatory process and that personal interpretations establish the channels through which anyone's anticipations must run. We can reduce these channels to a basic psychological unit, the *personal construct*. I discussed the logical and mathematical properties of such a unit and then turned to the *Repertory Grid*, in terms of which an individual's whole personal construct system can be represented.

This Repertory Grid portrays the interdependent relationships between two orders of experience—events as personally identified, and personal constructs. In terms of the Grid, an event assumes its individuality, not from its concrete discontinuity with other events, but from the variegated ways constructs are applied to it. And a construct acquires palpability, not from its verbalized definition, but from the differential way in which it is applied to referent events.

Revising Interpretations

While anything that can be interpreted can certainly be reinterpreted, this fact should not be taken to mean that nature is so compliant as to be equally acquiescent to all constructions we happen to place upon her. Nature does what she has a mind to, and some constructions of her antics work out a lot better than others. They are better because they are more compatible with what the future has in store.

Sometimes it is their greater precision that makes them so; sometimes it is because they are more comprehensive; and sometimes they simply enable one to peer further ahead. The fortunate thing about it is that one can always act on the assumption that whatever his present interpretation of events may be, it is not necessarily the ultimate one. His reinterpretation may turn out to be worse—that is not hard to accomplish—but also it can be better, and that is something worth striving for.

It is quite proper and useful to look at the human experience as a series of rounds, each comprising construction, followed by anticipation, followed by realization, and then by the reconstruction of events. The reconstruction is the beginning of the next round. Experience, then, is not to be measured by the number of things that have happened to a person, but rather by the number and extent of the rounds he has spiraled through.

And it is spiraled experience that goes to make the mature man. If we come to understand the nature of human experience in psychological terms—and by that I certainly mean something more than the roster of stimulus-events that play a part in human affairs—we shall have laid the groundwork for understanding the essential nature of the psychotherapeutic process.

In the preceding paper I invited attention mainly to the first stage of the experiential round—the construction or interpretation stage. Now, as we turn to the problem of man's reinterpretations, I need to say something about what intervenes—about what happens when one's anticipations materialize, or fail to materialize. Broadly speaking, of course, the confirmation of one's anticipations tends to validate the constructions on which they were based; and disconfirmation has an invalidating effect. But in either case the effect is complex, and it is by no means as simple a matter as changing one's mind whenever he finds he has guessed wrong, or slumping in his tracks whenever he sees nothing other than what he expected to see.

For example, a certain man relies on a personal construct—say, one he calls "thrift vs. extravagance"—in deciding what to do with his money. Since, let us suppose, he is both inept in handling the construct abstractly and unable to see matters in terms of other dimensions, he is left with no means of handling his financial affairs with moderation. With him each act of his life has to be simply and concretely one or the other—either thrifty or extravagant. So he tosses his one conceptual coin and it comes up "thrifty."

His wife and his therapist think he is altogether too tight-fisted and one or the other of them maneuvers him into a neat invalidating experience. They trip him up. As soon as he gets up off the ground he can make any one of a number of more or less cogent remarks. He can say, for example, "I was wrong. I was sure I was doing something thrifty, but it turned out to be extravagant. After this I'll have to be more careful and make certain that what I do is absolutely and unequivocally thrifty." Or, instead of rattling the specific act in the slot, he can rattle himself in the slot and say, "Okay, okay. You've convinced me. Where I have been thrifty I must now try being extravagant." Needless to say, neither his wife nor his therapist is likely to be any more pleased with the outcome in one case than in the other.

While the main thing that has happened is that the man has kept his construct and merely changed its application to one or the other of the elements, it is true, as I have already pointed out, that even this much revision has some measure of effect on the functional meaning of the construct. The man's personal notion of "thrift vs. extravagance" is itself altered somewhat, now that a certain act he once called thrifty must now be called extravagant or the thrifty man he once saw himself to be is now to act extravagantly. In terms of our grid, one cannot make changes in an event column without making at least minimal changes in a construct row.

The example we have given is, of course, more schematic than real, but it illustrates the simplest type of reinterpretation. Psychotherapists will recognize such a form of behavior change and many will recall the exasperation of having a client respond this way. On the other hand, those who have to do with mass behavior control, sometimes called "discipline," may have given up hoping for any other kind of human readjustment.

Circumspection as a Step toward Reinterpretation

A person who has had an invalidating experience may, if he is not being rushed, back off and look at the situation in terms of other constructs. We can call this circumspection. It is a matter of looking at the situation from other angles. He may find that another construct or combination of constructs now seems more applicable. Again, in terms of our grid, instead of changing one cell entry only, he reexamines the identity of his event column in terms of its pattern as it crosses a number of other rows.

It takes time to do this and while one is doing it he has to disengage himself from the events being reconstrued. If, however, one is threatened by the immediate outcome of what is going on, he may feel that he has to hold on tightly with whatever constructs he presently uses to grasp the situation, rather than reaching for other conceptual tools.

Perhaps here is as good a place as any to say what *threat* is, from the standpoint of personal construct theory. To feel threatened is to sense that one is on the brink of an important change in his make-up. In more formal terms it may be stated as the awareness of imminent and comprehensive change in the core of one's construct system. When one senses, then, that developments are imminent that will lead to such deep changes—that is, when he is *threatened*—he is likely to clutch at what he already has in his grasp, rather than assuming a more poised position from which he can examine the matter from various angles. Moreover, if a person is in a situation where it seems that he may be called upon to act or commit himself at any moment, he is bound to keep his attention on what is about to happen rather than let his eyes cast about for different ways of construing the situation.

In this connection it would be helpful to point out that psychotherapy, if it is taken seriously by the client, is bound to be threatening. It can scarcely be otherwise. The client believes that he is on the verge of something that will shake him right down to his toes.

The fact that he is uncomfortable with the way things have been going and wants to do something drastic about them does not make therapy any less threatening. He still clutches. He still finds it difficult to be detached and circumspect. It is still easier to rattle about in the most obvious slots.

But if one can succeed in looking at matters in terms of constructs he had not applied to them before, it becomes possible for his behavior ventures to become less abortive. Seeing things in terms of more constructs gives one a more finely graduated way of behaving. It permits him to make minor adjustments, to deal with the more delicate aspects of his life, to see things both in long range and short range perspective. Circumspection also gives new dimensions to his world, opens up new vistas, and provides latitude for his patterns of behavior.

Forming New Constructs

But there are other levels of reacting to an invalidating experience. Suppose, instead of slot rattling or rummaging about in one's ready-made construct cupboard, a person reacts to an invalidating experience by forming a brand new construct. This, of course, would be the most profound outcome of the three. This is generally what deep psychotherapy seeks to achieve. Therapy is not the only means of forming genuinely new constructs—the healthy person is working away at that kind of project all the time—but it is at best a particularly formidable undertaking, especially when one must work in areas where prior constructions are in the way, where there is threat, or where the events to be reconstrued are inaccessible.

The formation of new constructs nearly always requires the consideration of fresh elements or events in the context of the old. It is very difficult to take a single invalidating experience and say, "In what new way can I look at this particular thing? In what new way can I see it that is different—different from any way I have ever looked at anything before?"

Nor is it likely to be enough to say "Now let me look at this again in relation to all the things that I already know go with it; perhaps I will see a brand new relationship in this context of familiar things." Only when new events are unexpectedly brought into the display is it likely that genuinely new insights can be instigated. A therapy that rehashes familiar events or goes over and over the same ground is not likely to produce significant reinterpretations. Or, to state the case more generally, the person who attends only to what is familiar is not likely to become psychologically mature, nor can it be said that his life experience is enriched.

A new construct, which we can envision as a new row on a person's Repertory Grid, not only changes the identity of the single event it crosses, but it also has the effect of changing the significance of *all* the other events to which it is applied. Thus a genuinely new insight does what all experienced therapists have long known that it does; it changes not only the way a particular problematic event is seen, but also the way many other things are seen. It changes them so that the client often refers to them as if they all had somewhat different identities now. A new row in the grid has the effect of changing all the columns.

But another matter has to be noted too. The construct rows in the Repertory Grid tend to fall into factorial clusters. A new row, then, if it is really unlike any previous row, is difficult to subsume within a factorial cluster, or it may even have the effect of changing the distribution of the factorial cluster. This is a way of saying that a new construct may prove to be alien to the system and that it tends to alter the balance between other constructs and even substantially change the construct system as a whole.

Both these far-reaching effects of adding a new row to the Repertory Grid—the effect upon the character of events construed and the effect upon other constructs—may constitute obstacles in the way of developing and explicating a new construct. If a man sees his wife as a somewhat different person as a result of reconstruing his mother, or if his new outlook affects the established dimensions in terms of which he has successfully structured his job, he may have to take his new insight with a grain of salt. Thus, even new and obviously improved ways of dealing with troublesome matters may have to be boxed in because of the implications they extend to outside areas where a changed outlook does not seem to be called for or even desirable. This is one reason why people do not always seem to learn what it seems they should learn from experience, and why clients so often fail to go ahead and develop what seem to be their most brilliant therapy-room insights.

Failures of Prediction That Do Not Result in Reinterpretation

Sometimes it seems that events cannot be predicted. If they happen to be events that are particularly important to us, we are likely to be pretty unhappy about them, especially if they keep popping up unexpectedly. It is not, of course, that we cannot construe them at all—if that were so we would be paying little attention to them—but it is rather that we are unable to construe them adequately for our purposes. We cannot bring them within our system of anticipation. Not only can we not control them, but we cannot even get ready for them. We are caught flat footed with our constructs down. There is a word for this—anxiety. This is anxiety, stated in personal construct terms. As can be readily seen, it is quite a different view of anxiety and it includes some things that other theories do not and significantly excludes some things that are often identified as anxiety symptoms.

More simply stated, anxiety is the sense of confusion. On the other hand, more schematically stated in terms of the Repertory Grid, anxiety occurs whenever a given event column has too many vacillating or uncertain cell entries as it crosses those construct rows we depend upon to make our immediate predictions or to maintain our equilibrium.

We could say, along with a number of other theorists, that anxiety serves a purpose. Yet I would say it more generally and more emphatically this way: It is *the nature* of man to try to do something about his anxieties. He seeks to anticipate where, so far, he has been unable to anticipate successfully. He places structure on events to extricate them from confusion. When his structure crumbles, he experiences anxiety to a degree proportional to the importance of the events, and he sets about to remedy the situation. Of course, anxiety stirs up the person who is alive! If it did not, it would be time to bury him. This is an inference that falls into place as a result of our basic assumption about psychological processes.

But to be anxious about something is not necessarily to set about reinterpreting or reconstruing it. The person may thrash around in other ways. One way is to constrict. When one constricts he pushes more and more events out of his field of vision. He tries to ignore everything he cannot foresee. He goes only to those places where predictable things will happen to him. He cuts down the horizontal dimension of his grid by eliminating those columns which have too many uncertain cells in them. He may also cut it down the other way, by using only those constructs that seem to order events adequately, even if this restriction of multidimensionality makes for concretism.

Another reaction to invalidation, and a means of escaping the ensuing anxiety, is to do just the opposite of constrict—to dilate. Here the person frantically grasps for more and more events—whole handfuls of them—as if in the sheer grasping of more and more reality the course of troublesome events would become more clear. Sharper awareness and closer contact with more things is substituted for wisdom about things.

Even though dilation, of itself, is not necessarily the answer, the introduction of new unexpected elements, as I have already said, often is necessary to the formulation of new constructions. Similarly, I might add, constriction can serve a legitimate purpose. By limiting one's field of awareness, he can sometimes deal with matters more precisely. When he knows what he is doing, he can re-dilate and extend his new precisely-formed construct across wider ranges of events.

The extremes of constriction and dilation are the easily recognized poles between which the cycloid personality vacillates. Often suicide is most clearly and helpfully understood as an extremely constrictive effort. Moreover, both phases of cycloid behavior can be seen as employing the same kind of tactical principle—the notion that somehow by turning the flow of events on and off one can replace anxiety with structure and render events predictable.

There are many ways in which the human personality responds to invalidating experience, short of doing something constructive about it. Without trying to catalog all of them, let me mention two more in particular. A construct can be *loosened*. By this I mean it can be inconsistently applied to a number of events. What is "plus" at one time is "minus" the next. This inconsistency can characterize an entire construct row on the Repertory Grid. Yet the row may retain enough of its identity still to be called the same construct. This loosening gives an apparent flexibility to the construct dimension and allows a kind of second-guessing of events that were mis-predicted. If a person construes loosely enough he can hedge his bets with inconsistency and make it seem to himself that he had guessed right, whichever of two alternatives turns up.

One can also *tighten* up his construction. He can make his constructs more precise, more literal, more inflexible, and, when he does this, he is likely to make them more concrete and less abstract. The construct rows apply to a given set of columns definitely and to no others. The constructs are not only given operational definition by the cell entries as they cross the different event-columns; they are the cell entries, the concrete arrangement of events.

This kind of inflexible and consistent explicitness becomes legalistic and often is called "objectivity." It results in the person's needing a great many different construct rows in order to keep his filing system in order. It facilitates testing of one's interpretations. But carried too far, one may find himself kept terribly busy just keeping matters lined up properly. Once the system breaks down, as it occasionally does with the overly compulsive person, we witness a shift that is frequently referred to as the "decompensation" of the compulsive neurotic patient. Sometimes it breaks down into the shambles of anxiety. Sometimes the process reverses itself and we see the characteristic loosening of the schizoid personality.

Guilt, Hostility and the Societal Man

There is another order of construing which I have not mentioned so far. It is one thing to construe events—but something a little different to construe those events as if they themselves were construction systems. Yet this is what we have been doing here in these pages. As psychologists concerned with our own construction systems we have been talking about those human events which are, in turn, the varying construction systems of other persons—our subjects or clients—who are faced with invalidating outcomes to their anticipatory ventures. We have been applying constructs of our own; such as anxiety, constriction, and loosening; to these personal construction systems, and yet keeping in mind how the world must look to those who construe it in terms of their personal repertories. We have been construing constructions, not just physical things.

In looking at the world through other people's eyes, and at the same time trying ourselves to grasp some overview of the varying ways the world appears through them, we have not been doing anything especially remarkable. Remarkable for psychologists, perhaps, but not for normal human beings! Or perhaps I should say it would be unusual for a psychologist *to admit* that he was looking through another person's glasses. Yet a humane society does a lot of this sort of thing—this trying to see how something looks through other eyes. Children try to see things from their parents' point of view, and sometimes parents reciprocate and try to understand the personal construct systems of their children. A psychotherapist will often try very hard to get his clients to see things the way he does, calling it "interpretation" usually, and sometimes, if he doesn't have too many patients to see that day, he makes a magnanimous effort to see things the way they do.

All of this is as it should be. It makes for a society which, taken together, adds up to more wisdom than any one member is fortunate enough to have on his own. When one construes events that are primarily the outlooks of others, and in personal terms that provide him with a course of action of his own in relation to those persons, we say that he has *role constructs*. When he *acts* in accordance with those dimensions in some kind of social enterprise, we say he is enacting a *role*. This is a somewhat different definition of role, different from other currently used definitions, but it fits neatly into our theory and it throws a lot of human behavior into a new kind of perspective.

Now role constructs can be invalidated too. People around us, even when so sympathetically perceived, can do things we didn't expect them to. When things come to such a pass, we can revise our notions of people just as we can revise our interpretations of other events. Or we can simply become anxious. Or we can dilate, constrict, go loose, tighten up, or do any of the things that occur to us as a way of coping with the turn of events.

But there are some additional special terms we would like to use here for dealing with some of the more conspicuous non-reconstructive patterns of behavior we run into. When a person's role constructs collapse, he not only becomes anxious in the area of his interpersonal relations, but he also runs the danger of losing his way in his social actions. If he senses that he has lost his way—has lost his role in its most important respects—he suffers a particular kind of discomfort we may call *guilt*.

The person who feels himself displaced in this particular way is likely to find it hard to sustain life. Moreover, if there are those to whom he has entrusted the definition of his role and who, therefore, are in a position to make him feel that he has lost it, they are the ones who can lead him around by the nose. This is one of the most important facts about human society.

But when we talk about guilt as the sense of loss of role we must keep in mind what we mean by role; that it is a course of action based on one's construction of others' outlooks. It is not enough to accuse a person of failing to do what was expected of him; he may never have intended to. The accusation may make him feel more amused than guilty. What strikes him deeply is the realization that he has failed to do what he had intended to do and had indeed thought he was doing with respect to human outlooks. To be struck this way is to feel the full impact of guilt.

Another outcome of invalidation may be *hostility*. Here again we need to see the psychological construct in terms of the personal construction, rather than in the traditional terms of hedonism or social sanction. Our line of philosophical and psychological reasoning throws hostility into an entirely different light. Instead of being seen as the urge to hurt or destroy, as the hostile person's victim tends to see it, it should be seen as the hostile person's unique effort to pursue an already invalidated enterprise to which he has irrevocably committed himself.

When one's anticipations of others' behavior fail to materialize, whether these anticipations are based on role constructs or on others, he is likely to feel trapped on many sides. If it seems that there is too much at stake for him to revise his interpretations in the light of developing events, he may seek to keep his faulty interpretations intact by forcing the interpreted events to conform to his too well laid expectations. This Procrustean device is the essence of hostility. The fact that others are injured by one's hostility is of secondary psychological importance. The main effort in hostility is to get people to be what one always insisted they were—and what he dares not now admit that they aren't—even if they have to be stretched out or cut down to a size to fit his only conceptual bed.

The person who uses hostility to hold back the flood of anxiety does so by attempting to extort evidence in confirmation of wagers he knows are already lost in fact. Thus hostility is essentially unrealistic, not so much because it does a poor job of revising unproductive interpretations, but more because it forcibly distorts reality in order to save the vestiges of interpretations known to be outmoded. The therapist who observes hostility directed toward himself from his client is witnessing the last ditch stand of one who, now that his therapist has been admitted to the joint custodianship of a crumbling system, must try desperately to force the therapist to join him in confirming what he dares not disbelieve. The therapist often rightly construes this hostility as evidence that the client has been trapped both by his own insights and by the alliance he has formed with the therapist. Therapy is not merely a matter of letting the hostility blow itself out behind the protective walls of the therapy room. Instead, the client must somehow be allowed to see for himself if the hostile device will work whenever his rationale appears not to.

There are a number of interrelationships here—relationships between dependency, the transference of figure identifications, etc.—but there is no need to spell them all out. Yet there is one I would like to mention in particular. Where role constructs have been widely invalidated and the person is suddenly on the verge of overwhelming guilt feelings, hostility is often the quickest and most obvious answer for him. Thus hostility and guilt are often found wrapped up in the same pathological package.

We have been talking about conditions in which a genuine reinterpretation does not occur following an invalidating experience—guilt, hostility, and often anxiety. But let us remind ourselves that reinterpretations sometimes serve as blocks against further reinterpretations. The therapist who sheds light on his client's behavior by showing him how wide-spread his hostility is, may serve no other purpose than to turn the hostility back onto the client himself, and thus paralyze his capacity for further therapeutic movement.

Similarly, other interpretations may, by their too eager acceptance, block further progress, even though they may seem realistic enough both to client and therapist. Progress in therapy may not lie so much in seeing things as they really are, or in seeing the full sweep of new insights, but in cutting out the client's therapeutic task in pieces of a right size for him to handle one at a time. If contact with reality were all that a person needed to keep him on the right track, very few of us would ever get derailed. And certainly there would be no shortage of willing helpers, if outside suggestions were all that it took. It is, instead, the ponderous investment we all have in our construct systems and the self-contradictory complexity of those construct systems that slow down the attainment of psychological stature and social maturity.

Revising Interpretations That Have Proved Useful

We can express the directional feature of human motivation—as opposed to the force or energy feature—in terms of the choices a person makes. Generally speaking a person makes two kinds. Since life is characterized by its tendency to reach out and grasp the future, he may either seek to extend his interpretative system to cover outlying events or he may seek to define his system so he can make more specific predictions about everyday matters.

Take our hypothetical tight-wad who construes the world mainly with the single construct of *thrift vs. extravagance*. Having decided that this is the single issue at stake and that it pre-empts the field of decision, he must next choose which pole of the construct is for him. Whether to be thrifty or extravagant; that is the question. Which will he choose? Since he is human and alive, we shall say that he will make whichever choice seems to bring the future more firmly into his grasp. If it appears that he is about to be confronted with strange and exotic events that, if met unexpectedly, would prove threatening, he will, other things being equal, make that choice which will appear to *extend* his construct system further, so as to cover the exigencies. On the one hand, if it appears that thrift is the best way to be prepared for the unknown, he will choose thrifty ways of living so as to have clearer expectations of the likely outcomes. On the other hand, if it appears that extravagance—or the investment in more fluid or effervescent values—is the best way to meet unexpected eventualities, he will move in the opposite direction.

But our tight-wad may have something else in mind. It may be that it is not the strange things that threaten him, but the exasperatingly familiar goings on that keep eluding his grasp. In that case, his choice will be directed toward more clear-cut *definition* of his construct system. Often this is a matter of maintaining its organization, of resolving its dissonances. If thrift will help clarify the system, he will be thrifty. If extravagance will put his knickknacks in orderly array on the shelf, he will choose extravagance.

Now the point I want to make is that this sort of choice-making goes on all the time, regardless of whether one's predictions are confirmed or disconfirmed. The part that confirmation and disconfirmation play is not that of a traffic light—confirmation meaning "stop, you have arrived," and disconfirmation meaning "go, you are still in the wrong place." In either case it is always "go." Disconfirmation points to something that has gone wrong and ought to be fixed before you advance on too wide a front. Confirmation clears the way for further general improvements. But the word is always "go." Even in suicide something is envisioned as going on after death and as a result of it.

It is important, then, to see confirmation, or the validation of one's constructs, as securing a base upon which one can build major revisions of his construct system. This is why we so often cite security as necessary for broad advancement, whether in a person or in a society. This is why the arts and sciences flourish at a higher level when nations and peoples are led to believe they are mainly on the right track—not necessarily that they have arrived yet—and to believe that their mistakes are no bigger than they are. But if all were confirmation, our efforts would lack direction. If we were to extend our construct system into the unknown, and still, because of our inability to face up to stern realities, pretend that we were getting successive confirmation for every forecast we made our construct systems would soon start flapping about pretty loosely. We would not be likely to get anywhere.

In the case of the client it becomes obvious that two things are needed. He needs a broad base of confirmation, often at the rather generalized level of value or dependency constructs, in order to trust himself to undertake major revisions of his system. But he also needs disconfirmation to point out the spots where he needs to get busy. Clinicians have long known that it is the child who feels most certain that his mother will still be home when he returns who ventures into the next block, and it is the child who needs to make sure that his capricious mother has not gone off somewhere who keeps running in from play. So with the adult client in psychotherapy; the fellow who has some secure investments is the one who experiments outside the therapy room, while the one who is caught off-guard by everything that happens is the one who clings to the therapist. Reinterpretation, as a fact of everyday life, depends as much upon confirmation of one's expectations as it does upon their disconfirmation.

Reinterpretations and the Generalization of Experience

It has often been assumed—and there is some evidence for it—that when one changes his behavior in one respect he tends also to change it in similar respects. The same holds true for what is commonly believed about the interpretation of events—when one event is reinterpreted similar events are also reinterpreted. In stimulus-response psychology's terminology these effects are called *response generalization* and *stimulus generalization,* respectively. In both instances the key to the generalization is the notion of "similarity."

But who construes the similarity? Certainly when one deals with the subtle meanings of the human outlook he finds construed similarities that are by no means apparent in any physicalistic construction of either the stimuli or the responses. Are these the similarities that determine the baseline for a gradient of generalization? Or does generalization operate only against a baseline of what the physicalists construe as similarity?

This is an important question for the psychologist, and particularly for the psychotherapist. If a person reinterprets his mother, does he tend to reinterpret all persons who are like her, in proportion to the degree of their similarity? And, if so, "like her" in whose terms—the therapist's? This is one kind of gradient question.

There is another kind of gradient question that has to do with the shape of the gradient. If the mother is reinterpreted, what kind of generalization is likely to be extended to the person who is construed to be most like the mother? Will this second, similarly construed figure standing next to her be reconstrued in the same way the mother was reconstrued? Will it likely be in some other way? Or will it not be still more likely that the adjacent figure will be construed all the more rigidly?

A person finds that he was wrong about his mother. He must start seeing her in a different way. How about his older sister? Must he come to see her as somewhat like the new mother; or will he say, in effect, I was wrong about my mother, but at least I know what kind of person my sister is and I will not risk the entertainment of any new fangled notions about her?

Or suppose the question were put this way: How could a psychotherapist best help a client reinterpret his older sister—by first getting him to reinterpret a mother who closely resembles the sister? Or would this only make him cling more tightly to his image of his sister? Would the therapist do better to help the client first confirm the more important expectations he has built up about his mother and thus give him the kind of secure base from which he can venture a reinterpretation of his sister? As can be seen, I am still talking about the roles of confirmation and disconfirmation and their bearing on the reinterpretations with which life's experience is measured out bit by bit to each of us.

We can state our problem in a more mathematical form by using our model of the Repertory Grid. If the columns of the Grid represent persons—a kind of event—and the rows represent constructs, what happens to the column representing the client's sister when he finds it necessary to change the entries in the column representing his mother? If the two columns are initially patterned quite similarly, will they therefore both tend to be changed in step with each other; or will he freeze the entries in the sister column the moment the mother column is shaken up? Which is likely to be more important to him; to preserve the construed similarity between his mother and his sister, or to maintain the stability of one in the face of the instability of the other? Should a therapist not seek to reinterpret a client's mother to him unless he is willing to have the client become, for the time being, more rigidly fixed in his ideas about his sister?

Without trying to answer these questions about therapeutic strategy at the moment, let us bring out the issues in as basic a form as possible. We have been talking about generalization of one's reinterpretation among similarly construed figures, using the model of the Repertory Grid and its columns. We can flip the question over on its side and ask it this way; what happens to rows when columns are revised? Are similar constructs, that is, constructs whose rows are similar as they run across the figure columns, likely to be changed when one of them is changed? Or is one more likely to hold fast to a given notion when he finds that similar notions are being uprooted? Will our tight-wad person who, let us say, believes that thrift and honesty are highly correlated, be likely to become dishonest when he finds that his notion of thrift does not make as much sense as he thought it would? Or will he tend to become more rigidly honest in his dealings and more fixed in his judgments about who is honest and who is not. These are questions the psychotherapist needs to ask himself before attempting either to validate or invalidate the poor fellow's construct of thrift vs. extravagance.

Our problem of the generalization of reinterpretation has still another dimension. Take the client with the mother and the sister. Suppose he has four elder sisters all very maternal toward him. Will this make any difference? Will he be as likely to reconstrue all of them as he would if he had had only the one other person who seemed like a mother to him? Will having four such sisters make it easier to re-evaluate his mother?

Or, to flip the problem on its side again, will our tight-wad friend find it easier or harder to revise his ideas of thrift as well as his ideas of honesty if it should happen that he has several other important constructs which are closely related to these two basic constructs? Or we may ask if it will be easier to get him to reconsider thrift if we first help him build up a number of related constructs? Or will this have only the effect of making the whole structure more ponderous and each of the related parts more rigidly maintained?

At first it may seem that personal construct theory would offer no systematic hypotheses as to what would happen in the kinds of instances we have been mentioning. Yet we must keep in mind that it is as important for a person to keep his conceptual tools in working order as it is to make correct predictions. The mother whose construction is an anchor point in a person's construct system will not likely be reconstrued unless there is another person or a group of persons who serve the same function. If she must be reconstrued then there is more reason for stable reliance upon the others who are in the best position to serve as similar anchors. The more of them, of course, the less rigidly one would need to cling to his ideas about any one of them. Similarly for constructs; these, too, must be kept in working order. If thrift vs. extravagance and honesty vs. crookedness were the only two ways of dealing with a large portion of one's world, the invalidation of thrift would leave our friend with honesty alone to guide him.

So the theory gives us hypotheses and the Grid gives us a practical way of explicating these hypotheses so they may be systematically tested. The empirical evidence is still sketchy, but it tends to confirm the theory rather than the usual hypotheses about stimulus or response generalization gradients. In Bieri's data it turned out that a figure about whom one's predictions seemed to be confirmed was as ordinarily expected construed much the same way after the confirmation. But similar figures, as is not ordinarily expected were likely to be revised considerably. In a symmetrical fashion, a figure about whom one's predictions seemed to be disconfirmed was widely reconstrued, but adjacent figures tended to be firmly fixed. Thus the generalization gradient instead of running in a straight line from the point of validation to the poiint of invalidation tended to take the form of an *S* with greater freedom to change one's notions of other people in areas adjacent to the point of validation, and less freedom in areas adjacent to the point of invalidation. His data indicated a similar area effect with respect to construct rows on the Repertory Grid.

Instead of envisioning a concrete analog of construct parts being changed or maintained in proportion to their overlapping elements, we can use another model to envision the effect we have been talking about. Suppose each of the persons represented by the columns of the Grid is a pier supporting a superstructure—say a bridge. Persons who were construed as similar to each other could be represented by piers standing close together. Suppose a given pier is loosened or dislodged; the adjacent pier is put under greater stress in order to maintain the structure and it becomes harder to dislodge. Suppose another pier is confirmed or stiffened; then the adjacent piers can be more easily altered. In this fashion we can get some notion of the overall structural effects of reinterpretation and their relation to the acceptance or rejection of further reinterpretations in adjacent areas, whether these reinterpretations are offered directly by the therapist or undertaken by the client on his own.

Levy's data throw light on the other dimension of the problem, the dimension I mentioned a while ago as the matter of how many related constructs are involved. Here again we can use our bridge pier paradigm. If there are several piers in the area of the one being re-built, it will be easier to make the repair and less occasion to become rigid at the point of any one of the substitute piers. If the pier being repaired stands out by itself, then whatever piers must take over the shift in load must be stiffly maintained.

Conclusion

Since personal construct theory is a reality-based theory that sees interpretation as the basic psychological process, it is important to see how events and constructs are related. In this second paper I have dealt mainly with what happens to constructs when the events they lead one to expect either appear or fail to appear as scheduled. The round of interpretation, prediction, and validation is the basic cycle of human experience and the succession of such rounds constitutes a measure of personality growth. This is the growth that goes on all the time. Psychotherapy has no monopoly on it. Yet it is this inherent growth process, based on spiraling experience, that psychotherapy must seek to exploit. In the next paper, the third and last of this series, I shall discuss the psychotherapeutic techniques for making use of man's natural interpretative talents.

Techniques of Psychotherapeutic Reinterpretation

In the first paper of this series I outlined an epistemological position that I think needs to be clearly understood if one is to approach the problem of interpretation in psychotherapy. Psychotherapy is for the client a supreme ontological venture. The methodological procedures he uses lie deep in the ways of man. The psychologist must therefore face up to his own epistemological assumptions whenever he attempts to join his client in such an undertaking.

I proposed in this first paper the erection of a psychological unit called the personal construct as a methodological way of understanding the psychological processes of mankind. In originally proposing such a unit several years ago, I placed the major emphasis of my theorizing on what has turned out to be the topic of this series—interpretation. I also proposed the use of the Repertory Grid as a way of representing a construct system and the functional relationship between events and constructs.

In the second paper I dealt with the effects of anticipated and unanticipated events both on the construct and on the construction system. I discussed anxiety, threat, hostility, guilt, constriction, dilation, loosening, and tightening, all in the new framework of personal construct theory. I dealt with experience in terms of reinterpretation cycles and pointed to it as a measure of personal growth.

Now I would like to talk about psychotherapeutic technique within the framework of the theory I have tried to describe. What I have to say may make some sense regardless of its theoretical reference, but mainly it is dependent upon what I have theoretically assumed to be the psychological make-up of man.

Elaboration As a Step Toward Reinterpretation

Psychotherapy usually starts with a complaint, either the client's or someone else's who has to live with him. The therapist encourages the client to elaborate the complaint and then to follow through by elaborating the personal construct system within which the two of them must initially deal with the complaint. In the course of these two elaborations some changes are bound to take place. In a measure, these changes amount to reinterpretations on the part of the client.

For example, a client who complains about feelings of inadequacy cannot help but reconstrue his inadequacy when he is required to spell it out. Not only that, but his whole system for putting people and events together becomes altered as he attempts to put matters into words the therapist can understand. What is it he is inadequate for? What kind of adequacy does he envision as being denied him? Does it now seem like one kind of inadequacy and then another; is it free-floating? These are questions which cannot be answered without affecting the experience itself.

There are seven basic questions for the initial elaboration of a complaint. They can be posed in various forms. Let us state them as follows:

1 What is the difficulty?
2 When was it first noticed?
3 Under what conditions was it first noticed?
4 What has been done about it?
5 What changes have come with treatment or the passing of time?
6 Under what conditions is it most noticeable?
7 Under what conditions is it least noticeable?

The purpose of this kind of elaboration is two-fold: to provide a context of relevant events and to bring the complaint into perspective as something that changes. Expressing this in terms of the Repertory Grid we may say that we set up event columns around the complaint column so that we may have external anchor points for the constructs in terms of which the complaint is to be understood. For the client simply to sit there and describe his complaint over and over is to give the therapist only one column of his Grid and hence very little understanding of the meanings of the terms used. The complaint begins to make sense only as it is interlaced with constructs which are anchored in other events also.

Suppose we sketch a simple one-sentence answer to each of our seven questions. A client says he feels inadequate—his answer to the "difficulty" question. He first noticed it when he was in the ninth grade—his answer to the second question. Next, that was the year his companions started having dates. From time to time he sought the solace of his teachers. He became increasingly discouraged about the prospects for his career. As long as someone took a special interest in him things were not so bad. But when he was expected to make it on his own it became clear how inadequate he really was.

With the initial answers to our seven basic questions we now have something to construe along with the complaint; that is to say, we have six columns in our Repertory Grid, in addition to the complaint column, and we can start asking in what ways the columns can be related. What are the similarities and contrasts between his companions having dates and the solace of considerate teachers? What are some of the similarities and contrasts between having a career and having someone take a special interest in him? How do these constructs relate to the feeling of inadequacy?

But our questions, as we have noted, also invite the client to look at his complaint as if it were something that at one time is different from what it is at another. This is to set up the complaint itself, not as one column, but as several different columns, each representing the difficulty at a different point in time. Now the constructs can be interwoven so as to bring out the construed differences between these columns as well as between the other columns with which the complaint has been surrounded.

As long as a client deals with his complaint concretistically, that is to say, as an insular whole unrelated to other events, therapy is at a standstill and there certainly is little point in the therapist's offering any suggestions or reinterpretations. Furthermore, as long as he deals with his complaint as a single entity having no internal variations, there is little chance of getting the client to experiment to see what can be done about it. Analysis into both external and internal variants is necessary if one is to set the reconstruing process into motion again.

A Distinctive Approach

Now let us note how this approach, growing as it does out of personal construct theory, differs from the realist-determinist approach commonly associated with modern science—the approach exemplified, for example, by stimulus-response psychology. The conventional approach is a sort of witchhunt that starts out with either the inadequacy or the feeling of inadequacy as a concretely given event that must be accounted for. Here it is—inadequacy. It is perfectly obvious that we are stuck with it. Now who—or what—do you suppose put it here? Something did it. The question is, what! So runs the realist-determinist line of reasoning.

The personal construct approach is based on the notion that anything that exists can be construed. Here is the difficulty as currently construed by the client. Here are other relevant events in his life, some of which, for the time being, we shall take as obvious in the form they are now seen. Here are some of the different shapes the difficulty assumes. Now what are the operating constructs that give this difficulty its present individuality? And what new modes of construing will serve to give it new form in relationship to the other experiences of life? Out of the new relationships we are able to invent we may well hope to devise methods of altering conditions or taking them in our stride. As one can readily see, this is a far cry from stimulus-response psychology. Indeed, it is a far cry from what many people believe modern science has to be.

Yet actually this sort of thing goes on all the time in human psychology. Our fixed notions of science unfortunately keep us from recognizing it. But at a clinical level, where our scientific formulas are so often abandoned, I am sure we have all seen it. How often have we heard the recovered client say that realistically nothing has changed especially, that he has not put his finger on any particular cause to be removed, but that the meanings of things have changed and he is prepared to go about his business without getting all stirred up.

Sometimes this kind of remark is taken as an indication of "gut insight," as distinguished from "intellectual insight." True, there may be no new nouns or adjectives to act as verbal guideposts for him; and, for some psychologists, this seems to mean that there is no new conceptualization. But reconceptualization, or reconstruction as we prefer to call it, is not synonymous with verbalization, the concretistic realists notwithstanding. In the paradigm of the Repertory Grid a row pattern representing a construct is much better defined operationally by cell entries as it crosses the event columns than it is by the words used to label it. Our client who offers no new words for his insights may just as clearly—indeed even more clearly—peg his new constructs by the fresh ways he links and distinguishes events. His new constructions are not the causes of his new behavior; they are an essential feature of it. This is a point hard for a stimulus-response psychologist to understand. The therapist, on the other hand, because he is likely to be a stimulus-response psychologist only when he goes to his particular church, is in a good position to see how this works.

Construct Elaboration

The initial elaboration of the client's complaint, starting with our seven types of inquiry and continuing into further material, can be seen as an attempt to delineate the Repertory Grid by specifying event columns to serve as reference points for the constructs that must be holding the complaint in its present individual form. This gives the Grid greater horizontal breadth. But we shall soon be in a position to work the other way too. We can start inquiring about constructs. When we do this we shall be adding to the Grid's vertical dimension. This we must do if the events our client has described are to be understood psychologically.

The client said he sought comfort from his teachers from time to time. Do we think we know what this means as soon as it is stated as a fact? Suppose we ask him to construe it in relation to other things he has said. He says this seems like something quite different from running as a child to his mother; much more like playing the part of a man companion to his female peers. Using this same construct of frightened child versus man companion we look to see how it is applied to other events in his life. As he weaves it in and out among the facts of his daily living we can begin to understand what those facts amount to—what kind of individuality they have. Without knowing the client's personal construction of them we can understand them only in the terms we ourselves would have ascribed to them. This is not enough.

But there are other ways in which the client may construe his relations with his teachers. With each new construct dimension a new role is added to the Grid and the fabric of his construction system becomes clearer too. As it comes to be seen in multidimensional perspective it assumes individuality. But, as we have already indicated, for an event to assume individuality is not the same as becoming concretely unique. Thus, as new construct rows are added to the Grid and these constructs lace themselves through the client's complaint, there is increased possibility of dealing with the problem in new ways. A matter that can be seen from various angles can also be approached through various avenues, including new ones. This is what the client needs to see and do.

What Is Interpretation?

It should be clear by now that interpretation is more than a matter of pinning word labels on events, or even on constructs, though such labeling is often an important step in the psychotherapeutic process. Nor is interpretation simply a means of generalizing the client's perception of the events surrounding him or of the various behaviors that catch him unawares. It involves construing, and construing, as we tried to explain as clearly as we could in the first of these three papers, involves the attribution of similarity and differentiation both—equally and simultaneously. Similarity makes no sense unless it implies differentiation and differentiation makes no sense unless, in the very same terms, it implies similarities. Thus interpretation, in starting with construction, is much more than a simple matter of generalizing the client's perceptions of stimuli or his tendencies to make responses. For one thing, interpretation calls for new discriminations by the very same tokens. But it calls for other things too.

Proper interpretation requires the development of context—events against which the complaint can be compared and contrasted by one's constructs. In terms of the Repertory Grid, this means the addition of columns. It also may require some analysis of the complaint into constituent parts—expressing the complaint as several event columns, rather than as one column only. But we must go on from here. Event columns simply erected side-by-side contribute nothing to the understanding of each other unless they are construed—that is to say unless their likenesses and differences are formulated in several different dimensions. They must be related to each other by construct rows.

So the next step in interpretation is to construe the columns in terms of construct rows. But this still does not complete the process of interpretation. Only when new events are picked up in terms of constructs is the interpretative process fully expressed. In terms of our Grid model, this is to say that interpretation means getting over into the right hand quadrants by extending the construct rows. In terms of the clients, this means his application of ideas to new events of the sort he meets in daily life, or possibly, in some cases, to chronologically old events which, because they were once half-forgotten, now can serve as fresh elements for interpretation.

May I point out that technically, as the term is used by the more precise writers in the philosophy of science, such as Bertrand Russell, this is the proper meaning of "interpretation." The term is also used this way in the field of law. Only its imprecise use in the writings of psychotherapists and others has led us to think of it merely as an effort to set up generalizations by verbal means.

I am so eager to make this point clear that, at the risk of being monotonous, I want to say it again. In fact, if I fail to make the point clear, some of the things I want to say about the recall of half-forgotten experiences will fall flat. The psychotherapist and his client lay out the complaint as a column on the Grid. They then lay out other event columns, even though such columns may not at first appear to be particularly relevant to the complaint, or to offer any quick and easy way of alleviating the difficulty. Then they interweave the constructions, row upon row, to give the fabric texture. The columns, if left free-standing and independent of each other, serve little purpose. There must be constructs, too. But, eventually, after the fabric begins to assume body and patterns, the constructs are extended to fresh events and the client says, "Aha, we have been talking all this time about passivity, and I understood, of course, that this and that and the other things I have done have really been what we call 'passive.' But last night, let me tell you, I started to say something to my friends and there it was, just as clear as sin—passivity! I didn't have to tell myself it was 'passivity,' or wait until after it had happened in order to look back at it before I could see it as passivity. There it was. I was being passive—just like I have so many times. You don't have to tell me what passivity is any more, and I don't have to keep reminding myself, either. Believe me I know it now the instant it happens. And I feel that I would know the instant I was not being passive, too. Not only that, but 'passivity' isn't just a term to describe my behavior with; it is what I myself, do. It's the game I play whenever I get in a tight spot. I, entirely on my own, do things the passive way. How obvious it is! I don't have to think about it. I know it *when* I do it—when I'm *about* to do it—when I *set out* to do it—and not just afterwards when I back off and criticize myself, or when I come in here to talk to you."

Now, in terms of client remarks, this is interpretation par excellence! Indeed it is the kind of verbal discharge that is likely to brighten up a psychotherapist's whole weekend, especially when it appears in this kind of a client who has probably been engaging the therapist in a long winter's struggle. Certainly it is one thing to hash over things that have happened and to put them together in construct dimensions; but it is a fresh and exhilarating experience when genuine interpretative extension takes place and new events loom up in terms of the construct dimensions that have long been in the process of being worked out.

In terms of our Grid model, the upper left hand quadrant is routine, because it involves coming to know the client as he is; the upper right hand quadrant is discouraging, because it involves the extension of old constructs to events that deserve something better; the lower left hand quadrant is strenuous, because it requires seeing things in new lights that have long been firmly entrenched in old modes of thought; but the lower right hand quadrant is where the fun starts, because it involves facing new events with fresh ideas. This is the interpretative pay off.

This is interpretative extension, yes, but let me hasten to add that the psychotherapeutic process does not end with fourth quadrant extension of rows and columns. Only in the limited sense of interpretative extension does it end there. There was the validation cycle I talked about in the second of this series of papers. Constructs have to be tested by using them as wagers on the future. They may not pay off when so used. When they fail one must go back to his lower left hand quadrant and reconstrue the events that clutter up his life with confusion. Our client with the burst of insight may find that his notion of passivity still does not point as sharply to subsequent events as it should.

Interpretation in Reverse

We have said that interpretation proper starts with construing but is, properly speaking, a completed act only when a construction is applied to new elements. Or, to say it better, interpretative extension comes about when a new event makes its appearance in terms of a given construction. Seeing it in this way makes a difference. It means that the therapist does not think of his interpretative role so much as a matter of plying his client with words in order to set up new meanings as it is a matter of helping him find new experiences looming up in dawning light of new constructions. In fact, a reconstruction of events rarely takes proper hold in a client's mind until he has given it operational definition in terms of new events which, before the reconstruction, would probably have been overlooked altogether. Our client with the interpretation of "passivity," for example, would scarcely have had this insight if he had spent all his time going back over acts that were to be reconstrued as "passive." It was the fresh experience of last night, the one that emerged in the new light, that made the whole thing make sense.

Now let us see what goes on. It is a classic feature of psychotherapy that the client, during the course of the interviews, begins to recall events that he had long since put out of his mind. The psychoanalytic notion is that such buried facts have been stirring up trouble all the time and have to be brought to light in order to be neutralized. Of course, the psychoanalyst sees them this way. How else would one view such matters if he were implicitly committed to the stimulus-response paradigm?

But we have a different commitment. Because we do, the whole matter shapes up differently. The new constructs the client has been forming are indeed what make it possible for him to see things he had previously overlooked. And as he sees them in terms of the new construction, interpretation gives those constructs new roots. Where, then, does interpretation come from—from constructs being applied to new events, or from new events arising in recollection to meet the constructs that give them form? From both, I think!

So with dreams also. They also entwine themselves on the framework provided for them. It is sometimes a profitable exercise for the therapist, as he observes emerging constructs, to guess when the client will take advantage of the new structure to dream, and what such dreams will be about. This is not too difficult and the therapist can feel more certain of his understanding of his client when he finds he can make such predictions successfully. In fact, here is a little rule that I often propound to beginning therapists: When you can make discriminating predictions about what a client will do in the next interview, you can be more venturesome in the therapeutic effort; but when your predictions start to fail, play the game more conservatively. The dream that arises to meet the constructs set for it serves an extension function, among others, and anchors wavering constructs more securely. It thus stabilizes the client's new formulations, and no less the therapist's new formulations also. So with memories. So with behaviors, too. All serve client and therapist alike. Each of these teammates has his own grid. For each the new columns to which the construct rows are successfully extrapolated give greater length and precision to those construct rows.

Types of Therapeutic Content

Sometimes a client fills his hour with abstractions, analogies, explanations, and logical sequences. When he does this we say he is intellectualizing. Often, though not always, such a client seems to fit into the obsessive-compulsive category. In terms of our Grid, we can see this as an effort to build construct rows without adding columns. Some columns, of course, have to appear. But for the most part they are used over and over. Perhaps the columns mentioned are anecdotal citations of past events, each of which is interpreted as a single instance intercepting the given construct row and not having any depth in terms of other construct dimensions. Thus the instance serves only to anchor the single construct being talked about. Because it is not adequately woven into the Grid, it gives the therapist little more than a superficial notion of what the client's interpretative extension means.

Sometimes the intellectualizer insists on limiting his events to those which are remote or hypothetical, and attempts to explain his constructs in terms of such safe material. Again, this serves the same purpose—it makes sure that the event columns will not be seen in depth; instead, will be seen only as the columnar intercepts of a few constructs.

When the psychotherapist envisions his interpretative job as one of supplying authentic verbal generalizations for his client's experiences, he is likely to fall into the intellectualizer's trap. Sometimes in demanding that the client get down to bedrock experiences he finds that there is a lack of properly extended structure to contain such experiences adequately and that the client becomes threatened or anxious as a result of the therapist's demands. The intellectualizing client may desperately need some kind of structure, erected on neutral grounds and made available for his coming emergencies, before he dares plunge into chaotic material. So, from the standpoint of personal construct theory, intellectualizing is essentially a failure to make an adequate interpretative extension and yet it is occasionally a useful kind of preliminary to more comprehensive interpretation.

Now take the other kind of problem—the client who cites events but never strings them together. Or better still, take the client who creates events in the therapy room and elsewhere—who "acts out." This is a dilational kind of enterprise. He adds columns upon columns to his Grid without knitting them together adequately with constructs. In his way, he is engaging in extensional analysis—applying his notions to new events. But the interpretations are unidimensional and prevent him from putting his events into perspective.

Here again, instead of saying merely that the client's acting out tendencies should be squelched in the therapy room, it is often profitable to accept or even to develop them in a controlled manner. Role play is an example of the frank utilization of acting out. It has its place, too.

Sometimes the effort to add columns to the Grid without providing adequate row structure takes the form of an endless citation of anecdotes. This may be a genuine effort to recall something important. The client who does this sort of thing often thinks of the events as autonomous determiners of what has happened to him. If he were a personal construct psychologist, he would not, of course, make this mistake. Yet even the anecdotalist, in a limited way, is interpreting. It is up to the therapist to help him extend more of his construct rows to the new material he cites, and thus give him a better idea of what is worth talking about when he comes for his hour of therapy.

What Can the Therapist Say?

There are some who believe that a catalog of a therapist's remarks will identify the school of thought to which he belongs. In some cases this is true. Both psychoanalysis and non-directivism are clinically derived theories and, as such, they started out as techniques. Later they assumed the proportions of methodologies, then of personality theories, and finally of positions in social philosophy. Because of their origins and the kinds of protests they represented it is possible, to some degree, to identify them in terms of the isolated therapeutic remarks of their exponents.

Personal construct theory, on the other hand, represents an attempt at the outset to meet both the requirements of the clinical situation and of scientific methodology. It does this partly by noting the parallels between the problems of the researcher and of the client. It attempts to comprehend them both as human beings relying upon basic psychological method common to all human beings. What the therapist says, then, is limited only by what can profitably be said by anyone in the various stages of his explorations into the ways of life.

By starting out in this way personal construct theory offers wide latitude in the techniques used, probably wider than does any other systematic position. The personal construct therapist envisions his task as comprising various objectives and stages. What he says and does by way of interpretation, or by way of any other psychotherapeutic effort, depends on the objectives he envisions for his particular client and the stage he envisions their team enterprise to be in at the moment.

I have already said that the first job in a psychotherapeutic series is usually the partial elaboration of the complaint. I suggested seven types of questions, and then went on to show how the kind of material they might elicit could be structured in terms of the Repertory Grid. I talked of adding columns by eliciting facts and "acting out" behaviors and I talked of adding rows by linking and discriminating between such facts and behaviors. This weaving of warp and woof helps both client and therapist tie events together with constructs and, in turn, anchors constructs in palpable facts.

In simplest terms, then, what the psychotherapist does is try to bring into the therapy room either one or the other of two kinds of things; events or constructs. The events can be either old or new, and so can the constructs. Eventually, of course, the therapist will be interested primarily in new events and constructs; that is to say, events that will be different because of the new construction that is laid for them, and constructs that derive their novel meaning from fresh everyday experiences.

But the therapist can go too far in one direction, if he is not careful. Take the complaint. By elaborating events related to the complaint in great detail the therapist may find that both he and the client have more factual material laid out on the table between them than either is prepared to handle. There are two alternatives. One can ask for material that seems more remote and hence, possibly, better woven with constructs, or he can attempt to hold the troublesome material together with constructs, often temporary ones. The anxious client caught up in a welter of feelings and experiences that he can not tie together can often be helped temporarily by construing the likenesses and differences between these events in several different construct dimensions.

In the first instance the therapist may say something like this: "What you have been telling me is important and it is something we shall want to talk about after you know me better and after we have got a better idea of how such problems can be handled. But, for the present, let us hold off until we have some other facts in hand. Now, for example, suppose you tell me about—." This, as can be seen, is a matter of turning to other events.

In the second instance, when it is a matter of tying things together in order to keep them from flapping around and causing damage, one may say something like this: "Now before you tell me any more about your experiences and how you feel, let us see something of what we can make out of just these few things you have told me. We may change our minds later, but let us see if we can fit these things together temporarily. You mentioned A… and B…. Just what was it that made these two seem alike to you? …And C…, was that alike in the same way, or did it have a different quality to it? …And now let us see if we can put these together or set them apart in some other way."

Sometimes it seems the client at first can respond only by wailing about still other events. The therapist can either ask the client to come back to the question, or he can say, for example: "You have gone on to tell me about still another thing that happened. Is this related to what you had told me before? … How? … But is it not different in some ways, too?"

These are not, of course, the only kinds of remarks the therapist can make when the client appears to be bogging down in the facts of life. The kinds of remarks I have mentioned are those which have a direct bearing on interpretation—the particular topic of this series. There are, it should be pointed out, other relevant kinds of therapeutic intervention. There are, for example, acceptance remarks. In personal construct theory acceptance is construed as the readiness to see matters through the client's eyes, not necessarily to agree with him or to disagree, but to try to see what he sees. The therapist may or may not do it well, but he tries, and to the extent that he tries, he is accepting. Acceptance, then, is an experience of the therapist, not necessarily a type of verbal exchange.

The therapist may attempt to communicate acceptance by making such remarks as, "I see," "Of course," "You really felt …, didn't you." He may reflect those statements of the client that are particularly personal or are particularly unstructured, and thus show his effort to understand what most of the client's associates would let pass by as incomprehensible. He may even say, "I don't understand. Would you go back and help me understand better how you feel about …?" Even this is an accepting remark if it is not used as a preliminary to rejection of what the client has tried to express.

There are also other types of remarks the therapist may make—reassuring remarks, supportive remarks, validating remarks—but here we are concerned primarily with the function of interpretation in psychotherapy, and the many other kinds of things that go on, even though related to interpretation, are not within the scope of these three papers.

Can the Therapist Offer Interpretations of His Own?

Yes, indeed! The client and the therapist should establish themselves as a team, and it is as appropriate for one of them to suggest an interpretation of what has been said as it is for the other. If this cannot be done successfully it suggests that they have failed to work out a team relationship.

Perhaps this is as good a place as any to point out that personal construct theory views man as a dependent being. He achieves independence, not by ceasing to be dependent, but by structuring his dependencies—learning how to discriminate between them and how to allocate them appropriately. The psychotherapeutic team concept takes into account this notion of differentiated dependency. This client depends upon the therapist, wholistically, perhaps, at first, and then with increasing discrimination. The therapist perceptively depends upon the client for the successful outcome of the therapeutic venture. Eventually the team ceases to exist as a proximate unit. That can happen at the proper time because the client has learned how to allocate his dependencies among the normal facilities of his life and the therapist, supposedly, already knew how before he became a therapist.

There is another point in understanding how it is that the therapist can offer interpretations of his own. As I have already pointed out, personal construct theory does not take the naive realist's position that facts carry their interpretations written on their backs. The therapist, even though he is well trained and knows a lot about successful ways to interpret the client's experiences, should not reckon that he has the ultimate word of truth about such matters. His notions, as well as those of the client, are open to reconstruction. He, too, is a seeker after valid ways of anticipating events. He sees psychotherapy, not as a way of getting his client to see things the way he himself does, but as a research exploration in which both of them engage as a team. What he has to offer by way of reinterpretations, then, are just as much experimental hypotheses as such offerings would be in any other kind of scientific team enterprise. They need to be seen as such by both members of the team and, no less importantly, dealt with as such. In the light of personal construct theory this is how the human enterprise works.

Personal construct theory, following the scientific paradigm, emphasizes the testing of construct hypotheses in terms of their utility in forecasting future events. So should therapy. Personal construct theory, continuing to follow the scientific paradigm, emphasizes the reformulation of construct hypotheses in the light of the success or the failure of the predictions they dictate. So should therapy. Whatever the therapist, or his client, suggests as a possible construction to be placed upon the events of life, needs to be tried out—indeed, will be tried out—as grounds for prediction. Its fate should rest on its ability to produce valid predictions, not on the prestige or acumen of the person who utters the interpretation.

This view of psychotherapy in general, and of the function of interpretation in particular, is at variance with the whole notion of medical practice and of psychotherapy as a form of applied psychology. What happens in the therapy room is no less an ontological venture than what happens in the laboratory. It has to do with the nature of being itself. It is subject to the same tests of substance that we must inevitably apply to any human venture into the realm of what is unknown and unrealized. It is a matter of practicing psychology, or of applying psychological laws discovered in the pure atmosphere of the laboratory. Psychotherapeutic inquiry *is* psychological inquiry. The therapy room *is* a laboratory.

So the therapist offers interpretations whenever it appears that the team is ready to experiment with them. They are not offered as pronouncements of oracular truth, but as working hypotheses about which facts can be assembled and in terms of which predictions can be made and tested. The client who accepts his therapist's constructs in this way is not as likely to be upset by them, nor is he as likely to be led astray by his therapist's inevitable mistakes.

Often the therapist's reinterpretation can be prefaced by such phrases as, "What do you suppose would happen if … ?" or he may say, "If you had thought of it as …, how would it have turned out?" "Suppose you were to look at it this way next time." "Now tell me if this fits in any way." "Suppose, for the moment, we try looking at it this way."

Pursuing the Client's Interpretations

The client member of the psychotherapeutic team also formulates hypotheses. At first he may not see them so much as hypotheses subject to test as realities to be removed or resisted. But the therapist can help structure the client's constructs as hypotheses, thereby applying the principle of constructive alternativism, just as his own suggestions are structured as hypotheses. He may say, "Now what you have described is a way of looking at things. We know that there are many ways of looking at things; this happens to be yours at the moment. Now let us see how it works out, what this way of seeing things would lead one to expect. For example, from this point of view, one thing we would expect to happen would be …. Let's see if it does."

Sometimes the therapist helps the client piece together a number of constructs in order to understand their general directionality. He may say, "You said that A … and B … were both 'Alphas'. C … was not. Do 'Alpha' and 'Beta' add to about the same thing as far as you are concerned? Do you suppose we could check this out and see if this is the way it works?"

Sometimes the therapist invites reinterpretation by some such remark as, "Let's pull this whole business apart and see if we can look at it from an entirely different angle. It may not work, but whether it works or not is not as important as seeing just what happens when we deal with it a different way." In this way, even somewhat preposterous interpretations are invited and the client may arrive at what is even more important than a "right" interpretation—the fact that when matters are seen in different ways they turn out differently. In fact, from the standpoint of personal construct theory, the formulation and testing of "wrong" hypotheses is just as important as stumbling across "right" ones. After all, the task of therapy is not merely to supply the client with a bag full of "right" answers, but rather to teach him how to test and revise his constructs, even the ones he has not yet thought of.

Inviting Reinterpretations

Often the most effective way of achieving reinterpretation is by laying events out side-by-side. The basic formula is expressed by such phrases as, "You mentioned A …, and then you talked about B …, and then about C …. What is the connection?" Or, "If you had wanted A …, then it would have meant that you would B … and …." "This reminds me of what you said about A …."

There is a principle that plays a part in psychotherapeutic discourse. It is often helpful for the therapist to apply it. *The client may readily change the topic, but he rarely changes the theme.* The therapist who is aware of this principle is not so likely to dismiss his client's topical meanderings as "resistance." In fact, the shift of context may be precisely what the therapist needs to separate out the theme from the interesting "material" the client has brought to the interview.

Now this principle can be applied in reverse. By laying different topics down side by side the client also may be able to pick up a new theme that otherwise might be overlooked. Often this can be accomplished without using words to express the relationship. The mere fact that the client has examined certain events in context with each other may give him the beginnings of an interpretation, although he may find no words for the relationships he has begun to see. In fact, it is often better not to try to force words upon the relationships invited by the new display. If the client himself later suggests words or brings up similar material in context, either in free association or in dreams, the therapist may be assured that the reinterpretation has taken some kind of root.

Loosening of Conceptualization

Let me mention very briefly something that is closely related to the reinterpretative art—the *Creativity Cycle*. Some people's thinking is loose; that is to say, what is seen one way at one moment appears to be seen another way at the next. This wavering characteristic is likely to be observed in thinking that is poorly or strangely symbolized, and it is characteristic of certain types of schizophrenic thinking. It is also characteristic of one's dreams. In fact, for a client to be able to report his dreams at all requires him to loosen up his thinking, a task that he may find hard to accept.

Out of such loosened ideation it is possible to shape up preposterously novel concepts. But the shaping up requires one to pull himself together and think tightly about what has just come to mind. And if the new idea is tightened up enough it may be put to test and its validity determined. Thus the Creativity Cycle calls for a broad span of thinking, starting with what is conceptually loose and swinging over to what is conceptually tight and testable.

Many of the psychotherapeutic techniques are designed to aid the loosening process. Especially is this so of psychoanalysis which emphasizes dream recall, vague free association, phantasy, disconnected statements, etc. But the person who goes loose and cannot come back up with some of the ideas in his grasp and ready to be tightened is likely to be disturbed by this psychoanalytic effort. He may become more schizophrenic than he was before. In fact, the schizophrenic hazard is the principal one faced by the psychoanalyst.

It is for the psychotherapist to judge how far into the loosening phase of the Creativity Cycle he may properly ask his client to go in his effort to find reinterpretations of his circumstances. Certainly he should never ask his client to overreach himself. Always he should make sure that the cyclical swing back to tightened construction takes place. Loose construction cannot be tested; tight construction can. Yet tight construction has its hazard too, for it often leaves the person with the feeling that he has no alternatives when he finds his precise formulations do not work out.

Conclusion

These three papers on the role of interpretation in psychotherapy have attempted to show how a novel epistemological position will affect not only one's theorizing about the human personality, but how also it has implications for the way reinterpretation functions in the therapy room. It is quite possible and thoroughly reasonable for a personal construct approach to psychology to lend itself to the requirements of empirical science. Indeed, if the notion of science is taken seriously as a refinement of the psychology of man, something like the psychology of personal constructs is a natural consequence. Moreover, such a notion extends from the experimental laboratory to that special kind of a laboratory we call the therapy room. It makes the therapist and his client teammates in a scientific venture, just as a graduate student and his dissertation directors are teammates. It turns interpretations into testable hypotheses, rather than letting them remain as authoritative dicta. It enables the therapist either to stop sitting on his hands or to stop twirling his Sigma Xi key, whichever of the two it is he has been doing. In short, it admits mankind to the mysteries of scientific endeavor.

70

Is Treatment a Good Idea?[1]

"Is treatment a good idea?" When one poses a question like this to an audience like this—an audience dedicated to the mission of treating patients—he opens himself immediately to one of three charges: Perhaps he has nothing more to offer than the traditional answer and everyone hopes he will sit down as soon as he has said what he has to say. If not that, he must be a diehard hereditarian who doesn't think crazy people can be helped and who is optimistic enough to think that his pessimism will be listened to. Or, perhaps, he is merely employing a speech-maker's sensationalism in order to get folks to listen to what otherwise is going to be a very dull talk.

Now let me say at the outset that I do not want to be placed into any of these categories. What I have posed is an honest question that I believe is worth examining carefully. Moreover, to show my good faith and make clear that I am not merely dangling a question in front of you in order to make you keep your eyes open, let me say at the outset that my answer to this question is going to be "no." "No, treatment is not a good idea."

Now, will you examine, along with me, the notion of treatment itself—what it means—what it implies about the nature of man—and, in addition, some of the serious mistakes the idea of treatment has led us to make. I am inviting you to do this because I am convinced that a re-examination of the concept of treatment will have a salutary effect on what we all do as professional people.

First of all, I would like to say that, along with most of you, I still think it is good for people who are sick to get well. In addition, I still think there are things each of us can do to help them get well. And I think some of those things are already being done here and there—not as often as they should be, perhaps, and maybe only in the out-of-the-way corners of hospitals and clinics, but still they are being done. Sometimes they are done by professional or administrative intent, and sometimes, you all would agree, in spite of it.

During the past century the notions of modern science have been extended to the realm of human behavior. One of those notions is that everything that happens can be explained in terms of what preceded it. More particularly, this means that if we know everything that is going on today we can put it together and tell exactly what will happen tomorrow. Of course, in a down-to-earth practical sense, it is impossible to know absolutely everything that is going on today. Besides, as some scientists have recently argued, even if today's events are known, their consequences can be predicted only probabilistically. But I am not here concerned with either of these two interesting reservations on scientific reasoning. What I am concerned about is the effect such reasoning has on the human enterprise, particularly when the human enterprise begins to involve itself with the alteration of human behavior.

Most psychologists, when they try to think scientifically about human behavior, boil it down to two notions—something that goes on independently of the person, usually outside his skin, and something he does which is attributable to that outside event. The former the psychologist calls a "stimulus" and the latter, once he has invoked the notion of "stimulus" the psychologist has no choice but to call a "response".

This little solipsistic invention of "stimulus and response" underlies the major portion of psychology's scientific efforts to figure out what people are up to. While these efforts have by no means proved futile, the reasoning upon which they are based forces a strong bias on what men try to do for each other. If a person's behavior is faulty, change the stimulus—change the stimulus, for are not his responses attributable to events which preceded them? Once we start to think this way the net result is inevitably to focus our attention upon the treatment rather than upon the person who is in trouble, as if something inherent in the treatment itself carries the seeds that will sprout into behavior.

Let us approach treatment from another angle. Suppose, instead of abstracting the constructs of "stimulus" and "response," we talk about persons in "dynamic" terms. In psychiatric circles this is supposed to be good and if you are wise you will always be careful to use such language in the presence of properly educated people, unless you happen to be one of those poor benighted creatures known as a "state hospital" psychiatrist. It has for some time been a matter of interest to me why it is that people who can afford to pay private fees always have "dynamics,"

[1] Address to a Conference on Treatment, U. S. Veterans Administration Hospital, Sheridan, WY, 1958. Published in Howard, A. R. (Ed.). (1959), *Therapeutic roles in patient treatment* (pp. 20–25). Veterans Administration Hospital. Republished in *Constructs (The Newsletter of the Centre for Personal Construct Psychology)*, 1983, 2(2), 1–3. Republished in Fransella, F. (Ed.), (2003), *International handbook of personal construct psychology* (pp. 233–236). Wiley. Published here by permission of Nick Reed and Wiley.

Collected Papers of the Pioneer of Constructivist Psychology: George A. Kelly, First Edition. Edited by David A. Winter and Nick Reed.

while those who can't have "diagnoses." I have observed also that the more fees you can afford to pay the more dynamics you are likely to have. But, then, this is not what I came here to talk about.

Dynamic interpretations explain human behavior in terms of such notions as motives, needs, and incentives, or, if you have invested in the Freudian lexicon, in terms of such artistic inventions as Oedipal strivings, hostility, libidinal cathexes, etc. While, as a model of human thought, this is more primitive than the stimulus-response model—in fact, if the truth is to be known, even more primitive than Aristotelean thinking—it does provide certain advantages over its competitors. For example, the dynamic model envisions the determinants of human behavior as residing within the person, a more helpful way of looking at the matter if you hope to see him accomplish anything.

Treatment, under the aegis of dynamic thinking, becomes a matter of uncovering psychological forces and mechanisms, of venting pent-up impulses, of supporting some self-critical evaluations and undermining others, and various other interventions in the turmoil of the person's psyche. But still, even under this system of thought, the determinants of behavior, while now residing within the person, are abstracted from him as extra-personal entities and not altogether his own doings. Treatment continues to be undertaken as something imposed from without—something done to juggle the patient's dynamics. The person is still a "patient" with all the inert passivity that that unfortunate term has implied throughout its long history.

May I approach my thesis from still another angle. Mankind has a long history of intolerance and brutality. Over the centuries this history has been unfolding itself alongside an equally impressive story of expanding humanitarianism. For a long time it has been firmly believed that when a person went off his rocker he should first be given loving admonishment, and if that did not work he should be punished good.

In the meantime, medical science had made great progress in treating illness. Naturally enough it occurred to some physicians like Pinel that it might be better to treat certain kinds of misbehavior as if they were symptoms of illness rather than outcroppings of devilment. This way of thinking has led to the employment of far more humane methods of dealing with certain people. Incidentally, it has served to create an enormous paradox in our system of social thought; some people get solicitous treatment for their misbehavior while others, judged to be ineligible, get punishment measured out to them. Thus we try to live under two quite different and quite incompatible psychological systems for explaining human behavior and for deciding what we ought to do about misbehavior.

Treatment, of course, seems to hold more promise than punishment. It seems more civilized to say that a person is ill than to say he is bad. But illness implies that a person is acted upon by forces over which he has no control and that therefore the corrective measures must likewise be provided by an external agency. By this line of reasoning any person who finds he has done something he shouldn't is constrained to start looking for someone who will treat him. Of course, while he is waiting for the doctor to come he may apply a little first aid, such as figuring out how it happened his mother—the witch—made him into the kind of a person he turned out to be. He won't get far with this on his own, of course, because it requires some pretty time-consuming rationalization, and some kind of treatment, at least in the big cities nowadays, is not likely to be long in arriving.

Now what has all this to do with the topic of this symposium: "Therapeutic Roles in Patient Treatment." As you have probably already guessed I am for assigning the most important role to the patient himself—only, I would prefer not to call him a "patient." This means developing a kind of psychology that is not especially popular these days, a psychology that envisions human behavior as something initiated by the person who does the behaving. As I see it, such a psychology would have to abandon such notions as "stimulus" and "response" as well as a lot of psychodynamic constructs, at least abandon those uses of psychodynamic constructs that imply that the determinants of human behavior are independent operants within the psyche. Personally, I would just plain throw them all out, but I would be willing to settle for a compromise if psychodynamic concepts were used differently.

Something else follows from this line of thought. From our present vantage point in the course of human thinking it now seems to be a historical misfortune that psychological problems were ever placed in the medical context of illness. That twentieth century institution which has emerged as "the hospital" is so conceived, organized, and committed that it represents altogether too much that is unwholesome for the troubled mind. The societal structure of a hospital typically illustrates nearly all of those features which enlightened mankind seeks to reform—a rigid class structure stratifying both staff and patients, listlessness, futility, anonymity, loss of family and community relationships, irrational authoritarianism, regimentation, economic helplessness, endless waiting for something to happen, and passive conformity to what the straw boss says is "good for you," to mention only a few.

Most of what I have said thus far will seem negative and destructive. If treatment is such an inappropriate idea what then, one may well ask, are the roles that are to be played by those who want to help? Certainly one thing becomes clear about such roles: they are to be played out as person-in-relation-to-person roles rather than as specialist-in-relation-to-illness roles. The primary question to answer about a staff member is what do disturbed persons do with him. His area and degree of competence, when the chips are down, are operationally defined not so much by his education and list of former job incumbencies as by the practical uses to which he is put by those who need his help.

Mankind's approaches to its psychological problems are in for some drastic revision. The notion of treatment, derived as it is from our fumbling efforts to apply notions of scientific determinism to human troubles, misplaces the emphasis on the various external roles to be played. But restoration of the wholesome life is something done by the person whose life it is. His, then, is the principal role, and any system of psychological thought which envisions other roles as more important than his will serve only to stagnate mankind's efforts and turn out, for somebody to take care of, a generation of helpless creatures who seek "treatment" every time they slip up, rather than doing something about it themselves.

71

Suicide: The Personal Construct Point of View[1]

Personal construct theory assumes that life's vicissitudes do not thrust their singular meanings upon us; rather that it is we ourselves who must contrive to make sense out of whatever happens. If there seems to be genuine singularity in life's meanings, it stems primarily from the singularity of our own thinking. The events, on their part, never cease to be open to a host of alternative constructions.

Truth as a Human Invention

From this point of view human truth is never something discovered and wrapped up to keep; it is always invented and subject to day-by-day improvement. All that is discovered is some practical consistency between one's anticipations and their apparent outcomes. It runs like this: We invent a meaning. We impose it upon some events that happen in our immediate vicinity. This is fun, and we are often content to stop at this point. But if we have a skeptical streak in us and want to test validity, as well as enjoy the ecstasies of appreciation, we use our meaning to make a flat prediction; and then we stand back to see what happens.

Testing Truth by Making Predictions

A series of successful predictions is likely to lead us to believe, though not always, that our meaning has a substance all its own. We may even forget how it was derived and claim that we ran across it one day, quite by accident, lurking amid the predicted events. Yet, as a plain matter of fact, all that we ought to say is that what happened looked enough like what we expected to happen to satisfy our sense of similarity. And, as for the degree of truth to be credited to our invention, the safest thing to say is simply "so far, so good."

The matching of predictions against outcome is the essential feature of scientific method. More specifically, the method involves the generation of hypotheses out of theory or prior observations, conceptualization or abstraction, occasional experimental manipulations (controls) in order to maximize or minimize certain variations in events, explicit predictions, observation of outcomes at as low a conceptual level as possible (objectivity), reconciliation of predictions with outcomes, revision of constructs, and continual repetition of part or all of the cycle. One way of stating it is to say that science requires the reconciliation of predictive principles, abstracted at as high a conceptual level as possible, with concrete outcomes, identified at as low a conceptual level as possible.

As we see it, science is but a special case of human enterprise, and scientific method is but a special instance of human psychological method. Personal construct theory is an effort to get at the heart of the matter by stating the general case for human psychological method. If personal construct theory succeeds, its full statement will embrace the whole range of human psychological effort, from scientific progress, on the one hand, to existentialistic anguish, on the other.

Validation

If we look at man as an inventor of truths or, perhaps better, as a construer of events, we are bound to wonder if this means that he has any obligations except to his own whims. Or do the hard facts of life occasionally intervene to bring him back to his senses? From the position of personal construct theory we would argue that the facts never intervene. Perhaps we had better say that the *events* never intervene, since we are talking about raw reality.

[1] First published as Kelly, G.A. (1961). Suicide: The personal construct point of view. In N.L. Farberow & E.S. Schneidman (Eds.), *The cry for help* (pp. 255–280). McGraw-Hill. Republished by permission of McGraw-Hill, who hold the copyright.

Collected Papers of the Pioneer of Constructivist Psychology: George A. Kelly, First Edition. Edited by David A. Winter and Nick Reed.

It is the person himself who intervenes on behalf of reality. He makes his prediction of things he expects to happen. This has to be based on relatively high levels of abstraction. When he sees what actually does happen, according to his own lights, of course, he has something at hand that he can perceive at a relatively low level of abstraction. Now he can *validate* his construction of events. If what appeared to happen seems to be inconsistent with what he expected, he usually concludes that his expectations were at fault and sets about to correct them. Thus he checks his thinking against reality. But this validation is of his own doing. Reality, itself, goes its own way, oblivious, and lets him fret as he pleases over his ability to predict it.

What Truths Did A. S. Invent?

When we undertake to base a psychological theory on this kind of logic, interesting things begin to happen. Take the biographical events in the life of A. S. Under such theorizing, these events—the actual events—suddenly loom up not as themselves forces molding the outlook of the young man but as the grounds he used for the meanings he invented and as the outcomes against which, over the years, he must so often have checked his anticipations. The recollections he reported to his interviewer, recollections that presumably paralleled certain actual occurrences, were the verbalizable explications that most readily came to mind in his effort to lend verisimilitude to what he now felt and believed.

The events he described were important not because of what they did to him but because of what he had made out of them and what he was then making out of them. Always it was he who invented the meanings, whether verbalized or unverbalized. From such personalized constructs he projected his versions of what was about to happen next. Always he altered his own course to fit, right up to the very last.

Suicide as a Validating Act

It is often helpful to strip human behavior of pathological interpretations. Health and illness are exceedingly prejudicial terms, and more often than not, when we use them, we succeed only in beclouding the relevant issues. It is much more enlightening to look at any human act in terms of how and what it fits and the ends it accomplishes.

Take suicide, for example. Instead of treating it as something evil, pathological, or nonsensical, we can understand it far better if we look at the act itself and what it accomplishes from the point of view of the person who performs it.

Death as an Implicit Choice in Everyday Life

Suppose we examine suicide first in the context of a basic question about death. Let us state it this way: Under what conditions of outlook would anyone seek death rather than life? By stating our question in this manner, we shall be inquiring after a psychological principle rather than a simple situational determinant.

Certainly it is not so unusual for persons to stack their cards in favor of death. Some do it for a social cause. Some do it because it is expected of them, as in battle. Some do it for fun, as on the highway. Some do it to avoid the guilt of being a few minutes late for an appointment. Some do it in sheer exasperation. Some do it in beautiful resignation. Mothers often risk their lives to bear children, and it is not uncommon to find both parents risking their health, and lives, to support those children in competitive luxury. Indeed, if one looks around him, he can see lives being sacrificed on every hand, and for little reasons as well as for big ones.

Socrates, according to the political logic of his time, had his choice between conceding his error in order to bargain with the court in the matter of his sentence or reaffirming his convictions intact by voluntarily taking his own life. If he accepted the verdict of guilt in order to save his skin, it meant that he had been talking through his hat. He could then no longer live as if truth were his principal pursuit. If he drank the hemlock, it meant that he still was reaching into the future for truth and that others were invited to dedicate their lives to the same quest. And they did. His choice was to validate what he had taught, and thus to validate the life he had lived. Would we otherwise have had a Plato, followed by an Aristotle? Was not Socrates' suicide, in the light of these great lives that followed, an act of sublime anticipation?

Jesus, who undoubtedly was greatly influenced by Socrates' example, validated his life in much the same way. It appears that he too could have avoided what happened to him. Yet he deliberately made up his mind to accept crucifixion. To do so seemed to him altogether necessary if he was to make it perfectly clear that the way he lived was more vital than the mere fact of personal survival. Thus he, like Socrates, invited death to validate his life. He is consistently reported by his biographers to have put the general proposition this way: "For whoever wants to preserve his life will lose it, and whoever loses his life for me will preserve it. What good does it do a man to gain the whole world and lose or forfeit himself?"

Socrates and Jesus certainly are not unique in their use of death to validate the essentials of their lives. Thousands upon thousands of others, in all the succeeding centuries, have used death in the same way. They, too, have seen their concluding acts as the natural outcomes of their convictions, expressed under the circumstances in which they found themselves.

When Is It Suicide?

Probably, when it comes right down to it, we are apt to say that a person has committed a mere suicide, rather than performed a dedicated act, when it seems clear by our own lights that the problem he faced had a better solution. We think *we* would have known better. Perhaps so. Nevertheless, the fact remains that none of the alternatives that beckon so clearly in our own minds was quite so visible in his. So the suicide makes *his* choice, and not *ours*. We say it was a bad one? We are possibly right; it might have been a "bad" choice. But that does not tell us much. To understand his act we need to know what he died for. What personal constructions of life and truth, what anticipations formulated from his structured world seemed to be validated by so drastic an act.

In a broad sense, each of us gives his life for something, something noble or something ignoble, though mostly something in between. Some do it decisively in one abrupt and frightening gesture. Some do it slowly and unobtrusively, sacrificing themselves little by little. Some face death outright; others stumble in its general direction. To seek to die well is an object of the full life, and those who fail to live well never succeed in finding anything worth dying for. Thus life and death can be made to fit together, each as the validator of the other.

What Was There in A. S.'s Life That Was Worth Dying For?

Shall we not look at A. S.'s suicidal attempt in these validational terms? What was it his effort appeared to validate? There is no indication that he was ever asked this question in any of its forms. Apparently the event was interpreted clinically from the outset as an incident in some way characteristic or inevitable in his style of life.

But if we are to employ the style-of-life paradigm, where do we look for the style?; in the bare record of events?; in deviations from the way we ourselves would have dealt with such events if we had been in A. S.'s shoes?; or do we look for deviations from the way we think "normal" persons would have handled such events? Perhaps, in place of style, we would prefer to look for some alien psychopathology or disease process that invaded this young man's psyche. Since personal construct theory leads us to deal with A. S.'s problems in terms quite different from any of these, and thus to ponder over questions never put to him, we shall have to be content only to speculate about what it was his act sought to validate or at most to make precarious inferences from the slimmest of available evidence.

Two Limiting Conditions: Realism and Indeterminacy

We have seen how a suicidal attempt can be regarded as an act designed to validate one's life. As such, it is a bid to extend life rather than actually terminate it; to extend its essential meaning, that is. But there are two conditions of personal construction under which the actual abandonment of one's life seems like the sensible thing to do. The first is when the course of events seems so obvious that there is no point in waiting around for the outcome. The score has become so lopsided there is no reason to stay through to the end of the game. The other is when everything seems so utterly unpredictable that the only definite thing one can do is abandon the scene altogether. It has ceased to be a game with perceptible rules.

The former condition is one where realism has been carried to its ultimate conclusion: fatalism. Suicidal attempts under this condition are often successful. The latter is the condition of total anxiety, and the suicidal attempt, not so often successful in this instance, is a desperate bid for some kind, any kind, of certainty. It is indeed striking that these should be the two limiting conditions for the sustenance of life; on the one hand, the sense of knowing everything worth knowing and, on the other, knowing nothing worth knowing. Yet, since the very essence of life is the use of the present to bridge the past with the future, any construction that makes such an undertaking futile serves psychologically to destroy life. Once this destruction has already taken place, the question of whether the person keeps on breathing or not becomes a side issue. Psychologically he is already dead.

To be sure, there are other considerations that contribute to the psychological understanding of suicide, hostility, impulsivity, guilt, etc., but these we can treat as secondary matters. Before we take up some of these other theoretical constructs, let us speculate on how the two limiting conditions of realism and indeterminacy might have affected A. S.

What Did A. S.'s Personal Construct System Lead Him to Expect?

In any effort to understand a suicidal attempt we look first to see what we can learn about the personal construct system of the person involved. Did A. S. see himself in the clutches of fate, or was he so hopelessly uncertain about what was to become of him that any kind of certainty seemed better than utter chaos? If his attempt was an effort to abandon his life, rather than validate something in it, which of the two life-destroying constructions did he employ?

We have said that A. S.'s personal constructs served to project his day-to-day anticipations. That is the basic assumption of personal construct theory. Pursuant upon these anticipations there were undoubtedly some rude discoveries—a whole succession of them. But did they confirm his worst expectations and thus lead him to realistic despair? Or did they continually confound him and thus leave him overwhelmed with uncertainty?

In either case he might have been challenged by the outcomes to devise new meanings and so to come to grips with life. But in this he seems to have failed, although there is some possibility that he tried to find new meanings in his study of sociology during the few weeks between leaving the Army and making his trip to South America. In any event, he at last made his ultimate bid for certainty, whether to foil his fate or to forge it with his own hand. But, as chance would have it, even this dismal prediction was to fail to materialize. Or did it? The reported interviews give no clear clue as to what he really expected to happen.

So let us say that it was not the events of his life that led A. S. to the crossroads. He arrived there as the result of a series of perceived relationships; relationships between what he was able to construe and predict, on the one hand, and what he discovered was happening, on the other. It was the result of how little he was able to reconstrue after the outcomes of all his earlier expectations became apparent.

Whether life, up to this point, had treated A. S. well or not is quite beside the point. Even the question of reinforcements in his series of learning trials is not an issue. Indeed, such a line of reasoning would probably lead us to the logical conclusion that he could not possibly have done what he did. What is important is his personal construction of the world about him and the fact that the sequence of events appeared either to invest that construction with inexorable validity or to threaten its utter collapse. There could even have been some of both features.

For him the decision to commit suicide was, at that moment in the cheap hotel room, the most obvious thing to do. Of course, he may have thought otherwise later. What matters here, as in all psychological problems, is that one's personal constructions at the time of decision seem so completely dictated by the obvious that there are no practical alternatives left to explore.

Well-Known Words that Vanish

Learning and Reinforcement

Perhaps it would be helpful to mention some of the conventional psychological notions that one soon abandons along the way when one sets out to pursue the implications of personal construct theory. It is already clear that *biographical events* are not seen as having any meaning, except as meaning is imposed upon them, as in the case of A. S.'s biography and the personal meanings he must have imposed. So *reinforcement*, as a construct, must be abandoned also. In some respects *validation* in personal construct theory takes the place of *reinforcement*, although it is a construct of quite a different order. *Validation* is the relationship one senses between anticipation and realization, whereas in conventional theory *reinforcement* is a value property attributed to an event. Even *learning* as a construct gets sloughed off, partly because it has become so badly cluttered with ambiguous meanings and partly because there seems to be no segment of the life process that one can properly isolate from the rest and designate specifically as *learning*.

Motivation

Personal construct theory has a peculiar relationship to the so-called dynamic theories in psychology. Because it starts with the assumption that man's being is measured in the dimension of time rather than in the dimension of space only, any special set of terms formulated to rationalize the fact that one is alive is simply redundant. Constructs of *motivations, drives, forces, needs*, and even *stimuli*, together with the whole class of *psychodynamics*, drop out of the system of discourse. This makes personal construct theory, in one sense, an all-out dynamic system. Movement is built into its underlying assumptions about the essential nature of man. But for those to whom a dynamic theory can be identified only by a liberal sprinkling of terms implying forces operating upon the person, either from within him or from without, personal construct theory will seem as nondynamic as Kraepelin, or even more so.

Feeling and Emotion

The constructs of *feeling* and *emotion*, for more than two thousand years so deeply entrenched in all our European systems of discourse, also drop out when we apply the assumptions of personal construct theory rigorously. Furthermore, the semantic division we customarily make between *affect* and *intellect* is no longer required, a feature of the theory that greatly disturbs some psychologists, possibly because it threatens to put them into the uncomfortable position of having nothing left to talk about or because they interpret this development as signifying a return to pre-Freudian ways of describing human behavior.

A Cognitive Theory?

Yet personal construct theory sustains no necessity for distinguishing sharply between those psychological processes that appear to follow classic formulas of reasonableness and those that do not, nor between those that are signalized by words and those that can only be portrayed by enactment, nor even between those that appear to be soundly organized and those that appear to be disorganized. It assumes that the only logic we have available to us is that which is devised by human minds; thus what is logical is an extension of what is psychological. It would therefore disclaim being either a *cognitive* theory or a *noncognitive* theory. It would be as much misunderstood if it were classed as *behavioristic* as it would be if it were classed as *rationalistic*. In brief, the point of departure in personal construct theory is at such a philosophical level that none of the usual pigeonholes for the quick and easy filing of all new psychological theories as fast as they appear will serve as a neat container for it.

New Terms of Reference for Understanding Suicide

Having abandoned so many of the terms customarily employed in talking about suicidal behavior *(feelings, emotions, needs, psychodynamics, motivation, learning, reinforcement, stimulus, cognition, irrationality, disorganization)* we seem to have little left from conventional psychology to draw verbal pictures with. Before we can come up with anything very illuminating about A. S., we shall have to replenish our vocabulary. To a considerable extent we shall depend upon refurbished terms, old words with revised meanings. But some words will have to be new, at least new in the context of precise psychological discourse. Fortunately we can limit ourselves here to those terms that need to be applied to the case at hand and leave the rest of the lexicon of personal construct theory to our more persistent readers.

Let me say a word in general about the kind of dimension used by personal construct theory. The emphasis is placed on the use of axes of reference that are abstract, i.e., mathematical in the broad sense, rather than concrete. The theoretical task is to place the problems of psychology within the framework of meaningful dimensions rather than into nosological back wards. Only thus can one properly envision directions of change and movement.

So our terms, although they inevitably categorize our ways of looking at a patient, do not presume to categorize the patient himself, nor do they even pre-empt his behaviors. For example, if we construe him in reference to *hostility*, it is the construct of *hostility* that is impounded, and not the patient or his acts. Certainly we do not say that the patient is to be stuffed alive into the *hostility* bin. Nor do we say that he has come down with an attack of *hostility*. *Hostility* is our own axis of reference, like length or height, along which a measurement can be taken in order to get a clearer idea of the proportions of human behavior.

Dilation versus Constriction

Since we have already defined *validation* in connection with our rejection of the constructs of reinforcement and learning, let us turn next to another systematic construct that is important in the understanding of suicide: *dilation* versus *constriction*. In his search for personal constructs upon which to base his anticipations, a person sometimes broadens his area of concern, hoping that by grasping at more and more things he can come across something that will help him make better sense out of the onrush of events. Often his outreaching is indiscriminate. Whether it is or not, we still describe it as *dilation*.

When he moves in the opposite direction, we call it *constriction*. A person *constricts* when he attempts to shrink his world to manageable size, as when he pulls the bedcovers over his head or attempts to stop the clock by committing suicide. It is not uncommon to find a person exhibiting violent movement along this axis. Often such movement is taken to indicate the so-called manic depressive psychosis by those who think behavior is a disease.

Anxiety

Anxiety, from the standpoint of personal construct theory, is the sense of chaos. More specifically, it is the sweeping awareness of events for which it seems one has no adequate constructs. Lacking constructs for anticipating them, one seems helplessly caught up in events, with no idea of what posture to assume while waiting for them or what to do after they arrive. Clinically, anxiety has long been described as having a free-floating quality, not ever being clearly identified with one object or one set of objects.

Threat

Threat, the subjective experience, is distinguished from *anxiety*. A person is *threatened* when he finds himself on the brink of a deeply significant change in himself. Often the impending state of affairs is all too plausible, as in the case of the reformed alcoholic who knows too well what will happen to him if he takes the first drink. Often the sense of threat is identified with what appears likely to be the precipitating cause of the metamorphosis, but the threat experience itself has to do with what seems about to happen in the region of one's core construct system. Quite often, for example, a patient is deeply threatened by a realization of what is likely to occur to him as a result of therapy. The therapist finds this hard to understand. Even the realization that the change will be for the better and result in his being happier does not necessarily make it less threatening to the patient.

Basic Postulate and Choice Corollary

Personal construct theory does not use the notion of motivation. Because man is conceived from the outset as inhabiting the dimension of time, that is to say, conceived as alive and in motion, one does not need to conjure up motivating forces to push him around. We are then left with the task of explaining only the directions his motion will take.

But this also falls into place neatly enough, once we have ventured the initial leap to a *basic postulate*. That postulate is that a person's processes are psychologically channeled by the ways in which he anticipates events. We can elaborate this statement by a series of ensuing corollaries.

The channels for anticipating events are called *constructs*. They are guides to the future, and anybody who wants to face up to life had better have an ample stock of them on hand at all levels of consciousness. When it comes down to making everyday choices, it seems obvious that a person will choose those alternatives that promise to provide either of two things: greater extension of his construct system or better definition of it. This is what we call the *choice corollary*, and it takes care of what is left over after the *basic postulate* drops the bottom out from under motivation.

This is not to say that a person will behave according to classical laws of logic. Far from it. We can be sure that neither Aristotle nor Thomas Aquinas behaved that way in their private lives. Rather, he behaves according to his own system, and that is something that has to be understood in psychological, not logical, terms. Nor does it add anything to say that he behaves in response to pleasure and pain, unless one wants to define pleasure tautologically as what we seek and pain as what we try to avoid. Moreover, constructs are not necessarily put into words, either symbolically or explicatively. Indeed, one is always impressed with how extensively persons anticipate the future in terms for which they have no speech.

Hostility

Now we can talk about *hostility*. Sometimes matters come to such a pass that one finds himself on the brink of an overdue and far-reaching revision of his construct system. His predictions have gone awry. Evidence against the validity of his constructs mounts in overwhelming proportions. In desperation he may have tried dilation to see if, in a broader context, he could grasp the elusive veridity in his way of construing the world. He may have tried constriction to see if he could find localized confirmation of his outlook. A. S. appears to have tried both. But if neither of these nor any of the other exploratory methods works, he may be confronted with a difficult choice: either to revise the very foundations of his construct system or somehow to force events to prove him right. When, on the one hand, his deeply shaken constructions have to do with his understanding of other persons and, on the other, he chooses to extort confirming evidence from them, we call it *hostility*.

This, of course, is a strikingly unusual definition of *hostility*. But *hostility*, as any psychological term, ought to help us understand the predicament in which a person has found himself and not be used merely to label a person as dangerous. The construct's referent, from this point of view, is not the desire to injure someone; the injury is incidental; it is rather an extortioner's trick designed to preserve the psychological status quo and to relieve him of the responsibility of revising his outlook. *Hostility* may, of course, be directed against a threatening object, threatening because it appears on the verge of precipitating a deep-seated change in oneself. Certainly it is often found in the reactionary person who must shore up a crumbling system of values. But it may be found as well in the radical reformer who demands that the world at large furnish him with what he thinks his home in particular did not.

Guilt

There is one term yet to go: *guilt*. The definition is a little more complex. To get at it we first have to understand *role* from the standpoint of the psychology of personal constructs. Let us suppose that one person attempts to understand another, not merely as a behaving object or merely in terms of stimulus input and response output, but as another person who himself has an outlook tingeing all his perceptions of the world about him. If, seeing the other person in this manner, a person goes on to regulate his own behavior in reference to such a subsuming construction, then he is enacting a social *role*.

In the course of his life a civilized man is likely to base a considerable proportion of his behavior on such an interpretation of those with whom he lives. It becomes a key to his expectations for himself. His own life makes sense in terms of such *role* constructs. It loses sense when they are invalidated. If the turn of events seems to leave him high and dry with no true *role* left to him, he suffers in a peculiar way. We call that experience *guilt*.

A. S.'s Personal Construct System

Two recurrent themes stand out from the details reported in the protocol provided in the case of A. S.: his inability to understand why it was his parents crossed him for the first time when he tried to establish a close relationship with Mary, and his frequent recall of fighting during childhood. In elaborating the first of these he says, "It was the first time that they had ever crossed me. . . .. And I didn't know what to do. I couldn't go against my parents, and I couldn't see why they were so mean." This theme is repeated in later sections of the protocol.

Anxiety in the System

The extent of his perplexity (the full range of events involved) is not elaborated in the protocol, but we may reasonably infer that he was pinpointing an illustrative instance in a construction that ranged much further than the particular events he emphasized. In personal construct theory a widespread sense of such confusion is called anxiety. Certainly it becomes clear as one reads the protocol that there must have been many areas in which he felt the undercurrent of confusion: in school, in looking for something to do in South America, and during his half-hearted search for employment in Los Angeles. They were all caught up in the same chaos. Let us, therefore, not be too hasty in saying that the particular domestic events in which this confusion seems focused were the material causes of his anxiety. As we have already said, personal construct theory does not deal with events of this order as if they were psychological causes.

Invalidation Deep in the System

The likeliest interpretation of the anxiety is that his anticipations were invalidated on a large scale, so large, in fact, that the truth of some very basic constructs had to be called into question. Since such basic constructs are often not couched in words, he was probably confronted with a revision of outlook for which he had inadequate verbal tools.

But how did the invalidation happen on so vast a scale? For one thing, it seems, as he reported it, that he had long looked to his mother as a principal source of validation. Validation seems to have been a function she was ready and eager to serve, both in her family and in her community. She enjoyed responsibility. This service as a personal validator for his ventures seems to be what they both meant when they agreed that he seemed "closest" to her.

A. S. puts his finger on this matter when he says, "I think my sister turned out lazy because mother would never let anyone else do anything. I know I resented this at times." At this point the interviewer reports that he became somewhat tearful and said, "I feel all confused. Mother spent as much time with us as any other mother did—" and then was silent.

In this passage A. S. seems to be about to come to grips with the fact that somehow his mother had become the custodian of all his validational evidence, thus shutting off any venture designed to check reality elsewhere. This, of course, was precisely what led up to the sense of confusion. He says he was "confused" in just so many words. Yet he cannot quite put the blame on her for he vaguely senses that it was not what she did that produced the turn of events. What he does not quite understand is how it was that his own use of his mother as a validator made him so vulnerable to the collapse of all that he had built on the evidence she supplied.

To be sure, he had long tried to validate his anticipations elsewhere: the frequent fights are evidence enough of that; but the outcomes generally seem to have run against his expectations. Only in interaction with his mother did his constructions seem to lead to consistent outcomes. And the only adventures of which she seemed to disapprove, prior to Mary, were the fights. By the time he became an adult these simple aggressive attempts had been quite thoroughly invalidated, both because he lost the fights and because his parents failed to take his side in them.

A. S. did not give up. To say that would be to fall back on traditional motivational doctrine, which, from the standpoint of personal construct theory, is obsolete. He was alive and hence active. If his aggression appeared to fail him, it was because the alternatives he construed for himself turned it off into ineffectual channels.

By the end of high school he says he was "desperately trying to be popular." Even though his mother was "always trying to build me up and brag about me," he was still looking elsewhere for validity. At last he seems to have made intimate contact with the outside world when he met Mary. Now he had a project of his own that he was successfully testing out on its independent merits. Moreover, Mary's own aggressiveness (". . . when I wanted to take Mary out and Mary would call up") provided him with validation firm enough to test his weight on. So he inched his way out on new ground.

It was at this point that he was overwhelmed with invalidational evidence from home. It was not merely that his parents disapproved; what was vastly more threatening than that was their apparent metamorphosis. They also became unpredictable. Everything he thought he knew about them and his relationship to them fell apart. They not only withheld the keys to the car; they took away his keys to the truth. He could no longer understand them. Indeed, how could he now understand anything? The fact that they invalidated his understanding of them was far more devastating than their mere disapproval.

And so it always is. To face disapproval, punishment, pain, or a dismal succession of unrewarding outcomes is one thing. These are matters man can partly understand and hence often bears without complaint. But to face chaos is another thing. Even the bravest shudder on the brink of utter emptiness. What worse chaos can one face than sudden chaos where always before there has been firm certainty and the loving confidence of one's home.

To dwell on A. S.'s loss of Mary would be to miss the point. The void was not the place that Mary had filled; it was the place his parents had filled. Moreover, this was no physical place that had been emptied. Even the death of both of his parents would have disturbed him less. What he had lost was something that could never be restored, even by abandoning Mary, even by receiving daily comfort from his parents, even by marrying a girl of whom they approved. He had lost a deep sense of validity for the way he had once ordered his world. This is what he seems to be saying to his interviewer.

Dimensions of Threat

Threat, the sense of imminent change in one's core construct system, often lies at the roots of disturbed behavior. Although there must have been moments when A. S. felt that there were deep changes in the immediate offing (certainly on the eve of suicide he must have felt so), there is very little in the protocol to suggest exactly what he thought was about to happen to him. The story is, instead, primarily one of chaos or anxiety with little so clearly structured as threat looming up before him.

To be sure, the frequent fights throughout childhood and early adolescence imply threat. Yet, except to say he fought when he found he was not liked, he gives us little clue as to any consistent type of taunt or hazard that occasioned the fights. Then, too, there was the superior in the Army. In this case the dimensions of threat are more clearly spelled out: "This man was everything I hated. He was tall, domineering, didn't know what he was doing, but acted as if he knew everything. He always tried to humiliate me, and I couldn't disagree with him. I couldn't stick up for myself; he would always win."

Look at the constructs used and then at the contrasts they implied. The implication was that A. S. was about to be cast in a part that was "short," "dominated," in which he might "know what he was doing but could not act that way," "humiliated," "unable to disagree," "unable to stick up for himself," and "always the loser." This passage probably describes better than any other the axes along which he felt himself always in danger of being transformed. More than that, they suggest some of the well-defined slots in which he might try to rattle back and forth himself.

Later, if he felt that he had achieved some basic changes in his way of life by leaving the orbit of his family, and if then also he saw himself about to slip back into that all too plausible orbit, he would have sensed threat and might have taken extraordinary measures to stave off the relapse. But there is no clear indication of this or, indeed, that he later saw himself on the verge of any clear shift in psychological position. Yet threat is never something to be overlooked in a case where violent action has been taken, and it certainly would be a mandatory topic of psychotherapeutic exploration in the case of A. S.

Vacillation Between Dilation and Constriction

A.S.'s movements along the axis of dilation and constriction are important for his therapist to note. For the most part, the record seems to indicate that his method of dealing with perplexity was to constrict; that is to say, he tended to limit rather than to expand his world of concern. But there were marked exceptions. His shift to the study of sociology certainly suggests dilation, although the protocol does not say what had been his previous plan. Certainly his trip to South America seems not only to have been an impulsive venture with little systematic planning behind it, but also a combination of dilation and constriction; dilation because it would open up a whole world of new experiences, and constriction because it would shut him off from present matters he felt he could not handle.

The trip seems to have been his last desperate bid to deal with his problems en masse. If he could have found some semblance of structure there, as he had found the time before when he packed himself off to the Army, the effort might have succeeded. But there was no ready-made way of life waiting for him in South America; only more chaos.

All this suggests one of the problems that would continually have to be faced in therapy. As long as his dependence on his therapist was safe and his world of important realities constricted to the therapy room, matters might be expected to go along smoothly. When the time came to venture out of doors there would be the danger of impulsive movements along the old dilation-constriction axis. Such movements would confront both himself and his therapist with unanticipated developments and catch both of them unaware.

On the face of it, suicide is always a constrictive gesture. What needs to be kept in mind is that constriction is movement toward one end of an axis, the other end of which denotes dilation. To be free to move in one direction along this axis implies freedom also to move readily in the opposite direction. Together these poles define an avenue of movement, sometimes almost the only avenue of movement clearly open to a disturbed person.

Interlocking Relations Between Guilt and Hostility

Not all psychological systems employ the constructs of guilt and hostility. Among those that do, an interlocking relationship is usually assumed to exist between them. Hostility is often seen as a way of alleviating one's feelings of guilt; guilt, in turn, commonly follows the realization that one has acted in a hostile fashion.

Personal construct theory, as we have seen, conceptualizes these two types of experience in its own particular way; a way consistent with the assumptions and structure of its systematic position. For one thing, hostility and aggression are kept clearly distinct from each other. Clinical descriptions, therefore, come out in a somewhat different form.

Distinguishing Between Hostility and Aggression

Aggression, in personal construct theory, is more nearly synonymous with adventuresomeness, especially adventuresomeness involving high stakes and persistent action along a single chosen line. Hostility, as we have already said, is a last-resort effort to achieve validation in one's interpersonal realm by means of extortion, by a misleading manipulation of the data rather than by revision of the constructs that have proven themselves faulty.

Both A. S. and his father appear to have been threatened by A. S.'s mother. A. S. speaks of their "resenting" her efficiency. Better stated, they were threatened by the form her aggression took. For father as well as for son, she served as a constant reminder of their precarious hold upon life's initiative and the ever-present possibility of finding themselves to be confirmed incompetents. Undoubtedly they were threats to each other too, for each could see in the other an image of himself that was much too plausible for comfort.

In the presence of this sense of threat they could have been anxious, aggressive, or hostile; perhaps a little of each. With A. S. it seems to have been mostly anxiety, the feeling of chaos. But to the extent that he expressed his experience as resentment and took active measures to cope with the threat, he was aggressive. And not to be overlooked are the evidences of sporadic aggressiveness that appear all through the biographical record. The indications of hostility are less clear, but then hostility is usually hard to detect from bare protocol.

The Interviewer's Impression of Passivity

The interviewer was impressed with A. S.'s emphasis of the "passive role." He also notes that it was difficult for A. S. to request an interruption in the interview, even though he was apparently in severe pain at times. But how shall we interpret these two observations? Was he simply assuming the position that doctors expect of patients in hospitals? Was it a gesture of helplessness or of aggressive eagerness to get a job done by being a doctor's patient if necessary? The clinical evidence on this point would come more from the way he led out in steering the course of the interviews than from the posture he assumed or his failure to complain. He seems to have complained ("griped") enough in the service. Besides, there are cultural differences here that often mislead a clinician.

Another matter must also be taken into account. A clinician's theoretical orientation affects the way he sees things. Since personal construct theory makes a clean distinction between hostility and aggression, A. S.'s failure to show obvious hostility in the clinical situation would not weigh against the perception of aggressive tendencies or of impulsive vacillation along this axis. But still A. S.'s range of positions with reference to the axis of aggression remains undetermined. It is left for the psychotherapeutic series to clarify this critical point.

We must not neglect still another consideration. The protocol reports "some slight signs of organic brain illness, such as inability to concentrate and some impairment of memory, but these seemed gradually to improve as time went on." From what we know generally about organic brain involvements of this type, we are led to expect associated changes with respect to aggression, changes more marked than those taking place with respect to hostility, which is an additional reason for keeping the two constructs separate in our thinking. We have to remind ourselves that A. S. may behave more aggressively as he recovers. If so, some of the conspicuously missing evidences of hostility may come to light also.

Signs of Hostility

Whenever a clinician deals with a suicidal attempt, he most certainly has to be alert to the hostile strivings that may be expressed in the act. Too often the suicidal person uses both his verbal warning and his actual suicidal attempt to extort validating evidence from those upon whom he has come to depend for the confirmation of his social outlook. One can never be quite sure about this until one has examined closely the case at hand.

Of course, the conclusion is quite simple, if one always assumes that hostility is the tendency to hurt or destroy something. In that case we say that the suicide was obviously a matter of hostility turned inward. Usually we go further and say that it turned inward because it could not successfully turn itself outward. This is perfectly painless logic; any clinician can follow it.

But personal construct theory does not lead one to reason this way. The definition of hostility is different; furthermore, it is not envisioned as a directive force but rather as a reference axis in terms of which behavior can be judged. When we look at A. S.'s act in this manner, we seek to discover what he was trying to achieve. What did he expect would happen? If he thought his act would force his parents to concede to his position, there would be evidence of hostility. If, in some remote way, the act was perceived as producing a kind of artificial validity for his construction of life, that also would be evidence of hostility. Perhaps he was trying to prove his mother a murderer. But we have no such evidence at hand. There is not even a report of a suicidal warning being expressed by A. S. Besides, as we said before, hostility is a matter that is hard to elaborate adequately during the early stages of clinical contact.

Control by Guilt

To feel that one has ordered one's life by understanding the outlooks of others—that is awareness of role. To sense that one's role has been lost—that is guilt. This is not to say that a person feels guilty when he fails to conform to the expectations of others; it is rather when he fails to conform to those expectations of himself that he has based on his perception of what others believe and understand.

Guilt resembles anxiety, although personal construct theory makes a qualitative distinction between them. The loss of social role, the role one has defined for oneself in the light of genuine social perceptions, is what lies at the core of guilt. A person does not face conceptual chaos, as anxiety, but social excommunication in his own realm of values. Thus, in guilt, he senses himself being cut off from the means of interpersonal confirmation and hence from his contact with social reality.

Perhaps the clearest instance of guilt in A. S.'s anamnesis is the experience of finding that his mother's sister had died in the New York hospital before he had got around to calling on her. We have to infer this experience, of course, but his quick ensuing shift of attitude and his immediate effort to adapt to his mother's wishes regarding Mary strongly suggests that he suffered sharp pangs of guilt on this occasion.

Here, too, we see the classic relation between guilt and hostility. In response to the guilt feelings he had written Mary to "break it off," and he had asked for his ring to be returned. When it became apparent that there was still a tie between himself and Mary, he says he was resentful. Guilt had tricked him. How could he handle his mother so he would not be tricked again? Thus he felt guilty because he had aggressively deserted his mother at a time when her sister was dying, and he felt hostile because the guilt feeling had brought him back into tow.

There is no evidence in the protocol to indicate how he felt about the effect of his suicidal attempt on his role. He had tried to kill his mother's son; did he feel guilty about that? Or did it seem as if he could thus restore a childhood role, exemplified, perhaps, by the nourishment of his mother's attention or even by the two malted milks that seem to play such a symbolic part of his portrayal of deeper cravings.

We must keep in mind also that he had begun to structure his role in terms of other figures. Mary and the girl with whom he felt himself in love during the last year of service were doubtlessly involved. So was his sister, presumably. Even his sister's divorce could have been involved in some way. Certainly his failure to marry either Mary or the other girl must have given him some sense of having fallen below the standards he had recently erected for himself founded on his feelings for them.

One sentence in this part of the protocol seems worth exploring much further. In speaking of the second girl he is quoted as saying, "I felt myself falling in love with her and it was very hard for me to tell her that it was love, but as time went on I knew that that was so." Had he reached a point where the sense of being in love was threatening, or could he not speak of such feelings without experiencing guilt? Later, in Los Angeles, was this remembered inability to admit a loving relationship between himself and another person a contributor to his loss of role, his sense of guilt? Perhaps he could not tell her that he loved her because to do so would be to conform to his parents' outlook toward Mary, and the substitute mate would always be a living reminder of his failure to confirm his own way of life.

Questions

Was He Trying to Terminate His Life or Validate It?

We return to the fundamental issues posed earlier. Is there anything that would lead us to believe that A. S. had dedicated his life to some purpose that would have to be abandoned if he remained alive? Certainly we have little to go on, but if there was such a purpose, it might have been to establish his independence as a person. He was broke; he had just spent his last quarter. He could have asked for help, but that seems to be the thing that he was determined not to do. To go without food would have brought persons clattering to his relief, and he probably was already acutely aware of doctor bills. If, indeed, there was a firm line that he was continuing to follow, it seems that it must have been the line of independence. Whatever we infer from the protocol at hand, however, the matter is one that only the subsequent psychotherapeutic series could clarify.

Consider the two limiting conditions for terminating one's own life: complete realism or complete chaos. Of the two, the latter seems to be much the more likely condition in A. S.'s case. He must have felt himself confronted with inexorable reality at the moment he bought his last malted milk, but the picture as a whole is one of chaotic outlook, or anxiety, as it would be called in terms of personal construct theory. It seems likely that he was trying to terminate his life more than to validate it.

Interestingly enough, two of his last acts, the purchase of the malted milk and the bath, seem to be directed by deep-seated constructions. The constructs involved were probably preverbal; that is to say, they were not of an order that could easily be labeled or even easily talked about. He remembers the malted milk as one of the good things he was brought to eat after his tonsillectomy at age eleven. There is also a passage in the protocol that seems to express preverbal constructs: the one that tells of getting up early in the morning and running downstairs to get dressed in front of a warm stove. Somewhere among these elements the clinician might expect to find vaguely formulated constructions that would help him to reconstruct A. S.'s state of mind just before swallowing the barbiturate capsules. Such a reconstruction might throw light on A. S.'s basic structure and hence upon his basic resources.

"Something Bigger than Myself"

The expression "needing something bigger than oneself" is an overworked cliché in inspirational discourse, but A. S. gives it a personal meaning by following it with the appositional phrase "a feeling of understanding from home." He had come to depend upon this feeling of understanding as his evidence in hand for most of his construction of life and particularly for his construction of role relations. To say that one feels the need for something bigger than oneself is to say what is probably true of all of us. What is bigger than self is the whole world of reality and the sense of being validly in touch with it. To be out of touch with it is to be out of touch with the future and to realize that life's bridging of past and future has failed to cross the chasm. In the broadest possible sense, A. S. was saying that he needed the restoration of the only sure contact he had ever felt with the world of reality.

But Why Didn't He Get a Job?

If A. S. had been able to establish for himself the single purpose of becoming independent, matters might not have turned out as they did. Such a purpose wavers badly when one's whole system of truths appears to have lost its validity. He says, "I would look in the papers and try to get a job, but it would seem as if I just couldn't get started. I would look at them, but wouldn't do any more. . .. And all the time my mood was getting worse, and I still had the feeling that I wanted to sever relations with my family." Under these conditions his efforts were much too much taken up with the internal struggle to allow him to shine his shoes and put up a proper front to an employment interviewer. The task that confronted him could not be reduced to the dimension of job hunting.

Why Did He Go to South America?

The one role relationship outside his family that seems to have taken any kind of root at all was with the girl of South American extraction. Moreover, his parents' objection to her was on stereotyped grounds; they made it plain that their way of life could not be reconciled with her presumed way of life. If he was to abandon his old stakes altogether, what more likely place was there to go than the one identified with the antithetical way of life.

To be sure, it was an ill-considered venture. He admits himself that he decided upon it all one afternoon. Besides, one must remember that by this time Mary had become inconsiderate and that he felt this was his folks' fault. Perhaps in South America there was more of the kind of person Mary once was.

Psychotherapeutic Plans

Psychotherapeutic plans always have to take into account the personal constructs of the therapist as well as of the client. Perhaps it is even more important to take the therapist into account, because clients cannot always be depended upon to keep their therapists in line. This is by way of saying that, if A. S.'s therapist is a psychoanalyst, it would be best to lay out the therapeutic plans in analytic terms rather than to risk the confusion of trying to follow personal construct plans seen through psychoanalytic spectacles.

From the standpoint of the psychology of personal constructs the task of psychotherapy is to restore and accentuate those universal psychological processes that characteristically make life an ongoing proposition. The client needs enough structure to lay his wagers, channel his aggressive efforts, and accept his losses. He needs to experiment with some idea of what is at stake. He needs access to various forms of reality to be used as validational evidence. He needs to have a methodology for dealing with his world piecemeal instead of in catastrophic terms. He needs role relationships so he can sift out social outcomes and maintain himself as a distinct individual, related to but distinguishable from other persons. He needs basic structure that will not be too much shaken by life's daily vicissitudes. Finally, he needs to look upon the objective of his therapy not as a terminal state of well-being but as a course of action to be embarked upon and continuously replotted throughout his life.

Immediate Therapeutic Issues to Be Faced

In this case there is the matter of medical rehabilitation. The schedule for whatever structural repair is required following the tracheotomy will have to be fitted into the psychotherapeutic plans. Presumably there will also be physical medicine treatment required. Assuming all treatment will soon move from an intramural to an extramural basis, there will be the matter of living arrangements and employment to be considered. There will also be immediate adjustment problems to be faced: the way he will account for himself to employment interviewers and to new acquaintances; how he will make use of recreational and educational resources; how he will manage his psychotherapeutic interview appointments.

If he is to be treated in a Veterans Administration mental hygiene clinic he must be labeled a service-connected disability case. Whether or not his military service was in any way involved, the very notion of service-connected disability is prejudicial to psychotherapy, especially in a case of this sort and especially as psychotherapy is understood from the position of personal construct psychology. It suggests, most unfortunately, that his psychological difficulties were caused by external events rather than by the way he had dealt with those events.

If all these practical assumptions are correct, we think of A. S.'s psychotherapeutic program being set up on an outpatient basis. Ideally the program should be initiated immediately and the long-range plans laid out as definitely as possible, while A. S.'s recent experience is still fresh in his mind and before the beginning of another type of adjustment takes shape. Certainly the relationship to his therapist, so important in this particular case, needs to be established immediately, and it should be clear to him that it will be maintained even after he is shifted to an outpatient basis. In some ways the experience he has had serves the function of shock treatment, and, as with shock treatment, the sooner the psychotherapeutic relationship is established the better. Too often there is a tendency to wait until the patient is in contact. But this is a mistake; one should start before the patient has come back into full contact with the everyday world.

Elaboration of the Construct System

At the present stage we know too little about A. S.'s personal construct system to be able to anticipate accurately what reformulations will be needed and how he will come to make them. Personal construct psychology leads us to try to work out these matters on the client's own terms rather than in terms of dogmatized versions of reality or psychodynamics. This makes the task less technical and more one of creative conceptualization. Client and therapist work as a construing team rather than having the therapist wait patiently for the client to come around to his way of thinking.

A. S. seems to be articulate enough to be able to express large portions of his outlook in words. In addition, he seems willing to venture into areas of confusion where words fail him but in which he can at least express himself by gesture and tears. With this combination of useful skills, so valuable in any client undergoing therapy, it should not be too difficult to get some of the preverbal constructs expressed at a precise enough level to be examined and tested.

This is only our surmise. If he begins to deal with matters in sweeping terms of unworthiness and generalized hostility, the therapist will be in for a long, long series. If it appears that there is danger of this happening, it will be important to keep the elaboration of the construct system well compartmentalized and approach any kind of sweeping insight with caution. Especially must one keep in mind the two slots already mentioned in which he might impulsively vacillate: dilation-constriction and aggression. Until the nature of these two construct dimensions is more fully known, the therapist will have to be doubly alert.

Establishment of Working Relations with Parents

One difficult issue will have to be settled by the therapist early in the game. Will he and the client try to establish a working role relationship with the parents, or will they keep the field constricted to minimize interaction with the parents? This decision can be postponed for a time, until there is a further exploration of the client's social resources, but not for long.

The chances are that therapy cannot reach down to a stable construct foundation unless the former course is taken. There is so much construing at the level of nourishment and primitive guilt that it is hard to imagine a simple substitution of an adult world of role relationships. Even if the therapist undertakes to accept a heavily dependent transference role, the parents, both mother and father, are still much too clearly part of A. S.'s world to be ignored.

A. S. will not like this, I suspect. He will object, especially when he begins to feel that he has got a fresh grip on life. Every time the relations with the parents are explored he will perceive the old threats standing there before him: the mother keeping tight possession of the keys to reality and truth and the hapless father with whom he must identify in spite of himself. It will not be a comfortable picture, and he will probably become quite annoyed with his therapist for holding it up in front of him.

But the picture is one he painted; it is not a photograph of his family; and this he must come to understand. It can be painted in other ways that are no less accurate and far more revealing. Furthermore, the new picture can be validated by aggressive exploration of the two parental personalities. It will take skill on the part of both members of the psychotherapeutic team, but it will be the way to make sense out of the new outlook and it will provide deep roots for the new personality structure.

It is customary for therapists to take a dim view of parents, especially of mothers. Because mothers play an important part in the personality development of clients, it is easy for therapists to imagine themselves in competition with them. Clients often anchor their inadequate construction in their mothers, and thus it seems to client and therapist both that those constructions were foisted upon this poor mortal by a designing witch.

Personal construct theory by its basic position permits us to see through this subject-predicate error. Let us hope the theory can be used to avoid the error in the case of A. S. as he is helped to reconstrue his mother. Besides, it is quite likely that the person who has suffered most in this case is not A. S. but his mother. She has both guilt and anxiety to cope with. As she is an aggressive person, she may try to handle her situation by aggressive hostility and thus cut herself off from sympathy and support. But that will not mean she is to be abandoned by a wise therapist or by a perceptive son. So it is with the father too. What more did he need to confirm the picture of his own inadequacy?

This is not the place to elaborate on the techniques that are derived from personal construct theory. Certainly, each therapist will use the theory to invent techniques that would not occur to others. Under a personal construct regimen clients often devise their own techniques. This is as it should be; for what good is therapy if it turns out clients who are mentally aseptic and unable to conceptualize for themselves any new ways of coping with life, either good or bad? What good would it do A. S. to be extricated from his present confusion if he were to be left high and dry without the ingenuity to invent his way out of the next mess he gets into? Let us hope that psychotherapy will land him on his feet and arunning—forward, that is.

72

Innovations in Psychotherapy[1]

The premises underlying the much-used constructs of "disease," "illness," and "health" are how being openly questioned. This is particularly true in the psychological realm of discourse. Such terms suggest that what ails a person psychologically is something other than himself. The time may not be far off when we will no longer speak of "mental illness" or of "mental health."

When that time comes we will also probably stop talking about "treatment" and "psychotherapy," because these, too, are prejudicial terms suggestive of the idea that one's life is to be subjected to the management of some external agency. Does this mean that persons in distress will be left alone in their misery? Not at all! It will more likely mean that they will be given new challenges, put in possession of new resources, freed to attempt new experiments, and given new tools for solving their problems.

What are some of the new models of psychologizing out of which new approaches to psychotherapy may emerge? One cannot say for sure, but here are some possibilities.

1. There seems to be a line of thinking developing which would place emphasis upon ontological approaches to behavioral change in man. The Rogerian movement is definitely going in this direction. American existentialism, while still pretty vague as to its psychotherapeutic implications, is quite likely to generate new types of psychotherapeutic effort.
2. Role theory, in its various forms, suggests new approaches to behavioral change via placing persons in a new social position where there are different expectancies for them to meet.
3. Somewhat related to role and ontological lines of thinking are those which emphasize the purposive nature of man. The later thinking of the French philosopher, Camus, in which attention is drawn to "commitment" as that quality that keeps man alive, is likely to be translated into new technical approaches to psychotherapy.
4. There are models of man built on the concept of man-the-scientist, that is to say, a being who formulates theories, generates hypotheses, experiments, ventures, and generally seeks to predict and control himself and his world. Such theorizing leads to quite a different relationship between the "therapist" and his client. It, furthermore, opens the door to a wide spectrum of therapeutic activities and envisions no end to the therapeutic process while the person is alive. Therapy, according to this model, is simply an accelerated way of getting on with the human enterprise.
5. There are learning models of therapy, various types of which keep cropping up here and there. In America these are mostly based on connectionistic notions of behavioral change. In the Soviet Union they are based on the interaction of signal systems as originally envisioned by Pavlov. While these approaches tend to be couched in physiological terms, they need not remain so in the future.
6. There are self-actualization models of behavioral change. To some extent they appear to be related to the thinking of the ontologists I have mentioned—the Rogerians and the existentialists. But the movement is possibly aimed in a somewhat different direction. The thesis that man should become what he is sounds redundant, but the idea is capable of developing some concepts of operations. The philosophy of Zen is still a long way from the kind of formulation that Western minds can grasp, but this does not mean that it will remain so. It seems reasonable to expect that Oriental types of thought will come to have some influence on Western philosophy in general and upon psychotherapy in particular. Already there is some experimentation with the tendency of some persons to conform to outside forces, that is, to see themselves victimized by external agencies, and the tendency of others to see themselves as the agents of life or as having the potentiality of merging themselves with the universe.
7. Certainly the development of language psychology in general and communication theory in particular is likely to result in new ways of approaching distressed persons. If, as some are now suggesting, mental disorder is an expression in terms of some particular form of protolanguage, it would seem reasonable to expect that psychotherapy might develop systems of iconic semiotics for helping persons cope with their problems.

[1] Contribution to the Symposium on Innovations in Clinical Psychology, New York State Psychological Association Meetings, May 13, 1962. Published by permission of Jacqueline Aldridge.

Collected Papers of the Pioneer of Constructivist Psychology: George A. Kelly, First Edition. Edited by David A. Winter and Nick Reed.

8 Games theory is bound to have an influence on the psychotherapy of the future. Some have suggested that everyone is now playing the exciting and expensive game of "Doctor and Patient" and that it has caught on like Bingo. But if mental distress is the playing of a non-recreational game, there may be ways of changing the game, either by changing the ground rules or by changing the games strategies of the players.

These are a few of the possibilities for new departures in psychotherapy for the future. It is probably unfortunate that there is so much reluctance to get on with the active exploration, research, and development needed to bring these ideas into a state of technological formulation.

73

A Doctoral Program in Clinical Psychology[1]

Points of Departure

Launching the Scholarly Career

If education were simply a matter of doing something to a student, the planning of a doctoral program in clinical psychology would be a relatively simple affair. The student could be stimulated, instructed, lectured at, guided, disciplined, motivated and therapized until he became a facsimile of the current year's model of a respectable clinical psychologist.

But it does not work that way. The scholarly person educates himself as he goes. Scholarship, whether literary or scientific, is a career, not a posture. It has its beginnings before the student leaves the university and it is a way of life pursued by him on his own, not by others on his behalf. He presses forward along this line of endeavor through thick and thin, in the company of professors, though often in spite of them, and toward objectives that always turn out to be too ephemeral and much too small.

For the clinical psychologist, how is such a career launched? To answer this question is to say what a doctoral program in clinical psychology should be. On the face of it there are involved the following elements: (1) a place of ferment where scholarly enterprises are spontaneously designed and vigorously pursued for their own sake, and not merely as parts of a curriculum, (2) a community of scholars where juniors and seniors alike intimately share their scholarly thoughts and enthusiasms, (3) library resources, the essential units of which are immediately available in the room where one works, (4) participation in clinical activities involving genuine services to persons, (5) space and equipment optimally designed for the implementation of one's scholarly efforts, and (6) freedom from the necessity of dissipating one's efforts in non-productive activities that can better be performed by clerical or technical personnel.

Half-Baked Doctoral Programs

If there is one complaint voiced more frequently than any other by those who are invited by universities to come and evaluate doctoral programs, it is that from the moment they arrive on a campus they are confronted with a diffuse array of courses embellished with such a versatile lack of imagination as could be achieved only by the most rigorous self-discipline. Over and over, visiting committees say that the doctoral programs they see are designed in imitation of the most obsolete programs to be found in the larger universities. While the written reports handed to university administrators are often toned down to protect our colleagues, the private remarks of the visitors are often couched in much more colorful terms. The general opinion can be summed up in a phrase one visitor used: "There is nothing more stuffy than a university with an aspiration to become respectable, and nothing more exciting than a university determined to make others obsolete!"

Specifically, the charge of stuffiness is likely to be leveled at doctoral programs that are designed in terms of courses, prerequisites, credits, marks and hurdles, rather than in terms of students, staff, interpersonal communication, experiences, resources, scholarly milieu, and the aggressive advancement of human knowledge beyond its present limited frontiers. A second specific objection is likely to be directed at the narrowness of the viewpoints of those "who want to sire Ph.D's. of their own." This refers on the one hand, to "experimental psychologists" who believe that experimentation takes place only in areas familiar to them, and, on the other, to "clinical psychologists" who fancy themselves as irreproachable white-coat technicians rather than adventuresome scholars. There is a third complaint one hears. It is against programs in which research is a requirement added to the training program to make it "scientific," but without any essential relationship to what the student is required to learn in his contact with persons. When research

[1] Rough draft, prepared as a basis for discussion, for the Department of Psychology, City College, New York, March 22, 1962. Published by permission of Jacqueline Aldridge.

Collected Papers of the Pioneer of Constructivist Psychology: George A. Kelly, First Edition. Edited by David A. Winter and Nick Reed.

is not conceptually bound up with the central theme about which the student educates himself, it is not likely to contribute much of lasting significance to his career.

There is a fourth criticism, not so often heard, but, nonetheless, one that may well be taken into account. It is that certain fields of psychology, such as clinical psychology, are often regarded as "applied psychology." The term "applied" suggests that there is some basic science of psychology which is exploited by those who are incapable of creative or rigorous thinking, and to which they have no obligation to contribute. That there is a science of psychology emerging today need not be doubted, but that those who concern themselves with persons in distress can never be more than modern sophists, can well be questioned.

Seizing the Initiative

Suppose we assume that the following six conditions will maximize the development of advanced scholarship and that we can use them as points of departure for planning doctoral training in clinical psychology:

A *Communication*. Scholarship tends to thrive when there is frequent and informal communication between students, and between students and teachers. This means they should work, if possible, in adjacent rooms and should be in daily contact with each other.

B *Functional relations*. Scholars tend to be more productive when they join in their efforts to solve important problems. This is true, not only when they have mutual research interests, but when they assist each other in the early stages of hypothesis formation and creative thinking.

C *Independent scholarship*. Scholarship thrives when there is proper recognition of achievement growing out of independent study. Advanced students should have the privilege of learning on their own and should never be required to sit through courses they are capable of mastering independently.

D *Scientific methodology rather than professional technology*. In the area of a student's specialization, say, clinical psychology, the theory, the systematic information, and the methodology should never be taught separately from each other. This is to say, no lecture without laboratory, and no laboratory without lecture. Or, to put it in other words: when dealing with a scholar's specialty there should be *no whys without how, and no hows without the why*. The scholar who specializes in clinical psychology learns clinical methodology, and he is able to assign it its rightful place in the spectrum of scientific method: he does not learn technique merely, and wander through life imagining that scientific method is something altogether different.

E *Frontiers always*. A scholar is never far from the frontiers of human knowledge. This means that provision should be made to ensure that both students and staff members have intimate contact with the most exciting new ventures in the field of psychology, whether those ventures are to be found within the university or outside. Every possible provision should be made to assist staff members to attack the frontiers themselves, through research, through teaching in other universities, through scholarly production, through participation in important governmental decision-making bodies, and through other advanced scholarly enterprises.

F *After the Ph.D., what?* If the program is to stand at the top of those available in the country, the image of the student who has received the Ph.D. degree should be consonant with that objective. Graduates should not only be prepared for positions of scholarly responsibility, but steps should be taken to make sure that they are considered seriously for appointment. A program geared to the production of practitioners who aspire only to hang up the shingle of private practice, or who will fill only the ready-made slots of the State's Civil Service roster, can scarcely be regarded as a serious bid for scholarly leadership. Not only will it be essential that the doctoral candidates be well trained, but positive steps will have to be taken to make the quality of the doctoral program widely known and respected.

Five Channels of Scholarly Endeavor

Following is a five channel program whose design stems from the foregoing assumptions about how scholarship happens.

1 *Channel One: The Core Activity*. The main channel of this program is what may be called the *Core Activity*. It involves the formation of *Research Cadres* under the leadership of selected professors in clinical psychology. This channel is designed to provide the optimal fulfillment of Conditions A and B, Communication and Functional Relations, respectively, as described in the preceding section.

2 *Channel Two: Independent Study of Fundamentals, and* (3) *Channel Three: Independent Choice of Courses*. These two channels are complementary to each other. By allowing the student to master certain fundamentals of psychology on his own, and, at his convenience, to demonstrate his acquired competencies by examination, the stage is set for him to select freely, as a self-respecting scholar should, from the rich offerings available in the various units of the university. This part of the plan stems from Condition C, Independent Scholarship.

3 *Channel Four: The Professional Sequence*. This is a five course series to be taken in order, with each course embodying both practical and academic features welded into a coherent theme of instruction.

4 *Channel Five*: *Frontiers of Scholarship Program*. Conditions E, Contemporary Frontiers, and F, The Doctoral Image, suggest the fifth and last channel to scholarship to be opened to graduate students seeking the doctoral degree in clinical psychology in this university. Here the approach is different. Instead of starting with the special needs of partially educated students, this program starts with the current enthusiasms and the most advanced achievements of the outstanding scholars in the university, as well as in arenas outside the university. These scholars are invited to share their richest thoughts and experiences with students, utilizing whatever systems of communication are most suitable—lectures, workshops, field visits, seminars, etc. These events are scheduled ad hoc as the occasions may arise.

Another feature of this program, and one most important to the healthy development of doctoral training in the university, is the adoption of policies, devices, and work patterns designed to encourage and implement the advanced efforts of those staff members whose own scholarly careers are supposed to serve as models for the students.

Briefly, then, these are the five channels to be provided for students who are in the course of launching their careers in clinical psychology. While the plan for doctoral training may at first appear to be radical, particularly in the role assigned to formal courses, none of it is actually untried. The *Research Cadre* device has been the dominant feature of the clinical psychology training program in the Ohio State University for the past fifteen years, and it has been adapted wholly or in part by other areas of the department of psychology there, as well as by other universities. The *Professional Sequence*, a special kind of course arrangement with its welding of theory, content, and methodology, has also been a feature of the Ohio State Program. However, in the light of the new challenges to which clinical psychologists must now address themselves, certain improvements are suggested for inclusion in the program of the City University of New York. The other features cited here have their counterparts in a number of successful doctoral programs. It cannot be said, therefore, that any major part of this proposed program is so untried that its adoption would constitute an undue risk. Indeed, while this is novel as doctoral programs go, it is by no means a wild-eyed fantasy, but is an integrated program solidly built out of mutually supportive elements that in practice have proved to be sound.

In the second part of this proposal each of the channels will be discussed in turn and in greater detail.

The Five Channels in Detail

The Core Activity

This activity is not a course or a seminar. It is, rather, a setting, a team of scholars, and an enterprise. It is also a foretaste of the career of a creative scholar.

Suppose we start by describing how this channel to scholarship functions in the clinical psychology program at the Ohio State University, and then suggest ways in which it could be improved for adoption at the City University of New York.

The incoming graduate student is assigned provisionally to a *Research Team* under the leadership of one of the clinical psychology professors. In the first meeting, often at the professor's home, the student meets the other members of the team, some of whom are newcomers such as himself, but most of whom are old hands—second, third, and fourth year students—and of these a number are "regular" members. The regular members are those who have chosen this team as the one in which they will do their masters or doctoral research. The team discussion centers around research in progress, professional problems, new developments in psychology, and the faint glimmers of ideas which team members hope may materialize into a research project.

While the team has regularly scheduled meetings, it functions continually throughout the week as a cooperative work and study unit. Students and the leader assist each other in formulating research plans and in keeping up with current developments in the field of psychology. Members of the team often serve as subjects for each other's pre-experimental explorations. Older members of the team often help others with statistical problems or answer questions about concepts and techniques.

Much of the instruction that in a conventional university program must proceed from professor to student takes place, in the case of the research team, in informal communications between students. In this respect the development of scholarship parallels what happens in non-university research laboratories where senior scientists work together. While each member is free to develop his research ideas along his own line of interest, there is a tendency for students to formulate problems along cognate lines of inquiry. Members of the team consider it their privilege to drop into their team leader's office for coffee and conversation as frequently as they like.

If, by the end of the first quarter, the new student has not made any plans for his masters research, he is rotated to another team where he again becomes a provisional member. This rotation takes place each quarter until he has formulated some research plans and has asked for regular assignment to one of the teams for completion of his project. He may go to any team he likes and at any time, provided the team leader agrees to the arrangement. Usually he will make his choice after visiting some of the weekly meetings of other teams and discussing mutual interests with the leaders.

On completion of the masters thesis the student is again rotated among teams as a provisional member, until he makes the decision as to where he will do his doctoral research.

In this program the research team is the core activity of the student's doctoral training. The team is his "home base." It serves tutorial functions, with both fellow students and the leader serving as tutors. Sometimes the team holds a "kangaroo oral examination" for a student about to take the doctoral qualifying examination. The team leader and fellow members of the team advise the student as to whether they think he is ready to undertake the qualifying examination, or if they think he should delay it until he has informed himself in areas of psychology he has neglected.

The team is also a place where "integrative" learning takes place. It is here that the student reconciles as best he can the varying points of view he observes among his professors—such matters as the relation between profession and science, the principles that link experimental and clinical psychology, and the implications of the philosophy of science in understanding a variety of personality theories. The team is a place where creative thinking takes place: vague ideas are tolerated on a "trial run" basis.

The team is also a place where the student learns most about applied experimental design and statistical methods. It is, finally, the setting in which his doctoral research is completed and the initial pattern of his career as a scholar is established.

In this program, proposed for the City University of New York, it is suggested that the team be called the "Research Cadre," for no particular reason other than that it is a new term and that improvements on the Ohio State University scheme are anticipated. It is proposed that members of each cadre have their desks, books, and working space in a room or rooms next to their leader's office, with ready access to the leader during considerable parts of each working day. Each cadre room, at a minimum, should be equipped with student desks, typewriters, calculator, coffee pot, and a cadre conference table. It should be close to the departmental library. It should be open for students' use seven days a week. Research rooms used by the cadre members should be nearby.

Once or twice a year the cadre should go "on retreat" for a weekend. As much as possible the cadre should be used as an instructional unit, replacing formal lectures and courses, whenever possible. It should be the student's introduction to the kind of mature scholarly enterprise into which his career should eventually lead him.

Independent Scholarship: Fundamentals by Examination

Since one of the important objectives of this proposed doctoral program is to clear the way for independent scholarship, an arrangement is suggested for allowing the student to master whatever fundamentals of psychological science he can by independent study. To the maximum extent feasible, his competency in these more formal academic areas will be measured by examination, rather than by counting hours and credits. Let us say there are seven such areas in which the student might, with a minimum amount of guidance, suggested reading lists, and occasional discussions, be able to develop competence on his own, and to have his competency measured by examination.

1 Philosophy of Science
2 Statistics and Experimental Design
3 Basic Cognitive and Behavioral Processes
4 Physiological Psychology
5 Developmental Psychology
6 Personality
7 Social Psychology

It need not be assumed that *all* students can meet minimum requirements in all of these areas through independent study. Indeed, it is quite likely that most students will choose to take or audit formal courses in one or more areas.

Opportunity to take one or more of the seven *Fundamentals Examinations*, as the individual student may elect, should be provided each semester. It is anticipated that most students would be able to pass all of the examinations by the end of the second year, and that some will complete the series in their first year. The examinations should be prepared, administered, and evaluated by a committee representing the Department of Psychology as a whole.

The Proseminar

To assist those students who may wish to take advantage of it, a year-long proseminar series, corresponding to the seven topical areas of the Fundamentals Examinations, should be offered. Since this would be envisioned as an adjunctive service to students pursuing independent study of the topical areas, rather than a course, attendance would not be required, nor would there be any occasion to take attendance records. Students would simply attend sessions to the extent they found them useful.

The basic selected reading list for each of the seven areas would be made available, and for each topic a series of four to six semi-weekly sessions would be held. In these sessions the bibliography would be annotated and the students given suggestions for their independent study. Each month an additional topic in the seven-topic series would be introduced by a professor or professors who are familiar with the area. After the four to six initial presentations of annotations, the regular semi-weekly sessions can be discontinued for that month, while students pursue their reading. However, once a week for the following six weeks or so a qualified professor should hold open-house colloquies for students who have encountered difficulties in their reading or who have formulated special questions in the topical area.

On the next to the last session of the open-house colloquy series the professor may offer a voluntary "take-home" examination covering the proseminar topic for which he is responsible. This would be for advisory purposes only. If the student returns his answers at the next session, the professor may go over them with him, criticize them either privately or within the discussion group, and express an opinion as to whether or not he believes the student is prepared to take the Fundamentals Examination in that area.

Course Offerings for the Independent Student

In the areas of the fundamentals of psychological science there would be no courses required by name. However, course offerings, most of them open to graduate students exclusively, would be made available throughout the university. These offerings should be designed for two purposes: One would be to provide intensive instruction in the fundamentals of psychological science for those who may find themselves unable to master certain topical areas by independent study alone, or who prefer to use this means of preparing themselves for the fundamentals examinations. (See Appendix for detailed suggestions regarding courses.)

The Professional Sequence

There are three areas of clinical psychology that can be adequately covered by programs of independent study similar to those outlined in the proseminar. These are: (1) the nosology of psychological disorders—largely the list of disorders and symptoms covered by the statistical guide of the American Psychiatric Association, and a standard textbook in psychiatry, (2) the literature of assessment, including differential psychology research on the efficacy of tests of various sorts, and the array of tests and scales on the market, and (3) experimental psychopathology, including literature of the sort covered by Eysenck's recent book on abnormal psychology. There is no particular reason why this material has to be taught in formal courses. The student's familiarity with it can be covered by examinations administered by the clinical psychology staff. As for a special seminar, that should not be necessary either. The *Cadres*, with the assistance of their leaders, should be able to handle what discussions are necessary.

The clinical sequence is an arrangement of intensive courses which must be taken in order. The student is admitted to successive courses only on recommendation of the professor who taught the preceding course. He consults with the other members of the clinical psychology staff in making his recommendations. The pattern is, generally, two hours of lecture and discussion per week and approximately eight hours of actual laboratory work per week. The series runs four semesters and a summer as follows:

First Semester

1 Clinical Methodology

Second Semester

2 Psychopathology

Summer

3 Dynamics of Behavior Change

Third Semester

4 Prediction of Behavior Change

Fourth Semester

5 Control of Behavioral Change

1 *Clinical Methodology*. In this course the student will be introduced to clinical psychology primarily as a method in the spectrum of methods employed by psychologists in scientific inquiry. He will start his laboratory work with the basic methods of psychology, observation of free behavior and the interview, which, in various ways are combined into the more complicated methods, techniques, and instruments used by clinical psychologists. From this introduction he will move to the so-called objective tests, particularly those used for assessing intellectual functioning, and these will be learned as special cases of the basic clinical methodology of observation and interview. He will learn that as a scientist he should never presume to report "findings" as a laboratory technician does, but *hypotheses*. He will learn to alert fellow clinicians to possibilities in their clients that might otherwise be overlooked, to generate "low-level" hypotheses, as well as "high-level" hypotheses for which there is a greater weight of evidence, to present in a lucid fashion the supporting evidence for and against clinical hypotheses, and to suggest ways in which further observations, say those made by a psychotherapist, a social worker, a teacher, a parent, or a hospital manager, can be used to adduce further evidence bearing on the hypotheses—either for or against. In this way the student will learn to be of assistance in a clinical situation while remaining faithful to his role as a scientist.

2 *Psychopathology*. In this course the student will be introduced to the institutional setting for disturbed persons. He will continue developing his laboratory skills, using observation, interview, tests, and hypotheses development in connection with the so-called "clinical types." He will be introduced to "the status examination" and the use of informal psychological tests, such as those described in the Wells-Ruesch Handbook. It is expected that, having first had training in clinical methodology, he will be alerted to the possible fallacies in "disease entity classifications," and will see these classifications, not as established content in the discipline of psychology, but as current hypotheses with varying amounts of supportive evidence. It is in the laboratory portion of this course that he will become somewhat familiar with problems of institutionalization and patient management.

3 *Dynamics of Behavior Change*. This course is designed for the summer session. The student learns personality theory in a setting involving persons. Instead of understanding psychodynamics as an assumed complex of forces bound up inside the individual, the student is brought into contact with persons whose lives are actually in the process of changing and he uses his clinical skills to observe the changes as they occur. The laboratory setting is one in which he can devote at least half time and it is a clinic or institution where patients, preferably children, are under psychological treatment and where the changes are obvious enough to be observed. During this period the lectures and discussions deal with applied personality theory and in the laboratory he increases his skill in basic clinical methodology.

4 *The Prediction of Behavior Change*. This course would come in the fall of the second year. It would include what is usually called psychodiagnostics, but instead of teaching differential diagnosis into the usual categories, the student is taught to use his clinical skills to predict and plan behavioral change, such as the change that is sought through psychotherapy. Projective and concept formation methods are introduced and the laboratory includes intensively supervised practice with these more complex instruments. Tests are taught in terms of basic psychological processes. For example, the Rorschach Test would be taught as a special case of perception and the student would approach it from the standpoint of perception theory, as well as from the standpoint of the logic of science and the dynamics of behavioral change.

5 *The Control of Behavior Change*. In this course the student would continue his study of clinical methodology, using those skills in observation, interview, and testing, as a basis for moving into the area of behavior control. This is where psychotherapy, as we commonly understand it, would be introduced. But it is to be noted where psychotherapy fits into this particular sequence and how it is regarded as an extension of the clinical methodology the student has been learning through the preceding sixteen months. The laboratory would involve intensive supervision in the control of behavioral change through interview, group processes, and activity therapy. Not more than five students would be assigned to one professor for the laboratory part of the course. Following the first semester of the course the student would be expected to continue for another semester, in the laboratory either before or after his internship, where he would be supervised by a professor with a different theoretical orientation.

6 *The Internship*. During the third year of doctoral training the student takes twelve months of an approved internship in an institutional setting, either intra-mural or extra-mural. Not only should the internship be one accredited by the American Psychological Association, but it should also be especially accredited by the university with an explicit understanding of the syllabus to be followed and the progress reports to be made available to the clinical staff of the Department of Psychology. The standards required should include the following as a minimum:

   1 A highly competent setting where psychology functions as a scientific and professional discipline, and not merely as an adjunctive technology.
   2 A superior staff of clinical psychologists with some of them assigned actual teaching duties with interns.
   3 An interdisciplinary staff involving capable representatives of at least two disciplines other than psychology.
   4 A syllabus designed for the superior training of doctoral candidates.
   5 An organized training program in psychodiagnostics, psychotherapy, interdisciplinary communication, institutional management, and applied research.
   6 A variety of clinical material.
   7 Access of interns to staff meetings where professional and administrative decisions regarding patients are made.
   8 A weekly seminar series dealing with theoretical and academic matters. This is in addition to seminars dealing with case disposition and techniques.
   9 Individual consultation with interns on a scheduled basis.
   10 Opportunity for the intern to pursue research activities at least twenty percent of the time.
   11 Reports to the clinical staff of the university regarding each intern's progress. The last report should include recommendations to the university as to what further training the student should receive before completing his degree requirements, and what restrictions should be placed on his further practice of clinical psychology.

7 *The Research Year*. During the fourth year of the program—though in most cases it will likely turn out to be the fifth—the student spends nearly all of his time in Research Cadre activities. His doctoral dissertation is completed. There is intensive planning of his career, particularly during the immediate post-doctoral years. These plans should include the development of a study prospectus to be used as a basis for requesting a grant for a year abroad within the first two or three post doctoral years. They should also include

preparation for achieving diplomate status in clinical psychology within five years after graduation. During this year he should present at least one scientific paper at a national or regional scientific meeting and he should meet the outstanding psychologists of the country, including those with whom he may expect later to associate himself.

8 *The Frontiers Program.* The fifth channel to scholarship is one which provides the student with opportunities to see psychology in action at the very frontiers of its enterprise. Local staff members, who are judged to have made an outstanding contribution to psychology, or who are about to make such a contribution, will be asked to give one or more lectures, or perhaps one-day workshops, to let students know what they are doing and what difficulties are being encountered. But this should by no means be limited to local psychologists. There should be a continuing program of invited guests who describe their frontier efforts in psychology. The doctoral students should be given particular opportunity to become acquainted with these men and to learn directly from them what such frontier effort involves.

9 *The Four Year Program in Sequence.*
   1 First Year. The student is introduced to a career in psychology primarily via the Research Cadre activities. He undertakes preliminary work on his thesis, he passes as many of the fundamentals examinations as he can, and he is introduced to his specialty of clinical psychology via the first three courses of the professional sequence. He completes his language requirements.
   2 Second Year. The student continues his study of psychology in general through the enrichment courses made available to him by his completion of the fundamentals examinations. He finishes his thesis and he continues the study of clinical psychology.
   3 Third Year. The student takes his internship and passes his doctoral qualifying examination. He makes preliminary studies leading to the formulation of final plans for his doctoral dissertation.
   4 Fourth Year. The student completes his doctoral dissertation and engages in intensive career planning. He begins the implementation of this career planning by participating in scientific meetings and making the acquaintance of outstanding psychologists.
   5 First Post-Doctoral Year. The student, now a psychologist with the Ph.D. Degree, undertakes full-time employment in a setting where advanced psychological work is being done and where there are adequate resources to enable him to advance his career along scholarly lines. He assumes professional responsibilities and meets practical challenges. This employment will be considered temporary in most instances.
   6 Second Post-Doctoral Year. The psychologist spends the year abroad, preferably concentrating his scholarly efforts at one or two universities.
   7 Third to Fifth Post-Doctoral Years. The psychologist establishes himself as a scholar in a setting where advanced scholarly undertakings are not only possible, but are considered an essential part of his duties. He acquires diplomate status with the American Board of Examiners in Professional Psychology.

10 *The Thesis.* During the first two years of the training program the student should complete a minor study of publishable quality. This may or may not be considered a part of Masters Degree requirements. In any case, the purpose of the project is not only to make a scientific contribution, but to learn how to formulate scientific issues, to plan realistically for the completion of a research project, and to write a report that meets scientific and literary standards. It will be written in journal format, rather than in the usual padded style of MA theses. It should be directed at scientific issues whose relevance to clinical psychology can be clearly demonstrated by the Cadre leader and the oral examination should be conducted by the Cadre leader and two other professors, at least one of whom should be outside the specialty of clinical psychology.

11 *The Dissertation.* The final doctoral dissertation should be a fully rounded study, a section or sections of which should be of publishable quality. The study should be conducted in the Research Cadre setting with the Cadre leader serving as director. However, the director should have two professorial advisors assisting him, at least one of whom should be outside the specialty of clinical psychology. The dissertation should be concerned with scientific issues whose relevance to clinical psychology can be clearly demonstrated. The final oral examination should be open to all questions the committee considers relevant, not merely to issues embodied in the dissertation. The dissertation should meet both scientific and literary standards.

Appendix I

Independent Study and the Fundamentals Examinations

In order to implement the "Channels to Scholarship" we have called, *Independent Study of Fundamentals* and *Independent Choice of Courses* it is recommended that approximately seven areas of fundamentals of psychological science be identified and that approximately twice a year a student be permitted to take *Fundamentals Examinations* in as many of the areas as he wishes. It is anticipated that his decision to take any of the *Fundamentals Examinations* will be partly guided by the advice of his Cadre Leader and the Proseminar professors.

These *Fundamentals Examinations* should be formulated, administered, and appraised by a committee of the Department as a whole, and not by individual professors having veto authority. The standards should be high enough to guarantee a minimum level of achievement in each of the fundamentals of psychological science, but they should not be so high that students will be driven to take extensive courses in order to prepare themselves. In other words, it should be feasible for a student to prepare himself in most of the seven fundamentals, depending only on his independent study of the reading lists provided by the Department, on informal discussions in his Research Cadre, and on the Proseminars.

It would be hoped that a student would complete most of his *Fundamentals Examinations* by the end of his first graduate year, and that only in exceptional cases would he have any of the *Examinations* remaining to be taken at the end of his second year. It would also be hoped that the student would prepare himself to pass the *Examinations* with a minimum amount of formal course work. If this can be achieved it will mean that students will have more freedom to make selections from a wide variety of courses, according to their various interests. It will mean also that professors will have to teach fewer routine courses dealing with fundamentals only, and can direct their teaching to the more exciting aspects of psychology.

The Proseminars as a Way of Supporting Independent Study

As a support for students engaging in independent study, *and not as a course for cramming the student with what he ought to know*, the Department should conduct a year-long Proseminar Series each year, open on an optional basis to all students in the doctoral program. The Proseminar would deal, in succession, with each of the seven Fundamentals of Psychological Science. The typical pattern would be for a professor or professors in one of the Fundamentals areas to present a carefully selected reading list in that area and to spend four to six semi-weekly sessions annotating the reading list and in suggesting study plans and objectives.

Following this, an open-house colloquy every week or two over a period of six or eight weeks to answer questions that have arisen in the minds of the students who are pursuing the independent study of the reading lists. Near the end of the colloquy series students should be given a "take-home" examination. The purpose of this examination would be primarily self appraisal. If the student answers the questions and returns them, the professor may go over his answers with him and advise him as to whether he appears to be ready to attempt the Department's Fundamentals Examination in that area, or he should extend his preparation further in certain directions.

Proseminars should be introduced at approximately one month intervals, that is to say, the Proseminar on the next topic would be started before the colloquies on the preceding topic had been concluded. The student should be free to attend whatever Proseminar sessions he wishes, using his own judgment as to their value in helping him with his independent study. The Proseminar Series should not involve credit, but some lump amount of "credit," if credit must be hoarded, may be assigned for successful completion of the Fundamentals Examinations.

The Role of Courses in a Program Emphasizing Independent Scholarship

It is said that to play pool well is to disclose one's misspent youth. If this may be paraphrased, one might go on to say that a "straight A" record is evidence of indiscriminate scholarship, for in the course of one's academic career there must have been a number of occasions when time required to earn an "A" might have been spent more productively. May we assume, therefore, that the quality of one's attainment in well chosen courses is a better test of mature scholarship than is a record of minimum marks in all courses, especially in the dreary ones that so often trap the unwary student. Working on this assumption, then, it is suggested that the doctoral candidate show a record of "A" in half the graduate courses he takes, rather than a minimum grade of "B" in all courses. This would mean that his marks in some courses might be as low as "F," and no questions asked! If he found himself enrolled in a course where some of the lectures were of interest, but the assignments were not worth carrying out, he might attend what lectures he pleased, complete what assignments he pleased, and let the semester grade follow the natural course of such academic events.

But what happens to "standards?" Obviously such a liberal policy regarding "grades" must assume that minimum standards are protected by some other device. In the program suggested here the minimum standards in general psychology are protected by the *Fundamentals Examinations*. Without such examinations, such a liberal "grade" policy might be hazardous, although the question might well be raised as to the appropriateness of the indiscriminate scholarship by which we normally maintain "standards."

In this program a careful distinction must be made between courses that serve different functions. In an earlier part of this working paper it has been said that in the area of one's professional specialty it is pointless to teach the why without the how, and irresponsible to teach the how without the why. This suggests that in the clinical specialty certain courses would be "required" and that each course of this type would involve both the whys and the hows.

But what about areas in which closely supervised learning of methodology is not required? Cannot these be mastered by independent study, and achievement measured by formal examination only? The answer suggested in this doctoral education proposal is "yes." Still there are some special cases to be taken into account. In clinical psychology, the professional specialty field of this proposed program, there are also certain subject matter areas that might be covered by examination only. As indicated earlier, these areas may be "basic nosology," "the literature of assessment, differential psychology, and psychometrics," and "experimental psychopathology." It is suggested that these are areas in which no special courses need be given, assuming that a well-selected bibliography and well-led Research Cadres will take care of the student's needs.

There is a converse situation in the case of statistics and experimental design. This is a topical area suggested for inclusion in the Fundamentals Examinations for which the student prepares on his own. But here, quite definitely, is an area in which both whys and hows must be conjoined. Do we not need, therefore, to require a course with a laboratory, as in the case of the professional courses? Perhaps so, but it may be worth a try to see if the computational aspects of the area cannot be handled in the Research Cadre where applied research is actually in progress at all times.

Next we face more particularly the question as to what role "courses," as we academicians know them, play in this proposed doctoral program. They do play an important part, and radical as the proposals have been up to this point, there is no reason to believe that good courses are not essential to the program. Indeed, in this program it should be possible to have better courses, and even less excuse for having mediocre ones. Let us see how this works.

Some students will find it inexpedient to depend wholly upon independent study to prepare for all the Fundamentals Examinations. They will need to take courses, and suitable courses should be provided, either at City College or other colleges in the university. This is to say that there should be perhaps one seminar or course in each of the seven fundamentals designed for such students.

But beyond this bare minimum, the course offerings serve solely to provide the maximum amount of enrichment an enlightened faculty can provide and need never be routine presentations of ordinary subject matter, simply to get it taught. They should be designed to challenge the best students and should represent the very best that the faculty member has to offer in his own field. In no case should a course be taught by a faculty member who has no more than a passing interest in it, simply because the course is scheduled. In this program when a course is offered it should represent a genuine and current enthusiasm on the part of the faculty member, and an area where he is outstandingly competent. If these two conditions cannot be met, there is no excuse for offering the course to doctoral students. Indeed it should be canceled forthwith! There is no provision in this proposed enrichment program for teaching courses simply to extend curricular coverage or to fill out professorial teaching loads.

As suggested before, a certain amount of "credit" might be assigned to those who complete the Fundamentals Examinations—perhaps ten credits. Assuming that the professional sequence will represent a segment of the student's training equivalent to twenty-five credits, this leaves about twenty-five credits to be obtained by courses or seminars. It is suggested that the student be allowed to acquire these credits at the graduate level in any college of the university and in any advanced subject of any department. In fact, the more widely students forage for enrichment the more they will contribute to each other's education through their Cadre discussions.

Appendix II

Concrete Proposals Regarding Proseminars in Psychological Science

Typically at the end of the first year, and no later than the end of the second year, a written qualifying examination is required on the basic topics in psychological science indicated below. Those entering with advanced standing probably will already have sufficient background in several of the content areas. Entering students may prepare for this examination either through independent study or participation in the proseminar.

The proseminar program will be introduced with a presentation of the problems inherent in developing a philosophy of science. The exploration of assumptions underlying the application of a scientific approach to psychology will be the unifying theme throughout the year's proseminar program. The professor presenting this introductory unit will also serve as coordinator of the proseminars to provide articulation between the topic units and to place these areas in historical perspective to show their contributions to the development of psychological science. Particular attention will be devoted to demonstrating the role of conceptual bias in providing both theoretical unification and a constriction of the perceptual field.

Responsibility for each of the areas will be assumed by a different faculty member. At the beginning of the period for consideration of each topic, the instructor will present copies of a bibliography covering representative as well as historically and conceptually important material published in that area. At the first meeting he will comment on each of these articles or books to provide the students with an understanding of why he feels they are important and to place them within a conceptual framework so that their study will be more meaningful. Most topics will be under consideration for about four weeks. During that time students will be encouraged to work in small groups as they develop knowledge of the literature. Each week the proseminar leader for that topic will meet with the students at least once to stimulate discussion of the basic issues in the area. The readings will be assumed as a common background so that there may be an intensive effort to see implications of the experimental literature rather than simply review it. Emphasis will be on the clash of theoretical viewpoints and their resultant impact on contemporary thinking. At the end of each unit there will be a diagnostic test so that the student may be appraised of his deficiencies in the area before he takes the qualifying examination.

Proseminar 1: Philosophy of Science
The evolution of a scientific view of man will be presented as it evolved from earlier metaphysical concepts. The role of logical processes will be examined particularly in regard to the problems of making experimental inferences. Changing uses of the deductive and inductive methods will be reviewed in relation to the process of developing hypotheses. A broad perspective of systematic approaches to psychological problems will be included to provide a background for detailed study of the various areas. Attention will be devoted to the problem of creativity both as a personality function and as a challenge to accelerating the maturation of psychological science.

Proseminar 2: Applied Experimental Design
After developing an understanding of scientific method and the role of experimentation, it is necessary to examine the assumptions underlying selection of various experimental designs. This involves the limitations of "proof" as well as those inherent in various statistical procedures. Techniques, formulae and computational procedures will be included as parts of descriptive statistics and statistical inference. There will be an introduction to various laboratory methods such as psychophysical procedures and conditioning.

Proseminar 3: Physiological Psychology
Emphasis will be on an understanding of the functional role of the organism's structures in determining the expression and limitations of behavior. This will include study of the neuroendocrine system, the autonomic nervous system and the brain with the recent experimental data on the control functions of the brain stem. Specific applications will be presented in the study of disruption in the higher integrative functions due to organic brain disorders, and in the study of the role of stress in psychosomatic reactions.

Proseminar 4: Developmental Psychology
This area will review the psychological and physiological factors which contribute to the growth of the organism toward maturity and the eventual decline in functioning. Data on genetic factors, current concepts of instinct and prenatal influences will be studied to understand the limitations on behavior already imposed at birth. The growth from infancy to adulthood will be looked at both from the view of physical maturation and from an awareness of the perceptual and interpersonal environmental influences on psychogenic development. Problems of adolescence and aging will be included.

Proseminar 5: Basic Cognitive and Behavioral Processes
Although there will be recognition of the role of Behaviorist, Gestalt, Transactional and other "school" viewpoints in sharpening the analysis of basic psychological processes, the emphasis will be on the problems inherent in understanding the processes themselves. This will be an attempt to avoid the artificial dichotomization of activities as either involving perception or learning, and instead will show the interrelationship between sensation, perception, learning, motivation and the mediating processes. Modification of the organism's behavior by the environment will be studied in relation to the development of complex thought processes and activities.

Proseminar 6: Personality
The view of man held by varied personality theorists will be examined to show how this image determines the conceptual systems they develop and its implications in the treatment process. In view of the claims made for each personality theory, an effort will be made to determine underlying common factors which might account for their mutual effectiveness. The remaining differences will be studied in relation to the limitations and applications of the different approaches. The experimental literature will be reviewed not only as it applies to the evaluation of techniques for control of behavior, but also as it contributes to an understanding of specific problems in the determination of personality functions. Reference will also be made to the description and prediction of personality traits.

Proseminar 7: Social Interactions and Forces
This section will start with an examination of the individual's interaction with others and will culminate in the interaction among cultures. The formation of groups in play, school, work and community will be examined along with their effect on the individual's behavior. Interpersonal relations and interaction will be viewed both as processes in personality development and communication. The role of institutions within the community will be studied in relation to the sociopathology of prejudice and delinquency. Material from cultural anthropology will show varied solutions used by societies to meet the needs of man as a social creature.

An Alternative Proposal for Proseminar 7

Dr. Hartley has suggested the following draft revision for the Proseminar in Social Psychology. This revision is built around the theme of *communication*. It is hoped that this document will arouse others to offer alternative proposals in this and other areas, and in various other features of this proposed doctoral program.

Proseminar 7: Social Psychology

The point of departure for the study of social psychology will be the nature of communication, the process of interpersonal influence. The various approaches to such study from the linguistic, statistical, semantic, and psychological process orientations will be examined and the relevant research scrutinized. Structural features of human social organizations will be reviewed and integrated with the studies of the social processes. The difference between a social psychological approach and the approach to social phenomena through multiple individual psychologies will be examined. The nature of group processes and the "social" components of individual behavior will be considered. Selected problems in deviant behavior and in the behavior of deviant individuals will be studied.

Appendix III

Tentative Suggestions for Enrichment Seminars

The following seminars deal with specific topics in general and clinical psychology. They are both more extensive and intensive in their coverage of content than the proseminars, but some students may elect to take them in preparation for portions of the departmental qualifying examination. Many will be offered in different years on a rotating basis.

301 *Physiological Psychology I.* The interrelation of structure and behavior of the organism and the physiological background of various processes: structure and function of nervous system, problems relating to the concept of "reflex," the organization, development and coordination of motor activities, perceptual and cognitive functions, and the physiological basis of emotions.
2 lec., 2 lab. hrs. wk.

302 *Physiological Psychology II.* The biology of motivation and the analysis of instinctive behavior: the problem of behavioral genetics, endocrinological aspects of behavior, and the physiological basis of sensation, perception and learning. A critical examination of specific techniques used in the comparative study of animal behavior.
2 lec., 2 lab. hrs. wk.

305 *Theories of Learning.* Perceptual, motor and verbal learning, retention and forgetting, transfer of training, mediational processes.

306 *Theories of Perception.* Physiological, Gestalt and transactional approaches. Role of perception in individual and social behavior.

310 *Child and Adolescent Psychology.* Individuality in growth patterns, critical periods in development, methods for studying personality development, problems of role learning, delinquency.

311 *Differential Adult Psychology and Human Abilities.* Analysis of individual differences in human abilities, creativity and talent.

312 *Psychology of Aging.* Physiological and behavioral changes with age, problems of advancing maturity and old age, economic problems.

315 *Personality and Society.* A systematic analysis of theory and data relating to individual behavior and the functioning of social institutions. Social ecology and epidemiology of social illness, cultural and class differences. The social life of a mental hospital.

316 *Psychology of Intergroup Relations.* An examination of theory and data related to status relationship among various racial, color, nationality and ethnic groups comprising the American society. Special examination of the stresses and strains involved in competition for status, demands for and resistance to change and the techniques for change.

320 *Statistical Research Methods in Psychology I.* Review of sampling, probability and parameter estimation, tests of statistical hypotheses, correlation analysis. Analysis of variance and covariance.

321 *Statistical Research Methods in Psychology II.* Study of experimental designs and statistical assumptions. Non-parametric techniques, machine programming, multiple correlation and factor analysis.

331 *Development of Psychological Theory.* Antecedents of modern psychological science in ancient Greek thinking to beginnings of contemporary psychology.

332 *Contemporary Psychological Viewpoints.* Survey of recent trends and special areas of study such as semantics, information theory, E.S.P., and existentialism.

350 *Psychometric Methods.* Construction and evaluation of psychological tests. Theory of measurement, psychological scaling in psychophysics, differential and social psychology.

352 *Psychodiagnostics: Intelligence and Related Abilities.* Individual and group appraisal of intelligence and related abilities.

353 *Psychodiagnostics: The Rorschach Method.* Use of the Rorschach method for differential diagnosis and understanding of personality dynamics, analysis of records of normal, neurotic, psychotic, and organic subjects.

354 *Psychodiagnostics: Thematic Apperception Test and other Projective Techniques.* The concept of projection in personality evaluation as applied to the T.A.T. and other tests such as the M.A.P.S. and figure drawings.

375 *Freudian Personality Theory.* Analysis of Freud's contributions to the understanding of behavior with its historical-chronological approach.

376 *Recent Developments in Psychoanalytic Theory.* Particular stress on the emergence of ego psychology.

377 *Non-Freudian Theories of Personality.* The contributions of Jung, Adler, Rank, Horney, Fromm, Sullivan, and Rogers.

378 *Role of Learning and Motivation in Control of Behavior.* The contributions of Pavlov, Wolpe, Dollard, Miller, Mowrer and Cameron.

Alternatives

Following is an alternative suggestion for a seminar in social psychology:

315 *Social Behavior.* A systematic analysis of theory and data analyzing the behavior of the individual as it is influenced as determined by his participation in a structured society. Selected problems in the analysis of human behavior and social change will be examined from a social psychological point of view.

Appendix IV

Miscellaneous Proposals Regarding Procedures

A *Admission Requirements for the Doctoral Program in Clinical Psychology. Departmental Requirements:*
Since only a limited number of students can be accepted for graduate training, admission will be on a competitive basis. Evaluation of applicants will be based on all available data such as undergraduate records, letters of recommendation, test scores and interview.

B *General Requirements for the Masters in Psychology:*
The program is designed for students with the ability and motivation to complete doctoral training. In the process some may elect to meet the requirements for the Masters and others may need to terminate at this point. The Masters is not intended as a prerequisite to the Doctoral Program, but rather an indication that a portion of it has been completed.

1 *Credit and residence:* A minimum of 30 resident credits.
2 *Language requirement:* The candidate will be expected to show evidence of ability to read professional literature with the aid of a dictionary in at least one language which has a body of research literature relevant to his program of studies.
3 *Scholarship:* Students will receive a grade of "pass" or "fail" in each course or seminar. The grade of "pass" is required for degree credit. Further discrimination among students will be on the basis of departmental examination and assessment.
4 *Departmental Qualifying Examination:* All candidates must pass a written departmental examination on the fundamentals of psychological science and on the understanding of clinical problems. Reexamination will be permitted at the discretion of the Graduate Committee.
5 *Masters Thesis:* A research investigation must be completed within two years after passing the Qualifying Examination, and in no case later than the fourth year after admission to the program. It shall be presented in the form of a publishable paper with whatever supplementary materials are deemed necessary by the student's committee.
6 *Committee:* Each student shall have a committee which will supervise his program and thesis research and will conduct his final oral examination. It shall be composed of a chairman who will assume direct responsibility for thesis supervision, and two other members. One of these shall be kept closely informed of the research progress, and one of them shall represent an area different from that represented by the chairman.
7 *Oral Examination:* Upon completion of all other requirements, an oral examination must be passed. It will be based primarily on the thesis and related subjects. It shall be conducted by the student's committee in the presence of members of the student body and other interested faculty members.

C *General Requirements for the Doctorate in Psychology:*

1 *Credit and residence:* A minimum of 60 credits exclusive of internship, practicum and research requirements. At least 30 shall be in residence.
2 *Language requirement:* The candidate will be expected to show evidence of language skills relevant to his program of study and research. He may meet this requirement by demonstrating the ability to read professional literature in two languages with the aid of a dictionary, or by demonstrating higher-level, comprehensive skills in a single language. This must be met before the preliminary oral examination.

3 *Scholarship:* Students will receive a grade of "pass" or "fail" in each course or seminar. The grade of "pass" is required for degree credit. Further discrimination among students will be on the basis of departmental examination and assessment.

4 *Departmental Qualifying Examination:* All candidates must pass a written departmental examination on the fundamentals of psychological science and on the understanding of clinical problems. Students may take the entire examination or portions of it as soon as they feel prepared, but in no case later than the end of their second year in residence. Reexamination will be permitted, but the examination must be passed before the student may begin his internship.

5 *Committee:* By the end of the first year each student shall arrange for the appointment of a committee which will supervise his research and program of studies. It shall be composed of a chairman who will assume direct responsibility for dissertation supervision, and four other members. Two of these shall be kept closely informed of the research in progress, and at least one of them shall represent an area different from that represented by the chairman. The committee may require additional study or experience in areas where they feel the student is deficient.

6 *Clinical Assessment:* At the end of each semester that the student is engaged in clinical activities, his clinical supervisors shall meet with his committee chairman to assess the candidate's competence and maturity in dealing with clients. This judgment must be satisfactory if the student is to proceed with his clinical experience.

7 *Preliminary Oral Examination:* Upon completion of the first two years of the doctoral program or its equivalent, all candidates must pass a preliminary oral examination based on the integration of the student's preparation in psychological science and clinical psychology. Should a student fail, he may apply for reexamination within a year.

8 *Clinical Experience:* During the first two years of the program the student will participate in the clinical practice offered in conjunction with the clinical core program. During his first summer he will work at least thirty hours a week for two months in a clinical setting approved by the department. An internship of 2000 hours is required at approved institutions or organizations which provide adequately supervised, diverse experience appropriate to the candidate's training needs. The internship normally will be completed with a full-time assignment during the third year of the program. In some cases it may be taken over a two year period of half-time service.

74

Sin and Psychotherapy[1]

Everyman's Eden

Not so many years ago a man was recalling a childhood experience. His maternal grandfather, a clergyman, had died and his grandmother had recently come to live with the family. Her addition to the household required some readjustments all around. It was decided that his mother should undertake full-time employment to help bear the increased financial burden and the grandmother should assume the household duties, including supervision of the children. He recalled one evening in particular when he was nine years old. He and his grandmother were alone and he was preparing for his evening bath. She expressed shock at the exposure of his naked body, and in that instant there had come over him the most awful feeling of isolation he had ever experienced in his life.

At the time the man related this experience he had been in psychotherapy for more than a year. While he had mentioned the incident several times before, it was not until this particular session that he was able to express the force he attached to its impact and to reflect clearly the way he had come to construe the experience in subsequent years. I should add that, with him as with other persons who have underscored similar experiences in their autobiographies, it was his construction of many experiences that gave this incident its semiotic place in the chain of events that were to follow.

At the age of thirty my client had accumulated a remarkable series of failures in his life. In the university he had failed in course after course, and outside the university he had failed in job after job. He had neither been able to establish himself away from home nor had he been able to work out a comfortable relationship within the household where he lived with his aging parents. Only in recent months had his sense of unworthiness eased enough to permit him to have his first dates with girls.

Nor had the psychotherapeutic relationship been all that one might hope for. While there had often been moments when he had spoken of the anguish he felt, of his sense of helplessness, and of his apprehension about the confrontations psychotherapy might thrust upon him, there had been only fleeting instants when his communication with me had been unguarded. I was not the person he had been looking for.

Notwithstanding the tenuous relationship between us there had been some few occasions when he had gone beyond mere expressions of distress and had spoken with depth of feeling and insight. The interview I have mentioned was one of them. After telling me of the incident with his grandmother and how things had never been quite the same afterward, he fell silent. Then quickly he said, "It has always seemed as if that night I was thrown out of my Garden of Eden and through all these barren years I have been wandering about trying to find my way back in."

Ordinarily, I presume, when a therapist hears a remark like this he wonders if his patient has been going in for existentialism. But in this case, strangely enough, there was no evidence, either before or after, that his man had been reading in the existential vein, unless, of course, you consider certain passages from the Book of Genesis to be existential writing. To turn the inference around, it might be more cogent to speculate as to whether that ancient author of the Book of Genesis had been listening to my patient—or to someone like him.

The Penalty for Knowing Too Much

What about this knowledge of good and evil, this fruit that Adam and Eve ate? And what does it have to do with psychotherapy? Was—is—the exile Adam and Eve—and my patient—experienced to be regarded as a petulant retaliation for their dabbling in matters reserved for a superhuman being? Or do we face here a basic principle of human life, as true for the individual now as it was for the most

[1] Originally presented at the Temple University Symposium on Psychotherapy, Philadelphia, Pennsylvania, March 9, 1962. First published in Mowrer, O.H. (Ed.). (1966). *Morality and mental health* (pp. 365–381). Rand McNally. Republished in Vinacke, W.E. (Ed.). (1968). *Readings in general psychology* (pp. 123–139). American Book Co., and in Maher, B. (Ed.). (1969). *Clinical psychology and personality: The selected papers of George Kelly* (pp. 165–188). Wiley. Republished by permission of Wiley.

Collected Papers of the Pioneer of Constructivist Psychology: George A. Kelly, First Edition. Edited by David A. Winter and Nick Reed.

ancient progenitors of the human race; that with knowledge come responsibilities and with responsibilities comes trouble? Adam and Eve, in this remarkably insightful story, sought the knowledge of good and evil, and that is precisely what they got, for they lived to see one of their sons grow to be a good man, and the other his murderer.

Modern man, no less tragic in his plight, has also sought the knowledge of many things that have proved too much for him. Some have sought sexual knowledge—not too difficult an achievement. But they usually found out more than they wanted to know. Others, somewhat more intellectually inclined, no doubt, have searched for the secret of nuclear fission. That was harder, but they found it. And, like the sons of Adam, they found there was a lot more wrapped up in that tiny little affair than they had any intention of being responsible for.

While we all have Eves to titillate our curiosity, none of us, neither scholar, businessman, labor unionist, nor clergyman, can claim that he himself has not had an active part in welding the chain of events that has led up to where we are. And now all of us face the terror of an impatient and ruthless enemy who is held in check only by his own fears and his tenuous hope of gaining a less costly victory over us.

The realities come even closer home than that. We see our sons impressed into the uniformed roles into which society ordains its killers and its martyrs. These youngsters of ours will try to hold off catastrophe a little longer by the only means we know. Is it worth it? Well, of course it is worth it! It is the alternative that is not worth it!

So, confronted with all the terrifying varieties of knowledge they have sought—little things, big things, childish things, adult things—men everywhere, just like my client, are scampering hither and thither, from couch to picket line, from picket line to couch, trying to find their way back into the Garden of Eden, and altogether willing—even eager—to abandon all the good mankind has gradually achieved over the centuries in order to escape the bad that threatens to engulf them. For so many men and women today, whether it is from the fear of nuclear fission or from the dread of personal exile, the only way back to the amoral contentment of Eden seems to be through psychotherapy. They foresee no way of coping with the problems they face, other than to lie down and be treated for them.

Eden as a Psychological Problem

I hope it is clear that I am talking about a psychological problem and I intend to deal with it as best I can in a psychological manner, even though this is not the kind of undertaking most psychologists have any stomach for. The rather lurid title I have chosen for this paper is as exact a statement of the topic of my remarks as I could render. I make no apology for that!

I suppose I could offer an apology for making such a serious thing out of that spicy little story from Genesis. Forgive me for *that*, if you like. But I have reasons for it, too. First of all, it was a story used by a person in deep distress to let a psychologist know what he was experiencing. If his troubles had seemed to him to be more superficial or localized I doubt that he would have invoked the Eden metaphor. The depth of his perplexity opened the way for him to say something profound, and to voice the cry, not of himself alone, but of all lonely mankind. And, rather than take down what he said and discount it in proportion to his psychological disturbance, which is what psychologists usually do with such remarks, I am inclined to take what was said all the more seriously because it came from a deeply troubled man.

I shall want to say more about this point presently, but first let me go on to my second reason for talking about Eden. I am well aware that there is little precedence in scientific discourse for talking about sin, and much less for talking about the Garden of Eden. Scientists are reluctant to talk about things they cannot put their fingers on, or are not sure really happened the way they have been reported. But when a story has been told and retold through the centuries and it challenges, as this story does, generation after generation of scholars, then only the scientist who is willfully blind to human nature can ignore what is currently going on. Certainly the psychologist, least of all scientists, cannot[2] afford to ignore it altogether.

So I have two reasons for talking about Eden; one because it was a focal image in the experience of a troubled person whom I know rather intimately, the other because it is a story that men seem unable to forget. There it is, an experiential phenomenon, just the sort of thing psychologists are supposed to look into—or, if you insist, a behavioral phenomenon, if the word "behavioral" makes it any more legitimate. As a psychologist it is up to me to make something out of it if I can.

But how? Shall I approach the psychological phenomenon of Eden by the classical methods of scriptural exigesis? Shall I use the methods of protocol analysis—the verb-adjective ratio, the proportions of self-reference and notself-reference, the balance between feelings of strength and threat, some kind of confabulation index, or an abstract-concrete typology? While all these are analytic devices that might throw some psychological light on the problems of man, permit me to explore with a somewhat different method, one that grows out of the philosophical and psychological assumptions underlying personal construct theory.

[2] Editors' note: "can" in the original.

Personal Construct Analysis

Personal construct theory assumes, among other things, that any construct used by man is, psychologically speaking, a bi-polar affair. One does not understand a personal construct simply by apprehending some basis of *similarity* between objects; he must understand the basis of *distinction* as well. Both similarity and contrast are involved. So we look for the grounds upon which certain matters can be judged as similar to each other, and, by the same token, stand in meaningful contrast to certain other objects within the construct's range of convenience. Stated in Hegelian terms this is to say no thesis is complete without its antithesis. Perhaps I should add that I am aware that this dialectical form goes back a good deal further than Hegel, perhaps as far as the pre-Socratic philosopher Anaximander. Be that as it may, I am not so much concerned with the classical logic of the dialectic as I am with its psychological appropriateness in describing how man characteristically functions.

So let us approach the age-old story of Eden, and the up-to-the-minute version blurted out by my patient, as psychologists. Moreover, let us approach it from the standpoint of this particular theory. Specifically, this is to say we will *not* look for motives to explain the preoccupation of Adam, Eve, and my patient, for personal construct theory completely abandons the notion of motivation. We shall, instead, attempt to understand how the writer of Genesis, and all those who through the centuries have followed the same channels of thought, came to grips with that perplexing something that makes man human. What were the personal constructs in terms of which he, my patient, and all the millions in between erected to cope with an existence they could no longer take for granted?

There appear to be at least three essential constructs in the Eden story, each, in succession, offering man a pair of alternatives. The first is the distinction between loneliness and companionship. Against this axis man made a choice; he chose companionship. Having made this choice it was not long before he was confronted with a second, this one based on the construct of innocence versus knowledge. We all know how that one turned out; with a little gentle nudging he chose knowledge. No sooner had he done so than he was faced with the third dimension of choice, the construct of good versus evil. He is still hung up on that issue. Good and evil have proved to be extremely elusive values, so elusive, in fact, that man now spends a good deal of his time trying to renege on one or the other of his previous choices in the hopes that he can return to Eden and not have to face the issue any longer.

Three Ways to Escape

Personal construct theory has something else to say about psychological processes. Not only do men erect constructs to guide their way through what otherwise would be undifferentiated confusion, and not only do they often find it necessary to make personal choices in terms of these constructs, they also select from their personal repertories the constructs they intend to apply to the situation at hand. So it is with the three constructs of the Eden story. Finding themselves confronted with the perplexing construct of good and evil, men have attempted to back up a step and reconsider their choice between the preceding pair of alternatives—innocence versus knowledge. This time they will choose innocence. Will it work? Can man make his mind run in reverse?

No, it turns out to be well nigh impossible to find one's way back into Eden and live with one's companions in the way he might once have lived—in sheer innocence. Not that many haven't tried—psychopaths, for example! Nor is it easy to go back to man's lonely beginning and live without companionship altogether, though many, including my patient, have tried that too. So, if both the front and the back gates to Eden are boarded up, then what devices remain for avoiding the awful responsibility for distinguishing good from evil amidst shifting circumstances, and then making a firm choice between them? One way would be to reduce the construct to obsolescence by devising some transcendent principle that goes beyond good and evil. Philosophers, patients, and a lot of the rest of us have had an occasional go at this one. Scientists are always trying it, I've noticed. They seem to think that if they just keep their minds occupied with research, they will hit on something and the problem of good and evil will go away and stop bothering them. But as far as I can tell, none of these dodges has ever worked, and man is just as much plagued as ever with the imminent necessity for distinguishing one from the other and for making up his mind daily which to choose.

I hope it is clear that what I am saying does not have to do with formal philosophy only or with distinguished philosophers only, such as Thoreau, who tried getting in the back door to Eden, and Nietzsche, who tried to outrun the issue by reaching for a transcendent principle. The writings of such people we treat well enough with awe. But the efforts to get unsnagged are much more common than that. Just about everyone tries it. And when ordinary folks seem to try too hard we are likely to treat their efforts, not with awe, but with—psychotherapy.

Psychologists Too!

This is where psychologists themselves come into the picture. Even the people who treat people are likely to try to wriggle out of the dilemma. Some attempt it by pretending to avoid moral judgments where their patients are concerned. They end up making medical judgments instead! They don't feel so guilty about making medical judgments, for all they have to do is conform to the latest medical dogma and keep up their dues to the local medical society. There are a lot of psychologists who are clamoring for an invitation to that kind of club.

There are some who go further in their efforts to avoid the issue of good and evil. They talk about absolute permissiveness in their relations with others, and this, they would like to assume, is, in turn, the foundation of a democratic society, that is to say, Eden reentered by the front door. Thus, they seek both to enjoy the warmth of human companionship and the safety of a regulated society, without once venturing to do anything for which they might later feel guilty.

And, of course, some psychologists try to run around to the back door. They advocate complete self-acceptance as the primary principle of life. Presumably they think they don't even need companionship, and, if they don't need it, their patients don't either. There is no Eve in their Eden, or, if there is, she stays over on her side of the Garden and minds her own business. The self-sufficient Adam doesn't need her, he never gets hungry for apples, and he is never caught weeping parental tears of guilt and remorse over his beloved sons, Cain and Abel.

Thus far I have mentioned three types of escape from the issues of good and evil. I have called them, respectively, the front and the back door attempts to return to Eden, and the attempt to outrun the issue. I may be mistaken, but I am going to assume that it is not necessary to cite illustrations of these attitudes from the case records of our clients or from the writings of our colleagues in psychology and psychiatry. In a group of clinicians, such as yourselves, a sufficient number of illustrations will surely spring to mind.

Four Strategies

Let me go on, therefore, and describe some of the strategies mankind has employed for coping with the construct of good and evil on those occasions when he actually does try to face up to it. These, too, are as much the strategies of lowly persons, such as ourselves, as they are the formalized solutions of philosophers or societies.

Here personal construct theory has something else to say. Personal constructs are not abstractions that float around in thin air. They represent the ways we deal with things. If there were no elements to which the constructs were ever applied, there would be no constructs. The constructs of the individual man have to be understood both by his intentions and by his extensions. This applies to understanding one's own constructs as well as to understanding the constructs of the other fellow.

If a man has trouble distinguishing between good and evil he may try to straighten himself out by looking at cases. Look here; is this particular thing good? Is that particular thing to be called bad? How can I get the things here in front of me sorted out? Let us see how this works.

Law

First, I think we had better talk about the experience of the man who has done something he believes is wrong. This is not as simple a confrontation as many would have us believe. It might be simple if good and evil could be contained, once and for all, in a set of rules. A lot of people have thought of that strategy. But if you lay down a set of legalisms for governing future thought and action there can be only one outcome, and that is this: Tomorrow's vast challenges will be met with nothing more astute than yesterday's petty restraints. And the day after that, when you look back at what you have done, you discover, much too late, the evil you have allowed to infiltrate the world that has been entrusted to your care.

It is not so much the wrong that they have wanted to do that sends men to their psychotherapists, guilt-ridden and confused, as it is the wrong that has crept up on their blind side. I think most psychotherapists are aware of this now. Rules are useful enough as handrails for the morally nearsighted, and that, of course, includes most of us. But what we need to remember is that the man who willingly relies upon rules and laws to distinguish good from evil in his behalf is only seeking to avoid the foresight of what, in the end, good and evil will turn out to be. It is not going to be much comfort to him in the future, when he finds he has made a mess of things, to recall that he had closed his eyes and conformed to the rules.

What is this unctuous phrase that men so often quote once they have safely ensconced themselves in positions of legal power—"No man is above the law?" It sounds like the epitaph of an unsuccessful gangster. Indeed, for those who deign to accept this as the guiding principle of their lives, I suspect it is—even more appropriately so—an incriminating epitaph; it is their own! And for how many more of us, those of us who are certainly not the *visible* Eichmanns of this world and who have only tacitly accepted legalized power as the sufficient embodiment of good and evil, might not this well be the concluding statement: "Here lies a man, long since deceased, whose spirit, in its quest to separate the evil from the good, never thought to rise above the law!"

Authority

A second way to deal with good and evil is by subordination to authority. If I cannot distinguish between good and evil myself, I will hang on to the coattails of someone who can. In turning myself over for safekeeping, I may take account of the man's credentials—whether he has been educated in such matters, whether he has been a devout follower of certain long-standing principles or an institution, or whether he has been properly ordained in some kind of apostolic succession. I may, if I wish, use other criteria. If he seems strong, I can assume that he will not involve me with failure. If he seems to have an untroubled conscience, I can assume that he must be free from sin and hence a pretty good sort of fellow to take after. If he asserts that he has no doubts, it must be because he has a clear perception of where the whole business is going to end up. If he seems protective, he may bail me out of trouble.

By making these less complex judgments we simplify the crucial issue into one of obedience and disobedience. If it is obedience, it is good; if it is disobedience, it has got to be evil! Now it is not so hard to tell when you have been disobedient. In fact, the fellow who has your dossier will often, for no more than a nominal fee, agree to remind you of your obligations whenever you step out of line.

Conscience

Without stopping to comment on the effectiveness of this method of meeting mankind's crucial issue, other than to say that it probably provides the greatest freedom from guilt feelings, let me go on to a third strategy. This is to rely upon conscience. Some say this is the same as running back to mother, and one psychoanalyst—I've forgotten who it was—Fenichel perhaps—has said that the voice of conscience sounds suspiciously like the voice of mother. Knowing the current bad feeling between analysts and mothers, you can probably guess what *he* had to say about conscience as a guide to human conduct.

Reliance upon conscience places the responsibility for distinguishing good from evil squarely on the shoulders of the individual man. The other two strategies I have mentioned burden him only with the responsibility for obedience to law or authority, leaving the more difficult task of distinguishing essential good from evil to the law-making process or to persons entrusted with authority. The law-making process is inclined to lag behind the times, as we have already pointed out, while persons entrusted with authority are always inclined to exploit their powers arbitrarily.

But what about conscience? How up to date is it in meeting tomorrow's challenges, and how selfless is it in addressing itself to the searching task of distinguishing good from evil? Certainly our psychotherapeutic experience with conscience—or the superego, if you prefer— leads us to suspect that it too can be both out of date and biased. In fact, it may serve only to make the kinds of distinctions between good and evil that parents make for their children. The outcome may be that one who tries to be guided by his conscience may still be dependent upon antiquated rules and arbitrary authority via the vaguely remembered admonishments of his parents. Certainly if one is looking for the ultimate distinction between good and evil he will fail to find it in the present conscience of individual men, just as he has failed to find it in laws or embroidered in the robes of ecclesiastical potentates.

Purpose

There is a fourth strategy I suppose I should mention. If we decide what kind of world is scheduled to appear in the future, we can say that anything we can do to hasten it is good, and anything we do to delay it is evil. Everything hinges on making progress toward Utopia. It is fatal to change one's mind about the nature of that Utopia or to admit that one's efforts have been extended in the wrong direction. Psychologists do not often have experience with this kind of morality on this side of the Iron Curtain, though I have occasionally seen something like it here. When one is confronted with this point of view in a patient undergoing psychotherapy, he may expect a great tenacity, right up to the breaking point, then possibly a sudden collapse of the moral system.

Thus far I have not said anything especially helpful to the troubled mind. I have tried to show that Eden is a valid metaphor and that it expresses something in personal construct form that the psychologists who deal with distressed individuals ought to take seriously. I have mentioned the bipolar nature of psychological construing, and I have made a very simple analysis of the Eden story in terms of three such constructs—solitude versus companionship, innocence versus knowledge, and good versus evil. I have said that man selects his constructs from those he has at hand, as well as makes choices between the alternatives they offer. Some men, perhaps all of us at one time or another, try to renege on the choices we have made and attempt to reinstate a previous issue. That is to say, we try to reenter Eden by the back or the front door. Some try to replace the good-versus-evil construct with one that transcends it. Finally, I have spoken of four strategies—I suppose I could just as well have made it a dozen—by which men see the meaning of the good and evil dimension of life through the method of extension.

I hesitate to mention it, but complete candor would require me to point out the fact that the four strategies I have discussed—*law*, *authority*, *conscience*, and *purpose*—correspond to four of the great ethical systems now of concern to the Western World—*Judaism*, *Catholicism*, *Protestantism*, and *Communism*. But I must hasten to add to such a volatile statement, that the methods employed by one group are often used by others.

The strategies change somewhat with the years. I doubt, for example, that nowadays the Jesuits would very much mind relinquishing their historical claim to the notion that the end justifies the means, although I do doubt that the Communists, in turn, would be so gracious as to acknowledge the contribution. I have another thought. Since the Communists take such delight in reading the history of things that haven't happened yet, it might be that the Calvinists could be persuaded to put predestination into the missionary barrel. They have always felt a little ridiculous about it anyway, so I am sure they would find it highly amusing to see men running around inside the Kremlin trying to reach their predestinations. I suppose, too, the Jews might have something to offer, something they would be glad to get rid of, but at the moment I don't know what it would be.

As for making additions to their ethical systems, I suspect, as a whole, the Protestants, splintered into goodness knows how many sects by their emphasis upon the democracy of the individual conscience, would now just as soon lay claim to some of Judaism's traditionalism. Not because it necessarily makes sense to them, but for the sake of moral unity! Judaism, in turn, recently confronted as never before by the issue of exclusive nationalism versus exclusive nationalism[3], certainly is calling the attention of all of us in this country at least, to the far-reaching possibilities of a brotherhood of man.

So much for cross-fertilization! I brought the matter up only because I was afraid my earlier attempt to clarify the prototypical ways man has distinguished good from evil appeared to oversimplify the issues to the point of stereotypy.

What I have said so far may suggest that man simply cannot distinguish good from evil. In the sense of making an ultimate distinction in time to enjoy the weekend, that is true; he cannot. But man does distinguish the two after a fashion. He may not do it well enough, but nonetheless, he does it. Through the ages he has undoubtedly improved his perceptiveness and, while circumstances seem to keep increasing in complexity faster than he can keep up, it would be a mistake to argue that he should give up the quest. His laws have improved, on the whole, and his ecclesiastical authorities are a good deal more decent lot than they were a few generations back. So I don't see any reason for believing the state of affairs is absolutely hopeless.

The Psychology of Sin

Let us examine sin still more intimately, and from a psychological point of view. I am aware of the fact that up to now I have not even attempted to define the term, as would be mandatory if this were a discussion of formal ethics or theology. Yet, it will be sufficient for my purposes this afternoon merely to discuss sin as a personal experience.

A man is walking across a busy street holding the hand of his little girl and keeping a sharp lookout for the speeding traffic. Half way across he inadvertently steps into an open manhole, fractures his leg, cracks several ribs, and loses the sight in his left eye. This is what you might call a traumatic experience. He is likely to have a psychological reaction to it, as well as a physiological one. Or to state it more accurately in personal construct terms, it is an experience he will be inclined to make something out of, psychologically. He may feel foolish. He may thereafter jump two feet into the air every time he hears an automobile horn. He may berate himself for paying so much attention to the cars that he overlooked the hazard beneath his feet. He may wonder if he is losing his faculties and attempt rigid countermeasures against that eventuality. He may even cast about in his mind to recall if he has done something for which Providence would be disposed to punish him. But however he may construe the incident, whether at a cortical level or a reflex level, it would not be like him to dismiss it as something inconsequential.

Be that as it may, and distressed and anxious as he may be over the inferences he may draw from his mistake, I think one thing is clear; his feelings are quite different from what they would be if he had allowed his child to step into that open manhole, fracture her little leg, crack several ribs, and lose the sight of her left eye. I am sure that one does not need to have the empirical evidence that comes from experience as a psychotherapist to verify the probable psychological difference between the two experiences. Moreover, the difference cannot be attributed merely to the fact that it is against the law of Moses to drop your children into open manholes, or that the clergy generally take a dim view of that sort of mistake, or that it tends to be counterrevolutionary. The difference is pretty much a matter of the fact that the man's mistake has seriously involved someone other than himself. And more than that, it has involved someone to whom he, in his role as a parent, is deeply committed.

Guilt

Here we have what I believe are sufficient grounds for reaching a psychological understanding of sin. They may not be sufficient for an ethical understanding; as a matter of fact, I am sure they are not, but that is another matter. It is precisely at this point that personal construct theory comes into the psychological analysis of the problem.

Now you may be surprised to hear me say at this juncture that I do not regard personal construct theory as a phenomenological system. Phenomenology is an ontology and a psychology of private and noninterdependent worlds. I do not see one's personal construct system as wholly private, nor do I see it as free to regenerate itself into some monstrosity completely oblivious to external reality.

But I would say that the feelings of the man who had dropped his child into the open manhole are typically the feelings that go with the realization of sin. We call this experience *guilt*, and personal construct theory would want to make it clear that guilt is distinguishable from the other forms of anxiety and from the mere realization that one has made a mistake.

To experience guilt one must have a construction of himself in a role. In my illustration it was a parental role, one I calculated to be important enough to make my illustration vivid. But when I talk about role in this connection. I must insist upon a special definition. The definition of role as a set of expected behaviors anticipated by one's self or others will not serve to systematize our clinical observations. Nor is it enough to say that role is merely the performance of some function in an articulated social system. These definitions, and the several others like them

[3] Editors' note: [sic]

that are in current use among social scientists, do not provide us with the kind of scientific construct we can use for coming to grips with the problems of persons in deep distress. The definitions are largely couched in terms of extrapersonal operants, and it makes little sense to talk to a psychotherapy patient in such terms or their derivatives.

Let us say that a person copes with the world by erecting constructs or guidelines—verbal ones or reflexive ones—in terms of which he can fathom it and gain some sense of where he and it are going. Some of the constructs are erected for coping with the interpersonal aspects of his world. As long as these take no account of the outlooks of other persons, but only of their manifest behavior, we make no distinction between such constructs and others. But when his constructs provide the person with some notion of how matters appear to the other person, then we give them a special name, *role constructs*. This is to say, whatever one does in the light of his understanding of others' outlooks may be regarded as his role[4].

Now for guilt in terms of personal construct theory. I am obviously talking about the personal experience of guilt, not about moral culpability. Culpability is something else, and may or may not be involved, as most every psychotherapist's observations would probably attest. Nevertheless, if you should disagree with this observation, I would not be inclined to press the issue, for reasons that will be more clear when I come to talk about the psychotherapeutic task of helping patients come to grips with the problem of sin.

Guilt, in the personal construct theoretical system, then, becomes the sense of loss of role. The father in my illustration experienced guilt because he found himself a failure in the parental role. He suffered to the extent he was committed to that role, assuming he did not construe the incident as the culmination of a chain of other failures. And, to come back immediately to my other point, I see no reason to insist that a therapist would have to conclude that he was morally reprehensible for his mistake.

Loss of role can occur because of some sudden shift in one's construction of others' outlooks, leaving him the possessor of an invalidated life history. This is the sort of thing that happens when overeager young psychotherapists try to take on the problems of elderly clients. Fortunately, most elderly clients can stand up to them. One may feel guilty because of inconsistencies within his system. For example, it is a common experience to hear a client say, "I feel guilty because I don't feel guilty." One client a good many years ago, a Catholic girl, said she did not feel guilty for having extramarital sex relations, but she was overwhelmed with guilt feelings when she discovered the man was using a contraceptive. She was acutely aware of the speciousness of her judgment, and that, in turn, led her to wonder if she had any real moral sense at all, which led to another round of feelings of role loss, encompassing a good deal more than sex.

One may feel guilty because he remembers choosing to do something against his better judgment, or he may feel guilty simply because his judgment was faulty, as in my illustration of the unfortunate father. Moreover, since role constructs can just as well relate to one's interpretation of the outlook of a divine Being, one can feel as guilty for falling out of that role as for separation from a role based on an interpretation of more palpable personages.

Feeling Guilty for Being Good

One type of guilt manifestation that has proved most puzzling to those clinicians who are perceptive enough to observe it in their clients, is the feeling of the delinquent youngster who finds himself tricked into being "a good boy." In order to understand this well-documented phenomenon we need to make sure of our notion of role. I did not say that one plays a role only when he conforms to what he thinks others expect of him, nor did I say that he performs a role only to the extent that he correctly perceives the outlook of other persons. His role can just as well be designed to stand people on their heads and his interpretations of others may be wholly fallacious. Our unhappily good exdelinquent can put in hours of remorse and feel a great emptiness once he has found himself unfaithful to his role, antisocial and distorted as it may be. Indeed, it is not uncommon to find such a youngster attempting suicide, an act that makes both psychoanalysts and moralists turn themselves inside out to devise a coherent explanation. Sometimes it is said that such a person is upset because he has been disloyal to the delinquent society of which he is a member. But this is a crude oversimplification, based on the naive belief that morality is a simple matter of social identification.

There is a very interesting variant of this feeling-guilty-for-being-good. It turns up with increasing frequency in psychotherapy these days, and has become somewhat identifiable as a feature of our mid-century culture. The central idea seems to be that people should be themselves—an interesting kind of solipsism. Tell a young lady that she is a virtuous woman, and she is likely to start worrying right away. She will probably think you have accused her of being abnormal, bigoted, inhibited, intellectually dishonest, artificial, and not fit to associate with. It is pretty nearly as bad as telling a psychoanalyst he is neat and clean. Her construction undergirds a role when she takes the view that she must never appear to be anything other than what she has been at her worst. And her anxiety reaches the point of role loss and guilt when something happens to invalidate this position. Since psychotherapy is usually directed toward getting people to be something other than what they have thought themselves to be, it may become the occasion for acute guilt feelings in simple-minded men. The situation reminds me of the famous wood carving of the three monkeys in the Shinto Shrine at Nikko, Japan—"See no evil. Hear no evil. Speak no evil." The fourth monkey, "Do no evil," is conspicuously absent. After all, they are only monkeys, and there is no reason to expect monkeys to be anything but themselves!

[4] In my original definition of *role* I included the specification that there must be a conjoint enterprise involved. I now suspect that I was stepping outside the necessary implications of personal construct theory when I wrote that definition, though it seemed defensible enough at the time.

After Sin, What?

Let us turn our attention away from the person who believes he has sinned, and who feels guilty, to the persons who point accusing fingers at each other. The most primitive way to deal with a person who has done something evil is to retaliate. He does something bad, therefore, something bad can be done to him. This makes nearly everybody happy, except, of course, the fellow who starts the trouble. This procedure has two psychological effects: it extends coveted privileges to those who haven't had the nerve to try the same thing, and it serves warning on others who might be similarly tempted to start something.

An incident in the life of Jesus is a case in point. You remember He came upon a group of men about to stone a girl to death. She had been caught in the local parking lot at a rather inconvenient moment in her emotional life. Jesus suggested to the gang that if they really wanted to do it in an orderly fashion the fellow who had never sinned should heave out the first stone. I have the feeling that being the kind of punks they were they all had a pretty specific idea of what he meant, and that none of them wanted to admit in front of the others that he was innocent of that sort of thing—though I suspect some of them might have been innocent in this respect. The upshot was that they decided to give up the project, perhaps to go off and get into some mischief on the other side of town. But up to that point none of the goings on really had much to do with the girl and the sin she had committed.

I suppose retaliation may have another function. After an orgy of reprisals it may be that folks are satisfied to go back home and behave themselves a little longer. But neither does this have much to do with the person who sinned in the first place. As a matter of fact everyone should feel rather grateful to him for giving so many people a good excuse for doing what they so much wanted to do anyway. A good deal of our social interaction, both formal and informal, is still pitched at this level of treatment, though I doubt if the sinner often receives all the gratitude he deserves.

A somewhat more socialized approach is to demand restitution. Assuming that when a person sins he injures someone, he ought to do what he can to restore matters to their original state. Often a prisoner is encouraged to regard the serving of his sentence as a "payment of his debt to society," though it is a little hard to see how his imprisonment, which rarely returns a profit to society, can be considered the payment of a debt. Sometimes the restitution is even more labored. A man does something regarded as a sin against God. He is told to take twenty laps around the track and repeat a prayer two hundred times. It is difficult to imagine how this could make God feel any better, unless you imagine a God who likes to sit and listen to the same prayer over and over. If restitution is the objective, it might be more to the point to suggest to the man that he stop praying for a week or two so as to make less of a nuisance of himself.

Punishment

By far the most common way of treating sinners is to punish them. In psychological circles this is known as negative reinforcement. Throughout our culture it is pretty generally believed that behavior is controlled by red and green lights, known as punishment and rewards. There is the benign form of punishment that we use when we want to control the act of sin without bothering our heads about the personal constructs in terms of which the act made sense. This is the kind of thing we often do with children. From it they learn to keep a wary eye on parents, teachers, and policemen. Personal construct theory, which approaches behavior in terms of the constructions persons place upon their circumstances, would not consider this a very basic kind of psychological approach to the problems of human conduct.

And the same game is played under theological rules. Man makes a mistake. That upsets the Almighty. There is some disagreement on just how it upsets Him. Some say it makes Him furious and others say it depresses Him. Whichever it is, it is up to man to do something to restore the Almighty's peace of mind. So man punishes himself, or whoever it was who made the mistake. The Almighty wholeheartedly approves of this, and it makes Him feel so warm and permissive that He is disposed to forget the whole thing. He may even offer to pick up the tab for the damages caused by the sinful act. Under these theological rules man plays the classical role of a court fool in the Kingdom of Heaven.

A somewhat more mystical view, ably expressed by Elijah, is that punishment purifies the soul and enables the tortured individual to see the difference between good and evil with twenty-twenty vision. But lest you think that my simple way of stating this argument is intended to dismiss it, let me hasten to add that there is plenty of psychological evidence that some persons do make use of adversity to come to a deeper understanding of what is good and bad. I even suspect that the experience of sin is itself often just the thing to be woven into something constructive, though this is not the sort of remark one is supposed to make in front of the children.

As you can readily see, I don't think, taking all these methods into account, that we have yet found very good answers to the question of how to distinguish good from evil, nor to the question of how to get sinners straightened out. Some of the methods of treating sin turn out to be no more than methods of treating its guilt symptoms, and hence may work against their intended objectives. How often do we see the patient in psychotherapy who uses punishment to salve his guilty discomfort, yet scarcely gives a thought to how he got himself into trouble. Some patients even use punishment as a kind of prepayment for sins they think they might like to commit later on. This pay-as-you-go system may keep sinners from living beyond their means, but it contributes nothing to wisdom.

Assistance for the Troubled Man

Let us assume that, by and large, man was serious when he ate that apple; he really intended to gain the knowledge of good and evil. This is to say he has clearly embarked on an enterprise, and the task of those who wish to assist him is not to badger him into being good in spite of himself or to keep rapping his knuckles every time he reaches for something fragile. It is rather to accept his quest as legitimate and do what can be done to help him contrive a deeper understanding of how the distinctions between good and evil can be clarified. This is his task. He may not be up to it, but it is still his task, and it will be for generations to come.

We must concede, of course, that some men have lost interest in the quest. This is quite understandable when we consider the fact that most of the systems for dealing with good and evil are designed to circumvent the necessity for coming to grips with the problem. Why struggle with a perplexity for which you can never hope to devise more than a partial solution, when this culture, or that religion, will provide you with a thumb-indexed set of answers in tomorrow's mail, or, at the latest, during next Sunday's morning church service?

How to be Sick

But, as I have said, mankind, by and large, means to get this matter of good and evil straightened out to his satisfaction, even if it takes from now to eternity, as it likely will. In the meantime he can at least make progress. So let us turn now to the ways he has developed over the ages for assisting himself in his quest. There are a number of religious devices—prayer, penance possibly; certainly sharing the misfortunes of others is one device. These can be more than mere gimmicks for keeping your nose clean; they can be genuinely exploratory approaches to the much more challenging problem of understanding the real difference between right and wrong. There are also secular devices of a philosophical nature, and there are physical devices, one of which, in particular, I want to mention.

Man has always wondered if there isn't a relationship between evil and illness. At first he wondered if illness wasn't a symptom of evil. You remember Job decided that it wasn't, but was out-voted by his neighbors. More recently men have turned this hypothesis end-for-end and explored the possibility that evil is a symptom of illness. Understand and treat the illness, and the evil that tortures men's minds will evaporate. The only trouble with that apple that Adam ate was that it had worms in it. Treat his stomach ache and he will be as good as new.

There is some scientific evidence for this conclusion that I think we will have to accept as conclusive. Alcohol, tranquilizers, prefrontal lobotomy, will undoubtedly cause evil as experienced by the tortured mind to fade. As a matter of fact, there is nothing like a thorough-going topectomy to reduce the whole issue to inconsequentiality. Most of us use sleep more or less for this same purpose, though some find that sleep doesn't work and insist they can treat the ailment better if they stay awake and keep very, very busy. Move up in your job, keep up the payments, give the kids a little spending money while they're young enough to enjoy it, keep up the payments—or did I say that before? Above all, keep up the payments! You will find that is quite enough good and evil to worry about.

But I would like to talk about illness. Illness is a conceptual mode of thought that has proved to have wide utility. The use of this conceptual model has enabled mankind to accomplish many things that had long been believed impossible. Now I don't think this fact, important though it may be, obviates the possibility that many of these same benefits might better have been accomplished by other means. Even a few medical men have thought of this, and are genuinely concerned about it, though the drug manufacturers, whose advertising finances the most important "scientific" medical journals, have found effective ways to make it abundantly clear that reputable doctors should keep such thoughts to themselves.

Which Is It: Illness or Crime?

Illness is one thing; crime is another. Yet both of these are, in essence, conceptual models for dealing with man's failings. How man has come to apply one model to some things and the other model to others is a fascinating story of the history of thought. A woman screams at her husband from ten o'clock to midnight, and raises goose pimples on her neighbors' necks; that is sinful; apply the crime model and punish her. But if she has read anything at all in the women's magazines about psychiatry lately, she will realize that midnight is no time to stop. She should keep it up until six A.M., if her lungs will hold out. No one will punish her for that. They will take her to a place where there is a bed with crisp clean sheets, the same neighbors will send flowers, and the nicest man will come and talk to her! And the really ecstatic thing about it is that her husband—*her husband*, mind you—will have to pay that man fifty dollars an hour! All this, and heaven too!

So we have developed a culture where two distinct conceptual models are concurrently employed, one that says sin should be punished, the other that it should be treated. Our courts have the casuistic responsibility for determining which model to apply to whom. This can be a bit sticky when you are dealing with women whose husbands can't pay fifty dollars an hour, though the issue is less complex if you take into account the fact that if a woman had been the right kind of person in the first place, she would have married a man who could afford to pay fifty dollars an hour.

Well, the upshot is that the people who can afford it, as well as a lot of folks who can't, have decided that a problem is not something you solve, but is something you lie down and are treated for. The idea is catching on fast.

Stifling Man's Quest

I don't think that either punishment or treatment has much to do with man's basic undertaking, and it is unfortunate that these should be the only apparent alternatives for dealing with the more urgent matters of personal conduct. It is unfortunate that our psychological approaches to such matters were ever identified with medicine or illness, just as unfortunate, in the long run, as it would have been if they had remained identified with a punitive social system or a stimulus-response psychology. I even think it is unfortunate that we must use the term "therapy" for psychological assistance.

There is a further misfortune—perhaps even more far-reaching in its deleterious effects. Men who want to take this matter into their own hands and conclude the question in their own terms of morality or insight, have learned how to produce and alleviate guilt feelings. The device of excommunication, whether employed by a church, a political party, a sorority, a household, or a psychotherapist who unnecessarily invokes a dependency transference, is the most powerful device man has ever invented for bringing about individual conformity and cutting short man's personal quest for distinguishing good from evil. When this is combined with the devices men have contrived to alleviate the pangs of guilt—man's natural clue to sin—through religious confession, Communist self-criticism, sorority pledging, family reinstatement, or psychotherapeutic replacement of the superego, the suppression of man's enterprise can become very nearly absolute.

When the Psychotherapist Shares the Enterprise

The important thing to remember is, despite all the blatant claims that are made on every hand, no one has yet constructed the final answer to the question of what is good and what is evil, and that the moment man gives up the enterprise he is lost. The psychologist who attempts to assist his fellow man should keep this truth central to his system of practice. The task is to assist the individual man in what is singularly the most important undertaking in his life, the fullest possible understanding of the nature of good and evil. This is not to say that man must always steer clear of sin; it is to say, rather, that he should learn from it, and not blindly allow himself to repeat it.

It will occur to you that some of this might have been inferred from the teachings of Jesus and his concept of realistic confession followed by repentance, a concept that is quite different from penance, and quite different from the current interpretations of confession and repentance. Jesus suggested that if you do something bad you should not run from the scene of the crime screaming, "I've sinned, I've sinned. I'll make up for it! I'll never do it again!" he suggests instead that you stop, turn around and look at what you have done, acknowledge that it was you rather than the Devil, society, or your ulcers, examine the mistake, and reconstrue the situation so that the possibilities of making a similar mistake in the future are minimized.

What, then, are the steps in the psychotherapeutic process of a person who finds himself overwhelmed by a sense of sin—the sense of the loss of a great and important role? Logic, I suppose, would dictate that you should find out whether he had actually sinned or not. But here personal construct theory, being the psychology of the human enterprise rather than a substitute for it, takes issue with logic, which claims to be the foolproof process by which valid conclusions are always reached. Let the person tell you exactly what he thinks he did; yes. Speculate with him on whether it will be judged in the end as something evil; to do less would be hypocritical and evasive. But most of all, open the matter to inquiry—yours and his. This inquiry is the chosen quest of all mankind, and that includes both you and your client. Don't abandon it under any conditions—whether guilt, fear, or laziness. Don't abandon it for any set of prefabricated conclusions. Above all, don't let your client abandon it!

Therapy is not likely to get off to a good start with the therapist saying, "Yes, you did," or "No, you didn't." He may, in some cases, say, however, "I agree, that does sound like it was the wrong thing to do, but simply to call it wrong does not really tell us much unless we go back over the experience much more carefully than you have apparently been able to do so far. Besides, we need to have a much better sense of how matters seemed to you at the time the incident occurred."

Here we have illustrated in a very simplified form two of the essential psychotherapeutic steps in a case where the client's sense of guilt is a presenting symptom. We can call them *confession* and *repentance*, if we prefer the religious terms, or we can call them *observing incidents* and *formulating constructions*, if personal construct terms are preferred. To be sure, these are not standardized remarks to be used in all cases; indeed, in this particular form they might be quite inappropriate in some cases.

There is more to psychotherapy than the exploration of salient incidents. The client will have to reconstrue his role, experiment with it, and keep it open to continuing revision. Keeping in mind the special meaning of *role* in personal construct theory, the task is to press forward to develop and test role constructs experimentally. For role constructs are more than constructions of impersonal objects; they are efforts to understand the outlooks of others. One must find a way to put these man-made hypotheses into a comprehensive framework that will transcend the little stratagems of everyday social manipulation.

Throughout all this the psychotherapist has another kind of objective. Not only does he want to restore the resources of his clients and help him make his own determinations of the difference between good and evil in ways that are both valid and comprehensive, he wants also to restore the client as an on-going person. It is not enough for the client to be set back on his feet and given firm ground to stand on; he needs to prepare himself to advance into further explorations that we hope will not turn out so badly. But if he sins again, as he most certainly will if he is earnest in his quest, he should be able to profit from the next experience rather than be overwhelmed by it.

But this is enough to say about psychotherapeutic technique. After all, I promised you this would not be a how-to-do-it handbook for counselors who want to make people behave themselves without having to go into the grubby business of understanding them.

To come back to Jesus; do you remember what He said to the girl who had been so rudely exposed? He asked her where her accusers were and she said they were gone. Neither was He one of her accusers. She was on her own. Then He gently suggested that she might make something out of the experience so as not to repeat it. He didn't even forgive her; that sort of unction didn't seem to be called for. Notwithstanding all the words I have put into this paper, this that Jesus briefly said, or implied, is the substance of what I have to say about sin and psychotherapy. But, at that, I think it is quite a bit to say!

75

Psychotherapy and the Nature of Man[1]

A long time ago, so the story goes, Man made a fateful decision. He chose to live his life by understanding, rather than obedience. This was doing it the hard way. The outcome, as most of you know from the story—if not from making such a decision yourselves—was not a particularly happy one. Because the story didn't have a happy ending, a good many people, including the theologians who regard him as better off before the so-called fall from grace, think Adam bungled things. I presume they must be joined in this appraisal by the economists and other people who are impressed by the abundance of essentials with which he is supposed to have been supplied. Certainly the stimulus-response psychologists—at least those who worry about such things—must concur, since it seems clear that our ancestor did not act very realistically in terms of all his surrounding reinforcements. In any case, Man, the poor fellow, chose the toil and confusion of knowledge instead of the pleasant and obvious rewards of unquestioning obedience.

It should be said, I suppose, that Man probably would not have had the initiative to take this fateful step if he hadn't had some encouragement from his girlfriend. Without her he would probably have been content to do what he was told, as men are inclined to be when they are part of an all-male society, such as a football team, a monastery, or The United States Marine Corps. But when women are around, or you can't get your mind off them, material security and inner contentment don't always add up to the same thing. No matter how much happiness is available at hand, you are likely to become restless and itchy to test the limits of your instructions. We wonder just what would happen if . . .? All the luminous possibilities of the future become so fascinating that we are soon blinded to the obvious rewards of the present.

In any event, there was a woman around in the place called Eden. Apparently, if we can believe the story, she was not part of the initial experimental design. She had been introduced as a last minute concession without much thought to the problems of experimental control she might pose. The result was that things did not work out the way the Principal Investigator had specified in his original project proposal. In any event, while this may have been the first instance of a principal investigator adopting a punitive attitude toward his subjects for not confirming his hypotheses, it certainly was not the last.

Now, about this woman! She was not altogether a disobedient young thing herself, but she had had her feelings stirred up by something or other she had interpreted as rather suggestive—something symbolic, no doubt. And while, as frequently seems to be true of the opposite sex, she was disinclined to take any improper action herself—a fact that must be held to her credit—she was, nonetheless, disposed to drop the intriguing issue into the midst of Adam's idyllic contentment, just to see if he might not want to do something about it. This bit of domestic strategy is known as "sharing your problems." The upshot was that Adam did do something about it, and, as a dutiful mate, she went along with the deal. And, I am sure, something like this is what still makes man's world go round and round instead of standing still in obedient contentment, and what, more and more, turns it into the fascinating and fearsome puzzle it has come to be.

So notwithstanding all the psychology books whose authors hypothesize one kind of human nature and stay up nights with their typewriters demonstrating another—when they could just as well be in bed dreaming or otherwise occupied with drive reduction—the nature of man seems to be that he would rather coach the game than collect its winnings. This is to say that, in spite of all the solicitous admonishments and dire threats of the theologians and in spite of all the psychological reprints showing the conformity of rats and college freshmen to their reinforcements, man is pretty much inclined to end up choosing his own tenuous knowledge in preference to externally guaranteed happiness. At least he does this when women are around posing fuzzy issues in that irresponsible way of theirs—which is a good deal of the time. To be sure, he may start out acting like a rat or a college freshman, if that is what is expected of him, but before he gets through he is likely to be found usurping the role of The Creator Himself by hurling spheres into outer space, or, what may be worse, disengaging himself from the psychology of human behavior in order to act like a psychologist.

[1] Delivered at the annual meeting of the American Psychological Association, 1963. Published in Maher, B. (Ed.). (1969). *Clinical psychology and personality: The selected papers of George Kelly* (pp. 207–215). Wiley. Republished by permission of Wiley.

Collected Papers of the Pioneer of Constructivist Psychology: George A. Kelly, First Edition. Edited by David A. Winter and Nick Reed.

Sometimes it seems as if man is bent on doing everything he can to disrupt the regular operation of this lawful universe of ours. His persistent meddling with the future, rather than perpetuating the past or enjoying the present luxuries of The American Way of Life, reveals him as a perennial Adam who doesn't know that he is supposed to be himself, what his real motivations are, or when he is well off. There are, indeed, moments when I deeply suspect that man's only purpose in discovering the laws of human behavior is to contrive some way to escape them. This is certainly not the sort of thing psychologists are likely to talk about in public—at least not the scientific psychologists.

None of this is very sensible, particularly if you are supposed to "be yourself," always staying in your natural orbit, and revolving on your own unique axis. As in the case of Adam, who didn't perform according to his Designer's specifications, it is just this sort of nonconformity that drives the moralists to invoke the notion of "sin" and the psychologists the notion of a "neurotic paradox"—both notions representing essentially the same expression of frustration on the part of those who think man's behavior should follow the laws formulated to explain it, rather than vice versa. Worse than that, this tendency of man to cut loose from both his biography and his rewards, in order to reach out for the future and seize it in his own two fists, puts most of us scientists in an embarrassing position. It appears we must concede that human nature is disorganized, right after we have made a big case for science's supposedly most essential proposition: "All nature is organized."

What I have said so far about Adam frustrating his Creator to the point of exasperation and being called sinful for it, and the rest of mankind frustrating the psychologists to the point of being diagnosed as having come down with an attack of neurotic paradox, may make it appear that I am about to make a case for anarchy. But this is not my intention at all. If human nature does not work out the way it is supposed to, there is no reason to jump to the conclusion that it is either sinful or paradoxical. Nor need we conclude that it is unlawful—or lawful either, for that matter. But it does mean that our psychology is in difficulty. While I am not too sure, I think I can put my finger on what that difficulty is.

For my part, I am quite ready to assume—indeed it seems important to assume—that there is a reality out there, or, if you prefer, a truth deep inside all of us. If you are talking about psychology, I suppose it helps to think of its being inside. Just where it is probably does not matter much at this stage of the game. The point is that our grasp of it is approximate only. Moreover, it may be a little further out there, or a little deeper inside, than we have led ourselves to believe. This sort of thing has proved to be true before in science.

If this is so, then it may be that we have been taking the story of Genesis, or the findings of our psychological laboratories, a little too literally. To be sure, learning takes place under conditions of reinforcement. At least, it looks like a fact when we examine it with our Hullian spectacles. But how much of the truth is represented in this fact, or how close an approximation to the nature of man are we able to derive from this observation seen through the spectacles of current American Psychology? We don't really know. If we are making a mistake, it is not in assuming that there is a truth, or even in hoping that we can get closer to it than we are, but in claiming we have caught up with it, and especially in fostering the impression that we have nailed it at the one percent level of confidence.

For my own part, I would even go for the proposition that there is really such a thing as sin. But I am likely to recoil if someone knocks on my door, hands me a catalog, and says, "Bless you brother; I hear you believe in sin. and here it is, with a glossary at the back." When this sort of thing happens, I am inclined to suggest that he inquire into the matter more deeply before publishing his findings, though I may not hand his catalog back until I have thumbed through the pages and looked at the pictures. I might even say, after looking at it, "By golly, this is the most up-to-date compendium on sin I have ever seen, and, until I see a better one, I shall try to be guided by it." But, just as in the case of science, what we shall come to realize as sinful a thousand years from now may bear no more resemblance to the evils that preachers talk about today than does the morality of a thousand years ago—or even of a hundred years ago—resemble 1963's emerging sense of decency, especially as it applies to such matters as the equality of racial opportunity.

So the same goes for science in general and for psychology in particular. Let us hope we can keep getting a little closer to the truth. So, as a psychological experiment, Eden didn't work out as expected. Now whose fault was that? Adam's, for disobeying? Eve's, for posing a feminine question? The Serpent's, for his short-sighted version of the truth—"Relax. Honey, it won't *kill* you!" Or the Creator's, for molding one kind of being and then demanding that he act like another? Or is there a fault in our own persistent failure to find a better interpretation of what goes on in the affairs of man? I am willing to assume that it is our fault, if for no other reason, because, pursuant to such an assumption, we may be led to reexamine the presumed nature of man—and of God, too, for that matter—and then take more realistic steps to get our affairs straightened out.

Well, let's see; I said the same approach to truth holds for the scientist as for the moralist, and then I went on to talk about the psychology of Eden, as if that had something to do with the psychology of man. Well, it does, but perhaps I should bring my illustrations up to date and talk about the psychology of the laboratory and the clinic, since you can't find much on Eden in the *Psychological Abstracts*. Nevertheless, I shall end up saying about the same thing as I said about the fellow who is rumored to be the original man.

So, just as in the Eden project, our experiments, also, fail to confirm predictions, our women get neurotic, our nations go berserk. Now whose fault is that? The subjects', for disobeying the laws of human nature? Is it the fault of those who go on posing questions when it would be a lot safer to remain ignorant? Is it the fault of the shortsighted politicians and advertisers who peddle glowing promises to gullible people—"Come on, Honey, it'll be good for you!" Is it the fault of those who create one kind of society and then lay down rules designed for another? Or is it ours, in taking it for granted that human nature resides not in man but in the psychological systems erected so ingeniously by Freud, or Hull, or Jefferson, or Marx, or in the statistically tempered conclusions of psychological experimentation? As before, I am willing to assume that wherever the fault lies, the responsibility continues to be ours, and that the nature of man, howsoever it may ultimately turn out, is to be sought in the lives of the men, women, and children who inhabit the earth—on both sides of the Iron Curtain, as well as on both sides of the tracks. From such an assumption, which is central to what I want to say here, we may launch our psychological efforts in directions most likely to bring us closer to the truth than we have so far been.

With all respect to the psychologists who erect systems between themselves and their fellow men, among whom I am as guilty as any, the next step in this discussion is to point out that the closer one gets to persons the closer he gets to the nature of man. Granted, of course, that getting close to a person does not guarantee that you will understand him! But, on the other hand, if you never get close to him it is doubtful that you can ever develop a very perceptive scheme for understanding him. This is precisely why I believe that clinical psychology is basic to a science of psychology.

To the extent that psychology fails to touch the intimate life of man it makes the same mistake that was made in Eden, a mistake compounded by the religionists who make all those legalistic and punitive interpretations of what happened there. The official rulebook said that Adam and Eve would be content as long as their bellies were full. But the point is Adam and Eve were not content! Somebody goofed! Oh, I am sure that if you had persuaded them to volunteer as subjects in a simple reward type of experiment they would have behaved according to specifications. They were probably polite and cooperative in such matters. But when it came to crucial matters, it would have taken a lot more perceptiveness than has so far been displayed, either by the narrator of the story or the theologians, to understand why indeed these two inquisitive persons on one crucial occasion chose to know what life was all about rather than to obey blindly and pick their daily supply of juicy reinforcements off the trees of the garden.

It is sometimes argued that a person in distress does not behave as he does when things are going well. This is true. When things are going well he tends to behave like other people, or according to the way the cultural anthropologist has written up the manners of his home town. But, for the psychologist who wants to understand the nature of man, which is better, to observe a person when he is conforming to the local rulebook, or to try to understand him when he has been thrown back on his own resources and no official rulebook seems to apply?

Of course, coming to the psychotherapist can be listed in the local rulebook. When it is, I fear that seeking psychotherapeutic aid turns out to be no more than a reflection of conformity and the clinical psychologist is as much misled by it as is the experimental psychologist who insists on having "normal" subjects for his research.

It may be inferred from what I have said so far that I do not have much enthusiasm for applied psychology. But, in case the point has been missed, let me emphasize it—I do have very little enthusiasm for applied psychology. And that is why I think clinical psychology, and especially psychotherapy, is so important. But perhaps the point is obvious.

In Eden, it seems to me, there was a mistaken effort to deal with the tenants in terms of applied psychology. The Creator, having had a lot of recent experience with making things, had a pretty clear idea of what the norm for created things was. In fact, He had the advantage of being able to use total population statistics, if we can believe the story. He didn't have to worry about probability theory, a fact that must have relieved Him considerably. In terms, therefore, of His well-established means, or even His working means for related subspecies, it was perfectly reasonable to expect His latest creative effort to conform to the norms. So, at this point He turned Himself into an applied psychologist and laid down the law, being careful to back it up with an optimal reinforcement schedule. At least this is what we are told.

Now the Serpent appears also to have approached the situation from the standpoint of an applied psychologist. He may have been trained as one from the very first—I don't really know. However that may be, he was at the disadvantage of having to fall back on small sample statistics, for up to that time he had had no successful experience with the "temptation technique," or "rational therapy," or anything of that sort. The story is explicit on this point. He had to base his predictions on a hypothetical construct. This, as every doctoral candidate knows, is not nearly as good as basing it on an intervening variable. Probably accounts for his short-sightedness! In any case, he used his small sample statistics, took a chance at ten percent level of confidence, and told Eve she would not die, as she had been led to believe she would if she ate of the Tree of Knowledge of Good and Evil.

Within their own theoretical frameworks both the Creator and the Serpent were right. Yet both were wrong. The Creator was right in believing that most of the time, in fact, *normally*, in a scientific statistical sense man does do what is expected of him. He conforms to the prevailing social norms and responds to his reinforcements. If he doesn't, we throw him out of the experiment, a procedure which you can see has an ancient and honorable precedent. Psychologists have been proving God right about the normal nature of man for some time now, and I must say the evidence is overwhelming. There appears to have been only one occasion in Eden when this doctrinal application of validated psychological research findings failed. And when you stack this up against what must have been the thousands of previous occasions when the prediction had held, you come up with a confidence level that must have reached the .0001 level—at least—and that should satisfy the most rigorous experimentalist.

But the one occasion when the prediction didn't hold appears to have been a crucial one, or else the Creator was an absolute determinist, for the confidence level did not seem to have satisfied Him at all. If we are to believe the story, He went into a huff, punished

His subjects most ingeniously, and threw them out of the experiment. According to one account, He didn't make any serious effort to put Himself into Man's shoes until 4004 years later—in the Year Four B.C., when he began to approach the problem from the standpoint of the psychology of personal constructs.

The Serpent's experiment checked out pretty well, too, at least there is no report of his being dissatisfied. In fact it was an outright triumph for small sample statistics. Eve ate the apple, and, just as the experimenter suspected, nothing happened. Certainly she did not die right away, as she was afraid she might, and when she did die a good many years later, the Serpent had already published his results and had been made Chairman of the Department. Besides it was too late by that time to get a verbal report on her reactions. So, for all practical intents and purposes, the temptation turned out a grand success and has been quoted in the reviews ever since.

But, from another point of view, the Serpent was dead wrong, for man has been knocking himself out over this matter of the knowledge of good versus evil ever since. Wars, persecutions, family discords, intolerance, suppression of his own creative efforts have followed continually, as man has tried to impose on himself and others his dogmatic notions of what is psychologically good and has tried to destroy everything and everyone he regarded as evil. Good has been defined in terms of conformity rather than sought out in terms of understanding. This, of course, is applied psychology, and, as I have indicated, I believe one of the ways we can correct the situation is to study the nature of man through psychotherapy and thus achieve a more perceptive science.

I am not saying that the nature of man is the nature of the extraordinary man. What I am saying is that the nature of man is revealed in his extraordinary moments, moments that may be illuminated in the course of his psychotherapy. And it is for this reason that I have no desire to be an applied psychologist or to agree that the mean of man's behavioral reactions in a conformity situation is an adequate measure of his basic nature. For to agree with this tenet is to agree that the psychology of man is a psychology of norms and static mediocrity. It is to concede that truth lies with the majority, and to join, I fear, in the clamor for a unified theory of psychology, as if truth were to be achieved by negotiations.

Psychotherapy, it must be conceded, may not provide us with the only opportunity to see man in the crucial moment when conventionalities have failed him and he is left with no resources other than his own nature. The nature of man may be exposed to observation on other occasions. Perhaps we can see his nature equally well when he faces death and looks back regretfully on a life of normal and conforming behavior. Perhaps we can see it as we look back over two or three thousand years of history in which the myriad of average, normal, conforming behaviors have been mercifully overshadowed by the signal achievements of men and peoples. Perhaps it can be seen in a kindergarten before discipline and socialization have set in. Perhaps it can be seen even in the laboratory, though the chances are that if it shows up there the subjects will be thrown out of the experiment, just as Adam and Eve were thrown out when they failed to confirm a certain experimental hypothesis having to do with the efficacy of reinforcements.

But wheresoever the nature of man may be observed in its nascent form, I am sure that the psychologist is nowhere more likely to run into its puzzling complexities and exasperating perversities than in his efforts to accomplish psychotherapy. It is there that one hopes to see the person struggling with changes in himself as he attempts to draw some compromise between the normalized psychological doctrines of the world around him and his own natural eagerness to reach out for what he is unable to attain. To cope with this problem is not always a very comfortable experience for a would-be scientist. Certainly it is not a very practical way for him to extend his bibliography, and this is perhaps the reason that clinical psychologists do not publish more than they do and why what they do publish seems so inconclusive. But dissatisfied as I am with the progress of clinical psychology, I am even more pessimistic about any science of psychology that cuts itself loose from the perplexing realities of psychotherapy. As Mark Twain once said, "Every dog should have some fleas, lest he forget that he's a dog."

76

A Psychology of the Optimal Man[1]

Any discussion of the goals of psychotherapy is likely to proceed in both of two directions. First it will lead its participants to speculate about the kind of creature man ought to make of himself. Then against this ideal, often so vaguely formulated that it provides no clear guidelines for continuing the discourse, the discussants usually feel they must turn about and assess as realistically as they can those internal limitations of man that may prevent the attainment of this, or any other human objective.

While these are the directions such a discussion ordinarily takes, there are many twists and turns that may be attempted in order to avoid or re-shape the two issues. Among these is the especially attractive argument that man need seek only to become himself. By taking this position some psychologists attempt to resolve both matters at once—the question of what man should become and the question of what there is about his own self that blocks the fulfillment of his aspirations. Their stand, they hope, permits them to go on and say that psychotherapy needs no direction other than that spontaneously taken by their clients. Psychotherapy is something to be encouraged but never directed.

Although this posture of absolute respect for human nature in all its present forms appears to remove the onus of deciding what man should do with himself—and along with it the awful sense of responsibility for what is happening in human affairs everywhere—it seems to me to beg the question each of us asks himself sooner or later. In the end, man, the person, is left wondering in his loneliest hours what on earth he has been doing with himself, and man, the psychotherapist, who has acquired an easy virtue with his clients by lapsing into permissiveness, will come to hold himself no less accountable for the outcome of his efforts.

This is the way I see it. Yet it is only fair to say that before this chapter is finished I may find myself accused of using this same psychological dodge. *Accused*, that is! But I shall not accede to the charge!

Psychotherapy as an Ontological Venture

The statement, *to become oneself*, makes sense only if you believe that man is presently something that he has not yet managed to become. The reasoning is a little tricky, for it requires that we distinguish between what is existing in some active state of being and what exists only latently, and, therefore, remains to be realized. The whole of oneself is presumed to include both levels of reality, but *being*, in its strictly ontological sense, refers only to the former—to what is actually now existing.

The teleological construct of a human potentiality that has no actual "being," yet manages to serve as the sole activator of human destiny—and therefore as the infallible guide to psychotherapy as well—is more than a mite confusing. At worst, it encourages us to go around peering into dark corners looking for something which, by our own definition, isn't there. At best, it sets us out in pursuit of something we would not be able to see even if we were lucky enough to catch up with it.

Now there is no harm in talking about things that cannot be seen. We do it all the time. But when we do it we are depending on inferences rather than direct observations. Even the modem materialists, with all their emphasis upon keeping one's cycs open to what is going on, are caught "observing" their inferences now and then, as if, like the dachshund who chased a "strange animal" around a tree, they had bumped into their own constructs. Indeed, if they, or any of us for that matter, were to take full account of themselves from beginning to end they too would likely come to the conclusion that their "direct observations" follow hard on the heels of their own adventures. Thus, in some degree, the observations of the most wide-eyed observer must be regarded as inferential—and therefore constructive—in nature.

[1] Dated 1963. First published as Kelly, G.A. (1967). A psychology of the optimal man. In A. R. Maher (Ed.), *The goals of psychotherapy* (pp. 238–258). Appleton-Century-Crofts. Republished in Landfield, A. W., & Leitner, L. M. (Eds.). (1980). *Personal construct psychology: Psychotherapy and personality* (pp. 18–35). Wiley-Interscience. Published here by permission of Wiley.

Collected Papers of the Pioneer of Constructivist Psychology: George A. Kelly, First Edition. Edited by David A. Winter and Nick Reed.

It is when we forget this psychological fact that our inferences get in the way of our efforts, for constructs need to be evaluated not so much in terms of their visibility as in terms of what they lead us to do. It is against this criterion that the notion of a guiding human potentiality does us a disservice. We are tempted to go around looking for a certain golden key which, once it has been discovered, will unlock the door to all of human destiny.

Instead of arguing that man's potentialities are the guiding force behind his achievements, it seems more forthright to turn the proposition around and say that man is continually in the process of re-defining his potentialities through the sheer audacity of his achievements. Having put the proposition in this way we can take a good look at what man has accomplished thus far and then venture to say something about what generally happens to human hopes and how it is that man's presumed limitations can so effectively block his efforts.

One thing we can say, after looking at the unfolding record of man's achievement, is that, whatever the range of human potentialities may ultimately turn out to be, there are probably a lot more of them than any individual can, even in his most expansive moments, reasonably hope to exploit in a lifetime. Some possibilities, therefore, have to be abandoned outright. Then there are some talents that one never suspects, although they might have been inferred from his achievements. Or if he does suspect them, they are conceived too late in life for him to do anything about them. Then again, besides these, some objectives are pretty likely to get in the way of others. Any attempt to achieve them negates the contrary ones. This forces the abandonment of still more of one's potentialities. In the end, even if a man carefully defines his objectives in terms of what seem to be his emerging potentialities, there still are limiting choices to. be made.

Who is to make them? Stephen Leacock's man, who mounts his horse to ride off in all directions, will eventually find that some of his choices have been made by his horse. In the course of his headlong ride he, willy-nilly, abandons some of his brightest prospects in his galloping pursuit of the obvious. This is a common tragedy, as many a man past sixty-five realizes now that he has taken the time to think about it.

Ever since Eden it has been clear that man has capacities for both good and evil, and with them the burdensome yet exciting responsibility of distinguishing between the two, as well as between a lot of more transitive alternatives. The post-Eden man is held responsible even for the decisions of his horse. Most people, I am sure, are more or less convinced of this, in spite of the empathic amorality of their psychotherapists.

But the ontological decision that man must make—the decision to be something—need not be hemmed in by what he presumes are his potentialities, anymore than it can be foreordained by them. Just how broad his field of choice is man will never know until he assails the impossible. One thing is sure, if he starts his venture into reality by circumscribing himself with prior assumptions about potentialities, or lack of them, nothing very exciting is going to happen. Rather, the initial question—the point of departure for the genuinely adventuresome person—is what should he try to be. Or simply, what ought he to be?

I am well aware of the allergy psychologists have for *oughts*. This is because many of them regard all commitments as coercive. Perhaps in too many cases their own early commitments proved to be intolerable. But to state our problem the way we have is far less coercive than to argue that man can aspire to nothing more than to be himself. The *ought* we propose is a venturesome *ought*—an audacious *ought*. It becomes coercive only when one surrenders his right to state the predicates of his sentences and resigns himself to the *oughts* that others impress upon him. In any case, the initiative in man's enterprises lies with decision and commitment rather than with impulse and fulfillment.

Psychotherapeutic movement can thus be said to get under way when a man starts questioning for himself what his immediate objectives may be and is thus led to initiate actions that challenge whatever previous notions he may have held as to what his limitations were. This is the first step in re-defining his potentialities. He sets out to be what he is not.

The long range objective of the psychotherapeutic effort is an extension of this first step. It, as well as that of any other worthwhile human undertaking, is not to conform to oneself—whole or fragment, or to society—lay or ordained, or to nature—whatever the latest version of that happens to be, but for man continually to determine for himself what is worth the price he is going to end up paying for one thing or another anyway, to keep moving toward what he is not—surmounting obstacles as best he can, and to keep on doing both as long as he has anything to invest. To render and utilize technical aid in this ontological venture is the special transaction we call *psychotherapy*.

Experience and Vitality

The human enterprise does not follow a Euclidean line from Point A to Point B. No matter how carefully a man lays his plans and no matter how earnestly he announces his commitments, both plans and commitments are, almost from the very moment they are initiated, subject to reappraisal. An adolescent seeking to become a man, or a student aspiring to become a scholar, will change his notions about manhood or scholarship many times before he attains much of the status of either. This is not to say that his original plans were futile or that he must be unfaithful to his commitments. Even a plan which is abandoned outright may have served a purpose in leading one to the point where he could see more clearly what he should have planned instead.

So also with a commitment. A person who, from experience, knows what it means to be dedicated to a cause—even a bad one—may thus come to judge for himself what on earth is worth the ultimate price he must pay—that price being, of course, his own life. It is hard to say this of one who has never ventured to have the experience of commitment, although he too will certainly end up paying the same ultimate price, whether he wants to or not. And suppose, from his vantage point, the experienced man sees for the first time what lies beyond his original objectives and then commits himself to that instead—thus discarding the ill-phrased literalisms of his earlier commitments; can it be said that he has proved disloyal to his undertakings? I think not.

I am not saying that it is experience that changes man. I am saying, rather, that man changes himself through a process called experience. Nor would I want to say, as the stimulus-response psychologists do, that external events shape the man. That denies human vitality altogether and reduces life to a prolonged reverberation of outside occurrences.

Psychotherapy needs to be understood as an experience, and experience, in turn, understood as a process that reflects human vitality. Thus to define psychotherapy as a form of treatment—something that one person does to another—is misleading. Psychotherapy takes place when one person makes constructive use of another who has offered himself for that purpose. The professional skills of the therapist, as well as much of his repertory as an experienced human being, are brought into the transaction. He offers as much of both as he thinks can be used. But it is the client who weaves them into the fabric of his own experience.

Just as human progress, as we have said, follows a circuitous course rather than a Euclidean line, so should personal experience be regarded as a circuitous affair. The teacher who had had only one year of experience—repeated twenty-nine times—had indeed made little headway in life. Human progress is not accomplished so much by the persistence of effort along a single line as by the exploration of paths leading to fresh vantage points from whence one may chart and re-chart his course.

Experience, then, is not measured by years or the accumulation of events all handled in the same way, but by the revisions of one's outlook—revisions, of course, that take into account the outcomes of prior commitments. If one merely vacillates without taking into account what has occurred as a result of his previous ventures, or if he fails to put forth any serious effort to gain new perspectives, he may, to be sure, acquire some interesting scars to show his grandchildren, but he will end up surrendering his life without ever having experienced it.

What we have said about experience and the essential role of human vitality goes for psychotherapy too. Being a form of experience, it, too, follows an exploratory course with many reappraisals based on the outcomes of yesterday's commitments. Goals get changed and changed again. Yesterday's useful insights become today's stubborn resistances and tomorrow's trivial clichés. The enterprise into which the client plunged himself last week may mark a crucial turning point in his life, long awaited by his therapist, yet it may be something that ought never to be repeated. Indeed, some of life's most precious moments ought never to be repeated. This, too, is one of the considerations to be kept in mind in any attempt to state the goals of psychotherapy.

Historicism in the Psychology of the Optimal Man

To put it simply, it is not what the past has done to a man that counts—so much as it is what the man does with his past. The psychotherapist can scarcely fail to be amazed at how differently two of his clients may make use of what has happened to them. If he is alert he will be aware of wide differences in the way they make use of him too. Men are not so much shaped by events—including what the psychotherapist says during interviews—as they are shaped by the meaning they ascribe to such noises. This is not to say that one is perfectly free to ignore what is going on. He is not. But man is always free to reconstrue that which he may not deny.

It is true that events of the past intrude themselves into our present and that, to some extent, what we experience at any one moment is only the current phase of a process that began a long time ago, and will likely continue for a long time to come. But, more and more, man takes a hand in directing the course the process takes. The history of things that happened before he was born may point to the circumstances in which one now finds himself, but they do not dictate what he may do about them. What a man does with his history and its legacies is up to his own ingenuity and whether or not he wishes to exercise it.

The phenomenological psychologists, of whom I certainly am not one, usually take the view that it is only the experience of the passing instant that is of essential psychological significance. But I would argue that it is the whole story of mankind that is of greatest psychological significance. It is significant, not because it tells us what has happened to man, but because it tells us what has happened by the hand of man. I am talking about a history that tells us what man has done, not one that claims to say what he was made to do. Once history is interpreted in this way we need not limit ourselves to the phenomenal moment in order to see man in dynamic perspective.

While the historical record provides us with a version of what man has actually done, it does not set the limits on what he could have done, nor on what he can do, nor on what he will do. The story of all science, for example, is, as I see it, a story of man's past psychological efforts, unfolded in vast perspective. Those efforts produced, among other great things, what we know as the body of science—in itself an amazing display.

But this is not the most exciting part of the story that history has to tell us. This is only prologue. Infinitely more exciting is what potentiality these audacious feats suggest is locked up in the unrealized future of man. While the man of yesterday was developing a physicalistic science that tested itself by experiments and its ability to predict their outcomes, he was, without intending to do so, stating the basic postulates of a psychology for the man of tomorrow. Slowly he demonstrated, not merely that events could be predicted, but, what was vastly more important, that *he was a predictor*. It was not only that hypotheses could be generated, experiments controlled, anticipations checked against realizations, and theories revised, but that he—*man*—was a hypothesizer, an experimenter, an anticipator, a critical observer, an artful composer of new systems of thought. What he did, physically, portrayed what he was, psychologically.

Out of the saga of human achievement we can shape a postulate for a massive psychology of man. It runs like this: *A person's processes are psychologically channelized by the ways in which he anticipates events.* The bold pursuit of inferences that follow upon this postulate can serve to trace for us the outlines of a theory of personality we may call, *the psychology of personal constructs.*

None of this is to say that the factual substance of our present day science draws any outer boundaries around man's capabilities, nor does it convince me that the scientists I know are optimal men. On the contrary, if examined closely, what man has accomplished in science, and in other forms of scholarly enterprise, points to the presence of psychological processes that have never been fully unleashed. The history of mankind, whether particularly scientific or generally literary, throws psychological light on the processes of man; it is not an iron chain of events that binds him forever to what he is—that, and no more.

Some students, impressed by the accomplishments of scientists, try to make the most of themselves by acting like their heroes. Acting like a scientist is child's play. What one observes in scientific effort is not something to be imitated outright but is something to be examined and construed. Properly construed it may open new vistas that no scientist has yet envisioned.

As one abandons child-like imitation of scientists and launches into the exploration of the horizons opened up by them he is not likely to be regarded as a fellow-scientist. Especially is he not likely to be so regarded by the psychologists of our day who are themselves still pretty much in the imitative stage of their mental development. But no matter; whatever one does that turns out well in the end is likely to be claimed by the "scientists" eventually.

Making use of the record of past events, whether in one's own biography or in the history of human progress, is not, then, a matter of looking for something to imitate, any more than it is a matter of reading the writing on the wall. The value of the record lies in its being subject to construction, for it is by construing events, not by subordinating oneself to them, that light is thrown on human possibilities not yet envisioned.

In psychotherapy particularly it makes a great deal of difference how the historical past is used. A therapist who is aware of the sweep of man's accomplishments, as well as what particular men have done about their handicaps, will envision the goals of his efforts quite differently from one who thinks in terms of disease entities, childhood traumata, or the closed economies of psychodynamic systems. As for the client, if he is one who regards his past as the successively emerging phases of his personal experience, each leading to a new outlook, he will make use of his therapeutic opportunities in a much different way than will one who recounts his past only to show what it has done to him and who looks at other men only to see who can tell him what to do.

Theories of Psychologists and Men

So far what has been said is that the goals of psychotherapy cannot be taken as self-evident, that man must determine them for himself, that they are subject to continual revision—even during the course of the interview series, and that, in any effort to reach goals, the past is something to be utilized rather than undone. This is background for saying, next, that the goals of psychotherapy cannot be entirely separated from the human processes and stages through which they are to be pursued. But in saying that we have simply elaborated our basic postulate; *a person's processes are psychologically channelized by the ways in which he anticipates events.*

Perhaps it is clear by now that we see no valuable distinction between the theorizing of psychologists, who may want to be seen as scientists, and their clients, who usually prefer to be seen as human. Both may be regarded as scientists, if you please, as well as men, for both seek to anticipate events. Both have their theories in terms of which they attempt to structure the on-rush of occurrences. Both hypothesize. Both experiment. Both observe. Both reluctantly revise their predictions in the light of what they observe, on the one hand, and the extent of their theoretical investment, on the other.

Nor do we see psychotherapists as *applied* scientists, in the sense of exploiting what the pure scientists have found out, i.e., using science in an un-scientist-like manner. For us the course of therapy, like the course of all human enterprise, including scientific enterprise, is essentially exploratory—exploratory both for the therapist and for his client. This means that therapy is fraught with revisions, revisions that are undertaken by both client and therapist and by the two of them together. In short, psychotherapy is itself a form of experience, as we have defined experience.

Thus it is that the objectives of the psychotherapist must include the skillful facilitation of those human processes upon which all of us—"scientist" and "client" alike—depend as we move from stage to stage in the great human adventure. Goals, processes, and stages are often indistinguishable from each other. Indeed, the initiation and continuation of a lifetime effort to conjure up ever fresh visions of what is worthwhile is itself a goal of psychotherapy. This is not the kind of goal at which you can hope to arrive and then stop looking further. It is, instead, a continuing series of commitments and revisions of commitments. Most of all it is a commitment to experience, with the stock taking that honest experience requires. The person who profits from the therapeutic transaction is a fellow who has started to make headway in this ceaseless enterprise.

Furthermore, it is probably futile, without due allowance for the circuitous routes man must follow, to specify the ultimate goals he hopes to attain, except, possibly, in some such imprecise terms as "heaven," "brotherhood of man," or "Utopia." Who knows where man will eventually arrive? Certainly not the certified therapists! Thus for man, whether he is seen as on his own or as clutching the hand of his somewhat befuddled therapist, ends and means often turn out to be indistinguishable from each other.

Put it this way: The tangible end of therapy is to implement the means by which the ultimate and intangible end of mankind's efforts can hope to be achieved. This is to say that, while the therapist cannot quite put his finger on what his client should eventually achieve, he can, at least, put his finger on the processes by which his client might hope to achieve it. And he can implement those processes without knowing their ultimate outcome. To do this much is a perfectly tangible end of his psychotherapeutic effort.

For what kind of a therapist would claim he knew where the ultimate end of man lies, or even what epitaph should be written on his client's tombstone? At best, all the wise therapist can hope to say is, "There, at last I think my client and I are hot on the trail of something." As for the client, at the end of his last psychotherapeutic session he can hope to say little more than something like this himself. Indeed, if he tries to say too much more than this, he probably needs to schedule some further sessions—with another therapist.

So the way a person lives his life cannot be divorced from how he anticipates the future (our basic postulate again), and vice versa. A man spends his time making as much money as he can. What does it mean? Perhaps he is trying to insure his family against every conceivable hazard, or himself from the haunting fear of disclosing his own insufficiency. Whatever it is, his money-making makes sense only in the light of his anticipations. But it also works the other way around. He may end up his life as a wealthy grasping man, himself his family's worst hazard and, as a person, revealed as insufficient in more ways than when he started. The goal he so faithfully pursued turns out to be defined, not only by his ambition, but also by what he did to fulfill it. So for us all! The events we attempt to anticipate may turn out to be contaminated by what we did to anticipate them. In the words of our fundamental postulate, a person's processes are channelized by the ways in which he anticipates events.

The same goes for psychologists, who are known to have human characteristics too. Two therapists may state their goals in a similar way, yet have little in common, either in their methods or in what they eventually accept as confirming their predictions. For example, one American psychologist I know places primary psychological value on human "efficiency," while another says he hopes to aid in the fruition of a "fully functioning person." The two statements appear to be similar. Yet from listening to the two men I am convinced that what they would do to achieve their goal and when they would think they had reached it, differ vastly between them. Indeed, what one would do to his client would, I am sure, be considered unconscionable by the other—and, perhaps, vice versa. My point, therefore, is that psychotherapeutic goals have to be understood as part of the psychologist's functional involvement with a theoretical position in which his working assumptions about the nature of mankind, and of his client, have been made to stand out as clearly as possible. Now what I am saying about understanding the psychotherapist is very similar to what I said about understanding man in general.

So how shall we state the objectives, of psychotherapy? It is obvious by now that I have no stomach for making up a list of "goals" to be checked off against the names of my colleagues who also write about psychotherapy, though from other points of view. Without a clear understanding of their theoretical positions it is impossible to know what they mean when they recite their own "lists." So also for me. So also for my client. Without some clear understanding of the fellow's outlook, that is to say, without some notion of the way he personally construes events of his past and present, it is uncertain what he will be doing to attain the goals either he or I envision, and what contaminated meaning those goals will eventually come to have. Goals can be distorted in the most grotesque ways by the means one employs in his effort to achieve them.

One Psychologist's Assumptions

We turn now to the things that must be said before any further statement of my own therapeutic goals can be fully understood. This is what I think: Everything man does follows lines laid down in his effort to anticipate what will happen. We have already stated this as our basic postulate, though in somewhat different words.

Since this is our logical point of departure it is important that there be no misunderstanding about what such a statement means to us. One's anticipation of the onrush of events may not be expressed definitively; it may be expressed as a posture toward the future, possibly a future we would prefer not to portray too clearly or too realistically. A friend of mine while driving her car customarily closes her eyes when she gets caught in a tight spot. This is an anticipatory act; she suspects something may happen that she would prefer not to see. So far, it hasn't happened, though I can't understand why. Fortunately, in recent years she has given up driving a car; and that, too, is an anticipatory posture. Neither of her postures can be said to be very practical, but it would be hard to say neither of them was anticipatory in nature. As a matter of fact they seem very clearly to me to be anticipatory.

Most people anticipate death in a somewhat similar manner. This certainly does not mean that they go shopping for bargains in coffins. If they did I am sure it would have a salutary effect on the mortician business—and I would be for that! But in some persons especially we can see a great deal of what they do and say as an anticipatory posture toward death. Like my friend, they seem both to invite it to come and get them and to try to postpone it as long as possible, even to the extent of denying themselves the full life.

If we press this part of our theorizing into areas at the fringe of psychology's normal range of convenience we can say that contractions of the stomach, the beating of the heart, or the drooling of Pavlov's dog can easily enough be regarded as anticipatory. There is no reason to limit the notion of anticipation to what can be verbally communicated or logically projected.

We can, if we wish, extend this construct of anticipation to some other frontiers. We can speculate about the implications of saying that anticipation is one of the characteristic features of man, or saying that man is such and such a creature who does his best to cement the future to the past and thus grasp time in his own two fists, a Herculean task if ever there was one!

Some people are led to believe that man, in letting himself be guided by his ways of anticipating events, renders himself subservient to things that have not happened yet. But this is not true. Events do not control man's behavior before they occur, any more than they do afterward. The control of his behavior remains man's own prerogative, though limited, of course, by the amount of ingenuity he brings into play. If events, either past or expected, appear to manipulate a man it is only because, so far, he has figured out only one way to cope with them. He will continue to dance to the tune he thinks he hears them play until he contrives some other way of listening for the succession of notes.

Man never *waits* to see what will happen; he always *looks* to see what will happen. Even my motorist friend is looking for something, though she shuts her eyes to it. Many of us close our eyes when we are looking for something, though not usually when we are looking for an opening in freeway traffic. While man always looks to see what will happen, he is occasionally surprised out of his wits by what turns up. But if he had merely waited I doubt that he could ever have been surprised—not even faintly amused. Sometimes, to be sure, he is caught looking intently in the wrong direction. And there is many a time when he fails to be surprised because he overlooks what is going on under his nose.

All of this is, clearly enough, I suppose—particularly to those who disagree with me—my own particular assumption about the nature of man. Moreover, it is the way I, too, look to see what will happen, for, unlike most psychologists I know, who view themselves as scientists and their subjects as something else, my theory of personality applies to me as well as to people I don't like. It is the way I look to see what is going on in psychotherapy. It works moderately well, so far. I *anticipate*—yes, *anticipate*—it will work better after I have explored its implications further.

While right now this anticipatory approach seems like a particularly reasonable way to go about the job of being a psychologist, especially a psychotherapist, undoubtedly I will change my mind in some ways, for changing one's mind as a result of pursuing his commitments is, as I have already said, an essential feature of honest human experience. Just where I will end up with this business I cannot foresee, but at least, as the reader may all too readily agree, my posture is one of anticipating some changes I cannot yet spell out. But if I am to describe the goals of psychotherapy as I see them today, it is imperative that the reader know something about my present assumptions, tentative though they may be. But, please, do not accuse me of failing to make any commitment to these assumptions. I am determined to see where they lead, and, having seen where they lead, I am equally determined to modify or abandon them in the light of what my quest reveals.

A Little about Life

While our topic is the psychology of the optimal man, with particular reference to the goals of psychotherapy, it will do no harm to extend ourselves for a few moments and talk about life. This takes us outside the range of our assignment, and perhaps outside the range of psychology. But if we can venture a definition of life, whether human or otherwise, perhaps we can introduce an assumption of such far-reaching significance that what we attempt to say later about man in particular will be enhanced and clarified.

Let us start out with a definition—or an assumption, if you prefer, though all definitions are assumptions. Let us say that life is a way of using the present to link the future with the past in some original fashion. Now that we have started, let us pursue the implications of what we have said. We can say next that without life the present makes no difference in the future; only the past governs what will happen. Since, without life, there is no active anticipation of the future, the notion of a future does not even stand for anything until after it is too late to call it "future" anymore. And without a future the present makes no sense either, for what is the present but the boundary between past and future. No future, no present! And without a present there is no point of observation from which to differentiate time.

Already we can see some psychotherapeutic implications of these extra-psychological inferences. Some clients do make only minimal use of the present for anticipating their future. Most psychotherapists have dealt with such a client. He seems to have only the most precarious foothold on this vantage point for looking out on what goes on. He is disengaged from reality. Even his life appears to be held in a state of suspension.

But to return to our extra-psychological discussion of the nature of life. We could define it otherwise. We could describe it, as many psychologists describe man's behavior, simply as the outcome of past events. But to do this is to lose one's grip on the future, particularly the future of human affairs, and, through the concurrent loss of the present, to deny oneself the vantage point for viewing or doing anything at all. I don't like the idea of giving up all this, not even to be called a "scientist." It is too much like giving up the human enterprise in order to make of man something utterly predictable. But if the human enterprise is to be abandoned to the sequelae of past events, why bother to predict anything? If I am to give up one or the other, I would prefer to give up stimulus-response psychology, except, possibly, for explaining trivialities, or in those moments when I am in too much of a hurry to pay attention to what I am saying.

Everything we try to say about life seems to reflect upon psychology. Let us continue, therefore, to speculate about life. Suppose we were to take our fundamental postulate, the one we intended as a starting point for a psychology of man, and make a biological postulate out of it. Let us have a try. We shall then say something like this: *It is the nature of life to be channelized by the ways events are anticipated.* While I am not prepared to defend this assumption with great skill or the weight of much evidence, it does intrigue me and I cannot help but wonder where we would be led if we ventured to start from such a premise. Particularly, I wonder what a psychotherapist would be led to do or what goals he would envision for the outcomes of his efforts.

Salivation, for example, takes place in a manner that suggests the anticipation of food—or perhaps hunger—I am not sure which. Perhaps what is anticipated is an activity we call eating. Whatever it indicates, Pavlov seems to have demonstrated it and there is no reason we should not be grateful even though we are not quite sure what it was he demonstrated. The momentary rest the heart takes between beats can be construed as preparing it for its next effort. That, also, is consistent with observation. So far, so good.

But we must keep it clear in our noggins, as long as we are following the implications of our tentative biological postulate, that it is not the impending events that make a creature's mouth water or its heart rest up. It is the beast itself which does those things, and it does them as it does because this is in line with its particular ways of anticipating events. If the events were anticipated differently its heart and glands might very well function differently. Whether the anticipated events later actually do take place or not, e.g., whether the food arrives or the next beat occurs, is another matter.

This is s not the place to press any argument about "lower order processes" in great detail, or to answer the frequently asked question, "But does personal construct theory have any practical application to rats?" It is sufficient for a paper dealing with the goals of psychotherapy merely to suggest the notion that possibly, quite apart from psychology, life itself is essentially an anticipation of events to come. This is a more venturesome postulate than the one from which the psychology of personal constructs was launched. But from it may spring some additional ideas about the whole of psychology, as well as about the goals of psychotherapy.

It follows, for example, from such a super-assumption that an over-all technical goal of psychotherapy might be to enhance this essential feature of life by making the most of man's moment-to-moment expectations. This is to say that psychotherapy should make one feel that he has come alive. This, presumably, would be a good thing to have happen. But the expression really doesn't mean much unless behind it lies some assumption about the nature of life, such as is embodied in the biological postulate we have suggested.

One may, of course, question the appropriateness of our assumption on the grounds that it does not seem to correspond to our personal experience. For example, what about those rare and delectable hours when we can lie in the grass and look up at the fleecy summer clouds. Do we not then take life savoring each moment as it comes without rudely trying to outguess it? Does one not feel very much alive on such occasions? Certainly! But this, too, is an anticipatory posture. To be sure, it is not the frantic apprehension of popping little events. It is rather a composed anticipation of a slowly drifting universe of great and benign proportions.

Still, what we have managed to say about the anticipatory nature of life, and the goal of therapy it implies, remains much too general. Perhaps the specifics it embraces will become clearer after we have returned to the line of inference stemming directly from our psychological postulate. Let us see.

Criteria for a Good Theory: Scientific or Personal

A theory is a useful device, useful because one can derive from it all sorts of consistent notions about how to proceed in a variety of situations. Everybody has at least one of these gadgets tucked away somewhere, although many are reluctant to exhibit them, and some even deny that they have them—insisting, instead, that all their notions are revealed to them by direct observation of nature. I suppose one could regard this claim as itself a theory, but I intend to avoid any dispute that might ensue from pressing the point.

Generally it is supposed that a theory must be a comprehensive formulation; that is to say, it should be a statement of the essential feature of a large family of assumptions. There is some difference of opinion as to whether these assumptions all have to be logically inescapable in the theoretical formulation, or if the theory need serve only to provoke a fresh lot of semi-educated guesses about the nature of things, without coming right out and saying precisely what these guesses should be.

But whatever the opinion, the fact of the matter is that every theory, scientific or personal, has embedded in it a great many assumptions that are not initially apparent to those who read it—or even very clear at first to the person who formulates it. These embedded assumptions are likely to have much to do with what eventually happens to the theory and the people who use it. And this is true, whether it is a theory used publicly by a group of scientists or is a personal one used intuitively by a certain man in managing his daily affairs. All of this makes one of the objectives of psychotherapy the exploration of hidden assumptions in the client's construct system.

I suppose any of us would be tempted to say that the foremost requirement of a good theory is that it should be true. But, in any literal sense, this is an impractical specification. We already know that most of the theories formulated in the past have served their times and proponents only to be displaced by others which, at some later juncture in the course of human thought, seemed better. We have reason to suspect, therefore, that almost any theory we formulate today is going to end up like its predecessors and, sooner or later, be supplanted. If we rejected all theories that were not known to be accurate portrayals of bed rock truth we would find ourselves with nothing to live by.

This is not quite the same as saying there is no truth. It is rather grounds for the stand that, whatever the truth is, no one—least of *all* a scientifically trained psychotherapist—ought to claim that he has quite caught up with it yet. But even if we don't catch up with it, each of us can gain on it. And that, too, is something that may hopefully be said of personal theories as well as scientific ones. Clients approach truth by the same kind of successive approximations that scientists employ. Psychotherapy helps them do it.

Good theorizing does not unwind itself endlessly without being checked. To test a theory one acts in accordance with its implications to see what will happen. In a broad sense, this is what we mean by scientific experimentation, though to be good science we think there should also be appropriate controls to discipline the conclusions we draw. If, under the aegis of a certain new theory, events become more predictable and many desirable things can be made to happen that failed to occur before, we are justified in saying the theory has a good measure of truth in it.

But experimentation is no special prerogative of the accredited scientist. It is, first of all, man's device. And because it is a human technique for getting closer to truth—employed more or less by all of us—it becomes the concern of any proper psychotherapeutic effort.

A theory, then—scientific or personal—ought to cover a lot of situations, to be fertile with coherent practical suggestions about what one might do in those situations, to be a reasonable approximation to the truth—serving the person at his present stage of development, and it should always lead to constructive experimentation and revision. When we say specifically that these are the criteria of a good personal theory we are establishing some further objectives for psychotherapy to attain.

It should be noted that we have not said that *insight* is a goal of psychotherapy. That implies catching up with the truth. Too often, when such a notion is impressed upon a client, he functions well enough for awhile after "completion of his analysis," but eventually bogs down in some orthodoxy.

Psychotherapeutic Goals and Psychological Processes

Already the point has been made that psychotherapeutic goals cannot be appraised independently of the processes by which one seeks to attain them. Nor can either processes or goals be fully understood apart from the deeply underlying constructions employed by the client and his therapist. We have therefore discussed the underlying theories that men live by, whether they claim to be scientists or not. Then we discussed our own, and the emphasis it places upon anticipatory processes, very broadly conceived, in the life of man. And we have mentioned, too, the part that experimentation plays in checking one's construction of events, whether that construction is scientific or personal.

But our discussion has necessarily been very general, for when one brings up the matter of goals in psychotherapy he immediately involves himself in making value judgments and these tend to be more philosophical than technical in nature. Nevertheless, it should be helpful in understanding what goals I value most for me to mention more of the particular processes through which I think they can be attained.

In generating the theory of the psychology of personal constructs out of its basic postulate we are led, by a series of inferences that need not be detailed here, to say that one's ways of anticipating events can be regarded as his personal constructs. Each construct is a two-ended affair; that is to say, it is a reference axis rather than a punctate designation of an object or an entity. When events are plotted against such an axis, or within a system of such personal axes, alternatives become identified and it becomes possible for a person to make some choices between them.

Only within his personal system is one ever free to make a choice in his own behalf, and only along the coordinate lines he himself has managed to erect is he ever free to initiate movement. Man's freedom, then, can be said to have ontological meaning only within the anticipatory framework he has devised; his personal construct system defines the only liberties he is ever able to claim. Adam and his girl friend found this out when they decided to look into the matter of good and evil. They shifted the basis of their actions from obedience to knowledge, thus achieving freedom—and all the responsibilities that go with it.

There is no sense in prodding a client toward the choice of a therapeutic goal that does not yet fall within his coordinate system of personal constructs, any more than it would have made sense before "The Fall" to drag Adam and Eve off to a revival meeting—they wouldn't have known what all the shouting was about. One of the intermediate goals of psychotherapy, then, is to help the client devise a construct system through which he is free to move toward something worthwhile.

Given a pair of alternatives adequately defined within a client's personal construct system, how does one know which he will choose? It may seem doubtful at first, but I am inclined to believe he will always make what may be called, *the elaborative choice*. That is to say he will choose that alternative, aligned to one of his construct dimensions, which appears to provide the greater opportunity for the further elaboration of his anticipatory system.

Two men will not necessarily make the same choice, even though they may construe the alternatives the same way, nor will one man make the same choice at one time that he makes at another. It is still the man that makes the choice, not the alternatives that dictate it to him. At a certain stage in one's development it may be more promising to choose to do something that will help him define his position more clearly and thus consolidate his gains, just as a military commander who has seized the initiative must often pause to consolidate his position. But at other times one will choose to extend his system so it will embrace more of the unknown and bring more of the future within his grasp. The two kinds of action, because they are both efforts to develop the anticipatory system, are really not so different. Both are examples of the psychological principle of *the elaborative choice*. Of course, it seems that some clients are always consolidating their positions and others are always overextending them. But these are differences in strategy; the basic process remains the same.

Another process question! Finding himself caught up in shifting circumstances, how does one decide what to do? This is the fix that most clients are in when they come running for psychological assistance. But in a less spectacular way it is a fix in which each of us finds himself a thousand times a day.

The first step, of course, is to construe what we see. To do this we go through a *circumspection* phase, sometimes in a split second without actually spelling out anything to ourselves, and sometimes in a period unduly prolonged by see-saw efforts to define the issue. This is a period of "trying on for size" the various constructs available in our personal repertory.

If one does not have many constructs *circumspection* may not take long, and he may achieve the somewhat enviable reputation of being "a man of action." If circumstances appear to be changing faster than he can keep up with them one may plunge through this phase of his *decision cycle*. This is the way to get the reputation of being impulsive. The Hamlets of this world, with their complex repertories, may not be able to tolerate the delay a full exploration of their repertories would require, and sometimes they may unexpectedly act on impulse before their complex *circumspection* process has finished weighing the issues.

In any case, the next step in the *decision cycle* is *preemption*. One construct is allowed to preempt the situation and define the pair of alternatives between which the person must make his choice. From then on, unless he backs up, the issue appears—whatever else may have some applicability to the situation—to be "this and this only."

Finally comes the commitment, and at this point the principle of the *elaborative choice* takes over. The whole *decision cycle* may be called the *C-P-C Cycle*, after the terms we have used for its phases: *Circumspection, Preemption, and Choice*. One of the intermediate objectives of psychotherapy is to help the client make appropriate use of this cycle whenever important action is required.

New Constructs for Old

New constructs are obviously invented, not discovered. But how? There are several ways, but one of the most interesting is through a process we have termed the *creativity cycle*. Here a warning is in order. If one defines construing as a process that follows conventional principles of logic and conceptualization, or if he has already classified the psychology of personal constructs in his own mind as "a cognitive theory," what follows won't make much sense.

Some construing is consistent. It may not be logical but it can still be consistent. Of two objects one is always construed as darker than the other, or heavier, or more beautiful; that is to say, whenever the construct dimension is applied to a pair of objects the outcome is the same. This is tight construction. Language labels, for example, once they are pinned on constructs, tend to *tighten t*heir usage. Mathematics is a particular language system that seems to have the maximum *tightening* effect. Of course, mathematics is supposed to be logical, too; but that is another matter.

Tightening may, or may not, be a good thing. So may language. Certainly there are moments in psychotherapy when the conventionalities of language get in the way of the client's efforts, and there are other moments when they establish just the base he needs for extending his probe of the unknown.

But there is *loosened* construction too. The inconsistency of the dreams one tries to recall in the morning is a good example. Language may play a part in such dreams but it usually fails to keep their construction *tight*. Some of us don't have to be asleep to construe *loosely*. We can even make our spoken words clatter along with our *loose* construction in a way that would give Noah Webster the jitters.

Actually, construction can be *tight* or *loose*, regardless of whether words are tied to constructs or not. Many of the so-called physiological processes, which follow construction to our way of thinking just as much as the so-called conscious processes do, involve very *tight* construing—the regular beating of the heart for example. On the other hand, free association—a supposedly conscious verbal process—has a *loosening* effect that many of us have found quite helpful in our short-sighted moments.

When we construe *tightly* we can subject our constructs to experimentation and to various other kinds of tests, but it is very hard to rotate them into new positions so as to get any new slant on our personal affairs. A *tight* construct tends to be brittle, and it stands firm or is shattered by the outcome of the predictions it invokes.

It is almost impossible to test a *loose* construct, or, to put it better, a construct *loosely* used. In an elastic sort of way it seems to apply to almost everything—or to almost nothing—that happens. That, too, can be good, for if every idea we ever laid hold of remained rigid and either stood firm or collapsed in the face of every test it got, mental process would all be guesswork and any progress that happened to take place in human thinking would depend on the sheer accident of hitting on something useful.

The *creativity cycle* we envision is one that employs both loosening and *tightening* in a coordinated fashion. The cycle starts with a *loosened* phase in which construction is vague, elastic, and wavering. Out of this fertile chaos shapes begin to emerge and one seeks patiently to give them definite form until they are *tight* enough to talk about and to test.

This notion of creativity does not suggest that one simply alternates between *loose* thinking and *tight t*hinking, as he may appear to alternate between nighttime thinking and daytime thinking. These are not simply two separate exercises, but phases of the same creative process, just as I am convinced dreaming and alert critical thinking are essential phases of the basic process by which we keep ourselves from ending up as schizophrenics or automatons. It is when man tries too hard to separate his loosened construction from his tightened construction that he becomes unhinged and loses his ability to live creatively.

None of this has anything much to do with "creativity" as a particular trait possessed by "gifted" people, or that stultifying preoccupation which has been mis-named "the psychology of individual differences." We are talking about a human process, not about discriminable classes of mankind. Of course, we are willing to concede that some of us reach further into the outer chaos that surrounds us, and some further into the cosmos we have carved for ourselves, than others. And it is true, we know, that some go *loose* and stay that way, as, for example, those patients of early psychoanalytic technique who succumbed to its persistent *loosening* demands. It is true, also, that some of us get so *tight* and literal that when our thinking is finally shattered by its predictive failures we collapse into a protective *looseness* from which we dare not recover. But these are not traits; these are predicaments. They are some of the unfortunate outcomes of the psychological process all of us invoke when we try to solve our problems.

One of the important interim goals of psychotherapy is to help the client make optimal use of his ability to think both *loosely* and *tightly* and to employ those two phases of the *creativity cycle* in a proper relationship to each other. Moreover, therapy should enable a person to span an optimal range of *loosening* and *tightening* without breaking up the process into disjunctive thinking.

Orchestration of Psychotherapeutic Techniques

Unlike most personality theories, the psychology of personal constructs does not limit itself to any pet psychotherapeutic technique. More than any other theory, it calls for an orchestration of many techniques according to the therapist's awareness of the variety and nature of the psychological processes by which man works toward his ends.

In presenting the goals of psychotherapy as we see them we have laid initial stress on man as a creature who forges his own destiny rather than allows himself to drift with the tide of human affairs. The term *personal constructs*, refers to the guidelines by which he pinpoints anticipated events and along which he establishes the dimensions of the freedom he hopes to exercise and the pathways of movement he seeks to follow. There are many interesting processes man uses in reaching his ends, some of which we have attempted to describe. All of them fall within the purview of the technically versatile psychotherapist.

Man uses many kinds of resources too. One of the resources men occasionally find useful is a psychotherapist. And—speaking of therapists—in addition to the goals his client ought to seek, the therapist needs to have a goal of his own; he ought to try to be made good use of.

77

The Psychotherapeutic Relationship[1]

I have been so puzzled over the early labeling of personal construct theory as "cognitive" that several years ago I set out to write another short book to make it clear that I wanted no part of cognitive theory. The manuscript was about a third completed when I gave a lecture at Harvard University with the title, "Personal Construct Theory as a Line of Inference." Following the lecture, Professor Gordon Allport explained to the students that my theory was not a "cognitive" theory but an "emotional" theory. Later the same afternoon, Dr. Henry Murray called me aside and said, "You know, don't you, that you are really an existentialist."

Since that time I stepped into almost all the open manholes that psychological theorists can possibly fall into. For example, in Warsaw, where I thought my lecture on personal construct theory would be an open challenge to dialectical materialism, the Poles, who had been conducting some seminars on personal construct theory before my arrival, explained to me that "personal construct theory was just exactly what dialectical materialism stood for." Along the way also I have found myself classified in a volume on personality theories as one of the "learning theorists," a classification that seems to me so patently ridiculous that I have gotten no end of amusement out of it.

A few years ago an orthodox psychoanalyst insisted, after hearing me talk about psychotherapy, that, regardless of what I might say about Freud, and regardless even of my failure to fall in the apostolic succession to which a personal psychoanalysis entitled one, I was really "a psychoanalyst." This charge was repeated by a couple of psychoanalytically sophisticated psychiatrists in London last fall, and nothing I could say would shake their conviction.

I have, of course, been called a Zen Buddhist, and last fall one of our former students, now a distinguished psychologist, who was invited back to give a lecture, spent an hour and a half in a seminar corrupting my students with the idea that I was really a "behaviorist."

I think I should tell you all this at the outset, so that a little later on when you find that you are hopelessly confused by what I have to say, you will not be overly critical of yourselves or me.

While it seems perfectly clear to me that personal construct theory is not a cognitive theory, I am a little more puzzled about the question of whether or not it is a dynamic theory. Generally I have claimed that it is completely nondynamic. It is utterly innocent of any forces, motives, or incentives and, so far as I have been able to observe, all the other gremlins have been properly exterminated. But then, I may be quite mistaken about this, because I start with the assumption that something is going on, rather than the traditional assumption that the world is filled with a number of things that must be prodded into action by forces. And, since I assume that we start with a process, I am struck with the disturbing thought that personal construct theory may be the only truly dynamic theory available to psychology. So you can take your choice; this is either an all-out dynamic theory or an all-out nondynamic theory. I don't really much care which point of view you take, just so you take one or the other and not something in between.

Suppose we start out by making a distinction between what is man and what is his environment. There are some advantages in making such a distinction, although if you look at it too closely we will both have to admit that *man versus environment* is a somewhat fuzzy notion, especially when you realize that most of us have about as much trouble living with ourselves as we have living with other people—or, if you want to think of it that way, each of us represents a rather large chunk of his own environment.

Be that as it may, let us erect a construct of *man versus environment*, and then see what we can do with it. We must keep it clearly in mind that we invented this construct and must hold ourselves responsible for it. It would be improperly unctuous of us to claim that it was revealed to us—either on Mount Sinai or in a laboratory. It is my notion that if it doesn't turn out well there is nobody we can blame except ourselves.

[1] Presented at a symposium on "Cognitive and analytic conceptions of the therapeutic relationship," University of Houston, Texas, May 19, 1965. First published in Maher, B. (Ed.). (1969). *Clinical psychology and personality: The selected papers of George Kelly* (pp. 216–223). Wiley. Republished by permission of Wiley.

Collected Papers of the Pioneer of Constructivist Psychology: George A. Kelly, First Edition. Edited by David A. Winter and Nick Reed.

Now, in seeking to understand man, we can, as most psychologists do, say that something is initiated within the environment which results in a response from the person who inhabits it. This is stimulus-response psychology. The cycle in which we are interested starts with a stimulus and ends with a response. The role of the person is to mediate between the two. In this model man's job is to process events in the environment into behaviors. The model serves very well the purposes of those people who want to see the world running on an orderly course with each event carrying full responsibility for its progeny. Some people are sure that science is nothing but this kind of construction of the world. Of course I don't agree.

Now you can go at it another way and say, from man's point of view, the world is known only through his perception of it. Since he has only his perceptions to go by, the world is, for any human practical purposes, what he construes it to be. What it really is, outside of his perceptions, is a purely academic question and, according to the logic of the logical positivists, it is unanswerable and therefore foolish. Well, this is the phenomenological point of view. I am not a phenomenologist, and therefore, of course, am not a logical positivist, although I read somewhere—in the Koch volumes, I believe it was—that personal construct theory was a phenomenological theory.

Or you can take another point of view toward man in his environment. You can say he is what he is because of his cultural context. This is to say that the environment assigns him his role, makes him good or bad by contrast, appropriates him to itself, and, indeed, his whole existence makes sense only in terms of his relationship to the times and the culture. This is not personal construct theory either, and as far as I know, no one has yet claimed that it is.

Now there are dynamic theories. I am afraid I am the fellow who has said that motivation—or psychodynamics—is the kind of explanation we resort to when we don't want to bother to understand a person. We simply say that man does what he does not as an expression of his construction of the world, but because he has been pushed into it by the agents which inhabit his psyche. This is a very ancient kind of theory, antedating by thousands of years the Greek mythology from which Freud drew his models of explanation. The fact that it is based upon notions of demoniacal possession does not necessarily discredit it. As a matter of fact, one might argue that psychodynamic theory, because it is so deeply primitive, must also be deeply humanistic. In terms of the model of man in his environment, psychodynamic theory sees man as driven by internal forces to strike out against and for his environment.

Now we come to personal construct theory. As in phenomenology, personal construct theory sees man looking out on his environment, but, unlike phenomenology, does not portray that environment as a figment of his imagination. It's a real world that he lives in. The trick is for him to make something out of it.

Personal construct theory envisions man as devising constructions to place upon the events of the environment—even constructions to place upon himself. These constructions are essentially dimensions of appraisal rather than categories or entities, but basically they are not scalar constructions; they are, rather dichotomous grounds for discriminating events and assigning similarity to them. Out of such basic constructs one may, in turn, build scales, even though the constructs themselves are not scalar in nature.

The difficulty in understanding personal construct theory as a non-cognitive theory arises out of our assumption that all discrimination, as well as all of our sense of identity, is essentially cognitive. But human discrimination may take place also at levels which have been called "physiological" or "emotional." Nor is discrimination necessarily a verbalized process. Man discriminates even at a very primitive and behavioral level. For example, for him to be afraid on two different occasions suggests that he has somehow or other linked them or identified them as constructively the same object of danger.

There is another point—out of many—that should be mentioned in this connection before proceeding to the particular problem of the psychotherapeutic relationship. The languages of Western Europe are constructed so as to imply that the logic of explaining behavior is based on the S-R unit. This is to say that the behavioral cycle with which we are concerned is one that starts with a stimulus and asks the question, "What response will ensue?" In effect this means that the stimulus is the question and the response is the answer. This model is implicit in Freudian theory and indeed it is implicit in most dynamic theories. Behavior is the answer; it is the thing we are seeking to produce. In psychotherapy the object is to get the patient to change his behavior. In learning, also, the object is to get the student to change his behavior. In industry the object is to get the employee to do his job. In politics the object is to get the citizen to support the leadership. Once you are able to produce the behavior you are seeking, you have your answer. Indeed, most psychologists like to say that they are primarily concerned with the production of behavior. I think this is very sad.

But, from the standpoint of personal construct theory, behavior is not the answer, it is the question. The personal construct theorist who serves in the psychotherapeutic capacity does not consider his objective the production of certain classes of behavior. He is concerned, rather, with the constructions that man, including himself and his patient, places upon the world and how these constructions are tested out. For him, behavior is not the answer, it is the principal way in which man may inquire into the validity of his constructions. Thus the time-linked unit in which the personal construct theorist is interested is not one that starts with a stimulus and ends with a response, but rather one that starts with a behavior—which is man's way of posing a question—and ends with an outcome which may or may not confirm the prediction which the behavior was designed to test.

And in this theory, then, the task of the therapist is to join with his client in exploring, by the only means available to man—by behavior—the implications of the constructions he has devised for understanding reality. From this point of view therapy becomes an experimental process in which constructions are devised or delineated and are then tested out. Psychotherapy is not an applied science, it is a basic science in which the scientists are the client and his therapist. Moreover, the answers at which they arrive during the course of formal therapy are never the final answers. What, hopefully, the therapy has demonstrated is a way of getting on with one's life, not an answer to the question of "how shall I behave?"

But now let me go further into the problem of the psychotherapeutic relationship. I often tell my students that a psychopath is a stimulus-response psychologist who takes it seriously. This is to say that our classic model of the psychopath (whether anyone actually conforms to that model altogether or not is another question) describes a man who thinks he can get along with his fellow man by producing the right stimuli in order to invoke accommodating behavior. In other words, he thinks of his fellow man only as an organism which mediates between stimulus and response, and he is continually looking for the stimulus which will produce the response he wants.

But personal construct theory, as well as clinical experience, suggests that there are other ways of relating ourselves to our fellow men. If we see a fellow man simply as a behaving mechanism, our treatment of him will differ very little from our treatment of an infrahuman animal or even our treatment of an inanimate object. But if we understand our fellow man as a creature who himself has an outlook—who invents and tests and revises in terms of his outlook—our own interaction with him will be of a different order. In this case, our construction of him will be a construction of a creature who himself devises constructions. If we are to understand the person then we must seek out some interpretation of his construction rather than of his behavior merely.

Once we see man as a construing being, as personal construct theory does, of course, we have grounds for what I have chosen to call a "role relationship" with him. Our constructions of his outlook may not be accurate and, to the extent that they are not accurate, our role relationship may not be either predictive or effectual, but, accurate or not, our psychological construction of him will be quite different from what it would be if we regarded only his behavior as a matter of psychological concern.

Let me add further that our psychological construction of another person's outlook, while it does provide the basis for our having a role relationship with him, does not mean necessarily that we must conform to his expectations. Indeed, we may continually upset his expectations and may do so all the more effectively because we understand the outlook upon which they are based.

What I am saying, then, is that the development of that level of human relationship which I call a role relationship does not require mere accuracy or conformity and it may, indeed, lead to controversy and turmoil. But, nonetheless, it is what I would like to call a role relationship, in order to distinguish it from the psychopathic stimulus-response relationship advocated by most psychologists.

From the personal construct point of view, then, the task of the psychotherapist is to develop a role relationship with his client, and the task he poses for himself—to develop a reasonable number of role relationships with the people who constitute the client's most important surroundings. Often this task can be facilitated by encouraging the client to construe his therapist, not as a mediator of stimulus and response, but as a creature having an outlook.

I am suggesting that the psychotherapeutic relationship is not behaviorally standardized any more than the object of therapy is to produce a standardized behavior. The psychotherapeutic relationship is designed to get things done—the sort of things that all men have to do if they are to devise constructions of the world around them and are to check out those constructions by their use in prediction and by observation of the relation between predictions and outcomes.

Personal construct psychotherapy is a way of getting on with the human enterprise and it may embody and mobilize all of the techniques for doing this that man has yet devised. Certainly there is no one psychotherapeutic technique and certainly no one kind of interpersonal compatibility between psychotherapist and client. The techniques employed are the techniques for living and the task of the skillful psychotherapist is the proper orchestration of all of these varieties of techniques. Hence one may find a personal construct psychotherapist employing a huge variety of procedures—not helter-skelter, but always as part of a plan for helping himself and his client get on with the job of human exploration and checking out the appropriateness of the constructions they have devised for placing upon the world around them.

Now let me turn to one of the problems in psychotherapy of concern to nearly all experienced psychotherapists—the problem of "transference." As you might suspect at this point in our discussion, the psychology of personal constructs, because it sees man devising constructions to impose upon his fellow man, would be inclined to place a great deal of emphasis upon transference. Indeed, from this theoretical point of view, transference of one sort or another is the only device by which one may approach a stranger. This is to say that constructs must be employed which were originally devised for dealing with others, and it is to be anticipated that they will, at best, be an imperfect fit. But how else can we start?

A very young child meets a stranger. How shall he approach him? Being human, and a child at that, he can probably do no better than to construe the stranger as like one or the other of his parents. But how right is he? This is a question which he can pose only through his own behavior. Thus for the child his behavior at this point is the posing of a question arising out of his construction of the stranger. The behavioral question he poses may be badly put, and he may get an ambiguous or a shocking answer.

But whatever answer the child gets, he will normally try some reconstruction of the situation—transferring from his past experience in somewhat different ways—and pose another behavioral question.

Transference becomes a problem in psychotherapy, however, when a person keeps imposing the same transferred construction upon his therapist and is unable to make anything of the disconfirming evidence that is elicited by his behavioral questions. The problem of transference, as I see it then, is not that a person construes his therapist in terms of transferred constructions, but that he is unable to complete the experiential cycle and devise new constructions so as to get on with his interpersonal relationships with the psychotherapist and others.

There is another kind of transference, or perhaps I should say transference may take place in a somewhat different way. Instead of approaching the stranger as a total replica of some figure construed in one's past, one may erect his construction of the stranger one dimension at a time. This, in fact, is what the more mature person is able to do, and one of the signs of transition from childhood construction to mature construction is this movement from "whole figure transferences" to "propositional construct transferences." Let me illustrate. I may approach my psychotherapist as another father. This is applying the whole figure construction of my father to my therapist. A discontinuation of this kind of hypothesis is likely to imply a sweeping revision of my interpersonal outlook and hence may pose for me some threat to my total construction system.

But I can approach my therapist in another way. I may, for example, have seen my father as a strong figure. I may also have seen him as intellectual, as energetic, and in other ways. I can, however, transfer to my therapist only the construction of strength and reserve my construction of him in the other dimensions for later exploration. If now I find that he is not strong in the sense that I remember my father being strong, I experience disconfirmation in one dimension only. I may then revise my axis of reference, or my construct dimension, or I may turn to other constructs in order to get a more complete picture of my therapist in multidimensional psychological space, or "in depth."

What I have tried to do here is to suggest that personal construct theory, because of its particular way of viewing man's relationship to his environment, offers a distinctive approach to human relationships, and particularly to the psychotherapeutic relationship. I have tried to indicate that the task of psychotherapy is not to produce behavior, but rather to enable the client, as well as his therapist, to utilize behavior for asking important questions. In fact, the task of psychotherapy is to get the human process going again so that life may go on and on from where psychotherapy left off. There is no particular kind of psychotherapeutic relationship—no particular kind of feelings—no particular kind of interaction that is in itself a psychotherapeutic panacea, nor is there any particular set of techniques that are the techniques of choice for the personal construct theorist. The relationships between therapist and client and the techniques they employ may be as varied as the whole human repertory of relationships and techniques. It is the orchestration of techniques and the utilization of relationships in the on-going process of living and profiting from experience that makes psychotherapy a contribution to human life.

78

The Role of Classification in Personality Theory[1]

A theory is a device to enable man to deal comprehensively with what might otherwise be an overwhelming variety of events. Some of the events may not even yet have occurred. Moreover, there are myriads of them—some fascinating, some propitious, some perhaps catastrophic—that may indeed never occur unless a theory prompts someone to undertake them.

Strictly speaking, man invents his theory; he never discovers it. What he discovers, often to his dismay, is how well the theory works. But even that, as I suspect every venturesome theorist is painfully aware, often turns out to be a matter of taste and momentary convenience. But whether or not it works to suit its users, the theoretician must hold himself responsible for what he has contrived. Much as he might like to shift the responsibility, he cannot ever claim that his theory was dictated by the facts it seeks to explain. The facts tell him only when he is wrong—and not always that. And besides, there simply are too many ways of explaining the same facts—including a lot of ways that haven't turned up yet—for any of us to claim privileged communication with either God or Nature.

The process by which a theory is devised is known as abstraction, and the complementary process by which it is extended to events is known as generalization. Both may properly be regarded as psychological processes, or even as aspects of the same psychological process. That is to say, to understand them one may, instead of relying upon the principles of logic, employ some notion of man's style of life. Thus meaning is not extracted from nature, but projected by man upon it.

Neither abstraction nor generalization has ever been computerized, nor can either be realized by any unimaginative obedience to the canons of rationality, or by performing the symbolic transformations of mathematics, useful as these procedures may otherwise be. What can be computerized, for example, is the elimination of redundancy in a construction matrix. The resultant shrinkage in the matrix is sometimes mistaken for abstraction, for it appears to result in the expression of a great deal in relatively few terms. But the contribution the computer makes is to the economy of the language employed, not to conceptualization; albeit one must grant that linguistic parsimony may serve to clear away the clutter that stands in the way of fresh thinking. But housecleaning is not abstraction, and economizing does not constitute theoretical thinking. Occam's razor is a surgical instrument, not a creative tool.

A Construction Matrix

By a *construction matrix* I mean a postulated grid in which events and abstractions are so interlaced that whatever appears to occur independently of one's intention is given meaning in depth by being plotted against whatever coordinate reference axes he has intentionally erected. And in this psychological hyperspace the humanly contrived axes of reference, in turn, acquire whatever objective significance they have through extension—or through "operationalizing," if one prefers a term that has more current usage.

This is to say that human constructions derive their objectivity wholly from the way they cast events into varying arrays—or simply from the lines of perspective they provide. Actually it is in terms of such arrays that consensual judgment becomes psychologically possible. Consensus itself, while often cited as the criterion of objectivity, does not properly define the psychological grounds on which objectivity rests. Only sociological grounds are implied.

But now, since we are talking about human experience, including our own particular experience as scientists, it may be more precise, instead of saying that the matrix is a schema in which events and abstractions are interlaced, to say it is man's observations and his constructs that are woven into the fabric of experience—the one ascribing meaning to the other and the other lending

[1] Prepared for a conference convened by the American Psychiatric Association on "The role and methodology of classification in psychiatry and psychopathology" in Washington, D.C., November 19-21, 1965. First published in Katz, M., Cole, J.O. & Barton, W.E. (Eds.). (1968). *Classification in psychiatry and psychopathology*. U.S. Public Health Service. Republished by permission of the U.S. Public Health Service in Maher, B. (Ed.). (1969). *Clinical psychology and personality: The selected papers of George Kelly* (pp. 289–300). Wiley. Published here by permission of Wiley.

Collected Papers of the Pioneer of Constructivist Psychology: George A. Kelly, First Edition. Edited by David A. Winter and Nick Reed.

palpability to the one. And in this more phenomenological sense the grid might better be characterized as a "repertory grid," since it expresses one's own finite system of cross-references between the personal observations he has made and the personal constructs he has erected. I suppose it is apparent that all of us must have quite limited repertories, for the events we encounter are experienced only in such depth as our constructions will plumb, and our constructs have only that scope which is provided by the ranges of events to which we undertake to apply them.

A Theory as a Psychological Venture

In these few sentences I have tried to sketch the principles that are involved when one seeks to understand a theory as a psychological venture, rather than as a logical entity. Perhaps I have tried to say too much in altogether too little space. Obviously the far-flung implications of this psychological approach to human theorizing have not yet been mentioned. Nor do I have any intention of trying to spell them all out, except as they bear upon the problem addressed by this conference—"The role and methodology of classification in psychiatry and psychopathology."

What I have said is that a theory is a human contrivance, not something for which a man can escape personal responsibility by claiming he discovered it somewhere, that the abstraction process by which he fabricates his theory is a reflection of his own strategy for coping with events, and not a means of distilling truth out of the events themselves, that the condensation of a construction matrix—or *information net*, if you prefer a more limited and mechanistic notion—through the elimination of superfluous data and redundant terms is not to be confounded with abstraction, that man comes to grips with his existence by plotting his observations against his constructs and by testing his constructs against his observations, that meaning in the human role each man plays is limited by the variety of constructs he is able to devise, and that our constructions have no more substance to them than the extent of the events to which they are applied.

The Scientist as a Man, or Man as Scientist

There is something interesting that happens when one examines theorizing as a psychological process. He finds himself describing his own psychological efforts in the same terms he uses to account for those persons about whom he is psychologizing. This can be disconcerting, and, depending on the amount of cynicism built into his favorite personality theory, can lead to his having some very grave doubts about the validity of his efforts.

Most psychologists get around this by using different theoretical frameworks to explain the behavior of the scientist and the behavior of the ordinary man. For example, the scientist, they will say, systematically formulates his outlook, generates hypotheses from it, boldly ventures to make predictions, undertakes audacious experiments, courageously pits speculations against outcomes, candidly observes what happens, and completes the experiential cycle by humbly revising his outlook from the fresh vantage point to which his earlier naive commitments have led him. But ordinary men are held accountable in quite different terms. They are believed to be conditioned by the events that impinge upon them, sucked into the vacuums created by their needs, propelled by drives that invade their otherwise placid lives, caught up in the wake of their cultures, locked into the orbits of their biographies—lacking the imagination to attempt anything they have not rehearsed—or kept alive and kicking only by yielding to the persistent nagging of external stimuli.

But whatever we say about the behavior of the scientist is itself a personality theory, even though we may seek to limit its application to licensed scientists, or to other classes of "white folks." On the other hand, whatever we choose to say about human behavior in general is a personality theory that must deal not only with man's indiscretions, but hold itself accountable also for the structure of the scientific edifice that man, and man only, is known to have produced.

Categories as Obstacles to Theoretical Development

What happens when we undertake either to view the scientist as a man or man as a scientist? We get into categorical difficulties. And it is to just such difficulties imposed by categorization on theoretical thinking that a conference on classification, such as this one, should address itself.

If we view the scientist as a man we must regard his science with the same incredulity we apply to human behavior in general. This is to say that most of us would then have to claim that one's science is a symptom of his psychodynamics, or perhaps a product of his operant conditioning, though modulated, to be sure, by the psychodynamics—or the conditioning—of those with whom he is dynamically identified, or to whom he is conditioned. Thus, if we were to persist in accounting for scientists in terms of current psychological theories about men, I think we would soon be led to the conclusion that science is more a human predicament than a vital undertaking. On the other hand, if we apply the scientist paradigm to man, we someday are going to catch ourselves saying, in the midst of a heated family discussion, that our child's temper tantrum is best understood as a form of scientific inquiry.

In the one case—in the case of understanding science psychologically—we are limited by current personality theories that have never had to bridge the categorical boundaries customarily set up between natural logic and human behavior. Thus, by holding to the stubborn belief that science is human only when it is in error, we perpetuate some preposterous myths about the pure scientific enterprise. In the other case we are blocked by the ancient barriers that in Western culture seal off the classical categories of cognition, affect, and action. So we argue that since a temper tantrum has been categorized as an eruption of affect, one need accept no obligation to explain it in terms consistent with cognition. In each case, therefore, instead of using our constructs as reference axes in terms of which events can be seen in multidimensional depth, we continue to use them to construct pigeonholes in which events are tucked away and rendered inaccessible to other dimensions of appraisal.

But why not go all out and suggest that science, as we know it today, may be a reasonably apt—perhaps a tragically apt—statement of this century's human predicament? Or, if we may be permitted to take science itself as the model of a personality theory, why not then regard the child's temper tantrum as a frantic experimental effort to articulate some urgent question about human relationships for which no one so far has been willing to give him a candid answer? Why not? Why, in the first place, we say, because science "obviously" is a logical statement about nature itself, and therefore could not possibly be a Twentieth Century illusion created by man! Why not? Why, in the second place, we say, "a temper tantrum is an emotional outburst," and therefore clearly could not be a cognitive inquiry! Thus we see examples of the categorical barriers that block the free use of theory in the extension of human inquiry.

A Theory as an Aid to Creative Thinking

One of the unique functions of a theory is to enable man to reach beyond what he already knows. Having devised a system of constructs, and given it anchorage in his observations, one may state the parameters of some event he has never seen, but which might reasonably be expected to occur under certain conditions. Thus a good theory is fertile soil for producing something new, whether a new way of coping with mental disorder or a fresh approach to the education of the child. For my own part, I would place fertility at the top in any list of criteria for a good theory, particularly for a good personality theory. This, however, is not to overlook the importance of coherence, relevance, comprehensiveness, parsimony, verifiability, rigor, and predictive efficiency in theory construction.

From this point of view, categorization, helpful as it may be for certain practical purposes, proves itself to be almost completely sterile in suggesting something new to be looked for. It rarely leads to experimentation, and while at times it may challenge one's legalistic ingenuity in reaching a "diagnosis," it fails to set one's imagination on fire. It does, of course, tend to narrow down a scientist's field of inquiry, and on some occasions that may be just what he needs in order to develop a new construct more precisely within some limited range of convenience. Yet "hardening of the categories," a common affliction among scientists, usually marks the end of the creative phase of a distinguished career.

Efforts to Escape Categorical Restraints

From time to time in the history of human thought men have been acutely aware of the barriers that categorization has raised against their efforts to do creative thinking. It is no accident that dogmatism, the moat that surrounds all bastions of classical ignorance, is characteristically categorical in its logical form.

Among the obstacles produced by categorical thinking probably none has been more frequently assailed than that imposed by the dualism of mind versus body—or the spiritual versus the material. Typically the efforts to transcend this duality have taken the form of placing everything into one category or the other, as, for example, in idealism and materialism, or by envisioning some sort of interaction between mental things and physical things, as when we speak of psychosomatic disorders. But rarely in science have we given thoughtful considerations to the implications of categorization itself, and to the occasions when it would be better to structure our scientific efforts in other ways.

But now this conference has been called, and I am sure there is more afoot here than merely another updating of the approved system of psychiatric nomenclature. The notion of mental illness has itself been seriously challenged for the first time since the days of the Nancy School. Even the continued use of the so-called medical model in psychiatry is being thoughtfully questioned. Social psychiatry has brought fresh attention to the nature of psychological processes and has given relatively little play to pathological categories. Almost every new contribution to personality theory or to methods of treatment—from psychoanalysis to tranquilizers—has downgraded the importance of categorization of disorders and substituted some abstracted notions about how man copes with his circumstances. The new emphasis is upon what man does, rather than upon what happens to him—upon what he undertakes, rather than the state he is in.

Constructs as Reference Axes Rather Than as Denominations of Events

Up to this point I have been comparing and contrasting the aims of theorizing with the effects of categorization. I have pointed out that they usually serve different ends and that they too often get in the way of each other. But categorization, with its preemptive claim to the events it structures, is only one of the forms of classification, and since this conference has to do with the role of classification in general rather than categorization in particular, we may ask ourselves if there is not some other way to engage in classification without obstructing the development of better personality theories.

The key to our problem lies, I believe, in distinguishing clearly between the events we wish to control and the constructs we devise for understanding them. In terms of the repertory grid I have invited you to envision, this means differentiating sharply between what is warp and what is woof. This is to say that any clinical observation we make has meaning only in terms of the constructs with reference to which we choose to plot it. And our constructs, in turn, are not homologous with the events they enable us to understand, even though our language is grammatically constructed to make them appear that way.

We observe a patient's behavior. But it makes no sense until we plot it with reference to some such notion as, say, *anxiety*. This does not mean that what we have observed is of itself an anxiety. It means, instead, that if we construe it in terms of anxiety it begins to make sense. Similarly anxiety is not to be regarded as a particular collection of behaviors, but rather as a notion we have invented in terms of which the events observed in a patient's life appear to fall into some orderly array. Anxiety, then, is not a category of patients, nor is it even a category of symptoms, but it is a contrived reference axis against which any behavioral observation may be plotted, even including observations that may stand out much more clearly in the light of other constructs.

Propositional Rather Than Constellatory Relationships

In this kind of epistemology constructs are propositionally related to each other rather than bearing constellatory obligations to each other, or preemptively excluding each other. Let me explain what I mean. I observe a bit of behavior. It makes sense, it seems to me, to regard it as an expression of anxiety. That is to say I have made a proposition about its position in relation to my notion of anxiety. But does this mean that I must also regard it as neurotic? Not necessarily, for I may, if I wish, devise a construct of neuroticism which does not embrace all forms of anxiety. The two constructs thus need not be constellatorily related in my chain of inference. And certainly I do not need to insist that my diagnosis of anxiety precludes all other considerations. This would be preemptive construction, and it represents the worst of what can happen in a system of diagnostic categories—the worst, that is, from the point of view of a theoretician who is always hoping to see things in a new and better light.

Theory building relies heavily upon the propositional use of constructs. Thus the theoretician, no less than the dedicated psychotherapist, keeps himself alert to potentialities not yet realized in a patient's life. But the more practical and decision-oriented a clinician becomes the more he hastens to group his constructs into constellations, making inferences from his placement of an event on one reference axis to its probable placement on another. He might, for example, say that because his patient's behavior looms up so clearly in the light of his anxiety axis he had better go ahead and regard it as neurotic too. And in hospital management, where so frequently the most urgent decision made during the first week is to which of the overcrowded wards the patient should be sent, the clinical director is only too happy to have the fellow tentatively, but preemptively, consigned to a diagnostic category before the intake staff takes off for the day.

So far I have described the theoretician's constructs as reference axes for appraising objects, rather than as names for objects or groups of objects. And I have pointed to the theoretical advantage of using them propositionally, so that the full range of implications of each construct dimension can be explored separately without being encumbered by the implications of other constructs previously assumed to be related to it. For example, we can examine empirically all the implications arising out of the construct of anxiety, without necessarily having to concern ourselves with neuroticism.

The Noncategorical Use of Classification: Cluster Referents

Now it is possible to employ classification in science without resorting to categorization. Biologists, who are oldtimers in the categorization game, are just beginning to catch on to this notion, but librarians and efficient secretaries have known about it for a long time. Used in this way classification becomes a system of cross-referencing or indexing. Of course the books are physically located on some shelf and the papers have been put in some particular folder, and that much of it is categorical. But you don't keep track of the books and papers by running from shelf to shelf and from file to file. In this sense the classes not only overlap, but cut across each other, as the terms of classification are rotated into alignment with other axes of reference.

When we use classification in this noncategorical way the classes are retained as abstractions and are not walled off concretistically to encapsulate events. Though they have the logical form of classes, they are actually used as nonparametric reference axes. A particular set of behavior observations, for example, can then be described all at once as "anxious," "fragmented," "flattened," and "hallucinatory"—assuming that these classes can be clinically distinguished. Nor does this require that any of these be regarded as a subset of another.

In describing the observations in this way we have plotted them according to their proximity to certain criterion events whose projections have been clustered along four parametric reference axes—anxiety, fragmentation, flattening, and hallucination. But the behavior observations we are to classify are not, in this usage, related to the reference axes directly; instead, they are understood in terms of their proximity to clusters of other observations which have been so rated. This is what we do, for example, when we use a ward behavior rating scale and come up with a "diagnostic" profile of each patient's behavior. This procedure permits some retention of the abstractness of the classification system, although it sacrifices a certain amount of conceptual precision and flexibility. Moreover, one need not find himself hopelessly confronted with the barriers that are erected by disease entity thinking or by other forms of categorization that raise dogmatic obstacles to creative or analytic inquiry.

Facilitating the Clinician-Theoretician Exchange

Ideally, from the point of view of a personality theorist, it is most important for any system we use to maintain a clear distinction between events and reference axes—or between observations and constructs—keeping in mind particularly the postulated nature of the latter, and keeping in mind also the interplay between the two in producing meaning for events, and tangibility for constructs. If, for example, a clinician speaks of anxiety, the theoretician will shudder at any implication that anxiety was what was observed, instead of being the postulated dimension of reference for the clinician's observations—or the cluster of behavioral criterion referents he judged to be similar.

The theoretician is always concerned with envisioning fresh ways of looking at man, and if what is brought to his attention comes all sealed up in some clinician's favorite conceptual wrappers with a note that it must be taken or left in the state in which it was delivered, he is likely to feel that there is nothing he can now contribute except, possibly, to bundle up the packages into gross cartons without breaking their seals. This is precisely what happens to the research psychologist when he is asked to "come in and do research" on a twenty-year accumulation of clinical records. All he can find in the files are the wrappings within which the original observations were once classified. The observations themselves, which might have provided some grounds for reconstruing patients and their behaviors, have long since been lost—probably never got beyond the interviewing rooms where they originally occurred. "Doing research" on case files has, in my experience, always proved to be a waste of time as far as personality theory is concerned. In fact I am inclined to argue that the nosological system in current use does more to impede the development of improved personality theories than to accelerate it. If we cannot replace it, we ought, at least, to abandon it.

Universal Reference Axes—Now, If Possible

But if the convocation of this conference means we have now reached that stage of scientific and philosophical enlightenment where we can stop erecting categorical barriers in dealing with patients, and can regard the patient as the entity rather than the disease as the entity, and, furthermore, if we are at a point where we can use our constructs as multiple reference axes—plotting each set of observations against a set of key constructs, as physicists do with their notions of *mass*, *time*, and *energy*, then this conference may prove to be most timely.

Perhaps I should have attempted to suggest what such a key set of constructs for psychiatrists might be. I don't know whether *anxiety*, for example, could be made a universal reference axis against which psychiatric records would project all diagnosed cases. Certainly it is a notion widely employed in diagnosis, and in spite of the variety of notions about its derivation, seems to lend itself to considerable consensus in clinical observation. The construct of *projection* also suggests itself, though it may have picked up too much of a constellation of other constructs. It therefore might better be replaced by a more propositional reference axis, such as the I-E axis—internal versus external perception of the locus of control. Certainly *schizophrenia* is much too constellated in current usage to serve as a reference axis but *loosened construction*, often used in one form or another as a term in putting together a diagnosis of thought-disordered schizophrenia, might have possibilities.

There are many others that might be candidates for a universal system of reference axes, but I have here limited myself rather strictly to the topic assigned me in this conference—the role and function of classification in personality theory. Besides, the proposal of a complete set of significant constructs is a rather large undertaking. I doubt that I am up to it.

Even if it does not prove practicable for the participants in this conference to go all the way and recognize the appropriateness of postulated reference axes that give the best theoretical structure to clinical observations, and if we must, instead, temporize by endorsing the notion of a noncategorical classification system based on relating our observations to two or more clusterings of events, we shall have made some worthwhile progress. Simply to look at a bit of behavior, first in terms of its gross similarity to one type of criterion cluster—or set, if you prefer to relate this to mathematical set theory—and then to view it in terms of its similarity to other sets, is at least to put it in a concrete perspective. Certainly a concrete perspective is better than none at all. Each concrete referent set can be used as a vantage point from which to view the behavior of the man, and while we may be pretty fuzzy about what abstract constructs are being invoked, perhaps at long last we can break out of our categories and come to see the man from the perspective provided by simultaneously having more than one viewing angle.

79

Needs and Uses of Space in Clinical Psychology[1]

This memorandum has to do with a situation that is rapidly getting out of hand. The essential functions of the Clinical Psychology Area of the Department of Psychology are not and cannot be carried out in the space and with the equipment now available for them. As an inescapable result of this state of affairs the time and efforts of staff and students are being wastefully dissipated, the reputation of the University and the Department is being jeopardized, professional services to clients of the Clinic are downgraded, scholarship—particularly in research and in the development of clinical skills—is not approaching levels commensurate with the capacities of staff and students, and graduate students are delayed in the completion of their doctoral degrees. Moreover, the situation has deteriorated in the past two years and, due to increasing pressures for clinical instruction, the prospect is for a more rapid deterioration in the coming year.

The staff of the Clinical Area normally comprises about twenty-three persons as follows:

Professors	7
Visiting Professor (Spring)	1
Lecturers (Part Time)	1-3
Assistant Instructors	4
Secretaries	3
Assistants	7

In addition fifteen to twenty-five graduate students are, at any one time, serving as part time staff members rendering clinical services to the public under senior staff supervision. This number does not include other graduate students receiving laboratory instruction, nor does it take account of those students who are engaged in laboratory research requiring the regular assignment of space and equipment.

Offices

The office space needed for proper functioning of this staff requires, at a minimum, the following:

Single Occupancy Offices	
Professors	7
Visiting Professor or Lecturer	1
Ass't Instructor for Clinic Intake	1
Total	9
Multiple Occupancy Offices	
Three Assistant Instructors	1
Three Secretaries	1
Seven Assistants	2
Fifteen to twenty-five Part Time Clinicians (who must work on confidential case notes and records which may not be taken out of the Clinic)	1
Total	5
Total Offices	14

[1] Dated February 1st, 1965. Published by permission of Jacqueline Aldridge.

Collected Papers of the Pioneer of Constructivist Psychology: George A. Kelly, First Edition. Edited by David A. Winter and Nick Reed.

Research Space

Graduate students in the Clinical Area are normally organized into seven research teams of five to seven members each. Each team is led by a senior staff member who makes himself available to members of his team on an informal basis without appointments, as well as in scheduled meetings. Effective functioning of these teams requires for each of them a room equipped with table space for working on data and discussion of team projects, at least one typewriter, and a calculator. In addition, there should be at least ten research rooms where equipment may be set up and left undisturbed during the periods when subjects are being "run" in particular experiments. These rooms should not be used for clinical interviewing, for two important reasons: (a) The clutter of research equipment is professionally inappropriate in a room where a person in great personal distress is hoping to have his problems considered in a dignified and professional manner, and (b) research equipment which has been carefully set up is likely to be rendered inoperable if persons other than the researcher have free access to the room.

The needs for research space add up as follows:

Research Team Rooms	7
Research Project Rooms	10
TOTAL RESEARCH ROOMS:	17

Teaching and Service Space

The Clinical Area offers a clinical service to the public to the extent of the training needs of graduate students. The pattern of services varies somewhat from quarter to quarter during the academic year, depending on the stage of the students' training.

In the autumn fourth year students are conducting psychotherapeutic interviews, second year students are receiving training in psychodiagnostics, and 30-35 first year students are under laboratory instruction in basic interviewing methods, including individual psychological examination procedures. More than half of the first year students are from other areas of the Department. Each interview or examination must, of course, be conducted privately, and, in the case of the psychotherapeutic interviews, two adjacent rooms are required for each interview, one of them for monitoring. Psychotherapy interviews are recorded and each clinician spends about two hours going over each recording. This playback must be conducted in a private room.

In the winter the emphasis shifts to psychotherapeutic interviewing, as the second year class progresses from psychodiagnosis to psychotherapy, and the first year class begins to do more of its laboratory work in local institutions. In the spring the first year class does nearly all of its laboratory work in local institutions, though its members still need the workroom listed under "offices" for handling confidential case notes and records. But in the spring also the general introductory course in clinical psychology for undergraduates and non-clinical graduates must be provided extensive laboratory space. This is in addition to the couplets of rooms needed for the ongoing psychotherapeutic services. By careful articulation of courses it is possible to make maximum use of the available laboratory space throughout the academic year.

In order to offer professional service at a level the public has a right to expect of its tax supported University certain physical standards must be met. There is no need for luxurious appointments but rooms must be suitably furnished and equipped for the functions they are supposed to serve. The present rooms are downright shabby and the inordinately expensive monitoring equipment, which was improperly installed over the protests of the Clinic Staff, scarcely works at all. Moreover, the rooms now used must double as research rooms, a state of affairs that adds to the clutter and disreputable appearance of the Clinic. The rooms should be acoustically adapted to recording. This requires carpeting for these particular rooms, as well as acoustical treatment of the walls. It is often impossible to make intelligible recordings under the present conditions.

There must be a suitable waiting room for clients, and there must be a junior staff room where clinicians may wait for their clinical appointments without having to stand around in the hall. Our attempts to use the secretarial office for this latter purpose resulted in a great deal of distraction and loss of office efficiency. Two rooms adapted to specialized types of psychotherapy are needed, one equipped for children—considerably larger than the present one which serves both as a therapy room and as a storage room for children's specialized equipment—and one equipped for group psychotherapy—including family therapy. Each of these rooms must have adjacent monitoring space.

The Clinic must take care of checking a large amount of equipment in and out each day to the forty or more students who are receiving human laboratory instruction. During peak periods this involves about 100 items a day, including test kits, tape recorders, stop watches, etc. In addition, 50-100 books and manuals are checked out at any one time, on a one to seven day basis. Handling this equipment is a major responsibility of one of the secretaries, the one whose salary is paid under a training grant from the National Institute of Mental Health. By storing office equipment and supplies in a separate room, and by keeping the most used laboratory equipment in the office instead, it has been possible to make maximum use of an extremely limited amount of space.

The Clinic also requires appropriate space for its confidential files. Many of them now stand in the hallway—which is no place for confidential records. If the workroom mentioned under "offices" were large enough it could be used for this purpose, as well as for working on case records and reports.

In summary it must be said that the Clinical Area of the Department conducts a much more extensive laboratory teaching and public service program than is likely to be recognized. Each of the five core courses in the two and a half year clinical sequence includes intensive human laboratory experience, and the demand on the part of non-clinical majors for this high level type of instruction has increased rapidly in the last two years and is urgently pressed upon the Area both by the students and their advisers. Aside from other types of human laboratory interviewing, there are about forty psychotherapeutic interviews a week, each requiring space for the interview, for monitoring, and for play-back analysis of the tape recording. Our present efforts to carry on this program in a manner that will reflect credit upon the University and the Department are already faltering to a most discouraging degree, and new unsurmountable obstacles now loom in the way of continuing the program next fall unless determined steps are taken at higher administrative levels.

Altogether the teaching and clinical service space required for functioning of the program at a reasonable—though austere—professional level is as follows:

Psychotherapeutic interviewing (four pairs)	8 rooms
Other laboratory interviewing	8
Children's room with monitor room	2
Group psychotherapy room with monitor room	2
Clients' waiting room	1
Junior staff waiting room	1
Equipment room	1
Confidential file room	1
TOTAL	24 rooms

Summary of Space Needs for Next Fall

Assuming that the graduate training program in clinical psychology, in spite of the fact that its selection ratio of qualified applicants is by far the lowest in the Department, is still not to be enlarged to bring it into balance with the other areas, and disregarding the rapidly growing undergraduate program and the pressure from other areas for some clinical training for their graduate majors, the minimum space needs for effective operation of the Clinical Area's teaching, research, and service obligations in the Fall of 1965 are as follows:

Single Occupancy Offices (Each used for clinical interviewing)		
Professors	7	840 sq. ft.
Visiting Professor or Lecturer	1	140
Assistant Instructor for Clinic Intake	1	100
Sub-totals	9	1080 sq. ft.
Multiple Occupancy Offices		
Three Assistant Instructors	1	140
Three secretaries	1	324
Seven Assistants	2	324
Fifteen Part Time Clinicians (who must work on confidential records and reports which may not be removed from the Clinic)	1	180
Sub-totals	5	968
Research Rooms		
Research Team Rooms	7	1400
Research Project Rooms	10	920
Sub-totals	17	2320
Laboratory Teaching and Service Space		
Psychotherapeutic Interviewing (4 pairs)	8	512
Other Laboratory Interviewing	8	512
Children's Room, with Monitor	2	220
Group Psychotherapy Room with Monitor	2	388
Clients' Waiting Room	1	120
Junior Staff Waiting Room	1	120
Equipment Room	1	160
Confidential File Room	1	180
Sub-Total	24	2212
Total Rooms Needed	55 rooms	
Total Area Needed		6580 sq. ft.

Space Currently Available		
Room	*Area*	
Arps	401	140 sq. ft.
	402A	93
	402B	170
	402C	62
	403	96
	404	107
	406	62
	407	324
	408A	62
	408B	60
	408C	94
	406D	94
	408E	62
	408F	62
	412	62
	418A	100
	418B	87
	418D	61
	415	98
	419	44
	TOTAL AREA	1940 sq. ft

With the pressures bearing upon it the Clinical Area has been forced to do everything humanly possible to make optimal use of the space available. But no amount of ingenuity can overcome the seventy percent space deficit, no amount of enthusiasm can gloss over the fact that our professional services are rendered under physical conditions that make them professionally suspect and no juggling of credits and class enrollments can make up for the decrement in the quality of laboratory instruction that results from the cancellation of laboratory sessions for lack of space.

80

Space Needs for Clinical Psychology: 1965–1975[1]

The following space needs for clinical psychology are estimated for the decade, 1965–1975. The acute needs for the fall of 1965 are the subject of an earlier memorandum. (See "Needs and Uses of Space in Clinical Psychology," February 1, 1965.)

The proposed specifications derive themselves, in the main, from a particular style of graduate education which was originated at this University and developed here over the past twenty years. It is one which has proved itself remarkably effective in supplying scholarly leadership throughout American clinical psychology. (See memoranda, "Progress Report in Clinical Psychology," April 5, 1965, and "Academic Policy and the Scholarly Career," February 1, 1965.)

Two major principles undergird this development: The first is a philosophical one. It has to do with the logic of scientific development, particularly in psychology. Clinical psychology is not regarded in this program as an "applied" science, but as a form of psychology which restores the basic methods of observation and inference to their proper place in the spectrum of scientific methodology. To put it very simply, the clinician is presumed to be at his best when he, in honest collaboration with his client and as best they can, makes full use of the basic principles of scientific method for solving the problems the two of them have joined in confronting. He is not at his best when he imposes an externally derived psychology upon his client in a managerial sense—that is to say, when he indulges in "applied psychology."

Conversely, the scientifically minded psychologist is at his best when he bases his inquiries upon a disciplined familiarity with man—with particular men and with particular groups of men—on the most intimate terms. This is why clinical psychology is chosen as the arena best calculated to produce a truly humanistic psychology of man. Thus, hopefully, it may provide an alternative to the prevailing psychological notion of man as an organism to be manipulated in the society, exploited in the economy, and, when these fail to work, to be treated in an institution.

The other principle upon which the graduate program in clinical psychology is based is a practical one, though a certain affinity to the first principle can readily be detected. It is that the relationship between professors and their students, and within small groups of students themselves, should be close enough to maximize scholarly exchanges at truly penetrating levels. But this does not mean that scholarship should be so global as to seduce the student continually in "interdisciplinary cross-fertilizations," nor so persistent as to prevent him from pursuing independent and vaguely sensed lines of thought in the quiet of his own cubicle or amidst the clutter of his own research equipment.

The Basic Teaching Unit

Students in clinical psychology are grouped into research teams, each comprising a professor and eight to ten graduate students. The teams meet regularly and their members assist each other in developing the ideas and methods, as well as the research designs, employed in preparing their theses and dissertations. Communication and collaboration between members of a team is facilitated in every way possible. Every graduate student in clinical psychology is assigned to a research team on his arrival, rotates from team to team until he has selected the team in which he wishes to do his research, and is kept active in research team projects until he completes his doctoral program.

In support of each professor is an office staff sharing responsibility for meeting his stenographic and clerical needs and making sure that he is not diverted from his scholarly duties by having to do work for which he is neither fitted nor paid. Furthermore each professor is supported by graduate assistants, whose partial training in psychology permits them to perform academic chores for which the office staff is not qualified.

[1] Dated April 20th., 1965. Published by permission of Jacqueline Aldridge.

Collected Papers of the Pioneer of Constructivist Psychology: George A. Kelly, First Edition. Edited by David A. Winter and Nick Reed.

The space required for the proper functioning of this basic teaching unit includes the professor's office—which must be arranged and equipped for clinical interviewing as well as for conferences with students—and a research team room—equipped with a small desk, bookshelves, and a data file for each student, as well as with a conference table for team meetings and assembling data. Each team room should have also the basic equipment used by clinical psychologists in preparing and processing their research data—typewriters, Ditto machine, electric calculator, tape recorders. Normally, also it will house a portion of the professor's personal library of books and journals which he makes available to his students. This room should be adjacent to the professor's office so that he and his team members may have immediate access to each other.

Adjacent also, but separated from the team room, should be the professor's supporting staff—his secretarial and graduate assistants. The space for this staff may be shared with one to three other professors and would serve as a reception facility, for making appointments, as a buffer against too frequent interruptions by casual visitors, and to serve the needs of undergraduates who when the professor is responsible for a large lecture section make endless inquiries about assignments and marks. This arrangement is designed to provide an optimal working relationship between the professor and those students to whom he has a primary responsibility, while enabling him to serve appropriately the needs of those students to whom he should always recognize his secondary responsibility.

In addition to this space each team will require research space in varying amounts. Some of the clinical interviewing rooms, discussed in a later section, can serve certain research needs at times when they are not employed for their primary purpose. But some research requires setting up apparatus which should not be disturbed between sessions with subjects and which, moreover, would present a clutter not appropriate for a room used for clinical interviewing. This research space need not be adjacent to the team room, but it should not be far away. Furthermore it should be arranged so that subjects reporting for various projects may use a common waiting room.

Each basic teaching unit therefore requires the following space:

Research Team Room (8–12 persons)	288 sq.
Professor's Office (single occupancy)	140
Supporting Staff Office Space (1 graduate assistant, 1/2 secretary, waiting space for 2 1/2 persons)	140
Two Research Project Rooms	184
TOTAL	752 sq. ft.

Extent of the Graduate Effort in Clinical Psychology, 1965–1975

Since 1946 the number of graduate students in clinical psychology has remained nearly constant at around fifty, while the undergraduate enrollments in the University as a whole have doubled. Graduate enrollments in other areas of the Department of Psychology have also increased. It is appropriate at this point to consider as realistically as possible what would constitute a proper enrollment balance between the graduate effort in clinical psychology and the extent of the University's undergraduate commitment. It also is appropriate to give some thoughtful attention to the balance of graduate students within the Department.

The clinical psychology area of the Department accepts about one out of ten applicants who meet Entrance Board requirements. In other areas of the Department this ratio varies from about one out of two down to one out of one. If we accept the University's undergraduate growth as a criterion of the amount of expansion that should have been undertaken in clinical psychology, the enrollment in this area of graduate study should now be 100. Of course, if the University is to shift its emphasis from undergraduate to graduate study, the figure should perhaps be higher.

Another criterion that might be employed is the selection ratio of one out of two qualified applicants, a ratio which is often cited as ideal for maintaining a high quality program. Moreover, this would balance the clinical psychology area's selection ratio with others in the Department. Either of these two criteria would give clinical psychology an enrollment figure of approximately 250 instead of its present fifty.

Another criterion that might be employed is the increase in the public demand for the services of clinical psychologists. That figure has increased roughly four-fold since 1946.

The most conservative of these estimates—merely keeping up with undergraduate increases—would suggest a current figure of 100 for clinical psychology at this University. This is the figure assumed as a basis for this estimate of space needs for 1965-1975.

During the past decade the number of students electing undergraduate psychology courses in this University has increased enormously. Moreover, its ratio to the University's undergraduate enrollment has also increased markedly. The teaching staff of the clinical psychology area of the Department must share the added load for this teaching. So far it has met its responsibility by consolidating courses, abandoning specialized offerings for undergraduates, and shifting some courses to other areas of the Department. But classes taught by the usual methods have become unmanageable and serve little more of a higher educational function than a public lyceum course would offer.

Furthermore, this mounting load of undergraduate teaching would, if we permitted it, immobilize our professors as far as graduate teaching is concerned. We have, therefore, developed a teaching format which permits us to employ those advanced graduate students in clinical psychology who have completed their internships and who are in their fourth year of graduate training. By combining the talents of these well trained persons with the professional competence of the professors we have a way of keeping the matter under control. Moreover, this is precisely the kind of experience most needed by the students to round out their present training, just before receiving their Ph.D. degrees.

Assuming the orderly expansion of the graduate program in proportion only to the University's already achieved increase in undergraduate enrollment, and taking into account the large number of qualified applicants for graduate training in clinical psychology, together with the very conservative selection ratio we wish to maintain, the graduate students and staff in mid-decade 1965–1975 should add up as follows.

First Year	Graduate Majors	25
Second Year		22*
Third Year	(Internship Year)	21
Fourth Year		20
Fifth Year		12**
Total Major Students		100

* First year attrition is higher than these figures might suggest, but transfers from other areas of the Department largely compensate for it.
** Students employed on assistant instructorships during their fourth year are frequently unable to complete their training in the minimum time and must remain for a fifth year of study.

Total Minor Students—all levels	50
Senior Staff (Professors)	12
Visiting Professor from Abroad	1
Lecturers (Part Time)	4–8
Junior Teaching Staff (Assistant Instructors) (Included above under Fourth and Fifth Year Students)	15
Secretaries	7
Research and Graduate Assistants (Included above under First and Second Year Students)	24
Students Providing Clinical Services under Supervision of Senior Staff (Included above under Second and Fourth Year Majors and Minors)	55

These figures do not include other graduate students receiving laboratory instruction requiring clinical types of interviewing, but not regarded as services of the Psychological Clinic, nor do they take account of those students who are engaged in laboratory research requiring the regular assignment of space and equipment.

New Areas of Research and Development

It must be anticipated that new areas of research will be opened up during the next decade and new services undertaken as part of the essential training of clinical psychologists. Already our program in clinical psychology is entering into the field of community mental health. This new facet of the program, as well as others which cannot be foreseen at the moment, will create new space needs of a different order. Such programs may require the assembling of groups of varying size and the use of specialized equipment not mentioned elsewhere in this prospectus. It is therefore recommended that approximately 800 sq. ft. of space be allotted for future subdivision appropriate to the needs that develop during the decade.

In addition, the community program will probably require off-campus space in community locations in order to carry out research in various social settings. Such space could, perhaps, be leased in churches and in other community buildings.

Finally, it may become highly desirable to do what has been done by clinical psychologists at Stanford University and purchase trailers equipped with research apparatus. These may be taken to schools and other community locations where both children and adults may be studied under well controlled laboratory conditions and both visual and auditory data properly recorded.

Service Activities

For the past nineteen years the services of the Psychological Clinic have been strictly limited to those which serve a teaching function. No client is admitted unless he meets the training needs of a particular graduate student at a particular point in his curriculum. This training requires well-designed monitoring equipment and space arrangement. The monitoring equipment includes TV monitoring of some rooms, and direct visual and sound monitoring of all other rooms used for clinical services. The proper acoustical treatment of the system is of crucial importance.

Based on current experience the clinical service interviewing per week would involve fifty-five student therapists averaging 2.5 hours of interviewing, 2.5 hours of monitoring, and 2.5 hours of recorder playback (in privacy) each week. Assuming it will be possible to schedule the use of rooms efficiently up to 25 hours a week, this adds up to a clinical service interviewing room requirement of 16.5 rooms. If we add to these the less well equipped non-service laboratory clinical interviewing needs mentioned above this figure the estimate comes to 22 interviewing rooms altogether.

In addition certain specialized types of clinical rooms are required as indicated below.

Summary of Space Needs

Use	*No. Rooms*	*Area*
Basic Teaching Units (Sec. 1)	12	9,024 sq. ft.
Visiting Professor (suitable for small informal group conferences)	1	140
Assistant Instructor for Clinic Intake	1	100
Assistant Instructors (14)	5	700
Lecturers (4–8)	2	320
Service Clinical Interviewing and Monitoring	16	1,600
Non-Service Clinical Interviewing	8	384
Children's Psychotherapy with Storage and		
One Monitor Room	3	680
Family Psychotherapy with Monitor	2	220
Group Psychotherapy (Monitor Shared)	1	280
Research in Group Processes Special		
Intra-Room Communication Equipment	1	280
Isolation Room with Monitor	2	192
Research Equipment	1	180
Office Equipment	1	140
Confidential Files and Work Space for Clinicians Working on Confidential Reports	1	240
Colloquium Lounge (Open 14 hours a day)	1	240
Recording and Monitoring Center	1	196
Client Waiting Room	1	240
Subject Waiting Room	1	196
Junior Staff Waiting Room (Clinicians without assigned space)	1	150
Case Conference Room	1	196
Library (Manuals, Guides, and Check-Out Materials Needed Directly in Clinic Services or Research)	1	196
New Research and Development (on Campus)	1	800
New Research and Development (on Campus)	1	800
Research Trailers	2	
Total Usable Space Required	69	17,494 sq. ft.

Progress Report: Ohio State University's Graduate Program in Clinical Psychology[1]

The Ohio State University has been distinguished by its graduate program in clinical psychology for nearly half a century. Beginning in 1946 a series of significant revisions was undertaken. Within five years Ohio State training had become recognized, it is reasonably safe to say, as the best in the country. During the next decade, some deterioration in the program was allowed to set in. But the leading reputation of the Ohio State Ph.D. in clinical psychology was largely maintained—the increasing stature and visibility of the faculty tending to offset the gradual lapse in programmatic quality.

Outcomes of the Post-War Program

Standards of student selection and achievement are, however, high in comparison with those elsewhere. About one out of ten applicants who complete their applications and survive the Entrance Board's scholarship screening is accepted for training. About forty-six percent are successful in securing the Ohio State Ph.D. in clinical psychology, and another eight percent succeed elsewhere, or in another specialty of psychology. Altogether, since 1946, there have been 292 graduate students carried on the rolls. Currently the number is fifty-two, including those on internship. See Table 1. On the average a successful student takes a little more than five years to complete his degree requirements.

Altogether there have been 111 Ph.D. degrees awarded in clinical psychology since 1946. See Table 2. To an extent probably not approached by those of any other university our graduates have been employed in university graduate teaching. See Table 3. Currently nearly seventy percent are principally employed in the prestige categories of graduate teaching, research, and administration. See Table 4. In these positions they constitute a major influence in the doctoral training of clinical psychologists in this country. See Table 5.

Meeting the Crisis of 1963

In 1963 a retirement, a death, and the late spring resignation of three key faculty members—two of them full professors—precipitated a crisis in clinical psychology's seven-position staff. While these events were of themselves enough to precipitate a crisis, there were, nevertheless, factors behind them, both in the University community and in clinical psychology itself, which made the program vulnerable.

In this crisis the Administration of the College and of the University quickly rallied to the support of the Department of Psychology. A revised program was designed to correct some of the defects that had been allowed to take root in the previous one—particularly to correct the growing doctrinaire cynicism toward novel contributions to the central discipline of psychology, and also to dissolve the professional parochialism which had all but cut off scholarly intercourse with other departments of the University. But especially the new program was intended to follow imaginative lines which would carry this University on to a fresh position of leadership during the coming two decades, a position no less distinctive for the times than the one it had held in the field during the 1950s.

[1] Report dated April 5, 1965 by George A. Kelly, Professor of Psychology and Director of Clinical Psychology, to the President of the University, the Vice President for Instruction and Dean of Faculties, the Dean of the Graduate School, the Dean of the College of Education, and the Chairman of the Department of Psychology. Published by permission of Jacqueline Aldridge.

Collected Papers of the Pioneer of Constructivist Psychology: George A. Kelly, First Edition. Edited by David A. Winter and Nick Reed.

Table 1 Successful Completions

All students carried on rolls of The Ohio State University program in clinical psychology, 1946–1965 (Rev. April 5, 1965)

Total carried on rolls			292
Men		195	
Women		97	
Completed Ph.D. in clinical psychology at O.S.U.			111
Men		88	
Women		23	
Known to have completed doctoral degree elsewhere or in another specialty			20
Men		16	
Women		4	
Remaining in program			52
Men		36	
Women		16	
Total receiving doctoral degrees, or still in program			183
Percent of admissions		63%	
Men	72%		
Women	45%		
Total receiving doctoral degrees			131
Percent of total enrollments, less current students		55%	
Men	65%		
Women	33%		
Failure rate		45%	

Table 2 Ph.D. Degrees in Clinical Psychology Granted by the Ohio State University, 1946–1965 (Rev. April 5, 1965)

Year	*No. Ph.D. 's*	*Year*	*No. Ph.D.'s*
1948	2	1956	8
1949	3	1957	4
1950	5	1958	2
1951	11	1959	6
1952	11	1960	6
1953	8	1961	5
1954	14	1962	4
1955	8	1963	10
		1964	4
	TOTAL: 111		

The Plan

The plan for a revised program in clinical psychology, as it emerged during the succeeding months, embodied eight principal features.

1 The recruitment of a highly qualified staff. Except for the junior position in the seven-man staff, each faculty member was to be fully qualified as a clinician through post-doctoral training or experience in a highly rated clinical facility. Moreover, he was to be every inch a scientist, and particularly one who was disposed to use his clinical perceptiveness, not as a practical sideline, but to develop a more intimate and more basic science of man than psychologists ordinarily manage to do. In other words, he was not to be an "applied" scientist, but a perceptive one.

2 The practical improvement of standards of scholarship. Some graduate students had bogged down in their studies and it seemed obvious that they should either complete them or revise their plans.

Table 3 Types of Appointments (Past and Current)

One hundred and eleven clinical psychologists graduated from The Ohio State University, 1946–1965 (Rev. April 5, 1965)

Type of Principal Appointment	*Number*
Appointments to faculties of universities with graduate programs in clinical psychology	130
Appointments to faculties of other institutions of higher education	4
Appointments to clinical positions in institutions and agencies, exclusive of military and U.S. Public Health commissions	32
Military commissions, active duty	10
U.S. Public Health commissions, active duty	3
Research, other than that incidental to university teaching	19
Industry	4
Administration	7
Private practice	7
Post doctoral training fellowship	4

Table 4 Current Positions

Psychologists receiving the Ph.D. degree in clinical psychology from The Ohio State University, 1946—1965 (Rev. April 5, 1965)

Type of Primary Appointment	*Number*
Members of faculties of universities offering graduate training in clinical psychology	63
Clinical positions in institutions and agencies, exclusive of military and U.S. Public Health commissions	16
Military commissions, active duty	1
U.S. Public Health commissions, active duty	2
Research, other than that incidental to university teaching	7
Industry, other than research	1
Administration, other than categories above	7
Private practice	7
Post doctoral training fellowship	3
Inactive or deceased	4
TOTAL	111
Total currently employed principally in graduate teaching, research, or administration	77
Percent of graduates	69%

3 Improvement of teaching in the major clinical psychology study sequence. Serious gaps and inconsistencies between lecture and laboratory instruction had been allowed to appear, in spite of the fact that the close integration of these two aspects of scholarship had been one of the points of unusual strength in this University's post-war program. Senior faculty members would be asked to assume greater responsibility for the quality of laboratory instruction associated with their courses.

4 A more economical and better integrated use of courses offered undergraduates and casual graduate students. The number of ancillary courses in clinical psychology would be reduced, and those which were retained would be rescued from the status of tri-weekly lyceum offerings. Their teaching would be integrated into the training of advanced graduate students in clinical psychology. That is to say, training in teaching at university levels would be provided students who had passed their qualifying examinations and had successfully completed clinical internships.

5 An extended program for launching the scholarly career. Students would be encouraged to spend their first post-doctoral year abroad at one of ten selected university centers of which we had first-hand knowledge and with whom we had continuing scholarly relations. Following this they would be helped to obtain a post-doctoral training fellowship in some outstanding professional institute in this

Table 5 Current and Past Faculty Appointments in Universities Offering Graduate Education in Clinical Psychology

Graduates receiving the Ph.D. degree in clinical psychology, 1946 to 1964
(Rev. April 5, 1965)

University	*All Appts.*	*Current Principal Appts.*	*University*	*All Appts.*	*Current Principal Appts.*
*Arizona	1	1	*North Carolina	2	1
*Arkansas	1	1	Northern Illinois	2	2
Baylor	1	1	*Northwestern	2	1
Bowling Green State	1	1	*Ohio State (8 temp., 1 reg.)	9	2
Brigham Young	1	1			
Brooklyn, UCNY	1		Oklahoma State	2	2
Buffalo	2	2	*Oregon	1	1
*Chicago	1		*Peabody	2	
City College, UCNY	1		*Penn State	5	2
*Colorado	4	3	*Pittsburgh	2	
*Columbia	1		Princeton	1	1
*Connecticut	1	1	*Purdue	2	1
Dartmouth	1		*Rochester	1	1
Emory	1	1	Rutgers	1	1
*Florida	1	1	Sacramento State	1	1
*Florida State	2		San Fernando State	1	1
*Fordham	1	1	San Francisco State	1	1
*Harvard	5	3	San Jose State	1	1
*Houston	1	1	*Southern Illinois	6	2
Humboldt State	1	1	*Stanford	3	1
*Illinois	5	1	St. Louis	2	2
*Indiana	2	1	*Syracuse	3	3
*Iowa	5		*Temple	1	
Kansas State	1	1	*Tennessee	2	
*Kentucky	1		*Texas	3	2
*Louisiana State	2		*UCLA	5	
Louisville	1	1	*USC	1	
*Loyola (Chicago)	1	1	*Vanderbilt	1	1
Maryland	1		*Washington State	2	1
Merrill-Palmer	1		*Washington University	1	1
*Michigan State	2		Waterloo	1	1
*Missouri	2	2	*Wayne State	1	1
*Nebraska	1		Western Illinois	1	1
Nevada	1		*Wisconsin	3	1
N.Y. Upstate Med. Ctr.	1	1	*Yale	2	
			TOTAL APPOINTMENTS	130	63
			TOTAL UNIVERSITIES	69	49
			APA-APPROVED UNIVERSITIES APPOINTING OSU GRADUATES	42	29
			TOTAL APA-APPROVED UNIVERSITIES	59	

* Doctoral programs in clinical psychology approved by American Psychological Association.

country. Such a program should better prepare them to undertake the kinds of responsibilities that Ohio State graduates seem to have thrust upon them prematurely.

6 Doors opened to scholars from abroad. Not only would selected scholars be invited as visiting professors from abroad, but certain features of modern European scholarship not yet well known in this country would be infused into the Ohio State Program by bringing a distinguished European scholar onto our regular staff.

7 Selective use of lecturers and seminar leaders from disciplines other than psychology. Scholarship in the university community would be tapped.

8 A fresh look at the arena in which clinical psychology serves society. The nation's current massive mental health movement shifts clinical psychology's focus of professional attention from the hospital and the individual treatment clinic to the local community, the

family, groups, and institutions. Yet the basic scholarship in this particular psychology of socially adaptive behavior, a scholarship which must undergird the national effort if it is to be effective, is still in a primitive state of development. Our University, because of its established scientific position in clinical psychology, would consider itself particularly obligated to undertake leadership in developing the basic scholarship needed.

Progress since 1963

It is appropriate at this time to review the progress made in actualizing the plans developed during the months following the spring of 1963, so that the University's Administration may now decide whether to implement them further, or allow the program to lapse into less ambitious patterns, or abandon it altogether.

First it may be helpful to review progress under each of the eight points listed in the preceding section.

1 Recruitment of Staff. This has proved to be much more difficult than anticipated. However, all but one of the positions have been filled. The quality of the men we now have is, without exception, superb. A visiting faculty member from Harvard recently exclaimed, "We keep talking about what we are going to do in community mental health, but you have gone ahead and stolen a march on us and on every other university in the country."

Unfortunately, however, the one position we have been unable to fill is a crucial one. We need a man whose seniority and reputation will enable him to continue to place our graduates in top positions, and, furthermore, one who can take over the directorship of the program. At first it seemed as if the University's publicity during the spring of 1962 was the main obstacle to recruiting such a person. But concern over that matter seems now to have subsided. Currently the difficulty seems to be the policy of waiting for competitive offers before giving faculty members substantial raises in recognition of their productivity. Established scholars would prefer to be recognized for their contributions rather than their market value. And it is an established scholar that we need.

2 Standards of Scholarship. The response to this feature of the 1963 plans was immediate and unmistakable. Already students are accomplishing as much in two years as they formerly did in three. Most of them are now making their first attempt in the qualifying examination a year earlier than before.

Two years ago, half the students were unable to complete their masters theses before going away on their third year internship. This year all of them will. Student morale is higher than at any time in recent years. Today one student remarked, "Now everyone seems less defensive and much more humble about what he thinks he knows. Faculty members do not disparage each other or the members of other professions. Nor do students. Yet our thinking is no less critical than before."

3 Improvement of Teaching. By the autumn of 1964 the quality of instruction had so obviously improved that the pressure from advisers of graduate students in other areas of the Department, who wanted their students to minor in clinical psychology, had more than doubled the enrollment in the basic clinic course sequence. We were strained to the limit to accommodate them. The greater responsibility that senior faculty members take for the quality of laboratory instruction has clearly brought about higher levels of scholarship.

4 Use of Ancillary Courses for Advanced Training. This program is just now getting under way. Instead of letting such courses drain off the energies of the clinical psychology staff we have developed a plan which will combine the contributions of the staff with supervised teaching experience for those advanced graduate students who have passed their qualifying examinations and have successfully met their internship requirements. It is clear that this kind of opportunity for supervised teaching at the university level is precisely one of the things needed by Ohio State University doctoral candidates, especially so, since it is our students particularly who eventually flock into university teaching at graduate levels.

The rapidly growing number of students enrolled in the courses which can be taught with the help of these student teachers can thus be made to contribute to the graduate program in clinical psychology rather than detract from it. Furthermore, the format we have developed provides admirably for the identification and early nurturance of undergraduate students who may themselves continue into graduate study in psychology.

5 The Post-Doctoral Years. While we have been able to implement partially the idea of a post-doctoral year abroad, this feature of the program is slow in developing. Our attempt to have this element of the program underwritten in the training grant received annually from the National Institute of Mental Health failed in the first try on the grounds that Ohio State would first have to demonstrate that it could hold its top staff in clinical psychology. We were, instead, given two years support at the old level—$55,787—with a promise that we would be visited and reappraised in the autumn of 1965 before an increased annual grant, with the usual five year forward commitment, would be considered.

6 Scholars from Abroad. This part of the program has worked unusually well, although it is being run on a shoestring. Last spring Dr. Hardi Fischer of Zurich was a visiting professor. His work was so impressive that he was offered a regular professorship. Limitations of the Visitor Exchange Act will probably prevent him from coming before the autumn of 1966, but last summer he accepted our offer. This spring our visiting professor is Dr. Don Bannister of London whose seminars will deal with disorders in thinking.

7 Teachers from Other Disciplines. This feature of the program has also worked remarkably well, to a large extent due, no doubt, to careful selection of men and the creation of an intellectual climate among our students which makes them more open minded. Four psychiatrists have participated in this program, each extending himself far beyond what it would be reasonable to expect from a visiting lecturer. The response of students has been warm and enthusiastic.

8 New Directions in Clinical Psychology. The addition of Dr. James Kelly to our staff, while it was a severe loss to the National Institute of Mental Health where he was developing demonstrations of community mental health programs, has put this University into a position of leadership, in a newly emerging area. He chose Ohio State over a number of other universities who sought his services because he saw it as a place where new scholarship could be developed in the basic psychology of social adaptation. Already he has made his mark in community mental health planning in Ohio.

The Future

Gratifying as the progress has been in the past two years, the future of the program is not bright. It may be that we can fill the remaining vacancy in our staff with a senior person who meets our particular needs, but the hope of doing so is rapidly waning. But even if we are successful, new obstacles loom ahead much more formidably than two years ago. Since the spring of 1963, with our space needs increasing, we have lost square footage rather than gained it. To carry on our present activities at a minimally respectable level we need to have three times the space we now have—6580 sq. ft. as against a present 1950 sq. ft. If our program were to grow no more than in proportion to the undergraduate enrollment in the university in the past ten years, and if it were to be provided space commensurate with its needs and stature, the figure would 13,000 sq. ft. And if it were to combine certain features of its training with the Area of Developmental Psychology or the Area of Social Psychology in the Department, as it should, an amount of space approximately equivalent to that in the old Chemical Abstracts Building would be required. Nothing like this is in sight.

Next year the number of graduate assistants and assistant instructors in clinical psychology will be reduced. We should have more, as many as six to ten new assistant instructorships, if we are to combine and serve the need for more ancillary instruction with the needs of our advanced graduate students for supervised teaching experience. This part of the program is going backwards.

Equipment cannot be repaired. Expensive interview monitoring equipment, improperly installed over our protests when the Arps Hall addition was built, has never worked satisfactorily. Over and over during the past two years I have tried to get work orders approved which would put it into some kind of usable condition. I had tried during the years before too. The equipment is ninety percent unusable and, so far, the ingenuity exhibited in keeping it that way has exceeded my ingenuity for getting things done.

We need additional senior staff to meet the sharp increases in ancillary teaching loads. There is no likelihood that we can get them in the foreseeable future, and, even if suitable positions were to be budgeted, it would take months to recruit the caliber of men we would need to fill them.

But what really needs to be considered at this point is what is to be the University's overall stake in clinical psychology. The fact that the program has been the best in the country, and that it survived the crisis of 1963 to forge ahead in the past two years, may not be of importance in the University's overall plans, nor may it merit the University's recognition of the achievements of the clinical psychology faculty. The fact that our graduates are continuing to secure prestige appointments—last fall one to an assistant professorship in Harvard's Department of Social Relations, and next fall another, last fall one to a post-doctoral fellowship, one to Penn State University, and one to Buffalo State University—may not be grounds for guaranteeing clinical psychology's future in our own University. But, one way or the other, it would be nice to know.

82

Experimental Dependency[1]

What I am about to say is the outcome of a determined effort to illuminate the internal processes invoked by psychotherapeutic counseling. The point of departure has been a theoretical position I attempted to articulate a number of years ago and described as the *psychology of personal constructs*. The theory is only one of several possible embodiments of a philosophical assumption called—after a discouraging search for a better term—*constructive alternativism*.

Before outlining the theoretical position and proceeding to an examination of psychological processes, let me say as succinctly as I can what I mean by constructive alternativism. If I can make this philosophical assumption clear I may be able to forestall the kind of footless polemics with which new and untried theories are likely to be greeted. Let us assume that science—and indeed all forms of human understanding, including the so-called gut insights of psychotherapy—progresses only fitfully by accumulating fragments of information. For the distance, man makes his greatest forward strides instead by venturing to place sweeping new constructions upon events. Constructive alternativism thus stands in contrast to what we might call the assumption of accumulative fragmentalism—also a rather inelegant term; but one that I think says what I mean.

When a man places a vastly new construction on his circumstances much of the factual information he has accumulated up to that point becomes obsolete or meaningless to him. Sometimes the resultant loss of what once was considered important information is enormous, as when a nation adopts a new code of laws, or science begins to think in terms of a germ theory of disease, or an individual perceives the source of life within himself rather than in his circumstances. Yet the possibilities of alternative constructions are, as far as we know, infinite in number, and, hence, the likelihood of present circumstances becoming obsolescent at some future point in time approaches inevitability. Moreover, this may be as true for the individual as it is for politics or science, and perhaps more immediate, since the cycles between reconstructions are shorter in the case of an emerging personality.

But none of this is tantamount to saying that since all beliefs are open to revision one alternative construction is as good as another. That is the philosophy of cynicism, the trap into which all dogmatists must fall the moment they are confronted with a continuously changing universe. I am not a cynic. Nor have I said that there can never be a convergence of human constructions and reality. I have been careful, furthermore, to leave open the tangible possibility that man's construction of the world around him—and within him—will lead him to alter that world and, perhaps, even to change his own nature.

The net effect of assuming the position of constructive alternativism is to enable man to accept a great variety of new theories as tenable enough for experimental exploration, no matter how much at odds they may be with older theories, or how well the older theories may appear to be supported by known facts. The crux of the matter is that one need not discredit one theory in order to pursue the implications of another. Nor does his effort to test one outlook on life by committing it to experimental action mean necessarily that he has broken faith with what he has long believed to be true.

An Invitation to Pursue a New Line of Inquiry

It is in the light of this particular philosophical assumption that the personality theory, the psychology of personal constructs, is proposed. It is not so much a question of whether the facts gathered under the aegis of older theories will substantiate this new one, as it is a question of what will happen when the new theory is put into action. Facts have a way of reflecting the outlook of the person who perceives them.

We know, of course, a good many facts that emerge from the application of psychoanalytic method. And the more fashionable psychoanalysis becomes the more spontaneously people couch their complaints in the newly fashionable idiom, indeed the more they follow guidelines laid down by Freud himself in creating their predicaments. The complaints emerge as facts, so it appears clear enough that what ails us is precisely what the psychoanalysts have been saying all along.

[1] Unfinished and unpublished manuscript, Brandeis University, 1966. Published by permission of Jacqueline Aldridge.

Collected Papers of the Pioneer of Constructivist Psychology: George A. Kelly, First Edition. Edited by David A. Winter and Nick Reed.

We know also a great deal about how people describe their own actions and the actions of others in the language systems of Western Europe. And it should take no more than a small amount of linguistic nudging to remind ourselves that the sentence structure of those languages is built upon a grammar of stimulus-response couplets. It should come as no great surprise, then, that the "objective," "verifiable," "observable," and "repeatable" descriptions of human behavior should turn out to be various juxtapositions of stimulus and response, just as the distresses of man in the more "intellectual" circles of our society turn out to be psychoanalytic "facts."

But while a language may be used to come to terms with one's experience, it does not follow that one's present language sets an outer limit on what that experience may come to be. It is appropriate to ask, therefore, what it is man attempts to accomplish by means of his language, as well as by other means. If we can formulate some general notion of what that objective may be we may go on to search for better means of achieving it.

This is a scientific undertaking. I think it is particularly a psychological undertaking, although, I am sorry to say, the psychologists who are the most pretentious about being scientists, appear to be the least interested in devising alternative means of achieving human ends. Their experiments seem to envision man as a creature who has not alternatives once he is beset by stimuli, and who seeks to create none. That kind of psychology, may I suggest, is more committed to its epistemological ancestry than to its ontological posterity. Or perhaps, instead of using such fancy philosophical terminology, I should say that it is too bad that so much of psychology is bent on knowing what circumstances have made man do what he has done, and so little of it with what man can make his circumstances do for him.

What I am proposing, then, is a change of emphasis for science, particularly for psychology. Let us commit ourselves more to the exploration of new constructions of our world, not so much to see if they offer more parsimonious explanations of old facts as to see what unexpected new facts can thus be made to emerge. A sense of human history seems to me to suggest that the progress of art and science is much more kaleidoscopic than we have allowed ourselves to suspect. If we shake the kaleidoscope of human outlook new patterns of variegated relationships burst into view. It happens. Psychologists have seen it happen in psychotherapy. Well may we wonder, then, if the facts the sanest men have taken as the inescapable givens of science and personal life will not turn out to be reflections of our linguistic and scientific illumination systems cast back at us from a dark and restless sea of reality—a sea much too vast to be comprehended definitively in our times.

Now, may I invite you to look at psychology in a new way, more particularly at counseling in a new way, and especially at interpersonal dependency. This is not an attempt to proselyte. You may continue to be as loyal as ever you like to whatever you believe to be true of the psychotherapeutic process in general, and of dependency in particular. This is, instead, a proposal to explore the implications of a new viewpoint, even to the extent of experimenting with it actively.

Now let me see if I can shake the kaleidoscope for you. Watch closely. See what happens.

[2]One way to attain some notion of what man may be trying to accomplish is to look at him in the perspective of the centuries of science, paying attention mainly to its forward strides rather than to its journalistic accumulations.

If there's a rose that cannot be known
Then how it may smell I won't ask.
I may know what I don't
But to know what I won't
Becomes my millennial task.

What is is so joined by an is
Unto words which my talk has defined
Without language traditions
There are no rose conditions
And smells remain all of a kind.

I know that I think what I think
And I think I know what I know
And that is for me
Quite singularly
A "rose," as it's known to be so.

I think thus in order to know
What will make me to smell as I ought
Though thought's implication
Should prove the negation
Of roses my smell might have caught.

[2] Editors' note: The manuscript contains numerous reworkings, together with the following material. Several variants of the poem, which may or may not have been meant to be included in the paper, have been crossed out, including a five-verse version entitled "Episteme" in which the verses have the following titles: "Gertrude Aristotle;" "The Saint of Aquinas;" "Husserl Himself;" "Wittgenstein's Second Thoughts;" and "Now I'll Try."

A rose is a rose is a rose
And it smells as it smells as it smells
If it wasn't and didn't
I'd think that it sin't[3]
Though what then I'd know I can't tell

Ring around the Vienna Rosy.
Ring around the rosy, Viennese

I smell in the ways I devise
And without them no sweetness I'll know
And as scents become clearest
I'll bring you, my Dearest,
The loveliest rose I can grow.

I know in the ways that I know
Though what I thus know I smell not
The rose that may be
Is quite beyond me
But the smell is what I have got.

[3] Editors' note: [sic]

83

Clinical Psychology[1]

Clinical psychology is concerned with the assessment and alleviation of the problems of persons who are defective or emotionally ill. It can be understood properly in any one of three ways: as a type of personal service performed by psychologists; as a professional subgroup of psychologists having commonly recognized and self-imposed standards of training and practice together with sanctions designed to ensure compliance with those standards; or as a special area of scholarship within the main body of psychological knowledge.

History

Clinical psychology emerged at the beginning of the 20th century with the establishment of individualized treatment programs for disturbed or handicapped children. At first the emphasis was upon sensory handicaps and basic defects in muscular skills. The clinic established by Witmer in 1896 had such an emphasis and, moreover, it dealt with children whose problems arose primarily in school.

The practice of clinical psychology in hospitals and in collaboration with physicians dates also from the turn of the century. A psychological "laboratory" was established by Shepherd Ivory Franz at the MacLean Hospital in Waverley, Mass., in 1904 and was continued under Frederic Lyman Wills. In 1909 William Healy, a physician, founded the Juvenile Psychopathic Institute—later the Institute for Juvenile Research—in Chicago. In the beginning Healy, a psychiatrist who also had psychological training under William James at Harvard, and Grace M. Fernald, a psychologist, constituted the entire professional staff. Clinical psychology as practiced in the tradition established by these two ventures has been characterized both by its mutually supportive collaboration with advanced medical practice and by its attention to the so-called dynamic or motivational factors in the human personality.

Another current in the stream of clinical psychology started with the publication of the first successful intelligence scale by Binet and its subsequent adaptations by Goddard and Terman. Through these events the practice of clinical psychology came to be characterized by the use of relatively objective measures of psychological functions with, nonetheless, continued emphasis on dealing with troubled persons one at a time and taking into account those personal factors still requiring, in large measure, the psychologist's judgment.

At the beginning of World War II there were between 400 and 600 trained clinical psychologists in the United States. In other countries, except for the fact that the numbers are disproportionately smaller, the figure is difficult to estimate, primarily because in other countries the clinical psychologist is more difficult to identify. By 1943 the armed services of the United States were employing 1,500 persons as psychologists, a third of them in assignments that might be termed clinical; a large proportion of these persons, however, had had inadequate training. At the end of the war the U.S. Veterans Administration adopted a policy of employing clinical psychologists in all its hospitals and clinics; the U.S. Public Health Service and the various state mental health authorities moved in a similar direction; and child guidance clinics, as well as public and private schools, created new positions. By 1964 clinical psychologists in the United States numbered more than 7,000. In Great Britain most clinical psychologists are employed in the National Health Service. In 1964 there were 356 established posts.

In addition to the types of positions mentioned above, there are also places for clinical psychologists in industry, where some specialize in services to emotionally disturbed employees and others in services for managerial officials who need psychological consultation to help them cope with work stresses and interpersonal problems. Other clinical psychologists serve the courts in assessing psychological factors that bear upon judicial decisions; others serve prisons; some are employed by the armed services; and some teach. Many, in all types of positions, are engaged in research. A small proportion are in private practice.

[1] This is a section, written by Kelly, of an entry on Applied Psychology in the Encyclopedia Britannica in 1967, which had also appeared in previous editions of the encyclopedia. It is republished by permission of Jacqueline Aldridge.

Collected Papers of the Pioneer of Constructivist Psychology: George A. Kelly, First Edition. Edited by David A. Winter and Nick Reed.

Activities

Clinical psychologists generally classify their essential activities under three headings: psychodiagnosis, psychotherapy, and research. In psychodiagnosis emphasis is placed on skill in the administration and interpretation of psychological tests, particularly those administered to one person at a time. Such tests are described in the article *Psychological Tests and Measurements*. Less formal diagnostic procedures also are employed, including the psychodiagnostic interview. In psychotherapy, a variety of methods is used (see *Psychotherapy*). Research generally is considered to be a further obligation for the clinical psychologist, but it is often crowded out of his schedule; in some cases, where research is undertaken as a primary service to the client, it continues to be, because of the skills employed, a clinical service.

A considerable number of clinical psychologists perform their services in hospitals and clinics. The patterns of collaboration between clinical psychologists and their colleagues in medicine and social work vary greatly among such institutions. The variations are most marked with respect to psychotherapy; some institutions assign most psychotherapeutic duties, particularly work in behavior therapy, to clinical psychologists, others to psychiatrists only. Institutional collaboration with pediatricians follows a more regular pattern, the clinical psychologist being more likely to be held responsible for services requiring his clinical skills.

Professional Aspects

Clinical psychology gradually is assuming organized responsibility for its own standards of training and practice. The development was considerably delayed because of the conviction, widespread among psychologists, that the sanctions and restraints of a profession are antithetical to liberal scholarship and that they would impede the advancement of psychology as a science. Because of the threat of restrictions imposed from organized psychiatry, however, clinical psychologists were reluctantly joined by their colleagues in an effort to establish standards of training and practice and to provide legal refuge for the continuing development of psychology as a whole. Thus U.S. psychology, and especially clinical psychology, sought to achieve a body that was at once both science and profession.

In Britain the development of clinical psychology is less formal, and this is enabling the clinical psychologist to extend his work to many departments in general hospitals as well as in mental hospitals, especially in the field of rehabilitation.

Training

The pattern of training for clinical psychologists in the United States was established by a committee headed by David Shakow during the 1930s. A broad training in psychology as a science and in related disciplines, as well as demonstration of research competence, was recommended for the doctor of philosophy degree, to which were to be added practicum courses and a fourth year of graduate training to allow time for internship in an interdisciplinary setting.

The American Psychological Association, through its Education and Training Board, annually identifies universities and internship agencies that meet its standards. The American Board of Examiners in Professional Psychology certifies selected advanced specialists in psychological practice, including clinical psychologists, after examination. As a general guide to the practice of professional psychology the association developed a code of ethical standards, which was accepted by its membership and is used as a basis for disciplinary action against those who fail to perform[2].

[2] The section concludes with a paragraph on clinical psychology training in Great Britain, but this is not attributed to Kelly.

84

Fixed Role Therapy[1]

Fixed role therapy is an experimental procedure which may be followed in cases where one wishes to activate psychotherapeutic processes without resorting to applied psychology. This is to say that it represents a form of inquiry designed to shed light on an urgent problem, rather than a treatment warranted only by previous research. It is essentially experimental, not simply because it is novel, but because it involves the client in a calculated venture whose extended outcomes he must assess. In a strict sense it is not even a form of treatment, but an investigative project in which the client is himself the principal investigator—and knows it!

Constructive Alternativism

The form of the procedure is embedded in personal construct theory, which, in turn, is anchored in an epistemological position called *constructive alternativism.* Constructive alternativism holds that man understands himself, his surroundings, and his potentialities by devising constructions to place upon them and then testing the tentative utility of these constructions against such *ad interim* criteria as the successful prediction and control of events. It assumes that man's construction of events may ultimately converge upon reality, in the manner of non-Euclidean parallel lines, but that it is presumptuous to claim the convergence has already taken place. Any present construction is then open to an undetermined amount of reconsideration, no matter how obvious it may appear to be or how objective the evidence which supports it at the moment. Constructive alternativism stands in contrast to a view we may call *accumulative fragmentalism*, the notion that knowledge is a growing collection of substantiated facts—when we get all the facts we shall find ourselves arrived at the truth.

Personal Construct Theory

Personal construct theory starts with the postulate that a person's processes are psychologically channelized by the ways in which he anticipates events. It goes on to propose that one anticipates events by construing the manner in which future occurrences can be thought to replicate past ones. The unit of construction is the *personal construct*, which is defined as a way in which two or more events can be regarded as similar and in contrast to one or more other events. The personal construct is not a representation of an event or a group of events, as is sometimes said of a *concept*. It is, instead, a referent devised by the person upon which he may project events in order to cope with them. It need not be verbalized and it may be regarded as structuring smooth muscle and glandular processes, as well as skeletal muscle or verbal enactments.

The development of a personal construct system for the anticipation of events poses a minimax problem for the person—how to achieve maximum differentiation of events with a minimum of dichotomous discrimination units, or constructs. It also involves problems of ordinal relations between constructs, the employment of constructs in experience, commitment to behavioral inquiry, and the revision of constructs in the light of particular outcomes and the integrity of the system as a whole.

[1] Dated 1966 and first published as Kelly, G.A. (1973). Fixed role therapy. In R.M. Jurjevich (Ed.). *Direct psychotherapy: 28 American originals* (pp. 394–422). University of Miami Press. Republished in Groves, J. E. (Ed.). (1996). *Essential papers on short-term dynamic therapy* (pp. 202–229). New York University Press. Published here by permission of University of Miami Press.

Collected Papers of the Pioneer of Constructivist Psychology: George A. Kelly, First Edition. Edited by David A. Winter and Nick Reed.

The Science Paradigm

For purposes of understanding fixed role therapy there are two features of personal construct theory that must be kept clearly in mind. Both represent wide departures from the views of other personality theories. The first is the notion of *the scientist as the paradigm of man*. The second is the notion that *one enacts a role*—in the personal construct theoretical sense—*only to the extent that he is guided by a construction of another person's outlook*. Both notions require a little explaining.

A description of scientific method as it is practiced by scientists can quite properly be regarded as a personality theory—applied, of course, to persons who happen to be scientists. But the basic features of scientific method can be considered as basically human too. One can scarcely say the scientist does anything a human being cannot do, though he may do some things that not all his fellow humans do as well. But the behavior of the scientist is altogether human behavior, and a construction of his actions can provide guidelines for understanding all human behavior. Moreover, the tactics that scientists follow in pursuing their investigations are no less available to other men who have inquiries to pursue.

The thoughtful exploration of this line of theorizing suggests, then, that what a scientist does, man can do, and what a scientifically minded psychologist does, his client can do. It suggests, furthermore, that it may be as inept to try to get a client up on his feet by treating him or conditioning him as it would be to try to get a psychologist to make a monumental contribution by ordering him to do precisely what he is told. But if a client can begin to use the better methods of inquiry himself, if he can experiment appropriately, and if he can reformulate his hypotheses in the light of the relationships between his predictions and his observation of occurrences, he may be on his way to living his life in a manner that leads somewhere, rather than going round and round in "healthy" orbits prescribed by his psychiatrist. Fixed role therapy casts the client in the role of a scientist intent on inquiring into his most perplexing problems. It casts his psychotherapist in the role of a colleague who has as much to learn as he does.

Role

The other feature of personal construct theory that must be particularly well understood is its definition of role. The two conventional notions of role—a course of action articulated with the actions of others, and a set of behavioral expectations imposed upon a man—are both externalized definitions. That is to say their determinants are outside the person. Personal construct theory, however, makes every effort to employ terms which refer to the outlook of the person himself. The theory's definition of role represents such an effort.

If I attempt to understand another man mechanistically or behavioristically, it probably means that I am not concerned with the construction he is placing on me or the other events in his life, but only with those actions which I can observe and how I myself choose to construe them. For all I care, he could just as well be a combination of levers and wires. I may even refer to him as "an organism," rather than as "a person," in the manner of psychologists who think there is something unscientific about being a person. To be sure, I may be able to anticipate some of his behavior better by construing him in this way than if I listen to him too intently. This may turn out to be particularly true if I make the mistake of assuming that the words he uses have only the meanings attributed to them by the dictionary,

But however efficient may be this manner of construing my friend, personal construct theory would not call any of my ensuing behavior a role. On the other hand, if I make an attempt to see the world through his spectacles—through his constructs, I mean—and I structure my own actions in the light of what I think I see, what I do then is, for me, a role. This is not to say that my interpretation of his viewpoint is accurate, or even that I shall then choose to act in a manner compliant with his wishes. Indeed, my perception may be grossly inaccurate—which could result in considerable confusion—and I may even choose to use my version of his outlook to undo him—which also could have chaotic consequences. But in any case, my actions would constitute a role.

Implications of Role Enactment

However badly I may choose to act, or some other individuals may choose to act, it should not be necessary to go into great argumentative detail to suggest that, notwithstanding, it is in role relationships that men may hope to combine their ingenuities as well as their labors. Thus they may advance mankind's cultural achievements beyond what can be accomplished simply by assembly line divisions of labor or by the imposition of regularized behavioral expectations upon the masses. On the other hand, a socialization of human institutions which is based on the two conventional notions of role is all too likely to lead to the suppression of human ingenuity, as, in the case of one of the notions, it did in the early stages of the industrial revolution, or as, in the case of the other, it has done in the headlong rush of ideological socialism.

The notion of role as a man's course of action articulated with the actions of others leads one to envision a society populated with a species of *economic man*. The notion of role as a set of expectations conjures up an image of a society of *ideological man*. I suppose we could add that, if the current notions of psychotherapy continue to catch on, we may look forward to a society of the *self-conscious man*. But personal construct theory envisions a different kind of society, a society of the *inquiring man*. Fixed role therapy depends greatly upon both client and therapist understanding the meaning of role in this personal construct sense, rather than in the sense of either of the conventional definitions, or in the implied sense that emerges out of present-day psychotherapeutics,

Having said only this much it would be easy to break off the discussion and leave the reader with the impression that fixed role therapy is going to turn out to be no more than an epistemological pastime of gentle people. But this might be misleading. Fixed role therapy is as much an ontological venture as it is a perceptive psychoanalysis of one's neighbors. Personal construct theory is not a cognitive theory, but a theory about how the human process flows, how it strives in new directions as well as in old, and how it may dare for the first time to reach into the depths of newly perceived dimensions of human life.

Personal construct theory's epistemology is an epistemology of creative actions. Man understands his world by finding out what he can do with it. And he understands himself in the same way—by finding out what he can make of himself. Man is what he becomes. What he becomes is a product of what he undertakes—expected or by surprise. The peculiar genius of psychology, if it has one, is to see man in this perspective—as what the continuing effort of living can make of him. Here, beyond epistemology, lies the ontological rationale of fixed role therapy.

Other Forms of Psychotherapy within Personal Construct Theory

While fixed role therapy embodies the principles of personal construct theory, the reader should not be left with the impression that it is the only form of psychotherapy that may do so. It stands out as an example of the theory in action primarily because, on the face of it, it appears to disregard so much of what other systems hold to be essential. Psychoanalysis probes and strives for insight, yet fixed role therapy offers no necessary interpretations of the client's present problem. Behavior therapy prescribes a cure, yet fixed role therapy may propose an enactment no client or therapist would want to see continued. The client-centered therapist must offer his client "an unconditional positive regard" for the feelings he has so long experienced in dread, but fixed role therapy recognizes no such autonomy of feelings. Yet fixed role therapy is articulate about what it undertakes, it ventures to undertake unfamiliar modes of behavior, and it relies upon acute sensitivity to feelings arising out of one's own experimentation.

But however much at odds with better known approaches fixed role therapy appears to be, its rationale does not rest on any necessary conviction that they are wrong. The philosophical position—constructive alternativism—which underlies the theory and the method, does not require one to discredit one set of assumptions before daring to examine the implications of others. Indeed, this is, in effect, just what is proposed to the client. He need not invalidate his "neurotic" outlook before actively exploring what other outlooks have to offer. He has only to undertake psychotherapy as an ontological venture rather than as an epistemological exercise designed to convince himself of what he does not feel is so. All of this is a way of saying that one's personality is not altogether shaped by what he knows and what he accepts, but emerges continuously through his modes of pursuing what he hopes to be and what he would like to find out.

Personal construct theory, more than any other system of psychotherapy I know, envisions an orchestration of techniques—perhaps as wide a variety of techniques as the human armamentarium stocks. Unlike psychoanalysis, in which Freud precisely combined the techniques of his mentor Charcot and his colleague Breuer, personal construct theory does not prescribe for the therapist a single orthodox procedure. Nor does it see the salivating dog as the prototype of the client, or an abiding faith in man as the climate in which all good things grow. Yet what the psychoanalyst does to help his client articulate what has remained estranged from language, the personal construct theorist may do also. He may, as well, see conditioning as an experiment the client performs rather than an operation performed on him, and he may offer his client the acceptance of feelings as a hypothesis worth experimenting with.

Appropriateness of Fixed Role Therapy

One thing more; for my own part I do not employ fixed role therapy in the majority of cases I see—perhaps in no more than one out of fifteen. There are too many other orchestral possibilities for one to sit and hum the same therapeutic tune to his clients morning, noon and night. Sometimes I employ the procedure when I can see the client for less than a month, but can have him come in several times a week. I may resort to fixed role therapy when a client has become surfeited with other therapeutic efforts, including my own. It can be used to break through over-intellectualization, and it can serve to direct the client to resources outside the therapy room which are not for hire. Now and then I use it to prepare the client for a protracted psychotherapeutic sequence, and sometimes to finish off such a sequence. Occasionally it proves useful when a psychotherapist whom I am supervising becomes preoccupied with the "interesting material" that accumulates in session after session, and starts "peeling his onion."

As for the appropriateness of fixed role therapy in various diagnostic categories, our experience so far does not permit us to put our finger precisely on the outer boundaries. My early apprehension about using it with "schizophrenics" has been allayed; it does not foster the delusions I was afraid it might. I am also less reluctant to employ it with mild "paranoid schizophrenics," now that I have had some experience with it. Handled properly it seems to offer some stabilization for the aura of urgency that "manics" display. "Depressives," of course, experience difficulty mobilizing themselves for the continued enactment, but, since continued mobilization of their efforts is generally judged to be a good thing, this difficulty need not be taken as a contraindication for the method. I have even seen it work rather well in "conversion" cases and in cases of "immature personality." It has been tried with some success in cases of mental retardation, though not to "cure" the symptoms of mental deficiency itself, of course. Thus far I have not approached a "phobic case" through fixed role therapy. I must try that the next time a client comes in complaining of his inability to get along with snakes.

The Sequence of Steps in Fixed Role Therapy

It would perhaps be helpful at this point to turn from rationale to technique, starting with a sketch of the process as a whole, and then following with a step-by-step account of the sequence of procedures. The client—call him Quinn McQuirk—is asked to write a character sketch of himself from a particular point of view. The therapist then studies this sketch in consultation with colleagues, and, with their help, prepares an *enactment sketch*, one that might have been written by a hypothetical "Ernest Seeman" in response to a similar request.

In the next therapy session Quinn McQuirk is shown the "Ernest Seeman" sketch and his superficial reaction to it is tested. If the test is passed satisfactorily he is asked to pretend that he, Quinn, "has gone to the mountains to enjoy himself," and that, in his stead, "Ernest Seeman" materializes. The client is to enact as best he can, twenty-four hours a day, all that "Ernest Seeman" might do, say, think, or even dream. At least three therapy sessions a week are scheduled, and in them client and therapist rehearse the enactment, plan critical tests of its effectiveness, and examine outcomes. At the end of the period Quinn McQuirk "comes back," whether he wants to or not, and is invited to appraise the experience in whatever ways make sense to him.

The undertaking is not as simple as it probably sounds. Our experience—the experience of my colleagues and myself—suggests many points at which variation in the procedure can lead to trouble—especially in the hands of a therapist who thinks of fixed role therapy as a form of "treatment." While the method does not require one to make the usual psychoanalytic "interpretations," it is scarcely any the less vulnerable to the blunders of clinically insensitive therapists. It is neither easy nor routine. Clinical skill and perceptiveness are as crucial as they are known to be in a psychoanalytic relationship where volatile transference involvements are present. But, of course, the terms of reference are different.

The Self-Characterization

At first glance it may appear that the self-characterization the client is asked to write is not essential to the experiment. I am convinced, however, that it is an important step in the process. The particular way in which the self-characterization is elicited is intended to imply that neither psychodiagnosis nor the ensuing psychotherapy is based on "confession." Moreover, having written the self-characterization, the client should be better prepared to see the "Ernest Seeman" sketch as having both subjective and objective authenticity. "Ernest Seeman" is a man, such as Quinn himself is, who can see himself as a man, just as Quinn has been asked to see himself, who faces human problems too, and who makes no pretense of psychological perfection. Furthermore, Quinn may begin to see that there is a sense in which one may credit a man with being what he represents himself to be, this being an application of the principle of the *credulous approach*, about which personal construct theory has a great deal to say.

As I write these sentences I recall that last night—by an actual count of candy bars—exactly seventy goblins, witches, and sundry suspicious characters of assorted sizes came to our door, some of them piping in small voices, "Trick or treat, trick or treat!" To be sure, you and I might be constrained to say that "they were not goblins, or witches, or even very suspicious," both of us being quite willing to assume that we know what real spooks look like. But if we agree to make such a denial, do we approach the psychological truth about these visitors, or do we retreat from it? Which, psychologically, is the real child: The child behind the mask, or the child "un-masked," standing bare-faced in the bright light of the living room, surrounded by adults, and saying proper "pleases" and "thank yous?" Do I understand the child half as well if I refuse to see the part he is enacting? I think not!

A man becomes the President of the United States. But come now, between us psychologists, is he really the President? Or must we not diagnose him as the small time politician who has been playing "trick or treat" most of his life? No, I think that if he now undertakes to enact the part, he is, indeed, *The President*. If we are to understand psychologically a man who enacts such a commitment, we can do so only by empathizing the commitment—by being credulous to it. Of course, this does not mean that he will play the part the way we think we might, or the way we think Abraham Lincoln or George Washington played it.

Altogether, psychological perceptiveness does not depend upon the precision with which we can fit our client into one of our own preconceived categories, but in our grasp of his construction of events and of the part it leads him to take in coping with them. The therapist, too, has a role to enact—a role in the personal construct theoretical sense—one that comes to life only after he puts the client's glasses on over his own and sees as best he can what the client sees.

Eliciting the Self-Characterization

"I want you to write a character sketch of Quinn McQuirk, just as if he were the principal character in a play. Write it as it might be written by a friend who knew him very *intimately* and very *sympathetically*, perhaps better than anyone ever really could know him. Be sure to write it in the third person. For example, start out by saying 'Quinn McQuirk is ....'" This is the way Quinn McQuirk is asked to write a character sketch of himself.

The phrasing of this request has been carefully chosen and has gone through a good many revisions in the light of experience with it. The term, "character sketch" seems to work best in suggesting to the client that he is to present himself as a coherent whole, rather than to catalog his faults and virtues. The object is to see how he structures himself, and within what kind of framework, not to force him to diagnose himself within a psychologist's framework. He may find it difficult to present himself as an integral person. If so, it is worth knowing, and, furthermore, an appreciation of this fact should help the clinician structure his own role. A responsible therapist will seek to know something of how both Quinn's self and his outside world are seen through those glasses he wears.

It is easy to see that the therapist cannot suggest an outline for the sketch, though he may be asked to prescribe one. It is Quinn's outline—his own structural framework, however inadequate that may be—that is sought, not a burlesque of a man vainly juggling words to present himself in the alien language of a presumed expert. Nor is Quinn expected to encapsulate himself in the terms of any particular friend, as the phrase, "perhaps better than anyone ever really could know him," is intended to suggest.

To be sure, Quinn may find himself at a loss for words. If so, then that may be how it is with him—a self held together without the structure of language. Or he may say only, "I live at 35 1/2 Commercial Street. I am five feet two inches tall, I am 32 years old, and I weigh 190 pounds." Can we then say he has offered us nothing of psychological importance? I think no sensitive clinician would say that! He may thus indeed have put his identity in the most poignant perspective.

Or suppose he says only, "I am of medium height and build, I live in an average community, and I have never been in trouble." Can we allow ourselves to think for one moment that this tells us nothing of his inner experience or of the illusive issues that plague his daily life?

There are occasions when a client will protest he is quite incapable of writing down anything about himself. Ordinarily one suggests then that he give it a try and come in next time with whatever he has managed to write. But the therapist can add, if he wishes, "Just suppose I have never seen Quinn McQuirk or talked to him. How could this friend, who knows him so much more intimately and sympathetically than anyone really does know him, write the character sketch? You and I need his help." It does not seem advisable to go further than this, if indeed to go even this far. After all, the success of therapy rarely hinges on the client's avoiding all confrontation with his own unproductiveness.

Preparing the Enactment Sketch: An Experiment

There is much more to be said about systematic methods of analyzing the self-characterization. But that is a whole chapter in itself, and the reader, if he plans to have a go at fixed role therapy, is urged to read what is written elsewhere about it (Kelly, 1955). The analysis should be carried to the point where the therapist has some notions of the principal construct dimensions the client uses in identifying himself, of how he utilizes experience, and of the directions in which his sense of movement appears to carry him. One can begin to infer also what his words mean, although finding out precisely what a client's language means is an undertaking not likely to get very far in the brief course of a fixed role therapy sequence.

It may seem trite to say that "Ernest Seeman" must, first of all, present himself as human. The image of mental health that most psychotherapists manage to project is not of a person that most of us would warm up to, much as we might admire his stark realism, his overpowering release of libidinal energy, and his unfailing competence in manipulating his associates. Such realism robs the world of mystery, the energy makes all obstacles trivial, and the competence eliminates any exciting risk of failure. Certainly personal construct theory does not for one moment paint such a picture of mental health.

There is no implicit guarantee of success in the character of "Ernest Seeman." Like Quinn, he is a man of dreams, striving, and uncertainty. His answers turn out to be questions in another form, and his questions, if they are to lead him anywhere in his life, must be posed in judicious behavior, not in words merely. Any attempt to portray "Ernest" as a walking solution to Quinn's problems makes him into a Madison Avenue advertiser's layout, rather than an honest experiment. It would be as fraudulent as most applied psychology turns out to be, whether on Madison Avenue or in a practitioner's office.

Hypotheses Imbedded in "Ernest Seeman"

The task one faces in writing the enactment sketch is, then, to design a genuine experiment in which both client and therapist are active participants, and both are prepared to be surprised by the outcomes. That means there should be at least one hypothesis to be tested, and it should be stated explicitly in the "Ernest Seeman" sketch. The hypothesis may be one Quinn has already set up in his characterization of himself. Since, in human affairs, there is nothing that corresponds to the statistician's null hypothesis, we can examine Quinn's hypothesis only by testing its substantial alternatives. For example, if he has described himself as "meticulous," the alternative—from his point of view—might be to play the part of an "Ernest" who was "casual," and then to see what would happen.

But more often than not the psychotherapist will want to cast the enactment in a new dimension, one that has never occurred to Quinn, and, indeed, one he may not initially be able to visualize. "Ernest," for example, may be characterized as "generous," and the implications of being so, versus being "grasping," explored by actually playing the part. By structuring his behavior with respect to a new axis, the whole of living begins to take shape in a world he never suspected was there.

Contrast this kind of undertaking with one in which the client would simply play the part of a person who is "casual," as against Quinn's "meticulousness." He may even have tried it before; most clients have rattled back and forth in their slots. But to launch out in an altogether new dimension, through successive rehearsals and field trials, is to find a new kind of life space and to break out of the ruts which have too long channeled his life. The novel products of such a venture can, if properly recognized as outcomes of his initiative, be woven into the fabric of Quinn's life experience.

But without such sallies in new directions, life is no more than a series of accidental collisions with events, and the outcomes can be judged only as fortunes or misfortunes. The impact of an event, when no venture has been risked, leaves one's personality intact or bruised, but, in either case, essentially unchanged. But a true commitment, whose outcomes are reflected back upon its design, recreates personality by carrying it through the full cycle of human experience.

"Ernest Seeman" is a Role

The reader may recall my early insistence that one must keep two features of personal construct theory in mind when he employs fixed role therapy—the science paradigm and the notion of role. Let us hope I have now said enough about the science paradigm to make it clear that fixed role therapy is a genuine experiment in which client and therapist are co-investigators and the major hypotheses are stated in the "Ernest Seeman" sketch.

Now it will come as no surprise for me to say also that the enactment sketch must embody a role—a role in the personal construct sense. This is to say that "Ernest Seeman" is to be depicted as a man who acts in the light of his continuing attempt to catch a glimpse of the way things seem to others. Not only, then, is he an anthropomorphized hypothesis for Quinn to test, but he is such a man as would attempt to try on other men's glasses and to discover through experimentation if what he observed by looking through them was indeed what other men observe. Perhaps I had better say that "Ernest" actively concerns himself with the outlooks of others, not with their behaviors merely, and he is prepared to verify his perception of how the world looks to them. Whether his friends perceive accurately or not is another matter, and this he realizes too.

Sometimes I am asked if the client himself should not write—or at least take part in writing—the enactment sketch. This would seem to follow from the view of the client as a participating scientist. But when I have tried this approach I have noted that he does not often introduce a novel construct dimension. Probably it is not easy for him to express on the spur of the moment what has never before occurred to him. What he does then—if he tries anything new at all—is propose a reversal of his position on one of his prevailing construct axes. While this may eventually lead him to a new vantage point in construing his circumstances, it does not offer the dramatic possibilities that an experiment initially designed by an imaginative therapist might disclose. Nor is it likely to open up a world proportioned in new dimensions.

Nevertheless, there are stages and forms of therapy in which the client's design of his own experiments is not only valuable, but essential. Indeed, we may hope that the design and calculated execution of experiments is something he will be doing for the rest of his life.

What I have found space to mention here does not by any means exhaust the considerations that should be taken into account when one attempts fixed role therapy in a particular case. A therapist should be prepared to consider not only the wealth of his own clinical experience, but also the skills, the perceptions, the weaknesses, the perplexities, and the preoccupations of his client with "causes" and "circumstances." Moreover, he must respect the integrity of the Quinn personality, lest, by invalidating particular neurotic approaches to life, he destroys the man himself.

Illustrative Enactment Sketches

A few years ago the following enactment sketch was used in a fixed role therapy sequence:

> Kevin Malloy is a man whose basic integrity governs all his daily acts. Never are his actions incompatible with his convictions. He has found from experience that this kind of integrity enables him to rise above life's vexing obstacles and personal handicaps. This quality in his personal make-up may not always be noted by others, yet it subtly flavors all of his interpersonal relations.
>
> One of the conspicuous features of Mr. Malloy's character is his obvious respect for the personalities of other people, even those who do not meet the standards he applies to himself. It is his basic integrity that makes him unique in this respect. While he is always free to express his own point of view, it would never occur to him that, by doing so, he would be trying to compel others to conform to his views. When he expresses himself it is meant as a sincere invitation to others to express their own particular viewpoints also. Thus he interacts with people without feeling he must either teach or concede.

When Mr. Malloy was an adolescent his relations with his parents were sometimes strained, because of their rigid insistence that he look at certain situations from their viewpoint. Out of this experience has developed the point of view which now has become the characteristic feature of his personality.

Sometimes his friends find him a stimulating companion—willing both to give and to take. At other times he falls silent to the company of others, perhaps because he is hesitant to stifle another's self-expression. While on these latter occasions he gives the impression of being withdrawn and reticent, actually he always remains an alert, though sometimes quiet, participant in any social situation.

The above sketch was prepared for enactment by a client who was easily threatened by persons who did not subscribe to his "upright" virtues and often became disputatious. The initial "integrity" theme in the sketch was designed to maintain this feature of his perception of himself—or his pose, if you prefer—but to derive from it a mode of action which lent itself to the development of rudimentary role constructs. His experiences—as he remembered them—with his parents made the development of role constructs a tricky matter. It seemed best to incorporate somewhat similar "experiences" when writing the enactment sketch. It will be noted that the sketch also tried to provide grounds for his keeping his mouth shut while still "participating" in a group.

Following is a self-characterization written by a client for whom an enactment sketch was later prepared. The misspellings in her typewritten manuscript are reproduced.

In my opinion C.N. is not a shy girl by no means. She mixes well with both sexes but is frequently moody and therefore is irritable to those surrounding her. Carrie lies quite often; knowing she is doing wrong, but continues to do so. She exaggerates about things concerning herself which she feels would like to be true but are not. I find she's becomes dissatisfied with herself and the things she is doing quite often. For example, she gets disgusted with school and wants to quit and has no desire to study. Also she feel as if she wants to go to a new environment to meet new people. I also feel she possess a selfish character at times and other times quite generous depending upon her so-called mood. She has a strong desire to be happy and satisfied with the things she has and therefore have peace of mind. She sometimes has the feeling that she wants everything to come her way without working for it and she would like to possess of feeling of wanting to give as much as receive. She would like very much to fall in love and not only look for what he could give her, now but first look for how ambitious he is and what he will have in the future. She is dead set against marry a doctor because of that life a doctor's wife leads. She feels she requires constant attention and love in order not to have that sense of insecurity she so frequently feels.

The following enactment sketch was prepared for this client and used in fixed role therapy.

Julie Dornay is a good person to have for a friend. She is spontaneously and sympathetically interested in people. She is a good listener. She is sensitive to the ways other people feel. People value her friendship, not only because of the things she can give them or the favors she can do, but more because of the encouragement and strength her friendship gives them. Having had problems of her own she is well equipped to play a sympathetically supporting role to the people who confide in her. While she does not feel that all her own problems are solved, when others come to her, she lays her own problems aside in order to be of help. Basically she believes that all people are worthwhile in their own right, regardless of their accomplishments or worldly successes. Because of this fundamental belief in people her own worthwhileness is simply and naturally taken for granted.

There is an undercurrent of impatience in Julie's way of life. She is quick to express her liking for her friends. She is always ready to speak up in their behalf. When she sees someone being pushed around she really stands up and lets her voice be heard. But this impatience never seems to come into conflict with her underlying feeling of kindliness and sensitivity for others. Indeed, one might almost say that her impatience is a result of this feeling.

Julie's capacity to be a good friend leads her into many new and interesting adventures. While some people pick and choose the friends who conform to their own narrow specifications, Julie selects a tremendous variety of friends, no two of whom fit precisely the same set of specifications. Thus her own life is enriched and widened and new horizons are continually opening up before her.

When you talk to Julie you soon become aware of the fact that she is interested in you because, first of all, she fundamentally accepts you as you are and wholeheartedly believes that you are genuinely a worthwhile person. She responds to you spontaneously and takes your acceptance of her for granted. But most of all you discover that she is ready and eager to know you as a unique and different personality among her many and varied friends.

In this enactment sketch the role construction is frankly stated, though in a concrete, behavioral form. As can be seen, the enactment is designed to involve her in commitments—perhaps even premature ones. Her search for a Lochinvar is not invalidated, but she is to be kept busy attending to lesser characters along the way.

Presenting the Enactment Sketch to the Client

The usual procedure is to present a copy of the enactment sketch to the client and ask him to follow as the therapist reads a copy of it. Then the therapist asks two questions: (1) "Has Ernest Seeman described himself in a manner that makes him seem genuine?" and (2) "Does he sound like a person you would like to know?" If the answer to both questions is "yes," the enactment can proceed.

If the answer to the first question is "no" the therapist should ask what there is about the sketch that makes "Ernest Seeman" seem artificial. Sometimes this calls for re-writing a part of the sketch, but more often "an interpretation" will suffice. Sometimes the interpretation can be composed on the spot as an addendum to the sketch.

If the answer to the second question is negative the therapist can seek to find out what feature of the sketch is. threatening. Sometimes this difficulty, too, can be handled by "an interpretation" of "Ernest." In any case, unless the sketch can be made acceptable in terms of both questions, it is better to start over by writing another characterization before attempting the enactment.

The enactment can be proposed somewhat in the following manners: "During the next two weeks, instead of dealing directly with your problems, I would like to suggest that we do something altogether different. Let us suppose that Quinn McQuirk is going to have a two weeks vacation in the mountains, and, in his place, you are going to be 'Ernest Seeman.' You will act like 'Ernest Seeman,' talk like him, think like him, do the things you think he might do, eat the way you think he would eat, and, if you can, even have the dreams you think he might have.

"Here is another copy of 'Ernest's' character sketch. Keep one copy with you all the time and read it at least four times a day—particularly at night when you go to bed, and again in the morning. Read it also whenever you have difficulty playing the part.

"During these two weeks I'll be seeing you every other day, so we can rehearse. We'll try to anticipate some of the situations that will arise so that you can be ready to be as much like 'Ernest' as possible.

"Don't worry about Quinn. We don't even need to think about him. Besides, he is going to be away enjoying himself, and we can assume he doesn't want to be bothered. In any case, he will be coming back two weeks from today and that will be time enough to see what he has on his mind.

"Now, let's see, your supervisor is who? Angus McGillicuddy? OK, let us suppose it will be 'Ernest Seeman' who shows up for work this afternoon. How would 'Mr. Seeman' greet Mr. McGillicuddy? I'll be Mr. McGillicuddy. Good afternoon, 'Mr. Seeman'!"

It is important to get the enactment under way immediately. Rather than attempting to persuade Quinn that he should be "Ernest," the client is treated as if he actually was "Ernest," with the therapist expressing surprise or disbelief at any expression that is out of character. Even though Quinn is speechless, or fails to play the part convincingly, his confrontation with a therapist who sees him as "Ernest," and as "Ernest" only, cannot be ignored. Somehow he must cope with the novel situation in which he now finds himself. Though he may run the gamut of familiar manipulative devices to get out of it altogether, the most obvious pathways for movement are those staked out by the constructs "Ernest" envisions.

During this stage of the enactment the therapist may feel quite as strange as the client does. In fact, I find it generally more difficult to persuade therapists to commit themselves to the undertaking than to get clients to give it an honest experimental trial. I suppose that is because most clients expect to invest something in therapy, while all too many therapists, being applied psychologists rather than scientists, want little more than to be successful in the easiest possible manner. Perhaps we should remember that there is a great deal of difference between coming to a session to wager one's way of life, and coming only to put in an hour of professional time.

Perhaps the most difficult thing for the therapist to realize is that, even when his client says nothing, a few moments of being perceived as "Ernest" rather than Quinn will stick in the troubled mind long after the session is ended. A man can scarcely fail to wonder, amidst all the tortured doubts about ever being anything other than his miserable self, what it would be like—what it really would be like—to walk out into the world and be recognized, not as Quinn, but as "Ernest." Certainly—unless our observations have been quite misleading—the effectiveness of the therapeutic effort does not depend upon the glibness with which the part is played. Indeed, it seems to me that the reverse may be true—the client who finds the experience disruptively novel, and his first words in the part labored and inept, may be the one most deeply affected by the experience. He is the one who invests himself, who performs an experiment—not the skilled actor who makes a burlesque of the part, and risks nothing.

Protecting the Integrity of Quinn

Important as it is not to become embroiled in a debate with the client about whether he can or cannot enact the part of "Ernest," there are some questions that should be answered. The one most likely to be asked first is what the purpose of the enactment is, or how it "will help." It is a fair question and must be answered honestly, as I believe all questions must be in a psychotherapeutic relationship. While I have not settled on any particular phraseology, as I have for some of the other steps in the sequence, something like the following is appropriate.

"We both need to know right off just how much you are prepared to invest in developing a new way of life for yourself. Sometimes people think they can simply close their eyes and have the therapist do something to them that will take all their troubles away without their having to take any risks themselves. But psychotherapy is not simply a matter of going to the doctor to be treated and then going back home to continue acting and thinking in the same old way. That won't work. Besides, life is an adventure from beginning to end, and right here is where we start. *I'm* ready; are *you*?"

Sometimes the client will persist: "But I don't see how *this* can help." The answer can be brief: "Of course not; you haven't tried it. Neither of us knows for sure what will happen. The only thing we know for sure is that nothing much is likely to happen until we start to experiment as thoughtfully as we can and keep our eyes open to what happens as a result. The first thing to find out is what happens this afternoon."

Now and then at this point the client may say, "But I'm afraid." The therapist may respond, "You mean, *Quinn* is afraid. But '*Ernest Seeman*' isn't. So let's send Quinn to some place where he will have nothing to fear, and *you* simply be 'Ernest." I'll do everything I can to *help*. Now, 'Ernest' at what time did you say you expect to arrive at work this afternoon?"

The second most common question is, "You mean 'Ernest' is the kind of person I should be?" Again, the answer must be candid. "No! At this point neither of us knows what kind of person you should be. That is something that will have to be developed as we go along, and let us hope it will continue to develop long after you stop seeing me. As far as you and I are concerned 'Ernest' is simply an experiment and the important thing for both of us to observe is exactly what happens when a man lives his life this way—what happens both inside his skin and what happens outside."

What is so important for the therapist to keep in mind—and so difficult for most of us brought up in the traditions of realism, determinism, and stimulus-response psychology—is that the object of therapy is not to eradicate Quinn in order to replace him with some kind of "Ernest." Quinn's integrity is neither criticized nor questioned. It is treated with respect and even reaffirmed. Certainly the client is never told that he is at odds with himself, and thereby led to wonder what gremlins infest his psyche. The fact that "Ernest," by his contrast with Quinn, is so clearly make-believe rather than "real," is a key to the success of the venture, not a handicap.

And let us make no mistake about the basic methodology of science. For the genius of science is not its *realism*, but its calculated ventures into the world of make-believe—which scientists like to call "testing *hypotheses*." I doubt that an out-and-out realist could ever bring himself to test a hypothesis, any more than he could ever work himself out of a neurosis or a psychosis.

The "Quinn" the client has come to know is a hypothesis too. But how can a simple-minded realist know that? So he comes to the therapist for help. Since he can visualize no alternatives to the "Quinn" he knows, he cannot see that personality as hypothetical. All he can see are some of the outcomes of being "Quinn"—its "reinforcements"—and he rarely needs a therapist to point out to him how unhappy those particular events are or that he is exhibiting a "neurotic paradox." Without constructive alternatives—without hypotheses—"reinforcements" can serve only as palliatives and irritants.

But "Ernest" is so clearly a make-believe character—assuming the therapist is not too much of a realist himself to present him so, or too much of an applied psychologist to risk an honest experiment—that he can be treated as a hypothesis indeed. From the moment the client experiences "Ernest" as a hypothesis, science can have its day in the therapy room. And if "Ernest" is a hypothesis the client finds he can test, the thought can scarcely escape him that there must be others too.

Initiating the Rehearsals

Let us turn back to where we left off—the beginning of the first rehearsal. The therapist can hardly expect that his own initial attempt to play the part of "Ernest's" supervisor will portray that person accurately enough to provide strong support for the enactment of "Ernest." After a few sentences the client is likely to say, "But old Gillie wouldn't say that." "All right," says the therapist, "let me play the part of 'Ernest' and you play the part of his supervisor. Good afternoon, Mr. McGillicuddy."

The exchange of parts which follows is important to the experiment. If the client does not say something which suggests it, the therapist should take the initiative and propose it himself. In any rehearsal the client is likely to see one part as dominant over the other, and, if he finds himself in an awkward position, he will wonder if the therapist is not taking unfair advantage of the inequity by casting himself in the dominant part. Exchanging parts is therefore a good practice in all psychotherapeutic enactments, and especially so with children. Besides, being engaged in what must be both a true experiment and a true role enactment, it is almost as essential for the client to reach for the outlooks of others as it is to get the knack of being "Ernest." The exchange facilitates this attempt.

The effectiveness of the rehearsals probably depends as much upon the therapist's ingenuity as it does upon the client's cooperation. If the therapist is inept it will be painfully obvious to both of them. He cannot hide behind esoteric terminology or owlish expressions of hidden wisdom. He, no less than the client, is caught up in an experiment whose outcomes cannot be accurately forecast. Both must take the risk that goes with being scientists. Fixed role therapy is a strenuous and demanding undertaking, as anyone who attempts it seriously will find out soon enough. It is not a job for drop-outs who have taken up "psychotherapy," rather than continue to face the perplexities and frustrations of scientific inquiry.

The Sequence of Sessions

Generally we have planned the therapy sessions to emphasize, in succession, rehearsals for five kinds of interpersonal situations: (1)"Ernest's" interaction with a supervisor on the job or with a teacher, (2) his interaction with his peers, (3) interaction with his spouse or with someone to whom he has an affectionate attachment, (4) interaction with parents or their surrogates, and (5) interaction in a situation involving religious experience. While the therapist must continually call attention to the need for playing the part at all times, and not merely in the situations which have been previously rehearsed, the ventures can be somewhat scaled to the depth and difficulty of the anticipated enactment.

Sessions should be frequent. It is particularly urgent to schedule the second session within one or two days of the first. A minimum of three sessions a week seems to be essential if the project is not to be abandoned by the client in the face of his first obstacles.

He is usually discouraged during all of the first week, and he will ordinarily come to the second session with a flat announcement that he cannot play the part. The therapist who thinks behavior is simply the pursuit of pleasant rewards will be easily "taken in." But he will have to remind himself that the client and he are scientists, and that the object of the enterprise is to see precisely what happens under the conditions they have set up, not to scratch an itchy ego.

What is undertaken in fixed role therapy is a vigorous experiment, not a hit-and-miss search for the elixir of painless existence. Nothing short of persistent and ingenious effort is effective. This means frequent and arduous sessions which will tax the resources both of client and therapist.

While many clients will maintain that their relations with their supervisors are more uncomfortable than with others, it seems best to point the first rehearsals specifically at this kind of enactment situation. Supervisory relations, even when strained, tend to be simple. This is to say they involve relatively few personal construct dimensions, and those that are necessarily involved tend to be ones which can be more easily put into words, or, as some might say, are more "cognitive." Personal construct theory is not, of course, a cognitive theory, as anyone who senses the depth of its personal involvements must surely realize. But as "cognition" goes, the relatively articulate and structured relationship between a work supervisor and an employee—or between, a teacher and a pupil—can be considered to fit the category better than do most other important relationships.

There is another advantage in starting with this relationship. Playing out the first specific situation for which a rehearsal has been held usually proves to be a strenuous experience. It is just as well to make it one from which the client can withdraw before he becomes overwhelmed. Supervisory or student-teacher relationships usually lend themselves to this kind of touch-and-go dialog.

The relations with one's peers, which usually mean with a group of persons of the same age and often of the same sex, are not so highly and articulately structured. To be sure, one may not feel himself under as much restraint in dealing with friends, but the complexities of interaction and the subtle invitations to impulse are greater, making one's unfamiliar enactment of a new role considerably harder to keep under precisely structured control. Moreover, it is in this particular enactment that the client is most likely to be told for the first time that he is "behaving strangely." For this reason the specific rehearsal for a peer enactment is scheduled after the one pointing toward a supervisory enactment, rather than before.

Initiating Enactments

The client is often at a loss to think of some way he can precipitate a situation in which he can play the part of "Ernest." In rehearsing the supervisory situation the therapist may suggest that the enactment could start with some form of "shop talk." Usually that will be a question or a comment dealing with a matter of common concern between them. If the interaction is to be with a teacher, a brief after-class conversation on a topic recently discussed by the teacher is appropriate. Moreover, in this kind of situation it is quite reasonable for the client to play a role—in the personal construct sense. That is to say the interaction can be directed toward grasping the other person's point of view. Moreover, the feedback is immediate, thus lending itself to the purposes of a truly experimental venture.

As the first rehearsal gets under way the therapist can begin to show the client how hypotheses can be used as a basis of interaction. What does the client think the supervisor will say? How will he say it? Can the client play the part, during the exchange, in the way he suspects the supervisor will play it? What variations might occur, and what clues should be particularly observed? What will his own feelings be at each stage of the enactment? Having raised such questions, the client may be urged to look for all deviations from the hypothesized responses of the supervisor and to make note of them, perhaps in writing as soon after the interaction as possible. He can, at the same time, make notes describing his own feelings.

When the second session is held the client and therapist will want to go over the results of this particular enactment as well as what may have happened in others. The results may be reflected upon the hypotheses formulated in the previous session, though usually the therapist will not be as rigorous in comparing hypotheses with outcomes at this stage of therapy as later. When it comes to reporting feelings it will be necessary to have the client make clear whether those feelings were ones that might be attributed to "Ernest," or whether Quinn is sneaking back from his vacation. Therapists who are used to exploring the "true feelings" of their clients are likely to get into trouble at this point, and I have seen some of them let the session deteriorate into an exploration of Quinn, rather than "Ernest."

Usually a re-play of the supervisor enactment is in order during the second session. It can be played as it happened and again as it might have happened if the part of "Ernest" were played to the hilt. Exchanges of parts between the client and the therapist are again in order. Subtle variations in feeling tone and in the trend of the dialog can now be noted during the re-plays. The therapy session itself is part of the experiment, and its outcomes can be noted on the spot. What happens in the therapy room is a test-tube experiment; what happens outside is a field trial. Both are component parts of the experimental undertaking.

But the second session must not bog down in post mortems. The next two days of enactment must be planned, and the peer interaction rehearsed. Here the problem is not likely to be so much a matter of initiating a conversation as contributing to it in the role of "Ernest." The client will have to be alert to how the conversation is going and say what he has to say before it has gone off and left him. The rehearsal should prepare him for the quickened pace of the exchanges he may expect among a group of friends.

As I have already suggested, the enactment which follows the second session may confront the client with the reaction that he is acting strangely. It is just as well to prepare him for it. Rather than being disconcerted by his friends' surprise, he should take it as evidence that he has portrayed "Ernest" as a person unlike Quinn. It is "Ernest" with whom his friends must cope, and it will be important to him to note the various ways in which they attempt to do it. He may even ask them what they regard as "strange." Certainly it is an important part of any experiment to observe closely relevant changes in the dependent variables.

Support for the Enactment

Often a client will ask if he should not tell some of his friends that he is enacting a role. He may particularly want to tell his wife. What this request usually means is that he is *anxious*—in personal construct terms, confused—and he is willing to sacrifice some of the realistic feedback that he might obtain from the enactment in order to acquire support. If others know that he is "only playing a part," what he does may appear to have more structure. He wants to say, "Look, I am not really this incoherent. Disregard what I am doing, and continue to see me as Quinn. Quinn may not be the most effectual person in the world, but at least he makes a kind of sense."

But there is little to be gained by the enactment if one's friends are invited to ignore the experiment's independent variable—"Ernest." The enactment becomes an exercise rather than an experiment. As an exercise it does little more than put the client through the motions prescribed by the enactment sketch. And only the most insensitive of "learning" theories would attribute much of psychological importance to that!

In personal construct theory support has a specific meaning, and it is distinguished from reassurance. *Support is a broad response on the part of the therapist which permits the client to experiment widely and successfully.* Successful experimentation, in terms of the theory's basic assumptions, is that which leads to clear-cut answers to the questions he poses behaviorally, thus tending to dispel anxiety. Success is thus not defined in any of the usual ways—reward, drive reduction, satiation, feeling tone, need fulfillment, etc.

In fixed role therapy the therapist does supply support, and it is important that he do so. He offers candid comments on the client's enactment. He joins the client in predicting what may happen, and shares the client's surprise when unexpected results arise. He lends himself to the enactment by playing, as best he can, the wide variety of parts required by the rehearsals. He joins the client in seeking ways to put enactment experiences into words, or in clarifying them through reenactment in the therapy room. If the therapist performs his part of the task well he will minimize the client's urge to divulge the "Ernest" role prematurely, as the poor fellow may in an effort to find elsewhere the support he craves.

After all, the client should soon discover that he can experiment much more successfully—that is to say, elicit more definitive answers to his behaviorally posed questions—if he lets the enactment of "Ernest" speak for itself, rather than asking his friends what they think of the enactment sketch. The object of "being Ernest" for two weeks is not to amuse his friends or to see if he has at last "found himself," but to realize here and now that his innermost personality is something he creates as he goes along, rather than something he discovers lurking in his insides, or has imposed upon him from without. What others may say about the "Ernest" sketch is of much less therapeutic concern than what they think and do when confronted with "Ernest" in the flesh. Besides, the client is committed to "being Ernest" for no more than the brief period of the enactment, and he needs to get the most out of the experience.

The Deeper Enactments

When it comes to confronting his wife with "Ernest" the client has a more difficult task on his hands. Marriages can fall into rigid patterns, and often the partners, having struck a balance, after years of painful interaction, are reluctant to risk breaking the uneasy truce. Yet each of them may wish he could refresh the relationship, and each may doubt the other's willingness to take chances.

It has been my experience that a client is often eager enough to have a different role relation to his wife, but dreads what she may say when he attempts it. She may ridicule his fumbling efforts or tell him that he is doing only what he should have started a long time ago. But it has also been my experience that wives (or husbands) find the enactments of their spouses as exciting as they may be disconcerting. Susie McQuirk may be a little nervous about living with "Ernest Seeman" for two weeks, while her husband is "away on a holiday," but that isn't the same as saying she wouldn't like to give it a whirl. Making love as "Ernest Seeman" can make one feel like a different man, but being made love to by "Ernest Seeman" can make one feel like a different woman. It is a dull client indeed who, having plunged into this phase of the enactment, does not sense that his life could be very, very different.

For his enactments with a supervisor or with peers the client can prepare himself thoroughly for a limited series of relatively brief encounters. But keeping up the enactment with his experienced spouse requires sustained attention. Moreover, theirs is a relationship which may long since have settled into a routine. Now he must innovate continually, often violating the unwritten rules by which he and his wife have been unwittingly playing the marriage game. The third rehearsal is designed to meet this condition of sustained role enactment.

There is another matter to be confronted in this rehearsal, and in the two which follow. Many of the constructs in terms of which a client has structured his marriage may be preverbal. He cannot represent them as precisely by symbols as he can the more intellectualized dimensions of his life. He therefore cannot point to them and say, "There, that is a dimension in which I shall discontinue making distinctions;" or, "This is a notion I shall now apply to my daily circumstances in a different way." It is expecting too much of fixed role therapy to hope that the use of preverbal constructions can be so deliberately altered.

But it is not expecting too much to hope that the events produced by the enactment will be different. And when events are different, there is occasion to reflect them upon the reference axes of one's construct system in positions where previous events have not been plotted. Gradually the construct system—verbal and preverbal—adapts itself in some manner to that with which it must cope, and the intentionality of a personal construct slowly aligns itself to the shifts in its extensionality. Changes in operational definitions erode and enrich essential definitions, and one's definition of his marriage or of his spouse is no exception.

Extending the enactment to a situation involving one's parents often runs into a practical difficulty. The parents may be deceased, or may live too far away for a day's visit. Sometimes a letter embodying the enactment can be sent to the parents. And, indeed, if it is written, it must be sent, else we shall have indulged in an intellectual exercise without venturing the commitment which makes it into an enactment.

It is all too easy, both for client and therapist, to let fixed role therapy degenerate into intellectualism, on the one hand, or dissolve into expressionism, on the other. The method does not strive for "insight" nor does it invite "self-expression." Personal construct theory, by the way, generally takes a dim view of "insight," observing that it is a term more appropriate to naive realism than to a constructive outreach to the world. The theory is a little more tolerant of "self-expression," though that, too, seems often to be predicated on the notion of an inescapable "real self," rather than a self one creates through the process of experimenting with his life.

As with one's spouse, relations with parents involve preverbal constructions, and often stalemated interactions. The fourth rehearsal, which is directed particularly at this arena of enactment, must make maximum use of the temporary disengagement of the Quinn personality from the situation, and the commitment, instead, to an enactment of "Ernest." My experience suggests that a great deal of the value of the parental enactment accrues from the rehearsal in which the client exchanges parts and undertakes to feel and act as one or both of his parents would experience their relationship with him. The therapist can make a great deal of this opportunity by speeding up the tempo of this rehearsal, and by playing it out in a number of presumed settings. Since role, in the personal construct theoretical sense, is based on a construction of another person's outlook, here, in this particular rehearsal, is an opportunity to take a long delayed second look through the parental spectacles. The client is likely to be surprised by what he sees, even before he has confronted his parents, in the experimental role of "Ernest."

The final situation, for which a specific enactment is rehearsed, is the one involving religion. Now and then someone who has had little or no experience with fixed role therapy protests that this is much too intimate a matter to be approached as an enactment of any part other than that of the vacationing Quinn himself. But the therapist need not prescribe any particular religious doctrine. He and his client can work out together the inferred religious outlook that would characterize such a man as "Ernest Seeman" is. And why not? Must religion be a reluctant concession to the inevitable, or might it not be a commitment to an undertaking reaching far beyond the present self?

Just how the role is enacted through its religious implications will depend somewhat upon the situation available for its trial. At a minimum this will amount to holding a discussion of religious and ethical matters with others who have similar areas of concern. But I think the therapy works out best if the client takes the pains to search deeply for the implications of the part he has been playing. If he has had an incipient tendency to burlesque the part of "Ernest Seeman"—the man—the religious enactment should bring the client to the point of realizing that any man's commitment to behavior carries with it the profoundest of implications for the meaning his life will have, and the deepest of obligations to take account of what happens as a result of his acts.

Terminating the Enactment

In the end, of course, Quinn must come home. The therapist should see that he does, and that he takes responsibility for appraising what has happened, and for what he himself will choose to undertake. We hope Quinn will see his life open to fresh undertakings, and that he will not be unwilling to take candid account of what happens when he embarks upon them. It will be just as well if he decides to discontinue acting the part of "Ernest," valuable as he may feel the experience turned out to be. His next urgent task is to create the new *Quinn*, and that will take a little time—say, a lifetime. But if there was once an "Ernest" who, in the course of a mere two weeks, took on the flesh and vision of a man, there can be a "Quinn," and after him a "'Quinn,'" and a "'*Quinn*!'"

Perhaps it is not necessary to remark at the end of this discussion that there is much more to be said. The reader who is impatient to get on to other matters may think I have tried to say too much. The therapist who undertakes fixed role therapy will certainly wish I had said more.

Let us hope I have not focused so sharply upon fixed role therapy as to leave the impression that it is the only therapeutic method to be derived from personal construct theory. There are so many other implications of the theory it would be a pity if this particular method I happen to have used in no more than ten percent of my therapeutic efforts over the years were to be regarded as the definitive explication of personal construct psychotherapeutics.

It would also be a misfortune if I were to leave the impression that the steps I have outlined are the only ones that can profitably be followed. I have reported simply a part of what my experience seems to show, omitting, I fear, some of the interesting variants, such as fixed role therapy with groups of three to a hundred persons. But what experience I have reported I hope has been described in such a way as to make clear underlying assumptions about the nature of man, and how he goes about making himself into what he is.

Bibliography

Bannister, D. (1966). A new theory of personality. In B.M. Foss (Ed.), *New horizons in psychology* (pp. 361–380). Penguin.

Bonarius, J.C.J. (1965). Research in the personal construct theory of George A. Kelly. In B.A. Maher (Ed.), *Progress in experimental personality research, Vol. 2* (pp. 1–46). Academic Press.

Kelly, G.A. (1955). *The psychology of personal constructs*. 2 Vols. Norton.

Kelly, G.A. (1961). Theory and therapy in suicide: The personal construct point of view. In E. Shneidman & N. Farberow (Eds.), *The cry for help* (pp. 255–280). McGraw-Hill.

Kelly, G.A. (1964). The language of hypothesis: Man's psychological instrument. *Journal of Individual Psychology*, *20*, 137–152.

Kelly, G.A. (1965). The strategy of psychological research. *Bulletin of the British Psychological Society*, *18*, 1–15,

Kelly, G.A. (1966). Sin and psychotherapy. In O.H. Mowrer (Ed.), *Morality and mental health* (pp. 365–381). Rand-McNally.

Kelly, G.A. (1967). A psychology of the optimal man. In A. Mahrer (Ed.), *The goals of psychotherapy* (pp. 238–258). Appleton-Century-Crofts.

Patterson, C.H. (1966). *Theories of counseling and psychotherapy*. Harper and Row.

Sechrest, L. (1963). The psychology of personal constructs: George Kelly. In J.M. Wepman and R.W. Heine (Eds.), *Concepts of personality* (pp. 206–233). Aldine.

Section VI

Education

Kelly's earliest writing in the field of education was *A plan for socializing Friends University with respect to student participation in school control*. The university in question was one that Kelly credited with contributing more to his education than any other institution. His plan involved "a shift from the narrow classroom conception of education to the broad 'total activity' conception of education," in which students assume the responsibility for problem-solving that is traditionally held by staff. Indeed, it included a vision that "school participation groups will be able to invade the classroom to the extent that the very discussions will be maintained by the students, and the teacher will be requested to take a side seat and speak only when asked to do so."

In *Social inheritance*, Kelly offers early reflections on the nature-versus-nurture debate in relation to school achievement and the content of the school curriculum. He concludes that "social inheritance should be a free store upon which all . . . can draw."

The place of the psychologist in the small school system is the abstract of a conference paper in which Kelly argues for the role of the psychologist as a "teacher without curriculum."

In *Observations made in a search for dynamic and accessible factors in intellectual development*, Kelly examines the vectors that may influence intellectual development, as well as the methods through which such development may be facilitated.

Papers discussing the role of television in the classroom (*A preliminary enquiry leading to a plan for a comprehensive experimental study of the uses of television in teacher education; Report on classroom television; Television and the teacher*) constitute some of the earliest research on remote teaching, a method that is now prevalent, particularly when instruction is delivered to a geographically dispersed audience or when an event, such as a pandemic, prevents face-to-face teaching. Among the advantages identified by Kelly regarding the utilization of television in education are its ability to foster intimacy and enhance intercommunication. He underscores the importance of tailoring instructional approaches to the talents of each individual teacher and reflects on the transformation in the role of the classroom teacher that this method facilitates. Of particular interest from a personal construct psychology perspective is the statement in *Report on classroom television* that

> "Local teachers may not greatly influence WHAT pupils believe, but they do have a lot to do with pupils' FREEDOM TO EXPRESS their beliefs."

In *Teacher–student relations at the university level*, Kelly examines how educators can assist students in establishing new types of relationships with knowledge, authority, truth, and peers. Among the illustrations he provides are the "Thursday evening" sessions in which his students were invited to listen to and comment on drafts of *The psychology of personal constructs*, which involved "a remarkable shift in the authority relationship." This included teaching students how to ask questions rather than simply provide answers, as well as the process of "taking people who come as students and changing them into colleagues."

The poem *Nursery rhymes for older tots (To all you kettles, from all us pots)* essentially provides a description of Kelly's perspective on what a teacher should not be like.

Collected Papers of the Pioneer of Constructivist Psychology: George A. Kelly, First Edition. Edited by David A. Winter and Nick Reed.

85

A Plan for Socializing Friends University with respect to Student Participation in School Control[1]

Preface

Friends University holds a warm spot in the hearts of many who have had contact with its spirit. A Quaker institution, it has become imbibed with the humble spirit and sincere friendliness of a great people. The closing words of the University Hymn whose words and music were written by one of its graduates, now dean of the college, express the deep idealism inspired within the soul of every student of Friends.

"O Father, hear her children pray
That we may all hold true,
And that our lives, full noble, may
Bring honor to F. U."

Although the author of this paper does not hold a degree from Friends, three of his undergraduate years were spent there and he believes that the school has contributed more to his education than has any other institution. The author had very intimate relationships with its problems of student participation. He was a member of the Student Council, Chairman of a committee for revision of the Student Government Association Constitution, chairman of the Constitutional Committee for the Universal Club which sought to fill a unique social need, and member of numerous other project groups. He has faced in an intimate and personal way, the problems with which this paper deals.

G.A.K.

Chapter I What is Meant by Socializing a School?

Traditional Methods of School Control

The old concepts of learning made distinction between the teacher and the one taught. Knowledge was thought to be imparted from one possessing the fund by some sort of intellectual shute into the storage bin of a pupil's head. Schools, although originally organized as a cooperative effort involving scholars of greater and lesser accomplishments, became institutions for the propagandizing of the intellectually meek with academic literature and thought. The young must be taught the Jewish Law; the irresponsible ones must be fortified with platitudes of Confucius; the embryonic orators must mouth the stagnant phrases of Jefferson, meaningless that they are taken out of their day with its issues and implications. The traditional idea of education conceived it as "of the children, by the schools, and for the teachers."

It goes without saying that such a concept left no place for student expression, much less for student control of their own propagandizement. Teachers controlled and regulated, and the more they could control, and the more they could regulate, the more they thought they were educating. In order to aid the teachers in aspiration for autocratic power, students were segregated from society and taken to villages out of the line of contacts, there to be under the direct supervision of the instructors. The environment was controlled by these administrators of education until matters reached the point where restless youths began to break their bonds and do all manner of unprecedented things. Some of these youths grew up and then turned to investigate the system which had nurtured them.

[1] Previously unpublished manuscript, Kansas University, May 23, 1927. Published by permission of Jacqueline Aldridge.

Collected Papers of the Pioneer of Constructivist Psychology: George A. Kelly, First Edition. Edited by David A. Winter and Nick Reed.
 Published 2026 by John Wiley & Sons Ltd.

Objective Research

They found that the largest contributors to society had not always been among the honored during their school days. They found that students learned things when out of earshot of an instructor, and they also found that sometimes they learned more efficiently in this manner the very things which instructors had tried to pry into their heads.

Incidental notice of such facts encouraged the more curious ones to experiment with teaching methods. Results were startling. Improvement of teaching method has added and is still adding considerable increments to the learning capacity of students. It is easier to be a scholar now than it was fifty, twenty or even ten years ago.

The new methods developed are based upon activity. The students learn by doing in as nearly the same situations as possible, the things which they hope to do later on. They learn by doing the things which their own spontaneous impulses urge them to do. Child activities are better training for adult activities, as far as children are concerned, than the adult activities themselves. Training is best carried out in the most natural environment possible.

Laboratory Method

The first contribution was that of introducing laboratory methods. The highly developed and specialized fields of the sciences were compelled to adopt more efficient methods of teaching. The physics lecturer found himself incapable of describing his findings without the presence of apparatus and found the students incapable of learning without actually repeating the experiment and learning in the same way the lecturer had learned. Laboratory method marked the first step in student participation—participation in handling the actual apparatus used in demonstrating scientific facts.

Project Method

The natural outgrowth of the laboratory method was the project method. Some articles in the curriculum did not involve the handling of physical apparatus but involved in no less an important way the handling of materials in order to demonstrate a conclusion The overcoming of an obstacle which involves orientation and a search for method of attack is the essence of a project. It requires full participation on the part of the student with respect to that particular project. He cannot rely upon the teacher's judgment nor can he shift the responsibility of bringing forth a solution to one who might be more capable. It is his problem and he has no choice but to face it squarely and employ his own initiative for solution. The project represents participation carried to the point of *responsibility*.

But the project method as usually practiced has a defect; it encourages participation only with respect to a limited field. A project in an English class might involve the comparing of Shakespeare and Browning but it does not usually go to the extent of building a good English precedent on the campus. If participation is carried out to the full extent of its possibilities, the whole educational career of the student will become a vital project in which he can secure practice, advice and instruction just as he now receives in his Shakespeare-Browning projects.

Supervised Study

Although the activity of the student is important, and its spontaneity and responsibilities are of great value in the educative process, the part which the teacher performs is of no less value. The teacher must direct and supervise the attempts of the student to solve his project so that the solution will come most readily and with maximum educational by-product and training. It would be useless for the pupil to repeat all the trials and errors which the race performed in reaching the solution; he should be guided in such a manner that his experiments will be efficiently carried on. The provision for making this guidance available to the pupil when he wants it, is the teacher.

Supervised study is almost universal in high school education. It is part and parcel of the project method although it may be practised where the project method is not used. Supervised study is taking the place of recitation, and rightly so, for recitation is valuable only as a measure of progress, and measurement is not the most important function of a teacher. Furthermore, measurement does not require as much time or as detailed procedure as it once did, leaving more time for the teacher to devote to educating. The expression, "supervised study" should become the true meaning of formal education. Education at its best and in its highest sense, is simply supervised study.

Socialized Recitation

The interplay of thoughts and gestures which makes up the human life and creates the human mind is a process of utmost significance. The words of a lecturer or teacher depend upon the response of the audience or class for their meaning. In general, it might be said, the freer the response, or interplay of ideas, the more meaningful a teacher's efforts become. Development of the social self depends not only upon interplay with one individual such as the teacher, but with all individuals and groups with which one has contact such as classmates and class groups. Thus the social self will be more adequately developed when the class discussion is carried on between pupils and teacher. The socialized recitation is the name used for this means of education. It represents an opportunity for the pupil to participate in controlling the course of the class discussion and thus have a voice in determining the content of the course of study. The teacher becomes one of a group of students each contributing to a common pool of experiences. The socialized recitation is a valuable asset to the cause of student participation.

Dewey's principle of participation is bound to become of great significance in the new educational reorganization. He points out that all life is participation and that the individual or group that does not participate is committing suicide—or failing to grow. It means more than cooperation; it implies a common goal, a common interest, a common motivation. More of the sense of mutual ownership is contained in its connotation. Students must do more than cooperate in school control; they must participate in it, if they would become educated.

Kindergarten Viewpoint

The idea of participation was carried out in the kindergarten schools which were recently established in this country. The children who were considered too young to take up the "serious task of becoming educated" were sent to "play schools." In consequence, they were not hampered by the classical teacher-pupil technique and came fairly in the way of real education. The games they played and the songs they sang together furnished them with freer interplay of ideas on their own level of life and the result was that the kindergartens became the most efficient educating institutions in the school system. Even today, the lower grades of the public schools are more efficiently conducted than any other portion of the educational structure. Education on the level of child-life with intensified play as a basis is the contribution of the kindergarten to our school system.

Organization Around Student Life

When this contribution is utilized, it will mean that a school together with its curriculum, teachers, and equipment will be organized about student life. The natural interests of college students will become the basis of the college course of study instead of vague whims of men and women long past the age of adolescent interests. Those educators who believe football to be opposed to the best interests of their subjects will be informed that if their subjects are antagonistic to the student life as expressed in such activities as football, they must re-adapt their subject matter or omit it from the curriculum. Student life as expressed in football should be considered more important than adult life as expressed in Rhetoric.

But this principle does not mean that colleges will become what some wit has termed,"stadiums with classrooms annexed." Normal student life, when freed from "arrested development" in Rhetoric caused by overzealous and impractical teachers, will find an actual need for that subject. It will demand that training and information in Rhetoric be made available. The study of English is just as truly an interest of student life, in its normal form, as is football. Educators need not fear to organize education about the normal interests of student life. Those interests are often more sound than the artificial rulings regarding pre-requisites and majors.

Students Rather than Materials are the Subjects of Instruction

The basis upon which some educationists of the old order will oppose the new changes will be the claim that certain materials of great value will not be studied nor knowledge in certain fields conserved, if the content of education be left to the judgment of those being educated. The answer to this argument is that, even if such might be the case, the real subjects of instruction are not materials, but students. If materials must be conserved at the expense of society it is pertinent to ask; of what value are the materials? Knowledge which is a burden on society rather than an enlightenment might better even be lost. A school has no moral right to make of itself a catch-pocket where youth can be cornered and propagandized with iambic pentameters and ablative cases. It might be of great value to the cause of progress in education for some bold soul to stand out and forbid the use of the word,"subject" except as it refers to students. Mathematics and chemistry have too long been *subjects* of instruction; it is time that students be made the subjects.

The Problem in the College and University

Reforms in education seem to develop in the humbler institutions and affect only secondarily the higher institutions where the teachers are chosen because "they know their subject." There have been few changes in college methods of instruction in the past decade while the same period has witnessed marked development in elementary methods of instruction. Grade schools are carefully planned and equipped to allow for proper lighting, ventilation *et cetera* but college buildings are still built as models of castles, cathedrals, or mountains, as if their educational value depended upon their impracticability. While experiments are being conducted and information compiled and utilized with regard to student participation in elementary and secondary school control, the colleges and universities are just beginning to "recognize" and accredit such activities as inter-collegiate debate, dramatics, glee clubs and travel. This does not mean that these educative activities, and many more, have only recently entered the college student's life. It means rather that whereas the students have created these activities for their own education and have developed them to a point where the faculties can no longer overlook their educative significance, recognition is being reluctantly granted. The initiative for modern progress has not come from those who are called leaders but from those who are called students and pupils.

Whereas student participation in school control has been instigated in elementary and secondary schools by teachers, it has been tolerated in most colleges after having been instigated by students. The problem in the colleges and universities is to make available the superior scholastic training of professors for use in developing student participation. If the students can develop the plan to its present status with the opposition of authorities, how much better could they do in the future with the assistance of authorities? The problem is one of changing from "outlaw" student control to "bona fide" student *participation* in control.

Objectives of a Socialized School

The objectives of a socialized school should be the same as the general objectives of education. Dewey says, growth. Counts says, adjustment. Others say, social efficiency. The N.E.A. has enumerated six objectives. A socialized school has opportunity for greater emphasis on fitting the subjects for efficient community life. It should make as one of its objectives, the orientation of the student in the society of which he is a part and then it should make an objective of fitting him to play that part, whether he be a diplomat with a thousand friendships to be kept, or scientist with few primary contacts with society. It is to be borne in mind that the scientist holds just as an important place in society as does the diplomat, and needs just as careful socialized training to fit him for his place, although his primary relationships with people may be few. It is just as important for one to become oriented as the other.

The socialized school should educate student society in such a manner that it will live its own life more intensely and consequently prepare it for living an adult life more intensely. A progressive society will be the reward.

Chapter II The Present Status of Student Participation in School Control

Every school has its own problems to be dealt with. It would be erroneous to assume that because one system of school control has been successful in one school, it would be successful in another. Schools vary widely in their traditions, problems, student clientele, and supply of personality leadership. Participation is still in the elementary stages of experiment and there are few set rules which have been proved most useful. The school that attempts to become socialized must place more emphasis upon a knowledge of its own traditions and the results of its own experience than upon the experiences of others. It must develop its own system. Such development can be made freer from disastrous mistakes, however, if proper cognizance is taken of the successful plans now in operation. A thorough knowledge of the educational principles discussed in the last chapter together with familiarity with the present methods of carrying out those principles should be obtained by all those who expect to attempt socialization of a school.

The following agencies represent the current practices in socialized and partially socialized schools:

The Student Council

In spite of numerous objections by critics of democratic or representative government in the school, the fact remains that students are no more susceptible to the faults of democracy than are their elders. Lack of efficient leadership, indifference, license mistaken for liberty, officers elected on basis of popularity rather than ability, favoritism, and a social precedent which frowns upon students disciplining and reporting on each other, are all difficulties which arise in every phase of adult government and are by no means confined to student governing associations.

The federal government of the United States is often used as a model for miniature school governments and junior republics. Of course, modifications and simplifications are made. "At the De Witt Clinton High School, which is typical of many of the New York City high schools, the General Organization, generally called the G.O., is made up of all students who pay the regular dues. Most members are affiliated with one or more of the clubs, associations, or other activities which must be chartered by the G.O., through its Executive Council. This Council is made up of teachers and pupils representing the "forms" or half-grades and three student officers of the school, president, vice-president, and secretary. One of the teacher-members is the treasurer. A second controlling body is the Board of Governors composed of three faculty members and one student representing the Executive Council."[2]

"At the Washington Junior High School in Rochester, New York, there were in 1919 fifty-two home-rooms which were the core of the democratic organization. Each home-room had several class-officers through which its activities in the class-rooms, corridors, assemblies, and school grounds were controlled under the guidance and counsel of home-room and associated home-room teachers. The groups of student officers met with faculty directors to be instructed in their duties and to maintain their interest in their work. Class meetings were held in charge of these student-officer groups."[3]

At the Walla Walla High School the principal is an ex-officio member of all committees and governing bodies. The Student Council is used to taking charge of some of the disciplinary problems as well as some of the problems of boosting the interest in school projects. When a student learns of an offense against the school government he drops a notice in the Student Council box whereupon the

[2] Cox, P.W.L. (1927). *Creative school control*. J.B. Lippincott.

[3] Cox, P.W.L. (1927). *Creative school control*. J.B. Lippincott.

Council takes the matter up at its next session. If the student committing the offense pleads guilty, the Council imposes sentence; if he pleads innocent, witnesses are called and a regularly conducted trial is made. Sentence can only be imposed by a two-thirds majority or more.

The William George Junior Republic has attracted a great deal of attention as a model of school government. It was established in Ithaca, New York under the supervision of William R. George, a successful social worker. The republic consists of 350 acres of land owned by the Republic and controlled by the citizens of the Republic. Citizenship is limited to those boys or girls under sixteen years of age. The government is modeled very closely after the government of the United States with a President and his Cabinet, Legislature, etc. All citizens of the republic must work at some occupation. The village maintains a hotel, general store, bank, school, chapel, factories—on a miniature scale, and a city hall. Aluminum money is used which is interchangeable for silver currency at the bank.

Other junior republics have since arisen modeled after the George Junior Republic. Their work is judged very successful. Citizens tend to accept those responsibilities which fall upon them and the mistakes that are made cannot be considered as more serious evidence against their plan's feasibility than the mistakes of adult government are serious evidence against democracy.

These different types of government for school control represent the Student Council types among the secondary and elementary schools and students of those ages. Nearly every college now maintains a student council in conjunction with what is usually called the "honor system." Students are said to pe placed upon their "honor," hence the term "honor system." The representatives to the councils must usually be approved by the faculty before election. Councils are given varied responsibilities and different degrees of power. In some places, they are used by the well meaning faculty as spies upon their fellow students. Where such conditions are felt to be existent by students, the councils are not successes. It is very tempting to use a self-governing organization as a "goat" upon which the faculty can shift all responsibility for enforcing decisions which are really made by social pressure from the faculty themselves. Where the faculty possesses a final veto power upon all decisions of the Council and uses that power frequently, the situation tends to become a farce and it takes a very short time for the average college student to see through the situation. Failure to really place the student upon their "honor" is really the cause of many of the unsuccessful attempts to use the "honor system." Often the faculty makes campus rules and then puts the students and student council "on their honor" to enforce the rules. Such is not self-government. True responsibility can exist only when the government has both the responsibility of formulating and of enforcing their own rules.

The Home-Room

Public schools have contributed to the field of student participation in developing the home room unit of government. It provides a small enough unit to provide for those personal contacts said to be the basis of the usefulness of fraternity life in the colleges. The two are different, however, in that the home room is directly provided for in the school program while the fraternity is an attempt of the students to provide a feature of education overlooked or frowned upon by the school administrators. The technique of teacher supervision of projects can be utilized by sponsors of college clubs and societies.

Societies and Clubs

Often clubs and societies are maintained outside of the curriculum and tolerated rather than encouraged by those in control of the schools. The students have developed the club and society almost without aid from their teachers. These organizations represent a tendency to band together those of common interest in order to cooperate better in furthering this common interest. If the common interest is mathematics, we have a mathematics club which allows itself a wider scope of freedom than does the classroom where mathematics is "taught." If the common interest is social superiority of a snobbish nature, we find a society which is pursuing non-social ends. It is and rightly should be a problem of the educator to use all the educative agencies and to encourage them in their social ends. Too large an amount of supervision, however, or the wrong nature of supervision will destroy the most valuable features of the club processes. Their great contribution to the education of many students has been made greater because of the little attention which the old-time teachers paid them. Through the clubs and societies, the students shouldered real responsibilities, both of making rules and of enforcing them afterwards.

Assemblies

It has been said that nowhere is the real life of the school so well expressed as in the assembly. On the other hand the assembly may be the most deceitful in its appearance of any of the agencies of student-life expression. When students are trained to march down aisles to martial music and to recite orders of service and to follow a regulation procedure, the appearance may seem to show a well ordered school with good balance of judgment and a good spirit of solidarity. In such cases, however, the appearances may merely cover a lack of solidarity which enables the faculty to force the students to submit to standardized procedures.

On the other hand, those assemblies which are responsive to the interests of the student body tend to express in better form than any other agency the real under-current of school life. The chapel or…[4]might be used for forums conducted by groups who have studied the materials on the subjects. The athletic or debating teams may be cheered on to victory in the coming games or contests. The group spirit of control generated in the assembly yelling and cheering is a valuable social asset to the impression which a school makes upon

[4] Editors' note: two illegible words.

a student. That elusive thing called, "school spirit" can be developed better through the proper use of the assembly than through the use of any other one of the agencies. It is here that the school hears itself and sees itself, and thereby comes to know itself and feel itself.

Publications

With the great place of importance which the newspaper holds in creating group spirit in the nation, that agency cannot be overlooked as a medium for creating group spirit in the school. Nearly all schools which are able to maintain a newspaper, are doing so. The use of the newspaper gives valuable training in the use of that agency in future life as well as training in the management of publicity in school life. Other publications are often used—school art magazines, wild-cat publications, and annuals. The extensive use of these agencies for socializing the education of the student, should be encouraged.

Athletics

The present status of college athletics has recently been the cause of much concern. Football is said to be ruining our schools. No doubt, the professionalization of that game has been detrimental to the training of the college student. But football is like many of the activities of adult life and the fact that it might have been carried to extremes by student bodies merely proves that students are like adults; they go wild over transatlantic flights and other spectacular occurrences. The student should learn to maintain a balanced interest in football or any of the athletics if he is to learn to maintain a balanced interest in many of adult sports; and the way to create this ability for balanced interest is not by the abolition of footbal l. Athletics forms a means of expression of the group spirit created in the assembly, on the sport level. It is one of the many natural interests of the students about which real education must be built.

Other Methods

These are but a few of the agencies now in use by students for educating themselves in a socialized manner. They do not represent the only methods nor do they necessarily represent the best possible methods. The *spirit* of the socialized school is the element that counts. Whether that spirit finds expression through athletics or through assemblies, the loyalties involved, and the training in citizenship are the educative factors which are to be considered of greater value. School spirit is just as necessary to progress as scientific investigation. No doubt time will soon find other means of expressing and developing this newly valued objective of the curriculum.

Chapter III The Situation at Friends

The History and Location

In 1884 a Garfield University was established at Wichita, Kansas. The equipment provided for one building in which to house all the activities of a highly developed university. It was, at the time, the largest university under one roof in the world. About three years later the Society of Friends took over the property and established a school under the name of Friends University. The building has never been finished and the large amount of room contained under its roof allows comparatively easy expansion in that respect.

There were, last year, about five hundred students enrolled. The school maintains a dormitory for girls while the girls of the upper classes and the men find rooms in the vicinity surrounding the school. The neighborhood about the university is centered in a Friends church nearby and the neighborhood spirit is unusually well developed, due, probably, to the fact that the Quakers have a tradition for friendliness.

The Traditions and Customs

Friends is not void of sacred and valuable traditions. They prize their spirit of unity and family-like attitudes toward one another. The chapel singing has become a tradition. They believe that they excel in chapel singing. Among their sports they place football far above the others in point of interest and their sportsmanship in that particular is unusually well developed. The Quaker reputation for clean play is a pride of the school.

An incident will show the spirit of unity with which it has been customary for the student body to act. About 1912 a body of students went to the Administration and asked for a new gymnasium. The one in which they were compelled to play was merely an enlarged basement room of the main building. Supporting posts stood out in the middle of the basketball court and these had to be padded during the games to keep from injuring the players. The school was finding it hard to secure basketball games with the larger and more important schools of the conference. The Administration, being short of funds at that time, turned down the request. Student enthusiasm ran high and although the enrollment at that time was scarcely half of the present enrollment and the number of graduates few and of scanty means, the student body decided to build a gymnasium of their own. Plans were drawn up for a twenty-thousand dollar building and a campaign was started in spite of efforts of the Faculty and Administration to curb the enthusiasm. In four months, they had raised twelve thousand dollars and construction on the building began. Students took time from their studies to help in the work and some even cut classes to make the project a success. Today the gymnasium stands as worthy monument to the ambition of those few students who were willing to carry out a project in spite of opposition from those who were supposed to be their teachers of citizenship.

Dancing and smoking are taboo on the campus although these rules are never enforced by any other agency than by social pressure. It is not an infrequent sight to see a student smoking on the campus during the first two weeks of school but after that the spirit of the institution is such that smoking is an extremely rare sight.

Friends traditions should be a very valuable asset to the program of socialization of the school.

The Equipment and Financial Situation

Like all denominational schools, the equipment of Friends is limited. The buildings consist of an administration building in which nearly all of the activities take place, a gymnasium, a music conservatory, and a girls' dormitory. The Friends endowment is slightly past the four-hundred-thousand mark with a vigorous campaign now in progress for the raising of two hundred and fifty thousand more. Ninety thousand have already been raised of this amount and the remaining will be covered in bond by one of the local agencies. The need of increased funds is due to a raise in standards by the North Central Association of which Friends has been a member. It seems probable that membership will be restored by the time commencement exercises take place.

A small amount of tuition is charged each student, $4 per semester hour. The money raised in this manner together with that appropriated by the Society of Friends represents the income of the school which is used to cover running expenses.

The Alumni

The alumni of the institution do not represent the richest or most prominent men of the country. Most of them are men of very modest means; teachers, ministers, foreign missionaries, and farmers. The graduating classes have always been small so that the alumni body does not represent a very powerful force in a financial way.

The University Woman's Club

The University Woman's Club is an organization of women who are immediately interested in the school. They are helpful in doing those things which only a personal interest can appreciate. They furnish rest rooms, redecorate and refinish recreation rooms, and help the morale of the school by many such acts of consideration for the comfort of the students and faculty. Each year the Woman's Club gives a reception for the whole student body where students may make personal acquaintance with their faculty professors before forming any ideas of their personal nature from mere classroom contacts. The Woman's Club is a body to which one might appeal for help in making minor changes about the campus.

The Faculty

The faculty is not especially strong from a teaching standpoint, but they are a well unified body. Most of the men are progressive in their ideas and would be willing to cooperate with any plan they believed a forward step in the policy of the school. There are almost no petty jealousies existing between individual members.

The President is a man of whom one hears nothing but praise from faculty and students alike. The writer has spent three years on the campus during his administration and never has he heard a single word from a student or faculty member given in slighting reference to the President. The man's quiet air and sincere force do more toward changing the Friends' student's attitude toward life than any other influence in the school. He is progressive and has done much thinking upon the lines of socializing the activities of the school.

The Student Body

Until the last three years the students have seen recruited from the rural areas of western Kansas. Lately, however, the local resident students have begun to patronize the University. These two groups represent a problem and often lines of dissension on different issues follow the division points of these two groups. The rural students resent the invasion of the school by the town students who live scattered over the city, are usually in better financial situations, do not take as active an interest in social affairs of the school, and have friendships and circles of acquaintances before entering the school. The difference has never interfered with harmonious school spirit, however, and no serious evils have resulted therefrom.

The Student Government[5] Association

The so-called honor system is in effect at Friends with a Student Governing Association supposedly in charge of discipline. All students are members of the association and have a right to vote in the spring elections for Council representatives and class officers. The Freshman Class is allowed one representative on the Council, the Sophomore Class two representatives, the Junior Class three

[5] Editors' note: (sic)

representatives, and the Senior Class four representatives. The President of the Council and of the Student Governing Association is elected by the council and must be one who has had one year's experience and must be a member of the Senior Class. Candidates are submitted by petition signed by a number of students.

A "point system" is used by which outside activities of students are limited and equalized. All the offices of the student body and of the clubs are classed in the order of their importance, and points assigned accordingly. For instance the office of Council member carries with it three points while the office of President of an organization carries with it five points. Membership of play casts and special groups also carry with them a specified number of points according to the importance of the project. The total number of points which one student may carry at any one time is nine. This system has been very valuable in distributing the responsibility for leadership

The problems of discipline of the school rarely come before the Council except in a very general way. They are handled by the Faculty which also makes the rulings. The duties of the Council are mostly limited to the regulation of athletics, planning of social events, disciplining the societies, and taking charge of a Student Chapel once a week.

Clubs and Societies

Next to the Student Council in importance is the Booster Club of which every student is a member and liable for draft to special service at any time. The purpose of the club is to create enthusiasm for intercollegiate contests.

The Calendar Committee is a committee composed of one faculty member, a representative from the Student Council and a representative from each class. Its purpose is to avoid conflicts of time in meetings held by the different organizations and classes and to keep too many activities from occurring at one time. It has proven to be a very valuable committee.

There are three honorary clubs for those who have won letters in school intercollegiate contests. The Q club is for those men who have won letters in athletics. The Gold Q is for those who have won the gold Q for work in debate or oratory and is open to both men and women. The Zeta Phi is an honorary society for those women who have won Qs under the regulations prescribed by the Woman's Athletic Association.

The Commerce Guild is a national organization started at Friends University with an elaborate system of ranks and degrees. It has been successful as a Department organization.

A Journalism Club has been started with membership depending upon previous activity in journalistic lines. The candidate must have had so many galleys of copy printed in the school paper before he is eligible.

The Woman's Athletic Association provides for all women's athletics, including hiking, archery, baseball, basketball, track, tennis, swimming, and the training for these activities. The W.A.A. athletics are carried on the intramural basis.

There are several departmental clubs including the Science Club, the Spanish Club, and the German Club. Their aim is the supplementing of classroom work with laboratory training in these subjects.

There are four literary societies; the Kiononian (men's) and its sister society, the Alethian, the Ithone, and the Philenthian (both women's). Their activity is usually confined to two or three social functions during the year although their membership is chosen competitively by tryouts in literary accomplishment.

The Universal Club is a men's organization with the specific aim of developing leadership for the school. The plan of action provides for the accomplishment of one project per year of general school interest. Only those who carry no other major official duties can be leaders in this club. Membership is chosen by tryouts which show the candidates' ambition and attitude.

The Alpha Kappa Tau and Delta Sigma Rho are brother and sister dramatic societies. They are active in giving high class plays…[6]

The Y.M.C.A. and Y.W.C.A. hold weekly meetings with outside speakers and forums on topics of interest. All students of the university are members.

The Glee Clubs are part of the regular accredited curricular course of study. Tryouts are held each fall and a musical program is prepared and a trip made to neighboring towns each spring.

Chapel

There is a regular half-hour period each day set apart for special activities. On Mondays and Wednesdays there is a chapel exercise planned by the Faculty; on Fridays the Student Council takes charge of chapel (this was granted them upon their own insistent demand); on Tuesdays there are class meetings and Freshman Orientation Assembly; on Thursdays the Y.M.C.A. and Y.W.C.A. hold meetings. Attendance is required on Mondays, Wednesdays, and Fridays, and for the Freshmen on Tuesdays.

The Student Chapels on Fridays are usually a source of great interest. Very often they are conducted as a forum on some particular phase of the school life on which members of the Council have done research.

[6] Editors' note: Illegible sentence.

Freshmen Orientation

This is a course of lectures by professors in different departments on the fields of activities which they represent, a general series by the President and Dean on the ideals and traditions of the school, and the fostering of a strong class organization. The Faculty takes great pains creating class consciousness and unity of spirit in the Freshman Class.

Publications

Each year the Council appoints an Editor and Business Manager for the University Life, the weekly school paper. These men are financially responsible for the success of the paper and share the profits made therefrom. The Journalism Department assumes the responsibility of furnishing copy, but the Editor has final word regarding the choice of material and make-up of the paper.

Every other year an annual is published, called The Talisman. The Junior Class is responsible but may draft help from any one of the other classes.

Debate

Friends maintains a place in the Kansas Intercollegiate Debate Association and the Kansas Intercollegiate Oratorical Association. Both these organizations hold contests each year and choose a state championship team. In addition, the University maintains a Freshman debate squad, and sends representatives to the oratorical contests of the Kansas Peace Oratorical Association and the Kansas No-Tobacco Oratorical Association. The university also sends a representative to the State Extempore Contest. Twice each year tryouts are held for an extempore speaking contest held in chapel for the temporary possession of a large loving cup. Winners have their names engraved upon the cup.

Athletics

Friends belongs to athletic conferences and competes for championships each year in football, cross-country, basketbal l, tennis, soccer, track, and golf. A schedule of intramural contests in which any man may compete on a team is held in basketball. Each class maintains a track team before the varsity track season starts and each club or special group wishing to do so maintains a baseball team. Every student has an opportunity to participate in intramural athletics whether he has ability or not.

Student Centers

A small café is maintained in the basement of the Administration Building and is operated by a student. The "Canteen," as it is called is a general congregating place for students. There is a large recreation hall with long tables and a piano open at all times. The women have a well-furnished rest room and the library is not overcrowded. On the edge of the campus is a drug store where students often congregate after evening entertainments. Although there are a number of boarding places, two are traditional and it is with them that all out-of-town students who are leaders of the school take their meals. The names of the clubs are significant; Kerr's and Hare's. The religious activity of the school centers in the University Friends Church, a beautiful new building just off the campus. Not all students attend but the majority of out-of-town students make it their church home.

Chapter IV Initiating a School Control Program

Securing the Support of Controlling Bodies

No new program of school control by students could be harmoniously effective unless sanctioned by those bodies which now control the school. The Board of Trustees and the Kansas Yearly Meeting feel that Friends is their school and should be conducted however they wish it conducted. The first part of the program for socializing the school should be a thorough enlistment of the support of the Board of Trustees for such a program. They must be shown that the school will serve the Kansas Yearly Meeting better if the students partictpate in its control.

The first step should be conducted under the leadership of the President and the Dean. They, better than any others, can win the confidence of the Board members. It should be pointed out by them that school control will only be given the students as they demand it, but that the new purpose of the Faculty and authorities will be nourishment of those potential citizenship qualities among the students until they have grown to the place where they will demand more responsibilities and more opportunity for responsibility education.

The Faculty should be given opportunity to discuss and study the problem of school control and to formulate a Faculty attitude toward the project. They should not be allowed to assume initiative and responsibility for creating school machinery, but the matter should be presented to them in such a manner that they will see the need for arousing that sort of divine discontent among the students that will grow into a thorough investigation of the responsibilities of social citizenship and a demand for actual training for its duties. The school control idea is not something for the Faculty to "put over" on the Student Body but something which will be a natural outgrowth of the right sort of teaching and influence both in and out of the classroom. The Faculty should make the matter one of intense study and research for several weeks before the students should become aware of any change in the Faculty attitude.

Securing the Support of Students

It has been intimated above that the school control project is not an "over the top" campaign or drive for some set situation but a change from the attitude of "outside activities" to the attitude of expansion of the curriculum to include all interests of the students. It is a shift from the narrow classroom conception of education to the broad "total activity" conception of education.

The students can be educated to this broader conception of education wherever they meet one who has it. The classroom, the chapel, the University Life, the athletic field, the recreation hall, the Canteen, the clubroom, the campus walk, the community drug store, the Sunday School class, the President's office, the Dean's front porch, are all places where opportunities occur for directive education of the sort that will lead to a demand for student participation in school control. The whole attitude of the teachers should be so permeated with the broader conception that it will crop out wherever contacts are made with students.

Securing the Support of Leadership

There are always some students in every student body that are constructively critical of the educational system. They are wise enough to see through to the core of the matter and take enough interest to make a real study of educational problems when opportunity affords. Very often this group of students contains some able personality leaders who might well assist the Faculty in spreading the broad conception of education. Such students could be given opportunity to discuss the more philosophic problems of education and to study the development of the school control idea in forums. They can be brought face to face with the problems of finding the best methods of educating themselves.

The leaders in the group may form an intelligent and well-prepared nucleus around which organizational leadership can be developed. Those minds in the Student Body which demand more than superficial study of the new proposition can be given such opportunity in special forums.

Chapter V Arousing Discontent

Building on Problems Rather than on Organizations

The aim of a program of student participation in school control is not organization, but practical experience in solving problems. After a certain amount of sentiment has been established in favor of the broader education which participation represents, the next problem is that of making the need for readjustments about the campus felt by the students. The whole system of participation must be built upon problems which actually exist and are felt to exist. The students should be aroused to a point where they will not be content with anything less than a whole-hearted attempt to find solutions. They must assume the responsibility for the solving of problems which the Faculty has hitherto assumed. Because one student takes upon himself a personal concern of the way a class is conducted, is no reason the instructor should feel that the student is intruding. In fact, the method of conducting a class is of more vital importance to the student than to the teacher. It is his education and he is giving valuable time and energy, why shouldn't he be concerned? If the participation program is to be successful, such prying interests must be capitalized and directed as a truly educative process. The program must be built upon just such interests in problems which actually exist and affect the student, not upon some distant problems which the teachers set up or do not consider worthy of their own interest and direction. Most classroom problems concern the student a great deal more vitally than the teachers and they should be allowed to build their participation program upon the very problems which the teachers have hitherto considered sacred to their own circle.

If the spirit of the Faculty at Friends would so permeate the classroom and other points of contact that the need for solution of such problems would be felt by the students as one of their own problems, it would not be long before students would be demanding an opportunity to take a hand in making readjustments.

Use of Publications

Of the many influences which might be used in arousing this divine discontent, the school publications furnish some of the most effective. The editorials of the school paper can easily be made the subject of conversation at Kerr's and Hare's, the corner drug store, and the Canteen. Arousing public interest is one of the functions of any live newspaper and the Editor of the University Life should be glad to keep interest stimulated on problems existing around the campus.

Employment

The first proposition that faces most Friends students on the campus is that of employment, for nearly eighty percent of the Friends men must work their way through school. Jobs which are more than simple drudgery and "blind alley" affairs are hard to find. The pay very meager and the hours usually very poor. A large number of Friends men work at jobs which require them to rise at two-thirty in the morning and when their school work is completed there is no chance for advancement and the student must start all over again and find another "bottom rung of the ladder" upon which to start his career. The problem of employment is one of the most vital to the Friends Student Body and should be made a concern of the whole school.

Assimilation of Freshmen

Another problem upon which a participation program might be based is that of assimilation of Freshmen. The Y.M.C.A. and Y.W.C.A. have both assumed student responsibility in this matter but the whole problem could be made one of concern of everyone. Making the incoming Freshman feel the necessity for conforming in some degree to the social pressure built up through years of history and rich traditions is a problem which both students and Faculty must study. The orientation course given once a week during the first semester of the year is not enough; the problem is not so easily solved.

Football

Interest in the great college game is a natural phase of every normal college student's life. The Friends football team furnishes an interest about which the most wholesome of play-life can be developed. Loyalty to the team, good sportsmanship which has been traditional at Friends, rivalry with other schools, furnish social spirit and broadness of interest. Intercollegiate activities acquaint students with other colleges and help them to understand that their school, while worthy of their utmost in loyalty, is not the only worth-while school in the universe.

Scholastic Attainments

Until a few weeks ago Friends was a member of the North Central Association. Due to a deficiency in endowment, they were dropped from the list of members. Student activity and Administration policy have banded together in raising sufficient funds to reinstate the school. Friends students positively refuse to have...[7]

Vocational Guidance

Each year the Y.M.C.A. and others foster some lectures on vocational guidance. This practice could be improved upon and the type of lecturers could be bettered if the faculty would join hands in assuming responsibility for the vocational guidance of each student at Friends.

Improvement of Chapel Exercises

About three years ago the Student Council took up the matter of chapel programs. There had been some complaint concerning the quality of the programs which then, were all managed by the faculty. So much interest and constructive suggestion was resultant that the Council demanded that the Faculty offer better speakers and programs in chapel. The Faculty accepted the challenge and the result was a definite improvement of the chapel exercises. Later the Council requested opportunity to present school problems in chapel with the result that every Friday, chapel was given over to the Council in presenting matters of student interest. Thus it has been shown that the improvement of chapel exercises is a problem about which student participation can be built.

Campus Appearance

Each year the students have a day set apart for cleaning the campus. Every student. works at the project with the result that they are more careful of its appearance on all occasions. At present, the campus is undeveloped. It might be a very interesting problem upon which to base a program of participation, to beautify the Friends University campus.

Other Problems

The participation program should be so constructed that new problems will be continually suggesting themselves. Students must have opportunity to express their interests in a variety of problems and in new problems. These problems which have been mentioned are only suggestions and do not pretend to cover all the problematical fields at Friends. The proper solution of one problem will reveal another problem which needs solution. The bases which underlie participation should be constantly changing. There should be no objection to the assuming of new responsibilities on the part of the students.

Chapter VI Creating Machinery

Kinds of Machinery Depend upon Problems

Since problems are the basis upon which the participation program should be built, the kinds of machinery used in the participation program should also be dependent upon those problems. Too often organizations are created to satisfy students who merely want the name of "being in something." Literary societies are often formed which place great emphasis upon "getting in," and building up an

[7] Editors' note: missing text.

elaborate constitution and set of ideals, which no one takes seriously, then initiating gullible neophytes into the inner circle of the "chosen." The activity of the organization often closes with this impressive ceremony, to reopen again in the spring with a farewell banquet.

The kinds of machinery which should be used at Friends cannot be set forth in this paper as only the students and the problems which they choose to confront can determine the nature of the organization.

Utilizing Existing Machinery

It is a better policy, however, to utilize those organizations which already exist for carrying out the projects of participation. The stabilizing influence and the group consciousness which exist in an organization which has history and tradition back of it should be of value in determining more sane methods of procedure. Many of the organizations at Friends have very worthy traditions back of them and it would be folly to create new machinery for doing things which these organizations can do just as well themselves

Eliminating Dead Machinery

About three years ago the Student Council took steps to compel organizations to function. It was required that each organization should present an outline of its work to the Council and pass satisfactory examination regarding its usefulness before its charter could be re-granted for another year. The raising of the number of points involved with holding an office in a club also tended to free the officers of each club from other activities and consequently make them more anxious to distinguish themselves in their limited field.

If proper ambition and social control were built up in the student body, the regulations which the Council has already made will eliminate dead machinery. Machinery which has no usefulness and has died a natural death will be afforded a decent burial.

Universality of Participation

With increased activity in school control comes the danger of over-working those who are wiling to accept responsibility and are capable of leadership, while those who are less talented or less ambitious lose the opportunities for education. Every student should be required to carry some outside activity. Perhaps the point system already in effect could be modified so that it would require a minimum number of points to be carried as well as a maximum. Some method should be devised of measuring the amount of each student's participation. When the students of Friends feel that the participation in school and intramural affairs is part of the regular education for which they are paying, and that it is evaluated and measured as such, they will begin to concern themselves with those activities which they have thought be in interference with their education. Every means should be used to bring social pressure to bear upon those students who neglect their responsibilities for school control. The Student Council and other organizations make numerous appointments each year and it would behoove each student to make himself worthy of one of these appointments. Jobs should not be arbitrarily assigned students, just because they would otherwise not have them; the students should actually be held responsible for making themselves popular or respected enough to receive responsibility. Complaints that they are not popular should not excuse the backward students. Teachers should encourage such students, help them find out what is wrong with themselves, and see that they win the respect of their fellow students enough to be recipients of positions of honor and responsibility. The student, himself, should be held responsible if he does not receive the election.

Coordination

With the increased activity of the school and student body there will be a danger of conflict and over-stressing of certain activities. All organizations should receive the sanction of the Student Council before they attempt any considerable project that involves more than their own memberships. The Calendar Committee must work over-time in distributing events of general interest. Non-cooperating groups must be whipped into line and made to function. The leaders of different societies must meet in their Literary Society Council and coordinate their programs. The new program of socialization will lead to greater conflicts but the danger can be kept at a minimum by careful manipulation on the part of the Student Council.

The School Calendar

What the students propose to do and when they propose to do it should be their own responsibility. The calendar should be in the hands of the students with faculty advice available. Every event should be scheduled and the interest of the student body should be allowed to surge from one field to another without such over-emphasis upon one field as to cause reaction. The natural enthusiasms of the student body should be given opportunity to swing between limits. A week of music, or a week of parties do not represent unbalanced emphasis but rather, a spicy diversion;

Time of Meetings

Meetings might be scheduled for any time during the day or week but they should not be pushed off into the undesirable odds and ends of time in order to make room for classes. Perhaps it would be best to reserve a certain period each day for meetings of major importance. Students should be willing, however, to meet at times outside the customary school hours, such as noon-time, after the last class, in the evening and after school. In considering all these times the necessity of some students having time off in which to earn their way through school should be considered just as important as the participation activity time.

Faculty Supervision

The faculty of institution should be composed of those individuals who are most capable in guiding and inspiring students in their lives. They should be the advisors to whom the students can turn for instruction and advice concerning the best methods of educating themselves. The classroom part of their teachers' work should not be the most important. If the Faculty at Friends would so conduct itself that the students will come to respect their advice, the teachers need not fear that the students will make unadvised decisions. The faculty should consider themselves responsible for making their influence appreciated by the students. Students should not be compelled to accept the advice of individuals whose judgment they do consider of value. The participation program should be a program of the students conducted for the purpose of educating those most concerned with the education, namely, the students themselves.

Chapter VII Student Participation in Operation

Conservative Influence

After the program of participation has been set in operation at Friends the next problem will be the use of conservative influence on the part of those who are more far-sighted than the rest. The first influence must be that of arousing desire for change while the second, not in opposition, will be the encouragement of caution. Youthful enthusiasm makes both more violent mistakes and brilliant successes than mature age. For the school control to be all control and no ballast would be fatal to itself. The students must be influenced to conserve the best practices and traditions of former student bodies for reference and use in the formulating of their own new policies. There must be both unrest and conservatism in the influences which play upon the student mind.

Real Projects

Likewise, conservatism must be used in sifting the real projects from the too ambitious or too superfluous ones. The projects which the students undertake must be those which they are, in a measure, prepared to undertake. It is important that the first attempts of the students be successful. In order to assure this, those upon whom the students depend for advice must be careful to advise those activities which are important enough to challenge the enthusiasm of the participants and yet be easy enough to make success reasonably sure. When a job has been finished the students must be able to look back and feel that they have really accomplished something worth while. It is important that the student participation control program involve real projects.

Thoroughness of Investigation

If the first attempts of the students have been successful there will be a temptation for them to declare a project before thoroughly investigating its implications. No group of students should be allowed to present a program of participation until all important materials and involved issues have been studied. The different organizations should be constantly investigating the possibilities of new projects and the number investigated should be several times the number chosen. Thorough investigation should be encouraged at all times to prevent unnecessary failures, and at the same time train the students in a method of procedure which will always be of great value to them.

Assuming Responsibility

As the plan progresses more and more of the responsibility should be shifted from those faculty members which have been drafted into service, to the students themselves. Students should begin to feel the responsibility for well conducted classroom procedures and should be able to proceed with a course of study whether a teacher is present or not. The whole educating process should be made the responsibility of the students. Students might even recommend the employment of special advisors or teachers in certain fields.

Raising Finances

Every privately owned school has a particular kind of financial problem. It must depend upon the benevolence of its patrons for the largest part of its operating funds, except where the endowment has been raised to a large sum. The students should feel the responsibility for raising finances for the maintenance of the school just as they have done in the past few weeks. When the funds are raised, the students should have the responsibility of properly distributing part of them. The school should furnish equipment for the social laboratory out of the same fund that equipment for the physical laboratory is purchased. The participation projects should be figured as part of the regular running expenses of the school although the students should have responsibility in raising certain minor funds for special purposes.

Chapter VIII Recognition of Student Participation

Requiring Participation

Aside from the social pressure mentioned in a previous chapter for requiring participation, there should be some way of including participation activities in the regular school curriculum. Courses of study in certain departments might make certain types of student. participation prerequisite. The President of the University has already expressed a wish that the outside activities of each senior upon graduating could be mentioned on the diploma and that diplomas could be evaluated by the range and effectiveness of the these activities. It would not be impractical to require active participation of all those majoring in Sociology, in some specific sociological projects. Those majoring in a modern language might be required to have carried so many points in a certain language club for so long a time. These different requirements might be made prerequisite to graduation from Friends.

Accrediting Participation

The formal accrediting of student participation involves a larger problem. The North Central Association would probably be slow to recognize credit given in Student Council or in Cheer leading. The accrediting of these different activities in such a manner that they will be recognized in transfer by other schools is a problem for which there is no immediate solution as far as Friends University is concerned. Friends would have to be a pioneer in the field and prove by some sort of measurement of results that the process is fully as worthy of recognition as the formal courses under a teacher "who knows his subject," instead of his students.

But the fact that the North Central Association might not recognize the educational value of managing the May Day Fête does not mean that the courses of study mentioned in the catalog cannot be liberally construed. A course in dramatic interpretation could easily be extended to include the presentation of a May Day pageant or the Junior Play. The courses in Methods of Teaching in Secondary Schools could include the problems relating a Booster Club. Liberal construction of the formal courses of the curriculum will furnish a means of partially accrediting student participation in school control.

Invasion of the Classrooms

The applications of a subject being taught in a particular classroom to projects being conducted in the student life can always be placed in the foreground. The class in surveying can take upon itself the whole problem of draining the campus so that landscaping can be done. It is not improbable that in the future school participation groups will be able to invade the classrooms to the extent that the very discussions will be maintained by the students and the teacher will be requested to take a side seat and speak only when asked to do so. Other teachers might be requested to lecture upon topics of interest while the regular teacher discretely listens or is excused from attendance. Such ideas of classroom procedure seem visionary but after all, a college education is of more vital concern for the student than for the teacher. Why shouldn't students control their own classes, when they are the ones whose success or failure depends upon the kind of education which they receive?

Future Possibilities

The whole idea of student participation in school control is destined to great development in the next few years. Every school which now attempts the program is a pioneer and must prove that some certain procedure is workable or useless. In order to make this proof, some method of measuring the results of the system must be developed. What that method will be cannot be prophesied at the present writing. The author contemplates a thesis study of the personality leadership results of different types of education with the hope that those activities which have been classed as "outside" will prove of more value in developing personality leadership than the "recognized" activities. Perhaps the study will reveal methods of measuring results which can be applied before students have reached obscurity or have risen to the heights of success.

If Friends University, or any other school should take upon itself the carrying out of such a program as has been outlined here, and is wise enough to quickly make adaptations when these principles fail, it would be placing itself in the role of a pioneer and not improably would be able to make some real contribution to the field of socialized education within a few years.

Bibliography[8]

Satchel, J.K.,Student Participation in School Administration.
Cronson, B., Pupil Self-Government.
George, W.R. & Stowe, L. B., Citizens Made and Re-made.
Willing, R., Self-Government, Proceed. N.E.A., 1915

[8] Editors' note: The bibliography has been left largely in the way that it was originally presented.

Cox, Philip, The Ben Blewett Junior High School, an experiment in democracy, School Review, May 1919.
George, W. R., The George Junior Republic
Fowler, B. P., The social organization of a high school, School and Society, Oct. 30, 1920
Jones, H.W., Student cooperation in school government, School and Society, Feb. 26, 1921
Clapp, H. L., Pupil self-government, Education, April, 1918
Bowden, A. O., Student self-government, School and Society July, 27,1918
Abbott, W. C., The Guild of Students, Atlan Monthly, 6 Nov. 1921, pp 618–25
Dewey, John, Moral Principles in Education
Scott, C.A., Social Education
Robbins, C. L, The School as a Social Institution
Morehouse, F.M., The Discipline of the School
Bagley, W. C., School Discipline
Rae, W. S., Some Student Body Problems
Gilbert, C.B., The School and its Life
Briggs, Thomas, H., Curriculum Problems
Carlton, F.T. Education and Industrial Evolution
Cox, Philip W. L, Creative School Control
Cox, Philip W. L., Curriculum-Adjustment in the Secondary School
Foghy, H. W., The Danish Folk. High Schools, U.S. Bureau of Education Bulletin No:22, 1914
Miller, H. L. & Hargraves, R.T., The Self -Directed School
Sisson, E.O., Education for Freedom
Sisson, E.O., Moral education again to the front, School and Society, May 9, 1925
Smith, W.R., Constructive School Discipline
Snedden, David, Sociological Determination of Objectives in Education.
Tildsley, J.L., Are our schools successfully preparing for citizenship?, School and Society. Dec., 1923
Yeomans, Edward, Shackled Youth
Coe, George A., What Ails Our Youth?
Fryer, Douglas, Vocational Self-Guidance
Lindsey B.B., and Evans, Wainwright, The Revolt of Modern Youth
Palmer, Jasper T., Democratizing influences of the school of to-day, Elementary School Journal, Feb., 1924
Paul, Francis J.H., The growth of character through participation in extra-curriculum activities, Fifth Yearbook, N.A.S.S.P. 1921
Glueck, Benard, Some extra-curriculum problems of the classroom, School and Society, Feb, 9, 1924
Fretwell, E. K., Education for leadership, Teachers College Record, Sept. 1919.
Mitchel, E.D., Intramural Athletics
Holch, K.E., The Social Basis of Extra-Curricular Activities, Jan, 1926
Stern, Renee B., Club Making and Management
Spain, C. L., The auditorium as a socializing unit, Detroit Educational Bulletin, No.2, Jan.,1923
Fretwell, Elbert K., and O' Neill, Marion, School publications, Teachers College Record, Sept., 1924
Reavis, W.C., Student publications, Twenty-fifth Yearbook N.S.S.E. 1926 Part II, pp. 141 ff
Archer, C.P., School government as an educative agency, School Review, June, 1923
Jones, H. W., Student cooperation in school government. School and Society, Feb 26, 1923
Lewis, Grace, T., Centralizing student activities, School Review, Oct., 1923
Parmenter, Ethel N., Student government, a project method, School Review, Feb., 1925
Thomas-Tindal, E.V., and Myers, J.D. Student Participation in School Government
Geiger, J.R., Educational value of the Honor System, School and Society, May 2, 1925
Horst, H.M., Student participation, School Review, May 1924
Vaughan, T. H., A point system and record card for extra-curricular activities, School and Society December 30,1922
Wiley, Will E., Organization of extra-curricular activities as a device for training in citizenship, School Review, Jan., 1925

86

Social Inheritance[1]

The term, "Social Inheritance," is a new coinage in man's system of thought exchange. It is so-called because it is to be compared and contrasted with biological inheritance. Yet there have been many terms used which imply the same meaning. Herbert Spencer called it "the superorganic" inheritance; that inheritance which is dependent upon the existence of the organic, and yet, which is not transmitted organically. C. H. Judd calls it " … the accumulation of social capital or culture complexes … that not inherited by wild animals or plant life. "Culture" is a term which in its true meaning is synonymous with "Social Inheritance." The trouble with using "culture" is the fact that the term has a false connotation. Culture originally meant cultivatedness. A cultured man was one whose mental faculties were scrubbed and burnished until they reflected without the distortion of originality all the abstractions of the day. A man so afflicted is still considered by some to be a cultured man.

Then there is the rather popular idea that our social inheritance includes only the aristocracy of learning, that it is a sort of title conferred upon that knowledge of ancient and noble lineage. A mathematics professor once told us that he hoped none of us would ever find his course useful. He was decidedly successful in persuading me that I had no use for the stuff from then on. He had given his particular branch of study a crest and a coat-of-arms and had attempted to withdraw it from productive toil.

The Germans had a term, "kultur" which had a slightly different meaning. To them it meant the German mode of life, the sum-total of things German. With the exception of the provincialism which they read into the term, their conception was very close to the real meaning.

Human institutions, language, tools, methods, governments, schools, manners of living, are the elements which make up our social inheritance. All our folkways, mores, and fads are to be included in this classification. Without excluding any development of the human mind which is transmissible, culture becomes the sum and total of things human. This interpretation of culture avoids the controversy as to which parts of our social inheritance merit the term "culture," and which do not. Here, knowledge of the steam engine becomes just as truly a part as are the meditations of Marcus Aurelius, and every bit as complex. Which of the two is the more valuable, is another question upon which we hope to throw some light later on. The important thing at this point is to recognize that both are contained in society's inheritance.

To Auguste Comte should be given credit for the first use of the term "Sociology" which has now become generally recognized as the study of the phenomena of social inheritance. In his "Positive Philosophy" published in 1839 the term first appears. The study represents the newest off-shoot from that study of the unknown and irrelevant which we call, "philosophy".

There are at least two problems in education, rather distinct problems, to which a study of the social inheritance is related. Educators want to know, in the first place, how much school achievement can ever be expected from a child who makes a certain score on an intelligence test. Can anything be done to increase that child's educability? Can the test score be raised? Will an alteration in the environment of early childhood help any? Are the differences in ability as we find them in our schools attributable to variations in the home environment or to variations in the biological heredity? These belong to the first type of questions which educators want answered.

The second problem is one of determining what the curriculum should contain. To be sure, the choice is not as great for the dull pupils as for the brighter ones, and, to that extent, the two problems over-lap. But the curricular content is not automatically determined, even by an IQ as low as 70. Dr Ogburn of Chicago University once told us that "It is at the activities required by culture and the activities occasioned by the original nature of man where the planes of the super-organic and the organic meet". Thus, to the educator, the problems present themselves in such a fashion as this: Should little Nancy Dugan from down on the High Street "whose father's a drunkard, whose mother is dead" be conscripted for service in Caesar's Gaelic Wars, armed only with a modest IQ to help her in the fray? Will her industry compensate for her lack of mental alertness? That is the first type of problem. Then, supposing she should enlist with Caesar and emerge with the flag of victory clutched in her eager fingers; what of it? Now, what is the value of that classic barbecue in her social

[1] Written in 1930. First published in Stringer, P., & Bannister, D. (Eds.). (1979), *Constructs of sociality and individuality*. Academic Press (pp. 4–17). Republished by permission of Jacqueline Aldridge.

Collected Papers of the Pioneer of Constructivist Psychology: George A. Kelly, First Edition. Edited by David A. Winter and Nick Reed.
 Published 2026 by John Wiley & Sons Ltd.

sphere? Of course, little Nancy likes it. Her cheeks will glow with true Scottish pride when the eyes of her friends come to rest on the "D.P." now framed and hung above the kitchen grate. I'm assuming that "D.P." stands for "Discharge Papers" or whatever Caesar was in the habit of awarding his faithful legionnaires. Yes, and in his sober moments, even Old Man Dugan himself will be proud of Nancy's achievement. Well, to be sure, this is all hypothetical, because, as things are, Nancy would have been tried in an Advanced Division and condemned to a technical school. There would be no Roman coat-of-arms above the Dugans' kitchen grate and on Saturday nights Old Dugan would still have difficulty in making the three flights of stairs under his own power. There seems magic in the fact that "*Omnia Gallia in partes tres divisit*" and the second problem for the educator is to discover the true secret of that magic.

Is Environment Principally Responsible for Variation in School Achievement?

The nature versus nurture problem is not so much a question of which is the more potent as one of discovering the spheres of influence which these two factors dominate. Although we may ardently attempt to prove the supremacy of nature over nurture, or vice versa, little graphite is wasted computing the relative importance of food and cook and few rural debating societies spend a Friday night haggling over the relative value of seed and soil. When it comes to the more practical situations we find that nature seems to demand constant nutrition and nurture is a part of the natural order.

It will do no harm at this point to refresh our minds on the classic arguments on this question. The following account is given by Starch in his "Educational Psychology", p. 77.

Similarities of Abilities Among Related Defective and Low Grade Persons

Quite a number of studies have been made in recent years concerning the frequency with which defective persons are either distantly or closely related. One of the first studies was that of the Jukes reported by R. G. Dugdale in 1877. Max Juke, born in 1720 was a shiftless truant, who married an equally worthless woman. Up to 877 there had been five generations with approximately 1,200 descendants among whom have been traced the following types of persons: 310 paupers, 7 murderers, 60 habitual thieves, 50 prostitutes, 130 convicted of crime, 300 died in infancy, 440 physical wrecks from debauchery, only 20 learned a trade, and 10 of these learned it in prison. The estimated cost to the State of New York has been put at approximately $1,000 a person. In contrast with this lineage, a comparison has been suggested with the Jonathan Edwards family, which had approximately 1,400 descendants in the same period of time. Among them there have been 120 graduates of Yale alone, 14 college presidents, over 100 professors, 135 books of merit have been written by various members of the family, and 118 journals have been edited by them. Aaron Burr was the only black sheep among them and he can certainly not be classed as an intellectually defective person. (Winship '00)

Poellman of Bon (Guyer '16, p. 271) made a study of a family called the Zeros in which 800 descendants were traced through six generations back to a female drunkard. Among them were found 102 professional beggars, 107 illegitimate offspring, 181 prostitutes, 54 inmates of almshouses, 76 convicted of crime, and 7 murderers. The cost to the state was placed at $1,206,000.

More recently a very interesting study was conducted by Dr Goddard of the Training School of Vineland, New Jersey. Dr Goddard ('12) traced the ancestry of a young girl who had been brought to his institution. It was found that the lineage went back to a man, Martin Kallikak, a soldier in the Revolutionary War, who was the progenitor of two lines of descendants. (See Figure 31). He had an illegitimate son whose mother was feeble-minded. This was the establishment of a line -- A -- which had, down to the time of the study, 480 direct descendants among whom were found the following: 143 feeble-minded, 292 unknown, 36 illegitimates, 33 prostitutes, 24 alcoholics, 3 epileptics, 82 died in infancy, 3 criminals, 8 keepers of disreputable houses, and only 46 normal individuals. Apparently human nature does not gather grapes of thorns or figs or thistles. After his return from the war, Martin married a woman of normal intelligence and from this lineage -- B -- there had come during the same period of time 496 direct descendants, of whom all were normal individuals with the exception of five, one of whom was reported as mentally defective, two as alcoholics, one as sexually immoral, and one as a case of religious mania. There were no epileptics or criminals and only 15 died in infancy. The remainder were good citizens, including doctors, lawyers, educators, judges, and business men.

One thing seems to stand out very conspicuously from the numerous facts of family histories that have been unraveled in recent years, namely that much defective mentality, degeneracy, and crime is a matter of ancestry. General opinion among persons in charge of institutions for defectives is that two-thirds of all cases are due to heredity and one-third to environmental or unknown causes.

No one can listen to these accounts without being profoundly impressed with the potency of inheritance and yet it is only fair to point out that there was both biological and social inheritance operative. The hotel in which Martin Kallikak met the feeble-minded mother of the line A, was not a comparable environment to that established by Martin for the children of his line, B.

To continue with Starch's argument:

Pearson has shown that the resemblance in physical characteristics among brothers and sisters is approximately 0.50. He gives the following coefficients of correlation for various physical traits.

	Brother and Sister
Hair Color	0·55
Cephalic index	0·49
Height	0·50
Eye Color	0·52

Starch continues by showing similar correlations between mental abilities of brothers and sisters, from a study which he made himself:

Reading-speed	0·51
Reading-comprehension	0·64
Writing-speed	0·72
Writing-quality	0·46
Size of reading vocabulary	0·07
Spelling	0·05
Arithmetical reasoning	0·38
Addition-attempts	0·71
Addition-rights	0·44
Subtraction-attempts	0·43
Subtraction-rights	0·29
Multiplication-attempts	0·37
Multiplication-rights	0·25
Division-attempts	0·46
Division-rights	0·56
Average	0·42

Memory	0·31
A-test	0·50
Geometrical form test	0·07
Tapping	0·65
Average	0·38

Starch concludes from this, first, that "the resemblance of siblings is apparently no greater in those mental traits which are directly affected by school work than in those which are not so affected." And secondly, "the resemblance of siblings is approximately as great as in mental traits as in physical traits."

Odin, in his study of 5,233 noted French men of letters living during the period 1400 to 1830 inferred that if France as a whole had been as fertile as Paris in the production of genius there would approximately be 54,000 great men of letters instead of less than 6,000. But here again the complimentary aspect of biological and social heredity was not sufficiently taken into account to make the results conclusive.

At this point a few moments might well be taken to repeat Professor Thomson's citation of Miss Burk's paper on the variability of intelligence.

The general plan of inquiry was to correlate (1) true children with their true parents, and (2) foster-children with their foster-parents. Clearly if heredity is the main factor the former correlations should be high and the latter zero, whereas if environment is the main factor the correlations should be equal in the two cases. Both the true parents of the control group were white, non-Jewish, American, British, or North European born, and so also were the true parents of the foster-children, as far as this could be traced or inferred. The children were all legally adopted, and not merely in a less responsible relationship to the foster-parents. Great care was taken in equating the control-group and the foster-group in every relevant point that could be conceived of. The Stanford-Binet test was used in obtaining the mental ages of both the parents and the children, and various other measures and observations were recorded, including an assessment of the home conditions by means of the Whittier Scale, and of cultural conditions of the home, separately, by means of a special scale devised for the purpose, based on such matters as the speech of the parents, their education, the size of the home library, the artistic taste apparent in the home, and the like. Probably the following table best sums up the quantitative side of the work:

Correlations of Child's IQ with	*Foster-Group*		*Control-Group*	
	r	*N*	*r*	*N*
Father's M.A.	0.09	178	0.55	100
Mother's M.A.	0.23	204	0.57	105
Father's vocabulary	0.14	181	0.52	101
Mother's vocabulary	0.25	202	0.48	104
Whittier index	0.24	206	0.49	104
Culture index	0.29	186	0.49	101
Income	0.26	181	0.26	99

Heredity is shown to account for differences of as much as five times those accounted for by environment.

I cannot help but quote Starch's general conclusion at this point:

> Nature predominates enormously over nurture only in the relative and not in the absolute sense. This distinction must always be borne in mind in studies of heredity. In fact, in the absolute sense, nurture predominates enormously over nature.

I don't think Starch himself quite understands what he has said but he apparently has realized in attempting to sum up his argument that there are two spheres which nature and nurture dominate respectively. Obviously, when one variable does not vary, it can scarcely be said to be the cause of variation in another: however, the non-varying factor may be a potential cause in that it may be necessary to the existence of the other. Starch's statement is at least a partial recognition of the fact that for a given culture level, nature is more significant, but for a given biological level, culture is more significant. In other words, when we limit our study to Edinburgh school children in the year 1930, we have chosen a very narrow range on the scale of culture, but the scale of biological inheritance has scarcely been shortened. Again, if we limit our study to, say, the great navigators of history, we shall find that their social inheritance has made all the difference in the world in determining their achievement, while we have good reason to believe that the quality of their biological inheritances remained approximately constant. Why, Angus McIntosh, with an IQ of 88 is obviously better off than Yon Yat Sun, whose father is a tribal leader on the northern slopes of the Himalayas. Angus, who has no hopes of entering the Royal High School, can do problems in mathematics that would have stumped Pythagoras and can solve domestic problems that would have driven Solomon into the regions beyond Jordan. What is the difference? There is little reason for believing that the biological inheritance has so favored Angus. The reverse is more likely true. Yet Solomon was a king and Angus will be a plumber—the educators have told him so. Evidently, one's station in society is finally determined somewhat by the relative amount of culture at his command. This relative amount of culture wielded by an individual in a particular society seems to be a function of his intelligence.

From the data now available we are led to the tentative conclusion that the variation in school achievement as the educator finds it in his classroom is due principally to variation in the biological heredity of the pupils. But the educator wants to know more nearly the exact relative weights of heredity and environment. Although several authors have attempted to assign exact percentages to these weights, obviously, it is impossible to do so with any great degree of certainty, at least at the present time. The educator wants a working hypothesis, however, and in giving him that hypothesis it is better to make the errors come out on the conservative side. What is the conservative side? The teacher who has had considerable classroom experience will tell you that there are few things as exasperating as a dull pupil. "Try as I will", says Miss Tress at the Friday night teachers' whist drive, "I simply can't get Nancy to see the difference between a gerund and a gerundive." Now tell Miss Tress that Nancy's failure to register impressions is not due to any fault of her teacher but to an unfortunate array of genes. There will be a sigh of relief: but will you not have furnished that school mistress with a too convenient alibi? If environment is to be conceived as playing a minor role, why be so concerned about home conditions, kindergarten, and playgrounds? Although over-emphasis upon the potency of environment may lead educators to attempt the impossible, over-emphasis upon the potency of heredity may turn the school into a mere sorting machine. From the standpoint of the pupil the conservative estimate should favor the environment.

What Should the Curriculum Contain?

This is the second problem in education upon which a discussion of the social inheritance has a direct bearing.

The social inheritance is composed of innumerable elements which have been accruing since the day the grandson of the pithecanthropus taught his offspring that women could be temporarily brought to submission by means of a stick grasped near one end. The development of a method of making fire and the transmission of that institution from one generation to the next is an interesting illustration. Just how fire was first discovered, no one knows, nor is it known how the first firemakers plied their craft. We do know, however, that in some tribes a priesthood was established for the firemakers, so revered were they. Yet who of us, by rubbing sticks together as did those aboriginal clerics, can produce fire? In fact, the very skill of stoking a fire seems to have been lost to some of us. The point to be inferred is that not all our social inheritance need be transmitted to every member of society. Even those elements which are most important historically need not necessarily be included in the accoutrement of a classically educated man. If the end of education is to pass on selected elements of the social inheritance, then evidently, the selection is not entirely upon the basis of historical significance.

Again, there is the persistent belief that certain of the culture elements when studied are effective as mental discipline. In the light of recent investigation this contention becomes doubtful.

Then there is the argument that certain culture traits are to be selected because few people have the imagination, the muscular skill, or the sensory equipment to acquire them. Not so many years ago while I was sitting in a Philosophy of Education class, it occurred to me that few people could wiggle their ears. I also observed that there were occasions when the possessor of that highly specialized skill attained a certain degree of social recognition. Whereupon, I set apart that hour of the day for practice. Fortunately, the examination included no questions on ear-wiggling, else my grade might have been even more hazardous than it was.

Should selection be based upon the difficulty of mastery? Yes, say some. But then why do we study Latin instead of Chinese? Evidently difficulty is not the final criterion.

Then, there is the argument that certain elements are to be selected because of their broad applicability. An artist implants form and color onto a strip of coarse cloth. We gaze at the dried paint and experience a new pattern of feelings. A musician touches our ears and fancy is set swinging across the whole range of human experience. A poet with the home-made tool of language carves the most delicate details of thought. A philosopher, a mathematician, a scientist, touches the length and breadth of human experiences, but with a sweeping gesture that takes little notice of the third dimension in which the different strata of society lie. It would be interesting to compute, if possible, the effect the steam engine has produced upon thought. Then it would be interesting to trace its development. What we would find would be that the steam engine, although important, is not a single invention but an accumulation of social capital to which three rather obscure men, working independently, in three different countries, added its final increment. For centuries men had wanted to fly. Great minds which were in possession of this broadly applicable culture had attacked the problem. Suddenly, two small-town bicycle mechanics with grease on their hands and dirty handkerchiefs in their pockets added the last increment to the accumulation of social capital. But they were none too quick, for simultaneously, others were doing the same thing. A knowledge of the details of bicycle making, as well as of a few of the general principles of aerodynamics was essential to the final production of the airplane. The point to be gotten is that progress demands the transmission of both broad and narrow principles. And on what basis should the selection be made? On the basis of applicability, not necessarily broad applicability, but on the basis of applicability to the creation of new culture elements! There are many unfinished accumulations of social capital needing only a few more small increments for completion. There are many half-finished accumulations and others scarcely started upon which each generation will cast its offering. Now, who is a cultured man? Not necessarily the one who has sopped up the most of his social inheritance, but the one who has partaken liberally of what he needs and sparingly of what he does not need in order to make his contribution.

I trust this hasty treatment of the criteria upon which culture elements are to be selected for transmission has not caused us to lose sight of Nancy, or of Angus McIntosh. It has a very direct relation to them, for it is very important that Nancy and Angus produce. You may say that what they produce is not of lasting value; can scarcely be dignified by the name of culture. Yet their very continuance in housework and plumbing under changing conditions compels them to make, along with others, new adjustments, new institutions, new culture. But we shall come back to this argument later.

How is culture formed? What are the related variables? Several theories have been suggested. There is the theory that civilizations go through a sort of cycle of definite changes. This is called the Successive Stages Theory. Then, there is the argument that biological factors are the causes of social change. Mutation, mixture, and selection, according to this argument, produce biological changes which, in turn, cause social change. It has often been suggested that changes in environment, such as climate, have produced physiological improvement. More recently it has been suggested that Endocrinology can explain the growth of culture. Then too, there is the saying that necessity is the mother of invention.

To discuss thoroughly the possibilities of these suggested explanations would require considerable time and patience, neither of which we are fortunate enough to possess.

True, there seem to be periods of excitation and depression in the history of society. The Golden Age of Pericles was followed by a period of political chaos. Rome fell. The Dark Ages came, and so on. But at no point in history is there exact similarity with the situation in a previous age. The changes are somewhat cyclical, the path of progress would appear to follow a helix. If the Successive Stages Theory is to be interpreted as meaning that for a given stage the culture level is constant and that the social inheritance is parceled out to us according to the stage we have reached, we must admit some truth in the theory. The difficulty, however, is that these stages have to be rather arbitrarily set off and that even within a particular stage the culture level varies steadily. Observe the rapid increase in culture during the last fifty years, especially in the newer sciences. Looking back we can observe that in a larger sense the social inheritance has been, not only increasing, but steadily accelerating. The lapses in the process have been momentary compared with the whole advance. As a final criticism it should be pointed out that the Successive Stages Theory is more a description of the rise of culture than an explanation of the related variables.

As regards mutations, mixtures and selection there is little reason to believe that they have influenced mental traits more than physiological traits. To be sure, physiological traits have been somewhat changed during the period of history. Armor used by Tenth Century warriors fits with uncomfortable snugness upon undersized men of today. But vastly more ill-fitting is the cultural accoutrement of those Tenth Century warriors. While physiological changes have been slight and uncertain, there has been nothing uncertain about the cultural changes which have taken place during the last thousand years. So we can scarcely consider these biological phenomena as causes if they have failed to influence physiological traits in any proportion to the changes undergone in the social inheritance.

Climate certainly has something to do with the way men live. Hottentots could scarcely be expected to devise the igloo nor could the Esquimaux be expected to invent the fly-swatter. On the other hand, the American Indians lived in an invigorating climate for many centuries without building a civilization as great as that existing under this abominable Scotch mist. True, the Aztecs had a calendar that was nearly as perfect as our own, and the Incas had a system of compulsory labor for everyone under a highly organized scheme of regimentation, but we can scarcely give climate the whole credit for that.

The hormones secreted from the endocrine glands have a great deal of effect upon the emotional making-up of an individual but no one has been successful in showing a progressive change in these secretions that would sufficiently account for the social progress of the race.

"Necessity is the mother of invention," is a little metaphor which is used in the same careless way in which most metaphors are used. One can think of hundreds of instances when it was more necessitous that men should fly than that day when the Wright brothers drew lots to see which should be the first to pilot their new flying contraption. It is hard to conceive of a necessity for a motor car any greater now than a hundred years ago, unless it be the fact that our neighbor now has one makes it necessary. As far as the race is concerned, necessity seems to be pretty fairly constant. Of course, radical changes in the social adjustment such as war may direct progress into certain lines, but mostly to the exclusion of other lines, so that the rate of total production is increased comparatively little. A notable instance of the effect of necessity on invention is that of the German development of the glider. Just after the war the Germans were prohibited from constructing high-powered airplanes. Immediately, they turned to the construction of gliders, and it was not long before Germans were accomplishing feats such as staying aloft for hours in motorless planes while the inventors of other nations were scarcely getting their machines off the ground. While engineers in other countries were still installing 90 horsepower engines in two passenger training planes, German pilots were going aloft carrying four passengers behind a 35 horsepower, three cylinder engine. Gliders had taught them how to use a long slender tapering wing. But while German genius was being directed in these lines, British and American inventors were perfecting the welded steel fuselage and the radial aircooled motor. Apparently necessity steers rather than stimulates invention.

Ethnological classification of peoples is first made on the basis of language. The dividing line between the savage and the barbarian is the attainment of a written language and between the barbarian and the civilized man it is the possession of a phonetic alphabet. The tools of communication, both of language and transportation are the most accurate index of the height of culture attained by a society. The argument to be advanced at this point is that tools of communication not only help pass down the social inheritance but are essential in making acquisitions to it. If we should stop all communication today, I fancy it would have the same effect on the construction of culture as it did on the construction of the Tower of Babel. Only upon the interplay of ideas in new and changing situations can culture be built. Where there is ready and quick intercommunication which takes place as soon as ideas are crystallized, there is ready and quick selection and adoption of those ideas which are useful. Culture consists, in one sense, of adopted ideas, ideas which have been selected by a process of interplay. Once the selection is made and adopted it is retained until it is forgotten or replaced by a more desirable idea. The new idea will probably be an improvement upon the old and will include a more complex array of elements, some of which will have been carried over from before. On the other hand, if a culture trait is forgotten, that is, not transmitted to the succeeding generation, the selection must be made all over again. Thus the speed of accumulation of social capital is a function of both the culture base and the facilities for interplay. The latter, in turn is probably a function of the culture base. If this assumption is valid, then the increase of culture should follow an exponential curve and should be practically independent of individual genius. This is very nearly what we find. Genius seems to be fairly constant in society at all times and the rate of increase of culture appears to be in a state of acceleration. It has been suggested that the formula for compound interest -- $P_t = \phi_0 (1 + r)^n$ might hold. Some studies have been made along this line. An attempt was made in the University of Minnesota to follow up the inventions subsequent upon the adoption of the plow sulky. For a short period the exponential formula held true until the influence of the tractor and the re-adaptation of the disc plow either submerged or replaced the influence of the plow sulky invention. Another study in the same school was made of the adoption of the city-manager type of municipal government. The results showed an ogive curve. Adoptions of the system were infrequent at first, then gradually became more frequent only to drop off again, apparently as modifications of the mayoral system became more popular. What little study has been made on these phenomena tends to show that for a given culture trait both the improvement and scope of adoption follow the exponential curve until the influence is submerged by multiple modifications and selections.

If then we accept the contention that the function of education, in a broad sense, is to facilitate accretion of social capital both for the sake of the individual and of society, the task of the educator becomes more than just handing down the social heritage. Not only must the social heritage be passed down but the legatees must be taught how to manipulate it, how to use it, how to select from it, and how to build upon it. In short, they must be put into the great game of interplay and taught how to give, take, and select. Isolate them, and they hide their one talent till you return, while the men to whom were given five talents have with them made five more. What we arrive at is a doctrine of education closely resembling that of Dewey, but which I believe, was partially devised in America before Dewey's time.

One more point needs to be taken up before we return to Angus and Nancy. There is in America a new theory bearing on democratic education developed since Dewey wrote his "Democracy and Education." It is that a comparatively small amount of culture is actually contributed by the class of people who are termed "geniuses." the people whose names are in print. Leaders are leaders, only in the Rooseveltian sense, people who can observe which way the crowd is going and who run and get in front. Professor Walter Robinson Smith of the University of Kansas has taken the initiative in teaching this theory. His argument runs something like this: three things contribute to a great leader, a great occasion, a great personality, and a great following. The leader simply adds a large increment to an already massive structure in order to complete an invention, whether it be social or physical. The main structure is supplied by the average and mediocre people, each of whom brings his little contribution and throws it onto the pile.

Take Dewey, himself, and his doctrine of tentative ends in education and free interplay of ideas in the school-room. The American pioneer was like that, long before Dewey was born. It was the average American who discovered that he had to change his mind frequently if he was ever to build up his country. It was the average American schoolboy who would not be silenced when he wished to express his ideas in the school-room. A president of an older American university gets the credit for introducing the elective system now so widely used in America. But it was the students who had first conceived it, and not the brilliant ones at that. It was the ones of mediocre intelligence from the farms and small villages who were determined to get their money's worth from "that thar new state university place, that dad's tax money is goin' tew," Imagine young fellows like that, fellows of mediocre intelligence, to whom a lone fence on the prairie "clutters things all up," being told that what they want is an original knowledge of the Sanskrit to take back to the cows. It was useless to refuse them entrance because the university belonged to those fellows. It was through their self-sacrifice that a university was possible. Now the educational philosophers and leaders in the field are coming to the conclusion that a flexible curriculum and non-bookish education is alright.

Suppose we make the assumption that one's ability to contribute to culture varies in direct linear ratio to his intelligence. With a distribution seven sigmas in length and with 2% of the population in each of the outside compartments, 10% in each of the next, 23% in the next, and 30% in the middle compartment, let us assume that the upper 2% produce twenty-six units of culture. The number of units produced by each of the other groups runs as follows, 110 units, 221 units, 210 units, 115 units, 30 units and 2 units. The middle 76% of individuals have produced exactly 72% of the total culture. It remains to be proved by those who hold to this theory that the relationship between intelligence and the ability to produce culture is linear. It is not hard to imagine that the proof might be forthcoming.

Now, what is the magic of the fact that "Gaul, as a whole, is divided into three parts?" There are many culture-elements which Nancy can use in her selection process, but Latin is very probably not one of them. Give little Nancy the social inheritance which she needs for turning her talents into social capital. Divide it into three parts, if necessary, just like Gaul. Place psychoanalysis in her hands, if there's really anything to the stuff, and who knows but that Old Man Dugan may sober up yet. Give her home making, nursing, a practical kind of child psychology, but above all, give her a Roman coat-of-arms with all the status it implies to hang above the kitchen grate.

And as for Angus, already he knows something that most of the boys at the Royal High School have overlooked. He knows of the appalling need for bath tubs in Edinburgh. It would be worthwhile to spend years in putting Angus in possession of that part of his social inheritance which would enable him not merely to install bath tubs, but to sell bath tubs, to create a market for them, to create a demand for the most practical and inexpensive kind of bath tubs. He may have an IQ of 88 but from one viewpoint his period of schooling needs to be the longer for it.

There are many of those who will argue that this interpretation of human needs is narrow, low, and vulgar and who will point with admiration to the great souls of the age who live "not by bread alone" but who, I may venture to say, will grudgingly buy one of Angus's bath tubs and be the better soul for it. If psychological science has shown anything it has shown that the millions of humanity never will and never can be "great souls." The tide of mankind has advanced slowly and steadily while these sorts are like waves on the surface which have rushed hither and left you in the sunlight of the upper atmosphere. The ocean of humanity is not to be stirred by the same winds that splash its surface. The masses of men are continually with us and we gain nothing by ignoring them. The social inheritance should be a free store upon which all the little Nancy Dugans and Angus McIntoshes can draw, a store in which the small parcels are wrapped with care and presented without stigma.

87

The Place of the Psychologist in the Small School System[1]

Attempts to increase the annual production of the school plant have resulted in a type of organization in which administrators are removed from pupils and teachers and compelled to recognize greater responsibilities to administrative regulations and to curricula and less responsibility for the welfare of individual pupils. If the school psychologist is simply to be another specialist, we cannot justify his existence in a small school system. The place of the psychologist should be envisaged as that of a teacher without curriculum, whose major responsibility is to assist individual pupils and teachers. An outline of the typical activities of such a psychologist in a small system is presented, together with suggested plans for including his salary in the budget.

[1] Abstract published as Kelly, G. A. (1938). The place of the psychologist in the small school system. In P. Weatherwax (Ed.), *Proceedings of the Indiana Academy of Science*, *48,* 183. Republished by permission of the Indiana Academy of Science.

Collected Papers of the Pioneer of Constructivist Psychology: George A. Kelly, First Edition. Edited by David A. Winter and Nick Reed.

88

Observations Made in a Search for Dynamic and Accessible Factors in Intellectual Development[1]

Methods of Increasing the Resultant Vectorial Projection on the Line of Intellectual Development

Regardless of our acceptance or rejection of any of the conflicting theories of the intrinsic nature of intelligence—Spearman's *G* and *s* theory, Thomson's composite view, Thurstone's primary ability theory, Kelley's ample factor view, or others—it is possible to view intellectual development as the resultant of a number of vectors. These vectors vary in strength and direction. They vary from time to time. They vary from person to person. It may not be necessary for all of us to envisage them in the same way. They could be considered, in turn, as themselves partial resultants in the force system.

According to this view it ought to be possible to facilitate intellectual development in three ways:

1 Increase all of the vectors which have projections upon the line of intellectual development,
2 Modify the system so that the resultant becomes a maximum for a given vectorial total, or
3 Increase a selected vector which does not have too great an angular separation from the line of intellectual development.

See Figure 1. The first method would increase the internal strain upon the system, but would have the advantage of not requiring any preliminary analysis of the system. The second method would decrease the internal strain but, if improperly applied, would retard intellectual development. The third method would increase the internal strain to some extent, depending upon the vector selected, but would require a clinical diagnosis of each case in order to find a vector which was both related to intellectual development and susceptible to stimulation.

An application of the first method would be the general stepping up of intellectually stimulating conditions for a child. The second method would require the reduction of unfavorable tensions, perhaps the reduction of all external stimulation, so that the naturally favorable internal trends might manifest themselves. The third method would require a clinical study of each case so that a key factor could be singled out and suitable stimulation applied.

In connection with the third method it should be said that the stimulation of a given factor, such as silent reading ability, could scarcely be expected to cause a statistically reliable acceleration of intellectual development in an unselected population any more than the general application of hearing aids could help a group of people most of which could already hear well enough. There are two ways of applying the third method:

1 Diagnose each case in an unselected population and apply the remedial devices indicated to be appropriate in each individual case, or
2 Select by diagnostic methods a group which may be expected to respond to a certain therapy, eliminating by partial or complete diagnoses those who appear not to be susceptible to the given treatment.

Clinical observations and some of the research attempted in the past four years at the Fort Hays Psychological Clinic may throw some light upon the efficacy of these methods. Wellman's encouraging results at the Iowa Child Welfare Research Station have inspired at least two of these studies.

[1] First published as Kelly, G.A. (1940). Observations made in a search for dynamic and accessible factors in intellectual development. *Fort Hays Kansas State College, Studies in Clinical Psychology*, *1*, 5–10. Republished by permission of Forsyth Library Special Collections, Fort Hays State University.

Collected Papers of the Pioneer of Constructivist Psychology: George A. Kelly, First Edition. Edited by David A. Winter and Nick Reed.

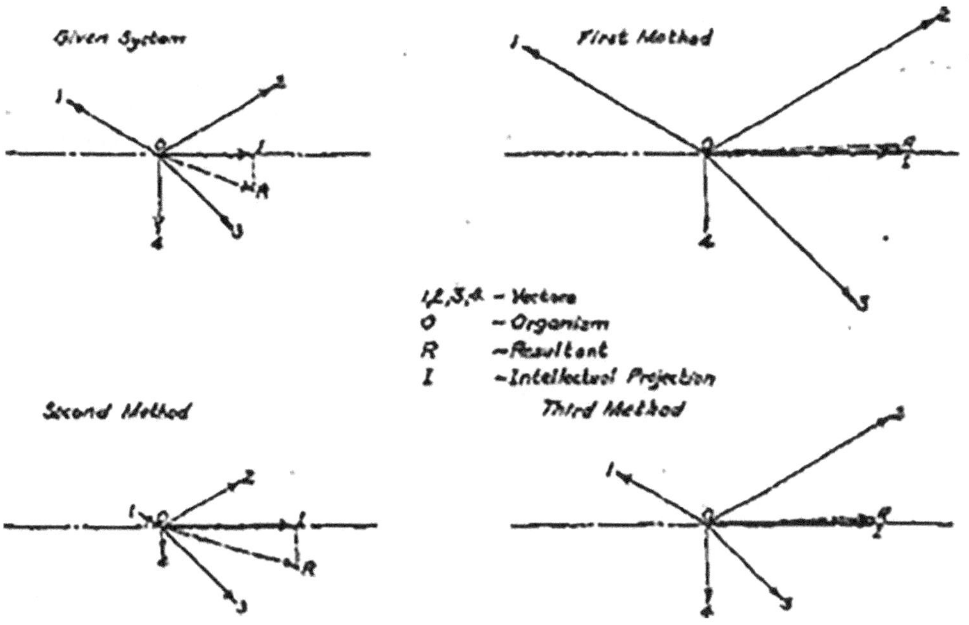

Figure 1

Isolating Vectors

There is the task of isolating some of the vectors. During the school year of 1935-36 Martinson[2] made a comparison of the results obtained by mathematical factor analysis of certain intelligence test results with those obtained by a clinical analysis of some of the cases in the same population. In general the clinical analyses substantiated the factor analyses. The study revealed what should have been perfectly obvious in the first place: that mathematical factor analysis discovers only those factors which are rather conspicuously measured by the test battery. Of course, such substantiation by hindsight is probably the hallmark of any valid research. Certainly it appears reasonable to suppose that by the time one has progressed far enough to construct a test battery which will measure the wanted factors he will have gone far beyond the point where he should have been able to recognize the presence of those factors clinically. Emmons[3], continuing the study of factor analysis in a clinical setting, found certain factors which clinical analysis showed beyond any question of doubt to be operative in a given situation, measured these known dynamic vectors, and yet found no method of mathematical factor analysis which revealed their presence in the lines along which they were known to have projections. It appears that we shall be somewhat dependent upon clinical methods for the present in isolating our vectors.

Accessible Vectors

But suppose we do find, either clinically or statistically, vectors which project upon any given line of development, say the line of intellectual development; how can we be sure that they possess dynamic properties or that they are not merely inaccessible resultants of more deeply seated and more dynamic vectors? While we have no evidence dealing directly with the development of intelligence in this connection, a study by Pankaskie[4] throws some light upon the problem. She made a clinical study of some of the factors affecting the employability of nonschool youth who were working on a National Youth Administration work project. The factors which she found immediately bearing upon their employability were, in turn, the resultants of familial trends; still back of these were other forces, and others back of those, etc. There was a point in her investigation when it appeared that Catherine the Great of Russia was the prime cause of their difficulty because she invited some Germans to the lower Volga region to raise wheat; but there were probably factors behind that, too. In seeking a factorial solution of unemployment, and perhaps of intellectual improvement too, it appears that our real problem is the determination of accessible factors rather than the seeking of a comprehensive statistical or psychological vocabulary in which precisely to summarize a situation.

[2] To be published in a later number of the *Studies*.

[3] *Loc. Cit.*

[4] *Loc. Cit.*

Breakdown of Factorial Composition

Along this same line, Downs[5], continuing the study of the psychological factors affecting unemployment, found some interesting contrasts between attitudinal factors as revealed in a questionnaire or interview situation and those exhibited by the same person later when he is suddenly offered an unexpected job. Such a terrifying experience may break down entirely the factorial composition of his attitudes. Probably in our study of intellectual development we may also have some difficulty in discovering the truly dynamic vectors.

Dynamic and Static Vectorial Formulations

Mason[6] in a study of teachers' use of cathartic methods found that teachers described and evaluated their pupils' problems in terms of school annoyances, superficial symptoms, their own maladjustments, and various other static concepts. And this was with cases in which they were doing intensive work, hence could not have been due to an ordinary casual attitude. Mason found that the formulation of these static concepts marked the point from which there was failure to make further progress with their cases.

Clinical Manipulation of the Vectorial Matrix

Turning now to the actual manipulation of the vectorial matrix, let us consider a clinical study by Hadley (1938). It bears upon the method of facilitating development by the reduction of certain vectorial components. He made several case and group studies of the role of relaxation in rational psychotherapeutics. In some cases relaxation appeared to remove tensions and to foster directly better adjustment. In some cases it formed a protective frame which permitted a freer catharsis and the formulation of a more reasonable picture of the patient's problem. In other cases the removal of superficial tensions by relaxation simply enabled the patient to confirm his original undesirable formulation of his personality problem, In fact, there was one case in which relaxation played all of these roles, but at different stages in the treatment.

From Hadley's work it would appear that where pathological mechanisms are already deeply seated and partly satisfying to the patient, relaxation may crystallize the static mental state and prevent active progress toward a solution. Again, it appears from his study that relaxation of the accessible tensions in an individual may permit unwanted tendencies to manifest themselves. In a college class where nearly all of the other students were finding their training in differential relaxation helpful while taking a strenuous test, one individual reported that he had not permitted himself to relax because he always did careless work when he was not keyed up. Perhaps the method of reducing stimulation could be expected to have more wholesome results among young children who have not become so dependent upon such crystalized patterns of self-discipline. In adult cases where the patterns are crystallized it may be more practical to use the third method, that of lengthening a certain accessible vector, unless, of course, a complete, program of psychotherapy is to be undertaken. Studies now being conducted in the Clinic have developed out of this line of reasoning. Ames[7] used the reduction-of-unfavorable-tension method with nursery school children. No attempt was made to introduce into their program any artificial stimulation or to enrich experience beyond the usual area of a child's curiosity. Freedom of action, integration of efforts, and the reduction of social and academic tensions was the order of their day. The more or less internal developmental vectors—maturation forces, perhaps—were carefully protected from opposition. The findings indicate that such a program is more likely to be successful in the cases of children who have not come to rely too much upon the artificial control of adults. Ames used change in I.Q. as a measure of intellectual acceleration.

G. Thompson, Birrer, Bryan, F. Wright and Kelly[8], working with college students and using the method of selecting cases clinically which give promise of responding to a given treatment, showed some significant rises in intelligence test scores following the application of individualized and integrated remedial reading techniques.

The statistical significance of individual gains rather than that of the group gain was computed. All cases showed gain after a relatively short period of treatment. With the exception of cases in which clinically there could be little doubt of the presence of a factor other than silent reading disability which was prejudicing the intelligence test result, the treated showed gains represented by a reliability of 99.40 to 99.95 chances out of 100. While the study is preliminary and exploratory, the results certainly justify setting up a program of intensive investigation along this line.

New vectors projecting upon the line of intellectual development need to be discovered, tested for accessibility, and checked in various situations to discover their dynamic properties. J. Wright[9] has shown a distinctive uniqueness in the pattern of transient

[5] *Loc. Cit*

[6] Published in the same monograph as this paper.

[7] Published in the same monograph as this paper.

[8] Unpublished.

[9] To be published later.

aphasic cycles of different individuals. His results suggest that there are ways of controlling them. Others are studying the bearing of this factor upon intellectual output.

Reference

Hadley, J. (1938). Various roles of relaxation in psychotherapeutics. *Journal of General Psychology*, *19*, 191–203.

89

A Preliminary Inquiry Leading to: A Plan for a Comprehensive Experimental Study of the Uses of Television in Teacher Education[1]

Section A

Assigned Mission of this Inquiry

Authorization by the New Jersey State Commissioner of Education

The New Jersey State Teachers College at Montclair is interested in making a comprehensive experimental study of the uses of television in teacher education.

In authorizing such a study the New Jersey State Commissioner of Education stated three major objectives as follows:

1. To find ways to increase the effectiveness of classroom teaching by the use of television.
2. To find ways to enrich the school curriculum through television.
3. To find ways to extend the influence of master teachers through the use of television.

In order to plan and organize The Comprehensive Experimental Study the College was further authorized to undertake the present Preliminary Inquiry with the following objectives:

1. To formulate plans for making an experimental study in the use of television in the education of teachers.
2. To develop plans for measuring the value of using television in educating teachers.
3. To survey the facilities available for conducting experimental projects in using television in educating teachers.
4. To list additional facilities and personnel needed to conduct the experimental projects in using television in the education of teachers in New Jersey.
5. To estimate carefully the cost of conducting experimental projects in using television in the education of teachers in accord with the formulated plan.

The Grant from The Fund for The Advancement of Education

The Fund for the Advancement of Education of the Ford Foundation has expressed an interest in the study of television as it specifically relates to the national shortage of qualified teachers. The College, therefore, asked it to support the present preliminary investigation which was described as "an investigation leading to the design and implementation of an intensive study of television in relation to the shortage of competent teachers."

[1] Report to Dr. E. D. Partridge, President, The New Jersey State Teachers College at Montclair, November 10, 1953. Published by permission of Jacqueline Aldridge. An Appendix, consisting of descriptions of equipment, budgetary requirements, and a list of consultants, has been omitted from this chapter, but is available from the editors on request.

Collected Papers of the Pioneer of Constructivist Psychology: George A. Kelly, First Edition. Edited by David A. Winter and Nick Reed.

It was stated explicitly that, on the basis of such a grant from the Fund, the College would conduct an investigation of the following:

1 The relevant educational issues.
2 The available information bearing on these issues.
3 The resources which might be employed in the further investigation of these issues.

Moreover, it was specified that an integral feature of the report of the preliminary investigation would be:

4 A design for the three to five year intensive study of the issues as formulated.

The Relation between the Authorization and the Grant

It is to be noted that the Commissioner's authorization was handed down within an administrative framework and that it cleared the way for the college to pursue certain operational plans and objectives. The grant from the Fund for the Advancement of Education was then used by the College to clarify certain basic issues relevant to educational television.

Moreover, it is quite clear that the Fund was concerned with these issues primarily in the hope that they might throw some light on educational problems which have grown out of the teacher shortage. The Commissioner, on the other hand, did not try to define the *problem area*, but he did set up certain *operating* areas: the classroom, the curriculum, the master teacher, and teacher education.

Both the Commissioner and the Fund expected preliminary investigation to lead to the development of a detailed plan for the further intensive study of educational television.

The report of the College's Consultant is prepared in partial fulfillment of the College's commitment to the Fund. The full implementation of the Commissioner's authorization is a larger matter, extending much beyond the proper domain of the Consultant.

Section B

Persons and Places Visited

At the request of the College the following places were visited during the autumn of 1953. The names of key persons with whom conferences were held appear in the list below.

1 **Cleveland Ohio**
September 7 and 8
Dr. Jay Otis, Director, Personnel Research Institute, Western Reserve University. Director of research relating to University's telecourse program.
Dr. John F. White, Vice-President, Western Reserve University. Chairman, University Broadcasting Council.
Symposium on Teaching Psychology by Means of Television Participants:
Dr. Richard I. Evans, University of Houston
Dr. Martin Frits, Iowa State college
Dr. Wilbert J. McKeachie, University of Michigan
Dr. Eleroy Stromberg, Western Reserve University

2 **Montclair and New Brunswick, New Jersey, and New York City**
September 14, 15 and 16
Mr. R. T. Cavanagh, Assistant to Director of Research, Allen B. Du Mont Laboratories, Inc.
Dr. Thomas T. Goldsmith, Jr., Vice-President in Charge of Research, Allen B. Du Mont Laboratories, Inc.
Dr. Herbert B. Gooden, New Jersey State Department of Education.
Dr. Clarence Hinchey, Superintendent, Montclair Public Schools.
Dr. Robert H. Morrison, Assistant Commissioner for Higher Education in New Jersey.
Mr. Edward C. Rasp, Director, New Jersey Educational Television Station at New Brunswick.
Dr. Robert T. Rock, Jr., Professor of Psychology, Fordham University. Director of Joint Navy-Air Force Television Evaluation Project.
Members of the staff of the New Jersey State Teachers College at Montclair.

3 **Mt. Pleasant and Bay City, Michigan**
September 24 and 25
Dr. Charles L. Anspaugh, President, Central Michigan College of Education.

Mr. Paul Briggs, Superintendent, Bay City Public Schools.
Dr. Julian Foust, Vice-President, Central Michigan College of Education.
Dr. Charles B. Park, Co-Director, Cooperative Study for the Better Utilization of Teacher Competencies.
Dr. Woodward C. Smith, Co-Director, Cooperative Study for the Better Utilization of Teacher Competencies.
Miss Harriet Van Antwerp, Director of Elementary Education, Bay City Public Schools.
Mr. Toby Welbourne, Educational Specialist, Bay City Public Schools.
Mr. Harold Wilcox, Educational Specialist, Central Michigan College of Education.
Principals, teachers and teachers' aides of the Bay City Public Schools.

4 **Minneapolis, Minnesota**
October 7 and 8
Dr. Asher Christensen, Professor of Political Science, University of Minnesota.
Dr. John G. Darley, Associate Dean, Graduate School, University of Minnesota.
Dr. Marcia Edwards, Assistant Dean, College of Education, University of Minnesota.
Dr. Robert Keller, Head of Research Committee in Education, University of Minnesota.
Dr. Sterling Mitchell, Principal, University High School, University of Minnesota.
Students and Members of the Staff of the University High School.

5 **Ames, Iowa**
October 9
Mr. James Davis, Operating Supervisor, Television School Service, Station WOI.
Mr. Merritt Ludwig, Assistant to the Director, Station WOI, Iowa State College.
Dr. William Owens, Chairman, Department of Psychology, Iowa State College.
Mrs. Helen Seagraves, Producer of Social Studies Programs, "Iowa TV Schooltime", Station WOI.
Mr. Edward Wegoner, Director, Program Development, Station WOI.
Mr. George Zimbalman, Director of Art Department, Station WOI.
Members of technical staff of station WOI.

6 **Montclair, New Jersey**
October 15
Mr. Keeton Arnett, General Assistant to the President, Allen B. Du Mont Laboratories, Inc.
Dr. Ronald Doll, Director of Instruction, Montclair Public Schools.
Dr. Thomas T. Goldsmith, Jr., Vice-President in Charge of Research, Alan B. Du Mont Laboratories, Inc.
Dr. Clarence Hinchey, Superintendent, Montclair Public Schools.
Mr. Clifton Marshall, Principal, the Bradford School, Montclair.
Mr. Jacob Ruiter, Director of Public Relations, Allen B. Du Mont Laboratories, Inc.
Members of the staff of the New Jersey State Teachers College.

7 **Philadelphia, Pennsylvania and Washington, DC.**
October 16
Miss Martha Cable, Assistant Director of Public Relations, Philadelphia Public Schools, in charge of educational television.
Dr. Edgar Fuller, American Council on Education. Chairman, Joint Committee on Educational Television. Member of Steering Committee of National Citizens Committee for Educational Television. Member of American Council on Education Committee on Educational Television.
Dr. Ray Maul, Assistant Director, Research Division, National Education Association.

8 **State College, Pennsylvania**
October 17
Dr. C. R. Carpenter, Chairman, Department of Psychology, Pennsylvania State College. Director, Pennsylvania State College Instructional Film Research Program.
Members of the staff of the Instructional Film Research Program.

9 **Trenton and Montclair, New Jersey**
November 4
Mr. Keeton Arnett, General Assistant to the President, Allen B. Du Mont laboratories, Inc.
Dr. Alan B. Du Mont, President, Allen B. Du Mont Laboratories, Inc.
Dr. Thomas T. Goldsmith, Jr., Vice-President in Charge of Research, Allen B. Du Mont Laboratories, Inc.
Dr. Charles W. Hamilton, Executive Secretary, New Jersey State Commission on Educational Television and Director of the Administrative Division of the New Jersey State Department of Education.
Mr. William King, Coordinator, Audio-Visual Education, New Jersey State Department of Education.
Dr. Robert H. Morrison, Assistant Commissioner of Higher Education in New Jersey.
Mr. Edward Rasp, Director, New Jersey Educational Television Station at New Brunswick.

10 **Trenton, New Jersey Stanford, Connecticut**
November 5
Dr. F. M. Raubinger, New Jersey State Commissioner of Education.
Dr. Jack Dunlap, President, Dunlap and Associates.
11 **New York City**
November 6
Dr. Frank Stanton, President, The Columbia Broadcasting System.
Members of the staff, New Jersey State Teachers College at Montclair.

Other Sources of Information

In addition to information acquired through conference with individuals this Preliminary Inquiry made use of the following sources:

1 Reports and personal accounts of the development of educational television by the Television Committee of the New Jersey State Teachers College at Montclair.
2 Published reports of activities and research relating to other specific educational television projects.
3 Published reports dealing with the supply and demand for trained teachers, with recent developments in the training of teachers, and with emergency provisions which are now being used where qualified teachers are not available.
4 Informally prepared information relating to television equipment and problems of production in educational television.

Section C

Perspectives

Television's Educational Role

Television has already arrived on the American scene. To those who are lately concerned with its impact the realistic question which its advent poses is not whether it shall be allowed to stay but what its roles shall be.

On the commercial side, television's role is rapidly becoming apparent to everyone who owns a receiving set. It is bringing to the home entertainment for which everyone used to sally forth; and it admits everyone without distinction to the halls and theaters and arenas. It brings information on all kinds of topics to the notice of all citizens, young and old. It brings cultural experiences that were formerly unattainable, and gives us, literally, our pick of the world's most gifted personalities and performers.

But does television have an educational role, quite apart from all this? Can television be used by the alert teacher to teach what needs to be learned, just as he skillfully uses a blackboard, a textbook, or a scale model? Or is educational television simply a matter of "leaving out the commercials."

In order to seek the answers to these questions it is necessary to disentangle ourselves from that resounding phrase, "mass communication media" and look at television in fresh perspective.

Suppose we started out by considering television as a *way of looking over the teacher's shoulder*. We might even call it a device for eliminating the back row of seats from any classroom.

Or suppose we conceptualized television as *a you-can-see-it-now device*, before which each viewer can share, moment-by-moment, the adventures of distant companions.

Then again, as we note television's capacity for packaging and presenting all conceivable combinations of sights and sounds, we might see it as *the new picture window built into the classroom*, through which even the most underprivileged child can look out on a breath-taking view of the world in which he lives.

And what if educational television should prove to be *the way to catch those rare and precious glimpses of the great teacher* at his best, teaching what he knows best in a moment of high enthusiasm?

But if educational television were to prove itself to be none of these, might it not still become *a visitor's card for all who seek admittance to the classroom*, a card for the parent who is interested in the 10 o'clock presentation of her child's history lesson, a card for the school administrator whose round of duties make him feel more and more out of touch with teaching, a card for the temporarily certificated teacher who has no other opportunity to take the teacher training course he needs.

All of this adds up to a simple proposition. Is educational television simply to be today's commercial television divested of its merchandizing endeavors, or is it to be approached afresh with wide-angled vision, vivid imagination, and keen criticism.

The Educational Scene

We have been talking about the possible role of educational television. Let us turn now and look at the scene in which it is to play its part—the schools.

Throughout the country the schools are being hard-pressed to keep their doors open to the unprecedented numbers of children who are swarming upwards through the grades. More classrooms and more trained teachers are urgently needed. But not nearly enough are available.

What are the schools doing about the situation?

1 They have created over-sized classes. For example, in New Jersey 39% of elementary schoolchildren were enrolled in classes during 1952–53 which contained thirty or more pupils.
2 They have employed teachers with sub-standard training. For example, The National Education Association estimates that 60,000 of the 160,000 new teachers needed this year should be taking the places of inadequately trained teachers who are already pressed into service. New Jersey reports that in 1952 approximately one teacher in eleven failed to meet the certification requirements of her job.
3 And in many instances the schools have put their teachers on double shifts, assigned classes to old schools and warehouses, or abandoned important features of their curricula.

There is no longer any point in talking about whether oversized classes can be taught as well as normal classes, or about whether partially trained teachers can do their job well enough to meet the standards of an enlightened society.

We already have oversized classes and, whether we like it or not, we are going to have many more of them.

We have already put a large proportion of education in the hands of teachers with sub-standard training and, inevitably, that proportion is going to increase.

These are harsh facts which will shatter any educational ideals which do not take them into account. So let's face them and see what defenses our ingenuity can provide.

The Role of the Teachers College

The teachers colleges of the country are the gateways through which teachers enter the teaching profession. They carry the principal responsibility for helping teachers achieve adequate standards of competence and, in a large measure, for recruiting young people to the profession. They hold a key position in helping education meet the challenge of increased enrollments.

Every oversized class which is organized creates a heavier teaching burden for which someone must eventually be trained. Every partially qualified teacher who is employed creates an urgent in-service training problem in the educational community.

The teachers colleges must not only train teachers who can carry these heavier teaching burden but they must actively concern themselves with all ingenious means of making those burdens bearable.

This is the point at which the more alert teachers colleges will start to inquire into the possibilities of educational television in all of its classroom aspects.

The present inquiry has to do with educational television in all of its classroom aspects. It is most particularly concerned with the elementary and secondary school levels and it approaches the various problems involved within the framework of the legitimate responsibilities of teacher education.

The Role of the New Jersey State Teachers College at Montclair

The New Jersey State Teachers College at Montclair has taken the initiative in exploring the educational possibilities of television in the schools. During the past three years it has developed certain preliminary educational television procedures, skilled personnel, and liaison relationships with schools and with the television industry.

The Du Mont Company has not only subsidized the College's efforts but has contributed its executive talents, its technical skill, and its technical training facilities to the initial development of the program. At one stage in the program the Kliegl Brothers Company lent the College valuable studio equipment.

Within the College the development was carried out through the cooperative efforts of a considerable proportion of the faculty and with the assistance of students. The faculty participants organized themselves into a Committee on Television in Education. In addition to exploring the uses of television in the classroom the Committee organized workshops for teachers in the area.

In the schools and cooperating communities the Committee organized special Area Committees to coordinate the efforts of the College. Certain school systems, notably those of Bloomfield, Clifton, and Montclair took steps to participate in the project officially.

Through this experience and this organization of resources the New Jersey State Teachers College at Montclair has established itself as a pioneer in the field of educational television in the classroom, a position which may be used as an appropriate springboard for a series of definitive studies of educational television.

Section D

Impact Areas

1 The Direct Impact of Educational Television on the Pupil

What is Being Done

There are numerous plans and rumors of plans shaping up for the use of television in the classrooms of the elementary and high schools. Very few of them have yet been put into operation. The programs of the Iowa State College at Ames and the Philadelphia Board of Education are two clear-cut examples of contrasting approaches.

The Ames program has developed long grass-roots lines. It is designed around the syllabus of the upper grades and the expressed wishes of the teachers who make use of it in their classrooms. The College keeps in continuous touch with teachers and pupils through a visiting representative. In spite of initial skepticism, communities were quick to make use of the broadcasts and there was a mad scramble to get television receiving sets into classrooms soon after the program got underway last year. It is estimated that 75,000 pupils now make use of the daily forty-five minute broadcast.

The Philadelphia program is an arm of the Public Relations Department and its composition reflects the mission of that Department. Emphasis is upon the enlistment and wide utilization of organized community resources. There is evidence indicating that the broadcasts are viewed in schools over a wide area adjacent to Philadelphia.

What is Known

Neither the Iowa program nor the Philadelphia program embodies any systematic plan for measuring the impact of educational television on the pupil-viewer.

As far as is known only university extension programs embody this feature. Iowa State College, Western Reserve University, and the University of Houston are examples. Their results are still inconclusive, primarily because of the viewer sampling biases and the novelty value of the medium. The trend of data, however, is in favor of the television viewer rather than the classroom participant. The trend is consistent with the results of Army and Navy studies.

Issues

1 *Learning and retention.* These are the conventional issues which are envisioned whenever some new instructional device is proposed. They have to do with speed, efficiency and accuracy of rote learning and the retention of content.
2 *Generalization of learning.* These issues have to do with the pupil's ability to make use of learned contents in various contexts, his perception of relationships to other content, his development of relevant skills, his application of the content to problem solving behavior, and his induction of principles.
3 *Motivation.* These issues have to do with the learner's acceptance of the instructional device, his spontaneous use of it, his interest in the material taught by means of the device, and his extra curricular application of the content.
4 *Action.* These issues have to do with the learner's decision-making and his choice of a stand to take when controversial social issues arise. With whom will he identify? What moral and ethical stand will be take? How will he commit himself? How will he express and act upon his convictions?
5 *Individual differences.* Which children respond best to the use of the device? How are the individual differences defined—in terms of intellectual ability, educational background, sensory capacity such as visual acuity, age, sex, vocational aspirations, etc.?

2 The Impact of Educational Television on the Individual Teacher

What is Being Done

A considerable number of television workshops have been organized for teachers during the past summer season. If the trend continues the number will increase greatly next year. Aside from these workshops there is no indication that there are any programs which are primarily designed to reach the individual teacher.

What is Known

In general teachers seem to be more receptive than are administrators and parents to the idea of using television in the classroom to lighten their load and improve their efficiency, if we may believe that the Iowa experience is representative. Moreover, attendance at workshops thrives when teachers have had access to television presentations and when they have been called upon to help plan programs for the ensuing year.

When we turn to university adult extension programs we find some examples of an interesting outcome, Western Reserve University has lost three of its television instructors to commercial television programs.

Issues

1. *Training for use.* What training and information needs to be provided to the individual teacher in order for her to make maximum use of the television presentation?
2. *Attitude.* What will be the individual teacher's response to the notion of television teacher? Will she initially resist it and then accept it? To what extent will she see herself in competition with the televised teacher? Will she spontaneously turn the set on?
3. *Capacity for use.* How much television presentation can the teacher absorb? What kinds of presentations can she utilize? To what extent can she adapt her procedures to the material made available by television? How do teachers differ from each other in respect to the use of television?
4. *Improvement of teaching.* To what extent will the individual teacher be motivated and assisted in the improvement of her own classroom techniques through having an opportunity to observe her children respond to televised presentations?

3 The Impact of Educational Television on the Teaching Profession

What is Being Done

The Central Michigan College of Education is conducting a project on the utilization of teacher competencies. The initial stage of the study involved a stop-watch time study of teachers' classroom activities. Upon the basis of the results it was hypothesized that, where classes were over-sized, "teachers' aides" might be employed to perform duties which might be less focal to the educational process. Nine teachers' aides are now employed in selected elementary school classrooms of Bay City, Michigan. The effects are currently being studied.

As far as is known there is, as yet, no parallel attempt to aim educational television at the teaching profession and the urgent problems which are currently confronting it.

What is Known

Three of the makeshift measures which are being employed because of the growing teacher shortage have profound implications for the morale of the teaching profession.

1. Large classes often make the teaching load unbearable. This fact is frequently cited by teachers who decide to abandon the profession in spite of the need for their services.
2. The employment of semi-trained teachers on an equal basis with teachers who have trained themselves seriously is demoralizing.
3. The abandonment of the more liberal arts in the curriculum reduces the teacher to teaching only the *what* of life but not the *why*. This tends to degrade the basic character of the professional services rendered in the classroom.

Some members of the teaching profession have mixed feelings toward the advent of educational television. Any suggestion that television might be used as a way of maintaining professional values in the face of makeshift emergency measures is met with apprehension lest it prove itself to be a robot competitor for the jobs of well-qualified teachers.

In some quarters this apprehension is so near panic proportions that it may lead to efforts to block both disinterested experimentation with educational television and the critical analysis of its actual classroom potentialities.

Except for these apprehensions, which are based wholly on speculation, there is very little actually known about educational television's impact on the teaching profession.

Issues

1. *Relation to the use of the teacher's time and competencies.* How may television presentations help the teacher redistribute her time among activities which are more central to her professional role? How may television make better use of the competencies of the more professionally advanced teacher? How may television make better use of the specialist teacher?
2. *Relation to excessively large classes.* What may television do to assist the teacher who has been assigned an oversized class? What kinds of presentation are most suited to the oversized class?
3. *Recognition for the better qualified teachers.* Can television add a vertical dimension to the teaching profession? Can it make it possible for a teacher to receive promotion on the basis of her teaching skills, rather than on the basis of administrative competence only?
4. *Professional prestige.* What will happen to the prestige of the teaching profession as the public is given a better chance to observe televised examples of the teacher at her best? Will it improve recruitment, as young people become intrigued with the skills and accomplishments of good teaching instead of being recruited, as they now are, by the rumored angelic values of the profession?

4 The Impact of Educational Television on Methods of Teacher Education

What is Being Done

The University High School of the University of Minnesota has been designed and equipped to enable teachers-in-training to observe classrooms from a remote point. The innovation was, in part, dictated by economic considerations; they had to choose between making the classrooms large enough to accommodate twenty-five to fifty observers in addition to the high school class and the use of television. They chose television.

Except for teacher training measures which are centered around demonstrating television to teachers, the Minnesota plan appears to be the only one which is directly concerned with the use of television to train teachers.

What is Known

The Minnesota plan has, at this writing, not yet mastered its technical problems. They are still hoping to use projection receivers with five or six foot screens. They also are limited to one camera, a limitation which prevents televising both the pupils' faces and what the pupils are looking at. Moreover, they are not yet able to use their camera to produce satisfactory pictures.

Neither the staff of the University School nor the Department of Education has yet given any thought to the experimental analysis of the effectiveness of their new procedure. When the question was raised, however, they clearly recognized that this was a defect in their approach and they indicated that they intended to get busy and design some experimental studies.

Issues

1 *Class observation.* To what extent can television be used to supplant direct observation of classrooms? Will there be less awareness of the response of individual members of the observed class or will it be possible for the observers to examine and discuss the individual reactions of pupils in greater detail? Will television enable the observer to observe more different classrooms in the same amount of time? Can kinescopes be used more effectively in this connection?

2 *Observation of the practice teacher.* Can television, either with or without kinescopes, contribute as much to the analysis and correction of the practice teacher's faults as sound recording has contributed to the training of interviewers? What may be the effect of teachers-in-training seeing each other's efforts kinescoped and criticized in staff conference? Can television enable one critic teacher to supervise several practice teachers more effectively?

3 *Training teachers to use television in their classrooms.* What kind of training programs need be installed in order to prepare teachers to use television presentations effectively?

4 *In service training.* How can television be used to provide in-service training for teachers? Can television courses be used to help a partially trained teacher to complete her training? Will the daily presentations in her classroom help bring the partially trained teacher up to an acceptable standard?

5 The Impact of Educational Television on the School Administrator

What is Being Done

The television program of the Philadelphia Board of Education is one type of approach to the problems of the school administrator. In this instance television is managed in the department of public relations and the presentations are designed with a keen eye on community reactions.

There is no indication that television is being used anywhere as a means to bring the administrator into closer contact with the classroom or the classroom teacher. The nearest parallel of such a usage comes from the published accounts of the Army's using television as a way of keeping field commanders in touch with developments during practice maneuvers.

What is Known

Even in Philadelphia, where there appears to be considerable sensitivity to community reactions, there is no body of precise information regarding the effectiveness of television in achieving their purposes. Perhaps the recent stampede to get an educational television station on the air is a clear enough indication that the program has been successful.

Issues

1 *Public relations.* What public relations problems may television help the school administrator to solve? What kind of school programs should he allow to be broadcast on open circuits? What amount of controversial material may be covered in a televised presentation? For example, are differences between the educational viewpoints of public and parochial schools likely to be accentuated by televised teaching? Will television give the superintendent a better access to the public when an educational issue is at stake?

2 *Supervision.* Will television enable the supervisors to keep in touch with the classroom problems of their teachers? Will television enable the superintendent to know more about what goes on in classrooms?

3 *Organization.* What kind of an administrative organization will the schools have to invent in order to carry on television activities? Who should be given the responsibility of developing educational television? What qualifications are needed in one who is to be given charge of the television program of the local schools? How should an evaluation program be organized locally?

4 *Cost.* What will be the cost of an adequate television program in a local school system? Can the cost be justified by the face-validity of the program? How should the cost of equipment be amortized?

6 The Impact of Educational Television on the Committee

What is Being Done

For the most part educational television is being directed toward the adult viewer. Universities are perceiving educational television within the framework of their extension courses for adults or in terms of their public service for special interest and occupational groups. Commercial television has directed some educational television toward the child viewer: Ding Dong School, Zoo Parade, Mr. Wizard, etc.

What is Known

Educational television which is designed for classrooms and which is broadcast may have some impact upon the community. The broadcasts of the Iowa State College are known to be having some effect upon the community. For one thing, they have aroused enough interest to lead many communities to scrounge for television receivers for which the regular school budget had made no provision. Yet this effect has not been systematically studied.

Issues

1 *Acceptance.* What will be the initial reaction of the public to the notion of installing television in the schools? What features of educational television will win general public acceptance? What kind of communications will be effective in bringing serious public appraisal of television?
2 *Attitudes toward the schools.* How will attitudes toward the schools be affected by the use of educational television in the classrooms? Can television be used effectively as a means of letting parents "visit" school? What will the community discover about what goes on in the schools from the use of television?
3 *Pre-school preparation.* Can television be used during the summer to prepare youngsters for their first days in school? Can they be given a preview of what school is like? Can television be used to help parents prepare their six-year old children for school? Can it be used to help parents set up an at-home nursery and pre-school program for their children?
4 *Parent education.* Can television be used to prepare parents to adjust to the changes which school may bring about with their children? Can it be used to show parents how they may best cooperate with the school in such matters as home-work, social adjustment, problems, participation in extra-mural activities, etc.?

7 The Impact of Educational Television on Ancillary Educational Specialties

What is Being Done

In the elementary and secondary school fields the coming of educational television has obviously had some effect upon the activities of the audio-visual aids specialist. In some schools television is simply classified as an audio-visual aid and let go at that. Where it is so conceived its field of usefulness has been correspondingly constricted.

Speech and dramatics specialists have been intrigued by television since it invites them to develop a new expressive form.

Intercollegiate sports are already feeling the impact of television. It is likely that any television station which is operated by the local schools will be expected to televise the local high school games. This raises, of course, financial issues for the athletic departments.

What is Known

While the speech people and the public relations people are showing some signs of reconceptualizing their jobs in the light of what television can do there is still little indication that audio-visual aids people, athletic coaches and other ancillary specialty groups have yet reconsidered their tasks in the light of television's possibilities—except, perhaps, to envision more hardware, bigger budgets, and larger cheering sections. Certainly there is no indication that any specialty group has yet been prodded into giving more than a passing thought to the systematic re-study of its ancillary functions.

Issues

1 *Audio-visual aids specialists.* What changes in the service functions of the audio-visual aids specialist will come about through the use of television? Will there be less emphasis upon packaged films and displays and more emphasis upon picking up "footage" for incorporation in forthcoming presentations and upon serving in a consultant capacity for the televised teacher? Will the artist become a part of the A-V Aids Specialist's staff? Will the film library be moved to the central Board of Education Office?
2 *Speech and dramatics specialists.* To what extent will speech and dramatics specialists be required in the production aspects of educational television? What new emphasis will be placed upon speech and dramatics training for all teachers who aspire to make television presentations? What contributions to studio design and equipment will be expected of members of this specialty?
3 *Fine arts specialists.* What part will fine arts specialists need to play in the production of classroom presentations? Can the three-dimensional possibilities of television be utilized to examine three-dimensional art? What part will music play?
4 *All specialists.* To what extent can television be used to bring special instruction to the classroom? Can the art supervisor who now spends half an hour a semester in each classroom use television to teach two half-hour sessions a week in every classroom?

8 The Impact of Educational Television on the Curriculum

What is Being Done

There is a slight trend, though still feeble, to plan educational television presentations in terms of a syllabus. Teachers occasionally point out the advantages of *syllabus programming* over *spot programming*.

The teachers in the Iowa State College viewing area occasionally mention the disadvantage of presenting each television course only once a week. However, there are production problems involved in presenting lessons in the same syllabus every day which have not yet been surmounted.

Experiments in educational television are still not far enough advanced to make use of kinescopes from the preceding curriculum cycle to fill in the syllabus.

There is no indication so far of any effort to re-conceptualize any part of the curriculum in the light of television, e.g., developing courses in current affairs.

What is Known

Educators appear to be generally unaware of the possibility that educational television has implications for the curriculum. Hence there is no indication that anyone is asking what the impact will be, much less planning any systematic inquiry. This is surprising in view of the emphasis that progressive educators usually place upon re-conceptualizing the curriculum in terms of contemporary culture.

Issues

1 *What subjects.* What subjects can best be taught by television? What modes of presentation are suitable for different subjects? What limitations in subject matter must be recognized? What new subjects become feasible in the light of television? Can tests be satisfactorily administered by television, as in one military experiment?

2 *Design of syllabi.* What is the effect of *syllabus planning* of educational television versus the *spot program* or "one show package?" How should syllabi be planned? Can last year's kinescopes be used? Is it necessary to stick with the sacred one-year cycle in spiraling the curriculum? Can a single syllabus be planned for two, three or four grades to be spanned in the same presentation? Will it be necessary to transmit several presentations simultaneously in order to span all grade levels during the hours of the school day?

3 *Reflection of teacher opinion.* Can television presentations be organized around a continuous feed-back of responses from the teachers who use them? How can this teacher reaction best be sounded? How can it best be incorporated into the television syllabus? Can the presenting teacher be kept in touch with a sample of viewing teachers on a day-by-day basis?

4 *Study guides.* What is the role of study guides for the teacher who uses television? How should such guides be prepared? Should they be in the nature of pupil workbooks? How far in advance should they be distributed?

5 *Preparation and discussion.* What forms of preparation are necessary to enable the pupil to make the most out of a televised presentation? What kinds of subsequent discussion and activity are needed to give him closure on the presentation?

6 *Length of presentation.* How long should presentations be? How much total viewing time per day is desirable? Should a subject be presented daily or once a week only?

7 *Relation to the regular curriculum.* How closely should the televised presentations be tied to the syllabi of the grade for which they are planned? Can the presentations be timed to correspond to classroom assignments? To what extent can the teacher rely wholly upon televised presentations to expound a given topic?

9 The Impact of Educational Television on School Architecture

What is Being Done

Here is an area where the impact of television is producing some new ideas. Mr. Frank Lloyd Wright, in a recent telecast, took cognizance of the influence of educational television on the architectural design of schools. Already provision is being made for co-axial cable installations in some new buildings.

The new University High School Building at the University of Minnesota shows the possible effects of television plans on the lighting of classrooms both artificial and natural, upon the shape of classrooms—deep and square rather than rectangular—location of stairways—to keep traffic noise down—, and the space planning for transmitter equipment.

What is Known

A cursory survey of the completed building at the University of Minnesota suggests that it will require considerable experimentation and much more thought before the problems of architectural design for television-equipped school buildings will be solved. Experience thus far suggests that the most difficult problems will be those of lighting in rooms where cameras are used. There also will be problems in providing satisfactory camera angles and in moving cameras from room to room. The acoustical problems may not be so difficult but they are still a long way from being solved.

Issues

1 *Space.* What sizes and shapes of classrooms lend themselves to the use of television, both for televising and receiving? What arrangement of rooms is required? What additional space is required for the equipment? What studio space is needed?

2 *Lighting.* How should natural light be controlled? What artificial lighting fixtures should be installed? Can the needs of television and the visual needs of pupils be compromised?

3 *Acoustics*. What design and materials should be used in the classroom to meet the acoustical requirements of television? How should traffic noise be controlled? How can operations noises be controlled, e.g., noise of machines in a shop class?
4 *Wiring*. What electrical circuits must be installed to provide for television? What roof antennae are needed? How can the needs of television be combined with the needs of an intercommunication system?
5 *Building location*. If reception is to be by microwave or some other closed-circuit device location of the building may be a consideration.

10 The Impact of Educational Television on the Design and Packaging of Transmitting, Receiving and Studio Equipment

What is Being Done

Television transmission equipment is still undergoing comparatively rapid technological changes. This seems to be even more true in the area of kinescope equipment. Except for the imminent color receivers, it is somewhat less true of receiving equipment.

School budgets are badly strained these days and the cost of television transmitting and studio equipment seems both prohibitive and wholly unjustifiable to most school boards. Moreover the rapid technological advances add enormously to the depreciation of any equipment purchased.

The result is that the relationship between manufacturers of equipment and the vast number of potential purchasers of educational television equipment is relatively at a stalemate.

What is Known

Schools are not convinced that the cost of equipment is justified by its probable contribution to education. Manufacturers lack the basic human engineering data to design equipment, plan studios, and put together merchandising packages which are specifically designed for educational use and educational pocketbooks. The usual manufacturer's procedure of letting the consumer purchase equipment and seeing how he gets along with it may not work in this case or at this stage of the game. A more systematic human engineering study of the problem may be needed.

Issues

1 *Receivers*. How large a tube face is needed in the classroom? Can multiple receivers be used in the same classroom? Can projection screens be used effectively? What kind of cabinet design will meet the classroom's need for mobility, safety from shock protection, protection from theft, and teacher control of tuning?
2 *Transmitters*. What kind of transmitter equipment can be packaged for school systems of different sizes? Can the equipment be designed so that the school may add on piece by piece? Can equipment be designed which can be operated and maintained by semi-skilled technicians and teachers? What kind of equipment is best suited to educational presentations?
3 *Studios*. What kind of studio equipment is needed for educational television? How mobile can the studio equipment be made and still provide for acceptable production and transmission? Can studio equipment be designed which can be used in existing space and with existing electrical circuits?

11 Technical Problems in Educational Television Transmission and Reception

What is Being Done

For the most part the technical headaches of television transmission are now being borne by commercial studios. They have the technical equipment and personnel and, for the most part, do not have to get along with a bare minimal supply of either.

When we turn to educational television equipment which is owned and operated by educational institutions we encounter difficulties. There are problems of installation, operation and maintenance which schools appear to be disposed to handle with non-specialized personnel. In most instances students are being used or, at least, are expected to be used.

What is Known

The Iowa State College experience is largely negative with respect to the use of student technical personnel. They have students but they say the students actually make no contribution to the operation of the station—even get in the way. Yet most plans for educational television contemplate the use of students or teachers with audio-visual aid backgrounds.

As for the transmission of television over closed circuits there are problems of public right-of-way and use of micro-wave equipment about which almost nothing is known, except that the rental of common carrier-owned circuits is quite costly.

Issues

1 *Personnel*. What kind of personnel are needed for the operation and maintenance of equipment? Can such personnel be trained locally? What union jurisdictional problems are involved?

2 *Signal.* To what extent can satisfactory signals be originated in local schools? Can all the receivers be kept operative at all times?
3 *Repair equipment.* What kind of repair and shop equipment is needed in a school television set-up? What is the cost of maintenance? How much stand-by equipment is needed?
4 *Kinescopes.* It may be that the use of kinescopes will be a particularly important feature of educational television. Can these be produced locally? What kind of personnel would be needed? What would be the cost?
5 *Special displays.* Educational television may make considerable use of slides, film and opaque projections. What problems of personnel and equipment arise when the school undertakes to transmit this kind of material?
6 *The use of closed versus open circuits.* If the demands of a multi-level curriculum require the simultaneous presentation of several programs by a school system, what technical facilities and what special adaptations of them must be undertaken? Will multiple studio facilities be required or may it be possible to use one studio for "live" shows while other channels are transmitting kinescopes which have been prepared previously?

12 Production Problems in Educational Television

What is Being Done

For the most part educational television is making use of "talent" from its own classrooms—teachers and students. The Army and Navy experience, together with the experience of nearly all other ventures emphasizes the drift away from the use of "actors" or "personalities." Western Reserve University opinion is particularly emphatic in this regard. An experienced research worker in still another context said,

> "The first consideration is to have a teacher who knows what he is talking about and can talk about what he knows."

There is also a trend in some quarters away from the rehearsed presentation. This puts the cameraman and the director in a new role—more like that of the news cameraman who cannot demand that things happen in certain ways but must make sure that he captures what is actually going on.

What is Known

The Army and Navy research indicates that dramatization, as contrasted with demonstration and exposition, has questionable educational value. It also suggests that "fluffs" add, rather than detract, from the teaching effectiveness of the presentation.

The planning of educational presentations, even though they are not rehearsed, requires a great deal of production staff time. At the Iowa State College it requires approximately 10 times as much staff to produce an hour of television as it does to produce an hour of radio program. In television, instead of "script writers" one has "production teams." This contrast is particularly marked in educational television vs. educational radio.

In educational television which is *syllabus planned* the typical production for the upper grades requires a weeks's preparation by a teacher assisted by a team comprised of part-time assistants. One teacher who is regularly engaged in preparing and presenting educational telecasts said that the team should be comprised of the following:

1 A television man who knows the medium
2 A television technician
3 A librarian and resources consultant
4 A teacher who is familiar with teachers' general needs, e.g., a teacher training supervisor
5 An artist for preparing displays
6 An educational principles man who understands the curriculum and the development of an educational philosophy

Issues

1 *The production team.* How should the production team be organized? What should be the role of the teacher? What consultant services are required in preparing a presentation?
2 *Types of effective production.* What kinds of presentation lend themselves to the television medium? Which are easiest to produce? How much rehearsal is desirable? Should pupils play a part in the presentation?
3 *The televised teacher.* Should an attempt be made to build up the "personality" of the teacher in the televised series? What kind of a person makes the best presentation? Should the televised teacher have a full-time assignment to television or should she be assigned on a part-time or intermittent basis?
4 *Budgeting productions.* How can productions be budgeted? How good a presentation can be offered on a given budget?
5 *Coordination with technical staff.* Does the educational presentation require the camera operator and the technical director to redefine their roles? What should be the emphasis upon technical and production perfection? Do "fluffs" interfere with the educational effectiveness of the presentation?
6 *Kinescope versus "live" productions.* Is it necessary to use "live" productions at all? If kinescopes can be used exclusively for classroom presentation will it solve the problem of staffing the studio with teachers who are regularly on duty in their own classrooms

during school hours? How soon does a kinescope film become obsolete for classroom use? What kinds of material must be presented in a "live" program and what kind may be presented year after year in the same kinescope film?

Section E

Approach to Research

Experimentation or Evaluation

One way to approach educational research is to get up early on Monday morning and say, "Let's see what would happen if......?" Another is to wait until late Friday afternoon, wake up and mumble, "Wha' happen'd?"

The former leads to *experimentation*, the latter to what is loosely called, *evaluation*. Both procedures have their proper place. But experimentation is ordinarily the more dependable approach if one expects to do something as a result of what he finds out.

The proposed project has been envisioned as an *experimental project*. This means that much of it will be based on Monday morning questions. It also means that the design will employ both statistical and experimental controls and that some of the variables, such as the type of television production, types of classroom procedures, etc. will be deliberately and systematically manipulated.

From such a study one learns, not whether educational television is vaguely "a good thing" or not, but exactly *which* of certain specifically defined procedures are better in exactly *what* ways.

What to Test

The preceding sections on the impacts of educational television do not cover all the issues but they should suffice to indicate the scope and variety of problems which are tied up with educational television.

It will not be feasible for any given research project to try to give a specific practical answer to all questions which have been raised. Rather, it must do two things:

1 Abstract the complex technical issues and restate them in terms of simple alternative principles.
2 Test the principles with well-designed experiments.

Example

For example, a research team might be assigned the topical area of "teaching arithmetic by means of television." Instead of designing an elaborate experiment around all the permutations of arithmetic topics, grade levels, teachers, modes of presentation, and pupil IQ, the team might decide on the basis of preliminary study to *abstract two rival hypothetical principles*, such as the following:

1 "Formalized abstractions, such as those involved in fourth, fifth and sixth grade arithmetic, can be learned solely from a carefully ordered series of concrete presentations, such as it is possible to make over television."
2 "Formalized abstractions, such as those involved in fourth, fifth and sixth grade arithmetic, cannot be learned from concrete presentations, such as it is possible to make over television, except as provision is made for the pupil to manipulate the symbols actively in a problem-solving situation."

Having set up two rival but testable hypotheses it then becomes feasible to design a straight-forward experiment to determine which of them best explains the facts. The experimenters would use, of course, a television presentation and mathematical content.

The operating design of the experiment would be somewhat more complicated than our illustration might imply on first reading. Our point is, however, that unless such an approach is used by the research teams participating in this project, the whole undertaking may bog down in a mass of particulars.

The Nucleus of Good Research

Research is not merely a technical job of amassing data and subjecting it to *post hoc* mathematical analysis. The key to good research is the ability to formulate *ad hoc* hypotheses which are at once both significant and testable.

This requires the preliminary study of the practical setting of the issues and the combined efforts of imaginative research workers. Once the hypotheses are formulated by such thoughtful people and the experiments built around them by individuals who are skilled in the logic of experimental design, the systematic collection of data begins to take on meaning.

In the light of these research concepts it becomes clear that the nucleus of any comprehensive research project is a staff of competent research workers organized into teams to attack problem areas.

Experimental Designs

The writing of experimental designs follows upon the definition of relevant variables and hypotheses. Where several comparable variables and hypotheses are tested on comparable sub-samples it is ordinarily possible to economize by employing *Analysis of Variance* designs. In a project of this type, where there is a complex of related issues, it should be possible to use the *Latin Square* design to test a number of hypotheses simultaneously.

Fortunately, many of the more concrete problems in educational television should be solvable in terms of simple counting of cases. Such data often do not need any more complicated statistical treatment than the use of *Chi-Square*.

It should be possible to report some of the outcomes of the experiment in terms of *qualitative description* only. Whenever this can be done reliably it is, economically, the procedure of choice. For example, some of the production and human engineering issues might be resolved by means of descriptive reports only.

As much as possible in this type of research the staff member should avoid highly theoretical issues in the field of social science, except as those issues must inevitably be faced in providing dependable information to their sponsors. The interrelationships which are finally reported should be of such a level of simplicity and manageability as to be readily applied by all persons who need to make use of the results of the study.

Measurement Techniques

In a comprehensive project of this type the experimental and control variables come in all shapes and sizes. The yardsticks with which they are measured must therefore be tailored to the precision of measurement required and to the concrete palpability of the things measured.

For example, in measuring the effect of television instruction on pupil acceptance and retention, it may be necessary to determine *precisely* the differential amounts of information retained following a lesson but to measure *in gross units only* the pupils' acceptance of the lesson presentation. As for adjusting the yardsticks to palpability, one might use conventional academic test items to measure the retention of *rote content* but be forced to resort to the more subtle projective approaches in assessing the retention of the more elusive *attitudes*.

It is not desirable, therefore, to specify in advance the precise nature of the yardsticks which shall be used. The designing of measuring instruments is a major task of scientific conceptualization and should always proceed apace with the emerging ideas of the research staff.

Section F

Recommendations

1 First Recommendation: Feasibility

It is recommended that the College continue with its plans and efforts to study the uses of educational television in the classroom but that it envisions budget requirements which will more realistically reflect inevitable costs.

Discussion of the First Recommendation

First of all, the minimum investment in technical equipment would have to be greater than anything thus far perceived by the College. Once this equipment is purchased and installed it would be economically unwise not to make proper use of it in finding the answers to the basically important questions about educational television in the classroom.

This means, therefore, that the investment in equipment should be balanced by a commensurate effort along research lines. The facts which are now apparent indicate that, in launching a program extending, say, five years, one should foresee a possible total outlay approaching a million and a half dollars.

(Detailed breakdowns of estimated costs are presented as part of a later recommendation.)

2 Second Recommendation: Definition and Objectives

It is recommended that the College propose that the television project be defined as follows:

A Study of the Effectiveness of Television in Relation to Current Problems in Teaching

and that the following stated objectives be pursued:

a To formulate and test basic principles relating to the impact of television in the following 12 problem areas:

1 The pupil
2 The individual teacher
3 The teaching profession
4 Methods of teacher education
5 School administration
6 The constituent community
7 Ancillary educational specialties
8 The curriculum

9 School architecture
10 Educational television equipment
11 Educational television transmission
12 Educational television production

b To inquire specifically into the ways in which the above principles may be applied to correct educational malpractices growing out of the rapidly expanding people enrollments or applied to alleviate the effects of such malpractices.
Four types of malpractice would be given explicit attention:
1 The creation of over-sized classes under conditions which are clearly detrimental to the educational progress of the pupil and to the professional needs of the teacher.
2 The employment of teachers with sub-standard qualifications under conditions which are incompatible with good teaching.
3 The assignment of teachers to double shifts of duty which demonstrably interfere with the proper discharge of their professional obligations to individual pupils.
4 The abandonment of important features of the curriculum.

c To make all findings of the study available to the teaching profession in a maximally usable form.

Discussion of the Second Recommendation

It has become abundantly clear during this Preliminary Inquiry that the College should exercise considerable caution and foresight in defining the project. In scientific inquiry the definitions of questions not only limit the scope of their answers but may actually cause the answers to imply distortions of basic truths.

If this project is defined, say, as, "a study of how television can replace teachers," or even as, "a study of television in relation to the shortage of teachers," it will be immediately interpreted in some important educational quarters as being the effort of a pressure group to produce distorted answers through a narrow definition of the research problem.

For example, under either of these definitions, any finding of the usefulness of television would imply that less emphasis need now be placed on the recruitment, training and employment of teachers. But perhaps the basic truth behind the findings would be that television requires a shift in the teacher's role from that of a rostrum lecturer and blackboard artist to that of a skilled educational adviser to the individual pupil.

The public relations, both of the College and of the Fund for the Advancement of Education, would suffer immensely as a result of adopting either of these definitions. Moreover, the research itself would suffer because of its limitation to matters of purely technical facilitation.

But this need not happen. The long-range aspirations of the teaching profession and the public service objectives of the Fund lie in exactly the same direction—better education for the pupil. It is only necessary to make entirely clear with what levels of scientific conceptualization and with what degree of public responsibility the matter of educational television is being approached.

The project is to be a *research* project. As such it is concerned with the formulation and testing of basic principles involved in the classroom use of television, followed by the experimental application of those principles to the solution of certain acute problems which confront American education today. This approach to a problem is the way of science and it stands in sharp contrast to the partisan hit-and-miss efforts to reduce school taxes or to demonstrate that teachers can be purchased at the local furniture store.

From the researcher's point of view the study might eventually accomplish both of these partisan ends or it might accomplish neither; that remains to be seen. He will insist only that the problem should be initially defined in terms which will permit the specific technological issues to be spelled out as the study progresses.

Relation to the "Bay City" Project

The project now underway at the Central Michigan College of Education and the Bay City (Michigan) Public Schools is dealing with closely related problems. The project is entitled, "A cooperative study of the utilization of teacher competences" and is subsidized by the Fund for the Advancement of Education.

The "Bay City Project" is viewed in some quarters with a skepticism which approaches downright suspicion. The managers of the project have done a good job of translating much of the skepticism into testable hypotheses and persuading the skeptics to let the answers ride on the experimental outcomes.

In order to do this they have had to convene, at considerable expense, a large "advisory panel" representing a great variety of educational interests, and sell the members on the idea of letting the experiment answer their misgivings. The size of the advisory panel is, of course, grossly out of proportion to the amount and kinds of advice actually needed. Indeed the study has several times as many advisers as it has experimental subjects. Public relations hazards, however, make the investment in the advisory panel necessary.

The proposed television study must and should be carried out in close liaison with the "Bay City Project" because of its correlated issues. But for the time being, this liaison must be accepted as a public relations hazard, both for the Fund and for the College.

3 Third Recommendation: Development

It is recommended that the College confine its initial television presentations to closed circuits leading to a limited number of selected classrooms and that it gradually expands its operations to include more classrooms, more grade levels, and more subjects of instruction only as the research requirements dictate.

Discussion of the Third Recommendation

a Closed Circuits

Even if it were possible to establish an educational television broadcasting station at the College at the present time it would not be advisable, from the standpoint of the research project, to do so. The operation of a broadcasting station involves certain public responsibilities for keeping a program going all day, for giving everybody a little bit of something rather than dealing intensively with a selected group, and for making the broadcasts equally available to all viewers. All of these requirements militate against controlled experimental research.

b Fifth Grade Social Studies at the Bradford School

The College originally planned the project to start with social studies at the fifth grade level. This is a good choice. Children of the fifth grade are at an age when they are articulate about what they observe. The area of social studies also provides subject matter about which children can easily express their reactions. These facts suggest the advantage of starting with fifth grade social studies in exploring the effectiveness of classroom television.

The Bradford School of Montclair, being close to the College campus, is a logical choice for the first school to be involved in the experiment. It should be relatively easy to carry on the initial exploratory interviewing of pupils, teachers and parents in this community.

c Subsequent Grades, Subjects and Schools

As the experiment progresses other grade levels may be brought into the study. The experimentation may be extended both upward and downward through the grades. As high school grade levels are incorporated into the study the experimenters should have already acquired experience with additional kinds of subject matter in the upper elementary grades.

d Use of Kinescope Films

The experiment will need to make extensive use of kinescopes. This will permit the more careful experimental control of features which go into the presentations. It also will permit the re-running of presentations under varying classroom conditions.

e Use of Other Educational Television Facilities

When it becomes necessary to present certain programs to larger viewing groups it would be advisable for the College to utilize the facilities of such stations as the New Jersey State Station at New Brunswick or Station WOI-TV at Ames, Iowa. Selected kinescopes prepared at Montclair can be presented to large-N samples through such stations as these. In this way the Research Project can avoid the distracting burden of having to undertake large-scale operations itself.

4 Fourth Recommendation: Organization

It is recommended that the staff of the project be organized into five operating units—research, professional relations, production, technical operations, and sub-contracts—an administrative unit, a panel of *expert consultants, and a policy advisory board.*

The following table of organization is recommended:

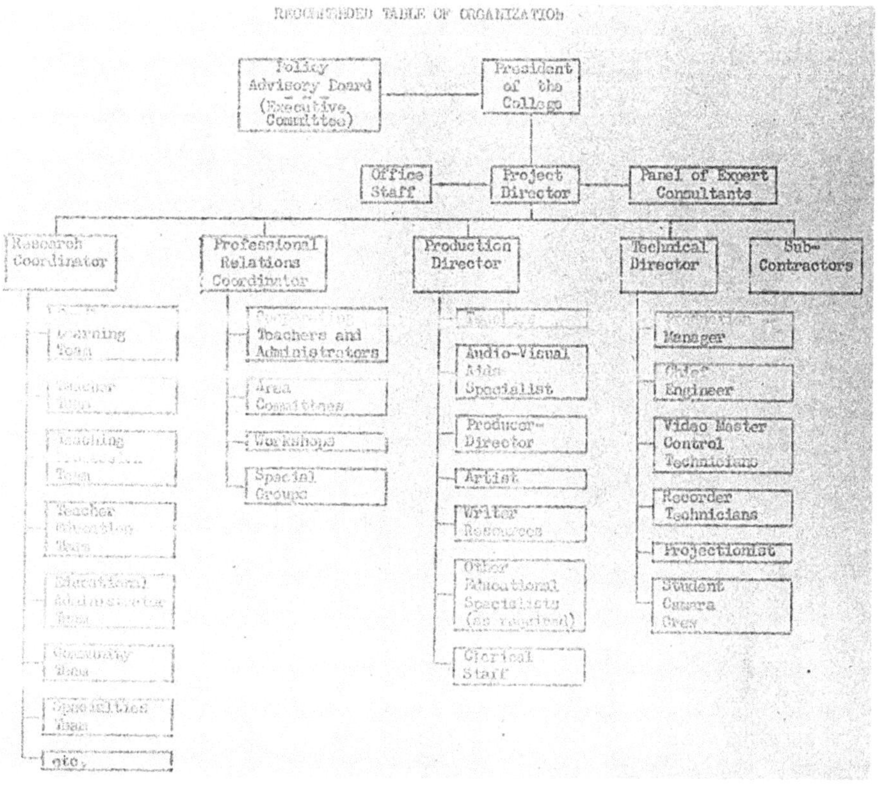

Discussion of the Fourth Recommendation

Policy Advisory Board

It is recommended that this Board be advisory to the President in matters of policy. It is recommended that three members of the Board, each representing a different interest group, constitute an "executive committee" which would be advisory to the President in matters of interim policy.

It is recommended that this Board be comprised of twenty to thirty members representing the following interest groups:

1 The Education Profession
  a The National Education Association
  b The American Council on Education and N.J.E.A.
  c The American Association of Colleges of Teacher Education
  d The New Jersey State Department of Education
  e The American Federation of Teachers
2 The Television Industry
3 Organized Research Agencies
4 Related Special Projects in Current Operation
  a The "Bay City" Project

Administrative Unit

The Administrative Unit would have responsibility for implementing policy as defined by the President of the College. The Project Director would define the areas of activity of the subordinate units, coordinate that activity in the interest of the project as a whole, and facilitate the work of the units by budgeting funds, by authorizing purchases of equipment and supplies, and by employing expert consultants when needed. The Project Director would be directly responsible to the President.

Panel of Expert Consultants

It is recommended that a panel of expert consultants in various specialties be developed as the project progresses. Individuals from this panel may be asked to spend certain amounts of time in service to the project as required by the Project Director.

Research Unit

The recommended primary emphasis of this project is research which is competently conceived and skillfully executed. The task of the other units in the table of organization will be to provide the Research Unit with an adequate background of competent advice and to make sure that experimental designs which it prepares are faithfully executed.

As suggested before the Research Unit should be comprised of a staff of competent research workers organized into teams and assigned to problem areas. A team would normally be comprised of a senior scientist and two half-time graduate assistants.

It is recommended that the Research Unit be established as a *departmentalized staff type of organization* with each research team functioning relatively autonomously within its assigned problem area. The activities of the teams would be coordinated by the Research Director. The Research Director would approve and recommend to the Project Director the implementation of experimental designs proposed by the various teams.

1 The crucial task of these teams would be to formulate, within their assigned problem areas, rival hypothetical principles which will be both educationally significant and experimentally testable.
2 The secondary task of these teams would be to design experiments around these hypotheses.
3 The final task of these teams would be to collect and analyze relevant data.

Professional Relations Unit

We have mentioned the necessity for making preliminary studies of the practical setting in which the issues arise. Since the project cannot be expected to move ahead on all fronts at once, it will be necessary to maintain these studies of the practical setting on a continuing basis.

One of the services which will be needed by the research teams is an active *Professional Relations Unit.*

It is recommended that the Professional Relations Unit be established as a *conference staff type of organization.* Subordinate units would be fluid and the emphasis would be upon the formulation and exchange of ideas.

1 The primary task of the Professional Relations Unit would be to keep the research teams fully aware of all practical problems relating to educational television as they arise in the schools, in the committees, among administrators, and in the teaching profession at large. The Unit would be responsible for keeping the staff alert to issues arising both on a local and on a national scale.

2 The Unit would be responsible for keeping in contact with all persons and groups who have a particular stake in the outcome of the project, for making sure that such groups are articulate in expressing their reactions to representatives of the project, and for communicating the results of all its inquires to the coordinator of the Research Unit.
3 The Unit would have the task of keeping in contact with the teachers who use television in their classrooms and of making sure that the productions are utilized in the schools in accordance with the experimental design.

Production Unit

There must be a phenomenon to be evaluated and in order to produce that phenomenon in its best possible form the project will need an effective Production Unit. The Unit would be built around the most competent teachers available, together with Consultants in various specialties such as audio-visual aids, speech, etc. Part of the Unit would be organized into production teams.

It is recommended that the Production Unit be established as a *departmentalized line type of organization*. Production teams would be organized but would operate under the immediate direction of the Production Director.

1 The primary task of the Production Unit would be to implement the experimental designs required by the project's mission.
2 The Unit would plan, package, and present instructional lessons.
3 The Unit would be expected to conceive and develop new techniques of television instruction.
4 The Unit would keep the Research Unit advised regarding the feasibility of making certain types of presentations.
5 The Unit would staff and plan the syllabi for teachers' workshops in educational television.

Technical Unit

Research, professional relations and production would all fail in their purpose if the television signal did not reach the viewer. The Technical Unit will need to assume a rather broad range of responsibilities in that connection.

It is recommended that the Technical Unit be established as a *straight line type of organization*. Each member of the Unit should be assigned within a clear administrative hierarchy and the Unit should be organized for immediate and effective action at all times.

1 The primary task of the Technical Unit would be to see that what is produced appears on designated receiving sets.
2 The Unit would be responsible for coordinating its efforts with the Production Unit in accordance with the experimental design.
3 The Unit would install, operate, and maintain studio, transmitting and receiving equipment.
4 The Unit would be expected to conceive and develop new techniques appropriate to educational television.
5 The Unit would keep the Research Unit advised regarding new technical developments and the feasibility of transmitting certain types of productions.

Sub-Contractors

It is recommended that wherever an organization is prepared to conduct a study of some phase of the problem of educational television economically arrangements be made a write such a sub-contract.

For example, it appears likely that the University of Minnesota is prepared to study certain phases of teacher education in its new television-equipped high school. The Iowa State College has the staff and the large viewing population for conducting certain large sample studies of pupil response and community reaction. The Pennsylvania State College has a laboratory and trained staff for evaluating kinescopes. Dunlap and Associates have the experience and the know-how to design and execute human engineering studies of television equipment.

5 Fifth Recommendation: Operating Schedules and Budget

It is recommended that the following operating schedules and budget be tentatively adopted and revised from time to time in the light of experience.

Recommended
Operating Schedules
Fiscal years ending June 30

Item	*1954*	*1955*	*1956*	*1957*	*1958*
Hours of production	16	78	134	134	54
Hours camera time	230	900	1100	1100	440
Hours kinescope recording	16	60	100	100	27
Hours kinescope presentation	0	18	148	148	60
Schools in Montclair closed circuits	1	3	5	8	8
Hrs. kines. farmed out for large N	0	9	36	36	18
Research terms activated full time	0	2	4	4	4
Research teams activated part time	2	4	4	4	4
Sub-contracts in operation	0	3	4	3	0

Summary of Recommended Budget Requirements
(Details on following pages)
Fiscal Years Ending June 30

Item	*1954*	*1955*	*1956*	*1957*	*1958*	*Total*
Administrative Unit						
Equipment	1,400	500	250	250	100	2,500
Operations	40,360	90,760	92,200	90,940	83,280	397,540
Research Unit						
Equipment	1,800	2,400	2,400	1,050	1,000	8,650
Operations	9,250	50,550	74,600	79,800	84,250	298,450
Production Unit						
Equipment	6,320	3,550	2,850	2,000	600	15,320
Operations	8,740	22,700	30,170	31,070	15,510	108,190
Technical Unit						
Equipment	171,560	20,000	21,000	21,000	3,000	236,560
Operations	23,850	66,000	77,000	83,600	41,800	292,250
Professional Relations Unit						
Equipment						
Operations	790	1,820	1,820	2,020	2,820	9,270
Sub-contracting Unit						
Operations		30,000	50,000	40,000		120,000
TOTALS	264,070	288,280	352,290	351,730	232,360	1,488,730

Remaining value of technical equipment	50,000
Remaining values of other equipment	5,350
	55,350

NET TOTAL COST 1,433,380

Recommendation: Operative Schedules and Budget
Recommended Budget For
Administrative Unit
Fiscal Years Ending June 30

Item	*1954*	*1955*	*1956*	*1957*	*1958*
Equipment					
Office furniture ($100/person)	600	100			
Typewriters	450	150			
Duplicator	250				
Files	50	50			
Equipment contingency	50	200	250	250	100
TOTAL BY YEARS	1,400	500	250	250	100
TOTAL FOR 4½ YRS. OPERATION					2,500

Operations					
Director	11,200	22,400	22,400	22,400	22,400
Coordinator of Research		12,000	12,300	12,600	12,900
Director of Production	5,000	10,300	10,600	11,200	5,900
Technical Director	3,000	6,250	6,500	6,750	3,500
Coordinator Prof. Relations	3,000	6,250	6,500	6,750	7,000
Clerical Staff	2,860	5,960	6,200	6,440	6,680
Travel	5,000	8,600	8,600	8,600	8,600
Advisory Board					
Conferences	1,500	3,000	3,000	3,000	3,000
Coordination with Bay City Project	2,000	3,000	3,000		
Supplies, postage, telephone	300	500	600	700	800
Fiscal & inventory clerical costs	1,500	2,500	2,500	2,500	2,500
General contingency	5,000	10,000	10,000	10,000	10,000
TOTALS BY YEARS	40,360	90,760	92,200	90,940	83,280
TOTALS FOR 4½ YRS. OPERATION					397,540

Recommended Budget For
Research Unit
Fiscal Years Ending June 30

	1954	1955	1956	1957	1958
Equipment					
Office furniture ($100/person)	200	900	600		
Calculators	750		750		
Typewriters	300	450			
Files	50	50	50	50	
Equipment contingency	500	1,000	1,000	1,000	1,000
TOTALS BY YEARS	1,800	2,400	2,400	1,050	1,000
TOTAL FOR PROJECT					8,650
Operations					
Full-time research teams (One full-time sr. scientist & two half-time grad. assistants)		20,000	40,600	41,800	43,000
Part-time research teams	5,000	20,000	20,600	21,200	21,800
Interviewers & test technicians	200	1,000	2,000	4,000	2,000
Statistical clerks			500	1,000	3,000
Secretarial assistance	1,100	4,600	5,000	5,400	7,600
IBM services			500	1,000	1,000
Local travel for surveys, etc.	100	300	500	500	500
Memberships, books, periodicals	150	150	150	150	100
Research consultants	2,000	3,000	3,000	3,000	3,000
Supplies	200	500	750	750	750
Operations contingency	500	1,000	1,000	1,000	1,500
TOTALS BY YEARS	9,250	50,550	74,600	79,800	84,250
TOTAL FOR PROJECT					298,450

Recommendations: Operating Schedules and Budget
Recommended Budget For
Professional Relations Unit
Fiscal Years Ending June 30

Item	*1954*	*1955*	*1956*	*1957*	*1958*
Operations					
Area Committee Meetings	300	600	600	600	600
Workshops	100	300	300	300	300
Local mileage 7c/ml.	140	420	420	420	420
Printing and postage	250	500	500	700	1,500
Equipment (none)					
TOTALS BY YEARS	790	1,820	1,820	2,020	2,820
TOTAL FOR 4½ YRS. OPERATION					9,270

Recommendations: Operating Schedules and Budget
Recommended Budget For
Production Unit
Fiscal Years Ending June 30

Item	*1954*	*1956*	*1956*	*1957*	*1958*
Equipment					
Sets and props.	1,000	1,800	1,800	1,200	500
Art equipment	500	500	250	250	
Motion picture equipment	3,920	500	500	250	
Office furniture ($100/person)	400	300			
Typewriters	300	150			
Equipment contingency	200	300	300	300	100
TOTALS BY YEARS	6,320	3,550	2,850	2,000	600
TOTAL FOR 4½ YRS. OPERATION					15,320

Recommendations: Operating Schedules and Budget
Recommended Budget For
Production Unit
Fiscal Years Ending June 30

Item	*1954*	*1956*	*1956*	*1957*	*1958*
Operations (Supplies)					
Film supplies	1,830	1,830	1,200	600	
Art supplies	200	150	150	150	100
Audio-visual rentals	100	500	500	500	100
Local mileage at 7c	210	420	420	420	210
Operations contingency	300	500	500	500	200
(Personnel)					
Teachers	2,500	10,200	10,600	11,200	5,600
Audio-visual specialists	1,000	2,100	4,400	4,600	2,400
Producer-Directors		1,500	3,200	3,400	1,800
Artists	750	1,600	3,400	3,600	1,900
Writers and sources	750	1,600	3,400	3,600	1,900
Clerical	1,100	2,300	2,400	2,500	1,300
TOTALS BY YEARS	8,740	22,700	30,170	31,070	15,510
TOTALS FOR 4½ YRS. OPERATION					108,190

Recommended Budget for Technical Unit
Fiscal Years Ending June 30

Item	*1954*	*1955*	*1956*	*1957*	*1958*
Equipment					
Central control equipment	22,410				
Dual studio camera equipment	33,760				
Film & opaque projection & pickup	34,900				
Video recording & developing	27,900				
Audio equipment	10,400				
Test equipment	4,200				
Accessories	9,350				
Miscellaneous equipment	2,730				
Lighting facilities	8,980				
Acoustical treatment	1,000				
Studio equipment	5,000				
Installation	3,930	1,000	1,000	1,000	
Vidicon camera equipment		9,000			
Technical equipment contingency	7,000	10,000	10,000	20,000	3,000
TOTALS BY YEARS	171,560	29,000	21,000	21,000	3,000
TOTAL FOR 4½ YRS OPERATION					236,560

Item	*1954*	*1955*	*1956*	*1957*	*1958*
Operations (Supplies)					
Film supplies	2,000	5,500	5,500	5,500	1,000
Trucking & freight	500	300	300	300	500
Local mileage at seven cents	700	1,400	1,400	1,400	700
Fire and theft insurance	500	500	500	500	250
Orthicon tube replacement		3,600	3,600	3,600	1,200
Replacement of other parts	1,500	5,000	7,500	10,000	5,000
Transmission lines and service	5,000	8,000	10,000	10,000	5,000
Maintenance	1,500	5,000	7,500	10,000	5,000
Operations (Personnel)					
Studio Production Mgrs.	2,750	5,800	6,100	6,400	3,350
Chief Engineers	2,750	5,800	6,100	6,400	3,350

Item	*1954*	*1955*	*1956*	*1957*	*1958*
Video Master Control Technicians	2,250	8,000	9,600	10,000	5,250
Recorder Technicians	2,200	9,000	9,400	9,800	5,100
Projectionists	1,000	3,000	3,200	3,400	3,600
Crew (Student)	1,200	5,100	6,300	6,300	2,500
TOTAL BY YEARS	23,850	66,000	77,000	83,600	41,800
TOTAL FOR 4½ YEARS OPERATION					292,250

Item	*1954*	*1955*	*1956*	*1957*	*1958*
Subcontracts relating to the spontaneous use of television by the schools and community response to classroom television (e.g., Iowa State College)		10,000	10,000	10,000	
Subcontracts dealing with televised classrooms (e.g., Univ. Minnesota)		10,000	10,000		
Subcontracts dealing with kinescope analysis (e.g., Pennsylvania State College)			10,000	10,000	
Subcontracts dealing with test construction (e.g., Educational Test Service)		10,000	10,000	10,000	
Subcontracts dealing with human engineering problems (e.g., Dunlap and Associates)			10,000	10,000	
TOTALS BY YEARS		30,000	50,000	40,000	
TOTAL FOR 4½ YRS OPERATION					120,000

Section G

Draft of a Proposal for A Study of the Effectiveness of Television in Relation to Current Problems in Teaching addressed to The Fund for the Advancement of Education by the New Jersey State Teachers College at Montclair

It is proposed that the Fund for the Advancement of Education provide a grant-in-aid to the New Jersey State Teachers College at Montclair in order to conduct a study of the effectiveness of television in relation to current problems in teaching.

The study would be initiated immediately and designed for completion by June 30th, 1958. Except for sub-contracts with agencies which are especially equipped to perform certain aspects of the study, the research will be conducted at the New Jersey State Teachers College at Montclair and in the neighboring communities.

The Need for the Study

American education is currently meeting serious difficulty in providing adequate instruction for the unprecedented numbers of pupils which are swarming upwards through the grades. More classrooms and more teachers are urgently needed. In attempting to meet the emergency the schools have often found it necessary to create over-sized classes, to employ teachers with sub-standard qualifications, to assign teachers to double shifts of duty, and to abandon important features of the curriculum.

It seemed important for serious students of the educational scene to inquire into other ways in which the emergency may be met—ways which involve less hazard to the educational welfare of the pupil and the professional status of the teacher. One such study is that now being pursued at Bay City, Michigan. It has to do with the better utilization of teacher competencies or, in other words, with the conservation of one of the school's principal resources—the competent teacher. At the moment the project at Bay City is approaching this problem through reconsideration and experimentation with new personnel and work assignment policies.

But there are other approaches. It is not inconceivable that recent technological advances may have as profound an effect upon education as they have had in other social areas. If mismanaged, these advances may cause ill effects; if intelligently controlled, they may help to solve some of education's problems.

Educational television is on the horizon. A basic and urgent problem is whether or not it can be intelligently employed to meet current emergencies which are arising in the field of teaching. Or will it be allowed to seek its own level of influence? It must not be allowed to develop into an instrument for making the classroom into a theater of entertainment. Nor should it be looked upon by taxpayers merely as a scheme for employing robot teachers and thus reducing education budgets. Perhaps it will be exploited by the schools solely as a public relations medium. Before it becomes "typed" and the educational channels tentatively reserved for it are committed to a haphazard kind of use, it seems advisable to make a thorough analysis of what its potentialities are and what kind of public servant it should become.

This is a proposal that television's potentialities be investigated immediately and that its bearing upon certain current problems in teaching given explicit consideration.

Objectives of the Study

A To formulate and test basic principles relating to the impact of television in the following 12 areas:
1 The pupil
2 The individual teacher
3 The teaching profession
4 Methods of teacher education
5 School administration
6 The constituent community
7 Ancillary educational specialties
8 The curriculum
9 School architecture
10 Educational television equipment
11 Educational television transmission
12 Educational television production

B To inquire specifically into the ways in which the above principles may be applied to correct educational malpractices growing out of the rapidly expanding pupil enrollments or applied to alleviate the effects of such malpractices.
Four types of malpractices would be given explicit attention:
1 The creation of over-sized classes under conditions which are clearly detrimental to the educational progress of the pupil and to the professional needs of the teacher.
2 The employment of teachers with sub-standard qualifications under conditions which are incompatible with good teaching.
3 The assignment of teachers to double shifts of duty which demonstrably interfere with the proper discharge of their professional obligations to individual pupils.
4 The abandonment of important features of the curriculum.

C To make all findings of the study available to the teaching profession in a maximally usable form.

Operation of the Project

The project is conceived as a research project. As such the College would exercise great care in its experimental and statistical design. The production and technical operations would be kept strictly subservient to the requirements of research and every effort would be made to resolve issues in terms of facts rather than in terms of opinions. Closed television circuits would be used primarily in order to maintain experimental control over uniformity of presentation and the viewer conditions. Technical facilities would be developed only as the experimental design would have use for them.

During the first six months of the project equipment would be installed and placed in operation, production teams would develop exploratory procedures with social science teaching in the fifth grade of the Bradford School in Montclair, and research teams would start their work in the design of fixed experiments. Survey types of investigations would be activated. About March first it should be possible to present one production a week. By May first it may be possible to step up the production rate to three a week.

During the summer of 1954 productions will be designed around closely written research specifications and the productions kinescoped for later presentation under controlled conditions. In the fall of 1954 it should be possible to add further viewer groups and start to expand the range of grade levels and subject matter. A tentative list of operating schedules is presented in the following table.

Operating Schedule
Fiscal Years Ending June 30

Item	*1954*	*1955*	*1956*	*1957*	*1958*
Hours of production	16	78	134	134	54
Hours camera time	230	900	1100	1100	440
Hours kinescope recording	16	60	100	100	27
Hours kinescope presentation	0	18	148	148	60
Schools in Montclair and vicinity closed circuits	1	3	5	8	8
Hrs. kines. farmed out for large N	0	9	36	36	18
Research teams activated full-time	0	2	4	4	4
Research teams activated part-time	2	4	4	4	4
Sub-contracts in operation	0	3	4	3	0

Organization of Staff

The staff of the project would be organized into eight units as follows: (1) an advisory policy board, (2) a panel of expert consultants, (3) an administrative unit, (4) a research unit, (5) a professional relations unit, (6) a production unit, (7) technical unit, and (8) a sub-contracting unit. The table of organization appears in the Consultant's Report which is appended to this proposal.

Budget Requirements

The estimated cost of the project during the first fiscal year ending June 30th, 1954, would be $264,070. The total estimated cost of the project for 4 and a half years of operation is $1,488,730. A summary of budget estimates appears in the following table. A break-down of these estimates by units appears in the Consultant's Report which is appended to this proposal.

90

Report on Classroom Television[1,2]

Part One: Report and General Evaluation

Report of Research Activity in Educational Television—February 1st to July 1st, 1954—Conducted by the Television in Education Project at the Montclair State Teachers College With the Support of The Fund for the Advancement of Education

A **The Scope of the Study**

6 ***The Proposed Five-Year Project***

In November, 1953, the College offered to the Fund for the Advancement of Education a proposal for a five-year study that would cost approximately a million and a half dollars, to be called

A STUDY OF THE EFFECTIVENESS OF TELEVISION IN RELATION TO THE CURRENT PROBLEMS IN TEACHING

in which the College would undertake to formulate and test basic principles relating to the impact of television on the following twelve impact areas:

1 the pupil
2 the individual teacher
3 the teaching profession
4 methods of teacher education
5 school administration
6 the constituent community
7 ancillary educational specialties
8 the curriculum
9 school architecture
10 educational television equipment
11 educational television transmission
12 educational television production

7 ***The Limited Study for the Spring of 1954***

The Fund made, in succession, two small grants to aid us in defining the field and scope of our study, and to enable us to find other sources of equipment and of funds. And then, in February, 1954 the Fund made a substantial preliminary grant to enable the college to explore "the educational feasibility of televising the outstanding teacher under conditions which simulate her normal classroom setting, and teaching units of instruction that form a part of the school curriculum."

The following pages constitute a report of the study of this problem.

B **The Stages of Our Spring Activity**

1 We studied other teacher-centered TV operations, to learn what light they might throw upon our problem.

[1] Co-authored in 1954 with Lawrence H. Conrad of the Television in Education project at the direction of President E. D. Partridge, N.J. State Teachers College at Monclair. Published by permission of Jacqueline Aldridge.

[2] Editors' note: The original report includes the following Appendices, which are not included in this volume but are available from the editors on request: Appendix A. The people who were involved in these operations; Appendix B. The Teacher's Guide and related documents.

Collected Papers of the Pioneer of Constructivist Psychology: George A. Kelly, First Edition. Edited by David A. Winter and Nick Reed.

a Dr. E. DeAlton Partridge visited a studio rehearsal of Ding Dong School in Chicago, conferring with "Miss Frances" and with the producer, Reinold Werrenrath, Jr., to learn something of the simplicity of the format of that highly successful program; of the absence of drill techniques; and of the importance of spontaneity and of sincere understanding between teacher and pupils. His findings were communicated to the staff of the Project.

b Prof. Lawrence H. Conrad spent a week at Station WOI-TV at Ames, Iowa, studying the history of their classroom productions, participating in their studio operations, and visiting schools where the programs were received and put to use as lesson material. He viewed manifold kinescopes of programs of the State Teachers College and the State University as well as of the State College. He conferred at length with all levels of school personnel and with the psychology and the education people at the Iowa State College, as well as with the producers of these programs, in preparation for his own duties as Director of Production for the Montclair Spring Operations.

Prof. Conrad also spent several days at the University of Minnesota, studying the use of television equipment in promoting observation of demonstration teaching in the University High School. Here, too, he conferred at length concerning all of the classroom angles of the use of television.

The findings of these conferences were communicated to the staff of the Project, and were put to use as shown herein.

c Dr. George A. Kelly, Project Director, Prof. Conrad and Thaddeus J. Sheft, Director of Studio Operations, spent considerable time on repeated occasions in the studio of Station WTLV at New Brunswick, where every courtesy was extended them to pore over the reports of school broadcasts, to confer with any and all personnel, and even to carry out limited experiments in educational television, by courtesy of the Department of Education of the State of New Jersey. This experience gave added dimensions to the work we were all to undertake at Montclair.

d Mr. Sheft attended sessions in Cleveland and in East Lansing during the same period, studying the use of television in the schools of Cleveland, and conferring at length with officials at Western Reserve University concerning their problems of cooperation with a commercial studio in presenting college credit courses by television. At East Lansing Mr. Sheft participated in the Annual Television Institute at Michigan State College.

2 We made a "base-line" study of our problem.

a We studied fifteen outstanding teachers.

School authorities in five communities (including New York City) were asked seriously to select their outstanding fifth-grade teachers, so that we might commence with teachers who had demonstrated superior skill and capacity in classroom teaching. No other criterion was used. Fifteen teachers came to us in this way. Only one of them had ever been before a television camera; most of them had never given any thought to the possibility of teaching by television.

Promptly upon assembling them, we gave them a talk about our interest in experimenting with classroom television; *then we asked whether each of them would be willing that very day and hour to get up before the cameras and "teach" some lesson recently taught, using the camera-lens for a class.* They agreed readily enough. Our Producer then took each one of them before the cameras for two minutes, to help them to avoid any feeling of strangeness; then the studio was cleared, and each one in turn was brought in for his or her lonely performance. With no warning, each "lesson" was cut off after ten or twelve minutes. The studio had been set up to resemble the front of a classroom. There was a blackboard, an eraser, some chalk. On a side wall, quite by chance, hung an outline map of the United States. All had the same equipment, the same handicaps. We suggested that the lesson be in the area of the social studies if there was a choice to be made; otherwise the lesson should be whatever that teacher felt best qualified to handle. None of these teachers knew that the performance was being recorded on sound film—a video recording, or "kinescope"—which remains now as a permanent record of this experiment.

In the judgment of all who later saw this record, every one of the fifteen appeared to be a fully competent teacher teaching a class in a schoolroom. No one of them broke down or broke off or became embarrassed or frightened. Each appeared to be launched for a full class period.

All made some use of the blackboard.

Several of them found and made use of the map.

Most of them carried on some exchange with the "pupils" who weren't there at all. Some called pupils by name in asking questions, and then confirmed or rejected a supposed answer. Some said,

"I can see that you are all thinking such-and-so." One even reprimanded a pupil for inattention, and went back over what she had just said, to insure its being heard and understood. One or two filled up the blackboard with quick entries that were made during quite illuminating instruction. Some gave information, merely. Some provoked thought. More than one carried on class discussion the whole time, with a class that wasn't there! It is not difficult to see that these are good teachers.

One would be tempted to say at once that really good classroom teachers have at the outset most of the more important qualities required for television classroom teaching.

We studied a total sample of twenty-five teachers under these same conditions.

To test whether all teachers, or even most teachers, might show up as well under these conditions, we wanted a sample that would contain good, bad, and indifferent teachers in about the proportion that these are likely to be encountered.

We chose a North Jersey community in which there are twenty-eight teachers of the fifth and sixth grade in the system, feeling that thus we would have a convincing across-the-board sample. By a careful piece of organizing, we were able to bring twenty-five of them together on one day (a Saturday) in the studio. Among them were the oldest teachers in that system, and the youngest. But there was no one among them who had been selected by a supervisor; all were on an even footing.

We gave to these candidates precisely the same briefing, given by the same person, and precisely the same "interview" before the cameras. They had exactly the same equipment with which to work. But we gave each one of them a completely free choice as to which field of subject-matter he might want to teach.

Many were nervous. Some were suspicious of us and our motives. Some wanted to be very sure that their colleagues would not be watching them while they taught.

Among the twenty-five are a few who would rank, we feel sure, with the better ones in our earlier sample. But among them also are a number of very poor performers.

Though we held the length of each trial down to a ten-minute maximum for this group, several simply could not continue for that long, and were mercifully cut off at an earlier juncture. A few broke down, with no more to say. At least one, though he had chosen his own subject, simply did not know the facts with which he was dealing. Some were loquacious without being enlightening. In all, this trial reinforced our growing belief that while the general run of teachers would probably require some special training in order to teach well on television, the best classroom teachers are already possessed of most of the skills and capacities that make good television teachers.

We have still a further trial we want to make with the kinescopes of these "base-line" samples of teaching. We want to cut the film into its proper segments, and then reassemble it so that "good" teachers will not be all in one cluster and "ordinary" teachers in another. Mixing them all up on the reel, we want to offer it to groups of educators, teacher-trainers, school executives, and even future teachers, and ask them to designate the "outstanding' teachers" among these samples. If their choices should correspond even roughly with the selections with which we commenced, we would then feel pretty confident that a really good classroom teacher would make a pretty plausible teacher on television. To this end, we have contacted the Superintendent who furnished us the twenty-five unselected teachers, and have asked him to provide a confidential list of the ones he would designate as "outstanding" teachers. So that for forty teachers, we have twenty-one who are designated as superior on the basis of their regular classroom work; and nineteen who have not won such a rating from their supervisors. The problem thus becomes simple. If educators can in general see the differences and can pick the superior ones out of a mixed sample on our kinescope, we then know that the superior teacher in the classroom will handle with some competence the task of teaching by television.

3 We explored several problems of TV teaching techniques.

a The Two-Teacher Arrangement

All of our study and observation having led us to believe that classroom television will involve a cooperation among teachers, we undertook some informal experimentation on our home ground, with the role to be played by each of the two most important teachers involved—the "visiting" teacher, who comes into the school via the TV screen, and the "local" teacher, who was there with her class all the time, but must now have an altered relationship with her pupils. Our demonstration high school at Montclair State provides an excellent ground for such an exploration. We had merely to add television to an existing situation in order to study this problem.

For our purpose, we used coaxial cable to create a closed circuit between our studio and two of the classrooms of College High School. In one of these rooms is a social studies class on an "integrated" program which employs two teachers—one in social studies, the other in speech. It was not difficult to put one teacher on the TV screen and to leave the other one in the classroom; nor to change them about whenever we wished. Thus it was possible to see the "local" teacher being assisted by the "visiting" teacher; and again to see the "visiting" teacher handle the class with only some assistance from the "local" teacher. Continued experimentation with these subordinate-coordinate roles served to teach us a great deal about how to plan our lessons for television presentation.

The other classroom that we wired for closed-circuit work was an English classroom in which the tenth grade class happened to have two teachers available: one who had just given them up in order to carry on television work, and the replacement teacher who had taken over his work. The two teachers were equal in skill and training; both were on intimate terms with the problems of this group, and both knew every individual in the class. Again we were able to try one in the studio while the other one met with the class; and then to reverse them when we pleased. We tried them with literature, with composition, and with "class discussion." Besides learning many of the small devices we would have to use in solving the problems of the teacher-from-the-screen, we were deeply impressed in these experiments with the degree of pupil-participation that is possible for a thoughtful teacher to attain. But this problem is carried further in another angle of our study, which follows.

b The Effort to Pierce the "Sound Barrier"

One of the serious problems of television teaching seems to be this: that the pupils may be spoken to, but seemingly they cannot speak back to the teacher on the screen. Many of us feel that this may be a shortcoming which, in the long run, may restrict this method of education quite seriously. A whole study of this problem alone needs to be undertaken. But we felt the need to explore the problem in preparation for our planned series of television lessons, and so we moved far enough into the study to satisfy ourselves that there may not be a permanent barrier here.

Using a graduate workshop group in our studio, we spent several weeks trying out every suggestion anyone could make for promoting participation *or a sense of participation* on the part of the pupils, with what was being offered from the screen. Several quite fruitful techniques were developed. Of these, the ones that seemed most likely to be immediately useful were these three:

1 The mind-reading approach, which is possible when the teacher on the screen knows children so well that she is able to take into account *what they are thinking*, and is quick to respond to the questions they would want to ask, and to the suggestions they would be likely to make if they could reach through to her.

2 The co-operative approach; in which the teacher on the screen is cast pretty largely in a *presentation* role, leaving discussion, judgment, and the disposal of open choices to the teacher who is present with the class in their own room; but in which the teacher on the screen, by mentioning these other aspects of the lesson, becomes a party to the more highly social part of the lesson which takes place after the screen is dark.

3 The illusion of representation; in which someone belonging to the same age-group as do members of the class, takes some part in the program on the screen—someone with whom the class can identify, and who they may suppose could speak up in terms of their interests. This is an illusion, to keep them, merely, from feeling shut out. The youngster or youngsters in the program must not be there *being taught*; they must be taking part in an instructional program.

Through the use of such devices as these, we have reason to suppose, a higher degree of pupil-participation can be attained than is ever reached by the ordinary teacher in an ordinary classroom. Pupils cut off from communication with the screen during the first half of a classroom lesson, frequently come storming through, the moment the screen goes dark, the more eager to participate because of the length of time they have held themselves repressed. It has never been shown, anyway, that the one good way to teach is to ask children what it is they want to know.

4 But most of all, we planned and taught a series of television lessons, and put them to use in the schools.

a We selected and organized a "team" of six teachers, and laid out an intensive schedule covering fifteen weeks. Our teachers were selected from the list of "outstanding teachers" certified to us by the school authorities in several communities. We chose six teachers for the team, because we thought that a sufficient number for one person—our Producer—to direct, and because we thought the job to be done would require that many workers. We paid these teachers on a consulting basis, as they were working for us one evening each week and all day Saturday each week, besides the study and planning that had to be done between sessions.

The members of this team, and their sponsors, are listed here.

Raymond A. Hoch	Bloomfield Public Schools
Beatrice Rubin	Clifton Public Schools
Alice Waud	Long Branch Public Schools
Teresa Relihan	Montclair Public Schools
Lawrence J. Ossi	Bloomfield Public Schools
Elizabeth Vreeken	New York City Schools

b We undertook to prepare a syllabus and a teacher's guide for a unit of ten daily lessons in the social studies, fifth grade level. No daily lessons constituting a series based upon the regular school curriculum had ever been prepared and taught by television. We wanted to use such a series for our study, in order to discount the factors of novelty and excitement which usually attend the showing of television programs in the schools. The novelty would soon wear off if the lessons continued daily for a period of two weeks.

The syllabus would be an important part of our work because in it the whole unit would be comprehended and fitted into its proper relationship with the year's work. Moreover, the syllabus would develop each lesson in full—both the part that would be seen on the screen, and the part that would be handled by the local teacher, before and after the television presentation. Our plan, in short, was an organic plan, using two teachers who might never see each other, working in close co-operation on a lesson which they both understand.

Our team of teachers would be unable to teach any one of the lessons until the overall plan of the series had been determined, and until each member of the team had a good grasp of the educational purposes to be served by the unit.

We studied the syllabi of many school systems, including the five school systems from which members of the team were recruited. And at last, wishing to have a unit that would be likely to be presented at the end of May—when our work would be finished and ready for the schools—we chose a unit of American history, the beginnings of the Westward movement, and labeled our series, "The Pioneer in American Life." The material is worth two weeks of treatment; and it is customarily given that much time in the schools. Accordingly, we planned ten lessons, which were later cut down to nine when an honest appraisal of lesson number one convinced us that most of its material could be distributed among the other lessons.

We did not decide who was to teach each lesson until we had made quite detailed plans for all of the lessons in the series. Thus all members of the team worked on all of the lessons—a plan we heartily recommend.

First we decided on the overall objectives for the series. Then as we began setting up objectives for each individual lesson, it became apparent that *only a part of each lesson would appear on the screen*, but that we had to prepare the whole lesson before we could choose the items or phases that would call for television treatment. Our Teacher's Guide, accordingly, was the first full outcome of our collaboration. Once that work was completed in its length and breadth, we were ready to turn to television.

c Meanwhile, we had to equip and staff our studio for a full-fledged operation. Equipment came from an unexpected source. With the failure of the State Legislature to authorize funds, the New Jersey Television Project at New Brunswick had to close down about May 1st, cutting off, among other things, our hope of preparing our kinescopes with the help of the equipment and the engineers who served there in Station WTLV. But the State Department of Education intervened in our behalf and enabled us to borrow much of the equipment that had been held at New Brunswick on a loan basis; so that, just when we needed it most, we found ourselves possessed, momentarily, of a well-equipped studio, including an excellent video recorder and film processor.

While our teachers were at work preparing lessons, our Studio Operations unit was busy expanding our studio, redesigning our control room, and putting our new video recorder into operation.

For the program that lay immediately ahead, we needed a greatly augmented technical staff; and fortunately many of those who had belonged to the project at New Brunswick—at loose ends for the moment—were available for employment. Our Studio Operations unit succeeded in assembling a most remarkably cohesive and responsive and talented staff—and to hold them together through the month of May, by which time our great labor of the Spring was finished.

Let no one who takes an interest in educational television underestimate the crucial importance of good equipment and a finely co-ordinated team of studio workers. First class results can come only out of sensitive co-operation between the studio people and the educators with whom they have to deal. A critical point, in fact, is the point of articulation between the techniques of education on the one hand, and the techniques of the TV studio on the other. The TV crew says, in effect, "We know how to handle anything that comes into the studio." But of course they don't. And the educator is likely to say, "We were old in this game before you fellows ever started." It is well if neither side is stubborn about it. For if television is to deal with this essentially new body of subject-matter, it must be prepared to learn—and to invent—new techniques for the purpose. And if education is to make use of this new medium, it must be prepared to adapt its techniques to new requirements—and to new advantages. The crucial person in all this tense relationship is the television director who actually puts on the program.

He is not directing a show, and he must realize that fact at once. This is one part of television that is not "show business." It stems from different impulses, and it aims at different results. It has a different service to render to society, in the long run. When educational television gets into its stride, this fact will come to be appreciated more fully. Just now it is the director who has to co-ordinate the forces on the two sides of the camera. If the director is himself disciplined, and is sympathetic toward the aims of education, he can make, at this current stage, an important contribution in setting a pattern for a new profession.

By the time our programs were ready for production at Montclair, we had an augmented technical staff and an expanded studio crew, ready to handle the programs.

d Our "team" of six teachers now prepared to teach before the cameras. Each teacher chose his or her own lesson, with the advice and consent of the group. In two of the cases, we "tried out" more than one teacher on a given lesson, before deciding which one should teach it. With nine lessons and only six teachers, we felt free to switch people around. The choice as to which of the teachers were to teach two lessons was made pretty largely on the basis of the degree of enthusiasm each one felt for the subject-matter of those three extra lessons. The choice was made by the whole team.

Rehearsals in teaching these lessons were held not in the studio, but in a classroom. Members of the team offered comment and made suggestions after each of the rehearsals. It was not until the lesson was well in hand, that rehearsals were moved into the studio, and the consequent adjustments began. At the last, before production, a final, polished performance was held, with everything exactly as it should be in the finished program; and then the production was recorded on sound film for later use and evaluation.

In our production schedule, we used about two hours for each twenty-minute program. Two of the lessons were produced in evening sessions, between eight and ten-thirty P.M. In one Saturday session, operating all day long, we produced three programs; and in another, we produced four. The nine programs were produced and kinescoped within one week. If we do this again, we are agreed we want to take a slower pace.

e In the meantime, we were taking advantage of a standing offer of co-operation by Mr. Walter Reade, owner of Station WRTV, Channel 58, RHF, at Asbury Park, New Jersey to broadcast our lessons to the schools *via* his UHF channel. Conferences were held with Mr. Earl B. Garrison, County Superintendent of Schools of Monmouth County, and through him, arrangements were made to offer the lessons to fifth (and some sixth) grade classes in the two towns of Red Bank and Long Branch, both in Monmouth County, where the television station is also located. Further conferences with the local Superintendents in these two towns, and then with the teachers of the grades in question, brought about an arrangement whereby only those teachers who wished to do so, would use these lessons for their regular class work for the last week in May and the first week in June. Thirteen teachers volunteered, and agreed to help us in evaluating the educational results—seven in Long Branch, and six in Red Bank. Local television dealers equipped the thirteen classrooms with 21-inch receivers adapted to Channel 58, and mounted antennae on the schools.

The two school systems chose the hour at which they wished to have the programs shown; and the station willingly broadcast at that chosen hour each school day. As there was one school holiday (May 31) during the broadcast period, the nine lessons covered each of the school days in a two-weeks' period, May 24 to June 4, from 10:00 to 10:30 each day. The schedule and arrangement of programs, together with the names of the teachers involved, are given herewith.

Monday, May 24	How the Pioneers Travelled to their New Homes—Miss Alice Waud
Tuesday, May 25.	How the Pioneers Built their Homes—Miss Elizabeth Vreeken
Wednesday, May 26.	How Pioneer Families Helped Each Other—Miss Teresa Relihan
Thursday, May 27.	How Pioneer Children Spent their Time—Mr. Raymond A. Hoch
Friday, May 28.	Early Pioneer Schools—Miss Beatrice Rubin
Tuesday, June 1st.	Fun and Amusements of Pioneer Days—Miss Alice Waud
Wednesday, June 2nd.	Food and Clothing in Pioneer Days—Miss Teresa Relihan
Thursday, June 3rd.	How the Pioneer Earned a Living—Mr. Lawrence J. Ossi
Friday, June 4th.	Pioneering in Our Own Day—Miss Beatrice Rubin

The school Superintendents in Monmouth County who participated in this experiment with us, were: in Red Bank, M. Gregg Hibbs, Jr., and in Long Branch, Harmon M. Bradford, Their teachers:

In Long Branch	*In Red Bank*
(The Grammar School)	(The Mechanic Street School)
Mrs. Elsie Ayres	Miss Myrtle Cook
Miss Kaye Brooks	Miss Dorothy Metzgar
Mrs. Betty Churchin	(The Oakland Street School)
Mrs. Ruth Cooper	Mrs. Joyce Wyler
Mr. Conrad De la Motte	(The River Street School)
Miss Dora Joffe	Miss Eleanor Wright
Miss Lena Neely	(The Fort Monmouth School)
	Mrs. Frances Stern

In addition, pupils in charge of these teachers also participated:
In Red Bank: Miss Emily Reedy, Bedside Teacher
In Long Branch: Miss Helen Immen, Special Teacher

The Teacher's Guide that was prepared for these lessons, was furnished to each of these teachers and to their supervisors, so that a maximum use might he made of the lessons in each classroom. In addition, each teacher was supplied with nine copies of a Teacher's Evaluation Form, on which to report the effectiveness of each day's lesson.

These forms were mailed in to our office at the close of each day by all of the teachers involved in the experiment. There was furnished also about four hundred copies of a Pupil's Evaluation Form, on which the pupils were to be invited at the close of the whole series to express themselves on the effectiveness of the lessons, by replying to a series of thirty-six questions of a quite provocative sort. Copies of these evaluation forms and the instruction sheet will be found in the Teacher's Guide that is bound with this report. One hundred thirty of the teacher's Evaluation Forms were received from the teachers—the maximum number. From the pupils, 308 replies were received, filled out generally in full, and often accompanied by a letter supplementing the child's formal responses by an attempt at discussion of some of the values.

5 What were the results of this television teaching *in the classroom*?

a The children were enthusiastic about these lessons. They maintained an eager attitude throughout the two weeks' period.

b The children were aware of learning, and were ready to tell what it was they had learned. They could discriminate the important from the unimportant.

c The children were more deeply affected by ideas when they had *seen* the situations that produced them.

d They remembered things vividly, and were able to refer back to the different lessons, *usually by making a visual reference.*

e The children responded to these "visiting teachers." In most of the rooms, they sang with the television teacher, without specific invitation. In some of the rooms, they called out answers when the television teacher asked such questions as: "I think that would be worth while, don't you?" And the observers saw hands go up more than once when the teacher said, "I wonder how many of you know how to do a square dance."

f The children felt fully as close to the television teacher as to any teacher. *They were as much in communication with this teacher* as they are with their own "regular" teacher over a comparable period of time.

g The teachers who used these lessons in their own rooms were all willing to have some more. All feel sure there is a place for television in the classroom.

h The teachers all made—on invitation—very frank comments; not one of them found anything seriously damaging to say about the effectiveness of the medium.

i The lessons were a great success; nevertheless, we all feel already how far they fell short of the ideal. We have the kinescopes to study at our leisure; we have had thorough evaluation sessions with the teachers who used the lessons, with the teachers who made up and taught the lessons, and with various educators to whom we have shown the series. And we are involved in a never-ending follow-up evaluation of the whole experience. One of the most important results, it may be, is what the experience has taught us about planning, teaching, producing, and using classroom television. That value will be observable and measurable as time goes by; we know it now only as a feeling of inner certainty that we could surely do better another time.

The General Evaluations

Classroom Television Through the Eyes of Teachers Who Have Made Use of It

I All of the issues are there on the classroom screen.

In all of the clamor of discussion on the use of television in the schools, there is one group of voices to which we should surely harken: the voices of those who have actually had the experience of using televised lessons in their classes as a part of the regular work of the school. There are not many who have had this experience. The number grows smaller if you confine the inquiry to those who have used in their classes lesson-material that was designed for their own school grade-level. It grows smaller still if you ask only for those who have used *lessons that were deliberately prepared by other teachers of that same grade-level*, and were taught by "regular" public school teachers. Finally, if you asked for teachers who had used lessons that persistently followed the curriculum for a period of two weeks of daily lessons in one unit of work—you would be able to get views and opinions from *only fifteen teachers in the United States*. But it would certainly be worth-while to hear their testimony, and to compare it with the great wealth of mere speculation that is available on this subject.

In the last week of May and the first week of June, 1954, there was broadcast from Station WRTV in Asbury Park, New Jersey, over UHF Channel 58, a daily series of lessons designed for the fifth grade, and geared to the social studies unit of work that would normally be covered during those weeks in the schools. The lessons were received in thirteen classrooms in Long Branch and Red Bank, New Jersey, for these classrooms and these alone had been provided with television receivers adapted to the ultra-high-frequency impulses of Channel 58. These particular classrooms were so fitted out because the teachers in them had offered to accept the lessons and use them as a regular part of their daily instruction. The broadcast was made at the hour chosen by the teachers, namely, ten o'clock in the morning. Though only thirteen classrooms were involved, and thirteen "regular" fifth or sixth grade classes, fifteen teachers in those schools were involved, two of them with "special", not "regular" school grades. So there are fifteen teachers who are qualified to speak on the questions that are constantly raised concerning classroom lessons brought in day after day by means of television.

There were nine lessons in all; and in the two-week period covered, there were nine regular school days, because of the Memorial Day holiday. Hence a full two weeks of work.

The lessons were prepared and produced at the New Jersey State Teachers College at Montclair where, as an experiment in one of the educational uses of television, a group of six outstanding fifth grade teachers was enlisted to serve for two months in studying the curriculum, organizing a unit, preparing a prospectus, and designing the nine lessons in great detail. At the conclusion, having prepared a Teacher's Guide for the use of the teachers in Red Bank and Long Branch, these six outstanding teachers then proceeded, among them, to teach the nine lessons before the television cameras in the studios of the Montclair Television in Education Project. The nine lessons were thereupon recorded as "kinescopes," and so made available for later use. Funds for the operations were provided by the Fund for the Advancement of Education.

During the nine days of the broadcasts, the fifteen teachers filled out daily reports on the effectiveness of the lessons, and of the uses that were made of them. We have all of these reports—about 130 of them; and they are the only evidence of this precise kind that has ever been gathered up to now. At the close of the series, we took our six "television teachers" out to Red Bank for a full-dress conference with the teachers who had used the lessons in that town; and on another day, we took them to Long Branch for the same purpose. Needless to say, supervisory and administrative officers of the school systems in these two towns attended the conferences. And the present writer, who conducted these sessions kept a record of the views and ideas that were expressed.

We cannot answer the question, "What do teachers think of educational television?" But we can give as good a set of answers as anyone can, of what these particular teachers thought of the experience they had with this particular phase of that subject: namely, daily lessons designed for the classroom and brought into the classroom *via* television.

They were genuinely and thoughtfully impressed with the prospect which this demonstration opened up. They had thought in general, that it wouldn't be as good as it was. They had thought it would be a much longer time before it ever got around to their own schools. They had thought that everything might go wrong, whereas only a few things went wrong. They had thought the children might take a difficult attitude—though they weren't very sure as to what it would be. For all of this, though, they were a very "game" group of teachers whom no one could describe as provincial or as lacking in the kind of enlightenment that belongs in our better schools. Not all of the teachers in the fifth grade classrooms of the two towns took the lessons: only the ones who thought they would really like to have them. And we admitted a few sixth grade teachers who were eager to take part in the experiment.

We should note about this report, that these teachers were summing up at the close of each day—and mailing off that summary—for two whole weeks. Attitudes changed, and we were able to note those changes. Some reversed their own judgments as they went along. Some put the finger upon a vital point at the outset and found themselves still pointing at that area when the series closed. The reports filed for the final days of the field-trial were steady and moderate and highly constructive. The experience of nearly two weeks of using television lessons had given these teachers a respect for the medium and a sobering sense of its potentialities—not only on what they had seen, but on what they had themselves begun to plan for the future. Heretofore, television has come into the schools mostly as a one-shot treatment, unrelated to what lies about it in the curriculum. School stops for such a broadcast. But in the series of May-June, 1954, school goes right along and the television lessons fall into step because they have been built to match that stride. Whatever excitement the teachers and pupils felt on the first day, had cooled a good deal by the time of the seventh or the eighth lesson. Whatever hysteria may have infected their responses at the outset, had receded before the end of the series. So it may be that the final judgments on this series will be soberer (i.e., not so wild) than much that has been written about educational television; but it will be nearer to a sound estimate, on the basis of which money that is now being withheld can be spent for education.

II What they liked about it was the good teaching.

Here were teachers capable of appreciating first-class teaching when they saw it; and they did see it (though not at all points by any means) in many places in this series of lessons. They were frank and quick in giving credit both for themselves and on behalf of their pupils, whose reactions they were able to watch. Whenever in the series a quite strikingly fine piece of work was done, the teachers' reports that came in next day would show a warm response to it. They were equally discriminating among all values; but were both generous and uninhibited in giving praise for teaching skills. Such words as "excellent," "wonderful," and "splendid" were freely used; and even the teacher whose lesson was not proceeding to their full satisfaction, would win a "Bravo!" for something well done in passing.

These teachers are not trained critics, perhaps, but they should be very good judges of what some other teacher is able to do with their own classes, in their own classrooms.

They were able to appreciate that the television lesson is a product of the preparation and the planning of a number of good teachers; that it is planned and then replanned; that it is built out of materials gathered by the research and the experience of several people; and that it is enriched by several rehearsals, each followed by a session of further discussion and planning. Such preparation takes us far beyond what is possible in the ordinary run of daily lessons.

They spoke their appreciation also of the prodigious use of physical properties of all kinds. No such combing of the museums, the libraries, and the historical collections is possible when a lone teacher tries to get up a lone lesson on any subject. Here were items of historical interest to which the ordinary teacher does not have access. Why? Because the items are comparatively rare, and the teachers are so very numerous. There will be twenty to a hundred fifth grade classrooms in an ordinary city; each will have its teacher; and each teacher will want to show his class as many as possible of the authentic items that attest the color and flavor of life in the past. In this situation, nothing is quite so efficient—and inexpensive—as television. The teachers who used these lesson-programs in their classes were quite fully taken with the fact that the *realia* shown were far beyond what is regularly available for teaching purposes.

These classroom teachers were quick to detect also the occasional flash of ingenuity in teaching: and they gave professional admiration to the television teacher who had devised a better way of saying or of showing the truth that was to be learned. We ourselves knew that often this "master touch" was the product of group thinking and group planning on the part of the "team" that stood behind all of these lessons. Yet it was something for which "television teaching" can take much credit; for it is only when there is a prospect of using the lessons to teach a number of classes at once, that education can afford to spend the care and the time necessary to get up superior lessons. What was most admirable in these cases was:

(I) The situation in which the teacher had prepared some special device in advance that would further the clarity and assist the understanding of the thing to be taught; or, (II) the situation in which the teacher did something before the camera that advanced the lesson by furnishing one of those quick insights into the essence of the lesson. This latter might be something the teacher did quite unaided; or it might be something done with the collaboration of pupils drawn from the same age-level as those being taught; or it might be something demonstrated by such a pupil or group of pupils quite by themselves and apart from the teacher who is handling the lesson. It might even be done by a group of pupils from the class that is being taught, selected for the purpose by their own classroom teacher, and directed in what they are to do, by the "television teacher" who speaks to them from the screen.

A study of the appreciations of the fifteen teachers who used these lessons and commented upon them freely, leads to the conclusion *that top success in television teaching comes when the pupils who are being taught are watching a process and are having it explained or commented upon by a teacher at the same time.* Here concentration is at its height; and what is imparted in such a moment, if it is understood, has an excellent chance of being retained as though it had come to the pupil out of his own life-experience. Not more than twenty minutes of such concentration, it would seem, should be attempted in any class hour at the grammar school level.

III Their critical suggestions were directed toward a job of teaching, and not toward a television performance.

It is singular that no one of the teachers made any comparison between these lessons and the television programs with which many of them are surely familiar. It is as though they all instinctively regarded all "regular" television programs as fiction, and this series as non-fiction; preserving the kind of distinction that everybody makes in his responses to these two divisions of literature. One of the youngsters may have crystallized the distinction when he said of the lessons: "These people on the screen are real people."

In most of the evaluation sheets that these teachers sent in, you would not know that what they are discussing is shadows on a screen. They are talking about a teacher and a lesson and its relation to their own class. It is only when something goes wrong, either with the teaching or with the transmission to the screen, that the critic remembers that he is dealing with a moving, talking picture. This being the case, the critic's discussion is all the more remarkable. For she is discussing another teacher whom she has had the rare opportunity to observe at the closest possible range. This is a visiting teacher who has come into her own classroom and offered a lesson to her own well-known pupils. Any teacher who could do that—and survive the professional scrutiny—would have to be good! It is remarkable that the attitude shown by these classroom teachers in evaluating the "visiting teachers" should have been so uniformly friendly and constructive. A great moment came, surely, when after the series had finished, we brought the two groups of teachers together and had them discussing around a table the lessons the one group had taught and the other group had used as material in the classroom. The whole atmosphere was most remarkably co-operative and helpful, with not a little wonder on both sides of the table at their being so close together in the common enterprise of teaching. Of course all were experienced teachers, with much that is common in their training and in their attitudes. They met quite definitely as members of one profession, not two. It should not be difficult to imagine the roles of the two groups being reversed—perhaps during the next school term.

They found justification for preserving some of the old rules of teacher-deportment. They told our teachers not to turn toward the blackboard while telling something to the class. Not only does this muffle what is said—as in an ordinary classroom—but in television it sometimes loses contact with the microphone, and so loses what is said, quite entirely. They told us also to be more careful of diction and enunciation on television than we are accustomed to being when we do not have television. Because of mechanical reproduction, only the clearest enunciation comes through entirely clear. These were not fussy remarks, but testimony out of the experience of using this series of lessons. They told us further to take greater pains with personal appearance when teaching from the screen, than when teaching from the front of a classroom *because you come under closer scrutiny when on the screen.*

In the same spirit, they asked us for more careful choice—and use—of the visual items to be shown on the screen as a part of the lesson. One of our maps had too much detail in it, and those in the back of the room had difficulty seeing on it the designated points of interest. Some of our pictures—black and white line drawings—were artistically stylized just enough to make them difficult for direct-minded youngsters. And they suggested that we take care not to crowd too many things into one lesson, lest we merely bewilder the pupils with a visual display about which they have scarcely time to think.

They asked further for more use of photography to bring authentic scenes into the lessons; and for filmstrips and motion pictures on occasion to put the pupils into the visual presence of the scenes with which the lesson is dealing. Then they asked us to study the problem of introducing the new teacher—having her name said, and having her hold still long enough to let the pupils "size her up" before she whirls into her opening of the lesson. All this was in the very finest spirit; and we found every word of it most helpful.

IV Finally, they made some shrewd estimates of their own part in the final success of classroom television.

Both in their daily evaluations, and in the sessions we held with them in their own home communities, these teachers exhibited a newly-awakened alertness to *ways of doing things.* To say that something is not fully satisfactory when done one way is to give yourself the challenge to say how it might otherwise have been done to better effect. The round-table discussions were very lively conferences on educational method, with almost everyone saying better things than he ever said before. *Some of the best things said were invented, then and there.* They grew out of the necessity of filling up the vacuum created by rejecting something which everyone had seen and hadn't liked very well.

Continued long enough, these experiences with lessons that come into the school *via* television, would surely result in upgrading most teachers. They would be a challenge to the best teachers to keep employing their best, and to continue growth from year to year. They would be invaluable as in-service training for teachers who have not attained their maximum of knowledge, skill, and professional attitude. Well-planned lessons produced by a team of high-grade teachers would supply the full content of professional training for teachers who are seeking to improve. Such lessons would teach by example, and by funnelling a host of ideas into a minimum of viewing-time. Our sessions with people who are really good teachers convinced us of that. They got so much out of dealing with these lessons, that surely less able teachers, discussing the lessons with competent supervisors, would be able to use them for the precise training they might most require.

Many of their best points implied the desire to see a closer working relationship between the teacher on the screen and the pupils in the classroom. They were delighted with every contact our teachers seemed to make with their pupils; and they wished to further this relationship by their own help. It was out of our final conferences that the idea arose which should make a further series of lessons at once more intimate and more effective. For we have studied plans for making contact between the teacher on the screen and her new class that is found in each classroom in which the lessons are used. But we had made no sort of contact between the "visiting teacher" and the "classroom teacher" who is on her home ground with her own pupils. We had only addressed this classroom teacher through the medium of our *Teacher's Guide*, to tell her how she might help *before* the lesson, and how she might help *after* the lesson. From our discussions with these teachers, we learned of her desire to help *during* the lesson, and of her willingness to lend her services in the actual teaching that is initiated from the screen.

Of course the classroom teacher can know in advance how the teaching is to proceed. And if she can, then she can be given a part to play in its unfolding. Some part of the lesson from the screen can be directed to the classroom teacher—or through the class to her—setting up the precise conditions of co-operation between these two teachers on this one lesson about which they have both advance knowledge, and for which they both should have made advance preparation. Once put this scheme into operation, and down will go the last barrier that has made the television teacher seem inaccessible. *Two* teachers are teaching this lesson; the pupils may direct their remarks to the one that stands nearest and can respond most quickly. Co-operative teaching; an enterprise that should make many of the finest blessings of education available to even the poorest community. It may not be cheaper in cost per unit; but if it is higher quality, and more of it is imparted in the same space of time, then it will save us billions of dollars in a very few years of use.

The fifteen teachers who alone know what it is like to have their classes taught from a television screen day after day have given no indication that they regard classroom television as a threat to their security. Not one of them seems to have wondered what will eventually become of her job. They see in classroom television an added richness that should make school a more thrilling enterprise than ever, with a stronger appeal to all those who are seeking preparation for a work and a station in life. They see in classroom television a new boost for school-teaching, a "shot in the arm" that will enable them to get better results with their teaching than they were able to get when they were working alone.

Through the Eyes of the Pupils

Boys and girls of the fifth grade age-level are not very good at weighing issues and making difficult choices. But they can answer questions like mad. And if you can devise the proper questions, you can get from their answers more evaluation and discrimination than they are aware of giving forth. Hence we gave a good deal of thought to devising a questionnaire that would elicit from the pupils some choices among the values presented in our series of lessons, and some measurement of the degree to which these children were affected by the teaching that was offered. When we were satisfied with the question form, we struck off 400 copies and gave them out to the co-operating teachers together with a kind of warning notice, asking the teachers to encourage independence on the part of each pupil answering the questions.

Promptly following the series of lessons, the pupils took up our questionnaire and answered it. We have 308 answers, many of them with additional letters attached, expressing some further thought or estimate of the experience. Tabulation and study of all of these answers has taken a little time, as there were well over ten thousand possible items. And we are ready now to discuss only the broader (and more certain) of the findings.

The broadest discovery of all is that the pupils liked these lessons, and liked them not because they suspended school work, but because they made school work more interesting and rewarding. Their enthusiasm is not of a wild sort, but is controlled, as behooves anyone who has been asked to give you his best judgment. But the enthusiasm is there, unmistakably. Learning took place, almost constantly, and the awareness of learning remained after the experience had concluded. This much we can say without citing any count of the answers given.

One of the best-attested findings of the study is that the level of conviction—the question whether the learning goes deep enough to change the learner's attitudes—fluctuated from classroom to classroom. This would show two things, both of some importance to educational television. First, that the classroom teacher remains a dominant figure in education, though her material may be piped in to her from some deep well or reservoir in the community. Second, that what is done, locally, to develop the lesson with the children in a given room, is as vital and important as what is done in presenting it from the screen. Hence the work that was done in preparing a Teacher's Guide for this series of lessons, was right and proper; but the great area for further development will be to devise more extensive two-teacher participation from the very beginning in bringing the lessons to the minds and lives of the pupils. The classroom teacher, we know by proof, will continue to have the key to the more profound effects of any instruction, however offered. She must be built into the lesson and into the series of lessons.

We have a puzzling array of differences in response to lesson-topics, with some fine distinctions to be drawn eventually. But just taking the choices that fall at the bottom and the top of the scale of pupil-choice, it seems apparent that single topics or few topics in one presentation, will be more impressive and better remembered, than scattered topics, however well and engagingly presented. It may be that we knew this all along. But we now know that this unity of theme or topic has more to do with impressing the pupils than does any other factor except the personality of the teacher. A lesson that "has everything" will pile up a big tally on separate counts; but it will not be the one chosen for top honors. The most powerfully-delivered lesson—on television—is also the one that makes the neatest package. It needn't be simple, but it should all fall under one label.

On teacher personality, the top honors for fifth grade would go to a man, probably because most of these pupils have had only women teachers, and they find the change refreshing. But beyond that choice, they look for geniality and understanding before they look for handsome features. And they'll trade off some pretty important qualities for a little sparkle: a smile, a humorous word, a pleasant expression. The warmth of the teacher—if it is there—pervades the whole lesson. We found it difficult to account for some of the views and choices of these pupils, until we realized that the youngsters' attraction for a teacher was swaying all of their judgments. Here was an area of positive conviction. The most popular of our six teachers was chosen by these youngsters eight times as often as the least popular. And they were choosing a *teacher as such*—to help them plan and do some teaching—not as a friend or a matinee idol.

We were impressed, too, by the possibility of teaching ideas by means of television. The experience of producing and using this series seemed not only to show that it could readily be done, but that fifth grade children are definitely on the lookout for ideas and are ready to receive them. A striking occurrence in the course of the pupils' evaluation gives support to this view. The class lesson which they ranked highest for its having the most interesting displays and actions in it, turned up in another tabulation as the one they rated lowest of all for the importance of the idea around which it was built. Here is a clear capacity to discriminate. And then, in the aggregate rating, that program, which "had everything" to interest the eye and the ear, was ranked well below the ones built about important ideas. Hence we feel encouraged about the capacity of this medium to convey serious intellectual content; and about the ability of fifth grade boys and girls to seek something beyond mere display in the lessons. Aggregate ratings seemed clearly to be based on *what you learned*, rather than on *what you saw*.

Anyone who has not had experience with classroom television *designed for the classroom* would say off-hand that pupils would certainly make comparisons with their favorite programs. And we have a whole series of reflections that grow out of this supposition. Well, all such reflections fell to the ground as we inspected the responses of these 308 pupils. *We find no evidence that they are thinking of this as television at all.* This is school. This is education. This is a teacher and a lesson. Their comparisons—sometimes quite shrewd—are comparisons with their own classroom and how things are done there. They like things that move, and they don't much care for "just talk." But this taste is merely extended from their classroom to the screen. They don't ask for excitement. They would surely object to any liveliness that was staged in order to secure an effect. When two children who were used in one of the lessons, were alone before the camera, doing a pantomime dramatization of pioneer life, the almost unanimous cry that went up was, "Make them talk. Bring the teacher in, and let him talk to them, and let them talk back." The pantomime struck these pupils as unnatural as a means of teaching a lesson. They wanted these children to be *real children*. They didn't want anybody putting on a play in order to teach them something they could grasp easily enough, if you just showed them and told them about it. We feel quite relieved as a result of this experience. We feel it is clear that classroom television does not have to compete with television, but only with classroom teaching; and with that, it should co-operate rather than to compete, for it is a branch of the same plant.

But a truly large question that is raised stems from the fact that in classroom television one teacher enters several classrooms simultaneously, to teach a lesson that has been prepared by a group of teachers. But the atmosphere is not the same in Room A as in Room B. It is easy enough, we believe, to set up a lesson that will have a proper appeal to the normal range of pupils; but it is a fact that *the tone one takes in teaching* will be one tone, when it comes from the television set, whereas each of the rooms it enters is accustomed to a slightly different tone as its customary mode of address. Of course, we are not talking about *tone of voice* at all. In some classrooms, the atmosphere is filled with electrically-charged particles; in others, the air is always clear. Some pupils find a sparkling personality on the screen to be quite the natural thing; some find it a great novelty. Some can never again be the same after experiencing it.

We found these pupils learning facts about equally well, in one classroom as in another. We found them with interests about the same in one classroom as in another. We even found them grasping and appreciating ideas about as readily in one atmosphere as in another, only exhibiting the usual ranges of individual capacity. But in what they dared to accept, to believe, and to express, we found a distinct cleavage as the lesson offered itself in Room A and in Room B. If these differences in teachers are of value and are worth preserving, they would seem to be threatened, mildly, by the incursions of classroom television. For a particular atmosphere—if it is markedly different—can be preserved only if the children do not know that another atmosphere is possible. The experience of a different class atmosphere—which is itself educational—would be upsetting only in a situation in which there is actual tyranny in the room. And regular visits from a fellow-teacher, even on the screen, would tend to reduce the tensions in any room in which tension is artificially maintained.

By planning all lessons with committees or panels of teachers, the danger can be avoided that the "visiting teacher" may bring to the classroom a freedom of spirit that would disrupt any of the local classroom values that ought to be preserved.

Oddly, in all of this, the boys and girls clearly showed that they were judging the worth and value of a teacher by direct comparison with their own current teachers; and those who were very different from their own, they tended to reject. In fact one of the surest confirmations arising out of this series of lessons is that educational television simply could not be imposed from above. To be effective, it would have to come at the invitation of the classroom teacher, and would have to have her sympathy and co-operation if it is to succeed.

Our Own Summary Evaluation

1 We now feel it is clear that television may be used not only for introducing educational specialties and occasional lessons into the classroom, but for teaching purposes day after day.
2 We feel sure that the television lesson will seldom carry the whole burden of instruction in a given unit of work, or even in a given lesson. The classroom teacher is not replaced by it; but her time and her talents may be redistributed.
3 In the *presentation* of certain types of material, television is definitely a superior teaching method.
4 Television is not necessarily a "one-way" medium. Skillful teachers are able to develop a good deal of intercommunication with the class.
5 Really high grade classroom teachers have many if not most of the skills required for successful television teaching.
6 Classroom television calls for superior teaching; it calls for no more dramatic talent than is required for "regular" classroom work.
7 Television teachers need not be beautiful; they should have interesting personalities. So should regular classroom teachers.
8 The keynote for television teaching is *friendliness*; it cannot be faked, but can be achieved only by someone who knows and likes boys and girls of the age-group that is being taught.
9 Lessons employing television constitute richer experiences than are regularly attainable in the various departments of school work.
10 Classroom television need not replace films, filmstrips, slides, or radio in the schools. On occasion, it should make masterful use of all of these media of instruction.
11 A television lesson can be produced for a small fraction of the cost of a motion picture film on the same subject; it can be local in its origin and in all of its references; and it can be distributed to any and all classrooms simultaneously, or be repeated next day or next hour as the need arises.
12 "Closed circuit" television transmission throughout a local school system may be had at a modest cost.
13 Non-commercial (UHF) television broadcasting is likely to remain quite local, giving its best service within a radius of twenty-five miles of its tower, thus insuring that any regimentation of lessons and schedules will not be imposed "from outside."
14 Children are accustomed to learning by watching television. They accept that kind of instruction in the schools without a murmur.
15 Children do not ask for excitement or glamor in their school television lessons. They like best the ones from which they learn most.
16 A television lesson in the classroom gives the pupils all the advantage of contact with a new teacher-personality, without having to give up the old one.
17 Pupils like best those television teachers who are most nearly like their regular teachers, and care least for the ones who do not seem like any teacher they ever had.
18 Good teachers need very little instruction before going before the cameras. They need mostly to know how the camera works and what it can do. This they can learn in a few hours' time.
19 We see little likelihood that teacher-education will undergo any serious overhauling in order to produce "television teachers" for the future. The introduction of one course involving practical studio experience would probably be all that is needed for years to come.
20 Classroom television uses *two* teachers for each lesson. But for certain kinds of material, it is *completely* effective; that is, it teaches a lesson that should not ever need to be taught again.

Part Two: Report of the Separate Studies

The Baseline Study

To what extent is the television camera able to capture the qualities of the outstanding teacher?

This question represents a particular aspect of the gross feasibility problem around which the present group of studies is centered. Specifically it has to do with the matter of whether or not good teachers are distinguishable from poor teachers when they appear on the television screen. If they are not distinguishable from poor teachers it would suggest that any attempt to spread their influence by means of television would have to find some way of utilizing certain less obvious professional qualities, such as ability to plan lessons, assemble teaching materials, deal with classroom emergencies, adjust to individual differences among pupils, etc. If these were the qualities to be captured it might well be that the outstanding teacher would be used only as a member of the production team and not as the studio performer.

If the outstanding teacher is clearly distinguishable on the television screen, even when she teaches impromptu, the task of the educational television producer is immensely simplified. In that case his principal objective is to find outstanding classroom teachers and develop appropriate ways of turning his cameras on them. Whatever he does in addition to this to make the teaching effective is frosting on his cake.

Procedure

In connection with the Fifth Grade Syllabus Study, the Project Staff invited supervisory personnel in each of several neighboring school systems to nominate their outstanding fifth grade teachers. From the panels of nominees a team of six teachers, four women and two men, was selected to produce a unit of the fifth grade curriculum on television. With one exception none of these teachers had had any television experience.

In order to record a baseline performance of each teacher, before he had had an opportunity to familiarize himself with television as a teaching medium, the group was taken to a television studio and told to stand up and teach. Each teacher was given about two hours warning but no opportunity to prepare what he would say. It was suggested that he might teach a lesson he had recently taught in his own classroom. A classroom set, including desk, blackboard, chalk, eraser, and a map of the United States, was provided in the studio. In addition the Project Production Director gave each teacher a brief indoctrination interview before the cameras.

Although all the teachers were apprehensive, none of them failed to turn in a highly plausible performance. The studio staff, with two years of educational television behind them, were amazed at the uniformly high level of performance and noted how much better it was than many of the highly rehearsed performances they had had a part in producing. Teachers talked as if they were in their own classrooms, calling pupils by name, anticipating and answering questions and generally making enlightened educational noises.

The uniformly and unexpectedly high performance of this group of six teachers immediately raised certain important questions relating to the central topic of the spring series of studies. Had we merely run onto an exceptionally talented group of potential television performers? Was it the kind of briefing they had had? Was it the lack of rehearsal? Was it because they were highly selected classroom performers anyway, and hence qualified for television performance of this type? Or was it that all teachers might be expected to show television talent?

In order to answer the first of these questions nine additional teachers were selected from the panels of nominees and put through the same experimental procedure. Again the same poised performance was recorded in every case.

In order to answer the question of whether or not their classroom proficiency was the unexpected variable operating, the staff turned next to the problem of recording the performances of teachers who were not selected for their teaching proficiency. But how does one go about getting such a group invited into the studio? In order to solve this problem a school system was chosen which had twenty-eight fifth and sixth grade teachers. Thinking that there might be as many as three who could not possibly schedule a trip to the campus, an invitation was issued for twenty-five of this group of teachers to come to the studio. The same type of briefing and impromptu performances was employed.

Now a variety of performances was observed. Some of them clearly exhibited the now familiar pattern which had been observed in the poised performances of teachers who were already known to be outstanding. The most noticeable difference, however, was in the greater insecurity and suspicion apparent in certain members of this group. Some of the actual performances before the camera were also inferior, but the principal differences were in the contextual behavior of some of the teachers.

It was a comparatively simple matter to secure informed judgments of who the outstanding classroom teachers in the last group of twenty-five were. These teachers were then added to the original two groups of six and nine, respectively, giving a sub-sample of twenty-one outstanding teachers and a subsample of nineteen who were not judged to be outstanding. It should be kept in mind that the nineteen were not necessarily poor teachers, nor necessarily even mediocre; they simply were not among those nominated as outstanding. Furthermore, some of the nineteen undoubtedly were competent teachers whose classroom performance had not yet come to the attention of their supervisors. Similarly, it should be borne in mind that some of those nominated as outstanding might not have been judged to be outstanding by the pupils who faced them in the classroom every day. In other words, the criterion differentiation between the two sub-samples is subject to some measure of unreliability.

A ten-minute kinescope recording of each teacher's baseline performance was taken. When additional research funds become available it will be a relatively straight-forward matter to copy the film and edit it in such a manner that the samples can be presented in random order to panels of educators and pupils to see if they make the same selections from the filmed performances that supervisors made from classroom performances. If they do, it will be strong evidence that, even without production facilities and the features of curriculum planning which go with good teaching, the television camera is able to capture certain palpable features of the outstanding classroom teacher. Of course, certain other questions will remain to be answered, such as whether the qualities which the camera successfully captured are those which actually contribute to classroom efficiency or whether they are merely by-products of the greater personal security which the capable teacher enjoys when her capability is recognized by her supervisors.

Tentative Conclusion

The television situation, though not necessarily the camera, elicits an observable differential between the behavior of outstanding and non-outstanding teachers. The outstanding teachers, when asked to perform impromptu under the conditions employed in this study, exhibit poised performances and appear to be altogether effective in the presentation of didactic material. Non-outstanding teachers may often do as well, but there is more indication of a tendency among them to become disturbed and suspicious under television direction. The study strongly suggests that this latter group might not he able to stand the strain of continuous television production.

The Gross Feasibility Study

Will teachers who are selected solely because of their superior performance in the classroom teach successfully in the studio, or does television require a special talent?

If classroom television is to be conceived as a way of spreading the influence of the superior teacher, it becomes important to discover whether or not the superior teacher is still superior when she is taken out of her live classroom and asked to teach before bright lights, into the lens of a camera, with no one in the crowded and cluttered studio paying the slightest attention to what she has to say. A considerable proportion of those who are experienced in commercial production say that teachers cannot be selected for television in this way. Educators, on the other hand, take a dim view of any plan for turning the classroom into an actor's stage. If television, through the practical demands of its studios, frustrates the very talent which it seeks to distribute, then the future of educational television may well lie along a rough and winding road, and may be a long way in the future.

Procedure

1 *The Production Panel*

The superintendents of Bloomfield, Clifton, and Montclair, New Jersey, and of New York City were asked to select their outstanding fifth grade teachers and to permit their employment by the Project in a consultant capacity in order to produce a unit in the fifth grade curriculum for television. In addition, one teacher from Long Branch, New Jersey, who had previously been recommended to the New Jersey State Educational Station, WTLV-TV, at New Brunswick, was included in the panel. Superintendents were asked not to speculate on their nominees' photogenic or histrionic potentialities but to make their recommendations solely on the basis of classroom effectiveness.

The top teacher on the list was contacted first; then, if necessary, the second teacher and the third. After five teachers had been selected, the working panel included only one man. The next nominated male teacher was then added to the panel. This accounts for the fact that two members of the panel came from the same system.

The panel was given the task of preparing, under the leadership of an experienced educational television producer, a unit of the fifth grade curriculum in the area of the social studies. Since the pioneer period of American history is commonly studied in the spring of the fifth grade year, an instructional unit dealing with this topic was selected by the panel.

The assignment, furthermore, was to develop a two-weeks daily series, and to make the television teaching carry as much of the classroom instructional burden as possible. This was to be an experiment in *maximum teaching*, in an all-out effort to attain every educational objective of the pioneer unit, and not merely an *enrichment* program to supplement classroom instruction. As such it was an ambitious undertaking. Yet it is important that the serious researcher test the outside limits of the medium. The full development of educational television's maximum possibilities calls for a bold approach, but one in which the risks are thoughtfully calculated and the results objectively appraised.

The panel normally met all day on Saturdays and on one evening each week. The first meeting was held on March twentieth and the last lesson of the series was kinescoped on May twenty-second. Each presentation was approximately a half hour in length. There were nine lessons in the series. Each lesson was prepared by the panel as a group, and the teacher who taught it was selected by the panel only after a considerable proportion of the preparation had been completed. Three teachers taught two lessons each and three taught one lesson each. There was no attempt within the panel to decide which of them was the best television teacher, and it was purely a matter of working convenience as to who was selected to teach two lessons and who, one lesson only.

2 *Studio Operations*

The lessons were produced and kinescoped in the College Studio. The facilities were augmented by equipment recently transferred from Station WTLV-TV after that project was abandoned by the State. Studio facilities included state-owned equipment and equipment on loan from the General Precision Laboratories, the Allen B. DuMont Laboratories, the Kliegl Brothers Lighting Company, and the Radio Corporation of America. In addition, some key personnel were made available on the WTLV-TV payroll.

The studio set-up, as actually employed in this series, was a two-camera studio chain with a sixteen millimeter video-recorder and hot processor producing positive film. For the most part, classroom sets were used, although there was one venture into set-making with a log cabin interior. Models, both of sets and props, were used extensively. Props were loaned by the Newark Museums, the Newark City Library, the New Jersey Historical Society, the Monmouth County Historical Association, and the

Montclair Board of Education. A television director, experienced in educational television, directed the studio production, under the general supervision of the Production Director.

Efforts were made to economize on studio time in order to keep payroll and other operating costs at a minimum. Inevitably this may have reduced the quality of the eventual product somewhat, although, as compared with other educational productions which have been seen by the Project Staff, the finished productions were excellent, both educationally and technically.

Altogether, thirty-six hours of on-camera studio rehearsal time were required. This, together with actual studio production time, time for emergency repairs, etc. added up to a total of approximately forty-two hours of live studio time required for the series. This total, of course, does not include studio time consumed in the Baseline, Intercommunication, and other Studies conducted during the spring. The estimated cost of the commercial equivalent of this studio time is $18,600 to $24,000, for the Pioneer Series alone.

3 *Classroom Utilization*

Earlier surveys in this research series have indicated that quite as much preparation may be required for the proper utilization of television in the classrooms as for the productions themselves. With this in mind the panel of consultant teachers prepared a Teacher's Guide. This was placed in the hands of each classroom teacher, in a meeting which preceded the field trial.

In addition, the classroom teachers were given an opportunity to discuss the utilization of the series with the Educational Production Director before the telecasts were even scheduled for the field trial. Such matters as the time of day when the telecasts could best be utilized, the type of analysis to be submitted by teachers, the educational objectives of the series, and the visiting of classrooms during telecasts, were settled in face-to-face consultation in which the wishes of the classroom teachers were sought and were respected.

4 *The Field Trial*

Arrangements were made for a field trial of the Pioneer Series. Through the Superintendent of Schools of Monmouth County, New Jersey, and the Superintendents of the respective City Schools, two groups of fifth grade teachers and their principals were assembled, one in Long Branch and the other in Red Bank.

In these sessions the educational objectives of the Pioneer Series were discussed and the research objectives of the field trial were outlined. Teachers agreed to use the Series as a regular part of their class work, insofar as their schedules would permit. They recommended that the lessons be broadcast at ten o'clock in the morning. That recommendation was accepted. Teacher's Guides and daily report forms were distributed.

Thirteen fifth grade classrooms were involved in the field trial. In one of the classrooms there were both fifth and sixth grade pupils. In another, pupils from a special class of slower learning pupils visited during the broadcasts. Two classes missed two of the lessons because of conflicting arrangements made previously, and one class missed one of the lessons. There is a possibility that there may have been one or two other gaps; our records are somewhat uncertain as to this point. In addition, allowance should be made for the fact that not all receivers worked satisfactorily on all days and that, on two days, difficulty with the projection equipment in the broadcasting station cut down markedly on the intelligibility of the audio portion of the signal. Three hundred and eight pupils returned Pupil Evaluation Forms, so it is certain that at least this number saw a major portion of the lessons.

Station WRTV (UHF) of Asbury Park volunteered to present the broadcasts. Daily broadcasts from film recordings were presented each school day for two weeks beginning Monday, May twenty-fourth. Monday, May thirty-first, being a school holiday, was omitted from the broadcast schedule. Arrangements were made by the Project Staff for the installation and servicing of special UHF receivers and antennae in each of the thirteen classrooms. In this connection it should be mentioned that UHF transmission and reception involves some special engineering problems which had to be overcome by alert monitoring during the field trial.

Representatives of the Project made spot visits to various classrooms to observe the reception and classroom utilization of the Series. At the outset some of the teachers requested that visits not be made in their classrooms but, as it became clear that it was television and not teachers which was on trial, this apprehensiveness seemed to disappear.

After the close of the field trial, each group of classroom teachers met with the panel of televised teachers and with representatives of the Project to discuss their evaluation of the experiment. At this time arrangements were made for each pupil to make an appraisal of the Series as a whole, using a special report form.

5 *Evaluation Procedure*

It is important to bear in mind that none of the studies conducted during the Spring of 1954 was a controlled experiment. All of them were either exploratory or concerned with gross issues only. In the case of the Gross Feasibility Study, evaluation is based upon the following kinds of information:

a The experiences of the production and studio staffs in preparing the series.
b The judgment of the panel of teachers who prepared the series.
c The daily reports of classroom teachers who received the broadcasts of the kinescoped lessons.
d The considerable number of informal letters and reports from pupils.

e The reports of visitors who observed the use of lessons in the classrooms.
f The terminal reports of pupils.
g The group discussions between classroom and televised teachers at the conclusion of the series.

The form prepared for the classroom teacher's daily reports was designed around issues rather than categories of response. It is a relatively open-ended questionnaire and the teachers' use of it indicated that, as such, it was successful. Six issues were presented:

a The clarity of the lesson objectives (the objectives had also been stated in the Teacher's Guide).
b The technical quality of the presentation.
c The apparent teaching abilities of the televised teacher.
d The respondent's feeling of communication with the televised teacher.
e The reaction of pupils.
f Suggestions for improvement.

The Pupil's Evaluation Form employed both categorization of response and open-ended structure. Five levels of evaluation were attempted, although the loose nature of the experimental design did not permit the definitive isolation of variables for testing purposes. The five levels were as follows:

a Information
b Interest
c Ideas
d Convictions
e Integration and utilization

Compilation of Results

Field notes were kept during the production and field trial of the Pioneer Series. The reproduction of these notes in a report of this sort, even in an appendix, would involve an unmanageable bulk of manuscript. No such attempt to reproduce them has therefore been undertaken. A descriptive account of the content of these notes appears in the narrative section of the Report (Part One).

The data which could readily be categorized were, for the most part, thrown into contingency tables from which levels of statistical significance could be readily computed. Host tests of significance were made in terms of the *Chi Square Technique*; a few utilized *Fisher's t*.

The following compilations were made:

1 Pupil evaluations were compiled of the three topics about which they learned most. Contingencies between classrooms and lessons were compiled and each of the 117 cells, as well as each of the two distributions, was checked for statistically significant deviation,
2 Pupil lists of what three actions and objects were most interesting to them were distributed by classes. The 1118 contingency cells were inspected for significance and a descriptive evaluation was made. Items were allocated between lessons. Evaluation of interest level of lessons in terms of this concrete criterion was made.
3 Pupil evaluations of the three most important ideas were compiled and distributed in contingency tables between classes and lessons. Tests were made of statistical significance of each of the 117 cells and each of the two distributions.
4 Contingencies between selections of televised teachers and ideas were compiled and statistical significance checked for the 54 cells and the two arrays.
5 Pupils' expressions of conviction which met the criterion level built into the measuring instrument were distributed by convictions and classes. The 117 contingency cells were checked for statistical significance. The two arrays—type of conviction and classroom—were also checked.
6 Mean level of pupil conviction (number of items chosen by each pupil for denial) was computed by classes and assembled separately for the two school systems involved in the field trial. *Analysis-of-variance* procedures were employed and *t-tests* were made between each of the 78 pairs of classes, as well as between the two systems. The mean level of each class was also checked by *t-test* against the sample as a whole.
7 Pupil selections of television teachers to assist them in a hypothetical project were distributed by classes and the 78 contingencies inspected for significance.
8 Pupil selections of topics about which they learned most, and ideas which they considered to be most important were distributed in a contingency table to see if there was a relation between them. The 81 cells were checked for statistical significance as was the table as a whole.

9 Those teacher evaluations which were categorical answers to each of the six daily questions were distributed by question and by lesson.

10 Qualitative comments of teachers were condensed and recorded separately by lessons. There were 422 separate types of comments, some of which were, of course, repeated by different teachers when describing the same lesson.

11 Summaries of prevailing criticisms for each lesson and for the series as a whole were compiled.

Primary Conclusions

1 *It is feasible to use outstanding classroom teachers as talent in educational television produced for classroom use, but this conclusion implies a number of conditions.*

Condition A. In the first place, the television teacher should be genuinely outstanding in his own face-to-face classroom work. Teachers who are merely satisfactory and who are chosen because they like the idea of teaching by television may not perform satisfactorily. It requires a clear and subsuming perception of one's teaching objectives, both in general and with respect to a given lesson for one to do a good job of teaching pupils who are not present, amidst the ever-present clutter and distractions of a studio. Any teacher whose primary motivation is other than educational, and who fails to subordinate her own aspirations to the needs of real-life children, is likely to lead the whole enterprise astray.

In this connection there is a special problem, that of selecting teachers who are genuinely outstanding. The administrative selection method used in this study appeared to work quite satisfactorily in general, but there was some indication that a combination of selection methods might, in some cases, point more accurately to the best teachers. As long, however, as the selection is aimed at the very top, the administrative choice is not likely to fall too far down the competency scale.

Condition B. In the second place, the television teacher should ordinarily not be too remote from her own classroom and her own pupils. A teacher who was a good fifth grade teacher two years ago may still be a good fifth grade teacher when she is restored to her classroom, but when she conjures up the pupil faces in order to talk to them in the studio, her retrospective perception is likely to be distorted. Moreover, such a teacher is likely to be criticized by the viewing pupils as talking over their heads or, as one pupil wrote, "treating us like babies."

Condition C. In the third place, outstanding classroom teachers are likely to be effective in educational television only if they recognize the cooperative role of the teacher in the classroom where the lesson in being received. This is a new facet of teaching responsibility which both production people and the televised teacher are likely to overlook. The televised teacher is talking not only to pupils; he is also talking to the pupils' teachers and, unless he enlists their intelligent cooperation, the lesson is likely to fail. There is informal evidence in support of the conclusion that where particular classroom teachers liked particular televised teachers, much more was done to develop the lesson objectives in the classroom.

Condition D. In the fourth place, the generalization of this conclusion about the television effectiveness of outstanding teachers is subject to qualifications based on the individual differences among the outstanding teachers. What makes one teacher an outstanding success in the classroom is likely to be quite different from what makes another effective. This was abundantly exemplified among the six different teachers who comprised the panel which produced the Pioneer Series. The differences between them were not merely subtle shades of skill and outlook; they were gross, conspicuous, and educationally important. One teacher could do what the other five could not do well at all, and yet each of the others had particular classroom skills which were far beyond the capacity of that one.

Condition E. In the fifth place, the exploitation of the superior teacher's abilities on television is a complex production problem which requires educational insight both in the production staff and in the studio staff. The teacher is not an actor in this kind of production. He does not read lines from a professional writer's script. Instead, the producer and the studio director must adjust themselves to each teacher's unique talents in ways which would be inconceivable in commercial television. Each teacher must be studied as a special kind of production problem. Plans for capturing his particular classroom competence must be ingeniously contrived, even in relation to such matters as lesson objectives, program format, and camera shots.

Failure to adapt television to the individual teacher may destroy otherwise effective television teaching. For example, in one or two of the Pioneer Series Lessons, failure to adapt production to the particular skills of the teacher resulted in an almost complete loss of effectiveness, even though all the basic elements of a good program were present, including a successful and likable teacher. In another case, a careful study of the teacher's talents and potentialities resulted in a highly effective presentation, even though the original prospects for this teacher were very dim. In this connection, the production staff should make maximum use of the "baseline" kinescopes, for guidance in directing each teacher toward maximum effectiveness.

2 *Classroom television will require as much attention to its classroom utilization as to its studio production.*

This conclusion is borne out, both by observation of other educational television operations, their failures and successes, and by the studies at Montclair during the past spring. The neglect of this aspect of educational motion pictures, for example, may partially account for their failure to mature as primary teaching devices, although there are ample other reasons to account for this disappointment. While the development of the Pioneer Series was accompanied by the careful preparation of a Teacher's Guide, it was apparent, from the results of the field trial, that much more should be done along this line. Teachers need to be alerted as to the potentialities of using the television presentations in their classrooms, and they need to be helped to adapt themselves to this new educational resource. The classroom teacher still holds the key to learning, and her utilization of a televised lesson generally makes the difference between success and failure of its objectives.

Teaching is much more than didactics, the enthusiasms of educational television proponents notwithstanding. For example, the television teacher needs to be continually aware of what may be going on in the classroom during his presentations and even between presentations. He should make every effort to fit his teaching to the probable activity program of the local classroom. This means suggesting a reasonable number of projects which may be carried out during the teaching of the unit, and well-timed references to these projects in progress. There should be a realistic perception of the correlative materials the local teacher may have available. The probable skills and limitations of various classroom teachers must likewise be kept in mind.

Secondary Conclusions

1 *When a pupil is asked to select topics about which he has learned the most, it appears that the local classroom development of those topics has as much to do with his selection as has their television presentation.*

One class in the field trial, in which the teacher was judged to be unusually competent, distributed its choices of highly informative lessons quite differently from other classes. Moreover, certain lessons had quite atypical distributions. In the Pioneer Series the most frequently chosen lesson was selected three times as frequently as was the least frequently chosen lesson. These facts, together with less formal observations, suggest that the choice of informative lessons was strongly influenced by what went on in the classroom where the lesson was used.

This indicates that it will be important to determine whether or not the classroom statistical variance exceeds individual pupil variance or studio variance. Unfortunately, in an uncontrolled experiment of this kind, it is impossible to make this determination statistically. A controlled experiment along these lines should provide more definite evidence as to just how important the role of the classroom teacher is, when educational television is employed. Such a study would naturally call for a further follow-up study of how to increase the variance attributable to the studio performance.

2 *Classroom utilization appears to have much to do with pupils' selection of objects and actions which they consider to be most interesting.*

Classes distributed themselves atypically in what pupils chose to be the most interesting objects and actions. This, too, suggests an important local factor in the effectiveness of television teaching. It is curious that what is shown on the screen can be made more interesting by what is done with it in the classroom.

3 *There is a very great range of interest in what is presented, even at a single grade stratum.*

Altogether, eighty-four different objects and actions were selected by pupils as among the three each considered most interesting. Fifty-six of these were mentioned by more than one pupil. Again, something indigenous to the viewing classroom is suggested. Objects and activities mentioned by more than half of the pupils in one classroom might be mentioned by no more than one or two in another class, where the same presentation was seen.

4 *Demonstration of practical use and the showing of live children seemed to be the general factors which tended to account for choices of interesting items.*

This conclusion is verified by interviews with classroom teachers and by comments written by pupils, as well as by statistical compilation. The most frequently chosen items in this section of the Pupil Evaluation Form were, in order:

a Method of building log cabins (94 choices)
b Children dancing (83 choices)
c The making of clothes (47 choices)
d The activities of the pioneer classroom (45 choices)
e The use of tools in different vocations (45 choices)
f Pioneer games (38 choices)
g Children helping their families (32 choices)
h Songs (31 choices)

5 *The basic ideas pupils select from televised lessons seem to be affected very little by individual classroom teachers.*

Taken altogether, the pupils chose the basic ideas of Lessons One and Three as among the three each considered most important. These ideas were:

(1) To be a pioneer one must be brave and not give up too easily.

(3) When people are faced with hardships and danger they must learn to help each other, just as the pioneers did.

The ideas from Lessons Four and Six were least frequently chosen. They were:

(4) Children can really help their families get along, just as pioneer children helped their families.

(6) A child can have fun playing with the simplest of everyday things, just as pioneer children had fun playing with what they had.

Idea One was selected five times as frequently as Idea Four.

Admittedly, the study had no statistical controls for the level of generality of each of the ideas which were abstracted from the lessons. The question, therefore, of which lesson was the most effective from this point of view cannot be answered. But there are more important questions which can be answered from the class distribution of choices.

In contrast to the class distribution of choices of topics about which the most had been *learned*, the choices of *ideas* were uniformly distributed among the classes, within the limits of statistical probability. No class showed a tendency to distribute itself atypically with respect to the nine ideas as a group, and no idea, with possibly the exception of Number Seven, showed a tendency to be distributed atypically among the thirteen classes as a group. Idea Seven was:

(7) Like the pioneers, we must always make sure that our families have the food and clothing they need before we try to get other things for them.

The distribution of classes with respect to this item is one which would be expected approximately once out of ten times under random sampling conditions. It is therefore only slightly suggestive of a trend.

In our analysis of pupils' attitudes toward *facts*, we inferred that the viewpoint of the local teacher had a great deal to do with what the pupil learned. But in the realm of *ideas* the situation seems to be different. The viewpoint of the local teacher does not appear to affect the differential learning of *ideas*.

This conclusion must be considered tenuous; we do not know for sure that the opinions of the teachers in this study materially differed from each other, we do not know what their personal viewpoints were, and it is entirely possible that some leveling factor was operating across all the classrooms, in spite of the teachers.

Yet this conclusion, if it continues to hold up, is astounding. We have long been arguing that the outlook of the classroom teacher subtly affects the thinking of the pupil at the abstract, as well as at the concrete level. The teacher is supposed to teach ideas, rather than facts merely. Yet does she? Our study points a tentative finger of doubt at this bright hope of the educator's profession.

6 *The idea a pupil selects as important is not necessarily the one which is developed by his favorite television teacher.*

One may state this same conclusion another way: The pupil does not necessarily choose the teacher who develops what he considers to be an important idea. It may be, of course, that pupils at this level do not clearly associate importance of ideas with what goes on in the classroom or on the television screen. It is quite likely that pupils consider it more important to select teachers on other grounds, such as warmth of personality, resourcefulness, or working skill.

7 *The particular convictions pupils select after seeing televised lessons seem to be affected very little by individual classroom teachers.*

Here we have another finding in which there are no statistically significant differences among classes. Moreover, there is no statistically significant tendency for a particular conviction to be distributed atypically among the classes. This may be due to the fact that the convictions listed were ones about which all educators would have a uniform opinion. Again, it may be due to some other leveling factor.

The statement which was most frequently denied by pupils came from Lesson Five:

(5) In the pioneer schools pupils got a better education than they do today.

The least frequently denied statement came from Lesson Six:

(6) The person who has the true pioneer spirit does not waste his time trying to amuse himself.

But, again, the phrasing of the items has a great deal to do with their tendency to be selected. What we concern ourselves with statistically, therefore, is the *distribution of the choices in relation to other factors*.

We have just said that particular convictions did not appear to be biased by classes. But there is more to this conviction business than this, as we shall see in the following section.

8 *The level of conviction which pupils are inclined to express varies greatly from class to class.*

This is one of the most exciting outcomes of the study. There were nine statements, one based on each lesson, which a pupil could deny, in spite of assurance that he would be going against a popular viewpoint when he did so. On the average, pupils ventured to deny 5.56 of them. But the averages of certain classes differed from this group average to a highly significant extent. For example, the class taught by the outstanding teacher mentioned in a previous section averaged 6.71 denials, a deviation which would occur less than once in 30,000 times under random conditions.

Analysis of variance yielded an *F-ratio* of 2.94 which, for 12 and 291 degrees of freedom, gives a *p-value* of approximately .02. Five of the classes deviated significantly from the group as a whole in level of conviction. When each of the thirteen classes was compared with each of the other twelve, nearly half the seventy-eight paired contrasts were statistically significant.

Apparently there are great differences between classrooms *in the willingness of pupils to venture the expression of a personal conviction which might be criticized*. If we put this conclusion together with the one in the previous section, we come up with something like this: *Local teachers may not greatly influence WHAT pupils believe, but they do have a lot to do with pupils' FREEDOM TO EXPRESS their beliefs*. Educational television must take account of the great extremes of intellectual climate in which its effectiveness will be tested.

9 *Televised teachers are subject to marked differences in popularity.*

Pupils in the field trial were given an opportunity to select the televised teacher whom they would most want to help them on a project. Three of the six televised teachers received 82% of the choices on this item.

10 *Pupils claimed to have learned the most in topical areas where they judged the corresponding ideas to be important.*

While, as we have already reported, there was no significant contingency between classrooms and ideas, there was a significant contingency between the perceived information value of the different television lessons, and the ideas which were considered to be important. This suggests that the television lessons really carried ideational freight somewhat commensurate with their informational loading. Television's great potentiality for organizing facts and mobilizing rich visual displays may, therefore, offer improved opportunities for teaching important ideas in the classroom. There is the possibility that it may even surpass the local teacher in this respect.

11 *Teachers generally agreed that the educational objectives were clearly apparent in all the televised lessons and that the objectives were successfully attained by the televised teachers.*

The vote on clarity of objectives was almost unanimous, there being only two qualified votes on one lesson and one on another. With respect to success in attaining objectives, there were 101 categorically affirmative votes, two qualified affirmatives, two categorically negative votes, and three qualified negatives.

No attempt is made to summarize at this point the comments which accompanied these teacher assessments.

12 *There were technical difficulties which interfered with the effectiveness of the presentations.*

Forty-six votes categorically affirmed the audio-visual success of particular lessons, and twenty-four votes categorically denied the audio-visual success of particular lessons. There were thirty-two reports calling attention particularly to poor audio reception and twenty calling attention to poor video reception.

The distribution of reports of failure, together with what is known from direct observation, indicates that most of the failures were attributable to the unsatisfactory operation of the classroom receiving sets. The sets were installed especially for the field trial and it required some servicing of several sets and their antennae before operation became satisfactory. If the series had continued, it is likely that nearly all of the technical difficulties would have been overcome.

But there were technical difficulties which were a function of studio direction technique, such as the difficulty of picking up the voice of a strange teacher when she turned to write something on the blackboard. In one area, however, the technical quality of the productions was surprisingly satisfactory—that of the film recording. The "kinescopes" were excellent, although the making of film recordings is generally regarded among television engineers as a high art.

There were many comments regarding technical aspects of the studio production which are not summarized in this report, since they have importance, primarily, for the non-educational aspects of television.

13 *Teachers generally agreed that the outstanding classroom abilities of the televised teacher were captured by the camera.*

Eighty-five out of 105 comments were affirmative on this point and seventy-four of these were categorically affirmative. There were only fifteen categorically negative responses and these tended to be associated, with presentations in which there were technical difficulties. No attempt is made here to summarize the kinds of abilities which the viewing teachers thought they detected in the televised teachers, although there were 166 such estimates of abilities, together with a number of comments on disabilities and suggestions for improvement.

14 *The viewing teachers found the televised teachers highly acceptable as professional colleagues and as persons.*

When asked if they would predict that the televised teacher would spontaneously enrich and add to what had already been offered on the television screen, the viewing teachers gave 107 categorically affirmative answers, seven qualified answers, and one categorically negative answer. Only six times did viewing teachers not give an answer to this question.

When asked if they thought it would seem awkward to talk to the televised teacher about the effectiveness of the presentation, only six gave a categorically affirmative answer, ninety-one gave a categorically negative answer, none gave a qualified answer, and nineteen did not answer. It should be said in this connection that the teachers filled out their reports anonymously and before they had an opportunity to meet any of the televised teachers face to face.

This conclusion is bolstered by direct observation. When the classroom teachers finally met the televised teachers in the post-series meetings they cordially greeted them as old friends, somewhat to the surprise of the televised teachers. Yet it could easily have been otherwise, for television brings into the classroom a rival teacher who may be perceived as either a guest or an over-privileged intruder.

15 *It is very difficult for television to make everything clear to the viewing pupil.*

It is easy to underestimate the educational and technical problems which must be solved in the projection of outstanding teachers into classrooms by means of television. It involves much more than turning a candid television camera on an outstanding teacher at work. In spite of the care taken by the panel of teachers, their personal skill, and meticulous technical direction, there was much that was puzzling to the pupils. In each lesson there was at least one teacher who reported that the pupils were puzzled about something, and in some lessons the majority of teachers reported difficulties of this sort among the pupils. Some of this may be due to the natural arousal of further curiosity, but, for the most part, the comments indicate that the skill to make matters clear on the television screen is an accomplishment not easily attained.

16 *Viewing teachers do not consider educational television to be directly competitive with commercial television, but they do tend to be critical of certain features which are inherent in the medium.*

In the pre-series meetings, the viewing teachers, as do many others, expressed some apprehension that educational television would have to compete with commercial television for the interest of the pupils. But after the televised lessons began to come to the classrooms, nothing more was heard of this problem. Apparently, neither teachers nor pupils consider the presentation of a lesson by television as anything which needs to be directly compared with commercial television. The issue is probably entirely academic.

The teachers did offer many criticisms, however. One group of criticisms had to do with the use of illustrations. They wanted illustrative material blown up larger. Maps were sometimes too detailed—a common problem in educational television. The line drawings, which it was hoped would prove particularly suitable for television, were generally unsatisfactory.

Viewing teachers were insistent that the televised teachers should look directly into the camera more of the time. Yet it had seemed to the directors during production that considerable emphasis had already been placed on this point. The viewing teachers also criticized other movements, particularly the televised teacher's blackboard behavior.

The personal appearance of the televised teachers was criticized. It had been agreed that no studio make-up would be used on the teachers in these productions and there was occasional criticism of their appearance. When the classroom teachers met the televised teachers in conference at the end of the series they commented spontaneously on how much better they looked in real life than on the television screen. One teacher said, "Why, you've all lost at least ten pounds."

The viewing teachers thought more time should be spent in introducing the television teachers to the pupils. They wanted more sustained close-ups of the televised teacher. They generally wanted the television teacher to become better known to the pupils as a person.

There was a general tendency among teachers and pupils to ask for more action, particularly action of other children, shown on the screen. They asked for live models, rather than pictures and dolls. Some thought it would be better to show the television teacher's own class on the screen, but there was a shift of opinion on this point as the series progressed. Some suggested that more "sparkling" language be used.

The voices and diction of the television teachers were often criticized. Partly this was a reflection on technical difficulties, partly a reflection on the amateur status of the teachers as television performers.

There was a tendency of some programs to contain too much material and, at the same time, to progress too slowly. These criticisms represent a real challenge to the educational television producer, whose task, in the light of this study, looms up as more and more important. In fact, it would appear that the entire role of a director of educational production must be conceptualized in ways which are quite different from anything comparable in commercial television. On him rests much of the responsibility for the failure or success of classroom television. This is particularly important if outstanding classroom teachers are to be employed to teach in the studio.

Finally—and this is probably most important of all—the receiving teachers insisted that much more be done to integrate the pupil's activities and learning in the classroom with the television lesson. They felt that this was as much a responsibility of the educational television producer as it was their own. They said their children wanted more active parts in the lessons, that they wanted evidence of co-operation between the viewing pupil and the televised teacher, and that television should take more effective steps to mobilize the pupil's initiative.

There are many other tentative conclusions of a minor nature which can be drawn from the Gross Feasibility study, but they are related primarily to the particular kinds of production efforts which entered into the individual lessons of the Pioneer Series. They have meaning only in relation to the contexts of particular lesson-productions. It does not seem appropriate, therefore, to report them here. Extensive use will be made of all the knowledge gained in this study, when the opportunity is made for extending it to include all of the "impact areas" noted on the first page of this Report.

The Intercommunication Study

How can the intercommunication aspects of learning and teaching be preserved when television is used extensively in the classroom?

In contrast to the views of a century ago, the modern educator sees learning as taking place through *intercommunication*. Teaching is no longer conceived as a constant stream of talk funneled from the mouth of the teacher into the ear of the pupil. In the enlightened school of today ideas are exchanged back and forth between pupil and teacher, between pupil and pupil, and between pupil and society. The classroom is envisioned as a system of reverberating circuits, through which ideas are amplified by their free exchange, and brought into clear focus for all to see. The effectiveness, both of the teacher as a teacher and of the learner as a learner, is measured by their sensitivity to each other and to the incipient strivings of the society in which they enact their roles.

But television, physically at least, would seem to be a one-way street. The viewer-listener cannot talk to the speaker. Nor can he readily exchange places with him in order to clear up a subtle point or reconcile a divergent view. Therefore, will not classroom television, if used as a primary instructional device, tend to suppress freedom of communication? And will it not condemn millions of pupils to sitting with their hands folded before an implacable sheet of phosphorescent glass? A more alarming phrasing of the issue is to say that television, employed in an improper context, may do more to destroy the enlightened educational developments of the last century than any of us would care to imagine.

It is easy to come up with too-hasty answers when the stakes are so high and fundamental values appear to be threatened. This is as true of the modern educator who is convinced of the importance of classroom intercommunication as it is of the social planner who thinks it would be a good idea to economize on teachers. Let us, therefore, be as sensible as possible; let us resolve this intercommunication issue into four basic questions.

1 It might be smart to ask ourselves just how much verbal intercommunication actually does take place in the modern classroom. How often does Johnny, who is one of forty pupils, talk to his teacher; what does he say, and what response does he get?
2 Does the extensive use of television in the classroom diminish the intercommunication aspects of what goes on there? May not television, instead, give both teachers and pupils more fascinating things to talk to each other about, and hence enrich the intercommunicative aspects of learning? May it not take the teacher away from her blackboard and seat her at her pupils' elbows?
3 Just how does intercommunication function in learning? Is it an integral part of all phases of the learning process or does it play a primary role at certain stages only?
Are all types of learning equally dependent upon it?
4 What measures may one employ, both in studio production and in classroom utilization, to preserve the learning values which are presumed to be inherent in intercommunication? There are exciting possibilities here. For example, viewers of educational television sometimes claim that they feel themselves to be in more intimate communication with the televised teacher than with the one who stands at the front of their classroom.

The problem of intercommunication in the classroom is only secondarily related to the gross feasibility problem which was the primary target for the spring. The problem area is a large one and what was accomplished amounted to little more than some imaginative speculation followed by trial productions in the studio and adjacent viewing rooms. Operations were conducted in the graduate workshop without the aid of Project funds. They centered around part of the last of the four basic questions mentioned above: the question of studio techniques for preserving intercommunication values.

Studio Techniques for Stimulating or Simulating Intercommunication

We have taken the liberty of assigning picturesque names to some of the studio techniques which may be employed to preserve the intercommunication values in learning.

1 *Mind Reading.* This is the use of the simulated question or remark of the viewer. It is used extensively by "Miss Frances" of NBC's *Ding Dong School* series. Its effectiveness depends upon one's faithful perception of the world through the viewer's eyes, a perception which none but the most sensitive of classroom teachers is likely to have, and which is quickly lost when the teacher is promoted to an administrator's desk.
2 *Intercession.* This is the reportorial or interviewer approach which commercial news programs use extensively. The interviewer tries to ask questions in behalf of the viewer, and thus serve as his surrogate. Again, the interviewer must have the ability to phrase the questions the pupil would want to have answered. Most interviewers succeed in making the verbal exchange amusing, but they usually get in the way of its being educational.
3 *Panel of Peers.* If the pupil cannot ask questions or discuss the lesson, perhaps a group of his peers, being generally like him, can be depended upon to say, out loud, what he is thinking. But is this equivalent to having the pupil speak his thoughts for himself?
4 *Real People.* The study this spring has turned up some surprises. One of them is this: Children do not think of television actors as being real people. They are, instead, glamorous creatures from a phantasy world. When the pupil discovers that the televised person is what he calls "real", his attitudes turn a flip-flop. The televised person becomes plausible, and the pupil studies his behavior in a new and realistic light.
5 *Emergent Personality.* The feeling of intercommunication is more likely to occur if the pupil hears a familiar voice and sees a familiar face. There are many steps which can be taken to make the televised teacher emerge as a familiar personality in the child's social milieu. One of them, of course, is to use the same televised teacher with some regularity.
6 *Disembodied Voice.* Here we get into the subtleties of studio technique. The viewer feels a sound barrier between himself and the teacher. How can he pierce it? An off-camera voice seems to be having the same difficulty in "getting through" to the teacher to ask a question. The pupil establishes a "common threat" type of identification with the disembodied voice. After this is accomplished psychologically, the disembodied voice succeeds in penetrating the sound barrier and the viewer, too, feels that he has succeeded in establishing intercommunication.
7 *Heckling.* The hypothetical communication axis ordinarily extends from the televised teacher to the viewing pupil. One of the achievements of intercommunication is the placing of the pupil, from time to time, on the same end of the axis as his teacher. A heckler, either shown on or off-camera apparently can do much to accomplish this. The pupil may either identify with the heckler or with the teacher.
8 *Roving Eye.* This is a studio technique in which the camera is made to behave as would a visitor in the teacher's office or classroom. It may be combined with the disembodied voice approach.

9 *Teacher's Lap*. Television's "capacity for intimacy" is often mentioned. The use of close camera shots may give the pupil the same view of his teacher's face as he would get if he were sitting on the teacher's lap. Cues of facial expression and voice intonation may thus be picked up which might be lost in the case of a teacher standing in the front of a classroom.

10 *Interlude*. The televised lesson may be broken up with an interlude for the pupils to raise questions with their own classroom teacher, to prepare working materials, or to perform related tasks. During the interlude, pupils in the viewing class may perform exercises competitively with pupils shown on the television screen.

11 *Hog Fattening*. The frustration caused by the impenetrable sound barrier may be used to stimulate greater intercommunication in the classroom as soon as the television set is turned off. We have named the technique after Dr. Herbert Toops' method of fattening hogs. Since, during the latter part of the fattening period, the task is to get the hogs to consume as much feed as possible, he suggests dividing the feed pen in two and then feeding half the herd while the other half squeals hungrily on the other side of the barrier. When the first group is satisfied, their appetites are quickly revived when they see and hear the gusto with which their hungry neighbors take their turn.

Procedure

There were forty-one productions, exclusive of baseline samples, which were designed during the spring. Of these, thirty-four were actually produced in the studio and twenty-eight presented to pupils, either in their regular classrooms or in special viewing groups.

To some extent, all of these productions involved designed experimentation with studio solutions to the intercommunication problem. However, those which concerned themselves primarily with the problem were limited to seven, of which four were viewed in a tenth grade classroom, two were viewed by specially assembled fourth graders, and one was viewed by the graduate workshop group only. All of the studio techniques mentioned in the preceding section were tried in one form or another, usually in combinations of two or more.

Tentative Conclusions

Conclusions drawn from the intercommunication study are to be classed as little more than enlightened observations. Each of the studio techniques has certain palpable advantages, disadvantages and practical difficulties.

1 *Mind Reading*. This works remarkably well when it is skillfully employed with younger pupils. The viewer feels that his unuttered questions are being sensed, that there is, therefore, a bond of understanding between himself and the teacher whom he has never met. But only the most psychologically perceptive teachers dare try the technique amidst the clutter of a television studio. It demands of them an unshakably accurate perception of their pupils' outlooks. Certainly they must have taught the same lesson many times to children of the same age, and of the same intellectual and cultural level. Otherwise they will not know how the pupil would ask his question, and they will, as one viewing pupil complainingly wrote, "treat us like babies." An off-pitch impugned to the viewer by the teacher can completely destroy the pupil's feeling of being in communication with her. Our experience also strongly suggests that if a teacher is only a few months away from the live classroom, that fact may so dim his understanding of the pupil's outlook that he will soon misuse the technique.

Another note should be made, and this is important to those who are concerned with the evaluation of classroom television. When this technique is used, other teachers who view the presentation are likely to complain that the questions are off-key or that they are distracting. But only the children themselves can make a proper evaluation and, to an unexpected extent, they do not agree with adults. An example of this is the common adult response to the technique when it is used in the *Ding Dong School* program. They find the pace too slow, the questions bizarre, and little grounds for rapport. Yet the youngsters do not agree at all. The results suggest that Dr. Horowitz[3] knows her youngsters better than their parents or their teachers do.

2 *Intercession*. This is one of the most commonly used and, perhaps, the least effective of the methods of securing a sense of intercommunication. Neither the person interviewed nor the interviewer emerges as a palpable personality in the mind of the pupil. They get in each other's way, become involved with each other, and the viewer is quickly elbowed out of the picture. It is a makeshift expedient to be used only when television is used to bring the "expert," who cannot talk the pupils' language, momentarily into the classroom for display.

3 *Panel of Peers*. This method has real possibilities when used in connection with *Hog Fattening* (11). However, it is important that the panel discussion be completely spontaneous if it is to tempt the viewer to take part. There must be explosive remarks, ejaculations, puzzled expressions on faces, competition for the listener's ear, and all the other features which characterize a genuine clash of ideas.

Yet this may be more than the studio crew can handle. Unexpected and unartistic things happen. The director scarcely knows how to set up his shots and the boom operator is likely to start swinging wildly all over the talent area. The result is that the receiving sets fail to reproduce the essential features of the panel exchange. In order to get things under control, the studio crew will insist that the program be rehearsed, for participants to take their allotted turns, and for everyone to "sit pretty for the camera man." This turns the discussion into a kind of amateur dramatic performance. No one is much surprised at what happens, no one is really puzzled, and everyone speaks in measured tones. Thus, much of the intercommunication value is lost when priority is given to technical studio requirements.

[3] Editors' note: This should probably be Dr. Horwich, who was known as "Miss Frances."

4 *Real People*. Even when pantomime is used, pupils often prefer to have the make-believe stripped away and the actors reveal themselves in their natural roles. This may destroy the phantasy, but they say it makes the point of the pantomime clearer and gives a much more intimate feeling of participation in the lesson.

This was illustrated in the Pioneer Series where one teacher used two children from his own classroom to demonstrate, in costume, some of the activities of pioneer children. The viewing children complained that they would have preferred to have the "television children" talk to the teacher and perhaps have the lesson show them getting ready for the pantomime. This applied to the log cabin "set" too. Instead of adhering rigidly to the illusion of a log cabin, the viewing children felt themselves in better communication when it was pointed out how the set was made *to look like* a log cabin.

Undoubtedly there is much more to be learned about this matter of realism *versus* illusion, and its bearing upon the intercommunicative aspects of learning. It may be that here we are being biased by some of our motion picture traditions.

We could even speculate that the pupil learns most about what is being taught in a dramatized lesson if he views it as if he were in the wings rather than in the orchestra.

5 *Emergent Personality*. The evidence in favor of this technique is rapidly mounting, although it is still informal in nature. It takes time to become familiar with a teacher's voice, verbal pace, and facial cues. This argues strongly for one teacher to appear daily throughout a series of lessons. In our Pioneer Series there was some informal evidence that the pupils responded more spontaneously to a teacher when she reappeared to teach a second lesson. Moreover, the teacher who teaches all of a series can do a much better job of integrating the material, that is, calling attention to the relation between what was said yesterday and what is implied today. A series, all taught by the same teacher, would seem to be more of one piece.

6 *Disembodied Voice*. Experimentation with this technique was tried in several ways. It can easily degenerate to the level of *Intercession* but our informal evidence indicates that it has some exciting possibilities, provided it can be properly developed.

7 *Heckling*. This was combined, in one of our productions, with the technique of the *Disembodied Voice*. It is little more than a passing trick, and not something to be developed for repeated or continuous use.

8 *Roving Eye*. This, too, can be combined with the *Disembodied Voice*. Our experience indicates that it can be used effectively to give the viewer the sense of participation. The camera work required, however, is complex and it would take a remarkably skillful studio crew to develop the technique adequately.

9 *Teacher's Lap*. Here is where television can take advantage of one of its natural capabilities to produce the feeling of intercommunication. The close-up shot is clearly an effective device, especially when it is used in connection with a teacher whose personal warmth is such that the pupil would want to get close to her. We experimented with this technique in our Pioneer Series with highly encouraging, though tentative, results. More is involved, of course, than mere camera work. The teacher has to teach as if the pupil were on her lap and she must accept the value of this kind of teaching. For example, if the camera is in close, the teacher should ordinarily be paying attention more to the viewer than to any object in the studio.

10 *Interlude*. Experimentation with this technique suggests that much more should be done with it. Broadcast television, of course, might question this use of station time, but closed circuit television would not find the technique administratively unfeasible. This technique further opens the door to pupil participation and it also provides another way for the classroom teacher to coordinate her teaching efforts with those of the televised teacher.

11 *Hog Fattening*. This technique requires the use of open-ended presentations—presentations in which questions are raised and only partly answered, where controversial viewpoints are expressed, and where, if possible, there is a great deal of the kind of activity in the studio which can be duplicated in the classroom. When some or all of these conditions are met, excitement runs high in the classroom and, as our experience clearly indicates, pupils can hardly wait until the set is turned off and they can get both front feet into the trough. The technique will probably fail, however, if the classroom teacher fails to participate or tries to steer the discussion away from the points toward which psychological pressure has directed it.

General Conclusion

Educational television need not destroy the intercommunication values of teaching and learning if proper ingenuity is used in the studio and good sense is used in the classroom. But it could destroy them, particularly if it is used merely as a "medium of mass education," or as an inexpensive substitute for cooperative learning.

91

Television and the Teacher[1]

Television is a marvelous electronic device but it has not yet become an educational instrument. Between now and the day it becomes educationally mature a lot of important things will have to happen. For one thing, the people who manipulate the gadget will have to end their preoccupation with the little technical rules that now regiment the studio and turn their attention broadly to the educational process and the role they can play in it. For another, educators are going to have to open their minds to unheard-of curricular developments—developments which, for the first time, television makes possible.

But before we get too much involved with television's academic road ahead, let us see for ourselves how it feels to be a television teacher. Those of us who have come face to face with that four-eyed studio monster, the camera, are not likely to forget our first experience. The hot lights come on. You not only see them; almost instantly you feel the dry heat on your face and on the backs of your hands. It is as if you are yourself a lamp bulb that has just been turned on. In one creeping moment the studio clutter and all its mumbling activity are overrun by the converging shadows. The boom "mike" hovers just overhead like a Sword of Damocles. A crouching figure on the floor in front of you swings its arm in a wide arc and points an accusing finger. Now! Start teaching!

There is no class. The studio is filled with people—busy people—but none of them is concerned with what you are saying; they have other work to do, their own little jokes to laugh at. There are no questions from the class, no puzzled expressions on the faces of students, not even the familiar signs of boredom or disagreement. You are there but you do not exist as a social being. Your imagination catches a flitting glimpse of a disembodied ghost standing by the clock in Grand Central Station trying to expound an idea of intricate and desperate importance to the scurrying crowds. No one hears. No one sees. So you wanted to teach on television! In the words of two popular TV clichés, you asked for it, so there you are!

If we were to stop at this point in our discussion of educational television, it could only be to conclude that here is something which is ominously impersonal, artificial, and inherently nonintercommunicative. We would have made it appear that the automation that will as surely touch our classrooms as it will our factories must produce a generation of wooden teachers and putty pupils. But nothing could be farther from the truth.

In spite of all that may be said against it, television has a peculiar capacity for intimacy. Paradoxically this capacity stems from a mechanical limitation of the television tube itself. The image we see on our screens is composed of fine polka dots of light spotted there by the scanning beam as it swings rapidly across the face of the tube, line by line. But the dots are not as fine, nor are there as many of them as the engineers would like. The image produced has a coarse quality that makes it compare unfavorably with a photograph or with a motion-picture film projected on a screen. We say the television image has limited *definition*.

Because of television's limited definition, production directors have had to forego the staging of "production numbers" requiring the reproduction of large amounts of detail in one shot. The engulfing excitement of a live seven-ring circus performance, or Cinerama, is not for television—at least not yet. Instead, studios have had to make more use of candid close-ups, and have had to ask their talent to rub noses when talking to each other before the camera.

But out of this, as well as out of certain flexible features of camera coordination not possible with motion pictures, has come television's "capacity for intimacy." The viewer is brought up close to the speaker's face. No longer is the pupil seated at a desk 30 feet away from his shrill-voiced teacher; he is taken up and seated on the teacher's lap, and she speaks into his ear with the soft voice of understanding. Now, for the first time, he catches the twinkle in her eye, senses the lines about her mouth as she speaks, hears the overtones of gentleness in what she has to say. No longer is the blackboard a shiny black expanse on the far side of the room; instead, what he is expected to examine is brought up to reading distance and set down before him at the center of his attention.

But what about intercommunication? Here again, if we look at television's educational capacities rather than at its present commercial practices, we find encouraging answers. An analogy may help. Before the days of newspapers, news was spread inaccurately

[1] First published as Kelly, G. A. (1955). Television and the teacher. *American Psychologist, 10* (10), 590–592. Now in the public domain, and republished by permission of Jacqueline Aldridge.

Collected Papers of the Pioneer of Constructivist Psychology: George A. Kelly, First Edition. Edited by David A. Winter and Nick Reed.

by word of mouth and the town crier passed on his meager information by bellowing up and down the street at his neighbors. When newspapers came, people ceased to depend wholly upon the chatter of gossip and the town crier was silenced. People withdrew to their homes and absorbed the printed information in passive silence.

But the newspapers did not turn us into a society of inarticulate introverts. If anything, face-to-face discussions became all the more animated, they covered a wider range of topics, and, because they made use of better information, they became more profitable. Intercommunication in the age of newspapers actually improved.

An experiment performed last year at the New Jersey State Teachers College at Montclair throws light on the intercommunicative aspect of educational television. A tenth-grade class was coming to grips with a curricular unit in literary criticism. One day the period was divided into two half-hour parts. During the first half-hour a panel discussion of certain assigned books was presented by closed-circuit television. During the presentation there was an obvious mounting tension among members of the class. The several experimental observers in the room were ignored. Even the exploding flash bulbs of certain enthusiastic data seekers attracted no more than an irritated glance. The instant the television presentation was concluded the class went into action in a manner that would warm the heart of any discussion-minded teacher. The students were ready. They were informed. The issues were partially drawn. Not even a fire drill or a football holiday could have blocked the educative process which had been set in motion by the timely telecast.

The Montclair 1954 series of experiments furnished evidence of a similar nature at other grade levels and with other topical content. Those who fear that educational television will create passivity in the pupil have nothing to worry about, *provided* television is developed in the larger context of teaching and learning and not simply as a device for reproducing the faces of half-scared teachers in the local high school auditorium.

The development of television as an educational device hinges on a kind of psychological study that has rarely been mentioned. The talents of the teacher must be understood if they are to be captured in the camera's eye. The electronic gadgetry that makes up television is not a teaching machine. It may become the arm of teaching, but not the brain. Teaching and learning are human processes, not electronic processes. If educational television is to be developed to the limit of its versatile capacities, we must find those talents of the live teacher that it can capture, as well as those lower-order classroom activities it can be expected to replace.

Here is where psychology comes in. What is it about a good teacher? One teacher is good because she carries around in her head a crystal-clear picture of everything she is expected to explain. Her presentations are lucid. Another is a good teacher because she can make the facts and characters of history or contemporary thought spring to life, another because she can picture the day's lesson through the eyes of a puzzled child, another because she understands how differently the various children in the room approach the learning task, and still another because of her tenderness and sympathy for schoolroom distresses.

If television is to become educational, it must learn how to turn its camera on each teacher's peculiar talents and not, as so often happens, stifle those talents with its chalk marks on the studio floor and its meticulous hours of camera rehearsals. Teaching—great teaching—is something that takes place on certain precious occasions. It is for television, with the help of psychological studies of teachers and teaching, to catch these great moments when and where they occur.

Again the Montclair studies have made some preliminary progress along this line. In one study six fifth-grade teachers (four women and two men) in the Metropolitan New York area were chosen for their outstanding classroom performance but without regard for any "telegenic" talents. As might be expected, they turned out to represent six quite different kinds of professional competence. Apparently each had attracted attention to his classroom work for quite different reasons.

This panel of teachers, working as a team, produced a two-weeks series of daily lessons comprising a fifth-grade unit on "The Pioneer in American Life." Each teacher taught one or two of the lessons before the camera. As production got under way it became more and more evident that the talents of each teacher would have to be captured in a special way. This was a problem for the producer who helped translate each lesson into the video medium, as well as for the director who called the camera shots during live "takes." One teacher who was initially assessed as having "no telegenic talent at all" became, through recognition of her special teaching talents, one of the most effective television teachers, as judged by the pupils and teachers who used the broadcast series.

We have been talking about the teacher in the studio. There is also the teacher in the classroom where the television presentation is received. The effect of television upon the classroom teacher's role is more subtle but just as profound. When a classroom teacher is first asked to use televised lessons, she is likely to be apprehensive. Will the TV lessons fit in with the objectives of her particular classroom? Will the youngsters actually be encouraged to learn, to do their homework? Will her own efforts appear to be drab and uninteresting in comparison with the glamorized television presentations? Will the pupils wish they had the studio teacher instead of the one they now have? These are the thoughts that actually run through teachers' minds when regular classroom telecasts are first proposed.

Television teaching is a team job. Not only must the studio teacher and the classroom teacher function together as a teaching team, but curriculum planning and studio production have to go hand in hand. A good deal of the failure of educational television—and there has been plenty of it up to this point—has been due to inability to accomplish this. Stephens College is now developing a kind of educational television program embodying this kind of teamwork. The local faculty develops the basic outline of the television syllabus. An invited scholar-in-residence serves as the studio teacher. Small discussion groups are assembled at many points throughout the campus. Together with their local faculty leader, these groups view the telecast, and then, over coffee, proceed immediately to an intimate discussion of the studio teacher's lecture. Between times the guest scholar mingles with staff and students to get feedback of ideas. This is the program, at least as it is now envisioned.

In the coming era of classroom television the classroom teacher will be drawn more and more away from her blackboard at the front of the room and stationed at the pupil's elbow. Television can and should take over most of the blackboard and lecture job, thus freeing the teacher's time for the more intimate and psychological tasks of teaching. There should be more time for dealing with individual learning problems, more identification with the individual pupil as teacher and pupil mull over the same presentation, and more sharing of the learner's point of view. When a perplexed child asks a question, the teacher will be less likely to exclaim, "But I just got through making that *perfectly clear* to the class. Weren't you listening?" Instead, she may be more likely to say, "I know what you mean. I don't think the television teacher made that point as clear as she should have. Let's you and me work it out together."

The change in the role of the classroom teacher that may come from the proper use of televised presentations may be far-reaching and altogether for the good. The teacher may be restored to her proper place at the learner's elbow. To be sure, this may call for a new kind of teacher and a new kind of teacher training. It may call for much more emphasis upon a psychological understanding of the child and the various ways of helping him develop his capabilities.

The full development and utilization of television may affect the teacher in many more ways. Not only may it call for new appraisal of her talents and way of capturing them in the studio, not only may it subtly change the role of the classroom teacher, but it also promises to open up new possibilities for training her and developing higher levels of professional status and competence. Television can provide better in-service training right in her own school building in the late afternoon. It can also be used by her supervisor or training director as a way of visiting her classroom.

But there is a particularly intriguing way in which television can be used to educate a new kind of teacher. At the new University of Minnesota High School television cameras can be brought right into the demonstration classrooms. The camera can be inconspicuously brought to bear upon the strained expressions of individual pupils and the close-ups can be reproduced in the viewing room. The camera thus becomes an instrument of intimate psychological study. In the hands of an insightful supervisor it becomes a way of showing student teachers in the viewing room what is taking place. Moreover, it focuses the attention of all the viewers on a central topic and makes it possible for a running comment to be carried on in the viewing room. It is amazing what a different slant this gives the classroom observer on what is actually going on—*psychologically*—in the demonstration classroom.

What we have said about television and the teacher is partly based on experimental ventures—our own as well as those of others—and partly on speculation. Right now educational television needs to have some creative imagination applied to it. The chi squares can come later!

92

Teacher-Student Relations at the University Level[1]

But I believe this, that every individual has a right to choose the persons to whom he will relate himself. This means that, *by and large*, I think students have the right to choose their professors, to choose their universities, to choose the subjects in which they will do well and to choose the subjects in which they will do poorly. Now, the choices may not always be wise. Some of you are going to disagree with me on this. But I believe that one's education is his own responsibility, primarily; and you cannot have responsibility without, at the same time, risking authority. Thus, if a student is to be held responsible for his education, he then must have some authority for it, some right to choose it.

I think the student should exercise considerable initiative in determining what he should study, what he should not study, with whom he should study and with whom he will not study, and what he should think and what he shall choose not to think.

What I am saying is this. That the patterns of student-professor relationships will have to be varied. And what I have been saying about students I think also can be said about professors. Perhaps less so because professors are employed and they are supposed to be more flexible in dealing with different students.

Let me put my main points under four headings. The task of the university professor who is meeting students coming to the university for the first time is to establish four new kinds of relationships. I think he wants to help the student establish new kinds of relationship to knowledge itself. Second, new relationships to authority. Third, new relationships to truth itself. And last, new relationships to the students' own colleagues.

As for the new relationships to knowledge, this requires the university professor to do some shifting on his own. He takes the students in the Fall. He sees them in one kind of relationship to knowledge and he has to shift that relationship so that by the end of the year it's a somewhat different kind of relationships. It's a very subtle thing and a very important thing. Perhaps I can put it this way. You have, in the Spanish language, I believe, a way of punctuating questions. You put the question mark upside down at the beginning of the question and then, just in case you forget that it is a question, you put it right side up at the end of the question. It strikes me that this is a very good thing because you warn a person in advance that it's going to be a question, and when you get through you remind him that it is a question. Now I think this is a good deal like what we need to do in university teaching. Perhaps I can put it figuratively this way. All statements in the classroom should start with this inverted question mark and conclude with a question mark. It means then, that while in high school there were declarative sentences ending with periods and often with exclamation points, in the university, nearly all of the sentences are implicitly sentences which start with a question mark, so there is the implied inflexion of the question mark in everything that is said. Now, this can be very distressing to students and it can be very distressing to professors: for to tell that everything you are saying ends with a question mark is sometimes to feel that you are saying nothing, that you are giving nothing firm. And sometimes your students embarrass you because of this and they hold up their hands and they say "Don't you know anything?" And they'll trap you into putting exclamation points after your remarks instead of question marks, because they get so disgusted with you and with your question marks!

I suppose another way of saying the same thing is that you teach students in the university how to ask questions whereas the high school has often tried to teach them how to give answers or to regurgitate answers, to throw them back out of their mouths. Now the task is to teach them how to ask questions. In lots of instances they ask very bad questions, questions which can't be answered. So, I think, often the problem of the university professor, in trying to establish new relationships to knowledge, not only is to teach the asking of questions but to teach people how to relinquish questions as badly posed, as poor issues, as poor dichotomies. We can set up these "either or" types of questions and get ourselves into a lot of difficulty.

There's another shift, and this is a hard one for many a professor to make. It is a shift from controlling students, from managing them, to challenging them. It is the shift in the role of the professor. In high school perhaps you try to control students; you try to get them to

[1] Lecture given at Faculty of General Studies, University of Puerto Rico, 1958. Spanish translation published as Kelly, G. A. (1959). Las relaciones entre el profesor y el estudiante en el nivel universitario. *Revista de la Facultad de Estudios Generales, Universidad de Puerto Rico*, *2*(3–6), 18–19. Published by permission of Jacqueline Aldridge.

Collected Papers of the Pioneer of Constructivist Psychology: George A. Kelly, First Edition. Edited by David A. Winter and Nick Reed.

do the things they ought to do; you try to get them to wash behind their ears, or to use the dictionary, or to discover the encyclopedia or to read a book that has not been assigned. You try to control them. But in the university the task becomes one of shifting from that, over to challenging them, to making them so miserable with their present state of knowledge that out of sheer exasperation with you or with their own ignorance, or with something else, they go out and they find out something. So, the task is to stop controlling and to challenge instead. But sometimes when we attempt to challenge, we only destroy. Sometimes our efforts to challenge really degenerate into a kind of negative hostile control; and this is of course a pitfall for us. We have to teach our students how to replace certainty with uncertainty. There's a line in the musical play "The King and I" where it says that people fight most violently for the things they are not quite sure are so, but which they don't want to admit they are questioning. The things that you really feel comfortable about you don't usually get quite so violent over. But things which you feel you must believe even though you doubt, those are the things we become unreasonable about. And so I think we have to teach students how to live with uncertainty.

Basically, this is a problem of taking people who come as students, and changing them into colleagues. Does this seem like a radical idea? In a way it is like saying. "You come to me as students sitting in the classroom before me. I am up here on the pedestal. But I am here to destroy this relationship we have between us. And when we get through I want us to be sitting around a table, and I want you as my colleagues upon whom I can lean, who will support me, who will keep me from making mistakes and slap me down when I get out of line. This is the transition that I want to take place. And I am going to destroy your present attitude toward me as an authority, as an authoritative person."

Now you see, this is a very difficult thing for a teacher to do. It means essentially that the teacher takes his own status, and there before the eyes of the students he destroys himself as an authority, and he asks the students to come up and sit with him and to join him as a colleague. Now this is humiliating. Sometimes I say that there's nothing more humiliating than being a university professor. If you don't want to be humiliated, then teach kindergarten. If you want to be an authority, if you want to be "boss," then get way, way down the line; because the university professor destroys his own status by the very nature of his teaching. One way of thinking of it is this. We are teaching, we are interacting with the very people who a generation from now, or perhaps sooner, will be proving us wrong. These are the people who will be giving the lie to many of the things we are saying in the classroom. There they are, sitting around, looking at us. To be sure, now we have the advantage of them. But sometime that rascal back there, who is so dumb that he just can't get one of my points, sometime that fellow is going to write a book that will tear my writings all to pieces, and he'll destroy me. And I'm here to help him do it. These are the people who will undo what we are doing today. These are the people who will stand up before the world and prove us wrong.

It means also, I think, that we have to share our perplexities with students, if we are genuinely worried about something, if we are genuinely perplexed, if we have our own doubts, I think we have to transmit those doubts, admit them to our students. And I think in the long run they'll appreciate it. At least my students seem to. They take advantage of me at first. If I tell them I'm not sure about certain things, they do indeed take advantage of me! And there are a lot of things that I'm skeptical about. One of the sacred cows of psychology, for example, is this concept of learning. Every textbook in psychology has chapter after chapter on learning. As I read those chapters I get more and more disturbed, because it seems as if the verb "to learn" has degenerated simply into the verb "to become." "Learning" has become such a broad concept that I think it is nothing but a form of the verb "to become," *or* "to be." And so I say to my students, "I doubt if this concept of learning means anything. It just bothers me. I am perplexed about it." So they set about to try to tell me what *learning* is. And they say "Well, you should read this and this." And they bring in articles for me to read. My students are always bringing in things for me to read, to take care of my education. Most of them do it very gracefully. They say, "Well, I know you've been very busy. I know it will take you some time to get this out of the library. So I've checked it out for you, and I've marked the places I thought you might like to read." They're always doing that. I've got one student who brings in a paper-backed book, or something for me to read just every couple of weeks or so, and they are somewhat stacked up, I'm afraid, on the edge of my desk.

I am perplexed and I think it is all right for students to learn that professors are perplexed. And as they learn this they will discover that professors are not very good authorities. I think also we need to teach students not to teach. (I guess none of this is teaching, is it?) We need to invite students to share in our own efforts if we are trying to solve a problem, if we are doing a piece of research, if we are preparing a manuscript. I think it is very *helpful* to ask students to help work out the ideas; but I warn you it is also very painful.

Like many of you, I thought years ago that I wanted to write a book. Most of you, I suspect, are planning to write a book, or feel that you should write a book. Well, years ago, I came down with this disease, too; and I kept telling myself I was going to write a book. I would potter around with it and I wrote notes and tried writing chapters. And they were horrible things. So, finally, the years went by and I got older and older, and I got lazier. Then I began to be afraid I would never get this book written. So finally I took myself in hand and I said, "I am going to get this book written, good, bad, or indifferent. I have to get it out of my system." So I sat down and I really began writing it. I hated what I wrote, but I was going to write it anyway.

I did something else. I invited anybody who wanted, including my students, to come every Thursday evening to listen to me read what I had written during the week and to make comments on it. Now this was a very rugged experience. Sometimes we covered as much as one page of manuscript and sometimes we covered much more. But they forced me to rewrite. Some of them told me that what I had written made no sense at all. They couldn't understand it. Besides, I didn't really believe all that nonsense, they were sure. They enjoyed this and I have never had a stronger group of students come through a program. Not all of them were students. Some of my colleagues came too, to listen to this monstrosity of an author reading his own manuscript. Some time later, some of the students said, "Do you know, when you were doing that, (this happened over a three year period, by the way, it was a long torture for me) we would go out together afterwards, and sit around the table and say 'Now do you think we hit him too hard tonight? Do you think maybe he'll quit writing?'" And some of them were worried for fear they may have hit me too hard and I might give up the project. So then, they would come around to me individually and say "Now, don't give up just because the rest have criticized. Come on, keep going, I'm on your side." And then they would usually decide as a group that they would hit me again the next week, until it really looked as if I was going to go down. Then, they would pick me up. Now this really went on among my students. And while it was a painful experience, it turned out to be a very good learning experience for them. While nearly all of them have their Ph.D's now, as a group, they are very loyal to me and to this experience, and I feel I have colleagues to whom I can go for advice. There was a remarkable shift in the authority-relationship there. ....

It is unfortunate for a student to go through the university without sharing his professor's efforts. I think he needs to see his professor as one who is striving as a scholar, and it is just too bad that a student can't sit at the professor's elbow and the two of them together puzzle about the problem that the professor is interested in. We have, in our own Department of Psychology (in the clinical psychology area, where I teach) what we call "seminars," and these seminars are not student centered, nor curriculum centered. They are deliberately professor centered. They are taught for the amusement of the professor, and we announce them this way. But they are this. They are invitations for the students, for any student who wants to come in and join the professor as he puzzles about problems that he is interested in. And it is not expected that the professor will try to teach them anything at all, but that only he will share his questions, share his quest with them. And students like this. They come in; the professor says, "I am worried about this. I am trying to solve this. I am going to have a series of discussions on this topic. I invite you to come with me as I explore this area of the unknown that I am puzzling about. Come join me." And so he puzzles about it, thinks out loud, questions out loud, and they chime in and react to him. I think these are very important kinds of classes. They are different, you see. I think it is too bad for a student not to have a chance to join with a professor in this quest for knowledge.

My third new-relations topic is new relations to truth, new relations to truth itself. I separate this from new relations to knowledge, knowledge being more of a factual nature, truth being presumably something which is basic and general. How shall we say this? I think, first of all, it means something like this: That the University professor has to teach the student, or help the student understand, that the truth that is capsulated in words, that is packaged in words or formulated in words, is only a partial truth, that the great truths have not yet been reduced to words. Thus, when you ask most young students how they would discover some truth that was not in the library, that had never been enunciated, never been said, which had never been put into words, most of them are confused. And yet, this is the task of University education, I think—to go beyond mere words and to seek out truth which exists in the amorphous, unverbalized form. One of the students yesterday asked me something like this. He asked whether a certain kind of a student organization would work. He was asking me to put in words the answer to his question, and I said, "I don't know." "Where could I find out?" he asked. I answered, "I doubt if anyone knows whether this would work." Then it seemed for the moment as if he was completely blocked. If truth had not yet been reduced to words, how can you find it? And I suggested that one of the ways we find truth is by experimentation, by trying things, by observing, by exploring, for there is the vast world of truth that does not exist in words, and yet is still open for exploration. And this I think is a real challenge to teaching to get youngsters to go after truth which is beyond words. Sometimes it means a formulation of programs of inquiry, sometimes it means a formulation of hypotheses, sometimes a formulation of experimentation, sometimes it means, only going to where the truth may be, except that you don't know how you will find it. A very good research professor that I know once told me that if you don't know how to break open a problem, don't sit behind your desk and try to break it open. Go to where the problem is, you may not know for sure what the problem is, but go to its locus, get in the midst of it, and sit there in the midst of it, or act in the midst of it, and then maybe you will find a way to get hold of it.

One of the greatest examples of this kind of grasping of a very difficult problem is the problem faced by Binet, the psychiatrist and psychologist in Paris at the beginning of this century, known for the Binet intelligence testing. There had been efforts to measure intelligence after some manner or another for approximately a century before this. And most of them had fallen flat on their faces. In 1903, the city commissioners of Paris got worried about the tax problem and got worried about the question of the school budget, and whether they were educating a lot of youngsters who really didn't have the mental ability to be educated. Sounds like 1958, doesn't it? And so they appointed a commission of two men, Simon and Binet, to make a study, to find out whether funds were being used to educate youngsters who were worth educating. Simon, having been an army physician no doubt, decided that the proper approach was to give all the children a physical examination. In the army, every time you turn around, you get a physical examination. So, he got busy with that right away, and this left Binet with nothing to do. He wished he had thought of that first. But Simon got the jump on him and so he had to think of something different. He sat in his office and puzzled day after day. How do I get at this question of children's ability? And not knowing what else to do, finally he just put on his hat and went out and went to the school. He asked teachers if he could sit in the back of the classroom and he just sat in classroom after classroom. "How do I do this?" he asked himself, "Puzzling!" He was going where the problem was. He talked to children. He couldn't get anywhere. He talked to teachers. He asked them if they could measure mental ability. "Of course"-- you know how teachers are. They all said they could. So he asked them how they did it. One of them said, "Why yes, I give them problems in arithmetic because mathematics really tests the mind." Another said, "I take an opportunity to feel their heads, to feel where the bumps are, and that's the way I tell." Another said, "I just get one good look at the light in their eyes; that's the way I tell." He felt rather badly about this, but he still wanted to be with the problem. So he said to these teachers: "Look. Can you spare some time on Saturdays, and come down to my office? I'll have some children there that you haven't seen before. If you don't mind I'll sit in the back of the office while you look at these children, interview them, do with them whatever you want to do with them. I'll see if I get any ideas from that." So he watched teachers facing children for the first time, right in his office, and he took notes. And then the idea began to dawn on him. And it was out of this kind of immersion in the problem, going to where the problem was, that he developed his concept of intelligence. Of course, after we got it over in the United States we rode it into the ground. But his is an example of a kind of scholarship that breaks open problems that have not yet been cast in words. This is one of the great teaching responsibilities.

And finally, the task of the University professor is to help the students establish new relations to their own colleagues. I think this is one of the most frequently overlooked functions of the University education. A number of years ago, twelve and a half years ago, to be exact, I went to the Ohio State University to direct the clinical psychology program. I got myself immersed in a little bit of administrative responsibility, from which I was able later to extricate myself, and I've been trying ever since to avoid administrative responsibility. But that is another matter. When I first went there, there were a great many students who wanted to become clinical psychologists. We started holding special seminars. I'm a great believer in doing your teaching in non-credit courses. I don't think it is possible to teach very much in a course that has credit, or where roll is taken. I think the best teaching is done where people don't have to come, and where there is no standard syllabus....Anyway, in some of these special seminars, when I would mention statistics, for example, or a mathematical computation applied to human data, there would be a very dull silence around the room. They would look away, look at each other and murmur, "Clinical psychologists, must know statistical methods?" It was a very discouraging thing. And then I would talk about something else, or one of the other professors would talk about another topic. But always there would be a sort of a silence and a cringing away from these erudite topics.

The situation is different now. Rarely do we have to teach statistical concepts to the students. Why? They teach them to each other. Most of the teaching that goes on in our graduate program is teaching that goes on from student to student. The first year students go to the second or third or fourth year students. All we, as professors, have to do is to present them with the new stuff, stuff that has just come out in the past two or three years. Students themselves mainly take responsibility for teaching each other the standard things. And it takes a great deal of the load off our shoulders. Moreover, I think they do a better job of it, because in the student-teacher relationship it gets pretty stiff and formal sometimes, especially if the teacher doesn't know it too well himself. So, I think one of the great tasks of the University is to create a kind of community in which a great deal of education goes on between students, to create a climate of interactive scholarship, so students know what other students to go to in order to get help on something. For if you depend upon education to take place in the classroom or in the library, or at home at the desk, you are missing one of the great resources of education. Think what happens after students go out. Then they will have to depend upon colleagues for educational resources. I think this is one of our tasks: to teach students how to use their own colleagues as instructors.

93

Nursery Rhymes for Older Tots[1]

(To all you kettles, from all us pots)

Teacher, Teacher—teacher taught,
What you teach is what I ought.
Keep it simple, make it plain;
Big ideas are too much strain.

Mark the pages I must scan;
Read them to me when you can.
Tell me only what I need;
Ask me only what I've seed.

Now add my hours. I made the team,
Got in no scrape, dreamed up no dream.
So graduate me by the rules,
And recommend me to the schools.

Dear Teacher, Teacher, I've been bought,
And what I teach is what you taught.
An education I can claim;
But why were all *your* efforts vain?

****

Teacher, Teacher, you've been taught
Intellectual tommyrot.
Get this straight—if you remain:
You are here to play our game!

Teach the brats to spell and figger,
Snatch their fortunes, bloat them bigger.
Don't talk theoretically;
Make them want things they can see.

Avoid the controversial,
For they must buy what we must sell.
Historic values thus they'll gain,
While strange ideas are never sane.

[1] Dated 1963. Published by permission of Jacqueline Aldridge.

Collected Papers of the Pioneer of Constructivist Psychology: George A. Kelly, First Edition. Edited by David A. Winter and Nick Reed.

So Teacher, Teacher, you've been hired
To worship all that we've acquired.
What more in life *is* there to know
Than that what *we* believe is so?

****

Teacher, Teacher—strict upbrought,
Truth is that which you've been taught.
All that contradicts is sin;
Therefore man needs discipline.

Never question any saint;
Question only those who ain't.
Never seek an answer new;
Only answers old are true.

Install a monolithic faith
To guide each step a man may take.
Thus, tuned to your authority,
His life shall run perpetually.

And Teacher, Teacher—orthodox,
Abolish dreams and stop all clocks,
For hopes and hours do *press* us so
We sometimes *question* what we know.

****

Teacher, Teacher, vainly sought,
Noble skeptic, bold in thought,
Keen assayer of all man's gains,
Where stand you amidst these claims?

Down these halls where pupils learn
Voices—stupid, strident, stern,
Teaching children codes of cowards—
Much too much resemble ours.

Still, you are part of us, the part
Denied when safer lusts our heart
Desired, and in us gaped instead
A dark, where truth is raped by dread.

But Teacher, Teacher, if our will
To comprehend shall dare not fill
This void in our society,
Then in what sense *can* we be free?

****

Critics, teachers, kettles, pots,
Boobies, bullies, and bigots,
Whilst flushing freedoms down the drain,
Cry, "*Education* is to blame!"

Section VII

Professional Issues

In *Standardization of techniques in clinical psychology*, Kelly emphasizes the uniqueness of the psychologist within the multidisciplinary team due to their "grounding in the evaluation of objective evidence," and he makes an early call for what has come to be known as evidence-based practice. In his view, techniques should only be accepted as standard by the psychologist if they are supported by evidence.

The next paper in this section is Lieutenant Commander Kelly's *Foreword* to a compilation of papers from a conference held shortly after the conclusion of the Second World War, for which he chaired the program committee, and which involved contributions from members of a different branch of the psychology profession: military psychologists. Interestingly, Kelly frames these contributions as likely to be "useful in the pursuits of peace," rather than warfare.

Practices in interdisciplinary collaboration examines the relationships among the various professionals that comprise the "mental hygiene team," emphasizing the importance of each profession not only providing its own distinctive construction of a case, but also striving to comprehend the constructions of other professionals rather than, for example, dismissing them as "wrong." The paper considers, in some detail, the role of the psychologist within the team.

In *Single level* versus *legislation for different levels of psychological training and experience*, Kelly advocates for a diversified profession of psychology. *The organization of an agency*, which appears to be part of a psychology lecture series, offers valuable guidance on the establishment and management of a clinical agency. *The place of psychology in Southern Illinois University* is a report that Kelly was commissioned to produce regarding the role of psychology within the total program of the university. Of greater significance than its specific recommendations are a set of guiding principles for the future. *Doctoral training in psychology in Southern Illinois University* presents observations on the progress that had been made when he visited the university six years later.

In *Training for professional function in clinical psychology. 2. Principles of training in clinical psychology*, the principles that Kelly enumerates arguably possess as much relevance to contemporary clinical psychology training as they did in 1951, when the paper was first published. They are the principles of training for professional adjustment to a world of emerging ideas rather than to a world of fixed doctrines, training for cooperative effort, and training for administrative competence. As Kelly states in this paper, "A clinician trained in this way will not need to feel that his whole training has been wasted the day the American Psychiatric Association publishes its newest nosological system." Regarding interdisciplinary work, he also emphasizes the importance of "learning to think in other people's terms."

In *Requirements of Training and Competence for Psychological Participation in Rehabilitation*, Kelly articulates his view of the development of the clinical psychology student as one that involves progression from taking a purely technical perspective through a theoretical perspective and a professional perspective to the research perspective of the scientist practitioner. He also emphasizes the therapeutic significance of "communication without words."

Next steps for the profession of psychology delineates a nine-step plan through which, in Kelly's view, the Ohio Psychological Association could enhance its position as a representative of psychology within the community. This plan, which possesses broader applicability beyond Ohio, had not been discussed with his colleagues in the Association prior to his presentation. Like other papers in this section, it serves as a reminder of the professional context in which Kelly was operating, amidst pressures such as avoiding "the obviously growing contempt of our local sister professions."

Collected Papers of the Pioneer of Constructivist Psychology: George A. Kelly, First Edition. Edited by David A. Winter and Nick Reed.

I itch too examines the conflict between being a clinician and being a scientist. *Interdisciplinary collaboration* articulates the perspective that different disciplines offer alternative coordinate axes for plotting human behavior, while also advocating for the principle of *habeas mentem*, which denotes an individual's right to the possession of their own mind. In *Emerging concepts that affect interprofessional alignments in psychology (Discussion of the findings of the Psychology Commission)*, Kelly addresses the "chasm" between psychology and medicine regarding their understanding of individuals presenting with problems, while also positing that psychology and biology merely provide alternative constructions of the person. Furthermore, it argues (as does *Knowledge: Discovery or invention?*) that no profession should be regarded as the privileged custodians of truth. The relationship between psychology and psychiatry is further explored in *Issues: Hidden or mislaid?*

Problems of clinical psychology in an industrial setting expresses some of Kelly's concerns regarding what he perceived as the opportunistic application of psychology in this context, without, for example, consideration of the long-term implications of this development. In the paper, he portrays himself as "the last of a line of dust-bowl empiricists," employing metaphors derived from reminiscences of his early life in the Kansas dust bowl.

Post-doctoral training appears to consist of headings for a presentation that Kelly delivered on this topic.

Comments on Special Areas Reviews Committee contains Kelly's reflections on a committee of which he was a member that reviewed project proposals. It concludes with a statement that surely reflects not only his perspective on the committee, but also on life itself, namely that the "program is in a state of flux, and none of us knows exactly where he is going. And that's what I like about it."

In *Training for professional obsolescence*, Kelly argues against training clinical psychologists in outdated practices but rather as "scientist–practitioners." *Issues in the professional training of clinical psychologists*, co-authored with other members of a committee concerned with such training, articulates various alternative positions on this and other related matters, along with different models of training that remain relevant to current debates in this field. *Epilogue: Moments I remember* looks back on the evolution of a profession of psychology grounded in science, independent of medicine, with clear standards of training and accreditation, all of which were initiatives in which Kelly was significantly involved.

94

Standardization of Techniques in Clinical Psychology[1]

With the establishment of the mental hygiene team, comprised of social worker, psychiatrist, and psychologist, as a basic operating unit, the Neuropsychiatric Service of the Veterans Administration has laid an unaccustomed responsibility upon the psychological profession. It is appropriate that, at the outset, we examine the implications of this policy and ourselves impose the limitations of practice and responsibility which someone's good professional judgment will eventually require.

Membership in an in-group may involve responsibilities for which a long association in an outgroup status may be poor preparation. Psychology is in! Now what is it going to do about it. Now we shall see whether psychology is able to transfer its boasted scientific precision and caution to a clinical situation where the stakes are high enough to mean something. That well-known line we hand students in the elementary course about psychology being a science is now going to be open to examination in the light of a public record. I do not think there is any possible way in which our profession can evade the position of responsibility to which the course of national events has led us. Regardless of what degree of responsibility we wish to assume, the record of psychology in the Veterans Administration during the next few years is going to be a conspicuous part of the whole public record of our profession. Once you are recognized as having a social responsibility there isn't much you can do about it except assume it as gracefully as possible.

It is inevitable that with its increased responsibility the clinical psychology profession is faced with the need to establish some sort of standardization of the services which it claims to render. Obviously such standardization should not interfere with the freedom of action and inquiry which should characterize a liberally educated group of scholars. This paper, then, concerns itself, not with technical details, but rather with an inquiry into the basic problems that must arise when members of three professions must work in the close collaborative relationship. From such an inquiry we may be able to find the common ground upon which any standardization of techniques must ultimately stand.

Let us consider the mission of the mental hygiene team. Right now Neuropsychiatric Service is concerned with staffing three main types of activities. There are neuropsychiatric hospitals, about thirty-three are in operation. There are nineteen neurosis centers attached to general hospitals. These handle both inpatients and out-patients. Finally there are thirty-three mental hygiene clinics for outpatients. These are generally located in down-town office buildings and they handle out-patients only. Some of their work is done in the evenings so as not to interfere with the working hours of patients who are regularly employed. In each of these activities positions for social workers and psychologists have been established as well as for psychiatrists. It is understood that one or more psychologists is not only desirable in each of these activities but that he is an essential member of the professional staff. Without the psychologist the neuropsychiatric unit would be incomplete and not qualified to function.

In this setting the concept of the mental hygiene team implies equal professional status for the psychologist. The psychologist is not merely a psychometrist, on a level with the laboratory technician, he is a full-fledged member of the team with an area of responsibility which cannot be wholly subsumed under that of any other member of the team. This, as I understand it, is basic to the idea of the mental hygiene team.

Of course, none of us expects that all Veterans Administration personnel will take up with this notion with equal enthusiasm or support it with an unbroken singleness of purpose. There will be local and isolated instances of resistance to it. But the war has done much to teach psychologists and psychiatrists how to work together and the pressure of the Veterans Administration case load should be scarcely less effective in getting professional people to work with a singleness of purpose. The idea of the mental hygiene team has a real chance of catching on.

New areas of authority also carry with them new kinds as well as amounts of responsibility. Not all psychologists have been taught to place the welfare of their subjects above the outcomes of their experiments. Psychology's laboratory traditions have always placed the emphasis upon data and generalized conclusions rather than upon the outcome of individual cases. This was perfectly proper when

[1] Paper read at Veterans Administration meeting of University Training Directors, Summer, 1946. Published by permission of Jacqueline Aldridge.

Collected Papers of the Pioneer of Constructivist Psychology: George A. Kelly, First Edition. Edited by David A. Winter and Nick Reed.

considered in the light of the traditional purposes which were being served. Now, we must make sure that the clinician does not reverse his logic and chop up his cases into small bits of data in order to apply psychological generalizations. It is probably a vague apprehension of this danger that causes the impressionistic clinician to scream that he wants no statistics in his research and no quantitative methods in his diagnosis. An amusing example of this apprehension came to our attention a few weeks ago when there was a request to recommend some psychoneurotic inventories for use in selecting personnel at a certain activity. It was specified that the inventories must be *non-quantitative*.

There are at least three legitimate levels of abstraction to which the psychologist may reduce his patient. First, the patient may be considered as a datum. As such he helps to give meaning to many data of the same kind, but he himself is seen with a minimum of internal structuralization. He exists only as a point on a scale, a knot on a string, an event on a time line. His degrees of freedom are sharply limited and, like the dwellers in the mythical Realm of Flatland, he lives a very restricted life. After all there isn't much that a datum can do except just sit on its own continuum. That is all right for psychological research but it is no position to put a patient in if you want to help him.

Second, the patient may be considered as a case. This lower order of abstraction permits internal structuralization, at least within the limits of the area which is conceived to be in the field of neuropsychiatry. This order of abstraction permits the clinician to make rather loose generalizations on the basis of similarity of patterns, profiles, etc. It has clinical usefulness but is a very difficult kind of abstraction to do research with.

Finally, the patient may be considered as a person. This, as all of us can readily recognize, represents the lowest order of abstraction. With the person, internal structuralization is complex, and each person is unlike any other. It is to the person, the individual patient who is like no other, that the clinical psychologist bears his primary responsibility. If the psychologist abstracts in the higher orders of *case* or *datum* that abstraction must serve a purpose which is subordinate to the welfare of the *person*. This represents a fundamental problem in the orientation of the psychologist toward the people with whom he works. Simply stated, it means that the welfare of Joe Heffelfinger must come first even if it wrecks a beautiful experimental design.

Let me add a footnote to what may already be an overlabored point. We psychologists are usually willing to accept generalizations which are at the 99% level of confidence. In turning these generalizations around and applying them to the guidance of individuals it is easy to make two kinds of errors. First, if the stakes are high and the penalty for error is psychological ruin for the individual patient, the 99% level of confidence is not high enough. If I should ever be considered for a lobotomy I certainly want the alternatives weighed against each other, and not merely against the statistical chances of the lobotomy being successful. Furthermore, if I have anything to say about it, I want more than a 99% level of confidence. A second error that bears mentioning is a simple statistical one. A certain type of generalization, such as a mean, may be contained within a certain range with a 99% level of confidence, but the confidence with which we may forecast an individual score is much lower than that with which we forecast a mean. Of course all of us know this, but it is easy to forget it in dealing with patients.

Let us suppose now that we have our clinical psychologist ready to assume a social responsibility and let us suppose he is no longer confused in his thinking about persons, cases, and data. What shall he consider himself qualified to do!

At the risk of oversimplification let us compare the training and points of view of each of the three professions represented on the mental hygiene team. First there is the social worker. As a profession social workers have been trained from the beginning to accept social responsibility. For some time they have maintained a professional society with well-enforced standards of membership. The Association of Schools of Social Work has set up a two-year masters curriculum to which all of its accredited schools must rigidly conform. The social worker is taught to recognize the ever-changing social forces which buffet the individual.

She is alerted to the signals which betray these forces, the across-the-tracks community, the furniture in the living room, the migrations from state to state, the misdirected allotment checks. She is taught to fit together the epic story of a little man in a big world.

The psychiatrist has been trained from the outset as a clinician. His background of medical practice has thrown him with a lot of sick people whom he has tried to make well by whatever methods his medical training and native ingenuity could devise. He has been taught to weigh alternatives against each other rather than against a null hypothesis, to consider all cues which could possibly have any bearing on a case, to seek corroborative evidence, to make a decision where a decision must be made.

The psychologist is born in an atmosphere of research and scientific skepticism. The null hypothesis is the point of departure for all of his thinking. He designs experiments, amasses quantities of normative data and calculates his level of confidence for everything he believes. At least this is the model of a psychologist.

And now we have clinical psychologists, people who are trained first as psychologists and who then, with a supposedly engrained background of scientific skepticism, go forth to make urgent decisions in the case of Joe Heffelfinger. The outcome is interesting, to say the least! Let us examine it before we try to answer the question of what the clinical psychologist is qualified to do.

All of us have seen the varying effects of this impact upon students. We have all seen the able and rigidly indoctrinated student preoccupy himself with psychometrics because that was the only service he could render in which he himself had any confidence. We have all seen the graduate in psychology who shored up his fill of scientific ideas and rapidly became a convert to the latest ink-blot, set of blocks, or semantic syntax. Then we have all seen the clinical psychologist who, with the impact of seeing a psychiatrist make decisions in real cases, stood in awe and wistfully pondered upon the thought that if he had studied anatomy, and physiology, and neural pathways he too would have had the background for making decisions in real cases. Finally there are those students who adapt their background of training and attitude to the problems at hand. They learn to sift for the best evidence. They quickly recognize that agreement between psychologist and psychiatrist regarding a diagnosis is not evidence of validity in the diagnostic procedure of either of them. They do not confuse reliability with validity. They recognize interim evidence in support of a partially standardized technique. They can evaluate the practically significant results of free research as well as the definitive results of fixed research. In the absence of the completely validated techniques they are able to distinguish between those which are significantly better and those which have only face validity. And this is what well-trained clinical psychologists ought to be able to do. If there is one thing that is unique to the training of a clinical psychologist it is his grounding in the evaluation of objective evidence.

We are now ready to attempt a first approximation to an answer for the question of what the psychologist ought to be qualified to do in the Veterans Administration Mental Hygiene Team. In this particular government service he ought to be qualified to accumulate and evaluate objective psychological evidence, thus leaving to the social worker the necessarily subjective evaluation of the case history and to the psychiatrist both the medical evaluation of the case and all those necessarily impressionistic formulations which immediately precede the making of major decisions regarding the case.

In such an arrangement psychologists will lose nothing that it is to their advantage to retain. Psychologists have always insisted upon objective evidence in their own field of practice and have always sought to avoid impressionism in dealing with their problems. Nor by such an arrangement will psychiatrists lose anything that they might desire to keep. In general, psychiatrists have always welcomed the submission of objective evidence by collaborating professions. The only thing they wish to reserve for themselves is the final psychiatric judgment wherein they may take into account all special bits of evidence or structuralize discrete items of evidence. Of the three members of the mental hygiene team the psychiatrist's predominantly clinical background should normally identify him as the best prepared to make such decisions. Moreover, considering the kind of evidence he frequently has to use in reaching a final decision, the psychiatrist who is willing to take this overall responsibility should be given a clear field and a Godspeed by the psychologist.

So far we have said nothing about standardization of clinical techniques in the ordinary sense. We have not suggested that the Wechsler-Bellevue be given to all cases or that the Klopfer system of scoring the Rorschach be used in preference to the Beck. What we have tried to get at is something more fundamental, namely that clinical psychologists in the Veterans Administration accept as standard only those techniques for whose validity they are able to mobilize suitable objective evidence. It is suggested that *uncritical acceptance* of any technique *not* be considered standard for clinical psychologists in the Veterans Administration.

This kind of standardization of clinical techniques has a direct implication for the training program. It can be stated simply: Train in any technique whose validity is supported by reasonable evidence, and *as a part of that training* teach the student what that evidence is and how to evaluate it for himself. Let those who wish to teach the Rorschach go ahead and teach it but, if they do, let us hope that their students are given simultaneous training in evaluating the evidence for and against its validity.

Society has, indeed, placed a large order for clinical psychologists. Let us hope that, in our mass production of this commodity, we will continue to emphasize a uniform awareness of underlying scientific evidence rather than merely insisting on a standard bag of tricks.

95

Foreword[1]

During the war of 1941–1945 American psychologists were asked to help solve a great variety of practical problems relating to national defense. Many of the on-the-spot methods which were developed in the course of fulfilling this assignment should prove useful in the pursuits of peace.

It was with this thought in mind that the Military Division of the American Psychological Association accepted the invitation of the University of Maryland to hold a conference on military contributions to methodology in applied psychology.

The Maryland Conference was held on the College Park Campus, November 27–28, 1945. About 150 military psychologists were in attendance. The program was comprised of papers which had been prepared at the invitation of the program committee whose names appear below.

Cdr. W. A. Hunt, USNR, Secretary of the Division and Member *Ex Officio*
Lt. Cdr. Ray Faulkner, USNR
Col. J. C. Flanagan, AAF
Lt. Col. M. W. Richardson, AUS
Col. M. A. Seidenfeld, AUS
Capt. C. P. Sparks, AUS
Lt. (jg) Iris Stevenson, USNR
Lt. Cdr. D. B. Stuit, USNR
Lt. Cdr. G. A. Kelly, USNR, Chairman

The papers in this volume have been arranged for the convenience of the reader rather than in the order of their original presentation.

Special acknowledgement is gratefully extended to Capt. J. Jenkins, USNR for his advice and assistance in connection with editing the manuscript.

[1] First published as Kelly, G. A. (1947). Foreword. In Kelly, G. A. (Ed.), *New methods in applied psychology: Proceedings of the Maryland Conference on Military Contributions to Methodology in Applied Psychology held at the University of Maryland, November 27–28, 1945 under the auspices of the Military Division of the American Psychological Association* (p. iii). University of Maryland. Republished by permission of Jacqueline Aldridge.

Collected Papers of the Pioneer of Constructivist Psychology: George A. Kelly, First Edition. Edited by David A. Winter and Nick Reed.

96

Practices in Interdisciplinary Collaboration[1]

Multiple Approach as a Principle in Mental Hygiene

The conceptual systems under which various professions operate may lead them to construe their observations in quite different ways. It is not a simple matter to resolve all of their contradictions. At first glance it may appear that, with respect to any given set of observations, one construction must be "right" and all inconsistent constructions must therefore of necessity be "wrong." This would be correct if the "right" construction stemmed from a knowledge of ultimate truth regarding all things. But men do not have knowledge of ultimate truth regarding all things and so their workings must be confined to the separate and often inconsistent systems by which truth is approximated in our times. Thus in practice it becomes impossible for the professional man to banish *all* "wrong" conclusions in favor of *one* "right" conclusion.

Those who become unhappy at the thought of living in an adolescent world of inconsistencies may seek an ultimate answer in terms of authority. Their solution is to have someone designated to utter the truth; then what he says will *be* the truth. Even among men of scientific bent there has been more than a little of this attitude. There are those who believe that membership in a profession endows one with this kind of authority. This solution to the problem of inconsistencies tends to block scientific progress by defining as "wrong" any notion which deviates from the dicta of the profession.

Research and the other activities which compose scientific endeavor represent a third approach to the problem of contradictory systems. Slowly but surely scientific progress brings about clarity and harmony in those areas toward which its efforts have been directed. It is practical. The issues it solves, with minor exceptions, tend to stay solved. Even authority tends to be drawn into its wake. No society and, specifically, no program of professional services can profitably operate over an appreciable period of time without investing a substantial portion of its effort in scientific enterprise.

There is a further approach which may be employed in meeting the immediate problems of professional service. It is to explore the individual case from the differing viewpoints of different professions. Applied to cases in the field of mental hygiene it calls for the organization of mental hygiene teams composed of representatives of different disciplines or professions. The usual combination is that of social work, psychiatry, and psychology, though other combinations may be utilized. The effectiveness of this multiple approach to problems of mental hygiene depends upon two conditions: on the one hand, the maintenance of systematically distinct points of view by the different team members and on the other hand the cultivations of flexibility in planning treatment in individual cases.

If the representative of one of the contributing professions abandons his systemic point of view and attempts to emulate one of the other professions the advantages of a multiple approach are lost. This loss of the capacity to effectuate an interdisciplinary approach in the mental hygiene team may even stem from a man's training. If his training embodied more of the point of view of another discipline than of his own he may be rendered incapable of making a distinct contribution to any team of which he may be a member.

Along with the ability to represent a distinctive point of view the individual team member must show a capacity for understanding and cooperating with practical plans formulated in the light of other points of view. This capacity does not require compromising with one's conscience nor does it require a complete familiarity with the whole systematic position of the other participating disciplines. It is a capacity which develops with one's increasing recognition of the tentativeness of all knowledge and of the limitations which he must accept in himself in attempting to extend his own horizons.

[1] Dated 1948. Published by permission of Jacqueline Aldridge.

Collected Papers of the Pioneer of Constructivist Psychology: George A. Kelly, First Edition. Edited by David A. Winter and Nick Reed.

Three Professional Approaches to Mental Hygiene

The mental hygiene team principle ordinarily implies an attempt to utilize at least three separate approaches in dealing with the individual patient. The essence of this principle can be summed up in the statement that the best psychological service to an individual client embodies the collaborative and interactive approaches of psychology with at least two of the following: social work, medicine and teaching. Moreover, if less than three of these approaches is not adequately represented in the services given a psychological patient then those services must be considered incomplete and, possibly, inadequate.

While this principle is not unfamiliar to the informed reader its present incorporation into a large scale working policy is sufficiently novel to call for a reiteration of its basic premises. These premises arise out of certain interesting historical developments in mankind's quest for an explanation of his own mental aberrations.

Three Professional Approaches to Mental Hygiene: The Medical Approach

The mental hygiene team principle represents the confluence of three courses of events which respectively trace the development of three professions, psychiatry, psychology, and social work.

Following its labored emergence from the disciplines of theology and philosophy the medical profession gradually developed more precise methods for differentiating and healing a variety of maladies. As medicine's methods became more precise there was a corresponding tendency for medicine to cut its cake to suit its knife. Whenever new techniques were invented there was an increase in the frequency with which the corresponding diagnoses were used. This tendency to force all clinical observations into familiar patterns was a perfectly natural one which has its counterparts in other disciplines.

In the field of mental disorders this tendency has expressed itself in certain fixed ideas, which have been persistent enough in some quarters to prove a real obstacle to the free development of the medical approach to mental hygiene, for example, the idea that any mental disorder which has no demonstrable organic pathology is not real, that "it is all in the patient's head." Even now, this denial of the real existence of a functional disorder is likely to be an implicit factor in the antipathy or hostility which is sometimes expressed toward the field of neuropsychiatry.

Another fixed idea is that no real understanding of a mental disorder can be reached at the psychological or social levels of abstraction. Those who hold to this view believe that the organic level of abstraction is the only level at which any primary meaning can be adduced.

A third idea which has often marred the medical approach is the semantic pitfall which Korzybski has sought to illuminate. Mental disorders are usually given names whose roots denote supposed pathologies. Once these names are fixed their etymology prejudices any attempt to explore further the raw phenomena with which they are associated. For example, the term *schizophrenia* means, etymologically, a shattered mind. But a shattered mind is not something which one can observe directly: the choice of the word was only an early investigator's attempt to coin an expression which would be both a name and an explanation. The explanation may be all wrong. Yet no matter how wrong the explanation, as long as the word is used, the phenomenon stays frozen to the etymology of its word. In the lexicon of all literal minded men, *schizophrenia* will continue to mean *shattered mind*.

While suffering from misconceptions which were an outgrowth of its own rapid progress, medicine nevertheless attempted actively to extend its healing arts to all patients who were mentally disturbed. In the ears of the medical profession the cries of such patients could never be completely ignored. It was inevitable that the basic approach of the medical psychiatrist should become that of the healer.

The Social Work Approach

The second course of events is that which traces the development of social work. The beginnings of sociology lie in such awakenings as the philosophy of Auguste Comte, the studies of the social phenomena of the industrial revolution, and the systematic theories of Herbert Spencer. The approach of the sociologist has been that of a systematizer of the world of human relations.

Characteristically, the applied sociologist, the social worker, has interested himself in the social forces which impinge upon the individual. The patient is seen at the focal point in a matrix of interpersonal strains and his behavior interpreted as the resultant of all the forces bearing upon him. The social worker has sought to write the epic story of the little man in a big world.

Like psychiatry, social work also has had its growing pains. In his attempt to trace all of the lines of social force bearing upon a patient, the early social worker tended to run case histories into endless recordings of uninterpretable facts. Narrative sketches quickly grew into stories, and stories into biographies, and biographies into compendia of human experience. It soon became apparent that criteria would have to be established by which the more relevant facts could be selected and the social worker could avoid being drowned in his own sea of anecdotes.

By contrast, the modern social worker, trained as he is in the selection of relevant facts out of a maze of anecdotal material, is able to contribute both to the setting in which a diagnosis must be made and to the control of the social influences with which the recuperating patient must contend. Because of his understanding of the social milieu the social worker may provide the basis for helping the patient understand his own role in the various social groups of which he is a voluntary or involuntary member.

The Educational Approach

The teaching profession in America has largely broken its ties with classicism and humanism. Pestalozzi, Rousseau, Horace Mann, John Dewey, Kilpatrick, and Ellsworth Collings have left their mark here. While the training given American teachers is all too brief and the investment generally a short-time one the teacher has come to represent a potent liberal force in the American cultural movement. The fact that the teachers are not always aware of the roots of their profession does not prevent them from making a distinct and consistent contribution.

In the main the teacher is oriented toward expecting and accentuating growth in children. Of all of the four professional groups hers is characteristically the most optimistic. She expects children to grow to master their maladjustments, to improve through her efforts. She usually feels that she has failed professionally if any child does not respond to her efforts.

The teacher is characteristically eager to learn from other professions and, to a much lesser degree than the physician and social worker, depends upon a closed system of theoretical constructs. She tends to be eclectic, uncertain, and socially motivated. Her professional training tends to emphasize the importance of a great variety of knowledge, much of it loosely organized, to be sure. Her relation to the community tends to keep her constantly aware of its emerging cultural needs and to develop in her a growing intellectual but non-militant liberalism.

Teachers tend to underestimate their own professional skill. They will listen most attentively to the patronizing attempts of physicians and psychologists to tell them how to handle a classroom situation and then go back to their work and handle with consummate skill the kaleidoscopic problems of a room full of children, a feat which would drive members of other professions to distraction. Here is the one profession whose contribution to interdisciplinary teamwork is most likely to be under-evaluated.

The Psychological Approach

Modern clinical psychology has its roots in the perceptual studies of the late Nineteenth Century Wundtians and in the mental testing movement, beginning with Galton, Ebbinghaus, and Cattell, rejuvenated by Binet, and cultivated by the American school psychologists. The physiological psychology of the behaviorists during the second and third decades of this century also left its imprint, especially upon our understandings of human development. Clinical psychology furthermore has been profoundly influenced through its parent discipline, general psychology and by the developments in applied probability theory which have taken place in this century.

Psychology has suffered from its own over-eagerness much as its sister professions have suffered from theirs. For nearly a half century the fledgling discipline sought to attain one principal goal, to become known as a member of the fraternity of sciences, "to make Sigma Xi." Efforts were bent toward keeping psychology "pure." *Fixed* rather than *free* research was conducted. *Neat* rather than *urgent* problems were formulated. Definitive answers rather than useful approximations to answers became the goal of all the bright young graduate students. Science was spelled with a capital "S" and psychologists were on the point of forgetting that scientific progress must take place by successive approximations.

In this atmosphere of Science (with the capital "S") graduate students were not taught to develop their clinical insight or to appreciate their professional responsibility to people in need. On the positive side, their training did teach them to weigh their conclusions against a null hypothesis and to substitute p-values for adjective assertions.

Misconceptions of the Psychologist's Role

It has not been easy for scholars reared on critical ratios to fit themselves into a world where sick people must be made well. It has been hard to reconcile scientific rigor with the daily use of incompletely validated clinical techniques. Faced with this apparent dilemma, psychologists have sometimes chosen between two undesirable courses of action: (1) while restricting themselves to the purely technical duties of intelligence testing and inventory scoring, they bemoaned the fact that if *they* had only studied medicine, they too might be able to understand the mental life of the patient, or while (2) walling off all of their research training and setting themselves up as "little psychiatrists," they imitated the psychiatrist's many improvised techniques and contributed nothing that the psychiatrist could not do better.

The Psychologist's Contribution to the Mental Hygiene Team

In a team comprised of (1) a social worker who has been trained to recognize the social forces which impinge upon the patient, (2) a psychologist who has been trained to isolate behavior patterns and to determine by experimental means the validity of specific techniques, and (3) a psychiatrist who is trained both to understand the medical aspects of a case and to take responsibility for the final decisive leap from symptoms to treatment, the role of the psychologist begins to take shape. *Broadly stated, the role of the psychologist is to carry forward all psychological evaluations as far as they can be reasonably supported on the basis of their objectivity and established validity.* Between that point and the point of ultimate decision regarding a patient, there may be a void, across which no wise man should be too eager to leap. But because that void must be spanned by someone, the assignment falls to the member of the team whose training and intuitive experiences best fit him for this grave duty. Thus the final responsibility for adding the inevitably subjective elements of judgment and estimating what should be done in a given case, normally falls to the psychiatrist.

This division of labor should not restrict any member of the team in following his normal professional aspirations. Psychologists have always been reluctant to interpret observations without statistical knowledge of the probability of error. For them to go all out for the use of incompletely validated interpretations would be out of line with the scientific tenets of modern experimental psychology. The modern psychiatrist, on the other hand, is eager to have objectively validated evidence to support his decisions. His serious pursuit of the healing arts prompts him to heed all kinds of scientific evidence whenever they are applicable and where-ever they are found.

The Psychologist's Recognized Areas of Competence

There is a sense in which psychology is not just one profession but a whole group of professions and disciplines. There are very few academic courses or bodies of knowledge which are uniformly required of all graduate students. One study, conducted some years ago, indicated that *statistical methods* was the only specified course which was uniformly required for the Ph.D. in psychology. (Since University facilities subsume the subject matter of psychology under different course names and also leave much of the basic coverage to the independent study of the student, one should not leap to the conclusion that there is no solid core of basic knowledge required of all graduates.)

The professional activities of psychologists are almost as varied as their research interests. Clinical psychologists, rat psychologists, ape psychologists, physiological psychologists, personnel psychologists, human engineering psychologists, aviation psychologists, industrial psychologists, market research psychologists, child psychologists, systematic psychologists, test psychologists, statistical psychologists, educational psychologists, represent, in practice, a markedly divergent group of disciplines. The following recognized areas of competence need to be interpreted with corresponding caution.

The Psychologist's Presumed Areas of Competence

a The analysis and measurement of mental abilities, aptitudes, and achievements.
b The analysis of the learning processes and the development of techniques for the optimum production of ideational, motor, and social learning.
c The isolation, definition, and precise observation of normal behavior patterns.
d The measurement of individual and group attitudes.
e The development of techniques for analyzing jobs and of selecting and guiding personnel in relation to them.
f The design of surveys and experimental research in problems of human behavior so as to permit clear-cut interpretation of the outcomes.
g The application of statistical and biometric methods, in the light of what is known regarding probability theory, to such problems as the reliability and validity of clinical techniques, the measurement of individual differences and the assessment of social trends.

The Psychologist's Responsibility for Making Good his Professional Label

While the listed items in the preceding paragraph represent the psychologist's supposed areas of competence, there is so much diversity in training that one cannot be sure that all psychologists are equally prepared to assume responsibility in any given area. Psychologists who are already admitted to professional status, either on a temporary or permanent basis, should consider it their professional responsibility to keep themselves informed in all of the areas where they are presumed to be qualified by reason of their professional label.

The Psychologist's Role in the Assessment of Mental Ability

A long history of study in the field of intelligence testing gives the psychological profession a clear title to leadership in this area. It should be borne in mind, however, that nearly all psychological studies of the validity of intelligence measurement have been made against some educational criteria. As long as psychologists were dealing with school children or university students this type of validation was good enough. When it comes to dealing with adult patients in a mental hygiene clinic or hospital, the problem of assessing mental ability takes on an altogether different form. It is no longer of primary importance to predict whether or not a given individual can get A's in college or receive a failing grade in engineering. Rather, the clinician is interested in assessing one aspect of the individual's ability to react to various types of therapy, to make adjustments to rapidly changing social situations, keep pace with his own aspirations, or to recover the use of intellectual functions which have become overlaid with the scars of traumatic experiences. These are not the conventional uses of intelligence tests and the psychologist who comes to the team out of an academic atmosphere should be prepared to recognize these new functions and learn to make his test interpretations accordingly.

The Psychologist's Role in the Assessment of Personality

Psychologists and psychiatrists have both undertaken serious studies of the measurement of personality. Characteristically they have approached the problem in different ways, psychologists seeking differentiable variables which could be subjected to reliable measurement in the population at large and psychiatrists seeking clinical manipulatable classifications which would enable them to plan better treatment for the more disturbed types of patients with whom they normally come in contact. During the war the military services repeatedly discovered that this difference in approach could be utilized and correlated. Psychologists were found useful in psychiatric screening where large numbers had to be dealt with and standardized methods developed. Psychiatrists were found to be best prepared to deal with the problems which arose when individual deviates had to be treated clinically. In the light of these differences in training and the practical experience of the military services, it should be possible to state a first approximation of the role of the V.A. clinical psychologist in assessing personality. *In the assessment of personality the role of the psychologist is to develop and apply biometrically validated measures of personality structure while to the psychiatrist is left the responsibility for evaluating those observations whose usefulness rests primarily upon clinical evidence and intuitive skill.*

The Psychologist's Role in Diagnosis

With neuropsychiatric service conceived as an integrated series of clinical contacts culminating in an improved adjustment for the patient, the functions of testing and diagnosis assume positions subordinate to the overall rehabilitative process. In this scheme diagnosis can never be considered as an end in itself but rather as the planning stage of therapy. It may even be carried on concurrently with therapy, as in the rational psychotherapies. Diagnosis thus sloughs off its traditional function of classification for its own sake. Whenever a psychologist administers a test or pieces together a diagnosis he must envisage his task as that of setting the stage for therapy. *To the extent that the diagnosis must be formulated to meet the practical needs of therapy, each member of the mental hygiene team must be prepared to subordinate his role to that of the member who is to shoulder responsibility for treatment of the patient.*

The Psychologist's Role in Therapy

Just as the concept of the mental hygiene team implies that the diagnostic phase of the neuropsychiatric service calls for cooperative effort, so also, the therapeutic phase of the service should be a team undertaking. Everything that happens to a patient during the time he is under neuropsychiatric care has therapeutic implications. It is a mistake to suggest that therapy is limited to what goes on in a conference between a clinician and a patient. If the principle of the mental hygiene team is properly followed no clinician can properly speak of "my patient," he can speak only of "our patient." This is true even where the patient has a close transference relationship to one member of the team.

Experience thus far indicates that there is some tendency for psychologists and other members of the mental hygiene team to slight diagnostic duties in order to reap the ego-satisfying rewards of "doing therapy." This is probably the result of a narrow concept of therapy in the minds of all local staff members. As neuropsychiatric team services are conceived, all members of the mental hygiene team must inevitably participate in the planning phase of therapy, otherwise they are only classifiers and pigeonholers. The psychologist should be especially eager, through his peculiar skills and insight, to make an optimum contribution to the planning stage of therapy. Thus, with all aspects of therapy properly conceived, there should be no intense feeling of need, on the part of any member of the team, to "horn in on" therapy.

The division of labor in the mental hygiene team is probably as much a matter of tradition as of specific skill or scientific training.

1 Obviously, therapeutic procedures which involve the close correlative control of medical factors fall in the psychiatrist's or neurologist's area of responsibility. A psychologist would want to attempt only specifically delegated duties in such cases.
2 Similarly, those procedures involving so-called "depth" therapy fall, by long tradition at least, to the psychiatrist with psychoanalytic experience. The intuitive elements involved in the successful conduct of such therapy would, in the light of the premises already stated in this chapter, normally put the responsibility upon the psychiatrist. In general, research has been unable to remove psychologists' doubts regarding the theoretical constructs of psychoanalytic systems, and, for that reason alone, if for no other, cautious psychologists will not ordinarily find depth therapy a wholly congenial assignment.
3 Group psychotherapy, a recent development, seems to be settling down in the recognized area of the clinical psychologist. There is comparatively little known regarding the rationale of the technique and, fortunately, so far the area has not become badly rutted by partisan schools of thought. The psychologist's presumed competence in the teaching skills together with his supportive knowledge of social psychology may provide justification for this division of labor.
4 Hypnotherapy involves skills and dangers which are well known to comparatively few clinicians, whether psychiatrists or psychologists. There are some systematic contributions to the literature of hypnosis which are authored by psychologists (e.g., Hull's *Hypnosis and Suggestibility*) and there are some psychiatrists who have developed outstanding skill in the use of this technique in diagnosis and therapy. In the light of these facts it seems advisable to leave the allocation of responsibility for hypnotherapy to local decision regarding local talent rather than to state hard and fast rules.
5 Occupational therapy comprises a wide range of rehabilitative devices reaching all the way from the conventional handcraft activities to the carefully planned daily routine of work and recreation. In its broadest sense, it involves the systematic control of all social stimulation affecting the patient. There is a sense, then, in which occupational therapy may be considered to embrace nearly all of what is done to make the patient well. In this frame of reference, occupational therapy is even more a team responsibility than are the previously mentioned special forms of therapy. It is not only reasonable that the psychologist should have a part in outlining this therapeutic regimen, but that he should consider himself responsible for pointing up all of his work so as to clarify all such therapeutic implications. Certainly this is one type of therapy which is not the exclusive property of any one professional group.
6 In speech rehabilitation it is generally recognized that speech pathologists who are trained both in speech correction and clinical psychology are normally best prepared to control the learning problems involved. Where there is a neuropathology to be surmounted by learning, it is obvious that the intimate collaboration of the neurologist should be sought. Where there is structural malformation, the contribution of the otolaryngologist is important.
7 The psychologist's background in the field of learning should normally enable him to make valuable contributions to the planning and execution of most types of re-training therapy.
8 The term "counseling" seems to cover a considerable range of conference techniques. For the purposes of this discussion it may be considered to refer to procedures which do not involve appreciable amounts of catharsis or phantasy nor require protracted periods of treatment. Emphasis is placed upon fairly simple interpretations which are offered the patient or worked out in collaboration with him on the basis of issues which the patient can verbalize and which the therapist is willing to deal with. Counseling in the areas of vocational guidance is a familiar task for psychologists. Counseling in the area of family relations is a familiar task for the social worker. Counseling in the area of psychodynamics and unconscious mechanisms is familiar ground for the psychiatrist who is experienced in handling neurotics. It does not seem to be either possible or desirable to try to classify counseling wholly within the professional area of any one member of the mental hygiene team.
9 One form of counseling is frequently known as "interpretative therapy." It involves explaining the behavior of the people in the patient's world so that he can understand them and feel some degree of sympathy with their motives. In a more or less simple form this sort of therapy touches the patient every day, in the wards, in relations with attendants, in the dining hall, on visiting days, and whenever instructions are given in group activities. Much of what the social worker does, both in his contact with the patient and in his contact with the patient's family, is interpretive therapy. This particular form of counseling is an essential skill in the social worker's bag of tricks. Normally, the social worker's contribution is an essential part of the planning of such therapy even in the cases where he does not conduct the fixed series of conferences in which the method is employed.

The Psychologist's Role in Research

There is no doubt but that the crucial requirement for the Ph.D. degree in psychology is the successful prosecution of research. This one hurdle eliminates more candidates than all others combined.

It can therefore be presumed that, as a group, psychologists are positively selected as to their research capabilities. The parent discipline, general psychology, is so traditionally research minded that all psychologists whether in clinical or in other applied areas should feel obligated to keep their research competences up-to-date.

Psychologists should be able particularly to contribute to the planning of research involving the validity and reliability of clinical techniques, the establishment of criteria against which the experimental effectiveness of techniques can be measured, the design of experiments so as to provide the quantitative basis for defending conclusions, the treatment of numerical data, and the weighing of results against the statistical probabilities of chance.

The Transitional Nature of Inter-Professional Relations

While the purpose of this chapter is to clarify the relationship between different members of the mental hygiene team, it must be recognized that the practical operating relationship between the professions of clinical psychology, psychiatry, and social work is still in the early stages of development. What is written now specifically may prove either to be too restrictive or too permissive after the operating relationship becomes widely stabilized. In the light of this fact, what is projected here must be taken for what it is: an attempt to find and delineate as much common ground for agreement as the present stage of this adventure in friendship will permit. With common ground under our feet and a sincere desire to render professional services to one deserving class of citizens, we should be able to inaugurate a new era of cooperative neuropsychiatric progress in which, eventually, all humanity will benefit.

97

Single Level Versus Legislation for Different Levels of Psychological Training and Experience[1]

Any plan for development of our psychological profession should reflect the spirit of the times. We have the advantage of starting our profession in the middle of this Twentieth Century, and we should be able to develop its conceptualization along new lines; lines which are more socially useful and more flexible than the lines which characterized the development of professions during the last century. The older concept of a profession retained some of the authoritarianism of a priesthood. Now it should be possible for us with our scientific attitudes to develop a new kind of profession which is not a priesthood, but rather an occupational structure which recognizes various kinds of social responsibilities within it and various types of services rendered by its members. It is not so much a question of a hierarchy of levels of professional prestige; it is rather a question of differentiation of professional responsibilities.

I think we are very fortunate now to have this chance for psychology to develop a new kind of a profession with scientific attitudes as well as service skills playing an essential role as never before in any profession. Certainly we ought to be at the place where we can see that scientific thinking, scientific experimentation, and scientific flexibility in the adoption of new ideas is not restricted to a privileged few who happen to be endowed by some sort of superior intellect. The time has come for the scientific attitude to be incorporated as an essential element in a profession and, in turn, to be reflected in the occupational structure of a large section of our society. So, let us think in terms of a new kind of profession whose responsibility stems not from a priestly authority but from scientific advancement and wisdom. Society's occupational structure is becoming much more complicated, and it is possible in the new type of society which we are developing to have a new kind of profession as an essential component.

In the first place we all realize that much of the psychological work of the country is being carried on by people who do not claim to be psychologists and might even be surprised if they were called psychologists. Certainly our teachers are using applied psychology, our physicians are using applied psychology, and psychology is much used by people who would not be called or would not attempt to be called psychologists. In addition, there are a number of people with some more or less specialized psychological training who have cut out for themselves areas of responsibility in which they are well prepared to function in socially useful ways. Most of them have limited their responsibilities to areas of such a size and nature as they can handle efficiently, with dignity and with great social usefulness. These people constitute an important occupational subdivision of psychology.

In the second place we have the so-called *profession of psychology*, with a Ph.D training program patterned somewhat after the old notion of a profession. Finally, we have the occupational concept of a high level specialist with which the American Board of Examiners in Professional Psychology is currently concerned. It was probably rather unfortunate that this professional category was underscored by the American Board's work before the other two categories were given certified status. From the standpoint of the whole occupational group, specialty certification was not nearly as important as some of the other problems now confronting state psychological societies.

As I see it, in developing this new profession and in developing certification or licensing, whether legislative or voluntary within a state psychological association, we should provide for flexibility in the emerging concepts of psychological vocations. It might be well to continue with licensing at the level of the Ph.D and a year of internship. But if we stop there or stop with that plus the American Board certification, we are going to miss a lot of opportunity to be socially useful through establishing accurate descriptions of other types of psychological vocations which are more specialized.

It seems to me then that we have to help define, plan, and conceive psychological vocational patterns in more diversified forms in which people can be socially useful, responsible, and can operate with dignity. We may want to recognize some of these as *technical specialties*, although the word "technician" sometimes carries with it the undesirable idea of subordination. It should be possible for a

[1] First published as Kelly. G. A. (1950). Single level versus legislation for different levels of psychological training and experience. *American Psychologist, 5*, 109, 111. Republished by permission of the American Psychological Association.

Collected Papers of the Pioneer of Constructivist Psychology: George A. Kelly, First Edition. Edited by David A. Winter and Nick Reed.

person to be (usefully) trained with a year of graduate work plus a very carefully supervised practicum in his specific area. For example, there is a very useful technical area of operation in the schools, say, in dealing with the psychological problems of teaching handicapped children. There are other kinds of technical specialties which can be defined and for which the universities can train many competent people in a one- or two-year curriculum. Such technical occupations should be recognized in any freezing of the social structure of psychology through legislation or through voluntary certification. If such a thing is done, technical areas might be much more diversified and specific than the specialties recognized by the American Board. They might even be more flexible, changing from year to year, or from decade to decade.

Certainly, in this post-war era, we should be able to conceptualize a new kind of profession which has many ramifications, which has many kinds of social responsibilities, and which provides for the useful activity of many people with varied training.

98

The Organization of an Agency[1]

The Planning Stage

If the agency is to be a public or semi-public agency its organization needs to be preceded by wide-spread discussion of the needs which the agency is to meet. These needs should be expressed in terms of factual data—a survey of delinquency, an analysis of the effectiveness of the schools, a compilation of data regarding the numbers of people who have been unable to procure certain types of services, etc. In this stage a certain amount of publicity is desirable but the main factor is the participation of a great number of individuals who stand up and have their say and who publicly commit themselves to a point of view.

The initiators of the movement which is to eventuate in the establishment of an agency must keep a few steps ahead of the public trend but should always keep their plans sensitive to the public trend. When people start to say, "Let's not just talk. Let's do something," the initiators need to be prepared to suggest a course of action. In the early stages this course of action is simply to go out and organize more wide-spread interest in the topics. In the later stages the course of action is to elect representatives to a central planning committee which is to propose a course of action.

The central planning committee ordinarily takes the initial steps toward the formal enlistment of the support of various established organizations and proposes various alternative means of financing the agency. These proposals are ordinarily a part of their first report back to the informal groups which are represented on the central planning committee. The central planning committee also proposes the proper widening of the basis for support of the social action. For example, they may propose that certain established organizations be formally represented on their committee.

Once the social action of establishing some kind of agency has been widely approved by the informal groups the central planning committee should be re-constituted with representatives from all the organizations which are to have a permanent interest in the program. Let us call this the organizing committee. Its job is to set up the formal administrative structure, the basic policy regarding what kind of services are to be rendered and to whom they are to be rendered, the method of maintaining financial support, and proceed to the formal establishment of the first board of directors. This is the committee that writes the constitution, the by-laws, and designates the incorporators.

Administrative Structure

Community services rendered by the type of agency in which psychologists ordinarily serve should always involve the formation of a flexible and representative policy board. Continued community support for the program of the agency requires such a board. The board should be comprised of a changing or shifting membership in order to avoid the criticism of becoming a vested interest of a limited number of people. It should be representative of a wide variety of interests and a considerable number of formal organizations who must therefore feel some responsibility for the continued functioning of the agency.

The board of trustees of an agency should incorporate under the laws of the state. This not only protects the individual trustees from certain kinds of personal financial loss but also helps guarantee that constitutional procedures will always be followed in maintaining the agency. A properly incorporated agency is also likely to be a better place for a psychologist to be employed. Psychological work is often precarious because one is dealing with disturbed people. The responsibility for what is done professionally and administratively should be shared widely in order to protect the individual psychologist.

In the by-laws there should be a clear separation of the policy-making and executive functions. The policy-making functions should be widely distributed, the executive functions should be in the hands of not more than half a dozen people. Policies should always be a matter of

[1] Unpublished MS, Ohio State University, 1950. Published by permission of Jacqueline Aldridge.

Collected Papers of the Pioneer of Constructivist Psychology: George A. Kelly, First Edition. Edited by David A. Winter and Nick Reed.

discussion by the entire board of directors and should frequently be referred back informally to the organizations who are represented on the board of directors. Policies should always be put into writing for the protection of the people who must execute the policies. An unwritten policy is always a hazard to an executive.

Finance

The financial support of the agency should be set up in such a way that there is reasonable assurance that the agency will be continuously maintained. An agency that is dependent upon solicitation of funds by its own representatives is likely to be short-lived. It has a better chance of survival if it is supported by several organizations who recognize that they have a permanent stake in the agency. In general tax sources are the most stable of all sources of financial support.

An agency must be very cautious in using contingent funds. These are funds which are made available to the agency a year or two at a time without any commitment of continuing responsibility on the part of the giver. Ordinarily it is not practical to refuse to accept such funds but they should never be used for the salaries of staff members who are considered to have tenure. They are best used for the purchase of new equipment, for repairs, for temporary appointments of interns, special research workers, temporary clerks, etc.

The financial structure of the agency should be set up in such a way that will give it resiliency. If one source of support is cut off the agency should not be forced to go out of business. It is important that the use of funds always be planned with this in mind.

The fee structure of a social agency is always a ticklish matter. The public has become accustomed to expect certain social types of services which appear to be related to the services of the schools to be free. This is in contrast to what is expected of medical services. Psychiatrists working in social agencies are likely to be surprised to discover that even the most modest partial fees are resented by their patients. The fee scale or scales should be explicit. No public agency should attempt to administer a fee system which cannot be clearly understood by the public.

Professional Structure

In addition to a policy board, which is ordinarily the board of directors, there should be a professional advisory board to establish and keep track of professional standards and practices. This board should be comprised exclusively of professional people. It should pass on the professional qualifications of all professional people employed by the agency. It should determine policy regarding interdisciplinary collaboration. It should sit in on occasional case conferences. Complaints regarding the professional services of the agency should be given consideration by the professional advisory board. It is practically impossible for a high quality of professional service to be maintained for long without a system of regular case conferences. The more full the participation of various professional people in these case conferences the more likely it will be that high standards of professional service will be maintained. When a person attempts to keep his professional procedures to himself, he soon degenerates and develops eccentricities in his practice.

The team approach to mental hygiene practice has long been advocated by mental hygienists. It has frequently been advocated but unfortunately it tends to break down in practice. The team is frequently considered to be comprised of a psychologist, a psychiatrist, and a social worker. There are other interdisciplinary combinations which are more effective in certain situations. The psychologist may team up with a pediatrician and a teacher in order to deal with certain types of problems. Psychiatrists do not like this kind of teamwork and some of them appear to be even more annoyed by it than by the psychologist omitting the medical member of the team altogether.

The team approach is not the complete answer to the mental hygiene practice issue. Three people of different backgrounds who work together over a long period of time eventually discover that they have become more like each other than like other members of their profession. Eccentricities of practice can easily develop in such teams. Furthermore, in order to establish intercommunication on the team, each member tends to simplify his conceptual scheme. At first this is good for him because he has to reconsider his whole professional stand. Later, however, his simplified conceptual system and vocabulary results in a simplified and limited professional outlook and he may find that his colleagues in his own profession have left him far behind.

In practice the interdisciplinary problem is more frequently handled by the method of departmentalization. In such a case the psychologists are all put into one department and are asked to collaborate with other professional people on a case-to-case basis. The larger the agency the more likely it is that this will have to be the solution to the interdisciplinary problem.

Accreditation and Recognition

Most states and cities have some form of accreditation or licensing for public agencies which render social service. The American Hospital Association, the American Medical Association, and the American Psychological Association's committee on psychological services are also concerned. In urban communities the Council of Social Agencies concerns itself with agency quality. If an agency is to support itself by public solicitation of funds the Community Chest Organization also makes a careful investigation of the agency's program.

An agency needs to be concerned with the professional accreditation of its staff. Certificates and licenses should be displayed by staff members in their offices. The agency should take an active part in encouraging and assisting its professional people in making professional advancement and in securing appropriate accreditation for their advancement. Attendance at professional meetings should not only be encouraged but financed by the agency. The preparation and reading of papers should be actively supported by the agency. The agency should see that all important papers prepared by their staff are published and the agency should take steps to see that reprints are widely distributed. This is a good investment on the part of the agency and will pay off financially.

Staffing

All permanent staff members should have written contracts. The best procedure with professional staff is to have a period of one, two, or three years of provisional appointments, following which the staff member is given tenure.

The agency should be careful not to try to work at the minimum level of salary for a maximum level of paper qualifications. That is a sure way of collecting social misfits on one's staff. If the salary level must be below the average for a given level of paper qualifications it is better to lower the paper qualifications in order to get someone who is competent and personally acceptable but who does not have the paper qualifications to compete for a higher priced job.

Credentials should always be evaluated by someone in the profession of the applicant. A physician who tries to pass judgment upon a psychologist's credentials is likely to make some very bad mistakes. The same is true of the psychologist who tries to pass judgment upon a physician's or social worker's credentials. The professional advisory board should always have distinguished representatives of each of the professions who work in the agency. These representatives can pass on the credentials of applicants in their respective professions. Letters of recommendation should not be given any credence when they are not addressed to the reader or when they are written without the writer's knowledge of what specific job situation the applicant is seeking. Ordinarily, they are most useful when the writer knows the addressee, knows the hazards and demands of the job, has recently seen the applicant functioning in a similar type of position, wants to keep the professional respect of the addressee, and are written in response to a direct inquiry from the addressee.

Recruitment is usually most effective when the agency is able to show the prospect that he will have opportunities for professional recognition both within the agency and within the community. Professional people like to go where their national reputations have some chance of being established. If there is a university in the community it is much easier to recruit professional people. Opportunities and facilities for research and publication are important to the prospective professional member of an agency staff.

Verbal commitments to candidates should always be followed up immediately by properly authenticated written commitments. The written communication should embody all of the essential features of the verbal assurances which were the basis of the candidate's verbal acceptance of the position. The agency should never ask the candidate to make a written acceptance of a verbal offer.

Scheduled Activities

There are approximately four different types of staff conferences that have a proper place in an agency's calendar of activities. There is the administrative staff conference which has to do with housekeeping and procedural issues. The responsible secretarial staff should ordinarily participate in such staff conferences. There is the inter-disciplinary staff conference which helps keep each discipline aware of the thinking of the other disciplines and the ways in which they can collaborate in the handling of a case. There is the intra-disciplinary staff conference which tends to be much more theoretical in nature, and there is the more informal staff conference by means of which each professional person shares with at least one other professional person his problem in dealing with a case. The hospital ward-round falls in this category.

An agency needs to develop a carefully controlled procedure for making client appointments. The person who handles calls from prospective clients needs to be alert to suicidal tendencies and needs to be able to avoid having clients spill clinical material on the telephone or in the front office. Ordinarily all clinical work should be done by appointment only but there are occasions when the agency must act quickly in an emergency case. Client appointments should be spaced so that the clinician may make adequate notes immediately following a conference.

Any community agency must recognize a certain measure of responsibility for maintaining adequate non-professional contacts. The staff will have to expect to render a certain amount of free community service in the form of lectures, appearing before study groups, serving on community committees, etc. If the staff do not do this the community support will soon dry up. Participation in preventive mental hygiene activities also falls into this category.

An agency must be prepared to provide a certain amount of adjunctive assistance to other agencies who need collaboration on certain cases and on certain projects. This means that a part of the agency's time must be set aside for collaboration with other agencies and that effective channels and vocabularies for inter-agency communications must be established.

The agency should set aside a certain amount of time for study activities. A journal club which meets during working hours is a partial answer. There should also be some more intensive professional study. A good agency soon sets up a program of speakers and institutes which attracts the more competent professional people in the community. An experienced visitor can soon determine the professional quality of an agency by listening to the level of discourse which takes place among staff members.

Members of the professional staff should be encouraged to take refresher training. For the more mature staff members this may be replaced by their teaching at a high level in other places, by their serving as institute instructors elsewhere, and by exchanges of staff personnel with similar agencies in other places.

Public Relations

The maintenance of adequate public relations means not only that the agency shall enjoy the approval of the community but that its work shall be well understood so that the community will refer the right types of cases to it. This takes time. The agency needs to be very careful to avoid making statements either orally or in the press which will be interpreted by the over-eager listener as a claim. The agency should not go into detail as to the kinds of diagnostic categories into which their clients fall. Rather they can give the public a better idea of where they fit into the social scheme by indicating what types of staff are employed, the numbers of cases seen, the duration of treatment, the agencies with which the agency collaborates, etc.

The announcement of services should ordinarily be confined to a single statement rather than a list of types of problems. For example it is much better to say,

"*The Mental Health Center.*
Children's Adjustment Problems."

than it is to say,

"*The Mental Health Center.*
Psychiatrists, psychologists, social workers, teachers.
Assistance for Children and Parents.
Speech Disorders. Educational Deficiencies.
Emotional Problems. Development of Personality."

Of course, such statements as "Expert Consultants" or "Skilled Psychotherapists" should never be used.

The reception of clients has a great deal of bearing upon the effectiveness of the agency in dealing with them. The quarters should be attractive, quiet, dignified, and unconfused. Personnel who are informally dressed, chatter, and noise all tend to destroy the confidence of the person who has come to seek help on intimate and disturbing problems.

99

The Place of Psychology in Southern Illinois University[1]: A Report of a Study Made at the Request of President Delyte W. Morris

Nature of the Study

In April, 1950 President Morris invited the writer to Carbondale to make a study of the place of psychology in the total program of the University. The following problems were specifically mentioned:

a Should there be a department or departments of psychology? If so, how should they be organized into the administrative structure of the University? If not, how should psychological activities be organized?
b What kinds of psychological activities and services should be sustained or initiated by the University?
c What kinds of personnel should be procured for the various psychological activities and services of the University?
d Any other matters relating to the place of psychology in the University.

During the week of May eighth to twelfth the writer visited Carbondale and conferred with members of the Board of Trustees, members of the University Administration, members of the Faculty, students of the University, alumni, and citizens prominent in the economic and cultural life of the community. Thirty-three scheduled conferences were held with forty-nine different persons. Without a single exception the writer was received with the greatest cordiality, and the topics of discussion were pursued with delightful frankness and vigor.

Approach to the Study

An Advisory Committee

Prior to his visit to Carbondale a communication was sent to the President indicating the proposed general approach to the study and asking for the assistance of a local committee to "....guide...both in making the proper interpersonal contacts and in keeping facts in the proper perspective." A bibliography was attached to the letter for the convenience of those who wished more extensive information regarding recent professional and curricular developments in the field of psychology. Copies of the letter and bibliography are contained in the appendix to this report.

The advisory committee met on three different days and served most competently in the manner which had been anticipated. In addition they provided most thoughtful and penetrating criticism in the early stages of formulating the principles upon which this report is based.

Six Basic Questions

Interviews were conducted with a view to obtaining useful answers to six basic questions.

a What are the special relations and obligations of Southern Illinois University to its constituency?
b What overall developments are generally expected in the University and in the community during the coming decade?

[1] Unpublished report to the President, Southern Illinois University, 1950. Published by permission of Jacqueline Aldridge.

Collected Papers of the Pioneer of Constructivist Psychology: George A. Kelly, First Edition. Edited by David A. Winter and Nick Reed.

c What is the nature and scope of psychological activities and services which are now provided or envisioned by individuals in the university community?
d What undeveloped opportunities exist for useful psychological activities which are not yet clearly perceived by representatives of the university community?
e What is the nature and scope of the psychological training now effectively provided to students in the University?
f What channels of communication and execution are now most effectively operated by personnel who perform psychological duties?

Formulation and Preliminary Discussions of Principles

It was believed that this report would have far greater significance as a basis for administrative action if, in addition to suggesting immediate measures, it developed more generalized statements in the form of principles. Such principles could be incorporated into the President's master plan for the University. As a part of that master plan they could guide the Administration in the future by suggesting practical steps to be taken in situations which cannot now be wholly foreseen. In addition they should help provide the President with some relief from the mental strain of trying to administer the psychological activities of the University on an opportunistic or circumstantial basis.

Since no statement of a principle is very effective unless it makes good sense to those who are expected to use it, several principles were tentatively formulated and "tried on for size." The responses proved to be most discriminating. It is believed therefore that the principles as now stated herein are compatible with the educational philosophy of those for whose guidance they were derived.

Recommendation of Specific Measures

On the basis of the guiding principles, on the one hand, and the current circumstances, on the other, the final step in the study was conceived to be the recommendation of specific measures which appeared to be feasible at the time of the study. New developments in the University's relations with its constituency, expanding physical facilities, and the usual turnover of staff will eventually make it necessary to reconsider the specific measures undertaken at any particular time.

What is Psychology?

The Psychologist's Orientation

Modern psychology dates back about seventy-five years to the first experimental attempts to study human behavior. Prior to that time psychology was based solely on philosophical speculation. Now modern training in psychology places great stress upon the practicability of marshaling facts to explain human behavior. Using this humble approach psychologists have been able to make increasingly significant contributions to man's knowledge and basic understanding of himself.

The well-trained student in psychology, when asked a question regarding human behavior, is not likely to say, "I, personally, insist on the following answer." He is more likely to say, "So far the evidence seems to support the following answer." Or he may say, "Here is a way to let facts rather than opinions answer the question."

Among psychologists there is surprisingly little reliance upon the authoritative status of their colleagues. A prominent psychologist loses face rapidly if he falls into the habit of stating psychological conclusions without citing scientific evidence. There are, of course, individual exceptions to this generalization but, on the whole, psychologists are investigation-minded rather than authority-minded.

Working Relationships

In most instances the services of psychologists are most effective when they are performed in collaboration with representatives of other disciplines and professions. In the schools, the psychologists who have actively participated in teachers' staff conferences have been most effective. In industry, psychologists have done their best work where they have been in frequent contact with the line organization even though, for administrative purposes, they may have been attached to the staff organization. In hospitals and clinics, the use of psychological services has become almost synonymous with the introduction of the mental hygiene team principle.

Keeping Abreast of New Developments

While psychological services are usually best performed in a team-work situation, the psychologist whose communications with his fellow psychologists are cut soon becomes antiquated. Psychological developments of a profound and practical nature are crowding on each other's heels. There are over thirty professional journals of direct concern to psychologists. New areas of psychological endeavor are being opened up each year. The psychologist who does not maintain close academic association with other psychologists will find, sooner or later, that not even the momentum of his own enthusiasm will keep him up to date for long. For psychologists the only satisfactory insurance against obsolescence is a close academic association with other psychologists both within their own administrative organization and through regular attendance at professional meetings.

Psychology as a Profession

Psychologists are now engaged in an important attempt to establish for themselves some of the controls on practices which characterize a profession. Some of the states now have modern licensing laws for psychologists. The American Board of Examiners in Professional Psychology now awards its diplomas to psychologists who evidence high professional competence in one of three specialties: industrial psychology, counseling and guidance, and clinical psychology.

There is an increasing demand for the services of psychologists. One well-informed source estimates that the country has only eight percent of the number of clinical psychologists it needs. Graduate training programs normally require a minimum of four years of intensive training leading to the Ph.D. degree. The programs are badly overcrowded. At some of the better known universities the selection ratio has dropped as low as three percent of qualified applicants. Yet industry, public agencies, and even universities are having difficulty procuring well-trained psychologists for their staffs.

Some of the Things Psychologists Do

Unlike some other professional groups, psychologists are employed in such a great variety of undertakings that it is difficult to say where a psychologist will *not* be found. The following outline may give some idea of the scope of psychological activities.

1 General Psychology
  a Measurement of and experimentation with human variability, both individual and group.
  b Problems of perception, learning, development, social phenomena, and personality.
2 Educational Psychology
  a Classroom learning.
  b Diagnosis, remediation, and adjustment to defects and deficiencies.
  c Social problems of the school. The classroom and playground from the standpoint of interaction dynamics. The community from the standpoint of learning and adjustment.
  d Measurement and testing.
  e Evaluation of educational programs.
  f Pupil personnel administration.
  g Teacher selection and personnel administration.
  h Career planning and occupational follow-up services.
  i Inter-community relations and interpretation of differences through the school.
  j Clinical services for pupils and parents.
  k Consultative services for teachers.
3 Home and Community Life Services
  a Child development research and education.
  b Preventive mental hygiene.
  c Interpretation of interpersonal relations.
  d Studies of adult life. Gerontology.
  e Marital counseling.
  f Parent guidance services.
4 Business and Industry
  a Job analysis and personnel selection.
  b Industrial training, both workman and foreman.
  c Industrial morale.
  d Administrative organization and channelizing of communication for maximum psychological effectiveness.
  e Interpretation of interpersonal relationships in supervision and management.
  f Work simplification.
  g Market research.
  h Biomechanics.
  i Quality control.

5 Special Fields
 a Psychoacoustics
 b Systems research (military).
 c Analysis of attitudes and potentialities of national groups in relation to problems of national defense.
 d Opinion studies.
6 Clinical Psychology
 a Clinics.
 b Hospitals.
 c Personality conflict in the community.

This list is not exhaustive nor are most of the fields mentioned the exclusive hunting grounds of psychologists. This section of the report is included simply to make clear the fact that Southern Illinois University may extend its psychological activities in any number of a great variety of directions if it chooses to do so.

The Southern Illinois University Situation

The answers to the six basic questions which were sought through interviews comprise the factual substance of this report. The recommendations with which the report concludes represent the outcome of considering this factual substance in the light of certain principles. The following are re-statements of the six basic questions together with the answers, as far as the writer was able to determine them.

What are the Special Relations and Obligations of Southern Illinois University to its Constituency?

There was remarkable agreement among all people interviewed as to the directness of the responsibility of the University to the people of the thirty-one counties of southern Illinois. This responsibility includes meeting what appear to be the most urgent economic and social needs as well as the more general educational needs of the community. It is unfortunate for the morale of citizens in general and students in particular that the area is regarded by many of its residents as "the thirty-one blighted counties of Illinois." Yet most people feel that local fortunes will change and many believe that the University will play a leading role in bringing about the change. There was one exception. A representative of an industry recently relocated in the Crab Orchard Lake area spoke in enthusiastic terms *both* of the present and of the future. He had not found the people to be backward nor the local leadership of organized labor to be unreasonable.

Relations between organized labor on the one hand and outside capital and local business on the other have not been sufficiently wholesome to support much-needed economic progress. The local labor program, largely organized along lines designed to protect the workers' interests on an industry-wide basis, apparently has not always been adapted to the recovery needs of southern Illinois. Labor's successes in its struggles have therefore tended to be transitory and scattered rather than solid and far-reaching.

Outside capital in some instances appears to have been able to establish wholesome working relations with local organized labor. In other notable instances, however, representatives of outside capital, responding to the invitations of Southern Illinois, Inc. to locate in the area, have misjudged the determination of local labor to maintain its standards of working conditions and union recognition.

Local business appears to have failed entirely in its attempts to establish wholesome working relations with organized labor although there seem to have been a number of efforts recently made in this direction. It may be some time before the condition is corrected.

In the midst of this field of social conflict the University appears to be the one enterprise which has, up to the present moment, enjoyed the full confidence and support of all factions. This fact alone bears the weight of a solemn obligation which the University cannot ignore. While neither organized labor, which is indigenous in the community, nor recently recruited capital, upon which the industrial recovery of the community is said to be dependent, appear to be formally represented at the policy-forming level of the University's administration, the University is still in a position to learn to speak with the voice of a united economic community. The challenge of this opportunity is alone enough to give the University a high sense of its mission and a meaningful direction to its program of community services.

Agriculture in the area appears to be the victim of apathy more than of conflict. A tally of the occupational structure of the area compared with a list of the occupations of the parents of students attending the University suggests that the children of farmers are only half as likely to be enrolled in the University as are the children of miners, for example. Yet there seems to be common agreement that the University must concern itself with the recovery of agriculture. The task may prove to be discouraging.

The University has a long-standing commitment to the public schools. Its leadership in public school affairs and teacher training is unquestioned. Many of the social developments which the University is not in a position to promote directly may be promoted indirectly through the public schools. The improvement of agricultural practices is an example. Adult educational programs in child care are another.

Recently the University has given considerable attention to its obligations in the field of medicine and its allied professions. The establishment of pre-clinical medical training at the University has been strongly urged. Yet it is clinical and preventive services which are most urgently needed. There appears to be some excellent medical leadership in these latter phases of medicine which are already established in the area. It might be easier to establish advanced training opportunities, even residencies, in these phases of medicine than it would be to organize, equip, and staff a two-year undergraduate medical program which would necessarily be confined to the campus.

There are both advantages and disadvantages in the unusually intimate relationship between Southern Illinois University and the total social and economic life of the constituency which it serves. Certainly the relationship should give both staff and students a high sense of social responsibility. Certainly the stimulation of research, the most virile type of scholarship in any university, should lend impetus to the University's program of expansion. Yet the University may, in bending its program to urgent and provincial demands, depreciate the value of that same education by which it hopes to raise the status of its students. University education is by nature universal and broadly useful, not provincial and restrictively technical. A university, if it is to be a seat of learning in its community, must set its horizons far beyond the boundaries of the thirty-one counties of southern Illinois. It cannot serve its local constituency well unless it concerns itself with the problems of all of mankind. Southern Illinois will have a university in both fact and spirit only if it contributes to all of society through the operation of its university. It will have something less than a university if it seeks merely to use the tokens of culture for trading with the local natives.

What Overall Developments are Generally Expected in the University and in the Community During the Coming Decade?

While many special difficulties and problems were mentioned during the course of the writer's visit to the Carbondale area, there were no exceptions to the firm belief that the University would expand into an important cultural center and that the economy of southern Illinois would grow apace. Estimates of the University's probable enrollment ten years hence varied from 5000 to 15,000. A group of professional colleges was envisioned by some. Graduate training leading to the doctoral level was seen for the immediate future by certain individuals who are well able to appreciate the significance of such a development. The University's plant is undergoing a belated expansion. A master plan of building development has been prepared. Whatever restraints on the development of the University may be operating, hopelessness is not one of them.

The development of peacetime industry in the Crab Orchard Lake area has already started. So far the plant space, power, and labor resources which were used during the war have been only partially converted to peacetime industry. The coming decade should see a significant development in this part of the University's front yard.

It is expected that agricultural developments will take place principally along the lines of improved subsistence farming and soil conservation. There is a likelihood that new and more profitable crops will be produced. Timber resources suggest the feasibility of light industrial production of hard-wood products.

In the commercial field there is a recognized need for improved merchandising. Professional services are at the point of being established upon new bases. Group medical practice will probably be undertaken more extensively in the future. Public health education and services must be expected to make significant strides in the immediate future. Labor leadership and practices will inevitably respond to changing concepts of social responsibility, perhaps as a direct result of the training given students in the University who are its potential leaders. Already there is an expressed need on the part of industry for extension of curricular offerings in the field of labor relations.

In general it is expected that southern Illinois will become a much better place to live in. Home life will be stabilized and enriched. Schools and communities will be better places for the rearing of children. The responsibilities of parenthood and marriage will be borne with greater wisdom and dignity. The careers open to youth as well as the processes by which careers are chosen and developed will become the common knowledge every high school youngster will have available.

What is the Nature and Scope of Psychological Activities and Services which are Now Provided or Envisioned by Individuals in the University Community?

Psychology at Southern Illinois University is now principally conceived in relation to its contribution to child clinical psychological services, remedial education, guidance and counseling procedures, and personnel practices. There is an awareness in some quarters of its potentialities in relation to community education programs and in relation to child development and nursery education. The use of psychological survey techniques for evaluating the results of the University's program in the community also appeared novel.

The present program in the Department of Guidance and Special Education is being pursued with enthusiasm and obvious high morale among staff and students. The program is definitely service oriented but the field is pretty well limited to the public schools. Graduate students are recruited mainly from among the teachers of the area, a fact which tends to give assurance that their training will be put to immediate use, but which rather restricts the outlook of the training program. In most instances the research phases of graduate study have been abandoned and presumably in their place more attention is given to counseling practice. The training now embraces "internship" or supervised field work and this feature appears in a large measure to account for the enthusiasm of the students.

The child guidance clinic continues to provide more or less intensive services to a limited number of clients both on and off the campus. This program has operated over a number of years and appears to be comparable in quality to the best psycho-educational clinic services offered anywhere. Like all good services it makes heavy demands upon the time of the staff.

The counseling and personnel services in the offices of the Dean of Men and of the Dean of Women are organized along ambitious lines. The advisory relationships which in many universities are considered to be basically student-teacher relationships are here largely centralized in the offices of the student deans. The counseling duties undertaken by these offices, if fully discharged, would be tremendous and would require substantial outlays of staff time and office space.

The work of the advisement center operated under contract with the Veterans Administration is at the point of being discontinued. As everywhere, this program has played an important part in the occupational readjustment of veterans. To be sure, as the post war years have gone by, these centers have more and more had their time taken up by those who are chronically maladjusted. But occupational maladjustment is not limited to veterans nor to the immediate post war period. Moreover, efforts spent in working out a reasonable occupational adjustment for a disturbed young man may serve to prevent a more devastating personality break requiring expensive public support for him at a later date.

In the college of Liberal Arts there is a recognized need for academic instruction in psychology. Members of other departments have expressed the need for such instruction as an adjunct to their own instructional efforts. It is believed that the student with some background in psychology is in a position to react more intelligently to some of the concepts presented in economics, for example. This is indeed a point of view which is consistent with the best traditions of liberalism.

In the Department of Home Economics there appears to be an excellent opportunity for psychological collaboration in a congenial setting. The field of child development and nursery education lends itself readily to the joint endeavors of home economists, teachers and psychologists.

In the field of speech therapy there is an expressed interest in securing the active collaboration of a clinical psychologist. Even in the field of public speaking there is a recognized area of cooperation in studying audience opinion and the dynamics of group interaction.

What Undeveloped Opportunities Exist for Useful Psychological Activities which are Not Yet Clearly Perceived by Representatives of the University Community?

No university can mount its horse and ride off in all directions, no matter how many opportunities may beckon. There are, however, for Southern Illinois some further opportunities which may be well worth exploring.

The coming of new industry to the area, with the attendant problems of interpreting the skills and attitudes of the southern Illinois worker to his new employers, offers a challenge to the University. There is much that could be done through thoughtful unbiased studies of the problems of labor relations in the area. If these studies could be translated into personnel services for newly located industrial plants the University would thereby make a substantial contribution to the economic recovery of the community.

While in no way the exclusive skill of the psychologist, the making of evaluative surveys to support and guide administrative policy is a skill in which many psychologists have been trained. Since Southern Illinois University policy involves a constantly developing and changing program of services to the community it is mandatory that the Administration maintain an active organization and program for surveying the results of its efforts. The writer believes that this need cannot be overemphasized.

While the idea may come as a surprise to some, every progressive university needs to maintain an educational program for its own staff. Professors soon lose their keenness and fall into careless habits if they are not constantly kept alert by the impact of new ideas. This is particularly true of their relations with students. There is always the temptation to divest a teacher of his guidance relationships with his students as soon as he shows signs of becoming "narrow and encapsulated."

One of the ways in which a university can render a real service to itself and to its instructors is to set up most of its guidance services in a "staff" relationship to instructors rather than in a "line" relationship. In this relationship the guidance specialists assist the instructor in his relationships with his students by providing technical information in the form of test results, personnel records, etc. In addition they may assist the instructor by conducting special interviews, suggesting approaches to the student, and generally helping the instructor improve his relationships with his students. This takes skill of a high type. It is well worth trying.

What is the Nature and Scope of the Psychological Training now Effectively Provided to Students in the University?

Psychological course offerings seem to be subject to the same proliferations at Southern Illinois University that are found in other American universities. One cannot help but compare this tendency in our country with the practices in European universities where the courses are frequently limited to two, an elementary course and an advanced course. The writer's experience with both practices leads him to believe that the tendency to excessive course offerings tends to becloud rather than enrich our educational offerings.

The confusion probably arises out of certain implicit assumptions upon which American university practices are based. One is that generalized knowledge is irrelevant to the practical world in which we live and hence should be lumped with traditionalism and other relics that might better be forgotten. Another is that students come to the university with specific questions and the job of the instructor is to answer them in the form in which they are put. Still another implicit assumption is that students are not interested in the content of higher education and therefore we must titillate them with highly specific course titles to catch their passing fancies. But knowledge that is irrelevant to the practical world is certainly not generalized, and the questions that students bring to the campus must be reconstructed before sensible answers can be given, and students do respond to instruction pretty much in proportion to the vision of the instructor.

The University catalog lists twenty-six courses that might be considered psychological in nature. The record of courses actually offered in the Department of Guidance and Special Education during the winter, spring, and summer quarters of this year lists twenty-nine different course numbers and sixty-four different class sections. The Department has an informal listing of thirty-nine courses under its cognizance. With five regular members of the Department's instructional staff it is difficult to see how this program of course offerings can be maintained without reducing much of the psychological instruction to the level of uninspired mumblings out of the dry mouth of an overworked teacher.

There appear to be fifty-six graduate students enrolled in the Department, of whom twenty expect to receive advanced degrees at the spring and summer commencements. The total course enrollments in psychology were 580 and 597 for the winter and spring quarters, respectively. With the exception of clinical psychology, in which about one fourth of the graduate students of the Department are enrolled, training involves very little research. Even with the substitution of technique for methodology which this arrangement implies, it is difficult to see how the staff can have time to give graduate training which is comparable with that given in the better universities. Even if there were no undergraduate teaching responsibilities, the ratio of eleven graduate students for each instructor would be excessive. Certainly the self-sacrificing efforts of the staff of this department in attempting to spread the advantages of graduate training to all those who deserve it are to be commended. Yet students who later find reason to believe that their training was watered-down may not express the degree of gratitude that the instructors deserve.

In some respects the curriculum for advanced students in psychology is the best the writer has seen. The practicum or internship program makes excellent use of the opportunity for practical experience in connection with the various resources which the campus provides. There is no doubt but that this program is reflected in the high enthusiasm for their work which the writer observed in the students. The close tie-up between the graduate program and in-service teachers might well be imitated by other departments of psychology.

Altogether the present training program in psychology adds up long on specialized technique and enthusiasm, short on generalized instruction and basic psychological methodology.

What Channels of Communication and Execution are Now Most Effectively Operated by Personnel who Perform Psychological Duties?

Most of the instructional activities of a psychological nature are now organized within the Department of Guidance and Special Education. It is understood that this department was formed as a tentative solution to the problem last year.

In addition to the activities organized under the Department of Guidance and Special Education there is a great deal of psychological activity in the offices of the Deans of Students. There appears to be a reasonably effective arrangement for collaboration between these offices and the Department in the matter of practicums for advanced students.

There is a question which commonly arises when counseling services are associated with disciplinary services. What is the appropriate relationship between the counselor and the administration on the one hand, and between the counselor and his client on the other? When the counselor is directly subordinate to an official who carries a heavy load of disciplinary responsibility, both counselor and client may develop a confused idea of their relationship with each other. Psychological counseling, if it is to be effective at anything more than a superficial level, must have the status of "privileged communication." Unless a student is willing to yield the most intimate direction of his life to a university official and to play a passive role of childlike dependency upon a governmental agency he is likely to look upon psychological counseling in a dean's office as more of a threat than an opportunity.

The Department of Guidance and Special Education appears to have a keen sense of its mission. It is oriented toward services to the community as few university departments are. In working through the public schools it is utilizing channels to the community which have already been cleared and are ready for peak capacity operation. It has shown itself ready to collaborate with other activities of the University in such matters as the practicum training of graduate students. No one could fail to be impressed with the way it has directed its service efforts along the very lines in which the University as a whole must move. Morale among staff members and major students appears to be high. They like the new set-up. They feel it opens up opportunities for them. They feel they are participating in a "going concern."

Yet as service-oriented as the Department's program is, it is not broad enough. The Department is not organized to develop the University's psychological opportunities except insofar as they are recognized within the purview of education. The need for psychological enterprise is more extensive than the organization of the present Department of Guidance and Special Education is prepared to cope with.

Principles

Every administrator who carries out a long-term program of developing his organization must distinguish between the principles by which he has chosen to guide his actions and the measures through which his decisions are expressed. If this report is to have more than temporary value it should suggest guiding principles for the future as well as measures for the present. The following principles are suggested as having more or less permanent applicability to psychological activities at the University of Southern Illinois.

The Principle of Building Permanent Organizations of Scholars on the Basis of Permanent Common Interests

If a scholar is to build his career upon successive attainments in the discipline of his choice he must be prepared to alter and refresh his viewpoint in the light of the most advanced developments in that discipline. Scholarship must be nourished if it is to thrive. This is particularly true of the psychologist whose discipline of psychology is undergoing such rapid transition that each decade makes obsolescent the training one has received in the decade before. The psychologist needs close academic association with his psychological colleagues if his own scholarship is to keep abreast of the times. While he may be useful for a time in an organization where he is the sole representative of the psychological approach, his usefulness will diminish in direct proportion to his loss of contact with his fellow psychologists. Intra-disciplinary interaction is essential to healthy scholarship.

The Principle of Interdisciplinary Approach to Practical Problems

This is not the antithesis of the first principle but rather a kind of corollary to it. More correctly, the first principle is a corollary to the second. We may borrow from military science the notion of the "task force" which is organized for a specific mission and in its best form combines the characteristic methods of attack of various corps and services. If men who are sufficiently well grounded in their different basic disciplines can unite in a common practical task there is always a better chance that the job will be well done. This is just as true for a university as it is for a military command. It is particularly applicable to Southern Illinois University where there are so many action missions of a practical nature to be performed during the next decade.

The Principle of Using Temporary Organizations for Reaching Short-Range Objectives. Again the Task Force Analogy is Relevant

Who knows what missions psychologists, or anyone for that matter, will be called upon to perform during the coming years. The University is presumably entering upon a period of far-reaching and kaleidoscopic changes. If it builds permanent organizations especially to do the jobs which now seem urgent it may find those organizations are maladapted to the jobs which will loom before it in the future. Moreover the established leadership in a permanent organization has a well-known propensity for growing old and rigid, a fact which serves better to keep events in historical perspective than to get a particular job done by six months from next Tuesday. The use of temporary organizations for reaching specified short-range objectives permits the use of youthful and energetic leadership without concessions to seniority and academic rank.

This principle also implies that there shall be frequent evaluation of progress toward the specified objectives together with an attendant freedom of the University's Administration to change tactics in the light of experience. If the writer senses the temper of the present administration correctly it not only needs this kind of flexibility of organization in order to operate with maximal effectiveness, but it will make full use of such organizations in carrying out its program.

The Principle of Building Maximal Student-Professor Relationships on the Grounds of Common Scholarly Pursuits

This principle is rooted not only in a philosophy of education but in a theory of mental hygiene itself. The view that advanced learning requires the interchange of ideas between student and teacher is not new. A modern state university with its punch card personnel system and its professional counselors is likely to throw many obstacles in the way of this type of relationship. When it does so the student is likely to miss the adventure of pursuing knowledge in the company of scholarly men. As undergraduate enrollments become excessively large this type of companionship tends to be reserved for graduate students. Now that graduate training is reaching the mass education stage it may be that one will be forced to acquire a Ph.D. before he can enjoy the company of advanced scholars.

The situation is not hopeless. If it is recognized that the student-professor relationship is the one basic inter-personal relationship in the university, it should be possible to build counseling and personnel programs which maximize that relationship.

The building of inter-personal relationships on the grounds of common scholarly pursuits has important mental hygiene implications. The personal stability and the social usefulness that characterize the mature mind are achieved only as one is able to turn his attention away from himself to problems which exist independently of himself. Even if we accept the fact that, in order to reach this level of maturity, some of us must take a lot of time out to set our personal houses in order, we could scarcely argue that continued preoccupation with one's own feelings and moods is the ultimate basis for a healthy social adjustment. Good mental hygiene requires that one must transcend this kind of autistic preoccupation. In this sense, then, any learning which is objectively pursued may serve a hygienic function. This is a fact which mental hygienists should not overlook. It argues strongly for using the common interests of professors and students in scholarly topics as a primary and practical basis for improving students' outlook on life as a whole.

The Principle of Combining Generalized Instruction with Service Training

In one respect the students of this generation at Southern Illinois University have a rare opportunity. They are where they can see scholarship in action, see it transforming the community, witness its ways of solving human problems, even participate in the transition. It would be a serious loss to the students of the University not to be associated actively with every one of the service projects through which the institution is to serve its community. Whatever the University does for southern Illinois should involve the participation of students. To do otherwise would be to deny them opportunities which lie at their doorsteps.

Instruction should not stop with participation in the service program of the University, nor with the technical training which develops a student's skill in rendering services. Students should not be trained merely to render the services required in the 1950s. Rather they should be given, in addition, a firm grasp of the generalizations, the principles, the basic concepts within the structure of which the techniques of the ensuing decade will make as much sense as the skills of the present. This is not an argument for abstruse teaching—quite the opposite. Generalized learning cannot take place if the student is unaware of any of the things from which generalizations are drawn. The combination of generalized instruction with service training should make theories come alive and turn abstract principles into ever-meaningful ways of life.

The Principle of Stressing the Methodology of Inquiry

The instructional problem of a university is not so much how to give a student an education as it is how to insure his education against obsolescence. The student who is taught how to pose his questions in the form in which they are answerable has some protection against the creeping ignorance that attacks so many educated people in the prime of life.

It is unfortunate that research is regarded as esoteric by so many educators. Yet, in one form or another, research represents a basic approach to the novel problems which confront all of us. The methodology of research can be described simply as the art of asking questions that can be answered. There is nothing impractical about that kind of art. Certainly it deserves a better fate than dismissal from the graduate curriculum. And the student who has some familiarity with the methodology of inquiry should, over the years, be better able to serve his community by guiding its progress in the light of new knowledge.

Recommended Organizational Structure for Psychological Activities

A Single Department of Psychology

It is recommended that there be organized a single department of psychology in the University with all psychologists attached to it. It is recommended that the department have a chairman elected for a five year term from among the members holding tenure and the rank of assistant professor and above. It is recommended that the electorate be comprised of the entire instructional staff of the department and the graduate majors in the department; the combined vote of the latter being weighted equally with the combined vote of the former.

It is recommended that the department be authorized to propose curricular offerings within the fields of competence of its members and, for such offerings as are approved by the Administration, be held responsible for adequate instruction.

It is recommended that the salaries of all psychologists in the University be budgeted wholly within the department of psychology. It is recommended that the department's secretarial staff, graduate assistantships, and instructional equipment and supplies also be budgeted wholly within the department of psychology.

Fractional Time Assignments

It is recommended that each member of the psychology department have a dual assignment, one an assignment to the department covering all of his academic duties in psychology, the other an assignment to non-academic services or to collaboration in the instructional program of another department. It is recommended that the proportion of the staff member's time to be devoted to each of these two types of assignment be stipulated at the beginning of each academic year.

Task Force Organization

It is recommended that the services of psychologists be freely used in interdisciplinary programs undertaken by the University. It is recommended that, in view of the University's need for flexible organization in developing its community-centered program, task forces be organized from time to time and given specified missions to be accomplished by given dates. The accomplishments of these temporary organizations should be surveyed regularly, perhaps every six months, and the administration should be in a position to reorganize the personnel as the need for new missions and objectives becomes apparent.

Operating budgets for task force organizations should be established on a year-to-year basis. It is recommended that task force operations make maximum use of graduate students through practicum assignments to the task force or through research collaboration.

It is recommended that taskforces be headed by directors appointed by the Administration. In general these directors should be chosen from among the most vigorous members of the University faculty. Competence for the task at hand should be given foremost consideration; rank and seniority need not enter into the selection.

Some task force organizations might be expected to have a greater degree of permanence than others. For example, the Child Guidance Clinic, which has been in successful operation for a number of years, might be considered a type of task force organization whose mission one might expect to be renewed for a series of three-year terms. A bureau of guidance might be established as a task force organization to undertake certain phases of counseling now conducted in the offices of the Deans of Students and in the Veterans Advisement Center. A more temporary type of task force might be organized to survey industrial personnel programs in the area and to draft a plan for University participation in such programs. Such a mission might be scheduled for completion in six months or a year. Another short-time task force might be assigned the task of developing an approach to soil conservation demonstrations in the area. Another might set as its objective the establishment of twenty active child-development study groups in the surrounding communities.

The extensive use of the flexible task force type of organization to carry out the rapidly developing program of the University would require a central administrative unit to coordinate task forces. Assignment of personnel, formulation of missions, review of periodic evaluations of results, allocation of operating budgets, and similar matters would fall under the cognizance of this central unit. It would also be the responsibility of this unit to see that task force assignments were formulated in such a manner as to give optimal support to the President in planning activities and that reports of missions completed were made available to him in the most useful form.

Tenure, Salaries, and Promotions

The proposed plan for the organization of psychological activities is designed to give each psychologist academic security through his identification with a department of psychology. Even though task force assignments may change, tenure need in no way be affected.

Since salaries would be budgeted entirely through the department of psychology, changes in task force assignments would have no essential effect on funds available for salaries.

Since the task force plan should provide more than usual opportunity for younger men to demonstrate their organizing and executive ability, it should be possible to make promotions in rank on the basis of observed relevant performance. Moreover, with an elected chairmanship in the department of Psychology, it should be possible for the leadership of that department to fall to young but task-force-experienced hands.

In what College?

Since this report recommends a type of organization which is utterly flexible as far as psychological services are concerned the question of what college should claim the department of psychology is of minor importance. Certainly the curricular offerings of the department should serve the needs of the University as a whole. Presumably most of the courses offered by the department would be relevant to the curricula of all three colleges. Courses which were considered to be of such a nature as to be appropriate to the curriculum of one college only could easily be tagged by a suitable subscript on the identifying number in the catalog. The writer can see no substantial objection to placing the department of psychology in any of the three colleges.

Recommended Instructional Policies in Psychology

Alignment of the Curriculum with a Broader Conception of the Field of Psychology

It is recommended that the number of course offerings in psychology be reduced, perhaps to as few as twenty. While curricular revision must always be considered a local undertaking perhaps the following suggested arrangement might be taken as a point of departure for discussion.

Undergraduate Courses

Introductory Psychology I
- Adjustment
- Development
- Ranges of Individual Capacity

Introductory Psychology II
- Social Interaction
- Perception
- Learning

Undergraduate and Graduate Courses

Quantitative Methodology I
- Experimentation
- Measurement and Tests

Quantitative Methodology II
- Testing Significances

Clinical Methodology I
- Observation
- Interview

Clinical Methodology II
- Individual Testing
- Communication of Psychological Information
- Advanced Psychology of Adjustment
- Advanced Psychology of Development
- Advanced Psychology of Individual Capacity (including occupational information and psychology of the handicapped)
- Advanced Social Psychology
- Advanced Perception and Physiological Psychology
- Advanced Learning
- Reading

Graduate Courses

Seminar in Personnel
Seminar in Clinical Psychology
Seminar in Social and Industrial Psychology
Seminar in Special Education
Group Counseling
Psychodynamics and Psychotherapy
Advanced Psychological Methodology
Practicum

It is recommended that instruction in service techniques be largely consigned to the practicum courses rather than to the classroom courses. It is recommended that the syllabi of classroom courses be written in such a manner as to give effective generalized support to the training of industrial and social psychologists as well as counselors and clinicians. It is recommended that the seminar series be left as flexible as possible and that students be permitted to repeat seminars for additional credit.

Teaching Load

It is recommended that in psychology the normal teaching load not exceed six class hours a week but that this load be considered approximately half of the total load borne by a psychologist in his service to the University.

It is recommended that six fully active graduate advisees be considered a maximum load for an instructor but that this load be considered approximately half the total load borne by a psychologist in his service to the University.

Extending the Instructional Services of the Psychological Staff

It is recommended that where necessary to bring the teaching load into line with the above recommendations the sizes of class sections be enlarged indefinitely. While ideally a class section should be small enough to encourage individual attention on the part of the instructor it is unrealistic to expect such individual attention if the instructor is bogged down with other classes and other duties. It is far more important that an instructor comes before his class prepared, alert, and inspired than that he be able to give each student an individual pat on the head.

Recommended Services and Projects

Guidance Services

It is recommended that the guidance services which have been so well developed in the University be sustained and encouraged. It is recommended that the work of the Veterans Advisement Center be incorporated into the guidance service program of the University and that the combined services be made available to the community both through the schools and through self-referrals.

It is recommended that guidance services be rendered through a bureau of guidance and special education services. Such a bureau should be organized as a task force. It is recommended that as a general policy the bureau of guidance and special education services accept voluntary referrals only and that it does not directly involve itself with the administrative measures which are a necessary part of the University's personnel program.

Personnel Services

It is recommended that personnel services, insofar as they involve uniform psychological testing of all students be retained in the office of the Dean of Men, or the Director of Student Personnel, if the Klein report is put into effect. It is recognized that it would be impractical to separate all counseling functions from the Deans' offices since the judicious handling of most student affairs requires a measure of skillful counseling. It is recommended, however, that psychological counseling, as it is possible to distinguish it from social or academic counseling, be separated as far as possible from any office where coercive influences may be felt by the student.

It is further recommended that academic advisement as far as possible be placed in the hands of the instructional staff and that it be based upon the solid ground of a common scholarly interest, whether that interest be in pottery or fish culture.

It is recommended that both in the case of guidance services and the case of personnel services every effort be made to support the relationship between students and instructional staff. Psychologists may find themselves most useful in serving their professorial colleagues by supplying psychological data regarding their advisees and suggesting psychologically sound approaches to professors who have difficulty with their advisees.

Child Guidance Services

It is recommended, for the present at least, that the clinical psychology services be offered under the aegis of the bureau of guidance and special education services. A similar association seems now to be working out happily for all concerned.

It is recommended that a representative of the present Department of Guidance and Special Education get in touch with Dr. Phyllis Wittman, State Psychologist, Elgin State Hospital, Elgin, Illinois and explore the possibility of establishing internship facilities in clinical psychology at the Anna State Hospital. It is understood that the pending appointment of a chief psychologist at Anna might be worked out in collaboration with Southern Illinois University, perhaps with a joint appointment to both staffs.

Industrial Personnel Services

It is recommended that a task force be organized to explore, on a one year basis, the feasibility and necessary procedures for offering local industrial plants a cooperative personnel service. It is suggested that the advice of Mr. C.W. Borden, Manager of the Hoosier Cardinal Plant would be valuable in this connection.

A Community Mental Hygiene Clinic

It is suggested that a representative of the University get in touch with Dr. Jerry Carter, National Institute of Mental Health, Washington, D.C., to explore the possibility of using U.S. Public Health funds which have been allotted to the State of Illinois for the establishment of a community mental hygiene clinic in Carbondale. Such a clinic would normally involve the appointment of a full mental hygiene team, comprised of a psychiatrist, a clinical psychologist, and two psychiatric social workers.

Appendix

Copy of Letter

29 April 1950

Dr. Delyte Morris, President
Southern Illinois university
Carbondale, Illinois

Dear Delyte,

Following our telephone conversation a few minutes ago, I believe everything is set for me to arrive in Carbondale Monday noon, May eighth. As soon as I arrive I shall get in touch with your office.

If you consider it appropriate I would very much like to have a local committee with whom I could meet daily to discuss my observations. Such a committee could guide me both in making the proper interpersonal contacts and in keeping facts in the proper perspective. Perhaps we could arrange to meet for an hour and a half in the late afternoon of each day, or perhaps the group would prefer a dinner meeting that would close early enough for them to keep late evening engagements.

The composition of such a committee is a matter in which I am wholly dependent upon your judgment. Presumably you would want your administration represented, probably also your teaching faculty. Representation of the non-university community is probably highly desirable; perhaps a local member of your Board of Trustees, a member of the Alumni Association, or an actively interested citizen would be willing to take time for the five meetings. It might be very stimulating to have students represented.

Enclosed is a bibliography which should be of interest to those who are concerned with my visit. With the exception of the Harvard Report, the references are quite brief. All are quite readable. On the guess that this report may not have reached your library, I have wired for a copy to be sent directly to you.

During the first day I should like to have an opportunity to visit individually with your administrative officers, particularly those who might be expected to have some concern with psychological activity in the university.

Presumably the second day should be spent in conferences with the teaching staff. In addition to individual conferences I would be grateful for an opportunity to participate in any departmental staff meetings where the topic of "psychology in relation to the needs of the university" would be of common interest.

During the week I shall want also to have an opportunity to talk with students, both singly and in groups. I hope to have a number of visits with community leaders and alumni. It is my conviction that such persons frequently have an uncluttered view of the role of the University in the community.

Would your secretary mind doing two things for me: (1) Send me a copy of your catalog together with copies of any recent committee reports you have bearing on curriculum planning or community services and (2) reserve a room at your local hotel for four nights beginning May eighth.

I am looking forward to this visit. I hope it will be as profitable for your organization as I anticipate it will be for me.

Yours very truly,
George A. Kelly

Bibliography

Gregg, A., et al. *The place of psychology in an ideal university*. Cambridge: Harvard University Press, 1947. Pp 42

Sanford, F. H. and Fleishman, E. A. A survey of undergraduate psychology courses in American colleges and universities. *American Psychologist*, 1950, 5. 33–37

Shartle, C. L. Occupations in psychology. *American Psychologist*, 1946, 1, 559–582

Watson, G. Psychological contributions to world understanding. *American Psychologist*, 1949, 4, 65–68

Wolfle, D. The sensible organization of courses in psychology. *American Psychologist*, 1947, 2, 445–447

American Psychological Association, Policy and Planning Board. Annual Reports 1947. *American Psychologist*, 1947, 2, 191–198

Berrien, F. K. A new type of elementary course. *American Psychologist*, 1947, 2, 148–150

Black, J. D. A survey of employment in psychology and the place of personnel without the Ph.D. *American Psychologist*, 1950, 4, 38–42

Bryan, A. I. and Boring, E. G. Women in American psychology: Statistics from the OPP questionnaire. *American Psychologist*, 1946, 1, 71–79

Cantril, H. Psychology working for peace. *American Psychologist*, 1949, 4, 69–73

Gregg, A. The profession of psychology as seen by a doctor of medicine. *American Psychologist*, 1948, 3, 397–401

Hall, M. E. Current employment requirements for school psychologists. *American Psychologist*, 1949, 4, 519–525

Henry, E. R. A survey of courses in psychology offered by undergraduate colleges of liberal arts. *Psychological Bulletin*, 1938, 35, 430–435.

Horrocks, J. E. State certification requirements for school psychologists. *American psychologist*, 1946, 1, 399–401

McQuitty, L. L. Developing applied psychologists. *American Psychologist*, 1948, 3, 16–19

Pressey, S. L. The place and functions of psychology in undergraduate programs. *American Psychologist*, 1949, 4, 148–150

100

Doctoral Training in Psychology in Southern Illinois University[1]

Assignment

A visit to the Southern Illinois campus was made on February eighth and ninth at the invitation of Dr. Noble H. Kelley, Chairman of the Department of Psychology. The assignment was to evaluate the University's readiness to initiate doctoral training in psychology.

Six years ago I made a survey of the local situation in order to offer suggestions regarding the organization of a new department of psychology. Since that time there have been rapid developments in the department as well as over the entire campus. The visit this year provided an opportunity to observe the progress that has taken place since the original recommendations were submitted.

In formulating the following observations and appraisals I have tried not only to cover the major issues upon which the University Administration must base its decisions but also to discuss a few of the special problems that are likely to arise when a new doctoral program gets under way.

Summary of Major Conclusions

1 The present Psychology Department staff is, as a group, qualified to offer doctoral training in selected fields of applied psychology. It is not prepared to offer doctoral training focused upon the theoretical aspects of psychology.
2 The Department, under its present leadership, will probably establish sound policies for its doctoral program. It seems inclined to resist the incipient growth of those practices that so often work to defeat the purposes of doctoral education.
3 The University Library is now operating under purchase and subscription policies which, if followed consistently over the years, will adequately provide essential sources of information for graduate study in psychology.
4 The Graduate Council has not yet established the framework of policy within which the departments of the University will operate their doctoral programs. While there is always the possibility that an overly self-conscious committee will initially draft hamstringing regulations when it sets out to espouse high academic standards, there is no present indication that the Council will attempt to create scholarship by fiat.
5 The graduate program will be handicapped for several years by the lack of scholarly traditions among the students of the University. This handicap can be partially offset by measures designed to help graduate students create their own intellectual climate and cultural controls.
6 The current allocations of space, both in amount and in functional utility, are not adequate to sustain an integrated doctoral program in psychology. They do not provide sufficient opportunity for laboratory and practicum work in applied psychology, nor are they suited to the needs of individual doctoral candidates who must conduct independent research and study during the latter part of their training period.
7 The opportunities for the employment of psychologists with sound training in certain new applied fields are good and appear to be improving. If the University emphasizes such fields as modern school psychology, community life, and services for small industry, its graduates will be able to compete favorably with graduates whose training has been along conventional lines.
8 Formal lecture courses need not be added to the curriculum at the present time. A continuing seminar with flexible topics and flexible credits will take care of any new formal content that needs to be introduced. Formal courses can emerge out of this as needed. In addition, there should be some provision for the full accreditation of a student's practicum training, particularly his internship, so as to keep that part of his experience firmly controlled as an integral and academically respectable part of his doctoral program.

[1] Consultant's report, March 20, 1956. Published by permission of Jacqueline Aldridge.

Collected Papers of the Pioneer of Constructivist Psychology: George A. Kelly, First Edition. Edited by David A. Winter and Nick Reed.

Comments

The Psychology Staff

Most of the ten members of the Psychology Department staff are still young and have received their doctoral degrees from good universities during the post-war period. This represents certain advantages. The major universities have reorganized their doctoral training programs in psychology during the past ten years. Students are now much better selected. Curricula in clinical and counseling psychology are subject to special accreditation by the Education and Training Board of the American Psychological Association. Internships have been added and the quality of recent Ph.D. graduates is considerably above what it was before the war. By having staff members who have been trained in the revised psychological curricula, especially in clinical and counseling psychology, the University has an advantage over those institutions whose staffs have not received the more professional type of doctoral training.

There are, of course, disadvantages in having a young staff, even though well trained. Young staff members are often less adept in handling students. They are sometimes more punitive than inspiring in their efforts to maintain high academic standards. They are also more inclined to exaggerate the range of their own specialties. Occasionally their self-consciousness and lack of personal security make them defensive in their relations both with students and with administrative personnel.

While embodying the advantages of modern training, the Southern Illinois Department of Psychology Staff also is liable to some of the disadvantages of youth and inexperience. There is some tendency for members to think their own areas of specialization encompass a major portion of the whole field of psychology. In those areas where a staff member is the sole representative of his special field of psychology there is, understandably, some tendency that he alone can take over a major portion of the doctoral training of a student.

But whatever the disadvantages of having a young and relatively inexperienced staff, they are largely offset by the excellent leadership under which the Department has had its initial growth. This leadership has exercised special care and good judgment in the selection of new staff members. As long as this aspect of departmental administration is handled well the staff will continue to grow in quality as well as in numbers. If, however, presumed administrative emergencies force the employment of new staff members at the last minute or as part of a "crash" program, the quality of staff will undoubtedly suffer. It is most important, therefore, to operate under policies which guarantee that professors will be selected with the same deliberate care that has characterized the Department's administration in the past five years. It is far better to let a position lie fallow than to fill it with a person whose rank will prove to be more conspicuous than his competence.

The Department compensates for its inexperience in another important way. There is a high level of intellectual communication between staff members. This means that new ideas will likely be brought to the attention of all staff members and that they will be subject to group criticism and evaluation. In part, this is a reflection of the quality of leadership in the Department and, in part, it is a reflection of the keen personalities of individuals who now compose the Department Staff. Altogether, it represents a built-in deterrent against the insularity and compartmentalization that have ruined the quality of doctoral training in more than one other university.

One could wish that there were some members of the Department with extensive experience in directing doctoral dissertations. But this is a form of experience that is not easy to graft onto a new department. If one seeks to purchase experience outright he is likely to end up with itinerant professors whose previous record has already proved them to be inferior. It seems better, therefore, to try to compensate for inexperience by other means.

One way in which the Department might compensate for the lack of doctoral training experience among the staff is to set up a plan for using outside consultants in connection with the later stages of each doctoral candidate's training. A consultant might be invited to the campus to participate in preliminary and final doctoral examinations and to hold a faculty seminar during his visit. Such a consultant might also be a corresponding member of a candidate's dissertation committee, serving both in the development of the initial experimental design and in the final appraisal. In addition, it might be possible, in the early stages of the program, to have students spend a term at another university, perhaps taking seminars with persons who might later be used as visiting consultants.

The present psychology staff is rather heavily weighted in the direction of clinical and counseling psychology. It seems therefore that the new doctoral program should recognize this balance of strength and not presume to offer intensive training in the more classical areas of psychology. Instead, even in the clinical and counseling fields, it would not appear to be wise to attempt to prepare students in direct competition to well-established training programs in other universities. The best course would be to develop training with specialization along applied psychology lines that are not so clearly drawn elsewhere. Moreover, the University might well emphasize a brand of psychological specialization which would make maximum use of some of the local needs and resources. This could include community-life, counseling services, gerontology, school psychology, industrial counseling, and other under-developed areas of applied psychology adjacent to the clinical and counseling fields.

Departmental Policies

In planning its program, the Department will need to take into account not only the quality of the training it is prepared to offer but also the potential advantages and disadvantages of Southern Illinois training from the graduate's point of view. Even if his training were comparable in quality the student would scarcely be either loyal or grateful if he found that his Southern Illinois Ph.D. would not open the employment doors for him that a degree from a better-known university would open. This makes it especially important that the doctoral program not be conceived as a minimum standard program for training along conventional lines, but rather as one developed along lines in which the present department can hope to establish obvious supremacy. It is most important that students who receive their degrees at Southern Illinois will be glad they did so. Otherwise the training program will ultimately fail.

It will be helpful if the University keeps in touch with the emerging standards of the Education and Training Board of the American Psychological Association. This Board is not a self-styled accrediting agency of the type some professional societies have set up, but an arm of the psychology profession that is genuinely interested in helping departments improve their programs in creative and imaginative ways. When required to do so the Board does indicate to subsidizing agencies which universities have the most mature programs in specified areas, but its primary mission is constructive rather than restrictive. In addition to his regular duties the Executive Officer of the Board is authorized to accept a limited number of invitations each year from universities who want formal advisory visits. At some time in the future the University may wish to take advantage of this service.

The addition of doctoral training to the curriculum of the Department will principally involve two new educational features: a) the direction of advanced research and b) the development of independent scholarship outside the framework of courses. The first addition requires that the Staff learn to foster and advise independent research efforts without resorting to the actual management of the student's inquiries. This is a skill that is both a matter of technique and of mature attitude on the part of the professors. Not all professors acquire it. The program should be set up so that students are not forced to work under the direction of those who are incapable of this kind of teaching. Each student should be able to choose his dissertation adviser from among several professors without having to shift his area of research interest.

In this kind of graduate teaching milieu the teacher teaches as much by example and the sharing of enthusiasm as by precept. If the Department believes it is ready to direct doctoral dissertations it can quite properly check this impression of itself by looking at its own spontaneous research activities. Staff members who are not themselves pursuing inquiries are not likely candidates for the direction of students' inquiries. Moreover, Staff members whose present students are not already pursuing independent study with some spontaneity may not be prepared to direct doctoral study, even though they themselves are active researchers.

As for independent scholarship, the Department will have to create a climate of informal scholarship that cuts the student free from course credits and reading assignments. Again, the professor teaches by example and by sharing enthusiasms. If the present Staff is active on this front and if students are already sharing the spontaneous scholarly interests of their professors, the climate may be right for undertaking doctoral training. If, on the other hand, there is now very little scholarly exchange between students and professors outside classes and if students and staff move in independent academic circles, then the time may not be ripe for the introduction of doctoral training. In short, one of the criteria of whether or not a department is ready to offer doctoral training is the presence or absence of spontaneous doctoral-type activities among both staff and students. Doctoral education cannot be legislated into being; it has to exist in an incipient form beforehand.

It is easy for students to become too busy to think. Because a doctoral training program is supposed to be "hard" there is a tendency for departments to load the student down with activities and requirements. If these demands are real challenges to his intellect and energies they may serve to bring him to a mature level of scholarship. But if they induce him to the status of an over-worked clerk they may stifle all his scholarly impulses. It is important that the Department look to the scholarship that its program produces rather than to the difficulties it places in the way of its students. The more able students will eliminate themselves from a pesterous training program whereas the persistent drudges will thrive on it.

The Department will have to give considerable thought to its recruitment of graduate students. Students who have done their undergraduate work at one university should always be encouraged to go to another for their graduate work. This would mean that the Department ought to send its graduate majors elsewhere for doctoral training and should recruit its doctoral candidates from other colleges and universities.

The field of psychology is highly competitive in certain respects. While there are more positions than there are psychologists, there is severe competition for the better positions in the field and many of the conspicuously vacant positions are not really professionally desirable. Moreover, the bottle-neck in university training facilities for psychologists throughout the country has had a screening effect upon the yearly crop of Ph.D.'s. Only the most competent students have been able to get into doctoral training, and they, when they graduate, tend to be a highly select lot. A university that does not recruit such top-caliber students for its doctoral program is therefore likely to find its graduates eking out their careers in second-rate jobs.

It would be highly desirable to establish a number of generous stipends for graduate students in psychology. These will not only tend to attract students who are promising enough to have their choice of admission to any of several first-rate universities, but they will make it financially possible for more mature students with families to come to Carbondale. Without such inducements the candidates are likely to be mediocre students whom other universities will not accept or else youngsters who dare not adventure beyond the familiar environs of Egypt.

The curriculum should emphasize selected aspects of psychology, particularly those which are not well developed in the established universities and which the local staff is prepared to work out without too much adherence to traditions. It should be professional as well as scientific in its emphasis. By this is meant an emphasis on making the student competent to serve clients, a competency which is over and beyond scientific competence. Yet the curriculum should not be allowed to degenerate into a "do-it-yourself kit" for students who want to use psychological tools on their fellowmen. The professionalism should emphasize responsibility in relation to clients but it should be firmly anchored in liberal scholarship and rigorous scientific inquiry.

The doctoral curriculum should include a year of well-organized internship. This will mean a minimum of four years beyond the baccalaureate degree. Most students in such curricula need a little more time than this. The internship should not be merely a working experience but should be a well-organized training situation where the intern is not exploited and the training agency correlates its work closely with the syllabus of the Department. The internship should have a teaching curriculum and should be approved by the Department. Certain kinds of internships are accredited by the Education and Training Board of the American Psychological Association. Where applicable this accreditation should be required by the Department.

While it may seem more cautious not to admit more than one or two graduate students to the doctoral program at first, actually it is better to admit more than this or else none at all. Graduate students need to create for themselves a scholarly society in which there can be informal but challenging intellectual discourse. This argues for the admission of at least four to six students in the first class.

Library

The field of psychology is developing rapidly. While books are important to the graduate student it is relatively more important that he have immediate access to journals and monographs. Certain new books need to be put on the shelves as soon as they are reviewed; some others even sooner. Students need to have an opportunity to learn of the appearance of new books and to examine them in their own work rooms. Moreover, there needs to be provision for use of typewriters in the library. The Library needs to make provision for procuring the loan of documents and research reports as quickly as possible after the student discovers that he needs to examine them in connection with his studies. It is gratifying to learn that the Library has anticipated these special needs of graduate students and has already taken steps to meet them.

Administrative Framework

Competent teaching staff and enthusiastic students are the two principal ingredients that go to make up a good doctoral training program. Some administrative regulation may help to steady the program but, in general, administrative measures should be designed primarily to expedite graduate study rather than to police it. With this in mind it might be well for the Graduate Council to consider an initial policy under which it would not undertake to make any restrictive regulation until after a situation had arisen which clearly indicated its desirability. Until there was evidence to the contrary each department might be expected to conduct its program with appropriate standards in mind and with respect for the best academic traditions.

In general it is better to control the quality of the educational product rather than the accumulation of credits. This might mean that the emphasis would be placed on bringing competent judgments to bear upon the scholarship of individual students rather than laying down rules as to what and how many courses should be taken. Foreign language requirements, load limitations, majors and minors are all matters that may well be left to the judgment of those who must evaluate the individual doctoral candidate. It is helpful to keep in mind that if one wishes to appraise the caliber of a doctoral training program he usually finds it more profitable to sit for a time at the seminar table rather than go to the registrar's files. It is in the exchanges between students and students and between students and faculty that scholarly standards are reached and maintained.

Viewed from the standpoint of expenditure of staff time, doctoral training is extremely costly. Any staff member who does good work with doctoral students will spend many hours beyond the amount listed on his record of academic load. In part, this is because students and staff work together spontaneously on projects of genuine mutual interest. In part, it is because graduate teaching, especially in research and advanced seminars, is a labor of love. It cannot, therefore, be subjected to the same cost-accounting that one applies to other teaching.

In the long run the presence of a virile graduate program pays secondary dividends. It enables the university to attract and retain faculty members who are active on the frontier of their professions and, if there are not too many leveling influences on the campus, it tends to arouse scholarly interests among undergraduates.

Space

The present allocations of space are not well suited to the conduct of an advanced graduate program. Whilst space is becoming a more and more acute problem on campuses there are considerations which will enable a university to make better use of its limited resources. A major portion of a graduate psychology student's education takes place in a) informal discussions with fellow students and advisers, b) experience in research project rooms, and c) professional practicum activities. Advanced graduate students need to have a small informal discussion room which will be immediately accessible to them at all times, a place where they can go to discuss difficulties that arise in their research as well as one where they can spend evening hours in stimulating discussion of theoretical topics. It is also important that their own research work rooms be located nearby, preferably in the same building. The staff members who are their immediate advisers should also be close to this room so that they, too, can participate in the informal discussions. The practicum training facilities need not be so centrally located. The present Child Study Laboratory for example, while located at some distance from the probable center of advanced graduate student activities, offers no more than a minor inconvenience.

Curriculum

The further a student goes in his doctoral training the less his reliance on formal courses and credits. One of the real advantages of a small department is its ability to bring staff and students close together in the kind of intimate working relationship that produces advanced scholarship. It therefore seems inadvisable for the Department at Southern Illinois University to manufacture courses merely to have something to show on a student's transcript. It would be better to offer a continuing seminar with varying topics adjusted to the needs of the particular students enrolled. Students might be allowed to accumulate an unlimited number of credits in such a seminar and to enroll for any number of credits at a time.

Such a plan assumes that credits will not be used as either a measure of the breadth of a student's training or of its depth. Such measurement might better be based on other kinds of appraisal, such as comprehensive examinations and periodic Departmental staff ratings of overall progress. The seminar would be designed primarily for teaching rather than for record-keeping purposes.

As the comprehensive seminar series develops it may appear that certain topical content has to be repeated in a regular fashion. When this becomes clear it may become desirable to formulate such content into a standard course for advanced doctoral candidates. However, it should be kept in mind that such a course tends to deteriorate in pedagogical quality over the years. It may, therefore, be appropriate to approve it for only three to five years at a time.

Placement of Doctoral Graduates

Psychology is a rapidly expanding field, both in numbers and in the range of activities in which psychologists engage. At the end of World War II the membership of the American Psychological Association, a fairly good measure of the number of active psychologists in the country, stood at around 4000. During the current year it will probably pass the 15,000 mark. During the decade the balance has shifted from the campus to the field and from traditional psychology to applied psychology.

The major accredited universities are turning away from seventy to ninety percent of the students who want to pursue graduate training in such applied fields as clinical psychology. While this involves some duplicate applications and not all the candidates for admission are as well qualified as the universities would like, there is a real bottle-neck in training facilities for certain kinds of applied psychologists.

Generally speaking, it seems desirable for a new doctoral program not to see itself as merely taking the overflow of graduate students. Such a program condemns itself to an inferior rating among universities and its candidates to second class citizenship in the profession. It would be far better to look particularly to those areas of the emerging profession which are growing but for which the established departments have not yet geared their training programs. School psychology, not in the traditional mental testing and vocational guidance pattern but in the comprehensive modern sense, is such a field. The growth of school enrollments in the coming years should reinforce this development. There is also a movement toward the use of applied psychologists in the field of community life. Sometimes this is called community mental health programming; sometimes it takes on other forms and other emphases. But there is a field there, it is emerging, and it is ready to take on trained leadership. There is also the need for the increasing use of industrial psychologists who are broadly enough trained to serve the all-around needs of small industry. The large industries tend to use their psychologists in specialized ways. But small industries cannot afford such specialization and have therefore delayed their appointment of psychological services. Now there is an increasing opportunity and demand for comprehensively trained applied psychologists who can adapt themselves to the local industrial situation.

In general the program at Southern Illinois University should reflect the youth and progressiveness of the University itself. To the extent that youth and lack of commitments to tradition are stimulants to scholarship, the Department should take fresh and full advantage of them in planning its doctoral program.

The Department appears to be ready to shoulder the responsibilities of developing a sound doctoral training program. If it is kept from hamstringing regulations and subservience to academic traditions that have outlived their usefulness, it may be depended upon to develop a first-rate program in certain applied specialties of psychology. The University will need to place its confidence primarily in the confidence and mature judgments of the staff and not attempt to produce quality by legislation merely.

101

Training for Professional Function in Clinical Psychology: 2. Principles of Training in Clinical Psychology[1]

The occupational structure of twentieth-century society is undergoing some very marked developmental changes. Not only is it becoming immensely more complicated, but the concepts of responsibility of one occupation to the others are undergoing important changes. In no other group of occupations is this change as apparent as it is in the professions.

At the turn of the century the concept of a profession was an admixture of three traditional occupational roles: the role of priest who exercised authority that the layman had no right to question, the role of the scholar whose library was filled with large books and whose mind was filled with encyclopedic information, and the role of the skilled technician. In the case of the lawyer, for example, it was the technical skill of forensic dispute that was thus conjoined; in the case of the physician it was, among other things, the technical skill of the barber. Both of these professions had the advantage or disadvantage, depending upon how one looks at the values of a profession, of emerging as entities in our social structure at an early date. Both of these professions have had difficulty incorporating the points of view of the sciences (biological, social, political and psychological) upon which their continuing claims to authority must depend. It is not easy for any professional group to reconcile its claims to authoritative status with the modern scientific notion of the tentativeness of all professional knowledge. Yet it is precisely this embodiment of the humbling qualities of science that is required if a profession is to adapt itself to the changing scenes of this century.

As clinical psychology begins to take on the stature and responsibilities of a professional occupation in our societal structure it must give the most thoughtful attention to the role it is to play. It would indeed be tragic if clinical psychology were able to envision its role only as a counterpart of those professions which have grown to be large and powerful, but whose roots are embedded in the concepts of an earlier and less enlightened generation. It is not only that clinical psychology is now ready to emerge as a profession but, more important from the standpoint of society, it is that a new concept of a professional occupation is now ready to emerge and that clinical psychology may be one of the first professions to exemplify it.

Let us consider three principles which may well govern the training of clinical psychologists if we are to make full use of this moment in the history of social thought. The first is the principle of *training for professional adjustment to a world of emerging ideas* rather than to a world of fixed doctrines. This is somewhat analogous at the social level to the modern emphasis upon understanding the individual patient's mental health in terms of dynamic changes rather than in terms of pathological states. The clinical psychologist must be trained not merely to occupy a present status of professional adjustment through the acquisition of contemporary sophistication, but he must be made ready to relinquish some of the very concepts in which he is being trained, and to embrace new ideas as they may emerge.

The application of this principle implies an ordering of the relationship between psychological methodology and psychological content. It implies understanding that the so-called facts of psychology are the outcomes of the methodology which has been used to highlight them: that facts are prejudiced by the methodological constructs in terms of which they were first formulated. For example, the fact of a child's having the level of intelligence of a five-year-old is indeed the outcome of a psychologist's methodological prejudice. That prejudice started with the assumption that what it takes to get along in today's schools is a developmental property of the child's organism. One might contemplate how different the so-called facts of intelligence would have been today if we had based our mental testing methodology upon a different assumption, say, that it is society that expects different reactions from its children at different ages. Our tests would then probably be standardized in terms of different age roles in specified societies.

[1] First published in 1951 in *American Journal of Orthopsychiatry, 21*, 312–318. Reproduced by permission of the American Psychological Association.

Collected Papers of the Pioneer of Constructivist Psychology: George A. Kelly, First Edition. Edited by David A. Winter and Nick Reed.

The norms would be stated in terms of classrooms, teachers and communities and a child's intellectual attainments might be described in some such terms as the following: "Willie conforms to the expectancies of a ninth-grade Latin teacher in a New England private school. If everything goes well during the next two years he may be ready to make an optimal adjustment to the expectancies of the kindergarten at the Merrill-Palmer School." Of course, for the sake of brevity, we would reduce the yardsticks to generalized forms. Willie would be described as being currently adapted to Society Type NEPS Sub-Nine, for example.

All of this is suggested not as a serious undertaking for our profession at the present moment but to make clear that the content of psychology is the outcome of certain original assumptions and the methodology which grew out of them. This, the student, whose career is to span three or four decades of rapidly emerging ideas, must understand at the outset. If he does not, his investment in professional training will be rapidly depreciated and perhaps ultimately reduced to complete obsolescence.

The principle of training for professional adjustment to a world of emerging ideas rather than to a world of fixed doctrines implies a continuing emphasis upon ways of changing our versions of truth. There is a methodology for changing methodologies. A study of the philosophy of science should give the student a new perspective toward his own research, toward his reading of research reports and even toward his own clinical observations. But more than this he needs the personal experience of changing his ideas as a direct result of experimentation. This may be as painful to the psychologist as it is to the neurotic patient who undergoes a similar process in therapy. To stake one's beliefs on the outcome of a series of experiments requires courage. It is this courage which is the essence of the so-called rare talent for research rather than the commonly supposed superintellectual powers of abstraction. Almost any student will take up research spontaneously once he musters up the courage to transfer his ego investment from a given anticipated outcome to the anticipation of outcomes in general and of whatever nature they may be. Thus one of the most essential aspects of any training program for clinical psychologists is removal of their fear of changing the facades of truth. This reassurance cannot be accomplished secondhand. The university teacher who persuades his classroom student to accept a new version of truth has not necessarily given that student the courage to look for new ideas; he has only supported him in facing predigested ideas. Training students in the ways of change is much more than this. It can mean nothing less for the student than the firsthand experience of standing alone and seeing the visage of truth gradually take shape out of the clouds and storms of his own experience.

Modern training in clinical psychology has another use for the point of view of science. The clinical study of the individual patient is best pursued with that same flexibility of thought which properly characterizes the scientist's pursuit of conclusions and generalizations. The modern clinician is careful to interpret his clinical observations in terms of constructs rather than in terms of entities. His test results and interview observations are no longer considered to be fixed findings pointing to the presence or absence of whole disease entities, but rather as grounds for formulating clinical hypotheses which, taken together, permit one to construe, in a reasonably systematic way, as much of the patient's behavior as possible and to plan a logically meaningful program for his rehabilitation. A clinician trained in this way will not need to feel that his whole training has been wasted the day the American Psychiatric Association publishes its newest nosological system.

In addition to implying new emphasis upon psychological methodology rather than upon content, new emphasis upon ways of changing our versions of truth, and new emphasis upon interpreting clinical experience in terms of constructs rather than in terms of entities, the principle of training for professional adjustment to a world of emerging ideas rather than to a world of fixed doctrines also implies that the student shall learn how to formulate and develop meaningful hypotheses. Here we refer both to clinical hypotheses regarding the individual patient and experimental hypotheses. The two types of hypotheses have much more in common than most people have been led to believe. Both types of hypotheses must be stated in critical form if they are to be of any practical use; that is, both must be stated in such a: way that they tend either to stand or fall with the data. For example, to hypothesize that a patient's problem is characterized by strong tendencies toward aggression, and then to claim that the hypothesis is substantiated (a) if the patient has lived like a mouse or (b) if the patient has not lived like a mouse is pointless. It may make the clinician feel good to have his hypothesis stand regardless of what the facts are, but such reasoning contributes no more to the development of a differential treatment for the individual patient than it does to the development of a precise science.

The student of clinical psychology must be taught where to seek hypotheses as well as how to state them. All of us are familiar with the kind of graduate student whose conception of research is to test merely the factual nature of certain miscellaneous statements he has encountered in his reading. He has not learned to take into account the range of generality of the statements, their place in theoretical structure, or their plausibility in terms of practical clinical experience. There are, of course, some hypotheses in experimental psychology which are derived almost directly from personality theory. For the most part, however, our most useful hypotheses in clinical psychology are formulated out of the impact of firsthand clinical experience upon explicitly stated theory. Thus the research worker will always suffer a remoteness from reality if he is not also a clinician, and the clinician who is aware of his theoretical biases will be in the best position to propose experimental hypotheses. Any attempt to draw a sharp line between the training of clinicians and the training of research psychologists will be disadvantageous for both and will only prolong the nineteenth-century myth that scientific inquiry is not a functional part of a professional man's role. So much for the principle of training clinical psychologists to live in a world that won't stand still.

The second principle I should like to discuss is that of *training for cooperative effort*. The notion of cooperative effort has taken hold in scientific and professional circles. It is doubtful if we will ever go back to the prewar emphasis upon egocentric effort. The student of clinical psychology needs to be trained to participate in this new type of working relationship.

Now interdisciplinary cooperation is a complicated business. It is not achieved simply by calling a luncheon meeting of heads of three different departments or designing a research project in a two-day meeting of a panel of consultants in a Washington conference room. Nor is it obtained in the mental hygiene team, as some would have us believe, by a general admixture of the syllabi of courses in psychology, psychiatry and social work. Such homogenized training may make for smooth-running staff conferences in which each member of the mental hygiene team accepts the prejudices of his colleagues because they are the same as his own, but it does not necessarily exploit the unique resources of the different professions comprising the team.

Basically, cooperative effort requires that problems, both research problems and clinical problems, be approached from varied and distinct viewpoints. But more than this, cooperative effort requires that each member of the cooperating professions be particularly prepared for his cooperative role in three ways: First he must be prepared to use both intramural and extramural languages in communicating his professional observations. For the psychologist this means the development of precise uses of psychological terminology. For example, if he uses such a term as "transference" he should be clear as to which of the several current meanings of that term he wishes to convey; whether the generalized meaning as that term is used by psychoanalysts to describe the etiological process that takes place in psychasthenia, a particular relation between patient and therapist, the process of "transfer" in learning, or the process of "transformation" in statistical computation. The graduate of one university's training program in clinical psychology must be prepared to communicate in precise psychological language with graduates of other training programs. That is intramural communication.

In most clinics and hospitals where the mental hygiene team approach is used there is a tendency to hold two types of weekly staff conferences: one, an intramural staff conference where, say, the psychologists discuss their cases in the more specialized language of their discipline; and the other, an interdisciplinary staff conference, where a more generalized extramural language must be used. It is in this latter type of staff conference that the young clinical psychologist frequently finds difficulty in playing his role.

If the psychiatric members of the mental hygiene team are psychoanalytically indoctrinated the psychologist may have difficulty communicating his clinical observations without feeling that his own participation is circumscribed by the same doctrines. Students should be trained not to be disturbed by this problem of interdisciplinary communication. They should be taught to translate from their intramural psychological language to an extramural mental hygiene language with a minimum loss of precision.

This brings us to the second way in which the student of clinical psychology may be taught to perform a cooperative role. Students sometimes become confused as to the distinction between intellectual honesty and cooperative flexibility. A psychological intern will say, "I can't honestly follow this procedure as advised by the mental hygiene team because I don't believe in the Rogerian growth principle." At this point it may be necessary for the student to be reminded of the tentativeness of all theoretical formulations, including his own. With this awareness he may be able to perform the practical role assigned to him by the mental health team even though he may entertain some doubt of its ultimate validity. This flexibility in viewpoint as regards practical matters does not, of course, absolve any professional man from responsibility for the outcomes of measures which have been thoughtlessly prescribed.

Perhaps all of what we have tried to say regarding the preparation of clinical psychologists for the performance of cooperative roles could be subsumed under the phrase, "learning to think in other people's terms." If this is true then basic training in psychotherapeutic skill should teach us to operate within the conceptual systems of our fellow professions as well as within the private conceptual systems of our patients.

There is a third principle which should be considered in a modern training program for clinical psychologists. As far as I know it is not explicitly embodied in any of the current training programs in clinical psychology. It is the principle of *training for administrative competence*.

As clinical psychology assumes the social responsibilities and stature of a profession there will be more and more occasions on which psychologists will be asked to apply their skills and experience in administrative roles. For some psychologists this may involve such a sudden reversal of perspective that they may find themselves in a state of confusion or be forced to regress to adolescent patterns of leadership.

If we agree that the first responsibility of an administrator is to organize and implement the strivings of a group we should train students to perform this type of service. They should have experience in helping individuals adjust to established institutional controls by helping them find real personal freedom of psychological movement within that system of institutional controls.

By and large psychologists, and especially clinical psychologists, have not been noted for their skill in this latter respect. But whatever rebel note we may voice while we are students, and whatever novel system we may institute in our first administrative post, sooner or later, the task of the administrator will involve persuading people that "the system is not so bad, that they really are not slaves to it, and that they can find freedom in it if they only look."

Training for administrative competence requires the acquisition of personal skill in handling threat, both the threat of authority as the student experiences it in himself and the threat which he represents to others when he must play a leadership role. Perhaps the best way to carry out this requirement is through group psychotherapy with graduate students and with a professor as leader. There is no doubt but that we clinical psychologists tend to be uncomfortable in our relations with authority figures. Our traditional attitude of skepticism toward all untested doctrines probably aggravates the situation. There is no doubt but that the psychologist's background in this respect is different from that of his fellows on the mental hygiene team. The personal history experiences which lead the psychologist to choose and continue in the field of psychology, to take up research and to thumb his nose at the high elimination rate of the Ph.D. curriculum certainly imply different attitudes toward authority and prestige than those which lead another student to get himself into medical school and later branch out into psychiatry, or those which lead a third student to find himself in the recognition of the human misery with which casework must deal and to develop the tender skills of psychiatric social work. Modern training will have to do something about the psychologist's traditional perversity and teach him how to handle threat.

One other set of attitudes must be especially nourished, if the clinical psychologist is to be a successful administrator. These are the attitudes which enable one to be impersonal without being inconsiderate in discharging his administrative responsibilities. This problem in various forms is continually brought up by graduate students for discussion. Sometimes it is mentioned in connection with a student's relation with a patient, as in the remarks, "I feel I may be getting too involved in my patient's problem." Again it appears in such a remark as the following: "I discussed my criticisms of my friend's paper with him privately rather than in the seminar," or "Now that I've become more sensitive to people's feelings I find that I can phrase my criticism of their ideas in such a way as not to make them 'go rigid.'"

Whatever the training techniques may be which will ultimately prove effective, modern training for clinical psychologists must include fundamental preparation for administrative roles. If we can incorporate this kind of preparation together with a kind of dynamic ongoing conception of clinical psychology theory and put it to work in a cooperative enterprise, the youngsters who are getting their Ph.D.'s nowadays should really make clinical psychology progress between now and the time they are ready to retire!

102

Requirements of Training and Competence for Psychological Participation in Rehabilitation[1]

The training of a modern clinical psychologist is both long and costly. He must have a university degree before he can even be considered for admission to the graduate curriculum. When he applies for admission he finds that his record must be outstanding if he is to be given any consideration at all. While all of the professional branches of psychology are short of training facilities these days—industrial psychology, personnel psychology, human engineering, counselling and guidance, experimental psychology, and clinical psychology—since the war it has been clinical psychology that has had the lowest selection ratio. That ratio at our university, for example, has, in some years, dropped as low as two percent of the academically qualified applicants.

Once admitted, the student finds that it is not the completion of courses or the serving out of residency requirements that takes the measure of his competence. Theoretically, under the postwar curriculum, he can complete the requirements for the Ph.D. in clinical psychology in as little as four years. Rather it is his capacity to adjust his thinking to the rigorous methodology of research where the variables are not the kind of things he can hold in his hands or see in a test tube but are things which must always be precisely defined in terms of operations and behaviors and their mathematical probabilities.

But not only must the clinical psychologist train himself in the scholarly disciplines which have so recently brought psychology to a new point of usefulness in our free society; he must also prepare himself in the arts and skills of the professional person. Clinical psychology, in contrast with the other branches of psychology, not infrequently involves a close working collaboration with medicine and those other professions which are closely allied with it in the pursuit of the healing arts. For this reason the modern clinical psychologist is trained both as a scientist and as a practitioner. That is a double order which makes heavy demands, not only on the student's time but upon his flexibility of thinking and upon his all-around competence. It is not surprising, then, that even amongst the small select minority who are admitted to training, only two out of three are successful—and it is a rare student who gets his Ph.D. degree in the space of four years of graduate study. Even then he is not through. Nowadays even the successful doctoral candidate in the specialties of clinical psychology, industrial psychology, or counselling and guidance faces a minimum of another five years of qualifying experience before he can be admitted to the American Board Examinations, a sequence of written and oral examinations spread over a several months' period.

Psychology is a new profession. Being new, its members must be especially sensitive to human problems and broad in social outlook. Students in the clinical branch of psychology must always be on the lookout for new facets in this problem of human behavior. The student who takes the technical aspects of his training so seriously that he misses the broad sweep of new ideas will not render great service to his fellow man.

There are new freedoms in the air. There are freedoms from man's incapacitating anxieties and destructive hostilities. Psychology promises to implement these freedoms. Yet the implementation of these freedoms of the future is a service to humanity which simply cannot be envisioned by the narrowly trained student whose outlook is staked to the scoring of some test or to the exposition of some psychotherapeutic dogma that has begun to outlive its usefulness.

Let me illustrate. In recent years clinical psychology has made much use of a general type of approach to the patient which is known as the projective tests. No doubt you are familiar with some of them—the Rorschach, the Thematic Apperception Test, the Incomplete Sentences Test, etc. The essential feature of the projective test is that it puts the patient on grounds where social convention provides him with no ready-made answers and he is free to read into the test any of his own personal biases. Sometimes these biases appear to be reflected more or less in all of the patient's living.

Following the war many technically minded students were deeply impressed with the practical usefulness of the projective approach to the understanding of a patient's personality structure. It seems to me that hardly a week went by but that some student came in to announce

[1] Address at the Milwaukee Conference on Rehabilitation, July 8, 1952. Published by permission of Jacqueline Aldridge.

Collected Papers of the Pioneer of Constructivist Psychology: George A. Kelly, First Edition. Edited by David A. Winter and Nick Reed.

breathlessly that he had just discovered a new projective technique. Gradually, however, all of our advanced students came to appreciate a basic psychological principle—the principle that people express their underlying personality structure more or less in everything they think and do, in the stories they see unfolding in the background of a picture, the turbulence they see in the looming shadows of a cloud, the embellishments of their handwriting, the noises that they make at a baseball game or at a political convention, the way they walk, or even in the way they look at their finger nails. To be sure, it is difficult to draw broadly generalized conclusions from observing some of these behaviors but nevertheless each does in a measure reflect the uniqueness of an individual's personality.

Take, for example, the movie which preceded this panel discussion. Everything that the patient did was an expression of his outlook in life; the way he sat, the way he spoke or refused to speak, the way he played basketball, the way he struck out against the encroaching world. Moreover, as the patient's outlook began to change, that change was reflected in his activities quite as much, and perhaps even more, than in his words. Rather than expressing his personality in the words of a textbook, he acted out his personality and its changes. Most of what he had to express could not be put into ordinary words. The feelings which were welling up within him probably had roots which reached far back beyond the time of his life when he could talk with words. Yet he did express himself in the private language of activity. And at this hospital he was able to find people who were willing to try to communicate with him in that private language.

Now if the graduate students in clinical psychology whom I help to train were to see this movie, I would hope they would respond to it in various ways. I would hope there might be some who would say, "Ah hah, take that bit of behavior there. I have an idea! Why not set up that particular situation as a new kind of projective test. We could standardize it." That would be a first year graduate student talking. Another might say, "I see the ingredients of a learning situation there—See! There are the secondary reinforcements, notice the extinctions, and throughout it all note the partial reinforcements. And now I see how this activity business might be placed on a more general procedural basis." Or another graduate student might say, "Now look, that is all noted but if we approached this problem from the standpoint of perceptual theory rather than stimulus-response theory, it should give us some new angles. We then could say that this patient was actually trying out his interpretations of the world throughout the story. He was really putting his biases to test. Now there may be one of the keys to the rehabilitation process, to get the patient to lay his ideas on the line by acting them out, by testing them in a genuinely social situation." Now both of these students might be, say, second year students.

The third year student might approach the problem differently. While the first year student approached the problem as a technician, and the second year students might have approached the problem from varying and flexible systematic points of view, the third year student might be said to approach the problem from a professional point of view. He might say, "Yes, I see several angles to this. What I want to do is get close to this thing and get a good look at some of the features of this activity business which were not portrayed in the film." The fourth year student, in the final stage of his research training, might react in a still more advanced way. He might say, "Sure, I agree with the first student's observation. That patient's activity did express what his outlook was and I agree that there are some fertile systematic approaches to the exploration of what went on. Moreover, I have seen first hand this kind of rehabilitation taking place in different ways with different patients. But what we need now is to get this business pinned down so we know just what it is that works in these cases and why it works. Then we can hope to put together some new methods which will work better." As soon as the fourth year student is able to demonstrate unmistakably that he can follow up his remark, we like to award him a Ph.D. degree in clinical psychology and recommend that he make himself as useful as possible at this enlightened level of service.

Perhaps this series of illustrative remarks from graduate students at different levels of outlook and training will serve to indicate what I believe to be the essential requirements for training and competence for psychological participation in rehabilitation. As some of you have no doubt detected, most of what I have said might have been said about the training of psychologists for participation in any kind of a program. There is, however, something psychologically special about physical rehabilitation. The film illustrated it. Not only did the patient in the film act out his version of himself in a stifling world and not only did he portray his new outlook when he found people who were willing to try to communicate with him in his own pre-verbal language, but he actually learned his lessons in the terms of a language that had no abstract words. To be sure, people spoke to him but the words they used were not such terms as "security," "acceptance," "insight," etc. They talked to him. They responded to him with sounds. Yet to him the words were things only, not really ideas. They were not themselves the liberating ideas—not even the symbols of them. Rather the words spoken to him were the raw material out of which the new ideas began to take shape. His therapists were communicating the ideas in a language which had no words for what he needed to know. Thus the mental rehabilitation of this patient involved more than an acting out on his part, or a willingness to listen to the therapists; it involved the therapists themselves acting out what the patient needed to be told. There may be other patient relationships as well as those occurring in physical and mental rehabilitation where such a skill is useful, yet I think that the psychologist who is to collaborate with the rehabilitation worker needs especially to be aware of the value of this particular approach.

In summary, it seems to me that the film we have seen points up the needs for the training of clinical psychologists at various levels from the early technological level, through the theoretical level then the professional level, and finally the research level or the "let's know what we're doing" level. Moreover physical and mental rehabilitation of the type portrayed points up the need for psychologists to understand the "communication without words" approach to therapy.

103

Knowledge: Discovery or Invention?[1]

Man has a tendency to be mystified by his knowledge, even when it is his own. He is likely to think of it, not so much as a product of his own venturesome efforts, but as something that happens to him, like the wind and the rain. Often he sees the swirling events as imbued with their own unique knowledgeability, their own rationale. He seeks to discover this knowledge that they are so reluctant to disclose, or, failing this, he seeks to find a god, a priest or a doctor who will let him in on the secret. It is terribly hard for most of us to be convinced that knowledge is something that we can and often do create for ourselves.

Take an example. For centuries men wished that they could ride on magic carpets. Some men asked their gods to give them magic carpets, and were more than a little annoyed to find their requests ignored. Others, a little more venturesome, packed their suitcases or saddled up their horses and went out looking for a place where magic carpets were in the retail market. It rarely occurred to ancient man that if he really wanted a magic carpet to ride on, it was up to him to figure out how to make one. Thus for centuries man has looked upon his quest for knowledge as a persistent solicitation for a gift or as a tedious search for something that was hidden—a golden fleece, perhaps, or a holy grail, or a lost Europa. The notion that knowledge is something more to be invented than discovered has itself been one of his only more recent inventions.

What people believe about the basic nature of things has a lot to do with the kind of society they create for themselves. If knowledge is something that lurks in mysterious places it is presumed to be available only to those who go poking around in dark comers and making mysterious noises. Such people came to be regarded as a special class. They are priests, or Levites, or medicine men or, in the modern scene, simply members of a profession. The validity of the priest's dicta inhered in his presumed superior ability to hold conversations with the gods. The validity of the more recent professional man has rested upon two somewhat similar assumptions: his superior training as evidenced by his diplomas, his certificates and his licenses; and his superior motivation as evidenced by the organized groups to whose sanctions he subjects himself.

And now we are up to the end of the nineteenth century. The twentieth century finds men still restive about this matter of knowledge. Science has started to examine itself. It is beginning to see itself not so much as a body of true facts, jealously inventoried under such headings as biology, physics, medicine, as it is a methodology—a way of creating knowledge. The idea that one profession and no other has a right to a portion of their fellow-man is beginning to seem obsolete. It is quite out of tune with the basic tenets of science itself. And it is not surprising that those disciplines, such as psychology, whose emphasis has been upon the development of the methodology of science rather than the filing of its facts, are beginning to challenge nineteenth-century professionalism and its preemptive attitudes toward facts and knowledge. Men are growing increasingly skeptical of the special claims that others place upon the world's wisdom.

At this mid-point in the twentieth century the emergence of psychology as a profession seems to be based upon different grounds from that upon which any previous profession has established itself. It has sought to rest its authority upon its scientific method of developing knowledge, rather than upon its special privileges or even a given body of prior knowledge.

(At this point this unfinished article concludes with the following headings:)

The scientific clinician.
New notions, both of practice and of science itself.
The hypothesis in clinical practice.
The hypothesis in psychotherapy: for the clinician, for the patient.
The place of the null hypothesis in therapy.
The C-P-C Cycle.
Concept-formation in clinical practice.
Every man his own scientist.

[1] Fragment of Kelly's writing, marked Louisville VA Hospital, circa 1954. Published by permission of Jacqueline Aldridge.

Collected Papers of the Pioneer of Constructivist Psychology: George A. Kelly, First Edition. Edited by David A. Winter and Nick Reed.

104

Next Steps for the Profession of Psychology[1]

Several years ago the Ohio Psychological Association began to take a series of steps to strengthen its position as the state-wide representative organization of psychology in Ohio. It developed reciprocal relations with the Psychology Section of the Ohio Academy of Science. It maintained that reciprocal relation until the Psychology Section was dissolved. At the same time it developed a similar affiliate relationship with the School Psychologists of Ohio. Its relations to the state employed psychologists of Ohio were not formalized but steps were taken to tie the two groups closer together.

All of these moves were designed to enable the Ohio Psychological Association to be in a position to represent all of the psychologists in the state and to represent them not only as scientists but in their professional capacities as well. It was hoped that thus the Association would become an important functioning part of the professional and social structure of our state and that it would be able to make psychology a useful and self-disciplined profession in whom our fellow-citizens might come to have increased confidence.

At the same time the Association put on a membership drive which brought on to its rolls the names of a considerable proportion of the active psychologists of the state. This membership drive was never carried through as far as it might have been but it did move forcefully in the right direction.

The Ohio Psychological Association at this time also redesigned its by-laws. It made the meeting of professional as well as scientific standards a rigid requirement for membership and for continuation in good standing. The Association developed a code of ethics even before the American Psychological Association published theirs. It incorporated itself under the laws of Ohio. It set up a Board of Examiners under a far-sighted and progressive plan which has become known in other states as the "Ohio Plan." Under this plan we set up our own certification Board certifying at two professional levels and we gradually developed the confidence of our membership in the standards upon which the Board based its appraisals. That Board has done an excellent job and its activities might well be given much wider publication.

But while psychology in Ohio made some fine steps forward a few years ago there are mounting signs of its having lost ground on certain important local fronts. In the State Civil Service the position of psychology with respect to pay raises has been weaker than that of any comparable profession. Psychology has also lost certain important positions in the state, including the directorship of the Bureau of Juvenile Research. There have also been losses in connection with the projected professional training program of the Columbus Receiving Hospital and with respect to personnel policy in the State Division of Mental Hygiene. At the Midwestern Governor's Conference on Mental Hygiene last year Ohio's delegation was conspicuous for its omission of psychology both in its membership and in its contribution to the Conference. We are also developing some problems in relation to school psychology in Ohio, problems which ought to be straightened out before they cause friction.

But while Ohio has been losing ground since its professional efforts of several years ago, professional psychology on the national scene has been moving forward. In the South, psychologists have been an accepted and active group in the development of the cooperative mental hygiene program developed by the governors of the states. The relations of the American Psychological Association with the American Psychiatric Association have notably improved in the past year and the way is now clear, as far as the American Psychiatric Association is concerned, for the kind of legislation that psychologists believe to be essential for the protection of the public and for the proper protection of their profession. The Veterans Administration has recently opened the door to the utilization of all kinds of psychology—not clinical merely—in the mental hygiene effort of their hospitals and clinics. Everywhere on the national scene we may see signs of psychology's professional progress. Yet Ohio's recent developments do not permit us to share wholly in the national optimism.

[1] Summary of an address presented to the Ohio Psychological Association, Columbus, Ohio, November 19, 1955. Published by permission of Jacqueline Aldridge.

Collected Papers of the Pioneer of Constructivist Psychology: George A. Kelly, First Edition. Edited by David A. Winter and Nick Reed.

If the profession of psychology in Ohio is to avoid the obviously growing contempt of our local sister professions and begin to keep pace with the development of psychology on the national scene, it must give serious consideration to some strong positive steps to strengthen its position in the state. Last spring a committee on legislation was appointed with Dr. Frank Fletcher as Chairman but it has become increasingly clear that for Dr. Fletcher's committee to move aggressively into a legislative program at this time would probably do nothing but arouse the animosity of those who believe that such a program is not in the public interest and, indeed, might provide a welcome opportunity to those who hold psychology in contempt. Dr. Fletcher's committee simply does not have the kind of backing from our own organization that he would need to carry on a successful campaign. Moreover, legislation, while desirable, is not our biggest professional need in Ohio. It even has its hazards. After all, psychologists in Ohio might even find themselves in the same position that psychologists find themselves in the city of Miami, Florida where they are licensed; but by the same licensing board that licenses the fortune tellers. Legislation is by no means a sure way to gain professional status or to guarantee that the public will not be hoodwinked. Indeed, the public in the State of Ohio is probably being hoodwinked in its mental hygiene hopes by the very professions that have the most secure legal status.

In my opinion there are nine specific steps that ought to be taken by the Ohio Psychological Association in order to strengthen its position as a representative of psychology in the community. I have not discussed these nine steps with the officers of the Ohio Psychological Association and what I propose is strictly my own idea. There is nothing official about these proposals. The Board of Directors will be as much surprised to hear them as anyone of you may be.

1 *A central office for the Ohio Psychological Association with a paid executive secretary.*
The job of maintaining public relations is far too important and far too complicated to be done satisfactorily by volunteer workers. We need a central office with communication facilities and we need a paid executive secretary employed for a large enough fraction of his time to guarantee that he will be on the job at least part of every day,

2 *An advisory board on the employment of psychologists.*
There are a good many potential employers of psychologists in the state, and yet we have, as an organization, no central clearing house for helping employers, such as school superintendents and representatives of industry, to find the people they want. Or, indeed, even to help them set up standards on which to judge applicants for employment. An advisory board should undertake an active program in calling the attention of employers to the qualifications of psychologists. It should distribute a list of certified psychologists in Ohio, the list of diplomates in psychology in Ohio, and the places where young graduate psychologists may be found. It also should take a continuing and active interest in civil service standards for psychologists. It should never expect the state employed psychologists to take the principal initiative in this matter. Standards and salary scales are a concern to all psychologists in the state even though we may not ourselves be employed by the civil service. These standards have a great deal to do indirectly with the esteem in which our own positions are held.

3 *An advisory board on psychological research.*
The Ohio Psychological Association should set up an advisory board to make the research of psychologists available to the consumers of research data in the most useful possible form. This applies not only to research done within the State of Ohio but also to research reported in the psychological literature of the national journals. This should be a real service to the local consumers of psychology from housewives to industrialists. It should make the state organization a respected and influential body.

4 *Advisory board on psychology in schools.*
Since the Thayer Conference in 1954 we have a blueprint of the development of psychological services in the schools in the country. The Thayer Conference was financed by the National Institute of Mental Health and conducted by the Selection and Training Board of the American Psychological Association. In that conference representatives of school administration, teaching, social work, psychiatry, psychology and other groups interested in education came together to discuss how psychology might best serve the interests of the schools. Ohio should take advantage of the outcome of this conference and make sure that the ideals and services envisioned by the Thayer conference become widely known among school people. This board should also take steps to support the activities of the school psychologists of Ohio and do everything possible to strengthen their program.

5 *A public information service, including a speakers bureau.*
The Ohio Psychological Association should provide a public information service describing the activities of psychologists and the nature of the contribution of psychology to our public life. It should also maintain a speakers bureau which would make available to the colleges of the state, as well as to other interested groups such as local mental hygiene societies, speakers who could speak with authority on the contributions of psychology. In the mental hygiene movement altogether too little is known about what psychologists are contributing. Indeed some people are surprised to find that psychologists have contributed anything at all.

6 *Membership.*
There appear to be about five hundred psychologists in Ohio of whom only about 60% belong to our association. The representation in our Association should be nearer 90% and we should look forward to an expansion in the next few years perhaps

reaching a thousand or more. Only if the Ohio Psychological Association fully represents professional psychology in Ohio can it expect to be an influential force on behalf of psychology or can we as individual psychologists expect to participate effectively in the social growth of the commonwealth.

7 *Legislation.*
The Ohio Psychological Association should move forward with a legislative program along the lines which have now been cleared by the Committee on Relations with Psychiatry of the American Psychological Association.

8 *Dues consistent with professional aspirations.*
Several years ago I had occasion to tell a business meeting of the Ohio Psychological Association that our dues should be raised from one dollar to something in the neighborhood of thirty dollars if we were to become a truly professional organization. Shortly thereafter the dues were raised to two dollars. It now is abundantly clear that no two-dollar-a-year outfit is ever going to hold its own as the arm of a profession. It will not get either state legislation in favor of certification or decent recognition for psychologists now in the state employ. A minimum of twenty-five dollars a year for members of the Association will be required if we are to gain and maintain the respect of those whose respect is essential for our profession's well-being. Moreover, these dues should be tied into certification in such a way that certificates will be revoked if the person does not maintain himself as a member in good standing of the Ohio Psychological Association.

9 *A broadened basis of leadership for the Ohio Psychological Association.*
The center of emphasis of psychology in Ohio is shifting from college teachers to those in professional practice. This shift should be recognized at this time and the base of leadership of the Association should be made as broad as possible with more and more reliance being placed in those younger psychologists who are pioneering in the field of human service outside the academic walk.

The Ohio Psychological Association is in a crucial period but it is not the welfare of the organization, as an organization, that is primarily at stake. Rather, it is the welfare of psychology itself that is at stake. Every psychologist in Ohio is involved in the professional scene whether he realizes it or not. The Association is merely the agency through which we all can hope to achieve some of the objectives toward which we are striving. What I have to say is directed really at all Ohio Psychologists regardless of whether or not they are members of this Association. The nine points I have listed seem to me to be the next steps we must take if we are to move forward.

105

I Itch Too[1]

Man, the ingenious creature, has invented many ways of torturing himself. Perhaps the most clever technique is to raise an itchy rash of doubts all over himself. Just let any of us start to doubt what he earnestly believes, or to question the true value of what he is doing, or to lie awake wondering what sort of a person he really is, and the urge to scratch becomes almost unbearable. During such restless hours many of us have asked, as one of the articulate writers of the two preceding communications has asked, if a soothing ointment of ignorance might not bring on some kind of relief. Or, if ignorance cannot be made to cover all the elusive spots, perhaps a sharp restriction in our diet of knowledge will give us immunity against the recurring attacks.

We psychologists are particularly susceptible to this allergy of modem man. That may be because we have not localized our itches yet. Among our group the clinician in us is continually doubting the humane value of the scientist in us. And the scientist in us is forever nagging about the moral validity of our sympathetic efforts on behalf of patients. This makes the whole profession downright miserable in spots, both as a self-doubting collection of individuals and, as the second writer points out, as a colleague-doubting confederation of specialists.

So one writer urges that we avoid intrapsychic conflict by letting clinicians be clinicians and experimentalists be experimentalists. That way the clinicians would supposedly scratch only clinical itches and experimentalists would scratch whatever it is that makes them itch. And the other writer makes it clear enough that this would by no means relieve the irritation. As long as they are within earshot of each other the clinicians will scream at the experimentalists for being irrelevant and the experimentalists will rail against the clinicians for being immaterial. So it is that we psychologists make ourselves miserable, either by doubting ourselves or by doubting each other.

What would happen, ideally, if the clinician ego could effectively ignore the scientist superego, and the scientist superego could remain oblivious to pressing clinical realities? Would ego and superego then live happily side by side and in full spiritual communion with reality? Would all the itchy doubts disappear? Or would there not be a lingering tickle of curiosity, half pain half enticement, that both one's clinician-self and one's scientist-self would impulsively reach up to scratch?

It is interesting to speculate on whether "the fifty top-notch clinicians," mercifully kept in ignorance of scientific method, would be grateful to their mentors after discovering that they had only one hand with which to scratch their curiosities. Or "the fifty excellent experimentalists," with minds uncluttered by clinical insights—what will they think of an education that leaves them with no fingers to scratch another man's itch in those wee inaccessible places he cannot reach on his own? Which is better for scratching; which is worse: the bimanual incoordination of a whole man or the one-handed dexterity of an amputee?

The writer who identifies himself as a student has a legitimate complaint. Now if there were only some place he could take it! On Mondays, Wednesdays, and Fridays he is expected to be an experimentalist, albeit one who knows only how to manipulate the things that experimentalists have grown so fond of. On Tuesdays, Thursdays, and Saturdays he is supposed to float along in his patient's unconscious. Two alternating careers; two systems of values! Each morning he wakes up in a rash about the value of what he did the day before; each night he goes to bed to try to get his mind off the lessons the day's experience has taught. Can he balance the seesaw? The future of our kind of profession hinges on the outcome.

Certainly there is no nice man with the rank of full professor who can solve the student's problem for him. The present generation of professors have itching curiosities themselves, but still too few of them have more than one hand to scratch with. The student's predicament is not merely the result of his being a student; it is the predicament of the profession as a whole. Psychologists have yet to learn how to test in the laboratory the induced hypotheses of the therapy room. And our discipline has yet to build a theoretical framework that will deductively support both clinical insight and experimental inquiry. Both of these accomplishments will undoubtedly come to pass, and the self-doubting, rather than the colleague-doubting, students who are being trained today are the ones who will eventually do the job. Meanwhile, I itch too!

[1] First published in 1955 in *The American Psychologist*, *10*, 172–173. Now in the public domain and published by permission of Jacqueline Aldridge.

Collected Papers of the Pioneer of Constructivist Psychology: George A. Kelly, First Edition. Edited by David A. Winter and Nick Reed.

106

Interdisciplinary Collaboration[1]

This address will be an attempt to build a conceptual bridge between two remote incidents and to see if such a bridge can be used to walk dry-footed across some of the turbulent waters that threaten to engulf psychology and some of its sister professions.

In the upper left hand drawer of my desk is a bulging folder of materials and correspondence relating to the work of the Committee on Relations with Psychiatry. Two years ago, when I set up the file in a moment of skeptic whimsy, I labeled the folder "APA *versus* APA" (American Psychological Association *versus* American Psychiatric Association). Every time I open the drawer my attention is drawn to this lurking paradox and I have a nagging feeling of discomfort. Several times I have been on the point of changing the label in order to remove the discomfort—changing it, perhaps, to something like "The Medicine Man's Burden" or "Pax Vobiscum, Psychiatreia." But the label has remained unchanged, either because of some intransigent devotion to realism or a legalistic reluctance to mix Latin with Greek.

In any case that is one of the two incidents. Now for the other. On the night of November tenth (or shortly thereafter—the records are not altogether clear) in the Year 1619, René Descartes had three dreams. In the first dream he was a cripple seeking shelter in a church; in the second he heard thunder and saw fire; and in the third he was reading the words, "What way of life shall I follow." What is, perhaps, more important than his dream thoughts is the notion which he claimed preceded them. That notion was that the methods of analytic geometry might be broadly applied to other disciplines. Hardly enough to scare one into church, we would suppose, but then Descartes was a very well educated man whose intellectual ventures penetrated far deeper than the superficial mimicry that ordinarily passes for cognition—and, besides, the year was 1619.

Here are my two incidents. Now the conceptual bridge. While analytic geometry is perceived by most of us as a graphic way of representing algebraic equations, it is, more properly, perceived as an algebraic way of solving geometric problems. A crucial step in the method is the erection of reference axes against which to reflect the variation of the unknowns. In deference to Descartes the orthogonal axes most commonly used in analytic geometry are called "Cartesian Coordinates." Once these axes are assumed all the possible geometric lines in space can, presumably, be consistently represented. But without such axes, or with the axes rotated, the geometric facts of life take on quite different algebraic meanings.

Descartes' hunch about analytic geometry, which he chose to punctuate with three dreams—a dash, an explanation point, a quote, and a final question mark—can be applied to much of what psychologists do today. While we may not draw lines on paper, as we used to do in high school and college, we do erect convenient psychological reference axes as a first step toward the solution of human problems by algebraic or other precisely logical procedures. This is what we do when we take up a problem of social relations, or a problem of learning, or a problem of mental health. First the axes. Without them we cannot even visualize the problem. With them we think we know what we are dealing with.

But the axes we erect need not remain forever fixed. They are not the reality that intrudes itself upon us—only the framework within which we represent that reality to ourselves. If they cast our psychological problems in forms which are too complex for us to manage, we can always rotate them—or even consider an entirely different system of coordinates. In the statistical laboratory it is an everyday practice to rotate the axes in order to shift the basis of understanding a complex of psychometric data. So also in the clinic. When we attempt psychotherapy we really do the same thing; for it is quite appropriate and helpful to view psychotherapy as an effort to get the client to rotate his personal axes of understanding—rotate them so that more precise and rational methods of solution can be applied to the geo-social problems he encounters. Like Descartes, he too is likely to do some dreaming in connection with this shaking up of his frames of reference. And, as with Descartes, the rotation of reference axes will be, for him, no mere mimicry of current professional talky-talk, but an earth-shaking personal experience that leads him, too, to ask, "What way of life shall I take."

[1] Presidential address at Division 13 (Consulting Division), American Psychological Association, San Francisco, CA, September 1, 1955. Published in *Newsletter of Division*, 1955, 13. Republished by permission of Jacqueline Aldridge.

Collected Papers of the Pioneer of Constructivist Psychology: George A. Kelly, First Edition. Edited by David A. Winter and Nick Reed.

Now the conceptual bridge which I proposed a few moments ago is the idea that the convenient rotation of coordinate axes may be, for me as well as for patients in deep psychotherapy, a way to solve the nagging problem in the upper left-hand drawer of my desk. This is an intriguing thought. I would like to share it, not merely because I happen to be preoccupied with it, but because I think there are a lot of psychologists, and physicians, and educators who have got "*versus*" folders in their professional pigeonholes.

In another paper, which I understand will be published shortly in the Proceedings of the New York Academy of Science, I have tried to develop the notion that psychology as a profession is making a noble and utterly modern effort to base its professionalism, not on the Levitical idea of God-given authority over the minds of fellow men, nor on the Nineteenth Century ideas wherein law and medicine claimed the right to make decisions for their clients on the basis of superior educational training, but rather, on the idea that a professional psychologist serves his client by helping him discover for himself important truths about himself and the things that trouble him. Thus the psychologist is a fellow-explorer to his client, not a purveyor of superior wisdom. The psychologist's professionalism is not grounds for taking over some part of the client's right to make decisions—he makes no parallel claim to the medical man's oft-repeated insistence on "medical responsibility." Yet he serves his client no less faithfully, and he is no less devoted to his task. This is a new concept of professional relationship to clients. But, then, psychology is a new profession—and this is already past the middle of the twentieth century. Society could stand some renovation in its notions about who does the thinking for whom.

The upshot of this kind of twentieth century thinking is that we take another look at the patient. Carl Rogers expresses it succinctly when he stops calling people patients and dignifies the relationship as that of a client. Responsibility—medical, legal, psychological, or otherwise—can no more be wrested from a client than it can be shrugged off by the psychologist who serves him. Responsibility is something we are all stuck with. One does not take responsibility from another; the assuming of responsibility is not a game of buck-passing that leaves the client morally and psychologically disenfranchised.

Let us look at the roots of our idea in this manner. It was the dawn of a great day in the Anglo-Saxon world when the concept of *habeas corpus* began to penetrate our legal thinking. The right of a man to his own person became the stepping stone to human dignity, and its jealous protection is the first concern of a politically self-governing people. To be sure, there are those who say that most people do not know what to do with themselves, and really ought to be managed by their superiors. But the principle of *habeas corpus* still prevails, and poor managers or not, the people who follow the principle find their neighbors more congenial to live with.

In three paragraphs I have jumped from psychology as a new-type profession to the new look at the client, and thence to the principle of *habeas corpus*. What I am saying in all three paragraphs is this: we need—desperately need—among the professions that deal with the mental problems of mankind, a new application of the principle of *habeas corpus*. Like the citizen of the Anglo-Saxon state, the patient's right to his own mind, his right to do his own thinking, even when under medical or psychological care, should be considered basic to the mental well-being of the nation. Let us call this the principle of psychological *habeas corpus*, or perhaps better, the principle of *habeas mentem*, man's right to the possession of his own mind. If we accept this principle, there may be far-reaching outcomes, not the least of which might be the happy discontinuation of the APA versus APA scramble for possession of patients' minds and the special privilege of exercising medical responsibility.

Now the question arises, if the principle of *habeas mentem* does prevail, will both psychology and psychiatry be left holding empty professional bags? Can neither of them thereafter make executive decisions? Can neither of them "integrate" the findings of the other? Can neither of them lay claim to the "over-view", the broad outlook? The answer is simple. It comes all the way from Descartes. It isn't that medicine is more comprehensive than psychology or that psychology is more modern than medicine. Medicine and psychology are no more than sets of coordinate axes, like Descartes envisioned, that provide grounds upon which precise symbolic thinking can be adapted to the behavior of man. Sometimes a person's behavior, when plotted with respect to medical axes, for example, turns out to be too difficult to understand—our equations for dealing with the behavioral curves generated against those axes are too complex for us to handle. So, we rotate the axes—or apply the polar coordinates of psychology—and see if that step reduces the problem to a form simple enough for us to deal with it. Straightforward enough, it might seem. But, like Descartes, a lot of people still have nightmares when they try it. And there will be some who will keep whimpering in their sleep, "But isn't it really a medical problem?"

The question of which is the senior profession—psychology or psychiatry—is really quite irrelevant to the issue of who should take the initiative in helping a client get well. The assignment of the initiative should never be made on the basis of professional identification, for that would assume that one set of coordinates was naturally superordinate to another. As in any good administration, initiative action should be assigned to men, not to a social class of men. As in business, as in politics, as in any of the more normal human enterprises, the proper selection of the given clinician for the given client hinges on which mathematical plot of the particular behavior curve makes it more amenable to algebraic solution, the question of what individual is best able to assume leadership. Stated in less mathematical language, it is a question of which man's viewpoint will be most useful to the patient in finding a sensible solution to his problems.

We have been talking about psychology and psychiatry, and how they can get along together under the principle of *habeas mentem*. We need not stop here. Any discipline is properly regarded as a set of coordinate axes, against which human behavior can be plotted, We make our mistakes only when we get to thinking that the behavior is the private possession of the axes, that the curve belongs to the coordinates with respect to which we have chosen to plot it. Thus a man's traffic behavior does not really belong to the policeman on the motorcycle behind him, nor the child's multiplication tables to his teacher, nor a delusion to a psychologist. The person's behavior is his own—the policeman, the teacher and the psychologist simply have their own special ways of looking at it. Which is best? Which has the over-over-view? Well, let's take a closer look at the individual case. And while we're examining the behavior more closely, we may still have to live through some Cartesian nightmares.

107

Emerging Concepts that Affect Interprofessional Alignments in Psychology[1]: (Discussion of the Findings of the Psychology Commission)

In discussing this paper, I should like to do three things. Some points I should like to underscore to make sure their significance is not overlooked. Then I should like to add documentation to others. Finally, I should like to draw certain generalizations from the report that seem to indicate how, in the next decade, psychotherapy will most certainly be increasingly developed and practiced by psychologists.

Psychology as a discipline brings to our civilized society certain important new concepts. Some of these, as the report suggests, have ancient roots in the "tradition of philosophical and ethical concern with man's problems." Some, as the report also points out, are rooted in the experimentalism of the late 19th century. But it is proper to say that none of the important new concepts that psychology is now bringing into our public life is rooted in the medical tradition. Indeed, many of the convictions of psychologists are so antithetical to medical traditions and to medical concepts of the necessary relationship between a professional man and his client that a vast chasm has opened up between psychology and medicine. That chasm is threatening now to engulf both professions in a chaotic dispute.

This is a strong and revolutionary statement. One who hears it for the first time will immediately find his thoughts turning to the significant psychological contributions of Freud, Jung, Adler, and others, many of them physicians. But these were the men who broke with the medical tradition of their times, and the essential cleavage between what they sought to grasp and what modern medicine still believes is as wide and clean as it ever was. Psychoanalysis exists in the framework of organized medicine today only as another of those paradoxes that arise when an insecure new group finds it expedient to ally itself with a powerful agency whose views it secretly abhors. The strange alliance is as puzzling to most legitimate physicians as it is to psychologists. One cannot help wondering if any profession, thus misallied, will ever produce a whole generation of thinkers whose thoughts will be as unfettered by medical tradition as Freud's were.

Thus the report we have laid before us acknowledges the indebtedness of modem psychology to the theoretical and technical contributions of Freud, Jung, and others, but it claims no specific roots in the medical tradition. Whether good or ill, this is correct. Perhaps the authors of the report would not have emphasized this cleavage as sharply as I have, but there it is, and it is one which is often recognized and genuinely respected by nonpsychiatric medical men with whom psychologists frequently collaborate so successfully.

So, as the report points out, the new concepts of psychology have roots, roots in philosophy and ethics, roots in experimental research, and roots among those individuals who have had the courage and intellectual vigor to break out of the biological framework of medical thinking. Most psychologists are only too happy to acknowledge some spiritual kinship with these men, and they wish that the field of psychotherapy today might be more widely occupied by men of equally venturesome spirit.

Briefly, what are the new concepts that psychology brings into our society? Systematic empiricism is one. When the report speaks of empiricism, experimental research, and the outright emphasis that therapy-practicing psychologists place upon the logical processes of science, it is not referring to any fly-by-night opportunistic clinical intuition. We note, for example, the following statement in the report: "There is a common notion of a categorical distinction between 'cold' science and the 'warm' human relating that moves psychotherapy forward. Let it be said at once that this distinction is not only false but mischievous."

[1] First published as Kelly, G.A. (1955). Emerging concepts that affect interprofessional alignments in psychology (Discussion of the findings of the Psychology Commission). *Annals of the New York Academy of Sciences, 63*, 359–364. Republished by permission of Wiley.

Collected Papers of the Pioneer of Constructivist Psychology: George A. Kelly, First Edition. Edited by David A. Winter and Nick Reed.

This statement of the commission carries a considerable freight of meaning. As long as the biological point of view was considered to be the essential model of all behavioral science there was, indeed, an essential and categorical distinction between what could be conceived as science and what was viewed as a matter of warm human relationships. A professional man could establish warm human relationships only by laying aside his biological science for the moment. Biology quite obviously provided no framework for understanding such phenomena as human relationships. This laying aside of scientific outlook in which he has been disciplined is what many a skillful physician has learned to do after he has got away from the environment of the medical school. Often he does it with a guilty conscience; he knows he is not being scientific. Yet most of us here would say that it is a credit to the medical profession that so many of them have discovered when to stop being the kind of biological scientists they were trained to be, and have struck up warm, though unscientific, human relationships with their patients. And it is also a credit to the vast majority of practitioners that, when they have done so, they have made no pretense of being scientific. They have admittedly played by ear.

Now the science of biology, upon which medical practice is based, is a marvelous system of human thought. It has served humanity well and it will, no doubt, continue to make great strides into the future. Let us not, therefore, underestimate its stature. But biology is not a magic mirror in which human behavior can be seen in all its true aspects. There are other scientific ways of examining human behavior, and, lately, psychology has become one of these. Psychology is a vastly different kind of intellectual framework. Within its system of illumination, many brilliant new facets of man's behavior come to view, facets that never catch the light of biology.

So, which gives the better view of man, biology or psychology? Certainly, both are ways of looking at the very same man. Both are ways of making scientific predictions about his behavior. The answer is simple enough. Each way discloses, in its own particular manner, certain facets of the same human truth. There are occasions when some biological approach leads one to make more accurate predictions about man; others in which a psychological slant opens the way to a better understanding of what man is up to. It is not that man is himself a hyphenated combination of psychology and biology— a mind glued tightly onto a body—man is simply man; himself neither the property of biology nor of psychology. But he may be looked at through the spectacles of the biologist or through the spectacles of the psychologist, and, may I add, he may be looked at through other spectacles too, through those of theology, for example. As we successively try on new spectacles, each fresh viewpoint opens up to us a magnificent view of humanity.

Now what does this have to do with patients and the psychotherapeutic role of the psychological profession? Certainly this: the patient's discomfort, or the patient's behavior if you prefer, is not itself a biological thing, nor is it a psychological thing. It is the way that we look at it, the way we look at that discomfort, that is biological or psychological. Once we recognize this simple truth about human construction of reality, a lot of things begin to fall into place, including, I think, the proper relationships between the five professions who have contributed to this monograph.

Now let me come back to the quotation from the report which was the starting point of this excursion into epistemology. The statement was, "There is a common notion of a categorical distinction between 'cold' science and the 'warm' human relating that moves psychotherapy forward." The report adds, "Let it be said at once that this distinction is not only false but mischievous." By conceptualizing psychotherapy within the framework of psychology, rather than within the biological framework of medicine, it becomes possible for the psychotherapist to be scientific—and warm—without having to resort to the vagaries of psychiatric intuition.

The psychologist who practices psychotherapy does across his desk essentially the very same thing that he so painstakingly learned to do in performing the research required for his doctoral dissertation. He formulates hypotheses, both deductively from theory and inductively from the seemingly incoherent murmurings of his client. He tests the hypotheses in the interview room and listens attentively to the evidence with that quiet courageous humility that rabidly doctrinaire persons find so hard to accept and therefore brand as sheer naivete. But this is the scientist now sitting in the therapist's chair, and one may be sure that his techniques will often seem new and strange.

It is said that Carver, the distinguished research chemist and teacher, was wont to say something like this at the beginning of an experiment, "Students, we are about to ask God a little question. This is our particular way of asking it but we must be sure that it is a question we ask and not a reward that we demand, for it will be precisely the question we ask that will be answered, while the reward we demand may never be granted." What better statement of the essentials of experimental design could any scientist ever formulate!

But scientific method is not solely for the man sitting in the psychotherapist's chair. When the client and the psychologist walk into the interview room, they enter together a laboratory of human relations. Both become researchers. Both offer themselves as subjects for the experiment about to be performed. Both observe the client's reactions. Both take careful note of the therapist's responses. And with this new concept of psychotherapy, psychology's break with certain medical—and ecclesiastical—traditions becomes complete. For, by tradition, the medical man must place his patient in a horizontal position and ask him to assume an attitude of hopeful submission, while the concept of the client as a partner in research construes him in a vertical position. Together, these two persons, client and psychologist, who walk into the psychotherapeutic laboratory, comprise a test tube of human relations and, in each scheduled hour of interview, an experiment is performed by them. Each observes the experimental outcomes. Sometimes the mixture proves unexpectedly explosive. But this has been anticipated. Laboratory precautions have been taken, the test tube is small, and the blast damage is localized to keep it under control.

Sometimes, then, it is man the client, but it is always man the researcher. Perhaps we might well express this new psychological concept of the client role by paraphrasing one of the protestant cries of the Reformation and say, "We conceive that every man has the right to be his own scientist." The client needs only to discover how to ask God little questions. He does not merely collect official interpretations from his psychotherapist. Here is a notion of a client that, to say the least, is not in the medical tradition, and let us not underestimate the upheaval that will ensue from its adoption. Nor should we misjudge the consternation already arising in the ranks of those professional colleagues to whom the concept of "medical responsibility" has become a traditional and cherished rite to be performed upon incompetent patients.

But let us hasten on now with the underscoring of this comprehensive report. Perhaps this is the moment to talk about collaboration with our colleagues in other disciplines. It may serve to soften the harsh criticism unavoidably inferred from what has just been said. Yet I would remind any listener who might have been offended that one cannot speak from great conviction about a vastly new idea without reflecting vivid contrasts upon certain things that have grown old and treasured. May I say, especially to our psychiatric colleagues who may feel at this point that their noses have been tweaked, that there is no occasion for offense. This bold new venture into the therapeutic application of psychology as a science is one in which they might well join us, even though it would mean the open abandonment of those pretenses by which they now retain nominal membership in the medical fraternity. We wish they would stop talking about "medical responsibility," which to us is beginning to sound like "the white man's burden" of British colonialism, and make up their minds to join us in the development of a science upon which psychotherapy can be responsibly based.

We should like to have them on our side. We think they would enjoy doing research. We think they would find the psychologist's framework of scientific thinking deeply satisfactory and something into which they could get their teeth. We think they would find the social outlook of our professional group refreshing and, more, we think their erstwhile medical colleagues would respect them for it.

The report says that psychologists do collaborate with other disciplines. Of course they do! The fact that they do so stems from the very scientific assumptions we have been talking about, and not from timidity, as some would like to imply. Now we have just made a point of the fact that psychologists believe in collaborating with their clients. Psychologists believe that this is a sensible and humanly decent way of getting on with the psychotherapeutic process. It would be a strange contradiction for psychologists to urge collaboration with their clients while fearing or disbelieving in collaboration with their colleagues.

The report says that collaboration is spelled out in the psychologists' official code of ethics. I might add that I have not seen it so spelled out in any other discipline's code of ethics. Not only that, but I am sure that no other professional group, with perhaps the exception of social work, collaborates half so much in the conduct of their psychotherapeutic and counseling services as do psychologists. Certainly, the proportion of psychiatrists who seek psychological advice when it is urgently needed is still an insignificant minority.

We might perhaps say that psychologists collaborate because they are gregarious, or because they are trained to be articulate, explicit, and open to the testimony of objective evidence. To say so would be correct in part. But the reason goes deeper than this. It lies in the philosophical position that we have already sketched that man is not assigned to the jurisdiction of any particular system of thought, that he is himself neither psychological, nor biological, nor psychobiological. He is simply himself. It is the viewpoint from which he is seen that is intrinsically psychological, biological, economic, and so on. It is this position on the nature of man that makes it possible for the psychologist to collaborate with colleagues with different viewpoints and makes the psychologist cry out against the jurisdictionalism of the medical profession. Here was the underlying premise from which stemmed the action of the Council of the American Psychological Association, quoted by the report, that reads: "Psychology, therefore, does not favor narrowly restrictive legislation, which provides that only psychologists (or teachers, or physicians, etc.) may engage in certain applications of psychological knowledge and techniques." The philosophical background of psychologists causes them to believe in collaboration between the professions. In the language of psychodiagnostic concept-formation testing, they attempt to adopt the enlightened abstract outlook on life rather than the concretistic, jurisdictional outlook.

There is much more in this report that might be underscored and documented further, but let me turn from its individual topics to an over-all view of what is going on in psychology these days and where it is likely to lead in the next decade or two.

Let us look at the rise of psychology, not in the competitive context of medicine, of social work, or of religion merely, but rather in the context of society's emerging structure. From the time of the Levites, if not earlier, society has expected certain groups of men to prepare themselves for special kinds of services and to impose upon themselves certain sanctions and controls by which the quality of those services might be sustained at an optimal level. In recent generations, we have called such self-disciplined groups of specialized servants "professions." But professions have also taken it upon themselves to demand a special kind of authority over the affairs of their fellow men. In a domination-submission form of society, or a leader-follower type of society, if one prefers less vigorous terminology, this assumption of authoritarian prerogatives was tolerated. In the priesthood, the authority was presumed to have been conferred by God. But during the last century, when medicine emerged as a profession, the authority was conceived in a somewhat different way. It was an authority conferred by virtue of one's training—in the case of medicine, of course, medical training. This authority was encoded in our laws of medical practice. To a considerable extent, it must be said, the clergy also has come to rest its claim to authority upon this new kind of professional foundation. We might mention the rise of other professions too, but the point is probably clear enough as it stands.

But now it is the middle of the 20th century. Society is struggling with some powerful new concepts of social organization and questioning the propriety of having one class of men staring down their fellow men into intellectual submission, and it is asking itself on every hand, "Is this the only way men can build their society so as to make it safe and wholesome? What is authority anyway, and whence does it really stem?"

It is in this climate of inquiry and soul searching that a new profession called "psychology" is arising. Will this new profession be patterned along the lines of the medical profession of nearly a century ago? Or does it have the opportunity, as no profession before it has ever had, to establish itself on a new kind of foundation, a foundation of tested but continuing inquiry? Is it possible to build, for the first time, a profession based upon scientific understanding, with no claim to any kind of superior custody of truth, with no insistence upon privileged control of the persons whom it serves? We psychologists think it is now possible, for the first time, to build a profession upon such grounds. But the challenge is not merely a challenge to psychologists. It is a challenge to all. We psychologists should particularly like to enlist the collaboration of the members of the five groups represented in this monograph. There are some who say it cannot be done. But would it not be a splendid adventure to try?

108

Issues: Hidden or Mislaid[1]

A much respected professional colleague of mine has stoutly maintained, during the ten or more years I have known him, that the only good psychiatrist is a dead one and the surest way to get dependable medical service is to keep the physician under threat of blackmail. My friend is perfectly right. Only death will prevent a psychiatrist, or anyone else who must work in the half-light of present human knowledge, from making bad mistakes. And any professional person's jealous regard for his reputation is what makes him strive to do the best he can.

Yet in spite of this earthy appraisal of psychiatrists in particular and doctors in general, my friend has not, as far as I am able to observe, achieved very much improvement in his relations with the medical profession. Of course it may be that he has failed to act in terms of his neatly drawn issues. But I suspect the difficulty lies deeper than that. What I really suspect is that somewhere back along his line of reasoning he must have misplaced an issue.

Ausubel also has had a fling at the troubles psychology and psychiatry are having with each other. In construing these matters he also has set out before us some very straightforward and attractive issues. Of course, his formulations are not quite as simple and action oriented as those of my friend, but they do have that same salty flavor that we all enjoy so much when we are on the sidelines of a good rough game. Anyone who has been driven to the point of distraction trying to find decent common cause with psychiatry, or who has been exasperated by psychology's self-disciplining efforts, will find them most tempting.

These are issues, says Ausubel, that have really been with us all the time but they have been kept in hiding. He does not say whether he, being aware of them, has, unlike my friend, gone ahead and acted on them or, if he has acted, what resulting improvement in interprofessional relations he has observed. He merely says that they have been hidden, and he does a vigorous job of exposing them. But are these the fateful issues in terms of which psychology must inevitably square off with psychiatry? Or are they not humanly fallible constructions that are badly mislaid indeed?

When two professions find themselves working at cross purposes they can, if they look closely, observe that there are several courses open to them. They can shoot it out, using those weapons a polite society reserves for such affairs of honor. They can wait it out, each hoping that time will improve his position. They can stalemate the controversy by reducing it to terms that defy further exploration. Or, by joint effort, they can keep trying to reconstrue the issues into a form that offers each of them some freedom of movement—at least enough so that its members can get on with their business.

In their disputes with psychiatry psychologists have followed, in part, all of these courses. But mostly they have waited, assuming that sooner or later their overwhelmingly greater emphasis upon research and their wider use of scientific methodology in everyday affairs would align both time and enlightenment on their side. Psychiatrists, too, have generally waited, depending, perhaps, upon their protective alliance with legalized medicine to keep them in supervisory control of psychologists' activities.

But on both sides there is a growing impatience with waiting. "Psychiatric supervision" is proving to be an empty phrase, too often a cloak for both psychiatric and psychological malpractice and often an inversion of the order of competence. There are psychiatrists who are honestly embarrassed by its legalistics. Among psychologists there are some who are impatient because they are anxious. To be sure, the most anxious are those who see very little in their daily work to which they can apply scientific methodology to an advantage. Naturally, they do not expect to win out with their research.

Recently it has been possible to supplement the waiting policy with renewed effort on the part of both APA's—the American Psychological Association and the American Psychiatric Association—to recast the issues over which disputes have arisen.

After two years of intensive effort the committees representing the two associations have restated one set of issues and have come up with a sensible agreement. As a result the Council of the American Psychiatric Association has gone on record as being in

[1] First published as Kelly, G.A. (1956). Issues: Hidden or mislaid? *American Psychologist, 11 (2)*, 112–113. Republished by permission of the American Psychological Association.

Collected Papers of the Pioneer of Constructivist Psychology: George A. Kelly, First Edition. Edited by David A. Winter and Nick Reed.

Published 2026 by John Wiley & Sons Ltd.

agreement with the kind of legislation that the Council of the American Psychological Association has voted to recommend. There are still some local misunderstandings in certain states, largely growing out of the ambiguity of such terms as "licensing" and "certification." But unless matters get fogged over again, the way should remain clear, as far as the American Psychiatric Association is concerned, for all states to go ahead with legislation for psychologists along the lines recommended by the Council of the American Psychological Association. This does not, however, imply any working agreement yet with the American Medical Association or with all state medical and psychiatric groups.

Now it would have been possible for the two committees to have approached the interprofessional controversy on legislation in terms of the issues my colleague so stoutly defends. The psychologists' committee could have seen the solution in terms of intimidated physicians and dead psychiatrists. Or, if a somewhat more humane formulation were preferred, the committee might have chosen to deal with the problem in terms of the hidden issues Ausubel propounds. Since the committee did not choose to use either of these formulations it is impossible to say exactly what would have happened. Perhaps our psychiatric colleagues could give us some idea of how they would have reacted to either of these formulations.

There are other disputes still smoldering between psychologists and psychiatrists. Some of the squabbles have to do with the right to administer the sacrament of psychotherapy. This issue may prove difficult to reformulate into manageable terms. Yet the fact that neither profession has a very clear notion of what psychotherapy is and neither uniformly requires its members to be trained for it may ultimately make the redesigning of issues easier. Perhaps we shall fail. Perhaps we shall end up in deadlock over some such formulations as "financial competition" or "medical omniscience." But let us hope we can do better.

What we have been saying may appear to have to do with tactics merely. But it is more than that. It is an alternative philosophical position, quite different from that which Ausubel employs. He believes that issues are born, not made. He believes that in the course of shuffling human affairs they sometimes get hidden. When they get hidden he thinks someone ought to go out and find them.

It is possible to look at issues another way. Issues, like the quarrels that rage around them, are made by human beings. And since they are so made they can be remade, tested, remodeled, and eventually put to good use. It is a tedious job but we need to keep testing and remodeling our issues with psychiatry until we construct those upon which our mutual difficulties can be intelligently resolved.[2]

[2] In describing the application of the "grandfather clause" by the American Board of Examiners in Professional Psychology, Ausubel says, "To qualify for such status, all that was necessary was a Ph.D in psychology granted prior to a certain limiting date and training that was tangentially related to clinical psychology, e.g., experience in constructing psychological tests. In this way numerous completely untrained and inexperienced clinical psychologists were foisted upon the general public." Actually the Board refused to accept test construction as qualifying experience for the clinical diploma, except when associated with bona fide clinical activities involving responsibility for patients. The definition of qualifying experience for "grandfathers" was the same as it is today for "nongrandfathers" except that the Board has been gradually increasing the proportion of experience that must be postdoctoral.

Ausubel's language also implies, although it is not clear that he intended for it to do so, that the "grandfather clause" is still in effect. The provisions of the clause expired in 1949. He says also that, "To qualify as a 'grandfather' in psychiatry, many years of clinical experience in mental hospitals or in private psychiatric practice had to be demonstrated." The bylaws of ABEPP relating to "grandfathers" were patterned after the bylaws of various medical specialty boards, particularly the board in pathology. In general, the experience provisions were made parallel, both in regard to years of practice and in regard to the clinical nature of the experience. The parallel goes even further; the complaints against "grandfathers" proved to be just about as bitter as the experience with psychiatric "grandfathers" led us to expect.

109

Problems of Clinical Psychology in an Industrial Setting[1]

There is a thin line between empiricism and opportunism, and nowhere is that line more tenuously drawn than in the world of business. Empiricism says that if an idea works it is true. Opportunism says that if it works to your advantage it is good. The difference is very slight. The trouble with both of these positions is that a little truth, however neatly and explicitly verified, is, in this practical and actuarial world of ours, often taken as implicit grounds for concocting what—too late—proves to be a monstrous falsehood.

Now that is really all I have to say. However, since Starke Hathaway, who is the next speaker, will obviously want to come to the defense of empiricism and actuarialism—as well as goodness knows how many other things—it is only fair to give him a few minutes to sit and compose his reply. Besides, he is a very conscientious sort of fellow and I wouldn't want to put him in a spot where he might say something nasty he would be sorry for later. So let me drag this out a little by illustrating the point I have already made.

May I say that I fancy myself as something of an authority on dust-bowl empiricism. In fact, as one who lived in Western Kansas throughout the dust-bowl thirties—actually as one who has lived most of his life in Kansas—I have found it difficult to understand why the University of Minnesota, so pleasantly located in the land of the sky-blue waters, should ever have been identified with the dust-bowl—identified with empiricism, yes, but how come with dust-bowl empiricism?

Quite recently, through a rather personal experience, I think I have come to understand. Several months ago, after a lapse of some forty-five years, I had an opportunity to re-visit one of the scenes of my childhood. It was this personal experience that seemed to throw this whole business of dust-bowl empiricism into a strange new perspective and spread out before me a breath-taking view of the future possibilities of clinical psychology in industry. While my colleagues from Minnesota and Kansas are making last-minute revisions of their remarks, let me tell you about it.

When I was a youngster the federal government opened up a vast area of grass land in East Colorado to settlement. My father, in the tradition of his family who in succeeding generations had migrated first from Pennsylvania to Illinois, then to Iowa, and then to Kansas, immediately began to make plans to file claim to a half-section, to homestead on it, and, after the required three years of residence, to "prove up"—the phrase used for the last step in procuring a deed to the land. This new homestead was to be his legacy to me and, doubtless at the time, he would have expected me by the time I had reached my present age to have moved on with new frontiers on behalf of my own children.

So he sent off to Montgomery Ward for the ash bows and the tarpaulin with the draw strings at each end to convert his wagon into what he called a "mover wagon." (I can't remember the term covered-wagon ever being used any more than I can remember anyone ever calling a coyote a coy 'o 'te, or a revolver a gun). The wagon was not, of course, a Conestoga. I can't remember for sure but it was a Studebaker, the Studebaker people having taken over from the Conestoga people by that time and turned out a lighter and more maneuverable vehicle.

Well, in any case, we said good-bye to the Kansas farm and the new agricultural community which had changed the complexion of the landscape. The old Chisholm Trail which ran some two-hundred yards west of the house had been plowed over for several years now and there was a dwindling number of neighbors who could remember the days when cattle had been driven on it to the rail-head at Wichita—and very few who could remember herds being driven as far as Abilene.

The new land in Colorado was a world of open promise. There were vast horizons and in the distance on a clear day one could see Pike's Peak, a hundred miles away. The soil was ideal. I can remember the U.S. Department of Agriculture had determined that by scientific tests based on the very best of empirical methods. The annual rainfall was low, to be sure, but enough to sustain a mat of nutritious Buffalo Grass that covered as far as one could see the open range on which cattle were allowed free grazing. Only a claim here and there fenced in the crops to protect them from the herds roaming the open range. So my father built his shack—eight by sixteen feet. Being a practical man he used multiples of four feet to save lumber. And he registered his brand with the state capital in Denver. Being practical in that also he devised a brand which would require only one straight iron which, by a succession of applications would spell out his initials—TVK. And then he set out to locate and drill a water well. At this point the story comes to an abrupt end. There was no water.

[1] Paper presented at an American Psychological Association symposium, 1958. Published by permission of Jacqueline Aldridge.

Collected Papers of the Pioneer of Constructivist Psychology: George A. Kelly, First Edition. Edited by David A. Winter and Nick Reed.

Well, as I was saying, I revisited this vividly remembered scene of my childhood a few months ago. It was not too hard to find. The reservoir my father had dug in a last desperate effort to trap run-off water for the cattle was drifted nearly full, but still where I remembered it. There was a depression where the cistern had been, the one to which we hauled drinking water from a well a good many miles away. But the velvet mat of Buffalo Grass with the white dots of buffalo horns had gone and in its place a sea of hillocks of drifted silt covered with ugly tumbleweed, and for miles in every direction, not a sign of life.

Even the prairie dog town, where I used to throw clods at the sassy little creatures, was gone. The buffalo chips that it used to be my chore to gather for the cooking fire were deeply covered by the new desolation. I found myself watching the ground closely each time I took a step, just as I had been taught to do as a child, but even the prairie rattlers appeared to have deserted the place. The sun was beating down. The temperature was at 115°. The insistent wind tugged at my shirt-sleeves as if to remind me that I was unwelcome there, and I, the last of a breed of dust-bowl empiricists, got the hell out of there.

About the time my father was loading us up in his mover wagon there was a fellow over in Paris, a very practical sort of fellow, who took on a clinical consulting job of determining which children in the Paris schools were worth spending taxpayers' money on. He developed an instrument and a technique for doing this, validated it actuarially against the little stuffed shirts that were making good with Paris school teachers those days, and left his life's work as a legacy to the U.S. Army in World War I. As a result of his work, or more particularly as a result of his followers' loyal devotion, intelligence, as defined by model children of the regimented classroom, has become the scientific criterion of everything that is good, true, and rigorously standardized in our word-bound society. And anybody who doesn't think so had better not try to go to college or attempt to crash into the social set that manages modern industry.

Not so very many years ago somebody hit upon the notion that people in certain occupational groups might have tastes different from those in other occupational groups. They tried it out and, sure enough, it was true. Now there were two possible conclusions that might have been drawn from this interesting evidence: (1) that the natural models for dentists, YMCA secretaries, and auto-mechanics were actuarially shaping up and the youngsters who had already fallen into these natural molds could be identified early enough to keep them from falling prey to any other instance or (2) that it was high time certain occupational groups started putting some fresh ideas into their orbits and taking steps to diversify the members of their ranks. As I say, either of these conclusions could have been drawn. Of course, as matters turned out, only one of them was drawn—the opportunistic one or, if you prefer, the empirical one.

About the time of World War II someone made the astute observation that people in positions of top management in industry were not the paragons of self-confidence and composure that most of us had always thought they were. Some of these fellows in the carpeted offices were downright anxious and upset over the fact that they were not universally beloved by all their employees. Here was a chance for clinical psychology to be of service, and you can be sure that clinical psychology always stands ready to be of service to such worthy citizens.

Now there is something basically valid about doing psychotherapy across the selfsame desk at which the ulcers are made. In fact, one might generalize further and say that psychotherapy might always be most effectively conducted *in the situation*, although I can envision some awkwardness in the application of this principle in the case of certain problems arising in the context of marital counseling and the like. Be that as it may, I am sure that this application of the clinical psychologist's prestige to industry works—that it meets many of the criteria of empiricism and, if I read the signs aright, of opportunism too. Executives everywhere, in all kinds of unsuspected places, attest the value and personal comfort that comes to them from engaging this kind of personal service.

What disturbs me, as the last of a line of dust-bowl empiricists—one who has actually returned to look at his dust-bowl—is the fleeting picture I get of what the future could be when the industrial soil wears thin, the rain cycle of psychology in industry sinks into its drought phase, and psychologists are asked to look at their staked out claims to industry in a larger, and more scientific, and professionally responsible perspective. Where are the clinical psychologists in industry who have given serious thought to the long-range implications of their work, the systematic position into which they have gravitated, or to research inquiries designed to substantiate their activities?

110

Post-Doctoral Training[1]

- A Psychology's venture into becoming both science and profession
  - 1 Authority—Priesthood to Education to Science
  - 2 Replacing the notion of "applied science"
  - 3 Seeing science as embracing the spectrum of inquiry, from loose hypothesis formulation to tight formulation and empirical testing
  - 4 Psychotherapy as a special instance of the scientific method
- B Post-doctoral training must not be limited to what is merely technical
  - 1 Science, including research
  - 2 Theory
  - 3 Skill
- C The ethic of post-doctoral training
  - 1 Professional responsibility rather than prestige, merely
  - 2 Training to contribute to a) science b) clients
  - 3 To operate in the public domain
- D Role of universities
  - 1 Will lag, but will furnish integrity
  - 2 In-service training
  - 3 Full-time training
- E Organization of Agency
  - 1 Policy
    - a Investment in policy board insulated from immediate operations
    - b Protection from special interest control
    - c Spreading the sources of nominations
    - d Continuity of membership
    - e Drawing upon established agencies
    - f Avoid identification of program with doctrinism (but individuals may represent unique views)
  - 2 Operations
    - a Specified responsibility for administration
    - b Curriculum
    - c Laboratory
    - d Multiple language of discourse
    - e Public relations
  - 3 Staff
    - a Competencies
    - b Images
    - c Evaluation of
  - 4 Students
    - a Selection
    - b De-selection
    - c Evaluation of progress
    - d Follow-up in terms of career development

[1] Los Angeles, Jan 17, 1959. Published by permission of Jacqueline Aldridge and Archives and Special Collections, University of Nebraska – Lincoln Libraries.

Collected Papers of the Pioneer of Constructivist Psychology: George A. Kelly, First Edition. Edited by David A. Winter and Nick Reed.

111

Comments on Special Areas Review Committee[1]

The Special Areas Review Committee of the Community Research and Service Branch reviews project proposals in mental retardation, school mental health, aging, alcoholism and drug abuse, and in various other areas not specifically within the provinces of the three other committees serving the Branch. Proposals are now coming to the Committee at the rate of about 150 a year and are reviewed in three annual meetings, each lasting about three and a half days. In its most recent meeting the Committee approved twenty proposals out of fifty-six and, in addition, dealt with various policy matters relating to such issues as the support of projects in so-called have-not areas, re-demonstration of programs in different geographical areas, continued support of approved projects where key staff have resigned, and consultation visits to applicants whose proposals have not been recommended for approval by the National Mental Health Council.

In addition to its review of submitted project proposals at meetings, the Committee, through its various individual members, conducts site visits for the purpose of getting firsthand information needed to make sound appraisals, for passing on "bureaucratic wisdom" to the fortunate souls whose proposals we have approved, and for discussion of projects that have been disapproved but which might be redesigned to serve some particular need in the Branch's overall program.

It should be said that the Committee now and then finds itself required to make decisions in areas where policy is not clearly defined by NIMH. Occasionally a member will mumble something about getting a clearer mandate from upstairs so that he may restrict his appraisals to those professional matters in which he is sure of his competence. For my own part, I have resisted these attempts to seek outside definition of our task, except where clear legal or organizational issues are at stake. There are always those "executive types" who love to make decisions for people who go around looking puzzled. However, it seems to me it is better for those of us who are face to face with the practical issues to develop our own guidelines, based on a more intimate knowledge of the effect such decisions are likely to have. I believe the Committee is in general agreement with my position in this matter.

As I look back over my brief period of service with the Committee, I believe I am most impressed with the rapidity with which new issues are emerging and developments in mental health practices are taking place on the national scene. Two years ago, I had the impression that a considerable proportion of our applicants were experienced researchers, though, of course, we have always had more than our share of crackpot proposals. Now, it seems to me that we are receiving more applications from persons whose professional backgrounds are more distinctly in the field of services rather than in research. Partly as a result of this, I fear we are able to approve a smaller proportion of applications. But this is not to say we are losing ground. The service-oriented people are the ones who *should* be designing projects. As they get the hang of it they will be able to get practical programs under way in a manner that the conventional researchers would find it difficult to envision.

I suppose one might venture to say that a new breed of mental hygiene worker is being developed, one which fits neither the stereotype of the scientist, on the one hand, nor of the practitioner, on the other. If this happens it will be good. The scientists of the past century have been much too preoccupied with research technology to be humanistic, and the practitioners have either been too priestly to admit their own ignorance or too tender-hearted to forge ideas. Let us hope the new breed of community mental health worker will be one whose members will exercise well-informed imagination, perform bold experimentation, and risk candid appraisal of their failures. I think our review committee can help bring this about—unless, of course, they make the mistake of asking someone to tell them exactly what they should be doing.

One feature of this transitional period impresses me particularly. New ideas are being tested and demonstrated in local communities but more and more we are being asked to support re-demonstrations in other communities. And, more and more, what was once a demonstration seeks the continuing support of federal funds long after it has served its demonstrative purpose. Should we discontinue support after this stage is reached? Should we take action that will turn the hands of the clock backward in a community that has not been able to mobilize local support to carry on a good thing? From now on, we will be faced with the temptation to conduct such "holding operations," lest expensively acquired gains in a community will be lost entirely.

[1] Dated April 10, 1964. Published by permission of Jacqueline Aldridge.

Collected Papers of the Pioneer of Constructivist Psychology: George A. Kelly, First Edition. Edited by David A. Winter and Nick Reed.

But if we undertake many of these "holding operations" we shall, in the course of time, be committing NIMH resources to the support of mediocrity, just as many of our State resources are committed to the support of mediocrity—or worse. The bold new approach to mental health problems, made possible by new Federal funds in the post-war era, may find itself operating at a bare subsistence level, and the program will go the dismal way of the Veterans Administration, an enterprise which also once held bright new hopes for mental health.

It is a harsh decision, but my own answer to this question is to suggest that NIMH abandon any project, new or old, the moment it sinks into mediocrity. Our commitment should be to advancement in mental health, not mere maintenance. This is not to say we should abandon a project that appears to be in temporary difficulty, but we should be prepared to write off programs that are not good, even though the immediate effect will be a deterioration in a certain community's services.

For my own part, I am inclined to view the Title V Program in the paradigm of industry. On the one hand, a progressive industrial organization takes pains to keep its research program far ahead of its current production. But on the other, it works energetically to bring its products up to the levels that research suggests are possible. To do this industry develops a variety of programs, generally known as "development programs." The men who run these programs are knowledgeable as to what research has revealed and yet are practical enough to anticipate the problems of production. Their task is to translate research into design and design into pilot projects that can be copied by the out-and-out production men. The staff of the Community Research and Services Branch are, as I see it, just such people.

But this is not an easy task, nor are professional people reared in the models of nineteenth century science and twentieth century professionalism likely to be prepared for this kind of translation of ideas into practices. To do their unaccustomed task they need to make sure the outcomes of their pilot ventures are formulated into terms the production people can easily understand. As one who has been loaded down with bulky project reports when coming home from site visits, I can testify to the obscurity of such reports. They are dull, rambling, and often misleading. Except in unusual instances they would not prove helpful to persons setting up a community program in another setting.

But this is not to say the reports are useless. Far from it! They need the kind of processing that the staff of this Branch can give them. They need formulation into blue-print terms that community services people can read and adapt to their own needs. They need to be subjected to critical appraisal—not summarized in the kind of generalized and depersonalized ambiguities we ordinarily use to protect the feelings of our friends or to maintain our role as the tactful public servant, but in the harsh, blunt, articulate, and disparate terms of independent minds. Professional people usually dread this sort of thing, especially when it approaches the level of general public disclosure, but I believe that something of this sort is necessary to make the new mental health developments come alive sufficiently to mean something to the people who have to put the show on the road.

Along this same line let me add that I think that the experience now being gained from projects now supported by this Branch should be translated into "how-to-do-it-kits." This, let me hasten to say, does not mean that any project can be picked up lock stock and barrel and plunked down in another community. But unless something transferable comes out of our community projects this whole business is going to turn out to be inordinately expensive. Certainly the "how-to-do-it kits" should prove mighty useful to our regional people when they try to spread the word in one of their "technical assistance" projects.

One of the things our committee has urged upon the central office staff is the preparation of a prospectus in each of the principal areas served by the committee. I believe the time is about ripe for such an undertaking, at least in such areas as school mental health, alcoholism, and mental retardation. I see two functions to be served by such a prospectus—to disclose the suspected gaps in the array of projects now being supported, and to bring us up to date on the best methodologies that are emerging from contemporary experience. Such a prospectus would give the Committee a better idea of what should be supported with the limited funds available in a given field of endeavor. Moreover, it should be of some help to regional office personnel in giving advice to would-be applicants.

But perhaps I should add something at this point. I would not like to see NIMH put itself in the position of straightjacketing project applications. Even if we do have a prospectus in such an area as that of aging, for example, there should be full and open-minded consideration given to proposals that fall outside Central Office's normal range of imagination. The purpose of the prospectus should be primarily to provide information, not to legislate the directions in which inquiry should go.

This paper is already too long and some of the things I had thought of mentioning are probably not of sufficient importance to justify making it longer. However, there is a project I would like to propose for Bert Black. I would like to have him submit a proposal to study the flow of mental health information to those who must enact local and State legislation and initiate community programs. I would like to know where the information goes, when it is picked up, who picks it up, and who, in the course of time, does something about it. This is not intended to be a project on how to influence legislation—not that at all. It is intended as a project dealing not only with "the right to know" but with nature of the information transmitted and where it makes a difference. I would suggest that Bert, as he carries out this project, not allow himself to be burdened with the customary assumption that communication should always be directed toward the community "power structure." I suspect, rather, that useful information put in the hands of "uninfluential people" often results, in the course of time, in certain highly motivated individuals becoming "influential." In other words, this should not be a study in propaganda or in the virtuous peddling of influence by all the "right people," but, rather, in the flow of information and its relation to human decisions affecting the mental health effort. Incidentally, the study will inevitably involve the flow of misinformation, and the people who are particularly susceptible to it.

Mostly what I would like to say in this report is that the Branch's program is in a state of flux and none of us knows exactly where he is going. And that's what I like about it.

112

Training for Professional Obsolescence[1]

There is a problem which, sooner or later, confronts every profession, though few of them do much about it until too late to plan any constructive solution. It is the problem of professional obsolescence. As I see it, this problem arises, not late in a man's career—as one might expect—but early, and at two successive stages. Shortly after graduation he finds that his employment makes demands upon him which his professors apparently did not anticipate. Then, no sooner than he has voiced his complaint against the impracticalities of the academic mind, he discovers that those same practical demands of employment, for which he thought he should have been better prepared, are themselves structured in such a way as to preclude his doing what needs to be done. In short, his training does not fit his job, and his job does not fit his responsibilities!

Right now there are a lot of young clinical psychologists who are in one or the other of these two stages of disillusionment. Those who are in the first stage are still complaining that nobody told them about administrative procedures, that they had no instruction in governmental fiscal policies relating to mental health, that they did not have a course in how to manage a hospital ward, that they failed to receive enough supervised experience in long-term deep psychotherapy, that they are still unfamiliar with the big words "real doctors" use, that they cannot make a differential diagnosis that will stand up in a psychiatric staff meeting, that they do not understand the legalisms by which a court divests one man of his human rights and responsibilities and places them in the possession of another, that they do not know the economics of private practice, or even how to fill out a U.S. Civil Service Form 57 consistently with the way they filled it out the last time.

But all of these practices—literally all of them—are badly out of date, and those who insist that clinical psychologists be mass-produced to conform to them are imposing a terrible obsolescence both upon our profession and upon our society. Moreover, there is an increasing number of young members of our profession who have become aware of this fact. For example, they have begun to see that the administrative procedures under which they are employed serve to put persons in charge of mental health activities on the basis of the economic power of professional organizations rather than on the basis of clinical competence to meet patients' needs, that mental hospital wards are a blight to be eliminated as fast as community enlightenment can be made to provide the alternatives, that current fiscal policies in the mental health field are wasteful and are getting us deeper and deeper into chaos, that long-term psychotherapy is not a constructive answer to our mounting psychological problems, that medical nomenclature only perpetuates the crude belief that man is a precocious animal rather than a human being, that differential diagnosis in the psychological realm is a hostage to the Nineteenth Century notion of scientific determinism—a notion that our leading cosmologists have already abandoned— and that the economics of private practice are, in the long run, probably going to have to be worked out with the insurance companies, Medicare, and Social Security, rather than with one's clients, his professional competitors, and his interior decorators.

Now that we are "staffing-up" for the long-advertised drive on the nation's mental health problems, psychologists in administrative positions are having to give urgent attention to their local man-power problems. There are altogether too many positions that remain unfilled, and the number is increasing rapidly—though not as fast, it appears, as the number of psychologists who don't want them. A good many university departments of psychology are under pressure, or think they are, to mass-produce the kind of professionals the current job specifications call for. In other words, they are ready, at last, to meet the kinds of complaints voiced by young clinical psychologists in the first stage of their disillusionment, but not the kinds of complaints expressed by the more thoughtful ones who have taken a second look at their daily routines. What is being proposed is as much out of harmony with the needs of the times as the graduate training of the 1930s was out of touch with the developments that were to come in the 1940s.

I am well aware of the fact that doctoral research experience, as now provided in most universities, does not very well prepare psychologists to advance the cause of mental health. As a matter of fact, I have been aware of it for a good many years, and have even tried to

[1] A paper presented to the Conference of Chief State Psychologists at Los Angeles, California on September 2, 1964, as part of a symposium on "Emerging Roles for Psychology in State Mental Health Programs." Published by permission of Jacqueline Aldridge.

Collected Papers of the Pioneer of Constructivist Psychology: George A. Kelly, First Edition. Edited by David A. Winter and Nick Reed.

do something about it. But then I don't think it very well prepares them to advance the cause of science either. As a matter of fact, I have a very dim view of psychology's scientific progress during the past twenty years, the volume of its publications notwithstanding. It seems that we have produced a generation of small-time research technicians during a period when the history of human thought might have expected something more significant than a mass of technical notes to appear on the scene.

Perhaps I should confess also that I have very little use for "applied psychology," and that is why, throughout most of my career, I have identified myself primarily as a "clinical psychologist." To me a clinical psychologist is one who is willing to take the pains to try to understand man intimately; I mean a real man—not a "patient" or a "subject"—an actual person; to try to understand some poor dope who has given up pretending that he is nothing but a student, a doctor, or a Rotarian, and who is struggling with the problem of being human, of loving, of hating, of being loved or hated, of living, or of dying. Now *that*, in my opinion is not *applied psychology*—at least it should never be treated so. The *applied psychologists*, it seems to me, are those who "administer" tests, who "practice" psychotherapy, who "set up" learning experiments, or who engage themselves in other varieties of animal husbandry. There seems to be an awful lot of those around.

The Boulder Conference of 1949 more or less resulted in agreement that clinical psychologists should be trained both as scientists and as clinicians. And that is pretty much what most universities attempt to do. Some of our colleagues have pointed out that the effort has not been very successful as far as producing scientists is concerned, because so few of them "publish." We could probably draw the same conclusion from the fact that so many of them do publish. Yet it is true that psychologists, despite the fact that so many of them occupy service positions, are more likely to execute and publish research than are physicists, for example. I am not sure how to generalize from this fact, either. At least I think we ought to be a little cautious in concluding that the Boulder decisions put American psychology into a stalemate. I think it was something else that got in our way.

I hope you will forgive me if I burden you with a description of what we have tried to do in our own university. At the risk of being parochial I think I can best say what I think by describing what we have done. Back in 1946, before the Boulder Conference was even planned, we too decided to pursue the notion that a psychologist could be both a clinician and a scientist. But we went at it in quite a different way, at least we tried to. The notion, with which my colleagues more or less agreed, was that being a clinician and being a scientist were not two different kinds of undertakings, requiring minimal amounts of two different kinds of talent. It seemed to me, at least, that a psychologist might be at his scientific best when he was able to understand a fellow human being in depth; I mean understand how he felt, how he experienced his world, and how he construed it.

I was not thinking about empathic understanding merely, comforting as that kind of understanding may be in a world of tension and bitterness. I had in mind a kind of understanding that would take shape eventually in structured terms, that would range from empathy, on the one hand, to instrumentation of that empathy on the other, and, eventually, to rigorous scientific test. I saw the whole spectrum as one integral process of human inquiry, and, because I saw it so, I did not see how psychology could ever become a great discipline if it continued to insist that the clinician and the scientist had to be different, or even to suggest that the clinical psychologist try to wear two *different* hats.

I remember trying very hard to convey this idea in the Miami Conference—in 1957, I believe it was—after being invited by vote of the Conference the evening before to prepare a paper along these lines, and after staying up all night to write it. It did not, may I say, turn out to represent the consensus of the meeting. As a matter of fact I don't think I even succeeded in clarifying the issue on which I hoped they would take action.

To come back to the Ohio State University program which was developed with the loyal help of my colleagues during the academic year, 1946–47: We re-built the clinical training program completely. We would teach no course in clinical psychology without a concurrent and integrated lab, and we would teach no lab that was not tied to basic lectures. The first course, for example, was to be a philosophy of science course in which the basic scientific methods of observation and interview would be developed in the laboratory, and beginning testing would be introduced as a special case of these basic methodologies. Moreover, no professor would teach clinical psychology who did not expose himself to his students as a clinician. It was hoped that research hypotheses would be generated out of the interaction between theory, research literature, and intimate clinical experience. We set up research teams for this purpose, and centered the student's whole program around them. This was to say that students were not urged to get their hypotheses from the journals, on the one hand, nor were they to content themselves with the little technical exercises commonly called "clinical research," on the other.

Now I don't want to leave you with the impression that we were completely successful in carrying out this program. The temptation to do the kinds of research that other psychologists do can be overwhelming, especially when you want to get your dissertation completed by next summer. Moreover, my colleagues felt themselves under pressure to do what is expected of rising young geniuses, and I think they should be forgiven if, from time to time, one of them might have set up an experiment to fill a little theoretical gap without much thought about whether or not it had anything to do with man.

But one thing in my opinion, is certain, after eighteen years of this kind of curriculum, it *is* possible to train clinical psychologists in this way—I mean, under the implemented philosophy that the scientist at his best is a clinician, and the clinician, at his best, is a scientist. Do you mind if I cite the record? Last summer—a year ago—I attempted to account for the 265 graduate students we had carried on the rolls in clinical psychology since 1946. One hundred and four had received doctoral degrees in clinical psychology at our university and 19 others had received doctoral degrees elsewhere or in another psychological specialty. Disregarding those still in the program, 66% of the men and 35% of the women eventually received their Ph.D.'s (Some of the women, I should add at this point, were very attractive.)

Altogether, seven out of ten are now principally employed on the faculties of universities offering graduate training in clinical psychology or are primarily employed in research. The other 30% are employed in clinical positions in institutions and agencies, are themselves in post-doctoral training, are on active duty with the U.S. Public Health Services or the military services, or are serving in other capacities. As of last summer, five persons were in private practice.

I cite these data to give some idea of where a training program, based on this kind of outlook, may lead. While there is plenty of room for finding fault with the outcomes, I don't think it can be said that such a program produces graduates of whom the right wing of the American Psychological Association will feel ashamed, nor do I think that the more humanitarian liberals among us can say that these graduates have abandoned their concern for mankind.

Speaking of fault-finding; I have some fault-finding of my own. I sense a kind of smugness among too many of these gifted young people, and a provincialism for American psychology. Moreover, from now on I am determined that all of our graduates plan more carefully the first two post-doctoral years of their careers, going abroad, for example, during the first of those two years, and getting some high level clinical training in a post-doctoral institute during the second. And I want a European scholar on our clinical psychology staff each year, just to knock some of the *reinforcement* nonsense out of our youngsters. As a matter of fact; we have already started sending our graduates abroad and bringing European psychologists into our program.

Now what has this to do with meeting the current tables of organization in the U.S. mental health drive? To me it means that all this business about the scientist and the clinician being two different kinds of persons; or that there are two kinds of hats to be worn, is a nonsense that properly belongs to Nineteenth Century folklore, and serves only to hold back psychology, both as a science and as a profession. I think it means also that we will make a serious mistake if we start training clinical psychologists to fit the job specifications now on the state mental health department books. And I think it means also that there is room for some courageous thinking and action in our universities, regardless of what all the clever people seem to be saying, or the rumors about how the fiscal winds are blowing out of the National Institute of Mental Health in Bethesda, Maryland.

113

Issues in the Professional Training of Clinical Psychologists[1]

The statement to follow attempts to present the major issues in the professional training of clinical psychologists. While the focus is on the objectives and methods of doctoral training, issues in postdoctoral and subdoctoral training are also examined. It seems likely that issues in all three areas must be faced before a satisfactory solution to clinical training problems can be reached.

In preparing the statement the Committee had available to it thoughtful suggestions received from psychologists throughout the country. These were of great value in choosing major questions and in enumerating the pros and cons of each.

The intent of the statement is to make available to the Conference participants an organized collection of those questions which are being widely debated by the psychological profession. This is done with no claim to completeness and with every expectation that additional issues will be introduced by the conferees themselves.

Stuart Cook, Chairman
Roger Bibace
Sol Garfield
George Kelly
Milton Wexler

Many issues confront the profession of psychology with respect to the training of clinical psychologists. Among these one stands out as a central theme. This is the question of uniformity or diversity in the goals of professional training.

Since the Boulder Conference in 1949, we have shared one broad training objective, that of producing the doctoral-level, clinical psychologist who is prepared to combine the roles of scientist and professional. While universities have differed greatly in the effort and methods with which they pursued this objective, such differences exist within the framework of at least a superficial commitment to it.

Increasingly, in recent years, dissatisfactions have been voiced with the state of clinical psychology and with programs for training clinical students. This has led to a questioning not only of the training model advocated at the Boulder Conference, but also of the concept of broad uniformity of training goals which it exemplifies. Do we wish to retain this basic uniformity or do we wish to experiment with greater diversity? Do we wish to continue varying our approach to clinical training within the limits set by a single model of the clinical psychologist, or has the time come to recognize more than one conception of the clinical psychologist and adjust our training programs accordingly?

Whether we are for continued uniformity (and variations within it) or for legitimized diversity, we face the task of formulating and evaluating some of the possible alternatives available to us. This statement attempts to bring together some of the major considerations relevant to this task. It should be emphasized that in offering this statement the Committee is not presenting a list of possibilities to be acted upon at the Conference. Rather, the purpose is to pull together some of the major ideas which are being advocated and

[1] Presented by Cook, S.W., Bibace, R., Garfield, S., Kelly, G.A., & Wexler, M. at the Chicago Conference on the Professional Preparation of Psychologists, 27 August – 1 September, 1965, and excerpted from a fuller statement published in *Preconference materials*. Published in Hoch, E. L., Ross, A. O., & Winder, C. L. (Eds.). (1966). *Professional preparation of clinical psychologists* (pp. 29–36). American Psychological Association. Published here by permission of the American Psychological Association.

Collected Papers of the Pioneer of Constructivist Psychology: George A. Kelly, First Edition. Edited by David A. Winter and Nick Reed.

organize them in a way which would be helpful to their discussion. We assume that the Conference participants will not only modify the proposals we have summarized but will introduce still others.

Nature of this Statement

As indicated above, the statement to follow will concentrate on training alternatives. In this context we will necessarily be concerned with what the clinical psychologist does and what he should do. However, such questions will be discussed in relation to the goals of the broad training programs to which they are relevant. To some this presentation of alternative training programs as a context for the discussion of training objectives may appear to put the cart before the horse. Logically, choice of objectives precedes choice of programs. We have chosen to reverse this order for two reasons: First, questions of objectives, i.e., what the clinical psychologist is and what he should be, have been widely debated; this should permit the conference participants to move rather quickly to examining the implications of differences in objectives for training programs. Second, the task of the conference is to organize, clarify, and, perhaps, make recommendations with respect to training alternatives. Hence this statement will be most useful if it is helpful in this task.

Despite this general orientation, the statement begins not with training alternatives but with the national debate now in progress regarding clinical psychology. General themes, such as emphasis on treatment versus emphasis on prevention, recur in this debate. They represent the salient dimensions on which discussions of clinical psychology polarize. A number of such major themes are presented in the section to follow. However, the implications for one's view of training are not always clear from the position he takes on one of these themes. His position becomes more meaningful to others when introduced in support of or in opposition to a given training proposal.

Hence, while it seems appropriate to present first the major issues we so often hear debated, we do not believe that it will be necessary to devote much of the conference time to discussing them in this form. Thus, following the description of these issues the remainder of the statement is devoted to some alternatives which the profession might consider as possible training models and which may serve as a basis for delineation of such other alternatives as the conferees may wish to formulate.

General Themes in the Debate About Clinical Psychology

Presented below are what appear to be the most widely debated issues pertaining to training in clinical psychology. While each could be debated at length, we have limited ourselves to brief comments. Although the issues overlap to some extent, each emphasizes a particular theme of importance.

As an aid to defining the dimension on which positions differ, the issues have been formulated in the form of either-or questions. Such a formulation suggests there is no position between the extremes presented; this, of course, is not the case.

1 *Should the training of clinical psychologists include the conduct of research or should their training be concentrated upon preparation for professional practice?*
The relevance of research training is assumed in our present training of the clinical psychologist. The intent is to prepare him to contribute to theory, to develop new clinical methods, and to be capable of sophisticated appraisal of clinical theories and methods advanced by others. Whether these objectives are achievable and meaningful is now under debate. Claims that they have led to a highly useful research orientation on the part of clinical psychologists are countered by other claims that the clinician has neither time for nor interest in doing research. Some argue that the present pattern leads to inadequate preparation for both research and practice, and that if the former were de-emphasized, additional time would be gained for the latter. Those who support the present pattern of training argue that the fault lies not with the objective but with the inadequate manner in which training both for research and for practice is currently carried out. A version of this argument is that research training for the clinical student is often inappropriate in that it is tailored to the problems and methods of students in nonclinical areas. Some opponents of research training in its present form argue that students being trained for professional practice should be trained primarily in the use of the clinical situation as a research tool.
Proponents of research training for clinical psychologists point to one consideration which they feel is crucial. They argue that competence in research is responsible for the uniqueness of the clinical psychologist among the group of professions working in the general mental health area. Moreover, the argument goes, it has been the scientific· and research components of the clinical psychologist's training which have been his principal link to the field of psychology. If research is eliminated from all training in clinical psychology or even if additional training programs without a research component are introduced, we face significant changes not only in future patterns of practice but also in the nature of psychological organizations.

2 *Should training in clinical psychology stress individual psychotherapy or should it include (or stress) other approaches to behavior modification such as group therapy, sociotherapy, behavior therapy, sensitivity training, consultation, etc.?*

The basic training of clinical psychologists characteristically has included an introduction to the use of psychotherapy with the emotionally disturbed. More recently the advisability of concentrating training on individual psychotherapy has been questioned. Some argue that its time-consuming character make it impractical in view of the number of persons needing help. They illustrate with the overcrowded and understaffed situation prevailing in many hospitals and residential institutions. Others argue that it is ineffective. Meanwhile newer therapeutic approaches have gained prominence. Among these are group therapy, sociotherapy, and behavior modification based on learning principles. Moreover, new practice settings require new competencies in such methods as consultation with individuals, groups, organizations, and communities. In opposition, supporters of individual psychotherapy as the basic therapeutic technique argue that the problem lies with the inadequacy of current training. This, rather than the potential of the method, they feel to be responsible for the ineffectiveness of much psychotherapeutic work. They, in turn, recommend increased training in individual psychotherapy rather than less training.

The development of new approaches points a distinct challenge to the traditional view of the one-to-one therapist-client relationship evident in much of our clinical training. Some feel that the one-to-one relationship is already outmoded and that in training our graduate students in this way we are already training for obsolescence. By contrast, others stress their belief that there will always be individuals needing individual treatment and their conviction that group methods, short-cut procedures and techniques cut to the mold of social need are ineffective and often potentially dangerous. Still others stress the scientific value of individual psychotherapy in providing an understanding of human personality. They also insist that experience in individual psychotherapy as both patient and therapist is a necessary part of learning to understand self and others, i.e., is essential to development into a clinical psychologist.

3 *Should the training of clinical psychologists continue to have a treatment orientation, or should training stress knowledge and techniques needed for prevention?*

As the enormity of the problem of psychological disorder has been recognized our current emphasis on diagnosis and treatment is being reexamined. It appears to some psychologists that the effort to assist any substantial proportion of those persons in psychological trouble is doomed to failure. They feel that the incidence of new problems far outruns the rate at which existing ones are alleviated. This leads naturally to an examination of the possibility that spending our time on prevention would represent a more realistic approach. Accordingly, many clinical psychologists are devoting themselves to what is being called community mental health. They point to the success of public health work in other problem areas and argue that this is the direction in which the training of clinical psychologists should be turned.

4 *Should decisions about the nature of training be responsive to current social needs, or should they be based on judgments as to how best to meet the social needs of the future?*

The fact that clinical psychologists are in heavy demand is evident. This is reflected in hundreds of unfilled jobs in schools, institutions, and clinics. Should training departments be responsive to needs of this sort and direct their energies to the preparation of the needed clinicians? Should training emphasize the skills and techniques currently demanded, or would it be more meaningful to minimize this in favor of preparing students who are geared to respond to changing needs and opportunities? Should we train for the present or should we turn out the kind of person we feel will make the greatest contribution in the long run?

5 *Should clinical psychologists be trained to the doctoral level only, or should some also be trained for practice at a subdoctoral level?*

For some years most psychologists have held to the ideal of the doctoral-level clinician. This was motivated partly by the need to create an unambiguous public image of the psychologist and partly by the conviction that clinical problems are too complex to be worked with by persons with less than doctoral training. However, the number of jobs available to psychologists has by now far outrun the number trained and, given our present resources for and patterns of doctoral training, predictions for the future offer little hope for correcting this situation. Should we meet this problem either by training persons for practice at a subdoctoral level or by encouraging others to do so? Is this a feasible and socially worthwhile solution? What impact might it have on current modes of practice? Are we being professionally ethnocentric and socially unresponsive by limiting our training programs to those requiring a doctorate?

Whether or not persons trained at a subdoctoral level are to be identified as psychologists or by some other title is considered important by many. The working relationships between such subdoctoral clinicians and doctoral-level psychologists is also a matter at issue. Would they work independently or as technician groups supervised by the psychologist? These and many parallel questions arise in considering the issue of adhering to or departing from the ideal of the doctoral-level clinician. Possible practical alternatives which might be considered in relation to subdoctoral training are presented later.

6 *Should training in professional techniques be offered in university settings by psychology faculty members or in clinical settings by practicing clinicians?*

There has been considerable variation in the manner in which students in clinical training have received their training in professional techniques. In some cases the full-time clinical faculty have been responsible while, in others, practicing clinicians have been brought to the university on part-time assignments. In still others the training has been done largely by psychologists in clinical settings away from the university.

Those who believe that full-time faculty should be responsible for professional training stress the role of the teacher in serving as a functioning model for the student. Their position is that if the student learns his professional skills from someone he identifies as a research-oriented clinician he will incorporate this ideal for himself. If, however, his teachers of research do no practice and his teachers of practice do no research, he will be inclined to choose one or the other rather than both as the model after which he patterns himself.

Those who believe that practicing clinicians should provide the professional training, stress the added experience which such persons bring to the instruction. They feel the student will get more pertinent instruction here than from faculty members with limited clinical experience. Those who oppose this view feel that a preferable corrective for this situation, where it exists, would be to insure the continuation of clinical experience as a regular part of the faculty member's professional activity.

7 *Should clinical training be given within a graduate school or should it be offered in a professional school?*
As clinical psychology has grown in importance, it has assumed a prominent place in psychology departments. Characteristically, half or more of the graduate students within a department are in the clinical specialty. They share courses, examinations, dissertation standards, etc., with students from nonclinical specialties. Should this be continued or would the training of clinical psychologists be more effective if carried out in another setting, such as a professional school or separate department? In such a school or department some of the requirements appropriately made of other graduate students in psychology could be modified and additional practical professional training could be added. More specifically, the relevance for clinicians of the present type of training in research and in foreign languages has been raised and the possibility advanced of dropping these requirements—and the Ph.D—in favor of some type of professional degree (e.g., Doctor of Psychology, Doctor of Psychotherapy). The latter type of training program would also lend itself more easily to interdisciplinary training than is true in conventional departments of psychology. Among the arguments against this approach is the feeling among many psychologists that clinical subject matter and the feedback from clinical experience enriches the whole of psychology and the training of all psychologists.

8 *Should the clinical psychologist receive his practicum experience in a medical setting, in a psychologically administered clinic, or in other settings?*
To date, much of the field experience of the clinical student has been gained in medical settings. Among some psychologists there has developed a tendency to regret this fact.

There are three points at issue. One has to do with the client population deemed appropriate for the psychologist. Some psychologists would emphasize work with the seriously disturbed, and are led by this to practice in hospitals and residential institutions. Others would place the emphasis on work with the less disturbed who are not in need of confinement. For them the clinic, the guidance center, the school, are the preferred work settings.

The second point relates to the type of professional practice to which emphasis is given. Those who stress remedial work—by whatever method—are likely to give continued emphasis to practicum experience in institutions or clinics. By contrast, those who stress prevention will advocate experience in community settings.

The third point in dispute relates to the implications of the setting for the type of training the student receives and the professional identity he forms. Medical settings are by definition medically administered. It is argued by some that restrictions may be placed on what psychologists do in such settings and that this limits the student's training experience. Another difficulty seen in the medically administered setting is the tendency of the psychology student to mimic psychiatrists. The claim is that this tendency blinds the student to the potential contributions of psychological science to practice.

Those who support the medical setting as a location for practicum experience point to many advantages. Among these are the great variety of types of patients and problems, ranging from emotional stress prior to surgery through the family dynamics of hospitalized psychotics to a wide variety of neuroses. They argue also for the increasing need for closer collaboration with a wide variety of physicians and point to the rapidly growing role of psychologists in the education of medical students, interns, and residents.

Alternative Patterns of Doctoral Training

As we have said, we do not believe it would be productive for the conference to address itself more than momentarily to issues of the type just presented. The implication of one's position on such issues, we believe, is best communicated in a discussion of alternative plans for training.

This leads us to proceed immediately to the training patterns available to the profession. We begin with the focal problem of doctoral-level training. We shall present first the major training patterns which have attracted support—the scientist-professional pattern and three alternatives to it. However, interlocking with this set of alternatives for doctoral training is another, namely, alternatives with respect to the location of clinical training. Should it be located in psychology departments, professional schools, or clinical centers? The alternatives here combine with those above to produce a number of training combinations. These are, of course, not mutually exclusive. As indicated earlier the Conference may wish to endorse a number of training patterns.

We should note also, before reviewing alternative plans for doctoral training, that these can no longer be meaningfully discussed in isolation from undergraduate, subdoctoral, and postdoctoral training. One may take a given position with respect to doctoral training in part because of his views regarding the nature of undergraduate training, the function of postdoctoral training, and the role of subdoctoral clinical technicians. Hence, while components of the total problem must necessarily be discussed separately, it is quite likely that all components will be represented in the formulation of comprehensive approaches to clinical training of the future.

Four Models for Doctoral Training

1 ***The Scientist-Professional***

The distinctive feature of doctoral training is the effort to train the same individual to be both a practicing clinician and a research scientist. The former objective implies competence in both diagnostic and remedial work. The latter calls for competence in the substance and methods of psychological science. In theory at least we expect adequate preparation on both fronts.

We anticipate that a clinical psychologist trained in this manner will devote a substantial share of his time to practice. For most types of practice we assume he will need additional professional training either on the job or in formal postdoctoral programs. This was the conclusion of the Boulder Conference at which the Scientist-Professional model was formulated. It has subsequently been incorporated in ABEPP requirements.

We also expect him to contribute to the improvement of methods for facilitating change in individuals, groups and, perhaps in the future, larger social systems, using both his research and clinical skills to this end. Further we expect him to contribute to the development of psychological knowledge and theory, utilizing for this purpose both his clinical experience and the outcomes of his research. We assume that his scientific training will prepare him for such functions.

2 ***The Professional Psychologist***

The distinctive feature of this pattern of doctoral training would be the effort to prepare a broadly trained psychological clinician prepared to intervene in a wide variety of settings for the purpose of fostering change and forestalling psychological problems. His training would include psychological science but would stress those areas in which clinical methods find their support. It would also include relevant material from related disciplines such as medicine and sociology. He would be introduced to a variety of diagnostic, remedial and preventive procedures. His training would include analysis of the manner in which clinical methods are developed with the intent to make him a sophisticated evaluator of new methods developed in the future. Because he would not carry out a doctoral dissertation or learn foreign languages, he would have more time available for professional training and experience. Should he wish to develop the competence of a specialist in specified diagnostic, remedial, or preventive procedures he will need additional training—either on the job or in formal postdoctoral training programs.

We would expect a clinical psychologist trained in this manner to devote full time to professional practice oriented toward treatment, prevention, or both. He would use diagnostic instruments, carry out psychotherapy, engage in milieu therapy, use behavior therapy, consult in community mental health projects, work with groups, organizations, and communities—as the occasion demanded. He would, as far as his limited scientific training would permit, keep abreast of new methods as they developed and critically appraise them prior to adoption. He would contribute to the development of methods of practice by exchanging his professional experience with that of his clinical colleagues.

3 ***The Psychologist-Psychotherapist***

The distinctive feature of training under this pattern is the effort to train an adequately prepared psychotherapist. His training would include relevant aspects of psychology such as personality, developmental psychology, social psychology, etc. It would also include material from related fields such as sociology, cultural anthropology, literature, and comparative religion. It would include the study of psychosomatic phenomena and an introduction to neurology and physiology.

Principal stress would, of course, be given to psychological theory on which therapy is based. Great emphasis would be placed also upon supervised therapeutic experience. This would start relatively early in the training period. The student might himself have to undergo psychotherapy as a part of his preparation to work with others.

He would acquire familiarity with diagnostic techniques particularly those based upon psychodynamic theory. However, he would not be trained to a high level of competence in their use.

Like the clinical student trained in line with the Professional Psychologist model, the psychologist-psychotherapist would not carry out a research dissertation nor would he fulfill the usual foreign language requirements.

We would expect a clinical psychologist trained in this manner to devote full time to the practice of psychotherapy. From his clinical experience he might contribute to the further development of theory and methods in this area.

Before leaving this pattern of possible doctoral training, we should note that it may be generalizable to specialists in other clinical functions. Thus with an appropriate change in course content a diagnostician or sociotherapist might be trained in similar fashion.

4 ***The Research-Clinician***

Under this pattern of training the psychologist would be trained for a career of research on problems in clinical psychology. His training would stress the substance of general psychological science with an emphasis on personality and psychopathology. He would take the training in research methods expected of the Ph.D in psychology.

His clinical training would be at the level of that offered under the scientist-professional pattern with the exception that he would spend less time in supervised clinical experience. His internship would stress supervised research in a clinical setting.

We would expect the research clinician to work in clinical settings but to devote full time to research and writing. He might concentrate either upon the improvement of clinical methods or upon the development of psychodynamic theory.

114

Epilogue: Moments I Remember[1]

Looking back over the years it seems incredible that so much could have happened to one's profession in the brief course of his own career. I recall a December not so long ago—1930, it was—when the American Psychological Association held its meetings, the first for me, in two moderately sized classrooms. They were located at the north end of the hallway, across from each other, in East Hall of the State University of Iowa.

It is curious that I should remember best a moment during those meetings when I stood alone in the hallway trying to decide which of the two sessions to attend. Yet perhaps it is not so strange, for don't the moments we remember stand out because they epitomize a present perplexity not yet resolved? Behind the door on one side Professors Hunter and Lashley were having it out with each other in a controversy now regarded as a classic. On the other, the clinical psychologists were mathematicizing the Stanford-Binet in the hope of catching a glimpse of the potentialities of man. Which session should I attend?

That was a day when at last psychology was altogether scientific. It had got that way, we students had allowed ourselves to believe, by disentangling itself from the unrealities of philosophy and personal experience, and by poking around to see how the organism was wired up. Furthermore, clinical psychology was what you were advised to go in for if you were ready to quit bucking for scientist, first class. And vice versa! It went with a terminal M.A. Also vice versa!

As for psychoanalysis, that was something that appealed to quack doctors and society dilettantes, not a matter likely ever to be taken seriously by psychologists. Then there was *Gestalt*, a German word for a new party game recently imported from Europe. You played it by demonstrating that any well-meant conversation could be reduced to incoherence by making the cryptic remark, "But, of course, the whole is more than the sum of the parts." I still prefer this way of breaking up a conversation that has gotten beyond me, over the currently popular device of "interpreting the speaker's motivation;" though I must confess 1 occasionally do get erotic satisfaction from peeking at carelessly exposed psychodynamics.

Five years later there was another moment I remember well—two successive moments, in fact. The Great Depression had begun to make it clear that a viable profession shares the hardships of its society, and that psychology, in turn, was a new facet of our culture. Some psychologists had started to argue that the American Psychological Association had a responsibility for helping its younger members find positions. And the first of the moments I remember is when the tall and austere figure of one of psychology's elder statesmen rose to make his contemptuous reply.

Not many hours later, in that same lecture hall, I saw the Executive Secretary of the Association walk forward on the platform to announce that the Board of Directors had voted against permitting the Clinical Section to impose standards of professional competence and conduct on its members. This was the decision that led to The Great Split in American Psychology and the formation of a second national organization. I should add, also, that it was at this Ann Arbor meeting that plans for the Society for the Psychological Study of Social Issues were formulated. But the name was misleading. It quickly became an action group. So even psychology was caught up in the Twentieth Century's great dilemma: Can the cause of liberalism afford itself the luxury of being liberal?

Now my area of indecision was being enlarged. Caught between the two doors, I must ask myself; might it not be that psychology, at its best, was another way of expressing concern for mankind? But I was not alone now; there were others standing with me in the hallway, and they, too, were trying to decide where to go.

That was September, 1935. Within a month there was war. It started in Ethiopia and it ended—if it may be said that such an event has an end—ten years later in Tokyo Bay. When peace returned nothing else was quite the same. In helping win the war psychologists had become citizens, and after the August it ended no science could ever again be so pure or innocent it could enjoy academic privileges without risking mortal consequences. Scholars might still be free, if they chose, but never again immune. Psychology was not a

[1] Prepared for the Master Report of the Proceedings of the 1965 Chicago Conference on the Professional Preparation of Clinical Psychologists. First published as Kelly, G.A. (1966). Moments I remember. In E. L. Hoch, A. O. Ross, & C. L. Winder (Eds.), *Professional preparation of clinical psychologists* (pp. 97–99). American Psychological Association. Published by permission of the American Psychological Association.

Collected Papers of the Pioneer of Constructivist Psychology: George A. Kelly, First Edition. Edited by David A. Winter and Nick Reed.

game, but an undertaking. Professor Adam had taken a large bite out of his apple. The American Psychological Association could no longer meet behind the academic walls of two classrooms.

There were uncertain moments shortly after the end of the war. I remember one in particular. The Veterans Administration had found itself in urgent need of clinical psychologists to staff its hospitals and clinics. It was obvious there were not enough to go around, and they would have to be trained. A large and politically influential private psychiatric institution had announced, on its own, that it would train them under subsidy from the Veterans Administration, and what was more, it would see to it that none of them was contaminated by university departments of psychology or by academic degrees. At least forty trainees had already been recruited, and some had already arrived for training. But the scheme had not been discussed with the Central Office, much less authorized by it. As the psychology consultant to that Office I advised against approval. But it had been a close call for the wobbly profession, The pendulum was swinging wildly. It was a time when Hamlets who hesitated to make decisions had them made for them,

A moment for men to act! My hallway was more crowded now. So the 1949 Boulder Conference was called. The men who came were young, many of them only recently out of uniform. Some of those who were to make the most important proposals were still assistant professors, and some, called upon to make decisions about graduate training, had yet to direct their first doctoral dissertations. The question they faced was if and how to train the thousands of clinical psychologists a newly mental health-oriented society would demand.

There were few precedents and almost no guidelines to be followed. What were to be the relations with the established medical profession whose code of ethics, according to one study, was preponderantly directed at protecting doctors from competition rather than protecting patients from doctors? Should clinical psychology subscribe to the dogmas of psychiatry, or should it continue to try to educate scholars and scientists who would think for themselves, even when trying to be helpful to others? Was psychology being caught up in the cross currents of an unstable post-war society? How could these inexperienced men be expected to find the answers to such questions? And who would listen to them if they did?

Yet the Boulder outcome was a document of discretion. A pattern of training that had been proposed in 1947 in the far-sighted Shakow Report, a pattern that combined scientific, theoretical, and practical training together with a third-year internship, was adopted. The American Psychological Association backed up the report by stabilizing the accreditation efforts it had tentatively undertaken after the war, thus retaining the initiative in a field where, otherwise, Federal subsidizing agencies would have had to step in and set standards. Psychology was to become a profession based on science, rather than unction or privilege, and, in this respect, unlike any that had ever been. In spite of their doubts, their inexperience, the lack of precedents, and the swirling eddies of post-war schemes, these men had built boldly and well.

Between Boulder and Chicago lie sixteen years during which other conferences were held. At Palo Alto, at Miami, and then at Chicago I noted to myself how much my colleagues had grown older and grayer, and walked with a heavier tread. I am not sure we were wiser, but most of us managed to look as if we were. The men I saw in Chicago displayed the poise of successful careers and the quiet pride of membership in a respected profession. Many had distinguished administrative experience behind them.

Unlike Boulder this was a conference of scholars who knew where they stood, who had far clearer ideas of what psychology can achieve, who wasted almost no time at all wondering what the medical profession might say, who rarely mentioned psychiatry, and who had confidence that the decisions they made would carry weight wherever necessary and encourage innovation whenever responsibly undertaken.

To be sure, the months before the Conference had been marred by raucous and unprecedented invective from dissident and rumor-ridden local groups in the now massive psychological community. The dates of the Conference had even had to be set back several months to allow tempers to cool down, and give the normal processes of professional intercommunication a chance to function. But the Conference itself, when it occurred, was a model of dignified and intense discussion. Its outcomes appear elsewhere in these pages. But at least it can be said here that what was accomplished exemplifies professional psychology today.

Now the length of my hallway is filled with colleagues young and old, as far as I can see. And why not? Isn't *this* where the meetings are being held?

Section VIII

Book Reviews

Kelly reviewed a few books on clinical issues for *Contemporary Psychology*, published by the American Psychological Association, as well as one for *Educational Research Bulletin*. In *The clinical psychologist as navigator*, Kelly offers little opinion on William Hunt's *The clinical psychologist*, only noting that Hunt argues for clinical psychology being a science, but one that should be rooted in physiology. In *Cry of an exasperated crusader*, he seems disappointed in Mike Gorman's *Every other bed*, at least for the failure of the author, a journalist and activist for mental health reform, to discover who (presumably psychologists, in Kelly's view) might be on his side; and he is not significantly more enthusiastic about Louis Kaplan's *Mental health and human relations in education*. While one might expect Kelly to have been sympathetic to the views of a leading critic of the coercive use of psychiatry, Thomas Szasz, in *Muddles, myths, and medicine*, his review of Szasz's *The myth of mental illness* expresses disappointment that, in his view, Szasz is a dualist who does not question the construct of illness. In *Look who's talking*, Kelly is notably more enthusiastic about Eric Berne's *Transactional analysis in psychotherapy*, not least because it presents a systematic approach to group psychotherapy. *Clinical psychology afoot and abroad* is a brief review of H.P. David's *International resources in clinical psychology*.

Collected Papers of the Pioneer of Constructivist Psychology: George A. Kelly, First Edition. Edited by David A. Winter and Nick Reed.

115

The Clinical Psychologist as Navigator[1]

This is more than a description of psychology's lusty subdiscipline by a well-informed clinician; it is an amplified statement of the credo of one of psychology's most respected scholars. Hunt believes that psychology has been scientific only so far as it has anchored its thinking in physiological concepts, and that the ultimate language for coming to terms with human behavior will be a physiological language. In spite of the trends of recent years, he believes this to be no less true of clinical psychology than it is of the psychology of learning, or of experimental psychology, or of physiological psychology.

One is reminded of the early Christian ecclesiastics who, after dedicating their lives to a spiritual kingdom and missing no opportunity to denounce the flesh, were still unable to conclude the Apostles' Creed without affirming an essential belief in the resurrection of the body. While it may not be quite appropriate to speak of the author's life-long devotion to psychology in ecclesiastical terms, it is true that, in spite of his distinguished record, he pins his ultimate faith on the kind of stuff physiologists see through their glasses rather than on what psychologists see through theirs. He sees, of course, no inconsistency in this choice.

The author is the chairman of the department of psychology at Northwestern University. His research contribution to experimental psychology over the past three decades has been equaled by few others. He is a long-time member of psychology's most exclusive club, the Society of Experimental Psychologists. But he is also a former president of the clinical division of the American Psychological Association and he identifies himself solidly with clinical psychology. For a number of years he has served the Administrator of Veterans Affairs at the policy-forming level as a member of the Special Medical Advisory Group, a body specifically established by law. What many of his colleagues who are familiar with his record of research and public service may not know is that his career has embraced formal training in clinical procedures, including early schooling in psychotherapy. Not many of the clinical psychologists of his generation were so systematically trained for practical work, nor can many of them lay so strong a claim to the right to speak for clinical psychology.

In this book Hunt has indeed spoken for clinical psychology. His opportunity came when he was invited to give the Salmon Lectures during the autumn of 1954. The three discourses were obviously prepared for medical listeners and were delivered before a predominantly nonpsychological audience in New York. In their printed form they are considerably expanded beyond their original texts.

To lay the groundwork for understanding the clinical psychologist Hunt points to a fundamental difference in the ways psychology and medicine have dealt with the problem of pure vs. applied science. On its part, medicine has generally conceded itself to be an applied science and has looked to the disciplines of biology and physiology for basic information. Psychiatry has separated itself even further from basic research.

Psychology, on the other hand, began as a pure science. But because it was a science of human behavior it had to pay attention to human affairs. American psychology, especially, has been a functional psychology and, because it was so, it has openly functioned everywhere. Thus it happened that psychology's own subject-matter and American psychology's theoretical position forced the new discipline to come to grips with all its practical implications. In this way American clinical psychology developed as an essential elaboration of psychology as a whole. Clinical psychology's relation to pure science is thus intrinsic, rather than extrinsic as in the case of medicine or, more especially, as in the case of psychiatry.

Psychodiagnostic procedures today owe what precision and validity they have primarily to the clinical psychologist. The contribution rests upon his use of the research methodology in which every clinical psychologist is trained and the sound application of the scientific method with which every student in clinical psychology is required to be familiar. Nor does the clinical psychologist's competency in diagnosis stop here. It extends to his skilled use of the interview, the evaluation of case history material and even to the integration of medical findings with other relevant data. He is no mere technician, and the author makes this point clear.

[1] Review of Hunt, W.A. (1956). *The clinical psychologist*. Charles C. Thomas. First published as Kelly, G.A. (1957). The clinical psychologist as navigator. *Contemporary Psychology, 2,* 183–184. Republished by permission of the American Psychological Association.

Collected Papers of the Pioneer of Constructivist Psychology: George A. Kelly, First Edition. Edited by David A. Winter and Nick Reed.

The clinical psychologist also functions in the field of psychotherapy. Here the procedures are obviously rooted in his own discipline. But as psychiatry has departed further and further from medicine proper and has placed less and less reliance on the specific techniques and training given in medical school, psychology has been drawn more and more into jurisdictional controversies with it.

As long as psychiatry was medically oriented toward illness, it seemed proper for psychiatrists to accept medical supervision when dealing with the ill person. But now that so much of psychiatry has abandoned medicine, has so often asserted that illness is anything and everything, and has claimed exclusive jurisdiction over all interviews in which there is "subsequent benefit to the interviewee," trouble is afoot.

The author returns to the problem of interdisciplinary relations in his third lecture as he discusses the future of clinical psychology. He points out that contemporary psychiatry at times is dangerously close to mysticism. It is this fact that makes it difficult both for medicine and clinical psychology to make common cause with psychiatry. This mysticism, moreover, when it takes the form of ultimate and omniscient authority over the patient under the guise of medical responsibility, troubles the author.

Clinical psychology, on the other hand, "is full of probabilities rather than authoritative absolutes. It offers knowledge, with statistical evaluation attached, for the client's selection and use." Hunt continues by saying that psychology's responsibility, in contrast to the psychiatrist's "medical responsibility," is "for the authenticity of its knowledge, and for the correctness of its translation into terms of the client's need." And he insists the responsibility for the use of knowledge remains with the client. It is on this dimension that Hunt primarily differentiates the role of clinical psychology.

Hunt's second lecture on "how the clinical psychologist came to be" is a masterful discourse on the streams of thought which have enriched contemporary clinical psychology. He gives unreserved credit to Freud as a great human naturalist, but declines to call him a scientist in any sophisticated sense of the word. He points out that Watson, by lifting the siege of instinctualism, heralded an era in which "destiny becomes not a fate to be accepted, but a goal to be created." He observes that Gestalt psychology did not accept its configural properties "as irreducible emergents, outside the realm of science," but showed them "to be logical, orderly phenomena reducible to an observable and measurable set of relationships." Thus the author defends the status and traditions of clinical psychology as a science, a science that is soundly logical, vigorously hopeful, and, above all, physiologically palpable.

116

Cry of an Exasperated Crusader[1]

If there is an angry note of impatience in this book, it is long accumulated and difficult to restrain. "Eleven years ago, when as a newspaperman on *The Daily Oklahoman* I started waving the reek and stench of our state mental hospitals under the public's nostrils, I thought American know-how would make short work of the deficiencies in the system. I reckoned little with either the stifling hold of comfortable tradition or the granite power of professional intransigence."

Thus the author aptly introduces a volume jam-packed with frightening facts and ringing quotes about the nation's problem of mental illness. In the pages that follow, the worrisome theme is developed in a high-pitched journalistic key. Occasionally the reader is provided with anecdotes from the author's extensive experiences with legislative committees and governors' conferences—experiences he has had in his influential capacity as Executive Director of the National Mental Health Committee. In conclusion, there is a very fast run-down on what he believes medical research has produced in the field of psychiatry.

It soon becomes apparent that the problem of mental illness, as Mr. Gorman sees it, is the problem of patients' occupying mental hospital beds, how they are dosed, and how soon they are sent home to be cared for otherwise. He is skeptical of psychotherapy in general and he lumps all psychological approaches with psychoanalytic doctrinarism, for which he has an ill-concealed contempt. Preventative mental health and psychological maladaptation to a complex society are outside his range of concern.

Within his narrow definitions of mental illness, the author sees research as holding the key to progress. With this view psychologists will agree. He believes that getting research done is a matter of appropriating funds for it, lack of competent researchers notwithstanding. With this view psychologists will disagree. It turns out that Gorman is talking about physicians and the kind of research that is oriented toward discovering the schizococcus or tracing the neuromanic pathway. Psychology, the only profession in the field that emphasizes research training for all its members and the one that, from the best information available, is actually conducting the bulk of relevant research nowadays, is scarcely mentioned at all. But at least the man believes in research, as will the readers of this review, and that clearly is something to be grateful for.

There are features of the book for which ungrudging credit should be given. There is the plain fact that a big battle is on to clean up a mess that the nation has allowed to reach disastrous proportions. Mike Gorman is in the thick of that fight every day, flailing away right and left. In this book he has provided his fellow crusaders with an arsenal of words, phrases, and facts that ought to scare the living daylights out of a lot of legislators and make some of the ladies of the current-events club drop stitches in their knitting. But why—and this still sticks in the reviewer's craw—does not a man employed in this key position of leadership have an obligation to discover who is on his side! Or would that be a fatal deviation from medicine's party line?

[1] Review of Gorman, M. (1956). *Every other bed*. World Publishing Company. First published as Kelly, G.A. (1957). Cry of an exasperated crusader. *Contemporary Psychology, 2,* 47. Republished by permission of the American Psychological Association.

Collected Papers of the Pioneer of Constructivist Psychology: George A. Kelly, First Edition. Edited by David A. Winter and Nick Reed.

117

Kaplan, Louis. *Mental Health and Human Relations in Education*. New York: Harper and Brothers, 1959. xiv + 476 pp.[1]

Most talk about mental health quickly degenerates into talk about mental "ill" health. Mr. Kaplan's book is no exception. But at least he has done this: he has taken the present accumulation of lore about "psychoses," "neuroses," and "plupathic personalities" and has added to it some information gained from scholarly research.

In the first of the book's four parts the author includes statistical information on the incidence of maladjustment among children, adults, and teachers. For one who rarely reads newspapers or news magazines, the facts may come as a surprise. College students ought to be downright amazed.

Part II contains a good discussion of family relations. Part III briefly involves the reader with the mysteries of psychodynamics, and Part IV confronts him with dynamics in the classroom. Ever since Freud, it has been suggested as a good idea to think in terms of dynamics if possible. Actually it is not very hard to do, since the dynamic mode of human thought, of which demonology is a better known example, is one of the most primitive ways of looking at things.

Mr. Kaplan has done a conscientious job of gleaning the research literature for relevant information. To be sure, a lot of what he has turned up was originally extorted from poor souls who were willing to do almost anything to get an advanced degree. Still, the material probably represents their moments of most disciplined thinking. Research may not be as colorful as the psychiatric phantasies that are so often used to perk up a manuscript, but, from whatever quarter it stems, it tends to have an honest substance to it. Research and speculation, fact and phantasy—the author puts it all together and drones it out with the flattened affect of a professional textbook writer.

No one will deny that the schools need wise suggestions on how to improve mental health and human relations. Nor will anyone discount the hypothetical advantages of a simply written textbook telling education students all they need to know about human nature. Unfortunately this book does not go very far in accomplishing either objective. But considering the current shortages in both wisdom and scholars, one finds himself constrained to defend Kaplan's effort in terms of the well-known quip that ends, "... But it's the only poker game in town."

[1] Review by Kelly published in 1960 in *Educational Research Bulletin*, *39 (3)*, 76 (journal website: https://www.tandfonline.com/). Republished by permission of Taylor and Francis.

Collected Papers of the Pioneer of Constructivist Psychology: George A. Kelly, First Edition. Edited by David A. Winter and Nick Reed.

118

Muddles, Myths and Medicine[1]

Readers of the *American Psychologist*, which includes most of those who read *CP*[2], already have an inkling of what Doctor Szasz is up to. His fellow psychiatrists are probably less well informed, and it is a fair guess they will choose to remain so. No one, not even as scholarly a psychoanalyst as the author of this book, can expect to challenge the basic premises of our flourishing psychiatric economy and still manage to collect royalties from his industrious, privately enterprising colleagues. Indeed it is safe to say that this is one dust jacket that will not be used to impress the fifty-dollar-an-hour customers.

Let us admit at the outset that this book did not turn out quite the way your reviewer expected. For one thing, while the author quotes extensively from the logical positivists, he has not actually abandoned the thinking of the nineteenth century dualists. To him what is describable physiologically is essentially physiological, and what can be seen psychologically is itself psychological. For another, he does not question the concept of illness; that remains a venture of bolder minds. He simply points out that what is called "mental illness" is not truly illness, or else that physical and psychological languages are too often confounded in our discourses on this topic.

The story Doctor Szasz tells has its setting in the late nineteenth century. The two principal characters are the imaginative but clinically inept Prof. Jean Martin Charcot, physician at Paris's famed Salpêtrière, and his impressionable student, Dr. Sigmund Freud, who turns out to be equally imaginative. The plot unfolds out of the medical sociology of the times. That sociology demanded, above all else, that a clear-cut distinction be drawn between illness and malingering. If it was malingering, even out of utmost desperation, the doctor had no business trying to be helpful; but illness—that was something to challenge his most humanitarian impulses! Moreover, to make sure no nonsense slipped in, it was important to classify the illness in terms of disease categories. While this was not too difficult for anyone with a smattering of Greek or Latin, to fail to find a name was to be guilty of malpractice, just as it is today.

In this climate of opinion Charcot was by temperament and opportunity a man of the times. His interests were academic rather than clinical and he did love to classify things. Besides, he was the unchallenged Head Man at the Salpêtrière and no one dared question his morning's pronouncements. His assistants readily learned to select and work up his demonstration cases to fit his favorite diagnostic categories. In no time at all he had added "hysteria" to the lexicon of disease entities, the notion of a nosology of mental disease caught fire, wide-eyed young Freud was more than convinced, and the couch-side search for psychopathodynamics in the twilight zones of the mind was on.

In this headlong enterprise there was a lot of confusion, and Doctor Szasz points it out in great detail—great detail indeed. Surely very little that was ever misstated by Charcot or Freud has escaped his semantic eye. The conversion hysteric, he notes, "had a physical disorder"—and she "didn't have a physical disorder." The anxiety hysteric "had a symbol only"—but he "had the real thing too." Causes got mixed up with purposes, symptoms played hide-and-seek with pathologies, and by the time Sullivan rediscovered the lost ego the whole discipline of psychiatry had become a jumble of physical, psychological, and sociological jargon. All of this was a great disservice to psychiatry which, with its tacit claim to the humanitarian traditions of medicine, deserved a better fate.

The author makes a convincing case. In fact, he makes his case so well that before one is through the first section of the book he is amazed that any two people could be as incoherent as Charcot and Freud. By the end of the indictment, however, he is likely to find himself rooting for these two semantic illiterates who blundered onto some of the most exciting finds of our times.

Hereabouts lies the reason for this reviewer's faint feelings of disappointment. He would like to go all-out in support of a treatise that debunks mental illness—both "mental" and "illness." But the author accepts both constructs. His thesis is merely that they do not go together, that what is mental cannot be illness, and what is illness cannot be mental. But why make Charcot and Freud the scapegoats? The villainy is not the imperfect logic of these two early pioneers—pioneers always have trouble saying what they mean while language remains the ever-potent tool of conventional men. The real villainy is in the cultism that has grown up in the name of Freud, psychiatry, and medicine and which resists by every means, fair and foul, all efforts to inquire into its premises. Why blame Charcot and Freud for that!

[1] A review of Szasz, T.S. (1961). *The myth of mental illness: Foundations of a theory of personal conduct.* Harper. First published as Kelly, G.A. (1962). Muddles, myths, and medicine. *Contemporary Psychology, 7,* 363–365. Republished by permission of the American Psychological Association.
[2] *Contemporary Psychology*

Collected Papers of the Pioneer of Constructivist Psychology: George A. Kelly, First Edition. Edited by David A. Winter and Nick Reed.

But perhaps we are paying too much attention to Szasz's characters and not enough to his plot. He says that nineteenth century sociology expected doctors to separate malingerers from those who were genuinely ill. But what about the distress that leads to malingering? That is genuine too. Charcot and Freud saw malfunction in this kind of feeling, and, wisely or not, they choose to call it a form of illness. Otherwise, how could they, while remaining faithful to their role as physicians, afford to be caught treating persons so afflicted? The sociology of the twentieth century is not much different in this respect. Psychiatrists still think they are, or should be, doctors.

But if Charcot and Freud were trapped by the sociology of their times, how much more were their patients forced to make concessions to contemporary ontology and to the subject-predicate relationship in the language of deterministic materialism. Could a person point to his experience and say that was what hurt? Certainly not! To be taken seriously he must point to the thing that causes the experience. In communicating he must use the words that stand for objects, not the cry that arises out of his own personal existence. This is the game; this is the language. The rules are hard, fast, and "scientifically" enforced. The patients of a generation ago stuck to the rules as best they could. Charcot and Freud also stuck to the rules. Patients developed game strategies and skills. So did Charcot and Freud.

And now the Game of Doctor and Patient has become one of America's most popular pastimes. The price of admission is high and a lot of people cannot afford to participate as much as they would like. But liberal government subsidies will eventually give everyone who wants to play a chance to join in. It should be fun. Some say it is even more fun than sex, but that is hard to believe.

But to come back to Szasz, who does not actually carry things as far as the preceding paragraph suggests. The major part of his book has to do with models which may be used to replace the illness model in dealing with problems psychologically. First, there is language. We must distinguish protolanguage, a pre-logical language form, from language proper, which includes object language and metalanguage. Protolanguage has to be understood in terms of semiotics. In dealing with hysteria, for example, it is particularly useful to be aware of a particular class of semiotics—iconic signs.

Here the author sets a task for himself. Having agreed with Susanne K. Langer that semantic analysis need not stop where discursive language leaves off he points out that "her work in this regard remained mostly programmatic." He says, "One of the purposes of this book is to implement this program by providing a *systematic semiotical analysis of a language-form hitherto regarded as purely expressive,* i.e., *the language of certain bodily signs.*" (The italics are Szasz's.)

Such an analysis gives a clue to the nature of psychotherapy and why "talking often helps people to cope with their problems in living." He says, "The transformation (for it cannot properly be called translation) of presentational symbols in conventional signs (ordinary words), such as occurs in the course of psychoanalysis and some forms of psychotherapy, is thus seen as itself constituting a process of personality change ('treatment')." Nor does the author stop with an analysis of the psychotherapeutic process; he is concerned with personality change in general, and he extends his semiotic analysis to the development of the child through different language stages.

In the last two parts of his book the author sketches the theory of games, from the casuistic rule-following systems of the moralists to the logical games that mathematicians and scientists play. Having done so, he comes back to hysteria, the only disorder he discusses extensively in his book, and shows how it conforms to the game model.

In conclusion he points out that there is "no transcendentally valid (God-given) game," an insight that often leads Western man to the brink of despair. Yet man can choose "to rise to the challenge of the unceasing need to learn and relearn ... Some require a personal instructor for this; others do not."

119

Look Who's Talking[1]

If the reviewer had not made a prior commitment to *CP*[2] this book would have been laid aside after the preface and introduction had been scanned. That would have been a pity. As it turned out, every word was read.

In spite of the author's off-beat way of expressing himself he has come up with a delightful book about live persons caught up in the act of being themselves. Most psychiatrists, perhaps more keenly aware than he of what their profession expects of them, would have ground out a discourse about case histories, psychodynamics, or—nowadays—even such things as intervening variables. Yet with a bright-eyed Gallic sensitivity to what is childlike and what is tragic in our daily conversational exchanges, this man has contrived to produce a lucid paperback manual for group psychotherapists. Readers who insist that a book which is simple must also be trivial can save $3.95 by not buying this one.

The volume's title notwithstanding, *transactional analysis* is only one phase of the therapeutic program the author describes, and, at that, perhaps not the most important one. He starts off with *structural analysis*. There is a sense in which each of us speaks with the voices of three selves. There is my *Adult* self—capitalized because it is used as a proper noun—I, my *Adult*. Then, sometimes, it is I, my *Child* self, or what I retain of him, who speaks. Sometimes it is neither, for I am not altogether a unique being either as I was as a child or as I pretend to be as an adult, but I am also my *Parent*.

If I say to myself, as I sometimes do, "I cannot understand why 1 do such irrational things," I am probably identifying, at the moment, with myself as the *Adult* I, yet I, in the sense that I am still a certain child—just as I have always been—volunteered the deeds I momentarily regard as puzzling. If I say to myself, "Come now! You oughtn't to do such things," it may be I, my *Parent*, who is sounding off. And if I say to myself, "I am fully aware of the futility of such acts," it may be I, the *Adult*, standing up to my two other selves—the *Child* who reached for what he wanted, and the *Parent* who disapproves of such goings-on.

Normally, one keeps the initiative in the hands of his *Adult*, although both *Parent* and *Child* have something to contribute to the full life and should not be *decommissioned*. The first step in Berne's psychotherapy program is to help the person analyze his structure so that he is in no doubt about which of his selves says what. This structural analysis has, in fact, three ad interim functions; to *decontaminate* the *Adul*t of *Child* and *Paren*t mannerisms, to define boundaries between the three, and to stabilize the situation so that the Adult can maintain a minimum of social control.

Now comes the next step—*transactional analysis*—but before we get involved with that perhaps we should say that what Berne describes as *Child*, *Adult*, and *Parent* are not equivalents of *Id*, *Ego*, and *Super-Ego*, but are all three *ego states*. Besides, they are not intended as psychodynamic abstractions, for the term, *Child* refers not to what may be childish in one's personality but to what he actually was as a child and still is. His *Parent*, similarly, refers to what his parent actually was and what there is of that particular parent that sticks with him. The terms refer to particulars, not to generalities labeled as traits.

Things begin to get interesting in Berne's groups when the participants start to realize whose *Child* is talking to whose *Parent*, and when they can tell the moment a person shifts the initiative to one of his other selves. During this phase the therapist does not necessarily confine his participation to that of his *Adult*. In advanced transactions he may invoke his own *Child* and invite a *Child-to-Child* interplay between himself and another member of the group.

It is at this stage that participants begin to understand which selves are involved in their long-term relations with others. An interpersonal relationship based entirely on transactions between one person's *Child* and another's *Adult* is not likely to last indefinitely, unless, I suppose, the *Child* is a patient and the *Adult*, if adult he is, is a well-paid therapist. Transactions can get crossed, too. For example, one person's *Adult* may address another's *Adult* but get a response addressed from the other's *Parent* to his *Child*. This does not make for a comfortable relationship at any age.

[1] Review of Berne, E. (1961). *Transactional analysis in psychotherapy: A systematic individual and social psychiatry*. Grove Press. First published as Kelly, G.A. (1963). Look who's talking. *Contemporary Psychology, 8*, 189–190. Republished by permission of the American Psychological Association.

[2] Editors' note: *Contemporary Psychology*.

Collected Papers of the Pioneer of Constructivist Psychology: George A. Kelly, First Edition. Edited by David A. Winter and Nick Reed.

But if *transactional analysis* is interesting, then the fun really starts when *games analysis* gets underway. Games such as *Wooden Leg*, *Run in My Stocking*, *Let's You and Him Fight*, *PTA*, *Ain't It Awful*, *Yes... But*, and *Rapo* ("Whaddya mean, I seduced you!") are widely played and group psychotherapy nails them for what they are.

Finally, there is *script analysis* and *relationship analysis*. Scripts are made up of sequences of scenes and the person with the script acts as his own casting director. The show goes on the road with repeated performances, although box office receipts are not always encouraging. Husbands who don't play their parts according to the script are likely to be dismissed from the cast. So are wives. Group psychotherapy, if successful, helps one abandon a bad script and improve his repertory.

This book is important not only because it has something to say, but also because group psychotherapy is probably the only form of intensive treatment that is economically practical for society's large-scale mental health efforts. Systematic approaches to group psychotherapy have been slow in developing. But Berne has devised a way of programming group efforts that makes a lot of sense.

A concluding note to the prospective reader: It would be a good idea to have an unabridged dictionary handy when reading this book. In spite of his ability to state the simple case, the author goes on a word binge every now and then. And when he does he comes up with some whoppers.

120

Clinical Psychology Afoot and Abroad[1]

With the support of the Human Ecology Fund the author has compiled reports on clinical psychology from fifth-eight nations. In some cases the original documents he used were prepared by psychologists who are nationals of the respective countries; in others by visitors from abroad. Typically a country's resources are described very briefly under the headings: "general situation," "graduate university training," "supervised practicum experience," "professional roles" of clinical psychologists, "emerging trends," and, of course, the inevitable "relations with psychiatry." In some instances, however—e.g., The Cameroons, Ecuador, and Vietnam—descriptions are limited to one paragraph.

The volume contains also a section listing educational facilities and financial assistance for graduate students in the United States, together with doctoral programs and internships approved by the American Psychological Association. Standards for approval of programs are cited.

While the accounts the author provides are sketchy and admittedly open to the suspected biases of his informants, they do offer a useful source of information for clinical psychologists who must know something of the settings in which their colleagues abroad are trained and must serve. One is impressed, in reading the accounts, with the variety of academic standards. The PhD, for example, appears in some countries to represent little more than the completion of an undergraduate major. Yet in others it is awarded only midway in a distinguished career. There are also similarities one might not expect or wish to find; for example, the incessant jostling between psychiatry and psychology, arising, perhaps, out of Western Society's current ambivalence toward realism and nominalism.

The past two decades have seen among psychologists a rapidly growing awareness of their international scientific position. This has not been an unpleasant position to contemplate. But now their professional position as well is beginning to take shape. That may not be so much fun. I suspect that David's effort describing the latter will prove to be an early and significant milestone in a development culminating in psychologists' bearing more responsibility for tomorrow's crowded and cantankerous society than many of them, at their present level of maturity, care to assume.

[1] Review of David, H.P. (1964). *International resources in clinical psychology*. McGraw-Hill. First published as Kelly, G.A. (1966). Clinical psychology afoot and abroad. *Contemporary Psychology, 11,* 20–22. Republished by permission of the American Psychological Association.

Collected Papers of the Pioneer of Constructivist Psychology: George A. Kelly, First Edition. Edited by David A. Winter and Nick Reed.

Section IX

Miscellaneous

How I spent my seventy-fifth birthday provides an illustration of Kelly's whimsical anticipations, and his writing ability, as a young adolescent.

Psychology versus fate is a witty tale about surreptitiously testing the intelligence of a potential fiancée.

Understandable psychology is an unpublished psychology textbook in which Kelly's skills in explaining psychological concepts in a clear and engaging way is very apparent. There are few hints of the particular psychology that Kelly was to go on to develop over 20 years later, although he does remark that "The problem of how things come to have meaning to us is one of the most interesting in the whole galaxy of psychology's half-answered questions' and that 'the dividing lines between action, cognition, and affection are very difficult to place."

How to read a psychological dictionary between the lines, which was almost certainly written by Kelly, contains typically witty redefinitions of a range of psychological terms.

Inductive trigonometry consists of sections of a programmed learning book with W.G. Warnock that was never published. Of more interest than the numerous examples of trigonometric problems is likely to be the advice provided to readers on study skills.

Notes on perceptual integration in the design of aircraft instrument panels, complete with cartoons by Kelly, was written while he worked for the U.S. Navy. Also from this period is *Design of Critical Difference Computer*, which presents a method of checking the reliability of the difference between two proportions.

Collected Papers of the Pioneer of Constructivist Psychology: George A. Kelly, First Edition. Edited by David A. Winter and Nick Reed.

121

How I Spent My Seventyfifth Birthday[1]

It was the eve of my seventyfifth birthday. My grandchildren swarmed about me by the dozens. The day had been an enjoyable one for all of the family except me.

My fifteenth grandchild came to me for a story. "Why do you want a story?" I asked "Well", said he, "I cannot explain why, I just want one."

By that time several grandchildren of various ages and calibers had caught the drift of our conversation and also begged for a story.

"I have forgotten all the stories I ever knew" I said. "And if I could remember them they would be too old-fashioned for you."

"Tell us about those queer people who used to ride around in automobiles," said grandchild number twentythree.

"Those people," said I, "who rode in automobiles, did not care to travel fast. One hundred miles per hour was a fair speed and they would often be contented with sixty miles. The noise of the auto was very unpleasant and made it necessary to talk above a whisper to be heard."

"How odd, how did people ever get anywhere if they traveled so slowly?" "They did not go much," I said. "Some were known to remain for days in one country and I knew a man who stayed throughout an entire week." "My, how tiresome" said number twentythree. "Yes, but those people did not know any better then." Our conversation was abruptly ended by a loud snore from the couch which reminded us that we had better go to bed and since our bedroom was in Mars, we started at once.

[1] Dated 1918. Published by permission of Jacqueline Aldridge.

Collected Papers of the Pioneer of Constructivist Psychology: George A. Kelly, First Edition. Edited by David A. Winter and Nick Reed.

122

Psychology versus *Fate*[1]

He was in love—both his ego and his id had been aware of it for quite a while, but he restrained his urge to propose—in the interests of future generations.

Was her I.Q. above suspicion? That was the question which haunted him night and day. He knew that he was himself a superior adult, having made that momentous discovery in the psychological laboratory at Moray House. What a risk to think of entrusting his future happiness to one whose intelligent quotient was, perhaps, a bare ninety, or even approaching moron level. Certainly she was pretty and looked intelligent, but he knew very well that the external aspect is no criterion of the inner soul.

At last, he devised a scheme though he had to admit it was by no means foolproof. *He would test her intelligence*—not openly of course, that was rather crude and might offend her—but with the aid of a Terman and his own common sense he would adapt and alter the questions, so that he might be able to make a rough estimate of her inherent abilities.

He ventured his first question on the golf course. His approach was subtle, but his opponent laid him a dead stymie. He began by reading aloud his outgoing score—"9, 6, 7, 6, 5, 8, 6, 8, 9," he read out, nonchalantly. "Could you repeat that backwards, Mary?" Mary gave him a glance of scorn. "If I had a score like that I would keep it dark," she said in withering tones. He froze—"Minus on that test, anyway, you little beast," he reflected inwardly.

But he had relented by the time they were eating ices in the Palais that night. He laughed softly as he chased the last remnant of his ice around the dish. "I heard rather an ingenious problem the other day," he remarked casually. "Suppose the dish were a round field and I had lost a ball in it, how would you set out to find it?" "That's easy," and Mary took firm hold of the spoon and performed the correct snake-like circular movements in the shortest possible time. "Now, where's the puzzle?" "The puzzle?—oh—er—well, I mean to say—you know—that's it—that just it."

"Are you trying to make a fool of me?" said Mary, as she swam off in the arms of another man.

He mopped his brow—he must take better care in future and plan his experiments more carefully. He had not expected a girl to be quite so ++ in that test. "If she could do *that*, she could do anything."

He determined to try only one other test that day. If she passed that satisfactorily he would then proceed to really searching questions. On the way home he would ask her some of the "What would you do's?"—they were topics quite suitable to such an occasion, he thought.

They had talked of many things on the way, but there had been no opportunity for his psychological investigation. Just as they reached Mary's house he asked desperately, "Mary, what would you do if I were to ask you a question and you weren't sure how you ought to answer?"

Mary stopped short and turned to him with a beaming face. "Why, John, you dear old goose!—don't be so shy about it, there's no *ought* about it at all. I would answer 'yes' right away, just as I am doing now! And mind I insist on a Church wedding—no dusty Registry offices for me!"

At any rate, he reflected afterwards in bed, such an answer showed that her intelligence must positively amount to genius.

[1] Published in *Moray House Magazine*, 1930, *XXIII*, 36–37 under the pseudonym Mongrel. Although it is not certain that it was written by Kelly, it seems very likely that it was since it was published at a time when he was studying at Moray House in Edinburgh and in an issue of the magazine that includes the following reference to him: "Mr. Kelly's lecture to the IIc women on American Schools was greatly appreciated. Mr. Kelly is adept in the use of 'that little human touch' " Republished by permission of Jacqueline Aldridge.

Collected Papers of the Pioneer of Constructivist Psychology: George A. Kelly, First Edition. Edited by David A. Winter and Nick Reed.

123

Understandable Psychology[1]

Chapter 1

On The Definition of Psychology

Since it is the customary thing to do we shall start our discussion by defining *psychology*. Of course, the psychologists may not agree with our definition but that will not disturb us for everyone knows that they rarely agree among themselves as to their own definitions. There is that thing about psychologists; they are always disagreeing!

The trouble is that so little is known about psychology nobody can prove he is right. Six blind men went to see an elephant; and you know what became of that! But we shall have to grab somewhere so let us grab the tail and be with those who go to the end of the matter.

The field of psychology comprises a series of half-solved problems. If, then, we simply must define this phonetic atrocity which is spelled with a "p" we can probably do no better than to say that *psychology is what the psychologists talk about*. Definitions are rather unsatisfactory matters anyhow. We believe that once one knows what the psychologists talk about he will no longer have a need of a definition.

For one thing, the psychologists are very much concerned about whether or not psychology is to be called a science. *A science*, you know, *is a body of knowledge built up upon exacting investigations*. Everyone agrees that it would be a very fine thing if all psychologists would adhere strictly to scientific methods but some of the fellows are a little "off color." Yes, psychology really should be called a science, if that means anything to us!

There are three principal questions which psychologists talk about; (1) *how does a person act*, (2) *how does a person know*, and (3) *how does a person feel*? Re-phrased these questions might read, (1) how can you classify a person's behavior, (2) how does a person become aware of things, and (3) how do emotions and sentiments affect a person?

Besides these three big problems which comprise the basis of all psychology there are the problems; *how do abnormal people get that way*, *how do people learn*, *how do people's minds grow*, *how do people's minds differ*, *how do people behave in groups*, and other questions involving the application of psychological principles.

Grasp these problems and you have psychology by the tail!

[1] Unpublished MS, Fort Hays Kansas State College, 1932. Published by permission of Jacqueline Aldridge. Several of the figures are missing.

Collected Papers of the Pioneer of Constructivist Psychology: George A. Kelly, First Edition. Edited by David A. Winter and Nick Reed.

Chapter 2

A Note About the Nervous System

Already most of us know that living bodies are comprised of cells. Some cells go to make up muscle, others to make up bone, and still others to make up various special kinds of body tissue. It is convenient to think of the nervous system as another one of the things that are constructed of cells. The cells of the nervous system are called *neurons*.

Neurons are, for the most part, laid end to end and form the links in an extremely complicated system of nerve chains. The curious thing about the way these cells fit together is that they do not touch each other where they meet. There is a little space between the end of one neuron and beginning of the next called the *synapse*. What happens in that space when messages start romping down the nerve chains is, as one can easily imagine, one of the problems which cause so much speculation. *Speculation* is a very good word for it too because the psychologists (and the physiologists too) have no very satisfactory solution for the problem.

Nevertheless this much is known; *nerve impulses*, or messages, are continually traveling along the nerve chains. Once an impulse arrives at a neuron it is supposed to go all through the neuron—nothing can hinder it—but when an impulse is to jump a gap (the correct term is *synapse*) there may be complicating factors. For one thing, some of these synapses are harder to jump across than others; again, a synapse may be harder to jump across at one instant than it was a moment before. The latter is what happens when the surgeon gives his patient an anesthetic; some of the important synapses become blocked so that no nerve message can get to the patient's brain to inform him of the pain.

Now this nervous system, as you have already guessed, is no more or less than a very complicated system of neuron chains with cross-links and knots, and, for the most part, appearing to end nowhere in particular. However some of the ends lie in muscles, glands, skin surfaces, and so on. These ends are of two kinds. Some of them are "beginning ends," ends from which a nerve impulse can start out to travel along to the different nerve chains. Others are ends indeed for with them impulses coming out of the net-work must stop. This fact gives us an opportunity to use two big words, "*afferent*," a word relating to nerve conduction to the central net-work and "*efferent*," a word relating to nerve conduction away from the central net-work.

Suppose Jimmy's teacher does sit on the tack he has carefully prepared for her. The point of the tack is sensed by an *end-organ* which sets off an afferent nervous impulse (message) into the net-work of nerve chains which comprises the spinal cord and the brain. Within a very brief interval of time an efferent impulse comes out again, bouncing from neuron to neuron across synapses at the rate of four hundred feet per second, and goes to certain muscles—the ones used in getting Teacher off the pin!

Suppose Jimmy's teacher does sit on the pin...

That is the way the nervous system works!

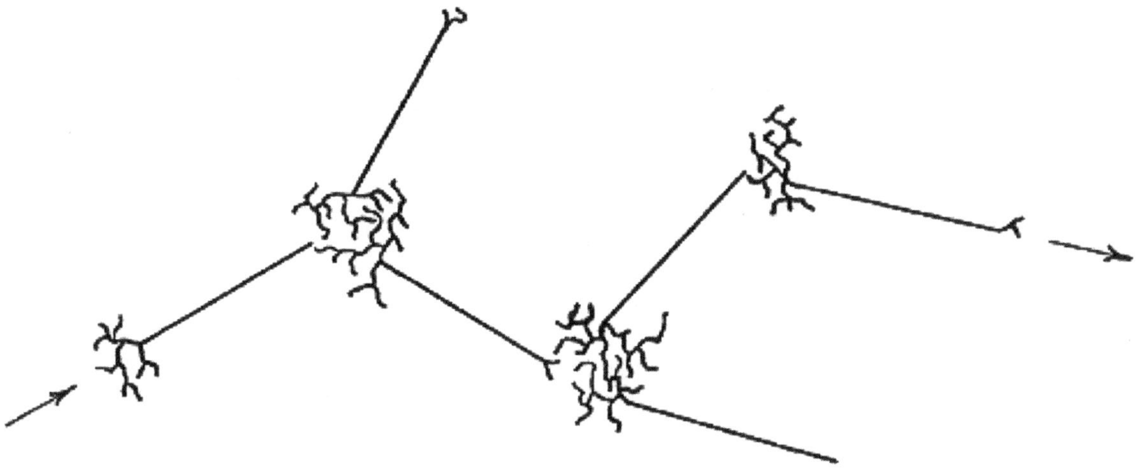

Chapter 3

Something One Ought to Know About Kinds of Nervous Systems

The psychologist, like the rest of us, is inclined, upon attempting to treat a matter which he does not understand, to divide the question up, name the different parts (usually with big names) and then claim intimate back-door acquaintance with the whole matter. It is one thing to know the parts of the nervous system and quite another to know how it works. Let us not fool ourselves; our task at the present is no more than to present a description of the kinds of nervous systems. Later we shall take up the more important task of describing how the nervous system works.

Take the nervous system of a flea. A flea's nervous system is not nearly as big or as complicated as that of a man. Man has all the nervous system that a flea has and a great deal more beside. As a general rule the more complex the nervous system the more complex and intelligent the behavior of the animal who possesses it. While this is a helpful rule to know (because it shows that a man is more intelligent than a flea) one must understand that it applies only between kinds of animals and not between animals of the same kind. A dog with a particularly large brain may be no more intelligent than a dog with an average sized brain. A man who has a brain of 2000 grams is not necessarily more intelligent than a man who has a normally sized brain (1400 grams). The brain of Anatole France, the great novelist, weighed far less than the average; the brain of Goethe, the German scholar, weighed far more. However, when it comes to a brain weighing more than 2000 grams or less than 900 grams the possessor is likely to be feebleminded.

Sizes of brains and nervous systems are not nearly as important as complicatednesses. A cat-fish has a larger brain than a humming-bird, but not such a complicated one, nor is the cat-fish as intelligent as the humming-bird. A dog, having a rather complicated nervous system, is more intelligent than a cray-fish which has a much simpler nervous system.

One may roughly divide the animal kingdom into seven groups according to the amount of nervous system involved. (1) Some animals have no nervous system at all. They move about but quite automatically. The sponge is an example. (2) Then there is a group of animals who have only the beginnings of a nervous system—just neurons but no synapses. A nervous impulse just goes from the end of one neuron to the other and that is all there is to it; there is no other place for it to go. The sea anemone is an example of this *asynaptic level.* (3) There is the *ganglionated cord level* of nervous system such as that of the cray-fish. In this level there are neurons and synapses and nerves to and from the different parts of the body. At the center of the nerve net is a slight trace of a centralized mass of neurons. They are somewhat bunched into two rows, one on either side of the body. The bunches are called *ganglia*. Now it may be surprising to learn that man has a ganglionated cord level of nervous system, but it is true. Right down on either side of the back bone are bunches of ganglia arranged like knotted cords. These, together with the system of nerves to which they are connected, comprise man's *autonomic nervous system*. The function of this system, as the name implies, is of a rather low order—the operation is practically the same every time the system is set going. Fortunately, man possesses other nervous systems superimposed upon this one, else our lives would be largely matters of eating, sleeping and getting angry. (4) Next above this is the *spinal cord level* represented by the amphioxus. Here are to be found the same ganglia with the addition of a string of neurons arranged in a somewhat more complicated fashion and located between the two spinal ganglia. This new addition to the nervous system represents the beginning of a spinal cord. Now the important thing to remember is that each time we find a new grouping of the neurons such as this spinal cord the new group is the principal authority on what the animal does. In the amphioxus the highest executive authority resides in the newly acquired spinal cord. (5) The next level is represented by the birds and reptiles. The newly added portion is a little knob on the front (*anterior*) end of the spinal cord. The accretion is called the mid-brain and this level of nervous system is called the *mid-brain level.* (6) Mammals, that is to say all animals which carry their young inside their bodies until the time of birth, have a brain much similar to man's. They have the mid-brain of the birds and reptiles plus a superimposed cortex. This represents the *primary cortical level.* (7) Man's brain has one thing more—a large bulge near the top of the forehead which has been called an associational area, and two bulges, one above either ear. In these newly acquired areas most of the heavy thinking is supposed to take place.

One thing more is significant; the brains of the last three types of animals, birds and reptiles, mammals and man, are partly divided through the middle longitudinally. The two halves of *cerebral cortex* (surface of the part of the brain called the *cerebrum*) are called *hemispheres.* The left hemisphere is principally connected to the right side of the body and the right hemisphere is principally connected to the left side of the body.

Now the important thing about this chapter is the fact that the new parts of the nervous system are in control of the older parts and that the higher the controlling part the more complicated is the nervous system and the more intelligent is the animal's behavior.

Knowing these few elementary facts about the nervous system we may turn our attention to psychology proper.

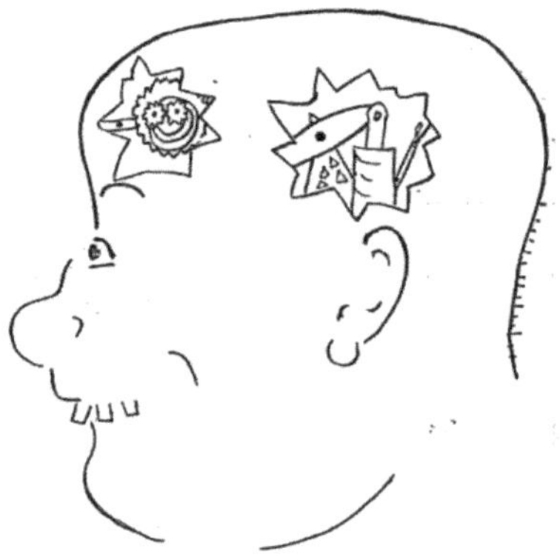

In these new areas most of the heavy thinking is supposed to take place.

Chapter 4

Introducing the First Great Psychological Problem: "How Does a Person Act?"

How does a person act? This may appear to be a very simple question and quite out of place in any serious discussion of psychology. Our best defense is that this is not intended to be a particularly solemn discussion. But, you will insist, is it not quite obvious that the way a person behaves depends entirely upon the character of the person and the circumstances into which he has been placed? To be sure, each person is somewhat different from every other person who ever lived; there is such a thing as individuality, and furthermore each situation that one may find himself projected into is like no other situation which ever existed. Adolf Spoonerheim is certainly an individual entirely different from Jackie O'Leary and the Spoonerheim lawn is not like the O'Leary alley. One may be tempted to assert that these two boys act in no way alike, *but they do*!

James eats; so does Jackie! James gets angry; so does Jackie! James blinks his eyes; so does Jackie! It is entirely a matter of viewpoint. Looking at the problem of *action* in a broad way it may be seen that all people act very much alike indeed, in fact, all the higher animals act very much alike. The biggest differences in the actions of animals are those between animals who have simple nervous systems and those who have complex nervous systems. While at this point we shall consider all forms of animal behavior as essentially similar; later we shall consider the matter of how people differ from each other or the problem which is known to psychologists as the problem of *individual differences.*

Now there are many different ways of classifying action. One could make the dichotomy, *voluntary* and *involuntary.* Again one might say that all action is either *hereditary* or *acquired*, and then present a discussion of heredity *versus* environment just as the Friday Night Literary Society used to do at the school house. One might use the classification, *reflexive*, *instinctive*, *voluntary*, the reflexive action being something like the beating of the heart, or the peristaltic motion of the intestines during digestion; the instinctive action being something like crying or running away when we are afraid; and the voluntary action being anything that we do intentionally. There are many other ways of classifying *action.* Nearly every psychologist has his own pet classification, and so let us play psychologist and set forth our own. Ours will be much like the common classifications in use at the present time.

James Whipplespoonerheim is a different individual from Jackie O'Leary.

Let us say that there are five general types of action as follows:

1 tropistic action
2 reflexive action
3 impulsive action
4 voluntary action
5 purposive action

Those are such nice little words that we shall have to take up one at a time.

Chapter 5

Tropistic Action

On the border-line between the vegetable and animal kingdoms is probably to be found the very lowest and simplest kind of action. It is called *tropism.* In the plant certain parts (the roots) are *geotropic*; that is to say, their action is in the direction of the ground. Other parts are *phototropic*, that is to say, they turn toward the light. Some small animals carry out tropistic actions of various sorts. An animal which is positively phototropic will, when it has to make a choice between two paths, choose the one which leads toward the light. An animal which is negatively phototropic will choose the path which leads away from the light. Many insects are positively phototropic and on a summer night one can see them wheeling madly about the street lamps. To some extent a very young child is positively phototropic; he will follow with his eyes and perhaps reach for a lighted object. Later the amorous youth may seek dimly lit paths—but that is not tropism.

Let us say that the following are the characteristics of tropistic action: The pattern of the response is unitary. By that we simply mean that in a tropism there is one and only one way (or pattern) in which the action (or response) can take place. The animal either turns toward the light or does not. The plant root either turns toward the ground or does not. There is only one alternative form of behavior. Another point is that the tropistic action is a very simple affair. It is no more than a turning of the body toward or away from something. Anything more than that is a different kind of action. Let us say that the *pattern* is very simple. Again, in most cases, the tendency to act in a tropistic manner is very deeply seated and is hard to change. A fourth point is that the tendency to act tropistically is very definitely a neural affair—that is, it is there because of the very arrangement of the nervous system. The last point is that consciousness does not have much to do with it. Thinking about it does not make any difference, in fact; when we act tropistically we may never be conscious of the act at all.

Now there are five characteristics of the tropism. We shall see how they contrast with the characteristics of each of the other kinds of action. Then when we have finished, we can sum it all up in a table.

Chapter 6

Reflexive Action

Now cross your legs and with the edge of your hand strike just below the knee cap of the upper leg. You will likely make a sudden kick which you cannot control. The action which you have seen is probably the most frequently demonstrated form of reflex—the *patellar reflex*. The *Achilles reflex*, a similar *skeletal* reflex, is elicited by striking the Achilles tendon when the toe of the foot has been drawn upward.

If you direct a beam from a flashlight into your friend's eyes his pupils will grow smaller. This *pupillary reflex* is a simple automatic form of action which is valuable in protecting his eyes from bright lights.

There are a great many examples of reflexes; the beating of the heart, the expulsion and inhalation of air by the lungs when stimulated by carbon dioxide, swallowing when food becomes thrust toward the back of the mouth, sneezing, coughing, and winking. All these are reflexes when they are not intentionally done.

If one were to make a classification of reflexes he might select any number of characteristics as the basis of distinction. There are *simple* reflexes. The simple reflex is one which takes place when the nerve impulse goes from the *receptor* or *end-organ* (the place where the stimulus is applied) into some central part of the nervous system and then out again through just one efferent nerve or chain of neurons to the *effector* (the organ of action).

We may call the reflex *compound* if the impulse comes out in two or more places. Then again we might speak of *allied* reflexes, meaning a kind of compound reflexes in which the different impulses come out to effectors which work in harmony with each other. We might call reflexes *antagonistic* if the impulses come out to muscles which oppose each other. There are *alternating* reflexes; when one walks the right foot is lifted up and forward quite automatically as soon as the left foot touches the ground.

Not all reflexes are the actions of muscles. There are in the human body a great number of glands—*salivary* glands, *intestinal* glands, *reproductive* glands and *ductless* or *endocrine* glands. The endocrine glands secrete the fluids which they produce right back into the blood; the other glands, the ones which have little tubes or *ducts*, secrete their products into the mouth, intestinal tract, or wherever their particular ducts lead. Now some reflexes are simply a matter of the activity of the glands. When you think of delicious pie topped off with a liberal helping of ice cream your mouth waters. That is a glandular reflex.

There is a term used in this connection with which we should all be familiar. While it does not appear in psychological literature as frequently as at one time it still describes the basic concept in many systems of psychology. The term is *reflex arc* and while it has to do with reflexes it appears to have nothing to do with arcs. The reflex arc is no more or less than the name applied to the route or path which the nervous impulse takes in going from the receptor to the effector. It includes an afferent or *sensory* neuron, a connecting or *associational* neuron, and an efferent or *motor* neuron. The neural path in the case of the reflex is supposed to be very short; in other words, the impulse may be routed back upon reaching the spinal cord without bothering to go up to the cortex or higher brain. Now here we have a little controversy on our hands. Some psychologists are beginning to say that it is not quite fair to speak of a reflex arc in this way for the impulse, to a certain extent, goes all through the nervous system. To be sure it may reach the effector before it reaches the cortex but that does not mean that the cortex had nothing to do with the affair. It is pointed out that the cortex exercizes a continual vigilance over the lower nervous centers and controls their actions by predisposing them to function in various ways. This new view of the activity of the nervous system is called the *mass response theory* as opposed to the *reflex arc* or traditional theory.

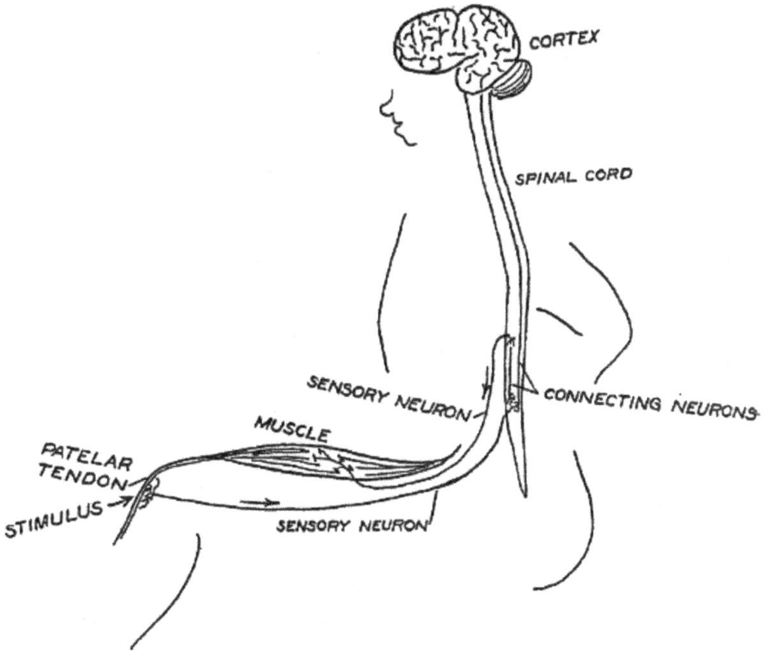

The manner in which impulses run through the nervous system is really a subject in neurology and not properly a concern of psychology. However, if the psychologist waited for other scientists to develop their own fields before applying the results to his own he might be seriously handicapped. Rather he enquires into fields other than his own to find basic material upon which to found psychology. An example is to be seen in the foregoing account; the discussion of the reflex arc theory *versus* the mass response theory is really a neurological discussion, not a psychological one. To be purely psychological the issue should be confined to the mental aspect of the situation.

Now we have said that the tropism involves a unitary response but we cannot be so definite in the case of reflex. Let us say that as compared with the tropism the reflex involves a *specific tendency*. The saliva may not always flow at the sight of pumpkin pie but it usually does! In the case of the tropism we had a simple response pattern, just a matter of turning or orienting the body; now we have a little more complex affair, shall we say, *slightly complicated*. The peristaltic action of the oesophagus is slightly complicated for it involves a rather nice synchronization of the smooth muscles in the walls of that tract. Furthermore we may say of the reflex what we could not say of the tropism; it is *slightly modifiable*. We may teach ourselves not to cry when our chair slips out from under us although to a young child crying would be reflexive in such a situation. We may teach ourselves to refrain from winking when someone thrusts his hand toward our eyes. Again we say that the basic organization of the reflex, or the arrangement of it, is not entirely neural. The *set*, the predisposing factor, the attitude toward the matter in hand, the understood task, or, to use a nice German word, the *Aufgabe*, is partly a matter of the state of our mind, somewhat psychic, we might say. We will probably wink when the grape fruit misbehaves—it is in our nervous system to do so—but we may also wink partly because we know what it is to have grape fruit juice in the eye. Let us say the set of the reflex is *mostly neural*. And as for consciousness, in the case of the reflex it is rather characteristic to realize that we have acted reflexively after the affair is over. Consciousness is *successive*.

Now our kinds of action are fitting into a systematic scheme. See the outline at the end of Chapter 9.

Chapter 7

Impulsive Action

It is very difficult to draw hard and fast lines between the different kinds of action for the reason that there are so many border-line varieties. To put out our hands when going through a dark room may be a reflexive action, that is, a *specific tendency*, *slightly complicated*, *slightly modifiable*, with a set that is *mostly neural* and with consciousness playing a *successive role*; or it might be no more than a *general tendency*, *more complex than the reflex, considerably modifiable, with either a neural or a psychic set* and with consciousness *definitely consenting to the action*. Probably it is the latter kind of action; *impulsive* we shall call it. But suppose the end of the chair rocker connects with our left shin bone. We drop a remark—a more or less emphatic one. That is probably an impulsive action. We grasp the injured member. Is that an impulsive action? Well, it is difficult to say. The best guess is that it is reflexive because grasping a wounded member of the body is a very deep-seated kind of response, more so than putting out one's hand in the dark.

We drop a remark... That is probably an impulsive act

It should not be difficult to see that there are many bases for classifying action. Every now and then a psychologist pops up with an idea as to the distinguishing features upon the basis of which classification should be made but the whole matter is still an open issue.

In naming impulsive action as one of the principal kinds we deviate from the usual practice. Most psychologists include "instincts" in their classification. Now it is perfectly all right to talk about instincts, but the thing that sets them off from other kinds of action is the fact that they are *inherited*, not *learned.* Such a distinction is a biological one. Since we are making a *psychological* rather than a *biological* classification, we set off our kinds of action on the basis of *mental* characteristics. That does not keep us from saying that some kinds of impulsive action are determined before birth—are instinctive—and other kinds of impulsive action are determined by the environment—are acquired. But the principal psychological characteristic of such activities is their impulsiveness.

Making out lists of instincts has been more or less of a Sunday afternoon pastime among psychologists. Most psychologists who have any originality about them make out their own individual lists. Here are some samples of their efforts:

William McDougall, *Outline of Psychology*

1 The parental or protective instinct
2 The instinct of combat
3 The instinct of curiosity
4 The food-seeking instinct
5 The instinct of repulsion
6 The instinct of escape
7 The gregarious instinct
8 The instincts of self-assertion and submission
9 The mating instinct
10 The acquisitive instinct
11 The constructive instinct
12 The instinct of appeal
13 Other special instinctive tendencies which are more specific

E. L. Thorndike, *Educational Psychology*

1 Sensitivities
2 Attentiveness
3 Bodily control
4 Food, habitation
5 Fear, fighting

6 Social instincts, gregariousness
7 Manipulation
    Visualization
    Vocalization
8 Expression of emotions
9 Learning, remembering

R. S. Woodworth, *Psychology*

1 Responses to organic needs
    Thirst, hunger, breathing, heat and cold, shrinking from injury, crying, fatigue, sleep
2 Responses to other persons
    Herd or gregariousness
    Mating or sex
    Parental or mothering
3 Non-specific or play instincts
    Kicking, running, etc.
    Locomotion
    Vocalization
    Manipulation, exploration
    Laughter
    Fighting
    Self-assertion
    Submission, docility

H. C. Warren and L. Carmichael, *Elements of Human Psychology*

1 Nutritive
2 Reproductive
3 Defensive
4 Aggressive
5 Social
6 Individual development

James Drever

Innate Tendencies

I Appetitive
    A General
        1 Pleasure
        2 Pain
    B Specific
        1 Hunger
        2 Thirst
        3 Sleep
        4 Sex
        5 Nausea
II Indistinct
    A General
        1 Play
        2 Experimentation
        3 Imitation
        4 Sympathy
        5 Suggestibility

- B Specific
  - 1 Pure—probably they are very numerous, although difficult to distinguish and may perhaps be classified as:
    - a Reactions of adjustment and attention
    - b Reactions of prehension
    - c Reactions of locomotion
    - d Reactions of vocalization
  - 2 Emotional
    - a Fear
    - b Anger
    - c Hunting
    - d Acquisitive
    - e Curiosity
    - f Gregariousness
    - g Courtship
    - h Self-display
    - i Self-abasement
    - j Parental

Another classification almost universally used is that of *habit*. Habit is frequently placed opposite instinct—the one acquired, the other inherited. Then, there are some psychologists who say habit is simply made up of a chain of reflexes—that is a bunch of reflexes organized into a plan of action. You see there are all sorts of ways of classifying action.

Well, the psychological characteristic of most of these acts is impulsiveness, and as such we shall classify them. The question of to what extent they are inherited we shall not try to answer just now; it is a pretty "stiff" question.

Our table of action is growing. The plan or *pattern* of impulsive action is *more general* than either of those we have mentioned before. It is also *more complex* than either of the others. We can *change it considerably*. The set may be *either neural or psychic*; that is, either nervous or mental. And finally we may be conscious of the act right *at the time it is made*. That does not mean that we do the thing voluntarily, but it does mean at least that we *acquiesce* to it. See the end of Chapter 9.

Chapter 8

Voluntary Action

Now we come to a kind of action that is very easy to understand. Sometimes we do things intentionally but without any ulterior motive. We do not do them *impulsively* nor on the other hand have we any particular end in view. If there is an *impulsiveness* involved, we are not aware of it. If we have any particular purpose in mind, neither are we aware of that.

I decide to shift the position of my chair: I do it. Why I did it, I cannot tell. I do know this much; I did it intentionally and *voluntarily*. The act was neither *impulsive* nor *purposive*. It was just a voluntary act. Now a great many of the things we do are done just like that. We walk around the room intentionally but without any particular motive. We may eat a meal without any particular impulse and without any particular consideration for our purpose in doing so. We simply eat. That is a *voluntary* kind of action.

A voluntary action pattern represents a rather *vague tendency*. It may differ greatly from time to time. There is nothing particularly set about the plans of our voluntary acts. These plans may be *very complex*, involving many different muscles. Since such an act is voluntary, we can say that whatever tendency is present is *completely modifiable*; we change our plan of action at will. The *mind set* or *Aufgabe* is *mostly psychic*, with perhaps only a touch of the influence of our neural make-up involved. Most important of all is the fact that consciousness *precedes* the act. We know what we are going to do before we do it.

Chapter 9

Purposive Action

There are very few tropisms, there are more reflexes, the number of impulsive acts is limited, the voluntary acts of man are numerous, but the purposes of man are as innumerable as are the situations in which he finds himself. We can count off man's reflexes. We can attempt to list his impulsive acts. We can have considerable insight into his voluntary acts, even predict them, in many instances. But man's purposive acts are events about which we can do little but conjecture. We know of *no set pattern* for them. When they appear, they usually involve the most intricate series of movements. Their pattern is *ultra-complex*. Having no set pattern they are not only modifiable but perfectly *plastic*. The set or *Aufgabe* is entirely psychic, and consciousness not only precedes the act, but is the sole *determinant* of it. There is a purpose, an intentional plan of action all thought out, and the purposive act is the attempt to set the plan in motion. I may voluntarily shift my chair or my position without any particular end in view, but if I perform that act *for the purpose* of avoiding shadows on my paper and easing my eyes, I have made a purposive act.

Some purposive acts are comparatively simple and others are most remarkably complex. Adjusting my chair so the light will fall upon my paper is a purposive act, but not nearly as complicated as the act of preparing a lecture. Later on we shall see what a wide variation there is between individuals with regard to the complicatedness of their purposive acts. We shall see that some people are capable of acting far more purposefully than others. When we meet people of that sort, we call them *intelligent*.

Now so far about all we have done is define and classify terms, psychological terms. Have we said anything that will give one an insight into human nature? Alas, we have said very little. Psychology is the science of half-solved problems—its concepts are the things the psychologists talk about. However in every line of work, in every science, there is a "lingo," a "shop vocabulary," a group of terms. It is pretty hard to get on in a job unless we learn its shop talk. The same is true with regard to the psychologist's layout of terms. Here are the words we have studied so far. From now on we are going to use them freely.

57 varieties of terms and concepts you should understand:

1 nervous system.
2 neurons
3 synapse
4 nerve impulse
5 afferent
6 efferent
7 end-organ
8 ganglia
9 ganglionated cord level of nervous systems
10 autonomic nervous system
11 spinal cord level of nervous system
12 mid-brain
13 cortex
14 associational area
15 hemispheres
16 action
17 tropism, tropistic
18 positively photo-tropic, geotropic, etc.
19 "pattern of response is unitary"
20 "pattern is simple"
21 neural affair
22 reflexive action
23 patellar reflex
24 Achilles reflex
25 knee-jerk reflex
26 pupillary reflex
27 simple reflex
28 compound reflex
29 allied reflex
30 antagonistic reflex
31 alternating reflex
32 endocrine glands
33 glandular reflex
34 reflex arc
35 effector
36 receptor
37 reflex arc theory
38 mass response theory
39 specific tendency
40 reflex is slightly modifiable

41 set, *Aufgabe*
42 psychic
43 consciousness is successive
44 impulsive action
45 general tendency
46 instinct
47 habit
48 consciousness is acquiescent
49 voluntary action
50 vague tendency
51 mind-set
52 consciousness is precedent
53 purposive action
54 pattern is ultra-complex
55 purposive actions are plastic
56 consciousness is determinant
57 intelligent

This is the way our table of action looks when completed:

Action

Action	*Definiteness of pattern*	*Complexity of pattern*	*Modifiability of pattern*	*Set or* Aufgabe	*Relation of consciousness*
tropistic	unitary response	simple	practically unmodifiable	entirely neural	sub-conscious
reflexive	specific tendency	slightly complicated	slightly modifiable	mostly neural	successive
impulsive	general tendency	complex	considerably modifiable	either neural or psychic	acquiescent (contemporary)
voluntary	vague tendency	very complex	completely modifiable	mostly psychic	precedent
purposive	no tendency	ultra-complex	plastic	entirely psychic	determinant

Chapter 10

Introducing the Second Great Psychological Problem: "How Does a Person Know?"

At this moment you are undergoing an experience! That mass of physical matter which is *you* is becoming aware of the meaning of these printed lines. How in the world is it done?

"Why", you reply, "I *look* at this printed page, I *see* those black symbols there, and I *know* what they mean".

Yes, that analysis is essentially correct, and the whole process is a process of cognition and comprises an experience.

How does a person know?

Our first great psychological problem was *action*, and now our second great psychological problem is to be called *cognition*. These two great problems are the basic problems of psychology. Other problems which we shall study later are the specific problems of *applied psychology*.

There are three levels of cognition, and they are just as you stated them a moment ago, only in order to be perfectly correct and psychological we must call them by big names. Here are the names we shall use: (1) *sensation*, (2) *apprehension*, (3) *comprehension*. We shall devote a chapter to each of these topics.

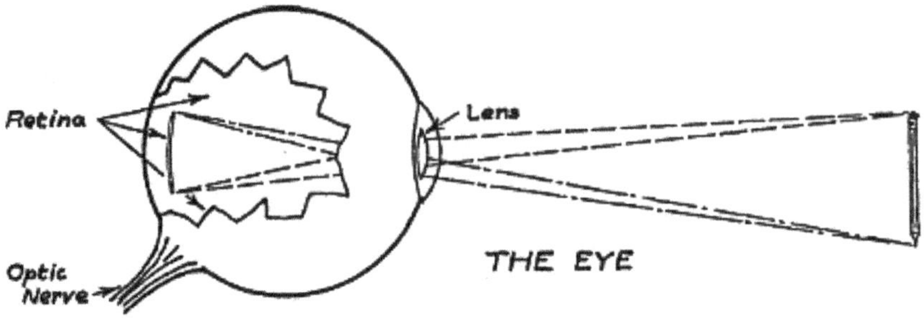

Chapter 11

The First Level of Cognition: Sensation

There are a number of organs of the body which are susceptible to different kinds of stimulation. Each one has its own specialty. The eye specializes in receiving light stimulations, the ear specializes in receiving sound stimulations, the nose is sensitive to the different chemical gases we call odors, and so on.

Most people think there are only five senses, but of course, strictly speaking, there are thousands of them. However, if one says there are five groups of senses, he is not far off. Most psychologists nowadays recognize about seven distinct groups of senses.

Here are the names of the seven groups of senses, the names of the organs in which they are aroused, and the kind of stimulation which arouses them.

Senses

Group Classification (Mode)	*Kind of Stimulation (Adequate Stimulus)*	*Location of the receiving mechanism (End Organs or Receptors)*	*Kinds of sensations received (Sensation)*
Visual (Seeing)	Light—ether waves which vary in length from about 16 millionths to 30 millionths of an inch	"Rods" and "cones" in the retina of the eye	Patterns of various forms, colors of various hues, saturations, and tints
Auditory (Hearing)	Sound—air pressure waves which vary in length from about 0.8 inch to 69 feet.	"Hair cells" in the cochlea of the ear	Patterns including rhythms, melodies, and pitch patterns (timbers) tones of various pitches, intensities, volumes, brightnesses, tonalities, and vocalities
Olfactory (Smelling)	Certain chemical gases and particles soluble in oil or water	"Spindles" in the mucous membrane of the nose	Odors of which the following are the fundamental ones: fragrant, fruity, putrid, spicy, resinous, burnt
Gustatory (Tasting)	Certain chemicals when dissolved by the action of the saliva	"Taste buds" in the mucous lining of the tongue and palate	Tastes of which the following are the fundamental ones: sour, sweet, bitter, salty
Cutaneous (Touching)	Contact with objects of various contours and temperatures	Various "corpuscles," "free nerve endings," and "hair roots" in the skin	Cold, warmth, pain, and pressure patterns, local signatures
Kinesthetic	Change in position and movement of parts of the body	"End plates" in the muscles	Muscular ache, tendinous strain articular friction
Organic	Mechanical and chemical condition existing in viscera (internal organs)	Exact nature of receiving mechanisms unknown	Pain, fatigue, sex, nausea, hunger, appetite, thirst, vascular and respiratory senses, and perhaps "feeling tone"

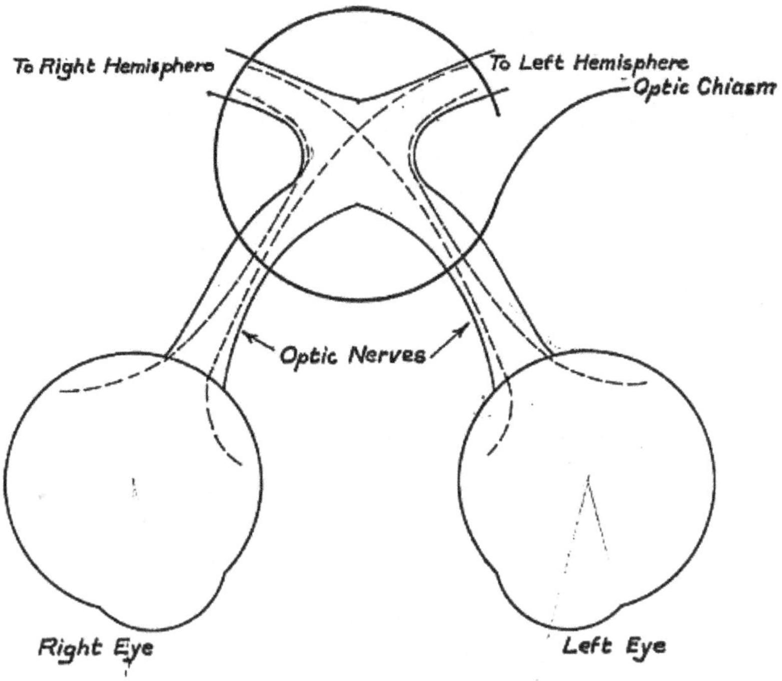

As far as we know the only way we can become aware of anything in this world about us is through one or more of these sense organs. Let's look them over one at a time.

The Eye and the Visual Sensations

Now it is one thing to look at something and quite another to really *see* it. You may be looking at these words, but if your mind is far afield you may not have any notion of what you are looking at. You may *sense* these patches of ink spots which make up a printed page, but that doesn't mean that you recognize them. In order to know what you are looking at, you have both to sense and to recognize or apprehend. (Stop! Read this last paragraph again—sense it, apprehend it, and then, be sure you comprehend what it means.) Now do you see why we call *sensation* the first of the three levels of cognition?

Before we begin talking about that group of sensations which we call *visual sensations*, let us take time briefly to describe the organ of vision—the eye. Imagine a hollow marble with a hole in it. In the hole a convex lens has been placed so that light from the outside is focused on the opposite wall on the interior side of the marble. That's about all there is to it, except that the eye is a little more delicate and complicated than a hollow marble with a lens stuck in one side of it. (See Figure 3.)

Probably the most important part of the eye from the standpoint of psychology is the *retina*, that part of the inside surface of the eye-ball upon which the rays of light from the outside are focused. From a point near the center of the retina the optic nerve, whose fibers are interlaced with the cells of the retina, leads out of the rear of the eyeball and back to the brain. (See Figure 3 again.)

Now look at Figure 4. This is a diagram of the eyes and optic nerves as you would see them if you looked down from above. Notice that the optic nerves apparently cross at the optic chiasm. Actually, however, they do not entirely cross; only the fibers from the inside (nasal) halves of the two retinas cross. (See dotted lines) From the optic chiasm the nerve fibers lead on back to the two *cerebral hemispheres* of the brain, one pair of fibers to the left hemisphere and the other to the right hemisphere. Now the cerebrum, you will remember, is the highest division of the brain, and the cortex, or outer surface of the cerebrum, is the highest authority in the nervous system. After the optic nerve fibers lead into the hemispheres, the path of the nervous impulses from the retinas is lost, but this we know, when a certain part of the cortex is removed, the individual become blind. From this we are led to believe that a certain area which is more or less indefinitely marked off is the *arrival platform* for visual sensations.

Figure 5 shows the brain and the location of the visual *arrival platform.*

So much for the eye and the related parts of the nervous system.

The important thing from the standpoint of psychology is the nature of the sensations, not the nervous system which conducts them to the brain. When the lens of the eye brings light to a focus on the retina, it causes an image of the object we are looking at to be formed on the retina. This image or picture has two kinds of characteristics; it has *pattern* and it has *color*. Now a pure visual sensation has *pattern* and *color*, too, and the pattern and color correspond quite closely to the picture on the retina. The pattern of a visual sensation may be in any sort of shape, but we don't know what that shape represents until we get to the second level of cognition. As far as sensation is concerned, why it's just another shape. So much for the pattern aspect of the visual sensation. We'll have more to say about patterns when we come to the second level of cognition— apprehension.

Now as to the color aspect of the visual sensation we have a great deal of information which has been compiled from the researches of many psychologists and physiologists. The sensation of color may, in turn, be divided up into three qualities: *hue*, *tint*, and *saturation*. By the hue quality we mean whether or not a color sensation is red, yellow, or green, etc. By the tint of a color sensation we mean whether or not we sense a light quality, a dark quality, or a medium quality, etc. By *saturation* is meant the "depth" or "strength" of a color. Thus we may look at a bit of colored paper and sense it as a square (pattern), blue (hue aspect of color), dark (tint aspect of color), and as a bit "weak" or "watery" (saturation aspect of color).

To illustrate these three aspects of color sensation pour some beet juice into a tumbler. There you have a color of a red hue. To decrease the saturation add water to the beet juice; to decrease both saturation and tint add black ink.

Now hues can be diagramed in a series around a circle like this. Red is placed opposite to green because red and green are complementary colors; in fact, we have arranged the names of the hues around the circumference so that complementary colors are opposite to each other. Thus yellow can be seen to be the complementary hue of blue, etc. Maybe you haven't heard of complementary hues; never mind, we'll make it all clear in a moment. Before we say any more about complementary colors, however, let us see how our diagram can be made to show saturation, too. (It has been shown that it is possible to get sensations of greater saturation with the following hues: red, yellow, green, and blue.) If we let the center of the circle represent a color of no saturation and no hue, the points on the circumference representing these four *primary hues* should be pushed out further from the center than other points and our diagram will look like this. Now if you mix a fairly highly saturated sensation of yellow (indicated by (1) in the diagram) and an equally highly saturated blue sensation (2) the resulting sensation is of no hue at all. You can illustrate it by drawing a line between (1) and (2), and the point midway along the line represents the resulting sensation. In this case the midpoint is in the center of the square and represents gray—a color with no hue or saturation. That is the reason yellow and blue are complementary hues—because they give gray when mixed in equal amounts. Likewise, and for the same reason, red and green, orange and greenish blue, etc. are complementary colors.

Suppose you mix the color sensation (1) with (3), what do you have? Well, you have a sensation of orange hue but of mediocre saturation. But, you may say, "I see very well how you diagram hue and saturation, but how is tint diagrammed?" In order to answer your question we must expand our diagram into a spindle-like affair, which is often called by the name "color pyramid." It is really a hectohedron. If a color is bright or "light" tint, we indicate it by a point in the hectohedron near the top, if a color is "dark", we indicate it in the lower half of the hectohedron. If you mix a light color sensation with a dark color sensation, the resulting sensation is of a medium tint. If you mix a very light gray or white with a very dark gray or black, the resultant sensation is a medium gray. The diagram is made pointed at the end to indicate the fact that with the very light or very dark colors it is impossible to have very saturated hue sensations. Furthermore the yellow and green sides of the hectohedron are tilted upwards to indicate the fact that the maximum saturation for these two hues is obtained when the tint is more nearly white. Taking into account all the different combinations of hue, saturation, and tint, there are about 35,000 different colors that can be distinguished by the ordinary human eye.

We have been talking about "mixing" colors. When we said that yellow and blue make gray when together, you may have made an emphatic vocal footnote; perhaps you threw this weighty volume into the waste-basket, in which case your act was in vain—for here we are again!

Of course, everybody who has dabbled with water-colors knows that when you mix yellow paint and blue paint, you get green paint. Here is the difference: it is one thing to mix paints and another to mix sensations. There is an interesting little experiment you can perform to show how color sensations can be mixed. If you want to try it, borrow your little brother's top and cut some discs of colored paper to fit the top of it, like this. Then fit two or more of the colored discs on the top so that only a sector of each disc is showing. Then spin the top and look down on it. If you have half of your top yellow and the other half blue—and your yellow and blue are of equal saturation, the resulting sensation will be one of gray.

There is another interesting experiment you can perform. It illustrates *negative after-sensations*. Lay one of your colored bits of paper in the center of a plain white sheet of writing paper. Put a dot in the center of your colored bit of paper, then look fixedly at the dot until you count 30; then look at a spot on the white paper. You will see a patch of color of the same shape as your colored paper except that it will not be of the same hue as your paper; rather it will be of a *complementary* hue. That is why it is called a *negative after-sensation*. You can also get a negative after-sensation in which black is substituted for white, and white for black. Look fixedly at the dot in the center of the accompanying picture, then look at the dot in the middle of the vacant picture frame at the right. Your negative after-sensation will fill the frame with a picture of a man prominent in public life. It is possible to get *positive after-sensations* too. They are of the same color as the original but do not last so long and are harder to get.

If you place a red card on a green background, it will look more saturated near the edges; likewise the green will look more saturated where it is next to the red. Then again if you look at green a while and then look at red, the red will appear more saturated than it ordinarily would. These two facts are true with any pair of complementary hues, also with black and white. There is still another thing we should know about visual sensations of color; it is *adaptation*. This is only a name for the fact that if you look fixedly at a hue for some time, it begins to lose its saturation and comes more and more to look like gray.

Perhaps you know someone who is color-blind. Probably your color-blind friend is a man, for there are about three times as many color-blind men as there are color-blind women. The most common kind of color-blindness is red-green blindness. People who are troubled in this way cannot distinguish between red and green hues—in other words they do not have red and green sensations. They can distinguish different *tints* of red or green but not the hues themselves. Then there are those who cannot distinguish between blue and yellow—and right here notice that red, green, blue, and yellow are the four colors which are primary.

There are a number of theories which attempt to explain color vision and color-blindness. One, the Ladd-Franklin theory, is that there are six kinds of *photo-chemical substances* in the retina of the eye, one corresponding to each of the primary color sensations, one for black, and one for white. The substances corresponding to red and green are scattered over just a small part of the retina—and indeed we cannot distinguish red from green unless we look almost directly at it. The yellow and blue chemical substances are distributed over a larger area, but the black-white substances are scattered over all the retina. To prove this point take a small bit of green paper about the size of the tip of your finger and hold it directly in front of you. Close one eye and them move the bit of paper over toward one side of your field of vision. You won't have to move it very far before it will lose all of its greenish tinge and become just a bright spot. If you try red, you will find that it loses its hue at about the same place as the green. If you try yellow or blue, you will find that you can distinguish their hues over a much greater part of your field of vision.

There are two more facts that are interesting. In the retina of the eye there are two kinds of cells, *rods* and *cones*. These cells are supposed to be directly affected by light. The cones are particularly sensitive to bright lights, and the rods are apparently used only when the light is very faint. These *rods* and *cones* are scattered over most of the retina except at the spot where the optic nerve comes into the eye-ball. At that place the retina is not sensitive to light; hence the name, *blind spot*. To illustrate this fact, close your left eye and look fixedly at the small cross in the accompanying diagram. Next, move the book slowly to and from you until you find a position at which the large black circle disappears. Yes, it will disappear all right!

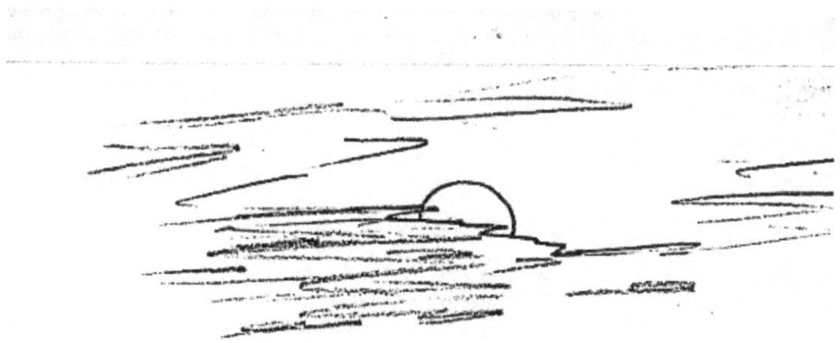

The other interesting fact is that at the *fovea* we have no *rods*. Now the fovea is a small spot in the middle of the retina immediately in line with the lens. At the fovea it is impossible to see very dimly lighted objects. When you pass the deserted cemetery on a dark night and you think you see a peculiar dark object straight in front of you, don't look directly at it! Look just a little to one side of it so the light will not fall on the fovea. If you do that, you may recognize your "ghost" as a clump of weeds. So much for visual sensation. See if you know what the following words mean; we have described them all in connection with visual sensations.

1 sensation
2 apprehension
3 comprehension
4 cognition
5 the seven groups of senses
6 retina
7 optic chiasm
8 optic nerve
9 cerebral hemispheres
10 arrival platform for visual sensations
11 pattern
12 color
13 hue, saturation, tint
14 complementary hues
15 primary hues
16 color pyramid (hectohedron)
17 color mixing
18 negative after-sensations
19 positive after-sensations
20 adaptation
21 kinds of color-blindness
22 Ladd-Franklin theory of color vision
23 photo-chemical substances
24 rods and cones
25 blind spot
26 fovea

The Ear and the Auditory Sensations

You'd never guess that the ear is the most complicated sense organ of the body; but it is—more complicated even than the eye. It consists of many winding passageways, some of them filled with salty water and lined with peculiar membranes. There are window-like openings, some of then closed with membranes or piston-like bones; there are spirals and circular canals and a labyrinth of nerves running this way and that. Small wonder is it that physiologists have found difficulty in locating the exact place where sound is changed into nervous impulse.

In the first place, we should know that sound waves are not in any way like light waves. Sound waves are vibrations in the air. If our sense of touch were delicate enough, we could feel the air rapidly beating against us whenever there was a loud sound. Look at the diagram of the ear; see where the air from the outside is admitted. Notice that it can go in no further than the *ear drum* (*tympanic membrane*). But this does not mean that the *ear drum* has anything to do with hearing; as a matter of fact it is not nearly so important as most people think. Just inside of the *ear drum* there are three small bones, *ossicles*, held together in a sort of tandem arrangement by little ligaments. Air vibrations beating against the ear drum jiggle these ossicles backward and forward. The third of the little bones thrusts its blunt end into the small *oval window* like the plunger in a squirt gun. Just inside the oval window is a labyrinthine-like series of cavities filled with liquid. There are two groups of these cavities: the *semi-circular canals* and the *cochlea*. The semi-circular canals are the organ for keeping our balance and have nothing to do with hearing. The organs of hearing are located in the cochlea, a spiral-like affair. The coiled tube which forms the cochlea has stretched across its interior two membranes which really divide the tube into three channels or canals. The upper-most canal leads directly from the oval window, continues to the apex of the cochlea, then doubles back and becomes the lower-most or descending canal. At the lower end of the descending canal is the *round window* which is closed by an elastic membrane (See diagram). Both of these canals are filled with perilymph, a salty liquid. The middle canal in the cochlea is called the *cochlear duct* and is filled with *endolymph* (see Figure 13). The cochlear duct is rather remotely connected with the three semi-circular canals which, too, are filled with *endolymph*.

Now look at Figure 14 which shows a cross-section of the tube which forms the cochlea. See the three channels or canals? Now look closely at the part marked *basilar membrane*. This membrane is really imbedded in a soft tissue. Do you see the *hair cells* pointing upwards toward the hood-like *tectorial membrane*? Well, those hair cells are the true sound receptors. They run nearly the entire length of the cochlear duct in five rows. Of course, in the diagram, you see only the end cell in each of these rows. Well, that's enough to say about the ear for the present. Let's say some psychological things for a change.

Take an *auditory sensation*—not an auditory apprehension just a simple sensation, an event occurring on the first level of cognition. Like a visual sensation this auditory sensation has a number of irreducible qualities. It has *pattern*, for one. You may wonder how a sound sensation has as one of its qualities, "pattern." Well, it has not only pattern but two kinds of pattern. Rhythm is one kind of pattern; it refers to the way in which sounds are "spaced out." Melody is another example of the same kind of pattern; it refers to the way in which sounds of different pitches are arranged in sequence. Rhythm and melody both may be called *time patterns* or *temporal* patterns. There are other kinds of temporal patterns. The second general type of pattern may be called "*pitch pattern*," although it may involve more than an arrangement of pitches. A better name might be "space patterns," although a critically minded psychologist would very quickly see that such a term is not very accurate. Well, let's not get ourselves "in" too deeply, let's just say that when you sound several different notes together, what you get, among other things, is a *pitch pattern*; and here is the important point—the so-called "quality" of a tone is really its pitch pattern, the way it has been fused with other higher tones, most of them one or more octaves above it. By listening carefully an expert can hear these infused high notes or *over-tones*. The tone of a violin is different from that of a piano, principally because its main or *fundamental tone* has combined with it a peculiar galaxy of over-tones; hence we say that a violin has its own peculiar *timber* or *pitch-pattern*.

Sound is really a jiggling of the air. If that jiggling occurs at a fairly uniform rate, it is called a *tone* and we get a *tone sensation*; if not, it's a *noise*. If the jiggling of the air is very rapid, we say that our tone or noise is very *high pitched*; if not, it is *low pitched*. Tone sensations cannot be gotten by the human ear if the jiggling rate or vibration rate is less than 16 a second or more than 17,000 a second. In this range there are about 11,000 pitches that can be distinguished by the human ear. If the jiggling of the air is very strong and violent, we usually say that the noise is *loud*, or *intense*.

There are probably other characteristics of the auditory sensations. It has been claimed that there is such a thing as *volume*, outside of *intensity* and *timber*. Then there are some psychologists who claim that some tones are *brighter* than others. Perhaps *brightness* is just the reverse of *volume*. Again there are some who say that auditory sensations have the quality of *tonality*, that all the *c's* on a piano have some peculiar characteristic in common which is not merely a matter of *pitch*. Likewise, all the *d's*, *e's*, *f's*, *etc.* have their own *tonalities*. But wait, there is still another quality suggested—*vocality*. Some say that certain notes have something in common with the vowels, which can't be explained in terms of any of the other qualities suggested. "Do, re, mi, fa, sol, la, ti, do" suggest the notes C, D, E, F, G, A, B, C, because of their *vowel qualities* or *vocality*. It has been suggested that perhaps some day it will be shown that vocality and tonality are the same quality or attribute.

Now let us see if we can't combine some of these qualities into a diagram like we did some of the qualities of visual sensations. The hectohedron we used for visual sensations is largely the work of a man by the name of Titchener. The diagram we will next use is largely the work of Ruckmick, one of Titchener's pupils. It is called "Ruckmick's Tonal Bell". Here it is with Ruckmick's own explanation.

Auditory sensations, then, have the following kinds of qualities:

1 *Temporal patterns* including rhythms and melodies
2 *Pitch patterns* or *Timbers*—what the musician calls "qualities"
3 *Pitches*
4 *Intensities* or *Loudnesses*
5 *Volumes* and their opposites, *Brightnesses*
6 *Tonalities* or *Vocalities*

Besides these terms, see if you recognize what these mean.

1 tympanic membrane
2 ossicles
3 oval window
4 round window
5 semi-circular canals
6 cochlea
7 perilymph
8 endolymph
9 cochlear duct
10 basilar membrane
11 hair cells
12 tectorial membrane
13 fundamental tone
14 overtone
15 tones

16 noises
17 Ruckmick's Tonal Bell

The Nostrils and the Olfactory Sensations

The organs for smell are located high up in the nasal cavities. They are little cells called "spindles," which are sensitive to certain chemical gases or chemicals soluble in oil or water. These spindles are embedded in the lining of the nostrils and form a direct connection between the nasal cavities and the *olfactory bulbs* of the brain which lie just on top of them. In the case of the *smell*, or *olfactory receptors* the connection with the brain is shorter than in the case of any of the other receptors.

Smell is not a very important sense in man, although it is probably more important than most people realize. Most of the differences in the "tastes" of foods are really a matter of smell. Frequently, olfactory sensations play a large part in our apprehensions, or even in our so-called "intuitions." "Intuitions" are really apprehensions which take place without our being conscious of the sense which brings them.

There are six primary types of odor sensations. All other odor sensations can be produced by combining two or four of certain of the stimuli which produce these six primary sensations. The primary olfactory sensations are:

1 ethereal
2 fragrant
3 burnt
4 foul
5 spicy
6 resinous

They can be arranged into a diagram in the following manner:

The Tongue and the Gustatory Sensations

The organs for taste are *taste buds* embedded in the surface of the tongue. Unless chemicals are partly dissolved they cannot reach the taste buds. Look at the figure and you will see why. There are only four primary kinds of taste sensations. They are *sweet*, *sour*, *bitter, salty*. Most of the differences in flavors of foods are matters either of smell or of general "feel" of the substances in the mouth. If you chop up raw onion into real fine particles so that you cannot "feel" its "grainy" quality in your month, then put a clothes-pin over your nose, you will find it very difficult to distinguish raw onion from many other foods.

The elementary tastes may be put into a tetrahedron as follows:

The Skin and the Cutaneous Sensations

There are four kinds of cutaneous sensations: *touch*, *warmth*, *cold*, and *pain*. It seems that the organs for these sensations are located in the skin; at least a number of tiny organs have been found there which seem to be related to these sensations. Just which organ goes with which sense hasn't been definitely determined yet. What we shall do is describe the organs briefly and tell what the purpose of each appears to be.

It has been fairly definitely established that the sensation of *pain* has no definite organ but rather is brought about by any stimulation which tends to destroy the nervous tissue. A sudden jab with a sharp pin will probably pinch or disturb one of the *free nerve endings* in the surface of the skin and cause a pain sensation. There are millions of these nerve endings in the skin and in other parts of the body. If you care to try it, you can locate spots on the back of your hand which are more sensitive to pain than others. Probably there are free nerve endings just under these spots.

The sensation of *touch* or *pressure* probably can be produced in two ways: either by bending one of the fine hairs which protrude from most parts of the body or by pressing the skin near one of the *Meissner corpuscles*. Around the roots of the body hairs there is wound the tiny fibers of nerves. Perhaps the bending of the hair causes it to act as a lever against one of these fibers thus stimulating it. On the other hand the Meissner corpuscles, too, have nerve fibers connected to them.

There are a number of other corpuscles in the skin. They are named after their respective discoverers. The *Ruffini Corpuscles* are most likely the warmth receptors. The *End Bulbs of Krause* are probably the cold receptors. The *Vater-Pacini Corpuscles* may be another kind of pressure receptor. Besides these there are the *Corpuscles of Merkel* and others.

You can discover the locations of some of these sense organs yourself. To discover the location of the *cold spots* take an ordinary lead pencil and move its point slowly across the back of your hand. Touch the surface of the skin very lightly as you go. At certain places you will get distinctly cool sensations. These are called the *cold spots*. To discover the location of the *warm spots* move the point of a slightly warmed curling iron lightly over the surface of the skin. The iron should be no more than a few degrees warmer than the skin itself. If you move a hot object over the skin, you will get a pain sensation as well as a warmth sensation. In cold spots on the skin, however, a hot object will give a sensation of biting cold. In fact the sensation of heat is caused by stimulating a warmth spot and a cold spot at the same time with a rather hot object. A very cold object may stimulate a *pain spot* and cause a sensation like that of burning heat.

Now it makes all the difference in the world what the temperature of the skin is when one is trying these experiments. If your skin is very warm, then the warm curling iron may not affect your warmth spots at all. If your skin is cold, then the pencil lead may not give a cool sensation at all. There is an old experiment to illustrate the importance of the temperature of the skin itself. If you hold one hand in a pan of very warm water and the other in a pan of very cold water until each becomes well adapted to the temperature, then put both hands into a pan of luke-warm water, the luke-warm water will seem warm to one hand and cool to the other.

There are other qualities of cutaneous sensations but just which qualities are primary and which qualities are combination qualities is not known. There are "bright pressures" and "dull pressures," "aches," "clear pains," "drags," and "pricks." The "tickle" and "itch" are probably fusions of certain qualities of the cutaneous group of sensations with certain qualities of another group of sensations which we have not yet discussed, the *kinesthetic* group. The quality of *local signature* in the cutaneous mode is particularly unique; by some quality distinction one can distinguish the locality of the body from which a sensation originates. One author has tentatively arranged a number of these sensations into the following diagram.

The Organs of Bodily Movement and the Kinesthetic Group of Sensations

There is a large group of rather indefinitely defined sensations which may roughly be grouped under the head of *kinesthetic*. Most of these sensations may be correctly called "muscle sensations," since they are concerned with the movements and tension of the muscles. Just how to classify these sensations has always been a problem for the psychologists. Perhaps the best thing for us to do here is to describe these sensations and their organs as far as they are known and not bother about putting them into a system.

In the striped muscles there are little *end-plates* imbedded among the fibers. From the end-plates there are nerve fibers leading out. There are also nerve fibers leading out of the tendons and joints. Presumably these endings correspond to the three elementary sensations of *muscular* ache, *tendinous* strain, and *articular friction*.

People sometimes speak of the "sense of balance" but the sense of bodily position or the sense of the change of bodily position is probably a blend of two or more of the elementary kinesthetic sensations together with sensations of the *organic* group. We have no separate sense of balance aside from other senses. However, there is a very important reflex mechanism which enables us automatically to keep our balance. We do not sense anything directly through this mechanism, but we do sense very definitely the muscular and internal changes which it brings about.

The receiving end of this mechanism is located in the *semi-circular canals* of the inner ear. The canals are three in number and are placed at right angles to each other in three different planes. The canals contain membrane tubes which are filled with endolymph and are surrounded by perilymph. The membrane tubes are lined with hair-like cells which sway in the wash of the endolymph. When the head is moved in any direction, these cells start a nerve impulse which results in a reflexive adjustment of the body or parts of it so as to maintain equilibrium. The actual movement of the head is probably recorded by similar hair-like cells in the *vestibule* or cavity into which the three semi-circular canals open.

There are a number of other reflex mechanisms in the body which have their own receiving organs but which do not directly give us any sensations. The only way we become aware of their activity is indirectly through the kinesthetic and organic sensations which are aroused when their reflexes start to operate.

The Viscera and the Organic Sensations

Of all the group of senses there is less concrete information available on the organic group. Men who have studied this group have resorted to a number of devices for investigating the sensations that are gotten with different kinds of internal stimulation. They have thrust tubes and electric heaters down the throat and into the rectum. There are probably two important sub-groups of organic sensations—the *thoracic* and the *abdominal*. In the thoracic group there are a number of *respiratory sensations* most of which can be analyzed into *pains* and *pressures*. However, it has been suggested that there is a sensation of *expansion* and its opposite, *stuffiness*, which is more than a matter of pressure and pain sensations. In the thoracic group we should include the *vascular* group of sensations, sensations of blood circulation, many of which can be reduced to sensations of *warmth*, *cold*, *pressure*, and *pain*. With the abdominal group of organic sensations we should include *digestive*, *excretory*, and *sexual* sensations, all of which can probably be reduced to the elementary sensations of *warmth*, *cold*, *pressure*, and *pain*.

Facts Applicable to All Sensations

All sensations have their peculiar *qualities* and their time of *duration*, their *intensity*, their *spatial* and *temporal patterns*, their *modalities*, and, in most cases, their *extensities*. To illustrate; the *qualities* of visual sensations are matters of color, the *qualities* of auditory sensations are matters of pitch, tonality, etc., the *qualities* of cutaneous sensations are matter of warmth, cold, pain, etc. Again it should not be hard to understand that a sensation has its own time of *duration* and its own degree of *intensity*. It is a little harder to explain the exact nature of *spatial* and *temporal patterns*. When a number of sensations of either the same or different qualities occur, at the same time, we sense their arrangement or spatial pattern. Likewise, if a number of sensations occur in a certain sequence or with different intervals between them, we sense their rhythm or melody—that is, their *temporal pattern*. Probably most important of all, nearly all sensations have their *modality*; we do not ordinarily confuse a visual sensation with an auditory sensation, although there are some people who have *synesthesia* and when they hear a note see it as a color. The mode of an olfactory sensation is distinct from the mode of kinesthetic sensation, although it may be confused with a gustatory sensation. Some of the groups of sensations have *extensity*. For instance, a visual sensation may represent a broad expanse in the field of vision. Some psychologists believe that the volume aspect of the auditory sensation is really a matter of extensity.

In connection with our discussion of visual sensations we described *after-sensations*. Now after-sensations are not confined to the visual mode. We can, under certain circumstances, have auditory, cutaneous, and other modes of after-sensations. However, the after-sensations in the visual mode are the most easily obtained.

Closely related to after-sensations is the fact that if a sensation is elicited time after time without giving the sense organ an opportunity to rest, the intensity of the sensation becomes weaker and weaker in relation to the intensity of the stimulus. Look steadily at a piece of red paper, and within a few seconds the sensation you get is a markedly less saturated red. *Adaptation* of this sort may be obtained in almost any sense mode. Adaptation appears to be related to negative after-sensation in the visual mode because as soon as one's red sensation becomes partially adapted, he may look away and see a green patch taking the place of the red sensation. Remember that green is the complementary hue of red. *Sensory adaptation* is another fact which is generally applicable to all sensations.

There is one further important fact in connection with sensations. Some sensations may *blend* with each other, while others may be completely *fused* with each other. Auditory pitch sensations may so completely blend with each other as to be recognized as one sensation, but they can never completely lose their identity as sensations. In fact a skilled observer, such as an orchestra director, can isolate the component sensations in a most intricately blended harmony. On the other hand visual color sensations not only *blend* but they completely *fuse* in the case of the whirling top. You can make red and green fuse into a gray and also make yellow and blue fuse into the same gray. In the fusions which are thus produced it is impossible to isolate the component sensations; in fact, one cannot tell which gray is made up of red and green and which is made up of blue and yellow. Blends may take place between sensations of different modes, but it is doubtful if a fusion can take place between two sensations of different modes.

At this point you should understand the meaning of the following terms:

1 olfactory
2 spindles
3 olfactory bulbs
4 the six primary types of olfactory sensations
5 the olfactory prism
6 gustatory
7 the taste buds
8 the four primary types of gustatory sensations
9 the gustatory tetrahedron
10 cutaneous
11 the four kinds of cutaneous sensations
12 free nerve endings
13 Meissner corpuscles
14 Ruffini corpuscles
15 End bulbs of Krause
16 Vater-Pacini corpuscles
17 cold spots
18 warm spots
19 pain spots
20 the touch pyramid
21 kinesthetic
22 end plates
23 the three elementary kinesthetic sensations
24 semi-circular canals
25 vestibule
26 viscera
27 organic
28 thoracic

29 abdominal
30 respiratory sensations
31 expansion and stuffiness
32 vascular
33 digestive, excretory, and sexual sensations
34 duration
35 intensity
36 spatial and temporal patterns
37 modality
38 synesthesia
39 extensity
40 after-sensations
41 blend
42 fuse

Chapter 12

The Second Level of Cognition—Apprehension

Now we know how events in this world about us are recorded by our sense organs. We also know something of the sense organs which record changes occurring within the body itself. It is one thing to *sense* these events, but it requires something more to *apprehend* them. The process of apprehending belongs to the second level of cognition.

There are two rather important facts about the way the human organism works. We can express them as two laws. They are: (1) *The Law of Continuity: Any process of the organism tends to follow a continuous temporal course.* (2) *The Law of Differentiation: The course of any process of the organism is in the direction of differentiation.* These laws need a bit of explaining.

The Law of Continuity calls attention to the fact that mental processes tend to be continuous even though something may occur to deflect them from their logical course. If you are reading a book, as you are now, certain mental processes are going on. If you stop reading the book, those processes will continue to carry out a more or less logical chain of thought unless something draws your attention elsewhere. Now that doesn't mean that you keep thinking about the same thing until some other thing happens to take your attention away from it, no, not at all: it means that all your thoughts tend to be connected no matter what they are. You are reading a book, the telephone rings, you answer it, carry on a conversation, return to your book, your mind wanders away from what you are reading; well, it's all one great big continuous process from beginning to end—that is what our mind is. Mind is not a thing; it is a course of events. Your mind is not your brain, it is the *pattern* of your cognitive processes, and since any process of the organism tends to follow a continuous temporal course that pattern is a continuous one. The experiences of life retrace and enhance that pattern, giving it new form as each day passes. Such is mind, and as the great psychologist James said of consciousness the chief thing about it is that it *goes on*.

James made another apt remark which bears upon our second law. He said that the child is born into a world where all is "one big, blooming, buzzing confusion." As one's life goes on, he begins to single out certain aspects from that big mass of experience, he *differentiates*. The better able a person is to single out important facts from the mass of sensory data at his disposal the better able he is to face life with all of its complexity. You may say that some mental processes go to "build up ideas," but no, we do not "build up ideas;" we *extract* them. Mental process is a discriminating process, a "tearing apart" process; it is an analytic rather than a synthetic process. Sometimes by mental process we learn to distinguish certain principles or forms which appear in a large number of situations, but even that is not a "building up" process. The Law of Differentiation is really a fundamental law. There are other laws of fundamental importance in psychology; there is probably one that governs the process by which things come to have meaning to us, but for the present our limited knowledge makes it impossible to make an exact statement of it or of other fundamental laws.

Now it is possible for the organism, or at least parts of it, to pursue somewhat separate processes. These processes cannot be entirely distinct and individual, however. For instance, it has long been known that if a person glances for a moment at a handful of marbles lying on the table, he is able to attend to or notice as many as five or six of them at the same time. That means that a person may really apprehend about six of such items simultaneously, or to state the same fact in psychological terms, the process of the organism may be partially subdivided into six relatively independent courses. Sometimes this is spoken of as the "limited span of apprehension." But it all depends upon how similar the mental courses are as to how many can be followed at the same time. Try reading the following two stories at the same time and you will see that it is extremely difficult to divide your apprehending process into even so few as two courses when these two courses are not in any way consistent with each other.

John and Mary had a little red wagon which they played
In a narrow street situated in the less respectable
with every day. John used to pull the wagon while Mary rode,
quarter of the city of Edinburgh there is an old stone house
and then Mary would pull John. However, John was so much
which has become a popular show place of the town. We paused
heavier than Mary that she could not pull him as far as he
there one foggy winter morning and delved into the damp book-
could pull her. One day they started out for the woods to
shelves that surround the place. The shop keeper's assistant
pick berries. On the way out John let Mary ride in the wagon
came to wait on us, but in response to our inquiries called the
while he tugged away. When they got to the woods, they found
shop keeper himself, a man dressed in badly worn but neatly
ever so many berries and filled their wagon full. So full
kept clothes. We bought a set of volumes on "The London Poor"
did they fill their wagon that it took both of them pulling with
upon his recommendation, while outside the thick fog dripped off
all of their strength to get their load back home, and John
the eves of the house where John Knox's stern shadow still
got no ride at all.
lurks.

As you read the above stories, it is not difficult to *look* at both of them at the same time; the difficulty comes when you try to *recognize* both of them at the same time. To say the same thing in psychological terms, the sensing process is inclusive enough but the apprehending process, being a higher process, differentiates and follows only a limited number of courses. The higher the process involved the more finely are things differentiated and the more limited is the span of apprehension. The Law of Differentiation accounts for the limited span of apprehension.

As you read those stories, you soon notice that once you have read a phrase of one story, it is much easier and more natural for you to go right on and apprehend what comes next in the same story than to change the course of your apprehension and consider a phrase from the other story. This is where your Law of Continuity comes in; any process of the organism tends to follow a continuous temporal course. Since the course of apprehension is a more specific course than the course of sensation, that law just made you want to go on *apprehending* the first story even though you begun to *sense* the second story.

There is still another thing that your experience with the stories illustrates. Perhaps already you have asked, "Well, if we go right on thinking in the same vein, how in the world do we ever get off the subject? Why did I even attempt to read the second story, once I had gotten started on the first?" The answer is simple when you take into consideration the course of your mental processes even before you started to read the first story; why, you were following a minute train of thought in which the reading of the stories was only an incident. You may raise another objection, and quite rightly, too. You may say, "Well, does that mean that all our higher mental processes are determined by what goes before, and if so, what starts us off in the first place?" No, things are continually happening to us, and many of them tend to deflect the course of our higher processes. The way it all works out is this: something happens; our senses, usually being on the lookout for such things, make a continuous report of what goes on. This continuous report we call "*sensation*." Now there are certain aspects in the course of sensation which tend to deflect the course of the higher processes. Our next task is to enumerate and explain these.

Aspects in the Course of Sensation which Tend to Deflect the Course of the Higher Processes:

(1) Contrast in Quality—Temporal

When something suddenly changes the course of sensation, we are apt to notice it. If you are looking at your friend's face while he tells of an interesting experience, you will probably not apprehend details of his features, but if a fly suddenly starts to crawl across his nose, the course of your apprehending process will change due to the new quality in the course of your sensation; you notice the fly. If when you fumble under the doorstep for your latch-key, you are thinking of the exciting events of the evening, the course of your higher mental processes will suddenly be altered by the sensation of a long, wiggling body in place of the expected latch-key.

(2) Contrast in Quality—Spatial

The sensing process, being a lower process, is necessarily broad in scope and undifferentiated in nature. Sensation takes in many things, while apprehension can take in but a few at a time. The higher the mental process the narrower its span at any given time. On all the things which are sensed at a certain time those which contrast most strikingly with their surroundings are usually apprehended. A picture on the wall will usually be apprehended in preference to the vague pattern of the wall paper. If your shoe pinches, the resulting sensation of pain will command your apprehension at the expense of all the myriads of other interesting items of sensation going on at the same time.

In place of the expected latch key...

If your shoe pinches...

In addition to these two kinds of contrasts in quality—temporal and spatial—there are temporal and spatial contrasts in *intensity*, in *extensity*, in *protensity* and in *repetition*. If your sensation of a buzzing sound suddenly grows louder, it will likely attract your apprehending process. There you have contrast in intensity. If you are driving along the road, you will probably notice those billboards which are largest and occupy the largest extensity in your field of sensation. If your alarm clock continues to ring in the morning, the continued ringing—the *protensity*—wakes you up. However, some manufacturers of alarm clocks so construct those unholy instruments of torture that they ring intermittently. You fumble with one of the things trying to find the gadget that shuts off the racket; it stops, and you lean back with the restful consciousness that you have succeeded. But no sooner than you resume your favorite nightmare, the blamed thing goes off again and you come to a full realization of what it is all about. *Repetition* is another one of the aspects in the course of sensation which tend to deflect the course of the higher mental processes.

We should not get the notion from all this that every one of the twists and turns in the course of the higher mental processes is caused by some quality in the sensory process. Oh, no, indeed; that would be very unpsychological! Our sensations do not govern the course of our thoughts; they do not even have complete control over the course of our apprehensions. What we apprehend is largely determined by what we "have on our minds." If I am thinking about a terrifying ghost story, the flapping of the bedroom curtain will come to my attention, when otherwise it might have remained entirely unapprehended. Our point is that aspects in the course of higher processes may themselves deflect the course of higher processes and of lower processes, too.

"The course of any process of the organism is in the direction of differentiation;" that is our Law of Differentiation. We have seen that apprehension is built upon only a part of the sensation, and we have just finished mentioning some of the things that influence that selection or differentiation. Now within the course of apprehension there are a series of differentiations, too. The first differentiation that is made can be more or less accurately described; beyond that we can not conveniently generalize.

Within the course of apprehension we shall call the first or lowest form of differentiation "the primary differentiation." The primary differentiation divides the apprehension into two courses, *figure and ground*. It happens like this: from the mass of sensation we select some aspect and apprehend it. As we apprehend that aspect, certain parts begin to stand out upon the background of the other parts. Look at Figure 22. Don't you apprehend a black square standing out on a white square background? You apprehend both of them at once, don't you? Now look at Figure 23. On the left you will likely apprehend a border or frame-like affair; on the right you will likely apprehend a square standing out of a plain background. If you try, you may be able to interchange the figure and ground in each of these figures. Figures 24, 25, 26 may be apprehended either with the black parts as figures or the white parts as figures. Figure 27 is the old well-known reversible staircase. At one time you may apprehend it as below you, and at another time you may apprehend it as above you.

Certain aspects in the course of sensation influence the primary differentiation. Figure 28 illustrates the effect of *relative proximity of certain parts*. Figure 29 illustrates the effect of *relative similarity of certain parts*. Figure 30 illustrates the effect of continuity of pattern. Figure 31 illustrates the effect of *inclusiveness of pattern*. Besides these there are at least two aspects in the course of higher processes which influence the primary differentiation. One is the *immediate course of the mental processes* and the other is *meaning*. If you are told to look for the facial profiles in Figure 32, a higher mental process will be set up whose immediate course will probably influence your apprehensive differentiation in such a manner that the black portion will be apprehended as figure and the light portion as ground. Figure 33 illustrates the influence of meaning on the primary differentiation. The shaded areas would probably fail to be apprehended as figure if it weren't for the fact that such a pattern has meaning to us.

The problem of how things come to have meaning to us is one of the most interesting in the whole galaxy of psychology's half-answered questions. Perhaps we should take up a discussion of it here, but there are a number of simpler processes involved which need to be described beforehand. We shall take up the question of meaning in the chapter on learning.

Already we have described the fundamental process of apprehending along with some of the things which influence it. We have yet to consider some of the simpler specific types of apprehending. These involve more than the primary differentiation; they involve secondary differentiations, tertiary differentiations, and so on. The first is the apprehension of *surfaces*.

Of all the tactile sensations which are going on at one time we are usually able to apprehend and distinguish those which come from the limbs, the trunk, the head, etc. The process of apprehension brings out the *local sign* with respect to the different sensations. An apprehended touch sensation from the tip of the finger has a different local sign from an apprehended touch sensation from the end of the nose. It is possible to give the apprehensions of these two touch sensations a different local sign because the sensations themselves fit into the *total pattern* of our touch sensations differently. That is why we can distinguish two different points on the surface of the skin. The same principle applies to distinguishing different points which are visually sensed. We also get some idea of the *size* and *direction* of things by this same local sign characteristic of apprehension. So much for the apprehension of surfaces.

How do we apprehend *depth* or distance *away* from us? That is the next specific question. Well, for the most part it is a matter of using the data from our visual and kinesthetic groups of sensations. Here is the way it is done. For one thing, when we look at a distant object, the lens of the eye is reflexively adjusted to focus an image of that object on the retina. Little muscles, called *cilliary muscles*, tend to this. Much of our apprehension of depth is merely a matter of isolating the kinesthetic sensations from these little muscles. Then again, this *distinctness* of visual sensation gives one a clue as to the distance of objects. *Shading* also gives a clue to distance. An artist, by the use of shades, can make us apprehend the flat surface of his picture as a thing of depth. *Superposition* aids in depth apprehension as Figure 36 illustrates. Size and shape also aid us when we are familiar with the objects seen. We know the child in Figure 37 must be closer than the man because we know the relative size of a child. We use one of the kinesthetic senses to apprehend distance when we focus our eyes on an object. The kinesthetic sensation from the muscles used in adjusting the eyeballs gives us a clue as to the nearness of the object focused upon. Hold a book about fifteen inches in front of you with its edge toward you; close one eye and then the other. Notice that the sensations gotten from the two eyes are different. This difference or *retinal disparity* is one of the most important clues used in depth apprehension.

Another specific instance of apprehending which is interesting is the apprehension of *time*. Not all is known that should be on this subject. Intervals of time less than three-fourths of a second appear to be apprehended as part of the temporal pattern or rhythm quality of the different sensations. Intervals between three-fourths of a second and four seconds in length appear to be apprehended according to the nature of the mental processes going on. Longer intervals are apprehended differently, depending upon whether or are not they "filled." If an interval is crammed with experiences it is likely to be overestimated, although in some instances "filled" intervals are markedly underestimated. Much of our apprehension of the time of day, however, is a matter of responding to little noises, light, etc. which occur regularly at about the same time each day. Many of us can awaken from an apparently sound slumber at any predetermined time in the morning. This is principally a matter of responding to customary morning sounds—all unconsciously, of course.

It is interesting to discover that apprehension of movement may take place when the objects sensed are entirely stationary. If you flash in rapid succession two bright lights which are near to each other, it will appear as if one light were moved from the first position. This illusion of movement is called the *Phi phenomenon*. It is because of this fact that the series of pictures we see in the movie appears as a continuous motion picture. The Phi phenomenon has attracted quite a bit of investigation among psychologists.

...responding to customary morning sounds...

Man's limited ability to discriminate between different stimuli has long been a topic of research. This field of psychology is called *psycho-physics*, so called because of its apparent bearing upon the relationship between the mental and the physical world. How closely can you apprehend the difference between two weights? How far apart do two points on the skin have to be before you can distinguish them from one point? How closely can you estimate the comparative length of two lines? What is the lowest note you can hear? These are the types of problems with which psycho-physics deals. Elaborate mathematical methods have been worked out for averaging a series of measurements of these facts. When the minimum difference between the two stimuli which one can apprehend has been worked out, that difference is called the *difference threshold* or *difference limen*. When it is a matter of determining the minimum stimulus which can be apprehended, the name used is simply *limen*. Here are some samples of difference limens for distinguishing two points from one point on different parts of the body.

There is a much referred to law in psycho-physics, Fechner-Weber Law. It has been found that the *just noticeable difference* or *difference limen* between two stimuli is proportional to the intensity of the stimuli which are to be distinguished. For instance it has been found that the difference limen for distinguishing weights is about two or three per cent of the size of the weights used, whatever the size might be. From that we would expect that if one can just distinguish between the weight of a 10 gram object and a 10.2 gram object he can likewise just distinguish between the weight of a 100 gram object and a 102 gram object, or a 1000 gram object and a 1020 gram object—the proportion remaining always the same. That is the Fechner-Weber Law. One should remember that the Fechner-Weber Law does not hold perfectly true for all kinds of stimuli, however

The study of illusions has long been of interest. Nearly every book in psychology refers to Aristotle's discovery that if you cross your middle fingers and hold a pea between them the pea is apprehended as two objects. Figure 39 shows a few of the better known types of illusions. These are, of course, in the visual mode. Illusions are of interest to the psychologist because they represent erroneous apprehension—a wrong interpretation of the sensations. These wrong interpretations are brought about by the unique way in which we have *learned* to interpret different sensations. We have come to attribute particular kinds of meanings to these sensations.

Let us go back now and think of apprehension as a process again. That process goes on and on, but sometimes it returns and retraces an old course or combination of old courses. Perhaps it would be better to say that there is always in the course which apprehension pursues some semblance of previous routes. Especially this is true when our apprehending is not at all based upon the sensing which is going on at the same time. When we apprehend without sensing we are usually following in old trains of apprehending; we are *imagining*. Imagination is a particular kind of apprehension. It takes place independently of the immediate sensation. Like other kinds of apprehension imagination usually has a direct reference to some sense mode. Perhaps most of us think of an image as being a representation of a visual sensation, that it is a visual picture, but no, we also have auditory, kinesthetic, olfactory and other images. Sometimes our imagination refers to more than one sense department. When we imagine eating a raw onion, reference is made to the smell, the taste, the grainy cutaneous sensation which characterizes an onion—all these are rolled into a more or less simple image.

Surprising as it may seem, it is almost impossible to distinguish between a sensation and an image. Take the case of the negative after-sensations which we described in the last chapter. Such sensations occur after the stimulus has been removed, yet we have been inclined to believe that they are due to continued activity in the sense organ. But now consider what is called the *memory after-image*. If you are reading aloud to someone, you may notice that your eyes are continually ahead of your voice, yet you have no difficulty is reproducing words which you have stopped sensing.

Or take the case of the experienced stenographer who makes shorthand notes from dictation. Her pencil flies along in response to her memory after-image of what just has been said. Such imagery is more definite than that involved in ordinary memory imagery. It is but a short step removed from after-sensation. Then there is imagination that is so vivid that one is inclined to believe that the corresponding sensation is actually present. Such imagination is called *hallucinatory imagination*. The habitual drunkard who winds up in delirium tremens experiences a great deal of hallucinatory imagination. Then there is the *eidetic image* which some people, notably artists and a few children are able to summon up. It differs from the hallucination in that it is never mistaken for a sensation, yet so vivid is the imagination that details can be noticed which cannot be recalled by means of the ordinary *memory-image* method of recollection. If a person who possesses ability in eidetic imagery is allowed to look at a picture for a few seconds and then asked to describe what he has seen it will be found that he can report only a few of the details of the picture. If, however, he is allowed to close his eyes or fixate them on a blank sheet of paper, he can recall a very nearly exact image of the picture and will be able to enumerate and pick out objects that he could not otherwise recall. In addition to this eidetic image there are the *hypnogogic images* such as occur during sleep. These constitute our dreams. There are other kinds of imagination but the most common are those involved in memory, reverie, day-dreaming, and constructive imagination.

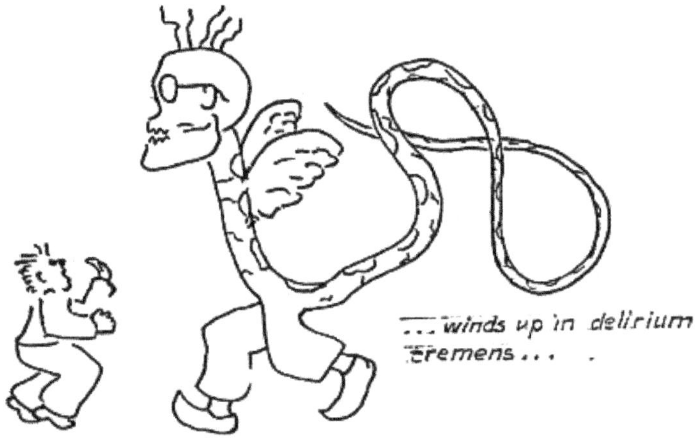

It is interesting to note at the end of this chapter that some people differ considerably in the ways of imagining. Some people, in fact, most of us, imagine in terms of visual sensations. Of course, we may have other types of images but for the most part we recall sights rather than sounds, odors, tastes, etc. Such people are called *visiles* and they comprise about three-fourths of the population-at-large. Practically all the remainder of the population may be classed as *audiles* for most of their imagination is of an auditory type. It has been suggested that most audiles are really *motiles* also. People who think in terms of sounds usually think in terms of the sound of their own voice together with the kinesthetic experience of forming those sounds. The thinking of such people is characterized by *incipient speech*—little movements of the muscles of the tongue and throat. Sometimes their lip movements are so pronounced as to be visible to an observer.

Sir Francis Galton, a famous English scientist, once performed this experiment. Instead of thinking of the numbers 1, 2, 3, 4, etc. either as visual symbols or as sounds, he taught himself to think of them in terms of certain odors. After considerable practice he was able to perform certain simple arithmetic operations by means of olfactory imagery alone. The odor "2" plus the odor "3" came to signify the odor "5." It must have been an arduous task, but it proved that number concepts can be couched in various sensory terms, that it is all a matter of how we learn them.

So much for the topic of apprehension, at least for the present. We shall come back to it later when we discuss some of the particular problems of special branches of psychology. Now see if you can remember what the following expressions mean.

1 the second level of cognition
2 apprehension
3 the Law of Continuity
4 the Law of Differentiation
5 mind
6 We do not build up ideas; we extract them
7 the limited span of apprehension
8 The sensing process is inclusive - but the apprehending process - differentiates
9 contrast in quality—temporal
10 contrast in quality—spatial
11 intensity, extensity, protensity, repetition
12 figure and ground
13 the primary differentiation
14 local sign
15 cilliary muscles
16 binocular difference or retinal disparity
17 Phi phenomenon
18 psycho-physics
19 difference threshold or difference limen
20 limen
21 Fechner-Weber Law
22 imagination and images
23 memory after-image
24 hallucinatory imagination
25 eidetic image
26 memory image
27 hypnogogic image
28 visiles, audiles, and motiles
29 incipient speech

Chapter 13

The Third Level of Cognition—Comprehension

It will be more difficult to draw a dividing line between the second and third levels of cognition than it was to draw a line between the first and second. Comprehension is very like apprehension. We have no new laws with remarkable names to begin this chapter with—we shall have to make the old ones do. If the laws of continuity and differentiation are at all basic they should be applicable to more than one level of mental process. Let us see how well they can be made to apply to this situation.

Before we become too deeply involved in abstractions let us take time to remind ourselves how similar the processes of cognition and action are. Take apprehension, for instance; apprehension is really a kind of action which this organism, the human being, carries on. Apprehension is not a state which the organism find itself in from time to time; it is not something which simply happens to the organism; rather it is something that the organism does. We cannot say whether the apprehension of something is a reflexive action, an impulsive action or any other particular kind of action—all we know is that it is something which the organism carries out. The three levels of cognition, from one standpoint, represent no more than another basis for classifying action. A certain school of psychologists, called *Behaviorism*, deals with all cognitive processes as a matter of reflexes, etc. but this plan is not altogether satisfactory.

Perhaps it would be better to say that they avoid the whole problem of cognition except as it can be looked upon as a question of action. There are very few psychologists, however, who take this extreme view.

Perhaps it would be easier to show that sensation is, in a way, a kind of action. To be sure, it is principally an action of end-organs and nerves, but it is an action. Well, the third level of cognition, comprehension, is probably a kind of action, a level of nervous activity. Of course, there is probably very little muscle activity involved in the comprehending process, but we must remember that action is action, whether of muscles, glands, or nerves. Action may be chemical or electrical as well as mechanical. To this extent we can think of the process of cognition as being a kind of action.

Now we do know this much; right along with certain sensing and apprehending processes there are reflexes, impulsive acts, and voluntary acts. For instance, you sense a bright glaring light; while you may not apprehend it at all, the pupils of your eyes will contract reflexively. Again, you apprehend that the door-bell is ringing; impulsively you may start for the door. Oh, we know a better illustration than that; suppose, oh just suppose that your sweetheart is resting in your arms. The warm night wind is gently blowing, and a great silver moon sails majestically overhead. All set? Sweetheart lifts two lips close to yours—ah! Is the ensuing action merely impulsive or is it so inevitable as to be reflexive? Yes, apprehensions have their action correlates—especially *some* apprehensions.

Much of our thinking involves a sort of half-whispered speech activity. Look at the child working a problem in arithmetic. Frequently his lips move as he calls into play the concepts of the multiplication tables. Perhaps you are one of those people who experience a tightness in your throat as you try to solve knotty problems. Some people's *incipient speech* is so marked that their friends are continually noticing it. Now if you are an extreme behaviorist you will say that thinking *is* incipient speech—nothing more—and you will spend a lot of time talking about such "*postural reactions.*"

We should realize that postural reactions such as incipient speech are an aid rather than a hindrance to thinking. With every comprehensive course as well as with every apprehensive and sensational course there are certain complementary reflexive and impulsive acts. Perhaps along with this certain thought there occurs a release of adrenalin from the adrenal glands. The chemistry of the blood is changed by this adrenalin. The heart beats faster. Certain muscles contract, and the sensation resulting from all this adds individuality, adds significance to the otherwise commonplace thought. Each thought, however abstract or definite, is the nucleus about which a whole constellation of subtle reflexes and impulses are grouped. The more pronounced and well defined these correlated visceral actions are, the more vivid and distinct is the mental process with which they are associated; and everyone knows that vivid and distinct comprehension is synonymous with clear thinking. Thought, then, is a comprehensive process which receives much of its distinctive coloring from little incipient acts which accompany it.

Now we are ready to describe the process of comprehending itself. *Understanding* is the nearest equivalent of comprehending. *Thinking* is often taken as the process of elaborating upon our apprehensions. *Insight* is another term which is frequently applied to a process on this level of cognition. When we apprehend something, it takes on form and significance to the extent that we recognize it. Something stands out from the mass of sensory process, and we suddenly know it is there. Or perhaps it stands out in the form of an image—some process which is following an old course. Perhaps the apprehension is quite minutely differentiated; if so, it may almost be said to be comprehension. That is the principal difference between apprehension and comprehension; comprehension is a much more highly differentiated process.

First let us illustrate just what we mean by all this. Let us take for an example the development of a child's concept of a dog. Suppose today you show him a dog—a little poodle. "Dog, dog, see the dog," you say. The child strokes the little poodle's soft hair, attempts to take it in his arms, steps on its tail, and generally makes its acquaintance. All that experience is "dog" to him. That is what "dog" is. With a very young child the *feeling tone* of the experience is very important. He likes "dog" or he dislikes "dog." He "loves" "dog" or perhaps he screams in rage at the animal. Perhaps he is afraid of "dog" and runs for protection. All this is the *feeling tone* of the experience. Incidentally it helps him recognize "dog" on future occasions. Like the incipient actions which accompany so much of our thinking this more or less emotional feeling tone lends individuality and vividness to our experiences. Well, our child has seen a dog. Now suppose that tomorrow we bring him a large police dog. "Dog, dog, see the dog", you say. The child looks puzzled for a moment; then he querulously strokes the large animal's coarse hair. "Dog," says the child, "dog? . . .. Dog." With a little less questioning in the voice this time. Then our child tries to lift the new "dog" and is somewhat bewildered when this part of yesterday's performance cannot be repeated. Presently he falls to stroking the dog's hair again. "Dog, nice dog," he says, "love dog." On the third day the child's mother is putting on her coat, a coat with a fur collar. The child touches the soft fur. "Dog," he says again, "nice dog."

What has happened is very nearly typical of all comprehensive processes. At first the child did very little more than differentiate "dog" from its surroundings. "Dog" was a more or less conglomerate experience, involving the hearing of his instructor say, "Dog," repeating the sounds, stroking some softness, lifting a wriggling body, seeing certain things, and hearing certain things, notably after the stepping-on-tail episode. Of course the child doesn't think of all these aspects separately; he doesn't even recognize them as different aspects—it's all one big whole experience.

Comes the second day's events. So this is "dog," too? The child does not understand; he does not comprehend "dog." It is confusing at first. Oh, this softness, that is familiar. But this heaviness, that is strange. "Dog—dog;" the softness is "dog." On the third day we are surprised to find the child calling another softness—the fur collar—dog." What has taken place is a differentiation. When the child is confronted with a new experience with the same name "dog," he casts about differentiating this and that until he arrives at something which tallies with some part of the image of yesterday's experience. In this case he seizes upon the softness aspect and associates that with "dog." But on the third day he finds that he was wrong; he must differentiate even further. Finally he is able to differentiate out of an experience with a dog the "dogness" aspect, the "poodleness" aspect, the "softness" aspect, and all the rest of the "nesses." In order to arrive at this concept many things had to be eliminated. The concept was *extracted*, not *built up*. "Dog" did not come to mean the first experience *plus* the second experience. "Dog" at the end of the second day did not mean a poodle *plus* a police dog; it meant something in the second experience which was *like* something in the first experience. The mental process required that this "something" be picked out. When, on the third day, the child called the fur collar "dog," it did not mean that he had put the first, second and third day's experience together and called them all "dog." It meant rather that only one aspect of those experiences was now being called "dog." The child was making progress in his differentiation. If, on the third day, we had shown the child the poodle again, the child would have been inclined to call only the softness "dog." We would very likely have distinguished between the experience as a whole and what he conceived to be the "dog-ness" aspect of it.

When we comprehend we react to a relatively minute aspect of our experience. It may seem strange to say that, because we are accustomed to think of comprehension as a matter of seeing the broad significance of a thing. Well, that is true; comprehension is frequently just that. But the broad significance we speak of is not a gross thing as far as cognition is concerned. What we do is observe a certain aspect in some course of our lower processes and discover that that same aspect can be observed in a great many other courses of our lower processes. It *tallies* with aspects of other situations. Yes, that is the way it works; we observe something so closely that we can differentiate out from the mass of it something which has broad significance. The *facts* with which we deal in comprehension are broad and . . .[2], but the comprehending *process* is one of discriminating differentiation.

There is something more about this that needs explaining. Do you remember where we said that on the second day our hypothetical child selected something from the experience with the police dog and saw that it tallied with something which he was able to select from his image of the experience with the poodle? What we have so far neglected to explain is, "*How did he know that it tallied*?" Here is where we call attention to those *incipient movements* and that *feeling tone* again. The kinesthetic and organic sensations from the incipient movements together with whatever feeling tone may be present are what furnish the cue in this *tallying*. We might say that our child, by paying attention to the softness aspect of the image of yesterday's poodle, found that it recalled the same sort of sensations and feeling tones as the softness of the police dog. We can very correctly say, "He *sensed* the similarity." That is not a very clear explanation, is it?

Let's try again. The experience with the poodle included a certain amount of action and perhaps a little feeling tone. As a result of this action and feeling tone the child gets more or less vague sensations. On the second day the child finds that the only way to get these vague sensations again is to differentiate out the softness aspect of the police dog experience. When he does that, the same little actions start up and go through the same performance as on the previous day. If today's experience is enough like yesterday's they will "click" along quite smoothly; for the law of continuity carries them right along. If, however, today's experience does not quite tally with yesterday's there will be little "hitches" in the course of this incipient action. In order to iron out the little hitches we must differentiate out the aspects which are exactly similar and pay attention only to them. That is how it works.

Much of what we have been talking about you yourself can verify. For instance, you can probably remember how you solved some knotty problem. Perhaps, at first, you thought you could understand it, that it tallied or fitted in to something you had done before. When you attempted to solve the problem, however, you found that it didn't quite fit; your further differentiation revealed a slight discrepancy. For a moment, perhaps you were "stuck." Then perhaps it appeared to fit into another vaguely familiar experience. You started to check. The further you checked the more sure you became that somehow you would solve it. Just how the solution would come about you could not quite foresee, but you *knew* you would get it. You had *insight*. That was the tallying process. Somehow or other the problem at hand *checked* with something familiar. This *insight* we have is frequently mistaken for *premonition*, so subtle it is. In fact, premonition is no more than insight, the "feeling" that the situation at hand tallies with some past experience.

Now sometimes our insight leads us to suppose that we are on the right track when we aren't. Try the puzzle in Figure 40. It's an old timer. Think you can solve it, don't you? Well you can't, unless you superimpose one line upon another. Most of us would almost have sworn that the problem could be worked by a straight-forward method when we first started out. Here is a case of our insight being wrong.

Comprehension is the further differentiation of the lower thought processes to the point where they tally with familiar experience. The tallying itself is largely a matter of apprehending the sensations aroused by complementary kinesthetic and visceral processes and the corresponding feeling tone.

[2] Editors' note: Illegible text.

Chapter 14

Introducing The Third Great Psychological Problem: "How Does A Person Feel?"

We might have tried to construct a very pretty little system of the general field of psychology into two parts, action and cognition. It would have worked very nicely and many psychologists would have approved. The great difficulty, however, arises from the fact that there is a great deal that we do not know and it is therefore quite impossible to describe some psychological facts satisfactorily in terms of action or cognition. There is the life of feeling and emotions—*affect* is the technical name. Where shall it be classified or how shall it be described? No one is quite sure just what emotions are. There is this curious thing about them; they disappear when you try to differentiate them in yourself. Just as soon as you start observing your own emotional state all the richness of the emotion vanishes and leaves you there in the ridiculous position of trying to turn around and catch yourself in your own tracks. Of course, we can remember something of our emotions after they have fled but on the whole they are the will-o-the-wisps of the psychologists.

Some psychologists, notably those of the British school, have accepted the mental life of man as divided into three more or less distinct categories; the *cognitive life* or life of knowing, the *conative life* or life of willing and the *affective life* or life of feelings and emotions. We have observed essentially the same classification but with some typically American variations. There is, to be sure, the cognitive life; we have described that. The conative life or life of wills and volitions we have really treated under the head of action. We believe that volition is very largely an attribute of action tendencies. The third division, the affective life, we have had to mention in connection with comprehension and *feeling tone*. You may have noticed that we avoided any description of feeling tone. That was because feeling tone is only one factor in the whole problem of affect. In this chapter we shall attempt to describe the affective life and its relation to action and cognition.

Before we go on let us remind ourselves of the fact that one school of American psychologists, the behavioristic school, accepts only one of the above three divisions of mental life. They say that psychology should only be considered as a study of the *behavior* or actions of man and animals. They do not believe that psychology as a science can afford to accept any evidence of mental life except as it manifests itself in behavior. Many of the things we have been saying are supported only by *introspection*; that is, *self-observation*. These things the behaviorist would not be willing to accept as scientific. Such a view seems rather extreme to most psychologists, although it would be perfectly justified if it were possible to look into other people's minds and observe what is going on there just as clearly as we can observe what is going on in our own minds.

Now before we get too deep into this business, let us define some of these terms, such as *feeling tone*, *affect*, and *emotion*. *Affect* is really a very broad term which includes all the experiences in this phase of our mental life. *Feeling tone* refers to milder forms of our affective life. It refers to our likes and our dislikes. It is usually thought of as varying from pleasantness on the one hand to unpleasantness on the other, although the great experimental psychologist, Wundt listed three dimensions in which *feeling* might vary: from *pleasantness* to *unpleasantness*, *excitement* to *numbness*, and *tension* to *release*—all at the same time. We must not say that feeling varies from pleasantness to *pain* because pain is a kind of sensation, not a kind of feeling tone. Of course a pain sensation is usually accompanied by an unpleasant feeling tone, unless indeed it be something in the nature of an itch.

Emotion is a very violent form of affect. It may involve more than merely pleasantness and unpleasantness; each emotion is inclined to have its own peculiar quality. Fear, rage, and love are typical emotions; in fact the behaviorist Watson maintains that they are the three primary emotions from which all other emotions are derived.

The British psychologist Drever speaks of three levels of the affective life which correspond roughly to the three levels of the cognitive life. The lowest level, emotion, corresponds to sensation; the second level, feeling, corresponds to apprehension; and the highest level, sentiment, corresponds to comprehension. This classification, however, is not entirely satisfactory because it appears that both emotion and sentiment are capable of more complex qualities than feeling appears to be capable of. Still we can scarcely make any improvement upon Drever's classification because no one is quite sure about this question.

Affects, especially emotions, appear to have both cognitive and action aspects. Fear, for instance, is an emotion which is usually brought about in connection with some apprehensive process—we usually fear something which has been brought to our attention. Love is an emotion which usually has a cognitive aspect to it—we love something we know about. This cognitive aspect of emotions and other affects is frequently of minor importance, however. Sometimes it appears as if emotion were chiefly a matter of impulsive and reflexive action. When we are afraid we are apt to tremble, to run, to cry out, to breathe rapidly, and to undergo a number of definite physiological changes. For one thing the endocrine[3] glands pour their product into the blood with far-reaching results. Particularly do the adrenal glands, endocrine glands which are particularly operative in situations of fear and rage, secrete their hormone, an autocoid substance called adrenin[4]. Once this adrenin is placed into the blood stream the digestive processes are inhibited, the liver puts sugar into the blood so that the muscle cells may act up to their maximum capacity, and the whole organism is placed on edge. It is the sensations from these visceral changes which occur when we apprehend dangerous or antagonizing situations that give to the emotions of fear and rage their characteristic disturbing effects. It is the violent action aspect of the emotion which makes it so vivid.

[3] Editors' note: Spelt "endocrine" by Kelly.

[4] Editors' note: [sic]

Such action is reflexive for the most part—at least impulsive. That is why an emotion seems so elemental and primitive. In the case of a feeling tone, on the other hand, the action aspect is not so apparent. At least, not so violent. We can better distinguish between the cognitive and action aspect of the situation. Hence we say, in the case of a feeling tone, that it is *pleasurable* or *unpleasurable*. But who can altogether say that a certain emotion is either pleasurable or unpleasurable? Emotions with all their violent reflexive and impulsive action concomitants are experienced as huge all-engrossing situations. Once we differentiate out of an emotional experience certain characteristics we have nothing left but a feeling tone which overcasts anything we do. Let us illustrate; suppose you are in a state of rage at your dog who has torn up your evening newspaper. The rage is not merely an apprehension of the situation, but it is characterized by visceral sensations, kinesthetic sensations, mechanical and chemical changes—all experienced as one more or less unitary experience. Now try to analyze the experience—is it a pleasant or unpleasant experience? "Unpleasant!" you say after a moment's hesitation. Stop! The instant you made that differentiation the emotion disappeared. Perhaps it returns presently as you stop differentiating; perhaps there is nothing left now but a rather general unpleasant feeling tone which will carry over into everything you do during the remainder of the evening. There is the difference between an emotion and a feeling tone. Just as an apprehension is a differentiation of the sensation, so is feeling tone a differentiation of the emotion.

Now it should be fairly easy to describe a sentiment; a sentiment is a more highly differentiated feeling tone. It is the essence of a feeling tone lifted out of its immediate setting and generalized so as to become applicable to many different situations. Our feeling of disgust for a thief becomes a sentiment against thievery in any form. Our emotion of rage at being betrayed by a hypocrite, on differentiation, becomes a feeling of displeasure in the betrayal, and on further differentiation and generalization, becomes a sentiment opposed to hypocrisy.

There is a much spoken-of theory regarding emotions. It is called the James-Lange theory. The great American psychologist William James and the Danish physiologist Lange both propounded it at about the same time. According to this theory the emotion *is* the sensation of our action; the action which characterizes an emotion *precedes* the feeling of an emotion. James suggested that we do not run from a bear in the woods because we are afraid, we run and then become afraid because of our running: the act precedes the emotion.

Walter Cannon of Harvard has recently done considerable experimentation upon the chemical changes which take place in the blood of animals during emotional states. As a result he has accepted the James-Lange theory in a somewhat modified form. He has been led to believe that while an emotion may be considerably "colored" or *characterized* by visceral reflexes, impulsive actions, etc., the essence of the emotion, the underlying feeling, is not a matter of visceral changes. The view that we have presented in the foregoing pages is in line with Cannon's interpretation.

The psychologist William McDougall has an interesting theory in connection with emotions. He claims that each instinct or inherited impulsive activity has its characteristic emotion. Thus the instinct of flight is characterized by the emotion of fear; the instinct of pugnacity is characterized by the emotion of anger; the mating instinct is characterized by the emotion of love, etc. McDougall is criticized by other psychologists, however, who maintain that his theory is invalidated by the fact that fear may accompany either flight or concealment, or that various emotions may characterize a given instinct.

Some psychologists emphasize the view that the emotional state is characterized by conflicting tendencies trying to gain control of the organism at the same time. To them, the essential characterization of an emotion is *conflict*. They say that emotion is most apt to result when we are thwarted in something.

Throughout our whole discussion of psychology we must bear in mind that the dividing lines between action, cognition, and affection are very difficult to place. There are so many reflexes and impulsive actions which accompany both cognition and affection; there are so many sensations and apprehensions which definitely accompany action and affection; and there are so many emotions, feelings, and sentiments that accompany both actions and cognitions; in fact, we have attempted to point out that all of the affective life probably can be reduced to a matter of cognition and action. What else we study in psychology is no more than an amplification and application of the facts we have learned about action and cognition. Oh, yes, we'll make some remarks about the nervous system as we go along but those will be of secondary importance.

Chapter 15

Abnormal and Clinical Psychology

Don't mistake us: abnormal psychology is the psychology of abnormal people, not abnormal psychology. It is of value and interest because it throws light upon the psychology of normal people. Abnormal people are just like normal people, only more so; so much more so that we can see magnified in them many essentially human characteristics which the normal person skillfully covers up.

Long ago a great philosopher by the name of Descartes thought that a certain little gland in the center of the head was the point of contact between the world of spirit and the world of flesh. Succeeding discoveries made his theory appear ridiculous. Nevertheless there remains a certain element of truth in the conjecture. That little gland which we call the pineal gland and a number of other *endocrine* glands similar to it have a great deal to do with the way we feel and think.

Endocrine glands differ from the ordinary glands in that they are not supplied with tubes or *ducts*. Salivary glands, as everyone knows, are supplied with little ducts which carry the saliva to the mouth. Endocrine glands make their products and release them right back into the blood and lymph which bathe their cells. These products are called *hormones* and differ from each other according to the function of the corresponding glands. Some of these hormones are terrific stimulants changing the whole course of bodily processes and one's very outlook on life.

The accompanying diagram (Figure 41) shows the locations of the principal endocrine glands.

The *pineal gland* is not as well understood as some of the others. It seems to wither up or atrophy as the individual reaches sexual maturity. Probably it has no other function than to hold the development of the sex organs in check until other physical organs have reached a certain measure of maturity.

The *pituitary gland* or *hypophysis cerebri* is divided into two lobes, front and rear, or *anterior* and *posterior*. The anterior lobe secretes a hormone which stimulates growth. Excess of this hormone may result in the individual becoming a giant. The posterior lobe seems to secrete a tonic for smooth muscles. Excessive secretion may result in irritability and early sexual maturation.

The *thyroid gland* is probably the best understood of the endocrines. Deficiency of *thyroxin*, the thyroid's product, results in *cretinism*, a pitiful state of affairs. The victim, if young, is stunted in growth and without physical stamina. His skin is dry and puffy, and his hair is dry and brittle. Mental activity is sluggish and greatly retarded.

When certain substances such as iodin are lacking in an individual's diet the thyroid increases in size to take care of the deficiency. This enlargement of the thyroid constitutes *exophthalmic goiter*—the ordinary garden variety of goiter. Excess of thyroxin results in unusual excitability on the part of the individual.

The *parathyroid glands* are four in number and are buried in the tissue of the thyroid gland. Their hormone appears to act as a stabilizing agent, holding in check the effect of the thyroid's hormone. The parathyroids are absolutely essential to life and the removal of some of them results in muscular spasms and trembling. The parathyroids appear to stimulate calcium mobilization, and their failure can contribute to epileptic attacks.

The function of the *thymus gland* is not well understood. It is largest at the time of puberty but degenerates thereafter. From this we might assume that it has a function similar to that of the pineal.

The *adrenal glands* are located one above each kidney. Another name for them is the "suprarenal." Each gland contains two kinds of tissue or parts—a *medulla* and a *cortex*. The cortex stimulates sexual development, but of its function we can say little more. The medulla secretes a powerful hormone called *adrenin*. Synthetic preparations of this hormone are called *adrenalin* or *epinephrin*. The secretion of the adrenal medulla is of especial value in case of fear or anger. In such experiences the tonus of the striped muscles is tremendously increased. The chemical composition of the blood is so changed that it clots readily, and the liver is forced to release its stored up fuel in the form of sugar for ready consumption. Injection of adrenalin directly into the muscles of the heart may revive that organ even after it has ceased to function. In some cases human life has been maintained in this manner.

The sex glands proper are duct glands, but much of the tissue which surrounds them is called *interstitial tissue* in the case of the male, *corpus luteum* in the case of the female, and produces a hormone. For this reason we refer to the *gonad* glands as part of the endocrine apparatus. The hormone of the gonads plays a large part in the determination of secondary sex characteristics—the differences in growth of hair, mammary glands, weight, etc.

...temporarily restoring his secondary sex characteristics with corresponding rejuvenescence!

It has long been known that interstitial tissue from one animal may be grafted into another. Around this information has been built up another sort of graft the—rejuvenation graft. Tissue which has been grafted into a degenerate animal may function and furnish that animal with the necessary hormone for restoring temporarily his secondary sex characteristics with corresponding vitalization. It is even possible to change the sex of an individual by such a process. Many people have sought a "fountain of youth" in the laboratory of the "goat gland specialist" who uses the method of grafting, when the sex glands proper are tied off and not allowed to secrete, they atrophy. The result is a temporary increase in the amount of interstitial tissue and a corresponding rejuvenescence. Neither the method of grafting nor that of "tying off" have proved satisfactory and after their temporary effects have disappeared the patient may find himself worse off than before his "operation."

The liver deserves to be classed as one of the endocrine group since much of its product is delivered directly to the blood stream. However, the conditions under which sugar is released are largely governed by the activity of the adrenal, parathyroid, and pancreatic glands.

Parts of the *pancreas* have an endocrine function. The active substance in their secretion has recently been discovered and named *insulin*. In this discovery there appears to have been found a cure for diabetes.

In conclusion we can say that the endocrine glands have a great deal to do with our moods and, indirectly, with our attitudes toward life. The glands make up a very complicated system of checks and cross checks, drives and counter drives. To disturb the function of one gland is to alter the working of all the others. Truly Descartes was not so far wrong when he located the link between the spiritual and physical worlds in one of the endocrine glands.

Have you ever had your head examined for "bumps?" At the beginning of the last century the scientists, Gall and Spurzheim made quite a "splash" by claiming that that they could locate different mental faculties in the bumps of bone on the head. Perhaps the heads of their particular clients were principally bone. However, this new semi-science was called "phrenology," and in spite of its odd name has persistently refused to die the death it well merits. Phrenology has nothing but the pocketbooks of the credulous to support it, for the contour of the outside of the head bears little resemblance to the contour of the brain cavity. Furthermore, the areas of the brain have been pretty well divided off according to their functions and the new division corresponds in no way to the phrenologists' bumpy divisions.

We must acknowledge a debt to the original phrenologists, however, for they at least emphasized the point that there were certain parts of the brain given over to certain functions. Perhaps we can forgive them for being wrong in their methods and classifications even though we find little excuse for their successors.

In the accompanying diagram of the brain (Figure 42) you will notice that there are three principal fissures in the cerebral cortex. The great *longitudinal fissure* divides the right hemisphere from the left. The *central fissure* divides either hemisphere into front and rear portions. The *fissure of Sylvius* separates an area called the *temporal lobe* from the *parietal lobe*. The *frontal lobe* is separated from the parietal lobe by the central fissure and the *occipital lobe* lies back of the temporal and parietal lobes. Notice that just back of the central fissure in the parietal lobe are a lot of little areas given over to the reception of sensations from different parts of the body. It might be said that these areas are *arrival platforms* for the new incoming sensations. Notice that just across the central fissure are a number of other little areas called motor areas. These may be said to be the *loading platforms* for outgoing messages. Notice that the arrival platform for visual sensations is set off by itself in the occipital lobe and that the arrival platform for auditory sensations is down in the temporal lobe. The loading platform for muscular control when one is writing is located somewhat in front of the regular motor areas, and the loading platform for control of vocal speech organs is somewhat below it.

The exact locations of the places where the different brain functions are carried out are hard to determine. The areas seem to be rather elastic. If you destroy one of them, the cells surrounding the destroyed part may take over the function. If you destroy tissue adjacent to one of the areas, the ability to recognize and interpret sensations arriving in that area may be partially impaired. The cells of the brain truly represent the members of a closely organized, highly cooperative colony.

There is an interesting fact in connection with the way the brain works. You will remember that there are two hemispheres which are practically identical except that one is the left hemisphere and the other the right hemisphere. They are really mirrored counterparts of each other. But not only are they mirrored counterparts of each other structurally—they are mirrored counterparts of each other functionally. For a person to turn his head to the right requires one kind of enervation from one hemisphere, but from the other hemisphere it requires the opposite kind of enervation. Thus the two sides of the brain are really antagonistic to each other. When one of them wants to do one thing, the other wants to do the opposite thing. Now one can see that in order to get anything done one hemisphere must dominate the other and take the lead. In right-handed people the dominant hemisphere is the left hemisphere. The reason can be readily seen when we know that the left side of the brain is more directly connected with the right side of the body. Now then, this development of cerebral dominance—for that is what this fact is called—is partly a matter of training but very largely a matter of inheritance. It is well-known that left-handedness tends to run in families, although it is a recessive trait and very rare it is that a majority of one family will be left handed. Now suppose a young child who has not yet developed a consistent "sidedness" to his brain is to learn the symbol "3" when the left hemisphere or cerebrum is dominant. A little later he is confronted with the symbol "E" which is the mirrored counterpart of the first symbol. If there is any tendency for the right hemisphere to be dominant for the moment, he will think that he recognizes the same symbol as before. The memory images as retained by the two sides of the brain tend to be just backwards from each other. It is not uncommon for a child whose margin of cerebral dominance is not definitely established in favor of one or the other side to write whole words and sentences backwards without noticing what is wrong with them.

Now what happens when cerebral dominance fails to become established? Well, it can be seen that an individual in such a situation will frequently have difficulty in reading and recognizing symbols. Congenital "*word blindness*" often found among children apparently is this sort of difficulty. Such an individual will confuse "b" with "d" and "p" with "q". Indeed to mind one's "p's" and "q's" involves a rather well organized brain. Another difficulty resulting from lack of cerebral dominance is stuttering, and many a child's "habit" of stuttering dates from the time his teacher forced him to write with his right hand when nature intended that he use his left. The coordination of muscles involved in speaking is probably the most complex and delicately organized system in the whole body, and any interfering nerve impulses arising from a rival side of the brain block and chop up the whole speaking process. Causes other than lack of cerebral dominance may also contribute to stuttering, but they are apt to be immediate causes rather than basic ones.

Sometimes one side of the brain becomes dominant due to unnatural causes. Chronic alcoholism, syphilis, high fevers, and other ailments may put poisons—*toxins*—into the system and destroy parts of the brain. In some cases the function of one hemisphere may become so impaired because of these *lesions* or destroyed areas that the other hemisphere has to take over as much of its function as possible. Such a change may lead to a change in handedness. In other cases tissue may become destroyed in the lower parts of the brain with paralysis on one or both sides of the body as a result. When the lesion is due to syphilis, the name given to this paralysis is *paresis*.

Sometimes lesions are caused by mechanical injury to the brain, that is, by concussion, severe blows, blood clots, birth injuries, etc. The head of the first born child may be partly crushed by the pelvic bones of the mother at the time of delivery. Instrumental delivery unless carefully carried out may also be partly responsible for birth injuries.

The effect of a lesion upon the mental life of an individual depends entirely upon its location. If it is located in one of the lower parts of the brain or nervous system, there will be little more than a paralysis of certain muscles or a faulty coordination of muscles. If it is large and located in certain parts of the cerebral cortex, while no paralysis may result, there may be a general reduction in mental efficiency.

Probably, in dealing with mental disorders one should always classify them into two groups, *organic* and *functional*. Organic disorders are those which have known physical bases—lesions or something of that sort. Functional disorders are those which apparently have no organic or physical bases. Heretofore we have been speaking of some of the organic bases for mental disorders.

Some functional disorders are remarkably interesting. Sometimes a person will declare that he is blind in one eye, but when an examiner resorts to subtle methods of testing, normal vision will be discovered in both eyes. Functional anesthesias are more or less common. An individual will declare that his hand is absolutely numb, that he can feel nothing in that hand. However, when the anesthetic or numb areas are investigated, it is found that they correspond to popularly known divisions of the body such as hand, arm, wrist, etc. rather than to the areas which correspond to different nerves. Sometimes functional anesthesias are temporary, and at other times relatively permanent ones are found.

Many of the symptoms of marked hysteria are functional in nature. Hallucinations, anxiety, undiagnosed physical illnesses, and many other symptoms belong to this group. It is safe to say that every physical disorder is somewhat complicated by functional factors. To say, however, that a person with a functional disorder is not sick at all, but just "imagines" he is sick is to disregard the truth. The functionally ill person suffers as does no other person. His illness is real. Illness of the mind may be most painful, and its ravages may disintegrate the whole morale and personality of the individual. "Faith healing" finds its successful patients among these people. So strong is the suggestive effect of the Christian Science philosophy that many of the members of that body are saved the pain of functional illness. It is difficult to tell whether or not the number who are saved this pain offsets the number who suffer from improperly treated organic disorders. Certain it is that correct care of both body and mind are essential to health and happiness.

There are some people who, all unintentionally, are remarkably susceptible to *superstition*. Let them pay strict attention to the action of a friend, and they are able to interpret many little movements the exact nature of which they are not directly aware of. Thus people are sometimes accredited with "mind reading" or "mental telepathic" powers. Even animals have been taught to interpret the incipient little gestures by which we all give our thoughts away. When this suggestion is carried to the extreme so that the person has his attention riveted upon the other it is termed hypnotism. Hypnotism is no more than that—some extreme state of attention and suggestibility. It is weird and hard to reconcile with the everyday . . .[5] of the mind, but in it there is certainly nothing supernatural.

The term intelligence is frequently misused. To the psychologist the term has a slightly different meaning than to most of the rest of us. To him it means more specifically the ability to think and learn in an abstract and symbolic way. To be sure, such an ability is pretty fundamental to success in this world, but it is not everything. Motivation, likability, enthusiasm, and idealism are also important if a person is to make good in life. Since 1905 when a Frenchman by the name of Binet who had been commissioned with the task of measuring the ability of pupils in Parisian schools published the first successful intelligence scale we have had reasonably accurate tests for measuring intelligence as the psychologist defines that commodity. Intelligence is usually measured in terms of *mental age* or in terms of the *intelligence quotient* (I.Q.). If a child makes a score on an intelligence test which is equivalent to the average score of twelve year-old children we say he has a mental age of twelve years. The I.Q. is simply the percentage that his mental age is of what it should be normally; thus if our child is only ten years old chronologically his I.Q. would equal 120. If the child is twelve years old chronologically we can say that his mental age is exactly 100 per cent of what it should be and the I.Q. equals 100. The I.Q. is gotten by dividing the mental age by the chronological age. For a child who develops normally the I.Q. will remain nearly constant.

Now about 60 per cent of the general child population have I.Q.'s between 90 and 110. About 1 per cent have I.Q.'s below 70, and about 1 per cent more have I.Q.'s above 130. The remaining 38 per cent have I.Q.'s between 70 and 90 and between 110 and 130.

A child who has an I.Q. below 70 can scarcely hope to get to the higher grades in the elementary school unless his deficiency is truly a temporary one. People whose I.Q. falls below 25 can safely be classed as idiots, those whose I.Q. is between 25 and 50 are classed as imbeciles, and those with I.Q.'s between 50 and 70 are classed as morons. These are rough general classifications and it is sometimes found that an individual may possess a few isolated capacities which measure up to the standard for people of better general mental ability.

There are certain kinds of feeblemindedness which carry with them marked physical features. One kind, called *microcephaly*, is characterized by an abnormally small head and brain. There is nothing that can be done to correct the defect and adequate training is often difficult because of the individual's ability to adjust to even the most rudimentary of life situations. Another kind of feeblemindedness which has marked physical symptoms is *macrocephaly*. Its symptom is an unusually large head. It may be due to too much *cerebro-spinal fluid*—the fluid which bathes the cells of the higher nerve centers—or to too many of a certain kind of cell in the brain tissue itself. If the enlargement is due to an excess of cerebro-spinal fluid, the disorder is called *hydrocephaly*. Something in a family where all the other children are normal there will be born a child possessing certain oriental-like features. The face is flat, the eyes are small and slanting like those of an oriental. The tongue is usually large and sometimes peculiarly marked. This type of feeblemindedness is called *mongolianism*. Another type of feeblemindedness called *cretinism* we have discussed earlier in this chapter in connection with thyroid deficiency.

The kinds of feeblemindedness which we have mentioned thus far belong to the classification of *amentia*, so called because they represent mental deficiency from the beginning of life. Another broad classification is that of *dementia*, so called because it represents a decline in mentality. Many mental disorders which do not in themselves represent deficient intelligence do, in their more severe state, bring about dementia. *Epilepsy* is an example. The milder forms of this disease may leave the intelligence of the individual perfectly intact, but the more severe forms affect all mental processes.

[5] Editors' note: Illegible word

General paresis, the result of syphilis, belongs to the dementia group. The disease is organic, not functional, toxic and not mechanical in nature. Early stages may exhibit no more than a general moral deterioration—a destruction of the highest of mental functions. Later the more elementary mental functions such as memory and ability to concentrate are impaired, and finally there is a complete nervous breakdown together with a loss of muscular coordination and general disability.

Chronic alcoholism is frequently accompanied by hallucinations, delirium, tremors, and sometimes by chemical destruction of brain tissue with resultant mental deterioration. Emotional disorders are probably the first symptoms of the deterioration of the alcoholic. Fits of temper, periods of elation and depression, inability to face the reality of unpleasant situations are both causes and results of excessive drinking. The release from restraint and the dulling of one's appreciations appeals to the self pity of the individual who feels he is being worsted in his battle with the stern realities of life. Restraints, social or legal, are thrown to the winds. Self pity, that breaker down of character, is the parasite in many a drunkard and potential drunkard's life. There are some who maintain that legal prohibition always drives people into intemperance. This doctrine has had wide advertisement in connection with the prohibition of alcoholic beverages in this country. The idea, on the face of it, is ridiculous. *It is not restraint that makes men rebellious but sympathy.* The Mark Anthony of Shakespeare made the populace suddenly rebellious simply by sympathizing with them and lamenting their loss. Many a law-abiding citizen is perfectly adjusted to his restraints, proud to be master of his appetites, and mentally healthy and happy until some fellow comes along and says, "Oh, ho! Why, you poor fellow, they won't let you drink anymore, will they?"

It is not within the province of this book to enter into a discussion of the social and legal phases of American prohibition laws except as they furnish illustrations of psychological facts. It is within our province to say that we have every reason to believe that alcoholism is neither a fundamental human weakness nor is it inherited as a habit from one generation to the next. The thing which is fundamental is the common desire to escape from reality and to play the part of a "suffering hero" in an imagined "melodrama of life!"

Mental disorders of the insanity type are frequently classed into two divisions, the *neuroses* or *psychoneuroses* and the *psychoses.* Under neuroses we would place such disorders as *somnambulism*, *fugue*, *anxieties*, *compulsions*, *hysteria* and others of the more specific forms of mental maladjustments. One should not include feeblemindedness under this heading although many mental diseases terminate in a demented condition. The rather definite distinction that should be made between feeblemindedness and insanity is not always observed. The most intelligent person may be "queer"—the subject of odd whims. On the other hand, a moron may be normal in his mode of behavior but deficient in the effectiveness of his behavior. The psychoses and the neuroses are not to be considered as mental deteriorations but more definitely as mental abnormalities.

A psychosis refers to a general personality make up as contrasted to the somewhat specific nature of the neurosis. Generally speaking there are those individuals who face reality directly and those who resort to mental reconstruction. The former are sometimes called *extroverts* because they live in a world of real things and people, they live outside of themselves; the latter are sometimes called *introverts* because they live in a world of reverie and imagination. The former are social; the latter nonsocial. When faced with a situation to which they find themselves inadequate to adjust, the former alternate between periods of elation and depression. The extreme form of this state is called the *manic-depressive* or *cycloid* form. The latter, the introverts, when unable to adjust to the difficulties tend to withdraw into themselves and are called *schizoid* or *schizophrenics*. Schizophrenia is the most common type of insanity, usually exhibiting its first symptoms during early adolescence. For this reason it has sometimes been called *dementia praecox*. In the latter stages the individual appears to lose all interest and awareness of things going on around him, sometimes becomes *catatonic* that is possesses abnormal muscular rigidity. This type of psychosis seems to be incurable as contrasted with the manic-depressive type which is somewhat susceptible to treatment.

Another type of psychosis should be mentioned. Frequently it is a complication of schizophrenia. It is called *paranoia*. It is characterized by delusions of persecution. The patient justifies himself in everything that he does and at the same time maintains that everyone is bent on persecuting him. It is not uncommon for people afflicted with this disease to have delusions of grandeur. A patient will tell you that he is the Emperor of Japan and that he is being treated miserably for political reasons.

Of course all of us have symptoms which suggest one or all of the psychoses, but it must be remembered that the abnormal people, as we said at the beginning of this chapter, are just like normal people but with certain traits accentuated.

The so called *rationalizations* of everyday life symptomize an inability to face reality. When one employs this method or mechanism, he is really setting up an *irrational* reason in support of an unworthily motivated act. Two kinds of rationalization are probably employed by everyone. One, the *sour grape* attitude is like that of the fox in the fable who after failing to reach a luscious bunch of grapes, argued that they were sour anyway! Another similar attitude may be called the *sweet lemon* or *Pollyanna* rationalization. It is the attitude of meeting misfortune by saying that it might have been worse.

Other everyday types of mental adjustment include *identification*, *projection*, and *empathy*. Identification refers to placing one's self into another's shoes and "living with" that person. It is the basis of entertainment at motion picture shows—the audience identifies itself with the hero and in a vicarious way "lives out" the episode. Projection refers to attaching an idea to some other object. I may say that a certain cat is jealous or apprehensive. In doing so I project an idea which I have created and make it appear as if it belonged to some other creature or object. Empathy is of considerable value in appreciation of art. It has been called "feeling into" an inanimate object or situation. Take the accompanying illustration showing the same figure in two orientations. We can say that the first figure "feels" solid and secure, while the second figure "feels" tipsy and insecure. We empathize the situation and "feel into" it. Why do you clamp your right foot firmly on the floor boards when your neighbor takes you for an auto ride? Why do you strain every muscle at a football game? Empathy!

As we have stated before, many functional disorders can be alleviated by suggestion and hypnosis. Some years ago Sigmund Freud, a German[6], advocated a modification of this method which he subsequently called *psychoanalysis*. Briefly, his method of treatment involves getting the patient to relax, release himself form all restraints and inhibitions, and report whatever train of thought which appears significant. Freud maintained that all neuroses were the result of improperly restrained desires or complexes. In some cases these desires were so restrained, perhaps because of judged unworthiness, that they were repressed below the level of consciousness, and the individual was unaware of the exact nature of the forces which were ravaging his life. By getting the patient to relax and report frankly everything which came into his mind, particularly dreams, Freud claimed to be able to detect the source of many of the common functional difficulties. Once the underlying sources of a maladjustment are brought to light the individual experienced less difficulty in adjusting to them. Freud found that most of these desires which had been suppressed into the dungeon of people's unconscious were of a sexual nature. He has maintained that the *libido* or general reproductive urge underlies all human motivation, and that to refuse to give it some sort of outlet is to deny ourselves the very elixir of life. The Freudian doctrine has sometimes led to abuses, especially on the part of those who have wished to rationalize their own lustful tendencies. There has been some difficulty in determining just how narrowly Freud intends to define his term libido. If it is to be defined as lustful sexual gratification, then many of us will feel that life cannot be reduced to such an elementary term. However, if we look at these "lower" impulses as simply the elements from which a rich fabric of life may be woven into a sublime pattern, then we can experience little philosophic difficulty. Even our Bible tells us that man was created from the "dust of the earth."

The real controversy, of course, lies in the question of to what extent the sexual urge shall be allowed unrestrained freedom. At this point one should take careful stock of the true Freudian view. For a master fabric to be streaked with the bare outlines of the threads out of which it has been woven is to have its beauty coarsened and marred. We must remember that the psychoanalytic method is really a method of unraveling and tearing apart the personality until the first snags and mistakes have been bared. A patient may be shown the bare sexual urge in its primitive form and told that he must incorporate it into the warp and woof of his life. However, after the elements of his life have thus been bared, it should not, in our opinion, be implied that there shall be no progress from that point on. The highest form of life is that which is most complex and unified. In order for an individual to rehabilitate himself he must re-differentiate and recognize the basic pattern of his life processes. It is in the re-differentiation and reorganization which follows psychoanalysis that personality is restored.

When an impulse is allowed to run its course for the purpose of "getting it out of the system," the method is called *catharsis*. The older view that a young man "must sow his wild oats" before he could hope to "settle down" was consistent with the cathartic principle. The need for cathartic methods is a delicate subject. Modern psychology, but probably not modern public opinion, has tended to shy away from the view in its extreme form. Yet it must be admitted that a cathartic outlet for a not too undesirable impulse is a simple and effective way of dealing with an emergency situation. A good cry has a soothing effect on overwrought nerves if not engaged in too frequently. A "confession is good for the soul" provided that it does not happen too often and in too public a manner. A violent turn at the lawn mower may permit a fit of irritability to run its course and so avoid domestic friction. But when it comes to an impulse to go on a drinking 'spree' the cathartic outlet may be more difficult to adjust to than the original ungratified wish. Here we can profitably resort to vicarious catharsis. Let the individual picture himself as vividly as he can going on the 'spree.' Let him dwell upon the feeling of freedom and exhilaration which would come. Let him picture no less vividly—really experience vicariously—the after effects, the neighbor's gossip, the wife's humiliation, the morning of remorse, the possible loss of position, and he will find that in proportion to his ability to make vivid the entire experience will he have sufficient emotional control to make a wise decision.

Probably no popular treatment of abnormal psychology should omit the much talked of *complex*. Certainly we should not forget our old familiar friend the *inferiority complex*. Of all the human strivings the striving[7] for personal self-respect is one of the most universal. Let this[8] be denied one and he will go to no end to regain it. The "suffering hero," the self-pitying paranoic, and the rationalizing, gossiping neighbor of every day life are individuals who have taken an indirect method of maintaining self-respect. It can be seen how, in a sense, all their naïve devices have origin in a feeling of inferiority.

Other complexes of specific nature may be enumerated to fit all the difficult situations of life. The dislike or *arrested development* of a child for arithmetic, a dislike which dates from an unfortunate experience with an arithmetic teacher, is an example.

There is something more we should know of the way the mind works. The study of aphasia has been an interesting and fruitful one. *Aphasia* means the temporary or somewhat permanent loss of a certain kind of higher function. One kind of aphasia is *amnesia*—loss of memory. Another is *alexia*, loss of the ability to read. *Aphonia*, loss of ability to speak, and *agraphia*, loss of ability to write, are other varieties. The more permanent kinds of aphasia are caused either by brain lesions or by severe psychotic complexes. Not a few cases appear to be due to the same causes as stuttering. In fact, the stutterer is frequently aphasic. It appears that aphasia in a transient form is more or less common to all of us. Sudden losses of memory or of the trend of thought of a conversation in which we have been

[6] Editors' note: [sic]

[7] Editors' note: "strife" in the original

[8] Editors' note: Illegible word

engaging are known to nearly all of us. Sometimes we forget the thought of a sentence before we have a chance to finish it. Our mind goes blank when we are asked a simple question. Sometimes these momentary lapses are due to distraction from outside sources, and at others they appear to be due to organic or subjective factors entirely. A man driving a car testifies that he did not see another car approaching until it was upon him, although he is certain he was wide awake and was closely observing the road. Such a testimony may incite ridicule, but it is perfectly plausible. The human mind normally works in a series of short stops and starts. The stops are normally less than a second in duration, although in case of fatigue they may be longer. Perhaps it would be accurate to say that the normal individual "sleeps" for a short fraction of a second at more or less uniform intervals. The frequency of his "naps" appears to depend upon the task which he is performing, his state of fatigue, and distracting stimuli. There seems reason to believe that they may occur as frequently as two or three a second and as infrequently as two or three in a half minute. The length and frequency of these *transient aphasia* periods seems to vary considerably from one individual to another. Perhaps they represent momentary conflict between the cerebral hemispheres. Perhaps they are due to momentary lack of blood supply to certain neurons in essential brain tracts. Perhaps they are due to momentary fatigue of certain neurons, a condition which is known to exist and which has been described as their refractory phase. One view is that the little electric currents which are set up by the passage of neural impulses, get cross-circuited in such a way as to induce counter currents in adjacent neural tracts to impede the passage of neural impulse. Whatever the cause the mind seems to be a fitful worker ill adapted to monotony.

Chapter 16

More About Psychoanalysis

In the year 1885 a young German[9] physician left Vienna for Paris to study under the great French psychiatrist, Charcot. A few years before Charcot had succeeded in describing and setting forth a method of partial treatment for a disease which had puzzled physicians for hundreds of years. Patients had become deaf but without injury to their ears; they had become blind and then suddenly regained their sight in miraculous fashions; some had become paralyzed and yet none of the ordinary explanations would apply; in fact, the symptoms of every known disease were so accurately simulated that only the most careful diagnosis could distinguish them from the real thing. Charcot had worked upon the hypothesis that all of these pseudo-symptoms might be the result of a single disease, *hysteria*. He came to the conclusion that the cause of the disease was a vicious idea in the mind of the patient. In order to discover the nature of the idea he resorted to hypnotism. It was already known that a patient under hypnosis was able to remember events and names which he could not recall during the normal state. By the use of suggestion while the patient was hypnotized Charcot found that he sometimes was able to remove the hysterical symptom. Sometimes the patients renewed their symptoms later but Charcot was on the right track. He tried telling his patients that their symptoms were imaginary and did not really exist. Sometimes that worked.

Sigmund Freud, for that was the young physician's name, studied in Paris for a year. During that time he learned a great deal from Charcot although it appears that his master took little notice of the German student. Freud returned to Vienna and to his old friend, Breuer. One day while the two of them were discussing psychotherapy Breuer brought out from his desk some notes which he had taken some six years before. The notes related to the case of a young woman who had had marked hallucinations. She had stopped "seeing things" apparently as the result of recalling some disturbing experiences which had been forgotten, reliving them and working out the explanations to logical and reassuring conclusions. The patient had expressed the opinion that she had simply talked herself out of the abnormal mental state. It might almost be said that this patient was the true discoverer of the psychotherapeutic treatment which was later to make the name of Freud famous.

For some time Freud and Breuer worked together upon the theory that the resolution of old half-forgotten infantile experiences (*abreaction*) and the purging of the mind (*catharsis*) would bring relief to sufferers of mental disease. Later these two colleagues separated and Freud developed his method of *psychoanalysis* with the aid of a few students who rallied about him. At first the method of treatment was little more than that of gaining the confidence of the patient and encouraging him to unburden himself. All kinds of mental cases were treated including hysterics. Hypnotism as a method was soon abandoned because it failed to help the patient integrate his experiences while in the waking state. Rather the patient was asked to tie the threads of his childhood experiences together while in a relaxed *twilight state*. The psychoanalyst sat quietly, sometimes behind a screen, and listened.

Out of a wide experience Freud has developed his theories and methods far beyond this crude but auspicious beginning. To tell the whole story would require a large, but surely interesting, volume. Let us do no more than summarize the doctrines in their present state. It will be important for anyone receiving his first impression of the Freudian doctrines to keep in mind the fact that Freud's work is clinical, not speculative; practical, not primarily theoretical. While much of his work is philosophical it is philosophy arrived at inductively. His doctrines are formulated from the psychoanalysis of actual cases not from any code of ethics or system of rational philosophy. Many of the theories are not scientifically verified as yet, they only form a working basis which many a psychiatrist has found to be of inestimable practical value.

[9] Editors' note: [sic]

In the first place, according to Freudian doctrine, there are three great elemental problems which the individual successively attacks during his lifetime. The first is the problem of nourishment, the second the problem of social approval and the third the problem of reproduction. Life energy is the force of love which in its elemental form is largely sexual. This elemental drive is called *libido*. In the young infant the libido is localized about the mouth. The mouth is most sensitive in order that the important act of nursing will not lose any of its significance. While libido is localized at the mouth the child is said to be in the *oral stage*. The problem of social approval is first met when social pressure is brought to bear upon the child to compel him to control his bowel movements. It is in effecting this achievement that the will of the mother is first superimposed upon that of the child and the child is made to feel social obligation. In this self-imposed restraint conscience is born. Perhaps this accounts for the fact that the voice of conscience sounds so much like the voice of mother. During this stage the libido of the child must be mobilized about the anus, hence the name, *anal stage*. The third stage is called the *genital stage* and is entered into immediately after the libido has been freed from the conscious control of the anus. It is during this stage that the child develops an interest in his own sex organs and later in the social problems of sex. Even in the young child the mysteries of sex are likely to be the cause of vague apprehensions. The coming of another child into the family is nearly always a disturbing factor.

According to the Freudian doctrine there are three levels of consciousness in which ideas may reside. A small area will suffice to represent the *conscious* mind. Just below that is the *foreconscious* in which ideas are stored until raised to the level of the conscious. The lowest level is that of the *unconscious* mind where vague memories of racial experiences, fetal experiences, and all repressed thoughts reside. These unconscious ideas exert a profound influence upon the behavior of the individual. While they are never directly brought into consciousness they are continually active and many of the slips of tongue, dreams and phantasies are masked expressions of repressed thoughts.

It is convenient to look upon the psychic activity of the individual as the interplay between three personalities who inhabit the various levels of the mind. The *Ego* is the "I" within us. He is the one with whom we are accustomed to identify ourselves. He inhabits the higher levels of consciousness and rarely hides any part of his nature. The *Id* is the "me," the primitive giant who inhabits the regions of the unconscious. He has a tremendous reservoir of energy and is never thoroughly tamed. He continually seeks expression. Time and logic mean nothing to him and in his greed for primitive satisfactions he may ride rough-shod over the Ego causing no end of remorse and unhappiness. The third personality is partly conscious and partly unconscious. It is the *Super-ego* who partly corresponds to that part of ourselves commonly known as our conscience. Among his other tasks the Super-ego must perform the all-important function of protecting the Ego from the depredations of the Id. How he does this has much to with the happiness of the whole family. If Super-ego is tyrannical, refusing to grant any form of expression to Id the personality as a whole will likely lack vital energy and will be given to perverted methods of meeting the demands of Id. If Super-ego is weak Ego may lose status and the demands of a civilized society may not be met. If Super-ego is wise the power of Id will be harnessed to serve the ends of the whole personality. In that case we say that the individual is *integrated* or in good mental health.

One of the concessions that Id is likely to insist upon is sexual gratification. The libido, or power which he possesses, is largely sexual unless properly diverted or *sublimated* into other channels. Sex attraction is likely to be directed toward the parent of the opposite sex. It is not long, however, before Super-ego makes it clear that sex gratification should not be obtained from that quarter. Sometimes the whole idea is immediately repressed into the unconscious and not even allowed a hearing before the Ego. When this happens there is conflict and danger of disintegration. Sometimes the utter dependence of a child upon the parent of the opposite sex will appear to have none of the sex element in it. That is because the sex element is repressed and the child has no way of understanding why it is so difficult to cast away and direct his libidinal forces elsewhere—into vocational channels—toward his mate. The constellation of ideas surrounding this problem is called the *Oedipus* complex after the young man in the Greek myth who killed his father and married his own mother. Sometimes the corresponding complex in girls is called the *Electra* complex. Strictly speaking these complexes are never outgrown; they are resolved only through insight into one's own self or through the avoidance of aggravating circumstances. Time alone can never effect a solution.

Another Greek myth is pressed into service by the Freudians to characterize libidinal perversion. Narcissus was a youth who, according to the story, fell in love with his own reflection in a pool of water. When the libidinal force is principally directed toward one's own body a condition of *Narcissism*[10] is said to be present. Narcissism is not unusual in young children with a newly awakened interest in their own bodies but when the tendency persists the individual becomes too self-centered for his own good. Many physical diseases are simulated because of the excessive concern of the patient for his own body.

According to Freudian doctrine there are two instincts or patterns of life purpose; *Eros* or life instinct and the death instinct. That is another way of saying that there are both constructive and destructive instincts. While we are in the habit of saying that everyone seeks life it would be just as correct to add that everyone also seeks death, destruction and escape from life.

The technique of psychoanalytic treatment requires first that the analyst gain the utter confidence (*rapport*) of the patient. Usually nothing more than a willingness to listen, to take the problems of the patient seriously and to avoid dogmatic comment is necessary to gain the patient's intimacy. The strictly Freudian method forbids any attempt to make explanations to the patient before the third or fourth month of treatment. Other psychoanalytic schools admit the patient to explanation earlier.

The night dream is considered the royal road to the unconscious. During sleep the censor of our thoughts dozes and the Id presents to consciousness a great deal of partly disguised material. If the thoughts presented by Id are not properly disguised the sleeper

[10] Editors' note: "Narcism" in the original

awakes and Ego trembles with a vague fear and a feeling of insecurity. The censor awakes too and prevents the most significant elements of the dream from being remembered.

Sometimes, in order to pass the censor during sleep, the drama which Id wishes enacted (*latent dream content*) is so distorted, condensed, inverted, symbolized and the characters so interchanged (dream work) that the dream itself (*manifest dream content*) is extremely difficult to interpret. The dream, however, is always to be considered a concession to the wishes of Id and, in part, a compensation for the inadequacies of the day's experience. Frequently the material out of which the dream is woven is local and inconsequential; the plot of the dream is the significant thing.

The Freudian practitioner asks his patient to tell and retell his dreams. Sometimes a patient will claim to have had no dreams. The analyst then points out that the dreams have occurred but have been forgotten and that the patient should, immediately upon rising in the morning make a note of his dreams. Usually this is sufficient to make the patient remember his dreams. After the dream has been recalled the patient is allowed to discuss, re-live and elaborate the associations which arise in connection with the experience. Sometimes the patient is permitted to drift off into phantasy speaking his mind without any attempt to be logical or systematic. Now and then these recitations assume peculiarly emotional trends; the patient becomes depressed and sad, tears come to his eyes; again he becomes angry and lashes himself into a fury apparently directed at the psychoanalyst. These storms of emotion are likely to be short-lived, however, and if the analyst is forbearing he will find that his companionship has become indispensable to the patient. The explanation of this emotional behavior is that the patient is reenacting in a somewhat vague sort of way the childhood scenes out of which his neurosis was born. By allowing this outlet (*catharsis*) the analyst is enabling the patient to tease out the tangled threads back at the place where the first knot was made. The analyst plays the parts of many characters in this re-enacted drama and it may not always be apparent to him what part he plays at the moment. When the analyst in the eyes of the patient assumes the role of different *dramatis personae* the phenomenon of *transference* is said to take place. If the analyst takes a too positive stand at the beginning of the psychoanalysis, or if he already bears some set relationship to the patient such as that of neighbor, husband, or old acquaintance the transference becomes difficult and the patient fails to cast him in the different roles necessary to the re-enactment of childhood scenes. At the end of the psychoanalysis when the disturbing problems have all been resolved, the explanations made, and the materials of life reintegrated the patient finds himself no longer dependent upon the psychoanalyst and the companionship between the two becomes casual or disappears entirely. The complete psychoanalysis may occupy three to twenty-four months. During this time conferences may be held from two to seven times a week.

Two psychoanalytic schools have branched off from the Freudian school. The first is led by C. J. Jung of Zurich and differs from the Freudian school mostly in its lesser emphasis upon childhood complexes, especially the Oedipus, and the sexual implication of the libido. Jung is more concerned with the synthesis of life impulses than with the cathartic analysis of traumatic experiences. If the life interest is principally turned inward upon the patient's self (*introversion*) personality becomes inverted or if the force is turned outward upon the world of real things (*extraversion*) the more one's capacities are realized. Jung has many followers, especially among those who treat the less specific disorders such as the psychoses, among those who find it necessary to give guidance in a limited number of conferences and among those whose moral and esthetic compunctions prohibit them from going all the way with Freud.

Another essential psychoanalytic school is led by Alfred Adler of Vienna. According to its doctrine the great human need is that of social superiority. When illness occurs it comes as a form of *inferiority complex*. These tenets are aligned with certain Germanic movements and, to some extent, with the views of sociologists in this country. The system is called *individual psychology*.

Mental disease is both an individual problem and a social problem. There is no pain so severe and no defect so incapacitating as this. Socially the disease is more menacing to the progress of society than is physical disease. It requires more painstaking supervision; it demands the sacrificing service of more practitioners for its effectual control. One psychiatrist cannot treat more than twenty major cases in a year. While our limited technical knowledge of therapeutic methods indicates that professional training might be relatively simple such is not the case for the psychiatrist must undergo an unusually rigid discipline before he can be entrusted with his task. To a greater extent than in medicine each patient represents a unique problem which must be met in an individual way. Combine with these facts the fear that most of us retain against a mental diagnosis and the startling information that today there are more hospital beds being occupied by patients with mental disorders than by patients with physical disorders and one may begin to grasp the significance of the problem.

Chapter 17

Educational Psychology

The course of American psychology has largely been determined by two factors, our love of individualism and our interest in the practical application of scientific facts to everyday human needs. The result has been a definite American leadership in the fields of the psychology of individual differences and the psychology of learning. In the former field, however, the pioneer work of the great English scientist, Sir Francis Galton, must not be overlooked. It was he who established a laboratory in London where a visitor might, by paying a nominal fee, have all sorts of measurements made of his height, weight, strength, etc. Thus the resourceful Galton was able to gather data of various kinds on a great many different individuals. His interest in individual differences was by no means limited to the work of this laboratory. Imagery, color preferences, inheritance of mental and physical characteristics, paranoia, and the psychology of religious experience all fell within the realm of interest of this "free-lance" scientist.

Probably the most important fact concerning individual differences is that which we touched upon in the last chapter. There we observed that intelligence is distributed among the population in a known characteristic fashion. Now we can go further and say that with regard to *any* mental trait people tend to distribute themselves in a characteristic fashion. If in the accompanying figure one lets different measures of a given trait be represented along the horizontal base and at the same time lets the numbers of people who conform to the different measurements be represented by height above the base line, the popularity of the different measures will generally fall into a typical curve such as we have shown. Notice that there are many people who receive average or nearly average measures and that there is a decline in numbers of people, indicated by a falling away of the curve, as one goes either direction from the average. The falling away becomes less marked as one reaches the outer limits of the range of measurements. Of course, when insufficient numbers of people are measured, the above curve is no more than approximated. The interesting part of all this is that apparently *all* human traits fall into this sort of distribution.

The *normal curve*, as this curve is called, furthermore represents almost a philosophy, a way of looking at all problems of human difference. How frequently we find in unscientific literature such statements as, "The man lives by reason, but the woman is a creature of intuition," "The negro is the white man's inferior," or "There are two (or three or more) kinds of people in the world, those who—," etc. Indeed one psychologist has humorously quoted the saying that there are two kinds of people in the world: those who divide the world into two kinds of people and those who do not. In making any comparison between groups the important fact to be observed is not the difference between their averages but the tremendous overlapping of the traits of individuals. Take the question of sex differences. The weight of evidence leads us to believe the difference in mental ability supposed to exist between men and women is totally absent. The overlapping of the two groups is almost 100 per cent. Of course there are superficial mental differences which are laid down by the society in which the man and woman are reared, but there is nothing like the marked qualitative differences that certain popular and careless authors attempt to capitalize upon. Or take the question of the negro's *versus* the white man's intelligence. The significant thing is not the slight difference in the averages as measured by a white man's intelligence test but the practically 100 per cent overlapping in the ranges of negro and white intelligence measures. We cannot attempt to divide human beings into two distinct classes and meet anything but failure. People differ only in the amount of what they possess, not in the kinds of things they possess. We can better say in describing an individual that he possesses *more* or *less*, not that he possesses *this* or *that*.

In order to express human traits in quantitative terms psychology has employed a number of interesting statistical methods. For instance, in describing an individual's performance on a certain test we may say that he ranked at the *sixty-third percentile*. By that we mean that his performance was such that it would normally be superior to that of sixty-three per cent of the people and inferior to the upper thirty-seven per cent of the people. A person ranking at the *fiftieth percentile* would be average with respect to that particular trait—superior to the lower fifty per cent of the population and inferior to the upper fifty per cent.

In order to describe groups of people averages are, of course, used. In addition to the average it is sometimes necessary to express the spread or range of performances. The whole range may be used in which case we might say that scores on a certain test ranged from 10 to 200; however, on examining the test more closely we might find that there were only one or two people who got scores anywhere nearly as low as 10 or anywhere nearly as high as 200. In order to express the range or spread of scores more accurately only part of the total range is taken, in some cases, the range of the middle fifty per cent. Such a range would be divided in two and called the *semi-interquartile range* (Q) or the *probable error* (P.E.). The measure of spread which is generally conceded to be most significant from a mathematical point of view is called the *standard deviation*. It is gotten by taking the difference between each of a series of scores and their average, then squaring these differences separately, averaging them, and finally taking the square root of their average. Normally such a procedure will yield a measure which represents about one sixth of the total range.

For the student of individual differences the problem of to what extent relationship exists between certain mental traits is important. To what extent does the person who is good in one thing tend to be good in other things? Is there a relationship between logical memory and ability in mathematics? Is there a relationship between ability in school and ability to succeed in a certain kind of vocation? Such questions can be answered with mathematical accuracy once the two traits have been properly measured. The degree of relationship is expressed in terms of a coefficient of correlation. If there is an absolutely perfect relationship between the two traits, the coefficient of correlation will be stated as +1.00. If the relationship is perfect but inverse, that is, a high amount of one trait being always associated with a correspondingly low amount in another, the coefficient of correlation will be -1.00. If there is no relationship whatever between the two traits in question, the coefficient of correlation will be 0. Various degrees of correlation are represented by decimals between 0 and +1.00 or -1.00. Thus if we should say that the correlation between intelligence and school marks is +.62, it would mean that there is a considerable but by no means perfect relationship between these two measures of human traits.

The quantitative view of human personality has been particularly fruitful in the production of all sorts of mental tests. Those purporting to measure *native* intelligence are best known. Such tests as these attempt to measure a person's *ability* to learn without regard for *what* he has learned. Obviously it would be nigh impossible to adhere strictly to this ideal, for the best of tests must assume at least a beginning of learning in the rudiments of life experience common to us all. Many tests have, nevertheless, gone far in arriving at a direct measure of a person's capacity regardless of what previous use he has made of that capacity.

Other tests designed chiefly for use in schools where all pupils have had approximately the same opportunities to learn are made so as to be a direct measure of what the pupil has achieved. Such tests are useful in determining the grade or class in which a pupil should be placed.

A third type of test is designed for measuring special aptitudes. Mechanical aptitude, musical aptitude, mathematical aptitude, scales for judging children's drawings, scales for evaluating sewing stitches, in fact nearly everything that is susceptible to measurement or judgment has been incorporated into some test or scale, levels of performance standardized, and norms published by means of which the percentile standing of any child in the population at large can be determined.

A fourth type of test is the diagnostic test, so called, because it attempts to measure the different aspects of mental ability and single out those particular ones in which an individual needs special aid. Diagnostic tests in arithmetic have been markedly successful in this respect.

As a fifth type of test we might list the prognostic or remedial exercise. The purpose of such a test is not so much to measure as to give a pupil special training in some skill in which he is known to be weak. Usually a diagnostic test is followed up by such remedial exercises.

There are many special varieties of tests, some of which are devised with the utmost pains and standardized by the most accurate of statistical methods, others of which are little more than a conglomeration of short-answer questions thrown together in haphazard fashion, published and sold as "standardized tests." Among the former there are available valuable instruments and tools which, if properly used and understood, would fairly revolutionize the educational efficiency of our schools. The difficulty has been the unfamiliarity of teachers with the tests and the inability properly to interpret their results. The latter difficulty has been made greater by the tendency of many enthusiastic but poorly informed educators to make claims for any and all standardized tests which even their authors could not have hoped for. Another difficulty has been due to the overemphasis upon intelligence and achievement tests. Measures have been made of these traits, the results elaborately, at least painfully, compiled, articles published, and nothing done about it. Psychologists and educators of better repute recently have tended to turn their efforts toward the diagnostic and remedial types of tests, and it is in such a movement that the immediate problems of the school are touched upon. The work of F.B. Knight of the University of Iowa is representative of this new movement. He was one of the first to make of the standardized test a teaching device instead of a mere measuring device. However even with the availability of such valuable teaching materials the reaction on the part of administrators has been slow. The interpretation of test data requires technical training which few teachers possess. With the rise of a new generation of teachers who possess the requisite statistical and clinical training together with a quantitative view of individual differences we can expect the new era of educational efficiency which the work of psychological and educational scientists now so brilliantly forecasts.

We said at the beginning of this chapter that the American disposition has directed American psychologists into the fields of individual differences and learning. If we are to recognize a patron saint in the latter field as we have in the former, we should mention the name of Johann Friedrich Herbart. Although he made his contribution a hundred years ago, his influence still is felt in the routine of many a classroom. He listed five formal steps in the development of an inductive lesson: *preparation* of pupils for the material which is to be presented, *presentation* of the materials of the lesson, *association* of new material with the old, *systematization*, that is, definition of terms, and finally *application* on the part of the learner to everyday situations.

If modern educational psychology has changed this plan at all, it has changed little more than the viewpoint under which such a procedure is followed. Where Herbart's five formal steps were rules of teaching, modern educational psychology has concerned itself with rules of learning. The work of Edward L. Thorndike of Columbia University in formulating laws of learning stands preeminent in the annals of modern educational psychology. Thorndike began early, publishing his doctorate thesis at the age of twenty-three. His three-volume work on educational psychology has been a standard reference for nearly twenty years.

Thorndike has listed three primary and five secondary laws of learning, as follows:

Primary Laws

1 *Readiness*: When a bond is ready to act, to act gives satisfaction and not to act gives annoyance. When a bond which is not ready to act is made to act, annoyance is caused. Thorndike thinks of all responses whether physical or mental as activity of certain neural paths or bonds; hence we roughly say this law means that for the organism to have to do something for which it is unready or unprepared is fundamentally annoying or dissatisfying.

2 *Effect*: "When a modifiable connection between a situation and a response is made or followed by a satisfying state of affairs, that connection's strength is increased: When made and accompanied or followed by an annoying state of affairs, its strength is decreased." That is to say satisfaction increases our tendency to repeat an act while annoyance makes us tend to avoid it.

3 *Exercise*: This law may be divided into two parts, *use* and *disuse*.

3a *Use*: "When a modifiable connection is made between a situation and response, that connection's strength is, other things being equal, increased . . .."

3b *Disuse*: "When a modifiable connection is not made between a situation and a response during a length of time, that connection's strength is decreased." These two laws are simply more exact ways of saying that practice normally leads to improvement and prolonged lack of it leads to forgetting.

Secondary Laws

1 *Multiple Response to the Same External Situation*: The three primary laws make it clear enough what factors govern improvement of connections, but the question arises as to how it comes about that the correct responses are made in the first place. Well, this law states that when confronted with any novel situation the individual experiments, manipulates, makes a great number of various tentative responses until he finally hits upon a satisfying one.
2 *Attitude*, *Set*, or *Disposition*: This frequently determines the particular response that shall be made as well as whether it shall be satisfying or annoying.
3 *Partial Activity*: Another way a response may get started is for the stimulating situation to contain some part, element, or aspect of some familiar situation for which there is a predisposition to respond in a certain way. A stranger with a prominent nose, blue eyes, red hair, and familiar features comes to the door, and at first glance we greet him as our old friend Bill Jones because we have seen in him some traits which belong to Bill Jones.
4 *Assimilation and Analogy*: Like the previous law this law states that we tend to react in similar ways to similar situations.
5 *Associative Shifting*: Sometimes this law is called the law of conditioning. If one stimulus will elicit a certain response, all you have to do is present another stimulus at the same time you present the first one and pretty soon it, too, will produce the same response by itself.

We quote these laws, not because we accept them but because they are so generally known and referred to that no one can be ignorant of them and pretend to be well informed in current educational psychology.

Right here we find ourselves in the midst of an inferno of psychological controversy. On the one hand we have Thorndike and his rapidly thinning ranks; on the other we have a motley throng of rebels representing nearly as many versions of the learning process as there are people to write them. A few of these rebels have banded themselves together under a banner recently imported from Germany. This band is known as the *Gestalt* school. Gestalt is not the name of a man but a word meaning "pattern," "shape," or "form." A common English translation is "configuration." The members of this school are continually emphasizing the fact that the total configuration, plan, or setting in which activity takes place is the important thing to be considered. In learning it is the "insight," not the repetition or effect, that counts. "Insight" is the recognition of the "whole" or "Gestalt" involved. There are larger "wholes" and there are smaller "wholes." Understand it? Neither do I! Yet many of the principles which we have laid down, especially those in the chapters on apprehension and comprehension are compatible with the *Gestalt* theory. Perhaps the essential difference between our view and that of *Gestalt* psychology is that our view is a quantitative one and theirs somewhat qualitative. But this discussion gets us nowhere!

Much of the controversy over the laws of learning has arisen out of the fact that the contending parties have failed properly to analyze the problem. When the *Gestalt* people set their law of insight over against Thorndike's law of exercise, they fail properly to recognize that the one is particularly applicable to the mental processes involved in solving problems and that the other bears upon memorizing already solved problems. There are really three phases or aspects of learning, and it would be well if in all controversies on the subject a clear distinction between them were kept in mind. They are:

1 Problem Solution
2 Habituation
3 Memorization

The first of the three is technically termed *higher thought process* and corresponds to the processes which we discussed in the chapter on comprehension. Habituation is the automatization of actions which have previously been worked out. Memorization is much like habituation except that no muscular movement need take place. In discussing the conditions under which these three learning processes take place we shall do little more than apply the laws of continuity and differentiation to a specific problem.

PROBLEM SOLUTION: There are at least three factors which must be respected in accounting for the appearance of a solution to a problem: the problem itself, or rather, the individual's version of it, the method of attack, and the judgment of the fitness of possible solutions. The first we shall call *disposition*, the second *conditioning*, and the third the effect.

The first factor in problem solution, *Disposition*: The way a person will act in a given situation depends largely upon what he is doing or thinking at the moment it confronts him. Thus a child who has been adding a series of numbers when confronted with the expressions "two" and "five," will probably respond by attempting to add them. If he has been multiplying and is confronted with these two stimuli, he will probably respond by telling you what their product is. If he has been repeating digits after you, he will probably respond by saying "two, five." If he has been repeating digits backwards after you, he will be disposed to say "five, two." All of us are like that; we are disposed to meet situations in the fashion in which we have been accustomed to meet them. Our disposition, mental set, or *Aufgabe*, whatever you wish to call it, is no more or less than the tendency to continue what we are already or have been doing. The law which governs disposition is the First Law which we stated: *The Law of Continuity*: Any process of the organism tends to follow a continuous temporal course.

Now some of the things we do are largely foreshadowed by the way we are made. Our physical make-up lends itself quite readily to such an activity as, say, walking. On the other hand the body which we have been presented with lacks the proper streamlining and other characteristics necessary for good flying. Many of our dispositions to act are determined by relatively permanent factors such as our physical make-up as well as by transient moods and momentary occupations. We have a set of glands whose chemical products are pretty well standardized. We have a set of muscles and sense organs whose very structure and location largely determine their function. And our nerves—why some of our neural circuits are leased wires making permanent connections between permanent subscribers. Why does a baby cry when he hears a loud noise? Why, it is because he was born with that sort of a "hook-up" already established.

Sometimes psychologists call these more or less permanent dispositions, "urges," or "tensions." It's all the same; an urge is no more than the tendency to continue an activity which has gotten started. Frequently the deep set urges involve internal organs or *viscera*, and from them we get sensations which we interpret as deep cravings. But they are no more than deep seated dispositions—actions seeking fruition. Their law is the law of continuity.

The second factor in problem solution, *Conditioning*: If our tendency is to keep on doing what we have started out to do, how do we ever get new responses started?

The answer to this question is found in an experiment now become classic. Ivan Petrovitch Pavlov, a Russian, reported in 1903 an experiment which later became known as the conditioned reflex experiment. Apparatus was constructed by means of which the flow of a dog's saliva could be recorded. At feeding time a bell was rung when the food was presented. After a number of trials the dog became so *conditioned* that the ringing of the bell alone was sufficient to start the flow of saliva.

Nearly all learning is similar to this. Like the dog who responded only to a part of the dinner situation (the bell) so do we frequently respond to familiar parts or aspects of new situations. Suppose we are confronted with the expression "2+5=." Suppose we have never seen that particular expression before. We have seen the "2," the "+," the "5," and the "=" separately but never together. What do we do? We tend to respond to the familiar parts. The "=" suggests that an answer is required, the "+" suggests that a sum shall be taken, etc. Thus we meet a "new" situation in a "new" way.

Sometimes the conditioning process has been generalized in this way. Suppose a certain stimulus—S_1—results in a certain response—R_1. We wish to condition ourselves so that we can produce R_1 when confronted with S_2 without having to resort to S_1. We do exactly what Pavlov did: present S_1 and S_2 together a few times and soon S_2 alone will be sufficient to produce R_1. Suppose you wish to learn how to make a cake. You are hungry for cake. Let us call your hunger S_2. Let us call the cook book S_1. R_1 is not a very good name for a cake, but it will have to do. First you let your hunger and the cook book work together a few times with resulting cakes; then pretty soon you will be able to make a cake every time you get hungry without referring to the cook book. You have learned to respond to a small aspect of the former situation. That is the efficient way to solve all problems—pick out the familiar aspects and react to them. That is the normal way for the mind to work. It is the law of differentiation which we have talked about. The course of any process of the organism is in the direction of differentiation.

Sometimes we are confronted with a situation in which there is nothing familiar. Try as we will we cannot differentiate out of it anything for which we have a formula. We are completely baffled. But solve it we must. There is an urge, a tension, a drive within us that demands satisfaction. Our disposition is such that we cannot overlook it. Continuity demands that the problem be met. It is a law of life that we must go on some way. How do we act? We act every way, using a few selected acts at first, but as the problem becomes more pressing, resorting to a wide variety of acts or movements. We try everything. Sometimes we meet with accidental success. Such a method of learning has been termed trial and error or trial and accidental success. It is not the most efficient method of attack, but it is sometimes a useful one.

But wait, does one ever attack a problem by a purely trial and error method? It is doubtful. There is always some recognizable aspect in the most novel of situations. Our own presence in the situation is certainly not a totally strange thing to be reacted to in a random fashion. There is nearly always a familiar sense involved. Perhaps we can classify the new situation as one having visual aspects. There may be wheels that go round, personalities that act, but certainly there is never but one totally novel situation in the life of a human being—his birth—and there are some psychologists who would have us believe that even birth has its precursory experiences and recollections.

In conclusion let us say that all conditioning is brought about by a process of differentiating familiar aspects out of novel situations, though sometimes the differentiating process is rather inefficiently carried out.

The third factor in problem solution, *The Effect*: How do we know when we have struck the right solution to a problem? The answer to this question is that we do not necessarily know when we have struck the right solution. All we can say of a solution is that it *satisfies*, leaves no unanswered questions, neutralizes our tensions, consummates the continuity of our mental processes—or whatever way you wish to say it. We judge a projected solution by its *effect* upon ourselves. We judge by the changes that take place within us. It may truthfully be said that we sense and apprehend that our solution is a satisfactory one. We have located the satisfying element, the missing link in our continuity of activity. Yes, you have guessed it; *we have differentiated out of a projected solution its aspect of fitness*! The problem is solved!

HABITUATION: The organism rarely is satisfied with the mere solution of a problem, especially if it is a problem which is likely to reoccur. Particularly valuable solutions tend to be made automatic. Take the instance of the child who is learning to write the word "the." The first time he attempts to write the word the task is highly problematical. His muscular acts definitely belong to the level of the *purposive acts* which we described in an earlier chapter. But later on the act of writing the word "the" becomes automatized; the child habituates the action. No longer can we classify his writing of that simple word as a purposive act. It is not even *voluntary*, for it represents no more than an unconscious link in the process of setting down his thoughts. It has been thrust down the scale of action to the level of an *impulsive act*. The seat of its *Aufgabe* has become as much neural as psychic and the mind has been left free to carry out more complex and highly differentiated processes. Isn't that convenient? What a lot of bother and worry it saves us! Truly this would be a humdrum world filled with tedious details if we had not habit to come to our rescue and relieve our troubled minds of minor tasks.

Many of the well known "laws of learning" are factors governing habituation. For an up-to-date clear statement of these factors we feel that we cannot improve upon that given by William Clark Trow of the University of Michigan. They are as follows:

"1. Exercise: Varying amounts of practice or drill tend to produce a corresponding improvement in performance.
2. Interval: Practice interspersed with periods of no practice tends to (a) eliminate fatigue and (b) shorten the total learning time, though (c) longer intervals may lower the level of performance.
3. Maturation: Progress in learning under constant conditions follows the concave-convex or S curve, but as usually measured displays a rapid initial rise, minor fluctuations and, often, plateaus.
4. Motivation: Improvement is more rapid when the learner comprehends his task or Aufgabe and recognizes its harmony with his desires and needs."

The first factor is simply the basis for the old saying that practice is necessary to perfection. The factor of *interval* accounts for the fact that periods of rest are necessary not only to eliminate fatigue, but also to facilitate learning. The great psychologist James has said that we do learn to skate in summer and to swim in winter. There seems to be value in periods of inactivity even though there is no conscious attempt to learn. Perhaps it is because there is a loss of interest when practice is maintained regularly. A more likely explanation is that most improvement involves more than merely habituation. There are stages of the game when new methods must be worked out; that is, new problems present themselves for solution. In the case of the child habituating the muscular movements necessary to write the word "the" there comes a stage when he can perfectly form each of the letters, but when he continues to form them by separate acts. He has reached his maximum possibility of improvement for that particular method. In order for him further to automatize the action he must learn to write the word as a whole. Here is a new problem for him to solve. He has habituated the old solution, and he is now ready for a more advanced type of activity. Perhaps it is some time before the problem is solved. In the meantime he appears to be standing still in his learning process. We say he has reached a "plateau" in his learning. (See Fig. 45). No, he is simply taking time out to solve a new problem. Perhaps that is what happens during the winter when we have no opportunity to swim; we solve new problems of swimming so that when summer comes we can start right in habituating an improved solution to the swimming problem.

The factor of *maturation* accounts for the typical habituation curve. Such a curve is shown in Figure 46. Why does not the typical habituation curve rise rapidly at first as does the curve in Figure 47? The answer is found in the preceding paragraph. At the start the problem solving aspect has not been carried along far enough for any real habituation to set in. The problem solution and the habituation are somewhat telescoped in the early stages, and it is some time before the habituation breaks away into the clear. In Figure 47 the problem has been rather well solved—perhaps because it was an easy one—before any measurements were taken of the improvement of habituation. Notice in both curves the tendency to level off at the top. That is the "ceiling effect" of the so-called *physiological limit*. The physiological limit is the hypothetic limit above which it is physically impossible for a person to attain. Of course there is no way of determining exactly where the physiological limit lies with regard to any function because there is always the possibility of finding a new and better method of attack with a higher physiological limit. It stands to reason, of course, that as one begins to approach the physiological limit the rate of improvement must be correspondingly reduced.

To continually practise an activity requires motivation. To stick at a job is a problem within itself and like problem solution requires a disposition to do so. That disposition is no more or less than the tendency to continuity which we have mentioned so frequently. The factor of *motivation* is that the task memorizing must be recognized as a proper solution to some felt need or urge. Thus the problem of the worthwhileness of my enterprise must be settled before habituation can be effectively carried on.

MEMORIZATION: We believe that Trow's four principles apply equally well to the third aspect of learning, memorization. Indeed we cannot draw such a hard and fast line between habituation and memorization as we attempted to draw between these two aspects of learning and problem solution. Of course we cannot say that memorization is the automatization of a once purposive act until it is reduced to the level of an impulsive act. Memory belongs to the life of cognition as contrasted with habituation which we classified under the life of action. To remember well is to have a facility for summoning accurate images. Memorization is so to control one's cognitive processes that certain apprehensions may be retraced or *recalled*. The automatization tends to reduce a comprehensive process to the level of an apprehensive process. Thus, a word whose meaning once had to be dwelt upon separately now is no more than apprehended as a link in a sentence.

It is common to make a distinction between three aspects of memorization. First there is the *memorizing process* proper, following that there is *retention*, and finally there is *recollection*. A specific application of the law of motivation to memorization is interesting to consider at this point. It has been found that the best method of memorizing a piece of poetry, a lesson, or any other series is to learn it by the *part-progressive method*. In using this method the individual divides the lesson into convenient parts, memorizes the first part, then the second, then the first and second together. Next he will memorize the third part and follow it up by memorizing the first, second and third parts together. Thus he can frequently orient himself and see just what relation the particular part which he is memorizing bears to the whole task. It follows directly from the law of motivation that one should never allow himself to become too far removed from the larger purposes into which his separate acts must fit.

Let us illustrate, finally, the entire process of learning. Suppose you are confronted with a lesson. First of all there must be an urge, a disposition to solve the problem of the lesson set before you. Your attack must be a continuity of what you have been doing. It will not do for your period of study to be an interruption of the continuity of your thoughts. The *disposition* must be right. Secondly there must be *conditioning*. Reading the material of the lesson will normally elicit the desired mental responses, that is, S_1 (the reading of the lesson) will be sufficient to elicit R_1 (the proper corresponding mental processes). But there is to be conditioning. That means that we wish to set up a state of affairs wherein questions asked by our instructor or arising in life situations alone will be sufficient to elicit R_1. Let us call these questions or cues S_2. Now we are ready to set the conditioning process into operation. We present S_1 (the reading of the lesson) and S_2 (the questions) *together* and thereby elicit R_1 (the proper corresponding mental processes). The law of effect shows us how to fit the two together. Thus the original solution to the problem is worked out. But notice, woe to the conditioning process if no S_2 is worked out and presented with S_1! The person who reads with no questions in his mind does a sorry job of conditioning himself. For him there is no problem solving process. When he finally is confronted with real questions, it may be too late for him to recall his reading experience and the accompanying mental processes.

After the problem has been solved satisfactorily, that is, the questions answered, the learner sets about memorizing the solution and perhaps habituating certain responses. Here he must consider the factors of *exercise* (frequent reviews and rehearsals), *interval* (well spaced reviews and rehearsals), and *motivation* (recognition of the purpose of his efforts). He may expect progress involving the factor of *maturation* with such fluctuations as are entailed by slight alterations of his solution which he may find it necessary to make from time to time.

That is how we learn.

Chapter 18

Genetic Psychology

Genetic psychology is a point of view as much as it is a field of psychology. Up to this point we have been trying to picture the cross-section of behavior of the organism as it exists at any one time. Now we shall attempt to strike through the other way and view its development. Genetic psychology is the study of the development of the human individual.

It is convenient for us to divide that period of existence between "the womb and the tomb" into five periods: infancy, childhood, adolescence, adulthood, and senescence. Just what ages each of these periods includes is rather difficult to determine. Infancy probably includes the period from birth to the age of three or four, when the child begins to talk well enough to make his own individuality felt in the family circle. To be sure he possesses individual traits before this time, but it is probably not until his vocabulary is developed that he is able to claim his individual heritage. The period of childhood may be considered as lasting from three or four until the onset of puberty or sexual maturation. Adolescence includes the remainder of the years in which physical growth normally takes place. Adulthood, representing the longest of these arbitrary divisions of life, is considered as lasting from the age of twenty-one until the onset of sexual impotence. The last period, senescence, includes the rest of life. These periods are not to be thought of as constituting separate epochs in the life history of the individual but as convenient divisions based upon observable physiological changes. In no way are they to be recognized as logical divisions of mental development.

Our last statement in the preceding paragraph might not have been accepted twenty or thirty years ago. At that time genetic psychology was making its bow to the public. With its introduction there came the influence of a great personality which was largely responsible for the widespread popularity granted this new study. G. Stanley Hall is a name not soon to be forgotten by psychologists. G. Stanley Hall had a theory, a theory that accounted for the changes which take place in the early part of life much more adequately than they needed to be accounted for. This *Recapitulation* theory or doctrine was not original with Hall, but little would have been heard of it by the public if it had not been for his influence. This doctrine states that the development of the individual is typical of that of the race. It draws an analogy from the fact that during the prenatal stage the human fetus bears resemblance successively to forms of life representing different levels on the evolutionary scale. It further holds that the human child repeats typical epochs through which primitive and civilized man has passed. The child has his stone age, his bronze age, and his iron age. He is first a savage, then a barbarian, and finally a civilized man. He passes through his classic humanitarian period, his "dark ages" and his period of chivalry. For him to fail to relive any of these periods is to omit a necessary link in his chain of development. Hall went further and said that the innate and primitive instincts which characterized these different periods of human development must be given outlet or *catharsis* else they would be forever cropping out in the mature man in the form of primitive and unacceptable behavior. Jean Jacques Rousseau, a Frenchman who lived about the middle of the eighteenth century and whose treatment of educational subjects has become a classic in the field of teaching method, expressed a similar doctrine with regard to the necessity of a cathartic outlet for primitive instincts and passions. We have met such a doctrine in the philosophical psychology of the psychoanalyst Freud. One is apt to meet such a cathartic doctrine whenever too much emphasis is placed upon the "drives," "instincts," and "mainsprings" of human action. Probably no other tendency has made it so hard for psychologists to see things placed right in front of their noses as the tendency to interpret all life in terms of "vital urges," "great underlying human forces," "fundamental purposes" and what not. It is difficult to be a philosopher and a scientist in the same breath—at least to be a very pretentious philosopher and a very objective scientist. To have a theory is to see the world through colored glasses; to have none is to be nearsighted. G. Stanley Hall had a theory and no one can accuse him of being nearsighted. The only trouble with his theory was that it accounted for too much—it accounted for things that weren't there. We have no reason to believe that the child must learn the culture of the stone age nor the intolerance of the chivalric period. The hunting occupations of the primitive man were not instincts that craved outlet but merely activities incidental to his primitive state. The so-called "innate cruelty" of the eight-year-old youngster is merely a by-product of a naive and simple mind. Nothing more! There is no metamorphosis of the mind at the time of puberty. The youth's soul does not deepen with his voice, though his squeaking vocal cords may cause him some embarrassment and make him feel conspicuous. Sometimes it would seem that the remarkable thing about the human mind is not that it is so complex but that it is so simple—and effective.

The question of what the child brings with him when he enters this world is one which has been variously answered. There are some who still believe that he has packed away in his luggage a great many specific ideas and attitudes. To them the instinctive equipment of the child is all sorted, labeled and classified. They believe that there are inborn habits, intuitions and concepts. Such a view is not in accord with the facts. The new-born child brings with him only the vaguest of tendencies together with a few reflex connections. If all children exhibit the same specific attitudes as they grow older, it is because the organization of their nerves, glands, muscles, etc. when met with environmental influences of a certain sort produces such specific attitudes. Rather than to say that we inherit certain tendencies, it is far more accurate and truthful to say that we inherit a physical make-up which develops a certain way of behaving when confronted with the sort of environment which most of us have. I was not born a gregarious creature, but the way I was put together and the circumstances under which I was reared made it quite natural that I should become so. I may go further and say that my very physical makeup was determined by a rather fortunate sort of environment—the environment of a certain sperm cell at a certain time. To go to the other extreme I may say that my home surroundings have been inherited—they were passed on to me without my having much to do with it. Why all this argument about heredity and environment, anyhow? What difference does it make which way the argument is settled so long as all heredity is determined by environment and all environment is inherited?

The answer to these questions is that the psychologists, sociologists, and educationists have been hoping that by evaluating the influence of environment and heredity they might answer the practical question of to what extent the human personality might be altered or controlled. Now we have the real question. Can an unfortunate selection of grandparents ever be mitigated? Can you keep a good man down? Is education a process of training people's minds or a process of grading, stamping, and labeling? Such questions are not to be answered in qualitative terms of yes or no, for it all depends upon the strength of our grip upon the conditions under which the human organism develops. Let us rephrase the questions to read: *How much* will old Zack Horsethief's grand-daughter benefit by a change of homes, an operation, or a sound spanking? *How much* can little Willie Wumpzitz get out of life under the combined influence of an I.Q. of 140 and a drunken father? *How much* can be expected of the future school?

The development of the child follows the laws of continuity and differentiation. It tends to be continuous with that aspect of his environment which we call his ancestry. It tends to be consistent with what he has been in his early years. There are no real breaks in the life of the child. The reasoning faculty of the mature adult is foreshadowed in the plasticity and activity of the infant. Personality does not suddenly blossom forth, but like the flower is temporarily concealed from those who do not take the pains to look closely. The giggly, boy-struck, inquisitive girl does not suddenly become the mature, self-possessed, and queenly woman. No, the giggles simply become smiles, the inquisitiveness becomes "understanding" and "sympathy", and the weakness for males becomes "it." The woman has learned to differentiate the graceful smile that matches her features and company from the silly girlish titter, the "sympathetic interest" that inspires confidence and yields rich morsels of information from the curiosity that all men abhor. The development has been continuous and in the direction of differentiation. We may truthfully say of human individual development what Herbert Spencer said of evolution, that it is ". . .a change from an indefinite, incoherent homogeneity to a definite coherent heterogeneity. . .." The child faces a world in which there are few recognizable distinctions; all furry objects are "kitty," all rhythmic motions are "horsey," and all emergencies are "mamma." The youth who has not differentiated the little rights and wrongs, permissibles and taboos of highly organized society is over-prone to use the epithets of "hypocrisy" and "sham." The mature man who is able to tease out the threads of personal ambition and greed in modern society may use the same epithets but with greater insight.

In conclusion we should mention the fact that both physical and mental traits tend to follow similar growth curves. A theoretical growth curve which is fairly typical of all human traits is shown in Figure 49. Notice its resemblance to the habituation curves show in the last chapter. It resembles the s-shaped curve except in one respect, it does not have the flat place at the beginning. You will remember that in the case of habituation we attributed that initial slow rise to a hang-over of the problem solving aspect of the learning process. Here, then, we have a truer picture of the development of any single trait. Figures 50 to 53 show some samples of growth curves for certain traits.

Chapter 19

Comparative Psychology

Comparative psychology is the study of different kinds of minds and largely resolves itself into a study of animal minds. Strictly speaking, it should also include a study of the minds of different racial groups.

The animal mind—is there such a thing? Can animals reason? Do dogs go to heaven? If so, to which one—ours? But let us confine our answers to the first two questions.

If you accept our definition of mind as given in Chapter 12, that mind is the basic pattern of cognitive processes, you will have little difficulty with the first question. In that case it only remains to be shown what evidences there are of cognitive processes and of their stability.

We have divided the cognitive aspect of psychology into three principal divisions: sensation, apprehension, and comprehension. We shall observe those divisions in describing the animal mind. We work under a handicap, however; the animal cannot give us very accurate introspective reports of his mental processes. He does give us some reports of those activities, but they are not in our language, hence we must take into account the light which animal actions or behavior throw upon our question. In order to interpret animal cognition we are dependent upon such manifestations as he chooses to exhibit for our observation. In observing animal behavior we cannot fail to notice one thing, that the behavior of creatures is largely limited in scope by the complexity of their nervous systems. When the form of life is so low that the individual experiences of the organism have little to do with the way it behaves, we are inclined to say that the nervous system lacks plasticity. Perhaps it would be better to say that it lacks the complexity necessary to make more than one sort of adjustment to a given situation. The insect will make the same mistake over and over again, even though it always leads to discomfiture. His behavior is susceptible to variation only to the extent that his nervous system is complicated enough to meet the vicissitudes of the situation. Take the sponge. At the top of the sponge is an opening which we might call a mouth. This mouth contracts whenever stimulated without regard for what it is enclosing. The sponge must behave so as long as it lacks a nervous system which is capable of differentiating between kinds of stimulation. Presumably man's complicated nervous system is absolutely essential for carrying on the differentiation which characterizes his thinking.

Sense organs may be found, as everyone knows, rather highly developed among animals. Even the insect has an eye, although his possession of a specialized ear may be doubted. The spider can detect sounds but only by means of what might be called his *tactual* sense. He senses the contact of the air waves beating against his body. His ears have not yet become entirely distinct from his cutaneous sense organs. So it is throughout the scale. Sense organs with special tasks develop out of older more generalized sense organs. By the time we get to the mammals we find sense organs rather well developed, in some cases even better than those of man. The olfactory organs of the dog are quite well developed. Scents form a large part of his environment. In some respects his auditory sense is superior to ours. He can distinguish finer differences in pitch than a normal human child will ordinarily notice. He can also sense higher pitches than we can hear. The dog howls when a high pitched siren or whistle is sounded near him because he hears piercing sounds which are practically inaudible to the human ear. The greater specificity of sense organs is the trait which gives the higher animal minds advantage over the lower animal minds.

To distinguish between the minds of the higher animals themselves we must abandon the criterion of the sense organ and repair to the second level of cognition, apprehension. The superiority of the dog over the cat lies not so much in any difference in sensitivity to his environment as in his ability to recognize or apprehend sensations. Here we have the factor of the dog's better memory in certain situations. W.S. Hunter has shown that after the animals had learned to find food back of a lighted space, dogs could react properly to the light after as much as one to three minutes had elapsed, while cats apparently could retain the memory or apprehensive image no more than sixteen to eighteen seconds. Such an experiment involves memory of the simplest sort. It is no more than an ability to repeat an apprehensive process after a lapse of time. It is not to be confused with logical memory which involves processes of the comprehensive sort. Simple apprehension may be found quite well developed among the higher types of mammals. Sometimes we find them recognizing and reacting to events which the human has difficulty in teaching himself to notice. The following extract from G. D. Higginson illustrates such an instance.

"The behavior of the horse, *Clever Hans*, was carefully studied by several scientifically trained persons, with a view to determining how the animal could perform so remarkably. But it was left to Pfungst to discover the true nature of the animal's performances. When Pfungst began his study of *Hans* it was generally claimed that the horse was capable of inner speech and thus cold count the taps of his foot (in terms of which he gave his answers); that he was quite familiar with the fundamental arithmetical processes; that he could readily read written or printed German; that he had very keen vision and could count the windows of the distant houses; and that he had a mind equal to that of a normal child of 13 or 14 years of age. With all these and many other claims before him, Pfungst began. He found that the horse could respond correctly even when the owner and the trainer were both absent. But he also shortly found that *Hans* could not add, multiply, divide or subtract, unless the questioner or some spectator within the range of vision of the animal knew the answer to the problem given him. For instance, when the experimenter turned his back to the horse and reaching behind pushed aside a number of balls in a box (the number not known to him) the horse failed every time to count them correctly; although sometimes the number was quite small. Neither could he read nor tell the time of day. When cards bearing simple words, or when clocks were shown him in such a way that no one, not even the experimenter, knew the answer to the problem being presented until after the horse had made his calculation, he generally failed. He was able to solve approximately ten per cent. When the questioner, however, knew the answer, his accuracy was as high as 98 per cent. The ten per cent reported correctly was to be explained partly in terms of chance, and partly in terms of an assumption that in some cases, at least, there had been a sufficient degree of training on some problems to secure a kind of habituated performance. The animal had simply learned to paw so many times to a few situations.

The large percentage of correct responses, when the questioner knew the answer, is to be attributed to the ability of the animal to use such visual cues as very slight head movements of the questioner. These movements were so slight that they were not perceived, either by the various experimenters or by the spectators, until Pfungst made his study. The horse, then, did not think; it merely perceived and pawed. Human beings unconsciously gave the animal the cue to the solution. There were certain characteristic features of the animal's behavior which tended to show that it was really responding to such human cues. Among these we wish to point out that the animal made errors; (1) when the questioner computed correctly but did not move at the proper moment to cue the horse, (2) when the questioner made a mistake in computation, and (3) when the number shown the horse differed from that shown the spectators. Let us illustrate the last. The experimenter wrote a number such as 1+6 on a slate. He then showed this to the spectators, groom, stable boy, and so on. But as he turned to show it to the horse he added a stroke so that it was now 7+6. The horse replied in terms of the problem, 1+6. Moreover, the horse appeared to need no more time for the difficult than for the easy problems. Finally, the animal did not appear to scrutinize the problem carefully as the human individual would have done. He immediately started to paw out his answers."

It is fundamental that one should recognize the difference between this sort of mental process and that which involves the differentiation of abstract principles and aspects out of apprehended data. By careful training a man can learn to apprehend slight differences in the tint of playing cards, incipient gestures—the "stop and go" signs—of his friends and all manner of other data which, though available to all of us in sensory form, are not apprehended. Many animals can make this sort of discrimination, but it requires a highly developed creature to "put two and two together" even in the most simple fashion.

It is only on the level of comprehension, then, that we can find any great superiority of the human mind over the minds of the lower forms. The dog may recognize symbols, but he cannot manipulate them in anything like a logical manner. In finding his way through a maze a child may strike upon the abstract principle that he will make no mistakes if he takes alternately the right and left openings. He may be able to carry over that principle to other mazes. The dog may learn the maze but not by the application of any such principle. He is incapable of this higher type of differentiation. He must solve the problem of the maze by accident or by means of cues which he can apprehend, such as colored lights or geometrical figures.

The beginning of the World War found a German physicist and psychologist by the name of Wolfgang Köhler on the island of Tenerife, where there was a station for the study of apes. The island was under the control of Spain, and Köhler was interned. During the years which followed he gathered the materials for a study which was to make him famous and eventually bring him to America as a professor of psychology. At the same time an American by the name of Robert M. Yerkes, who had already made contributions to the field of animal psychology was turned from his course by the same influence which redirected Köhler's. Yerkes was called upon to help administer the mental testing program of the American army during the World War. The names of these two men have become inseparably connected with research in anthropoid ape behavior.

In the apes we find about the only example of ability to devise and use tools that can be found below the level of man. The ape will devise a clumsy pyramid of boxes from which he can reach a banana suspended from the roof of a cage. He may also use a stick to pull a banana which has been placed out of his reach through the bars of the cage. He has even been observed to fit two sticks together in order to have a tool long enough to reach such a prize. Here we have something like a primitive comprehension. Köhler would say that it is *insight*. Such behavior cannot be satisfactorily explained as mere accident. The ability to "put two and two together" is definitely present. There is some differentiation of the aspect of usefulness out of the situation that does not involve mere habit. There has been a problem solved by "seeing in" the situation an aspect which fits and then recognizing its fitness even before it is tried.

We can truly say that from the lowest of animals on up to man there is marked continuity. There is no "missing link." The links are all there, and it only remains for man to observe them. The problem is not so much to find an animal which is almost human as it is to find how much like the animal's is our own mode of thought. To say the same thing in philosophical terms our task is not so much to bridge the gap which lies behind us as to confront the opening which lies before.

Chapter 20

Social Psychology

Man lives in groups. This is characteristic of him. One question which has confronted the social psychologist is the proposition that the group precedes the individual. That is a hard concept to swallow. It is something like saying that the chicken precedes the egg, yet from one standpoint it is true. We believe that it would be more accurate to say that *you can have no such thing as an individual unless* you have a group. That is equivalent to saying that there is no egg without a chicken.

It is only because of his social contacts that man acquires status as an individual. It is through a social or inter-individual relationship that he is able to come into existence in the first place. If there were no courtships, there would be no parents. The very existence of the individual is preceded by such a social grouping.

The single-celled animal divides and becomes two. It is both father and mother, although those two aspects of its function are not individualized. As you go up the animal scale you find that the father and mother aspects of life become individualized. Can you say which precedes the other, the socialization or the individualization? Can you imagine one without the other? Of course not! If you are to choose, you might say that the *social function* of mating is carried on in the unicellular animal *before* any individualization has taken place. But that is to overlook the meaning of socialization. But why the argument, you say—granted that individualization and socialization do appear simultaneously as two different aspects of the same thing—what of it? The argument is to clear a popular notion that man was first a solitary animal and that society was formed when certain individuals banded themselves together because some could hunt, some could cook, and some could make weapons. What we want to show is that this division of labor or individualization of members of the group was as much the *result* of living in groups as it was the *cause* of men banding together. The women *learned* to cook because of their status in the family group. The men learned to hunt because of their position in the group. Some individuals became proficient in making weapons because they had to. Some became leaders, not because they were leaders beforehand, but because their situation in the group made it possible to have a following. Their individual trait of leadership appeared simultaneously with the group trait of followership. Thus it goes. Modern society individualizes its members in proportion to its gain in complexity. It is only in the highly organized society that a child aspires to such a specialized vocation as that of street car conductor, radio electrician, or landscape engineer. The group precedes him and compels him to be different, to be specialized, to be a distinct individual. It is as much a fallacy to say that society is formed by a number of individuals getting together for a common purpose as it is to say that a president, a secretary, a treasurer, and a few members get together to organize a club and elect officers. There are no individuals until there are other individuals for them to be related to and distinguished from. The group and individual are two aspects of the same thing.

Another puzzling question is that of the *group mind*. Some psychologists and sociologists have spoken of the group mind as if it were something distinct from the minds of the individuals comprising the group. They have described the mob mind as a terrific force sweeping men off their feet and leading all of them against their wills and better judgments. Is there such a thing as a group mind?

Again we ask ourselves, what is mind? The underlying pattern of cognitive processes! Can there be an underlying pattern of cognitive processes of a group? What are the cognitive processes of a group? These processes consist in moving this man here and that man there, in jockeying this man into a certain relation with that group of men over there, in circumscribing one group with another and so on. The pawns in the game are not moved by some super hand but under their own power. The influences by which they are guided are those of time and circumstance. We can answer the last question: The cognitive processes of the group are no other than the organic processes of the individual members. But is there an underlying pattern for these processes which is not to be seen in any one member? Yes! The Irishman who reported that single-handed he captured twenty of the enemy by "surrounding them" might be the only exception. A lone soldier cannot do a "squads right" or a "left front into line." A lone voter cannot deadlock an election. A bride does not go on a honeymoon alone. The process of group behavior is nothing but the behavior of individual members, although the pattern may be super-individual. In this sense, then, we can say there is a group mind. But wait, we should be careful not to jump at conclusions. *The group mind is not a separate organism, not a separate process, not a separate will, not a separate force from that of the individual. It is a super-pattern into which the individual sub-patterns fit.* If we had defined mind as force or as will or as behavior, we should have had to deny the existence of such a thing as a group mind. We have been careful not to fall into the error which so many of the older psychologists and sociologists have fallen. Where they made the mistake of assuming that the group mind was at once a force and a super-individual mechanism, we have strictly adhered to the doctrine that the group mind is only a mechanism through which the energies of individual members may be felt in particularly potent ways. *The group mind is a situation into which individual tendencies are so combined as to make their effect violently felt by all.*

The social life of certain animals especially that of the so-called social insects has been one of the intriguing problems of the psychologist. How do ants come to recognize authority? How do they communicate with each other? Why is it that the ant is able to domesticate other insects and make slaves of them much as man has domesticated the horse and the cow? Did you know that some ants keep the aphid, feed, herd, and milk it as we do the cow? Answer such questions and you have begun to acquire insight into the forces which hold human society together. Obviously we can not say that the ant possesses refined comprehensive ability. As a matter of fact he does not. What he does is act in a certain way to certain stimuli. Cover an ant with the odor of an enemy colony and he will instantly be attacked. Two swarms of bees may be made to live peaceably with each other simply by changing their odor. Perhaps it would be analogous to say that the negro and the white might sit down at the same table if their colors could be made to match. What passes for comprehension is frequently no more than apprehension. Group life and social coordination are both fundamental and primitive.

What is personality? There you have a question. Is it an individual trait or a kind of reputation? The sociologist is apt to say that personality is individuality in a social setting. A human creature living alone on an island would not, according to this definition, be a person; he would lack the social setting. He would not be a personality until he possessed a reputation. Are we, then, to say that our true personality is no more than what our associates think us to be? Some people say that they can detect "personality" immediately.

They say that personality cannot be hid, that it is revealed by the expression on the face, the intonation of the voice, and the "light in the eye." Are we, then, to say that personality is the muscular convulsions which occur in that part of the anatomy which sticks up above the collar? Is personality an "inner self?" Is it the real "I" residing within the "inner chambers of the soul?" Is the personality separate from the mind? We shall make our answer short. If there is ever a necessity to distinguish between mind and personality, we can probably do no better than to say that *personality is that aspect of the mind which has social significance*. The expression of the face is part of the pattern of organic processes. To the extent that it represents a pattern of socially significant cognitive processes it represents personality. The intonation of the voice may reveal a cognitive process of a certain kind. To the extent that social significance is represented it is a part of personality. Personality is not a strictly psychological term, for it must be partially defined in terms of conditions external to the individual. It is a coinage of the social psychologist and the psychiatrist.

To the extent that an individual is able to cooperate with other members of his group and generally behave in a socially acceptable way we say that he possesses *sociality*. Some individuals are not very wealthy in terms of this commodity. The young child is not. The hobo is not. The process of building up sociality is called *socialization*. One of the principal aims of the modern school is to socialize the pupils. Cooperativeness and tolerance—especially tolerance of the majority—are important virtues in a highly organized society. We attempt to teach them with vim and vigor. The trouble is that it is one thing to cooperate with people whom you meet in a face to face relationship and quite another to cooperate with such abstractions as "the government," "the state," "the city," or "the plant." Downright old fashioned fire and brimstone morality with its definitely personal implication seems to bear greater psychological significance than impersonal abstractions. It would be extremely difficult to be patriotic if there were no such things as flags, anthems, uniforms, battleships, automobiles, wealth, catch phrases, etc. in terms of which we can crystallize the meaning of such an abstraction as patriotism. "Out of sight out of mind" is an unforgettable epitaph to the glories of the human mind.

The sociologist distinguishes two general types of groups, the primary and the secondary group. The primary group is such a group as the family, the gang, the neighborhood, which is characterized by face-to-face contacts. The secondary group is such a group as the ward, the association, the corporation which is characterized by a lack of face-to-face relations but is held together by a common purpose or a community of interest. The primary group is comprised of individuals who are usually thrown together unintentionally. It is more of a spontaneous grouping. The secondary group is more apt to be consciously formed, intentionally brought together. One might think that, this being true, the individual would be more loyal to the secondary group, but it is not necessarily so. It is the face-to-face contacts that are real. We had no choice as to the home into which we were born, yet the face-to-face relationships, the intimate reality of our experience there makes us loyal to the home as to no other group. It is paradoxical that we should be so loyal to a group in which we have not sought membership.

Psychology pure and proper deals with the mechanisms of human behavior. It is not a study of the stimuli which play upon man's sense organs or of the different predicaments in which he finds himself. It goes no further than to say what happens when he undergoes certain experiences. In order to have a complete picture of human behavior we must examine the forces which impinge upon man. In order to understand the behavior of an automobile it is necessary to know the condition of the road, the gasoline, the driver, and the other forces external to the machine as well as the mechanism of the machine itself. As the social psychologist, Kimball Young, has said, "In brief, to understand any social behavior it is necessary to know *what* lies in the mind as well as *how* the brain, the muscles, and the glands operate." Social psychology then is a supplementary study to psychology proper. Many of its terms are not purely psychological but rather carry some reference to conditions external to the individual. "Personality," as we have defined it, is such a term.

Another problem of social psychology is that of the development of language. The kind of language which a people possess has a great deal to do with the efficiency of their thinking. For instance there are some people in the southern Pacific who have words for only four numbers, one, two, three, and many. Thinking is handicapped when a language is so limited. Of course you may say that language is merely a means of communicating thought and that as soon as the people are able to comprehend such a number as five they will invent a name for it. That is not altogether the truth. Language is as much a producer of thought as it is an expression of it. Give a child or a savage a name for the thing which he holds in his hand and you have clarified his thinking about that object.

As we write the newspapers are carrying accounts of some strange meteoric disturbances. Observers are reporting that they hear strange thunder out of a clear sky and are seeing brilliant flashes of light in mid-afternoon. What a difference it makes when you can calmly read in your newspaper that the noises and flashes are caused by *perseids* and are to be expected during a two-day period at this time of year. What a difference it makes just to have a name for it! Language is more than a tool for communication; it is a stabilizer and clarifier of thought.

The races of man are frequently divided into three groups according to the culture which they are supposed to possess. The lowest level, savagery, merges into barbarism at the point a written language is developed. Civilization emerges from barbarism with the development of a phonetic alphabet. This basis of distinction is open to criticism, but it is generally accepted. There is no better cue to the cultural status of a race than the status of its language.

The forerunner of language is supposed to be the gesture. When man stood upon his hind legs for the first time, his whole perspective was changed. His range of view was widened. His forefeet became hands with which he could move objects. He was no longer required to manipulate his food with his snout. The musculature of his face became more finely developed. A changing expression to fit a changing mood became possible. A variety of vocal sounds was made possible. The hands were available for gestures. At first gestures were no more than the beginnings of acts. A belligerent posture, an angry snarl, a clenched fist, suggested the attack which would normally follow. It became unnecessary to complete the series in order to convey the meaning. In such a fashion a sort of gesture language was developed. This stage is called the pre-human or subjective stage. The signs used were merely spontaneous expressions of the subjective condition of the actor. They did not stand for things outside. In this stage there was no sign or gesture meaning "sun" or "tree" or "food." The gestures merely proclaimed that the actor was awake or safe or hungry. Such a prehuman language is found among certain species of birds, who have a particular call corresponding to particular subjective states. The apes also employ such a language.

The next step was the development of an objective gesture language. Certain gestures or sounds began to stand for different things out in the environment. There was a projection of thought to the outside. Here we have the beginning of the human language. There are four theories which have been advanced to account for the way particular sounds became associated with different situations or objects. They are the "bow-wow" theory, the "pooh-pooh" theory, the "ding-dong" theory, and the "yo-he-ho" theory. The first holds that primitive man began his objective language by naming animals according to the sound which they made. Thus a dog would be a "bow-wow," a cat a "meow," a donkey a "hee-haw." The second theory holds that certain situations began to be described in terms of vocal emotional utterances. Thus the "pooh-pooh" was a sort of forerunner to the "oh-yeah" of modern times. The "ding-dong" theory holds that there is a natural connection between certain objects and certain sounds. The very nature of the object is supposed to suggest certain sounds. The last theory holds that certain sounds came to stand for the rhythm of certain group activities. Thus the expression "yo-he-ho" might be developed out of the rhythm of rowing a boat or dragging a carcass.

Language may be likened to an extra chromosome for the transmission of the social inheritance. By it there is a continuity of custom and thought maintained from one generation to the next. It has been argued that it is foolish for us to keep on having many different languages in this age of enlightenment. Why not all express our ideas in the same language? Such a plan would undoubtedly clarify many an international situation and save the tourist considerable embarrassment. On the other hand it would mean a loss of the little niceties of expression, the cherished bits of rhyme and verse, the rhythmic swing of majestic prose, and the dry swaggering humor of American slang which so well expresses the American philosophy of life. To change language would not be merely to alter the medium of thought exchange, it would revolutionize thought itself.

Man's social inheritance is his worldly asset. It is his wealth of ideas accumulated by his patrician fathers. It has been designated as his *culture*. Culture in this sense does not mean an aristocracy of manners, etiquette, etc. It has meaning more like the German word "*Kultur*" had during the World War. Just as "*Kultur*" came to mean the sum total of things German, so we might say that culture means the sum total of things human. Ways of doing things, ideas about nature, rituals and customs, all go to make up our social inheritance or culture. W.G. Sumner has made a classification of culture traits which is generally accepted. He has called them folkways and mores. The folkways are the ways of folk in a literal sense. The mores are those folkways which have become so engrained into society that one cannot disregard them without bringing down upon his head the wrath of his fellows. The notch in the lapel of my coat collar represents a folkway, and I could dispense with it without inciting any indignation. To wear clothing on the street is to conform to the code of mores—I dare not rebel. Customs of moral significance are the mores. All customs and popular modes of behaving are folkways.

If we were to distinguish the folkways further, we might mention fashions, fads, and crazes. These represent the less stable folkways. They change from time to time, and the value of our culture is not particularly altered. Sometimes a craze will temporarily eclipse the more stable folkways. A panic, a boom, or a flood of patriotism may shake the very foundations of our social structure for a time, even destroy a part of the social inheritance. Such was the case when the Spanish conquerors of Mexico burnt the records which may have held the secret of the population of the western hemisphere.

Finally, culture is like capital lent out at compound interest. The more you have the faster you can acquire it. True, there have been setbacks in the growth of human culture, but these have been relatively temporary. The sweep of human progress goes forward with gathering momentum.

The science of social psychology lies between that of sociology, anthropology, and ethnology on the one hand and that of psychology on the other. It is a study, not merely of the individual mind, but of the influences which play upon the individual mind, particularly other human minds to which adjustment must be made. Its terms are less well defined than those of psychology, and it cannot lay claim to being such an exact science. Its field, however, is infinitely broad—and infinitely interesting.

Chapter 21

Some Other Forms of Applied Psychology

The Psychology of Salesmanship

To hear some people talk you would think that psychology was the science of making people do what you want them to do. Thank heavens that is not true—at least not yet! If some upshot psychologist ever does discover the "key to the human mind," let us hope he will keep it to himself and allow it to be buried with his odious carcass. The international crook of the serial movie who attempts to steal the professor's secret formula for blowing up the world would be a savior of society by comparison. Think of it—a salesman would take a three month's course in "the mind of the buyer" and come out all prepared to "sell us" anything. All our human vulnerable points would be exposed, and we would be haunted by a horrible feeling of helplessness. We suspect that what the world needs is not improved insight into the mind of the buyer but improved insight into the mind of the "go gettum salesman."

One way to make sales is to locate the people who want to buy the particular article that you are representing and talk to them. The good salesman is one who conserves his energy and makes his sales talks count. A large percentage of any salesman's time may profitably be spent in locating prospective buyers, advance advertising, and similar preparatory tasks.

Another point to be borne in mind is that the article to be sold must be partially identified with the salesman who represents it. Otherwise there is no true salesmanship. It is useless for a salesman to "sell himself" unless he has made it clear that he is inseparably bound up with the article he wishes to sell. Familiarity with the goods, apparent loyalty to and confidence in the firm are means of bringing about this identification in the mind of the buyer.

There are two general ways for a salesman to "sell himself." He can either exhibit such traits as the prospective buyer would like to possess or he can present himself in such a way that the prospective buyer's own personality is supplemented and enhanced. Let a self-confident salesman come around to the fellow who feels that he has lost every vestige of personality, and the chances are that the victim will seize anything which looks like an opportunity to put himself in the salesman's shoes. On the other hand, the deferential, courteous salesman who treats you as if you were the king of Siam and who apparently does nothing to encroach upon your individuality is the one who supplements your character. Both men "sell themselves."

Finally, the salesman has the task of showing that the goods meet the needs of the buyer. Self-esteem, rivalry, social approval, power, and mastery are some of the generally dependable motives. Most of the task at this point is a matter of meeting quickly and conclusively the individual questions which arise concerning the particular fitness of the goods to the particular situation. No specific rules of salesmanship will cover this point. The salesman simply must know what his commodity is good for and what his prospective buyer wants.

The Psychology of Advertising

The psychology of advertisement is based largely upon the principles of attention. This field of psychology has been studied quite carefully, and we shall do no more than to summarize some of the more important findings. An advertisement has as its first task the securing of attention. Attention is secured by contrast—either temporal or spatial. A man driving along a "billboard alley" by means of which he hopes to gain access to one of our cities, will scarcely notice the forty-seventh sign on the right hand side of the road. There is insufficient temporal contrast. He has been looking at billboards so long that he has turned his attention to something else. On the other hand, the chances are that the accompanying "fake ad" appearing in such an unusual context will attract the attention of every reader of this book even before he reaches this explanation.

We have mentioned five kinds of spatial and temporal contrasts: contrasts in quality, intensity, extensity, protensity, and repetition. The large type displayed in the accompanying advertisement represents an aspect in the course of sensation which tends to deflect the course of the higher mental processes. In this case it is a temporal contrast in extensity. Large things attract more attention than small things. The attention value of a sign is not in direct proportion to its area but more nearly in proportion to the length of one of its sides. That is to say that a square advertisement two inches on a side will be worth approximately twice as much as a square advertisement one inch on a side, although its area is four times as great. Another point to be borne in mind is that the extensity of an object presented to the sense is not so much a matter of the size of the object itself as of the area of the retina which it subtends. A two-inch advertisement in a newspaper held a few inches from the reader's face will subtend a larger area of his retina than will an eight-foot billboard a quarter of a mile away. Its extensity will be greater and under normal conditions its extensity contrast will be greater unless it is placed along with a number of larger displays. The position of an advertisement on a page is a very significant matter. The upper lefthand corner is many times as valuable as the lower righthand corner. The reason is obvious enough; we usually begin perusing a page from its upper lefthand corner. If it were our purpose to make a complete exposition of the value of the different kinds of contrast, we could take up each of the others in turn and illustrate how they could be utilized as principles in advertising.

One thing must always be borne in mind. The advertisement must do more than catch the attention; it must leave the reader with a favorable impression of the article advertised. If the picture accompanying the display is obnoxious, if the advertisement is annoying either because of its content or location, the value of the advertisement is greatly diminished. Some advertisers are able to combine annoyance and satisfaction in such a way that the satisfaction becomes definitely tied up with the article advertised. Many other advertisers in trying to copy them fail to make this distinction clear in the casual reader's mind. An example of such advertisement is shown in the accompanying illustration. It is of little more use than to attract attention and to fix the name of the product in the reader's mind. Unless he reads the entire advertisement with a view to purchasing the product immediately, the name will be vaguely connected with an unfavorable impression.

Many of the better advertisers display the name of their product and the picture of an attractive woman in such a manner that the casual reader who does not take the pains to read the copy through will see the two as part of the same context. A certain manufacturer of automobile bodies makes admirable use of this principle. There may even be a subtle connection between the use of the term "body" and the display of a graceful human female form. Certainly few of his advertisements illustrate any other kind of "body".

The Psychology of Employment

Another phase of applied psychology deals with the problem of *personnel*, the selecting of men for certain positions. There is probably no phase of industrial psychology in which there are so many helpful scientific developments and so little use made of them. The smug conceit of employers is principally to blame for this condition. It is almost a universally accepted rule that a neatly dressed young man will be neat in his work, while a carelessly dressed young man will be slovenly. Bumps on the head, large ears, sensuous mouths, ambling gaits, all enter into the employment situation, although they have as little relation to the situation as the wart on the nose of a grand uncle. Aside from the effect upon the applicant for a position many employers would be far better off if they dispensed with the personal interview and hired "sight unseen." Probably the only kind of position for which the personal interview has any objective value is such a position where the usefulness of the candidate will depend upon exactly such a showing as he is able to make before an employer on his first visit. Salesmen whose success must depend upon their ability to meet people for the first time rather than to keep friendships might be selected according to their showing in a personal interview because of its similarity to the conditions under which they are to work.

Even in the hands of experienced sales managers the personal interview is a very uncertain and questionable device. The following well known experiment illustrates this point in a conclusive way. Twelve sales managers of high standing were asked to interview and rank fifty-seven candidates for a certain position. A sample of the results is given in the accompanying table.

"Position 1 means the best candidate and Position 57 means the poorest candidate. Reading across the table discloses the different ratings given a candidate by the various judges. Candidate C, for example, is rated as best by one manager and as poorest by another. Other candidates made almost equally discordant impressions. In actual practice such errors are not discovered directly and immediately on account of the lack of any adequate check upon selections. Not only is there no means of discovering the good candidates who failed to be employed, but there is no tendency to attribute rapid turnover to the selection of the wrong individuals."

If there is such unreliability in the selection of salesmen for whom the interview closely approximates the working situation, what must be the error in attempting to select other types of employees by means of the interview?

The other side of the picture is more hopeful. There are available some quite reliable intelligence tests which can be administered to a candidate without supervision in half an hour or so. One of these tests will measure a candidate's native ability to learn more accurately than a whole regiment of employment managers working overtime asking all manner of unstandardized questions and making all sorts of unstandardized judgments. There are a few special aptitude tests which measure a candidate's aptitude in special lines of work. The number of such tests available is rapidly increasing. Many employers are engaging the services of technicians experienced in test construction and are being well repaid for their confidence.

There are a few personality tests on the market, but so far they have not been developed to a point where they are of great value to industry. Personality, inasmuch as it represents something apart from intelligence, is a rather illusive trait and not as important as many are led to believe. Select an employee with high intelligence, adequate technical training, emotional stability, and a genuine interest in the work he is offered, and that illusive thing we call personality will take care of itself. Intelligence and technical training can be measured quite accurately, emotional stability can be roughly estimated from the number of different positions held, and interest is a matter of the nature of the particular occupation. Some employers make the mistake of attempting to secure the most intelligent employees available and to place them in positions in which they cannot possibly sustain interest. It is safe to say that most employers over-estimate the opportunities for advancement which they offer their employees. On the other hand most employees are

Table 1 Poffenberger

Applicant	*Sales Managers*											
	1	2	3	4	5	6	7	8	9	10	11	12
A . . .	33	46	6	56	28	32	12	38	23	22	22	9
B . . .	36	50	43	17	51	47	38	20	38	55	39	9
C . . .	53	10	6	21	16	9	20	2	57	28	1	26
D . . .	44	25	13	48	77	8	43	11	17	12	20	9
E . . .	54	41	33	19	28	48	8	10	56	8	19	26
F . . .	18	13	13	8	11	15	15	31	32	18	25	9
G . . .	33	2	13	16	28	46	19	32	55	4	16	9
H . . .	13	40	6	24	51	49	10	52	54	29	21	53
I . . .	2	36	6	23	11	7	23	17	6	5	6	9
J . . .	43	11	13	11	37	40	36	46	25	15	29	1
K . . .	18	5	55	37	57	16	34	6	46	13	38	26
L . . .	7	20	6	1	1	10	3	7	17	2	2	26
M . . .	18	45	26	9	51	43	33	29	46	32	37	26
N . . .	2	15	6	28	7	45	24	40	40	17	30	48
O. . . .	18	42	19	2	16	4	14	51	32	45	31	26

led to under-estimate their opportunities for advancement. Intelligent employees are apt to become trouble makers in a stable organization where promotions are made largely on the basis of seniority. Employers should not expect proficiency in a position in which only a lazy unambitious person could be contented.

The Psychology of Industry

Another psychological problem of industry is that of getting the maximum amount of work out of an employee with a reasonable amount of fatigue. Probably the greatest gain which will be made in the near future toward the solution of this problem will be from suitable recognition of the fact of individual differences. There may be a tremendous difference in the amount of work which two men can do with a given amount of fatigue. A lock-step system in a factory assembling line represents a great improvement over some of the older systems, but it is not the ultimate solution of the problem of efficient human labor.

Another psychological fact which the well-organized industry of the future will take into consideration is that the age of sixty-five is not necessarily the time for a man to retire. Many a man has made his greatest contribution after he has attained the age of seventy or even eighty. The old saying that you cannot teach an old dog new tricks is not supported by the facts. To retire some men at the age of sixty-five is to rob them of their most fruitful years.

For a long time psychologists have sought some adequate measure of fatigue. The acidity of the saliva, the carbon dioxide content of the breath and the blood, the electrical resistance of certain areas of the skin have all been tried and have met with only partial success. Fatigue is not a condition which increases steadily and gradually throughout the day; it may be so severe after a moment's work that continuation of that task is completely blocked. As soon as any neuron has conducted a neural impulse, it undergoes a *refractory phase* during which it strongly resists the passage of any other impulse. This refractory phase is essentially the same as fatigue. Groups of neurons undergo somewhat the same sort of periods of fatigue except that the periods are longer. Periodicity of various duration is the rule of organic activity. A man who does but one thing becomes far more fatigued than the man who does many things but who does the same number of foot-pounds of work. Furthermore his fatigue is not merely confined to one part of the body; it is transmitted to all parts of the body in the form of poisons in the blood. The following summary by G. D. Higginson of the findings of another investigator illustrates the point.

"The introduction of rest periods within the working day appears to decrease fatigue and to increase the degree of achievement. The individual has an opportunity during such periods to recover partially from the effects of fatigue. There are no arbitrary periods at which such rest intervals should occur. Their number, distribution, and length appear to depend largely upon the type of work. Heavy and quickly exhausting labor is assumed to be best performed in short working periods interspersed with longer rest periods. This assumption finds confirmation in the results of several studies. Those made by Taylor on men engaged in loading pig iron are perhaps most interesting. Taylor found that where men handled pigs weighing 92 pounds, the optimum working period was seven minutes followed by a rest period of ten minutes. Under such distribution of rest and working periods, the men were actually active only about 43 % of the time, yet the final results showed an increase in output of more than 260 %. Whereas before each man handled 12½ tons per day, he now handled 47½ tons. Moreover, while the wages were increased 70 %, the actual cost of loading decreased 66 %. The recognition of short-time fatigue as well as the exhaustion which comes at the end of a day's work is another way in which the industrialist may apply the findings of psychology."

Distraction is another enemy of efficient labor. While some forms of distraction, such as regular, but not too monotonous, noise, may actually increase the output of a worker, certainly all distraction increases fatigue and lowers *capacity* for output. A worker in a noisy room has to exert himself more to keep his mind on his work. After a time individual noises blend into the general hubbub until he does not notice them. This is an application of the Fechner-Weber Law—*The just noticeable difference between two sensations is proportional to their absolute size.* If noises about one are loud, a certain increase in loudness will not be as noticeable as it would be if they were faint. It is the contrast that counts. It is an inefficient practice to attempt to increase workers' productivity by putting them in distracting circumstances. Far greater productivity can be gotten by judicious choice of incentives.

The Psychology of Jurisprudence

Psychological findings are being applied to legal problems. Recognition is now being made of the fact that many petty crimes are the result of feeblemindedness, although the diagnosis of mentality is still left to physicians and judges who have a "broad insight into human nature" and no technical training for the task. It seems that many a professional man considers himself a natural expert in "sizing up people" just because he meets some of the creatures every day. Little progress will be made in this form of diagnosis until the people who judge the mentality of others by the "look in the eye" are supplanted by people who have the rather simple technical training required for the task.

Another rather simple psychological fact needs to be recognized in connection with the crime situation. Much disrespect and antagonism toward the law is due to the undesirable personal traits of many of our policemen. One discourteous or cowardly policeman can create an attitude of mind which fifty courteous and efficient policemen cannot correct. The personal abuse with which many officers are allowed to administer warnings against minor infractions of the law is one of the most important factors in the whole problem of law enforcement. There is no force in the whole gamut of human motives which compares to a man's resentment of personal abuse. A man will calmly take the consequences of an untoward act and go his way resolved to do better in the future, but let his personal status be brought into the picture and he will fight against the representatives of society to the bitter end. If police departments were made welfare organizations as well as law enforcement agencies, the effect upon both officers and citizenry would doubtless be gratifying. A different class of men would be drawn into the police departments and the citizen might call his officers "Bobby" instead of "Bully."

Laboratory methods of detecting crime are interesting. Of course there is no such thing as a "lie detector," but there are some very clever methods of detecting emotional responses. The oldest method is the "word association test." A suspected individual is asked to respond to a series of words orally presented by saying the first word that comes into his mind. Most of the words which are given him are ordinary words such as chair, green, music, sky, water, picture, etc. Some of the words, however, have definitely to do with the crime of which he is suspected. When he is confronted with such a word, he must do one of two things, answer by giving the first word which comes into his mind or hesitate long enough to think of a word which he is sure will not "give him away." There are two ways of evaluating his responses: examine the response words themselves to see if they reveal any peculiar connection with the situation of the crime, and compare the reaction times for the "crime words" with the reaction times for the ordinary words.

Now, as we have said before, this method is not a "lie detector" but simply an "emotion detector." The most innocent of individuals will become "flustrated" when confronted with a word which he knows is connected with the crime of which he is accused. The value of the method depends upon the number of words available which will appear as ordinary words to the innocent man but which are known to be connected with the crime situation by the guilty man. There must be unique information concerning the crime which is known only to the experimenter and to the guilty man.

Another method is that of the psycho-galvanic reflex. The activity of the sweat glands is very susceptible to momentary emotional changes. For this reason the electrical resistance of the skin is continually fluctuating. By putting two electrodes on a person's skin these fluctuations may be accurately measured. The psycho-galvanic reflex is practically beyond the individual's control. It is practically impossible intentionally to budge the galvanometer with which his skin resistance is being measured. On the other hand the most stoic of individuals even when he knows that a certain word is coming will find it quite impossible to stop the galvanometer deflection which inevitably accompanies an emotionally significant word. This method has the advantage of being entirely independent of the individual's willingness to reply to the words or questions put to him.

Another aspect of psychology as applied to law is that which reveals the inaccuracy of testimony. Witnesses who are requested to report the most simple of observations on the very next day after an exciting event exhibit the most astounding inaccuracies. Couple with this the complexity of the testimony asked of some witnesses, and the lapse of time between the event and the testimony and you have a rather discouraging picture. Prompt trials and the use of notes on the witness stand will tend to improve the accuracy of the testimony of well-meaning witnesses.

The Psychology of Aesthetics

Psychology has been applied to aesthetics. Even the artistic quality of music has been brought under the analytic scrutiny of the psychologist. After all, what better field is there for a student of human nature than the study of human appreciations? In this country the work of Carl E. Seashore is pre-eminent in the psychology of music. From the beginning he has been faced with the active opposition of a certain group of unscientifically minded musicians. When he brought out his tests for certain specific phases of musical talent he was criticized because his tests did not measure all phases of musical talent. His test for pitch discrimination was criticized because the tones used were nearly pure tones without the complication of overtones. Musicians of good repute reported that they had "flunked" the tests. The reason was probably that the tests measured the traits so finely that even the best of musicians found himself confronted with situations in which he could not make a judgement. The temperament of the unscientific and self-conscious man in such a predicament leads him to "give up" and rationalize afterwards by criticizing the test. It is significant that few of the criticisms of Seashore's tests have been couched in exact and quantitative terms.

Seashore's recent work has dealt with the vibrato. Here his findings have been more convincing, even to the die-hard "artistic" musicians. By apparatus in his laboratory he is able to photograph the human voice or the tone of a violin. The developed records are a revelation. It takes objective evidence to convince people that their favorite grand opera star is really singing a half-tone off pitch with a vibrato that is actually two to four times as great as it is heard by the trained vocal critic. Truly there is no field in which the scientist finds the going so rough as in those fields which have been the domain of the aestheticists—those souls who "know" and "do" without knowing how or why or wishing to learn how or why.

Psychology has many uses. We have mentioned only a few which have been experimentally treated. Many other fields of application are awaiting the inquiring gaze of the skillful investigator.

Chapter 22

The History and The Systems of Psychology

Psychology as a separate science is new, but its roots are grounded in the same soil out of which all the other sciences have sprung. It is customary to trace most sciences, especially the biological sciences, back to Aristotle. Not that Aristotle would have conformed to the present ideal of a scientist—he even refused to perform any experiments—but that he believed in careful observation and systematic interpretation of the results. Of course, his chief bent was in the direction of philosophy, but considering his time and his lights the work of Aristotle is unquestionably epochal. He believed with a number of others of his time that the earth was a sphere. That was nearly two thousand years before Columbus was born (384-322, B. C.). Great man—Aristotle!

For our next great personality we must come to Descartes (1596-1650). René Descartes was a Frenchman—soldier, philosopher, physician, and mathematician. We have mentioned him at the beginning of our chapter on abnormal psychology. His contribution was that of accounting for mental states in physiological terms. Do not mistake us, he did not maintain that the mind and the body were the same by any means.

John Locke (1632-1704) was a teacher and a physician who, one day after witnessing the futility of a discussion among his friends, decided to write a short criticism of human understanding. About one page would be enough, he thought. Well, it was twenty years before he had it finished—which in itself is a criticism of human understanding. Locke's *Essay Concerning Human Understanding* was published when he was fifty-seven years old, and it represented his first and only bid to fame. But what a bid it was! And what student of philosophy or psychology could afford to overlook the name of John Locke! Locke said that all information came to the individual by means of his senses. The human mind was to be looked upon as a blank slate upon which the experiences of life are written. The characters in which the experiences are written are *ideas*. According to him all mental states can be analyzed into a group of ideas, and one of the problems of psychology is to discover the ways in which these ideas are associated. This notion of the "content" of the mind has been responsible for much of the unproductivity of British psychology and has persisted to the present day in popular thinking. It is easy to think of the mind as a place where a flock of separate ideas are stored. A better view, psychology has found, is to think of ideas simply as ways the mind has of behaving. Locke's most helpful contribution was his defense of exact methods for arriving at conclusions and his emphasis of the fact that all knowledge comes to us by way of the senses; that is, that sensation is the primary level of cognition.

Locke's philosophy was the forerunner of a trend of psychology called British Associationism. More particularly this trend became a definite doctrine with the writing of David Hartley (1705-1757). Two contemporary British philosophers, George Berkeley (1685-1753) and David Hume (1711-1776), had done much to develop the concept, but with Hartley the association of ideas became association*ism*. He did what many near-great men have done. He took one concept and built a whole philosophy around it. British Associationism is to be traced through the writings of James Mill (1773-1836) and his precocious son John Stuart Mill (1806-1873) properly concluding with Alexander Bain (1818-1903).

Another trend of thought which has tremendously influenced British psychology is the theory of evolution as advocated and ably supported by Charles Darwin (1809-1882). The storm of criticism which broke about Darwin's head was his reward for amassing a greater amount of accurate evidence in support of the theory than any of his predecessors had done. It is difficult to realize what a remarkable influence this theory has had. Nearly every British writer in psychology even to the present day seeks to show the phylogenetic or evolutionary implication of the subject with which he concerns himself. It may safely be said that the unproductive British Associationism which was centered about the concept of the mind as a place where ideas were stuffed has been largely supplanted by the more fertile doctrine of evolution with its broad genetic implications.

In olden days it used to be possible for a great scholar to have a mastery of practically all human knowledge. The last great scholar to attempt such a mastery was Herbert Spencer (1820-1903). He attempted to systematize all the knowledge of the world in a series of ten volumes. The remarkable thing about it is that he came so close to reaching his goal. Spencer's work, although largely eclipsed by the striking Darwinian theory, represented a broader view of the evolutionary process than that of any other man of the nineteenth century. Spencer's work was neither so thorough nor so original, but it was better systematized. He was not as well appreciated in his own country, Britain, as he was in the United States. It is not until recent years that British writers have begun to recognize fully the debt which they owe to their talented fellow-countryman.

We have roughly traced the ancestral line of British psychology from Locke to Spencer. Let us turn now to German psychology. Perhaps we should start with Gottfried Wilhelm Leibnitz (1646-1716), although he can scarcely be placed in the list of experimental scientists, even for his time. His name is to be remembered, however, for his invention of the calculus and for his philosophical doctrine of *monads*. All existence is divided up into independent units or monads which have absolutely no relation to each other. If these units of existence do appear to concur or to act in relation to each other, it is because the laws of the universe cause them to act synchronously. They cannot affect each other. They are like a series of clocks wound up and set going at the same time; one clock has nothing to do with the other clocks, yet it is so perfectly regulated that it will always show the same time. Well, that part of the doctrine is interesting, but it does not have much to do with psychology. The part that does have psychological significance is that these monads, or units of existence, are not to be considered as objects but as courses of action. Here we have the beginning of a different trend of thought from that of the British psychologists. Locke made the mistake of envisaging the idea as an object or thing rather than as a course of mental activity, while Leibnitz went to the other extreme and said that not only are ideas activities but matter itself is no more than a group of activities—monads of motion. Such is the German tradition. Is it any wonder that England produced its Spencer and Germany its Einstein?

Immanuel Kant (1724-1804), the great German philosopher, discarded Leibnitz's theory of monads and concentrated his attention on the nature of mind before experience touches it. This lack of interest in the part which experience plays tended to divorce his philosophy from the psychological train. An interesting fact concerning Kant's personal life is frequently cited. He lived all his life in Königsberg without ever being farther away from the city than his recreational tramps might carry him; some say, never more than ten miles.

Johann Friedrich Herbart (1776-1841) was both a philosopher and a scientific pedagogue. He was one of the first to attempt to apply psychology to the problems of teaching. According to his doctrine of the *apperceptive mass* the mind could not accept a new idea unless it fitted into the ideas which were conscious at the time. In trying to recall or set up an idea the apperceptive mass, or background of previous experience, must always be taken into consideration. Our perceptions are then really more than perceptions, they are apperceptions, experiences into which all past experiences are fused as well as the object of the moment. This doctrine became one of the canons of good pedagogy.

Johannes Müller (1801-1858) was not a philosopher but a physiologist. He once predicted that the velocity of the nervous impulse could never be measured, but six years later one of his students, Hermann von Helmholtz (1821-1894) made quite accurate calculations of the velocity of nervous conduction in the frog. Helmholtz investigated many subjects. He was both a physiologist and a physicist. Much of his experimentation in the field of sensation still stands. His description of the physiology and the function of the ear and eye has scarcely been improved upon except in minor details.

Gustav Theodor Fechner (1801-1887), a German, was both philosopher and physicist. In 1860 he published his *Elemente der Psychophysik* in which he set forth the experimental method of determining the relation between mind and body which was to become known as the Fechner-Weber law. The law itself is not so important for our purposes here except as it marked the beginning of an attitude toward the relation between these two aspects of our existence without which psychology as it exists today could never have come into being. There is a relation between the two, and it is only through physical manifestations that we are ever able to predict the nature of mind.

Wilhelm Wundt (1832-1920) is probably the greatest name in the history of psychology. In 1873 and 1874 he published his most important book, *Grundzüge der physiologischen Psychologie*. In 1879 he established the first psychological laboratory at Leipzig. Many of the earlier American psychologists received their training in this laboratory, some of whom we shall have cause to mention when we take up American psychology. Wundt's *Grundzüge* went through six revisions in the period from 1873 to 1911. It is not to be supposed that Wundt's only contribution was contained in the book. It has been said that he wrote or revised his writings at an average rate of 2.2 pages a day for the sixty-seven years of his productive life. We now leave Wundt for the moment to return to him when we have cause to study his system.

Second to the great experimentalist Wundt we must mention Georg Elias Müller (1850-) and his laboratory at Göttingen. His principal contributions have been in line with Fechner in psycho-physics (the experimental study of the mind-body relation).

Franz Brentano (1838-1917) of Italian descent was born and lived in Germany. He is important because we may directly trace to him one of the important systems of psychology of the last century. Following in the train which we have hinted at from the philosophy of Leibnitz he maintained that mental phenomena are to be thought of as acts; hence the name given this system of psychology—act psychology. We do not see the color green, but we *act* in such a way as to imply such a phenomenon. The sensation of sound is not sound itself, but it is an *act* in which sound is imminent. Notice the distinction between the sensation and the thing which is sensed. The former is an *act*; the latter is a *content*. Of course the content is the intention of the act. The act stands for the content.

Brentano tremendously influenced Carl Stumpf (1848-) who is next in the line of the act psychologists. Stumpf's principal interest was in music, but he combined his interest and his academic vocation. He became a philosopher, for in Germany psychology has always been considered a branch of philosophy, and made his principal contributions in the field of the psychology of music—acoustics, tone perception, esthetics. Since 1894 he has held a professorship in the University of Berlin, a most distinguished position in an ideal location for a man of Stumpf's interests.

Stumpf carried forward the Brentano tradition of *act* psychology, but one of his students, Husserl (1859[11]-), altered the doctrine slightly. He distinguished between the acts and the phenomena. There grew up around this distinction a system of psychology called *phenomenology*. In the pure act psychology it was the act of the organism that was the subject of psychology; in phenomenology it was the event toward which the act was directed. Roughly we might say that the one studied the organic process, and the other studied the stimulation.

This psychology was to be particularly contrasted with the psychology of Wundt which was branded as elementalism. Wundt attempted to analyze the processes of the mind into sensations or units, a thing which the act psychologists and the phenomenologists argued could not be done. Here we have the fundamental difference between the systems of act and content. Of course, Wundt was quite aware that sensation, perception, etc. were not states but were processes. It was the situation into which he as an experimentalist found himself thrust that made it hard to avoid analysis and elementalism.

Oswald Külpe (1862-1915) is to be known for the work of himself and his students at Würtzburg. Their subject of investigation was the higher thought processes. Is there such a thing as thought which does not take into account sensory impressions or images? Their answer was, yes, there are conscious attitudes in thought which are not imaginal in nature. These psychologists became known as the Würtzburg school of imageless thought. Needless to say, they made quite a stir in the field which was so dominated by the Wundtian type of analysis.

To return to act psychology: Christian von Ehrenfels (1859-) like Stumpf had studied under Brentano but at Vienna. He created the concept of form-quality (Gestaltqualität). It is not alone the object or its parts that we sense; we also sense the form or pattern.

[11] Date inserted by editors.

That is a new quality in the situation. He distinguished two general kinds of form-qualities, the temporal and the non-temporal. The non-temporal corresponded to what we have referred to as *spatial patterns* in an earlier chapter of this book.

Max Wertheimer (1880-) further modified this system by denying that the form or pattern was sensed in addition to the other qualities. He said that any experience comes to us as a whole, as a form in itself, as a *Gestalt*, not as a bundle of sensations of which the sensation of form is only one. The paper in which this doctrine was set forth appeared in 1912, and it established Wertheimer as the originator of the new and much talked of school of *Gestalt* psychology. Kurt Koffka (1886-) and Wolfgang Köhler (1887-) have become known as the twin priests of the new sect.

We turn now to mention the last of the long list of important German psychologists, Hermann Ebbinghaus (1850-1909). Impressed by the psycho-physics of Fechner this talented scholar set about applying the new science to the problem of memory. It was his own memory that he experimented upon, often learning long and tedious lists of nonsense syllables. Much of Ebbinghaus's work was done without connection with any university. Later he became professor at Berlin, then at Breslau, and finally at Halle. His name does not belong to the history of any one system of psychology, but his work opened up an important field.

We turn again to British psychology. Sir Francis Galton (1822-1911) investigated wherever his interests led him. He was motivated in his psychological work mainly by the contribution of his half cousin, Charles Darwin. He wished to study human evolution and inheritance from a quantitative point of view. We remember him because of his contribution to mental tests, individual differences, and statistical method. While Galton laid the foundation for statistical methods, it is to Karl Pearson (1857-) that we turn for the mathematical formulation of many of the devices now in use. It was he who gave us the present formula for correlation as well as a number of other practical applications of statistical theory. More recent British names in this field of psychology are G. Udny Yule (1871-), Charles Spearman (1863-) and Godfrey Thomson (1881-). Thomson, following the British tradition as set by Spencer and Galton, has turned his talents into many productive channels. Turning from his interest in music, he trained himself in science at Leipzig. Later his interest shifted from physics to psycho-physics, from psycho-physics to statistical method, from statistical method to the problem of the statistical analysis of intelligence where he confuted Spearman's doctrine of the general factor underlying all mental ability, from problems of intelligence to problems of character formation, and finally from problems of character to problems of education. His latest book, *A Modern Philosophy of Education*, presents a progressive view which only a man with broad experiences extending from Leipzig to Columbia and back again to England and Scotland could be expected to express. He is now professor of education at the University of Edinburgh and director of the Edinburgh Provincial Training College for teachers.

French psychology with perhaps two exceptions does not bear the systematic relation to modern American psychology that we have seen in the case of the German and the British psychologies. Those exceptions, however, are important ones. French psychologists have always been interested in abnormality and the problems of mental disease. Pierre Janet (1859-) is noted for his descriptions of hysteria. Systematically his point of view is about as mechanistic as that of any of the students of abnormal psychology. To explain what we mean by the term mechanistic let us take up the doctrines of Sigmund Freud (1856-[12]). Freud was really influenced more by the French school than the German, although he was a German[13] by nationality and his connection has been with the University of Vienna. Freud said that instincts are really *forces* which play upon us. That idea of *forces* is important. It serves to distinguish his brand of psychology from the mechanistic brand. Where Janet would describe the mind as a stream of sensations or reactions—a *mechanistic* view—Freud would describe it as a place where forces are brought into play—a *dynamic* view. Freud's theories have made quite a stir. We have mentioned some of the difficulties which the layman has in accepting them in our chapter on abnormal psychology. In spite of his technical difference, Freud, the German[14], really belongs systematically to the French school. I think we would be justified in placing all psychologists who adopt the dynamic point of view in abnormal psychology in that lineage.

Theodule Armand Ribot (1839-1916) is another French psychologist to whom we are indebted. While his principal interests were in psychopathology, he did more than any other man to interpret the German, British, and American viewpoints for the French psychologists.

Aside from this systematic angle psychology, and especially that of America, owes French psychology a debt by way of Alfred Binet (1857-1911). Binet constructed the first successful intelligence test while working with the school children of Paris. What school, wherever it may be, has not heard of the Binet test? The "Binet scale" was first published in 1905, an important date to be remembered by every educator.

From Europe we turn to America where the seat of experimental psychology now is indisputably located. America has her psychological roots in the classic writings of the great William James (1842-1910). While James was primarily a philosopher and while most of American experimental psychology was imported from Germany by students who went to Leipzig to study under Wundt, it is in James that we find our psychological tradition. James's psychology was definitely physiological; so is present American psychology. James's psychology was functional; so is most of American psychology. His *Principles of Psychology* published in 1890 are worthy of study even by him who would be ultra-modern in this most fadistic of sciences.

[12] Date inserted by editors.

[13] Editors' note: [sic].

[14] Editors' note: [sic].

John Dewey (1859-) developed James's functional psychology. Dewey is probably the greatest of living philosophers, at least the greatest of living educational philosophers.

James McKeen Cattell (1860-) was one of the Americans who studied under Wundt. He took with him to Leipzig the problem of individual differences, but he brought it back again to America with the result that American applied psychology has been largely a study of this problem, and Cattell has been aptly named the dean of American psychologists.

G. Stanley Hall (1844-1924) was a great founder of institutions and journals. We have met him in our discussion of genetic psychology. Hall started many lines of investigation but left them to his students to complete while he went on to other fields of interest. His stimulating influence on American psychology is sometimes under-estimated by those who disagree with his views.

One of Cattell's students, Edward L. Thorndike (1874-) entered psychology by way of animal psychology. The problem of animal learning yielded for him the basis of an exhaustive treatment of educational psychology which has largely been responsible for making Columbia University the mecca for educational study in the United States.

American psychologists have turned to the interesting problem of neuro-physiology or the problem of the function of nervous tissue. The work of some younger psychologists must be mentioned here. Such men as K. S. Lashley (1890-) and more lately L. E. Travis (1896-) have adopted the view of mass responsiveness in the nervous system, a view which is in line with the new *Gestalt* psychology (we touched upon "mass responsiveness" in an early chapter). In opposition we find W. S. Hunter (1889-) representing a mild form of behaviorism.

We must mention a figure which stands picturesquely alone. Edward Bradford Titchener (1867-1927) was educated at Oxford but made the mistake—at least from the standpoint of the Oxford tradition—of completing his study in physiological psychology under Wundt at Leipzig. He would like to have returned to Oxford, but there was no opportunity there for a man of his interests, so he was forced to come to America finally to settle down at Cornell, where he remained the rest of his life. Systematically he represents the Wundtian tradition in America, a tradition which is scarcely compatible with the functionalism of the James tradition. His system has been called *structuralism*. It is really the psychology of content which we have mentioned above. The American version of the German controversy between the psychologies of act and content is the controversy between functionalism and structuralism.

Like their master, most of Titchener's students stand alone unperturbed by the storms of mental testers, functionalists, selfists, Freudian psychoanalysts, behaviorists, and *Gestalt* psychologists. Their psychology is systematically complete, analytic, and thoroughly scholarly in form.

Another Englishman, William McDougall (1871-) came to America. His contribution has rested largely in the field of social psychology, but his most striking doctrine bears upon abnormal psychology, which, by the way, is properly quite closely related. According to his view instincts are drives (in that he agrees with Freud) and each instinct has its characteristic emotion. He has probably met his most able critic in James Drever (1873-) of the University of Edinburgh, a mechanist of the British school with an unusual analytic talent.

We may recognize four principal systems in American psychology: *functionalism*, *structuralism*, *behaviorism*, and *Gestalt psychology*. Functionalism is the truly American psychology following James. The term has been somewhat variously used, but in general it stands for the type of psychology which studies mental processes rather than mental states. Structuralism is not necessarily the antithesis of functionalism, although the two schools have commonly been cited as opposites. It emphasizes the study of the manner in which concepts or mental phenomena are built up. It is thus an analytic and synthetic type of psychology. Behaviorism really comes from the Russian psychologist, Ivan Petrovitch Pavlov (1849-) who performed the first conditioned reflex experiment. Behaviorism is essentially a method rather than a theory in psychology. Many people make the mistake of treating it as a philosophical theory and criticizing it accordingly. The behaviorist discards all experimental evidence except that which is most objective and easily verified. He accepts no terms such as mind, consciousness, or instinct on the grounds that they are not verifiable by the method of observation of overt behavior. The method is no more or less than that of animal psychology applied to human psychology. Although not the first to advocate the method or the term in this country, John B. Watson (1878-) has been the most noticeable exponent of this "ism." *Gestalt* psychology we have briefly described before. It was imported from Germany largely by the twin priests, Köhler and Koffka. American psychology seems to have proved to be even more fertile soil for its development than its native Germany. A newer and more complete version of this system has been propounded by Raymond Wheeler (1892-) under the name of *organismic* psychology.

We said in our introductory chapter that psychologists were always disagreeing among themselves. We hope that we have made it clear that the bases of their disagreement have been highly technical and difficult points—not short-sighted and personal prejudices. It is only when one reaches the frontier of a science that he finds well trained and sincere scientists disputing as to which road to take next.

Psychology is what the psychologists talk about. Perhaps you thought we were merely being facetious in making that remark at the beginning of this book. Well, now that you have read the bit of psychological gossip which we have recorded on these pages, how would you define it?

Chapter 23

What To Read Next

We shall assume that you wish to read further in this subject of psychology. That may be an unwarranted assumption.

If you wish to read a more advanced book of the survey type, a book covering such fields as we have discussed in Chapters 15 to 21 of the present volume, we suggest G.D. Higginson's new book, *Fields of Psychology*, Henry Holt and Company, New York, 1931. You will find it a little stiffer to handle than some other books but if you are anxious to make another rapid survey of the field you probably cannot do better.

In the field of introductory general psychology, such a field as you would study if you were to take a first course in psychology at a university, we are going to suggest two out of a large number of available texts. Howard C. Warren and Leonard Carmichael have a very carefully written and illustrated text called, *Elements of Human Psychology*, Houghton Mifflin Company, New York, 1930. The view-point taken is pretty well in the middle of the road as far as modern systems of psychology are concerned. These authors have done some very good work in systematizing and classifying terms. Another good book is J.F. Dashiell's *Fundamentals of Objective Psychology*, Houghton Mifflin Company, New York, 1928. It is written definitely from the behavioristic standpoint. It contains a good deal of neuro-physiology and cites the results of a great many experiments. Either of these texts will give you a thorough grounding in the field of general psychology.

For a thorough description of cognition it is pretty hard to beat E.B. Titchener's *A Textbook of Psychology*, Macmillan Company, New York, 1909. The point of view is analytic, following in the track of Wundt. You will find it pretty tough going. If you wish to read a more elementary book, and you probably will, we suggest a little book by one of Titchener's pupils, C.A. Ruckmick. It is called *The Mental Life*, Longmans, Green and Company, New York, 1928. It is written in a very readable style but it is thoroughly scholarly.

If you wish to read from the classic writings of William James we suggest his book, *Psychology*, Henry Holt and Company, New York, 1893. You will be surprised to see how little of his work has been superseded.

In abnormal psychology our opinion is that the outstanding textbook is J.J.B. Morgan's *Psychology of Abnormal People*, Longmans, Green and Company, New York, 1928. His description of mental disorders is given from the conservative psychological point of view. Little is said about psychoanalysis and Freudian doctrines. If you wish to study these see the book by William Healy, Augusta F. Bronner, and Anna Mae Bowers, *The Structure and Meaning of Psychoanalysis*, Alfred A. Knopf, New York, 1930. It is a large volume and difficult reading, but you cannot expect to understand the doctrine of psychoanalysis without some very tedious study. We do not believe that this topic can be well covered in a survey type of book. That is our personal opinion.

The best book on the psychology and neurology of speech is L.E. Travis' *Speech Pathology*, Appleton Company, New York, 1931. In our opinion it is not only the best but the only thorough book of its kind. You will find his treatment of the problem of stuttering particularly satisfactory.

In the field of educational psychology we recommend as a general text W.C. Trow's *Educational Psychology*, Houghton Mifflin Company, New York, 1931 although there are a number of good texts in the field. You may want to read one of L.E. Thorndike's books. In that case we recommend his recent book, *Human Learning*, The Century Company, New York, 1931. It is a short book and deals entirely with the problem of learning. It consists of a defense and restatement of his laws of learning. Another good systematic book dealing with the problem of learning is W.H. Pyle's *Psychology of Learning*, Warwick and York, Inc., Baltimore, 1925.

In the field of statistical method we recommend H.E. Garrett's much used *Statistics in Psychology and Education*, Longmans Green and Company, New York, 1926, although for a very brief and simple treatment one may prefer to read Harold Rugg's *A Primer of Graphics and Statistics*, Houghton Mifflin Company, New York, 1925.

In the field of standardized tests it is hard to make a selection. Personally we are rather partial to the type of intelligence test which A.S. Otis constructs. Its principal advantage is its ease and speed of administration. The World Book Company of New York handles them although the state university of nearly every state maintains a test bureau or department of service through which all of the modern standardized tests may be obtained. For diagnostic and remedial tests we recommend the series in which F.B. Knight has collaborated, *The Compass Tests*, Scott Foresman and Company, Chicago. For a thorough text on the psychology of elementary school subjects the author would like to recommend his colleague's book, *The Psychology of Elementary School Subjects*, by H.B. Reed, Ginn and Company, New York, 1927.

In genetic psychology J.J.B. Morgan's *Child Psychology*, Richard R. Smith, Inc., New York, 1931 and F.D. Brooks' *Psychology of Adolescence*, Houghton Mifflin Company, New York, 1929 are both good books.

In animal psychology Margaret F. Washburn's *The Animal Mind,* Macmillan Company, New York, 1909 has long been a standard text. You may like to read Wolfgang Köhler's *The Mentality of Apes* (Translated by E. Winter.) Harcourt Brace, New York, 1925. It is certainly an interesting book.

We believe that the most through treatment of social psychology is that by Kimball Young in his two volume work, *Social Psychology*, F.S. Crofts and Company, New York, 1930 and *Source Book for Social Psychology*, F.S. Crofts, New York, 1927. The treatment is apt to be tedious at times but we can assure you that little of importance in social psychology has been left out. A briefer volume written from the sociological point of view but not so good from the psychological point of view is E.S. Bogardus' *Fundamentals of Social Psychology*, The Century Company, New York, 1931. If you want to read a classic but thoroughly interesting book, look up W.G. Sumner's *Folkways*, Ginn and Company, Boston, 1906. For a recent book in educational sociology you will find W.R. Smith's *Educational Sociology*, Houghton Mifflin Company, New York 1929 one in which a number of unique and stimulating ideas are expressed.

In applied psychology look for A.T. Poffenberger's *Applied Psychology*, D. Appleton and Company, New York, 1927. Carl E. Seashore's book, *The Psychology of Musical Talent*, Silver, Burdett and Company, 1919, is certainly worth reading if you are interested in the psychology of music. A more recent volume is one edited by Seashore which consists of a report of the laboratory studies conducted under his supervision. See Volume 1 of the University of Iowa Studies in the Psychology of Music, *The Vibrato*, University of Iowa, 1932.

Finally, in the history of psychology we recommend E.G. Boring's *A History of Experimental Psychology*, The Century Company, New York, 1929. While it is a rather large volume the style is most readable and clear. We recommend it highly.

124

Aggravating Aphorisms: How to Read a Psychological Dictionary Between the Lines[1]

Intervening Variable	A psychic apparition flapping between two fixed observations.
Objectivity	The fine print in a psychological transaction.
Reliability	A characteristic of any test which fails to detect variation in the person tested[2].
Validity	A property of human judgment often erroneously attributed to a test.
Stimulus	Something invented to account for a response.
Response	Something invented so a stimulus could be made accountable for something.
Operational definition	A fact allowed to stand in lieu of an idea. Characteristically found in the thinking of brain-injured patients.
Pavlov	An early Muscovite who was the first of several to demonstrate a practical way of making a person's mouth water without giving him anything to eat. (Note: This eventually results in widespread extinction, *vide* Hungary, 1956.)
Reinforcement	An experimentalist's effort to apply the Golden Rule to his subject.
Learned	The past participle of the verb, *to become*.
Construct	A type of hurdle used in intra-scholastic competition. (Note: If it is knocked down or bypassed the student is considered disqualified.)
Empirical finding	A fact that makes no sense. A lonely fact wandering about in search of meaning.
Scientific inference	A sense that makes no fact. A lonely (innocent) meaning wandering about in search of a vulgar fact.
Event	Something that comes out of nowhere and ends in oblivion.
Null hypothesis	A hostage to chaos.
Authoritarian personality	Anyone I can blame for my ineffectuality. A person I haven't the courage to disagree with.
Equalitarian personality	Anyone I can ignore. A person who doesn't bother to disagree with me.
Human nature	The only part of nature people are reluctant to change.
Schizophrenic	A person to whom one must listen with a split mind.
Anxiety	A disorienting clutter of impulses[3].

[1] Dated 1936. Published by permission of Jacqueline Aldridge.
[2] A previous definition of this in the manuscript was 'A characteristic of any test which fails to measure change.'
[3] Kelly's alternative definition of this, which was deleted, was 'Psychological garbage that psychiatrists are willing to collect regularly for fifty dollars an hour.'

Collected Papers of the Pioneer of Constructivist Psychology: George A. Kelly, First Edition. Edited by David A. Winter and Nick Reed.

125

Inductive Trigonometry[1]

Assignment 1

Introduction

With the development of civilization has come the need for measurement. Everything that exists exists in some amount and this is particularly true of distance. When man first found it necessary to measure the distance between two points he probably did it by pacing off the distance. Later, when more accurate means were needed he devised such linear units as "foot," "meter," and "mile." However, it is not always possible to measure directly even with exact and accurate units; oftentimes an obstacle is in the way. Swiftly flowing rivers, sheer cliffs, distant stars caused man to cast about for some indirect method of measuring distances.

More than 2000 years before the Christian era Egyptian and Babylonian mathematicians used their knowledge of the properties of angles in devising indirect means of mensuration. They found that by taking into account the angles between "lines of sight" great distances could be ascertained in relation to a smaller and more readily measured distance. During the ages which have intervened between their times and ours the science of trigonometry has become symbolic of the natural orderliness and symmetrical beauty of the universe. It has also become an indispensable tool of the engineer, the carpenter, the surveyor, the glass-cutter, the thoretical physicist, the landscape architect, the mathematician, and all the rest of the human artisans whose crafts depend upon a knowledge of the natural order in space.

An Angle Defined

In reading this work the exact trigonometric notion of an angle must be clearly understood. *An angle is the amount of rotation of a line (l) about a point (0) from an initial position (OX) to a terminal position (OP)* (Fig. 1). There is no limitation on the amount of rotation of the line about 0. The angle may represent any part of a complete revolution or it may represent several complete revolutions. This definition of an angle is more comprehensive and practical than the popular conception of an angle.

If the rotation is in a counter-clockwise direction, that is, in the direction opposite to that of the hands of a clock when one faces it, the angle is said to be positive. A clockwise direction of rotation makes the angle negative (Fig. 1[2]).

Sexagesimal and Radian Measure

Now that the definition of an angle is understood a unit of measurement must be considered. If we divide one complete revolution into 360 equal parts we have the most common unit of angle measure, *the degree*. Ninety degrees, written "90°," form a right angle. One hundred eighty degrees form a flat angle or half a revolution. If we divide the degree into sixty equal parts we have *minutes* and if we divide the minute into sixty equal parts we have *seconds*. Thus there are sixty seconds in a minute, sixty minutes in a degree and three hundred sixty degrees in a complete revolution. This system is called "sexagesimal measure." An angle thirty-nine degrees, forty-five minutes and fifty-four seconds in size is written $39^\circ\ 45'54''$.

Another measure of angularity which is frequently used and which possesses some technical and theoretical advantages over the sexagesimal measure is the *radian*. If we lay off along the circumference of a circle a distance exactly equal to the radius of the circle the resulting arc will subtend an angle one radian in size (Fig. 2). Since the circumference of a circle equals $2\pi r$ we see that there are 2π radians in a complete revolution. We have seen that one complete revolution equals 360 degrees.

Therefore: $2\pi \text{ Rad} = 360^\circ$.

and: $1 \text{ Rad} = 360/2\,\pi^\circ$ or $57^\circ\ 17'\ 45''$

(when π is given the value 3.1416)

Likewise: 1° equals $2\pi/360$ Rad or $\pi/180$ Rad or 0.01745 Rad.

[1] Sections of an unpublished programmed learning book with W.G. Warnock, dated 1935. Published by permission of Jacqueline Aldridge.

[2] Editors' note: The Figures are missing from the manuscript.

Collected Papers of the Pioneer of Constructivist Psychology: George A. Kelly, First Edition. Edited by David A. Winter and Nick Reed.

In designating an angle with radian measure the radian symbol is frequently omitted. Thus the expression A = 4 is read, "Angle A equals four radians."

Coordinate System

Before our knowledge of angles can aid us in making indirect measurements of distances it is necessary that we know something about the relations between angles and straight-line distances. Consider the line, XOX′. (Fig. 3.) Begin at 0 and mark off equal distances in both directions. Number these, "1, 2, 3, 4," etc. Those to the right of 0 are taken as positive; those to the left, negative. In this way a simple geometric notion of algebraic numbers is formed. If we place two such scales mutually perpendicular to each other to intersect at 0, as shown in Fig. 3, we obtain a coordinate system on which any point in the plane may be located by giving its horizontal and vertical distances from 0. The horizontal distances are known as x-distances or *abscissas* and the vertical distances are known as y-distances or *ordinates*. The line XOX′ is known as the x-axis or axis of abscissas and the line YOY′ is known as the y-axis or axis of ordinates. The point, P (3, 3) is three units to the right and three units up while the point, Q (4,-1) is four units to the right and one unit down. The first number in the parentheses always indicates the x-distance or horizontal distance from 0 while the second number in the parentheses always indicates the y-distance or vertical distance from 0. The diagonal distance from 0 directly to P is called the *radius vector, vector*, or *r*. Since r is really the hypotenuse of a right angled triangle whose other sides are x and y we can infer the length of r from the equation $r^2 = x^2 + y^2 \; or \; r = \sqrt{x^2 + y^2}$. This system of coordinates in a plane is known as *Cartesian Rectangular Coordinates* after René Descartes (1596-1650).

The Fundamental Functions of Trigonometry

The characteristics of an angle which make it possible to measure distances indirectly are based upon the six possible ratios of abscissa, ordinate, and vector (x, y, and r). The angle described is the one lying between OP and OX. These characteristics are called the *trigonometric functions* of an angle and are designated as follows (Fig. 4):

1 The *sine* of an angle.

$$\sin \text{AOP} = \frac{\text{Ordinate of P}}{\text{Vector of P}} = \frac{y}{r}$$

2 The *cosine* of an angle.

$$\cos \text{AOP} = \frac{\text{Abscissa of P}}{\text{Vector of P}} = \frac{x}{r}$$

3 The *tangent* of an angle.

$$\tan \text{AOP} = \frac{\text{Ordinate of P}}{\text{Abscissa of P}} = \frac{y}{x}$$

4 The *cotangent* of an angle,

$$\cot \text{AOP} = \frac{\text{Abscissa of P}}{\text{Ordinate of P}} = \frac{x}{y}$$

5 The *secant* of an angle,

$$\sec \text{AOP} = \frac{\text{Vector of P}}{\text{Abscissa of P}} = \frac{r}{x}$$

6 The *cosecant* of an angle.

$$csc \; \text{AOP} = \frac{\text{Vector of P}}{\text{Ordinate of P}} = \frac{r}{y}$$

Because these functions are defined in ratios any point on the terminal side could serve as P. That is, the various other functions are independent of the point P provided only d is on the terminal side…

Notice (Fig. 4) that while the vector is always positive the abscissa and ordinate may be either positive or negative, The area XOY is called the *first quadrant*, the area X′OY is called the *second quadrant*, the area X′OY′ is called the *third quadrant*, and the area XOY′ is called the *fourth quadrant* (see roman numerals in Fig. 4).

It will be observed that the trigonometric functions themselves have different signs according to the quadrant in which P lies. The student should verify the following table at this point by substituting in the formulae above the appropriate positive and negative values of x and y according to the quadrant in which P lies.

SIGNS OF TRIGONOMETRIC FUNCTIONS ACCORDING TO QUADRANTS

	Quadrant in which P is located			
Function	*First*	*Second*	*Third*	*Fourth*
Sine	+	+	-	-
Cosine	+	-	-	+
Tan gent	+	-	+	-
Cotangent	+	-	+	-
Secant	+	-	-	+
Cosecant	+	+	-	-

Simple Trigonometric Relations

Trigonometry is nothing more than the study and application of the relationships between the six functions of an angle (except in rare instances when other functions are added to the list). Following are a few relations which appear directly from the definitions of the functions. The student should learn them well, for they are involved in the solution of nearly every trigonometric problem. This group is known as the *reciprocal relations.*

Since: $\sin A = \frac{y}{r}$ and $\csc A = \frac{r}{y}$, $\sin A = \frac{1}{\csc A}$, $\csc A = \frac{1}{\sin A}$, and $\sin A \csc A = 1$

Also: $\cos A = \frac{x}{r}$ and $\sec A = \frac{r}{x}$, $\cos A = \frac{1}{\sec A}$, $\sec A = \frac{1}{\cos A}$, and $\cos A \sec A = 1$

And: $\tan A = \frac{y}{x}$ and $\cot A = \frac{x}{y}$, $\tan A = \frac{1}{\cot A}$, $\cot A = \frac{1}{\tan A}$, and $\tan A \cot A = 1$

Another simple relation may be shown as follows:

$$\sin A = \frac{y}{r}, \cos A = \frac{x}{r}, \therefore \frac{\sin A}{\cos A} = \frac{\frac{y}{r}}{\frac{x}{r}} = \frac{y}{x} = \tan A, \tan A = \frac{\sin A}{\cos A}, \text{and } \cot A = \frac{\cos A}{\sin A}$$

Three other simple relations may be shown as follows:

$$x^2+y^2 = r^2, \sin^2 A = \frac{y^2}{r^2}, \cos^2 A = \frac{x^2}{r^2}, \sin^2 A+\cos^2 A =$$

$$\frac{y^2}{r^2}+\frac{x^2}{r^2} = \frac{x^2+y^2}{r^2} = \frac{r^2}{r^2} = 1 \text{ or } 1\text{-}\sin^2 A = \cos^2 A \text{ and } 1\text{-}\cos^2 A = \sin^2 A$$

$$r^2\text{-}y^2 = x^2, \tan^2 A = \frac{y^2}{x^2}, \sec^2 A = \frac{r^2}{x^2}, \sec^2 A\text{-}\tan^2 A = \frac{r^2}{x^2}-\frac{y^2}{x^2}$$

$$= \frac{r^2-y^2}{x^2} = \frac{x^2}{x^2} = 1, \text{ or } \tan^2 A+1 = \sec^2 A \text{ and } \sec^2 A\text{-}1 = \tan^2 A$$

$$r^2\text{-}x^2 = y^2, \cot^2 A = \frac{x^2}{y^2}, \csc^2 A = \frac{r^2}{y^2}, \csc^2 A - \cot^2 A = \frac{r^2}{y^2}-\frac{x^2}{y^2} =$$

$$\frac{r^2-x^2}{y^2} = \frac{y^2}{y^2} = 1, \text{ or } \cot^2 A+1 = \csc^2 A \text{ and } \csc^2 A\text{-}1 = \cot^2 A$$

These relations may be summarized as follows:
The Reciprocal Relations

$$\sin A = \frac{1}{\csc A}, \csc A = \frac{1}{\sin A}, \sin A \csc A = 1$$

$$\cos A = \frac{1}{\sec A}, \sec A = \frac{1}{\cos A}, \cos A \sec A = 1$$

$$\tan A = \frac{1}{\cot A}, \cot A = \frac{1}{\tan A}, \tan A \cot A = 1$$

The Three-Function Relation

$$\tan A = \frac{\sin A}{\cos A}, \cot A = \frac{\cos A}{\sin A} \underline{\text{etc.}}$$

The Other Simple Relations

$$\sin^2 A + \cos^2 A = 1 \ \underline{\text{etc.}}$$

$$\sec^2 A - \tan^2 A = 1 \ \underline{\text{etc.}}$$

$$\csc^2 A - \cot^2 A = 1 \ \underline{\text{etc.}}$$

Practice Exercises

To the student: Do not attempt to solve the following practice exercises until you have carefully read the following instructions. This is important!

1 Answer all of the questions. Do not omit a single one. These questions are not simply thrown together; they are a carefully compiled and correlated series of practice exercises. Every unnecessary question has been taken out of the lists. The ones which remain are designed to give you just the proper balance of practice in handling each idea presented in the text.
2 Answer the questions in the order in which they have been numbered. Start with number 1 and complete it before going to Number 2, and so on. The questions have been arranged in a logical and systematic order and, in general, each answer prepares the student for the succeeding questions. This is what is called the inductive method. It will save you more time than you realize.
3 Learn actively, not passively. Simply finding the correct answers to the questions is not enough. It is possible for a student to answer all the questions and know little more then when he started. Make up your mind that you will master this course. You have at your disposal some of the best teaching devices that can be provided but they are useless unless you take an aggressive attitude toward your work.
4 Have regular periods of study. It is difficult to study during an hour which you have customarily employed in recreation or sleep.
5 Study intensively. Study periods should be short enough to enable you to avoid the habit of half-hearted study. Thirty-minute periods are not too short. Some students may find it advantageous to use even shorter periods. Never let your attention wander from your task during a regular study period.
6 Think frequently about your work when not actually studying. Casually turn over in your mind principles and questions which have confronted you, even when on the way to classes, during recreation periods, or in odd moments. This is in accordance with the psychological principle of maturation which is nothing more or less than the old adage "never make an important decision until you have slept on it." Your study periods should be so arranged that you will have plenty of time for maturation before attending class sessions. The student who goes over his lesson and then throws his book aside and "forgets it" does just that—he forgets it!
7 Following the numbers of most of the practice exercises are other numbers. The second number refers you to an illustrated solution of a similar exercise. The list of illustrated solutions follows the list of practice exercises.
When you find a problem which you cannot solve turn to the illustrated solutions and read the solution of a similar problem.
8 Notice that a systematic plan of continuous review is maintained throughout the practical assignments. This means that you may have frequently to refer to previous assignments.
9 Most of the questions are of the multiple choice type. Notice that in some cases more than one answer is to be chosen.

Remember that your task is *to teach yourself trigonometry* not merely to answer questions.

1 Which of the following are indirect methods of measuring distance?
  a Apply the measuring instrument to the straight line along which the distance is measured.
  b Estimate the distance by measuring "with the eye."
  c Find the distance by observing its relation to other known distances and the angles between them.
  d Rotate the distance about a point.

2 Which of the following can ordinarily best be measured by some indirect method?
  a The height of a tall chimney.
  b The height of a door
  c The height of Niagara Falls.
  d The length of a pencil.
  e The distance to the moon.
  f The latitude of a ship at sea.

3 About how early are the first records of the use of trigonometry?
  a 1832 A.D.
  b 1754 A.D.
  c 663 A.D.
  d 63 B.C.
  e 2000 B.C.
  f 17000 B.C.

4 Which of the following is a trigonometric definition of an angle?
  a A space between two intersecting lines.
  b The distance a line moves about a point.
  c The amount of rotation of a line about a point.
  d The sharp point where two things meet.

5 Which of the following represent negative angles?
  a The angle through which the hands of a clock move.
  b The left front wheel of a forward moving motor car when viewed from the outside.
  c Screwing a lamp into a light socket.
  d Lifting the right hand end of a board.

6 Why is it said that a sexagesimal system is used in measuring angles?
  a Because it takes sixty of a smaller unit to make a larger unit.
  b Because rotation rather than distance is measured.
  c Because the system was devised by Sextus.
  d Sexagesimal measure is not used in measuring angles.

7 Which of the following relations defines the sine function of an angle?
  a x/y
  b y/x
  c r/x
  d x/r
  e r/y
  f y/r

8 Which of the above relations defines the cosine function of an angle?

9 Which of the above relations defines the secant function of an angle?

10 Which of the above relations defines the cosecant function of an angle?

11 Which of the above relations defines the tangent function of an angle?

12 Which of the above relations defines the cotangent function of an angle?

13 Which of the following are impossible relations?
- a -x/y
- b -y/r
- c -x/-r
- d -r/y
- e x/-y
- f -y/-x

14 In which of the following quadrants is the abscissa negative?
- a First
- b Second
- c Third
- d Fourth

15 In which of the above quadrants is the sine function negative?

16 In which of the above quadrants is the cosine function negative?

17 In which of the above quadrants is the secant function negative?

18 In which of the above quadrants is the cosecant function negative?

19 In which of the above quadrants is the tangent function negative?

20 In which of the above quadrants is the cotangent function negative?

21 Which of the following equations gives the correct relationship between x, y, and r?
- a $2x = 2r - 2y$
- b $x = \pm\sqrt{r^2 - y^2}$
- c $r = x^2 + y^2$
- d $x^2y^2 = r^2$

22 When the vector is in the third quadrant which of the following are negative?
- a sine
- b cosine
- c secant
- d cosecant
- e tangent
- f cotangent

23 What part of the Cartesian coordinate system is always considered the initial side of the angle?
- a OY
- b OY′
- c OX
- d OX′

24 Which use of the following trigonometric functions is equal to 1/sin A?
- a sin A
- b cos A
- c sec A
- d csc A
- e tan A
- f cot A

25 Which of the above trigonometric functions is equal to 1/cos A ?

26 Which of the above trigonometric functions is equal to 1/sec A ?

27 Which of the above trigonometric functions is equal to 1/csc A ?

28 Which of the above trigonometric functions is equal to 1/tan A ?

29 Which of the above trigonometric functions is equal to 1/cot A ?

30 Which of the above trigonometric functions is equal to sin A/cos A ?

31 Which of the above trigonometric functions is equal to cos A/sin A ?

32 Which of the above trigonometric functions is equal to $\pm\sqrt{1-\cos^2 A}$?

33 Which of the above trigonometric functions is equal to $\pm\sqrt{\sec^2 A-1}$?

34 Which of the above trigonometric functions is equal to $\pm\sqrt{\cot^2 A+1}$?

What are the sizes of the following angles in degrees, minutes and seconds?

35 An angle described by a line rotated from an initial position, OX through $+\frac{1}{4}$ of a complete revolution to a terminal position, OP?
- a 25°00′00″
- b 57°32′15″
- c 100°00′00″
- d 90°00′00″

36 - - if rotated $+\frac{1}{4}$ of a complete revolution?
- a 90°00′00″
- b 180°00′00″
- c 270°00′00″
- d 45°00′00″

37 -- $+1\frac{1}{4}$ of a complete revolution?
- a 90°00′00″
- b 75°00′00″
- c 450°00′00″
- d 360°00′00″

38 --+5 5/8 of a complete revolution?
- a 2025°00′00″
- b 558°45′15″
- c 58°45′15″
- d −180°30′30″

39 - - if rotated $-\frac{1}{4}$ of a complete revolution?
- a 90°00′00″
- b 270°00′00″
- c −90°00′00″
- d 57°32′15″

40 - - if rotated -1 7/8 of a complete revolution?
- a −675°00′00″
- b 675°00′00″
- c −45°00′00″
- d 45°00′00″

41 -- +0.38 of a complete revolution?
- a 136°00′80″
- b 136°48′00″
- c 380°00′00″
- d −380°00′00″

42 --if rotated −1.30 of a complete revolution?
- a 108°00′00″
- b −108°00′00″
- c −468°00′00″
- d 130°00′00″

43 --if rotated +0.011 of a complete revolution?
- a 3°57′36″
- b 5°76′00″
- c 1°10′00″
- d 0°01′10″

44 --if rotated -3.61 of a complete revolution?
- a $-1220°24'00''$
- b $-1299°36'00''$
- c $-219°36'00''$
- d $-219°6'00''$

Express the following angles in radians.

45 The angle expressed in #35.
- a 1.75 Rad.
- b 2π Rad.
- c $\pi/2$ Rad.
- d 90 Rad

46 The angle expressed in #44.
- a -6.838π
- b -6.12π
- c -7.16π
- d 8.76π

Assignment 3

Discussion

Finding other Functions when the Value of one Function is Given

If the value of one function of an angle is given it is possible to find the values of the other functions. Suppose sin A is given equal to 3/5. This is the same as saying that the ratio $\frac{y}{r} = \frac{3}{5}$. If y is 3 r must be 5. If y is 6 r must be 10, etc. Furthermore, since the expression, 3/5 is positive in this example and the radius vector is always positive it follows that y must be positive and that the angle A must be terminate either in the first or in the second quadrant.

Let us first consider the case when the angle terminates in the first quadrant (Fig. 17). When y is 3 and r is 5, x must be 4, since $x^2 = r^2 - y^2$. This makes it possible to find the other functions of the angle as may be seen from the figure.

$$\cos A = \frac{4}{5};$$

$$\sec A = \frac{5}{4};$$

$$\tan A = \frac{3}{4};$$

$$\csc A = \frac{5}{3};$$

$$\cot A = \frac{4}{3}.$$

Next consider the case when the angle terminates in the second quadrant (Fig. 18). In this case $x = -4$ so the other functions have the following values:

$$\cos A = -\frac{4}{5};$$

$$\sec A = -\frac{5}{4};$$

$$\tan A = -\frac{3}{4};$$

$$\csc A = \frac{5}{3};$$

$$\cot A = -\frac{4}{3}.$$

We see, then, that when sinA = 3/5. each of the other functions may have one of two values. Let us see what values the other functions would have if sinA = −3/5. Since r can never be negative it must be that in this case y is negative and the vector is in the third or fourth quadrant. If the angle terminates in the third quadrant (Fig. 19) both x and y are negative and the other functions have the following values:

$$\cos A = -\frac{4}{5};$$

$$\sec A = -\frac{5}{4};$$

$$\tan A = \frac{3}{4};$$

$$\csc A = -\frac{5}{3};$$

$$\cot A = \frac{4}{3}.$$

When the angle terminates in the fourth quadrant (Fig. 20) the other functions are:

$$\cos A = \frac{4}{5};$$

$$\sec A = \frac{5}{4};$$

$$\tan A = -\frac{3}{4};$$

$$\csc A = -\frac{5}{3};$$

$$\cot A = -\frac{4}{3}.$$

The student will notice, in general, that for any allowable value of a function there are two, and only two, possible positions of the angle. There are exceptions to this rule. These occur in the case of the sine when the angle is 90° or 270°, in the case of the cosine when the angle is 0° or 180°, etc. The interested student will find this easy to prove. He will notice also that all of the other functions of an angle may be obtained if only one function is given.

Functions of Angles Possessing Similar Trigonometric Properties

Consider a 30° angle. For such an angle the length of the ordinate is always equal to one half the length of the vector. The truth of this statement is made clear by considering the angle AOB in the equilateral triangle AOC in Fig. 21. Since each of the angles in such a triangle is equal to 60° (from plane geometry) and since the line OB bisects both the angle AOC and the side AC it is shown that the angle AOB is 30° and AB is exactly half of AO. From this simple geometric consideration it follows that in the case of the 30° angle the ordinate is equal to one half the vector. We may write, then (Fig. 22):

$$\sin 30^\circ = \frac{1}{2}$$

$$\cos 30^\circ = \frac{3}{2}$$

etc.

From Fig. 23 we see that the 150° angle has similar properties except that the abscissa is negative. Likewise, 210° and 330° angles have similar properties (Figs. 24 and 25). By following the figures we see that these angles have functions as follows:

$\sin 30° = \frac{1}{2}$	$\sin 150° = \frac{1}{2}$	$\sin 210° = -\frac{1}{2}$	$\sin 330° = -\frac{1}{2}$
$\cos 30° = \frac{\sqrt{3}}{2}$	$\cos 150° = -\frac{\sqrt{3}}{2}$	$\cos 210° = -\frac{\sqrt{3}}{2}$	$\cos 330° = \frac{\sqrt{3}}{2}$
$\tan 30° = \frac{1}{\sqrt{3}}$	$\tan 150° = -\frac{1}{\sqrt{3}}$	$\tan 210° = \frac{1}{\sqrt{3}}$	$\tan 330° = -\frac{1}{\sqrt{3}}$
$\cot 30° = \sqrt{3}$	$\cot 150° = -\sqrt{3}$	$\cot 210° = \sqrt{3}$	$\cot 330° = -\sqrt{3}$
$\sec 30° = \frac{2}{\sqrt{3}}$	$\sec 150° = -\frac{2}{\sqrt{3}}$	$\sec 210° = -\frac{2}{\sqrt{3}}$	$\sec 330° = \frac{2}{\sqrt{3}}$
$\csc 30° = 2$	$\csc 150° = 2$	$\csc 210° = -2$	$\csc 330° = -2$

The student should now be able to demonstrate to his own satisfaction the similar trigonometric properties of such angles as 60°, 120°, 240°, and 300°, or 45°, 135°, 225°, and 315°.

Functions of Angles which Require Special Consideration

Angles of 0°, 90°, 180°, 270°, and 360° require special consideration. In the case of 0° (Fig. 26) we may think of a point P on....[2]the angle POX is becoming smaller and smaller until it becomes infinitesimally small or 0°. If r, the radius vector, is kept constant while the angle is decreasing, y approaches 0 and x approaches the length of r. The trigonometric functions of 0° then, are:

$$\sin POX = \sin\ 0° = \frac{\pm y}{r} = \frac{0}{r} = 0$$

$$\cos\ POX = \cos\ 0° = \frac{x}{r} = \frac{r}{r} = 1$$

$$\tan POX = \tan 0° = \frac{\pm y}{x} = \frac{0}{r} = 0$$

Before stating the value of the cotangent the student should be reminded of what happens when the denominator of a fraction becomes smaller and smaller while the numerator remains constant.

Consider the following successive values:

$$\frac{1}{10} = .1, \frac{1}{1} = 1, \frac{1}{.1} = 10, \frac{1}{.01} = 100, \frac{1}{.0001} = 10{,}000, \frac{1}{.0000001} = 10{,}000{,}000$$

As the denominator becomes smaller the value of the fraction becomes larger and if the process were continued indefinitely the value of the fraction would become infinitely great. Returning now to our discussion of the zero angle we will notice that the cotangent of $POX = \frac{x}{y}$. Since y becomes smaller and smaller as the angle approaches 0° and since x never gets greater than r we have just such a fraction as we have described and the value of the cotangent may be expressed:

$$\cot POX = \cot\ 0° = \frac{x}{\pm y} = \frac{x}{0} = \pm\infty \qquad \text{(since } y \to 0)$$

also:

$$\sec POX = \sec\ 0° = \frac{r}{x} = \frac{r}{r} = 1 \qquad \text{(since } x \to r)$$

and:

$$\csc POX = \csc\ 0° = \frac{r}{\pm y} = \frac{r}{0} = \pm\infty \qquad \text{(like the cotangent)}$$

[2] Editors' note: illegible text.

In the case of 90° the angle in Fig. 25 may be used. It will be observed that when r is fixed the y becomes equal to r and the x becomes zero as the angle POX approaches 90°. It follows by reasoning similar to that given above that:

$$\sin 90° = 1 \qquad \cot 90° = 0$$

$$\cos 90° = 0 \qquad \sec 90° = \pm\infty$$

$$\tan 90° = \pm\infty \qquad \csc 90° = 1$$

Similar arguments give the values of the functions of the 180° and the 270° angles. Those of 360° will be seen to be the same as those of 0°.

Line Values of Functions

It is possible to determine the numerical value of any function of an angle by geometric construction and the measurement of the lengths of lines. If we consider the vector in Fig. 28 as one unit long (say, an inch), we may write:

$$\sin A = \frac{y}{r} = \frac{y}{1} = y$$

and:

$$\cos A = \frac{x}{r} = \frac{x}{1} = x$$

Remember that this is true only when r = 1.

If we construct our figure so that the abscissa is one unit long we may write (Fig. 29):

$$\tan A = \frac{y}{x} = \frac{y}{1} = y$$

and:

$$\sec A = \frac{r}{x} = \frac{r}{1} = r$$

If we construct our figure so that the ordinate is one unit long we may write (Fig. 30):

$$\cot A = \frac{x}{y} = \frac{x}{1} = x$$

and:

$$\csc A = \frac{r}{y} = \frac{r}{1} = r$$

A convenient way to combine all of these constructions is to use the "unit circle" (Fig. 31). A circle is drawn with a radius one unit long. By continuing the vector and constructing a perpendicular at Y as shown in the figure, the line values of the different trigonometric functions of the angle may be determined graphically.

Assignment 7

Discussion

The Meaning of Logarithms

Logarithms are used to simplify long processes of multiplication and division. The logarithm of a number, to a given base, is the exponent to which the base number has to be raised in order to equal the number. Thus, the logarithm of 100. to the base 10. (written, $\log_{10}100.$) is the power to which 10 must be raised to give 100. Thus we would write:

$$\log_{10}100. = 2., \text{ and } \log_{10}1000. = 3., \text{ and } \log_6 216 = 3., \text{ and } \log_2 64 = 6.$$

More exactly we may say that if $a^x = N$, $\log_a N = x$, where a is a positive number not equal to 1. The exponent x may be thought of as being a logarithm. Similarly, any exponent may be considered as a logarithm. We may write:

$$c^n = M \text{ then } \log_c M = n.$$

Since logarithms are exponents it is well to recall a few of the properties of exponents.

1. $a^x a^y = a^{(x+y)}$ To multiply a number raised to an exponent by the same number raised to an exponent simply raise the number to an exponent equal to the sum of the exponents.
2. $\frac{a^x}{a^y} = a^{(x-y)}$ To divide a number raised to an exponent by the same number raised to an exponent raise the number to a power equal to the exponent of the numerator less the exponent of the denominator.
3. $(a^x)^y = a^{xy}$ To raise a powered number to a power simply multiply the exponents and raise the number to that power.
4. $\sqrt[y]{a^x} = a^{\frac{x}{y}}$ To find the root of a powered number divide the exponent by the root and raise the number to that power.

Interpreting these statements into terms of logarithms we have respectively:

1. The logarithm of a product equals the sum of the logarithms of the factors.
   For if: $N = a^x$, $\log_a N = x$
   And: $M = a^y$ $\log_a M = Y$
   then: $NM = a^{(x+y)}$, $\log_a NM = x + y = \log_a N + \log_a M$
2. The logarithm of a quotient equals the logarithm of the numerator minus the logarithm of the denominator.
   From above: $\frac{N}{M} = a^{(x-y)}$, $\log_a\left(\frac{N}{M}\right) = x - y = \log_a N - \log_a M.$
3. The logarithm of a number raised to an exponent equals the product of the exponent and the logarithm of the number.
   If: $N = a^x$, $\log_a N = x$
   then: $N^y = a^{xy}$ $\log_a N^y = xy = y\log_a N$
4. The logarithm of a root of a number is equal to the logarithm of the number divided by the root.
   From the above: $\sqrt[y]{N} = \sqrt[y]{a^x} = a^{\frac{x}{y}}$ $\log_a \sqrt[y]{N} = \frac{x}{y} = \frac{1}{y}\log_a N$

Common Logarithms

The further development of the theory of logarithms does not belong to a course in trigonometry and we shall proceed directly to the applications of logarithms. Any positive number except unity may be used as a base of logarithms but because our number system is a decimal system it is customary to use a base of ten in practical arithmetic computations. Since Henry Briggs (1561 - 1631) first suggested this practice it is customary to designate logarithms with base ten as Briggian or common logarithms. In theoretical work, however, Naperian (after John Napier,1550 -1617, the inventor of logarithms) or natural base logarithms are employed. The base of these logarithms is designated as *e* and its numerical value is approximately 2.71838. Having found this constant and the logarithms which employed it as a base it was possible to find the value of common logarithms by the formula: $\log_{10} x = \frac{\log_e x}{\log_e 10}$.

The following table illustrates the use of the base 10 in common logarithms:

Since:	$10^{-3} = .001$	$\log_{10}.001 = -3$
	$10^{-2} = .01$	$\log_{10}.01 = -2$
	$10^{-1} = .1$	$\log_{10}.1 = -1$
	$10^0 = 1$	$\log_{10}1. = 0$
	$10^1 = 10.$	$\log_{10}10. = 1$
	$10^2 = 100.$	$\log_{10}100. = 2$
	$10^3 = 1000.$	$\log_{10}1000. = 3$
also:	$10^{.30103} = 2.0$	$\log_{10}2 = 0.30103$
	$10^{.47712} = 3.0$	$\log_{10}3 = 0.47712$
	$10^{.60206} = 4.0$	$\log_{10}4 = 0.60206$
	$10^{.69875} = 5.0$	$\log_{10}5 = 0.69875$
	$10^{.09132} = 1.234$	$\log_{10}1.234 = 0.09132$

From this point on, unless otherwise indicated, all logarithms considered will be common logarithms and the base will not be specifically indicated. We shall write $\log_{10}N$ simply as logN.

Use of Tables

From the tables above we see that:

$$10^{.09132} = 1.234, \text{ then } \log 1.234 = 0.09132$$

Suppose we desire to find log12.34.

$$12.34 = 10 \times 1.234 = 10^1 \times 10^{.09132} = 10^{1.09132} \qquad \text{(From 7.1(1))}$$

$$\therefore \log 12.34 = 1.09132$$

Likewise: $123.4 = 100 \times 1.234 = 10^2 \times 10^{.09132} = 10^{2.09132}$

$$\therefore \log 123.4 = 2.09132$$

Similarly it may be shown that:

$$\log 1234. = 3.09132$$

If log.1234 is required the following proof may be used:

$$.1234 = \frac{1.234}{10} = 10^{-1} \times 10^{.09132} = 10^{(-1+.09132)}$$

$$\therefore \log .1234 = -1 + .09132$$

Likewise: $.01234 = \frac{1.234}{100} = 10^{-2} \times 10^{.09132} = 10^{(-2+.09132)}$

$$\therefore \log .01234 = (-2 + .09132)$$

Similarly it may be shown that

$$\log .0001234 = (-4 + .09132)$$

The student will notice that a logarithm of a number consists of two parts, an integer and a decimal. Log N = (integer + decimal). The integer is called the characteristic of the logarithm. The decimal is called the mantissa of the logarithm and is the part found in the tables of logarithms of numbers. We may say that

$$\log N = (\text{characteristic} + \text{mantissa}).$$

Examine carefully the logarithm of the numbers 1.234, 12.34, 123.4, 1234., .1234,.01234,.0001234 above. The mantissas are all the same equal to .09132. This is because the mantissa of the logarithm of a number depends only upon the digits which make up that number and does not at all upon the position of the decimal point. Decimal points are important in computation however and must be considered. This is done by evaluating the characteristic part of the logarithm. Examine the characteristics of the logarithms of the numbers given above:

When the number is 123.4 the characteristic is 2.

"	"	"	"	12.34	"	"	"	1.
"	"	"	"	1.234	"	"	"	0.
"	"	"	"	.1234	"	"	"	-1.
"	"	"	"	.01234	"	"	"	-2.
"	"	"	"	.0001234	"	"	"	-4.

The first three numbers are greater than 1 and the characteristics of their logarithms are positive. The last three numbers are less than 1 and the characteristics of their logarithms are negative. The rule for finding the characteristic may be stated as follows:

RULE

The characteristic of log 1 is 0.

The characteristic of the logarithm of any number greater than 1 is positive and one less than the number of digits to the left of the decimal point. The characteristic of the logarithm of any number less than 1 is negative and one more than the number of zeros between the decimal point and the first digit.

To illustrate: in the number 123.4 there are three digits to the left of the decimal point so the characteristic of the logarithm is 2. We may write $\log 123.4 = 2.09132$. In the number .01234 there is one zero between the decimal point and the first digit so the characteristic of the logarithm is -2. We may write $\log .01234 = (-2 + .09132)$.

The student will notice that in all of these examples the mantissa of the logarithm was allowed to remain positive. Adjustments due to the position of the decimal point in the number were made in the characteristics. If the subtraction operation in $\log .01234 = (-2 + .09132)$ had been completed the logarithm would appear as follows:

$$\log .01234 = (-2 + .09132) = -1.90868$$

While this is the true logarithm of .01234 it is more convenient to keep the mantissa positive. Rather than requiring two tables of logarithms, one with positive mantissas and the other with negative mantissas, it is customary to use only a table of positive mantissas and attach negative signs to the characteristics when necessary. The student must keep in mind the fact that all mantissas given in the tables are positive. Logarithms which have a negative characteristic and a positive mantissa may be designated in either of two ways as may be seen from the following:

first way second way

$$\log .2000 = (-1 + .30103) = (9.30103 - 10) \text{ or } \bar{1}.30103$$

$$\log .01234 = (-2 + .09132) = (8.09132 - 10) \text{ or } \bar{2}.09132$$

$$\log .0005 = (-4 + .69875) = (6.69875 - 10) \text{ or } \bar{4}.69875$$

The first way is somewhat more commonly employed while the second way possesses advantages which in the opinion of the authors makes it preferable.

The student will understand from this discussion that the logarithm of any number can easily be obtained as soon as the mantissa is determined. Tables of common logarithms such as Table 2 in this text show such mantissas. The logarithm of any number may be found by locating the mantissa in the table and adding the appropriate characteristic. Suppose one is to find the logarithm of 385.0. The mantissa of 3850 is found in the table. It is .58546. Since there are three places to the left of the decimal the characteristic must be 2. We may then write:

$$\log 385.0 = 2.58546$$

Similarly: $\log .3850 = \bar{1}.58546$

etc.

If our number had been 385.1 instead of 385.0 we would have had to read the value of the mantissa in the column headed "l" and to the right of "385". This would have given us a mantissa of .58557. This method of tabulating saves space and makes the table accurate for four-place numbers. If we wish to find the mantissa of a five-place number we may resort to the method of interpolation. Suppose we are to find the mantissa of 385.12. This number lies between 385.10 whose mantissa is .58557 and 385.20 whose mantissa is .58569. The difference between these two mantissas is .00012. By referring to the small table of "proportional parts" in the margin one may read in the column headed "12" (the difference between the two mantissas) opposite the number 2 (the fifth place in the number whose mantissa is to be found) "2.4". If this number is added to the last place in the mantissa of 385.10 we obtain the mantissa of 385.12.

mantissa of	385.10	=	.58557	
proportionalpart of	.02	=	24	
mantissa of	385.12	=	.585594	= .58559 ("rounded")

Application of Logarithms to Arithmetic Computations

Suppose the following arithmetic operation is to be completed.

$$\frac{326.70\times .45808^2\times 35897000\times \sqrt[3]{.0000004500}}{-76834\times .00047631\times 400.01\times 100.02^{-5}}$$

Since the logarithm of a quotient is equal to the logarithm of the numerator less the logarithm of the denominator we add the logarithm of the numerator and denominator separately and then subtract the sum of the latter from the sum of the former. For convenience numbers with negative exponents should be treated as the corresponding reciprocals with positive exponents; thus, in our problem we shall treat 100.02^{-5} as if it were 100.05^5 in the numerator.

Numerator:

$\log 326.70 =$	2.514150
$\log .45808 = \overline{1}.660942$	
$\log .45808^2 = 2\times \overline{1}.660942 =$	$\overline{1}.321884$
$\log 35897000 =$	7.555054
$\log .0000004500 = \overline{7}.653210$	
$\log \sqrt[3]{.0000004500} = \left(\overline{9}+2.653210\right)\div 3 =$	$\overline{3}.884403$
$\log 100.02 = 2.000086$	
$\log 100.02^5 = 2.000086\times 5 =$	10.000430
$\log(\text{numerator}) =$	17.273921
Denominator:	
$\log 76834 =$	4.885554
$\log .00047651 =$	$\overline{4}.677889$
$\log 400.01 =$	2.862071
$\log(\text{denominator}) =$	4.165514

Subtract the logarithm of the denominator from the logarithm of the numerator:

$$\begin{aligned}\log(\text{numerator}) &= 17.275921\\ \log(\text{denominator}) &= 4.165514\\ \log(\text{fraction}) &= 13.1104047\end{aligned}$$

$$\log^{-1} 13.110407 = 12{,}895{,}000{,}000{,}000$$

From inspection of the problem we know that the answer must be negative. We write it then as:

$-12{,}895{,}000{,}000{,}000$ answer

We cannot expect to get the answer to more than five significant places unless we use a table with more places in it. If the numbers in the problem are known to be exact and not approximate this is justifiable. Otherwise since one of the numbers of the numerator is significant to only four places we "round off" our answer to four significant places.

$-12{,}9\underline{0}0{,}000{,}000{,}000$

A number of features in the above solution are to be observed. The mantissa of each logarithm we kept positive although finding $\log \sqrt[3]{.0000004500}$ required some manipulation.

$$\log \sqrt[3]{.0000004500} = \frac{1}{3}\log .0000004500$$

$$= \frac{\overline{7}.653210}{3}$$

One does not care to divide -7 by 3 for the decimal part of the quotient would be negative and it is better to avoid negative decimals in logarithms. To overcome this difficulty one replaces -7 by $-9+2$ or by any negative number which is a multiple of 3 plus a suitable positive number to give a -7 . Thus $-12+5$ would do.

So: $$\frac{\bar{7}.653210}{3}=\frac{9+2.653210}{3}=\frac{\bar{9}}{3}+\frac{2.653210}{3}=\bar{3}.884403$$

Negative numbers need not confuse the student for the arithmetic value of the product or quotient may be computed without considering the signs, then the proper sign affixed to the answer according to the combination of negative signs in the original expression.

The term $\log^{-1}$ 13.110407 is read "antilogarithm 13.110407". It means "the number whose logarithm is 13.110407". Obviously the evaluation of the antilogarithm is the last step in the solution since the logarithm must be converted back into numbers.

The student who is skeptical about the economy of using logarithms should attempt to solve the above problem by common arithmetic.

Logarithms of Trigonometric Functions

Table 3 gives the logarithms of trigonometric functions directly. This table is convenient to use when trigonometric functions are used as factors. In this table the integer 9 before the decimal means 9._____ 10, or simply $\bar{1}$._____ Thus, 25° is found as 9.66867 which means

$$\log\tan 25°=(9.66867-10)\text{ or }\bar{1}.66867$$

The -10 is omitted in order to save space in the tables. It is understood. If the result is 8.13871 it means 8.13871 - 10 or $\bar{2}$.13871. When the characteristic given in these tables is 0, 1, 2, or 3 the -10 is *not* implied. Thus, $\log\cot 25°$ is given as 0.33133 which means exactly that.

Cologarithms

Some mathematicians make use of cologarithms in computations. The cologarithm of a number is the logarithm of a reciprocal of a number and may be added to another logarithm in place of subtracting the original logarithm. The following computation illustrates the use of the logarithm and the cologarithm.

Find: $\frac{389.4}{4169.}$

Solution with logarithms only

log 389.4 = 2.59040

log 4169. = <u>3.62003</u>

<u>subtracting:</u> $\bar{2}$.97037

$\log^{-1}\bar{2}.97037=.09340$

Solution with cologarithm

log 389.4 = 2.59040

(log 4169. = 3.62003)

$$[\text{illegible text}]\ \text{colog}\,4169.\begin{array}{l}(10.00000-10\\ \underline{-(3.62003}\\ =6.37997-10\end{array}$$

Add log 389.4 and colog 4169.

2.59040

<u>6.37997 − 10</u>

8.97037 − 10

$\log^{-1}8.97037-10=0.9340$

126

Notes on Perceptual Integration in the Design of Aircraft Instrument Panels[1]

The Perceptual Problem

The function of aircraft instruments is to provide ready data from which the pilot may construct a picture of his plane in flight. The form in which the data are presented has a great deal to do with the pilot's facility for knowing what is going on.

By itself, each flight instrument responds only to one aspect of the plane's attitude or motion. The pilot's perceptual job is to keep the constantly changing readings properly pieced together.

To do this he rapidly turns his attention from one dial to another, making readings, sometimes identifying numerals—more often, short-circuiting such verbal symbols. As he makes these visual excursions from dial to dial he must make up-to-the moment revisions in the composite picture. Each revision must embody, at least implicitly, all of the elements essential to safe flight.

The inexperienced pilot finds it hard to keep the pattern intact. His perceptual structure is continually being broken up and he must make new configurations emerge from the clock faces before him before he can tell what to do about it. If he concentrates his attention on one needle, another, over on the other side of the panel, gets out of hand. He tries to learn each instrument's characteristic "all-is-well" signal under each different maneuvering condition. He must recognize its meaning without traversing a chain of verbal translations. Thus, it requires many hours of instrument time before the pilot's attention can span the whole panel at once.

Psychological research has provided abundant evidence that the span of human attention is increased many-fold when the stimulus elements are fixed in a well-organized master pattern. This simple principle has an inescapable meaning for the designer of aircraft instrument panels.

The solution to the perceptual problem in aircraft instrumentation is to design the whole panel so that the complex indicator readings can all be fixed within a few simple perceived-as-a-whole configurations.

Current Approaches to the Perceptual Problem

Most of the attempts to improve instrument dials have been directed toward clearer presentation of each instrument's own particular kind of data rather than toward bridging the perceptual gaps between the different kinds of data.

Uniform Dials and Markings

This approach has probably aggravated the perceptual problem rather than alleviated it. The typical instrument now in use has a clock face approximately three inches in diameter with sixty to one hundred forty graduations and ten to fifteen numerals marked on the periphery. The pilot who comes aboard a new plane may be confronted with an unfamiliar arrangement of instruments which is made all the more confusing by the similarity between the dials. Perceptual interference results.

[1] Notes for a Report to Aviation Psychology Branch, Division of Aviation Medicine, Bureau of Medicine and Surgery, U. S. Navy, 1945. Published by permission of Jacqueline Aldridge.

Collected Papers of the Pioneer of Constructivist Psychology: George A. Kelly, First Edition. Edited by David A. Winter and Nick Reed.

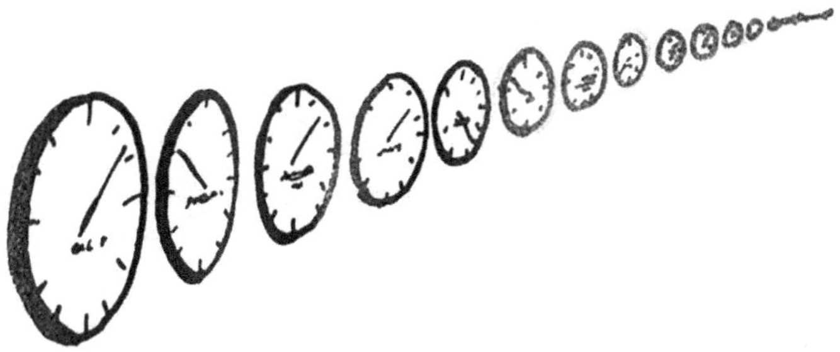

Legibility of Figures

If it were essential that all instrument readings be put into words, the legibility of numerals and markings would be a crucial consideration. Most of the pilot's reading of instruments, however, is not reading at all—in the verbal sense. Mostly the pilot does what may be called "check reading."

For example, the man on the street who has just looked at his watch probably cannot tell you the time, yet it would be incorrect to say that he has forgotten what he looked at his watch to see. He simply did not read his watch in terms of words. He may have used his watch to assure himself that he was not too late for dinner or that a dreaded appointment was still a long time off. To do that he did not need to say numbers to himself and then perform mental arithmetic. He got the particular kind of answer he needed without all that. He *check read* his watch. Now you make him look at it again and say the words for what time it is.

Similarly the instrument pilot gradually learns to get the kind of assurances he needs from his instruments without continually tossing up digits in his mind. He reads his instruments as he would the faces of old friends.

Only to the extent that the pilot has occasion to read instruments in terms of numbers is legibility an important problem.

Considerable information regarding the legibility of type is to be found in the publications of M.A. Tinker and D.G. Paterson of the University of Minnesota. F.C. Bartlett of Cambridge University has prepared a memorandum, now available to the Navy, covering the more general topic of controls and display.

Parsimonious use of Markings

It is possible to approach the perceptual problem from the standpoint of simplification, with simplification considered to be the reduction of the number of dial markings.

Night flying has precipitated some attempts along this line. In order to preserve dark adaptation in the pilot's eyes it has been thought to be desirable to reduce panel lighting to a minimum, both as to lighted area and as to intensity of illumination. This has led to the policy of using radioactive paint on a limited number of markings only.

The spacing of markings, whether luminous or not, can well be based upon an analysis of the maximum tolerable errors in reading the dials.

In some cases it is practicable to reduce the entire indicator to a warning signal which enters the sensory field only when an unusual situation arises.

Similarly, a mechanical display can be designed which, when set for a given condition, provides a series of dichotomous readings aligned so as to constitute a kind of check list.

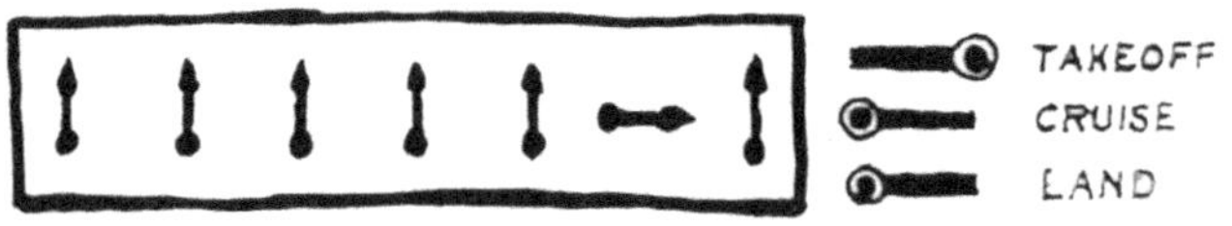

A combination of the warning signal system and the maximum tolerable error criterion is found in the kind of dial on which certain crucial points are marked. An example is the airspeed indicator which has "do not exceed," "cruise," and "power approach" markings.

Alignment of Indicators

Instruments which require attention only when out of their normal operating range, may be rotated and calibrated so that their needles will all normally point in the same direction. Thus the oil pressure gauge, fuel pressure gauge, head temperature gauge, etc. may be arranged so that their needles all line up along a single horizontal lubber line when operating conditions are normal.

This scheme provides for quick "all-is-well" checks but the row of similar dials may cause confusion (*perceptual interference*) if maneuvers require differential *check reading* of the instruments.

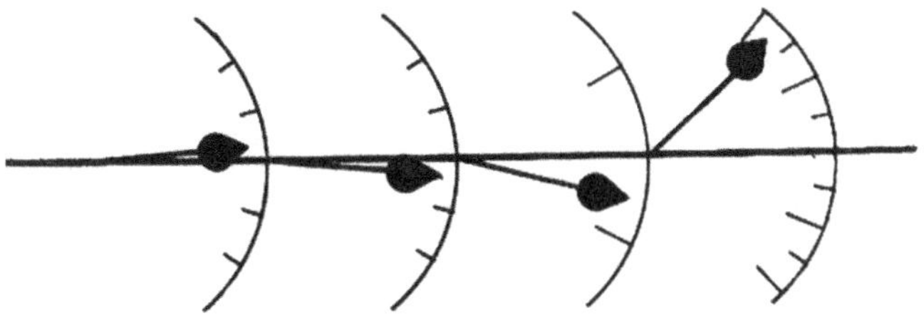

Logical Grouping of Clock-Face Instruments

There is a tendency of designers now to group engine instruments together, navigation instruments together, flying instruments together, etc. Superficially such grouping may appear to have a real functional basis. Actually, however, it may be functional only with respect to the physics of the airplane and not at all with respect to the behavior of the pilot.

For example, if the pilot is to make a let-down, new readings both on the manifold pressure gauge (an engine instrument) and the rate of climb indicator (a flight instrument) must be correlated. Again, if a level turn is required, a truly functional grouping would be dictated by the need for associating new readings on the compass, the rate of turn, and the gyro-horizon. In addition, airspeed, altitude, and slip-skid must be *check read*. A logical grouping based on the machinery back of the instruments rather than on the job of piloting cannot be considered relevantly functional.

Arrangement in Relation to Eye-Movements

It is possible to place instruments on the panel on the basis of the pilot's usual eye-movements. Photographs of eye-movements show which instruments are looked at most frequently, how long the fixations are, and the pattern of eye-movements for different maneuvers.

The Navy has conducted one study along this line. The report indicates that instruments placed in the center or upper center position in a rectangular group of nine tend to be more frequently observed. The implication is that these positions are preferable for instruments which should be read more frequently. The study was not intended to answer the question of which instruments ought to be more frequently consulted.

Selective Display of Instruments

Under the Civil Aeronautics Administration there has been developed a scheme for illuminating only those instruments toward which the pilot turns his head. This is accomplished by coating dial markings and needles with very small plastic beads which are cut in such a way as to cause internal reflection of outside light. Red light from a small lamp on the pilot's forehead causes the coated markings to light up. Only those instruments toward which the pilot has turned his head are lighted. The arrangement reduces the amount of light on the panel, thus both protecting the pilot's dark adaptation and practically eliminating all distracting stimuli in his peripheral field of vision.

Another scheme, proposed by a returned combat pilot, is to provide selector switches by which the dials of any combination of instruments would be projected onto the windshield. For example, during a dive-bombing attack, the pilot may choose to project his airspeed and ball bank indicators onto the windshield beside the gunsight.

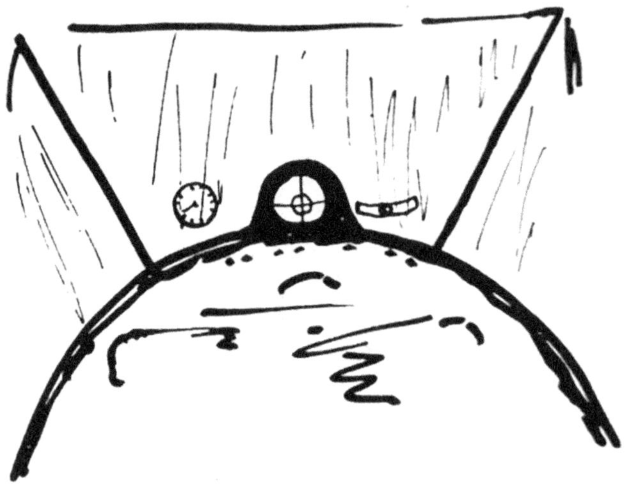

Simulation of Contact Conditions

A cleverly designed device by G.W. Hoover combines a non-tumbling gyro-horizon with a gyro-compass. The pilot looks into a lighted recess and sees what appears to be a landscape in panorama as it might appear from an altitude of 1500 feet. Ahead of him is a plane which banks in response to his own controls. As he changes his heading the horizon appears to turn as in actual flight. Thus the device simulates the organized stimulus pattern of contact flying. This is one way, though by no means the only one, of facilitating truly integrative perception.

There is a possibility that the verisimilitude of the instrument may be overdone to the extent that the display implies flight data which are not measured. The pilot who fails fully to discount the invalid aspects of the display can quickly place himself in a dangerous position.

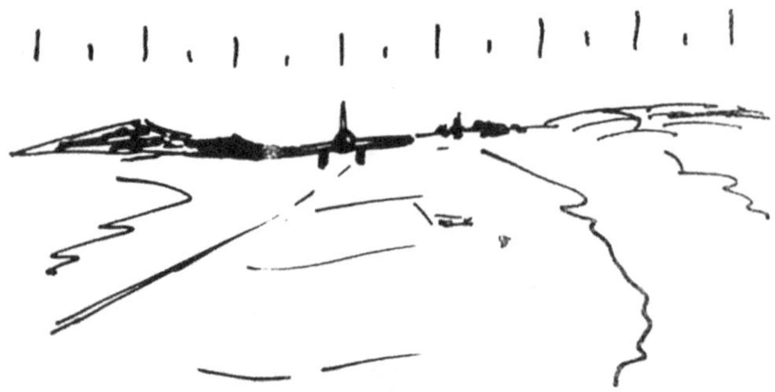

For example, the photograph appears to have been taken from an altitude of approximately 1500 feet. It still looks like 1500 feet, even if one is losing altitude rapidly. The pilot who uses the instrument must be fully and constantly aware of the fallibility of the terrain illusion and be sure to integrate no more into his perception than the factual data warrant.

Notwithstanding this criticism, Hoover's development is a far step toward better perceptual integration.

Consideration needs to be given to the hypothesis that simulation of contact conditions may still not be the best way of achieving perceptual integration.

Criterion Specifications for the Design of an Improved Instrument Panel

Maximum Use of Spatial Relations

This point is exemplified by the gyro-horizon which employs the same indicator to show both angle of bank and angle of incidence.

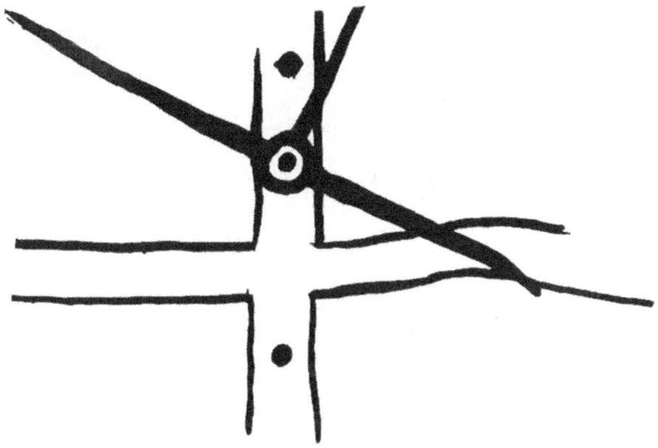

Superposition of Functionally Related Dials and Pointers

The combination of gyro-horizon and ball illustrates this principle. When the ball is in a normal position it is perceptually fused with the gyro-horizon indicator into a simple configuration. When a slip or skid takes place the pattern breaks up and produces a new configuration.

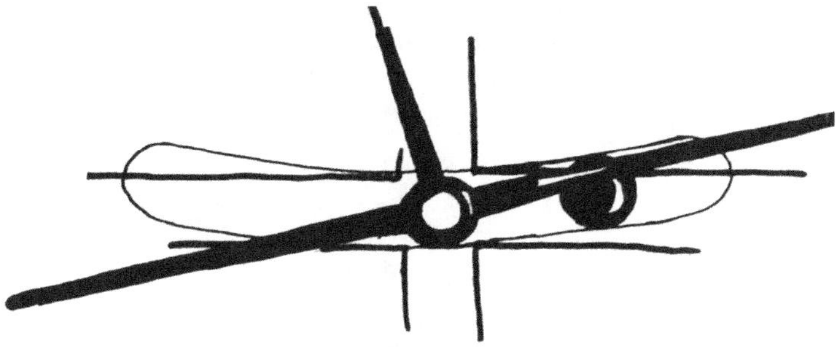

Juxtaposition of Functionally Related Indicators

For example, a level turn involves correlation of readings on the compass, rate-of-turn, and gyro-horizon. A simple configuration can be produced by calibrating the rate-of-turn so that it is aligned with the gyro-horizon during standard turns at cruising speed. Both can then be read in relation to approaching points on the compass.

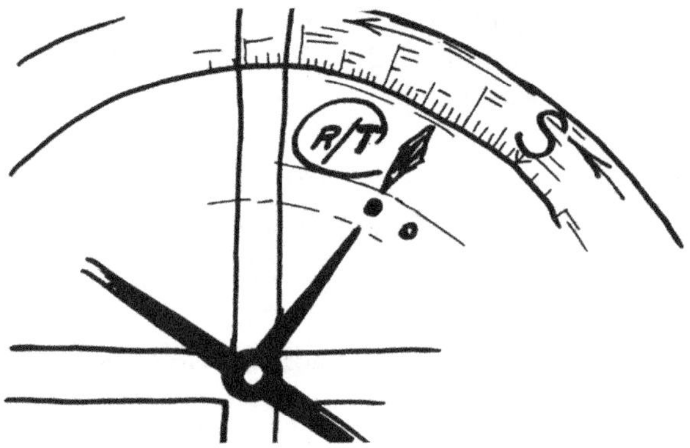

Alignment of Several Indicators Along the Same Lubber Lines

The use of lubber lines to control the sweep of eye-movements clear across the panel and the alignment of instrument hands along these paths of observation tends to facilitate *check reading*.*

* See previous discussion of *check reading*.

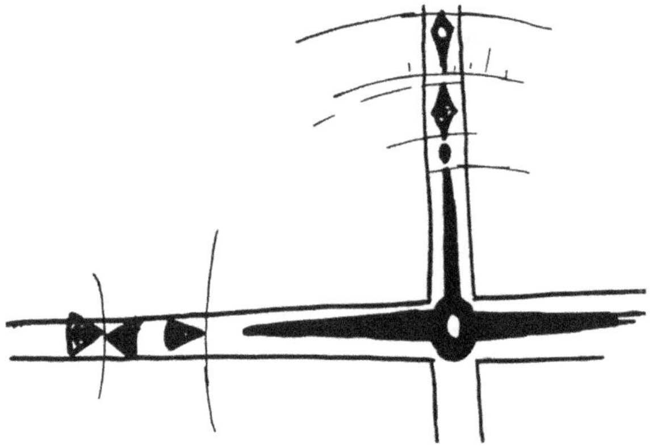

Spacing of Graduations Determined in Relation to the Maximum Tolerable Reading Error

For example, if the maximum tolerable error in reading the altimeter under the most exacting instrument flying conditions is shown by investigation to be plus or minus sixty-five feet, the graduations on the altimeter scale should be spaced with regard for this fact. A one-to-one ratio between the two is probably adequate, i.e., graduations at sixty-five-foot intervals—probably reduced to fifty-foot intervals for the sake of "round" numbers.

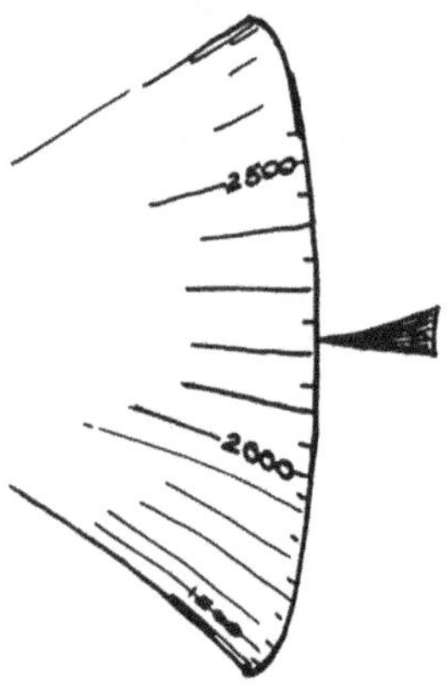

Utilization of On-Off Signals and Marking of Critical Points on Dials

The use of warning lights or other attention-getting devices is particularly suitable for such instruments as fuel gauges, radio altimeters, pressure gauges, and temperature gauges. One must bear in mind, however, that a single light, in contrast to a dial, does not furnish enough information on the trend of conditions to enable the pilot to anticipate a critical condition before it takes place. On dials, the marking of certain critical points, such as power-approach airspeed, is certainly justified. Standard rates of climb and let-down, tied in with their corresponding manifold pressure settings, also lend themselves to this type of instrumentation.

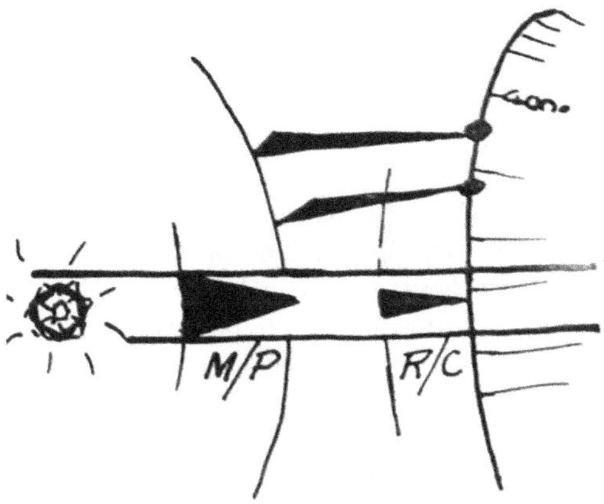

Minimum Accommodation Difficulty

When the pilot looks at his instruments after looking at distant objects his perception is delayed until ocular accommodation takes place. The use of relatively large indicators, involving only coarse discriminations, will facilitate perception under such conditions.

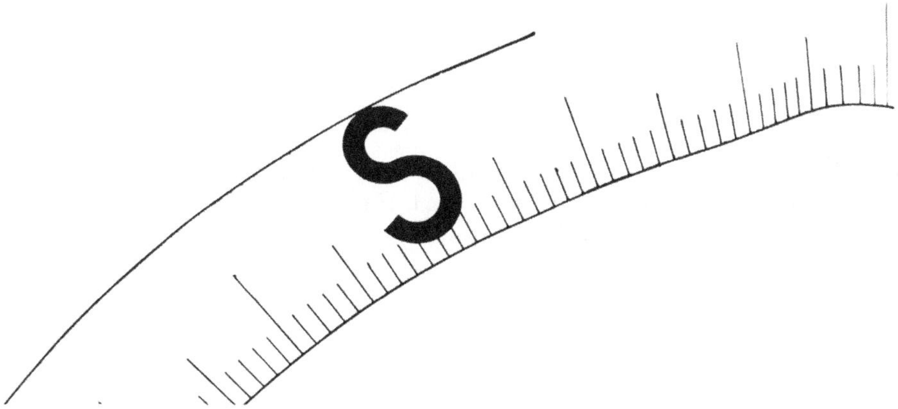

Use of Peripheral Vision

There are 3 considerations here:

1 Indicators which require occasional check reading only should be arranged so as to appear normally in the peripheral visual field. Particular care should be taken to make sure such displays are easily organized into the total instrument configuration.

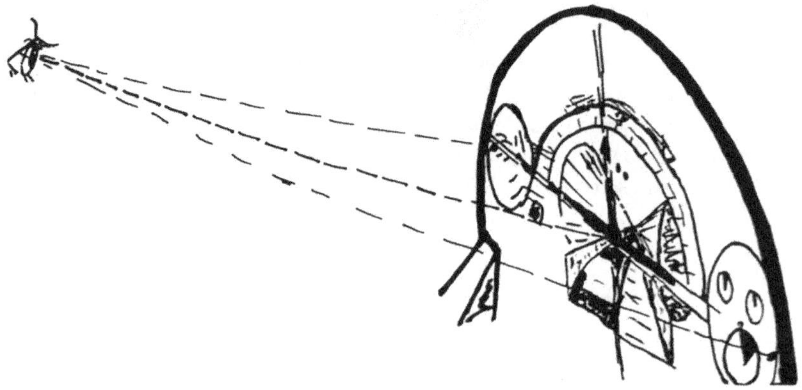

2 By taking account of the acuity of peripheral vision at various angles eccentric to the line of sight the sizes of indicators can be determined in relation to their positions on the panel. The diagram below is a full scale templet based upon available evidence on visual acuity in the periphery. It shows how large, relatively, indicators should be when placed at various distances from the usual fixation point on a panel 24 inches from the eye. The diameters of the circles are ten times the minimum which can be resolved by normal vision (based upon space between resolvable parallel lines). The larger circles correspond to the decrease in acuity at points away from the point of fixation.

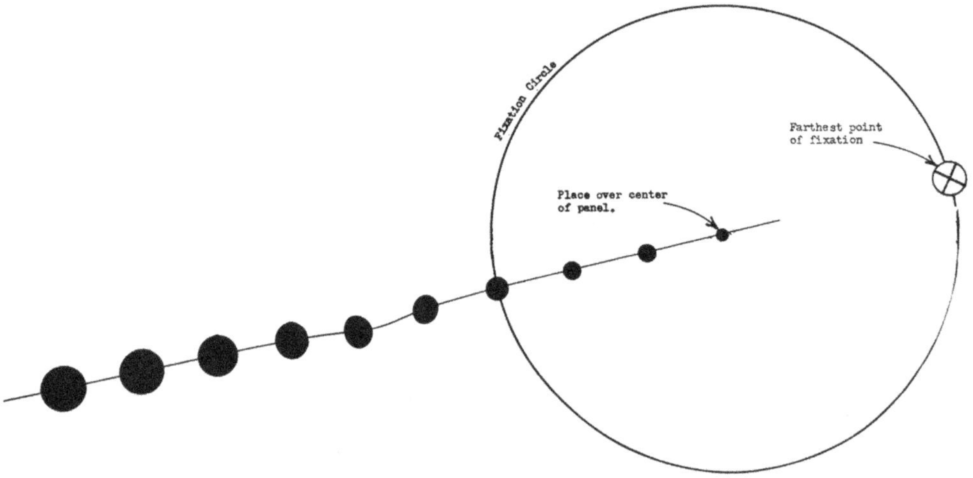

3 If the pilot who has been looking out of his cockpit takes a quick look at his panel his glance may not fall precisely on the instrument he is looking for. The panel should be designed so that if his glance falls anywhere within a general area his peripheral vision will pick up all the necessary readings. This area may be called the "fixation circle."

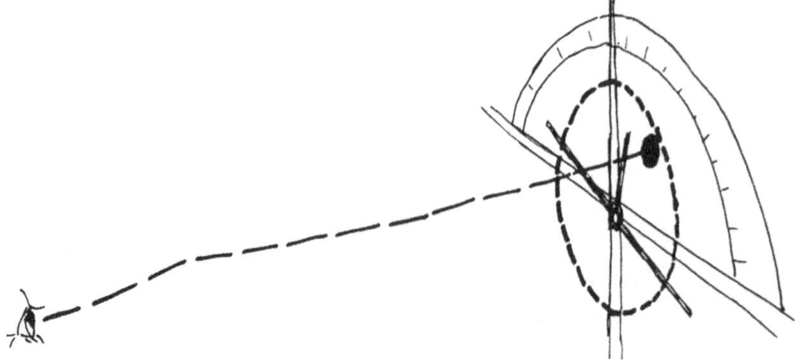

Optimum Legibility

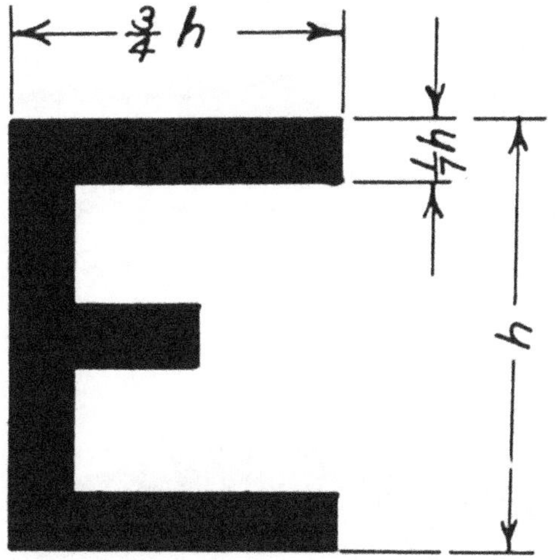

Consideration of the Relative Frequency with which Different Instruments are Normally Read and the Quickness with which they Must be Perceived

For example, if airspeed must be read very rapidly or very frequently, the airspeed indicator should be made conspicuous and located within the fixation circle. On the other hand, if temperature changes take place relatively slowly and need only be read in-between-times, the temperature dials can be made less conspicuous and well out in the normal field of peripheral vision.

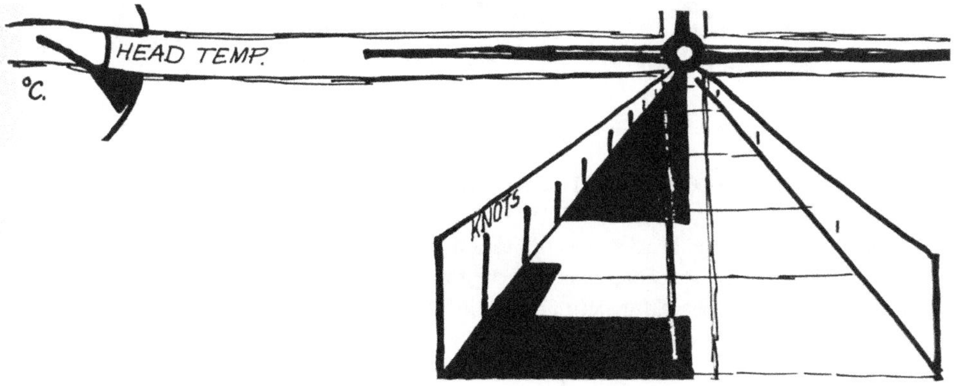

Use of Patterns of Movement

Not all configurational simplification needs to be confined to spatial dimensions, instrument displays can also be organized within temporal configurations.

The pilot, of course, needs more than a succession of "still pictures" in his mind, he needs "movies" of his plane flying. He must grasp the course of events. He must know not only where he stands but *what is going on*. This requires perceptual integration in the dimension of time as well as in the three spatial dimensions of height, breadth, and length.

It is possible to design instrument displays so that the movements of their indicators are read rather than the positions. Data such as airspeed and altitude, which are subject to rapidly occurring crucial changes, must be immediately perceived in their temporal perspective. It may be desirable to design the airspeed and altitude indicators so as to facilitate this course-of-events perception. Both movement readings and position readings could be provided in the same display.

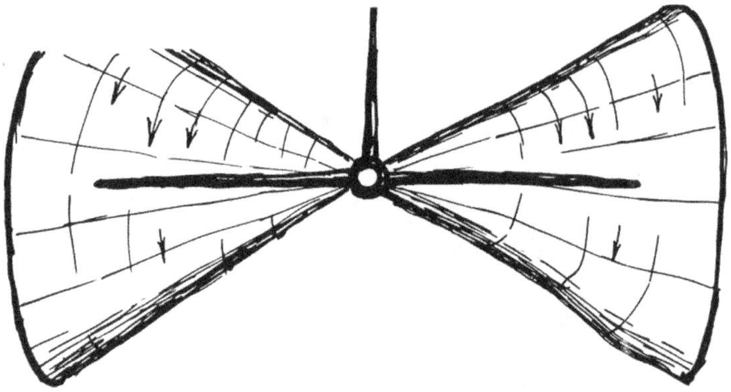

Preliminary Drafts of a Revised Instrument Panel Display

The panel design shown above is intended to illustrate the application of the proposed specifications. Obviously it is not based upon the preliminary studies recommended in the earlier paragraphs of these notes. It must therefore be considered as a first approximation of the proposed criterion specifications. It should serve, furthermore, to illustrate how extensively panel revisions might be carried out.

Compasses

Gyro-compass and magnetic compass dials are mounted concentrically to simplify comparing their readings and re-setting the gyro. The gyro-compass dial is marked with larger figures and is displayed nearer the center of the panel since it probably is more frequently referred to in instrument flying.

A heading marker (shown in a 30° off-heading position) is used to make check reading easier. The marker is controlled through the direction indicator at the lower left corner of the panel.

A movable variation scale (shown in position for VAR. 12° WEST) is set by a knob which turns by one-degree clicks. A course marker (shown in position for DRIFT 5° RIGHT) indicates magnetic course on the magnetic compass dial.

Lubber Lines

Double lubber lines are spaced so that, in relation to the width of the indicators, they provide for adequate tolerance in reading the instruments.

Rate-of-Turn

The rate-of-turn indicator moves through an arc approximately concentric with the compass dials. It is geared so that, when two and three-needle-width turns are made at cruising speed, it continues in alignment with the gyro-horizon indicator.

Gyro-horizon

The indicator (little airplane) rotates clockwise with respect to the lubber lines when a right bank is executed, counter-clockwise when a left bank is executed. The horizontal pair of lubber lines represents the horizon. The width of the indicator is such as to provide proper reading tolerance between the lubber lines.

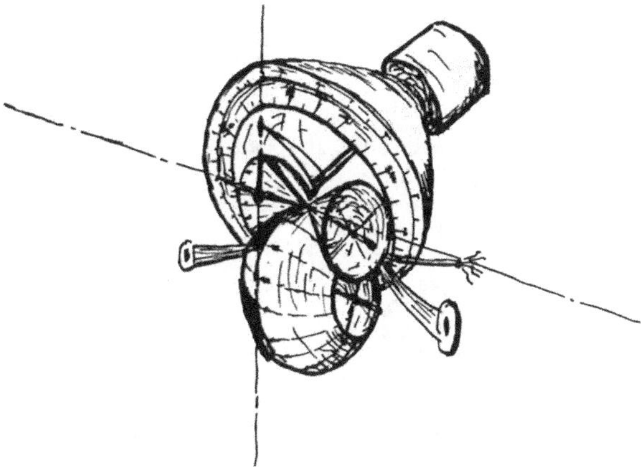

A column of dots between the vertical pair of lubber lines indicates graduations in the plane's angle of incidence.

Ball

The ball, or slip-skid indicator, is arranged behind the gyro-horizon indicator. When unequal transverse forces act upon the airplane the ball rolls out and changes the gross configuration of the gyro-horizon indicator. The ball is small enough not to be conspicuous when it moves only a short distance off-center.

Altimeter

Two kinds of indicators are shown in this preliminary panel design: a veedometer dial for specific altitudes, as used in navigation and procedural flight, and a moving dial for check reading during maneuvers.

The moving dial is comprised of two cones with their apices touching so as to give a vista effect. The graduations simulate horizontal lines in space parallel to the line of flight. Changes in altitude are detected by movement over a considerable area of the visual field. Furthermore, this movement is easily integrated into the familiar temporal configuration of a climbing plane.

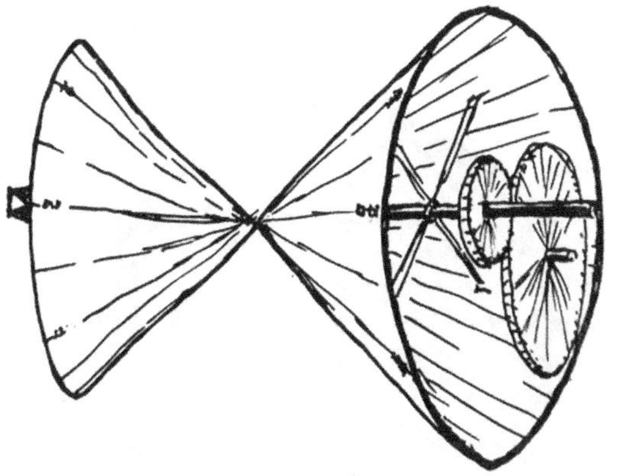

The configuration is as if one were flying along between a pair of level wires stretched along his path just beyond his wing tips. Altitude is maintained by keeping even with a pair of these "wires." If one wishes to fly at an altitude 200 feet higher, he climbs until he comes up to the level of the next pair of "wires."

When executing maneuvers which should not be accompanied by changes of altitude, the pilot need not think of altitude as an isolated datum, he needs merely to maintain the level-flight configuration on the dial. Any departure from level flight should immediately break up that configuration and crash his field of attention.

Rate-of-Climb

The rate-of-climb indicator appears on one side of the altimeter dial. Its movements are calibrated so that it points to the *altitude where you will be one minute from now at your present rate of climb or descent.*

Airspeed

Again, both veedometers and a moving dial are employed in the tentative design. The moving part is an ellipsoid which turns on its major axis. It turns continually during flight at a rate proportional to the airspeed.

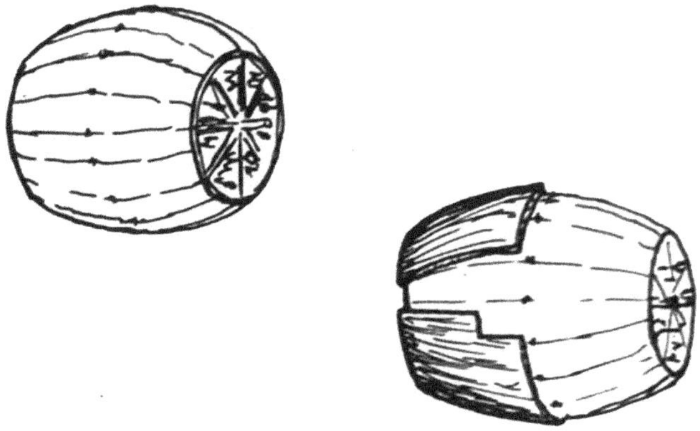

The exposed portion of the ellipsoid surface appears behind a window which, in turn, is designed to augment the vista effect already mentioned. Longitudinal markings on the surface of the ellipsoid are spaced to correspond to one-mile intervals. Thus the illusion is one of flying over "section lines" as the ellipsoid slowly rotates toward the observer.

The "section lines" are labeled so that the pilot can pick out, say, the "ten-mile line" and fly until he appears to arrive over it. He thus eliminates that part of procedural flying which requires him to multiply airspeed by time or to make calculations for fluctuating airspeed.

In order to provide a conspicuous indicator of airspeed fluctuations the ellipsoid is partially covered by a movable shell. The shell is mounted coaxially with the ellipsoid and rotates away from the observer as airspeed is increased. Its nearer edge indicates airspeed readings on the calibrated scale. That edge also indicates the "section line" at which the plane will arrive in one minute (at the present airspeed), e.g., in the drawing on page 942 the pilot can expect to arrive just beyond the 10-mile line 60 seconds from now. The right hand scale indicates that this check point is about three and a third miles away.

Stalling speeds are indicated by the two off-set upper edges of another shell. One edge shows where a stall can be expected with flaps up, the other shows stalling speed with flaps down. As long as there is a gap between these upper edges of the stall shell and the lower edge of the airspeed shell the pilot has a proportional margin of safety in his airspeed.

The stall shell operates as an accelerometer, rising to indicate increased stalling speeds when the plane is put into a turn.

Manifold Pressure

Manifold pressure readings for standard rates of climb and descent are tied into the appropriate rate-of-climb readings by heavy tie-lines.

The altimeter setting dial is placed across the rate-of-descent tie-lines.

Fuel Gauges and Tank Selector Valve

Three fuel gauges are exposed through holes in the face plate of the tank selector valve. The largest hole is over the gauge corresponding to the tank from which fuel is being taken. The indicators on the fuel gauges are helical disks of which larger and larger segments are exposed as fuel is used up. A warning light flashes when a tank becomes nearly empty.

Around the periphery of the instrument are two rings which indicate total fuel consumption and elapsed time, respectively. They are geared so that they turn at equal rates under normal cruising conditions. A radius-of-action marker can be preset according to expected wind conditions.

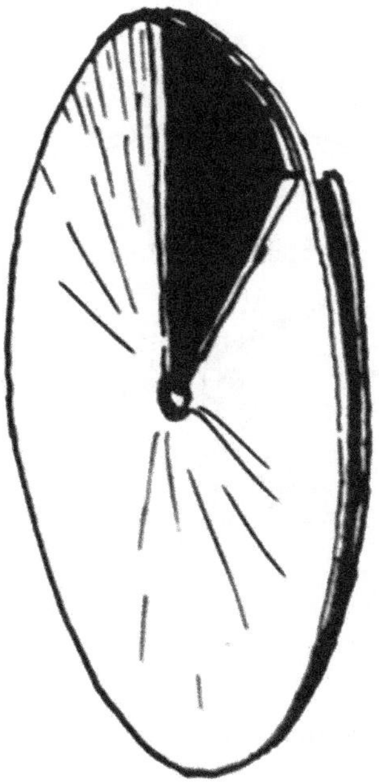

Illustrative Situations

Straight and Level Flight

For the most part this is a matter of keeping all markers aligned between the major horizontal and vertical lubber lines (course marker, rate-of-turn, ball, gyro-horizon, rate-of-climb, manifold-pressure, tachometer, head temperature, fuel and oil pressure gauges). Desired altitude readings are also maintained between the major lubber lines. The whole altitude field is kept as nearly motionless as possible.

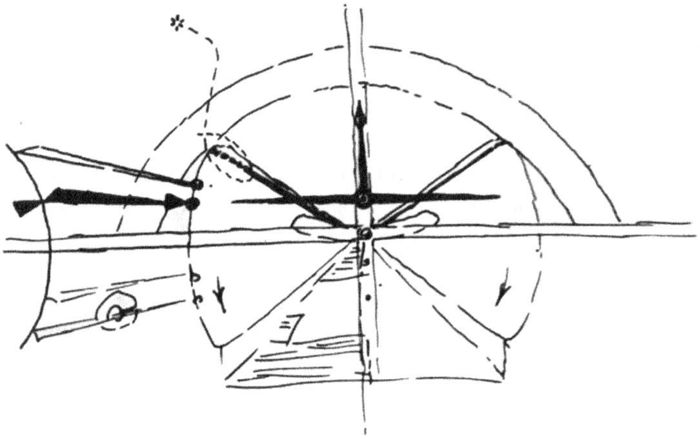

A safe gap is maintained between the airspeed shell and the stall shell. Occasional check is made on discrepancies between the elapsed-time and rate-of-consumption rings.

Straight Climb

The configuration for level flight is maintained except that three indicators—rate-of-climb, angle-of-incidence (gyro-horizon), and manifold-pressure—rise together. The R/C pointer is conceived as reaching up for the desired new altitude reading, which, in turn, starts crawling down to meet it. In leveling off they are brought down to the lubber lines together and secured there.

The M/P pointer is coordinated with the R/C pointer through the appropriate tie-line. A/I calibration is shown by round black dots located between the vertical lubber lines. The ring in the center of the A/I indicator is made to encircle one of these dots or to ride between two of them.

Straight Descent

The configuration is analogous to that maintained in a straight climb. The altimeter setting dial is placed across the descent tie-lines to remind the pilot to check his pressure setting before approaching the ground.

Two-Needle-Width Turn to Starboard

The straight-and-level configuration is maintained except that the rate-of-turn pointer reaches out for the desired new compass reading. The new reading rises to meet it. Both are brought back together and secured between the vertical lubber lines.

The angle-of-bank indicator (gyro-horizon) is maintained in alignment with the rate-of-turn pointer and the first (two-needle-width) dot.

Especial care is taken to make sure that the altitude field remains stationary and that the airspeed shell does not creep back against the stall shell.

Power Approach

The main consideration is to keep a line of "daylight" between the airspeed and stall shells.

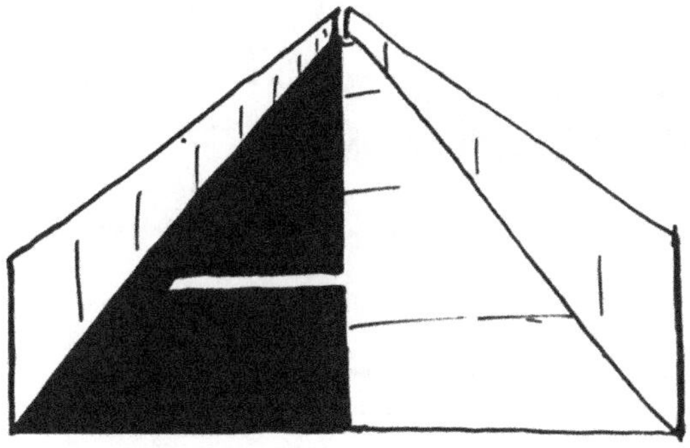

Use of Plotting Board

Direction indicator, trip veedometer, clock, elapsed time ring, and fuel consumption ring provide the principal data. They are mounted close to the plotting board to facilitate reading.

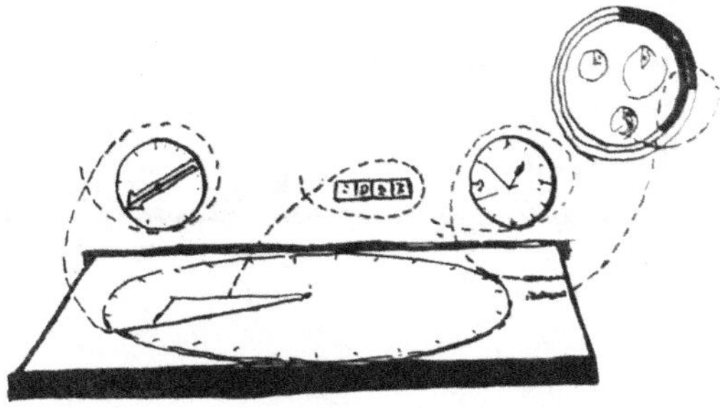

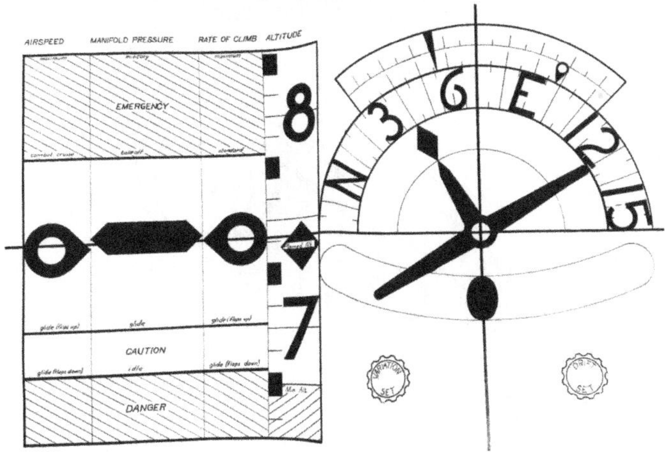

An Alternative Design

An alternative panel design appears on the preceding page. Since manifold pressure is ordinarily used either to increase airspeed or rate-of-climb, the manifold pressure marker is located between the airspeed marker and the rate-of-climb marker.

To increase airspeed one moves the M/P and A/S markers up the dial together.

To increase climb one moves the M/P and R/C markers up the dial together. As in the case of the other panel, the altitude readings start marching down the dial to meet the raised R/C marker.

Two special markers can be set on the altitude scale, a minimum altitude marker to indicate the height of obstacles which must be cleared on the trip, and a planned altitude marker which is conspicuous enough to be easily kept on the lubber line.

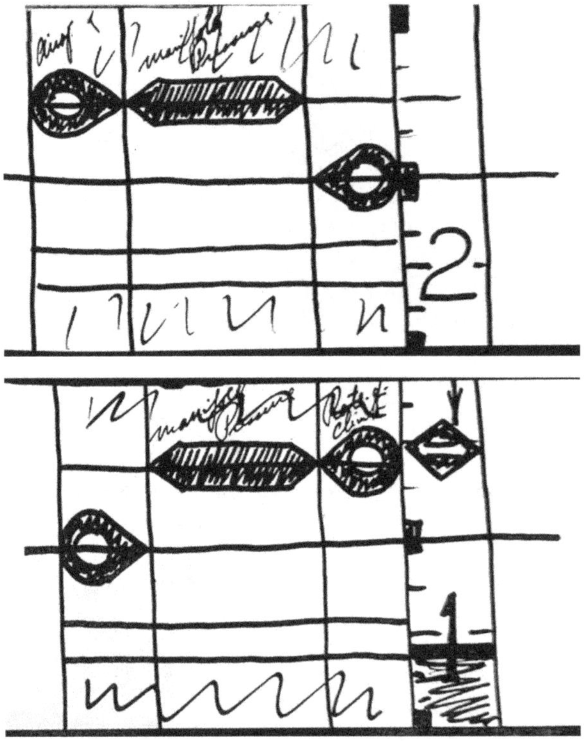

A/S, M/P, R/C, and Alt. markers are mounted on flexible bands. The bands are actuated by sprockets mounted immediately behind the horizontal lubber line.

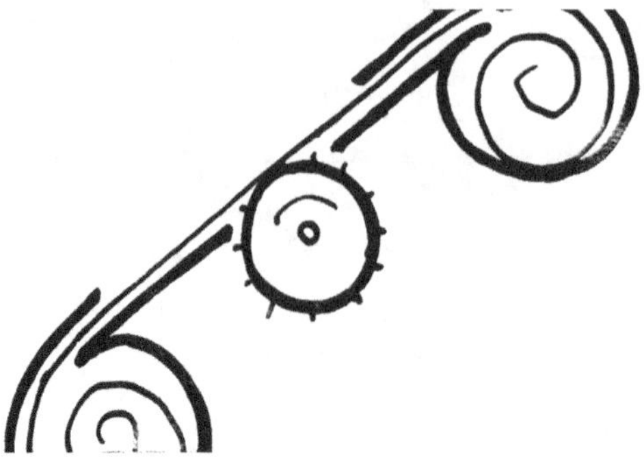

A Comprehensive Program for Developing a Better Panel *(Tentative Outline)*

Thus far these notes have attempted to convey two general ideas: (1) an idea of the perceptual principles which may be invoked in panel design, (2) an idea of the lengths to which the designer is free to go. Against the background of these two ideas it is now intended to sketch, in broad outline only, a comprehensive program for developing a better panel.

The suggested program naturally divides itself into three phases: (1) survey, (2) design, (3) experiment. Parts of these phases may be conducted concurrently.

This three-phase type of development is in accord with what has, out of necessity, emerged as the applied psychologist's basic strategy in attacking any new human engineering problem.

Survey

Step 1. Identification of the practical problems from the standpoint of the instrument panel user.

The *free interview method* would be advisable in this initial step of the program. This method is employed because at this point the object is not to acquire precise statistical data but to make an initial descriptive formulation of all the recognized practical problems.

The raw data would be the freely expressed experiences, opinions and suggestions of those people in whose environment aircraft instrument panels play a recognized functional role. Such people as the following:

Direct Users of Panels

1 Pilots who frequently fly on instruments.

They have a vested interest in the skill they have acquired but they know how to use conventional panels.

2 Pilots who should fly on instruments more frequently than they do.

Why haven't they learned?

3 Students of instrument flight.

The whole panel looks screwy to them.

4 Instrument flight instructors.

They know about obstacles to learning.

5 Potential students of instrument flight.

How much are they ready to tackle?

6 Night flyers.

They must avoid distractions.

7 Owners and potential owners.

What do they expect of their airplanes?

8 Aircraft salesmen.

Why do people balk at buying instrument-equipped planes?

Indirect Users of Panels

1 Accident statisticians.

For perspective on difficulties.

2 Insurance investigators.

To get down to cases.

3 CAB representatives.

Who gets into trouble?

4 Military safety board members.

Where instrument flying is not practical.

5 Operations officers.

What is maximum performance?

6 Traffic control officers.

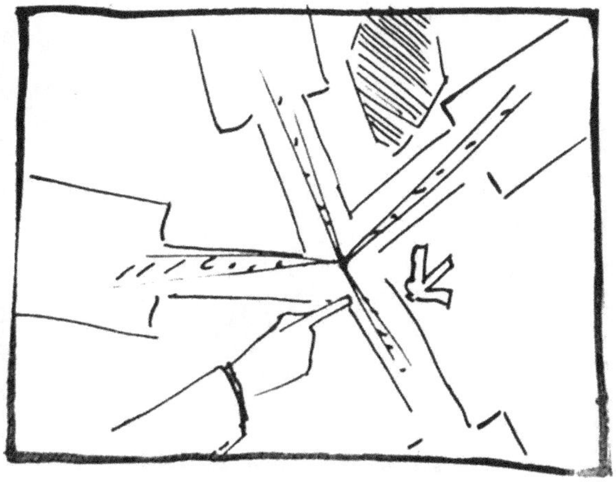

What about instrument flying in traffic?

7 Tower operators.

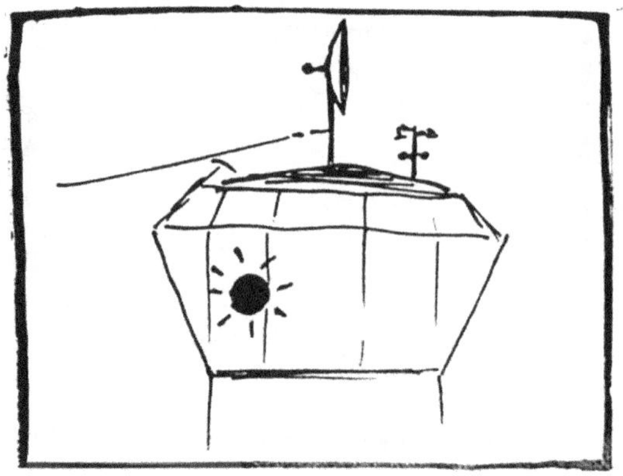

What about instrument flying close to the airport?

8 Meteorologists.

What meteorological conditions must be surmounted?

9 Instrument maintenance men.

What are the bugs?

10 Instrument engineers.

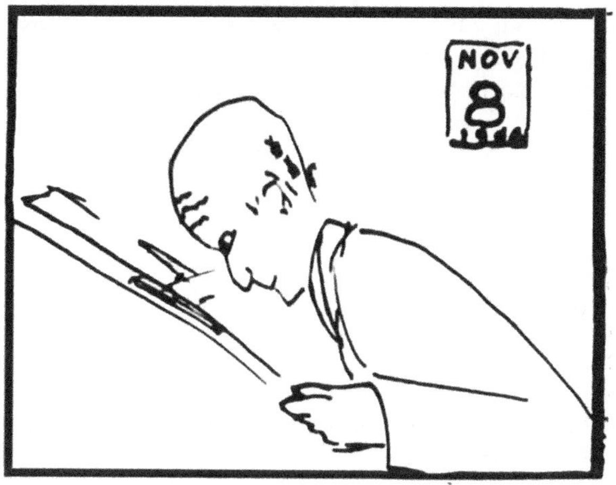

What are the unsolved problems?

11 Aircraft engineers.

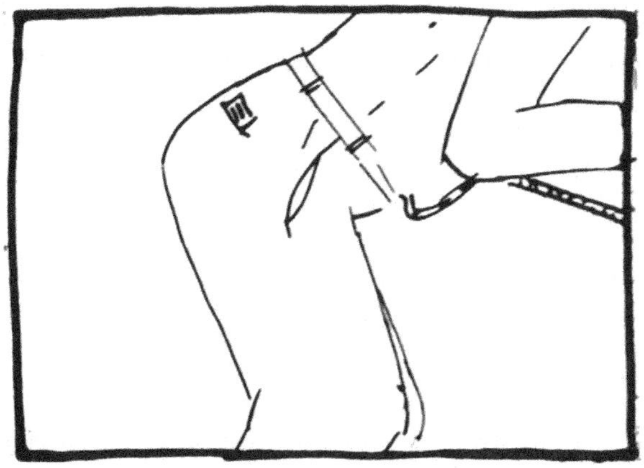

Instruments needed in the new designs.

Step 2. Partial quantification of the practical problems of instrument flying.
Controlled methods of obtaining data would be used in this step of the program in contrast with the *free interview method* used in the first step. This would include the controlled interview, questionnaire, interpretation of available statistics, etc.

The objective of this step would be to obtain quantitative data on accidents, faults, pilot errors, instrument errors, difficulties, criticisms, limitations, and instrument flying situations. The specific areas subjected to quantification would be those indicated in the first step of the investigatory program.

The data would not necessarily be complete nor would they be subjected to any detailed statistical analysis. Their usefulness would lie in the light which they would shed upon the comparative importance of the various specific problems uncovered in the first step. They should keep the investigator from going overboard in attempting to correct some minor fault whose incidence does not justify its figuring greatly in the overall evaluation. At the same time the investigator must not be misled into accepting incidence as a sole criterion of importance.

As a result of this second step the investigator's conception of the whole problem of instrument design may be altered radically and in ways which cannot be predicted before the step is completed. It is to be expected that the subsequent course of the investigation would hinge on the outcome of this step.

Step 3. First hand observation of the specific problems whose relevance and importance were established in Steps 1 and 2.
The purpose of this step would be to enable the investigator to envision, insofar as possible, each specific problem in its context. The *general method of observation* would be used in this step.

Step 4. Field study.
Systematically planned and recorded observations of flying functions would be undertaken in this step *(The method of systematically controlled observation).*

This would be a first hand study of flying procedures as they are actually practiced on airlines, in military services, and by private operators rather than a study of official or nominally accepted procedures. It would be an attempt to describe accurately the wider context of the more specifically contextual elements seen in Step 3. The following should be objectively described:

1 Types of maneuvers used.
2 Instruments used in each maneuver.
3 Instrument readings used.
4 Variants in manner of using instruments.
5 Use of substitute instruments.
6 Integral perception of combinations of readings.
7 Exceptions to each of the above.

Step 5. Analysis of maneuvers.
The records obtained in Step 4 would be analyzed. This analysis would include functional classification, frequency tabulations, and determination of inter-relations. The purpose of the step would be to organize the data into a simple comprehensible system. The result should be a usable statement of the fundamental flying evolutions.

Step 6. Analysis of fundamental instrument readings.
Instrument readings would be analyzed according to the fundamental maneuvers revealed in Step 5. This should indicate precisely what readings must be read, when they must be read, in what combinations they must be read, and what the tolerable errors are.

Collateral Studies

Study 1. Accommodation time.
This would be a laboratory study of ocular accommodation time required of men of different ages under conditions of alternating near and far fixation such as those encountered by the pilot when he looks back and forth from instrument panel to horizon. The results should indicate how much additional visibility, over that required for ordinary visual perception, is required in instrument faces which must be seen with distance-accommodated eyes.

Study 2. Acuity in the periphery.
This study should also throw light upon the extra margin of visibility required in instrument faces. In order to get "pattern reading" it would be desirable for some readings to be picked up out of the "corner of the eye." Furthermore in giving the panel a "stroke of the eye" the fixation point may not coincide precisely with the center of the dial. The visibility of the dials should be such that such off-center vision would be effective.

Study 3. Accuracy of fixations.
This would be a study of the amount of angular error that is likely to occur on the first fixation after the attention is turned from the horizon to the panel. This should be a fairly simple eye-movement camera study conducted in conjunction with Study 2.

Study 4. Uniqueness of Instrument Face Gestalten.
If the principle of perceptual integration is used as suggested in the earlier part of this manuscript, it would be well to make some enquiries into the variety of perceptual patterns which can be readily distinguished from each other.

Design

The steps in this phase of the program would be largely determined by the results of the earlier part of the investigation. Here is the principal point at which engineering and psychological considerations must be reconciled.

Validation

Step 1. Reading time and accuracy studies.
This step would involve use of cardboard mockups of the initial experimental design and of a conventional design. Simple laboratory studies of comparative reading time and accuracy would be conducted. Unless the new design showed definite superiority in both respects when used on non-pilot subjects, redesign should be considered before proceeding further.

Step 2. Studies of learning time.
Subjects who have flown light planes but who have seen very little of complicated instrument panels would be used. Learning problems would be set up. Learning time for the problems would be compared for experimental and conventional panels. The group of subjects would be split and rotated in the experimental design.

Step 3. Face validation.
Experienced pilots would be shown the mockup of the experimental panel and asked for comments and suggestions.

Step 4. Synthetic trainer installation.
The new design should be checked by installing it in a synthetic trainer. If advanced synthetic trainers such as those developed by the Navy for F6F night fighter training cannot be used, at least a Link trainer installation should be undertaken. Steps 2 and 3 should then be repeated with such modifications as the installation required.

Step 5. Experimental plane installation.
Shakedown flights with the new panel should be systematically planned, starting with general orientation flights and continuing on through flights which simulate civil and military operating conditions.

Step 6. Limited adoption.
The last step would be limited adoption of the panel in a specified sample group of planes. The sample group should be selected so that it would be properly compared with a control group in which standard installations were used. Operating records on the two groups should be carefully maintained over a period of time both to establish the superiority of the new panel and to indicate needed modifications.

127

Design of Critical Difference Computer[1]

1 The purpose of the Critical Difference Computer is to provide a ready means of checking the reliability of the difference between two proportions. The basic formula is:

$$cr = \frac{p_1 - p_2}{\sigma_{diff}}$$

Where: cr is the critical ratio

p_1 is the first proportion

p_2 is the second proportion

σ_{diff} is the standard error of the difference

2 The computer is essentially a parallel line nomograph with variable outside scales and alternative central scales. The general equation for the parallel line nomograph (Fig. 1) is:

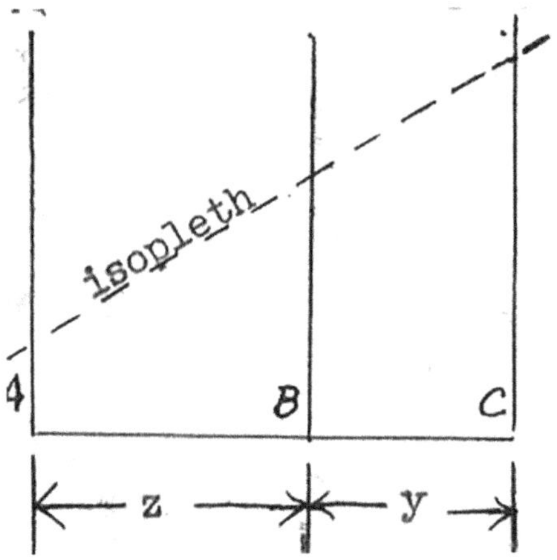

Fig. 1

$$B = \frac{yA + zC}{y + z}$$

When z = y this becomes

$$2B = A + C$$

3 In designing the computer the equation for σ_{diff} was reduced to the form of the equation for a parallel line nomograph in which the outer lines are equidistant from the center line. The equation for σ_{diff} is :

$$\sigma_{diff} \sqrt{\sigma^2_{p_1} + \sigma^2_{p_2}}$$

[1] Dated March, 1945. Published by permission of Jacqueline Aldridge.

Collected Papers of the Pioneer of Constructivist Psychology: George A. Kelly, First Edition. Edited by David A. Winter and Nick Reed.

Where: σ_{p_1} is the standard error of the first proportion
σ_{p_2} is the standard error of the second proportion

but $\sigma_p = \sqrt{\frac{pq}{N}}$
where: p is the proportion of the population responding to a given item
q is the proportion of the population not responding to the given item
N is the size of the population
since: $q = 1 - p$
we may write: $\sigma_p^2 = \frac{p - p^2}{N}$
The equation for the standard error of the difference may then be written:

$$\sigma_{\text{diff}}^2 = \frac{p_1 - p_1^2}{N_1} + \frac{p_2 - p_2^2}{N_2}$$

an equation which is of the same form as that for the parallel line nomograph.

4 The A and C scales are laid out on the wings of the Computer. The measurements are scalar values of $\frac{p-p^2}{N}$ and the entries are simply values of p expressed per cent. The scalar values increase to a maximum as p approaches .50. The scalar value for an entry of 60 is the same as that for 40, for 70 the same as that for 30, etc.

5 The wings are designed to represent a family of scales in which equal values of $\frac{p-p^2}{N}$ for various p's and N's are shown as equal scalar values. The scalar values are all measured along radii from the center of rotation of the wing. Thus an appropriate scale for a given N can be rotated into position along the side of the nomograph. The lengths of the scales are inversely proportional to the N's they represent.

6 Parallel lines representing equal values of p for various N's are drawn on the wings.

7 The construction of a wing for N's ranging between 25 and 100 is as follows (Fig. 2):

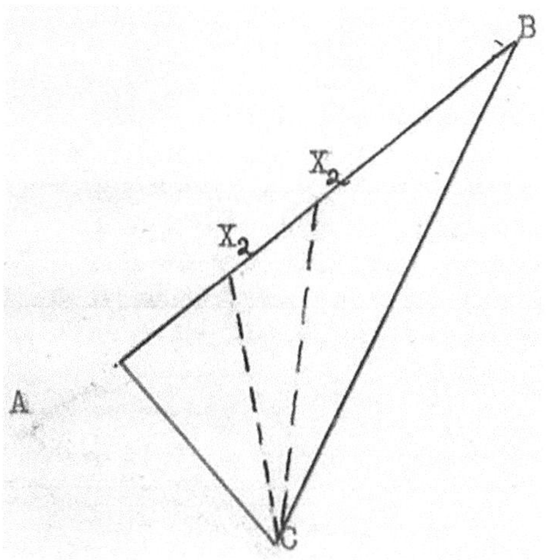

Fig. 2

The wing is pivoted at C. By rotation various scales, CB, CX_1, CX_2, CA, etc., can be laid up to the edge of the nomograph. The scale, CB, being the longest, is used for an N of 25. The scale, CA, being one fourth as long, is used for the N which is four times as great, i.e., 100. The entry at B is "25" and at A, "100". Intermediate entries may be determined by laying off the reciprocals of the N's from C. In practice, however, this method of locating the points is not very accurate. The scalar values can better be obtained by the equation:

$$\overline{AX} = \frac{\overline{AC}}{\tan \text{arc} \sin \frac{N_X}{N_L}}$$

where N_X is the entry
N_L is the largest entry (in this case, $N_L = 100$)

8 The lines representing equal values of p are drawn parallel to AB through points located on BC. The scalar values are the solutions of $\frac{p-p^2}{N}$ and the entries are the values of p. In the present case N is 25.

9 Different "B" or central scales are constructed to correspond to several useful levels of confidence. The levels selected in this case are the p = .07, p = .05, p = .01, and p = .0014 (3 σ) levels. Corresponding critical ratios are computed

From # 1, $cr = \frac{p_1 - p_2}{\sigma_{diff}}$

From # 3, $\sigma^2_{diff} = \frac{p_1 - p_1^2}{N_1} + \frac{p_2 - p_2^2}{N_2}$

Substituting: $\frac{(p_1 - p_2)^2}{CR^2} = \frac{p_1 - p_1^2}{N_1} + \frac{p_2 - p_2^2}{N_2}$

Which is in the form of the nomograph equation mentioned in # 2:

$$2B = A + C$$

Thus the "B" scalar values are determined by the expression:

$$2B = \frac{(p_1 - p_2)^2}{CR^2} \text{ or, } B = \frac{1}{2}\frac{(p_1 - p_2)^2}{CR^2}$$

Where: B is the scalar value on the central scale
cr is the critical ratio
p_1 is the first proportion
p_2 is the second proportion
The entries on the central scale are values of $p_1 - p_2$.

10 The wings may be used with other ranges of N's, e.g., if the longest scale is made to represent an N of 50 instead of 25 all the other N entries may be multiplied by two. This amounts to doubling the scalar values both for the wings and the central scales. This further requires the construction of alernative central scales for use when the wings are read in this way. The alternative central scales can be constructed directly from the table of entries and scalar values used for the regular central scale. The equation is:

$$\frac{S_1}{S_2} = \frac{N_1}{N_2}$$

where S_1 is the scalar value on the regular scale
S_2 is the scalar value on the alternative scale
$\frac{N_1}{N_2}$ is the ratio between the populations represented on a given wing scale.

If the regular central scale is used with wings entered with N's ranging from 25–100 the alternative central scale to be used with the wings read for N's ranging from 50–200 will have scalar values just twice as great for given entries.

11 In order to have a convenient combination of scales it was decided to construct wings with the front sides entered for populations of 25–100 and the back sides for populations of 200–800. By use of alternate central scales and halving or doubling the wing N readings the following ranges would be covered:

(front)	$12\frac{1}{2}$ to 50	(alternative central scale)
"	25 to 100	(regular central scale)
"	50 to 200	(alternative central scale)
(back)	100 to 400	(alternative central scale)
"	200 to 800	(regular central scale)
"	400 to 1600	(alternative central scale)

12 Following are tables of entries and scalar values for the particular scales employed. Units of 1/50 inch were used in drawing original design.

Table 1 Entries and Scalar Values for

N Scales on Front Sides of Wings

$$S = \frac{25}{\tan \sin^{-1} \frac{N}{100}}$$

Entry	*Scalar Value*	*Entry*	*Scalar Value*	*Entry*	*Scalar Value*
25	9678	51	4216	76	2137
26	9276	52	4106	77	2071
27	8913	53	4000	78	2005
28	8567	54	3896	79	1940
29	8245	55	3796	80	1874
30	7945	56	3699	81	1809
31	7663	57	3603	82	1745
32	7400	58	3511	83	1679
33	7152	59	3422	84	1615
34	6912	60	3333	85	1549
35	6692	61	3248	86	1483
36	6478	62	3163	87	1416
37	6276	63	3081	88	1348
38	6085	64	3001	89	1281
39	5903	65	2923	90	1211
40	5726	66	2845	91	1139
41	5562	67	2770	92	1064
42	5402	68	2695	93	988
43	5249	69	2622	94	907
44	5103	70	2549	95	821
45	4959	71	2479	96	729
46	4826	72	2410	97	626
47	4695	73	2340	98	507
48	4569	74	2272	99	356
49	4448	75	2205	100	-
50	4330				

Table 2 Entries and Scalar Values for N Scales on Back Sides of Wings

$$S = \frac{25}{\tan \sin^{-1} \frac{N}{800}}$$

Entry	*Scalar Value*	*Entry*	*Scalar Value*
200	9678	510	3022
210	9191	520	2923
220	8737	530	2826
230	8328	540	2733
240	7953	550	2641
250	7598	560	2550
260	7274	570	2463
270	6974	580	2375
280	6693	590	2290
290	6429	600	2205
300	6183	610	2121
310	5947	620	2039
320	5727	630	1957
330	5522	640	1875
340	5325	650	1794
350	5137	660	1713
360	4960	670	1631
370	4792	680	1549
380	4630	690	1467
390	4476	700	1383
400	4330	710	1298
410	4188	720	1210
420	4053	730	1121
430	3922	740	1027
440	3796	750	928
450	3674	760	822
460	3557	770	704
470	3443	780	570
480	3346	790	399
490	3227	800	0
500	3122		

Table 3 Entries and Scalar Values for Per Cent Scales both for Fronts and Backs of Wings (Scalar values measured along N = 25 scale on fronts and along N = 400 scale on backs)

$$S = \frac{p - p^2}{N}$$

Entry	*Scalar Value*	*Entry*	*Scalar Value*
.01	.000396	26	.007696
.02	784	27	7884
.03	1164	28	8064
.04	1536	29	8236
.05	1900	30	8450
.06	2256	31	8556
07	2604	32	8704
08	2944	33	8844
09	3276	34	8976
10	3600	35	9100
11	3916	36	9216
12	4224	37	9324
13	4524	38	9424
14	4816	39	9516
15	5100	40	9600

Table 3 (Continued)

Entry	*Scalar Value*	*Entry*	*Scalar Value*
16	5376	41	9676
17	5644	42	9744
18	5904	43	9804
19	6156	44	9856
20	6400	45	9900
21	6636	46	9936
22	6864	47	9964
23	7084	48	9984
24	7296	49	9996
25	7500	50	10000

Table 4 Entries and Scalar Values for the 3 σ (p = .0014)

Scales on Front of Computer

$$S_2 = \frac{1}{2}\frac{(p_1 - p_2)^2}{3^2}$$

Scalar Values

	Range $12\frac{1}{2} - 50$	*Range 25–100*	*Range 50–200*
Entry $(p_1 - p_2)$	$S_1 = \frac{1}{2}S_2$ *(Alt. Scale)*	S_2 *(Reg. Scale)*	$S_3 = 2S_2$ *(Alt. Scale)*
01	.00000276	.00000552	.0000 1104
02	001112	002225	004450
03	002510	005020	010040
04	004450	008900	017800
05	0074	0139	0278
06	0100	0200	0400
07	0136	0272	0544
08	0178	0356	0712
09	0225	0450	0900
10	0278	0557	1114
11	0336	0672	1344
12	0400	0800	1600
13	0470	0940	1880
14	0542	1085	2170
15	0625	1250	2500
16	0710	1420	2840
17	0805	1610	3220
18	0900	1800	3600
19	0995	1990	3980
20	1110	2220	4440
21	1225	2450	4900
22	1347	2695	5390
23	1470	2940	5880
24	1600	3200	6400
25	1735	3470	6940
26	1875	3750	7500
27	2025	405	810
28	2175	435	870
29	2335	467	934
30	2500	500	1000
31	.002665	533	
32	2850	570	
33	3040	608	

(Continued)

Table 4 (Continued)

	Range $12\frac{1}{2}-50$	*Range 25–100*	*Range 50–200*
Entry $(p_1 - p_2)$	$S_1 = \frac{1}{2}S_2$ *(Alt. Scale)*	S_2 *(Reg. Scale)*	$S_3 = 2S_2$ *(Alt. Scale)*
34	3215	643	
35	3400	680	
36	3610	722	
37	3805	761	
38	4005	801	
39	4225	845	
40	4450	890	
41	4675	935	
42	4910	982	
43	5136		
44	5377		
45	5625		
46	5877		
47	6136		
48	6400		
49	6669		
50	6944		
51	7225		
52	7511		
53	7802		
54	8100		
55	8402		
56	8711		
57	9025		
58	9344		
59	9669		
60	10000		

Table 5 Entries and Scalar Values for the 2.33 σ (p = .01)

Scales on Front of Computer

$$S_2 = \frac{1}{2}\frac{(p_1 - p_2)^2}{2.33^2}$$

Scalar Values

	Range $12\frac{1}{2}-50$	*Range 25–100*	*Range 50–200*
Entry $(p_1 - p_2)$	$S_1 = \frac{1}{2}S_2$ *(Alt. Scale)*	S_2 *(Reg. Scale)*	$S_3 = 2S_2$ *(Alt. Scale)*
01	.0000046	.0000092	.0000184
02	00184	00369	00738
03	00415	00830	01660
04	00735	01470	02940
05	01150	02300	04600
06	0166	0332	0664
07	0226	0452	0904
08	0295	0590	1180
09	0375	0750	1500
10	0465	0921	1842
11	0565	1120	2240

Table 5 (Continued)

	Range $12\frac{1}{2}-50$	Range 25–100	Range 50–200
Entry (p_1-p_2)	$S_1=\frac{1}{2}S_2$ (Alt. Scale)	S_2 (Reg. Scale)	$S_3=2S_2$ (Alt. Scale)
12	0665	133	266
13	078	156	312
14	090	180	360
15	104	208	416
16	118	236	472
17	133	266	532
18	149	299	598
19	166	332	664
20	184	369	738
21	203	406	812
22	223	446	892
23	244	488	976
24	265	531	
25	287	575	
26	311	623	
27	336	672	
28	361	722	
29	388	777	
30	415	830	
31	443	886	
32	471	943	
33	500	1000	
34	532		
35	564		
36	596		
37	630		
38	664		
39	700		
40	736		
41	774		
42	812		
43	851		
44	891		
45	932		
46	974		

Table 6 Entries and Scalar Values for the 1.645 σ (p = .05)

Scales on Front of Computer

$$S_2=\frac{1}{2}\frac{(p_1-p_2)^2}{1.645^2}$$

Scalar Values

	Range $12\frac{1}{2}-50$	Range 25–100	Range 50–200
Entry (p_1-p_2)	$S_1=\frac{1}{2}S_2$ (Alt. Scale)	S_2 (Reg. Scale)	$S_3=2S_2$ (Alt. Scale)
01	.0000092	.0000184	.0000368
02	00369	740	0148
03	00830	1660	0332

(Continued)

Table 6 (Continued)

	Range $12\frac{1}{2}-50$	Range 25–100	Range 50–200
Entry (p_1-p_2)	$S_1=\frac{1}{2}S_2$ (Alt. Scale)	S_2 (Reg. Scale)	$S_3 = 2S_2$ (Alt. Scale)
04	01475	2950	0590
05	0231	462	0924
06	0331	663	1326
07	0451	903	1804
08	0590	1180	2360
09	0745	1490	298
10	0920	1840	368
11	1115	2230	446
12	1330	2660	532
13	1565	3130	626
14	1800	360	720
15	2075	415	830
16	236	472	944
17	266	532	
18	300	600	
19	333	667	
20	369	738	
21	406	812	
22	449	898	
23	489	979	
24	532		
25	577		
26	625		
27	674		
28	724		
29	777		
30	832		
31	888		
32	946		

Table 7 Entries and Scalar Values for the 1.476 σ(p = .07)

Scales on Front of Computer

$$S_2 = \frac{1}{2}\frac{(p_1 - p_2)^2}{1.476^2}$$

Scalar Values

	Range $12\frac{1}{2}-50$	Range 25–100	Range 50–200
Entry (p_1-p_2)	$S_1=\frac{1}{2}S_2$ (Alt. Scale)	S_2 (Reg. Scale)	$S_3 = 2S_2$ (Alt. Scale)
01	.0000114	.0000228	.0000456
02	00460	00920	01840
03	0103	0206	0412
04	0183	0366	0732
05	0286	0573	1146
06	0413	0825	1650
07	0562	113	226
08	0735	147	294
09	0930	186	372
10	1150	230	460

Table 7 (Continued)

	Range $12\frac{1}{2}-50$	*Range 25–100*	*Range 50–200*
Entry (p_1-p_2)	$S_1=\frac{1}{2}S_2$ *(Alt. Scale)*	S_2 *(Reg. Scale)*	$S_3=2S_2$ *(Alt. Scale)*
11	138	277	554
12	165	330	660
13	194	388	776
14	225	450	900
15	259	517	
16	294	588	
17	331	663	
18	371	742	
19	414	828	
20	460	920	
21	506		
22	555		
23	607		
24	661		
25	717		
26	775		
27	836		
28	899		
29	965		

Table 8 Entries and Scalar Values for the 3 σ (p = .0014)

Scales on Back of Computer

$$S_2=\frac{1}{2}\frac{(p_1-p_2)^2}{3^2}$$

Scalar Values

	Range 100–400	*Range 200–800*	*Range 400–1600*
Entry (p_1-p_2)	$S_4=4S_2$ *(Alt. Scale)*	$S_5=8S_2$ *(Reg. Scale)*	$S_6=16S_2$ *(Alt. Scale)*
.005	.000006	.000011	.000022
.010	0022	0044	0088
.015	0050	0100	0200
.020	0089	0178	0356
.025	0139	0278	0555
.030	0200	0400	0800
.035	0272	0544	1089
.040	0355	0711	1422
.045	0450	0900	1800
.050	0555	1111	2222
.055	0672	1344	2689
.060	0800	1600	3200
.065	0939	1878	3755
.070	1089	2178	4356
.075	1250	2500	5000
.080	1422	2844	5688
.085	1605	3211	6422
.090	1800	3600	7200
.095	2005	4011	8022
.100	2222	4444	8888

(Continued)

Table 8 (Continued)

	Range 100–400	*Range 200–800*	*Range 400–1600*
Entry (p_1–p_2)	*$S_4 = 4S_2$ (Alt. Scale)*	*$S_5 = 8S_2$ (Reg. Scale)*	*$S_6 = 16S_2$ (Alt. Scale)*
.105	2450	4900	9799
.110	2688	5377	
.115	2939	5877	
.120	3199	6399	
.125	3472	6944	
.130	3755	7510	
.135	4050	8099	
.140	4355	8710	
.145	4672	9344	
.150	5000	10000	
.155	5338		
.160	5688		
.165	6049		
.170	6422		
.175	6805		
.180	7200		
.185	7605		
.190	8021		
.195	8449		
.200	8888		
.205	9338		
.210	9799		

Table 9 Entries and Scalar Values for the 2.33 σ (p = .01)

Scales on Back of the Computer

$$S_2 = \frac{1}{2}\frac{(p_1 - p_2)^2}{2.33^2}$$

Scalar Values

	Range 100–400	*Range 200–800*	*Range 400–1600*
Entry (p_1–p_2)	*$S_4 = 4S_2$ (Alt. Scale)*	*$S_5 = 8S_2$ (Reg. Scale)*	*$S_6 = 16\,S_2$ (Alt. Scale)*
.005	.000009	.000018	.000037
.010	0036	0073	0146
.015	0083	0166	0332
.020	0148	0295	0590
.025	0230	0461	0923
.030	0332	0663	1326
.035	0451	0902	1805
.040	0588	1179	2357
.045	0746	1492	2984
.050	0920	1842	3683
.055	1114	2228	4458
.060	1326	2652	5305
.065	1557	3113	6225
.070	1805	3610	7221
.075	2072	4144	8288
.080	2357	4714	9429
.085	2661	5323	
.090	2984	5968	
.095	3324	6649	
.100	3683	7367	
.105	4061	8123	

Table 9 (Continued)

	Range 100–400	*Range 200–800*	*Range 400–1600*
Entry (p_1-p_2)	$S_4 = 4S_2$ *(Alt. Scale)*	$S_5 = 8S_2$ *(Reg. Scale)*	$S_6 = 16\ S_2$ *(Alt. Scale)*
.110	4456	8913	
.115	4872	9742	
.120	5303		
.125	5756		
.130	6225		
.135	6714		
.140	7219		
.145	7745		
.150	8288		
.155	8849		
.160	9429		
.165	10027		

Table 10 Entries and Scalar Values for the 1.645 σ (p = .05) S

Scales on Back of the Computer

$$S_2 = \frac{1}{2}\frac{(p_1 - p_2)^2}{1.645^2}$$

Scalar Values

	Range 100–400	*Range 200–800*	*Range 400–1600*
Entry (p_1-p_2)	$S_4 = 4S_2$ *(Alt. Scale)*	$S_5 = 8S_2$ *(Reg. Scale)*	$S_6 = 16\ S_2$ *(Alt. Scale)*
.005	.000020	.000037	.000073
.010	0073	0146	0293
.015	0166	0333	0665
.020	0296	0592	1184
.025	0462	0925	1846
.030	0665	1331	2661
.035	0905	1810	3622
.040	1181	2365	4730
.045	1497	2994	5987
.050	1846	3696	7391
.055	2235	4471	8944
.060	2661	5322	
.065	3123	6247	
.070	3622	7245	
.075	4158	8316	
.080	4730	9460	
.085	5339		
.090	5987		
.095	6669		
.100	7391		
.105	8149		
.110	8941		
.115	9776		

Table 11 Entries and Scalar Values for the 1.476 σ (p = .07)

Scales on Back of the Computer

$$S_2 = \frac{1}{2}\frac{(p_1 - p_2)^2}{1.476^2}$$

Scalar Values

	Range 100–400	*Range 200–800*	*Range 400–1600*
Entry (p_1–p_2)	$S_4 = 4S_2$ *(Alt. Scale)*	$S_5 = 8S_2$ *(Reg. Scale)*	$S_6 = 16\,S_2$ *(Alt. Scale)*
.005	.000025	.000045	.000091
.010	0091	0182	0364
.015	0207	0413	0827
.020	0368	0736	1471
.025	0575	1149	2294
.030	0827	1653	3306
.035	1124	2248	4501
.040	1467	2939	5877
.045	1860	3720	7440
.050	2294	4592	9184
.055	2777	5555	
.060	3306	6613	
.065	3881	7762	
.070	4501	9002	
.075	5166		
.080	5877		
.085	6634		
.090	7440		
.095	8287		
.100	9184		

Appendix

Writings by Kelly that cannot be traced or are not included in these volumes for other reasons.

Kelly, G. A. (1926). *The call to arms.*[1] Unpublished manuscript.
Kelly, G. A. (1928). *One thousand workers and their leisure.*[2] Unpublished master's thesis, University of Kansas.
Kelly, G. A. (1929). *Fuselage stress analysis and design specifications for Skylark Model 1.* Report to the U.S. Bureau of Aeronautics in support of an application for a manufacturing license for the Watkins Aircraft Co., Wichita, KS.
Kelly, G. A. (1930). *Prediction of teaching success.* Unpublished B.Ed. thesis, University of Edinburgh.
Kelly, G. A. (1931). *Common factors in reading and speech disabilities.*[3] Unpublished PhD dissertation, State University of Iowa.
Kelly, G. A. (1937). *Report to the president of Fort Hays Kansas State College concerning psychological clinical services.* Fort Hays Kansas State College.
Kelly, G. A. (1938). *Outline for the study of a child.* Fort Hays Kansas State College.
Kelly, G. A. (1941). *Outline for a clinical case study.* Fort Hays Kansas State College.
Kelly, G. A. (1944). *Problems in the aviation training of British Royal Navy Cadets. Report to U.S. Navy.*
Kelly, G. A. et al. (1945). *Attrition in U.S. Naval Aviation.*
Kelly, G. A. et al. (1945). *War weariness in U.S. Naval Aviation.*
Kelly, G. A., & Moore, B. V. (1950). *Report of survey of psychology at the University of Louisville.*
Kelly, G. A. (1951). *The psychological construction of life.* Psychology Clinic Library, Ohio State University.
Kelly, G. A. (1953). *A plan for a comprehensive experimental study of the uses of television in teacher education.* Annual reports, 1953–1954, New Jersey State Teachers College at Montclair.
Conrad, L. H., & Kelly, G. A. (1954). *Television in a time of educational crises.*[4] Unpublished book.
Kelly, G. A. (1955). *Television at the classroom door.* Unpublished manuscript.
Kelly, G. A. (1957). *Contemporary problems in clinical psychology.*
Kelly, G. A. (1962). *A further explanation of the factor analysis of repertory grids.* Ohio State University.
Kelly, G. A. (1963). *Clinical psychology at The Ohio State University: A critical appraisal.*[5] Unpublished manuscript.
Kelly, G. A. (1964). *Evaluation of U.S. Air Force Retraining Program.* Chairman's report of findings of Evaluation Board appointed by U.S. Air Force.

[1] This is a novel that Kelly's family does not wish to be published.
[2] Available from the editors upon request.
[3] This has not been included, as much of its content is covered in papers in the section on Research, Measurement, and Experimental Psychology. A copy is available from the editors upon request.
[4] Not included, as much of the content is repeated in other papers in the Education section. Available from the editors upon request.
[5] Not included, as it is labeled "Privileged communication."

Collected Papers of the Pioneer of Constructivist Psychology: George A. Kelly, First Edition. Edited by David A. Winter and Nick Reed.

Index